WHO WAS WHO

VOLUME X

1996–2000

WHO'S WHO

An annual biographical dictionary
first published in 1849

WHO WAS WHO

Volume I	1897–1915
Volume II	1916–1928
Volume III	1929–1940
Volume IV	1941–1950
Volume V	1951–1960
Volume VI	1961–1970
Volume VII	1971–1980
Volume VIII	1981–1990
Volume IX	1991–1995
Volume X	1996–2000

A CUMULATED INDEX 1897–1990

WHO'S WHO 1897–1998

The complete text of
WHO WAS WHO and WHO'S WHO 1998
on CD-ROM

WHO WAS WHO

1996–2000

A COMPANION TO

WHO'S WHO

CONTAINING THE BIOGRAPHIES
OF THOSE WHO DIED DURING
THE PERIOD 1996–2000

A & C BLACK
LONDON

FIRST PUBLISHED 2001
BY A & C BLACK (PUBLISHERS) LIMITED
37 SOHO SQUARE LONDON W1D 3QZ

COPYRIGHT © 2001 A & C BLACK (PUBLISHERS) LTD

ISBN 0 7136 5439 2

Typeset, printed and bound in Great Britain by William Clowes Ltd, Beccles and London

PREFACE

This, the tenth volume of biographies removed from *Who's Who* on account of death, contains the entries of those who died between 1996 and 2000. Those whose deaths were not notified until after this volume went to press are listed as Addenda at the beginning of the biographical section.

The entries are as they last appeared in *Who's Who*, with the date of death added and in some cases further information, such as posthumous publications. It has not always been possible to ascertain the exact date of death, and the editors will welcome such information for inclusion in the next edition of this volume.

CONTENTS

ABBREVIATIONS USED IN THIS BOOK

Some of the designatory letters in this list are used merely for economy of space and do not necessarily imply any professional or other qualification.

A

AA — Anti-aircraft; Automobile Association; Architectural Association; Augustinians of the Assumption
AAA — Amateur Athletic Association; American Accounting Association
AAAL — American Academy of Arts and Letters
AA&QMG — Assistant Adjutant and Quartermaster-General
AAAS — American Association for the Advancement of Science
AAC — Army Air Corps
AACCA — Associate, Association of Certified and Corporate Accountants (now see ACCA)
AACE — Association for Adult and Continuing Education
AAF — Auxiliary Air Force (now see RAux AF)
AAFCE — Allied Air Forces in Central Europe
AAG — Assistant Adjutant-General
AAI — Associate, Chartered Auctioneers' and Estate Agents' Institute (now (after amalgamation) see ARICS)
AAIL — American Academy and Institute of Arts and Letters (now see AAAL)
AAM — Association of Assistant Mistresses in Secondary Schools
AAMC — Australian Army Medical Corps (now see RAAMC)
A&AEE — Aeroplane and Armament Experimental Establishment
A and SH — Argyll and Sutherland Highlanders
AAPS — Aquatic and Atmospheric Physical Sciences
AAS — American Astronomical Society
AASA — Associate, Australian Society of Accountants (now see FCPA)
AASC — Australian Army Service Corps
AATSE — Australian Academy of Technological Sciences and Engineering
AAUQ — Associate in Accountancy, University of Queensland
AB — Bachelor of Arts (US); able-bodied seaman; airborne
ABA — Amateur Boxing Association; Antiquarian Booksellers' Association; American Bar Association
ABC — Australian Broadcasting Commission; American Broadcasting Companies; Amateur Boxing Club
ABCA — Army Bureau of Current Affairs
ABCC — Association of British Chambers of Commerce
ABCFM — American Board of Commissioners for Foreign Missions
ABI — Association of British Insurers
ABIA — Associate, Bankers' Institute of Australasia
ABINZ — Associate, Bankers' Institute of New Zealand
ABIS — Association of Burglary Insurance Surveyors
ABM — Advisory Board of Ministry
ABNM — American Board of Nuclear Medicine
ABP — Associated British Ports
Abp — Archbishop
ABPsS — Associate, British Psychological Society (now see AFBPsS)
ABRC — Advisory Board for the Research Councils
ABS — Associate, Building Societies' Institute (now see ACBSI)
ABSA — Association for Business Sponsorship of the Arts
ABSI — Associate, Boot and Shoe Institution
ABSM — Associate, Birmingham and Midland Institute School of Music
ABTA — Association of British Travel Agents
ABTAPL — Association of British Theological and Philosophical Libraries
AC — Companion, Order of Australia; Ante Christum (before Christ)
ACA — Associate, Institute of Chartered Accountants
Acad. — Academy

ACARD — Advisory Council for Applied Research and Development
ACAS — Advisory, Conciliation and Arbitration Service; Assistant Chief of the Air Staff
ACBSI — Associate, Chartered Building Societies Institute
ACC — Association of County Councils; Anglican Consultative Council
ACCA — Associate, Chartered Association of Certified Accountants
ACCEL — American College of Cardiology Extended Learning
ACCM — Advisory Council for the Church's Ministry (now see ABM)
ACCS — Associate, Corporation of Secretaries (formerly of Certified Secretaries)
ACDP — Australian Committee of Directors and Principals
ACDS — Assistant Chief of Defence Staff
ACE — Association of Consulting Engineers; Member, Association of Conference Executives
ACF — Army Cadet Force
ACFA — Army Cadet Force Association
ACFAS — Association Canadienne-Française pour l'avancement des sciences
ACFHE — Association of Colleges for Further and Higher Education
ACG — Assistant Chaplain-General
ACGI — Associate, City and Guilds of London Institute
ACGS — Assistant Chief of the General Staff
ACIArb — Associate, Chartered Institute of Arbitrators
ACIB — Associate, Chartered Institute of Bankers
ACII — Associate, Chartered Insurance Institute
ACIS — Associate, Institute of Chartered Secretaries and Administrators (formerly Chartered Institute of Secretaries)
ACIT — Associate, Chartered Institute of Transport
ACLS — American Council of Learned Societies
ACM — Association of Computing Machinery
ACMA — Associate, Chartered Institute of Management Accountants (formerly Institute of Cost and Management Accountants)
ACNS — Assistant Chief of Naval Staff
ACommA — Associate, Society of Commercial Accountants (now see ASCA)
ACORD — Advisory Committee on Research and Development
ACOS — Assistant Chief of Staff
ACOST — Advisory Council on Science and Technology
ACP — Association of Clinical Pathologists; Associate, College of Preceptors; African/Caribbean/Pacific
ACPO — Association of Chief Police Officers
ACRE — Action with Rural Communities in England
ACS — American Chemical Society; Additional Curates Society
ACSEA — Allied Command South East Asia
ACSM — Associate, Camborne School of Mines
ACT — Australian Capital Territory; Australian College of Theology; Associate, College of Technology; Association of Corporate Treasurers
ACTT — Association of Cinematograph, Television and Allied Technicians
ACTU — Australian Council of Trade Unions
ACU — Association of Commonwealth Universities
ACWA — Associate, Institute of Cost and Works Accountants (now see ACMA)
AD — Dame of the Order of Australia; Anno Domini (in the year of the Lord); Air Defence
aD — ausser Dienst
ADAS — Agricultural Development and Advisory Service

ADB	Asian Development Bank; Associate of the Drama Board (Education)
ADB/F	African Development Bank/Fund
ADC	Aide-de-camp
ADCM	Archbishop of Canterbury's Diploma in Church Music
AD Corps	Army Dental Corps (*now* RADC)
ADC(P)	Personal Aide-de-camp to HM The Queen
ADEME	Assistant Director Electrical and Mechanical Engineering
Ad eund	*Ad eundem gradum*; and *see under* aeg
ADFManc	Art and Design Fellow, Manchester
ADFW	Assistant Director of Fortifications and Works
ADGB	Air Defence of Great Britain
ADGMS	Assistant Director-General of Medical Services
ADH	Assistant Director of Hygiene
Adjt	Adjutant
ADJAG	Assistant Deputy Judge Advocate General
ADK	Order of Ahli Darjah Kinabalu
Adm.	Admiral
ADMS	Assistant Director of Medical Services
ADOS	Assistant Director of Ordnance Services
ADP	Automatic Data Processing
ADPA	Associate Diploma of Public Administration
ADS&T	Assistant Director of Supplies and Transport
Adv.	Advisory; Advocate
ADVS	Assistant Director of Veterinary Services
ADWE&M	Assistant Director of Works, Electrical and Mechanical
AE	Air Efficiency Award
AEA	Atomic Energy Authority; Air Efficiency Award (*now see* AE)
AEAF	Allied Expeditionary Air Force
AEC	Agriculture Executive Council; Army Educational Corps (*now see* RAEC); Atomic Energy Commission
AECMA	Association Européenne des Constructeurs de Matériel Aérospatial
AEE	Atomic Energy Establishment
AEEU	Amalgamated Engineering and Electrical Union
AEF	Amalgamated Union of Engineering and Foundry Workers (later AEU, *now see* AEEU); American Expeditionary Forces
aeg	*ad eundem gradum* (to the same degree—of the admission of a graduate of one university to the same degree at another without examination)
AEGIS	Aid for the Elderly in Government Institutions
AEI	Associated Electrical Industries
AEM	Air Efficiency Medal
AER	Army Emergency Reserve
AERE	Atomic Energy Research Establishment (Harwell)
Æt., Ætat.	*Ætatis* (aged)
AEU	Amalgamated Engineering Union (*now see* AEEU)
AF	Admiral of the Fleet
AFA	Amateur Football Alliance
AFAIAA	Associate Fellow, American Institute of Aeronautics and Astronautics
AFASIC	Association for All Speech Impaired Children
AFB	Air Force Base
AFBPsS	Associate Fellow, British Psychological Society
AFC	Air Force Cross; Association Football Club
AfC	Association for Colleges
AFCAI	Associate Fellow, Canadian Aeronautical Institute
AFCEA	Armed Forces Communications and Electronics Association
AFCENT	Allied Forces in Central Europe
AFD	Doctor of Fine Arts (US)
AFDS	Air Fighting Development Squadron
AFHQ	Allied Force Headquarters
AFI	American Film Institute
AFIA	Associate, Federal Institute of Accountants (Australia)
AFIAP	Artiste, Fédération Internationale de l'Art Photographique
AFIAS	Associate Fellow, Institute of Aeronautical Sciences (US) (*now see* AFAIAA)
AFICD	Associate Fellow, Institute of Civil Defence
AFIMA	Associate Fellow, Institute of Mathematics and its Applications
AFM	Air Force Medal
AFNORTH	Allied Forces in Northern Europe
AFOM	Associate, Faculty of Occupational Medicine

AFRAeS	Associate Fellow, Royal Aeronautical Society (*now see* MRAeS)
AFRC	Agricultural and Food Research Council (*now see* BBSRC)
AFV	Armoured Fighting Vehicles
AG	Attorney-General
AGAC	American Guild of Authors and Composers
AGARD	Advisory Group for Aerospace Research and Development
AGC	Adjutant General's Corps
AGH	Australian General Hospital
AGI	Artistes Graphiques Internationaux; Associate, Institute of Certificated Grocers
AGR	Advanced Gas-cooled Reactor
AGRA	Army Group Royal Artillery; Association of Genealogists and Record Agents
AGSM	Associate, Guildhall School of Music and Drama; Australian Graduate School of Management
AHA	Area Health Authority; American Hospitals Association; Associate, Institute of Health Service Administrators (*now see* AHSM)
AHA(T)	Area Health Authority (Teaching)
AHQ	Army Headquarters
AHSM	Associate, Institute of Health Services Management
AH-WC	Associate, Heriot-Watt College, Edinburgh
ai	*ad interim*
AIA	Associate, Institute of Actuaries; American Institute of Architects; Association of International Artists
AIAA	American Institute of Aeronautics and Astronautics
AIAgrE	Associate, Institution of Agricultural Engineers
AIAL	Associate Member, International Institute of Arts and Letters
AIArb	Associate, Institute of Arbitrators (*now see* ACIArb)
AIAS	Associate Surveyor Member, Incorporated Association of Architects and Surveyors
AIB	Associate, Institute of Bankers (*now see* ACIB)
AIBD	Associate, Institute of British Decorators
AIBP	Associate, Institute of British Photographers
AIBScot	Associate, Institute of Bankers in Scotland
AIC	Agricultural Improvement Council; Associate of the Institute of Chemistry (later ARIC, MRIC; *now see* MRSC)
AICA	Associate Member, Commonwealth Institute of Accountants; Association Internationale des Critiques d'Art
AICC	All-India Congress Committee
AICE	Associate, Institution of Civil Engineers
AIChE	American Institute of Chemical Engineers
AICPA	American Institute of Certified Public Accountants
AICS	Associate, Institute of Chartered Shipbrokers
AICTA	Associate, Imperial College of Tropical Agriculture
AID	Agency for International Development (USA)
AIDS	Acquired Immunity Deficiency Syndrome
AIE	Associate, Institute of Education
AIEE	Associate, Institution of Electrical Engineers
AIF	Australian Imperial Forces
AIG	Adjutant-Inspector-General
AIH	Associate, Institute of Housing
AIHort	Associate, Institute of Horticulture
AIIA	Associate, Insurance Institute of America; Associate, Indian Institute of Architects
AIIMR	Associate, Institute of Investment Management and Research
AIInfSc	Associate, Institute of Information Scientists
AIIRA	Associate, International Industrial Relations Association
AIL	Associate, Institute of Linguists
AILA	Associate, Institute of Landscape Architects (*now see* ALI)
AILocoE	Associate, Institute of Locomotive Engineers
AIM	Associate, Institution of Metallurgists (*now see* MIM); Australian Institute of Management
AIMarE	Associate, Institute of Marine Engineers
AIMC	Associate, Institute of Management Consultants
AIME	American Institute of Mechanical Engineers
AIMgt	Associate, Institute of Management
AIMSW	Associate, Institute of Medical Social Workers

AInstM	Associate Member, Institute of Marketing
AInstP	Associate, Institute of Physics
AInstPI	Associate, Institute of Patentees and Inventors
AIP	Association of Independent Producers
AIPR	Associate, Institute of Public Relations
AIProdE	Associate, Institution of Production Engineers
AIQS	Associate Member, Institute of Quantity Surveyors
AIRTE	Associate, Institute of Road Transport Engineers
AIRTO	Association of Independent Research and Technology Organizations
AIS	Associate, Institute of Statisticians (*later* MIS)
AISA	Associate, Incorporated Secretaries' Association
AIStructE	Associate, Institution of Structural Engineers
AITI	Associate, Institute of Translators and Interpreters
AITP	Associate, Institute of Town Planners, India
AJAG	Assistant Judge Advocate General
AJEX	Association of Jewish Ex-Service Men and Women
AK	Knight, Order of Australia; Alaska
AKC	Associate, King's College London
AL	Alabama
ALA	Associate, Library Association; Association of London Authorities
Ala	Alabama (US)
ALAA	Associate, Library Association of Australia
ALAI	Associate, Library Association of Ireland
ALAM	Associate, London Academy of Music and Dramatic Art
ALCD	Associate, London College of Divinity
ALCM	Associate, London College of Music
ALCS	Authors Lending and Copyright Society
ALFSEA	Allied Land Forces South-East Asia
ALI	Argyll Light Infantry; Associate, Landscape Institute
ALICE	Autistic and Language Impaired Children's Education
ALLC	Association for Literary and Linguistic Computing
ALP	Australian Labor Party
ALPSP	Association of Learned and Professional Society Publishers
ALS	Associate, Linnean Society
Alta	Alberta
ALVA	Association of Leading Visitor Attractions
AM	Albert Medal; Member, Order of Australia; Master of Arts (US); Alpes Maritimes
AMA	Association of Metropolitan Authorities; Assistant Masters Association (later AMMA, *now see* ATL); Associate, Museums Association; Australian Medical Association
AMARC	Associated Marine and Related Charities
Amb.	Ambulance; Ambassador
AMBDA	Associate Member, British Dyslexia Association
AMBIM	Associate Member, British Institute of Management (*now see* AIMgt)
AMBritIRE	Associate Member, British Institution of Radio Engineers (*now see* AMIERE)
AMC	Association of Municipal Corporations
AMCST	Associate, Manchester College of Science and Technology
AMCT	Associate, Manchester College of Technology
AME	Association of Municipal Engineers
AMEME	Association of Mining Electrical and Mechanical Engineers
AMet	Associate of Metallurgy
AMF	Australian Military Forces
AMGOT	Allied Military Government of Occupied Territory
AMIAE	Associate Member, Institution of Automobile Engineers
AMIAgrE	Associate Member, Institution of Agricultural Engineers
AMIBF	Associate Member, Institute of British Foundrymen
AMICE	Associate Member, Institution of Civil Engineers (*now see* MICE)
AMIChemE	Associate Member, Institution of Chemical Engineers
AMIE(Aust)	Associate Member, Institution of Engineers, Australia
AMIED	Associate Member, Institution of Engineering Designers
AMIEE	Associate Member, Institution of Electrical Engineers (*now see* MIEE)
AMIE(Ind)	Associate Member, Institution of Engineers, India
AMIERE	Associate Member, Institution of Electronic and Radio Engineers
AMIH	Associate Member, Institute of Housing
AMIMechE	Associate Member, Institution of Mechanical Engineers (*now see* MIMechE)
AMIMinE	Associate Member, Institution of Mining Engineers
AMIMM	Associate Member, Institution of Mining and Metallurgy
AMInstBE	Associate Member, Institution of British Engineers
AMInstCE	Associate Member, Institution of Civil Engineers (*now see* MICE)
AmInstEE	American Institute of Electrical Engineers
AMInstR	Associate Member, Institute of Refrigeration
AMInstT	Associate Member, Institute of Transport (*now see* ACIT)
AMInstTA	Associate Member, Institute of Traffic Administration
AMINucE	Associate Member, Institution of Nuclear Engineers
AMIRSE	Associate Member, Institute of Railway Signalling Engineers
AMIStructE	Associate Member, Institution of Structural Engineers
AMMA	Assistant Masters & Mistresses Association (*now see* ATL)
AMN	Ahli Mangku Negara (Malaysia)
AMP	Advanced Management Program; Air Member for Personnel
AMRINA	Associate Member, Royal Institution of Naval Architects
AMS	Assistant Military Secretary; Army Medical Services
AMSO	Air Member for Supply and Organisation
AMTE	Admiralty Marine Technology Establishment
AMTRI	Advanced Manufacturing Technology Research Institute
ANA	Associate National Academician (America)
ANAF	Arab Non-Arab Friendship
Anat.	Anatomy; Anatomical
ANC	African National Congress
ANECInst	Associate, NE Coast Institution of Engineers and Shipbuilders
ANGAU	Australian New Guinea Administrative Unit
Anon.	Anonymously
ANU	Australian National University
ANZAAS	Australian and New Zealand Association for the Advancement of Science
Anzac	Australian and New Zealand Army Corps
AO	Officer, Order of Australia; Air Officer
AOA	Air Officer in charge of Administration
AOC	Air Officer Commanding
AOC-in-C	Air Officer Commanding-in-Chief
AOD	Army Ordnance Department
AOER	Army Officers Emergency Reserve
APA	American Psychiatric Association
APACS	Association of Payment and Clearing Systems
APCK	Association for Promoting Christian Knowledge, Church of Ireland
APD	Army Pay Department
APEX	Association of Professional, Executive, Clerical and Computer Staff
APHA	American Public Health Association
APIS	Army Photographic Intelligence Service
APM	Assistant Provost Marshal
APMI	Associate, Pensions Management Institute
APR	Accredited Public Relations Practitioner
APS	Aborigines Protection Society; American Physical Society
APsSI	Associate, Psychological Society of Ireland
APSW	Association of Psychiatric Social Workers
APT&C	Administrative, Professional, Technical and Clerical
APTC	Army Physical Training Corps
AQ	Administration and Quartering
AQMG	Assistant Quartermaster-General
AR	Associated Rediffusion (Television); Arkansas
ARA	Associate, Royal Academy
ARACI	Associate, Royal Australian Chemical Institute
ARAD	Associate, Royal Academy of Dancing
ARAeS	Associate, Royal Aeronautical Society
ARAgS	Associate, Royal Agricultural Societies (*ie* of England, Scotland and Wales)
ARAIA	Associate, Royal Australian Institute of Architects
ARAM	Associate, Royal Academy of Music
ARAS	Associate, Royal Astronomical Society
ARBA	Associate, Royal Society of British Artists

ARBC	Associate, Royal British Colonial Society of Artists
ARBS	Associate, Royal Society of British Sculptors
ARC	Architects' Registration Council; Agricultural Research Council (later AFRC); Aeronautical Research Council
ARCA	Associate, Royal College of Art; Associate, Royal Canadian Academy
ARCamA	Associate, Royal Cambrian Academy of Art
ARCE	Academical Rank of Civil Engineer
ARCIC	Anglican-Roman Catholic International Commission
ARCM	Associate, Royal College of Music
ARCO	Associate, Royal College of Organists
ARCO(CHM)	Associate, Royal College of Organists with Diploma in Choir Training
ARCPsych	Associate Member, Royal College of Psychiatrists
ARCS	Associate, Royal College of Science
ARCST	Associate, Royal College of Science and Technology (Glasgow)
ARCUK	Architects' Registration Council of the United Kingdom
ARCVS	Associate, Royal College of Veterinary Surgeons
ARE	Associate, Royal Society of Painter-Printmakers (*formerly* of Painter-Etchers and Engravers); Arab Republic of Egypt; Admiralty Research Establishment
AREINZ	Associate, Real Estate Institute, New Zealand
ARELS	Association of Recognised English Language Schools
ARIAS	Associate, Royal Incorporation of Architects in Scotland
ARIBA	Associate, Royal Institute of British Architects (*now see* RIBA)
ARIC	Associate, Royal Institute of Chemistry (later MRIC; *now see* MRSC)
ARICS	Professional Associate, Royal Institution of Chartered Surveyors
ARINA	Associate, Royal Institution of Naval Architects
Ark	Arkansas (US)
ARLT	Association for the Reform of Latin Teaching
ARMS	Associate, Royal Society of Miniature Painters
ARP	Air Raid Precautions
ARPS	Associate, Royal Photographic Society
ARR	Association of Radiation Research
ARRC	Associate, Royal Red Cross
ARSA	Associate, Royal Scottish Academy
ARSC	Association of Recorded Sound Collections
ARSCM	Associate, Royal School of Church Music
ARSM	Associate, Royal School of Mines
ARTC	Associate, Royal Technical College (Glasgow) (*now see* ARCST)
ARVIA	Associate, Royal Victoria Institute of Architects
ARWA	Associate, Royal West of England Academy
ARWS	Associate, Royal Society of Painters in Water-Colours
AS	Anglo-Saxon
ASA	Associate Member, Society of Actuaries; Associate of Society of Actuaries (US); Australian Society of Accountants; Army Sailing Association; Advertising Standards Authority
ASAA	Associate, Society of Incorporated Accountants and Auditors
ASAI	Associate, Society of Architectural Illustrators
ASAM	Associate, Society of Art Masters
AS&TS of SA	Associated Scientific and Technical Societies of South Africa
ASBAH	Association for Spina Bifida and Hydrocephalus
ASC	Administrative Staff College, Henley
ASCA	Associate, Society of Company and Commercial Accountants
ASCAB	Armed Services Consultant Approval Board
ASCAP	American Society of Composers, Authors and Publishers
ASCE	American Society of Civil Engineers
ASCHB	Association for Study of Conservation of Historic Buildings
AScW	Association of Scientific Workers (*now see* ASTMS)
ASD	Armament Supply Department
ASE	Amalgamated Society of Engineers (later AUEW, then AEU; *now see* AEEU); Association for Science Education
ASEAN	Association of South East Asian Nations
ASH	Action on Smoking and Health
ASIAD	Associate, Society of Industrial Artists and Designers

ASIA(Ed)	Associate, Society of Industrial Artists (Education)
ASLE	American Society of Lubrication Engineers
ASLEF	Associated Society of Locomotive Engineers and Firemen
ASLIB or Aslib	Association for Information Management (*formerly* Association of Special Libraries and Information Bureaux)
ASM	Association of Senior Members
ASME	American Society of Mechanical Engineers; Association for the Study of Medical Education
ASO	Air Staff Officer
ASSC	Accounting Standards Steering Committee
ASSET	Association of Supervisory Staffs, Executives and Technicians (*now see* ASTMS)
AssocISI	Associate, Iron and Steel Institute
AssocMCT	Associateship of Manchester College of Technology
AssocMIAeE	Associate Member, Institution of Aeronautical Engineers
AssocRINA	Associate, Royal Institution of Naval Architects
AssocSc	Associate in Science
Asst	Assistant
ASTA	Association of Short Circuit Testing Authorities
ASTC	Administrative Service Training Course
ASTMS	Association of Scientific, Technical and Managerial Staffs (now part of MSF)
ASVU	Army Security Vetting Unit
ASWDU	Air Sea Warfare Development Unit
ASWE	Admiralty Surface Weapons Establishment
ATA	Air Transport Auxiliary
ATAE	Association of Tutors in Adult Education
ATAF	Allied Tactical Air Force
ATC	Air Training Corps; Art Teacher's Certificate
ATCDE	Association of Teachers in Colleges and Departments of Education (*now see* NATFHE)
ATCL	Associate, Trinity College of Music, London
ATD	Art Teacher's Diploma
ATI	Associate, Textile Institute
ATII	Associate Member, Chartered Institute (*formerly* Incorporated Institute, then Institute) of Taxation
ATL	Association of Teachers and Lecturers
ato	Ammunition Technical Officer
ATPL (A)or(H)	Airline Transport Pilot's Licence (Aeroplanes), or (Helicopters)
ATS	Auxiliary Territorial Service (*now see* WRAC)
ATTI	Association of Teachers in Technical Institutions (*now see* NATFHE)
ATV	Association TeleVision
AUA	American Urological Association
AUCAS	Association of University Clinical Academic Staff
AUEW	Amalgamated Union of Engineering Workers (later AEU, *now see* AEEU)
AUS	Army of the United States
AUT	Association of University Teachers
AVCC	Australian Vice-Chancellors' Committee
AVCM	Associate, Victoria College of Music
AVD	Army Veterinary Department
AVLA	Audio Visual Language Association
AVR	Army Volunteer Reserve
AWA	Anglian Water Authority
AWO	Association of Water Officers (*now see* IWO)
AWRE	Atomic Weapons Research Establishment
aws	Graduate of Air Warfare Course
AZ	Arizona

B

b	born; brother
BA	Bachelor of Arts
BAA	British Airports Authority
BAAB	British Amateur Athletic Board
BAAL	British Association for Applied Linguistics
BAAS	British Association for the Advancement of Science
BAB	British Airways Board

BAC	British Aircraft Corporation
BACM	British Association of Colliery Management
BACUP	British Association of Cancer United Patients
BAe	British Aerospace
BAED	Bachelor of Arts in Environmental Design
B&FBS	British and Foreign Bible Society
BAFO	British Air Forces of Occupation
BAFPA	British Association of Fitness Promotion Agencies
BAFTA	British Academy of Film and Television Arts
BAG	Business Art Galleries
BAgrSc	Bachelor of Agricultural Science
BAI	*Baccalarius in Arte Ingeniaria* (Bachelor of Engineering)
BAIE	British Association of Industrial Editors
BALPA	British Air Line Pilots' Association
BAO	Bachelor of Art of Obstetrics
BAOMS	British Association of Oral and Maxillo-Facial Surgeons
BAOR	British Army of the Rhine (formerly *on* the Rhine)
BAOS	British Association of Oral Surgeons (*now see* BAOMS)
BAppSc(MT)	Bachelor of Applied Science (Medical Technology)
BARB	Broadcasters' Audience Research Board
BARC	British Automobile Racing Club
BArch	Bachelor of Architecture
Bart	Baronet
BAS	Bachelor in Agricultural Science
BASc	Bachelor of Applied Science
BASCA	British Academy of Songwriters, Composers and Authors
BASEEFA	British Approvals Service for Electrical Equipment in Flammable Atmospheres
BASW	British Association of Social Workers
Batt.	Battery
BBA	British Bankers' Association; Bachelor of Business Administration
BB&CIRly	Bombay, Baroda and Central India Railway
BBB of C	British Boxing Board of Control
BBC	British Broadcasting Corporation
BBFC	British Board of Film Classification
BBM	Bintang Bakti Masharakat (Public Service Star) (Singapore)
BBS	Bachelor of Business Studies
BBSRC	Biotechnology and Biosciences Research Council
BC	Before Christ; British Columbia; Borough Council
BCAR	British Civil Airworthiness Requirements
BCC	British Council of Churches (*now see* CCBI)
BCE	Bachelor of Civil Engineering; Before the Christian Era
BCh or BChir	Bachelor of Surgery
BChD	Bachelor of Dental Surgery
BCIA	British Clothing Industries Association
BCL	Bachelor of Civil Law
BCMF	British Ceramic Manufacturers' Federation
BCMS	Bible Churchmen's Missionary Society
BCOF	British Commonwealth Occupation Force
BCom or BComm	Bachelor of Commerce
BComSc	Bachelor of Commercial Science
BCPC	British Crop Protection Council
BCS	Bengal Civil Service; British Computer Society
BCSA	British Constructional Steelwork Association
BCURA	British Coal Utilization Research Association
BCYC	British Corinthian Yacht Club
BD	Bachelor of Divinity
Bd	Board
BDA	British Dental Association; British Deaf Association; British Dyslexia Association
Bde	Brigade
BDQ	Bachelor of Divinity Qualifying
BDS	Bachelor of Dental Surgery
BDSc	Bachelor of Dental Science
BE	Bachelor of Engineering; British Element
BEA	British East Africa; British European Airways; British Epilepsy Association
BEAMA	Federation of British Electrotechnical and Allied Manufacturers' Associations (formerly British Electrical and Allied Manufacturers' Association)
BE&A	Bachelor of Engineering and Architecture (Malta)
BEAS	British Educational Administration Society
BEC	Business Education Council (*now see* BTEC)
BEc	Bachelor of Economics
BECTU	Broadcasting, Entertainment, Cinematograph and Theatre Union
BEd	Bachelor of Education
Beds	Bedfordshire
BEE	Bachelor of Electrical Engineering
BEF	British Expeditionary Force; British Equestrian Federation
BEM	British Empire Medal
BEMAS	British Education Management and Administration Society
BEME	Brigade Electrical and Mechanical Engineer
BEng	Bachelor of Engineering
BEO	Base Engineer Officer
Berks	Berkshire
BESO	British Executive Service Overseas
BEVA	British Equine Veterinary Association
BFI	British Film Institute
BFMIRA	British Food Manufacturing Industries Research Association
BFPO	British Forces Post Office
BFSS	British Field Sports Society
BFWG	British Federation of Women Graduates
BGS	Brigadier General Staff
BHA	British Hospitality Association
Bhd	Berhad
BHF	British Heart Foundation
BHRA	British Hydromechanics Research Association
BHRCA	British Hotels, Restaurants and Caterers' Association (*now see* BHA)
BHS	British Horse Society
BI	British Invisibles
BIBA	British Insurance Brokers' Association (*now see* BIIBA)
BIBRA	British Industrial Biological Research Association
BICC	British Insulated Callender's Cables
BICERA	British Internal Combustion Engine Research Association (*now see* BICERI)
BICERI	British Internal Combustion Engine Research Institute
BICSc	British Institute of Cleaning Science
BIEC	British Invisible Exports Council (*now see* BI)
BIEE	British Institute of Energy Economics
BIF	British Industries Fair
BIFU	Banking Insurance and Finance Union
BIIBA	British Insurance & Investment Brokers' Association
BIM	British Institute of Management
BIR	British Institute of Radiology
BIS	Bank for International Settlements
BISF	British Iron and Steel Federation
BISFA	British Industrial and Scientific Film Association
BISPA	British Independent Steel Producers Association
BISRA	British Iron and Steel Research Association
BITC	Business in the Community
BJ	Bachelor of Journalism
BJSM	British Joint Services Mission
BKSTS	British Kinematograph, Sound and Television Society
BL	Bachelor of Law; British Library
BLA	British Liberation Army
BLDSA	British Long Distance Swimming Association
BLE	Brotherhood of Locomotive Engineers; Bachelor of Land Economy
BLegS	Bachelor of Legal Studies
BLESMA	British Limbless Ex-Servicemen's Association
BLitt	Bachelor of Letters
BM	British Museum; Bachelor of Medicine; Brigade Major; British Monomark
BMA	British Medical Association
BMedSci	Bachelor of Medical Science
BMEO	British Middle East Office
BMet	Bachelor of Metallurgy
BMEWS	Ballistic Missile Early Warning System
BMG	British Military Government
BMH	British Military Hospital

BMilSc	Bachelor of Military Science
BMJ	British Medical Journal
BMM	British Military Mission
BMR	Bureau of Mineral Resources
BMRA	Brigade Major Royal Artillery
Bn	Battalion
BNAF	British North Africa Force
BNC	Brasenose College
BNEC	British National Export Council
BNF	British National Formulary
BNFL	British Nuclear Fuels Ltd
BNOC	British National Oil Corporation; British National Opera Company
BNP	Banque Nationale de Paris
BNSC	British National Space Centre
BNSc	Bachelor of Nursing Science
BOAC	British Overseas Airways Corporation
BomCS	Bombay Civil Service
BomSC	Bombay Staff Corps
BoT	Board of Trade
Bot.	Botany; Botanical
BOTB	British Overseas Trade Board
BOU	British Ornithologists' Union
Bp	Bishop
BPA	British Paediatric Association
BPG	Broadcasting Press Guild
BPharm	Bachelor of Pharmacy
BPIF	British Printing Industries Federation
BPMF	British Postgraduate Medical Federation
BPsS	British Psychological Society
BR	British Rail
Br.	Branch
BRA	Brigadier Royal Artillery; British Rheumatism & Arthritis Association
BRB	British Railways Board
BRCS	British Red Cross Society
BRE	Building Research Establishment
Brig.	Brigadier
BritIRE	British Institution of Radio Engineers (*now see* IERE)
BRNC	Britannia Royal Naval College
BRS	British Road Services
BRurSc	Bachelor of Rural Science
BS	Bachelor of Surgery; Bachelor of Science; British Standard
BSA	Bachelor of Scientific Agriculture; Birmingham Small Arms; Building Societies' Association
BSAA	British South American Airways
BSAP	British South Africa Police
BSC	British Steel Corporation; Bengal Staff Corps
BSc	Bachelor of Science
BScA, BScAgr	Bachelor of Science in Agriculture
BSc(Dent)	Bachelor of Science in Dentistry
BSc (Est. Man.)	Bachelor of Science in Estate Management
BScN	Bachelor of Science in Nursing
BScSoc	Bachelor of Social Sciences
BSE	Bachelor of Science in Engineering (US)
BSES	British Schools Exploring Society
BSF	British Salonica Force
BSFA	British Science Fiction Association
BSI	British Standards Institution
BSIA	British Security Industry Association
BSJA	British Show Jumping Association
BSME	Bachelor of Science in Mechanical Engineering; British Society of Magazine Editors
BSN	Bachelor of Science in Nursing
BSNS	Bachelor of Naval Science
BSocSc	Bachelor of Social Science
BSRA	British Ship Research Association
BSS	Bachelor of Science (Social Science)
BST	Bachelor of Sacred Theology
BSurv	Bachelor of Surveying
BT	Bachelor of Teaching; British Telecommunications
Bt	Baronet; Brevet
BTA	British Tourist Authority (*formerly* British Travel Association)
BTC	British Transport Commission

BTCV	British Trust for Conservation Volunteers
BTDB	British Transport Docks Board (*now see* ABP)
BTEC	Business and Technology (*formerly* Technician) Education Council
BTh	Bachelor of Theology
BTP	Bachelor of Town Planning
Btss	Baroness
Bty	Battery
BUAS	British Universities Association of Slavists
Bucks	Buckinghamshire
BUGB	Baptist Union of Great Britain
BUPA	British United Provident Association
BURA	British Urban Regeneration Association
BV	Besloten Vennootschap
BVA	British Veterinary Association
BVetMed	Bachelor of Veterinary Medicine
BVI	British Virgin Islands
BVM	Blessed Virgin Mary
BVMS	Bachelor of Veterinary Medicine and Surgery
BVSc	Bachelor of Veterinary Science
BWI	British West Indies
BWM	British War Medal

C

C	Conservative: 100
c	child; cousin; *circa* (about)
CA	Central America; County Alderman; Chartered Accountant (Scotland and Canada); California
CAA	Civil Aviation Authority
CAABU	Council for the Advancement of Arab and British Understanding
CAAV	(Member of) Central Association of Agricultural Valuers
CAB	Citizens' Advice Bureau; Centre for Agricultural and Biosciences (*formerly* Commonwealth Agricultural Bureau)
CACTM	Central Advisory Council of Training for the Ministry (later ACCM; *now see* ABM)
CAER	Conservative Action for Electoral Reform
CAFOD	Catholic Fund for Overseas Development
CALE	Canadian Army Liaison Executive
Calif	California (US)
CAM	Communications, Advertising and Marketing
Cambs	Cambridgeshire
CAMC	Canadian Army Medical Corps
CAMRA	Campaign for Real Ale
CAMS	Certificate of Advanced Musical Study
CAMW	Central Association for Mental Welfare
C&G	City and Guilds of London Institute
Cantab	*Cantabrigiensis* (of Cambridge)
Cantuar	*Cantuariensis* (of Canterbury)
CARD	Campaign against Racial Discrimination
CARE	Cottage and Rural Enterprises
CARICOM	Caribbean Community
CARIFTA	Caribbean Free Trade Area (*now see* CARICOM)
CAS	Chief of the Air Staff
CASI	Canadian Aeronautics and Space Institute
CAT	College of Advanced Technology; Countryside Around Towns
CATE	Council for the Accreditation of Teacher Education
Cav.	Cavalry
CAWU	Clerical and Administrative Workers' Union (later APEX)
CB	Companion, Order of the Bath; County Borough
CBC	County Borough Council
CBCO	Central Board for Conscientious Objectors
CBE	Commander, Order of the British Empire
CBI	Confederation of British Industry
CBIM	Companion, British Institute of Management (*now see* CIMgt)
CBiol	Chartered Biologist
CBNS	Commander British Navy Staff
CBS	Columbia Broadcasting System; Confraternity of the Blessed Sacrament
CBSA	Clay Bird Shooting Association
CBSI	Chartered Building Societies Institute (*now see* CIB)

CBSO	City of Birmingham Symphony Orchestra
CC	Companion, Order of Canada; City Council; County Council; Cricket Club; Cycling Club, County Court
CCAB	Consultative Committee of Accountancy Bodies
CCAHC	Central Council for Agricultural and Horticultural Co-operation
CCBE	Commission Consultative des Barreaux de la Communauté Européenne
CCBI	Council of Churches for Britain and Ireland
CCC	Corpus Christi College; Central Criminal Court; County Cricket Club
CCE	Chartered Civil Engineer
CCF	Combined Cadet Force
CCFM	Combined Cadet Forces Medal
CCG	Control Commission Germany
CCH	Cacique's Crown of Honour, Order of Service of Guyana
CChem	Chartered Chemist
CCHMS	Central Committee for Hospital Medical Services
CCIA	Commission of Churches on International Affairs
CCIS	Command Control Information System
CCJ	Council of Christians and Jews
CCPR	Central Council of Physical Recreation
CCRA	Commander Corps of Royal Artillery
CCRE	Commander Corps of Royal Engineers
CCREME	Commander Corps of Royal Electrical and Mechanical Engineers
CCRSigs	Commander Corps of Royal Signals
CCS	Casualty Clearing Station; Ceylon Civil Service; Countryside Commission for Scotland
CCSU	Council of Civil Service Unions
CCTA	Commission de Coopération Technique pour l'Afrique
CCTS	Combat Crew Training Squadron
CD	Canadian Forces Decoration; Commander, Order of Distinction (Jamaica); Civil Defence; Compact Disc
CDA	Co-operative Development Agency
CDEE	Chemical Defence Experimental Establishment
CDipAF	Certified Diploma in Accounting and Finance
Cdo	Commando
CDRA	Committee of Directors of Research Associations
Cdre	Commodore
CDS	Chief of the Defence Staff
CDU	Christlich-Demokratische Union
CE	Civil Engineer
CEA	Central Electricity Authority
CEC	Commission of the European Communities
CECD	Confédération Européenne du Commerce de Détail
CECG	Consumers in European Community Group
CEDEP	Centre Européen d'Education Permanente
CEE	Communauté Economique Européenne
CEED	Centre for Economic and Environmental Development
CEF	Canadian Expeditionary Force
CEFIC	Conseil Européen des Fédérations de l'Industrie Chimique
CEGB	Central Electricity Generating Board
CEI	Council of Engineering Institutions
CEIR	Corporation for Economic and Industrial Research
CEM	Council of European Municipalities (now see CEMR)
CEMA	Council for the Encouragement of Music and Arts
CEMR	Council of European Municipalities and Regions
CEMS	Church of England Men's Society
CEN	Comité Européen de Normalisation
CENELEC	European Committee for Electrotechnical Standardization
CEng	Chartered Engineer
Cento	Central Treaty Organisation
CEPT	Conférence Européenne des Postes et des Télécommunications
CERL	Central Electricity Research Laboratories
CERN	Organisation (formerly Centre) Européenne pour la Recherche Nucléaire
CERT	Charities Effectiveness Review Trust
Cert Ed	Certificate of Education
CertITP	Certificate of International Teachers' Program (Harvard)
CEST	Centre for Exploitation of Science and Technology
CET	Council for Educational Technology
CETS	Church of England Temperance Society
CF	Chaplain to the Forces

CFA	Canadian Field Artillery
CFE	Central Fighter Establishment
CFM	Cadet Forces Medal
CFR	Commander, Order of the Federal Republic of Nigeria
CFS	Central Flying School
CGA	Community of the Glorious Ascension; Country Gentlemen's Association
CGeol	Chartered Geologist
CGH	Order of the Golden Heart of Kenya (1st class)
CGIA	Insignia Award of City and Guilds of London Institute (now see FCGI)
CGLI	City and Guilds of London Institute (now see C&G)
CGM	Conspicuous Gallantry Medal
CGRM	Commandant-General Royal Marines
CGS	Chief of the General Staff
CH	Companion of Honour
Chanc.	Chancellor; Chancery
Chap.	Chaplain
ChapStJ	Chaplain, Order of St John of Jerusalem (now see ChStJ)
CHAR	Campaign for the Homeless and Rootless
CHB	Companion of Honour of Barbados
ChB	Bachelor of Surgery
CHC	Community Health Council
Ch.Ch.	Christ Church
Ch.Coll.	Christ's College
CHE	Campaign for Homosexual Equality
ChLJ	Chaplain, Order of St Lazarus of Jerusalem
CHM	Chevalier of Honour and Merit (Haiti)
(CHM)	See under ARCO(CHM), FRCO(CHM)
ChM	Master of Surgery
Chm.	Chairman or Chairwoman
CHN	Community of the Holy Name
CHSC	Central Health Services Council
ChStJ	Chaplain, Most Venerable Order of the Hospital of St John of Jerusalem
CI	Imperial Order of the Crown of India; Channel Islands
CIA	Chemical Industries Association; Central Intelligence Agency
CIAD	Central Institute of Art and Design
CIAgrE	Companion, Institution of Agricultural Engineers
CIAL	Corresponding Member of the International Institute of Arts and Letters
CIArb	Chartered Institute of Arbitrators
CIB	Chartered Institute of Bankers
CIBS	Chartered Institution of Building Services (now see CIBSE)
CIBSE	Chartered Institution of Building Services Engineers
CIC	Chemical Institute of Canada
CICB	Criminal Injuries Compensation Board
CICHE	Committee for International Co-operation in Higher Education
CICI	Confederation of Information Communication Industries
CID	Criminal Investigation Department
CIDEC	Conseil International pour le Développement du Cuivre
CIE	Companion, Order of the Indian Empire; Confédération Internationale des Etudiants
CIEx	Companion, Institute of Export
CIFRS	Comité International de la Rayonne et des Fibres Synthétiques
CIGasE	Companion, Institution of Gas Engineers
CIGRE	Conférence Internationale des Grands Réseaux Electriques
CIGS	Chief of the Imperial General Staff (now see CGS)
CIIA	Canadian Institute of International Affairs
CIL	Corpus inscriptionum latinarum
CIM	China Inland Mission
CIMA	Chartered Institute of Management Accountants
CIMarE	Companion, Institute of Marine Engineers
CIMEMME	Companion, Institution of Mining Electrical and Mining Mechanical Engineers
CIMgt	Companion, Institute of Management
CIMGTechE	Companion, Institution of Mechanical and General Technician Engineers
C-in-C	Commander-in-Chief
CINCHAN	Allied Commander-in-Chief Channel
CIOB	Chartered Institute of Building

CIPD	Companion, Institute of Personnel and Development
CIPFA	Chartered Institute of Public Finance and Accountancy
CIPL	Comité International Permanent des Linguistes
CIPM	Companion, Institute of Personnel Management (*now see* CIPD)
CIR	Commission on Industrial Relations
CIRES	Co-operative Institute for Research in Environmental Sciences
CIRIA	Construction Industry Research and Information Association
CIRP	Collège Internationale pour Recherche et Production
CIS	Institute of Chartered Secretaries and Administrators (*formerly* Chartered Institute of Secretaries); Command Control Communications and Information Systems; Commonwealth of Independent States
CISAC	Confédération Internationale des Sociétés d'Auteurs et Compositeurs; Centre for International Security and Arms Control
CIT	Chartered Institute of Transport; California Institute of Technology
CITB	Construction Industry Training Board
CIU	Club and Institute Union
CIV	City Imperial Volunteers
CJ	Chief Justice
CJC	Companions of Jesus Christ
CJM	Congregation of Jesus and Mary (Eudist Fathers)
CL	Commander, Order of Leopold
cl	*cum laude*
Cl.	Class
CLA	Country Landowners' Association
CLIC	Cancer and Leukemia in Children
CLIP	Common Law Institute of Intellectual Property
CLit	Companion of Literature (Royal Society of Literature Award)
CLJ	Commander, Order of St Lazarus of Jerusalem
CLP	Constituency Labour Party
CLRAE	Congress (*formerly* Conference) of Local and Regional Authorities of Europe
CLY	City of London Yeomanry
CM	Member, Order of Canada; Congregation of the Mission (Vincentians); Master in Surgery; Certificated Master; Canadian Militia
CMA	Canadian Medical Association; Cost and Management Accountant (NZ)
CMAC	Catholic Marriage Advisory Council
CMath	Chartered Mathematician
CMB	Central Midwives' Board
CMet	Chartered Meteorologist
CMF	Commonwealth Military Forces; Central Mediterranean Force
CMG	Companion, Order of St Michael and St George
CMLJ	Commander of Merit, Order of St Lazarus of Jerusalem
CMM	Commander, Order of Military Merit (Canada)
CMO	Chief Medical Officer
CMP	Corps of Military Police (*now see* CRMP)
CMS	Church Mission (*formerly* Church Missionary) Society; Certificate in Management Studies
CMT	Chaconia Medal of Trinidad
CNAA	Council for National Academic Awards
CND	Campaign for Nuclear Disarmament
CNI	Companion, Nautical Institute
CNO	Chief of Naval Operations
CNR	Canadian National Railways
CNRS	Centre National de la Recherche Scientifique
CO	Commanding Officer; Commonwealth Office (after Aug. 1966) (*now see* FCO); Colonial Office (before Aug. 1966); Conscientious Objector; Colorado
Co.	County; Company
C of E	Church of England
C of S	Chief of Staff; Church of Scotland
Coal.L or Co.L	Coalition Liberal
Coal.U or Co.U	Coalition Unionist
CODEST	Committee for the Development of European Science and Technology
COHSE	Confederation of Health Service Employees
COI	Central Office of Information
CoID	Council of Industrial Design (*now* Design Council)
Col	Colonel
Coll.	College; Collegiate
Colo	Colorado (US)
Col.-Sergt	Colour-Sergeant
Com	Communist
Comd	Command
Comdg	Commanding
Comdr	Commander
Comdt	Commandant
COMEC	Council of the Military Education Committees of the Universities of the UK
COMET	Committee for Middle East Trade
Commn	Commission
Commnd	Commissioned
CompAMEME	Companion, Association of Mining Electrical and Mechanical Engineers
CompICE	Companion, Institution of Civil Engineers
CompIEE	Companion, Institution of Electrical Engineers
CompIERE	Companion, Institution of Electronic and Radio Engineers
CompIGasE	Companion, Institution of Gas Engineers
CompIMechE	Companion, Institution of Mechanical Engineers
CompIWES	Companion, Institution of Water Engineers and Scientists
CompOR	Companion, Operational Research Society
CompTI	Companion of the Textile Institute
Comr	Commissioner
Comy-Gen.	Commissary-General
CON	Commander, Order of the Niger
Conn	Connecticut (US)
Const.	Constitutional
Co-op.	Co-operative
COPA	Comité des Organisations Professionels Agricoles de la CEE
COPEC	Conference of Politics, Economics and Christianity
COPUS	Committee on the Public Understanding of Science
Corp.	Corporation; Corporal
Corresp. Mem.	Corresponding Member
COS	Chief of Staff; Charity Organization Society
COSA	Colliery Officials and Staffs Association
CoSIRA	Council for Small Industries in Rural Areas
COSLA	Convention of Scottish Local Authorities
COSPAR	Committee on Space Research
COSSAC	Chief of Staff to Supreme Allied Commander
COTC	Canadian Officers' Training Corps
CP	Central Provinces; Cape Province; Congregation of the Passion
CPA	Commonwealth Parliamentary Association; Chartered Patent Agent; Certified Public Accountant (Canada) (*now see* CA)
CPAG	Child Poverty Action Group
CPAS	Church Pastoral Aid Society
CPC	Conservative Political Centre
CPEng	Chartered Professional Engineer (of Institution of Engineers of Australia)
CPhys	Chartered Physicist
CPL	Chief Personnel and Logistics
CPM	Colonial Police Medal
CPR	Canadian Pacific Railway
CPRE	Council for the Protection of Rural England
CPRW	Campaign for the Protection of Rural Wales
CPS	Crown Prosecution Service
CPSA	Civil and Public Services Association
CPSU	Communist Party of the Soviet Union
CPsychol	Chartered Psychologist
CPU	Commonwealth Press Union
CQSW	Certificate of Qualification in Social Work
CR	Community of the Resurrection
cr	created or creation
CRA	Commandor, Royal Artillery
CRAC	Careers Research and Advisory Centre
CRAeS	Companion, Royal Aeronautical Society
CRAG	Clinical Resources and Audit Group
CRASC	Commander, Royal Army Service Corps
CRC	Cancer Research Campaign; Community Relations Council
CRCP(C)	Certificant, Royal College of Physicians of Canada

CRE	Commander, Royal Engineers; Commission for Racial Equality; Commercial Relations and Exports	**DAAG**	Deputy Assistant Adjutant-General
Cres.	Crescent	**DA&QMG**	Deputy Adjutant and Quartermaster-General
CRMP	Corps of Royal Military Police	**DAC**	Development Assistance Committee; Diocesan Advisory Committee
CRNCM	Companion, Royal Northern College of Music		
CRO	Commonwealth Relations Office (*now see* FCO)	**DACG**	Deputy Assistant Chaplain-General
CS	Civil Service; Clerk to the Signet	**DAD**	Deputy Assistant Director
CSA	Confederate States of America	**DAdmin**	Doctor of Administration
CSAB	Civil Service Appeal Board	**DADMS**	Deputy Assistant Director of Medical Services
CSB	Bachelor of Christian Science	**DADOS**	Deputy Assistant Director of Ordnance Services
CSC	Conspicuous Service Cross; Congregation of the Holy Cross	**DADQ**	Deputy Assistant Director of Quartering
		DADST	Deputy Assistant Director of Supplies and Transport
CSCA	Civil Service Clerical Association (*now see* CPSA)	**DAG**	Deputy Adjutant-General
CSCE	Conference on Security and Co-operation in Europe	**DAgr**	Doctor of Agriculture
CSD	Civil Service Department; Co-operative Secretaries Diploma; Chartered Society of Designers	**DAgrFor**	Doctor of Agriculture and Forestry
		DAMS	Deputy Assistant Military Secretary
CSDE	Central Servicing Development Establishment	**D&AD**	Designers and Art Directors Association
CSEU	Confederation of Shipbuilding and Engineering Unions	**DAppSc**	Doctor of Applied Science
CSG	Companion, Order of the Star of Ghana; Company of the Servants of God	**DAQMG**	Deputy Assistant Quartermaster-General
		DArch	Doctor of Architecture
CSI	Companion, Order of the Star of India	**DArt**	Doctor of Art
CSIR	Commonwealth Council for Scientific and Industrial Research (*now see* CSIRO)	**DArts**	Doctor of Arts
		DASc	Doctor in Agricultural Sciences
CSIRO	Commonwealth Scientific and Industrial Research Organization (Australia)	**DATA**	Draughtsmen's and Allied Technicians' Association (later AUEW(TASS))
CSO	Chief Scientific Officer; Chief Signal Officer; Chief Staff Officer; Central Statistical Office	**DATEC**	Art and Design Committee, Technician Education Council
CSP	Chartered Society of Physiotherapists; Civil Service of Pakistan	**DBA**	Doctor of Business Administration
		DBE	Dame Commander, Order of the British Empire
CSS	Companion, Star of Sarawak; Council for Science and Society	**DC**	District Council; District of Columbia (US)
		DCAe	Diploma of College of Aeronautics
CSSB	Civil Service Selection Board	**DCAS**	Deputy Chief of the Air Staff
CSSp	Holy Ghost Father	**DCB**	Dame Commander, Order of the Bath
CSSR	Congregation of the Most Holy Redeemer (Redemptorist Order)	**DCC**	Diploma of Chelsea College
		DCCH	Diploma in Community Child Health
CStat	Chartered Statistician	**DCDS**	Deputy Chief of Defence Staff
CSTI	Council of Science and Technology Institutes	**DCE**	Diploma of a College of Education
CStJ	Commander, Most Venerable Order of the Hospital of St John of Jerusalem	**DCG**	Deputy Chaplain-General
		DCGRM	Department of the Commandant General Royal Marines
CSU	Christlich-Soziale Union in Bayern		
CSV	Community Service Volunteers	**DCGS**	Deputy Chief of the General Staff
CSW	Certificate in Social Work	**DCh**	Doctor of Surgery
CT	Connecticut	**DCH**	Diploma in Child Health
CTA	Chaplain Territorial Army	**DCIGS**	Deputy Chief of the Imperial General Staff (*now see* DCGS)
CTB	College of Teachers of the Blind		
CTC	Cyclists' Touring Club; Commando Training Centre; City Training College	**DCL**	Doctor of Civil Law
		DCLI	Duke of Cornwall's Light Infantry
CText	Chartered Textile Technologist	**DCLJ**	Dame Commander, Order of St Lazarus of Jerusalem
CTR(Harwell)	Controlled Thermonuclear Research	**DCM**	Distinguished Conduct Medal
CU	Cambridge University	**DCMG**	Dame Commander, Order of St Michael and St George
CUAC	Cambridge University Athletic Club	**DCMHE**	Diploma of Contents and Methods in Health Education
CUAFC	Cambridge University Association Football Club	**DCnL**	Doctor of Canon Law
CUBC	Cambridge University Boat Club	**DCO**	Duke of Cambridge's Own
CUCC	Cambridge University Cricket Club	**DComm**	Doctor of Commerce
CUF	Common University Fund	**DCP**	Diploma in Clinical Pathology; Diploma in Conservation of Paintings
CUHC	Cambridge University Hockey Club		
CUMS	Cambridge University Musical Society	**DCS**	Deputy Chief of Staff; Doctor of Commercial Sciences
CUNY	City University of New York	**DCSO**	Deputy Chief Scientific Officer
CUP	Cambridge University Press	**DCT**	Doctor of Christian Theology
CURUFC	Cambridge University Rugby Union Football Club	**DCVO**	Dame Commander, Royal Victorian Order
CV	Cross of Valour (Canada)	**DD**	Doctor of Divinity
CVCP	Committee of Vice-Chancellors and Principals of the Universities of the United Kingdom	**DDes**	Doctor of Design
		DDGAMS	Deputy Director General, Army Medical Services
CVO	Commander, Royal Victorian Order	**DDH**	Diploma in Dental Health
CVS	Council for Voluntary Service	**DDL**	Deputy Director of Labour
CVSNA	Council of Voluntary Service National Association	**DDME**	Deputy Director of Mechanical Engineering
CWA	Crime Writers Association	**DDMI**	Deputy Director of Military Intelligence
CWGC	Commonwealth War Graves Commission	**DDMO**	Deputy Director of Military Operations
CWS	Co-operative Wholesale Society	**DDMS**	Deputy Director of Medical Services
CWU	Communication Workers Union	**DDMT**	Deputy Director of Military Training
		DDNI	Deputy Director of Naval Intelligence
		DDO	Diploma in Dental Orthopaedics
		DDOS	Deputy Director of Ordnance Services

D

D	Duke	**DDPH**	Diploma in Dental Public Health
d	died; daughter	**DDPR**	Deputy Director of Public Relations
DA	Dame of St Andrew, Order of Barbados; Diploma in Anaesthesia; Diploma in Art	**DDPS**	Deputy Director of Personal Services
		DDR	Deutsche Demokratische Republik
DAA&QMG	Deputy Assistant Adjutant and Quartermaster-General	**DDRA**	Deputy Director Royal Artillery

DDS	Doctor of Dental Surgery; Director of Dental Services
DDSc	Doctor of Dental Science
DDSD	Deputy Director Staff Duties
DDSM	Defense Distinguished Service Medal
DDST	Deputy Director of Supplies and Transport
DDWE&M	Deputy Director of Works, Electrical and Mechanical
DE	Doctor of Engineering; Delaware
DEA	Department of Economic Affairs
decd	deceased
DEconSc	Doctor of Economic Science
DEd	Doctor of Education
Del	Delaware (US)
Deleg.	Delegate
DEME	Directorate of Electrical and Mechanical Engineering
DEMS	Defensively Equipped Merchant Ships
(DemU)	Democratic Unionist
DenD	Docteur en Droit
DEng	Doctor of Engineering
DenM	Docteur en Médicine
DEOVR	Duke of Edinburgh's Own Volunteer Rifles
DEP	Department of Employment and Productivity; European Progressive Democrats
Dep.	Deputy
DERA	Defence Evaluation and Research Agency
DES	Department of Education and Science (now see DFE)
DèsL	Docteur ès lettres
DèS or DèsSc	Docteur ès sciences
DesRCA	Designer of the Royal College of Art
DFA	Doctor of Fine Arts
DFAS	Decorative and Fine Art Society
DFC	Distinguished Flying Cross
DFE	Department for Education
DFH	Diploma of Faraday House
DFLS	Day Fighter Leaders' School
DFM	Distinguished Flying Medal
DG	Director General; Dragoon Guards
DGAA	Distressed Gentlefolks Aid Association
DGAMS	Director-General Army Medical Services
DGEME	Director General Electrical and Mechanical Engineering
DGLP(A)	Director General Logistic Policy (Army)
DGMS	Director-General of Medical Services
DGMT	Director-General of Military Training
DGMW	Director-General of Military Works
DGNPS	Director-General of Naval Personal Services
DGP	Director-General of Personnel
DGPS	Director-General of Personal Services
DGS	Diploma in Graduate Studies
DGStJ	Dame of Grace, Order of St John of Jerusalem (now see DStJ)
DGU	Doctor of Griffith University
DH	Doctor of Humanities
DHA	District Health Authority
Dhc	Doctor honoris causa
DHEW	Department of Health Education and Welfare (US)
DHL	Doctor of Humane Letters; Doctor of Hebrew Literature
DHM	Dean Hole Medal
DHMSA	Diploma in the History of Medicine (Society of Apothecaries)
DHQ	District Headquarters
DHSS	Department of Health and Social Security (now see DoH and DSS)
DHum	Doctor of Humanities
DHumLit	Doctor of Humane Letters
DIAS	Dublin Institute of Advanced Sciences
DIC	Diploma of the Imperial College
DICTA	Diploma of Imperial College of Tropical Agriculture
DIG	Deputy Inspector-General
DIH	Diploma in Industrial Health
DIMP	Darjah Indera Mahkota Pahang
DIntLaw	Diploma in International Law
Dio.	Diocese
DipAA	Diploma in Applied Art
DipAD	Diploma in Art and Design
DipAe	Diploma in Aeronautics
DipArch	Diploma in Architecture

DipASE	Diploma in Advanced Study of Education, College of Preceptors
DipAvMed	Diploma of Aviation Medicine, Royal College of Physicians
DipBA	Diploma in Business Administration
DipBS	Diploma in Fine Art, Byam Shaw School
DipCAM	Diploma in Communications, Advertising and Marketing of CAM Foundation
DipCC	Diploma of the Central College
DipCD	Diploma in Civic Design
DipCE	Diploma in Civil Engineering
DipEcon	Diploma in Economics
DipEd	Diploma in Education
DipEE	Diploma in Electrical Engineering
DipEl	Diploma in Electronics
DipESL	Diploma in English as a Second Language
DipEth	Diploma in Ethnology
DipFD	Diploma in Funeral Directing
DipFE	Diploma in Further Education
DipGSM	Diploma in Music, Guildhall School of Music and Drama
DipHA	Diploma in Hospital Administration
DipHSM	Diploma in Health Services Management
DipHum	Diploma in Humanities
DipLA	Diploma in Landscape Architecture
DipLib	Diploma of Librarianship
DipM	Diploma in Marketing
DipN	Diploma in Nursing
DipNEC	Diploma of Northampton Engineering College (now City University)
DipPA	Diploma of Practitioners in Advertising (now see DipCAM)
DipPSA	Diploma in Public Service Administration
DipREM	Diploma in Rural Estate Management
DipSMS	Diploma in School Management Studies
DipSoc	Diploma in Sociology
DipTA	Diploma in Tropical Agriculture
DipT&CP	Diploma in Town and Country Planning
DipTh	Diploma in Theology
DipTMHA	Diploma in Training and Further Education of Mentally Handicapped Adults
DipTP	Diploma in Town Planning
DipTPT	Diploma in Theory and Practice of Teaching
DIS	Diploma in Industrial Studies
DistTP	Distinction in Town Planning
DIur	Doctor of Law
Div.	Division; Divorced
Div.Test	Divinity Testimonium (of Trinity College, Dublin)
DJAG	Deputy Judge Advocate General
DJPD	Dato Jasa Purba Di-Raja Negeri Sembilan (Malaysia)
DJStJ	Dame of Justice, Order of St John of Jerusalem (now see DStJ)
DJur	Doctor Juris (Doctor of Law)
DK	Most Esteemed Family Order (Brunei)
DL	Deputy Lieutenant
DLC	Diploma of Loughborough College
DLES	Doctor of Letters in Economic Studies
DLI	Durham Light Infantry
DLit or DLitt	Doctor of Literature; Doctor of Letters
DLittS	Doctor of Sacred Letters
DLJ	Dame of Grace, Order of St Lazarus of Jerusalem
DLO	Diploma in Laryngology and Otology
DM	Doctor of Medicine
DMA	Diploma in Municipal Administration
DMD	Doctor of Medical Dentistry (Australia)
DME	Director of Mechanical Engineering
DMet	Doctor of Metallurgy
DMI	Director of Military Intelligence
DMin	Doctor of Ministry
DMiss	Doctor of Missiology
DMJ	Diploma in Medical Jurisprudence
DMJ(Path)	Diploma in Medical Jurisprudence (Pathology)
DMLJ	Dame of Merit, Order of St Lazarus of Jerusalem
DMO	Director of Military Operations
DMR	Diploma in Medical Radiology
DMRD	Diploma in Medical Radiological Diagnosis
DMRE	Diploma in Medical Radiology and Electrology
DMRT	Diploma in Medical Radio-Therapy

DMS	Director of Medical Services; Decoration for Meritorious Service (South Africa); Diploma in Management Studies
DMSc	Doctor of Medical Science
DMSSB	Direct Mail Services Standards Board
DMT	Director of Military Training
DMus	Doctor of Music
DN	Diploma in Nursing
DNB	Dictionary of National Biography
DNE	Director of Naval Equipment
DNI	Director of Naval Intelligence
DO	Diploma in Ophthalmology
DOAE	Defence Operational Analysis Establishment
DObstRCOG	Diploma of Royal College of Obstetricians and Gynaecologists (*now see* DRCOG)
DOC	District Officer Commanding
DocEng	Doctor of Engineering
DoE	Department of the Environment
DoH	Department of Health
DoI	Department of Industry
DOL	Doctor of Oriental Learning
Dom.	*Dominus* (Lord)
DOMS	Diploma in Ophthalmic Medicine and Surgery
DOR	Director of Operational Requirements
DOrthRCS	Diploma in Orthodontics, Royal College of Surgeons
DOS	Director of Ordnance Services; Doctor of Ocular Science
Dow.	Dowager
DP	Data Processing
DPA	Diploma in Public Administration; Discharged Prisoners' Aid
DPD	Diploma in Public Dentistry
DPEc	Doctor of Political Economy
DPed	Doctor of Pedagogy
DPH	Diploma in Public Health
DPh or **DPhil**	Doctor of Philosophy
DPharm	Doctor of Pharmacy
DPhilMed	Diploma in Philosophy of Medicine
DPhysMed	Diploma in Physical Medicine
DPLG	Diplômé par le Gouvernement
DPM	Diploma in Psychological Medicine
DPMS	Dato Paduka Mahkota Selangor (Malaysia)
DPP	Director of Public Prosecutions
DPR	Director of Public Relations
DPS	Director of Postal Services; Director of Personal Services; Doctor of Public Service
DPSA	Diploma in Public and Social Administration
DPSE	Diploma in Professional Studies in Education
DPsych	Doctor of Psychology
DQMG	Deputy Quartermaster-General
Dr	Doctor
DRA	Defence Research Agency (*now see* DERA)
DRAC	Director Royal Armoured Corps
DRC	Diploma of Royal College of Science and Technology, Glasgow
DRCOG	Diploma of Royal College of Obstetricians and Gynaecologists
DRD	Diploma in Restorative Dentistry
Dr ing	Doctor of Engineering
Dr jur	Doctor of Laws
DrŒcPol	*Doctor Œconomiæ Politicæ* (Doctor of Political Economy)
Dr rer. nat.	Doctor of Natural Science
Dr rer. pol.	Doctor of Political Science
DRS	Diploma in Religious Studies
DRSAMD	Diploma of the Royal Scottish Academy of Music and Drama
DS	Directing Staff; Doctor of Science
DSA	Diploma in Social Administration
DSAC	Defence Scientific Advisory Council
DSAO	Diplomatic Service Administration Office
DSC	Distinguished Service Cross
DSc	Doctor of Science
DScA	Docteur en sciences agricoles
DSCHE	Diploma of the Scottish Council for Health Education
DScMil	Doctor of Military Science
DScPol	Doctor of Political Sciences
DSc (SocSci)	Doctor of Science in Social Science

DSD	Director Staff Duties
DSF	Director Special Forces
DSIR	Department of Scientific and Industrial Research (later SRC; then SERC)
DSL	Doctor of Sacred Letters
DSLJ	Dato Seri Laila Jasa (Brunei)
DSM	Distinguished Service Medal
DSNB	Dato Setia Negara Brunei
DSNS	Dato Setia Negeri Sembilan (Malaysia)
DSO	Companion of the Distinguished Service Order
DSocSc	Doctor of Social Science
DSP	Director of Selection of Personnel; Docteur en sciences politiques (Montreal)
dsp	*decessit sine prole* (died without issue)
DSS	Department of Social Security; Doctor of Sacred Scripture
Dss	Deaconess
DSSc	Doctor of Social Science
DST	Director of Supplies and Transport
DStJ	Dame of Grace, Most Venerable Order of the Hospital of St John of Jerusalem; Dame of Justice, Most Venerable Order of the Hospital of St John of Jerusalem
DTA	Diploma in Tropical Agriculture
DTD	Dekoratie voor Trouwe Dienst (Decoration for Devoted Service)
DTech	Doctor of Technology
DTH	Diploma in Tropical Hygiene
DTh or **DTheol**	Doctor of Theology
DThPT	Diploma in Theory and Practice of Teaching
DTI	Department of Trade and Industry
DTM&H	Diploma in Tropical Medicine and Hygiene
DU	Honorary Doctor of the University
Dunelm	*Dunelmensis* (of Durham)
DUniv	Honorary Doctor of the University
DUP	Democratic Unionist Party; Docteur de l'Université de Paris
DVA	Diploma of Veterinary Anaesthesia
DVH	Diploma in Veterinary Hygiene
DVLA	Driver and Vehicle Licensing Authority
DVLC	Driver and Vehicle Licensing Centre
DVM	Doctor of Veterinary Medicine
DVMS or **DVM&S**	Doctor of Veterinary Medicine and Surgery
DVR	Diploma in Veterinary Radiology
DVSc	Doctor of Veterinary Science
DVSM	Diploma in Veterinary State Medicine

E

E	East; Earl; England
e	eldest
EAA	Edinburgh Architectural Association
EACR	European Association for Cancer Research
EAGA	Energy Action Grants Agency
EAHY	European Architectural Heritage Year
EAP	East Africa Protectorate
EAW	Electrical Association for Women
EBC	English Benedictine Congregation
Ebor	*Eboracensis* (of York)
EBRD	European Bank for Reconstruction and Development
EBU	European Broadcasting Union
EC	Etoile du Courage (Canada); European Community; European Commission; Emergency Commission
ECA	Economic Co-operation Administration; Economic Commission for Africa
ECAFE	Economic Commission for Asia and the Far East (*now see* ESCAP)
ECCTIS	Education Courses and Credit Transfer Information Systems
ECE	Economic Commission for Europe
ECGD	Export Credits Guarantee Department
ECLA	Economic Commission for Latin America
ECLAC	United Nations Economic Commission for Latin America and the Caribbean
ECOVAST	European Council for the Village and Small Town
ECSC	European Coal and Steel Community

ECU	English Church Union
ED	Efficiency Decoration; Doctor of Engineering (US); European Democrat
ed	edited
EdB	Bachelor of Education
EDC	Economic Development Committee
EdD	Doctor of Education
EDF	European Development Fund
EDG	European Democratic Group; Employment Department Group
Edin.	Edinburgh
Edn	Edition
EDP	Executive Development Programme
Educ	Educated
Educn	Education
EEC	European Economic Community (*now see* EC); Commission of the European Communities
EEF	Engineering Employers' Federation; Egyptian Expeditionary Force
EEIBA	Electrical and Electronic Industries Benevolent Association
EETPU	Electrical Electronic Telecommunication & Plumbing Union (*now see* AEEU)
EETS	Early English Text Society
EFCE	European Federation of Chemical Engineering
EFTA	European Free Trade Association
eh	ehrenhalber (honorary)
EI	East Indian; East Indies
EIA	Engineering Industries Association
EIB	European Investment Bank
EICS	East India Company's Service
E-in-C	Engineer-in-Chief
EIS	Educational Institute of Scotland
EISCAT	European Incoherent Scatter Association
EIU	Economist Intelligence Unit
ELBS	English Language Book Society
ELSE	European Life Science Editors
ELT	English Language Teaching
EM	Edward Medal; Earl Marshal
EMBL	European Molecular Biology Laboratory
EMBO	European Molecular Biology Organisation
EMP	Electro Magnetic Pulse; Executive Management Program Diploma
EMS	Emergency Medical Service
Enc.Brit.	Encylopaedia Britannica
Eng.	England
Engr	Engineer
ENO	English National Opera
ENSA	Entertainments National Service Association
ENT	Ear Nose and Throat
EO	Executive Officer
EOC	Equal Opportunities Commission
EOPH	Examined Officer of Public Health
EORTC	European Organisation for Research on Treatment of Cancer
EP	European Parliament
EPP	European People's Party
EPSRC	Engineering and Physical Sciences Research Council
er	elder
ER	Eastern Region (BR)
ERA	Electrical Research Association
ERC	Electronics Research Council
ERD	Emergency Reserve Decoration (Army)
ESA	European Space Agency
ESCAP	Economic and Social Commission for Asia and the Pacific
ESF	European Science Foundn
ESL	English as a Second Language
ESNS	Educational Sub-Normal Serious
ESRC	Economic and Social Research Council; Electricity Supply Research Council
ESRO	European Space Research Organization (*now see* ESA)
ESTA	European Sciences and Technology Assembly
ESU	English-Speaking Union
ETA	Engineering Training Authority
ETH	Eidgenössische Technische Hochschule
ETUC	European Trade Union Confederation
ETUCE	European Trade Union Committee for Education
EU	European Union

EUDISED	European Documentation and Information Service for Education
Euratom	European Atomic Energy Community
EurChem	European Chemist
Eur Ing	European Engineer
EUROM	European Federation for Optics and Precision Mechanics
EUW	European Union of Women
eV	eingetragener Verein
Ext	Extinct

F

FA	Football Association
FAA	Fellow, Australian Academy of Science; Fleet Air Arm
FAAAI	Fellow, American Association for Artificial Intelligence
FAAAS	Fellow, American Association for the Advancement of Science
FAAO	Fellow, American Academy of Optometry
FAAP	Fellow, American Academy of Pediatrics
FAARM	Fellow, American Academy of Reproductive Medicine
FAAV	Fellow, Central Association of Agricultural Valuers
FAAVCT	Fellow, American Academy of Veterinary and Comparative Toxicology
FABE	Fellow, Association of Building Engineers
FACC	Fellow, American College of Cardiology
FACCA	Fellow, Association of Certified and Corporate Accountants (*now see* FCCA)
FACCP	Fellow, American College of Chest Physicians
FACD	Fellow, American College of Dentistry
FACDS	Fellow, Australian College of Dental Surgeons (*now see* FRACDS)
FACE	Fellow, Australian College of Education
FACerS	Fellow, American Ceramic Society
FACI	Fellow, Australian Chemical Institute (*now see* FRACI)
FACMA	Fellow, Australian College of Medical Administrators (*now see* FRACMA)
FACMG	Fellow, American College of Medicinal Genetics
FACOG	Fellow, American College of Obstetricians and Gynæcologists
FACOM	Fellow, Australian College of Occupational Medicine
FACP	Fellow, American College of Physicians
FACR	Fellow, American College of Radiology
FACRM	Fellow, Australian College of Rehabilitation Medicine
FACS	Fellow, American College of Surgeons
FACVT	Fellow, American College of Veterinary Toxicology (*now see* FAAVCT)
FADM	Fellow, Academy of Dental Materials
FAeSI	Fellow, Aeronautical Society of India
FAFPHM	Fellow, Australian Faculty of Public Health Medicine
FAGO	Fellowship in Australia in Obstetrics and Gynaecology
FAGS	Fellow, American Geographical Society
FAHA	Fellow, Australian Academy of the Humanities
FAI	Fellow, Chartered Auctioneers' and Estate Agents' Institute (*now* (after amalgamation) *see* FRICS); Fédération Aéronautique Internationale
FAIA	Fellow, American Institute of Architects
FAIAA	Fellow, American Institute of Aeronautics and Astronautics
FAIAS	Fellow, Australian Institute of Agricultural Science
FAIB	Fellow, Australian Institute of Bankers
FAIBiol	Fellow, Australian Institute of Biology
FAICD	Fellow, Australian Institute of Company Directors
FAIE	Fellow, Australian Institute of Energy
FAIEx	Fellow, Australian Institute of Export
FAIFST	Fellow, Australian Institute of Food Science and Technology
FAII	Fellow, Australian Insurance Institute
FAIM	Fellow, Australian Institute of Management
FAIP	Fellow, Australian Institute of Physics
FAMA	Fellow, Australian Medical Association
FAMI	Fellow, Australian Marketing Institute
FAmNucSoc	Fellow, American Nuclear Society
FAMS	Fellow, Ancient Monuments Society
F and GP	Finance and General Purposes
FANY	First Aid Nursing Yeomanry

FANZCA	Fellow, Australian and New Zealand College of Anaesthetists
FANZCP	Fellow, Australian and New Zealand College of Psychiatrists (*now see* FRANZCP)
FAO	Food and Agriculture Organization of the United Nations
FAOrthA	Fellow, Australian Orthopaedic Association
FAPA	Fellow, American Psychiatric Association
FAPHA	Fellow, American Public Health Association
FAPI	Fellow, Australian Planning Institute (*now see* FRAPI)
FAPM	Fellow, Association of Project Managers
FAPS	Fellow, American Phytopathological Society
FArborA	Fellow, Aboricultural Association
FARE	Federation of Alcoholic Rehabilitation Establishments
FARELF	Far East Land Forces
FAS	Fellow, Antiquarian Society; Fellow, Nigerian Academy of Science; Funding Agency for Schools
FASA	Fellow, Australian Society of Accountants (*now see* FCPA)
FASc	Fellow, Indian Academy of Sciences
fasc.	fascicule
FASCE	Fellow, American Society of Civil Engineers
FASI	Fellow, Architects' and Surveyors' Institute
FASME	Fellow, American Society of Mechanical Engineers
FASPOG	Fellow, Australian Society for Psychosomatic Obstetrics and Gynaecology
FASSA	Fellow, Academy of the Social Sciences in Australia
FAusIMM	Fellow, Australasian Institute of Mining and Metallurgy
FAustCOG	Fellow, Australian College of Obstetricians and Gynæcologists (*now see* FRACOG)
FBA	Fellow, British Academy; Federation of British Artists
FBCO	Fellow, British College of Optometrists (*formerly* of Ophthalmic Opticians (Optometrists)) (*now see* FCOptom)
FBCS	Fellow, British Computer Society
FBEC(S)	Fellow, Business Education Council (Scotland)
FBES	Fellow, Biological Engineering Society
FBHA	Fellow, British Hospitality Association
FBHI	Fellow, British Horological Institute
FBHS	Fellow, British Horse Society
FBI	Federation of British Industries (*now see* CBI); Federal Bureau of Investigation
FBIA	Fellow, Bankers' Institute of Australasia (*now see* FAIB)
FBIAT	Fellow, British Institute of Architectural Technicians
FBIBA	Fellow, British Insurance Brokers' Association (*now see* FBIIBA)
FBID	Fellow, British Institute of Interior Design
FBIIBA	Fellow, British Insurance and Investment Brokers' Association
FBIM	Fellow, British Institute of Management (*now see* FIMgt)
FBINZ	Fellow, Bankers' Institute of New Zealand
FBIPP	Fellow, British Institute of Professional Photography
FBIRA	Fellow, British Institute of Regulatory Affairs
FBIS	Fellow, British Interplanetary Society
FBKS	Fellow, British Kinematograph Society (*now see* FBKSTS)
FBKSTS	Fellow, British Kinematograph, Sound and Television Society
FBOA	Fellow, British Optical Association
FBOU	Fellow, British Ornithologists' Union
FBPICS	Fellow, British Production and Inventory Control Society
FBPsS	Fellow, British Psychological Society
FBritIRE	Fellow, British Institution of Radio Engineers (later FIERE)
FBS	Fellow, Building Societies Institute (later FCBSI; *now see* FCIB)
FBSI	Fellow, Boot and Shoe Institution (*now see* FCFI)
FBSM	Fellow, Birmingham School of Music
FC	Football Club
FCA	Fellow, Institute of Chartered Accountants; Fellow, Institute of Chartered Accountants in Australia; Fellow, New Zealand Society of Accountants; Federation of Canadian Artists
FCAI	Fellow, New Zealand Institute of Cost Accountants; Fellow, Canadian Aeronautical Institute (*now see* FCASI)
FCAM	Fellow, CAM Foundation

FCAnaes	Fellow, College of Anaesthetists (*now see* FRCA)
FCASI	Fellow, Canadian Aeronautics and Space Institute
FCBSI	Fellow, Chartered Building Societies Institute (*now see* FCIB)
FCCA	Fellow, Chartered Association of Certified Accountants
FCCEA	Fellow, Commonwealth Council for Educational Administration
FCCS	Fellow, Corporation of Secretaries (*formerly* of Certified Secretaries)
FCCT	Fellow, Canadian College of Teachers
FCEC	Federation of Civil Engineering Contractors
FCFI	Fellow, Clothing and Footwear Institute
FCGI	Fellow, City and Guilds of London Institute
FCGP	Fellow, College of General Practitioners (*now see* FRCGP)
FCH	Fellow, Coopers Hill College
FChS	Fellow, Society of Chiropodists
FCI	Fellow, Institute of Commerce
FCIA	Fellow, Corporation of Insurance Agents
FCIArb	Fellow, Chartered Institute of Arbitrators
FCIB	Fellow, Corporation of Insurance Brokers; Fellow, Chartered Institute of Bankers
FCIBS	Fellow, Chartered Institution of Building Services (*now see* FCIBSE); Fellow, Chartered Institute of Bankers in Scotland
FCIBSE	Fellow, Chartered Institution of Building Services Engineers
FCIC	Fellow, Chemical Institute of Canada (*formerly* Canadian Institute of Chemistry)
FCIH	Fellow, Chartered Institute of Housing
FCII	Fellow, Chartered Insurance Institute
FCIJ	Fellow, Chartered Institute of Journalists
FCILA	Fellow, Chartered Institute of Loss Adjusters
FCIM	Fellow, Chartered Institute of Marketing; Fellow, Institute of Corporate Managers (Australia)
FCIOB	Fellow, Chartered Institute of Building
FCIPA	Fellow, Chartered Institute of Patent Agents (*now see* CPA)
FCIPS	Fellow, Chartered Institute of Purchasing and Supply
FCIS	Fellow, Institute of Chartered Secretaries and Administrators (*formerly* Chartered Institute of Secretaries)
FCISA	Fellow, Chartered Institute of Secretaries and Administrators (Australia)
FCIT	Fellow, Chartered Institute of Transport
FCIWEM	Fellow, Chartered Institution of Water and Environmental Management
FCM	Faculty of Community Medicine
FCMA	Fellow, Chartered Institute of Management Accountants (*formerly* Institute of Cost and Management Accountants)
FCMSA	Fellow, College of Medicine of South Africa
FCNA	Fellow, College of Nursing, Australia
FCO	Foreign and Commonwealth Office
FCOG(SA)	Fellow, South African College of Obstetrics and Gynæcology
FCollH	Fellow, College of Handicraft
FCollP	Fellow, College of Preceptors
FCommA	Fellow, Society of Commercial Accountants (*now see* FSCA)
FCOphth	Fellow, College of Ophthalmologists (*now see* FRCOphth)
FCOptom	Fellow, College of Optometrists
FCP	Fellow, College of Preceptors
FCPA	Fellow, Australian Society of Certified Practising Accountants
FCPath	Fellow, College of Pathologists (*now see* FRCPath)
FCPS	Fellow, College of Physicians and Surgeons
FCP(SoAf)	Fellow, College of Physicians, South Africa
FCPSO(SoAf)	Fellow, College of Physicians and Surgeons and Obstetricians, South Africa
FCPS (Pak)	Fellow, College of Physicians and Surgeons of Pakistan
FCRA	Fellow, College of Radiologists of Australia (*now see* FRACR)
FCS	Federation of Conservative Students
FCS or **FChemSoc**	Fellow, Chemical Society (now absorbed into Royal Society of Chemistry)
FCSD	Fellow, Chartered Society of Designers
FCSHK	Fellow, College of Surgeons of Hong Kong
FCSLT	Fellow, College of Speech and Language Therapists

FCSP	Fellow, Chartered Society of Physiotherapy
FCSSA or	
FCS(SoAf)	Fellow, College of Surgeons, South Africa
FCSSL	Fellow, College of Surgeons of Sri Lanka
FCST	Fellow, College of Speech Therapists (*now see* FCSLT)
FCT	Federal Capital Territory (*now see* ACT); Fellow, Association of Corporate Treasurers
FCTB	Fellow, College of Teachers of the Blind
FCU	Fighter Control Unit
FCWA	Fellow, Institute of Costs and Works Accountants (*now see* FCMA)
FDA	Association of First Division Civil Servants
FDF	Food and Drink Federation
FDI	Fédération Dentaire Internationale
FDP	Freie Demokratische Partei
FDS	Fellow in Dental Surgery
FDSRCPSGlas	Fellow in Dental Surgery, Royal College of Physicians and Surgeons of Glasgow
FDSRCS or	Fellow in Dental Surgery, Royal College of Surgeons
FDS RCS	of England
FDSRCSE	Fellow in Dental Surgery, Royal College of Surgeons of Edinburgh
FE	Far East
FEAF	Far East Air Force
FEANI	Fédération Européenne d'Associations Nationales d'Ingénieurs
FEBS	Federation of European Biochemical Societies
FECI	Fellow, Institute of Employment Consultants
FEE	Fédération des Expertes Comptables Européens
FEF	Far East Fleet
FEFC or	
FEFCE	Further Education Funding Council for England
FEI	Fédération Equestre Internationale
FEIDCT	Fellow, Educational Institute of Design Craft and Technology
FEIS	Fellow, Educational Institute of Scotland
FELCO	Federation of English Language Course Opportunities
FEng	Fellow, Royal Academy (*formerly* Fellowship) of Engineering
FES	Fellow, Entomological Society; Fellow, Ethnological Society
FESC	Fellow, European Society of Cardiology
FF	Fianna Fáil; Field Force
FFA	Fellow, Faculty of Actuaries (in Scotland); Fellow, Institute of Financial Accountants
FFAEM	Fellow, Faculty of Accident and Emergency Medicine
FFARACS	Fellow, Faculty of Anaesthetists, Royal Australasian College of Surgeons (*now see* FANZCA)
FFARCS	Fellow, Faculty of Anaesthetists, Royal College of Surgeons of England (*now see* FRCA)
FFARCSI	Fellow, Faculty of Anaesthetists, Royal College of Surgeons in Ireland
FFAS	Fellow, Faculty of Architects and Surveyors, London (*now see* FASI)
FFA(SA)	Fellow, Faculty of Anaesthetists (South Africa)
FFB	Fellow, Faculty of Building
FFCM	Fellow, Faculty of Community Medicine (*now see* FFPHM)
FFCMI	Fellow, Faculty of Community Medicine of Ireland
FFDRCSI	Fellow, Faculty of Dentistry, Royal College of Surgeons in Ireland
FFF	Free French Forces
FFFP	Fellow, Faculty of Family Planning of the Royal College of Obstetricians and Gynaecologists
FFHC	Freedom from Hunger Campaign
FFHom	Fellow, Faculty of Homœopathy
FFI	French Forces of the Interior; Finance for Industry
FFOM	Fellow, Faculty of Occupational Medicine
FFOMI	Fellow, Faculty of Occupational Medicine of Ireland
FFPath, RCPI	Fellow, Faculty of Pathologists of the Royal College of Physicians of Ireland
FFPHM	Fellow, Faculty of Public Health Medicine
FFPHMI	Fellow, Faculty of Public Health Medicine of Ireland
FFPM	Fellow, Faculty of Pharmaceutical Medicine
FFPS	Fauna and Flora Preservation Society
FFR	Fellow, Faculty of Radiologists (*now see* FRCR)
FG	Fine Gael
FGA	Fellow, Gemmological Association
FGCL	Fellow, Goldsmiths' College, London

FGCM	Fellow, Guild of Church Musicians
FGDS	Fédération de la Gauche Démocratique et Socialiste
FGGE	Fellow, Guild of Glass Engineers
FGI	Fellow, Institute of Certificated Grocers
FGS	Fellow, Geological Society
FGSM	Fellow, Guildhall School of Music and Drama
FGSM(MT)	Fellow, Guildhall School of Music and Drama (Music Therapy)
FHA	Fellow, Institute of Health Service Administrators (*formerly* Hospital Administrators; *now see* FHSM)
FHAS	Fellow, Highland and Agricultural Society of Scotland
FHCIMA	Fellow, Hotel Catering and Institutional Management Association
FHFS	Fellow, Human Factors Society
FHKIE	Fellow, Hong Kong Institution of Engineers
FHMAAAS	Foreign Honorary Member, American Academy of Arts and Sciences
FHS	Fellow, Heraldry Society; Forces Help Society and Lord Roberts Workshops
FHSA	Family Health Services Authority
FHSM	Fellow, Institute of Health Services Management
FH-WC	Fellow, Heriot-Watt College (*now* University), Edinburgh
FIA	Fellow, Institute of Actuaries
FIAA	Fellow, Institute of Actuaries of Australia
FIAAS	Fellow, Institute of Australian Agricultural Science
FIAA&S	Fellow, Incorporated Association of Architects and Surveyors
FIAgrE	Fellow, Institution of Agricultural Engineers
FIAgrM	Fellow, Institute of Agricultural Management
FIAI	Fellow, Institute of Industrial and Commercial Accountants
FIAL	Fellow, International Institute of Arts and Letters
FIAM	Fellow, International Academy of Management
FIAP	Fellow, Institution of Analysts and Programmers
FIArb	Fellow, Institute of Arbitrators (*now see* FCIArb)
FIArbA	Fellow, Institute of Arbitrators of Australia
FIAS	Fellow, Institute of Aeronautical Sciences (US) (*now see* FAIAA)
FIASc	Fellow, Indian Academy of Sciences
FIAWS	Fellow, International Academy of Wood Sciences
FIB	Fellow, Institute of Bankers (*now see* FCIB)
FIBA	Fellow, Institute of Business Administration, Australia (*now see* FCIM)
FIBD	Fellow, Institute of British Decorators
FIBiol	Fellow, Institute of Biology
FIBiotech	Fellow, Institute for Biotechnical Studies
FIBMS	Fellow, Institute of Biomedical Sciences
FIBP	Fellow, Institute of British Photographers
FIBScot	Fellow, Institute of Bankers in Scotland (*now see* FCIBS)
FIC	Fellow, Institute of Chemistry (*now see* FRIC, FRSC); Fellow, Imperial College, London
FICA	Fellow, Commonwealth Institute of Accountants; Fellow, Institute of Chartered Accountants in England and Wales (*now see* FCA)
FICAI	Fellow, Institute of Chartered Accountants in Ireland
FICD	Fellow, Institute of Civil Defence (*now see* FICDDS); Fellow, Indian College of Dentists; Fellow, International College of Dentists
FICDDS	Fellow, Institute of Civil Defence and Disaster Studies
FICE	Fellow, Institution of Civil Engineers
FICeram	Fellow, Institute of Ceramics (*now see* FIM)
FICFM	Fellow, Institute of Charity Fundraising Managers
FICFor	Fellow, Institute of Chartered Foresters
FIChemE	Fellow, Institution of Chemical Engineers
FICI	Fellow, Institute of Chemistry of Ireland; Fellow, International Colonial Institute
FICM	Fellow, Institute of Credit Management
FICMA	Fellow, Institute of Cost and Management Accountants
FICorrST	Fellow, Institution of Corrosion Science and Technology
FICS	Fellow, Institute of Chartered Shipbrokers; Fellow, International College of Surgeons
FICT	Fellow, Institute of Concrete Technologists
FICW	Fellow, Institute of Clerks of Works of Great Britain
FIDA	Fellow, Institute of Directors, Australia
FIDCA	Fellow, Industrial Design Council of Australia

FIDE	Fédération Internationale des Echecs; Fellow, Institute of Design Engineers; Fédération Internationale pour le Droit Européen
FIDEM	Fédération Internationale de la Médaille
FIEAust	Fellow, Institution of Engineers, Australia
FIEC	Fellow, Institute of Employment Consultants
FIED	Fellow, Institute of Engineering Designers
FIEE	Fellow, Institute of Electrical Engineers
FIEEE	Fellow, Institute of Electrical and Electronics Engineers (NY)
FIEHK	Fellow, Institution of Engineering, Hong Kong
FIElecIE	Fellow, Institution of Electronic Incorporated Engineers (*now see* FIEIE)
FIEI	Fellow, Institution of Engineering Inspection (*now see* FIQA); Fellow, Institution of Engineers of Ireland
FIEIE	Fellow, Institution of Electronics and Electrical Incorporated Engineers
FIEJ	Fédération Internationale des Editeurs de Journaux et Publications
FIERE	Fellow, Institution of Electronic and Radio Engineers (*now see* FIEE)
FIES	Fellow, Illuminating Engineering Society (later FIllumES; *now see* FCIBSE); Fellow, Institution of Engineers and Shipbuilders, Scotland
FIET	Fédération Internationale des Employés, Techniciens et Cadres
FIEx	Fellow, Institute of Export
FIExpE	Fellow, Institute of Explosives Engineers
FIFA	Fédération Internationale de Football Association
FIFF	Fellow, Institute of Freight Forwarders
FIFireE	Fellow, Institution of Fire Engineers
FIFM	Fellow, Institute of Fisheries Management
FIFor	Fellow, Institute of Foresters (*now see* FICFor)
FIFST	Fellow, Institute of Food Science and Technology
FIGasE	Fellow, Institution of Gas Engineers
FIGCM	Fellow, Incorporated Guild of Church Musicians
FIGD	Fellow, Institute of Grocery Distribution
FIGO	International Federation of Gynaecology and Obstetrics
FIH	Fellow, Institute of Housing (*now see* FCIH); Fellow, Institute of the Horse
FIHE	Fellow, Institute of Health Education
FIHM	Fellow, Institute of Housing Managers (later FIH; *now see* FCIH)
FIHort	Fellow, Institute of Horticulture
FIHospE	Fellow, Institute of Hospital Engineering
FIHT	Fellow, Institution of Highways and Transportation
FIHVE	Fellow, Institution of Heating & Ventilating Engineers (later FCIBS and MCIBS; *now see* FCIBSE)
FIIA	Fellow, Institute of Industrial Administration (later CBIM and FBIM); Fellow, Institute of Internal Auditors
FIIB	Fellow, International Institute of Biotechnology
FIIC	Fellow, International Institute for Conservation of Historic and Artistic Works
FIIDA	Fellow, International Interior Design Association
FIIM	Fellow, Institution of Industrial Managers
FIInfSc	Fellow, Institute of Information Scientists
FIInst	Fellow, Imperial Institute
FIIP	Fellow, Institute of Incorporated Photographers (*now see* FBIPP)
FIIPC	Fellow, India International Photographic Council
FIIPE	Fellow, Indian Institution of Production Engineers
FIL	Fellow, Institute of Linguists
FILA	Fellow, Institute of Landscape Architects (*now see* FLI)
FILDM	Fellow, Institute of Logistics and Distribution Management (*now see* FILog)
FilDr	Doctor of Philosophy
Fil.Hed.	Filosofie Hedersdoktor
FILLM	Fédération Internationale des Langues et Littératures Modernes
FIllumES	Fellow, Illuminating Engineering Society (*now see* FCIBSE)
FILog	Fellow, Institute of Logistics
FIM	Fellow, Institute of Materials (*formerly* Institution of Metallurgists, then Institute of Metals)
FIMA	Fellow, Institute of Mathematics and its Applications
FIMarE	Fellow, Institute of Marine Engineers
FIMatM	Fellow, Institute of Materials Management (*now see* FILog)
FIMBRA	Financial Intermediaries, Managers and Brokers Regulatory Association
FIMC	Fellow, Institute of Management Consultants
FIMCB	Fellow, International Management Centre from Buckingham
FIMechE	Fellow, Institution of Mechanical Engineers
FIMfgE	Fellow, Institution of Manufacturing Engineers (*now see* FIEE)
FIMFT	Fellow, Institute of Maxillo-facial Technology
FIMgt	Fellow, Institute of Management
FIMGTechE	Fellow, Institution of Mechanical and General Technician Engineers
FIMH	Fellow, Institute of Materials Handling (later FIMatM); Fellow, Institute of Military History
FIMI	Fellow, Institute of the Motor Industry
FIMinE	Fellow, Institution of Mining Engineers
FIMIT	Fellow, Institute of Musical Instrument Technology
FIMLS	Fellow, Institute of Medical Laboratory Sciences (*now see* FIBMS)
FIMLT	Fellow, Institute of Medical Laboratory Technology (later FIMLS)
FIMM	Fellow, Institution of Mining and Metallurgy
FIMMA	Fellow, Institute of Metals and Materials Australasia
FIMS	Fellow, Institute of Mathematical Statistics
FIMT	Fellow, Institute of the Motor Trade (*now see* FIMI)
FIMTA	Fellow, Institute of Municipal Treasurers and Accountants (*now see* IPFA)
FIMunE	Fellow, Institution of Municipal Engineers (now amalgamated with Institution of Civil Engineers)
FIN	Fellow, Institute of Navigation (*now see* FRIN)
FINA	Fédération Internationale de Natation Amateur
FInstAM	Fellow, Institute of Administrative Management
FInstArb(NZ)	Fellow, Institute of Arbitrators of New Zealand
FInstB	Fellow, Institution of Buyers
FInstBiol	Fellow, Institute of Biology (*now see* FIBiol)
FInstD	Fellow, Institute of Directors
FInstE	Fellow, Institute of Energy
FInstEnvSci	Fellow, Institute of Environmental Sciences
FInstF	Fellow, Institute of Fuel (*now see* FInstE)
FInstFF	Fellow, Institute of Freight Forwarders Ltd (*now see* FIFF)
FInstHE	Fellow, Institution of Highways Engineers (*now see* FIHT)
FInstLEx	Fellow, Institute of Legal Executives
FInstM	Fellow, Institute of Meat; Fellow, Institute of Marketing (*now see* FCIM)
FInstMC	Fellow, Institute of Measurement and Control
FInstMSM	Fellow, Institute of Marketing and Sales Management (later FInstM; *now see* FCIM)
FInstMet	Fellow, Institute of Metals (later part of Metals Society; *now see* FIM)
FInstNDT	Fellow, Institute of Non-Destructive Testing
FInstP	Fellow, Institute of Physics
FInstPet	Fellow, Institute of Petroleum
FInstPI	Fellow, Institute of Patentees and Inventors
FInstPS	Fellow, Institute of Purchasing and Supply (*now see* FCIPS)
FInstSM	Fellow, Institute of Sales Management (*now see* FInstSMM)
FInstSMM	Fellow, Institute of Sales and Marketing Management
FInstW	Fellow, Institute of Welding (*now see* FWeldI)
FINucE	Fellow, Institution of Nuclear Engineers
FIOA	Fellow, Institute of Acoustics
FIOB	Fellow, Institute of Building (*now see* FCIOB)
FIOH	Fellow, Institute of Occupational Hygiene
FIOM	Fellow, Institute of Office Management (*now see* FIAM)
FIOP	Fellow, Institute of Printing
FIOSH	Fellow, Institute of Occupational Safety and Health
FIP	Fellow, Australian Institute of Petroleum
FIPA	Fellow, Institute of Practitioners in Advertising
FIPD	Fellow, Institute of Personnel and Development
FIPDM	Fellow, Institute of Physical Distribution Management (later FILDM)
FIPENZ	Fellow, Institution of Professional Engineers, New Zealand
FIPG	Fellow, Institute of Professional Goldsmiths
FIPHE	Fellow, Institution of Public Health Engineers (*now see* FIWEM)
FIPlantE	Fellow, Institute of Plant Engineers (*now see* FIIM)

FIPM	Fellow, Institute of Personnel Management (*now see* FIPD)
FIPR	Fellow, Institute of Public Relations
FIProdE	Fellow, Institution of Production Engineers (later FIMfgE; *now see* FIEE)
FIQ	Fellow, Institute of Quarrying
FIQA	Fellow, Institute of Quality Assurance
FIQS	Fellow, Institute of Quantity Surveyors
FIRA	Furniture Industry Research Association
FIRA(Ind)	Fellow, Institute of Railway Auditors and Accountants (India)
FIRE(Aust)	Fellow, Institution of Radio Engineers (Australia) (*now see* FIREE(Aust))
FIREE(Aust)	Fellow, Institution of Radio and Electronics Engineers (Australia)
FIRI	Fellow, Institution of the Rubber Industry (later FPRI)
FIRM	Fellow, Institute of Risk Management
FIRSE	Fellow, Institute of Railway Signalling Engineers
FIRTE	Fellow, Institute of Road Transport Engineers
FIS	Fellow, Institute of Statisticians
FISA	Fellow, Incorporated Secretaries' Association; Fédération Internationale des Sociétés d'Aviron
FISE	Fellow, Institution of Sales Engineers; Fellow, Institution of Sanitary Engineers
FISITA	Fédération Internationale des Sociétés d'Ingénieurs des Techniques de l'Automobile
FISM	Fellow, Institute of Supervisory Managers
FISOB	Fellow, Incorporated Society of Organ Builders
FISP	Fédération Internationale des Sociétés de Philosophie
FIST	Fellow, Institute of Science Technology
FISTC	Fellow, Institute of Scientific and Technical Communicators
FISTD	Fellow, Imperial Society of Teachers of Dancing
FIStructE	Fellow, Institution of Structural Engineers
FISW	Fellow, Institute of Social Work
FITD	Fellow, Institute of Training and Development (*now see* FIPD)
FITE	Fellow, Institution of Electrical and Electronics Technician Engineers
FIW	Fellow, Welding Institute (*now see* FWeldI)
FIWE	Fellow, Institution of Water Engineers (later FIWES; then FIWEM; *now see* FCIWEM)
FIWEM	Fellow, Institution of Water and Environmental Management (*now see* FCIWEM)
FIWES	Fellow, Institution of Water Engineers and Scientists (later FIWEM; *now see* FCIWEM)
FIWM	Fellow, Institution of Works Managers (*now see* FIIM)
FIWPC	Fellow, Institute of Water Pollution Control (later FIWEM; *now see* FCIWEM)
FIWSc	Fellow, Institute of Wood Science
FIWSP	Fellow, Institute of Work Study Practitioners (*now see* FMS)
FJI	Fellow, Institute of Journalists (*now see* FCIJ)
FJIE	Fellow, Junior Institution of Engineers (*now see* CIMGTechE)
FKC	Fellow, King's College London
FKCHMS	Fellow, King's College Hospital Medical School
FL	Florida
FLA	Fellow, Library Association
Fla	Florida (US)
FLAA	Fellow, Library Association of Australia
FLAI	Fellow, Library Association of Ireland
FLAS	Fellow, Chartered Land Agents' Society (*now* (after amalgamation) *see* FRICS)
FLCM	Fellow, London College of Music
FLHS	Fellow, London Historical Society
FLI	Fellow, Landscape Institute
FLIA	Fellow, Life Insurance Association
FLS	Fellow, Linnean Society
Flt	Flight
FM	Field-Marshal
FMA	Fellow, Museums Association
FMAAT	Fellow Member, Association of Accounting Technicians
FMANZ	Fellow, Medical Association of New Zealand
FMES	Fellow, Minerals Engineering Society
FMF	Fiji Military Forces
FMI	Foundation for Manufacturing and Industry
FMS	Federated Malay States; Fellow, Medical Society; Fellow, Institute of Management Services

FMSA	Fellow, Mineralogical Society of America
FNA	Fellow, Indian National Science Academy
FNAEA	Fellow, National Association of Estate Agents
FNCO	Fleet Naval Constructor Officer
FNECInst	Fellow, North East Coast Institution of Engineers and Shipbuilders
FNI	Fellow, Nautical Institute; Fellow, National Institute of Sciences in India (*now see* FNA)
FNIA	Fellow, Nigerian Institute of Architects
FNM	Free National Movement
FNZEI	Fellow, New Zealand Educational Institute
FNZIA	Fellow, New Zealand Institute of Architects
FNZIAS	Fellow, New Zealand Institute of Agricultural Science
FNZIC	Fellow, New Zealand Institute of Chemistry
FNZIE	Fellow, New Zealand Institution of Engineers (*now see* FIPENZ)
FNZIM	Fellow, New Zealand Institute of Management
FNZPsS	Fellow, New Zealand Psychological Society
FO	Foreign Office (*now see* FCO); Field Officer; Flying Officer
FODA	Fellow, Overseas Doctors' Association
FODC	Franciscan Order of the Divine Compassion
FOIC	Flag Officer in charge
FOMI	Faculty of Occupational Medicine of Ireland
FONA	Flag Officer, Naval Aviation
FONAC	Flag Officer Naval Air Command
FOR	Fellowship of Operational Research
For.	Foreign
FOREST	Freedom Organisation for the Right to Enjoy Smoking Tobacco
FOX	Futures and Options Exchange
FPA	Family Planning Association
FPC	Family Practitioner Committee (*now see* FHSA)
FPEA	Fellow, Physical Education Association
FPHM	Faculty of Public Health Medicine
FPhS	Fellow, Philosophical Society of England
FPI	Fellow, Plastics Institute (later FPRI)
FPIA	Fellow, Plastics Institute of Australia
FPMI	Fellow, Pensions Management Institute
FPRI	Fellow, Plastics and Rubber Institute (*now see* FIM)
FPS	Fellow, Pharmaceutical Society (*now see* FRPharmS); Fauna Preservation Society (*now see* FFPS)
FPhysS	Fellow, Physical Society
f r	fuori ruole
FRA	Fellow, Royal Academy
FRACDS	Fellow, Royal Australian College of Dental Surgeons
FRACGP	Fellow, Royal Australian College of General Practitioners
FRACI	Fellow, Royal Australian Chemical Institute
FRACMA	Fellow, Royal Australian College of Medical Administrators
FRACO	Fellow, Royal Australian College of Ophthalmologists
FRACOG	Fellow, Royal Australian College of Obstetricians and Gynaecologists
FRACP	Fellow, Royal Australasian College of Physicians
FRACR	Fellow, Royal Australasian College of Radiologists
FRACS	Fellow, Royal Australasian College of Surgeons
FRAD	Fellow, Royal Academy of Dancing
FRAeS	Fellow, Royal Aeronautical Society
FRAgS	Fellow, Royal Agricultural Societies (*ie* of England, Scotland and Wales)
FRAHS	Fellow, Royal Australian Historical Society
FRAI	Fellow, Royal Anthropological Institute of Great Britain & Ireland
FRAIA	Fellow, Royal Australian Institute of Architects
FRAIB	Fellow, Royal Australian Institute of Building
FRAIC	Fellow, Royal Architectural Institute of Canada
FRAIPA	Fellow, Royal Australian Institute of Public Administration
FRAM	Fellow, Royal Academy of Music
FRAME	Fund for the Replacement of Animals in Medical Experiments
FRANZCP	Fellow, Royal Australian and New Zealand College of Psychiatrists
FRAPI	Fellow, Royal Australian Planning Institute
FRAS	Fellow, Royal Astronomical Society; Fellow, Royal Asiatic Society
FRASB	Fellow, Royal Asiatic Society of Bengal
FRASE	Fellow, Royal Agricultural Society of England

FRBS	Fellow, Royal Society of British Sculptors; Fellow, Royal Botanic Society
FRCA	Fellow, Royal College of Art; Fellow, Royal College of Anaesthetists
FRCCO	Fellow, Royal Canadian College of Organists
FRCD(Can.)	Fellow, Royal College of Dentists of Canada
FRCGP	Fellow, Royal College of General Practitioners
FRCM	Fellow, Royal College of Music
FRCN	Fellow, Royal College of Nursing
FRCO	Fellow, Royal College of Organists
FRCO(CHM)	Fellow, Royal College of Organists with Diploma in Choir Training
FRCOG	Fellow, Royal College of Obstetricians and Gynaecologists
FRCOphth	Fellow, Royal College of Ophthalmologists
FRCP	Fellow, Royal College of Physicians, London
FRCPA	Fellow, Royal College of Pathologists of Australasia
FRCP&S (Canada)	Fellow, Royal College of Physicians and Surgeons of Canada
FRCPath	Fellow, Royal College of Pathologists
FRCP(C)	Fellow, Royal College of Physicians of Canada
FRCPE or FRCPEd	Fellow, Royal College of Physicians, Edinburgh
FRCPGlas	Fellow, Royal College of Physicians and Surgeons of Glasgow
FRCPI	Fellow, Royal College of Physicians of Ireland
FRCPSGlas	Hon. Fellow, Royal College of Physicians and Surgeons of Glasgow
FRCPsych	Fellow, Royal College of Psychiatrists
FRCR	Fellow, Royal College of Radiologists
FRCS	Fellow, Royal College of Surgeons of England
FRCSCan	Fellow, Royal College of Surgeons of Canada
FRCSE or FRCSEd	Fellow, Royal College of Surgeons of Edinburgh
FRCSGlas	Fellow, Royal College of Physicians and Surgeons of Glasgow
FRCSI	Fellow, Royal College of Surgeons in Ireland
FRCSoc	Fellow, Royal Commonwealth Society
FRCUS	Fellow, Royal College of University Surgeons (Denmark)
FRCVS	Fellow, Royal College of Veterinary Surgeons
FREconS	Fellow, Royal Economic Society
FREI	Fellow, Real Estate Institute (Australia)
FRES	Fellow, Royal Entomological Society of London
FRFPSG	Fellow, Royal Faculty of Physicians and Surgeons, Glasgow (*now see* FRCPGlas)
FRG	Federal Republic of Germany
FRGS	Fellow, Royal Geographical Society
FRGSA	Fellow, Royal Geographical Society of Australasia
FRHistS	Fellow, Royal Historical Society
FRHS	Fellow, Royal Horticultural Society (*now see* MRHS)
FRHSV	Fellow, Royal Historical Society of Victoria
FRIAS	Fellow, Royal Incorporation of Architects of Scotland; Royal Institute for the Advancement of Science
FRIBA	Fellow, Royal Institute of British Architects (*and see* RIBA)
FRIC	Fellow, Royal Institute of Chemistry (*now see* FRSC)
FRICS	Fellow, Royal Institution of Chartered Surveyors
FRIH	Fellow, Royal Institute of Horticulture (NZ)
FRIN	Fellow, Royal Institute of Navigation
FRINA	Fellow, Royal Institution of Naval Architects
FRIPA	Fellow, Royal Institute of Public Administration (the Institute no longer has Fellows)
FRIPHH	Fellow, Royal Institute of Public Health and Hygiene
FRMCM	Fellow, Royal Manchester College of Music
FRMedSoc	Fellow, Royal Medical Society
FRMetS	Fellow, Royal Meteorological Society
FRMIA	Fellow, Retail Management Institute of Australia
FRMS	Fellow, Royal Microscopical Society
FRNCM	Fellow, Royal Northern College of Music
FRNS	Fellow, Royal Numismatic Society
FRPharmS	Fellow, Royal Pharmaceutical Society
FRPS	Fellow, Royal Photographic Society
FRPSL	Fellow, Royal Philatelic Society, London
FRS	Fellow, Royal Society
FRSA	Fellow, Royal Society of Arts
FRSAI	Fellow, Royal Society of Antiquaries of Ireland
FRSAMD	Fellow, Royal Scottish Academy of Music and Drama
FRSanI	Fellow, Royal Sanitary Institute (*now see* FRSH)
FRSC	Fellow, Royal Society of Canada, Fellow, Royal Society of Chemistry
FRS(Can)	Fellow, Royal Society of Canada (used when a person is also a Fellow of the Royal Society of Chemistry)
FRSCM	Hon. Fellow, Royal School of Church Music
FRSC (UK)	Fellow, Royal Society of Chemistry (used when a person is also a Fellow of the Royal Society of Canada)
FRSE	Fellow, Royal Society of Edinburgh
FRSGS	Fellow, Royal Scottish Geographical Society
FRSH	Fellow, Royal Society for the Promotion of Health
FRSL	Fellow, Royal Society of Literature
FRSM or FRSocMed	Fellow, Royal Society of Medicine
FRSNZ	Fellow, Royal Society of New Zealand
FRSSAf	Fellow, Royal Society of South Africa
FRST	Fellow, Royal Society of Teachers
FRSTM&H	Fellow, Royal Society of Tropical Medicine and Hygiene
FRTPI	Fellow, Royal Town Planning Institute
FRTS	Fellow, Royal Television Society
FRVA	Fellow, Rating and Valuation Association (*now see* IRRV)
FRVC	Fellow, Royal Veterinary College
FRVIA	Fellow, Royal Victorian Institute of Architects
FRZSScot	Fellow, Royal Zoological Society of Scotland
FS	Field Security
fs	Graduate, Royal Air Force Staff College
FSA	Fellow, Society of Antiquaries
FSAA	Fellow, Society of Incorporated Accountants and Auditors
FSAE	Fellow, Society of Automotive Engineers; Fellow, Society of Art Education
FSAI	Fellow, Society of Architectural Illustrators
FSAIEE	Fellow, South African Institute of Electrical Engineers
FSAM	Fellow, Society of Art Masters
FSArc	Fellow, Society of Architects (merged with the RIBA 1952)
FSaRS	Fellow, Safety and Reliability Society
FSAScot	Fellow, Society of Antiquaries of Scotland
FSASM	Fellow, South Australian School of Mines
FSBI	Fellow, Savings Banks Institute
fsc	Foreign Staff College
FSCA	Fellow, Society of Company and Commercial Accountants
FScotvec	Fellow, Scottish Vocational Education Council
FSCRE	Fellow, Scottish Council for Research in Education
FSDC	Fellow, Society of Dyers and Colourists
FSE	Fellow, Society of Engineers
FSG	Fellow, Society of Genealogists
FSGT	Fellow, Society of Glass Technology
FSI	Fellow, Chartered Surveyors' Institution (*now see* FRICS); Fellow, Securities Institute
FSIAD	Fellow, Society of Industrial Artists and Designers (*now see* FCSD)
FSLAET	Fellow, Society of Licensed Aircraft Engineers and Technologists
FSLCOG	Fellow, Sri Lankan College of Obstetrics and Gynaecology
FSLTC	Fellow, Society of Leather Technologists and Chemists
FSMA	Fellow, Incorporated Sales Managers' Association (later FInstMSM, then FInstM)
FSMC	Freeman of the Spectacle-Makers' Company
FSME	Fellow, Society of Manufacturing Engineers
FSMPTE	Fellow, Society of Motion Picture and Television Engineers (USA)
FSNAD	Fellow, Society of Numismatic Artists and Designers
FSNAME	Fellow, American Society of Naval Architects and Marine Engineers
FSRHE	Fellow, Society for Research into Higher Education
FSRP	Fellow, Society for Radiological Protection
FSS	Fellow, Royal Statistical Society
FSTD	Fellow, Society of Typographic Designers
FSVA	Fellow, Incorporated Society of Valuers and Auctioneers
FT	Financial Times
FTAT	Furniture, Timber and Allied Trades Union
FTC	Flying Training Command; Full Technological Certificate, City and Guilds of London Institute
FTCD	Fellow, Trinity College, Dublin

FTCL	Fellow, Trinity College of Music, London
FTI	Fellow, Textile Institute
FTII	Fellow, Chartered Institute (*formerly* Incorporated Institute, then Institute) of Taxation
FTMA	Fellow, Telecommunications Managers Association
FTP	Fellow, Thames Polytechnic
FTS	Fellow, Australian Academy of Technological Sciences and Engineering; Flying Training School; Fellow, Tourism Society
FTSC	Fellow, Tonic Sol-fa College
FUCUA	Federation of University Conservative and Unionist Associations (*now see* FCS)
FUMIST	Fellow, University of Manchester Institute of Science and Technology
FVRDE	Fighting Vehicles Research and Development Establishment
FWAAS	Fellow, World Academy of Arts and Sciences
FWACP	Fellow, West African College of Physicians
FWCMD	Fellow, Welsh College of Music and Drama
FWeldI	Fellow, Welding Institute
FWSOM	Fellow, Institute of Practitioners in Work Study, Organisation and Method (*now see* FMS)
FZS	Fellow, Zoological Society
FZSScot	Fellow, Zoological Society of Scotland (*now see* FRZSScot)

G

GA	Geologists' Association; Gaelic Athletic (Club); Georgia
Ga	Georgia (US)
GAI	Guild of Architectural Ironmongers
GAP	Gap Activity Projects
GAPAN	Guild of Air Pilots and Air Navigators
GATT	General Agreement on Tariffs and Trade (*now* World Trade Organisation)
GB	Great Britain
GBA	Governing Bodies Association
GBE	Knight or Dame Grand Cross, Order of the British Empire
GBGSA	Governing Bodies of Girls' Schools Association (*formerly* Association of Governing Bodies of Girls' Public Schools)
GBSM	Graduate of Birmingham and Midland Institute School of Music
GC	George Cross
GCB	Knight or Dame Grand Cross, Order of the Bath
GCBS	General Council of British Shipping
GCCC	Gonville and Caius College, Cambridge
GCFR	Grand Commander, Order of the Federal Republic of Nigeria
GCH	Knight Grand Cross, Hanoverian Order
GCHQ	Government Communications Headquarters
GCIE	Knight Grand Commander, Order of the Indian Empire
GCLJ	Grand Cross, St Lazarus of Jerusalem
GCLM	Grand Commander, Order of the Legion of Merit of Rhodesia
GCM	Gold Crown of Merit (Barbados)
GCMG	Knight or Dame Grand Cross, Order of St Michael and St George
GCON	Grand Cross, Order of the Niger
GCSE	General Certificate of Secondary Education
GCSG	Knight Grand Cross, Order of St Gregory the Great
GCSI	Knight Grand Commander, Order of the Star of India
GCSJ	Knight Grand Cross of Justice, Order of St John of Jerusalem (Knights Hospitaller)
GCSL	Grand Cross, Order of St Lucia
GCStJ	Bailiff or Dame Grand Cross, Most Venerable Order of the Hospital of St John of Jerusalem
GCVO	Knight or Dame Grand Cross, Royal Victorian Order
gd	grand-daughter
GDBA	Guide Dogs for the Blind Association
GDC	General Dental Council
Gdns	Gardens
GDR	German Democratic Republic
Gen.	General
Ges.	Gesellschaft
GFD	Geophysical Fluid Dynamics

GFS	Girls' Friendly Society
ggd	great-grand-daughter
ggs	great-grandson
GGSM	Graduate in Music, Guildhall School of Music and Drama
GHQ	General Headquarters
Gib.	Gibraltar
GIMechE	Graduate, Institution of Mechanical Engineers
GL	Grand Lodge
GLAA	Greater London Arts Association (*now see* GLAB)
GLAB	Greater London Arts Board
GLC	Greater London Council
Glos	Gloucestershire
GM	George Medal; Grand Medal (Ghana)
GMB	(Union for) General, Municipal, Boilermakers
GMBATU	General, Municipal, Boilermakers and Allied Trades Union (*now see* GMB)
GmbH	Gesellschaft mit beschränkter Haftung
GMC	General Medical Council; Guild of Memorial Craftsmen; General Management Course (Henley)
GMIE	Grand Master, Order of the Indian Empire
GMSI	Grand Master, Order of the Star of India
GMWU	General and Municipal Workers' Union (later GMBATU; *now see* GMB)
GNC	General Nursing Council
GOC	General Officer Commanding
GOC-in-C	General Officer Commanding-in-Chief
GOE	General Ordination Examination
Gov.	Governor
Govt	Government
GP	General Practitioner; Grand Prix
GPDST	Girls' Public Day School Trust
GPMU	Graphical, Paper and Media Union
GPO	General Post Office
GQG	Grand Quartier Général
GR	General Reconaissance
Gr.	Greek
GRSM	Graduate of the Royal Schools of Music
GS	General Staff; Grammar School
gs	grandson
GSA	Girls' Schools Association
GSM	General Service Medal; (Member of) Guildhall School of Music and Drama
GSMD	Guildhall School of Music and Drama
GSO	General Staff Officer
GTCL	Graduate, Trinity College of Music
GTS	General Theological Seminary (New York)
GUI	Golfing Union of Ireland
GWR	Great Western Railway

H

HA	Historical Association; Health Authority
HAA	Heavy Anti-Aircraft
HAC	Honourable Artillery Company
HACAS	Housing Association Consultancy and Advisory Service
Hants	Hampshire
HARCVS	Honorary Associate, Royal College of Veterinary Surgeons
Harv.	Harvard
HAT	Housing Action Trust
HBM	His (or Her) Britannic Majesty (Majesty's); Humming Bird Gold Medal (Trinidad)
hc	*honoris causa* (honorary)
HCEG	Honourable Company of Edinburgh Golfers
HCF	Honorary Chaplain to the Forces
HCIMA	Hotel, Catering and Institutional Management Association
HCO	Higher Clerical Officer
HCSC	Higher Command and Staff Course
HDA	Hawkesbury Diploma in Agriculture (Australia)
HDD	Higher Dental Diploma
HDFA	Higher Diploma in Fine Art
HDipEd	Higher Diploma in Education
HE	His (or Her) Excellency; His Eminence
HEA	Health Education Authority

HEC	Ecole des Hautes Etudes Commerciales; Higher Education Corporation
HEFCE	Higher Education Funding Council for England
HEFCW	Higher Education Funding Council for Wales
HEH	His (or Her) Exalted Highness
HEIC	Honourable East India Company
HEICS	Honourable East India Company's Service
Heir-pres.	Heir-presumptive
HEO	Higher Executive Officer
HEQC	Higher Education Quality Council
Herts	Hertfordshire
HFARA	Honorary Foreign Associate of the Royal Academy
HFEA	Human Fertilisation and Embryology Authority
HFRA	Honorary Foreign Member of the Royal Academy
HG	Home Guard
HGTAC	Home Grown Timber Advisory Committee
HH	His (or Her) Highness; His Holiness; Member, Hesketh Hubbard Art Society
HHA	Historic Houses Association
HHD	Doctor of Humanities (US)
HI	Hawaii
HIH	His (or Her) Imperial Highness
HIM	His (or Her) Imperial Majesty
HJ	Hilal-e-Jurat (Pakistan)
HKIA	Hong Kong Institute of Architects
HKIPM	Hong Kong Institute of Personnel Management
HLD	Doctor of Humane Letters
HLI	Highland Light Infantry
HM	His (or Her) Majesty, or Majesty's
HMA	Head Masters' Association
HMAS	His (or Her) Majesty's Australian Ship
HMC	Headmasters' Conference; Hospital Management Committee
HMCIC	His (or Her) Majesty's Chief Inspector of Constabulary
HMCS	His (or Her) Majesty's Canadian Ship
HMHS	His (or Her) Majesty's Hospital Ship
HMI	His (or Her) Majesty's Inspector
HMIED	Honorary Member, Institute of Engineering Designers
HMMTB	His (or Her) Majesty's Motor Torpedo Boat
HMOCS	His (or Her) Majesty's Overseas Civil Service
HMS	His (or Her) Majesty's Ship
HMSO	His (or Her) Majesty's Stationery Office
HNC	Higher National Certificate
HND	Higher National Diploma
H of C	House of Commons
H of L	House of Lords
Hon.	Honourable; Honorary
HPk	Hilal-e-Pakistan
HQ	Headquarters
HQA	Hilali-Quaid-i-Azam (Pakistan)
HRCA	Honorary Royal Cambrian Academician
HRGI	Honorary Member, The Royal Glasgow Institute of the Fine Arts
HRH	His (or Her) Royal Highness
HRHA	Honorary Member, Royal Hibernian Academy
HRI	Honorary Member, Royal Institute of Painters in Water Colours
HROI	Honorary Member, Royal Institute of Oil Painters
HRSA	Honorary Member, Royal Scottish Academy
HRSW	Honorary Member, Royal Scottish Water Colour Society
HSC	Health and Safety Commission
HSE	Health and Safety Executive
HSH	His (or Her) Serene Highness
Hum.	Humanity, Humanities (Classics)
Hunts	Huntingdonshire
HVCert	Health Visitor's Certificate
Hy	Heavy

I

I	Island; Ireland
IA	Indian Army; Iowa
Ia	Iowa (US)
IAAF	International Amateur Athletic Federation
IAC	Indian Armoured Corps; Institute of Amateur Cinematographers

IACP	International Association of Chiefs of Police
IADB	Inter American Development Bank
IADR	International Association for Dental Research
IAEA	International Atomic Energy Agency
IAF	Indian Air Force; Indian Auxiliary Force
IAHM	Incorporated Association of Headmasters
IAM	Institute of Advanced Motorists; Institute of Aviation Medicine
IAMAS	International Association of Meteorology and Atmospheric Sciences
IAMC	Indian Army Medical Corps
IAMTACT	Institute of Advanced Machine Tool and Control Technology
IAO	Incorporated Association of Organists
IAOC	Indian Army Ordnance Corps
IAPS	Incorporated Association of Preparatory Schools
IAPSO	International Association for the Physical Sciences of the Oceans
IARO	Indian Army Reserve of Officers
IAS	Indian Administrative Service; Institute for Advanced Studies; International Academy of Science
IASC	International Arctic Science Committee
IASS	International Association for Scandinavian Studies
IATA	International Air Transport Association
IATUL	International Association of Technological University Libraries
IAU	International Astronomical Union
IAWPRC	International Association on Water Pollution Research and Control
ib. or ibid.	*ibidem* (in the same place)
IBA	Independent Broadcasting Authority; International Bar Association
IBCA	International Braille Chess Association
IBG	Institute of British Geographers (*now see* RGS)
IBRD	International Bank for Reconstruction and Development (World Bank)
IBRO	International Bank Research Organisation; International Brain Research Organisation
IDTE	Institution of British Telecommunications Engineers
i/c	in charge; in command
ICA	Institute of Contemporary Arts; Institute of Chartered Accountants in England and Wales (*now see* ICAEW)
ICAA	Invalid Children's Aid Association
ICAEW	Institute of Chartered Accountants in England and Wales
ICAI	Institute of Chartered Accountants in Ireland
ICAO	International Civil Aviation Organization
ICBP	International Council for Bird Preservation
ICBS	Irish Christian Brothers' School
ICC	International Chamber of Commerce
ICCROM	International Centre for Conservation at Rome
ICD	*Iuris Canonici Doctor* (Doctor of Canon Law); Independence Commemorative Decoration (Rhodesia)
ICE	Institution of Civil Engineers
ICED	International Council for Educational Development
ICEF	International Federation of Chemical, Energy and General Workers' Unions
Icel.	Icelandic
ICES	International Council for the Exploration of the Sea
ICF	International Federation of Chemical and General Workers' Unions (*now see* ICEF)
ICFC	Industrial and Commercial Finance Corporation (later part of Investors in Industry)
ICFTU	International Confederation of Free Trade Unions
ICHCA	International Cargo Handling Co-ordination Association
IChemE	Institution of Chemical Engineers
ICI	Imperial Chemical Industries
ICJ	International Commission of Jurists
ICL	International Computers Ltd
ICM	International Confederation of Midwives
ICMA	Institute of Cost and Management Accountants (*now see* CIMA)
ICME	International Commission for Mathematical Education
ICOM	International Council of Museums
ICOMOS	International Council of Monuments and Sites
ICorrST	Institution of Corrosion Science and Technology
ICPO	International Criminal Police Organization (Interpol)

ICRC	International Committee of the Red Cross
ICRF	Imperial Cancer Research Fund
ICS	Indian Civil Service
ICSA	Institute of Chartered Secretaries and Administrators
ICSD	International Council for Scientific Development
ICSID	International Council of Societies of Industrial Design; International Centre for Settlement of Investment Disputes
ICSS	International Committee for the Sociology of Sport
ICSTIS	Independent Committee for Supervision of Telephone Information Services
ICSTM	Imperial College of Science, Technology and Medicine, London
ICSU	International Council of Scientific Unions
ICT	International Computers and Tabulators Ltd (_now see_ ICL)
ID	Independence Decoration (Rhodesia); Idaho
Id	Idaho (US)
IDA	International Development Association
IDB	Internal Drainage Board; Industrial Development Board
IDC	Imperial Defence College (_now see_ RCDS); Inter-Diocesan Certificate
idc	completed a course at, or served for a year on the Staff of, the Imperial Defence College (_now see_ rcds)
IDRC	International Development Research Centre
IDS	Institute of Development Studies; Industry Department for Scotland
IEA	Institute of Economic Affairs
IEC	International Electrotechnical Commission
IEE	Institution of Electrical Engineers
IEEE	Institute of Electrical and Electronics Engineers (NY)
IEEIE	Institution of Electrical and Electronics Incorporated Engineers (_now see_ IEIE)
IEETE	Institution of Electrical and Electronics Technician Engineers (later IEEIE; _now see_ IEIE)
IEI	Institution of Engineers of Ireland
IEIE	Institution of Electronics and Electrical Incorporated Engineers
IEME	Inspectorate of Electrical and Mechanical Engineering
IEng	Incorporated Engineer
IERE	Institution of Electronic and Radio Engineers
IES	Indian Educational Service; Institution of Engineers and Shipbuilders in Scotland; International Electron Paramagnetic Resonance Society
IExpE	Institute of Explosives Engineers
IFAC	International Federation of Automatic Control
IFAD	International Fund for Agricultural Development (UNO)
IFAW	International Fund for Animal Welfare
IFBWW	International Federation of Building Woodworkers
IFC	International Finance Corporation
IFIAS	International Federation of Institutes of Advanced Study
IFIP	International Federation for Information Processing
IFL	International Friendship League
IFLA	International Federation of Library Associations
IFORS	International Federation of Operational Research Societies
IFPI	International Federation of the Phonographic Industry
IFRA	World Press Research Association
IFS	Irish Free State; Indian Forest Service
IG	Instructor in Gunnery
IGasE	Institution of Gas Engineers
IGPP	Institute of Geophysics and Planetary Physics
IGS	Independent Grammar School
IGU	International Geographical Union; International Gas Union
IHA	Institute of Health Service Administrators
IHospE	Institute of Hospital Engineering
IHSM	Institute of Health Services Management
IHVE	Institution of Heating and Ventilating Engineers (later CIBS)
IIExE	Institution of Incorporated Executive Engineers
IILS	International Institute for Labour Studies
IIM	Institution of Industrial Managers
IIMR	Institute of Investment Management and Research
IIMT	International Institute for the Management of Technology
IInfSc	Institute of Information Scientists
IIS	International Institute of Sociology
IISI	International Iron and Steel Institute
IISS	International Institute of Strategic Studies
IIT	Indian Institute of Technology
IL	Illinois
ILA	International Law Association
ILEA	Inner London Education Authority
ILEC	Inner London Education Committee
Ill	Illinois (US)
ILO	International Labour Office; International Labour Organisation
ILP	Independent Labour Party
ILR	Independent Local Radio; International Labour Review
IM	Individual Merit
IMA	International Music Association; Institute of Mathematics and its Applications
IMCB	International Management Centre from Buckingham
IMCO	Inter-Governmental Maritime Consultative Organization (_now see_ IMO)
IME	Institute of Medical Ethics
IMEA	Incorporated Municipal Electrical Association
IMechE	Institution of Mechanical Engineers
IMechIE	Institution of Mechanical Incorporated Engineers
IMEDE	Institut pour l'Etude des Méthodes de Direction de l'Entreprise
IMF	International Monetary Fund
IMGTechE	Institution of Mechanical and General Technician Engineers
IMinE	Institution of Mining Engineers
IMM	Institution of Mining and Metallurgy
IMMLEP	Immunology of Leprosy
IMMTS	Indian Mercantile Marine Training Ship
IMO	International Maritime Organization
Imp.	Imperial
IMRO	Investment Management Regulatory Organisation
IMS	Indian Medical Service; Institute of Management Services; International Military Staff
IMTA	Institute of Municipal Treasurers and Accountants (_now see_ CIPFA)
IMU	International Mathematical Union
IMunE	Institution of Municipal Engineers (now amalgamated with Institution of Civil Engineers)
IN	Indian Navy; Indiana
INASFMH	International Sports Association for People with Mental Handicap
Inc.	Incorporated
INCA	International Newspaper Colour Association
Incog.	Incognito
Ind.	Independent; Indiana (US)
Inf.	Infantry
INFORM	Information Network Focus on New Religious Movements
INSA	Indian National Science Academy
INSEA	International Society for Education through Art
INSEAD or Insead	Institut Européen d'Administration des Affaires
Insp.	Inspector
Inst.	Institute
InstBE	Institution of British Engineers
Instn	Institution
InstSMM	Institute of Sales and Marketing Management
InstT	Institute of Transport (_now see_ CIT)
INTELSAT	International Telecommunications Satellite Organisation
IOB	Institute of Banking (_now see_ CIOB)
IOC	International Olympic Committee; Intergovernmental Oceanographic Commission
IOCD	International Organisation for Chemical Science in Development
IODE	Imperial Order of the Daughters of the Empire
I of M	Isle of Man
IOGT	International Order of Good Templars
IOM	Isle of Man; Indian Order of Merit
IOOF	Independent Order of Odd-fellows
IOP	Institute of Painters in Oil Colours
IOTA	(Fellow of) Institute of Transport Administration
IoW	Isle of Wight
IPA	International Publishers' Association
IPCS	Institution of Professional Civil Servants

IPFA	Member or Associate, Chartered Institute of Public Finance and Accountancy
IPHE	Institution of Public Health Engineers (*now see* IWEM)
IPI	International Press Institute; Institute of Patentees and Inventors
IPlantE	Institution of Plant Engineers (*now see* IIM)
IPM	Institute of Personnel Management
IPPA	Independent Programme Producers' Association
IPPF	International Planned Parenthood Federation
IPPR	Institute for Public Policy Research
IPPS	Institute of Physics and The Physical Society
IProdE	Institution of Production Engineers (later Institution of Manufacturing Engineering; *now see* IEE)
IPS	Indian Police Service; Indian Political Service; Institute of Purchasing and Supply
IPU	Inter-Parliamentary Union
IRA	Irish Republican Army
IRAD	Institute for Research on Animal Diseases
IRC	Industrial Reorganization Corporation; Interdisciplinary Research Centre
IRCAM	Institute for Research and Co-ordination in Acoustics and Music
IRCert	Industrial Relations Certificate
IREE(Aust)	Institution of Radio and Electronics Engineers (Australia)
IRI	Institution of the Rubber Industry (*now see* PRI)
IRO	International Refugee Organization
IRPA	International Radiation Protection Association
IRRV	(Fellow/Member of) Institute of Revenues, Rating and Valuation
IRTE	Institute of Road Transport Engineers
IS	International Society of Sculptors, Painters and Gravers
Is	Island(s)
ISBA	Incorporated Society of British Advertisers
ISC	Imperial Service College, Haileybury; Indian Staff Corps
I3CM	International Society for Contemporary Music
ISCO	Independent Schools Careers Organisation
ISE	Indian Service of Engineers
ISI	International Statistical Institute
ISIS	Independent Schools Information Service
ISJC	Independent Schools Joint Council
ISM	Incorporated Society of Musicians
ISMAR	International Society of Magnetic Resonance
ISME	International Society for Musical Education
ISMRC	Inter-Services Metallurgical Research Council
ISO	Imperial Service Order; International Organization for Standardization
ISSA	International Social Security Association
ISSTIP	International Society for Study of Tension in Performance
ISTC	Iron and Steel Trades Confederation; Institute of Scientific and Technical Communicators
ISTD	Imperial Society of Teachers of Dancing
IStructE	Institution of Structural Engineers
IT	Information Technology; Indian Territory (US)
It. or Ital.	Italian
ITA	Independent Television Authority (later IBA)
ITAB	Information Technology Advisory Board
ITB	Industry Training Board
ITC	International Trade Centre; Independent Television Commission
ITCA	Independent Television Association (*formerly* Independent Television Companies Association Ltd)
ITDG	Intermediate Technology Development Group
ITEME	Institution of Technician Engineers in Mechanical Engineering
ITF	International Transport Workers' Federation
ITN	Independent Television News
ITO	International Trade Organization
ITU	International Telecommunication Union
ITV	Independent Television
ITVA	International Television Association
IUA	International Union of Architects
IUB	International Union of Biochemistry (*now see* IUBMB)
IUBMB	International Union of Biochemistry and Molecular Biology

IUC	Inter-University Council for Higher Education Overseas (*now see* IUPC)
IUCN	World Conservation Union (*formerly* International Union for the Conservation of Nature and Natural Resources)
IUCW	International Union for Child Welfare
IUGS	International Union of Geological Sciences
IUHPS	International Union of the History and Philosophy of Science
IULA	International Union of Local Authorities
IUP	Association of Independent Unionist Peers
IUPAC	International Union of Pure and Applied Chemistry
IUPAP	International Union of Pure and Applied Physics
IUPC	Inter-University and Polytechnic Council for Higher Education Overseas
IUPS	International Union of Physiological Sciences
IUTAM	International Union of Theoretical and Applied Mechanics
IVF	In-vitro Fertilisation
IVS	International Voluntary Service
IWA	Inland Waterways Association
IWEM	Institution of Water and Environmental Management
IWES	Institution of Water Engineers and Scientists (*now see* IWEM)
IWGC	Imperial War Graves Commission (*now see* CWGC)
IWM	Institution of Works Managers (*now see* IIM)
IWO	Institution of Water Officers
IWPC	Institute of Water Pollution Control (*now see* IWEM)
IWS	International Wool Secretariat
IWSA	International Water Supply Association
IWSOM	Institute of Practitioners in Work Study Organisation and Methods (*now see* IMS)
IWSP	Institute of Work Study Practitioners (*now see* IMS)
IY	Imperial Yeomanry
IYRU	International Yacht Racing Union
IZ	I Zingari

J

JA	Judge Advocate
JACT	Joint Association of Classical Teachers
JAG	Judge Advocate General
Jas	James
JCB	*Juris Canonici* (or *Civilis*) *Baccalaureus* (Bachelor of Canon (or Civil) Law)
JCR	Junior Common Room
JCS	Journal of the Chemical Society
JCD	*Juris Canonici* (or *Civilis*) *Doctor* (Doctor of Canon (or Civil) Law)
JCI	Junior Chamber International
JCL	*Juris Canonici* (or *Civilis*) *Licentiatus* (Licentiate in Canon (or Civil) Law)
JCO	Joint Consultative Organisation (of AFRC, MAFF, and Department of Agriculture and Fisheries for Scotland)
JD	Doctor of Jurisprudence
jd	*jure dignitatis* (by virtue of status)
JDipMA	Joint Diploma in Management Accounting Services
JG	Junior Grade
JInstE	Junior Institution of Engineers (*now see* IMGTechE)
jl(s)	journal(s)
JMB	Joint Matriculation Board
JMN	Johan Mangku Negara (Malaysia)
JMOTS	Joint Maritime Operational Training Staff
Jno. or Joh.	John
JP	Justice of the Peace
Jr	Junior
jsc	qualified at a Junior Staff Course, or the equivalent, 1942–46
JSD	Doctor of Juristic Science
JSDC	Joint Service Defence College
jsdc	completed a course at Joint Service Defence College
JSLS	Joint Services Liaison Staff
JSM	Johan Setia Mahkota (Malaysia)
JSPS	Japan Society for the Promotion of Science
JSSC	Joint Services Staff College
jssc	completed a course at Joint Services Staff College
jt, jtly	joint, jointly

JUD   *Juris Utriusque Doctor* (Doctor of Both Laws (Canon and Civil))

Jun.   Junior

Jun.Opt.   Junior Optime

JWS or jws   Joint Warfare Staff

K

KA   Knight of St Andrew, Order of Barbados

Kans   Kansas (US)

KAR   King's African Rifles

KBE   Knight Commander, Order of the British Empire

KC   King's Counsel

KCB   Knight Commander, Order of the Bath

KCC   Commander, Order of the Crown, Belgium and Congo Free State

KCH   King's College Hospital; Knight Commander, Hanoverian Order

KCHS   Knight Commander, Order of the Holy Sepulchre

KCIE   Knight Commander, Order of the Indian Empire

KCL   King's College London

KCLJ   Knight Commander, Order of St Lazarus of Jerusalem

KCMG   Knight Commander, Order of St Michael and St George

KCSA   Knight Commander, Military Order of the Collar of St Agatha of Paternò

KCSG   Knight Commander, Order of St Gregory the Great

KCSHS   Knight Commander with Star, Order of the Holy Sepulchre

KCSI   Knight Commander, Order of the Star of India

KCSJ   Knight Commander, Order of St John of Jerusalem (Knights Hospitaller)

KCSS   Knight Commander, Order of St Silvester

KCVO   Knight Commander, Royal Victorian Order

KCVSA   King's Commendation for Valuable Services in the Air

KDG   King's Dragoon Guards

KEH   King Edward's Horse

KEO   King Edward's Own

KG   Knight, Order of the Garter

KGCSS   Knight Grand Cross, Order of St Silvester

KGStJ   Knight of Grace, Order of St John of Jerusalem (*now see* KStJ)

KH   Knight, Hanoverian Order

KHC   Hon. Chaplain to the King

KHDS   Hon. Dental Surgeon to the King

KHNS   Hon. Nursing Sister to the King

KHP   Hon. Physician to the King

KHS   Hon. Surgeon to the King; Knight, Order of the Holy Sepulchre

K-i-H   Kaisar-i-Hind

KJStJ   Knight of Justice, Order of St John of Jerusalem (*now see* KStJ)

KLJ   Knight, Order of St Lazarus of Jerusalem

KM   Knight of Malta

KORR   King's Own Royal Regiment

KOSB   King's Own Scottish Borderers

KOYLI   King's Own Yorkshire Light Infantry

KP   Knight, Order of St Patrick

KPM   King's Police Medal

KRRC   King's Royal Rifle Corps

KS   King's Scholar; Kansas

KSC   Knight of St Columba

KSG   Knight, Order of St Gregory the Great

KSJ   Knight, Order of St John of Jerusalem (Knights Hospitaller)

KSLI   King's Shropshire Light Infantry

KSS   Knight, Order of St Silvester

KStJ   Knight, Most Venerable Order of the Hospital of St John of Jerusalem

KStJ(A)   Associate Knight of Justice, Most Venerable Order of the Hospital of St John of Jerusalem

KT   Knight, Order of the Thistle

Kt   Knight

KY   Kentucky

Ky   Kentucky (US)

L

L   Liberal

LA   Los Angeles; Library Association; Literate in Arts; Liverpool Academy; Louisiana

La   Louisiana (US)

LAA   Light Anti-Aircraft

Lab   Labour

LAC   London Athletic Club

LACSAB   Local Authorities Conditions of Service Advisory Board

LAE   London Association of Engineers

LAMDA   London Academy of Music and Dramatic Art

LAMSAC   Local Authorities' Management Services and Computer Committee

LAMTPI   Legal Associate Member, Town Planning Institute (*now see* LMRTPI)

L-Corp. or Lance-Corp.   Lance-Corporal

Lancs   Lancashire

LAPADA   London & Provincial Antique Dealers' Association

LARSP   Language Assessment, Remediation and Screening Procedure

Lautro   Life Assurance and Unit Trust Regulatory Organisation

LBC   London Broadcasting Company

LBHI   Licentiate, British Horological Institute

LC   Cross of Leo

LCAD   London Certificate in Art and Design (University of London)

LCC   London County Council (later GLC)

LCh   Licentiate in Surgery

LCJ   Lord Chief Justice

LCL   Licentiate of Canon Law

LCP   Licentiate, College of Preceptors

LCSP   London and Counties Society of Physiologists

LCST   Licentiate, College of Speech Therapists

LD   Liberal and Democratic; Licentiate in Divinity

LDDC   London Docklands Development Corporation

LDiv   Licentiate in Divinity

LDS   Licentiate in Dental Surgery

LDV   Local Defence Volunteers

LEA   Local Education Authority

LEDU   Local Enterprise Development Unit

LEP   Local Ecumenical Project

LEPRA   British Leprosy Relief Association

LèsL   Licencié ès lettres

LG   Lady Companion, Order of the Garter

LGSM   Licentiate, Guildhall School of Music and Drama

LGTB   Local Government Training Board

LH   Light Horse

LHD   *Literarum Humaniorum Doctor* (Doctor of Literature)

LHSM   Licentiate, Institute of Health Services Management

LI   Light Infantry; Long Island

LIBA   Lloyd's Insurance Brokers' Association

Lib Dem   Liberal Democrat

LIBER   Ligue des Bibliothèques Européennes de Recherche

LicMed   Licentiate in Medicine

Lieut   Lieutenant

LIFFE   London International Financial Futures and Options Exchange

Lincs   Lincolnshire

LIOB   Licentiate, Institute of Building

Lit.   Literature; Literary

LitD   Doctor of Literature; Doctor of Letters

Lit.Hum.   *Literae Humaniores* (Classics)

LittD   Doctor of Literature; Doctor of Letters

LJ   Lord Justice

LLA   Lady Literate in Arts

LLB   Bachelor of Laws

LLCM   Licentiate, London College of Music

LLD   Doctor of Laws

LLL   Licentiate in Laws

LLM   Master of Laws

LM   Licentiate in Midwifery

LMBC   Lady Margaret Boat Club

LMC   Local Medical Committee

LMCC   Licentiate, Medical Council of Canada

LMed	Licentiate in Medicine
LMH	Lady Margaret Hall, Oxford
LMR	London Midland Region (BR)
LMS	London, Midland and Scottish Railway; London Missionary Society
LMSSA	Licentiate in Medicine and Surgery, Society of Apothecaries
LMRTPI	Legal Member, Royal Town Planning Institute
LNat	Liberal National
LNER	London and North Eastern Railway
LOB	Location of Offices Bureau
L of C	Library of Congress; Lines of Communication
LP	Limited Partnership
LPH	Licentiate in Philosophy
LPO	London Philharmonic Orchestra
LPTB	London Passenger Transport Board (later LTE; now see LRT)
LRAD	Licentiate, Royal Academy of Dancing
LRAM	Licentiate, Royal Academy of Music
LRCP	Licentiate, Royal College of Physicians, London
LRCPE	Licentiate, Royal College of Physicians, Edinburgh
LRCPI	Licentiate, Royal College of Physicians of Ireland
LRCPSGlas	Licentiate, Royal College of Physicians and Surgeons of Glasgow
LRCS	Licentiate, Royal College of Surgeons of England
LRCSE	Licentiate, Royal College of Surgeons, Edinburgh
LRCSI	Licentiate, Royal College of Surgeons in Ireland
LRFPS(G)	Licentiate, Royal Faculty of Physicians and Surgeons, Glasgow (now see LRCPSGlas)
LRIBA	Licentiate, Royal Institute of British Architects (now see RIBA)
LRPS	Licentiate, Royal Photographic Society
LRT	London Regional Transport
LSA	Licentiate, Society of Apothecaries; Licence in Agricultural Sciences
LSE	London School of Economics and Political Science
LSHTM	London School of Hygiene and Tropical Medicine
LSO	London Symphony Orchestra
Lt	Lieutenant; Light
LT	London Transport (now see LRT); Licentiate in Teaching
LTA	Lawn Tennis Association
LTB	London Transport Board (later LTE; now see LRT)
LTCL	Licentiate of Trinity College of Music, London
Lt Col	Lieutenant Colonel
LTE	London Transport Executive (now see LRT)
Lt Gen.	Lieutenant General
LTh	Licentiate in Theology
LU	Liberal Unionist
LUOTC	London University Officers' Training Corps
LVO	Lieutenant, Royal Victorian Order (formerly MVO (Fourth Class))
LWT	London Weekend Television
LXX	Septuagint

M

M	Marquess; Member; Monsieur
m	married
MA	Master of Arts; Military Assistant; Massachusetts
MAA	Manufacturers' Agents Association of Great Britain
MAAF	Mediterranean Allied Air Forces
MAAT	Member, Association of Accounting Technicians
MACE	Member, Australian College of Education; Member, Association of Conference Executives
MACI	Member, American Concrete Institute
MACM	Member, Association of Computing Machines
MACS	Member, American Chemical Society
MADO	Member, Association of Dispensing Opticians
MAE	Member, Academia Europaea
MAEE	Marine Aircraft Experimental Establishment
MAF	Ministry of Agriculture and Fisheries
MAFF	Ministry of Agriculture, Fisheries and Food
MAI	Magister in Arte Ingeniaria (Master of Engineering)
MAIAA	Member, American Institute of Aeronautics and Astronautics
MAICE	Member, American Institute of Consulting Engineers
MAIChE	Member, American Institute of Chemical Engineers

Maj. Gen.	Major General
MALD	Master of Arts in Law and Diplomacy
Man	Manitoba (Canada)
M&A	Mergers and Acquisitions
MAO	Master of Obstetric Art
MAOT	Member, Association of Occupational Therapists
MAOU	Member, American Ornithologists' Union
MAP	Ministry of Aircraft Production
MAPsS	Member, Australian Psychological Society
MARAC	Member, Australasian Register of Agricultural Consultants
MArch	Master of Architecture
Marq.	Marquess
MASAE	Member, American Society of Agricultural Engineers
MASC	Member, Australian Society of Calligraphers
MASc	Master of Applied Science
MASCE	Member, American Society of Civil Engineers
MASME	Member, American Society of Mechanical Engineers
Mass	Massachusetts (US)
MATh	Master of Arts in Theology
Math.	Mathematics; Mathematical
MATSA	Managerial Administrative Technical Staff Association
MAusIMM	Member, Australasian Institute of Mining and Metallurgy
MB	Medal of Bravery (Canada); Bachelor of Medicine
MBA	Master of Business Administration
MBASW	Member, British Association of Social Workers
MBC	Metropolitan/Municipal Borough Council
MBCS	Member, British Computer Society
MBE	Member, Order of the British Empire
MBES	Member, Biological Engineering Society
MBFR	Mutual and Balanced Force Reductions (negotiations)
MBHI	Member, British Horological Institute
MBIFD	Member, British Institute of Funeral Directors
MBIM	Member, British Institute of Management (now see MIMgt)
MBKS	Member, British Kinematograph Society (now see MBKSTS)
MBKSTS	Member, British Kinematograph, Sound and Television Society
MBOU	Member, British Ornithologists' Union
MBPICS	Member, British Production and Inventory Control Society
MBritIRE	Member, British Institution of Radio Engineers (later MIERE; now see MIEE)
MBS	Member, Building Societies Institute (now see MCBSI)
MBSc	Master of Business Science
MC	Military Cross; Missionaries of Charity
MCAM	Member, CAM Foundation
MCB	Master in Clinical Biochemistry
MCBSI	Member, Chartered Building Societies Institute
MCC	Marylebone Cricket Club; Metropolitan County Council
MCCDRCS	Member in Clinical Community Dentistry, Royal College of Surgeons
MCD	Master of Civic Design
MCE	Master of Civil Engineering
MCFP	Member, College of Family Physicians (Canada)
MCh or MChir	Master in Surgery
MChE	Master of Chemical Engineering
MChemA	Master in Chemical Analysis
MChOrth	Master of Orthopaedic Surgery
MCIBS	Member, Chartered Institution of Building Services (now see MCIBSE)
MCIBSE	Member, Chartered Institution of Building Services Engineers
MCIH	Member, Chartered Institute of Housing
MCIM	Member, Chartered Institute of Marketing
MCIOB	Member, Chartered Institute of Building
M.CIRP	Member, International Institution for Production Engineering Research
MCIS	Member, Institute of Chartered Secretaries and Administrators
MCIT	Member, Chartered Institute of Transport
MCIWEM	Member, Chartered Institution of Water and Environmental Management
MCL	Master in Civil Law
MCMES	Member, Civil and Mechanical Engineers' Society

MCom	Master of Commerce
MConsE	Member, Association of Consulting Engineers
MConsEI	Member, Association of Consulting Engineers of Ireland
MCOphth	Member, College of Ophthalmologists (*now see* MRCOphth)
MCP	Member of Colonial Parliament; Master of City Planning (US)
MCPA	Member, College of Pathologists of Australia (*now see* MRCPA)
MCPath	Member, College of Pathologists (*now see* MRCPath)
MCPP	Member, College of Pharmacy Practice
MCPS	Member, College of Physicians and Surgeons
MCS	Madras Civil Service; Malayan Civil Service
MCSD	Member, Chartered Society of Designers
MCSEE	Member, Canadian Society of Electrical Engineers
MCSP	Member, Chartered Society of Physiotherapy
MCST	Member, College of Speech Therapists
MCT	Member, Association of Corporate Treasurers
MD	Doctor of Medicine; Military District; Maryland
Md	Maryland (US)
MDC	Metropolitan District Council
MDes	Master of Design
MDS	Master of Dental Surgery
MDSc	Master of Dental Science
Me	Maine (US)
ME	Mining Engineer; Middle East; Master of Engineering; Maine
MEAF	Middle East Air Force
MEC	Member of Executive Council; Middle East Command
MEc	Master of Economics
MECAS	Middle East Centre for Arab Studies
Mech.	Mechanics; Mechanical
MECI	Member, Institute of Employment Consultants
Med.	Medical
MEd	Master of Education
MEF	Middle East Force
MEIC	Member, Engineering Institute of Canada
MELF	Middle East Land Forces
Mencap	Royal Society for Mentally Handicapped Children and Adults
MEng	Master of Engineering
MEO	Marine Engineering Officer
MEP	Member of the European Parliament
MESc	Master of Engineering Science
MetR	Metropolitan Railway
MetSoc	Metals Society (formed by amalgamation of Institute of Metals and Iron and Steel Institute; now merged with Institution of Metallurgists to form Institute of Metals)
MEXE	Military Engineering Experimental Establishment
MF	Master of Forestry
MFA	Master of Fine Arts
MFC	Mastership in Food Control
MFCM	Member, Faculty of Community Medicine (*now see* MFPHM)
MFGB	Miners' Federation of Great Britain (*now see* NUM)
MFH	Master of Foxhounds
MFHom	Member, Faculty of Homœopathy
MFOM	Member, Faculty of Occupational Medicine
MFPaed	Member, Faculty of Paediatrics, Royal College of Physicians of Ireland
MFPHM	Member, Faculty of Public Health Medicine
MGA	Major General in charge of Administration
MGC	Machine Gun Corps
MGDSRCS	Member in General Dental Surgery, Royal College of Surgeons
MGGS	Major General, General Staff
MGI	Member, Institute of Certificated Grocers
MGO	Master General of the Ordnance; Master of Gynaecology and Obstetrics
Mgr	Monsignor
MHA	Member of House of Assembly
MHCIMA	Member, Hotel Catering and Institutional Management Association
MHK	Member of the House of Keys
MHort (RHS)	Master of Horticulture, Royal Horticultural Society
MHR	Member of the House of Representatives
MHRA	Modern Humanities Research Association
MHRF	Mental Health Research Fund
MHSM	Member, Institute of Health Services Management
MI	Military Intelligence; Michigan
MIAeE	Member, Institute of Aeronautical Engineers
MIAgrE	Member, Institution of Agricultural Engineers
MIAM	Member, Institute of Administrative Management
MIAS	Member, Institute of Aeronautical Science (US) (*now see* MAIAA)
MIBC	Member, Institute of Business Counsellors
MIBF	Member, Institute of British Foundrymen
MIBiol	Member, Institute of Biology
MIBritE	Member, Institution of British Engineers
MIB(Scot)	Member, Institute of Bankers in Scotland
MICE	Member, Institution of Civil Engineers
MICEI	Member, Institution of Civil Engineers of Ireland
MICFor	Member, Institute of Chartered Foresters
Mich	Michigan (US)
MIChemE	Member, Institution of Chemical Engineers
MICM	Member, Institute of Credit Management
MICorrST	Member, Institution of Corrosion Science and Technology
MICS	Member, Institute of Chartered Shipbrokers
MIDPM	Member, Institute of Data Processing Management
MIE(Aust)	Member, Institution of Engineers, Australia
MIED	Member, Institution of Engineering Designers
MIEE	Member, Institution of Electrical Engineers
MIEEE	Member, Institute of Electrical and Electronics Engineers (NY)
MIEEM	Member, Institute of Ecology and Environmental Management
MIEI	Member, Institution of Engineering Inspection
MIEIE	Member, Institution of Electronics and Electrical Incorporated Engineers
MIE(Ind)	Member, Institution of Engineers, India
MIEnvSc	Member, Institute of Environmental Science
MIERE	Member, Institution of Electronic and Radio Engineers (*now see* MIEE)
MIES	Member, Institution of Engineers and Shipbuilders, Scotland
MIET	Member, Institute of Engineers and Technicians
MIEx	Member, Institute of Export
MIExpE	Member, Institute of Explosives Engineers
MIFA	Member, Institute of Field Archaeologists
MIFF	Member, Institute of Freight Forwarders
MIFireE	Member, Institution of Fire Engineers
MIFM	Member, Institute of Fisheries Management
MIFor	Member, Institute of Foresters (*now see* MICFor)
MIGasE	Member, Institution of Gas Engineers
MIGeol	Member, Institution of Geologists
MIH	Member, Institute of Housing (*now see* MCIH)
MIHM	Member, Institute of Housing Managers (later MIH)
MIHort	Member, Institute of Horticulture
MIHT	Member, Institution of Highways and Transportation
MIHVE	Member, Institution of Heating and Ventilating Engineers (later MCIBS)
MIIA	Member, Institute of Industrial Administration (later FBIM)
MIIM	Member, Institution of Industrial Managers
MIInfSc	Member, Institute of Information Sciences
MIL	Member, Institute of Linguists
Mil.	Military
MILGA	Member, Institute of Local Government Administrators
MILocoE	Member, Institution of Locomotive Engineers
MIM	Member, Institute of Metals (*formerly* Institution of Metallurgists)
MIMarE	Member, Institute of Marine Engineers
MIMC	Member, Institute of Management Consultants
MIMechE	Member, Institute of Mechanical Engineers
MIMEMME	Member, Institution of Mining Electrical & Mining Mechanical Engineers
MIMgt	Member, Institute of Management
MIMGTechE	Member, Institution of Mechanical and General Technician Engineers
MIMI	Member, Institute of the Motor Industry
MIMinE	Member, Institution of Mining Engineers
MIMM	Member, Institution of Mining and Metallurgy
MIMunE	Member, Institution of Municipal Engineers (now amalgamated with Institution of Civil Engineers)

MIN	Member, Institute of Navigation (*now see* MRIN)
Min.	Ministry
Minn	Minnesota (US)
MInstAM	Member, Institute of Administrative Management
MInstBE	Member, Institution of British Engineers
MInstCE	Member, Institution of Civil Engineers (*now see* FICE)
MInstD	Member, Institute of Directors
MInstE	Member, Institute of Energy
MInstEnvSci	Member, Institute of Environmental Sciences
MInstF	Member, Institute of Fuel (*now see* MInstE)
MInstHE	Member, Institution of Highway Engineers (*now see* MIHT)
MInstM	Member, Institute of Marketing (*now see* MCIM)
MInstMC	Member, Institute of Measurement and Control
MInstME	Member, Institution of Mining Engineers
MInstMet	Member, Institute of Metals (later part of Metals Society, *now see* MIM)
MInstP	Member, Institute of Physics
MInstPet	Member, Institute of Petroleum
MInstPI	Member, Institute of Patentees and Inventors
MInstPkg	Member, Institute of Packaging
MInstPS	Member, Institute of Purchasing and Supply
MInstR	Member, Institute of Refrigeration
MInstRA	Member, Institute of Registered Architects
MInstT	Member, Institute of Transport (*now see* MCIT)
MInstTM	Member, Institute of Travel Managers in Industry and Commerce
MInstW	Member, Institute of Welding (*now see* MWeldI)
MInstWM	Member, Institute of Wastes Management
MINucE	Member, Institution of Nuclear Engineers
MIOA	Member, Institute of Acoustics
MIOB	Member, Institute of Building (*now see* MCIOB)
MIOM	Member, Institute of Office Management (*now see* MIAM)
MIOSH	Member, Institution of Occupational Safety and Health
MIPA	Member, Institute of Practitioners in Advertising
MIPD	Member, Institute of Personnel and Development
MIPlantE	Member, Institution of Plant Engineers (*now see* MIIM)
MIPM	Member, Institute of Personnel Management (*now see* MIPD)
MIPR	Member, Institute of Public Relations
MIProdE	Member, Institution of Production Engineers (*now see* MIEE)
MIQ	Member, Institute of Quarrying
MIQA	Member, Institute of Quality Assurance
MIRE	Member, Institution of Radio Engineers (later MIERE)
MIREE(Aust)	Member, Institution of Radio and Electronics Engineers (Australia)
MIRO	Mineral Industry Research Organisation
MIRT	Member, Institute of Reprographic Technicians
MIRTE	Member, Institute of Road Transport Engineers
MIS	Member, Institute of Statisticians
MISI	Member, Iron and Steel Institute (later part of Metals Society)
MIS(India)	Member, Institution of Surveyors of India
Miss	Mississippi (US)
MIStructE	Member, Institution of Structural Engineers
MIT	Massachusetts Institute of Technology
MITA	Member, Industrial Transport Association
MITD	Member, Institute of Training and Development (*now see* MIPD)
MITE	Member, Institution of Electrical and Electronics Technician Engineers
MITI	Member, Institute of Translation & Interpreting
MITT	Member, Institute of Travel and Tourism
MIWE	Member, Institution of Water Engineers (later MIWES; then MIWEM; *now see* MCIWEM)
MIWEM	Member, Institution of Water and Environmental Management (*now see* MCIWEM)
MIWES	Member, Institution of Water Engineers and Scientists (later MIWEM; *now see* MCIWEM)
MIWM	Member, Institution of Works Managers (*now see* MIIM)
MIWPC	Member, Institute of Water Pollution Control (later MIWEM; *now see* MCIWEM)
MIWSP	Member, Institute of Work Study Practitioners (*now see* MMS)
MJA	Medical Journalists Association
MJI	Member, Institute of Journalists
MJIE	Member, Junior Institution of Engineers (*now see* MIGTechE)
MJS	Member, Japan Society
MJur	*Magister Juris* (Master of Law)
ML	Licentiate in Medicine; Master of Laws
MLA	Member of Legislative Assembly; Modern Language Association; Master in Landscape Architecture
MLC	Member of Legislative Council
MLCOM	Member, London College of Osteopathic Medicine
MLitt	Master of Letters
Mlle	Mademoiselle
MLM	Member, Order of the Legion of Merit (Rhodesia)
MLO	Military Liaison Officer
MLR	Modern Language Review
MM	Military Medal; Merchant Marine
MMA	Metropolitan Museum of Art
MMB	Milk Marketing Board
MMD	Movement for Multi-Party Democracy
MME	Master of Mining Engineering
Mme	Madame
MMechE	Master of Mechanical Engineering
MMet	Master of Metallurgy
MMGI	Member, Mining, Geological and Metallurgical Institute of India
MMin	Master of Ministry
MMM	Member, Order of Military Merit (Canada)
MMS	Member, Institute of Management Services
MMSA	Master of Midwifery, Society of Apothecaries
MN	Merchant Navy; Minnesota
MNAS	Member, National Academy of Sciences (US)
MNECInst	Member, North East Coast Institution of Engineers and Shipbuilders
MNI	Member, Nautical Institute
MNSE	Member, Nigerian Society of Engineers
MNZIS	Member, New Zealand Institute of Surveyors
MNZPI	Member, New Zealand Planning Institute
MO	Medical Officer; Military Operations; Missouri
Mo	Missouri (US)
MoD	Ministry of Defence
Mods	Moderations (Oxford)
MOF	Ministry of Food
MOH	Medical Officer(s) of Health
MOI	Ministry of Information
MOMI	Museum of the Moving Image
Mon	Monmouthshire
Mont	Montana (US); Montgomeryshire
MOP	Ministry of Power
MOrthRCS	Member in Orthodontics, Royal College of Surgeons
MoS	Ministry of Supply
Most Rev.	Most Reverend
MoT	Ministry of Transport
MOV	Member, Order of Volta (Ghana)
MP	Member of Parliament
MPA	Master of Public Administration; Member, Parliamentary Assembly, Northern Ireland
MPBW	Ministry of Public Building and Works
MPH	Master of Public Health
MPhil	Master of Philosophy
MPIA	Master of Public and International Affairs
MPMI	Member, Property Management Institute
MPO	Management and Personnel Office
MPP	Member, Provincial Parliament
MPRISA	Member, Public Relations Institute of South Africa
MPS	Member, Pharmaceutical Society (*now see* MRPharmS)
MR	Master of the Rolls; Municipal Reform
MRAC	Member, Royal Agricultural College
MRACP	Member, Royal Australasian College of Physicians
MRACS	Member, Royal Australasian College of Surgeons
MRAeS	Member, Royal Aeronautical Society
MRAIC	Member, Royal Architectural Institute of Canada
MRAS	Member, Royal Asiatic Society
MRC	Medical Research Council
MRCA	Multi-Role Combat Aircraft
MRCGP	Member, Royal College of General Practitioners
MRC-LMB	Medical Research Council Laboratory of Molecular Biology

MRCOG	Member, Royal College of Obstetricians and Gynaecologists
MRCOphth	Member, Royal College of Ophthalmologists
MRCP	Member, Royal College of Physicians, London
MRCPA	Member, Royal College of Pathologists of Australia
MRCPath	Member, Royal College of Pathologists
MRCPE	Member, Royal College of Physicians, Edinburgh
MRCPGlas	Member, Royal College of Physicians and Surgeons of Glasgow
MRCPI	Member, Royal College of Physicians of Ireland
MRCPsych	Member, Royal College of Psychiatrists
MRCS	Member, Royal College of Surgeons of England
MRCSE	Member, Royal College of Surgeons of Edinburgh
MRCSI	Member, Royal College of Surgeons in Ireland
MRCVS	Member, Royal College of Veterinary Surgeons
MRE	Master of Religious Education
MRES or MREmpS	Member, Royal Empire Society
MRHS	Member, Royal Horticultural Society
MRI	Member, Royal Institution
MRIA	Member, Royal Irish Academy
MRIAI	Member, Royal Institute of the Architects of Ireland
MRIC	Member, Royal Institute of Chemistry (now see MRSC)
MRIN	Member, Royal Institute of Navigation
MRINA	Member, Royal Institution of Naval Architects
MRPharmS	Member, Royal Pharmaceutical Society
MRSanI	Member, Royal Sanitary Institute (now see MRSH)
MRSC	Member, Royal Society of Chemistry
MRSH	Member, Royal Society for the Promotion of Health
MRSL	Member, Order of the Republic of Sierra Leone
MRSM or MRSocMed	Member, Royal Society of Medicine
MRST	Member, Royal Society of Teachers
MRTPI	Member, Royal Town Planning Institute
MRurSc	Master of Rural Science
MRUSI	Member, Royal United Service Institution
MRVA	Member, Rating and Valuation Association
MS	Master of Surgery; Master of Science (US); Mississippi
MS, MSS	Manuscript, Manuscripts
MSA	Master of Science, Agriculture (US); Mineralogical Society of America
MSAAIE	Member, Southern African Association of Industrial Editors
MSAE	Member, Society of Automotive Engineeers (US)
MSAICE	Member, South African Institution of Civil Engineers
MSAInstMM	Member, South African Institute of Mining and Metallurgy
MS&R	Merchant Shipbuilding and Repairs
MSAutE	Member, Society of Automobile Engineers
MSC	Manpower Services Commission; Missionaries of the Sacred Heart; Madras Staff Corps
MSc	Master of Science
MScD	Master of Dental Science
MSD	Meritorious Service Decoration (Fiji)
MSE	Master of Science in Engineering (US)
MSF	(Union for) Manufacturing, Science, Finance
MSH	Master of Stag Hounds
MSI	Member, Securities Institute
MSIAD	Member, Society of Industrial Artists and Designers (now see MCSD)
MSINZ	Member, Surveyors' Institute of New Zealand
MSIT	Member, Society of Instrument Technology (now see MInstMC)
MSM	Meritorious Service Medal; Madras Sappers and Miners
MSN	Master of Science in Nursing
MSocIS	Member, Société des Ingénieurs et Scientifiques de France
MSocSc	Master of Social Sciences
MSocWork	Master of Social Work
MSR	Member, Society of Radiographers
MSt	Master of Studies
MSTD	Member, Society of Typographic Designers
MT	Mechanical Transport; Montana
Mt	Mount, Mountain
MTA	Music Trades Association
MTAI	Member, Institute of Travel Agents
MTB	Motor Torpedo Boat

MTCA	Ministry of Transport and Civil Aviation
MTD	Midwife Teachers' Diploma
MTech	Master of Technology
MTEFL	Master in the Teaching of English as a Foreign or Second Language
MTh	Master of Theology
MTIRA	Machine Tool Industry Research Association (now see AMTRI)
MTPI	Member, Town Planning Institute (now see MRTPI)
MTS	Master of Theological Studies
MUniv	Honorary Master of the University
MusB	Bachelor of Music
MusD	Doctor of Music
MusM	Master of Music
MV	Merchant Vessel, Motor Vessel (naval)
MVEE	Military Vehicles and Engineering Establishment
MVO	Member, Royal Victorian Order
MVSc	Master of Veterinary Science
MW	Master of Wine
MWA	Mystery Writers of America
MWeldI	Member, Welding Institute
MWSOM	Member, Institute of Practitioners in Work Study Organisation and Methods (now see MMS)

N

N	Nationalist; Navigating Duties; North
n	nephew
NA	National Academician (America)
NAACP	National Association for the Advancement of Colored People
NAAFI	Navy, Army and Air Force Institutes
NAAS	National Agricultural Advisory Service
NAB	National Advisory Body for Public Sector Higher Education
NABC	National Association of Boys' Clubs
NAC	National Agriculture Centre
NACAB	National Association of Citizens' Advice Bureaux
NACCB	National Accreditation Council for Certification Bodies
NACETT	National Advisory Council for Education and Training
NACF	National Art-Collections Fund
NACRO	National Association for the Care and Resettlement of Offenders
NADFAS	National Association of Decorative and Fine Arts Societies
NAE	National Academy of Engineering
NAEW	Nato Airborn Early Warning
NAHA	National Association of Health Authorities (now see NAHAT)
NAHAT	National Association of Health Authorities and Trusts
NALGO or Nalgo	National and Local Government Officers' Association
NAMAS	National Measurement and Accreditation Service
NAMCW	National Association for Maternal and Child Welfare
NAMH	MIND (National Association for Mental Health)
NAMMA	NATO MRCA Management Agency
NAPT	National Association for the Prevention of Tuberculosis
NARM	National Association of Recording Merchandisers (US)
NAS	National Academy of Sciences
NASA	National Aeronautics and Space Administration (US)
NASDIM	National Association of Security Dealers and Investment Managers (later FIMBRA)
NAS/UWT	National Association of Schoolmasters/Union of Women Teachers
NATCS	National Air Traffic Control Services (now see NATS)
NATFHE	National Association of Teachers in Further and Higher Education (combining ATCDE and ATTI)
NATLAS	National Testing Laboratory Accreditation Scheme
NATO	North Atlantic Treaty Organisation
NATS	National Air Traffic Services
Nat. Sci.	Natural Sciences
NATSOPA	National Society of Operative Printers, Graphical and Media Personnel (formerly of Operative Printers and Assistants)
NAYC	Youth Clubs UK (formerly National Association of Youth Clubs)
NB	New Brunswick; Nebraska

NBA	North British Academy
NBC	National Book Council (later NBL); National Broadcasting Company (US)
NBL	National Book League
NBPI	National Board for Prices and Incomes
NC	National Certificate; North Carolina (US)
NCA	National Certificate of Agriculture
NCARB	National Council of Architectural Registration Boards
NCB	National Coal Board
NCC	National Computing Centre; Nature Conservancy Council (now see NCCE); National Consumer Council
NCCE	Nature Conservancy Council for England (English Nature)
NCCI	National Committee for Commonwealth Immigrants
NCCL	National Council for Civil Liberties
NCD	National Capital District, Papua New Guinea
NCDAD	National Council for Diplomas in Art and Design
NCET	National Council for Educational Technology
NCH	National Children's Homes
NCLC	National Council of Labour Colleges
NCOPF	National Council for One Parent Families
NCSE	National Council for Special Education
NCSS	National Council of Social Service
NCTA	National Community Television Association (US)
NCTJ	National Council for the Training of Journalists
NCU	National Cyclists' Union
NCVCCO	National Council of Voluntary Child Care Organisations
NCVO	National Council for Voluntary Organisations
NCVQ	National Council for Vocational Qualifications
ND	North Dakota
NDA	National Diploma in Agriculture
NDak	North Dakota (US)
ndc	National Defence College
NDD	National Diploma in Dairying; National Diploma in Design
NDH	National Diploma in Horticulture
NDIC	National Defence Industries Council
NDP	New Democratic Party
NDTA	National Defense Transportation Association (US)
NE	North-east
NEAB	Northern Examinations and Assessment Board
NEAC	New English Art Club
NEAF	Near East Air Force
NEARELF	Near East Land Forces
NEB	National Enterprise Board
Neb	Nebraska (US)
NEBSS	National Examinations Board for Supervisory Studies
NEC	National Executive Committee
NECCTA	National Education Closed Circuit Television Association
NECInst	North East Coast Institution of Engineers and Shipbuilders
NEDC	National Economic Development Council; North East Development Council
NEDO	National Economic Development Office
NEH	National Endowment for the Humanities
NEL	National Engineering Laboratory
NERC	Natural Environment Research Council
Nev	Nevada (US)
New M	New Mexico (US)
NFC	National Freight Consortium (formerly Corporation, then Company)
NFCG	National Federation of Consumer Groups
NFER	National Foundation for Educational Research
NFHA	National Federation of Housing Associations
NFMS	National Federation of Music Societies
NFS	National Fire Service
NFSH	National Federation of Spiritual Healers
NFT	National Film Theatre
NFU	National Farmers' Union
NFWI	National Federation of Women's Institutes
NGO	Non-Governmental Organisation(s)
NGTE	National Gas Turbine Establishment
NH	New Hampshire (US)
NHBC	National House-Building Council
NHS	National Health Service
NI	Northern Ireland; Native Infantry

NIAB	National Institute of Agricultural Botany
NIACRO	Northern Ireland Association for the Care and Resettlement of Offenders
NIAE	National Institute of Agricultural Engineering
NIAID	National Institute of Allergy and Infectious Diseases
NICEC	National Institute for Careers Education and Counselling
NICG	Nationalised Industries Chairmen's Group
NICS	Northern Ireland Civil Service
NID	Naval Intelligence Division; National Institute for the Deaf; Northern Ireland District; National Institute of Design (India)
NIESR	National Institute of Economic and Social Research
NIH	National Institutes of Health (US)
NIHCA	Northern Ireland Hotels and Caterers Association
NII	Nuclear Installations Inspectorate
NILP	Northern Ireland Labour Party
NIMR	National Institute for Medical Research
NISTRO	Northern Ireland Science and Technology Regional Organisation
NJ	New Jersey (US)
NL	National Liberal; No Liability
NLCS	North London Collegiate School
NLF	National Liberal Federation
NLYL	National League of Young Liberals
NM	New Mexico
NMR	Nuclear Magnetic Resonance
NNMA	Nigerian National Merit Award
NNOM	Nigerian National Order of Merit
Northants	Northamptonshire
NOTB	National Ophthalmic Treatment Board
Notts	Nottinghamshire
NP	Notary Public
NPA	Newspaper Publishers' Association
NPFA	National Playing Fields Association
NPk	Nishan-e-Pakistan
NPL	National Physical Laboratory
NRA	National Rifle Association; National Recovery Administration (US); National Rivers Authority
NRAO	National Radio Astronomy Observatory
NRCC	National Research Council of Canada
NRD	National Registered Designer
NRDC	National Research Development Corporation
NRPB	National Radiological Protection Board
NRR	Northern Rhodesia Regiment
NS	Nova Scotia; New Style in the Calendar (in Great Britain since 1752); National Society; National Service
ns	Graduate of Royal Naval Staff College, Greenwich
NSA	National Skating Association
NSAIV	Distinguished Order of Shaheed Ali (Maldives)
NSF	National Science Foundation (US)
NSM	Non-Stipendiary Minister
NSMHC	National Society for Mentally Handicapped Children (now see Mencap)
NSPCC	National Society for Prevention of Cruelty to Children
NSQT	National Society for Quality through Teamwork
NSRA	National Small-bore Rifle Association
N/SSF	Novice, Society of St Francis
NSTC	Nova Scotia Technical College
NSW	New South Wales
NT	New Testament; Northern Territory (Australia); National Theatre (now see RNT); National Trust
NT&SA	National Trust & Savings Association
NTDA	National Trade Development Association
NTUC	National Trades Union Congress
NUAAW	National Union of Agricultural and Allied Workers
NUBE	National Union of Bank Employees (now see BIFU)
NUFLAT	National Union of Footwear Leather and Allied Trades (now see NUKFAT)
NUGMW	National Union of General and Municipal Workers (later GMBATU)
NUHKW	National Union of Hosiery and Knitwear Workers (now see NUKFAT)
NUI	National University of Ireland
NUJ	National Union of Journalists
NUJMB	Northern Universities Joint Matriculation Board
NUKFAT	National Union of Knitwear, Footwear and Apparel Trades

NUM	National Union of Mineworkers
NUMAST	National Union of Marine, Aviation and Shipping Transport Officers
NUPE	National Union of Public Employees
NUR	National Union of Railwaymen (*now see* RMT)
NUS	National Union of Students
NUT	National Union of Teachers
NUTG	National Union of Townswomen's Guilds
NUTN	National Union of Trained Nurses
NUU	New University of Ulster
NV	Nevada
NVQ	National Vocational Qualification
NW	North-west
NWC	National Water Council
NWFP	North-West Frontier Province
NWP	North-Western Province
NWT	North-Western Territories
NY	New York
NYC	New York City
NYO	National Youth Orchestra
NZ	New Zealand
NZEF	New Zealand Expeditionary Force
NZIA	New Zealand Institute of Architects
NZRSA	New Zealand Retired Services Association

O

O	Ohio (US)
o	only
OA	Officier d'Académie
OAM	Medal of the Order of Australia
O & E	Operations and Engineers (US)
O & M	organisation and method
O & O	Oriental and Occidental Steamship Co.
OAS	Organisation of American States; On Active Service
OASC	Officer Aircrew Selection Centre
OAU	Organisation for African Unity
OB	Order of Barbados
ob	*obiit* (died)
OBE	Officer, Order of the British Empire
OBI	Order of British India
OC	Officer, Order of Canada (equivalent to former award SM)
OC or	
o/c	Officer Commanding
oc	only child
OCA	Old Comrades Association
OCC	Order of the Caribbean Community
OCDS or	
ocds Can	Overseas College of Defence Studies (Canada)
OCF	Officiating Chaplain to the Forces
OCS	Officer Candidates School
OCSS	Oxford and Cambridge Shakespeare Society
OCTU	Officer Cadet Training Unit
OCU	Operational Conversion Unit
OD	Officer, Order of Distinction (Jamaica)
ODA	Overseas Development Administration
ODI	Overseas Development Institute
ODM	Ministry of Overseas Development
ODSM	Order of Diplomatic Service Merit (Lesotho)
OE	Order of Excellence (Guyana)
OEA	Overseas Education Association
OECD	Organization for Economic Co-operation and Development
OED	Oxford English Dictionary
OEEC	Organization for European Economic Co-operation (*now see* OECD)
OF	Order of the Founder, Salvation Army
OFEMA	Office Française d'Exportation de Matériel Aéronautique
OFFER	Office of Electricity Regulation
OFM	Order of Friars Minor (Franciscans)
OFMCap	Order of Friars Minor Capuchin (Franciscans)
OFMConv	Order of Friars Minor Conventual (Franciscans)
OFR	Order of the Federal Republic of Nigeria
OFS	Orange Free State
OFSTED	Office for Standards in Education

OFT	Office of Fair Trading
Oftel	Office of Telecommunications
OGS	Oratory of the Good Shepherd
OH	Ohio
OHMS	On His (or Her) Majesty's Service
O i/c	Officer in charge
OJ	Order of Jamaica
OK	Oklahoma
OL	Officer, Order of Leopold; Order of the Leopard (Lesotho)
OLJ	Officer, Order of St Lazarus of Jerusalem
OLM	Officer, Legion of Merit (Rhodesia)
OM	Order of Merit
OMCS	Office of the Minister for the Civil Service
OMI	Oblate of Mary Immaculate
OMM	Officer, Order of Military Merit (Canada)
ON	Order of the Nation (Jamaica)
OND	Ordinary National Diploma
Ont	Ontario
ONZ	Order of New Zealand
OO	Order of Ontario
OON	Officer, Order of the Niger
OP	*Ordinis Praedicatorum* (of the Order of Preachers (Dominican)); Observation Post
OPCON	Operational Control
OPCS	Office of Population Censuses and Surveys
OPSS	Office of Public Service and Science
OQ	Officer, National Order of Quebec
OR	Order of Rorima (Guyana); Operational Research; Oregon
ORC	Orange River Colony
Ore	Oregon (US)
ORGALIME	Organisme de Liaison des Industries Métalliques Européennes
ORL	Otorhinolaryngology
ORS	Operational Research Society
ORSA	Operations Research Society of America
ORSL	Order of the Republic of Sierra Leone
ORT	Organization for Rehabilitation through Training
ORTF	Office de la Radiodiffusion et Télévision Française
os	only son
OSA	Order of St Augustine (Augustinian); Ontario Society of Artists
OSB	Order of St Benedict (Benedictine)
osc	Graduate of Overseas Staff College
OSFC	Franciscan (Capuchin) Order
O/Sig	Ordinary Signalman
OSNC	Orient Steam Navigation Co.
osp	*obiit sine prole* (died without issue)
OSRD	Office of Scientific Research and Development
OSS	Office of Strategic Services
OST	Office of Science and Technology
OStJ	Officer, Most Venerable Order of the Hospital of St John of Jerusalem
OSUK	Ophthalmological Society of the United Kingdom
OT	Old Testament
OTC	Officers' Training Corps
OTL	Officer, Order of Toussaint L'Ouverture (Haiti)
OTU	Operational Training Unit
OTWSA	Ou-Testamentiese Werkgemeenskap in Suider-Afrika
OU	Oxford University; Open University
OUAC	Oxford University Athletic Club
OUAFC	Oxford University Association Football Club
OUBC	Oxford University Boat Club
OUCC	Oxford University Cricket Club
OUDS	Oxford University Dramatic Society
OUP	Oxford University Press; Official Unionist Party
OURC	Oxford University Rifle Club
OURFC	Oxford University Rugby Football Club
OURT	Order of the United Republic of Tanzania
Oxon	Oxfordshire; *Oxoniensis* (of Oxford)

P

PA	Pakistan Army; Personal Assistant; Pennsylvania
Pa	Pennsylvania (US)
PAA	President, Australian Academy of Science

pac	passed the final examination of the Advanced Class, The Military College of Science
PACE	Protestant and Catholic Encounter
PAg	Professional Agronomist
P&O	Peninsular and Oriental Steamship Co.
P&OSNCo.	Peninsular and Oriental Steam Navigation Co.
PAO	Prince Albert's Own
PASI	Professional Associate, Chartered Surveyors' Institution (now see ARICS)
PBS	Public Broadcasting Service
PC	Privy Counsellor; Police Constable; Perpetual Curate; Peace Commissioner (Ireland); Progressive Conservative (Canada)
pc	per centum (in the hundred)
PCC	Parochial Church Council
PCE	Postgraduate Certificate of Education
PCEF	Polytechnic and Colleges Employers' Forum
PCFC	Polytechnics and Colleges Funding Council
PCL	Polytechnic of Central London
PCMO	Principal Colonial Medical Officer
PdD	Doctor of Pedagogy (US)
PDG	Président Directeur Général
PDR	People's Democratic Republic
PDRA	post doctoral research assistant
PDSA	People's Dispensary for Sick Animals
PDTC	Professional Dancer's Training Course Diploma
PE	Procurement Executive
PEI	Prince Edward Island
PEN	Poets, Playwrights, Editors, Essayists, Novelists (Club)
PEng	Registered Professional Engineer (Canada); Member, Society of Professional Engineers
Penn	Pennsylvania
PEP	Political and Economic Planning (now see PSI)
PER	Professional and Executive Recruitment
PEST	Pressure for Economic and Social Toryism
PETRAS	Polytechnic Educational Technology Resources Advisory Service
PF	Procurator Fiscal
PFA	Professional Footballers' Association
pfc	Graduate of RAF Flying College
PFE	Program for Executives
PGA	Professional Golfers' Association
PGCE	Post Graduate Certificate of Education
PH	Presidential Order of Honour (Botswana)
PHAB	Physically Handicapped & Able-bodied
PhB	Bachelor of Philosophy
PhC	Pharmaceutical Chemist
PhD	Doctor of Philosophy
Phil.	Philology, Philological; Philosophy, Philosophical
PhL	Licentiate of Philosophy
PHLS	Public Health Laboratory Service
PhM	Master of Philosophy (USA)
PhmB	Bachelor of Pharmacy
Phys.	Physical
PIA	Personal Investment Authority
PIARC	Permanent International Association of Road Congresses
PIB	Prices and Incomes Board (later NBPI)
PICAO	Provisional International Civil Aviation Organization (now ICAO)
pinx.	pinxit (he painted it)
PIRA	Paper Industries Research Association
PITCOM	Parliamentary Information Technology Committee
PJG	Pingat Jasa Gemilang (Singapore)
PJK	Pingkat Jasa Kebaktian (Malaysia)
Pl.	Place; Plural
PLA	Port of London Authority
PLC or plc	public limited company
Plen.	Plenipotentiary
PLI	President, Landscape Institute
PLP	Parliamentary Labour Party; Progressive Liberal Party (Bahamas)
PMA	Personal Military Assistant
PMC	Personnel Management Centre
PMD	Program for Management Development
PMG	Postmaster-General
PMN	Panglima Mangku Negara (Malaysia)
PMO	Principal Medical Officer
PMRAFNS	Princess Mary's Royal Air Force Nursing Service

PMS	Presidential Order of Meritorious Service (Botswana); President, Miniature Society
PNBS	Panglima Negara Bintang Sarawak
PNEU	Parents' National Educational Union
PNG	Papua New Guinea
PNP	People's National Party
PO	Post Office
POB	Presidential Order of Botswana
POMEF	Political Office Middle East Force
Pop.	Population
POUNC	Post Office Users' National Council
POW	Prisoner of War; Prince of Wales's
PP	Parish Priest; Past President
pp	pages
PPA	Periodical Publishers Association
PPARC	Particle Physics and Astronomy Research Council
PPCLI	Princess Patricia's Canadian Light Infantry
PPE	Philosophy, Politics and Economics
PPInstHE	Past President, Institution of Highway Engineers
PPIStructE	Past President, Institution of Structural Engineers
PPITB	Printing and Publishing Industry Training Board
PPP	Private Patients Plan
PPRA	Past President, Royal Academy
PPRBA	Past President, Royal Society of British Artists
PPRBS	Past President, Royal Society of British Sculptors
PPRE	Past President, Royal Society of Painter-Printmakers (formerly of Painter-Etchers and Engravers)
PPRIBA	Past President, Royal Institute of British Architects
PPROI	Past President, Royal Institute of Oil Painters
PPRP	Past President, Royal Society of Portrait Painters
PPRTPI	Past President, Royal Town Planning Institute
PPRWA	Past President, Royal Watercolour Association
PPS	Parliamentary Private Secretary
PPSIAD	Past President, Society of Industrial Artists and Designers
PQ	Province of Quebec
PR	Public Relations; Parti républicain
PRA	President, Royal Academy
PRBS	President, Royal Society of British Sculptors
PRCS	President, Royal College of Surgeons
PRE	President, Royal Society of Painter-Printmakers (formerly of Painter-Etchers and Engravers)
Preb.	Prebendary
PrEng.	Professional Engineer
Pres.	President
PRHA	President, Royal Hibernian Academy
PRI	President, Royal Institute of Painters in Water Colours; Plastics and Rubber Institute
PRIA	President, Royal Irish Academy
PRIAS	President, Royal Incorporation of Architects in Scotland
Prin.	Principal
PRISA	Public Relations Institute of South Africa
PRO	Public Relations Officer; Public Records Office
Proc.	Proctor; Proceedings
Prof.	Professor; Professional
PROI	President, Royal Institute of Oil Painters
PRO NED	Promotion of Non-Executive Directors
PRORM	Pay and Records Office, Royal Marines
Pro tem.	Pro tempore (for the time being)
Prov.	Provost; Provincial
Prox.	Proximo (next)
Prox.acc.	Proxime accessit (next in order of merit to the winner)
PRS	President, Royal Society; Performing Right Society Ltd
PRSA	President, Royal Scottish Academy
PRSE	President, Royal Society of Edinburgh
PRSH	President, Royal Society for the Promotion of Health
PRSW	President, Royal Scottish Water Colour Society
PRUAA	President, Royal Ulster Academy of Arts
PRWA	President, Royal West of England Academy
PRWS	President, Royal Society of Painters in Water Colours
PS	Pastel Society; Paddle Steamer
ps	passed School of Instruction (of Officers)
PSA	Property Services Agency; Petty Sessions Area
psa	Graduate of RAF Staff College
psc	Graduate of Staff College († indicates Graduate of Senior Wing Staff College)

PSD	Petty Sessional Division; Social Democratic Party (Portugal)
PSGB	Pharmaceutical Society of Great Britain (*now see* RPSGB)
PSI	Policy Studies Institute
PSIAD	President, Society of Industrial Artists and Designers
PSM	Panglima Setia Mahkota (Malaysia)
psm	Certificate of Royal Military School of Music
PSMA	President, Society of Marine Artists
PSNC	Pacific Steam Navigation Co.
PSO	Principal Scientific Officer; Personal Staff Officer
PSOE	Partido Socialista Obrero Español
PSSC	Personal Social Services Council
PTA	Passenger Transport Authority; Parent-Teacher Association
PTE	Passenger Transport Executive
Pte	Private
ptsc	passed Technical Staff College
Pty	Proprietary
PUP	People's United Party
PVSM	Param Vishishc Seva Medal (India)
PWD	Public Works Department
PWE	Political Welfare Executive
PWO	Prince of Wales's Own
PWR	Pressurized Water Reactor

Q

Q	Queen; Quartering
QAIMNS	Queen Alexandra's Imperial Military Nursing Service
QALAS	Qualified Associate, Chartered Land Agents' Society (*now* (after amalgamation) *see* ARICS)
QARANC	Queen Alexandra's Royal Army Nursing Corps
QARNNS	Queen Alexandra's Royal Naval Nursing Service
QBD	Queen's Bench Division
QC	Queen's Counsel
QCVSA	Queen's Commendation for Valuable Service in the Air
QEH	Queen Elizabeth Hall
QEO	Queen Elizabeth's Own
QFSM	Queen's Fire Service Medal for Distinguished Service
QGM	Queen's Gallantry Medal
QHC	Honorary Chaplain to the Queen
QHDS	Honorary Dental Surgeon to the Queen
QHNS	Honorary Nursing Sister to the Queen
QHP	Honorary Physician to the Queen
QHS	Honorary Surgeon to the Queen
Qld	Queensland
Qly	Quarterly
QMAAC	Queen Mary's Army Auxiliary Corps
QMC	Queen Mary College, London (*now see* QMW)
QMG	Quartermaster-General
QMW	Queen Mary and Westfield College, London
QO	Qualified Officer
QOOH	Queen's Own Oxfordshire Hussars
Q(ops)	Quartering (operations)
QOY	Queen's Own Yeomanry
QPM	Queen's Police Medal
Qr	Quarter
QRIH	Queen's Royal Irish Hussars
QRV	Qualified Valuer, Real Estate Institute of New South Wales
QS	Quarter Sessions; Quantity Surveying
qs	RAF graduates of the Military or Naval Staff College
QSM	Queen's Service Medal (NZ)
QSO	Queen's Service Order (NZ)
QUB	Queen's University, Belfast
qv	*quod vide* (which see)
qwi	Qualified Weapons Instructor

R

(R)	Reserve
RA	Royal Academician; Royal (Regiment of) Artillery
RAA	Regional Arts Association
RAAF	Royal Australian Air Force

RAAMC	Royal Australian Army Medical Corps
RABI	Royal Agricultural Benevolent Institution
RAC	Royal Automobile Club; Royal Agricultural College; Royal Armoured Corps
RACDS	Royal Australian College of Dental Surgeons
RACGP	Royal Australian College of General Practitioners
RAChD	Royal Army Chaplains' Department
RACI	Royal Australian Chemical Institute
RACO	Royal Australian College of Ophthalmologists
RACOG	Royal Australian College of Obstetricians and Gynaecologists
RACP	Royal Australasian College of Physicians
RACS	Royal Australasian College of Surgeons; Royal Arsenal Co-operative Society
RADA	Royal Academy of Dramatic Art
RADAR	Royal Association for Disability and Rehabilitation
RADC	Royal Army Dental Corps
RADIUS	Religious Drama Society of Great Britain
RAE	Royal Australian Engineers; Royal Aerospace Establishment (*formerly* Royal Aircraft Establishment)
RAEC	Royal Army Educational Corps
RAeS	Royal Aeronautical Society
RAF	Royal Air Force
RAFA	Royal Air Force Association
RAFO	Reserve of Air Force Officers (*now see* RAFRO)
RAFRO	Royal Air Force Reserve of Officers
RAFVR	Royal Air Force Volunteer Reserve
RAI	Royal Anthropological Institute of Great Britain & Ireland; Radio Audizioni Italiane
RAIA	Royal Australian Institute of Architects
RAIC	Royal Architectural Institute of Canada
RAM	(Member of) Royal Academy of Music
RAMC	Royal Army Medical Corps
RAN	Royal Australian Navy
R&D	Research and Development
RANR	Royal Australian Naval Reserve
RANVR	Royal Australian Naval Volunteer Reserve
RAOC	Royal Army Ordnance Corps
RAPC	Royal Army Pay Corps
RARDE	Royal Armament Research and Development Establishment
RARO	Regular Army Reserve of Officers
RAS	Royal Astronomical Society; Royal Asiatic Society; Recruitment and Assessment Services
RASC	Royal Army Service Corps (*now see* RCT)
RASE	Royal Agricultural Society of England
RAuxAF	Royal Auxiliary Air Force
RAVC	Royal Army Veterinary Corps
RB	Rifle Brigade
RBA	Member, Royal Society of British Artists
RBC	Royal British Colonial Society of Artists
RBK&C	Royal Borough of Kensington and Chelsea
RBL	Royal British Legion
RBS	Royal Society of British Sculptors
RBSA	(Member of) Royal Birmingham Society of Artists
RBY	Royal Bucks Yeomanry
RC	Roman Catholic
RCA	Member, Royal Canadian Academy of Arts; Royal College of Art; (Member of) Royal Cambrian Academy
RCAC	Royal Canadian Armoured Corps
RCAF	Royal Canadian Air Force
RCamA	Member, Royal Cambrian Academy
RCAS	Royal Central Asian Society (*now see* RSAA)
RCDS	Royal College of Defence Studies
rcds	completed a course at, or served for a year on the Staff of, the Royal College of Defence Studies
RCGP	Royal College of General Practitioners
RCHA	Royal Canadian Horse Artillery
RCHM	Royal Commission on Historical Monuments
RCM	(Member of) Royal College of Music
RCN	Royal Canadian Navy; Royal College of Nursing
RCNC	Royal Corps of Naval Constructors
RCNR	Royal Canadian Naval Reserve
RCNVR	Royal Canadian Naval Volunteer Reserve
RCO	Royal College of Organists
RCOG	Royal College of Obstetricians and Gynaecologists
RCP	Royal College of Physicians, London

RCPath	Royal College of Pathologists
RCPE or	
RCPEd	Royal College of Physicians, Edinburgh
RCPI	Royal College of Physicians of Ireland
RCPSG	Royal College of Physicians and Surgeons of Glasgow
RCPsych	Royal College of Psychiatrists
RCR	Royal College of Radiologists
RCS	Royal College of Surgeons of England; Royal Corps of Signals; Royal College of Science
RCSE or	
RCSEd	Royal College of Surgeons of Edinburgh
RCSI	Royal College of Surgeons in Ireland
RCT	Royal Corps of Transport
RCVS	Royal College of Veterinary Surgeons
RD	Rural Dean; Royal Naval and Royal Marine Forces Reserve Decoration
Rd	Road
RDA	Royal Defence Academy
RDC	Rural District Council
RDF	Royal Dublin Fusiliers
RDI	Royal Designer for Industry (Royal Society of Arts)
RDS	Royal Dublin Society
RE	Royal Engineers; Fellow, Royal Society of Painter-Printmakers (*formerly* of Painter-Etchers and Engravers); Religious Education
REACH	Retired Executives Action Clearing House
react	Research Education and Aid for Children with potentially Terminal illness
Rear Adm.	Rear Admiral
REconS	Royal Economic Society
Regt	Regiment
REME	Royal Electrical and Mechanical Engineers
REngDes	Registered Engineering Designer
REOWS	Royal Engineers Officers' Widows' Society
REPC	Regional Economic Planning Council
RERO	Royal Engineers Reserve of Officers
RES	Royal Empire Society (*now* Royal Commonwealth Society)
Res.	Resigned; Reserve; Resident; Research
RETI	Association of Traditional Industrial Regions
Rev.	Reverend; Review
RFA	Royal Field Artillery
RFC	Royal Flying Corps (*now* RAF); Rugby Football Club
RFD	Reserve Force Decoration
RFH	Royal Festival Hall
RFN	Registered Fever Nurse
RFPS(G)	Royal Faculty of Physicians and Surgeons, Glasgow (*now see* RCPSG)
RFR	Rassemblement des Français pour la République
RFU	Rugby Football Union
RGA	Royal Garrison Artillery
RGI	Royal Glasgow Institute of the Fine Arts
RGJ	Royal Green Jackets
RGN	Registered General Nurse
RGS	Royal Geographical Society
RGSA	Royal Geographical Society of Australasia
RHA	Royal Hibernian Academy; Royal Horse Artillery; Regional Health Authority
RHAS	Royal Highland and Agricultural Society of Scotland
RHB	Regional Hospital Board
RHBNC	Royal Holloway and Bedford New College, London
RHC	Royal Holloway College, London (*now see* RHBNC)
RHF	Royal Highland Fusiliers
RHG	Royal Horse Guards
RHistS	Royal Historical Society
RHQ	Regional Headquarters
RHR	Royal Highland Regiment
RHS	Royal Horticultural Society; Royal Humane Society
RHV	Royal Health Visitor
RI	(Member of) Royal Institute of Painters in Water Colours; Rhode Island
RIA	Royal Irish Academy
RIAI	Royal Institute of the Architects of Ireland
RIAM	Royal Irish Academy of Music
RIAS	Royal Incorporation of Architects in Scotland
RIASC	Royal Indian Army Service Corps
RIBA	(Member of) Royal Institute of British Architects
RIBI	Rotary International in Great Britain and Ireland
RIC	Royal Irish Constabulary; Royal Institute of Chemistry (*now see* RSC)
RICS	Royal Institution of Chartered Surveyors
RIE	Royal Indian Engineering (College)
RIF	Royal Inniskilling Fusiliers
RIIA	Royal Institute of International Affairs
RILEM	Réunion internationale des laboratoires d'essais et de recherches sur les matériaux et les constructions
RIM	Royal Indian Marines
RIN	Royal Indian Navy
RINA	Royal Institution of Naval Architects
RINVR	Royal Indian Naval Volunteer Reserve
RIPA	Royal Institute of Public Administration
RIPH&H	Royal Institute of Public Health and Hygiene
RIrF	Royal Irish Fusiliers
RLC	Royal Logistic Corps
RLSS	Royal Life Saving Society
RM	Royal Marines; Resident Magistrate; Registered Midwife
RMA	Royal Marine Artillery; Royal Military Academy Sandhurst (*now* incorporating Royal Military Academy, Woolwich)
RMB	Rural Mail Base
RMC	Royal Military College Sandhurst (*now see* RMA)
RMCM	(Member of) Royal Manchester College of Music
RMCS	Royal Military College of Science
RMedSoc	Royal Medical Society, Edinburgh
RMetS	Royal Meteorological Society
RMFVR	Royal Marine Forces Volunteer Reserve
RMIT	Royal Melbourne Institute of Technology
RMLI	Royal Marine Light Infantry
RMN	Registered Mental Nurse
RMO	Resident Medical Officer(s)
RMP	Royal Military Police
RMPA	Royal Medico-Psychological Association
RMS	Royal Microscopical Society; Royal Mail Steamer; Royal Society of Miniature Painters
RMT	Rail, Maritime and Transport Union
RN	Royal Navy; Royal Naval; Registered Nurse
RNAS	Royal Naval Air Service
RNAY	Royal Naval Aircraft Yard
RNC	Royal Naval College
RNCM	(Member of) Royal Northern College of Music
RNEC	Royal Naval Engineering College
RNIB	Royal National Institute for the Blind
RNID	Royal National Institute for Deaf People (*formerly* Royal National Institute for the Deaf)
RNLI	Royal National Life-boat Institution
RNLO	Royal Naval Liaison Officer
RNR	Royal Naval Reserve
RNS	Royal Numismatic Society
RNSA	Royal Naval Sailing Association
RNSC	Royal Naval Staff College
RNT	Registered Nurse Tutor; Royal National Theatre
RNTNEH	Royal National Throat, Nose and Ear Hospital
RNUR	Régie Nationale des Usines Renault
RNVR	Royal Naval Volunteer Reserve
RNVSR	Royal Naval Volunteer Supplementary Reserve
RNXS	Royal Naval Auxiliary Service
RNZAC	Royal New Zealand Armoured Corps
RNZAF	Royal New Zealand Air Force
RNZIR	Royal New Zealand Infantry Regiment
RNZN	Royal New Zealand Navy
RNZNVR	Royal New Zealand Naval Volunteer Reserve
ROC	Royal Observer Corps
ROF	Royal Ordnance Factories
R of O	Reserve of Officers
ROI	Member, Royal Institute of Oil Painters
RoSPA	Royal Society for the Prevention of Accidents
(Rot.)	Rotunda Hospital, Dublin (after degree)
RP	Member, Royal Society of Portrait Painters
RPC	Royal Pioneer Corps
RPE	Rocket Propulsion Establishment
RPMS	Royal Postgraduate Medical School
RPO	Royal Philharmonic Orchestra
RPR	Rassemblement pour la République
RPS	Royal Photographic Society
RPSGB	Royal Pharmaceutical Society of Great Britain

RRC	Royal Red Cross
RRE	Royal Radar Establishment (*now see* RSRE)
RRF	Royal Regiment of Fusiliers
RRS	Royal Research Ship
RSA	Royal Scottish Academician; Royal Society of Arts; Republic of South Africa
RSAA	Royal Society for Asian Affairs
RSAF	Royal Small Arms Factory
RSAI	Royal Society of Antiquaries of Ireland
RSAMD	Royal Scottish Academy of Music and Drama
RSanI	Royal Sanitary Institute (*now see* RSH)
RSAS	Royal Surgical Aid Society
RSC	Royal Society of Canada; Royal Society of Chemistry; Royal Shakespeare Company
RSCM	Royal School of Church Music
RSCN	Registered Sick Children's Nurse
RSE	Royal Society of Edinburgh
RSF	Royal Scots Fusiliers
RSFSR	Russian Soviet Federated Socialist Republic
RSGS	Royal Scottish Geographical Society
RSH	Royal Society for the Promotion of Health
RSL	Royal Society of Literature; Returned Services League of Australia
RSM	Royal School of Mines
RSM or	
RSocMed	Royal Society of Medicine
RSMA	Royal Society of Marine Artists
RSME	Royal School of Military Engineering
RSMHCA	Royal Society for Mentally Handicapped Children and Adults (*see* Mencap)
RSNC	Royal Society for Nature Conservation
RSO	Rural Sub-Office; Railway Sub-Office; Resident Surgical Officer
RSPB	Royal Society for Protection of Birds
RSPCA	Royal Society for Prevention of Cruelty to Animals
RSRE	Royal Signals and Radar Establishment
RSSAf	Royal Society of South Africa
RSSAILA	Returned Sailors, Soldiers and Airmen's Imperial League of Australia (*now see* RSL)
RSSPCC	Royal Scottish Society for Prevention of Cruelty to Children
RSTM&H	Royal Society of Tropical Medicine and Hygiene
RSUA	Royal Society of Ulster Architects
RSV	Revised Standard Version
RSW	Member, Royal Scottish Society of Painters in Water Colours
RTE	Radio Telefis Eireann
Rt Hon.	Right Honourable
RTL	Radio-Télévision Luxembourg
RTO	Railway Transport Officer
RTPI	Royal Town Planning Institute
RTR	Royal Tank Regiment
Rt Rev.	Right Reverend
RTS	Religious Tract Society; Royal Toxophilite Society; Royal Television Society
RTYC	Royal Thames Yacht Club
RU	Rugby Union
RUC	Royal Ulster Constabulary
RUI	Royal University of Ireland
RUKBA	Royal United Kingdom Beneficent Association
RUR	Royal Ulster Regiment
RURAL	Society for the Responsible Use of Resources in Agriculture & on the Land
RUSI	Royal United Services Institute for Defence Studies (*formerly* Royal United Service Institution)
RVC	Royal Veterinary College
RWA or	
RWEA	(Member of) Royal West of England Academy
RWAFF	Royal West African Frontier Force
RWF	Royal Welch Fusiliers
RWS	(Member of) Royal Society of Painters in Water Colours
RYA	Royal Yachting Association
RYS	Royal Yacht Squadron
RZSScot	Royal Zoological Society of Scotland

S

(S)	(in Navy) Paymaster; Scotland
S	Succeeded; South; Saint
s	son
SA	South Australia; South Africa; Société Anonyme
SAAF	South African Air Force
SABC	South African Broadcasting Corporation
SAC	Scientific Advisory Committee
sac	qualified at small arms technical long course
SACEUR	Supreme Allied Commander Europe
SACIF	sociedad anónima commercial industrial financiera
SACLANT	Supreme Allied Commander Atlantic
SACRO	Scottish Association for the Care and Resettlement of Offenders
SACSEA	Supreme Allied Command, SE Asia
SA de CV	sociedad anónima de capital variable
SADF	Sudanese Auxiliary Defence Force
SADG	Société des Architectes Diplômés par le Gouvernement
SAE	Society of Automobile Engineers (US)
SAMC	South African Medical Corps
SARL	Société à Responsabilité Limitée
Sarum	Salisbury
SAS	Special Air Service
Sask	Saskatchewan
SASO	Senior Air Staff Officer
SAT	Senior Member, Association of Accounting Technicians
SATB	Soprano, Alto, Tenor, Bass
SATRO	Science and Technology Regional Organisation
SB	Bachelor of Science (US)
SBAA	Sovereign Base Areas Administration
SBAC	Society of British Aerospace Companies (*formerly* Society of British Aircraft Constructors)
SBS	Special Boat Service
SBStJ	Serving Brother, Most Venerable Order of the Hospital of St John of Jerusalem
SC	Star of Courage (Canada); Senior Counsel; South Carolina (US)
sc	student at the Staff College
SCA	Society of Catholic Apostolate (Pallottine Fathers); Société en Commandité par Actions
SCAA	School Curriculum and Assessment Authority
SCAO	Senior Civil Affairs Officer
SCAPA	Society for Checking the Abuses of Public Advertising
SCAR	Scientific Committee for Antarctic Research
ScD	Doctor of Science
SCDC	Schools Curriculum Development Committee
SCF	Senior Chaplain to the Forces; Save the Children Fund
Sch.	School
SCI	Society of Chemical Industry
SCIS	Scottish Council of Independent Schools
SCL	Student in Civil Law
SCM	State Certified Midwife; Student Christian Movement
SCONUL	Standing Conference of National and University Libraries
Scot.	Scotland
ScotBIC	Scottish Business in the Community
SCOTMEG	Scottish Management Efficiency Group
SCOTVEC	Scottish Vocational Education Council
SD	Staff Duties; South Dakota
SDA	Social Democratic Alliance; Scottish Diploma in Agriculture; Scottish Development Agency
SDak	South Dakota (US)
SDB	Salesian of Don Bosco
SDF	Sudan Defence Force; Social Democratic Federation
SDI	Strategic Defence Initiative
SDLP	Social Democratic and Labour Party
SDP	Social Democratic Party
SE	South-east
SEAC	South-East Asia Command
SEALF	South-East Asia Land Forces
SEATO	South-East Asia Treaty Organization
SEC	Security Exchange Commission
Sec.	Secretary
SED	Scottish Education Department
SEE	Society of Environmental Engineers
SEFI	European Society for Engineering Education

SEN	State Enrolled Nurse
SEPM	Society of Economic Palaeontologists and Mineralogists
SERC	Science and Engineering Research Council (*now see* EPSRC and PPARC)
SERT	Society of Electronic and Radio Technicians (*now see* IEIE)
SESO	Senior Equipment Staff Officer
SFA	Securities and Futures Authority
SFInstE	Senior Fellow, Institute of Energy
SFInstF	Senior Fellow, Institute of Fuel (*now see* SFInstE)
SFTA	Society of Film and Television Arts (*now see* BAFTA)
SFTCD	Senior Fellow, Trinity College Dublin
SG	Solicitor-General
SGA	Member, Society of Graphic Art
SGBI	Schoolmistresses' and Governesses' Benevolent Institution
Sgt	Sergeant
SHA	Secondary Heads Association; Special Health Authority
SHAC	London Housing Aid Centre
SHAEF	Supreme Headquarters, Allied Expeditionary Force
SH&MA	Scottish Horse and Motormen's Association
SHAPE	Supreme Headquarters, Allied Powers, Europe
SHEFC	Scottish Higher Education Funding Council
SHHD	Scottish Home and Health Department
SIAD	Society of Industrial Artists and Designers (*now see* CSD)
SIAM	Society of Industrial and Applied Mathematics (US)
SIB	Shipbuilding Industry Board; Securities and Investments Board
SICOT	Société Internationale de Chirurgie Orthopédique et de Traumatologie
SID	Society for International Development
SIESO	Society of Industrial and Emergency Services Officers
SIMA	Scientific Instrument Manufacturers' Association of Great Britain
SIME	Security Intelligence Middle East
SIMG	Societas Internationalis Medicinae Generalis
SinDrs	Doctor of Chinese
SIROT	Société Internationale pour Recherche en Orthopédie et Traumatologie
SIS	Secret Intelligence Service
SITA	Société Internationale de Télécommunications Aéronautiques
SITPRO	Simpler Trade Procedures Board (*formerly* Simplification of International Trade Procedures)
SJ	Society of Jesus (Jesuits)
SJAB	St John Ambulance Brigade
SJD	Doctor of Juristic Science
SJJ	Setia Jubli Perak Tuanku Ja'afar
SL	Serjeant-at-Law; Sociedad Limitada
SLA	Special Libraries Association
SLAC	Stanford Linear Accelerator Centre
SLAET	Society of Licensed Aircraft Engineers and Technologists
SLAS	Society for Latin-American Studies
SLD	Social and Liberal Democrats
SLP	Scottish Labour Party
SM	Medal of Service (Canada) (*now see* OC); Master of Science; Officer qualified for Submarine Duties
SMA	Society of Marine Artists (*now see* RSMA)
SMB	Setia Mahkota Brunei
SME	School of Military Engineering (*now see* RSME)
SMHO	Sovereign Military Hospitaller Order (Malta)
SMIEE	Senior Member, Institute of Electrical and Electronics Engineers (New York)
SMIRE	Senior Member, Institute of Radio Engineers (New York)
SMMT	Society of Motor Manufacturers and Traders Ltd
SMN	Seri Maharaja Mangku Negara (Malaysia)
SMO	Senior Medical Officer; Sovereign Military Order
SMP	Senior Managers' Program
SMPTE	Society of Motion Picture and Television Engineers (US)
SMRTB	Ship and Marine Requirements Technology Board
SNAME	Society of Naval Architects and Marine Engineers (US)
SNCF	Société Nationale des Chemins de Fer Français
SND	Sisters of Notre Dame

SNH	Scottish Natural Heritage
SNP	Scottish National Party
SNTS	Society for New Testament Studies
SO	Staff Officer; Scientific Officer; Symphony Orchestra
SOAS	School of Oriental and African Studies
Soc.	Society
Soc & Lib Dem	Social and Liberal Democrats (*now see* Lib Dem)
SocCE(France)	Société des Ingénieurs Civils de France
SODEPAX	Committee on Society, Development and Peace
SOE	Special Operations Executive
SOGAT	Society of Graphical and Allied Trades (*now see* GPMU)
SOLACE or Solace	Society of Local Authority Chief Executives
SOLT	Society of London Theatre
SOM	Society of Occupational Medicine
SOSc	Society of Ordained Scientists
SOTS	Society for Old Testament Study
sowc	Senior Officers' War Course
SP	Self-Propelled (Anti-Tank Regiment)
sp	*sine prole* (without issue)
SpA	Società per Azioni
SPAB	Society for the Protection of Ancient Buildings
SPARKS	Sport Aiding Medical Research for Children
SPCA	Society for the Prevention of Cruelty to Animals
SPCK	Society for Promoting Christian Knowledge
SPCM	Darjah Seri Paduka Cura Si Manja Kini (Malaysia)
SPD	Salisbury Plain District; Sozialdemokratische Partei Deutschlands
SPDK	Seri Panglima Darjal Kinabalu
SPG	Society for the Propagation of the Gospel (*now see* USPG)
SPk	Sitara-e-Pakistan
SPMB	Seri Paduka Makhota Brunei
SPMK	Darjah Kebasaran Seri Paduka Mahkota Kelantan (Malaysia)
SPMO	Senior Principal Medical Officer
SPNC	Society for the Promotion of Nature Conservation (*now see* RSNC)
SPNM	Society for the Promotion of New Music
SPR	Society for Psychical Research
SPRC	Society for Prevention and Relief of Cancer
sprl	société de personnes à responsabilité limitée
SPSO	Senior Principal Scientific Officer
SPTL	Society of Public Teachers of Law
SPUC	Society for the Protection of the Unborn Child
Sq.	Square
sq	staff qualified
SQA	Sitara-i-Quaid-i-Azam (Pakistan)
Sqdn or Sqn	Squadron
SR	Special Reserve; Southern Railway; Southern Region (BR)
SRC	Science Research Council (later SERC); Students' Representative Council
SRCh	State Registered Chiropodist
SRHE	Society for Research into Higher Education
SRIS	Science Reference Information Service
SRN	State Registered Nurse
SRNA	Shipbuilders and Repairers National Association
SRO	Supplementary Reserve of Officers; Self-Regulatory Organisation
SRP	State Registered Physiotherapist
SRY	Sherwood Rangers Yeomanry
SS	Saints; Straits Settlements; Steamship
SSA	Society of Scottish Artists
SSAC	Social Security Advisory Committee
SSAFA or SS&AFA	Soldiers', Sailors', and Airmen's Families Association
SSBN	Nuclear Submarine, Ballistic
SSC	Solicitor before Supreme Court (Scotland); Sculptors Society of Canada; *Societas Sanctae Crucis* (Society of the Holy Cross); Short Service Commission
SSEB	South of Scotland Electricity Board
SSEES	School of Slavonic and East European Studies
SSF	Society of St Francis
SSJE	Society of St John the Evangelist
SSM	Society of the Sacred Mission; Seri Setia Mahkota (Malaysia)

SSO	Senior Supply Officer; Senior Scientific Officer
SSRC	Social Science Research Council (*now see* ESRC)
SSSI	Sites of Special Scientific Interest
SSStJ	Serving Sister, Most Venerable Order of the Hospital of St John of Jerusalem
St	Street; Saint
STA	Sail Training Association
STB	*Sacrae Theologiae Baccalaureus* (Bachelor of Sacred Theology)
STC	Senior Training Corps
STD	*Sacrae Theologiae Doctor* (Doctor of Sacred Theology)
STh	Scholar in Theology
Stip.	Stipend; Stipendiary
STL	*Sacrae Theologiae Lector* (Reader or a Professor of Sacred Theology)
STM	*Sacrae Theologiae Magister* (Master of Sacred Theology)
STP	*Sacrae Theologiae Professor* (Professor of Divinity, old form of DD)
STRIVE	Society for Preservation of Rural Industries and Village Enterprises
STSO	Senior Technical Staff Officer
STV	Scottish Television
Subst.	Substantive
SUNY	State University of New York
Supp. Res.	Supplementary Reserve (of Officers)
Supt	Superintendent
Surg.	Surgeon
Surv.	Surviving
SW	South-west
SWET	Society of West End Theatre (*now see* SOLT)
SWIA	Society of Wildlife Artists
SWPA	South West Pacific Area
SWRB	Sadler's Wells Royal Ballet
Syd.	Sydney

T

T	Telephone; Territorial
TA	Telegraphic Address; Territorial Army
TAA	Territorial Army Association
TAF	Tactical Air Force
T&AFA	Territorial and Auxiliary Forces Association
T&AVR	Territorial and Army Volunteer Reserve
TANS	Territorial Army Nursing Service
TANU	Tanganyika African National Union
TARO	Territorial Army Reserve of Officers
TAS	Torpedo and Anti Submarine Course
TASS	Technical, Administrative and Supervisory Section of AUEW (now part of MSF)
TAVRA or TA&VRA	Territorial Auxiliary and Volunteer Reserve Association
TC	Order of the Trinity Cross (Trinidad and Tobago)
TCCB	Test and County Cricket Board
TCD	Trinity College, Dublin (University of Dublin, Trinity College)
TCF	Temporary Chaplain to the Forces
TCPA	Town and Country Planning Association
TD	Territorial Efficiency Decoration; Efficiency Decoration (T&AVR) (since April 1967); Teachta Dala (Member of the Dáil, Eire)
TDD	Tubercular Diseases Diploma
TE	Technical Engineer
TEAC	Technical Educational Advisory Council
TEC	Technician Education Council (*now see* BTEC); Training and Enterprise Council
Tech(CEI)	Technician
TEFL	Teaching English as a Foreign Language
TEFLA	Teaching English as a Foreign Language to Adults
TEM	Territorial Efficiency Medal
TEMA	Telecommunication Engineering and Manufacturing Association
Temp.	Temperature; Temporary
TEng(CEI)	Technician Engineer (*now see* IEng)
Tenn	Tennessee (US)
TeolD	Doctor of Theology
TES	Times Educational Supplement

TESL	Teaching English as a Second Language
TESOL	Teaching English to Speakers of other Languages
TET	Teacher of Electrotherapy
Tex	Texas (US)
TF	Territorial Force
TFR	Territorial Force Reserve
TFTS	Tactical Fighter Training Squadron
TGEW	Timber Growers England and Wales Ltd
TGO	Timber Growers' Organisation (*now see* TGEW)
TGWU	Transport and General Workers' Union
ThD	Doctor of Theology
THED	Transvaal Higher Education Diploma
THELEP	Therapy of Leprosy
THES	Times Higher Education Supplement
ThL	Theological Licentiate
ThSchol	Scholar in Theology
TIMS	The Institute of Management Sciences
TLS	Times Literary Supplement
TMMG	Teacher of Massage and Medical Gymnastics
TN	Tennessee
TNC	Theatres National Committee
TOSD	Tertiary Order of St Dominic
TP	Transvaal Province
TPI	Town Planning Institute (*now see* RTPI)
Trans.	Translation; Translated
Transf.	Transferred
TRC	Thames Rowing Club
TRE	Telecommunications Research Establishment (later RRE)
TRH	Their Royal Highnesses
TRIC	Television and Radio Industries Club
Trin.	Trinity
TRRL	Transport and Road Research Laboratory
TS	Training Ship
TSB	Trustee Savings Bank
tsc	passed a Territorial Army Course in Staff Duties
TSD	Tertiary of St Dominic
TSSA	Transport Salaried Staffs' Association
TUC	Trades Union Congress
TULV	Trade Unions for a Labour Victory
TUS	Trade Union Side
TV	Television
TVEI	Technical and Vocational Education Initiative
TWA	Thames Water Authority
TX	Texas
TYC	Thames Yacht Club (*now see* RTYC)

U

U	Unionist
u	uncle
UAE	United Arab Emirates
UAR	United Arab Republic
UAU	Universities Athletic Union
UBC	University of British Columbia
UBI	Understanding British Industry
UC	University College
UCAS	Universities and Colleges Admissions Service
UCCA	Universities Central Council on Admissions
UCCF	Universities and Colleges Christian Fellowship of Evangelical Unions
UCET	Universities Council for Education of Teachers
UCH	University College Hospital (London)
UCL	University College London
UCLA	University of California at Los Angeles
UCLES	University of Cambridge Local Examinations Syndicate
UCMSM	University College and Middlesex School of Medicine
UCNS	Universities' Council for Non-academic Staff
UCNW	University College of North Wales
UCRN	University College of Rhodesia and Nyasaland
UCS	University College School
UCSD	University of California at San Diego
UCW	University College of Wales; Union of Communication Workers (*now see* CWU)
UDC	Urban District Council; Urban Development Corporation

UDF	Union Defence Force; Union démocratique française
UDR	Ulster Defence Regiment; Union des Démocrates pour la Vème République (now see RPR)
UDSR	Union Démocratique et Socialiste de la Résistance
UE	United Empire Loyalist (Canada)
UEA	University of East Anglia
UED	University Education Diploma
UEFA	Union of European Football Associations
UF	United Free Church
UFAW	Universities Federation for Animal Welfare
UFC	Universities' Funding Council
UGC	University Grants Committee (later UFC)
UIAA	Union Internationale des Associations d'Alpinisme
UICC	Union Internationale contre le Cancer
UIE	Union Internationale des Etudiants
UISPP	Union Internationale des Sciences Préhistoriques et Protohistoriques
UITP	International Union of Public Transport
UJD	Utriusque Juris Doctor (Doctor of both Laws, Doctor of Canon and Civil Law)
UK	United Kingdom
UKAC	United Kingdom Automation Council
UKAEA	United Kingdom Atomic Energy Authority
UKCC	United Kingdom Central Council for Nursing, Midwifery and Health Visiting
UKCIS	United Kingdom Chemical Information Service
UKERNA	United Kingdom Education and Research Networking Association
UKIAS	United Kingdom Immigrants' Advisory Service
UKISC	United Kingdom Industrial Space Committee
UKLF	United Kingdom Land Forces
UKMF(L)	United Kingdom Military Forces (Land)
UKMIS	United Kingdom Mission
UKOOA	United Kingdom Offshore Operators Association
UKPIA	United Kingdom Petroleum Industry Association Ltd
UKSLS	United Kingdom Services Liaison Staff
ULCI	Union of Lancashire and Cheshire Institutes
ULPS	Union of Liberal and Progressive Synagogues
UMDS	United Medical and Dental Schools
UMIST	University of Manchester Institute of Science and Technology
UN	United Nations
UNA	United Nations Association
UNCAST	United Nations Conference on the Applications of Science and Technology
UNCIO	United Nations Conference on International Organisation
UNCITRAL	United Nations Commission on International Trade Law
UNCSTD	United Nations Conference on Science and Technology for Development
UNCTAD or Unctad	United Nations Commission for Trade and Development
UNDP	United Nations Development Programme
UNDRO	United Nations Disaster Relief Organisation
UNECA	United Nations Economic Commission for Asia
UNEP	United Nations Environment Programme
UNESCO or Unesco	United Nations Educational, Scientific and Cultural Organisation
UNFAO	United Nations Food and Agriculture Organisation
UNFICYP	United Nations Force in Cyprus
UNHCR	United Nations High Commissioner for Refugees
UNICE	Union des Industries de la Communauté Européenne
UNICEF or Unicef	United Nations Children's Fund (formerly United Nations International Children's Emergency Fund)
UNIDO	United Nations Industrial Development Organisation
UNIDROIT	Institut International pour l'Unification du Droit Privé
UNIFEM	United Nations Development Fund for Women
UNIFIL	United Nations Interim Force in Lebanon
UNIPEDE	Union Internationale des Producteurs et Distributeurs d'Energie Electrique
UNISIST	Universal System for Information in Science and Technology
UNITAR	United Nations Institute of Training and Research
Univ.	University
UNO	United Nations Organization
UNRRA	United Nations Relief and Rehabilitation Administration

UNRWA	United Nations Relief and Works Agency
UNSCOB	United Nations Special Commission on the Balkans
UP	United Provinces; Uttar Pradesh, United Presbyterian
UPGC	University and Polytechnic Grants Committee
UPNI	Unionist Party of Northern Ireland
UPU	Universal Postal Union
UPUP	Ulster Popular Unionist Party
URC	United Reformed Church
URSI	Union Radio-Scientifique Internationale
US	United States
USA	United States of America
USAAF	United States Army Air Force
USAF	United States Air Force
USAID	United States Agency for International Development
USAR	United States Army Reserve
USC	University of Southern California
USDAW	Union of Shop Distributive and Allied Workers
USM	Unlisted Securities Market
USMA	United States Military Academy
USN	United States Navy
USNR	United States Naval Reserve
USPG	United Society for the Propagation of the Gospel
USPHS	United States Public Health Service
USPS	United States Postal Service
USR	Universities' Statistical Record
USS	United States Ship
USSR	Union of Soviet Socialist Republics
USVI	United States Virgin Islands
UT	Utah
UTC	University Training Corps
UU	Ulster Unionist
UUUC	United Ulster Unionist Coalition
UUUP	United Ulster Unionist Party
UWCC	University of Wales College of Cardiff
UWE	University of the West of England
UWIST	University of Wales Institute of Science and Technology
UWT	Union of Women Teachers

V

V	Five (Roman numerals); Version; Vicar; Viscount; Vice
v	versus (against)
v or vid.	vide (see)
VA	Virginia
Va	Virginia (US)
VAD	Voluntary Aid Detachment
V&A	Victoria and Albert
VAT	Value Added Tax
VC	Victoria Cross; Voluntary Controlled
VCAS	Vice Chief of the Air Staff
VCDS	Vice Chief of the Defence Staff
VCGS	Vice Chief of the General Staff
VCNS	Vice Chief of the Naval Staff
VD	Royal Naval Volunteer Reserve Officers' Decoration (now VRD); Volunteer Officers' Decoration; Victorian Decoration
VDC	Volunteer Defence Corps
Ven.	Venerable
Vet.	Veterinary
VG	Vicar-General
VHS	Hon. Surgeon to Viceroy of India
VIC	Victoria Institute of Colleges
Vice Adm.	Vice Admiral
Visc.	Viscount
VM	Victory Medal
VMH	Victoria Medal of Honour (Royal Horticultural Society)
Vol.	Volume; Volunteers
VP	Vice-President
VPP	Volunteer Political Party
VPRP	Vice-President, Royal Society of Portrait Painters
VQMG	Vice-Quartermaster-General
VR	Victoria Regina (Queen Victoria); Volunteer Reserve
VRD	Royal Naval Volunteer Reserve Officers' Decoration
VSO	Voluntary Service Overseas

VT	Vermont
Vt	Vermont (US)
VUP	Vanguard Unionist Party

W

W	West
WA	Western Australia; Washington
WAAF	Women's Auxiliary Air Force (later WRAF)
WAOS	Welsh Agricultural Organisations Society
Wash	Washington State (US)
WCC	World Council of Churches
W/Cdr	Wing Commander
WCMD	Welsh College of Music and Drama
WDA	Welsh Development Agency
WEA	Workers' Educational Association; Royal West of England Academy
WES/PNEU	Worldwide Education Service of Parents' National Educational Union
WEU	Western European Union
WFSW	World Federation of Scientific Workers
WFTU	World Federation of Trade Unions
WhF	Whitworth Fellow
WHO	World Health Organization
WhSch	Whitworth Scholar
WI	West Indies; Women's Institute; Wisconsin
Wilts	Wiltshire
WIPO	World Intellectual Property Organization
Wis	Wisconsin (US)
Wits	Witwatersrand
WJEC	Welsh Joint Education Committee
WLA	Women's Land Army
WLD	Women Liberal Democrats
WLF	Women's Liberal Federation
Wm	William
WMO	World Meteorological Organization
WNO	Welsh National Opera
WO	War Office; Warrant Officer
Worcs	Worcestershire
WOSB	War Office Selection Board
WR	West Riding; Western Region (BR)
WRAC	Women's Royal Army Corps
WRAF	Women's Royal Air Force
WRNS	Women's Royal Naval Service

WRVS	Women's Royal Voluntary Service
WS	Writer to the Signet
WSAVA	World Small Animal Veterinary Association
WSPA	World Society for the Protection of Animals
WSPU	Women's Social and Political Union
WUS	World University Service
WV	West Virginia
WVa	West Virginia (US)
WVS	Women's Voluntary Services (*now see* WRVS)
WWF	World Wide Fund for Nature (*formerly* World Wildlife Fund)
WY	Wyoming
Wyo	Wyoming (US)

X

X	Ten (Roman numerals)
XO	Executive Officer

Y

y	youngest
YC	Young Conservative
YCNAC	Young Conservatives National Advisory Committee
Yeo.	Yeomanry
YES	Youth Enterprise Scheme
YHA	Youth Hostels Association
YMCA	Young Men's Christian Association
YOI	Young Offenders Institute
Yorks	Yorkshire
YPTES	Young People's Trust for Endangered Species
yr	younger
yrs	years
YTS	Youth Training Scheme
YVFF	Young Volunteer Force Foundation
YWCA	Young Women's Christian Association

Z

ZANU	Zimbabwe African National Union
ZAPU	Zimbabwe African People's Union

ADDENDA I

The following biographies are of those whose deaths occurred before 31 December 1995, but were not reported until after the volume of *Who Was Who* covering the years 1991–1995 had been published.

BEHNE, Edmond Rowlands, CMG 1974; Managing Director, Pioneer Sugar Mills Ltd, Queensland, 1952–76; *b* 20 Nov. 1906; *s* of late Edmund Behne; *m* 1932, Grace Elizabeth Ricketts; two *s* one *d*. *Educ:* Bendigo Sch. of Mines; Brisbane Boys' Coll.; Univ. of Queensland. BSc and MSc (App.); ARACI. Bureau of Sugar Experiment Stations, 1930–48 (Director, 1947); Pioneer Sugar Mills Ltd, 1948–80. *Recreation:* bowls. *Address:* Craigston, 217 Wickham Terrace, Brisbane, Qld 4000, Australia. *T:* (7) 38315657. *Club:* Johnsonian (Brisbane).
Died 29 Dec. 1994.

BENSON, Horace Burford; *b* 3 April 1904; *s* of Augustus W. Benson and Lucy M. (*née* Jarrett); *m* 1930, Marthe Lanier; one *s* one *d*. Called to Bar, Gray's Inn, 1936; practised as Barrister, Seychelles Islands, 1936–46; District Magistrate, Ghana, 1946; Puisne Judge, Ghana, 1952–57; retired, 1957; Temp. Magistrate, Basutoland, 1958–60; Puisne Judge, Basutoland, Bechuanaland Protectorate and Swaziland, 1960–61; Chief Justice, Basutoland (later Lesotho), 1965; Puisne Judge, Malawi, 1967–69. *Recreations:* bowls, bridge. *Address:* c/o Barclays Bank, West Norwood, SE27 9DW.
Died 26 May 1995.

BEWICK, Herbert; retired barrister; *b* 4 April 1911; *s* of late James Dicker and Elizabeth Inne Dewick. *Educ:* Whitehill Secondary Sch., Glasgow; Royal Grammar Sch., Newcastle upon Tyne; St Catharine's Coll., Cambridge. Called to Bar, Gray's Inn, 1933, Recorder of Pontefract, 1961–67; Chm. of Industrial Tribunal (Newcastle upon Tyne), 1967–72; practised in common law, 1972–84. *Address:* Flat 38, Cranlea, 1 Kingston Park Avenue, Kingston Park, Newcastle upon Tyne NE3 2HB.
Died Aug. 1995.

BRADLEY, Sir Burton Gyrth B.; *see* Burton-Bradley.

BREADALBANE AND HOLLAND, 10th Earl of, *cr* 1677; **John Romer Boreland Campbell;** Mac Chailein Mhic Dhonnachaidh (celtic designation); Viscount of Tay and Paintland; Lord Glenorchy, Benederaloch, Ormelie and Weik, 1677; Bt of Glenorchy; Bt of Nova Scotia, 1625; *b* 28 April 1919; *o s* of 9th Earl of Breadalbane and Holland, MC and Armorer Romer, *d* of Romer Williams, JP, DL, and *widow* of Capt. Eric Nicholson, 12th Royal Lancers; *S* father, 1959; *m* 1949, Coralie (marr. diss.), *o d* of Charles Archer. *Educ:* Eton; RMC, Sandhurst; Basil Patterson Tutors; Edinburgh Univ. Entered Black Watch (Royal Highlanders), 1939; served France, 1939–41 (despatches); invalided, 1942. *Recreations:* piobaireachd, Scottish highland culture. *Address:* House of Lords, SW1A 0PW; 29 Mackeson Road, Hampstead, NW3 2LU.
Died 15 Dec. 1995.

BROWN, Hon. George Arthur, CMG 1962; Governor, Bank of Jamaica, 1967–78 and 1989–92; *b* 25 July 1922; *s* of Samuel Austin Brown and Gertrude Brown; *m* 1st, 1951, Jean Farquharson; one *s* one *d*; 2nd, 1964, Leila Leonie Gill; two *d*. *Educ:* St Simon's College, Jamaica; London School of Economics. Jamaica Civil Service: Income Tax Dept, 1941; Colonial Secretary's Office, 1951; Asst Secretary, Min. of Finance, 1954; Director, General Planning Unit, 1957; Financial Secretary, 1962; Dep. Administrator, 1978–84, Associate Administrator, 1984–89, UNDP. *Publications:* contrib. Social and Economic Studies (University College of the West Indies). *Recreations:* hiking, boating, fishing. *Address:* c/o Bank of Jamaica, PO Box 621, Kingston, Jamaica. *Club:* Jamaica (Jamaica).
Died 2 March 1993.

BURTON-BRADLEY, Sir Burton (Gyrth), Kt 1990; OBE 1982; MD; FRCPsych; Clinical Professor of Psychiatry, University of Hawaii, 1978; *b* 18 Nov. 1914; *s* of Alan Godfrey and Ruby Malvina Burton-Bradley; *m* 1950, Ingeborg Roeser (*d* 1972). *Educ:* Univs of Sydney, Melbourne, NSW; RCPsych. MD (NSW), BS. FRANZCP, FRACMA, DPM, DTM&H, DipAnth. MO, Western Suburbs Hosp., Sydney, 1945–46; GP, NSW, 1946–48; MO, Aust. Mil. Mission in Germany and Austria, 1949–50; Psychiatrist, Brisbane Mental Hosp., 1950–57; Colombo Plan Psychiatrist, Singapore, 1957–59; Lectr in Psychol Med., Univ. of Malaya, Singapore, 1957–59; Chief, Mental Health, Papua New Guinea, 1959–75; Hon Associate Prof., Medical Faculty, Univ. of PNG, 1972–75. Wenner-Gren Res. Fellow in Psychol Anthropol., 1970; Travelling Fellow, Fund for Res. in Psych., 1975–76. Advr in Ethno-Psychiatry, S Pacific Commn, 1967. World Health Organization: Mem., Expert Adv. Panel, 1978; Advr, Solomon Is, 1979; Rockefeller Scholar, Italy, 1979. Abraham Flexner Lectr, Vanderbilt Univ., USA, 1973; Special Lectr, Pacific Rim Coll. of Psychiatrists, Tokyo, 1986; Ext. Examr, Dept of Tropical Medicine, Univ. of Sydney. Chm., first Conf., Asian Chapter of Internat. Coll. of Psychosomatic Medicine, Tokyo, 1984; Counsellor, Soc. Internat. de Psychopathologie de l'Expression, 1982; Pres., PNGPsych. Assoc., 1978; Vice Pres., Asian Chapter, Internat. Coll. of Psychosomatic Medicine, 1991. Fellow, Orgn Internationale de Psychophysiologie, Montreal, 1981; Mem., NY Acad. of Scis; Hon. Mem., Sociedad Internat. de Nuevas de la Conducta Argentina, 1982. Mem. Editl Cttee, PNG Med. Jl, 1976. Benjamin Rush Bronze Medal, APA, 1974; Sen. Organon Res. Award, RANCP, 1980. Papua New Guinea Independence Medal, 1975. *Publications:* Longlong, 1973; South Pacific Ethnopsychiatry, 1967; L'Examen Psychiatrique de Autochtone de Papuasie et Nouvelle Guinée, 1967; Mixed-race Society in Port Moresby, 1968; Psychiatry and the Law in the Developing Country, 1970; Stone Age Crisis, 1975; Crisis en la edad de piedra, 1988; (ed) History of Medicine in Papua New Guinea, 1990; Kavakava, the Irrational Vector: perspectives of trans-cultural psychiatry in Papua New Guinea, 1992; over 200 sci. papers in learned jls. *Recreations:* patrolling, historical research in PNG. *Address:* PO Box 111, Port Moresby, Papua New Guinea. *T:* 255245.
Died Feb. 1994.

CAVALLERA, Rt Rev. Charles; *b* Centallo, Cuneo, Italy, 8 Jan. 1909. *Educ:* International Missionary College of the Consolata of Turin; Pontifical Univ. of Propaganda Fide of Rome (degree in Missionology). Sec. to Delegate Apostolic of British Africa, 1936–40; Vice-Rector, then Rector, of Urban Coll. of Propaganda Fide of Rome,

1941–47; formerly Titular Bishop of Sufes; Vicar-Apostolic of Nyeri (Kenya), 1947–53; RC Bishop of Nyeri, 1953–64; RC Bishop of Marsabit, 1964–81. *Address:* Missioni Consolata, Viale Mura Aurelie 12, 00165 Rome, Italy. *Died 22 Sept. 1990.*

CAYFORD, Dame Florence Evelyn, DBE 1965; JP; Mayor, London Borough of Camden, 1969; *b* 14 June 1897; *d* of George William and Mary S. A. Bunch; *m* 1923, John Cayford (*d* 1989); two *s. Educ:* Carlton Road Sch.; St Pancras County Secondary Sch.; Paddington Technical Institute. Alderman, LCC, 1946–52; Member: LCC for Shoreditch and Finsbury, 1952–64; GLC (for Islington) and ILEA, 1964–67; Chm., LCC, 1960–61. Chairman: Hospital and Medical Services Cttee LCC, 1948; Health Cttee, Division 7, 1948–49, Division 2 in 1949; Health Cttee, 1953–60; Welfare Cttee, 1965; Metropolitan Water Bd, 1966–67 (Vice-Chm., 1965–66). Mem. Hampstead Borough Council, 1937–65 (Leader of Labour Group, 1945–58), Councillor for Kilburn until 1945, Alderman, 1945–65; Dep. Mayoress, Camden Borough Council, 1967–68. Chairman: (Hampstead), Maternity and Child Welfare Cttee, 1941–45; Juvenile Court Panel, 1950–62; Probation Cttee, 1959; Leavesden Hosp. Management Cttee, 1948–63; Harben Secondary Sch., 1946–61. Member: Co-operative Political Party (ex-Chm. and Sec.); Co-operative Soc.; Labour Party; National Institute for Social Work Training, 1962–65; Min. of Health Council for Training of Health Visitors, 1962–65; Min. of Health Council for Training in Social Work, 1962–65. Chm., YWCA Helen Graham Hse, 1972. JP Inner London, 1941. Freeman, London Borough of Camden (formerly Borough of Hampstead), 1961. Noble Order, Crown of Thailand, 3rd Class, 1964. *Address:* 26 Hemstal Road, Hampstead, NW6 2AL. *T:* (0171) 624 6181. *Deceased.*

COOK, Rt Rev. Henry George; retired; *b* Walthamstow, London, England, 12 Oct. 1906; *s* of Henry G. Cook and Ada Mary Evans; *m* 1935, Opal May Thompson, Sarnia, Ont, *d* of Wesley Thompson and Charity Ellen Britney; two *s* one *d. Educ:* Ingersoll Collegiate Inst., Ont; Huron Coll. (LTh); Univ. of Western Ont, London, Canada (BA). Deacon, 1935, priest, 1936; Missionary at Fort Simpson, 1935–43; Canon of Athabasca, 1940–43; Incumbent S Porcupine, Ont, 1943–44; Archdeacon of James Bay, 1945–48; Principal, Bp Horden Sch., Moose Factory, 1945–48; Mem., Gen Synod Exec., 1943–47; Supt of Indian Sch. Admin, 1948–62; Bishop Suffragan of the Arctic, 1963–66, of Athabasca, 1966–70 (the area of Mackenzie having been part first of one diocese and then of the other, constituted an Episcopal District, 1970); Bishop of Mackenzie, 1970–74. RCNR Chaplain, 1949–56. Hon. DD Huron Coll. and Univ. of Western Ont, 1946. *Recreations:* fishing, coin collecting, model carving. *Address:* 15 Plainfield Court, Stittsville, Ont K2S 1R4, Canada. *Died 18 Oct. 1995.*

COOPER, Wing Comdr Geoffrey; free-lance writer; architect; Member, Pornography and Violence Research Trust (formerly Mary Whitehouse Educational and Research Trust), since 1985; *b* 18 Feb. 1907; *s* of Albert Cooper, Leicester, and Evelyn J. Bradnam, Hastings; *m* 1951, Mrs Tottie Resch, Jersey, CI. *Educ:* Wyggeston Grammar Sch., Leicester; Royal Grammar School, Worcester. Accountancy, business management. Auxiliary Air Force, 1933; BOAC, 1939; Royal Air Force 1939–45, Pilot (mentioned in despatches). MP (Lab) Middlesbrough West Div., 1945–51. Farming in Jersey, CI, 1951–61; founder and one of first directors, Jersey Farmers' Co-operative; Chm. Jersey Branch, RAFA; architecture and land develt, Bahama Is, 1962–77; Pres., Estate Developers Ltd; writing and social welfare voluntary work in S London, 1977–84; former Mem., Gideons; Captain, 56th London Boys' Brigade. *Publications:* Cæsar's Mistress

(exposé of BBC and nationalisation); Christ Will Come Again, 1994; articles in England, Bahamas and USA on civil aviation, business management and government methods. *Recreations:* portrait and landscape painting, swimming. *Address:* 91 Connor Court, Battersea Park, SW11 5HG. *Club:* Royal Air Force.
Died 10 April 1995.

COPLESTON, Ernest Reginald, CB 1954; Secretary, Committee of Enquiry into the Governance of the University of London, 1970–72; *b* 16 Nov. 1909; *s* of F. S. Copleston, former Chief Judge of Lower Burma, and 2nd wife, Norah, *d* of Col Colhoun-Little, MD, IMS; *m* 1945, Olivia Green. *Educ:* Marlborough Coll.; Balliol Coll., Oxford. Inland Revenue Dept, 1932; Treasury, 1942; Under-Sec., 1950; Dep. Sec., 1957–63, Sec., 1963–69, UGC; retired. *Address:* Arden, Bears Lane, Lavenham, Suffolk CO10 9RT. *T:* (01787) 247470.
Died 29 Nov. 1993.

CRANE, Sir James (William Donald), Kt 1980; CBE 1977; HM Chief Inspector of Constabulary, 1979–82; *b* 1 Jan. 1921; *s* of late William James Crane and Ivy Winifred Crane; *m* 1942, Patricia Elizabeth Hodge; one *s* one *d. Educ:* Hampshire schs. Served RE, RA, Royal Hampshire Regt, 1939–46. Joined Metrop. Police, 1946; Comdr and Dep. Asst Comr, Fraud Squad and Commercial Br., 1970–76; Inspector of Constabulary, 1976–79. Member: Parole Bd, 1983–85; Fraud Trials Cttee, 1984–85. Mem. Council, Univ. of Wales Coll. of Cardiff, 1988–. *Recreations:* gardening, walking, reading. *Address:* c/o Home Office, 50 Queen Anne's Gate, SW1H 9AT. *Club:* Commonwealth Trust. *Died 29 Nov. 1994.*

DAULTANA, Mumtaz Mohammad Khan; Ambassador of Pakistan to the Court of St James's, 1972–78; *b* 23 Feb. 1916; *o s* of Nawab Ahmadyar Daultana; *m* 1943, Almas Jehan; one *s* one *d. Educ:* St Anthony's Sch., Lahore; Government Coll., Lahore (BA Hons); Corpus Christi Coll., Oxford (MA). Called to Bar, Middle Temple, 1940; 1st cl. 1st position in Bar exam. Joined All India Muslim League, 1942; unopposed election as Mem. Punjab Legislative Assembly, 1943; Gen. Sec., Punjab Muslim League, 1944; Sec., All India Muslim League Central Cttee of Action, 1945; Elected Member: Punjab Assembly, 1946; Constituent Assembly of India, 1947; Constituent Assembly, Pakistan, 1947; Finance Minister, Punjab, 1947–48; Pres., Punjab Muslim League, 1948–50; Chief Minister of Punjab, 1951–53; Finance Minister, West Pakistan, 1955–56; Defence Minister, Pakistan, 1957; Pres., Pakistan Muslim League, 1967–72. Elected Member: Nat. Assembly of Pakistan, 1970; Constitution Cttee of Nat. Assembly, 1972. *Publications:* Agrarian Report of Pakistan Muslim League, 1950; Thoughts on Pakistan's Foreign Policy, 1956; Kashmir in Present Day Context, 1965. *Recreations:* music, squash. *Address:* 8 Durand Road, Lahore, Pakistan. *T:* (42) 302459, (21) 532387. *Clubs:* United Oxford & Cambridge University; Gymkhana (Lahore). *Died 30 June 1995.*

DAVIES, Harry, JP; DL; Member, Greater Manchester County Council, 1973–86 (Chairman, May 1984–1985); *b* 5 March 1915; *s* of Herbert Jacob Davies and Mary Elizabeth Johnson; *m* 1941, Elsie Gore; three *d. Educ:* Bedford Methodist Primary School; Leigh Grammar School; Padgate Teacher Training College. 6th Royal Tank Regt, 1941–46. Dep. Head, Westleigh C of E School, 1958; Headmaster, Bedford Methodist School, 1964–77. Mem., Leigh Borough Council, 1959; Mayor, Borough of Leigh, 1971–72. JP Leigh, 1969; DL Greater Manchester, 1987. Silver Jubilee Medal, 1977. *Recreations:* gardening, bread baking, wine making. *Address:* 45 Edale Road, Leigh WN7 2BD. *T:* (01942) 672583.
Died Sept. 1993.

EAST, Sir (Lewis) Ronald, Kt 1966; CBE 1951; Chairman, State Rivers and Water Supply Commission, Victoria, 1936–65, and Commissioner, River Murray Commission, Australia, 1936–65, retired; *b* 17 June 1899; *s* of Lewis Findlay East, ISO, Evansford, Vic, Australia and Annie Eleanor (*née* Burchett), Brunswick, Vic; *m* 1927, Constance Lilias Keil, MA, Kilwinning, Ayrshire; three *d. Educ:* Scotch Coll., Melbourne; Melbourne Univ. BCE (Melbourne) 1922; MCE (Melbourne) 1924. Mem., Snowy Mountains Council, until 1965. Pres., Instn of Engrs, Aust., 1952–53; Mem. Council, Instn of Civil Engrs, 1960–62; Vice-Pres., Internat. Commn on Irrigation and Drainage, 1959–62. Hon. Fellow, Instn of Engineers, Australia, 1969; FRHSV 1983. Coopers Hill War Meml Prize and Telford Premium, ICE, 1932; Kernot Memorial Medal, University of Melbourne, 1949; Peter Nicol Russell Memorial Medal, Instn of Engineers, Australia, 1957. Hon. DEng Melbourne, 1981. *Publications:* River Improvement, Land Drainage and Flood Protection, 1952; A South Australian Colonist of 1836 and his Descendants, 1972; The Kiel Family and related Scottish Pioneers, 1974; More Australian Pioneers: the Burchetts and related families, 1976; (ed) The Gallipoli Diary of Sergeant Lawrence, 1981; More About the East Family and Related Pioneers, 1988; many technical papers on water conservation and associated subjects in Proc. Instn Engrs Aust., Proc. Instn Civil Engrs, Amer. Soc. Civil Engrs and other jls. *Recreation:* handicrafts (model engineering). *Address:* 57 Waimarie Drive, Mt Waverley, Victoria 3149, Australia. *T:* (3) 92774315. *Died 9 March 1994.*

EDDLEMAN, Gen. Clyde Davis; DSM with oak leaf cluster (US); Silver Star; Legion of Merit; Bronze Star; Philippines Distinguished Service Star; Vice-Chief of Staff, US Army, 1960–62; *b* 17 Jan. 1902; *s* of Rev. W. H. Eddleman and Janie Eddleman (*née* Turcman), *m* 1926, Lorraine Heath; one *s* (and one *s* decd). *Educ:* US Military Academy, West Point, New York. Commissioned 2nd Lieut of Infantry upon graduation from US Military Academy, 1924; advanced, through the ranks, and reached grade of Gen. 1959; Comdr, Central Army Group (NATO), and C-in-C, US Army, Europe, at Heidelberg, Germany, 1959–60. Knight Commander's Cross, Order of Merit (Germany); Kt Grand Cross of the Sword (Sweden). *Recreations:* hunting, fishing.

Died 19 Aug. 1992.

FRANCIS, Sir Laurie (Justice), Kt 1982; New Zealand High Commissioner to Australia, 1976–85; barrister and solicitor, High Court of New Zealand, as Consultant to Farry & Co., Solicitors, Dunedin, since 1985; Commissioner of Oaths for Australian States, including Northern Territory, since 1985; *b* 30 Aug. 1918; *s* of Bernard Francis and Isabel Hampton (*née* Justice); *m* 1952, Heather Margaret McFarlane; three *d. Educ:* Otago Boys High Sch.; Victoria University of Wellington; Univ. of Otago (LLB). Practised law as barrister and solicitor, Winton, Southland, until 1964; Senior Partner, Dunedin firm of Gilbert, Francis, Jackson and Co., Barristers and Solicitors, 1964–76. Hon. Life Mem., RSL, 1984. *Recreations:* golf occasionally, follower of Rugby and cricket, lover of jazz. *Address:* 42 Glengyle Street, Dunedin, New Zealand. *Club:* Dunedin (Fernhill).

Died 3 Aug. 1993.

FRANKS, Air Vice-Marshal John Gerald, CB 1954; CBE 1949; Royal Air Force, retired 1960; *b* 23 May 1905; *e s* of late James Gordon Franks (*e s* of Sir John Hamilton Franks, CB), and Margaret, *y d* of Lord Chief Justice Gerald Fitz-Gibbon, Dublin; *m* 1936, Jessica Rae West (decd); two *d. Educ:* Cheltenham Coll.; RAF Coll., Cranwell. RAF: commissioned from Cranwell, 1924; No 56 Fighter Sqdn, Biggin Hill, 1925–26; flying duties with FAA HMS Courageous, Mediterranean, 1928–29; India,

1930–35; Middle East, 1936; RAF Staff Coll., 1939; Air Armament Sch., Manby, 1941; Experimental Establishment, Boscombe Down, 1944; Dir Armament Research and Development, 1945–48; idc 1951; Comdt RAF Technical Coll., Henlow, 1952; Air Officer Commanding No 24 Group, Royal Air Force, 1952–55; Pres. of Ordnance Board, 1959–60. Comdr American Legion of Merit, 1948. *Recreations:* motoring and walking in the west of Ireland. *Died 23 Sept. 1995.*

GANDAR, Hon. Leslie Walter; JP; Chairman: Capital Discovery Place, since 1988; Andrews Environmental (NZ) Ltd; Andrews Environmental (Australia) Ltd; *b* 26 Jan. 1919; *s* of Max Gandar and Doris Harper; *m* 1945, M. Justine, *d* of T. A. Smith and Florence Smith; four *s* one *d* (and one *d* decd). *Educ:* Wellington College; Victoria Univ., Wellington (BSc 1940). FNZIAS, FInstP. Served RNZAF and RAF, 1940–44. Farming, 1945–. MP, Ruahine, 1966–78; Minister of Science, Energy Resources, Mines, Electricity, 1972; Minister of Education, Science and Technology, 1975–78; High Comr for NZ in UK, 1979–82. Chairman, Pohangina County Council, 1954–69. Chancellor, Massey Univ., 1970–76. Chairman: NZ Social Adv. Council, 1982–87; NZ SSRC, 1984–89; Queen Elizabeth II Nat. Trust of NZ, 1983–87; NZ Royal Society Prince and Princess of Wales Science Award Liaison Cttee; NZ Cttee, C. A. Baker Trust (UK), 1982–. Mem., Waitangi NT, 1992–. Pres., Friends of Turnbull Library, 1984–91. JP 1958. Hon. DSc Massey, 1977. *Recreations:* music—when not watching cricket; wood-carving, work. *Address:* 34 Palliser Road, Wellington, New Zealand.

Died 16 Dec. 1994.

GARDINER, Robert (Kweku Atta); Commissioner for Economic Planning, Ghana, 1975–78; *b* Kumasi, Ghana, 29 Sept. 1914; *s* of Philip H. D. Gardiner and Nancy Torraine Ferguson; *m* 1943, Linda Charlotte Edwards; one *s* two *d. Educ:* Adisadel Coll., Cape Coast, Ghana; Fourah Bay Coll., Sierra Leone; Selwyn Coll., Cambridge (BA), New Coll., Oxford. Lectr in Economics at Fourah Bay Coll., 1943–46; UN Trusteeship Dept, 1947–49; Dir, Extra Mural Studies, University Coll., Ibadan, 1949–53; Dir, Dept of Social Welfare and Community Development, Gold Coast, 1953–55; Perm. Sec., Min. of Housing, 1955–57; Head of Ghana Civil Service, 1957–59; Dep. Exec. Sec., Economic Commn for Africa, 1959–60; Mem. Mission to the Congo, 1961; Dir Public Admin. Div., UN Dept of Economic and Social Affairs, 1961–62; Officer-in-Charge, UN Operation in the Congo, 1962–63; Exec. Sec., UN Economic Commn for Africa, Addis Ababa, 1962–75. Chm., Commonwealth Foundation, 1970–73. Reith Lectures, 1965; David Livingstone Vis. Prof. of Economics, Strathclyde, 1970–75; Vis. Prof. of Economics, 1974–75, and Consultant, Centre for Development Studies, 1974–77, Univ. of Cape Coast. Lectures: Gilbert Murray Meml, 1969; J. B. Danquah Meml, 1970; Aggrey-Fraser-Guggisberg Meml, 1972. Mem. professional socs, and activities in internat. affairs. Hon. Fellow: Univ. of Ibadan; Selwyn Coll., Cambridge. Hon. DCL: East Anglia, 1966; Sierra Leone, 1969; Tuskegee Inst., 1969; Liberia, 1972; Hon. LLD: Bristol, 1966; Ibadan, 1967; E Africa, 1968; Haile Sellassie I Univ., 1972; Strathclyde, 1973; Hon. PhD Uppsala, 1966; Hon. DSc: Kumasi, 1968; Bradford, 1969. *Publications:* (with Helen Judd) The Development of Social Administration, 1951, 2nd edn 1959; A World of Peoples (BBC Reith Lectures), 1965. *Recreations:* golf, music, reading, walking. *Address:* PO Box 9274, The Airport, Accra, Ghana. *Died 1993.*

GREENSMITH, Edwin Lloydd, CMG 1962; *b* 23 Jan. 1900; *s* of Edwin Greensmith and Isabella Cleland (*née* Lloydd); *m* 1932, Winifred Bryce; two *s* two *d. Educ:* Victoria Univ., Wellington, NZ. MCom (Hons), 1930.

Accountant; Solicitor. Chief Accountant, Ministry of Works, New Zealand, to 1935; then Treasury (Secretary, 1955–65). Chm., NZ Wool Commn, 1965–72. *Recreation:* gardening. *Address:* Unit 42, Crestwood Village, Titirangi, Auckland, New Zealand. *Club:* Wellington (Wellington NZ). *Died 8 Aug. 1993.*

GWANDU, Emir of; Alhaji Haruna Muhammadu Basharu, CFR 1965; CMG 1961; CBE 1955; 18th Emir of Gwandu, 1954; Member, North Western State House of Chiefs, and Council of Chiefs; Member, and Chairman, Executive Council, State Self-Development Funds Council; President, former Northern Nigeria House of Chiefs, since 1957 (Deputy President 1956); *b* Batoranke, 1913; *m* 1933; fifteen *c. Educ:* Birnin Kebbi Primary Sch.; Katsina Training Coll. Teacher: Katsina Teachers Coll., 1933–35; Sokoto Middle Sch., 1935–37; Gusau Local Authority Sub-Treasurer, 1937–43; Gwandu Local Authority Treasurer, 1943–45; District Head, Kalgo, 1945–54. Member former N Reg. Marketing Board. *Recreations:* hunting, shooting. *Address:* Emir's Palace, PO Box 1, Birnin Kebbi, North Western State, Nigeria. *Died Aug. 1995.*

HARKIN, Brendan; Chairman, Industry Matters (Northern Ireland) Ltd, 1987–90; *b* 21 April 1920; *s* of Francis and Catherine Harkin; *m* 1949, Maureen Gee; one *s* two *d. Educ:* St Mary's Christian Brothers' Primary and Grammar Schs, Belfast. Apprentice electrician, 1936. Asst Sec. 1953, Gen. Sec. 1955–76, NI Civil Service Assoc. (which after amalgamations became Public Service Alliance, 1971); Chm. and Chief Exec., Labour Relations Agency, 1976–85. Chm., Strathearn Audio Ltd, 1974–76; Deputy Chairman: NI Finance Corp., 1972–76; NI Development Agency, 1976. Mem., EEC Economic and Social Cttee, 1973–76. Chm., Industry Year. Pres., Irish Congress of Trade Unions, 1976. Member: Council, NUU, later Univ. of Ulster, 1982– (Chm., Staffing Cttee, 1993–); Council, Co-operation North, 1984–. Pres., NI Hospice, 1985–. MUniv Open, 1986. *Publications:* contrib. on industrial relations. *Recreations:* theatre, music, reading. *Address:* 113 Somerton Road, Belfast, Northern Ireland BT15 4DH. *T:* (01232) 774979. *Died 17 Sept. 1995.*

HENRISON, Dame (Anne) Rosina (Elizabeth), DBE 1984; *b* 7 Dec. 1902; *d* of Julius Marie and Amelina Marie (*née* Malepa); *m* 1st, 1931, Charles Duval; three *s* one *d*; 2nd, 1943, Edward Henrison. *Educ:* Loreto Convent, Port Louis. Hon. Citizen, Town of Bangui, Central Africa, 1975; Ordre de Mérite, Centre Africaine; Mother Gold Medal. *Recreations:* reading, travelling. *Address:* Melville, Grandgaube, Mauritius. *T:* 039518. *Club:* Port Louis Tennis (Mauritius). *Died 17 Sept. 1989.*

HINES, Sir Colin (Joseph), Kt 1976; OBE 1973; President: NSW Returned Services League Clubs Association, 1971–90; NSW Branch, Returned Services League of Australia, 1971–90; Vice-President of the National Executive, Returned Services League of Australia, 1971–90 (Deputy National President, 1974–90); *b* 16 Feb. 1919; *s* of J. Hines and Mrs Hines, Lyndhurst, NSW; *m* 1942, Jean Elsie, *d* of A. Wilson, Mandurama, NSW; two *s. Educ:* All Saints' Coll., Bathurst, NSW. Farmer and grazier. Army, 1937–45. Hon. Officer, Returned Services League of Aust., 1946–, Trustee, 1990–. State Comr, Aust. Forces Overseas Fund, 1971–; Trustee, Anzac Meml Trust, 1971–. Pres., War Veterans Homes, Narrabeen, 1976– (Chm., 1971–76); Chm., Clubs Mutual Services Ltd, 1972–. *Recreations:* rifle shooting, golf. *Address:* The Meadows, Lyndhurst, NSW 2741, Australia. *T:* (63) 675151. *Club:* Imperial Services (Sydney, NSW). *Died 29 Dec. 1992.*

HU DINGYI; Secretary-General, All-China Federation of Industry & Commerce, 1988; *b* Dec. 1922; *m* Xie Heng;

one *s* one *d. Educ:* Central Univ., Sichuan Province, China (graduate). 3rd Secretary, Embassy of People's Republic of China in India, 1950–54; 2nd Sec., Office of the Chargé d'Affaires of People's Republic of China in UK, 1954–58; Section Chief, Dept of Western European Affairs, Min. of Foreign Affairs, 1958–60; 1st Sec., Ghana, 1960–66; Division Chief, Dept of African Affairs, 1966–71; 1st Sec., then Counsellor, UK, 1972–79; Consul General, San Francisco, 1979–83; Minister, US, 1983–85; Ambassador to UK, 1985–87. *Recreation:* reading. *Address:* c/o All-China Federation of Industry & Commerce, 93 Bei He Yan Dajie, 100006, Beijing, China. *Died 15 Oct. 1994.*

HUNTE, Joseph Alexander; Senior Community Relations Officer, Tower Hamlets, 1968–82, retired; *b* 18 Dec. 1917; *s* of Clement and Eunice Hunte; *m* 1967, Margaret Ann (formerly Jones); three *d* (and one *d* decd). *Educ:* Swansea University Coll., 1962–65 (BA Politics, Economics, Philosophy); PRO, 1964–65. West Indian Standing Conference: PRO, Sec., Chairman 1958–80; Executive Member: Jt Council for Welfare of Immigrants, 1968–74; CARD, 1969–70 (Grievance Officer); Anne Frank Foundn, 1965–70; Chm., Presentation Housing Assoc., 1981–; Governor, St Martin-in-the-Fields Girls' Sch., SW2, 1982–. Silver Jubilee Medal (for services in community relations), 1977. *Publication:* Nigger Hunting in England, 1965. *Recreations:* reading, watching television. *Address:* 43 Cambria Road, SE5 9AS. *T:* (0171) 733 5436. *Died 8 Oct. 1983.*

IBRAHIM, Sir (Shettima) Kashim, GCON 1963; KCMG 1962; CBE 1960 (MBE 1952); Governor of Northern Nigeria, 1962–66; Chancellor, Lagos University, 1976–84; *b* 10 June 1910; *s* of Mallam Ibrahim Lakkani; *m* 1st, 1943, Halima; 2nd, 1944, Khadija; 3rd, 1957, Zainaba; four *s* three *d* (and two *d* decd). *Educ:* Bornu Provincial Sch.; Katsina Teachers' Trng Coll. Teacher, 1929–32; Visiting Teacher, 1933–49; Educn Officer, 1949–52; Federal Minister of Social Services, 1952–55; Northern Regional Minister of Social Develt and Surveys, 1955–56; Waziri of Bornu, 1956–62. Advr to Military Governor, N Nigeria, 1966. Chm. Nigerian Coll. of Arts, Science and Technology, 1958–62; Chancellor, Ibadan Univ., 1967–75; Chm. Provisional Council of Ahmadu Bello Univ. Hon. LLD: Ahmadu Bello, 1963; Univ. of Ibadan; Univ. of Nigeria (Nsukka); University of Lagos. *Publications:* Kanuri Reader Elementary, I-IV; Kanuri Arithmetic Books, I-IV, for Elementary Schs and Teachers' Guide for above. *Recreations:* walking, riding, polo playing. *Address:* PO Box 285, Maiduguri, Bornu State, Nigeria. *Died 26 July 1990.*

JACOBS, Sir Wilfred (Ebenezer), GCMG 1981; GCVO 1985 (KCVO 1977); Kt 1967; OBE 1959; QC 1959; Governor-General of Antigua and Barbuda, 1981–93; *b* 19 Oct. 1919; 2nd *s* of late William Henry Jacobs and Henrietta Jacobs (*née* Du Bois); *m* 1947, Carmen Sylva, 2nd *d* of late Walter A. Knight and Flora Knight (*née* Fleming); one *s* two *d. Educ:* Grenada Boys' Secondary Sch.; Gray's Inn, London. Called to the Bar, Gray's Inn, 1946; Registrar and Additional Magistrate, St Vincent, 1946; Magistrate, Dominica, 1947, and St Kitts, 1949; Crown Attorney, St Kitts, 1952; Attorney-Gen., Leeward Is, 1957–59, and Antigua, 1960. Acted Administrator, Dominica, St Kitts, Antigua, various periods, 1947–60. MEC and MLC, St Vincent, Dominica, St Kitts, Antigua, 1947–60; Legal Draftsman and Acting Solicitor-Gen., Trinidad and Tobago, 1960; Barbados: Solicitor-Gen., and Actg Attorney-Gen., 1961–63; PC and MLC, 1962–63; Dir of Public Prosecutions, 1964; Judge of Supreme Court of Judicature, 1967; Governor of Antigua, 1967–81. KStJ. *Recreations:* swimming, gardening, golf. *Address:* c/o

Governor-General's Office, St John's, Antigua, West Indies. *Club:* Royal Commonwealth Society.

Died 5 March 1995.

JIMÉNEZ DE ARÉCHAGA, Eduardo, DrJur; President, Court of Arbitration for the Delimitation of Maritime areas between Canada and France, 1989–92; *b* Montevideo, 8 June 1918; *s* of E. Jiménez de Aréchaga and Ester Sienra; *m* 1943, Marta Ferreira; three *s* two *d. Educ:* Sch. of Law, Univ. of Montevideo. Prof. of Internat. Law, Montevideo Law Sch., 1946; Under-Sec., Foreign Relations, 1950–52; Sec., Council of Govt of Uruguay, 1952–55; Mem., Internat. Law Commn of UN, 1961–69 (Pres., 1963); Cttee Rapporteur, Vienna Conf. on Law Treaties, 1968–69; Minister of the Interior, Uruguay, 1968; Pres. of the International Ct of Justice, The Hague, 1976–79 (Judge of the Ct, 1970–79). Pres., World Bank Admin. Tribunal, 1981–90. *Publications:* Reconocimiento de Gobiernos, 1946; Voting and Handling of Disputes in the Security Council, 1951; Derecho Constitucional de las Naciónes Unidas, 1958; Curso de Derecho Internacional Público, 2 vols, 1959–61; International Law in the Past Third of a Century, vol. I, 1978; Derecho Internacional Contemporáneo, 1980. *Address:* Casilla de Correo 539, Montevideo, Uruguay. *Died 4 April 1994.*

KEKEDO, Dame Mary (Angela), DBE 1987 (CBE); BEM; formerly Headmistress and Manageress of schools in Kokoda; retired from active public service, 1981; *b* 12 July 1919; *d* of Alphonse Natera and Lucy Silva; *m* 1939, Walter Gill Kekedo; two *s* six *d* (and two *s* decd). *Educ:* St Patrick's Sch., Yule Island, PNG. Certificated teacher. Began first sch. in Kokoda, in own private home, and first women's club in Kokoda, 1949; Headmistress of Kokoda Sch. (first female apptd in PNG), 1956; founded first Vocational Sch. in Kokoda, 1974, Manageress, 1976. Member: Kokoda Area Authority, 1975; (first) Interim Northern Province Provincial Assembly, 1978. Cross Pro Ecclesia et Pontifice (Holy See), 1987. *Address:* Post Office Box 10, Kokoda, Northern Province, Papua New Guinea. *Died 15 Jan. 1993.*

KELSICK, Osmund Randolph, DFC 1944; Chairman and Managing Director, Carib Holdings Ltd (owning and operating The Blue Waters Beach Hotel), 1979–85, retired; Director: Caribbean Consultants Ltd; T. H. Kelsick Ltd (Montserrat); Caribbean Hotel Association; Antigua Hotel Association; *b* 21 July 1922; *s* of T. H. Kelsick; *m* 1950, Doreen Avis Hodge; one *s* (and one *s* decd), and two step *d. Educ:* private preparatory sch.; Montserrat Grammar Sch.; Oxford Univ. (Devonshire Course). RAF, Fighter Pilot, 1940–46. ADC and Personal Sec. to Governor of the Leeward Islands, 1946–47; District Commissioner, Carriacou, 1947–51; Asst Chief Sec., Governor's Office, Grenada, 1951–52; Asst Administrator and Administrator, St Vincent, 1952–57; in 1956 seconded for short periods as Asst Trade Commissioner for British West Indies, British Guiana and British Honduras in UK, and Executive Sec. of Regional Economic Cttee in Barbados; Chief Sec., Leeward Islands, 1957–60. Past Pres., Caribbean Hotel Assoc. FRSA 1973. *Recreations:* fishing, gardening, tennis. *Address:* PO Box 454, Antigua, Leeward Islands, West Indies. *Clubs:* Commonwealth Trust; New (Antigua). *Died 4 Sept. 1992.*

KENNEDY, Sir Clyde (David Allen), Kt 1973; Chairman of Sydney (New South Wales) Turf Club, 1972–77 and 1980–83 (Vice-Chairman, 1967–72); company director; *b* 20 Nov. 1912; *s* of late D. H. Kennedy; *m* 1937, Sarah Stacpoole; two *s* one *d*. Member, NSW Totalisator Agency Board, 1965–82; Chairman, Spinal Research Foundation, 1977. *Address:* 13A/23 Thornton Street, Darling Point, NSW 2027, Australia. *Clubs:* Australian Jockey, Sydney Turf, Rugby, Tattersalls (all NSW).

Died 2 July 1991.

KING, Sir Albert, Kt 1974; OBE 1958; Leader, Labour Group, Leeds Metropolitan District Council, 1975–78, retired (Leader of the Council with one break, 1958–75); *b* 20 Aug. 1905; *s* of George and Ann King; *m* 1928, Pauline Riley; one *d. Educ:* Primrose Hill, Leeds. Full-time officer, engrg, 1942–70, retd. Hon. Freedom of the City of Leeds, 1976. *Recreations:* walking, reading. *Address:* 25 Brook Hill Avenue, Leeds LS17 8QA. *T:* Leeds (0113) 268 4684. *Clubs:* Beeston Working Men's, East Leeds Labour (Leeds). *Died 30 Jan. 1995.*

LACKEY, Rt Rev. Edwin Keith; Archbishop and Metropolitan of Ontario, 1991–93; Bishop of Ontario, 1981–93; *b* 10 June 1930. *Educ:* Bishop's Univ., Lennoxville (BA 1953). Deacon 1953, priest 1954, Ottawa; Curate of Cornwall, 1953–55; Incumbent of Russell, 1955–60, Vankleek Hill, 1960–63; Rector of St Michael and All Angels, Ottawa, 1963–72; Director of Programme, dio. Ottawa, 1972–78; Hon. Canon, 1972–78; Archdeacon of the Diocese, 1978–81. Hon. DCL Bishop's Univ., 1988. *Address:* Archbishop's Office, 71 Bronson Avenue, Ottawa, Ontario K1R 6G6, Canada.

Died 9 Jan. 1993.

LARSON, Frederick H, DFM 1943; General Manager, Business Development, Alberta Opportunity Co., Edmonton, Alberta (Alberta Crown Corporation), 1974–90; *b* 24 Nov. 1913; *s* of Herman B. and Martha C. Larson; *m* 1941, Dorothy A. Layng; one *s. Educ:* University of Saskatchewan. Observer, RCAF, 1941–43. Member for Kindersley, Parliament of Canada, 1949–53; Delegate to UN, Paris, 1952. Ten years in oil and gas business, production refining and sales, domestic and offshore; eight years in financial trust business, representing financial interests, Canada and Jamaica; three years in construction and engineering; agricultural interests, Saskatchewan; Agent-Gen. for Province of Saskatchewan in London, 1967–73. *Recreation:* golf. *Address:* c/o Alberta Opportunity Co., PO Box 1860, Ponoka, Alberta T0C 2H0, Canada. *Clubs:* Ranchmen's (Calgary); Mayfair Golf (Edmonton, Alta).

Died Feb. 1994.

le FLEMING, Sir Quentin (John), 12th Bt *cr* 1705, of Rydal, Westmorland; Taxi Proprietor, Palmerston North Taxis Ltd, since 1982; *b* 27 June 1949; *s* of Sir William Kelland le Fleming, 11th Bt and of Noveen Avis, *d* of C. C. Sharpe; *S* father, 1988; *m* 1971, Judith Ann, *d* of C. J. Peck; two *s* one *d. Recreations:* flying modern and vintage aircraft (private pilot), Scouting, caravanning, restoration of vintage cars. *Heir: s* David Kelland le Fleming, *b* 12 Jan. 1976. *Address:* 147 Stanford Street, Ashhurst, Manawatu, New Zealand. *T:* (63) 268406.

Died 4 March 1995.

LLOYD, James Monteith, CD 1979; CMG 1961; Deputy Chairman, Industrial Disputes Tribunal, Jamaica, 1976–78; *b* 24 Nov. 1911; *s* of late Jethro and Frances Lloyd; *m* 1936, Mavis Anita Frankson; two *s* two *d. Educ:* Wolmer's High Sch., Jamaica. Called to Bar, Lincoln's Inn, 1948. Jamaica: entered Public Service as Asst, Registrar-General's Dept, 1931 (2nd Class Clerk, 1939, 1st Class Clerk, 1943, Asst Registrar-General, 1947); Asst Secretary, Secretariat, 1950; Principal Asst Secretary, Secretariat, 1953 (seconded to Grenada on special duty, Dec. 1955–May 1956); Permanent Secretary, Jamaica, 1956; Administrator, Grenada, 1957–62; Permanent Secretary, Jamaica, 1962–72; Chm., Ombudsman Working Party, Jamaica, 1972; retired from Civil Service, 1975. Chief Comr, Scouts, Jamaica, 1973–78. Coronation Medal, 1953; Jamaica Independence Medal, 1962. *Recreations:* cricket, tennis, golf. *Clubs:* Jamaica; Kingston CC; YMCA. *Died 6 April 1995.*

McCARTHY, Adolf Charles; HM Diplomatic Service, retired; *b* 19 July 1922; *s* of Herbert Charles McCarthy and Anna Schnorf; *m* 1949, Ursula Vera Grimm; one *s* two *d*. *Educ:* London Univ. (BScEcon). Served War, RN, 1942–46. Min. of Agriculture, Fisheries and Food, 1939–64; Min. of Overseas Develt, 1964–66; HM Diplomatic Service, 1966; First Secretary: (Economic), Pretoria, 1968–70; (Commercial), Wellington, 1971–74; Asst Head of Western European Dept, FCO, 1974–77; Consul-Gen., Stuttgart, 1977–82; Hon. Consul at Freiburg, 1985–92. *Publication:* Robert Grimm: the Swiss revolutionary, 1990. *Recreations:* music, modern political history. *Address:* Engeriedweg 17, Bern 3012, Switzerland. *T:* (31) 3013440. *Club:* Rotary (Freiburg i. Br.). *Died 2 Oct. 1995.*

McCUSKER, Sir James (Alexander), Kt 1983; Founder, Town and Country Permanent Building Society, 1964, Foundation Chairman 1964–83; *b* Perth, WA, 2 Dec. 1913; *s* of James McCusker; *m* Mary Martindale McCusker; three *c*. *Educ:* Perth Modern Sch. Served War of 1939–45, 2½ years with 1st Armoured Div. (Sgt). 30 years with Commonwealth Bank of Aust.; resigned 1959, as Sen. Branch Manager in Perth. Chm., State Cttee of Inquiry into Rates and Taxes, 1980. Councillor: WA Permanent Building Socs Assoc., 1964–83 (former Pres.); Aust. Assoc. of Permanent Building Socs; Fellow, Aust. Inst. of Valuers; Member: Council of Rural and Allied Industries; WA Indicative Planning Cttee (Housing). Patron, Paraplegic Assoc. of WA. *Address:* 47 Birdwood Parade, Dalkeith, WA 6009, Australia.
Died 30 Sept. 1995.

McDONALD, Hon. Sir William (John Farquhar), Kt 1958; *b* 3 Oct. 1911; *s* of John Nicholson McDonald and Sarah McDonald (*née* McInnes); *m* 1935, Evelyn Margaret Koch; two *d*. *Educ:* Scotch Coll., Adelaide, South Australia. Served AIF, 1939–45, Capt. Councillor, Shire of Kowree, 1946–61. MLA, electorate of Dundas, Victoria, 1947–52, 1955–70; Speaker, Legislative Assembly, Victoria, 1955–67; Minister of Lands, Soldier Settlement, and for Conservation, 1967–70. Mem., Exec. Council, Victoria. Trustee, Shrine of Remembrance, 1955–70. Victoria State Pres., Poll Shorthorn Soc. of Aust., 1962–72; Trustee, Royal Agricultural Soc. of Victoria, 1968–. Trustee, Victoria Amateur Turf Club, 1969. *Address:* Brippick, 102 St Georges Road, Toorak, Vic 3142, Australia. *T:* (3) 98275839. *Clubs:* Hamilton (Hamilton, Victoria); Australian, Naval and Military, Melbourne (Melbourne). *Died 13 Sept. 1995.*

McGILVRAY, Prof. James William; Professor of Economics, University of Strathclyde, since 1988; *b* 21 Feb. 1938; *m* 1966, Alison Ann Wingfield; one *s* one *d*. *Educ:* St Columba's Coll., Dublin; Univ. of Edinburgh (MA); Trinity Coll., Dublin (MLitt). Lectr in Econs, TCD, 1962–69; Res. Fellow, Harvard Univ., 1969–70; Sen. Lectr, Univ. of Stirling, 1970–75; Res. Prof., 1975–80, Dir, 1980–85, Fraser of Allander Inst., Univ. of Strathclyde; Dir of Econs, Dar Al-Handasah Consultants, 1985–88. *Publications:* Irish Economic Statistics, 1968, 2nd edn 1983; Use and Interpretation of Medical Statistics (with G. J. Bourke), 1969, 4th edn 1991; articles in Econometrica, Economic Jl, Rev. of Econs and Statistics, Jl of Reg. Sci., etc. *Recreations:* golf, gardening. *Address:* Gartinstarry Lodge, Buchlyvie, Stirling FK8 3PD. *Club:* Fitzwilliam (Dublin). *Died 19 Nov. 1995.*

MAHON, Peter, JP; *b* 4 May 1909; *s* of late Alderman Simon Mahon, OBE, JP, Bootle, Liverpool; *m* 1935, Margaret Mahon (*née* Hannon); three *s* one *d*. *Educ:* St James Elementary Sch.; St Edward's Coll. (Irish Christian Brothers). One of the longest serving Local Govt representatives in GB (42 years); Bootle Borough Council, 1933–70 (Mayor, 1954–55); Liverpool City Council,

1970–75; Liverpool DC, 1973–80 (Mem. (L) Old Swan Ward); Chm. or Dep. Chm. numerous cttees; Mem. Nat. Cttee of TGWU. Prospective Parly Candidate (Lab) Blackburn, 1952–54, contested (Lab) Preston, 1962–64; MP (Lab) Preston South, 1964–70; contested Liverpool Scotland, April 1971, as first Against Abortion candidate in UK; expelled from Labour Party. Talked out first Abortion Bill, House of Commons, 1966. *Recreations:* football and swimming enthusiast, fond of music. *Address:* Seahaven, Burbo Bank Road, Blundellsands, Liverpool L23 8TA. *Died 29 Sept. 1980.*

MATTHEWS, Prof. Ernest, DDS, PhD, MSc, DIC; ARCS, FDSRCS; Director of Prosthetics, University of Manchester, 1935–70, then Professor Emeritus; *b* 14 Dec. 1904; *s* of James Alfred Matthews, Portsmouth; *m* 1st, 1928, Doris Pipe (decd); one *d* (two *s* decd); 2nd, 1992, Pauline Mary Bates. *Educ:* Imperial Coll., London; Cambridge; Guy's Hospital, London. Demonstrator and Lecturer, Guy's Hospital Medical and Dental Schs, 1926–34; Dean and Dir, Turner Dental Sch., 1966–69. Prosthetic Dental Surgeon, Manchester Royal Infirmary, 1937; Cons. Dental Surgeon, Christie Hosp., 1945; Hon. Adviser in Dental Surgery to Manchester Regional Hospital Board, 1951. Silver Jubilee Medal, 1977. *Recreation:* gardening. *Address:* 16 The Spain, Petersfield, Hants GU32 3LA. *Died 17 Aug. 1995.*

MELCHIOR-BONNET, Christian; author; Director and founder, Historia, since 1946; *b* Marseille, 10 April 1904; *s* of Daniel-Joseph Melchior-Bonnet and Geneviève (*née* de Luxer); *m* 1930, Bernardine Paul-Dubois-Taine (*g d* of the historian Taine, herself a historian, author of several historical works, recipient of Grand Prix Gobert of Académie Française); two *s* one *d*. *Educ:* St Jean de Béthune, Versailles; Ecole du Louvre, Faculté de droit de Paris. Secretary to Pierre de Nolhac, de l'Académie française, historian, at Jacquemart-André museum, 1927–36; formerly, Editor-in-Chief, Petit Journal, 1936–45 and Flambeau; Dir, historical and religious series of Editions Flammarion, 1932–46; Literary Dir, Fayard editions, 1946–67; Director of the reviews: Oeuvres Libres, 1946–64; Historia, 1946–; A la Page, 1964–69; Co-dir, Jardin des Arts; Dir and Ed.-in-Chief, Journal de la France, 1969–80. Literary Adviser to Nouvelles Littéraires, 1946–70. Privy Chamberlain to every Pope, 1946–, incl. Pope John Paul II. Membre du jury: Prix Historia; Prix de la Fondation de France; Prix des Ambassadeurs. Prix du Rayonnement, Académie française, 1963. Officier de la Légion d'honneur; Commandeur de l'Ordre national du Mérite; Officier des Arts et des Lettres; et décorations étrangères. *Publications:* Scènes et portraits historiques de Chateaubriand, 1928; Les Mémoires du Comte Alexandre de Tilly, ancien page de la reine Marie-Antoinette, 1929; Les Mémoires du Cardinal de Retz, 1929; Principes d'action de Salazar, 1956; Le Napoléon de Chateaubriand, 1969; et nombreuses éditions de mémoires historiques. *Address:* 17 Boulevard de Beauséjour, 75016 Paris, France.
Died 23 July 1995.

MILLER, Sir John Holmes, 11th Bt *cr* 1705, of Chichester, Sussex; *b* 1925; *er s* of 10th Bt and of Netta Mahalah Bennett; *S* father, 1960; *m* 1950, Jocelyn Robson Edwards, Wairoa, NZ; two *d*. *Heir: b* Harry Miller [*b* 15 Jan. 1927; *m* 1954, Gwynedd Margaret Sherriff; one *s* two *d*]. *Died 27 Dec. 1995.*

MILNE, Kenneth Lancelot, CBE 1971; chartered accountant; *b* 16 Aug. 1915; *s* of F. K. Milne, Adelaide; *m* 1st, 1941, Mary (*d* 1980), *d* of E. B. Hughes; two *s* one *d*; 2nd, 1982, Joan Constance, *d* of Claude W. J. Lee. *Educ:* St Peter's Coll., Adelaide. Served with RAAF, 1940–45, attaining rank of Flt Lieut. Entered Public Practice as Chartered Accountant, 1946; elected to State

Council, 1951 (Chm., 1958–60), Mem. Gen. Council, 1956–60, Inst. of Chartered Accountants in Australia Municipality of Walkerville: Councillor, 1960; Mayor, 1961–63; Municipal Assoc., 1961–65 (Pres. 1964–65). MLC (Australian Democrat) SA, 1979–85 (Parlt Leader, 1983–85). Mem. Faculty of Economics, University of Adelaide, 1963–65; Agent Gen. and Trade Comr for S Aust. in UK, 1966–71. President: SA Br., Aust. Inst. of Internat. Affairs, 1958–60; SA Branch, Royal Overseas League, 1975–; Royal Life Saving Soc. of SA, 1977–. Chm., State Govt Insce Commn, 1971–79; Member: Commn on Advanced Educn, 1973–77; Universities Commn, 1977. Chm., Stirling Dist Bicentennary Cttee, SA, 1987–89. Freeman, City of London, 1970. *Publications:* Ostrich Heads, 1937; Forgotten Freedom, 1952; The Accountant in Public Practice, 1959. *Recreations:* rowing, tennis, conchology. *Address:* 50 Birch Road, Stirling, SA 5152, Australia. *T:* (8) 3393674. *Clubs:* Naval, Military and Air Force (Adelaide); Adelaide Rowing (Pres., 1986–). *Died 27 Dec. 1995.*

MOOKERJEE, Sir Birendra Nath, Kt 1942; Partner of Martin & Co. and Burn & Co.; Managing Director, Martin Burn Ltd, Engineers, Contractors, Merchants, Shipbuilders, etc; Chairman, Steel Corporation of Bengal Ltd; President, Calcutta Local Board of Imperial Bank of India; Director, Darjeeling Himalayan Railway Co. Ltd and many other companies; *b* 14 Feb. 1899; *s* of late Sir Rajendra Nath Mookerjee, KCIE, KCVO, MIE (India), FASB, DSc (Eng); *m* 1925, Ranu Priti Adhikari, *d* of Phani Bhusan Adhikari, late Professor Benares Hindu Univ.; one *s* two *d. Educ:* Bishop's Collegiate Sch., Hastings House, Calcutta; Bengal Engineering Coll.; Trinity Coll., Cambridge (MA). MIE (India). Formerly Mem., Viceroy's Nat. Defence Council; Adviser, Roger Mission; Mem. Munitions Production Adv. Cttee. Fellow Calcutta Univ.; Sheriff of Calcutta 1941. *Address:* 7 Harrington Street, Calcutta 700071, India; Martin Burn Ltd, Martin Burn House, 12 Mission Row, Calcutta 1, India. *Clubs:* National Liberal, Calcutta, Calcutta Polo, Royal Calcutta Turf, Calcutta South, Cricket Club of India (Calcutta), etc. *Died 4 Nov. 1982.*

MORRIS, Ivor Gray, CMG 1974; former Chairman and Managing Director, Morris Woollen Mills (Ipswich) Pty Ltd; Chairman, Queensland Export Advisory Committee; *b* 28 March 1911; *s* of John and Annie Morris, Talybont, Cards, and Ipswich, Qld; *m* 1944, Jessie Josephine Halley; two *d. Educ:* Scotch Coll., Melbourne; Scots Coll., Warwick, Qld; Ipswich Grammar Sch., Qld; Leeds Univ. Founded Morris Woollen Mills (Ipswich) Pty Ltd, 1934. Former Mem. Exec., Wool Textile Manufrs Assoc. of Australia; Life Mem., Nuclear Physics Foundn; Former Mem., Trade Develt Council, Canberra. Former Chm. of Trustees, Ipswich Grammar Sch.; Vice-Pres., Qld Museum Trust, 1970–; Patron, St David's Welsh Soc.; Foundn Mem. and District Governor, Ipswich Apex Club (1st Apex Club formed in Aust.), 1938. *Recreations:* music, reading. *Clubs:* Tattersall's (Brisbane); Ipswich, Ipswich North Rotary (Ipswich, Qld). *Deceased.*

MUNRO, Charles Rowcliffe; *b* 6 Nov. 1902; *s* of Charles John Munro, CA, Edinburgh, Hon. Sheriff Substitute, County of Selkirk, and Edith Rowcliffe; *m* 1942, Moira Rennie Ainslie, *d* of Dr Alexander Cruickshank Ainslie; two *s. Educ:* Merchiston Castle Sch., Edinburgh. Hon. Treasurer W Edinburgh Unionist Assoc., 1945–61; Hon. Treas. Scottish Nat. Cttee English-Speaking Union of the Commonwealth 1952–64; Pres. Edinburgh Union of Boys' Clubs, 1957–66. *Recreation:* fishing. *Address:* 66 Murrayfield Avenue, Edinburgh EH12 6AY. *T:* (0131) 337 2139. *Died 9 May 1995.*

MURRAY, Sir Rowland William Patrick, 14th Bt *cr* 1630, of Dunerne, Fifeshire; retired hotel general manager; *b* 26

Oct. 1910; *s* of late Rowland William Murray (2nd *s* of 12th Bt) and Gertrude Frances McCabe; *s* uncle 1958; *m* 1944, Josephine Margaret Murphy; four *s* two *d*. Served in US Army during War of 1939–45; Captain. *Heir: s* Rowland William Murray [*b* 22 Sept. 1947; *m* 1970, Nancy Diane, *d* of George C. Newberry; one *s* one *d*]. *Died 1994.*

NEDD, Sir (Robert) Archibald, Kt 1985; Chief Justice of Grenada, 1979–86; *b* 7 Aug. 1916; *s* of late Robert and Ruth Nedd; *m* 1941, Annis (*née* McDowall); two *s* one *d. Educ:* King's Coll. London (LLB). Called to the Bar, Inner Temple, 1938. Registrar of High Court, and Addtl Magistrate, St Vincent, 1940–41, Dominica, 1941–43; Magistrate, St Lucia, 1943–44 (acted Crown Attorney); Crown Attorney, Dominica, 1944–49 (Officer administering Govt of Dominica, March 1945–Nov. 1946); Magistrate, full powers, Nigeria, 1949–53; private practice, Nigeria, 1953–70; Principal State Counsel, Rivers State, Nigeria, 1970–71 (exercising functions of legal draftsman); Legal draftsman, Rivers State, Nigeria, 1971–74 (occasionally perf. functions of Solicitor-Gen.); Puisne Judge of Supreme Court of Associated States of W Indies and Grenada, at Antigua, 1974–75, at Grenada, 1975–79. *Recreation:* reading. *Address:* Old Fort, St George's, Grenada, West Indies. *T:* 1225. *Died 20 June 1992.*

O'REGAN, Hon. Sir (John) Barry, Kt 1984; Judge of the Court of Appeal, Cook Islands, since 1986; *b* 2 Dec. 1915; *s* of John O'Regan; *m* 1941, Catherine, *d* of John O'Donnell; four *s* one *d. Educ:* Sacred Heart College, Auckland; Victoria University, Wellington (LLB). Army service, 1941–45 (Captain). Partner, Bell O'Regan & Co., 1945–73; Judge of High Court, NZ, 1973–84; Judge of Ct of Appeal, Fiji, 1983–87. Chairman: Prisons Parole Bd, 1977–83; War Pensions Appeal Bd, 1984–90. Member: Council, Wellington Law Soc., 1959–69 (Pres., 1968); Council, NZ Law Soc., 1967–69; Council of Legal Education, 1969–73; Legal Aid Board, 1970–73. Consul-Gen. for Ireland, 1965–73. *Address:* Apt A/4 Lincoln Courts, 1 Washington Avenue, Wellington 2, New Zealand. *Died 23 Sept. 1995.*

ORMOND, Sir John (Davies Wilder), Kt 1964; BEM 1940; JP; Chairman: Shipping Corporation of New Zealand Ltd, 1973; Container Terminals Ltd, 1975; Exports and Shipping Council, 1964; *b* 8 Sept. 1905; *s* of J. D. Ormond and Gladys Wilder; *m* 1939, Judith Wall; four *s* one *d. Educ:* Christ's Coll., Christchurch, New Zealand. Chairman, Waipukurau Farmers Union, 1929; President, Waipukurau Jockey Club, 1950; Member, New Zealand Meat Producers Board, 1934–72, Chm., 1951–72. Active Service Overseas (Middle East), 1940. JP, NZ, 1945. DSc (*hc*), 1972. *Recreations:* tennis, polo, Rugby Union football. *Address:* Wallingford, Waipukurau, New Zealand. *T:* (6) 8554701. *Club:* Hawke's Bay (New Zealand). *Died 8 March 1995.*

PANDEY, Ishwari Raj, Hon. GCVO 1986; Prasiddha Prabala Gorakha-Dakshina Bahu, 1982; Vikhyata Trishakti-Patta, 1974; Additional Foreign Secretary to HM's Government, Kingdom of Nepal, 1988–91; *b* 15 Aug. 1934; *s* of Rajguru Sri Hem Raj Panditgue and Nayab Bada Guruma Khaga Kumari Pandit; *m* 1953, Gita Rajya Laxmi Devi Rana; three *s* two *d. Educ:* Bombay Univ. (MA); Univ. of Pittsburgh (MPIA). Planning Officer, Min. of Planning and Develt, 1959; Under Sec., Min. of Finance (Foreign Aid Co-ordination), 1961; Dir, Dept of Industries, 1964; Head of Section for Econ. Relations, Min. of Foreign Affairs, 1966; First Secretary: Royal Nepalese Embassy, London, 1968; Perm. Mission of Kingdom of Nepal to UN, New York, 1972; Head of Section for Neighbouring Countries, Min. of For. Affairs, 1974; Chargé d'Affaires (Counsellor), Royal Nepalese

Embassy, Tehran, 1975; Jt Sec., Div. for Europe and the Americas, Min. of For. Affairs, 1979; Minister, Royal Nepalese Embassy, New Delhi, 1980; Ambassador to the UK, 1983–88 (concurrently Ambassador to Denmark, Finland, Norway, Iceland and Sweden). Coronation Medal, Bhutan, 1975. *Publications:* The Economic Impact of the Tourist Industry (with special reference to Puerto Rico and Nepal), 1961 (Univ. of Pittsburgh); contrib. to many jls. *Recreations:* reading, travelling. *Address:* Bharatee Bhawan, Dhokatole, Kathmandu, Nepal. *T:* 211297. *Club:* Hurlingham. *Died June 1995.*

PATERSON, Sqdn-Ldr Ian Veitch, CBE 1969; JP; DL; Deputy Chairman, Local Government Boundary Commission for Scotland, 1974–80; *b* 17 Aug. 1911; *s* of Andrew Wilson Paterson; *m* 1940, Anne Weir, *d* of Thomas Brown; two *s* one *d. Educ:* Lanark Grammar School; Glasgow University. Served RAF, 1940–45. Entered local govt service, Lanark, 1928; Principal Legal Asst, Aberdeen CC; Lanarkshire: Dep. County Clerk, 1949; County Clerk, 1956, resigned 1974. Chm., Working Party which produced The New Scottish Local Authorities Organisation and Management structures, 1973. DL Lanarkshire (Strathclyde), 1963; JP Hamilton (formerly Lanarkshire). *Address:* 12 Fairfield Lodge, Green Street, Bothwell, Glasgow G71 8RJ. *Died 1994.*

PERCIVAL, Robert Clarendon, FRCS, FRCOG; Consulting Obstetric Surgeon, The Royal London Hospital; *b* 16 Sept. 1908; British; *m* 1st, 1944, Beryl Mary Ind (*d* 1967); one *d*; 2nd, 1972, Beatrice Myfanwy Evans, FFARCS. *Educ:* Barker College, NSW; Sydney University; The London Hospital (qualified 1933). Resident appointments: Poplar Hospital; Hosp. for Sick Children, Gt Ormond St; The London Hosp.; Southend Gen. Hosp. Obstetric and Gynæcological 1st Asst, The London Hosp., 1937–41; Surgeon-Lt-Comdr, RNVR, 1941–45 (Surgical Specialist); Obstetric Surgeon, The London Hospital, 1947–73, Director, Obstetric Unit, 1968–73. Chm., Obst. Adv. Cttee, NE Region Met. Hosp. Bd, 1967–73; President: Section of Obst. and Gyn., RSocMed, 1973–74; The London Hosp. Clubs' Union, 1965 (Treasurer, 1955–73); United Hosps RFC, 1969–72; London Hosp. Cricket Club, 1946–72. *Publications:* (jtly) Ten Teachers' Midwifery, 1958, new edition as Ten Teachers' Obstetrics, 1972; (jtly) Ten Teachers' Diseases of Women, 1965, new edition as Ten Teachers' Gynæcology, 1971; (jtly) British Obstetric Practice, 1963; (ed) Holland and Brews Obstetrics, 1969, 14th edn 1979; contribs to Lancet, British Jl of Obst. and Gynæcol. *Recreations:* fishing, golf. *Address:* Coker Wood Cottage, Pendomer, near Yeovil, Somerset BA22 9PD. *T:* Corscombe (01935891) 328. *Clubs:* Gynaeological Travellers' of GB and Ireland; Royal Navy Ski. *Died 13 Aug. 1995.*

PETERS, Prof. Raymond Harry; Professor of Polymer and Fibre Science, University of Manchester, 1955–84, then Emeritus; *b* 19 Feb. 1918. *Educ:* County High Sch., Ilford; King's Coll., London Univ.; Manchester Univ. BSc (London) 1939, PhD (London), 1942, in Chemistry; BSc (Manchester), 1949, BSc (London), 1949, in Mathematics; DSc (London), 1968. Scientist at ICI Ltd, 1941–46 and 1949–55. Visiting Professor: UMIST, 1984–86; Univ. of Strathclyde, 1984. President, Society of Dyers and Colourists, 1967–68. *Publications:* Textile Chemistry: Vol. I, The Chemistry of Fibres, 1963; Vol. II, Impurities of Fibres: Purification of Fibres, 1967; Vol. III, Physical Chemistry of Dyeing, 1975; contributions to Journals of Chemical Society, Society of Dyers and Colourists, Textile Institute, British Journal of Applied Physics, etc. *Recreation:* gardening. *Address:* 1 Vale Road, Pownall Park, Wilmslow, Cheshire SK9 5QA.
Died 15 July 1995.

PHILLPOTTS, (Mary) Adelaide Eden, (Mrs Nicholas Ross); writer; *b* Ealing, Middlesex, 23 April 1896; *d* of late Eden Phillpotts; *m* 1951, Nicholas Ross. *Publications: novels:* The Friend, 1923; Lodgers in London, 1926; Tomek, the Sculptor, 1927; A Marriage, 1928; The Atoning Years, 1929; Yellow Sands, 1930; The Youth of Jacob Ackner, 1931; The Founder of Shandon, 1932; The Growing World, 1934; Onward Journey, 1936; Broken Allegiance, 1937; What's Happened to Rankin?, 1938; The Gallant Heart, 1939; The Round of Life, 1940; Laugh with Me, 1941; Our Little Town, 1942; From Jane to John, 1943; The Adventurers, 1944; The Lodestar, 1946; The Fosterling, 1949; Stubborn Earth, 1951; Village Love, 1988; The Beacon of Memory, 1990; *plays:* Arachne, 1920; Savitri the Faithful, 1923; Camillus and the Schoolmaster, 1923; Akhnaton, 1926; (with Eden Phillpotts) Yellow Sands, 1926; Laugh With Me, 1938; *poetry:* Illyrion, and other Poems, 1916; A Song of Man, 1959; *travel:* Panorama of the World, 1969; *miscellaneous:* Man, a Fable, 1922; (selected with Nicholas Ross) Letters to Nicholas Ross from J. C. Powys (ed A. Uphill), 1971; A Wild Flower Wreath, 1975; Reverie: an Autobiography, 1981. *Address:* Trelana Home, Poughill, near Bude, Cornwall EX23 9EL. *Died 4 June 1993.*

PLENDERLEITH, Thomas Donald; Hon. Fellow, Royal Society of Painter-Etchers and Engravers, 1987 (RE 1961 (retd); ARE 1951); Senior Art Master, St Nicholas Grammar School, Northwood, 1956–85, retired; *b* 11 March 1921; *s* of James Plenderleith and Georgina Ellis; *m* 1949, Joyce Rogers; one *s. Educ:* St Clement Danes; Ealing Sch. of Art; Hornsey Sch. of Art. Art Teacher's Diploma, 1947. Pilot, Bomber Command, RAF, 1941–46. Art Master, Pinner County Grammar Sch., 1948–56. *Recreations:* cricket, badminton. *Address:* Homelea, Tresean, Cubert, Newquay, Cornwall TR8 5HN.
Died 27 Oct. 1995.

PYATT, Rt Rev. William Allan, CBE 1985; MA; Bishop of Christchurch, 1966–83, retired; *b* Gisborne, NZ, 4 Nov. 1916; *e s* of A. E. Pyatt; *m* 1942, Mary Lilian Carey; two *s* one *d. Educ:* Gisborne High Sch.; Auckland Univ.; St John's Coll., Auckland; Westcott House, Cambridge. BA 1938 (Senior Schol. in Hist.); MA 1939. Served War of 1939–45: combatant service with 2 NZEF; Major, 2 i/c 20 NZ Armd Regt 1945. Ordained, 1946; Curate, Cannock, Staffs, 1946–48; Vicar: Brooklyn, Wellington, NZ, 1948–52; Hawera, 1952–58; St Peter's, Wellington, 1958–62; Dean of Christchurch, 1962–66. *Publications:* contribs to NZ Jl of Theology. *Recreations:* Rugby referee; political comment on radio, golf, wood turning, caravanning, lecturing on current affairs, study of Maori language and racial issues in New Zealand. *Address:* 55a Celia Street, Christchurch 8, New Zealand.
Died 24 Nov. 1991.

RAE, Robert Wright; Civil Service, retired; Clerk to the General Commissioners of Income Tax, Blackheath Division, 1977–88 (Clerk, Bromley Division, 1977–85); *b* 27 March 1914; *s* of Walter Rae and Rachel Scott; *m* 1st, 1945, Joan McKenzie (*d* 1966); two *s*; 2nd, 1977, Marjorie Ann Collyer. *Educ:* George Heriot's Sch., Edinburgh; Edinburgh Univ. MA 1st cl. hons. Asst Inspector of Taxes, 1936; Dep. Chief Inspector of Taxes, 1973–75; Dir Personnel, Inland Revenue, 1975–77. *Recreations:* gardening, walking. *Address:* Oak Lodge, Blackbrook Lane, Bickley, Bromley BR1 2LP. *T:* 0181–467 2377. *Died 25 May 1995.*

REED, Most Rev. Thomas Thornton, CBE 1980; MA, DLitt, ThD; Archbishop of Adelaide and Metropolitan of South Australia, 1973–75; *b* Eastwood, South Australia, 9 Sept. 1902; *s* of Alfred Ernest Reed, Avoca, Vic; *m* 1932, Audrey Airlie, *d* of Major Harry Lort Spencer Balfour-Ogilvy, MBE, DCM, Tannadice, Renmark, South

Australia; two *d* (and one *d* decd). *Educ:* Collegiate Sch. of St Peter, Adelaide; Trinity College, University of Melbourne (Hon. Schol., BA, MA); St Barnabas' Theol Coll., Adelaide. ThL, ATC, 1st cl. hons. Fred Johns Schol. for Biography, Univ. of Adelaide, 1950. Deacon, 1926; priest, 1927; Curate, St Augustine's, Unley, 1926–28; Priest in Charge, Berri Mission, 1928–29; Resident Tutor, St Mark's Coll., Univ. of Adelaide, and Area Padre, Toc H, 1929–31; Asst Chaplain, Melbourne Grammar Sch., 1932–36; Rector, St Michael's, Henley Beach, 1936–44; Asst Tutor, St Barnabas' Coll., 1940–46; Rector, St Theodore's, Rose Park, 1944–54; Rural Dean, Western Suburbs, 1944; Priest Comr, Adelaide Dio. Centenary, 1947; Canon of Adelaide, 1947–49; Archdeacon of Adelaide, 1949–53; Dean of Adelaide, 1953–57; Bishop of Adelaide, 1957–73. Pres., Toc H, S Aust., 1960; Pres., St Mark's Coll., Univ. of Adelaide, 1961–74, Hon. Fellow, 1973. Hon. ThD, Australian Coll. of Theology, 1955; DLitt, Univ. of Adelaide, 1954. Chaplain and Sub Prelate of Venerable Order of St John of Jerusalem, 1965. Chaplain, Australian Mil. Forces, 1939–57; Chaplain, AIF with HQ, New Guinea Force, 1944–45; Senior Chaplain, RAA, HQ, C Command, South Australia, 1953–56. Editor, Adelaide Church Guardian, 1940–44. *Publications:* Henry Kendall: a Critical Appreciation, 1960; Sonnets and Songs, 1962; (ed) The Poetical Works of Henry Kendall, 1966; A History of the Cathedral Church of St Peter, Adelaide, 1969; Historic Churches of Australia, 1978. *Recreations:* golf, research on Australian literature, heraldry, genealogy. *Address:* 44 Jeffcott Street, North Adelaide, SA 5006, Australia. *T:* 2674841; PO Box 130, North Adelaide, SA 5006, Australia. *Clubs:* Adelaide, Naval, Military and Air Force, Royal Adelaide Golf (Adelaide).

Died 19 Aug. 1995.

RICHARDS, Rt Rev. Ronald Edwin, MA, ThD (*jd*); Bishop of Bendigo, 1957–74; *b* Ballarat, Vic, 25 Oct. 1908; *s* of Edward and Margaret Elizabeth Richards, Ballarat; *m* 1937, Nancy, *d* of W. E. Lloyd Green; one *d*. *Educ:* Ballarat High Sch., Trinity Coll., Melbourne Univ. BA 2nd Cl. Hons Phil., 1932, MA 1937. Asst Master, Ballarat C of E Grammar Sch., 1926, Malvern C of E Grammar Sch., 1927–28; deacon, 1932; priest, 1933; Curate of Rokewood, 1932–33, Priest-in-charge, 1934; Priest-in-charge, Lismore, 1934–41 and 1945–46; Chaplain AIF, 1941–45; Vicar of Warrnambool, 1946–50; Archdeacon of Ballarat, and Examining Chap. to Bp of Ballarat, 1950–57; Vicar-Gen., 1952–57. *Address:* Madron, 119 Dare Street, Ocean Grove, Vic 3226, Australia. *Clubs:* Royal Automobile of Victoria (Melbourne); Barwon Heads Golf.

Died 18 Nov. 1994.

RINFRET, Hon. Gabriel-Edouard, OC 1983; PC (Can.) 1949; Chief Justice of Québec, 1977–80, retired; *b* St-Jérôme, PQ, 12 May 1905; *s* of Rt Hon. Thibaudeau Rinfret, Chief Justice of Canada, and Georgine, *d* of S. J. B. Rolland; *m* 1929; two *s*; *m* 1982, Marcelle Landreau. *Educ:* Collège Notre-Dame, Côte des Neiges, PQ; Petit Séminaire, Montréal; Collège Ste-Marie (BA with distinction); McGill Univ., Montréal (LLM with distinction); pupil of Hon. J. L. Perron. Admitted to practice, 1928; joined law office of Campbell, McMaster, Couture, Kerry and Bruneau; partner, Campbell, Weldon, MacFarlane and Rinfret, 1945; KC 1943. Sec. or Legal Adviser to various provincial govt commns of enquiry, 1934–45. Pres., Jeunesse Libérale de Montréal, 1934; Co-founder and 1st Pres., Assoc. de la Jeunesse Libérale de la Province de Québec, 1934–35; MP (L) Outremont, 1945–49, Outremont-St Jean 1949–52, House of Commons of Canada; Postmaster General in St Laurent Cabinet. A Judge of the Court of Appeal of Québec, 1952–80. Pres. or Director: Concerts Symphoniques de Montréal; Inst. Internat. de Musique; Grands Ballets Canadiens; Dominion Drama Festival (organised Montréal Festival, 1961; Pres., W Québec Region, and Mem., Nat. Exec. Cttee, 1962–68; Canadian Drama Award, 1969); Vice Pres., Conservatoire Lassalle, 1967–. Hon. LLD Univ. of British Columbia, 1979. *Publications:* Répertoire du théâtre canadien d'expression française, vol. 1, 1975, vol. 2, 1976, vol. 3, 1977, vol. 4, 1978; Histoire du Barreau de Montréal, 1989. *Recreations:* cabinet-work, Canadian paintings; formerly baseball, lacrosse, tennis, hockey, skiing. *Address:* 121 Melbourne Avenue, Town of Mount Royal, Québec H3P 1G3, Canada.

Died 12 Jan. 1994.

ROSS, (Mary) Adelaide Eden, (Mrs Nicholas Ross); *see* Phillpotts, M. A. E.

ROWLANDS, Maldwyn Jones, OBE 1979; FLA, FRGS, FLS; Head of Library Services, British Museum (Natural History), 1965–81, retired; *b* 7 March 1918; *s* of Thomas and Elizabeth Rowlands; *m* 1941, Sybil Elizabeth Price; two *s* one *d*. *Educ:* Newtown Grammar Sch., Montgomeryshire; University Coll. London. Served in Army, 1940–46: commnd 1941 (Lieut); HQ 21 Army Gp (Staff Captain), 1944–46 (C-in-C's Cert. 1945). Asst Librarian, Science Museum Library, 1946–54; Deputy Librarian: British Museum (Natural History), 1954–63; Patent Office, 1963–65. *Recreations:* old books and bindings, Welsh history and folk-lore. *Address:* Llys Hafren, Caersws, Powys SY17 5JA.

Died 29 Dec. 1995.

RYDBECK, Olof; Comdr 1st Class, Order of the Star of the North, Sweden, 1973; Commissioner-General, United Nations Relief and Works Agency, 1979–85; *b* Djursholm, 15 April 1913; *s* of Oscar Rydbeck and Signe Olson; *m* 1940, Monica Schnell; one *s* one *d*. *Educ:* Univ. of Uppsala, Sweden (BA 1934, LLB 1939). Attaché, Min. for Foreign Affairs, 1939; Berlin, 1940; Ankara, 1941; Stockholm, 1942; Second Sec., 1943; Washington, 1945–50 (First Sec., 1946); Bonn, 1950; Head of Press Sect., Min. for For. Affairs, 1952; Dir Gen., Swedish Broadcasting Corp., 1955–70; Perm. Rep. to UN, 1970–76; Rep. of Sweden to Security Council, 1975–76; Special Rep. of Sec. Gen. on Western Sahara, 1976; Ambassador of Sweden to the UK, 1977–79. Chairman: Adv. Cttee on Outer Space Communications, UNESCO, 1966–70; Working Gp on Direct Broadcast Satellites, UN Cttee on Peaceful Uses of Outer Space, 1969–75; Cttee of Trustees, UN Trust Fund for S Africa, 1970–75; Prep. Cttee, World Food Conf., 1974; Second Cttee, 30th Gen. Assembly, 1975. Chairman: Assoc. of Royal Swedish Nat. Defence Coll., 1957–70; Internat. Broadcasting Inst., Rome, 1967–70; Hon. Pres., EBU, 1964– (Pres., 1961–64). Member: Central Cttee, Swedish Red Cross; Nat. Swedish Preparedness Commn for Psychol Defence, 1954–70 (Vice Chm., 1962–70); Royal Swed. Acad. of Music, 1962–. Member Boards: Swed. Inst., 1953–55; Amer. Swed. News Exchange, 1953–55; Swed. Tourist Traffic Assoc., 1953–55; Stockholm Philharmonic Soc., 1955–62; Swed. Central News Agency, 1967–70; Swed. Inst. of Internat. Affairs, 1967– King's Medal, 12th size, Sweden, 1980; Medal of Serahims, Sweden, 1987; Commander 1st Class: Order of the White Rose (Finland); Order of the Falcon (Iceland); Comdr, Order of the Dannebrog (Denmark); Verdienstkreutz (FRG). *Recreations:* music, books. *Address:* 3 avenue Charles de Gaulle, 69260 Charbonnières-les-Bains, France.

Died 23 Dec. 1995.

ST GEORGE, Sir George (Bligh), 9th Bt *cr* 1766 (Ire.), of Athlone, Co. Westmeath; *b* 23 Sept. 1908; *s* of Sir Theophilus John St George, 6th Bt and Florence Emma Vanderplank; *S* brother, 1989; *m* 1935, Mary Somerville, *d* of John Francis Fairby Sutcliffe; two *s* three *d*. *Educ:* Christian Bros Coll., Kimberley; Natal Univ. (BA). Natal

Provincial Administration, 1929–73, last appointment Dep. Dir (Admin), Addington Hospital, Durban. *Recreations:* music, bowls. *Heir: s* John Avenel Bligh St George [*b* 18 March 1940; *m* 1st, 1962, Margaret Carter (marr. diss. 1979); two *d*; 2nd, 1981, Linda, *d* of Robert Perry; two *s*]. *Address:* Hatley Cottage, 28 Waterfall Gardens Village, Private Bag X01, Link Hills 3652, Natal, South Africa. *T:* (31) 7633299.

Died 19 April 1995.

SINHA, 4th Baron *cr* 1919, of Raipur; **Susanta Prasanna Sinha;** *b* 1953; *s* of 3rd Baron and Madhabi, *d* of late Monoranjan Chatterjee; *S* father, 1989; *m* 1972, Patricia Orchard; one *d* (and one *s* one *d* decd). *Heir: uncle* Anindo Kumar Sinha [*b* 18 May 1930; *m* 1965, Lolita, *d* of late Deb Kumar Das; two *s* two *d*]. *Address:* 7 Lord Sinha Road, Calcutta, India. *Died 25 July 1992.*

SKINNER, Thomas Monier, CMG 1958; MBE; MA Oxon; *b* 2 Feb. 1913; *s* of late Lt-Col and Mrs T. B. Skinner; *m* 1st, 1935, Margaret Adeline (*née* Pope) (*d* 1969); two *s*; 2nd, 1981, Elizabeth Jane Hardie, *d* of late Mr and Mrs P. L. Hardie. *Educ:* Cheltenham Coll.; Lincoln Coll., Oxford. Asst District Officer (Cadet), Tanganyika, 1935; Asst District Officer, 1937; District Officer, 1947; Senior Asst Secretary, East Africa High Commission, 1952; Director of Establishments (Kenya), 1955–62, retired 1962. Member, Civil Service Commission, East Caribbean Territories, 1962–63; Chairman, Nyasaland Local Civil Service Commission, 1963; Salaries Commissioner, Basutoland, The Bechuanaland Protectorate and Swaziland, 1964. Reports on Localisation of Civil Service, Gilbert and Ellice Islands Colony and of British National Service, New Hebrides, 1968. Chairman: Bear Securities, 1962–73; Exeter Trust, 1973–79; Edinburgh Mortgage Corp., 1988–92; Dir, Business Mortgages Trust, 1979–87. *Recreation:* fishing. *Address:* 2 Parsonage Street, Bradninch, near Exeter, Devon EX5 4NW. *Club:* Army and Navy. *Died 29 Aug. 1995.*

SLADE, Leslie William, JP; Agent General for Western Australia in London, 1978–82; *b* 17 July 1915; *s* of Leonard Barrington Slade and Gwendoline (*née* Fraser); *m* 1942, Marion Joan, *d* of V. J. Devitt, Perth, WA; (one *d* decd). *Educ:* Scotch Coll., Melbourne, Australia. Accountant, Myer Emporium Ltd, Melbourne, 1933–39; served RAN (Lieut-Comdr), 1939–46; Proprietor of import/export business, Perth, WA, 1947–61; Export Consultant, W Australian Govt, Perth, 1962–68; Official Rep., Govt of W Australia for Far East, Tokyo, 1968–78. Freedom of City of London, 1978. JP WA, 1978. *Recreations:* golf, cricket, fishing, sailing. *Address:* Unit 8, Kyamala, 19 Broome Street, Mosman Park, WA 6012, Australia. *Clubs:* Weld, West Australian Cricket Association, Royal Perth Yacht, Nedlands Golf (Perth); Tokyo (Tokyo). *Died 26 Oct. 1995.*

SLEVIN, Brian Francis Patrick, CMG 1975; OBE 1973; QPM 1968; CPM 1965; *b* 13 Aug. 1926; *s* of late Thomas and Helen Slevin; *m* 1972, Constance Gay (*d* 1991), *e d* of late Major Ronald Moody and of Amy Moody; one *s*. *Educ:* Blackrock Coll., Ireland. Palestine Police, 1946–48; Royal Hong Kong Police, 1949–79; Directing Staff, Overseas Police Courses, Metropolitan Police Coll., Hendon, London, 1955–57; Director, Special Branch, 1966–69; Sen. Asst Comr of Police, Comdg Kowloon Dist, 1969–70; Dir, Criminal Investigation Dept, 1971; Dep. Comr of Police, 1971, Comr of Police, 1974–79; Hong Kong; retired 1979. *Recreations:* walking, golf, reading, painting. *Address:* Lantau Lodge, 152 Coonanbarra Road, Wahroonga, Sydney, NSW 2076, Australia. *T:* (2) 4896671. *Clubs:* East India, Royal Automobile; Hong Kong, Royal Hong Kong Golf, Royal Hong Kong Jockey (Hong Kong).

Died 11 Sept. 1995.

SMAILES, George Mason; retired barrister; *b* 23 Jan. 1916; *s* of late Thomas and Kate Smailes; *m* 1939, Evelyn Mabel Jones; one *s* two *d*. *Educ:* The Leys Sch., Cambridge; Leeds Univ. (LLB); Metropolitan Police College. Served RAF, 1944–45. Solicitor's articled clerk, 1933–37; Station Inspector, Metropolitan Police, 1937–47; called to Bar, Gray's Inn, 1946; practised on North-Eastern Circuit, 1947–67; acted as Deputy County Court Judge and Deputy and Asst Recorder of various boroughs, 1967–68. Part-time legal member of tribunals: Mental Health Review, 1960–67; National Insurance, Local, 1962–65; Medical Appeal (Industrial Injuries), 1965–67; Industrial, 1966–67; Regional Chm. of Industrial Tribunals, Leeds, 1967–82. Associate, Wellington Dist Law Soc. (NZ). *Recreations:* listening to music, gardening. *Club:* Masterton (Masterton). *Died 23 Oct. 1988.*

SMITH, Donald Charles; a Master of the Supreme Court of Judicature (Chancery Division), 1969–73; *b* 23 Jan. 1910; *o s* of Charles Frederic Smith and Cecilia Anastasia Smith (*née* Toomey); *m* 1941, Joan Rowsell, twin *d* of Richard Norman Rowsell Blaker, MC. *Educ:* Stonyhurst College. Articled, Peacock & Goddard, Gray's Inn, 1927–31; admitted Solicitor, 1932; Solicitor with Thorold, Brodie & Bonham-Carter, Westminster, 1931–34; Legal Staff of Public Trustee Office, 1934–39; joined Chancery Registrars' Office, 1939; Chancery Registrar, 1952; Chief Registrar, 1963; first Chancery Registrar to be appointed a Master. Pres., Stonyhurst Assoc., 1969. Served in RNVR, Fleet Air Arm, 1943–46; Lieut, 1944–46. *Publications:* Atkin's Encyclopaedia of Court Forms, (Revising Editor) 1st edn, (Advisory Editor) 2nd edn; contribs to Law Jl. *Recreations:* cricket, walking, theatre, philately. *Address:* Reading Hall, Denham, Eye, Suffolk IP21 5DR. *T:* Eye (01379) 870500.

Died 21 June 1995.

SMITH, William Frederick Bottrill, CBE 1964; Accountant and Comptroller General of Inland Revenue, 1958–68; Principal, Uganda Resettlement Board, 1972–74; *b* 29 Oct. 1903; *s* of late Arthur and Harriet Frances Smith; *m* 1926, Edyth Kilbourne (*d* 1970); *m* 1971, M. Jane Smith, Washington, DC. *Educ:* Newton's, Leicester. Entered the Inland Revenue Dept, Civil Service, 1934. President, Inland Revenue Staff Federation, 1945–47. Vice-Pres., CS Fedn Drama Socs. Church Warden, Holy Trinity Church, Las Palmas. *Address:* 17 Bridge Avenue Mansions, Bridge Avenue, Hammersmith, W6 9JB. *T:* (0181) 748 3194.

Died 11 June 1995.

SOMERSET, Sir Henry Beaufort, Kt 1966; CBE 1961; *b* 21 May 1906; *s* of Henry St John Somerset; *m* 1930, Patricia Agnes Strickland; two *d*. *Educ:* St Peter's Coll., Adelaide; Trinity Coll., University of Melbourne; MSc 1928. Director: Humes Ltd, 1957–82 (Chm., 1961–82); Goliath Cement Hldgs Ltd, 1947–82 (Chm., 1967–82); Associated Pulp & Paper Mills Ltd, 1937–81 (Man. Dir, 1948–70; Dep. Chm., 1970–81); Electrolytic Zinc Co. of Australasia Ltd, 1953–78; Perpetual Exors Trustees Ltd, 1971–81 (Chm., 1973–81); Tioxide Australia Pty Ltd, 1949–82 (Chm., 1953–76); Central Norseman Gold Corp. Ltd, 1977–82. Chancellor, University of Tasmania, 1964–72; Member: Council, Australasian Inst. of Mining and Metallurgy, 1956–82 (President, 1958 and 1966); Exec., CSIRO, 1965–74; Council, Nat. Museum of Victoria, 1968–77; Pres., Australian Mineral Foundn, 1972–83. FRACI; FTS. Hon. DSc Tasmania, 1973. *Clubs:* Melbourne, Australian (Melbourne).

Died 15 Sept. 1995.

STARKE, Hon. Sir John Erskine, Kt 1976; Judge of Supreme Court of Victoria, Australia, 1964–85; Trustee, Australian War Memorial, Canberra; *b* 1 Dec. 1913; *s* of Hon. Sir Hayden Starke, KCMG and Margaret Mary, *d* of

Hon. John Gavan Duffy; *m* Elizabeth, *d* of late Colin Campbell. Admitted to Victorian Bar, 1939; QC 1955; Judge, 1946. *Address:* 16 Jacksons Road, Mount Eliza, Vic 3930, Australia. *Died 22 Nov. 1994.*

STIFF, Rt Rev. Hugh Vernon; retired; *b* 15 Sept. 1916; unmarried. *Educ:* Univ. of Toronto (BA); Trinity Coll., Toronto (LTh). BD General Synod; Hon. DD, Trinity Coll., Toronto. Bishop of Keewatin, 1969–74; Rector of St James Cathedral and Dean of Toronto, 1974–86; Asst Bishop, Diocese of Toronto, 1977–86. *Address:* Apt #207, 83 Elm Avenue, Toronto, Ontario M4W IP1, Canada.
Died 24 Sept. 1995.

STONHOUSE, Sir Philip (Allan), 18th Bt *cr* 1628, and 14th Bt *cr* 1670, of Radley, Berkshire; Assessor and Land Appraiser, Government of Alberta; *b* 24 Oct. 1916; *s* of Sir Arthur Allan Stonhouse, 17th Bt, and Beatrice C. Féron; *S* father, 1967; *m* 1946, Winnifred Emily Shield; two *s. Educ:* Western Canada Coll.; Queen's Univ., Kingston, Ontario. Gold mining, 1936–40; general construction, 1940–42; ranching, 1942–54; assessing, 1954–68. Freemason. *Recreations:* water-fowl and upland game hunting, tennis, ski-ing. *Heir: s* Rev. Michael Philip Stonhouse, BA, LTh [*b* 4 Sept. 1948; *m* 1977, Colleen Coueill, Toronto; three *s*]. *Address:* 521–12 Street SW, Medicine Hat, Alberta, Canada. *T:* (403) 5265832. *Club:* Medicine Hat Ski. *Died 15 Oct. 1993.*

SUMMERS, (Sir) Felix Roland Brattan, 2nd Bt *cr* 1952, of Shotton, co. Flint; did not use the title and his name was not on the Official Roll of Baronets; *b* 1 Oct. 1918; *s* of Sir Geoffrey Summers, 1st Bt, CBE; *S* father, 1972; *m* 1945, Anna Marie Louise, *d* of Gustave Demaegd, Brussels; one *d. Educ:* Shrewsbury.
Died 1993 (ext).

TAYLOR, Nicholas George Frederick, CMG 1970; FIPR; Development Director, East Caribbean, Higgs & Hill (UK) Ltd, 1973–80; Chairman: Higgs & Hill (St Kitts) Ltd, 1973–80, West Indies General Insurance Co., since 1979; Caribbean (East) Currency Authority, 1983 (Director, since 1981); Director, Caribluc Hotels Ltd, St Lucia, since 1968; Local Adviser, Barclays Bank International, St Lucia, since 1974; *b* 14 Feb. 1917; 3rd *s* of Louis Joseph Taylor and Philipsie (*née* Phillip); *m* 1952, Morella Agnes, *e d* of George Duncan Pitcairn and Florence (*née* La Guerre); two *s* two *d. Educ:* St Mary's Coll., St Lucia; LSE, London; Gonville and Caius Coll., Cambridge. Clerk, various Depts, St Lucia, 1937–46; Asst Social Welfare Officer, 1948–49; Public Relations and Social Welfare Officer, 1949–54; District Officer, and Authorised Officer, Ordnance Area, St Lucia, 1954–57; Dep. Dir St Lucia Br., Red Cross Soc., 1956–57; Perm. Sec., Min. of Trade and Production, 1957–58 (acted Harbour Master in conjunction with substantive duties); Commn for W Indies in UK: Administrative Asst, 1959; Asst Sec.-Chief Community Development Officer, Migrants Services Div., 1961; Commn in UK for Eastern Caribbean Govts: Officer-in-Charge, 1962–63; Actg Comr, 1964–66; Comr for E Caribbean Govts in UK, 1967–73. Dir, St Lucia (Co-operative) Bank Ltd, 1973–74. Mem., Civil Service Appeals Bd, 1973–77. Vice-Chm. Commonwealth Assoc., Bexley, Crayford and Erith, 1965–67; a Patron, British-Caribbean Assoc., 1962–73. Member: West India Committee Executive, 1968–; Bd of Governors, Commonwealth Inst., 1968–73. Assoc. Mem. 1951, Mem. 1962, Fellow, 1973, (British) Inst. of Public Relations. Chairman: Central Library Bd, 1973–81, Nat. Insurance Scheme, 1979–81, St Lucia; Central Housing Authority, St Lucia, 1975–77; Income Tax Comrs Appeals Bd, 1980–; St Lucia Boy Scouts Assoc., 1977–79. Vice-Chm., Nat. Develt Corp., 1979–. Founder Life Mem., Cambridge Soc., 1976. JP 1948. Coronation Medal, 1953; British Red

Cross Medal, 1949–59. *Recreations:* cricket, lawn tennis, reading. *Clubs.* Royal Commonwealth Society, Travellers'. *Deceased.*

TEUSNER, Hon. Berthold Herbert, CMG 1972; JP; solicitor, 1931–71; Speaker, South Australian Parliament, 1956–62; *b* 16 May 1907; *s* of Carl Theodor Teusner and Agnes Sophie Elisabeth Teusner (*née* Christian); *m* 1934, Viola Hilda Kleeman; two *s. Educ:* Immanuel Coll., Adelaide; Univ. of Adelaide (LLB). Legal Practice at Tanunda, SA, 1932–71. MP for Angas, S Australian Parlt, 1944–70; Govt Whip, 1954–55; Dep. Speaker and Chm. of Cttees: 1955–56, 1962–65 and 1968–70. Councillor, Dist Council of Tanunda, 1936–56 (Chm. for 17 years); JP 1939. Member: Bd of Governors, Adelaide Botanical Gdns, 1956–70; SA Nat. Fitness Council, 1953–70; Royal Adelaide Hosp. and Queen Elizabeth Hosp. Advisory Cttees (Chm., 1962–65); Immanuel Coll. Council, 1933–71; Hon. Assoc. Life Mem., SA Br. of Commonwealth Parly Assoc.; Mem., Transport Control Bd of SA, 1971–74. *Recreations:* bowls, gardening. *Address:* 18 Elizabeth Street, Tanunda, SA 5352, Australia. *T:* 632422. *Died 7 Aug. 1992.*

TURBERVILLE, Geoffrey, MA; Principal, Leulumoega High School, Samoa, 1959–62, (retired); *b* 31 March 1899; *o s* of A. E. Turberville, FCA, Stroud Green, London; *m* Jane Campbell Lawson. *Educ:* Westminster Sch. (King's Scholar), Trinity College, Cambridge (Exhibitioner). 2nd Lieut, Queen's Royal West Surrey Regt, 1917–19; Senior Classical Master, Liverpool Collegiate School, 1921–25; Senior Classical Master, Epsom College, 1925–30; Headmaster of Eltham College, 1930–59. Chm. Dorset Congregational Assoc., 1970–71. *Publications:* Cicero and Antony; Arva Latina II; Translation into Latin. *Address:* 4 Spiller's House, Shaftesbury, Dorset SP7 8EP.
Died 23 June 1993.

TYDEMAN, Col Frank William Edward, CMG 1966; CIE 1945; port consultant; *b* 20 Jan. 1901; *s* of Harvey James and Kate Mary Anne Tydeman; *m* 1924, Jessie Sarah Mann (*d* 1947); one *s* (and one *s* decd). *Educ:* London University. BSc (Eng) London, 1920. Chartered Civil Engineer. FICE, FIMechE, FIStructE, FIEAust, FCIT. Served Palestine; Haifa Harbour, 1930; Jaffa Port, 1934; Singapore Harbour Board, 1937; Indian Army, 1942; Colonel, Deputy Director Transportation, India, Burma and Malaya, 1944; reconstructed Bombay Port and Town after disastrous explosion, 1945; Port Consultant, Australia, to Commonwealth and WA govts and port authorities, on develt of ports of Fremantle, Bunbury, Townsville, Davenport, Mackay, Lae, Tjilatjap, 1946; Gen. Man., Fremantle Port Authy, 1950; retired 1965. *Recreation:* music. *Address:* c/o ANZ Banking Group Ltd, 77 St George's Terrace, Perth, WA 6000, Australia. *Club:* Naval and Military (Perth).
Died 8 May 1995.

UATIOA, Dame Mere, DBE 1978; *b* 19 Jan. 1924; *d* of Aberam Takenibeia and Bereti Bamatang; *m* 1950, Reuben K. Uatioa, MBE (*d* 1977); three *s* one *d. Educ:* Hiram Bingham High School, Beru Island. Widow of Reuben K. Uatioa, MBE, a leading Gilbertese nationalist and former Speaker, House of Assembly, Gilbert Islands; supported her husband throughout his long public service, demonstrating those qualities of wife and mother which are most admired in the Pacific; after his death, she devoted herself to her family. *Recreations:* social and voluntary work for Churches. *Address:* Erik House, Antebuka, Tarawa, Kiribati. *Died June 1979.*

VINCENT, Maj.-Gen. Douglas, CB 1969; AM 1994; OBE 1954; Director, Alcatel Australia, 1973–93; *b* Australia, 10 March 1916; *s* of William Frederick Vincent, civil engineer, and Sarah Jane Vincent; *m* 1947, Margaret Ector, *d* of N. W. Persse, Melbourne; two *s* one *d. Educ:* Brisbane State High School; Royal Military Coll., Duntroon. Commissioned, Dec. 1938; Middle East (7 Div.), 1940–42; BLA, 1944; NW Europe (30 Corps); Borneo Campaign, 1945; Brit. Commonwealth Forces, Korea, 1954; Dir of Signals, 1954–58; Dir of Staff Duties, 1958–60; Chief of Staff, Eastern Command, 1960–62; Commander, Aust. Army Force, 1962–63 (Singapore, Malaya); idc 1964; Commander: 1 Task Force, 1965; 1st Div., 1966; Aust. Force, Vietnam, 1967–68; Head, Aust. Jt Services Staff, Washington, DC, USA, 1968–70; Adjutant General, Australian Army, 1970–73. Mem. Nat. Exec., RSL (Defence Adviser, 1975). Sen. Mem., Instn of Radio and Electronics Engrs, Aust. *Recreations:* golf, swimming. *Address:* 41 Hampton Circuit, Yarralumla, Canberra, ACT 2600, Australia.　　　　　　　　*Died 8 Oct. 1995.*

WALKER, Philip Gordon, FCA; Chairman, Chapman Industries PLC, 1968–83; *b* 9 June 1912; *s* of late William and Kate Blanche Walker; *m* 1st, 1938, Anne May (marr. diss.); one *s* two *d*; 2nd, 1962, Elizabeth Oliver. *Educ:* Epworth Coll., Rhyl, North Wales. Bourner, Bullock & Co., Chartered Accountants, 1929–35; Walkers (Century Oils) Ltd, 1935–40; Layton Bennett, Billingham & Co., Chartered Accountants, 1940, Partner, 1944–51 (later Arthur Young McLelland Moore); Albert E. Reed & Co Ltd (later Reed International), Man. Dir, 1951–63; Chm. and Man. Dir, Philblack Ltd, 1963–71; Chm., Sun Life Assurance Soc. Ltd, 1971–82 (Exec. Chm. 1976–82). Part-time Mem. Monopolies Commn, 1963–65; Member: Performing Right Tribunal, 1971–83; Restrictive Practices Court, 1973–83. *Recreation:* golf. *Address:* The Garden Flat, Scotswood, Devenish Road, Sunningdale, Berks SL5 9QP. *Clubs:* Brooks's; Wildernesse (Sevenoaks); Rye; Berkshire.　　　　　　　　　　*Died 16 April 1994.*

WALLIS, Victor Harry; Assistant Under Secretary of State, Police and Fire Department, Home Office, 1980–82; *b* 21 Dec. 1922; *s* of Harry Stewart Wallis, MBE, and Ada Elizabeth (*née* Jarratt); *m* 1948, Margaret Teresa (*née* Meadowcroft); one *s* three *d. Educ:* Wilson's Grammar School. Served Royal Scots and Indian Army (Major), 1941–47 (War, Burma and Defence medals); RARO, 1947–48; Territorial Army and TARO (Int. Corps), 1948–77. Entered Home Office, Immigration Service, 1947; Regional Officer, 1952; Policy Div., 1958; Chief Trng Officer, 1967; Establishments, 1968. Chm., various cttees, Fire Brigades Adv. Council, 1980–82; Chm., Residents' Assoc., 1989–. *Recreations:* philately, military history, painting. *Clubs:* Civil Service, St Stephen's Constitutional, Royal British Legion.

　　　　　　　　　　Died 18 May 1995.

WALTER, Hon. Sir Harold (Edward), Kt 1972; QC (Mauritius) 1985; Barrister-at-law; Minister of External Affairs, Tourism and Emigration, Mauritius, 1976–82; *b* 17 April 1920; *e s* of Rev. Edward Walter and Marie Augusta Donat; *m* 1942, Yvette Nidza, MBE, *d* of James Toolsy; no *c. Educ:* Royal Coll., Mauritius. Served in HM Forces, 1940–48, Mauritius Sub-Area; E Africa Comd, GHQ MELF. Called to Bar, Lincoln's Inn, 1951. Village Councillor, 1952; Municipal Councillor, Port Louis, 1956; MLA Mauritius, 1959–82. Minister: of Works and Internal Communications, 1959–65; of Health, 1965–67 and 1971–76; of Labour, 1967–71; mem. numerous ministerial delegns. Chm., Commonwealth Med. Conf., 1972–74; Dep. Leader, UN General Assembly, NY, 1973, 1974, 1975; Pres., Security Council, UN, 1979; Mem. Exec. Bd, WHO, 1973–75, Pres., 1975–76. Chm., Council of Ministers, Organisation of African Unity, 1976–77; Vice Pres., Internat. Cttee for the Communities of Democracy (Washington), 1985. Trustee, Child Alive Program (Geneva), 1984–. Hon. DCL Univ. of Mauritius, 1984.

Commandeur de l'Ordre National Français des Palmes Académiques, 1974; Comdr de la Légion d'Honneur (France), 1980; Diplomatic Order of Merit (Korea), 1981. *Recreations:* shooting, fishing, swimming, gardening. *Address:* La Rocca, Eau Coulée, Mauritius. *T:* 860300. *Clubs:* Wings, Racing (Mauritius).

　　　　　　　　　　Died 25 July 1992.

WARD, William Kenneth, CMG 1977; Under-Secretary, Department of Trade, retired; *b* 20 Jan. 1918; *e s* of late Harold and Emily Ward; *m* 1949, Victoria Emily, *d* of late Ralph Perkins, Carcavelos, Portugal; three *s* one *d. Educ:* Queen Elizabeth's Grammar Sch., Ashbourne; Trinity Coll., Cambridge. 1st class Hons Modern and Medieval Langs Tripos. Entered Ministry of Supply, 1939; Board of Trade, 1955; HM Principal Trade Commissioner, Vancouver, BC, 1959–63; Under-Sec., BoT, 1966–69; Min. of Technology, later DTI and Dept of Trade, 1969–78; Sec., BOTB, 1973. *Recreation:* gardening. *Address:* 31 Plough Lane, Purley, Surrey CR8 3QG. *T:* (0181) 660 2462.　　　　　　　　*Died 7 July 1995.*

WATTON, Rt Rev. James Augustus, BA, DD; *b* 23 Oct. 1915; *s* of George A. Watton and Ada Wynn; *m* 1st, 1941, Irene A. Foster; one *s* two *d*; 2nd 1986, Janet Miller. *Educ:* Univ. of Western Ontario (BA); Huron Coll. (STh); Post graduate Univ. of Michigan. Deacon 1938; priest 1939. Bishop of Moosonee, 1963–80; Archbishop of Moosonee and Metropolitan of Ontario, 1974–79; retired 1980. DD (*jure dig.*), 1955. *Address:* 124 Meadow Heights Drive, Bracebridge, Ontario P1L 1A3, Canada.

　　　　　　　　　　Died 14 Aug. 1995.

WHEELER, Sir Frederick (Henry), AC 1979; Kt 1967; CBE 1962 (OBE 1952); Secretary to the Treasury, Australia, 1971–79; *b* 9 Jan. 1914; *s* of late A. H. Wheeler; *m* 1939, Peggy Hilda (*d* 1975), *d* of Basil P. Bell; one *s* two *d. Educ:* Scotch College; Melbourne University (BCom). State Savings Bank of Victoria, 1929–39; Treasury: Research Officer, 1939; Economist, 1944; Asst Sec., 1946; First Asst Sec., 1949–52; Treasurer Comptroller, ILO, Geneva, 1952–60; Chm., Commonwealth Public Service Bd, Canberra, 1961–71. Member: Aust. delegn to various British Commonwealth Finance Ministers' Conferences; Aust. Delegn Bretton Woods Monetary Conf.; UN Civil Service Adv. Bd, 1969–72; Commonwealth Govt Defence Review Cttee, 1981–82. Director: Amatil Ltd, 1979–84; Alliance Holdings Ltd, 1979–86. Dir, Winston Churchill Meml Trust (Aust.), 1965– (Nat. Pres., 1992–). *Address:* 9 Charlotte Street, Red Hill, ACT 2603, Australia. *T:* (6) 2959888. *Clubs:* (Pres. 1966–69) Commonwealth (Canberra); Royal Canberra Golf.

　　　　　　　　　　Died 5 Aug. 1994.

WICKREMESINGHE, Dr Walter Gerald, CMG 1954; OBE 1949; *b* 13 Feb. 1897; *s* of Peter Edwin Wickremesinghe and Charlotte Catherine Goonetilleka; *m* 1931, Irene Amelia Goontilleka; two *s* two *d. Educ:* Royal College, Colombo; Ceylon Medical College; London University (the London Hospital); Harvard University (School of Public Health). Licentiate in Medicine and Surgery (Ceylon), 1921; MRCS, LRCP 1923; Master of Public Health (Harvard), 1926; Dr of Public Health (Harvard), 1927. Director of Medical and Sanitary Services, Ceylon, 1948–53. Chief Delegate from Ceylon at WHO Assembly and Executive board, Geneva, 1952; Mem. UN Health Planning Mission to Korea, 1952; WHO Consultant, Manila, 1965; Chairman, Committee of Inquiry into Mental Health Services, Ceylon, 1966. Hon. FAPHA 1952. OStJ. *Publications:* contributions to Brit. Med. Jl, Ceylon Med. Jl, Trans Soc. of Med. Officers of Health, Ceylon, Amer. Jl of Public Health. *Recreations:* golf, tennis, riding, swimming. *Address:* 48 Buller's Lane, Colombo 7, Sri Lanka. *T:* Colombo (1) 581374. *Clubs:*

Otter Aquatic, Royal Colombo Golf (Colombo); Nuwara Eliya Golf, Nuwara Eliya Hill; (Life Mem.) Health Dept Sports. *Died 30 May 1986.*

WILHELM, Most Rev. Joseph Lawrence, MC; DD, JCD; Former Archbishop of Kingston, Ontario, (RC); *b* Walkerton, Ontario, 16 Nov. 1909. *Educ:* St Augustine's Seminary, Toronto; Ottawa Univ., Ottawa, Ont. Ordained priest, Toronto, 1934. Mil. Chaplain to Canadian Forces, 1940–46 (MC, Sicily, 1943). Auxiliary Bishop, Calgary, Alberta, 1963–66; Archbishop of Kingston, Ont, 1967–82. Hon. DD Queen's Univ., Kingston, Ont, 1970. *Address:* The Anchorage, Belleville, Ont K8N 5K7, Canada.
Died 25 June 1995.

WILLIS, Charles Reginald; Director, Tiverton Gazette & Associated Papers Ltd, since 1971; Member, Press Council, 1967; *b* 11 June 1906; *s* of Charles and Marie Willis, Tiverton, Devon; *m* 1929, Violet Stubbs; one *d.* *Educ:* Tiverton Grammar Sch. Tiverton Gazette, 1922–27; North Western Daily Mail, 1927–29; Evening Chronicle, Newcastle upon Tyne, 1929–35; Evening Chronicle, Manchester, 1935–42; Empire News, London, 1942–43; The Evening News, London, 1943 (Editor, 1954–66); Dir, Associated Newspapers Ltd, 1961–71; Editorial Dir, Harmsworth Publications, 1967–70. *Recreation:* cricket. *Address:* Howden Heyes, Ashley, Tiverton, Devon EX16 5PB. *T:* Tiverton (01884) 254829.
Died 12 Nov. 1995.

WILSON, Prof. John Graham; Cavendish Professor of Physics, 1963–76 (Professor, 1952–63), Pro-Vice-Chancellor, 1969–71, University of Leeds; then Emeritus Professor; *b* 28 April 1911; *er s* of J. E. Wilson, Hartlepool, Co. Durham; *m* 1938, Georgiana Brooke, *o d* of Charles W. Bird, Bisley, Surrey; one *s* one *d.* *Educ:* West Hartlepool Secondary Sch.; Sidney Sussex Coll., Cambridge. Member of teaching staff, University of Manchester, 1938–52; Reader in Physics, 1951. University of York: Member, Academic Planning Board, 1960–63; Member of Council, 1964–84; Chairman, Joint Matriculation Board, 1964–67. DUniv York, 1975; Hon. DSc Durham, 1977. *Publications:* The Principles of Cloud Chamber Technique, 1951; (ed) Progress in Cosmic Ray Physics, 1952–71; (with G. D. Rochester), Cloud Chamber Photographs of the Cosmic Radiation, 1952; papers on cosmic ray physics, articles in jls. *Recreation:* gardening. *Address:* 23 Newall Hall Park, Otley, West Yorks LS21 2RD. *T:* Otley (01943) 465184.
Died 24 Aug. 1994.

WILSON, Prof. Richard Middlewood; Professor of English Language, University of Sheffield, 1955–73; *b* 20 Sept. 1908; *e s* of late R. L. Wilson, The Grange, Kilham, Driffield, E Yorks; *m* 1938, Dorothy Muriel, *y d* of late C. E. Leeson, Eastgate House, Kilham, Driffield; one *d.* *Educ:* Woodhouse Grove School; Leeds University. Asst Lecturer, Leeds Univ., 1931, Lecturer, 1936; Senior Lecturer and Head of Dept of English Language, Sheffield Univ., 1946. *Publications:* Sawles Warde, 1939; Early Middle English Literature, 1939; (with B. Dickins) Early Middle English Texts, 1951; The Lost Literature of Medieval England, 1952; (with D. J. Price) The Equatorie of the Planetis, 1955; (contrib.) A Dictionary of English Surnames, 2nd edn 1976, 3rd edn 1991; articles and reviews. *Recreation:* cricket. *Died 23 May 1995.*

ADDENDA II

The following biographies are of those whose deaths occurred between 1996 and 2000 but were not reported until after the main part of this volume had gone to press.

BELLAMY, Alexander (William); retired; Senior Legal Assistant, Council on Tribunals, 1967–76 (temporary Legal Assistant, 1963–67); *b* Aug. 1909; *m* 1931, Lena Marie Lauga Massy. *Educ:* Mill Hill Sch.; Clare Coll., Cambridge. Called to Bar, Gray's Inn, 1934; practised at Bar, London, 1934–38; Magistrate, Straits Settlements and FMS, 1938; Penang & Province Wellesley Volunteer Force, 1940–42; escaped from Singapore in 1942; seconded as District Magistrate, Gold Coast, 1942; legal staff, Malaya Planning Unit, WO, 1944; SO2 (Legal) SEAC, 1944; SO1 British Mil. Admin (Malaya), 1945; Pres., Superior Court, Penang, 1945; released from mil. service overseas, 1946, with Hon. rank of Lt Col; Crown Counsel, Singapore, 1946; District Judge (Civil), Singapore, 1948; District Judge and 1st Magistrate, Singapore, 1952; actg Puisne Judge, Fed. of Malaya, 1953–54; Puisne Judge, Supreme Court, Nigeria, 1955; Actg Chief Justice, High Court of Lagos and Southern Cameroons, 1959, 1960; Actg Chief Justice, High Court of Lagos, 1961; a Judge of High Court of Lagos and Southern Cameroons, 1955–62.
Died 3 Dec. 1999.

BROUGHTON, Leonard, DL; Member, Lancashire County Council, 1974–89 (Chairman and Leader, 1974–81); *b* 21 March 1924; *s* of Charles Cecil Broughton and Florence (*née* Sunman); *m* 1949, Kathleen Gibson; one *d. Educ:* Kingston-upon-Hull. Served RASC, 1942–47. Estates Manager, Bedford Borough Council, 1957; business man. Member: Blackpool County Borough Council, 1961–74 (Leader, 1968–73); Blackpool Bor. Council, 1974–79; NW Co. Boroughs' Assoc., 1968–74; NW Economic Planning Council, 1970–72; Assoc. of Co. Councils, 1973–77; Board, Central Lancs Develt Corp., 1976–84. Mem. Courts, Lancaster and Salford Univs, 1974–81; Vice-President: Lancs Youth Clubs Assoc., 1974–81; NW Arts Assoc., 1974–81; Blackpool Social Service Council, 1974–84; Chm., Blackpool and Fylde Civilian Disabled Soc., 1964–84. Freeman, Co. Borough of Blackpool, 1973. DL Lancs, 1975; High Sheriff of Lancashire, 1983–84. *Recreations:* gardening, overseas travel. *Address:* 14 The Grove, Cleveleys, Blackpool, Lancs FY5 2JD. *T:* (01253) 822886. *Died 29 May 2000.*

ELSE, John, MBE 1946; TD 1946; Regional Chairman of Industrial Tribunals, Eastern Region, Bury St Edmunds, 1980–84; *b* 9 Aug. 1911; *s* of late Mr and Mrs A. G. Else; *m* 1937, Eileen Dobson; one *d. Educ:* Cowley Sch., St Helens; Liverpool Univ. (LLB 1930). Admitted as solicitor, 1932. Commnd TA, 1932; served War: UK and BEF, 1939–41 (despatches, 1940); Iraq, 1942; India, 1942–45 (ADS GHQ, 1944–45). Practised in St Helens, London and Birmingham, 1932–39; Partner, Beale & Co., London and Birmingham, 1946–61; Mem., Mental Health Review Tribunal, 1960–61; Chm., Traffic Comrs and Licensing Authority for Goods Vehicles, W Midlands Traffic Area, 1961–72; Indust. Tribunals Chm., Birmingham, 1972–76; Cambridge, 1976–80. *Recreations:* photography, gardening. *Address:* The Cottage, Long Lane, Fowlmere, Royston, Herts SG8 7TA. *T:* (01763) 208367. *Died 8 Sept. 1996.*

FISHER, Harold Wallace; Director, 1959–69, and Vice-President, 1962–69, Exxon Corporation, formerly Standard Oil Company (New Jersey) New York, retired; *b* 27 Oct. 1904; *s* of Dean Wallace Fisher and Grace Cheney Fisher; *m* 1930, Hope Elisabeth Case (*d* 1989); one *s*; *m* 1989, Janet Wilson Sawyer. *Educ:* Massachusetts Institute of Technology (BSc). Joined Standard Oil Company (NJ), 1927; Dir Esso Standard Oil Co. and Pres. Enjay Co. Inc., 1945. Resided in London, 1954–59. UK Rep. for Standard Oil Co. (NJ) and Chm. of its Coordination Cttee for Europe, 1954–57; Joint Managing Dir, Iraq Petroleum Co. Ltd and Associated Companies, 1957–59. Mem., Marine Bd, Nat. Acad. of Engineering, 1971–74; Vice-Chm., Sloan-Kettering Inst. for Cancer Research, 1974–75 (Chm., 1970–74); Mem., MIT Corp. Develt Cttee, 1975; Vice-Chm., and Chm. Exec. Cttee, Community Blood Council of Greater New York, 1969–71. Hon. DSc 1960, Clarkson Coll. of Technology, Nat. Acad. of Engrg. *Publications:* various patents and technical articles relating to the Petroleum Industry. *Recreations:* golf, photography, horology. *Address:* 68 Goose Point Lane, PO Box 1792, Duxbury, MA 02331, USA. *Club:* Duxbury Yacht. *Died 8 Dec. 2000.*

HOWD, Mrs Isobel; Regional Nursing Officer, Yorkshire Regional Health Authority, 1973–83; *b* 24 Oct. 1928 (*née* Young); *m* 1951, Ralph Howd. SRN, RMN, BTA Cert. Matron, Naburn Hosp., York, 1960–63; Asst Regional Nursing Officer, Leeds Regional Hosp. Bd, 1963–70; Chief Nursing Officer, South Teesside Hosp. Management Cttee, 1970–73. Mem., Mental Health Act Commn, 1983–87. *Address:* Yew Tree Cottage, Upper Dunsforth, York YO26 9RU. *T:* (01423) 322534.
Died 11 Dec. 2000.

HYDE, W(illiam) Leonard, FCIB; Director, Leeds Permanent Building Society, 1972–90 (Chief General Manager, 1973–78; Vice-President, 1978–81; President, 1981–83); *b* 1914. Joined Leeds Permanent Building Soc., 1936. Member Council: Building Socs Assoc., 1973–78; Nat. House Builders, 1973–78; Chm., Yorkshire County Assoc. of Building Socs, 1978–80. *Recreations:* golf, walking. *Address:* 5 Burn Bridge Road, Harrogate, Yorks HG3 1NS. *T:* (01423) 871748. *Club:* Pannal Golf.
Died 11 Nov. 2000.

JOHNSTON, John Douglas Hartley; Under Secretary (Legal), Solicitor's Office, Inland Revenue, 1986–95; Assistant Editor, Simon's Tax Cases; *b* 19 March 1935; *s* of John Johnston and Rhoda Margaret Hartley. *Educ:* Manchester Grammar Sch.; Jesus Coll., Cambridge (MA, LLB, PhD); Harvard Law Sch. (LLM). Called to the Bar, Lincoln's Inn, 1963. Practised at Bar, 1963–67; joined Solicitor's Office, Inland Revenue, 1968; Asst Solicitor, 1976–86. *Recreations:* reading, music, gardening. *Address:* Butterworths, Halsbury House, Chancery Lane, WC2A 1EL. *Died 10 March 2000.*

KENNAWAY, Prof. Alexander, MA; FIM; Senior Researcher and Lecturer, Conflict Studies Research Centre, Royal Military Academy, Sandhurst, since 1993; *b* 14 Aug. 1923; *s* of late Dr and Mrs Barou; *m* 1st, 1947, Xenia

Rebel (marr. diss. 1970); one *s* one *d*; 2nd, 1973, Jean Simpson. *Educ:* Downsend Sch., Leatherhead; St Paul's Sch., London; Pembroke Coll., Cambridge (MA). CEng, FIMechE 1962, FIM (FPRI 1968). Engr Officer, RN: active list, 1942–47; reserve, 1970. Imperial Chemical Industries Ltd, 1947–58; Metal Box Co., 1958–60; Director: BTR Industries, 1960–66; Allied Polymer Gp, 1972–78; Thomas Jourdan, 1976–83; Imperial Polymer Technology, 1984–86. Chm., Terrafix, 1983–90. Mem. Bd, CAA, 1979–83. Hon. medical engrg consultant, various hosps and charities, 1950–. Mem., Standing Adv. Cttee on artificial limbs, DHSS, 1964–70. Vis. Prof. of Mech. Engrg, Imp. Coll. of Science and Technology, 1976–97. Interim Sec., Nat. Fedn of Zool Gardens of GB and Ireland, 1984–86. Pres., English Chess Assoc., 1988–92. For. Mem., Ukrainian Acad. of Transport, 1994. *Publications:* (contrib.) Advances in Surgical Materials, 1956; (contrib.) Polythene—technology and uses, 1958, 2nd edn 1960; Engineers in Industry, 1981; (contrib.) The British Malaise, 1982; some 30 papers on biomechanics, technology of use and production of rubbers and plastics, and on design of specific aids for disabled living; 55 papers on Soviet and Post-Soviet economy, defence industries, science, technologies, culture and history. *Recreations:* sailing, chess, music. *Address:* 12 Fairholme Crescent, Ashtead, Surrey KT21 2HN. *T:* (01372) 277678. *Died 1 May 2000.*

KENNEDY, Eamon, MA, BComm, PhD; Special Adviser, with rank of Ambassador, Permanent Mission of Ireland, United Nations, New York, since 1987; *b* 13 Dec. 1921; *s* of Luke William Kennedy and Ellen (*née* Stafford); *m* 1960, Barbara Jane Black, New York; one *s* one *d*. *Educ:* O'Connell Schools, Dublin; University Coll., Dublin (MA, BComm); National University of Ireland (PhD 1970). Entered Irish Diplomatic Service, 1943; 2nd Sec., Ottawa, 1947–49; 1st Sec., Washington, 1949–50; 1st Sec., Paris, 1950–54; Chief of Protocol, Dublin, 1954–56; Counsellor, UN Mission, New York, 1956–61; Ambassador to: Nigeria, 1961–64; Federal Republic of Germany, 1964–70; France, OECD and UNESCO, 1970–74; UN, 1974–78; UK, 1978–83; Italy, Turkey, Libya, and FAO Rome, 1983–86. Grand Cross: German Order of Merit, 1970; French Order of Merit, 1974. *Recreations:* golf, theatre, music. *Address:* 525 East 86th Street, Apartment 17-D, New York, NY 10028, USA; 6730 Nassau Point Road, Cutchogue, NY 11935, USA. *Club:* North Fork Country (Long Island, NY). *Died 12 Dec. 2000.*

KNOWLES, Sir Leonard (Joseph), Kt 1974; CBE 1963; barrister; Chief Justice of the Bahamas, 1973–78; *b* Nassau, 15 March 1916; *s* of late Samuel Joseph Knowles; *m* 1939, Harriet Hansen, *d* of John Hughes, Liverpool; two *s*. *Educ:* Queen's Coll., Nassau, Bahamas; King's Coll., Univ. of London (LLB); first Bahamian student to take and pass Higher Sch. Certif. in Bahamas, 1934; LLB Hons 1937, 1st cl. in Final Bar Examinations; BD London, 1985. Called to the Bar, Gray's Inn, London, 1939; Lord Justice Holker Scholar, Gray's Inn, 1940; practised law in Liverpool for some years. Served War of 1939–45, Royal Air Force (radar). Returned to Nassau, 1948, and was called to local Bar; Attorney-at-Law and Actg Attorney-Gen. of the Bahamas, 1949; Registrar-Gen., 1949–50. Past Stipendiary and Circuit Magistrate. Chm., Labour Board, Bahamas, 1953–63; MLC (Upper House of Legislature), 1960–63; President, Senate, 1964; re-elected, 1967, 1968, and continued to hold that office until 1972; returned to private law practice, 1978. Methodist local preacher. *Publications:* Elements of Bahamian Law, 1978, 2nd edn 1989; Financial Relief in Matrimonial Cases, 1980; Bahamian Real Property Law, 1989; My Life (autobiog.), 1989; Introduction to Bahamian Company Law, 1993; Law of Dower and Curtesy, 1994; Law of Executors and Administrators, 1996; Seven Greatest Events of All Time,

1998; Happy Birthday, Jesus; Stories From the Bahamas; compilations of Bahamian Statutes 1981–94. *Recreations:* music, motion photography, swimming. *Address:* 4684 South Beechwood Drive, Macon, GA 31210, USA. *Fax:* (912) 7410070. *Died 23 Sept. 1999.*

KOLANE, John Teboho, ODSM, OL; LLD; Speaker of the National Assembly, Lesotho, 1973–86 and since 1990; *b* 22 Feb. 1926; *s* of Elizabeth and Zacharia Kolane; *m* 1955, Julia; two *s* three *d*. *Educ:* National University of Lesotho; Cambridge Univ.; BA South Africa; attorney's admission, Pretoria. Interpreter, District Comr's Court and Judicial Comr's Court, Lesotho, 1950–59; Registrar of Births, Marriages and Deaths, and Registrar of Deeds, 1959–63; Clerk of Senate, 1965–67; Permanent Secretary: Min. of Justice, 1967–69; Cabinet Office, 1969–70; Min. of Justice, 1970–73; High Comr to UK, 1986–89; Dir of Parly Affairs, Lesotho, 1990–92; Speaker of Constituent Assembly, 1992–93. LLD 1985. *Recreations:* golf, gardening, walking. *Address:* National Assembly, PO Box 190, Maseru, Lesotho. *Club:* Maseru Golf. *Died 1999.*

MACKLIN, Sir Bruce (Roy), Kt 1981; OBE 1970; FCA; company director; Chairman: Standard Chartered Bank Australia Ltd, since 1987; Hyundai Automotive Distributors Australia Pty, since 1990; *b* 23 April 1917; *s* of Hubert Vivian Macklin and Lillian Mabel Macklin; *m* 1944, Dorothy Potts, Tynemouth, England; two *s* one *d*. *Educ:* St Peter's Coll., Adelaide; St Mark's Coll., Univ. of Adelaide (AUA Commerce). Served RAAF (Aircrew), 1941–45. Practising chartered accountant, 1947–69. Pres., Aust. Chamber of Commerce, 1967–69. Hon. Consul in S Aust. for Fed. Republic of Germany, 1968–94; Leader, Aust. Govt Mission to Papua New Guinea, 1971. Mem. Council of Governors, St Peter's Coll., 1962–69; Mem. Council, Univ. of Adelaide, 1965–71. A Founder, Adelaide Festival of Arts, 1958, Chm. Bd of Governors, 1972–78; Dep. Nat. Chm., Queen Elizabeth II Silver Jubilee Trust for Young Australians. Silver Jubilee Medal 1977; Commander's Cross, Order of Merit of Fed. Republic of Germany, 1986. *Recreations:* tennis, gardening, music. *Address:* Unit 221, 242–266 Greenhill Road, Glenside, SA 5065, Australia. *T:* (8) 83387848. *Clubs:* Adelaide, Naval, Military and Air Force (South Australia). *Died 29 Aug. 2000.*

MAGUIRE, Rt Rev. Robert Kenneth, MA, DD; Hon. Assisting Bishop: Diocese of Western New York, 1984–86; Diocese of Southeast Florida, 1984–89, retired; *b* 31 March 1923; *s* of late Robert Maguire and late Anne Crozier; unmarried. *Educ:* Trinity Coll., Dublin (BA 1945; Divinity Testimonium, 1947). Deacon, 1947; priest, 1948; Curate of: St Mark, Armagh, 1947–49; St James the Apostle, Montreal, 1949–52; Dean of Residence, Trinity Coll., Dublin, 1952–60; Curate-in-charge of St Andrew's, Dublin, 1954–57; Minor Canon of St Patrick's Cathedral, Dublin, 1955–58; Dean and Rector of Christ Church Cathedral, Montreal, 1961–62; Bishop of Montreal, 1963–75. Co-ordinator: Canadian Conf., Theology '76, 1975–76; North American Consultation on the Future of Ministry, 1979–80. Assistant to the Primate, Anglican Church of Canada, 1980–84. DD (*jure dig.*): Dublin Univ., 1963; Montreal Diocesan Theol Coll., 1963; DCL (*hc*) Bishop's Univ., Lennoxville, Qué., 1963. *Address:* 4875 Dundas Street West, Apt 304, Islington, ON M9A 1B3, Canada. *Died 14 Oct. 2000.*

MARTIN, Samuel Frederick Radcliffe, CB 1979; First Legislative Draftsman, 1973–79; *b* 2 May 1918; 2nd *s* of late William and Margaret Martin; *m* 1947, Sarah, *y d* of late Rev. Joseph and Margaret McKane; three *s*. *Educ:* Royal Belfast Academical Instn; Queen's Univ., Belfast (LLB). Called to Bar, Gray's Inn, 1950. Examr, Estate Duty Office, NI, 1939; Professional Asst, Office of Parly

Draftsmen, 1956. Legal Adviser to Examiner of Statutory Rules, NI, 1979–81; Asst Comr, Local Govt Boundaries' Commn, 1983–84. Northern Ireland Editor, Current Law, 1979–90. *Publications:* articles in NI Legal Qly and Gazette of Incorp. Law Soc. *Recreation:* golf. *Address:* Brynburn, 196 Upper Road, Greenisland, Carrickfergus, Co. Antrim BT38 8RW. *T:* (028) 9086 2417.

Died 20 Nov. 2000.

MURDOCH, William Ridley Morton, CBE 1963; DSC 1940 and Bar, 1942; VRD 1949; Sheriff of Grampian, Highland and Islands (formerly Ross and Cromarty), at Dingwall and Tain, 1971–78; *b* 17 May 1917; *s* of William Ridley Carr Murdoch and Margaret Pauline Mackinnon; *m* 1941, Sylvia Maud Pearson; one *s* one *d. Educ:* Kelvinside Academy, Glasgow; Glasgow Univ. (MA, LLB). War Service in Navy, 1939–45; Captain, RNR, 1959. Solicitor in private practice, 1947–71; Dir, Glasgow Chamber of Commerce, 1955–71; Dean, Royal Faculty of Procurators in Glasgow, 1968–71. DL, County of City of Glasgow, 1963–75. OStJ 1976. *Recreations:* sailing, gardening. *Address:* Seaview, Shore Street, Gairloch, Ross-shire IV21 2BZ. *T:* (01445) 712481.

Died 31 July 2000.

OLIVIER, Henry, CMG 1954; Order for Meritorious Service (Gold), 1992; DScEng, PhD London, DEng; FICE, FASCE, Beit Fellow; FRSA; specialist consulting engineer in water resources engineering, Henry Olivier & Associates, since 1974; *b* 25 Jan. 1914; *s* of J. Olivier, Umtali, S Rhodesia; *m* 1st, 1940, Lorna Renée Collier; one *d* (one *s* decd); 2nd, 1979, Johanna Cecilia van der Merwe. *Educ:* Umtali High Sch.; Cape Town Univ. (BSc 1936; MSc 1947); University College, London (PhD 1953); DEng Witwatersrand, 1967. Beit Engineering Schol., 1932–38; Beit Fellow for two Rhodesias, 1939. Engineering post-grad. training with F. E. Kanthack & Partners, Consulting Engineers, Johannesburg, 1937; Sir Alex. Gibb & Partners, Cons. Engineers, London: training 1938, Asst Engineer, 1939. Experience covers design and construction of steam-electric power-stations, hydro-electric, floating harbour, irrigation, and water resources development schemes in UK, Africa, Middle East, and USA; Chief Engineer in charge civil engineering contracts, Owen Falls Hydro-Electric Scheme, Uganda, 1950–54; Partner in firm of Sir Alexander Gibb and Partners (Africa), 1954–55; Resident Director and Chief Engineer (Rhodesia), in firm of Gibb, Coyne & Sogei (Kariba), 1955–60; Consultant (mainly in connection with Indus Basin Project in Pakistan) to Sir Alexander Gibb and Partners, London, 1960–69 (Sen. Consultant, 1967); Partner, Gibb Hawkins and Partners, Johannesburg, 1963–69, associated with design and construction of Hendrik Verwoerd and P. K. le Roux dams on Orange River, RSA; Chm. LTA Ltd and LTA Engineering Ltd, 1969–73; major projects: Cahora Bassa Hydro-electric Scheme in Mozambique as mem. of Internat. Consortium Zamco; Orange-Fish Tunnel in South Africa; Sen. Partner, Henry Olivier and Associates, 1974–86, acting for Dept of Water Affairs, RSA, on concept plans for water and power projects in Lesotho, Transkei, Swaziland and Botswana; major concept plans accepted and implemented Lesotho Highlands Water Scheme. Mem., Exec. Cttee, SA Nat. Cttee on Large Dams, 1972–81. Hon. Fellow, SA Inst. of Civil Engineers, (Pres., 1979). Hon. DSc: Cape, 1968; Rhodesia, 1977; Orange Free State, 1992. *Publications:* Irrigation and Climate, 1960; Irrigation and Water Resources Engineering, 1972; Damit, 1975; Great Dams in Southern Africa, 1977; Papers to Institution Civil Engineering Journal; Int. Commn on Irrigation and Drainage; Water for Peace Conference, Washington, DC. *Recreation:* bowls. *Club:* Country (Johannesburg).

Died 1994.

ROWELL, Sir John (Joseph), Kt 1980; CBE 1974; BA; Chairman, Legal Aid Commission of Queensland, 1979–90; Consultant, Neil O'Sullivan & Rowell, Solicitors, Brisbane (Senior Partner, 1968–88); *b* 15 Feb. 1916; *s* of Joseph Alfred Rowell and Mary Lilian Rowell (*née* Hooper), both born in England; *m* 1947, Mary Kathleen (*née* de Silva); three *s* two *d. Educ:* Brisbane Grammar School; Univ. of Queensland (BA). Served AIF, 1940–46; Captain 2/10 Fd Regt (Efficiency Medal, 1946). Admitted Solicitor, 1939; Notary Public, 1959. Pres., Queensland Law Soc. Inc., 1964–66 (Mem. Council, 1956–67); Treas., Law Council of Aust., 1961–63 (Mem. Exec., 1960–67); Mem. Bd, Faculty of Law, Univ. of Queensland, 1959–78; Chm., Legal Assistance Cttee of Queensland, 1966–79; Member: Law Reform Commn of Qld, 1967–89; Commonwealth Legal Aid Commn, 1980–85. Chairman: Qld Bulk Handling Pty Ltd; Gas Corp. of Qld Ltd, 1974–90; Qld Bd, Capita Financial Gp (formerly City Mutual Life Assce Soc. Ltd), 1986–88 (Mem. Bd, 1971–88); Concrete Constructions (Qld) Pty, until 1993; Dir of Principal Bd, Boral Ltd and Boral Resources Ltd, 1974–87; Dir, Castlemaine Tooheys Ltd, 1980–85. Former Hon. Consul of Qld for Federal Repub. of Germany, 1963–86; Dean, Consular Corps of Qld, 1978–80. Pres., Qld Br., Australia-Britain Soc., 1988–94; Vice Pres., Qld Br., ESU, 1990–93. Officer's Cross, 1st class, 1979, Comdr's Cross, Order of Merit, 1986, FRG. *Recreations:* golf, fishing, reading. *Address:* Edgecliffe, 48 Walcott Street, St Lucia, Brisbane, Qld 4067, Australia. *T:* (7) 8709070. *Clubs:* Australian (Sydney); Brisbane, United Service, Tattersall's, Queensland Turf (Brisbane).

Died 5 May 1996.

A

ABBOTT, Morris Percy; Chief Executive, 1974–83, Chairman, 1977–83, Hogg Robinson Group Ltd; *b* 3 May 1922; *s* of Harry Abbott and Agnes Maud Breeze; *m* 1944, Marjorie Leven; one *s* one *d*. *Educ:* Rothesay Academy. MIB(Scot). Served War as Pilot, 1941–46; Flight Lieut, RAF; seconded to US Navy at Pensacola Naval Air Station, Florida. Bank of Scotland, 1939–49; Senior Executive with National Bank of India (later Grindlays Bank) in India and East Africa, 1949–59. Managing Director: Credit Insurance Assoc. Ltd, 1969; Hogg Robinson & Gardner Mountain Ltd, 1971; Group Man. Dir, Hogg Robinson Group Ltd, 1973. *Recreations:* music, golf, tennis, sailing. *Address:* Abbey Oak, 5 North Trade Road, Battle, East Sussex TN33 0HA. *Clubs:* Caledonian; Royal and Ancient Golf, Rye Golf, Royal Calcutta Golf.
Died 25 Jan. 1998.

ABBOTT, Trevor Michael, FCA; Director, Virgin Group of Companies, since 1997 (Managing Director, 1989–97); Chairman, Passport Alliance Group, since 1997; *b* 25 May 1950; *s* of late Stephen Sharrah Abbott, OBE and of Sheila Ann Jane Abbott; *m* 1st, 1971 (marr. diss. 1985); one *s* two *d*; 2nd, 1989, Claire Margaret Mclaughlin; one *s* one *d*. *Educ:* Priory Sch., Jamaica; Parkside Sch., Surrey; Cranleigh Sch. FCA 1972; FCCA 1980; FCT 1984. Articled, Roffe Swayne & Co., 1967–71; Dept Supervisor, KPMG, 1971–74; Chief Financial Officer, Gp Treas. and Dir, operating subsidiaries, MAM plc, later merged with Chrysalis Gp plc, 1974–84; Gp Finance Dir, Virgin Gp of Cos, 1985–89. Gov., Cranleigh Sch., 1995–. Council Mem. and Dir, Wooden Spoon Soc. (Rugby Union charity), 1995–. FIMgt (FBIM 1979); FRSA 1990. *Recreations:* golf, tennis, boating. *Clubs:* Wisley Golf, Hindhead Golf (Surrey). *Died 9 Dec. 1997.*

ABEL-SMITH, Prof. Brian; Professor of Social Administration, University of London, at the London School of Economics, 1965–91; *b* 6 Nov. 1926; *s* of late Brig.-Gen. Lionel Abel-Smith and Genevieve, *d* of Robert Walsh, Armagh. *Educ:* Haileybury Coll.; Clare Coll., Cambridge. MA, PhD 1955. Served Army: Private 1945; commissioned Oxford and Bucks Light Inf., 1946; Mil. Asst to Dep. Comr, Allied Commn for Austria (Capt.), 1947–48. Res. Fellow, Nat. Inst. of Economic and Social Res., collecting economic evidence for Guillebaud Cttee (cost of NHS), 1953–55; LSE: Asst Lectr in Social Science, 1955; Lectr, 1957; Reader in Social Administration, University of London, 1961. Assoc. Prof., Yale Law Sch., Yale Univ., 1961. Consultant and Expert Adv. to WHO on costs of med. care, 1957–; Consultant: to Social Affairs Div. of UN, 1959, 1961; to ILO, 1967 and 1981–83; Special Adviser: to Sec. of State for Social Services, 1968–70, 1974–78; to Sec. of State for the Environment, 1978–79; Adviser to Comr for Social Affairs, EEC, 1977–80. Member: SW Metrop. Reg. Hosp. Bd, 1956–63; Cent. Health Services Council Sub-Cttee on Prescribing Statistics, 1960–64; Sainsbury Cttee (Relationship of Pharmaceut. Industry with NHS), 1965–67; Long-term Study Group (to advise on long-term develt of NHS), 1965–68; Hunter Cttee (Functions of Medical Administrators,) 1970–72; Fisher Cttee (Abuse of Social Security Benefits), 1971–73. Chm., Chelsea and Kensington HMC, 1961–62; Governor: St Thomas' Hosp., 1957–68; Maudsley Hosp. and Inst. of Psychiatry, 1963–67. Hon. MD Limburg, 1981. *Publications:* (with R. M. Titmuss) The Cost of the National Health Service in England and Wales, 1956; A History of the Nursing Profession, 1960; (with R. M. Titmuss) Social Policy and Population Growth in Mauritius, 1961; Paying for Health Services (for WHO), 1963; The Hospitals, 1800–1948, 1964; (with R. M. Titmuss *et al.*) The Health Services of Tanganyika, 1964; (with K. Gales) British Doctors at Home and Abroad, 1964; (with P. Townsend) The Poor and the Poorest, 1965; (with R. Stevens) Lawyers and the Courts, 1967; An International Study of Health Expenditure (for WHO), 1967; (with R. Stevens) In Search of Justice, 1968; (with M. Zander and R. Brooke) Legal Problems and the Citizen, 1973; People Without Choice, 1974; Value for Money in Health Services, 1976; Poverty Development and Health Policy, 1978; National Health Service: the first thirty years, 1978; (with P. Grandjeat) Pharmaceutical Consumption, 1978; (with A. Maynard) The Organisation, Financing and Cost of Health Care in the European Community, 1979; Sharing Health Care Costs, 1980; (with E. Mach) Planning the Finances of the Health Sector, 1984; Cost Containment in Health Care, 1984; (with Marios Raphael) Future Directions for Social Protection, 1986; (ed with Kay Titmuss) The Philosophy of Welfare: selected writings of Richard M. Titmuss, 1987; (with Andrew Creese) Recurrent Costs in the Health Sector, 1989; (jtly) Health Insurance for Developing Countries, 1990; Cost Containment and New Priorities in Health Care, 1992; (with E. Mossialos) Cost Containment and Health Care Reform, 1994; (jtly) Policy Options and Pharmaceutical Research and Development in the European Community, 1994; (ed jtly) Cost Containment, Pricing and Financing of Pharmaceuticals in the European Community, 1994; An Introduction to Health: policy, planning and financing, 1994; (jtly) Choices in Health Policy: an agenda for the European Union, 1995; pamphlets for Fabian Soc., 1953–; articles. *Recreations:* skiing, swimming. *Address:* London School of Economics, Houghton Street, WC2A 2AE. *T:* 0171–405 7686.
Died 4 April 1996.

ABELES, Sir (Emil Herbert) Peter, AC 1991; Kt 1972; Chairman, Abakus/Transabakus Group; *b* 25 April 1924; *s* of late Alexander Abel and Mrs Anna Deakin; *m* 1969, Katalin Ottilia (*née* Fischer); two *d*. *Educ:* Budapest. Scrap metal industry, Hungary; emigrated to Australia, Sept. 1949; formed Alltrans Pty Ltd, 1950; Man. Dir and Chief Exec., 1967–92, Dep. Chm., 1967 93, TNT (formerly Thomas Nationwide Transport Ltd), Australia, and associated cos; Jt Man. Dir, 1980–92 and Jt Chm., 1981, Ansett Transport Industries Ltd. Trustee and Founder, Australian Cancer Foundn for Medical Res. *Recreations:* swimming, bridge. *Address:* PO Box 473, Kings Cross, NSW 2011, Australia. *Clubs:* Carlton; American National (Sydney). *Died 25 June 1999.*

ABERGAVENNY, 5th Marquess of, *cr* 1876; **John Henry Guy Nevill,** KG 1974; OBE 1945; JP; Baron Abergavenny 1450; Earl of Abergavenny and Viscount Nevill 1784; Earl of Lewes 1876; Lieutenant-Colonel, late Life Guards; Lord-Lieutenant of East Sussex, 1974–89 (Vice-Lieutenant of Sussex, 1970–74); Chancellor, Order of the Garter, 1977–94; *b* 8 Nov. 1914; *er s* of 4th Marquess of Abergavenny and Isabel Nellie (*d* 1953), *d* of James Walker Larnach; *S* father, 1954; *m* 1938, Patricia, *d* of late Lt-Col John Fenwick Harrison, Royal Horse Guards; three *d* (and one *s* one *d* decd). *Educ:* Eton; Trinity Coll., Cambridge. Joined Life Guards, 1936; served War of 1939–45 (despatches, OBE); Lt-Col, retired 1946; Hon. Col, Kent & Co. of London Yeomanry, 1948–62. Director: Massey-Ferguson Holdings Ltd, 1955–85; Lloyds Bank Ltd, 1962–85; Lloyds Bank UK Management, 1962–85; Lloyds Bank SE Regional Bd (Chm.), 1962–85; Whitbread Investment Co. Trustee, Ascot Authority, 1953–82; HM Representative at Ascot, 1972–82; President: Royal Assoc. of British Dairy Farmers, 1955 and 1963; Assoc. of Agriculture, 1961–63; Royal Agricl Soc. of England, 1967 (Dep. Pres. 1968, 1972); Hunters' Improvement Soc., 1959; British Horse Soc., 1970–71; Vice-Chm., Turf Bd, 1967–68; Mem. Nat. Hunt Cttee, 1942 (Senior Steward, 1953 and 1963); Mem. Jockey Club, 1952. Member: E Sussex CC, 1947–54 (Alderman, 1954–62); E Sussex Agric. Cttee, 1948–54. JP Sussex, 1948; DL Sussex, 1955. KStJ 1976 (Pres. Council, Order of St John, Sussex, 1975). *Heir: nephew* Christopher George Charles Nevill [*b* 23 April 1955; *m* 1985, Venetia, *er d* of Frederick Maynard; one *d* (one *s* decd)]. *Address:* (seat) Eridge Park, Tunbridge Wells, East Sussex TN3 9JT. *T:* (01892) 527378. *Club:* White's. *Died 23 Feb. 2000.*

ABLESON, Frank; *see* Vaughan, Frankie.

ABRAHAM, Sir Edward (Penley), Kt 1980; CBE 1973; DPhil; FRS 1958; Fellow of Lincoln College, Oxford, 1948–80, Honorary Fellow, since 1980; Professor of Chemical Pathology, Oxford, 1964–80, then Emeritus Professor; *b* 10 June 1913; *s* of Albert Penley Abraham and Mary Abraham (*née* Hearn); *m* 1939, Asbjörg Harung, Bergen, Norway; one *s. Educ:* King Edward VI School, Southampton; The Queen's College, Oxford (1st cl. Hons Sch. of Natural Science; MA, DPhil; Hon. Fellow 1973). Rockefeller Foundation Travelling Fellow at Universities of Stockholm, 1939 and California, 1948. Reader in Chemical Pathology, Oxford, 1960–64. Founder: Edward Penley Abraham Res. Fund; Edward Penley Abraham Cephalosporin Fund. FRSA. Lectures: Ciba, Rutgers Univ., NJ, 1957; Guest, Univ. of Sydney, 1960; Rennebohm, Univ. of Wisconsin, 1966–67; Squibb, Rutgers Univ., 1972; Perlman, Univ. of Wisconsin, 1985; A. L. P. Garrod, RCP, 1986; Sarton, Univ. of Gent, 1989. Hon. Fellow: Linacre Coll., Oxford, 1976; Lady Margaret Hall, Oxford, 1978; Wolfson Coll., Oxford, 1982; St Peter's Coll., Oxford, 1983. For. Hon. Mem., Amer. Acad. of Arts and Scis, 1983. Hon. DSc: Exeter, 1980; Oxon, 1984; Strathclyde, 1989. Royal Medal, Royal Soc., 1973; Mullard Prize and Medal, Royal Soc., 1980; Scheele Medal, Swedish Academy of Pharmaceut. Sciences, 1975; Chemical Soc. Award in Medicinal Chemistry, 1975; Internat. Soc. Chemotherapy Award, 1983; Sarton Medal, Gent, 1989. *Publications:* Biochemistry of Some Peptide and Steroid Antibiotics, 1957; Biosynthesis and Enzymic Hydrolysis of Penicillins and Cephalosporins, 1974; contribs to: Antibiotics, 1949; The Chemistry of Penicillin, 1949; General Pathology, 1957, 4th edn 1970; Cephalosporins and Penicillins, Chemistry and Biology, 1972; scientific papers on the biochemistry of natural products, incl. penicillins and cephalosporins; contrib. Biographical Memoirs of Fellows of Royal Society (Lord Florey, 1971; Sir Ernst Chain, 1983). *Recreations:* walking, ski-ing. *Address:* Badger's Wood, Bedwells Heath, Boars Hill, Oxford OX1 5JE. *T:* (01865) 735395; Sir William Dunn School of Pathology, South Parks Road, Oxford OX1 3RE. *T:* (01865) 275571. *Club:* Athenæum. *Died 9 May 1999.*

ABRAHAMS, Gerald Milton, CBE 1967; President, Aquascutum Group plc, 1991 (Chairman and Managing Director, 1947–91); *b* 20 June 1917; *s* of late Isidor Abrahams; *m* 1st, 1946, Doris, *d* of Mark Cole, Brookline, Mass, USA; two *d;* 2nd, 1972, Marianne Wilson, *d* of

David Kay, London. *Educ:* Westminster Sch. Served War of 1939–45, Major HAC, RHA, in Greece, W Desert and Ceylon. Member: Council, FBI, 1962–65, CBI, 1965–87; British Menswear Guild (Chm., 1959–61, 1964–66); Clothing Export Council (Chm., 1966–70; Vice-Pres., 1970–87); Clothing Manufacturers Fedn of GB, 1960–82 (Chm., 1965–66); EDC for Clothing Industry, 1966–69; British Clothing Industry Assoc., 1982–87; BNEC Cttee for Exports to Canada, 1965–70; North American Adv. Gp, BOTB, 1978–87 (Vice Chm., 1983–87). FRSA 1972; CIMgt (CBIM 1973). *Recreations:* golf, tennis. *Address:* 100 Regent Street, W1A 2AQ. *T:* (020) 7734 6090. *Club:* Buck's. *Died 9 July 1999.*

ADAM SMITH, Janet Buchanan, (Mrs John Carleton), OBE 1982; author and journalist; *b* 9 Dec. 1905; *d* of late Very Rev. Sir George Adam Smith, Principal of Aberdeen Univ. and Lilian, *d* of Sir George Buchanan, FRS; *m* 1st, 1935, Michael Roberts (*d* 1948); three *s* one *d;* 2nd, 1965, John Carleton (*d* 1974). *Educ:* Cheltenham Ladies' College; Somerville College, Oxford. BBC, 1928–35; Asst Editor, The Listener, 1930–35; Asst Literary Editor, New Statesman and Nation, 1949–52, Literary Editor, 1952–60. Virginia Gildersleeve Vis. Prof., Barnard Coll., New York, 1961 and 1964. Trustee, National Library of Scotland, 1950–85; Pres., Royal Literary Fund, 1976–84. Hon. LLD Aberdeen, 1962. *Publications:* Poems of Tomorrow (ed), 1935; R. L. Stevenson, 1937; Mountain Holidays, 1946, 2nd edn 1996; Life Among the Scots, 1946; (ed) Henry James and Robert Louis Stevenson, 1948; (ed) Collected Poems of R. L. Stevenson, 1950; (ed) Faber Book of Children's Verse, 1953; (ed) Collected Poems of Michael Roberts, 1958; John Buchan: a Biography, 1965; John Buchan and his World, 1979. *Recreation:* mountain walking. *Address:* 57 Lansdowne Road, W11 2LG. *T:* (020) 7727 9324. *Club:* Alpine (Vice-Pres., 1978–80; Hon. Mem., 1993). *Died 11 Sept. 1999.*

ADAMS, Rt Rev. (Albert) James; Acting Vicar, Ridgeway Team Ministry, Diocese of Salisbury, 1984–87; *b* 9 Nov. 1915; *s* of James and Evelyn Adams, Rayleigh, Essex; *m* 1943, Malvena Jones; three *s. Educ:* Brentwood Sch.; King's Coll., London; Community of St Andrew, Whittlesford, Cambridge. Ordained deacon, 1942; priest, 1943; Curate of Walkley, Sheffield, 1942–44; Succentor, 1944, Precentor, 1945–47, Sheffield Cathedral; Rector of Bermondsey, 1947–55; Rural Dean of Bermondsey, 1954–55; Rector of: Stoke Damerel, Devonport, 1955–63; Wanstead, 1963–71; Sub-Dean, Wanstead and Woodford, 1968–69; Asst Rural Dean, Redbridge, 1970–71; Archdeacon of West Ham, 1970–75; Bishop Suffragan of Barking, 1975–83. *Address:* 89 Hardens Mead, Chippenham, Wilts SN15 3AQ. *T:* (01249) 660728. *Died 11 May 1999.*

ADAMS, (Charles) Christian (Wilfred), CMG 1992; HM Diplomatic Service; Ambassador to Thailand and (non-resident) to Laos, since 1992; *b* 2 June 1939; *s* of Flying Officer Wilfred Sydney Charles Adams, RAF (killed in action 1940) and of Katherine (*née* Hampton); *m* 1965, (Elinor) Pauline Lepper; three *s* one *d. Educ:* King's Sch., Canterbury; New Coll., Oxford (BA 2nd cl. Hons Mod. Hist.). Joined CRO, 1962; Asst Private Sec. to Commonwealth Sec., 1965–66; Rio de Janeiro, 1966–70; ODA, 1970–72; CSCE, Helsinki, 1972–74; Dep. Pol Advr, British Mil. Govt, Berlin, 1974–78; Head, Mech. and Electrical Engrg Br. I (Robotics, Machine Tools and Flexible Manufacturing Systems), DoI, 1979–82; Sen. British Trade Comr, Hong Kong, 1982–85; Head: SE Asia Dept, FCO, 1986–88; Project Exports Policy Div., DTI, 1988–91. *Recreations:* history, music, sailing, tennis, mountain walking, dogs, Scottish dancing. *Address:* c/o

Foreign and Commonwealth Office, SW1A 2AH. *Clubs:* Athenæum; Hong Kong; Royal Varuna Yacht (Pattaya) *Died 10 July 1996.*

ADAMS, Frank Alexander, CB 1964; Member, Public Health Laboratory Service Board, 1968–79; *b* 9 July 1907; *m* 1928, Esther Metcalfe (*d* 1988); two *d. Educ:* Selhurst Grammar Sch.; London School of Economics, Univ. of London. HM Inspector of Taxes, 1928; Assistant Secretary, Board of Inland Revenue, 1945; Counsellor (Economic and Financial), UK Delegation to OEEC, Paris, 1957–59; Director, Civil Service Pay Research Unit, 1960–63; Under-Sec. (Finance) and Accountant-General, Min. of Health, 1963–67. Mem. Council, Hosp. Saving Assoc., 1968–89. *Address:* 31 Cardinal Court, Cardinal Avenue, Borehamwood WD6 1EP. *Clubs:* Climbers'; Swiss Alpine (Geneva). *Died 30 June 1998.*

ADAMS, Gerald Edward, PhD, DSc; Director, Medical Research Council Radiobiology Unit, Chilton, Oxon, 1982–95; Editor-in-Chief, British Journal of Cancer, since 1995 (Member, Editorial Board, 1981–95); Chairman, Gray Laboratory Cancer Research Trust, since 1995; *b* 8 March 1930; *m* 1955, Margaret Ray; three *s. Educ:* Royal Technical Coll., Salford (BSc London, 1955); Univ. of Manchester (PhD 1958, DSc 1970). Post-doctoral Fellow, Argonne National Lab., USA, 1958–60; Vis. Scientist, Centre d'Etude Nucléaire, Saclay, France, 1961–62; Lectr, 1962–66, Sen. Lectr, 1966–70, Cancer Campaign Res. Unit in Radiobiol., Mount Vernon Hosp. (later CRC Gray Lab.); Dir of Molecular Radiobiol., 1970–72, Dep. Dir of Lab., 1972–76, CRC Gray Lab.; Prof. of Physics as Applied to Medicine, Inst. of Cancer Res. (Univ. of London), Sutton, 1976–82. Hon. Vis. Prof., Dept of Pharmacy, Univ. of Manchester, 1984–; Vis. Prof. of Radiobiol., Shanghai Med. Univ., 1986–87. Adrian Fellow, Univ. of Leicester, 1986–. Lectures: 2nd Milford Schulz Annual, Harvard Med. Sch., 1979; Maurice Lenz Annual, Columbia Univ., NY, 1981. Pres., British Inst. of Radiology, 1995–96. Hon. FACR 1981. Hon. doctorate, Univ. of Bologna, 1982. Radiation Res. Award, 1969; Failla Gold Medal, 1990, Radiation Res. Soc., USA; David Anderson-Berry Prize, RSE, 1969; Silvanus Thompson Medal, British Inst. of Radiol., 1979; Röntgen Medal, Soc. of Friends of German Röntgen Mus., 1989; Henry Kaplan Medal, Internat. Assoc. of Radiation Res., 1995; Klaas Breur Medal, Eur. Soc. for Therapeutic Radiol. and Oncol., 1996. Specialist Editor, Encyc. of Pharmacology and Therapeutics, 1975–; Member Editorial Board: Internat. Jl of Radiation Oncology, Biology and Physics, 1978–; Internat. Jl of Radiation Biology, 1983–91; Radiation Research, 1987–90. *Recreations:* music, golf, walking. *Address:* c/o Gray Laboratory Cancer Research Trust, Mount Vernon Hospital, Northwood, Middlesex HA6 2JR. *T:* (01923) 828611. *Died 6 June 1998.*

ADAMS, Hervey Cadwallader, RBA 1932; FRSA 1951; landscape painter; lecturer on art; *b* Kensington, 15 Feb. 1903; *o s* of late Cadwallader Edmund Adams and Dorothy Jane, *y d* of Rev. J. W. Knight; *m* 1928, Iris Gabrielle, (*d* 1984), *y d* of late F. V. Bruce, St Fagans, Glamorgan; two *s. Educ:* Charterhouse. Studied languages and singing in France and Spain, 1922–26; studied painting under Bernard Adams, 1929. Art Master, Tonbridge Sch., 1940–63. *Publications:* The Student's Approach to Landscape Painting, 1938; Art and Everyman, 1945; Eighteenth Century Painting, 1949; Nineteenth Century Painting, 1949; The Adventure of Looking, 1949. *Address:* Priory Nursing Home, Horsley, near Stroud, Glos GL6 0PT. *Died 25 May 1996.*

ADAMS, Rt Rev. James; *see* Adams, Rt Rev. A. J.

ADAMS, John Nicholas William B.; *see* Bridges-Adams.

ADAMSON, Sir (William Owen) Campbell, Kt 1976; Chairman, Abbey National plc (formerly Abbey National Building Society), 1978–91; *b* 26 June 1922; *o s* of late John Adamson, CA; *m* 1st, 1945, Gilvray (*née* Allan) (marr. diss. 1984; she *d* 1998); two *s* two *d*; 2nd, 1984, Mrs J., (Mimi), Lloyd-Chandler. *Educ:* Rugby Sch.; Corpus Christi Coll., Cambridge (Hon. Fellow, 1996). Royal Inst. of Internat. Affairs, 1944–45; Baldwins Ltd as Management Trainee, 1945; successive managerial appts with Richard Thomas & Baldwins Ltd and Steel Co. of Wales Ltd, 1947–69; Gen. Man. i/c of construction and future operation of Spencer Steelworks, Llanwern; Dir, Richard Thomas & Baldwins Ltd, 1959–69, seconded as Dep. Under-Sec. of State, and Co-ordinator of Industrial Advisers, DEA, 1967–69; Dir-Gen., CBI, 1969–76. Director: Imperial Group, 1976–86; Renold, 1976–86 (Dep. Chm., 1981–82; Chm., 1982–86); Revertex Chemicals, 1977–82 (Chm., 1979–82); Lazard Bros & Co., 1977–87; Tarmac, 1980–90; Yule Catto, 1983–84. Member: BBC Adv. Cttee, 1964–67 and 1967–75; SSRC (on formation), 1965–69; NEDC, 1969–76; Council, Industrial Soc.; Design Council, 1971–73; Council, Iron and Steel Inst., 1960–72; Iron and Steel Industry Delegn to Russia, 1956, and to India, 1968; Vice-Chm., National Savings Cttee for England and Wales, 1975–77. Chairman: Family Policy Studies Centre, 1984–; Independent Broadcasting Telethon Trust, 1988–; Third Age Challenge Trust (formerly Re-Action Trust), 1991–; Changing Faces, 1993–99; Pres., NCVO, 1992–98; Trustee: Horticultural Therapy, 1978–; SANE, 1991–. Visiting Fellow: Lancaster Univ., 1970–90; Nuffield Coll., Oxford, 1971–79. Governor: Rugby Sch., 1979–93; Bedford Coll., London Univ., 1983–85. Hon. DSocSc Birmingham, 1993. *Publications:* various technical articles. *Recreations:* walking, music, arguing. *Address:* Abbey National plc, 1st Floor, 138 Kings Road, SW3 4XB. *T:* (020) 7581 8669. *Died 21 Aug. 2000.*

ADDISON, Dr Philip Harold, MRCS, LRCP; Hon. Consulting Secretary, The Medical Defence Union, since 1974 (Secretary, 1959–74); *b* 28 June 1909; 2nd *s* of late Dr Joseph Bartlett Addison and Mauricia Renée Addison; *m* 1934, Mary Norah Ryan; one *s* one *d. Educ:* Clifton Coll., Bristol; St Mary's Hosp. Medical Sch. MRCS, LRCP 1933; Gold Medallist, Military Medicine and Bronze Medallist Pathology, Army Medical Sch., 1935. Permanent Commission, IMS, 1935; served Burma Campaign, 1943–45 (despatches). Chm., Ethical Cttee of Family Planning Assoc., 1956–60; Vice-Pres., Medico-Legal Soc., 1965–74. *Publications:* Professional Negligence, in, Compendium of Emergencies, 1971; The Medico-Legal Aspects of General Anaesthesia, in, Clinical Practice of General Anaesthesia, 1971; contrib. Brit. Med. Jl, Irish Med. Jl, Proc. RSocMed, Medico-Legal Jl, Lancet. *Recreations:* fishing, golf, bridge. *Address:* Red-Wyn-Byn, Monkmead Lane, West Chiltington, Pulborough, West Sussex RH20 2PF. *T:* (01798) 813047. *Clubs:* East India, Devonshire, Sports and Public Schools; Shark Angling Club of Gt Britain; West Sussex Golf; BMA Bridge (Founder Mem.). *Died 27 Nov. 1996.*

AGER, Rear-Adm. Kenneth Gordon, CB 1977; retired Royal Navy, 1977; *b* 22 May 1920; *s* of Harold Stoddart Ager and Nellie Maud (*née* Tate); *m* 1944, Muriel Lydia Lanham; one *s* one *d. Educ:* Dulwich Central Sch. and Royal Navy. Called up for War Service, RN, 1940; Sub Lt (Special Br.) RNVR, 1943; Lieut (Electrical) RN, 1944; Weapons and Elect. Engr; Comdr (WE) 1958; Captain (E) 1966; Fleet Weapons and Elect. Engr Officer, 1969–71; Sen. Officers' War Course, 1971–72; CSO (Eng) to Flag Off. Scotland and NI, and Captain Fleet Maintenance, Rosyth, 1972–75; Rear-Adm. (E) 1975; Flag Officer, Admiralty Interview Bd, 1975–77. *Recreations:* bowls, reading. *Died 20 May 1998.*

AGNEW, Spiro Theodore, (Ted); *b* Baltimore, Md, 9 Nov. 1918; *s* of Theodore S. Agnew and Margaret Akers; *m* 1942, Elinor Isabel Judefind; one *s* three *d. Educ:* Forest Park High Sch., Baltimore; Johns Hopkins Univ.; Law Sch., Univ. Baltimore (LLB). Served War of 1939–45 with 8th and 10th Armd Divs, 1941–46, Company Combat Comdr in France and Germany (Bronze Star). Apptd to Zoning Bd of Appeals of Baltimore County, 1957 (Chm., 1958–61); County Executive, Baltimore County, 1962–66; Governor of Maryland, 1967–68; Vice-President of the United States, 1969–73. Republican. With Pathlite Inc., Crofton, Md, 1974. *Publication:* The Canfield Decision, 1976. *Recreations:* golf, tennis.

Died 17 Sept. 1996.

AHERN, Most Rev. John James; *b* 31 Aug 1911; *s* of James Ahern and Ellen Mulcahy. *Educ:* St Colman's Coll., Fermoy; St Patrick's Coll., Maynooth; Irish Coll., Rome. Ordained, 1936. Professor: St Colman's Coll., Fermoy, 1940–44; St Patrick's Coll., Maynooth, 1946–57; Bishop of Cloyne, 1957–87. *Address:* Nazareth House, Mallow, Co. Cork, Ireland. *Died 25 Sept. 1997.*

AINSWORTH, Sir (Thomas) David, 4th Bt *cr* 1916, of Aidanaiseig, co. Argyll; *b* 22 Aug. 1926; *s* of Sir Thomas Ainsworth, 2nd Bt, and Marie Eleanor, (May) (*d* 1969), *d* of Compton Charles Domvile; *S* half-brother, 1981; *m* 1957, Sarah Mary, *d* of late Lt-Col H. C. Walford; two *s* two *d. Educ:* Eton. Formerly Lieut 11th Hussars. *Recreations:* shooting, fishing. *Heir:* *s* Anthony Thomas Hugh Ainsworth, *b* 30 March 1962. *Address:* 80 Elm Park Gardens, SW10 9PD; Ashley House, Wootton, Woodstock, Oxon OX20 1DX.

Died 24 Nov. 1999.

AIREDALE, 4th Baron *cr* 1907; **Oliver James Vandeleur Kitson;** Bt 1886; Deputy Chairman of Committees, House of Lords, since 1961; Deputy Speaker, House of Lords, since 1962; *b* 22 April 1915; *o s* of 3rd Baron Airedale, DSO, MC, and Sheila Grace (*d* 1935), *d* of late Frank E. Vandeleur, London; *S* father, 1958; unmarried. *Educ:* Eton; Trinity College, Cambridge. Major, The Green Howards. Called to the Bar, Inner Temple, 1941. *Heir:* none. *Address:* (seat) Ufford Hall, Stamford, Lincs PE9 3BH. *Died 19 March 1996 (ext).*

AITKEN, Sir Robert (Stevenson), Kt 1960; MD (New Zealand), DPhil (Oxford); FRCP, FRACP; retired; *b* NZ, 16 April 1901; *s* of late Rev. James Aitken; *m* 1929, Margaret G. Kane (*d* 1991); one *s* two *d. Educ:* Gisborne High School, Gisborne, NZ; University of Otago, Dunedin, NZ; Oxford Univ. Medical Qualification in New Zealand, 1922. Rhodes Scholar, Balliol College, Oxford, 1924–26; attached to Medical Unit, The London Hospital, 1926–34; Reader in Medicine, British Post-Graduate Medical School, Univ. of London, 1935–38; Regius Prof. of Medicine, Univ. of Aberdeen, 1939–48; Vice-Chancellor, Univ. of Otago, Dunedin, NZ, 1948–53; Vice-Chancellor, Univ. of Birmingham, 1953–68. Vice-Chm. Association of Univs of the British Commonwealth, 1955–58; Dep. Chm., UGC, 1968–73; Chairman: Committee of Vice-Chancellors and Principals, 1958–61; Birmingham Repertory Theatre, 1962–74. DL Co. Warwick, 1967, West Midlands, 1974–93. Hon. FRCPE; Hon. FDSRCS; Hon. DCL Oxford; Hon. LLD: Dalhousie, Melbourne, Panjab, McGill, Pennsylvania, Aberdeen, Newfoundland, Leicester, Birmingham, Otago; Hon. DSc: Sydney, Liverpool. *Publications:* papers in medical and scientific journals. *Address:* 6 Hintlesham Avenue, Birmingham B15 2PH. *Died 10 April 1997.*

ALBERT, Sir Alexis (François), Kt 1972; CMG 1967; VRD 1942; Chairman: Albert Investments Pty Ltd, since 1962; J. Albert & Son Pty Ltd, Sydney, since 1962; The Australian Broadcasting Company Pty Ltd, Sydney, since 1962; *b* 15 Oct. 1904; *s* of late M. F. and M. E. Albert, Sydney; *m* 1934, Elsa K. R. (decd), *d* of late Capt. A. E. Lundgren, Sydney; three *s. Educ:* Knox College, Sydney; St Paul's College, University of Sydney. BEc 1930. Director: Amalgamated Television Services Pty Ltd, 1955–87; Australasian Performing Right Association Ltd, 1946–76. Underwriting Member of Lloyd's, 1944–74. President, Royal Blind Soc. of NSW, 1962–78; Fellow of Council, St Paul's Coll., Univ. of Sydney, 1965–95; Mem. Council, Nat. Heart Foundn of Aust., NSW Div. 1959. RANR, 1918–49; Lt-Comdr, retd. Hon. ADC to Governors of NSW, 1937–57. KStJ 1985. *Recreations:* swimming, yachting. *Address:* 25 Coolong Road, Vaucluse, NSW 2030, Australia; (office) 175 Macquarie Street, Sydney, NSW 2000. *T:* (2) 92322144. *Clubs:* Naval and Military; Australian (Sydney); Royal Sydney Golf, Royal Sydney Yacht Squadron (Commodore, 1971–75); New York Yacht. *Died 10 Oct. 1996.*

ALBERT, Carl (Bert); Speaker, US House of Representatives, 1971–77; Member, Third Oklahoma District, 1947–77 (Democratic Whip, 1955–62; Majority Leader, 1962–71); *b* McAlester, Oklahoma, 10 May 1908; *s* of Ernest Homer and Leona Ann (Scott) Albert; *m* 1942, Mary Sue Greene Harmon; one *s* one *d. Educ:* Univ. of Oklahoma (AB 1931); Oxford Univ. (Rhodes Scholar, BA 1933, BCL 1934). Served US Army, 1941–46. Admitted Oklahoma Bar, 1935; Legal Clerk, Fed. Housing Admin, 1935–37; attorney and accountant, Sayre Oil Co., 1937–38; legal dept, Ohio Oil Co., 1939–40. Practised law: Oklahoma City, 1938; Mattoon, Ill, 1938–39; McAlester, Oklahoma, 1946–47. Bronze Star, USA, 1945. *Recreation:* reading. *Address:* 1831 Wood Road, McAlester, OK 74501, USA. *Died 4 Feb. 2000.*

ALBROW, Desmond; an Assistant Editor, Sunday Telegraph, 1976–87; *b* 22 Jan. 1925; *er s* of Frederick and Agnes Albrow; *m* 1950, Aileen Mary Jennings; one *s* three *d. Educ:* St Bede's Grammar Sch., Bradford; Keble Coll., Oxford (MA). RN, 1944–47. On the Editorial Staff of the Yorkshire Observer, 1950–51, Manchester Guardian, 1951–56, Daily Telegraph, 1956–60; Sunday Telegraph, 1960–66: Chief Sub-Editor, News Editor, and Night Editor; Editor, Catholic Herald, 1966–71; Features Editor, Sunday Telegraph, 1971–76. *Recreations:* drinking in moderation and talking to excess, watching other people cultivate their gardens. *Address:* Totyngton Cottage, 18 Victoria Road, Teddington, Middx TW11 0BG. *T:* (0181) 977 4220. *Club:* Garrick. *Died 16 Jan. 1998.*

ALDINGTON, 1st Baron *cr* 1962 of Bispham, in Co. Borough of Blackpool; **Toby Austin Richard William Low,** KCMG 1957; CBE 1945 (MBE 1944); DSO 1941; TD and clasp, 1950; PC 1954; DL; Baron Low (Life Peer), 1999; *b* 25 May 1914; *s* of Col Stuart Low, DSO (killed at sea by enemy action, Dec. 1942), and Hon. Lucy Gwen (later Hon. Mrs Spear), *e d* of Baron Atkin; *m* 1947, Araminta Bowman, *e d* of Sir Harold MacMichael, GCMG, DSO; one *s* two *d. Educ:* Winchester; New Coll., Oxford (Hon. Fellow 1976). Called to the Bar, Middle Temple, 1939. Rangers, KRRC (TA), 2nd Lieut 1934; Brig. BGS 5 Corps Italy, 1944–45; served Greece, Crete, Egypt, Libya, Tunisia, Sicily, Italy, Austria (DSO, MBE, CBE, Croix de guerre avec palmes, Commander of Legion of Merit, USA); Hon. Col 288 LAA Regt RA (TA), 1947–59. MP (C) Blackpool North, 1945–62; Parliamentary Secretary, Ministry of Supply, 1951–54; Minister of State, Board of Trade, 1954–57; Dep. Chm., Cons. Party Organisation, 1959–63; Chairman: H of L Select Cttee on Overseas Trade, 1984–85; Sub-Cttee A, H of L European Communities Select Cttee, 1989–92. Chm., GEC, 1964–68, Dep. Chm. 1968–84; Chairman: Grindlays Bank Ltd, 1964–76; Sun Alliance and London Insurance Co., 1971–85; Westland Aircraft, 1977–85 (Pres., 1985);

Director: Lloyds Bank, 1967–85; Citicorp, 1969–84. Chairman: Port of London Authority, 1971–77; Jt Special Cttee on Ports Industry, 1972. Chairman: Cttee of Management, Inst. of Neurology, 1962–80; BBC Gen. Adv. Council, 1971–78; ISJC, 1986–89; Leeds Castle Foundn, 1984–94; Kent Foundn, 1986–94; President: BSI, 1986–89; Brain Res. Trust, 1987– (Chm., 1974–87). Fellow, Winchester Coll., 1972–87 (Warden, 1979–87). DL Kent, 1973. *Recreation:* golf. *Heir: s* Hon. Charles Harold Stuart Low [*b* 22 June 1948; *m* 1989, Regine, *d* of late Erwin von Csongrady-Schopf; one *s* two *d* (twins)]. *Address:* Knoll Farm, Aldington, Ashford, Kent TN25 7BY. *T:* (01233) 720292. *Club:* Carlton.

Died 7 Dec. 2000.

ALEPOUDELIS, Odysseus; *see* Elytis, O.

ALEXANDER, Anthony Victor, CBE 1987; Director, Sedgwick Group, 1978–89; *b* 17 Sept. 1928; *s* of Aaron and Victoria Alexander; *m* 1958, Hélène Esther, *d* of late Victor Adda; one *d. Educ:* Harrow School; St John's Coll., Cambridge (BA, LLB, Mod. Langs and Law). FINucE. Sedgwick Collins & Co: joined 1954; Exec., UK Co., 1954–64; Dir, 1964–68; Sedgwick Collins Holdings Ltd: Dir, 1968–73, and Chm., SCUK; Sedgwick Forbes Holdings: Dir and Chm., SFUK, 1973–77; Dep. Chm., Sedgwick Forbes, 1977–78; Sedgwick Group: Chm., Underwriting Services and Special Services, 1978–84; Director: Securicor Group and Security Services, 1976–96; ARV Aviation, 1985–88. Member: Overseas Projects Bd, 1978–79; British Invisible Exports Council, 1983–90; Marketing of Investments Bd, 1985–86; Dir, Securities and Investments Bd, 1986–89. Chm., Trustees, Victor Adda Foundn and Fan Museum Trust; Chm., British Insurance Brokers Assoc., 1982–87 (Dep. Chm., 1981–82). *Recreations:* gardening, sailing, fishing, forestry, antique collecting. *Address:* 1 St Germans Place, Blackheath, SE3 0NH. *T:* (020) 8858 5509. *Clubs:* Lloyd's Yacht, Bar Yacht, Medway Yacht.

Died 17 Aug. 1999.

ALEXANDER, Sir (John) Lindsay, Kt 1975; Deputy Chairman, Lloyds Bank PLC, 1980–88 (Director, 1970–91); Director: British Petroleum Co. PLC, 1975–91; Hawker Siddeley plc, 1981–91; *b* 12 Sept. 1920; *e s* of Ernest Daniel Alexander and Florence Mary Mainsmith; *m* 1944, Maud Lilian, 2nd *d* of Oliver Ernest and Bridget Collard; two *s* one *d. Educ:* Alleyn's Sch.; Brasenose Coll., Oxford (Thomas Wall Schol.; MA; Hon. Fellow 1977). Royal Engineers, 1940–45 (Capt.); served Middle East and Italy. Chairman: The Ocean Steam Ship Co. Ltd, later Ocean Transport and Trading Ltd, 1971–80 (Man. Dir, 1955–71; Dir, 1955–86); Lloyds Bank Internat., 1980–85 (Dir, 1975–85; Dep. Chm., 1979–80); Lloyds Merchant Bank Hldgs, 1988 (Dep. Chm. and Dir, 1985–88). Director: Overseas Containers Holdings Ltd, 1971–82 (Chm., 1976–82); Jebsens Drilling PLC, 1980–86; Wellington Underwriting Holdings Ltd, 1986–96; Wellington Underwriting Agencies Ltd, 1986–98; Britoil, 1988–90; Abbey Life Gp, later Lloyds Abbey Life, 1988–91. Chairman: Liverpool Port Employers' Assoc., 1964–67; Cttee, European Nat. Shipowners' Assocs, 1971–73; Vice-Chm., Nat. Assoc. of Port Employers, 1965–69; President: Chamber of Shipping of UK, 1974–75 (Vice-Pres., 1973–74); Gen. Council, British Shipping Ltd, 1974–75. Hon. Mem., Master Mariners' Co., 1974. FCIT (MInstT 1968); CIMgt (CBIM 1980; FBIM 1972). JP Cheshire, 1965–75. Comdr, Royal Order of St Olav, Norway. *Recreations:* gardening, music, photography. *Address:* Lloyds TSB, 71 Lombard Street, EC3P 3BS. *T:* (020) 7626 1500.

Died 15 May 2000.

ALEXANDER, Sir Norman (Stanley), Kt 1966; CBE 1959; *b* 25 Oct. 1906; *s* of late Charles Monrath Alexander;

m 1st, 1935, Frances Elizabeth Somerville (*d* 1958), *d* of late K. S. Caldwell; one *s* two *d*; 2nd, 1959, Constance Lilian Helen (*d* 1990), *d* of late H. V. Geary. *Educ:* Univ. of Auckland, NZ (MSc); Trinity Coll., Cambridge (PhD). Professor of Physics: Raffles Coll., Singapore, 1936–49; Univ. of Malaya, Singapore, 1949–52; University Coll., Ibadan, Nigeria, 1952–60; Vice-Chancellor, Ahmadu Bello Univ., Nigeria, 1961–66.

Died 26 March 1997.

ALLAN, John Clifford, RCNC; Director, Manpower, Dockyards, 1975–79; *b* 3 Feb. 1920; *s* of James Arthur and Mary Alice Allan; *m* 1947, Dorothy Mary (*née* Dossett); two *d. Educ:* Royal Naval Coll., Greenwich. Entered Royal Corps of Naval Constructors, 1945; service at HM Dockyards: Portsmouth, Chatham, Devonport, Gibraltar, Singapore, 1950–75; Chief Constructor, Chief Executive Dockyard HQ, 1967–69, Asst Dir, 1969, Dir, 1975. *Recreations:* painting, tennis, bridge, squash (Pres., Lansdown Lawn Tennis & Squash Racquets Club, 1985–95). *Address:* 21 Henrietta Street, Bath, Avon BA2 6LP. *T:* (01225) 446570.

Died 24 March 1997.

ALLARD, General Jean Victor, CC 1968; CBE 1946; DSO 1943 (Bars 1944, 1945); ED 1946; CD 1958; Chief of Canadian Defence Staff, 1966–69; Representative of the Province of Quebec in New York, Sept. 1969–June 1970; *b* Nicolet, PQ, 12 June 1913; *s* of late Ernest Allard and Victorine Trudel; *m* 1939, Simone, *d* of Gustave Piche, OBE; two *d* (one *s* decd). *Educ:* St Laurent Coll., Montreal; St Jerome Coll., Kitchener, Ont. Joined Three Rivers Regt, 1933; Capt., 1938; Major, 1939; War of 1939–45: Co. of London Yeomanry, 1940–41; Canadian Army Staff Coll., Kingston, 1941–42 (Instructor, 1942); 5th Canadian Armoured Div.; second in command: Régt de la Chaudière, Royal 22e Regt, 1943 (Italy); Lt-Col 1944; CO Royal 22e Regt; Brig. 1945; Comd 6th Canadian Infantry Brigade, 1945 (Holland); Military Attaché Canadian Embassy, Moscow, 1945–48; Comd Eastern Quebec Area, 1948–50; idc 1951; Vice Quarter-Master Gen., Canada, 1952; Comdr, 25th Canadian Infantry Brigade Group, in Korea, 1953; Comdr 3rd Canadian Infantry Brigade, 1954; Comd Eastern Quebec Area, 1956; Maj.-Gen. 1958; Vice Chief of the General Staff, Canada, 1958; Comdr 4th Division, BAOR, 1961–63 (first Canadian to command a British Div.); Maj. Gen. Survival, Ottawa, 1963; Lt-Gen. 1964; Chief of Operational Readiness, Canada, 1964–65; Comdr, Mobile Command, Canada, Oct. 1965–June 1966; General, 1966; Col Comdt, 12 Regt Blindé du Canada; Col, Royal 22e Regt, 1985. Member: Royal 22e Regt Assoc.; La Régie du 22e; Royal Canadian Air Force Assoc.; Royal Canadian Naval Service Assoc.; Cercle Universitaire d'Ottawa; Chm. Bd of Governors, Ottawa Univ., 1966–69; Member Bd, 1969–. Hon. DSS Laval, 1957; Hon. LLD: Ottawa, 1959; St Thomas, 1966; St Mary's, Halifax, 1969; Hon. DScMil RMC Canada, 1970. FRSA. Bronze Lion (Netherlands), 1945; Légion d'Honneur and Croix de Guerre (France), 1945; Legion of Merit (US), 1954. Kt of Magistral Grace, Sovereign and Military Order of Malta, 1967. *Publication:* Mémoires, 1985. *Recreation:* music. *Address:* 3265 Boulevard du Carmel, Trois-Rivières, Quebec, Canada.

Died 23 April 1996.

ALLEN, Prof. Harry Cranbrook, MC 1944; Professor of American Studies, 1971–80, then Emeritus, and Dean of the School of English and American Studies, 1974–76, University of East Anglia; *b* 23 March 1917; *s* of Christopher Albert Allen and Margaret Enid (*née* Hebb); *m* 1947, Mary Kathleen Andrews (*d* 1992); one *s* two *d. Educ:* Bedford School; Pembroke College, Oxford (Open Scholar; 1st cl. hons Modern History; MA). Elected Fellow, Commonwealth Fund of New York, 1939 (held Fellowship, Harvard Univ., Jan.-Sept. 1946). Served War of 1939–45, with Hertfordshire and Dorsetshire Regts, in France and Germany (Major); Comdt 43rd Division Educational Coll., June-Nov. 1945. Fellow and Tutor in Modern History, Lincoln College, Oxford, 1946–55; Commonwealth Fund Prof. of American History, University Coll., 1955–71, and Dir, Inst. of United States Studies, 1966–71, Univ. of London. Senior Research Fellow, Aust. Nat. Univ., Canberra, and Visiting Scholar, Univ. of California, Berkeley, 1953–54; Schouler Lecturer, The Johns Hopkins University, April 1956; American Studies Fellow, Commonwealth Fund of New York, 1957, at the University of Virginia; Vis. Mem., Inst. for Advanced Study, Princeton, NJ, 1959; Vis. Professor: Univ. of Rochester, New York, 1963; Univ. of Michigan, Ann Arbor, 1966. Member: Dartmouth Royal Naval College Review Cttee, 1958, Naval Education Adv. Cttee, 1960–66; Academic Planning Board, Univ. of Essex, 1962; Chm., British Assoc. for American Studies, 1974–77; Pres., European Assoc. for American Studies, 1976–80. *Publications:* Great Britain and the United States, 1955; Bush and Backwoods, 1959; The Anglo-American Relationship since 1783, 1960; The Anglo-American Predicament, 1960; The United States of America, 1964; Joint Editor: British Essays in American History, 1957; Contrast and Connection, 1976. *Recreation:* retirement. *Address:* 929 Merion Square Road, Gladwyne, PA 19035–1509, USA.   *Died 21 June 1998.*

ALLEN, John; *see* Allen, W. J. G.

ALLEN, John Hunter, OBE 1978; company director; District Councillor, Antrim, since 1963 (Mayor, 1973–90); *s* of John Allen and Jane Kerr Hunter; *m* 1952, Elizabeth Irwin Graham; three *d. Educ:* Larne Grammar Sch., NI; Orange's Acad., NI. Served RAF, pilot, 1942–47. Civil Service Excise, 1947–59; Proprietor: Ulster Farm Feeds Ltd, 1959–76; Antrim Feeds Ltd, 1959–76; Roadway Transport Ltd, 1959–; Aldergrove Farms Ltd, 1965–; A.B. Fuels, 1969–; Downtown Developments Ltd, 1975–; Allen Service Stns, 1977–; Century Supplies, 1984–. Chm., NI Sports Council, 1977–84. Chm., Antrim Royal British Legion. Member: Ulster Games Foundn, 1983–; NI Gen. Consumers Council, 1984–. Life Mem., Royal Ulster Agricl Soc, 1972. *Recreations:* Rugby, sailing, boxing, tennis. *Clubs:* Royal Air Force; Antrim Rugby (Pres.); Antrim Hockey (Pres.); Antrim Boxing (Pres.); Antrim Boat (Trustee); Muckamore Cricket (Life Member).
Died 17 April 1997.

ALLEN, Prof. Joseph Stanley; (first) Professor and Head of Department of Town and Country Planning, University of Newcastle upon Tyne (formerly King's College, Durham University), 1946–63 (developing first University Degree Course in Town and Country Planning); then Professor Emeritus; *b* 15 March 1898; *s* of late Harry Charles Allen and Elizabeth S. Allen; *m* 1931, Guinevere Mary Aubrey Pugh (*d* 1974); one *s* one *d*; *m* 1977, Meryl (*d* 1992), *d* of late Charles and Eveline Watts. *Educ:* Liverpool Collegiate School; Liverpool University; post-graduate study in USA. RIBA Athens Bursar. Lectr, Liverpool Univ., 1929–33; Head, Leeds School of Architecture, 1933–45; founded Leeds Sch. of Town and Country Planning, 1934. Vice-Chm. RIBA Bd of Architectural Education and Chm. Recognised Schools Cttee, 1943–45; Member of Council, RIBA, 1943–50; Pres. Royal Town Planning Institute, 1959–60 (Vice-Pres. 1957–59). Architect and town planning consultant; undertakings include: Develt Plan for Durham Univ.; Quadrangle, King's College, Newcastle; Courthouse, Chesterfield; Nat. Park Residential Study Centre, Maentwrog; Science Wing, Durham Univ.; Consultant, Snowdonia National Park, 1957–74; Member, North of England Regional Advisory Committee, Forestry Commission, 1951–74; Member Diocesan Committees

for Care of Churches: Ripon, Newcastle and York Dioceses. Hon. DLitt Heriot-Watt, 1978. *Publications:* (with R. H. Mattocks): Report and Plan for West Cumberland; Report and Plan for Accrington (Industry and Prudence), 1950. Founder-Editor, Planning Outlook (founded 1948); contrib. to professional journals on architecture and town and country planning. *Recreations:* motoring and walking in the countryside, music, farming, breeding Welsh ponies. *Address:* Bleach Green Farm, Ovingham, Northumberland NE42 6BL. *T:* (01661) 832340.   *Died 15 March 1997.*

ALLEN, Sir Kenneth; *see* Allen, Sir W. K. G.

ALLEN, Prof. Kenneth William; Professor of Nuclear Structure, 1963–91, Professor Emeritus, since 1991, and Head of Department of Nuclear Physics, 1976–79 and 1982–85, University of Oxford; Fellow, 1963–92, Emeritus Fellow, since 1992, Balliol College, Oxford (Estates Bursar, 1980–83 and 1991–93); *b* 17 Nov. 1923; *m* 1947, Josephine E. Boreham; two *s. Educ:* Ilford County High School; London University (Drapers' Scholar); St Catharine's College, Cambridge University. PhD (Cantab) 1947. Physics Division, Atomic Energy of Canada, Chalk River, 1947–51; Leverhulme Research Fellow and Lecturer, Liverpool University, 1951–54; Deputy Chief Scientist, UKAEA, 1954–63. Sen. Vis. Scientist, Lawrence Berkeley Lab., Univ. of California, 1988–89. Mem., Nuclear Physics Bd, SRC, 1970–73. *Publications:* contribs to Nuclear Physics, Physical Review, Review of Scientific Instruments, Nature, etc. *Recreations:* music, chess. *Address:* Ridgeway, Lincombe Lane, Boars Hill, Oxford OX1 5DZ. *T:* (01865) 739327.
Died 2 May 1997.

ALLEN, Sir Richard (Hugh Sedley), KCMG 1960 (CMG 1953); retired; *b* 3 Feb. 1903; *s* of late Sir Hugh Allen, GCVO and Winifred, *d* of Oliver Hall, Dedham; *m* 1945, Juliet Home Thomson (*d* 1983); one step *s* (and one *s* decd). *Educ:* Royal Naval Colleges, Osborne and Dartmouth; New College, Oxford. Junior Asst Sec., Govt of Palestine, 1925–27; entered Foreign Office and Diplomatic Service, 1927; Second Sec., 1932; First Sec., 1939; Counsellor, 1946; Minister, British Embassy, Buenos Aires, 1950–54; Minister to Guatemala, 1954–56; British Ambassador to Burma, 1956–62. *Publications:* Malaysia: Prospect and Retrospect, 1968; A Short Introduction to the History and Politics of Southeast Asia, 1970; Imperialism and Nationalism in the Fertile Crescent, 1974. *Recreation:* sailing. *Address:* 42 Somerstown, Chichester, Sussex PO19 4AL. *T:* Chichester (01243) 781182. *Club:* Bosham and Itchenor Sailing.
Died 16 Jan. 1996.

ALLEN, (Walter) John (Gardener); Controller, Capital Taxes Office (formerly Estate Duty Office), Inland Revenue, 1974–78; *b* 8 Dec. 1916; *s* of late John Gardiner Allen and Hester Lucy Allen, Deal, Kent; *m* 1944, Irene (*d* 1983), *d* of late John Joseph and Sarah Henderson, Lisburn, N Ireland; one *s* one *d. Educ:* Manwoods, Sandwich; London Univ. (LLB). Entered Inland Revenue, 1934. Served RAF, 1940–46 (Flying Officer). FGS 1982. *Recreations:* amateur geologist, gardening. *Address:* c/o Greenbank, 57 Main Street, Kinoulton, Notts, NG12 3EL.   *Died 11 Feb. 1999.*

ALLEN, William Alexander, CBE 1980; RIBA; Founder Chairman, Bickerdike Allen Partners, architects, 1962–89, retired; *b* 29 June 1914; *s* of late Professor Frank Allen, FRSC and Sarah Estelle, *d* of late D. S. Harper, NB; *m* 1938, Beatrice Mary Teresa Pearson; two *s* one *d. Educ:* public schools in Winnipeg; University of Manitoba. Royal Architectural Inst. of Canada Silver Medal, 1935; Univ. Gold Medal in Architecture, 1936; ARIBA 1937; FRIBA 1965. Appointed to Building Research Station,

Watford, 1937; Chief Architect, Bldg Res. Stn, 1953–61; Principal of the Architectural Assoc. School of Architecture, 1961–66. Advr for Building Res. to US Govt, 1966–91. Mem. Council, RIBA, 1953–72, 1982–89 (Chm. various cttees); Chm., Fire Research Adv. Cttee, 1973–83, Visitor, 1983–88; President: Institute of Acoustics, 1975–76; Ecclesiastic Arch. Assoc., 1980. Hon. Associate NZIA, 1965; Hon. Fellow: Inst. of Acoustics, 1978; American Inst. of Architects, 1984; CIBSE, 1996. Hon. LLD Manitoba, 1977. Commander, Ordem do Mérito, Portugal, 1972. *Publications:* (with R. Fitzmaurice) Sound Transmission in Buildings, 1939; Envelope Design for Buildings, 1997; papers, etc, on scientific and technical aspects of architecture and urban design, professionalism, and modern architectural history and education. *Recreations:* writing, drawing, music, archaeology. *Address:* 4 Ashley Close, Welwyn Garden City, Herts AL8 7LH. *T:* (01707) 324178, *Fax:* (01707) 391992. *Club:* Athenæum.   *Died 14 Dec. 1998.*

ALLEN, Sir (William) Kenneth (Gwynne), Kt 1961; *b* 23 May 1907; *er s* of Harold Gwynne Allen and Hilda Allen, Bedford; *m* 1931, Eleanor Mary (*née* Eeles) (*d* 1990); one *s* one *d*. *Educ:* Westminster Sch.; Univ. of Neuchâtel, Switzerland. Started as engineering pupil, Harland & Wolff Ltd, Glasgow and Belfast; subsequently at W. H. Allen, Sons & Co. Ltd, Bedford; Dir, 1937–70, Man. Dir, 1946–70, Chm., 1955–70, W. H. Allen, Sons & Co. Ltd; Chm., Amalgamated Power Engineering, 1968–70; Director: Whessoe Ltd, 1954–65; Electrolux, 1970–78. Chm., Brit. Internal Combustion Engine Manufacturers' Assoc., 1955–57; Pres., British Engineers' Assoc., 1957–59 (later British Mechanical Engineering Fedn); Chm., BEAMA, 1959–61; Pres., Engineering Employers' Fedn, 1962–64; Chm., Labour and Social Affairs Cttee of CBI, 1965–67. FIMarE; MRINA. Freeman of City of London. Liveryman, Worshipful Company of Shipwrights. Mem. Beds CC, 1945–55; High Sheriff Beds, 1958–59; DL, Beds, 1978–91. *Address:* Amesbury Abbey, Amesbury, Wilts SP4 7EX. *T:* (01980) 624048.
                                                 Died 4 April 2000.

ALLEN-JONES, Air Vice-Marshal John Ernest, CBE 1966; Director of Legal Services, Royal Air Force, 1961–70, retired; *b* 13 Oct. 1909; *s* of Rev. John Allen-Jones, Llanyblodwel Vicarage, Oswestry; *m* 1st, 1937, Margaret Rix (*d* 1973; Sawbridgeworth; one *s* two *d*; 2nd, 1973, Diana Gibbons. *Educ:* Rugby; Worcester Coll., Oxford (MA). Solicitor (Honours), 1934; Partner with Vaudrey, Osborne & Mellor, Manchester. Joined RAF, 1939; Air Vice-Marshal, 1967. Gordon-Shepherd Memorial Prizeman, 1963. *Recreations:* tennis, bridge. *Address:* Hartfield, Duton Hill, Dunmow, Essex CM6 2DX. *T:* (01371) 870554.   *Died 24 July 1999.*

ALLEY, Ronald Edgar; art historian; Keeper of the Modern Collection, Tate Gallery, London, 1965–86; *b* 12 March 1926; *s* of late Edgar Thomas Alley; *m* 1955, Anthea Oswell, painter and sculptor (marr. diss. 1973, remarried 1993; *d* 1993); two *d*. *Educ:* Bristol Grammar School; Courtauld Institute of Art, London University. Tate Gallery staff as Asst Keeper II, 1951–54; Deputy Keeper, 1954–65. Member: Museum Board, Cecil Higgins Art Gallery, Bedford, 1957–; Art Cttee, Ulster Museum, Belfast, 1962–70; Art Panel of Arts Council, 1963–66; Trustee, Graham Sutherland Gall., Picton, 1984–89. *Publications:* Tate Gallery: Foreign Paintings, Drawings and Sculpture, 1959; Gauguin, 1962; William Scott, 1963; Ben Nicholson, 1963; (with Sir John Rothenstein) Francis Bacon, 1964; British Painting since 1945, 1966; Picasso's "Three Dancers", 1967, rev. and enlarged edn, 1986; Barbara Hepworth, 1968; Recent American Art, 1969; Portrait of a Primitive: the art of Henri Rousseau, 1978; Catalogue of the Tate Gallery's Collection of Modern Art,

other than works by British Artists, 1981; Forty Years of Modern Art 1945–1985, 1986. *Recreation:* ornithology. *Address:* 61 Deodar Road, SW15 2NU. *T:* (020) 8874 2016.   *Died 25 April 1999.*

ALLFORD, David, CBE 1984; FRIBA; architect, retired; Senior Partner, YRM Partnership, 1975–87 (Partner since 1958); Chairman, YRM plc, 1987–89; Visiting Professor, Bartlett School of Architecture, University College London, since 1989; *b* 12 July 1927; *s* of Frank Allford and Martha Blanche Allford; *m* 1953, Margaret Beryl Roebuck; one *s* two *d* (and one *d* decd). *Educ:* High Storrs Grammar Sch., Sheffield; Univ. of Sheffield (BA Hons Architecture, 1952). FRIBA 1969. Served RAF, 1945–48. Joined Yorke Rosenberg Mardall, Architects (later YRM plc), 1952; Partner i/c architectural projects: schools, univs (principally Univ. of Warwick), Newcastle Airport, hosps and commercial projs in UK and overseas. Mem. Council, Architectural Assoc., 1970–71 and 1977–78. Hon DLitt Sheffield, 1994. *Publications:* articles in architectural press and related jls. *Recreations:* drawing, painting, following Sheffield Wednesday Football Club. *Address:* Studio B, Mica House, Barnsbury Square, N1 1RN. *T:* (0171) 607 0418. *Clubs:* Arts, MCC.
                                                 Died 10 Aug. 1997.

ALLHUSEN, Major Derek Swithin, CVO 1984; DL; farmer; Standard Bearer, HM's Body Guard of Honourable Corps of Gentlemen at Arms, 1981–84; *b* 9 Jan. 1914; 2nd *s* of late Lt-Col F. H. Allhusen, CMG, DSO, Fulmer House, Fulmer, Bucks, and Enid, *d* of Comdr Harold W. Swithinbank; *m* 1937, Hon. Claudia Violet Betterton, *yr d* of 1st and last Baron Rushcliffe, GBE, PC (*d* 1949); one *s* one *d* (and one *s* decd). *Educ:* Eton; Chillon Coll., Montreux, Switzerland; Trinity Coll., Cambridge (MA). Lieut, 9th Queen's Royal Lancers, 1935. Served War of 1939–45: France, 1940, North Africa, Italy (wounded twice) (Silver Star Medal of USA, 1944); Major 1942; 2 i/c 1945–47, retired, 1949. One of HM's Body Guard of Hon. Corps of Gentlemen at Arms, 1963–84. Chm., Riding for the Disabled, Norwich and Dist Gp, 1968– (Vice-Pres., Eastern Region); President: Royal Norfolk Agric. Assoc., 1974; Nat. Pony Soc., 1982; Cambridge Univ. Equestrian Club; Norfolk Schs Athletic Assoc.; British Horse Soc., 1986–88 (Mem. Council, 1962–). Freeman, City of London; Hon. Yeoman, Worshipful Co. of Saddlers, 1969; Hon. Freeman, Worshipful Co. of Farriers, 1969. High Sheriff, 1958, DL 1969, Norfolk. Represented GB: Winter Pentathlon, Olympic Games, 1948; Equestrianism European Championships Three-Day Event, 1957, 1959, 1965, 1967, 1969 (Winners of Team Championship, 1957, 1967, 1969); Olympic Games, Mexico, 1968 (Gold Medal, Team; Silver Medal, Individual); lent his horse Laurieston to British Olympic Equestrian Team, Munich, 1972 (individual and team Gold Medals). *Recreations:* riding, shooting, skiing. *Address:* Manor House, Claxton, Norwich, Norfolk NR14 7AS. *T:* (01508) 480228.
                                                 Died 24 April 2000.

ALLSOPP, (Harold) Bruce, FSA; author and artist, *b* Oxford, 4 July 1912; *s* of Henry Allsopp and Elizabeth May Allsopp (*née* Robertson); *m* 1935, Florence Cyrilla Woodroffe, ARCA (*d* 1991); two *s*. *Educ:* Manchester Grammar Sch.; Liverpool School of Architecture. BArch (1st Cl. Hons), Liverpool, 1933; Rome Finalist, 1934; Diploma in Civic Design 1935; ARIBA 1935; MRTPI (AMTPI 1936); FRIBA 1955; FSA 1968. War Service 1940–46, N Africa, Italy, Captain RE. Asst Architect in Chichester and London, 1934–35; Lecturer, Leeds Coll. of Art, 1935–40; Lecturer in Architecture, 1946, Sen. Lecturer, 1955, Durham Univ.; University of Newcastle upon Tyne: Sen. Lecturer, 1963; Dir of Architectural Studies, 1965–69; Sen. Lecturer in History of Architecture, 1969–73; Reader, 1973–77; Member: Senate, 1964–65,

1974–77; Court, 1974–77. Chm., Oriel Press Ltd, 1962–87; Dir, Routledge & Kegan Paul Books Ltd, 1974–85. Chairman: Soc. of Architectural Historians of GB, 1959–65; Independent Publishers Guild, 1971–73; Master, Art Workers Guild, 1970; Pres., Fedn of Northern Art Socs, 1980–83. Presenter, TV films, including: Fancy Gothic, 1974; The Bowes Museum, 1977; Country Houses and Landscape of Northumberland, 1979. *Publications:* Art and the Nature of Architecture, 1952; Decoration and Furniture, Vol. 1 1952, Vol. 2 1953; A General History of Architecture, 1955; Style in the Visual Arts, 1957; Possessed, 1959; The Future of the Arts, 1959; A History of Renaissance Architecture, 1959; The Naked Flame, 1962; Architecture, 1964; To Kill a King, 1965; A History of Classical Architecture, 1965; Historic Architecture of Newcastle upon Tyne, 1967; Civilization, the Next Stage, 1969; The Study of Architectural History, 1970; Modern Architecture of Northern England, 1970; Inigo Jones on Palladio, 1970; Romanesque Architecture, 1971; Ecological Morality, 1972; The Garden Earth, 1973; Towards a Humane Architecture, 1974; Return of the Pagan, 1974; Cecilia, 1975; Inigo Jones and the Lords A'Leaping, 1975; A Modern Theory of Architecture, 1977; Appeal to the Gods, 1980; Should Man Survive?, 1982; The Country Life Companion to British and European Architecture, 1985; Social Responsibility and the Responsible Society, 1985; Guide de l'Architecture, 1985; Larousse Guide to European Architecture, 1985; Patronage and Professionalism, 1993; Spirit of Europe, 1997; (contrib.) Artists and Authors at War, 1999; (with Ursula Clark): Architecture of France, 1963; Architecture of Italy, 1964; Architecture of England, 1964; Photography for Tourists, 1966; Historic Architecture of Northumberland, 1969; Historic Architecture of Northumberland and Newcastle, 1977; English Architecture, 1979; (with U. Clark and H. W. Booton) The Great Tradition of Western Architecture, 1966; *as Simon Grindle:* The Loving Limpet, 1964; *as Rielo:* Blow up the Ark, 1964; What to do with Beetles, 1964; articles in Encyclopedia Americana, Encyclopaedia Britannica, Jl of RSA, Didaskalos, etc. *Recreations:* piano and organ, gardening. *Address:* Ferndale, Mount View, Stocksfield, Northumberland NE43 7HL. *T:* (01661) 842323. *Club:* Athenæum. *Died 22 Feb. 2000.*

ALPORT, Baron *cr* 1961 (Life Peer), of Colchester, co. Essex; **Cuthbert James McCall Alport,** TD 1949; PC 1960; DL; *b* 22 March 1912; *o s* of late Prof. Arthur Cecil Alport, MD, FRCP, and Janet, *y d* of James McCall, Dumfriesshire; *m* 1945, Rachel Cecilia (*d* 1983), *o d* of late Lt-Col R. C. Bingham, CVO, DSO, and Dorothy Louisa Pratt; one *s* one *d* (and one *d* decd). *Educ:* Haileybury; Pembroke Coll., Cambridge. MA History and Law; Pres., Cambridge Union Society, 1935. Tutor, Ashridge Coll., 1935–37. Barrister-at-Law, Middle Temple, 1944. Joined Artists Rifles; served War of 1939–45 (Hon. Lt-Col). Director, Conservative Political Centre, 1945–50. MP (C) Colchester division of Essex, 1950–61. Asst Postmaster-General, Dec. 1955–Jan. 1957; Parliamentary Under-Secretary of State, Commonwealth Relations Office, 1957–59; Minister of State, Commonwealth Relations Office, Oct. 1959–March 1961. Chm., Joint East and Central African Board, 1953–55. British High Commissioner in the Federation of Rhodesia and Nyasaland, 1961–63; Mem. of Council of Europe, 1964–65; British Govt Representative to Rhodesia, June–July 1967. A Dep. Speaker, House of Lords, 1971–82, 1983–94. Adviser to the Home Secretary, 1974–82. Chm., New Theatre Trust, 1970–83; Pres., Minories Art Gall., Colchester, 1978–91. Governor, Charing Cross Hosp., 1954–55; Life Governor, Haileybury Coll. Master, Skinners' Co., 1969–70, 1982–83. Pro-Chancellor, City Univ., 1972–79. Chm., Acad. Adv. Cttee, Gresham Coll.,

1984–86. DL Essex, 1974; High Steward of Colchester, 1967–; Hon. Freeman, Colchester, 1992. Hon. DCL City Univ., 1979; DU Essex 1997. *Publications:* Kingdoms in Partnership, 1937; Hope in Africa, 1952; The Sudden Assignment, 1965. *Address:* The Cross House, Layer de la Haye, Colchester, Essex CO2 0JG. *T:* (01206) 734217. *Club:* Farmers'. *Died 28 Oct. 1998.*

AMBARTSUMIAN, Victor Amazaspovich; National Hero of Republic of Armenia; Hero of Socialist Labour (twice); Order of Lenin (five times); Order of Labour Red Banner (twice); Hon. President, Academy of Sciences of Armenia, since 1993 (President, 1947–93); *b* 18 Sept. 1908; *s* of Amazasp and Hripsime Ambartsumyan; *m* 1931, Vera Ambartsumian; two *s* two *d*. *Educ:* Univ. of Leningrad. Lecturer in Astronomy, 1931–34, Prof. of Astrophysics, 1934–44, Univ. of Leningrad; Prof. of Astrophysics, Univ. of Erevan, 1944–. Full Mem., Russian Academy of Sciences, 1953–. Pres., Internat. Council of Scientific Unions, 1968–72. Hon. Dr of Science Univs of: Canberra, 1963; Paris, 1965; Liège, 1967; Prague, 1967; Torun, 1973; La Plata, 1974; Foreign Member of Academies of Science: Washington, Paris, Rome, Vienna, Berlin, Amsterdam, Copenhagen, Sofia, Stockholm, Boston, New York, New Delhi, Cordoba, Prague, Budapest; Foreign Member of Royal Society, London. *Publications:* Theoretical Astrophysics, 1953 (in Russian; trans. into German, English, Spanish, Chinese); about 100 papers in learned jls. *Address:* Academy of Sciences of Armenia, Marshal Bagramian Avenue 24, Erevan, Armenia. *Died 12 Aug. 1996.*

AMBLER, Eric Clifford, OBE 1981; novelist and screenwriter; *b* 28 June 1909; *s* of Alfred Percy and Amy Madeleine Ambler; *m* 1st, 1939, Louise Crombie (marr. diss. 1958); 2nd, 1958, Joan Harrison (*d* 1994). *Educ:* Colfe's Grammar Sch.; London Univ. Apprenticeship in engineering, 1927–28; advertisement copywriter, 1929–35; professional writer, 1936–. Served War of 1939–45: RA, 1940; commissioned, 1941; served in Italy, 1943; Lt-Col, 1944; Asst Dir of Army Kinematography, War Office, 1944–46. US Bronze Star, 1946. Wrote and produced film, The October Man, 1947 and resumed writing career. Diamond Dagger Award, CWA, 1986. Hon. DLitt City, 1992. *Screenplays* include: The Way Ahead, 1944; The October Man, 1947; The Passionate Friends, 1948; Highly Dangerous, 1950; The Magic Box, 1951; Gigolo and Gigolette, in Encore, 1952; The Card, 1952; Rough Shoot, 1953; The Cruel Sea, 1953; Lease of Life, 1954; The Purple Plain, 1954; Yangtse Incident, 1957; A Night to Remember, 1958; Wreck of the Mary Deare, 1959; Love Hate Love, 1970. *Publications:* The Dark Frontier, 1936; Uncommon Danger, 1937; Epitaph for a Spy, 1938; Cause for Alarm, 1938; The Mask of Dimitrios, 1939; Journey into Fear, 1940; Judgment on Deltchev, 1951; The Schirmer Inheritance, 1953; The Night-comers, 1956; Passage of Arms, 1959; The Light of Day, 1962; The Ability to Kill (essays), 1963; (ed and introd) To Catch a Spy, 1964; A Kind of Anger, 1964 (Edgar Allan Poe award, 1964); Dirty Story, 1967; The Intercom Conspiracy, 1969; The Levanter, 1972 (Golden Dagger award, 1973); Doctor Frigo, 1974 (MWA Grand Master award, 1975); Send No More Roses, 1977; The Care of Time, 1981; Here Lies (autobiog.), 1985; The Story So Far, 1993. *Address:* 14 Bryanston Square, W1H 7FF. *Club:* Garrick. *Died 23 Oct. 1998.*

AMBROSE, Prof. Edmund Jack, MA (Cantab), DSc (London); Professor of Cell Biology, University of London, Institute of Cancer Research, 1967–76, then Emeritus Professor; Staff of Chester Beatty Research Institute, Institute of Cancer Research: Royal Cancer Hospital, 1952–75; *b* 2 March 1914; *s* of Alderman Harry Edmund Ambrose and Kate (*née* Stanley); *m* 1943, Andrée (*née* Huck), Seine, France; one *s* one *d*. *Educ:* Perse Sch., Cambridge; Emmanuel Coll., Cambridge. Wartime research for Admiralty on infra-red detectors, 1940–45; subseq. research on structure of proteins using infra-red radiation at Courtauld Fundamental Research Laboratory. Formerly Convener of Brit. Soc. for Cell Biology. Formerly Special Adviser in Cancer to Govt of India at Tata Meml Centre, Bombay; Special Adviser in Leprosy, Foundn for Med. Res., Bombay, 1978– (awarded St Elizabeth Meml Medal, Order of St John, Paris, 1981 for leprosy work); Adviser, Regional Cancer Centre, Kerala, India, 1984–. Pres., Internat. Cell Tissue and Organ Culture Group. Research on structure of proteins, on structure of normal and cancer cells, and on characteristics of surface of cancer cells, cell biology and microbiology of leprosy, using labelled metabolites. *Publications:* Cell Electrophoresis, 1965; The Biology of Cancer, 1966, 2nd edn 1975; The Cancer Cell *in vitro*, 1967; (jtly) Cell Biology, 1970, rev. edn 1976; Nature of the Biological World, 1982; The Mirror of Creation, 1990; publications on protein structure and cell biology, in Proc. Royal Soc., biological jls. *Recreation:* sailing. *Address:* The Mill House, Westfield, Hastings, E Sussex TN34 4SU. *Clubs:* Chelsea Arts; Royal Bombay Yacht.

Died 14 Jan. 1996.

AMERY OF LUSTLEIGH, Baron *cr* 1992 (Life Peer), of Preston, in the County of Lancashire and of Brighton in the County of East Sussex; **(Harold) Julian Amery;** PC 1960; *b* 27 March 1919; *s* of late Rt Hon. Leopold Amery, CH, PC and Florence (CI 1945), *d* of John Hamar Greenwood, Ont; *m* 1950, Lady Catherine (*d* 1991), *d* of 1st Earl of Stockton, OM, PC, FRS; one *s* three *d*. *Educ:* Summer Fields; Eton; Balliol Coll., Oxford. War Corresp. in Spanish Civil War, 1938–39; Attaché HM Legation, Belgrade, and on special missions in Bulgaria, Turkey, Roumania and Middle East, 1939–40; Sergeant in RAF, 1940–41; commissioned and transferred to army, 1941; on active service, Egypt, Palestine and Adriatic, 1941–42; liaison officer to Albanian resistance movement, 1944; served on staff of Gen. Carton de Wiart, VC, Mr Churchill's personal representative with Generalissimo Chiang Kai-Shek, 1945. Contested Preston in Conservative interest, July 1945; MP (C): Preston North, 1950–66; Brighton Pavilion, 1969–92; Parly Under-Sec. of State and Financial Sec., War Office, 1957–58; Parly Under-Sec. of State, Colonial Office, 1958–60; Sec. of State for Air, Oct. 1960–July 1962; Minister of Aviation, 1962–64; Minister of Public Building and Works, June-Oct. 1970; Minister for Housing and Construction, DoE, 1970–72; Minister of State, FCO, 1972–74. Delegate to Consultative Assembly of Council of Europe, 1950–53 and 1956. Member Round Table Conference on Malta, 1955. Hon. LLD Westminster Coll., Fulton, Miss, 1994. Kt Comdr, Order of Phœnix, Greece; Grand Cordon, Order of Skanderbeg, Albania; Order of Oman, first class. *Publications:* Sons of the Eagle, 1948; The Life of Joseph Chamberlain: vol. IV, 1901–3: At the Height of his Power, 1951; vols V and VI, 1901–14: Joseph Chamberlain and the Tariff Reform Campaign, 1969; Approach March (autobiog.), 1973; articles in National Review, Nineteenth Century and Daily Telegraph. *Recreations:* ski-ing, mountaineering, travel. *Address:* 112 Eaton Square, SW1W 9AE. *T:* 0171–235 1543; Forest Farm House, Chelwood Gate, East Sussex RH17 7DA. *Clubs:* White's, Beefsteak, Carlton, Buck's. *Died 3 Sept. 1996.*

AMES, Rachel, (Mrs Kenneth Ames); *see* Gainham, Sarah.

AMOORE, Rt Rev. Frederick Andrew; Provincial Executive Officer, Church of the Province of South Africa, 1982–87, retired; *b* 6 June 1913; *s* of Harold Frederick Newnham Amoore and Emily Clara Amoore, Worthing; *m* 1948, Mary Dobson; three *s*. *Educ:* Worthing Boys'

High Sch.; University of Leeds. BA Hons Hist. Leeds, 1934. Deacon 1936, priest 1937; Curate of: Clapham, London, 1936; St Mary's, Port Elizabeth, S Africa, 1939; Rector of St Saviour's, E London, S Africa, 1945; Dean of St Albans Cathedral, Pretoria, 1950; Exec. Officer for Church of Province of S Africa, 1962–67; Bishop of Bloemfontein, 1967–82. *Recreations:* music, italic script. *Address:* 6 Regency Park, Main Road, Kenilworth, CP, 7700, South Africa. *Died 11 June 1996.*

ANDERSON, Dr Arthur John Ritchie, (Iain), CBE 1984; MA; MRCGP; general medical and hospital practitioner, trainer, 1961–94; final year Tutor, Royal Free Hospital, 1985–94; *b* 19 July 1933; *s* of Dr John Anderson and Dorothy Mary Anderson; *m* 1959, Janet Edith Norrish; two *s* one *d*. *Educ:* Bromsgrove Sch.; Downing Coll., Cambridge; St Mary's Hospital Medical Sch. MA, MB BChir (Cantab). MRCS; LRCP; DCH; DObstRCOG. Various hospital posts, 1958–61. Hemel Hempstead RDC, 1967–74, Vice-Chm., 1970–74; Councillor (C), Hertfordshire CC, 1973–, Vice-Chm., 1985–87 (Leader, 1977–83), Chief Whip, Cons. Gp, 1989–. Member: Herts Police Authority, 1973–87 and 1993– (Chm., 1985–87); NW Thames Regional Health Authority, 1978–84; Regional Planning Council for South East, 1977–79; Police Cttee, ACC, 1977–87. President, Hertfordshire Branch, BMA, 1973–74. Member, various governing bodies of primary, secondary, further and higher educn instns. Chm., Crouchfield Trust, 1989–. FRSM 1985. *Publications:* numerous articles, mainly in periodicals. *Recreations:* writing, hockey, walking. *Address:* Leaside, Rucklers Lane, King's Langley, Herts WD4 9NQ. *T:* (01923) 262884. *Club:* Herts 100.

Died 1 July 1996.

ANDERSON, Brig. David William, CBE 1976 (OBE 1972); Chief Executive, Cumbernauld Development Corporation, 1985–88; *b* 4 Jan. 1929; *s* of David and Frances Anderson; *m* 1954, Eileen Dorothy Scott; one *s* two *d*. *Educ:* St Cuthbert's Grammar Sch., Newcastle upon Tyne. Black Watch, 1946; RMA, Sandhurst, 1947; commnd HLI, 1948; served ME and Malaya; RHF, Staff Coll., Trucial Oman Scouts, Sch. of Inf., 1 RHF, Germany, and HQ NORTHAG, 1959–66; Instr, Staff Coll., 1967–69; CO 1 RHF, Scotland, N Ireland, Singapore, 1969–72; Colonel GS: MoD, 1972–73; HQ Dir of Inf., 1974; Comdr, 3 Inf. Bde, N Ireland, 1975–76; Comdt, Sch. of Infantry, 1976–79; Comdr, Highlands, 1979–81, Comdr 51 Highland Bde, 1982; ADC to the Queen, 1981–82. Chief Exec., NE Fife DC, 1982–85. Hon. Colonel: Aberdeen Univ. OTC, 1982–87; 1/52 Lowland Vol., 1987–88; Member: RHF Council, 1970–88; Highland TA&VRA, 1984–88; Lowland TA&VRA, 1987–88. Chm., Fife Area Scout Council, 1985–86. Mem., St John Assoc., 1984–85. Hon. Vice-Pres., Cumbernauld Br., Royal British Legion (Scotland), 1985–88. *Recreation:* moving house.

Died 5 Feb. 1999.

ANDERSON, Iain; *see* Anderson, A. J. R.

ANDERSON, Prof. John Allan Dalrymple, TD 1967; DL; FRCP, FRCPE, FRCGP, FFPHM, FFOM; Professor of Community Medicine, University of London, at United Medical and Dental Schools (Guy's Campus), 1975–90, then Professor Emeritus; Consultant Emeritus, Guy's Hospital, since 1990; *b* 16 June 1926; *s* of John Allan Anderson and Mary Winifred (*née* Lawson); *m* 1965, Mairead Mary MacLaren; three *d*. *Educ:* Loretto Sch.; Worcester Coll., Oxford (MA); Edinburgh Univ. (MD 1964); London Univ. (DPH); DObstRCOG 1953. FFPHM (FFCM 1974); FRCGP 1984; FRCP 1987; FFOM 1990. Lectr in gen. practice, 1954–59, Dir, Industrial Survey Unit, 1960–63, Univ. of Edinburgh; Sen. Lectr, Social Medicine, LSHTM, 1963–69; Dir, Dept of Community Medicine, Guy's Hosp. Med. Sch., 1970–90; Hon.

Consultant, Guy's Hosp., 1970–90; Prof. and Chm., Dept of Public Health and Occupational Medicine, Univ. of the UAE, 1990–94. Dir, Occupational Health Service, Lewisham and N Southwark HA, 1984–90. Acad. Registrar, FCM, RCP, 1983–89. OC London Scot. Co. 1/ 51 Highland Vol., TA, 1967–70; CO 221 Fd Amb. (TA), 1978–81; TA Col HQ Lond. Dist, 1981–84; Regtl Col Lond. Scot. Regt, 1983–89. Hon. Civilian Consultant to the Army in Public Health Medicine, 1990–96. Elder, Ch of Scotland, 1977–; Area Surg., SJAB, SW Lond., 1984–90. DL Greater London, 1985; Rep. DL, Borough of Richmond, 1986–90. *Publications:* A New Look at Community Medicine, 1965; Self Medication, 1982; (with Dr R. Grahame) Bibliography of Low Back Pain, 1982; Epidemiological, Sociological and Environmental Aspects of Rheumatic Diseases, 1987; sci. papers on public health and occupational med. and rheumatology. *Recreations:* golf, bridge. *Address:* The Lanterns, 11D Ettrick Road, Edinburgh EH10 5BJ. *T:* (0131) 229 0433. *Clubs:* New, Royal Scots (Edinburgh). *Died 21 Oct. 2000.*

ANDREWS, Raymond Denzil Anthony, MBE 1953; VRD 1960; Consultant, Andrews, Downie & Partners, Architects, since 1990 (Senior Partner, 1960–90); *b* 5 June 1925; *s* of Michael Joseph Andrews, BA, and Phylis Marie Andrews (*née* Crowley); *m* 1958, Gillian Whitlaw Small, BA (Hons); one *s* one *d. Educ:* Highgate Sch.; Christ's Coll., Cambridge; University Coll. London (DipArch, DipTP); Univ. of Michigan (MArch). RIBA. Lieut, Royal Marines, 1943–46; RM Reserve, 1948–68 (Major). King George VI Meml Fellow of English-Speaking Union of US, 1954–55. Chm., Fest. of Architecture, 1984; Dir, Westminster Cathedral Centenary Exhibn, 1995–96. Chm., London Region, 1968–72, Vice-Pres., 1972–74, 1978–81, RIBA; Pres., Architectural Assoc., 1975–77. Civic Trust Award, 1971 and 1978; 1st Prize, Royal Mint Square Housing Competition, GLC, 1974. Order of Al Rafadain (Iraq), 1956. *Recreation:* sailing. *Address:* 34 Clarendon Road, W11 3AD. *T:* (020) 7727 4129. *Club:* RIBA Sailing (Cdre, 1983–87). *Died 28 Oct. 1999.*

ANGLIN, Eric Jack; HM Diplomatic Service, retired; Consul-General, Melbourne, 1979–83; *b* 9 Aug. 1923; *m* 1954, Patricia Farr; three *s*. Joined Foreign Service (subseq. Diplomatic Service), 1948; FO, 1948–52; HM Missions in: Damascus, 1952–56; Rangoon, 1956–59; Madrid, 1960–64; FO, 1964–67; La Paz, 1967–70; Khartoum, 1970–72; Inspector, Diplomatic Service, FCO, 1973–76; Buenos Aires, 1976–78; Chargé d'Affaires and Consul-Gen., Santiago, 1978–79. *Recreations:* auctions, food. *Address:* 20 Gainsborough Drive, Sherborne, Dorset DT9 6DR. *T:* (01935) 817364. *Died 4 April 1999.*

ANNAN, Baron, *cr* 1965 (Life Peer), of Royal Burgh of Annan, co. Dumfries; **Noël Gilroy Annan,** OBE 1946; Chairman, Board of Trustees, National Gallery, 1980–85 (Trustee, 1978–85); *b* 25 Dec. 1916; *s* of late James Gilroy Annan and Fannie Mildred, *y d* of Thomas Sylvester Quinn, NY, USA; *m* 1950, Gabriele, *d* of Louis Ferdinand Ullstein, Berlin; two *d. Educ:* Stowe Sch.; King's Coll., Cambridge (Exhibitioner and Scholar). Served War of 1939–45: WO, War Cabinet Offices, and Military Intelligence, 1940–44; France and Germany, 1944–46; GSO1, Political Div. of British Control Commn, 1945–46. University of Cambridge: Fellow of King's Coll., 1944–56, 1966; Asst Tutor, 1947; Lectr in Politics, 1948–66; Provost of King's Coll., 1956–66; Provost of University Coll., London, 1966–78 (Hon. Fellow, 1968); Vice-Chancellor, Univ. of London, 1978–81. Romanes Lectr, Oxford, 1965. Chairman: Departmental Cttee on Teaching of Russian in Schools, 1960; Academic Planning Bd, Univ. of Essex, 1965–70; Cttee on Future of Broadcasting, 1974–77, report published 1977. Member: Academic Adv. Cttee, Brunel Coll., 1966–73; Academic Planning Bd, Univ. of

East Anglia, 1964–71; Public Schools Commn, 1966–70. Chm., Enquiry on the disturbances in Essex Univ. (report published 1974). Sen. Fellow, Eton Coll., 1956–66. Governor: Stowe Sch., 1945–66; Queen Mary Coll., London, 1956–60. Trustee: Churchill Coll., Cambridge, 1958–76; British Museum, 1963–80; Pres., London Library, 1980–96. Dir, Royal Opera House, Covent Garden, 1967–78; Gulbenkian Foundation: Mem., Arts Cttee, 1957–64; Chm., Educn Cttee, 1971–76. FRHistS; Fellow, Berkeley Coll., Yale, 1963; Hon. Fellow, Churchill Coll., Cambridge, 1988; Emer. Fellow, Leverhulme Trust, 1984. For. Hon. Mem., Amer. Acad. of Arts and Sciences, 1973. Hon. DLitt: York, Ontario, 1966; New York, 1981; London, 1997; DUniv Essex, 1967; Hon. LLD Pennsylvania, 1980. Le Bas Prize, 1948; Diamond Jubilee Medal, Inst. of Linguists, 1971; Clerk Kerr Medal, Univ. of Calif, Berkeley, 1985. Comdr, Royal Order of King George I of the Hellenes (Greece), 1962. *Publications:* Leslie Stephen: his thought and character in relation to his time, 1951 (James Tait Black Memorial Prize, 1951), rev. edn 1984; The Intellectual Aristocracy, in Studies in Social History, a tribute to G. M. Trevelyan, 1956; The Curious Strength of Positivism in English Political Thought, 1959; Kipling's Place in the History of Ideas, in Kipling's Mind and Art, 1964; Roxburgh of Stowe, 1965; Our Age: portrait of a generation, 1990; Changing Enemies: the defeat and regeneration of Germany, 1995; The Dons, 1999; articles in NY Rev. of Books and other periodicals. *Recreation:* writing English prose. *Address:* 45 Ranelagh Grove, SW1W 8PB. *Club:* Brooks's.

Died 21 Feb. 2000.

ANNIS, Philip Geoffrey Walter; Manager, Regimental History Project, Royal Regiment of Artillery, since 1986; *b* 7 Feb. 1936; *s* of Walter and Lilian Annis; *m* 1967, Olive, *d* of Mr and Mrs E. W. A. Scarlett; one *s. Educ:* Sale Grammar Sch.; Kelsick Grammar Sch., Ambleside; Manchester Univ. FSA 1973; FRHistS 1975. Served RA, 1957–59, and RA (TA), 1961–66. Board of Inland Revenue, 1959–62; joined National Maritime Museum, 1962; Head of Museum Services, 1971; Dep. Dir, 1979–86. Mem., British Commn, Internat. Commn for Maritime History, 1980–88. Alfred Burne Meml Award, Royal Artillery Instn, 1995. Comdr, Order of Lion of Finland, 1986. *Publications:* Naval Swords, 1970; (with Comdr W. E. May) Swords For Sea Service, 1970; articles on the history of naval uniform. *Recreation:* gardening. *Address:* The Royal Artillery Institution, Old Royal Military Academy, Woolwich, SE18 4DN. *T:* (020) 8781 5613. *Died 12 Nov. 1998.*

ANSTEY, Brig. Sir John, Kt 1975; CBE 1946; TD; DL; President and Chairman, National Savings Committee, 1975–78 (a Vice-Chairman, 1968–75); retired as Chairman and Managing Director, John Player & Sons; Director, Imperial Tobacco Co., Ltd, 1949–67; *b* 3 Jan. 1907; *s* of late Major Alfred Anstey, Matford House, Exeter, Devon; *m* 1935, Elizabeth Mary (*d* 1990), *d* of late William Garnett, Backwell, Somerset; one *s* one *d. Educ:* Clifton; Trinity Coll., Oxford; Harvard Univ. (MBA 1952). Served War of 1939–45: N Africa, France, SEAC (despatches); Lt-Col 1944; Brig. 1944. Mem. Council, Nottingham Univ., 1948–93 (Treasurer, 1979–81; Pro-Chancellor, 1982–93); Member: (part-time) East Midlands Gas Board, 1968–72; Univ. Authorities Panel, 1979–82. Governor, Clifton Coll. Mem. Council, The Queen's Silver Jubilee Appeal, 1976. High Sheriff of Nottinghamshire, 1967; DL Notts, 1970. Hon. LLD Nottingham, 1975. Legion of Honour (France); Croix de Guerre (France); Legion of Merit (USA). *Address:* Southwell, Notts. *Died 17 Sept. 2000.*

ANTONIO; *see* Ruiz Soler, Antonio.

APLEY, Alan Graham, FRCS; Consulting Editor, Journal of Bone and Joint Surgery, since 1989 (Editor, 1983-89); *b* 10 Nov. 1914; *s* of Samuel Apley and Mary Tanis, *m* 1st, 1939, Janie Kandler (decd); one *s* one *d*; 2nd, 1988, Violet Chambers. *Educ:* Regent Street Polytechnic; University Coll. London; University College Hosp., London (MB BS). MRCS, LRCP 1938, FRCS 1941; Hon. FRCSE 1987. Served RAMC, 1944-47. Cons. Surg., Rowley Bristow Orthopaedic Hosp., Pyrford, 1947; Dir of Accident and Emergency Centre, St Peter's Hosp., Chertsey, 1964; Hon. Dir, Dept of Orthopaedics, St Thomas' Hosp., London, 1972; Mem. Council, 1973-85, Vice-Pres. 1984-85, RCS; Pres., Orthopaedic Sect., RSM, 1979. *Publications:* System of Orthopaedics and Fractures, 1959, 7th edn 1993; (jtly) Replacement of the Knee, 1984; (jtly) Atlas of Skeletal Dysplasias, 1985; (ed) Recent Advances in Orthopaedics, 1969; (ed) Modern Trends in Orthopaedics, 1972; (jtly) A Concise System of Orthopaedics and Fractures, 1988, 2nd edn 1994; various articles in surg. jls. *Recreations:* music, ski-ing, travelling. *Address:* Singleton Lodge, West Byfleet, Surrey KT14 6PW. *T:* (019323) 43353.
Died 20 Dec. 1996.

APPLEBY, Robert, CBE 1969; Chairman, Black & Decker Ltd, 1956-75 (Managing Director, 1956-72); *b* 1913; *s* of Robert James Appleby; *m* 1936, Muriel Valmai Jones (*d* 1994); two *d*; partner, Elisabeth Friederike (*d* 1975), *d* of Prof. Fidmann; one *s* one *d*. *Educ:* Graham Sea Training and Engineering Sch., Scarborough. Dep. Chm., Black & Decker Manufacturing Co., Maryland, 1968-72. Mem., Post Office Bd, 1972-73. CEng, FIEE; CIMgt.
Died 15 Nov. 1996.

ap REES, Prof. Thomas; Professor of Botany and Head of Department of Plant Sciences, University of Cambridge, since 1991 and Fellow of Gonville and Caius College, Cambridge; *b* 19 Oct. 1930; *s* of Elfan Rees and Frances Rees (*née* Boston); *m* 1955, Wendy Ruth, *d* of late Reginald and Marjorie Holroyde, three *s*. *Educ:* Llandovery Coll., Dyfed; Lincoln Coll., Oxford (BA 1955; MA, DPhil 1958); ScD Cantab 1983. Nat. service, commnd Royal Signals, 1949-51. Lectr in Mycology, Univ. of Sydney, 1959-61; Res. Officer and Sen. Res. Officer, CSIRO, 1961-64; University of Cambridge: Lectr in Botany, 1964-91; Reader in Plant Biochem., 1991; Gonville and Caius College: Fellow, 1965-91, Professorial Fellow, 1991-; College Lectr, 1965-91; Dir of Studies in Biol Scis, 1986-91. Science and Engineering Research Council: Mem., Plant Sci. and Microbiol. Cttee, 1982-87 (Chm., 1985-87); Mem., Biol Scis Cttee, 1984-87; Biotechnology and Biological Sciences Research Council: Mem., Sci. and Engrg Base Bd, 1994-; Chm., Plant and Microbiol Scis Cttee, 1994-. Trustee, Llandovery Coll., 1966-94. *Publications:* (jtly) Plant Biochemistry, 1964; sci. papers in learned jls. *Recreations:* mountaineering, gardening. *Address:* Department of Plant Sciences, Downing Site, Downing Street, Cambridge CB2 3EA. *T:* (01223) 333900; The Elms, High Street, Little Eversden, Cambridge CB3 7HE.
Died 3 Oct. 1996.

ARCHER, Gen. Sir (Arthur) John, KCB 1976; OBE 1964 (MBE 1959); Chief Executive, Royal Hong Kong Jockey Club, 1980-86, retired; *b* 12 Feb. 1924; *s* of Alfred and Mildred Archer, Fakenham; *m* 1950, (Cynthia) Marie, *d* of Col Alexander and Eileen Allan, Swallowcliffe, Wilts; two *s*. *Educ:* King's Sch., Peterborough; St Catharine's Coll., Cambridge. Entered Army, 1943; commnd 1944; regular commn Dorset Regt, 1946; psc 1956; jssc 1959; GSO1 3rd Div., 1963-65; CO 1 Devon and Dorset Regt, 1965-67; Comdr Land Forces Gulf, 1968-69; idc 1970; Dir of Public Relations (Army), 1970-72; Comdr 2nd Div., 1972-74; Dir of Army Staff Duties, 1974-76; Comdr British Forces Hong Kong, 1976-78 and Lt-Gen. Brigade

of Gurkhas, 1977-78; C-in-C, UKLF, 1978-79. Col, Devonshire and Dorset Regt, 1977-79. Mem. Council, Officers' Pension Soc., 1989- (Pres., 1994-). *Recreations:* light aviation, gliding, sailing. *Address:* c/o Lloyds Bank, 38 Blue Boar Row, Salisbury, Wilts SP1 1DB. *Clubs:* Army and Navy; Royal Motor Yacht (Sandbanks, Dorset); Hong Kong, Hong Kong Jockey (Hong Kong).
Died 12 March 1999.

ARCHIBALD, Barony of, *cr* 1949, of Woodside, Glasgow; title disclaimed by 2nd Baron and became extinct on his death; *see under* Archibald, George Christopher.

ARCHIBALD, (George) Christopher, FRSC 1979; Professor of Economics, University of British Columbia, 1970-91, then Emeritus; *b* 30 Dec. 1926; *s* of 1st Baron Archibald, CBE, and Dorothy Holroyd Edwards (*d* 1960); *S* father, 1975, as 2nd Baron Archibald, but disclaimed his peerage for life; *m* 1st, 1951, Liliana Barou (marr. diss. 1965); 2nd, 1971, Daphne May Vincent. *Educ:* Phillips Exeter Academy, USA; King's Coll., Cambridge (MA); London Sch. of Economics (BSc Econ.). Served in Army, 1945-48, Captain RAEC. Formerly: Prof. of Economics, Univ. of Essex; Lectr in Economics, Otago Univ. and LSE; Leon Fellow, London Univ. Fellow, Econometric Soc., 1976. *Publications:* (ed) Theory of the Firm, 1971; (with R. G. Lipsey) Introduction to a Mathematical Treatment of Economics, 1973; Information, Incentives and the Economics of Control, 1992. *Address:* Cumbria.
Died 27 Feb. 1996.

ARCHIBALD, Dr (Harry) Munro, CB 1976; MBE 1945; Deputy Chief Medical Officer (Deputy Secretary), Department of Health and Social Security, 1973-77; *b* 17 June 1915; *s* of James and Isabella Archibald; unmarried. *Educ:* Hillhead High Sch.; Univ. of Glasgow. MB, ChB 1938; DPH 1956. War Service: RAMC, 1940-43; IMS/IAMC, 1943-46; Lt-Col; Italian Campaign (despatches). Colonial Medical Service, Nigeria, 1946-62. Senior Specialist (Malariologist), 1958; Principal Med. Officer, Prevent. Services, N Nigeria, 1960; Med. Officer, Min. of Health, 1962; Sen. Med. Off., 1964; Principal Med. Off., DHSS, 1970; Sen. Principal Med. Off., 1972. Mem. Bd, Public Health Laboratory Service, 1975-77. Fellow, Faculty of Community Medicine, 1973. *Recreation:* travel. *Address:* 1 Camborne House, Camborne Road, Sutton, Surrey SM2 6RL. *T:* (0181) 643 1076. *Club:* Caledonian.
Died 13 Oct. 1996.

ARGYLE, His Honour Major Michael Victor, MC 1945; QC 1961; a Circuit Judge (formerly an Additional Judge of the Central Criminal Court), 1970-88; *b* 31 Aug. 1915; *e s* of late Harold Victor Argyle and Elsie Marion, Repton, Derbyshire; *m* 1951, Ann Norah (*d* 1994), *d* of late Charles Newton and M. Newton, later Mrs Jobson; three *d*. *Educ:* Shardlow Hall, Derbyshire; Westminster Sch.; Trinity Coll., Cambridge (MA). Served War of 1939-45: with 7th Queen's Own Hussars in India, ME and Italy (immediate MC), 1939-47. Called to Bar, Lincoln's Inn, 1938, Bencher, 1967, Treasurer, 1984; resumed practice at Bar, 1947 (Midland Circuit); Recorder of Northampton, 1962-65, of Birmingham, 1965-70; Dep. Chm., Holland QS, 1965-71; Lay Judge, Arches Court, Province of Canterbury, 1968-92. General Elections, contested (C) Belper, 1950, and Loughborough, 1955. Master, Worshipful Co. of Makers of Playing Cards, 1984-85. *Publications:* (ed) Phipson on Evidence, 10th edn. *Recreations:* chess, boxing. *Address:* The Red House, Fiskerton, near Southwell, Notts NG25 0UL. *T:* (01636) 830530. *Club:* Kennel.
Died 4 Jan. 1999.

ARKELL, John Heward, CBE 1961; TD; Director of Administration, BBC, 1960-70; *b* 20 May 1909; *s* of Rev. H. H. Arkell, MA, and Gertrude Mary Arkell; *m* 1st, 1940, Helen Birgit (marr. diss.), *d* of Emil Huitfeldt, formerly

Norwegian Ambassador to Denmark, and Dorothy Huitfeldt; two *s* one *d;* 2nd, 1956, Meta Bachke Grundtvig (marr. diss.; she *d* 1996); one *s. Educ:* Dragon Sch.; Radley Coll.; Christ Church, Oxford (MA). Sir Max Michaelis (Investment) Trust, 1931–37; Asst Sec., CPRE, 1937–39, Mem. of Exec. Cttee, 1945–75, Vice-Chm., 1967–74, Vice-Pres., 1975–. Commissioned Territorial Officer, 1st Bn Queen's Westminsters, KRRC, 1939; Instructor, then Chief Instructor, Army Infantry Signalling Sch., 1940; served in BLA as special infantry signalling liaison officer, 1944; demobilised 1945, Major. Personnel Manager, J. Lyons, 1945–49; BBC: Controller, Staff Admin, 1949–58; Dir, Staff Admin, 1958–60. Director: The Boots Co. Ltd, 1970–79; UK Provident Instn, 1971–80; Sen. Associate, Kramer Internat. Ltd, 1980–86. Chm., Air Transport and Travel ITB, 1970–80. Lay Mem., Nat. Industrial Relations Ct, 1971–74. Lectr on indust. subjects; occasional indep. management consultancies included P&O and Coates Group of Cos (Dir, 1970–76). Founder, 1932, Exec. Pres., then Jt Pres., and former Gen. Hon. Sec., then Chm., Christ Church (Oxford) United Clubs (Community Centre, SE London). Chm. Council, British Institute of Management, 1972–74 (Vice-Chm., 1966–72; Chm. Exec. Cttee, 1966–69; Vice Pres., 1974–); Chm. BIM/CBI Educl Panel, 1971–72; Dir, BIM Foundn, 1976–81; Member Council: CBI, 1973–75; Industry for Management Educn, 1971; Foundn for Management Educn, 1971–75; National Trust, 1971–84 (Chm., NT Council's Adv. Cttee on the Trust, its members and public, which produced the Arkell Report, 1982–83); Adv. Council, Business Graduates Assoc., 1973–85; Action Resources Centre, 1975–86 (special advr, 1986–90). Mem., later Dir, Christian Frontier Council, 1955–65; Chm., Cttee of British Council of Churches responsible for report on further educn of young people, 1960–61; Member: Finance Cttee, C of E Bd of Finance, 1960–68; CS Deptl Cttee to consider application of Fulton Report to Civil Service, 1968–70; Final Selection Bd, CS Commn, 1978–81. Trustee, Visnews, 1960–69; Vis. Fellow, Henley Management Coll. (formerly Administrative Staff Coll.), 1971–90; Governor, Radley Coll., 1965–70 (Chairman: Social Services Cttee, 1960–74; War Meml Cttee, 1963–88). Chm., Ringstead Bay Protection Soc., 1983–96 (Life Pres.). Inherited Lordship of the Manor, Fawley, 1992; patron of living, 1992. FIPM; CIMgt (FIMgt 1964). FRSA. Olaf Medal, Norway, 1945. *Publications:* composer of light music (The Leander Waltz, Bless Them Lord, Seringa, Candlelight and others); contrib. to jls on management and indust. subjects. *Recreations:* walking, swimming, music. *Address:* Fawley Manor, Pinnocks, Fawley Bottom, Henley-on-Thames, Oxon RG9 6JH. *T:* (01491) 573017; Glen Cottage, Ringstead Bay, Dorchester, Dorset DT2 8NG. *T:* (01305) 852686. *Clubs:* Savile, Lansdowne; Leander. *Died 28 July 1999.*

ARKFELD, Most Rev. Leo, Hon. CBE 1976; Archbishop of Madang, (RC), 1976–87; *b* 4 Feb. 1912; *s* of George Arkfeld and Mary Siemer. *Educ:* St Mary's Seminary, Techny, Ill, USA (BA). Bishop of Wewak, Papua New Guinea, 1948–76; Administrator Apostolic of Wewak, 1976. *Address:* PO Box 107, Wewak, Papua New Guinea. *Died 21 Aug. 1999.*

ARMITAGE, Maj.-Gen. Geoffrey Thomas Alexander, CBE 1968 (MBE 1945); *b* 5 July 1917; *s* of late Lt-Col H. G. P. Armitage and Mary Madeline (*née* Drought); *m* 1949, Monica Wall Kent, widow (*née* Poat); one *s*, and one step *d. Educ:* Haileybury Coll.; RMA, Woolwich (Sword of Honour). Commissioned Royal Artillery, 1937; served War of 1939–45 (despatches, MBE), BEF, Middle East, Italy, NW Europe; transferred to Royal Dragoons (1st Dragoons), 1951, comd 1956–59; Instructor (GSO1), IDC, 1959–60; Col GS, War Office, 1960–62; Comdt RAC Centre, 1962–65; Chief of Staff, HQ1 (BR) Corps,

1966–68; Dir, Royal Armoured Corps, 1968–70; GOC Northumbrian Dist, 1970–72; retd 1973. Dir, CLA Game Fair, 1974–80. *Recreations:* writing, some field sports. *Address:* Clyffe Cottage, Tincleton, near Dorchester, Dorset DT2 8QR. *Clubs:* Army and Navy, Kennel. *Died 23 June 1996.*

ARMSTRONG, Sir Andrew (Clarence Francis), 6th Bt *cr* 1841, of Gallen Priory, King's County; CMG 1959; Permanent Secretary, Ministry of Mines and Power, Federation of Nigeria, retired; *b* 1 May 1907; *s* of E. C. R. Armstrong (*d* 1923) (*g s* of 1st Bt), FSA, MRIA, Keeper of Irish Antiquities and later Bluemantle Pursuivant, Heralds' Coll., and Mary Frances (*d* 1953), *d* of Sir Francis Cruise; *S* cousin, 1987; *m* 1st, 1930, Phyllis Marguerite (*d* 1930), *e d* of Lt-Col H. Waithman, DSO; 2nd, 1932, Laurel May (*d* 1988), *d* of late A. W. Stuart; one *s* (and one *s* decd). *Educ:* St Edmund's Coll., Old Hall, Ware; Christ's Coll., Cambridge (BA). Colonial Administrative Service : Western Pacific, 1929; Nigeria, 1940. *Recreation:* croquet. *Heir: s* Christopher John Edmund Stuart Armstrong, MBE, Lt-Col RCT [*b* 15 Jan. 1940; *m* 1972, Georgina Elizabeth Carey, *d* of Lt-Col W. G. Lewis; three *s* one *d*]. *Address:* No 5 Thamesfield Court, Wargrave Road, Henley-on-Thames, Oxon RG9 2LX. *T:* (01491) 577635. *Club:* Phyllis Court. *Died 21 Dec. 1997.*

ARMSTRONG, Prof. (Arthur) Hilary, MA; FBA 1970; Emeritus Professor: University of Liverpool, since 1972; Dalhousie University, Halifax, Nova Scotia, since 1983; *b* 13 Aug. 1909; *s* of Rev. W. A. Armstrong and Mrs E. M. Armstrong (*née* Cripps); *m* 1933, Deborah (*d* 1986), *d* of Alfred Wilson and Agnes Claudia Fox Pease; two *s* two *d* (and one *d* decd). *Educ:* Lancing Coll.; Jesus Coll., Cambridge (MA). Asst Lectr in Classics, University Coll., Swansea, 1936–39; Professor of Classics, Royal University of Malta, Valletta, 1939–43; Classical VIth Form Master, Beaumont Coll., Old Windsor, Berks, 1943–46; Lectr in Latin, University Coll., Cardiff, 1946–50; Gladstone Professor of Greek, Univ. of Liverpool, 1950–72; Vis. Prof. of Classics and Phil., Dalhousie Univ., Halifax, NS, 1972–83. Killam Sen. Fellow, Dalhousie Univ., 1970–71. *Publications:* The Architecture of the Intelligible Universe in the Philosophy of Plotinus, 1940, repr. 1967 (French trans. with new preface, 1984); An Introduction to Ancient Philosophy, 1947 (American edn, 1949, 4th edn, 1965, last repr. 1981); Plotinus, 1953 (American edn, 1963); Christian Faith and Greek Philosophy (with R. A. Markus), 1960 (American edn, 1964); Plotinus I–VII (Loeb Classical Library), 1966–88; Cambridge History of Later Greek and Early Mediæval Philosophy (Editor and part author), 1967, repr. 1970; St Augustine and Christian Platonism, 1968; Plotinian and Christian Studies, 1979; Classical Mediterranean Spirituality (Vol. 15 of World Spirituality) (Editor and part author), 1986; Hellenic and Christian Studies, 1990; contribs to Classical Qly, Jl Hellenic Studies, Jl Theological Studies, etc. *Recreations:* travel, gardening. *Address:* Minia, Livesey Road, Ludlow, Shropshire SY8 1EX. *T:* (01584) 872854. *Died 16 Oct. 1997.*

ARMSTRONG, Rt Hon. Ernest; PC 1979; *b* 12 Jan. 1915; *s* of John and Elizabeth Armstrong; *m* 1941, Hannah P. Lamb; one *s* one *d. Educ:* Wolsingham Grammar Sch. Schoolmaster, 1937–52; Headmaster, 1952–64. Chm., Sunderland Educn Cttee, 1960–65. MP (Lab) NW Durham, 1964–87. Asst Govt Whip, 1967–69; Lord Comr, HM Treasury, 1969–70; an Opposition Whip, 1970–73; Parly Under-Sec. of State, DES, 1974–75, DoE, 1975–79; Dep. Chm., Ways and Means and Dep. Speaker, 1981–87. Vice-Pres., Methodist Conf., 1974–75. Pres., Northern Football League, 1982–. *Recreation:* walking. *Address:*

Penny Well, Witton-le-Wear, Bishop Auckland, Co. Durham DL14 0AR. T: Witton-le-Wear (01388) 488397.
Died 8 July 1996.

ARMSTRONG, Hilary; *see* Armstrong, A. H.

ARMSTRONG, Dr Terence Edward; Founder Fellow, 1964–87, then Emeritus Fellow, and Vice-President, 1985–87, Clare Hall, and Reader in Arctic Studies, 1977–83, then Emeritus, Cambridge University; *b* 7 April 1920; *s* of Thomas Mandeville Emerson Armstrong and Jane Crawford (*née* Young); *m* 1943, Iris Decima Forbes; two *s* two *d*. *Educ:* Winchester; Magdalene Coll., Cambridge (BA 1941; MA 1947; PhD 1951). Served Army, 1940–46 (Intelligence Corps, parachutist, wounded at Arnhem). Scott Polar Research Institute: Res. Fellow in Russian, 1947–56; Asst Dir of Res. (Polar), 1956–77; Actg Dir, 1982–83; Tutor, Clare Hall, Cambridge, 1967–74. Extensive travel in Arctic and sub-Arctic, incl. voyage through NW Passage, 1954. US Nat. Sci. Foundn Sen. For. Scientist Fellowship, Univ. of Alaska, 1970; Vis. Prof. of Northern Studies, Trent Univ., Ontario, 1988. Chm., Wkg Gp on Arctic Science Policy, NERC, 1987–88. Jt Hon. Sec., Hakluyt Soc., 1965–90. Hon. LLD McGill, 1963; Hon. DSc Alaska, 1980. Cuthbert Peek Award, RGS, 1954; Victoria Medal, RGS, 1978. *Publications:* The Northern Sea Route, 1952; Sea Ice North of the USSR, 1958; The Russians in the Arctic, 1958; Russian Settlement in the North, 1965; (ed) Yermak's Campaign in Siberia, 1975; (jtly) The Circumpolar North, 1978; contribs to jls on socio-economic problems of Arctic and sub-Arctic regions. *Recreations:* making music, walking, foreign travel. *Address:* Harston House, Harston, Cambridge CB2 5NH. *T:* Cambridge (01223) 870262.
Died 21 Feb. 1996.

ARMYTAGE, Prof. Walter Harry Green; Professor of Education, University of Sheffield, 1954–82, then Emeritus Professor; Gerald Read Professor of Education, Kent State University, Ohio, 1982–85; *b* 22 Nov. 1915; *e s* of Walter Green Armytage and Harriet Jane May Armytage; *m* 1948, (Lucy) Frances Horsfall (*d* 1996); one *s*. *Educ:* Redruth County School; Downing Coll., Cambridge. 1st Cl. Hist. Trip. 1937, Cert. in Educn 1938. History Master, Dronfield Grammar Sch., 1938–39; served War of 1939–45 (despatches); Captain, London Irish Rifles; Univ. of Sheffield: Lectr, 1946; Sen. Lectr, 1952; Pro-Vice-Chancellor, 1964–68. Visiting Lecturer: Univ. of Michigan, USA, 1955, 1959, 1961, 1963, 1975; Newcastle, NSW, 1977; Lectures: Ballard-Matthews, University Coll. of North Wales, 1973; Cantor, RSA, 1969; Hawkesley, IMechE, 1969; S. P. Thompson, IEE, 1972; Galton, Eugenics Soc., 1974; Clapton, Leeds Univ., 1979. Hon. DLitt: NUU, 1977; Hull, 1980; Hon. LLD Sheffield, 1991. *Publications:* A. J. Mundella 1825–1897: the Liberal background of the Labour Movement, 1951; (with E. C. Mack) Thomas Hughes: the life of the author of Tom Brown's Schooldays, 1953; Civic Universities: aspects of a British tradition, 1955; Sir Richard Gregory: his life and work, 1957; A Social History of Engineering, 1961; Heavens Below: Utopian experiments in England 1560–1960, 1962; Four Hundred Years of English Education, 1964; The Rise of the Technocrats, 1965; The American Influence on English Education, 1967; Yesterday's Tomorrows: a historical survey of future societies, 1968; The French Influence on English Education, 1968; The German Influence on English Education, 1969; The Russian Influence on English Education, 1969; (ed jtly) Perimeters of Social Repair, 1978. *Recreations:* walking, gardening. *Address:* 3 The Green, Totley, Sheffield, South Yorks S17 4AT. *T:* (0114) 236 2515. *Club:* University Staff (Sheffield).
Died 13 June 1998.

ARNOLD, Rt Rev. George Feversham; *b* 30 Dec. 1914; *s* of Arnold Feversham and Elsie Mildred Arnold; *m* 1940, Mary Eleanor Sherman Holmes; one *s* one *d*. *Educ:* Univ. of King's Coll., Halifax, NS (LTh 1937, BD 1944); Dalhousie Univ. (BA 1935, MA 1938). Diocese of Nova Scotia: Rector: Louisbourg, 1938–41; Mahone Bay, 1941–50; St John's, Fairview, 1950–53; Windsor, 1953–58; Clerical Sec. and Diocesan Registrar, 1958–67; Exam. Chaplain to Bishop of Nova Scotia, 1947–70; Hon. Canon of All Saints Cathedral, 1959–63, Canon, 1963–67; Bishop Suffragan of Nova Scotia, 1967–75, Bishop Coadjutor, May-Sept. 1975; Bishop of Nova Scotia, 1975–79. Hon. DD King's Coll., Halifax, 1968. *Recreation:* yachting. *Address:* 56 Holmes Hill Road, Hantsport, NS B0P 1P0, Canada.
Died 31 Jan. 1998.

ARNOTT, Sir (William) Melville, Kt 1971; TD (and clasps) 1944; MD; FRCP, FRCPE, FRCPath; FRSE; British Heart Foundation Professor of Cardiology, University of Birmingham, 1971–74, then Emeritus Professor of Medicine; Consultant Physician, United Birmingham Hospitals, 1946–74; Hon. Consultant Physician, Queen Elizabeth Hospital, Birmingham, since 1974; *b* 14 Jan. 1909; *s* of Rev. Henry and Jeanette Main Arnott; *m* 1938, Dorothy Eleanor (decd), *er d* of G. F. S. Hill, Edinburgh; one *s*. *Educ:* George Watson's Coll., Edinburgh; Univ. of Edinburgh. MB, ChB (Hons), 1931, BSc (1st Cl. Hons Path.), 1934, MD (Gold Medal and Gunning Prize in Path.), 1937, Edinburgh; Murchison Scholar, 1931, McCunn Res. Schol. in Path., 1933–35, Crichton Res. Schol. in Path., 1935, Shaw Macfie Lang Res. Fellow, 1936–38, Edinburgh; MD Birmingham, 1947. 2nd Lieut RA, 1929; TA, 1929–39; War of 1939–45, served as specialist physician; five years foreign service (China, Malaya, Middle East, Siege of Tobruk; despatches, NW Europe); Lt-Col 1942. Asst Physician, Edinburgh Municipal Hosps, 1934–36; Hon. Assistant Physician, Church of Scotland Deaconess Hosp., Edinburgh, 1938–46; Edinburgh Royal Infirmary, 1946; Dir, Postgrad. studies in Medicine, Edinburgh Univ., 1945–46; William Withering Prof. of Medicine, Univ. of Birmingham, 1946–71. Consultant Adviser in Research to W Midlands RHA, 1974–79. Associate Examr in Medicine, London Univ., 1948–49; Examr in Medicine, to Univs of Cambridge, 1950–56, London, 1951–54, Wales, 1954–57, Queen's, Belfast, 1956–59, Edinburgh, 1959–62, Leeds, 1959–62, St Andrews, 1961–63, Oxford, 1961–68, Newcastle, 1964–67, Manchester, 1964–67, Singapore, 1965, East Africa, 1965, Malaysia, 1973, NUI, 1975–77. Member: UGC, 1954–63; MRC, 1965–69; Council, University Coll. of Rhodesia, 1964–70; UGC Hong Kong, 1966–75; Home Office Cttee (Brodrick) on Death Registration and Coroners, 1965–71; Tropical Medicine Res. Bd, 1967–71. Dep. Pres., First Internat. Conf. on Med. Educn, 1953. Editor, Clinical Science, 1953–58; Member, Editorial Board: Brit. Jl of Social Medicine; Brit. Jl of Industrial Medicine and Cardiovascular Research. Royal College of Physicians of Edinburgh: Mem., 1933; Fellow, 1937; John Matheson Shaw Lectr, 1958; Cullen Prize, 1958. Royal College of Physicians: Mem., 1947; Fellow, 1951; Mem. Council, 1954–56; Oliver-Sharpey Lectr, 1955; Examr for Membership, 1957–66; Croonian Lectr, 1963; Censor, 1969–71; Sen. Vice-Pres., and Sen. Censor, 1973. Foundation Fellow, Royal Coll. of Pathologists, 1963. FRMedSoc 1929 (late Senior Pres.); Hon. FRCPC 1957; Hon. FACP 1968 (Lilly Lectr, 1968); FRSE 1971. Member: Assoc. of Physicians; Physiological Soc.; Pathological Soc.; Med. Res. Soc.; Cardiac Soc.; Thoracic Soc.; Internat. Soc. of Internal Medicine. Sir Arthur Sims Commonwealth Trav. Prof. of Medicine, 1957. Lectures: Frederick Price, Trinity Coll., Dublin, 1959; Hall, Cardiac

Soc. of Aust. and NZ, 1962; Henry Cohen, Hebrew Univ. of Jerusalem, 1964; Alexander Brown Meml, Univ. of Ibadan, 1972; John Snow, Soc. of Anaesthetists, 1973. President: Edinburgh Harveian Soc., 1955; British Lung Foundation, 1984–87. Research: originally into experimental path. of renal hypertension and peripheral vascular disease; latterly, into physiology and path. of cardio-respiratory function. Hon. DSc: Edinburgh, 1975; Chinese Univ. of Hong Kong, 1983; Hon. LLD: Rhodesia, 1976; Dundee, 1976. *Publications:* some 50 scientific papers, principally in Lancet, Jl of Physiol., Jl of Path., Brit. Jl of Social Medicine, Edinburgh Med. Jl, etc. *Recreation:* travel. *Address:* Flat 20, Bushwood, 32 St James Road, Edgbaston, Birmingham B15 2NX. *T:* (0121) 440 2195. *Club:* Naval and Military.

Died 17 Sept. 1999.

ARONSON, Geoffrey Fraser, CB 1977; retired solicitor; Legal Adviser and Solicitor to Ministry of Agriculture, Fisheries and Food, to Forestry Commission, and to (EEC) Intervention Board for Agricultural Produce, 1974–79; *b* 17 April 1914; *er s* of late Victor Rees Aronson, CBE, KC, and Annie Elizabeth Aronson (*née* Fraser); *m* 1940, Marie Louise, *e d* of late George Stewart Rose-Innes; one *s* two *d. Educ:* Haileybury. Solicitor (Honours) 1936. Legal Dept, Min. of Agriculture and Fisheries, 1938; served War of 1939–45, Flying Control Officer, RAFVR; agricl employment and animal health legislation, MAFF, 1950–59; promoted Asst Solicitor, MAFF, 1960; Under-Sec. (Principal Asst Solicitor), 1971, when chiefly concerned with UK accession to EEC. Part-time consultant to Law Commn, 1979–84. Co-Founder, 1959, and Chm., 1959–74, Epsom Protection Soc. *Recreations:* environmental, travel, gardening. *Address:* 4 The Oaks, Downs Avenue, Epsom, Surrey KT18 5HH. *T:* (01372) 722431. *Club:* Royal Automobile.

Died 15 March 1998.

ARTHUR, Allan James Vincent, MBE 1948; DL; Vice Lord-Lieutenant of Essex, 1978–85; *b* 16 Sept. 1915; *s* of late Col Sir Charles Arthur, MC, VD, and Lady (Dorothy Grace) Arthur; *m* 1st, 1940, Joan Deirdre Heape (marr. diss. 1948); 2nd, 1949, Dawn Rosemary Everil, *d* of Col F. C. Drake, OBE, MC, DL; two *s* two *d. Educ:* Rugby Sch.; Magdalene Coll., Cambridge (MA). CU swimming team, 1935–38 (Capt. 1937); CU water polo team, 1937–38. Indian Civil Service (Punjab), 1938–47; Sub Divl Officer, Murree, 1941, Kasur, 1942–43; Dep. Comr, Attock, 1944–46, Multan, 1946–47; Sudan Political Service, 1948–54; District Comr, Khartoum, 1949–51, Shendi, 1951–54; Dep. Governor, Northern Province, 1954; J. V. Drake and Co. Ltd, Sugar Brokers, 1954–60; Woodhouse, Drake, and Carey Ltd, Commodity Merchants, 1960–75 (Chm., 1972–75). Member, Chelmsford Borough Council, 1973–79; Mayor, 1977–78; Governor: London Hosp. Med. Coll., 1956–74; Chigwell Sch., 1972–82; Brentwood Sch., 1973–85. Pres., Chelmsford Medical Educn and Res. Trust, 1981–88. Trustee, Friends of Essex Youth Orchestras, 1985–94. Member: Bd of Visitors, HM Prison, Chelmsford, 1973–79; Council, Univ. of Essex, 1980–87. President: Old Rugbeian Soc., 1982–84; Indian Civil Service (Retired) Assoc., 1997–. High Sheriff of Essex, 1971–72; DL Essex, 1974. *Publications:* contrib. to: The District Officer in India, 1930–47, 1980; Set under Authority, by K. D. D. Henderson, 1987. *Recreations:* swimming, shooting, gardening. *Address:* Mount Maskall, Boreham, Chelmsford CM3 3HW. *T:* (01245) 467776. *Clubs:* Oriental; Hawks (Cambridge). *Died 22 May 1998.*

ARTHUR, Peter Bernard; Deputy Chairman and Chairman of the Sub-Committees of Classification, Lloyd's Register of Shipping, 1976–84; *b* 29 Aug. 1923; *s* of Charles Frederick Bernard Arthur and Joan (*née* Dyer); *m* 1954,

Irène Susy (*née* Schüpbach); one *s* two *d. Educ:* Oundle Sch. Commnd 1943; Mahratta LI, 1943–47 (mentioned in despatches, Italy, 1945); RA, 1947–53. Mem. Cttee, Lloyd's Register of Shipping, and Vice-Chm., Sub-Cttees of Classification, 1967. Dir, Bolton Steam Shipping Co. Ltd, 1958–84; Chairman: London Deep Sea Tramp Shipowners' Assoc., 1970–71; Deep Sea Tramp Sect., Chamber of Shipping of UK, 1972–73; Bolton Maritime Management Ltd, 1982–83. *Recreations:* music, water colour painting, gardening. *Address:* Lower Terrace, 37A Peter Avenue, Oxted, Surrey RH8 9LG. *T:* (01883) 712962. *Died 20 May 1998.*

ARTHURE, Humphrey George Edgar, CBE 1969; MD; FRCS, FRCOG; Consulting Obstetric and Gynæcological Surgeon: Charing Cross Hospital; Queen Charlotte's Hospital; Mount Vernon Hospital; *b* 22 Jan. 1906; *s* of Rev. H. E. E. Arthure, Vicar of Mickleton, Glos; *m* 1936, Phyllis Edith Maxwell, (Dickie), (*d* 1993), *d* of James Munro. MRCS, LRCP 1931; MB, BS 1933; FRCS 1935; MD London 1938; FRCOG 1950 (Hon. Sec. 1949–56; Vice-Pres. 1964–67). Formerly Resident Obstetric Officer and Obstetrical Registrar, Charing Cross Hospital; Resident Medical Officer, Chelsea Hospital for Women. FRSocMed (Pres., Section of Obstetrics and Gynaecology, 1969); co-opted Mem. Council, RCS 1960; Pres., West London Medico-Chirurgical Soc., 1964; formerly: Chm., Central Midwives Board, and Adviser, Obstetrics and Gynæcology, DHSS; Mem., Standing Maternity and Midwifery Advisory Cttee. Served War of 1939–45, temp. Lt-Col, RAMC. *Publications:* Simpson Oration, 1972; (jtly) Sterilisation, 1976; contribs med. jls. *Address:* 12 Eyot Green, Chiswick Mall, W4 2PT. *T:* 0181–994 7698.

Died 29 Jan. 1996.

ARTON, Major Anthony Temple B.; *see* Bourne-Arton.

ARTUS, Ronald Edward, CBE 1991; non-executive Director: Electrocomponents plc, since 1990; GEC, since 1990; The Solicitors Indemnity Fund Ltd, since 1990; CLM Insurance Fund plc, since 1993; (independent) Member of Board, Securities and Futures Authority (formerly Securities Association Ltd), since 1990 (Deputy Chairman, since 1996); *b* 8 Oct 1931; *s* of late Ernest and of Doris Artus; *m* 1st, 1956, Brenda M. Touche (marr. diss.); three *s* one *d*; 2nd, 1987, Joan M. Mullaney, MD. *Educ:* Sir Thomas Rich's Sch., Gloucester; Magdalen Coll., Oxford (MA). Joined Prudential, 1954; Head of Economic Intelligence Department, 1958–71; Senior Assistant Investment Manager, 1971–73; Dep. Investment Manager, 1973–75; Jt Sec. and Chief Investment Manager, 1975–79; Dep. Chm., 1985–90; Prudential Corp. PLC: Gp Chief Investment Manager, 1979–90; an Exec. Dir, 1984–90, non-exec. Dir, 1990–93; Chairman: Prudential Portfolio Managers, 1981–90; Prudential Property Services, 1986–90; a Dir of various cos, Prudential Gp, until 1990. Director: Keyser Ullmann Holdings Ltd, 1972–80; Charterhouse Gp Ltd, 1980–82; Celltech Ltd, 1980–91; Imperial Cancer Res. Technology Ltd, 1988–98. Member: City Capital Markets Cttee, 1982–90 (Chm., 1988–90); Accounting Standards Cttee, 1982–86; Financial Law Panel, 1993–; Council, Inst. for Fiscal Studies, 1988–94; CBI City Industry Task Force, 1987; Lloyd's Task Force, 1991. Mem. Finance Cttee, 1975–, Mem. Council, 1994–, ICRF. Hon. Fellow, IIMR (formerly Soc. of Investment Analysts), 1980 (Mem. Council, 1964–76; Chm., 1973–75). *Publications:* contrib. various jls on economic and investment matters. *Recreations:* music (esp. opera), learning about art (esp. British Sch. and English watercolours). *Address:* GEC, 1 Stanhope Gate, W1A 1EH. *Club:* MCC.

Died 17 July 1999.

ASAAD, Prof. Fikry Naguib M.; *see* Morcos-Asaad.

ASFA WOSSEN HAILE SELLASSIE, HIH Merd Azmatch, Hon. GCMG 1965; Hon. GCVO 1930; Hon. GBE 1932; Crown Prince of Ethiopia, since 1930; *b* 27 July 1916; *e s* and *heir* of late Emperor Haile Sellassie, KG, and Empress Menen; *m* 1st, Princess Wallatta Israel (marr. diss.); (one *d* decd); 2nd, Princess Madfariash Wark Abebe; one *s* three *d. Educ:* privately; Liverpool Univ. Governor of Wollo province; Mem., Crown Council. Fought in Italo-Ethiopian War, 1935–36. Grand Cross: Légion d'Honneur; Belgian Order of Leopold; Order of the Netherlands; Order of Rising Sun, Japan; Order of White Elephant, Siam. *Heir: s* Prince Zara Yacob, *b* 18 Aug. 1953. *Died 17 Jan. 1997.*

ASH, Rear-Adm. Walter William Hector, CB 1962; WhSch; CEng; FIEE; *b* Portsmouth, Hants, 2 May 1906; *s* of Hector Sidney and Mabel Jessy Ash; *m* 1932, Louisa Adelaide Salt, Jarrow-on-Tyne; three *d. Educ:* City & Guilds Coll., Kensington; Royal Naval Coll., Greenwich. Whitworth Scholar, 1926; John Samuel Scholar, 1927. Asst Elect. Engr, Admiralty (submarine design), 1932–37; Elect. Engr, Admiralty (battleship design), 1937–39; Fleet Elect. Engr, Staff C-in-C Med., 1939–40; Supt Elect. Engr, Admiralty (supply and prod.), 1940–45; Supt Elect. Engr, HM Dockyard, Hong Kong, 1945–48; Supt Elect. Engr, Admiralty Engineering Lab., 1948–49; Comdr RN, HMS Montclare, 1950–51; Capt. RN, Admiralty (weapon control design), 1951–54; Capt. RN, Elect. Engr Manager, HM Dockyard, Devonport, 1954–58; Capt. RN, Ship Design Dept, Admiralty, 1959–60; Rear-Adm. 1960; subseq. Ship Dept Directorate, Admty, retd Aug. 1963. Vis. Lectr in electrical machinery design, RN Coll., Greenwich, 1934–37. Chairman IEE, SW Sub Centre, 1957–58. ADC to the Queen, 1958–60. *Recreation:* music (piano and organ). *Address:* 4 Vavasour House, North Embankment, Dartmouth, Devon TQ6 9PW. *T:* (01803) 834630. *Died 26 May 1998.*

ASHBURNHAM, Captain Sir Denny Reginald, 12th Bt *cr* 1661, of Broomham, Sussex; Captain South Staffordshire Regiment; *b* 24 March 1916; *o surv. s* of Sir Fleetwood Ashburnham, 11th Bt, and Elfrida, *d* of late James Kirkley, JP, Cleadon Park, Co. Durham; *S* father, 1953, *m* 1946, Mary Frances, *d* of Major Robert Pascoe Mair, Wick, Udimore, Sussex; two *d* (one *s* decd). *Heir: g s* James Fleetwood Ashburnham, *b* 17 Dec. 1979. *Address:* Little Broomham, Guestling, Hastings, East Sussex TN35 4HS. *Died 21 June 1999.*

ASHCROFT, James Geoffrey, CB 1988; Deputy Under Secretary of State, Finance, Ministry of Defence, 1985–88; *b* 19 May 1928; *s* of James Ashcroft and Elizabeth (*née* Fillingham); *m* 1953, Margery (*née* Barratt); one *s. Educ:* Cowley Sch., St Helens; Peterhouse, Cambridge (BA Hons Hist.). Min. of Supply, 1950–59; Min. of Aviation, 1959–61, 1964–65; Min. of Defence, 1961–64, 1965–68, 1970–73; Inst. of Strategic Studies, 1968–70; Under-Sec., Pay Board, 1973–74; Asst Under Sec. of State, Management Services, PE, 1974–76; Asst Under Sec. of State, Gen. Finance, MoD, 1976–84. *Publications:* papers on international collaboration in military logistics. *Recreation:* golf. *Address:* 1 Hawthorn Way, Shipston-on-Stour CV36 4FD. *T:* (01608) 663800. *Died 21 July 2000.*

ASHCROFT, Ven. Lawrence; Archdeacon of Stow and Vicar of Burton-on-Stather, 1954–62; *b* 1901; *s* of Lawrence Ashcroft; *m* 1927, Barbara Louise Casson; two *s* three *d. Educ:* University Coll., Durham; Lichfield Theological Coll. Deacon, 1926; priest, 1927; Curate of Ulverston, 1926–29, of Egremont, 1929–30; District Sec., Brit. and Foreign Bible Society, 1930–33; hon. mem. of staff, Southwell Minster, 1930–33; Vicar of St Saviour's, Retford, 1934–40; Chaplain to the Forces (Emergency Commission), 1940–43, then Hon. Chaplain; Rector of St Michael's, Stoke, Coventry, 1943; Rural Dean of Coventry, 1949–53; Hon. Canon of Coventry, 1952–53; Hon. Canon of Lincoln, 1954–62; Proctor in Convocation, Canterbury, 1955–62; Chaplain to High Sheriff of Lincolnshire, 1958, to British Embassy, Oslo, 1967, Luxembourg, 1968; Rector, St Philip's, Antigua, 1969, Manvers St Crispin, Toronto, 1970–79. Mem., Church Assembly, 1955–62. Governor, De Aston Grammar Sch., 1955–62; Founder and Chm., Brigg Church Sch., 1956–62. *Died 18 May 1996.*

ASHE, Sir Derick (Rosslyn), KCMG 1978 (CMG 1966); HM Diplomatic Service, retired; Ambassador and Permanent UK Representative to Disarmament Conference, Geneva, 1977–79 and Permanent Head of UK Delegation to UN Special Session on Disarmament, New York, 1977–78; *b* 20 Jan. 1919; *s* of late Frederick Allen Ashe and Rosalind Ashe (*née* Mitchell); *m* 1957, Rissa Guinness, *d* of late Capt. Hon. Trevor Tempest Parker, DSC, Royal Navy (*e s* of Baron Parker of Waddington, PC, a Lord of Appeal in Ordinary) and Mrs Marie Louise Parker; one *s* one *d. Educ:* Bradfield Coll.; Trinity Coll., Oxford. HM Forces, 1940–46 (despatches 1945). Joined HM Diplomatic Service; Second Sec., Berlin and Frankfurt-am-Main, 1947–49; Private Sec. to Permanent Under-Sec. of State for German Section of FO, 1950–53; First Sec., La Paz, 1953–55; FO, 1955–57; First Sec. (Information), Madrid, 1957–61; FO, 1961–62; Counsellor and Head of Chancery: Addis Ababa, 1962–64; Havana, 1964–66; Head of Security Dept, FCO (formerly FO), 1966–69; Minister, Tokyo, 1969–71; Ambassador to: Romania, 1972–75; Argentina, 1975–77. Knight of the Order of Orange-Nassau (with swords) (Netherlands), 1945. *Recreations:* gardening, antiques. *Address:* Dalton House, Hurstbourne Tarrant, Andover, Hants SP11 0AX. *T:* (01264) 736276. *Clubs:* Travellers, Beefsteak. *Died 4 May 2000.*

ASHE LINCOLN, Fredman; *see* Lincoln, F. A.

ASHFORD, George Francis, OBE 1945; retired; *b* 5 July 1911; *s* of G. W. Ashford and L. M. Redfern; *m* 1950, Eleanor Vera Alexander; two *s. Educ:* Malvern Coll.; Trinity Hall, Cambridge; Birmingham Univ. Served War of 1939–45, Army, N Africa and Italy (despatches 1944). Distillers Co. Ltd, 1937–67: Solicitor, 1937; Legal Adviser, 1945; Dir, 1956; Management Cttee, 1963–67; Dir, BP Co. Ltd, 1967–73, Man. Dir, 1969–73; Dir, Albright & Wilson Ltd, 1973–79. Mem., Monopolies and Mergers Commn, 1973–80. Pres., British Plastics Fedn, 1966–67; Vice-President: Soc. of Chemical Industry, 1966–69; Chem. Ind. Assoc., 1967–70. Mem., Economic Policy Cttee for Chemical Industry, 1967–74; Chm., Working Party on Industrial Review, 1973. Organiser, Meals on Wheels, Woodley and Sonning, 1983–86. *Recreation:* gardening. *Address:* The Old House, Sonning, Berks RG4 0UR. *T:* (01734) 692122. *Died 18 Nov. 1998.*

ASHFORD, Ven. Percival Leonard; Chaplain to the Queen, 1982–97; *b* 5 June 1927; *s* of late Edwin and Gwendoline Emily Ashford; *m* 1955, Dorothy Helen Harwood; two *s. Educ:* Kemp Welch Sch., Poole; Bristol Univ.; Tyndale Hall Theol Coll., Bristol. Deacon 1954, priest 1955; Asst Curate, St Philip and St James, Ilfracombe, 1954; Curate-in-Charge, Church of Good Shepherd, Aylesbury, 1956; Vicar, St Olaf's, Poughill, Bude, 1959; HM Prison Service: Asst Chaplain, Wormwood Scrubs, 1965; Chaplain: Risley Remand Centre, 1966; Durham, 1969; Wandsworth, 1971; Winchester, 1975; SW Reg. Chaplain of Prisons, 1977; Chaplain General of Prisons, 1981–85; Archdeacon to the Prison Service, 1982–85; Vicar of Hambledon, 1985–87; Permission to officiate, dio. Sarum, 1991–. Mem. Gen. Synod, C of E, 1985. Exam. Chaplain to Bishop of Portsmouth, 1986. Selector Chm., ACCM,

1988–89. *Publications:* contribs to: Dining with the Famous, 1995; By Royal Command, 1997. *Recreations:* choral and classical music, reading. *Address:* 45 Windsor Way, Alderholt, near Fordingbridge, Hants SP6 3BN. *T:* (01425) 655493. *Died 11 Oct. 1998.*

ASHLEY, Prof. Francis Paul, PhD; FDSRCS; Professor of Periodontology and Preventive Dentistry, since 1984 and Head, Guy's, King's and St Thomas' Dental Institute, King's College, since 1998, London University; *b* 21 July 1942; *s* of late George Francis Ashley and Mary (*née* McIntyre); *m* 1967, Carolyn Patricia Whittenbury; one *s* one *d. Educ:* De La Salle Coll., Pendleton; Turner Dental Sch., Univ. of Manchester (BDS 1964); Guy's Hosp. Dental Sch. (PhD 1974). FDSRCS 1969. FKC 2000. House Surgeon, Manchester Dental Hosp., 1965; Gen. Dental Practitioner, 1965–68; Guy's Hospital Dental School: Res Asst in Preventive Dentistry, 1968–71; Lectr in Periodontology and Preventive Dentistry, 1971–73; Sen. Lectr, 1973–79; Hon. Consultant, 1975; Reader in Periodontology and Preventive Dentistry, Univ. of London, 1979–84; Dean, Dental Sch., UMDS of Guy's and St Thomas' Hosps, 1991–98. Member: Health Educn Council, 1984–87; Standing Dental Adv. Cttee, 1998–; Chairman: Dental Health Adv. Panel, 1984–90; Dentifrice Accreditation Panel, BDA, 1990–; Mem., GDC, 1994– (Chairman: Health Cttee, 1997–; Central Examining Bd for Dental Hygienists, 1997–). Chm., Periodontal Res. Gp, Brit. Soc. for Dental Res., 1984–86; Pres., British Soc. of Periodontology, 1998–99 (Chm., Teachers' Sect., 1980–83); Hon. Sec., Assoc. of Profs of Dentistry, 1990–93. Scientific Advr, British Dental Jl, 1980–95 (Scientific Asst Ed, 1980–85); Mem. Editl Bd, Jl Clinical Periodontology, 1996–. *Publications:* various contribs to scientific literature. *Recreations:* gardening, walking, reading, opera. *Address:* GKT Dental Institute, Guy's Hospital, SE1 9RT. *Died 3 Sept. 2000.*

ASHTON, Prof. Norman (Henry), CBE 1976; DSc; FRS 1971; FRCP, FRCS, FRCPath, FRCOphth; Professor of Pathology, University of London, 1957–78, then Emeritus; Director, Department of Pathology, Institute of Ophthalmology, University of London, 1948–78; Consultant Pathologist, Moorfields Eye Hospital, 1948–78; *b* 11 Sept. 1913; 2nd *s* of Henry James and Margaret Ann Ashton. *Educ:* West Kensington Central Sch.; King's Coll. and Westminster Hosp. Med. Sch.; Univ. of London; DSc London, 1960. FRCPath 1963; FRCP 1967; FRCS 1976; FRCOphth 1989. Westminster Hospital: Prize in Bacteriology, 1938; Editor Hosp. Gazette, 1939–40; House Surg., House Phys., Sen. Casualty Officer and RMO, 1939–41; Asst Pathologist, Princess Beatrice Hosp., 1939; Dir of Pathology, Kent and Canterbury Hosp., and Blood Transfusion Officer of East Kent, 1941; Lt-Col RAMC, Asst Dir of Pathology and Officer i/c Central Pathological Lab., Middle East, 1946; Pathologist to the Gordon Hosp., 1947; Reader in Pathology, Univ. of London, 1953; Fellow in Residence, Johns Hopkins Hosp., Baltimore, 1953, and Visiting Prof. there, 1959. Emeritus Fellow, Leverhulme Trust; Vis. Research Fellow, Merton Coll., Oxford, 1980. Lectures: Walter Wright, 1959; Banting, 1960; Clapp (USA), 1964; Proctor (USA), 1965; Bradshaw, RCP, 1971; Montgomery, 1973; Foundation, RCPath, 1974; Jackson (USA), 1978; Foundn, Assoc. of Clinical Pathologists, 1985. Member: Brit. Nat. Cttee for Prevention of Blindness, 1973–78; Royal Postgrad. Med. Sch. Council, 1977–80; Council, RCPath, 1963–66 and 1976–78 (Founder Fellow); Governing Body, Brit. Postgrad. Med. Fedn, 1967–82, and Cent. Acad. Council, 1957–78 (Chm., 1967–70); Council, RSM, 1971–79, and Exec. Cttee, 1976–81; Med. Adv. Bd, British Retinitis Pigmentosa Soc.; Pathological Soc. of Great Britain and Ireland; European Assoc. for Study of Diabetes; Chapter Gen. and

Hosp. Cttee of St John; Oxford Ophthalmological Congress; Medical Art Soc.; Member, Committee of Management: Inst. of Ophthalmology, 1953–78, 1984–92; Inst. of Child Health, 1960–65; Cardio-Thoracic Inst., 1972–78; Inst. of Rheumatology, 1973–77; Member, Board of Governors: Moorfields Eye Hosp., 1963–66 and 1975–78; Hosp. for Sick Children, Gt Ormond St, 1977–80; Royal Nat. Coll. for the Blind, 1977–92; Brendoncare Foundn, 1984. President: Ophth. Sect., RSM, 1972–74; Assoc. of Clinical Pathologists, 1978–79; Ophth. Soc. of UK, 1979–81. Chairman: Brit. Diab. Assoc. Cttee on Blindness in Diabetes, 1967–70; Fight for Sight Appeal, 1980–91. Fellow, Inst. of Ophthalmology; FRSocMed. Hon. Life Mem., British Diabetic Association; Life Pres. European Ophth. Pathology Soc.; Pres. Brit. Div. Internat. Acad. of Pathology, 1962. Hon. Member: Assoc. for Eye Research; Hellenic Ophth. Soc.; British Div., Internat. Acad. of Pathology; Amer. Ophth. Soc.; Amer. Assoc. of Ophthalmic Pathologists; Gonin Club. Hon. Fellow: RSocMed; Royal Coll. of Ophthalmologists; Royal Coll. of Pathologists; Coll. of Physicians, Philadelphia; Amer. Acad. Ophthal. and Otolaryng. Mem. Editl Bd, Brit. Jl Ophthalmology, 1963–78, and Jl Histopathology. Trustee, Sir John Soane's Mus., 1977–82. Master, Soc. of Apothecaries of London, 1984–85; Freeman, City of London. Hon. Steward, Westminster Abbey, 1969–84. Hon. DSc Chicago. KStJ. Edward Nettleship Prize for Research in Ophthalmology, 1953; BMA Middlemore Prize, 1955; Proctor Medal for Research in Ophthalmology, USA, 1957; Doyne Medal, Oxford, 1960; William Julius Mickle Fellow, Univ. of London, 1961; Bowman Medal, 1965; Donder's Medal, 1967; Wm Mackenzie Memorial Medal, 1967; Gonin Medal, 1978; 1st Jules Stein Award, USA, 1981; Francis Richardson Cross Medal, 1982; Lord Crook Gold Medal, Spectacle Makers' Co., 1989; Internat. Pizart Vision Award, USA, 1991; Buchanan Medal, Royal Soc., 1996; Helen Keller Internat. Prize for Vision Res., 1998. *Publications:* contrib. to books; numerous scientific articles in Jl of Pathology and Bacteriology, Brit. Jl of Ophthalmology, and Amer. Jl of Ophthalmology. *Recreations:* painting, gardening. *Address:* 4 Blomfield Road, Little Venice, W9 1AH. *T:* (020) 7286 5536. *Clubs:* Athenæum, Garrick.

Died 4 Jan. 2000.

ASHWORTH, Sir Herbert, Kt 1972; Chairman: Nationwide Building Society, 1970–82 (Deputy Chairman, 1968–70); Nationwide Housing Trust, 1983–87; *b* 30 Jan. 1910; *s* of Joseph Hartley Ashworth; *m* 1936, Barbara Helen Mary, *d* of late Douglas D. Henderson; two *s* one *d. Educ:* Burnley Grammar Sch.; London Univ. (LLB, BSc (Econ)). General Manager, Portman Building Soc., 1938–50; General Manager, Co-operative Permanent Building Soc., 1950–61; Director and General Manager, Hallmark Securities Ltd, 1961–66. Dep. Chm., 1964–68, Chm., 1968–73, Housing Corp. Dir, The Builder Ltd, 1975–80. Chm., Surrey and W Sussex Agricl Wages Cttee, 1974–87. Vice-Pres., Building Socs Assoc., 1975–. *Publications:* Housing in Great Britain, 1951; Building Society Work Explained, 1942, 18th edn 1987; The Building Society Story, 1980. *Address:* 38 Mountford Close, Wellesbourne, Warwicks CV35 9QQ.

Died 29 Dec. 2000.

ASKEW, John Marjoribanks Eskdale, CBE 1974; *b* 22 Sept. 1908; *o s* of late William Haggerston Askew, JP, Ladykirk, Berwicks, and Castle Hills, Berwick-on-Tweed; *m* 1st, 1933, Lady Susan Egerton (marr. diss. 1966), 4th *d* of 4th Earl of Ellesmere, MVO; one *s* one *d*; 2nd, 1967, Rona Trotter, Clenghhead, Berwicks, *widow* of Major H. R. Trotter; 3rd, 1976, Priscilla Anne, *e d* of late Algernon Ross-Farrow. *Educ:* Eton; Magdalene Coll., Cambridge (BA). Lieut 2 Bn Grenadier Guards, 1932; Capt. 1940; Major 1943; served NW Europe 1939–40 and 1944–45.

Brigadier, Royal Company of Archers, Queen's Body Guard for Scotland. Convener: Berwicks CC, 1961; Border Regional Council, 1974–82. *Address:* Ladykirk, Berwicks TD15 1SU. *T:* (01289) 82229; Castle Hills, Berwick-on-Tweed TD15 1PB. *Clubs:* Boodle's; New (Edinburgh).   *Died 29 Nov. 1996.*

ASPINALL, John Victor; Chairman of the Trustees, Howletts and Port Lympne Foundation, since 1984; *b* 11 June 1926; *s* of late Col Robert Aspinall and Mary (*née* Horn, later Lady Osborne); *m* 1st, 1956, Jane Gordon Hastings (marr. diss. 1966); one *s* one *d*; 2nd, 1966, Belinda Musker (marr. diss. 1972); 3rd, 1972, Lady Sarah Courage (*née* Curzon); one *s. Educ:* Rugby Sch.; Jesus Coll., Oxford. Founded: Howletts Zoo Park, 1958; Clermont Club, 1962; Port Lympne Zoo Park, 1973; Aspinall's Club, 1978; Aspinall Curzon Club, 1984; Aspinalls, 1992–. Won gaming case Crown *v* Aspinall, 1958. Contested (Referendum), Folkestone and Hythe, 1997. *Publications:* The Best of Friends, 1976, Amer. edn 1977, German edn 1978; contributor to numerous publications. *Recreations:* wild animals, gambling. *Address:* 64 Sloane Street, SW1X 9SH. *T:* (020) 7235 2768, *Fax:* (020) 7235 4701.   *Died 29 June 2000.*

ASTON, Hon. Sir William (John), KCMG 1970; JP; Speaker, House of Representatives, Australia, 1967–73; *b* 19 Sept. 1916; *s* of Harold John Aston and Dorothea (*née* McKeown); *m* 1941, Beatrice Delaney Burrett; one *s* two *d. Educ:* Randwick Boys' High School. Served War, 1939–45, AIF in New Guinea, Lieut. Mayor of Waverley, 1952–53. MP (L) Phillip, 1955–61, 1963–72; Dep. Govt Whip, 1959–61 and 1963–64; Chief Govt Whip, 1964–67. Trustee, Parlt Retiring Allowances, 1964–67; Mem. and Dep. Chm., Joint Select Cttee on New and Perm. Parlt House, 1965–72; Chairman: House of Reps Standing Orders Cttee, 1967–72; Joint House Cttee, 1967–72; Library Cttee, 1967–72; Joint Cttee on Broadcasting of Parly Proceedings, 1967–72; Jt Chm., Inter-Parliamentary Union (Commonwealth of Aust. Br.) and Commonwealth Parly Assoc. (Aust. Br.), 1967–72. Leader, Aust. Delegn to IPU Conf., Ottawa, 1964; Convenor and Chm., First Conf. of Aust. Presiding Officers, 1968; rep. Australia at: opening of Zambian Parlt Bldg; IPU Symposium, Geneva, 1968; Funeral of Israeli Prime Minister Eshkol, 1969; Conf. of Commonwealth Presiding Officers, Ottawa, 1969, New Delhi, 1971; opened Aust. House, Mt Scopus, Univ. of Israel, 1971; led Parly delegn to Turkey, Yugoslavia, UK and to Council of Europe, 1971. JP NSW, 1954. Korean Order of Distinguished Service Merit (1st Class), 1969. *Recreations:* cricket, golf, football, fishing, bowls. *Address:* 55 Olola Avenue, Vaucluse, NSW 2030, Australia. *T:* (2) 93375992. *Clubs:* Royal Automobile of Australia (Sydney); Waverley Bowling, Royal Sydney Golf.   *Died 21 May 1997.*

ASTOR, Hon. Hugh Waldorf; JP; Director, Hutchinsons Ltd, 1959–78; *b* 20 Nov. 1920; 2nd *s* of 1st Baron Astor of Hever and Lady Violet Mary Elliot, *y d* of 4th Earl of Minto and *widow* of Major Lord Charles Mercer Nairne; *m* 1950, Emily Lucy, *d* of Sir Alexander Kinloch, 12th Bt; two *s* three *d. Educ:* Eton; New Coll., Oxford. Served War of 1939–45; Intelligence Corps, Europe and SE Asia (Lt-Col). Joined The Times as Asst Middle East Correspondent, 1947; elected to Board of The Times, 1956; Dep. Chm., 1959, resigned 1967 on merger with Sunday Times; Chm., The Times Book Co. Ltd, 1960, resigned 1967 on merger with Sunday Times. Chairman: Times Trust, 1967–82; Trust Houses Forte Council, 1971–97 (Mem. Council, 1962–97); Trusthouse Charitable Foundn, 1997–; Exec. Vice Chm., Olympia Ltd, 1971–73; Director: Hambro's plc, 1960–91; Winterbottom Energy Trust plc, 1961–86; Phoenix Assurance plc, 1962–85. Dep. Chm., Middlesex Hosp., 1965–74; Chm., King

Edward's Hospital Fund for London, 1983–88. Governor, Peabody Donation Fund, 1973–92 (Chm., 1981–92); Hon. Treasurer: Franco-British Soc., 1969–76; Marine Biol Assoc. UK, 1968–78; served on Council or governing body of RNLI, RYA, RORC, Air League. Mem. Ct of Assts, Fishmongers' Co. (Prime Warden, 1976–77). In partnership with Sir William Dugdale participated in air races, London-Sydney 1969, London-Victoria 1971. JP Berks, 1953; High Sheriff of Berks, 1963. *Recreations:* sailing, flying, shooting, diving. *Address:* Folly Farm, Sulhamstead, Berks RG7 4DF. *T:* (01734) 302326; 79 Ashley Gardens, Thirleby Road, SW1P 1HG. *T:* (020) 7976 6818. *Clubs:* Brooks's, Buck's, Pratt's; Royal Yacht Squadron, Royal Ocean Racing.
                              Died 7 June 1999.

ASTOR, Major Hon. Sir John (Jacob), Kt 1978; MBE 1945; ERD 1989; DL; Major, Life Guards; *b* 29 Aug. 1918; 4th *s* of 2nd Viscount Astor and Nancy Witcher, (Viscountess Astor, CH, MP), *d* of James W. Paul, Philadelphia, USA; *m* 1st, 1944, Ana Inez (marr. diss. 1972; she *d* 1992), *yr d* of late Señor Dr Don Miguel Carcano, KCMG, KBE; one *s* one *d* (and one *s* decd); 2nd, 1976, Susan Sheppard (marr. diss. 1985; she *d* 1997), *d* of late Major M. Eveleigh; 3rd, 1988, Marcia de Savary. *Educ:* Eton; New Coll., Oxford. Served War of 1939–45 (MBE, Legion of Honour, French Croix de Guerre). Contested (C) Sutton Div. of Plymouth, 1950; MP (C) Sutton Div. of Plymouth, 1951–Sept. 1959. PPS to Financial Sec. of Treasury, 1951–52. Chairman: Governing Body of Nat. Inst. of Agricultural Engineering, 1963–68; Agricl Res. Council, 1968–78; NEDC for Agricultural Industry, 1978–83. Member: Horserace Totalisator Bd, 1962–68; Horserace Betting Levy Bd, 1976–80. Steward of Jockey Club, 1968–71 and 1983–85. DL 1962, JP, 1960–74, Cambs. *Address:* The Dower House, Hatley Park, Hatley St George, Sandy, Beds SG19 3HL. *T:* (01767) 650266. *Club:* White's
                              Died 10 Sept. 2000.

ASTWOOD, Lt-Col Sir Jeffrey (Carlton), Kt 1972, CBE 1966 (OBE (mil.) 1946); ED 1942; Speaker of House of Assembly, Bermuda, 1968–72, retired; *b* 5 Oct. 1907; *s* of late Jeffrey Burgess Astwood, Neston, Bermuda, and Lilian Maude (*née* Searles); *m* 1928, Hilda Elizabeth Kay (*née* Onions); one *s* one *d. Educ:* Saltus Grammar School, Bermuda. Served local TA, 1922–60; retired as Lt-Col, having commanded, 1943–60. House of Assembly, Bermuda, 1948–72; Minister of Agriculture, Immigration and Labour, and Member of Exec. Council; Dep. Speaker, 1957–68. President: Exec. Cttee, Sandys Grammar Sch., 1950–57 (Chm. Trustees, 1950); Bermuda Sea Cadet Assoc., 1974–78; Chm., St James' Church Vestry. President: Atlantic Investment and Development Co. Ltd; J. B. Astwood & Son Ltd; Belfield-in-Somerset Ltd; Aberfeldy Nurseries Ltd. FInstD. *Recreations:* theatre, horticulture. *Address:* Greenfield, 6 Long Bay Lane, Somerset MA 03, Bermuda. *T:* (business) Hamilton 2922245; (home) 2341729. *Clubs:* Royal Bermuda Yacht, Sandys Boat, Somerset Lawn Tennis (Bermuda).   *Died 25 Dec. 1996.*

ATHOLL, 10th Duke of, *cr* 1703; **George Iain Murray;** DL; Lord Murray of Tullibardine 1604; Earl of Tullibardine 1606; Earl of Atholl 1629; Marquess of Atholl, Viscount of Balquhidder, Lord Murray, Balvenie and Gask, 1676; Marquess of Tullibardine, Earl of Strathtay and Strathardle, Viscount Glenalmond and Glenlyon, 1703—all in the peerage of Scotland; Representative Peer for Scotland in the House of Lords, 1958–63; *b* 19 June 1931; *s* of Lieut-Col George Anthony Murray, OBE, Scottish Horse (killed in action, Italy, 1945), and Hon. Mrs Angela Campbell-Preston (*d* 1981), *d* of 2nd Viscount Cowdray (she *m* 2nd, 1950, Robert

Campbell-Preston of Ardchattan, OBE, MC, TD); *S* kinsman, 1957. *Educ:* Eton; Christ Church, Oxford. Director: Westminster Press (Chm., 1974–93); BPM Holdings, 1972–83; Pearson Longman Ltd, 1975–83. Pres., Scottish Landowners Fedn, 1986–91 (Vice-Convener, 1971–76, Convener, 1976–79); Chm., RNLI, 1979–89 (Dep. Chm., 1972–79); Member: Cttee on the Preparation of Legislation, 1973–75; Exec. Cttee, Nat. Trust for Scotland (Vice-Pres., 1977–); Red Deer Commn, 1969–83. DL Perth and Kinross, 1980. *Heir: cousin* John Murray [*b* 19 Jan. 1929; *m* 1956, Margaret Yvonne, *o d* of late Ronald Leonard Leach; two *s* one *d*]. *Address:* Blair Castle, Blair Atholl, Perthshire PH18 5TJ; 31 Marlborough Hill, NW8 0NG. *Clubs:* Turf, White's; New (Edinburgh).
Died 27 Feb. 1996.

ATKINS, family name of **Baron Colnbrook.**

ATKINS, Leonard Brian W.; *see* Walsh-Atkins.

ATKINSON, Leonard Allan, CMG 1963; *b* 6 Dec. 1906; *s* of L. Atkinson; *m* 1933, Annie R., *d* of A. E. Wells; one *s* two *d. Educ:* Wellington Coll.; Victoria Univ. of Wellington, New Zealand. Joined Customs Dept, 1924; Inspector, Public Service Commission, 1941–44; Sec., 1944–47; Asst Comr, 1947–54; Commission Member, 1954–58; Chm., 1958–62; Chm., State Services Commission, NZ, 1963–66. *Recreation:* bowls. *Address:* 181 The Parade, Island Bay, Wellington, NZ. *Club:* Wellington (NZ). *Died 14 Jan. 1998.*

ATWELL, Sir John (William), Kt 1976; CBE 1970; FREng; FIMechE, FRSE; Chairman, Omega Software Ltd, 1982–84; *b* 24 Nov. 1911; *s* of William Atwell and Sarah Workman; *m* 1945, Dorothy Hendry Baxter (*d* 1996), *d* of J. H. Baxter and Janet Muir; no *c. Educ:* Hyndland Secondary Sch., Glasgow; Royal Technical Coll., Glasgow (ARTC); Cambridge Univ. (MSc). General Management, Stewarts and Lloyds Ltd, 1939–54; Dir 1955–61, Man. Dir 1961–68, G. & J. Weir Ltd; Dir, The Weir Group Ltd, 1961–74, and Chm., Engineering Div., 1968–74; Mem., BRB (Scottish), 1975–81. Chm., Scottish Offshore Partnership, 1975–81; Director: Anderson Strathclyde Ltd, 1975–78; Govan Shipbuilders Ltd, 1975–79. Mem., Bd of Royal Ordnance Factories, 1974–79. Chm., Requirements Bd for Mechanical Engineering and Machine Tools, DTI, 1972–76. Member: University Grants Cttee, 1965–69; NEDC Mech. Eng Cttee, 1969–74; Court, Strathclyde Univ., 1967–83 (Chm., 1975–80); Council, RSE, 1974–85 (Treas., 1977–82; Pres., 1982–85); Exec. Cttee, Scottish Council of Develt and Industry, 1972–77; Adv. Council for Applied R&D, 1976–80; Scottish Hosps Res. Trust, 1972–84; Council, Scottish Business Sch., 1972–80. Vice-Pres., IMechE, 1966–73, Pres., 1973–74; Vice-Chm., 1977–78, Chm., 1978–79, CEI. Hon. Fellow, Strathclyde Univ., 1990. Hon. LLD Strathclyde, 1973. *Recreation:* golf. *Address:* Malin Brae Cottage, Malin Court, Maidens, Girvan, Ayrshire KA26 9PB. *T:* (01655) 331285. *Clubs:* New (Edinburgh); Western (Glasgow).
Died 5 July 1999.

AUBREY, John Melbourn, (Peter), CBE 1979; *b* 5 March 1921; *s* of Melbourn Evans Aubrey and Edith Maria Aubrey; *m* 1949, Judith Christine Fairbairn; two *s* two *d* (and one *s* decd). *Educ:* St Paul's Sch.; Corpus Christi Coll., Cambridge (Mech. Sciences Tripos). FCIPA 1952. Armstrong Siddeley Motors Ltd, 1942–43; RE, 1943–47; Tootal Broadhurst Lee Co., 1947–49; Gill Jennings and Every, Chartered Patent Agents, 1949–55; Courtaulds Ltd, 1955–81, Consultant 1982–86. Chm., Baptist Insurance Co. Ltd, 1980– (Dir, 1971–); Mem. Council, Baptist Union of GB and Ireland, 1970–89. *Recreations:* gardening, sailing, swimming, skiing. *Address:* Clarence Cottage, 45 Clarence Hill, Dartmouth TQ6 9NY. *T:* (01803) 833194. *Clubs:* United Oxford & Cambridge University, Ski of GB; Dartmouth Yacht.
Died 27 Dec. 1996.

AUCKLAND, 9th Baron *cr* 1789 (Ire), 1793 (GB); **Ian George Eden;** non-executive Director: C. J. Sims & Co. Ltd; George S. Hall & Co. Ltd; *b* 23 June 1926; *s* of 8th Baron Auckland and Evelyn Vane, *d* of Col Arthur William Hay-Drummond; *S* father, 1957; *m* 1954, Dorothy Margaret, *d* of H. J. Manser, Eastbourne; one *s* two *d. Educ:* Blundell's Sch. Royal Signals, 1945–48; 3/4 County of London Yeomanry (Sharpshooters) (TA), 1948–53. Underwriting Mem. of Lloyd's, 1956–64. Pres., Inst. of Insurance Consultants, 1977–89. Chm., Anglo-S Pacific Group, CPA, 1985–. Member: New Zealand Soc.; Anglo-Finnish Parly Gp, 1965–. Pres., Surrey Co., Royal British Legion, 1983–; Council, RoSPA. Master, Broderers' Co., 1967–68; Hon. Mem., Court of Assistants, Blacksmiths' Co. Knight, 1st cl., White Rose (Finland), 1984. *Recreations:* music, theatre, tennis, walking. *Heir: s* Hon. Robert Ian Burnard Eden [*b* 25 July 1962; *m* 1986, Geraldine Caroll; one *d*]. *Address:* Tudor Rose House, 30 Links Road, Ashtead, Surrey KT21 2HF. *T:* (01372) 274393. *Clubs:* City Livery, World Traders.
Died 28 July 1997.

AUDLEY, 25th Baron *cr* 1312–13; **Richard Michael Thomas Souter;** Director, Graham Miller & Co. Ltd, retired 1983; *b* 31 May 1914; *s* of Sir Charles Alexander Souter, KCIE, CSI (*d* 1958) and Charlotte Dorothy Souter (*née* Jesson) (*d* 1958), aunt of 23rd Baron; *S* kinswoman, Baroness Audley (24th in line), 1973; *m* 1941, Pauline, *d* of D. L. Eskell; three *d. Educ:* Uppingham. FCILA. Military Service, 1939–46; Control Commission, Germany, 1946–50. Insurance Broker until 1955; Loss Adjuster, 1955–84. *Recreations:* shooting, gardening. *Co-heiresses presumptive: daughters* Hon. Patricia Ann Mackinnon [*b* 10 Aug. 1946; *m* 1969, Carey Leigh Mackinnon; one *s* one *d*]; Hon. Jennifer Michelle Carrington [*b* 23 May 1948; *m* 1978, Michael William Carrington; two *s* one *d*]; Hon. Amanda Elizabeth Souter, *b* 5 May 1958. *Address:* Friendly Green, Cowden, near Edenbridge, Kent TN8 7DU. *T:* (01342) 850682.
Died 27 June 1997.

AUSTERBERRY, Ven. Sidney Denham; Archdeacon of Salop, 1959–79, then Archdeacon Emeritus; *b* 28 Oct. 1908; *s* of late Mr and Mrs H. Austerberry; *m* 1934, Eleanor Jane Naylor; two *s* two *d. Educ:* Hanley High Sch.; Egerton Hall, Manchester. Deacon 1931, priest 1933; Curate, Newcastle-under-Lyme Parish Church, 1931–38; Vicar of S Alkmund, Shrewsbury, 1938–52; Vicar of Brewood, 1952–59; Hon. Clerical Sec., Lichfield Diocesan Conf., 1954–70; Rural Dean of Penkridge, 1958–59; Vicar of Great Ness, 1959–77. Hon. Canon, Lichfield Cathedral, 1968–79. *Address:* 6 Honeysuckle Row, Sutton Park, Shrewsbury SY3 7TW. *T:* (01743) 368080.
Died 22 March 1996.

AUSTICK, David; Chairman, Austicks Bookshops Ltd, since 1991 (Senior Partner, 1964–91); *b* 8 March 1920; *s* of Bertie Lister Austick and Hilda (*née* Spink); *m* 1944, Florence Elizabeth Lomath. Dir, James Miles (Leeds) Ltd, antiquarian bookseller, 1970–. Member: Leeds City Council (for W Hunslet), 1969–74, Hon. Alderman, 1988; Leeds Metropolitan District Council (for Hunslet), 1969–75; W Yorkshire County Council (for Otley and Lower Wharfedale), 1974–79. MP (L) Ripon, July 1973–Feb. 1974; contested (L) Ripon, 1974, (L) Cheadle, 1979, (L) Leeds, European Parlt, 1979. Vice Pres., Electoral Reform Soc. (Exec. Chm., 1984–86; Co-Sec., 1985–92); Member: European Movement; Fellowship of Reconciliation. Co. and Financial Sec., E. R. Ballot Services Ltd, 1989–91. *Address:* Austicks Bookshops, 16 Oxford Street, Harrogate HG1 1SN; Clarence House,

Clarence Place, Burley in Wharfedale, Ilkley LS29 7DW. *Club:* National Liberal. *Died 9 Feb. 1997.*

AUTY, Richard Mossop, CBE 1978 (OBE 1968); retired British Council officer; *b* 29 Jan. 1920; *s* of Rev. Thomas Richard Auty and Mrs Edith Blanche Auty (*née* Mossop); *m* 1st, 1944, Noreen Collins (marr. diss. 1949); one *d;* 2nd, 1956, (Anne) Marguerite Marie Poncet; one *s* one *d. Educ:* Hanley High Sch.; LSE, Univ. of London. Planning Br., Min. of Agriculture and Fisheries, 1942–46; Bureau of Current Affairs, 1946–49; Lectr, Goldsmiths' Coll. and Morley Coll., 1947–49; British Council, 1949–80: Lectr, Milan, 1949–57; Head, Overseas Students Centre, London, 1957–61; Reg. Rep., S India, 1961–65; Cultural Attaché, Brit. Embassy, Budapest, 1965–68; Director: S Asia Dept, 1968–70; Personnel Dept, 1970–72; Controller, European Div., 1972–76; Rep., France, and Cultural Counsellor, British Embassy, Paris, 1976–80. *Recreations:* literature, theatre, cinema. *Address:* 4 Thurlow Road, NW3 5PJ. *T:* (0171) 435 8982. *Died 26 Jan. 1996.*

AVELING, Alan John, CB 1986; Consultant, Mott Macdonald Group, 1988–95; Under Secretary, Director of Home Regional Services, Property Services Agency, Department of the Environment, 1980–88; *b* 4 Jan. 1928; *s* of late Herbert Ashley Aveling and Ethel Aveling; *m* 1960, Stella May Reed; one *s* one *d. Educ:* Fletton Grammar Sch.; Rugby Technical Coll. CEng; FIEE, FIMechE, FCIBSE. Air Min. Works Dir, Newmarket, 1951–52; RAF Airfield Construction, 2nd Allied Tactical Air Force, 1952–55; Air Min. HQ, 1955–61; Sen. Engr, War Office Works Dept, 1961–63; BAOR Services, Germany, MPBW, 1963–66; Directorate Personnel, MPBW, 1966–67; Superintending Engr, Overseas Defence and FCO Services, 1967–72; Reg. Works Officer, later Regional Dir, British Forces, Germany, PSA/DoE, 1972–76; Dir of Estate Management Overseas, 1976–78; Dir Eastern Region, PSA/DoE, 1978–80. *Recreations:* aviculture, ski-ing. *Club:* Royal Air Force. *Died 3 Feb. 1997.*

AVERY, Percy Leonard; Chairman, staff side, Civil Service National Whitley Council, 1977–80; General Secretary, Association of Government Supervisors and Radio Officers, 1951–79; *b* 10 March 1915; *s* of Percy James Avery and Frances Elisabeth Avery; *m* 1940, Joan Mahala Breakspear; one *s* one *d* (and one *d* decd). *Educ:* Woolwich Polytechnic. Served War: Navigator, RAF Bomber Comd, 1941–45; Flt Lieut. Exec. Sec., Internat. Fedn of Air Traffic Electronics Assoc., 1972–79. Member: Kent Area Health Authority, 1973–79; MoD Management Review Body, 1975–76; Civil Service Pay Rev. Board, 1978–79; CS Deptl Whitley Councils (various), 1949–77. Dir of Admin, British Karate Bd, 1979–82; Dir, Internat. Amateur Karate Fedn, 1983; Treasurer: English Karate Council, 1981–82; European Amateur Karate Fedn, 1982. Governor, Ruskin Coll.; Mem., Kent Age Concern, 1980–83. *Recreations:* athletics, Rugby, music, gardening. *Died 7 Jan. 2000.*

AVERY JONES, Sir Francis, Kt 1970; CBE 1966; FRCP; retired; Consulting Physician, Gastroenterological Department, Central Middlesex Hospital (Physician, 1940–74); Consulting Gastroenterologist: St Mark's Hospital (Consultant, 1948–78); Royal Navy (Consultant, 1950–78); Hon. Consulting Physician, St Bartholomew's Hospital, 1978; *b* 31 May 1910; *s* of Francis Samuel and Marion Rosa Jones; *m* 1st, 1934, Dorothea Pfirter (*d* 1983); one *s;* 2nd, 1983, K. Joan Edmunds. *Educ:* Sir John Leman Sch., Beccles; St Bartholomew's Hosp. Baly Research Scholarship, St Bart's, 1936; Julius Mickle Fellowship, University of London, 1952. Goulstonian Lecturer, Royal College of Physicians, 1947; Lumleian Lectr, RCP; Nuffield Lectr in Australia, 1952; First Memorial Lectr, Amer. Gastroenterological Assoc., 1954;

Croonian Lectr, RCP, 1969; Harveian Orator, RCP, 1980; Caroline Walker Meml Lectr, Caroline Walker Trust, 1992. Formerly Examiner: RCP; Univ. of London; Univ. of Leeds. Chairman: Emergency Bed Service, 1967–72; Med. Records Cttee, Dept of Health and Social Security; Medical Adv. Cttee, British Council, 1973–79; Member: Med. Sub-cttee, UGC, 1966–71; Brent and Harrow AHA, 1975–78; Dep. Chm., Management Cttee, King Edward VII Hosp. Fund, 1976–79; Mem. Council, Surrey Univ., 1975–82. Pres., United Services Section, RSM, 1974–75 (formerly Pres., section of Proctology); 2nd Vice-Pres., RCP, 1972–73; President: Medical Soc. of London, 1977–78; Medical Artists Assoc., 1980–91; British Digestive Foundn, 1981–92. Editor of Gut, 1965–70. Hon. FRCS 1981; Hon. FACP 1985; Hon. Mem., Amer., Canadian, French, Scandinavian and Australian Gastroenterological Assocs. Master, Worshipful Co. of Barbers, 1977–78. Hon. MD Melbourne, 1952; DUniv Surrey, 1980. Ambuj Nath Bose Prize, RCP, 1971; Moxon Medal, RCP, 1978; Fothergillian Gold Medal, Med. Soc., London, 1980; Henry L. Bockus Medal, World Orgn of Gastroenterology, 1982. *Publications:* Clinical Gastroenterology (jtly), 2nd edn 1967; (ed) Modern Trends in Gastroenterology First Series, 1952, Second Series, 1958; many articles on gastroenterology in the Medical Press. *Recreation:* water-side and herb gardening. *Address:* 19 Peter Weston Place, Chichester, West Sussex PO19 2PP. *T:* (01243) 773951.

Died 30 April 1998.

AVONSIDE, Rt Hon. Lord; Ian Hamilton Shearer; PC 1962; a Senator of the College of Justice in Scotland, 1964–84; *b* 6 Nov. 1914; *s* of Andrew Shearer, OBE, and Jessie Macdonald; *m* 1st, 1942; one *s* one *d;* 2nd, 1954, Janet Sutherland Murray (OBE 1958). *Educ:* Dunfermline High Sch., Glasgow Univ.; Edinburgh Univ. MA Glasgow, 1934; LLB Edinburgh, 1937. Admitted to Faculty of Advocates, 1938; QC (Scot.) 1952. Served War of 1939–45, RA; Major. Standing Counsel: to Customs and Excise, Bd of Trade and Min. of Labour, 1947–49; to Inland Revenue, 1949–51; to City of Edinburgh Assessor, 1949–51; Junior Legal Assessor to City of Edinburgh, 1951; Sheriff of Renfrew and Argyll, 1960–62; Lord Advocate, 1962–64. Mem., Lands Valuation Court, 1964 (Chm., 1975–84). Chm. Nat. Health Service Tribunal, Scotland, 1954–62; Mem. Scottish Cttee of Council on Tribunals, 1958–62; Chm. Scottish Valuation Advisory Council, 1965–68; Mem., Scottish Univs Cttee of the Privy Council, 1971–. Pres., Stair Soc., 1975–87. *Publications:* Purves on Licensing Laws, 1947; Acta Dominorum Concilii et Sessionis, 1951. *Recreations:* golf, gardening. *Address:* The Mill House, Samuelston, East Lothian EH41 4HG. *T:* Haddington (01620) 822396. *Club:* New (Edinburgh). *Died 22 Feb. 1996.*

AWDRY, Rev. Wilbert Vere, OBE 1996; Church of England clergyman, and author; *b* 15 June 1911; *s* of Rev. Vere Awdry and Lucy Louisa (*née* Bury); *m* 1938, Margaret Emily (*née* Wale) (*d* 1989); one *s* two *d. Educ:* Dauntsey's, W Lavington, Wilts; St Peter's Hall, Oxford (MA); Wycliffe Hall, Oxford (DipTh). Asst Master, St George's Sch., Jerusalem, 1933–36; deacon 1936, priest 1937; Curate: Odiham, Hants, 1936–38; W Lavington, 1938–40; King's Norton, Birmingham, 1940–46; Rector, Elsworth with Knapwell, Cambs, 1946–53; Rural Dean, Bourn, Cambs, 1950–53; Vicar, Emneth, Wisbech, 1953–65; authorised to officiate in Dio. of Gloucester, 1965–. *Publications: for children:* The Three Railway Engines, 1945; Thomas the Tank-engine, 1946; James the Red Engine, 1948; Tank-engine Thomas again, 1949; Troublesome Engines, 1950; Henry the Green Engine, 1951; Toby the Tram Engine, 1952; Gordon the Big Engine, 1953; Edward the Blue Engine, 1954; Four Little Engines, 1955; Percy the Small Engine, 1956; The Eight

Famous Engines, 1957; Duck & the Diesel Engine, 1958; Belinda the Beetle, 1958; The Little Old Engine, 1959; The Twin Engines, 1960; Branch Line Engines, 1961; Belinda beats the Band, 1961; Gallant Old Engine, 1962; Stepney the Bluebell Engine, 1963; Mountain Engines, 1964; Very Old Engines, 1965; Main Line Engines, 1966; Small Railway Engines, 1967; Enterprising Engines, 1968; Oliver the Western Engine, 1969; Duke the Lost Engine, 1970; Tramway Engines, 1972; Thomas' Christmas Party, 1984; *non fiction:* Map of the Island of Sodor, 1958, 4th edn 1988; (ed) Industrial Archaeology in Gloucestershire, 1973, 3rd edn 1983; (jt ed) A Guide to Steam Railways of Great Britain, 1979, 3rd edn 1984; (jtly) The Island of Sodor: its people, history and railways, 1987; (jtly) The Birmingham and Gloucester Railway, 1987. *Recreation:* reading. *Address:* Sodor, 30 Rodborough Avenue, Stroud, Glos GL5 3RS. *T:* (01453) 762321.

Died 21 March 1997.

AYLMER, Dr Gerald Edward, FBA 1976; Master of St Peter's College, Oxford, 1978–91, Hon. Fellow, 1991; *b* 30 April 1926; *s* of late Captain E. A. Aylmer, RN, and Mrs G. P. Aylmer (*née* Evans); *m* 1955, Ursula Nixon; one *s* one *d. Educ:* Winchester; Balliol Coll., Oxford (MA, DPhil). Served RN, 1944–47. Jane Eliza Proctor Vis. Fellow, Princeton Univ., NJ, USA, 1950–51; Jun. Res. Fellow, Balliol Coll., Oxford, 1951–54; Asst Lectr in History, Univ. of Manchester, 1954–57, Lectr, 1957–62; Prof. of History and Head of Dept of History, Univ. of York, 1963–78; Mem., Oxford History Faculty, 1978–. Vis. Mem., Inst. for Advanced Study, Princeton, 1975. Mem., Royal Commn on Historical Manuscripts, 1978– (Chm., 1989–94). Pres., RHistS, 1984–88 (Hon. Vice Pres., 1988–); Hon. Vice-President: Cromwell Assoc., 1991–; Historical Assoc., 1992–. Mem., Editorial Bd, History of Parliament, 1969–98 (Chm., 1989–98). Hon. DLitt Exeter, 1991; Hon. LittD Manchester, 1991. *Publications:* The King's Servants, 1961, 2nd edn 1974; (ed) The Diary of William Lawrence, 1962; The Struggle for the Constitution, 1963, 5th edn 1975; (ed) The Interregnum, 1972, 2nd edn 1974; The State's Servants, 1973; (ed) The Levellers in the English Revolution, 1975; (ed with Reginald Cant) A History of York Minster, 1978; Rebellion or Revolution?: England 1640–1660, 1986; articles and revs in learned jls. *Address:* The Old Captains, Hereford Road, Ledbury, Herefordshire HR8 2PX. *T:* (01531) 670817; 18 Albert Street, Jericho, Oxford OX2 6AZ. *T:* (01865) 512383. *Died 17 Dec. 2000.*

AYOUB, John Edward Moussa, FRCS; Consulting Surgeon, Moorfields Eye Hospital, since 1973 (Surgeon, 1950–73); Consulting Ophthalmic Surgeon: London Hospital (later Royal London Hospital), since 1973 (Surgeon, 1947–73); Royal Masonic Hospital, since 1973 (Consultant, 1967–73); Royal Navy; *b* 7 Sept. 1908; British; *m* 1939, Madeleine Marion Coniston Martin; one *s* one *d. Educ:* St Paul's Sch.; Lincoln Coll., Oxford; St Thomas' Hospital. BM, BCh Oxon 1933; FRCS 1935. Fellow, and Past Vice-Pres. Section of Ophthalmology, RSM; Past Mem. Council, Faculty of Ophthalmologists (Vice-Pres., 1959–). Served War of 1939–45, Surg. Lieut-Comdr RNVR, specialist in ophthalmology. Visiting Consultant Ophthalmologist to Western Memorial Hosp.,

Newfoundland, 1974. *Publications:* contributions to medical journals. *Recreation:* gardening. *Address:* 2 Clarendon Road, Boston Spa, near Wetherby, West Yorks LS23 6NG. *Clubs:* Leander; Royal Cruising.

Died 6 July 1999.

AZIKIWE, Rt Hon. Nnamdi, GCFR 1980; PC 1960; LLD, DLitt, MA, MSc; Ndichie Chief Owelle of Onitsha, 1973; Leader, Nigeria People's Party, 1979–83; (First) President of the Federal Republic of Nigeria, 1963–66; Governor-General and Commander-in-Chief of Nigeria, 1960–63; *b* Zungeru, Northern Nigeria, 16 Nov. 1904; *s* of Obededom Chukwuemeka and Rachel Chinwe Azikiwe; *m* 1936, Flora Ogbenyeanu Ogoegbunam, *d* of Chief Ogoegbunam, the Adazia of Onitsha (Ndichie Chief); three *s* one *d. Educ:* CMS Central Sch., Onitsha; Methodist Boys' High Sch., Lagos; Storer Coll., Harpers Ferry, W Va, USA; Howard Univ., Washington, DC; Lincoln Univ., Pa; Univ. of Pennsylvania. Overseas Fellow, Inst. Journalists, London, 1962 (Mem., 1933–). Editor-in-Chief, African Morning Post, Accra, 1934–37; Editor-in-Chief, West African Pilot, 1937–45; Correspondent for Associated Negro Press, 1944–47; Gen. Sec., Nat. Council of Nigeria and the Cameroons, 1944–46 (Pres., 1946–60); Correspondent for Reuter's, 1944–46; Chm. African Continental Bank Ltd, 1944–53. MLC Nigeria, 1947–51; Mem. Foot Commission for Nigerianisation of Civil Service, 1948. Leader of Opposition in the Western House of Assembly, 1952–53; Mem. Eastern House of Assembly, 1954–59; MHR 1954; Minister, Eastern Nigeria, 1954–57; Leader, Educational Missions to UK and USA, for establishment of Univ. of Nigeria, 1955 and 1959; Premier of Eastern Nigeria, 1954–59; Pres., Exec. Council of Govt of E Nigeria, 1957–59; President of Senate of Federation, Jan.-Nov. 1960. NPP Candidate, Presidential Election, 1979. Mem., Council of State, 1979–83. Ndichie Chief Ozizani Obi of Onitsha, 1963–72. Chm., Provisional Council of Univ. of Nigeria, 1960–61; Chancellor of Univ. of Nigeria, 1961–66, of Univ. of Lagos, 1970–76. Jt Pres., Anti-Slavery Soc. for Human Rights, London, 1970– (Vice-Pres., 1966–69). (Life) FREconS; (Life) FRAI; (Life) Mem. British Association for Advancement of Science; Member: American Soc. of International Law; American Anthropological Assoc. Pres. numerous sporting assocs and boards, 1940–60; Mem., Nigerian Olympic Cttee, 1950–60. Hon. DCL Liberia, 1969; Hon. DSc Lagos, 1972. KStJ 1960–66. *Publications:* Liberia in World Politics, 1934; Renascent Africa, 1937; The African in Ancient and Mediaeval History, 1938; Land Tenure in Northern Nigeria, 1942; Political Blueprint of Nigeria, 1943; Economic Reconstruction of Nigeria, 1943; Economic Rehabilitation of Eastern Nigeria, 1955; Zik: a selection of speeches, 1961; Meditations: a collection of poems, 1965; My Odyssey, 1971; Military Revolution in Nigeria, 1972; Dialogue on a New Capital for Nigeria, 1974; Treasury of West African Poetry; Democracy with Military Vigilance, 1974; Onitsha Market Crisis, 1975; Civil War Soliloquies: further collection of poems, 1976; Ideology for Nigeria, 1978. *Recreations:* athletics, boxing, cricket, soccer, swimming, tennis, reading. *Address:* Onuiyi Haven, PO Box 7, Nsukka, Nigeria.

Died 11 May 1996.

B

BABINGTON, William, CBE 1972; QFSM 1969; Chief Officer, Kent County Fire Brigade, 1966–76, retired; *b* 23 Dec. 1916; *s* of William and Annie Babington; *m* 1940, Marjorie Perdue Le Seelleur; one *d. Educ:* King Edward's Grammar Sch., Birmingham. Addtl Supt of Police, Assam, India, 1942–44; Instructor, Fire Service Coll., 1951–53; Divl Officer, Hampshire Fire Service, 1954–59; Asst Chief Officer, Suffolk and Ipswich Fire Service, 1959–62; Dep. Chief Officer, Lancashire Fire Brigade, 1962–66. *Recreations:* sailing, travel. *Address:* Alpine Cottage, Grouville, Jersey JE3 9AP. *T:* Jersey (01534) 852737.
Died 26 Oct. 1998.

BADDELEY, Very Rev. William Pye; Dean Emeritus of Brisbane, 1981; *b* 20 March 1914; *s* of W. H. Clinton-Baddeley and Louise Bourdin, Shropshire; *m* 1947, Mary Frances Shirley, *d* of Col E. R. C. Wyatt, CBE, DSO; one *d. Educ:* Durham Univ. (BA 1940); St Chad's Coll., Durham; Cuddesdon Coll., Oxford. Deacon, 1941; priest, 1942; Curate of St Luke, Camberwell, 1941–44; St Anne, Wandsworth, 1944–46; St Stephen, Bournemouth, 1946–49; Vicar of St Pancras (with St James and Christ Church from 1954), 1949–58; Dean of Brisbane, 1958–67; Rector of St James's, Piccadilly, 1967–80; RD of Westminster (St Margaret's), 1974–79; Commissary to: Archbishop of Brisbane, 1967–81; Bishop of Wangaratta, 1970–81; Archbishop of Papua New Guinea, 1972–80; Bishop of Newcastle, NSW, 1976–81. Member: London Diocesan Synod, 1970–80; Bishop of London's Council, 1975–80. Chaplain: Elizabeth Garrett Anderson Hospital, London, 1949–59; St Luke's Hostel, 1952–54; Qld Minty Anglican Soc., 1960–64; St Martin's Hosp., Brisbane, 1960–67; London Companions of St Francis, 1968–80; Lord Mayor of Westminster, 1968–69 and 1974–75; Actors' Church Union, 1968–70, Royal Acad. of Arts, 1968–80; Vis. Chaplain, Westminster Abbey, 1980–. Hon. Chaplain to: Archbishop of Brisbane (Diocesan Chaplain, 1963–67); Union Soc. of Westminster, 1972–80. President: Brisbane Repertory Theatre, 1961–64; Qld Univ. Dramatic Soc., 1961–67; Qld Ballet Co., 1962–67; Dir, Australian Elizabethan Theatre Trust, 1963–67; Mem. Council of Management, Friends of Royal Academy, 1978–; Chairman: Diocesan Radio and Television Council, 1961–67; weekly television Panel "Round Table", 1962–66; monthly television Panel "What Do YOU Think", 1960–67; Pres., Connard and Seckford Players, 1984. Governor: Burlington Sch., 1967–76; Archbishop Tenison's Sch., 1967–80; Chairman: Assoc. for Promoting Retreats, 1967–80; Malcolm Sargent Cancer Fund for Children, 1968–92 (Hon. Consultant, 1992–); Cttee for Commonwealth Citizens in China, 1970–73; Mem. Council, Metropolitan Hosp. Sunday Fund, 1968–78; Vice-Pres., Cancer Relief Appeal, 1977–. Life Governor of Thomas Coram Foundation, 1955. Mem. Chapter-Gen., OStJ, 1974–. ChStJ 1971 (SBStJ 1959). *Recreations:* theatre, music, photography. *Address:* Cumberland House, Woodbridge, Suffolk IP12 4AH. *T:* (01394) 384104. *Clubs:* East India, Carlton, Arts.
Died 31 May 1998.

BADENOCH, Sir John, Kt 1984; DM; FRCP, FRCPE; Hans Sloane Fellow, Royal College of Physicians, 1985–91; Emeritus Fellow, Merton College, Oxford University, 1987; *b* 8 March 1920; *s* of William Minty Badenoch, MB, and Ann Dyer Badenoch (*née* Coutts); *m* 1944, Anne Newnham, *d* of Prof. Lancelot Forster; two *s* two *d. Educ:* Rugby Sch.; Oriel College, Oxford. MA;

DM 1952; FRCP 1959; FRCPE 1982. Rockefeller Med. Studentship, Cornell Univ. Med. Coll., 1941. Res. Asst, Nuffield Dept of Clin. Medicine, Oxford, 1949–56; Dir, Clin. Studies, Univ. of Oxford, 1954–65; Consultant Phys., Oxfordshire HA, 1956–85; Univ. Lectr in Medicine, Univ. of Oxford, 1956–85. Former Mem., Board of Governors of United Oxford Hosps; Mem. Board, Oxford AHA(T), 1974–83; Mem., GMC, 1984–89. Royal College of Physicians: Pro-Censor and Censor, 1972–73; Sen. Censor and Sen. Vice-Pres., 1975–76; Goulstonian Lectr, 1960; Lumleian Lectr, 1977. Examiner in Medicine at various times for the Universities of Oxford, Cambridge, Manchester, QUB and NUI. Member: Assoc. of Physicians of GB and Ireland; Med. Res. Soc.; British Soc. of Haematology; British Soc. of Gastroenterology. Liveryman, Soc. of Apothecaries. *Publications:* (ed jtly) Recent Advances in Gastroenterology, 1965, 2nd edn 1972; various papers in the field of gastroenterology and medicine. *Recreations:* reading, walking, natural history. *Address:* 21 Hartley Court, 84 Woodstock Road, Oxford OX2 7PF. *T:* Oxford (01865) 511311.
Died 16 Jan. 1996.

BAELZ, Very Rev. Peter Richard; Dean of Durham, 1980–88, then Dean Emeritus; *b* 27 July 1923; 3rd *s* of Eberhard and Dora Baelz; *m* 1950, Anne Thelma Cleall-Harding; three *s. Educ:* Dulwich Coll.; Cambridge Univ. (BA 1944, MA 1948, BD 1971); DD Oxon 1979. Deacon 1947, priest 1950; Asst Curate: Bournville, 1947–50; Sherborne, 1950–52; Asst Chap., Ripon Hall, Oxford, 1952–53; Rector of Wishaw, Birmingham, 1953–56; Vicar of Bournville, 1956–60; Fellow and Dean, Jesus Coll., Cambridge, 1960–72; University Lectr in Divinity, Cambridge, 1966–72; Canon of Christ Church and Regius Prof. of Moral and Pastoral Theology, Univ. of Oxford, 1972–79. Hon. Prof., Univ. of Wales, 1993–98. Hulsean Lectr, 1965–66; Bampton Lectr, 1974. Hon. DD Durham, 1993. *Publications:* Prayer and Providence, 1968; Christian Theology and Metaphysics, 1968; The Forgotten Dream, 1975; Ethics and Belief, 1977; Does God Answer Prayer?, 1982; contributor to: Traditional Virtues Reassessed, 1964; Faith, Fact and Fantasy, 1964; The Phenomenon of Christian Belief, 1970; Christianity and Change, 1971; Christ, Faith and History, 1972; Is Christianity Credible?, 1981; God Incarnate: story and belief, 1981; Ministers of the Kingdom, 1985; By What Authority?, 1987; Embracing the Chaos, 1990; The Weight of Glory, 1991; Tradition and Unity, 1991; Using the Bible Today, 1991; Companion to Contemporary Architectural Thought, 1993; This Sumptuous Church, 1993; Veritatis Splendor: a response, 1994; Preaching from the Cathedrals, 1997; The Last Judgement, Sculpture by Anthony Caro, 1999. *Recreations:* walking, motoring. *Address:* 36 Brynteg, Llandrindod Wells, Powys LD1 5HB. *T:* (01597) 825404.
Died 15 March 2000.

BAGGLEY, (Charles) David (Aubrey), CBE 1980; MA; Headmaster of Bolton School, 1966–83; *b* 1 Feb. 1923; *s* of A. C. and M. Baggley, Bradford, Yorks; *m* 1st, 1949, Marjorie Asquith Wood (marr. diss. 1983), *d* of M. H. Wood, Harrogate; one *s* one *d*; 2nd, 1983, Julia Hazel Yorke, *d* of S. Morris, Sonning-on-Thames. *Educ:* Bradford Grammar Sch.; King's Coll., Cambridge (1942 and 1945–47) (Exhibitioner in Classics, Scholar in History: Class I, Part II of Historical Tripos, 1947; BA 1947, MA 1952). Temp. Sub Lieut, RNVR, 1942–45. History Master, Clifton Coll., 1947–50; Head of History Side, Dulwich

Coll., 1950–57; Headmaster, King Edward VII Sch., Lytham, 1957–66. Chm., HMC, 1978. Schools Liaison Advr, Salford Univ., 1983–91. Mem., Bolton Civic Trust, 1968–94. Gov., Giggleswick School, 1985–94. *Recreations:* walking, gardening, reading. *Address:* Masters, Thames Street, Sonning-on-Thames, Reading RG4 6UR. *Died 22 Oct. 1999.*

BAGNALL, Richard Maurice, MBE 1945; Deputy Chairman, Tube Investments Ltd, 1976–81, Managing Director, 1974–81, Director, 1969–81; *b* 20 Nov. 1917; *s* of late Francis Edward Bagnall, OBE and Edith Bagnall; *m* 1946, Irene Pickford; one *s* one *d. Educ:* Repton. Served War, 1939–45: RA, Shropshire Yeomanry, 1939–43 (despatches); Bde Major, 6 AGRA Italy, 1943–45. Joined Tube Investments Ltd, 1937. Chm., Round Oak Steel Works Ltd, 1976–81 (Dir, 1974–81). Governor, King's Sch., Worcester, 1977–81. Bronze Star, USA, 1945. *Recreations:* golf, gardening, photography. *Address:* Apartment 29A, Alto Club, Alvor, 8500 Portimao, Algarve, Portugal. *Club:* MCC.

Died 22 April 1997.

BAILEY, His Honour Desmond Patrick; a Circuit Judge (formerly Judge of County Courts), 1965–79; *b* 6 May 1907; 3rd *s* of Alfred John Bailey, Bowdon, Cheshire, and Ethel Ellis Johnson; unmarried. *Educ:* Brighton Coll.; Queens' Coll., Cambridge (BA, LLB). Called to Bar, Inner Temple, 1931. Northern Circuit; Recorder of Carlisle, 1963–65. Served War of 1939–45: Rifle Brigade, Lancashire Fusiliers, Special Operations Executive, North Africa, Italy (Major). *Address:* c/o Davies Wallis Foyster, 37 Peter Street, Manchester M2 5GB.

Died 29 Jan. 1996.

BAILEY, Eric; Director, Plymouth Polytechnic, 1970–74, retired; *b* 2 Nov. 1913; *s* of Enoch Whittaker Bailey, Overton Hall, Sandbach, Cheshire; *m* 1942, Dorothy Margaret Laing, Stockport; one *s* one *d. Educ:* King's Sch., Macclesfield; Manchester Univ. BSc Hons; CEng, FRIC, MIChemE; DipEd. Lectr, Stockport Coll. of Technology, 1936–41; industrial chemist, 1941–45; Lectr, Enfield Coll. of Technology, 1945–46; Vice-Principal, Technical Coll., Worksop, 1946–51; Principal: Walker Technical Coll., Oakengates, Salop, 1951–59; Plymouth Coll. of Technology, 1959–69. *Recreations:* putting colour into gardens, photography, pursuing leisure and voluntary activities. *Address:* 3 St Bridget Avenue, Crownhill, Plymouth, Devon PL6 5BB. *T:* (01752) 771426. *Club:* Rotary (Plymouth). *Died 14 July 1997.*

BAILEY, Fiona Mary; *see* Macpherson, F. M.

BAILEY, Sir Harold (Walter), Kt 1960; MA, W Aust.; MA, DPhil Oxon; FBA 1944; Professor of Sanskrit, Cambridge University, 1936–67, Professor Emeritus, 1967; Life Fellow, Queens' College, Cambridge, 1956 (Fellow, 1936–56; Hon. Fellow, 1967); *b* Devizes, Wilts, 16 Dec. 1899. Was Lecturer in Iranian Studies at Sch. of Oriental Studies. Member of: Danish Academy, 1946; Norwegian Academy, 1947; Kungl. Vitterhets Historie och Antikvitets Akademien, Stockholm, 1948; Governing Body, SOAS, Univ. of London, 1946–70; L'Institut de France (Associé étranger, Académie des Inscriptions et Belles-Lettres) 1968. President: Philological Soc., 1948–52; Royal Asiatic Society, 1964–67 (Gold Medal, 1972; Denis Sinor Medal for Inner Asian Studies, 1993); Soc. for Afghan Studies, 1972–79; Soc. of Mithraic Studies (1971), 1975–; Corpus Inscriptionum Iranicarum, 1987– (Mem., 1954; Chm., 1967–87); Chm., Anglo-Mongolian Soc., 1979–81. Chm., Ancient India and Iran Trust, 1978–91. FAHA 1971; Hon. Fellow: SOAS, London Univ., 1963; Queens' Coll., Cambridge, 1967; St Catherine's Coll., Oxford, 1976. Hon. Mem., Bhandarkar Oriental Res. Inst., Poona, 1968. Hon. DLitt: W Aust.,

1963; ANU, 1970; Oxon, 1976; Hon. DD Manchester, 1979. *Publications:* Zoroastrian Problems in the Ninth Century Books, 1938; Indo-Scythian Studies, Khotanese Texts, I–VIII, 1945–85; Khotanese Buddhist Texts, 1951, 2nd edn 1981; Saka Documents I–IV (portfolios) 1960–67; Saka Documents V (text vol.), 1968; Dictionary of Khotan Saka, 1979; The Culture of the Sakas in Ancient Iranian Khotan, 1981; numerous articles, 1930–. *Address:* Queens' College, Cambridge CB3 9ET.

Died 11 Jan. 1996.

BAILEY, John Everett Creighton, CBE 1947; Executive Chairman, Difco Laboratories (UK) Ltd, 1970–75; Chairman and Managing Director, Baird & Tatlock Group of Cos, 1941–69; *b* 2 Nov. 1905; *s* of late John Edred Bailey and Violet Constance Masters; *m* 1928, Hilda Anne Jones (*d* 1982); one *s* four *d. Educ:* Brentwood Sch. Peat Marwick Mitchell & Co., 1925–31; Director: Derbyshire Stone Ltd, 1959–69; Tarmac Derby Ltd, 1969–70; G. D. Searle & Co., 1969–70, and other companies. Pres. Scientific Instrument Manufacturers Assoc., 1945–50; Chm., British Laboratory Ware Assoc., 1950–52, Pres., 1974–83; Chm., British Sci. Instr. Research Assoc., 1952–64 (Pres. 1964–71; first Companion, SIRA Inst.); Mem., Grand Council FBI, 1945–58; Mem., Admty Chemical Adv. Panel, 1940–50; Mem., BoT Exhibns Adv. Cttee, 1957–65, and Census of Production Adv. Cttee, 1960–68; formerly Special Member, Prices and Incomes Board. Freeman of City of London, 1955; Master: Co. of Scientific Instrument Makers, 1957–58, 1974–75; Co. of Needlemakers, 1981–83. Fellow, Inst. of Export, 1955; MRI; CIMgt (CBIM 1961). *Address:* 9 Sibthorpe Road, North Mymms, Hatfield, Herts AL9 7PH. *Club:* Athenæum. *Died 21 Dec. 2000.*

BAILEY, Reginald Bertram, CBE 1976; Member, Employers' Panel, Industrial Tribunals in England and Wales, 1977–85; *b* 15 July 1916; *s* of late George Bertram Bailey and Elizabeth Bailey, Ilford; *m* 1942, Phyllis Joan Firman (decd); one *s* one *d. Educ:* Owen's School. Served War of 1939–45: RAPC, 1940–42; RE, 1942–46 (Captain). Entered Post Office as Exec. Officer, 1935; Higher Exec. Officer, 1947; Sen. Exec. Officer, 1948; Principal, 1950; Instructor, Management Trng Centre, 1957; Staff Controller, SW Region, 1958; Comdt, Management Trng Centre, 1962; Asst Sec., 1965; Dir, Wales and the Marches Postal Region, 1967; Dir, South-Eastern Postal Region, 1970–76. *Recreations:* walking, gardening, old railway timetables. *Address:* 21 Preston Paddock, Rustington, Littlehampton, West Sussex BN16 2AA. *T:* (01903) 772451. *Died 26 Feb. 1999.*

BAINES, Anthony Cuthbert, DLitt; FBA 1980; *b* 6 Oct. 1912; *s* of Cuthbert Edward Baines and Margaret Clemency Lane Poole; *m* 1960, Patricia Margaret Stammers. *Educ:* Westminster Sch. (KS); Christ Church Oxford; Royal College of Music. BA 1933, MA 1970, DLitt 1977, Oxon. Commissioned Royal Tank Regt, 1940–45. Member, London Philharmonic Orchestra, 1935–39, 1946–49; Associate Conductor, International Ballet Co., 1950–53; Member, Music Staff: Uppingham Sch., 1954–65; Dean Close Sch., 1965–70; Curator, Bate Collection of Historical Wind Instruments, Oxford Univ., 1970–80, retired. Fellow, University Coll., Oxford, 1974–80, retired. Editor, Galpin Society Jl, 1956–63 and 1970–84. Hon. DMus Edinburgh, 1994. *Publications:* Woodwind Instruments and their History, 1957, 5th edn 1977; Bagpipes, 1960, 4th edn 1979; (ed and contrib.) Musical Instruments through the Ages, 1961, 6th edn 1978; European and American Musical Instruments, 1966, 2nd edn 1981; Victoria and Albert Museum, Catalogue of Musical Instruments, vol. II, Non-Keyboard, 1968; Brass Instruments, their History and Development, 1976, 3rd edn 1980; The Oxford Companion to Musical Instruments,

1992. *Recreations:* painting, wild life. *Address:* 18 Bridge Square, Farnham, Surrey GU9 7QR
Died 3 Feb. 1997.

BAIRD, Sir David Charles, 5th Bt *cr* 1809, of Newbyth, Haddingtonshire; *b* 6 July 1912; *s* of late William Arthur Baird (2nd *s* of 3rd Bt), Lennoxlove, and Lady Hersey Baird, *d* of 4th Marquess Conyngham; *S* uncle, 1941. *Educ:* Eton; Cambridge. *Heir: nephew* Charles William Stuart Baird [*b* 8 June 1939; *m* 1965, Jane Joanna, *d* of late Brig. A. Darley Bridge; three *d*]. *Address:* Novaar, Barrhill Road, Dalbeattie DG5 4JB.
Died 15 Nov. 2000.

BAIRD, Sir James Richard Gardiner, 10th Bt *cr* 1695, of Saughton Hall, Edinburghshire; MC 1945; *b* 12 July 1913; *er s* of Captain William Frank Gardiner Baird (killed in action 1914) (2nd *s* of 8th Bt) and Violet Mary (*d* 1947), *d* of late Richard Benyon Croft; *S* uncle, Sir James Hozier Gardiner Baird, 9th Bt, 1966; *m* 1941, Mabel Ann, (Gay), *d* of A. Algernon Gill; two *s* one *d*. *Educ:* Eton. Served War of 1939–45: Lieut, Royal Artillery, 1940; Captain, Kent Yeomanry, 1944. *Heir: s* James Andrew Gardiner Baird [*b* 2 May 1946; *m* 1984, Jean Margaret (marr. diss. 1988), *yr d* of Brig. Sir Ian Jardine, 4th Bt; one *s*]. *Address:* Church Farm House, Guist, Norfolk NR20 5AJ. *Club:* Naval and Military. *Died 13 March 1997.*

BAIRD, Ronald; Vice-Chairman, Saatchi & Saatchi Advertising, 1992–97 (Director, 1974–97); *b* 9 Dec. 1930; *s* of Richard Baird and Emma Baird (*née* Martin); *m* 1957, Helen Lilian (*d* 1996), *d* of His Honour Judge John and Lilian Charlesworth. *Educ:* Grammar School, Blyth, Northumberland; King's College, Univ. of Durham. 13th/18th Royal Hussars (QMO), 1949–51. Saward Baker & Co., 1954–63; Chief Exec. Officer, Stuart Advtg, 1963–68; Man. Dir, Holmwood Advtg, 1968–74; Dir, Notley Advtg, 1970–74. Member: Derwent Howe Steering Group (Cumbria), 1982–90; Council, Think British, 1980–91; Board, Nat. Theatre, 1984–91 (Vice-Chm , Nat. Theatre Develt Council, 1985); Royal Life Saving Soc. (Vice-Pres.); London Fedn of Boys' Clubs. *Recreations:* Irish wolfhounds, music, painting, fell walking, field sports. *Address:* Berry Corner, Berry Lane, Chorleywood, Herts WD3 5EY. *T:* (01923) 283251; Spout House, Gosforth, Cumbria CA20 1AZ. *Died 15 Aug. 1999.*

BAIRD, Dr Thomas Terence, CB 1977; Chief Medical Officer, Department of Health and Social Services, Northern Ireland, 1972–78, retired; *b* 31 May 1916; *s* of Thomas Baird, Archdeacon of Derry, and Hildegarde Nolan; *m* 1st, 1940, Joan Crosbie; two *d;* 2nd, 1982, Mary Wilson Powell. *Educ:* Haileybury Coll.; Queen's Univ. of Belfast. MB, BCh, BAO 1939; DPH 1947; FFPHM (FFCM (RCP), 1972); MRCPI 1973, FRCPI 1975; MRCPEd 1975, FRCPEd 1994; FFCM Ireland (Founder Fellow), 1977; Fellow, Royal Acad. of Medicine in Ire., 1991. Served War, RNVR, 1940–46. Ho. Surg./Ho. Phys., North Lonsdale Hosp., Barrow-in-Furness, 1939–40; Queen's Univ. of Belfast, DPH course, 1946–47; Berks CC: Asst MO, 1947–49; Dep. County MO and Dep. Principal Sch. MO, 1949–54; Welsh Bd of Health: MO, 1954–57; Sen. MO, 1957–62; Min. of Health and Local Govt, Northern Ireland: PMO, 1962–64; Dep. Chief MO, 1964–68; Min. of Health and Social Services, NI, Sen. Dep. Chief MO, 1968–72. Chairman: NI Med. Manpower Adv. Cttee; NI Adv. Cttee on infant mortality and handicaps. Member: GMC, 1973–79; Faculty of Medicine, QUB; NI Council for Postgrad. Med. Educn; Bd, Faculty of Community Medicine, RCPI. Chief Surgeon for Wales, St John Ambulance Bde, 1959–62. QUB Boat Club: Capt. of Boats, 1937–38; Vice-Pres., 1989–90. QHP 1974–77. CStJ 1959. *Publications:* (jtly) Infection in Hospital—a code of practice, 1971; papers in various learned jls. *Recreations:* fishing, forestry. *Address:* Port-a-Chapel,

Greencastle, Co. Donegal. *T;* Greencastle (077) 81038. *Club:* Carlton. *Died 18 May 1996.*

BAKER, Geoffrey Hunter, CMG 1962; HM Diplomatic Service, retired; *b* 4 Aug. 1916; *s* of late Thomas Evelyn Baker and Gladys Beatrice Baker (*née* Marsh); *m* 1963, Anita Sirmay (*née* Wägeler); one *d. Educ:* Haberdashers' Aske's Hampstead Sch.; Royal Masonic Sch., Bushey, Herts; Gonville and Caius Coll., Cambridge (Scholar). Joined Consular Service, 1938; Vice-Consul at Hamburg, 1938, Danzig, 1939, Bergen, 1939; captured by German forces there, April 1940; Vice-Consul, Basra, 1942, Jedda, 1942; Foreign Office, 1945–47; First Sec., Rangoon, 1947–51, Tehran, 1951–52; FO, 1953–54; NATO Def. Coll., Paris, 1954; Consul-Gen., Hanoi, 1954–56; UK Delegation, UN, 1956–57; Cabinet Office, 1957–60; UK Delegation to the European Free Trade Association, Geneva, 1960–66; Consul-General, Munich, 1966–71, Zagreb, 1971–74. Order of Merit (Bavaria), 1971. *Recreation:* listening to music. *Address:* 10 Leigh Road, Highfield, Southampton SO17 1EF. *Clubs:* United Oxford & Cambridge University; Cambridge University Cruising (Cambridge). *Died 6 Oct. 1999.*

BAKER, George William, CBE 1977 (OBE 1971); VRD 1952 (Clasp 1979); HM Diplomatic Service, retired; *b* 7 July 1917; *e s* of late George William Baker and of Lilian Turnbull Baker; *m* 1942, Audrey Martha Elizabeth, *e d* of Harry and Martha Day; two *d. Educ:* Chigwell Sch.; Hertford Coll., Oxford (Colonial Service Second Devonshire Course). London Div., RNVR, 1937–62; served War, RN, 1939–45. Colonial Admin. Service, Tanganyika, 1946–62: Asst Colonial Attaché, Washington (incl. service in UK Delegn to Trusteeship Council at UN), 1957; Defence Sec., Tanganyika, 1959; Head of Tanganyika Govt Information Dept, 1959–62; retd after Tanganyika Independence, 1962; joined CRO, 1962; Head of Chancery, First Sec. (Information) and Dir of British Inf. Services, British High Comm, Freetown, 1962–65; served in FCO (Consular and Defence Depts), 1965–69; First Sec. and Head of Chancery, Kinshasa, 1969–72; Dep. British Govt Rep., St Vincent and Grenada, Windward Is, 1972–74; British Commissioner, Port Moresby, Papua New Guinea, 1974–75; High Comr to Papua New Guinea, 1975–77. Mem., E Sussex Cttee, VSO, 1984– (Chm., 1980–84). A Vice-Pres., Royal African Soc., 1973–92 (Hon. Vice-Pres., 1992–); Hon. Mem. and Foreign Affairs Advr, Scientific Exploration Soc., 1965–; Consultant to Operation Raleigh, 1987–. Chm., Heathfield Cttee, Sussex Housing Assoc. for Aged, 1979–84; Chm., Waldron Br., Wealden Cons. Assoc. and Vice-Chm., Constituency Political Cttee, 1983–84. Mem. Guild of Freemen of City of London, 1980–94; Freeman, City of London, 1980; Liveryman, Clockmakers' Co., 1984– (Mem., 1981–; Steward, 1987–; Ed., Clockmaker's Times, 1987–93). Mem., Queenhithe Ward Club, City of London, 1970–93. Member: Exeter Flotilla (Chm., 1987–90); Hertford Soc.; Cttee, Devon Br., Oxford Soc.; E Devon Luncheon Club (Chm., 1989–); sundry E Devon clubs and socs. *Publications:* official booklets and contribs to learned jls. *Recreations:* photography, fishing, sailing, climbing, tennis, Rugby Union, cricket, flying, clock and cabinet-making. *Address:* Crosswinds, Coreway, Sidford, Sidmouth, Devon EX10 9SD. *T:* Sidmouth (01395) 578845. *Club:* MCC. *Died 20 Aug. 1996.*

BAKER, John B.; *see* Brayne-Baker.

BAKER, His Honour John Burkett; QC 1975; a Circuit Judge, 1978–96; *b* 17 Sept. 1931; *s* of Philip and Grace Baker; *m* 1955, Margaret Mary Smeaton; two *s* seven *d* (and one *s* decd). *Educ:* Finchley Catholic Grammar Sch.; White Fathers, Bishops Waltham; UC Exeter. LLB London. RAF, 1955–58. Called to Bar, Gray's Inn, 1957; practised from 1958. Prosecuting Counsel to Dept of

Health and Social Security, 1969–75; Dep. Chm., Shropshire QS, 1970–71; a Recorder of the Crown Court, 1972–78. Mem. Cttee, Council of Circuit Judges, 1991–95. Marriage Counsellor, Catholic Marriage Adv. Council, 1970–87 (Chm., 1981–83); Pres., Barnet, Haringey and Hertsmere Marriage Guidance Council, 1982–92. Governor: Bedford Coll., London, 1983–85; Holy Family Convent, Enfield, 1984–89. Papal Cross Pro Ecclesia et Pontifice, 1986. *Recreation:* theatre. *Address:* 43 The Ridgeway, Enfield, Middx EN2 8PD.

Died 17 April 1997.

BAKER, Maurice Sidney; Managing Director, F. W. Woolworth & Co. Ltd, 1967–71, retired; *b* 27 Jan. 1911; *s* of Sidney B. Baker and Ellen Elizabeth (*née* Airey); *m* 1st, 1935, Helen Johnstone (*née* Tweedie) (*d* 1977); one *s*; 2nd, 1978, Kirsten Randine (*née* Haugen). *Educ:* Lowestoft Grammar School. Trainee Manager, F. W. Woolworth & Co. Ltd, 1928; RAOC, 1940–46 (Major); rejoined company, 1946; Dir 1962. Officer, Legion of Merit (US), 1945. *Recreation:* bowls (Pres., 1975, Hon. Life Mem., 1983, Surrey County Bowling Assoc., Founder and Chm., Patrons Assoc., 1971).

Died 11 July 1998.

BAKER, Sir Nicholas Brian, Kt 1997; MP (C) North Dorset, since 1979; *b* 23 Nov. 1938; *s* of late Col Harold Stanley Baker, OBE; *m* 1970, Penelope Carol d'Abo; one *s* one *d*. *Educ:* Clifton Coll.; Exeter Coll., Oxford (MA). Partner in Frere Cholmeley, subseq. Frere Cholmeley Bischoff, solicitors, EC4, 1973–94. Parliamentary Private Secretary to: Minister of State for the Armed Forces, 1981–83, for Defence Procurement, MoD, 1983–84; Sec. of State for Defence, MoD, 1984–86; Sec. of State for Trade and Industry, 1987–88; an Asst Govt Whip, 1989–90; a Lord Comr of HM Treasury (Govt Whip), 1990–94; Parly Under–Sec. of State, Home Office, 1994–95. *Publications:* pamphlets. *Recreations:* exercise, music, English countryside. *Address:* House of Commons, SW1A 0AA. *Clubs:* Wimborne Conservative; Blandford Constitutional. *Died 25 April 1997.*

BAKER, Very Rev. Thomas George Adames; Dean of Worcester, 1975–86, Dean Emeritus since 1986; *b* 22 Dec. 1920; *s* of late Walter and Marion Baker, Southampton; unmarried. *Educ:* King Edward VI Sch., Southampton; Exeter Coll., Oxford (MA); Lincoln Theological Coll. Deacon 1944, priest 1945; Curate of All Saints, King's Heath, Birmingham, 1944–47; Vicar of St James, Edgbaston, 1947–54; Sub-Warden of Lincoln Theological Coll., 1954–60; Principal of Wells Theological College and Prebendary of Combe II in Wells Cathedral, 1960–71; Archdeacon of Bath, 1971–75. Canon Theologian of Leicester Cathedral, 1959–66. Select Preacher, Univ. of Cambridge, 1963, Univ. of Oxford, 1973. Recognised Teacher, Bristol Univ., 1969–74. DD Lambeth, 1987. *Publications:* What is the New Testament?, 1969; Questioning Worship, 1977. *Recreation:* music. *Address:* Charterhouse, EC1M 6AN. *Died 25 Sept. 2000.*

BAKER, Willfred Harold Kerton, (Bill), TD; *b* 6 Jan. 1920; *o s* of late W. H. Baker; *m* 1st, 1945, Kathleen Helen Sloan (*née* Murray Bisset) (marr. diss. 1976; she *d* 1987); one *s* two *d*; 2nd, 1978, Jean Gordon Scott (*née* Skinner). *Educ:* Hardye's Sch.; Edinburgh Univ.; Cornell Univ., USA. Joined TA, and served War of 1939–45 (Major). Edinburgh Univ. (BSc Agriculture), 1946–49. MP (C) Banffshire, 1964–Feb. 1974. *Recreations:* golf, philately. *Address:* 42 Southfield Avenue, Paignton, South Devon TQ3 1LH. *T:* (01803) 550861.

Died 9 Nov. 2000.

BAKER-CARR, Air Marshal Sir John (Darcy), KBE 1962 (CBE 1951); CB 1957; AFC 1944; Controller of Engineering and Equipment, Air Ministry, 1962–64,

retired; *b* 13 Jan. 1906; *s* of late Brigadier-General C. D. B. S. Baker-Carr, CMG, DSO and Sarah Quinan; *m* 1934, Margery Dallas; no *c*. *Educ:* England and USA. Entered RAF as Pilot Officer, 1929; No 32 Fighter Sqdn 1930, Flying Officer; Flying Boats at home and overseas, 1931; Armament Specialist Course, 1934; Flight-Lieut; Armament and Air Staff appts, 1935–38; Sqdn Ldr, 1938; Armament Research and Development, 1939–45 (AFC); Wing Comdr, 1940; Gp Captain, 1942; Central Fighter Estab., 1946–47; Dep. Dir Postings, Air Min., 1947–48; Air Cdre, 1948; Dir of Armament Research and Development, Min. of Supply, 1948–51 (CBE); idc 1952; Comdt RAF St Athan, 1953–56; Senior Technical Staff Officer, HQ Fighter Command, RAF, 1956–59; Air Vice-Marshal, 1957; Air Officer Commanding, No 41 Group, Maintenance Command, 1959–61; Air Marshal, 1962. *Recreations:* sailing, carpentry. *Address:* Thatchwell Cottage, King's Somborne, Hants SO20 6PH. *Club:* Royal Air Force Yacht (Hamble, Hants).

Died 9 July 1998.

BALCOMBE, Rt Hon. Sir (Alfred) John, Kt 1977; PC 1985; a Lord Justice of Appeal, 1985–95; *b* 29 Sept. 1925; *er s* of late Edwin Kesteven Balcombe; *m* 1950, Jacqueline Rosemary, *yr d* of late Julian Cowan; two *s* one *d*. *Educ:* Winchester (schol.); New Coll., Oxford (exhibnr; BA 1949 (1st class Hons Jurisprudence), MA 1950). Served, 1943–47: Royal Signals; commnd 1945. Called to the Bar, Lincoln's Inn, 1950 (Bencher, 1977; Treas., 1999); practised at Chancery Bar, 1951–77; QC 1969; Judge of the High Court of Justice, Family Div., 1977–85; Judge of the Employment Appeal Tribunal, 1983–85. Mem., Gen. Council of the Bar, 1967–71. Mem., Steering Cttee for Revenue, Tax Law Rewrite, 1997–98. Lectures: Maccabæan, British Acad., 1993; Stevens, RSocMed, 1995. Chm., London Marriage Guidance Council, 1982–88. Pres., SW London Br., Magistrates' Assoc., 1993–2000. Pres., The Maccabaeans, 1990–2000. Master, Co. of Tin Plate Workers, 1971–72. Sen. Grand Warden, United Grand Lodge of England, 1996–98. Hon. Fellow, Hebrew Univ. of Jerusalem, 1996. *Publications:* Exempt Private Companies, 1953; (ed) Estoppel, in Halsbury's Laws of England, 4th edn. *Address:* Alban Place, 1A Lingfield Road, Wimbledon, SW19 4QA. *T:* (020) 8947 0980. *Club:* Garrick. *Died 9 June 2000.*

BALCOMBE, Frederick James; Lord Mayor of Manchester, 1974–75, Deputy Lord Mayor, 1975–76; *b* 17 Dec. 1911; *s* of late Sidney and Agnes Balcombe; *m* 1st, 1936, Clarice (*née* Cassel) (*d* 1949); two *s* (and two *c* decd); 2nd, 1956, Rhoda (*née* Jaffe) (*d* 1989); one *d*. *Educ:* St Anthony's RC Sch., Forest Gate; West Ham Secondary Central Sch., Stratford, London. Served War of 1939–45, RAF (commnd). Chm., family co. of insurance loss assessors. Mem. Manchester City Council, Crumpsall Ward, subseq. St Peter's Ward, Collegiate Church Ward, 1958–82; served as Chm. Central Purchasing Cttee, 1964–67, Gen. and Parly (later Policy), Markets, 1958–82, Airports, 1971–82 (Chm.), Parks, 1958–67, and Finance, 1964–73, Cttees (Dep. Chm.). Mem. Council, Manchester and Salford Police Authority, 1968–74; Mem., AMC Rating Cttee, 1973–74. Chm., Manchester Internat. Airport, 1975–79. Mem., Airport Owners' Assoc., 1979–82. Founder, Hillel House, Manchester Univ, 1958 (Hon. Sec., 1958–68; Sen. Life Vice-Pres.); Chm. of Governors, Coll. of Building, Manchester, 1964–67; Mem. Council, BBC Radio Manchester, 1970–76. President: Manchester and District Fedn of Community Assocs, 1962–78; Manchester and District Allotments Council, 1963–78; Higher Blackley Community Assoc., 1963; Vice-Pres., Blackley Prize Band, 1964; Mem., League of Friends, and Cttee, and Hon. Treas., Crumpsall Hosp., 1964–72. Mem., Bd of Deputies of British Jews, 1956–64; Mem. Council, Manchester and Salford Jews, 1958 (Exec.

Mem., 1963–68); Founder Mem., Manchester Jewish Blind Soc., 1956– (Hon. Sec, 13 years; Vice Pres.); Adjutant, Jewish Lads' Brigade and Club, Manchester, 1946–49, Chm. 1972–78. Trustee/Mem., NW Liver Research, 1986–96. Governor, King David Schs, Manchester, 1954–84; Vice-Pres., Fedn of Boys' Clubs, 1969–; connected with 199th Manchester Scout Gp. President: Manchester Cttee, Central British Fund, 1969–96; RAFA Manchester South, 1981–84; Manchester City Swimming Club, 1981–90. Founder Mem., Variety Club of Israel, 1972; Barker of Variety Club, 1970– (Chm. Manchester Cttee, 1976). JP Manchester, 1967. Mem. Jewish Faith. Life long blood donor. *Recreations:* family, communal endeavour, swimming, walking. *Address:* Flat 3, Filleigh Park Road, Bowdon, Cheshire WA14 3JG. *T:* (0161) 929 0847; (office) (0161) 941 6231.
Died 1 July 2000.

BALCOMBE, Rt Hon. Sir John; *see* Balcombe, Rt Hon. Sir A. J.

BALFOUR, Rear-Adm. (George) Ian (Mackintosh), CB 1962; DSC 1943; *b* 14 Jan. 1912; *yr s* of late Dr T. Stevenson Balfour, Chard, Som, and Mrs Balfour; *m* 1939, Pamela Carlyle Forrester, *y d* of late Major Hugh C. C. Forrester, DL, JP, Tullibody House, Cambus, and Mrs Forrester; one *s* one *d* (and one *s* decd). *Educ:* Royal Naval Coll., Dartmouth. Served in China, 1930–32; South Africa, 1935–37; commanded Destroyers for most of War of 1939–45, on various stations; Mediterranean, 1948; Far East, 1949–50; USA 1951–53; Captain (D) 2nd Destroyer Flotilla, 1956–58; Dir of Officer Appointments, 1958–59; Senior Naval Mem., Imperial Defence Coll., 1960–63; retired list, 1963. Chief Appeals Officer, Cancer Res. Campaign, 1963–77. *Address:* Westover, Farnham Lane, Haslemere, Surrey GU27 1HD. *T:* (01428) 643876.
Died 23 Oct. 1999.

BALFOUR, Rear-Adm. Hugh Maxwell, CB 1990; LVO 1974; consultant on communications and information systems, *b* 29 April 1933; *s* of Ronald Hugh Balfour and Ann Smith; *m* 1958, Sheila Ann Weldon; one *s* two *d. Educ;* Ardvreck; Crieff; Kelly College, Tavistock. Joined RN, 1951; qualified as Signal Officer, 1959; commanded HM Ships Sheraton, Phoebe, Whitby and Fifth Destroyer Squadron in HMS Exeter, to 1985 (Exec. Officer, HM Yacht Britannia, 1972–74); Comdr, Sultan of Oman's Navy, 1985–90. Order of Oman, 1990. *Recreations:* fishing, shooting, gardening. *Club:* Naval and Military.
Died 29 June 1999.

BALFOUR, Rear-Adm. Ian; *see* Balfour, Rear-Adm. G. I. M.

BALFOUR, Nancy, OBE 1965; President, Contemporary Art Society, since 1984 (Chairman, 1976–82); *b* 1911; *d* of Alexander Balfour and Ruth Macfarland Balfour. *Educ:* Wycombe Abbey Sch.; Lady Margaret Hall, Oxford (MA). Foreign Office Research Dept, 1941–45; BBC N American Service, 1945–48; Economist Newspaper, 1948–72: Asst Editor with responsibility for American Survey, 1954–72; Fellow, Inst. of Politics, Kennedy Sch. of Govt, Harvard Univ., 1973–74. Member: Council, RIIA, 1963–84; Bd, British–American Arts Assoc., 1980–; Hon. Treasurer, Contemporary Art Soc., 1971–76; Chm., Art Services Grants, 1982–89; Vice-Chm., Crafts Council, 1983–85 (Mem., 1980–85); Chairperson, Southern Arts Craft Panel, 1986–90; Chm., Arts Research Ltd, 1990–. Trustee, Public Art Develt Trust, 1983–91. FRSA 1985. *Recreations:* sightseeing, ancient and modern; viewing work by living artists. *Address:* 36E Eaton Square, SW1W 9DH. *T:* (0171) 235 7874. *Club:* Arts.   *Died 29 Aug. 1997.*

BALL, Michael George; JP; farmer since 1969; Vice Lord–Lieutenant of the Isle of Wight, since 1996; *b* 22 Aug. 1937; *s* of late Stanley George Ball and Nesta, *y d* of

James Pilling, Deeplish Hall, Rochdale; *m* 1966, Jane, 2nd *d* of late Col David E. Baird, St Andrews; one *s* one *d. Educ:* Charterhouse; Highbury Tech. Coll., Cosham. MIBritE 1965. Commission, 13/18 Royal Hussars (QMO), Germany and Malaya, 1958–60; Killick Martin & Co., and Ben Line (Hong Kong and Japan), 1960–64; Director: James Ball & Son, 1965–74; Arnold Heal Ltd, 1969–85. Founding Mem. and Dir, IoW Grain Storage Co-operative, 1978–97; Mem., Agric. Lands Tribunal, SE Area, 1991–; County Chm., NFU, 1982. Gov., Osborne Middle Sch., 1992–. Chm., IoW Magistrates, 1989–93 (Chm., Courts Cttee, 1981–88); Area Criminal Justice Liaison Cttee, Hants, Dorset and IoW, 1993–; JP 1968, DL 1984, High Sheriff 1994, IoW. *Address:* Ashengrove, Calbourne, Isle of Wight PO30 4HU. *T:* (01983) 531209.
Died 12 June 1998.

BALLARD, Prof. Clifford Frederick; Professor Emeritus in Orthodontics, University of London; Hon. Consultant, Eastman Dental Hospital, London; *b* 26 June 1910; *s* of Frederick John Ballard and Eliza Susannah (*née* Wilkinson); *m* 1937, Muriel Mabel Burling; one *s* one *d. Educ:* Kilburn Grammar Sch.; Charing Cross Hosp. and Royal Dental Hospital. LDS 1934; MRCS, LRCP 1940; FDS 1949; Diploma in Orthodontics, RCS, 1954; FFDRCSI 1964. Hd of Dept of Orthodontics, Inst. of Dental Surgery, British Post-Grad. Med. Fedn, Univ. of London, 1948–72; Prof. of Orthodontics, London Univ., 1956–72; Dental Surgeon, Victoria Hosp. for Children, SW3, 1948–64, Tooting, 1964–71. Pres. of Brit. Soc. for the Study of Orthodontics, 1957, Senior Vice-Pres., 1963, 1964; Mem. Council of Odontological Section of Royal Society Med., 1954–56, 1959–62 (Sec., 1957, Vice-Pres., 1969–72); Mem. Board, Faculty of Dental Surgery, RCS, 1966–74. Charles Tomes Lectr, RCS, 1966; Northcroft Memorial Lectr, Brit. Soc. for Study of Orthocortics, 1967. Hon. Life Mem., British Dental Assoc., 1982; Hon. Member: British Soc. for Study of Orthodontics; Israel Orthodontic Soc.; NZ Orthodontic Soc., European Orthodontic Soc.; Membre d'Honneur, Société Française d'Orthopédie Dento-faciale. Colyer Gold Medal, RCS, 1975; (first recipient) C. F. Ballard Award, Consultant Orthodontists' Gp, 1990. *Publications:* numerous contributions to learned journals, 1948–. *Recreation:* indoor bowls. *Address:* Flat 20, The Maltings, Salisbury, Wilts SP1 1BD, *T:* (01722) 335099.
Died 16 July 1997.

BAMFORD, Prof. Clement Henry, PhD, ScD; FRS 1964; CChem, FRSC; Hon. Senior Fellow, Department of Clinical Engineering (formerly Institute of Medical and Dental Bioengineering), University of Liverpool, 1980–96; Campbell Brown Professor of Industrial Chemistry, University of Liverpool, 1962–80, then Emeritus Professor; *b* 10 Oct. 1912; *s* of Frederic Jesse Bamford and Catherine Mary Bamford (*née* Shelley), Stafford; *m* 1938, Daphne Ailsa Stephan, BSc Sydney, PhD Cantab, Sydney, Australia; one *s* one *d. Educ:* St Patrick's and King Edward VI Schs, Stafford; Trinity Coll., Cambridge (Senior Scholar, 1931, MA, PhD, ScD). Fellow, Trinity Coll., Cambridge, 1937; Dir of Studies in Chemistry, Emmanuel Coll., Cambridge, 1937; joined: Special Operations Executive, 1941; Fundamental Research Laboratory of Messrs Courtaulds Ltd, Maidenhead, 1945; Head of Laboratory, 1947–62; Liverpool University: Dean, Faculty of Science, 1965–68; Pro-Vice-Chancellor, 1972–75; Hd, Dept of Inorganic, Physical and Industrial Chemistry, 1973–78. Member: Council, Chem. Soc., 1972–75; Council, Soc. Chem. Ind., 1974–75. Pres., British Assoc. Section B (Chemistry), 1975–76; Vice-Pres., 1977–81; Pres., 1981–85, Macromolecular Div., Internat. Union of Pure and Applied Chemistry. Visiting Professor: Kyoto Univ., 1977; Univ. of NSW, 1981. Mem. Editl Bd, Polymer, 1958; European

Ed., Jl of Biomaterials Sci., 1988–96 (Founder Mem., 1986). Hon. Mem., Soc. of Polymer Sci., Japan, 1996. Hon. DSc: Bradford, 1980; Lancaster, 1988. Meldola Medal, Royal Inst. of Chemistry, 1941; Macromolecules and Polymers Award, Chemical Soc., 1977; Award for dist. service in advancement of polymer science, Soc. of Polymer Science, Japan, 1989; George Winter Award, European Soc. for Biomaterials, 1992. *Publications:* Synthetic Polypeptides (with A. Elliott and W. E. Hanby), 1956; The Kinetics of Vinyl Polymerization by Radical Mechanisms (with W. G. Barb, A. D. Jenkins and P. F. Onyon), 1958; (ed with C. F. H. Tipper and R. G. Compton) Comprehensive Chemical Kinetics, 26 vols, 1969–86; papers on physical chemistry, polymer science and biomaterials science in learned journals. *Recreations:* music, especially violin playing, hill walking, gardening. *Address:* Broom Bank, Tower Road, Prenton, Birkenhead CH42 8LH. *T:* (0151) 608 3979.

Died 7 Nov. 1999.

BANCROFT, Baron *cr* 1982 (Life Peer), of Coatham in the county of Cleveland; **Ian Powell Bancroft,** GCB 1979 (KCB 1975; CB 1971); Head of the Home Civil Service and Permanent Secretary to the Civil Service Department, 1978–81; *b* 23 Dec. 1922; *s* of A. E. and L. Bancroft; *m* 1950, Jean Swaine; two *s* one *d. Educ:* Coatham Sch.; Balliol Coll., Oxford (Scholar; Hon. Fellow 1981). Served Rifle Brigade, 1942–45. Entered Treasury, 1947; Private Secretary: to Sir Henry Wilson Smith, 1948–50; to Chancellor of the Exchequer, 1953–55; to Lord Privy Seal, 1955–57; Cabinet Office, 1957–59; Principal Private Sec. to successive Chancellors of the Exchequer, 1964–66; Under-Sec., HM Treasury, 1966–68, Civil Service Dept, 1968–70; Dep. Sec., Dir Gen. of Organization and Establishments, DoE, 1970–72; a Comr of Customs and Excise, and Dep. Chm. of Bd, 1972–73; Second Permanent Sec., CSD, 1973–75; Permanent Sec., DoE, 1975–77. Mem., Adv. Council on Public Records, 1983–88. Dep. Chm., Sun Life Corp. plc, 1987–93 (Dir, 1983–93; a Vice-Chm., 1986–87); Director: Rugby Group (formerly Rugby Portland Cement), 1982–93; Bass Plc, 1982–93; ANZ Grindlays Bank plc, 1983–93; Bass Leisure Ltd, 1984–93. Pres., Building Centre Trust, 1987–93. Vis. Fellow, Nuffield Coll., Oxford, 1973–81; Chm. Trustees, Mansfield Coll., Oxford, 1988–95 (Chm. Council, 1981–88; Hon. Fellow, 1995). Chm., Royal Hosp. and Home, Putney, 1984–88 (Mem., Management Board, 1988–); Governor, Cranleigh Sch., 1983–92; Mem., Corp. of Cranleigh & Bramley Schs, 1983–. Patron, Friends of Public Record Office, 1993–. *Address:* House of Lords, SW1A 0PW. *T:* (0171) 219 3000. *Clubs:* United Oxford & Cambridge University, Civil Service.

Died 19 Nov. 1996.

BAND, David; Chief Executive, Barclays de Zoete Wedd, since 1988; Director: Barclays PLC, since 1988; Barclays Bank PLC, since 1988; *b* 14 Dec. 1942; *s* of David Band and Elisabeth Aitken Band; *m* 1973, Olivia Rose (*née* Brind); one *s* one *d. Educ:* Rugby; St Edmund Hall, Oxford (MA). Joined J. P. Morgan & Co. in London, 1964; General Manager: Singapore, 1976; Paris, 1978; Sen. Vice Pres., Morgan Guaranty Trust Co., New York, 1981; Man. Dir, Morgan Guaranty Ltd, London, 1986; Exec. Vice Pres., Morgan Guaranty Trust Co., and Chm., J. P. Morgan Securities Ltd, London, 1987. Dep. Chm., Securities Assoc., 1986–88. *Recreation:* tennis. *Address:* c/o BZW, Ebbgate House, 2 Swan Lane, EC4R 3TS. *T:* 0171–956 4007. *Died 28 March 1996.*

BANDA, Hastings Kamuzu, MD, **(Ngwazi Dr H. Kamuzu Banda);** President of Malaŵi, 1966–94; Chancellor, University of Malaŵi, 1965–94; Life President, Malaŵi Congress Party; *b* Nyasaland, 14 May 1898. *Educ:* Meharry Medical Coll., Nashville, USA (MD);

Universities of Glasgow and Edinburgh. Further degrees: BSc, MB, ChB, LRCSE; and several hon. degrees awarded later. Practised medicine in Liverpool and on Tyneside during War of 1939–45 and in London, 1945–53; returned to Africa, 1953, and practised in Gold Coast. Took over leadership of Nyasaland African Congress in Blantyre, 1958, and became Pres.-Gen.; was imprisoned for political reasons, 1959; unconditionally released, 1960; Minister of Natural Resources and Local Government, Nyasaland, 1961–63; Prime Minister of Malaŵi (formerly Nyasaland), 1963–66. *Address:* Blantyre, Malaŵi.

Died 25 Nov. 1997.

BANDARANAIKE, Sirimavo Ratwatte Dias; Prime Minister of Sri Lanka (Ceylon until 1972), 1960–65, 1970–77 and 1994–2000; President, Sri Lanka Freedom Party, since 1960; *b* 17 April 1916; *d* of Barnes Ratwatte, Ratemahatmaya of Ratnapura Dist, Mem. of Ceylon Senate, and Rosemund Mahawalatenne Ratwatte; *m* 1940, Solomon West Ridgeway Dias Bandaranaike (*d* 1959), Prime Minister of Ceylon, 1956–59; one *s* two *d. Educ:* Ratnapura Ferguson Sch.; St Bridget's Convent, Colombo. Assisted S. W. R. D. Bandaranaike in political career. Campaigned for Sri Lanka Freedom Party in election campaigns, March and July 1960. Formerly Pres. and Treasurer, Lanka Mahila Samiti. MP, 1960–80, and 1989–; Minister of Defence and External Affairs, 1960–65; Minister of Information and Broadcasting, 1964–65; Leader of the Opposition, 1965–70, and 1989–94; Minister of Defence and Foreign Affairs, of Planning and Econ. Affairs, and of Plan Implementation, 1970–77. Chm., Non Aligned Movt, 1976–77. Ceres Medal, FAO, 1977. *Address:* 65 Rosmead Place, Colombo 7, Sri Lanka.

Died 10 Oct. 2000.

BANKOFF, George; *see* Sava, G.

BANKS, Baron *cr* 1974 (Life Peer), of Kenton in Greater London; **Desmond Anderson Harvie Banks,** CBE 1972; *b* 23 Oct. 1918; *s* of James Harvie Banks, OBE and Sheena Muriel Watt; *m* 1948, Barbara Wells (OBE 1987); two *s. Educ:* Alpha Prep. Sch.; University College Sch. Served with KRRC and RA, 1939–46, Middle East and Italy (Major); Chief Public Relations Officer to Allied Mil. Govt, Trieste, 1946. Joined Canada Life Assce Co., subseq. Life Assoc. of Scotland; life assce broker, 1959; Director: Tweddle French & Co. (Life & Pensions Consultants) Ltd, 1973–82; Lincoln Consultants Ltd, 1982–89. Liberal Party: Pres., 1968–69; Chm. Exec., 1961–63 and 1969–70; Dir of Policy Promotion, 1972–74; Chm. Res. Cttee, 1966; Vice-Chm., Standing Cttee, 1973–79; Hon. Sec., Home Counties Liberal Fedn, 1960–61; Chairman: Working Party on Machinery of Govt, 1971–74; Liberal Summer Sch. Cttee, 1979–92; Member: For. Affairs Panel, 1961–88 (sometime Vice-Chm.); Social Security Panel, 1961–88; Hon. Sec., Liberal Candidates Assoc., 1947–52; contested (L): Harrow East, 1950; St Ives, 1955; SW Herts, 1959. Dep. Liberal Whip, House of Lords, 1977–83; spokesman on: social security, 1975–89; social services, 1977–83. Pres., Liberal European Action Gp, 1971–87; Vice-Pres., European Atlantic Gp, 1985– (Vice Chm., 1979–85); a Pres., British Council, European Movement, 1986–94 (Vice-Chm., 1979–86). Elder, United Reformed Church. *Publications:* Clyde Steamers, 1947, 2nd edn 1951; numerous political pamphlets. *Recreations:* pursuing interest in Gilbert and Sullivan opera and in Clyde river steamers, reading. *Address:* Lincoln House, The Lincolns, Little Kingshill, Great Missenden, Bucks HP16 0EH. *T:* (01494) 866164. *Club:* National Liberal (President, 1981–93).

Died 15 June 1997.

BANKS, Alan George; HM Diplomatic Service, retired; *b* 7 April 1911; *s* of George Arthur Banks and Sarah Napthen; *m* 1946, Joyce Frances Telford Yates; two *s.*

Educ: Preston Grammar Sch. Served: in HM Forces, 1939–43; at Consulate-Gen., Dakar, 1943–45; Actg Consul, Warsaw, 1945–48; HM Vice-Consul: Bordeaux, 1948–50; Istanbul, 1950–52; Zagreb, 1952–55; FO, 1955–58; HM Consul, Split, 1958–60; 1st Sec. and Consul, Madrid, 1960–62; 1st Sec., FO, 1962–67; Consul-General, Alexandria, 1967–71. *Recreations:* classical music, gardening, photography. *Address:* Reigate Beaumont, Colley Lane, Reigate, Surrey RH2 9JB. *T:* (01737) 237251. *Died 15 June 2000.*

BANKS, Richard Alford, CBE 1965; *b* 11 July 1902; *s* of William Hartland Banks, Hergest Croft, Kington, Hereford; *m* 1st, 1937, Lilian Jean (*d* 1974), *d* of Dr R. R. Walker, Presteigne, Radnorshire; two *s* one *d*; 2nd, 1976, Rosamund Gould. *Educ:* Rugby; Trinity Coll., Cambridge (BA). Dir of Imperial Chemical Industries Ltd, 1952–64; Chm. of the Industrial Training Council, 1962–64; Mem., Water Resources Bd, 1964–74. Veitch Meml Medal, RHS, 1983. JP Hereford, 1963–73. *Recreations:* arboriculture, gardening, travel. *Address:* Haywood Cottages, Kington, Herefordshire HR5 3EJ. *Died 26 Feb. 1997.*

BANKS, William Hartley; Member, West Yorkshire County Council, 1977–86 (Chairman, 1982–83); *b* 5 July 1909; *s* of Hartley and Edith Banks; *m* 1935, Elsie Kendrew; four *s* one *d* (and one *s* decd). *Educ:* Holbeck Technical Sch. Entered local politics, 1947; Mem., Divl Educn Exec., 1948; Mem., Rothwell UDC, 1959–74 (Chm., 1972–73). Hd, Woodwork Dept, 1964–74, Vice-Chm., Consultative Cttee, 1960–74, Rothwell Colliery. Pres., Yorks Mines Allied Trades Assoc., 1965–70. Chairman: Sch. Governors, Rothwell, 1964–68; Rothwell Primary Schs, 1974–; Rothwell Secondary Schs, 1982–. Chairman: Rothwell Accident Prevention Cttee, 1960–72; Rothwell Road Safety Cttee, 1987 (Vice-Chm., 1974–87); Secretary: Rothwell and Dist Civic Soc., 1974–77; Rothwell and Dist Histl Soc., 1994–; President: Rothwell Athletic Club, 1974– (Treasurer, 1951 74); Rothwell Cricket Club, 1960–; Rothwell Civic Soc., 1980–; Rothwell Pensioners' Assoc., 1986–; Chairman: Rothwell Gateway Club 1980 (?); Rothwell Theatre Gp, 1986–; Rothwell and Dist Probus Club, 1992–; Rothwell Methodist Church Men's Supper Club, 1992–; Leader, Rothwell Windmill Youth Club, 1950–55. Accompanist and on Preaching Plan, Rothwell Methodist Church, 1984–; talks to local schs and orgns on aspects of life in 1920s. *Publication:* The History of Rothwell Cricket Club 1875–1990, 1991. *Recreations:* classical music, most sports. *Address:* 6 Prospect Place, Rothwell, Leeds LS26 0AL. *T:* (0113) 282 1502. *Died 26 Dec. 1998.*

BANTOCK, Prof. Geoffrey Herman; Emeritus Professor of Education, University of Leicester, 1975; *b* 12 Oct. 1914; *s* of Herman S. and Annie Bantock; *m* 1950, Dorothy Jean Pick; no *c*. *Educ:* Wallasey Grammar Sch.; Emmanuel Coll., Cambridge. BA 1936, MA 1942, Cantab. Taught in grammar schs, training coll.; Lectr in Educn, University Coll. of Leicester, 1950–54; Reader in Educn, University Coll., Leicester, later Univ. of Leicester, 1954–64; Prof. of Educn, 1964–75; Leverhulme Emeritus Fellow, 1976–78. Vis. Prof., Monash Univ., Melbourne, 1971. *Publications:* Freedom and Authority in Education, 1952 (2nd edn 1965); L. H. Myers: a critical study, 1956; Education in an Industrial Society, 1963 (2nd edn 1973); Education and Values, 1965; Education, Culture and the Emotions, 1967; Education, Culture and Industrialization, 1968; T. S. Eliot and Education, 1969 (paperback 1970); Studies in the History of Educational Theory: Vol. I, Artifice and Nature 1350–1765, 1980, Vol. II, The Minds and the Masses 1760–1980, 1984 (Book Prize, Standing Conf. on Studies in Educn, 1985); Dilemmas of the Curriculum, 1980; The Parochialism of the Present, 1981.

Recreations: music, art, foreign travel. *Address:* c/o The University, Leicester. *Died 1 Sept. 1997.*

BARCLAY, Sir Roderick (Edward), GCVO 1966 (KCVO 1957; CVO 1953); KCMG 1955 (CMG 1948); HM Diplomatic Service, retired; *b* 22 Feb. 1909; *s* of late J. Gurney Barclay and Gillian (*née* Birkbeck); *m* 1934, Jean Cecil (*d* 1996), *d* of late Sir Hugh Gladstone; one *s* three *d*. *Educ:* Harrow; Trinity Coll., Cambridge. Entered Diplomatic Service, 1932; served at HM Embassies at Brussels, Paris, Washington and in FO; Counsellor in FO, 1946; Principal Private Sec. to Sec. of State for Foreign Affairs, 1949–51; Asst Under-Sec. of State, 1951; Dep. Under-Sec. of State, 1953–56; HM Ambassador to Denmark, 1956–60; Adviser on European Trade Questions, Foreign Office, and Dep. Under-Sec. of State for Foreign Affairs, 1960–63; Ambassador to Belgium, 1963–69. Director: Slough Estates, 1969–84; Barclays Bank SA, 1969–79 (Chm., 1970–74); Barclays Bank Internat., 1971–77; Banque de Bruxelles, 1971–77. Knight Grand Cross of the Dannebrog (Denmark) and of the Couronne (Belgium). *Publication:* Ernest Bevin and the Foreign Office 1932–69, 1975; contrib. Country Life, etc. *Recreations:* shooting, fishing. *Address:* Garden Cottage, Great White End, Latimer, Chesham, Bucks HP5 1UJ. *T:* (01494) 765919. *Club:* Brooks's. *Died 24 Oct. 1996.*

BARCROFT, Prof. Henry, MA; MD; FRCP; FRS 1953; Professor of Physiology, St Thomas's Hospital Medical School, London, 1948–71, Emeritus since 1971; a Wellcome Trustee, 1966–75; *b* 18 Oct. 1904; *s* of late Sir Joseph Barcroft, CBE, FRS and Mary Agnetta, *d* of Sir Robert S. Ball; *m* 1933, Bridget Mary (*d* 1990), *d* of late A. S. Ramsey; three *s* one *d*. *Educ:* Marlborough Coll.; King's Coll., Cambridge. Exhibitioner, 1923; Natural Science Tripos Class I, Parts I and II; Harold Fry and George Henry Lewes studentships at Cambridge, 1927–29; Gedge Prize, 1930. Harmsworth Scholar, St Mary's Hospital, London, 1929–32; Lectr in Physiology, University Coll., London, 1932–35; Dunville Prof. of Physiology, Queen's Univ., Belfast, 1935–48. Arris and Gale Lectr, RCS, 1945; Bertram Louis Abrahams Lectr, RCP, 1960; Robert Campbell Meml Orator, Ulster Med. Soc., 1975; Bayliss-Starling Meml Lectr, Physiological Soc., 1976; Vis. Prof., Univ. of Adelaide, 1963. Chairman: Editorial Bd, Monographs of Physiological Soc., 1957–65; Research Defence Soc., 1968–71, Sec. 1972–77, Vice-Pres., 1978–. FUMDS 1995. Hon. Member: British Microcirculation Soc., Société Française d'Angiologie; Japanese Coll. of Angiology; Czechoslovak Med. Soc. J. E. Purkinje. Hon. DSc Univ. Western Australia, 1963; Hon. MD Leopold-Franzens Univ., Innsbruck, 1969; Hon. DSc QUB, 1975. *Pro meritis* medal in silver, Karl Franzens Univ., Graz. *Publications:* (with H. J. C. Swan) Sympathetic Control of Human Blood Vessels, 1953; papers in the Journal of Physiology. *Recreations:* sailing, golf. *Address:* 73 Erskine Hill, NW11 6EY. *T:* (0181) 458 1066. *Died 11 Jan. 1998.*

BARFETT, Ven. Thomas; Archdeacon of Hereford and Canon Residentiary of Hereford Cathedral, 1977–82, then Emeritus; Prebendary of Colwall and Treasurer of Hereford Cathedral, 1977–82; Chaplain to the Queen, 1975–86; *b* 2 Oct. 1916; *s* of Rev. Thomas Clarence Fairchild Barfett and Dr Mary Deborah Barfett, MA, LRCP, LRCS; *m* 1945, Edna, *d* of Robert Toy; one *s* one *d*. *Educ:* St John's Sch., Leatherhead; Keble Coll., Oxford (BA 1938; MA 1942); Wells Theol Coll. Ordained deacon, Portsmouth, 1939; priest, 1940; Curate: Christ Church, Gosport, 1939–44; St Francis of Assisi, Gladstone Park, London, 1944–47; St Andrew Undershaft with St Mary Axe, City of London, 1947–49; Asst Sec., London Diocesan Council for Youth, 1944–49; Vicar, St Paul,

Penzance, dio. of Truro, 1949–55; Rector of Falmouth, 1955–77; licensed to officiate, dioceses of Bermuda, 1984, Europe, 1986. Sec., Truro Diocesan Conf., 1952–67; Proctor in Convocation, dio. of Truro, 1958–76; Hon. Canon, Truro, 1964–77; Chm., House of Clergy, and Vice-Pres., Truro Diocesan Synod, 1970–76; Mem., Gen. Synod, 1977–82. Officiating Chaplain, 1102 Marine Craft Unit, RAF, 1957–75; Chaplain to lay Sheriff, City of London, 1976–77. Church Comr, 1975–82; Mem. C of E Central Bd of Finance, 1969–77, Pensions Board, 1973–86. Chairman: Missions to Seamen, Cornwall, 1957–77; Cornwall Family History Soc., 1985–88 (Pres., 1994–95). Mem., St John Council for Cornwall, 1983–93. Freeman, City of London, 1973; Freeman and Liveryman, Scriveners' Co., 1976. ChStJ 1995 (Sub ChStJ 1971; Asst ChStJ 1963). Silver Jubilee Medal, 1977. *Publications:* Trebarfoote: a Cornish family, 1975, 2nd edn 1989; ed Cornish section, Hatchments in Britain, 1988. *Recreations:* heraldry, genealogy. *Address:* Treberveth, 57 Falmouth Road, Truro, Cornwall TR1 2HL. *T:* (01872) 73726. *Club:* United Oxford & Cambridge University.

Died 22 June 2000.

BARKER, Sir Alwyn (Bowman), Kt 1969; CMG 1962; CEng, FIEE, FIEAust; Chairman, Kelvinator Australia Ltd, 1967–80 (Managing Director, 1952–67); *b* 5 Aug. 1900; *s* of late A. J. Barker, Mt Barker, South Australia; *m* 1926, Isabel Barron Lucas (decd), *d* of late Sir Edward Lucas; one *d* (one *s* decd). *Educ:* St Peter's Coll., Adelaide; Geelong C of E Grammar Sch.; Univ. of Adelaide (BSc, BE). British Thomson Houston Co. Ltd, England, 1923–24; Hudson Motor Car Co., Detroit, 1924–25; Production Manager, Holden's Motor Body Builders Ltd, Adelaide, 1925–30; Works Manager, Kelvinator Aust. Ltd, Adelaide, 1931–40; Gen. Man., Chrysler Aust. Ltd, Adelaide, 1940–52. Chm., Municipal Tramways Trust SA, 1953–68; Dir, public companies. Mem. Faculty of Engineering, Univ. of Adelaide, 1937–66 (Lectr in Industrial Engineering, 1929–53). Chm., Industrial Develt Adv. Council, 1968–70; Member: Manufacturing Industries Adv. Council, 1958–72; Res. and Develt Adv. Cttee, 1967–72. Hon. Life Mem., Australian Mineral Foundn; FIAM. Hon. FAIM (Federal Pres., 1952–53, 1959–61; Pres. Adelaide Div., 1952–54); Pres., Australian Council, Inst. of Prodn Engrs, 1970–72. John Storey Meml Medal, 1965; Jack Finlay Nat. Award, 1964. *Publications:* Three Presidential Addresses, 1954; William Queale Memorial Lecture, 1965. *Recreations:* pastoral. *Address:* 30 Ninth Avenue, St Peters, Hackney, SA 5069, Australia. *T:* (8) 83622838. *Club:* Adelaide.

Died 25 Sept. 1998.

BARKER, Edward, OBE 1966; QPM 1961; Chief Constable of Sheffield and Rotherham Constabulary, 1967–72; *b* 1 Nov. 1909; *s* of George and Gertrude Barker; *m* 1935, Clare Garth; one *d*. *Educ:* The Grammar School, Malton. Joined Preston Borough Police, 1931; transf. Lancs Constabulary, 1938; Inspector/Chief Inspector, Comdt of Constabulary Trng Sch., 1946–51; Supt 1954; Vis. Lectr to Bermuda Police, 1955; Chief Supt 1956; Asst Comdt, Police Coll., Bramshill, 1956–57; Chief Constable: Bolton Borough Police, 1957; Sheffield City Police, 1964. Hon. Fellow, Sheffield Poly., 1973. Police Long Service and Good Conduct Medal, 1953. SBStJ. *Recreations:* golf, gardening, watching field sports. *Address:* 21 Woodstock Road, Aberdeen AB2 4ET. *T:* (01224) 318484. *Club:* Deeside Golf.

Died 7 Jan. 1999.

BARKLEY, Rev. Prof. John Montieth; retired; Principal, Union Theological College, Belfast, 1978–81; *b* 16 Oct. 1910; *s* of Rev. Robert James Barkley, BD, and Mary Monteith; *m* 1st, 1936, Irene Graham Anderson (*d* 1987); one *d*; 2nd, 1988, Caroline Margaret Barnett. *Educ:* Magee

University Coll., Derry; Trinity Coll., Dublin; The Presbyterian Coll., Belfast. BA 1934, MA 1941, BD 1944, PhD 1946, DD 1949, Trinity Coll., Dublin; BA 1952, MA 1953, Queen's Univ., Belfast. Thompson Memorial Prizeman in Philosophy, 1934; Larmour Memorial Exhibitioner in Theology, 1944; Paul Memorial Prizeman in History, 1953; Carey Lecturer, 1954–56. Ordained, Drumreagh Presbyterian Church, 1935; installed in II Ballybay and Rockcorry, 1939; installed in Cooke Centenary, Belfast, 1949. Lecturer in Ecclesiastical History, Queen's Univ., Belfast, 1951–54; Prof. in Ecclesiastical Hist., 1954–79, Vice-Principal, 1964–76, Principal, 1976–78, Presbyterian Coll., Belfast, until amalgamated with Magee Coll. to form Union Theological Coll. FRHistS. *Publications:* Handbook on Evangelical Christianity and Romanism, 1949; Presbyterianism, 1951; Westminster Formularies in Irish Presbyterianism, 1956; History of the Presbyterian Church in Ireland, 1959; Weltkirchenlexikon (arts), 1960; History of the Sabbath School Society for Ireland, 1961; The Eldership in Irish Presbyterianism; The Baptism of Infants, 1963; The Presbyterian Orphan Society, 1966; Worship of the Reformed Church, 1966; St Enoch's 1872–1972, 1972; (ed) Handbook to Church Hymnary, 3rd edn, 1979; Fasti of the Presbyterian Church in Ireland 1840–1910, 1987; Blackmouth and Dissenter (autobiog.), 1991; articles in Scottish Journal of Theology, Verbum Caro, Biblical Theology, Dictionary of Worship. *Recreations:* bowls, golf. *Address:* 14 Clonallon Park, Belfast BT4 2BZ. *T:* (01232) 650842.

Died 20 Dec. 1997.

BARLOW, Margaret, (Lady Barlow); *see* Rawlings, M.

BARNARD, Hon. Lance Herbert, AO 1979; retired; Director, Office of Australian War Graves, Department of Veterans' Affairs, Commonwealth of Australia, 1981–83; *b* 1 May 1919; *s* of Hon. H. C. Barnard and M. M. Barnard (*née* McKenzie); *m* 2nd, 1962, Jill Denise Carstairs, *d* of Senator H. G. J. Cant; one *s* two *d* (and one *d* decd); also one *d* by a former marriage. *Educ:* Launceston Technical Coll. Served War, overseas, AIF 9th Div., 1940. Formerly teacher, Tasmanian Educn Dept. Mem. for Bass, House of Representatives, 1954–75; Dep. Leader, Federal Parliamentary Labor Party, 1967–72; Deputy Prime Minister, 1972–74; Minister for Defence (Navy, Army, Air), 1972–75, and for Supply, 1973–75; also sometime Postmaster-Gen., Minister for Labour and National Service, Immigration, Social Services, Repatriation, Health, Primary Industry, National Development, and of the Interior, 1972–75; Australian Ambassador to Sweden, Norway and Finland, 1975–78. Captain, Aust. Cadet Corps, post War of 1939–45. State Pres., Tasmanian Br., Aust. Labor Party; Tasmanian deleg., Federal Exec., Aust. Labor Party. *Publication:* Labor's Defence Policy, 1969. *Recreation:* gardening. *Address:* 6 Bertland Court, Launceston, Tasmania 7250, Australia.

Died 6 Aug. 1997.

BARNES, Dame (Alice) Josephine (Mary Taylor), (Dame Josephine Warren), DBE 1974; FRCP, FRCS, FRCOG; Consulting Obstetrician and Gynaecologist, Charing Cross Hospital and Elizabeth Garrett Anderson Hospital; President, Women's Nationwide Cancer Control Campaign, since 1974 (Chairman, 1969–72; Vice-President, 1972–74); *b* 18 Aug. 1912; *er d* of late Rev. Walter W. Barnes, MA (Oxon), and Alice Mary Ibbetson, FRCO, ARCM; *m* 1942, Sir Brian Warren (marr. diss. 1964; he *d* 1996); one *s* two *d*. *Educ:* Oxford High Sch.; Lady Margaret Hall, Oxford (Hon. Fellow, 1980); University College Hosp. Med. Sch. BA 1st class Hons Physiology, Oxford, 1934; MA, BM, BCh 1937; DM 1941. FRCS 1939; FRCOG 1952; FRCP 1967. University College Hospital: Goldschmid Scholar; Aitchison Scholar; Tuke Silver Medal; Fellowes Silver Medal; F. T. Roberts

Prize; Suckling Prize. Various appointments at UCH, Samaritan Hosp., Queen Charlotte's Hosp., and Radcliffe Infirmary, Oxford; Dep. Academic Head, Obstetric Unit, UCH, 1947–52; Surgeon, Marie Curie Hosp., 1947–67. Medical Women's Federation: Hon. Sec., 1951–57; Pres., London Assoc., 1958–60; Pres., 1966–67. Royal Society of Medicine: Mem. Council, 1949–50; Pres., Sect. of Obstetrics and Gynaecology, 1972–73; Pres., Sect. of History of Medicine, 1995–96; Hon. Editor, Sect. of Obstetrics, 1951–71; Hon. Fellow, 1988. President: W London Medico-Chirurgical Soc., 1969–70; Nat. Assoc. of Family Planning Doctors, 1976–93; Obstetric Physiotherapists Assoc., 1976–94; BMA, 1979–80 (Pres.-elect, 1978–79; Life Mem., 1994); Union Professionnelle Internationale de Gynécologie et d'Obstétrique, 1977–79; Royal Medical Benevolent Fund, 1982–97; Royal British Nurses Assoc., 1997–. Examiner in Obstetrics and Gynaecology: Univ. of London; RCOG; Examining Bd in England, Queen's Univ., Belfast; Univ. of Oxford; Univ. of Kampala; Univ. of Ibadan; Univ. of Maiduguri. Member: Council, Med. Defence Union, 1961–82 (Vice-Pres. 1982–87; Hon. Fellow 1988); Royal Commn on Med. Educn, 1965–68; Council, RCOG, 1965–71 (Jun. Vice-Pres., 1972–74; Sen. Vice-Pres., 1974–75); MRC Cttee on Analgesia in Midwifery; Min. of Health Med. Manpower Cttee; Medico-Legal Soc.; Population Investigation Cttee, Eugenics Soc.; Cttee on the Working of the Abortion Act, 1971–73; Standing Med. Adv. Cttee, DHSS, 1976–80; Council, Advertising Standards Authority, 1980–93; DHSS Inquiry into Human Fertilisation and Embryology, 1982–84; Vice-Pres., Nat. Union of Townswomen's Guilds, 1979–82; President: Nat. Assoc. of Family Planning Nurses, 1980–; Osler Club of London, 1988–89; Friends of GPDST, 1988–. Mem. of Honour, French Gynaecological Soc., 1945; Hon. Member, British Paediatric Assoc., 1974; Italian Soc. of Obstetrics and Gynaecology, 1979; Nigerian Soc. of Gynaecology and Obstetrics, 1981; Corresp. Mem., Royal Belgian Soc. of Obstetricians and Gynaecologists, 1949. Governor; Charing Cross Hosp.; Chelsea Coll. of Science and Technology, 1958–85; Member Council; Benenden Sch., 1966–91, Bedford Coll., 1976–85; King's Coll., London, 1985–93 (FKC 1985); Mem. Court of Patrons, RCOG, 1984. Lectures: Fawcett, Bedford Coll., 1969; Rhys-Williams, Nat. Birthday Trust, 1970; Winston Churchill Meml, Postgrad. Med. Centre, Canterbury, 1971; Bartholomew Mosse, Rotunda Hosp., Dublin, 1975; Annual, Liverpool Med. Instn, 1979; Sophia, Univ. of Newcastle upon Tyne, 1980; Ann Horler, Newcastle upon Tyne, 1984; Helena Wright Meml, 1988; Margaret Jackson Meml, 1988. Simpson Oration, RCOG, 1977; Hunterian Orator, Hunterian Soc., 1994. Hon. FRCPI 1977; Hon. Fellow, Edinburgh Obstetrical Soc., 1980; Hon. FCSP 1991; Hon. FRCOG 1994; Hon. Fellow, RHBNC, London Univ., 1985. Hon. MD: Liverpool, 1979; Southampton, 1981; Hon. DSc: Leicester, 1980; Oxon, 1990. Hon. Bencher, Gray's Inn, 1992. Commandeur du Bontemps de Médoc et des Graves, 1966. Publications: Gynaecological Histology, 1948; The Care of the Expectant Mother, 1954; Lecture Notes on Gynaecology, 1966; (ed jtly) Scientific Foundations of Obstetrics and Gynaecology, 1970; Essentials of Family Planning, 1976; numerous contribs to med. jls, etc. Recreations: music, gastronomy, motoring, foreign travel; formerly hockey (Oxford Univ. Women's Hockey XI, 1932, 1933, 1934). Address: 1 Chartwell House, 12 Ladbroke Terrace, W11 3PG. T: (020) 7727 9832. Died 28 Dec. 1999.

BARNES, Daniel Sennett, CBE 1977; CEng, FIEE; Chairman, Berkshire and Oxfordshire Manpower Board, 1983–88; b 13 Sept. 1924; s of Paula Sennett Barnes and John Daniel Barnes; m 1955, Jean A. Steadman; one s. Educ: Dulwich Coll.; Battersea Polytechnic (BScEng, 1st

Cl. Hons). Apprenticeship at Philips, 1941–46; served REME, 1946–48; Battersea Polytechnic, 1948 51; Sperry Gyroscope, 1951–82: Dir of Engineering, 1962–68; Manager, Defence Systems, 1968–70; Gen. Manager, 1970–71; Man. Dir, 1971–82; British Aerospace PLC (formerly Sperry Gyroscope): Man. Dir, Electronic Systems and Equipment Div., 1982–85; HQ Dir, 1985–86; Director: Sperry Ltd UK, 1971–82; Sperry AG Switzerland, 1979–83. Pres., Electronic Engrg Assoc., 1981–82. Recreations: sailing, joinery, music and ballet, gardening. Died 10 Dec. 1996.

BARNES, Francis Walter Ibbetson; Chairman, Industrial Tribunals, 1976–87 (Resident Chairman, Exeter, 1984–87); b 10 May 1914; e s of late Rev. Walter W. Barnes, MA (Oxon) and Alice Mary Ibbetson, FRCO, ARCM; m 1st, 1941, Heather Katherine (marr. diss. 1953), d of Frank Tamplin; two s; 2nd, 1955, Sonia Nina, (Nina Walker, pianist), d of late Harold Higginbottom; two s one d. Educ: Dragon Sch., Oxford; Mill Hill Sch.; Balliol Coll., Oxford. BA Jurisprudence (Hons), Oxford, 1937; MA 1967. Called to the Bar, Inner Temple, 1938. Profumo Prize, Inner Temple, 1939. Served War, 1939–46 in Army (Middlesex Regt) and Home Office and Military Fire Services; Sen. Company Officer NFS and Capt. comdg military Fire Fighting Co., BLA; later Staff Capt. in Amsterdam, and in JAG (War Crimes Section), GHQ Germany; after release from Army, functioned as Judge Advocate or Prosecutor in various trials of war criminals in Germany, 1947–48. Recorder of Smethwick, 1964–66; Dep. Chm., Oxfordshire QS, 1965–71; Recorder of Warley, 1966–71, Hon. Recorder, 1972; a Recorder of the Crown Court, 1972–76. Elected to Bar Council, 1961. Bar Council's rep. (observer) on Cons. Cttee of Lawyers of the Common Market countries, 1962–71; contrib. to Common Market Law Review. Union Internationale des Avocats: Mem. Council, 1964; Rapporteur Général at Vienna Congress, 1967; Rapporteur National at Paris Congress, 1971. Life Governor, Mill Hill Sch., 1939, Mem., Dame Henrietta Barnett Bd (Educnl Trust), 1951. Mem., Exec. Cttee, Friends of Farnham Park Rehabilitation Centre, 1988–93; Dir, Farnham Park Ltd, 1989–93. Freeman, City of London, 1991. Recreations: music, languages, gardening. Address: 83 St George's Drive, Ickenham, Middx UB10 8HR. T: (01895) 672532.
Died 4 Feb. 2000.

BARNES, Dame Josephine; see Barnes, Dame A. J. M. T.

BARNES, Peter Robert, CB 1982; Deputy Director of Public Prosecutions, 1977–82; President, Video Appeals Committee, since 1985; b 1 Feb. 1921; s of Robert Stanley Barnes and Marguerite (née Dunkels); m 1955, Pauline Belinda Hannen; two s one d. Educ: Eton Coll.; Trinity Coll., Cambridge (BA). Called to Bar, Inner Temple, 1947. Dir. of Public Prosecutions: Legal Asst, 1951; Sen. Legal Asst, 1958; Asst Solicitor, 1970; Asst Director, 1974; Principal Asst Dir, 1977. Recreation: bridge. Address: 28 The Paddock, Godalming, Surrey GU7 1XD.
Died 4 Jan. 1996.

BARNES, Roland, CBE 1970; FRCS, FRCSE, FRCSGlas; Professor of Orthopaedic Surgery, University of Glasgow, 1959–72, then Professor Emeritus; b 21 May 1907; y s of Benjamin Barnes and Mary Ann Bridge, Accrington, Lancs.; m 1938, Mary Mills Buckley; one s two d. Educ: University of Manchester. BSc 1927; MB, ChB 1930; Medical and Surgical Clinical prizes. Usual resident appointments; Resident Surgical Officer, Manchester Royal Infirmary, 1934–35; Dickinson Travelling Scholar, Univ. of Manchester, 1935–36; visited orthopaedic clinics in USA; Fellow, Hospital for Ruptured and Crippled, New York; Chief Asst to Sir Harry Platt, Bt, Orthopaedic Department, Royal Infirmary, Manchester, 1937–39; Surgeon in Charge of Orthopædic and Peripheral Nerve

Injury Centre, EMS Hospital, Winwick, Lancs, 1940–43; Orth. Surgeon, Western Infirmary, Glasgow, and Killearn Hosp., Stirlingshire, 1943–72. Past Pres., British Orthopædic Assoc.; Hon. Mem. French, Finnish, German and S African Orthopædic Assocs; Corresp. Mem. Amer. Orthopædic Assoc. *Publications:* papers on injuries of the peripheral nerves and spine, fractures of neck of femur, and on tumours of bone. *Recreation:* gardening. *Address:* 12 St Germains, Bearsden, Glasgow G61 2RS. *T:* (0141) 942 2699. *Died 15 Nov. 1998.*

BARON, (Joseph) Alexander; writer; *b* 4 Dec. 1917; *s* of Barnet Baron and Fanny Levinson; *m* 1960, Delores Salzedo; one *s. Educ:* Hackney Downs Sch., London. Served War of 1939–45, Army. Asst Editor, The Tribune, 1938–39; Editor, New Theatre, 1946–49. Hon. Fellow, QMW, 1992. *Publications:* novels: From the City, From the Plough, 1948; There's No Home, 1950; Rosie Hogarth, 1951; With Hope, Farewell, 1952; The Human Kind, 1953; The Golden Princess, 1954; Queen of the East, 1956; Seeing Life, 1958; The Lowlife, 1963; Strip Jack Naked, 1966; King Dido, 1969; The In-Between Time, 1971; Gentle Folk, 1976; Franco is Dying, 1977; also film scripts and television plays. *Address:* c/o Unna and Durbridge, 24 Pottery Lane, W11 4LZ.
Died 6 Dec. 1999.

BARR, A(lbert) W(illiam) Cleeve, CBE 1972; architect, retired; *b* 5 Oct. 1910; *s* of Albert John Barr and Ellen (*née* Cleeve); *m* 1st, 1935, Edith M. Edwards, BA (*d* 1965); one *s* one *d* (and one *s* decd); 2nd, 1966, Mrs Mary W. Harley (*widow*). *Educ:* Borlase, Marlow; Liverpool Univ. Private offices (Charles Holden and Paul Mauger); Herts CC (schools) and LCC (housing); Dep. Housing Architect, LCC, 1956–57; Development Architect, Ministry of Education, 1957–58; Chief Architect, Min. of Housing and Local Govt, 1959–64; Dir, Nat. Building Agency, 1964–77 (Man. Dir, 1967–77); Dir, Nat. Building Agency Film Unit, 1977–80; Vice-Pres., UK Housing Trust, 1981–89. Hon. Sec., RIBA, 1963–65. *Recreation:* painting. *Address:* New Park House, Chivelstone Grove, Trentham, Stoke-on-Trent ST4 8HN.
Died 30 May 2000.

BARRER, Prof. Richard Maling, PhD Cantab; DSc NZ; ScD Cantab; FRS 1956; FRSC (FRIC 1939); Senior Research Fellow, Imperial College of Science and Technology, since 1977; Professor of Physical Chemistry, Imperial College of Science and Technology, University of London, 1954–77, then Emeritus; Head of Department of Chemistry, 1955–76; *b* 16 June 1910; *s* of T. R. Barrer, 103 Renall Street, Masterton, New Zealand; *m* 1939, Helen Frances Yule, Invercargill, NZ; one *s* three *d. Educ:* Canterbury University Coll., NZ (MSc); Clare Coll., Cambridge (1851 Exhibition Scholar). PhD Cantab, 1935; DSc NZ, 1937; ScD Cantab, 1948. Major Research Student, 1935–37, Research Fellow, 1937–39, Clare Coll., Cambridge; Head of Chemistry Dept, Technical Coll., Bradford, 1939–46; Reader in Chemistry, London Univ., 1946–49; Prof. of Chemistry, Aberdeen Univ., 1949–54. Dean, Royal Coll. of Science, 1964–66. Member Council: Faraday Soc., 1952–55; Chemical Soc., 1956–59, 1974–77; Royal Institute of Chemistry, 1961–64; Soc. of Chemical Industry, 1965–68. Governor, Chelsea Coll. of Sci. and Technol., 1960–81. Hon. Pres., Internat. Zeolite Assoc., 1994–. Hon. ARCS 1959; Hon. FRSNZ 1965; Hon. FNZIC 1987; Hon. DSc: Bradford, 1967; Aberdeen, 1983. *Publications:* Diffusion in and through Solids, 1941; Zeolites and Clay Minerals as Sorbents and Molecular Sieves, 1978; Hydrothermal Chemistry of Zeolites, 1982; research papers in British and foreign scientific journals. *Recreations:* tennis, interest in athletics (Full Blue and winner Oxford–Cambridge cross-country, 1934; winner UAU cross-country, 1935). *Address:* Flossmoor,

Orpington Road, Chislehurst, Kent BR7 6RA. *Clubs:* Hawks (Cambridge); Achilles.
Died 12 Sept. 1996.

BARRETT, Sir Dennis Charles T.; *see* Titchener-Barrett.

BARRETT, Ernest; Chairman: Henry Barrett & Sons Ltd, 1982–87 (Joint Managing Director, 1968–85); Steel Stockholding Division, Henry Barrett & Sons Ltd, 1967–85; Henry Lindsay Ltd, 1974–87; *b* 8 April 1917; *s* of Ernest Barrett and Marian Conyers; *m* 1940, Eileen Maria Peel; one *d. Educ:* Charterhouse. Served War, RA, and commissioned, 1940; served in Mediterranean Theatre, with 1st Army, 1943–46 (despatches, 1944); Major 1945. Joined Henry Barrett & Sons Ltd, Bradford, 1934; apptd Dir, 1946. Pres., Nat. Assoc. of Steel Stockholders, 1977–79 (Chm., Yorks Assoc., 1964–66; Vice-Pres., 1975–77); Pres., Engineering Industries Assoc., 1971 (Chm. Yorks Region, 1960–65; Vice-Pres. of Assoc., 1965–71). *Recreation:* gardening. *Address:* West Ghyll, Victoria Avenue, Ilkley, W Yorks LS29 9BW. *T:* (01943) 609294. *Died 10 June 1998.*

BARRETT, Jack Wheeler, CBE 1971; PhD; FEng 1976; CChem; FIC; Chairman, Cole Group plc, 1979–86 (Director, 1978); *b* 13 June 1912; *s* of John Samuel Barrett, Cheltenham; *m* 1935, Muriel Audley Read; two *s* two *d. Educ:* Cheltenham Grammar Sch.; Imperial Coll., Univ. of London. BSc, PhD; FRSC, FIChemE. Chief Chemist, London Essence Co. Ltd, 1936–41; joined Monsanto Chemicals Ltd, 1941; Dir of Research, 1955–71; Dir, Monsanto Ltd, 1955–78; Chm., Info-line Ltd, 1976–80. President: IChemE, 1971–72; Chem. Soc., 1974–75; IInfSc, 1976–79; ICSU Abstracting Bd, 1974–77; Chm., Chemical Divl Council, BSI, 1973–79; Mem., British Library Bd, 1973–79. *Publications:* articles in Jl Chem. Soc., Chemistry and Industry, Jl ASLIB, Chemistry in Britain. *Recreation:* gardening. *Address:* West Manor House, Bourton-on-the-Water, Cheltenham, Glos GL54 2AP. *T:* (01451) 820296. *Club:* Athenæum.
Died 27 Feb. 1998.

BARRY, Maj.-Gen. Richard Hugh, CB 1962; CBE 1953 (OBE 1943); *b* 9 Nov. 1908; *s* of Lt-Col Alfred Percival Barry and Helen Charlotte (*née* Stephens); *m* 1st, 1940, Rosalind Joyce Evans (*d* 1973); one *s* two *d*; 2nd, 1975, Elizabeth Lucia Middleton (*d* 1994). *Educ:* Winchester; Sandhurst. 2nd Lieut Somerset LI, 1929; Staff Coll., Camberley, Capt., 1938; served War of 1939–45: BEF, SOE, AFHQ, Algiers; Military Attaché, Stockholm, 1947; Deputy Chief of Staff Western Europe Land Forces, 1948; Dir, Standing Group, NATO, 1952; Chief of Staff, HQ British Troops in Egypt, 1954–56; Imperial Defence Coll., 1957; Standing Group Representative, North Atlantic Council, 1959–62; Maj.-Gen. 1959; retired, 1962. Africa Star, 1943; 1939–45 Star; Defence, Victory Medals, 1945. *Recreation:* hunting. *Address:* Room 3, Blue Wing, Brendoncare Alton, Adams Way, Alton, Hants GU34 2UU. *T:* (01420) 593727. *Club:* Army and Navy.
Died 30 April 1999.

BART, Lionel; composer, lyricist and playwright; *b* 1 Aug. 1930. Wrote lyrics for Lock Up Your Daughters, 1959; music and lyrics for Fings Ain't Wot They Used T'be, 1959; music, lyrics and book for Oliver!, 1960; music, lyrics and direction of Blitz!, also co-author of book with Joan Maitland, 1962; music and lyrics of Maggie May, 1964; music of Lionel, 1977. Also wrote several film scores and many individual hit songs. *Films:* Serious Charge; In the Nick; Heart of a Man; Let's Get Married; Light up the Sky; The Tommy Steele Story; The Duke Wore Jeans; Tommy the Toreador; Sparrers Can't Sing; From Russia with Love; Man in the Middle; Oliver (gold disc for sound track, 1969); The Optimists of Nine Elms. Tony (Antoinette Perry) Award, etc (for Oliver!), best composer and lyricist, 1962; Ivor Novello Awards as a song writer: three in 1957; four in 1959; two in 1960; for best original theme, radio and TV, 1989; Ivor Novello/Jimmy Kennedy Award, for life long achievement, 1985; Golden Break Award, 1990. Variety Club Silver Heart as Show Business Personality of the Year, 1960, Broadway, USA; Variety Club Silver Heart for contribution to the world's Musical Theatre, 1997. *Address:* c/o 65 New Cavendish Street, W1M 7RD. *Died 3 April 1999.*

BARTLETT, Sir John (Hardington David), 4th Bt *cr* 1913, of Hardington Mandeville, Somerset; Director of various companies; *b* 11 March 1938; *s* of Sir (Henry) David (Hardington) Bartlett, 3rd Bt, MBE and of Kathleen Rosamund, *d* of late Lt-Col W. H. Stanbury; *S* father, 1989; *m* 1st, 1966, Susan Elizabeth Waldock (*d* 1970); one *d*; 2nd, 1971, Elizabeth Joyce, *d* of George Raine: two *s. Educ:* St Peter's Grammar Sch., Guildford. Career in engineering and construction. FRSA. Freeman: City of London; Pattenmakers' Co. *Recreations:* joinery, woodwork, fine wine. *Heir: s* Andrew Alan Bartlett, *b* 26 May 1973. *Address:* Hardington House, Ermyn Way, Leatherhead, Surrey KT22 8TW. *Club:* Naval.
Died 8 April 1998.

BARTON, Sir Derek Harold Richard, Kt 1972; FRS 1954; FRSE 1956; Dow Distinguished Professor of Chemical Invention, Texas A and M University, since 1995; *b* 8 Sept. 1918; *s* of William Thomas and Maude Henrietta Barton; *m* 1st, 1944, Jeanne Kate Wilkins; one *s;* 2nd, 1969, Christiane Cognet (*d* 1992); 3rd, 1993, Judith Von-Leuenberger Cobb. *Educ:* Tonbridge Sch.; Imperial Coll., Univ. of London (Fellow, 1980). BSc Hons (1st Class) 1940; Hofmann Prizeman; PhD (Organic Chemistry) 1942; DSc London 1949. Research Chemist: on Govt project, 1942–44; Albright and Wilson, Birmingham, 1944–45; Asst Lectr, Dept of Chemistry, Imperial Coll., 1945–46, ICI Research Fellow, 1946–49; Visiting Lectr in Chemistry of Natural Products, Harvard Univ., USA, 1949–50; Reader in Organic Chemistry, 1950–53, Prof. of Organic Chemistry, 1953–55, Birkbeck Coll.; Regius Prof. of Chemistry, Glasgow Univ., 1955–57; Prof. of Organic Chem., 1957–70, Hofmann Prof. of Organic Chem., 1970–78, Imperial Coll.; Emeritus Prof. of Organic Chem., Univ. of London, 1978; Dir, Institut de Chimie des Substances Naturelles, CNRS, France, 1977–85; Distinguished Prof. of Chem., Texas A and M Univ., 1986–95. Arthur D. Little Vis. Prof., MIT, 1958; Karl Folkers Vis. Prof., Univs of Illinois and Wisconsin, 1959; Cecil H. and Ida Green Vis. Prof., Univ. of British Columbia, 1977; Firth Vis. Prof. in Chemistry, Univ. of Sheffield, 1978. Lectures: Tilden, Chem. Soc., 1952; Max Tischler, Harvard Univ., 1956; First Simonsen Memorial, Chem. Soc., 1958; Falk-Plaut, Columbia Univ., 1961; Aub, Harvard Med. Sch., 1962; Renaud, Michigan State Univ., 1962; Inaugural 3 M's, Univ. of Western Ontario, 1962; 3 M's, Univ. of Minnesota, 1963; Hugo Müller, Chem. Soc., 1963; Pedler, Chem. Soc., 1967; Sandin, Univ. of Alberta, 1969; Robert Robinson, Chem. Soc., London, 1970; Bakerian, Royal Society, 1970; Bose Endowment, Bose Inst., Calcutta, 1972; Stieglitz, Chicago Univ., 1974; Bachmann, Michigan, 1974; Woodward, Yale, 1974; First Smissman, Kansas, 1976; Benjamin Rush and Priestley, Pennsylvania State Univ., 1977; Romanes, Edinburgh, 1979; (first) Hirst, St Andrews Univ., 1980; Kharasch, Univ. of Chicago, 1987; Nelson Leonard, Illinois Univ., 1988; C. B. Purves, McGill Univ., 1988; Janôt, France, 1989; Rayson Huang, Hong Kong Univ., 1994. President: Section B, British Assoc. for the Advancement of Science, 1969; Organic Chemistry Div., Internat. Union of Pure and Applied Chemistry, 1969; Chem. Soc., 1973–74 (Pres., Perkin Div., 1971). Mem., Council for Scientific Policy, 1965–68. Hon. Member: Sociedad Quimica de Mexico, 1969; Belgian Chem. Soc.,

1970; Chilean Chem. Soc., 1970; Polish Chem. Soc., 1970; Pharmaceutical Soc. of Japan, 1970; Royal Acad. Exact Scis, Madrid, 1971; Acad. of Pharmaceutical Scis, USA, 1971; Danish Acad. Scis, 1972; Argentinian Acad. Scis, 1973; Società Italiana per il Progresso delle Scienze, 1977; Chem. Soc. of Japan, 1982; Acad. des Scis, France, 1983; Royal Irish Acad. of Sci., 1985; Corresp. Mem., Argentinian Chem. Soc., 1970; Foreign Member: Acad. das Ciencias de Lisboa, 1971; Academia Nazionale dei Lincei, Rome, 1974; Indian Nat. Sci. Acad., 1990; Foreign Hon. Member: American Academy of Arts and Sciences, 1960; Kitasato Inst. of Japan, 1990; Foreign Associate: Nat. Acad. of Sciences, USA, 1970; l'Académie des Sciences, Institute de France, 1978. Hon. Fellow: Deutsche Akad. der Naturforscher Leopoldina, 1967; Birkbeck Coll., 1970; ACS Centennial Foreign Fellow, 1976; Hon. FRSC 1985. Hon. DSc: Montpellier Univ., 1962; Dublin, 1963; St Andrews, Columbia NYC, 1970; Coimbra, 1971; Oxon, Manchester, 1972; South Africa, 1973; La Laguna, Western Virginia, 1974; Sydney, 1976; Valencia, Sheffield, Western Ontario, Weizman Inst. of Sci., 1979; London, 1984; Debrechen, 1986; Shanghai Inst. of Organic Chemistry, 1991; Marseille III, Nova de Lisboa, Cordoba (Argentina), Nacionel de Sur (Argentina), 1993; Hong Kong, 1994; Puebla, Salamanca, Conception, Tokushima, Munich, 1995; Hon. Dr: Frankfurt, 1980; Metz, 1981; Lyon, Uruguay, 1983; Paris-Sud, 1988; Hon. DrEng Stevens Inst. of Technol., 1984. Harrison Memorial Prize, Chem. Soc., 1948; First Corday-Morgan Medallist, Chemical Soc., 1951; Fritzsche Medal, Amer. Chem. Soc., 1956; First Roger Adams Medal, Amer. Chem. Soc., 1959; Davy Medal, Royal Society, 1961; Nobel Prize for Chemistry (jointly), 1969; First award in Natural Product Chemistry, Chem. Soc. of London, 1971; Longstaff Medal, Chem. Soc., 1972; B. C. Law Gold Medal, Indian Assoc. for Cultivation of Science, 1972; Medal, Soc. of Cosmetic Chem. of GB, 1972; Royal Medal, Royal Soc., 1972; Second Centennial of Priestley Chemistry Award, Amer. Chem. Soc., 1974; Medal of Union of Sci. Workers, Bulgaria, 1978; Univ. of Sofia Medal, 1978; Acad. of Scis, Bulgaria Medal, 1978; Copley Medal, Royal Soc., 1980; Hanbury Mcml Medal, PSGB, 1981; first May & Baker Award, RSC, 1987; Chemical Pioneers award, Amer. Inst. of Chem., 1993; Priestley Medal, Amer. Chem. Soc., 1995; Lavoisier Medal, French Chem. Soc., 1995. Order of the Rising Sun (2nd class), Japan, 1972; Officier, Légion d'Honneur, 1985 (Chevalier, 1974). *Publications:* numerous, in Journal of Chemical Society and Tetrahedron. *Address:* Chemistry Department, Texas A and M University, PO Box 300012, College Station, TX 77842–3012, USA. *Died 16 March 1998.*

BARWICK, Rt Hon. Sir Garfield (Edward John), AK 1981; GCMG 1965; Kt 1953; PC 1964; QC (Aust.); Chief Justice of Australia, 1964–81; *b* 22 June 1903; *s* of late Jabez Edward Barwick and Lilian Grace Ellicott; *m* 1929, Norma Mountier Symons; one *s* one *d. Educ:* Fort Street Boys' High Sch., Sydney; University of Sydney. BA 1923; LLB (Hons) 1926. New South Wales Bar, 1927; KC (NSW) 1941; Victorian Bar, 1945; KC (Vic) 1945; Queensland Bar, 1958; QC (Queensland) 1958. Practised extensively in all jurisdictions: Supreme Court, High Court of Australia and Privy Council. Attorney-Gen. Commonwealth of Australia, Dec. 1958–Feb. 1964; Minister for External Affairs, Dec. 1961–April 1964. Judge *ad hoc,* Internat. Court of Justice, 1973–74. President: NSW Bar Assoc., 1950–52 and 1955–56; Law Council of Australia, 1952–54; Australian Inst. of Internat. Affairs, 1972–83. Hon. Bencher, Lincoln's Inn, 1964. Leader: Australian Delegation, SEATO Council, Bangkok, 1961, Paris, 1963; UN Delegation, 1960, 1962–64; Australian Delegation to ECAFE, Manila, 1963; Australian Delegation, ANZUS, Canberra, 1962,

Wellington, 1963. Chancellor, Macquarie Univ., 1967–78. Vice–Patron, Royal NSW Inst. for Deaf and Blind Children, 1995– (Pres., 1976–95). Hon. LLD: Sydney, 1972; Macquarie, 1987. *Publications:* Sir John Did His Duty, 1983; A Radical Tory – reflections and recollections, 1995. *Recreations:* fishing, yachting. *Address:* 71 The Cotswolds, Curagul and Bobbin Head Roads, North Turramurra, NSW 2074, Australia. *Clubs:* Australian (Sydney); Royal Sydney Yacht Squadron; Hon. Member: Pioneers' (Australasian); Tattersalls; City Tattersalls; Middle Harbour Yacht. *Died 13 July 1997.*

BASINSKI, Prof. Zbigniew Stanislaw, OC 1985; DPhil, DSc; FRS 1980; FRSC; Research Professor, Department of Materials Science and Engineering, McMaster University, Ont, 1987–92, then Professor Emeritus; *b* Wolkowysk, Poland, 28 April 1928; *s* of Antoni Basinski and Maria Zofia Anna Hilferding Basinska; *m* 1952, Sylvia Joy Pugh; two *s. Educ:* Lyceum of Krzemieniec, Poland; Polish Army Cadet Sch., Camp Barbara, Palestine, 1943–47; Univ. of Oxford (BSc, MA, DPhil, DSc). Research Asst, Univ. of Oxford, 1951–54; Staff Member, Dept of Mech. Engrg (Cryogenic Lab.), Massachusetts Inst. of Technol., 1954–56; Nat. Res. Council of Canada, 1956–87, latterly as Principal Res. Officer and Head of Materials Physics (Div. of Physics). Ford Distinguished Vis. Prof., Carnegie Inst. of Technol., Pittsburgh, USA, 1964–65; Commonwealth Vis. Prof., Univ. of Oxford, Fellow of Wolfson Coll., Oxford, 1969–70; Adjunct Prof., Carleton Univ., Ottawa, 1975–77; Overseas Fellow, Churchill Coll., Cambridge, 1980–81. Dr *hc* Acad. of Mining and Metallurgy, Stanislaw Staszic Univ., Krakow, 1991. *Publications:* many original research papers, mainly related to crystal defects and the mechanical properties of metals, in learned jls. *Recreations:* computer design, the stock market, winemaking, general reading. *Clubs:* Oxford Union, Halifax House (Oxford).

Died 12 Aug. 1999.

BASSET, Lady Elizabeth, DCVO 1989 (CVO 1976); Extra Woman of the Bedchamber to Queen Elizabeth the Queen Mother, 1959–81 and since 1993 (Woman of the Bedchamber, 1981–93); *b* 5 March 1908; *d* of 7th Earl of Dartmouth, GCVO, TD and Ruperta, Countess of Dartmouth; *m* 1931, Ronald Lambart Basset (*d* 1972); one *s* (and one *s* decd). *Educ:* at home. *Publications:* anthologies: Love is My Meaning, 1973, 2nd edn 1988; Each in His Prison, 1978; The Bridge is Love, 1981; Interpreted by Love, 1994; Beyond the Blue Mountains, 1999. *Recreations:* riding, gardening, reading, writing, needlework. *Address:* 67 Cottesmore Court, Kelso Place, W8 5QW. *T:* (020) 7937 1803.

Died 30 Nov. 2000.

BATCHELOR, Prof. George Keith, FRS 1957; Emeritus Professor of Applied Mathematics, University of Cambridge, 1983; Fellow of Trinity College, Cambridge, since 1947; *b* Melbourne, 8 March 1920; *s* of George Conybere Batchelor and Ivy Constance Batchelor (*née* Berneye); *m* 1944, Wilma Maud Rätz, MBE (*d* 1997); three *d. Educ:* Essendon and Melbourne High Schs; Univ. of Melbourne (BSc 1940, MSc 1941); PhD 1948, Adams Prize, 1951, Cambridge. Research Officer, Aeronautical Research Laboratory, Melbourne, 1940–44; Lectr, Univ. of Cambridge, 1948–59, Reader in Fluid Dynamics, 1959–64, and Head of Dept of Applied Mathematics and Theoretical Physics, 1959–83; Prof. of Applied Maths, Univ. of Cambridge, 1964–83. Chairman: European Mechanics Cttee, 1964–87; Nat. Cttee for Theoretical and Applied Mechanics, 1967–72. Editor, Cambridge Monographs on Mechanics and Applied Mathematics, 1953–; Editor, Journal of Fluid Mechanics, 1956–. Mem. Council, Royal Soc., 1986–87; Mem., Royal Soc. of Sciences, Uppsala, 1972. Foreign Hon. Member: Amer.

Acad. of Arts and Scis, 1959; Polish Acad. of Scis, 1974; French Acad. of Sci., 1984; Aust. Acad. of Sci., 1989; Emeritus MAE, 1990; For. Associate, US Nat. Acad. of Scis, 1994. Dr *hc*: Grenoble, 1959; Tech. Univ. of Denmark, 1974; McGill, 1986; Michigan, 1990; Melbourne, 1994; Stockholm, 1995. Agostinelli Prize, Accad. Nazionale dei Lincei, Rome, 1986; Royal Medal, Royal Soc., 1988; Timoshenko Medal, Amer. Soc. Mech. Engrs, 1988; Taylor Medal, Soc. of Engrg Sci., 1997. *Publications:* The Theory of Homogeneous Turbulence, 1953; An Introduction to Fluid Dynamics, 1967; (ed) The Scientific Papers of G. I. Taylor, vol. 1, 1958, vol. 2, 1960, vol. 3, 1963, vol. 4, 1971; The Life and Legacy of G. I. Taylor, 1996; papers on fluid mechanics and its applications in scientific jls. *Address:* Trinity College, Cambridge CB2 1TQ. *T:* (01223) 339920.

Died 30 March 2000.

BATE, Sir (Walter) Edwin, Kt 1969; OBE 1955; Barrister, Solicitor and Notary Public, Hastings, New Zealand, since 1927; *b* 12 March 1901; *s* of Peter and Florence Eleanor Bate; *m* 1925, Louise Jordan; two *s* one *d. Educ:* Victoria Univ., Wellington (LLM (first class hons), 1922). Admitted Barrister and Solicitor, 1922; practised: Taumarunui, NZ, 1923; Hastings, NZ, 1927. Mayor, City of Hastings, NZ, 1953–59; Chm., Hawke Bay Hosp. Bd, 1941–74; Pres., Hosp. Bds Assoc. of NZ, 1953–74; Pres., Associated Trustee Savings Banks of NZ, 1968 and 1969. OStJ 1961. Grand Master of Freemasons in NZ, 1972–74. *Recreation:* gardening. *Address:* 38 Busby Hill, Havelock North, New Zealand. *T:* (6) 8777448. *Died 12 Sept. 1999.*

BATE, Prof. Walter Jackson; Kingsley Porter University Professor, Harvard University, since 1980; *b* 23 May 1918; *s* of William George Bate. *Educ:* Harvard Univ. AB 1939, PhD 1942. Harvard University: Associate Prof. of English, 1949–55; Prof. of English, 1955–62; Chm., Dept of English, 1955–62; Abbott Lawrence Lowell Prof. of the Humanities, 1962–80. Corresp. Fellow, British Acad., 1978. Member: Amer. Acad. of Arts and Sciences; Amer. Philosophical Soc.; Cambridge Scientific Soc. Christian Gauss Award, 1956, 1964, 1970; Pulitzer Prize for Biography, 1964, 1978; Nat. Book Award, 1978; Nat. Book Critics Award, 1978. *Publications:* Stylistic Development of Keats, 1945; From Classic to Romantic, 1946; Criticism: the Major Texts, 1952; The Achievement of Samuel Johnson, 1955; Prefaces to Criticism, 1959; Yale Edition of Samuel Johnson, Vol. II, 1963, Vols III-V, 1969; John Keats, 1963; Coleridge, 1968; The Burden of the Past and The English Poet, 1971; Samuel Johnson, 1977; (ed) Coleridge, *Biographia Literaria,* 1982; (ed) British and American Poets: Chaucer to the present, 1985; Harvard Scholars in English 1890–1990, 1992. *Recreation:* farming. *Address:* 781 Widener Library, Cambridge, MA 02138, USA. *Club:* Saturday (Boston, Mass). *Died 26 July 1999.*

BATEMAN, Sir Cecil (Joseph), KBE 1967 (MBE 1944); Chairman, G. Heyn & Sons Ltd, 1971–87; Director: Nationwide Building Society, 1970–84; Allied Irish Banks, 1970–80; Allied Irish Investment Bank Ltd, 1971–80; *b* 6 Jan. 1910; *s* of Samuel and Annie Bateman; *m* 1938, Doris M. Simpson; one *s* one *d. Educ:* Queen's Univ., Belfast. Served War of 1939–45, Royal Artillery (Major). Entered NI Civil Service, Nov. 1927; Dir of Establishments, Min. of Finance, 1958–63; Sec. to Cabinet and Clerk of Privy Council of N Ireland, 1963–65; Permanent Sec., Min. of Finance, and Head of Northern Ireland Civil Service, 1965–70. *Recreations:* golf, reading. *Address:* 26 Schomberg Park, Belfast BT4 2HH. *T:* (01232) 763484. *Died 26 March 1997.*

BATEMAN, Sir Geoffrey (Hirst), Kt 1972; FRCS; Surgeon, Ear, Nose and Throat Department, St Thomas' Hospital, London, 1939–71; *b* 24 Oct. 1906; *s* of Dr

William Hirst Bateman, JP, Rochdale, Lancs; *m* 1931, Margaret, *d* of Sir Samuel Turner, Rochdale; three *s* one *d*. *Educ*: Epsom Coll.; University Coll., Oxford. Theodore Williams Schol. in Anat., Oxford Univ., 1926; BA Oxon, Hons sch. Physiol., 1927; Epsom schol. to King's Coll. Hosp., 1927; BM, BCh Oxon, 1930; FRCS 1933; George Herbert Hunt Trav. Schol., Oxford Univ., 1933. RAFVR, Wing Comdr, 1939–45. Formerly Hon. Cons. on Oto-rhino-laryngology to the Army; Cons. Adviser in Otolaryngology, Dept of Health and Social Security. Mem., Bd Governors, St Thomas' Hosp., 1948; Mem. Collegium Otolaryngologica Amicitiæ Sacrum, 1949; Hon. Corresp. Mem. Amer. Laryngological Assoc., 1960; Past Mem. Council, RCS; Editor, Jl of Laryngology and Otology, 1961–77; Pres., British Assoc. of Otolaryngologists, 1970–71 (Vice-Pres., 1967–70). Hon. FRSocMed 1978. *Publications:* Diseases of the Nose and Throat (Asst Editor to V. E. Negus, 6th edn), 1955; contributor various jls, etc. *Recreations:* golf, fishing. *Address:* Thorney, Graffham, Petworth, West Sussex GU28 0QA. *T:* (01798) 867314.

Died 17 Sept. 1998.

BATEMAN, Sir Ralph (Melton), KBE 1975; MA Oxon; Chairman, Stothert and Pitt, 1977–85; President, Confederation of British Industry, 1974–76 (Deputy President, 1973–74); *b* 15 May 1910; 3rd *s* of William Hirst Bateman, MB, BCh, and Ethel Jane Bateman, Rochdale, Lancs; *m* 1935, (Barbara) Yvonne, 2nd *d* of Herbert Percy Litton and Grace Vera Litton, Heywood, Lancs; two *s* two *d*. *Educ*: Epsom Coll.; University Coll., Oxford. Turner & Newall Ltd: joined as management trainee, 1931; held various directorships in Group, 1942–76; Dir, 1957; Dep. Chm., 1959; Chm., 1967–76. Mem., NEDC, 1973–76. Mem. Council, Manchester Business Sch., 1972–76; Vice-Pres., Ashridge Management Coll.; Chm. of Council, University Coll. at Buckingham, 1976–79; Member Court: Manchester Univ.; Salford Univ. FCIS, CBIM; FRSA 1970. Hon. Fellow, UMIST, 1977. Hon. DSc: Salford, 1969; Buckingham, 1983. *Recreations:* family and social affairs. *Address:* 2 Bollin Court, Macclesfield Road, Wilmslow, Cheshire SK9 2AP. *T:* Wilmslow (01625) 530437.

Died 25 Jan. 1996.

BATES, Sir Dawson; *see* Bates, Sir J. D.

BATES, Eric, FIEE; Chairman, Midlands Electricity Board, 1969–72; *b* 1 Nov. 1908; *s* of late John Boon Bates and Edith Anne Bates; *m* 1933, Beatrice, *d* of late William Henry Herapath and Beatrice Herapath; one *s* two *d*. Trained Ilford Elec. Dept; Asst, County of London Elec. Supply Co., 1929–32; Consumers' Engineer: West Kent Electric Co., 1933–36; Isle of Thanet Elec. Supply Co., 1937–42; Elec. Engr, Kennedy & Donkin, 1942–44; Consumers' Engr, Luton Elec. Dept, 1944–48; Sect. Head, Eastern Elec. Bd, 1948–49; Dep. Chief Commercial Officer, Eastern Elec. Bd, 1949–57; North Eastern Electricity Board: Chief Commercial Officer, 1957–62; Dep. Chm., 1962–67; Chm., 1967–69. *Publications:* contribs to Proc. IEE. *Address:* Broadstairs, Kent.

Died 21 Jan. 1999.

BATES, Sir (John) Dawson, 2nd Bt *cr* 1937, of Magherabuoy, co. Londonderry; MC 1943; Regional Director of the National Trust, retired 1981; *b* 21 Sept. 1921; *o s* of Sir (Richard) Dawson Bates, 1st Bt, PC, and Muriel (*d* 1972), *d* of late Sir Charles Cleland, KBE, MVO, LLD; *S* father, 1949; *m* 1953, Mary Murray, *o d* of late Lieut-Col Joseph M. Hoult, Norton Place, Lincoln; two *s* one *d*. *Educ*: Winchester; Balliol Coll., Oxford (BA 1949). FRICS. Served War of 1939–45, Major, Rifle Brigade (MC). *Heir: s* Richard Dawson Hoult Bates, *b* 12

May 1956. *Address:* Butleigh House, Butleigh, Glastonbury, Somerset BA6 8SU.

Died 12 July 1998.

BATES, Ralph; writer; *b* Swindon, Wilts, 3 Nov. 1899; *s* of Henry Roy and Mabel Stevens Bates; *m* 1940, Eve Salzman; one *s*. *Educ*: Swindon and North Wilts Secondary Sch. After service in 16th Queen's Royal West Surreys, 1917–19, worked in Great Western Railway Factory at Swindon; in Spain, 1930–37; took active part in Republican politics in Spain; began literary career in 1933 as consequence of unemployment; Capt. in the Spanish Loyalist Army and in the International Brigade, Madrid sector, 1936–37; lecture tour in USA 1937–38; one year resident in Mexico, 1938–39; Adjunct Prof. of Literature, New York Univ. 1948–68, then Professor Emeritus of Literature. *Publications:* Sierra, 1933, Lean Men, 1934; Schubert, 1934; The Olive Field, 1936; Rainbow Fish, 1937; The Miraculous Horde, 1939; The Fields of Paradise, 1941; The Undiscoverables, 1942; The Journey to the Sandalwood Forest, 1947; The Dolphin in the Wood, 1949. *Recreations:* small boating, music. *Address:* 37 Washington Square West, New York, NY 10011–9123, USA. *T:* (212) 2544149.

Died 26 Nov. 2000.

BATES, His Honour Stewart Taverner; QC 1970; a Circuit Judge, 1989–95; *b* 17 Dec. 1926; *s* of John Bates, Greenock; *m* 1950, Anne Patricia, *d* of David West, Pinner; two *s* four *d*. *Educ*: Univs of Glasgow and St Andrews; Corpus Christi Coll., Oxford. Officers' Trng Sch., Bangalore, 1946, commnd Argyll and Sutherland Highlanders. Called to Bar, Middle Temple, 1954, Bencher, 1975, Lent Reader, 1992; a Recorder, 1981–89. Mem. Bar Council, 1962–66. Chm., Barristers' Benevolent Assoc., 1983–89; Member Goodman Cttee on Charity Law and Voluntary Organisations, 1976; Cttee of Management, Inst. of Urology, Univ. of London, 1978–89; Chm., St Peter's Hosp. Special Cttee, 1986 89 *Recreations:* theatre, sailing, ski-ing. *Address:* The Grange, Horsington, Templecombe, Somerset BA8 0EF. *T:* (01963) 370521. *Club:* Garrick.

Died 13 March 1999.

BATHURST, Joan Caroline, (Lady Bathurst); *see* Petrie, J. C.

BATTY, Christina Agnes Lillian, (Mrs Ronald Batty); *see* Foyle, C. A. L.

BAUM, Prof. (John) David, MD; FRCP, FRCPE, FRCPCH, FMedSci; Professor of Child Health, since 1985, and Founding Director, Institute of Child Health, since 1988, University of Bristol; *b* 23 July 1940; *s* of Isidor and Mary Baum; *m* 1967, Angela Rose Goschalk; four *s*. *Educ*: Univ. of Birmingham. MB ChB, MA, MSc, MD, DCH. Royal Postgrad. Med. Sch., 1967; Lectr, then Clinical Reader in Paed., Oxford, 1972; Professorial Fellow, St Catherine's Coll., Oxford, 1977. Vis. Prof., Univ. of Colorado Med. Center, 1969. Chm., Adv. Cttee, Winnicot Res. Unit, Cambridge, 1991–; President: RCPCH, 1997– (Dir, Res. Unit, 1993–97); Nat. Assoc. for Care of Children with Life Threatening Diseases and their Families, 1995– (Founding Chm., 1990–95); Chm., British Assoc. of Community Child Health, 1990–94; Mem., NICE Partners Council; Patron: Bristol Family Conciliation Service; Children's Hospice South West; Guardian, Helen House, Oxford; Gov., PPP Healthcare Med. Trust Bd. Inventor, Silver Swaddler, 1968; co-inventor, Human Milk Pasteuriser, 1976. Founder FMedSci 1998. Guthrie Medal, BPA, 1976. *Publications:* (ed jtly) Clinical Paediatric Physiology, 1979; (ed jtly) Care of the Child with Diabetes, 1985; (ed jtly) Listen, my child has a lot of living to do: caring for children with life-threatening conditions, 1990; numerous papers on preterm infants, childhood diabetes, palliative care for children, and internat. child health.

Recreations: visual arts, politics of child health, the environment. *Address:* 19 Charlotte Street, Bristol BS1 5PZ. *T:* (0117) 926 0448; *e-mail:* david.baum@bristol.ac.uk. *Clubs:* Royal Society of Medicine; Oxford University Choolent Society.										*Died 5 Sept. 1999.*

BAWDEN, Michael George, CMG 1995; Head, British Development Division, Caribbean, 1985–95; *b* 6 Dec. 1935; *s* of Sir Frederick Bawden, FRS, and late Marjorie Elizabeth Bawden; *m* 1960, Mary Roberta Jones; two *d. Educ:* St George's Sch., Harpenden; Emmanuel Coll., Cambridge (MA); Keele Univ. (MSc). Joined Colonial Office, 1959: Land Resources Div., Directorate of Overseas Surveys, 1959–73; Overseas Development Administration, Foreign and Commonwealth Office: Sci., Technol. and Medical Dept, 1973–75; E African Dept, 1975–76; Finance Dept, 1976–78; Estabt Officer, 1978–81; Hd, Latin American, Caribbean and Pacific Dept, 1981–85. *Recreations:* travel, walking, photography, current affairs. *Address:* 20 Thamespoint, Fairways, Teddington, Middx TW11 9PP. *T:* (020) 8943 3142; Brynmelyn, Bala, Gwynedd, N Wales LL23 7YA. *T:* (01678) 520251.										*Died 29 July 1999.*

BAYLEY, Dame Iris; *see* Murdoch, Dame J. I.

BAYLIS, Clifford Henry, CB 1971; Controller, HM Stationery Office, and Queen's Printer of Acts of Parliament, 1969–74; *b* 20 March 1915; *s* of late Arthur Charles and Caroline Jane Baylis, Alcester, Warwicks; *m* 1st, 1939, Phyllis Mary Clark; two *s*; 2nd, 1979, Margaret A. Hawkins. *Educ:* Alcester Grammar Sch.; Keble Coll., Oxford. Harrods Ltd, 1937–39; served with HM Forces, 1940–46: Major RASC; Principal, Board of Trade, 1947; Asst Sec., UK Trade Commissioner, Bombay, 1955; Export Credits Guarantee Dept, 1963–66; Under-Sec., Board of Trade, 1966–67; Under-Sec., Min. of Technology, 1967–69. Dir, Shipbuilders' and Repairers' Nat. Assoc., 1974–77; Clerk, Shipwrights' Co., 1977–86. *Address:* 38 Cleaver Street, SE11 4DP. *T:* (0171) 587 0817.										*Died 15 April 1998.*

BAYLISS, Sir Noel (Stanley), Kt 1979; CBE 1960; PhD; FRACI, FAA; Professor of Chemistry, University of Western Australia, 1938–71, Emeritus Professor, 1972; *b* 19 Dec. 1906; *s* of Henry Bayliss and Nelly Stothers; *m* 1933, Nellie Elise Banks; two *s*; *Educ:* Queen's Coll., Univ. of Melbourne (BSc 1927); Lincoln Coll., Oxford (BA 1930); Univ. of Calif, Berkeley (PhD 1933). FRACI 1942; FAA 1954. Victorian Rhodes Scholar, 1927–30; Commonwealth Fund (Harkness) Fellow, Univ. of Calif, 1930–33; Sen. Lectr in Chem., Univ. of Melbourne, 1933–37. Chm., Murdoch Univ. Planning Bd, 1970–73; Member: Australian Univs Commn, 1959–70; Hong Kong Univ. and Polytech. Grants Cttee, 1966–73. Hon. FACE 1965; Hon. DSc Univ. of WA, 1968; Hon. DUniv Murdoch Univ., 1975. *Publications:* over 70 original papers in scientific jls. *Recreations:* golf, music. *Address:* 62 Dorothy Genders Hostel, 99 McCabe Street, Mosman Park, WA 6012, Australia. *T:* (9) 3852987. *Club:* Royal Perth Yacht (WA).										*Died 17 Feb. 1996.*

BAYLY, Vice-Adm. Sir Patrick (Uniacke), KBE 1968; CB 1965; DSC 1944, and 2 bars, 1944, 1951; *b* 4 Aug. 1914; *s* of late Lancelot F. S. Bayly, Nenagh, Eire; *m* 1945, Moy Gourlay Jardine, *d* of Robert Gourlay Jardine, Newtonmearns, Scotland; two *d. Educ:* Aravon, Bray, Co. Wicklow; RN Coll., Dartmouth. Midshipman, 1932; Sub-Lieut, 1934; Lieut, 1935; South Africa, 1936; China station, 1938; Combined operations, 1941–44, including Sicily and Salerno; Lieut-Comdr 1944; HMS Mauritius, 1946; Comdr 1948, Naval Staff; Korean War, 1952–53, in HMS Alacrity and Constance; Captain 1954, Naval Staff; Imperial Defence Coll., 1957; Capt. (D) 6th Destroyer Sqdn, 1958; Staff of SACLANT, Norfolk, Va,

1960; Chief of Staff, Mediterranean, 1962; Rear-Admiral, 1963; Flag Officer, Sea Training, 1963; Adm. Pres., RN Coll., Greenwich, 1965–67; Vice-Adm., 1967; Chief of Staff, COMNAVSOUTH, Malta, 1967–70; retd, 1970. Dir, Maritime Trust, 1971–88. US Legion of Merit, 1951. *Recreation:* golf. *Address:* Dunning House, Liphook, Hants GU30 7EH.										*Died 1 May 1998.*

BAZLEY, Sir Thomas Stafford, 3rd Bt *cr* 1869, of Hatherop, co. Gloucester; *b* 5 Oct. 1907; *s* of Captain Gardner Sebastian Bazley, DL (*d* 1911) (*o s* of 2nd Bt) and Ruth Evelyn (she *m* 2nd, Comdr F. C. Cadogan, RN, retd, and *d* 1962; he *d* 1970), *d* of late Sir Edward Stafford Howard; *S* grandfather, 1919; *m* 1945, Carmen, *o d* of late J. Tulla; three *s* two *d. Educ:* Harrow; Magdalen Coll., Oxford. *Heir: s* Thomas John Sebastian Bazley, *b* 31 Aug. 1948. *Address:* Eastleach Downs Farm, near Eastleach, Cirencester, Glos GL7 3PX.										*Died 14 April 1997.*

BEALE, (Thomas) Edward, CBE 1966; JP; Chairman, Beale's Ltd, 1934–90; *b* 5 March 1904; *s* of late Thomas Henderson Beale, London; *m* Beatrice May (*d* 1986), *d* of William Steele McLaughlin, JP, Enniskillen; one *s. Educ:* City of London Sch. Mem. Bd, British Travel Assoc., 1950–70, Dep. Chm. 1965–70; Vice-Pres. and Fellow, Hotel and Catering Inst., 1949–71; Chm., Caterers' Assoc. of Gt Britain, 1949–52; Pres., Internat. Ho-Re-Ca (Union of Nat. Hotel, Restaurant & Caterers Assocs), 1954–64. Chm., Treasury Cttee of Enquiry, House of Commons Refreshment Dept, 1951. Master, Worshipful Co. of Bakers, 1955. Mem., Islington Borough Council, 1931–34. Gen. Comr of Income Tax, 1949–60. Creator, Beale Arboretum, West Lodge Park, 1965. JP Inner London, 1950 (Chm. EC Div., Inner London Magistrates, 1970–73). FRSH 1957; FRSA 1968; Hon FHCIMA 1974. Grant of Armorial Bearings and Crest, 1970. Médaille d'Argent de Paris, 1960. *Recreation:* arboriculture. *Address:* West Lodge Park, Hadley Wood, Herts EN4 0PY. *Club:* Carlton.										*Died 10 July 1998.*

BEAMISH, Air Vice-Marshal Cecil Howard, CB 1970; FDSRCS; Director of Dental Services, Royal Air Force, 1969–73; *b* 31 March 1915; *s* of Frank George Beamish, Coleraine; *m* 1955, Frances Elizabeth Sarah Goucher; two *s. Educ:* Coleraine Acad.; Queen's Univ., Belfast. Joined Royal Air Force, 1936; Group Capt., 1958; Air Cdre, 1968; Air Vice-Marshal, 1969. QHDS 1969–73. *Recreations:* Rugby football, golf, squash. *Address:* East Keal Manor, Spilsby, Lincs PE23 4AS.										*Died 21 May 1999.*

BEAR, Leslie William, CBE 1972; Editor of Official Report (Hansard), House of Commons, 1954–72; *b* 16 June 1911; *s* of William Herbert Bear, Falkenham, Suffolk; *m* 1st, 1932, Betsy Sobels (*d* 1934), Lisse, Holland; 2nd, 1936, Annelise Gross (*d* 1979), Trier, Germany; two *s. Educ:* Gregg Sch., Ipswich. Served War, Royal Air Force, 1943–44. Mem. of Official Reporting Staff, League of Nations, Geneva, 1930–36; joined Official Report (Hansard), House of Commons, 1936; Asst Ed., 1951. *Recreations:* music, reading.										*Died 2 April 2000.*

BEARD, Derek, CBE 1979; Assistant Director General, British Council, 1984–87; *b* 16 May 1930; *s* of Walter Beard and Lily Beard (*née* Mellors); *m* 1st, 1953, Ruth Davies (marr. diss. 1966); two *s*; 2nd, 1966, Renate Else, *d* of late W. E. Kautz, Berlin and Mecklenburg; two *s. Educ:* Hulme Grammar Sch., Oldham; Brasenose Coll., Oxford (MA, DipEd). Stand Grammar Sch., Whitefield, 1954–56; HMOCS, Nyasaland, 1956–59; Asst Educn Officer, WR Yorks, 1959–61; Sen. Asst, Oxfordshire, 1961–63; British Council, Pakistan, 1963–65; Producer, BBC Overseas Educnl Recordings Unit, 1965–66; British Council: Dir, Appts, Services Dept, 1966–70; Dep. Rep., India, 1970–73; Controller, Educn and Science Div.,

1973–77; Rep. in Germany, 1977–81, Belgium, 1981–84. Adviser, 21st Century Trust, 1987–88; Academic Dir, Oxford Internat. Summer Sch., 1988. MInstD. *Publications:* articles on educn and cultural relns. *Recreations:* sculpture, music, travel. *Address:* 3 College Avenue, Epsom, Surrey KT17 4HN.

Died 5 June 1999.

BEARSTED, 4th Viscount *cr* 1925, of Maidstone, Kent; **Peter Montefiore Samuel,** MC 1942; TD 1951; Bt 1903; Baron 1921; Banker; Director, Hill Samuel Group, 1965–87 (Deputy Chairman, after merger with Philip Hill, Higginson & Co., 1965–82); Chairman: Dylon International Ltd, 1958–84; Hill Samuel & Co. (Ireland) Ltd, 1964–84; *b* 9 Dec. 1911; second *s* of 2nd Viscount Bearsted and Dorothea, *e d* of late E. Montefiore Micholls; *S* brother, 1986; *m* 1st, 1939, Deirdre du Barry (marr. diss. 1942); 2nd, 1946, Hon. Elizabeth Adelaide Pearce Serocold (*d* 1983), *d* of late Baron Cohen, PC; two *s* one *d*; 3rd, 1984, Nina Alice Hilary, *widow* of Michael Pocock, CBE. *Educ:* Eton; New College, Oxford (BA). Served Warwickshire Yeo., Middle East and Italy, 1939–45. Director: M. Samuel & Co. Ltd, 1935 (Dep. Chm. 1948); Shell Transport & Trading Co. Ltd, 1938–82; Samuel Properties Ltd, 1961–86 (Chm., 1982–86); Mayborn Group PLC, 1946– (Chm., 1946–88); Trades Union Unit Trust Managers Ltd, 1961–82; General Consolidated Investment Trust Ltd, 1975–83. President, Norwood Home for Jewish Children, 1962–79; Hon. Treas., Nat. Assoc. for Gifted Children, 1968–81; Chairman: Council, Royal Free Hospital of Medicine, 1973–82 (Mem., 1948–); Bd of Governors, Royal Free Hosp., 1956–68 (Governor, 1939–). *Recreation:* shooting. *Heir: s* Hon. Nicholas Alan Samuel [*b* 22 Jan. 1950; *m* 1975, Caroline Jane, *d* of Dr David Sacks; one *s* four *d*]. *Address:* 9 Campden Hill Court, W8 7HX; Farley Hall, Farley Hill, near Reading, Berkshire RG7 1UL. *T:* Eversley (01734) 733242. *Club:* White's. *Died 9 June 1996.*

BEASLEY, John T.; *see* Telford Beasley.

BEASLEY-MURRAY, George Raymond, DD, PhD; Senior Professor of New Testament Interpretation, Southern Baptist Theological Seminary, Louisville, Kentucky, since 1980; *b* 10 Oct. 1916; *s* of George Alfred Beasley; *m* 1942, Ruth Weston; three *s* one *d. Educ:* City of Leicester Boys' Sch.; Spurgeon's Coll. and King's Coll., London (BD 1941; MTh 1945; PhD 1952; DD 1964); Jesus Coll., Cambridge (MA); DD Cambridge, 1989. Baptist Minister, Ilford, Essex, 1941–48; Cambridge, 1948–50; New Testament Lectr, Spurgeon's Coll., 1950–56; New Testament Prof., Baptist Theological Coll., Rüschlikon, Zürich, 1956–58; Principal, Spurgeon's Coll., 1958–73; Buchanan-Harrison Prof. of New Testament Interpretation, Southern Baptist Theol Seminary, Louisville, Ky, 1973–80. Pres., Baptist Union of Great Britain and Ireland, 1968–69. Hon. DD McMaster, 1973; Hon. LLD CNAA, 1989. *Publications:* Christ is Alive, 1947; Jesus and the Future, 1954; Preaching the Gospel from the Gospels, 1956, 2nd edn 1996; A Commentary on Mark Thirteen, 1957; Baptism in the New Testament, 1962; The Resurrection of Jesus Christ, 1964; Baptism Today and Tomorrow, 1966; Commentary on 2 Corinthians (Broadman Commentary), 1971; The Book of Revelation (New Century Bible), 1974; The Coming of God, 1983; Jesus and the Kingdom of God, 1986; Commentary on the Gospel of John (Word Commentary), 1987; Word Biblical Themes: John, 1989; Gospel of Life: theology in the Fourth Gospel, 1991; Jesus and the Last Days: the interpretation of the Olivet Discourse, 1993; (jtly) The Newell Lectureships II, 1993. *Recreation:* music. *Address:* 4 Holland Road, Hove, E Sussex BN3 1JJ. *Died 23 Feb. 2000.*

BEATTIE, Hon. Sir Alexander (Craig), Kt 1973; President, The Eryldene Trust, 1983–89; *b* 24 Jan. 1912, *e s* of Edmund Douglas and Amie Louisa Beattie; *m* 1st, 1944, Joyce Pearl Alder (*d* 1977); two *s*; 2nd, 1978, Joyce Elizabeth de Groot. *Educ:* Fort Street High Sch., Sydney; Univ. of Sydney (BA, LLB; Hon. LLD). Admitted to NSW Bar, 1936. Served War of 1939–45: Captain, 2nd AIF, Royal Australian Armoured Corps, New Guinea and Borneo. Pres., Industrial Commn of NSW, 1966–81 (Mem., 1955). Trustee, Royal Botanic Gardens and Govt Domain, Sydney, 1976–82, Chm. 1980–82. *Recreations:* gardening, bowls. *Club:* Australian (Sydney).

Died 30 Sept. 1999.

BEATTIE, Prof. Arthur James, FRSE 1957; Professor of Greek at Edinburgh University, 1951–81; Dean of the Faculty of Arts, 1963–65; *b* 28 June 1914; *e s* of Arthur John Rait Beattie. *Educ:* Montrose Academy; Aberdeen Univ.; Sidney Sussex Coll., Cambridge. Wilson Travelling Fellowship, Aberdeen, 1938–40. Served War, 1940–45: RA 1940–41; Int. Corps, 1941–45; Major GSO2; despatches, 1945. Fellow and Coll. Lectr, Sidney Sussex Coll., 1946–51; Faculty Asst Lectr and Univ. Lectr in Classics, Cambridge, 1946–51. Chm. Governors, Morrison's Acad., Crieff, 1962–75; Governor, Sedbergh Sch., 1967–78. Comdr, Royal Order of the Phœnix (Greece), 1966. *Publications:* articles contributed to classical jls. *Recreations:* walking, bird-watching. *Club:* New (Edinburgh). *Died 20 Feb. 1996.*

BEATTIE, Charles Noel; QC 1962; retired; *b* 4 Nov. 1912; *s* of Michael William Beattie and Edith Beattie (*née* Lickfold); *m*; three *d. Educ:* Lewes Grammar Sch. LLB (London). Admitted a solicitor, 1938. Served War of 1939–45 (despatches), Capt. RASC. Called to the Bar, Lincoln's Inn, 1946; Bencher 1971. *Publication:* My Wartime Escapades, 1987. *Address:* Leckhelm Estate, Loch Broom, Ullapool, Ross-shire IV23 2RL.

Died 12 Sept. 1998.

BEATTIE, Thomas Brunton, CMG 1981; OBE 1968; HM Diplomatic Service, retired 1982; Management Consultant, Control Risks Ltd, since 1982; *b* 17 March 1924; *s* of Joseph William Beattie and Jessie Dewar (*née* Brunton), Rutherglen; *m* 1st, 1956, Paula Rahkola (marr. diss. 1981); one *d*; 2nd, 1982, Josephine Marion Collins. *Educ:* Rutherglen Acad.; Pembroke Coll., Cambridge (MA). Served RAF, 1943–47. Jt Press Reading Service, British Embassy, Moscow, 1947; Finnish Secretariat, British Legation, Helsinki, 1951; FO, 1954; Second Sec., Madrid, 1956; FO, 1960; First Sec., Athens, 1964; First Sec., later Counsellor, FCO, 1969; Counsellor, Rome, 1977, FCO 1981. Mem., Inst. of Translation and Interpreting, 1991. Treas., Scottish Covenanter Memls Assoc., 1991–. Member: Management Cttee, Pembroke Coll. Cambridge Soc., 1995–98; Marie Stuart Soc.; Dumfries Burns Club, 1995–. Comr, Gen. Assembly, Church of Scotland, 1998–. Mem. Bd, Moniaive Sch., 1997–. MIL 1998. *Publications:* translated: Viktor Suvorov, Icebreaker, 1990; Vladimir Kuzichkin, Inside the KGB, 1990. *Recreations:* unremarkable. *Address:* Cairnside, Kirkland of Glencairn, Moniaive, Dumfriesshire DG3 4HD. *Clubs:* Carlton; Royal Scottish Automobile (Glasgow). *Died 28 May 2000.*

BEAUREPAIRE, Ian Francis, CMG 1967; Director, Pacific Dunlop Ltd (formerly Dunlop Olympic Ltd), 1980–92; Chairman, Olex Ltd, 1973–92; *b* 14 Sept. 1922; *s* of late Sir Frank and Lady (Myra) Beaurepaire; *m* 1946, Dame Beryl (Edith) Beaurepaire, AC, DBE (*née* Bedggood); two *s. Educ:* Carey Grammar Sch.; Scotch Coll., Melbourne; Royal Melbourne Inst. of Technology. Served RAAF (Flying Officer), 1942–45. Man. Dir, Beaurepaire Tyre Service Pty Ltd, 1953–55; Gen. Man., The Olympic Tyre & Rubber Co. Pty Ltd, 1955–61; Chm.,

1959–78, Man. Dir, 1959–75, Chief Exec., 1975–78, Exec. Chm., 1978–80, Olympic Consolidated Industries Ltd. Mem., Melbourne Underground Rail Loop Authority, 1971–83, Chm., 1981–83. Member: Melbourne City Council, 1956–75 (Lord Mayor of Melbourne, 1965–67); Management Cttee of Royal Victorian Eye and Ear Hosp., 1966–88 (Pres., 1982–88). *Recreations:* golf, grazing. *Address:* 18 Barton Drive, Mount Eliza, Vic 3930, Australia. *Clubs:* Athenæum, Naval and Military, Melbourne (Melbourne); Peninsula Country Golf (Frankston). *Died 24 June 1996.*

BECHER, Major Sir William Fane Wrixon-, 5th Bt *cr* 1831, of Ballygiblin, co. Cork; MC 1943; Temp. Major, Rifle Brigade (SRO); *b* 7 Sept. 1915; *o s* of Sir Eustace W. W. W. Becher, 4th Bt, and Hon. Constance Gough-Calthorpe, *d* of 6th Baron Calthorpe; *S* father, 1934; *m* 1st, 1946, Vanda (marr. diss. 1960; she *m* 1962, Rear-Adm. Viscount Kelburn, later 9th Earl of Glasgow; she *d* 1984), *d* of 4th Baron Vivian; one *s* one *d*; 2nd, 1960, Hon. Mrs Yvonne Mostyn. *Educ:* Harrow; Magdalene Coll., Cambridge (BA). Served War of 1939–45; Western Desert and Tunisian Campaigns, 1940–43 (MC, wounded twice); Liaison Officer to Comdr, 13th Corps, Lt-Gen. W. H. Gott, 1941 (taken prisoner at battle of Sidi Rezegh, Nov. 1941, and escaped); Italian Campaign, 1944; ADC to FM Lord Wilson, Supreme Allied Comdr Mediterranean. Lloyd's Underwriter, 1950. Member: British Boxing Bd of Control, 1961–82; Nat. Playing Fields Assoc., 1953–65 (Pres., Wiltshire Branch, 1950–56). *Recreations:* golf, cricket (played cricket for Sussex, 1939, captained Wiltshire, 1949–53), reading (biographies and autobiographies of famous men and women). *Heir: s* John William Michael Wrixon-Becher, *b* 29 Sept. 1950. *Address:* 13 Montpelier Crescent, Brighton BN1 3JF. *Clubs:* MCC, Royal Green Jackets; I Zingari (Sec., 1952–93). *Died 6 Jan. 2000.*

BECK, Prof. Arnold Hugh William; Professor of Engineering, 1966–83, Head of Electrical Division, 1971–81, University of Cambridge, then Emeritus Professor; Life Fellow of Corpus Christi College, Cambridge, 1983 (Fellow, 1962); Fellow of University College, London, since 1979; *b* 7 Aug. 1916; *y s* of Major Hugh Beck and Diana L. Beck; *m* Margaret Stewart MacIver (marr. diss. 1938); *m* 1947, (Katharine) Monica, *y d* of S. K. Ratcliffe; no *c*. *Educ:* Gresham's Sch., Holt; University Coll., London (BSc Eng); MA Cantab 1959. Research Engr, Henry Hughes & Sons, 1937–41; seconded to Admty Signal Estab., 1941–45; Standard Telephones & Cables, 1947–58; Lectr, Cambridge Univ., 1958–64; Reader in Electrical Engrg, 1964–66. FIEEE 1959. *Publications:* Velocity Modulated Thermionic Tubes, 1948; Thermionic Valves, 1953; Space-charge Waves, 1958; Words and Waves, 1967; (with H. Ahmed) Introduction to Physical Electronics, 1968; Handbook of Vacuum Physics, Vol. 2, Parts 5 and 6, 1968; Statistical Mechanics, Fluctuations and Noise, 1976; papers in Jl IEE, Inst. Radio Engrs, etc. *Address:* 18 Earl Street, Cambridge CB1 1JR. *T:* (01223) 362997. *Died 11 Oct. 1997.*

BECK, Sir Edgar (Charles), Kt 1975; CBE 1967; FREng; Chairman, John Mowlem & Company Ltd, 1961–79, President, since 1981; *b* 11 May 1911; *s* of Edgar Bee Beck and Nellie Stollard Beck (*née* Osborne); *m* 1933, Mary Agnes Sorapure (marr. diss. 1972); three *s* two *d*; *m* 1972, Anne Teresa Corbould. *Educ:* Lancing Coll.; Jesus Coll., Cambridge (MA). Joined John Mowlem & Co. Ltd as Engineer, 1933: Dir, 1940; Man. Dir, 1958. Director: Scaffolding Great Britain Ltd, 1942–85 (Chm., 1958–78); Builders' Accident Insce Ltd, 1959 (Dep. Chm., 1969). Mem., ECGD Adv. Council, 1964–69; President, Fedn of Civil Engrg Contractors, 1971–75 (Chm., 1958–59);

Chairman: Export Gp for the Constructional Industries, 1959–63; Brit. Hosps Export Council, 1964–75. Under-writing Mem. of Lloyd's, 1955–. FREng (FEng 1977). FICE. *Recreations:* golf, salmon fishing. *Address:* Mill Cottage, Wilsford-cum-Lake, near Salisbury, Wilts SP4 7BP. *Clubs:* Buck's; Swinley Forest Golf. *Died 29 July 2000.*

BECK, (Richard) Theodore, FRIBA, FSA; architect; *b* 11 March 1905; *s* of Alfred Charles Beck and Grace Sophia Beck (*née* Reading); *m* 1950, Margaret Beryl Page; one *s* one *d*. *Educ:* Haileybury; Architectural Association Sch. MRTPI; FRIBA. Past Mem. Council, Royal Archaeological Inst.; Past Master: Broderers' Company; Barber-Surgeons' Company; Parish Clerks' Co.; Mem. Court of Common Council, Corporation of London, 1963–82; Dep., Ward of Farringdon Within, 1978–82; Sheriff, City of London, 1969–70; former Dep. Chm., Central Criminal Court Extension Cttee. Chm., Governors, City of London Sch., 1971–75, Dep. Chm., 1976 (Hon. Mem., John Carpenter Club); Chm., Schools Cttee, Corporation of London, 1977, Dep. Chm., 1978. Former Governor: Bridewell Royal Hosp.; King Edward's Sch., Witley; Christ's Hospital (Aldermanic Almoner); Reeves Foundn. Vicary Lectr, 1969; Prestonian Lectr, 1975. Member: Soane Club, 1953–; Doric Club, 1992–. FRSA. Dep. Grand Supt of Works, United Grand Lodge of England. *Publication:* The Cutting Edge: early history of the surgeons of London, 1975. *Recreations:* gardening, archaeology. *Address:* Blundens House, Upper Froyle, Alton, Hants GU34 4LB. *T:* (01420) 23147. *Clubs:* Guildhall, City Livery. *Died 8 Jan. 2000.*

BECKETT, Prof. James Camlin, MA; Professor of Irish History, Queen's University of Belfast, 1958–75; *b* 8 Feb. 1912; 3rd *s* of Alfred Beckett and Frances Lucy Bushell. *Educ:* Royal Belfast Academical Instn; Queen's Univ., Belfast. History Master, Belfast Royal Academy, 1934; Lectr in Modern History, Queen's Univ., Belfast, 1945, Reader in Modern History, 1952. Fellow Commoner, Peterhouse, Cambridge, 1955–56; Cummings Lectr, McGill Univ., Montreal, 1976; Mellon Prof., Tulane Univ., New Orleans, 1977. Member: Irish Manuscripts Commn, 1959–86; Royal Commission on Historical Manuscripts, 1960–86. Hon. DLitt: New Univ. of Ulster, 1979; NUI, 1990; Hon. DLit Queen's Univ. of Belfast, 1980. FRHistS; MRIA. *Publications:* Protestant Dissent in Ireland, 1687–1780, 1948; Short History of Ireland, 1952; (ed with T. W. Moody) Ulster since 1800: a Political and Economic Survey, 1954; (ed with T. W. Moody) Ulster since 1800: a Social Survey, 1957; (with T. W. Moody) Queen's Belfast, 1845–1949, 1959; The Making of Modern Ireland 1603–1923, 1966; (ed with R. E. Glasscock) Belfast: the Origin and Growth of an Industrial City, 1966; (ed) Historical Studies VII, 1969; Confrontations, 1973; The Anglo-Irish Tradition, 1976; The Cavalier Duke, 1990; contrib. The Ulster Debate, 1972; articles, reviews, etc, in English Hist. Rev., History, Irish Hist. Studies and other jls. *Recreations:* chess, walking. *Address:* 19 Wellington Park Terrace, Belfast, N Ireland BT9 6DR. *Club:* Ulster Reform (Belfast). *Died 12 Feb. 1996.*

BECKINGHAM, Prof. Charles Fraser, FBA 1983; Professor of Islamic Studies, University of London, 1965–81, then Emeritus; *b* 18 Feb. 1914; *o c* of Arthur Beckingham, ARBA and Alice Beckingham, Houghton, Hunts; *m* 1st, 1946, Margery (*d* 1966), *o d* of John Ansell; one *d*; 2nd, 1970, Elizabeth (marr. diss. 1977), *y d* of R. J. Brine. *Educ:* Grammar Sch., Huntingdon; Queens' Coll., Cambridge (scholar, Members' English prizeman, 1934). Dept of Printed Books, British Museum, 1936–46; seconded to military and naval Intelligence, 1942–46; Foreign Office (GCHQ), 1946–51; Lectr in Islamic History, Manchester Univ., 1951–55, Sen. Lectr, 1955–58,

Prof. of Islamic Studies, 1958–65. Pres., Hakluyt Soc., 1969–72; Treas., Royal Asiatic Soc., 1964–67, Pres., 1967–70, 1976–79, Hon. Fellow, Sri Lanka Branch, 1978. Chm., St Marylebone Soc., 1980–84. Jt Editor, 1961–64, Editor, 1965, Jl of Semitic Studies; Editor, Jl of RAS, 1984–87; Internat. Dir, Fontes Historiae Africanae Project, Union Académique Internationale, 1986–95. Sir Percy Sykes Meml Medal, RSAA, 1987. *Publications:* contribs to Admiralty Handbook of Western Arabia, 1946; (with G. W. B. Huntingford) Some Records of Ethiopia, 1954; Introduction to Atlas of the Arab World and Middle East, 1960; (with G. W. B. Huntingford) A True Relation of the Prester John of the Indies, 1961; (ed and selected) Bruce's Travels, 1964; The Achievements of Prester John, 1966; (ed) Islam, in, Religion in the Middle East (ed A. J. Arberry), 1969; (with E. Ullendorff) The Hebrew Letters of Prester John, 1982; Between Islam and Christendom, 1983; (ed) The Itinerário of Jerónimo Lobo, 1984; (with H. A. R. Gibb) The Travels of Ibn Battuta, vol. IV, 1994; (ed with Bernard Hamilton) Prester John, the Mongols and the Ten Lost Tribes, 1996; articles in learned jls. *Address:* 3 Pipe Passage, Lewes, E Sussex BN7 1YG. *Clubs:* Travellers', Beefsteak.

Died 30 Sept. 1998.

BEDDALL, Hugh Richard Muir; formerly with Muir Beddall & Co. Ltd (Chairman, 1964); *b* 20 May 1922; *s* of Herbert Muir Beddall and Jennie Beddall (*née* Fowler); *m* 1946, Monique Henriette (*née* Haefliger); three *s* one d. *Educ:* Stowe; Ecole de Commerce, Neuchâtel, Switzerland. FCII. Served War of 1939–45; Royal Marines, 2nd Lieut, 1941; subseq. Captain A Troop 45 RM Commando and No 1 Commando Bde HQ; demob., 1946. Employee: Muir Beddall & Co., 1939–41; Muir Beddall, Mise & Cie, Paris, 1946–47; returned as employee of Muir Beddall & Co. Ltd, 1947; Dir, 1949; Dep. Chm., 1960; Chm., 1964; company taken over by C. T. Bowring, 1966. Dir, Muir Beddall Mise & Cie, Paris. Mem. of Lloyd's, 1943. *Recreations:* shooting, fishing, racing. *Address:* Flat 4, 53 Cadogan Square, SW1X 0HY. *T:* (020) 7235 9461. *Clubs:* Buck's, East India, Special Forces. *Died 10 Aug. 1999.*

BEDFORD, Alfred William, (Bill), OBE 1961; AFC 1945; FRAeS; aerospace consultant, since 1986; *b* 18 Nov. 1920; *s* of Lewis Alfred Bedford and Edith (*née* Lawrence); *m* 1941, Mary Averill; one *s. Educ:* Loughborough College School, Leics. Electrical engineering apprenticeship, Blackburn Starling & Co. Ltd; RAF 1940–51: served Fighter Sqdns, 605 (County of Warwick) Sqdn, 1941; 135 Sqdn, 1941–44; 65 Sqdn, 1945; qualified Flying Instructor, Upavon, 1945, and Instructor, Instrument Rating Examiner, until 1949; Graduate Empire Flying School all-weather course; awarded King's Commendation, 1949; Graduate and Tutor, Empire Test Pilots' School, 1949–50; Test Pilot, RAE Farnborough, 1950–51; Experimental Test Pilot, Hawker Aircraft Ltd, 1951–56; Chief Test Pilot, Hawker Aircraft Ltd, 1956–63; Chief Test Pilot (Dunsfold), Hawker Siddeley Aviation Ltd, 1963–67; Sales Man., Hawker Siddeley Aviation, 1968–78; British Aerospace: Divisional Mktg Manager, 1978–83; Regional Exec., SE Asia, 1983–86. London-Rome and return world speed records, 1956; made initial flight, Oct. 1960, on the Hawker P1127 (the World's first VTOL strike fighter), followed by first jet V/STOL operations of such an aircraft from an Aircraft Carrier (HMS Ark Royal) on 8 Feb. 1963; Harrier first flight, Aug. 1966; first UK holder of Internat. Gold 'C' with two diamonds; held eight British and UK national gliding records of 257 miles and altitude of 21,340 ft (19,120 ft gain of height); awarded British Gliding Association trophies: de Havilland (twice), Manio, and Wakefield, 1950–51. Approved Air Registration Bd glider test pilot. Chm. and founder Mem., Test Pilots' Group, RAeS, 1964–66. Member SBAC Test Pilots' Soc.,

1956–67. Fellow, Society of Experimental Test Pilots. RAeS Alston Memorial Medal, 1959; Guild of Air Pilots and Air Navigators Derry Richards Memorial Medal, 1959–60; Segrave Trophy, 1963; Britannia Trophy, 1964; Air League Founders Medal, 1967; C. P. Robertson Meml Trophy, Air Pubns Assoc., 1987; Gold Medal, Soc. British Aviation Consultants, 1994. First Class Wings, Indonesian Air Force, for services to the Republic, 1982. *Recreations:* squash, sail-plane flying. *Address:* The Chequers, West End Lane, Esher, Surrey KT10 8LF. *T:* (01372) 462285. *Clubs:* Royal Air Force; Esher Squash.

Died 20 Oct. 1996.

BEEBY, Clarence Edward, ONZ 1987; CMG 1956; PhD; International Consultant, 1969–87, and Director Emeritus, since 1986, New Zealand Council for Educational Research; *b* 16 June 1902; *s* of Anthony and Alice Beeby; *m* 1926, Beatrice Eleanor, *d* of Charles Newnham; one *s* one *d. Educ:* Christchurch Boys' High Sch.; Canterbury Coll., University of NZ (MA); University Coll., London; University of Manchester (PhD). Lectr in Philosophy and Education, Canterbury University Coll., University of NZ, 1923–34; Dir, NZ Council for Educational Research, 1934–38; Asst Dir of Education, Education Dept, NZ, 1938–40; Dir of Education, NZ, 1940–60 (leave of absence to act as Asst Dir-Gen. of UNESCO, Paris, 1948–49); NZ Ambassador to France, 1960–63; Research Fellow, Harvard Univ., 1963–67; Commonwealth Visiting Prof., Univ. of London, 1967–68; Consultant: to Australian Govt in Papua and New Guinea, 1969; to Ford Foundn in Indonesia, 1970–77; to UNDP in Malaysia, 1976; to World Bank, Washington, DC, 1983; to Aga Khan Foundn, Tanzania, 1987; External Consultant to Univ. of Papua New Guinea, 1982. Leader of NZ Delegs. to Gen. Confs of UNESCO, 1946, 1947, 1950, 1953, 1954, 1956, 1958, 1960, 1962; Hon. Counsellor of UNESCO, 1950; Mem., Exec. Bd, UNESCO, 1960–63 (Chm., Exec. Bd, 1963); Mem., Council of Consultant Fellows, Internat. Inst. for Educnl Planning, Paris, 1971–77. For. Associate, US Nat. Acad. of Educn, 1981. Hon. Fellow, NZ Educnl Inst., 1971. Hon. LLD Otago, 1969, Hon. LittD Wellington, 1970; Hon. LittD Canterbury, 1992. Mackie Medal, ANZAAS, 1971; Educn Award, We Care Foundn, NZ, 1995. Grand Cross, Order of St Gregory, 1964. *Publications:* The Intermediate Schools of New Zealand, 1938; (with W. Thomas and M. H. Oram) Entrance to the University, 1939; The Quality of Education in Developing Countries, 1966; (ed) Qualitative Aspects of Educational Planning, 1969; Assessment of Indonesian Education: a guide in planning, 1978; The Biography of an Idea: Beeby on Education, 1992; articles in educational periodicals. *Recreations:* gardening, fishing, cabinet-making. *Address:* 39A Lucknow Terrace, Khandallah, Wellington 4, New Zealand. *T:* (4) 4795058. *Died 10 March 1998.*

BEER, Patricia, (Mrs J. D. Parsons); freelance writer; *b* 4 Nov. 1919; *yr d* of Andrew William and Harriet Beer, Exmouth, Devon; *m* 1st, P. N. Furbank; 2nd, 1964, John Damien Parsons. *Educ:* Exmouth Grammar Sch.; Exeter Univ. (BA, 1st cl. Hons English); St Hugh's Coll., Oxford (BLitt). Lecturer in English, Univ. of Padua, 1947–49; British Inst., Rome, 1949–51; Goldsmiths' Coll., Univ. of London, 1962–68. *Publications: poetry:* Loss of the Magyar, 1959; The Survivors, 1963; Just Like The Resurrection, 1967; The Estuary, 1971; (ed) New Poems 1975, 1975; Driving West, 1975; (ed jtly) New Poetry 2, 1976; Selected Poems, 1980; The Lie of the Land, 1983; Collected Poems, 1989; Friend of Heraclitus, 1993; Autumn, 1997; *novel:* Moon's Ottery, 1978; *non-fiction:* Wessex, 1985; *autobiography:* Mrs Beer's House, 1968; *criticism:* Reader, I Married Him, 1974; contrib. The Listener, London Review of Books. *Recreations:*

travelling, cooking. *Address:* Tiphayes, Up Ottery, near Honiton, Devon EX14 9NZ. *T:* (01404) 861255.

Died 15 Aug. 1999.

BEESLEY, Prof. Michael Edwin, CBE 1985; PhD; Professor of Economics, 1965–90, and Director, PhD Programme, 1985–90, London Business School, then Emeritus Professor; *b* 3 July 1924; *s* of late Edwin S. and Kathleen D. Beesley; *m* 1947, Eileen Eleanor Yard; three *s* two *d. Educ:* King Edward's Grammar Sch., Five Ways, Birmingham; Univ. of Birmingham (BCom Div. 1, 1945; PhD 1951). Lectr in Commerce, Univ. of Birmingham, 1951–60; Rees Jeffreys Res. Fellow, LSE, 1961–64; Sir Ernest Cassel Reader in Econs, with special ref. to transport, Univ. of London tenable at LSE, 1964–65. Vis. Associate Prof., Univ. of Pennsylvania, 1959–60; Vis. Prof., Harvard Univ., 1974; Visiting Professor and Commonwealth Fellow: Univ. of BC, 1968; Macquarie Univ., Sydney, 1979–80. Chief Econ. Adviser, Min. of Transport, 1964–68; Special Adviser, Treasury and CS Cttee, Nationalised Industry Financing, 1981; Mem., Monopolies and Mergers Commn, 1988–94. Chm., Inst. of Public Sector Management, 1983–87 (Dir, 1978–83). Formerly Member: Cttee on Road Pricing (Smeed Cttee); Cttee on Transport in London; Cttee on Transport Planning (Lady Sharp Cttee); Urban Motorways Inter-Deptl Cttee; Standing Adv. Cttee on Trunk Road Assessment (Sir George Leitch Cttee). Managing Editor, Jl of Transport Economics and Policy, 1975–88; Ed., Regulating Utilities series, 1994–. Hon. LLD Birmingham, 1999. *Publications:* Urban Transport: studies in economic policy, 1973; (ed) Productivity and Amenity: achieving a social balance, 1974; (ed) Industrial Relations in a Changing World, 1975; (with T. C. Evans) Corporate Social Responsibility: a reassessment, 1978; Liberalisation of the Use of British Telecommunications Network: an independent economic enquiry, 1981; (with P. B. Kettle) Improving Railway Financial Performance, 1985; (with B. Laidlaw) The Future of Telecommunications, 1989; Privatisation, Regulation and Deregulation, 1992, 2nd edn 1998; (ed) Utility Regulation: challenge and response, 1995. *Recreations:* music, table tennis, golf. *Address:* 59 Canons Drive, Edgware, Middx HA8 7RG. *T:* (020) 8952 1320. *Club:* Reform. *Died 24 Sept. 1999.*

BEITH, Sir John (Greville Stanley), KCMG 1969 (CMG 1959); HM Diplomatic Service, retired; *b* 4 April 1914; *s* of late William Beith and Margaret Stanley, Toowoomba, Qld; *m* 1949, Diana Gregory-Hood (*d* 1987), *d* of Sir John Little Gilmour, 2nd Bt; one *s* one *d* (and one *d* decd), and one step *s* one step *d. Educ:* Eton; King's Coll., Cambridge. Entered HM Diplomatic Service, 1937, and served in FO until 1940; 3rd Sec., Athens, 1940–41; 2nd Sec., Buenos Aires, 1941–45; served Foreign Office, 1945–49; Head of UK Permanent Delegation to the UN at Geneva, 1950–53; Head of Chancery at Prague, 1953–54; Counsellor, 1954; Counsellor and Head of Chancery, British Embassy, Paris, 1954–59; Head of Levant Dept, FO, 1959–61; Head of North and East African Dept, Foreign Office, 1961–63; Ambassador to Israel, 1963–65; an Asst Sec.-Gen., NATO, 1966–67; Asst Under-Sec. of State, FO, 1967–69; Ambassador to Belgium, 1969–74. *Recreations:* music, racing, books. *Address:* Dean Farm House, Winchester SO21 2LP. *T:* (01962) 776326. *Clubs:* White's, Royal Anglo-Belgian. *Died 4 Sept. 2000.*

BEITH, John William, CBE 1972; Director Special Duties, Massey Ferguson Holdings Ltd, 1971–74, retired; *b* 13 Jan. 1909; *s* of John William Beith and Ana Theresia (*née* Denk); *m* 1931, Dorothy (*née* Causbrook) (*d* 1986); two *s. Educ:* Spain, Chile, Germany; Llandovery Coll., S Wales. Joined Massey Harris (later Massey Ferguson), 1927, London; occupied senior exec. positions in Argentina, Canada, France and UK; Vice-Pres., Canadian

parent co., 1963; Chm., Massey Ferguson (UK) Ltd, 1970. Pres., Agricl Engrs Assoc. Ltd, 1970. *Recreations:* ancient and contemporary history, follower of Rugby, swimming. *Address:* Torre Blanca, 22 Calle de S Hortet, 07669 Cala Serena, Mallorca. *T:* (71) 657830. *Club:* Oriental.

Died 4 Aug. 2000.

BELCH, Sir (Alexander) Ross, Kt 1992; CBE 1972; FRSE 1977; FRINA; Chairman, Kelvin Travel Ltd, since 1984; President, Altnamara Shipping plc, since 1998 (Chairman, 1993–98); *b* 13 Dec. 1920; *s* of Alexander Belch, CBE, and Agnes Wright Ross; *m* 1st, 1947, Janette Finnie Murdoch (*d* 1988); four *d*; 2nd, 1992, Dorothy West. *Educ:* Morrison's Acad., Crieff, Perthshire; Glasgow Univ. (BSc Naval Arch. 1st Cl. Hons). Lithgows Ltd: Dir and Gen. Manager, 1954–59; Asst Man. Dir, 1959–64; Man. Dir, 1964–69; Scott Lithgow Ltd: Man. Dir, 1969–80; Chm., 1978–80. Dir, Jebsen Carriers Ltd, 1990–97. Chm., Irvine Develt Corp., 1985–90. Pres., Shipbuilders and Repairers Nat. Assoc., 1974–76. Chm., Council of Trustees, Scottish Maritime Museum, 1983–98 (Hon. Pres., 1998–). CIMgt (CBIM 1981). Hon. LLD Strathclyde, 1978. *Address:* Westwinds, 158 Greenock Road, Largs KA30 8RX. *T:* and *Fax:* (01475) 689855.

Died 26 March 1999.

BELL, Ian Wright, CBE 1964; HM Diplomatic Service, retired; *b* Radlett, Herts, 21 Aug. 1913; *s* of late T. H. D. Bell; *m* 1940, (Winifred Mary) Ruth Waterfield, *y d* of late E. H. Waterfield, ICS; three *s. Educ:* Canford Sch.; St Peter's Hall, Oxford. Vice-Consul: Valparaíso, 1938; Montevideo, 1940; Foreign Office, 1946; First Sec., 1947; First Sec., Addis Ababa, 1949, Chargé d'Affaires, 1949, 1950, 1952 and 1953; Consul, Innsbruck, 1953; First Sec., Prague, 1954, Chargé d'Affaires, 1954 and 1956; Counsellor and Consul-Gen., Jedda, 1956; Counsellor and Official Sec., UK High Commission, Canberra, 1957; HM Consul-Gen., Lyons, 1960–65; Ambassador, Santo Domingo, 1965–69; Consul-Gen., Stuttgart, 1969–73. FRGS. *Publications:* The Scarlet Flower (poems), 1947; The Dominican Republic, 1981; reviews and articles in various periodicals. *Recreations:* painting, drama, music, walking. *Address:* 4A Fisher Lane, Bingham, Nottingham NG13 8BQ. *Died 2 April 1998.*

BELL, Joseph Denis Milburn; Chairman, North Western Electricity Board, 1976–85; *b* 2 Sept. 1920; *s* of John Bell, BEM, and Ann Bell; *m* 1949, Wilhelmina Maxwell Miller; one *s* one *d. Educ:* Bishop Auckland Grammar Sch.; St Edmund Hall, Oxford (MA). Served War, RAF, 1941–45. Contested (Lab) Canterbury, 1945. Lectr in Modern Econ. History, Univ. of Glasgow, 1946; National Coal Board: Indust. Relations Dept, 1954; Dep. Indust. Relations Dir, Durham Div., 1963; Electricity Council: Statistical Officer, Indust. Relations Dept, 1966; Dep. Indust. Relations Adviser (Negotiating), 1967; Indust. Relations Adviser, 1972. *Publications:* Industrial Unionism: a critical analysis, 1949 (repr. in Trade Unions: selected readings, ed W. E. J. McCarthy, 1972); (contrib.) The Scottish Economy (ed A. K. Cairncross), 1953; (contrib.) The System of Industrial Relations in Great Britain (ed A. Flanders and H. A. Clegg), 1954; (contrib.) The Lessons of Public Enterprise (ed M. Shanks), 1963. *Address:* Rossways, Broad Lane, Hale, Altrincham, Cheshire WA15 0DH. *T:* (0161) 980 4451. *Died 25 July 1997.*

BELL, Prof. Quentin (Claudian Stephen), FRSA; FRSL; Emeritus Professor of the History and Theory of Art, Sussex University; painter, sculptor, potter, author, art critic; *b* 19 Aug. 1910; 2nd *s* of late Clive and Vanessa Bell; *m* 1952, Anne Olivier Popham; one *s* two *d. Educ:* Leighton Park. Political warfare executive, 1941–43. Lectr in Art Education, King's Coll., Newcastle, 1952, Senior Lecturer, 1956; Prof. of Fine Art, University of Leeds, 1962–67 (Head of Dept of Fine Art, 1959); Slade Professor of Fine Art, Oxford Univ., 1964–65; Ferens Prof. of Fine Art, University of Hull, 1965–66; Prof. of History and Theory of Art, Sussex Univ., 1967–75. Exhibitions, 1935, 1947, 1949, 1972, 1977, 1981, 1982, 1986. Commissioned Sculpture for Univ. of Leeds. MA Dunelm, 1957. Regular contributor to Listener, 1951–60. *Publications:* On Human Finery, 1947, rev. edn 1976; Those Impossible English (with Helmut Gernsheim), 1951; Roger Montané, 1961; The Schools of Design, 1963; Ruskin, 1963; Victorian Artists, 1967; Bloomsbury, 1968; Virginia Woolf, a Biography, 2 vols, 1972 (James Tait Black Meml Prize; Duff Cooper Meml Prize); A New and Noble School, 1982; Techniques of Terracotta, 1983; The Brandon Papers (novel), 1985; Bad Art, 1989; Elders and Betters, 1995. *Address:* 81 Heighton Street, Firle, Sussex BN8 6NZ. *T:* (01273) 858201.   *Died 16 Dec. 1996.*

BELL, Ronald Percy, MA; FRS 1944; FRSE 1968; FRSC; Professor of Chemistry, University of Stirling, 1967–75, then Emeritus; Hon. Research Professor of Chemistry, University of Leeds, 1976–82; *b* 1907; *e s* of E. A. Bell, Maidenhead; *m* 1931, Margery Mary West; one *s. Educ:* County Boys' Sch., Maidenhead; Balliol Coll., Oxford. Bedford Lecturer in Physical Chemistry, Balliol Coll., 1932; Fellow of Balliol Coll., 1933 (Vice-Master, 1965; Hon. Fellow, 1967); Univ. Lecturer and Demonstrator, Oxford Univ., 1938; Univ. Reader, Oxford Univ., 1955. George Fisher Baker Lectr, Cornell Univ., 1958; Nat. Science Foundn Fellow, Brown Univ., 1964; Visiting Professor: Weizmann Inst. of Sci., Israel, 1973; Tech. Univ. of Denmark, Lyngby, 1976. President: Faraday Soc., 1956; Chemistry Section, British Assoc. Meeting, Durham, 1970; Vice-Pres. Chemical Soc., 1958 (Tilden Lectureship, 1941; Liversidge Lectureship, 1973–74; Spiers Meml Lectureship, 1975). Foreign Mem. Royal Danish Acad. of Arts and Sciences, 1962; Foreign Associate, Nat. Acad. of Sciences, USA, 1972; Foreign Hon. Mem., Amer. Acad. of Arts and Scis, 1974. Hon. LLD Illinois Inst. of Techn., 1965; Hon. DTech, Tech. Univ. of Denmark, 1969; Hon. DSc Kent, 1974; DUniv Stirling, 1977. Leverhulme Emeritus Fellow, 1976. Meldola Medal, Inst. of Chemistry, 1936; Chem. Soc. Award in Kinetics and Mechanism, 1974. *Publications:* Acid-Base Catalysis, 1941; Acids and Bases, 1952, 2nd edn 1969; The Proton in Chemistry, 1959, 2nd edn 1973; The Tunnel Effect in Chemistry, 1980; papers in scientific journals. *Address:* Flat 5, Park Villa Court, Roundhay, Leeds LS8 1EB. *T:* Leeds (0113) 266 4236.
Died 9 Jan. 1996.

BELL, William Rupert Graham, CB 1978; Under Secretary, Department of Industry, 1975–80; *b* 29 May 1920; *m* 1950, Molly Bolton; two *d. Educ:* Bradford Grammar Sch.; St John's Coll., Cambridge (Scholar). Served Royal Artillery, 1940–45 (despatches). Asst Principal, Min. of Fuel and Power, 1948; Principal, 1949; Asst Sec., 1959; Under-Sec., Min. of Power, 1966–70, DTI, 1970–72; Deputy Principal, Civil Service Coll., 1972–75. Imperial Defence Coll., 1965. *Address:* 47 Chiswick Staithe, Hartington Road, W4 3TP. *T:* (0181) 994 2545.   *Died 6 Oct. 1996.*

BELLINGHAM, Sir Noel (Peter Roger), 7th Bt (2nd creation) *cr* 1796, of Castle Bellingham, co. Louth; accountant; *b* 4 Sept. 1943; *s* of Sir Roger Carroll Patrick Stephen Bellingham, 6th Bt, and of Mary, *d* of late William Norman; *S* father, 1973; *m* 1977, Jane, *d* of late Edwin William and of Joan Taylor, Sale, Cheshire. *Heir: b* Anthony Edward Norman Bellingham, *b* 24 March 1947. *Address:* 20 Davenport Park Road, Davenport, Stockport, Cheshire SK2 6JS. *T:* (0161) 483 7168. *Club:* 64 Society (Cheshire).   *Died 7 July 1999.*

BELLIS, John Herbert; Regional Chairman of Industrial Tribunals, Nottingham Region, 1992–97 (Manchester

Region, 1984–92); *b* 11 April 1930; *s* of Thomas and Jane Bellis; *m* 1961, Sheila Helen McNeil Ford; two *s* one *d. Educ:* Friars Grammar Sch., Bangor; Liverpool Univ. (LLB). Admitted Solicitor, 1953. National Service, 1953–55. In practice as solicitor on own account, Penmaenmawr, N Wales, 1958–84. Parly Cand. (L) Conway, Caernarvonshire, 1959. *Recreations:* walking, gardening, horse racing. *Address:* Green Acre, Church Lane, Muston, Nottingham NG13 0FD. *T:* (01949) 842634.   *Died 25 Jan. 2000.*

BELOFF, Baron *cr* 1981 (Life Peer), of Wolvercote in the County of Oxfordshire; **Max Beloff,** Kt 1980; DLitt; FBA 1973; FRHistS; FRSA; *b* 2 July 1913; *er s* of late Simon and Mary Beloff; *m* 1938, Helen Dobrin; two *s. Educ:* St Paul's Sch.; Corpus Christi Coll., Oxford (Scholar; MA; Hon. Fellow, 1993); DLitt Oxon. Gibbs Schol. in Mod. Hist., 1934; 1st Cl. Hons, School of Modern History, 1935; Senior Demy, Magdalen Coll., Oxford, 1935. Junior Research Fellow, Corpus Christi Coll., 1937; Asst Lecturer in History, Manchester Univ., 1939–46; Nuffield Reader in Comparative Study of Institutions, Oxford Univ., 1946–56; Fellow of Nuffield Coll., 1947–57; Gladstone Prof. of Govt and Public Admin, Oxford Univ., 1957–74, then Professor Emeritus; Fellow, All Souls Coll., 1957–74, Emeritus Fellow, 1980–; Supernumerary Fellow, St Antony's Coll., Oxford, 1975–84; Principal, University Coll. at Buckingham, 1974–79. Hon. Prof., St Andrews Univ., 1993–98. War of 1939–45, Royal Corps of Signals, 1940–41. Governor, Haifa Univ.; Ex-Trustee and Ex-Librarian, Oxford Union Soc. Hon. Fellow, Mansfield Coll., Oxford, 1989. Hon. LLD: Pittsburgh, USA, 1962; Manchester Univ., 1989; Hon. DCL Bishop's Univ. Canada, 1976; Hon. DLitt: Bowdoin Coll., USA, 1976; Buckingham, 1984; Hon. DrUniv Aix-Marseille III, 1978. *Publications.* Public Order and Popular Disturbances, 1660–1714, 1938; The Foreign Policy of Soviet Russia, Vol. 1, 1947, Vol. 2, 1949; Thomas Jefferson and American Democracy, 1948; Soviet Policy in the Far East, 1944–51, 1953; The Age of Absolutism, 1660–1815, 1954; Foreign Policy and the Democratic Process, 1955; Europe and the Europeans, 1957, The Great Powers, 1959; The American Federal Government, 1959; New Dimensions in Foreign Policy, 1961; The United States and the Unity of Europe, 1963; The Balance of Power, 1967; The Future of British Foreign Policy, 1969; Imperial Sunset, vol. 1, 1969, 2nd edn 1988, vol. 2, Dream of Commonwealth 1921–42, 1989; The Intellectual in Politics, 1970; (with G. R. Peele) The Government of the United Kingdom, 1980, 2nd edn 1985; Wars and Welfare 1914–1945, 1984; An Historian in the Twentieth Century, 1992; Britain and European Union, 1996; edited: The Federalist, 1948, 2nd edn 1987; Mankind and his Story, 1948; The Debate on the American Revolution, 1949, 2nd edn 1989; On the Track of Tyranny, 1959; (jtly) L'Europe du XIXe et XXe siècle, 1960–67; (with V. Vale) American Political Institutions in the 1970's, 1975; articles in English, French, Italian and American journals. *Recreation:* watching cricket. *Address:* c/o House of Lords, SW1A 0PW. *T:* (020) 7219 6669. *Club:* Reform.
Died 22 March 1999.

BELOFF, Nora; author and journalist; *b* 24 Jan. 1919; *m* 1977, Clifford Makins (*d* 1990). *Educ:* King Alfred Sch.; Lady Margaret Hall, Oxford. BA Hons History 1940. Polit. Intell. Dept, FO, 1941–44; British Embassy, Paris, 1944–45; reporter, Reuters News Agency, 1945–46; Paris corresp., The Economist, 1946–48; Observer corresp., Paris, Washington, Moscow, Brussels etc, 1948–78; political correspondent, 1964–76, roving correspondent, 1976–78. Latterly engaged in research on internat. responsibilities for the conflict in former Yugoslavia. *Publications:* The General Says No, 1963; The Transit of Britain, 1973; Freedom under Foot, 1976; No Travel like

Russian Travel, 1979 (US, as Inside the Soviet Empire: myth and reality, 1980); Tito's Flawed Legacy: Yugoslavia and the West 1939–1984, 1985 (US, as Tito's Flawed Legacy: Yugoslavia and the West 1939 till now, 1986; trans. Italian, 1987, Slovene, 1990, Serbo-Croat, 1991). *Address:* 11 Belsize Road, NW6 4RX. *T:* and *Fax:* (0171) 586 0378.   *Died 12 Feb. 1997.*

BELPER, 4th Baron *cr* 1856, of Belper, co. Derby; **Alexander Ronald George Strutt;** formerly Major, Coldstream Guards; *b* 23 April 1912; *s* of 3rd Baron Belper and Hon. Eva Isabel Mary Bruce, DBE (*m* 2nd, 6th Earl of Rosebery; she *d* 1987), 2nd *d* of 2nd Baron Aberdare; *S* father, 1956; *m* 1940, Zara Sophie Kathleen Mary (marr. diss. 1949), *y d* of Sir Harry Mainwaring, 5th Bt; one *s. Educ:* Harrow. Served War with Coldstream Guards, 1939–44 (wounded). *Heir: s* Hon. Richard Henry Strutt [*b* 24 Oct. 1941; *m* 1st, 1966, Jennifer Vivian (marr. diss. 1979), *d* of late Capt. Peter Winser and of Mrs James Whitaker; one *s* one *d*; 2nd, 1980, Judith Mary de Jonge, *d* of Mr and Mrs James Twynam, Kitemore House, Faringdon, Oxon]. *Address:* c/o 12 Gough Square, EC4A 3DW.   *Died 23 Dec. 1999.*

BELSKY, Franta; sculptor; *b* Brno, 6 April 1921; *s* of Joseph Belsky, economist; *m* 1st, 1944, Margaret Constance Owen (cartoonist Belsky) (*d* 1989); 2nd, 1996, Irena Sedlecka. *Educ:* Acad. of Fine Arts, Prague; Royal Coll. of Art, London. ARCA, Hons Dip. 1950. Served War as gunner (France, 1940; Normandy, 1944; various decorations). Taught in art schs, 1950–55. FRBS (Mem. Council, 1958–92); Pres., Soc. of Portrait Sculptors, 1963–68, 1994–99; Governor, St Martin's Sch. of Art, 1967–88. Hon. Churchill Fellow, 1994–; Hon. DArts 1997, Westminster Coll., Fulton, Mo. Works in Nat. Portrait Gall. and collections in Europe and USA, and for numerous county councils, industrial, shipping and private cos and educn authorities; Paratroop Memorial, Prague, 1947; Lt-Col Peniakoff (Popski), Ravenna, 1952; statue of Cecil Rhodes, 8′, Bulawayo, 1953; statue of Sir Winston Churchill for Churchill Meml and Library in US, Fulton, Missouri and City of Prague, 1992 (bust in Churchill Archives, Cambridge, 1971 and Nat. Gall., Prague, 1990); RAF memorial, Prague, 1995; *groups:* Constellation, Colchester, 1953; Lesson, LCC housing develt, 1957–58; Triga, Knightsbridge, 1958; Joy-ride, Stevenage New Town Centre, 1958 (listed by English Heritage, 1998); Astronomer Herschel Memorial, 18′, Slough, 1969; Oracle, 18′, Temple Way House, Bristol, 1975 (RBS Sir Otto Beit Medal, 1976); Totem, 32′, Manchester Arndale Centre, 1975 (RBS Sir Otto Beit Medal, 1978); *fountains:* European Shell Centre, 30′, South Bank, 1961; Leap, 26′, Blackwall Basin, 1988; *reliefs:* Epicentre, Doncaster City Centre, 1965; 1978 Jean Masson Davidson Award for Dist. in Portrait Sculpture; *portraits* included: busts: Queen Mother, Birmingham Univ., 1962; Prince Philip, 1979 and HM the Queen, 1981, Nat. Portrait Gall.; Prince Andrew, 1963 and 1984; Prince William, 1985; Lord Cottesloe, Nat. Theatre, 1976; Harry S. Truman, bust, Presidential Library, Independence, Mo and figure, H. S. T. Dam, Osage River, Mo, 1972; Adm. Cunningham, half-figure, Trafalgar Square, 1969; Mountbatten Meml, Horse Guards Parade, 1983, and bust, Queen Elizabeth II Conf. Centre, Westminster, 1986; Adm. Lord Lewin, half-figure, HMS Dryad, 1985. Queen Mother 80th Birthday Crown coin. *Publications:* illus. and contrib. various books, jls and a monograph. *Address:* 4 The Green, Sutton Courtenay, Abingdon OX14 4AE.   *Died 5 July 2000.*

BENDER, Prof. Arnold Eric; Emeritus Professor, University of London; Professor of Nutrition and Dietetics, University of London and Head of Department of Food Science and Nutrition, Queen Elizabeth College, 1978–83 (Professor of Nutrition, 1971–78); *b* 24 July 1918; *s* of

Isadore and Rose Bender; *m* 1941, Deborah Swift; two *s. Educ:* Liverpool Inst. High Sch.; Univ. of Liverpool (BSc Hons); Univ. of Sheffield (PhD). FRSH, FIFST. Research, Pharmaceutical Industry, 1940–45 and 1950–54; Res. Fellow, National Inst. of Radiotherapy, Sheffield, 1945–47; Lectr, Univ. of Sheffield, 1947–49; Research, Food Industry, 1954–64; Teaching and Research, Univ. of London, 1965–83. Department of Health and Social Security: Gp Sec. of Working Party on Protein Requirements, 1963; Mem., Sub-cttee on Protein Requirements, 1967; Mem., Cttee on Toxic Chemicals in Food and the Environment, 1976–83; Mem., Cttee on Med. Aspects of Food Policy, 1978–85; Chm., Panel on Novel Foods, 1980–85. Ministry of Agriculture, Fisheries and Food: Mem., Cttee on Dietetic Foods, 1969–73 and on Composition of Foods, 1975–77; Mem., Adv. Cttee on Irradiated and Novel Foods, 1981–85 and on Naturally Occurring Toxic Substances in Foods, 1983–90. Society of Chemical Industry: Mem. Council, 1982–85; Food Group: Hon. Sec., 1955–60; Chm., 1979–80; Vice-Chm., 1980–82; Chm., Nutrition Panel, 1960–63 and 1976–78. Royal Society of Health: Mem. Council, 1974–89; Chm. Council, 1987–88; Chm., Examinations Cttee, 1983–85; Chm., Conf. and Meetings Cttee, 1985–86; Chm., Food and Nutrition Gp, 1968–70 (Vice Chm., 1967–68). Member: Royal Soc. British Nat. Cttee for Biochem., 1963–69, for Nutritional Scis, 1976–85; Eur. Cttee for Co-operation in Sci. and Technol. (COST 91), 1980–83 (Chm., Nutrition Sub-cttee, 1982–83); Cttee on Protein Quality Evaluation, ARC, 1955–66; Sector D Res. Cttee, CNAA, 1982–91; Pres., Inst. Food Sci. and Technol., 1989–91; Vice-Pres., Internat. Union of Food Sci. and Technol., 1983–87 (Mem. Exec., 1978–83). Hon. Treasurer, UK Nutrition Soc., 1962–67; Hon. Sec., UK Council for Food Sci. and Technol., 1964–77. Hon. DSc Univ. Complutense, Madrid, 1983. Mem. Editorial Board: Jl of Human Nutrition; Jl of Science of Food and Agriculture; Jl of Food Technol.; British Jl of Nutrition; Jl of Envmtl Mgt and Health. *Publications:* Dictionary of Nutrition and Food Technology, 1960, 6th edn 1990, Japanese edn 1965, Arabic edn 1985; Nutrition and Dietetic Foods, 1967, 2nd edn 1973; Value of Food, 1970, 3rd edn 1979, Spanish edn 1972; Facts of Food, 1975, Polish edn 1979; Food Processing and Nutrition, 1978, Japanese edn 1978; The Pocket Guide to Calories and Nutrition, 1979, 2nd edn 1986, Dutch, US, Italian and Spanish edns, 1981; Nutrition for Medical Students, 1982; Health or Hoax?, 1985, Spanish edn 1987; Food Tables, 1986; Food Labelling, 1992; Meat and Meat Products in Developing Countries, 1992; Dictionary of Food and Nutrition, 1995; Nutrition: a reference handbook, 1997; research papers and review articles in Brit. Jl of Nutrition, Biochem. Jl, BMJ, Jl Human Nutrition, Jl Science Food and Agric., and other professional jls, and reports. *Recreations:* writing, gardening, lecturing. *Address:* 2 Willow Vale, Fetcham, Leatherhead, Surrey KT22 9TE. *T:* (01372) 454702.   *Died 21 Feb. 1999.*

BENINGFIELD, Gordon George; artist, since 1966; *b* 31 Oct. 1936; *s* of George Robert Edward Beningfield and Emily Ellen (*née* McNally); *m* 1958, Elizabeth Boyce; two *d. Educ:* London Colney Secondary Sch. Ecclesiastical artist, 1952–65. President: Brit. Butterfly Conservation Soc., 1989–; Blackmore Vale Br., NT, 1989–. Designed and engraved 8 meml windows for the Guards Chapel, 1972–94; designed stamps for GPO: Butterfly, 1981; Insects, 1985; many philatelic designs worldwide. One-man exhibns, London, 1967–. Freeman, City of London, 1995; Liveryman, Glass Sellers' Co., 1995. Sir Peter Scott Meml Award, British Naturalists Assoc., 1997. *Publications:* Beningfield's Butterflies, 1978; Beningfield's Countryside, 1980; Hardy Country, 1983; Beningfield's English Landscapes, 1985; Beningfield's

English Farm, 1988; Hardy Landscapes, 1990; Beningfield's Woodland, 1993; Gordon Beningfield, the Artist and his Work: a pictorial autobiography, 1994; Beningfield's English Villages, 1996; *illustrator:* Darkling Thrush, 1985; Poems of the Countryside, 1987; Green and Pleasant Land, 1989; Poems of the Seasons, 1992. *Recreations:* enjoying the rural landscape, natural history, general British history. *Address:* 3 The Moor, Water End, near Hemel Hempstead, Herts HP1 3BL. *T:* (01442) 68356. *Died 4 May 1998.*

BENJAMIN, Pauline, (Mrs Joseph Benjamin); *see* Crabbe, P.

BENN, (Edward) Glanvill; Life President, Benn Brothers plc, Publishers, 1976, Chairman, 1945–75; *b* 31 Dec. 1905; 2nd *s* of late Sir Ernest Benn, 2nd Bt, CBE and Gwendoline, *d* of F. M. Andrews, Edgbaston; *m* 1931, (Beatrice) Catherine, MBE, *d* of Claude Newbald; one *s* one *d*. *Educ:* Harrow; Clare Coll., Cambridge. Served War of 1939–45: East Surrey Regt, 1940–45; Brigade Major, 138 Infantry Brigade, Italy, 1944 (despatches). Council Member: Nat. Advertising Benevolent Soc., 1937–61 (Trustee, 1951–80, and Pres., 1961–62); Advertising Assoc., 1951–67 (Hon. Treasurer, 1960–65); CPU, 1956 (Hon. Treasurer, 1967–77; Hon. Life Mem., 1975; Astor Award, 1982); Vice Pres., Readers' Pension Cttee, 1950; Life Vice Pres., Newspaper Press Fund, 1965 (Appeals Pres. 1971); Chm., Advertising Advisory Cttee, Independent Television Authority, 1959–64 (Mackintosh medal, 1967); Pres., Periodical Publishers Assoc., 1976–78. Dir, Exchange Telegraph Co. Ltd, 1960–72 (Chm. 1969–72). Master, Stationers' Company, 1977. *Address:* Crescent Cottage, Aldeburgh, Suffolk IP15 5HW. *Clubs:* Reform (Hon. Life Mem.); Tandridge Golf (Hon. Life Mem.). *Died 10 May 2000.*

BENNETT, Albert Joseph, CBE 1966; Secretary, National Health Service Staff Commission, 1972–75; Vice-Chairman, Paddington and North Kensington Health Authority, 1982–85; *b* 9 April 1913; *er s* of late Albert James Bennett and Alice Bennett, Stourbridge, Worcs; unmarried. *Educ:* King Edward VI Sch., Stourbridge; St John's Coll., Cambridge (MA). Mathematical Tripos (Wrangler). Admin. Officer, LCC, 1936–39; Central Midwives Board: Asst Sec., 1939–45; Sec., 1945–47; Instructor Lieut, later Lt-Comdr, RN, 1940–45; Sec., NW Met. Regional Hosp. Bd, 1947–65; Principal Officer, NHS Nat. Staff Cttee, 1965–72; Under-Sec., DHSS, 1972–75, seconded as Sec., NHS Staff Commn. Member: Nat. Selection Cttee for Recruitment of Trainee Hospital Admin. Staff, 1955–64; Cttee of Inquiry into the Recruitment, Training and Promotion of Admin. and Clerical Staff in Hospital Service, 1962–63; Adv. Cttee on Hospital Engineers Training, 1967–72; Admin. Training Cttee, Cttee of Vice-Chancellors and Principals, 1970–72; Kensington and Chelsea and Westminster AHA(T), 1977–82, and Family Practitioner Cttee, 1977–85. *Recreations:* walking, gardening. *Address:* 19 Garson House, Gloucester Terrace, W2 3DG. *T:* (0171) 262 8311. *Died 18 Sept. 1996.*

BENNETT, (Charles John) Michael, CBE 1974; FCA; Partner in Barton, Mayhew & Co., Chartered Accountants, 1937–71; *b* 29 June 1906; *e s* of late Sir Charles Alan Bennett (Hon. Mr Justice Bennett) and Constance Radeglance, *d* of Major John Nathaniel Still, KOSB; *m* 1931, Audrey (*d* 1990), *o d* of J. C. C. Thompson (killed in action, 1915), Scots Guards and Norah K. Davenport; two *d*. *Educ:* Clifton Coll.; Trinity Coll., Cambridge. Served with HM Forces, 1939–45: Major, RAPC, India, 1942–45. Member: Electricity Supply Companies Commn, 1959, in Hong Kong; Fiji Sugar Inquiry Commn, 1961; Commn of Inquiry (Sugar Industry) 1962, in Mauritius; Commn of Inquiry into Banana Industry of St Lucia, 1963; Commn of Inquiry (Chm.) into Sugar Industry and Agriculture of Antigua, 1965; Commn of Enquiry into Sugar Industry of Guyana, 1967; Cttee of Enquiry into the pricing of certain contracts for the overhaul of aero-engines by Bristol Siddeley Engines Ltd. Mem. of Council, Institute of Chartered Accountants, 1963–69. Part-time Mem., Commonwealth Development Corp., 1965–73, Dep. Chm. 1970–71, 1972–73; Independent Mem., NEDC for Chemical Industry, and Chm., Pharmaceuticals Working Party, 1969. Mem., E Anglian Regional Cttee of Nat. Trust, 1971–81. *Recreation:* talking, mainly about the future of the UK. *Address:* 2 The Beeches, Station Road, Holt, Norfolk, NR25 6AU. *T:* (01263) 713479. *Clubs:* Oriental; Royal West Norfolk Golf; Denham Golf. *Died 24 Oct. 1999.*

BENNETT, Sir Charles (Moihi), Kt 1975; DSO 1943; company director, retired; President, New Zealand Labour Party, 1972–76; *b* 27 July 1913; *s* of Rt Rev. Frederick August Bennett, Bishop of Aotearoa, 1928–50, and Rangioue Bennett; *m* 1947, Elizabeth May Stewart. *Educ:* Univ. of New Zealand; Exeter Coll., Oxford. MA, DipSocSci, DipEd. Director of Maori Welfare, 1954–57; High Comr for New Zealand to Fedn of Malaya, 1959–63; Asst Sec., Dept of Maori Affairs, 1963–69. Mem., NZ Prisons Parole Bd, 1974–76. Hon. LLD Canterbury Univ. of NZ, 1973. Hon. PMN (Malaysia), 1963. *Address:* 72 Boucher Avenue, Te Puke 3071, New Zealand. *Died 26 Nov. 1998.*

BENNETT, Sir Hubert, Kt 1970; FRIBA; architect in private practice; Architect to the Greater London Council (formerly London County Council) and Superintending Architect of Metropolitan Buildings, 1956–71; *b* 4 Sept. 1909; *s* of late Arthur and Eleanor Bennett; *m* 1938, Louise F. C. Aldred (*d* 1996); three *d*. *Educ:* School of Architecture, Victoria University of Manchester. Asst Lecturer, Leeds School of Architecture, 1933–35; Asst Lecturer, Regent Street Polytechnic Sch. of Architecture, 1935–40; Superintending Architect (Lands), War Dept, 1940–43; Borough Architect, Southampton, 1943–45, County Architect, W Riding of Yorks, 1945–56. Exec. Dir, English Property Corp. Ltd, 1971–79; Dir, Help the Aged Housing Assoc. (UK) Ltd. Pres., W Yorks Soc. of Architects, 1954–66; Chm., Technical Panel, Standing Conf. on London Regional Planning, 1962–64; Member: Building Res. Bd, 1959–66; Timber Res. and Develt Assoc. Adv. Panel, 1965–68; Housing Study Mission from Britain to Canada, 1968. Prof., Univ of NSW, 1973. Architect for the Hyde Park Corner–Marble Arch Improvement Scheme, Crystal Palace Recreational Centre and South Bank Arts Centre; Consulting Architect, Guest Palace for the Sultan of Oman, Muscat, 1982; architect to UNESCO Headquarters, Paris, 1980–85. RIBA Assessor, South Bank Competition, Vauxhall Cross, 1981; Assessor, City Polytechnic of Hong Kong, 1982–83. Royal Institute of British Architects: Mem. Council, 1952–55, 1957–62, 1965–66, 1967–69; Hon. Treas., 1959–62; Silver Medallist for Measured Drawings (Hon. Mention), 1932; Arthur Cates Prize, 1933; Sir John Soane Medallist, 1934; Neale Bursar, 1936; Godwin and Wimperis Bursar, 1948; London Architecture Bronze Medal, 1959; Bronze Medal, 1968. Royal Society of Arts Medal, 1934; Rome Scholarship Special Award, 1936; Min. of Housing and Local Govt Housing Medal, 1954, 1963, 1964, 1966, 1968; Civic Trust Awards; Sir Patrick Abercrombie Award (for planning project Thamesmead), Internat. Union of Architects, 1969; Fritz Schumacher Prize, 1970. Hon. Member: Architects in Industry Group; Inst. of Architects of Czechoslovakia; Soc. of Architects of Venezuela. *Address:* Broadfields, Liphook, Hants GU30 7JH. *T:* (01428) 724176. *Died 13 Dec. 2000.*

BENNETT, Sir John (Mokonuiarangi), Kt 1988; QSO 1978; Chairman: Maori Education Trust, since 1975; Te Kohanga Reo National Trust, since 1982; Takitimu School of Performing Arts Trust, since 1990; *b* 4 Sept. 1912; *e s* of Rt Rev. Frederick Augustus Bennett, sometime Bishop of Aotearoa, and Arihia Rangioue Bennett; *m* 1939, Moana Hineiwaerea (*d* 1975); two *s* two *d* (and two *s* decd). *Educ:* Clive Sch.; Te Aute Coll.; Christchurch Teachers' Coll. Various teaching positions, 1934–74. Mem., 1970–95, Chm., 1984–95, Nature Conservation Council. Vice Pres., New Zealand Maori Council, 1982 (Foundn Mem.). Adv. Council, Dictionary of NZ Biography, 1993. QSO awarded for Public Service, 1978; knighthood for services to education, 1988. *Address:* 70 Simla Avenue, PO Box 8486, Havelock North, Hawkes Bay, New Zealand. *T:* (6) 8777994. *Died 28 Oct. 1997.*

BENNETT, Michael; *see* Bennett, C. J. M.

BENNETT, Peter Ward, OBE; Chairman, W. H. Smith & Son Holdings Ltd, 1977–82; *b* Toronto, Ont, 7 Feb. 1917; *m* (Priscilla) Ann; one *s* three *d. Educ:* Upper Canada Coll.; Univ. of Toronto. Chartered Accountant. Served War of 1939–45, Canadian Army. *Address:* Dene House, Littledene, Glynde, Lewes, Sussex BN8 6LB. *Died 15 Sept. 1996.*

BENNETT, Sir Reginald (Frederick Brittain), Kt 1979; VRD 1944; company director and wine consultant; formerly psychiatrist and politician; *b* 22 July 1911; *e s* of late Samuel Robert Bennett and Gertrude (*née* Brittain); *m* 1947, Henrietta, *d* of late Capt. H. B. Crane, CBE, RN; one *s* three *d. Educ:* Winchester Coll.; New College, Oxford (sailing Blue, 1931–34; BM, BCh 1942; MA); St George's Hosp. Med. Sch., SW1. LMSSA 1937; DPM 1948. Oxford Univ. Air Squadron, 1931–34; RNVR, 1934–46; Fleet Air Arm, Medical Officer and Pilot; torpedoed twice. Maudsley Hosp., SE5, 1947–49. MP (C) Gosport and Fareham, 1950–74, Fareham, 1974–79; PPS to Rt Hon. Iain Macleod, 1956–63; Chairman: House of Commons Catering Sub-Cttee, 1970–74, 1976–79; Anglo-Italian Parly Gp, 1971–79 (Hon. Sec., 1961–71); Parly and Scientific Cttee, 1959–62. Vice-Pres., Franco-British Parly Relations Cttee, 1973–79; Mem. Council, Internat. Inst. of Human Nutrition, 1975–96. Helmsman: Shamrock V, 1934–35; Evaine, 1936–38; Olympic Games (reserve), 1936; in British-American Cup Team, 1949 and 1953 in USA; various trophies since. Chairman: Amateur Yacht Research Soc., 1972–90; World Sailing Speed Record Council, ISAF (formerly IYRU), 1980–; Portland/West Kirby Speed Sailing Cttee, RYA, 1980–92; RYA Nat. Match-Racing Championship Cttee, 1989–94. RYA Yachtsman's Award, 1999. Hon. Lt-Col, Georgia Militia, 1960; Hon. Citizen: Atlanta, Ga, 1960; Port-St Louis-du-Rhône, France, 1986. Grand Officer, Italian Order of Merit, 1977. Commandeur du Bontemps-Médoc, 1959; Chevalier du Tastevin, 1970; Galant de la Verte Marennes; Chevalier de St Etienne, Alsace, 1971; Chevalier Bretvin (Muscadet), 1973; Legato del Chianti, 1983. *Publications:* Three Chousing Reers (memoir), 1997; articles on wine, medicine, psychiatry, politics and yacht racing; videotapes of yacht racing in Shamrock V. *Recreations:* sailing, painting (exhib., RA Summer Exhibn, 1995), foreign travel, basking in the sun, avoiding exercise. *Address:* 19 Elm Lodge, River Gardens, SW6 6NZ. *Clubs:* White's; Imperial Poona Yacht (Cdre); Wykehamist Sailing (Cdre); Sea View Yacht, Sea View Buffs, etc. *Died 19 Dec. 2000.*

BENNETT, Ronald Alistair, CBE 1986; QC (Scot.) 1959; Vice-President for Scotland, Value Added Tax Tribunals, since 1977; *b* 11 Dec. 1922; *s* of Arthur George Bennett, MC and Edythe Sutherland; *m* 1950, Margret Magnusson, *d* of Sigursteinn Magnusson, Icelandic Consul-Gen. for Scotland; three *s* two *d* (and one *d* decd). *Educ:* Edinburgh Academy; Edinburgh Univ.; Balliol Coll., Oxford. MA, LLB Univ. of Edinburgh, 1942; Muirhead and Dalgety Prizes for Civil Law, 1942. Lieut, 79th (Scottish Horse) Medium Regt RA, 1943–45; Capt. attached RAOC, India and Japan, 1945–46. Called to Scottish Bar, 1947; Vans Dunlop Schol. in Scots Law and Conveyancing, 1948; Standing Counsel to Min. of Labour and National Service, 1957–59; Sheriff-Principal: of Roxburgh, Berwick and Selkirk, 1971–74; of S Strathclyde, Dumfries and Galloway, 1981–82; of N Strathclyde, 1982–83; Temp. Addtl Sheriff-Principal of Grampian, Highland and Islands, 1990–91. Lectr in Mercantile Law: Edinburgh Univ., 1956–68; Heriot-Watt Univ., 1968–75. Chairman: Med. Appeal Tribunals (Scotland), 1971–94; Agricultural Wages Bd for Scotland, 1973–95; Local Govt Boundary Commn for Scotland, 1974–90; Northern Lighthouse Bd, April-Sept. 1974; Industrial Tribunals, (Scotland), 1977–95; War Pension Tribunals, 1984–. Arbiter, Motor Insurers' Bureau appeals, 1975–; Mem., Scottish Medical Practices Cttee, 1976–88. *Publications:* Bennett's Company Law, 2nd edn 1950; Fraser's Rent Acts in Scotland, 2nd edn 1952; Editor: Scottish Current Law and Scots Law Times Sheriff Court Reports, 1948–74; Court of Session Reports, 1976–88. *Recreations:* crossword puzzles, reading, music, gardening. *Address:* Laxamyri, 46 Cammo Road, Barnton, Edinburgh EH4 8AP. *T:* 0131–339 6111. *Died 21 June 1996.*

BENNETT, Roy Grissell, CMG 1971; TD 1947; Chairman and Managing Director, Maclaine Watson & Co. Ltd, London and Singapore, 1970–72 (Director, 1958–72), retired; Chairman, Beder International Singapore and Beder Malaysia, since 1972; *b* 21 Nov. 1917; *s* of Charles Ernest Marklaw Bennett. *Educ:* privately and RMC Sandhurst. Served War of 1939–45, 17th/21st Lancers; seconded 24th Lancers, 1st Lothian and Border Horse, 2nd i/c, 1944–46; Major. Joined J. H. Vavasseur & Co. Ltd, Penang, 1946, Director, 1949; joined Maclaine, Watson & Co. Ltd, Singapore 1952: Dir London Board, 1958–72; Man. Dir, Eastern interests, 1960; Chm., Pilkington (SE Asia) Private Ltd and Fibreglass Pilkington Malaysia, 1972–89. Chairman: Singapore Internat. Chamber of Commerce, 1967–70; Singapore Chamber of Commerce Rubber Assoc., 1960–72; founder Chm., Rubber Assoc. of Singapore (Dep. Chm. 1966–72); Chm. Council, Singapore Anti-Tuberculosis Assoc., 1962; Founder Chm., 1972–78, and Governor, United World Coll., SE Asia (Chm. Governors, 1972–79); Chm., Racehorse Spelling Station, Cameron Highlands, Malaysia, 1976–. Riding for the Disabled Association of Singapore: Founder Chm., 1982–85; Mem. Cttee, 1982; Life Hon. Mem., 1989; Patron, 1992–. Patron, Nat. Kidney Foundn. FInstD. *Recreations:* economics, polo, racing, shooting, swimming, photography, motoring, safaris, camping, gardening, zoology, boating, reading, travelling, people especially of the East. *Address:* PO Box 49, Bukit Panjang, Singapore 9168; 22 Jalan Perdana, Johore Bharu 80300, Malaysia. *T:* Johore Bharu (7) 2234505, *Fax:* (7) 2249006; Oak Tree House, South Holmwood, Surrey RH5 4NF. *T:* Dorking (01306) 889414, *Fax:* (01306) 877604. *Clubs:* Cavalry and Guards; Tanglin, British, Turf (Dep. Chm.), Polo (Patron; Past Chm.; Pres. 1958–70), AA Sports (Singapore); Turf, Polo, Town, Swimming (Penang); Victoria Racing (Melbourne). *Died 16 Dec. 1996.*

BENSON, Jeremy Henry, OBE 1984; architect in private practice (Benson & Bryant, Chartered Architects), since 1954; *b* 25 June 1925; 3rd *s* of late Guy Holford Benson and Lady Violet Benson; *m* 1951, Patricia Stewart; two *s* three *d. Educ:* Eton; Architectural Assoc. (AADipl.); FRIBA. Royal Engineers, 1944–47. Pres., Georgian Gp, 1985–90 (Mem., Exec. Cttee, 1967–85; Chm., 1980–85); Chm., SPAB, 1989–90 (Vice-Chm., 1971–89; Mem. Exec.

Cttee, 1959–90, 1991–); Chm., Joint Cttee of SPAB, GG, Victorian Soc., Civic Trust, Ancient Monuments Soc. and Council for British Archaeology, 1989– (Mem., 1968–; Vice-Chm., 1972–89), and Chm. of its Tax Group; Member: Forestry Commn's Westonbirt Adv. Cttee, 1969–; Historic Buildings Council for England, 1974–84; Adv. Cttee on Trees in the Royal Parks, 1977–80; Council, Garden History Soc., 1994–. Historic Buildings and Monuments Commission for England: Comr, 1983–88; Mem., Historic Buildings and Areas (formerly Historic Buildings) Adv. Cttee, 1984–93; Chm., Gardens Cttee, 1984–92; Mem., Landscape Gardens Panel, 1992–. Chairman: Old Chiswick Protection Soc., 1993–; Chiswick House Friends, 1993–. *Recreation:* gardening. *Address:* (office) Walpole House, Chiswick Mall, W4 2PS. *T:* (020) 8994 1611; Field Barn, Taddington, Temple Guiting, Cheltenham, Glos GL54 5RY. *T:* (01386) 73228. *Club:* Brooks's. *Died 1 Dec. 1999.*

BENTINE, Michael, CBE 1995; actor, comedian, and writer; *b* 26 Jan. 1922; *m* 1st, 1941, Marie Barradell (marr. diss.); (one *d* decd); 2nd, 1947, Clementina Theresa Gadesden Stuart-McCall; one *s* one *d* (and one *s* one *d* decd). *Educ:* Eton. Stage début, Sweet Lavender, Cardiff, 1940; Robert Atkins' Shakespearian Co., Regent's Park; RAF, 1942–45; Starlight Roof, Windmill Theatre, 1946; *radio includes:* Round the Bend; Best of Bentine; The Goon Show (founder mem., The Goons, 1949); *television includes:* The Bumblies, 1954; The Cathode Ray Tube Show, 1957; It's a Square World, 1960, 1962, 1977; The Golden Silents (series), 1971; Potty Time (puppet series), 1976–77; *films include:* We Joined the Navy, 1962; The Sandwich Man, 1965; Bachelor of Arts, 1970. Internat. TV Concours, Montreux, 1963; Grand Prix de la Presse, 1963. *Publications:* Smith & Sons, Removers, 1981; Best of Bentine, 1983; Doors of the Mind, 1984; A Shy Person's Guide to Life, 1984; Open Your Mind, 1990; Reluctant Jester, 1992; *autobiography:* The Door Marked Summer, 1981; The Long Banana Skin, 1982. *Address:* c/o Jimmy Grafton Management, 26 Tavistock Court, Tavistock Square, WC1H 9HE. *Died 26 Nov. 1996.*

BENTLEY, Rev. Canon Geoffrey Bryan; Hon. Canon of Windsor, since 1982; *b* 16 July 1909; *s* of late Henry Bentley; *m* 1938, Nina Mary, *d* of late George Coombe Williams, priest; two *s* two *d*. *Educ:* Uppingham Sch.; King's Coll., Cambridge (Scholar); Cuddesdon Coll., Oxford. BA and Carus Greek Testament Prize, 1932; MA 1935. Ordained deacon 1933, priest 1934; Asst Curate, St Cuthbert's, Copnor, 1933–35; Tutor of Scholae Cancellarii, Lincoln, 1935–38; Lecturer, 1938–52; Priest Vicar of Lincoln Cathedral and Chaplain of Lincoln County Hosp., 1938–52; Proctor in Convocation, 1945–55; Rector of Milton Abbot with Dunterton, Dio. Exeter, 1952–57; Examg Chap. to Bp of Exeter, 1952–74; Commissary of Bp of SW Tanganyika, 1952–61; Canon of Windsor, 1957–82, President, 1962, 1971 and 1976. Member: Archbp's Commns on Atomic Power, 1946, and Divine Healing, 1953; Archbp's Group on Reform of Divorce Law, 1964 (author of report, Putting Asunder). William Jones Golden Lectr, 1965; Scott Holland Lectr., 1966. *Publications:* The Resurrection of the Bible, 1940; Catholic Design for Living, 1940; Reform of the Ecclesiastical Law, 1944; God and Venus, 1964; Dominance or Dialogue?, 1965; (contrib.) Sexual Morality: three views, 1965; (contrib.) Abortion and the Sanctity of Human Life, 1985. *Address:* 5 The Cloisters, Windsor Castle, Berks SL4 1NJ. *T:* (01753) 863001. *Died 12 Sept. 1996.*

BENTLEY, Sir William, KCMG 1985 (CMG 1977); HM Diplomatic Service, retired; Chairman: Society of Pension Consultants, since 1987; Coflexip Stena Offshore Holding Ltd (formerly Coflexip UK), since 1988; DUCO Ltd, since 1990; *b* 15 Feb. 1927; *s* of Lawrence and Elsie Jane Bentley; *m* 1950, Karen Ellen Christensen; two *s* three *d*. *Educ:* Bury High Sch.; Manchester Univ.; Wadham Coll., Oxford (1st cl. Mod. Hist.); Coll. of Europe, Bruges. HM Foreign (later Diplomatic) Service, 1952; 3rd (later 2nd) Sec., Tokyo, 1952–57; United Nations Dept, Foreign Office, 1957–60; 1st Sec., UK Mission to United Nations, 1960–63; Far Eastern Dept, FO, 1963–65; Head of Chancery, Kuala Lumpur, 1965–69; Dep. Comr-Gen., British Pavilion, Expo 70, Osaka, 1969–70; Counsellor, Belgrade, 1970–73; Head of Permanent Under-Sec.'s Dept, FCO, 1973–74; Head of Far Eastern Dept, FCO, 1974–76; Ambassador to the Philippines, 1976–81; High Comr in Malaysia, 1981–83; Ambassador to Norway, 1983–87. *Recreations:* fishing, shooting. *Address:* 48 Bathgate Road, SW19 5PJ; Les Terriers, Landivy, Mayenne, France. *Club:* Brooks's. *Died 10 June 1998.*

BENTON, Kenneth Carter, CMG 1966; HM Diplomatic Service, retired; *b* 4 March 1909; *s* of William Alfred Benton and Amy Adeline Benton (*née* Kirton); *m* 1938, Peggie (*d* 1992), *d* of Maj.-Gen. C. E. Pollock, CB, CBE, DSO; one *s* (and two step *s* decd). *Educ:* Wolverhampton Sch.; London Univ. Teaching and studying languages in Florence and Vienna, 1930–37; employed British Legation, Vienna, 1937–38; Vice-Consul, Riga, 1938–40; 2nd Sec., British Embassy, Madrid, 1941–43; 2nd, later 1st Sec., Rome, 1944–48; FO, 1948–50; 1st Sec., Rome, 1950–53; 1st Sec., Madrid, 1953–56; FO, 1956–62; 1st Sec. and Consul, Lima, 1963–64; FO, 1964–66; Counsellor, Rio de Janeiro, 1966–68; retd, 1968. *Publications:* Twenty-fourth Level, 1969; Sole Agent, 1970; Spy in Chancery, 1972; Craig and the Jaguar, 1973; Craig and the Tunisian Tangle, 1974; Death on the Appian Way, 1974; Craig and the Midas Touch, 1975; A Single Monstrous Act, 1976; The Red Hen Conspiracy, 1977; Ward of Caesar, 1986; The Plight of the Baltic States, 1986; as James Kirton: Time for Murder, 1985; Greek Fire, 1985. *Recreations:* writing, painting. *Address:* 2 Jubilee Terrace, Chichester, West Sussex PO19 1XL. *T:* (01243) 787148. *Club:* Detection. *Died 14 Oct. 1999.*

BERIOZOVA, Svetlana, ballerina; *b* 24 Sept. 1932; *d* of late Nicolas and of Maria Beriozoff (Russian); *m* 1959, Mohammed Masud Khan (marr. diss. 1974; he *d* 1989). *Educ:* New York, USA. Joined Grand Ballet de Monte Carlo, 1947; Metropolitan Ballet, 1948–49; Sadler's Wells Theatre Ballet, 1950–52; Sadler's Wells Ballet (later The Royal Ballet), 1952. Created leading rôles in Designs for Strings (Taras), Fanciulla delle Rose (Staff), Trumpet Concerto (Balanchine), Pastorale (Cranko), The Shadow (Cranko), Rinaldo and Armida (Ashton), The Prince of the Pagodas (Cranko), Antigone (Cranko), Baiser de la Fée (MacMillan), Diversions (MacMillan), Persephone (Ashton), Images of Love (MacMillan); classical rôles: Swan Lake, The Sleeping Beauty, Giselle, Coppélia, Sylvia, Cinderella; other rôles danced: Les Sylphides, The Firebird, The Lady and Fool, Checkmate, Fête Etrange, Ondine, Nutcracker. Danced with The Royal Ballet in USA, France, Italy, Australia, S Africa, Russia, and as guest ballerina in Belgrade, Granada, Milan (La Scala), Stuttgart, Bombay, Nervi, Helsinki, Paris, Vienna, New Zealand, Zurich. Played the Princess in The Soldier's Tale (film), 1966. Frequently appeared on television. *Relevant publications:* Svetlana Beriosova (by C. Swinson), 1956, Svetlana Beriosova (by A. H. Franks), 1958. *Recreation:* the arts. *Address:* 10 Palliser Court, Palliser Road, W14 9ED. *Died 10 Nov. 1998.*

BERKELEY, Frederic George; Chief Master of the Supreme Court Taxing Office, 1988–92 (Master,

1971–88); *b* 21 Dec. 1919; *s* of late Dr Augustus Frederic Millard Berkeley and Anna Louisa Berkeley; *m* 1964, Gillian Eugenie Louise Depreux (marr. diss.); one *s* one *d* (and one *d* decd); *m* 1988, Helen Kathleen Lucy; one step *s* one step *d*. *Educ:* Elstree Sch.; Aldenham Sch.; Pembroke Coll., Cambridge (MA). Admitted Solicitor, 1948. Served War of 1939–45, Leics Regt, Normandy (wounded); Major; DAD AWS Allied Land Forces SE Asia, 1945–46. Partner in Lewis & Lewis (from 1964 Penningtons and Lewis & Lewis), 1951–70. Mem. No 1 (London) Legal Aid Area Cttee (later No 14), 1954–70, Vice-Chm. 1964–70, Chm. 1970. General Editor and contributor, Butterworth's Costs Service, 1984–92. *Recreations:* reading, travel. *Address:* 10 Dover House, Abbey Park, Beckenham, Kent BR3 1QB. *T:* (020) 8650 4634.

Died 14 Nov. 1999.

BERLIN, Sir Isaiah, OM 1971; Kt 1957; CBE 1946; MA; FBA 1957; President of the British Academy, 1974–78; Fellow of All Souls College, Oxford, 1932–38, 1950–66 and since 1975; *b* 6 June 1909; *s* of Mendel and Marie Berlin; *m* 1956, Aline, *d* of Pierre de Gunzbourg. *Educ:* St Paul's Sch.; Corpus Christi Coll., Oxford. Lectr in Philosophy, New Coll., Oxford, 1932, Fellow, 1938–50; war service with Min. of Information, in New York, 1941–42, at HM Embassy in Washington, 1942–46, HM Embassy, Moscow, Sept. 1945–Jan. 1946; Chichele Prof. of Social and Pol Theory, Oxford Univ., 1957–67; Pres., Wolfson Coll., Oxford 1966–75, Hon. Fellow, 1975. Mem. Cttee of Awards: Commonwealth (Harkness) Fellowships, 1960–64; Kennedy Scholarships, 1967–79. Vice-Pres., British Academy, 1959–61; Pres. Aristotelian Soc., 1963–64. Mem., Academic Adv. Cttee., Univ. of Sussex, 1963–66. Visiting Professor: Harvard Univ., 1949, 1951, 1953, 1962; Bryn Mawr Coll., 1952; Chicago Univ., 1955; Princeton Univ., 1965; ANU, Canberra, 1975; Prof. of Humanities, City Univ. of NY, 1966–71. Lectures: Northcliffe, UCL, 1953; Mellon, Nat. Gall. of Art, Washington, DC, 1965; Danz, Washington Univ., 1971. Foreign Member: American Academy of Arts and Sciences; American Academy-Institute of Arts and Letters; American Philosophical Soc. Member, Board of Directors, Royal Opera House, Covent Garden, 1954–65, 1974–87; a Trustee, Nat. Gall., 1975–85. Hon. Pres., British Friends of the Univ. of Jerusalem. Hon. Fellow: Corpus Christi Coll., Oxford, 1967; Wolfson Coll., Cambridge, 1974; Wolfson Coll., Oxford, 1975; St Antony's Coll., Oxford, 1983; New Coll., Oxford, 1985. Hon. doctorates of the following universities: Hull, 1965; Glasgow, 1967; E Anglia, 1967; Brandeis, Mass, 1967; Columbia, NY, 1968; Cambridge, 1970; London, 1971; Jerusalem, 1971; Liverpool, 1972; Tel Aviv, 1973; Harvard, 1979; Sussex, 1979; Johns Hopkins, 1981; Northwestern, Ill, 1981; New York, 1982; Duke, NC, 1983; City, NY, 1983; New Sch. of Social Research, NY, 1987; Oxford, 1987; Ben Gurion, Israel, 1988; Yale, 1989; Toronto, 1994; Bologna, 1995. Erasmus Prize (jtly), 1983; Agnelli Internat. Prize for Ethics, 1987. *Publications:* Karl Marx, 1939, 4th edn 1978; (trans.) First Love by I. S. Turgenev, 1950; The Hedgehog and the Fox, 1953, 4th edn 1979; Historical Inevitability, 1954; The Age of Enlightenment, 1956; Moses Hess, 1958; Two Concepts of Liberty, 1959; Mr Churchill in 1940, 1964; Four Essays on Liberty, 1969; Fathers and Children, 1972; Vico and Herder, 1976; Russian Thinkers, 1978; Concepts and Categories, 1978; Against the Current, 1979; Personal Impressions, 1980; (trans.) A Month in the Country by I. S. Turgenev, 1980; The Crooked Timber of Humanity, 1990; The Magus of the North, 1993; The Sense of Reality, 1996; The Proper Study of Mankind, 1997; *relevant publication:* Isaiah Berlin, by Michael Ignatieff, 1998. *Address:* All Souls College, Oxford OX1 4AL. *Clubs:* Athenæum, Brooks's, Garrick; Century (New York).   *Died 5 Nov. 1997.*

BERMANT, Chaim Icyk; author, since 1966; *b* 26 Feb. 1929; *s* of Azriel Bermant and Feiga (*née* Daets); *m* 1962, Judy Weil; two *s* two *d*. *Educ:* Queen's Park Sch., Glasgow; Glasgow Yeshiva; Glasgow Univ. (MA Hons; MLitt); London School of Economics (MScEcon). Schoolmaster, 1955–57; economist, 1957–58; television script writer, 1958–61; journalist, 1961–66. *Publications:* Jericho Sleep Alone, 1964; Berl Make Tea, 1965; Ben Preserve Us, 1965; Diary of an Old Man, 1966; Israel, 1967; Swinging in the Rain, 1967; Troubled Eden, 1969; Here Endeth the Lesson, 1969; The Cousinhood, 1971; Now Dowager, 1971; Roses are Blooming in Picardy, 1972; The Last Supper, 1973; The Walled Garden, 1974; Point of Arrival, 1975; The Second Mrs Whitberg, 1976; Coming Home, 1976 (Wingate-Jewish Chronicle Book Award); The Squire of Bor Shachor, 1977; The Jews, 1978; Now Newman was Old, 1978; Belshazzar, 1979; (with Dr M. Weitzman) Ebla, 1979; The Patriarch, 1981; On the Other Hand, 1982; The House of Women, 1983; Dancing Bear, 1984; What's the Joke, 1986; Titch, 1987; The Companion, 1987; Lord Jacobovits: the authorised biography of the Chief Rabbi, 1990; Murmurings of a Licensed Heretic, 1990; *posthumous publication:* Genesis: a Latvian childhood, 1998. *Recreations:* walking, sermon-tasting.   *Died 20 Jan. 1998.*

BERNARD, Jeffrey Joseph; columnist, The Spectator, since 1976; *b* 27 May 1932; *s* of Oliver P. Bernard and Fedora Roselli Bernard; *m* 1st, 1951, Anna Grice (*d* 1955); 2nd, 1958, Jacki Ellis (marr. diss. 1964); 3rd, 1966, Jill Stanley (marr. diss. 1974); one *d*; 4th, 1978, Susan Ashley (marr. diss. 1981). *Educ:* Nautical College, Pangbourne. Odd jobs until 1958; film editor, 1958–62; actor, 1963; journalist and columnist, 1964–, for Sunday Times, New Statesman, Sporting Life and Spectator. 'Jeffrey Bernard is Unwell', a play by Keith Waterhouse based on 10 Spectator columns, Low Life, 1989. *Publications:* High Life – Low Life, 1982; Low Life, 1986; Talking Horses, 1987; More Low Life, 1989; Tales from the Turf, 1991; Reach for the Ground: the downhill struggle, 1996. *Recreations:* cricket, racing, cooking, Mozart. *Address:* c/o The Spectator, 56 Doughty Street, WC1N 2LL. *T:* (0171) 405 1706. *Clubs:* Groucho, Chelsea Arts.

Died 4 Sept. 1997.

BERNSTEIN, Prof. Basil Bernard; Karl Mannheim Professor of Sociology of Education, 1979–90, then Emeritus, and Head of Sociological Research Unit, 1963–90, University of London; *b* 1 Nov. 1924; *s* of Percival and Julia Bernstein; *m* 1955, Marion Black; two *s*. *Educ:* LSE (BScEcon); UCL (PhD). Teacher, City Day Coll., Shoreditch, 1954–60; Hon. Research Asst, UCL, 1960–62; University of London Institute of Education: Sen. Lectr, Sociology of Educn, 1963; Reader in Sociology of Educn, 1965; Prof., 1967; Senior Pro-Director, 1983–90. Hon. DLitt: Leicester, 1974; Rochester, 1989; E London, 1998; Fil H Dr Univ. of Lund, 1980; DUniv Open, 1983; Hon. PhD Athens, 1996. *Publications:* Class Codes and Control, Vol. I, Theoretical Studies Towards a Sociology of Language, 1971, 2nd edn 1974, (ed) Vol. II, Applied Studies Towards a Sociology of Language, 1973, Vol. III, Towards a Theory of Educational Transmissions, 1975, rev. edn 1977, Vol. IV, The Structuring of Pedagogic Discourse, 1990; (with W. Brandis) Selection and Control, 1974; (with U. Lundgren) Macht und Control, 1985; (with M. Diaz) Towards a Theory of Pedagogic Discourse, 1986; Poder, Educatión y Conciencia: sociología de la tranmisión cultural, 1988; Pedagogy, Symbolic Control and Identity: theory, research, critique, 1996. *Recreations:* music, painting, conversation, etc. *Address:* 90 Farquhar Road, Dulwich, SE19 1LT. *T:* (020) 8670 6411.

Died 24 Sept. 2000.

BERRILL, Prof. Norman John, PhD, DSc; FRS 1952; FRSC; FAAAS; lately Strathcona Professor of Zoology, McGill University, Montreal; *b* 28 April 1903. *Educ:* Bristol Grammar Sch., Somerset, England; Bristol Univ.; London Univ. BSc Bristol; PhD, DSc London. FRSC 1936; FAAAS 1979. *Publications:* The Tunicata, 1951; The Living Tide, 1951; Journey into Wonder, 1953; Sex and the Nature of Things, 1954; The Origin of Vertebrates, 1955; Man's Emerging Mind, 1955; You and the Universe, 1958; Growth, Development and Pattern, 1962; Biology in Action, 1966; Worlds Apart, 1966; Life of the Oceans, 1967; The Person in the Womb, 1968; Developmental Biology, 1971; Development, 1976. *Address:* 9 Orchard Drive, Durham, NH 03824, USA.
Died 16 Oct. 1996.

BERRY, Air Cdre Ronald, CBE 1965 (OBE 1946); DSO 1943; DFC 1940 and Bar, 1943; Royal Air Force, retired; Director of Control Operations, Board of Trade, 1965–68; *b* 3 May 1917; *s* of W. Berry, Hull; *m* 1940, Nancy Watson, Hessle, near Hull; one *d. Educ:* Hull Technical Coll. VR Pilot, Brough Flying Sch., 1937–39; 603 F Sqdn, Turnhouse/Hornchurch, 1939–41 (Battle of Britain); Sqdn Ldr, and CO 81 F Sqdn, North Africa, 1942; Wing Comdr, and CO 322 F Wing, North Africa, 1942–43; Camberley Army Staff Coll., 1944; CO, RAF Acklington, 1945–46; jssc 1955; various operational appts in Fighter and Bomber Comd; V Sqdn, 1957–59; Group Capt., Air Min. and HQ Bomber Comd, 1959. *Recreations:* motoring, gardening, flying. *Address:* Aldrian, Mereview Avenue, Hornsea HU18 1RR.
Died 13 Aug. 2000.

BERTRAM, (Cicely) Kate, PhD; President, Lucy Cavendish College, Cambridge, 1970–79 (Tutor, 1965–70; Hon. Fellow, 1982); *b* 8 July 1912; *d* of late Sir Harry Ralph Ricardo, FRS and Beatrice Bertha Hale; *m* 1939, Dr George Colin Lawder Bertram (Fellow and formerly Senior Tutor of St John's Coll., Cambridge); four *s. Educ:* Hayes Court, Kent; Newnham Coll., Cambridge. MA, PhD (Cantab), 1940, Jarrow Research Studentship, Girton Coll., Cambridge, 1937–40. Mem. Colonial Office Nutrition Survey, in Nyasaland, 1939; Adviser on Freshwater Fisheries to Govt of Palestine, 1940–43. Mem. Council, New Hall, Cambridge, 1954–66; Associate of Newnham Coll. FLS. JP: Co. Cambridge, and Isle of Ely, 1959; W Sussex, 1981. *Publications:* Lucy Cavendish College, Cambridge: a history of the early years, 1989; Letters from the Swamps, 1991; 2 Crown Agents' Reports on African Fisheries, 1939 and 1942; papers on African fish, in zoological jls; papers and articles on Sirenia (with G.C.L. Bertram). *Recreations:* foreign travel, gardening. *Address:* Ricardo's, Graffham, near Petworth, Sussex GU28 0PU. *T:* (01798) 867205. *Club:* English-Speaking Union.
Died 6 July 1999.

BEST, His Honour Giles Bernard; a Circuit Judge, 1975–91; *b* 19 Oct. 1925; *yr s* of late Hon. James William Best, OBE (*y s* of 5th Baron Wynford), and Florence Mary Bernarda, *e d* of Sir Elliott Lees, 1st Bt, DSO. *Educ:* Wellington Coll.; Jesus Coll., Oxford. Called to Bar, Inner Temple, 1951; Dep. Chm., Dorset QS, 1967–71; a Recorder, 1972–75. *Address:* Pitcombe, Little Bredy, Dorset DT2 9HG.
Died 27 Aug. 1997.

BETHELL, Richard Anthony; Lord-Lieutenant of Humberside, 1983–96; *b* 22 March 1922; *s* of late William Adrian Bethell and Cicely Bethell (*née* Cotterell); *m* 1945, Lady Jane Pleydell-Bouverie, *d* of 7th Earl of Radnor, KG, KCVO; two *s* two *d. Educ:* Eton. JP, ER Yorks, 1950; DL 1975, High Sheriff 1976–77, Vice Lord-Lieutenant 1980–83, Humberside. *Address:* Manor House Farm, Long Riston, Hull HU11 5JR. *T:* Hornsea (01964) 563245.
Died 20 July 1996.

BETHUNE, Sir Alexander Maitland Sharp, 10th Bt (NS), *cr* 1683, of Scotscraig, co. Fife; retired; Director; Copytec Services Ltd, 1964–86; Contoura Photocopying Ltd, 1952–86; *b* 28 March 1909; *o s* of Sir Alexander Sharp Bethune, 9th Bt of Scotscraig, JP, DL, Blebo, Cupar, Fife, and Elisabeth Constance Carnegie (*d* 1935), 3rd *d* of Frederick Lewis Maitland-Heriot of Ramornie, Fife; *S* father, 1917; *m* 1955, Ruth Mary, *d* of J. H. Hayes; one *d. Educ:* Eton; Magdalene Coll., Cambridge. *Recreations:* golf, Scottish history, nature. *Heir:* none. *Address:* 21 Victoria Grove, W8 5RW.
Died 20 May 1997 (ext).

BEVAN, (Andrew) David Gilroy; Principal, A. Gilroy Bevan, Incorporated Valuers & Surveyors; *b* 10 April 1928; *s* of Rev. Thomas John Bevan and Norah Gilroy Bevan; *m* 1967, Cynthia Ann Villiers Boulstridge; one *s* three *d. Educ:* Woodrough's Sch., Moseley; King Edward VI Sch., Birmingham. Served on Birmingham City Council and later W Midlands County Council, 1959–81; past Mem., Finance and Gen. Purposes Cttee, and Policy and Priorities Cttee; past Chm., City Transport Cttee, W Midlands PTA and Transport and Highways Cttee. MP (C) Birmingham, Yardley, 1979–92; contested same seat 1992. Jt Chm., Parly Road Passenger Transport Cttee, 1987–92; former Member, House of Commons Committees: Select Cttee on Transport, 1983–92; All Party Leisure and Recreation Industry (Jt Chm., 1979–92); Urban Affairs and New Towns (Jt Hon. Sec., 1980–87; Vice Chm., 1987–92); Tourism (Chm., 1984–92); Cdre, H of C Yacht Club, 1989. FIAA&S 1962 (Past Chm., W Midlands Br.); FRVA 1971; FSVA 1968 (Past Chm., W Midlands Br.); FFB 1972; FCIA 1954; MRSH 1957. *Recreations:* gardening, walking. *Address:* The Cottage, 12 Wentworth Road, Four Oaks Park, Sutton Coldfield, West Midlands B74 2RG. *T:* (home) 0121–308 3292; (business) 0121–308 6319. *Club:* Carlton.
Died 12 Oct. 1996.

BEVAN, Richard Thomas, MD; FRCP; Chief Medical Officer, Welsh Office, 1965–77, retired; *b* 13 Jan. 1914; *s* of T. Bevan, Bridgend; *m* 1940, Dr Beryl Bevan (*née* Badham) (*d* 1986); two *s* one *d. Educ:* Welsh Nat. Sch. of Medicine. MB, BCh 1939; DPH 1941; MD 1955; FRCP; FFCM. Resident Medical Officer, St David's Hosp., Cardiff; RAF, 1941–46; Lecturer, Welsh Nat. Sch. of Medicine, 1946–68; Deputy County MO, Glamorgan CC, 1948–62. QHP 1974–77. *Address:* 47 Chelveston Crescent, Solihull, W Midlands B91 3YH. *T:* (0121) 704 9890.
Died 3 July 1997.

BEVERIDGE, Sir Gordon (Smith Grieve), Kt 1994; FRSE; FREng; FIChemE; FRSA; MRIA; President and Vice-Chancellor, The Queen's University of Belfast, 1986–97; *b* 28 Nov. 1933; *s* of late Victor Beattie Beveridge and Elizabeth Fairbairn Beveridge (*née* Grieve); *m* 1963, Geertruida Hillegonda Johanna, (Trudy), Bruyn, *d* of late Gerrit Hendrik Bruijn and Johanna (*née* Breyaen); two *s* one *d. Educ:* Inverness Royal Academy; Univ. of Glasgow (BSc, 1st Cl. Hons Chem. Engrg); Royal College of Science and Technology, Glasgow (ARCST, 1st Cl. Hons Chem. Engrg); Univ. of Edinburgh (PhD). Asst Lectr, Univ. of Edinburgh, 1956–60; post-doctoral Harkness Fellow of Commonwealth Fund, New York, at Univ. of Minnesota, 1960–62; Vis. Prof., Univ. of Texas, 1962–64; Lectr, Univ. of Edinburgh and Heriot-Watt Univ., 1962–67; Sen. Lectr/Reader, Heriot-Watt Univ., 1967–71; Prof. of Chem. Engrg and Head of Dept of Chem. and Process Engrg, Univ. of Strathclyde, Glasgow, 1971–86. Consultant to industry. Chm., Radioactive Waste Mgt Adv. Cttee, DoE, 1995–. Institution of Chemical Engineers: Fellow, 1969–; Vice-Pres., 1979–81, 1983–84, Pres., 1984–85; Exec. Cttee, 1981–86; Hon. Librarian, 1977–84; Mem., Council, 1975–76, 1977–93; Scottish

Branch: Sec., 1963–71; Vice-Chm., 1972–74; Chm., 1974–76. Society of Chemical Industry, London: Mem. Council, 1978–88; Vice-Pres., 1985–88; Chm. of W of Scotland Section, 1978–86. Council of Engineering Institutions (Scotland): Member, 1977–82; Vice-Chm., 1979–80; Chm., 1980–81; Organiser of 1981 Exhibn, Engineering in the '80s, Edinburgh. Council for National Academic Awards: Chemical, Instrumentation and Systems Engrg Bd, 1976–81: Vice-Chm., 1979–81; Engineering Bd, 1981–84. Science and Engineering Research Council (formerly Science Research Council): various committees, 1973–76, 1980–83; Mem., Engrg Bd; Chm., Process Engrg Cttee (formerly Chemical Engrg Cttee), 1983–86. Engineering Council: Mem., 1981–95; Vice-Chm., 1984–85; Chm., Standing Cttee for Professional Instns, 1982–88; Chm., Standing Cttee for Regions and Assembly, 1989–95; Mem., Regl Orgn in NI, 1987–96. NEDO: Mem., Chemicals EDC, 1983–88; Chm., Petrochemicals Sector Wkg Gp, 1983–87; British Council: Member: Engrg and Technol. Adv. Cttee, 1986–92; CICHE, 1992–95; Bd, 1997–; Chm., NI Cttee, 1997–. Chairman: Local Organising Cttee, BAAS, Belfast, 1986–87; Organising Cttee of Celebration of Armagh and St Patrick, 1994–95; Dep. Chm., Armagh Observatory Bicentenary Cttee, 1990–91; Member: NI Partnership, 1987–; Educnl Adv. Cttee, Ulster TV, 1986–93; Adv. Council, ESDU Internat. Ltd, 1983–88 (Chm., 1983–86); Council, OU, 1988–93; Newcomen Soc., 1989–; Smeatonian Soc. of Civil Engrs, 1991–; European Sci. and Technol. Assembly, EC, 1994–95; Adv. Council, Ireland's Historic Science Centre, 1995–97. Royal Academy of Engineering (formerly Fellowship of Engineering): Fellow, 1984; Mem. Council, 1991–94, Standing Cttee for Engrg, 1991–94; Hon. Sec., Process Engrg, 1991–94. Chm., Navan Fort Initiative Gp, 1987–89; Director: NI Economic Res. Centre, 1987–95; NI Growth Challenge, 1996–97; Navan at Armagh, 1989–98 (Chm. 1989–98); Navan at Armagh Management Ltd, 1990–98 (Chm., 1990–98); Queen's University Bookbinding Ltd, 1989–97 (Chm., 1989–97); QUBIS Ltd, 1986–97 (Chm., 1991–97); The University Book Shop Ltd, 1986–97; Textflow Services Ltd, 1992–97 (Chm., 1992–97); Lennoxvale Developments Ltd, 1993–97; Cremer and Warner Ltd, 1984–91 (Chm., 1985–90); Opera NI, 1992–99; NI Quality Centre, 1993–96. Mem. Council, NI Chamber of Commerce and Industry, 1996–97. President: Retirement Assoc., NI, 1986–96; Queen's Univ. Assoc., 1989–90; Queen's Univ. Assoc. London, 1994–96; Trustee, Scotch–Irish Trust of Ulster, 1995–; Patron: Abercorn Trust, 1986–97; Linenhall Liby Appeal, 1989; John Whyte Trust Fund, 1990–97; NI Business Achievement Award Trust, 1993–97 (Vice Patron, 1990–92); NI Children's Holiday Scheme, 1994–95. Mem., TAVRA, NI, 1990–. Mem. Court, Univ. of Stirling, 1997–99. CIMgt (CBIM 1990). FRSA 1987; MRIA 1989. Hon. FRCSI 1995; Hon. FCGI 1997. Hon. LLD: Dublin, 1992; NUI, 1995; Limerick, 1995; QUB, 1998; Hon. DSc: Ulster, 1994; Connecticut Coll., 1995; Queen's Univ., Kingston, 1995; Hon. DAppSc Tech. Univ. of Lodz, Poland, 1995; DUniv Heriot-Watt, 1998. Associate Editor, Computers and Chemical Engineering, 1974–87. *Publications:* Optimization - theory and practice (with R. S. Schechter), 1970; multiple pubns in learned jls. *Recreations:* Irish, Scottish and Dutch history, Marlburian war-games, model railway system design, family golf, walking, the engineering profession. *Address:* 6 Brompton Road, Bangor, Northern Ireland BT20 3RE. *Club:* Caledonian. *Died 28 Aug. 1999.*

BEVINS, Rt Hon. John Reginald; PC 1959; *b* 20 Aug. 1908; *e s* of John Milton and Grace Eveline Bevins, Liverpool; *m* 1933, Mary Leonora Jones; three *s. Educ:* Dovedale Road and Liverpool Collegiate Schs. Served

War of 1939–45; gunner, 1940; Major, RASC, 1944; MEF and Europe. Mem. Liverpool City Council, 1935–50. Contested (C) West Toxteth Div., 1945, and Edge Hill (bye-election), 1947; MP (C) Toxteth Div. of Liverpool, 1950–64; PPS to the Minister of Housing and Local Government, 1951–53; Parliamentary Sec., Ministry of Works, 1953–57, Ministry of Housing and Local Govt, 1957–59; Postmaster-General, 1959–64. *Publication:* The Greasy Pole, 1965. *Address:* 37 Queen's Drive, Liverpool L18 2DT. *T:* (0151) 722 8484.

Died 16 Nov. 1996.

BEYNON, Prof. Sir (William John) Granville, Kt 1976; CBE 1959; PhD, DSc; FRS 1973; Professor and Head of Department of Physics, University College of Wales, Aberystwyth, 1958–81, then Emeritus Professor and Hon. Fellow; *b* 24 May 1914; *s* of William and Mary Beynon; *m* 1942, Megan Medi, *d* of Arthur and Margaret James; two *s* one *d. Educ:* Gowerton Grammar Sch.; University Coll., Swansea (Hon. Fellow). Scientific Officer, later Senior Scientific Officer, National Physical Laboratory, 1938–46; Lecturer, later Senior Lecturer in Physics, University Coll. of Swansea, 1946–58. Mem., SRC, 1976–80. Mem., Schools Council, 1965–76; Pres., 1972–75, Hon. Pres., 1981–, URSI; Hon. Mem., EISCAT Scientific Assoc. Hon. Professorial Fellow in Physics, UC Swansea, 1981. Hon. DSc Leicester, 1981. *Publications:* (ed) Solar Eclipses and the Ionosphere, 1956; (ed) Proceedings Mixed Commission on the Ionosphere, 1948–58; numerous publications in scientific jls. *Recreations:* music, cricket, tennis, Rugby. *Address:* Caebryn, Caergôg, Aberystwyth, Dyfed SY23 1ET. *T:* Aberystwyth (01970) 623947.

Died 11 March 1996.

BICKFORD SMITH, John Roger, CB 1988; TD 1950; *b* 31 Oct. 1915; *er s* of late Leonard W. Bickford Smith, Camborne, Cornwall, For. Man., ICI, and Anny Grete (*née* Huth); *m* 1st, 1939, Cecilia Judge Heath (marr. diss. 1971) (decd), *er d* of W. W. Heath, Leicester; two *s*; 2nd, 1972, Baronin (Joaise) Miranda (et Omnes Sancti) von Kirchberg-Hohenheim (*d* 1997). *Educ:* Eton (King's Schol.); Hertford Coll., Oxford (Schol.; BA 1937; MA 1952). Commnd in Duke of Cornwall's LI (TA), 1939; served 1939–46: UK, India, Burma and Germany; AJAG (Major), 1942; Lieut-Col 1944. Called to Bar, Inner Temple, 1942, Bencher, 1985. Practised at Common Law Bar in London and on Midland Circuit, 1946–67; Master of Supreme Court, QBD, 1967–88, Sen. Master and Queen's Remembrancer, 1983–88. Master, Bowyers' Co., 1986–88. *Publications:* The Crown Proceedings Act 1947, 1948; various contribs to legal pubns. *Recreation:* foreign travel. *Address:* 65 Gibson Square, N1 0RA. *Club:* Garrick. *Died 14 May 1998.*

BICKNELL, Christine Betty, CBE 1986; retired; *b* 23 Dec. 1919; *er d* of Walter Edward and Olive Isabelle Reynolds; *m* 1960, Claud Bicknell, OBE. *Educ:* St Martin-in-the-Fields High Sch. for Girls; Somerville Coll., Oxford (Exhibr; BA 1941; MA). Board of Trade, 1941–60: Principal, 1945; Asst Sec., 1958; Northern Regional Officer, Min. of Land and Natural Resources, 1965–67. Chairman: Prudhoe and Monkton HMC, 1966–70; Leavesden HMC, 1971–74; Kensington and Chelsea and Westminster AHA (T), 1973–77; Victoria HA, 1982–85; Member: Newcastle RHB, 1961–70, and NW Metrop. RHB, 1971–74; Nat. Whitley Council for Nurses and Midwives, 1962–70; Northern Econ. Planning Bd, 1965–67; Bd of Governors, Royal Vic. Infirm., Newcastle upon Tyne, 1965–70 and St Bartholomew's Hosp., 1971–74; Chm., CS Selection Bds, 1970–90; Member: Industrial Tribunals, 1977–88; Newspaper Panel, Monopolies Commn, 1973–83; British Library Board, 1979–82; Pres., Hosp. Domestic Administrators' Assoc.,

1970–74. *Recreations:* gardening, mountains, travel, sailing. *Address:* Aikrigg End Cottage, Burneside Road, Kendal LA9 6DZ. *Clubs:* Alpine, United Oxford & Cambridge University. *Died 4 March 1999.*

BIDWELL, Sydney James; *b* Southall, 14 Jan. 1917; *s* of late Herbert Emmett Bidwell; *m* 1941, Daphne, *d* of late Robert Peart, Southall; one *s* one *d. Educ:* Elementary sch., evening classes and trade union study. Railway worker (formerly NUR activist); Tutor and Organiser, Nat. Council of Labour Colls; TUC Reg. Educn Officer, London, 1963–66. Mem., TGWU (sponsored as MP by union). Mem., Southall Bor. Council, 1951–55. Contested (Lab): E Herts, 1959; Herts SW, 1964. MP (Lab) Southall, 1966–74, Ealing, Southall, 1974–92; contested (True Lab) Ealing, Southall, 1992. Mem., Parly Select Cttee on Race Relations and Immigration, 1968–79; Mem., Select Cttee on Transport, 1979–92. *Publications:* Red White and Black Book on Race-Relations, 1976; The Turban Victory, 1977; articles on Trade Union and Labour history. *Recreations:* soccer, painting, cartooning. *Died 25 May 1997.*

BIGNALL, John Reginald, FRCP; Physician, Brompton Hospital, 1957–79; *b* 14 Oct. 1913; *s* of Walter and Nellie Bignall; *m* 1939, Ruth Thirtle; one *s* three *d. Educ:* Nottingham High Sch.; St John's Coll., Cambridge (MA 1938; MD 1947); London Hospital. FRCP 1961. Served in RAMC, 1941–46, Middle East and Mediterranean (Major). *Died 15 Nov. 2000.*

BING, Sir Rudolf (Franz Joseph), KBE 1971 (CBE 1956); General Manager, Metropolitan Opera, New York, 1950–72; Distinguished Professor, Brooklyn College, City University of New York, 1972–75; Director Columbia Artists Management, since 1973; *b* Vienna, 9 Jan. 1902; *s* of Ernest Bing; *m* 1929, Nina (*née* Schelemskaja) (*d* 1983); *m* 1987, Carroll Lee Douglass (marr. annulled, 1989). *Educ:* Vienna. Hessian State Theatre, Darmstadt, 1928–30; Civic Opera, Berlin-Charlottenburg, 1930–33; Gen. Manager, Glyndebourne Opera, 1935–49; Artistic Director, Edinburgh Festival, 1947–49. Held hon. doctorates in music and in letters, from the US. Légion d'Honneur, 1958; Comdr's Cross of Order of Merit, Federal Republic of Germany, 1958; Grand Silver Medal of Honour, Republic of Austria, 1959; Comdr, Order of Merit, Republic of Italy, 1959, Grand Officer, 1970. *Publication:* 5000 Nights at the Opera, 1972. *Died 2 Sept. 1997.*

BINGHAM, Caroline Margery Conyers; professional writer; *b* 7 Feb. 1938; *o d* of Cedric and Muriel Worsdell; *m* 1958, Andrew Bingham (marr. diss. 1972); one *d. Educ:* Mount Sch., York; Convent de la Sagesse, Newcastle upon Tyne; Cheltenham Ladies' Coll.; Univ. of Bristol (BA Hons History). Res. Fellow, Dept of History, RHBNC, London Univ., 1985–87. *Publications:* The Making of a King: the early years of James VI and I, 1968 (USA 1969); James V, King of Scots, 1971; (contrib.) The Scottish Nation: a history of the Scots from Independence to Union, 1972; The Life and Times of Edward II, 1973; The Stewart Kingdom of Scotland, 1371–1603, 1974 (USA 1974); The Kings and Queens of Scotland, 1976 (USA 1976); The Crowned Lions: the Early Plantagenet Kings, 1978; James VI of Scotland, 1979; The Voice of the Lion (verse anthology), 1980; James I of England, 1981; Land of the Scots: a short history, 1983; History of Royal Holloway College 1886–1986, 1987; Beyond the Highland Line: Highland history and culture, 1991; Darnley, 1995. *Address:* Sheil Land Associates Ltd, 43 Doughty Street, WC1N 2LF. *Died 8 Jan. 1998.*

BINNEY, H(arry) A(ugustus) Roy, CB 1950; Director-General, 1951–70, Director-General, International, 1971–72, British Standards Institution; retired; *b* 18 May 1907; *s* of Harry Augustus Binney, Churston, Devon; *m* 1944, Barbara Poole (*d* 1975); three *s* one *d* (and one *d* decd). *Educ:* Royal Dockyard Sch., Devonport; London Univ. BSc(Eng). Entered Board of Trade, 1929, Under-Sec. 1947–51. Chairman: Standardization Cttee, European Productivity Agency, 1953–58; Cttee for European Standards (CEN), 1963–65; Mem. Council, 1951–72, Vice-Pres., 1964–69, ISO. UN Advr on Standards to Govt of Cyprus, 1974–77. Hon. Life Fellow, Standards Engrg Soc. of America; Hon. Life Mem., American Soc. for Testing and Materials. FKC; FRSA. *Recreation:* gardening. *Address:* Hambutts Orchard, Edge Lane, Painswick, Glos GL6 6UW. *T:* (01452) 813718. *Died 22 Aug. 1999.*

BINNS, His Honour (Geoffrey) John; a Circuit Judge, 1980–98; *b* 12 Oct. 1930; *s* of Rev. Robert Arthur Geoffrey Binns and Elizabeth Marguerite Binns; *m* 1964, Elizabeth Anne Poole Askew. *Educ:* Perse Sch.; Jesus Coll., Cambridge (MA). Admitted solicitor, 1956; Partner, Fraser, Woodgate & Beall, Wisbech, 1958–80; a Recorder, 1977–80. Chm., N Cambs Hosp. Management Cttee, 1970–74; Member: E Anglian Regl Hosp. Bd, 1972–74; E Anglian RHA, 1974–76; Panel of Chairmen, Cambridge Univ. Ct of Discipline, 1976–80. Registrar, Archdeaconry of Wisbech, 1972–80. *Publication:* Contributing Ed., Butterworths' County Court Precedents and Pleadings, 1985. *Recreations:* golf, gardening. *Club:* Norfolk (Norwich). *Died 13 Sept. 2000.*

BINNY, John Anthony Francis; *b* 13 Dec. 1911; *s* of late Lt-Col S. S. Binny, DSO, and Bertha Marjorie, *d* of late Henry Champion; *m* 1950, Diana Heather, *er d* of late John Buchanan Muir, Campden, Glos; two *d. Educ:* Wellington College. Supplementary Reserve of Officers, 15th/19th The King's Royal Hussars, 1936; served War of 1939–45, France and Burma (despatches). Chairman: Blue Circle Industries, 1975–78 (Dir, 1952); Law Debenture Corp., 1950–77 (Dir, 1948); Chm., Mercantile Investment Trust, 1971–77, Dep. Chm., Nat. Westminster Bank plc, 1972–81 (Dir, 1950); Dep. Chm., TI Group, 1975–79. *Recreations;* cricket, fishing, shooting, gardening. *Address:* Pollards Moor Farm, Pollards Moor Road, Copythorne, Cadnam, Southampton SO4 2NZ. *Clubs:* Cavalry and Guards, MCC. *Died 4 June 1996.*

BIRD, James Gurth, MBE 1945; TD 1951; *b* 30 Jan. 1909; *s* of Charles Harold Bird and Alice Jane Bird (*née* Kirtland); *m* 1940, Phyllis Ellis Pownall; one *s* two *d. Educ:* King William's Coll., Isle of Man (Scholar); St Catharine's Coll., Cambridge (Exhibnr). Classical Tripos Pts I and II, BA 1931, MA 1933. Asst Master, Rossall Sch., 1931–33; Asst Master and House Master, Denstone Coll., 1933–47 (interrupted by War Service); Head Master, William Hulme's Grammar Sch., Manchester, 1947–74. *Recreation:* gardening. *Address:* Ty Deryn, Ravenspoint Road, Trearddur Bay, Holyhead, Anglesey LL65 2AX. *Died 31 May 1999.*

BIRD, John Alfred William; Member (Lab) Midlands West, European Parliament, March 1987–1994; *b* 4 Feb. 1924; *s* of John and Elsie Bird; *m* 1946, Gwen Davies; two *s*. Member: Wolverhampton BC, 1962–73; Wolverhampton Metropolitan BC, 1973–88 (Chm., Educn Cttee, 1972–80; Leader, 1973–87); W Midlands CC, 1973–81; Vice-Chm., W Midlands Police Cttee, 1973–77. Chm., W Midlands DCs, 1986–87; Vice-Pres., AMA, 1987 (Mem. Council, 1974–87); Member: W Midlands EDC, 1973–81; W Midlands Regl Econ. Forum, 1986–87; Pres., Norwest Midlands Br., Chartered Inst. of Marketing, 1990–91. European Parliament: Chm., British Lab Gp, 1989–90; Mem., Ext. Econ. Relations Cttee, 1987–92; Mem., Develt and Co-operation Cttee, 1992–94. Hon. MEP, 1994. Mem., AEU, later AEEU, 1950– (Shop

Steward, 1953–63). Hon. Fellow, Faculty of Sci. and Technol., Wolverhampton Poly. Pres., W Mercia Scout Assoc., 1989–93. *Address:* 5 Giffard Road, Bushbury, Wolverhampton WV10 8EG.

Died 18 Nov. 1997.

BIRD, Rt Hon. Sir Vere (Cornwall), KNH 1999; OCC 1998; PC 1982; Prime Minister of Antigua and Barbuda, 1981–94; *b* 7 Dec. 1910; *m*; three *s* two *d. Educ:* St John's Boys' School, Antigua; Salvation Army Training School, Trinidad. Founder Mem. Exec., Antigua Trades and Labour Union, 1939 (Pres., 1943–67); Member: Antigua Legislative Council, 1945; Antigua Exec. Council, 1946 (Cttee Chm., 1951–56, land reform); Ministry of Trade and Production, 1956–60; first Chief Minister, 1960–67, first Premier, 1967–71; Founder (with reps from Barbados and Guyana), Caribbean Free Trade Assoc., 1965; led delegn to UK which achieved Associated Statehood for Antigua, 1966; re-elected to Parlt, 1976, Premier, 1976–81; Minister of Planning, External Affairs, Defence and Energy, 1981–82, of Finance and Defence, 1982–84; Leader, Antigua Labour Party, 1987. Hon. LLD St John Fisher Coll., Rochester, NY. *Address:* Tomlinsons, St John's, Antigua, West Indies.

Died 28 June 1999.

BIRD-WILSON, Air Vice-Marshal Harold Arthur Cooper, CBE 1962; DSO 1945; DFC 1940 and Bar 1943; AFC 1946 and Bar 1955; *b* 20 Nov. 1919; *s* of Harold Bird-Wilson and Victoria Mabel Cooper; *m* 1st, 1942, Audrey Wallace (*d* 1991); one *s* one *d*; 2nd, 1994, Margaret McGillivray Butler. *Educ:* Liverpool Coll. Joined RAF, Nov. 1937; No 17 Fighter Sqdn, Kenley, 1938; served War of 1939–45 (France, Dunkirk, Battle of Britain): Flt Comdr No 234 Sqdn, 1941; Sqdn Comdr Nos 152 and 66, 1942 (despatches); Wing Leader, No 83 Gp, 1943; Comd and Gen. Staff Sch., Fort Leavenworth, Kansas, USA, 1944; Wing Leader, Harrowbeer, Spitfire Wing and then Bentwater Mustang Wing, 1944–45; CO, Jet Conversion Unit, 1945–46; CO, Air Fighting Development Sqdn, CFE, 1946–47; Op. Staff, HQ, MEAF, 1948; RAF Staff Coll., Bracknell, 1949; Personal Staff Officer to C-in-C, MEAF, 1949–50; RAF Flying Coll., Manby, 1951; OC Tactics, later CO AFDS, CFE, 1952–54; Staff, BJSM, Washington, USA, 1954–57; Staff, Air Sec. Dept, Air Min., 1957–59; CO, RAF Coltishall, 1959–61; Staff Intell., Air Min., 1961–63; AOC and Comdt, CFS, 1963–65; AOC Hong Kong, 1965–67; Dir of Flying (Research and Develt), Min. of Technology, 1967–70; AOC No 23 Gp, 1970–73; Comdr, S Maritime Air Region, RAF, 1973–74, retired. BAC, Saudi Arabia, then British Aerospace, 1974–84, retired. Czechoslovak Medal of Merit 1st class, 1945; Dutch DFC, 1945.

Died 27 Dec. 2000.

BIRK, Baroness *cr* 1967 (Life Peer), of Regent's Park in Greater London; **Alma Birk,** JP; journalist; *b* 22 Sept. 1917; *d* of late Barnett and Alice Wilson; *m* 1939, Ellis Birk; one *s* one *d. Educ:* South Hampstead High Sch.; LSE. BSc Econ (Hons) London. Leader of Labour Group, Finchley Borough Council, 1950–53; contested (Lab): Ruislip-Northwood, 1950; Portsmouth West, 1951, 1955. Baroness in Waiting (Govt Whip), March-Oct. 1974; Parly Under-Sec. of State, DoE, 1974–79; Minister of State, Privy Council Office, 1979; Opposition frontbench spokesman H of L on: environment, 1979–86; arts, libraries, heritage and broadcasting, 1986–93. Mem., All Pty Penal Affairs Gp, 1983. Associate Editor, Nova, 1965–69. Dir, New Shakespeare Co. Ltd, 1979–. Formerly Lectr and Prison Visitor, Holloway Prison. Mem., Youth Service Develt Council, 1967–71; Chm., Health Educn Council, 1969–72; President: Assoc. of Art Instns, 1984–; Craft Arts Design Assoc., 1984–90; Vice-President: AMA, 1982–; Assoc. of District Councils, 1990–; Council for

Children's Welfare, 1968–75; H. G. Wells Soc., 1967–; Stamford Hill Associated Clubs, 1967–70; Redbridge Jewish Youth Centre, 1970–; Playboard, 1984–; Member: Fabian Soc., 1946– (Sec., Fabian Soc. Res. Cttee on Marriage and Divorce, 1951–52); Howard League for Penal Reform, 1948– (Exec., 1980–); Hendon Group Hosp. Management Cttee, 1951–59; Panel, London Pregnancy Adv. Service, 1968–; RCOG working party on the unplanned pregnancy, 1969–72; Exec., Council of Christians and Jews, 1971–77; Hon. Cttee, Albany Trust; Ct of Governors, LSE, 1971–; Council, British Museum Soc., 1979–; Council, RSA, 1981–87; Adv. Cttee on Service Candidates, 1984–; Council, Georgian Gp, 1985–; Chm. Arts Sub-Cttee, Holocaust Meml Cttee, 1979–. Trustee: Yorkshire Sculpture Park, 1980–; Health Promotion Res. Trust, 1983–95; Stress Syndrome Foundn, 1983–88; Theatres Trust, 1990–; Governor: BFI, 1981–87; Mander Mitchenson Theatre Collection, 1981–. FRSA 1980. JP Highgate, 1952. *Publications:* pamphlets, articles. *Recreations:* travelling, theatre, reading, talking, grandchildren. *Address:* Flat 1, 34 Bryanston Square, W1H 7LQ. *Died 29 Dec. 1996.*

BISCOE, Rear-Adm. Alec Julian T.; *see* Tyndale-Biscoe.

BISHOP, Sir George (Sidney), Kt 1975; CB 1958; OBE 1947; Director, Booker McConnell Ltd, 1961–82 (Vice-Chairman, 1970–71; Chairman, 1972–79); Director: Barclays Bank International, 1972–83; Barclays Bank Ltd, 1974–83; Ranks Hovis McDougall, 1976–84; International Basic Economy Corporation, USA, 1980–83; *b* 15 Oct. 1913; *o s* of late J. and M. Bishop; *m* 1st, 1940, Marjorie Woodruff (marr. diss. 1961); one *d*; 2nd, 1961, Una Padel. *Educ:* Ashton-in-Makerfield Grammar Sch.; London Sch. of Economics. Social service work in distressed areas, 1935–38; SW Durham Survey, 1939; Ministry of Food, 1940; Private Secretary to Minister of Food, 1945–49; Under-Secretary, Ministry of Agriculture, Fisheries and Food, 1949–59, Dep. Secretary, 1959–61. Leader, UK delegns to Internat. Wheat and Sugar Confs, 1955–58. Chm., Bookers Agricultural Holdings Ltd, 1964–70; Director: Food and Agricl Div., NATO Civil Supplies Agency, 1965–78; Nigerian Sugar Co. Ltd, 1966–70; Agricultural Mortgage Corp. Ltd, 1973–79. Chairman: Internat. Sugar Council, 1957; West India Cttee, 1969–71 (Pres., 1977–87); Industry Co-operative Programme, 1976–78; Council, Overseas Develt Inst., 1977–84; Vice-Chm., Internat. Wheat Council, 1959; Member: Panel for Civil Service Manpower Review, 1968–70; Royal Commn on the Press, 1974–77; Council, CBI, 1973–80; Dir, Industry Council for Develt, USA (Chm., 1979); Governor, Nat. Inst. for Economic and Social Research, 1968–. President: RGS, 1983–87 (Mem. Council, 1980–95; Hon. Fellow 1980; a Vice Pres., 1981; Hon. Vice Pres., 1987–); Britain-Nepal Soc., 1979–89; Mem., Management Cttee, Mount Everest Foundn, 1980–84 (Vice Chm. 1982; Chm. 1983). *Recreations:* mountaineering, motoring, photography. *Address:* Brenva, Eghams Wood Road, Beaconsfield, Bucks HP9 1JX. *T:* (01494) 673096. *Clubs:* Reform, Himalayan, Alpine, Royal Geographical Society, MCC. *Died 9 April 1999.*

BLACK, His Honour Iain James; QC 1971; a Circuit Judge, 1986–96. Called to the Bar, Gray's Inn, 1947, Bencher, 1985–86. Dep. Chm., Staffs QS, 1965–71; a Recorder, 1972–86. Member: Criminal Injuries Compensation Bd, 1975–86; Mental Health Review Tribunal, 1984–. *Address:* 3 Fountain Court, Steelhouse Lane, Birmingham B4 6DR. *T:* (0121) 236 5854. *Died 5 Sept. 2000.*

BLACK, Prof. Joseph, CBE 1980; PhD; FREng, FIMechE, FRAeS; Professor of Engineering, University of Bath, 1960–85, Head of School of Engineering, 1960–70 and 1973–85; *b* 25 Jan. 1921; *s* of Alexander and Hettie Black;

m 1946, Margaret Susan Hewitt; three *s* one *d. Educ:* Royal Belfast Academical Instn; QUB (BScEng, MSc); PhD Bristol. FRAeS 1961; FIMechE 1964; FREng (FEng 1981). Scientific Officer, RAE, 1941–44; Res. Fellow, QUB, 1944–45; Aerodynamicist, de Havilland Aircraft, 1945–46; Lectr/Sen. Lectr in Engrg, Univ. of Bristol, 1946–59. Gillette Fellow, USA, 1963. Pro-Vice-Chancellor, Univ. of Bath, 1970–73. Member: UGC, 1964–74 (Chm. Educnl Technol. Cttee); (founder) Council for Educnl Technol., 1974–; A/M Cttee, SRC, 1975–79; Design Council, 1977–82 (Chm. Engrg Components Awards 1976, Engrg Products Awards 1977); Mech. Engrg and Machine Tool Requirement Bd, DoI, 1979–81. SERC/Design Council Engrg Design Co-ordinator, 1985–89. Hon. DTech Loughborough, 1990; Hon. DSc City, 1991. Silver Jubilee Medal, 1977. *Publications:* Introduction to Aerodynamic Compressibility, 1950; contrib. aeronaut. and mech. engrg jls (UK and Europe). *Recreations:* photography, antiquarian books, silversmithing. *Address:* 20 Summerhill Road, Bath BA1 2UR. *T:* (01225) 423970. *Club:* Athenæum.

Died 3 Oct. 2000.

BLACK, Peter Blair; JP; Senior Partner, P. Blair Black & Partners, since 1948; *b* 22 April 1917; *s* of Peter Blair Black and Cissie Crawford Samuel; *m* 1952, Mary Madeleine Hilly, Philadelphia; one *s* three *d. Educ:* Sir Walter St John's, Battersea; Bearsden Acad.; Sch. of Building. CC 1949, Alderman 1961, Middlesex; Mem., GLC, 1963–86, Chm., 1970–71, Leader, Recreation and Community Services Policy Gp, 1977–81; motivator of Thames Barrier project; Chm., Cons. Group, GLC, 1982. Chm., Thames Water Authority, 1973–78; Pres., Pure Rivers Soc., 1976. Leader: GLC group to Moscow and Leningrad, 1971; British delegn to Washington, Potomac/Thames River Conf., 1977, Mem. Internat. team to Tokyo, Metropolitan Clean Air Conf., 1971. Former Member: Thames Conservancy Bd; Metrop. Water Bd; Jager Cttee on Sewage Disposal; PLA; Council, Nat. Fedn of Housing Socs; Founder Chm., Omnium Housing Assoc., 1962; Chm., 1972, Pres., 1983, Abbeyfield, London Region. Mem. Exec. Cttee, Nat. Union of Cons. and Unionist Assocs, 1987. Frequent performer on TV and radio. JP Thames Div., 1961. Freeman: City of London; Tucson, Arizona. *Recreations:* small boats, fishing. *Address:* The New House, 101A Limmer Lane, Felpham, W Sussex PO22 7LP. *T:* (01243) 582054. *Clubs:* Middleton Sports; Sewers Synonymous (Dir).

Died 27 March 1997.

BLACK, Sir Robert Brown, (Sir Robin), GCMG 1962 (KCMG 1955; CMG 1953); OBE 1949 (MBE (mil.) 1948); *b* 3 June 1906; *s* of late Robert and Catherine Black, formerly of Blair Lodge, Polmont, Stirlingshire; *m* 1937, (Elsie) Anne Stevenson, CStJ (*d* 1986); two *d. Educ:* George Watson's Coll.; Edinburgh Univ. Colonial Administrative Service, 1930; served in Malaya, Trinidad, N Borneo, Hong Kong; served War of 1939–45, commissioned in Intelligence Corps, 1942; 43 Special Military Mission; POW Japan, 1942–45; Dep. Chief Sec., N Borneo, 1946–52; Colonial Secretary, Hong Kong, 1952–55; Governor and C-in-C: Singapore, 1955–57; Hong Kong, 1958–64. Chancellor: Hong Kong Univ., 1958–64; Chinese University of Hong Kong, 1963–64. Mem., Commonwealth War Graves Commn, 1964–82. Chm., Clerical, Medical and General Life Assurance Soc., 1975–78. Chm., Internat. Social Service of GB, 1965–73; Pres., 1973–82. LLD (*hc*): Univ. of Hong Kong; Chinese Univ. of Hong Kong. KStJ. Grand Cross Order of Merit, Peru. *Recreations:* walking, fishing. *Address:* Mapletons House, Ashampstead Common, near Reading, Berks RG8 8QN. *Club:* East India, Devonshire, Sports and Public Schools.

Died 29 Oct. 1999.

BLACKBURN, Michael Scott; His Honour Judge Blackburn; a Circuit Judge, since 1986; *b* 16 Jan. 1936; *m* 1961, Vivienne (*née* Smith); one *s* one *d. Educ:* Dame Allan's Sch., Newcastle upon Tyne; William Hulme's Grammar Sch., Manchester; Keble Coll., Oxford (MA). Notary Public. A Recorder, 1981–86. President: Manchester Law Society, 1979–80; Manchester Medico-Legal Soc., 1986–88; Chairman, North Western Legal Services Cttee, 1981–85; Mem., Parole Bd, 1985–88. *Recreations:* squash rackets, hill walking, fishing, tennis. *Clubs:* Northern Lawn Tennis (Manchester); Bowdon Tennis, Cheshire Tally Ho, Hale Golf.

Died 9 Aug. 2000.

BLACKMUN, Hon. Harry A(ndrew); Associate Justice, United States Supreme Court, 1970–94; *b* Nashville, Illinois, 12 Nov. 1908; *s* of late Corwin Manning Blackmun and Theo Huegely (*née* Reuter); *m* 1941, Dorothy E. Clark; three *d. Educ:* Harvard Univ.; Harvard Law Sch. AB, LLB. Admitted to Minnesota Bar, 1932; private legal practice with Dorsey, Colman, Barker, Scott & Barber, Minneapolis, 1934–50: Associate, 1934–38; Jun. Partner, 1939–42; General Partner, 1943–50; Instructor: St Paul Coll. of Law, 1935–41; Univ. of Minnesota Law Sch., 1945–47; Resident Counsel, Mayo Clinic, Rochester, 1950–59; Judge, US Ct of Appeals, 8th Circuit, 1959–70. Member: American Bar Assoc.; Amer. Judicature Soc.; Minnesota State Bar Assoc.; 3rd Judicial Dist (Minn) Bar Assoc.; Olmsted Co. (Minn) Bar Assoc.; Judicial Conf. Adv. Cttee on Judicial Activities, 1969–79; Rep. of Judicial Br., Nat. Historical Pubns and Records Commn, 1975–82 and 1986–; Mem., Bd of Mems, Mayo Assoc. Rochester, 1953–60; Bd of Dirs and Mem. Exec. Cttee, Rochester Methodist Hosp., 1954–70; Trustee: Hamline Univ., St Paul, 1964–70; William Mitchell Coll. of Law, St Paul, 1959–74. Mem. Faculty, Salzburg Seminar in Amer. Studies (Law), 1989 (Chm., 1977); Co-moderator: Seminar on Justice and Society, Aspen Inst., 1979–93; Seminar on Constitutional Justice and Society, Aspen Inst Italia, Rome, 1986; participant, Franco-Amer. Colloquium on Human Rights, Paris, 1979; Vis. Instr on Constitutional Law, Louisiana State Univ. Law Sch.'s summer session, France, 1986 and 1992, Tulane Univ. Law Sch's summer session, Berlin, 1992. Hon. LLD: De Pauw Univ., Hamline Univ., and Ohio Wesleyan Univ., 1971; Morningside Coll., and Wilson Coll., 1972; Dickinson Sch. of Law, 1973; Drake Univ., 1975; Southern Illinois Univ., Pepperdine Univ., and Emory Univ., 1976; Rensselaer Polytech. Inst., 1979; Nebraska Univ., and New York Law Sch., 1983; McGeorge Sch. of Law, 1984; Vermont Law Sch., and Dartmouth Coll., 1985; Carleton Coll., and Luther Coll., 1986; Drury Coll., Tufts Univ., and Ill Inst. of Technol. (Chicago-Kent Coll. of Law), 1987; Northern Ill Univ., and Brooklyn Law Sch., 1988; New York Univ., 1989; Claremont Graduate Sch., 1991; Columbia Univ., Franklin and Marshall Coll., Univ. of Dist of Columbia, and Shippensburg Univ., 1992; New England Sch. of Law, 1993; Hon. DLitt Dickinson Sch. of Law, 1983; Hon. DPS Ohio Northern Univ., 1973; Hon. DHL: Oklahoma City, 1976; Massachusetts Sch. of Professional Psychology, 1984. *Publications:* contrib. legal and medical jls. *Recreations:* reading, music. *Address:* c/o Supreme Court Building, 1 First Street NE, Washington, DC 20543, USA. *Died 4 March 1999.*

BLACKWOOD, Wing Comdr George Douglas; Chairman, William Blackwood & Sons Ltd, publishers and printers, 1948–83; Editor of Blackwood's Magazine, and Managing Director of William Blackwood & Sons Ltd, 1948–76; *b* 11 Oct. 1909; *e s* of late James H. Blackwood and *g g g s* of Wm Blackwood, founder of Blackwood's Magazine; *m* 1936, Phyllis Marion, *y d* of late Sir John Caulcutt, KCMG; one *s* one *d. Educ:* Eton; Clare Coll., Cambridge. Short Service Commission in

RAF, 1932–38; re-joined 1939; formed first Czech Fighter Squadron, 1940–41; Battle of Britain (despatches); commanded Czech Wing of Royal Air Force 2nd TAF, 1944 (despatches); retired 1945. Czech War Cross, 1940; Czech Military Medal 1st class, 1944; Czech Medal of George of Podebrad, 1993. *Recreations:* countryside activities. *Address:* Airhouse, Oxton, Berwickshire TD2 6PX. *T:* (01578) 750225.   *Died 2 March 1997.*

BLAIR, Sir Alastair (Campbell), KCVO 1969 (CVO 1953); TD 1950; WS; *b* 16 Jan. 1908; 2nd *s* of late William Blair, WS, and Emelia Mylne Campbell; *m* 1933, Catriona Hatchard (decd), *o d* of late Dr William Basil Orr; four *s*. *Educ:* Cargilfield; Charterhouse; Clare Coll., Cambridge (BA); Edinburgh Univ. (LLB). Writer to the Signet, 1932; retired 1977 as Partner, Dundas & Wilson, CS. RA (TA) 1939; served 1939–45 (despatches); Secretary, Queen's Body Guard for Scotland, Royal Company of Archers, 1946–59; appointed Captain 1982; retired 1984. Purse Bearer to The Lord High Commissioner to the General Assembly of the Church of Scotland, 1961–69. Chm., subseq. Vice-Pres., Edinburgh Area Scout Council, 1964– (Silver Wolf, 1990). JP Edinburgh, 1954–96. *Recreation:* golf. *Address:* 7 Abbotsford Court, Colinton Road, Edinburgh EH10 5EH. *T:* (0131) 447 3095. *Club:* New (Edinburgh).   *Died 9 Jan. 1999.*

BLAKE, (Henry) Vincent; marketing consultant, retired; Secretary, Glassfibre Reinforced Cement Association, 1977–86; *b* 7 Dec. 1912; *s* of Arthur Vincent Blake and Alice Mabel (*née* Kerr); *m* 1938, Marie Isobel Todd; one *s*. *Educ:* King Edward's High Sch., Birmingham. Pupil apprentice, Chance Brothers, Lighthouse Engineers, Birmingham, 1931–34; subseq. Asst Sales Manager, 1937 and Sales Manager there, of Austinlite Ltd, 1945; Textile Marketing Manager, Fibreglass Ltd, 1951; Commercial Manager: Glass Yarns and Deeside Fabrics Ltd, 1960; BTR Industries Ltd, Glass and Resin Div., 1962–63, Plastics Group, 1963–66; Gen. Manager, Indulex Engineering Co. Ltd, 1966–71. Mem. Council and Chm., Reinforced Plastics Gp, British Plastics Fedn, 1959. Mem. Council, Royal Yachting Assoc., 1980– (Vice-Chm., Thames Valley Region, 1979–). *Publications:* articles in technical jls on reinforced plastics. *Recreations:* sailing, motoring, reading, waiting for my wife. *Address:* Little Orchard, Fern Lane, Little Marlow, Bucks SL7 3SD. *T:* (01628) 520252. *Clubs:* Datchet Water Sailing (Hon. Life Mem.), Cookham Reach Sailing (Hon. Life Mem.).
                    Died 3 June 1998.

BLAMEY, Norman Charles, OBE 1998; RA 1975 (ARA 1970); Senior Lecturer, Chelsea School of Art, London, 1963–79; *b* 16 Dec. 1914; *s* of Charles H. Blamey and Ada Blamey (*née* Beacham); *m* 1948, Margaret (*née* Kelly); one *s*. *Educ:* Holloway Sch., London; Sch. of Art, The Polytechnic, Regent Street, London. ROI 1952; Hon. ROI 1974. Exhibited at: RA, RHA, ROI, RBA, NEAC, and provincial galleries; retrospective exhibn, Norwich Gall., Victoria Art Gall., Bath, and Fine Art Soc., London, 1992; *mural decorations in:* Anglican Church of St Luke, Leagrave, Beds, 1956; Lutheran Church of St Andrew, Ruislip Manor, Middx, 1964; *works in permanent collections:* Municipal Gall., Port Elizabeth, S Africa; Beaverbrook Gall., Fredericton, NB; Beecroft Art Gall., Southend-on-Sea; Towner Art Gall., Eastbourne; Preston Art Gall.; Pennsylvania State Univ. Mus. of Art; La Salle Coll., Pa; V&A Museum; Tate Gall.; Chantry Bequest purchase, 1972, 1985; Govt Art Collection; Southampton Art Gall.; *portraits included:* Mrs Alison Munro; Dr Harry Pitt; Rev. Dennis Nineham; Sir Cyril Clarke; Prof. Graham Higman; Rt Hon. Bernard Weatherill, Speaker of H of C; Sir Alec Merrison, FRS; William Golding; Sir William Rees-Mogg; Sir Christopher Ball; George Richardson, Warden of Keble Coll., Oxford. Works in private

collections in UK and USA. RA Summer Exhibitions: Rowney Bicentenary Award, 1983; Charles Wollaston Award, 1984; Korn/Ferry/Carré Orban Picture of the Year Award, 1995. *Recreation:* walking. *Address:* 39 Lyncroft Gardens, NW6 1LB. *T:* (020) 7435 9250.
                    Died 17 Jan. 2000.

BLAND, Sir Henry (Armand), Kt 1965; CBE 1957; *b* 28 Dec. 1909; *s* of Emeritus Prof. F. A. Bland, CMG, and Elizabeth Bates Jacobs; *m* 1933, Rosamund (*d* 1995), *d* of John Nickal; two *d* (and one *d* decd). *Educ:* Sydney High Sch.; Univ. of Sydney. LLB (Hons) 1932. Admitted Solicitor Supreme Court of NSW, 1935. Entered NSW Public Service, 1927; Alderman, Ryde (NSW) Municipal Council, 1937–39; Acting Agent-Gen. for NSW in London, 1940–41; Adviser on Civil Defence to NSW and Commonwealth Govts, 1941; Prin. Asst to Dir-Gen. of Manpower, 1941–45; Asst Sec., First Asst Sec., 1946–51, Sec. 1952–67, Dept of Labour and National Service; Sec., Dept of Defence, Australia, 1967–70. Leader, Aust. Govt Delegns to Confs: 1948, 1953, 1957, 1960, 1962, 1963, 1964, 1966; Aust. Govt Rep. on the Governing Body of ILO, 1963–67; Adviser on industrial relations to Singapore Govt, 1958. Bd of Inquiry into Victorian Land Transport System, 1971; Chairman: Cttee on Administrative Discretions, 1972–73; Bd of Inquiry into Victorian Public Service, 1973–75; Commonwealth Admin. Rev. Cttee, 1976; ABC, 1976; Arbitrator between Aust. Nat. Railways and Tasmanian Govt, 1978. Chm. and Dir of numerous cos, 1970–90. *Address:* 54 Kenilworth Gardens, Kangaloon Road, Bowral, NSW 2576, Australia. *T:* (48) 613320. *Clubs:* Athenæum (Melbourne); Bowral Golf.
                    Died 8 Nov. 1997.

BLANDFORD, Heinz Hermann, CBE 1981; Fellow, Royal Postgraduate Medical School, Hammersmith Hospital, 1973 (Member Council, 1964–89; Treasurer, 1964–82; Vice Chairman, 1982–89); Chairman of Trustees, Blandford Trust for advancement of medical research and teaching, since 1964; *b* Berlin, Germany, 28 Aug. 1908; *s* of late Judge Richard Blumenfeld and Hedwig Kersten; *m* 1933, Hilde Kleczewer (*d* 1994); one *s* one *d*. *Educ:* Augusta Gymnasium; Univs of Berlin and Hamburg. Controller of continental cos in ceramic, pharmaceutical, iron and steel industries, 1933–39; Chm., Ulvir Ltd and various cos, 1936–76. Pioneered synthesis, manufacture and use of liquid fertilisers in the UK, 1945–60. School of Pharmacy, London University: Mem. Council, 1975–89; Treas., 1976–87; Vice-Chm., 1979–86; Hon. Fellow, 1988; British Postgraduate Medical Federation: Mem. Governing Body, 1969–86; Hon. Treas., 1969–84; Chm., 1977–79, Dep. Chm., 1980–85; Member: Management Cttee, Inst. of Ophthalmology, Moorfields, 1974–86; Court of Governors, LSHTM, 1982–89; Governor, London House for Overseas Graduates, 1977–80. Member: Org. Cttee, 6th World Congress of Cardiology, London, 1971; Board of Governors, Hammersmith and St Mark's Hospitals, 1972–74. *Recreations:* farming, gardening, walking. *Address:* Holtsmere Manor, Holtsmere End, Redbourn, Herts AL3 7AW. *T:* (01582) 792206. *Club:* Farmers'.
                    Died 5 Dec. 1996.

BLANKS, Howard John; Under-Secretary, Highways Policy and Programme, Department of Transport, 1985–88; *b* 16 June 1932; *s* of Lionel and Hilda Blanks; *m* 1958, Judith Ann (*née* Hughes). *Educ:* Barking Abbey Sch.; Keble Coll., Oxford (BA 1st Cl. Hons Music). National Service, RAF (Pilot), 1956–58. Air Traffic Control Officer, Min. of Aviation, 1958–64; Principal, Min. of Aviation (later Min. of Technology and Aviation Supply), 1964–71; Private Sec. to Chief Executive, Min. of Defence (Procurement Executive), 1972; Assistant Secretary: MoD, 1972–75; Cabinet Office, 1975–77; Dept of Trade, 1977–79; Under-Secretary, Head of Civil

Aviation Policy Div., Dept of Trade (subseq. Transport), 1980–85. *Recreations:* music, travel. *Address:* Withinlee, Hedgehog Lane, Haslemere, Surrey GU27 2PJ. *T:* (01428) 652468. *Died 13 March 1998.*

BLECH, Harry, CBE 1984 (OBE 1962); Musical Director, Haydn-Mozart Society, and Founder and Conductor, London Mozart Players, 1949–84; *b* 2 March 1910; British; *m* 1935, Enid Marion Lessing (marr. diss. 1957; she *d* 1977); one *s* two *d*; *m* 1957, Marion Manley, pianist; one *s* three *d*. *Educ:* Central London Foundation; Trinity Coll. of Music (Fellow); Manchester Coll. of Music (Fellow). Joined BBC Symphony Orchestra, 1930–36. Responsible for formation of: Blech Quartet, 1933–50 (Leader, 1935–50); London Wind Players, 1942 (conductor); London Mozart Players, 1949 (Conductor Laureate); Haydn-Mozart Soc., 1949; London Mozart Choir, 1952. Dir of Chamber Orchestra, RAM, 1961–65. Hon. RAM 1963. FRSA. *Address:* The Owls, 70 Leopold Road, Wimbledon, SW19 7JQ.
Died 9 May 1999.

BLISHEN, Edward William; author; *b* 29 April 1920; *s* of William George Blishen and Elizabeth Anne (*née* Pye); *m* 1948, Nancy Smith; two *s. Educ:* Queen Elizabeth's Grammar Sch., Barnet. Weekly Newspaper reporter, 1937–40; agricultural worker, 1941–46; teaching: Prep. Schoolmaster, 1946–49; Secondary Modern School Teacher, 1950–59. Presenter: Writers' Club, BBC African Service, 1959–72; The World of Books, BBC Topical Tapes, 1973–89; A Good Read, BBC Radio 4, 1989–. Soc. of Authors Travelling Scholarship, 1979. FRSL 1989. DUniv Open, 1995. *Publications:* Roaring Boys, 1955; This Right Soft Lot, 1969; (with Leon Garfield) The God Beneath the Sea, 1970 (Carnegie Medal, 1970); (with Leon Garfield) The Golden Shadow, 1972; *autobiography:* A Cackhanded War, 1972; Uncommon Entrance, 1974; Sorry, Dad, 1978; A Nest of Teachers, 1980; Shaky Relations, 1981 (J. R. Ackerley Prize); Lizzie Pye, 1982; Donkey Work, 1983; A Second Skin, 1984; The Outside Contributor, 1986; The Disturbance Fee, 1988; The Penny World, 1990; *edited:* Junior Pears Encyclopaedia, 1961–95; Oxford Miscellanies, 1964–69; Blond Encyclopaedia of Education, 1969; The School that I'd Like, 1969; The Thorny Paradise, 1975; *compiled:* Oxford Book of Poetry for Children, 1964; Come Reading, 1967; (with Nancy Blishen) A Treasury of Stories for Five Year Olds, 1989; (with Nancy Blishen) The Kingfisher Treasury of Stories for Children, 1992; Stand Up, Mr Dickens: a Dickens anthology, 1995; *posthumous:* Mind How You Go, 1997. *Recreations:* ambling, broadcasting, listening to music. *Address:* 12 Bartrams Lane, Hadley Wood, Barnet EN4 0EH. *T:* (0181) 449 3252.
Died 13 Dec. 1996.

BLISS, John Cordeux, QPM 1969; retired as Deputy Assistant Commissioner, Metropolitan Police, 1971 (seconded as National Co-ordinator of Regional Crime Squads of England and Wales from inception, 1964–71); *b* 16 March 1914; *s* of late Herbert Francis Bliss and Ida Muriel (*née* Hays); *m* 1947, Elizabeth Mary, *d* of Charles Gordon Howard; one *s* two *d. Educ:* Haileybury Coll. Metropolitan Police Coll., Hendon, 1936–37; Barrister, Middle Temple, 1954. Served in RAF, 1941–45, Flt Lt, 227 Sqdn, MEF. Various ranks of Criminal Investigation Dept of Metropolitan Police, 1946–62; seconded as Dir of Criminal Law at Police Coll., Bramshill, 1962–63; Dep. Comdr, 1963–64. Mem., Parole Bd, 1973–76 and 1978–81. Liveryman, Merchant Taylors' Company. Churchill Memorial Trust Fellowship, 1967. *Recreations:* gardening; formerly Rugby football, tennis. *Address:* Foxhanger Down, Hurtmore, Godalming, Surrey GU7 2RG. *T:* (01483) 422487. *Club:* Royal Air Force.
Died 18 Oct. 1999.

BLOCH, Prof. Konrad Emil; Higgins Professor of Biochemistry, Harvard University, 1954–82, then Emeritus; *b* 21 Jan. 1912; *s* of Frederick D. Bloch and Hedwig (*née* Striemer); US citizen, 1944; *m* 1941, Lore Teutsch; one *s* one *d. Educ:* Technische Hochschule, Munich; Columbia Univ., New York; MA Oxon 1982. Instructor and Research Associate, Columbia Univ., 1939–46; University of Chicago: Asst Prof., 1946–48; Associate Prof., 1948–50; Prof., 1950–54. Newton-Abraham Vis. Prof., and Fellow of Lincoln Coll., Oxford Univ., 1982. Foreign Mem., Royal Soc., 1982. Nobel Prize for Medicine (jointly), 1964; US Nat. Medal of Science, 1988. *Publications:* Lipide Metabolism, 1961; numerous papers in biochemical journals. *Address:* 16 Moon Hill Road, Lexington, MA 02173, USA. *T:* (617) 8629076; Department of Chemistry and Chemical Biology, Harvard University, 12 Oxford Street, Cambridge, MA 02138, USA.
Died 15 Oct. 2000.

BLOUNT, Bertie Kennedy, CB 1957; DrPhilNat; CChem, FRSC; *b* 1 April 1907; *s* of late Col G. P. C. Blount, DSO, and Bridget Constance, *d* of Maj.-Gen. J. F. Bally, CVO; unmarried. *Educ:* Malvern Coll.; Trinity Coll., Oxford (MA 1932, BSc 1929); Univ. of Frankfurt (DrPhilNat 1931). Ramsay Memorial Fellow, 1931; 1851 Senior Student, 1933; Dean of St Peter's Hall, Oxford, 1933–37. Served Army (Intelligence Corps), War of 1939–45; Capt. 1940; Major 1942; Col 1945. Messrs Glaxo Laboratories Ltd: Head of Chemical Research Laboratory, 1937; Principal Technical Executive, 1938–40. Asst Director of Research, The Wellcome Foundation, 1947; Director of Research Branch, Control Commission for Germany, 1948, and subsequently also Chief of Research Div. of Military Security Board; Director of Scientific Intelligence, Min. of Defence, 1950–52; Dep. Secretary, DSIR, 1952; Min. of Technology, 1964; retired 1966. Member Exec. Cttee, British Council, 1957–66. Royal Society of Arts: Armstrong Lecturer, 1955; Cantor Lecturer, 1963. Member, Parry Cttee to review Latin American Studies in British Universities, 1962. Pres., Exec. Cttee, Internat. Inst. of Refrigeration, 1963–71, Hon. Pres. 1971; Hon. Member: (British) Inst. of Refrigeration, 1971; Max-Planck-Ges. zur Förderung der Wissenschaften, 1984. Hon. Fellow, St Peter's Coll., Oxford, 1988. Golden doctorate, Frankfurt Univ., 1982. Minerva Award, Max Planck Inst., 1995. *Publications:* papers in scientific and other journals. *Recreations:* travel, walking, gardening. *Club:* Athenæum. *Died 18 July 1999.*

BLUMFIELD, Clifford William, OBE 1976; Director, Dounreay Nuclear Power Development Establishment, 1975–87, and Deputy Managing Director, Northern Division, UKAEA, 1985–87; *b* 18 May 1922; *m* 1944, Jeanne Mary; one *s* one *d* (and one *s* decd). *Educ:* Ipswich Boys' Central Sch. CEng, FIMechE, FINucE. With Reavell & Co. Ltd, 1938–44; served REME, 1944–47 (Major); Min. of Supply, Harwell, 1947–54; UKAEA, Harwell, 1954–58; Atomic Energy Estabt, Winfrith, 1958–68 (Group Leader, Design Gp, and Head of Gen. Ops and Tech. Div.); Asst Dir, Ops and Engineering, later Dep. Dir, Dounreay, 1968–75. *Address:* Rosebank, Janet Street, Thurso, Caithness KW14 7EG.
Died 11 July 1996.

BOATENG, Prof. Ernest Amano, GM 1968; environmental and educational consultant; Emeritus Professor of Geography, University of Ghana, since 1989; *b* 30 Nov. 1920; 2nd *s* of late Rev. Christian Robert and Adelaide Akonobea Boateng, Aburi, Ghana; *m* 1955, Evelyn Kensema Danso, *e d* of late Rev. Robert Opong Danso and of Victoria Danso, Aburi; four *d. Educ:* Achimota Coll.; St Peter's Hall, Oxford (Gold Coast Govt Schol.). Henry Oliver Beckit Meml Prize, 1949; BA

(Geog.) 1949, MA 1953, MLitt 1954. University College, Ghana: Lectr in Geography, 1950–57; Sen. Lectr, 1958–61; University of Ghana: Prof. of Geography, 1961–73; Dean, Faculty of Social Studies, 1962–69; Principal, 1969–71, Vice-Chancellor, 1972–73, University Coll., Cape Coast, later Univ. of Cape Coast, Ghana. Vis. Asst Prof., Univ. of Pittsburgh and UCLA, 1960–61; Smuts Vis. Fellow, Univ. of Cambridge, 1965–66; Vis. Prof., Univ. of Pittsburgh, 1966. Pres., Ghana Geographical Assoc., 1959–69; Foundn Fellow, Ghana Acad. of Arts and Sciences (Sec. 1959–62, Pres., 1973–76); Mem., Unesco Internat. Adv. Cttee on Humid Tropics Research, 1961–63; Mem., Scientific Council for Africa, 1963–80; Mem., Nat. Planning Commn of Ghana, 1961–64; Mem., Council for Scientific and Industrial Research, Ghana, 1967–75; Dir, Ghana Nat. Atlas Project, 1965–77; Deleg., UN Conf. on geographical names, Geneva, 1967; Chm., Geographical Cttee, Ghana 1970 population census; Chm., Environmental Protection Council, Ghana, 1973–81; Mem., 1974–78, and Vice-Chm., 1995–97, Nat. Economic Planning Council of Ghana; Alternate Leader, Ghana Delegn to UN Conf., Vancouver, 1976; Chm., Land Use Planning Cttee of Ghana, 1978–79; Pres., Governing Council of UNEP, 1979, Senior Consultant, 1980–92; Member: Constituent Assembly for drafting constitution for third Republic of Ghana, 1978–79; Presidential Task Force on Investments, Ghana, 1980; Nat. Council for Higher Educn, 1975–82; Chm., W African Exams Council, 1977–85. Pres., Ghana Wildlife Soc., 1974–87. Hon. Fellow, Ghana Inst. of Planners, 1984. FRSA 1973. Hon. DLitt: Ghana, 1979; Cape Coast, 1994. Nat. Book Award, Ghana, 1978. *Publications:* A Geography of Ghana, 1959; (contrib.) Developing Countries of the World, 1968; (contrib.) Population Growth and Economic Development in Africa, 1972; Independence and Nation Building in Africa, 1973; A Political Geography of Africa, 1978; African Unity: the dream and the reality (J. B. Danquah Memorial Lectures 1978), 1979; Crisis, Change and Revolution in Ghanian Education (Armstrong-Amissah Meml Lecture), 1996; Government and the People: outlook for democracy in Ghana, 1996; various pamphlets, Britannica and other encyclopaedia articles, and articles in geographical and other jls and reference works. *Recreations:* photography, gardening. *Address:* Environmental Consultancy Services, PO Box 84, Trade Fair Site, Accra, Ghana. *T:* Accra 777875; (home) 3 Aviation Road, Airport Residential Area, Accra, Ghana.   *Died 11 July 1997.*

BODEN, Leonard Monro, RP; portrait painter; *b* Greenock, Scotland, 31 May 1911; *s* of John Boden; *m* 1937, Margaret Tulloch (portrait painter, as Margaret Boden, PS, FRSA); one *d*. *Educ:* Sedbergh; Sch. of Art, Glasgow; Heatherley Sch. of Art, London. *Official portraits* included: HM Queen Elizabeth II; HRH The Prince Philip, Duke of Edinburgh; HM Queen Elizabeth the Queen Mother; HRH The Prince of Wales; The Princess Royal; HH Pope Pius XII; Field Marshals Lord Milne and Lord Slim; Margaret Thatcher; and many others. Vice-President: Artists' Gen. Benevolent Instn; St Ives Soc. of Artists; Governor, Christ's Hospital. Freeman, City of London; Liveryman, Painter-Stainers' Co. Gold Medal, Paris Salon, 1957. FRSA. *Work reproduced in:* The Connoisseur, The Artist, Fine Art Prints. *Address:* 36 Arden Road, N3 3AN. *T:* (020) 8346 5706. *Clubs:* Savage, Chelsea Arts.
Died 3 Nov. 1999.

BODILLY, Sir Jocelyn, Kt 1969; VRD; Chairman, Industrial Tribunals for London (South), 1976–86, retired; Chief Justice of the Western Pacific, 1965–75; *b* 1913; *s* of Comdr Ralph Bodilly, RN, Trenarren, Cornwall; *m* 1st, 1936, Phyllis Maureen (*d* 1963), *d* of Thomas Cooper Gotch, ARA; 2nd, 1964, Marjorie (*d* 1996), *d* of Walter Fogg. *Educ:* Munro Coll., Jamaica; Schloss Schule, Salem,

Baden; Wadham Coll., Oxford. Called to Bar, Inner Temple, 1937; engaged in private practice until War; Royal Navy until 1946; High Court Judge, Sudan, 1946–55; Crown Counsel, Hong Kong, 1955, Principal Crown Counsel, 1961–65. RNVR, 1937–56 (Lt-Comdr (S)); Lt-Comdr, RNR, Hong Kong, 1961–65. *Address:* Myrtle Cottage, St Peters Hill, Newlyn, Penzance, Cornwall TR18 5EQ. *Club:* Royal Ocean Racing.
Died 27 April 1997.

BOGARDE, Sir Dirk; *see* van den Bogaerde, Sir D. N.

BOGIE, David Wilson; Sheriff of Grampian, Highland and Islands at Aberdeen and Stonehaven, 1985–97; *b* 17 July 1946; *o s* of late Robert T. Bogie, Edinburgh; *m* 1st, 1983, Lady Lucinda Mackay (marr. diss. 1987), *o d* of 3rd Earl of Inchcape; 2nd, 1996, (Margaret) Jean Innes Leith, *yr d* of late Prof. John Lothian. *Educ:* George Watson's Coll.; Univ. of Grenoble; Edinburgh Univ. (LLB); Balliol Coll., Oxford (MA). Admitted to Faculty of Advocates, 1972; Temp. Sheriff, 1981. FSAScot. *Recreations:* architecture, heraldry, antiquities. *Address:* 22 Forest Road, Aberdeen AB15 4BS. *Clubs:* Brooks's; New (Edinburgh); Royal Northern and University (Aberdeen).
Died 9 Dec. 1999.

BOGLE, David Blyth, CBE 1967; WS; formerly Senior Partner, Lindsays, WS, Edinburgh; Member of Council on Tribunals, 1958–70, and Chairman of Scottish Committee, 1962–70; *b* 22 Jan. 1903; *s* of late Very Rev. Andrew Nisbet Bogle, DD and Helen Milne Bogle; *m* 1955, Ruth Agnes Thorley. *Educ:* George Watson's Coll., Edinburgh; Edinburgh Univ. (LLB). Writer to the Signet, 1927. Commissioned in the Queen's Own Cameron Highlanders, 1940, and served in UK and Middle East, 1942–45; demobilised, with rank of Major, 1945. *Recreation:* RNIB talking books. *Address:* 3 Belgrave Crescent, Edinburgh EH4 3AQ. *T:* (0131) 332 0047. *Club:* New (Edinburgh).
Died 31 Jan. 2000.

BOJAXHIU, Agnes Gonxha; *see* Teresa, Mother.

BON, Christoph Rudolf; Founder Partner, Chamberlin Powell & Bon, 1952; *b* 1 Sept. 1921; *s* of Rudolf Bon and Nelly Fischbacher. *Educ:* Cantonal Gymnasium, Zürich; Swiss Federal Inst. of Technology, Zürich (DipArch ETH 1946). Prof. W. G. Holford's Office, Master Plan for City of London, 1946; Studio BBPR, Milan, 1949–50; teaching at Kingston Sch. of Art, 1950–52. Work included: Golden Lane Estate; Expansion of Leeds Univ.; schools, housing and commercial buildings; New Hall, Cambridge; Barbican. *Address:* 60 South Edwardes Square, W8 6HL. *T:* (020) 7602 6462.
Died 21 Oct. 1999.

BONALLACK, Sir Richard (Frank), Kt 1963; CBE 1955 (OBE (mil.) 1945); MIMechE; *b* 2 June 1904; *s* of Francis and Ada Bonallack; *m* 1930, Winifred Evelyn Mary Esplen (*d* 1986); two *s* one *d*. *Educ:* Haileybury. War service in TA, 1939–45; transferred to TA Reserve, 1946, with rank of Colonel. Bonallack and Sons Ltd, subseq. Freight Bonallack Ltd: Chm., 1953–74; Pres., 1974–87; Dir, Alcan Transport Products, 1979–85. Chm., Freight Container Section, SMMT, 1967–83; Mem., Basildon Development Corporation, 1962–77. Chm., Working Party, Anglo-Soviet Cttee for Jt Technical Collaboration, 1961–65. *Recreation:* golf. *Address:* 4 The Willows, Thorpe Bay, Southend on Sea, Essex SS1 3SH. *T:* Southend (01702) 588180.
Died 4 Jan. 1996.

BOND, Godfrey William; Public Orator, Oxford University, 1980–92; Emeritus Fellow, Pembroke College, Oxford, since 1992 (Dean, 1979–92); *b* 24 July 1925; *o s* of William Niblock Bond, MC, Newry and Janet Bond (*née* Godfrey), Dublin; *m* 1959, Alison, *d* of Mr Justice T. C. Kingsmill Moore, Dublin; one *s* two *d*. *Educ:* Campbell Coll.; Royal Belfast Acad. Inst.; Trinity Coll. Dublin

(Scholar 1946; Berkeley Medal 1948; BA 1st Cl. Classics (gold medal); 1st Cl. Mental and Moral Sci. 1949); St John's Coll., Oxford (MA). Served War Office and Foreign Office (GCHQ), 1943–45. Fellow and Classical Tutor, Pembroke Coll., Oxford, 1950–92; Senior Tutor, 1962–72; Oxford University: Lectr in Classics, 1952–92; Senior Proctor, 1964–65; Gen. Bd of Faculties, 1970–76; Visitor, Ashmolean Museum, 1972–81. Mem., Inst. for Advanced Study, Princeton, 1969–70. *Publications:* editions of Euripides, Hypsipyle, 1963, Heracles, 1981; orations (mostly Latin) in OU Gazette, 1980–92; memorial addresses, articles and reviews. *Recreations:* people and places in Greece, France and Ireland; opera, dining, swimming. *Address:* Masefield House, Boars Hill, Oxford OX1 5EY. *T:* (01865) 735373. *Clubs:* Athenæum; Kildare Street and University (Dublin).

Died 30 Jan. 1997.

BONHAM-CARTER, John Arkwright, CVO 1975; DSO 1942; OBE 1967; ERD 1952; Chairman and General Manager, British Railways London Midland Region, 1971–75; *b* 27 March 1915; *s* of late Capt. Guy Bonham-Carter, 19th Hussars, and Kathleen Rebecca (*née* Arkwright); *m* 1939, Anne Louisa Charteris; two *s*. *Educ:* Winchester Coll.; King's Coll., Cambridge (Exhibitioner; 1st class hons Mech. Scis, 1936; MA 1970). Joined LNER Co. as Traffic Apprentice, 1936; served in Royal Tank Regt, 1939–46 (despatches, 1940 and 1942); subsequently rejoined LNER; held various appointments; Asst General Manager, BR London Midland Region, 1963–65; Chief Operating Officer, BR Board, 1966–68; Chm. and Gen. Manager, BR Western Region, 1968–71. Lieut-Col, Engrg and Transport (formerly Engr and Rly) Staff Corps RE (TA), 1966–71, Col 1971–95. FCIT. KStJ 1984; Comdr, St John Ambulance, Dorset, 1984–87. *Recreations:* theatre, foreign travel, cabinet making, carpentry. *Address:* Redbridge House, Crossways, Dorchester, Dorset DT2 8DY. *T:* (01305) 852669. *Club:* Army and Navy.

Died 9 Sept. 1998.

BONNER, Frederick Ernest, CBE 1974; Deputy Chairman, Central Electricity Generating Board, 1975–86; *b* 16 Sept. 1923; *s* of late George Frederick Bonner and Mrs Bonner, Hammersmith; *m* 1st, 1957, Phyllis (*d* 1976), *d* of late Mr and Mrs H. Holder and *widow* of W. A. Oliver; 2nd, 1977, Mary, *widow* of Ellis Walter Aries, AFC, ARICS. *Educ:* St Clement Danes Holborn Estate Grammar Sch.; BSc(Econ) London; DPA, JDipMA; FCA; CPFA. Local Govt (Fulham and Ealing Borough Councils), 1940–49; Central Electricity Authority: Sen. Accountant, 1949–50; Asst Finance Officer, 1950–58; Central Electricity Generating Board: Asst Chief Financial Officer, 1958–61; Dep. Chief Financial Officer, 1961–65; Chief Financial Officer, 1965–69; Member, 1969–75. Member: UKAEA, 1977–86; Monopolies and Mergers Commn, 1987–93. Chm., British Airways Helicopters, 1983–85; Dir (non-exec.), Nuclear Electric, 1990–93. Hon. Treas., 1989–97, Vice-Chm., 1993, Chm., 1994, BIEE; Chm., Uranium Inst., 1985–87. Mem., Public Finance Foundn, 1985–97. Hon. Treas., Chichester Counselling Services Ltd, 1995–99. CIMgt. *Recreations:* music, gardening, reading. *Address:* Joya, 20 Craigweil Manor, Aldwick, Bognor Regis, W Sussex PO21 4DJ. *Died 20 Oct. 2000.*

BONSER, Air Vice-Marshal Stanley Haslam, CB 1969; MBE 1942; CEng, FRAeS; Director, Easams Ltd, 1972–81; *b* 17 May 1916; *s* of late Sam Bonser and Phoebe Ellen Bonser; *m* 1941, Margaret Betty Howard (*d* 1994); two *s*. *Educ:* Sheffield University. BSc 1938; DipEd 1939. Armament Officer, Appts, 1939–44; British Air Commn, Washington, DC, 1944–46; Coll. of Aeronautics, 1946–47; RAE, Guided Weapons, 1947–51; Chief Instr (Armament Wing) RAF Techn. Coll., 1951–52; Staff Coll., Bracknell, 1953, psa 1953; Project Officer,

Blue Streak, Min. of Technology, 1954–57; Asst Dir, GW Engineering, 1957–60; Senior RAF Officer, Skybolt Development Team, USA, 1960–62; Dir, Aircraft Mechanical Engineering, 1963–64; Dir, RAF Aircraft Development (mainly Nimrod), 1964–69; Dep. Controller: of Equipment, Min. of Technology and MoD, 1969–71; Aircraft C, MoD, 1971–72. *Recreations:* scout movement, gardening. *Address:* Chalfont, Waverley Avenue, Fleet, Hants GU13 8NW. *T:* (01252) 615835.

Died 12 Nov. 1997.

BOON, John Trevor, CBE 1968; Chairman, Harlequin Mills & Boon (formerly Mills & Boon) Ltd, since 1972; *b* 21 Dec. 1916; 3rd *s* of Charles Boon and Mary Boon (*née* Cowpe); *m* 1943, Felicity Ann, *d* of Stewart and Clemence Logan; four *s*. *Educ:* Felsted Sch.; Trinity Hall, Cambridge (scholar). 1st Cl. Pts I and II History Tripos. Served War, 1939–45, with Royal Norfolk Regt and S Wales Borderers (despatches); Historical Section of War Cabinet, 1945–46. Joined Mills & Boon Ltd, 1938, Man. Dir, 1963. Dir, Wood Bros Glass Works Ltd, 1968, Chm., 1973–75, Dep. Chm., 1975–78. Vice Chm., Harlequin Enterprises Ltd, Toronto, 1972–83; Chairman: Harlequin Overseas, 1978–; Marshall Editions, 1977–95; Director: Harmex, 1978–82; Harlequin France, 1980–82 (Chm., 1978–80); Torstar Corp., Toronto, 1981–85; Open University Educational Enterprises, 1977–79. President: Soc. of Bookmen, 1981; Internat. Publishers Assoc., 1972–76 (Hon. Mem., 1982); Chairman: Publishers Adv. Panel of British Council, 1977–81; Book Trade Res. Cttee, 1978–82; Director: Book Tokens Ltd, 1964–84; Book Trade Improvements Ltd, 1966–84; Publishers Association: Mem. Council, 1953, Treas., 1959–61, Pres., 1961–63, Vice-Pres., 1963–65. Over-seas missions: for British Council, to SE Asia, USSR (twice), Czechoslovakia; for Book Development Council, to Malaysia, Singapore, and New Zealand. Mem. Management Cttee, Wine Soc., 1971–77. Hon. MA, Open Univ., 1983. *Recreations:* wine, books, friends. *Address:* Harlequin Mills & Boon Ltd, Eton House, 18–24 Paradise Road, Richmond, Surrey TW9 1SR. *Clubs:* Beefsteak, Garrick, Royal Automobile; Hawks (Cambridge). *Died 12 July 1996.*

BOON, Sir Peter Coleman, Kt 1979; Goodyear Professor of Business Administration, Kent State University, USA, 1983–86; *b* 2 Sept. 1916; *s* of Frank and Evelyn Boon; *m* 1940, Pamela; one *s* one *d*. *Educ:* Felsted. Stock Exchange, 1933–34; Lloyds & National Provincial Foreign Bank, 1934–35; Dennison Mfg Co., USA, 1936–39; Armed Services, War of 1939–45, 1939–46; Dennison Mfg, 1946; Hoover Ltd: graduate trainee, 1946; Managing Dir (Australia), 1955–65; Managing Dir, 1965–75; Chm., 1975–78. Dir, Belden & Blake UK Inc., 1985–. FIMgt; FRSA 1980. Hon. LLD Strathclyde, 1978. Chevalier de l'Ordre de la Couronne, Belgium. *Recreations:* horses, swimming, golf, theatre, economics, National Trust for Scotland, boys clubs, education. *Clubs:* Royal Wimbledon Golf; Western Racing, Australian, Imperial Services, American National, Royal Sydney Yacht Squadron, Australian Jockey, Sydney Turf (Australia).

Died 10 April 1997.

BOOTE, Col Charles Geoffrey Michael, MBE 1945; TD 1943; DL; Vice Lord-Lieutenant of Staffordshire, 1969–76; *b* 29 Sept. 1909; *s* of Lt-Col Charles Edmund Boote, TD, The North Staffordshire Regt (killed in action, 1916); *m* 1937, Elizabeth Gertrude (*d* 1980), *er d* of Evan Richard Davies, Market Drayton, Salop; three *s*. *Educ:* Bedford Sch. 2nd Lieut 5th Bn North Staffordshire Regt, 1927; served 1939–45, UK and NW Europe; despatches, 1945; Lt-Col, 1947. Director, H. Clarkson (Midlands) Ltd, 1969–75. Dir, Brit. Pottery Manufacturers' Fedn (Trustee) Ltd, 1955, retd 1969; Pres., Brit. Pottery Manufacturers' Fedn, 1957–58; Vice-Chm., Glazed and Floor Tile

Manufacturers' Assoc., 1953–57. Hon. Col 5/6 Bn North Staffordshire Regt, 1963–67; Mem. Staffs TAVR Cttee, retd 1976. JP, Stoke-on-Trent, 1955–65; DL 1958, JP 1959, High Sheriff, 1967–68, Staffordshire; Chm., Eccleshall PSD, 1971–76. Mem. Court of Governors, Keele Univ., 1957. *Recreations:* salmon fishing; British Racing Drivers' Club (Life Mem.); North Staffordshire Hunt (Hon. Sec., 1948–59). *Address:* Morile Mhor, Tomatin, Inverness-shire IV13 7YN. *T:* (01808) 511319. *Club:* Army and Navy.   *Died 3 Oct. 1999.*

BOOTH, Sir Angus Josslyn G.; *see* Gore-Booth.

BOOTH, Charles Leonard, CMG 1979; LVO 1961; HM Diplomatic Service, retired; re-employed in Foreign and Commonwealth Office, 1985–90; *b* 7 March 1925; *s* of Charles Leonard and Marion Booth; *m* 1958, Mary Gillian Emms; two *s* two *d. Educ:* Heywood Grammar Sch.; Pembroke Coll., Oxford Univ., 1942–43 and 1947–50. Served RA (Capt.), 1943–47. Joined HM Foreign Service, 1950; Foreign Office, 1950–51; Third and Second Secretary, Rangoon, 1951–55; FO, 1955–60 (Private Sec. to Parly Under-Sec. of State, 1958–60); First Sec., Rome, 1960–63; Head of Chancery, Rangoon, 1963–64, and Bangkok, 1964–67; FO, 1967–69; Counsellor, 1968; Deputy High Comr, Kampala, 1969–71; Consul-General and Counsellor (Administration), Washington, 1971–73; Counsellor, Belgrade, 1973–77; Ambassador to Burma, 1978–82; High Comr, Malta, 1982–85. Officer of Order of Merit of Italian Republic, 1961. *Recreations:* opera, reading biographies. *Address:* 7 Queen Street, Southwold, Suffolk IP18 6EQ. *Club:* Travellers'.
                            Died 21 March 1997.

BOOTH, His Honour James; a Circuit Judge (formerly a County Court Judge), 1969–84; *b* 3 May 1914; *s* of James and Agnes Booth; *m* 1954, Joyce Doreen Mather; two *s* one *d. Educ:* Bolton Sch.; Manchester Univ. Called to Bar, Gray's Inn, 1936 (Arden Scholar, Gray's Inn). Town Clerk, Ossett, Yorks, 1939–41. RAFVR, 1941–46 (Flt-Lieut). Contested (L): West Leeds, 1945; Darwen, 1950. Recorder of Barrow-in-Furness, 1967–69. *Address:* Spinney End, Worsley, Lancs M28 2QN. *T:* (0161) 790 2003.   *Died 31 Aug. 2000.*

BOOTH, Sir Robert (Camm), Kt 1977; CBE 1967; TD; Chairman, National Exhibition Centre Ltd, 1975–82 (Founder Director, 1970–82; Chief Executive, 1977–78); *b* 9 May 1916; *s* of late Robert Wainhouse and Gladys Booth; *m* 1939, Veronica Courtenay, *d* of late F. C. and Muriel Lamb; one *s* two *d* (and one *d* decd). *Educ:* Altrincham Grammar Sch.; Manchester Univ. (LLB). Called to Bar, Gray's Inn, 1949. War Service 8th (A) Bn Manchester Regt, France, Malta, Middle East, Italy, 1939–46. Manchester Chamber of Commerce, 1946–58; Sec., Birmingham Chamber of Industry and Commerce, 1958–65, Dir, 1965–78, Pres., 1978–79. Local non-exec. Dir, Barclays Bank, 1977–84; Member: W Midlands Econ. Planning Council, 1974–77; BOTB Adv. Council, 1975–82; Midlands Adv. Bd, Legal and General Assurance Soc., 1979–86; Midlands and NW Bd, BR, 1979–85; Bd, Inst. of Occupational Health, 1980–90. Trustee, Nuffield Trust for the Forces of the Crown, 1977–. Life Mem., Court of Governors, Birmingham Univ., 1969 (Mem. Council, 1973–78); Governor, Sixth Form Coll., Solihull, 1974–77; Hon. Mem., British Exhbns Promotions Council, 1982. Overseas travel with 20 trade missions and author of marketing and economic publications. Marketor and Freeman, City of London, 1978. Hon. DSc Aston, 1975; Hon. FInstM; FRSA 1975. Midland Man of the Year Press Radio and TV Award, 1970. Officier de la Légion d'Honneur, 1982. *Address:* White House, 7 Sandal Rise, Solihull B91 3ET. *T:* (0121) 705 5311.
                            Died 22 Oct. 1996.

BOOTH-CLIBBORN, Rt Rev. Stanley Eric Francis; Bishop of Manchester, 1979–92; *b* 20 Oct. 1924; *s* of late Eric and Lucille Booth-Clibborn; *m* 1958, Anne Roxburgh Forrester, *d* of late Rev. William Roxburgh Forrester, MC; two *s* two *d. Educ:* Highgate School; Oriel Coll., Oxford (MA); Westcott House, Cambridge. Served RA, 1942–45; Royal Indian Artillery, 1945–47, Temp. Captain. Deacon 1952, priest 1953; Curate, Heeley Parish Church, Sheffield, 1952–54, The Attercliffe Parishes, Sheffield, 1954–56; Training Sec., Christian Council of Kenya, 1956–63; Editor-in-Chief, East African Venture Newspapers, Nairobi, 1963–67; Leader, Lincoln City Centre Team Ministry, 1967–70; Vicar, St Mary the Great, University Church, Cambridge, 1970–79. Hon. Canon, Ely Cathedral, 1976–79. Member: Div. of Internat. Affairs, BCC, 1968–80; Standing Cttee, General Synod, 1981–90; BCC delegn to Namibia, 1981; Chm., Namibia Communications Trust, 1983–95; Pres., St Ann's Hospice, 1979–92. Moderator, Movement for Ordination of Women, 1979–82. Introduced to House of Lords, 1985. Hon. Fellow, Manchester Polytechnic, 1989. Hon. DD Manchester, 1994. *Publication:* Taxes—Burden or Blessing?, 1991. *Recreations:* photography, tennis, listening to music. *Address:* 9 Kirkhill Drive, Edinburgh EH16 5DH. *T:* 0131–662 0443.
                            Died 6 March 1996.

BOR, Walter George, CBE 1975; FRIBA, DistTP; FRTPI; Consultant: Llewelyn-Davies Planning, since 1984; Llewelyn-Davies Weeks, 1976–84; Partner, Llewelyn-Davies Weeks Forestier-Walker & Bor, London, 1966–76; *b* 1916, Czech parentage; father chemical engineer; *m* 1944, Dinah Allen (marr. diss. 1946); one *s*; *m* 1954, Glenys (*née* Conolly); one *s* one *d*; *m* 1984, Dr Muriel Blackburn. *Educ:* Prague Univ. (degree of Arch.); Bartlett Sch. of Architecture and Sch. of Planning and Regional Research, London (Dip.). Private architectural practice, London, 1946–57; Architectural Assoc., LCC Architect's Dept, 1947–62 (Dep. Planning Officer with special responsibility for civic design, 1960–62); Liverpool City Planning Officer, 1962–66. Mem. Minister's Planning Advisory Gp, 1964–65. In private practice as architect and planning consultant, 1966–. Pres., Town Planning Inst., 1970–71; Vice-Pres., Housing Centre Trust, 1971–98. Visiting Professor: Princeton Univ., 1977–79; Rice Univ., Houston, 1980–81. Mem., Severn Barrage Cttee, 1978–81; Consultant, UNDP, Cyprus, 1982–83; Advr, Shenzhen City Planning Commn, China, 1987–89; Consultant to: municipalities of Prague, Vienna and Beijing, 1990–94; Prague strategic plan Know How Fund, 1994–98. Pres., London Forum of Civic Socs, 1988–97; Vice-Pres., TCPA, 1997–. FRSA. *Publications:* Liverpool Planning Policy, 1965; (jtly) Liverpool City Centre Plan, 1966; (jtly) Two New Cities in Venezuela, 1967–69; (jtly) The Milton Keynes Plan, 1970; (jtly) Airport City (Third London Airport urbanisation studies), 1970; The Making of Cities, 1972; (jtly) Bogota Urban Development for UNDP, 1974; (jtly) Concept Plan for Tehran new city centre, 1974; Shetland Draft Structure Plan, 1975; (jtly) Unequal City: Birmingham Inner Area Study, 1977; (jtly) Shenzhen, China: airport and urban design reports, 1987; articles for jls of RTPI, RIBA, TCPA, and for Urbanistica, Habitat Internat., Ekistics. *Recreations:* music, theatre, sketching, sculpting, pottery. *Address:* 99 Swains Lane, Highgate, N6 6PJ. *T:* (020) 8340 6540. *Club:* Reform.
                            Died 4 Oct. 1999.

BORGES, Thomas William Alfred; Managing Director, Thomas Borges & Partners, since 1949; *b* 1 April 1923; *s* of Arthur Borges, Prague, and Paula Borges; *m* 1st (marr. diss.); 2nd, 1966, Serena Katherine Stewart (*née* Jamieson); two *s. Educ:* Dunstable Grammar Sch.; Luton Technical Coll. Served War, 1941–45. Trained in banking, shipping and industry, 1945–49; Dir, Borges Law & Co.,

Sydney and Melbourne, 1951; Chm., Smith Whitworth Ltd, 1974–80; Dir, Trust Co. of Australia (UK) Ltd, 1991–94. Governor, Royal National Orth. Hosp., 1968 (Dep. Chm., 1978–80, Chm., 1980–82); Dir, Inst. of Orths, Univ. of London, 1968 (Dep. Chm., 1978–80, Chm., 1980–82); Member: Grants Cttee, King Edward VII Hosp. Fund, 1975–80; Council, Professions Supp. to Medicine, 1980–88 (Dep. Chm., 1982–88); Sir Robert Menzies Centre for Australian Studies, 1993–97; Treasurer, Riding for Disabled Assoc., 1977–84. Chm., Australian Art Foundn, 1984–96. Trustee, Sir Robert Menzies Meml Trust, 1981–. FInstD. *Publication:* Two Expeditions of Discovery in North West and Western Australia by George Grey, 1969. *Recreations:* travel, collecting Australiana, riding, swimming. *Address:* Flat 2, 34 Phillimore Gardens, W8 7QF. *T:* (020) 7938 2976.

Died 26 Feb. 2000.

BORLAND, David Morton; former Chairman, Cadbury Ltd; Director, Cadbury Schweppes Ltd; *b* 17 Jan. 1911; *s* of David and Annie J. Borland; *m* 1947, Nessa Claire Helwig; one *s* one *d. Educ:* Glasgow Academy; Brasenose Coll., Oxford (BA). War service, Royal Marines (Lieut-Col), 1940–46. Management Trainee, etc, Cadbury Bros Ltd, Bournville, Birmingham, 1933; Sales Manager, J. S. Fry & Sons Ltd, Somerdale, Bristol, 1946; Sales Dir and a Man. Dir, J. S. Fry & Sons Ltd, 1948; a Man. Dir, British Cocoa & Chocolate Co. Ltd, 1959, and of Cadbury Bros Ltd, 1963. Mem. Govt Cttee of Inquiry into Fatstock and Meat Marketing and Distribution, 1962. Bristol University: Mem. Council, 1962–88; Pro-Chancellor, 1983–89; Hon. Fellow, 1989. Hon. LLD Bristol, 1980. *Recreation:* golf. *Address:* Garden Cottage, 3 Hollymead Lane, Stoke Bishop, Bristol BS9 1LN. *T:* Bristol (0117) 968 3978. *Clubs:* Achilles; Vincent's (Oxford).

Died 12 March 1996.

BORODIN, George; *see* Sava, G.

BORRETT, Ven. Charles Walter; Archdeacon of Stoke-upon-Trent and Hon. Canon of Lichfield Cathedral, 1971–82, then Archdeacon Emeritus; Priest-in-charge of Sandon, Diocese of Lichfield, 1975–82; a Chaplain to the Queen, 1980–86; *b* 15 Sept. 1916; *s* of Walter George Borrett, farmer, and Alice Frances (*née* Mecrow); *m* 1941, Jean Constable (*d* 2000), *d* of Charles Henry and Lilian Constable Pinson, Wolverhampton; one *s* two *d. Educ:* Framlingham Coll., Suffolk; Emmanuel Coll., Cambridge (MA); Ridley Hall, Cambridge. Deacon, 1941, priest, 1943; Curate: of All Saints, Newmarket, 1941–45; of St Paul, Wolverhampton, 1945–48; of Tettenhall Regis, 1948–49; Vicar of Tettenhall Regis, 1949–71; Rural Dean of Trysull, 1958–71; Prebendary of Flixton in Lichfield Cathedral, 1964–71. Chm., C of E Council for Deaf, 1976–86. Fellow, Woodard Schs, 1972–86. *Address:* Holly Lodge, Manor Road, Mildenhall, Bury St Edmunds IP28 7EL. *T:* (01638) 712718. *Club:* Hawks (Cambridge).

Died 30 Nov. 2000.

BORTHWICK, 23rd Lord *cr* 1450 (Scot.); **John Henry Stuart Borthwick of That Ilk,** TD 1943; DL, JP; Baron of Heriotmuir and Laird of Crookston, Midlothian; Hereditary Falconer of Scotland to the Queen; Chairman: Heriotmuir Properties Ltd, since 1965; Heriotmuir Exporters Ltd, since 1972; *b* 13 Sept. 1905; *s* of Henry Borthwick, *de facto* 22nd Lord Borthwick (*d* 1937) and Melena Florence, 4th *d* of Capt. James Thomas Pringle, RN, Torwoodlee, Selkirkshire; claim to Lordship admitted by Lord Lyon, 1986; *m* 1938, Margaret Frances (*d* 1976), *d* of Alexander Campbell Cormack, Edinburgh; twin *s. Educ:* Fettes Coll., Edinburgh; King's Coll., Newcastle (DipAgric 1926). Formerly RA TA, re-employed 1939; served NW Europe, Allied Mil. Govt Staff (Junior Staff Coll., SO 2), 1944; CCG (CO 1, Lt-Col), 1946. Dept of Agriculture for Scotland, 1948–50; farming own farms,

1950–71; Partner in Crookston Farms, 1971–79. National Farmers Union of Scotland: Mid and West Lothian Area Cttee, 1967–73 (Pres. 1970–72); Mem. Council, 1968–72; Member: Lothians Area Cttee, NFU Mutual Insurance Soc., 1969; Scottish Southern Regional Cttee, Wool Marketing Bd, 1966–87. Mem., Scottish Landowners' Fedn, 1937– (Mem., Land Use Cttee, 1972–83; Mem., Scottish Livestock Export Gp, 1972–83). Chm., Area Cttee, South of Scotland Electricity Bd Consultative Council, 1972–76. Chm., Monitoring Cttee for Scottish Tartans, 1976; Dir, Castles of Scotland Preservation Trust, 1985–. County Councillor, Midlothian, 1937–48; JP 1938; DL Midlothian (later Lothian Region), 1965; Member: Local Appeal Tribunal (Edinburgh and the Lothians), 1963–75; Midlothian Valuation Cttee, 1966–78. Member: Standing Council of Scottish Chiefs; Committee of the Baronage of Scotland (International Delegate); Mem. Corresp., Istituto Italiano di Genealogia e Araldica, Rome and Madrid, 1964; Hon. Mem., Council of Scottish Clans Assoc., USA, 1975. Hon. Mem., Royal Military Inst. of Canada, 1976. Patron for Scotland and Dep. Patron for England, Normandy Veterans Assoc., 1985–. KLJ; GCLJ 1975; Comdr, Rose of Lippe, 1971; Niadh Nask, 1982. *Recreations:* shooting, travel, history. *Heir: s* Master of Borthwick [*b* 14 Nov. 1940; *m* 1974, Adelaide, *d* of A. Birkmyre; two *d*]. *Address:* Crookston, Heriot, Midlothian EH38 5YS. *Clubs:* Carlton; New, Puffins (Edinburgh).

Died 30 Dec. 1996.

BORTHWICK, (William) Jason (Maxwell), DSC 1942; *b* 1 Nov. 1910; *er s* of late Hon. William Borthwick and Ruth (*née* Rigby); *m* 1937, Elizabeth Elworthy (*d* 1978), Timaru, NZ; one *s* three *d. Educ:* Winchester; Trinity Coll., Cambridge (BA). Called to Bar, Inner Temple, 1933. Commnd RNVR, 1940, Comdr (QO) 1945. Joined Thomas Borthwick & Sons Ltd, 1934, Dir 1946–76; Dir, International Commodities Clearing House Ltd and subsids, 1954–84; Dir, Commonwealth Develt Corp., 1972–78; Mem., Central Council of Physical Recreation, 1955–78; Chm., Nat. Sailing Centre, 1965–79. *Recreations:* yachting, shooting. *Address:* North House, Brancaster Staithe, King's Lynn, Norfolk PE31 8B1. *T:* (01485) 210475. *Clubs:* United Oxford & Cambridge University; Royal Thames Yacht. *Died 15 Jan. 1998.*

BOSTOCK, Rev. Canon Peter Geoffrey; Clergy Appointments Adviser, 1973–76; Deputy Secretary, Board for Mission and Unity, General Synod of Church of England, 1971–73; Canon Emeritus, Diocese of Mombasa, 1958; *b* 24 Dec. 1911; *s* of Geoffrey Bostock; *m* 1937, Elizabeth Rose; two *s* two *d. Educ:* Charterhouse; The Queen's Coll., Oxon (MA); Wycliffe Hall, Oxon. Deacon, 1935; priest, 1937; CMS Kenya, 1935–58; became Canon of Diocese of Mombasa, 1952; Archdeacon, 1953–58; Vicar-Gen., 1955–58; Examining Chaplain to Bishop of Mombasa, 1950–58; Chm., Christian Council of Kenya, 1957–58; Archdeacon of Doncaster and Vicar, High Melton, 1959–67; Asst Sec., Missionary and Ecumenical Council of Church Assembly, 1967–71. *Recreation:* home and family. *Address:* 6 Moreton Road, Oxford OX2 7AX. *T:* (01865) 515460. *Club:* Royal Commonwealth Society.

Died 28 May 1999.

BOTTINI, Reginald Norman, CBE 1974; General-Secretary, National Union of Agricultural and Allied Workers, 1970–78; Member, General Council of TUC, 1970–78; *b* 14 Oct. 1916; *s* of Reginald and Helena Teresa Bottini; *m* 1946, Doris Mary Balcomb (*d* 1996); no *c. Educ:* Bec Grammar School. Apptd Asst in Legal Dept of Nat. Union of Agricultural Workers, 1945; Head of Negotiating Dept, 1954; elected Gen.-Sec., Dec. 1969. Member: Agricultural Wages Bd, 1963–78; Agricultural Economic Development Cttee, 1970–78; (part-time) SE Electricity Bd, 1974–83; Food Hygiene Adv. Council,

1973–83; BBC Agric. Adv. Cttee, 1973–78; Econ. and Soc. Cttee, EEC, 1975–78; Clean Air Council, 1975–80; Adv. Cttee on Toxic Substances, 1977–80; Meat and Livestock Commn, 1977–86 (and Chm. of its Consumers Cttee); (Panel Mem.), Central Arbitration Cttee, 1977–86; Commn on Energy and the Environment, 1978–81; Waste Management Adv. Council, 1978–81; Employees' Panel, Industrial Tribunals, 1984–85. Formerly: Secretary: Trade Union Side, Forestry Commn Ind. and Trades Council; Trade Union Side, British Sugar Beet Nat. Negotiating Cttee; Chm., Trade Union Side, Nat. Jt Ind. Council for River Authorities; Member: Central Council for Agric. and Hort. Co-operation; Nat. Jt Ind. Council for County Roadmen. Chm., Market Harborough Volunteer Bureau, 1989–95, 1998–. *Recreations:* gardening, driving. *Address:* 43 Knights End Road, Great Bowden, Market Harborough, Leics LE16 7EY. *T:* (01858) 464229. *Clubs:* Farmers'; Probus (Market Harborough).

Died 5 May 1999.

BOTTOMLEY, Lady; Bessie Ellen Bottomley, DBE 1970; *b* 28 Nov. 1906; *d* of Edward Charles Wiles and Ellen (*née* Estall); *m* 1936, Arthur George Bottomley, later Baron Bottomley, OBE, PC (*d* 1995); no *c. Educ:* Maynard Road Girls' Sch.; North Walthamstow Central Sch. On staff of NUT, 1925–36. Member: Walthamstow Borough Council, 1945–48; Essex CC, 1962–65; Chm., Labour Party Women's Section, E Walthamstow, 1946–71, Chingford, 1973–. Mem., Forest Group Hosp. Man. Cttee, 1949–73; Mem., W Roding Community Health Council, 1973–76. Chm., Walthamstow Nat. Savings Cttee, 1949–65; Vice-Pres., Waltham Forest Nat. Savings Cttee, 1965 (Chm., 1975). Mayoress of Walthamstow, 1945–46. Mem., WVS Regional Staff (SE England), 1941–45. Past Mem., Home Office Adv. Cttee on Child Care. Chm. of Govs of two Secondary Modern Schools, 1948–68, also group of Primary and Infant Schools; Chm. of Governors of High Schools. Mem., Whitefield Trust. JP 1955–76 and on Juvenile Bench, 1955–71; Dep. Chm., Waltham Forest Bench. *Recreations:* theatre, gardening. *Address:* c/o 60 The Gardens, Doddinghurst, near Brentwood, Essex CM15 0LX. *Died 8 Sept. 1998.*

BOUGHEY, John Fenton C.; *see* Coplestone-Boughey.

BOULET, Gilles, OC 1985; Musée des arts et traditions populaires du Québec, since 1990; *b* 5 June 1926; *s* of Georges-A. Boulet and Yvonne Hamel; *m* 1971, Florence Lemire; one *s* one *d. Educ:* Coll. St Gabriel de St Tite; Séminaire St Joseph de Trois-Rivières; Laval Univ. (LTh 1951, DèsL 1954); Université Catholique de Paris (LPh, MA 1953). Prof. of Literature and History, Séminaire Ste Marie, Shawinigan, 1953–61; Centre d'Etudes Universitaires de Trois-Rivières: Founder, 1960; Dir, 1960–69; Prof. of Lit. and Hist., 1961–66; Laval University: Prof. of French, Faculty of Lit., 1955–62; Aggregate Prof., Fac. of Arts, 1959; Rector, Univ. du Québec à Trois-Rivières, 1969–78, Rector-Founder, 1979; Pres., Univ. of Quebec, 1978–88 (Asst to Pres., 1988–89). Founder and Pres., Inter-Amer. Orgn for Higher Educn, 1981. Dr *hc:* Universidade Federal de Rio Grande do Norte, Brazil, 1983; Univ. du Québec, 1992; Hon. Master of Administration, Univ. Autonoma de Guerrero, Mexico, 1984. Comdr, Assoc. Belgo-Hispanique, 1980; Comdr, Mérite et Dévouement Français, 1980; Officier de la Légion d'Honneur (France), 1988. Duvernay Award, Soc. St-Jean-Baptiste de Trois-Rivières (literature award), 1978; Gold Medal, Univ. Federal da Bahia, Brazil, 1983; Gold Medal of Merit (Sousandrade), Universidade Federal do Maranhâo, Brazil, 1986; Medal, Gloire de l'Escolle, Laval Univ., 1988. Personality of the Year, CKTM/TV, 1988. *Publications:* Nationalisme ou Séparatisme, Nationalisme et Séparatisme, 1961; (with Lucien Gagné) Le Français Parlé au Cours Secondaire, vols I and II, 1962,

vols III and IV, 1963; Textes et Préceptes Littéraires, vol. I, 2nd edn, 1967, vol. II, 1964; (with others) Le Boréal Express, Album no 1, 1965, Album no 2, 1967; De la philosophie comme passion de la liberté, 1984; Going Global, 1988. *Recreations:* reading, skiing, skating. *Address:* 3021 de la Promenade, Ste Foy, Quebec G1W 2J5, Canada. *T:* (418) 6574266. *Club:* Saint-Maurice Hunting and Fishing (Quebec). *Died 9 Oct. 1997.*

BOULTING, Sydney Arthur, (Peter Cotes); author, lecturer; stage, film and television producer and director; *b* Maidenhead, Berks, 19 March 1912; *e s* of Arthur Boulting and Rose Bennett; adopted stage name Peter Cotes; *m* 1st, 1938, Myfanwy Jones (marr. diss.); 2nd, 1948, Joan Miller (*d* 1988). *Educ:* Taplow; Italia Conti and privately. Was for some years an actor; made theatrical debut, Portsmouth Hippodrome, in the arms of Vesta Tilley; formed own independent play-producing co. with Hon. James Smith, 1949; presented Rocket to the Moon, St Martin's Theatre, and subsequently produced, in association with Arts Council of Great Britain, notable seasons in Manchester and at Embassy, Swiss Cottage and Lyric Theatres, Hammersmith; founded: New Lindsey, 1946; New Boltons, 1951. West-End productions included: Pick Up Girl, 1946; The Animal Kingdom, 1947; The Master Builder, 1948; Miss Julie, 1949; Come Back, Little Sheba, 1951; The Father, 1951; The Biggest Thief in Town, 1951; The Mousetrap, 1952; The Man, 1952; Happy Holiday, 1954; Book of the Month, 1955; Hot Summer Night, 1958; The Rope Dancers, 1959; Girl on the Highway, 1960; A Loss of Roses, 1962; The Odd Ones, 1963; What Goes Up. . .!, 1963; So Wise, So Young, 1964; Paint Myself Black, 1965; The Impossible Years, 1966; Staring at the Sun, 1968; Janie Jackson, 1968; The Old Ladies, 1969; Look, No Hands!, 1971; other productions included: A Pin to see the Peepshow, Broadway, 1953; Epitaph for George Dillon, Holland, 1959; Hidden Stranger, Broadway, 1963; films: The Right Person; Two Letters; Jane Clegg; Waterfront; The Young and the Guilty; prod and adapted numerous plays for BBC Television and ITV; Sen. Drama Dir, AR-TV, 1955–58; produced stage plays and films, 1959–60; Supervising Producer of Drama Channel 7, Melbourne, 1961; produced and adapted plays for Anglia TV, 1964; produced first TV series of P. G. Wodehouse short stories, on BBC; wrote George Robey centenary TV Tribute, BBC Omnibus series, 1969; wrote and dir. in One Pair of Eyes series, BBC TV, 1970; wrote, adapted and narrated many productions for radio incl. Back into the Light, The Prime Minister of Mirth, Mervyn Peake, Portrait of an Actor; collaborated 1980–81 on: The Song is Ended, Who Were You With Last Night, Who's Your Lady Friend, The Black Sheep of the Family (BBC); scripted and presented: Old Stagers, 1979–87; This Fabulous Genius (BBC), 1980; Wee Georgie Wood (BBC), 1980. FRSA; Member: Theatrical Managers' Assoc.; Medico-Legal Soc.; Our Society; Guild of Drama Adjudicators. Kt of Mark Twain, 1980. *Publications:* No Star Nonsense, 1949; The Little Fellow, 1951; A Handbook of Amateur Theatre, 1957; George Robey, 1972; The Trial of Elvira Barney, 1976; Circus, 1976; Origin of a Thriller, 1977; JP (The Man Called Mitch), 1978; Misfit Midget, 1979; Portrait of an Actor, 1980; (with Harold Atkins) The Barbirollis: a musical marriage, 1983; Dickie: the story of Dickie Henderson, 1988; Thinking Aloud (autobiog.), 1993; contrib. to The Field, Spectator, Queen, Guardian, etc. *Address:* 7 Hill Lawn Court, Chipping Norton, Oxon OX7 5NF. *Recreations:* book collecting, writing letters, criminology. *Clubs:* Savage, Our Society.

Died 10 Nov. 1998.

BOULTON, Sir (Harold Hugh) Christian, 4th Bt *cr* 1905, of Copped Hall, Totteridge, Herts; *b* 29 Oct. 1918; *s* of Sir (Denis Duncan) Harold (Owen) Boulton, 3rd Bt, and

Louise McGowan (*d* 1978), USA; *S* father, 1968; *m* 1944, Patricia Mary, OBE (who re-assumed by deed poll her maiden name of Maxwell-Scott, 1931; she *d* 1998), *d* ot Maj.-Gen. Sir Walter Joseph Constable Maxwell-Scott, 1st Bt, CB, DSO. *Educ:* Ampleforth College, Yorks. Late Captain, Irish Guards (Supplementary Reserve).

Died 12 July 1996 (ext).

BOULTON, Rev. Canon Peter Henry; Chaplain to the Queen, 1991–95; *b* 12 Dec. 1925; *s* of Harry Boulton and Annie Mary Penty Boulton; *m* 1955, Barbara Ethelinda Davies, SRN, SCM; three *s. Educ:* Lady Lumley's Grammar Sch., Pickering, N Yorks; St Chad's Coll., Univ. of Durham (BA Hons Theology); Ely Theol Coll., Cambs; LLM (Canon Law) Wales, 1996. RNVR, 1943–46. Ordained deacon, 1950, priest, 1951 (Chester). Asst Curate: Coppenhall S Michael, Crewe, 1950–54; S Mark, Mansfield, 1954–55; Vicar: Clipstone Colliery Village, Notts, 1955–60; St John the Baptist, Carlton, Nottingham, 1960–67; Worksop Priory, 1967–87; Hon. Canon of Southwell, 1975–87; Canon Residentiary of Southwell Minster and Diocesan Dir of Educn, 1987–92, Canon Emeritus, 1993. C of E Delegate: ACC, 1972–80; WCC Assembly, Nairobi, 1975. Proctor in Convocation and Mem., Gen. Synod of C of E, 1959–92; Prolocutor of York Convocation and Jt Chm., House of Clergy, Gen. Synod, 1980–90; Member: Howick Commn on Crown Appts, 1962–64; Standing Cttee of Gen. Synod, 1974–90; Churches' Council for Covenanting, 1978–82; Crown Appts Commn, 1982–87 and 1988–92; Legal Adv. Commn of Gen. Synod, 1985–91; Gen. Synod Bd of Educn, 1991–92; Gen. Cttee, Ecclesiastical Law Soc., 1991–. Mem., Notts County Educn Cttee, 1987–92; County Gov., local primary sch., 1993–. *Publications:* articles in learned and ecclesiastical jls. *Recreations:* crosswords, bridge, local history. *Address:* 3 Grasmere Drive, Holmes Chapel, Cheshire CW4 7JT.

Died 17 Nov. 1998.

BOURASSA, (Joseph Adrien Jean) Robert; Leader, Quebec Liberal Party, 1970–77 and 1983–94; Prime Minister of Québec, 1970–76 and 1985–94; Member of Québec National Assembly for St Laurent, 1986–94 (for Mercier, 1966–76 and for Bertrand, 1985); *b* 14 July 1933; *s* of Aubert Bourassa and Adrienne Courville; *m* 1958, Andrée Simard; one *s* one *d. Educ:* Jean-de-Brébeuf Coll.; Univs of Montreal, Oxford and Harvard. Gov.-Gen.'s Medal, Montreal, 1956. MA Oxford, 1959. Admitted Quebec Bar, 1957. Fiscal Adviser to Dept of Nat. Revenue and Prof. in Econs and Public Finance, Ottawa Univ., 1960–63; Sec. and Dir of Research of Bélanger Commn on Taxation, 1963–65; Special Adviser to Fed. Dept of Finance on fiscal and econ. matters, 1965–66; Prof. of Public Finance, Univs of Montreal and Laval, 1966–69; financial critic for Quebec Liberal Party; Minister of Finance, Quebec, May–Nov. 1970; Minister of Inter-govtl Affairs, 1971–72. Lectr, Institut d'Etudes Européennes, Brussels, 1977–78; Prof., Center of Advanced Internat. Studies, Johns Hopkins Univ., 1978; Prof., Univ. de Laval, Univ. de Montréal, 1979; Visiting Professor: INSEAD, Fontainebleau, 1976; Univ. of Southern Calif, 1981; Yale Univ., 1982. Hon. DPhil Univ. of Tel-Aviv, 1987. *Publications:* Bourassa/Québec!, 1970; La Baie James, 1973 (James Bay, 1973); Les années Bourassa: l'intégrale des entretiens Bourassa–St Pierre, 1977; Deux fois la Baie James, 1981; Power from the North, 1985; L'Energie du Nord: la force du Québec, 1985; Le défi technologique, 1985. *Died 2 Oct. 1996.*

BOURKE, Prof. Paul Francis, PhD; Professor of History, Australian National University, since 1985; President, Australian Academy of Social Sciences, 1994–97; *b* 6 July 1938; *s* of William and Mary Bourke; *m* 1960, Helen Prideaux; one *s* two *d. Educ:* Univ. of Melbourne (BA);

Univ. of Wisconsin (PhD). Lectr in History, Univ. of Melbourne, 1965–68; Prof. of American Studies, 1969–85, Pro Vice-Chancellor, 1980–82, Flinders Univ.; Director: Res. Sch. of Social Scis, ANU, 1985–92; Inst. of Advanced Studies, ANU, 1997–98. Vis. Prof., Smith Coll., USA, 1968–69, 1972, 1981; Charles Warren Fellow, Harvard, 1974; British Council Fellow, Sci. Policy Res. Unit, Univ. of Sussex, 1987. Pres., Aust. Historical Assoc., 1992–94. Hon. DLitt: Flinders, 1988; La Trobe, 1996. *Publications:* (with Linda Butler) A Crisis for Australian Science?, 1993; International Links in Australian Higher Education Research, 1994; (with Donald DeBats) Washington County: politics and community in antebellum America, 1995; numerous contribs to learned jls. *Recreations:* music, sport. *Address:* Research School of Social Sciences, Australian National University, Canberra, ACT 0200, Australia. *T:* (6) 2959617; 23 Borrowdale Street, Red Hill, ACT 2603, Australia. *Died 7 June 1999.*

BOURNE, Sir (John) Wilfrid, KCB 1979 (CB 1975); QC 1981; Clerk of the Crown in Chancery, and Permanent Secretary, Lord Chancellor's Office, 1977–82; *b* 27 Jan. 1922; *s* of late Captain Rt Hon. R. C. Bourne, PC, MP, and Lady Hester Bourne, *d* of 4th Earl Cairns; *m* 1958, Elizabeth Juliet, *d* of late G. R. Fox, Trewardreva, Constantine, Cornwall; two *s. Educ:* Eton; New Coll., Oxford (MA). Served War, Rifle Brigade, 1941–45. Called to the Bar, Middle Temple, 1948, Bencher 1977; practised at Bar, 1949–56; Lord Chancellor's Office, 1956–82, Principal Assistant Solicitor, 1970–72, Deputy Sec., 1972–77. *Address:* Povey's Farm, Ramsdell, Tadley, Hants RG26 5SN. *Club:* Leander (Henley-on-Thames).

Died 19 Oct. 1999.

BOURNE-ARTON, Major Anthony Temple, MBE 1944; *b* 1 March 1913; 2nd *s* of W. R. Temple Bourne, Walker Hall, Winston, Co. Durham, and Evelyn Rose, 3rd *d* of Sir Frank Wills, Bristol; assumed surname of Bourne-Arton, 1950; *m* 1938, Margaret Elaine, *er d* of W. Denby Arton, Sleningford Park, Ripon, Yorks; two *s* two *d. Educ:* Clifton. Served Royal Artillery, 1933–48; active service, 1936, Palestine; 1939–45: France, N Africa, Sicily and Italy (despatches, MBE); Malaya, 1947–48. MP (C) Darlington, 1959–64; PPS to the Home Sec., 1962–64. Gen. Commissioner Income Tax, 1952–80; served on Bedale RDC, and N Riding County Agric. Cttee; County Councillor, N Riding of Yorks, 1949–61; CC, W Riding of Yorks, 1967–70; Chm., Yorkshire Regional Land Drainage Cttee, 1973–80. JP N Riding of Yorks, 1950–80. *Recreations:* fishing, shooting. *Address:* The Old Rectory, West Tanfield, Ripon, N Yorks HG4 5JH. *T:* Bedale (01677) 470333. *Died 28 May 1996.*

BOVELL, Hon. Sir (William) Stewart, Kt 1976; JP; Agent-General for Western Australia, in London, 1971–74; *b* 19 Dec. 1906; *s* of A. R. Bovell and Ethel (*née* Williams), Busselton, Western Australia. *Educ:* Busselton, WA. Banking, 1923–40. Served War, RAAF, 1941–45, Flt Lt. MLA: for Sussex, WA, 1947–50; for Vasse, WA, 1950–71. Chief Govt Whip, WA, 1950–53; Opposition Whip, WA, 1953–57; Minister: for Labour, WA, 1961–62; for Lands, Forests and Immigration, WA, 1959–71. Rep., Australian States Gen. Council, at British Commonwealth Parly Assoc., Nairobi, Kenya, and Victoria Falls, S Rhodesia, 1954. Mem. Bd of Governors, Bunbury C of E Cathedral Grammar Sch., 1974 (Vice-Chm.). Hon. Lay Canon, St Boniface C of E Cathedral, Bunbury, WA, 1975. JP 1949, WA. Patron: Polocrosse Assoc. of WA; Geographe Bay Yacht Club. *Recreations:* swimming, tennis, walking. *Address:* Post Box 11, Busselton, WA 6280, Australia.

Died 15 Sept. 1999.

BOWERMAN, David Alexander; retired; *b* 19 April 1903; *s* of Frederick and Millicent Bowerman; *m* 1925, Constance Lilian Hosegood (*d* 1959); four *s* one *d; m*

1962, June Patricia Ruth Day. *Educ:* Queen's Coll., Taunton. Farmer, 1923–36; Wholesale Fruit and Potato Merchant (Director), 1936–60. Chairman, Horticultural Marketing Council, 1960–63. Director, 1963–75: Jamaica Producers Marketing Co. Ltd; JP Fruit Distributors Ltd; Horticultural Exports (GB) Ltd. *Publication:* Poems in time of war, 1991. *Recreations:* sailing, golf, gardens. *Address:* The Spinney, Brenchley, Kent TN12 7AE. *T:* (01892) 722149. *Clubs:* Lamberhurst Golf; Isle of Purbeck Golf. *Died 27 Aug. 1998.*

BOWLES, Rt Rev. Cyril William Johnston; Hon. Assistant Bishop, diocese of Gloucester, since 1987; *b* Scotstoun, Glasgow, 9 May 1916; *s* of William Cullen Allen Bowles, West Ham, and Jeanie Edwards Kilgour, Glasgow; *m* 1965, Florence Joan, *d* of late John Eastaugh, Windlesham. *Educ:* Brentwood Sch.; Emmanuel Coll., Jesus Coll. (Lady Kay Scholar) and Ridley Hall, Cambridge. 2nd cl., Moral Sciences Tripos, Pt I, 1936; 1st cl., Theological Tripos, Pt I, and BA, 1938; 2nd cl., Theological Tripos, Pt II, 1939; MA 1941. Deacon 1939, priest 1940, Chelmsford; Curate of Barking Parish Church, 1939–41; Chaplain of Ridley Hall, Cambridge, 1942–44; Vice-Principal, 1944–51; Principal, 1951–63; Hon. Canon of Ely Cathedral, 1959–63; Archdeacon of Swindon, 1963–69; Bishop of Derby, 1969–87. Mem. of House of Lords, 1973–87. Select Preacher: Cambridge, 1945, 1953, 1958, 1963; Oxford, 1961; Dublin, 1961. Exam. Chaplain to Bishop of Carlisle, 1950–63; to Bishops of Rochester, Ely and Chelmsford, 1951–63; to Bishops of Bradford, 1956–61; to Bishop of Bristol, 1963–69. Hon. Canon, Bristol Cathedral, 1963–69; Surrogate, 1963–69; Commissary to Bishop of the Argentine, 1963–69. Mem., Archbishops' Liturgical Commn, 1955–75. Pres., St John's Coll., Durham, 1970–84 (Hon. Fellow, 1991); Visitor of Ridley Hall, 1979–87. *Publications:* contributor: The Roads Converge, 1963; A Manual for Holy Week, 1967; The Eucharist Today, 1974. *Address:* Rose Lodge, Tewkesbury Road, Stow-on-the-Wold, Cheltenham, Glos GL54 1EN. *T:* (01451) 831965. *Died 14 Sept. 1999.*

BOWMAN, Maj-Gen. John Francis, (Jack), CB 1986; Director of Army Legal Services, 1984–86; Chairman, Principles and Law Panel, British Red Cross, 1988–94; *b* 5 Feb. 1927; *s* of Frank and Gladys Bowman; *m* 1956, Laura Moore; one *s* one *d*. *Educ:* Queen Elizabeth Grammar Sch., Penrith; Hertford Coll., Oxford (MA Hons). Called to the Bar, Gray's Inn, 1955. Served RN, 1943–48. Journalist and barrister, 1951–56; Directorate of Army Legal Services, 1956–86. Dir, Concepts Financial, 1991–. Mem. Council, BRCS, 1988–91 and 1992–94. Life Vice-Pres., Army Boxing Assoc., 1986. *Recreations:* sailing, ski-ing, mountain walking. *Address:* c/o Midland Bank, Newmarket Street, Ulverston, Cumbria LA12 7LH. *Died 26 March 1997.*

BOWMAN, William Powell, CBE 1995 (OBE 1972); Chairman, Covent Garden Market Authority, since 1988; *b* 22 Oct. 1932; *s* of George Edward and Isabel Conyers Bowman; *m* 1956, Patricia Elizabeth McCoskrie; two *s*. *Educ:* Uppingham School. MInstM 1964. Nat. Service, RAF, 1951–53; RAuxAF, 1953–57. Sales Manager: Goodall Backhouse & Co. Ltd, 1953–59; Cheeseboro Ponds Ltd, 1959–61; Marketing Manager, Dorland Advertising Ltd, 1961–63; United Biscuits UK Ltd: Marketing Manager, 1963–66; Man. Dir, Internat. Div., 1966–77; Gp Personnel Dir, 1977–84; Dir, The Extel Group PLC and Chm., Royds Advertising Gp, 1984–86; Chm., Royds McCann Ltd, 1986–87. Chairman: Trident Trust, 1985–94 (Hon. Life Vice Pres., 1994); Forum for Occupational Counselling and Unemployment Services Ltd, 1986–89; Van der Hass BV, 1987–89; Gibbson Blackthorn, 1989; Director: Harvey Bergenroth & Partners Ltd, 1987–89; Right Associates, 1989. Chairman: British

Food Export Council, 1971–73; Cake and Biscuit Alliance, 1975–77; London Enterprise Agency, 1983–84; Industry and Parliament Trust, 1983–84; Flowers and Plants Assoc., 1989–; St Peter's Res. Trust, 1990–92; Dir, Nat. Assoc. of Fresh Produce, 1989–93; Mem., Develt Trust, Zool Soc. of London, 1987–91. UK Pres., European Catering Assoc., 1995–97. Vice Pres., Weston Spirit, 1995–. Freeman: City of London, 1989; Fruiterers' Co., 1990; Mem., Guild of Freemen, 1989–. FIPM 1980; FIMgt (FBIM 1984); FInstD 1984; FZS 1986; Stamford Raffles Fellow, London Zool Soc., 1993. *Recreations:* gardening, music. *Address:* The Coach House, Shardeloes, Old Amersham, Bucks HP7 0RL. *T:* (01494) 724187. *Clubs:* Royal Air Force, Mosimann's. *Died 11 May 1998.*

BOWMAR, Sir (Charles) Erskine, Kt 1984; QSO 1977; JP; *b* 6 May 1913; *s* of Erskine Bowmar and Agnes Julia (*née* Fletcher); *m* 1938, Kathleen Muriel Isobel McLeod (*d* 1993); one *s* four *d* (and one *s* decd). *Educ:* Gore Public Sch.; Gore High Sch.; Southland Tech. Coll. Member: West Gore Sch. Cttee, 1952; Bd of Governors, Gore High Sch., 1961; Exec., NZ Counties Assoc. (former Vice-Pres.; PP, Otago and Southland Counties Assoc.); Nat. Roads Board; sometime Chairman: Southland County Council (Mem., 1953–86); Southland United Council; Mem., Gore Agricl and Pastoral Assoc., 1940, Life Mem., 1964. Mem., Southland Harbour, 1957–65; Vice-Pres., Southland Progress League; former Mem., NZ Territorial Local Govt Council. JP 1964. *Recreations:* mountaineering (Mem., NZ Alpine Club, 1933–), trout fishing, golf, gardening. *Address:* Waikaia Plains Station, RD6, Gore, Southland, New Zealand. *T:* (3) 2016201. *Died 15 Aug. 1996.*

BOWRING, Maj.-Gen. John Humphrey Stephen, CB 1968; OBE 1958; MC 1941; FICE; *b* 13 Feb. 1913; *s* of late Major Francis Stephen Bowring and Mrs Maurice Stonor; *m* 1956, Iona Margaret (*née* Murray); two *s* two *d*. *Educ:* Downside; RMA Woolwich; Trinity Coll., Cambridge. MA 1936. Commissioned, 1933; Palestine, 1936; India, 1937–40; Middle East, 1940–42; India and Burma, 1942–46; British Military Mission to Greece, 1947–50; UK, 1951–55; CRE, 17 Gurkha Div., Malaya, 1955–58; Col GS, War Office, 1958–61; Brig., Chief Engineer, Far East, 1961–64; Brig. GS, Ministry of Defence, 1964–65; Engineer-in-Chief, 1965–68. Col, The Gurkha Engineers, 1966–71; Col Comdt, RE, 1968–73. Dir, Consolidated Gold Fields, 1969–82. High Sheriff, Wiltshire, 1984. Kt SMO Malta, 1986. *Address:* The Manor, Coln St Aldwyns, Cirencester, Glos GL7 5AG. *T:* (01285) 750492. *Clubs:* Army and Navy, Royal Ocean Racing. *Died 14 Feb. 1998.*

BOX, Betty Evelyn, (Mrs P. E. Rogers), OBE 1958; film producer; *b* 25 Sept. 1915; *m* 1949, Peter Edward Rogers; no *c*. *Educ:* home. Director: Welbeck Film Distributors Ltd, 1958–; Ulster Television, 1955–85. *Films include:* Dear Murderer; When the Bough Breaks; Miranda; Blind Goddess; Huggett Family series; It's Not Cricket; Marry Me; Don't Ever Leave Me; So Long at the Fair; Appointment with Venus; Venetian Bird; A Day to Remember; The Clouded Yellow; Doctor in the House; Mad About Men; Doctor at Sea; The Iron Petticoat; Checkpoint; Doctor at Large; Campbell's Kingdom; A Tale of Two Cities; The Wind Cannot Read; The 39 Steps; Upstairs and Downstairs; Conspiracy of Hearts; Doctor in Love; No Love for Johnnie; No, My Darling Daughter; A Pair of Briefs; The Wild and the Willing; Doctor in Distress; Hot Enough for June; The High Bright Sun; Doctor in Clover; Deadlier than the Male; Nobody Runs Forever; Some Girls Do; Doctor in Trouble; Percy; The Love Ban; Percy's Progress. *Address:* Pinewood Studios, Iver, Bucks SL0 0NH. *Died 15 Jan. 1999.*

BOXER, Air Vice-Marshal Sir Alan (Hunter Cachemaille), KCVO 1970; CB 1968; DSO 1944; DFC 1943; *b* 1 Dec. 1916; *s* of late Dr E. A. Boxer, CMG, Hastings, Hawkes Bay, NZ; *m* 1941, Pamela Sword; two *s* one *d. Educ:* Nelson Coll., New Zealand. Commissioned in RAF, 1939; Trng Comd until 1942; flying and staff appts, Bomber Comd, 1942–45; RAF Staff Coll., 1945; Jt Staff, Cabinet Offices, 1946–47; Staff Coll., Camberley, 1948; Strategic Air Comd, USAF and Korea, 1949–51; Central Fighter Estabt, 1952–53; Mem. Directing Staff, RAF Staff Coll., 1954–56; CO No 7 Sqdn, RAF, 1957; Group Capt. and CO, RAF Wittering, 1958–59; Plans, HQ Bomber Comd, 1960–61; Air Cdre, idc, 1962; Senior Air Staff Officer: HQ No 1 Gp, RAF, 1963–65; HQ Bomber Comd, 1965–67; Defence Services Sec., MoD, 1967–70. Virtuti Militari (Polish); Bronze Star (US); Air Medal (US). *Died 26 April 1998.*

BOXER, Prof. Charles Ralph, FBA 1957; Emeritus Professor of Portuguese, University of London, since 1968; *b* 8 March 1904; *s* of Col Hugh Boxer and Jane Boxer (*née* Patterson); *m* 1st, Ursula Churchill-Dawes (marr. diss. 1937); 2nd, 1945, Emily Hahn (*d* 1997); two *d. Educ:* Wellington Coll.; Royal Military Coll., Sandhurst. Commissioned Lincs Regt, 1923; served War of 1939–45 (wounded, POW in Japanese hands, 1941–45); retired with rank of Major, 1947. Camoens Prof. of Portuguese, London Univ., 1947–51; Prof. of the History of the Far East, London Univ., 1951–53; resigned latter post and re-apptd Camoens Prof., 1953–67; FKC 1967; Prof. of History of Expansion of Europe Overseas, Yale Univ., 1969–72, then Emer. Prof. of History. Visiting Research Prof., Indiana Univ., 1967–79. Hon. Fellow, SOAS, 1974. A Trustee of National Maritime Museum, 1961–68. For. Mem., Royal Netherlands Acad. of Scis, 1976. Dr *hc* Universities of Utrecht (1950), Lisbon (1952), Bahia (1959), Liverpool (1966), Hong Kong (1971), Peradeniya (1980). Gold Medal, Instituto Histórico e Geográfico Brasileiro, 1986. Order of Santiago da Espada (Portugal), Grand Cross of the Order of the Infante Dom Henrique (Portugal); Kt Order of St Gregory the Great, 1969. *Publications:* The Commentaries of Ruy Freyre de Andrade, 1929; The Journal of M. H. Tromp, *Anno* 1639, 1930; Jan Compagnie in Japan, 1600–1817, 1936, 2nd edn 1950; Fidalgos in the Far East, 1550–1770, 1948; The Christian Century in Japan, 1549–1640, 1951, 2nd edn 1967; Salvador de Sá and the Struggle for Brazil and Angola, 1952; South China in the 16th Century, 1953; The Dutch in Brazil, 1624–1654, 1957; The Tragic History of the Sea, 1589–1622, 1959; The Great Ship from Amacon, 1959; Fort Jesus and the Portuguese in Mombasa, 1960; The Golden Age of Brazil, 1695–1750, 1962; Race Relations in the Portuguese Colonial Empire, 1415–1825, 1963; The Dutch Seaborne Empire, 1600–1800, 1965; Portuguese Society in the Tropics, 1966; Further Selections from the Tragic History of the Sea, 1969; The Portuguese Seaborne Empire, 1415–1825, 1969; Anglo-Dutch Wars of the 17th Century, 1974; Mary and Misogyny, 1975; João de Barros: Portuguese humanist and historian of Asia, 1981; From Lisbon to Goa 1500–1750, 1984; Portuguese Conquest and Commerce in Southern Asia 1500–1750, 1985; Portuguese Merchants and Missionaries in Feudal Japan 1543–1640, 1986; Dutch Merchants and Mariners in Asia 1602–1795, 1988; numerous articles in learned periodicals. *Address:* c/o Western House, 14 Rickfords Hill, Aylesbury, Bucks HP20 2RX. *Died 27 April 2000.*

BOYCOTT, Prof. Brian Blundell, FRS 1971; Visiting Professor, Institute of Ophthalmology, University College London, since 1997; Hon. Senior Research Fellow, Anatomy Department, Guy's Hospital, since 1990; Director, Medical Research Council Cell Biophysics Unit, 1980–89; Emeritus Professor of Biology, London University, 1990; *b* 10 Dec. 1924; *s* of Percy Blundell Boycott and Doris Eyton Lewis; *m* 1950, Marjorie Mabel Burchell; one *s* (and one *s* decd). *Educ:* Royal Masonic Sch. Technician, Nat. Inst. Medical Research, and undergraduate (BSc), Birkbeck Coll., London, 1942–46; University College London: Asst Lectr, Zoology, 1946–47; Hon. Res. Asst, Anatomy, 1947–52; Lectr, Zoology, 1952–62; Reader in Zoology, Univ. of London, 1962, Prof. of Zoology, 1968–70, Prof. of Biology by title, 1971–89. Vis. Lectr, Harvard Univ., 1963. Dep. Chm., Neuroscis and Mental Health Bd, MRC, 1989–91. Member: Adv. Council, British Library Board, 1976–80; Council, 1975–87, Acad. Consultative Cttee, 1989–93, Open Univ.; Council, Royal Soc., 1976–78; Univ. of London Cttee on Academic Organization, 1980–82; Comr, 1851 Exhibition, 1974–84. FKC 1990. DUniv Open, 1988. Scientific Medal, Zoological Soc. of London, 1965; Proctor Medal, Amer. Assoc. for Res. in Vision and Ophthalmology, 1999. *Publications:* various articles in learned jls on structure and function of nervous systems. *Recreations:* nothing of special notability. *Address:* c/o Department of Visual Science, Institute of Ophthalmology, 11–43 Bath Street, EC1V 9EL. *T:* (020) 7608 6879, *Fax:* (020) 7608 6850; *e-mail:* b.boycott@ucl.ac.uk. *Died 22 April 2000.*

BOYD, Arthur Merric Bloomfield, AC 1992 (AO 1979); OBE 1970; painter; *b* Melbourne, 24 July 1920; *s* of William Merric Boyd and Doris Lucy Eleanor Gough; *m* 1945, Yvonne Hartland Lennie; one *s* two *d. Educ:* State Sch., Murrumbeena, Vic, Australia. Was taught painting and sculpture by parents and grandfather, Arthur Merric Boyd. Served in Australian Army, 1940–43. Exhibited first in Australia, 1937; lived and exhibited in Europe and Australia, 1959–; first one-man exhibn painting, London, 1960; retrospective exhibn, Whitechapel Gall., 1962. Designed for ballet at Edinburgh Festival and Sadler's Wells Theatre, 1961, and at Covent Garden Royal Opera House, 1963; tapestry 30′×60′ designed for new Parliament House, Canberra, installed 1988. *Publications:* Etchings and Lithographs, 1971; (with T. S. R. Boase) Nebuchadnezzar, 1972, (illus.) Jonah (poems), by Peter Porter, 1973; Arthur Boyd Drawings, 1974; (illus.) The Lady and the Unicorn (poems), by Peter Porter, 1975; (illus.) Mars, by Peter Porter, 1988; *relevant publications:* Arthur Boyd, by Franz Philipp, 1967; Arthur Boyd Drawings, by Christopher Tadgell, 1973; Artist and River, by Sandra McGrath, 1983; Arthur Boyd—Seven Persistent Images, by Grazia Gunn, 1985; The Art of Arthur Boyd, by Ursula Hoff, 1986. *Died 24 April 1999.*

BOYD, James Fleming, CB 1980; Member, Civil Service Appeal Board, 1984–90; *b* 28 April 1920; *s* of late Walter and Mary Boyd; *m* 1949, Daphne Steer, Hendon; one *s* one *d. Educ:* Whitehill Sch., Glasgow. Tax Officer, Inland Revenue, 1937; served with HM Forces, RAF, 1940–46; Inspector of Taxes, 1950; Principal Inspector, 1964; Senior Principal Inspector, 1970; Dep. Chief Inspector of Taxes, 1973; Dir of Operations, Inland Revenue, 1975–77, Dir Gen. (Management), 1978–81. Financial Advr, B. & C. E. Holiday Management Scheme, 1981–86. *Recreations:* history, gardening. *Address:* 2A The Avenue, Potters Bar, Herts EN6 1EB. *Died 12 April 2000.*

BOYD, Dr (John) Morton, CBE 1987; FRSE; ecologist; Consultant: Scottish Hydro-Electric plc, since 1991 (North of Scotland Hydro-Electric Board, 1985–91); National Trust for Scotland, since 1985; Director, Scotland, Nature Conservancy Council, 1971–85; *b* Darvel, Ayrshire, 31 Jan. 1925; *s* of Thomas Pollock Boyd and Jeanie Reid Morton; *m* 1954, Winifred Isobel Rome; four *s. Educ:* Kilmarnock Acad.; Glasgow Univ. (BSc, PhD, DSc, DLitt). FRSE 1968. Served War, 1943–47: Flt Lieut RAF. Nature Conservancy Council: Reg. Officer, 1957–68; Asst

Dir, 1969–70. Consultant, Mirror Publishing, 1989. Nuffield Trav. Fellow, ME and E Africa, 1964–65; Leader, British Jordan Expedn, 1966; Mem., Royal Soc. Aldabra Expedn, 1967. Member: Council, Royal Zool Soc. of Scotland, 1963–69, 1980–85, 1986–93, 1994– (Mem., Adv. Cttee on Highland Wildlife Park, 1994–); Council, Azraq Internat. Biol Stn, Jordan, 1967–69; Council, National Trust for Scotland, 1971–85; Seals Adv. Cttee, NERC, 1973–79; BBC Scottish Agric. Adv. Cttee, 1973–76; Exec. Bd, Internat. Waterfowl Res. Bureau, 1976–78; Council, Royal Soc. of Edinburgh, 1978–81; Consultative Panel on Conservation of the Line and Phoenix Islands (Central Pacific), 1981–86. Internat. Union for Conservation of Nature and Natural Resources: British Rep., Kinshasa, 1975, Geneva, 1977, Ashkhabad, 1978, Christchurch, 1981, and Madrid, 1985; Mem. Commn on Ecology, 1976–92. Co-Chm., Area VI Anglo-Soviet Environmental Protection Commn, 1977–85; Chm., UK Internat. Conservation Cttee, 1980; Member: Cttee, Centre for Human Ecology, Edinburgh Univ., 1985–95; Panel on Scottish Popular Mountain Areas, CCS, 1989; Adv. Cttee on SSSIs, SNH, 1992–95; Vice-President: Scottish Conservation Projects Trust, 1985–; Scottish Wildlife Trust, 1995– (Mem., Council, 1985–91). Patron: Dynamic Earth, 1993–; Woodland Trust, 1995–; Dunbar John Muir Assoc., 1997–. Hon. Consultant, Forestry Commn, 1992– (Consultant, 1985–92). Lectures: Keith Entwistle Meml, Cambridge, 1968; British Council, Amman, Nicosia and Ankara, 1972, Jakarta, 1982, Delhi and Kuala Lumpur, 1983; Meml in Agricl Zool., W of Scotland Agricl Coll., 1976; Sir William Weipers Meml, Glasgow Univ. Vet. Sch., 1980; Nat. Trust for Scotland Jubilee, 1981; East African Tours, Swan (Hellenic) Ltd, 1972–94; Serenissima Travel Ltd, 1990–94; Noble Caledonia Ltd, 1991–. Gen. Editor, Island Biology Series, Edinburgh Univ. Press, 1985–92. FRSA 1985; Hon. FRZSScot (FRZSScot 1985); Hon. FRSGS (FRSGS 1987); CBiol 1987, FIBiol 1987. Neill Prize, Royal Soc. of Edinburgh, 1983. Church of Scotland Elder, 1959– (Rep., WCC Convocation on Justice, Peace and Integrity of Creation, Seoul, 1990). *Publications:* (with K. Williamson) St Kilda Summer, 1960; (with K. Williamson) Mosaic of Islands, 1963; (with F. F. Darling) The Highlands and Islands, 1964; Travels in the Middle East and East Africa, 1966; (with P. A. Jewell and C. Milner) Island Survivors, 1974; (ed) The Natural Environment of the Outer Hebrides, 1979; (ed with D. R. Bowes) The Natural Environment of the Inner Hebrides, 1983; Fraser Darling's Islands, 1986; (with I. L. Boyd) The Hebrides: a natural history, 1990; Fraser Darling in Africa, 1992; (trilogy) The Hebrides: a habitable land?, The Hebrides: a natural tapestry, The Hebrides: a mosaic of islands, 1996; scientific papers on nature conservation and animal ecology. *Recreations:* travel, painting, photography. *Address:* 57 Hailes Gardens, Edinburgh EH13 0JH. *T:* and *Fax:* (0131) 441 3220; Balephuil, Tiree, Argyll PA77 6UE. *T:* (01879) 220521. *Club:* New (Edinburgh).
Died 25 Aug. 1998.

BOYD, Leslie Balfour, CBE 1977; Courts Administrator, Central Criminal Court, 1972–77; *b* 25 Nov. 1914; *e s* of late Henry Leslie Boyd (Mem. of Lloyd's), Crowborough, Sussex, and Beatrix Boyd, *d* of Henry Chapman (for many years British Consul at Dieppe); *m* 1936, Wendy Marie (*d* 1997), *d* of George and Nancy Blake, Oswestry, Salop; one *s* one *d. Educ:* Evelyn's; Royal Naval College, Dartmouth. Invalided out of Royal Navy, 1931. Called to the Bar, Gray's Inn, 1939; joined staff of Central Criminal Court, 1941; Dep. Clerk of Court, 1948; Clerk of the Court, 1955–71; Dep. Clerk of Peace, 1949–55, Clerk of the Peace, 1955–71, City of London and Town and Borough of Southwark. Master, Worshipful Company of Gold and Silver Wyre Drawers, 1969. *Publications:*

contributor to Criminal Law and Juries titles, 3rd edn, Juries title, 4th edn, of Halsbury's Laws of England. *Recreation:* reading. *Address:* c/o B. Shephard, 7 Leigh Road, Bristol BS8 2DA.   *Died 18 Dec. 1998.*

BOYD, Morton; *see* Boyd, J. M.

BOYD-CARPENTER, Baron *cr* 1972 (Life Peer), of Crux Easton in the County of Southampton; **John Archibald Boyd-Carpenter;** PC 1954; *b* 2 June 1908; *s* of late Sir Archibald Boyd-Carpenter, MP and A. Dugdale, Harrowgate; *m* 1937, Margaret, *e d* of Lieut-Col G. L. Hall, OBE; one *s* two *d. Educ:* Stowe; Balliol Coll., Oxford. Pres. Oxford Union, 1930; BA (History, 1930); Diploma in Economics, 1931; toured USA with Oxford Union Debating Team, 1931. Harmsworth Law Scholar, Middle Temple, 1933; Council of Legal Education's Prize for Constitutional Law, 1934; called to Bar, Middle Temple, 1934, and practised in London and SE Circuit. Joined Scots Guards, 1940; held various staff appointments and served with AMG in Italy, retired with rank of Major. Contested (MR) Limehouse for LCC, 1934. MP (C) for Kingston-upon-Thames, 1945–72; Financial Sec., to the Treasury, 1951–54; Minister of Transport and Civil Aviation, 1954–Dec. 1955; Minister of Pensions and National Insurance, Dec. 1955–July 1962; Chief Sec. to the Treasury and Paymaster-Gen., 1962–64; Opposition Front Bench Spokesman on Housing, Local Government and Land, 1964–66; Chm., Public Accounts Cttee, 1964–70. Chairman: Greater London Area Local Govt Cttee, Conservative Party, 1968; London Members Cttee, 1966–72; Pres. Wessex Area, Nat. Union of Conservative and Unionist Assocs, 1977–80. Chairman: CAA, 1972–77; Rugby Portland Cement, 1976–84 (Dir, 1970–76); Orion Insurance Co., 1969–72; CLRP Investment Trust, 1970–72; Dir, TR Far East Income (formerly Australia Investment) Trust, 1977–, and other cos; Mem. Council, Trust House Forte Ltd, 1977. Governor, Stowe School; Chairman: Carlton Club, 1979–86; Assoc. of Cons. Peers, 1985–90 (Pres., 1991–); Mail Users' Assoc., 1986–90; Sort Out Sunday Cttee, 1986. High Steward, Royal Borough of Kingston-upon-Thames, 1973. DL Greater London, 1973–83. *Publications:* Way of Life, 1980; newspaper articles. *Recreations:* tennis, swimming. *Address:* 12 Eaton Terrace, SW1W 8EZ. *T:* (0171) 730 7765; Crux Easton House, Crux Easton, near Newbury, Berks. *T:* (01635) 253037. *Club:* Carlton.
Died 11 July 1998.

BOYLE, Archibald Cabbourn, MD; FRCP; Hon. Consultant Rheumatologist, King Edward VII Hospital for Officers, 1980–83; Hon. Consultant Physician, King Edward VII Hospital, Midhurst, 1984–87; Director, Department of Rheumatology, Middlesex Hospital, 1954–83; Hon. Clinical Adviser, Department of Rheumatological Research, Middlesex Hospital Medical School; *b* 14 March 1918; *s* of late Arthur Hislop Boyle and of Flora Ellen Boyle; *m* 1st, Patricia Evelyn Tallack (*d* 1944); one *d*; 2nd, Dorothy Evelyn (marr. diss. 1982), widow of Lieut G. B. Jones; one *s*; 3rd, 1983, June Rosemary Gautrey (*née* Pickett). *Educ:* Dulwich Coll.; St Bartholomew's Hospital. DPhysMed 1947; MD 1949; FRCP 1959. House Physician, St Bartholomew's Hosp., 1941–42. Served War of 1939–45 in Far East, and later as Command Specialist in Physical Medicine. Registrar and Sen. Asst, 1946–49, and Asst Physician, 1949–54, Middx Hosp.; Consultant in Physical Medicine, Bromley Gp of Hosps, 1950–54; Physician, Arthur Stanley Inst. for Rheumatic Diseases, 1950–65. Member: Bd of Governors, Middx Hosp.; Bd of Governors, Charterhouse Rheumatism Clinic; Bd of Studies in Medicine, Univ. of London; Council, British Assoc. for Rheumatology and Rehabilitation (Pres., 1973–74); British League against Rheumatism (Vice-Pres., 1972–77; Pres., 1977–81);

Council, Section of Physical Medicine, RSM, 1950 (Pres., 1956–58; Vice-Pres., 1970–); Heberden Soc.; Cttee on Rheumatology and Rehabilitation, RCP. Ernest Fletcher Meml Lectr, RSM, 1971. Formerly: Examnr in Physical Medicine, RCP; Examnr to Chartered Soc. of Physiotherapy; Editor, Annals of Physical Medicine, 1956–63; Sec., Internat. Fedn of Physical Medicine, 1960–64; Chm., Physical Medicine Gp, BMA, 1956–58; Pres., London Br., Chartered Soc. of Physiotherapy. Mem. Council, British Assoc. of Physical Medicine and Rheumatology, 1949–72 (Vice-Pres., 1965–68; Pres., 1970–72); fomer Member: Cttee on Chronic Rheumatic Diseases, RCP; Regional Scientific, and Educn, Sub-Cttees, Arthritis and Rheumatism Council; Physiotherapists Bd, Council for Professions Supplementary to Medicine; Central Consultants and Specialists Cttee, BMA; Med. Adv. Cttee, British Rheumatism and Arthritis Assoc. *Publications:* A Colour Atlas of Rheumatology, 1974; contribs to medical jls, mainly on rheumatic disease. *Recreation:* gardening. *Address:* Iping Barn, Iping, near Midhurst, West Sussex GU29 0PE. *T:* (01730) 816467.

Died 17 June 1998.

BOYNE, Sir Henry Brian, (Sir Harry), Kt 1976; CBE 1969; Political Correspondent, The Daily Telegraph, London, 1956–76; *b* 29 July 1910; 2nd *s* of late Lockhart Alexander Boyne, journalist, Inverness, and Elizabeth Jane Mactavish; *m* 1935, Margaret Little Templeton, Dundee; one *d. Educ:* Inverness High Sch.; Royal Academy, Inverness. Reporter: Inverness Courier, 1927; Dundee Courier and Advertiser, 1929; on active service, War of 1939–45, retiring with rank of Major, The Black Watch (RHR); Staff Correspondent, Glasgow Herald, at Dundee, 1945, and Edinburgh, 1949; Political Correspondent, Glasgow Herald, 1950. Dir of Communications, Conservative Central Office, 1980–82. Chairman: Parly Lobby Journalists, 1958–59 (Hon. Sec., 1968–71); Parly Press Gallery, 1961–62. Political Writer of Year, 1972. Mem., Police Complaints Bd, 1977–80; Chm., Bd of Visitors, HM Prison, Pentonville, 1980. Mem. Council, Savers' Union, 1982–86. *Publications:* The Houses of Parliament, 1981; Scotland Rediscovered, 1986. *Recreations:* reading, walking, watching cricket. *Address:* 122 Harefield Road, Uxbridge UB8 1PN. *T:* (01895) 255211. *Died 18 Sept. 1997.*

BOYS-SMITH, Captain Humphry Gilbert, DSO 1940; DSC 1943; RD; Royal Naval Reserve, retired; *b* 20 Dec. 1904; *s* of late Rev. Edward Percy Boys-Smith, MA, Rural Dean of Lyndhurst, Hants, and Charlotte Cecilia, *d* of late Thomas Backhouse Sandwith, CB, HM Consular Service; *m* 1935, Marjorie Helen (*d* 1981), *d* of Capt. Matthew John Miles Vicars-Miles, JP; no *c. Educ:* Pangbourne Nautical Coll. Joined Royal Naval Reserve, 1921; Merchant Navy, 1922–35; Extra Master's Certificate, 1930; HM Colonial Service, 1935–40 (Palestine) and 1946–50 (Western Pacific High Commission as Marine Supt); served War of 1939–45 (DSO and Bar, DSC, despatches and American despatches); Addnl Mem. RNR Advisory Cttee, 1949–51; War Course, Royal Naval Coll., Greenwich, 1950–51; placed on Retired List of RNR, 1952. Courtaulds Ltd, Central Staff Dept, 1951–68. Younger Brother of Trinity House, 1944; Mem. of Hon. Company of Master Mariners, 1946; Associate, Instn Naval Architects, 1948. *Address:* Dibben's, Semley, Shaftesbury, Dorset SP7 9BW. *T:* (01747) 830358.

Died 24 June 1999.

BOZZOLI, Guerino Renzo, DSc(Eng); Chairman, New Era (non-racial) Schools Trust, 1981–91; Vice-Chancellor and Principal, University of the Witwatersrand, Johannesburg, 1969–77; *b* Pretoria, 24 April 1911; *s* of late B. Bozzoli; *m* 1938, Cora Collins, *d* of late L. N. B.

Collins; one *s* three *d. Educ:* Sunnyside Sch. and Boys' High Sch., Pretoria; Witwatersrand Univ. BSc(Eng) 1933, DSc(Eng) 1948; PrEng, Major, SA Corps of Signals, 1940–45 (commendation 1944). Asst Engr, African Broadcasting Co., 1934–36; Jun. Lectr, Dept of Electrical Engrg, Witwatersrand Univ., Lectr, 1939, Sen. Lectr, 1942; apptd Prof. and Head of Dept of Electrical Engineering, 1948; Dean, Univ. Residence, Cottesloe, 1948–56; Dean, Faculty of Engrg, 1954–57 and 1962–65; Senate Mem., Council of the Univ., 1957–68; Deputy Vice-Chancellor, 1965–68. Chm. Council, Mangosuthu Technikon, Kwa Zulu, 1978–85. Member: Straszacker Commn of Enquiry into Univ. Educn of Engineers, 1957–68; de Vries Commn of Enquiry into SA Univs, 1968–75; Nat. Educn Council, 1975. President: AS&TS of SA, 1969–70; SA Assoc. for Advancement of Science, 1972. Hon. FSAIEE (Pres., 1955); Hon. FRSSAf 1976. Hon. LLD: Univ. of Cape Town, 1977; Univ. of Witwatersrand, 1978. *Publications:* Hear! Hear!: practical acoustics for amateur actors and producers, 1992; A Vice–Chancellor Remembers (memoirs), 1995; Forging Ahead: South Africa's Pioneering Engineers, 1997; numerous articles and papers on engineering education. *Recreations:* swimming, woodwork, electronics. *Address:* 121 Dundalk Avenue, Parkview, Johannesburg, 2193, South Africa. *T:* (11) 6461015. *Clubs:* 1926, Scientific and Technical (Johannesburg).

Died 27 Dec. 1998.

BRADBURY, Sir Malcolm (Stanley), Kt 2000; CBE 1991; FRSL; Emeritus Professor, University of East Anglia, since 1995 (Professor of American Studies, 1970–94; Professorial Fellow, 1994–95); *b* 7 Sept. 1932; *s* of Arthur Bradbury and Doris Ethel (*née* Marshall); *m* 1959, Elizabeth Salt; two *s. Educ:* University Coll. of Leicester (BA); Queen Mary Coll., Univ. of London (MA; Hon. Fellow, 1984); Univ. of Manchester (PhD). Staff Tutor in Literature and Drama, Dept of Adult Education, Univ. of Hull, 1959–61; Lectr in English Language and Literature, Dept of English, Univ. of Birmingham, 1961–65; Lectr (later Sen. Lectr and Reader) in English and American Literature, Sch. of English and American Studies, Univ. of East Anglia, 1965–70. Visiting Professor: Univ. of Zürich, 1972; Washington Univ., St Louis, 1982; Univ. of Queensland, 1983; Sen. Vis. Res. Fellow, St John's Coll., Oxford, 1994. Chairman of Judges: Booker McConnell Prize for Fiction, 1981; Whitbread Prize, 1997. Hon. DLitt: Leicester, 1986; Birmingham, 1989; Hull, 1994; Nottingham, 1996. Editor: Arnold Stratford-upon-Avon Studies series; Methuen Contemporary Writers series. Adapted for television: Tom Sharpe, Blott on the Landscape, 1985; Tom Sharpe, Porterhouse Blue, 1987 (Internat. Emmy Award); Alison Lurie, Imaginary Friends, 1987; Kingsley Amis, The Green Man, 1990; Stella Gibbons, Cold Comfort Farm, 1995; Reginald Hill, An Autumn Shroud, 1996; Reginald Hill, Ruling Passion and Killing Kindness, 1997; Mark Tavener, In the Red, 1998; television serials: Anything More Would Be Greedy, 1989; The Gravy Train, 1990; The Gravy Train Goes East, 1991 (Monte Carlo Award); television screenplays: A Touch of Frost (4 episodes), 1997–98; Kavanagh QC, 1998 (one episode); Inspector Morse, 1998 (one episode); Dalziel and Pascoe, 2000 (one episode); various television plays; stage play: Inside Trading, Norwich Playhouse, 1996. *Publications: non-fiction:* Evelyn Waugh, 1962; E. M. Forster: a collection of critical essays (ed), 1965; What is a Novel?, 1969; A Passage to India: a casebook, 1970; (ed with E. Mottram) Penguin Companion to Literature, vol. 3 USA and Latin America, 1971; The Social Context of Modern English Literature, 1972; Possibilities: essays on the state of the novel, 1973; (with J. W. McFarlane) Modernism, 1976; (ed) The Novel Today, 1977; (ed with H. Temperley) An Introduction to American Studies,

1981; Saul Bellow, 1982; All Dressed Up And Nowhere To Go (humour), 1982; The Modern American Novel, 1983; Why Come to Slaka? (humour), 1986; No, Not Bloomsbury (essays), 1987; (ed) Penguin Book of Modern British Short Stories, 1987; Mensonge (humour), 1987; The Modern World: ten great writers, 1987; Unsent Letters (humour), 1988; (with R. Ruland) From Puritanism to Postmodernism: a history of American literature, 1991; (ed with Judy Cooke) New Writing, 1992; (ed with Andrew Motion) New Writing 2, 1993; The Modern British Novel, 1993; Present Laughter: an anthology of modern comic fiction, 1994; Dangerous Pilgrimages: transatlantic mythologies and the novel, 1995; (ed) Class Work (anthology of UEA fiction), 1995; (ed) The Atlas of Literature, 1996; *fiction:* Eating People is Wrong, 1959; Stepping Westward, 1965; The History Man, 1975; Who Do You Think You Are? (short stories), 1976; The After Dinner Game (television plays), 1982; Rates of Exchange, 1982 (shortlisted, Booker Prize); Cuts: a very short novel, 1987; Dr Criminale, 1992; Inside Trading (play), 1997; To the Hermitage, 2000. *Recreations:* none. *Address:* c/o Curtis Brown, 4th Floor, Haymarket House, 28–29 Haymarket, SW1Y 4SP. *T:* (020) 7396 6600.
Died 27 Nov. 2000.

BRADBY, Edward Lawrence; Principal, St Paul's College, Cheltenham, 1949–72; *b* 15 March 1907; *y s* of late H. C. Bradby, Ringshall End, near Berkhamsted, Herts; *m* 1939, Bertha Woodall, *y d* of late Henry Woodall, Yotes Court, Mereworth, Maidstone; three *s* one *d. Educ:* Rugby Sch.; New College, Oxford (MA). Asst Master, Merchant Taylors' Sch., 1930–34; International Student Service, 1934–39: Secretary to Cttee for England and Wales, 1934–36; Asst General Secretary, Geneva, 1936–37; General Secretary, Geneva, 1937–39; Principal, Royal Coll., Colombo, Ceylon, 1939–46; Principal, Eastbourne Emergency Training Coll., 1946–49. Hon. MEd Bristol, 1972. *Publications:* (ed) The University Outside Europe (a collection of essays on university institutions in 14 countries), 1939; Seend, a Wiltshire Village Past and Present, 1981; The Book of Devizes, 1985; Seend Heritage, 1985. *Address:* 13 Hansford Square, Combe Down, Bath, Avon BA2 5LH. *T:* Bath (01225) 834092. *Club:* Commonwealth Trust. *Died 20 Aug. 1996.*

BRADFORD, Rt Hon. Roy Hamilton; PC (NI) 1969; Member (U) for East Belfast, Northern Ireland Assembly, 1973–75; Minister for the Environment, Northern Ireland Executive, 1974; *b* 7 July 1921; *s* of Joseph Hamilton Bradford, Rockcorry, Co. Monaghan, and Isabel Mary (*née* McNamee), Donemana, Co. Tyrone; *m* 1946, Hazel Elizabeth (*d* 1994), *d* of Capt. W. Lindsay, Belfast; two *s. Educ:* Royal Belfast Academical Institution; Trinity Coll., Dublin. Foundation Schol. 1940; First Class Hons (BA) German and French (with Gold Medal) 1942 (TCD). Army Intelligence, 1943–47 (France, Belgium, Germany). BBC and ITV producer and writer, 1950–. Dir, Geoffrey Sharp Ltd, 1962–. MP (U) for Victoria, Parlt of NI, 1965–73; Asst Whip (Unionist Party), 1966; Parly Sec., Min. of Educn, 1967; Chief Whip, Sept. 1968–April 1969; Minister of Commerce, NI, 1969–71; Minister of Develt, NI, 1971–72. Contested (Official U) North Down, 1974. Mem. Council, N Down (former Mayor). Pres., NI European Movt, 1987–. *Publications:* Excelsior (novel), 1960; The Last Ditch (novel), 1981; Rogue Warrior of the SAS: the Life of Lt-Col R. B. "Paddy" Mayne, DSO, 1987. *Recreations:* golf, architecture. *Address:* The Boathouse, Warren Road, Donaghadee, Co. Down, Ireland BT21 0PQ. *T:* (01247) 882487. *Club:* Royal and Ancient Golf (St Andrews). *Died 2 Sept. 1998.*

BRADING, Keith, CB 1974; MBE 1944; Chief Registrar of Friendly Societies and Industrial Assurance Commissioner, 1972–81; *b* 23 Aug. 1917; *s* of late Frederick C. Brading and Lilian P. Brading (*née* Courtney); *m* 1949, Mary Blanche Robinson, *d* of late William C. and Blanche Robinson. *Educ:* Portsmouth Grammar Sch. Called to Bar, Gray's Inn, 1950. Served War, Royal Navy, 1941–46 (Lieut RNVR). Entered Inland Revenue (Estate Duty Office), 1936; Solicitor's Office, Inland Revenue, 1950; Asst Solicitor, 1962; Asst Registrar of Friendly Societies and Dep. Industrial Assurance Commissioner, 1969. Vice-President: CBSI, 1981–; Bldg Socs Assoc., 1982–. Pres., Soc. for Co-operative Studies, 1983–. Chairman: Kensington Housing Trust, 1987–92 (Vice Chm., 1992–); UK Co-operative Council, 1991–92 (Hon. Pres., 1992–). FRSA 1986. *Publications:* contrib. Halsbury's Laws of England and Atkins Court Forms and Precedents. *Address:* 35 Chiswick Staithe, W4 3TP. *T:* 0181–995 0517. *Club:* Savile. *Died 2 Feb. 1996.*

BRADSHAW, Lt-Gen. Sir Richard (Phillip), KBE 1977; Director General, Army Medical Services, 1977–81; *b* 1 Aug. 1920; *s* of late John Henderson Bradshaw and May Bradshaw (*née* Phillips); *m* 1946, Estelle (*d* 1996), *d* of late Emile Meyer; one *d. Educ:* Newport High Sch.; London Univ.; Westminster Hosp. MRCS, LRCP 1945; DTM&H 1953; FRCPath 1967; FFCM 1977; FRSTM&H. House appts, Westminster and Kent and Canterbury Hosps. Commnd RAMC, 1946; appts as Hosp. Pathologist, Mil. Hosps in UK and Ceylon; Staff appts in Path., WO, 1950–52; Comd Cons. Pathologist, E Africa, 1954–57; Exch. Officer, Armed Forces Inst. of Path., Washington, 1959–60; Demonstr in Path., Royal Army Med. Coll., Millbank, 1961–63; Asst Dir of Path., BAOR, 1966–69; Prof. of Path., Royal Army Med. Coll., Millbank, 1969–71; CO, Cambridge Mil. Hosp., Aldershot, 1971–73; Comdt RAMC Trng Centre, 1973–75; DMS, BAOR, 1975–77. QHP 1975–81. FRSocMed; Mem., BMA. Member: Council, Sir Oswald Stoll Foundn, Fulham, 1977– (Chm., Management Cttee, 1983–94); Council, Phyllis Tuckwell Meml Hospice, Farnham, 1981–94; formerly HM Comr, Royal Hosp., Chelsea. CStJ 1977. *Publications:* articles and reports in professional jls. *Recreations:* bird-watching, gardening. *Died 12 Oct. 1999.*

BRAGGINS, Maj.-Gen. Derek Henry, CB 1986; Director General, Transport and Movements, Army, 1983–86; *b* 19 April 1931; *s* of late Albert Edward Braggins and of Hilda Braggins; *m* 1953, Sheila St Clair (*née* Stuart); three *s. Educ:* Rothesay Academy; Hendon Technical College. FCIT 1983. Commissioned RASC, 1950; RCT, 1965; regtl and staff appts, Korea, Malaya, Singapore, Ghana, Aden, Germany and UK; student, Staff Coll., Camberley, 1962, JSSC, Latimer, 1970; CO 7 Regt RCT, 1973–75; Col AQ Commando Forces RM, 1977–80; Comd Transport and Movements, BAOR, 1981–83. Col Comdt, RCT, 1986–93; Pres., RASC/RCT Assoc., 1987–95. Vice-Pres., Devon and Cornwall Br., British Korean Veterans, 1998–. Freeman, City of London, 1983; Hon. Liveryman, Worshipful Co. of Carmen, 1983. FIMgt (FBIM 1979). *Recreations:* shooting, fishing, gardening. *Died 16 Nov. 1999.*

BRAINE OF WHEATLEY, Baron *cr* 1992 (Life Peer), of Rayleigh in the County of Essex; **Bernard Richard Braine,** Kt 1972; PC 1985; DL; *b* Ealing, Middx, 24 June 1914; *s* of Arthur Ernest Braine and Elsa Hoffacker; *m* 1935, Kathleen Mary Faun (*d* 1982); three *s. Educ:* Hendon County Grammar Sch. Served North Staffs Regt in War of 1939–45: West Africa, SE Asia, NW Europe; Staff Coll., Camberley, 1944 (sc); Lt-Col. Chm., British Commonwealth Producers' Organisation, 1958–60. MP (C) Billericay Div. of Essex, 1950–55, South East Essex, 1955–83, Castle Point, 1983–92; Father of the House of Commons, 1987–92. Parly Sec., Min. of Pensions and National Insurance, 1960–61; Parly Under-Sec. of State for Commonwealth Relations, 1961–62; Parly Sec., Min.

of Health, 1962–64; Conservative front bench spokesman on Commonwealth Affairs and Overseas Aid, 1967–70; Chm., Select Cttees on Overseas Aid, 1970–71, on Overseas Develt, 1973–74; Treasurer, UK Branch of Commonwealth Parly Assoc., 1974–77 (Dep. Chm., 1964 and 1970–74). Chairman: British-German Parly Group, 1970–92; British-Greek Parly Group, 1979–92; All-party Pro Life Cttee, to 1991; Inter-Parly Council Against Antisemitism, 1993–; Founder and Chm., All-party Misuse of Drugs Cttee, 1984–88; Vice-Chm., Parly Human Rights Gp, 1979–92; Pres., All Party Parly Pro-Life Gp, 1991–. Chairman: Nat. Council on Alcoholism, 1973–82; UK Chapter, Soc. of Internat. Develt, 1976–83; President: UK Cttee for Defence of the Unjustly Prosecuted, 1980–88; River Thames Soc., 1981–87; Greater London Alcohol Adv. Service, 1983–; Falkland Is Assoc., 1993–. President, Cons. Clubs of Benfleet, Hadleigh and Canvey Is. Associate Mem., Inst. of Develt Studies, Univ. of Sussex, 1971–; Vis. Prof., Baylor Univ., Texas, 1987–91. A Governor, Commonwealth Inst., 1968–81, Trustee, 1981–. FRSA 1971. DL Essex, 1978. Hon. DH Dallas Baptist Univ., 1993. KStJ 1985; KCSG 1987; GCLJ 1987; GCMLJ 1988. Europe Peace Cross, 1979; Knight Comdr's Cross with Star, Order of Merit, 1984 (Comdr's Cross, 1974) (Germany); Grand Comdr, Order of Honour (Greece), 1987; Grand Cross, Order of Polonia Restituta, 1990 (Comdr's Cross with Star, 1983) (Poland). *Address:* House of Lords, SW1A 0PW.   *Died 5 Jan. 2000.*

BRAINE, Rear-Adm. Richard Allix, CB 1956; retired; *b* 18 Nov. 1900; *m* 1922, Lilian Violet (*d* 1985); one *s.* *Educ:* Dean Close Memorial Sch., Cheltenham. Joined RN as asst clerk, 1918; Comdr (S), Dec. 1938; Capt. (S), Dec. 1948; Rear-Adm. 1954. Command Supply Officer, Staff of Flag Officer Air (Home), 1954–56, Portsmouth, 1956–57. *Address:* The Old Cottage, Littlewick Green, near Maidenhead, Berks SL6 3RF.   *Died 5 Feb. 1998.*

BRAMALL, Sir (Ernest) Ashley, Kt 1975; DL; Member (Lab), Greater London Council, Bethnal Green and Bow, 1973–86 (Tower Hamlets, 1964–73); Chairman: GLC, 1982–83; ILEA, 1965–67 and 1984–86 (Leader, 1970–81), *b* 6 Jan. 1916; *er s* of late Major E. H. Bramall and Mrs K. B. Bramall (*née* Westby); *m* 1st, 1939, Margaret Elaine Taylor (marr. diss. 1950), OBE; two *s*; 2nd, 1950, Germaine Margaret, (Gery), Bloch; one *s.* *Educ:* Westminster and Canford Schs; Magdalen Coll., Oxford. Called to the Bar, Inner Temple, 1949. Served in Army, 1940–46; Major; psc 1945. Contested Fareham Div. of Hants, 1945; MP (Lab) Bexley, 1946–50; contested Bexley, 1950, 1951, 1959; Watford, 1955. Member (Lab): LCC, Bethnal Green, 1961; Westminster CC, 1959–68; Chm., Council of LEAs, 1975–76, 1977–78, Vice-Chm., 1976–77; Leader, Management Panel, Burnham Cttee (Primary and Secondary), 1973–78; Chm., Nat. Council for Drama Trng, 1981–89. Hon. Sec., Theatres Adv. Council, 1987–91. Mem. Council, City Univ., 1984–90; Chm., Westminster Further Educn Coll., 1992–99. Governor, Museum of London, 1981–. DL Greater London, 1981. Grand Officer, Order of Orange Nassau (Netherlands), 1982. *Address:* 2 Egerton House, 59–63 Belgrave Road, SW1V 2BE. *T:* (020) 7828 0973.
        Died 10 Feb. 1999.

BRANCKER, Sir (John Eustace) Theodore, Kt 1969; President of the Senate, Barbados, 1971–76; *b* 9 Feb. 1909; *s* of Jabel Eustace and Myra Enid Vivienne Brancker; *m* 1967, Esme Gwendolyn Walcott (OBE 1987). *Educ:* Harrison Coll., Barbados; Grad., Inst. of Political Secretaries; LSE (Certificate in Colonial Admin, 1933). Called to Bar, Middle Temple, 1933; in private practice; QC (Barbados) 1961. Mem., House of Assembly, Barbados, 1937–71 (Leader of Opposition, 1956–61; Speaker, 1961–71). Chm., 1973, Hon. Awards Liaison

Officer, 1978, Duke of Edinburgh Award Scheme. Mem., Medico-Legal Soc. Mem., CPA; Life Fellow, Royal Commonwealth Soc.; Life Mem., Barbados Mus. and Historical Soc.; Mem., Soc. of Friends of Westminster Cathedral. Charter Pres., Rotary Club, Barbados. Mem. Adv. Bd, St Joseph Hosp. of Sisters of the Sorrowful Mother. Hon. LLD Soochow Univ., 1973. FZS; FRSA (Life Fellow). Queen's Coronation Medal, 1953; Silver Jubilee Medal, 1977. *Recreations:* classical music, chess, drama. *Address:* 16 East Charlemont, Paradise Heights, St James's, Barbados. *T:* 4325563. *Clubs:* Royal Over-Seas League (Life Mem.), Challoner; Empire, Bridgetown, Sunset Crest (Barbados); Rotary International.
        Died 28 April 1996.

BRAND, Hon. Lord; David William Robert Brand; a Senator of the College of Justice in Scotland, 1972–89; *b* 21 Oct. 1923; *s* of late James Gordon Brand, Huntingdon, Dumfries, and Frances (*née* Bull); *m* 1st, 1948, Rose Josephine Devlin (*d* 1968); four *d*; 2nd, 1969, Bridget Veronica Lynch (*née* Russell), *widow* of Thomas Patrick Lynch, Beechmount, Mallow, Co. Cork. *Educ:* Stonyhurst Coll.; Edinburgh Univ. Served War of 1939–45: commissioned Argyll and Sutherland Highlanders, 1942; Capt. 1945. Admitted to Faculty of Advocates, 1948; Standing Junior Counsel to Dept of Education for Scotland, 1951; Advocate-Depute for Sheriff Court, 1953; Extra Advocate-Depute for Glasgow Circuit, 1955; Advocate-Depute, 1957–59; QC (Scot.) 1959; Senior Advocate-Depute, 1964; Sheriff of Dumfries and Galloway, 1968; Sheriff of Roxburgh, Berwick and Selkirk, 1970; Solicitor-General for Scotland, 1970–72; Judge of Appeal, High Court of Botswana, 1994. Chm., Medical Appeal Tribunal, 1959–70. Kt, SMO Malta. *Publications:* Joint Editor, Scottish Edn of Current Law, 1948–61; Scottish Editor, Encyclopedia of Road Traffic Law and Practice, 1960–64; An Advocate's Tale (autobiog.), 1995; contributor to Scots Law Times. *Recreation:* golf. *Address:* Ardgarten, Marmion Road, North Berwick, E Lothian EH39 4PG. *T:* North Berwick (01620) 3208. *Clubs:* New (Edinburgh); Highland Brigade; Honourable Company of Edinburgh Golfers.   *Died 11 April 1996.*

BRAND, David William Robert; *see* Brand, Hon. Lord.

BRANDON OF OAKBROOK, Baron *cr* 1981 (Life Peer), of Hammersmith in Greater London; **Henry Vivian Brandon,** Kt 1966; MC 1942; PC 1978; a Lord of Appeal in Ordinary, 1981–91; *b* 3 June 1920; *y s* of late Captain V. R. Brandon, CBE, RN, and Joan Elizabeth Maud Simpson; *m* 1955, Jeanette Rosemary, *e d* of late J. V. B. Janvrin; three *s* one *d. Educ:* Winchester Coll. (Scholar); King's Coll., Cambridge (Scholar 1938, Stewart of Rannoch Scholar 1939; BA 1946). Commnd 2nd Lieut RA 1939; Major 1944; served UK, 1939–42, Madagascar, 1942, India and Burma, 1942–45. Barrister, Inner Temple, 1946 (Entrance and Yarborough Anderson Scholar); Member Bar Council, 1951–53; QC 1961; Judge of the High Court of Justice, Probate, Divorce and Admiralty Division, 1966–71, Family Division, 1971–78; Judge of the Admiralty Court, 1971–78; Judge of the Commercial Court, 1977–78; a Lord Justice of Appeal, 1978–81. Member panel of Lloyd's arbitrators in salvage cases, 1961–66; Member panel from which Wreck Commissioners chosen, 1963–66. Hon. LLD Southampton, 1984. *Recreations:* cricket, bridge, travelling. *Address:* 6 Thackeray Close, SW19 4JL. *T:* (020) 8947 6344; House of Lords, SW1A 0PW. *Club:* MCC.   *Died 24 March 1999.*

BRANIGAN, Sir Patrick (Francis), Kt 1954; QC (Gold Coast) 1949; *b* 30 Aug. 1906; *e s* of late D. Branigan and Teresa, *d* of Thomas Clinton, Annagassan, Co. Louth; *m* 1935, Prudence, *yr d* of late Dr A. Avent, Seaton, Devon; one *s* one *d. Educ:* Newbridge Coll., Co. Kildare; Trinity

Coll., Dublin (BA 1st Class Hons in Law and Political Science and gold medallist, 1928). Called to the Irish Bar (Certificate of Honour), 1928 (1st Victoria Prize, 1927); called to the Bar, Gray's Inn, 1935. Practised at Irish Bar, 1928–30; Downing Coll., Cambridge, 1930–31; Colonial Administrative Service, Kenya, 1931; Crown Counsel, Tanganyika, 1934; Northern Rhodesia: Solicitor-General, 1938; Chairman, Man-power Cttee, 1939–41; Chairman, Conciliation Board, Copperbelt Strike, 1940; Member, Nat. Arbitration Tribunal, 1940–46; Member, Strauss Arbitration Tribunal, Bulawayo, 1944; Chairman, Road Transport Services Board and Electricity Board, 1939–46; Legal Secretary to Govt of Malta and Chairman, Malta War Damage Commission, 1946–48; periodically acting Lt-Gov. of Malta, 1947–48; Minister of Justice and Attorney-General, Gold Coast, 1948–54; retired, 1954. Dep. Chm., Devon QS, 1958–71; a Recorder, 1972–75. Chairman of Commission of inquiry into Copperbelt industrial unrest, Northern Rhodesia, 1956; Vice-Chm., and Ldr UK delegn to UN Seminar on Protection of Human Rights in Criminal Procedure, Vienna, 1960. Chairman: Pensions Appeal Tribunal, 1955–81; Agricultural Land Tribunal for SW Area of England, 1955–79; Nat. Insurance Med. Appeal Tribunal, SW Reg., 1960–78; Mental Health Review Tribunal, SW England, 1960–78; Mem., Industrial Disputes Tribunal, 1955–59. Knight Commander of Order of St Gregory the Great, 1956. *Address:* 17 Pyndar Court, Newland, near Malvern, Worcs WR13 5AX. *T:* (01684) 567761.

Died 2 Nov. 2000.

BRANSON, William Rainforth, CBE 1969; retired; *b* 2 Jan. 1905; *s* of late A. W. Branson, JP; *m* 1932, Dorothy Iris Green (*d* 1982); no *c*. *Educ:* Rydal Sch.; University of Leeds. BSc, 1st Class Hons (Fuel and Gas Engrg), 1927; MSc 1930. Asst Engineer, Gas Light & Coke Co., London, 1927–37; Asst Engineer, later Dep. Engineer, Cardiff Gas Light & Coke Co., 1937–45; Dep. Controller, later Controller, Public Utilities Br., Control Commn for Germany, 1945–49; Planning Engineer, Wales Gas Board, 1949–51; Technical Officer, E Midlands Gas Board, 1952–54; Dep. Chairman, W Midlands Gas Board, 1954–65; Chm., Scottish Gas Bd, 1965–68; Dir, Woodall-Duckham Group Ltd, 1969–73. President, Instn of Gas Engineers, 1964–65. *Recreation:* music. *Address:* Knappe Cross Nursing Home, Brixington Lane, Exmouth, Devon EX8 5DL. *Died 7 Nov. 1997.*

BRASS, John, CBE 1968; FREng, FIMinE; Member, National Coal Board, 1971–73; *b* 22 Oct. 1908; 2nd *s* of late John Brass, Mining Engineer, and Mary Brass (*née* Swainston); *m* 1934, Jocelyn Constance Cape, Stroud, Glos; three *s* (one *d* decd). *Educ:* Oundle Sch.; Birmingham Univ. (BSc Hons). Various appointments, all in mining; Chm., W Midlands Division, NCB, 1961–67; Regional Chm., Yorks and NW Areas, NCB, 1967–71. Chm., Amalgamated Construction Co., 1976–86. FREng (FEng 1978). FRSA. *Address:* Flat 6, The Old Mill, Scott Lane, Wetherby, W Yorks LS22 6NB.

Died 3 Nov. 1999.

BRASS, Prof. William, CBE 1981; FBA 1979; Professor of Medical Demography, 1972–88, then Emeritus, and Director of Centre for Population Studies, 1978–88, London School of Hygiene and Tropical Medicine (Hon. Fellow, 1997); *b* 5 Sept. 1921; *s* of John Brass and Margaret Tait (*née* Haig); *m* 1948, Betty Ellen Agnes Topp; two *d*. *Educ:* Royal High Sch., Edinburgh; Edinburgh Univ. (MA Hons Maths and Nat. Phil., 1943). Scientific Officer, Royal Naval Scientific Service, 1943–46; E African Statistical Dept, Colonial Service, 1948–55; Lectr in Statistics, 1955–64, Sen. Lectr 1964, Aberdeen Univ.; London School of Hygiene and Tropical Medicine: Reader in Med. Demography, 1965–72; Dir,

Centre for Overseas Population Studies, 1974–78; Head, Dept of Med. Stats and Epidemiology, 1977–82. Pres., Internat. Union for the Scientific Study of Population, 1985–89. For. Associate, US Nat. Acad. of Scis, 1984. Mindel Sheps Award for distinguished contribn to demography, Population Assoc. of America, 1978. *Publications:* The Demography of Tropical Africa, 1968; Metodos para estimar la fecundidad y la mortalidad en poblaciones con datos Limitados: selección de trabajos, 1974; Methods of Estimating Fertility and Mortality from Limited and Defective Data, 1975; Advances in Methods for Estimating Fertility and Mortality from Limited and Defective Data, 1985; about 100 papers in learned jls. *Recreations:* travel, observing art and archaeology. *Address:* 6 St Nicholas Close, Amersham, Bucks HP7 9NW. *T:* (01494) 765166. *Died 11 Nov. 1999.*

BRAY, Sir Theodor (Charles), Kt 1975; CBE 1964; Director, Queensland Arts Council, 1976–99; Chancellor, Griffith University, Brisbane, 1975–85; *b* 11 Feb. 1905; *s* of Horace and Maude Bray; *m* 1931, Rosalie (*d* 1988), *d* of Rev. A. M. Trengove; three *s* two *d* (and one *s* one *d* decd). *Educ:* state schs; Adelaide Univ. Apprentice Printer, Reporter, Register, Adelaide; Sub-editor, Chief Sub-editor, The Argus, Melbourne; Editor (26 yrs), Editor-in-Chief, Jt Man. Dir, Queensland Newspapers Pty Ltd, 1936–70, Dir, 1956–80; Chm., Australian Associated Press, 1968–70; Mem., Aust. Council for the Arts, 1969–73; Aust. Chm., Internat. Press Inst., 1962–70; Chm., Griffith Univ. Council, 1970–75. *Recreations:* bowls, travel. *Address:* 10/64 Macquarie Street, St Lucia, Qld 4067, Australia. *T:* (7) 38707442. *Clubs:* Queensland, Queensland University Staff (Brisbane).

Died 10 Aug. 2000.

BRAYNE-BAKER, John, CMG 1957; Colonial Administrative Service, Nigeria (retired); *b* 13 Aug. 1905; *s* of Francis Brayne-Baker and Dorothea Mary Brayne-Baker (*née* Porcher); *m* 1947, Ruth Hancock; no *c*. *Educ:* Marlborough Coll.; Worcester Coll., Oxford. Nigeria: Asst District Officer, 1928; District Officer, 1938; Senior District Officer, 1948; Resident, 1953; Senior Resident and Deputy Commissioner of the Cameroons, 1954–56; retired 1956. Member, Tiverton RDC, 1959–74, Tiverton DC, 1973–76. *Address:* 48 Markers, Uffculme, Cullompton, Devon EX15 3DZ. *T:* (01884) 840236. *Club:* Tiverton Golf (Tiverton). *Died 10 Jan. 1997.*

BRAYNE-NICHOLLS, Rear-Adm. (Francis) Brian (Price), CB 1965; DSC 1942; General Secretary, Officers Pensions Society, 1966–79; *b* 1 Dec. 1914; *s* of late Dr G. E. E. Brayne-Nicholls; *g s* of Sir Francis W. T. Brain; *m* 1st, 1939, Wendy (*née* Donnelly) (*d* 1983); one *d*; 2nd, 1986, Mimi M. Scott. *Educ:* RNC, Dartmouth. Sub-Lieut and Lieut, HMS Bee on Yangtse River, 1936–39; specialised in Navigation, 1939; Navigating Officer of HM Ships Nelson, Rodney, Cardiff, 1939–41, Manxman (during many mining ops, Malta convoys and Madagascar op.), 1941–42; Combined Ops, taking part in Sicily (despatches), Salerno, and Normandy landings; Navigating Officer: HMS Glory, 1944–46; HMS Vanguard, 1948; Comdr 1948; Comdg Officer: HMS Gravelines, 1952–53; HMS St Kitts, 1953–54; Capt 1954; Naval Asst to First Sea Lord, 1954–55; Comdg Officer, HMS Apollo, 1955–57; NATO Standing Group, Washington, 1957–59; Captain of Navigation Direction Sch., HMS Dryad, 1959–61; Admiralty, 1961–63; Rear-Adm. 1963; Chief of Staff to Commander, Far East Fleet, 1963–65. Younger Brother, Trinity House. *Recreation:* golf. *Address:* 3 Tedworth Square, SW3 4DU. *T:* (0171) 352 1681. *Club:* Naval and Military. *Died 4 March 1998.*

BREDIN, James John; specialist in television archives; Contributing Editor, Industry Week, American management magazine, since 1991; *b* 18 Feb. 1924; *s* of late John Francis and Margaret Bredin; *m* 1958, Virginia Meddowes, *d* of John Meddowes and Mrs K. Thomas; one *s* two *d. Educ.* Finchley Catholic Grammar Sch.; London University. Served Fleet Air Arm, RNVR, Sub Lieut, 1943–46. Scriptwriter, This Modern Age Film Unit, 1946–50; Producer, current affairs programmes, BBC TV, 1950–55; Sen. Producer, Independent Television News, 1955–59; Smith-Mundt Fellowship, USA, 1957; Producer of Documentaries, Associated Television, 1959–64; Man. Dir, Border TV Ltd, 1964–82. Chm., Guild of Television Producers and Directors, 1961–64. Director: Independent Television News Ltd, 1970–72; Independent Television Publications Ltd, 1965–82. FRTS 1983. Press Fellow, Wolfson Coll., Cambridge, 1987. *Address:* 25 Stack House, Cundy Street, SW1W 9JS. *T:* (020) 7730 2689. *Club:* Beefsteak. *Died 11 Nov. 1998.*

BRENNAN, Brian John, MC 1944; Chairman, Lloyd's of London Press Ltd, 1985–88; Deputy Chairman of Lloyd's, 1981–83 (Underwriting Member, since 1951); *b* 17 May 1918; *s* of Alfred Eric Brennan and Jean (*née* Wallace); *m* 1950, Mary Patricia Newbould; one *s* two *d. Educ:* Dulwich College. Member, HAC, 1938; commnd Cameronians (Scottish Rifles), 1939; India, 1/Cameronians, 1940–45; Burma, 1942; Burma, 1944; commanded 26 Column 1/Cameronians 111 Bde Special Force; Lt-Col 1/Cameronians, 1944–45. Joined E. W. Payne, Lloyd's Brokers, 1936; Director, E. W. Payne, 1947, Chm., 1966–74; Director, Montagu Trust, 1967–74; Dep. Chm., Bland Payne Holdings, 1974–78; Chm., Bland Payne Reinsurance Brokers, 1974–78; Dir, Sedgwick Forbes Bland Payne Holdings, 1979; Chm., Sedgwick Payne, 1979; Dir, Sedgwick Gp Ltd, 1980. Mem., Cttee of Lloyd's, 1975–80, 1981–84. *Recreations:* Rugby (Old Alleynians, Kent, London, Barbarians), sailing, tennis, gardening. *Address:* Weybank House, Meadrow, Godalming, Surrey GU7 3BZ. *Clubs:* Alderney Sailing, Alderney Golf. *Died 14 April 1998.*

BRENNAN, Hon. William Joseph, Jr; Legion of Merit, 1945; Associate Justice, Supreme Court of the US, 1956–90, retired; *b* 25 April 1906; *s* of William J. Brennan and Agnes McDermott; *m* 1st, 1928, Marjorie Leonard (*d* 1982); two *s* one *d;* 2nd, 1983, Mary Fowler. *Educ:* University of Pennsylvania; Harvard. BS Univ. of Pennsylvania, 1928; LLB Harvard, 1931. Admitted to New Jersey Bar, 1931; practised in Newark, New Jersey, 1931–49, Member Pitney, Hardin, Ward & Brennan; Superior Court Judge, 1949–50; Appellate Division Judge, 1950–52; Supreme Court of New Jersey Justice, 1952–56. Served War of 1939–45 as Colonel, General Staff Corps, United States Army. Hon. LLD: Pennsylvania, Wesleyan, St John's, 1957; Rutgers, 1958; Notre Dame, Harvard, 1968; Princeton, Columbia, Brandeis, NY Law Sch., John Marshall Law Sch., 1986; Ohio State, Yale, 1987; Glasgow, 1989; UC Dublin, 1990; Hon. DCL: New York Univ., Colgate, 1957; Hon. SJD Suffolk Univ., 1956. Hon. Bencher, Lincoln's Inn, 1985. ABA Medal, 1994. US Medal of Freedom, 1993. *Address:* c/o US Supreme Court, 1 First Street NE, Washington, DC 20543, USA. *Died 24 July 1997.*

BRESSON, Robert; Officier, Légion d'Honneur, 1971; Grand Croix, Ordre National du Mérite, 1986; Commandeur des Arts et des Lettres, 1974; film producer since 1934; *b* 25 Sept. 1901; *s* of Léon Bresson and Marie-Elisabeth (*née* Clausels); *m* 1st, 1926, Leidia van der Zee; 2nd, Marie-Madeleine van der Mersch. *Educ:* Lycée Lakanal, Sceaux. Started as painter; then producer of short films, Affaires Publiques; full-length films produced included: Les Anges du Péché, 1943; Les Dames du Bois de Boulogne, 1948; Journal d'un Curé de Campagne, 1951 (Internat. Grand Prix, Venice); Un Condamné à Mort s'est Echappé, 1956; Pickpocket, 1960; Procès de Jeanne d'Arc,

1962 (Jury's special prize, Cannes); Au Hasard Balthazar, 1966; Mouchette, 1967; Une Femme Douce, 1969; Quatre nuits d'un rêveur, 1971; Lancelot du Lac, 1974; Le diable, probablement, 1977; L'Argent, 1983. *Publication:* Notes sur le cinématographe, 1976. *Address:* 49 quai de Bourbon, 75004 Paris, France. *Died 18 Dec. 1999.*

BRETT, John Alfred, MA; Headmaster, Durham School, Durham, 1958–67; retired; *b* 26 Oct. 1915; *s* of Alfred Brett, Harrogate, Yorks; *m* 1939, Margaret Coode; one *s* three *d. Educ:* Durham School; St Edmund Hall, Oxford. MA (Hons Modern History). Temp. teacher, Stowe School, 1938; Teacher, Diocesan College, Rondebosch, South Africa, 1939; restarted Silver Tree Youth Club for non-Europeans, Cape Town; Army: Gunner to Major, RA, 1940–44; Instructor 123 OCTU Catterick; invasion of Normandy, 1944 (lost right eye); Military testing officer, WOSBs, finally Senior Military Testing Officer, War Office Selection Centre; returned to post at Diocesan College, Rondebosch, 1946; Housemaster, 1948; Temp. teacher, Canford School, Wimborne, Dorset, 1954; Headmaster, Shaftesbury Grammar School, 1954. Diocesan Lay Reader. Member Council: Brathay Hall Centre; McAlpine Educnl Endowments Ltd. Governor, Bernard Gilpin Society. *Recreations:* sport (Captain Oxford University Rugby Football Club, 1937, and Member British Touring XV to Argentina, 1936), travel, reading. *Address:* 32 Homefarris House, Bleke Street, Shaftesbury, Dorset SP7 8AU. *Died 10 Aug. 1996.*

BRETT, Prof. Raymond Laurence; G. F. Grant Professor of English, University of Hull, 1952–82; *b* 10 Jan. 1917; *s* of late Leonard and Ellen Brett; *m* 1947, Kathleen Tegwen, *d* of late Rev. C. D. Cranmer; one *s* (and two *s* decd). *Educ:* Bristol Cathedral School; University of Bristol (1st Class Hons BA, English and Philosophy, 1937; Taylor Prizeman, Hannam-Clark Prizeman, Haldane of Cloan Post-Grad. Studentship); University College, Oxford (BLitt 1940). Service in Admiralty, 1940–46, on Staff of First Lord; Lectr in English, Univ. of Bristol, 1946–52; Dean, Faculty of Arts, Hull Univ., 1960–62; Visiting Professor: Univ. of Rochester, USA, 1958–59; Kiel Univ., Osnabrück Univ., 1977; Baroda Univ., Jadavpur Univ., 1978; Univ. of Ottawa, 1981. Hon. DLitt Hull, 1983. *Publications:* Coleridge's Theory of Imagination (English Essays), 1949; The Third Earl of Shaftesbury: a Study in 18th Century Literary Theory, 1951; George Crabbe, 1956; Reason and Imagination, 1961; (with A. R. Jones) a critical edition of Lyrical Ballads by Wordsworth and Coleridge, 1963, 2nd edn 1991; (contrib.) The English Mind, 1964; (ed) Poems of Faith and Doubt, 1965; An Introduction to English Studies, 1965; Fancy and Imagination, 1969; (ed) S. T. Coleridge, 1971, 2nd edn 1978; William Hazlitt, 1978; (ed) Barclay Fox's Journal, 1979; (ed) Andrew Marvell, 1979; articles in The Times, Time and Tide, Essays and Studies, Review of English Studies, Modern Language Review, Philosophy, English, South Atlantic Qly, Critical Qly, etc. *Address:* 19 Mill Walk, Cottingham, North Humberside HU16 4RP. *T:* (01482) 847115. *Died 6 Dec. 1996.*

BREWER, Rear-Adm. George Maxted Kenneth, CB 1982; Flag Officer Medway and Port Admiral Chatham, 1980–82; *b* Dover, 4 March 1930; *s* of Captain George Maxted Brewer and Cecilia Victoria (*née* Clark); *m* 1989, Betty Mary, *o d* of Comdr C. H. Welton, RN and Elsie Gwendoline (*née* Harris). *Educ:* Pangbourne College. In Command: HMS Carysfort, Far East and Mediterranean, 1964–65; HMS Agincourt, Home, 1967; HMS Grenville, Far East and Mediterranean, 1967–69; HMS Juno, and Captain Fourth Frigate Sqdn, Home and Mediterranean, 1973–74; rcds 1975; In Command: HMS Tiger, and Flag

Captain to Flag Officer Second Flotilla, Far East, 1978; HMS Bulwark, NATO area, 1979–80. ADC to the Queen, 1980. *Recreation:* watercolour painting. *Address:* c/o National Westminster Bank, 2 West Street, Portchester, Fareham, Hants PO16 9XA. *Club:* Royal Navy of 1765 and 1785. *Died 5 Sept. 1998.*

BREWER, Rt Rev. John; Bishop of Lancaster, (RC), since 1985; *b* 24 Nov 1929; *s* of Eric W. Brewer and Laura H. Brewer (*née* Webster). *Educ:* Ushaw College, Durham; Ven. English College, Rome and Gregorian Univ. PhL, STL, JCL. Ordained priest, 1956; Parish Assistant, 1959–64; Vice-Rector, Ven. English Coll., Rome, 1964–71; Parish Priest of St Mary's, Middlewich, 1971–78; Auxiliary Bishop of Shrewsbury, 1971–83; Bishop Coadjutor of Lancaster, 1984. Officiating Chaplain, Royal Navy, 1966–71; Representative of RC Bishops of England and Wales in Rome, 1964–71. Chaplain to HH Pope Paul VI, 1965. FRSA. *Recreations:* reading, travel. *Address:* Bishop's House, Cannon Hill, Lancaster LA1 5NG. *T:* (01524) 32231, *Fax:* (01524) 849296.
Died 10 June 2000.

BRIAULT, Dr Eric William Henry, CBE 1976; Education Officer, Inner London Education Authority, 1971–76; Visiting Professor of Education, University of Sussex, 1977–81 and 1984–85; *b* 24 Dec. 1911; *s* of H. G. Briault; *m* 1935, Marie Alice (*née* Knight); two *s* one *d. Educ:* Brighton, Hove and Sussex Grammar Sch.; Peterhouse, Cambridge (Robert Slade Schol.). 1st cl. hons Geography, 1933; MA Cantab, 1937; PhD London, 1939. School teaching, 1933–47; Inspector of Schools, LCC, 1948–56; Dep. Educn Officer, ILEA, 1956–71. Dir. res. project on falling rolls in secondary schs, 1978–80. Hon. Sec., RGS, 1953–63. Freeman, City of London, 1935; Liveryman, Goldsmiths' Co., 1968–. Hon. DLitt Sussex, 1975. *Publications:* Sussex, East and West (Land Utilisation Survey report), 1942; (jtly) Introduction to Advanced Geography, 1957; (jtly) Geography In and Out of School, 1960; (jtly) Falling Rolls in Secondary Schools, Parts I and II, 1980; (ed jtly) Primary School Management, 1990. *Recreations:* travel, gardening, music, theatre, ballet; formerly athletics (Cambridge blue), cross-country running (Cambridge half-blue). *Address:* Woodedge, Hampers Lane, Storrington, W Sussex RH20 3HZ. *T:* Storrington (01903) 743919. *Died 14 Jan. 1996.*

BRICE, Geoffrey James Barrington Groves; QC 1979; barrister; a Recorder, since 1980; a Deputy High Court Judge, since 1996; *b* 21 April 1938; *s* of late Lt-Cdr John Edgar Leonard Brice, MBE and Winifred Ivy Brice; *m* 1963, Ann Nuala Connor; one *s. Educ:* Magdalen Coll. Sch., Brackley; University Coll., London (LLB). Called to the Bar, Middle Temple, 1960, Bencher, 1986; Harmsworth Scholar and Robert Garraway Rice Prize, 1960. Leader, Admiralty Bar, 1998–. Visiting Professor of Maritime Law: Tulane Univ., 1989–; Univ. of Natal, 1996–. Lloyd's Arbitrator, 1978–; Wreck Commissioner, 1979–. Chairman: London Bar Arbitration Scheme, 1986–; London Common Law and Commercial Bar Assoc., 1988–89; Member: UK Govt Delegn to IMO Legal Cttee, 1984–89; Gen. Council of the Bar, 1988–89. *Publications:* Maritime Law of Salvage, 1983, 3rd edn 1999; (contrib.) Limitation of Shipowners' Liability, 1986; articles in legal jls. *Recreations:* music, opera. *Address:* Yew Tree House, Spring Coppice, Newmer Common, Lane End, Bucks HP14 3NU. *T:* (01494) 881810; 15 Gayfere Street, Smith Square, SW1P 3HP. *T:* (020) 7799 3807; 4 Field Court, Gray's Inn, WC1R 5EA. *T:* (020) 7440 6900. *Clubs:* Athenæum; Phyllis Court (Henley-on-Thames).
Died 14 Nov. 1999.

BRIDGER, Pearl, MBE 1947; Director, Central Personnel, Post Office, 1968–72, retired; *b* 9 Dec. 1912; *d* of Samuel and Lottie Bridger. *Educ:* Godolphin and Latymer Girls'

Sch., London, W6. BA (Hons) Open Univ., 1978. Entered Post Office as Executive Officer, 1931; Asst Telecommunications Controller, 1938; Principal, 1947; Asst Sec., 1954. *Address:* St George's Retreat, Ditchling Common, Burgess Hill, West Sussex RH15 0SQ. *Club:* Civil Service. *Died 16 April 2000.*

BRIDGES-ADAMS, (John) Nicholas (William); a Recorder of the Crown Court, 1972–97; *b* 16 Sept. 1930; *s* of late William Bridges-Adams, CBE and Marguerite Doris, *y d* of W. H. Wellsted, JP; *m* 1962, Jenifer Celia Emily, *d* of David Sandell, FRCS. *Educ:* Stowe; Oriel Coll., Oxford (Scholar; MA, DipEd). Commnd Royal Artillery, 1949, transf. to RAFVR 1951 and served with Oxford and London Univ. Air Sqdn; Flying Officer, 2623 Sqdn RAuxAF Regt, 1980–82. Called to Bar, Lincoln's Inn, 1958 (Gray's Inn *ad eundem* 1979); Head of Chambers, 1979–92; Mem., Young Barristers Cttee, Bar Council, 1960–61; Actg Junior, Middx Sessions Bar Mess, 1965–67. Mem., Exec. Cttee, Soc. of Cons. Lawyers, 1967–69 (Chairman: Rates of Exchange sub-cttee, 1967–70; Criminal Law sub-cttee, 1983–87; Criminal Justice and Sentencing sub-cttee, 1987–92); Chm., Assoc. of Catholic Lawyers, 1997–; Mem., House of Lords Reform Cttee, CAER, 1982. Chm., panel from which Representations Cttees under Dumping at Sea Act 1974 drawn, 1976–85, and under Food and Environment Protection Act 1985, 1985–. Contested (C) West Bromwich West, Oct. 1974. Governor, St Benedict's Upper Sch., 1980–83. Member: RIIA; IISS; FCIArb (Mem. Cttee, 1995–, Chm., 1997–98, London Br.). *Publications:* contrib. on collisions at sea, 3rd edn of Halsbury's Laws of England, Vol. 35; articles in Arbitration. *Recreation:* from vain excess to clear the incumber'd laws. *Address:* 46 Essex Street, WC2R 3GH. *T:* (020) 7583 8899; Fornham Grange, Fornham St Martin, Bury St Edmunds, Suffolk IP31 1SP. *T:* (01284) 755307. *Clubs:* Savile, Garrick. *Died 26 Sept. 1998.*

BRIDGEWATER, Bentley Powell Conyers; Secretary of the British Museum, 1948–73; *b* 6 Sept. 1911; *s* of Conyers Bridgewater, OBE, Clerk to Commissioners of Taxes for City of London, and Violet Irene, *d* of Dr I. W. Powell, Victoria, BC. *Educ:* Westminster School (King's Schol.); Christ Church, Oxford (Westminster Schol., BA 1933, MA 1965). Asst Keeper, British Museum, 1937; Asst Sec., 1940; seconded to Dominions Office, 1941–42, and to Foreign Office, 1942–45; returned to British Museum, 1946; Deputy Keeper, 1950; Keeper, 1961; retired, 1973. *Recreation:* music. *Address:* 4 Doughty Street, WC1N 2PH. *Club:* Athenæum.
Died 17 Feb. 1996.

BRIGGS, Rear-Adm. Thomas Vallack, CB 1958; OBE (mil.) 1945; a Vice-Patron, Royal Naval Association (President, 1971–76); *b* 6 April 1906; *e s* of late Admiral Sir Charles John Briggs, KCB and Lady (Frances) Briggs (*née* Wilson); *m* 1947, Estelle Burland Willing (*d* 1997), Boston, USA; one step *s. Educ:* The Grange, Stevenage, Herts; Imperial Service College, Windsor. Joined Royal Navy, 1924; served HMS Thunderer, Hood, Wishart, Antelope, Wolsey, Nelson, Excellent, and Faulkner, 1924–37; Advanced Gunnery Specialist; served War of 1939–45: HMS Ark Royal, 1939–40; AA Comdr HMS Excellent, 1941–42; HMS Newcastle, 1943–44; staff of Flag Officer 2nd in Command, Eastern Fleet, 1944–45 (OBE and despatches twice); HMS Renown, Queen Elizabeth and Nelson; HMS Comus, 1945–46; US Naval War Coll., Newport, RI, 1946–47; Dep. Dir. of Naval Ordnance (G), 1947–49; commanded 5th Destroyer Flotilla, HMS Solebay, 1949–50, and HMS Cumberland, 1953–54; IDC, 1951; Chief of Staff: Plymouth, 1952–53; Home Fleet and Eastern Atlantic, 1956–57; Rear-Adm. 1956; Asst Controller of the Navy, 1958, retired. Director:

Hugh Stevenson & Sons Ltd, 1958–69; Hugh Stevenson & Sons (North East) Ltd, 1964; Bowater-Stevenson Containers Ltd, 1969–71; Free-Stay Holidays Ltd, 1971; Internat. Consumer Incentives Ltd, 1974–83; Meru Group Ltd, 1978–83. Vice-Chm., City of Westminster Soc. for Mentally Handicapped Children, 1969; Mem., Management Cttee, Haileybury and ISC Junior Sch., Windsor, 1959–80 (Chm., 1978–80); Life Governor, Haileybury and Imperial Service Coll., 1959 (Mem. Council, 1959–80); Pres., Haileybury Soc., 1973–74. Fellow, Inst. of Marketing, 1970–83. Chm., Aldeburgh Festival Club, 1979–80. DL Greater London, 1970–82 (Representative DL, Kingston upon Thames, 1970–79). *Recreations:* golf, shooting, bowling. *Address:* 630 Colonial Road, Guilford, CT 06437, USA. *Clubs:* Royal Naval Golfing Society, Aldeburgh Golf (Captain, 1981–82); Royal Naval Sailing Association; Royal Naval Ski; Madison Art. *Died 11 July 1999.*

BRILLIANT, Fredda, (Mrs Herbert Marshall); sculptor; *b* 7 April 1904; *d* of Mordechai and Raeisell Brilliant; *m* 1935, Herbert P. J. Marshall (*d* 1991). *Educ:* The Gymnasium (High Sch.), Lodz, Poland; Chelsea Art Sch. (drawing). Actress and singer, USA, 1930–33; actress and scriptwriter in England, 1937–50. Sculptor, 1934–; sculptures included: Nehru, Krishna Menon, Indira Gandhi, Paul Robeson, Herbert Marshall, Mahatma Gandhi (in Tavistock Square; Gandhi model in the Queen's Collection in Reading Room of St George's, Windsor Castle, 1983), Buckminster Fuller, Carl Albert, Sir Maurice Bowra, Lord Elwyn-Jones, Sir Isaac Hayward, Tom Mann, Dr Delyte Morris, Elie Wiesel, Pope John Paul II (work in progress). Exhibitions in London included: Royal Academy, Leicester Galls, Royal Watercolour Soc., Whitechapel Gall., St Paul's Cathedral; other exhibns in Melbourne, Moscow, Bombay and Washington. Work in permanent collections: Nat. Art Gall., New Delhi; Mayakovsky Mus., Moscow; Shevchenko Mus., Ukraine; Southern Illinois Univ. FRSA; FIAL. Mem. Soc. of Portrait Sculptors. *Publications:* Biographies in Bronze (The Sculpture of Fredda Brilliant), 1986; The Black Virgin, 1986, Women in Power, 1987; *short stories:* Truth in Fiction, 1986. *Recreations:* writing lyrics, composing songs and singing, attending classical concerts. *Address:* c/o Bonnie Owen, 816 East Main Street, Carbondale, IL 62901-3143, USA. *Died 25 May 1999.*

BRIND, Maj.-Gen. Peter Holmes Walter, CBE 1962 (OBE 1948); DSO 1945; DL; Vice President, Surrey Branch, British Red Cross Society, since 1984 (Deputy President, 1977–84); *b* 16 Feb. 1912; *yr s* of late General Sir John Brind, KCB, KBE, CMG, DSO and Dorothy M. S., *er d* of Col W. H. J. Frodsham, late E Surrey Regt; *m* 1942, Patricia Stewart Walker, *er d* of late Comdr S. M. Walker, DSC, RN, Horsalls, Harrietsham, Kent; three *s. Educ:* Wellington College; RMC, Sandhurst. Commissioned Dorset Regt, 1932; ADC to Governor of Bengal, 1936–39; Adjt, NW Europe, 1940; GSO 3 War Office, 1940–41; DAAG, HQ 12 Corps and Canadian Corps, 1941–42; Bde Major 1942; GSO 2 (MO) War Office, 1942; Comdt, Battle School, 1944; Comdg 2 Devons, NW Europe, 1944–45; GSO 1 (MT) War Office, 1946; GSO 1 (Ops), Palestine, 1948; GSO 1 (Plans), Egypt, 1949; GSO 1 (SD), War Office, 1950–54; Bt Lt-Col, 1952; Comdg 5th KAR (Kenya), 1954; Lt-Col, 1954; Col, 1955; Comdg 5 Inf. Bde Gp (BAOR), 1956; IDC 1959; Brig., 1960; Brig., AQ Middle East, 1960; BGS Eastern Comd, 1962; ADC to the Queen, 1964; Maj.-Gen., 1965; COS, Northern Comd, 1965–67. Dir, BRCS (Surrey Branch), 1968–77. Gov., public and preparatory schs, 1968–86. DL Surrey, 1970. *Recreations:* gardening, music. *Address:* Milestones, Hill Road, Haslemere, Surrey GU27 2JN.
Died 12 May 1999.

BRISE, Captain Guy Edward R.; *see* Ruggles-Brise.

BRISTOL, 7th Marquess of, *cr* 1826; **Frederick William John Augustus Hervey;** Baron Hervey of Ickworth, 1703; Earl of Bristol, 1714; Earl Jermyn, 1826; Hereditary High Steward of the Liberty of St Edmund; Governing Partner, Jermyn Shipping; Chairman, Estate Associates Ltd; *b* 15 Sept. 1954; *s* of 6th Marquess of Bristol and Pauline Mary, *d* of Herbert Coxon Bolton; *S* father, 1985; *m* 1984, Francesca (marr. diss. 1987), *d* of Douglas Fisher. *Educ:* Harrow; Neuchâtel Univ. Director: Guided Properties Ltd; Flintlock Hldgs Ltd. MInstD. *Heir:* half-*b* Lord Frederick William Augustus Hervey, *b* 19 Oct. 1979. *Clubs:* House of Lords Yacht; Travellers' (Paris); Monte Carlo Country. *Died 10 Jan. 1999.*

BRITTEN, Brig. George Vallette, CBE 1947 (OBE 1942, MBE 1940); HM Diplomatic Service, retired; *b* 19 March 1909; *s* of John Britten, Bozeat Manor, Northamptonshire, and Elizabeth Franziska Britten (*née* Vallette); *m* 1937, Shirley Jean Stewart Wink; three *s. Educ:* Wellingborough; RMC Sandhurst. Regtl duty in UK, 1929–38; Staff Coll., Camberley, 1938–39; served War: HQ 2 Corps, France and Belgium, 1939–40; Staff appts in UK, 1940–41; with 1st Airborne Div. in UK, N Africa and Sicily, 1942–43; DCS, 5 (US) Army, N Africa and Italy, 1943–44; HQ, 21st Army Gp, NW Europe, 1944–45; DCS, Brit. Military Govt, Germany, 1945–47; Regtl Duty, Berlin and Austria, 1947–49; WO, 1949–51; Comdt, Sch. of Infty, Hythe, 1952–54; Instr, US Army Staff Coll., Kansas, 1954–56; Planning Staff, NATO, Fontainebleau, 1956–58; Mil. Attaché, Brit. Embassy, Bonn, 1958–61; retired from Army, 1961; Ghana Desk, Commonwealth Office, 1961–62; with British High Commissions, Enugu, Kaduna, and Bathurst, 1962–66; Head of Chancery, British Embassy, Berne, 1967–71. American Legion of Merit, 1946; W German Grosses Verdienst Kreuz, 1959. *Recreation:* gardening. *Address:* 41 Bosville Drive, Sevenoaks, Kent TN13 3JA. *Died 5 Jan. 1997.*

BRITTEN, Rae Gordon, CMG 1972; HM Diplomatic Service, retired; *b* 27 Sept. 1920; *s* of Leonard Arthur Britten and Elizabeth Percival Taylor; *m* 1944, Mary Lynch; *m* 1952, Valentine Alms (marr. diss. 1974); one *s* three *d*; *m* 1977, Mrs Joan Dorothy Bull. *Educ:* Liverpool Institute High School; Magdalen College, Oxford. Served War 1941–45 (artillery and infantry). Research Assistant with Common Ground Ltd, 1947; apptd Commonwealth Relations Office, 1948; 2nd Sec., Brit. High Commn in India (Calcutta, 1948–49, Delhi, 1949–50); 1st Sec. Brit. High Commn, Bombay, 1955–58, Karachi, 1961–62; Deputy High Commissioner: Peshawar, March 1962; Lahore, June 1962–July 1964; Kingston, Jamaica, 1964–68; Head of Trade Policy Dept, FCO, 1968–71; Dep. High Comr, Dacca, and British Rep. to Bangladesh, 1971–72; Counsellor and Head of Chancery, Oslo, 1973–76; Head of SW Pacific Dept, FCO, 1976–78; Counsellor on Special Duties, FCO, 1978–80. *Address:* 4 Albany Crescent, Claygate, Esher, Surrey KT10 0PF. *Club:* Royal Commonwealth Society.
Died 3 April 1997.

BROACKES, Sir Nigel, Kt 1984; *b* Wakefield, 21 July 1934; *s* of late Donald Broackes and Nan Alford; *m* 1956, Joyce Edith Horne (*d* 1993); two *s* one *d. Educ:* Stowe. Nat. Service, commnd 3rd Hussars, 1953–54. Stewart & Hughman Ltd, Lloyd's Underwriting agents, 1952–55; various property developments, etc, 1955–57; Trafalgar House Ltd: Man. Dir, 1958; Dep. Chm. and Jt Man. Dir, 1968; Chm., 1969–92. Chm., Ship and Marine Technology Requirements Bd, 1972–77; Dep. Chm., Offshore Energy Technology Bd, 1975–77; Chm. Designate, then Chm., London Docklands Develt Corp., 1979–84; British Chm., EuroRoute, 1984–86; non-executive Director: Distillers Co., 1985–86; Eurotunnel plc, 1986–87; Channel Tunnel

Gp Ltd, 1986–87. Mem. Council, Nat. Assoc. of Property Owners, 1967–73. Governor, Stowe Sch., 1974–81. Trustee: Royal Opera House Trust, 1976–81; National Maritime Museum, 1987–96; Mem. Advisory Council, Victoria and Albert Museum, 1980–83. Dir, Horserace Totalisator Bd, 1976–81. Chm., Crafts Council, 1991–97. Mem., European Round Table, 1990–92. Freeman, City of London; Liveryman, Goldsmiths' Co. (Prime Warden, 1999–). Guardian Young Businessman of the Year, 1978. *Publication:* A Growing Concern, 1979. *Recreation:* silversmith. *Address:* 41 Chelsea Square, SW3 6LH; Checkendon Court, Checkendon, Oxon RG8 0SR.

Died 28 Sept. 1999.

BROADBRIDGE, 3rd Baron *cr* 1945, of Brighton, co. Sussex; **Peter Hewett Broadbridge;** Bt 1937; Deputy Speaker, House of Lords, 1994–99; Manager, Guild of Master Craftsmen, since 1993; *b* 19 Aug. 1938; *s* of 2nd Baron Broadbridge and Mabel Daisy (*d* 1966), *o d* of Arthur Edward Clarke; *S* father, 1972; *m* 1st, 1967, Mary (marr. diss. 1980), *o d* of W. O. Busch; two *d*; 2nd, 1989, Sally Finn. *Educ:* Hurstpierpoint Coll., Sussex; St Catherine's Coll., Oxford (MA, BSc). Unilever Ltd, 1963–65; Colgate Palmolive Ltd, 1966; Gallaher Ltd, 1967–70; Management Consultant: Peat, Marwick Mitchell & Co., EC2, 1970–78; Coopers and Lybrand and Associates Ltd, 1979–80; Dir, London Venture Capital Market Ltd, 1980–86. Pres., Nat. Assoc. of Leisure Gardeners, 1978–81. Freeman, City of London, 1980; Liveryman, Worshipful Co. of Goldsmiths, 1983. Brother, Art Workers Guild, 1997. *Recreations:* tennis, squash, antiques, silversmithing, watercolour painting, photography. *Heir:* cousin Martin Hugh Broadbridge [*b* 29 Nov 1929; *m* 1st, 1954, Norma (marr. diss.), *d* of late Major Herbert Sheffield, MC; one *s* one *d*; 2nd, 1968, Elizabeth, *d* of J. E. Trotman]. *Died 6 Feb. 2000.*

BROCKHOLES, Michael John F.; *see* Fitzherbert-Brockholes.

BROCKLEHURST, Maj.-Gen. Arthur Evers, CB 1956; DSO 1945; late RA; *b* 20 July 1905; *m* 1940, Joan Beryl Parry-Crooke; twin *d. Educ:* King's School, Canterbury; RMA Woolwich. 2nd Lieut, RA, 1925; CRA 6th Armoured Div., 1951; IDC 1954; DDPS (B) 1955; Chief of Staff, Malaya Comd, 1956–57; GOC, Rhine Dist, BAOR, 1958–59; Dep. Comdr BAOR, 1959–61; retired 1961. Chm., Devizes Constituency Cons. Assoc., 1963–65. *Recreation:* painting watercolours. *Address:* Downland Cottage, Bottlesford, Pewsey, Wilts SN9 6LU. *Club:* Army and Navy. *Died 2 Feb. 1998.*

BROCKMAN, Vice-Adm. Sir Ronald (Vernon), KCB 1965; CSI 1947; CIE 1946; CVO 1979; CBE 1943; Extra Gentleman Usher to the Queen, since 1979 (Gentleman Usher, 1967–79); *b* 8 March 1909; *er s* of late Engr Rear-Adm. H. S. Brockman, CB and Edith Mary Sheppard; *m* 1932, Marjorie Jean Butt (*d* 1994); one *s* three *d. Educ:* Weymouth Coll., Dorset. Entered Royal Navy, 1927; Assistant Secretary to First Sea Lord, Admiral of the Fleet Sir Roger Backhouse, 1938–39; Admiral's Secretary to First Sea Lord, Admiral of the Fleet Sir Dudley Pound, 1939–43; Admiral's Secretary to Admiral of the Fleet Lord Mountbatten in all appointments, 1943–59; Private Secretary to Governor-General of India, 1947–48; Principal Staff Officer to the Chief of Defence Staff, Min. of Defence, 1959–65. Lt-Comdr, 1939; Comdr, 1943; Captain, 1953; Rear-Admiral, 1959; Vice-Admiral, 1963; retired list, 1965. Mem., Rugby Football Union Cttee, 1956. DL Devon, 1968. KStJ 1985. Special Rosette of Cloud and Banner (China), 1946; Chevalier Legion of Honour and Croix de Guerre (France), 1946; Bronze Star Medal (USA), 1947. *Address:* Lympstone House,

Strawberry Hill, Lympstone, Devon EX8 5JZ. *T:* (01395) 268393. *Clubs:* Naval, MCC; Royal Western Yacht of England. *Died 3 Sept. 1999.*

BRODIE, Colin Alexander; QC 1980; *b* 19 April 1929; *s* of Sir Benjamin Collins Brodie, 4th Bt, MC, and late Mary Charlotte, *e d* of R. E. Palmer, Ballyheigue, Co. Kerry; *m* 1955, Julia Anne Irene, *yr d* of Norman Edward Wates; two *s. Educ:* Eton; Magdalen Coll., Oxford. 2/Lieut 8th KRI Hussars, 1949–50. Called to the Bar, Middle Temple, 1954. Bencher, Lincoln's Inn, 1988. *Recreation:* polo. *Address:* 24 Old Buildings, Lincoln's Inn, WC2A 3UJ. *T:* (020) 7404 0946. *Died 3 May 1999.*

BRODRICK, Elizabeth Ann, JP; FCCA; Chairman, Southampton University Hospitals NHS Trust, since 1992; *b* 12 July 1942; *d* of William Henry Hornby and Aldwyth Mary Hornby (*née* Collins); *m* 1963, Derek John Brodrick; two *d. Educ:* Wimbledon County Sch. for Girls. FCCA 1987. Trainee accountant, Cable and Wireless Ltd, 1960–65; Asst Accountant, Condé Nast Pubns Ltd, 1966; Roffe Swayne & Co., Chartered Accountants: Audit Senior, 1966–68; one-off assignments, 1968–74; Accountant and Company Sec., Manitou (Site Life) Ltd, 1974–80; freelance financial consultant, 1980–85; Manager, Coopers & Lybrand, Southampton, 1985–92. Mem., Electricity Consumers' Cttee, Southern Region, 1991–93. JP Eastleigh, Southampton, 1984. *Recreations:* friends and family, pet cats, light-hearted bridge and badminton, going to the theatre and concerts, reading, travelling. *Address:* Southampton University Hospitals NHS Trust, Trust Management Offices, Southampton General Hospital, Tremona Road, Southampton SO9 4XY. *Died 1 July 1996.*

BRODSKY, Joseph Alexandrovich; poet; *b* Leningrad, 24 May 1940; *s* of Alexander I. Brodsky and Maria M. Brodsky (*née* Volpert); one *s; m* 1990, Maria Sozzani; one *d. Educ:* Leningrad. Began writing poetry 1955; imprisoned as dissident, Arkhangelsk region, 1964–65; left for Vienna, 1972; went on to London and USA; poet in residence, Univ. of Michigan, 1972–73 and 1974–80; John and Catherine MacArthur Foundn Grant, 1981; teaching poetry and literature: Columbia Univ. (Russian Inst.); NY Univ. (Fellow, Inst. of Humanities); Mt Holyoke, Smith, Amherst and Hampshire Colls; Queen's Coll., City Univ. of NY. Hon. DLitt Yale, 1978 and other awards. Nobel Prize for Literature, 1987. *Publications:* Elegy for John Donne and other poems, 1967; Selected Poems, 1973; A Part of Speech, 1980; Less Than One, 1981 (Nat. Book Critics' Award, USA); To Urania, 1988; Watermark, 1992. *Address:* c/o Farrar, Straus & Giroux Inc., 19 Union Square West, New York, NY 10003, USA. *Died 28 Jan. 1996.*

BROMET, Air Comdt Dame Jean (Lena Annette), (Lady Bromet); *see* Conan Doyle, Air Comdt Dame J. L. A.

BROMLEY, His Honour Leonard John; QC 1971; a Circuit Judge, 1984–99; *b* 21 Feb. 1929; 2nd *s* of George Ernest and Winifred Dora Bromley; *m* 1962, Anne (*née* Bacon); three *d. Educ:* City of Leicester Boys' Sch.; Selwyn Coll., Cambridge (exhibnr). MA, LLM (Cantab). National Service: 2nd Lieut, RA, Hong Kong, 1947–49. Selwyn Coll., Cambridge, 1949–53; called to the Bar, Lincoln's Inn, 1954 (Greenland Scholar); Bencher, 1978; in practice, Chancery Bar, 1954–84; a Recorder, 1980–84. Chief Social Security Comr, 1984–90. General Council of the Bar: Mem., 1970–74; Chm., Law Reform Cttee, 1972–74; Mem., Exec. Cttee, 1972–74. Chm., Performing Right Tribunal, 1980–83. A Legal Assessor to: GMC, 1977–84; GDC, 1977–84. Governor, Latymer Sch., Edmonton, 1978–84. Chm., Selwyn Coll. Assoc., 1995–. Vice Cdre, Bar Yacht Club, 1971–75. *Recreations:* sailing, walking. *Address:* 1 Riverside Court, Chesterton Road, Cambridge CB4 3BB. *Died 2 Dec. 1999.*

BROOK, Helen Grace Mary, (Lady Brook), CBE 1995; Founder, 1963, and President, Brook Advisory Centre for Young People (Chairman, 1964–74); *b* 12 Oct. 1907; *d* of John and Helen Knewstub; *m* 1st, 1928, George Whitaker (marr. diss. 1930); one *d*; 2nd, 1937, Sir Robin Brook, CMG, OBE; two *d. Educ:* Convent of Holy Child Jesus, Mark Cross, Sussex. Voluntary worker: Family Planning Association, 1949– (Mem. Exec., Nat. Council, 1954–; Vice-Pres., 1987–); Family Planning Sales, 1972– (Chm., 1974–81); Dir, Marie Stopes Meml Clinic, 1958–64; Vice-Pres., Nat. Assoc. of Family Planning Nurses, 1980–. Freeman, City of London, 1993. Hon. DSc City, 1993. Galton Inst. Medal, 1994. *Recreations:* painting, gardening. *Died 3 Oct. 1997.*

BROOK, Sir Ralph Ellis, (Sir Robin), Kt 1974; CMG 1954; OBE 1945; Member: City and East London Area Health Authority, 1974–82 (Vice Chairman, 1974–79); City and Hackney District Health Authority, 1982–86; *b* 19 June 1908; *s* of Francis Brook, Harley Street, and Mrs E. I. Brook; *m* 1937, Helen (CBE 1995) (*d* 1997), *e d* of John Knewstub; two *d. Educ:* Eton; King's College, Cambridge. Served 1941–46; Brig., 1945 (OBE, despatches, Legion of Merit (Commander), Legion of Honour, Croix de Guerre and Bars, Order of Leopold (Officer), Belgian Croix de Guerre). Director, Bank of England, 1946–49. Formerly Chairman: Augustine Investments; Ionian Bank; Leda Inv. Trust; Jove Inv. Trust; W. E. Sykes; Truscon; Carclo; Sir Joseph Causton; Gordon Woodroffe; Vice-Chm., United City Merchants. Chm., 1966–68; Pres., 1968–72, London Chamber of Commerce and Industry; Pres., Assoc. of British Chambers of Commerce, 1972–74; Pres., Assoc. of Chambers of Commerce of EEC, 1974–76; Leader of Trade Missions: for HM Govt to Libya and Romania; for London or British Chambers of Commerce to France, Iran, China, Greece, Finland and Hungary; HM Govt Dir, BP Co., 1970–73; Deputy Chairman: British Tourist and Holidays Board, 1946–50; Colonial Development Corp., 1949–53. Mem., Foundn for Management Educn, 1975–82. Sports Council: Mem., 1971–78; Vice-Chm., 1974; Chm., 1975–78, Chm., Sports Develt Cttee, 1971–74; Mem. Governors and Exec. Cttee, Sports Aid Foundn, 1975–95. Mem., Cttee on Invisible Exports, 1969–74; Mem. Court, Council, Finance and Hon. Degrees Cttees, City Univ.; Hon. Treasurer: Amateur Fencing Assoc., 1946–61; CCPR, 1961–77 (also Mem. Exec.); Family Planning Association, 1966–75. High Sheriff of County of London, 1950; Mem. Council, Festival of Britain. Mem. Council and Exec. Cttee, King Edward's Fund; Pres., London Homes for the Elderly, 1980–91 (Chm., 1973–80). St Bartholomew's Hospital: Governor, 1962–74; Treasurer and Chm., 1969–74; Chm., Special Trustees, 1974–88; Pres., St Bartholomew's Med. Coll., 1969–88; Governor, Royal Free Hosp., 1962–74; former governor of schools. Past Master, Wine Warden, Haberdashers' Co. Hon. DSc City, 1989. *Recreation:* British Sabre Champion, 1936; Olympic Games, 1936, 1948; Capt. British Team, 1933 (3rd in European Championship), etc. *Address:* Flat 77, Rodney Court, 6–8 Maida Vale, W9 1TJ. *Died 25 Oct. 1998.*

BROOKE OF YSTRADFELLTE, Baroness *cr* 1964 (Life Peer), of Ystradfellte, co. Brecknock; **Barbara Muriel Brooke,** DBE 1960; *b* 14 Jan. 1908; *y d* of late Rev. Canon A. A. Mathews; *m* 1933, Henry Brooke, CH, PC (later Baron Brooke of Cumnor) (*d* 1984); two *s* two *d. Educ:* Queen Anne's School, Caversham. Joint Vice-Chm., Conservative Party Organisation, 1954–64. Member: Hampstead Borough Council, 1948–65; North-West Metropolitan Regional Hospital Board, 1954–66; Management Cttee, King Edward's Hospital Fund for

London, 1966–71; Chairman: Exec. Cttee, Queen's Institute of District Nursing, 1961–71; Governing Body of Godolphin and Latymer School, Hammersmith, 1960–78. Hon. Fellow, Queen Mary and Westfield College. *Address:* Romans Halt, Mildenhall, Marlborough, Wilts SN8 2LX. *Died 1 Sept. 2000.*

BROOKE, Prof. Bryan Nicholas, MD, MChir; FRCS; Emeritus Professor (Professor of Surgery, University of London, at St George's Hospital 1963–80); lately Consultant Surgeon, St George's Hospital; *b* 21 Feb. 1915; *s* of George Cyril Brooke, LitD, FSA (numismatist) and Margaret Florence Brooke; *m* 1940, Naomi Winefride Mills; three *d. Educ:* Bradfield College, Berkshire; Corpus Christi College, Cambridge; St Bartholomew's Hospital, London. FRCS 1942; MChir (Cantab.) 1944; MD (Birm.) with hons 1954. Lieut-Colonel, RAMC, 1945–46. Lecturer in Surgery, Aberdeen Univ., 1946–47; Reader in Surgery, Birmingham Univ., 1947–63; Hunterian Prof. RCS, 1951 and 1979. Examiner in Surgery, Universities of: Birmingham, 1951–63; Cambridge, 1958; Bristol, 1961; London, 1962; Glasgow, 1969; Oxford, 1970; Hong Kong, 1972; Nigeria, 1975; RCS, 1973; Chm., Ct of Examnrs, RCS, 1978. Member, Medical Appeals Tribunal, 1948–87. Founder Pres., Ileostomy Assoc. of GB, 1957–82. Chm., Malvern Girls' Coll., 1972–82. Copeman Medal for Scientific Research, 1960; Graham Award, Amer. Proctologic Soc., 1961; Award of NY Soc. of Colon and Rectal Surgeons, 1967. Hon. FRACS 1977, Hon. Fellow, Colo-Proctological Sect., RSM, 1989; Hon. Mem., British Soc. of Gastroenterology, 1979. Consultant Editor, World Medicine, 1980–82. *Publications:* Ulcerative Colitis and its Surgical Treatment, 1954; You and Your Operation, 1957; United Birmingham Cancer Reports, 1953, 1954, 1957; (co-editor) Recent Advances in Gastroenterology, 1965, (co-author) Metabolic Derangements in Gastrointestinal Surgery, 1966; Understanding Cancer, 1971; Crohn's Disease, 1977; The Troubled Gut, 1986; (jtly) A Garden of Roses, 1987; Editor, Jl Clinics in Gastroenterology; contrib. to various surgical works; numerous articles on large bowel disorder, medical education, steroid therapy. *Recreation:* painting. *Address:* The High House, 38 Kenley Lane, Kenley, Surrey CR8 5DD. *Club:* Athenæum. *Died 18 Sept. 1998.*

BROOKE, Sir Richard (Neville), 10th Bt *cr* 1662, of Norton Priory, Cheshire; *b* 1 May 1915; *s* of Sir Richard Christopher Brooke, 9th Bt, and Marian Dorothea (*d* 1965), *d* of late Arthur Charles Innes, MP, Dromantine, Co. Down; *S* father, 1981; *m* 1st, 1937, Lady Mabel Kathleen Jocelyn (marr. diss. 1959; she *d* 1985), *d* of 8th Earl of Roden; two *s*; 2nd, 1960, Jean Evison, *d* of late Lt-Col A. C. Corfe, DSO. *Educ:* Eton. Served as Lieutenant, Scots Guards, 1939–46; prisoner of war (escaped). Chartered Accountant (FCA), 1946; Senior Partner, Price Waterhouse & Co., European Firms, 1969–75; retired, 1975. *Recreations:* racing, fishing. *Heir: s* Richard David Christopher Brooke [*b* 23 Oct. 1938; *m* 1st, 1963, Carola Marion (marr. diss. 1978), *d* of Sir Robert Erskine-Hill, 2nd Bt; two *s*; 2nd, 1979, Lucinda Barlow, *o d* of late J. F. Voelcker and of Jean Constance Voelcker, Lidgetton, Natal]. *Address:* Pond Cottage, Crawley, near Winchester, Hants SO21 2PR. *T:* (01962) 776272. *Club:* Boodle's. *Died 9 Dec. 1997.*

BROOKES, Sir Wilfred (Deakin), Kt 1979; CBE 1972; DSO 1944; AEA 1945; *b* 17 April 1906; *s* of Herbert Robinson Brookes and Ivy Deakin; *m* 1928, Betty (*d* 1968), *d* of A. H. Heal; one *s. Educ:* Melbourne Grammar Sch.; Melbourne Univ. Exec., later Alternate Dir, Aust. Paper Manufacturers Ltd, 1924–38; Exec. Dir, Box and Container Syndicate, 1938–39. War Service, 1939–45; Sqdn Leader, RAAF, 1939–41 (despatches); CO 24 Sqdn, 1942 (despatches); CO 22 Sqdn, 1942; CO 7 Fighter

Section HQ; Comdr, 78th Fighter Wing, New Guinea Offensive, 1943–45; Dir of Postings, RAAF HQ, rank of Gp Captain, 1945. Chairman (retired): Associated Pulp and Paper Mills, 1952–78 (Dir, 1945–78); Colonial Mutual Life Soc., 1965–78 (Dir, 1955–78); Electrolytic Refining & Smelting Co. of Australia Ltd, 1956–80; Apsonor Pty Ltd, to 1983 (Dir, 1960–83); Collins Wales Pty Ltd, 1978–82 (Dir, 1974–82); Director (retired): BH South Group, 1956–82; North Broken Hill, 1970–82; Alcoa of Australia, 1961–83. Past Pres., Inst. of Public Affairs; former Chm. and Trustee, Edward Wilson Charitable Trust; Patron, Deakin Foundn, 1988–. Hon. Dr of Letters Deakin, 1982. Dep. Chm., Corps of Commissionaires, 1979–88 (Governor, 1975–90). *Recreations:* swimming, walking. *Address:* 20 Heyington Place, Toorak, Vic 3142, Australia. *T:* (3) 98224553. *Clubs:* Melbourne, Australian (Melbourne).   *Died 1 Aug. 1997.*

BROOKS, Eric Arthur Swatton; Head of Claims Department, Foreign Office, 1960 until retirement, 1967; *b* 9 Oct. 1907; *yr s* of late A. E. Brooks, MA, Maidenhead; *m* 1947, Daphne Joyce, *yr d* of late George McMullan, MD, FRCSE, Wallingford; one *s* one *d*. *Educ:* Reading Sch.; New Coll., Oxford (MA). 2nd cl. hons Jurisprudence, 1929. Solicitor, 1932; practised in London, 1932–39; Mem. Law Soc., 1934– (Mem. Overseas Relations Cttee, 1949). Served War of 1939–45 in Admty and Min. of Aircraft Production, and in Operational Research as Hon. Flt-Lieut RAFVR until 1944; Disposal of Govt Factories of Min. of Aircraft Production, 1944–Dec. 1945; Foreign Office, 1946; served on Brit. Delegns in negotiations with: Polish and Hungarian Governments, 1953, 1954; Bulgarian Government, 1955; Rumanian Government, 1955, 1956, 1960; USSR, 1964, 1965, 1966, 1967; British Representative on Anglo-Italian Conciliation Commn, until 1967. Councillor: Borough of Maidenhead, 1972–74; Royal Borough of Windsor and Maidenhead, 1973–87. Pres., Maidenhead Civic Soc., 1994. *Publications:* The Foreign Office Claims Manual, 1968; Maidenhead and its Name, 1985; Earlier Days of Maidenhead Golf Club, 1985; articles in legal jls, and on local history, local education, and flood prevention. *Recreations:* skating, study of birds, golf (Oxford Univ. team *v* Cambridge Univ., 1929; various later Amateur European Championships), gardening. *Address:* Kitoha, 116b Grenfell Road, Maidenhead, Berks SL6 1HB. *T:* (01628) 621621.   *Died 14 May 1997.*

BROOKSBY, John Burns, CBE 1973; FRS 1980; Director, Animal Virus Research Institute, Pirbright, 1964–79; *b* 25 Dec. 1914; *s* of George B. Brooksby, Glasgow; *m* 1940, Muriel Weir; one *s* one *d*. *Educ:* Hyndland Sch., Glasgow; Glasgow Veterinary Coll.; London University. BSc (VetSc) 1936; PhD 1947; DSc 1957; MRCVS 1935; FRCVS 1978. Research Officer, Pirbright, 1939; Dep. Dir, 1957; Dir, 1964. FRSE 1968. Hon. DSc Edinburgh, 1981. *Publications:* papers on virus diseases of animals in scientific jls. *Address:* The Burlings, 48 High Street, Swaffham Bulbeck, Cambridge CB5 0LX. *T:* (01223) 812607.   *Died 17 Dec. 1998.*

BROUGHTON, Air Marshal Sir Charles, KBE 1965 (CBE 1952); CB 1961; Royal Air Force, retired; Air Member for Supply and Organization, Ministry of Defence, 1966–68; *b* 27 April 1911; *s* of Charles and Florence Gertrude Broughton; *m* 1939, Sylvia Dorothy Mary Bunbury (*d* 1995); one *d* (and one *d* decd). *Educ:* New Zealand; RAF College, Cranwell. Commissioned, 1932; India, 1933–37; Flying Instructor, 1937–40; served War of 1939–45 in Coastal Command and Middle East (despatches four times); Flying Training Command, 1947–49; Air Ministry, 1949–51; Imperial Defence College, 1952; NATO, Washington DC, 1953–55; Far East, 1955–58; Transport Command, 1958–61; Dir-

General of Organization, Air Min. (subseq. Min. of Defence), 1961–64; UK Representative in Ankara on Permanent Military Deputies Group of Central Treaty Organization, 1965–66.   *Died 17 May 1998.*

BROWN, Alexander Cosens Lindsay, CB 1980; Chief Veterinary Officer, Ministry of Agriculture, Fisheries and Food, 1973–80; *b* Glasgow, 30 Jan. 1920; *s* of William Tait Brown and Margaret Rae; *m* 1945, Mary McDougal Hutchison; two *s*. *Educ:* Hutchesons' Grammar Sch., Glasgow; Glasgow Veterinary Coll. Diploma of RCVS; FRCVS 1980. Ministry of Agriculture, Fisheries and Food: appointed Vet. Officer to Dorset, 1943; Divisional Vet. Officer, HQ Tolworth, 1955; Divisional Vet. Officer, Essex, 1958–62; Dep. Regional Vet. Officer, W Midland Region, Wolverhampton, 1962–63; Regional Vet. Officer, Eastern Region, Cambridge, 1963; HQ Tolworth, 1967; Dep. Dir, Veterinary Field Services, 1969–70, Dir, 1970–73. Mem. ARC, 1975–80. *Publications:* contribs to Jl of Royal Soc. of Medicine, Veterinary Record, State Veterinary Jl. *Recreations:* gardening, swimming, reading. *Address:* 29 Ashwood Park, Fetcham, Leatherhead, Surrey KT22 9NT. *T:* (01372) 457997.

Died 23 July 1999.

BROWN, Sir Allen (Stanley), Kt 1956; CBE 1953; Australian Commissioner for British Phosphate Commissioners and Christmas Island Phosphate Commission, 1970–76; *b* 3 July 1911; *s* of Robert S. Brown, Hartwell, Vic; *m* 1936, Hilda May Wilke; one *s* two *d*. *Educ:* Wesley Coll., Univ. of Melbourne (MA; LLM 1933). Dir-Gen. of Post-War Reconstruction, 1948; Sec., Prime Minister's Dept and Sec. to Cabinet, Commonwealth Govt, 1949–58; Deputy Australian High Commissioner to UK, 1959–65; Australian Ambassador to Japan, 1965–70. *Address:* c/o 31 Uvadale Road, Kew, Vic 3101, Australia.   *Died 2 Aug. 1999.*

BROWN, Sir (Arthur James) Stephen, KBE 1967; CEng, MIMechE; Chairman: Stone-Platt Industries Ltd, 1968–73 (Deputy Chairman, 1965–67); Molins Ltd, 1971–78; Deputy Chairman, Chloride Group, 1965–73; *b* 15 Feb. 1906; *s* of Arthur Mogg Brown and Ada Kelk (*née* Upton); *m* 1935, Margaret Alexandra McArthur; one *s* one *d*. *Educ:* Taunton School; Bristol University (BSc(Eng)). Apprenticed British Thomson-Houston Co. Ltd, 1928–32; joined J. Stone & Co. Ltd, 1932, Dir, 1945; Man. Dir J. Stone & Co. (Deptford) Ltd (on formation), 1951; Divisional Dir, Stone-Platt Industries Ltd (on formation), 1958; Director: Fairey Co., 1971–76; Porvair Ltd, 1971–87. Pres., Engineering Employers' Fedn, 1964–65; Pres., Confedn of British Industry, 1966–68; Founder Mem., Export Council for Europe, 1960 (Dep. Chm., 1962–63); Mem., NEDC, 1966–71. Hon. DSc Aston Univ., 1967. *Address:* Martin Lodge, Church Street, Henfield, West Sussex BN5 9NR. *T:* (01273) 492881.

Died 26 Feb. 1998.

BROWN, Dame Beryl P.; *see* Paston Brown.

BROWN, Rev. Cyril James, OBE 1956; Rector of Warbleton, 1970–77; Chaplain to the Queen, 1956–74; *b* 12 Jan. 1904; *s* of late James Brown, Clifton, Bristol; *m* 1931, Myrtle Aufrère (*d* 1996), *d* of late Mark Montague Ford, London; no *c*. *Educ:* Westminster Abbey Choir School; Clifton College; Keble College, Oxford; St Stephen's House, Oxford. Deacon 1927, priest 1928; Curate of St Gabriel's, Warwick Square, 1927–31; Chaplain, Missions to Seamen, Singapore, 1931–34, Hong Kong, 1934–41; Chaplain, Hong Kong RNVR, 1941–46; Youth Secretary, Missions to Seamen, 1946–47, Superintendent, 1947–51, General Superintendent, 1951–59, General Secretary, 1959–69; Prebendary of St Paul's, 1958–69. *Publications:* contributions to East and West Review, World Dominion, etc. *Recreation:* choral

music. *Address:* Royal Alfred Seafarers Home, 5–11 Hartington Place, Eastbourne, East Sussex BN21 3BS.
Died 30 Jan. 1997.

BROWN, Denise Jeanne Marie Lebreton, (Mrs Frank Waters), RWA 1986 (ARWA 1980); RE 1959 (ARE 1941); artist; *b* 8 Jan. 1911; *d* of Frederick Peter Brown and Jeanne Lebreton; *m* 1938, Frank William Eric Waters (*d* 1986); one *s. Educ:* Lyzeum Nonnenwerth im Rhein; Royal College of Art. British Instn Schol. in Engraving, 1932; ARCA 1935; RCA Travelling Schol., 1936; *prox. acc.* Rome Scholarship in Engraving, 1936. Exhibited at: Royal Academy, regularly 1934–; Royal Society of Painter-Etchers and Engravers; Royal West of England Acad.; also in Canada, USA and S Africa; work represented in British, V&A, and Ashmolean Museums. *Publications:* books illustrated include: several on gardening; children's books, etc. *Recreations:* music, gardening. *Address:* c/o 7 Priory Lodge, Nightingale Place, Rickmansworth, Herts WD3 2DG. *Club:* Royal Air Force.
Died 22 July 1998.

BROWN, Denys Downing, CMG 1966; MM 1945; HM Diplomatic Service, retired; *b* 16 Dec. 1918; *s* of A. W. Brown, Belfast, and Marjorie Downing; *m* 1954, Patricia Marjorie, *e d* of Sir Charles Bartley; one *s* one *d. Educ:* Hereford Cathedral School; Brasenose College, Oxford (Scholar). Oxf. and Bucks LI, 1939–45 (prisoner-of-war, 1940; escaped, 1945). Entered Foreign Service, 1946; served in Poland, Germany, Egypt, Yugoslavia, Sweden, and FO; Minister (Economic), Bonn, retired 1971; Dir, P&O Steam Navigation Co., 1971–80. *Recreations:* reading, travel. *Address:* Step Cottage, 26 Shadyhanger, Godalming, Surrey GU7 2HR. *T:* (01483) 416635.
Died 7 Feb. 1997.

BROWN, Sir (Frederick Herbert) Stanley, Kt 1967, CBE 1959; BSc; FEng 1976; FIMechE; FIEE; retired; Chairman, Central Electricity Generating Board, 1965–72 (Deputy-Chairman, 1959–64); *b* 9 Dec. 1910; *s* of Clement and Annie S. Brown; *m* 1937, Marjorie Nancy (*née* Brown); two *d. Educ:* King Edward's School, Birmingham; Birmingham University. Corp. of Birmingham Electric Supply Dept, 1932–46; West Midlands Joint Electricity Authority, 1946–47; Liverpool Corporation Electricity Supply Department, 1947–48; Merseyside and N Wales Division of British Electricity Authority: Generation Engineer (Construction), 1948–49; Chief Generation Engineer (Construction), 1949–51; Deputy Generation Design Engineer of British Electricity Authority, 1951–54; Generation Design Engineer, 1954–57, Chief Engineer, 1957, of Central Electricity Authority; Member for Engineering, Central Elec. Generating Board, 1957–59. President: Instn of Electrical Engineers, 1967–68; EEIBA, 1969–70. Member: Council, City and Guilds of London Inst., 1969; Court of Govs, Univ. of Birmingham, 1969. Hon. DSc: Aston, 1971; Salford, 1972. *Publications:* various papers to technical institutions. *Recreation:* gardening. *Address:* Compton Suite, Northleach Court, High Street, Northleach, Glos GL54 3PQ. *T:* (01451) 860218.
Died 17 March 1997.

BROWN, George Mackay, OBE 1974; FRSL 1977; author; *b* 17 Oct. 1921; *s* of John Brown and Mary Jane Mackay. *Educ:* Stromness Acad.; Newbattle Abbey Coll.; Edinburgh Univ. (MA). Hon. MA Open Univ., 1976; Hon. LLD Dundee, 1977; Hon. DLitt Glasgow, 1985. *Publications: fiction:* A Calendar of Love, 1967; A Time to Keep, 1969; Greenvoe, 1972; Magnus, 1973; Hawkfall, 1974; The Two Fiddlers, 1975; The Sun's Net, 1976; Pictures in the Cave, 1977; Six Lives of Frankle the Cat, 1980; Andrina, 1983; Time in a Red Coat, 1984; Christmas Stories, 1985; The Golden Bird, 1987; The Masked Fisherman, 1989; The Sea King's Daughter, 1991;

Vinland, 1992; Beside the Ocean of Time, 1994; Winter Tales (short stories), 1995; *plays:* A Spell for Green Corn, 1970; Three Plays, 1984; The Loom of Light, 1986; A Celebration for Magnus (son et lumière), 1987; *poetry:* Loaves and Fishes, 1959; The Year of the Whale, 1965; Fishermen with Ploughs, 1971; Winterfold, 1976; Selected Poems, 1977, 2nd edn 1996; Voyages, 1983; Christmas Poems, 1984; Tryst in Egilsay, 1989; The Wreck of the Archangel, 1989; Selected Poems 1954–1983, 1991; Forresterhill, 1992; The Lost Village, 1993; Orfeo, 1995; *essays, etc:* An Orkney Tapestry, 1969; Letters from Hamnavoe, 1975; Under Brinkie's Brae, 1979; Portrait of Orkney, 1981; (ed) Selected Prose of Edwin Muir, 1987; Letters to Gypsy, 1990; Rockpools and Daffodils, 1993; *posthumous publications:* Following a Lark (poems), 1996; For the Islands I Sing (autobiog.), 1997. *Recreation:* reading. *Address:* 3 Mayburn Court, Stromness, Orkney KW16 3DH.
Died 13 April 1996.

BROWN, Prof. Sir (George) Malcolm, Kt 1985; FRS 1975; consultant geologist; Director: British Geological Survey (formerly Institute of Geological Sciences), 1979–85; Geological Museum, 1979–85; Geological Survey of Northern Ireland, 1979–85; *b* 5 Oct. 1925; *s* of late George Arthur Brown and Anne Brown; *m* 1st, 1963, Valerie Jane Gale (marr. diss. 1977); 2nd, 1985, Sally Jane Marston, *e d* of A. D. Spencer; two step *d. Educ:* Coatham Sch., Redcar; Durham Univ. (BSc, DSc); Oxford Univ. (MA, DPhil). RAF, 1944–47. FGS. Commonwealth Fund (Harkness) Fellow, Princeton Univ., 1954–55; Lectr in Petrology, Oxford Univ., 1955–66; Fellow, St Cross Coll., Oxford, 1965–67; Carnegie Instn Res. Fellow, Geophysical Lab., Washington DC, 1966–67; Prof. of Geology, Durham Univ., 1967–79, then Emeritus (Dean of Faculty of Science, 1978–79, and Pro-Vice-Chancellor, 1979). Vis. Prof., Univ. of Berne, 1977–78; Adrian Vis. Fellow, Univ. of Leicester, 1983. NASA Principal Investigator, Apollo Moon Programme, 1967–75; Geol Advr to ODA, 1979–85; Chm., Internat. Geol Correlation Prog. (IUGS–UNESCO), 1993–96. Member: Natural Environment Res. Council, 1972–75; Council, Royal Soc., 1980–81. Pres., Section C (Geology), British Assoc., 1987–88. Member: Council, RHBNC, Univ. of London, 1987–89; Adv. Bd, Sch. of Envmtl Scis, Univ. of E Anglia, 1991–94. UK Editor, Physics and Chemistry of the Earth, 1977–79. Hon. Foreign Fellow, Geol Soc. of America, 1993. Hon. DSc Leicester, 1984; DUniv Open, 1990. Daniel Pidgeon Fund Award, 1952, Wollaston Fund Award, 1963, Murchison Medal, 1981, Geol Soc. of London. *Publications:* (with L. R. Wager) Layered Igneous Rocks, 1968; (contrib.) Methods in Geochemistry, 1960; (contrib.) Basalts, 1967; (contrib.) Planet Earth, 1977; (contrib.) Origin of the Solar System, 1978; papers in several sci. jls. *Recreations:* travel and exploration, classical guitar playing. *Address:* 5 Horwood Close, Headington, Oxford OX3 7RF. *T:* (01865) 742464. *Club:* Royal Over-Seas League.
Died 27 March 1997.

BROWN, Dame Gillian (Gerda), DCVO 1981; CMG 1971; HM Diplomatic Service, retired; *b* 10 Aug. 1923; *er d* of late Walter Brown and Gerda Brown (*née* Grenside). *Educ:* The Spinney, Gt Bookham; Stoatley Hall, Haslemere; Somerville Coll., Oxford (Hon. Fellow 1981). FO, 1944–52; 2nd Sec., Budapest, 1952–54; FO, 1954–59; 1st Sec., Washington, 1959–62; 1st Sec., UK Delegn to OECD, Paris, 1962–65; FO, 1965–66; Counsellor and Head of Gen. Dept, FO, subseq. Head of Aviation, Marine and Telecommunications Dept, later Marine and Transport Dept, FCO, 1967–70; Counsellor, Berne, 1970–74; Under Sec., Dept of Energy, 1975–78; Asst Under Sec. of State, FCO, 1978–80; Ambassador to Norway, 1981–83. Mem., Panel of Chairmen, CSSB, 1984–88. Council Mem., Greenwich Forum, 1985–. Chm., Anglo-Norse Soc., 1988–98 (Mem. Council, 1998–). Hon. LLD Bath, 1981.

Grand Cross, Order of St Olav (Norway), 1981. *Address:* c/o HSBC, Central Hall, Westminster, SW1P 3AS.
Died 21 April 1999.

BROWN, Maj.-Gen. James, CB 1982; Administrative Manager (Projects), Mathematics and Statistics Department, Brunel University, since 1994; *b* 12 Nov. 1928; *s* of late James Brown; *m* 1952, Lilian May Johnson; two *s. Educ:* Methodist Coll., Belfast; RMA Sandhurst; psc, jssc, rcds. Commissioned RAOC, 1948; served UK (attached 1 Duke of Wellington's Regt), Egypt, Cyprus, War Office, 1948–58; Staff Coll., Camberley, 1959; BAOR, UK, 1960–64; JSSC, Latimer, 1964–65; HQ Gurkha Inf. Bde, Borneo, 1965–66 (despatches); MoD, 1966–67; Comdr RAOC, 4 Div., 1967–70; AA&QMG (Ops/Plans), HQ 1 (BR) Corps, 1970–72; Central Ordnance Depots, Donnington and Bicester, 1972–75; Dep. Dir, Ordnance Services, MoD, 1975; RCDS, 1976; Dep. Dir, Personal Services, MoD, 1977–80; Dir Gen. of Ordnance Services, 1980–83. Col Comdt, RAOC, 1983–85. Sec., Computer Centre, 1983–85, Dir, Management Inf. Services Div., 1985–89, London Univ.; Asst Dir (Projects), Numerical Algorithms Gp Ltd, 1989–95. *Address:* c/o Royal Bank of Scotland, 49 Charing Cross, SW1A 2DX. *Died 27 Jan. 2000.*

BROWN, His Honour James Alexander, TD 1948; QC 1956; Recorder of Belfast, 1978–82; *b* 13 June 1914; *s* of Rt Hon. Mr Justice (Thomas Watters) Brown and Mary Elizabeth Brown; *m* 1950, Shirley Wallace Sproule; one *s* two *d. Educ:* Campbell College, Belfast; Balliol College, Oxford (BA; Pres., Oxford Union Soc., 1936). Served 1/Royal Ulster Rifles, 1939–45 (wounded; Captain). Called Bar of NI, 1946; called English Bar (Gray's Inn), 1950. County Court Judge, Co. Down, 1967–78.
Died 19 May 1999.

BROWN, Sir John, Kt 2000; Deputy Chairman, John Brown & Co. Ltd, 1963–67, retired; *b* 6 May 1901; *m* 1st, 1940, Elizabeth Wright (*d* 1953); 2nd, 1956, Isobel Gibbon (*née* Turner) (*d* 1988). *Educ:* Hutchesons' Grammar Sch.; Glasgow Univ. (BSc Dist. Naval Architecture 1923). With John Brown & Co. Ltd, 1919–67: on secondment to Sociedad Española de Construcción Naval, 1927–29; Naval Architect, 1948; Local Dir, 1949–53; Technical Dir, 1953–59; Man. Dir, 1959–63. Major design projects included ships Queen Mary, Queen Elizabeth, QE2, and HMY Britannia. Pres., IES, 1959–61. Liveryman, Co. of Shipwrights, 1960–. Hon. LLD Glasgow, 1965. *Recreations:* sailing, bowls, golf. *Club:* Caledonian.
Died 27 Dec. 2000.

BROWN, Sir John (Douglas Keith), Kt 1960; Chairman, McLeod Russel plc, London, 1972–79 (Director, 1963–83), retired; Director of other companies; *b* 8 Sept. 1913; *s* of late Ralph Douglas Brown and Rhoda Miller Keith; *m* 1940, Margaret Eleanor (*d* 1995), *d* of late William Alexander Burnet; two *s. Educ:* Glasgow Acad. CA 1937. Joined Messrs Lovelock & Lewes, Chartered Accountants, Calcutta, 1937 (Partnership, 1946; retired 1948); joined Jardine Henderson Ltd as a Managing Director, 1949, Chairman, 1957–63. Pres., Bengal Chamber of Commerce and Industry and Associated Chambers of Commerce of India, 1958–60; Pres., UK Citizens' Assoc. (India), 1961. Member: Eastern Area Local Bd, Reserve Bank of India, 1959–63; Advisory Cttee on Capital Issues, Govt of India, 1958–63; Technical Advisory Cttee on Company Law, 1958–63; Companies Act Amendment Cttee, 1957; Central Excise Reorganisation Cttee, 1960. *Recreations:* gardening, walking. *Clubs:* Oriental; Bengal (Calcutta).
Died 13 Oct. 2000.

BROWN, Leslie; Deputy Chairman, Prudential Assurance Co. Ltd, 1970–74 (a Director, 1965–77); *b* 29 Oct. 1902;

s of late W. H. Brown and Eliza J. Fiveash; *m* 1930, Frances Vernon (*d* 1995), *d* of T. B. Lever; two *s* one *d. Educ:* Selhurst Grammar School. Joined Prudential Assurance Co. Ltd, 1919; Secretary and Chief Investment Manager, Prudential Assurance Co. Ltd, 1955–64 (Joint Secretary 1942); Chairman: Prudential Unit Trust Managers Ltd, 1968–75; Prudential Pensions Ltd, 1970–75. Member, Jenkins Committee on Company Law Amendment, 1960. Deputy-Chairman, Insurance Export Finance Co. Ltd, 1962–65. Inst. of Actuaries: FIA 1929; Vice-Pres., 1949–51. *Recreation:* bowls.
Died 8 March 1998.

BROWN, Rt Rev. Leslie Wilfrid, CBE 1965; Bishop of St Edmundsbury and Ipswich, 1966–78; *b* 10 June 1912; *s* of Harry and Maud Brown; *m* 1939, (Annie) Winifred (*d* 1999), *d* of R. D. Megaw, sometime Puisne Judge, NI; one *d. Educ:* Enfield Grammar School; London College of Divinity (London Univ.). BD 1936, MTh 1944, DD 1957. Deacon, 1935, priest, 1936; Curate, St James' Milton, Portsmouth, 1935–38; Missionary, CMS, Cambridge Nicholson Instn, Kottayam, Travancore, S India, 1938–43; Fellow Commoner and Chaplain, Downing College, Cambridge, 1943–44; Kerala United Theological Seminary, Trivandrum: tutor, 1945; Principal, 1946, and 1951–53; Chaplain, Jesus Coll., Cambridge, 1950–51; Bishop of Uganda, 1953–60, of Namirembe (following change of name of diocese), 1960–65; Archbishop of Uganda, Rwanda and Burundi, 1961–65. Chm., ACCM, 1972–76. Select Preacher before Univ. of Cambridge, 1950, 1967, 1979, Oxford, 1967. Hon. Fellow, Downing Coll., Cambridge, 1966. Hon. MA Cantab, 1953; DD (*hc*) Trinity Coll., Toronto, 1963. Chaplain and Sub-Prelate, Order of St John, 1968. *Publications:* The Indian Christians of St Thomas, 1956, 2nd edn 1982; The Christian Family, 1959; God as Christians see Him, 1961; Relevant Liturgy, 1965; Three Worlds, One Word, 1981; The King and the Kingdom, 1988. *Address:* Manormead Nursing Home, Tilford Road, Hindhead, Surrey GU26 6RA. *Club:* Royal Commonwealth Society.
Died 27 Dec. 1999.

BROWN, Sir Malcolm; *see* Brown, Sir G. M.

BROWN, Prof. Robert, DSc; FRS 1956; Regius Professor of Botany, Edinburgh University, 1958–77, then Emeritus Professor; *b* 29 July 1908; *s* of Thomas William and Ethel Minnie Brown; *m* 1940, Morna Doris Mactaggart. *Educ:* English School, Cairo; University of London (DSc). Assistant Lecturer in Botany, Manchester University, 1940–44; Lecturer in Botany, Bedford College, London, 1944–46; Reader in Plant Physiology, Leeds University, 1946–52; Professor of Botany, Cornell University, 1952–53; Director, Agricultural Research Council Unit of Plant Cell Physiology, 1953–58. *Publications:* various papers on plant physiology in the Annals of Botany, Proceedings of Royal Society and Journal of Experimental Botany. *Recreation:* gardening. *Address:* 5 Treble House Terrace, Blewbury, Didcot, Oxfordshire OX11 9NZ. *T:* (01235) 850415. *Died 13 July 1999.*

BROWN, Robert Crofton; DL; Member, Newcastle City Council, since 1988; Lord Mayor of Newcastle, 1994–95; *b* 16 May 1921; *m* 1945, Marjorie Hogg, Slaithwaite, Yorks; one *s* one *d. Educ:* Denton Road Elementary School; Atkinson Road Technical School; Rutherford Coll. War Service, 1942–46. Apprenticed plumber and gasfitter, Newcastle & Gateshead Gas Co., 1937; plumber, 1946; Inspector, 1949; in service of Northern Gas Board until 1966. Secretary of Constituency Labour Party and Agent to MP for 16 years. MP (Lab): Newcastle upon Tyne West, 1966–83; Newcastle upon Tyne North, 1983–87. Parly Sec., Ministry of Transport, 1968–70; Parly Under-Sec. of State, Social Security, March-Sept. 1974; Parly Under-Sec. of State for Defence for the Army,

1974–79. Vice-Chairman: Trade Union Gp of MPs, 1970–74; PLP Transport Gp, 1970–74; PLP Defence Gp, 1981–83; Member: Select Cttee on Nationalised Inds, 1966–68; Speakers Conf., 1966–68. Member Newcastle Co. Borough Council (Chief Whip, Lab. Gp), retd 1968. Nat. Chm., Community Transport, 1987. Pres., Lemington Male Voice Choir, 1987. DL Tyne and Wear 1988. *Recreations:* walking, reading, gardening, watching Association football. *Address:* 1 Newsham Close, The Boltons, North Walbottle, Newcastle upon Tyne NE5 1QD. *T:* 0191–267 2199. *Died 3 Sept. 1996.*

BROWN, Rear-Adm. Roy Stephenson F.; *see* Foster-Brown.

BROWN, Sir Stanley; *see* Brown, Sir F. H. S.

BROWN, Sir Stephen; *see* Brown, Sir A. J. S.

BROWN, Sir William, Kt 1996; CBE 1971; Chairman, Scottish Television plc, 1991–96; *b* 24 June 1929; *s* of Robert C. Brown, Ayr; *m* 1955, Nancy Jennifer, 3rd *d* of Prof. George Hunter, Edmonton, Alta; one *s* three *d. Educ:* Ayr Academy; Edinburgh University. Lieut, RA, 1950–52. Scottish Television Ltd: London Sales Manager, 1958; Sales Dir, 1961; Dep. Man. Dir, 1963; Man. Dir, 1966–90; Dep. Chm., 1974–91. Chm., Scottish Amicable Life Assurance Soc., 1989–94 (Dir, 1981–); Director: ITN, 1972–77, 1987–90; Scottish Radio (formerly Radio Clyde) Holdings Ltd, 1973–; Channel Four Co. Ltd, 1980–84; GMTV Ltd, 1992–94. Dir, Scottish Opera Theatre Royal Ltd, 1974–91. Member: Royal Commn on Legal Services in Scotland, 1976–80; Arts Council of GB, 1992–94; Chm., Scottish Arts Council, 1992–96. Chm., Council, Independent Television Cos Assoc., 1978–80. Trustee, Nat. Museums of Scotland, 1991–92. Dr *hc* Edinburgh, 1990; DUniv Strathclyde, 1992. Ted Willis Award (for outstanding services to television), 1982; Gold Medal, RTS, 1984. *Recreations:* gardening, golf, films. *Address:* Gean House, Horseshoe Road, Bearsden, Glasgow G61 2ST. *T:* (0141) 942 0115. *Clubs:* Caledonian; Prestwick Golf, Royal and Ancient Golf (St Andrews).
Died 29 Dec. 1996.

BROWN, William Eden T.; *see* Tatton Brown.

BROWNE, Rt Hon. Sir Patrick (Reginald Evelyn), Kt 1965; OBE (mil.) 1945; TD 1945; PC 1974; a Lord Justice of Appeal, 1974–80, retired; *b* 28 May 1907; *er s* of Edward Granville Browne (Sir Thomas Adams's Prof. of Arabic, Fellow of Pembroke Coll., Cambridge), and Alice Caroline (*née* Blackburne-Daniell); *m* 1st, 1931, Evelyn Sophie Alexandra (*d* 1966), *o d* of Sir Charles and Lady Walston; two *d*; 2nd, 1977, Lena, *y d* of late Mr and Mrs James Atkinson. *Educ:* Eton; Pembroke Coll., Cambridge (Hon. Fellow, 1975). Barrister-at-law, Inner Temple, 1931; Bencher, 1962. QC 1960; Deputy Chairman of Quarter Sessions, Essex, Co. Cambridge and Isle of Ely, 1963–65; a Judge of the High Court of Justice, Queen's Bench Div., 1965–74. Pres., Cambs Branch, Magistrates' Assoc., 1972–85. A Controller, Royal Opera House Development Land Trust, 1981–84. Served Army, 1939–45; GSO 1, Lt-Col. *Publication:* Judicial Reflections, in Current Legal Problems 1982. *Address:* Thriplow Bury, Thriplow, Royston, Herts SG8 7RN. *T:* (01763) 208234. *Clubs:* Garrick; Cambridge County. *Died 1 Oct. 1996.*

BROWNING, Prof. Robert, MA; FBA 1978; Professor Emeritus, University of London; *b* 15 Jan. 1914; *s* of Alexander M. Browning and Jean M. Browning (*née* Miller); *m* 1st, 1946, Galina Chichekova; two *d*; 2nd, 1972, Ruth Gresh. *Educ:* Kelvinside Academy, Glasgow; Glasgow Univ. (MA); Balliol Coll., Oxford. Served Army, Middle East, Italy, Balkans, 1939–46. Harmsworth Sen. Scholar, Merton Coll., Oxford, 1946; Lectr, University Coll. London, 1947, Reader, 1955; Prof. of Classics and

Ancient History, Birkbeck Coll., Univ. of London, 1965–81. Fellow, Dumbarton Oaks, Washington, DC, 1973–74, 1982, Long-Term Fellow 1983–. President, Soc for Promotion of Hellenic Studies, 1974–77; Life Vice-Pres., Assoc. Internat. des Etudes Byzantines, 1981; Chm., National Trust for Greece, 1985–. Corresponding Mem., Athens Acad., 1981. Hon. DLitt Birmingham, 1980; Hon. DPhil: Athens, 1988; Ioannina, 1996. Gold Medal for Excellence in Hellenic Studies, Onassis Center for Hellenic Studies, NY Univ., 1990; Gold Medal, City of Athens, 1994. Comdr of the Order of the Phoenix, Greece, 1984. *Publications:* Medieval and Modern Greek, 1969, rev. edn 1983; Justinian and Theodora, 1971, rev. edn 1987; Byzantium and Bulgaria, 1975; The Emperor Julian, 1976; Studies in Byzantine History, Literature and Education, 1977; The Byzantine Empire, 1980, rev. edn 1992; (ed) The Greek World, Classical, Byzantine and Modern, 1985; History, Language and Literacy in the Byzantine World, 1989; (with C. N. Constantinides) Dated Greek Manuscripts from Cyprus, 1993; articles in learned jls of many countries. *Address:* 17 Belsize Park Gardens, NW3 4JG. *Died 11 March 1997.*

BROWNLOW, Col William Stephen; Lord-Lieutenant of Co. Down, 1990–96; *b* 1991; *s* of late Col Guy J. Brownlow, DSO, DL, and Elinor H. G. Brownlow, *d* of Col George J. Scott, DSO; *m* 1961, Eveleigh, *d* of Col George Panter, MBE; one *s* two *d. Educ:* Eton; Staff Coll., Camberley (psc). Major, Rifle Bde, 1940–54 (wounded, despatches); Hon. Col 4 Bn Royal Irish Rangers, 1973–78. Member: Down CC, 1969–72; NI Assembly, 1973–75. Member: Irish Nat. Hunt Cttee, 1956–; Irish Turf Club, 1982–; Chairman: Downpatrick Race Club, 1960–90; NI Reg., British Field Sports Soc., 1971–90; Master, East Down Foxhounds, 1956–62. JP 1956, DL 1961, High Sheriff 1959, Co. Down. CStJ 1990. *Recreation:* field sports. *Address:* Ballywhite House, Portaferry, Co. Down BT22 1PB. *T:* (01247) 728325. *Club:* Army and Navy. *Died 30 April 1998.*

BROWNRIGG, Philip Henry Akerman, CMG 1964; DSO 1945; OBE 1953; TD 1945; *b* 3 June 1911; *s* of late Charles E. Brownrigg, Master of Magdalen Coll. Sch., Oxford, and 2nd wife, Valerie Margaret Elizabeth, *e d* of W. S. Akerman; *m* 1936, Marguerite Doreen Ottley (*d* 1992); three *d. Educ:* Eton; Magdalen Coll., Oxford (BA). Journalist, 1934–52; Editor, Sunday Graphic, 1952. Joined Anglo American Corp. of S Africa, 1953: London Agent, 1956; Dir in Rhodesia, 1961–63; Dir in Zambia, 1964–65; retd, 1969. Director (apptd by Govt of Zambia): Nchanga Consolidated Copper Mines Ltd, 1969–80; Roan Consolidated Mines Ltd, 1969–80. Joined TA, 1938; served War of 1939–45 with 6 R Berks, and 61st Reconnaissance Regt (RAC); Lieut-Col 1944; CO 4/6 R Berks (TA) 1949–52. Insignia of Honour, Zambia, 1981. *Publication:* Kenneth Kaunda, 1989. *Recreations:* golf, sport on TV. *Address:* Wheeler's, Checkendon, near Reading, Berks RG8 0NJ. *T:* (01491) 680328. *Died 17 Nov. 1998.*

BRUCE, Rt Hon. Sir (James) Roualeyn Hovell-Thurlow-C.; *see* Cumming-Bruce.

BRUCE, Robert Nigel (Beresford Dalrymple), CBE 1972 (OBE (mil.) 1946); TD; CEng, Hon. FIGasE; *b* 21 May 1907; *s* of Major R. N. D. Bruce, late of Hampstead; *m* 1945, Elizabeth Brogden, *d* of J. G. Moore; twin *s* two *d. Educ:* Harrow School (Entrance and Leaving Scholar); Magdalen College, Oxford (Exhibitioner). BA (Hons Chem.) and BSc. Joined Territorial Army Rangers (KRRC), 1931; Major, 1939; served Greece, Egypt, Western Desert, 1940–42; Lt-Col Comdg Regt, 1942; GHQ, MEF, Middle East Supply Centre, 1943–45; Col, Dir of Materials, 1944. Joined Gas, Light and Coke Co., as Research Chemist, 1929; Asst to Gen. Manager, 1937,

Controller of Industrial Relations, 1946; Staff Controller, 1949, Dep. Chm., 1956, North Thames Gas Bd; Chm., S Eastern Gas Bd, 1960–72. President: British Road Tar Assoc., 1964 and 1965; Coal Tar Research Assoc., 1966; Institution of Gas Engineers, 1968; Mem. Bd, CEI, 1968–80. Chm. Governing Body, Westminster Technical Coll., 1958–76. Sec., Tennis and Rackets Assoc., 1974–81. *Publications:* Chronicles of the 1st Battalion the Rangers (KRRC), 1939–45; contribs to Proc. Royal Society, Jl Soc. Chemical Industry, Jl Chemical Society. *Recreations:* fishing, military history. *Address:* Fairway, 57 Woodland Grove, Weybridge, Surrey KT13 9EQ. *T:* (01932) 852372. *Club:* Queen's (Hon. Mem.). *Died 20 May 1997.*

BRUCE-GARDNER, Sir Douglas (Bruce), 2nd Bt *cr* 1945, of Frilford, Berks; Director, Guest, Keen & Nettlefolds Ltd, 1960–82; *b* 27 Jan. 1917; *s* of Sir Charles Bruce-Gardner, 1st Bt and Gertrude Amy, *d* of C. Rivington Shill; *S* father, 1960; *m* 1st, 1940, Monica Flumerfelt (marr. diss. 1964), *d* of late Sir Geoffrey Jefferson, CBE, FRS; one *s* two *d*; 2nd, 1964, Sheila Jane, *d* of late Roger and Barbara Stilliard, Seer Green, Bucks; one *s* one *d. Educ:* Uppingham; Trinity College, Cambridge. Lancashire Steel, 1938–51; Control Commn, Germany, 1945–46; joined GKN, 1951; Dir, GKN Ltd, 1960, Dep. Chm., 1974–77; Dep. Chm., GKN Steel Co. Ltd, 1962, Gen. Man. Dir, 1963–65, Chm., 1965–67; Chairman: GKN Rolled & Bright Steel Ltd, 1968–72; GKN (South Wales) Ltd, 1968–72; Exors of James Mills Ltd, 1968–72; Parson Ltd, 1968–72; Brymbo Steel Works Ltd, 1974–77; Miles Druce & Co. Ltd, 1974–77; Exec. Vice-Chm., UK Ops, Gen. Products, GKN Ltd, 1972–74; Dep. Chm., GKN (UK) Ltd, 1972–75; Director: Henry Gardner & Co. Ltd, 1952–68; Firth Cleveland Ltd, 1972–75; BHP-GKN Holdings Ltd, 1977–78. Dep.-Chm., Iron Trades Employers' Insurance Assoc., 1984–87 (Dir, 1977–87); President: Iron and Steel Inst., 1966–67; British Indep. Steel Producers' Assoc., 1972; Iron and Steel Employers' Assoc., 1963–64. Prime Warden, Blacksmiths' Co., 1983–84. *Recreations:* fishing, photography. *Heir: s* Robert Henry Bruce-Gardner [*b* 10 June 1943; *m* 1979, Veronica Ann Hand-Oxborrow, *d* of late Rev. W. E. Hand and of Mrs R. G. Oxborrow, Caterham; two *s*]. *Address:* Stocklands, Lewstone, Ganarew, near Monmouth NP5 3SS. *T:* (01600) 890216. *Died 25 Nov. 1997.*

BRÜCK, Prof. Hermann Alexander, CBE 1966; DPhil, PhD; Astronomer Royal for Scotland and Regius Professor of Astronomy in the University of Edinburgh, 1957–75, then Professor Emeritus; *b* 15 Aug. 1905; *s* of H. H. Brück; *m* 1st, 1936, Irma Waitzfelder (*d* 1950); one *s* one *d*; 2nd, 1951, Dr Mary T. Conway; one *s* two *d. Educ:* Kaiserin Augusta Gymnasium, Charlottenburg; Universities of Bonn, Kiel, Munich (DPhil 1928) and Cambridge (PhD). Astronomer: Potsdam Einstein Inst., 1928; Potsdam Astrophysical Observatory, 1930–36; Lectr, Berlin University, 1935–36; Research Associate, Vatican Observatory, Castel Gandolfo, 1936; Asst Observer, Solar Physics Observatory, Cambridge, 1937; John Couch Adams Astronomer, Cambridge University, 1943; Asst Director, Cambridge Observatory, 1946; Director, Dunsink Observatory and Professor of Astronomy, Dublin Institute for Advanced Studies, 1947–57. Dean, Faculty of Science, Univ. of Edinburgh, 1968–70. Mem., Bd of Governors, Armagh Observatory, NI, 1971–84. MRIA 1948; FRSE 1958; Member, Pontif. Academy of Sciences, Rome, 1955 (Mem. Council, 1964–86); Corresp. Mem., Academy of Sciences, Mainz, 1955. Hon. DSc: NUI, 1972; St Andrews, 1973. GCSG 1995. *Publications* (ed jtly) Astrophysical Cosmology, 1982; The Story of Astronomy in Edinburgh, 1983; (with Mary T. Brück) The Peripatetic Astronomer: a biography of Charles Piazzi Smyth, 1988; scientific papers in journals and observatory publications. *Recreations:* music, history.

Address: Craigower, Penicuik, Midlothian EH26 9LA. *T:* (01968) 675918. *Died 4 March 2000.*

BRUNNER, Dr Guido; Grand Cross, Order of Federal Republic of Germany; German diplomat and politician; Ambassador of the Federal Republic of Germany in Madrid, 1982–92; *b* Madrid, 27 May 1930; *m* 1958, Christa (*née* Speidel). *Educ:* Bergzabern, Munich; German Sch., Madrid; Univs of Munich, Heidelberg and Madrid (law and econs). LLD Munich; Licentiate of Law Madrid. Diplomatic service, 1955–74, 1981–92; Private Office of the Foreign Minister, 1956; Office, Sec. of State for For. Affairs, 1958–60; German Observer Mission to the UN, New York, 1960–68; Min. for Foreign Affairs: Dept of scientific and technol relns, 1968–70; Spokesman, 1970–72; Head of Planning Staff, Ambassador and Head of Delegn of Fed. Rep. of Germany, Conf. for Security and Co-op. in Europe, Helsinki/Geneva, 1972–74; Mem., Commn of the European Communities, (responsible for Energy, Research, Science and Educn), 1974–80; Mem., Bundestag, 1980–81; Mayor of Berlin and Minister of Economics and Transport, Jan.-May 1981; Ambassador, Min. of Foreign Affairs, Bonn, 1981–82. Corresp. Member: Spanish Acad. of History, 1986; Spanish Royal Acad. of Arts, 1990. Hon. DLitt Heriot-Watt, 1977; Dr *hc:* Technical Faculty, Patras Univ., Greece; City Univ., London, 1980. Melchett Medal, Inst. of Energy, 1978. Hon. Citizen, City of Madrid, 1993. Grand Cross, Order of Civil Merit, Spain, 1978; Grand Cross, Order of Leopold, Belgium, 1981; Grand Cross, Order of Merit, FRG, 1981; Grand Cross, Order of Isabel la Católica, Spain, 1986. *Publications:* Bipolarität und Sicherheit, 1965; Friedenssicherungsaktionen der Vereinten Nationen, 1968; Stolz wie Don Rodrigo, 1982; El Poder y la Unión, 1989; contrib. Vierteljahreshefte für Zeitgeschichte, Aussenpolitik, Europa-Archiv. *Address:* Paseo de Eduardo Dato 13, 7°A, 28010 Madrid, Spain. *Died 2 Dec. 1997.*

BRYCE, Dame Isabel G.; *see* Graham-Bryce.

BUCHAN, Sir John; *see* Buchan, Sir T. J.

BUCHAN, Dr Stevenson, CBE 1971; Chief Scientific Officer, Deputy Director, Institute of Geological Sciences, 1968–71; *b* 4 March 1907; *s* of late James Buchan and Christian Ewen Buchan (*née* Stevenson), Peterhead; *m* 1937, Barbara, *yr d* of late Reginald Hadfield, Droylsden, Lancs; one *s* one *d. Educ:* Peterhead Acad.; Aberdeen Univ. BSc 1st cl. hons Geology, James H. Hunter Meml Prize, Senior Kilgour Scholar, PhD; FRSE, FGS. Geological Survey of Great Britain: Geologist, 1931; Head of Water Dept, 1946; Asst Dir responsible for specialist depts in GB and NI, 1960; Chief Geologist, Inst. of Geological Sciences, 1967. Mem. various hydrological cttees; Founder Mem., Internat. Assoc. of Hydrogeologists (Pres., 1972–77; Advr, 1980–; Hon. Mem., 1985–); Pres., Internat. Ground-Water Commn of Internat. Assoc. of Hydrological Sciences, 1963–67; British Deleg. to Internat. Hydrological Decade; Scientific Editor, Hydrogeological Map of Europe; Vis. Internat. Scientist, Amer. Geol Inst.; Pres. Section C (Geology), Brit. Assoc., Dundee, 1968. Hon. FCIWEM. Awarded Geol Soc.'s Lyell Fund, and J. B. Tyrell Fund for travel in Canada. *Publications:* Water Supply of County of London from Underground Sources; papers on hydrogeology and hydrochemistry. *Recreation:* oenology. *Address:* Southside Place, 122 The Street, Rockland St Mary, Norwich NR14 7HQ. *T:* Long Stratton (01508) 538092. *Died 24 July 1996.*

BUCHAN, Sir Thomas Johnston, (Sir John), Kt 1971; CMG 1961; FRAIA; Chairman, Buchan Laird International Planners, since 1982; Chairman and Chief Executive, Buchan, Laird and Buchan, Architects,

1957–82; *b* 3 June 1912; *s* of Thomas Johnston Buchan; *m* 1948, Virginia, *d* of William Ashley Anderson, Penn, USA, one *s* two *d*. *Educ:* Geelong Grammar School. Served Royal Aust. Engineers (AIF), 1940–44 (Capt.). Member, Melbourne City Council, 1954–60. Member Federal Exec., Liberal Party, 1959–62; President, Liberal Party, Victorian Division, Australia, 1959–62, Treasurer, 1963–67. Pres., Australian American Assoc., Victoria, 1964–68; Federal Pres., Australian American Assoc., 1968–70, Vice-Pres., 1971–82. Member: Council, Latrobe University, 1964–72; Cttee of Management, Royal Melbourne Hosp., 1968–78. Founding Mem., and Chm., Nat. Cttee for Youth Employment, 1992– (Dep. Chm., 1983–86); Co-Founder Apex Association of Australia. *Recreations:* golf, reading. *Address:* 14 Kent Court, Toorak, Vic 3142, Australia. *Club:* Melbourne (Melbourne). *Died 25 Oct. 1998.*

BUCHTHAL, Hugo, PhD; FBA 1959; Professor of Fine Arts, 1965–70, Ailsa Mellon Bruce Professor, 1970–75, then Emeritus Professor, New York University Institute of Fine Arts; *b* Berlin, 11 Aug. 1909; *m* 1939, Amalia Serkin; one *d*. *Educ:* Universities of Berlin, Heidelberg, Paris and Hamburg. PhD Hamburg, 1933. Resident in London from 1934. Lord Plumer Fellowship, Hebrew University, 1938; Librarian, Warburg Institute, 1941; Lecturer in History of Art, University of London, 1944; Reader in the History of Art, with special reference to the Near East, 1949; Professor of the History of Byzantine Art in the University of London, 1960. Visiting Scholarship, Dumbarton Oaks, Harvard University, 1950–51, 1965, 1974, 1978; Temp. Member Inst. for Advanced Study, Princeton, NJ, 1959–60, 1968, 1975–76; Visiting Professor Columbia University, New York, 1963. Guggenheim Fellow, 1971–72; Corresp. Mem., Oesterreichische Akad. der Wissenschaften, 1975; Hon. Fellow, Warburg Inst., 1975. Prix Schlumberger, Académie des Inscriptions et Belles Lettres, 1958, 1981; Presidential Medal, NY Univ., 1995. *Publications:* The Miniatures of the Paris Psalter, 1938; (with Otto Kurz) A Handlist of Illuminated Oriental Christian Manuscripts, 1942; The Western Aspects of Gandhara Sculpture, 1944; Miniature Painting in the Latin Kingdom of Jerusalem, 1957; Historia Trojana, studies in the history of mediaeval secular illustration, 1971; (jtly) The Place of Book Illumination in Byzantine Art, 1976; (with Hans Belting) Patronage in Thirteenth Century Constantinople: an atelier of late Byzantine illumination and calligraphy, 1978; The Musterbuch of Wolfenbüttel and its position in the art of the thirteenth century, 1979; Art of the Mediterranean World, AD 100 to AD 1400 (collected essays), 1983; numerous articles in learned journals. *Address:* 22 Priory Gardens, N6 5QS. *T:* (0181) 348 1664. *Died 10 Nov. 1996.*

BUCKLEY, Anthony James Henthorne; consultant; *b* 22 May 1934; *s* of late William Buckley, FRCS; *m* 1964, Celia Rosamund Sanderson, *d* of late C. R. Sanderson; one *s* two *d*. *Educ:* Haileybury and ISC; St John's Coll., Cambridge (MA, LLB). FCA. Peat Marwick Mitchell & Co., 1959–62; Rank Organisation Ltd, 1962–66; Slater Walker Securities Ltd, 1966–75, Man. Dir., 1972–75. *Address:* 6 Cambridge Road, Barnes, SW13 0PG. *Died 6 June 2000.*

BUCKLEY, Rt Hon. Sir Denys (Burton), Kt 1960; MBE 1945; PC 1970; a Lord Justice of Appeal, 1970–81; *b* 6 Feb. 1906; 4th *s* of 1st Baron Wrenbury and Bertha Margaretta, 3rd *d* of Charles Edward Jones; *m* 1932, Gwendolen Jane (*d* 1985), yr *d* of late Sir Robert Armstrong-Jones, CBE, FRCS, FRCP; three *d*. *Educ:* Eton; Trinity College, Oxford. Called to the Bar, Lincoln's Inn, 1928, Bencher, 1949, Pro-Treasurer, 1967, Treasurer, 1969; Pres., Senate of the Inns of Court, 1970–72. Served War of 1939–45, in RAOC, 1940–45; Temporary Major;

GSO II (Sigs Directorate), War Office. Treasury Junior Counsel (Chancery), 1949–60; Judge of High Court of Justice, Chancery Div., 1960–70. Member, Restrictive Practices Ct, 1962–70, President, 1968–70; Member: Law Reform Cttee, 1963–73; Cttee on Departmental Records, 1952–54; Advisory Council on Public Records, 1958–79. Hon. Fellow: Trinity Coll., Oxford, 1969; Amer. Coll. of Trial Lawyers, 1970. Master, Merchant Taylors' Co., 1972, First Upper Warden, 1986–87. CStJ 1966. Medal of Freedom (USA), 1945. *Died 13 Sept. 1998.*

BUCKLEY, Sir John (William), Kt 1977; FIEE; chairman and director of companies; Chairman, Davy Corporation (formerly Davy International Ltd), 1973–82, retired; *b* 9 Jan. 1913; *s* of John William and Florence Buckley; *m* 1st, 1935, Bertha Bagnall (marr. diss. 1967); two *s*; 2nd, 1967, Molly Neville-Clarke; one step *s* (and one step *s* decd). *Educ:* techn. coll. (Dipl. Engrg). MIEE 1933, FIEE 1976. George Kent Ltd, 1934–50 (Gen. Man., 1945–50); Man. Dir., Emmco Pty Ltd, 1950–55; Man. Dir, British Motor Corp. Pty Ltd, 1956–60; Vice Chm. and Dep. Chm., Winget, Gloucester Ltd, 1961–68; Man. Dir and Dep. Chm., Davy International Ltd, 1968–73. Chairman: Alfred Herbert Ltd, 1975–79; Oppenheimer International, 1983–89; Engelhard Industries, 1979–85; John Buckley Associates Ltd, 1983–92; Harman Ltd, 1985; Alexanders Laing & Cruickshank Mergers and Acquisitions Ltd, 1986–88; Amchem Ltd, 1989–92; Director: Engelhard Corp. Inc., USA, 1982–86; Fuerst Day Lawson, 1981–98; AWD Ltd, 1989–91. Dir, British Overseas Trade Bd, 1973–76. Mem., BSC, 1978–81. Hon. FIChemE 1975. FRSA 1978. Order of the Southern Cross (Brazil), 1977. *Recreations:* gardening, music, photography, fishing, painting. *Address:* Finlay House, 19 Phyllis Court Drive, Henley-on-Thames, Oxon RG9 2HS. *T:* (01491) 577793. *Clubs:* Boodle's; Phyllis Court (Henley). *Died 19 Nov. 2000.*

BUCKLEY, Major William Kemmis, MBE 1959; Vice Lord-Lieutenant of Dyfed, 1989–98; President, Buckley's Brewery Ltd, 1983–86 (Director, 1960, Vice-Chairman, 1963–72, Chairman, 1972–83); *b* 18 Oct. 1921; o *s* of late Lt-Col William Howell Buckley, DL, and Karolie Kathleen Kemmis. *Educ:* Radley Coll.; New Coll., Oxford (MA). Commd into Welsh Guards, 1941; served N Africa, Italy (despatches, 1945); ADC, 1946–47, Mil. Sec., 1948, to Governor of Madras; Staff Coll., Camberley, 1950; GSO2, HQ London Dist, 1952–53; OC Guards Indep. Para. Co., 1954–57; Cyprus, 1956; Suez, 1956; War Office, 1957; Mil. Asst to Vice-Chief of Imp. Gen. Staff, 1958–59; US Armed Forces Staff Coll., Norfolk, Va, 1959–60. Director: Rhymney Breweries Ltd, 1962–69; Whitbread (Wales) Ltd, 1969–81; Felinfoel Brewery Co., 1975; Guardian Assurance Co. (S Wales), 1966–83 (Dep. Chm., 1967–83). Mem. Council, Brewers' Soc., 1967; Chm., S Wales Brewers' Assoc., 1971–74; Dep. Chm. and Treas., Nat. Trade Develt Assoc., 1966 (Chm., S Wales Pancl, 1965); Lay Mem., Press Council, 1967–73. Chm., Council of St John of Jerusalem for Carms, 1966; Pres., Carms Antiquarian Soc., 1971–96 (Chm., 1968); Mem., Nat. Trust Cttee for Wales, 1962–70; Mem., T&AFA (Carms), 1962–82 and T&AFA (S Wales and Mon), 1967–83. Jt Master and Hon. Sec., Pembrokeshire and Carms Otter Hounds, 1962. High Sheriff of Carms, 1967–68, DL Dyfed (formerly Carms), 1969. KStJ 1984 (CStJ 1966). *Publications:* contributions in local history journals. *Recreations:* gardening, bee-keeping, tapestry work. *Address:* Briar Cottage, Ferryside, Dyfed, S Wales SA17 5UB. *T:* (01267) 267359. *Clubs:* Brooks's; Cardiff and County (Cardiff). *Died 12 March 2000.*

BUCKS, Ven. Michael William; Director General, Naval Chaplaincy Services, Chaplain of the Fleet and Archdeacon for the Royal Navy, 1993–97; *b* 2 June 1940;

s of William James Bucks and Dorothy Arkell Bucks (*née* Hill); *m* 1972, Maria Ines Currie; one *s* one *d*. *Educ:* Rossall Sch.; King's Coll. London (BD; AKC). Deacon 1964, priest 1965; Asst Curate, Workington Parish Church, 1964–68; Chaplain, Royal Navy, 1969–93: Temp. Addnl, HMS Victory and Eagle, 1969–70; Her Majesty's Ships: Raleigh, 1970–71; Albion, 1971–72; Neptune, 1972–74; Mauritius, 1974–76; Fearless, 1976–77; RNEC Manadon, 1977–81; Exchange Programme, US Navy, 1981–83; Staff Chaplain, MoD, London, 1983–86; HM Naval Base, Portsmouth, 1986–90; Staff Chaplain, C-in-C Fleet, HMS Warrior, 1990–93. QHC, 1993–97. *Recreations:* steam railways, model railways, country walking, organs and organ music, painting. *Address:* Tamarin, Brodick, Isle of Arran KA27 8BE. *T:* (01770) 302132. *Club:* Brodick Golf (Isle of Arran). *Died 20 July 1997.*

BUDGEN, Nicholas William; barrister; *b* 3 Nov. 1937; *s* of Captain G. N. Budgen; *m* 1964, Madeleine E. Kittoe; one *s* one *d*. *Educ:* St Edward's Sch., Oxford; Corpus Christi Coll., Cambridge. Called to Bar, Gray's Inn, 1962; practised Midland and Oxford Circuit. MP (C) Wolverhampton South West, Feb. 1974–1997. An Asst Govt Whip, 1981–82. *Recreations:* hunting, racing. *Address:* Malt House Farm, Colton, near Rugeley, Staffs WS15 3LN. *T:* (01889) 577059.
Died 26 Oct. 1998.

BUFFET, Bernard Léon Edmond; Officier de la Légion d'Honneur; painter; *b* Paris, 10 July 1928; *s* of Charles Buffet and Blanche-Emma (*née* Colombe); *m* 1st, Agnès Nanquette (marr. diss.); 2nd, 1958, Annabel May Schwob, Lure; one *s* two *d*. *Educ:* Lycée Carnot; Ecole Nat. Supérieure des Beaux-Arts. Annual exhibitions: Galerie Drouant-David, 1949–56; Galerie David et Garnier, 1957–67; Galerie Maurice Garnier, 1968–. Retrospective exhibitions: Paris, 1958; Berlin, 1958; Belgium, 1959; Tokyo and Kyoto, 1963; Musée d'Unterlinden, Colmar, 1969; Wieger Deurne, Holland, 1977; Musée postal, Paris, 1978; Zurich, 1983; Toulouse, 1985; Musée Pouchkine, Moscow and Musée de l'Hermitage, Leningrad, 1991; Musée Hyundai, Seoul, 1991; Musée Gustave Courbet, Ornans, 1993; Château de Chenonceau, 1993; documenta-Halle, Kassel, 1994; Musée Odakyu, Tokyo, 1995; Musée des Beaux-Arts, Kaoshiung, 1996. Buffet Museum founded in Japan, 1973; large room of his mystic works in Vatican Museum. Illustrator of books, engraver, lithographer and state designer. Grand Prix de la Critique, 1948. Officier des Arts et des Lettres; Mem., Acad. des Beaux-Arts, 1974. *Address:* c/o Galerie Maurice Garnier, 6 avenue Matignon, 75008 Paris, France; Domaine de la Baume, 83690 Tourtour, France.
Died 4 Oct. 1999.

BULGER, His Honour Anthony Clare, BA, BCL; a Circuit Judge (formerly County Court Judge), 1963–86; *b* 5 Oct. 1912; *s* of Daniel Bulger; *m* Una Patricia Banks (*d* 1992); one *s* one *d*. *Educ:* Rugby; Oriel Coll., Oxford. Called to the Bar, Inner Temple, 1936. Oxford Circuit; Dep Chm., 1958–70, Chm. 1970–71, Glos QS; Dep. Chm. Worcs QS, 1962–71; Recorder of Abingdon, 1962–63. *Address:* The Dower House, Forthampton, Glos GL19 4QW. *T:* Tewkesbury (01684) 293257. *Died 5 May 1996.*

BULLOCK, Hugh, Hon. GBE 1976 (Hon. KBE 1957; Hon. OBE 1946); FRSA 1958; President, Pilgrims of the United States, since 1955; Chairman and Chief Executive Officer, Calvin Bullock Ltd; retired 1984; Head of Bullock Investment Advisory Co., since 1984; *b* 2 June 1898; *s* of Calvin Bullock and Alice Katherine (*née* Mallory); *m* 1933, Marie Leontine, (Fleur), Graves (*d* 1986); two *d*. *Educ:* Hotchkiss Sch.; Williams Coll. (BA). Investment banker, 1921; President and Director: Calvin Bullock, Ltd, 1944–66; Bullock Fund, Ltd; Canadian Fund, Inc.; Canadian Investment Fund, Ltd; Dividend Shares, Inc.;

Chairman and Director: Carriers & General Corp.; Nation-Wide Securities Co.; US Electric Light & Power Shares, Inc.; High Income Shares Inc.; Money Shares Inc.; Pres., Calvin Bullock Forum. Trustee: Roosevelt Hospital, 1949–69; Estate and Property of Diocesan Convention of New York; Williams Coll., 1960–68. Member Exec. Cttee, Marshall Scholarship Regional Cttee, 1955–58. Member: Amer. Legion; Academy of Political Science; Amer. Museum of Nat. History; Acad. of Amer. Poets (Dir); Assoc. Ex-mems Squadron A (Gov. 1945–50); Council on Foreign Relations; Ends of the Earth; English-Speaking Union; Foreign Policy Assoc.; Investment Bankers Assoc. of Amer. (Gov. 1953–55); New England Soc.; Nat. Inst. of Social Sciences (Pres. 1950–53; Gold Medal, 1985); Newcomen Soc.; St George's Soc.; France America Assoc. Benjamin Franklyn Fellow, RSA. Hon. LLD; Hamilton Coll., 1954; Williams Coll., 1957. 2nd Lieut Infantry, European War, 1914–18; Lieut-Col, War of 1939–45 (US Army Commendation Ribbon); Civilian Aide to Sec. of the Army, for First Army Area, United States, 1952–53 (US Army Certificate of Appreciation). Distinguished Citizens' Award, Denver, 1958; Exceptional Service Award, Dept of Air Force, 1961; US Navy Distinguished Public Service Award, 1972. Assoc. KStJ 1961, and Vice-Pres. Amer. Society. Knight Comdr, Royal Order of George I (Greece), 1964. Episcopalian. *Publication:* The Story of Investment Companies, 1959. *Address:* (office) 40th Floor, 1 Wall Street, New York, NY 10005, USA. *T:* (212) 8091920; (home) 1030 Fifth Avenue, New York, NY 10028. *T:* (212) 8795858. *Clubs:* White's; Bond (former Gov.), Century, Racquet and Tennis, Down Town Association, River, Union, Williams, Church, New York Yacht (New York); Denver County (Denver); Chevy Chase, Metropolitan (Washington); Edgartown Yacht (Cdre), Edgartown Reading Room (MA); West Side Tennis (Forest Hills, NY); Mount Royal (Montreal).
Died 5 Nov. 1996.

BULLOCK, Richard Henry Watson, CB 1971; Consultant, Faulkbourn Consultancy Services; Director-General, Electronic Components Industry Federation, 1984–90 (Consultant Director, 1981–84); retired Civil Servant; *b* 12 Nov. 1920; *er s* of late Sir Christopher Bullock, KCB, CBE and Lady Bullock (*née* Barbara May Lupton); *m* 1946, Beryl Haddan, *o d* of late Haddan J. Markes, formerly Malay Civil Service; one *s* one *d*. *Educ:* Rugby Sch. (Scholar); Trinity Coll., Cambridge (Scholar). Joined 102 OCTU (Westminster Dragoons), Nov. 1940; commnd Westminster Dragoons (2nd County of London Yeo.), 1941; served in England, NW Europe (D-day), Italy, Germany, 1941–45; Instructor, Armoured Corps Officers' Training Sch., India, 1945–46; demobilized 1947, rank of Major. Established in Home Civil Service by Reconstruction Competition; joined Min. of Supply as Asst Principal, 1947; Principal, 1949; Asst Sec., 1956; on loan to War Office, 1960–61; Ministry of Aviation, 1961–64; Under-Sec., 1963; Min. of Technology, 1964–70, Head of Space Div., 1969–70, Dep. Sec., 1970; DTI, 1970–74; Dept of Industry, 1974–80; retired Nov. 1980. Mem., BOTB, 1975–78. Director: Berkeley Seventh Round Ltd, 1981–87; Grosvenor Place Amalgamations Ltd, 1981–95. Vice-Pres. (and Chm. 1978–82), Westminster Dragoons Assoc.; Chm. Trustees, Westminster Dragoons Benevolent Fund; Pres., Old Rugbeian Soc., 1984–86; Dir, Rugby Sch. Develt Campaign, 1981–86. *Publication:* (ed and contrib.) D-Day Remembered: personal recollections of members of the Westminster Dragoons, 1997. *Recreations:* fly-fishing, hockey (President: Dulwich Hockey Club, 1962–91; Rugby Alternatives HC, 1976–97; Civil Service Hockey Cttee/Assoc., 1978–84), lawn tennis, watching cricket.

Address: 12 Peterborough Villas, SW6 2AT. *T:* (0171) 736 5132. *Clubs:* MCC, Hurlingham; Union, Hawks (Cambridge). *Died 14 June 1998.*

BULTEEL, Christopher Harris, MC 1943; Director, GAP Activity Projects (GAP) Ltd, 1982–88; *b* 29 July 1921; *er s* of late Major Walter Bulteel and Constance (*née* Gaunt), Charlestown, Cornwall; *m* 1958, Jennifer Anne, *d* of late Col K. E. Previté, OBE and Frances (*née* Capper); one *s* two *d. Educ:* Wellington Coll.; Merton Coll., Oxford. Served War with Coldstream Guards, 1940–46 (MC). Assistant Master at Wellington Coll., 1949–61; Head of History Dept, 1959–61; Hon. Sec., Wellington Coll. Mission, 1959–61; Headmaster, Ardingly Coll., 1962–80. *Recreations:* natural history, sailing. *Address:* Street Farm Cottage, Park Street, Charlton, Malmesbury, Wilts SN16 9DF. *T:* (01666) 823764. *Died 11 Oct. 1999.*

BUNDY, McGeorge; Professor of History, New York University, 1979–89, then Emeritus; Scholar–in–residence, Carnegie Corporation of New York, since 1993; *b* 30 March 1919; *s* of Harvey Hollister Bundy and Katharine Lawrence Bundy (*née* Putnam); *m* 1950, Mary Buckminster Lothrop; four *s. Educ:* Yale Univ. AB 1940. Political analyst, Council on Foreign Relations, 1948–49; Harvard University: Vis. Lectr, 1949–51; Associate Prof. of Government, 1951–54; Prof., 1954–61; Dean, Faculty of Arts and Sciences, 1953–61; Special Asst to the Pres. for National Security Affairs, 1961–66; President of the Ford Foundation, 1966–79. *Publications:* (with H. L. Stimson) On Active Service in Peace and War, 1948; (ed) Pattern of Responsibility, 1952; The Strength of Government, 1968; Danger and Survival, 1988; (jtly) Reducing Nuclear Danger, 1993. *Address:* Carnegie Corporation of New York, 437 Madison Avenue, New York, NY 10022–7001, USA.
Died 16 Sept. 1996.

BUNKER, Albert Rowland, CB 1966; Deputy Under-Secretary of State, Home Office, 1972–75; *b* 5 Nov. 1913; *er* and *o* surv. *s* of late Alfred Francis Bunker and Ethel Trudgian, Lanjeth, St Austell, Cornwall; *m* 1st, 1939, Irene Ruth Ella (*d* 1996), 2nd *d* of late Walter and Ella Lacey, Ealing; two *s*; 2nd, 1996, Barbara Reece Pugh, *o d* of late Brig. H. C. Pugh, CBE, TD, MA and Betty Pugh (*née* Rickcord). *Educ:* Ealing Grammar Sch. Served in Royal Air Force, 1943–45. Service in Cabinet Office, HM Treasury, Ministry of Home Security and Home Office. *Recreation:* golf. *Address:* 34 Farm Avenue, NW2 2BH. *T:* (0181) 452 1321. *Clubs:* Royal Air Force; Denham Golf. *Died 20 May 1998.*

BUNTON, George Louis, MChir (Cantab); FRCS; Consultant Surgeon to University College Hospital, London, 1955–84, to Metropolitan Hospital, 1957–70, and to Northwood Hospital, 1958–84, retired; Emeritus Consulting Surgeon to University College and Middlesex Hospitals, 1986; *b* 23 April 1920; *s* of late Surg. Capt. C. L. W. Bunton, RN, and Marjorie Denman; *m* 1st, 1948, Margaret Betty Edwards (*d* 1988); one *d*; 2nd, 1993, Louise Phillippa Brooks. *Educ:* Epsom; Selwyn Coll., Cambridge; UCH. MB, BChir Cantab 1951; MRCS, LRCP 1944; FRCS 1951; MChir Cantab 1955. Served in RNVR, 1944–47. University of London: Examr in Surgery, 1974–78; Mem., Academic Council, 1975–77; University College Hospital, London: Chm., Med. Cttee, 1977–80; Mem., Academic Bd, Med. Sch., 1970–78; Mem., Sch. Council, Med. Sch., 1976–81; Mem., Bd of Governors, 1972–74; Mem., Bd of Trustees, UC Gp of Hosps, 1978–82. Chairman: Health Gp, Centre for Policy Studies, 1980–84; S Camden Dist Med. Cttee, 1980–83; Member: Exec., University Hosps Assoc. (England and Wales), 1975–89 (Treasurer, 1980–89); Court of Examiners, RCS, 1977–84 (Chm., 1984). Fellow, Assoc. of Surgeons; Fellow, British Assoc. of Pædiatric Surgeons.

Publications: contribs to journals and books on surgical subjects. *Recreations:* gardening, music. *Address:* Smarkham Orchard, Madgehole Lane, Shamley Green, Guildford, Surrey GU5 0SS. *T:* (01483) 892187.
Died 8 April 1997.

BURGES, (Margaret) Betty (Pierpoint), MBE 1937; Headmistress, Staines Preparatory School, 1973–88; Chairman, Surrey County Council Conservative Group, 1981–84; *d* of Frederick Eales Hanson and Margaret Pierpoint Hanson (*née* Hurst); *m* 1937, Cyril Travers Burges, MA (*d* 1975). *Educ:* Edgbaston High Sch., Birmingham. Civil Service, 1929–37 and 1940–45. Councillor, Surrey County Council, 1967–85; Chairman, General Purposes Cttee, 1974–84. *Recreations:* walking, travel. *Address:* 7 Gresham Road, Staines, Middx TW18 2BT. *T:* (01784) 452852. *Died 2 Sept. 1999.*

BURGESS, Claude Bramall, CMG 1958; OBE 1954; Minister for Hong Kong Commercial Relations with the European Communities and the Member States, 1974–82; *b* 25 Feb. 1910; *s* of late George Herbert Burgess, Weaverham, Cheshire, and Martha Elizabeth Burgess; *m* 1941, Sessan Lilian Fjord Christensen; *m* 1952, Margaret Joan Webb (marr. diss. 1965); one *s*; *m* 1969, Linda Nettleton, *e d* of William Grothier Beilby, New York. *Educ:* Epworth Coll.; Christ Church, Oxford. Eastern Cadetship in HM Colonial Administrative Service, 1932. Commissioned in RA, 1940; POW, 1941–45; demobilized with rank of Lt-Col, RA, 1946. Colonial Office, 1946–48; attended Imperial Defence Coll., London, 1951; various Government posts in Hong Kong; Colonial Secretary (and Actg Governor on various occasions), Hong Kong, 1958–63, retd; Head of Co-ordination and Develt Dept, EFTA, 1964–73. *Address:* 75 Chester Row, SW1W 8JL. *T:* (020) 7730 8758. *Died 2 Nov. 1998.*

BURGESS, Prof. Robert Arthur, PhD; Sir Alexander Stone Professor of Business Law and Practice, University of Strathclyde, 1989–97, then Emeritus; *b* 24 Feb. 1946; *s* of late John Burgess and of Joan Burgess (*née* Holland); *m* 1st, 1966, Frances Isobel Lydia Burns (*d* 1995); one *s* one *d*; 2nd, 1995, Glenys Pamela Betts. *Educ:* University Coll. London (LLB 1967); Edinburgh Univ. (PhD 1975). Bank Official, National Westminster Bank, 1967–69; Lecturer in Law: Southampton Univ., 1969–72; Edinburgh Univ., 1972–78; University of East Anglia: Sen. Lectr in Law, 1978–82; Reader in Law, 1982–89; Dean, Law Sch., 1987–89; Head, Law Sch., Univ. of Strathclyde, 1990–94. Chm., Glasgow Royal Infirmary Univ. NHS Trust, 1994–97. FRSA 1993. *Publications:* Perpetuities in Scots Law, 1980; Partnership Law in England and Scotland, 1980; Corporate Finance Law, 1985, 2nd edn 1992; Law of Loans and Borrowing, 1989, 12th issue 1998. *Recreations:* food, drink, travel. *Address:* 3 Lagarie House, Torwoodhill Road, Rhu, Helensburgh G84 8LF. *T:* (01436) 820389. *Died 30 Nov. 1999.*

BURKE, Adm. Arleigh Albert; Navy Cross; DSM (3 Gold Stars); Legion of Merit (with 2 Gold Stars and Army Oak Leaf Cluster); Silver Star Medal, Purple Heart, Presidential Unit Citation Ribbon (with 3 stars), Navy Unit Commendation Ribbon; Chief of Naval Operations, US Navy and Member of Joint Chiefs of Staff, 1955–61, retired; Member of Board of Directors, Freedoms Foundation, at Valley Forge; *b* 19 Oct. 1901; *s* of Oscar A. and Claire Burke; *m* 1923, Roberta Gorsuch; no *c. Educ:* United States Naval Academy; Univ. of Michigan (MSE). Commnd ensign, USN, 1923, advancing through grades to Admiral, 1955. USS Arizona, 1923–28; Gunnery Dept, US Base Force, 1928; Post-graduate course (explosives), 1929–31; USS Chester, 1932; Battle Force Camera Party, 1933–35; Bureau of Ordnance, 1935–37; USS Craven, 1937–39; USS Mugford, Captain, 1939–40; Naval Gun Factory, 1940–43; Destroyer Divs 43 and 44,

Squadron 12 Comdg, 1943; Destroyer Squadron 23 Comdg, 1943–44; Chief of Staff to Commander Task Force 58 (Carriers), 1944–45; Head of Research and Development Bureau of Ordnance, 1945–46; Chief of Staff, Comdr Eighth Fleet and Atlantic Fleet, 1947–48; USS Huntington, Captain, 1949; Asst Chief of Naval Ops, 1949–50; Cruiser Div. 5, Comdr, 1951; Dep. Chief of Staff, Commander Naval Forces, Far East, 1951; Director Strategic Plans Div., Office of the Chief of Naval Operations, 1952–53; Cruiser Division 6, Commanding, 1954; Commander Destroyer Force, Atlantic, 1955. Member: American Legion; American Soc. of Naval Engineers and numerous other naval assocs, etc; National Geographic Society; also foreign societies, etc. Held several hon. degrees. Ul Chi Medal (Korea), 1954; Korean Presidential Unit Citation, 1954. *Recreations:* reading, gardening. *Address:* The Virginian, Apt 323, 9229 Arlington Boulevard, Fairfax, VA 22031, USA. *Clubs:* Army-Navy Town, Metropolitan, Chevy Chase, Alfalfa, Circus Saints and Sinners, Ends of the Earth, etc (Washington, DC); Quindecum (Newport, US); The Brook, Lotos, Salmagundi, Inner Wheel, Seawanhaka Corinthian Yacht (New York); Bohemian (San Francisco).   *Died 1 Jan. 1996.*

BURKE, Rt Rev. Geoffrey Ignatius; Titular Bishop of Vagrauta; Auxiliary Bishop of Salford, (RC), 1967–88; *b* 31 July 1913; *s* of Dr Peter Joseph Burke and Margaret Mary (*née* Coman). *Educ:* St Bede's Coll., Manchester; Stonyhurst Coll.; Oscott Coll., Birmingham; Downing Coll., Cambridge (MA). Priest, 1937; taught History, St Bede's Coll., 1940–66 (Prefect of Studies, 1950); Rector, St Bede's Coll., 1966–67. Consecrated Bishop 29 June 1967. *Address:* 52 Plymouth Grove West, Manchester M13 0AR.   *Died 13 Oct. 1999.*

BURLEIGH, Thomas Haydon, CBE 1977; Director, John Brown & Co. Ltd, 1965–77; *b* 23 April 1911; *s* of late J. H. W. Burleigh, Great Chesterford; *m* 1933, Kathleen Mary Lenthall (*d* 1992), *d* of late Dr Gurth Eager, Hertford; two *s. Educ:* Saffron Walden Sch. RAF, short service commission, No 19 (F) Sqdn, 1930–35; Westland Aircraft Ltd, 1936–45; Thos Firth & John Brown Ltd, 1945–48; Firth Brown Tools Ltd, 1948–77. Pres., Sheffield Chamber of Commerce, 1963–64; Pres. Nat. Fedn of Engineers' Tool Manufacturers, 1968–70; Master of Company of Cutlers in Hallamshire in the County of York, 1970–71. *Recreations:* golf, gardening. *Address:* Kirkgate, Holme next Sea, Hunstanton, Norfolk PE36 6LH. *T:* (01485) 525387. *Clubs:* Royal Air Force; Royal and Ancient Golf (St Andrews).   *Died 6 Nov. 1999.*

BURMAN, Sir (John) Charles, Kt 1961; DL; JP; *b* 30 Aug. 1908; *o s* of Sir John Burman, JP and Elizabeth Vernon, *d* of C. H. Pugh, Penns, Warwicks; *m* 1936, Ursula Hesketh-Wright, JP; two *s* two *d. Educ:* Rugby Sch. City Council, 1934–66 (Lord Mayor of Birmingham, 1947–49); General Commissioner of Income Tax, 1941–73; Indep. Chm., Licensing Planning Cttee, 1949–60; Chm. Birmingham Conservative and Unionist Assoc., 1963–72; County Pres. St John Ambulance Brigade, 1950–63; Member, Govt Cttee on Administrative Tribunals, 1955; Member, Royal Commission on the Police, 1960. Director: Tarmac Ltd, 1955–71 (Chm., 1961–71); S Staffs Waterworks Co., 1949–82 (Chm. 1959–79). Life Governor, Barber Institute, at University of Birmingham (Trustee, 1936–90; Chm. Trustees, 1979–90). JP 1942; High Sheriff, 1958, DL 1967, Warwickshire. KStJ 1961. Hon. LLD Birmingham, 1986. *Address:* Little Bickerscourt, Danzey Green, Tanworth-in-Arden, Warwickshire B94 5BL. *T:* (01564) 742711.
                                Died 26 Dec. 1999.

BURNETT, Rear-Adm. Philip Whitworth, CB 1957; DSO 1945; DSC 1943, and Bar, 1944; *b* 10 Sept. 1908; *s* of

Henry Ridley Burnett; *m* 1947, Molly, *d* of H. M. Trouncer, and widow of Brig. H. C. Partridge, DSO; one *s* two *d. Educ:* Preparatory Sch., Seascale; Royal Naval Coll., Dartmouth. Served War of 1939–45: HMS Kelly, 1939–41; HMS Osprey, 1941–43; Western Approaches Escort Groups, 1943–45; Chief of Staff to Comdr-in-Chief, Portsmouth, 1955–57; retd list 1958. Lieut 1930; Comdr 1940; Capt. 1945; Rear-Adm. 1955.
                                Died 10 June 1996.

BURNS, Maj.-Gen. Sir (Walter Arthur) George, GCVO 1991 (KCVO 1962); CB 1961; DSO 1944; OBE 1953; MC 1940; retired; Lord-Lieutenant of Hertfordshire, 1961–86; *b* 29 Jan. 1911; *s* of late Walter Spencer Morgan and Evelyn Ruth Burns. *Educ:* Eton; Trinity Coll., Cambridge. BA Hons History. Commissioned Coldstream Guards 1932; ADC to Viceroy of India, 1938–40; Adjt 1st Bn, 1940–41 (MC); Brigade Major: 9 Inf. Bde, 1941–42; Special Gp Gds Armd Div., 1942; 32 Gds Bde, 1942–43; CO 3rd Bn Coldstream Gds, Italy, 1943–44 (DSO); Staff Coll., Camberley, 1945; Brigade Major, Household Bde, 1945–47; CO 3rd Bn Coldstream Gds, Palestine, 1947–50; AAG, HQ London Dist, 1951, 1952; Regimental Lt-Col Coldstream Gds, 1952–55; Comdg 4th Gds Bde, 1955–59; GOC London District and The Household Brigade, 1959–62. Col, Coldstream Guards, 1966–94. Steward, The Jockey Club, 1964–. Lay Canon, St Alban's Cathedral, 1992–. KStJ 1972. *Recreations:* shooting, racing. *Address:* Home Farm, North Mymms Park, Hatfield, Hertfordshire AL9 7TH. *T:* (01707) 645117. *Clubs:* Jockey, Pratt's, Buck's.   *Died 5 May 1997.*

BURRELL, Derek William; DL; Headmaster, Truro School, 1959–86; Chairman, Methodist Day Schools' Committee, since 1988; *b* 4 Nov. 1925; *s* of late Thomas Richard Burrell and Flora Frances Burrell (*née* Nash). *Educ:* Tottenham Grammar Sch.; Queens' Coll., Cambridge. Assistant Master at Solihull Sch. (English, History, Religious Instruction, Music Appreciation), 1948–52; Senior English Master, Dollar Academy, 1952–59. Vice-Pres., Methodist Conf., 1987–88. DL Cornwall, 1993. *Recreations:* music of any kind, theatre, wandering about London. *Address:* Flat 5, 2 Strangways Terrace, Truro, Cornwall TR1 2NY. *T:* (01872) 277733. *Club:* East India, Devonshire, Sports and Public Schools.
                                Died 3 April 1999.

BURRELL, Peter Eustace, CBE 1957; Director, The National Stud, 1937–71; *b* 9 May 1905; *s* of Sir Merrik R. Burrell, 7th Bt and 1st wife, Wilhemina Louisa, *d* of Walter Winans; *m* 1st, 1929, Pamela Pollen (marr. diss. 1940); one *s* (and one *s* decd); 2nd, 1971, Mrs Constance P. Mellon (*d* 1980). *Educ:* Eton; Royal Agricultural Coll., Cirencester. *Recreations:* shooting, stalking. *Address:* Long Hill, Moulton Road, Newmarket, Suffolk CB8 8QG. *T:* (01638) 662280.   *Died 31 July 1999.*

BURRENCHOBAY, Sir Dayendranath, KBE 1978; CMG 1977; CVO 1972; Governor-General of Mauritius, 1978–84; *b* 24 March 1919; *s* of Mohabeer Burrenchobay, MBE, and Anant Kumari Burrenchobay; *m* 1957, Oomawatee Ramphul; one *s* two *d. Educ:* Royal Coll., Curepipe, Mauritius; Imperial Coll., London (BScEng Hons); Inst. of Education, London (Postgrad. CertEd). Education Officer, Govt of Mauritius, 1951–60, Sen. Educn Officer, 1960–64, Chief Educn Officer, 1964; Permanent Secretary: Min. of Education and Cultural Affairs, 1964–68; Min. of External Affairs, Tourism and Emigration, also Prime Minister's Office, 1968–76; Secretary to Cabinet and Head of Civil Service, 1976–78. Attended various confs and seminars as Govt rep.; Chm., Central Electricity Bd, 1968–78. Hon. DCL Univ. of Mauritius, 1978. Chevalier, Légion d'Honneur, 1975; Grand Cross, 1st Cl., Order of Merit (Fed. Republic of

Germany), 1978. *Recreations:* swimming, walking. *Address:* S. Ramphul Street, Eau Coulée, Mauritius.
Died 29 March 1999.

BURROUGH, John Outhit Harold, CB 1975; CBE 1963; *b* 31 Jan. 1916; *s* of Adm. Sir Harold M. Burrough, GCB, KBE, DSO, and late Nellie Wills Outhit; *m* 1944, Suzanne Cecile Jourdan; one *s* one *d. Educ:* Manor House, Horsham; RNC Dartmouth. Midshipman, 1934; Sub-Lt 1936; Lieut 1938; Lt-Comdr 1944; RN retd 1947; Foreign Office (GCHQ), 1946–65; IDC 1964; British Embassy, Washington, 1965–67; Under-Sec., Cabinet Office, 1967–69; an Under Sec., FCO (Govt Communications HQ), 1969–76. Director: Racal Communications Systems Ltd, 1976–79; Racal Communications Ltd, 1979–82. *Address:* The Old Vicarage, Guiting Power, Glos GL54 5TY. *T:* Guiting Power (01451) 850596. *Club:* Naval and Military (Chm., 1969–72). *Died 15 Feb. 1996.*

BURY, John, OBE 1979; designer for theatre, opera and film; *b* 27 Jan. 1925; *s* of C. R. Bury; *m* 1st, 1947, Margaret Leila Greenwood (marr. diss.); one *s*; 2nd, 1966, Elizabeth Rebecca Blackborrow Duffield; two *s* one *d. Educ:* Cathedral Sch., Hereford; University Coll., London. Served with Fleet Air Arm (RN), 1942–46. Theatre Workshop, Stratford, E15, 1946–63; Associate Designer, Royal Shakespeare Theatre, 1963–73; Head of Design: RSC, 1965–68; NT, 1973–85. Arts Council: Designers' Working Gp, 1962–78; Mem., Drama Panel, 1960–68 and 1975–77. Chairman: Soc. of British Theatre Designers, 1975–85; Scenographic Commn, Organisation Internationale des Scenographs, Techniciens et Architectes du Théâtre, 1990–98. FRSA 1970. Hon. FRCA 1990. Co-winner, Gold Medal for Scene Design, Prague Quadrienale, 1975 and 1979; Antoinette Perry Awards (Best Set Design and Best Lighting), for Broadway prodn of Amadeus, 1981. *Address:* Burleigh House, Burleigh, Glos GL5 2PQ. *Died 12 Nov. 2000.*

BURY, Shirley Joan, FSA; Keeper of Metalwork, Victoria and Albert Museum, 1982–85; *b* 1925, *d* of Ernest Leslie Saxton Watkin and Florence Keen; *m* 1947, John Morley Bury; one *s. Educ:* University of Reading (BA Fine Arts 1946; MA 1960). FSA 1972. Joined V&A Mus., 1948: Research Asst, 1948, Senior Research Asst, 1961, Circulation Dept; Asst Keeper, Library, 1962–68, Metalwork Dept, 1968–72; Dep. Keeper, Dept of Metalwork, 1972–82. Mem., British Hallmarking Council, 1974–85. Liveryman, Goldsmiths' Co., 1982. *Publications:* Victorian Electroplate, 1972; V&A Jewellery Gallery Summary Catalogue, 1982; An Introduction to Rings, 1984; Sentimental Jewellery, 1985; Jewellery 1790–1910, 1988; (compiled and ed) Catalogue, Copy or Creation, Goldsmiths' Hall, 1967; (ed) Catalogue, Liberty's 1875–1975, V&A 1975; introd. to C. R. Ashbee, Modern English Silver, new edn 1974; contribs to Burlington Magazine, Connoisseur, Apollo, V&A Bulletin, Yearbook and Album. *Recreations:* theatre, walking, gardening. *Died 25 March 1999.*

BUTLER, Sir Clifford (Charles), Kt 1983; PhD; FRS 1961; FInstP; Vice-Chancellor of Loughborough University of Technology, 1975–85; *b* 20 May 1922; *s* of C. H. J. and O. Butler, Earley, Reading; *m* 1947, Kathleen Betty Collins; two *d. Educ:* Reading Sch.; Reading Univ. (BSc 1942; PhD 1946). FInstP 1996. Demonstrator in Physics, Reading Univ., 1942–45; Asst Lecturer in Physics, Manchester Univ., 1945–47, Lecturer in Physics, 1947–53; Imperial College of Science and Technology, London: Reader in Physics, 1953–57; Professor of Physics, 1957–63; Asst Dir, Physics Dept, 1955–62; Prof. of Physics and Head of Physics Dept, 1963–70; Dean, Royal Coll. of Science, 1966–69; Dir, Nuffield Foundn, 1970–75. Charles Vernon Boys Prizeman, London Physical Soc., 1956. Member: Academic Planning Board, Univ. of Kent,

1963–71; Schools Council, 1965–84; Nuclear Physics Board of SRC, 1965–68; University Grants Cttee, 1966–71; Council, Charing Cross Hosp. Med. Sch., 1970–73; Council, Open Univ., 1971–95 (Vice-Chm., 1986–94); Science Adv. Cttee, British Council, 1980–85; Chairman: Track Chamber Cttee, CERN, 1962–65; Standing Education Cttee, Royal Society, 1970–80; Council for the Educn and Training of Health Visitors, 1977–83; Adv. Council for Supply and Educn of Teachers, 1980–85; Steering Cttee, DES Educnl Counselling and Credit Transfer Information Service Project, 1983–89; ABRC/NERC Study Gp into Geol Surveying, 1985–87; Working Party on Res. Selectivity, Dept of Educn, NI, QUB and Univ. of Ulster, 1986–87. Pres., Internat. Union of Pure and Applied Physics, 1975–78 (Sec.-Gen., 1963–72; first Vice-Pres., 1972–75). Hon. DSc Reading, 1976; DUniv Open, 1986; Hon. DTech Loughborough, 1987. *Publications:* scientific papers on electron diffraction, cosmic rays and elementary particle physics in Proc. Royal Society and Physical Society, Philosophical Magazine, Nature, and Journal of Scientific Instruments, etc. *Address:* Low Woods Farm House, Belton, Loughborough, Leics LE12 9TR. *T:* (01530) 223125.
Died 30 June 1999.

BUTLER, Edward Clive Barber, FRCS; Surgeon: The London Hospital, E1, 1937–69; Harold Wood Hospital, Essex, 1946–69; retired; *b* 8 April 1904; *s* of Dr Butler, Hereford; *m* 1939, Nancy Hamilton Harrison (marr. diss. 1957), Minneapolis, USA; two *s* one *d. Educ:* Shrewsbury Sch.; London Hospital. MRCS, LRCP 1928; MB, BS London, 1929; FRCS 1931. Resident posts London Hosp , 1928–32; Surgical Registrar, London Hosp., 1933–36; Surgeon, RMS Queen Mary, Cunard White Star Line, 1936. Hunterian Prof., RCS, 1939; examinerships at various times to London Univ. and Coll. of Surgeons. Pres. section of Proctology, Royal Soc. of Medicine, 1951–52; Member: Medical Soc. London; Royal Soc. Medicine. *Publications:* chapter: on bacteraemia, in British Surgical Practice, 1948, on hand infections, in Penicillin (by Fleming), 1950; (jointly) on combined excision of rectum, in Treatment of Cancer and Allied Diseases (New York), 1952; articles on various surgical subjects in Lancet, BMJ, Proc. Royal Soc. Med., British Journal Surgery. *Recreations:* golf, gardening, yachting. *Address:* Flat 304, Enterprise House, Chingford, E4 7ND. *Club:* United Hospitals Sailing. *Died 25 Jan. 1999.*

BUTLER, Air Vice-Marshal Eric Scott, CB 1957; OBE 1941; Air Officer i/c Administration, HQ Fighter Command, Royal Air Force, 1957–61; *b* 4 Nov. 1907; *s* of Archibald Butler, Maze Hill, St Leonards-on-Sea, Sussex; *m* 1936, Alice Evelyn Tempest Meates (*d* 1985); three *s* one *d. Educ:* Belfast Academy. Commissioned RAF, 1933; Bomber Command European War, 1939–45; idc 1952; Director of Organisation, Air Ministry, 1953–56. *Address:* Camden Cottage, High Street, Pevensey, Sussex BN24 5JP. *T:* (01323) 762353. *Club:* Royal Air Force.
Died 8 Jan. 1997.

BUTLER, George, RWS 1958; RBA; NEAC; painter, principally in water-colour, in England and Provence; *b* 17 Oct. 1904; *s* of John George Butler; *m* 1933, Kcenia Kotliarevskaya (*d* 1992); one *s* one *d. Educ:* King Edward VII School, Sheffield; Central School of Art. Director and Head of Art Dept, J. Walter Thompson Co. Ltd, 1933–60. Vice Pres., Artists' General Benevolent Institution, 1977– (Mem. Council; Hon. Treas., 1957–77). Mem., Société des Artistes Indépendants Aixois. *Address:* Riversdale, Castle Street, Bakewell, Derbyshire DE45 1DU. *T:* (01629) 813133. *Club:* Arts. *Died 19 April 1999.*

BUTLER, Dr Rohan D'Olier, CMG 1966; MA, DLitt; FRHistS; Laureate, Institute of France; Fellow Emeritus of All Souls, Oxford, since 1984 (Fellow, 1938–84; Sub-

Warden, 1961–63; representative at 12th International Historical Congress at Vienna, 1965, at 11th Anglo-American Conference of Historians, 1982); *b* St John's Wood, 21 Jan. 1917; *o* surv. *s* of late Sir Harold Butler, KCMG, CB, MA, and Lady (Olive) Butler, *y c* of late Asst Inspector-General S. A. W. Waters, JP, RIC; *m* 1956, Lucy Rosemary (Lady of the Manor of White Notley, Essex), *y c* of late Eric Byron. *Educ:* Eton; abroad and privately; Balliol Coll., Oxford (Hall Prizeman, 1938). BA (1st Class Hons in Modern History), 1938. On International Propaganda and Broadcasting Enquiry, 1939; on staff of MOI, 1939–41 and 1942–44, of Special Operations Executive, 1941; served with RAPC, 1941–42, with HG, 1942–44 (Defence Medal, War Medal); on staff of FO, 1944–45; Editor of Documents on British Foreign Policy (1919–39), 1945–65 (with Sir Llewellyn Woodward, 1945–54; Senior Editor, 1955–65); Sen. Editor, Documents on British Policy Overseas, 1973–82. Leverhulme Res. Fellow, 1955–57, Emeritus Fellow, 1984–86. Governor, Felsted Sch., 1959–77, representative on GBA, 1964–77; Trustee, Felsted Almshouses, 1961–77; Noel Buxton Trustee, 1961–67. Historical Adviser to Sec. of State for Foreign Affairs, 1963–68, for Foreign and Commonwealth Affairs, 1968–82 (from 14th Earl of Home to 6th Baron Carrington). On management of Inst. of Hist. Research, Univ. of London, 1967–77; Mem., Lord Chancellor's Adv. Council on Public Records, 1982–86. Mem. Court, Univ. of Essex, 1971–91. *Publications:* The Roots of National Socialism (1783–1933), 1941; Documents on British Foreign Policy, 1st series, vols i-ix, 2nd series, vol. ix; The Peace Settlement of Versailles, 1918–33 (in New Cambridge Modern History); Paradiplomacy (in Studies in Diplomatic History in honour of Dr G. P. Gooch, OM, CH, FBA); Introduction to Anglo-Soviet historical exhibition of 1967; Choiseul, 1980 (special award, Prix Jean Debrousse, Acad. des Sciences Morales et Politiques, 1982); Documents on British Policy Overseas, series I, vol. i; The Secret Compact of 1753 between the Kings of France and of Naples (in Sovereignty in Early Modern Europe). *Recreation:* idling. *Address:* White Notley Hall, near Witham, Essex CM8 1RX. *Club:* Beefsteak.   *Died 30 Oct. 1996.*

BUTT, Sir (Alfred) Kenneth (Dudley), 2nd Bt *cr* 1929, of Westminster, co. London; Underwriting Member of Lloyd's, 1931–74; farmer and bloodstock breeder; *b* 7 July 1908; *o s* of Sir Alfred Butt, 1st Bt and Lady Georgina Mary Butt (*née* Say); *S* father, 1962; *m* 1st, 1938, Kathleen Farmar (marr. diss. 1948); 2nd, 1948, Marie Josephine, BA Oxon (*née* Bain), widow of Lt-Col Ivor Birts, RA (killed on active service). *Educ:* Rugby; Brasenose Coll., Oxford. Lloyd's, 1929–39. Royal Artillery, 1939–45, Major RA. Chairman, Parker Wakeling & Co. Ltd, 1946–54; Managing Director, Brook Stud Co., 1962–81. Pres., Aberdeen-Angus Cattle Soc., 1968–69; Chm., Thoroughbred Breeders Assoc., 1973. *Recreations:* shooting, horse-racing, travelling, paintings. *Address:* Wheat Hill, Sandon, Buntingford, Herts SG9 0RB. *T:* (01763) 287203. *Clubs:* Carlton, etc.

Died 10 Feb. 1999 (ext).

BUTTER, Prof. Peter Herbert; Regius Professor of English, Glasgow University, 1965–86; *b* 7 April 1921; *s* of Archibald Butter, CMG, and Helen Cicely (*née* Kerr); *m* 1958, Bridget Younger; one *s* two *d. Educ:* Charterhouse; Balliol Coll., Oxford. Served in RA, 1941–46. Assistant, 1948, Lecturer, 1951, in English, Univ. of Edinburgh; Professor of English, Queen's Univ., Belfast, 1958–65. *Publications:* Shelley's Idols of the Cave, 1954; Francis Thompson, 1961; Edwin Muir, 1962; Edwin Muir: Man and Poet, 1966; (ed) Shelley's Alastor and Other Poems, 1971; (ed) Selected Letters of Edwin Muir, 1974; (ed) Selected Poems of William Blake, 1982; (ed) The Truth of Imagination: uncollected prose of Edwin

Muir, 1988; (ed) Complete Poems of Edwin Muir, 1992; articles in periodicals. *Address:* Ashfield, Bridge of Weir, Renfrewshire PA11 3AW. *T:* (01505) 613139. *Club:* New (Edinburgh).   *Died 11 May 1999.*

BUTTERFIELD, Baron *cr* 1988 (Life Peer), of Stechford in the County of West Midlands; **William John Hughes Butterfield,** Kt 1978; OBE 1953; DM; FRCP; Regius Professor of Physic, University of Cambridge, 1976–87 (Deputy, since 1987); Master of Downing College, Cambridge, 1978–87; *b* 28 March 1920; *s* of late William Hughes Butterfield and Mrs Doris North; *m* 1st, 1946, Ann Sanders (*d* 1948); one *s*; 2nd, 1950, Isabel-Ann Foster Kennedy, *d* of Dr Foster Kennedy, NY and Mrs Isabel Stephenson McCann Kennedy, Belfast; two *s* one *d. Educ:* Solihull Sch.; Exeter Coll., Oxford (DM 1968; Hon. Fellow, 1978); Johns Hopkins Univ. (MD 1951); MA, MD Cantab 1975. Repr. Oxford University: Rugby football, *v* Cambridge, 1940–41; hockey, 1940–42 (Captain); cricket, 1942 (Captain). Major RAMC, Army Operational Research Group, 1947–50. Member, Scientific Staff, Medical Research Council, 1946–58: Research Fellow, Medical Coll. of Virginia, Richmond, Va, USA, 1950–52; seconded to Min. of Supply, 1952; seconded to AEA, 1956; Prof. of Experimental Medicine, Guy's Hospital, 1958–63; Prof. of Medicine, Guy's Hosp. Med. Sch., and Additional Physician, Guy's Hosp., 1963–71; Vice-Chancellor, Nottingham Univ., 1971–75; Professorial Fellow, Downing Coll., Cambridge, 1975–78; Vice-Chancellor, Cambridge Univ., 1983–85. Chairman: Bedford Diabetic Survey, 1962; Woolwich/Erith New Town Medical Liaison Cttee, 1965–71; SE Met. Reg. Hospital Board's Clinical Research Cttee, 1960–71; Scientific Advisory Panel, Army Personnel Research Cttee, 1970–76; Council for the Education and Training of Health Visitors, 1971–76; East Midlands Economic Planning Council, 1974–75; Medicines Commn, 1976–81; Member: UGC Medical Sub-Cttee, 1966–71; Council, British Diabetic Assoc., 1963–74 (Chm. 1967–74; Vice-Pres. 1974–); DHSS Cttee on Medical Aspects of Food Policy, 1964–80; DHSS Panel on Medical Research, 1974–76; MRC Cttee on General Epidemiology, 1965–74; MRC Clinical Res. Grants Bd, 1969–71; MRC, 1976–80; Anglo-Soviet Consultative Cttee; Minister of Health's Long Term Study Group; Health Educn Council, DHSS, 1973–77; Trent RHA, 1973–75; IUC Council and Exec. Cttee, 1973; British Council Med. Adv. Cttee, 1971–80; Northwick Park Adv. Cttee, 1971–76; Council, European Assoc. for Study of Diabetes, 1968–71 (Vice-Pres.); Hong Kong Univ. and Polytechnic Grants Cttee, 1975–83; House of Lords Sci. of Technology Cttee, 1987–88; St George's House Council, 1987–89; various H of L Select Cttees, 1987–99. Chairman: Trustees, Lucy Cavendish Coll., 1987–97; Council of Governors, UMDS, 1989–96; Trustees, Strangeways Res. Lab., Cambridge, 1994–97 (Trustee, 1997–); Med. Cttee, Tommy's Campaign, St Thomas' Hosp., 1996–99; Trustee, William Harvey Res. Inst., 1995–2000; Dir, Co. and Trustees, Hawks Charitable Trust, 1997– (Chm. Bd, Hawks Club, 1992–97). Chairman: Jardine Educnl Trust, 1982–90; Health Promotion Res. Trust, 1983–93; Croucher Foundn, Hong Kong, 1989–97 (Trustee, 1979–89; Pres., 1997–); GB-Sasakawa Foundn, 1992–97 (Trustee, 1985–); Trustee, Ely Cathedral, 1986. Consultant, WHO Expert Cttee on Diabetes, 1964–80; Visitor, King Edward's Hospital Fund, 1964–71; Examiner in Medicine: Oxford Univ., 1960–66; Univ. of E Africa, 1966; Cambridge Univ., 1967–75; Pfizer Vis. Professor, NZ and Australia, 1965; Visiting Professor: Yale, 1966; Harvard, 1978. Rock Carling Fellow, RCP, 1968; Lectures: Oliver-Sharpey, RCP, 1967; Banting, BDA, 1970; Linacre, Cambridge, 1979; Roberts, Med. Soc. of London, 1981; Claysmore, Blandford Forum, 1983; Northcott, Exeter, 1984; Cohen, Hebrew

Univ. of Jerusalem, 1985. Dir, Prudential Corp., 1981–92. Member: Editorial Board, Diabetaloga, 1964–69; Jl Chronic Diseases, 1968–. Hon. Fellow. NY Acad. Science, 1962; NY Acad. of Medicine, 1987; Hughes Hall, Cambridge, 1988; Hon. FDS RCS, 1992; Hon. FUMDS 1996; Hon. FRCDS 1997; Corres. FACP 1973. FKC 1998. Hon. Med. Adviser, Leeds Castle. Patron, Richmond Soc., 1968–71. FRSA 1971. Hon. LLD: Nottingham, 1977; Bristol, 1995; Hon. DMedSci Keio Univ., Tokyo, 1983; Hon. DSc Florida Internat. Univ., Miami, 1985; Hon. MD Chinese Univ., Hong Kong, 1989; Hon. DSc (Med) London, 1997; Hon. DHumLit Virginia Commonwealth Univ., 1999. Order of Sacred Treasure, Gold Rays and Neck Ribbon (Japan), 1999. *Publications:* On Burns (jtly), 1953; Tolbutamide after 10 years, 1967; Priorities in Medicine, 1968; Health and Sickness: the choice of treatment, 1971; (ed) International Dictionary of Medicine and Biology, 1986; over 100 contribs to med. and allied literature incl. books, chapters, official reports and articles on diabetes, health care and educnl topics. *Recreations:* tennis (not lawn), cricket (village), talking (too much). *Address:* 39 Clarendon Street, Cambridge CB1 1JX. *T:* (01223) 328854. *Clubs:* Athenæum, MCC, Queen's; Vincent's (Sec., 1942) (Oxford); CURUFC (Pres., 1984–); CUCC (Pres., 1979–90).   *Died 22 July 2000.*

BUTTERWORTH, Prof. George Esmond, DPhil; Professor of Psychology, University of Sussex, since 1991; *b* 8 Nov. 1946; *s* of late Reginald Esmond Butterworth and of Helen Butterworth; *m* 1st, 1970, Jonquil Delia Sandra Hale (*d* 1982); one *s* one *d*; 2nd, 1992, Margaret Harris; one *d. Educ:* Southern GS for Boys, Portsmouth; NE London Poly. (BSc London Ext. Psych.); Univ. of Birmingham (MSc Clinical Psych.); St John's Coll., Oxford (DPhil). FBPsS. Lectr and Sen. Lectr, Univ. of Southampton, 1974–85; Prof. of Psychology, Univ. of Stirling, 1985–91. Dist. Vis. Res. Fellow, La Trobe Univ., 1993; Hon. Prof. of Psychology, Univ. of East London, 1996–; Leverhulme Res. Fellow, 1998. Pres., European Soc. for Development Psychol., 1997–. Editor: British Jl of Developmental Psych., 1988–94; Developmental Sci., 1998–. *Publications:* (ed) The child's representation of the world, 1977; (ed) Infancy and epistemology, 1981; (ed jtly) Social cognition, 1982; (ed jtly) Evolution and developmental psychology, 1985; (ed) Infancy, 1985; (ed jtly) Causes of development, 1990; (ed jtly) Perspectives on the child's theory of mind, 1991; (jtly) Michotte's experimental phenomenology of perception, 1991; (ed jtly) Context and cognition, 1992; (with M. Harris) Principles of developmental psychology, 1994; (ed jtly) Infant Development: recent advances, 1996; (ed jtly) The development of sensory, motor and cognitive capacities in early infancy: from perception to cognition, 1998; (ed jtly) Imitation in Infancy, 1999; papers in learned jls. *Recreation:* antique shops. *Address:* Psychology in the School of Cognitive and Computing Sciences, University of Sussex, Brighton, E Sussex BN1 9QH. *T:* (01273) 678501.   *Died 12 Feb. 2000.*

BUTTERWORTH, Henry, CEng, MIMechE; retired; Managing Director, Ammunition Division (formerly Director General (Ammunition)), Royal Ordnance plc (formerly Royal Ordnance Factories), 1979–88; Chairman, Royal Ordnance (Speciality Metals) Ltd, 1986–88; *b* 21 Jan. 1926; *s* of late Henry and Wilhemena Butterworth; *m* 1948, Ann Smith; two *s. Educ:* St Mary's, Leyland, Lancs. DipProd Birmingham. Apprenticeship, 1940–47; draughtsman, 1947–52; technical asst, 1952–53; progressively, shop manager, asst manager, manager, 1953–71; Director ROF: Cardiff, Burghfield, Glascoed, 1971–79. *Recreation:* coarse fishing. *Address:* 5 Vicarsfield Road, Worden Park, Leyland, Lancs PR5 2BH. *T:* (01772) 436073.   *Died 13 Nov. 1996.*

BUXTON, Sir Thomas Fowell Victor, 6th Bt *cr* 1840, of Belfield, Dorsetshire; *b* 18 Aug. 1925; *s* of Sir Thomas Fowell Buxton, 5th Bt, and Hon. Dorothy Cochrane (*d* 1927), *yr d* of 1st Baron Cochrane of Cults; *S* father, 1945; *m* 1955, Mrs D. M. Chisenhale-Marsh (*d* 1965). *Educ:* Eton, Trinity Coll., Cambridge. *Heir: cousin* Jocelyn Charles Roden Buxton [*b* 8 Aug. 1924; *m* 1960, Ann Frances, *d* of late Frank Smitherman, MBE; three *d*].
                                    Died 14 Nov. 1996.

BYERS, Sir Maurice (Hearne), Kt 1982; CBE 1978; QC (Aust.) 1960; barrister; Solicitor-General of Australia, 1973–83; Chairman, Australian Constitutional Commission, 1986–88; *b* 10 Nov. 1917; *s* of Arthur Tolhurst Byers and Mabel Florence Byers (*née* Hearne); *m* 1949, Patricia Therese Davis; two *s* one *d. Educ:* St Aloysius Coll., Milson's Point, Sydney; Sydney Univ. (LLB). Called to the Bar, 1944. Mem., Exec. Council, Law Council of Australia, 1966–68; Vice-Pres., NSW Bar Assoc., 1964–65, Pres., 1965–67. Leader, Australian delegations to: UN Commn on Internat. Trade Law, 1974, 1976–82; Diplomatic Conf. on Sea Carriage of Goods, Hamburg, 1979. Chm., Police Bd of NSW, 1984–88. Member: Council, ANU, 1975–78; Australian Law Reform Commn, 1984–85. *Address:* 3 Kardinia Road, Clifton Gardens, NSW 2088, Australia. *T:* (2) 99698257.
                                    Died 16 Jan. 1999.

C

CADELL, Colin Simson, CBE 1944; Air Commodore, Royal Air Force, retired; Vice Lieutenant for West Lothian, 1972–88; *b* 7 Aug. 1905; *s* of late Lt-Col J. M. Cadell, DL, Foxhall, Kirkliston, W Lothian; *m* 1939, Rosemary Elizabeth, *d* of Thomas Edward Pooley; two *s* one *d. Educ:* Merchiston; Edinburgh Univ.; Ecole Supérieur d'électricité, Paris. MA; AMIEE; Ingénieur ESE. Commnd RAF, 1926; Dir of Signals, Air Min., 1944; retd 1947. Man. Dir, International Aeradio, 1947–58; Director: Carron Company, 1958–71; Royal Bank of Scotland, 1963–69. Mem., Edinburgh Airport Consultative Cttee, 1972 (Chm., 1972–82). Mem. Queen's Body Guard for Scotland (Royal Company of Archers). DL Linlithgowshire, 1963–72. Officer, US Legion of Merit, 1945. *Address:* 2 Upper Coltbridge Terrace, Edinburgh EH12 6AD. *Club:* New (Edinburgh).

Died 29 Oct. 1996.

CADELL, Vice-Adm. Sir John (Frederick), KBE 1983; District General Manager, Canterbury and Thanet Health Authority, 1986–94; *b* 6 Dec. 1929; *s* of Henry Dunlop Mallock Cadell and Violet Elizabeth (*née* Van Dyke); *m* 1958, Jaquetta Bridget Nolan; one *s* two *d. Educ:* Britannia Royal Naval Coll., Dartmouth. Served in HMS Frobisher, 1946, then Mediterranean, Persian Gulf, North and Baltic Seas; 2 years with RNZN, to 1960; served in HMS Ashton, Dartmouth, HMS Leopard, 9th Minesweeping Sqdn, SACLANT, HMS Bulwark, 1960–70; Naval Asst to First Sea Lord, 1970–72; HMS Diomede, 1972–74; RCDS 1974–75; RN Presentation Team, 1975–76; Comd, Sch. of Maritime Ops, 1976–79; Dir Gen. Naval Personal Services, 1979–81; COS to Comdr, Allied Forces Southern Europe, 1982–85. *Recreations:* tennis, skiing, chess. *Address:* Great Mongeham House, near Deal, Kent CT14 0HD.

Died 13 Aug. 1998.

CADELL, Simon John; actor; *b* 19 July 1950; *s* of John Cadell and Gillian (*née* Howell); *m* 1986, Rebecca Croft; two *s. Educ:* Bedales Sch., Petersfield. Bristol Old Vic Co., 1969–70; Nottingham Playhouse, 1971; Lloyd George Knew My Father, Savoy, 1972–73; Belgrade, Coventry, 1974; The Case in Question, Haymarket, 1975; Lies, Albery, 1975; Actors' Co., 1976, 1977; Private Lives, on tour, 1981; Noel and Gertie, King's Head, 1983; Hamlet, Birmingham Rep., 1984; Jumpers, Aldwych, 1985; Blythe Spirit, Vaudeville, 1985–86; Tons of Money, A Small Family Business, National, 1986–87; Double Act, Playhouse, 1988; Noel and Gertie, Comedy, 1989–90; Don't Dress for Dinner, Apollo, 1991; Travels with My Aunt, Wyndham's, 1992–93 (Olivier Award, Best Comedy Perf., 1993) . Work on radio and numerous TV appearances. *Recreations:* wine, travel. *Address:* c/o Caroline Renton, 23 Crescent Lane, SW4 9PT. *T:* 0171–498 7217. *Clubs:* Groucho, Tramps, MCC.

Died 6 March 1996.

CADOGAN, 7th Earl *cr* 1800; **William Gerald Charles Cadogan,** MC 1943; DL; Baron Cadogan, 1718; Viscount Chelsea, 1800; Baron Oakley, 1831; Lieutenant-Colonel Royal Wiltshire Yeomanry, Royal Armoured Corps; Captain Coldstream Guards Reserve of Officers, until 1964 (retaining hon. rank of Lieutenant-Colonel); *b* 13 Feb. 1914; *s* of 6th Earl and Lilian Eleanora Marie (who *m* 2nd, 1941, Lt-Col H. E. Hambro, CBE; she *d* 1973); *d* of George Coxon, Craigleith, Cheltenham; *S* father, 1933; *m* 1st, 1936, Hon. Primrose Lillian Yarde-Buller (marr. diss. 1959), *y d* of 3rd Baron Churston; one *s* three *d*; 2nd, 1961, Cecilia, *y d* of Lt-Col H. K. Hamilton-Wedderburn, OBE. *Educ:* Eton; RMC Sandhurst. Served War of 1939–45 (MC). Mem. Chelsea Borough Council, 1953–59; Mayor of Chelsea, 1964. DL County of London, 1958. *Heir: s* Viscount Chelsea [*b* 24 March 1937; *m* 1st, 1963, Lady Philippa Wallop (*d* 1984), *d* of 9th Earl of Portsmouth; two *s* one *d*; 2nd, 1989, Jennifer Jane Greig Rae (marr. diss. 1994), *d* of J. E. K. Rae; 3rd, 1994, Dorothy Ann Shipsey, MVO, *yr d* of late Dr W. E. Shipsey]. *Address:* 28 Cadogan Square, SW1X 0JH. *T:* (0171) 584 2335; Snaigow, Dunkeld, Perthshire PH1 4LJ. *T:* (01738) 710223. *Club:* White's.

Died 4 July 1997.

CADWALLADER, Air Vice-Marshal Howard George, CB 1974; RAF retd; Director of Purchasing, Post Office, 1978–79; *b* 16 March 1919; British; *m* 1950, Betty Ethel Samuels; no *c. Educ:* Hampton Sch., Middx. Sen. Equipment Staff Officer: HQ Transport Comd, 1963–65; HQ FEAF Singapore, 1965–68; Dep. Dir of Equipment 14 MoD (Air), 1968–69; Comdt of RAF Supply Control Centre, Hendon, 1969–72; Dir of Movts (RAF), MoD (Air), 1972–73; SASO HQ Support Comd, RAF, 1973–74. Controller of Contracts, PO, 1974–78. *Recreations:* golf, sailing. *Address:* Spain.

Died 12 June 1998.

CÆSAR, Irving; author-lyrist; Past President of Songwriters' Protective Association; Member Board of Directors, American Society of Composers, Authors and Publishers; *b* New York, 4 July 1895; *s* of Rumanian Jews. *Educ:* public school; Chappaqua Quaker Inst.; City Coll. of New York. Protégé of Ella Wheeler Wilcox, who, when he was a boy of nine, became interested in bits of verse he wrote and published at the time; at twenty became attached to the Henry Ford Peace Expedition, and spent nine months travelling through neutral Europe (during the War) as one of the secretaries of the Ford Peace Conference; returned to America, and became interested in writing for the musical comedy stage. *Publications:* most important work, No, No, Nanette; wrote hundreds of songs and collaborated in many other musical comedies; writer and publisher of Sing a Song of Safety, a vol. of children's songs in use throughout the public and parochial schools of USA; also Sing a Song of Friendship, a series of songs based on human rights; in England: The Bamboula, Swanee, Tea for Two (successive awards for being among the most performed ASCAP standards), I Want to be Happy, I Was So Young; author of "Peace by Wireless" proposal for freedom of international exchange of radio privilege between governments. *Recreations:* reading, theatre, swimming. *Address:* Irving Cæsar Music Corporation, 429 East 52nd Street, Apartment 31G, New York, NY 10022, USA. *Club:* Friars (New York).

Died 17 Dec. 1996.

CAFFIN, A(rthur) Crawford; a Recorder, 1971–82; solicitor, since 1932; *b* 10 June 1910; *s* of Charles Crawford Caffin and Annie Rosila Caffin; *m* 1933, Mala Pocock (decd); one *d. Educ:* King's Sch., Rochester. Assistant Solicitor: to Norfolk CC, 1933–37; to Bristol Corporation, 1937–46; Partner in firm of R. L. Frank & Caffin, Solicitors, Truro, 1946–72, Consultant, 1972–84. Pres., Cornwall Law Soc., 1960; Mem. Council, Law Society, 1966–76; Dep. Chm., Traffic Commissioners for Western Traffic Area, 1964–84. *Recreation:* swimming. *Address:* Cove Cottage, Portloe, Truro, Cornwall TR2 5QY.

Died 21 Sept. 2000.

CAHILL, Michael Leo; Head of Central and Southern Africa Department, Overseas Development Administration, 1983 88, retired; *b* 4 April 1928; *s* of John and Josephine Cahill, *m* 1961, Harriette Emma Clemency, *e d* of late Christopher Gilbert Eastwood, CMG and Catherine Eastwood; two *d. Educ:* Beaumont Coll.; Magdalen Coll., Oxford (Demy). National Service, Intelligence Corps, Trieste, 1950–52 (Lieut). FO, 1953; CO, 1955; Asst Private Sec. to Sec. of State, 1956–57; Private Sec. to Parly Under-Sec., 1957–58; Dept of Technical Co-operation, 1961; Asst Sec., ODM, 1969; UK Perm. Deleg. to Unesco, 1972–74. Chm., Woldingham Sch. Parents Assoc., 1981–83. *Recreations:* history of the arts, pianism. *Address:* 9 Murray Road, SW19 4PD. *T:* (020) 8947 0568. *Died 26 Dec. 1999.*

CAIN, Sir Edward (Thomas), Kt 1972; CBE 1966; Commissioner of Taxation, Australia, 1964–76; retired; *b* Maryborough, Qld, Australia, 7 Dec. 1916; *s* of Edward Victor and Kathleen Teresa Cain; *m* 1942, Marcia Yvonne Cain (*née* Parbery); one *s* one *d. Educ:* Nudgee Coll., Queensland; Univ. of Queensland (BA, LLB). Commonwealth Taxation Office in Brisbane, Sydney, Perth and Canberra, 1936–76. Served War, 2/9th Bn, AIF, 1939–43. *Recreations:* golf, fishing. *Address:* 99 Buxton Street, Deakin, Canberra, ACT 2600, Australia. *T:* (6) 2811462. *Clubs:* Commonwealth, Royal Canberra Golf (Canberra). *Died 26 April 1996.*

CAIN, Maj.-Gen. George Robert T.; *see* Turner Cain.

CAINE, Sir Michael (Harris), Kt 1988; Chairman, 1979–93, Vice Chairman, 1973–79, Chief Executive, 1975–84, Director, 1964–93, Booker plc; *b* 17 June 1927; *s* of Sir Sydney Caine, KCMG and Muriel Anne (*née* Harris); *m* 1st, 1952, Janice Denise (*née* Mercer) (marr. diss. 1987); one *s* one *d*; 2nd, 1987, Emma Harriet Nicholson (later Baroness Nicholson of Winterbourne); one adopted *s. Educ:* Bedales; Lincoln Coll., Oxford; George Washington Univ., USA. Joined Booker McConnell Ltd, 1952; Chairman: Five TV Ltd, 1991–96; Artisan Trust and Artisan Link Ltd, 1992–; Director: Arbor Acres Farm Inc., 1980–91; Booker Tate, 1993–; Commonwealth Equity Fund, 1990–95; Internat. Pepsi-Cola Bottlers (Africa) Ltd, 1996–; Chm., African Emerging Markets Fund, 1993–. Chairman: Council for Technical Educn and Training for Overseas Countries, 1973–75; UK Council for Overseas Student Affairs, 1980–93. Member: Council, Inst. of Race Relations, 1969–72; Council, Bedford Coll., London, 1966–85; IBA, 1984–89; Commonwealth Develt Corp., 1985–94 (Dep. Chm., 1989–94); Governing Body: Inst. of Develt Studies, Sussex Univ., 1975–95; NIESR, 1979–97; Queen Elizabeth House, Oxford, 1983–96; Chairman: Council, Royal African Soc., 1984–96 (Pres., 1996–); Africa '95, 1993–95; Africa Centre, 1995–; Commonwealth Scholarships Commn in the UK, 1987–96; One World Broadcasting Trust, 1987–96. *Address:* c/o Booker plc, 85 Buckingham Gate, SW1E 6PD. *T:* (020) 7411 5500. *Club:* Reform. *Died 20 March 1999.*

CAIRD, William Douglas Sime; Registrar, Family Division of High Court (formerly Probate, Divorce and Admiralty Division), 1964–82; *b* 21 Aug. 1917; *er s* of William Sime Caird and Elsie Amy Caird; *m* 1946, Josephine Mary, *d* of Peter and Elizabeth Seeney, Stratford on Avon; no *c. Educ:* Rutlish Sch., Merton. Entered Principal Probate Registry, 1937; Estabt Officer, 1954; Sec., 1959; Mem., Matrimonial Causes Rule Cttee, 1968–79. *Publications:* Consulting Editor, Rayden on Divorce, 10th edn 1967, 11th edn 1971, 12th edn 1974, 13th edn 1979. *Address:* 17 Pine Walk, Bookham, Surrey KT23 4AS. *T:* (01372) 456732. *Died 16 Dec. 1999.*

CAIRNCROSS, Sir Alexander Kirkland, (Sir Alec), KCMG 1967 (CMG 1950); FBA 1961; Chancellor, University of Glasgow, 1972–96; *b* 11 Feb. 1911; 3rd *s* of Alexander Kirkland and Elizabeth Andrew Cairncross, Lesmahagow, Scotland; *m* 1943, Mary Frances Glynn (*d* 1998), *d* of Maj. E. F. Glynn, TD, Ilkley; three *s* two *d. Educ:* Hamilton Academy; Glasgow and Cambridge Univs. Univ. Lectr, 1935–39; Civil Servant, 1940–45; Dir of Programmes, Min. of Aircraft Production, 1945; Economic Advisory Panel, Berlin, 1945–46; Mem. of Staff of The Economist, 1946; Mem. of Wool Working Party, 1946; Economic Adviser to: BoT, 1946–49; Organisation for European Economic Co-operation, 1949–50; Prof. of Applied Economics, Univ. of Glasgow, 1951–61; Dir, Economic Development Inst., Washington DC, 1955–56; Economic Adviser to HM Govt, 1961–64; Head of Govt Economic Service, 1964–69; Master of St Peter's Coll., Oxford, 1969–78, Hon. Fellow, 1978; Supernumerary Fellow, St Antony's Coll., Oxford, 1978–89, Hon. Fellow, 1989. Vis. Prof., Brookings Instn, Washington, DC, 1972; Leverhulme Vis. Prof., Inst. of Economic and Social Change, Bangalore, 1981; Leverhulme Emeritus Fellow, 1983–86. Chairman: independent advrs on reassessment of Channel Tunnel Project, 1974–75 (Adviser to Minister of Transport on Channel Tunnel Project, 1979–81); Commonwealth Secretariat Gp of Experts on Protectionism, 1982; Local Development Cttee, 1951–52; Member: Crofting Commn, 1951–54; Phillips Cttee, 1953–54; Anthrax Cttee, 1957–59; Radcliffe Cttee, 1957–59; Cttee on N Ireland, 1971; Cttee on Police Pay, 1978; Council of Mgt, NIESR, 1949–96; Court of Governors, LSE, until 1989 (Hon. Fellow, 1980); Council, Royal Economic Soc. (Pres., 1968–70). President: Scottish Economic Soc., 1969–71; British Assoc. for Advancement of Science, 1970–71 (Pres. Section F, 1969); Vice Pres., GPDST, 1992– (Pres., 1972–92). Houblon-Norman Trustee, 1982–86. Editor, Scottish Journal of Political Economy, 1954–61. Hon. Mem., Amer. Econ. Assoc., 1989; For. Hon. Mem., Amer. Acad. of Arts and Scis, 1973. Hon. LLD: Mount Allison, 1962; Glasgow, 1966; Exeter, 1969; Hon. DLitt: Reading, 1968; Heriot-Watt, 1969; Hon. DSc(Econ.): Univ. of Wales, 1971; QUB, 1972; DUniv Stirling, 1973. *Publications:* Introduction to Economics, 1944, 6th edn 1982; Home and Foreign Investment, 1870–1913, 1953; Monetary Policy in a Mixed Economy, 1960; Economic Development and the Atlantic Provinces, 1961; Factors in Economic Development, 1962; Essays in Economic Management, 1971; Control of Long-term International Capital Movements, 1973; Inflation, Growth and International Finance, 1975; Science Studies (Nuffield Foundn report), 1980; Snatches (poems), 1981; (with Barry Eichengreen) Sterling in Decline, 1983; Years of Recovery, 1985; The Price of War, 1986; Economics and Economic Policy, 1986; A Country to Play With, 1987; (ed) The Diaries of Robert Hall, Vol. I 1989, Vol. II 1991; (with Nita Watts) The Economic Section 1939–61, 1989; Planning in Wartime, 1991; The British Economy since 1945, 1992, 2nd edn 1995; (with K. Burk) Goodbye Great Britain, 1992; (ed with F. Cairncross) The Legacy of the Golden Age, 1992; Austin Robinson: the life of an economic adviser, 1993; Economic Ideas and Government Policy, 1995; Managing the British Economy in the 1960s, 1996; The Wilson Years 1964–69, 1997. *Recreation:* writing. *Address:* 14 Staverton Road, Oxford OX2 6XJ. *T:* (01865) 552358. *Died 21 Oct. 1998.*

CALDECOTE, 2nd Viscount *cr* 1939, of Bristol, co. Gloucester; Robert Andrew Inskip, KBE 1987; DSC 1941; DL; FREng; Chairman: Delta Group plc (formerly Delta Metal Co.), 1972–82; Investors in Industry (formerly Finance for Industry), 1980–87; *b* 8 Oct. 1917; *o s* of Thomas Walker Hobart Inskip, later 1st Viscount

Caldecote, CBE, PC, and Lady Augusta Orr Ewing (*d* 1967), *e d* of 7th Earl of Glasgow, and *widow* of Charles Orr Ewing, MP for Ayr Burghs; *S* father, 1947; *m* 1942, Jean Hamilla, *d* of late Rear-Adm. H. D. Hamilton; one *s* two *d*. *Educ:* Eton Coll.; King's Coll., Cambridge (BA 1939; MA 1944). RNVR, 1939–45; RNC Greenwich, 1946–47; an Asst Manager, Vickers-Armstrong Naval Yard, Walker-on-Tyne, 1947–48; Fellow, King's Coll., and Lectr, Engineering Dept, Cambridge Univ., 1948–55; Dir, English Electric Co., 1953–69; Man. Dir, English Electric Aviation, 1960–63; Dep. Man. Dir, British Aircraft Corp., 1961–67 (Dir, 1960–69); Chm., Legal and General Gp, 1977–80. Chairman: EDC Movement of Exports, 1965–72; Export Council for Europe, 1970–71. Mem., H of L Select Cttee for Sci. and Technol., 1988–92. President: Soc. of British Aerospace Cos, 1965–66; Internat. Assoc. of Aeronautical and Space Equipment Manufacturers, 1966–68; Parliamentary and Scientific Cttee, 1966–69; Fellowship of Engineering, 1981–86 (FREng (FEng 1977)); RINA, 1987–90 (FRINA 1987). Director: Consolidated Gold Fields, 1969–78; Lloyds Bank, 1975–88; Lloyds Bank International, 1979–85; Equity Capital for Industry, 1980–85; W. S. Atkins Ltd, 1985–92; Industry Ventures Ltd, 1989–93. Member: Review Bd for Govt Contracts, 1969–76; Inflation Accounting Cttee, 1974–75; Engineering Industries Council, 1975–82; British Railways Bd, 1979–85; Adv. Council for Applied R&D, 1981–84; Engrg Council, 1981–85. Chairman: Design Council, 1972–80; BBC Gen. Adv. Council, 1982–85; Mary Rose Trust, 1983–92; Crown Appts Commn, 1990. Pro-Chancellor, Cranfield Inst. of Technology, 1976–84. Mem., Church Assembly, 1950–55. Mem. UK Delegn to UN, 1952. Pres., Assoc. Sail Training Orgns, 1988–97. Fellow, Eton Coll., 1953–72; Pres., Dean Close Sch., 1960–90. Hon. Mem., Coll. of Teachers, 1998. DL Hants, 1991. Hon. FICE 1981; Hon. FIMechE 1982; Hon. FIEE 1984; Hon. FIM 1984; Hon. FCSD (FSIAD 1976). Hon. DSc: Cranfield, 1976; Aston, 1979; City, 1982; Bristol, 1982; Hon. LLD: London, 1981; Cambridge, 1985. *Recreations:* sailing, shooting, golf. *Heir: s* Hon. Piers James Hampden Inskip [*b* 20 May 1947; *m* 1st, 1970, Susan Bridget, *d* of late W. P. Mellen; 2nd, 1984, Kristine Elizabeth, *d* of Harvey Holbrooke-Jackson; one *s*]. *Address:* Orchard Cottage, South Harting, Petersfield, Hants GU31 5NR. *T:* (01730) 825529. *Clubs:* Athenæum, Royal Ocean Racing; Royal Yacht Squadron; Royal Cruising. *Died 20 Sept. 1999.*

CALDWELL, Surg. Vice-Adm. Sir (Eric) Dick, KBE 1969; CB 1965; MD; FRCP, FRCPE; Medical Director-General of the Royal Navy, 1966–69; Executive Director, Medical Council on Alcoholism, 1970–79; *b* 6 July 1907; *s* of late Dr John Colin Caldwell; *m* 1942, Margery Lee Abbott (*d* 1991). *Educ:* Edinburgh Acad.; Edinburgh Univ. MB, ChB Edinburgh 1933; MD Edinburgh 1950; MRCP 1956; FRCPE 1962; FRCP 1967. Joined Royal Navy, 1934; served War of 1939–45 in Atlantic, Mediterranean and Pacific; survivor from torpedoeing of HMS Royal Oak and HMS Prince of Wales; Medical Specialist, RN Hosp., Hong Kong, 1947; Sen. Med. Specialist at RN Hosp., Haslar, 1956–58; Surg. Captain 1957; MO i/c of RN Hosp., Plymouth, 1963–66. RN Consultant in Medicine, 1962; Surg. Rear-Adm. 1963; Surg. Vice-Adm. 1966. QHP 1963–69. Gilbert Blane Gold Medal, RCP, 1962. FRSocMed. CStJ. *Recreations:* reading, travelling, trying to write. *Address:* Flat 10 Woodsford, 14 Melbury Road, Kensington, W14 8LS. *T:* (020) 7602 2225. *Died 11 July 2000.*

CALLAGHAN, Rear-Adm. Desmond Noble, CB 1970; Director-General, National Supervisory Council for Intruder Alarms, 1971–77; *b* 24 Nov. 1915; *s* of Edmund Ford Callaghan and Kathleen Louise Callaghan (*née* Noble): *m* 1948, Patricia Munro Geddes; one *s* two *d*.

Educ: RNC Dartmouth. HMS Frobisher, 1933; RNEC Keyhan, 1934; HM Ships: Royal Oak, 1937; Iron Duke, 1938; Warspite, 1939; Hereward, 1941; Prisoner of War, 1941; HMS Argonaut, 1945; HMS Glory, 1946; RNC Dartmouth, 1947; Admiralty, 1949; C-in-C Med. Staff, 1950; HMS Excellent, 1953; HMS Eagle, 1956; RN Tactical Sch., 1958; Admiralty, 1960; HMS Caledonia, 1962; Admiralty, 1965; Vice-Pres. and Pres., Ordnance Board, 1968–71, retired. FRSA. *Recreations:* Rugby, tennis, swimming. *Address:* Bridge End, Abbotsbrook, Bourne End, Bucks SL8 5RE. *T:* (01628) 520519. *Died 28 May 2000.*

CALLARD, Sir Eric John, (Sir Jack), Kt 1974; FEng 1976; Chairman, British Home Stores Ltd, 1976–82 (Director 1975–82); *b* 15 March 1913; *s* of late F. and A. Callard; *m* 1938, Pauline M., *d* of late Rev. Charles Pengelly; three *d*. *Educ:* Queen's Coll., Taunton; St John's Coll., Cambridge (1st cl. Hons Mech. Sci. Tripos; BA 1935; MA 1973); Harvard Business Sch. (Adv. Management Programme, 1953). Joined ICI Ltd, 1935; seconded to Min. of Aircraft Prodn, 1942; ICI Paints Div., 1947 (Jt Man. Dir, 1955–59; Chm., 1959–64); Chairman: Deleg. Bd, ICI (Hyde) Ltd, 1959; ICI (Europa) Ltd, 1965–67; ICI Ltd, 1971–75 (Dir, 1964–75; Dep. Chm., 1967–71); Director: Pension Funds Securities Ltd, 1963–67; Imp. Metal Industries Ltd, 1964–67; Imp. Chemicals Insurance Ltd, 1966–70; Midland Bank Ltd, 1971–87; Ferguson Industrial Holdings, 1975–86; Commercial Union Assurance Co., 1976–83; Equity Capital for Industry, 1976–84. Member Council: BIM, 1964–69; Manchester Univ. Business Sch., 1964–71; Export Council for Europe, 1965–71; Member: CBI Steering Cttee on Europe, 1965–71; Cambridge Univ. Appointments Bd, 1968–71; CBI Overseas Cttee, 1969–71; Council of Industry for Management Educn, 1967–73; Royal Instn of GB, 1971–; Vice-Pres., Manchester Business Sch. Assoc., 1971– (Hon. Mem., 1966–; Pres., 1969–71); Pres., Industrial Participation Assoc., 1971–76 (Chm., 1967–71). Member: Hansard Soc. Commn on Electoral Reform, 1975–76; Cttee of Inquiry into Industrial Democracy, 1976–77. Trustee, Civic Trust, 1972–75; Governor, London Business Sch., 1972–75. Mem. Court, British Shippers' Council, 1972–75. FRSA 1970; CIMgt (FBIM 1966); Hon. FIMechE. Hon. DSc Cranfield Inst. of Technology, 1974. *Recreations:* games, fishing. *Address:* Crookwath Cottage, High Row, Dockray, Penrith, Cumbria CA11 0LG. *Club:* Flyfishers'. *Died 21 Sept. 1998.*

CALLEY, Sir Henry (Algernon), Kt 1964; DSO 1945; DFC 1943; DL; Owner and Manager of a stud, since 1948; *b* 9 Feb. 1914; *s* of Rev. A. C. M. Langton and Mrs Langton (*née* Calley); changed surname to Calley, 1974; unmarried. *Educ:* St John's Sch., Leatherhead. Taught at Corchester, Corbridge-on-Tyne, 1933–35; Bombay Burmah Trading Corp., 1935–36; teaching, 1936–38; Metropolitan Police Coll., and Police Force, 1938–41; Royal Air Force, 1941–48: Pilot in Bombers, Actg Wing Comdr, 1944. Mem. Wiltshire CC, 1955; Chm. Finance Cttee, 1959–68; Chm. of Council, 1968–73. Chm. Wessex Area Conservative Assoc., 1963–66. DL Wilts, 1968. *Died 12 Aug. 1997.*

CALTHORPE, 10th Baron *cr* 1796; **Peter Waldo Somerset Gough-Calthorpe;** Bt 1728; *b* 13 July 1927; *s* of Hon. Frederick Somerset Gough-Calthorpe (*d* 1935, *o s* of 8th Baron) and Rose Mary Dorothy, *d* of late Leveson William Vernon-Harcourt; *S* brother, 1945; *m* 1st, 1956, Saranne (marr. diss. 1971; she *d* 1984), *o d* of James Harold Alexander, Ireland; 2nd, 1979, Elizabeth, *d* of James and Sibyl Young, Guildford, Surrey. Formerly Lieut Welsh Gds. Pilot; founder, Mercury Airlines, 1960. *Publications:* (as Peter Somerset): The Sea Wraith, 1967; A Break in

the Clouds, 1968. *Heir:* none. *Address:* c/o Isle of Man Bank, 2 Athol Street, Douglas, Isle of Man.
Died 23 May 1997 (ext).

CALVIN, Prof. Melvin; University Professor of Chemistry, University of California, since 1971; Professor of Molecular Biology, 1963–80; *b* 8 April 1911; *s* of Rose and Elias Calvin; *m* 1942, Marie Genevieve Jemtegaard (*d* 1987); one *s* two *d*. *Educ:* Univ. of Minnesota, Minneapolis (PhD). Fellow, Univ. of Manchester, 1935–37. Univ. of California, Berkeley: Instr., 1937; Asst Prof., 1941–45; Assoc. Prof., 1945–47; Prof., 1947–71; Dir, Laboratory of Chemical Biodynamics, 1960–80; Associate Dir, Lawrence Berkeley Lab., 1967–80. Foreign Mem., Royal Society, 1959. Member: Nat. Acad. of Sciences (US); Royal Netherlands Acad. of Sciences and Letters; Amer. Philos. Society. Nobel Prize in Chemistry, 1961; Davy Medal, Royal Society, 1964; Virtanen Medal, 1975; Gibbs Medal, 1977; Priestley Medal, ACS, 1978; Amer. Inst. Chemists Gold Medal, 1979; Nat. Medal of Science, US, 1989; John Ericsson Award in Renewable Energy, US Dept. of Energy, 1991. Hon. degrees: Michigan Coll. of Mining and Technology, 1955; Univ. of Nottingham, 1958; Oxford Univ., 1959; Northwestern Univ., 1961; Univ. of Notre Dame, 1965; Brooklyn Polytechnic Inst., 1969; Rijksuniversiteit-Gent, 1970; Columbia Univ., 1979. *Publications:* very numerous, including (8 books): Theory of Organic Chemistry (with Branch), 1941; Isotopic Carbon (with Heidelberger, Reid, Tolbert and Yankwich), 1949; Chemistry of Metal Chelate Compounds (with Martell), 1952; Path of Carbon in Photosynthesis (with Bassham), 1957; Chemical Evolution, 1961; Photosynthesis of Carbon Compounds (with Bassham), 1962; Chemical Evolution, 1969; Following the Trail of Light: a scientific odyssey, 1992. *Address:* University of California, Berkeley, CA 94720, USA; (home) 2683 Buena Vista Way, Berkeley, CA 94708, USA. *Died 8 Jan. 1997.*

CAMBELL, Rear-Adm. Dennis Royle Farquharson, CB 1960; DSC 1940; *b* 13 Nov. 1907, *s* of Dr Archibald Cambell and Edith Cambell, Southsea; *m* 1933, Dorothy Elinor Downes; two *d*. *Educ:* Westminster Sch. Joined RN, 1925, HMS Thunderer Cadet Training; trained as FAA pilot, 1931; 1st Capt. of HMS Ark Royal IV, 1955–56; retired, 1960. *Address:* c/o National Westminster Bank, High Street, Petersfield, Hants GU32 3JF.
Died 6 April 2000.

CAMDEN, John; President, RMC Group plc (Chairman, 1974–93; Managing Director, 1966–85); *b* 18 Nov. 1925; *s* of late Joseph Reginald Richard John Camden and Lilian Kate McCann; *m* 1st, 1951, Helen Demel (marr. diss. 1959); one *s* one *d*; 2nd, 1959, Irmgard Steinbrink (marr. diss. 1971); one *d*; 3rd, 1972, Diane Mae Friese; two *d*. *Educ:* Worcester Royal Grammar Sch.; Birmingham Univ. (BSc). Royal Tank Corps and Intell. Corps, 1943–47. Joined RMC Group (formerly Ready Mixed Concrete Group), 1952; Dir responsible for Group's ops in Europe, 1962. Grand Decoration of Honour in Silver (Austria), 1978. *Recreations:* golf, gardening. *Address:* RMC Group plc, RMC House, Coldharbour Lane, Thorpe, Egham, Surrey TW20 8TD. *Died 15 May 1996.*

CAMERON, Hon. Lord; John Cameron, KT 1978; Kt 1954; DSC; HRSA; FRSGS; a Senator of The College of Justice in Scotland and Lord of Session 1955–85; *b* 8 Feb. 1900; *m* 1st, 1927, Eileen Dorothea (*d* 1943), *d* of late H. M. Burrell; one *s* two *d*; 2nd, 1944, Iris, *widow* of Lambert C. Shepherd. *Educ:* Edinburgh Acad.; Edinburgh Univ. Served European War, 1918–19, with RNVR; served with RNVR, Sept. 1939–1944 (despatches, DSC); released to reserve, Dec. 1944. Advocate, 1924; Advocate-Depute, 1929–36; QC (Scot.) 1936; Sheriff of Inverness, Elgin and Nairn, 1945; Sheriff of Inverness, Moray, Nairn and Ross

and Cromarty, 1946–48; Dean of Faculty of Advocates, 1948–55. Member: Cttee on Law of Contempt of Court, 1972; Royal Commn on Civil Liability and Compensation for Personal Injury, 1973–78. DL Edinburgh, 1953–84. Hon. FRSE 1983; Hon. FBA 1983. DUniv Edinburgh, 1983; Hon. LLD: Aberdeen; Glasgow; Edinburgh; Hon. DLitt Heriot-Watt. *Address:* 28 Moray Place, Edinburgh EH3 6BX. *T:* 0131–225 7585. *Clubs:* New, Scottish Arts (Edinburgh); Royal Forth Yacht.
Died 30 May 1996.

CAMERON, Dr Clive Bremner; Dean, Institute of Cancer Research, London, 1978–82; *b* 28 Sept. 1921; *s* of Clive Rutherford and Aroha Margaret Cameron; *m* 1958, Rosalind Louise Paget; two *s* one *d*. *Educ:* King's Coll., Auckland, NZ; Otago Univ., NZ (MD). Consultant in Clinical Pathology, Royal Marsden Hospital, 1961–82; Chairman, SW Thames Regional Cancer Council, 1976–81. Mem. Bd of Governors, Royal Marsden Hosp., 1977–82. *Publications:* papers on steroid biochemistry, biochemical and other aspects of cancer. *Recreation:* country pursuits. *Address:* East Kennett Manor, Marlborough, Wilts SN8 5ET. *T:* (01672) 861239.
Died 13 Nov. 1996.

CAMERON, Sir (Eustace) John, Kt 1977; CBE 1970; Tasmanian pastoralist, since 1946; *b* 8 Oct. 1913; *s* of Eustace Noel Cameron and Alexina Maria Cameron; *m* 1934, Nancie Ailsa Sutherland (OBE 1983) (*d* 1988); one *d*. *Educ:* Geelong Grammar Sch.; Trinity Coll., Cambridge (MA). Served RANVR, 1942–46. ICI, 1938–41. State Pres., Liberal Party, 1948–52. Pres., Tasmanian Stockowners Assoc., 1965–68; Vice-Pres., Aust. Graziers, 1968–71. University of Tasmania: Mem. Council, 1956–82; Dep. Chancellor, 1964–72; Chancellor, 1973–81. Member: Selection Cttee, Winston Churchill Fellowship, 1965–74; CSIRO Adv. Cttee, 1959–77; Housing Loan Insurance Corp., 1970–73. Hon. LLD Tasmania, 1982. *Publications:* contrib. Australian Dictionary of Biography. *Recreation:* reminiscences. *Address:* Lochiel, Ross, Tas 7209, Australia. *T:* (3) 63815253. *Club:* Tasmanian (Hobart).
Died 28 April 1998.

CAMERON, George Edmund, CBE 1970; retired; *b* 2 July 1911; *s* of William Cameron and Margaret Cameron (*née* Craig); *m* 1939, Winifred Audrey Brown; two *s*. *Educ:* Ballymena Academy. Chartered Accountant, 1933; Partner, Wright Fitzsimons & Cameron, 1937–79. Pres., Inst. of Chartered Accountants in Ireland, 1960–61. *Recreations:* golf, gardening. *Address:* Ardavon, Glen Road, Craigavad, Co. Down BT18 0HB. *T:* (01232) 422232. *Clubs:* Royal County Down Golf, Royal Belfast Golf. *Died 27 June 1997.*

CAMERON, Sir John; see Cameron, Hon. Lord, and Cameron, Sir E. J.

CAMERON, Sir John (Watson), Kt 1981; OBE 1960; President, J. W. Cameron & Co., since 1977; *b* 16 Nov. 1901; *s* of Captain Watson Cameron and Isabel Mann; *m* 1930, Lilian Florence Sanderson; one *s* two *d*. *Educ:* Lancing Coll. Commnd Durham RGA, 1920. Joined J. W. Cameron & Co., brewery co., 1922; Man. Dir, 1940; Chm., 1943–75. Mem., Northern Area, Economic League, 1950–80. Chm., 1964–69, Treasurer, 1967–72, Northern Area Cons. Party; Hartlepool Conservative Party: Chm., 1942–45; Pres., 1945–76; Patron, 1976–78; Pres. and Patron, 1978–. Chm., Hartlepools Hosp. Trust, 1973–80. *Recreations:* gardening, shooting, fishing. *Address:* Cowesby Hall, near Thirsk, N Yorks YO7 2JJ.
Died March 1997.

CAMPBELL, Prof. (Alexander) Colin (Patton), FRCPath, FRCPE; Procter Professor of Pathology and Pathological

Anatomy, University of Manchester, 1950–73, then Professor Emeritus (formerly Dean, Faculty of Medicine and Pro-Vice Chancellor); formerly Director of Studies, Royal College of Pathologists; *b* 21 Feb. 1908; *s* of late A. C. Campbell, Londonderry; *m* 1943, Hon. Elisabeth Joan Adderley, 2nd *d* of 6th Baron Norton; one *s* one *d* (and one *s* decd). *Educ:* Foyle Coll., Londonderry; Edinburgh Univ. MB, ChB (Hons) Edinburgh 1930; FRCPE 1939. Rockefeller Fellow and Research Fellow in Neuropathology, Harvard Univ., 1935–36; Lectr in Neuropathology, Edinburgh Univ., 1937–39; Lectr in Pathology, Edinburgh Univ., and Pathologist, Royal Infirmary, Edinburgh, 1939–50. War service, 1940–46, RAFVR (Wing-Comdr). Hon. MSc Manchester, 1954. *Publications:* papers on pathological subjects in various medical and scientific jls. *Recreations:* carpentry, cabinet-making. *Address:* The Priory House, Ascott-under-Wychwood, Oxford OX7 6AW.
Died 19 Nov. 1996.

CAMPBELL, Colin; *see* Campbell, A. C. P.

CAMPBELL, Sir Colin Moffat, 8th Bt *cr* 1667, of Aberuchill, Perthshire; MC 1945; Director, James Finlay plc, 1971–92 (Chairman, 1975–90); *b* 4 Aug. 1925; *e s* of Sir John Campbell, 7th Bt and Janet Moffat (*d* 1975); *S* father, 1960; *m* 1952, Mary Anne Chichester Bain, *er d* of Brigadier G. A. Bain, Sandy Lodge, Chagford, Devon; two *s* (one *d* decd). *Educ:* Stowe. Scots Guards, 1943–47, Captain. Employed with James Finlay & Co. Ltd, Calcutta, 1948–58, Nairobi, 1958–71, Dep. Chm., 1973–75. President, Federation of Kenya Employers, 1962–70; Chairman: Tea Board of Kenya, 1961–71; E African Tea Trade Assoc., 1960–61, 1962–63, 1966–67. Member: Scottish Council, CBI, 1979–85; Council, CBI, 1981–92; Commonwealth Develt Corp., 1981–89 (Dep. Chm., 1983–89). CIMgt (CBIM 1980); FRSA 1982. *Recreations:* gardening, racing, cards, travel. *Heir: s* James Alexander Moffat Bain Campbell, [*b* 23 Sept. 1956; *m* 1993, Carola Jane, *yr d* of George Denman; two *d*]. *Address:* Kilbryde Castle, Dunblane, Perthshire FK15 9NF. *T:* (01786) 823104. *Clubs:* Boodle's; Western (Glasgow); Royal Calcutta Turf, Tollygunge (Calcutta); Nairobi (E Africa).
Died 1 Dec. 1997.

CAMPBELL, Hugh, PhD; Industrial Adviser, Department of Trade and Industry, 1971–74, retired; *b* 24 Oct. 1916; *s* of Hugh Campbell and Annie C. Campbell (*née* Spence); *m* 1946, Sybil Marian Williams, MB, ChB (*d* 1988), *y d* of Benjamin and Sarah Williams; two *s*. *Educ:* University College Sch., London; St John's Coll., Cambridge (MA, PhD). Research, Dept of Colloid Science, Cambridge, 1938–45; Head of Physical Chem., Research Gp, May and Baker Ltd, 1945–61; Lectr, West Ham Techn. Coll., 1949–54; Research Manager, Chloride Electrical Storage Co. Ltd, 1961–65; Managing Director: Alkaline Batteries Ltd, 1965–67; Electric Power Storage Ltd, 1968–71; Dir, Chloride Electrical Storage Co. Ltd, 1968–71. Career consultant in Paris and London, 1974–78. *Publications:* papers on various subjects in scientific jls. *Recreations:* ski-ing, theatre, travelling. *Address:* 25 Kittiwake Drive, Kidderminster, Worcs DY10 4RS. *T:* (01562) 829626.
Died 5 Oct. 1998.

CAMPBELL, Maj.-Gen. Ian Ross, CBE 1954; DSO and Bar, 1941; *b* 23 March 1900; *s* of Gerald Ross Campbell, barrister, NSW, and Mary Stewart; *m* 1st, 1927, Patience Allison Russell (*d* 1961); one *d*; 2nd, 1961, Barbara, *widow* of Col E. A. McKewan; 3rd, 1967, Irene Cardamatis (*d* 1996). *Educ:* Wesley Coll., Melbourne; Scots Coll., Sydney; Royal Military College, Duntroon, Canberra (Sword of Honour, 1922). psc Camberley, 1936–37. Served War of 1939–45, Middle East Campaigns, Libya, Greece and Crete (DSO and Bar, Cross of Kt Comdr, Greek Order of Phœnix; POW, 1941–45); comd Aust.

forces in Korean War, 1951–53 (CBE); Comdt, Australian Staff Coll., 1953–54; Comdt, Royal Mil. Coll. Duntroon, 1954–57; retired, 1957. Mem. Federal Exec., RSL, 1955–56. Chm., NSW Div., Aust. Red Cross Soc., 1967–74. Pres., Great Public Schs Athletic Assoc., NSW, 1966–69. Hon. Col, NSW Scottish Regt, 1957–60. *Recreation:* reading. *Clubs:* Australian, Royal Sydney Golf (Sydney).
Died 31 Oct. 1997.

CAMPBELL, John Lorne, OBE 1990; owner of Heiskeir and Humla, of the Small Isles; formerly owner of Isle of Canna, which he presented to National Trust for Scotland, 1981; farmer (retired) and author; *b* 1 Oct. 1906; *e s* of late Col Duncan Campbell of Inverneill and Ethel Harriet, *e d* of late John I. Waterbury, Morristown, NJ; *m* 1935, Margaret Fay (author of Folksongs and Folklore of South Uist), *y d* of Henry Clay Shaw, Glenshaw, Pennsylvania (US); no *c. Educ:* Cargilfield; Rugby; St John's Coll., Oxford (Dipl. Rural Economy 1930; MA 1933, DLitt 1965). Sec., Barra Sea League, 1933–38. Curator of Woods on Isle of Canna for Nat. Trust for Scotland. FRSE 1989. Hon. LLD St Francis Xavier Univ., Antigonish, NS, 1953; Hon. DLitt Glasgow Univ., 1965. KSG 1992. *Publications include:* Highland Songs of the Forty-Five, 1933, 2nd edn 1984; The Book of Barra (with Compton Mackenzie and Carl Hj. Borgstrom), 1936; Sia Sgialachdan, 1938; Act Now for the Highlands and Islands (with Sir Alexander MacEwen, in which creation of Highland Develt Bd suggested for first time), 1939; Gaelic in Scottish Education and Life, 1945, 2nd edn 1950; Fr Allan McDonald of Eriskay, Priest, Poet and Folklorist, 1954; Tales from Barra, told by the Coddy, 1960; Stories from South Uist, 1961; The Furrow Behind Me, 1962; Edward Lhuyd in the Scottish Highlands (with Prof. Derick Thomson), 1963; A School in South Uist (memoirs of Frederick Rea), 1964; Gaelic Poems of Fr Allan McDonald, 1965; Strange Things (story of SPR enquiry into Highland second sight, with Trevor H. Hall), 1968; Hebridean Folksongs (waulking songs from South Uist and Barra) (with F. Collinson), vol. i, 1969, vol. ii, 1977, vol. iii, 1981; Canna, the Story of a Hebridean Island, 1984; Songs Remembered in Exile, traditional Gaelic songs from Nova Scotia, 1990; (contrib.) Dictionary of National Biography 1986–90, 1996; other pubns and articles on Highland history and Gaelic oral tradition, also on Hebridean entomology. *Recreations:* entomology, sea fishing, listening to old Gaelic stories. *Address:* Canna House, Isle of Canna, Scotland PH44 4RS.
Died 25 April 1996.

CAMPBELL, Sir Matthew, KBE 1963; CB 1959; FRSE; Deputy Chairman, White Fish Authority, and Chairman, Authority's Committee for Scotland and Northern Ireland, 1968–78; *b* 23 May 1907; *s* of late Matthew Campbell, High Blantyre; *m* 1939, Isabella (decd), *d* of late John Wilson, Rutherglen; two *s. Educ:* Hamilton Academy; Glasgow Univ. Entered CS, 1928, and after service in Inland Revenue Dept and Admiralty joined staff of Dept of Agriculture for Scotland, 1935; Principal, 1938; Assistant Sec., 1943; Under Sec., 1953; Sec., Dept of Agriculture and Fisheries for Scotland, 1958–68. *Address:* 10 Craigleith View, Edinburgh EH4 3JZ. *T:* (0131) 337 5168.
Died 7 March 1998.

CAMPBELL, Ronald Francis Boyd, ERD (2 clasps); MA; *b* 28 Aug. 1912; *o s* of Major Roy Neil Boyd Campbell, DSO, OBE and Effie Muriel, *y d* of Major Charles Pierce, IMS; *m* 1939, Pamela Muriel Désirée, *o d* of H. L. Wright, OBE, late Indian Forest Service; one *s* two *d. Educ:* Berkhamsted Sch.; Peterhouse, Cambridge. Asst Master, Berkhamsted Sch., 1934–39; War of 1939–45: Supplementary Reserve, The Duke of Cornwall's Light Infantry, Sept. 1939; served in England and Italy; DAQMG, HQ 3rd Div., 1943; demobilized with hon. rank of Lt-Col, 1945; Housemaster and OC Combined Cadet Force, Berkhamsted Sch., 1945–51; Headmaster, John Lyon Sch., Harrow, 1951–68; Dir, Public Sch. Appointments Bureau, later Independent Schs Careers Orgn, 1968–78. Hon. Assoc. Mem., HMC, 1969–. Walter Hines Page Travelling Scholarship to USA, 1960. 1939–45 Star, Italy Star, Defence and Victory Medals. *Recreations:* sailing, fishing. *Address:* 30 Marine Drive, Torpoint, Cornwall PL11 2EH. *T:* (01752) 813671. *Clubs:* East India, Devonshire, Sports and Public Schools, Royal Cruising. *Died 23 Oct. 1996.*

CAMPBELL, Ross; Director, International Military Services Ltd, 1979–83, retired; *b* 4 May 1916; 2nd *s* of George Albert Campbell and Jean Glendinning Campbell (*née* Ross); *m* 1st, 1939, Emmy Zoph (marr. diss. 1948); one *s* one *d*; 2nd, 1952, Dr Diana Stewart (*d* 1977); one *d* (and one *d* decd); 3rd, 1979, Jean Margaret Turner (*née* Ballinger) (marr. diss. 1984). *Educ:* Farnborough Grammar Sch.; Reading Univ. CEng, FICE. Articled to municipal engr; local authority engr, 1936–39; Air Min. (UK), 1939–44; Sqdn Ldr, RAF, Middle East, 1944–47; Air Min. (UK), 1947–52; Supt Engr, Gibraltar, 1952–55; Air Min. (UK), 1955–59; Chief Engr, Far East Air Force, 1959–62 and Bomber Comd, 1962–63; Personnel Management, MPBW, 1963–66; Chief Resident Engr, Persian Gulf, 1966–68; Dir Staff Management, MPBW, 1968–69; Dir of Works (Air), 1969–72; Under-Sec., and Dir of Defence Services II PSA, DoE, 1972–75; Dir, 1975–77, Dep. Chief Exec., 1977–79, Internat. Military Services Ltd. *Publications:* papers on professional civil engrg and trng in ICE Jl. *Recreations:* golf, music. *Address:* 41 Nightingale Road, Rickmansworth, Herts WD3 2DA. *T:* Rickmansworth (01923) 773744. *Clubs:* Royal Air Force; Denham Golf.

Died 5 Aug. 1996.

CAMPBELL, Sir Thomas C.; *see* Cockburn-Campbell.

CAMPBELL, Maj.-Gen. William Tait, CBE 1945 (OBE 1944); retired; *b* 8 Oct. 1912, *s* of late R. B. Campbell, MD, FRCPE, Edinburgh; *m* 1942, Rhoda Alice, *y d* of late Adm. Algernon Walker-Heneage-Vivian, CB, MVO, Swansea; two *d. Educ:* Cargilfield Sch.; Fettes Coll.; RMC Sandhurst. 2nd Lieut, The Royal Scots (The Royal Regt), 1933; served War of 1939–45: 1st Airborne Div. and 1st Allied Airborne Army (North Africa, Sicily, Italy and Europe); Lt-Col Commanding 1st Bn The Royal Scots, in Egypt, Cyprus, UK and Suez Operation (despatches), 1954–57; Col, Royal Naval War Coll., Greenwich, 1958; Brig. i/c Admin, Malaya, 1962; Maj.-Gen., 1964; DQMG, MoD (Army Dept), 1964–67; Col, The Royal Scots (The Royal Regt), 1964–74. Dir, Fairbridge Soc., 1969–78. US Bronze Star, 1945. *Recreations:* gardening, golf, shooting, fishing. *Address:* Ashwood, Boarhills, St Andrews, Fife KY16 8PR. *Died 7 Oct. 1999.*

CAMPBELL-JOHNSON, Alan, CIE 1947; OBE 1946; FRSA; MRI; public relations consultant; *b* 16 July 1913; *o c* of late Lieut-Col James Alexander Campbell-Johnson and Gladys Susanne Campbell-Johnson; *m* 1938, Imogen Fay de la Tour Dunlap; one *d* (one *s* decd). *Educ:* Westminster; Christ Church, Oxford (scholar; BA 2nd Cl. Hons Mod. Hist., 1935; MA). Political Sec. to Rt Hon. Sir Archibald Sinclair, Leader of Parly Lib. Party, 1937–40; served War of 1939–45, RAF; CO HQ, 1942–43; HQ SACSEA (Wing Comdr i/c Inter-Allied Records Section), 1943–46; Press Attaché to Viceroy and Gov.-Gen. of India (Earl Mountbatten of Burma), 1947–48. Chm., Campbell-Johnson Ltd, Public Relations Consultants, 1953–78; Dir, Hill and Knowlton (UK) Ltd, 1976–85. Contested (L) Salisbury and South Wilts Div., 1945 and 1950. Hon. Fellow Inst. of Public Relations, Pres. 1956–57. Hon. DLitt Southampton, 1990. Officer of US Legion of Merit, 1947. *Publications:* Growing Opinions, 1935; Peace

Offering, 1936; Anthony Eden: a biography, 1938, rev. edn 1955; Viscount Halifax: a biography, 1941; Mission with Mountbatten, 1951, repr. 1972. *Recreations:* watching cricket, listening to music. *Address:* 21 Ashley Gardens, Ambrosden Avenue, SW1P 1QD. *T:* (0171) 834 1532. *Clubs:* Brooks's, National Liberal, MCC.

Died 25 Jan. 1998.

CAMPBELL-PRESTON of Ardchattan, Robert Modan Thorne, OBE 1955; MC 1943; TD; DL; Vice-Lieutenant, Argyll and Bute, 1976–90; *b* 7 Jan. 1909; *s* of Colonel R. W. P. Campbell-Preston, DL, JP, of Ardchattan and Valleyfield, Fife, and Mary Augusta Thorne, MBE; *m* 1950, Hon. Angela Murray (*d* 1981), 3rd *d* of 2nd Viscount Cowdray and *widow* of Lt-Col George Anthony Murray, OBE, TD (killed in action, Italy, 1945); one *d. Educ:* Eton; Christ Church, Oxford (MA). Lieut Scottish Horse, 1927; Lt-Col 1945; Hon. Col, Fife-Forfar Yeo./Scottish Horse, 1962–67. Member Royal Company of Archers, Queen's Body Guard for Scotland. Joint Managing Director, Alginate Industries Ltd, 1949–74. DL 1951, JP 1950, Argyllshire. Silver Star (USA), 1945. *Recreations:* shooting, fishing, gardening. *Address:* Ardchattan Priory, by Oban, Argyll PA37 1RQ. *T:* Bonawe (0163175) 274. *Club:* Puffin's (Edinburgh). *Died 13 June 1996.*

CAMPION, Sir Harry, Kt 1957; CB 1949; CBE 1945; MA; Director of Central Statistical Office, Cabinet Office, 1941–67, retired; *b* 20 May 1905; *o s* of John Henry Campion, Worsley, Lancs. *Educ:* Farnworth Grammar Sch.; Univ. of Manchester. Rockefeller Foundation Fellow, United States, 1932; Robert Ottley Reader in Statistics, Univ. of Manchester, 1933–39. Dir of Statistical Office, UN, 1946–47; Mem. of Statistical Commission, United Nations, 1947–67. President: International Statistical Institute, 1963–67; Royal Statistical Society, 1957–59. Hon. LLD Manchester, 1967. *Publications:* Distribution of National Capital; Public and Private Property in Great Britain; articles in economic and statistical journals. *Address:* Rima, Priory Close, Stanmore, Mddx HA7 3HW. *T:* 0181–954 3267. *Club:* Reform. *Died 24 May 1996.*

CAMPS, William Anthony; Fellow, since 1933, and Master, 1970–81, Pembroke College, Cambridge; *b* 28 Dec. 1910; *s* of P. W. L. Camps, FRCS, and Alice, *d* of Joseph Redfern, Matlock; *m* 1953, Miriam Camp (*d* 1994), Washington, DC, *d* of Prof. Burton Camp, Wesleyan Univ., Connecticut. *Educ:* Marlborough Coll.; Pembroke Coll., Cambridge (Schol.). University Lectr in Classics, Cambridge, 1939; Temp. Civil Servant, 1940–45; Pembroke College, Cambridge: Asst Tutor, 1945; Senior Tutor, 1947–62; Tutor for Advanced Students, 1963–70; Pres., 1964–70. Mem., Inst. for Advanced Study, Princeton, 1956–57; Vis. Assoc. Prof., UC Toronto, 1966; Vis. Prof., Univ. of North Carolina at Chapel Hill, 1969. *Publications:* edns of Propertius I, 1961, IV, 1965, III, 1966, II, 1967; An Introduction to Virgil's Aeneid, 1969; An Introduction to Homer, 1980; sundry notes and reviews in classical periodicals. *Recreations:* unremarkable. *Address:* c/o Pembroke College, Cambridge CB2 1RF. *T:* (01223) 338100. *Died 17 Jan. 1997.*

CANDELA OUTERIÑO, Félix; engineer and architect; Professor, Escuela Nacional de Arquitectura, University of Mexico, since 1953 (on leave of absence); *b* Madrid, 27 Jan. 1910; *s* of Felix and Julia Candela; *m* 1940, Eladia Martin Galan (*d* 1964); four *d; m* 1967, Dorothy H. Davies. *Educ:* Univ. of Madrid, Spain. Architect, Escuela Superior de Arquitectura de Madrid, 1935. Captain of Engineers, Republican Army, Spanish Civil War, 1936–39. Emigrated to Mexico, 1939; Mexican Citizen, 1941; USA citizen, 1978. General practice in Mexico as architect and contractor; founded (with brother Antonio) Cubiertas ALA, SA, firm specializing in design and construction of reinforced concrete shell structures; work included Sports Palace for Mexico Olympics, 1968. Retrospective exhibn, Madrid, 1995; exhibn of pictures and models, Tokyo, 1996. Founding Mem., Internat. Acad. of Architecture, Sofia, 1986; Hon. Member: Sociedad de Arquitectos Colombianos, 1956; Sociedad Venezolana de Arquitectos, 1961; International Assoc. for Shell Structures, 1962; Acad. de Arquitectura de Mexico, 1983. Charles Elliot Norton Prof. of Poetry, Harvard Univ., for academic year, 1961–62; Jefferson Meml Prof., Univ. of Virginia, 1966; Andrew D. White Prof., Cornell Univ., 1969–74; Prof., Dept of Architecture, Univ. of Illinois at Chicago, 1971–78; William Hoffman Wood Prof., Leeds Univ., 1974–75; Prof. Honorario: Escuela Tecnica Superior de Arquitectura de Madrid, 1969; Univ. Nacional Federico Villareal, Peru, 1977. Gold Medal, Instn Structural Engineers, England, 1961; Auguste Perret Prize of International Union of Architects, 1961; Plomada de Oro, Soc. de Arquitectos Mexicanos, 1963; Alfred E. Lindau Award, Amer. Concrete Inst., 1965; Silver Medal, Acad. d'Architecture, Paris, 1980; Gold Medal, Consejo Superior de Arquitectos de España, 1981; Silver Medal, Union des Architects Bulgares, 1983; Gold Medal, Premio Antonio Camuñas, Madrid, 1985. Hon. Fellow American Inst. of Architects, 1963; Hon. Corresp. Mem., RIBA, 1963. Doctor in Fine Arts *hc*: Univ. of New Mexico, 1964; Univ. of Illinois, 1979; Dr Ing *hc* Univ. de Santa Maria, Caracas, 1968; Dr *hc*: Univ. of Sevilla, Spain, 1990; Univ. Politécnica of Madrid, Spain, 1994. Order of Civil Merit, Spain, 1978. *Publications:* En Defensa del Formalismo, 1985; several articles in architectural and engineering magazines all around the world; *relevant publications:* Candela, the Shell Builder, by Colin Faber, 1963; Felix Candela, by Yotaka Saito, 1995. *Address:* 6341 Wynbrook Way, Raleigh, NC 27612, USA. *T:* (919) 8483303, *Fax:* (919) 6762498; Avenida America 14–7, Madrid 2, Spain. *T:* 3560096, *Fax:* 2556365. *Died 7 Dec. 1997.*

CANET, Maj.-Gen. Lawrence George, CB 1964; CBE 1956; BE; Master General of the Ordnance, Australia, 1964–67, retired; *b* 1 Dec. 1910; *s* of late Albert Canet, Melbourne, Victoria; *m* 1940, Mary Elizabeth Clift, *d* of Cecil Clift Jones, Geelong, Victoria; one *s. Educ:* RMC Duntroon; Sydney Univ. (BE). Served War of 1939–45 with 7th Australian Div. (Middle East and Pacific); GOC Southern Command, 1960–64. Brigadier 1953; Maj.-Gen. 1957. *Address:* 37 The Corso, Isle of Capri, Surfers Paradise, Qld 4217, Australia.
Died 8 March 1996.

CANT, Robert Bowen; *b* 24 July 1915; *s* of Robert and Catherine Cant; *m* 1940, Rebecca Harris Watt; one *s* two *d. Educ:* Middlesbrough High Sch. for Boys; London Sch. of Economics. BSc (Econ.) 1945. Lecturer in Economics, Univ. of Keele, 1962–66. Member: Stoke-on-Trent City Council, 1953–76; Staffs CC, 1973–93 (Chm., Educn Cttee, 1981–89). Contested (Lab) Shrewsbury, 1950, 1951; MP (Lab) Stoke-on-Trent Central, 1966–83. *Publication:* American Journey. *Recreation:* bookbinding. *Address:* (home) 119 Chell Green Avenue, Stoke-on-Trent, Staffordshire ST6 7LA. *Club:* Chell Working Men's. *Died 13 Sept. 1997.*

CAPLAN, Daniel; Under-Secretary, Department of the Environment, 1970–71; *b* 29 July 1915; *y s* of Daniel and Miriam Caplan; *m* 1945, Olive Beatrice Porter; no *c. Educ:* Elem. and Secondary Schools, Blackpool; St Catharine's Coll., Cambridge. Asst Principal, Import Duties Adv. Cttee, 1938; Private Secretary to three Permanent Secretaries, Ministry of Supply, 1940; Principal, 1942; Ministry of Supply Representative and Economic Secretary to British Political Representative in Finland, 1944–45; Asst Secretary, Board of Trade, 1948; Adviser to Chancellor of Duchy of Lancaster, 1957–60; Under-

Secretary, Scottish Development Dept, 1963–65; Under-Secretary, National Economic Development Office, 1966; Asst Under-Sec. of State, DEA, 1966–69; Under-Sec., Min. of Housing and Local Govt, 1969–70. Consultant to Minister for Housing for Leasehold Charges Study, 1972–73. Indep. Review of Royal Commn on Historical Manuscripts, for HM Govt, 1980. *Publications:* People and Homes (indep. report on Landlord and Tenant Relations in England for British Property Fedn), 1975; Border Country Branch Lines, 1981; Report on the Work of the Royal Commission on Historical Manuscripts, 1981; The Waverley Route, 1985; The Royal Scot, 1987; The West Highland Line, 1988; numerous papers on religious and economic history in learned journals. *Recreations:* railways, historical research, gardening. *Address:* Knowle Wood, London Road, Cuckfield, West Sussex RH17 5ES. *T:* (01444) 454301.
Died 10 Jan. 1997.

CAPPER, Rt Rev. Edmund Michael Hubert, OBE 1961; LTh; Auxiliary Bishop in the Diocese of Gibraltar in Europe, since 1973; Assistant Bishop of Southwark, since 1981; *b* 12 March 1908; *e s* of Arthur Charles and Mabel Lavinia Capper; unmarried. *Educ:* St Joseph's Academy, Blackheath; St Augustine's College, Canterbury; LTh Durham, 1932. Deacon, 1932, priest, 1933. Royal Army Chaplains' Dept, 1942–46 (E Africa); Archdeacon of Lindi and Canon of Masasi Cathedral, 1947–54; Archdeacon of Dar es Salaam, 1954–58; Provost of the Collegiate Church of St Alban the Martyr, Dar es Salaam, Tanganyika, 1957–62; Canon of Zanzibar, 1954–62; Chaplain, Palma de Mallorca, 1962–67; Bishop of St Helena, 1967–73; Chaplain of St George's, Malaga, 1973–76. Member, Universities' Mission to Central Africa, 1936–62; Chairman, Tanganyika British Legion Benevolent Fund, 1956–62; President, Tanganyika British Legion, 1960–62. *Address:* Morden College, Blackheath, SE3 0PW. *T:* (0181) 858 9169. *Club:* Travellers'.
Died 6 March 1998.

CAREY, D(avid) M(acbeth) M(oir), CBE 1983; Joint Registrar to Faculty Office of Archbishop of Canterbury, since 1982; Legal Secretary to the Archbishop of Canterbury, 1958–82; Legal Secretary to the Bishops of Ely, 1953–82 and Gloucester, 1957–82; Registrar to the Diocese of Canterbury, 1959–82; *b* 21 Jan. 1917; *s* of Godfrey Mohun Carey, Sherborne, Dorset, and Agnes Charlotte Carey (*née* Milligan); *m* 1949, Margaret Ruth (*née* Mills), Highfield Sch., Liphook, Hants; two *s* one *d* (and one *s* decd). *Educ:* Westminster Sch. (King's Scholar); St Edmund Hall, Oxford (MA). Lt-Comdr (S) RNVR, 1940–46. Articled Clerk, Messrs Lee, Bolton & Lee, 1938–40; qualified Solicitor, 1947; Partnership with Lee, Bolton & Lee, 1948–82, Consultant, 1982–. Gov., Westminster Sch., 1960–92. DCL Lambeth, 1978. *Recreation:* fishing. *Address:* 34 Shepherds Way, Liphook, Hants GU30 7HF. *T:* (01428) 723452.
Died 21 Jan. 2000.

CAREY JONES, Norman Stewart, CMG 1965; Director, Development Administration, Leeds University, 1965–77; *b* 11 Dec. 1911; *s* of Samuel Carey Jones and Jessie Isabella Stewart; *m* 1946, Stella Myles (*d* 1990); two *s. Educ:* Monmouth Sch.; Merton Coll., Oxford. Colonial Audit Service: Gold Coast, 1935; Northern Rhodesia, 1939; British Honduras, 1946; Kenya, 1950; Asst Financial Sec., Treasury, Kenya, 1954; Dep. Sec., Min. of Agric., Kenya, 1956; Perm. Sec., Min. of Lands and Settlement, Kenya, 1962. *Publications:* The Pattern of a Dependent Economy, 1952; The Anatomy of Uhuru, 1966; Politics, Public Enterprise and The Industrial Development Agency, 1974; articles and reviews for: Journal of Rhodes-Livingstone Inst.; E African Economics Review; Africa

Quarterly; Geog. Jl. *Address:* Mawingo, Welsh St Donats, near Cowbridge, S Glam CF7 7SS. *Club:* Royal Commonwealth Society. *Died 26 Aug. 1997.*

CARLETON, Janet Buchanan, (Mrs John Carleton); *see* Adam Smith, J. B.

CARLILE, Rev. Edward Wilson; Liaison Officer, East Africa Church Army Appeal, 1981–84; *b* 11 June 1915; *s* of Victor Wilson and Elsie Carlile; *m* 1946, Elizabeth (*née* Bryant); two *s* one *d*. *Educ:* Epsom Coll.; King's Coll., London (BD). Chartered Accountant, 1939. Deacon, 1943; priest, 1944; Curate, All Saints, Queensbury, 1943–46; Hon. Asst Sec. of Church Army, 1946–49; Chief Sec. of Church Army, 1949–60; Vicar of St Peter's with St Hilda's, Leicester, 1960–73; Rector of Swithland, Leicester, 1973–76; Priest in Charge of St Michael and All Angels, Belgrave, Leicester, 1976–81. *Recreations:* race relations, evangelism, walking, travel, photography. *Address:* 120A Mount View Road, Sheffield S8 8PL. *T:* Sheffield (0114) 258 1098. *Died 26 June 1996.*

CARLILL, Vice-Adm. Sir Stephen Hope, KBE 1957; CB 1954; DSO 1942; *b* Orpington, Kent, 23 Dec. 1902; *s* of late Harold Flamank Carlill; *m* 1928, Julie Fredrike Elisabeth Hildegard (*d* 1991), *o d* of late Rev. W. Rahlenbeck, Westphalia; two *s*. *Educ:* Royal Naval Colleges, Osborne and Dartmouth. Lieut RN, 1925; qualified as Gunnery Officer, 1929; Commander 1937; commanded IIM Destroyers Hambledon, 1940, and Farndale, 1941–42; Captain 1942; Captain (D), 4th Destoyer Flotilla, HMS Quilliam, 1942–44 (despatches); Admiralty, 1944–46; Chief of Staff to C-in-C British Pacific Fleet, 1946–48; Captain, HMS Excellent, 1949–50; commanded HMS Illustrious, 1950–51; Rear-Admiral, 1952; Senior Naval Member, Imperial Defence Coll., 1952–54; Vice-Admiral, 1954; Flag Officer, Training Squadron, 1954–55; Chief of Naval Staff, Indian Navy, 1955–58, retired. Representative in Ghana of West Africa Cttee 1960–66; Adviser to W African Cttee, 1966–67. *Recreations:* walking, gardening. *Address:* Evendine House, Colwall, Malvern, Worcs WR13 6DT. *Club:* Naval and Military. *Died 9 Feb. 1996.*

CARMICHAEL, Sir John, KBE 1955; Chairman, St Andrews Links Trust, 1984–88; *b* 22 April 1910; *s* of late Thomas Carmichael and Margaret Doig Coupar; *m* 1940, Cecilia Macdonald Edwards; one *s* three *d*. *Educ:* Madras Coll., St Andrews; Univ. of St Andrews; Univ. of Michigan (Commonwealth Fund Fellow). Guardian Assurance Co., Actuarial Dept, 1935–36; Sudan Govt Civil Service, 1936–59; Member, Sudan Resources Board and War Supply Dept, 1939–45; Secretary, Sudan Development Board, 1944–48; Asst Financial Secretary, 1946–48; Dep. Financial Secretary, 1948–53; Director, Sudan Gezira Board, 1950–54; Chm., Sudan Light and Power Co., 1952–54; Acting Financial Secretary, then Permanent Under Secretary to Ministry of Finance, 1953–55; Financial and Economic Adviser to Sudan Government, 1955–59. Member: UK delegation to General Assembly of UN, 1959; Scottish Gas Board, 1960–70; Scottish Industrial Develt Adv. Bd, 1973–80; Dep. Chm., ITA, 1960–64, Acting Chm., ITA, 1962–63; Chm., Herring Industry Bd, 1962–65; Director: Fisons Ltd, 1961–80 (Chief Executive, 1962–66, Dep. Chm., 1965–71); Grampian Television, 1965–72; Jute Industries Ltd, later Sidlaw Industries Ltd, 1966–80 (Dep. Chm., 1969; Chm., 1970–80); Royal Bank of Scotland, 1966–80; Adobe Oil and Gas Corp., Texas, 1973–85. Mem., Social and Economic Cttee, EEC, 1972–77. Pres., Senior Golfers' Soc., 1982–85. *Recreations:* golf, gardening. *Address:* Hayston Park, Balmullo, St Andrews, Fife KY16 0AN. *T:* Balmullo (01334) 870268. *Clubs:* Honourable Company of Edinburgh Golfers; Royal and Ancient Golf (St

Andrews) (Captain, 1974–75); Augusta National Golf, Pine Valley Golf (USA). *Died 7 Jan. 1996.*

CARMICHAEL, Peter, CBE 1981; self-employed consultant and horological specialist; *b* 26 March 1933; *s* of Robert and Elizabeth Carmichael; *m* 1st; two *s* four *d*; 2nd, 1980, June Carmichael (*née* Philip). *Educ:* Glasgow Univ. (BSc 1st Cl. Hons Physics). Design Engineer with Ferranti Ltd, Edinburgh, 1958–65; Hewlett-Packard: Project Leader, 1965–67 (Leader of Project Team which won Queen's Award to Industry for Technical Innovation, 1967); Production Engrg Manager, 1967–68; Quality Assurance Manager, 1968–73; Engrg Manager, 1973–75; Manufacturing Manager, 1975–76; Division Gen. Man., 1976–82, and Jt Managing Director, 1980–82; Scottish Development Agency: Dir, Small Business and Electronics, 1982–88; Gp Dir (East), 1988–89. Chairman: Strathclyde Fabricators, 1989–93; Wolfson Microelectronics, 1990–93. Chm., Esmée Fairbairn Res. Centre, Heriot-Watt Univ., 1990–95. Hon. DSc Heriot-Watt, 1984. *Recreations:* fishing, antique clock restoration. *Address:* 86 Craiglea Drive, Edinburgh EH10 5PH. *T:* (0131) 447 6334; Marchbank Cottage, Ballantrae KA26 0LR. *T:* (01465) 831355. *Died 28 Aug. 1999.*

CAROE, Martin Bragg, FSA; conservation architect, specialising in the care of historic buildings; Partner, Caroe & Partners, since 1963; *b* 15 Nov. 1933; *s* of Alban Douglas Rendall Caroe and Gwendolen Mary (*née* Bragg); *m* 1962, Mary Elizabeth Roskill; one *s* three *d* (and one *s* decd). *Educ:* Amesbury Sch.; Winchester Coll.; Trinity Coll., Cambridge (BA); Kingston Sch. of Art (DipArch). Joined family firm of Caroe & Partners, 1961. *Works included:* St Davids Cathedral, 1966–; Wells Cathedral West Front sculpture conservation, 1981–86; Kingston Lacy on accession to NT, 1982–84; Rochester Cathedral, 1982–; Chatham Dockyard, Masthouse and Mould Loft, 1988–89; HM Tower of London, 1991–99. Pres., Ecclesiastical Architects and Surveyors Assoc., 1978–79; Mem., Exec. Cttee, Council for Care of Churches, 1986–89; Commissioner: Faculty Jurisdiction Comm, 1980–84; English Heritage, 1989–92; Commn on Faculties (Church in Wales), 1991–92; Cathedrals and Churches Commn, Ch in Wales, 1994–. FSA 1988. Master, Plumbers' Co., 1986. *Publications:* articles on conservation of Wells Cathedral West Front in Bull. of Assoc. of Preservation Technology (USA), preprints of Bologna Conf. of Internat. Inst. of Conservators, Trans ASCB; on Kingston Lacy in Trans ASCHB. *Recreations:* care and presentation to the public of a Jekyll garden, punting. *Address:* (office) 1 Greenland Place, NW1 0AP. *T:* (020) 7267 9348; Vann, Hambledon, near Godalming, Surrey GU8 4EF. *T:* (01428) 683413.

Died 19 Nov. 1999.

CARPENTER; *see* Boyd-Carpenter.

CARPENTER, Rev. Dr Edward Frederick, KCVO 1985; Dean of Westminster, 1974–85; Dean, Order of the Bath, 1974–85; *b* 27 Nov. 1910; *s* of Frederick James and Jessie Kate Carpenter; *m* Lilian Betsy Wright; three *s* one *d*. *Educ:* Strodes Sch., Egham; King's Coll., University of London (BA 1932, MA 1934, BD 1935, PhD 1943; AKC 1935; FKC 1951). Deacon, 1935; priest, 1936; Curate, Holy Trinity, Marylebone, 1935–41; St Mary, Harrow, 1941–45; Rector of Great Stanmore, 1945–51; Canon of Westminster, 1951; Treasurer, 1959–74; Archdeacon, 1963–74; Lector Theologiae of Westminster Abbey, 1958. Chairman Frances Mary Buss Foundation, 1956–85; Chairman Governing Body of: North London Collegiate Sch.; Camden Sch. for Girls, 1956–85; Chairman of St Anne's Soc., 1958–85; Joint Chm., London Soc. of Jews and Christians, 1960–85; Chm., CCJ, 1986–93; Member, Central Religious Advisory Cttee serving BBC and ITA, 1962–67; Chairman: Recruitment Cttee, ACCM, 1967;

Religious Adv. Cttee of UNA, 1969–95; President: London Region of UNA, 1966–67; Modern Churchmen's Union, 1966–91; World Congress of Faiths, 1966, 1992–95 (Patron, 1997–). Chm., Christian Consultative Council for Welfare of Animals, 1981–95. Hon. DD London, 1976; DD Lambeth, 1979. *Publications:* Thomas Sherlock, 1936; Thomas Tenison, His Life and Times, 1948; That Man Paul, 1953; (jtly) Nineteenth Century Country Parson, 1954; The Protestant Bishop, 1956; (jtly) History of St Paul's Cathedral, 1957; Common Sense about Christian Ethics, 1961; (jtly) From Uniformity to Unity, 1962; (jtly) The Church's Use of the Bible, 1963; The Service of a Parson, 1965; (jtly) The English Church, 1966; (jtly) A House of Kings, 1966; Cantuar: the Archbishops in their office, 1971, 2nd edn 1997; (contrib.) Man of Christian Action, ed Ian Henderson, 1976; (with David Gentleman) Westminster Abbey, 1987; Archbishop Fisher: his life and times, 1991. *Recreations:* walking, conversation, Association football. *Address:* 6 Selwyn Avenue, Richmond, Surrey TW9 2HA.

Died 26 Aug. 1998.

CARR, Air Marshal Sir John Darcy B.; *see* Baker-Carr.

CARR, Dr Thomas Ernest Ashdown, CB 1977; part-time medical referee, Department of Health and Social Security, 1979–87; *b* 21 June 1915; *s* of late Laurence H. A. Carr, MScTech, MIEE, ARPS, Stockport, and Norah E. V. Carr (*née* Taylor); *m* 1940, Mary Sybil (*née* Dunkey); one *s* two *d. Educ:* County High Sch. for Boys, Altrincham; Victoria Univ. of Manchester (BSc). MB, ChB 1939; FRCGP 1968; FFCM 1972; DObstRCOG. Jun. hosp. posts, Manchester and Ipswich, 1939–41; RAMC, UK and NW Europe, 1941–46 (Hon. Major, 1946); GP, Highcliffe, Hants, 1947; Mem. Hants Local Med. Cttee, 1952–55; Ministry of Health: Regional Med. Officer, Southampton, 1956; Sen. Med. Officer, 1963; Principal Med. Officer, 1966; SPMO in charge of GP and Regional Med. Service, DHSS, 1967–79. Founder Mem., RCGP, 1953 (Provost of SE England Faculty, 1962–64; Mem. Council, 1964–66); Chm., Guildford Div., 1988–89, Mem. Exec. Cttee, Lambeth and Southwark Div., 1975–79, BMA. FRSocMed (Mem. Council, Gen. Practice Section, 1977–79). Member: Camping Club of GB and Ireland, 1976–83; Southampton Gramophone Soc., 1956–63 (Chm., 1957–58); Guildford Philharmonic Soc., 1964–89; Guildford Soc., 1968–89; Putney Music, 1989–; Putney Soc., 1989–; Consumers' Assoc., 1974–; Nat. Soc. of Non-Smokers (QUIT), 1981– (Chm., 1982–86; Vice-Pres., 1987–93); British Humanist Assoc., 1965–; Fabian Soc., 1989–. *Publications:* papers on NHS practice organisation in Medical World, Practitioner, Update, Health Trends, faculty jls of RCGP, Proc. of RSM. *Recreation:* photography. *Address:* 17 Westpoint, Putney Hill, SW15 6RU. *T:* (020) 8788 9969. *Club:* Civil Service. *Died 9 Dec. 1999.*

CARREL, Philip, CMG 1960; OBE 1954; *b* 23 Sept. 1915; *s* of late Louis Raymond Carrel and Lucy Mabel (*née* Cooper); *m* 1948, Eileen Mary Bullock (*née* Hainworth); one *s* one *d. Educ:* Blundell's; Balliol Coll., Oxford. Colonial Admin. Service, 1938, Zanzibar Protectorate; E African Forces, 1940; Civil Affairs, 1941–47 (OETA); Civilian Employee Civil Affairs, GHQ MELF, 1947–49 (on secondment from Somaliland Protectorate); Colonial Admin. Service (Somaliland Protectorate), 1947; Commissioner of Somali Affairs, 1953; Chief Sec. to the Government, Somaliland Protectorate, 1959–60. Cttee Sec., Overseas Relns, Inst. of Chartered Accountants in England and Wales, 1961–77; retired. *Address:* Lych Gates, 51 Chiltley Lane, Liphook, Hants GU30 7HJ. *T:* (01428) 722150. *Died 29 Jan. 2000.*

CARRICK, Edward; *see* Craig, E. A.

CARRICK, Maj.-Gen. Thomas Welsh, OBE 1959; Specialist in Community Medicine, Camden and Islington Area Health Authority (Teaching), 1975–78; *b* 19 Dec. 1914; *s* of late George Carrick and Mary Welsh; *m* 1948, Nan Middleton Allison; one *s. Educ:* Glasgow Academy; Glasgow Univ.; London Sch. of Hygiene and Tropical Med. MB, ChB 1937; DPH 1951; DIH 1961. FFPHM (FFCM 1972). House appts in medicine, surgery and urological surgery at Glasgow Royal Infirmary, 1937–38; Dep. Supt, Glasgow Royal Infirmary, 1939–40; commissioned, RAMC, 1940; later service appts included: Asst Dir, Army Health, 17 Gurkha Div., Malaya, 1961–63; Asst Dir, Army Health, HQ Scotland, 1964–65; Dir, Army Personnel Research Estabt, 1965–68; Dep. Dir, Army Health, Strategic Command, 1968–70; Prof. of Army Health, Royal Army Med. Coll., 1970; Dir of Army Health and Research, MoD, 1971–72; Comdt and Postgraduate Dean, Royal Army Medical Coll., Millbank, 1973–75; retd. Col Comdt, RAMC, 1975–79. Blackham Lectr, RIPH&H, 1977. QHS 1973. Pres., Blackmore Vale and Yeovil Centre, National Trust, 1979–85. OStJ 1946. *Publications:* articles in Jl of RAMC, Army Review, Community Health. *Recreations:* gardening, theatre.

Died 4 Oct. 2000.

CARROLL, Maj.-Gen. Derek Raymond, OBE 1958; retired; *b* 2 Jan. 1919; *er s* of late Raymond and Edith Lisle Carroll; *m* 1946, Bettina Mary, *d* of late Leslie Gould; one *s* two *d.* Enlisted TA, 1939; commnd into Royal Engineers, 1943; served Western Desert, 1941–43, Italy, 1943–44; psc 1945; various appts, 1946–66, in War Office (2), Germany (2), Sudan Defence Force, Libya, Malaya; CRE 4 Div., 1962–64; comd 12 Engr Bde, 1966–67; idc 1968; Dir, MoD, 1969–70; Chief Engr, BAOR, 1970–73; RARO, 1973.

Died 9 Nov. 1996.

CARRUTHERS, Prof. Ian Douglas, PhD; Professor of Agrarian Development, Wye College, University of London, since 1984; Director, Wye External Programme, since 1988; *b* 30 Aug. 1938; *s* of William Walker Carruthers and late Kathleen Carruthers (*née* Irvin); *m* 1st, 1961, Barbara Price (marr. diss.); two *s* one *d*; 2nd, 1993, Sarah Ladbury. *Educ:* Chislehurst and Sidcup Grammar Sch.; Wye Coll., Univ. of London (BSc 1961); St Edmund Hall, Oxford (DipAgEcon 1962); Univ. of London (PhD 1976). Agricl Economist, Pakistan, 1963–67; Wye College: ODA Home-based Lectr, 1967–72 (Res. Fellow, Makerere Univ. Coll., Uganda, 1968–69; Res. Officer, Min. of Agric., Nairobi, 1971–72); Lectr in Agricl Econs, 1972–76; Reader in Agrarian Develt, 1976–84. Member: Council, ODI, 1991–; Bd, Commonwealth Develt Corp., 1992–. Consultant/adviser on rural develt and water resource economics: World Bank; FAO; ILO; UNDP; WHO; OECD; Commonwealth Secretariat; ODA; USAID; German Technical Assistance in Africa, ME and Asia. *Publications:* (with C. Clark) The Economics of Irrigation, 1981; (with L. Small) Farmer Financed Irrigation, 1991; (ed) Aid for Irrigation, 1986. *Recreation:* horticulture. *Address:* Wye College, Ashford, Kent TN25 5AH. *T:* Ashford (01233) 812401. *Club:* Railway (Lahore, Pakistan). *Died 24 May 1996.*

CARSTEN, Prof. Francis Ludwig, DPhil, DLitt Oxon; FBA 1971; Masaryk Professor of Central European History in the University of London, 1961–78; Emeritus Professor, School of Slavonic and East European Studies; *b* 25 June 1911; *s* of Prof. Paul Carsten and Frida Carsten (*née* Born); *m* 1945, Ruth Carsten (*née* Moses) (*d* 1994); two *s* one *d. Educ:* Heidelberg, Berlin and Oxford Univs. Barnett scholar, Wadham Coll., Oxford, 1939; Senior Demy, Magdalen Coll., Oxford, 1942. Lectr in History, Westfield Coll., Univ. of London, 1947; Reader in Modern History, Univ. of London, 1960. Co-Editor, Slavonic and

East European Review, 1966–84. *Publications:* The Origins of Prussia, 1954; Princes and Parliaments in Germany from the 15th to the 18th Century, 1959; The Reichswehr and Politics, 1918–1933, 1966; The Rise of Fascism, 1967, rev. edn, 1980; Revolution in Central Europe, 1918–1919, 1972; Fascist Movements in Austria, 1977; War against War: British and German Radical Movements in the First World War, 1982; Britain and the Weimar Republic, The British Documents, 1984; Essays in German History, 1985; The First Austrian Republic, 1986; A History of the Prussian Junkers, 1988; August Bebel und die Organisation der Massen, 1991; Eduard Bernstein, 1993; The German Workers and the Nazis, 1995; ed and contributor, The New Cambridge Modern History, vol. V: The Ascendancy of France, 1961; articles in English Historical Review, History, Survey, Historische Zeitschrift, etc. *Recreations:* gardening, climbing, swimming. *Address:* 11 Redington Road, NW3 7QX. *T:* (0171) 435 5522. *Died 23 June 1998.*

CARSWELL, John Patrick, CB 1977; FRSL; Secretary, British Academy, 1978–83, then Emeritus; Honorary Research Fellow, Department of History, University College London, since 1983; *b* 30 May 1918; *s* of Donald Carswell, barrister and author, and Catherine Carswell, author; *m* 1944, Ianthe Elstob; two *d. Educ:* Merchant Taylors' Sch.; St John's Coll., Oxford (MA). Served in Army, 1940–46. Entered Civil Service, 1946; Joint Sec., Cttee on Economic and Financial Problems of Provision for Old Age (Phillips Cttee), 1953–54; Asst Sec., 1955; Principal Private Sec. to Minister of Pensions and Nat. Insurance, 1955–56; Treasury, 1961–64, Under-Sec., Office of Lord Pres. of the Council and Minister for Science, 1964; Under-Sec., DES and Ministry of Health, 1964–74; Sec., UGC, 1974–77. Life Mem. Inst. of Historical Research, Univ. of London, 1984; FRSL 1984. *Publications:* The Prospector, 1950; The Old Cause, 1954; The South Sea Bubble, 1960, 2nd edn 1993; (ed with L. A. Dralle) The Diary and Political Papers of George Bubb Dodington, 1965; The Civil Servant and his World, 1966; The Descent on England, 1969; From Revolution to Revolution: English Society 1688–1776, 1973; Lives and Letters, 1978; The Exile: a memoir of Ivy Litvinov, 1983; Government and the Universities in Britain, 1986; The Porcupine: a life of Algernon Sidney, 1989; The Saving of Kenwood and the Northern Heights, 1992; contribs to Times Literary Supplement and other periodicals. *Address:* 5 Prince Arthur Road, NW3 6AX. *T:* (0171) 794 6527. *Club:* Garrick. *Died 12 Nov. 1997.*

CARTER, Sir Derrick (Hunton), Kt 1975; TD 1952; Vice-Chairman, Remploy Ltd, 1976–78 (Chairman, 1972–76; Director, 1967–79); *b* 7 April 1906; *s* of Arthur Hunton Carter, MD and Winifred Carter, Sedbergh; *m* 1st, 1933, Phyllis, *d* of Denis Best, Worcester; one *s* one *d*; 2nd, 1948, Madeline (*d* 1992), *d* of Col D. M. O'Callaghan, CMG, DSO; one *d. Educ:* Haileybury Coll.; St John's Coll., Cambridge (MA). 2nd Lieut, 27th (LEE) Bn RE, TA, 1936, mobilised Aug. 1939; in AA until Dec. 1941; 1st War Advanced Class; Major RA, Dept Tank Design; comd Armament Wing of Dept Tank Design; Lulworth, 1942–45 (Lt-Col). Civil Engr, Dominion Bridge Co., Montreal, 1927–28; Res. Engr, Billingham Div., ICI, 1928–33; Asst Sales Controller, ICI, London, 1933–38; Asst Sales Man., ICI, 1938–39 and 1945–47; Gen. Chemicals Div., ICI; Sales Control Man., 1947; Commercial Dir, 1951; Man. Dir, 1953; Chm., 1961; also Chm. Alkali Div., 1963; Chm. (of merged Divs as) Mond Div., 1964; retd from ICI, 1967. Chm., United Sulphuric Acid Corp. Ltd, 1967–71; Chm., Torrance & Sons Ltd, 1971–79; Director: Avon Rubber Co. Ltd, 1970–81; Stothert & Pitt Ltd, 1971–79; BICERI Ltd, 1967–90.

Mem. Exec. Cttee, Gloucestershire Council for Small Industries in Rural Areas, 1970–86. Mem. Council of Management, Nat. Star Centre for Disabled Youth, 1977–82; Vice-Pres., Glos Assoc. of Boys' Clubs. Freeman of City of London, 1973; Liveryman, Worshipful Co. of Coachmakers and Coach Harness Makers, 1973. *Recreations:* shooting, gardening. *Address:* Withington House, Withington, Cheltenham, Glos GL54 4BB. *T:* (01242) 890286. *Club:* Army and Navy. *Died 8 Dec. 1997.*

CARTER, Douglas, CB 1969; Under-Secretary, Department of Trade and Industry, 1970–71; *b* 4 Dec. 1911; 3rd *s* of Albert and Mabel Carter, Bradford, Yorks; *m* 1935, Alice (*d* 1986), *d* of Captain C. E. Le Mesurier, CB, RN; three *s* one *d. Educ:* Bradford Grammar Sch.; St John's Coll., Cambridge (Scholar), First Cl Hons, Historical Tripos Part I and Economics Tripos Part II; Wrenbury Research Scholarship in Economics, Cambridge, 1933. Asst Principal, Board of Trade, 1934; Sec., Imperial Shipping Cttee, 1935–38; Prin., BoT, 1939; Asst Sec., BoT, 1943; Chm., Cttee of Experts in Enemy Property Custodianship, Inter-Allied Reparations Agency, Brussels, 1946; Controller, Import Licensing Dept, 1949; Distribution of Industry Div., BoT, 1954; Industries and Manufactures Div., 1957; Commercial Relations and Exports Div., 1960; Under-Sec., 1963; Tariff Div., 1965. *Publications:* articles in bridge magazines. *Recreations:* reading, golf, bridge, travel. *Address:* 12 Garbrand Walk, Ewell Village, Epsom, Surrey KT17 1UQ. *Died 20 Jan. 1998.*

CARTER, Eric Bairstow, CEng, FIMechE, FRAeS, FIEE; Director-General (Engine Research and Development), Ministry of Technology, later Ministry of Defence (Aviation Supply), 1969–72; *b* 26 Aug. 1912; *s* of John Bolton Carter and Edith Carter (*née* Bairstow); *m* 1st, 1934, Lily (*d* 1981), *d* of John Charles and Ethel May Roome (*née* Bates); one *d*; 2nd, 1981, Olive Hicks Wright, *d* of Major William George and Olive Theresa Groombridge (*née* Hicks). *Educ:* Halifax Technical Coll.; BSc Eng. Staff appt, Halifax Tech. Coll., 1932; Supt and Lectr, Constantine Technical Coll., Middlesbrough, 1936; apptd to Air Min. (Engine Directorate), Sept. 1939; subseq. Air Min. appts to engine firms and at HQ; Asst Dir (Research and Develt, Ramjets and Liquid Propellant Rockets), 1955; Dir (Engine Prod.), 1960; Dir (Engine R&D), 1963. Chm., Gas Turbine Collaborative Cttee, 1969–70. *Recreations:* Spain, aviation history, bowls. *Address:* 15 Colyford Road, Seaton, Devon EX12 2DP. *Died 13 Sept. 1997.*

CARTER, Francis Jackson, CMG 1954; CVO 1963; CBE 1946; Under-Secretary of State of Tasmania and Clerk of Executive Council, also Permanent Head of Premier's and Chief Secretary's Department, 1953–64; *b* Fremantle, W Australia, 9 Sept. 1899; *s* of late Francis Henry Carter, formerly of Bendigo, Victoria; *m* 1926, Margaret Flora (*d* 1997), *d* of late William Thomas Walker, Launceston; two *s* one *d. Educ:* Hobart High Sch.; Univ. of Tasmania. Entered Tasmanian Public Service, 1916; transferred to Hydro-Electric Dept, 1925; Asst Secretary, Hydro-Electric Commn, 1934; Secretary to Premier, 1935–39; Dep. Under-Secretary of State, 1939–53; served War of 1939–45 as State Liaison Officer to Commonwealth Dept of Home Security; Official Secretary for Tasmania in London, 1949–50; State Director for Royal Visits, 1954, 1958, 1963, and Thai Royal Visit, 1962. Executive Member, State Economic Planning Authority, 1944–55; Chairman, Fire Brigades Commn of Tasmania, 1945–70. Grand Master GL of Tasmania, 1956–59. FCIS, FCIM. JP 1939. *Recreations:* music, golf, lawn bowls. *Address:* Bowditch Hostel, 3 Wellington Road, Lindisfarne, Tas

7015, Australia. *T:* (3) 62435975. *Clubs:* Royal Automobile of Tasmania, Masonic (Hobart).

Died 30 March 1999.

CARTER, John Arkwright B.; *see* Bonham-Carter.

CARTER, Air Vice-Marshal Wilfred, CB 1963; DFC 1943; international disaster consultant; *b* 5 Nov. 1912; *s* of late Samuel and Sarah Carter; *m* 1950, Margaret Enid Bray; one *d* (one *s* decd). *Educ:* Witney Grammar Sch. RAF, 1929; served War of 1939–45 with Bomber Command in UK and Middle East; Graduate, Middle East Centre for Arab Studies, 1945–46; Air Adviser to Lebanon, 1950–53; with Cabinet Secretariat, 1954–55; OC, RAF, Ternhill, 1956–58; Sen. RAF Dir, and later Commandant, Jt Services Staff Coll.; Asst Chief of Staff, Cento, 1960–63; Asst Commandant, RAF Staff Coll., 1963–65; AOA, HQ Bomber Command, 1965–67; Dir, Australian Counter Disaster Coll., 1969–78. Gordon Shephard Memorial Prize (for Strategic Studies), 1955, 1956, 1957, 1961, 1965, 1967. Officer, Order of Cedar of Lebanon, 1953. *Publications:* Disaster Preparedness and Response, 1985; Disaster Management, 1991. *Recreations:* walking, swimming. *Address:* Blue Range, Macedon, Vic 3440, Australia. *Died 19 Feb. 1999.*

CARTER, Sir William (Oscar), Kt 1972; Consultant, Eversheds, Solicitors, Norwich; *b* 12 Jan. 1905; *s* of late Oscar and Alice Carter; *m* 1934, Winifred Thompson. *Educ:* Swaffham Grammar Sch.; City of Norwich Sch. Admitted Solicitor of Supreme Court of Judicature, 1931. Served War, 1940–45, RAF (Wing Comdr), UK and Middle East. Mem. Council, The Law Society, 1954–75, Vice-Pres. 1970, Pres. 1971–72; President: East Anglian Law Soc., 1952–80; Norfolk and Norwich Incorporated Law Soc., 1959; Internat. Legal Aid Assoc., 1974–80; Life Mem. Council, Internat. Bar Assoc. (first Vice-Pres., 1976–78). Member: County Court Rules Cttee, 1956–60; Supreme Court Rules Cttee, 1960–75; Criminal Injuries Compensation Board, 1967–82 (Dep. Chm., 1977–82). Former Chm., Mental Health Review Tribunals for E Anglian and NE Thames RHA Areas. Upper Warden, 1984, Master, 1985–86, Co. of Glaziers. Hon. Mem., The Fellows of American Bar Foundn. *Recreations:* walking, foreign travel. *Address:* 83 Newmarket Road, Norwich NR2 2HP. *T:* (01603) 453772. *Clubs:* Army and Navy; Norfolk (Norwich). *Died 11 Dec. 2000.*

CARTLAND, Dame (Mary) Barbara (Hamilton), DBE 1991; authoress and playwright; *b* 9 July 1901; *d* of late Major Bertram Cartland, Worcestershire Regiment and Polly Cartland; *m* 1st, 1927, Alexander George McCorquodale (marr. diss. 1933; he *d* 1964), Cound Hall, Cressage, Salop; one *d*; 2nd, 1936, Hugh (*d* 1963), 2nd *s* of late Harold McCorquodale, Forest Hall, Ongar, Essex; two *s*. Published first novel at the age of twenty-one, which ran into five editions; designed and organised many pageants in aid of charity, including Britain and her Industries at British Legion Ball, Albert Hall, 1930; carried the first aeroplane-towed glider-mail in her glider, the Barbara Cartland, from Manston Aerodrome to Reading, June 1931; 2 lecture tours in Canada, 1940; Hon. Junior Commander, ATS and Lady Welfare Officer and Librarian to all Services in Bedfordshire, 1941–49; Certificate of Merit, Eastern Command, 1946; County Cadet Officer for St John Ambulance Brigade in Beds, 1943–47, County Vice-Pres. Cadets, Beds, 1948–50; organised and produced the St John Ambulance Bde Exhibn, 1945–50; Chm., St John Ambulance Bde Exhibn Cttee, 1944–51; County Vice-President: Nursing Cadets, Herts, 1951 (instigated a govt enquiry into the housing conditions of old people, 1955); Nursing Div., Herts, 1966; Pres., Herts Br. of Royal Coll. of Midwives, 1961. CC Herts (Hatfield Div.), 1955–64. Had Law of England changed with regard to sites for gypsies so that their children can go to school;

founded Cartland Onslow Romany Trust, with private site in Hatfield for family of Romany Gypsies. Founder and Pres., Nat. Assoc. for Health, 1964–. DStJ 1972 (Mem. Chapter Gen.; Pres., St John Council, Herts, 1992). FRSA. Bishop Wright Air Industry Award for contrib. to aviation in 1931, Kennedy Airport, 1984; Médaille de Vermeil de la Ville de Paris (Gold Medal of City of Paris) for Achievement, for sales of 25 million books in France, 1988. Bestselling author in the world (Guinness Book of Records), having completed 700 titles with worldwide sales of over 750 million copies; broke world record for 18 years, by writing an average of 23 books a year. Television: Portrait of a Successful Woman, 1957; This is Your Life, 1958, 1989; Success Story, 1959; Midland Profile, 1961; No Looking Back—a Portrait of Barbara Cartland, 1967; The Frost Programme, 1968; The Time of Your Life (prog. about first glider air mail 1931), 1985; radio: The World of Barbara Cartland, 1970; and many other radio and television appearances. *Publications: novels:* Jigsaw, 1923; Sawdust, 1926; If the Tree is Saved, 1929; For What?, 1930; Sweet Punishment, 1931; A Virgin in Mayfair, 1932; Just off Piccadilly, 1933; Not Love Alone, 1933; A Beggar Wished, 1934; Passionate Attainment, 1935; First Class, Lady?, 1935; Dangerous Experiment, 1936; Desperate Defiance, 1936; The Forgotten City, 1936; Saga at Forty, 1937; But Never Free, 1937; Bitter Winds of Love, 1938; Broken Barriers, 1938; The Gods Forget, 1939; Stolen Halo, 1940; Now Rough—Now Smooth, 1941; Open Wings, 1942; The Leaping Flame, 1942; A Heart is Broken, 1944; The Dark Stream, 1944; Sleeping Swords, 1944; Escape From Passion, 1945; Towards the Stars, 1945; Armour Against Love, 1945; Out of Reach, 1945; The Hidden Heart, 1946; Against the Stream, 1946; Again This Rapture, 1947; The Dream Within, 1947; Where is Love?, 1947; No Heart is Free, 1948; A Hazard of Hearts, 1949; A Duel of Hearts, 1949; The Enchanted Moment, 1949; The Knave of Hearts, 1950; The Little Pretender, 1950; A Ghost in Monte Carlo, 1951; Love is an Eagle, 1951; Love is Mine, 1952; The Passionate Pilgrim, 1952; Love is the Enemy, 1952; Cupid Rides Pillion, 1952; Blue Heather, 1953; Love me Forever, 1953; Elizabethan Lover, 1953; Wings on My Heart, 1954; Desire of The Heart, 1954; The Enchanted Waltz, 1955; The Kiss of the Devil, 1955; The Kiss of Paris, 1956; The Captive Heart, 1956; The Coin of Love, 1956; Love Forbidden, 1957; The Thief of Love, 1957; Stars in my Heart, 1957; Sweet Adventure, 1957; Lights of Love, 1958; The Sweet Enchantress, 1958; The Golden Gondola, 1958; The Kiss of Silk, 1959; Love in Hiding, 1959; The Smuggled Heart, 1959; The Price is Love, 1960; Love Under Fire, 1960; The Runaway Heart, 1961; The Messenger of Love, 1961; A Light to the Heart, 1962; The Wings of Love, 1962; Love is Dangerous, 1963; The Hidden Evil, 1963; Danger by the Nile, 1964; The Fire of Love, 1964; The Unpredictable Bride, 1964; The Magnificent Marriage, 1964; Love on the Run, 1965; Love Holds the Cards, 1965; Theft of a Heart, 1966; A Virgin in Paris, 1966; Love to the Rescue, 1967; Love is Contraband, 1968; The Enchanting Evil, 1968; The Unknown Heart, 1969; The Secret Fear, 1970; The Reluctant Bride, 1970; The Black Panther, 1970; The Pretty Horse-Breakers, 1971; The Audacious Adventuress, 1972; Halo for the Devil, 1972; The Irresistable Buck, 1972; Lost Enchantment, 1972; The Complacent Wife, 1972; The Odious Duke, 1973; The Wicked Marquis, 1973; The Daring Deception, 1973; The Little Adventure, 1974; No Darkness for Love, 1974; Lessons in Love, 1974; The Ruthless Rake, 1974; Journey to Paradise, 1974; The Karma of Love, 1974; The Dangerous Dandy, 1974; The Bored Bridegroom, 1974; The Penniless Peer, 1974; The Cruel Count, 1974; The Castle of Fear, 1974; Love is Innocent, 1975; The Mask of Love, 1975; A Sword to the Heart, 1975; Bewitched, 1975; The Impetuous

Duchess, 1975; The Shadow of Sin, 1975; The Tears of Love, 1975; The Devil in Love, 1975; The Frightened Bride, 1975; The Flame is Love, 1975; A Very Naughty Angel, 1975; Call of the Heart, 1975; As Eagles Fly, 1975; Say Yes, Samantha, 1975; An Arrow of Love, 1975; A Gamble with Hearts, 1975; A Kiss for the King, 1975; A Frame of Dreams, 1975; The Glittering Lights, 1975; Fire on the Snow, 1975; Fragrant Flowers, 1976; The Elusive Earl, 1976; Moon Over Eden, 1976; The Golden Illusion, 1976; No Time for Love, 1976; The Husband Hunters, 1976; The Slaves of Love, 1976; Passions in the Sands, 1976; An Angel in Hell, 1976; The Wild Cry of Love, 1976; The Blue-Eyed Witch, 1976; The Incredible Honeymoon, 1976; A Dream from the Night, 1976; Never Laugh at Love, 1976; The Secret of the Glen, 1976; The Dream and the Glory, 1976; The Proud Princess, 1976; Hungry for Love, 1976; The Heart Triumphant, 1976; The Disgraceful Duke, 1976; Conquered by Love, 1977; The Taming of Lady Lorinda, 1977; Vote for Love, 1977; The Mysterious Maidservant, 1977; The Magic of Love, 1977; Kiss the Moonlight, 1977; Love Locked In, 1977; The Marquis Who Hated Women, 1977; Rhapsody of Love, 1977; Look, Listen and Love, 1977; Duel with Destiny, 1977; The Wild Unwilling Wife, 1977; Punishment of a Vixen, 1977; The Curse of the Clan, 1977; The Outrageous Lady, 1977; The Love Pirate, 1977; The Dragon and the Pearl, 1977; The Naked Battle, 1977; The Hell-Cat and the King, 1977; No Escape from Love, 1977; A Sign of Love, 1977; A Touch of Love, 1978; The Temptation of Torilla, 1978; The Passion and the Flower, 1978; Love, Lords and Ladybirds, 1978; Love and the Loathsome Leopard, 1978; The Castle Made for Love, 1978; The Saint and the Sinner, 1978; A Fugitive from Love, 1978; Love Leaves at Midnight, 1978; The Problems of Love, 1978; The Twists and Turns of Love, 1978; Magic or Mirage, 1978; The Ghost Who Fell in Love, 1978; The Chieftain Without a Heart, 1978; Lord Ravenscar's Revenge, 1978; A Runaway Star, 1978; A Princess in Distress, 1978; The Irresistable Force, 1978; Lovers in Paradise, 1978; The Serpent of Satan, 1978; Love in the Clouds, 1978; The Treasure is Love, 1978; Imperial Splendour, 1978; Light of the Moon, 1978; The Prisoner of Love, 1978; Love in the Dark, 1978; The Duchess Disappeared, 1978; Love Climbs In, 1978; A Nightingale Sang, 1978; Terror in the Sun, 1978; Who Can Deny Love?, 1978; Bride to the King, 1978; The Judgement of Love, 1979; The Race for Love, 1979; Flowers for the God of Love, 1979; The Duke and the Preacher's Daughter, 1979; The Drums of Love, 1979; Alone in Paris, 1979; The Prince and the Pekinese, 1979; Only Love, 1979; The Dawn of Love, 1979; Love Has His Way, 1979; The Explosion of Love, 1979; Women Have Hearts, 1979; A Gentleman in Love, 1979; A Heart is Stolen, 1979; The Power and the Prince, 1979; Free From Fear, 1979; A Song of Love, 1979; Love for Sale, 1979; Little White Doves of Love, 1979; The Perfection of Love, 1979; Lost Laughter, 1979; Punished with Love, 1979; Lucifer and the Angel, 1979; Ola and the Sea Wolf, 1979; The Prude and the Prodigal, 1979; The Goddess and the Gaiety Girl, 1979; Signpost to Love, 1979; Money, Magic and Marriage, 1979; From Hell to Heaven, 1980; Pride and The Poor Princess, 1980; The Lioness and The Lily, 1980; A Kiss of Life, 1980; Love At The Helm, 1980; The Waltz of Hearts, 1980; Afraid, 1980; The Horizons of Love, 1980; Love in the Moon, 1980; Dollars for the Duke, 1981; Dreams Do Come True, 1981; Night of Gaiety, 1981; Count the Stars, 1981; Winged Magic, 1981; A Portrait of Love, 1981; River of Love, 1981; Gift of the Gods, 1981; The Heart of the Clan, 1981; An Innocent in Russia, 1981; A Shaft of Sunlight, 1981; Love Wins, 1981; Enchanted, 1981; Wings of Ecstasy, 1981; Pure and Untouched, 1981; In the Arms of Love, 1981; Touch a Star, 1981; For All Eternity, 1981; Secret Harbour, 1981;

Looking for Love, 1981; The Vibration of Love, 1981; Lies for Love, 1981; Love Rules, 1981; Moments of Love, 1981; Lucky in Love, 1981; Poor Governess, 1981; Music from the Heart, 1981; Caught by Love, 1981; A King in Love, 1981; Winged Victory, 1981; The Call of the Highlands, 1981; Love and the Marquis, 1981; Kneel for Mercy, 1981; Riding to the Moon, 1981; Wish for Love, 1981; Mission to Monte Carlo, 1981; A Miracle in Music, 1981; A Marriage Made in Heaven, 1981; From Hate to Love, 1982; Light of the Gods, 1982; Love on the Wind, 1982; The Duke Comes Home, 1982; Journey to a Star, 1983; Love and Lucia, 1983; The Unwanted Wedding, 1983; Gypsy Magic, 1983; Help from the Heart, 1983; A Duke in Danger, 1983; Tempted to Love, 1983; Lights, Laughter and a Lady, 1983; The Unbreakable Spell, 1983; Diona and a Dalmatian, 1983; Fire in the Blood, 1983; The Scots Never Forget, 1983; A Rebel Princess, 1983; A Witch's Spell, 1983; Secrets, 1983; The Storms of Love, 1983; Moonlight on the Sphinx, 1983; White Lilac, 1983; Revenge of the Heart, 1983; Bride to a Brigand, 1983; Love Comes West, 1983; Theresa and a Tiger, 1983; An Island of Love, 1983; Love is Heaven, 1983; Miracle for a Madonna, 1984; A Very Unusual Wife, 1984; The Peril and the Prince, 1984; Alone and Afraid, 1984; Temptation for a Teacher, 1984; Royal Punishment, 1984; The Devilish Deception, 1984; Paradise Found, 1984; Love is a Gamble, 1984; A Victory for Love, 1984; Look with Love, 1984; Never Forget Love, 1984; Helga in Hiding, 1984; Safe at Last, 1984; Haunted, 1984; Crowned with Love, 1984; Escape, 1984; The Devil Defeated, 1985; The Secret of the Mosque, 1985; A Dream in Spain, 1985; The Love Trap, 1985; Listen to Love, 1985; The Golden Cage, 1985; Love Casts Out Fear, 1985; A World of Love, 1985; Dancing on a Rainbow, 1985; Love Joins the Clans, 1985; An Angel Runs Away, 1985; Forced into Marriage, 1985; Bewildered in Berlin, 1985; Wanted—a Wedding Ring, 1985; Starlight Over Tunis, 1985; The Earl Escapes, 1985; The Love Puzzle, 1985; Love and Kisses, 1985; Sapphires in Siam, 1985; A Caretaker of Love, 1985; Secrets of the Heart, 1985; Riding to the Sky, 1986; Lovers in Lisbon, 1986; Love is Invincible, 1986; The Goddess of Love, 1986; An Adventure of Love, 1986; A Herb for Happiness, 1986; Only a Dream, 1986; Saved by Love, 1986; Little Tongues of Fire, 1986; A Chieftain Finds Love, 1986; The Lovely Liar, 1986; The Perfume of the Gods, 1986; A Knight in Paris, 1987; Revenge is Sweet, 1987; The Passionate Princess, 1987; Solita and the Spies, 1987; The Perfect Pearl, 1987; Love is a Maze, 1987; A Circus for Love, 1987; The Temple of Love, 1987; The Bargain Bride, 1987; The Haunted Heart, 1987; Real Love or Fake, 1987; A Kiss from a Stranger, 1987; A Very Special Love, 1987; A Necklace of Love, 1987; No Disguise for Love, 1987; A Revolution of Love, 1988; The Marquis Wins, 1988; Love is the Key, 1988; Free as the Wind, 1988; Desire in the Desert, 1988; A Heart in the Highlands, 1988; The Music of Love, 1988; The Wrong Duchess, 1988; The Taming of a Tigress, 1988; Love Comes to the Castle, 1988; The Magic of Paris, 1988; Stand and Deliver Your Heart, 1988; The Scent of Roses, 1988; Love at First Sight, 1988; The Secret Princess, 1988; Heaven in Hong Kong, 1988; Paradise in Penang, 1988; A Game of Love, 1988; The Sleeping Princess, 1988; A Wish Comes True, 1988; Loved for Himself, 1988; Two Hearts in Hungary, 1988; A Theatre of Love, 1988; A Dynasty of Love, 1988; Magic from the Heart, 1988; Windmill of Love, 1988; Love Strikes Satan, 1988; The Earl Rings a Belle, 1988; The Queen Saves the King, 1988; Love Lifts the Curse, 1988; Beauty or Brains, 1988; Too Precious to Lose, 1988; Hiding, 1988; A Tangled Web, 1988; Just Fate, 1988; A Miracle in Mexico, 1988; Warned by a Ghost, 1988; Terror from the Throne, 1988; The Cave of Love, 1988; The Peaks of Ecstasy, 1988; A Kiss in Rome, 1988; Hidden by Love, 1988; Walking to Wonderland, 1988;

Lucky Logan Finds Love, 1988; Born of Love, 1988; The Angel and the Rake, 1988; The Queen of Hearts, 1988; The Wicked Widow, 1988; To Scotland and Love, 1988; Love and War, 1988; Love at the Ritz, 1989; The Dangerous Marriage, 1989; Good or Bad, 1989; This is Love, 1989; Seek the Stars, 1989; Escape to Love, 1989; Look with the Heart, 1989; Safe in Paradise, 1989; Love in the Ruins, 1989; A Coronation of Love, 1989; A Duel of Jewels, 1989; The Duke is Trapped, 1989; Just a Wonderful Dream, 1989; Love and a Cheetah, 1989; Drena and the Duke, 1989; A Dog, a Horse and a Heart, 1989; Never Lose Love, 1989; The Eyes of Love, 1989; The Duke's Dilemma, 1989; Saved by a Saint, 1989; Beyond the Stars, 1990; The Spirit of Love, 1991; The Innocent Imposter, 1991; The Incomparable, 1991; The Dare-Devil Duke, 1991; A Royal Rebuke, 1991; Love Runs in, 1991; Love Light of Apollo, 1991; Love, Lies and Marriage, 1991; In Love in Lucca, 1991; Fascination in France, 1992; Something to Love, 1992; Three Days to Love, 1992; A Magical Moment, 1992; A Secret Passage to Love, 1992; An Icicle in India, 1992; Running from Russia, 1992; The Loveless Marriage, 1992; The Protection of Love, 1992; The Patient Bridegroom, 1992; A Train to Love, 1992; The Unbroken Dream, 1992; A Challenge of Hearts, 1993; The Man of her Dreams, 1993; The White Witch, 1993; Saved by the Duke, 1993; Captured by Love, 1993; Danger to the Duke, 1993; The King without a Heart, 1993; A Battle of Love, 1993; Lovers in London, 1993; Love or Money, 1993; Love Wins in Berlin, 1993; Learning to Love, 1993; One Minute to Love, 1993; Saved by an Angel, 1993; The Marquis is Deceived, 1993; A Princess Runs Away, 1993; A Change of Hearts, 1993; Love by the Lake, 1993; A Heart of Stone, 1993; Journey to Love, 1993; Love finds a Treasure, 1993; The Mountain of Love, 1993; Follow your Heart, 1993; A Kiss in the Desert, 1993; Love for Eternity, 1993; The Duke Disappears, 1993; The Earl Elopes, 1993; The King Wins, 1993; A Beauty Betrayed, 1993; Rivals for Love, 1993; The Earl's Revenge, 1993; A Golden Lie, 1993; Love and Apollo, 1993; A Princess Prays, 1993; The Battle of Brains, 1993; Ruled by Love, 1993; Wanted a Royal Wife, 1993; A Kiss of Love, 1993; Money or Love, 1993; The Marquis is Trapped, 1993; Pray for Love, 1993; Hide and Seek for Love, 1993; A Teacher of Love, 1993; The Gates of Paradise, 1993; The Tree of Love, 1993; Search for Love, 1993; Love is Magic, 1993; The Prince is Saved, 1993; Secret Love, 1993; Search for Love, 1994; Love is Magic, 1994; The Prince is Saved, 1994; Secret Love, 1994; Love in Egypt, 1994; The Kingdom of Love, 1994; The Healing Hand, 1994; A Miracle for Love, 1994; A Virgin Bride, 1994; A Royal Love Match, 1994; A Steeplechase for Love, 1994; Search for a Wife, 1994; A Shooting Star, 1994; The Duke is Deceived, 1994; The Queen Wins, 1994; Love and the Clans, 1994; The Winning Post is Love, 1994; Love and the Gods, 1994; Love Conquers War, 1994; A Sacrifice for Love, 1994; A Call of Love, 1994; A Heart Finds Love, 1994; She Wanted Love, 1994; A Prayer for Love, 1994; Wish Upon a Star, 1994; A Road to Romance, 1994; Soft, Sweet and Gentle, 1994; The Viscount's Revenge, 1994; An Archangel Called Ivan, 1994; Wanted a Bride, 1994; A Prisoner in Paris, 1994; Rescued by Love, 1994; Danger in the Desert, 1994; The Bride Runs Away, 1994; The Duke is Captured, 1994; Crowned by Music, 1995; Love Solves the Problem, 1995; An Icicle in India, 1995; The Loveless Marriage, 1995; A Magical Moment, 1995; Passage to Love, 1995; The Patient Bridegroom, 1995; The Protection of Love, 1995; The Daredevil Duke, 1996; Fascination in France, 1996; Love Runs In, 1996; The Love Light of Apollo, 1996; A Royal Rebuke, 1996; In Love in Lucca, 1997; Love Lies and Marriage, 1997; *philosophy:* Touch the Stars; *sociology:* You in the Home; The Fascinating Forties; Marriage for Moderns; Be Vivid,

Be Vital; Love, Life and Sex; Look Lovely, Be Lovely; Vitamins for Vitality; Husbands and Wives; Etiquette; The Many Facets of Love; Sex and the Teenager; Charm; Living Together; Woman the Enigma; The Youth Secret; The Magic of Honey; Health Food Cookery Book; Book of Beauty and Health; Men are Wonderful; The Magic of Honey Cookbook; Food for Love; Recipes for Lovers; The Romance of Food; Getting Older, Growing Younger; (jtly) Keep Young and Beautiful; The Etiquette of Romance, 1985; *biography:* Ronald Cartland, 1942; Bewitching Women; The Outrageous Queen; Polly, My Wonderful Mother, 1956; The Scandalous Life of King Carol; The Private Life of Charles II; The Private Life of Elizabeth, Empress of Austria; Josephine, Empress of France; Diane de Poitiers; Metternich, the Passionate Diplomat; *historical:* A Year of Royal Days, 1988; Royal Jewels, 1989; Royal Lovers, 1989; Royal Eccentrics, 1989; *autobiography:* The Isthmus Years, 1943; The Years of Opportunity, 1947; I Search for Rainbows, 1967; We Danced All Night, 1919–1929, 1971; I Seek the Miraculous, 1978; I Reach for the Stars, 1994; *general:* (ed) The Common Problem, by Ronald Cartland, 1943; Useless Information (foreword by Earl Mountbatten of Burma); Light of Love (prayers), 1978; Love and Lovers (pictures), 1978; Barbara Cartland's Book of Celebrities, 1982; Barbara Cartland's Scrapbook, 1980; Romantic Royal Marriages, 1981; (ed) Written with Love, 1981; (ed) The Library of Love; (ed) The Library of Ancient Wisdom; How to Write like Barbara Cartland, vols 1 and 2, 1994; *for children:* Princess to the Rescue; *verse:* Lines on Love and Life; *plays:* Blood Money, 1925; (with Bruce Woodhouse) French Dressing, 1943; *revue:* The Mayfair Revue; *radio play:* The Caged Bird. *Address:* Camfield Place, Hatfield, Herts AL9 6JE. *T:* (01707) 642612, 642657. *Died 21 May 2000.*

CARTWRIGHT, Rt Rev. (Edward) David; *b* 15 July 1920; *o c* of John Edward Cartwright, master butcher and grazier, and Gertrude Cartwright (*née* Lusby), North Somercotes and Grimsby, Lincs; *m* 1946, Elsie Irene, *o c* of Walter and Jane Elizabeth Rogers, Grimsby; one *s* two *d. Educ:* Grimsby Parish Church Choir Sch.; Lincoln Sch.; Selwyn Coll. and Westcott House, Cambridge. 2nd Cl. Hons Hist. Tripos Pt 1, 1940; 2nd Cl. Hons Theol. Tripos Pt 1, 1942; Steel Univ. Student in Divinity, 1941; BA 1941, MA 1945; Pres., SCM in Cambridge, 1941–42. Deacon, 1943; priest, 1944; Curate of Boston, 1943–48; Vicar: St Leonard's, Redfield, Bristol, 1948–52; Olveston with Aust, 1952–60; Bishopston, 1960–73; Secretary, Bristol Diocesan Synod, 1967–73; Hon. Canon of Bristol Cathedral, 1970–73; Archdeacon of Winchester and Vicar of Sparsholt with Lainston, 1973–84; Hon. Canon of Winchester Cathedral, 1973–88; Bishop Suffragan of Southampton, 1984–88. Dir of Studies, Bristol Lay Readers, 1956–72; Proctor in Convocation, Mem. of Church Assembly and General Synod, 1956–73, 1975–83. Member: Central Bd of Finance of C of E, 1970–73; C of E Pensions Bd, 1980–84. Church Commissioner, 1973–83 (Mem. Board of Governors, 1978–83); Member: Dilapidations Legislation Commn, 1958–64; Working Party on Housing of Retired Clergy, 1972–73; Differential Payment of Clergy, 1976–77. Secretary, Bristol Council of Christian Churches, 1950–61; Chm., Winchester Christian Council, 1976–77; Pres., Southampton Council of Churches, 1984–88. Chm., Christian Aid Cttee: Bristol, 1956–73; Winchester, 1974–81. Member: Anglican-Presbyterian Conversations, 1962–66; Convocations Jt Cttees on Anglican-Methodist Union Scheme, 1965. *Recreations:* book-hunting, rose-growing. *Address:* Bargate House, 25 Newport, Warminster, Wilts BA12 8RH. *T:* (01985) 216298. *Died 24 April 1997.*

CARTWRIGHT, Frederick; *see* Cartwright, W. F.

CARTWRIGHT, Dame Mary Lucy, DBE 1969; ScD Cambridge 1949; MA Oxford and Cambridge; DPhil Oxford; FRS 1947; Fellow of Girton College, Cambridge, 1930–49, and since 1968; *b* 17 Dec. 1900; *d* of late Rev. W. D. Cartwright, Rector of Aynhoe. *Educ:* Godolphin Sch., Salisbury; St Hugh's Coll., Oxford. Asst Mistress, Alice Ottley Sch., Worcester, 1923–24, Wycombe Abbey Sch., Bucks, 1924–27; read for DPhil, 1928–30; Yarrow Research Fellow of Girton Coll., 1930–34; Univ. Lectr in Mathematics, Cambridge, 1935–59; Mistress of Girton Coll., Cambridge, 1949–68; Reader in the Theory of Functions, Univ. of Cambridge, 1959–68, Emeritus Reader, 1968–. Visiting Professor: Brown Univ., Providence, RI, 1968–69; Claremont Graduate Sch., California, 1969–70; Case Western Reserve, 1970; Polish Acad. of Sciences, 1970; Univ. of Wales, 1971; Case Western Reserve, 1971. Consultant on US Navy Mathematical Research Projects at Stanford and Princeton Universities, Jan.-May 1949. Comdt, British Red Cross Detachment, Cambs 112, 1940–44. Fellow of Cambridge Philosophical Soc.; President: London Math. Soc., 1961–63; Mathematical Assoc., 1951–52 (later Hon. Mem.). Hon. FIMA 1972; Hon. FRSE. Hon. LLD Edin., 1953; Hon. DSc: Leeds, 1958; Hull, 1959; Wales, 1962; Oxford, 1966; Brown, USA, 1969. Sylvester Medal, Royal Soc., 1964; De Morgan Medal, London Mathematical Soc., 1968; Medal of Univ. of Jyväskylä, Finland, 1973. Commander, Order of the Dannebrog, 1961. *Publications:* Integral Functions (Cambridge Tracts in Mathematics and Mathematical Physics), 1956; math. papers in various journals. *Address:* Midfield Nursing Home, Cambridge Road, Oakington, Cambridge CB4 5BG.
Died 3 April 1998.

CARTWRIGHT, (William) Frederick, CBE 1977; DL; MIMechE; Director, BSC (International) Ltd; a Deputy Chairman, British Steel Corporation, 1970–72; Group Managing Director, South Wales Group, British Steel Corporation, 1967–70; Chairman, The Steel Co. of Wales Ltd, 1967 (Managing Director, 1962–67); *b* 13 Nov. 1906, *s* of Rev. William Digby Cartwright, Rector of Aynhoe; *m* 1937, Sally Chrystobel Ware; two *s* one *d. Educ:* Rugby Sch. Joined Guest, Keen and Nettlefold, Dowlais, 1929; gained experience at steelworks in Germany, Luxembourg and France, 1930; Asst Works Manager, 1931, Tech. Asst to Managing Director, 1935, Dir and Chief Engineer, 1940, Dir and General Manager, 1943, Guest, Keen and Baldwin, Port Talbot Works; Dir and General Manager, Steel Co. of Wales, 1947; Asst Man. Dir and General Manager of the Steel Div., The Steel Co. of Wales Ltd, 1954. Pres., Iron and Steel Inst., 1960. Dir, Lloyds Bank, 1968–77 (Chm., S Wales Regional Bd, 1968–77). Dir, Develt Corp for Wales. Freeman of Port Talbot, 1970. DL, County of Glamorgan; High Sheriff, Glamorgan, 1961. OStJ. Hon. LLD Wales, 1968. Bessemer Gold Medal, 1958; Frederico Giolitti Steel Medal, 1960. *Recreations:* riding, yachting. *Address:* Castle-upon-Alun, St Brides Major, near Bridgend, Mid Glam CF32 0TN. *T:* (01656) 880298. *Clubs:* Royal Ocean Racing, Royal Cruising; Royal Yacht Squadron.
Died 3 May 1998.

CARTWRIGHT SHARP, Michael; *see* Sharp, J. M. C.

CASALONE, Carlo D.; *see* Dionisotti-Casalone.

CASEY, Rt Rev. Patrick Joseph; former Bishop of Brentwood; *b* 20 Nov. 1913; *s* of Patrick Casey and Bridget Casey (*née* Norris). *Educ:* St Joseph's Parochial Sch., Kingsland; St Edmund's Coll., Ware. Ordained priest, 1939; Asst, St James's, Spanish Place, 1939–61; Parish Priest of Hendon, 1961–63; Vicar Gen. of Westminster, 1963; Domestic Prelate, and Canon of Westminster Cathedral, 1964; Provost of Westminster Cathedral Chapter, 1967; Auxiliary Bishop of Westminster and Titular Bishop of Sufar, 1966–69; Bishop of Brentwood, 1969–79, then Apostolic Administrator; Parish Priest, Our Most Holy Redeemer and St Thomas More, Chelsea, 1980–89.
Died 26 Jan. 1999.

CASEY, Dame Stella (Katherine), DBE 1990; *b* 22 May 1924; *d* of William Wright and Stella Hickey; *m* 1948, Maurice Eugene Casey (later Rt Hon. Sir Maurice Casey, PC); three *s* six *d. Educ.* Rahotu Sch.; Opunake Dist High Sch.; Victoria Univ. (BA). Voluntary service: Catholic Women's League of NZ, 1967–; Nat. Council of Women of NZ, 1976–; NZ Fedn of Univ. Women, 1969–; World Union of Catholic Women's Organisations, 1975–79; Hato Petra Coll. Assoc., 1968–73; Girl Guides Assoc., 1968–75; Bd of Governors, Sacred Heart Coll., 1976–82; Banking Ombudsman Commn, 1992–97. Member: Cttee on Secondary Educn, 1975–76; Working Party, Teacher Training Review, 1977–78; Christchurch Polytechnic Council, 1979–82; Nat. Adv. Cttee on Women and Educn, 1982–83; Dep. Chm., Adv. Cttee on Women's Affairs, 1981–84. Chm. Trustees, Natural Family Planning Foundn, 1992–97. Chm. Dirs, Dorchester Apartments, 1992–. *Publications:* Drugs and the Young New Zealander, 1968. *Address:* 5/144 Oriental Parade, Wellington, New Zealand. *T:* (4) 3843258.
Died 7 July 2000.

CASSELS, Field-Marshal Sir (Archibald) James (Halkett), GCB 1961 (CB 1950); KBE 1952 (CBE 1944); DSO 1944; Chief of the General Staff, Ministry of Defence, 1965–68; *b* 28 Feb. 1907; *s* of late General Sir Robert A. Cassels, GCB, GCSI, DSO and Florence Emily, *d* of Lt-Col H. Jackson; *m* 1st, 1935, Joyce (*d* 1978), *d* of late Brig.-Gen. Henry Kirk and Mrs G. A. McL. Sceales; one *s*; 2nd, 1978, Joy (Mrs Kenneth Dickson). *Educ:* Rugby Sch.; RMC, Sandhurst. 2nd Lieut Seaforth Highlanders, 1926; Lieut 1929; Capt. 1938; Major 1943; Col 1946; temp. Maj.-Gen. 1945; Maj.-Gen. 1948; Lieut-Gen. 1954; Gen. 1958; Field Marshal 1968. Served War of 1939–45 (despatches twice): BGS 1944; Bde Comd 1944; GOC 51st Highland Div., 1945, GOC 6th Airborne Div., Palestine, 1946 (despatches); idc, 1947; Dir Land/Air Warfare, War Office, 1948–49; Chief Liaison Officer, United Kingdom Services Liaison Staff, Australia, 1950–51; GOC 1st British Commonwealth Div. in Korea (US Legion of Merit), 1951–52; Comdr, 1st Corps, 1953–54; Dir-Gen. of Military Training, War Office, 1954–57; Dir of Emergency Operations Federation of Malaya, 1957–59 (PMN 1958); GOC-in-C, Eastern Command, 1959; C-in-C, British Army of the Rhine and Comdr NATO Northern Army Group, 1960–63; Adjutant-Gen. to the Forces, 1963–64. ADC Gen. to the Queen, 1960–63. Col Seaforth Highlanders, 1957–61; Col Queen's Own Highlanders, 1961–66; Colonel Commandant: Corps of Royal Military Police, 1957–68; Army Physical Training Corps, 1961–65. Pres., Company of Veteran Motorists, 1970–73. *Recreations:* follower of all forms of sport. *Address:* Hamble End, Barrow, Bury St Edmunds, Suffolk IP29 5BE. *Club:* Cavalry and Guards (Hon. Mem.).
Died 13 Dec. 1996.

CASSILLY, Prof. Richard; operatic tenor; Professor, School of Fine Arts, Boston University, since 1986; *b* Washington, DC, 14 Dec. 1927; *s* of Robert Rogers Cassilly and Vera F. Swart; *m* 1st, 1951, Helen Koliopoulos; four *s* three *d*; 2nd, 1985, Patricia Craig. *Educ:* Peabody Conservatory of Music, Baltimore, Md. New York City Opera, 1955–66; Chicago Lyric, 1959–; Deutsche Oper, Berlin, 1965–; Hamburgische Staatsoper, 1966–; San Francisco Opera, 1966–; Covent Garden, 1968–; Staatsoper, Vienna, 1969–; La Scala, Milan, 1970–; Staatsoper, Munich, 1970–; Paris Opera, 1972–; Metropolitan Opera, NY, 1973–; *television:* Otello, Peter Grimes, Fidelio, Wozzeck, Die Meistersinger; numerous recordings. Kammersänger, Hamburg, 1973;

Distinguished Alumni Award, Peabody, 1977; Gold Medal, Acad. of Vocal Arts, Philadelphia, 1984. *Address:* c/o Boston University School of Fine Arts, 855 Commonwealth Avenue, Boston, Mass 02215, USA.
Died 30 Jan. 1998.

CASSON, Sir Hugh (Maxwell), CH 1985; KCVO 1978; Kt 1952; RA 1970; RDI 1951; RIBA, FCSD; President of the Royal Academy, 1976–84; Professor of Environmental Design, 1953–75, Provost, 1980–86, Royal College of Art; Member, Royal Mint Advisory Committee, since 1972; *b* 23 May 1910; *s* of late Randal Casson, ICS; *m* 1938, Margaret Macdonald Troup, architect and designer; three *d*. *Educ:* Eastbourne Coll.; St John's Coll., Cambridge (MA). Craven Scholar, British Sch. at Athens, 1933. Started in private practice as architect, with Christopher Nicholson, 1937; served War of 1939–45, Camouflage Officer in Air Ministry, 1940–44; Technical Officer Ministry of Town and Country Planning, 1944–46; private practice, Sen. Partner, Casson Conder & Partners, 1946–76; Dir. of Architecture, Festival of Britain, 1948–51. Master of Faculty, RDI, 1969–71. Mem., Royal Fine Art Commn, 1960–83; Trustee: British Museum (Nat. Hist.), 1976–86; Nat. Portrait Gall., 1976–84; Mem. Bd, British Council, 1977–81. Mem., Royal Danish Acad., 1954; Hon. Associate, Amer. Inst of Architects, 1968; Hon. Mem., Royal Canadian Acad. of Arts, 1980. Hon. Dr: RCA 1975; Southampton, 1977; Hon. LLD Birmingham, 1977; Hon. DLitt Sheffield, 1986. Hon. Fellow University Coll. London, 1983. Albert Medal, RSA, 1984. Italian Order of Merit, 1980. Regular contributor as author and illustrator to technical and lay Press. *Publications:* New Sights of London (London Transport), 1937; Bombed Churches, 1946; Homes by the Million (Penguin), 1947; (with Anthony Chitty) Houses-Permanence and Prefabrication, 1947; Victorian Architecture, 1948; Inscape: the design of interiors, 1968; (with Joyce Grenfell) Nanny Says, 1972; Diary, 1981; Hugh Casson's London, 1983; Hugh Casson's Oxford, 1988; Japan Observed, 1991; Hugh Casson's Cambridge, 1992; The Tower of London: an artist's portrait, 1993. *Recreation:* drawing. *Address:* 6 Hereford Mansions, Hereford Road, W2 5BA. *T:* (office) (020) 7221 7774.
Died 15 Aug. 1999.

CASSON, Margaret MacDonald, (Lady Casson); architect, designer; Senior Tutor, School of Environmental Design, Royal College of Art, retired 1974; *b* 26 Sept. 1913; 2nd *d* of James MacDonald Troup, MD, and Alberta Davis; *m* 1938, Sir Hugh Maxwell Casson, CH, KCVO, RA (*d* 1999); three *d*. *Educ:* Wychwood Sch., Oxford; Bartlett Sch. of Architecture, University Coll. London; Royal Inst. of British Architecture. Office of Christopher Nicholson, 1937–38; private practice, S Africa, 1938–39; Designer for Cockade Ltd, 1946–51; Tutor, Royal Coll. of Art, 1952–72; private practice as architect and designer for private and public buildings and interiors, also of china, glass, carpets, furniture, etc. Design consultant to various cos; Member: Council for Design Council, 1967–73 (Chm. Panel for Design Council Awards for Consumer Goods, 1972); Three-Dimensional Design Panel of NCDAD, 1962–72 (Ext. Assessor for NCDAD, 1962–65); Council of RCA, 1970; Arts Council, 1972–75; Adv. Council of V&A Museum, 1975–80; Craft Adv. Cttee, 1976–82; Royal Soc. of Arts, 1977–82; Stamp Adv. Cttee, PO, 1980–95; Design Cttee, London Transport, 1980–88; Council, Zoological Soc. of London, 1983–86. Member, Board of Governors: Wolverhampton Coll. of Art, 1964–66; West of England Coll. of Art, 1965–67; BFI, 1973–79. FSIAD; Sen. Fellow RCA; Hon. Fellow, Royal Acad., 1985. Art photographer (as Margaret MacDonald): exhibited: London, 1984, 1985, 1986, 1993; RPS, Bath, 1989; Tokyo, 1989; NY, 1988, 1990, 1994.

Address: 6 Hereford Mansions, Hereford Road, W2 5BA. *T:* (020) 7727 2999. *Died 13 Nov. 1999.*

CATER, Sir John Robert, (Sir Robin), Kt 1984; Chairman, Distillers Co. Ltd, 1976–83; *b* 25 April 1919; *s* of Sir John Cater and Jessie Sheila MacDonald, *d* of Dr Robert Moodie, Stirling; *m* 1945, Isobel Calder Ritchie; one *d*. *Educ:* George Watson's Coll., Edinburgh; Cambridge Univ. (MA). Trainee, W. P. Lowrie & Co. Ltd, 1946; James Buchanan & Co. Ltd, 1949: Dir 1950; Prodn Dir 1959; Distillers Co. Ltd, Edinburgh: Prodn Asst, 1959; Dir, 1967–83 (Mem., Management Cttee); Dep. Chm., 1975–76; Man. Dir, John Haig & Co. Ltd, 1965–70; Non-Exec. Dir, United Glass, 1969, Chm. 1972. *Recreations:* music, theatre, fishing, golf (Walker Cup team, 1955; played for Scotland, 1952–56). *Address:* Avernish, Elie, Fife, Scotland KY9 1DA. *Clubs:* New (Edinburgh); Royal and Ancient (St Andrews); The Golf House (Elie).
Died 2 July 1997.

CATHCART, 6th Earl *cr* 1814; **Alan Cathcart,** CB 1973; DSO 1945; MC 1944; Lord Cathcart (Scot.) 1447; Viscount Cathcart, Baron Greenock 1807; Major-General; *b* 22 Aug. 1919; *o s* of 5th Earl and Vera, *d* of late John Fraser, Cape Town; *S* father, 1927; *m* 1st, 1946, Rosemary (*d* 1980), *yr d* of late Air Commodore Sir Percy Smyth-Osbourne, CMG, CBE; one *s* two *d*; 2nd, 1984, Marie Isobel, Lady Weldon. *Educ:* Eton; Magdalene Coll., Cambridge. Served War of 1939–45 (despatches, MC, DSO). Adjt RMA Sandhurst, 1946–47; Regimental Adjt Scots Guards, 1951–53; Brigade Major, 4th Guards Brigade, 1954–56; Commanding Officer, 1st Battalion Scots Guards, 1957; Lt-Col comd Scots Guards, 1960; Colonel AQ Scottish Command, 1962–63; Imperial Defence Coll., 1964; Brigade Comdr, 152 Highland Brigade, 1965–66; Chief, SHAPEX and Exercise Branch SHAPE, 1967–68; GOC Yorkshire District, 1969–70; GOC and British Comdt, Berlin, 1970–73; retd. A Dep-Chm. of Cttees and Dep. Speaker, House of Lords. Ensign, Queen's Body Guard for Scotland, Royal Company of Archers. Pres., ACFA, 1975–82; Dep. Grand Pres., British Commonwealth Ex-Services League, 1976–86. Pres., RoSPA, 1982–86. Cdre, RYS, 1974–80. GCStJ 1986 (KStJ 1985); Lord Prior, Order of St John of Jerusalem, 1986–88 (Vice Chancellor, 1984–86). *Heir:* s Lord Greenock, *b* 30 Nov. 1952. *Address:* Moor Hatches, West Amesbury, Salisbury, Wilts SP4 7BH. *Clubs:* Brooks's; Royal Yacht Squadron (Cowes).
Died 15 June 1999.

CATO, Sir Arnott Samuel, KCMG 1983; Kt 1977; President of the Senate of Barbados, 1976–86; *b* St Vincent, 24 Sept. 1912. *Educ:* St Vincent Grammar Sch. (St Vincent Scholar, 1930); Edinburgh Univ. (MB, ChB). Returned to St Vincent; Asst Resident Surgeon, Colonial Hosp., 1936–37; Ho. Surg., Barbados Gen. Hosp., 1937–41; private practice from 1941; Vis. Surgeon, Barbados Gen. Hosp., later Queen Elizabeth Hosp., and Chm. Med. Staff Cttee, 1965–70. Past Pres., Barbados Br. BMA; Chm., Barbados Public Service Commn, 1972–76. Prime Minister's Nominee, Senate of Barbados, following Gen. Election of Sept. 1976; Actg Governor Gen. for periods in 1976, 1980, 1981, 1983, 1984, 1985 and 1986; PC (Barbados) 1976–87. Hon. LLD Univ. of West Indies, 1978. *Address:* Little Kent, Kent, Christ Church, Barbados. *Died 19 Feb. 1998.*

CATO, Rt Hon. (Robert) Milton; PC 1981; barrister; Leader of the Opposition, St Vincent and the Grenadines, since 1984 (Prime Minister, 1979–84); *b* 3 June 1915; *m* 1951, Lucy Claxton. *Educ:* St Vincent Grammar Sch. Called to the Bar, Middle Temple, 1948; in private practice. Served War of 1939–45, Canadian Army. Leader, St Vincent Labour Party; Premier of St Vincent, 1967–72, 1974–79; former Minister of Finance. Mem., Kingstown

Town Bd, 1952–59 (Chm., 1952–53); former Mem., Public Service Commn. A Governor, Caribbean Reg. Develt Bank for St Vincent. Former Pres., St Vincent Cricket Assoc. *Address:* PO Box 138, Kingstown, St Vincent and the Grenadines. *Club:* Kingstown.
Died 10 Feb. 1997.

CATTELL, George Harold Bernard; Group Managing Director, FMC, 1978–84; Chief Executive, NFU Holdings Ltd, since 1978; Director, Agricultural Credit Corporation, since 1980; *b* 23 March 1920; *s* of H. W. K. Cattell; *m* 1951, Agnes Jean Hardy; three *s* one *d. Educ:* Royal Grammar Sch., Colchester. Served Regular Army, 1939–58; psc 1954; despatches, Malaya, 1957; retired as Major, RA. Asst Director, London Engineering Employers' Assoc., 1958–60; Group Industrial Relations Officer, H. Stevenson & Sons, 1960–61; Director, Personnel and Manufacturing, Rootes Motors Ltd, 1961–68; Managing Director, Humber Ltd, Chm., Hills Precision Diecasting Ltd, Chm., Thrupp & Maberly Ltd, 1965–68; Dir, Manpower and Productivity Services, Dept of Employment and Productivity, 1968–70; Dir-Gen., NFU, 1970–78. Member Council: Industrial Soc. 1965–84; CBI, 1970–84. FRSA; FIMgt. AMN 1958. *Recreations:* tennis, fishing. *Address:* Little Cheveney, Yalding, Kent ME18 6DY. *T:* Hunton (01622) 820365. *Club:* Institute of Directors. *Died 13 March 1996.*

CAUSEY, Prof. Gilbert, FRCS; retired; Sir William Collins Professor of Anatomy, Royal College of Surgeons, Professor of Anatomy, University of London, and Conservator of Hunterian Museum, 1952–70; *b* 8 Oct. 1907; 2nd *s* of George and Ada Causey; *m* 1935, Elizabeth, *d* of late F. J. L. Hickinbotham, JP, and Mrs Hickinbotham; two *s* three *d. Educ:* Wigan Grammar Sch.; University of Liverpool (MB, ChB (1st Hons), 1930; DSc 1964). MRCS, LRCP 1930; FRCS 1933; FDSRCS 1971. Gold Medallist in Anatomy, Surgery, Medicine, and Obstetrics and Gynæcology; Lyon Jones Scholar and various prizes. Member of Anatomical and Physiological Societies. Asst Surgeon, Walton Hospital, Liverpool, 1935; Lecturer in Anatomy, University College, London, 1948; Rockefeller Foundation Travelling Fellow, 1950. John Hunter Medal, 1964; Keith Medal, 1970. *Publications:* The Cell of Schwann, 1960; Electron Microscopy, 1962; contributions to various scientific texts and journals. *Recreation:* music. *Address:* West Gosland Down, near Winkleigh, Devon EX19 8DN. *T:* (01837) 83353.
Died 25 Aug. 1996.

CAVE, Sir Charles (Edward Coleridge), 4th Bt *cr* 1896, of Sidbury Manor, Sidbury, co. Devon; JP; DL; *b* 28 Feb. 1927; *o s* of Sir Edward Charles Cave, 3rd Bt, and Betty (*d* 1979), *o d* of late Rennell Coleridge, Salston, Ottery St Mary; *S* father, 1946; *m* 1957, Mary Elizabeth, *yr d* of late John Francis Gore, CVO, TD; four *s. Educ:* Eton. FRICS. Lieut The Devonshire Regt, 1946–48. CC Devon, 1955–64; High Sheriff of Devonshire, 1969. JP Devon 1972, DL Devon 1977. *Heir: s* John Charles Cave [*b* 8 Sept. 1958; *m* 1984, Carey Diana, *er d* of John Lloyd, Langport, Somerset; two *s* one *d*]. *Address:* Sidbury Manor, Sidmouth, Devon EX10 0QE. *T:* (01395) 597207. *Died 1 Nov. 1997.*

CAVE, Sir (Charles) Philip H.; *see* Haddon-Cave.

CAVE, John Arthur, FCIB; Chairman: Midland Bank Finance Corporation Ltd, 1975–79; Midland Montagu Leasing Ltd, 1975–79; Forward Trust Ltd, 1975–79; Director, Midland Bank Ltd, 1974–79; *b* 30 Jan. 1915; *s* of Ernest Cave and Eva Mary Cave; *m* 1937, Peggy Pauline, *y d* of Frederick Charles Matthews Browne; two *s* two *d. Educ:* Loughborough Grammar Sch. FCIB (FIB 1962). Served War, Royal Tank Regt, 1940–46. Entered Midland Bank, Eye, Suffolk, 1933; Manager,

Threadneedle Street Office, 1962–64; Jt Gen. Man., 1965–72; Asst Chief Gen. Man., 1972–74; Dep. Chief Gen. Man., 1974–75; Dir, Midland Bank Trust Co. Ltd, 1972–76. Mem. Council, Inst. of Bankers, 1967–75 (Dep. Chm., 1973–75). Hon. Captain and Founder, Midland Bank Sailing Club (Cdre, 1967–75). *Recreation:* sailing. *Address:* Dolphin House, Centre Cliff, Southwold, Suffolk IP18 6EN. *T:* (01502) 722232. *Club:* Royal Norfolk and Suffolk Yacht (Lowestoft). *Died 28 Jan. 1998.*

CAWLEY, Sir Charles (Mills), Kt 1965; CBE 1957 (OBE 1946); Chief Scientist, Ministry of Power, 1959–67; a Civil Service Commissioner, 1967–69; *b* 17 May 1907; *s* of John and Emily Cawley, Gillingham, Kent; *m* 1934, Florence Mary Ellaline (*d* 1996), *d* of James Shepherd, York; one *d. Educ:* Sir Joseph Williamson's Mathematical Sch., Rochester; Imperial Coll. of Science and Technology (Royal College of Sci.). ARCS, BSc (First Cl. Hons in Chem.) 1928; DIC, MSc 1929; PhD 1932; FRSC (FRIC 1943); DSc London, 1950; SFInstF (FInstF 1953). Fellow, Imperial Coll. of Science and Technology. Fuel Research Station, DSIR, 1929–53; Imperial Defence Coll., 1949; a Dir, Headquarters, DSIR, 1953–59. Chm., Admiralty Fuels and Lubricants Advisory Cttee, 1957–64. Melchett Medal, Inst. of Fuel, 1968. FRSA. *Publications:* papers in various scientific and technical journals.
Died 8 Nov. 2000.

CAWLEY, Prof. Robert Hugh, PhD; FRCP, FRCPsych; Professor of Psychological Medicine, University of London, at King's College School of Medicine and Dentistry (formerly King's College Hospital Medical School), and Institute of Psychiatry, and Consultant Psychiatrist, King's College Hospital, 1975–89; then Emeritus Professor; *b* 16 Aug. 1924; *yr s* of Robert Ernest Cawley and Alice Maud (*née* Taylor); *m* 1985, Elizabeth Ann, *d* of Eugene Malachy Doris and Mary Doris (*née* Crummie). *Educ:* Solihull Sch.; Univ. of Birmingham (BSc Hons Zool., PhD, MB, ChB); Univ. of London (DPM). FRCP 1975; FRCPsych 1971, Hon. FRCPsych 1990. University of Birmingham: Res. Scholar, 1947; Res. Fellow, 1949; Halley Stewart Res. Fellow, 1954; Honn Phys. and Surg., Queen Elizabeth Hosp., Birmingham, 1956–57; Registrar, then Sen. Registrar, Bethlem Royal and Maudsley Hosps, 1957–60; Clin. Lectr, Inst. of Psych., 1960–62; Sen. Lectr and First Asst in Psych., Univ. of Birmingham, and Hon. Consultant, United Birm. Hosps and Birm. RHB, 1962–67; Phys., 1967–75, and Consultant Psychiatrist, 1967–89, Bethlem Royal and Maudsley Hosps. Consultant Advr (Psychiatry) to DHSS, 1984–89; Civilian Advr in Psychiatry to RAF, 1986–89. Mem., MRC, 1979–83 (Chm., Neurosciences Bd, 1979–81). Chief Examnr, Royal Coll. of Psychiatrists, 1981–88. *Publications:* papers on biological, medical and psychiatric subjects in scientific books and jls. *Club:* Athenæum.
Died 21 April 1999.

CAWS, Genevra Fiona Penelope Victoria, (Mrs J. W. O. Curtis); QC 1991; *b* 21 Feb 1949; *d* of Richard Byron Caws, CVO, CBE, FRICS and Fiona Ruth Muriel Elton Caws; *m* 1985, James William Ockford Curtis, QC; one *d. Educ:* Notting Hill and Ealing High School; Lady Margaret Hall, Oxford (MA Jurisp.). Called to the Bar, Inner Temple, 1970, Bencher, 1996. *Recreations:* fishing, ski-ing, sheep breeding. *Address:* 4/5 Gray's Inn Square, Gray's Inn, WC1R 5AY. *T:* (0171) 404 5252.
Died 14 April 1997.

CAWS, Richard Byron, CVO 1997; CBE 1984; FRICS; Chairman, Caws & Morris Ltd, Chartered Surveyors, London, since 1987; Senior Property Adviser, BZW Property Advisory Group, since 1993; *b* 9 March 1927; *s* of Maxwell and Edith S. Caws; *m* 1948, Fiona Muriel Ruth Elton Darling; one *s* one *d* (and one *s* one *d* decd). FRICS 1949. Partner, Chartered Surveyors: Nightingale

Page & Bennett, Kingston upon Thames, 1944–60; Debenham Tewson & Chinnocks, 1961–87. Sen. Consultant (Real Estate), Goldman Sachs Internat. Corp. (London), 1987–93. Non-exec. Dir, Allied London Properties, 1995–. Crown Estate Comr, 1971–96. Member: Commn for the New Towns, 1976–96 (Chm., Property Cttee, 1978–94; Dep. Chm., CNT Land, 1994–96); Dobry Cttee on Review of the Develt Control System, 1973–75; DoE Adv. Gp on Commercial Property Develt, 1973–77; DoE Property Adv. Gp, 1978–88. Dir, British Sailors' Soc., 1965–. Gov., Royal Agricl Coll., 1985–88; Mem. Council, Queen's Coll., Harley St, 1984–. Master, Worshipful Co. of Chartered Surveyors, 1982–83; Chm., Jun. Orgn, RICS, 1959–60. *Recreations:* sailing, travel. *Address:* 36 Mount Park Road, Ealing, W5 2RS. *Clubs:* Boodle's, Royal Thames Yacht, Little Ship.

Died 13 May 1997.

CAYZER, Baron *cr* 1982 (Life Peer), of St Mary Axe in the City of London; **William Nicholas Cayzer;** Bt 1921; Chairman: British and Commonwealth Shipping Co. Ltd, 1958–87; Caledonia Investments PLC, 1958–94; *b* 21 Jan. 1910; *s* of Sir August Cayzer, 1st Bt, and Ina Frances (*d* 1935), 2nd *d* of William Stancombe, Blounts Ct, Wilts; *S* to father's baronetcy, 1943; *m* 1935, Elizabeth Catherine (*d* 1995), *d* of late Owain Williams and *g d* of Morgan Stuart Williams, Aberpergwm, Glamorgan; two *d*. *Educ:* Eton; Corpus Christi Coll., Cambridge. Director: Clan Line Steamers Ltd, 1938–87 (Chm.); Cayzer, Irvine & Co. Ltd, 1939–87 (Chm.); Union-Castle Mail Steamship Co. Ltd and associated cos, 1956–87 (Chm.); Air Hldgs Ltd, 1962–87 (Chm.); Meldrum Investment Trust, 1971 (Chm.). Chm. Liverpool Steamship Owners Association, 1944–45; Pres. Chamber of Shipping of the UK, 1959; Pres. Inst. of Marine Engineers, 1963. Chairman: Gen. Council of British Shipping, 1959; Chamber of Shipping's British Liner Cttee, 1960–63; Mem., MoT Shipping Adv. Panel, 1962–64; sometime Mem. Mersey Dock and Harbour Board; sometime Mem. National Dock Labour Board. Prime Warden, Shipwrights' Company, 1969. *Heir* (to baronetcy)*:* none. *Address:* The Grove, Walsham-le-Willows, Suffolk IP31 3AD. *T:* (01359) 259263; 95j Eaton Square, SW1W 9AQ. *T:* (020) 7235 5551. *Club:* Brooks's. *Died 16 April 1999 (Btcy ext).*

CELIBIDACHE, Sergiu; Chief Conductor, Munich Philharmonic Orchestra, since 1979; Composer and Guest Conductor to leading orchestras all over the world; *b* Rumania, 28 June 1912; *s* of Demosthene Celibidache; *m* Maria Celibidache. *Educ:* Jassy; Berlin. Doctorate in mathematics, musicology, philosophy and Buddhist religion. Conductor and Artistic Dir, Berlin Philharmonic Orchestra, 1946–51. Member: Royal Acad. of Music, Sweden; Acad. of Music, Bologna. German Critics' Prize, 1953; Berlin City Art Prize, 1955; Grand Cross of Merit, Federal Republic of Germany, 1954. *Recreations:* skiing, water-skiing. *Address:* Munich Philharmonic Orchestra, Gasteig-Kulturzentrum, Kellerstrasse 4/III, 81667 Munich, Germany. *Died 14 Aug. 1996.*

CHABAN-DELMAS, Jacques Pierre Michel; Commandeur de la Légion d'Honneur; Compagnon de la Libération; Deputy, Department of Gironde, 1946–97; Mayor of Bordeaux, 1947–95; *b* Paris, 7 March 1915; *s* of Pierre Delmas and Georgette Delmas (*née* Barrouin); *m* 1st, Odette Hamelin (marr. diss.); one *s* two *d*; 2nd, 1947, Mme François Geoffray (*née* Marie Antoinette Iōn) (*d* 1970); one *s*; 3rd, 1971, Mme Micheline Chavelet. *Educ:* Lycée Lakanal, Sceaux; Faculté de Droit, Paris; Ecole Libre des Sciences Politiques (Dip.). Licencié en droit. Journalist with l'Information, 1933. Served War of 1939–45: Army, 1939–40 (an Alpine Regt); joined the Resistance; *nom de guerre* of Chaban added (Compagnon de la Libération, Croix de Guerre); attached to Min. of Industrial Production, 1941; Inspector of Finance, 1943; Brig.-Gen., 1944; Nat. Mil. Deleg. (co-ord. mil. planning), Resistance, 1944; Inspector Gen. of Army, 1944; Sec.-Gen., Min. of Inf., 1945. Deputy for Gironde (Radical), 1946. Leader of Gaullist group (Républicains Sociaux) in Nat. Assembly, 1953–56; also Mem., Consultative Assembly of Council of Europe; Minister of State, 1956–57; Minister of Nat. Defence, 1957–58; Pres., Nat. Assembly, France, 1958–69, 1978–81 and 1986–88; Prime Minister, June 1969–July 1972. Président: Communauté urbain de Bordeaux, 1983–95; Conseil régional d'Aquitaine, 1985–88. *Publications:* L'ardeur, 1975; De Gaulle, 1980; La Libération, 1984; Les Compagnons, 1986; Aliénor d'Aquitaine, 1987; Montaigne, 1992; Mémoires pour Demain, 1997. *Address:* 1 rue de Lille, Paris 75007, France. *Died 10 Nov. 2000.*

CHACKSFIELD, Air Vice-Marshal Sir Bernard (Albert), KBE 1968 (OBE 1945); CB 1961; CEng, FRAeS; *b* 13 April 1913; *s* of Edgar Chacksfield, Ilford, Essex; *m* 1st, 1937, Myrtle, (*d* 1984), *d* of Walter Matthews, Rickmansworth, Herts; two *s* two *d* (and one *s* decd); 2nd, 1985, Mrs Elizabeth Beatrice Ody. *Educ:* Co. High Sch., Ilford; RAF, Halton; RAF Coll., Cranwell. CEng; FRAeS 1968. Service: NW Frontier, 1934–37; UK, India, Burma, Singapore, 1939–45 (OBE); Air Min., 1945–48; Western Union (NATO), Fontainebleau, 1949–51; RAF Staff Coll., 1951–53; Fighter Command, 1954–55; Director, Guided Weapons (trials), Min. of Supply, 1956–58; IDC, 1959; SASO, Tech. Trng Comd, RAF, 1960; AOC No 22 Group RAF Technical Training Command, 1960–62; Comdt-Gen., RAF Regiment and Inspector of Ground Defence, 1963–68; retired 1968. Chm., Burma Star Assoc. Council, 1977– (Vice-Chm., 1974–76). Chm., Bd of Management, Royal Masonic Hosp., 1988–92 (Mem., 1987–88); Pres., Bedstone College, 1991– (Governor, 1970–90; Chm. Govs, 1978–90); Chm. Govs, Wye Valley Sch. (formerly Deyncourt Sch.), 1978–89 (Governor, 1977). Pres., Bourne End Community Assoc., 1995–. Order of Cloud and Banner with special rosette (Chinese), 1941. *Recreations:* scouting (HQ Comr, Air Activities, 1959–72; Chief Comr for England, 1968–77), sailing, fencing (Pres. RAF Fencing Union, 1963–68), gliding, travel, model aircraft (Pres. British Model Flying Assoc. (formerly Soc. Model Aircraft Engrs, GB), 1965–), modern Pentathlon (Pres., RAF Pentathlon Assoc., 1963–68), shooting (Chm. RAF Small Arms Assoc., 1963–68), swimming, youth work, amateur dramatics. *Address:* 8 Rowan House, Bourne End, Bucks SL8 5TG. *T:* (01628) 520829. *Club:* Royal Air Force. *Died 27 Dec. 1999.*

CHADWICK, Helen; artist; *b* 18 May 1953. *Educ:* Brighton Poly.; Chelsea Sch. of Art. Solo exhibitions, 1990– include: Meat Lamps, Chicago and NY, 1990; Viral Landscapes, Canada, Germany and Mus. of Modern Art, Oxford, 1990; De Light, Philadelphia, 1991; Im Fleischgarten, Germany, 1992; Trophies, Austria, 1993; Effluvia, Germany, Spain and Serpentine Gall., 1994; Poesies, Austria, 1994; Bad Blooms, NY, 1995. *Address:* c/o Zelda Cheatle Gallery, 8 Cecil Court, WC2N 4HE. *T:* 0171–836 0506. *Died 15 March 1996.*

CHADWICK, John, LittD; FBA 1967; Perceval Maitland Laurence Reader in Classics, University of Cambridge, 1969–84; Hon. Fellow, Downing College, Cambridge, since 1984 (Collins Fellow, 1960–84); *b* 21 May 1920; *yr s* of late Fred Chadwick; *m* 1947, Joan Isobel Hill; one *s*. *Educ:* St Paul's Sch.; Corpus Christi Coll., Cambridge. MA, LittD. Editorial Asst, Oxford Latin Dictionary, Clarendon Press, 1946–52; Asst Lectr in Classics, 1952–54, Lectr in Classics, 1954–66, Reader in Greek Language, 1966–69, Univ. of Cambridge. Corresponding Member: Deutsches Archäologisches Inst., 1957; Austrian

Acad. of Scis, 1974; Associé étranger, Acad. des Inscriptions et Belles-Lettres, Institut de France, 1985; For. Mem., Accademia Nazionale dei Lincei, 1992. Pres., Swedenborg Soc., 1987–88; Hon. Councillor, Athens Archaeol Soc., 1988 (Hon. Fellow, 1974); Hon. Dr of Philosophical Sch., University of Athens, 1958; Hon. DLitt Trinity Coll., Dublin, 1971; Hon. Dr: Université Libre de Bruxelles, 1969; Euskal Herriko Unibertsitatea, Vitoria, Spain, 1985; Univ. of Salzburg, 1990. Medal of J. E. Purkyně Univ., Brno, 1966; Ehrenzeichen für Wissenschaft und Kunst, Austria, 1992; Antonio Feltrinelli Prize, Accademia Nationale dei Lincei, 1997. Comdr, Order of the Phoenix, Greece, 1984. *Publications:* (jtly) Documents in Mycenaean Greek, 1956, rev. edn 1973; The Decipherment of Linear B, 1958, 2nd edn 1967 (trans. into 13 languages); The Pre-history of the Greek Language (in Cambridge Ancient History), 1963; The Mycenaean World, 1976 (trans. into 6 languages); (ed jtly) Corpus of Mycenaean Inscriptions from Knossos, Vol. I, 1986, Vol. II, 1990, Vol. III, 1997; Linear B and Related Scripts, 1987; Lexicographica Graeca, 1996; *translations:* (jtly) The Medical Works of Hippocrates, 1950; E. Swedenborg, The True Christian Religion, 1988; E. Swedenborg, Conjugial Love, 1996; E. Swedenborg, The Worlds in Space, 1997; articles in learned jls on Mycenaean Greek. *Recreation:* travel. *Address:* 75 Gough Way, Cambridge CB3 9LN. *Died 24 Nov. 1998.*

CHADWICK, Robert Everard; Director, Leeds Permanent Building Society, 1974–86 (President, 1983–85); *b* 20 Oct. 1916; *s* of Robert Agar Chadwick and Aline Chadwick; *m* 1948, (Audrey) Monica Procter; two *s* one *d. Educ:* Oundle; Leeds Univ. (LLB). Served RA, 1939–46. Solicitor, 1938–82; Director: J. Hepworth & Son, subseq. Hepworth & Chadwick, 1946–81 (Chm., 1956–81); John Waddington, 1954–77 (Chm., 1969–77); Magnet Joinery, 1969–77; Robert Glew & Co., 1969–77; W Riding Reg. Bd, Barclays Bank, 1972–82. *Recreations:* hill walking, fishing. *Address:* Baxters Fold, Cracoe, Skipton, N Yorks BD23 6LB. *T:* (01756) 730233. *Club:* Leeds (Leeds). *Died 28 Jan. 2000.*

CHALDECOTT, John Anthony; Keeper, Science Museum Library, South Kensington, 1961–76; *b* 16 Feb. 1916; *o s* of Wilfrid James and Mary Eleanor Chaldecott; *m* 1940, Kathleen Elizabeth Jones; one *d. Educ:* Latymer Upper Sch., Hammersmith; Brentwood Sch.; Borough Road Coll., Isleworth; University College, London. BSc 1938, MSc 1949, PhD 1972. FInstP; CPhys. Meteorological Branch, RAFVR, 1939–45 (despatches). Lecturer, Acton Technical Coll., 1945–48; entered Science Museum as Asst Keeper, Dept of Physics, 1949; Deputy Keeper and Secretary to Advisory Council, 1957. Pres., British Society for the History of Science, 1972–74. *Publications:* Josiah Wedgwood: the arts and sciences united (with J. des Fontaines and J. Tindall), 1978; Science Museum handbooks; papers on the history of science. *Address:* 1 Saxon Court, Bull Lane, Maldon, Essex CM9 4HS. *Died 2 May 1998.*

CHALLIS, Dr Anthony Arthur Leonard, CBE 1980; consultant; Chief Scientist, Department of Energy, 1980–83; *b* 24 Dec. 1921; *s* of Leonard Hough Challis and Dorothy (*née* Busby); *m* 1947, L. Beryl Hedley; two *d. Educ:* Newcastle upon Tyne Royal Grammar Sch.; King's Coll., Univ. of Durham. 1st cl. hons BSc Chemistry; PhD. Imperial Chemical Industries: joined Billingham Div., 1946; Research Man., HOC Div., 1962; Research Dir, Mond Div., 1966; Head of Corporate Lab., 1967; Gen. Man. Planning, 1970; Sen. Vice-Pres., ICI Americas Inc., 1975–76; Dir, Polymer Engrg, SRC, subseq. SERC, 1976–80. Dir, Wyvern Waste Services, 1992–. Mem., SERC (formerly SRC), 1973–83; Pres., PRI, 1985–87 (Chm. Council, 1983–85). Associate Prof., Wolfson Unit

on Processing Materials, Brunel Univ., 1968–; lectr on energy, waste and polymer engrg, Dep. Chm., Watt Cttee on Energy. Mem. Somerset Br. Cttee, CPRE. Mem. Court, Univ. of Stirling, 1968–74. Mem., Horners' Co. *Publications:* contrib. chem, energy and managerial jls. *Recreations:* music, walking, narrow boat. *Address:* Classeys, Low Ham, Langport, Somerset TA10 9DP. *Died 5 March 1996.*

CHAMBERS, George Michael; Prime Minister and Minister of Finance and Planning, Trinidad and Tobago, 1981–86; *b* 4 Oct. 1928; *m* 1956, Juliana; one *d. Educ:* Nelson Street Boys' RC Sch.; Burke's Coll.; Osmond High Sch.; Wolsey Hall, Oxford. MP (People's National Movement), St Ann's, 1966–86; Parly Sec., Min. of Finance, 1966; Minister of Public Utilities and Housing, 1969; Minister of State in Min. of National Security and Minister of State in Min. of Finance, Planning and Develt, 1970; Minister of National Security, Nov. 1970; Minister of Finance, Planning and Development, 1971–73; Minister of Finance, 1973–75; Minister of Educn and Culture, 1975–76; Minister of Industry and Commerce and Minister of Agriculture, Lands and Fisheries, 1976–81. Formerly, Asst Gen. Sec. and Mem. Central Exec., Gen. Council, and Res. and Disciplinary Cttees, People's National Movement. Chm. Bd of Governors, World Bank and IMF, 1973; Governor, Caribbean Develt Bank, 1981. *Died 4 Nov. 1997.*

CHAMPERNOWNE, David Gawen, FBA 1970; Professor of Economics and Statistics, Cambridge University, 1970–78, then Emeritus; Fellow of Trinity College, Cambridge, since 1959; *b* Oxford, 9 July 1912; *s* of late F. G. Champernowne, MA, Bursar of Keble Coll., Oxford; *m* 1948, Wilhelmina Dullaert; two *s. Educ:* The College, Winchester; King's Coll., Cambridge (MA). Asst Lecturer at London Sch. of Economics, 1936–38; Fellow of King's Coll., Cambridge, 1937–40; University Lecturer in Statistics, Cambridge, 1938–40; temp. Civil Servant, 1940–45; Dir of Oxford Univ. Institute of Statistics, 1945–48; Fellow of Nuffield Coll., Oxford, 1945–59; Prof. of Statistics, Oxford Univ., 1948–59; Reader in Economics, Cambridge Univ., 1959–70. Editor, Economic Jl, 1971–76. *Publications:* Uncertainty and Estimation in Economics (3 vols), 1969; The Distribution of Income between Persons, 1973; Economic Inequality and Income Distribution, 1998; sundry articles on mathematics, statistics and economics in learned jls, 1933–. *Address:* Lower Eryl Mor, 22A Victoria Place, Budleigh Salterton, Devon EX9 6JP; Trinity College, Cambridge CB2 1TQ. *Died 19 Aug. 2000.*

CHAN, Chun Hung Jerome; Hon. Mr Justice Jerome Chan; Judge of the High Court of Hong Kong, since 1993; *b* 14 July 1951; *s* of Tan Thye Poh and Chih Pui Fan; *m* 1977, Tang Yiu Kin Grace; two *s* one *d. Educ:* Univ. of Hong Kong (LLB); Postgrad. Cert. in Laws, Dist.). Demonstrator, Dept of Law, Hong Kong Univ., 1974–75; Barrister in private practice, 1976–85; Permanent Magistrate, 1985–87; Presiding Officer, Labour Tribunal, 1987–89; Judge of Dist Court, 1989; Dep. Registrar of Supreme Court, 1990–93. Mem., Law Reform Commn, 1995–. Hong Kong University: Visitor, Faculty of Law, 1991; Hon. Lectr, Dept of Professional Legal Educn, 1992–; Chief External Examiner: Hong Kong and City Univs, 1995–; Dept of Prof. Legal Educn, Univ. of Hong Kong, 1995–; Overseas Lawyers Qualifying Exams, Hong Kong Law Soc., 1995–. *Recreations:* music, photography, sports. *Address:* High Court, Hong Kong. *Died 25 July 1997.*

CHANDLEY, Peter Warren, OBE 1995; MVO 1981; HM Diplomatic Service, retired; Deputy Head of Mission, Bogotá, Colombia, 1992–95; *b* 24 Nov. 1934; *s* of Samuel and Freda Chandley; *m* 1961, Jane Williams. *Educ:*

Manchester Warehousemen and Clerks Orphan School, Cheadle Hulme. Clerk, Min. of Fuel and Power, 1953; Nat. Service, RAF, 1953–55; FO, 1955; served Tripoli, 1955; Kabul, 1958; Havana, 1960; Phnom Penh, 1962; Madagascar, 1966; FCO, 1969; Nairobi, 1972; Kampala, 1976; Oslo, 1977; FCO, 1981; Chargé d'Affaires, Libreville, Gabon, 1984–85; Abidjan, 1986; Amb. to People's Republic of the Congo, 1990–91. Ridder 1st Class, Order of St Olav (Norway), 1981. *Recreations:* bird-watching, reading, conservation activities.

Died 27 June 1996.

CHAPLIN, (Arthur) Hugh, CB 1970; Principal Keeper of Printed Books, British Museum, 1966–70; *b* 17 April 1905; *er s* of late Rev. Herbert F. Chaplin and Florence B. Lusher; *m* 1938, Irene Marcousé (*d* 1990). *Educ:* King's Lynn Grammar Sch.; Bedford Modern Sch.; University Coll., London. Asst Librarian: Reading Univ., 1927–28; Queen's Univ., Belfast, 1928–29; Asst Keeper, Dept of Printed Books, British Museum, 1930–52; Dep. Keeper, 1952–59; Keeper, 1959–66. Exec. Sec., Organizing Cttee of Internat. Conf. on Cataloguing Principles, Paris, 1961; Mem. Council, Library Assoc. 1964–70; Pres., Microfilm Assoc. of GB, 1967–71; Mem. Senate, Univ. of London, 1973–79. Fellow UCL, 1969. *Publications:* Cataloguing Principles and Practice (contrib.), ed M. Piggott, 1954; Tradition and Principle in Library Cataloguing, 1966; GK: 150 Years of the General Catalogue of Printed Books, 1987; contribs to Jl Documentation, Library Assoc. Record, Library Quarterly. *Address:* 41 Ridgmount Gardens, WC1E 7AT. *T:* (0171) 636 7217.

Died 24 Dec. 1996.

CHAPMAN, Prof. Dennis, FRS 1986; Professor of Biophysical Chemistry, Royal Free Hospital School of Medicine, University of London, 1977–93, then Emeritus; *b* 6 May 1927; *s* of George Henry Chapman and Katherine Magnus; *m* 1st, 1949, Elsie Margaret Stephenson (*d* 1989); two *s* one *d*; 2nd, 1993, Françoise Nioukleen Ng. *Educ:* London Univ. (BSc; DSc); Liverpool Univ. (PhD); Cambridge Univ. Comyns Berkeley Fellow, Gonville and Caius Coll., Cambridge, 1960–63; Head of Gen. Research Div., Unilever Ltd, Welwyn, 1963–69; Professor Associate, Biophysical Chem., Sheffield Univ., 1968–76; Sen. Wellcome Trust Research Fellow, Dept of Chemistry, Chelsea Coll., Univ. of London, 1976–77; Royal Free Hospital School of Medicine, London University: Head, Dept of Protein and Molecular Biol., 1988–93; Head of Div. of Basic Med. Scis, 1988–89; Vice Dean, 1990–93. Associate Dir, IRC (Medical Biomaterials), Univ. of London, 1991–. Langmuir Lectr, Amer. Chem. Soc., US, 1992. Founder, and non-exec. Dir, Biocompatibles Ltd, 1984–. Hon. MRCP 1988; First Hon. Mem., Spanish Biophysical Soc., 1991. Hon. DSc: Utrecht, 1976; Meml, Canada, 1980; Pais Vasco, Spain, 1994; Cluj-Napoca, Romania, 1995; Ancona, 1997. Royal Free Hosp. Sch. of Medicine Medal, 1987; Interdisciplinary Award, RSC, 1992; Harden Medal, Biochemical Soc., 1995. *Publications:* Biological Membranes, vol. I–vol. V, 1968–84; 450 scientific publications in biochemical jls. *Recreations:* golf, walking. *Died 28 Oct. 1999.*

CHAPMAN, John Henry Benjamin, CB 1957; CEng; FRINA; RCNC; *b* 28 Dec. 1899; *s* of Robert Henry Chapman and Edith Yeo Chapman (*née* Lillicrap); *m* 1929, Dorothy Rowlerson (*d* 1991); one *s* one *d*. *Educ:* HM Dockyard Sch., Devonport; RNC Greenwich. Dir of Naval Construction, Admiralty, 1958–61. Dir, Fairfield S & E Co. Ltd, 1962–66; Consultant, Upper Clyde Shipbuilders, 1966–68. Mem. of Royal Corps of Naval Constructors, 1922–61; Hon. Vice-Pres., RINA. *Address:* Lordington Park, near Chichester, W Sussex PO18 9DX. *T:* (01243) 377273. *Club:* Bosham Sailing.

Died 25 Feb. 1997.

CHAPMAN, Kathleen Violet, CBE 1956; RRC 1953 (ARRC 1945); QHNS 1953–56; Matron-in-Chief, Queen Alexandra's Royal Naval Nursing Service, 1953–56, retired; *b* 30 May 1903; *d* of late Major H. E. Chapman, CBE, DL Kent, Chief Constable of Kent, and Mrs C. H. J. Chapman. *Educ:* Queen Anne's, Caversham. Trained St Thomas' Hospital, 1928–32. *Died 26 July 1996.*

CHARLES, Leslie Stanley Francis; Director, Birmid Qualcast plc, 1981–88, retired; *b* 28 July 1917; *s* of Samuel Francis Charles and Lena Gwendolyn (*née* Reed); *m* 1941, Henrietta Elizabeth Calvin Thomas; one *s*. *Educ:* Cardiff High Sch.; University Coll. of S Wales and Mon, Univ. of Wales (BScEng London, 1st Cl. Hons). Grad. Engr, Metropolitan Vickers Ltd, 1936–39; Regular Officer, REME, 1939–54; Consultant, Urwick Orr & Partners Ltd, 1954–60; Chief Engr Ops, UKAEA, 1960–63; Dir of Factories, Raleigh Industries Ltd, 1963–66; Man. Dir, Aluminium Wire & Cable Co. Ltd, 1966–68; British Aluminium Co. Ltd: Dep. Man. Dir, 1968–79; Man. Dir, 1979–82. Chm., European Aluminium Assoc., 1981–84. *Recreations:* golf, bridge, music. *Address:* Crana, Claydon Lane, Chalfont St Peter, Bucks SL9 8JU. *T:* (01753) 884290. *Died 12 Dec. 2000.*

CHARLISH, Dennis Norman; Panel Chairman, Civil Service Selection Board, 1978–88 (Resident Chairman, 1975–78); *b* 24 May 1918; *s* of Norman Charlish and Edith (*née* Cherriman); *m* 1941, Margaret Trevor (*d* 1995), *o d* of William Trevor and Margaret Ann Williams, Manchester; one *d*. *Educ:* Brighton Grammar Sch.; London Sch. of Economics (Rosebery Schol., 1947; BSc (Econ) 1st class hons, 1951). Joined Civil Service as Tax Officer, Inland Revenue, 1936; Exec. Officer, Dept of Overseas Trade, 1937; Dep. Armament Supply Officer, Admty, 1941; Principal, BoT, 1949; Asst Secretary, 1959; Imperial Defence Coll., 1963; Under-Sec., BoT, 1967–69; Min. of Technology, 1969–70; Head of Personnel, DTI, 1971–74; Dept of Industry, 1974–75. *Died 4 April 1999.*

CHARLTON, (Foster) Ferrier (Harvey), CBE 1986; DFC 1945; Partner, 1953–88, Senior Partner, 1985–88, Linklaters & Paines, Solicitors; *b* 26 March 1923; *s* of Foster Ferrier Charlton and Esther Naomi French Charlton (*née* Brown); *m* 1950, Doris Winnifred (Lola) Marson; one *s* three *d*. *Educ:* Rugby Sch.; Wadham Coll., Oxford (MA, PPE 1st Cl. 1947). RAFVR (Pilot), 1941–53; served W Africa, India, Ceylon, 8 Sqdn and 200 Sqdn, RAF, 1944–45. Articles with Linklaters & Paines, 1948; qualified as solicitor, 1950. Director: Short Bros, 1958–89; Law Debenture Corp., 1988–95. Member: City/Industry Task Force, CBI, 1987; DTI Companies Acts Wkg Party, 1993–95. *Publications:* legal and gardening articles. *Recreation:* gardening (Pres., Alpine Garden Soc., 1988–91). *Address:* 28 Witches Lane, Riverhead, Sevenoaks, Kent TN13 2AX. *T:* (01732) 453370.

Died 13 Jan. 1999.

CHARLTON, (Frederick) Noel, CB 1961; CBE (mil.) 1946; *b* 4 Dec. 1906; *s* of late Frederick William Charlton and Marian Charlton; *m* 1932, Maud Helen Rudgard; no *c*. *Educ:* Rugby School; Hertford Coll., Oxford Univ. (MA). War Service, 1939–46 (attained rank of Colonel, Gen. List). Admitted a Solicitor, 1932; in private practice as Solicitor in London, 1932–39; joined Treasury Solicitor's Dept, 1946; Principal Asst Solicitor (Litigation), Treasury Solicitor's Dept, 1956–71; Sec., Lord Chancellor's Cttee on Defamation, 1971–74; with Dept of Energy (Treasury Solicitor's Branch), 1975–81, retired. Chairman, Coulsdon and Purley UDC, 1953–54 and 1964–65; Hon. Alderman, London Borough of Croydon. Bronze Star (USA), 1945. *Recreations:* golf, travel. *Address:* 4 Newton Road, Purley, Surrey CR8 3DN. *T:* (020) 8660 2802. *Club:* Army and Navy.

Died 29 March 2000.

CHARLTON, Prof. Thomas Malcolm, FRSE 1973; historian of engineering science; Jackson Professor of Engineering, University of Aberdeen, 1970–79, then Emeritus; *b* 1 Sept. 1923; *s* of William Charlton and Emily May Charlton (*née* Wallbank); *m* 1950, Valerie, *d* of late Dr C. McCulloch, Hexham; two *s* (and one *s* decd). *Educ:* Doncaster Grammar Sch.; Doncaster Tech. Coll.; Derby Tech. Coll.; UC, Nottingham. BSc (Eng) London, 1943; MA Cantab, 1954. Premium apprentice, LNER, 1939–41; Junior Scientific Officer, Min. of Aircraft Prodn, TRE, Malvern, 1943–46; Asst Engr, Merz & McLellan, Newcastle upon Tyne, 1946–54; Univ. Lectr in Engrg, Cambridge, 1954–63; Fellow and Tutor, Sidney Sussex Coll., 1959–63; Prof. of Civil Engrg, Queen's Univ., Belfast, 1963–70; Dean, Faculty of Applied Science, QUB, 1967–70. Vis. Prof. of Civil Engineering, Univ. of Newcastle upon Tyne, 1982–89. FICE, 1964–83; Mem. Council, Instn of Civil Engrs of Ireland, 1965–69. For. Mem., Finnish Acad. of Technical Sciences, 1967. Personal Symposium, Turin Politecnico, 1989. Mem., Bd of Finance, Hereford Dio., 1980–82. *Publications:* Model Analysis of Structures, 1954, new edn 1966; (contrib.) Hydro-electric Engineering Practice, 1958; Energy Principles in Applied Statics, 1959; Analysis of Statically-indeterminate Frameworks, 1961; Principles of Structural Analysis, 1969, new edn 1977, Arabic edn 1983; Energy Principles in Theory of Structures, 1973; (contrib.) The Works of I. K. Brunel, 1976; A History of Theory of Structures in the Nineteenth Century, 1982; (contrib.) Encyclopaedia of Building Technology, 1986; Professor Emeritus (autobiog.), 1991; (contrib.) Rendicanti Lincei, 1991; contrib. Children's Britannica; papers on energy principles, hist. of structures. *Recreations:* ecclesiastical history, golf. *Address:* The Old School House, 72 North Street, Burwell, Cambridge CB5 0BB. *T:* (01638) 741351. *Club:* Royal Northern and University (Aberdeen).
Died 1 Feb. 1997.

CHARNOCK, Henry, CBE 1992; FRS 1976; Professor of Physical Oceanography, 1966–71 and 1978–86 (then Emeritus), Deputy Vice-Chancellor, 1982–84, Southampton University; *b* 25 Dec. 1920; *s* of Henry Charnock and Mary Gray McLeod; *m* 1946, Eva Mary Dickinson; one *s* two *d*. *Educ:* Queen Elizabeth's Grammar Sch., Blackburn; Municipal Techn. Coll., Blackburn; Imperial Coll., London. Staff, Nat. Inst. of Oceanography, 1949–58 and 1959–66; Reader in Physical Oceanography, Imperial Coll., 1958–59; Dir, Inst. of Oceanographic Scis (formerly Nat. Inst. of Oceanography), 1971–78. President: Internat. Union of Geodesy and Geophysics, 1971–75; RMetS, 1982–84; Vice-Pres., Scientific Cttee on Oceanic Res., 1980–82 (Sec., 1978–80); Mem., Royal Commn on Environmental Pollution, 1985–94. *Publications:* papers in meteorological and oceanographic jls. *Address:* 5 Links View Way, Southampton SO16 7GR. *T:* (01703) 769629. *Died 28 Nov. 1997.*

CHARTERIS OF AMISFIELD, Baron *cr* 1978 (Life Peer), of Amisfield, county of East Lothian; **Martin Michael Charles Charteris,** GCB 1977 (KCB 1972; CB 1958); GCVO 1976 (KCVO 1962; MVO 1953); QSO 1978; OBE 1946; PC 1972; Royal Victorian Chain, 1992; Provost of Eton, 1978–91; Chairman of Trustees, National Heritage Memorial Fund, 1980–92; *b* 7 Sept. 1913; 2nd *s* of Hugo Francis, Lord Elcho (killed in action, 1916) and Lady Violet Manners, *d* of 8th Duke of Rutland, KG; *g s* of 11th Earl of Wemyss; *m* 1944, Hon. Mary Gay Hobart Margesson, *yr d* of 1st Viscount Margesson, MC, PC; two *s* one *d*. *Educ:* Eton; RMC Sandhurst. Lieut KRRC, 1933; served War of 1939–45; Lt-Col, 1944. Private Secretary to Princess Elizabeth, 1950–52; Asst Private Secretary to the Queen, 1952–72; Private Secretary to the Queen and Keeper of HM's Archives, 1972–77; a Permanent Lord in Waiting to the Queen, 1978–. Director: Claridge's Hotel,

1978–95; Connaught Hotel, 1978–97; De La Rue Co., 1978–85; Rio Tinto Zinc Corp., 1978–84. Trustee, BM, 1979–89. Chm. of Trustees, Police Convalescence and Rehabilitation Trust, 1986–96. Pres., Prayer Book Soc., 1987–. Hon. RA 1981. Hon. DCL Oxon, 1978; Hon. LLD London, 1981. *Recreation:* sculpting. *Address:* Wood Stanway House, Wood Stanway, Cheltenham, Glos GL54 5PG. *T:* (01386) 584480; 11 Kylestrome House, Cundy Street, SW1W 9JT. *T:* (020) 7730 2959. *Club:* White's.
Died 23 Dec. 1999.

CHATER, Nancy, CBE 1974; Headmistress, Stanley Park Comprehensive School, Liverpool, 1964–75, retired; *b* 18 July 1915; *d* of William John and Ellen Chater. *Educ:* Northampton Sch. for Girls; Girton Coll., Cambridge (Math. Schol., Bell Exhibr, MA); Cambridge Trng Coll. for Women (CertEd). Asst Mistress, Huddersfield College Grammar Sch. for Boys, 1940–42; Asst Mistress, Fairfield High Sch. for Girls, Manchester, 1942–45; Sen. Maths Mistress, Thistley Hough High Sch., Stoke on-Trent, 1945–49; Sen. Lectr, Newland Park Trng Coll. for Teachers, 1949–55; Dep. Head, Whitley Abbey Comprehensive Sch., Coventry, 1955–63. *Publications:* contrib. Math. Gazette. *Address:* 18 Hardingstone Lane, Hardingstone, Northampton NN4 6DE. *Club:* Soroptimist International. *Died 14 June 2000.*

CHAUDHURI, Nirad Chandra, Hon. CBE 1992; FRSL; FRAS; author and broadcaster; *b* Bengal, 23 Nov. 1897; *s* of Upendra Narayan Chaudhuri and Sushila, Banagram, Bengal; *m* 1932, Amiya Dhar (*d* 1994); three *s*. *Educ:* Calcutta University. BA (Hons) 1918. Resident in UK, 1970–. University Lectures included: Chicago; Texas Univ. at Austin; Pennsylvania; Potsdam; Boston; Oxford; Canadian Univs. DUniv Stirling, 1978; Hon. DLitt Oxon, 1990. Broadcasting on radio and TV; television appearances included: A Brown Man in Search of Civilization (feature on life), 1972; Everyman, 1983; Springing Tiger, 1984. *Publications:* The Autobiography of an unknown Indian, 1951, A Passage to England, 1959; The Continent of Circe, 1965 (Duff Cooper Meml Prize, 1966); The Intellectual in India, 1967; Woman in Bengali Life, 1967 (in Bengali language); To Live or not to Live, 1970; Scholar Extraordinary: life of F. Max Muller, 1974; Clive of India, 1975; Culture in the Vanity Bag, 1976; Hinduism, 1979, Italian trans. 1980, Japanese trans. 1985; Thy Hand, Great Anarch!, 1987; Three Horsemen of the New Apocalypse, 1997; contribs to The Times, TLS, The Daily Telegraph, Guardian, London Magazine, Encounter, The New English Review, Spectator, The Atlantic Monthly (USA), Pacific Affairs (USA), major Indian newspapers and magazines. *Recreations:* music, gardening, walks. *Address:* 20 Lathbury Road, Oxford OX2 7AU. *T:* (01865) 557683. *Died 1 Aug. 1999.*

CHEETHAM, John Frederick Thomas, CB 1978; Secretary, Exchequer and Audit Department, 1975–79; *b* 27 March 1919; *s* of late James Oldham Cheetham, MA, BCom; *m* 1943, Yvonne Marie Smith; one *s* one *d*. *Educ:* Penarth Grammar Sch.; Univ. of Wales. War Service, Royal Artillery, 1939–46. Entered Exchequer and Audit Dept, 1938; Office of Parly Comr for Administration, 1966–69; Dep. Sec., Exchequer and Audit Dept, 1973–74. *Recreations:* tennis, food and wine. *Address:* 70 Chatsworth Road, Croydon, Surrey CR0 1HB. *T:* (020) 8688 3740. *Died 30 Nov. 1999.*

CHELMER, Baron *cr* 1963 (Life Peer), of Margaretting, co. Essex; **Eric Cyril Boyd Edwards,** Kt 1954; MC 1944; TD; JP; DL; *b* 9 Oct. 1914; *s* of Col C. E. Edwards, DSO, MC, TD, DL, JP, and Mrs J. Edwards; *m* 1939, Enid, *d* of F. W. Harvey; one *s*. *Educ:* Felsted Sch. Solicitor, 1937; LLB (London) 1937. Served Essex Yeomanry, 1940–54 (MC), Lieut-Col Commanding, 1945–46. Chm., Provident Financial Gp, 1976–83 (Dir, 1970–83); Chm. and Dir,

Greycoat Group, 1977–85; Director: NEM Group, 1970–86; NEL Assurance, 1970–86. National Union of Conservative Associations: Chm., 1956; Pres., 1967; Chm., Review Cttee, 1970–73; Chm., Nat. Exec. Cttee of Conservative and Unionist Assoc., 1957–65; Conservative Party: Jt Treas., 1965–77; Mem. Adv. Cttee on Policy, 1956–85. Member: Political Cttee, Carlton Club, 1961; Cttee of Musicians' Benevolent Fund; Ralph Vaughan Williams Trust. JP Essex, 1950; DL Essex, 1971. *Recreation:* "improving". *Address:* Peacocks, Margaretting, Essex CM4 9HY. *Clubs:* Carlton, Royal Ocean Racing. *Died 3 March 1997.*

CHELMSFORD, 3rd Viscount *cr* 1921, of Chelmsford, co. Essex; **Frederic Jan Thesiger;** Baron Chelmsford 1858; Lloyd's Insurance Broker, retired; Director, Willis Faber plc, 1979–91; *b* 7 March 1931; *s* of 2nd Viscount Chelmsford and Gilian (*d* 1978), *d* of late Arthur Nevile Lubbock; *S* father, 1970; *m* 1958, Clare Rendle, *d* of Dr G. R. Rolston, Haslemere; one *s* one *d.* Formerly Lieut, Inns of Court Regt. Dir, European Informatics Market, 1994–; Member: Bd, SITPRO, 1991–; Mgt Cttee, UK Confederation of Electronic Data Interchange Systems, 1995–; President: Inst. for Mgt of Information Systems, 1996–; Electronic Commerce Assoc., 1997–98; Ind. Financial Advrs Assoc., 1997–. *Publication:* L is for Limnet, 1992. *Heir: s* Hon. Frederic Corin Piers Thesiger, *b* 6 March 1962. *Address:* 26 Ormonde Gate, SW3 4EX. *Died 15 Dec. 1999.*

CHERMAYEFF, Serge, FRIBA, FRSA; architect, author, abstract painter; *b* 8 Oct. 1900; *s* of Ivan and Rosalie Issakovitch; named Sergius Ivanovitch Issakovitch; changed surname by deed poll to Chermayeff and adopted British nationality, 1927; became US citizen, 1945; *m* 1928, Barbara Maitland May; two *s. Educ:* Harrow Sch. Journalist, 1918–22; studied architecture, 1922–25; principal work in England, studios for BBC; Modern Exhibitions; Gilbey's Offices; ICI Laboratories; in Partnership: Bexhill Pavilion; Professor, Brooklyn Coll., 1942–46; Pres. and Dir, Inst. of Design, Chicago, 1946–51; Prof., Harvard Univ., 1953–62; Prof., Yale Univ., 1962–71, then Emeritus. Hon. Fellow, Assoc. of Columbian Architects. Hon. Dr of Fine Art, Washington Univ., 1964; Hon. Dr of Humanities, Ohio State Univ., 1980. Gold Medal, Royal Architectural Inst., Canada, 1974; AIA and Assoc. of Collegiate Schs 1980 Award for excellence in educn; Misha Black Meml Medal for significant contribn to design educn, SIAD, 1980; Gold Medal, NY State Univ. at Buffalo, 1982. *Publications:* Art and Architectural Criticism; ARP, 1939; Community and Privacy, 1963; Shape of Community, 1970; Design and the Public Good (collected works), 1982. *Address:* Box 1472, Wellfleet, MA 02667, USA. *Died 8 May 1996.*

CHERRY, Prof. Gordon Emanuel; Professor of Urban and Regional Planning, University of Birmingham, 1976–91, then Emeritus Professor; *b* 6 Feb. 1931; *s* of Emanuel and Nora Cherry; *m* 1957, Margaret Mary Loudon Cox; one *s* two *d. Educ:* Holgate and District Grammar Sch., Barnsley; QMC, Univ. of London (BA Hons Geog. 1953). Variously employed in local authority planning depts, 1956–68; Research Officer, Newcastle upon Tyne City Planning Dept, 1963–68; University of Birmingham: Sen. Lectr and Dep. Dir, Centre for Urban and Regional Studies, 1968–76; Dean, Fac. of Commerce and Social Science, 1981–86; Head, Sch. of Geography, 1987–91. Member: Local Govt Boundary Commn for England, 1979–89; Adv. Cttee on Landscape Treatment of Trunk Roads, 1984–94; Adv. Bd, Nat. Forest, 1991–94; Trustee, Bournville Village Trust, 1979–91 (Chm., 1992–). President: RTPI, 1978–79; Internat. Planning History Soc., 1993–. FRICS; FRSA 1991. Hon. DSc Heriot-Watt, 1984.

Publications: Town Planning in its Social Context, 1970, 2nd edn 1973; (with T. L. Burton) Social Research Techniques for Planners, 1970; Urban Change and Planning, 1972; The Evolution of British Town Planning, 1974; Environmental Planning, Vol. II: National Parks and Recreation in the Countryside, 1975; The Politics of Town Planning, 1982; (with J. L. Penny) Holford: a study in planning, architecture and civic design, 1986; Cities and Plans, 1988; Birmingham: a study in geography, history and planning, 1994; (with A. W. Rogers) Rural Change and Planning, 1995; Editor: Urban Planning Problems, 1974; Rural Planning Problems, 1976; Shaping an Urban World, 1980; Pioneers in British Planning, 1981; (with A. R. Sutcliffe) Planning Perspectives, 1986–. *Recreations:* work, professional activities, church ecumenism, reading, music, enjoyment of family life. *Address:* Quaker Ridge, 66 Meriden Road, Hampton in Arden, West Midlands B92 0BT. *T:* Hampton in Arden (01675) 443200. *Died 11 Jan. 1996.*

CHESTER JONES, Prof. Ian, DSc; Professor of Zoology, University of Sheffield, 1958–81, then Emeritus Professor; Independent Research Worker, Pathology, Sheffield Medical School, since 1987; *b* 3 Jan. 1916; *s* of late H. C. Jones; *m* 1942, Nansi Ellis Williams; two *s* one *d. Educ:* Liverpool Institute High Sch. for Boys; Liverpool Univ. BSc 1938; PhD 1941; DSc 1958. Served in Army, 1941–46 (despatches). Commonwealth Fund Fellow, Harvard Univ., 1947–49; Senior Lecturer in Zoology, Univ. of Liverpool, 1955; Milton Fellow, Harvard Univ., 1960. Vis. Prof., Coll. of William and Mary, Virginia, 1968–69. Ian Chester Jones Internat. Lectureship for Distinction in Comparative Endocrinology, triennium. Chm., Soc. for Endocrinology, 1966 (Sir Henry Dale medal, 1976, Hon. Fellow): Hon. FZS; Hon. FIBiol; Hon. Fellow: Amer. Soc. of Zoologists; NY Acad. of Scis. Dr de l'Université de Clermont (*hc*), 1967. *Publications:* The Adrenal Cortex, 1957; Integrated Biology, 1971; General, Comparative and Clinical Endocrinology of the Adrenal Cortex, vol. 1, 1976, vol. 2, 1978, vol. 3, 1980; Fundamentals of Comparative Vertebrate Endocrinology, 1987. *Address:* 36 Sale Hill, Sheffield S10 5BX. *Died 25 May 1996.*

CHESTERMAN, Sir (Dudley) Ross, Kt 1970; PhD; Warden of Goldsmiths' College (University of London), 1953–74 (Hon. Fellow, 1980); Master of the College of Design, Craft and Technology (formerly College of Craft Education), 1982 (Vice-Master, 1960–82; Dean, 1958–60); *b* 27 April 1909; *s* of late Dudley and Ettie Chesterman; *m* 1st, 1938, Audrey Mary Horlick (*d* 1982); one *s* one *d*; 2nd, 1985, Patricia Burns Bell. *Educ:* Hastings Grammar Sch.; Imperial College of Science, London (scholar). Acland English Essay Prizeman, 1930; 1st class hons BSc (Chem.), 1930; MSc 1932; PhD 1937; DIC. Lecturer in Chemistry, Woolwich Polytechnic; science master in various grammar schools; Headmaster, Meols Cop Secondary Sch., Southport, 1946–48; Chief County Inspector of Schools, Worcestershire, 1948–53. Educnl consultant to numerous overseas countries, 1966–73. Ford Foundation Travel Award to American Univs, 1966. Chairman: Standing Cttee on Teacher Trng; Nat. Council for Supply and Trng of Teachers Overseas, 1971; Adv. Cttee for Teacher Trng Overseas, FCO (ODA), 1972–74. Fellow *hc* Coll. of Handicraft, 1958. Liveryman and Freeman of Goldsmiths' Co., 1968. *Publications:* The Birds of Southport, 1947; chapter in The Forge, 1955; chapter in Science in Schools, 1958; Teacher Training in some American Universities, 1967; Golden Sunrise, 1996; scientific papers in chemical journals and journals of natural history; articles in educational periodicals. *Recreations:* writing, music, painting, travel, natural history. *Address:* The Garden House, 6 High Street, Lancaster LA1 1LA. *T:* (01524) 65687.

Died 24 March 1999.

CHOLMELEY, Sir Montague (John), 6th Bt *cr* 1806, of Easton, Lincolnshire; *b* 27 March 1935; *s* of 5th Bt and Cecilia, *er d* of W. H. Ellice; *S* father, 1964; *m* 1960, Juliet Auriol Sally Nelson; one *s* two *d*. *Educ:* Eton. Grenadier Guards, 1954–64. *Heir: s* Hugh John Frederick Sebastian Cholmeley [*b* 3 Jan. 1968; *m* 1993, Ursula, *d* of Hon. Sir H. P. D. Bennett; one *s*]. *Address:* Church Farm, Burton le Coggles, Grantham, Lincs. *T:* (0147684) 329. *Clubs:* White's, Cavalry and Guards.

Died 25 Nov. 1998.

CHRIMES, Henry Bertram; DL; Chairman, Liverpool Daily Post and Echo Ltd, 1976–85; *b* 11 March 1915; *s* of Sir Bertram Chrimes, CBE, and Mary (*née* Holder); *m* 1946, Suzanne, *d* of W. S. Corbett-Lowe, Sodylt Hall, Ellesmere; one *s* three *d*. *Educ:* Oundle; Clare Coll., Cambridge. Served War of 1939–45: RA, India and Burma, Bde Major (despatches). Cooper & Co.'s Stores Ltd, 1945–60 (Man. Dir, 1954–60); Ocean Transport & Trading Ltd, 1960–85 (Dep. Chm., 1971–75); Liverpool Daily Post & Echo Ltd, 1963–85; Member, Liverpool Bd, Barclays Bank Ltd, 1972–83. Member: Council, Univ. of Liverpool, 1951–87 (Pres., 1975–81; Pro-Chancellor, 1981–Nov. 1987); Univ. Authorities Panel, 1976–87; Dir, Univs Superannuation Scheme Ltd, 1980–85; Vice-Pres., Liverpool Sch. of Tropical Medicine, 1981–87; Mem., 1951–, Vice-Pres., 1973–, Liverpool Council of Social Service (Chm., 1964–70); President: Merseyside Pre-Retirement Assoc., 1977–87; Royal Liverpool Seamen's Orphan Instn, 1980–86. DL 1974, High Sheriff 1978–79, Merseyside. Hon. LLD Liverpool, 1987. *Recreations:* books, gardening. *Address:* Bracken Bank, Heswall, Merseyside L60 4RP. *T:* (0151) 342 2397. *Clubs:* Reform; Racquet (Liverpool). *Died 7 June 1997.*

CHRISTIAN, Clifford Stuart, CMG 1971; consultant in environmental matters, retired; *b* 19 Dec. 1907; *s* of Thomas William and Lily Elizabeth Christian; *m* 1933, Agnes Robinson; four *d*. *Educ:* Univ. of Queensland (BScAgr); Univ. of Minnesota (MS). Officer-in-charge: Northern Australia Regional Survey Section, 1946–50; Land Research and Regional Survey Section, CSIRO, 1950–57; Chief, Div. of Land Research, CSIRO, 1957–60; Mem. Executive, CSIRO, 1960–72. Adviser, Ranger Uranium Environmental Inquiry, 1975–76. Farrer Memorial Medal, 1969. FAIAS; FWA; Fellow, Aust. Acad. of Technological Sciences and Engrg. Hon. DScAgr Queensland, 1978. *Publications:* A Review Report, Alligator Rivers Study (with J. Aldrich), 1977; chapter contribs to books; articles in various pubns mainly concerning natural resources and regional surveying. *Recreation:* photography. *Address:* 6 Baudin Street, Forrest, ACT 2603, Australia. *T:* (2) 62952495.

Died 7 June 1996.

CHRISTIE, Prof. Ian Ralph, FBA 1977; Astor Professor of British History, University of London at University College, 1979–84, then Professor Emeritus; Hon. Research Fellow, University College London, since 1984; *b* 11 May 1919; *s* of John Reid Christie and Gladys Lilian (*née* Whatley); *m* 1992, Ann (*née* Hastings). *Educ:* privately; Worcester Royal Grammar Sch.; Magdalen Coll., Oxford, 1938–40 and 1946–48 (MA). Served War, RAF, 1940–46. University College London: Asst Lectr in Hist., 1948; Lectr, 1951; Reader, 1960; Prof. of Modern British History, 1966; Dean of Arts, 1971–73; Chm. History Dept, 1975–79. Ford Lectr, Oxford Univ., 1983–84. Jt Literary Dir, Royal Hist. Soc., 1964–70, Mem. Council, 1970–74. Mem. Editorial Bd, History of Parliament Trust, 1973–. *Publications:* The End of North's Ministry, 1780–1782, 1958; Wilkes, Wyvill and Reform, 1962;

Crisis of Empire: Great Britain and the American Colonies, 1754–1783, 1966; (ed) Essays in Modern History selected from the Transactions of the Royal Historical Society, 1968; Myth and Reality in late Eighteenth-century British Politics, 1970; (ed) The Correspondence of Jeremy Bentham, vol. 3, 1971; (with B. W. Labaree) Empire or Independence, 1760–1776, 1976; (with Lucy M. Brown) Bibliography of British History, 1789–1851, 1977; Wars and Revolutions: Britain, 1760–1815, 1982; Stress and Stability in Late Eighteenth Century Britain: reflections on the British avoidance of revolution, 1984; The Benthams in Russia 1780–1791, 1993; British 'Non-élite' MPs 1715–1820, 1995; contrib. to jls. *Recreation:* gardening. *Address:* 10 Green Lane, Croxley Green, Herts WD3 3HR. *T:* (01923) 773008.

Died 25 Nov. 1998.

CHRISTOPHERSON, Sir Derman (Guy), Kt 1969; OBE 1946; FRS 1960; FREng; DPhil; FIMechE; Master, Magdalene College, Cambridge, 1979–85; *b* 6 Sept. 1915; *s* of late Derman Christopherson, Clerk in Holy Orders, formerly of Blackheath, and Edith Frances Christopherson; *m* 1940, Frances Edith (*d* 1988), *d* of late James and Martha Tearle; three *s* one *d*. *Educ:* Sherborne Sch.; University Coll., Oxford (DPhil 1941; Hon. Fellow, 1977). MICE. Henry Fellow at Harvard Univ., 1938; Scientific Officer, Research and Experiments Dept, Ministry of Home Security, 1941–45; Fellow, Magdalene Coll., Cambridge, 1945 (Hon. Fellow 1969), Bursar, 1947; University Demonstrator, Cambridge Univ. Engineering Dept, 1945, Lecturer, 1946–49; Professor of Mechanical Engineering, Leeds Univ., 1949–55; Prof. of Applied Science, Imperial Coll. of Science and Technology, 1955–60; Vice-Chancellor and Warden, Durham Univ., 1960–78. Mem. Council of Institution of Mechanical Engineers, 1950–53; Clayton Prize, Instn of Mechanical Engineers, 1963. Chairman: Cttee of Vice-Chancellors and Principals, 1967–70; Central Council for Educn and Training in Social Work, 1971–79; CNAA (Chm., Educn Cttee), 1966–74; Board of Washington New Town Develt Corp., 1964–78; SRC, 1965–70; Jt Standing Cttee on Structural Safety, Instns of Civil and Structural Engrs, 1983–88. Member: Council, Royal Soc., 1975; British Library Adv. Council, 1984; Chm., Royal Fine Art Commn, 1980–85 (Mem., 1978). FREng (FEng 1976). Fellow, Imperial Coll. of Science and Technology, 1966. Hon. DCL: Kent, 1966; Newcastle, 1971; Durham, 1986; Hon DSc: Aston, 1967; Sierra Leone, 1970; Cranfield Inst. of Technology, 1985; Hon. LLD: Leeds, 1969; Royal Univ. of Malta, 1969; DTech Brunel, 1979. *Publications:* The Engineer in The University, 1967; The University at Work, 1973; various papers in Proc. Royal Soc., Proc. IMechE, Jl of Applied Mechanics, etc. *Address:* c/o 10 Hallam Road, Mapperley, Nottingham NG3 6HA.

Died 7 Nov. 2000.

CHUBB, John Oliver, CMG 1976; HM Diplomatic Service, retired; Counsellor, Foreign and Commonwealth Office, 1973–80; *b* 21 April 1920; *s* of Clifford Chubb and Margaret Chubb (*née* Hunt); *m* 1945, Mary Griselda Robertson (marr. diss. 1980); one *s* two *d*. *Educ:* Rugby; Oxford (MA). Served War, Scots Guards, 1940–46. Joined Diplomatic Service, 1946; Beirut, 1947; Bagdad, 1948–49; Canal Zone, 1950–52; Cyprus, 1953; FO, 1954–56; Tokyo, 1957–61; FO, 1961–63; Hong Kong, 1964–66; FO, 1967. Chm., St John's Wood Soc., 1978–83. *Recreations:* reading, spectator sports, golf, gardening, sailing. *Address:* Clayhill House, Clayhill, Beckley, near Rye, East Sussex TN31 6SQ. *T:* Northiam (01797) 252268. *Clubs:* Athenæum, MCC; Rye Golf, Senior Golfers' Society.

Died 19 July 1996.

CHURCH, Ronald James H.; *see* Harrison-Church.

CHURCHER, Maj.-Gen. John Bryan, CB 1952; DSO 1944, Bar 1946; retired; Director and General Secretary, Independent Stores Association, 1959–71; *b* 2 Sept. 1905; *s* of late Lieut-Col B. T. Churcher, Wargrave, Berks, and Beatrice Theresa Churcher; *m* 1st, 1937, Rosamond Hildegarde Mary (*d* 1993), *y d* of late Frederick Parkin, Truro Vean, Truro, Cornwall; one *s* two *d*; 2nd, 1995, Mrs Pauline Thompson. *Educ:* Wellington Coll., Berks; RMC Sandhurst. Commissioned DCLI, 1925; Lieut, 1927; Capt. KSLI, 1936; Staff Coll., 1939; served War of 1939–45 (despatches, DSO and Bar); commanded: 1 Bn Hereford Regt, 1942–44; 159 Inf. Bde, 1944–46; 43 Div., 1946; Northumbrian Dist, 1946; 2 Div., 1946; 3 Div., 1946–47; 5 Div., 1947–48; Brig., Imperial Defence Coll., 1948; BGS, Western Command, 1949–51; Chief of Staff, Southern Comd, 1951–54; GOC, 3rd Inf. Div., 1954–57; Dir of Military Training at the War Office, 1957–59; retired, 1959. ADC to King George VI, 1949–52; ADC to the Queen, 1952. *Address:* Godbolts Cottage, 187 Coggeshall Road, Marks Tey, Colchester, Essex CO6 1HS. *T:* (01206) 210196. *Died 2 Aug. 1997.*

CITRINE, 2nd Baron *cr* 1946, of Wembley; **Norman Arthur Citrine,** LLD; solicitor in general practice, retired 1984; author, editor, lecturer, advocate; *b* 27 Sept. 1914; *er s* of 1st Baron Citrine, GBE, PC, and Doris Helen (*d* 1973), *d* of Edgar Slade; *S* father, 1983; *m* 1939, Kathleen Alice (*d* 1993), *d* of George Thomas Chilvers; one *d*. *Educ:* University Coll. Sch., Hampstead; Law Society's Sch., London. Admitted solicitor of Supreme Court (Hons), 1937; LLB (London), 1938; LLD (London), 1993. Articled Clerk, Shaen, Roscoe, Massey & Co., 1934–37. Served War of 1939–45, Lieut RNVR, 1940–46. Legal Adviser to Trades Union Congress, 1946–51; re-entered general legal practice, 1951. Pres., Devon and Exeter Law Soc., 1971. Fellow, Inst. of Diagnostic Engrs, 1990. *Publications:* Union Leaders Vindicated, 1940; War Pensions Appeal Cases, 1946; Guide to Industrial Injuries Acts, 1948; Citrine's Trade Union Law, 1950, 3rd edn 1967; Citrine's ABC of Chairmanship, 1952–82; *Recreations:* yachting, camping, hiking, music, literature, art and numerous creative pursuits. *Heir: b* Dr the Hon. Ronald Eric Citrine [*b* 19 May 1919; *m* 1945, Mary, *d* of Reginald Williams]. *Address:* Casa Katrina, The Mount, Opua, Bay of Islands, New Zealand.

Died 18 March 1997.

CLAMAGERAN, Alice Germaine Suzanne; Director, School of Social Workers, Centre Hospitalier Universitaire de Rouen, 1942–73; President, International Council of Nurses, 1961–65; *b* 5 March 1906; *d* of William Clamageran, shipowner at Rouen, and Lucie Harlé. *Educ:* Rouen. Nursing studies: Red Cross School of Nurses, Rouen; Ecole Professionnelle d'Assistance aux Malades, Paris. Tutor, Red Cross Sch. for Nurses, Rouen, 1931–42 (leave, for course in Public Health at Florence Nightingale Internat. Foundn, London, 1934–35). War service (6 months), 1939–40. President: Bd of Dirs, Fondation Edith Seltzer (Sanatorium Chantoiseau, Briançon) for Nurses, Social Workers and Medical Auxiliaries; Assoc. Médico-Sociale Protestante de Langue Française; Hon. Pres. Nat. Assoc. of Trained Nurses in France. Hon. Fellow, Royal Coll. of Nursing of UK, 1977. Médaille de Bronze de l'Enseignement Technique, 1960; Officier dans l'Ordre de la Santé Publique, 1961; Chevalier, Légion d'Honneur, 1962. *Address:* Hautonne, 27310 Bourg-Achard, France.

Died 25 Nov. 1998.

CLAPHAM, His Honour Brian Ralph; arbitrator; a Circuit Judge, South East Circuit, 1974–85; *b* 1 July 1913; *s* of Isaac Clapham and Laura Alice Clapham (*née* Meech); *m* 1961, Margaret Warburg; two *s. Educ:* Tonbridge Sch.; Wadham Coll., Oxford; University Coll. London (LLB; LLM 1976); BA Open, 1981. FCIArb 1988. Called to Bar,

Middle Temple, 1936. Contested (Lab): Tonbridge, 1950; Billericay, 1951, 1955; Chelmsford, 1959. Councillor, Tonbridge and Southborough UDCs, 1947–74; Chm., Tonbridge UDC, 1959–60. Governor, West Kent Coll., 1972–95. Freeman of City of London, 1978. *Publications:* legal articles in various jls. *Recreations:* walking and talking. *Died 20 Dec. 1998.*

CLARK, Rt Hon. Alan (Kenneth McKenzie); PC 1991; MP (C) Kensington and Chelsea, since 1997; historian; *b* 13 April 1928; *s* of Baron Clark (Life Peer), OM, CH, KCB, CLit, FBA and late Elizabeth Martin; *m* 1958, (Caroline) Jane Beuttler; two *s. Educ:* Eton; Christ Church, Oxford (MA). Household Cavalry (Training Regt), 1945; RAuxAF, 1952–54. Barrister, Inner Temple, 1955. MP (C) Plymouth, Sutton, Feb. 1974–1992. Parly Under Sec. of State, Dept of Employment, 1983–86; Minister for Trade, 1986–89; Minister of State, MoD, 1989–92. Chm., Internal Market Council of EEC Ministers, 1986–87. Mem., Inst. for Strategic Studies, 1963; Mem., RUSI. *Publications:* The Donkeys: a History of the BEF in 1915, 1961; The Fall of Crete, 1963; Barbarossa: the Russo-German Conflict, 1941–45, 1965; Aces High: the war in the air over the Western Front 1914–18, 1973; (ed) A Good Innings: the private papers of Viscount Lee of Fareham, 1974; Diaries, 1993; The Tories: Conservatives and the nation state 1922–97, 1998; *posthumous publication:* Alan Clark Diaries: Into Politics, 2000. *Address:* Saltwood Castle, Kent CT21 4QU. *T:* (01303) 265446. *Clubs:* Brooks's, Pratt's.

Died 5 Sept. 1999.

CLARK, His Honour Albert William; a Circuit Judge, 1981–95; *b* 23 Sept. 1922; *s* of William Charles Clark and Cissy Dorothy Elizabeth Clark; *m* 1951, Frances Philippa, *d* of Dr Samuel Lavington Hart, Tientsin; one *s* one *d. Educ:* Christ's Coll., Finchley. War service, 1941–46, Royal Navy. Called to Bar, Middle Temple, 1949; Clerk of Arraigns, Central Criminal Court, 1951–56; Clerk to the Justices, E Devon, 1956–70; Metropolitan Magistrate, 1970–80; Acting Dep. Chm., Inner London QS, 1971; Dep. Circuit Judge, 1972–80. Mem., Central Council of Probation and After-Care Cttees, 1975–81. County Chm., W Sussex Abbeyfield Socs, 1997–. *Recreations:* fly-fishing, seafishing, walking, travel to remote places. *Address:* Pelham, 45 West Parade, Worthing, West Sussex BN11 5EF. *T:* (01903) 247472. *Club:* Royal Over-Seas League. *Died 26 May 1998.*

CLARK, David S.; *see* Stafford-Clark.

CLARK, Lt-Gen. Findlay; *see* Clark, Lt-Gen. S. F.

CLARK, His Honour (Francis) Leo; QC 1972; a Circuit Judge, 1976–93; Designated Judge and Liaison Judge, Oxford Combined Court Centre, 1983–93; *b* 15 Dec. 1920; *s* of Sydney John Clark and Florence Lilian Clark; *m* 1st, 1957, Denise Jacqueline Rambaud; one *s*; 2nd, 1967, Dr Daphne Margaret Humphreys. *Educ:* Bablake Sch.; St Peter's Coll., Oxford (MA). Called to Bar, Lincoln's Inn, 1947. Dep. Chm., Oxford County QS, 1970; a Recorder of the Crown Court, 1972–76. Hon. Recorder, City of Oxford, 1989–. *Recreations:* music, reading, travel. *Address:* The Ivy House, Charlbury, Oxon OX7 3PX. *Club:* Union (Oxford).

Died 5 Dec. 1998.

CLARK, Rev. Canon Robert James Vodden; *b* 12 April 1907; *s* of Albert Arthur Clark and Bessie Vodden; *m* 1934, Ethel Dolina McGregor Alexander; one *d. Educ:* Dalry Normal Practising Episcopal Church Sch., Edinburgh; Church Army Coll.; Coates Hall Theol Coll. Ordained, 1941. Men's Social Dept, Church Army, 1926; varied work in homes for men; special work in probation trng home under Home Office, 1934–39; St Paul and St George, Edinburgh, 1941–44; Rector, St Andrew's, Fort

William, 1944–47; seconded to Scottish Educn Dept as Warden-Leader of Scottish Centre of Outdoor Trng, Glenmore Lodge, 1947–49; Curate i/c St David's, Edinburgh, 1949–54; Rector of Christ Church, Falkirk, 1954–69; Rector of St Leonard's, Lasswade, 1969–79; Canon, Edinburgh, 1962; Dean of Edinburgh, 1967–76; Hon. Canon, Edinburgh, 1976; retd 1979. Mem., Royal Highland and Agric. Soc. *Recreations:* mountaineering, photography. *Address:* 15 North Street, St Andrews, Fife, Scotland KY16 9PW. *Died 25 Sept. 1998.*

CLARK, Lt-Gen. (Samuel) Findlay, CBE 1945; CD 1950; PEng; *b* 17 March 1909; *s* of James Clark, Winnipeg; *m* 1937, Leona Blanche Seagram. *Educ:* Univ. of Manitoba (BSc Elec. Eng); Univ. of Saskatchewan (BSc Mech. Eng). MEIC, MCSEE. Lieut, Royal Canadian Signals, 1933; Associate Prof. of Elec. and Mech. Engrg (Capt.) at RMC Kingston, 1938; overseas to UK, Aug. 1940 (Major); Comd 5th Canadian Armd Div. Sigs Regt (Lt-Col), 1941; GSO1 Can. Mil. HQ, London, 1942; Staff Course, Camberley, England (Col), 1942–43; CSO, HQ 2nd Canadian Corps until end of War (Brig. 1943); Dep. Chief of Gen. Staff, 1945; Imperial Defence Coll., 1948; Canadian Mil. Observer on Western Union Mil. Cttee; Maj.-Gen. 1949; Canadian Mil. Rep., NATO, London, 1949; Chm., Joint Staff, CALE, London, 1951; QMG of Canadian Army, 1951; GOC Central Comd, 1955; CGS, 1958–61. Chm., Nat. Capital Commission, 1961–67. Past Col Comdt, Royal Canadian Corps of Signals. Fellow, Royal Geographic Soc., Canada. Legion of Merit (USA), 1945; Comdr Order of Orange Nassau (Netherlands), 1945. OStJ 1975. *Address:* 301–1375 Newport Avenue, Victoria, BC V8S 5E8, Canada. *T:* (604) 5924338. *Club:* Union (Victoria). *Died 3 Sept. 1998.*

CLARKE, Prof. Sir Cyril (Astley), KBE 1974 (CBE 1969); MD, ScD; FRS 1970; FRCP, FRCOG; FIBiol; Emeritus Professor and Hon. Nuffield Research Fellow, Department of Genetics, and Hon. Research Fellow, Department of Geriatric Medicine, University of Liverpool (Professor of Medicine, 1965–72, Director, Nuffield Unit of Medical Genetics, 1963–72, and Nuffield Research Fellow, 1972–76); Consultant Physician, United Liverpool Hospitals (David Lewis Northern, 1946–58, then Royal Infirmary) and to Broadgreen Hospital, 1946; *b* 22 Aug. 1907; *s* of Astley Vavasour Clarke, JP, MD, and Ethel Mary Clarke, *d* of H. Simpson Gee; *m* 1935, Frieda Margaret Mary, (Féo) (*d* 1998), *d* of Alexander John Campbell Hart and Isabella Margaret Hart; three *s. Educ:* Wyggeston Grammar Sch., Leicester; Oundle Sch.; Gonville and Caius Coll., Cambridge (Hon. Fellow, 1974); Guy's Hosp. (Schol.). 2nd Class Hons, Natural Science Tripos Pt I; MD Cantab 1937; ScD Cantab 1963. FRCP 1949; FRCOG 1970; FFCM 1974; FRCPE 1975; FLS 1981. House Phys., Demonstr in Physiology and Clin. Asst in Dermatology, Guy's Hosp., 1932–36; Life Insurance practice, Grocers' Hall, EC2, 1936–39. Served, 1939–46, as Med Specialist, RNVR: HM Hosp. Ship Amarapoora (Scapa Flow and N Africa), RNH Seaforth and RNH Sydney. After War, Med. Registrar, Queen Elizabeth Hosp., Birmingham. Visiting Prof. of Genetics, Seton Hall Sch. of Med., Jersey City, USA, 1963; Lectures: Lumleian, RCP, 1967; Ingleby, Univ. of Birmingham, 1968; Foundn, RCPath, 1971; Inaugural Faculty, Univ. of Leeds, 1972; P. B. Fernando Meml, Colombo, 1974; Marsden, Royal Free Hosp., 1976; Linacre, 1978; New Ireland, UC Dublin, 1979; William Meredith Fletcher Shaw, RCOG, 1979; Harveian Oration, RCP, 1979; Sir Arthur Hall Meml, Sheffield, 1981; Ransom, Univ. of Nottingham, 1990. Examr in Med., Dundee Univ., 1965–69. Pres., RCP, 1972–77 (Censor, 1967–69, Sen. Censor, 1971–72; Dir, Med. Services Study Group, 1977–83; Dir, Med. Res. Unit, 1983–88); Pres., Liverpool Med. Instn, 1970–71 (Hon. Mem., 1981). Chairman:

British Heart Foundn Council, 1982–87; British Soc. for Res. on Ageing, 1987–92; Jt Cttee of Management, British Paediatric Surveillance Unit, 1990–; Member: MRC Working Party, 1966; Sub-Cttee of Dept of Health and Social Security on prevention of Rhesus hæmolytic disease, 1967–82 (Chm., 1973–82); Bd of Governors, United Liverpool Hosps, 1969; Assoc. of Hungarian Medical Socs, 1973; Res. Adv. Cttee, Royal Hosp. and Home, Putney, 1988–94; President: Harveian Soc.; Royal Entomological Soc. of London, 1991–92; Governor and Councillor, Bedford Coll., 1974, Chm. of Council, 1975–85. Chm., Cockayne Trust Fund, Natural History Museum, 1974–. Hon. Fellow: UMDS, 1992; British Blood Transfusion Soc., 1992; Leverhulme Emeritus Fellow, 1980; Fellow, Ceylon Coll. of Physicians, 1974. Hon. FRACP 1973; Hon. FRCPI 1973; Hon. FACP 1976; Hon. FRCPC 1977; Hon. FRCPE 1981; Hon. FRCPath 1981; Hon. FRSocMed 1982; Hon. FRCPCH 1997. Hon. DSc: Edinburgh, 1971; Leicester, 1971; East Anglia, 1973; Birmingham, Liverpool and Sussex, 1974; Hull, 1977; Wales, 1978; London, 1980; Coll. of William and Mary, Williamsburg, USA, 1992. Gold Medal in Therapeutics, Worshipful Soc. of Apothecaries, 1970; James Spence Medal, Brit. Paediatric Assoc., 1973; Addingham Medal, Leeds, 1973; John Scott Medal and Award, Philadelphia, 1976; Fothergillian Medal, Med. Soc., 1977; Gairdner Award, 1977; Ballantyne Prize, RCPEd, 1979; (jtly) Albert and Mary Lasker Foundn Award, 1980; Linnean Medal for Zoology, 1981; Artois-Baillet Latour Health Prize, 1981; Gold Medal, RSM, 1986; Buchanan Medal, Royal Soc., 1990; Duncan Medal, Faculty of Public Health Medicine, 1997. *Publications:* Genetics for the Clinician, 1962; (ed) Selected Topics in Medical Genetics, 1969; Human Genetics and Medicine, 1970, 3rd edn 1987; (with R. B. McConnell) Prevention of Rhesus Hæmolytic Disease, 1972; (ed) Rhesus Hæmolytic Disease: selected papers and extracts, 1975; many contribs to med. and scientific jls, particularly on prevention of Rhesus hæmolytic disease and on evolution of mimicry in swallowtail butterflies. *Recreations:* small boat sailing, breeding swallowtail butterflies. *Clubs:* Oxford and Cambridge Sailing Society (Pres., 1975–77); West Kirby Sailing; United Hospitals Sailing (Pres., 1977–92). *Died 21 Nov. 2000.*

CLARKE, Edwin (Sisterson), MD; FRCP; Hon. Curator, Sherrington Room, University Laboratory of Physiology, Oxford University, since 1985; Director, Wellcome Institute for the History of Medicine, 1973–79, retired; *b* Felling-on-Tyne, 18 June 1919; *s* of Joseph and Nellie Clarke; *m* 1st, 1949, Margaret Elsie Morrison (marr. diss.); two *s;* 2nd, 1958, Beryl Eileen Brock (marr. diss.); one *d;* 3rd, 1982, Gaynor Crawford. *Educ:* Jarrow Central Sch.; Univ. of Durham Med. Sch. (MD); Univ. of Chicago Med. Sch. (MD). Neurological Specialist, RAMC, 1946–48; Nat. Hosp., Queen Square, 1950–51; Postgrad. Med. Sch. of London, 1951–58; Lectr in Neurology and Consultant Neurologist to Hammersmith Hosp., 1955–58; Asst Sec. to Wellcome Trust, 1958–60; Asst Prof., History of Medicine, Johns Hopkins Hosp. Med. Sch., 1960–62; Vis. Associate Prof., History of Medicine, Yale Univ. Med. Sch., 1962–63; Med. Historian to Wellcome Historical Med. Library and Museum, 1963–66; Sen. Lectr and Head of Sub-Dept of History of Medicine, University Coll. London, 1966–72, Reader, 1972–73. *Publications:* (jtly) The Human Brain and Spinal Cord, 1968; (ed) Modern Methods in the History of Medicine, 1971; (jtly) An Illustrated History of Brain Function, 1972; (trans.) Die historische Entwicklung der experimentellen Gehirn- und Rückenmarksphysiologie vor Flourens, by M. Neuburger, 1981; (jtly) Nineteenth Century Origins of Neuroscientific Concepts, 1987; articles in jls dealing with neurology and with history of medicine. *Died 11 April 1996.*

CLAXTON, Maj.-Gen. Patrick Fisher, CB 1972; OBE 1946; General Manager, Regular Forces Employment Association, 1971–81; *b* 13 March 1915; *s* of late Rear-Adm. Ernest William Claxton and Kathleen O'Callaghan Claxton, formerly Fisher; *m* 1941, Jóna Gudrún Gunnarsdóttir (*d* 1980); two *d*. *Educ:* Sutton Valence Sch.; St John's Coll., Cambridge (BA). Served GHQ, India, 1943–45; Singapore, 1945–46; WO, 1946–48; British Element Trieste Force, 1949–51; HQ, BAOR, 1952–54; RASC Officers' Sch., 1955–56; Amphibious Warfare HQ and Persian Gulf, 1957–58; Col, WO, 1959–60; Brig., WO, 1961–62; DST, BAOR, 1963–65; Chief Transport Officer, BAOR, 1965–66; Comdt, Sch. of Transport, and ADC to the Queen, 1966–68; Transport Officer-in-Chief (Army), 1969–71, retired. Col Comdt, RCT, 1972–80. Governor and Mem. Administrative Bd, Corps of Commissionaires, 1977–90. FCIT. *Publication:* The Regular Forces Employment Association 1885–1985, 1985. *Address:* The Lodge, Beacon Hill Park, Hindhead, Surrey GU26 6HU. *T:* (01428) 604437. *Club:* MCC.
Died 8 Sept. 2000.

CLAYTON, Prof. Frederick William; Professor of Classics, 1948–75, and Public Orator, 1965–73, University of Exeter; *b* 13 Dec. 1913; *s* of late William and Gertrude Clayton, Liverpool; *m* 1948, Friederike Luise Büttner-Wobst; two *s* two *d*. *Educ:* Liverpool Collegiate Sch.; King's Coll., Cambridge (Members' Essay Prizes (Latin and English), Porson Prize, Browne Medal, 1933; Craven Scholar in Classics, 1934; Chancellor's Medal for Classics, 1935). Fellow of King's Coll., Cambridge, 1937–40; Lectr in Latin, Edinburgh Univ., 1946–48. Served War, Nov. 1940–Oct. 1946, Signals, Field Security, RAF Intelligence, India. *Publications:* The Cloven Pine, 1942; various articles. *Address:* Halwill, Clydesdale Road, Exeter, Devon EX4 4QX. *T:* (01392) 271810.
Died 8 Dec. 1999.

CLAYTON, Lucie; *see* Kark, E. F.

CLAYTON, Sir Robert (James), Kt 1980; CBE 1970 (OBE 1960); FEng 1977; FInstP, FIEE, FIEEE; Technical Director, 1968–83, Director, 1978–83, The General Electric Co. plc; *b* 30 Oct. 1915; *m* 1949, Joy Kathleen King (*d* 1997); no *c*. *Educ:* Christ's Coll., Cambridge (Scholar; MA; Hon. Fellow, 1983). GEC Research Labs, 1937; Manager, GEC Applied Electronics Labs, 1955; Dep. Dir, Hirst Research Centre, 1960; Man. Dir, GEC (Electronics), 1963; Man. Dir, GEC (Research), 1966. Member: Adv. Council for Applied R&D, 1976–80 (Chm. of Groups producing reports on Applications of Semiconductors, Computer Aided Design and Manufacture, and Inf. Technology); Adv. Council on R&D for Fuel and Power, 1976–83; NEB, 1978–80; Adv. Council, Science Mus., 1980–83, Trustee, 1984–90; British Library Bd, 1983–87; UGC, 1982–89; Monopolies and Mergers Commn, 1983–89; Chairman: Computer Systems and Electronics Requirements Bd, DoI, 1978–81; Open Technology Steering Gp, MSC, 1983–84; Policy Cttee, IT Skills Agency, 1985–88. Chm., Electronics Engrg Assoc., 1965; President: IEE, 1975–76 (Chm., Electronics Div., 1968–69); Inst. of Physics, 1982–84; Assoc. for Science Educn, 1983; IInfSc, 1985–86; Vice-President: Fellowship of Engineering, 1980–82; IERE, 1983–84. Vis. Prof., Electrical Engrg Dept, Imperial Coll. of Science and Technology, 1971–77; Lectures: Faraday, IEE; Graham Clarke, CEI; Christopher Hinton, Fellowship of Engineering. Hon. FIEE 1982. Hon. DSc: Aston, 1979; Salford, 1979; City, 1981; Oxon, 1988; Hon. DEng Bradford, 1985. *Publications:* The GEC Research Laboratories 1919–1984, 1989; (ed) A Scientist's War—the Diary of Sir Clifford Paterson, 1991; papers in Proc. IEE (premium awards). *Club:* United Oxford & Cambridge University. *Died 20 June 1998.*

CLEARY, Denis Mackrow, CMG 1967; HM Diplomatic Service, retired; *b* 20 Dec. 1907; *s* of late Francis Esmonde Cleary and Emmeline Marie Cleary (*née* Mackrow); *m* 1st, 1941, Barbara Wykeham-George (*d* 1960); 2nd, 1962, Mary Kent (*née* Dunlop), widow of Harold Kent; one step *d*. *Educ:* St Ignatius Coll. and St Olave's Sch.; St John's Coll., Cambridge (Major Schol.). 1st Class Hons Pts I and II, Math. Tripos; BA 1930; MA 1934. Asst Principal, India Office, 1931; Principal, 1937; seconded to Min. of Home Security, 1940–44; Dep. Principal Officer to Regional Commissioner, Cambridge, March 1943–Sept. 1944; seconded to Foreign Office (German Section) as Asst Sec., 1946–49; transferred to CRO and posted to Delhi as Counsellor, 1949–51; Dep. High Commissioner, Wellington, 1955–58; Mem. of British Delegn to Law of the Sea Conf., Geneva, 1960; Dep. High Comr, Nicosia, 1962–64; Head of Atlantic Dept, Commonwealth Office, 1964–68 (Mem., Cttee for Exports to the Caribbean, 1965–67); retd 1968; re-employed in Internat. Div., DHSS, 1968–72; UK Delegate to Public Health Cttees, Council of Europe, 1968–72; Chm., Council of Europe Med. Fellowships Selection Cttee, 1972–74. *Recreations:* gardening, walking. *Address:* High Gate, Burwash, East Sussex TN19 7LA. *T:* (01435) 882712.
Died 28 Aug. 1997.

CLEAVER, Air Vice-Marshal Peter (Charles), CB 1971; OBE 1945; *b* 6 July 1919; *s* of William Henry Cleaver, Warwick; *m* 1948, Jean, *d* of J. E. B. Fairclough, Ledbury; two *s*. *Educ:* Warwick Sch.; Coll. of Aeronautics (MSc); Staff Coll., Haifa, 1945; idc 1966. CEng, FRAeS, FIMechE. HM Asst Air Attaché, Bucharest, 1947–49; Coll. of Aeronautics, Cranfield, 1950–52; Structural Research, RAE Farnborough, 1952–55; Min. of Supply, 1955–57; HQ FEAF, 1957–60; Maintenance Comd, 1960–63; OC, Central Servicing Develt Estabt, 1963–64; Air Officer Engineering: HQ Flying Trng Comd, 1964–66; HQ FEAF, 1967–69; Air Support Command, 1969–72; retired 1972. Sec., Cranfield Inst. of Technology, 1973–78. Governor, Warwick Schs Foundn, 1978–85; Chm. Governors, Warwick Sch., 1980–85. *Recreation:* gardening. *Address:* Willow House, Watling Street, Little Brickhill, Milton Keynes MK17 9LS. *Club:* Royal Air Force. *Died 19 Dec. 1999.*

CLÉMENT, René; Officier de la Légion d'Honneur; Grand Officier, Ordre National du Mérite; Commandeur des Arts et des Lettres; film director; *b* Bordeaux, 18 March 1913; *s* of Jean Maurice Clément and Marguérite Clément (*née* Bayle); *m* 1st, 1940, Bella Gurwich (decd); 2nd, 1987, Johanna Harwood. *Educ:* Ecole nationale supérieure des beaux-arts. *Films:* Soigne ton Gauche (short), 1936; *documentaries:* L'Arabie Interdite, 1937; La Grande Chartreuse, 1938; La Bièvre, 1939; Le Triage, 1940; Ceux du Rail, 1942; La Grande Pastorale, 1943; Chefs de Demain, 1944; *feature films:* La Bataille du Rail, 1946 (Cannes Fest. Prize); Le Père Tranquille, 1946; Les Maudits, 1947 (Cannes Fest. Prize); Au-delà des Grilles, 1948 (US Academy Award, British award); Le Château de Verre, 1950; Jeux Interdits, 1952 (US Academy Award, British award and Grand Internat. Prize Venice Biennale); Monsieur Ripois, 1954 (Cannes Fest. Prize); Gervaise, 1955 (Venice Internat. Prize); Barrage contre le Pacifique, 1958; Plein Soleil, 1959; Quelle Joie de Vivre, 1961; Le Jour et l'Heure, 1962; Les Félins, 1964; Paris, Brûle-t-il?, 1966 (Prix Europa); Le Passager de la Pluie, 1969; La Maison sous les Arbres, 1971; La Course du lièvre à travers les champs, 1971; The Baby Sitter, 1975. Founder Mem., Institut des hautes études cinématographiques; Mem., Institut de France. *Publication:* (with C. Audry) Bataille du rail, 1947. *Recreations:* antiques, painting, yachting. *Address:* 5 Avenue de St Roman, 98000 Monte Carlo, Monaco. *Died 17 March 1996.*

CLEMITSON, Ivor Malcolm; *b* 8 Dec. 1931; *s* of Daniel Malcolm Clemitson and Annie Ellen Clemitson; *m* 1960, Janet Alicia Meeke; one *s* one *d*. *Educ:* Harlington Primary Sch.; Luton Grammar Sch.; London Sch. of Economics (BScEcon); Bishops Theol College. Deacon 1958, priest 1959. Curate: St Mary's (Bramall Lane), Sheffield, 1958–61; Christ Church, Luton, 1962–64; Industrial Chaplain, Dio. St Albans, 1964–69; Dir of Industrial Mission, Dio. Singapore, 1969–70; Research Officer, National Graphical Assoc., 1971–74. MP (Lab) Luton East, Feb. 1974–1979; contested (Lab) Luton South, 1983. *Publication:* (with George Rodgers) A Life to Live, 1981. *Recreations:* watching football, theatre, travel. *Address:* La Croix Haute, Pierrefitte 79–330, Deux Sèvres, France.
Died 24 Dec. 1997.

CLEMOES, Prof. Peter Alan Martin, PhD (Cantab); FRHistS; FSA; Elrington and Bosworth Professor of Anglo-Saxon, Cambridge University, 1969–82, Emeritus Professor since 1982; Official Fellow of Emmanuel College, Cambridge, 1962–69, Professorial Fellow 1969–82, Life Fellow since 1982; Fellow, Queen Mary and Westfield (formerly Queen Mary) College, London University, since 1975; *b* 20 Jan. 1920; *o s* of Victor Clemoes and Mary (*née* Paton); *m* 1956, Jean Elizabeth, *yr d* of Sidney Grew; two *s*. *Educ:* Brentwood Sch.; Queen Mary Coll., London; King's Coll., Cambridge. BA London (1st Cl. Hons English) 1950; Soley Student, King's Coll., Cambridge, 1951–53; Research Fellow, Reading Univ., 1954–55; PhD Cambridge 1956; LittD Cambridge. Lectr in English, Reading Univ., 1955–61; Lectr in Anglo-Saxon, Cambridge Univ., 1961–69; Emmanuel College, Cambridge: Coll. Lectr in English, 1963–69 and Dir of Studies in English, 1963–65; Tutor, 1966–68; Asst Librarian, 1963–69. Hon. Sen. Res. Fellow, KCL, 1987–89. Mem. Council of Early English Text Soc., 1971–. Pres., Internat. Soc. of Anglo-Saxonists, 1983–85; Dir, Fontes Anglo-Saxonici (a register of written sources used by authors in Anglo-Saxon England), 1985–93. Founder and Chief Editor, Anglo-Saxon England, 1972–89. *Publications:* The Anglo-Saxons, Studies . . . presented to Bruce Dickins (ed and contrib.), 1959; General Editor of Early English Manuscripts in Facsimile (Copenhagen), 1963–74, and co-editor of vol. XIII, 1966, vol. XVIII, 1974; Rhythm and Cosmic Order in Old English Christian Literature (inaug. lecture), 1970; England before the Conquest: Studies . . . presented to Dorothy Whitelock (co-ed and contrib.), 1971; Interactions of Thought and Language in Old English Poetry, 1995; textual and critical writings, especially on the works of Ælfric and Old English poetry; *festschrift:* Learning and Literature in Anglo-Saxon England: studies presented to Peter Clemoes on the occasion of his sixty-fifth birthday, ed Michael Lapidge and Helmut Gneuss, 1985. *Address:* 14 Church Street, Chesterton, Cambridge CB4 1DT. *T:* Cambridge (01223) 358655.
Died 16 March 1996.

CLEVERLEY FORD, Rev. Preb. Douglas William; Chaplain to the Queen, 1973–84; *b* 4 March 1914; *yr s* of late Arthur James and Mildred Ford; *m* 1939, Olga Mary (*d* 1993), *er d* of late Dr Thomas Bewley and Elizabeth Gilbart-Smith; no *c*. *Educ:* Great Yarmouth Grammar Sch.; Univ. of London. BD, MTh, ALCD (1st cl.). Deacon 1937, priest 1938. London Coll. of Divinity: Tutor, 1937–39; Lectr, 1942–43 and 1952–58; Lectr, Church Army Trng Coll., 1953–60. Curate of Bridlington, Yorks, 1939–42; Vicar of Holy Trinity, Hampstead, 1942–55; Vicar of Holy Trinity with All Saints Church, South Kensington, 1955–74; Senior Chaplain to Archbishop of Canterbury, 1975–80; Hon. Dir, Coll. of Preachers, 1960–73; Rural Dean of Westminster, 1965–74; Prebendary of St Paul's Cathedral, 1968, then Prebendary Emeritus; Provincial Canon of York, 1969–; Lectr, Wey Inst. of Religious Studies, 1980–84; Tutor, Southwark Ordination Course, 1980–86. Six Preacher, Canterbury Cathedral, 1982–91. Chm., Queen Alexandra's House, Kensington Gore, 1966–74; Mem. Governing Body, Westminster City Sch. and United Westminster Schs, 1965–74; Hon. Life Governor: British and Foreign Bible Soc., 1948; Church's Ministry among the Jews, 1955. Queen's Jubilee Medal, 1977. *Publications:* An Expository Preacher's Notebook, 1960; The Christian Faith Explained, 1962; A Theological Preacher's Notebook, 1962; A Pastoral Preacher's Notebook, 1965; A Reading of St Luke's Gospel, 1967; Preaching at the Parish Communion, Vol. 1 1967, Vol. 2 1968, Vol. 3 1969; Preaching Today, 1969; Preaching through the Christian Year, 1971; Praying through the Christian Year, 1973; Have You Anything to Declare?, 1973; Preaching on the Special Occasions, 1974, Vol. 2 1981; Preaching at the Parish Communion (Series III), 1975; New Preaching from the Old Testament, 1976; New Preaching from the New Testament, 1977; The Ministry of the Word, 1979; Preaching through the Acts of the Apostles, 1979; More Preaching from the New Testament, 1982; More Preaching from the Old Testament, 1983; Preaching through the Psalms, 1984; Preaching through the Life of Christ, 1985; Preaching on Devotional Occasions, 1986; From Strength to Strength, 1987; Preaching the Risen Christ, 1988; Preaching on Great Themes, 1989; Preaching on the Holy Spirit, 1990; God's Masterpieces, 1991; Preaching the Incarnate Christ, 1992; Preaching on the Crucifixion, 1993; Preaching on the Historical Jesus, 1993; Preaching What We Believe, 1995; Preaching on the Sayings of Jesus, 1996; Day by Day with the Psalms, 1996; contrib. Churchman's Companion 1967, Expository Times. *Recreations:* gardening, music, languages. *Address:* Rostrevor, Lingfield, Surrey RH7 6BZ. *Club:* Athenæum.
Died 4 May 1996.

CLIBBORN, Donovan Harold, CMG 1966; HM Diplomatic Service, retired; *b* 2 July 1917; *s* of Henry Joseph Fairley Clibborn and Isabel Sarah Jago; *m* 1st, 1940, Margaret Mercedes Edwige Nelson (*d* 1966); one *s* two *d*; 2nd, 1973, Victoria Ondiviela Garvi; one step *s* two step *d*. *Educ:* Ilford High Sch.; St Edmund Hall, Oxford (MA). Laming Travelling Fellow, Queen's Coll., Oxford, 1938–40; entered Consular Service, 1939; Vice-Consul, Genoa, 1939–40; Army Service, 1940–45: Intelligence Corps and Royal Signals, Western Desert, Sicily, Italy, NW Europe (despatches); Major, 1944; Foreign Office, 1945–46; Consul, Los Angeles, 1946–48; Foreign Office, 1948–50; 1st Sec. (UK High Commn, India), Madras, 1950–52; 1st Sec. (Information), Rio de Janeiro, 1952–56; 1st Sec. (Commercial), Madrid, 1956–60; Consul (Commercial), Milan, 1960–62; Counsellor (Economic), Tehran, 1962–64; Counsellor, Rio de Janeiro, 1964–66; Consul-General, Barcelona, 1966–70; Ambassador, El Salvador, 1971–75. *Recreations:* reading, music, perpetuating light verse. *Address:* Paseo del Dr Moragas 188, Atico 1A, Barberá del Vallés, Prov. Barcelona 08210, Spain. *T:* (3) 7185377.
Died 24 July 1996.

CLIBBORN, Rt Rev. Stanley Eric Francis B.; *see* Booth-Clibborn.

CLIFFORD, Clark McAdams; Special Counsel of the President of the United States, 1946–50; former Special Envoy of President Jimmy Carter; *b* 25 Dec. 1906; *s* of Frank Andrew Clifford and Georgia (*née* McAdams); *m* 1931, Margery Pepperell Kimball; three *d*. *Educ:* Washington Univ., St Louis (LLB). Served US Naval Reserve, 1944–46 (Naval Commendation Ribbon). Practised law in St Louis, 1928–43; specialised in trial cases, corporation and labour law; Senior Partner, Clifford & Miller, 1950–68; Secretary of Defense, USA, 1968–69;

Sen. Partner, Clifford & Warnke, 1969–91. Medal of Freedom with Distinction, USA, 1969. *Recreation:* golf. *Address:* 901 Fifteenth Street NW, Suite 400, Washington, DC 20005, USA.   *Died 10 Oct. 1998.*

CLIFFORD, William Henry Morton, CB 1972; CBE 1966; Legal Consultant, Civil Service College, 1974–79, retired; *b* 30 July 1909; *s* of Henry Edward Clifford, FRIBA, Glasgow, and Margaret Alice, *d* of Dr William Gibson, Campbeltown, Argyll; *m* 1936, Katharine Winifred (*d* 1995), *d* of Rev. H. W. Waterfield, Temple Grove, Eastbourne; one *s* two *d. Educ:* Tonbridge Sch.; Corpus Christi Coll., Cambridge. Admitted a solicitor, 1936. Entered Solicitor's Department, GPO, 1937; served in Army, 1939–45: Major GS, Army Council Secretariat, WO, 1944–45; transferred to Solicitor's Office, Min. of National Insurance, 1945; Assistant Solicitor, Min. of Pensions and Nat. Insurance (later Min. of Social Security), 1953; Solicitor, DHSS (formerly Min. of Social Security), 1968–74. *Recreations:* reading, listening to music (especially opera), genealogy, walking, sailing. *Address:* Woodbrook, 9 Lake Road, Tunbridge Wells, Kent TN4 8XT. *T:* (01892) 521612.   *Died 3 Sept. 1996.*

CLIFTON, Lt-Col Peter Thomas, CVO 1980; DSO 1945; JP; DL; Standard Bearer, HM Body Guard of Honourable Corps of Gentlemen at Arms, 1979–81; *b* 24 Jan. 1911; *s* of Lt-Col Percy Robert Clifton, CMG, DSO, TD, Clifton Hall, Nottingham, and 2nd wife, Evelyn Mary Amelia, *d* of Major Thomas Leith, Aberdeen; *m* 1st, 1934, Ursula (marr. diss. 1936), *d* of Sir Edward Hussey Packe; 2nd, 1948, Patricia Mary Adela, DStJ (who *m* 1935, Robert Cobbold, killed in action 1944), *d* of Major J. M. Gibson-Watt, Doldowlod, Radnorshire; two *d. Educ:* Eton; RMC Sandhurst. 2nd Lieut Grenadier Guards, 1931; served War of 1939–45: France, 1939–40; Italy, 1944–45; Lt-Col 1944; Palestine, 1945–47. Mem. HM Body Guard of Hon. Corps of Gentlemen at Arms, 1960–81 (Clerk of the Cheque and Adjutant, 1973–79). DL Notts 1954; JP Notts 1952–59, Hants 1964. *Address:* Dummer House, Basingstoke, Hants RG25 2AG. *T:* (01256) 397306. *Clubs:* Cavalry and Guards, White's; Royal Yacht Squadron.   *Died 5 Nov. 1996.*

CLOSE, Richard Charles, FCT; FCA; Group Finance Director (formerly Managing Director for Finance), Post Office, since 1993; *b* 3 Sept. 1949; *s* of Richard Alwen Close and Marjorie Ann Close; *m* 1973, Elizabeth Janet Beatrice Brown; one *s* one *d. Educ:* Canford Sch., Wimborne, Dorset; Sidney Sussex Coll., Cambridge Univ. (MA). Qualified Inst. of Chartered Accountants, 1974; FCA 1979; FCT 1990. Arthur Young & Co., Chartered Accountants, 1971–74; Arthur Young, Milan, Italy, 1974–81; Regional Dir Internal Audit, Europe, ME and Africa, Sperry Corp., 1981–84; European Treasurer, Sperry Corp., 1984–86; Finance Dir, Unisys Ltd, 1986–87; Post Office: Corporate Finance Dir, 1987–89; Bd Mem. for Corporate Finance and Planning, 1989–93. *Publications:* contribs to financial jls. *Recreations:* tennis, fishing, walking. *Address:* c/o The Post Office, 148 Old Street EC1V 9HQ.   *Died 6 April 2000.*

CLOUGH, (Arthur) Gordon; broadcaster and writer, freelance since 1973; *b* 26 Aug. 1934; *s* of late James Stanley Gordon Clough and Annie Clough; *m* 1959, Carolyn Stafford (marr. diss. 1991; remarried 1994); one *s* three *d. Educ:* Bolton Sch., Bolton, Lancs; Magdalen Coll., Oxford (William Doncaster Schol.; BA Mod Langs, French and Russian). National Service, RN, 1953–55. BBC: Studio Man., 1958–60; Russian Service, 1960–68 (Prog. Organiser, 1963–68); Radio News Features, Sen. Duty Ed., 1968–73; 1973–: freelance presenter, World at One, PM, World this Weekend, Europhile; co-chm. and question setter, Round Britain Quiz, Round Europe Quiz and Transatlantic Quiz; presenter, Twentyfour Hours,

BBC World Service. Writer/Reporter for many documentary progs for BBC Radio Four and World Service, notably: Let there be No More War, 1985; Revolution Without Shots, 1987; The Indissoluble Union, 1989 (Sony Award, Best Documentary Feature, Current Affairs, 1990); Whose shall be the Land?, 1990; Death of a Superpower, 1991; Ashes of Empire, 1991. Sony Award, Best Current Affairs Prog., World this Weekend,1984. *Publications:* translations from Russian: Years off my Life, General A. V. Gorbatov, (with Tony Cash), 1964; The Ordeal, V. Bykov, 1972; Hostages, G. Svirsky, 1976; The Yawning Heights, A. Zinoviev, 1979; The Radiant Future, A. Zinoviev, 1981; translations from French: The Elusive Revolution, Raymond Aron, 1971; The Art of the Surrealists, A. Alexandrian, 1972; (with Peter Sadecky) Octobriana, Progressive Political Pornography, 1972; occasional articles in The Listener, etc. *Recreations:* cooking, crossword puzzles, coarse chess. *Address:* 52 Ellerton Road, SW18 3NN. *T:* 0181–874 6514.

Died 6 April 1996.

CLOUGH, Prunella; painter; *b* 14 Nov. 1919; *d* of Eric Clough Taylor, poet and civil servant, and Thora Clough Taylor. *Educ:* privately; Chelsea Sch. of Art. Exhibited at Leger Gallery, 1947; Roland Browse & Delbanco, 1949; Leicester Galleries, 1953; Whitechapel Gallery, 1960; Grosvenor Gallery, 1964, 1968; Graves Art Gallery, Sheffield, 1972; New Art Centre, 1975, 1979; Serpentine Gallery, 1976; Warwick Arts Trust, 1982; Annely Juda Fine Art, 1989, 1993; Camden Arts Centre, 1996; Henie Onstad Kunstsenter, Oslo, 1997; Kettle's Yard, Cambridge (retrospective), 1999. City of London Midsummer Prize, 1977. *Address:* 19 Sherbrooke Road, SW6 7HX.

Died 26 Dec. 1999.

CLOUTMAN, Air Vice-Marshal Geoffrey William, CB 1980; FDSRCS; Director of Dental Services, Royal Air Force, 1977–80; *b* 1 April 1920; *s* of Rev. Walter Evans Cloutman and Dora Cloutman; *m* 1949, Sylvia Brown; two *d* (and one *d* decd). *Educ:* Cheltenham Grammar Sch.; Queen Mary Coll., and The London Hosp., Univ. of London. LDSRCS 1942, FDSRCS 1954. House Surg., London Hosp., 1942; joined RAFVR, 1942; War Service, UK and India; specialisation in preventive dentistry, 1948–55; dental hygiene trng; oral surgery appts, 1955–73; RAF Hosps, Fayid, Akrotiri, Aden, Wegberg, Wroughton, Uxbridge; Principal Dental Off., Strike Comd, 1973; QHDS, 1976–80. *Publications:* papers in Brit. Dental Jl and Dental Practitioner. *Recreations:* English church music, cricket, Rugby, Wells Cathedral (Sub-Deacon, 1984–), history of Wells Cathedral and Bishop's Palace. *Address:* Ivy Cottage, 27 Millers Gardens, Wells, Somerset BA5 2TN. *T:* (01749) 679477.

Died 2 March 2000.

CLUTTERBUCK, Maj.-Gen. Richard Lewis, CB 1971; OBE 1958; writer, lecturer and broadcaster; *b* London, 22 Nov. 1917; *s* of late Col L. St J. R. Clutterbuck, OBE, late RA, and Mrs I. J. Clutterbuck; *m* 1948, Angela Muriel Barford; three *s. Educ:* Radley Coll.; Pembroke Coll., Cambridge. MA Cantab (Mech. Scis); PhD (Econ. and Pol.), London Univ., 1971. Commd in RE, 1937; War Service: France, 1940; Sudan and Ethiopia, 1941; Western Desert, 1941–43; Italy, 1944; subseq. service in: Germany, 1946; Italy, 1946; Palestine, 1947; Germany, 1951–53; Instructor, British Army Staff Coll., 1953–56; service in: Malaya, 1956–58; Christmas Island (Nuclear Trials), 1958; Instructor, US Army Staff Coll., 1961–63; idc 1965; Chief Engr, Far East Land Forces, Singapore, 1966–68; Engr-in-Chief (Army), 1968–70; Chief Army Instructor, Royal Coll. of Defence Studies, 1971–72, retired. Col Comdt, RE, 1972–77. Sen. Lectr and Reader, Dept of Politics, Univ. of Exeter, 1972–83. FICE. *Publications:* Across the River (as Richard Jocelyn), 1957; The Long

Long War, 1966; Protest and the Urban Guerrilla, 1973; Riot and Revolution in Singapore and Malaya, 1973; Living with Terrorism, 1975; Guerrillas and Terrorists, 1977; Britain in Agony, 1978, rev. edn 1980; Kidnap and Ransom, 1978; The Media and Political Violence, 1981, rev. edn 1983; Industrial Conflict and Democracy, 1984; Conflict and Violence in Singapore and Malaysia, 1985; The Future of Political Violence, 1986; Kidnap, Hijack and Extortion, 1987; Terrorism and Guerrilla Warfare, 1990; Terrorism, Drugs and Crime in Europe after 1992, 1990; International Crisis and Conflict, 1993; Terrorism in an Unstable World, 1994; Drugs, Crime and Corruption, 1995; Public Safety and Civil Liberties, 1997; contribs to British and US jls. *Address:* Department of Politics, University of Exeter, Exeter EX4 4RJ. *Clubs:* Royal Commonwealth Society, Army and Navy.
Died 6 Jan. 1998.

CLYDESMUIR, 2nd Baron *cr* 1948, of Braidwood, co. Lanark; **Ronald John Bilsland Colville,** KT 1972; CB 1965; MBE 1944; TD; Lord High Commissioner to the General Assembly, Church of Scotland, 1971 and 1972; Lord-Lieutenant, Lanarkshire, 1963–92; a Captain, Royal Company of Archers, Queen's Body Guard for Scotland, 1985–88, Captain General 1988–96; *b* 21 May 1917; *s* of 1st Baron Clydesmuir, GCIE, TD, PC, and Agnes Anne (*d* 1970), CI 1947, Kaisar-i-Hind Gold Medal; *S* father, 1954; *m* 1946, Joan Marguerita, *d* of Lt-Col E. B. Booth, DSO, Darver Castle, Co. Louth; two *s* two *d. Educ:* Charterhouse; Trinity Coll., Cambridge. Served in The Cameronians (Scottish Rifles), 1939–45 (MBE, despatches); commanded 6/7th Bn The Cameronians, TA, 1953–56. Director: Colvilles Ltd, 1958–70; British Linen Bank (Governor, 1966–71); Bank of Scotland (Dep. Governor, 1971–72, Governor, 1972–81); Scottish Provident Instn, 1954 88; Scotbits Securities Ltd, 1960–78; The Scottish Western Investment Co., 1965–78; BSC Strip Mills Div., 1970–73; Caledonian Offshore Co. Ltd, 1971–87; Barclays Bank, 1972–82; Chm., North Sea Assets Ltd, 1972 87. President: Scottish Council (Development and Industry), 1978–86 (Chm., Exec. Cttee, 1966–78); Scottish Council of Physical Recreation, 1964–72; Scottish Br., National Playing Fields Assoc.; Chm., Council, Territorial, Auxiliary and Volunteer Reserve Assocs, 1969–73, Pres., 1974–81; Chm., Lanarkshire T&AFA, 1957–63, Pres. 1963–68; Pres., Lowland TA&VRA. Hon. Colonel: 6th/7th (Territorial) Bn, The Cameronians (Scottish Rifles), 1967–71; 52 Lowland Volunteers, T&AVR, 1970–75. Chm., Scottish Outward Bound Assoc. Trustee, MacRobert Trusts. DL Lanarkshire, 1955, Vice-Lieut, 1959–63. Hon. LLD Strathclyde, 1968; Hon. DSc Heriot-Watt, 1971. *Recreations:* shooting, fishing. *Heir: s* Hon. David Ronald Colville [*b* 8 April 1949; *m* 1978, Aline Frances, *er d* of Peter Merriam, Holton Lodge, Holton St Mary, Suffolk; one *s* two *d*]. *Address:* Langlees House, Biggar, Lanarkshire ML12 6NP. *T:* (01899) 20057. *Club:* New (Edinburgh). *Died 2 Oct. 1996.*

COALES, Prof. John Flavell, CBE 1974 (OBE 1945); FRS 1970; FREng; Professor of Engineering, Cambridge University, 1965–74, then Emeritus; Fellow of Clare Hall, Cambridge, 1964–74, then Emeritus; *b* 14 Sept. 1907; *s* of John Dennis Coales and Marion Beatrice Coales (*née* Flavell); *m* 1936, Mary Dorothea Violet, (Thea), *d* of Rev. Guthrie Henry Lewis Alison; two *s* two *d. Educ:* Berkhamsted Sch.; Sidney Sussex Coll., Cambridge (MA; ScD 1985). Admty Dept of Scientific Res., 1929–46; Res. Dir, Elliott Bros (London) Ltd, 1946; Engineering Department, Cambridge University: Asst Dir of Res., 1953; Lectr, 1956; Reader in Engrg, 1958. Part-time Mem., E Electricity Bd, 1967–73. Director: Tube Investments Technological Centre, 1955–60; TI R&D Bd, 1960–65; BSA Metal Components, 1967–73; BSA Gp

Res. Bd (Dep. Chm.), 1967–73; Delta Materials Research Ltd, 1974–77. Mackay Vis. Prof. of Electrical Engrg, Univ. of Calif, Berkeley, 1963. Internat. Fedn of Automatic Control: MEC, 1957; Vice-Pres., 1961; Pres., 1963. British Conference on Automation and Computation: Gp B Vice-Chm., 1958; Chm., 1960. UK Automation Council: Chm. Res. and Develt Panel, 1960–63; Chm. For. Relations Panel, 1960–64; Vice-Chm., 1961–63; Chm., 1963–66. Institution of Electrical Engineers: Mem. Council, 1953–55, 1964–77; Chm., Measurement Section, 1953; Chm., Control and Automation Div., 1965, etc; Vice-Pres., 1966–71; Pres., 1971–72. Council of Engineering Institutions: Vice-Chm., 1974; Chm., 1975 (Mem. Council for Envtl Sci. and Engrg, 1973–76); Chm., Commonwealth Bd for Engrg Educn and Training, 1976–80; Pres., World Environment and Resources Council, 1973–74. Pres., Soc. of Instrument Technology, 1958. Member: Gen. Bd and Exec. Cttee of Nat. Physical Laboratory, 1959–64; Adv. Council, RMCS, 1963–73; Educn Adv. Cttee for RAF, 1967–76; Trng and Educn Adv. Cttee of RAF, 1976–79; Court of Cranfield Inst. of Technology, 1970–82; Governing Body, Nat. Inst. of Agric. Engrg, 1970–75; Envtl Design and Engrg Res. Cttee, DoE Bldg Res. Estab., 1973–76; British Council Sci. Adv. Cttee, 1973–75; Engrg and Bldgs Bd, ARC, 1973–77; British Library Adv. Council, 1975–81; Chm., IFAC Pubns Managing Bd, 1976–87. Governor: Hatfield Coll. of Technology, 1951–68; Hatfield Polytechnic, 1969–70 (Hon. Fellow, 1971). FICE, FIEE (Hon. FIEE 1985), FIEEE, FInstP; Founder Fellow, Fellowship of Engineering, 1976 (Mem., Exec. Cttee and Chm., Activities Cttee, 1976–80); Hon. Mem., Inst. of Measurement and Control, 1971. For. Mem., Serbian Acad. of Scis, 1981. Hon. DSc City Univ., 1970; Hon. DTech Loughborough, 1977; Hon. DEng Sheffield, 1978. Harold Hartley Medal 1971; Giorgio Quazza Medal, IFAC, 1981 (first recipient); Honda Prize, 1982. *Publications:* (ed) Automatic and Remote Control (Proc. First Congress of Internat. Fedn of Automatic Control), 1961; original papers on radio direction finding, radar, information theory, magnetic amplifiers, automatic control, automation, technical education and econometrics. *Recreations:* mountaineering, gardening. *Address:* 14 Chesterford House, Southacre Drive, Cambridge CB2 2TZ. *Club:* Alpine. *Died 6 June 1999.*

COATES, Kenneth Howard, OBE 1993; CEng, FRAeS; Executive Chairman, Meggitt PLC, since 1984; Chairman, Southern Electric plc, 1996–98; *b* 13 May 1933; *s* of late Cecil Howard Coates and Frederica Margaret Coates (*née* Slaughter); *m* 1958, Jennefer Anne Holmes; one *s* two *d. Educ:* Royal High Sch., Edinburgh; Herriot-Watt Coll. MIMechE. Machinery Purchasing Agent, Ford Motor Co., 1961–69; Chief Exec., Marwin Holdings, 1969–73; Chief Exec., Kearney & Trecker Marwin, 1973–77; Man. Dir, Flight Refuelling, 1977–83. Hon. DTech Bournemouth, 1992. *Recreations:* golf, sailing. *Address:* Meggitt plc, Farrs House, Cowgrove, Wimborne, Dorset BH21 4EL. *T:* (0202) 841141. *Clubs:* Royal Motor Yacht; Ferndown Golf. *Died 4 April 1998.*

COBB, Richard Charles, CBE 1978; FBA 1967; Professor of Modern History, University of Oxford, 1973–84; Senior Research Fellow of Worcester College, Oxford, 1984–87; *b* 20 May 1917; *s* of Francis Hills Cobb, Sudan Civil Service, and Dora Cobb (*née* Swindale); *m* 1952, Françoise Richard; *m* 1963, Margaret Tennant; three *s* one *d. Educ:* Shrewsbury Sch.; Merton Coll., Oxford (Hon. Fellow 1980). Postmastership in History, Merton, 1934. HM Forces, 1942–46. Research in Paris, 1946–55; Lectr in History, UCW Aberystwyth, 1955–61; Sen. Simon Res. Fellow, Manchester, 1960; Lectr, University of Leeds, 1962; Fellow and Tutor in Modern History, Balliol Coll., 1962–72, Hon. Fellow, 1977; Reader in French Revolutionary History, Oxford, 1969–72. Vis. Prof. in the

History of Paris, Collège de France, 1971. Lectures: Ralegh, British Academy, 1974; Zaharoff, Oxford, 1976; Helmsley, Brandeis, 1981. DUniv Essex, 1981; Hon. LittD Leeds, 1988; Hon. DLitt Cambridge, 1989. Chevalier des Palmes Académiques, 1956; Officier de l'Ordre National du Mérite, 1977; Chevalier de la Légion d'Honneur, 1985. *Publications:* L'armée révolutionnaire à Lyon, 1952; Les armées révolutionnaires du Midi, 1955; Les armées révolutionnaires, vol. 1, 1961, vol. 2, 1963 (English trans., by Marianne Elliott, as The People's Armies: instrument of the Terror in the Departments, April 1793 to Floréal Year II, 1987); Terreur et Subsistances, 1965; A Second Identity: essays on France and French history, 1969; The Police and the People: French Popular Protest 1789–1820, 1970; Reactions to the French Revolution, 1972; Paris and its Provinces 1792–1802, 1975; A Sense of Place, 1975; Tour de France, 1976; Death in Paris 1795–1801, 1978 (Wolfson Prize, 1979); Streets of Paris, 1980; Promenades, 1980; French and Germans, Germans and French, 1983; People and Places, 1985; *autobiography:* Still Life: sketches from a Tunbridge Wells childhood, 1983 (J. R. Ackerley Prize); A Classical Education, 1985; Something to Hold Onto: autobiographical sketches, 1988; *posthumous publication:* The End of the Line, 1997 (memoir). *Address:* Worcester College, Oxford OX1 2HB.						*Died 15 Jan. 1996.*

COBBAN, Sir James (Macdonald), Kt 1982; CBE 1971; TD; DL; JP; MA; Headmaster of Abingdon School, 1947–70; *b* 14 Sept. 1910; *s* of late A. M. Cobban, MIStructE, Scunthorpe, Lincs; *m* 1942, Lorna Mary (*d* 1961), *er d* of late G. S. W. Marlow, BSc, FRIC, barrister-at-law, Sydenham; four *d* (one *s* decd). *Educ:* Pocklington Sch.; Jesus Coll., Cambridge (Scholar); Univ. of Vienna. Classical Tripos, Part I, 1931, Part II, 1932; Sandys Student, 1932: Thirlwall Medallist and Gladstone Prizeman, 1935; MA, Cambridge; MA, Oxford (Pembroke Coll.). Asst Master, King Edward VI Sch., Southampton, 1933–36; Class. Sixth Form Master, Dulwich Coll., 1936–40, 1946–47. Intelligence Corps (TA), 1941; GSO3, Directorate of Mil. Intelligence, 1941; Intermediate War Course, Staff Coll., 1943; DAQMG, Combined Ops HQ, 1943; Staff Officer, CCG, 1944 (Lt-Col 1945). Rep. Diocese of Oxford on Gen. Synod, 1970–85 (Panel of Chairmen 1979–81); Vice-Pres., Dio. Synod, 1975–82; Chm., Abingdon Co. Bench, 1964–74; Member: Cttee, GBA, 1972 (Dep. Chm., 1976–82; Hon. Life Mem., 1981); Direct Grant Schs Jt Cttee, 1966–80 (Chm., 1975–80); Cttee, GBGSA, 1976–81; Council, Ind. Schs Careers Orgn, 1972–80; Cttee, United Soc. Christian Lit., 1974–83; Thames Valley Police Authority, 1973–80; Vale of White Horse DC, 1973–76; Governor: Stowe Sch., 1970–83; Wellington Coll., 1970–81; Campion Sch., Athens, 1980–83; Sch. of St Helen and St Katharine, 1954–80, 1983–87 (Chm., 1958–67); Abingdon Coll. of Further Education, 1974–80; St Stephen's House, Oxford, 1982–85; Gloucester School of Ministry, 1984–86. JP Berks, 1950, Oxon, 1974; DL Berks, 1966, Oxon, 1974. *Publications:* Senate and Provinces, 78–49 BC, 1935; (in collaboration) Civis Romanus, 1936; Pax et Imperium, 1938; Church and School, 1963; Dulwich goes to War—and from it, 1995; One Small Head, 1998. *Address:* Tyndale, Preston Road, Yeovil BA21 3AQ.
						Died 19 April 1999.

COCKBURN-CAMPBELL, Sir Thomas, 6th Bt *cr* 1821; of Gartsford, Ross-shire; *b* 8 Dec. 1918; *e s* of Sir Alexander Thomas Cockburn-Campbell, 5th Bt, and Maude Frances Lorenzo (*d* 1926), *o d* of Alfred Giles, Kent Town, Adelaide, SA; *S* father, 1935; *m* 1st, 1944, Josephine Zoi (marr. diss. 1981), *e d* of Harold Douglas Forward, Curjardine, WA; one *s;* 2nd, 1982, Janice Laraine (marr. diss. 1990), *y d* of William John Pascoe, Bundoora, Vic. *Educ:* Melbourne C of E Grammar Sch.

Heir: s Alexander Thomas Cockburn-Campbell [*b* 16 March 1945; *m* 1969, Kerry Ann, *e d* of Sgt K. Johnson; one *s* one *d*]. *Address:* 21 Cardwell Street, York, WA 6302, Australia.						*Died 1999.*

COCKCROFT, Dr Janet Rosemary, OBE 1975; Chairman, Bottoms Mill Co. Ltd, Todmorden, 1980–96 (Director, 1961–96; Deputy Chairman, 1974–80); *b* 26 July 1916; *er d* of late Major W. G. Mowat, MC, TD, JP, Buchollie, Lybster, Caithness, Scotland, and Mary Mowat; *m* 1942, Major Peter Worby Cockcroft (*d* 1980); one *s* one *d* (and one *s* decd). *Educ:* Glasgow Univ. (MB, ChB 1938). Ho. Surg. and Ho. Phys., Glasgow Royal Infirmary, 1938–39; GP, 1939–43; Asst MOH, Co. of Caithness, 1943–46; MO, Maternity and Child Welfare, Halifax, 1950–53; Part-time MOH, WR CC, 1953–67; MO, Family Planning Assoc., 1947–75 (Halifax and Sowerby Bridge Clinics); MO, British Red Cross, Halifax, 1960–66; Chairman: N Midlands FPA Doctors' Gp, 1966–68; Halifax FPA Clinic, 1963–75. Mem., Food Additives and Contaminants Cttee, MAFF, 1972–81; Chm., Consumers' Cttees for England and Wales and for GB, MAFF, 1975–82; Vice-Pres., 1969–70, Pres., 1970–72, Nat. Council of Women of GB; Vice-Pres., Internat. Council of Women, 1973–76; UK Rep., UN Status of Women Commn, 1973–79 (Vice Chm., 1976; Chm., 1978–80); Member: BBC Northern Adv. Council, 1975–79; Gen. Adv. Council, BBC, 1980–87. Elder, United Reformed Church, 1973–. *Publication:* Not a Proper Doctor (autobiog.), 1986. *Recreations:* travel, reading. *Address:* Dalemore, Savile Park, Halifax, W Yorks HX1 3EA. *T:* (01422) 352621.						*Died 5 Jan. 2000.*

COCKCROFT, Sir Wilfred (Halliday), Kt 1983; Chairman, Educational Project Resources, 1989–99; *b* 7 June 1923; *s* of Wilfred Cockcroft and Bessie Halliday; *m* 1st, 1949, (Barbara) Rhona Huggan (*d* 1982); two *s*; 2nd, 1982, Vivien, *o d* of Mr and Mrs David Lloyd. *Educ:* Keighley Boys' Grammar Sch.; Balliol Coll., Oxford (Williams Exhibnr, 1941, Hon. Scholar, 1946; MA, DPhil). CMath, FIMA 1973. Technical Signals/Radar Officer, RAF, 1942–46. Asst Lectr, Univ. of Aberdeen, 1949, Lectr 1950; Lectr, Univ. of Southampton, 1957, Reader 1960; G. F. Grant Prof. of Pure Mathematics, Univ. of Hull, 1961; Vice-Chancellor, NUU, 1976–82; Chm. and Chief Exec., Secondary Exams Council, 1983–88. Vis. Lectr and Prof., Univs of Chicago, Stanford, State Univ. of NY, 1954, 1959, 1967. University Grants Committee: Mem., 1973–76; Mem., Math. Sciences Subcttee, 1967–72, Chm. 1973–76; Chm., Educn Subcttee, 1973–76; Mem., Management and Business Studies Subcttee, and Educnl Technology Subcttee, 1973–76. Science and Engineering Research Council (formerly Science Research Council): Mem., 1978–82; Mem., Maths Sub-Cttee, 1964–68 (Chm., 1969–73); Mem., Science Bd, 1969–73; Chm., Postgraduate Trng Cttee, 1979–82. Chairman: Nuffield Maths Project Consultative Cttee, 1963–71; Specialist Conf. on Maths in Commonwealth Schs, Trinidad, 1968; Cttee to review Rural Planning Policy, DoE, NI, 1977–78; Cttee to consider teaching of maths in schs in England and Wales, 1978–82; Standing Conference on Univ. Entrance, 1979–82; Nat. Foundn for Educnl Res., 1988–90; Royal Soc. Maths Curriculum Subcttee, 1991–94; Pres., British Accreditation Council for Ind. Further and Higher Educn, 1991–; Member: Computer Bd for Univs and Res. Councils, 1975–76; US/ UK Educnl Commn, 1977–80; Educn Cttee, Royal Soc., 1990–94. Member, Council: London Mathematical Soc., 1973–76; IMA, 1974–77, 1982–85. Hon. Fellow, Humberside Higher Educn Coll., 1987; Hon. Mem., CGLI, 1987. Hon. DSc: Kent, 1983; Southampton, 1986; Hull, 1988; Bradford, 1996; DUniv Open, 1984. *Publications:* Your Child and Mathematics, 1968; Complex Numbers, 1972. *Recreations:* mathematics textbook writing and editing, golf, swimming, sketching, bad piano playing. *Address:* The Old Rectory, Warmington, OX17 1BU. *T:* (01295) 690531. *Club:* Athenæum.

Died 27 Sept. 1999.

COCKERELL, Sir Christopher (Sydney), Kt 1969; CBE 1966; RDI 1987; FRS 1967; designer and inventor; *b* 4 June 1910; *s* of late Sir Sydney Cockerell and Florence Kate Kingsford; *m* 1937, Margaret Elinor Belsham (*d* 1996); two *d. Educ:* Gresham's; Peterhouse, Cambridge (Hon. Fellow, 1974). Pupil, W. H. Allen & Sons, Bedford, 1931–33; radio research, Cambridge, 1933–35; airborne and navigational equipment research and development (36 patents), Marconi Wireless Telegraph Co. Ltd, 1935–51 (designed, for Admiralty, long-range radar, which was fitted to cruiser, Suffolk, and used to locate Bismarck; designed, for Bomber Comd, equipment able to locate radar stns which were then bombed before D-Day); inventor of and engaged on hovercraft since 1953 (56 patents); Consultant (hovercraft), Ministry of Supply, 1957–58; Consultant: Hovercraft Development Ltd, 1958–70 (Dir, 1959–66); British Hovercraft Corp., 1973–79; Chm., Ripplecraft Co. Ltd, 1950–79; Founder and Chm., Wavepower Ltd, 1974–82 (3 patents), Consultant, 1982–88. Foundn Pres., Internat. Air Cushion Engrg Soc., 1971 (Vice-Pres., 1971–); Pres., UK Hovercraft Soc., 1972–; Member, Min. of Technology's Adv. Cttee for Hovercraft, 1968–70. A Trustee of National Portrait Gallery, 1967–79. Hon. Fellow: Swedish Soc. of Aeronautics, 1963; Soc. of Engineers, 1966; Manchester Inst. of Sci. and Tech., 1967; Downing Coll., Cambridge, 1969. Hon. Mem., Southampton Chamber of Commerce, 1967. Hon. DSc: Leicester, 1967; Heriot-Watt, 1971; London, 1975; Hon. Dr RCA, 1968. Hon. Freeman, Borough of Ramsgate, 1971. Viva Shield, Worshipful Co. of Carmen, 1961; RAC Diamond Jubilee Trophy, 1962; Thulin Medal, Swedish Soc. of Aeronautics, 1963; Howard N. Potts Medal, Franklin Inst., 1965; Albert Medal, RSA, 1966; Churchill Medal, Soc. of Engineers, 1966; Royal Medal, Royal Soc., 1966; Mitchell Memorial Medal, Stoke-on-Trent Assoc. of Engineers, 1967; Columbus Prize, Genoa, 1968; John Scott Award, City of Philadelphia, 1968; Elmer A. Sperry Award, 1968; Gold Medal, Calais Chamber of Commerce, 1969; Bluebird Trophy, 1969; James Alfred Ewing Medal, ICE, 1977; James Watt Internat. Gold Medal, IMechE, 1983. *Recreations:* the visual arts, gardening, fishing. *Address:* 16 Prospect Place, Hythe, Hants SO45 6AU.

Died 1 June 1999.

COCKIN, Rt Rev. George Eyles Irwin; Assistant Bishop, Diocese of York, since 1969; *b* 15 Aug. 1908; *s* of late Charles Irwin Cockin, solicitor, and Judith Cockin. *Educ:* Repton; Leeds University (BA); Lincoln Theological College. Tutor, St Paul's College, Awka, Nigeria, 1933–40; Supervisor, Anglican Schools, E Nigeria, 1940–52; deacon, 1953, priest, 1954; Curate, Kimberworth, Rotherham, 1953–55; Sen. Supervisor, Anglican Schools, E Nigeria, 1955–58; Canon, All Saints Cathedral, Onitsha, 1957; first Bishop of Owerri, 1959–69; Rector of Bainton, dio. York, 1969–78; Rural Dean of Harthill, 1973–78. *Died 18 Nov. 1996.*

COCKRAM, Sir John, Kt 1964; Director, 1952–79, General Manager, 1941–73, The Colne Valley Water Company; Director, 1970–86, Chairman, 1971–86, Rickmansworth Water Co. (formerly Rickmansworth and Uxbridge Valley Water Co.); *b* 10 July 1908; *s* of Alfred John and Beatrice Elizabeth Cockram; *m* 1937, Phyllis Eleanor (*d* 1994), *d* of Albert Henning; one *s* two *d. Educ:* St Aloysius Coll., Highgate. Chartered Accountant. Member: Herts CC, 1949–74 (Chm. 1961–65); Thames Conservancy, 1954–74; Exec. Cttee, British Waterworks Assoc., 1948–74 (Pres., 1957–58); Central Advisory Water Cttee,

1955–73; Thames Water Authy, 1973–76. Life Mem., Water Cos Assoc., 1985 (Mem., 1950–85; Chm , 1950–79; Dep. Pres., 1979–85) Life Governor, Haileybury. *Recreations:* fishing, gardening. *Address:* Rebels' Corner, The Common, Chorleywood, Hertfordshire WD3 5LT.

Died 30 Sept. 1999.

COCKS, Rt Rev. Francis William, CB 1959; *b* 5 Nov. 1913; *o s* of late Canon W. Cocks, OBE, St John's Vicarage, Felixstowe; *m* 1940, Irene May, (Barbara) (*d* 1989), 2nd *d* of H. Thompson, Bridlington; one *s* one *d. Educ:* Haileybury; St Catharine's Coll., Cambridge; Westcott House. Played Rugby Football for Cambridge Univ., Hampshire and Eastern Counties, 1935–38. Ordained, 1937. Chaplain RAFVR, 1939; Chaplain RAF, 1945; Asst Chaplain-in-Chief, 1950; Chaplain-in-Chief, and Archdeacon, Royal Air Force, 1959–65; Rector and Rural Dean of Wolverhampton, 1965–70; Bishop Suffragan of Shrewsbury, 1970–80. Hon. Chaplain to the Queen, 1959–65. Prebendary of S Botolph in Lincoln Cathedral, 1959; Canon Emeritus, 1965–70; Prebendary of Lichfield Cathedral, 1968–70; Hon. Canon of Lichfield Cathedral, 1970–. Select Preacher, Univ. of Cambridge, 1960. Dir, Mercia Television, 1980–81. Mem. of Council, Haileybury and Imperial Service Coll., 1949–87; Pres., Haileybury Soc., 1976–77. Fellow, Woodard Schools, 1970–83; Mem. Council: Denstone Sch., 1970–72; Shrewsbury Sch., 1971–80; Ellesmere Coll., 1971–80. Archbishops' Advr to IIMC, 1975–80. President: Shropshire Horticultural Soc., 1979; Shropshire and W Midlands Agric. Soc., 1980; Buccaneers CC, 1965–89. *Recreations:* playing golf, watching TV, reading. *Address:* 41 Beatrice Avenue, Felixstowe, Suffolk IP11 9HB. *T:* (01394) 283574. *Clubs:* MCC, Royal Air Force; Hawks (Cambridge). *Died 20 Aug. 1998.*

COFFER, David Edwin, CBE 1973 (OBE 1963); General Secretary, The Royal British Legion, 1959–78; *b* 18 Sept. 1913; *s* of David Gilbertson Coffer and Florence Ellen Gard, *m* 1947, Edith Mary Moulton; three *d. Educ:* Colfe Grammar Sch. Member: Supplementary Benefits Appeal Tribunals, 1978 85; Central Advisory Cttee on War Pensions, 1976–87; Bromley, Croydon and Sutton War Pensions Cttee, 1953–87, Chm., 1976–87; Patron, SE County, Royal British Legion, 1978–. *Address:* 47 Malvern Road, Orpington, Kent BR6 9HA. *T:* (01689) 829007. *Died 21 July 1998.*

COGGAN, Baron *cr* 1980 (Life Peer), of Canterbury and of Sissinghurst in the County of Kent; **Rt Rev. and Rt Hon. Frederick Donald Coggan;** PC 1961; Royal Victorian Chain, 1980; DD; Archbishop of Canterbury, 1974–80; *b* 9 Oct. 1909; *s* of late Cornish Arthur Coggan and Fannie Sarah Coggan; *m* 1935, Jean Braithwaite Strain; two *d. Educ:* Merchant Taylors' School; St John's College, Cambridge (schol.; 1st cl. Oriental Langs Trip. pt i, 1930; BA (1st cl. Oriental Langs Trip. pt ii) and Jeremie Septuagint Prize, 1931; Naden Divinity Student, 1931; Tyrwhitt Hebrew Schol. and Mason Prize, 1932; MA 1935); Wycliffe Hall, Oxford; BD Wycliffe Coll., Toronto, 1941. Asst Lectr in Semitic Languages and Literature, University of Manchester, 1931–34; ordained deacon, 1934, priest, 1935; Curate of St Mary Islington, 1934–37; Professor of New Testament, Wycliffe College, Toronto, 1937–44; Principal, London College of Divinity, 1944–56; Bishop of Bradford, 1956–61; Archbishop of York, 1961–74. Chairman of the Liturgical Commission, 1960–64. President, Society for Old Testament Studies, 1967–68; first Life President, Church Army, 1981. Pro-Chancellor, York Univ., 1962–74. Hull Univ., 1968–74. Prelate, Order of St John of Jerusalem, 1967–90. FKC 1975. DD Lambeth, 1957; Hon. DD: Wycliffe Coll., Toronto, 1944; Cambridge, 1962; Leeds, 1958; Aberdeen, 1963; Tokyo, 1963; Saskatoon, 1963; Huron, 1963; Hull,

1963; Manchester, 1972; Moravian Theol Seminary, 1976; Virginia Theol Seminary, 1979; Hon. LLD Liverpool, 1972; HHD Westminster Choir Coll., Princeton, 1966; Hon. DLitt Lancaster, 1967; STD (*hc*) Gen. Theol Seminary, NY, 1967; Hon. DCL Kent, 1975; DUniv York, 1975. Hon. Freeman, City of Canterbury, 1976. *Publications:* A People's Heritage, 1944; The Ministry of the Word, 1945; The Glory of God, 1950; Stewards of Grace, 1958; Five Makers of the New Testament, 1962; Christian Priorities, 1963; The Prayers of the New Testament, 1967; Sinews of Faith, 1969; Word and World, 1971; Convictions, 1975; On Preaching, 1978; The Heart of the Christian Faith, 1978; The Name above All Names, 1981; Sure Foundation, 1981; Mission to the World, 1982; Paul—Portrait of a Revolutionary, 1984; The Sacrament of the Word, 1987, rev. edn as A New Day for Preaching: the Sacrament of the Word, 1996; Cuthbert Bardsley: bishop, evangelist, pastor, 1989; God of Hope, 1991; Voice From the Cross, 1993; The Servant-Son, 1995; Meet Paul: an encounter with the Apostle, 1997; Psalms 1–72, 1999; Psalms 73–150, 2000; contributions to Theology, etc. *Recreations:* travel, motoring, music. *Address:* 28 Lions Hall, St Swithun Street, Winchester SO23 9HW. *T:* (01962) 864289. *Club:* Athenæum.
Died 17 May 2000.

COGHILL, Sir Egerton James Nevill Tobias, (Sir Toby), 8th Bt *cr* 1778 of Coghill, Yorkshire; *b* 26 March 1930; *s* of Sir Joscelyn Ambrose Cramer Coghill, 7th Bt and Elizabeth Gwendoline (*d* 1980), *d* of John B. Atkins; *S* father, 1983; *m* 1958, Gabriel Nancy, *d* of Major Dudley Claud Douglas Ryder; one *s* one *d*. *Educ:* Gordonstoun; Pembroke College, Cambridge. ESU Walter Hines Page Scholar to USA. Architectural Asst with Sir Frederick Gibberd & Ptnrs, 1952–55; Industrial Developer, 1955–58; Admin. Manager, McKinsey and Co. Inc., 1959–61; Supply teacher, LCC, 1961–62; Housemaster, Aiglon Coll., Switzerland, 1962–64; Headmaster, Aberlour House, 1964–89. Man. Dir, Wallcoatings Scotland Ltd, 1996–. Director: Aiglon Coll., Switzerland (Chm. Govs, 1991–99); The Gordonstoun Foundn Ltd, 1990–. Trustee: Scottish Dyslexia Trust, 1992–96; Cantraybridge Rural Skills College Trust, 1996–. *Recreation:* country sports. *Heir:* s Patrick Kendal Farley Coghill, *b* 3 Nov. 1960. *Club:* Royal Ocean Racing. *Died 23 Sept. 2000.*

COHEN, George Cormack; Sheriff-Substitute of the Lothians and Peebles at Edinburgh, 1955–66; *b* 16 Dec. 1909; *s* of J. Cohen and Mary J. Cormack, Melfort House, Bearsden, Dunbartonshire; *m* 1939, Elizabeth, *d* of James H. Wallace, Malvern; one *s* one *d*. *Educ:* Kelvinside Academy, Glasgow; Glasgow Univ. MA 1930, LLB 1934. Admitted to Scottish Bar, 1935; Sheriff-Substitute of Caithness at Wick, 1944–51; of Ayr and Bute at Kilmarnock, 1951–55. *Recreations:* travel, gastronomy, philately, gardening. *Address:* 37B Lauder Road, Edinburgh EH9 1UE. *T:* (0131) 668 1689.
Died 30 April 1999.

COHEN, Dr Louis; Executive Secretary, Institute of Physics, 1966–90, retired; *b* 14 Oct. 1925; *s* of late Harry Cohen and Fanny Cohen (*née* Abrahams); *m* 1948, Eve G. Marsh; one *s* two *d*. *Educ:* Manchester Central High Sch.; Manchester Univ.; Imperial Coll., London. BSc, PhD, FInstP. Research Physicist, Simon-Carves Ltd, 1953–63; Research Manager, Pyrotenax Ltd, 1963–66. Hon. Sec., Council of Science and Technology Insts, 1969–87; Treasurer, European Physical Soc., 1968–73; Corresp. Mem., Manchester Literary and Philosophical Soc., 1963. FRSA. *Publications:* papers and articles on physics and related subjects. *Recreations:* cooking, books, music, the theatre. *Address:* Flat 1, 21 Hamilton Road, W5 2EE. *T:* (0181) 579 2227.
Died 28 July 1997.

COHEN, Lt-Col Nathan Leslie, OBE 1990; CPM 1956; TD 1949; JP; *b* 13 Jan. 1908; *s* of Reuben and Maud Cohen; unmarried. *Educ:* Stockton-on-Tees Grammar Sch.; Clifton Coll. In private practice as a Solicitor until 1939; called to the Bar, Lincoln's Inn, 1954. War Service, Aug. 1939–May 1945. Senior Legal Officer (Lt-Col), Military Govt, Carinthia, Austria, 1945–49; Pres. of Sessions Courts, Malaya, 1949–57; Justice of the Special Courts, Cyprus, 1958–59; Judge of HM Court of Sovereign Base Areas of Akrotiri and Dhekalia, Cyprus, 1960–61; Adjudicator under Immigration Appeals Act, 1970–71. Mem., Cleveland Co. Social Services Cttee 1978–80. Dist Hd, Forces Relief Soc., Stockton, 1975–; Vice-President: Northern Area, Royal British Legion; Cleveland British Red Cross Soc.; Patron, Durham and Cleveland Royal British Legion, 1985–; President: Stockton Physically Handicapped Club, 1990–; St John Ambulance Assoc., Stockton and Thornaby. Hon. Mem., Stockton-on-Tees Rotary Club. JP Stockton-on-Tees, 1967. Freedom, Stockton-on-Tees, 1991. Diamond Jubilee Medal (Johore), 1955; Royal Brit. Legion Gold Badge, 1979; British Red Cross Badge of Honour, 1981, Voluntary Medical Service Medal, 1982; Service Medal, Order of St John, 1993; Paul Harris Fellowship Award, Rotary Club, 1997. SBStJ 1980. *Recreations:* travelling, reading. *Address:* 646 Yarm Road, Eaglescliffe TS16 0DH. *T:* (01642) 645485. *Club:* Royal Over-Seas League. *Died 27 Sept. 2000.*

COHEN, Dr Richard Henry Lionel, CB 1969; Chief Scientist, Department of Health and Social Security, 1972–73, retired; *b* 1 Feb. 1907; *y s* of Frank Lionel and Bertha Hendelah Cohen; *m* 1934, Margaret Clarkson Deas (*d* 1996); one *s*. *Educ:* Clifton Coll.; King's Coll., Cambridge; St Bartholomew's Hospital. Miscellaneous hosp. appts, 1940–46; MRC, 1948–62; Dep. Chief Med. Off., MRC, 1957–62; Dept of Health and Social Security (formerly Min. of Health), 1962–73. *Address:* The End House South, Lady Margaret Road, Cambridge CB3 0BJ.
Died 8 Jan. 1998.

COILEY, John Arthur, PhD; Keeper, National Railway Museum, York, 1974–92; *b* 29 March 1932; *o s* of Arthur George Coiley and Stella Coiley (*née* Chinnock); *m* 1956, Patricia Anne Coiley, BA (*née* Dixon); two *s* one *d*. *Educ:* Beckenham and Penge Grammar Sch.; Selwyn Coll., Cambridge (BA, PhD Metallurgy). Scientific Officer, UKAEA, Harwell, 1957–60; Aeon Laboratories, Egham, 1960–65; Development Manager, Fulmer Research Laboratories, 1965–73; Asst Keeper, Science Museum, 1973–74. Mem. Bd, Internat. Assoc. of Transport Museums, 1977–91 (Pres., 1983–86; Vice-Pres., 1986–91). *Publication:* (jtly) Images of Steam, 1968, 2nd edn 1974. *Recreations:* photography, motoring. *Address:* 4 Beech Close, Farnham, Knaresborough, N Yorkshire HG5 9JJ. *T:* (01423) 340497. *Died 22 May 1998.*

COLBERT, (Lily) Claudette, (Mrs Joel J. Pressman); Chevalier, Légion d'Honneur, 1988; stage and film actress; *b* Paris, 13 Sept. 1903; *d* of Georges Chauchoin and Jeanne Loew; *m* 1st, Norman Foster (marr. diss. 1935); 2nd, Dr Joel J. Pressman (*d* 1968). Went to America, 1908. First appearances: New York Stage, 1923; London stage, 1928; after success on Broadway, entered films, 1929; returned to Broadway stage, 1958–60. *Plays include:* Wild Westcotts, The Marionette Man, We've Got to Have Money, The Cat Came Back, Leah Kleschna, High Stakes, A Kiss in the Taxi, The Ghost Train, The Pearl of Great Price, The Barker, The Mulberry Bush, La Gringa, Within the Law, Fast Life, Tin Pan Alley, Dynamo, See Naples and Die, The Marriage-Go-Round, The Kingfisher, Talent for Murder, Aren't We All? *Films include:* For the Love of Mike, 1927; The Lady Lies, 1929; Manslaughter, 1930; The Smiling Lieutenant, 1931; Sign of the Cross, 1932; Cleopatra, It Happened One Night (Academy Award),

1934; The Gilded Lily, Private Worlds, 1935; I Met Him in Paris, Maid of Salem, 1937; Bluebeard's Eighth Wife, 1938; Zaza, Midnight, Drums Along the Mohawk, 1939; Skylark, Remember the Day, 1941; Palm Beach Story, 1942; No Time for Love, So Proudly We Hail, 1943; Since You Went Away, 1944; Without Reservations, The Secret Heart, 1946; The Egg and I, 1947; Sleep My Love, 1948; Three Came Home, The Secret Fury, 1950; The Planter's Wife, 1952; Daughters of Destiny, 1953; Royal Affairs in Versailles, 1954; Parrish, 1961; *film for television:* The Two Mrs Grenvilles, 1988 (Golden Globe award). Kennedy Center Honors Award, 1989. *Address:* Bellerive, St Peter, Barbados, West Indies.
Died 30 July 1996.

COLCHESTER, Nicholas Benedick Sparrowe, OBE 1993; Editorial Director, Economist Intelligence Unit, since 1993; *b* 30 Dec. 1946; *s* of Rev. Halsey Sparrowe Colchester, CMG, OBE and Rozanne Felicity Hastings Medhurst, *d* of late Air Chief Marshal Sir Charles Medhurst, KCB, OBE, MC; *m* 1976, Laurence Lucie Antoinette Schloesing; two *s. Educ:* Dragon Sch.; Radley Coll.; Magdalen Coll., Oxford (BA). Joined Financial Times, 1968: New York Corresp., 1970–73; Bonn Corresp., 1974–77; For. Editor, 1981–86; joined The Economist, 1986, Dep. Editor, 1989–93. Chm., Intermediate Technology Develt Gp, 1996–; Non-executive Director: 3i Smaller Quoted Co. Investment Trust, 1993–; Halifax Financial Services (Holdings), 1995–. Chevalier de l'Ordre National du Mérite (France), 1988. *Publication:* Europe Relaunched (jtly), 1990. *Recreations:* music, theatre. *Address:* 37 Arundel Gardens, W11 2LW. *T:* (0171) 221 2829. *Club:* Garrick.
Died 25 Sept. 1996.

COLDRICK, Albert Percival, (Percy), OBE 1974; FCIT 1972; Chairman: National Health Service SE Thames Appeals Tribunal, 1974–89; Executive Committee, Industrial Participation Association, 1974–93; *b* 6 June 1913; *s* of Albert Percival and Florence Coldrick; *m* 1938, Esther Muriel Blades; two *s* (and one *s* decd). *Educ:* Britannia Bridge Elementary Sch.; Wigan Mining and Technical College. Railway Controller, 1933–47; Transport Salaried Staffs' Association: full-time Officer, 1948–62; Sen. Asst Sec., 1962–66; Asst Gen. Sec., 1967; Gen. Sec., 1968–73. Member: General Council, TUC, 1968–73; Industrial Tribunal, 1975–84. Member: Southern Gas Bd, 1970–73; Midlands and West Region Rlys Bd, 1975–77. Chm., Foundn for Industrial Understanding, 1979–93; Vice Chm., Nat. Exam. Bd for Supervisory Management, 1969–96. Jt Editor, International Directory of the Trade Union Movement, 1977. *Recreations:* reading, golf, walking, photography. *Address:* 10 Murray Avenue, Bromley, Kent BR1 3DQ. *T:* (020) 8464 4089. *Club:* Royal Over-Seas League. *Died 4 Dec. 1999.*

COLE, Prof. Boris Norman, PhD; WhSch; CEng, FIMechE, FInstP; Professor of Mechanical Engineering, 1962–88, Head of Department of Mechanical Engineering, 1962–87, University of Leeds, then Professor Emeritus; *b* 8 Jan. 1924; *s* of James Edward Cole and Gertrude Cole; *m* 1945, Sibylle Duijts; two *s* one *d. Educ:* King Edward's Sch., Birmingham. Apprenticed to Messrs Belliss and Morcom Ltd, Engineers, Birmingham. Department of Mechanical Engineering, University of Birmingham: Lectr, 1949–55; Sen. Lectr, 1955–58; Reader, 1958–62; Chm. of Faculty Bd of Applied Sciences, Birmingham Univ., 1955–57 and 1959–62. Dir, Univ. of Leeds Industrial Services Ltd. Member: Smethwick Co. Borough Educn Cttee, 1957–60; Engrg Materials Res. Requirements Bd, 1974–78, and various other govt cttees; Governor, Engrg Industries Training Bd, Leeds Training Centre, 1967–82. Prizewinner, IMechE, 1953 and 1962. *Publications:* numerous in fields of solid and fluid

mechanics and in engineering education. *Recreations:* walking, music, social history of engineering. *Address:* 6 Wedgewood Grove, Leeds LS8 1EG. *T:* (0113) 266 4756. *Died 3 Sept. 1999.*

COLE, Sir David (Lee), KCMG 1975 (CMG 1965); MC 1944; HM Diplomatic Service, retired; *b* 31 Aug. 1920; *s* of late Brig. D. H. Cole, CBE, LittD, and Charlotte Cole (*née* Wedgwood); *m* 1945, Dorothy (*née* Patton); one *s. Educ:* Cheltenham Coll.; Sidney Sussex Coll., Cambridge. MA (1st Cl. Hons History). Served Royal Inniskilling Fusiliers, 1940–45. Dominions Office, 1947; seconded to Foreign Office for service with UK Delegn to UN, New York, 1948–51; First Sec., Brit. High Commn, New Delhi, 1953–56; Private Sec. to 14th Earl of Home, Sec. of State for Commonwealth Relations and Lord President of the Council (later Baron Home of the Hirsel), 1957–60; Head of Personnel Dept, CRO, 1961–63; British Dep. High Comr in Ghana, 1963–64; British High Comr in Malawi, 1964–67; Minister (Political), New Delhi, 1967–70; Asst Under-Sec. of State, FCO, 1970–73; Ambassador to Thailand, 1973–78. *Publications:* Thailand: Water Colour Impressions, 1977; Rough Road to Rome, 1983. *Recreation:* watercolour painting (exhibited RI, RBA). *Address:* 19 Burghley House, Somerset Road, Wimbledon, SW19 5JB. *Died 28 May 1997.*

COLE, Ven. Ronald Berkeley; Archdeacon Emeritus of Leicester; *b* 20 Oct. 1913; *s* of James William and Florence Caroline Cole; *m* 1943, Mabel Grace Chapman; one *s* one *d. Educ:* Bishop's Coll., Cheshunt. Registrar, London County Freehold and Leasehold Properties Ltd, 1934–40. Deacon, 1942; priest, 1943; Curate, Braunstone, Leicester, 1942–48; Succentor, Leicester Cathedral, 1948–50; Vicar of St Philip, Leicester, 1950–73; Archdeacon of Loughborough, 1953–63, of Leicester, 1963–80; Residentiary Canon of Leicester Cathedral, 1977–80. Hon. Chaplain, 1949–53, Examining Chaplain, 1956–80, to Bishop of Leicester. RD of Repps, dio. Norwich, 1983–86. Hon. DLitt Geneva Theol. Coll., 1972. *Recreations:* gardening, motoring. *Address:* Harland Rise, 70 Cromer Road, Sheringham, Norfolk NR26 8RT.
Died 19 July 1996.

COLE, William Charles, LVO 1966; DMus; FSA, FRAM, FRCM, FRCO; The Master of the Music at the Queen's Chapel of the Savoy, 1954–94, then Master of Music Emeritus; Member Council, Royal College of Organists, since 1960 (Hon. Treasurer, 1964–85; President, 1970–72); Member, Central Music Library Council (formerly Committee), 1964–95 (Chairman, 1973–93); *b* 9 Oct. 1909; *s* of Frederick George Cole and Maria (*née* Fry), Camberwell, London; *m* 1st, 1933, Elizabeth Brown Caw (*d* 1942); three *d*; 2nd, 1947, Winifred Grace Mitchell (*d* 1991); one *s. Educ:* St Olave's Grammar Sch.; RAM. Organist and Choirmaster, Dorking Parish Church, 1930; Music Master, Dorking County Sch., 1931; served War of 1939–45, in Air Ministry; Hon. Musical Dir, Toynbee Hall, 1947–58; Prof. of Harmony and Composition, and Lectr in History of Music, Royal Academy of Music, 1945–62; Royal Academy of Dancing: Lectr, 1948–62; Chm., Music Cttee, 1961–68; Mem., Exec. Council, 1965–68; Mem., Grand Council, 1976–88; Conductor: People's Palace Choral Soc., 1947–63; Leith Hill Musical Festival, 1954–77; Sec., Associated Bd of Royal Schools of Music, 1962–74; Hon. Sec., Royal Philharmonic Soc., 1969–80. President: Surrey County Music Assoc., 1958–76; London Assoc. of Organists, 1963–66. Member: Governing Cttee, Royal Choral Soc., 1972–92 (Chm., Music Cttee, 1975–78); Council, Musicians' Benevolent Fund, 1994– (Mem. Exec. Cttee, 1972–93). Mem. Education Cttee, Surrey CC, 1951–62. *Publications:* Rudiments of Music, 1951; chapter on Development of British Ballet Music, in The Ballet in Britain, 1962; The

Form of Music, 1969; A catalogue of Netherlandish and North European roundels in Britain, 1993; articles in various musical jls and in various learned jls on stained glass. *Recreation:* stained glass. *Address:* Barnacre, Wood Road, Hindhead, Surrey GU26 6PX. *T:* (01428) 734917. *Club:* Garrick. *Died 9 May 1997.*

COLEMAN, Arthur Percy; Deputy Director and Secretary to the Board of Trustees, British Museum (Natural History), 1976–82 (Museum Secretary, 1965–76); *b* 8 Feb. 1922; *s* of late Percy Coleman and Gladys May Coleman (*née* Fisher); *m* 1948, Peggy (*née* Coombs); two *d. Educ:* Wanstead Co. High Sch.; Bristol Univ.; King's Coll. London (MPhil). War Service in 1st King George V Own Gurkha Rifles, 1943–47; Min. of Public Building and Works, 1948–61; HM Treasury, 1961–64. *Publication:* A Special Corps: the beginnings of Gurkha service with the British, 1999. *Recreations:* wild life, music. *Address:* Candleford, Hurst, Beaminster, Dorset DT8 3ES. *T:* (01308) 862155.
Died 31 July 2000.

COLES, Prof. Bryan Randell, DPhil; FRS 1991; FInstP; Professor of Solid State Physics, Imperial College, University of London, 1966–91, then Emeritus Professor (Pro-Rector, 1986–91); Dean of the Royal College of Science, 1984–86; *b* 9 June 1926; *s* of Charles Frederick Coles and Olive Irene Coles; *m* 1955, Merivan Robinson; two *s. Educ:* Canton High Sch., Cardiff; Univ. of Wales, Cardiff (BSc); Jesus Coll., Univ. of Oxford (DPhil). FInstP 1972. Lectr in Metal Physics, Imperial Coll., London, 1950–60, Reader, 1960–65; Res. Fellow, Carnegie Inst. of Technol., Pittsburgh, 1954–56. Vis. Prof., Univ. of Calif, San Diego, 1962 and 1969; Hill Vis. Prof., Univ. of Minnesota, 1983. Vice-Pres., Inst. of Physics, 1968–72; Mem. Physics Cttee, SRC, 1972–76 (Chm. 1973–76); Chm., Neutron Beam Cttee, SERC, 1985–88. Chm. Bd of Dirs, Taylor & Francis Ltd (Scientific Publishers), 1976–96. Mem. Council, Royal Soc., 1996–. *Publications:* Electronic Structures of Solids (with A. D. Caplin), 1976; papers on structure, electrical properties, superconductivity and magnetic properties of metals and alloys in Philosoph. Magazine, Advances in Physics, Jl of Physics. *Recreations:* music, natural history, theatre. *Address:* 61 Courtfield Gardens, SW5 0NQ. *T:* (0171) 373 3539.
Died 24 Feb. 1997.

COLES, Norman, CB 1971; *b* 29 Dec. 1914; *s* of Fred and Emily Coles; *m* 1947, Una Valerie Tarrant; five *s. Educ:* Hanson High Sch., Bradford; Royal College of Science; City and Guilds Coll. Head, Armament Dept, RAE, 1959; Dir Gen. Equipment Research and Development, Min. of Aviation, 1962; Deputy Controller: of Aircraft (RAF), Min. of Technology, 1966–68; of Guided Weapons, Min. of Technology, 1968–69; Dep. Chief Adviser (Research and Studies), MoD, 1969–71; Dep. Controller, Establishments and Research, MoD, 1971–75. *Recreations:* carpentry, crossword puzzles. *Address:* Castle Gate, 27 Castle Hill, Banwell, Weston-super-Mare, Avon BS29 6NX. *T:* (01934) 822019.
Died 4 April 1999.

COLLIE, Alexander Conn, MBE 1979; JP; Lord Provost of the City of Aberdeen, 1980–84; Member (Lab), Aberdeen District Council, 1975–95; *b* 1 July 1913; *s* of late Donald and Jane Collie; *m* 1942, Elizabeth Keith Macleod (*d* 1985); two *s. Educ:* Ferryhill Sch., Aberdeen; Ruthrieston Sch., Aberdeen. Member: (Lab), Aberdeen Town Council, 1947–75; Aberdeen Harbour Board, 1947–74; North of Scotland Hydro-Electric Consultative Council, until Oct. 1980; Past Member: Scottish Sports Council; Scottish Bakers' Union Exec. Council. JP Aberdeen, 1956. Freedom, City of Aberdeen, 1995. Hon. LLD Aberdeen, 1996. OStJ 1981.
Died 27 Dec. 1999.

COLLIER, (Kenneth) Gerald; Principal, College of the Venerable Bede, Durham, 1959–75; *b* 24 March 1910; *m* 1938, Gwendoline Halford; two *s. Educ:* Aldenham Sch.; St John's Coll., Cambridge (MA 1935); Diploma in Education (Oxon) 1945. Technical translation, Stockholm, 1931–32; schoolmaster, 1933–41; Royal Ordnance Factories, 1941–44; Physics Master, Lancing Coll., 1944–49; Lectr, St Luke's Coll., Exeter, 1949–59. Editor, Education for Teaching, 1953–58. Chm., Assoc. Teachers in Colls and Depts of Education, 1964–65. Vis. Prof. of Education, Temple Univ., Philadelphia, 1965, 1968; Hon. Research Fellow, Univ. of East Anglia, 1978–81. Consultant to Council for Educational Technology, 1971–80. British Council tours, 1976–79: India, Brazil and Portugal; lecture tours, USA, 1979, 1990; study tour, Kenya, 1988. FSRHE 1993. *Publications:* The Science of Humanity, 1950; The Social Purposes of Education, 1959; New Dimensions in Higher Education, 1968; (ed) Innovation in Higher Education, 1974; (ed) Values and Moral Development in Higher Education, 1974; (ed) Evaluating the New BEd, 1978; (ed) The Management of Peer-Group Learning, 1983; A New Teaching, A New Learning: a guide to theological education, 1989; articles in educational and other jls. *Recreations:* local history, music, the film. *Address:* 4 Robson Terrace, Shincliffe, Durham DH1 2NL. *T:* (0191) 3841647.
Died 10 Aug. 1998.

COLLIGAN, John Clifford, CBE 1963 (OBE 1957); Director-General, Royal National Institute for the Blind, 1950–72; Secretary, British Wireless for the Blind Fund, 1950–84; Hon. Treasurer and Life Member, World Council for the Blind, since 1969 (British Representative, 1954–69); *b* 27 Oct. 1906; *s* of John and Florence Colligan, Wallasey, Cheshire; *m* 1st, 1934, Ethel May Allton (*d* 1948); one *s* one *d*; 2nd, 1949, Frances Bird (*d* 1988); 3rd, 1989, Beryl May Johns. *Educ:* Liscard High Sch., Wallasey. Dep. Sec., National Institute for the Blind, 1945–49. *Publications:* The Longest Journey, 1969; various articles on blind welfare. *Recreations:* watching cricket, walking, gardening. *Address:* 7 Grayburn Close, Back Lane, Chalfont St Giles, Bucks HP8 4NZ. *T:* (01494) 875193.
Died 6 July 1999.

COLLINS, Sir Arthur (James Robert), KCVO 1980; ERD 1989; *b* 10 July 1911; *s* of Col William Fellowes Collins, DSO, and Lady Evelyn Collins, OBE, *d* of 7th Duke of Roxburghe; *m* 1965, Elizabeth, *d* of Rear-Adm. Sir Arthur Bromley, 8th Bt, KCMG, KCVO, and widow of 6th Baron Sudeley (*died* on war service, 1941). *Educ:* Eton; Christ Church, Oxford (MA). Admitted a Solicitor, 1935; Partner, Withers, 1937, Sen. Partner, 1962–81, then Consultant. Served with Royal Horse Guards, 1938–46; Adjt, 2nd Household Cavalry Regt, 1940–44 (despatches); Major 1943. *Address:* Kirkman Bank, Knaresborough, N Yorks HG5 9BT. *T:* (01423) 863136. *Clubs:* Turf, White's.
Died 28 Dec. 2000.

COLLINS, Stuart Verdun, CB 1970; retired; Chief Inspector of Audit, Department of the Environment (formerly Ministry of Housing and Local Government), 1968–76; *b* 24 Feb. 1916; *s* of Herbert Collins; *m* 1st, 1942, Helen Simpson (*d* 1968); two *d*; 2nd, 1970, Joan Mary Walmsley (widow); one step *s* two step *d. Educ:* Plymouth Coll. Entered Civil Service as Audit Assistant in the District Audit Service of the Ministry of Health, 1934; appointed District Auditor for the London Audit District, 1958. IPFA, FBCS. *Recreations:* golf, do-it-yourself, sailing. *Address:* Kemendine, Court Wood, Newton Ferrers, Devon PL8 1BW.
Died 26 March 1997.

COLLINS, Brig. Thomas Frederick James, CBE 1945 (OBE 1944); JP; DL; *b* 9 April 1905; *s* of Capt. J. A. Collins and Emily (*née* Truscott); *m* 1942, Marjorie

Morwenna (*d* 1992), *d* of Lt-Col T. Donnelly, DSO; one *d. Educ:* Haileybury; RMC, Sandhurst. Gazetted to Green Howards, 1924; Staff College, 1938; served War of 1939–45 (despatches twice, OBE, CBE): France, 1940, NW Europe, 1944–45; retired, with rank of Brig., 1948. Essex County Council: CC, 1960; Vice-Chm., 1967; Chm., 1968–71. JP 1968, DL 1969, Essex. Comdr, Order of Leopold II (Belgium), 1945. *Recreation:* shooting. *Address:* Ashdon Hall, Saffron Walden, Essex CB10 2HF. *T:* (01799) 584232. *Club:* Army and Navy.

Died 28 May 1999.

COLNBROOK, Baron *cr* 1987 (Life Peer), of Waltham St Lawrence in the Royal County of Berkshire; **Humphrey Edward Gregory Atkins,** KCMG 1983; PC 1973; *b* 12 Aug. 1922; *s* of late Capt. E. D. Atkins, Nyeri, Kenya Colony; *m* 1944, Margaret, *d* of Sir Robert Spencer-Nairn, 1st Bt; one *s* three *d. Educ:* Wellington Coll. Special entry cadetship, RN, 1940; Lieut RN, 1943; resigned, 1948. MP (C): Merton and Morden, Surrey, 1955–70; Spelthorne, 1970–87. PPS to Civil Lord of the Admiralty, 1959–62; Opposition Whip, 1967–70; Treasurer of HM Household and Dep. Chief Whip, 1970–73; Parly Sec. to the Treasury and Govt Chief Whip, 1973–74; Opposition Chief Whip, 1974–79; Secretary of State for N Ireland, 1979–81; Lord Privy Seal, 1981–82. Chm., Select Cttee on Defence, 1984–87. Hon. Sec. Conservative Parly Defence Cttee, 1965–67; Pres., Nat. Union of Conservative and Unionist Assocs, 1985–86; Chm., Assoc. of Conservative Peers, 1990–94. Mem., Press Complaints Commn, 1991–94. Vice-Chm., Management Cttee, Outward Bound Trust, 1966–70; Chm., Airey Neave Trust, 1984–90 (Pres., 1990–). *Address:* Tuckenhams, Waltham St Lawrence, Reading, Berks RG10 0JH. *Club:* Brooks's.

Died 4 Oct. 1996.

COLQUHOUN, Maj.-Gen. Sir Cyril (Harry), KCVO 1968 (CVO 1965); CB 1955; OBE 1945; late Royal Artillery; Secretary of the Central Chancery of the Orders of Knighthood, 1960 68; Extra Gentleman Usher to the Queen since 1968; *b* 1903; *s* of late Capt. Harry Colquhoun; *m* 1930, Stella Irene (*d* 1996), *d* of late W. C. Rose, Kotagiri, India, and Cheam, Surrey; one *s. Educ:* RMA, Woolwich. Commnd RA, 1923; served War of 1939–45 (despatches, OBE); Palestine, 1946–48 (despatches); Comdr, 6th, 76th and 1st Field Regiments; CRA 61st Div., 1945; CRA 6th Airborne Div., 1947–48; CRA 1st Infantry Div., 1949–50; Comdt, Sch. of Artillery, 1951–53; GOC 50th (Northumbrian) Infantry Div. (TA), and Northumbrian District, 1954–56; GOC Troops, Malta, 1956–59; retired 1960. Col Commandant: Royal Artillery, 1962–69; Royal Malta Artillery, 1962–70. *Recreations:* gardening, shooting. *Address:* Longwalls, Shenington, Banbury, Oxon OX15 6NQ. *T:* Edge Hill (01295) 670246. *Died 5 June 1996.*

COLQUHOUN, Rev. Canon Frank, MA; Canon Residentiary of Norwich Cathedral, 1973–78, Canon Emeritus, since 1978; Vice-Dean, 1974–78; *b* 28 Oct. 1909; *s* of Rev. R. W. Colquhoun; *m* 1st, 1934, Dora Gertrude Hearne Slater; one *s* one *d*; 2nd, 1973, Judy Kenney. *Educ:* Warwick Sch.; Durham Univ. LTh 1932, BA 1933, MA 1937, Durham. Deacon, 1933; priest, 1934; Curate, St Faith, Maidstone, 1933–35; Curate, New Malden, Surrey, 1935–39; Vicar, St Michael and All Angels, Blackheath Park, SE3, 1939–46; Editorial Sec., Nat. Church League, 1946–52; Priest-in-Charge, Christ Church, Woburn Square, WC1, 1952–54; Vicar of Wallington, Surrey, 1954–61; Canon Residentiary of Southwark Cathedral, 1961–73; Principal, Southwark Ordination Course, 1966–72. Editor, The Churchman, 1946–53. *Publications:* The Living Church in the Parish (ed), 1952; Harringay Story, 1954; Your Child's Baptism, 1958; The Gospels, 1961; Total Christianity, 1962; The

Catechism, 1963; Lent with Pilgrim's Progress, 1965; Christ's Ambassadors, 1965; (ed) Parish Prayers, 1967; (ed) Hard Questions, 1967; Preaching through the Christian Year, 1972; Strong Son of God, 1973; Preaching at the Parish Communion, 1974; Contemporary Parish Prayers, 1975; (ed) Moral Questions, 1977; Hymns that Live, 1980; Prayers that Live, 1981; New Parish Prayers, 1982; Family Prayers, 1984; Fourfold Portrait of Jesus, 1984; A Hymn Companion, 1985; Preaching on Favourite Hymns, 1986; (ed) Your Favourite Songs of Praise, 1987; Sing to the Lord, 1988; Prayers for Today, 1989; More Preaching on Favourite Hymns, 1990; God of our Fathers, 1990; Prayers for All, 1991; My God and King, 1993. *Recreations:* writing, listening to music. *Address:* 21 Buckholt Avenue, Bexhill-on-Sea, East Sussex TN40 2RS. *T:* (01424) 221138. *Died 3 April 1997.*

COLVIN, Michael Keith Beale; MP (C) Romsey, since 1997 (Bristol North West, 1979–83, Romsey and Waterside, 1983–97); *b* 27 Sept. 1932; *s* of late Captain Ivan Beale Colvin, RN, and Mrs Joy Colvin, OBE; *m* 1956, Hon. Nichola, *e d* of Baron Cayzer; one *s* two *d. Educ:* Eton; RMA, Sandhurst; Royal Agricultural Coll., Cirencester. Served Grenadier Guards, 1950–57: Temp. Captain; served BAOR, Berlin, Suez campaign, Cyprus. J. Walter Thompson & Co. Ltd, 1958–63. Councillor: Andover RDC, 1965–72; Test Valley Bor. Council, 1972–74 (first Vice Chm.); Dep. Chm., Winchester Constituency Conservative Assoc., 1973–76; Mcm. (parttime), Cons. Res. Dept, 1975–79. PPS to Baroness Young, Dep. Foreign Sec., FCO, 1983–85, and to Richard Luce, Minister for Arts, 1983–87. Member, Select Committee: on Employment, 1981–83; on Energy, 1990–92; on Defence, 1992– (Chm., 1995–97; Vice Chm., 1997–); Chairman: British-Lithuanian All-Party Gp, 1983–; St Helena and Dependencies All-Party Gp, 1987 ; Conservative Aviation Cttee, 1982–83, 1987–92; Cttee of W Country Cons. MPs, 1982–83; Vice-Chairman: British-Gibraltar All-Party Gp, 1997– (Chm., 1987–97); Conservative Smaller Businesses Cttee, 1980 83; Cons. Foreign and Commonwealth Affairs Cttee, 1997– (Chm., 1992–97); Sec., Conservative Shipping and Shipbuilding Cttee, 1981–83; Parly Adviser to Play Board, 1983–86; Chm., H of C Shooting VIII, 1983–. Dir, Royal British Legion Trng Co., 1993–. President: Hampshire Young Farmers Clubs, 1973–74; Test Valley Br., CPRE, 1974–; Mem., Southern Sports Council, 1970–74; Vice-Chm., British Field Sports Soc., 1987–; Chm., Council for Country Sports, 1988–. Governor, Enham Village Centre. *Address:* Tangley House, near Andover, Hants SP11 0SH. *T:* (01264) 730215. *Clubs:* Kennel, Pratt's.

Died 24 Feb. 2000.

COLYTON, 1st Baron *cr* 1956, of Farway and of Taunton; **Henry Lennox d'Aubigné Hopkinson,** CMG 1944; PC 1952; *b* 3 Jan. 1902; *e s* of late Sir Henry Lennox Hopkinson, KCVO and Maric Ruan, *d* of Francis Blake du Bois, Virgin Is and New York; *m* 1st, 1927, Alice Labouisse (*d* 1953), *d* of Henry Lane Eno, Bar Harbor, Maine, USA; (one *s* decd); 2nd, 1956, Mrs Barbara Addams, *d* of late Stephen Barb, New York. *Educ:* Eton Coll.; Trinity Coll., Cambridge (BA History and Modern Languages Tripos). Entered Diplomatic Service, 1924; 3rd Sec., Washington, 1924; 2nd Sec., Foreign Office, 1929; Stockholm, 1931; Asst Private Sec. to Sec. of State for Foreign Affairs, 1932; Cairo, 1934; 1st Sec., 1936; Athens, 1938; War Cabinet Secretariat, 1939; Private Sec. to Permanent Under-Sec. for Foreign Affairs, 1940; Counsellor and Political Advr to Minister of State in the Middle East, 1941; Minister Plenipotentiary, Lisbon, 1943; Dep. High Comr in Italy, and Vice-Pres., Allied Control Commn, 1944–46; resigned from Foreign Service to enter politics, 1946; Head of Conservative Parly Secretariat and Jt Dir, Conservative Research Dept,

1946–50; MP (C) Taunton Div. of Somerset, 1950–56; Sec. for Overseas Trade, 1951–52; Minister of State for Colonial Affairs, 1952–Dec. 1955. Mem., Consultative Assembly, Council of Europe, 1950–52; Delegate, General Assembly, United Nations, 1952–55; Chairman: Anglo-Egyptian Resettlement Board, 1957–60; Joint East and Central African Board, 1960–65; Tanganyika Concessions Ltd, 1965–72. Royal Humane Society's Award for saving life from drowning, 1919. OStJ 1959. Grand Cross, Order of Prince Henry the Navigator (Portugal), 1972; Dato, Order of the Stia Negara (Brunei), 1972; Grand Star, Order Paduka Stia Negara (Brunei), 1978; Commander, Order of the Zaire (Congo) 1971. *Heir: g s* Alisdair John Munro Hopkinson [*b* 7 May 1958; *m* 1980, Philippa J., *yr d* of Peter J. Bell; two *s* one *d*]. *Address:* Le Formentor, avenue Princesse Grace, Monte Carlo, Monaco. *T:* 309296. *Clubs:* Buck's, White's, Beefsteak. *Died 6 Jan. 1996.*

COMBERMERE, 5th Viscount *cr* 1826; **Michael Wellington Stapleton-Cotton;** Bt 1677; Baron Combermere 1814; Lecturer in Biblical and Religious Studies, University of London, Department of Extra-Mural Studies, 1972–94; Senior Lecturer, Centre for Extra-Mural Studies, Birkbeck College, 1988–94; *b* 8 Aug. 1929; *s* of 4th Viscount Combermere and Constance Marie Katherine (*d* 1968), *d* of Lt-Col Sir Francis Dudley W. Drummond, KBE; *S* father, 1969; *m* 1961, Pamela Elizabeth, *d* of Rev. R. G. Coulson; one *s* two *d. Educ:* Eton; King's Coll., Univ. of London (BD, MTh). Palestine Police, 1947–48; Royal Canadian Mounted Police, 1948–50; short-service commn as gen. duties Pilot, RAF, 1950–58, retd as Flt-Lt; Sales Rep., Teleflex Products Ltd, 1959–62; read Theology, KCL, 1962–67. Chm., World Congress of Faiths, 1983–88. *Heir: s* Hon. Thomas Robert Wellington Stapleton-Cotton, *b* 30 Aug. 1969. *Address:* Vanners, Bucklebury, Reading, Berks RG7 6RU. *T:* (0118) 971 3336. *Club:* Royal Automobile.

Died 3 Nov. 2000.

COMFORT, Alexander, PhD, DSc; physician: poet and novelist; Adjunct Professor, Neuropsychiatric Institute, University of California at Los Angeles, 1980–91; Consultant, Ventura County Hospital (Medical Education), 1981–91; *b* 10 Feb. 1920; *s* of late Alexander Charles and Daisy Elizabeth Comfort; *m* 1st, 1943, Ruth Muriel Harris (marr. diss. 1973); one *s*; 2nd, 1973, Jane Tristram Henderson (*d* 1991). *Educ:* Highgate Sch.; Trinity Coll., Cambridge (Robert Styring Scholar, Classics, and Senior Scholar, Nat. Sciences); London Hospital (Scholar). 1st Cl. Nat. Sci. Tripos, Part I, 1940; 2nd Cl. Nat. Sci. Tripos, 1st Div. (Pathology), 1941; MRCS, LRCP 1944; MB, BCh Cantab 1944; MA Cantab 1945; DCH London 1945; PhD London 1949 (Biochemistry); DSc London 1963 (Gerontology). Refused military service in war of 1939–45. Lectr in Physiology, London Hospital Medical Coll., 1948–51; Hon. Research Associate, Dept of Zoology, 1951–73, and Dir of Research, Gerontology, 1966–73, UCL; Clin. Lectr, Dept of Psychiatry, Stanford Univ., 1974–83; Prof., Dept of Pathol., Univ. of Calif Sch. of Med., Irvine, 1976–78; Consultant Psychiatrist, Brentwood Veterans' Admin Hospital, LA, 1978–81. Pres., Brit. Soc. for Research on Ageing, 1967; Member: RSocMed.; Amer. Psychiatric Assoc. *Publications: fiction:* No Such Liberty, 1941; The Almond Tree, 1943; The Powerhouse, 1944; Letters from an Outpost (stories), 1947; On this side Nothing, 1948; A Giant's Strength, 1952; Come Out to Play, 1961; Tetrarch (trilogy), 1980; Imperial Patient, 1987; The Philosophers, 1989; *poetry:* France and Other Poems, 1942; A Wreath for the Living, 1943; Elegies, 1944; The Song of Lazarus (USA), 1945; The Signal to Engage, 1947; And All but He Departed, 1951; Haste to the Wedding, 1961; Poems, 1979; Mikrokosmos, 1994; *plays:* Into Egypt, 1942; Cities of the Plain (melodrama), 1943; Gengulphus, 1948; *songs:*

Are You Sitting Comfortably?, 1962; *translation:* The Koka Shastra, 1964; *non-fiction:* The Silver River (travel), 1937; Art and Social Responsibility (essays), 1947; First Year Physiological Technique (textbook), 1948; The Novel and Our Time (criticism), 1948; Barbarism and Sexual Freedom (essays), 1948; Sexual Behaviour in Society (social psychology), 1950; The Pattern of the Future (broadcast lectures), 1950; Authority and Delinquency in the Modern State (social psychology), 1950; The Biology of Senescence (textbook), 1956, 3rd edn 1978; Darwin and the Naked Lady (essays), 1961; Sex and Society (social psychology), 1963; Ageing, the Biology of Senescence (textbook), 1964; The Process of Ageing (science), 1965; Nature and Human Nature (science), 1966; The Anxiety Makers (medical history), 1967; The Joy of Sex (counselling), 1973; More Joy (counselling), 1974; A Good Age, 1976; (ed) Sexual Consequences of Disability, 1978; I and That: notes on the Biology of Religion, 1979; (with Jane T. Comfort) The Facts of Love, 1979; A Practice of Geriatric Psychiatry, 1979; What is a Doctor? (essays), 1980; Reality and Empathy, 1983; (with Jane T. Comfort) What about Alcohol? (textbook), 1983; The New Joy of Sex, 1991; Writings against Power and Death (essays), 1993. *Address:* Chacombe House, Chacombe, Banbury, Oxon OX17 2SL. *Died 26 March 2000.*

COMMAGER, Henry Steele, PhD; Professor of American History, 1956–72, Simpson Lecturer, 1972–92, Amherst College; Professor of History, Columbia University, 1938–56; Hon. Professor, University of Santiago de Chile; *b* 25 Oct. 1902; *s* of James W. Commager and Anna Elizabeth Dan; *m* 1st, 1928, Evan Carroll (decd); one *s* two *d*; 2nd, 1979, Mary Powlesland. *Educ:* Univ. of Chicago; Univ. of Copenhagen. AB Univ. of Chicago, 1923, MA 1924, PhD 1928; MA Oxon and Cantab. Scholar Amer-Scand. Foundation, 1924–25; taught History, New York Univ., 1926–29; Prof. of History, 1929–38. Lectr on American History, Cambridge Univ., 1942–43; Hon. Fellow, Peterhouse; Pitt Prof. of Amer. Hist., Cambridge Univ., 1947–48; Lectr, Salzburg Seminar in Amer. Studies, 1951; Harold Vyvyan Harmsworth Prof. of American History, Oxford Univ., 1952; Gotesman Lectr, Upsala Univ., 1953; Special State Dept Lectr to German Univs, 1954; Zuskind Prof., Brandeis Univ., 1954–55; Prof., Univ. of Copenhagen, 1956; Visiting Prof., Univ. of Aix-Provence, summer 1957; Lectr, Univ. of Jerusalem, summer 1958; Commonwealth Lectr, Univ. of London, 1964; Harris Lectr, Northwestern Univ., 1964; Visiting Prof., Harvard, Chicago, Calif, City Univ. NY, Nebraska, etc. Editor-in-Chief, The Rise of the American Nation, 50 vols. Consultant, Office War Information in Britain and USA; Mem. US Army War Hist. Commn; Mem. Historians Commn on Air Power; special citation US Army; Consultant US Army attached to SHAEF, 1945. Trustee: American Scandinavian Foundation; American Friends of Cambridge Univ. Member: Mass Historical Soc.; American Antiquarian Soc.; Colonial Soc. of Mass; Amer. Acad. of Arts and Letters (Gold Medal for History, 1972). Hon degrees: EdD Rhode Is; LittD: Washington; Ohio Wesleyan, Pittsburgh, Marietta, Hampshire Coll., 1970; Adelphi Coll., 1974; NY State, 1985; Rutgers, 1988; DLitt: Cambridge, Franklin-Marshall, W Virginia, Michigan State; LHD: Brandeis, Puget Sound, Hartford, Alfred; LLD: Merrimack, Carleton; Dickinson Coll., 1967; Franklin Pierce Coll., 1968; Columbia Univ., 1969; Ohio State, 1970; Wilson Coll., 1970; W. C. Post Coll., 1974; Alassa Univ., 1974; DHL: Maryville Coll., 1970; Univ. of Mass, 1972. Pepper Medal for contrib. to social democracy, 1984; Jefferson Medal, Council for Advancement and Support of Educn, 1987; Gold Medal for Arts, Brandeis Univ., 1988. Knight of Order of Dannebrog (Denmark), 1957 (1st cl.). *Publications:* The Growth of the American

Republic (with S. E. Morison) 1930, 2 vols 1939; (sub-ed with S. E. Morison) Documents of American History, 1934, 9th edn 1974; Theodore Parker, 1936; Heritage of America (with A. Nevins), 1939; America: Story of a Free People (with A. Nevins), 1943, new edn 1966; Majority Rule and Minority Rights, 1944; Story of the Second World War, 1945; The American Mind, 1950; The Blue and the Gray, 2 vols 1950; Living Ideas in America, 1951; Robert E. Lee, 1951; Freedom, Loyalty, Dissent, 1954 (special award, Hillman Foundation); Europe and America since 1942 (with G. Bruun), 1954; Joseph Story, 1956; The Spirit of Seventy-Six, 2 vols (with R. B. Morris); Crusaders for Freedom; History: Nature and Purpose, 1965; Freedom and Order, 1966; Search for a Usable Past, 1967; Was America a Mistake?, 1968; The Commonwealth of Learning, 1968; The American Character, 1970; The Use and Abuse of History, 1972; Britain Through American Eyes, 1974; The Defeat of America, 1974; Essays on the Enlightenment, 1974; The Empire of Reason, 1978; Commager on Tocqueville, 1992; edited: Tocqueville, Democracy in America, 1947; America in Perspective, 1947; The St Nicholas Anthology, 1947; Atlas of American Civil War, 1958; Winston Churchill, History of the English Speaking Peoples; Why the Confederacy Lost the Civil War; Major Documents of the Civil War; Theodore Parker, an Anthology; Immigration in American History, 1961; Lester Ward and the Welfare State; The Struggle for Racial Equality, 1967; Joseph Story, Selected Writings and Judicial Opinions; Winston Churchill, Marlborough, 1968; American Destiny, 12 vols. *Recreation:* music. *Address:* PO Box 2187, Amherst, MA 01004–2187, USA. *Clubs:* Lansdowne; Century (New York); St Botolph (Boston); (former Pres.) PEN (American Centre). *Died 2 March 1998.*

COMPSTON, Vice-Adm. Sir Peter (Maxwell), KCB 1970 (CB 1967); *b* 12 Sept. 1915; *s* of Dr G. D. Compston; *m* 1st, 1939, Valerie Bocquet (marr. diss.); one *s* one *d*; 2nd, 1953, Angela Brickwood (*d* 1994). *Educ:* Epsom Coll. Royal Navy, 1937, specialised in flying duties; served 1939–45, HMS Ark Royal, Anson, Vengeance; HMCS Warrior, 1946; HMS Theseus, 1948–50 (despatches); Directorate of RN Staff Coll., 1951–53; Capt. 1955; in comd HMS Orwell and Capt. 'D' Plymouth, 1955–57; Imperial Defence Coll., 1958; Naval Attaché, Paris, 1960–62; in comd HMS Victorious, 1962–64; Rear-Adm., 1965; Chief of British Naval Staff and Naval Attaché, Washington, 1965–67; Flag Officer Flotillas, Western Fleet, 1967–68; Dep. Supreme Allied Comdr, Atlantic, 1968–70, retired. Life Vice Pres., RNLI. *Recreations:* theatre, country life. *Address:* 10 Berehurst, Borovere Lane, Alton, Hants GU34 1PA. *Club:* Army and Navy. *Died 20 Aug. 2000.*

COMPTON, Denis Charles Scott, CBE 1958; professional cricketer, retired 1957; Sunday Express Cricket Correspondent, since 1950; BBC Television Cricket Commentator, since 1958; *b* 23 May 1918; *m* 1st, 1941, Doris Rich (marr. diss.); one *s*; 2nd, 1951, Valerie (marr. diss. 1968), *d* of Cecil Platt, Durban, South Africa; two *s*; 3rd, 1975, Christine Franklin Tobias; two *d*. *Educ:* Bell Lane Sch., Hendon. First played for Middlesex, 1936; first played for England *v* New Zealand, 1937; *v* Australia, 1938; *v* West Indies, 1939; *v* India, 1946; *v* S Africa, 1947; played in 78 Test matches; made 123 centuries in first-class cricket. Association Football: Mem. of Arsenal XI; England XI, 1943. Editor, Denis Compton's Annual, 1950–57. *Publications:* Playing for England, 1948; Testing Time for England, 1948; In Sun and Shadow, 1952; End of an Innings, 1958, repr. 1988; Denis Compton's Test Diary, 1964; (jtly) Cricket and All That, 1978; *relevant publication:* Denis: the authorised biography of the incomparable Compton, by Tim Heald, 1994. *Recreation:* golf. *Address:* c/o Sunday Express, Ludgate House, 245

Blackfriars Road, SE1 9UX. *Clubs:* MCC, Middlesex CC (Pres., 1990–91); Wanderers (Johannesburg). *Died 23 April 1997.*

COMYN, Hon. Sir James (Peter), Kt 1978; Judge of the High Court of Justice, Queen's Bench Division, 1979–85 (Family Division, 1978–79), resigned due to ill-health, Sept. 1985; *b* Co. Dublin, 8 March 1921; *o s* of late James Comyn, QC, Dublin and Mary Comyn; *m* 1967, Anne (solicitor), *d* of late Philip Chaundler, MC, solicitor, Biggleswade, and Mrs Chaundler; one *s* one *d*. *Educ:* Oratory Sch.; New Coll., Oxford (MA). Ex-Pres. of Oxford Union. With Irish Times (briefly), BBC and various wartime orgns, 1938–44. Called to the Bar, Inner Temple, 1942; called to Irish Bar, 1947, Hong Kong Bar, 1969; QC 1961. Recorder of Andover, 1964–71; Comr of Assize, Western Circuit, 1971; Hon. (life) Recorder of Andover, 1972; a Recorder of the Crown Court, 1972–77. Master of the Bench, Inner Temple, 1968; Mem. and Chm., Bar Council, 1973–74. Chairman: Court Line Enquiry, 1972–73; Solihull Hosp. Enquiry, 1974. Mem., Parole Bd, 1982–84, Vice-Chm. 1983–84. A Governor of the Oratory Sch., 1964–90; President: Oratory Sch. Assoc. (Sch. and Prep. Sch.), 1983–90; Oratory Sch. Soc. (old boys), 1984–. Owner of the "Clareville" herd of pedigree Aberdeen-Angus. *Publications:* Their Friends at Court, 1973; Irish at Law: a selection of famous and unusual cases, 1981; Lost Causes, 1982; Summing It Up (memoirs), 1991; Watching Brief (memoirs), 1993; Leave to Appeal (memoirs), 1995; various vols of light verse and books and articles on legal subjects. *Recreations:* cattle-breeding, farming, golf, planting trees. *Address:* Belvin, Tara, Co. Meath, Ireland. *Club:* Royal Dublin Society. *Died 5 Jan. 1997.*

CONAN DOYLE, Air Comdt Dame Jean (Lena Annette), (Lady Bromet), DBE 1963 (OBE 1948); AE 1949; Director of the Women's Royal Air Force, 1963–66, retired; *b* 21 Dec. 1912; *d* of late Sir Arthur Conan Doyle and Lady Conan Doyle (*née* Jean Leckie); *m* 1965, Air Vice-Marshal Sir Geoffrey Bromet, KBE, CB, DSO, DL (*d* 1983). *Educ:* Granville House, Eastbourne. Joined No 46 (Co. of Sussex) ATS, RAF Company, Sept. 1938; commnd in WAAF, 1940; served in UK, 1939–45; commnd in RAF, 1949; Comd WRAF Admin Officer: BAFO, Germany, 1947–50; HQ Tech. Trng Comd, 1950–52; Dep. Dir, WRAF, 1952–54; Inspector of the WRAF, 1954–56; OC, RAF Hawkinge, 1956–59; Inspector of the WRAF, 1959–60; Dep. Dir, WRAF, 1960–62; Comd WRAF Admin Officer, HQ Tech. Trng Comd, 1962–63. Hon. ADC to the Queen, 1963–66. A Governor, Royal Star and Garter Home, 1968–82; Mem. Council, Officers' Pensions Soc., 1970–75, a Vice-Pres. 1981–88; Mem. Cttee, Not Forgotten Assoc., 1975–91, a Pres. 1981–91. Holder of USA copyright on her father's published works. *Recreation:* attempting to paint. *Address:* Flat 6, 72 Cadogan Square, SW1X 0EA. *Clubs:* Naval and Military, Royal Air Force. *Died 18 Nov. 1997.*

CONNELL, John Morris, OBE 1991; Chairman, Noise Abatement Society, since 1964; *b* 13 Sept. 1911; *s* of late James and Florence Connell; *m* 1939, Gertrude, *d* of late Judge Johann Adler, Vienna; three *d*. *Educ:* BeckenhamTechnical Sch.; Goldsmiths' Coll. MInstM 1935; MIPR 1965. Wholesale meat salesman, Smithfield Market, 1930–39; dir, own meat business, 1939–56; RN, 1941–46; company directorships, 1956–. Founded Noise Abatement Soc., 1959, Hon. Sec., 1959–64; Co-Founder, and Hon. Treasurer, Instn of Environmental Scis, 1970–; Co-Founder, Internat. Assoc. Against Noise, Zürich, 1960. *Publications:* articles and letters in the press. *Recreations:* gardening, reading newspapers. *Address:* Chalkhurst, Upper Austin Lodge Road, Eynsford, Kent DA4 0HT. *T:* (01322) 862789. *Died 8 Sept. 1999.*

CONNELL, Dr Philip Henry, CBE 1986; Emeritus Physician, The Bethlem Royal Hospital and The Maudsley Hospital, 1986 (Physician, 1963–86); *b* 6 July 1921; *s* of George Henry Connell and Evelyn Hilda Sykes; *m* 1st, 1948, Marjorie Helen Gilham (marr. diss. 1973); two *s*; 2nd, 1973, Cecily Mary Harper. *Educ:* St Paul's Sch.; St Bartholomew's Hosp., London. MB BS 1951, MD 1957; MRCS, LRCP 1951, FRCP 1976, FRCPsych 1971; DPM (academic) 1956. St Stephen's Hosp., Fulham Road, 1951–53; Registrar and Sen. Registrar, The Bethlem Royal Hosp. and the Maudsley Hosp., 1953–57; Cons. Psychiatrist, Newcastle Gen. Hosp. and Physician i/c Child Psychiatry Unit, Newcastle Gen. Hosp. in assoc. with King's Coll., Durham Univ., and Assoc. Phys., Royal Victoria Infirm., 1957–63. Extensive nat. and internat. work on drug addiction and dependence (incl. work for WHO, Council of Europe and CENTO), and on maladjusted and psychiatrically ill children and adolescents. Mem. numerous adv. cttees and working parties, including: Standing Mental Health Adv. Cttee, DHSS (formerly Min. of Health), 1966–72 (Vice Chm., 1967–72); Standing Adv. Cttee on Drug Dependence (Wayne Cttee), 1966–71 (Mem., Hallucinogens Sub-Cttees on Cannabis, 1967–68, and on LSD and Amphetamines, 1968–70); Consultant Adviser (Addiction) to DHSS, 1965–71 and 1981–86; Pres., Soc. for Study of Addiction, 1972–75; Vice Pres., Internat. Council on Alcohol and Addictions, 1982–97 (Chm., Scientific and Prof. Adv. Bd, 1971–79, Mem., Bd of Management, 1984–88); Chairman: Inst. for Study of Drug Dependence, 1975–90; Adv. Council on Misuse of Drugs, 1982–88; Sec. of State for Transport's Hon. Med. Adv. Panel on Driving, Alcohol, Drug and Substance Misuse, 1988–95; Member: Council, RMPA, 1962–67; Cttee of Management, Inst. of Psychiatry, 1968–74; Trethowan Cttee on Role of Psychologists in Health Service, 1968–72; Standing Mental Health Adv. Cttee, DHSS, 1966–71; GMC, 1979–91 (Preliminary Screener for Health, 1982–84, 1989–91; Dep. Screener, 1984–89); Vice-Pres., RCPsych, 1979–81 (Mem. Council, 1971–81; Chm., Child and Adolescent Specialist Section, 1971–74; observer on Council as Coll. appointee to GMC, 1979–91). Dent Meml Lectr, KCL and Soc. for Study of Addiction, 1985. Member of Bd of Governors: Bethlem Royal and Maudsley Hosps, 1966–73; Mowden Hall Sch., 1976–82. Hon. FRCPsych 1992; Corresp. FAPA 1970. Mem., editorial bds, various jls. *Publications:* Amphetamine Psychosis (monograph), 1958; (ed jtly) Cannabis and Man, 1975; over 90 chapters in books, papers in sci. jls and proc. sci. confs. *Recreations:* theatre, bridge. *Address:* 25 Oxford Road, Putney, SW15 2LG. *T:* (0181) 788 1416. *Clubs:* Athenæum, Roehampton.

Died 26 July 1998.

CONSTANT, Antony; Group Management Development Executive, the Delta Group plc (formerly Delta Metal Co. Ltd), retired 1980 (Group Archivist, 1980–83); *b* 1916; *s* of Frederick Charles and Mary Theresa Constant; *m* 1947, Pamela Mary Pemberton (*d* 1989); one *s*. *Educ:* Dover Coll.; King's Coll., Cambridge. Asst Master, Oundle Sch., 1939–45; Staff of Dir of Naval Intelligence, Admiralty, 1940–44; Educational Adviser to the Control Commission, Germany, 1945; Asst Master, and Asst House Master of School House, Rugby Sch., 1945–49; Rector of Royal Coll., Mauritius, 1949–53; Dir of Studies, RAF Coll., Cranwell, 1953–59; Educnl Advr, RAF Benevolent Fund, 1953–78; Advr to MoD on officer recruitment, and Chm. of Joint-Services Working Party, 1959–62; joined Delta Group of Companies, 1963, as Head of Group Training Dept. Mem. Bd for Postgraduate Studies, and Mem. Faculty Bd, Management Centre, Univ. of Aston, 1973–77. *Publications:* The Percy Lane Group 1932–52, 1982; articles on local history, ships and shipping. *Recreations:*

genealogy, ornithology, ships, watching smoke. *Address:* Old Bonham's, Wardington, near Banbury, Oxon OX17 1SA. *Died 23 Sept. 1996.*

CONWAY, Most Rev. Dominic Joseph; Bishop of Elphin (RC), 1971–94, then Emeritus; *b* 1 Jan. 1918; *s* of Dominic Conway and Mary Hoare. *Educ:* Coll. of the Immaculate Conception, Sligo; Pontifical Irish Coll., Pontifical Lateran Univ., Pontifical Angelicum Univ., Gregorian Univ. (all in Rome); National Univ. of Ireland. BPh, STL, DEcclHist, Higher Diploma Educn. Missionary, Calabar Dio., Nigeria, 1943–48; Professor: All Hallows Coll., Dublin, 1948–49; Summerhill Coll., Sligo, 1949–51; Spiritual Dir, 1951–65, Rector, 1965–68, Irish Coll., Rome; Sec.-Gen., Superior Council of the Propagation of the Faith, Rome, 1968–70; Auxiliary Bishop of Elphin, 1970–71. *Address:* St Mary's, Sligo, Ireland. *T:* 62670. *Died 22 Aug. 1996.*

COOK, Maj.-Gen. Arthur Thompson, FRCP, FRCPE; Director of Army Medicine, 1977–81; *b* 21 Oct. 1923; *s* of Thomas and Mabel Elizabeth Cook; *m* 1960, Kathleen Lane; two *s* one *d*. *Educ:* China Inland Mission Sch., Chefoo, N China; City of London Sch.; St Thomas' Hosp., London (MB). FRCP 1955, FRCPE 1954. Joined RAMC, 1948. QHP, 1977–81. *Address:* The Old Cricketers, Cricket Hill Lane, Yateley, Hants GU46 6BA. *T:* (01252) 879452. *Died 10 Dec. 2000.*

COOK, Eric William; HM Diplomatic Service, retired; *b* 24 Feb. 1920; *s* of Ernest Gordon Cook and Jessie (*née* Hardy); *m* 1949, Pauline Elizabeth Lee; one *s*. *Educ:* various private estabts. RAF, 1940–46. GPO, 1947–49; FO (later FCO), 1949–80; Consul, Belgrade, 1961–64; Vice-Consul, Leopoldville, 1964–65; Consul, Cleveland, Ohio, 1967–69; also served at Rome, Moscow, Peking and Djakarta; Consul Gen., Adelaide, 1974–76; FCO, 1977–80. *Recreations:* music, writing, photography. *Address:* 11 St Ann's Court, Nizells Avenue, Hove, East Sussex BN3 1PR. *T:* (01273) 776100.

Died 28 Nov. 1998.

COOK, Francis John Granville, MA; Headmaster of Campbell College, Belfast, 1954–71; *b* 28 Jan. 1913; *o s* of late W. G. Cook and Nora Braley; *m* 1942, Jocelyn McKay, *d* of late John Stewart, Westholm, Dunblane, Perthshire; one *s* two *d*. *Educ:* Wyggeston Sch.; Downing Coll., Cambridge (MA). Historical Tripos, Law Tripos; Squire Scholar; Tancred Studentship, Lincoln's Inn. Asst Master, Rossall Sch., 1937; served War, 1940–46, with Royal Navy; Headmaster of Junior Sch., Rossall Sch., 1949–54. *Recreations:* gardening, books, people. *Address:* 49 Bryansford Village, Newcastle, Co. Down BT33 0PT. *T:* (013967) 25165. *Died 15 Sept. 1997.*

COOK, George Steveni L.; *see* Littlejohn Cook.

COOK, Harold James; a Metropolitan Stipendiary Magistrate, 1975–96; *b* 25 Jan. 1926; *s* of Harold Cook and Gwendoline Lydia (*née* List); *m* 1952, Mary Elizabeth (*née* Edwards); one *s*. *Educ:* The John Lyon Sch., Harrow; Edinburgh Univ. RN, 1943–47. Civil Service, 1947–52. Called to the Bar, Gray's Inn, 1952; Dep. Chief Clerk, Bow Street, and later Thames, Magistrates' Courts, 1952–54; Inner London QS, 1955; Dep. Clerk to Justices, Gore Div., Middx, 1956–60; Clerk to Justices, Highgate Div., 1961, and also Barnet and South Mymms Divs, 1968. *Publications:* contrib. legal jls. *Address:* The Coach House, Penketh Drive, Harrow-on-the-Hill, Middlesex HA1 3JX. *Died 1 July 1997.*

COOK, Reginald, FCA; Chairman, South Wales Electricity Board, 1977–81; Member, Electricity Council, 1977–81; *b* 29 Dec. 1918; *s* of Harold and Gwendolyn Cook, Birmingham; *m* 1945, Constance Irene Holt, Norden, Lancs; one *s* one *d*. *Educ:* Rochdale High Sch.; Manchester Univ. (BA); Admin. Staff Coll. Served War, 1939–46;

Staff Captain, RA. Local Govt Service with Corporations of Manchester, West Bromwich and York, 1946–52; Midlands Electricity Board: accountancy posts, 1952–59; Chief Accountant, 1959–69; Exec. Mem., 1964–69; Dep. Chm., S Wales Electricity Bd, 1969–77. CompIEE. Gold Medal, IMTA, 1949. *Recreations:* countryside activities, gardening, golf, bridge. *Address:* Heppleshaw, Itton, Chepstow, Mon NP6 6BZ. *T:* (01291) 641265.

Died 24 Dec. 1997.

COOK, Maj.-Gen. Robert Francis Leonard, MSc, MPhil; CEng, FIEE; CPhys; Director General, Federation of the Electronics Industry (formerly Electronic Engineering Association), since 1993; *b* 18 June 1939; *s* of Lt-Col Frank Leonard Cook and Louise Alicia (*née* Davis); *m* 1961, Gillian Margaret Lowry; one *s* two *d*. *Educ:* Karachi Grammar Sch., Pakistan; St John's Coll., Southsea; University Coll. of Wales; Welbeck Coll.; RMA Sandhurst; RMCS; Staff Coll., Camberley; NATO Defence Coll., Rome. BSc 1962, MSc 1964, London; MPhil (Strategic Studies) Wales, 1989. Commnd Royal Signals, 1959; served Germany, Malaysia, UK, 1959–70; Directorate of Manning (Army), MoD, 1972; OC 7 Armd Bde, Signal Sqn, 1973; Project Management Staff, MoD (PE), 1975; Lt-Col DS, RMCS, 1976; CO 4 Armd Div. HQ and Signal Regt, 1978; Logistics Staff, HQ BAOR, 1981; Colonel, MoD Operational Requirements Staff, 1982; Brig., Comd 1 Signal Bde, 1 (BR) Corps, 1983; Sec., NATO Mil. Cttee, NATO HQ, Brussels, 1986; Signal Officer-in-Chief (Army), 1989–92, and DG Comd, Control, Communications and Information Systems (Army), 1990–92. Col. Comdt, RCS, 1993–. MInstD. Freeman, City of London, 1989; Liveryman: Engineers' Co., 1990; Information Technologists' Co., 1993. Hon. DTech De Montfort Univ., 1994. *Recreations:* mountain walking, winter and water sports, music, travel, wine. *Address:* c/o Lloyds Bank, 8 Market Place, Faringdon, Oxon SN7 7HN. *Club:* Army and Navy.

Died 25 Feb. 1997.

COOK, Prof. Robert Manuel, FBA 1976; Laurence Professor of Classical Archaeology, University of Cambridge, 1962–76; *b* 4 July 1909; *s* of Rev. Charles Robert and Mary Manuel Cook; *m* 1938, Kathleen (*d* 1979), *d* of James Frank and Ellen Hardman Porter. *Educ:* Marlborough Coll.; Clare Coll., Cambridge (BA 1931). Walston Student, Cambridge Univ., 1932; Asst Lectr in Classics, Manchester Univ., 1934; Lectr, 1938; Sub-warden, St Anselm's Hall, Manchester, 1936–38; Min. of Works, 1939–46; Laurence Reader in Classical Archaeology, Cambridge Univ., 1945–62. Ord. Mem., German Archaeological Inst., 1953. Chm., Managing Cttee, British School at Athens, 1983–87. *Publications:* Corpus Vasorum Antiquorum, British Museum 8, 1954; Greek Painted Pottery, 1960, 3rd edn 1997 (3rd edn trans. Greek, 1994); The Greeks till Alexander, 1962; (with Kathleen Cook) Southern Greece: an archaeological guide, 1968; Greek Art, 1972; Clazomenian Sarcophagi, 1981; (with P. Dupont) East Greek Pottery, 1998. *Address:* 15 Wilberforce Road, Cambridge CB3 0EQ. *T:* (01223) 352863.

Died 10 Aug. 2000.

COOKE, Alexander Macdougall, DM; FRCP; Hon. Consulting Physician, United Oxford Hospitals, 1966; *b* 17 Oct. 1899; *s* of Arthur Clement Cooke, OBE and Isobel Gilles Macdougall; *m* 1928, Vera (*d* 1984), *d* of Charles Hermann Lea; one *s* two *d* (and one *d* decd). *Educ:* Merchant Taylors' School; Jesus College, Oxford; St Thomas's Hosp. (Mead Medal, 1923; Toller Prize). 1st Cl. Hons Nat. Sci. 1920; BM 1923; DM 1933; MRCP 1926, FRCP 1935. War Service, Royal Fusiliers, RFC and RAF, 1917–18. Resident Asst Physician, 1927–28, 1st Asst, Professorial Med. Unit, 1928–30 and Dep. Dir, 1930–32, St Thomas's Hosp.; Physician, Radcliffe Infirmary, 1932–66; May Reader in Medicine, 1933–47; Dir, Clinical Studies, Oxford Medical Sch., 1939–49; Fellow of Merton Coll., Oxford, 1942–66, Emeritus Fellow, 1966–. Lectures: Lumleian, RCP, 1955; Langdon-Brown, RCP, 1968; Litchfield, Oxford, 1964; Stopford Meml, Manchester, 1973. Royal College of Physicians: Examr, 1943–47 and 1952–62; Councillor, 1953–55; Censor, 1956–58; Sen. Censor, 1959–60; Oxford Univ. Rep., GMC, 1963–73. FRSocMed 1924, Hon. Fellow, 1972 (Pres., Section of Medicine, 1960–62); Mem., Assoc. of Physicians, 1936 (Exec. Cttee, 1950–53), Hon. Mem., 1966; Hon. Mem., Royal Coll. of Radiologists. Sec. to Editors, 1937–50 and Editor, 1951–65, Quarterly Jl of Medicine. *Publications:* A History of the Royal College of Physicians of London, Vol. III, 1972; Sir E. Farquhar Buzzard, Bt, KCVO, 1975; The Cookes Tale, 1991; My Seventy Five Years of Medicine, 1994; articles and papers on medicine and med. hist. *Recreation:* inertia. *Address:* Grove Cottage, St Cross Road, Oxford OX1 3TX. *T:* (01865) 242419.

Died 5 Jan. 1999.

COOKE, His Honour (Richard) Kenneth, OBE 1945; a Circuit Judge, 1980–92; *b* 17 March 1917; *s* of Richard and Beatrice Mary Cooke; *m* 1st, 1945, Gwendoline Mary Black (*d* 1985); no *c*; 2nd, 1986, E. A. Rowlands (*née* Bachmann). *Educ:* Sebright Sch., Wolverley; Birmingham Univ. Admitted Solicitor (Hons), 1939; Birmingham Law Soc. Prizeman. Sqdn Leader, RAFVR, 1939–45. Solicitor in private practice specialising in Magistrates' Courts, 1945–52; Clerk: to Prescot and St Helens Justices, 1952–57; to Rotherham County Borough and WR Justices, 1957–64; to Bradford City Justices, 1964–70; Metropolitan Stipendiary Magistrate, 1970–80; a Recorder of the Crown Court, 1972–80. Mem. Council, Magistrates' Assoc., 1973–89 (Chm. Legal Cttee; Hon. Sec., Inner London Branch, 1972–89; a Dep. Chm., 1981–82; Pres., SE London Br., 1985–89); Member: Lord Chancellor's Adv. Cttee on the Training of Magistrates, 1978–85; Adv. Bd, Crime Concern Trust, 1988–93. Chm., Nat. Benevolent Instn, 1997–. Chm., Bromley Talking Newspaper for the Blind, 1997–. Reader, Rochester Dio., 1970–. Hon. Mem., Justices' Clerks Soc., 1988. *Publications:* contribs to Criminal Law Review, Justice of the Peace and Local Govt Review, etc. *Recreations:* fishing, choral singing, sampling bin ends. *Address:* The Bridewell, 6 Liskeard Close, Chislehurst, Kent BR7 6RT. *T:* (020) 8467 3908.

Died 25 Oct. 2000.

COOKSON, Dame Catherine (Ann), DBE 1993 (OBE 1985); author, since 1950; *b* 20 June 1906; *d* of Catherine Fawcett; *m* 1940, Thomas Cookson. Member: Society of Authors; Writers' and Authors' Guild. Paul Harris Fellow, Rotary International, Hexham, 1985. Catherine Cookson Foundation, Newcastle Univ., established 1985. Hon. MA Newcastle upon Tyne, 1983; Hon. DLitt Sunderland Polytechnic, 1991. Freeman of South Shields, 1978. *Publications:* Kate Hannigan, 1950; The Fifteen Streets, 1951 (staged 1987, London 1988); Colour Blind, 1953; Maggie Rowan, 1954; A Grand Man, 1954 (filmed as Jacqueline, 1956); The Lord and Mary Ann, 1956; Rooney, 1957 (filmed 1958); The Menagerie, 1958; The Devil and Mary Ann, 1958; Slinky Jane, 1959; Fanny McBride, 1959; Fenwick Houses, 1960; Love and Mary Ann, 1961; The Garment, 1962; Life and Mary Ann, 1962; The Blind Miller, 1963; Hannah Massey, 1964; Marriage and Mary Ann, 1964; The Long Corridor, 1965; Mary Ann's Angels, 1965; Matty Doolin, 1965; The Unbaited Trap, 1966; Katie Mulholland, 1967; Mary Ann and Bill, 1967; The Round Tower, 1968 (RSL Winifred Holtby Award for Best Regional Novel); Joe and the Gladiator, 1968; Our Kate (autobiog.), 1969; The Nice Bloke, 1969; The Glass Virgin, 1970; The Invitation, 1970; The Nipper, 1970; The Dwelling Place, 1971; Feathers in the Fire, 1971; Pure as the Lily, 1972; Blue Baccy, 1972; The Mallen

Streak, 1973; The Mallen Girl, 1974; The Mallen Litter, 1974; Our John Willie, 1974; The Invisible Cord, 1975; The Gambling Man, 1975 (staged 1985); The Tide of Life, 1976; Mrs Flannagan's Trumpet, 1976; The Girl, 1977; Go Tell It To Mrs Golightly, 1977; The Cinder Path, 1978; The Man Who Cried, 1979; Tilly Trotter, 1980; Lanky Jones, 1980; Tilly Trotter Wed, 1981; Tilly Trotter Widowed, 1982; The Whip, 1983; Hamilton, 1983; The Black Velvet Gown, 1984; Goodbye Hamilton, 1984; A Dinner of Herbs, 1985; Harold, 1985; The Moth, 1986; Catherine Cookson Country (memoirs), 1986; Bill Bailey, 1986; The Parson's Daughter, 1987; Bill Bailey's Lot, 1987; The Cultured Handmaiden, 1988; Bill Bailey's Daughter, 1988; Let Me Make Myself Plain, 1988; The Harrogate Secret, 1989; The Black Candle, 1989; The Wingless Bird, 1990; The Gillyvors, 1990; My Beloved Son, 1991; The Rag Nymph, 1991; The House of Women, 1992; The Maltese Angel, 1992; The Year of the Virgins, 1993; The Upstart, 1996; The Branded Man, 1996; The Bonny Dawn, 1996; The Solace of Sin, 1998; *as Catherine Marchant:* Heritage of Folly, 1962; Fen Tiger, 1963; House of Men, 1964; Martha Mary Crawford, 1975; The Slow Awakening, 1976; The Iron Façade, 1977. *Recreations:* painting, gardening. *Address:* c/o Anthony Sheil Associates, 43 Doughty Street, WC1N 2LF. *Club:* PEN (English Centre).   *Died 11 June 1998.*

COOLEY, Sir Alan (Sydenham), Kt 1976; CBE 1972; FIE Aust; Secretary, Department of Productivity, 1977–80, retired 1981; *b* 17 Sept. 1920; *s* of Hector William Cooley and Ruby Ann Cooley; *m* 1949, Nancie Chisholm Young; four *d. Educ:* Geelong Grammar Sch.; Melbourne Univ. (BEngSc). Cadet Engr, Dept of Supply, 1940–43; Engrg Rep., London, 1951–52; Manager, Echuca Ball Bearing Factory, 1953–55; Supply Rep., Washington, 1956–57; Manager, Small Arms Factory, Lithgow, 1958–60; Dept of Supply: First Asst Sec. (Management Services and Planning), 1961–62; Controller-Gen. (Munitions Supply), 1962–66; Sec., 1966–71; Chm., Australian Public Service Bd, 1971–77. *Address:* PO Box 105, Milton, NSW 2538, Australia.   *Died 13 April 1997.*

COOMBS, Herbert Cole, (Nugget), MA, PhD; FAA; FAHA; FASSA; Visiting Fellow, Centre for Resource and Environmental Studies, Australian National University, since 1976; *b* 24 Feb. 1906; *s* of Francis Robert Henry and Rebecca Mary Coombs; *m* 1931, Mary Alice Ross; three *s* one *d. Educ:* Univ. of Western Australia, Perth, WA (MA); LSE (PhD; Hon. Fellow, 1961). School teacher, Education Dept, WA, 1929; Asst Economist, Commonwealth Bank of Australia, 1935; Economist to Commonwealth Treasury, 1939; Mem., Commonwealth Bank Board, 1942; Dir of Rationing, 1942; Dir-Gen. of Post-War Reconstruction, 1943; Governor, Commonwealth Bank of Australia, 1949–60; Chm., Commonwealth Bank Board, 1951–60; Governor and Chm. of Board, Reserve Bank of Australia, 1960–68; Chancellor, ANU, 1968–76. Chairman: Australian Elizabethan Theatre Trust, 1954–68; Australian Council for Arts, 1968–74; Australian Council for Aboriginal Affairs, 1968–76; Royal Commn on Australian Govt Admin, 1974–76. Hon. LLD: Melbourne; ANU; Sydney; Hon. DLitt WA; Hon. DSc NSW. AC 1975, relinquished 1977. *Publications:* The Fragile Pattern, 1970; Other People's Money, 1971; Kulinma: Listening to Aboriginal Australians, 1978; Trial Balance—issues in my working life, 1981; (jtly) A Certain Heritage: programs by and for Aborigines, 1983; Towards a National Aboriginal Conference, 1985; The Waitangi Treaty and Aborigines (Boyer Lect.), 1988; (jtly) Land of Promises—economic development and aborigines of the East Kimberly, 1989; The Return of Scarcity—Essays Economic and Ecological, 1989; Aborigines Made Visible—from Humbug to Politics (Myer Lect.), 1991; Aboriginal Autonomy, 1993.

Recreations: walking, cooking, listening to music. *Address:* 119 Milson Road, Cremorne, NSW 2090, Australia.   *Died 29 Oct. 1997.*

COOMBS, Nugget; *see* Coombs, H. C.

COOP, Sir Maurice (Fletcher), Kt 1973; solicitor; *b* 11 Sept. 1907; *s* of George Harry and Ada Coop; *m* 1948, Elsie Hilda Brazier. *Educ:* Epworth Coll., Rhyl; Emmanuel Coll., Cambridge (BA). Admitted Solicitor of Supreme Court, 1932. Sec., Dunlop Rubber Co. Ltd, 1948–68; Dir, Dunlop Rubber Co. Ltd, 1966–70. Chm., Standing Adv. Cttee to Govt on Patents, 1972–74. *Recreations:* Association football, cricket. *Address:* 39 Hill Street, Berkeley Square, W1X 7FG. *T:* 0171-491 4549. *Club:* United Oxford & Cambridge University.
                    Died 5 Jan. 1996.

COOPER, Very Rev. Alan; *see* Cooper, Very Rev. W. H. A.

COOPER, Rev. Albert Samuel; Moderator, Free Church Federal Council, 1973–74; *b* 6 Nov. 1905; *s* of Samuel and Edith Cooper; *m* 1936, Emily (*d* 1983), *d* of Hugh and Emily Williams; one *s* one *d. Educ:* Birkenhead Inst.; London Univ. (external student; BA Hons Philosophy); Westminster Coll., Cambridge (DipTh); Fitzwilliam House, Cambridge (BA Theol Tripos, MA). Ordained, 1936; pastoral charges: St Columba's Presbyterian Church, Grimsby, 1936–41; Blundellsands Presbyt. Ch., Liverpool, 1941–44; St Columba's Presbyt. Ch., Cambridge, 1944–60; St Columba's Presbyt. (later United Reformed) Ch., Leeds, 1960–72, retd 1972. Free Church Chaplain, Fulbourn Mental Hosp., Cambridgeshire, 1950–60. Moderator, Presbyt. Ch. of England, 1968–69. *Address:* Dundoran Nursing Home, Vyner Road South, Noctorum, Birkenhead, Merseyside L43 7PW.
                    Died 25 Dec. 1998.

COOPER, Joan Davies, CB 1972; Hon. Research Fellow, University of Sussex, since 1979; *b* 12 Aug. 1914; *d* of late Valentine Holland Cooper and Wynnefred Louisa Cooper; unmarried. *Educ:* Fairfield High Sch., Manchester; University of Manchester (BA). Asst Dir of Educn, Derbyshire CC, 1941; Children's Officer, E Sussex CC, 1948; Chief Inspector, Children's Dept, Home Office, 1965–71; Dir, Social Work Service, DHSS, 1971–76; Nat. Inst. for Social Work, 1976–77. Mem., SSRC, 1973–76. Vice Pres., Nat. Children's Bureau, 1964–; Chairman: Parents for Children, 1979–87; NACRO Adv. Council on Juvenile Crime, 1982–87; Central Council for Educn and Trng in Social Work, 1984–86; E Sussex Care for the Carers, 1985–91 (Pres., 1991–). Chm., Internat. Conf. on Data Protection, 1987. Trustee, Homestart, 1981–89. Vice-Chm., Lewes Tertiary Coll., 1990–93. FRAI 1972. *Publications:* Patterns of Family Placement, 1978; Social Groupwork with Elderly Patients, 1981; Creation of the British Personal Social Services 1962–74, 1983. *Recreation:* walking. *Address:* 44 Greyfriars Court, Court Road, Lewes, East Sussex BN7 2RF. *T:* (01273) 472604. *Club:* University Women's.   *Died 15 Jan. 1999.*

COOPER, John Newton, CBE 2000; Chairman, John Cooper Garages Ltd, since 1971; *b* 17 July 1923; *s* of Charles and Elsie Cooper; *m* 1947, Pauline Marie; one *s* one *d* (and one *d* decd). *Educ:* Surbiton Grammar Sch. Cooper Cars won Formula 1 World Manufacturers Championships, 1959, 1960; designed Mini Cooper, 1959–60, winner, Monte Carlo Rally, 1964, 1965, 1967. FIMI. Hon. FCGI. *Recreations:* motor racing, golf. *Address:* John Cooper Garages Ltd, 50 Ferring Street, Ferring, Worthing, Sussex BN12 5JP. *T:* (01903) 504455. *Clubs:* British Racing Drivers' at Silverstone (Vice Pres.); British Racing and Sports Car at Brands Hatch (Pres.).
                    Died 24 Dec. 2000.

COOPER, Peter James; QC 1993; a Recorder, since 1993; *b* 7 Oct. 1947; *s* of William James Cooper and Audrey (*née* Knight); *m* 1979, Jenifer Ann Redway; two *s. Educ:* Peter Symonds Sch., Winchester; Southampton Univ.; Council of Legal Educn. Called to the Bar, Gray's Inn, 1974; Asst Recorder, 1989–93. *Recreations:* golf, music. *Address:* 2 Harcourt Buildings, Temple, EC4Y 9DB. *T:* (020) 7353 2112. *Club:* Midfearn Open Golfing Society (Ardgay, Ross-shire). *Died 6 April 2000.*

COOPER, Sidney G.; *see* Grattan-Cooper.

COOPER, Very Rev. (William Hugh) Alan; Priest-in-charge of Chrishall, 1981–88; *b* 2 June 1909; *s* of William and Ethel Cooper; *m* 1st, 1940, Barbara (*née* Bentall); one *s* two *d*; 2nd, 1980, Muriel Barnes. *Educ:* King's Coll. Sch., Wimbledon; Christ's Coll., Cambridge (MA); St John's Hall, London. ALCD. Deacon 1932, priest 1933; Curate: St Margaret, Lee, 1932–36; Holy Trinity, Cambridge, 1936–38; CMS Missionary and Diocesan Missioner of Dio. Lagos, 1938–41; Curate of Farnham, 1941–42; Rector of Ashtead, 1942–51; Vicar of St Andrew, Plymouth, 1951–62; Preb. of Exeter Cathedral, 1958–62; Provost of Bradford, 1962–77; Hon. Assistant to Bishop of Karachi, 1977–80. Hon. MA Bradford, 1978. *Address:* 4 Eastgate Gardens, Guildford, Surrey GU1 4AZ. *Died 14 Oct. 1999.*

COOTE, Rt Rev. Roderic Norman, DD; *b* 13 April 1915; *s* of late Comdr B. T. Coote, RN and Grace Harriet (*née* Robinson); *m* 1964, Erica Lynette, *d* of late Rev. E. G. Shrubbs, MBE; one *s* two *d. Educ:* Woking County Sch.; Trinity Coll., Dublin; (DD 1954). Deacon 1938, priest 1939; Curate Asst, St Bartholomew's, Dublin, 1938–41; Missionary Priest in the Diocese of Gambia and the Rio Pongas, 1942; Bishop of Gambia and the Rio Pongas, 1951–57; Suffragan Bishop of Fulham, 1957–66; Suffragan Bishop of Colchester, 1966–87; Archdeacon of Colchester, 1969–72. Member, General Synod of Church of England, 1969–72. *Recreations:* walking, piano (composer and broadcaster); Irish Champion 120 yds hurdles. *Address:* Friday Woods, Stoke Road, Cobham, Surrey KT11 3AS. *Died 8 July 2000.*

COPE, Prof. F(rederick) Wolverson, DSc; CEng, FIMM, FGS; Professor of Geology and Head of Geology Department, University of Keele, 1950–76, now Professor Emeritus; *b* 30 July 1909; *e s* of late Fred and Ida Mary Cope (*née* Chappells), Macclesfield; *m* 1st, 1935, Ethel May Hitchens, BSc (*d* 1961); one *s* two *d*; 2nd, 1962, Evelyn Mary Swales, BA, AKC, *d* of late John Frederick and Ada Mary Swales, Kingston-upon-Hull; one *d. Educ:* The King's Sch., Macclesfield; Univs of Manchester (DSc 1946) and London. Brocklehurst Scholar, 1928; John Dalton Prize, 1930; BSc with First Class Honours in Geology, 1931; MSc, Mark Stirrup Res. Scholar, Manchester, 1932. Demonstrator in Geology, Bedford Coll., Univ. of London, 1933–34; Daniel Pidgeon Fund, Geol. Soc. of London, 1937; Prin. Geologist in Geological Survey of GB, 1934–50 (discoverer of Formby oilfield, 1937); Murchison Award of Geol. Soc. of London, 1948; Vis. Prof. of Geology, Univ. of Pisa, 1964. Sometime Examr, Univs of Bristol, Exeter, London, Manchester, Nottingham, Sheffield and Wales. FGS 1934 (Senior Fellow 1984); FIMinE 1968; CEng 1969. Chm., Essex Gp of Geologists' Assoc, 1980–99, Pres., 2000–; Life Mem., Geologists' Assoc., 1982 (Hon. Mem., 1994). Hon. DSc Keele, 2000. *Publications:* The North Staffordshire Coalfields, in Coalfields of Great Britain (ed by late Sir Arthur Trueman), 1954; Geologists' Association Guide to Geology Explained in the Peak District, 1976, rev. edn 1998; Geologists' Association Guide to Geology of the Peak District, 1999; various research publications mainly in the fields of stratigraphy and palaeontology. *Recreations:* hill walking, landscape sketching, servicing own cars, travel, geology, ornithology, Italy, reading and speaking Italian. *Address:* Willersley, 6 Boley Drive, Clacton on Sea, Essex CO15 6LA. *T:* (01255) 421829. *Died 4 May 2000.*

COPLESTONE-BOUGHEY, His Honour John Fenton; a Circuit Judge (formerly Judge of the County Courts), 1969–85; *b* 5 Feb. 1912; *o s* of late Comdr A. F. Coplestone-Boughey, RN; *m* 1944, Gilian Beatrice (*d* 1999), *e d* of late H. A. Counsell, Appleby; one *s* one *d. Educ:* Shrewsbury School; Brasenose Coll., Oxford (Open Exhibitioner, Matthew Arnold Prizeman). Inner Temple, Entrance Scholar 1934, Barrister 1935. Legal Assistant, Min. of Health, 1937–40. Royal Artillery, 1940–46; Advanced Class, Military Coll. of Science, 1945. Chester Chronicle & Associated Newspapers, Ltd: Dir, 1947–56; Dep. Chm., 1956–65. Chairman, Nat. Insurance Tribunals (SW London), 1951–69; Referee, Nat. Service and Family Allowances Acts, 1957–69. Member, 1960–69, Chairman, 1969–74, Battersea Hospital Management Cttee; Mem., Wandsworth AHA, 1973–82. Chm., Chelsea Housing Improvement Soc., 1981–84. Governor, St Thomas' Hosp., 1971–74; Special Trustee, St George's Hospital, 1974, Chm. of Trustees, 1980–84. Mem. Council, Queen's Coll., London, 1976, Vice-Chm. 1979–84, Chm. 1984. *Publications:* contrib. to Halsbury's Laws of England. *Recreations:* walking, travel. *Address:* 82 Oakley Street, SW3 5NP. *T:* (020) 7352 6287. *Club:* Athenæum. *Died 12 July 2000.*

COPP, Prof. (Douglas) Harold, CC 1980 (OC 1971); MD, PhD; FRCPC; FRS 1971; FRSC; Professor of Physiology, University of British Columbia, Canada, 1950–80, then Emeritus; *b* 16 Jan. 1915; *s* of Charles J. Copp and Edith M. O'Hara; *m* 1939, Winnifred A. Thompson; three *d. Educ:* Univ. of Toronto, Canada (BA, MD), Univ. of California, Berkeley, Calif (PhD); British Columbia College of Physicians and Surgeons (Lic.). Asst Prof. of Physiology, Calif, 1945–50; Head of Dept of Physiology, Univ. of British Columbia, 1950–80 (Co-ordinator, Health Scis, 1976–77). FRSC 1959 (Mem. Council, 1973–75, Vice-Pres., and Pres. Academy of Science, 1978–81); FRCP(C) 1974. Hon. LLD: Queen's Univ., Kingston, Ont, 1970; Univ. of Toronto, 1970; Hon. DSc: Univ. of Ottawa, 1973; Acadia Univ., 1975; Univ. of British Columbia, 1980. Inducted into Canadian Medical Hall of Fame, 1994. Discovered calcitonin (ultimobranchial hormone) and stanniocalcin (corpuscles of Stannius). *Recreation:* gardening. *Address:* 4755 Belmont Avenue, Vancouver, BC V6T 1A8, Canada. *T:* (604) 2243793. *Died 17 March 1998.*

COPPLESTONE, Frank Henry; Deputy Chairman, Westcountry Television Ltd, since 1991 (Director, since 1990); Managing Director, Southern Television Ltd, 1976–88; *b* 26 Feb. 1925; 2nd *s* of late Rev. Frank T. Copplestone; *m* 1st, 1950, Margaret Mary (*d* 1973), *d* of late Edward Walker; three *s*; 2nd, 1977, Penny Perrick (marr. diss. 1988); one step *s* one step *d*; 3rd, 1989, Fenella, *widow* of Prof. Gamini Salgado; one step *s* one step *d. Educ:* Truro Sch., Nottingham Univ. (BA). Royal Horse Artillery, 1943–47. Pres., Univ. of Nottingham Union, 1952–53; Pres., Nat. Union of Students, 1954–56; Internat. Research Fellow, 1956–58; Regional Officer, Independent Television Authority, 1958–62; Head of Regional Services, ITA, 1962–63; Head of Programme Services, ITA, 1963–67; Controller, ITV Network Programme Secretariat, 1967–73; Dir, ITV Programme Planning Secretariat, 1973–75; Director: Independent Television News Ltd, 1977–81; Independent Television Publications Ltd, 1976–81. Dir, Trevithick Trust, 1992–94. Mem., Broadcasters' Audience Res. Bd, 1981. FRSA 1994. *Recreations:* sailing, reading, music. *Address:* Pen an Mor, 39 Esplanade, Fowey, Cornwall PL23 1HY. *T:*

Fowey (01726) 832818. *Clubs:* Reform, Royal Over-Seas League; Royal Fowey Yacht, Fowey Gallants Sailing.
Died 30 April 1996.

COPPOCK, Prof. John Terence, (Terry), CBE 1987; FBA 1975; FRSE 1976; Secretary and Treasurer, 1986–2000, and Curator designate, Carnegie Trust for the Universities of Scotland; *b* 2 June 1921; *s* of late Arthur Coppock and Valerie Margaret Coppock (*née* Phillips); *m* 1953, Sheila Mary Burnett (*d* 1990); one *s* one *d. Educ:* Penarth County Sch.; Queens' Coll., Cambridge (MA); PhD, DSc London. Civil Servant: Lord Chancellor's Dept, Min. of Works, Board of Customs and Excise, 1938–47. Served War, Army, 1939–46 (commissioned Welch Regt, 1941). Cambridge Univ., 1947–50. University College London (Dept of Geography): successively, Asst Lecturer, Lecturer, Reader, 1950–65; Fellow, 1987; Ogilvie Prof. of Geography, Univ. of Edinburgh, 1965–86, Professor Emeritus, 1987–. Visiting Professor: Loughborough Univ., 1986–89; Birkbeck Coll., London, 1986–96. Chm., British Acad./British Liby review panel on information needs in the humanities, 1990–92. Member: Scottish Sports Council, 1976–87; Ordnance Survey Rev. Cttee, 1978–79. FRSA 1980; FRSGS 1988. Ed., Internat. Jl of Geographical Information Systems, 1986–93. Hon. DLitt Glasgow, 1999; Hon. DSc Edinburgh, 1999. *Publications:* The Changing Use of Land in Britain (with R. H. Best), 1962; An Agricultural Atlas of England and Wales, 1964, 2nd edn 1976; (ed with H. C. Prince) Greater London, 1964; An Agricultural Geography of Great Britain, 1971; (with B. S. Duffield) Recreation in the Countryside: a Spatial Analysis, 1975; (ed with W. R. D. Sewell) Spatial Dimensions of Public Policy, 1976; An Agricultural Atlas of Scotland, 1976; (ed) Second Homes: Curse or Blessing?, 1977; (ed with W. R. D. Sewell) Public Participation in Planning, 1977; (with L. F. Gebbett) Land Use and Town and Country Planning, 1978; (ed with M. F. Thomas) Land Assessment in Scotland, 1980; Agriculture in Developed Countries, 1984; (with W. R. D. Sewell and A. Pitkethly) Innovation in Water Management, 1986; (ed with P. T. Kivell) Geography, Planning and Policy Making, 1986; (ed) Information Technology and Scholarship, 1999; (ed) Making Information Available in Digital Format, 1999; numerous papers, mainly in geographical, but also historical, planning and agricultural periodicals, mainly on theme of rural land use in Great Britain. *Recreations:* listening to music, natural history. *Address:* Flat 45, 14 Maxwell Street, Edinburgh EH10 5HU. *T:* (0131) 447 3443.
Died 28 June 2000.

CORBET, Lt-Col Sir John (Vincent), 7th Bt *cr* 1808, of Moreton Corbet, Shropshire; MBE 1946; JP; DL; Royal Engineers, retired; *b* 27 Feb. 1911; *s* of Archer Henry Corbet (*d* 1950) (*g g s* of 1st Bt), and Anne Maria (*d* 1951), *d* of late German Buxton; *S* kinsman, Sir Gerald Vincent Corbet, 6th Bt, 1955; *m* 1st, 1937, Elfrida Isobel Francis; 2nd, 1948, Doreen Elizabeth Stewart (*d* 1964), *d* of Arthur William Gibbon Ritchie; 3rd, 1965, Annie Elizabeth Lorimer, MBE, MSc, Dunedin, NZ. *Educ:* Shrewsbury Sch.; RMA; Magdalene Coll., Cambridge. BA 1933, MA 1972. 2nd Lieut, RE, 1931; served North-West Frontier, India, 1935, and War of 1939–45 in India, Burma and Malaya (despatches, MBE); Lieut-Col, 1953; retd 1955. DL County of Salop, 1961; JP 1957; High Sheriff of Salop, 1966; CC Salop, 1963–81. OStJ. Mem., Church Assembly, later General Synod, 1960–75; former Chm., Board of Visitors, Stoke Heath Borstal. *Heir:* none. *Address:* Acton Reynald, near Shrewsbury, Salop SY4 4DS. *T:* Clive (01939) 220259. *Club:* Royal Thames Yacht.
Died 20 March 1996 (ext).

CORBETT, Prof. John Patrick; Professor of Philosophy, University of Bradford, 1972–76; *b* 5 March 1916; *s* of E. S. H. and K. F. Corbett; *m* 1st, 1940, Nina Angeloni; two

s ; 2nd, 1968, Jan Adams; two *d. Educ:* RNC, Dartmouth; Magdalen Coll., Oxford (MA). Lieut, RA, 1940; POW in Germany, 1940–45. Fellow of Balliol Coll., Oxford, 1945–61; Prof. of Philosophy, Univ. of Sussex, 1961–72; Jowett Lectr in Philosophy. Council of Europe Fellow, 1957; Visiting Lectr, Yale Univ., 1958; NATO Fellow, 1960; Vis. Prof., Univ. of Toronto, 1968. *Publications:* Europe and the Social Order, 1959; Ideologies, 1965.
Died 4 Dec. 1999.

CORLEY, His Honour Michael Early Ferrand; a Circuit Judge (formerly County Court Judge), 1967–82; *b* 11 Oct. 1909; *s* of late Ferrand Edward Corley, Christian College, Madras, and Elsie Maria Corley. *Educ:* Marlborough; Oriel Coll., Oxford. Called to Bar, Middle Temple, 1934. War Service, RNVR, 1940–46. *Publication:* At The Gates—Tomorrow, 1983. *Address:* The Old Rectory, Rectory Road, Broome, Norfolk NR35 2HU.
Died 25 Sept. 1998.

CORLEY SMITH, Gerard Thomas, CMG 1952; HM Diplomatic Service, retired; *b* 30 July 1909; *s* of late Thomas and Nina Smith; *m* 1937, Joan Haggard (*d* 1984); one *s* three *d. Educ:* Bolton Sch.; Emmanuel Coll., Cambridge. Gen. Consular Service, 1931; served in Paris, Oran, Detroit, La Paz, Milan, St Louis, New York, Brussels, and at various times in the Foreign Office; became 1st Sec. and Consul, on appt as Labour Attaché to Embassy in Brussels 1945; Counsellor UK Deleg. to UNO at New York and UK Alternate Rep. on UN Economic and Social Council, 1949–52; Press Counsellor, Brit. Embassy, Paris, 1952–54; Labour Counsellor, Brit. Embassy, Madrid, 1954–59; British Ambassador: to Haiti, 1960–62; to Ecuador, 1962–67. Sec. Gen., Charles Darwin Foundn for the Galapagos Islands, 1972–82. Grand Officer, Order of Merit (Ecuador), 1980. *Recreations:* music, mountains, birds. *Address:* Greensted Hall, Chipping Ongar, Essex CM5 9LD. *T:* (01277) 362031.
Died 7 Oct. 1997.

CORMACK, Prof. Allan MacLeod; University Professor, Tufts University, 1980–94, then Emeritus; *b* 23 Feb. 1924; *s* of George Cormack and Amelia MacLeod; *m* 1950, Barbara Jeanne Seavey; one *s* two *d. Educ:* Univ. of Cape Town (BSc, MSc). Research Student, St John's Coll., Cambridge (Hon. Fellow, 1993). Lecturer, Univ. of Cape Town, 1950–56; Research Fellow, Harvard Univ., 1956–57; Tufts University: Asst Prof., 1957–60; Associate Prof., 1960–64; Prof. of Physics, 1964–80; Chairman, Physics Dept, 1968–76. Nelson Medical Lectr, Univ. of Calif, Davis, 1985; Watkins Vis. Prof., Wichita State Univ., 1986. Fellow, Amer. Physical Soc., 1964; Fellow, Amer. Acad. of Arts and Sciences, 1980; Mem., Nat. Acad. of Sciences, 1983; Hon. Member: Swedish Neuroradiological Soc., 1979; S African Inst. of Physics, 1985; Amer. Assoc. of Physicists in Medicine, 1988; Foreign Fellow, Royal Soc. of S Africa, 1983; Hon. Foreign Fellow, Korean Acad. of Sci. and Technol., 1995. Hon. DSc Tufts Univ., 1980. Ballou Medallist, Tufts Univ., 1978; (jtly) Nobel Prize for Physiology or Medicine, 1979; Medal of Merit, Univ. of Cape Town, 1980; Mike Hogg Medallist, Univ. of Texas, 1981; US Nat. Medal of Sci., 1990. *Publications:* articles on nuclear and particle physics, computed tomography, and related mathematics. *Address:* 18 Harrison Street, Winchester, MA 01890, USA. *T:* (617) 7290735.
Died 7 May 1998.

CORNELL, Ward MacLaurin; retired; Deputy Minister, Ministry of Housing (formerly Ministry of Municipal Affairs and Housing), Province of Ontario, 1982–88; *b* London, Ont, 4 May 1924; *m* Georgina Saxon; three *s* two *d. Educ:* Pickering Coll.; Univ. of Western Ontario. Lectr in English and History, Pickering Coll., Ont, 1949–54; Gen. Manager, Broadcast Div. (Radio), Free Press Printing Co., 1954–67; Pres., Creative Projects in Communications,

1967–72; Agent-Gen. for Ont in UK, 1972–78; Gen. Manager, European Ops, Lenroc Internat. Ltd, 1978–80; Dep. Minister, Min. of Citizenship and Culture, Province of Ontario, 1980–82. Vis. Lectr, Conestoga Coll., 1968–72. *Recreations:* reading, tennis, travelling. *Address:* RR1, Uxbridge, ON L0C 1K0, Canada.

Died 5 Feb. 2000.

CORNER, Edred John Henry, CBE 1972; FRS 1955; FLS; Professor of Tropical Botany, University of Cambridge, 1966–73, then Emeritus; *b* 12 Jan. 1906; *s* of late Edred Moss Corner and Henrietta Corner (*née* Henderson); *m* 1953, Helga Dinesen Sondergoord; one *s* two *d* (by 1st *m*). *Educ:* Rugby Sch. Asst Dir, Gardens Dept, Straits Settlements, 1929–45; Principal Field Scientific Officer, Latin America, Unesco, 1947–48; Lecturer in Botany, Cambridge Univ., 1949–59, Reader in Plant Taxonomy, 1959–65; Fellow, Sidney Sussex Coll., Cambridge, 1959–73. Member: American Mycological Soc.; Brit. Mycological Soc.; French Mycological Soc.; Fellow, American Assoc. for the Advancement of Science; Corr. Member: Botanical Soc. of America; Royal Netherlands Botanical Soc.; Hon. Member: Japanese Mycological Soc.; Czechoslovak Scientific Soc. for Mycology; British Mycolog. Soc. Mem., Governing Body of Rugby Sch., 1959–75. Darwin Medal, Royal Soc., 1960; Patron's Medal, RGS, 1966; Gold Medal, Linnean Soc. of London, 1970; Victoria Medal of Honour, RHS, 1974; Allerton Award, Pacific Tropical Botanical Garden, Hawaii, 1981; Internat. Prize for Biology, Japan Acad., 1985. *Publications:* Wayside Trees of Malaya (2 vols), 1940, 3rd edn 1988; A Monograph of Clavaria and allied genera, 1950; Life of Plants, 1964; Natural History of Palms, 1966; Monograph of Cantharelloid Fungi, 1966; Boletus in Malaysia, 1972; Seeds of Dicotyledons, 2 vols, 1976; The Marquis: a tale of Syonan-to, 1981; Biographical Memoir of HM Hirohito, Emperor of Japan, 1990; Botanical Monkeys, 1992. *Address:* 91 Hinton Way, Great Shelford, Cambs CB2 5AH. *T:* (01223) 842167. *Died 14 Sept. 1996.*

CORNFORD, Sir (Edward) Clifford, KCB 1977 (CB 1966); FEng 1980; Chief of Defence Procurement, Ministry of Defence, 1977–80; *b* 6 Feb. 1918; *s* of John Herbert Cornford; *m* 1945, Catherine Muir; three *s* three *d*. *Educ:* Kimbolton Sch.; Jesus Coll., Cambridge (BA). Joined RAE, 1938; operational research with RAF, 1939–45; guided weapons res. at RAE, 1945–60; jssc 1951; Head of Guided Weapons Dept, RAE, 1956–61; Ministry of Defence: Chm., Def. Res. Policy Staff, 1961–63; Asst Chief Scientific Adviser, 1963–64; Chief Scientist (Army), and Mem. Army Board, 1965–67; Chm. Programme Evaluation Group, 1967–68; Dep. Chief Adviser (Research and Studies), 1968–69; Controller of Guided Weapons and Electronics, Min. of Technology, later Min. of Aviation Supply and MoD (Procurement Executive), 1969–72; Ministry of Defence (PE): Controller (Policy), 1972–74; Dep. Chief Exec., 1974–75; Chief Exec. and Permanent Under Sec. of State, 1975–77. Mem., PO Board, 1981–87. FRAeS. *Publications:* on aeronautical subjects in jls of learned socs and technical publications. *Recreation:* travelling. *Address:* The Spinney, 7 Ash Grove, Liphook, Hants GU30 7HZ. *T:* (01428) 722780. *Club:* Athenæum. *Died 6 May 1999.*

CORRIE, W(allace) Rodney, CB 1977; *b* 25 Nov. 1919; *o c* of late Edward and Mary Ellen Corrie; *m* 1952, Helen Margaret (*née* Morice), *widow* of Flt-Lt A. H. E. Kahn; one *s* one *d. Educ:* Leigh Grammar School; Christ's Coll., Cambridge (BA 1941, MA 1944). Served Royal Signals, 1940–46 (despatches). Entered Civil Service, Min. of Town and Country Planning, 1947; Min. of Housing and Local Govt, 1951; Asst Secretary, 1961; Assistant Under-Secretary of State, DEA, 1969; Under-Secretary: Min. of

Housing and Local Govt, 1969; Dept of the Environment, 1970; Chm., NW Econ. Planning Bd, 1969–80, and Regl Dir (NW), DoE, 1971–80, Dept of Transport, 1976–80. *Recreations:* exploring byways, catching up on things. *Address:* Brambledown, Chapel Lane, Hale Barns, Cheshire WA15 0AJ. *Died 4 Feb. 1997.*

CORRY, Lt-Comdr Sir William (James), 4th Bt *cr* 1885, of Dunraven, Co. Antrim; Royal Navy, retired; *b* 1 Aug. 1924; *s* of Sir James Perowne Ivo Myles Corry, 3rd Bt and Molly Irene (*d* 1996), *d* of Major O. J. Bell; *S* father, 1987; *m* 1945, Pamela Diana Mary, *d* of late Lt-Col J. B. Lapsley, MC; four *s* two *d. Educ:* RNC Dartmouth. Joined RN, 1938; Lt-Comdr 1953; retired, 1977. *Recreation:* beagling. *Heir:* *s* James Michael Corry [*b* 3 Oct. 1946; *m* 1973, Sheridan Lorraine, *d* of A. P. Ashbourne; three *s*]. *Address:* East Hillerton House, Spreyton, Crediton, Devon EX17 5AD. *T:* (01363) 82407.

Died 9 May 2000.

COTES, Peter; *see* Boulting, S. A.

COTTENHAM, 8th Earl of, *cr* 1850; **Kenelm Charles Everard Digby Pepys;** Bt 1784 and 1801; Baron Cottenham 1836; Viscount Crowhurst 1850; *b* 27 Nov. 1948; *s* of 7th Earl of Cottenham and Lady Angela Isabel Nellie Nevill, *d* of 4th Marquess of Abergavenny; *S* father, 1968; *m* 1975, Sarah, *d* of Captain S. Lombard-Hobson, CVO, OBE, RN; two *s* one *d. Educ:* Eton. *Heir:* *s* Viscount Crowhurst, *b* 11 Oct. 1983. *Died 20 Oct. 2000.*

COULSHED, Dame (Mary) Frances, DBE 1953 (CBE 1949); TD 1951; Brigadier, Women's Royal Army Corps, retired; *b* 10 Nov. 1904; *d* of Wilfred and Maud Coulshed. *Educ:* Parkfields Cedars, Derby; Convent of the Sacred Heart, Kensington. Served War of 1939–45 (despatches); North West Europe, 1944–45, with General Headquarters Anti-Aircraft Troops and at Headquarters Lines of Communications; Deputy Dir, Anti-Aircraft Command, 1946–50; Dep. Dir, War Office, July-Dec. 1950; Director, WRAC, 1951–54. ADC to the King, 1951, to the Queen, 1952–54. Order of Leopold I of Belgium with palm, Croix de Guerre with palm, 1946. *Died 28 Sept. 1998.*

COULSON, Sir John Eltringham, KCMG 1957 (CMG 1946); President, Hampshire Branch, British Red Cross Society, 1972–79; Secretary-General of European Free Trade Association, 1965–72, retired; *b* 13 Sept. 1909; *er s* of H. J. Coulson, Bickley, Kent; *m* 1944, Mavis Ninette Beazley; two *s. Educ:* Rugby; Corpus Christi Coll., Cambridge (Hon. Fellow 1975). Entered HM Diplomatic Service in 1932; served in Bucharest, Min. of Econ. Warfare, War Cabinet Office, Foreign Office and Paris; sometime Dep. UK representative to UN, New York; Asst Under-Sec., Foreign Office, 1952–55; Minister British Embassy, Washington, 1955–57; Asst to Paymaster-Gen., 1957–60; Ambassador to Sweden, 1960–63; Dep. Under-Sec. of State, Foreign Office, 1963–65; Chief of Administration of HM Diplomatic Service, Jan.-Sept. 1965. Director: Atlas Copco (GB), 1972–80; Sheerness Steel Co., 1972–84. Knight Grand Cross, Order of the North Star, Sweden, 1982. *Recreations:* fishing, golf. *Address:* The Old Mill, Selborne, Hants GU34 3LG. *Club:* Brooks's. *Died 15 Nov. 1997.*

COUSTEAU, Jacques-Yves; Commandeur, Légion d'Honneur; Croix de Guerre with Palm; Officier du Mérite Maritime; Chevalier du Mérite Agricole; Officier des Arts et des Lettres; Member of Académie Française, 1989; marine explorer; *b* 11 June 1910; *s* of Daniel and Elizabeth Cousteau; *m* 1st, 1937, Simone Melchior (*d* 1990); one *s* (and one *s* decd); 2nd, 1992, Francine Triplet; one *s* one *d. Educ:* Stanislas, Paris; Navy Academy, Brest. Lt de vaisseau, War of 1939–45. Inventor with Emile Gagnan, 1943, of the Aqualung, a portable breathing device for divers; with André Laban, perfected first underwater camera equipment for television transmission, 1951; with Jean Mollard, produced the diving saucer, 1959; development with Lucien Malavard and Bertrand Charrier of Turbosail (wind-propulsion system for ships), 1985. Established Undersea Research Group, 1946; Founder and President: Campagne Océanographiques Françaises, 1950; Centre d'Etudes Marines Avancées, 1952; made oceanographic expedns on his ships Calypso and Alcyone, and film records of his undersea expedns, 1951–; promoted Conshelf saturation dive programme, 1962–65; Founder, Cousteau Soc., 1973. Dir, Musée Océanographique, Monaco, 1957–88; Gen. Sec., Internat. Commn for Scientific Exploration of the Mediterranean Sea, 1966; Chm., Council on Rights of Future Generations, 1993–95. Fellow, BAFTA, 1975; For. Assoc. Mem., Nat. Acad. Scis, USA, 1968; Corresp. Mem., Hellenic Inst. of Marine Archaeology, 1975; Hon. Mem., Indian Acad. of Scis, 1978. Hon. DSc: California, 1970; Brandeis, 1970; Rensselaer Polytechnic Inst., 1979; Harvard, 1979; Ghent, 1983; Dr *hc* Univ. Autónoma de Guadalajara, 1989; Hon. DHL Amer. Univ. of Paris, 1994. Gold Medal, RGS, 1963; Pott's Medal, Franklin Inst., 1970; Gold Medal, Nat. Geographic Soc., and Gold Medal Grand Prix d'Océanographie Albert Ier, 1971; Grande Médaille d'Or, Soc. d'encouragement au Progrès, 1973; Award of New England Aquarium, 1973; Prix de la couronne d'or, 1973; Polena della Bravura, 1974; Gold Medal "Sciences" (Arts, Sciences, Lettres), 1974; Manley Bendall Prize, Marine Acad., 1976; Special Cervia prize, 1976; Internat. Pahlavi Environment Prize, 1977; (with Sir Peter Scott) UN Internat. Envmtl Prize, 1977; Jean Sainteny Prize, 1980; Kiwanis Internat. Europe Prize, 1980; Lindbergh Award, 1982; Neptune Award, Amer. Oceanic Orgn, 1982; Bruno H. Schubert Foundn Award, 1983; US Presidential Medal of Freedom, 1985; Founder's Award, Internat. Council of Nat. Acad. of Arts and Scis, 1987; Centennial Award, Nat. Geographic Soc., 1988; inducted into Diving Equipment Manufrs Assoc. Hall of Fame, 1989 (Reaching Out Award, 1989); Internat. Catalan Prize, 1991; CRISMA Prize, World Energy Award, Light at the End of the World (Argentina) Award, 1992; Tribute 21, Common Wealth Award, USA, 1994; J. Smithson Bicentennial Medal, 1996. *Films:* Par 18 mètres de fond, 1946; The Silent World, 1954 (Grand Prix, Gold Palm, Cannes 1956; Oscar, 1957); The Golden Fish (Oscar, best short film, 1959); World Without Sun, 1964 (Oscar, 1965); Voyage to the Edge of the World, 1975; Cries from the Deep, 1982; St Lawrence: stairway to the sea, 1982; Jacques Cousteau: the first seventy-five years, 1985; Riders of the Wind, 1986; Island of Peace, 1988; Outrage at Valdez, 1990; Lilliput in Antarctica, 1990; *TV film series:* The Undersea World of Jacques Cousteau, 1968–76 (numerous Emmy awards); Oasis in Space, 1977; The Cousteau Odyssey, 1977–82; Cousteau/Amazon, 1982–85; Cousteau/Mississippi, 1985; Cousteau/ Rediscovery of the World, 1985–. *Publications:* La Plongée en Scaphandre, 1950; (with Frederic Dumas) The Silent World, 1953 (New York and London), first published in English, then in 21 other languages; (ed with James Dugan) Captain Cousteau's Underwater Treasury, 1959 (London); The Living Sea, 1963 (London); World Without Sun, 1965; (with P. Cousteau) The Shark, 1970; (with P. Diolé) Life and Death in a Coral Sea, 1971; Diving for Sunken Treasure, 1971; The Whale: mighty monarch of the sea, 1972; Octopus and Squid, 1973; Galapagos, Titicaca, the Blue Holes: three adventures, 1973; The Ocean World of Jacques Cousteau (21 vol. encyclopedia), 1973; Diving Companions, 1974; Dolphins, 1975; Jacques Cousteau: the ocean world, 1979; The Cousteau Almanac, 1981; Jacques Cousteau's Calypso, 1983; (with Mose Richards) Jacques Cousteau's Amazon Journey, 1984; Jacques Cousteau: Whales, 1988; articles in National Geographical Magazine, 1952–66;

posthumous publication: The Man, the Octopus and the Orchid (autobiog.), 1997. *Address:* The Cousteau Society Inc., 870 Greenbrier Circle, Suite 402, Chesapeake, VA 23320–2641, USA.   *Died 25 June 1997.*

COUVE DE MURVILLE, Maurice Jacques; Commandeur de la Légion d'Honneur; Ambassadeur de France; *b* 24 Jan. 1907; *s* of Edouard Couve de Murville and Hermine (*née* Caesar); *m* 1932, Jacqueline Schweisguth; three *d. Educ:* Paris Univ. Inspecteur des finances, 1930; directeur des finances extérieures, 1940; membre du Comité français de la libération nationale (Alger), 1943; représentant de la France, Conseil consultatif pour l'Italie, 1944; Ambassador in Rome, 1945; directeur général des affaires politiques, Ministère des Affaires Etrangères, 1945–50; Ambassador in Egypt, 1950–54; French Permanent Rep., NATO, Sept. 1954–Jan. 1955; Ambassador in the US, 1955–56; Ambassador of France to the Federal Republic of Germany, 1956–58; Ministre des Affaires Etrangères, 1958–68, de l'Economie et des Finances, June-July 1968; Prime Minister of France, 1968–69; Deputy, French Nat. Assembly, Paris 8ème Arrondissement, 1973–86; Mem. of Senate, for Paris, 1986–95. *Publications:* Une Politique étrangère 1958–69, 1973; Le Monde en face, 1989. *Address:* 44 rue du Bac, 75007 Paris, France.   *Died 24 Dec. 1999.*

COVACEVICH, Sir (Anthony) Thomas, Kt 1978; DFC 1943; Senior Partner, MacDonnells, Solicitors and Notaries Public, Cairns, Queensland, Australia, 1963–92 (Partner, 1939); *b* 1 March 1915; *s* of Prosper and Ellen Covacevich; *m* 1944, Gladys Rose (*née* Bryant); one *s* one *d. Educ:* Townsville and Brisbane Grammar Schools. Admitted Solicitor, Supreme Court of Queensland, 1938. Formerly Director of five publicly listed Australian companies, including Foxwood Ltd, a timber company (Chm.). *Recreation:* fishing. *Address:* 17 Temora Close, Edge Hill, Cairns, Qld 4870, Australia. *T:* (70) 300600; Box 5046, Cairns Mail Centre, Qld 4870, Australia. *Clubs:* North Queensland (Townsville, Qld); Cairns Game Fishing (Cairns, Qld).   *Died 25 Aug. 1999.*

COVENTRY, Rev. John Seton, SJ; Master, St Edmund's House, Cambridge, 1976–85; *b* 21 Jan. 1915; *yr s* of late Seton and Annie Coventry, Barton-on-Sea, Hants. *Educ:* Stonyhurst; Campion Hall, Oxford. MA Oxon 1945. Entered Society of Jesus, 1932; ordained, 1947; Prefect of Studies, Beaumont, 1950; Rector, Beaumont, 1956–58; Provincial, English Province of Soc. of Jesus, 1958–64; Lectr in Theology, Heythrop Coll., 1965–76. *Publications:* Morals and Independence, 1946; The Breaking of Bread, 1950; Faith Seeks Understanding, 1951; The Life Story of the Mass, 1959; The Theology of Faith, 1968; Christian Truth, 1975; Faith in Jesus Christ, 1980; Reconciling, 1985; Our God Reigns, 1995. *Address:* 114 Mount Street, W1Y 6AH. *T:* (0171) 493 7811.

    Died 9 April 1998.

COWAN, Brig. (James) Alan (Comrie), CBE 1992 (MBE 1956); Secretary, Government Hospitality Fund, 1980–93; *b* 20 Sept. 1923; *s* of late Alexander Comrie Cowan and Helen May Isobel (*née* Finlayson); *m* 1948, Jennifer Evelyn Bland; two *s* one *d. Educ:* Rugby Sch., Warwicks. Commnd Rifle Bde, 1942; served War, Italy and Egypt, 1942–46; served Army, 1947–60: OU Trng Corps, BAOR, Army Staff Coll., WO, Kenya and Malaya; DS, Army Staff Coll., 1961–63; CO 1 Royal Leicesters, later 4 Royal Anglian, UK, Aden and Malta, 1964–66; GSO1 17 Div., Malaysia, 1966–67; Col GS MoD, 1967–69; Comd 8 Inf. Bde, NI, 1970–71; DAG HQ UKLF, 1972–75; entered Civil Service and joined NI Office, with responsibility for industrial, economic and social affairs, 1975; Principal, 1975–78; Asst Sec., 1978–80. *Recreations:* current affairs, music, theatre, the countryside. *Address:* c/o C. Hoare & Co., 37 Fleet Street, EC4P 4DQ. *Clubs:* Army and Navy, MCC. *Died 17 April 1999.*

COWAN, William Graham, MBE 1943; Chairman, J. H. Carruthers & Co. Ltd, since 1981 (Managing Director, 1981–84); *b* 29 April 1919; *s* of William Cowan, WS, Edinburgh, and Dorothy Isobel Horsbrugh; *m* 1st, 1960, Karen Wendell Hansen (marr. diss. 1991), Crestwood, NY; two *s* one *d*; 2nd, 1994, Ann, *d* of Col Noel Carington Smith and *widow* of G. L. B. Mundell. *Educ:* Edinburgh Academy; Cambridge Univ. (MA). CEng, FIMechE, FCSD, FSA(Scot), FRSA. Served 1940–46, Royal Engrs and Gen. Staff, Africa, Italy (Lt-Col). Asst Man. Dir, North British Locomotive Co. Ltd, 1947–50; Man. Dir, J. H. Carruthers and Co. Ltd, 1950–79. Dir, Glasgow Sch. of Art, 1979–82. Mem. Exec. Cttee, Scottish Council (Develt and Industry), 1972–74; Pres., Scottish Engrg Employers' Assoc., 1972. Member: Design Council, 1974–78 (Chm., Scottish Cttee, 1976–78); Council, Nat. Trust for Scotland, 1984–89; Dir, Scottish Transport Group, 1977–80. *Address:* The Old Inn, Fowlis Wester, Perthshire PH7 3NL. *T:* (01764) 683319. *Club:* New (Edinburgh). *Died 1 Jan. 1997.*

COWDREY OF TONBRIDGE, Baron *cr* 1997 (Life Peer), of Tonbridge in the co. of Kent; **Michael Colin Cowdrey,** Kt 1992; CBE 1972; Chairman, International Cricket Council, 1989–93; Director, Bilton plc, 1995–98; Consultant, Barclays Bank PLC, 1991–98; *b* 24 Dec. 1932; *s* of late Ernest Arthur Cowdrey and Kathleen Mary Cowdrey, BEM (*née* Taylor); *m* 1st, 1956, Penelope Susan (*née* Chiesman) (marr. diss. 1985); three *s* one *d*; 2nd, 1985, Lady Herries of Terregles. *Educ:* Homefield, Sutton, Surrey; Tonbridge; Brasenose Coll., Oxford. Cricket: 5 years Tonbridge Sch. XI (Capt., 1949–50); Public Schs (Lord's) (Capt. 1950); 3 years Oxford XI (Capt. 1954); Kent Cap, 1951 (Captain, 1957–71; Pres., 2000); 117 appearances for England, 1954–75; Capt. 23 times; 11 Overseas Tours; 107 centuries in first class cricket, of which 22 were Test centuries; on retirement in 1975, held record for most runs and most catches in Test Matches. Runner-up Amateur Rackets Title, Queen's Club, 1953 and Doubles, 1965. Chm., Internat. Cricket Conf., 1986–87. Member Council: British Heart Foundn, 1994–; Winston Churchill Meml Trust, 1969–88; Britain Australia Soc. Master, Skinners' Co., 1985; Freeman, City of London, 1962. *Publications:* Cricket Today, 1961; Time for Reflection, 1962; Tackle Cricket This Way, 1969; The Incomparable Game, 1970; MCC: the Autobiography of a Cricketer, 1976. *Recreation:* golf. *Address:* Angmering Park, Littlehampton, W Sussex BN16 4EX. *T:* (01903) 871423. *Clubs:* MCC (Mem. Cttee; Pres., 1986–87), Boodle's, Lord's Taverners (Pres., 1996–98); Royal & Ancient Golf. *Died 4 Dec. 2000.*

COWE, (Robert George) Collin; Fellow and Senior Bursar, Magdalen College, Oxford, 1970–80; *b* 24 Sept. 1917; *s* of Peter and Annie Cowe, Berwick-upon-Tweed; *m* 1943, Gladys May, *d* of William Greenwood Wright and Jessie Wright, Bingley, Yorks; one *d*. *Educ:* The Duke's Sch., Alnwick; The Grammar Sch., Berwick-upon-Tweed; Edinburgh Univ. (MA (Hons Classics) 1939); MA Oxon, 1970. Served Royal Regiment of Artillery, Field Branch, 1939–46; Major, RA, 1944–46; Instructor in Gunnery, Sch. of Artillery, UK, and CMF, 1943–46. National Coal Board, 1947–70; Private Sec. to Chm., 1947–49; Principal Private Sec. to Chm., 1949–52; Sec., East Midlands Div., 1952–55; Staff Dir, North-Eastern Div., 1955–58; Dep. Sec. to NCB, 1958–59; Sec., 1960–67; Man. Dir, Associated Heat Services Ltd (associate co. of NCB), 1967–69. Mem., Advisory Council, BBC Radio Oxford, 1985–88. *Recreation:* listening to overseas broadcasts, especially BBC World Service. *Address:* Brookside Cottage, Brook End, Chadlington, Oxford OX7 3NF. *T:* (01608) 676025. *Died 27 Sept. 1999.*

COWELL, John Richard; Secretary, Royal Horticultural Society, 1975–88; *b* 30 April 1933; *er s* of late Frank Richard Cowell, CMG, PhD, and Lilian Margaret (*née* Palin); *m* 1972, Josephine Suzanne Elizabeth, *d* of I. A. F. Craig, Nun Monkton, Yorks; two *s* one *d*. *Educ:* Westminster Sch.; Trinity Coll., Cambridge (MA). Secretariat: London Chamber of Commerce, 1957–58; Royal Horticultural Soc., 1958–88. Mem. Council, London Children's Flower Soc., 1988–. *Recreations:* gardening, fishing. *Address:* The Old House, Boreham Street, near Hailsham, E Sussex BN27 4SF. *T:* (01323) 832128. *Club:* Athenæum. *Died 16 July 1998.*

COWEY, Brig. Bernard Turing Vionnée, DSO 1945; OBE 1976; DL; *b* 20 Nov. 1911; *s* of late Lt-Col R. V. Cowey, DSO, RAMC and Mrs B. A. Cowey (*née* Blancke); *m* 1947, Margaret Heath Dean (*née* Godwin) (*d* 1994). *Educ:* Wellington; RMC Sandhurst. Commnd The Welch Regt, 1931; served War of 1939–45: N Africa, 1939–41 (despatches 1941); psc 1941; India, 1942–43; Burma, 1944–45; CO 2 York and Lancs, 1944; CO 2 Welch, 1945–47; Co. Comdr RMA Sandhurst, 1947–49; Chief Instructor, Staff Coll., Quetta, 1952–53; CO 1 Welch, 1953–56; Comd (Brig.) 9 Indep. Armd Bde Gp TA, 1956 and 148 Inf. Bde Gp TA, 1956–58; Inspector of Intelligence, 1961–63; retd 1963. Sec., Notts T&AFA, 1965–67; TAVR Council (formerly TA Council): Dep. Sec., 1967–72; Sec., 1973–75. Regional Organiser, Army Benevolent Fund, 1975–91; Regional Sec., British Field Sports Soc., 1976–83. DL Notts, 1973. *Recreations:* Rugby football (played for Wales, Barbarians and Army, 1934–35; Chm., Army Rugby Union Referees Soc., 1963–73), Arab horses (Hon. Show Dir, Arab Horse Show, 1968–81). *Address:* East Leake Hall, near Loughborough, Leics LE12 6LQ. *T:* (01509) 854009. *Clubs:* Army and Navy, British Sportsman's. *Died 20 Aug. 1997.*

COWIE, Mervyn Hugh, CBE 1960; ED 1954; FCA; *b* 13 April 1909; *s* of Capt. Herbert Hugh Cowie, JP; *m* 1st, 1934, Erica Mary Beaty (*d* 1956); two *s* one *d*; 2nd, 1957, Valori Hare Duke; one *s* one *d*. *Educ:* Brighton; Brasenose Coll., Oxford. Hon. Game Warden, 1932–; Mem. Nairobi District Council, 1932–36; KAR, Reserve of Officers, 1932–38 (3rd and 5th Battalions); Kenya Regt, 1939; served War of 1939–45: Abyssinia, Middle East, Madagascar (retd Lieut-Col). MLC Kenya, 1951–60; Dir of Manpower, Mau-Mau Emergency, 1953–56. Founder and Dir, Royal National Parks of Kenya, 1946–66. Vice-Pres. E African Tourist Travel Assoc., 1950–65; Mem. Nat. Parks Commn, Internat. Union for Conservation of Nature, 1959–66; Hon. Trustee, Uganda Nat. Parks, 1950–; Vice-Pres., Fauna Preservation Soc., London; Hon. Vice-Chm., East African Wild Life Soc.; Financial Dir, African Med. and Res. Foundn (Flying Doctor Services), 1972–79. TV and Radio (BBC Natural History Section). Editor, Royal Nat. Parks of Kenya Annual Reports, 1946–65. Lectures (tours USA and Britain). Gold Medal, San Diego Zool Soc., 1972. Order of the Golden Ark, Netherlands, 1975. *Publications:* Fly Vulture, 1961; I Walk with Lions (USA), 1964; African Lion, 1965; contributor to international journals and conferences. *Recreation:* wild life conservation. *Address:* Kikenni, Walnut Tree Farm, Benhall, Saxmundham, Suffolk IP17 1JB. *T:* Saxmundham (01728) 603397. *Clubs:* Shikar; Explorer's (New York); Muthaiga Country (Nairobi). *Died 19 July 1996.*

COWLEY, Kenneth Martin, CMG 1963; OBE 1956; *b* 15 May 1912; *s* of late Robert Martin Cowley, OBE, and Mabel Priscilla Cowley (*née* Lee); *m* 1948, Barbara Callow (*née* Tannahill) (decd); one step *s* (and one *s* decd). *Educ:*

Merchant Taylors' Sch., Crosby; Exeter Coll., Oxford (MA). District Officer, Kenya, 1935–44; Asst Sec., 1944–46; District Comr, 1946–49; Actg Native Courts Officer, 1949–53; Sec. for African Affairs, 1953–56; Provincial Commissioner, Southern Province, Kenya, 1956–63 (despatches, 1957); Sec., Kenya Regional Boundaries and Constituencies Commns, 1962; Sen. Administrative Manager, Express Transport Co. Ltd, Kenya, 1963–70. Sec., Overseas Service Pensioners' Assoc., 1971–79. *Recreation:* natural history. *Address:* Oakview Cottage, Cricket Green, Hartley Wintney, Hants RG27 8PZ. *T:* (01252) 844210. *Club:* Nairobi (Kenya).
Died 10 Nov. 1998.

COX; *see* Roxbee Cox, family name of Baron Kings Norton.

COX, Sir (Ernest) Gordon, KBE 1964; TD; DSc; FRS 1954; FRSC; FInstP; FIBiol; Secretary of the Agricultural Research Council, 1960–71; *b* 24 April 1906; *s* of Ernest Henry Cox (*d* 1987) and Rosina Ring; *m* 1st, 1929, Lucie Grace Baker (*d* 1962); one *s* one *d*; 2nd, 1968, Prof. Mary Rosaleen Truter, DSc, *d* of Dr D. N. Jackman. *Educ:* City of Bath Boys' Sch.; University of Bristol. Research Asst, Davy-Faraday Laboratory, Royal Institution, 1927; Chemistry Dept, Univ. of Birmingham, 1929–41 (Reader in Chemical Crystallography, 1940); Prof. of Inorganic and Structural Chemistry, University of Leeds, 1945–60. Commissioned in Territorial Army, 1936; special scientific duties, War Office, 1942–44; attached to HQ staff of 21 Army Group, France and Germany, as Technical Staff Officer, Grade I, 1944–45. Vice-Pres., Institute of Physics, 1950–53; Mem. Agricl Research Council, 1957–60. Hon. DSc: Newcastle, 1964; Birmingham, 1964; Bath, 1973; East Anglia, 1973; Hon. LLD Bristol, 1969; Hon. ARCVS 1972. *Publications:* numerous scientific papers in jls of various learned societies, chiefly on the crystal structures of chemical compounds. *Recreations:* music, gardening, natural history. *Address:* 117 Hampstead Way, NW11 7JN. *T:* 0181–455 2618. *Clubs:* Athenæum, English-Speaking Union, Lansdowne.
Died 23 June 1996.

COX, Dr Keith Gordon, FRS 1988; Reader in Petrology, Department of Earth Sciences, Oxford University, since 1990; Fellow of Jesus College, Oxford, since 1973; *b* 25 April 1933; *s* of Sir (Ernest) Gordon Cox, KBE, TD, FRS; *m* 1960, Gillian Mary Palmer; two *s* one *d*. *Educ:* Leeds Grammar Sch.; Queen's Coll., Oxford (MA); Leeds Univ. (PhD). Lectr in Geology, Univ. of Edinburgh, 1962–71; Lectr, Dept of Earth Scis, Oxford Univ., 1972–90. Editor: Earth & Planetary Science Letters, 1981–85; Jl of Petrology, 1981–83. *Publications:* (with J. D. Bell and R. J. Pankhurst) The Interpretation of Igneous Rocks, 1979; scientific papers, mainly in field of basalt petrology. *Recreation:* water colours. *Address:* 59 Bagley Wood Road, Kennington, Oxford OX1 5LY. *T:* (01865) 735590.
Died 27 Aug. 1998.

CRABBE, Pauline, (Mrs Joseph Benjamin), OBE 1969; JP; National Vice-Chairman, Brook Advisory Centres, 1980–86; *b* 1 April 1914; *y d* of Cyril and Edith Henriques, Kingston, Jamaica; *m* 1st, 1936, Geoffrey Henebery (marr. diss. 1948); one *d*; 2nd, 1949, Neville Crabbe (marr. diss. 1960); one *s*; 3rd, 1969, Joseph Benjamin; three step *s*. *Educ:* Highgate Convent; London Academy of Music and Drama; London Univ. (extra-mural course in Psychology). Actress and broadcaster, 1945–53; secretarial work with British Actors' Equity and WEA, 1953–56; then with Old People's Welfare and London Council of Social Service, 1956–57; Welfare Sec. and Dep. Gen. Sec. to Nat. Council for Unmarried Mother and her Child, 1957–69; Conciliation Officer for Race Relations Bd, 1969–71; Sec., 1971–76, Sen. Counsellor, 1976–80, London Brook Adv. Centres. Founder Mem., Haverstock Housing Trust for Fatherless Families, 1966; Mem. Bd, Housing Corp.,

1968–75; Member: Community Relations Commn, 1972–77; Standing Adv. Council on Race Relations, 1977; Parole Bd, 1978–82. Hon. Fellow, Manchester Polytechnic, 1979. Radio and TV broadcaster and panellist. JP London, 1967. FRSA 1972. *Publications:* articles and book reviews in social work jls. *Recreations:* entertaining, walking, indoor gardening, the theatre, the arts. *Address:* 88 Osprey House, Sillwood Place, Brighton, Sussex BN1 2NF. *Club:* Magistrates' Association.
Died 1 Nov. 1998.

CRABBE, Reginald James Williams, FIA, FSS; President for Life, Provident Life Association Ltd (Chairman, 1967–82, and President, 1982–86, Provident Life Association of London Ltd); Chairman: United Standard Insurance Co. Ltd, 1967–79; Vigilant Assurance Co. Ltd, 1970–79; *b* 22 June 1909; *e s* of late Harry James and Annie Martha Crabbe; *m* 1948, Phyllis Maud Smith; two *d*. *Educ:* Chigwell Sch., Essex. FIA 1933. Entered National Mutual Life Assurance Soc., 1926; joined Provident Life as Asst Actuary, 1935; Man. Dir, 1956–74; Dir, 1956–86; Dep. Chm., 1971–85, Chm., 1975–77, Cope & Timmins Holdings. Chm., Life Offices' Assoc., 1965, 1966. *Publication:* (with C. A. Poyser) Pension and Widows' and Orphans' Funds, 1953. *Recreations:* reading, gardening, music, art.
Died 28 Nov. 1996.

CRABBIE, (Margaret) Veronica, CBE 1977; *b* 26 Nov. 1910; *d* of late Hon. Lord Sands, Senator of the College of Justice, Scotland, and Lady Sands; *m* 1938, John Patrick Crabbie; two *s* one *d*. *Educ:* St Denis Sch., Edinburgh; Queen Margaret's Sch., Escrick, York. Chairman: Edinburgh Home for Mothers and Infants, 1951–66; Walpole Housing Assoc., 1969–72; Scottish Council for the Unmarried Mother and her Child, 1966–72; WRVS, Scotland, 1972–77. *Recreation:* curling. *Club:* New (Edinburgh).
Died 17 Aug. 1998.

CRADOCK-HARTOPP, Sir John Edmund; *see* Hartopp.

CRADOCK-HARTOPP, Lt-Comdr Sir Kenneth Alston, 10th Bt *cr* 1796, of Freathby, Leics; MBE 1946; DSC 1952; Royal Navy, retired; *b* 26 Feb. 1918; *s* of Maj. Louis Montague Cradock-Hartopp (*d* 1957) and Marjorie Somerville (*née* Watson; *d* 1971); *S* cousin, 1996; *m* 1942, Gwendolyn Amy Lilian (*née* Upton) (*d* 8 June 2000); one *d*. Served War, 1939–45 and Korea. Legion of Merit, USA, 1953. *Heir:* none. *Address:* Keepers, Yeovilton, Yeovil, Somerset BA22 8EX.
Died 8 June 2000 (ext).

CRAGG, Prof. James Birkett, DSc; Emeritus Professor of Environmental Science, University of Calgary, Alberta; *b* 8 Nov. 1910; *s* of late A. W. Cragg, N Shields; *m* 1937, Mary Catherine Macnaughtan (marr. diss. 1968); four *s* (and one *s* one *d* decd); *m* Jean Moore. *Educ:* private sch.; Tynemouth High Sch.; Durham Univ. BSc King's Coll., University of Durham, 1933; DThPT 1934; MSc 1937; DSc Newcastle, 1965. Demonstrator, Physiology Dept, Manchester Univ., 1935; Asst Lecturer, and later Lecturer, in Zoology, University Coll. of North Wales, 1937; seconded to Agricultural Research Council, 1942; Scientific Officer, ARC Unit of Insect Physiology, 1944; Reader in Zoology, Durham Colls, in University of Durham, 1946; Prof. of Zoology, University of Durham, 1950–61; Dir, Merlewood Research Station (Nature Conservancy, NERC), Grange-over-Sands, Lancs, 1961–66; Dir, Environmental Sciences Centre, and Prof. of Biology, 1966–72, Killam Meml Prof., 1966–76, Vice-Pres. (Academic), 1970–72, Univ. of Calgary, Alberta. Pres., British Ecol. Soc., 1960–61; former Chairman: Commn for Ecology; Internat. Union for Conservation of Nature; Convenor, Internat. Biological Programme PT Cttee; Mem., Internat. Biological Programme Cttees; Consultant, Ford Foundation, 1965. Commonwealth

Prestige Fellow (New Zealand), 1964. Jubilee medal, 1977. Hon. FIBiol 1981. *Publications:* papers in scientific periodicals; formerly Editor, Advances in Ecological Research. *Recreation:* books. *Address:* 2112 Uralta Road, Calgary, Alberta T2N 4B4, Canada. *Club:* Athenæum.
Died 12 Nov. 1996.

CRAGGS, Prof. John Drummond, PhD; FInstP; Professor of Electronic Engineering, University of Liverpool, 1955–82; *b* 17 May 1915; *s* of Thomas Lawson Craggs and Elsie Aidrienne Roberts; *m* 1941, Dorothy Ellen Margaret Garfitt; two *d. Educ:* Huddersfield Coll.; University of London (MSc, PhD). Research Student, King's Coll., London Univ., 1937–38; Metropolitan-Vickers High Voltage Research Laboratory, Manchester, 1938–48; University of California, Radiation Laboratory, 1944–45; apptd Sen. Lectr, 1948, and, later, Reader, Dept of Electrical Engineering, University of Liverpool. A Pro-Vice-Chancellor, Liverpool Univ., 1969–72. Hon. DSc NUI, 1986. *Publications:* Counting Tubes, 1950 (with S. C. Curran); Electrical Breakdown of Gases, 1953; (with J. M. Meek) High Voltage Laboratory Technique, 1954; (with J. M. Meek) Electrical Breakdown of Gases, 1978; papers in various professional jls.
Died 4 Sept. 1999.

CRAIG, Charles (James); opera singer (tenor); *b* 3 Dec. 1919; *s* of James and Rosina Craig; *m* 1946, Dorothy Wilson; one *s* one *d. Educ:* in London. Protégé of Sir Thomas Beecham; Principal Tenor with Carl Rosa Opera Co., 1953–56; joined Sadler's Wells Opera Co., 1956; appeared regularly at internat. opera houses, incl. Covent Garden, Milan, Rome, Vienna, Paris, Berlin, Buenos Aires, etc; repertoire of 48 operas, incl. Otello, Aida, Turandot, Norma, Andrea Chenier, Die Walküre, Götterdämmerung, Lohengrin, etc. Concerts, TV and radio, and records. International Opera Medal Award, 1962. *Recreations:* motoring, cooking. *Address:* Whitfield Cottage, Whitfield, Brackley, Northants NN13 5TF.
Died 23 Jan. 1997.

CRAIG, Edward Anthony, (Edward Carrick), FRSA; writer and lecturer, designer for film and theatre; independent film art director; *b* 3 Jan. 1905; *s* of late Edward Gordon Craig, CH and Elena Meo; *m* 1st, 1928, Helen Godfrey (*d* 1960); one *s* one *d*; 2nd, 1960, Mary, *d* of late Lt-Col H. A. Timewell, OBE. Studied art, the theatre and photography in Italy, 1917–26; discovered numerous documents of great value to the history of the theatre; Art Dir to the Welsh Pearson Film Co., 1928–29; Art Dir for Associated Talking Pictures, 1932–36; Supervising Art Dir, Criterion Film, 1937–39; established AAT Film Sch., 1937; Art Dir to the Crown Film Unit (Ministry of Information), 1939–46; Executive Art Dir, Independent Producers (Rank), 1947–49. Wood-engravings, oil paintings, and scene designs exhibited at: the St George's Gallery, 1927 and 1928; at the Redfern Gallery, 1929, 1931, 1938; The Grubb Group, 1928–38; also in the principal galleries of Canada and North America; designer of scenes and costumes for numerous London productions, and at Stratford-upon-Avon, 1949. *Official Purchasers:* the British Museum; Victoria and Albert Museum; Metropolitan Museum, New York; Yale Univ., USA; The University, Austin, Texas. *Publications:* Designing for Moving Pictures, 1941; Meet the Common People, 1942; Art and Design in British Films, 1948; Designing for Films, 1949; Gordon Craig, The Story of his Life, 1968, Polish trans., 1977, Amer. edn 1985; (in Italian) Fabrizio Carini Motta, 1972; William Nicolson's An Alphabet, 1978; Robinson Crusoe and Gordon Craig, 1979; William Nicolson's An Almanac, 1980; (ed) Gordon Craig: the last eight years, by Ellen Gordon Craig, 1983; Baroque Theatre Construction, 1982; *illustrations:* The Georgics of Virgil, 1931, etc; books of verse by John

Keats, Edith Sitwell, Edmund Blunden, W. H. Davies, etc. *Recreations:* books, music. *Address:* Southcourt Cottage, Long Crendon, Aylesbury, Bucks HP18 9AQ.
Died 21 Jan. 1998.

CRAIGMYLE, 3rd Baron *cr* 1929, of Craigmyle, co. Aberdeen; **Thomas Donald Mackay Shaw;** Chairman, Craigmyle & Co. Ltd; President, Catholic Union of Great Britain, since 1993; *b* 17 Nov. 1923; *s* of 2nd Baron Craigmyle and Lady Margaret Cargill Mackay (*d* 1958), *e d* of 1st Earl of Inchcape; *S* father, 1944; *m* 1955, Anthea Esther Christine, *y d* of late E. C. Rich; three *s* three *d. Educ:* Eton; Trinity Coll., Oxford (MA). Served RNVR, 1943–46. FRSA. Bailiff, Grand Cross of Obedience, SMO Malta, 1995, and Pres., British Assoc., 1989–95 (Hospitaller, 1962–73; Sec.-Gen., 1979–83; Vice-Pres., 1983–89). KStJ 1989. *Publication:* (ed with J. Gould) Your Death Warrant?, 1971. *Recreation:* home baking. *Heir: s* Hon. Thomas Columba Shaw [*b* 19 Oct. 1960; *m* 1987, Alice, 2nd *d* of David Floyd; three *s*]. *Address:* 18 The Boltons, SW10 9SY; Scottas, Knoydart, Inverness-shire PH41 4PL. *Clubs:* Caledonian, Royal Thames Yacht; Bengal (Calcutta).
Died 30 April 1998.

CRAIK, Duncan Robert Steele, CB 1979; OBE 1971; Auditor-General for Australia, 1973–81; *b* 17 Feb. 1916; *s* of Henry Steele Craik and Lilian Kate Ellis; *m* 1943, Audrey Mavis Ion; four *d. Educ:* Univ. of Sydney (BEc). FASA 1973–87; FAIM 1975–86; FRAIPA 1983. Commonwealth Bank, 1933–40; Taxation Br., 1940–60; Treasury: Asst Sec., 1960–66; First Asst Sec., 1966–69; Dep. Sec., 1969–73. Part-time Mem., Admin. Appeals Tribunal, 1981–86. Mem. Council, ANU, 1981–83. *Recreation:* gardening. *Address:* 78 Grayson Street, Hackett, ACT 2602, Australia.
Died 22 Aug. 1999.

CRAMPTON, (Arthur Edward) Seán, MC 1943; GM (mil.) 1944; TD 1946; PPRBS (FRBS 1965; ARBS 1952); sculptor; *b* 15 March 1918; *e s* of late Joshua Crampton, architect, and Ethel Mary (*née* Dyas); *m* 3rd, 1959, Patricia, *e d* of late L. J. Cardew Wood, one *s* one *d*, three *d* by former marriages. *Educ:* St Joseph de Cluny, Stafford; Vittoria Jun. Sch. of Art, Birmingham; Birmingham Central Coll. of Art; London; Paris. Served TA, London Irish Rifles, Western Desert, Sicily, Italy, 1938–46. Prof. de Sculpture, Anglo-French Art Centre, 1946–50. Served on juries for Thomas More and Winston Churchill meml statues. Member, Art Workers Guild, 1971 (Master, 1978); Pres., RBS, 1966–71. Mem., Accademia Italia, 1981. Governor: Camberwell Sch. of Arts and Crafts, 1970–88 (Chm., 1983–88); London Inst., 1986–88. FRSA 1973. *Exhibitions: general:* RA and RWA Galls; *one-man:* fourteen exhibns in London, 1948–82. *Major heroic size works:* Persephone, Crowmallie, Aberdeen; Horseman (RBS Silver Medal, 1965); Simon de Montfort, County Hall, Leics; Three Judges, Churchill Coll., Cambridge; Three Kings, Knochallachie, Aberdeen; Two Geese, Goose Green, Altrincham (Civic Trust Award, 1984); Bird Flight, St John's Coll., Cambridge; *works in churches:* St Mary and Child, Midhurst; Our Lady, St Michael and Crucifix, Wolverhampton; Crucifix, Church of Child Jesus, Birmingham; Risen Christ and sanctuary furniture, St Vincent's Convent, Mill Hill; Our Lady and Child, Convent of Sisters of Mercy, Brentwood; Crucifix, St Cedd's, Goodmayes; Our Lady, St Mary's Coll., Wallasey; Cross Motif, St Thomas More, Manor House; Risen Christ, St Albans, Derby; Stations of the Cross, St Edmunds, Calne (RBS Medal, 1986), etc. *Publication:* Humans, Beasts, Birds (with Hicks and Anderson), 1981. *Recreations:* gardening, painting, cooking. *Address:* Rookery Farmhouse, Calne, Wilts SN11 0LH. *T:* (01249) 814068. *Clubs:* Athenæum, Chelsea Arts.
Died 16 July 1999.

CRAWFORD, (Robert) Norman, CBE 1973; Chairman, R. N. Crawford & Co., Business Advisors, since 1968; Director, William Clark & Sons, 1983–88 (Chief Executive, 1983–87); *b* 14 June 1923; *s* of William Crawford and Annie Catherine (*née* Rexter); *m* 1948, Jean Marie Patricia (*née* Carson); one *s* five *d*. *Educ:* Foyle Coll., Londonderry; Queen's Univ., Belfast (BComSc). FCA. Sec./Accountant, John McNeill Ltd, 1948–60; Dep. Man. Dir, McNeill Group Ltd, 1960–66, Man. Dir 1966–68; Chm., N Ireland Transport Holding Co., 1968–75; Divisional Hd, NI Develt Agency, 1976–82. Pres., N Ireland Chamber of Commerce and Industry, 1966–67; Chairman: N Ireland Regional Bd, BIM, 1966–69; Nature Reserves Cttee, 1967–85; NI Outward Bound Assoc., 1969–76 (Pres., 1983–92); Open Door Housing Assoc., 1979–84; Retirement Assoc. of NI, 1982–83; Member: CEED, 1985–92; Solway Heritage, 1995–; Crichton Trust, 1996–; Crichton Develt Co. Ltd, 1996–. Member Senate, Queen's University, Belfast, 1968–93 (Pres., Queen's Univ. Assoc., 1982–83); Pres., Foyle Coll. Old Boys' Assoc., 1981–82. Chm., NI Wildlife Campaign, 1986–88. FRSA. *Address:* 23 Corberry Mews, Dumfries DG2 7AX. *T:* (01387) 261236. *Club:* Ulster Reform (Belfast). *Died 6 Jan. 1998.*

CRAWSHAW, 4th Baron *cr* 1892; **William Michael Clifton Brooks;** Bt 1891; DL; *b* 25 March 1933; *s* of 3rd Baron Crawshaw and Sheila (*d* 1964), *o d* of late Lieut-Col P. R. Clifton, CMG, DSO; *S* father, 1946. *Educ:* Eton; Christ Church, Oxford. Jt Master, Oxford Univ. Drag Hounds, 1952–53. Treasurer, Loughborough Div. Conservative Assoc., 1954–58; Pres., NW Leics Conservative Assoc., 1982–. County Commissioner, Leics Boy Scouts, 1958–77. Pres., Leics Assoc. of the Disabled; Chm., Quorn Hunt Cttee, 1971–91. Trustee, Henry Smith's Charity. Lord of the Manor of Long Whatton. Patron of the Living of Shepshed. DL Leics, 1992. *Heir: b* Hon. David Gerald Brooks [*b* 14 Sept. 1934; *m* 1970, Belinda Mary, *d* of George Burgess, Melbourne, and of Mrs J. P. Allen, Coleman's Hatch, Sussex; four *d*]. *Address:* Whatton, Loughborough, Leics LE12 5BG. *TA:* Kegworth. *Clubs:* Boodle's, MCC. *Died 7 Nov. 1997.*

CRAWSHAY, Col Sir William (Robert), Kt 1972; DSO 1945; ERD; TD; Vice Lieutenant of Gwent, 1979–95; *b* 27 May 1920; *o s* of late Captain J. W. L. Crawshay, MC, Caversham Park, Oxon, and Claire (who later *m* Hon. George Egerton, 2nd *s* of 5th Earl of Wilton), Brussels; *m* 1950, Elisabeth Mary Boyd Reynolds, CBE. *Educ:* Eton. Served Royal Welch Fus.(SR), 1939–46; SOE 1944 (DSO, despatches twice); TA, 1947–62, Parachute Regt, Welch Regt, SW Brigade. ADC to HM the Queen, 1966–71. Hon. Colonel: 3rd RRW (V) Bn, 1970–82; Cardiff Univ. OTC, 1977–85. Mem., Arts Council of GB, 1962–74; Chairman: Welsh Arts Council, 1968–74; Council, University Coll. of Cardiff, 1966–87; Member: Council and Court, Univ. of Wales, 1967; Welsh Council, 1966–69, 1970–; Council and Court, Nat. Museum of Wales, 1966–92 (Pres., 1977–82). Vice-Pres., Royal British Legion, 1989– (Pres., Wales Area, 1974–88). Mem., Crafts Adv. Council, 1974–78. Hon. LLD, Univ. of Wales, 1975. DL Glamorgan, 1964, Monmouthshire, 1970, Gwent, 1974. Chevalier, Légion d'honneur, 1956; Croix de Guerre (France) with Palms twice, 1944, 1945. KStJ (formerly KJStJ) 1969. *Address:* Llanfair Court, Abergavenny, Gwent NP7 9BB. *Clubs:* White's; Cardiff and County (Cardiff). *Died 24 Jan. 1997.*

CRAXTON, (Harold) Antony, CVO 1977 (MVO 1968); former television consultant; *b* 23 April 1918; 2nd *s* of late Harold Craxton, OBE, and Essie Craxton; *m* 1944, Anne Sybil Cropper (marr. diss. 1978); one *s* one *d*. *Educ:* St George's Chapel Choir Sch., Windsor; Royal Acad. of Music; Gordonstoun Sch., Scotland. Joined BBC Radio,

1941; Home and Overseas Announcer, 1942–45; joined TV Service as Outside Broadcast Producer, 1951; resp. for coverage of all major Royal occasions, 1953–77, Jubilee Day being 200th broadcast involving the Queen and Royal Family; retd, 1979. Helped pioneer presentation of internat. cricket, rugby and golf in early 50s; covered over 100 orchestral concert relays from many parts of country, 1953–71. Chief Royal Occasions: Queen's 1st Christmas Television Broadcast, and Prince Philip's 1st major TV appearance, Round the World in 40 Minutes, 1957; Princess Margaret's Wedding, 1960; Duke of Kent's Wedding, 1961; Princess Alexandra's Wedding, 1963; State Funeral of Sir Winston Churchill, 1965; Investiture of Prince Charles as Prince of Wales, 1969; Lying in State of Duke of Windsor, 1972; Queen's Silver Wedding Celebrations, 1972; Princess Anne's Wedding, 1973; Funeral of Duke of Gloucester, 1974; Funeral of Field-Marshal Montgomery, 1976; Queen's Silver Jubilee Day Celebrations, 1977; 10 State visits abroad and 19 visits by Foreign Heads of State to Britain, 1954–76. News Chronicle Readers' Award for Prince Philip's Round the World Documentary, 1957; Guild of TV Producers' Award for Princess Alexandra's Wedding, 1963; French TV Internat. Award for Investiture of Prince Charles, 1970; BAFTA Award for Jubilee Day (1977), 1978. Silver Jubilee Medal, 1977. *Recreations:* golf, cricket, classical music. *Club:* MCC. *Died 21 June 1999.*

CREE, Brig. Gerald Hilary, CBE 1946; DSO 1945; Colonel, The Prince of Wales's Own Regiment of Yorkshire, 1960–70; *b* 23 June 1905; *s* of late Maj.-Gen. Gerald Cree, CB, CMG and Isabella Sophie Alice, *o d* of Surg.-Gen. P. Broke Smith, AMS; *m* 1945, Joan Agnes, *d* of late Lt-Col W. R. Eden, RA; one *d. Educ:* Kelly Coll.; RMC Sandhurst. Commissioned, The West Yorks Regt, 1924; King's African Rifles, 1931–36; served Palestine, East Africa, Abyssinia, Western Desert, Iraq, Burma, 1938–45; comd 2nd Bn West Yorks Regt, 1942–44; 1st Bn 1946–48; Comdr 25 (East African) Infantry Bde, 1944–45 and Brig. 1953; Commander 127 (East Lancs) Infantry Brigade (TA), 1953–56; Col, The West Yorks Regt, 1956–57, Col, PWO Regt of Yorkshire, 1960–70, retd. *Address:* Laurels, Sharpham Drive, Totnes, Devon TQ9 5HE. *T:* (01803) 862902. *Died 21 Aug. 1998.*

CREIGHTMORE, Peter Beauchamp; Master of Supreme Court, Queen's Bench Division, 1975–96; *b* 15 Jan. 1928; *s* of late Maximilian Louis Creightmore, MRCS, LRCP and Mary Arnell Beauchamp; *m* 1957, June Patricia, *d* of Harold William Hedley, Captain Suez Canal Co. (Pilote Majeur), and Gwendoline Pugh; one *s* one *d. Educ:* Geelong Grammar Sch. (H. H. Whittingham Student, 1945); Worcester Coll., Oxford (MA). O/Sig, RNVR, 1952, commnd 1955. Called to Bar, Inner Temple, 1954; Oxford, later Oxford and Midland, Circuit. *Recreation:* music. *Address:* c/o Royal Courts of Justice, Strand, WC2A 2LL. *Died 15 May 1997.*

CRESWELL, Jack Norman; Deputy Chairman of Lloyd's, 1972, 1974; *b* 20 April 1913; *s* of late Sydney and Dora Creswell; *m* 1938, Jean (Lilian Jane) Maxwell (*d* 1998); two *s. Educ:* Highgate School. Served War, 1942–46, 2nd Household Cavalry Regt; Captain and Adjt, The Life Guards, 1945–46. Member of Lloyd's, 1940; Mem. Cttee, 1969–72, 1974; Mem. Cttee Lloyd's Underwriters Non-Marine Assoc., 1968–74, Chm. 1973. *Recreations:* photography, family croquet. *Address:* Lullington Court, near Polegate, E Sussex BN26 5QY. *T:* (01323) 870548. *Club:* Devonshire (Eastbourne).

Died 31 May 1999.

CREWE, Quentin Hugh; writer and journalist; *b* 14 Nov. 1926; *s* of Major Hugh Crewe (surname changed by Deed Poll from Dodds, 1945) and Lady Annabel Crewe, *d* of 1st and last Marquess of Crewe, KG; *m* 1st, 1956, Martha

Sharp; one *s* one *d*; 2nd, 1961, Angela Huth (marr. diss. 1970); one *d* (one *s* decd); 3rd, 1970, Susan Anne Cavendish (marr. diss. 1983); one *s* one *d*. *Educ:* Eton; Trinity Coll., Cambridge. Joined Evening Standard, 1953; subseq. worked for Queen, Vogue, Daily Mail, Sunday Mirror; freelance, 1970–, contrib. to Times, Sunday Times, Sunday Telegraph, and Spectator. Snowdon Award, 1982. *Publications:* A Curse of Blossom, 1960; Frontiers of Privilege, 1961; Great Chefs of France, 1978; Pocket Book of Food, 1980; In Search of the Sahara, 1983; The Last Maharaja, 1985; Touch the Happy Isles, 1987; In the Realms of Gold, 1989; Well, I Forget the Rest (autobiog.), 1991; Foods from France, 1993; Crewe House, the Royal Embassy of the Kingdom of Saudi Arabia, 1995; Letters from India, 1998. *Recreation:* travel. *Address:* 9 Bliss Mill, Chipping Norton, Oxon OX7 5JR. *T:* (01608) 642176, *Fax:* (01608) 642178.

Died 14 Nov. 1998.

CRICHTON, Charles Ainslie; film director; *b* 6 Aug. 1910; *s* of John Douglas Crichton and Hester Wingate Ainslie; *m* 1st, 1936, Vera Pearl Harman-Mills; two *s*; 2nd, 1962, Nadine Haze. *Educ:* Oundle; New Coll., Oxford (BA History). Pictures, 1944–88, included: Painted Boats, 1945; Hue and Cry, 1947; Against the Wind, 1947; Dance Hall, 1950; The Lavender Hill Mob, 1951 (Dirs' Guild Awards Nomination, 1953); Hunted, 1952; The Titfield Thunderbolt, 1953; The Love Lottery; The Divided Heart, 1954; The Man in the Sky, 1957; Battle of the Sexes, 1959; The Third Secret, 1964; He Who Rides a Tiger, 1965; A Fish Called Wanda, 1988 (Directors' Guild Awards Nomination, 1989; Oscar Nomination, 1989; BAFTA Award, 1989; Evening Standard Award, 1989). Television: Danger Man, The Avengers, Strange Report, Black Beauty, Space 1999, Dick Turpin, Smuggler; video arts shorts. *Recreations:* fishing, photography. *Address:* 1 Southwell Gardens, SW7 4SB.

Died 15 Sept. 1999.

CRICHTON, David George, LVO 1968; HM Diplomatic Service; Consul-General, Nice, 1970–74; *b* 31 July 1914; *e s* of late Col Hon. Sir George Crichton, GCVO and Lady Mary Dawson, *y d* of 2nd Earl of Dartrey; *m* 1st, 1941, Joan Fenella (*d* 1992), *d* of late Col D. W. Cleaver, DSO; one *s* one *d*; 2nd, 1994, Betty, *widow* of Andrew Hughes-Onslow. *Educ:* Eton. Worked as journalist, Reading and Manchester, and on Daily Telegraph, Paris and London, 1933–39; served War of 1939–45 in Derbyshire Yeomanry (despatches); Major 1944; entered Foreign Service, 1946; served in Belgrade, Singapore, Alexandria, Miami, La Paz and Santiago. *Address:* 29B Thorney Crescent, Morgan's Walk, SW11 3TT. *T:* (0171) 738 9694. *Club:* Boodle's.

Died 24 Jan. 1997.

CRICHTON-MILLER, Donald, TD; MA; *b* 7 Dec. 1906; *s* of late Hugh Crichton-Miller, MA, MD, FRCP and Eleanor Jane Campbell, *d* of Sheriff Lorimer, KC, Edinburgh; *m* 1931, Monica, *d* of late B. A. Glanvill, JP, Bromley, Kent; two *s* one *d*. *Educ:* Fettes Coll., Edinburgh; Pembroke Coll., Cambridge (Exhibitioner). Played Rugby Football for Cambridge and Scotland. Asst Master: Monmouth Sch., 1929–31; Bryanston Sch., 1931–34; Stowe Sch., 1934–36; Head Master: Taunton Sch., Somerset, 1936–45; Fettes Coll., 1945–58; Stowe Sch., 1958–63. Carried out education surveys in Pakistan, 1951, and Malta, 1956. *Recreations:* governing schools, managing properties. *Address:* Glencorse, Compton, Newbury, Berks RG16 0RE. *T:* (01635) 578384.

Died 5 Aug. 1997.

CRICKMAY, John Rackstrow, FRICS; Chairman, Percy Bilton PLC, 1984–89 (Director, 1980–89); *b* 16 May 1914; *s* of Edward John Crickmay and Constance May Bowyer; *m* 1939, Margaret Hilda Rainer (*d* 1993); one *s*. *Educ:* Brighton Coll. Artist Rifles, 1936; Royal Regt of Artillery, 1939–46, served in Far East, 1940–45 (POW, 1942–45); TEM 1946. Surveyor, 1936–46, Chief Estates Surveyor, 1946–74, Legal & General Assurance Society; Cons. to property interests, 1974–; Dir, Ecclesiastical Insce Office, 1980–84. President: British Chapter Real Property Fedn, 1966; Chartered Auctioneers & Estate Agents Inst., 1968; Mem. Council, RICS, 1972–85, Hon. Treas., 1980–85. Gov., Royal Star & Garter, Richmond, 1975–90; Dep. Chm., Christ's Hosp., 1984–89, Almoner, 1977–89. Pres., Pulborough Br., RBL, 1996. Amicable Soc. of Blues, 1990. Master, Ironmongers' Co., 1976–77. Hon. Fellow, Coll. of Estate Management, Reading, 1988. Medal of Internat. Real Estate Fedn, 1974; Silver Jubilee Medal, 1977. *Recreations:* cricket, golf. *Address:* Old Walls, Old Rectory Lane, Pulborough, West Sussex RH20 2AF. *T:* (01798) 872336. *Clubs:* Oriental, MCC.

Died 27 Nov. 1997.

CRIGHTON, Prof. David George, FRS 1993; Master, Jesus College, Cambridge, since 1997; Professor of Applied Mathematics, since 1986, and Head of Department of Applied Mathematics and Theoretical Physics, since 1991, University of Cambridge; *b* 15 Nov. 1942; *s* of George Wolfe Johnston Crighton and Violet Grace Crighton (*née* Garrison); *m* 1st, 1969, Mary Christine West (marr. diss. 1985); one *s* one *d*; 2nd, 1986, Johanna Veronica Hol. *Educ:* St John's College, Cambridge (BA 1964; MA 1980; ScD 1993); Imperial College London (PhD 1969). Research Asst, Imperial College London, 1967–74; Prof. of Applied Mathematics, Univ. of Leeds, 1974–85; Fellow, St John's Coll., Cambridge, 1986–97. President: EUROMECH, 1993–97; IMA, 1996–97. Hon. DSc: Loughborough, 1999; UMIST, 1999. *Publications:* papers on fluid mechanics and wave theory in jls, conf. proc. *Recreations:* music, opera. *Address:* The Master's Lodge, Jesus College, Cambridge CB5 8BL. *T:* (01223) 766218/339400.

Died 12 April 2000.

CRIPPS, Anthony Leonard; *see* Cripps, M. A. L.

CRIPPS, Sir (Cyril) Humphrey, Kt 1989; CChem, FRSC; Chairman, Pianoforte Supplies Ltd, Roade, Northampton, since 1979; Founder Member, Cripps Foundation, Chairman since 1979; Chairman: Velcro Industries NV, 1973–96; Air BVI, 1971–86; *b* 2 Oct. 1915; *o s* of Sir Cyril Thomas Cripps, MBE, and Lady (Amy) Cripps; *m* 1942, Dorothea Casson, *o d* of late Reginald Percy Cook, architect; two *s* (and one *s* one *d* decd). *Educ:* Northampton Grammar Sch. (schol.); St John's Coll., Cambridge (Nat. Sci. Prelim. Cl. 1, Tripos Pts I and II, Cl. 2; BA, MA). FCS 1935; FRIC 1977; FRSC 1979. Founder of private businesses in UK, Australia, Canada and Brit. Virgin Islands. Member, Northamptonshire CC, 1963–74 (Leader of Independents, to 1974; formerly Vice-Chm., Educn and Planning Cttees); Mem., (new) Northants CC, 1973–81; Board Mem., Northampton Develt Corp., 1968–85. Life Mem. Ct, Univ. of Nottingham, 1953; Governor: Northampton Grammar Sch., 1963–74; Northampton Sch. for Boys, 1977–81; (Vice-Chm., 1970–81, 1986–88, Chm., 1988–96, Foundn Trust); Northampton High Sch. for Girls, 1966–92 (Chm., 1972–84); Foundn Governor, Bilton Grange Prep. Sch., 1957–80. Trustee, Cripps Postgrad. Med. Centre, Northampton Gen. Hosp., 1969–74; Member of Trusts: Peterborough Cath., 1975–95; All Saints Church, Northampton, 1975–85; Trustee, Univ. of Nottingham Develt Trust, 1990–93. Hon. Fellow: Cripps Hall, Nottingham Univ., 1959; Cambridge University: St John's Coll., 1966; Magdalene Coll., 1971; Selwyn Coll., 1971; Queens' Coll., 1979. Hon. DSc Nottingham, 1975; Hon. LLD Cantab, 1976. Pres., Johnian Soc., 1966. Liveryman, Worshipful Co. of Wheelwrights, 1957, Mem. Court 1970, Master 1982; Liveryman, Worshipful Co. of Tallow Chandlers, 1983; Freeman, City of London (by redemption), 1957. High Sheriff, Northants,

1985–86; DL Northants, 1986–96. *Recreations:* travel, photography, natural history (entomology, espec. Rhopalocera), philately. *Address:* Bull's Head Farm, Stoke Goldington, Newport Pagnell, Bucks MK16 8LP. *T:* (01908) 551223. *Died 14 April 2000.*

CRIPPS, (Matthew) Anthony Leonard, CBE 1971; DSO 1943; TD 1947; QC 1958; a Recorder, 1972–85 (Recorder of Nottingham, 1961–71); Deputy Senior Judge, British Sovereign Base Areas, Cyprus, 1978–90; *b* 30 Dec. 1913; *s* of late Major Hon. Leonard Harrison Cripps and Miriam Barbara, *d* of Rt Hon. Sir Matthew I. Joyce; *heir-pres.* to 4th Baron Parmoor; *m* 1941, Dorothea Margaret (*d* 1992) (Surrey CC, 1965–67), *d* of G. Johnson Scott, Ashby-de-la-Zouch; three *s*. *Educ:* Eton; Christ Church, Oxford; Combined Army and RAF Staff Coll., Haifa, 1944–45. Royal Leicestershire Regt, TA, 1933; served War of 1939–45: Norway, Sweden, Finland, Iceland, N Africa, Italy, Egypt, 1939–44 (Capt. to Lt-Col); Staff Officer, Palestine and Syria, 1944–46. Barrister-at-law, Middle Temple, 1938 (Bencher 1965; Treasurer, 1983), Inner Temple, 1961, Hong Kong, 1974 and Singapore, 1987. Hon. Judge of Court of Arches, 1969–80. Comr for Local Govt Petitions, 1978–84. Chairman: Disciplinary Cttees, Milk Marketing Bd, 1956–90, Potato and Egg Marketing Bds, 1956–67; Isle of Man Govt Commn on Agricultural Marketing, 1961–62; Home Sec.'s Adv. Cttee on Service Candidates, 1966–94 (Dep. Chm., 1965); Nat. Panel, Approved Coal Merchants Scheme, 1972–89; Legal Adv. Cttee, RSPCA, 1978–90; Univ. of London Appeals Cttee, 1980–90. Member: Agricultural Wages Bd, 1964–67; Northumberland Cttee of Inquiry into Foot and Mouth Disease, 1968–69; Cttee of Inquiry, Export of Live Animals for Slaughter, 1973–74. Pres., Coal Trade Benevolent Assoc., 1983. Mem., Ct of Assts, Fuellers' Co., 1985– (Master, 1990). *Publications:* Agriculture Act 1947, 1947; Agriculture Holdings Act 1948, 1948; (ed) 9th edn, Cripps on Compulsory Purchase: Powers, Procedure and Compensation, 1950; Spice of Life, 1992; legal articles, especially on agricultural matters, for Law Jl and Encyclopaedia Britannica. *Recreations:* family life, writing, forestry. *Address:* Woodhurst, McCrae's Walk, Wargrave, Berks RG10 8LN. *T:* (01734) 403449. *Clubs:* Brooks's; Phyllis Court (Henley-on-Thames).
Died 22 Jan. 1997.

CRITCHLEY, Sir Julian (Michael Gordon), Kt 1995; writer, broadcaster and journalist; *b* 8 Dec. 1930; *s* of late Dr Macdonald Critchley, CBE; *m* 1st, 1955, Paula Joan Baron (marr. diss. 1965); two *d*; 2nd, 1965, Mrs Heather Goodrick; one *s* one *d*. *Educ:* Shrewsbury; Sorbonne; Pembroke Coll., Oxford (MA). MP (C) Rochester and Chatham, 1959–64; contested (C) same seat, 1966; MP (C) Aldershot and N Hants, 1970–74, Aldershot, 1974–97. Mem., Armed Forces Select Cttee, 1975–79; Vice-Chairman: Cons. Party Broadcasting Cttee, 1975; Cons. Party Defence Cttee, 1979–87; Chm., Cons. Party Media Cttee, 1976–81; Mem., One Nation Gp of Cons. MPs, 1989–97. Delegate to WEU and Council of Europe, 1973–79; Chm., WEU Defence Cttee, 1975–79; Deleg. to N Atlantic Assembly, 1979–83. Chm., Bow Gp, 1966–67; Pres., Atlantic Assoc. of Young Political Leaders, 1968–70. Steward, British Boxing Bd of Control, 1987–. *Publications:* (with O. Pick) Collective Security, 1974; Warning and Response, 1978; The North Atlantic Alliance and the Soviet Union in the 1980s, 1982; (jtly) Nuclear Weapons in Europe, 1984; Westminster Blues, 1985; (ed) Britain: a view from Westminster, 1986; Heseltine: the unauthorised biography, 1987, 2nd edn 1994; Palace of Varieties: an insider's view of Westminster, 1989; Hung Parliament, 1991; Floating Voter, 1992; Some of Us, 1992; Borderlands: Shropshire and the Welsh Marches, 1993; A Bag of Boiled Sweets (autobiog.), 1994, (jtly) Collapse of Stout Party: the decline and fall of the Tories,

1997; various Bow Group and CPC pamphlets. *Recreations:* watching boxing, the country, reading military history, looking at churches, collecting pottery and porcelain. *Address:* 19 Broad Street, Ludlow SY8 1NG. *T:* (01584) 877084. *Died 9 Sept. 2000.*

CRITCHLEY, Macdonald, CBE 1962; MD; FRCP; consulting neurologist; *b* 2 Feb. 1900; *s* of Arthur Frank and Rosina Matilda Critchley; *m* 1st, 1927, Edna Auldeth Morris (decd); two *s*; 2nd, Eileen Hargreaves. *Educ:* Christian Brothers Coll.; Univ. of Bristol (Lady Haberfield Scholarship in Medicine, Markham Skerritt Prize for Original Research; MB, ChB 1st Class Hons, 1922; MD 1925). Hon. Consulting Neurologist, King's Coll. Hosp.; Hon. Consulting Physician, National Hosp., Queen Square; formerly Dean, Inst. of Neurology; Neurological Physician, Royal Masonic Hosp.; formerly Neurologist to Royal Hosp. and Home for Incurables, Putney; Consulting Neurologist to Royal Navy, 1939–77. Hunterian Prof., RCS, 1935; Goulstonian Lectr, 1930, Bradshaw Lectr, 1942, Croonian Lectr, 1945, Harveian Orator, 1966, RCP; Long Fox Lectr, Univ. of Bristol, 1935; William Withering Lectr, Univ. of Birmingham, 1946; Tisdall Lectr, Univ. of Manitoba, 1951; Semon Lectr, Univ. of London, 1951; Sherrington Lectr, Univ. of Wisconsin; Orator, Medical Soc. of London, 1955; Hunterian Orator, 1957; Doyne Memorial Lectr, 1961; Wartenberg Lectr, 1961; Victor Horsley Memorial Lectr, 1963; Honyman Gillespie Lectr, 1963; Schorstein Lectr, 1964; Hughlings Jackson Lectr and Medallist, RSM, 1964; Gowers Lectr and Medallist, 1965; Veraguth Gold Medallist, Bern, 1968; Sam T. Orton Award for work on Dyslexia, 1974; Arthur Hall Memorial Lectr, 1969; Rickman Godlee Lectr, 1970; Cavendish Lectr, 1976. Visiting Prof., Univs of: Istanbul, 1949; California, 1950 and 1964; Hawaii, 1966; Vis. Prof., Winston-Salem State Univ., NC, 1983. President: Harveian Soc., 1947; World Fedn of Neurology, 1965–73; Assoc. of British Neurologists, 1962–64; Second Vice-Pres., RCP, 1964; Mem., GMC, 1957–73; Founder-Pres., Migraine Trust. Hon. FACP; Hon. Fellow: Faculty of History and Philosophy of Medicine and Pharmacy; Pan-African Assoc. of Neurological Scis; Hon. Mem., RSM; Hon. Corresp. Member: Académie de Médecine de France; Norwegian Academy of Science and Letters; Royal Academy of Medicine, Barcelona; Neurological Socs of France, Switzerland, Holland, Turkey, Uruguay, US, Canada, Australia, Brazil, Argentine, Germany, Chile, Spain, Roumania, Norway, Czechoslovakia, Greece, Italy, Bulgaria, Hungary, Peru, Poland and Sweden. MD *hc:* Zürich; Madrid; DenM *hc* Aix-Marseille. Master, Worshipful Soc. of Apothecaries, 1956–57. Served European War, 1917–18; Surgeon Captain RNVR, 1939–46. *Publications:* Mirror Writing; Neurology of Old Age; Observations on Pain; Language of Gesture; Shipwreck-survivors; Sir William Gowers; The Parietal Lobes; The Black Hole; Developmental Dyslexia; Aphasiology; The Dyslexic Child; Silent Language; (ed jtly) Music and the Brain, 1976; (jtly) Dyslexia defined, 1978; The Divine Banquet of the Brain, 1979; The Citadel of the Senses, 1986; The Ventricle of Memory, 1990; various articles on nervous diseases. *Address:* Hughlings House, Mill Lane, Nether Stowey, Bridgwater, Somerset TA5 1NL. *Died 15 Oct. 1997.*

CROCKATT, Lt Comdr (Douglas) Allan, OBE 1981 (MBE 1971); RD 1978; Royal Naval Reserve, retired; Vice Lord-Lieutenant of West Yorkshire, 1985–92; *b* 31 Jan. 1923; *s* of late Douglas Crockatt, JP, LLD and Ella Crockatt (*née* Lethem); *m* 1946, Helen Townley Tatton (*d* 1985), *d* of late Capt. T. A. Tatton, MC; one *d*. *Educ:* Bootham School, York; Trinity Hall, Cambridge; Dept of Navigation, Southampton Univ. RNVR, 1942–46, Western Approaches and N Russia; RNVSR, 1946–64; RNR active list, 1964–82. Director: Johnson Group

Cleaners, 1961–84 (Dep. Chm., 1976–84); Johnson Group Inc. (USA) (formerly Apparelmaster Inc.), 1975–84 (Dep. Chm., 1981–84); local Dir, Martins and Barclays Banks W Yorks Bd, 1964–84. Mem., Multiple Shops' Fedn Council, 1972–77. Life Vice-Pres., W Yorks Branch Magistrates' Assoc., 1980 (Hon. Sec., 1958–72; Chm., 1975–77; Pres., 1977–79); Mem. Council, Magistrates' Assoc., 1959–80 (Chm., Training Cttee, 1974–80); Member: Lord Chancellor's Adv. Cttee for training of Magistrates, 1964–79; Lord Chancellor's Magistrates' Courts Rule Cttee, 1979–81. CC, W Riding of Yorks, 1953–58; JP 1956, DL 1971, West (formerly WR) Yorks. Freeman, City of London, 1958; Liveryman, Dyers' Co., 1958. Hon. LLD Leeds, 1990. *Recreations:* cricket, sailing, fishing. *Address:* Paddock House, Sicklinghall, Wetherby, W Yorks LS22 4BJ. *T:* Wetherby (01937) 582844. *Club:* Army and Navy. *Died 15 Aug. 1996.*

CROFT, 2nd Baron *cr* 1940, of Bournemouth, co. Southampton; **Michael Henry Glendower Page Croft;** Bt 1924; *b* 20 Aug. 1916; *s* of 1st Baron Croft, CMG, PC, and Hon. Nancy Beatrice Borwick (*d* 1949), *y d* of 1st Baron Borwick; *S* father, 1947; *m* 1948, Lady Antoinette Fredericka Conyngham (*d* 1959), *o d* of 6th Marquess Conyngham; one *s* one *d. Educ:* Eton; Trinity Hall, Cambridge (BA). Served War of 1939–45, Capt. RASC. Called to the Bar, Inner Temple, 1952. Director: Henry Page & Co. Ltd, 1946–57; Ware Properties Ltd, 1958–65; Hereford and Worcester, Building Preservation Trust Ltd, 1986–. Underwriting Mem., Lloyd's, 1971–. Member Executive Cttee: Contemporary Arts Soc., 1960–68 and 1970–81 (Hon. Sec., 1971–76, Hon. Treasurer, 1976–80, Vice-Chm., 1980–81); British Museum Soc., 1969–76. Hon. Keeper of Contemporary Art, Fitzwilliam Museum, Cambridge, 1984. FRSA. OStJ. *Heir: s* Hon. Bernard William Henry Page Croft [*b* 28 Aug 1949; *m* 1993, Elizabeth Mary Richardson, *o d* of late James Richardson, Co. Tyrone]. *Address:* Croft Castle, near Leominster, Herefordshire HR6 9PW; 19 Queen's Gate Gardens, SW7 5LZ. *Club:* Athenæum. *Died 11 Jan. 1997.*

CROFT, Col (Noel) Andrew (Cotton), DSO 1945; OBE 1970; MA Oxon; Essex Regiment; retired; *b* 30 Nov. 1906; *s* of late Rev. Canon R. W. Croft, MA; *m* 1952, Rosalind (*d* 1996), 2nd *d* of late Comdr A. H. de Kantzow, DSO, RN; three *d. Educ:* Lancing Coll.; Stowe Sch.; Christ Church, Oxford; Sch. of Technology, Manchester. Cotton trade, 1929–32; Mem. British Trans-Greenland Expedition, 1933–34; ADC to Maharajah of Cooch Behar, India, 1934–35; Second-in-Command, Oxford Univ. Arctic Expedition to North-East Land, 1935–36; Ethnological Expedn to Swedish Lapland, 1938; Sec. to Dir of Fitzwilliam Museum, Cambridge, 1937–39; served War of 1939–45, Capt. 1939; WO Mission to Finno-Russian War, 1939–40; Bde Intelligence Officer Independent Companies, Norwegian Campaign, 1940; Combined Ops, 1940–41; Major, 1941; Asst Mil. Attaché, Stockholm, 1941–42; sea or parachute ops in Tunisia, Corsica, Italy, France, and Denmark, 1943–45; Lieut-Col 1945; Asst Dir Scientific Research, War Office, 1945–49; WO Observer on Canadian Arctic "Exercise Musk-Ox", 1945–46, and on NW Frontier Trials, India, 1946–47; attached Canadian Army, 1947–48; GSO1, War Office, 1949–51; Liaison Officer HQ Continental Army, USA, 1952–54; comd The Infantry Junior Leaders Bn, 1954–57; Col 1957; Comdt Army Apprentices Sch., Harrogate, 1957–60; Comdt, Metropolitan Police Cadet Corps, 1960–71. Vice-Pres., Women's Transport Service (FANY), 1987– (Chm., 1972–87). Corresp. Fellow, Arctic Inst. of North America; Mem., Reindeer Council of UK, 1949–89 (Chm., 1962–82). Polar Medal (clasp Arctic, 1935–36), 1942; Back Award, RGS, 1946 and 1947. *Publications:* (with A. R. Glen) Under the Pole Star, 1937; Polar Exploration, 1939, 2nd edn 1947; A Talent for

Adventure (autobiog.), 1991. *Recreations:* mountaineering, ski-ing, sailing, photography. *Address:* River House, Strand-on-the-Green, W4 3PD. *T:* (0181) 994 6359. *Clubs:* Alpine, Special Forces, Geographical.
Died 26 June 1998.

CROLY, Brig. Henry Gray, CBE 1958; JP; *b* 7 June 1910; *s* of late Lt-Col W. Croly, DSO, late RAMC, Ardvarna, Tralee; *m* 1939, Marjorie Rosanne, *er d* of late Major J. S. Knyvett, late Royal Warwickshire Regt, Clifford Manor Road, Guildford; two *s* two *d. Educ:* Sherborne Sch.; RMA Woolwich; BA Open Univ., 1993. 2nd Lieut RA, 1930; served in India: Mohmand Ops, 1935; Waziristan, 1936–37 (despatches); served War of 1939–45, mostly India and Burma; GSO1, British Mil. Mission to France, 1946–47; 2nd-in-Comd 26 Medium Regt RA, 1947–48; jssc 1949; GSO1, WO, 1950–51; Col GS, SHAPE, 1952; OC 26 Field Regt Suez Canal Zone, 1953–55; Dep. Sec., Chiefs of Staff Cttee, 1955–58; UK Nat. Mil. Rep. to SHAPE, 1959–61; retd 1962. Sec., Health Visitor Trng Council and Council for Trng in Social Work, 1963–66; Asst Sec. of Commns, Lord Chancellor's Office, 1966–74; Sec., Wolfenden Cttee on Voluntary Orgns, 1974–78. JP Surrey, 1968. *Recreations:* golf, reading. *Address:* 20 Middle Bourne Lane, Farnham, Surrey GU10 3NH. *T:* (01252) 714851. *Clubs:* Army and Navy, MCC; Hankley Common Golf. *Died 4 June 1998.*

CROMBIE, Alistair Cameron, MA, BSc, PhD; FBA 1990; Fellow, 1969–83, garden master, 1971–81, Trinity College, Oxford (Hon. Fellow, 1994); Lecturer in History of Science, University of Oxford, 1953–83; *b* 4 Nov. 1915; 2nd *s* of William David Crombie and Janet Wilmina (*née* Macdonald); *m* 1943, Nancy Hey (*d* 1993); three *s* one *d* (and one *s* decd). *Educ:* Geelong Grammar Sch.; Trinity Coll., Melbourne Univ.; Jesus Coll., Cambridge. Zoological Lab., Cambridge, 1941–46; Lectr in History and Philosophy of Science, University Coll., London, 1946–53, nominated Reader, resigned; All Soul's Coll., Oxford, 1954–69. Kennedy Prof. in the Renaissance, 1982, Prof. of History of Science and Medicine, 1983–85, Smith Coll., Mass. Visiting Professor: Technische Hochschule, Aachen, 1948; Univ. of Washington, 1953–54; Princeton Univ., 1959–60; Australian Univs (guest of Vice-Chancellors' Cttee), 1963; Tokyo Univ. (guest of Japan Soc. for Promotion of Sci.), 1976; All-India Inst. of Med. Scis, and guest of Indian Nat. Sci. Acad., 1976; Virginia Mil. Inst., 1977; Williams Coll., Mass (Bernhard Vis. Prof.), 1984; Prof. d'Histoire des Sciences, Sorbonne (Univ. of Paris I), 1982–83; Directeur Associé, Ecole des Hautes Etudes, Paris, 1989. Conseil Scientifique, Dépt d'Hist. et Philosophie de la Médecine, Univ. of Paris XII, 1981–85. Mem. Council, Science Museum, London, 1962–66; Mem., British Nat. Cttee for History of Science, 1963–69. Editor: Brit. Jl Philos. Sci., 1949–54; Hist. Sci., 1961; Dir, Oxford Univ. Symp. Hist. Sci., 1961; Pres., Brit. Soc. Hist. Sci., 1964–66; Pres., Internat. Acad. Hist. Sci., 1968–71; Member: Internat. Acad. Hist. Med.; Academia Leopoldina (Pontifical Acad. of Scis); FRHistS. Hon. DLitt Durham, 1979; Dr *hc* Université de Paris X, 1993. Galileo Prize, Domus Galileana, 1969; Alexander von Humboldt Res. Award, 1994. *Publications:* Augustine to Galileo, 1952, 4th edn 1979; Robert Grosseteste and the Origins of Experimental Science, 1953, 3rd edn 1971; Scientific Change, 1963; The Mechanistic Hypothesis and the Scientific Study of Vision, 1967; The Rational Arts of Living, 1987; Science Optics and Music in Medieval and Early Modern Thought, 1990; Styles of Scientific Thinking in the European Tradition, 1994; Science, Art and Nature in Medieval and Modern Thought, 1995; contrib. Annals of Sci., Brit. Jl Hist. Sci., EHR, Isis, Jl Animal Ecol., Physis, Proc. Royal Soc., Rev. de Synthèse, TLS, Dict. Sci. Biogr., Encyc. Brit., New Cambridge Modern Hist., etc. *Recreations:*

literature, travel, landscape gardening. *Address:* Orchardlea, Boars Hill, Oxford OX1 5DF. *T:* Oxford (01865) 735692. *Club:* Brooks's.

Died 9 Feb. 1996.

CROMBIE, Prof. Leslie, FRS 1973; CChem, FRSC; Sir Jesse Boot Professor of Organic Chemistry, University of Nottingham, 1969–88, then Emeritus (Dean of Science, 1980–83); *b* 10 June 1923; *s* of Walter Leslie Crombie and Gladys May Crombie (*née* Clarkson); *m* 1953, Winifred Mary Lovell Wood; two *s* two *d. Educ:* Portsmouth Municipal Coll.; King's Coll., London. PhD, DSc; FKC 1978. Admiralty Chemical Lab., Portsmouth Naval Dockyard, 1941–46. Lectr, Imperial Coll., London, 1950–58; Reader in Organic Chemistry, King's Coll., London, 1958–63 (Fellow, 1978); Prof. of Organic Chemistry, University Coll., Cardiff (Univ. of Wales), 1963–69. Pres., British Association, Section B, 1978; Chm., Phytochemical Soc. of Europe, 1986–88 (Vice-Chm., 1984–86, 1988–90). Member: British Libraries Chemical Inf. Review Panel, 1976–77; UGC Physical Scis Sub-Cttee, 1978–85; Royal Society: Govt Grants Cttee, 1976–77 (Chm., 1978–79); Sect. Cttee 3, 1977–78 (Chm., 1978–80); Chemical Educn Cttee, 1981–82 (Chm., 1983–87); Educn Cttee, 1983–85 (Chm., 1986–91); Travelling Expenses Cttee, 1984–86; Council, 1984–86; Higher Educn Study Gp, 1991–93; Science Research Council: Chem. Cttee, 1970–75; Enzyme Cttee, 1973–75; Chemical Society: Council, 1962–64 and 1972–80; Library Cttee, 1959–63; Primary Jls Cttee, 1964–69; Reports and Reviews Cttee, 1964–69 (Chm., 1969–73); Pub. Services Bd, 1969–77; Perkin Div. Council, 1971–85 (Pres., 1976–79); Presidents' Cttee, 1972–74; Tertiary Pub. Cttee, 1974–76; Exec. Cttee, 1976–79; Div. and Annual Congress Cttee, 1976–79; UKCIS Bd, 1972–77; Royal Inst. of Chemistry: Jt Cttee for HNC and HND quals, 1962–84; Council, 1975–78; Exams and Institns Cttee, 1976–78; Quals and Admissions Cttee, 1976–78; Royal Society of Chemistry: Council, 1980–81; Jls Bd, 1981–85; Quals and Exams Bd, 1983–86; Chm., Perkin Jls Editorial Bd, 1981–85; Pedler Lectr, 1982; Robert Robinson Lectr, 1993; Flintoff Medal, 1984. Lectures, Chemical Society: Tilden, 1970; Simonsen, 1975; Hugo Müller, 1977. Trustee, Uppingham Sch., 1994–98. Hon. Fellow, Portsmouth Polytechnic, 1983. Natural Products Chemistry award, RIC, 1980; Phytochem. Soc. of Europe medal, 1990; Agricl Chemistry award, ACS, 1998. *Publications:* (ed) Recent Advances in the Chemistry of Insect Control, Vol. II, 1990; Royal Soc. report on Beyond GCSE (Chm.); almost 400 original papers in learned chemical jls, especially those of RSC, London. *Recreation:* gardening. *Address:* 153 Hillside Road, Bramcote, Beeston, Nottingham NG9 3BD. *T:* (0115) 925 9412. *Club:* Athenæum. *Died 3 Aug. 1999.*

CROOM-JOHNSON, Rt Hon. Sir David Powell, Kt 1971; DSC 1944; VRD 1953; PC 1984; a Lord Justice of Appeal, 1984–89; *b* 28 Nov. 1914; 3rd *s* of late Hon. Sir Reginald Powell Croom-Johnson, sometime a Judge of the High Court, and Lady (Ruby) Croom-Johnson; *m* 1940, Barbara Douglas (*d* 1994), *y d* of late Erskine Douglas Warren, Toronto; one *d. Educ:* The Hall, Hampstead; Stowe Sch.; Trinity Hall, Cambridge (MA; Hon. Fellow, 1985). RNVR (London Div.), 1936–53; served with Royal Navy, 1939–46. Called to the Bar, Gray's Inn, 1938, Master of the Bench, 1964, Treasurer, 1981; Western Circuit; QC 1958; Recorder of Winchester, 1962–71; Judge of Courts of Appeal, Jersey and Guernsey, 1966–71; Judge of High Court of Justice, Queen's Bench Div., 1971–84. Member: Gen. Council of the Bar, 1958–62; Senate of Inns of Court, 1966–70. Conducted Home Office Inquiry concerning amalg. of Lancs Police Areas, 1967–68; Vice-Chm., Home Office Cttee on Mentally Abnormal Offenders, 1972–75; Chm., Crown Agents Tribunal,

1978–82. Mem., Council, Oakdene Sch., 1956–79; Chm., Knightsbridge Assoc., 1965–71. *Recreations:* books, music. *Address:* 59 Coleherne Court, Old Brompton Road, SW5 0EF. *Club:* Garrick. *Died 21 Nov. 2000.*

CROSBIE, William, RSA 1973; RGI 1977; artist; *b* Hankow, China, 31 Jan. 1915; *s* of Archibald Shearer Crosbie, marine engineer, and Mary Edgar, both Scottish; *m* 1st, 1944, M. G. McPhail (decd); one *d* (and one *d* decd); 2nd, 1975, Margaret Anne Roger. *Educ:* Chinese Tutor; Renfrew primary sch.; Glasgow Academy; Glasgow Sch. of Art, Glasgow Univ. (4 yrs under Forrester Wilson; BA; Hon. Fellow, 1996). Haldane Travelling Schol., 1935, for 3 yr period of study in British Schs in Athens, Rome and Paris (Académie des Beaux-Arts); studied history and theory of techniques, in Acad. des Beaux-Arts and Sorbonne, and finally took a post-grad. qualif. in these (continued to acquire craftsmanship); passed into studio of Fernand Leger, Paris, and remained until war declared; served War of 1939–45: ambulance service, WVS driving pool, and at sea. Exhibited, on average, every two yrs, 1946–; principally one-man exhibns: Glasgow, Edinburgh, London, etc; also in USA, Brussels, Hamburg, etc. *Works in:* Kelvingrove Galls, Glasgow; Scottish provincial galls; Edinburgh City Arts Centre (mural), 1980; Scottish Gall. of Modern Art, 1980; Nat. Portrait Gall. of Scotland, 1994; Sydney State Gall., Australia; Wellington, NZ; Royal collection, UK, etc; also in many private collections. *Recreation:* sailing. *Address:* Rushes House, 10 Winchester Road, Petersfield, Hants GU32 3BY. *Clubs:* Glasgow Art (Glasgow); Royal Northern and Clyde Yacht (Rhu). *Died 15 Jan. 1999.*

CROSS, (Alan) Beverley; playwright; *b* 13 April 1931; *s* of George Cross, theatrical manager, and Eileen Williams, actress; *m* 1st, 1955, Elizabeth Clunies-Ross (marr. diss.); two *d;* 2nd, 1965, Gayden Collins (marr. diss.); one *s;* 3rd, 1975, Maggie Smith (later Dame Maggie Smith, DBE). *Educ:* Nautical Coll., Pangbourne; Balliol Coll., Oxford. Mem. Shakespeare Memorial Theatre Company, 1954–56; then began writing plays. One More River, Duke of York's, 1959; Strip the Willow, Arts, Cambridge, 1960 (Arts Council Drama Award for both, 1960); The Singing Dolphin, Oxford, 1960; The Three Cavaliers, Birmingham Rep., 1960; Belle, or The Ballad of Dr Crippen, Strand, 1961; Boeing-Boeing, Apollo, 1962; Wanted On Voyage, Marlowe, Canterbury, 1962; Half A Sixpence, Cambridge, London, 1963; Jorrocks, New, London, 1966; The Owl on the Battlements, Nottingham, 1971; Catherine Howard, York, 1972; The Great Society, Mermaid, 1974; Hans Andersen, Palladium, 1974; Happy Birthday, Apollo, 1979; Haworth, Birmingham Rep., 1981; The Scarlet Pimpernel, Chichester, Her Majesty's, 1985; Miranda, Chichester Fest., 1987; The Ghostwriter, QE2, 1996; *libretti:* The Mines of Sulphur, Sadler's Wells, 1965; All the King's Men, 1969; Victory, Covent Garden, 1970; The Rising of the Moon, Glyndebourne, 1970; A Capital Transfer, British Council, London, 1981; *screenplays of:* Jason and the Argonauts, 1962; The Long Ships, 1963; Genghis Khan, 1965; Half A Sixpence, 1966; (with Carlo Lizzani) Mussolini: Ultimo Atto, 1973; Sinbad and the Eye of the Tiger, 1977; The Clash of the Titans, 1981; *television plays:* The Nightwalkers, 1960; The Dark Pits of War, 1960; Catherine Howard, 1969; March on, Boys!, 1975; A Bill of Mortality, 1975. *Directed:* Boeing-Boeing, Sydney, 1964; The Platinum Cat, Wyndham's, 1965. *Publications:* Mars in Capricorn, 1955; The Nightwalkers, 1956; Plays For Children, 1960. *Address:* c/o Write on Cue, 29 Whitcomb Street, WC2H 7EP. *T:* (0171) 839 3040. *Died 20 March 1998.*

CROSS, Alexander Galbraith, MA, MD; FRCS; ophthalmic surgeon; lately Dean of the Medical School, St Mary's Hospital; Civilian Consultant in Ophthalmology,

Royal Navy, 1946–76; Consultant Surgeon, Moorfields Eye Hospital, 1947–73; Consultant Ophthalmic Surgeon, St Mary's Hospital, 1946–73; Consultant Ophthalmic Surgeon, Royal National Throat, Nose, and Ear Hospital, 1954–73, Ophthalmic Surgeon, St Dunstan's, 1946–84; Hon. Consultant Ophthalmologist, Royal National Institute for the Blind, 1968–82; *b* 29 March 1908; *er s* of late Walter Galbraith Cross and Mary Stewart Cross, Wimbledon; *m* 1939, Eileen Longman, twin *d* of late Dr H. B. Corry, Liss, Hants; one *d. Educ:* King's Coll. Sch.; Gonville and Caius Coll., Cambridge; St Mary's Hosp., London (University Scholar). Meadows Prize, 1932, Broadbent and Agnes Cope Prizes, 1933, Cheadle Gold Medallist, 1933, St Mary's Hospital. House Phys. and House Surg., St Mary's, 1933–35; House Surg. and Sen. Res. Officer, Moorfields Eye Hosp., 1937–39; Ophthalmic Surgeon: West Middlesex Hosp., 1938–48; Tite Street Children's Hosp., 1939–48; Princess Beatrice Hosp., 1939–47; Royal Masonic Hosp., 1961–71. Wing Comdr, RAFVR, 1941–46 and Adviser in Ophthalmology, South-East Asia Air Forces. Examiner in Fellowship and in Diploma of Ophthalmology for RCS and in Ophthalmology for Univ. of Bristol; Recognised Teacher of Ophthalmology, University of London. Co-opted Mem. Council RCS, 1963–68. Mem. Paddington Group Hosp. Management Cttee, 1952–60. Pres. Ophthalmological Soc. of UK, 1975–77 (Sec. 1949–51; Vice-Pres., 1963–66); Member: RSocMed (Sec., Ophthalmic Section, 1951; Vice-Pres., 1960; Hon. Mem. 1979); BMA (Sec., Ophthalmic Section, 1948; Vice-Pres., 1957). Chm., Ophthalmic Gp Cttee, 1963–75; Mem. Council, Faculty of Ophthalmologists, 1963–72, Vice-Pres. 1964, Pres. 1968–71; Dean, Inst. of Ophthalmology, 1967–75 (Deputy Dean, 1966–67); Mem., Orthoptists Bd, 1970, Vice-Chm. 1971, Chm. 1972–75. Member Board of Governors: St Mary's Hosp., 1951–60; Moorfields Eye Hosp., 1962–65 and 1968–75. *Publications:* 12th edn, May and Worth's Diseases of the Eye; articles in British Jl of Ophthalmology, the Lancet, and other med. jls, dealing with ophthalmology. *Recreations:* gardening, lawn tennis, golf, squash racquets. *Address:* 4A Cottenham Park Road, Wimbledon, SW20 0RZ. *T:* 0181–946 3491. *Died 4 Feb. 1996.*

CROSS, Beverley; *see* Cross, A. B.

CROSS, Prof. Robert Craigie, CBE 1972; FRSE; Regius Professor of Logic, 1953–78, Vice-Principal, 1974–77, University of Aberdeen, *b* 24 April 1911; *s* of Matthew Cross and Margaret Dickson; *m* 1943, Peggy Catherine Elizabeth Vernon; two *d. Educ:* Glasgow Univ. (MA 1st Cl. Hons Classics, 1932); Queen's Coll., Oxford (1st Cl. Hons Classical Mods, 1934; 1st Cl. Lit. Hum., 1936; MA). Served War, 1941–45, Navy and Admiralty. Fellow, and Tutor in Philosophy, Jesus Coll., Oxford, 1938–53, Senior Tutor, 1948–53. Trustee, Scottish Hospital Endowments Research Trust, 1968–80; Mem., University Grants Cttee, 1965–74; Mem., North Eastern Regional Hospital Bd, 1958–65. *Publications:* (with A. D. Woozley) Plato's Republic: a Philosophical Commentary, 1964; contributions to learned jls. *Address:* Inverard, 46/22 Inverleith Gardens, Edinburgh EH3 5QF. *Died 13 Sept. 2000.*

CROSSLAND, Sir Leonard, Kt 1969; farmer since 1974; Chairman: Eaton Ltd (UK), 1972–88; Ford Motor Co. Ltd, 1968–72; Energy Research and Development Ltd (formerly Sedgeminster Technical Developments Ltd), since 1974; *b* 2 March 1914; *s* of Joseph and Frances Crossland; *m* 1st, 1941, Rhona Marjorie Griffin (marr. diss. 1962); two *d*; 2nd, 1963, Joan Brewer (*d* 1996); 3rd, 1997, Mrs Mary Head. *Educ:* Penistone Grammar Sch. Royal Army Service Corps, 1939–45 (despatches twice). Ford Motor Co. Ltd: Purchase Dept, 1937–39 and 1945–54; Chief Buyer, Tractor and Implement Dept,

1954–57; Chief Buyer, Car and Truck Dept, 1957–59; Asst Purchase Manager, 1959–60; Purchase Manager, 1960–62; Exec. Dir, Supply and Services, 1962–66; Dir, Manufacturing Staff and Services, 1966; Asst Man. Dir, 1966–67; Man. Dir, 1967; Dep. Chm., 1967, Chm., Autolite Motor Products Ltd; Director: Henry Ford & Son Ltd, Cork; Eaton Corp. (US), 1974–81. *Recreations:* shooting, fishing, golf. *Address:* Abbotts Hall, Great Wigborough, Colchester, Essex CO5 7RZ. *T:* (01206) 735456. *Clubs:* City Livery, Royal Automobile, British Racing Drivers', American. *Died 5 Aug. 1999.*

CROSSLEY, Harry; DL; Chief Executive, Derbyshire County Council, 1974–79, retired; *b* 2 Sept. 1918; *s* of late Percy Crossley and Nellie McMinnies Crossley, Burnley, Lancs; *m* 1949, Pamela, *e d* of late Ald. E. A. C. Woodcock, Kettering, Northants; two *s. Educ:* Burnley Grammar Sch. Solicitor. LAM RTPI. War service, RA, attached Indian Army (Major), 1939–46. Private practice and local govt service as solicitor; Derbyshire County Council: Dep. Clerk of Peace and of CC, 1960–69; Clerk of Peace and of CC, 1969–74; Clerk to Derbyshire Lieutenancy, 1969–79; Sec., Lord Chancellor's Adv. Cttee for Derbyshire, 1969–79. Clerk, Peak Park Planning Bd, 1969–74. DL Derbyshire, 1978. *Publications:* articles for legal and local govt jls. *Recreations:* golf, tennis, gardening. *Address:* Alpine, Bracken Lane, Holloway, Matlock DE4 5AS. *T:* (01629) 534382.
Died 17 Oct. 1997.

CROSSLEY, Sir Nicholas John, 4th Bt *cr* 1909, of Glenfield, Dunham Massey, Co. Chester; *b* 10 Dec. 1962; *s* of Sir Christopher John Crossley, 3rd Bt and of Carolyne Louise, *d* of late L. Grey Sykes; *S* father, 1989. *Heir: b* Julian Charles Crossley, *b* 11 Dec. 1964. *Address:* 331 Penn Street #1, El Segundo, CA 90245, USA.
Died 13 April 2000.

CROUCH, Sir David (Lance), Kt 1987, DL; Chairman, David Crouch & Co. Ltd, 1964–89; *b* 23 June 1919; *s* of late Stanley Crouch and Rosalind Kate Crouch (*née* Croom); *m* 1947, Margaret Maplesden, *d* of Major Sydney Maplesden Noakes, DSO and Norah Parkyns Maplesden Noakes (*née* Buckland), Shorne, Kent; one *s* one *d. Educ:* University Coll. Sch. Served in City of London Yeomanry (TA), 1938–39; served War of 1939–45, Royal Artillery: Major 1943; attached RAF Staff (GSO2), 1944–45. Joined British Nylon Spinners Ltd, 1946; ICI Ltd, 1950; Dir of Publicity, Internat. Wool Secretariat, 1962–64; formed own co., David Crouch & Co. Ltd, as international marketing and public relations consultants; Director: Pfizer Ltd, 1969–88; Burson Marsteller Ltd, 1972–83; Kingsway Public Relations (Hldgs) Ltd, 1985–89; Westminster Communications Gp Ltd, 1989–97. Contested (C) West Leeds, 1959. MP (C) Canterbury, 1966–87. Chairman: British-Egyptian Parly Gp, 1972–87; British-Algerian Gp, 1980–87 (represented HM Govt at 25th anniversary celebrations of estabt of State of Algeria, 1979); All-Party Gp for the Chemical Industry, 1970–85; All-Party Gp for Energy Studies, 1980–85; British Gp, Inter-Parly Union, 1985–87; Vice-Chm., Cons. Middle East Council, 1980–87; Member: Select Cttee for Nationalized Industries, 1966–74; Public Accounts Cttee, 1974–79; Speaker's Panel, 1982–87; Select Cttee for Social Services, 1983–84; Adv. Cttee on the Arts to Mr Speaker, 1970–87 (Chm., 1983–87). Life Pres., Theatres Trust, 1992 (Trustee, 1977–92; Dep. Chm., 1979–87; Chm., 1987–92); Chm., Channel Theatre Co., 1984–87. Member: SE Thames RHA, 1970–85; MRC, 1984–87; Soc. of Chemical Industry; Council, Univ. of Kent, 1971–95; Council, RSA, 1974–78 (Fellow, 1971). Pres., Kent Soc., 1987–94; Gov., Kent Inst. of Art and Design, 1988–93; Chm., Kent Wishing Well Appeal, 1988–89. DL Kent, 1992. Hon. DCL Kent, 1987. *Publication:* A Canterbury Tale, 1987.

Recreations: painting, golf. *Address:* The Oast House, Fisher Street, Badlesmere, Faversham, Kent ME13 0LB. *Clubs:* Athenæum; MCC; Kent and Canterbury (Canterbury); Royal St George's Golf.

Died 18 Feb. 1998.

CROWDER, F(rederick) Petre; QC 1964; a Recorder (formerly Recorder of Colchester), 1967–91; barrister; *b* 18 July 1919; *s* of late Sir John Ellenborough Crowder and Florence, *d* of Alfred R. Petre; *m* 1948, Hon. Patricia Stourton, *d* of 25th Baron Mowbray, MC (also 26th Baron Segrave and 22nd Baron Stourton); two *s. Educ:* Eton; Christ Church, Oxford. Served War of 1939–45: joined Coldstream Guards, 1939, and served in North Africa, Italy, Burma; attained rank of Major. Called to the Bar, Inner Temple, 1948 (Bencher, 1971; Reader, 1990; Treasurer, 1991); South Eastern Circuit; North London Sessions; Recorder of Gravesend, 1960–67; Herts Quarter Sessions: Dep. Chm., 1959–63; Chm., 1963–71. Chancellor, Primrose League, 1996–. Contested (C) North Tottenham, by-elec. 1945; MP (C) Ruislip-Northwood, 1950–74, Hillingdon, Ruislip-Northwood, 1974–79; PPS to Solicitor-Gen., 1952–54; PPS to Attorney General, 1954–62. *Recreation:* field sports. *Address:* 2 Harcourt Buildings, Temple, EC4Y 9DB. *T:* (020) 7353 2112; 8 Quarrendon Street, SW6 3SU. *T:* (020) 7731 6342. *Clubs:* Carlton, Pratt's, Turf. *Died 16 Feb. 1999.*

CROWE, Dame Sylvia, DBE 1973 (CBE 1967); landscape architect in private practice since 1945; *b* 1901; *d* of Eyre Crowe; unmarried. *Educ:* Berkhamsted; Swanley Hort. Coll. Designed gardens, 1927–39. Served FANY and ATS, 1939–45. Private practice as landscape architect included: work as consultant to: Harlow and Basildon New Town Corporations; Wimbleball and Rutland Water reservoirs; Central Electricity Generating Board, for Trawsfynydd and Wylfa Nuclear Power Stations; Forestry Commission; reclamation of land after 1952 floods and design of public gardens at Mablethorpe and Sutton on Sea; gardens for Oxford Univ., various Colls and Commonwealth Inst., London; design of Commonwealth Gardens, Canberra, Australia. Sec., Internat. Federation Landscape Architecture, 1948–59, Vice-Pres., 1964; Pres., Inst. Landscape Architects, 1957–59; Corresp. Mem., Amer. Soc. of Landscape Architects, 1960; Hon. Fellow, Aust. Inst. of Landscape Architects, 1978. Chm., Tree Council, 1974–76. Hon. FRIBA 1969; Hon. FRTPI 1970. Hon. DLitt: Newcastle, 1975; Heriot-Watt, 1976; Hon. LLD Sussex, 1978. VMH 1990. *Publications:* Tomorrow's Landscape, 1956; Garden Design, 1958, 3rd edn 1994; The Landscape of Power, 1958; Landscape of Roads, 1960; Forestry in the Landscape, 1966; The Landscapes of Forests and Woodlands, 1979; Patterns of Landscape, 1986. *Recreations:* walking, gardening. *Address:* 59 Ladbroke Grove, W11 3AT. *T:* (0171) 727 7794.

Died 30 June 1997.

CROWLEY, Rear-Adm. George Clement, CB 1968; DSC 1942, and Bar 1944; Official Fellow and Domestic Bursar of Corpus Christi College, Oxford University, 1969–75; *b* 9 June 1916; *s* of Charles Edmund Lucas Crowley and Beatrice Cicely Crowley; *m* 1948, Una Margaret Jelf (*d* 1991); two *s. Educ:* Pangbourne Coll. Cadet, HMS Frobisher, 1933; served in China and New Zealand, 1934–39; served War of 1939–45, destroyers; comdg HMS Walpole, 1943–45; comdg HMS Tenacious, 1945–46 (despatches); RN Staff Course, 1947; Staff appts, 1948–53; Exec. Off., HMS Newfoundland, 1953–55; Drafting Comdr, Chatham, 1955–57; Asst Dir Plans, 1957–59; Capt. (D) 7th Destroyer Sqdn, 1959–61; CO New Entry, Trng Estabt HMS Raleigh, 1961–63; Capt. of Fleet to Flag Off. C-in-C Far East Fleet, 1963–64; Staff of Jt Exercise Unison, 1964–65; Staff of Defence Operational Analysis Estabt, W Byfleet, 1965–66; Director-General,

Naval Personal Services, 1966–68. Capt. 1957; Rear-Adm. 1966. *Recreations:* fishing, tennis, gardening.

Died 14 Dec. 1999.

CROWLEY, Niall, Hon. CBE 1993; FCA; Deputy Chairman, Alliance & Leicester Building Society, 1991–97 (Director, 1990–97); Chairman, Allied Irish Banks Ltd Group, 1977–89; *b* 18 Sept. 1926; *s* of Vincent Crowley and Eileen (*née* Gunning); *m* 1953, Una Hegarty; five *s* one *d. Educ:* Xavier Sch.; Castleknock Coll. FCA 1955. Entered father's accounting firm, Stokes Kennedy Crowley & Co., as articled clerk, 1944: qualified, 1949; Partner, 1950, subseq. Managing Partner; Consultant to the firm, which also represented KPMG (formerly Peat Marwick Mitchell & Co.) in Ireland, 1977–84. Chm., Cahill May Roberts Gp, 1989–95; Director: Irish Life Assurance Co. Ltd, 1964–84 (Chm., 1974–83); Girobank, 1990–97; J. Rothschild International Assurance, 1992–. President: Inst. of Chartered Accountants in Ireland, 1971–72; Dublin Chamber of Commerce, 1983–84; Irish Bankers Fedn, 1985–87; Inst. of Bankers, 1987–88. Chairman: Financial Services Industry Assoc., 1984–88; British-Irish Assoc., 1994–97. Mem. Exec. Bd, Anglo-Irish Encounter Gp, 1983–. Member, Company of Goldsmiths of Dublin, 1973–. Hon. LLD NUI, 1982; Hon. DPhil Pontifical Univ., Maynooth, 1988. *Recreations:* bridge, golf. *Address:* (office) 46 Upper Mount Street, Dublin 2. *T:* (1) 6762474; (home) 18 Whitebeam Road, Clonskeagh, Dublin 14, Ireland. *T:* (1) 2694672. *Clubs:* Stephens Green; Portmarnock Golf; Milltown Golf; Fitzwilliam Lawn Tennis (Dublin).

Died 9 June 1998.

CROWLEY-MILLING, Air Marshal Sir Denis, KCB 1973; CBE 1963; DSO 1943; DFC 1941, Bar 1942; Registrar and Secretary, Order of the Bath, 1985–90 (Gentleman Usher of the Scarlet Rod, 1979–85); *b* 22 March 1919; *s* of T. W. and G. M. Crowley-Milling (*née* Chinnery); *m* 1943, Lorna Jean Jeboult (*née* Stuttard); two *d* (one *s* decd). *Educ:* Malvern Coll., Worcs. Rolls Royce apprentice and RAF Volunteer Reserve, 1937–39; Fighters and Fighter Bombers, Nos 615, 242, 610 and 181 Sqdns, 1939–44; Air Ministry Operational Requirements, 1945–47; OC No 6 Sqdn, Middle East, 1947–50; Personal Staff Officer C-in-C Fighter Comd, 1950–52; Wing Comdr Flying, RAF Odiham, 1952–54; Directing Staff, RAF Staff Coll., Bracknell, 1954–57; Flying Coll., RAF Manby, 1957–58; Plans Staff Fighter Comd, 1958–59; Group Capt. Operations Central Fighter Establishment, 1959–62; Station Comdr, RAF Leconfield, 1962–64; AOC RAF Hong Kong, 1964–66; Dir Operational Requirements, MoD (Air), 1966–67; Comdr, RAF Staff and Principal Air Attaché, Washington, 1967–70; AOC No 38 Gp, RAF Odiham, 1970–72; AOC 46 Gp RAF Upavon, 1973; UK Rep., Perm. Mil. Deputies Gp, Cento, 1974–75. Controller, RAF Benevolent Fund, 1975–81, Mem. Council, 1981–; Mem. Council, Malvern Coll., 1972–90. Pres., Malverian Soc., 1993–. Chm., Douglas Bader Foundn, 1988–. Master, GAPAN, 1992–93. *Recreations:* golf, shooting. *Address:* c/o Barclays Bank, 46 Park Lane, W1A 4EE. *Club:* Royal Air Force.

Died 1 Dec. 1996.

CROXTON-SMITH, Claude; Chartered Accountant in public practice, Bristol, 1946–83, retired; President, Institute of Chartered Accountants in England and Wales, 1970–71; *b* 24 Aug. 1901; *m* 1928, Joan Norah Bloss Watling (*d* 1989); two *d. Educ:* Dulwich Coll.; Gonville and Caius Coll., Cambridge. The Sales Staff, Anglo American Oil Co. Ltd, 1924–31; Articled Clerk, Inst. of Chartered Accountants in England and Wales, 1932–36; Chartered Accountant, 1936–39. Served War of 1939–45, RAOC (Major). *Recreations:* walking, reading. *Address:*

New Cote Rest Home, Cote House Lane, Westbury-on-Trym, Bristol BS9 3UW. *T:* (0117) 962 8341.
Died 6 Dec. 1996.

CRUDDAS, Rear-Adm. Thomas Rennison, CB 1974; CEng, FIMechE; *b* 6 Feb. 1921; *s* of late Thomas Hepple Wheatley Cruddas, MBE, and Lily (*née* Rennison); *m* 1943, Angela Elizabeth Baisley; one *s* one *d. Educ:* Queen Elizabeth Grammar Sch., Darlington; RN Engineering College, Keyham. Joined RN, 1938; RNEC, 1939–42; served War, 1939–45: in Mediterranean and E Indies, in HM Ships Unicorn and Valiant; HMS Cardigan Bay, 1948–50; specialised aeronautical engrg, 1950; RNAY Donibristle, 1951–53; Comdr, 1953; HMS Ark Royal, 1953–55; RNAY Fleetlands, 1956–58; Admiralty, 1958–61; Staff of Flag Officer Aircraft Carriers, 1961–63; Captain, 1963; Asst Dir Ship Prodn, 1964–66; service with USN, Washington, DC, as Programme Manager UK Phantom Aircraft, 1967–69; Comd Engr Officer, Staff FONAC, 1970–72; Rear-Adm. Engineering, Naval Air Comd, 1972; Dep. Controller Aircraft B, MoD (PE), 1973–76, retired. Dir, Pressure Vessels Quality Assurance Bd, 1977–86. *Recreation:* country living. *Address:* Beeches Close, Bishop's Waltham, Hants SO32 1FZ. *T:* (01489) 892335. *Died 22 Nov. 2000.*

CRUMP, (William) Maurice (Esplen), CBE 1959; *b* 13 Jan. 1908; *s* of William Hamilton Crump and Jean Morris Alan Crump (*née* Esplen); *m* 1946, Mary Arden (*d* 1995), *d* of Austin Stead, Montreal, PQ, Canada. *Educ:* Harrow; Oxford. Called to Bar, Inner Temple, 1931; practised Western Circuit. RAF Reserve, 1929–35; recommissioned RAF Volunteer Reserve, 1940; served War of 1939–45, as pilot, 1940–45; Capt. in Command on North Atlantic Return Ferry, 1944–45. In Dept of Dir of Public Prosecutions, 1945; Asst Dir, 1951–58, Deputy Dir, 1958–66. *Recreation:* flying, travelling. *Address:* No 2, 46 Elm Park Road, SW3 6AX. *T:* 0171–351 2126.
Died 2 July 1996.

CUBBON, Maj.-Gen. John Hamilton, CB 1962; CBE 1958 (OBE 1940); DL; *b* 15 March 1911; *s* of Joseph Cubbon; *m* 1951, Amelia Margaret Yates; two *s* one *d. Educ:* St Bees Sch.; RMC Sandhurst. 2nd Lieut Cheshire Regt, 1931; commanded: 1st Bn The Parachute Regt, 1946–49; 1st Bn The Cheshire Regt, 1951–54; 18th Infantry Bde, Malaya, 1956–57; Maj.-Gen. 1960; GOC SW Dist, 1960–63; GOC Land Forces, Middle East Command, 1963–65. DL Devon, 1969. *Recreation:* sailing. *Address:* Highfield, Harpford, Sidmouth, Devon EX10 0NJ. *Died 5 Jan. 1997.*

CUDLIPP, Baron *cr* 1974 (Life Peer), of Aldingbourne, W Sussex; **Hugh Kinsman Cudlipp,** Kt 1973; OBE 1945; Chairman: International Publishing Corporation Ltd, 1968–73 (Deputy Chairman, 1964–68); International Publishing Corporation Newspaper Division, 1970–73; Deputy Chairman (editorial), Reed International Board, 1970–73; Director, Associated Television Ltd, 1956–73; *b* 28 Aug. 1913; *s* of William Cudlipp, Cardiff; *m* 1st, 1938, Edith Parnell; 2nd, 1945, Eileen Ascroft (*d* 1962), 3rd, 1963, Jodi, *d* of late John L. Hyland, Palm Beach, Fla, and Mrs D. W. Jones, Southport. *Educ:* Howard Gardens Sch., Cardiff. Provincial newspapers in Cardiff and Manchester, 1927–32; Features Ed., Sunday Chronicle, London, 1932–35; Features Ed., Daily Mirror, 1935–37; Ed., Sunday Pictorial, 1937–40; Military Service, 1940–46: CO, British Army Newspaper Unit, CMF, 1943–46; Ed., Sunday Pictorial, 1946–49; Managing Ed., Sunday Express, 1950–52; Editorial Dir, Daily Mirror and Sunday Pictorial, 1952–63; Joint Managing Dir, Daily Mirror and Sunday Pictorial, 1959–63; Chm., Odhams Press Ltd, 1961–63; Chm., Daily Mirror Newspapers Ltd, 1963–68. Mem., Royal Commn on Standards of Conduct in Public Life, 1974–76. Exec.

Founder Chm., Chichester Festivities, 1975–80; Mem. Bd, Productions Co., Chichester Fest. Th., 1980–87; Vice-Pres., Chichester Fest. Th. Trust, 1987–96. *Publications:* Publish and be Damned, 1955; At Your Peril, 1962; Walking on the Water, 1976; The Prerogative of the Harlot, 1980. *Recreation:* music. *Address:* 14 Tollhouse Close, Avenue de Chartres, Chichester, West Sussex PO19 1SF. *Clubs:* Garrick; Chichester City.
Died 17 May 1998.

CULLEN OF ASHBOURNE, 2nd Baron *cr* 1920; **Charles Borlase Marsham Cokayne,** MBE 1945; a Lord in Waiting (Government Whip), 1979–82; Major, Royal Signals; *b* 6 Oct. 1912; *e s* of 1st Baron Cullen of Ashbourne and Grace Margaret (*d* 1971), *d* of Rev. Hon. John Marsham; *S* father, 1932; *m* 1st, 1942, Valerie Catherine Mary (marr. diss. 1947), *o d* of late W. H. Collbran; one *d*; 2nd, 1948, Patricia Mary (*d* 1996), *er d* of late Col S. Clulow-Gray and late Mrs Clulow-Gray, formerly of Clare Priory, Suffolk; 3rd, 1998, Mrs Filiz Zeynep Sargent, *yr d* of late Lt-Gen. Ali Merey, Kalam, Istanbul. *Educ:* Eton. Served War of 1939–45 (MBE). Amateur Tennis Champion, 1947, 1952. One of HM Lieutenants, City of London, 1969–. Chm., Osteopathic Educnl Foundn, 1969–94; President: Fedn of Ophthalmic & Dispensing Opticians (formerly Fedn of Optical Corporate Bodies), 1983–96; Gen. Council and Register of Osteopaths, 1987–89. Dep. Chm. of Cttees, H of L, 1982–91. *Heir: b* Hon. Edmund Willoughby Marsham Cokayne [*b* 18 May 1916; *m* 1943, Janet Manson, *d* of late William Douglas Watson and Mrs Louis Lauritson, Calgary]. *Address:* 75 Cadogan Gardens, SW3 2RB. *T:* (020) 7589 1981. *Club:* MCC.
Died 17 Dec. 2000.

CUMMING-BRUCE, Rt Hon. Sir (James) Roualeyn Hovell-Thurlow-, Kt 1964; PC 1977; a Lord Justice of Appeal, 1977–85; *b* 9 March 1912; *s* of 6th Baron Thurlow and Grace Catherine, *d* of Rev. Henry Trotter; *m* 1935, Lady (Anne) Sarah (Alethea Marjorie Saville) (*d* 1991), *d* of 6th Earl of Mexborough; two *s* one *d. Educ:* Shrewsbury; Magdalene Coll., Cambridge (MA; Hon. Fellow, 1977). Barrister, Middle Temple, 1937 (Harmsworth Scholar); Master of the Bench, 1959; Treasurer, 1975. Served War of 1939–45 (Lt-Col RA). Chancellor of Diocese of Ripon, 1954–57; Recorder of Doncaster, 1957–58; Recorder of York, 1958–61; Junior Counsel to the Treasury (Common Law), 1959–64; Judge of the High Court, Family Div. (formerly Probate, Divorce and Admiralty Div.), 1964–77; Judge of the Restrictive Practices Court, 1968; Presiding Judge, North Eastern Circuit, 1971–74. *Address:* Selaby Hall, Gainford, Darlington DL2 3HF. *Club:* United Oxford & Cambridge University. *Died 12 June 2000.*

CUNEO, Terence Tenison, CVO 1994; OBE 1987; portrait and figure painter, ceremonial, military and engineering subjects; *b* 1 Nov. 1907; *s* of Cyrus Cuneo and Nell Marion Tenison; *m* 1934, Catherine Mayfield Monro (*d* 1979), *yr d* of Major E. G. Monro, CBE; one *d. Educ:* Sutton Valence Sch.; Chelsea and Slade. Served War of 1939–45: RE, and as War Artist; special propaganda paintings for Min. of Information, Political Intelligence Dept of FO, and War Artists Advisory Cttee; representative of Illustrated London News, France, 1940. Royal Glasgow Inst. of Fine Arts; Pres. of Industrial Painters Group; Exhibitor, RA, RP, ROI, Paris Salon (Hon. Mention, 1957). Painted extensively in North Africa, South Africa, Rhodesia, Canada, USA, Ethiopia, Far East and Antarctica; one-man exhibition, Underground Activities in Occupied Europe, 1941; one-man exhibitions: RWS Galleries, London, 1954 and 1958; Sladmore Gall., 1971, 1972, 1974; Mall Galls, 1988. Best known works include: Meml Paintings of El Alamein and The Royal Engineers, King George VI at The Royal Artillery Mess, Woolwich, King

George VI and Queen Elizabeth at The Middle Temple Banquet, 1950; Meml Painting of The Rifle Brigade, 1951; Visit to Lloyd's of Queen Elizabeth II with the Duke of Edinburgh to lay Foundation Stone of Lloyd's New Building, 1952; Queen's Coronation Luncheon, Guildhall, The Duke of Edinburgh at Cambridge, 1953; Portraits of Viscount Allendale, KG, as Canopy Bearer to Her Majesty, 1954; Coronation of Queen Elizabeth II in Westminster Abbey (presented to the Queen by HM's Lieuts of Counties), 1955; Queen's State Visit to Denmark, Engineering Mural in Science Museum, 1957; Queen Elizabeth II at RCOG, 1960; Queen Elizabeth II at Guildhall Banquet after Indian Tour, 1961; Equestrian Portrait of HM the Queen as Col-in-Chief, Grenadier Guards, 1963; Garter Ceremony, 1964; Commonwealth Prime Ministers' Banquet, Guildhall, 1969; first official portraits of Rt Hon. Edward Heath, 1971, of Field Marshal Viscount Montgomery of Alamein, 1972; HM the Queen as Patron of Kennel Club, 1975; King Hussein of Jordan, 1980; Col H. Jones, VC, 1984; 40th Anniversary of D-Day, 1984. Set of stamps commemorating: the 150th anniv. of GWR; the Channel Tunnel, 1994. *Publications:* The Mouse and his Master (autobiog.), 1977; The Railway Painting of Terence Cuneo, 1984; articles in The Studio, The Artist; *relevant publication:* Terence Cuneo, Railway Painter of the Century, by Narisa Chakra, 1990. *Recreations:* writing, sketching, travel, riding. *T:* 0181–398 1986. *Died 3 Jan. 1996.*

CUNINGHAME, Sir William Henry F.; *see* Fairlie-Cuninghame.

CUNNINGHAM, Sir Charles (Craik), GCB 1974 (KCB 1961; CB 1946); KBE 1952; CVO 1941; *b* Dundee, 7 May 1906; *s* of late Richard Yule Cunningham, Abergeldie, Kirriemuir, and Isabella Craik; *m* 1934, Edith Louisa Webster (*d* 1990); two *d. Educ:* Harris Acad., Dundee; University of St Andrews. Entered Scottish Office, 1929; Private Sec. to Parliamentary Under Sec. of State for Scotland, 1933–34; Private Sec. to Sec. of State for Scotland, 1935–39; Asst Sec., Scottish Home Dept, 1939–41; Principal Asst Sec., 1941–42; Dep. Sec., 1942–47; Sec., 1948–57; Permanent Under-Sec. of State, Home Office, 1957–66; Dep. Chm., UKAEA, 1966–71; Chm., Radiochemical Centre Ltd, 1971–74; Dir, Securicor Ltd, 1971–81. Chm., Uganda Resettlement Bd, 1972–73. Mem., Nat. Radiological Protection Bd, 1971–74. Hon. LLD St Andrews, 1960. *Address:* 25 Regent Terrace, Edinburgh EH7 5BS. *T:* (0131) 556 9614. *Clubs:* Reform; New (Edinburgh). *Died 7 July 1998.*

CUNNINGHAM, Sir Josias, Kt 2000; DL; Chairman, Josias Cunningham & Co. Ltd, later Cunningham Coates Ltd, 1989–98; *b* 20 Jan. 1934; *s* of Josias Cunningham and Isobel Cunningham (*née* Mackie); *m* 1962, Grace Margaret Anne Webb; two *s* two *d. Educ:* Mourne Grange, Co. Down; Fettes Coll., Edinburgh; Clare Coll., Cambridge (BA 1956, MA 1960; DipAgr 1957). Joined Josias Cunningham & Co. (Stockbrokers), 1957, Partner, 1960, Sen. Partner, 1969. Chairman: Belfast Stock Exchange, 1972–73; Belfast Unit, Stock Exchange, 1973–76. Pres., Ulster Unionist Council, 1991–. Liveryman, Drapers' Co., 1969–. DL, 1988, High Sheriff, 1977, Co. Antrim. *Recreations:* natural history, shooting, farming. *Address:* Silversprings, Templepatrick, Co. Antrim. *Club:* Ulster Reform (Belfast). *Died 9 Aug. 2000.*

CUNNINGHAM, Robert Kerr, CMG 1983; PhD; FIBiol; FRSC; Chief Natural Resources Adviser, Overseas Development Administration, 1976–83, and Head of Natural Resources Department, 1980–83, retired; *b* 7 June 1923; *s* of John Simpson Cunningham and Agnes Stewart Cunningham; *m* 1947, Jean Sinclair (*née* Brown); one *s* one *d. Educ:* Bathgate Acad., Scotland; Edinburgh Univ. (BSc); London Univ. (PhD). FRSC (FRIC 1964). Served

War, RAF, 1942–46. Science Teacher, W Lothian County Educn Cttee, 1947–50; Science Lectr and Chemist, Govt of Bahamas, 1950–55; Colonial Res. Fellowship, Rothamsted Experimental Stn, 1955–56; Res. Off., W African Cocoa Res. Inst., Gold Coast and Ghana, 1956–60; Principal Scientific Off., Rothamsted Experimtl Stn, 1960–64; Prof. of Chemistry and Soil Science, Univ. of WI, Trinidad, 1964–67; Adviser on Res. and Nat. Resources, Min. of Overseas Develt, 1967–76. *Publications:* many scientific papers dealing mainly with soil chem. and plant nutrition in jls; several reports on organisation of R&D in developing countries; (co-author) reports on Brit. and internat. aid in natural resources field. *Recreations:* walking, reading, golf. *Address:* 19 Coleridge Court, Milton Road, Harpenden, Herts AL5 5LD. *T:* (01582) 460203. *Club:* Royal Air Force.

Died 22 June 2000.

CURLE, Sir John (Noel Ormiston), KCVO 1975 (CVO 1956); CMG 1966; HM Diplomatic Service, retired; *b* 12 Dec. 1915; *s* of Major W. S. N. Curle, MC, Melrose, Scotland; *m* 1st, 1940, Diana Deane (marr. diss. 1948); one *s* one *d*; 2nd, 1948, Pauline, *widow* of Capt. David Roberts; two step *d* (one step *s* decd). *Educ:* Marlborough; New Coll., Oxford. 1st Class Hons; MA; Laming Travelling Fellow of Queen's Coll. HM Diplomatic Service, 1939; Irish Guards, 1939; War Cabinet Secretariat, 1941–44; served in Lisbon, Ottawa, Brussels, Stockholm (Counsellor), Athens (Counsellor); Boston (Consul-Gen., 1962–66); Ambassador to: Liberia, 1967–70 and Guinea, 1968–70; the Philippines, 1970–72; Vice Marshal of Diplomatic Corps, 1972–75; retired 1975; Dir of Protocol, Hong Kong, 1976–85; Advr for coronation of the King of Swaziland, 1986. Liveryman, Masons' Company. *Recreation:* skiing (represented Oxford *v* Cambridge, and British Univs *v* Swiss Univs). *Address:* Appletree House, near Aston-le-Walls, Daventry, Northants NN11 6UG. *T:* (01295) 660211. *Clubs:* Cavalry and Guards, Beefsteak; Hong Kong. *Died 30 Sept. 1997.*

CURRAN, Sir Samuel (Crowe), Kt 1970; FRS 1953; FRSE 1947; FEng 1983; Principal and Vice-Chancellor, University of Strathclyde, 1964–80, Fellow, since 1990; *b* 23 May 1912; *s* of John Curran, Kinghorn, Fife, and Sarah Owen Crowe, Ballymena, Ulster; *m* 1940, Joan Elizabeth, *yr d* of Charles William Strothers and Margaret Beatrice (*née* Millington); three *s* one *d. Educ:* Glasgow Univ. (MA, BSc; PhD 1937; DSc 1950); St John's Coll., Cambridge (PhD Cantab, 1941; Hon. Fellow, 1971). Cavendish Laboratory, 1937–39; RAE, 1939–40; Min. of Aircraft Production and Min. of Supply, 1940–44; Manhattan Project (Min. of Supply), Univ. of California, 1944–45 (invention of scintillation counter, 1944); Natural Philosophy, Glasgow Univ., 1945–55 (invention of proportional counter, 1948); UK Atomic Energy Authority, 1955–58; Chief Scientist, AWRE, Aldermaston, Berks, 1958–59; Principal, Royal Coll. of Science and Technology, Glasgow, 1959–64. Vis. Prof. in Energy Studies, Univ. of Glasgow, 1980–88. Pres., Scottish Soc. for the Mentally Handicapped, 1954–. Member: Council for Scientific and Industrial Research, 1962–65; Science Research Council, 1965–68; Adv. Council on Technology, 1965–70; Chairman: Adv. Cttee on Med. Research, 1962–75; Adv. Bd on Relations with Univs, 1966–70; Electricity Supply Res. Council, 1978–80 (Dep. Chm., 1980–82); Dep. Chm., Electricity Council, 1977–79; Chief Scientific Adviser to the Sec. of State for Scotland, 1967–77; Member: Oil Develt Council for Scotland, 1973–78; Adv. Cttee on Safety of Nuclear Installations, 1977–80; Radioactive Waste Management Adv. Cttee, 1978–81; Adv. Council of A Power for Good (APG), 1978–; UK Nat. Commn for Unesco, and Educn Adv. Cttee, 1978–; Standing Commn on Scottish Economy, 1987–. Director: Scottish Television, 1964–82;

Hall Thermotank Ltd, 1969–76; Cetec Systems Ltd, 1965–77; Internat. Res. & Develt Co. Ltd, 1970–78; Gen. Steels Div., BSC, 1970–73; Nuclear Structures (Protection) Ltd, 1981–. Hon. Pres., Scottish Polish Cultural Assoc., 1972–; President: St Andrews' Soc., Glasgow, 1982–88; Inst. of Envmtl Safety, 1992. Hon. FRCPS 1964; Hon. FIEE 1989. Hon. LLD: Glasgow, 1968; Aberdeen, 1971; Hon. ScD Lodz, 1973; Hon. DSc Strathclyde, 1980; Hon. DEng Nova Scotia, 1982. Freeman: Motherwell and Wishaw, 1966; City of Glasgow, 1980. DL Glasgow, 1969. St Mungo Prize, 1976. Comdr, St Olav (Norway), 1966; Comdr, Order Polish People's Republic, 1976. *Publications:* (with J. D. Craggs) Counting Tubes, 1949; Luminescence and the Scintillation Counter, 1953; Alpha, Beta and Gamma Ray Spectroscopy, 1964; (jt) Energy Resources and the Environment, 1976; (with J. S. Curran) Energy and Human Needs, 1979; Issues in Science and Education, 1988; papers on nuclear researches and education in Proc. Royal Society. *Recreations:* horology, golf. *Address:* 93 Kelvin Court, Glasgow G12 0AH. *T:* (0141) 334 8329.
Died 25 Feb. 1998.

CURREY, Rear-Adm. Edmund Neville Vincent, CB 1960; DSO 1944; DSC 1941; *b* 1 Oct. 1906; *s* of Dr and Mrs E. F. N. Currey, Lismore, Co. Waterford, Ireland; *m* 1941, Rosemary Knight (*d* 1992); one *d. Educ:* Royal Naval Colls, Osborne and Dartmouth. Joined RNC Osborne, 1920; served in submarines and destroyers as junior officer; served War of 1939–45: commanded HM Ships Wrestler, Escapade and Musketeer; Comdr, 1942; Capt., 1949; subsequently served with British Naval Mission to Greece; Naval Asst to Adm. Commanding Reserves; in command of HMS Bermuda; Naval Asst to Second Sea Lord; Rear-Adm., 1958; Chief of Staff to C-in-C, Portsmouth, 1958–61, retired. Polish Gold Cross of Merit, with swords, 1943. *Recreation:* golf. *Address:* Owlswood House, Blakemere, Hereford HR2 9JY. *T:* (01981) 500116.
Died 2 May 1998.

CURREY, Prof. Harry Lloyd Fairbridge, FRCP; Arthritis and Rheumatism Council Professor of Rheumatology, University of London, 1983–87, then Emeritus Professor of Rheumatology; Director, Bone and Joint Unit, London Hospital Medical College, 1976–87; Consulting Rheumatologist, London Hospital, since 1988; *b* 5 June 1925; *s* of late Ronald Fairbridge Currey and of Dorothy (*née* White); *m* 1st, 1950, Chrystal Komlosy (decd); one *s* two *d*; 2nd, 1973, Jacqueline Harris. *Educ:* Cordwalles, S Africa; Michaelhouse, Natal; Univ. of Cape Town (MB, ChB 1950, MMed 1960). FRCP 1971 (MRCP 1962). Intern, Groote Schuur Hosp., and House Officer, City Hosp. and Peninsular Maternity Hosps, Cape Town, 1951–53; gen. practice, Port Elizabeth, 1953–58; Med. Registrar, Groote Schuur Hosp., Cape Town, 1959–61; Intern, Hammersmith Hosp., London, 1962; Registrar, Dept of Rheumatology, London Hosp., 1963–65; London Hospital Medical College: Sen. Lectr, 1965–70; Reader in Rheumatol., 1970–74; Prof of Rheumatol., 1974–83; Res. Fellow, Southwestern Med. Sch., Dallas, Texas, 1966. Philip Ellman Lectr, RCP, 1977. Pres., Heberden Soc., 1980–81; Heberden Round presented 1972. Editor, Annals of the Rheumatic Diseases, 1983–88. *Publications:* Mason and Currey's Clinical Rheumatology, 1970, 4th edn 1986; Essentials of Rheumatology, 1983, 2nd edn 1988; (with S. A. Hull) Rheumatology for GPs, 1987; articles on rheumatol topics in learned jls. *Recreations:* gardening, music, golf, fell-walking, inland waterways. *Address:* The Heights, Galloway Road, Bishop's Stortford, Herts CM23 2HS. *T:* (01279) 654717.
Died 30 Jan. 1998.

CURRIE, Sir Neil (Smith), Kt 1982; CBE 1977; Chairman, Coal & Allied Industries Ltd, 1988–93 (Director, 1987–93); *b* 20 Aug. 1926; *s* of Sir George (Alexander) Currie and Margaret, *d* of Alexander Smith; *m* 1951, Geraldine Evelyn; two *s* two *d. Educ:* Wesley Coll., Perth, W Australia; Univ. of Western Australia (BA), Department of External Affairs, Australia, 1948–59; Dept of Trade and Industry, 1959–71; Secretary: Dept of Supply, 1971–74; Dept of Manufacturing Industry, 1974–76; Dept of Industry and Commerce, 1976–82; Australian Ambassador to Japan, 1982–86. Dep. Chm., Westpac Banking Corp., 1991–92 (Dir, 1987–92). Chm., Australia Japan Foundn, 1989–93 (Mem., 1986–93). *Recreations:* golf, tennis. *Address:* 25 Denise Drive, Lilli Pilli, Batemans Bay, NSW 2536, Australia.
Died 30 July 1999.

CURRIE, Rev. Piers William Edward, MC 1945; Assistant Priest, St Mary in the Marsh, Norwich, 1990–96; Hon. Priest Vicar, Norwich Cathedral, 1993–96; *b* 26 Feb. 1913; *e c* of late P. A. and Mrs Currie; *m* 1956, Ella Rosaleen, *y c* of late Rev. W. and Mrs Bennett-Hughes; no *c. Educ:* Rugby Sch.; Brasenose Coll., Oxford (MA). Solicitor, admitted Dec. 1939. Served War, 1940–45, in 4th Regt RHA. Sen. Legal Asst, Nat. Coal Bd, 1946–53; Asst Sec., 1953–55; Sec., W Midlands Divisional Bd, 1955–60; Sec. and Legal Adviser, 1960–62; Dep. Sec., NCB, 1962–67; Legal Adviser, Land Commission, 1967–71; Deputy Master, Court of Protection, 1971–77. Ordained deacon, 1980; priest, 1981; Hon. Curate of Holt with Edgefield, 1980–82; permanent permission to officiate, dio. Norwich, 1982; Priest in charge of Baconsthorpe and Hempstead by Holt, dio. Norwich, 1983–85; Staff mem., Glaven Assoc. of Parishes, 1986–90 and 1997–. *Recreations:* gardening, natural history. *Address:* 10 Meadow Close, Holt, Norwich NR25 6JP.
Died 21 Jan. 1999.

CURRIE, Prof. Ronald Ian, CBE 1977; FIBiol; FRSE; Professorial Fellow, Grant Institute of Geology, University of Edinburgh, 1988–90; *b* 10 Oct. 1928; *s* of Ronald Wavell Currie and Elizabeth Currie; *m* 1956, Cecilia, *d* of William and Lilian de Giris; one *s* one *d. Educ:* The Univ., Glasgow (BSc 1st Cl. Hons Zool., 1949), Univ. of Copenhagen FIBiol 1967; FRSE 1969. Joined Royal Naval Scientific Service, 1949; seconded to National Inst. of Oceanography; Head of Biol. Dept, 1962–66; Dir and Sec., Scottish Marine Biological Assoc., 1966–87 (Hon. Mem., 1989). Hon. Prof., Heriot-Watt Univ., 1979–. William Scoresby Expedn, S Africa, 1950; Discovery Expedn, Antarctica, 1951; res. voyages, N Atlantic, 1955–64; Chm., Biol. Planning Cttee, Internat. Indian Ocean Expedn, 1960; Indian Ocean Expedn, 1963 and 1964. Secretary: Internat. Assoc. for Biol Oceanography, 1964–66 (Pres., 1966–70); Scientific Cttee on Oceanic Res., Internat. Council of Scient. Unions, 1972–78. Chm., NERC Adv. Cttee on Internat. Ocean. Affairs, 1981–87; Member: Scottish Cttee, Nature Conservancy Council; Council, N British Hotels Trust; Royal Nat. Mission to Deep Sea Fishermen; Chm., Kilmore Community Council, 1977–86; Hon. Sec., Challenger Soc., 1956–88; Hon. Mem., Challenger Soc. for Marine Sci., 1989. *Publications:* (with T. J. Hart) The Benguela Current (Discovery Report), 1960; scientific papers on organic prodn in the sea and fertility of the ocean. *Recreations:* cooking, gardening, local history. *Address:* Tigh-nan-Eala, Kilmore, by Oban, Argyll PA34 4XT. *T:* Kilmore (01631) 770248.
Died 19 Feb. 1996.

CURTIS, Most Rev. (Ernest) Edwin, CBE 1976; Hon. Assistant Bishop of Portsmouth, since 1976; *b* 24 Dec. 1906; *s* of Ernest John and Zoe Curtis; *m* 1938, Dorothy Anne Hill (*d* 1965); one *s* one *d*; *m* 1970, Evelyn Mary Josling. *Educ:* Sherborne; Foster's Sch.; Royal College of Science, London. BSc Hons Chem. London, 1927; ARCS 1927; Dipl. Educn London, 1928. Asst Master, Lindisfarne Coll., Westcliff, 1928–31; Wells Theol Coll., 1932–33; deacon 1933, priest 1934; Asst Curate, Holy Trinity,

Waltham Cross, 1933–36; Chaplain i/c parishes Rose Hill and Bambous, and Principal, St Paul's Theol Coll., Mauritius, 1937–44; Missions to Seamen Chaplain, Port Louis, 1944; Priest i/c St Wilfrid, Portsmouth, 1945–47; Vicar, All Saints, Portsmouth, and Chaplain, Royal Portsmouth Hospital, 1947–55; Priest i/c St Agatha, Portsmouth, 1954–55; Vicar, St John Baptist, Locks Heath, 1955–66; Warden of Readers, Dio. Portsmouth, 1956–66; Rural Dean of Alverstoke, 1964–66; Bishop of Mauritius and Seychelles, 1966–72, of Mauritius, 1973–76; Archbishop of the Indian Ocean, 1973–76; Priest-in-charge of St Mary and St Rhadagunde, Whitwell, 1976–82. *Recreations:* walking, hill-climbing, piano. *Address:* 5 Elizabeth Gardens, Havenstreet, Ryde, Isle of Wight PO33 4DU. *T:* (01983) 883049. *Club:* Flyfishers'.
Died 15 Aug. 1999.

CURTIS, Genevra Fiona Penelope Victoria, (Mrs J. W. O. Curtis); *see* Caws, G. F. P. V.

CURTIS, His Honour Philip; a Circuit Judge (formerly a Judge of County Courts), 1969–80; *b* 29 April 1908; *s* of James William and Emma Curtis; *m* 1937, Marjorie Lillian Sharp (*d* 1993); two *s* one *d. Educ:* St Mary's RC Primary Sch., Denton, Lancs; Manchester Grammar Sch.; Brasenose Coll., Oxford. Called to the Bar, Gray's Inn, 1944. *Address:* Mottram Hall Farm, Mottram St Andrew, Macclesfield, Cheshire SK10 4QT. *T:* (01625) 829509.
Died 9 May 1998.

CUSACK, Henry Vernon, CMG 1955; CBE 1947; HM Overseas Civil Service (retired); Deputy Director General of the Overseas Audit Service, 1946–55; *b* 26 June 1895; 2nd *s* of late Edward Cusack, Bray, Co. Wicklow, and Constance Louisa Vernon, *e d* of late Col Vernon, DL, JP, Clontarf Castle, Dublin; unmarried. *Educ:* Aravon Sch., Ireland. Served European War, 1914–19 (General Service and Victory medals), France, Belgium and North Russia, as Captain, RASC, attached RGA; entered Colonial Audit Service, 1920; Asst Auditor: Sierra Leone, 1920–22; Nigeria, 1922–28; Sen. Asst Auditor, Nyasaland, 1928–33; Asst Director, Central Office, Colonial Audit Dept London, 1933–37; Auditor, Gold Coast, 1937–46. A Governor of the King's Hospital Sch., Dublin (Chm., 1964–69). FRGS. Coronation Medal, 1953. *Address:* Our Lady's Manor, Bulloch Castle, Dalkey, Co. Dublin. *Clubs:* Naval and Military; Royal St George Yacht (Dun Laoghaire, Co. Dublin). *Died 20 March 1996.*

CUSTANCE, Michael Magnus Vere, CB 1959; *b* 3 Jan. 1916; *o s* of late Zeffirino Costanzo, Sicily, and (Margaret) Gabrielle (*née* Campbell; she *m* 2nd, Arthur Long), novelist (as Marjorie Bowen); changed name to Custance, 1926; *m* 1st, Margaret Joy Bulman; one *s* one *d;* 2nd, Katharine Patricia Mary Haslam (*née* Gregory). *Educ:* St Paul's (schol.); The Queen's Coll., Oxford (open hist. schol.; BA Hons 1st cl., Mod. Hist., 1937). Asst Principal, Board of Trade, 1938; Ministry of Shipping, 1939; Royal Air Force, 1941–45; Principal, Ministry of War Transport, 1943; Asst Sec., Min. of Transport, 1948; Under-Sec.,

Min. of Transport and Civil Aviation, 1956, Dep. Sec., 1958; in Ministry of Aviation, 1959–63; in Ministry of Transport, 1963–66; in Min. of Social Security, later DHSS, 1966–75; Chief Advr to Supplementary Benefits Commn, 1968–75. IDC (1952 Course).
Died 30 Jan. 1999.

CUTLER, Sir Horace (Walter), Kt 1979; OBE 1963; DL; Member of Greater London Council for Harrow West, 1964–86; Chairman, Branch Retirement Homes PLC, since 1985; *b* London, N16, 28 July 1912; *s* of Albert Benjamin and Mary Ann Cutler; *m* 1957, Christiane, *d* of Dr Klaus Muthesius; one *s* three *d* (and one *s* of previous marriage). *Educ:* Harrow Grammar Sch.; Hereford. Served War of 1939–45: RNVR, 1941–46, Lieut. Harrow Borough Council: elected 1952; Chm. Planning Cttee, 1954; Chm. Housing Cttee, 1955–58; Dep. Mayor, 1958; Alderman, 1959; Mayor, 1959–60; Leader of Council, 1961–65; Chm., Gen. Purposes Cttee, 1962–65; Middlesex CC: elected, 1955; Vice-Chm., Estates and Housing Cttee, 1957; Chm. Planning Cttee, 1961–65; Dep. Leader of CC, 1962; Leader, 1963–65; Greater London Council: Dep. Leader of Opposition, 1964–67 and 1973–74; Dep. Leader, 1967–73; Leader of Opposition, 1974–77 and 1981–82; Leader, 1977–81; Chm. Housing Cttee, 1967–70; Policy and Resources Cttee, 1970–73. Chm., Central Milton Keynes Shopping Management Co. Ltd, 1976–89; Member: Milton Keynes New City Develt Corp, 1967–86; Central Housing Adv. Cttee, Min. of Housing and Local Govt, 1967–74; Nat. Housing and Town Planning Exec. Cttee, 1967–74 (Vice-Chm., London Region, 1968). Dir, S Bank Theatre Bd; Mem., Nat. Theatre Bd, 1975–82; Trustee, Nat. Theatre, 1976–83. Contested (C) Willesden East, 1970; Pres., Harrow West Conservative Assoc., 1964 (Chm., 1961–64). Freeman of Harrow, and City of London. DL Greater London, 1981. FRSA. OStJ. *Publication:* The Cutler Files, 1982. *Recreations:* golf, ski-ing, classical music, travel. *Address:* Hawkswood, Hawkswood Lane, Gerrards Cross, Bucks SL9 7BN. *T:* (01753) 663182. *Clubs:* Constitutional, United & Cecil.
Died 2 March 1997.

CUTTS, Rt Rev. Richard Stanley; Assistant Bishop, diocese of Lincoln, since 1992; *b* 17 Sept. 1919; *s* of Edward Stanley and Gabrielle Cutts; *m* 1960, Irene Adela Sack; one *s* three *d. Educ:* Felsted School, Essex. Deacon 1951, priest 1952; Asst Curate, SS Peter and Paul, Godalming, 1951–56; Director of St Cyprian's Mission, Etalaneni and Priest-in-Charge Nkandhla Chapelry, Zululand, 1957–63; Director, Kambula Mission District, 1963–65; Rector, St Mary's, Kuruman and Director, Kuruman Mission District, 1965–71; Archdeacon of Kuruman, 1969–71; Dean of Salisbury, Rhodesia, 1971–75; Bishop in Argentina and Eastern South America, 1975; name of dio. changed to Argentina and Uruguay 1986, to Argentina 1988; retired 1989. *Address:* 37 King Street, West Deeping, Lincs PE6 9HP.
Died 12 April 1997.

D

DAHL, Robert Henry, TD 1950; MA; Head Master of Wrekin College, 1952–71; *b* 21 April 1910; *y s* of Murdoch Cameron Dahl, London, and Lilian May Edgcumbe; *m* 1936, Lois Helen Allanby (decd); three *s. Educ:* Sedbergh Sch.; Exeter Coll., Oxford (MA). Asst Master (Modern Langs) at Merchant Taylors' Sch., 1934–38; Asst Master and Housemaster at Harrow Sch., 1938–52. Served War of 1939–45: Intelligence Corps, Middle East, 1941–43; Major, 1943; Political Intelligence Dept of Foreign Office, 1943–46. FRSA 1969. *Publication:* (ed jtly) Selections from Albert Schweitzer, 1953. *Recreations:* music, painting. *Address:* Cornwallis Court, Hospital Road, Bury St Edmunds, Suffolk IP33 3NH.

Died 6 Nov. 1999.

DAICHES, Lionel Henry; QC (Scot.) 1956; *b* 8 March 1911; *s* of late Rev. Dr Salis Daiches, Edinburgh, and Mrs Flora Daiches; *m* 1947, Dorothy Estelle Bernstein (marr. diss. 1973); two *s. Educ:* George Watson's Coll., Edinburgh; Edinburgh Univ. (MA, LLB). Pres., Edinburgh Univ. Diagnostic Soc., 1931; Convener of Debates, Edinburgh Univ. Union, 1933; Editor, The Student, 1933. Served 1940–46 in N Stafford Regt and Major, JAG Branch in N Africa and Italy, including Anzio Beachhead. Admitted Scots Bar, 1946. Standing Junior Counsel to Board of Control, Scotland, 1950–56; Sheriff-Substitute of Lanarkshire at Glasgow, 1962–67. Fellow, Internat. Acad. of Trial Lawyers, 1976. Contested (L) Edinburgh South, 1950. *Publication:* Russians at Law, 1960. *Recreations:* walking, talking. *Address:* 10 Heriot Row, Edinburgh EH3 6HU. *T:* (0131) 556 4144. *Clubs:* New, Scottish Arts (Edinburgh). *Died 11 Nov 1999.*

DAINTON, Baron *cr* 1986 (Life Peer), of Hallam Moors in South Yorkshire; **Frederick Sydney Dainton,** Kt 1971; MA, PhD, ScD; FRS 1957; Chancellor, Sheffield University, since 1978; *b* 11 Nov. 1914; *y s* of late George Whalley and Mary Jane Dainton; *m* 1942, Barbara Hazlitt, JP, PhD, *o d* of late Dr W. B. Wright, Manchester; one *s* two *d. Educ:* Central Secondary Sch., Sheffield; St John's Coll., Oxford (MA, BSc); Sidney Sussex Coll., Cambridge (PhD, ScD). Open Exhibitioner, 1933; Casberd Prizeman, 1934, Casberd Scholar, 1935, Hon. Fellow 1968, St John's Coll., Oxford; Goldsmiths' Co. Exhibitioner, 1935, 1st class Hons Chemistry, 1937, University of Oxford; Research Student, 1937, Goldsmiths' Co. Senior Student, 1939, University Demonstrator in Chemistry, 1944, H. O. Jones Lecturer in Physical Chemistry, 1946, University of Cambridge. Fellow, 1945, Praelector, 1946, Hon. Fellow 1961, St Catharine's Coll., Cambridge. Prof. of Physical Chemistry, University of Leeds, 1950–65; Vice-Chancellor, Nottingham Univ., 1965–70; Dr Lee's Prof. of Chemistry, Oxford University, 1970–73; Chm., UGC, 1973–78. Vis. Prof., Univ. Toronto, 1949; Arthur D. Little Visiting Prof., MIT, 1959. Lectures: Tilden, 1950, Faraday, 1973, Chem. Soc.; Peter C. Reilly, Univ. of Notre Dame, USA, 1952; Lady Masson, Melbourne, 1959; George Fisher Baker, Cornell Univ., 1961; Boomer, Univ. of Alberta, 1962; Rede, Cambridge, 1981; Crookshank, RCR, 1981; Stamp, London Univ., 1983; Convocation, Newcastle Univ., 1986; Boyle, RSA, 1987; Dainton, British Liby, 1987; Gray Hartley, Manchester Univ., 1987; John Snow, Assoc. of Anaesthetists, 1987; Lee Kuan Yew, Singapore Univ., 1989. Chm., Cttee on Swing away from Science (report published as Enquiry into the Flow of Candidates in Science and Technology into Higher Education, Cmnd 3541, 1968). Chairman: Assoc. for Radiation Research, 1964–66; Nat. Libraries Cttee 1968–69; Adv. Cttee on Sci. and Tech. Information, 1966–70; Adv. Bd for Res. Councils, 1972–73; British Cttee, Harkness Fellowship, 1977–81 (Mem., 1973–); British Library Bd, 1978–85; Nat. Radiological Protection Bd, 1978–85. President: Faraday Soc., 1965–67; Chemical Soc., 1972–73 (Hon. Fellow, 1983); Assoc. for Science Education, 1967; Library Assoc., 1977; BAAS, 1980; Soc. of Designer Craftsmen, 1985–96; Arthritis and Rheumatism Council for Res., 1988–. Member: Council for Scientific Policy, 1965–79 (Chm. 1969–72); Central Advisory Council for Science and Technology, 1967–70; Council, Foundn for Science and Technol., 1987–94; Crafts Council, 1984–88; Museums and Galleries Commn, 1985–92; Trustee: Natural Hist. Museum, 1974–84; Wolfson Foundn, 1978–88; Patron, English Place Name Soc., 1993–. Chairman: Edward Boyle Meml Trust, 1982–; Council, RPMS, 1979–90 (Pres., 1990–97). Prime Warden, Goldsmiths' Co., 1982–83. Foreign Member: Swedish Acad. of Sci., 1968; Amer. Acad. of Arts and Scis, 1972; Acad. of Scis, Göttingen, 1975; Acad. Mediterranae della Scienze, 1982; Amer. Philos. Soc., 1991. Privelegeiate *hc,* St Hilda's Coll., Oxford, 1994; Hon. Fellow: Goldsmiths' Coll., London, 1985; Queen Mary Coll., London, 1985; Birkbeck Coll., London, 1986; RPMS, 1990; Hon. FRCP 1979; Hon. FRSC 1983; Hon. FRCR 1984; Hon. FLA 1986. Hon. ScD: Lódz, 1966; Dublin, 1968; Hon. DSc: Bath Univ. of Technology, 1970; Loughborough Univ. of Technology, 1970; Heriot-Watt, 1970; Warwick, 1970; Strathclyde, 1971; Exeter, 1971; QUB, 1971; Manchester, 1972; E Anglia, 1972; Leeds, 1973; McMaster, 1975; Uppsala, 1977; Liverpool, Salford, 1979; Ulster, 1980; Kent, 1981; Reading, 1996; Hon. LLD: Nottingham, 1970; Aberdeen, 1972; Sheffield, Cambridge, 1979; London, 1984; Lancaster, 1989; Hon. DCL Oxford, 1988; Hon. DLitt CNAA, 1991. Sylvanus Thompson Medal, BIR, 1958; Davy Medal, Royal Soc., 1969; Faraday Medal, RSC, 1974; Crookshank Medal, RCR, 1981; 1300 Years Bulgaria Medal, 1982; Curie Medal, Poland, 1983; John Snow Medal, Coll. Anaesthetists, 1987; Firth Medal, Forensic Science Soc., 1993; Semonov Centenary Medal, Russian Acad. Scis, 1996. Kt Comdr, Order of Merit (Poland), 1985. *Publications:* Chain Reactions, 1956; (ed and contrib.) Photochemistry and Reaction Kinetics, 1967; Choosing a British University, 1981; (contrib.) The Parliament of Science, 1981; Universities and the National Health Service, 1983; papers on physico-chemical subjects in scientific jls. *Recreation:* walking. *Address:* 36 Charlbury Road, Oxford OX2 6UX. *T:* (01865) 510568. *Club:* Athenæum. *Died 5 Dec. 1997.*

DALE, Sir William (Leonard), KCMG 1965 (CMG 1951); international legal consultant; Director, Centre for Legislation Studies, Institute of Advanced Legal Studies, since 1997; *b* 17 June 1906; *e s* of late Rev. William Dale, Rector of Preston, Yorks; *m* 1966, Mrs Gloria Spellman Finn, Washington, DC; one *d. Educ:* Hymers Coll., Hull; LLB London, 1931. Barrister, Gray's Inn, 1931. Asst Legal Adviser, Colonial and Dominions Offices, 1935; Min. of Supply, 1940–45; Dep. Legal Adviser, Colonial and Commonwealth Relations Offices, 1945; Legal Adviser, United Kingdom of Libya, 1951–53; Legal Adviser: Min. of Educn, 1954–61; CRO, subseq. CO, 1961–66. Special Asst to the Law Officers, 1967–68; Gen. Counsel, UNRWA, Beirut, 1968–73. Dir of Studies, Govt

Legal Advrs Course, 1976–99. Hon. LLD Hull, 1978. *Publications:* Law of the Parish Church, 1932, 7th edn 1998; Legislative Drafting: a new approach, 1977; The Modern Commonwealth, 1983; (ed) Anglo-French Statutory Drafting, 1987; Preparation and Accessibility of the Written Law in France, 1993; Time Past Time Present (autobiog.), 1994; contributions to journals. *Recreation:* music (except Wagner). *Address:* 20 Old Buildings, Lincoln's Inn, WC2A 3UP. *T:* (020) 7242 9365. *Club:* Travellers. *Died 8 Feb. 2000.*

DALHOUSIE, 16th Earl of, *cr* 1633; **Simon Ramsay,** KT 1971; GCVO 1979; GBE 1957; MC 1944; Baron Ramsay 1618; Lord Ramsay 1633; Baron Ramsay (UK) 1875; Lord Chamberlain to the Queen Mother, 1965–92; Lord-Lieutenant of Angus, 1967–89; Chancellor, Dundee University, 1977–92; *b* 17 Oct. 1914; 2nd *s* of 14th Earl (*d* 1928) and Lady Mary Adelaide Heathcote Drummond Willoughby (*d* 1960), *d* of 1st Earl of Ancaster; *S* brother, 1950; *m* 1940, Margaret Elizabeth (*d* 1997), *d* of late Brig.-Gen. Archibald Stirling, Keir and Hon. Margaret, *d* of 13th Lord Lovat; three *s* two *d.* *Educ:* Eton; Christ Church, Oxford. Served TA, Black Watch, 1936–39; embodied, 1939. MP (C) County of Angus, 1945–50; Conservative Whip, 1946–48 (resigned). Governor-General, Fedn of Rhodesia and Nyasaland, 1957–63. Hon. LLD: Dalhousie, 1952; Dundee, 1967. *Heir: s* Lord Ramsay, *b* 17 Jan. 1948. *Address:* Brechin Castle, Brechin, Angus DD9 6SH. *T:* (01356) 622176. *Club:* White's.
Died 15 July 1999.

DALLEY, Christopher Mervyn, CMG 1971; CEng; Director, London and Scottish Marine Oil Co. Ltd, 1979–84; *b* 26 Dec. 1913; *er s* of late Christopher Dalley; *m* 1947, Elizabeth Alice, *yr d* of late Lt-Gen. Sir James Gammell, KCB, DSO, MC; one *s* three *d.* *Educ:* Epsom Coll., Surrey; Queens' Coll., Cambridge (MA). Served in RN, 1939–45. Joined British Petroleum Co., 1946; joined Oil Operating Companies in Iran, 1954, Asst Gen. Managing Dir, 1958; joined Iraq Petroleum Co. and associated companies, 1962, Man. Dir, 1963, Chm., 1970–73; Chm., Oil Exploration Holdings Ltd, 1973–79. Dir, Viking Resources Trust, 1973–84. Pres., Inst. of Petroleum, 1970; Mem. Council, World Petroleum Congress, 1970. Mem., Governing Body, Royal Medical Foundn (Epsom Coll.), 1970–94. *Address:* Mead House, Woodham Walter, near Maldon, Essex CM9 6RD. *T:* (01245) 222404. *Club:* Athenæum.
Died 28 July 1999.

DANIEL, Prof. Peter Maxwell, DM, DSc; FRCP, FRCS, FRCPath (Founder Fellow), FRCPsych (Founder Fellow); FLS; FIBiol; Senior Research Fellow, Department of Applied Physiology and Surgical Science, Hunterian Institute, Royal College of Surgeons, 1976; Visiting Senior Research Fellow, St Thomas's Hospital Medical School, 1981; Professor of Neuropathology, University of London, at the Institute of Psychiatry, Maudsley Hospital, 1957–76, then Emeritus Professor; Emeritus Physician, Bethlem Royal and Maudsley Hospitals, since 1977; *b* 14 Nov. 1910; *s* of Peter Daniel, FRCS, surgeon to Charing Cross Hospital, and Beatrice Laetitia Daniel; *m* 1st, Sarah Shelford (marr. diss.) (decd); two *s* three *d*; 2nd, F. Dawn Bosanquet (marr. diss.); one *s*; 3rd, Marion F. Bosanquet. *Educ:* Westminster Sch.; St John's Coll., Cambridge (MA, MB, BCh); New Coll., Oxford (MA, DM); DSc London. Hon. Consultant Pathologist, Radcliffe Infirmary, 1948–56; Senior Research Officer, University of Oxford, 1949–56; Hon. Consultant in Neuropathology to the Army at Home, 1952–77; Hon. Consultant Neuropathologist, Bethlem Royal and Maudsley Hosps, 1956–76. Emeritus Fellow, Leverhulme Trust, 1978–80; Hon. Librarian, RCPath, 1981; Mem., Library Cttee, Linnean Soc., 1987. John Hunter Medal and Triennial Prize, 1946–48, and

Erasmus Wilson Lectr, 1964, RCS. President: British Neuropathological Society, 1963–64; Neurological Section, RSM, 1970–71; Harveian Soc. London, 1966 (Trustee, 1971; Hon. Mem., 1985); Section of Hist. of Med., RSM, 1979–82; Osler Club, 1979–82; Mem. Council: Royal Microscopical Soc., 1968–72; Neonatal Soc., 1959–61; Assoc. of British Neurologists, 1966–69 (Hon. Mem., 1985); Med. Soc. of London, 1981 (Hon. Librarian, 1984–90; Pres., 1987–88). Hon. Mem., Physiological Soc., 1981; Life Mem., Anatomical Soc. of GB. Member: Bd of Govs, Bethlem Royal and Maudsley Hosps, 1966–75; Council, Charing Cross Hosp. Medical Sch., 1972–85. Chm., Academic Bd, Inst. of Psychiatry, 1966–70; Vice-Chm., Central Academic Council, British Postgrad. Med. Fedn, 1975–76; Mem., Bd of Studies in Physiology, Univ. of London, 1981. Liveryman, Soc. of Apothecaries, 1952. Editorial Board of: Jl of Physiology, 1958–65; Jl of Neurology, Neurosurgery and Psychiatry, 1953–64; Journal of Neuroendocrinology, 1966–77; Brain, 1974–76; Qly Jl Exp. Physiol., 1980–84. *Publications:* (jtly) Studies of the Renal Circulation, 1947; The Hypothalamus and Pituitary Gland, 1975; papers in various medical and scientific journals. *Recreations:* books, medical history. *Address:* 5 Seaforth Place, Buckingham Gate, SW1E 6AB. *T:* (020) 7834 3087. *Clubs:* Athenæum, Garrick, Green Room. *Died 19 Nov. 1998.*

DANIELS, Prof. Henry Ellis, FRS 1980; Professor of Mathematical Statistics, University of Birmingham, 1957–78, then Emeritus Professor; Senior Research Associate, Statistical Laboratory, University of Cambridge, 1978–81; *b* 2 Oct. 1912; *s* of Morris and Hannah Daniels; *m* 1950, Barbara Edith Pickering; one *s* one *d.* *Educ:* Sciennes Sch., Edinburgh; George Heriot's Sch., Edinburgh; Edinburgh Univ. (MA 1933; PhD 1943); Clare Coll., Cambridge (BA 1935; Hon. Fellow, 1992); ScD Cantab 1981. Statistician, Wool Industries Research Assoc., 1935–47; Ministry of Aircraft Production, 1942–45; Lecturer in Mathematics, University of Cambridge, 1947–57; Fellow, King's Coll., Cambridge, 1975–76. Pres., Royal Statistical Soc., 1974–75; Fellow Inst. of Mathematical Statistics; elected Mem., 1956, Hon. Mem., 1993, Internat. Statistical Inst. Freeman, Clockmakers' Co., 1981, Liveryman 1984. Guy Medal (Silver) 1957, (Gold) 1984, Royal Statistical Society. *Publications:* papers in Journal of the Royal Statistical Society, Annals of Mathematical Statistics, Biometrika, etc. *Recreations:* playing the English concertina, repairing watches. *Address:* 12 Kimberley Road, Cambridge CB4 1HH. *T:* (01223) 313402. *Died 14 April 2000.*

DANILOVA, Alexandra Dionysievna; lecturer, teacher and choreographer, actress; *b* Pskoff, Russia, 20 Nov. 1903; *d* of Dionis Daniloff and Claudia Gotovzeffa; *m* 1st, 1931, Giuseppe Massera (*d* 1936); 2nd, 1941, Kazimir Kokic (marr. annulled, 1949). *Educ:* Theatrical Sch., Petrograd. Maryinski Theatre, Leningrad, 1923–24; Diaghileff Company, 1925–29; Waltzes from Vienna, 1931; Colonel de Basil Company, 1933–37; Prima Ballerina, Ballet Russe de Monte Carlo, 1938–58. Teacher (on Faculty) of School of American Ballet. Guest artist Royal Festival Hall, London, 1955; Ballerina in Oh Captain (musical), New York, 1958. Guest Choreographer Metropolitan Opera House, Guest Teacher and Choreographer, Germany (Krefeld Festival of Dance) and Amsterdam, 1959–60; choreographed Coppelia for La Scala di Milano, 1961; Guest Choreographer, Washington Ballet, 1962–64; choreographed Coppelia (with George Balanchine), NY City Ballet, 1975. With own Company toured West Indies, Japan, Philippines, USA, Canada and S Africa. Screen acting debut in film, The Turning Point, 1977. Lecture performances throughout US. Capezio Award, for outstanding services to Art of the Dance, 1958; Kennedy Center Honors Award, 1989; Handel Medal,

New York City, 1989, *Recreations:* needlework, ping-pong, gardening. *Address:* Carnegie House, 100 West 57th Street, New York, NY 10019, USA.
Died 13 July 1997.

DANKS, Sir Alan (John), KBE 1970; Chairman, New Zealand University Grants Committee, 1966–77; *b* 9 June 1914; *s* of T. E. Danks; *m* 1943, Loma Beryl Hall (*née* Drabble). *Educ:* West Christchurch High Sch.; Canterbury Coll. (MA). Teaching profession, 1931–43; Economics Dept, Univ. of Canterbury (formerly Canterbury University Coll.), 1943–66; Prof., 1962; Pro-Vice Chancellor, 1964. Chm., Information Authy, 1982–88. Hon. LLD Canterbury, 1973. *Address:* 116 Upland Road, Wellington 5, New Zealand. *Died 9 Dec. 1993.*

DARBY, Dr Francis John, TD 1964; MRCGP; MFOM; *b* 24 Feb. 1920; *o s* of Col John Francis Darby, CBE, late Royal Signals, and Georgina Alice (*née* Dean); *m* 1st, 1949, Joyce Helene Campbell Stewart (marr. diss.); one *s*; 2nd, 1969, Pamela Lisbeth, *o d* of Sydney Hill, Sutton Coldfield. *Educ:* Nottingham High Sch.; Edinburgh Acad.; Edinburgh Univ. (MB ChB 1950). MRCGP 1970; DIH 1963; DMJ 1965; MFOM RCP 1982; DPhilMed 1994. Commissioned, Royal Signals, 1939–46: N Africa (despatches), Italy and Egypt, 1942–46. Hospital and general practice, 1950–64; Department of Health and Social Security, 1964–82: Dep. Chief Medical Advr, 1978–80; Chief Medical Advr (Social Security), 1980–82; CMO and Consultant Physician, Cayman Is, 1983–85. Mem. BMA, 1950. Freeman, City of London, 1979; Liveryman, Soc. of Apothecaries of London, 1991 (Fellow, Faculty of History and Philosophy of Medicine, 1991). QHP, 1980–84, *Recreations:* sailing, swimming. *Address:* Ruardean, Captains Row, Lymington, Hants SO41 9RP. *T:* Lymington (01590) 677119. *Clubs:* Army and Navy; Royal Signals Yacht; Royal Lymington Yacht.
Died 19 May 1996.

DARESBURY, 3rd Baron *cr* 1927, of Walton, Co. Chester; **Edward Gilbert Greenall;** Bt 1876; *b* 27 Nov. 1928; *s* of 2nd Baron Dareshury and Josephine (*d* 1958), *y d* of Brig. Gen. Sir Joseph Laycock, KCMG, DSO; *S* father, 1990; *m* 1st, 1952, Margaret Ada (marr. diss. 1986), *y d* of late C. J. Crawford; three *s* one *d*; 2nd, 1986, Mary Patricia, *d* of late Lewis Parkinson. *Educ:* Eton. Chm., Randall & Vautier Ltd; formerly Chm., Grunhalle Lager Internat. *Heir:* *s* Hon. Peter Gilbert Greenall [*b* 18 July 1953; *m* 1982, Clare Alison, *d* of Christopher Weatherby; four *s*]. *Address:* Crossbow House, Trinity, Jersey, CI. *T:* (01534) 863316. *Died 9 Sept. 1996.*

DARLING, Gerald Ralph Auchinleck, RD 1967; QC 1967; QC (Hong Kong) 1968; DL; MA; Lieutenant-Commander, retired; Judge, Admiralty Court of the Cinque Ports, since 1979; *b* 8 Dec. 1921; *er s* of late Lieut-Col R. R. A. Darling and Moira (*née* Moriarty); *m* 1954, Susan Ann, *d* of late Brig. J. M. Hobbs, OBE, MC; one *s* one *d*. *Educ:* Harrow Sch. (Reginald Pole Schol.); Hertford Coll., Oxford (Baring Schol., Kitchener Schol.); MA 1948). Served with RNVR, 1940–46: Fleet Fighter Pilot with 807 Seafire Sqdn in HM Ships Furious, Indomitable, Battler and Hunter; Test Pilot, Eastern Fleet and Chief Test Pilot, British Pacific Fleet in HMS Unicorn; RNR until 1967. Called to Bar, Middle Temple, 1950 (Harmsworth Law Schol.), Bencher, 1972, Treasurer, 1991; Barrister, Northern Ireland, 1957, Hon. Bencher, 1992. Member: Panel of Lloyd's Arbitrators in Salvage Cases, 1967–78, Appeal Arbitrator, 1978–91; Panel of Wreck Commissioners, 1967. Trustee, Royal Naval Museum, 1985–90. DL Co. Tyrone, 1990; High Sheriff, Co. Tyrone, 1993. Freeman of City of London, 1968. Lloyd's Silver Medal, 1991. *Publications:* (contrib.) 3rd edn Halsbury's Laws of England (Admiralty and Ship Collisions), 1952; (contrib.) International Commercial and Maritime Arbitration, 1988; (with Christopher Smith) LOF90 and the New Salvage Convention, 1991, *Recreations:* fly fishing, shooting. *Address:* Crevenagh House, Omagh, Northern Ireland BT79 0EH; Queen Elizabeth Building, Temple, EC4Y 9BS. *T:* (0171) 353 9153. *Clubs:* Naval and Military; Tyrone County (Omagh).
Died 13 Sept. 1996.

DARLING, Sir James Carlisle S.; *see* Stormonth Darling.

DARLING, Gen. Sir Kenneth (Thomas), GBE 1969 (CBE 1957); KCB 1963 (CB 1957); DSO 1945; Commander-in-Chief, Allied Forces, Northern Europe, 1967–69, retired; *b* 17 Sept. 1909; *s* of late G. K. Darling, CIE and 1st wife, Mabel Eleanor, *d* of John Burgess; *m* 1941, Pamela Beatrice Rose Denison-Pender (*d* 1990). *Educ:* Eton; Royal Military College, Sandhurst. jssc 1946; idc 1953. Commissioned 7th Royal Fusiliers, 1929; served NW Europe, 1944–45; comd 5th Parachute Bde, 1946; comd Airborne Forces Depot, 1948; comd 16th Parachute Bde, 1950; Brig. AQ 1st (British) Corps, 1954; Chief of Staff 1st (British) Corps, 1955; Chief of Staff 2nd Corps, 1956; Dep. Dir of Staff Duties (D), WO, 1957–58; GOC Cyprus District and Dir of Ops, 1958–60; Dir of Infantry, 1960–62; GOC 1st (British) Corps, 1962–63; GOC-in-C, Southern Command, 1964–66. Colonel: The Royal Fusiliers (City of London Regt), 1963–68; The Royal Regt of Fusiliers, 1968–74; Col Comdt, The Parachute Regt, 1965–67. ADC Gen., 1968–69. *Recreation:* riding. *Address:* Vicarage Farmhouse, Chesterton, Bicester, Oxon OX6 8UQ. *T:* (01869) 252092. *Club:* Army and Navy.
Died 31 Oct. 1998.

DARLINGTON, Rear-Adm. Sir Charles (Roy), KBE 1965; Director of the Naval Education Service and Head of Instructor Branch, Royal Navy, 1960–65, retired; on staff of Haileybury, 1965–75; *b* 2 March 1910; *o s* of C. A. Darlington, Newcastle under Lyme, Staffs; *m* 1935, Nora Dennison Wright (*d* 1993), Maulds Meaburn, Westmorland; one *s* one *d*, *m* 1995, Lucille Patricia Bailey, Southsea. *Educ:* Orme Sch., Newcastle under Lyme; Manchester Univ. (BSc). Double First in Maths 1931. Sen. Maths Master, William Hulme's Grammar Sch., 1937–40; entered Royal Navy, 1941 (Instructor Lieut); served in: HM Ships Valiant and Malaya during War, and later in HM Ships Duke of York, Implacable, Vanguard and Tyne; on Staff of C-in-C Home Fleet, 1954–55, as Fleet Meteorological Officer; for various periods in Admty, HMS Excellent and HMS Collingwood; Rear-Adm. 1960. *Recreations:* cricket, hill-walking, mathematics, trying to avoid ignorance of the arts, and particularly of history.
Died 4 July 1998.

DARTMOUTH, 9th Earl of, *cr* 1711; **Gerald Humphry Legge;** Baron Dartmouth 1682; Viscount Lewisham 1711; *b* 26 April 1924; *s* of 8th Earl of Dartmouth, CVO, DSO and Roma, *e d* of Sir Ernest Horlick, 2nd Bt; *S* father, 1962; *m* 1st, 1948, Raine (marr. diss. 1976), *d* of late Alexander McCorquodale and of Dame Barbara Cartland, DBE; three *s* one *d*; 2nd, 1980, Mrs Gwendoline Mary Seguin. *Educ:* Eton. Served War, 1943–45, Coldstream Guards, Italy (despatches). FCA 1951. Dir, Rea Brothers Group PLC, Bankers, 1958–89. Chairman: Royal Choral Soc., 1970–92; Anglo-Brazilian Soc., 1975–94. Hon. LLD Dartmouth Coll., USA, 1969. Grand Officer, Order of the Southern Cross (Brazil), 1994. *Heir:* *s* Viscount Lewisham, *b* 23 Sept. 1949. *Address:* The Manor House, Chipperfield, King's Langley, Herts WD4 9BN. *Clubs:* Buck's (Pres., 1994–), Boodle's. *Died 14 Dec. 1997.*

DASHWOOD, Sir Francis (John Vernon Hereward), 11th Bt *cr* 1707, of West Wycombe, Buckinghamshire; Premier Baronet of Great Britain; *b* 7 Aug. 1925; *s* of Sir John Lindsay Dashwood, 10th Bt, CVO, and Helen Moira Eaton (*d* 1989); *S* father, 1966; *m* 1st, 1957, Victoria Ann

Elizabeth Gwynne de Rutzen (d 1976); one s three d; 2nd, 1977, Marcella (née Scarafia), formerly wife of Giuseppe Sportoletti Baduel and widow of Jack Frye, CBE; one step s (from wife's first m). Educ: Eton; Christ Church, Oxford (BA 1948, MA 1953); Henry Fellow, Harvard Business Sch., USA. Foreign Office, 1944–45. Aluminum Company of Canada Ltd, 1950–51; EMI Ltd, 1951–53. Member of Buckinghamshire County Council, 1950–51; Member of Lloyd's, 1956. Contested (C) West Bromwich, 1955, Gloucester, 1957. High Sheriff Bucks, 1976. SBStJ. Publications: The Dashwoods of West Wycombe, 1987; The Great Lloyd's Robbery, 1992. Heir: s Edward John Francis Dashwood [b 25 Sept. 1964; m 1989, Lucinda, d of G. H. F. Miesegaes; two s one d]. Address: Sawmill House, West Wycombe, High Wycombe, Bucks HP12 4AF. T: (01494) 523720. Club: White's.

Died 9 March 2000.

DAUBE, Prof. David, DCL, PhD, Dr jur; FBA 1957; Director of the Robbins Hebraic and Roman Law Collections and Professor-in-Residence at the School of Law, University of California, Berkeley, 1970–81, Emeritus Professor of Law, since 1981; Emeritus Regius Professor, Oxford University, since 1970; Member, Academic Board, Institute of Jewish Affairs, London, since 1953; b Freiburg, 8 Feb. 1909; 2nd s of Jakob Daube; m 1st, 1936 (marr. diss. 1964); three s; 2nd, 1986, Helen Smelser (née Margolis). Educ: Berthold-gymnasium, Freiburg; Univs of Freiburg and Göttingen (Dr jur 1932); PhD Cantab 1935; MA 1955, DCL 1956 Oxon. Fellow of Gonville and Caius Coll., Cambridge, 1938–46, Hon. Fellow, 1974; Lecturer in Law, Cambridge, 1946–51; Professor of Jurisprudence, Aberdeen Univ., 1951–55; Regius Prof. of Civil Law, Oxford Univ., and Fellow of All Souls Coll., 1955–70, Emeritus Fellow, 1980. Senior Fellow, Yale Univ., 1962; Ford Prof. of Political Science, Univ. of California, Berkeley, 1964; Vis. Prof. of History, 1966–78, Hon. Prof., 1980, Univ. of Constance. Lectures: Delitzsch, Münster, 1962; Gifford, Edinburgh, for 1962 and 1963 (lectures delivered, 1963–64); Olaus Petri, Uppsala, 1963; Riddell, Newcastle, 1965; Gray, Cambridge, 1966; Pope John, Catholic Univ. of America, Washington, 1966; Lionel Cohen, Jerusalem, 1970; inaug. Frosty Gerard, UC Irvine, 1981; G. Hitchings Terriberry, Tulane Univ., 1982; inaug. Gerald Goldfarb Meml, Univ. of Judaism, Los Angeles, 1991. President: Société d'Histoire des Droits de l'Antiquité, 1957–58; Classical Assoc. of GB, 1976–77; Jewish Law Assoc., 1983–85; Founder-Pres., B'nai B'rith Oxford, 1961. Corresp. Mem., Akad. der Wissenschaften, Göttingen, 1964, Bayer. Akad. Wiss., Munich, 1966; Hon. Mem. Royal Irish Acad., 1970; Fellow: Amer. Acad. of Arts and Sciences, 1971; World Acad. of Art and Sci., 1975; Amer. Acad. for Jewish Research, 1979; Amer. Soc. for Legal History, 1983; Hon. Fellow, Oxford Centre for Postgraduate Hebrew Studies, 1973. Hon. LLD: Edinburgh, 1960; Leicester, 1964; Cambridge, 1981; Aberdeen, 1990; Dr hc Paris, 1963; Hon. DHL: Hebrew Union Coll., 1971; Graduate Theol Union, Berkeley, 1988; Dr jur hc Munich, 1972; Dr phil hc Göttingen, 1987. Publications: Studies in Biblical Law, 1947; The New Testament and Rabbinic Judaism, 1956; Forms of Roman Legislation, 1956; (with W. D. Davies) Studies in honour of C. H. Dodd, 1956; (ed) Studies in memory of F. de Zulueta, 1959; The Exodus Pattern in the Bible, 1963; The Sudden in the Scriptures, 1964; Collaboration with Tyranny in Rabbinic Law, 1965; He that Cometh, 1966; Roman Law, 1969; Civil Disobedience in Antiquity, 1972; Ancient Hebrew Fables, 1973; Wine in the Bible, 1975; Medical and Genetic Ethics, 1976; Duty of Procreation, 1977; Typologie im Werk des Flavius Josephus, 1977; Ancient Jewish Law, 1981; Geburt der Detektivgeschichte, 1983; Das Alte Testament im Neuen, 1984; Sons and

Strangers, 1984; (with C. Carmichael) Witnesses in Bible and Talmud, 1986; Appeasement or Resistance and other essays on New Testament Judaism, 1987; Festschriften: Daube Noster, 1974; Studies in Jewish Legal History in Honour of D.D., 1974; Donum Gentilicium, 1978; Berkeley and Oxford Symposium in Honour of D.D., 1993; articles. Address: School of Law, University of California, Berkeley, CA 94720, USA.

Died 24 Feb. 1999.

DAUNT, Maj.-Gen. Brian, CB 1956; CBE 1953; DSO 1943; late Royal Artillery; b 16 March 1900; s of Dr William Daunt, Parade House, Hastings; m 1938, Millicent Margaret, d of Capt. A. S. Balfour, Allermuir House, Colinton, Edinburgh; two d (one s decd). Educ: Tonbridge; RMA, Woolwich. Commissioned RA, 1920; served NW Frontier, India, 1929–30; War of 1939–45: France, 1940, as 2 i/c Regt; CO Anti-Tank Regt, 1941; Italy, as CO 142 Field Regt, RA, Royal Devon Yeo., 1943 (DSO); CRA: 1st Armoured Div., 1944; 46 Div., 1944; 10 Indian Div., 1946; Italy, 1945 (despatches); various Brigadier's appts; Commandant Coast Artillery Sch. and Inspector Coast Artillery, 1950–53; General Officer Commanding Troops, Malta, 1953–Nov. 1956; retired, 1957; Controller, Home Dept, British Red Cross Society, 1957–66. Col Comdt RA, 1960–65. CStJ 1966. Recreations: gardening, music, drama. Address: 10 Church Lane, Wallingford, Oxon OX10 0DX. T: Wallingford (01491) 38111. Club: Army and Navy.

Died 18 March 1996.

DAVENPORT, Brian John; QC 1980; b 17 March 1936; s of Robert Cecil Davenport, FRCS, and Helen Elizabeth Davenport, MRCS, LRCP; m 1969, Erica Tickell, yr d of Prof. E. N. Willmer, ScD, FRS; two s one d. Educ: Bryanston Sch.; Worcester Coll., Oxford (MA). 2 Lieut RE, 1955–56. Called to the Bar, Gray's Inn, 1960 (Atkin Scholar); Bencher, 1983. Junior Counsel: to Export Credit Guarantees Dept, 1971–74; to Dept of Employment, 1972–74; (Common Law), to Bd of Inland Revenue, 1974–80; (Common Law), to the Crown, 1978–80; a Law Comr, 1981–88. Mem., Gen. Council of the Bar, 1969–73. Publications: (ed with F. M. B. Reynolds) 13th and 14th edns of Bowstead on Agency. Address: 43 Downshire Hill, NW3 1NU. T: (020) 7435 3332.

Died 23 Sept. 2000.

DAVENTRY, 3rd Viscount cr 1943; **Francis Humphrey Maurice FitzRoy Newdegate;** Lord-Lieutenant of Warwickshire, 1990–96; b 17 Dec. 1921; s of Comdr Hon. John Maurice FitzRoy Newdegate, RN (y s of 1st Viscountess Daventry; he assumed by Royal Licence, 1936, additional surname and arms of Newdegate and d 1976) and Lucia Charlotte Susan, OBE (d 1982), d of Sir Francis Alexander Newdigate Newdegate, GCMG; S uncle, 1986; m 1959, Hon. Rosemary, e d of 1st Baron Norrie, GCMG, GCVO, CB, DSO, MC; two s one d. Educ: Eton. Served War of 1939–45 with Coldstream Guards, N Africa and Italy; Captain 1943. ADC to Viceroy of India, 1946–48. JP 1960, DL 1970, High Sheriff 1970, Vice-Lieut, 1974–90, Warwickshire. KStJ 1991. Heir: s Hon. James Edward FitzRoy Newdegate [b 27 July 1960; m 1994, Georgia, d of John Lodge, Cirencester; one s one d]. Address: Temple House, Arbury, Nuneaton, Warwickshire CV10 7PT. T: (024) 7638 3514. Club: Boodle's.

Died 15 Feb. 2000.

DAVEY, David Garnet, OBE 1949; MSc, PhD; Research Director of Pharmaceuticals Division, Imperial Chemical Industries Ltd, 1969–75; b 8 Aug. 1912; y s of I. W. Davey, Caerphilly, Glamorgan; m 1938, Elizabeth Gale; one s two d. Educ: University Coll., Cardiff (1st cl. Hons Zoology; MSc 1935); Gonville and Caius Coll., Cambridge (PhD 1938); Harvard Univ. Med. Sch. (Research Fellow). Inst. of Animal Pathology, Univ. of Cambridge, 1938; Lectr, University Coll., Cardiff, 1939–40; Min. of Supply

(Radar), 1941; joined ICI 1942, Biological Research Manager, Pharmaceuticals Div., 1957–69. Pres., European Soc. for Study of Drug Toxicity, 1964–69; Member: MRC, 1971–75; Cttee on Review of Medicines, 1975–81; Sub-cttee on Toxicity, Clinical Trials, and Therapeutic Efficacy, Cttee on Safety of Medicines, 1976–81. Chalmers Gold Medal, Royal Soc. Tropical Medicine and Hygiene, 1947; Therapeutics Gold Medal, Apothecaries Soc., 1947. *Publications:* contribs to Annals Trop. Med., Trans Royal Soc. Tropical Medicine and Hygiene, British Med. Bulletin, Proc. European Soc. for Study of Drug Toxicity, etc. *Recreation:* gardening. *Address:* Flat 41, St Vincent Court, St Vincent Street, Broughty Ferry, Dundee DD5 2DA. *T:* (01382) 775744. *Died 6 April 1997.*

DAVEY, Idris Wyn; Under-Secretary, Welsh Office, 1972–77; Deputy Chairman, Local Government Boundary Commission for Wales, 1979–89; *b* 8 July 1917; 2nd *s* of late S. and M. Davey, Blaina, Mon; *m* 1943, Lilian Lloyd-Bowen; two *d.* Admiralty, 1940–47; Welsh Bd of Health: Asst Principal, 1948; Principal, 1951; Sec. Local Govt Commn for Wales, 1959–62; Welsh Office: Asst Sec. (in Min. of Housing and Local Govt), 1962; Establishment Officer, 1966–72; Under-Sec., 1972; seconded as Sec. and Mem., Local Govt Staff Commn for Wales and NHS Staff Commn for Wales, 1972–73. Mem., Sports Council for Wales, 1978–88. *Recreations:* University of the Third Age, watching Rugby football, gardening. *Address:* 4A Southgate Road, Southgate, Swansea SA3 2BT. *T:* (01792) 234320. *Died 19 Dec. 1996.*

DAVEY, John Trevor, FCA; Director 1968–91, and Deputy Chairman 1988–91, Thames Television PLC; *b* 20 March 1923; *s* of Clarence Reginald Davey and Ivy Ellender Davey (*née* Lippiatt); *m* 1962, Margaret June Cobby; two *d. Educ:* Richmond (Surrey) County Secondary Sch. Binder Hamlyn & Co., Chartered Accountants, 1939–55 (during which time served under Articles), Gp Accountant, British Lion Films Ltd, 1955–58; Co. Sec. and Financial Controller, Pulsometer Engrg Co. Ltd, 1958–61; British Electric Traction Co., later BET PLC, 1961–88: Chm. and/or Man. Dir, various subsids, and Main Bd Dir, 1978–88. *Address:* 20 Mulberry Hill, Shenfield, Brentwood, Essex CM15 8JS. *Died 8 May 1996.*

DAVID, Tudor, OBE 1984; freelance journalist and publisher; Publisher, Langham Legal Publishing, since 1998; *b* 25 April 1921; *s* of Thomas and Blodwen David; *m* 1st, 1943, Nancy Ramsay (*d* 1984); one *s* one *d*; 2nd, 1987, Margaret Dix. *Educ:* Barry Grammar Sch.; Univ. of Manchester (BA Hons); Univ. of Oxford. Technical Officer, RAF, 1942–47; Extra-mural Lectr, Univ. of Newcastle upon Tyne, 1947–49; Careers Officer, 1950–55; Asst Editor, Education, 1955–65; Editor, The Teacher, 1965–69; Managing Editor, Education, 1969–86. Mem., Welsh Acad., 1969–. FCP 1980. *Publications:* (ed) Scunthorpe and its Families, 1954; Defence and Disarmament, 1959; Church and School, 1963; (jtly) Perspectives in Geographical Education, 1973; (jtly) Education, the wasted years 1973–86, 1988. *Recreations:* Wales, the Isle of Dogs, opera. *Address:* 21 Pointers Close, Isle of Dogs, E14 3AP. *T:* (020) 7987 8631. *Club:* London Welsh. *Died 21 Feb. 2000.*

DAVIDSON, Francis, CBE 1961; Finance Officer, Singapore High Commission, London, 1961–71; *b* 23 Nov. 1905; *s* of James Davidson and Margaret Mackenzie; *m* 1937, Marial Mackenzie, MA (decd); one *s* one *d. Educ:* Millbank Public Sch., Nairn; Nairn Academy. Commercial Bank of Scotland Ltd, 1923–29; Bank of British West Africa Ltd, 1929–41; Colonial Service (Treasury), 1941–61; retired from Colonial Service, Nov. 1961, as Accountant-General of Federation of Nigeria. *Recreation:*

philately. *Address:* Woolton, Nairn, Scotland. *T:* (01667) 452187. *Club:* Royal Over Seas League. *Died 23 Dec. 1999.*

DAVIE; *see* Ferguson Davie.

DAVIES; *see* Llewelyn-Davies.

DAVIES; *see* Lloyd Davies.

DAVIES, Air Marshal Sir Alan (Cyril), KCB 1979 (CB 1974); CBE 1967; Co-ordinator of Anglo-American Relations, Ministry of Defence, 1984–94; *b* 31 March 1924; *s* of Richard Davies, Maidstone; *m* Julia Elizabeth Ghislaine Russell (*d* 1995); two *s* (and one *s* decd). Enlisted RAF, 1941; commnd 1943; comd Joint Anti-Submarine School Flight, 1952–54; comd Air Sea Warfare Development Unit, 1958–59; comd No 201 Sqdn, 1959–61; Air Warfare Coll., 1962; Dep. Dir, Operational Requirements, MoD, 1964–66; comd RAF Stradishall, Suffolk, 1967–68; idc 1969; Dir of Air Plans, MoD, 1969–72; ACAS (Policy), MoD, 1972–74; Dep. COS (Ops and Intell.), HQ Allied Air Forces Central Europe, 1974–77; Dep. C-in-C, RAF Strike Command, 1977; Dir, Internat. Mil. Staff, NATO, Brussels, 1978–81; Hd, Support Area Economy Review Team, RAF, 1981–83. Pres., Corps of Commissionaires, 1992 (Chm., 1989–92). *Address:* 10 Crispin Close, Caversham, Berks RG4 7JS. *Club:* Royal Air Force. *Died 27 Jan. 1998.*

DAVIES, Albert John; Chief Agricultural Officer, Agricultural Development and Advisory Service, Ministry of Agriculture, Fisheries and Food, 1971–79; *b* 21 Jan. 1919; *s* of David Daniel Davies and Annie Hilda Davies; *m* 1944, (Winnifred) Ivy (Caroline) Emberton; one *s* one *d. Educ:* Amman Valley Grammar Sch.; UCW Aberystwyth. BSc Hons Agric. 1940. FIBiol. Adv. Staff, UCW Aberystwyth, 1940–41; Asst Techn. Adviser, Montgomeryshire War Agricultural Cttee, 1941–44; Farm Supt, Welsh Plant Breeding Stn, 1944–47; National Agricultural Advisory Service: Crop Husbandry Adviser Wales, 1947–51; Grassland Husbandry Adviser Wales, 1951–57 and E Mids, 1957–59; Dep. Dir Wales, 1959–64; Regional Dir SW Region, 1964; Chief Farm Management Adviser, London Headquarters, 1964–67; Sen. Agric. Adviser, 1967–68; Dep. Dir, 1968–71. *Publications:* articles in learned jls and agric. press. *Recreations:* golf, Rugby, gardening. *Address:* Cefncoed, 38A Ewell Downs Road, Ewell, Surrey KT17 3BW. *T:* (020) 8393 0069. *Clubs:* Farmers'; Epsom Golf.

Died 30 April 1999.

DAVIES, Sir Alun Talfan, Kt 1976; QC 1961; *b* Gorseinon, 22 July 1913; *s* of late Rev. W. Talfan Davies, Presbyterian Minister, Gorseinon; *m* 1942, Eiluned Christopher, *d* of late Humphrey R. Williams, Stanmore, Middx; one *s* three *d. Educ:* Gowerton Grammar Sch.; Aberystwyth University Coll. of Wales (LLB; Hon. Professorial Fellow, 1971; Hon. Fellow, 1994); Gonville and Caius Coll., Cambridge (MA, LLB). Called to the Bar, Gray's Inn, 1939, Bencher, 1969. Recorder: of Merthyr Tydfil, 1963–68; of Swansea, 1968–69; of Cardiff, 1969–71; Hon. Recorder, 1972–86; Dep. Chm., Cardiganshire QS, 1963–71; a Recorder, 1972–85; Judge of the Courts of Appeal, Jersey and Guernsey, 1969–84. Member: Commn on the Constitution, 1969–73; Criminal Injuries Compensation Bd, 1977–85. President: Court of Nat. Eisteddfod of Wales, 1977–80; Court, Welsh Nat. Opera, 1978–80; Welsh Centre of Internat. Affairs, 1985–89; Wales Internat., 1991–. Dir, Cardiff World Trade Centre Ltd, 1985–97. Chm., Bank of Wales, 1991–96 (Dep. Chm., Commercial Bank of Wales, 1973–91; Dir, 1971–96); Dir, HTV Ltd, 1967–83 (Vice-Chm., and Chm. Welsh Bd, 1978–83); Vice-Chm., HTV (Group) Ltd, 1978–83. Chm. Trustees, Aberfan Fund (formerly Aberfan Disaster Fund), 1969–88. Mem. Court of University of

Wales and of Courts and Councils of Aberystwyth and Swansea University Colls. Hon. Fellow, Trinity Coll., Carmarthen, 1994. Hon. LLD Wales: Aberystwyth, 1973. Contested (Ind.) University of Wales (by-elec.), 1943; contested (L): Carmarthen Div., 1959 and 1964; Denbigh, 1966. *Address:* 18 The Grange, Baroness Place, Penarth, South Glam CF64 3UW. *T:* (029) 2070 1341. *Club:* Cardiff and County (Cardiff).

Died 11 Nov. 2000.

DAVIES, Prof. Arthur; Reardon-Smith Professor of Geography, University of Exeter, 1948–71; Deputy Vice-Chancellor, University of Exeter, 1969–71; Dean of the Faculty of Social Studies, 1961–64; *b* 13 March 1906; *s* of Richard Davies, Headmaster, and Jessie Starr Davies, Headmistress; *m* 1933, Lilian Margaret Morris (decd); one *d. Educ:* Cyfarthfa Castle Sch.; University Coll. of Wales, Aberystwyth. 1st cl. Hons in Geography and Anthropology, 1927; MSc Wales 1930. Fellow, University of Wales, 1929–30; Asst Lecturer in Geography, Manchester Univ., 1930–33; Lecturer in Geography, Leeds Univ., 1933–40. Served War of 1939–45: RA 1940–45, Normandy (despatches twice, Major; Lt Col, 1945); Mem., High Mil. Tribunal of Hamburg, 1945. Hon. FRGS 1982. *Publications:* Yugoslav Studies, Leplay Soc., London, 1932; Polish Studies, Leplay Soc., London, 1933; numerous papers in learned jls on Great Age of Discovery, Columbus, Drake (resolving California/San Francisco problem), John Lloyd's discovery of America in 1477, etc. *Recreations:* gardening, architecture. *Address:* Morlais, Winslade Park, Clyst St Mary, Devon EX5 1DA. *T:* (01392) 873296. *Died 15 April 1998.*

DAVIES, Sir David (Henry), Kt 1973; first Chairman, Welsh Development Agency, 1976–79; General Secretary, Iron and Steel Trades Confederation, 1967–75; *b* 2 Dec. 1909; *s* of David Henry Davies; British; *m* 1934, Elsie May Battrick; one *s* one *d* (and one *d* decd). *Educ:* Ebbw Vale, Mon. Organiser, 1950, Asst. Gen. Sec., 1953–66, Iron and Steel Trades Confederation. Chm., Jt Adv. Cttee on Safety and Health in the Iron and Steel Industry, 1965–67; Vice-Chm., Nat. Dock Labour Bd, 1966–68; Hon. Treas. WEA, 1962–69 (Mem. Central Council and Central Exec. Cttee, 1954–69); Hon. Treas., British Labour Party, 1965–67 (Chm., 1963; Mem. Nat. Exec., 1954–67); Hon. Sec., Brit. Sect., Internat. Metalworkers Federation, 1960; Member: Iron and Steel Operatives Course Adv. Cttee, City and Guilds of London Institute Dept of Technology, 1954–68; Iron and Steel Industry Trng Bd, 1964; Constructional Materials Gp, Economic Development Cttee for the Building and Civil Engrg Industries, 1965–68; Iron and Steel Adv. Cttee, 1967; English Industrial Estates Corporation, 1971; Vice-Pres., European Coal and Steel Community Consultative Cttee, 1975 (Pres., 1973–74). Governor: Ruskin Coll., Oxford, 1954–68; Iron and Steel Industry Management Trng Coll., Ashorne Hill, Leamington Spa, 1966. Member: Ebbw Vale UDC, 1945–50; TUC Gen. Council, 1967–75. Mem., RIIA, 1954. *Address:* 82 New House Park, St Albans, Herts AL1 1UP. *T:* (01727) 856513.

Died 6 April 1998.

DAVIES, Donald Watts, CBE 1983; FRS 1987; Consultant, Data Security, since 1984; *b* 7 June 1924; *s* of John and Hilda Davies; *m* 1955, Diane Lucy (*née* Burton); two *s* one *d. Educ:* Portsmouth Boys' Southern Secondary Sch.; Imperial Coll. of Science and Technology (ARCS, BSc (Physics, 1st cl. hons), 1943, BSc (Maths, 1st cl. hons), 1947). Wartime research, 1943–46; Nat. Physical Laboratory, 1947–84: pioneer of digital computing, 1947–50; pioneer of packet switching (data communication), 1965–70; Supt of Computer Science Div., 1966–78; Individual Merit DCSO, 1978–84. Consultant to financial insts for data security, 1976–. Vis.

Prof. RHBNC, London Univ., 1987–. Commonwealth Fund Fellow, 1954–55. Dist. Fellow, BCS, 1975. Hon. DSc Salford, 1989. Sir John Lubbock Prize in Maths, 1946; John Player Award, BCS, 1975; John von Neumann Award, J. v. Neumann Soc., Budapest, 1985. *Publications:* Digital Techniques, 1963; Communication Networks for Computers, 1973; Computer Networks and their Protocols, 1979; Security for Computer Networks, 1984, 2nd edn 1989; papers in learned jls. *Recreations:* mathematical games and puzzles, cipher machines of World War II, travel. *Died 28 May 2000.*

DAVIES, Glyn; see Davies, Thomas G.

DAVIES, Rev. Gwynne Henton; Principal, Regent's Park College, Oxford, 1958–72, Emeritus since 1973; *b* 19 Feb. 1906; *m* 1935, Annie Bronwen (*née* Williams), BA Wales; two *d. Educ:* Perse Sch., Cambridge; University College of South Wales, Cardiff (BD, MA); St Catherine's and Regent's Park Colls, Oxford Univ. (MLitt, MA); Marburg/Lahn, Germany. Minister, West End Baptist Church, London, W6, 1935–38; Tutor, Bristol Baptist Coll., 1938–51; Special Lecturer in Hebrew, University of Bristol, 1948–51; (first) Prof. of Old Testament Studies, Faculty of Theology, Durham Univ., 1951–58, Dean of Faculty, 1956. Select Preacher to the Universities of Cambridge and Oxford. Secretary, Society for Old Testament Study, 1946–62 (President, 1966). Vice-Pres., Baptist Union of GB and Ireland, 1970–71, Pres., 1971–72. OT Lecture, Pantyfedwen Foundn, 1975; Distinguished Visiting Professor: Meredith Coll., USA, 1978, 1979; William Jewell Coll., 1982, 1983. Vice Pres., Pembrokeshire History Soc., 1985–. Hon. Moderator, Penuel Baptist Ch., Manorbier, 1991–95. Hon. DD: Glasgow, 1958; Stetson, 1965. OT Editor, The Teachers' Commentary (revised 7th edn), 1955. *Publications:* (with A. B. Davies) The Story in Scripture, 1960; Exodus, 1967; Who's Who in the Bible, 1970; Deuteronomy, in Peake's Commentary on the Bible, rev. edn, 1962; 20 articles in The Interpreter's Bible Dictionary, 1962; The Ark in the Psalms, in Promise and Fulfilment (ed F. F. Bruce), 1963; essay in R. Goldman's Breakthrough, 1968; Genesis, in The Broadman Bible Commentary, 1969; Gerhard von Rad, in OT Theology in Contemporary Discussion (ed R. Laurin). *Address:* 50 Whitlow, Saundersfoot, Dyfed SA69 9AE. *T:* (01834) 813750. *Died 22 Oct. 1998.*

DAVIES, Dame Jean; see Lancaster, Dame J.

DAVIES, John Alun Emlyn; retired 1977; *b* 4 May 1909; *s* of Robert Emlyn and Mary Davies; *m* 1941, Elizabeth Boshier (decd); three *s. Educ:* Ruabon Grammar Sch.; Trinity Coll., Cambridge (Scholar). BA 1st cl. Pts I and II, History Tripos; MA 1984. Called to Bar, Lincoln's Inn, 1936. Served War of 1939–45: DAA&QMG 2nd Parachute Bde, 1943; DAAG 1st Airborne Div., 1944. Joined BoT, 1946; Asst Solicitor, 1963; Principal Asst Solicitor, DTI, 1968–72; Asst Solicitor, Law Commn, 1972–74; part-time Asst, Law Commn, 1974–77. Asst Sec. to Jenkins Cttee on Company Law, 1959–62. *Recreations:* gardening, walking. *Address:* 29 Crescent Road, Sidcup, Kent DA15 7HN. *T:* (0181) 300 1421.

Died 12 July 1997.

DAVIES, John Howard Gay; Editorial Director, Thomson Regional Newspapers Ltd, 1972–82; *b* 17 Jan. 1923; *er s* of late Edgar and Beatrice (Gay) Davies, Nicholaston, Gower; *m* 1st, 1948, Eira Morgan (marr. diss. 1953); 2nd, 1955, Betty Walmsley; one *s. Educ:* Bromsgrove Sch.; Wadham Coll., Oxford (Exhibnr; MA). Lieut, Welsh Guards, 1942–46 (despatches). Western Mail, 1950–52; Daily Telegraph, 1952–55; Deputy Editor, Western Mail, 1955–58; an Assistant Editor, Sunday Times, 1958–62; Exec. Assistant to Editorial Director, Thomson Newspapers Ltd, 1962–64; Editor, Western Mail, 1964,

1965. *Address:* 46 Coalecroft Road, SW15 6LP. *Club:* Naval and Military. *Died 3 Feb. 2000.*

DAVIES, Sir Oswald, Kt 1984; CBE 1973; DCM 1944; Director, AMEC plc (holding company of Fairclough Construction Group and William Press Group), since 1982 (Chairman, 1982–84); *b* 23 June 1920; *s* of George Warham Davies and Margaret (*née* Hinton); *m* 1942, Joyce Eaton; one *s* one *d. Educ:* Central Schs, Sale; Manchester Coll. of Technology. FIHT, FCIOB, FFB; CIMgt; FRGS; FRSA. Served War of 1939–45: Sapper, bomb disposal squad, RE, Europe and ME, from 1940 (DCM (ME) 1944); returned to Europe, where involved with his unit in clearance of waterways, port, docks and bridge reconstruction. Dir, 1948–, Jt Man. Dir, 1951, Chm., 1965–83, Fairclough Construction Group plc (formerly Leonard Fairclough Ltd). *Recreations:* gardening, sport. *Address:* (office) AMEC plc, Sandiway House, Northwich, Cheshire CW8 2YA. *T:* Northwich (01606) 883885. *Died 14 June 1996.*

DAVIES, (Thomas) Glyn, CBE 1966; *b* 16 Aug. 1905; *s* of Thomas Davies, Gwaelod-y-Garth, Cardiff; *m* 1935, Margaret Berry; one *d. Educ:* Pontypridd Grammar Sch.; Univ. of Wales, Cardiff (MA). Asst Master, Howard Gardens High Sch., Cardiff, 1927–37; Warden, Educational Settlement, Pontypridd, 1937–43; Director of Education: Montgomeryshire, 1943–58; Denbighshire, 1958–70, retd. Mem. ITA, later IBA, 1970–75. Mem., Court and Council, UC Bangor. Fellow, UC Cardiff, 1981. *Recreations:* travel, music. *Address:* 42 Park Avenue, Wrexham, Clwyd LL12 7AH. *T:* (01978) 352697. *Died 8 Jan. 1997.*

DAVIS, Rt Rev. Brian Newton, CNZM 1997; Primate and Archbishop of New Zealand, 1986–97; Bishop of Wellington, 1986–97, *b* 28 Oct. 1934; *s* of Leonard Luncelot and Ethel May Davis; *m* 1961, Marie Lynette Waters: four *d. Educ:* Stratford Primary and Technical High School; Ardmore Teachers' Training Coll., Auckland; Victoria Univ. of Wellington (MA 1st class Hons Geog.); Christchurch Theol Coll. (LTh). Teacher, Stratford Primary School, 1954; Laboratory Asst, Victoria Univ., 1958. Deacon 1960, priest 1961; Assistant Curate: St Mark's, Wellington, 1960–62; Parish of Karori West and Makara, 1962–64; Vicar: Karori West and Makara, 1964–67; Dannevirke, 1967–73; Cathedral Parish of St John the Evangelist and Dean of Waiapu, 1973; Vicar General of Waiapu, 1979–80; Bishop of Waikato, 1980–86. *Publications:* (contrib.) An Encyclopaedia of New Zealand, 1966; The Way Ahead: Anglican change and prospect in New Zealand, 1995. *Recreations:* tennis, wood carving and turning, water colour painting. *Address:* 1 Wells Place, Tamatea, Napier, New Zealand. *Died 22 June 1998.*

DAVIS, Sir Charles (Sigmund), Kt 1965; CB 1960; Counsel to the Speaker (European Legislation), (formerly Second Counsel), House of Commons, 1974–83; *b* London, 22 Jan. 1909; *y s* of late Maurice Davis (*b* Melbourne, Australia) and Alfreda Regina Davis; *m* 1940, Pamela Mary (*d* 1997), *er d* of late J. K. B. Dawson, OBE, and Phyllis Dawson; two *d. Educ:* Trinity Coll., Cambridge. Double 1st Cl. Hons, Law Tripos; Sen. Schol., Exhibitioner and Prizeman of Trinity, 1927–30; MA 1934. Called to the Bar, Inner Temple (Studentship and Certif. of Honour), 1930, and in Sydney, Australia, 1931; practised as barrister in London, 1931–34; entered Legal Branch, Ministry of Health, 1934; held legal posts in various public offices, 1938–46 (Corporal, Home Guard, 1940–45); Asst Solicitor, Min. of Agric. and Fisheries, 1946–55; Prin. Asst Solicitor, MAFF, 1955–57; Legal Adviser and Solicitor, MAFF, and Forestry Commission, 1957–74, retired. Vice-Pres., Macmillan Cancer Relief (formerly Nat. Soc. for Cancer Relief), 1989– (Chm.

Council, 1983–85; Trustee, 1985–89). *Recreations:* music (LRAM, ARCM) and much else. *Address:* 9 Beech Court, 33b Arterberry Road, SW20 8AG. *Died 25 May 1999.*

DAVIS, Chloë Marion, OBE 1975; Chairman, Consumer Affairs Group of National Organisations, 1973–79; Member: Council on Tribunals, 1970–79; Consumer Standards Advisory Committee of British Standards Institution, 1965–78 (Chairman 1970–73); *b* Dartmouth, Devon, 15 Feb. 1909; *d* of Richard Henry Pound and Mary Jane Chapman; *m* 1928, Edward Thomas Davis (*d* 1983), printer and sometime writer; one *s. Educ:* limited formal, USA and England. Various part-time voluntary social and public services from 1929; Birth Control Internat. Information Centre, 1931–38; voluntary activity in bombing etc emergencies, also cookery and domestic broadcasting during War of 1939–45; information service for Kreis Resident Officers, Control Commn for Germany, Berlin, 1946–48; regional Citizens Advice Bureaux office, London Council of Social Service, 1949–55; Sen. Information Officer to Nat. Citizens Advice Bureaux Council, 1956–69. Member: Nat. House-Building Council, 1973–76; Consumer Consultative Cttee, EEC, 1973–76; Exec. Cttee, Housewife's Trust, 1970–77. *Recreations:* reading present history in the morning in newspapers and past history in books in the evening, gardening, walking, talking with friends. *Address:* Auberville Cottage, 246 Dover Road, Walmer, Kent CT14 7NP. *T:* (01304) 374038. *Died 8 Jan. 2000.*

DAVIS, David; *see* Davis, William Eric.

DAVIS, Hon. Sir (Dermot) Renn, Kt 1981; OBE 1971; **Hon. Mr Justice Davis;** Chief Justice, Supreme Court of the Falkland Islands, since 1987; Judge, Supreme Court of the British Antarctic Territory, since 1988, Judge, Court of Appeal for Gibraltar, since 1989; of St Helena, since 1991; for the British Indian Ocean Territory, since 1991; *b* 20 Nov. 1928; *s* of Captain Eric R. Davis, OBE and Norah A. Davis (*née* Bingham); *m* 1984, Mary, *d* of late Brig. T. F. K. Howard, DSO, RA, and *widow* of William James Pearce. *Educ:* Prince of Wales Sch., Nairobi; Wadham Coll., Oxford (BA Hons). Called to the Bar, Inner Temple, 1953; Daly and Figgis, Advocates, Nairobi, 1953–56; Attorney-General's Chambers, Kenya, 1956–62; Attorney-General, British Solomon Islands Protectorate, and Legal Advr, Western Pacific High Commn, 1962–73; British Judge, New Hebrides Condominium, 1973–76; Chief Justice, Solomon Islands, 1976–80 and Chief Justice, Tuvalu, 1978–80; Chief Justice, Gibraltar, 1980–86. *Recreations:* music, walking. *Address:* The Supreme Court, Stanley, Falkland Islands; c/o Barclays Bank, 30 High Street, Hungerford, Berks RG17 0NQ. *Clubs:* United Oxford & Cambridge University; Muthaiga Country (Nairobi); Royal Gibraltar Yacht. *Died 6 June 1997.*

DAVIS, Godfrey Rupert Carless, CBE 1981; FSA; Secretary, Royal Commission on Historical Manuscripts, 1972–81; *b* 22 April 1917; *s* of late Prof. Henry William Carless Davis and Rosa Jennie Davis (*née* Lindup); *m* 1942, Dorothie Elizabeth Mary Loveband (*d* 1994); one *s* two *d. Educ:* Highgate Sch.; Balliol Coll., Oxford (MA, DPhil). Rome Scholar in Ancient History, 1938. Army Service, 1939–46, Devon Regt and Intell. Corps, Captain 1942. Dept of MSS, British Museum: Asst Keeper, 1947; Dep. Keeper, 1961–72. FRHistS 1954 (Treas. 1967–74); FSA 1974. *Publications:* Medieval Cartularies of Great Britain, 1958; Magna Carta, 1963; contrib. British Museum Cat. Add. MSS 1926–1950 (6 vols); learned jls. *Died 27 Sept. 1997.*

DAVIS, Hon. Sir Renn; *see* Davis, Hon. Sir D. R.

DAVIS, Sir Rupert Charles H.; *see* Hart-Davis.

DAVIS, William Eric, (professionally known as **David Davis**), MBE 1969; MA Oxon; LRAM, ARCM; *b* 27 June 1908; *s* of William John and Florence Kate Rachel Davis; *m* 1935, Barbara de Riemer (*d* 1982); one *s* two *d. Educ:* Bishop's Stortford Coll.; The Queen's Coll., Oxford (MA). Schoolmaster, 1931–35; joined BBC as mem. of Children's Hour, 1935; served with RNVR Acting Temp. Lieut, 1942–46; BBC, 1946–70; Head of Children's Hour, BBC, 1953–61; Head of Children's Programmes (Sound), BBC, 1961–64; Producer, Drama Dept, 1964–70, retired. *Publications:* various songs, etc including: Lullaby, 1943; Fabulous Beasts, 1948; Little Grey Rabbit Song Book, 1952; *poetry:* A Single Star, 1973; various speech recordings, including: Black Beauty; Just So Stories; The Wind in the Willows (complete text), 1986. *Recreations:* children, cats, growing roses. *Address:* 18 Mount Avenue, W5 2RG. *T:* 0181–997 8156. *Club:* Garrick.
Died 29 April 1996.

DAVSON, Sir Geoffrey Leo Simon, 2nd Bt; *see* Glyn, Sir Anthony, 2nd Bt.

DAWE, Donovan Arthur; Principal Keeper, Guildhall Library, London, 1967–73, retired; *b* 21 Jan. 1915; *s* of late Alfred Ernest and Sarah Jane Dawe, Wallington, Surrey; *m* 1946, Peggy Marjory Challen; two *d. Educ:* Sutton Grammar Sch. Associate, Library Assoc., 1938. Entered Guildhall Library as junior assistant, 1931. Served with Royal West African Frontier Force in Africa and India, 1941–46. Freeman of City of London and Merchant Taylors' Company, 1953. FRHistS 1954. *Publications:* Skilbecks: drysalters 1650–1950, 1950; 11 Ironmonger Lane: the story of a site in the City of London, 1952; The City of London: a select book list, 1972; Organists of the City of London 1666–1850, 1983; contribs professional literature, Connoisseur, Musical Times, Genealogists' Magazine, etc. *Recreations:* the countryside, local history, musicology. *Address:* 46 Green Lane, Purley, Surrey CR8 3PJ. *T:* 0181–660 4218.
Died 13 July 1996.

DAWES, Prof. Geoffrey Sharman, CBE 1981; FRS 1971; Director of Charing Cross Medical Research Centre, 1984–89; *b* 21 Jan. 1918; *s* of Rev. W. Dawes, Thurlaston Grange, Derbyshire; *m* 1941, Margaret Monk; two *s* two *d. Educ:* Repton Sch.; New Coll., Oxford. BA 1939; BSc 1940; BM, BCh 1943; DM 1947. Rockefeller Travelling Fellowship, 1946; Fellow, Worcester Coll., Oxford, 1946–85, Emeritus Fellow, 1985; University Demonstrator in Pharmacology, Oxford, 1947; Foulerton Research Fellow, Royal Society, 1948; Dir, Nuffield Inst. for Medical Research, Oxford, 1948–85. Mem., MRC, 1978–82; Chm., Physiological Systems and Disorders Bd, MRC, 1978–80. Chm., Lister Inst. for Preventive Medicine, 1988. Governor of Repton, 1959–88, Chm., 1971–85. A Vice-Pres., Royal Society, 1976, 1977. FRCOG, FRCP; Hon. FACOG. Max Weinstein Award, 1963; Gairdner Foundation Award, 1966; Maternité Award of European Assoc. Perinatal Medicine, 1976; Virginia Apgar Award, Amer. Acad. of Pediatrics, 1980; Osler Meml Medal, Oxford Univ., 1990. *Publications:* Foetal and Neonatal Physiology, 1968; various publications in physiological, pharmacological and obstetric journals. *Recreation:* fishing. *Address:* 8 Belbroughton Road, Oxford OX2 6UZ. *T:* Oxford (01865) 58131.
Died 6 May 1996.

DAWSON, Sir Anthony (Michael), KCVO 1993; MD; FRCP; Physician to the Royal Household, 1974–82, to the Queen, 1982–93, and Head of HM Medical Household, 1989–93; Physician, King Edward VII Hospital for Officers, since 1968; Consulting Physician, St Bartholomew's Hospital, since 1986 (Physician, 1965–86); *b* 8 May 1928; *s* of Leslie Joseph Dawson and Mabel Jayes; *m* 1956, Barbara Anne Baron Forsyth, *d* of late Thomas Forsyth, MB, ChB; two *d. Educ:* Wyggeston

Sch., Leicester; Charing Cross Hosp. Med. Sch. MB, BS 1951, MD 1959, London; MRCP 1954, FRCP 1964. Jun. appts, Charing Cross Hosp., Brompton Hosp., Royal Postgrad. Med. Sch., Central Middlesex Hosp., 1951–57; MRC and US Public Health Res. Fellow, Harvard Med. Sch. at Massachusetts Gen. Hosp., 1957–59; Lectr and Sen. Lectr in Medicine, Royal Free Hosp. Med. Sch., 1959–65; formerly Physician, King Edward VII Convalescent Home for Officers, Osborne. Hon. Sec., Assoc. of Physicians of Gt Britain and Ireland, 1973–78, Treasurer 1978–83. Examnr, London and Oxford, MRCP; Censor, RCP, 1977–78, Treasurer, 1985–91; Treasurer, St Bartholomew's Hosp. Med. Coll., 1976–79, Vice-Pres., 1979–84; Vice-Chm., Bd of Management, King Edward's Hosp. Fund for London, 1978–93; Chm., Med. Coll. of St Bartholomew's Hosp. Trust, 1986–. Chairman: Council, BHF, 1993–96; Exec. Cttee, Royal Med. Benevolent Fund, 1996–; Treas., British Digestive Foundn, 1992–; Trustee, Distressed Gentlefolk's Aid Assoc., 1994–; Special Trustee, St Bartholomew's and St Mark's Hosps, 1994–; Council, QMW, 1996–. *Publications:* contrib. med. books and jls. *Recreations:* music, gardening. *Address:* Thorpe View, The Green, Culworth, Banbury, Oxon OX17 2BB. *Club:* Garrick.
Died 25 Sept. 1997.

DAWSON, John Leonard, CVO 1992; FRCS; Surgeon: King's College Hospital, 1964–94; Bromley Hospital, 1967–94; King Edward VII Hospital for Officers, 1975–94; Dean of the Faculty of Clinical Medicine, King's College School of Medicine and Dentistry, 1988–92; *b* 30 Sept. 1932; *s* of Leslie Joseph Dawson and Mabel Annie Jayes; *m* 1958, Rosemary Brundle; two *s* one *d. Educ:* Wyggeston Boys' Grammar Sch., Leicester; King's College Hosp., Univ. of London. MB, BS 1955, MS 1964; FRCS 1958. Served RAMC, 1958–60. Surgeon to Royal Household, 1975–83; Surgeon to the Queen, 1983–90, Serjeant Surgeon, 1990–91. Nuffield Scholarship, Harvard Univ., 1963–64; Sir Arthur Sims Travelling Prof., Australasia, 1981. Examiner in Surgery: Univs. of London, 1966–94, and Cambridge, 1980–83; Soc. of Apothecaries; Primary FRCS, 1974–80; Mem. Ct of Examrs, RCS, 1981–89. Mem. Council, Med. Protection Soc., 1979–88. Vice-Chm., British Jl of Surgery, 1981–89. *Publications:* contribs to surgical textbooks and jls on abdominal surgery. *Recreations:* theatre, gardening, reading. *Address:* 107 Burbage Road, Dulwich, SE21 7AF. *T:* (020) 7733 3668.
Died 16 May 1999.

DAWSON-MORAY, Edward Bruce, CMG 1969; HM Diplomatic Service, retired; *b* 30 June 1909; *s* of late Alwyn Bruce Dawson-Moray and Ada (*née* Burlton); *m* 1st, 1933, Ursula Frances (*née* Woodbridge) (marr. diss. 1969); one *s* one *d* (and one *d* decd); 2nd, 1970, Beryl Barber (*d* 1998). *Educ:* Cranbrook Sch.; University of London (BA Hons). Housemaster, Chillon Coll., Switzerland, 1938–42; British Legation, Berne, 1942; 3rd Secretary, 1944; 3rd Secretary and Vice-Consul, Rome, 1947–48; Consul: Leopoldville, 1948–50; Detroit, 1950–51; 1st Secretary and Consul, Rangoon, 1952–54; Information Officer and Consul, Naples, 1954–56; Foreign Office, 1956–60; Consul, Casablanca, 1960–63; Chief Establishment Officer, Diplomatic Wireless Service, 1963–69; Civil Service Dept, 1969–74, retired; Dir, Pre-retirement Training, CSD, 1975–82. Senior Editor, Foreign Office List, 1957–60. *Recreations:* literature, photography, opera, travel. *Address:* West Winds, Lighthouse Road, St Margaret's Bay, Dover, Kent CT15 6EJ. *T:* (01304) 852805.
Died 17 July 1999.

DAY, John King, TD; MA; Principal, Elizabeth College, Guernsey, CI, 1958–71; *b* Ipoh, Perak, FMS, 27 Oct. 1909; *s* of Harold Duncan Day, mining engineer, and Muriel Edith Day; *m* 1935, Mary Elizabeth Stinton, *er d*

of late Tom Stinton, Headmaster of the High Sch., Newcastle-under-Lyme; three *s. Educ:* Stamford Sch.; Magdalen Coll., Oxford (Demy 1928–32; Honour School of Natural Science (Chemistry) Class 2, BSc 1935). Assistant Master, Kendal Sch., Westmorland, 1932; Asst Master and Housemaster, Gresham's Sch., 1933–57. Served Royal Norfolk Regt (7th Bn) and Military College of Science, 1939–45. *Recreations:* walking, fishing, sketching. *Address:* 1 Pearson's Road, Holt, Norfolk NR25 6EJ. *T:* (01263) 713435. *Died 8 Oct. 1997.*

DAY, Sir Robin, Kt 1981; television and radio journalist; *b* 24 Oct. 1923; *s* of late William and Florence Day; *m* 1965, Katherine Ainslie (marr. diss. 1986); two *s. Educ:* Bembridge Sch.; St Edmund Hall, Oxford (Hon. Fellow, 1989). Military service, 1943–47; commnd RA, 1944. Oxford, 1947–51: Union debating tour of American universities, 1949; President, Oxford Union, 1950; BA Hons (Jurisprudence), 1951; MA. Middle Temple: Blackstone Entrance Scholar, 1951; Harmsworth Law Scholar, 1952–53; called to the Bar, 1952; Hon. Bencher, 1990. British Information Services, Washington, 1953–54; BBC Talks Producer (radio), 1955; Newscaster and Parliamentary Correspondent, Independent Television News, 1955–59; columnist in News Chronicle, 1959; ITV programmes, 1955–59: Roving Report (ITN); Tell the People (ITN); Under Fire (Granada); BBC TV programmes, 1959–, included: Panorama, Gallery, People to Watch, Daytime, 24 Hours, Midweek, To-night, Sunday Debate, Talk-in, Newsday; Question Time, 1979–89; The Elder Statesmen, 1992, 1997; The Parliament Programme (ITN), 1992; Robin Day's Book Talk, 1997–98; BBC radio programmes: It's Your Line, 1970–76; Election Call, 1974, 1979, 1983, 1987; The World at One, 1979–87. Chm., Hansard Soc., 1981–83. Mem., Phillimore Cttee on Law of Contempt, 1971–74. Contested (L) Hereford, 1959. Hon. LLD: Exeter, 1986; Keele, 1988; DU Essex, 1988. Guild of TV Producers' Merit Award, Personality of the Year, 1957; Richard Dimbleby Award for factual television, 1974; Broadcasting Press Guild Award, for Question Time, 1980; RTS Judges' Award for 30 yrs TV journalism, 1985; RTS Hall of Fame, 1995. *Publications:* Television: a Personal Report, 1961; The Case for Televising Parliament, 1963; Day by Day, 1975; Grand Inquisitor—memoirs, 1989; … But With Respect—memorable interviews, 1993; Speaking for Myself, 1999. *Recreations:* reading, talking, walking. *Clubs:* Garrick, Royal Automobile. *Died 6 Aug. 2000.*

DEACON ELLIOTT, Air Vice-Marshal Robert, CB 1967; OBE 1954; DFC 1941; AE 1944 (2 mentions); *b* 20 Nov. 1914; *s* of Frank Deacon Elliott, Church Brampton, Northants; *m* 1948, Grace Joan Willes, Leamington Spa; two *s* one *d. Educ:* Northampton. 72 Fighter Sqdn (Dunkirk and Battle of Britain), 1939–41; HQ Fighter Comd, 1942–43; 84 Group 2 ATAF, 1944–46; Air Ministry (OR 5), 1946–48; OC Flying Wing and OC 26 Armoured Personnel Carrier in Cyprus, 1948–51; HQ Fighter Comd, Head of Admin. Plans, 1951–54; Army Staff Coll., on Directing Staff, 1954–56; CO, RAF Leconfield, 1956–57; CO, RAF Driffield, 1957–58; Air University USAF, Maxwell AFB, USA, 1958–61; Commandant, Officer and Aircrew Selection Centre, 1962–65; AOC, RAF Gibraltar, 1965–66; AOC, RAF Malta, and Dep. C-in-C (Air), Allied Forces Mediterranean, 1966–68, retd; Bursar, Civil Service Coll., 1969–79. *Recreations:* shooting, photography. *Address:* Thor House, Old Roar Road, St Leonards-on-Sea, E Sussex TN37 7HH. *T:* (01424) 752699. *Club:* Royal Air Force. *Died 5 June 1997.*

DEAN OF BESWICK, Baron *cr* 1983 (Life Peer), of West Leeds in the County of West Yorkshire; **Joseph Jabez Dean;** *b* 3 June 1922; *s* of John Dean; *m* 1945, Helen Hill

(*d* 1998). Engineer; formerly Shop Steward, AUEW. Formerly Leader, Manchester City Council. MP (Lab) Leeds West, Feb. 1974–1983; contested (Lab) same seat, 1983; PPS to Minister of State, CSD, 1974–77; an Asst Govt Whip, 1978–79; Opposition Pairing Whip, 1982–83; an Opposition Whip, H of L, 1983–97; Opposition spokesman on Energy, 1991–92; formerly Opposition spokesman on Nat. Heritage (Sport) and on Housing. *Address:* House of Lords, SW1A 0PW.
Died 26 Feb. 1999.

DEAR, Hon. Sir John (Stanley Bruce), KCMG 1996; CHB 1981; QC 1963; Attorney-at-Law; *b* 18 July 1925; *s* of Cyril Bruce Dear and Marie Elizabeth Dear (*née* Plummer); *m* 1949, Jeanne Dylis Rawlins; two *s* one *d. Educ:* Harrison Coll., Barbados; Pembroke Coll., Cambridge (MA). Called to the Bar, Middle Temple, 1947; admitted to practice in Barbados, 1948. *Recreations:* bridge, reading, seabathing. *Address:* Epworth Chambers, Pinfold Street, Bridgetown, Barbados. *T:* (246) 4296750. *Clubs:* Commonwealth Trust; Barbados Yacht, Summerhayes Tennis. *Died 2 April 1997.*

DEARNLEY, Christopher Hugh, LVO 1990; DMus; FRCO, FRSCM; Organist and Director of Music, St Paul's Cathedral, 1968–90; *b* 11 Feb. 1930; 3rd *s* of Rev. Charles Dearnley and Gertrude Dearnley (*née* Smith); *m* 1957, Bridget (*née* Wateridge); three *s* one *d. Educ:* Cranleigh Sch., Surrey; Worcester Coll., Oxford (Organ Scholar, 1948–52; BMus 1955; MA). FRCO 1954; FRSCM 1996. Asst Organist, Salisbury Cathedral, and Music Master, the Cathedral Sch., Salisbury, 1954–57; Organist and Master of the Choristers, Salisbury Cathedral, 1957–67; Acting Dir of Music, Christ Church, St Laurence, Sydney, 1990–91; Organist *locum tenens*, St David's Cathedral, Hobart, 1991; Dir of Music, Trinity Coll., Univ. of Melbourne, 1992–93; Organist and Master of Choristers, St George's Cathedral, Perth, 1993–94; Acting Organist and Master of Choristers: St Andrew's Cathedral, Sydney, 1995; Christ Church Cathedral, Newcastle, 1996. Pres., Incorporated Assoc. of Organists, 1968–70; Chairman: Friends of Cathedral Music, 1971–90 (Vice-Pres., 1990–); Harwich Festival, 1982–89 (Pres., 1989–); Percy Whitlock Trust, 1982–89 (Pres., 1989–). Dir, English Hymnal Co., 1970–94. Patron: Nat. Accordion Orgn, 1989–; Organ Historical Trust of Australia, 1990–; Hon. Gov., Corp. of Sons of the Clergy, 1989–. Hon. FGCM. *Publications:* The Treasury of English Church Music, Vol. III, 1965; English Church Music 1650–1750, 1970. *Recreations:* sketching, gardening, bush walking. *Address:* PO Box 102, Wilberforce, NSW 2756, Australia. *T:* (2) 45750453. *Died 15 Dec. 2000.*

de BOER, Anthony Peter, CBE 1982; Vice-Chairman, Royal Automobile Club, 1985–90, retired (Member, Committee, 1984–90); *b* 22 June 1918; *s* of Goffe de Boer and Irene Kathleen (*née* Grist); *m* 1942, Pamela Agnes Norah Bullock; one *s. Educ:* Westminster School. Served War of 1939–45: RE (AA), 1939–40; Indian Army, 6th Gurkha Rifles, 1940–43; RIASC, 1944–46; Major 1944. Joined Royal Dutch/Shell Gp, 1937: served in China, Sudan, Ethiopia, Egypt, Palestine, 1946–58; Area Co-ordinator, Africa and Middle East, 1959–63; Chm., Shell Trinidad, 1963–64; Man. Dir, Marketing, Shell Mex & BP, 1964–67; Deputy Chairman: Wm Cory & Son, 1968–71; Associated Heat Services Ltd, 1969–76; Chairman: Anvil Petroleum plc (formerly Attock Oil Co.), 1974–85; Tomatin Distillers plc, 1978–85; Steel Brothers Hldgs, 1980–87 (Dir, 1971–87); Channel Tunnel Develts (1981), 1981–84; Director: Nat. Bus Co., 1969–83; Tarmac plc, 1971–83; British Transport Advertising, 1973–83; Chloride Gp, 1976–85; Burmah Oil plc, 1978–85; Mem. Policy Cttee, Price Waterhouse, 1979–86. Chm., British Road Fedn, 1972–87 (Vice-Pres., 1987–); Dir, Internat.

Road Fedn, 1974–87. Mem., Bd, British Travel Assoc., 1965–67. Chm., Keep Britain Tidy Gp, 1969–79 (Vice-Pres., 1979–). Mem. Council, CBI, 1980–83; Mem. Court, Sussex Univ., 1991– (Mem. Council, 1969–91); Chm., Indep. Schools Careers Org., 1973–88 (Vice-Pres., 1988–); Pres., Fuel Luncheon Club, 1967–69; Dir, Brighton and Hove Albion Football Club, 1969–72. Freeman, City of London; Liveryman, Coach Makers' and Coach Harness Makers' Co. FIMgt (FBIM 1970; Mem. Council 1974). *Recreations:* racing, theatre, gardening. *Address:* Southmead, South Avenue, Hurstpierpoint, Hassocks, W Sussex BN6 9QB. *T:* (01273) 833068. *Club:* Royal Automobile. *Died 24 April 1999.*

de BOTTON, Gilbert; Chairman, Global Asset Management Ltd, since 1983; *b* 16 Feb. 1935; *s* of Jacques and Yolande de Botton; *m* 1st, 1962, Jacqueline (*née* Burgauer) (marr. diss. 1988); one *s* one *d*; 2nd, 1990, Hon. Mrs Janet Green, *d* of Baron Wolfson. *Educ:* Victoria College, Alexandria, Egypt; Hebrew Univ., Jerusalem (BA Econ 1955); Columbia Univ. (MA 1957). Ufitec SA Union Financière, Zürich, 1960–68; Managing Director, Rothschild Bank AG, Zürich, 1968–82. Trustee, Tate Gallery, 1985–92. *Address:* Global Asset Management (UK) Ltd, 12 St James's Place, SW1A 1NX. *T:* (office) (020) 7493 9990. *Clubs:* Athenæum, Carlton. *Died 27 Aug. 2000.*

DEBRÉ, Michel Jean-Pierre; Membre de l'Académie française, 1988; Deputy from La Réunion, French National Assembly, 1963–88 (re-elected 1967, 1968, 1973, 1978, 1981, 1982); *b* 15 Jan. 1912; *s* of late Prof. Robert Debré and Dr Jeanne Debré (*née* Debat-Ponsan); *m* 1936, Anne-Marie Lemaresquier; four *s*. *Educ:* Lycée Louis-le-Grand; Faculté de Droit de Paris (LLD); Ecole Libre des Sciences Politiques; Cavalry Sch., Saumur. Auditeur, Conseil d'Etat, 1934; French Army, 1939–40; Résistance clandestine, 1941–44; Commissaire de la République, Angers region, 1944–45; Saar Economic Mission, 1947; Secretary-General for German and Austrian Affairs, 1948. Senator from Indre et Loire, 1948, re-elected 1955; Minister of Justice, 1958–59; Prime Minister, 1959–62; Minister of Economic Affairs and Finances, 1966–68; Minister for Foreign Affairs, 1968–69; Minister for National Defence, 1969–73. Member, European Parliament, 1979–80. Mem. from Amboise, Conseil Général of Indre-et-Loire, 1951–70, 1976–82 and 1988; Mayor of Amboise, 1966–89. Member, Rassemblement pour la République. Officer Légion d'Honneur, Croix de Guerre, Rosette of Résistance, Free French Medal, Medal of Escaped Prisoners. *Publications:* La Mort de l'Etat Républicain, 1947; La République et son Pouvoir, 1950; La République et ses Problèmes, 1952; Ces Princes qui nous Gouvernent, 1957; Au Service de la Nation, 1963; Jeunesse, quelle France te faut-il?, 1965; (with Jean-Louis Debré) Le gaullisme, 1967; Une certaine idée de la France, 1972; Combat pour les Elections, 1973; Une Politique pour la Réunion, 1974; Ami ou Ennemi du Peuple, 1975; Français, choisissons l'espoir, 1979; Lettre ouverte aux Français sur la reconquête de la France, 1980; Peut-on lutter contre le chômage?, 1982; Trois Républiques pour une France (mémoires): vol. I, Combattre, 1984; vol. II, Agir, 1988; vol. III, Gouverner, 1988; vol. IV, Gouverner autrement, 1993; vol. V, Combattre toujours, 1994; Entretiens avec le Général de Gaulle, 1993; Entretiens avec Georges Pompidou, 1996; as de Jacquier (with M. Emmanuel Monick): Refaire la France, 1944; Demain la Paix, 1945. *Recreation:* equitation. *Address:* 20 rue Jacob, 75006 Paris, France. *Died 2 Aug. 1996.*

de BRUYNE, Dr Norman Adrian, FRS 1967; FEng 1976; Chairman, Techne Inc., 1973–88 (President, 1967–73); *b* 8 Nov. 1904; *s* of Pieter Adriaan de Bruyne and Maud de Bruyne (*née* Mattock); *m* 1940, Elma Lilian Marsh; one *s* one *d. Educ:* Lancing Coll.; Trinity Coll., Cambridge. MA 1930, PhD 1930. Fellow of Trinity Coll., Cambridge, 1928–44. Managing Director: Aero Research Ltd, 1934–48; Ciba (ARL) Ltd, 1948–60; Techne (Cambridge) Ltd, 1964–67. Dir, Eastern Electricity Bd, 1962–67. Awarded Simms Gold Medal, RAeS, 1937. FInstP 1944; FRAeS 1955; *Recreation:* inventing. *Address:* Pyne's House, 8 Chapel Street, Duxford, Cambridge CB2 4RJ. *T:* (01223) 832109; 3700 Brunswick Pike, Princeton, NJ 08540, USA. *T:* (609) 4529275.

Died 7 March 1997.

de COURCY, Kenneth Hugh; (Duc de Grantmesnil); Chancellor, Order of the Three Orders, since 1977; Chairman, Kilbrittain Newspapers, since 1987; *b* 6 Nov. 1909; 2nd *s* of late Stephen de Courcy (*s* of 8th Duc de Grantmesnil), Co. Galway and Hollinwood Mission, and Minnie de Courcy (*née* Schafer), *d* of late Frederick and Sophia Schafer-Andres, Schloss Kyburgh, Kirn am Nahe; *m* 1950, Rosemary Catherine (marr. diss. 1973), *o d* of late Comdr H. L. S. Baker, OBE, RN (retired), Co. Roscommon, Eire; two *s* two *d. Educ:* King's College Sch. and by travelling abroad. 2nd Lieut, 3rd City of London Regt (Royal Fusiliers) TA (Regular Army Candidate), 1927; 2nd Lieut Coldstream Guards (Supplementary Reserve), 1930; Lieut and resigned, 1931. Hon. Secretary to Sir Reginald Mitchell-Banks' unofficial cttee on Conservative policy, 1933; 1934, formed with Earl of Mansfield, Viscount Clive, Lord Phillimore, and Sir Victor Raikes, KBE, Imperial Policy Group and was Hon. Secretary, 1934–39; travelled as Group's chief observer of Foreign Affairs in Europe and America, 1935–39; special visit of enquiry to Mussolini, Doctor Beneš, Dr Schuschnigg, 1936; to King Boris of Bulgaria, etc, 1938; to Italy and King Boris, 1939–40; FCO released 45 secret reports from 1936–40 to PRO, 1972. Adviser on War Intelligence to United Steel Companies Ltd, 1944–45. Formerly published monthly serial memoranda on foreign affairs and strategy, (first published 1938); Proprietor of: Intelligence Digest, 1938–76; The Weekly Review, 1951–76; Director, Ringrone Newspapers Ltd, 1966–68. Editor: Bankers Digest, 1969–72; Special Office Brief, 1973.Trustee, Marquis de Verneuil Trust, 1971–. Hon. Citizen of New Orleans, La, USA, 1950; Hon. Life Mem., Mark Twain Soc., 1977; Companion of Western Europe, 1979. Gave collection of historic documents to Hoover Instn, Stanford Univ., 1983. *Publications:* Review of World Affairs (23 vols since 1938); Mayerling, 1983; Secret Reports of Prime Minister Chamberlain 1938–40, 1984; The Carolingian Crown of France, 1984; The Great Marshal Philippe Pétain, 1995; various articles on strategy and foreign affairs. *Recreation:* climbing. *Address:* Yeomans Cottage, Longborough, Moreton-in-Marsh, Glos GL56 0QG. *Fax:* (01608) 650540; (office) 37 Upper Mount Street, Dublin 2, Ireland. *T:* 760705, *Fax:* 766560. *Died 8 Feb. 1999.*

DEERHURST, Viscount; Edward George William Omar Coventry; *b* 24 Sept. 1957; *s* and *heir* of 11th Earl of Coventry. *Died 4 Oct. 1997.*

de LASTIC, Most Rev. Alan Basil; Archbishop of Delhi, (RC), since 1990; *b* Burma, 24 Sept. 1929. Ordained priest, 1958; Auxiliary Bishop of Calcutta, 1979–84; Bishop of Lucknow, 1984–90. *Address:* Archbishop's House, Ashok Place, New Delhi 11001, India. *T:* 343593, 343457, *Fax:* 3746575. *Died 20 June 2000.*

DELL, Rt Hon. Edmund; PC 1970; *b* 15 Aug. 1921; *s* of late Reuben and Frances Dell; *m* 1963, Susanne Gottschalk. *Educ:* elementary schs; Owen's Sch., London; Queen's Coll., Oxford (Open Schol.; 1st Cl. Hons Mod. Hist., BA and MA 1947). War Service, 1941–45, Lieut RA (Anti-tank). Lecturer in Modern History, Queen's Coll., Oxford, 1947–49; Executive in Imperial Chemical Industries Ltd,

1949–63; Simon Research Fellow, Manchester Univ, 1963–64. Mem., Manchester City Council, 1953 60. Pres., Manchester and Salford Trades Council, 1958–61. Contested (Lab) Middleton and Prestwich, 1955. MP (Lab) Birkenhead, 1964–79; Parly Sec., Min. of Technology, 1966–67; Jt Parly Under-Sec. of State, Dept of Economic Affairs, 1967–68; Minister of State: Board of Trade, 1968–69; Dept of Employment and Productivity, 1969–70; Paymaster General, 1974–76; Sec. of State for Trade, 1976–78. Chm., Public Accts Cttee, 1973–74 (Acting Chm., 1972–73). Mem., Cttee of Three apptd by European Council to review procedures of EEC, 1978–79. Chm. and Chief Exec., Guinness Peat Gp, 1979–82; Founder Chm., Channel Four TV Co., 1980–87; Dir, Shell Transport and Trading Co. plc, 1979–92. Pres., London Chamber of Commerce and Industry, 1991–92 (Dep. Chm., 1988–90; Chm., 1990–91; Chm., Commercial Educn Trust, 1989–92). Chairman: Hansard Soc. Commn on Financing of Politics, 1980–81; Public Finance Foundn, 1984–91; Working Party on Internat. Business Taxation, Inst. for Fiscal Studies, 1982; Wkg Pty on Company Political Donations (apptd by Hansard Soc. and Constitutional Reform Centre), 1985; Wkg Pty on 1992: Ownership, Productivity and Investment, 1988–89; Canada–UK Dalhousie Colloquium, 1987; Prison Reform Trust, 1988–93. Dep. Chm., Governing Body, Imperial Coll. of Science, Technology and Medicine, 1988–91. Boys' Chess Champion of London, 1936. FRHistS 1995. Hon. Fellow, Fitzwilliam Coll., Cambridge, 1986; Hon. Sen. Res. Fellow, UCL, 1998. *Publications:* (ed with J. E. C. Hill) The Good Old Cause, 1949; Brazil: the Dilemma of Reform (Fabian Pamphlet), 1964; Political Responsibility and Industry, 1973; (with B. Biesheuvel and R. Marjolin) Report on European Institutions, 1979; The Politics of Economic Interdependence, 1987; A Hard Pounding: politics and economic crisis 1974–76, 1991; Britain and the Origins of the European Monetary System, in Contemporary European History Vol. 3, Pt 1, 1994, The Schumann Plan and the British Abdication of Leadership in Europe, 1995; The Chancellors: a history of the Chancellors of the Exchequer 1945–90, 1996; articles in learned journals. *Posthumous publication:* A Strange Eventful History, 2000. *Recreation:* listening to music. *Address:* 4 Reynolds Close, NW11 7EA.

Died 1 Nov. 1999.

DELMAS, Jacques Pierre Michel C.; *see* Chaban-Delmas.

DENINGTON, Baroness *cr* 1978 (Life Peer), of Stevenage in the County of Hertfordshire; **Evelyn Joyce Denington,** DBE 1974 (CBE 1966); Chairman, Stevenage Development Corporation, 1966–80 (Member, 1950–80); Chairman, Greater London Council, 1975–76; *b* 9 Aug. 1907; *d* of Phillip Charles Bursill and Edith Rowena Bursill; *m* 1935, Cecil Dallas Denington. *Educ:* Blackheath High Sch.; Bedford Coll., London. Journalism, 1927–31; teacher, 1933–50; Gen. Sec., Nat. Assoc. of Labour Teachers, 1938–47. Member: St Pancras Borough Council, 1945–59; LCC, 1946–65 (Chm. New and Expanding Towns Cttee, 1960–65); GLC, 1964–77 (Chm. Housing Cttee, 1964–67; Dep. Leader (Lab), Opposition, 1967–73; Chm., Transport Cttee, 1973–75). Member: Central Housing Adv. Cttee, 1955–73 (Chm. Sub-Cttee prod. report Our Older Homes); SE Economic Planning Council, 1966–79; Chm., New Towns Assoc., 1973–75. Member: Sutton Dwellings Housing Trust, 1976–82; North British Housing Assoc., 1976–88; Sutton (Hastoe) Housing Assoc. Ltd, 1981–88. Freeman, City of London. Hon. FRIBA; Hon. MRTPI. *Address:* Flat 3, 29 Brunswick Square, Hove BN3 1EJ. *Died 22 Aug. 1998.*

DENISON, (John) Michael (Terence Wellesley), CBE 1983; actor; *b* 1 Nov. 1915; *s* of Gilbert Dixon Denison and Marie Louise (*née* Bain); *m* 1939, Dulcie Gray, CBE,

actress, playwright and authoress. *Educ:* Harrow; Magdalen Coll., Oxford (BA). Dramatic Sch., 1937–38; Westminster Theatre, 1938; Aberdeen Repertory, 1939; first film, 1940. Served War of 1939–45, Royal Signals and Intelligence Corps, 1940–46. Appeared in following plays (in London, unless stated): Ever Since Paradise, 1946; Rain on the Just, 1948; Queen Elizabeth Slept Here, 1949; The Four-poster, 1950; Dragon's Mouth, 1952; Sweet Peril, 1952; The Bad Samaritan, 1953; Alice Through the Looking Glass, 1953, 1955 and 1972; We Must Kill Toni, 1954; tour of S Africa, 1954–55; All's Well That Ends Well, Twelfth Night, Merry Wives of Windsor, Titus Andronicus, Stratford-on-Avon, 1955; prod and acted in Love Affair, 1956; A Village Wooing and Fanny's First Play (Edinburgh and Berlin festivals), 1956; Meet Me By Moonlight, 1957; Let Them Eat Cake, 1959; Candida, 1960; Heartbreak House, 1961; My Fair Lady (Melbourne); A Village Wooing (Hong Kong); Shakespeare Recital (Berlin Festival), 1962; Where Angels Fear to Tread, 1963; Hostile Witness, 1964; An Ideal Husband, 1965; On Approval, 1966; Happy Family; Number 10, 1967; Out of the Question, 1968; Three, 1970; The Wild Duck, 1970; Clandestine Marriage (tour), 1971; The Tempest, 1972; Twelfth Night, 1972, 1978, 1985; The Dragon Variation (tour), 1973; At the End of the Day, 1973; The Sack Race, 1974; Peter Pan, 1974; The Black Mikado, 1975; The First Mrs Fraser (tour), 1976; The Earl and the Pussycat (tour), 1976; Robert and Elizabeth (tour), 1976; The Cabinet Minister (tour), 1977; The Lady's Not For Burning, Ivanov, 1978; Bedroom Farce, 1979; The Kingfisher (tour), 1980–81; Venus Observed (Windsor), 1980; Relatively Speaking (Far and Near East tour), 1981; A Coat of Varnish, Captain Brassbound's Conversion, 1982; School for Scandal, 1982, 1983; See How They Run, 1984; There Goes the Bride (Near and Far East tour), 1985; Ring Round the Moon, 1985 and 1988; The Apple Cart, 1986; Court in the Act, 1986, 1987; You Never Can Tell, 1987; The Chalk Garden (tour), 1989; Dear Charles (tour), 1990; The Best of Friends (tour), 1990, 1991; The Importance of Being Earnest (tour), 1991; Bedroom Farce (tour), 1992; An Ideal Husband, 1992, 1996 (incl. début, NY), 1997; The Schoolmistress, Pygmalion, Chichester, 1994; Two of a Kind (tour), 1995; The Admirable Crichton, Chichester, 1997. *Films include:* My Brother Jonathan, 1947; The Glass Mountain, 1948; Landfall, 1949; The Franchise Affair, 1950; Angels One Five, The Importance of Being Earnest, 1951; The Truth About Women, 1957; Shadowlands, 1994. Many television appearances including title role Boyd, QC, 1956–61 and 1963. Director: Allied Theatre Productions, 1966–75; Play Company of London, 1970–74; New Shakespeare Company, 1971–. On Council British Actors Equity Assoc., 1949–76 (Vice-Pres. 1952, 1961–63, 1973); Mem. Drama Panel, Arts Council, 1975–78. FRSA. *Publications:* (with Dulcie Gray) The Actor and His World, 1964; memoirs: vol. 1, Overture and Beginners, 1973, vol. 2, Double Act, 1985; DNB articles on Sir Noël Coward and Sir Peter Daubeny, 1983, Peter Bridge, 1987, Glen Byam Shaw, 1994. *Recreations:* golf (Pres., Stage Golf Soc., 1991), painting, watching cricket, gardening, motoring. *Address:* Shardeloes, Amersham, Bucks HP7 0RL. *Clubs:* MCC, Middlesex County Cricket; Richmond Golf (Richmond). *Died 22 July 1998.*

DENMAN, Prof. Donald Robert; Professor of Land Economy, 1968–78 and Head of Department of Land Economy, 1962–78, Cambridge University, then Professor Emeritus; Fellow of Pembroke College, Cambridge, 1962–78, then Emeritus; *b* 7 April 1911; 2nd *s* of Robert Martyn Denman and Letitia Kate Denman, Finchley; *m* 1941, Jessica Hope, 2nd *d* of Richard H. Prior, Chichester; two *s. Educ:* Christ's Coll., Finchley; London Univ. (BSc 1938; MSc 1940; PhD 1945; MA Cantab. 1948). FRICS

1949. Dep. Exec. Off., Cumberland War Agricultural Exec. Cttee, 1939–46; University Lectr, Cambridge Univ., 1948–68. Land Management Cttee of Agricultural Improvement Council, 1953–60; Member: Church Assembly, 1957–69; Standing Cttee of Istituto de Diritto Agrario Internazionale e Comparato, Florence, 1960; Nat. Commn of Unesco, 1972–74; Advisor to Min. of Co-operation and Rural Affairs, Iran, 1968–75; Mem., Commn on Ecology, IUCN, 1987. Mem. Council, University Coll. at Buckingham, 1973–81. Chm., Commonwealth Human Ecology Council, 1984–88; Mem., Land Decade Educnl Council, 1981. Patron, Small Farmers' Assoc. Hon. Fellow, Ghana Instn of Surveyors, 1970; Fellow, Royal Swedish Acad. of Forestry and Agriculture, 1971. Hon. DSc Univ. of Sci. and Technol., Kumasi, Ghana, 1979. Gold Medal, RICS, 1972. Distinguished Order of Homayoun of the Imperial Court of Persia, 1974. *Publications:* Tenant Right Valuation: in History and Modern Practice, 1942; Tenant Right Valuation and Current Legislation, 1948; Estate Capital: the Contribution of Landownership to Agricultural Finance, 1957; Origins of Ownership: a Brief History of Landownership and Tenure, 1958; Bibliography of Rural Land Economy and Landownership 1900–1957 (*et al*), 1958; Farm Rents: a Comparison of Current and Past Farm Rents in England and Wales, 1959; (ed and contrib.) Landownership and Resources, 1960; (ed and contrib.) Contemporary Problems of Landownership, 1963; Land in the Market, 1964; (jtly) Commons and Village Greens: a Study in Land Use, Conservation and Management, 1967; (ed and contrib.) Land and People, 1967; Rural Land Systems, 1968; Land Use and the Constitution of Property, 1969; Land Use: an Introduction to Proprietary Land Use Analysis, 1971; Human Environment: the surveyor's response, 1972; The King's Vista (Persian Land reform), 1973; Prospects of Co-operative Planning (Warburton Lecture), 1973; Land Economy: an education and a career (British Assoc. lecture), 1975; The Place of Property, 1978; Land in a Free Society, 1980; The Fountain Principle, 1982; Markets under the Sea?, 1984; Survival and Responsibility, 1987; After Government Failure?, 1987; (jtly) Planning Fails the Inner Cities, 1987; A Half and Half Affair: the chronicles of a hybrid don, 1993; (jtly) The Idea of Property, 1997; numerous monographs, articles and papers in academic and professional jls and nat. press in Britain and abroad. *Recreation:* travel. *Address:* Pembroke College, Cambridge CB2 1RF; 12 Chaucer Road, Cambridge CB2 2EB. *T:* (01223) 357725. *Clubs:* Carlton, Farmers'.   *Died 2 Sept. 1999.*

DENNING, Baron (Life Peer) *cr* 1957, of Whitchurch, co. Southampton; **Alfred Thompson Denning,** OM 1997; Kt 1944; PC 1948; DL; Master of the Rolls, 1962–82; *b* 23 Jan. 1899; *s* of Charles and Clara Denning; *m* 1st, 1932, Mary Harvey (*d* 1941); one *s*; 2nd, 1945, Joan (*d* 1992), *d* of J. V. Elliott Taylor, and *widow* of J. M. B. Stuart, CIE. *Educ:* Andover Grammar Sch.; Magdalen Coll., Oxford (Demy; Hon. Fellow, 1948). 1st Class Mathematical Moderations; 1st Class Mathematical Final School; 1st Class Final Sch. of Jurisprudence; Eldon Scholar, 1921; Prize Student Inns of Court. Called to the Bar, Lincoln's Inn, 1923, Bencher, 1944, Treas., 1964; KC 1938; Judge of the High Court of Justice, 1944–48; a Lord Justice of Appeal, 1948–57; a Lord of Appeal in Ordinary, 1957–62. Chancellor of Diocese of London, 1942–44, and of Southwark, 1937–44; Recorder of Plymouth, 1944; Nominated Judge for War Pensions Appeals, 1945–48. Chm. Cttee on Procedure in Matrimonial Causes, 1946–47; Chm., Royal Commission on Historical MSS, 1962–82. Held inquiry into circumstances of resignation of Mr J. D. Profumo, Sec. of State for War, 1963. Chairman: Cttee on Legal Education for Students from Africa, 1960; British Institute of International and Comparative Law, 1959–86.

Pres., Birkbeck Coll., 1952–83. Hon. Fellow, Nuffield Coll., Oxford, 1982. Hon. Bencher: Middle Temple, 1972; Gray's Inn, 1979; Inner Temple, 1982. Dimbleby Lectr, BBC TV, 1980. Hon. FBA 1979. Hon. LLD: Ottawa, 1955; Glasgow, 1959; Southampton, 1959; London, 1960; Cambridge, 1963; Leeds, 1964; McGill, 1967; Dallas, 1969; Dalhousie, 1970; Wales, 1973; Exeter, 1976; Columbia, 1976; Tilburg (Netherlands), 1977; W Ontario, 1979; British Columbia, 1979; Sussex, 1980; Buckingham, 1983; Nottingham, 1984; Hon. DCL Oxford, 1965. DL Hants, 1978. Served in RE 1917–19 (BEF, France). Chevalier, Légion d'Honneur (France), 1998. *Publications:* (ed jtly) Smith's Leading Cases, 1929; (ed jtly) Bullen and Leake's Precedents, 1935; Freedom under the Law (Hamlyn Lectures), 1949; The Changing Law, 1953; The Road to Justice, 1955; The Discipline of Law, 1979; The Due Process of Law, 1980; The Family Story, 1981; What Next in the Law, 1982; The Closing Chapter, 1983; Landmarks in the Law, 1984; Leaves from my Library, 1986. *Address:* The Lawn, Whitchurch, Hants RG28 7AS. *T:* (01256) 892144.

Died 5 March 1999.

DENNIS, Maxwell Lewis, CMG 1971; Chairman, South Australia Totalizator Agency Board, 1973–79; *b* 19 April 1909; *s* of Frank Leonard and Ethel Jane Dennis; *m* 1935, Bernice Abell Symons; one *d* (one *s* decd). *Educ:* Gladstone High Sch., South Australia. FCPA 1990. Entered South Australian Public Service, 1924; Public Service Commissioner, 1965; Chm., Public Service Bd, 1968–73. Life Governor, Royal Soc. for the Blind. *Address:* Apartment 34, Carinya Park, 2 Plantation Street, Mount Lawley, WA 6050, Australia.

Died 5 July 1999.

DENNISON, Brig. Malcolm Gray; Lord-Lieutenant of Orkney, since 1990; *b* 19 March 1924; *s* of John Reid Dennison, Shapinsay and Margaret Gray, Roeberry. *Educ:* Lincoln Sch.; Edinburgh Univ. RAF, 1942–52: Bomber Comd, 1944–45; Sen. Intell. Officer, 219 and 205 Groups, 1946–47; MECAS, 1947–48; HQ Middle East Air Force, 1948–51; retired 1952. Bahrain Petroleum Co., 1953–55; Sultan's Armed Forces, Intelligence, 1955–83. Pres., SSAFA (Orkney). Chm., Orkney Historic Bldgs Trust. Sultan's Commendation, 1970; DSM (Oman), 1972; Order of Oman (Military), 1974. *Recreation:* book collecting. *Address:* Roeberry House, St Margaret's Hope, Orkney KW17 2TW. *T:* (01856) 831228, *Fax:* (01856) 831544. *Clubs:* Royal Air Force, Special Forces, Royal Over-Seas League; New (Edinburgh).   *Died 30 Aug. 1996.*

DENNY, Margaret Bertha Alice, (Mrs E. L. Denny), OBE 1946; DL; Under Secretary, Ministry of Transport and Civil Aviation, 1957–58; *b* 30 Sept. 1907; *o d* of late Edward Albert Churchard and Margaret Catherine (*née* Arnold), and step *d* of late William Ray Lenanton, JP; *m* 1957, Edward Leslie Denny, JP, formerly Chm., William Denny Bros, Shipbuilders, Dumbarton. *Educ:* Dover County Sch.; Bedford Coll. for Women, London Univ. (BA Hons, PhD). Entered Civil Service as Principal, Ministry of Shipping, 1940; Asst Sec., 1946. Gov., Bedford Coll., University of London. Member: Scottish Adv. Council for Civil Aviation, 1958–67; Western Regional Hospital Board, Scotland, 1960–74; Scottish Cttee, Council of Industrial Design, 1961–71; Gen. Advisory Council, BBC, 1962–66; Gen. Nursing Council, Scotland, 1962–78; Board of Management, State Hosp., Carstairs, 1966–76; Vice-Chm., Argyll and Clyde Health Bd, 1974–77. National Trust for Scotland: Mem. Council, 1973–81; Mem. Exec. Cttee, 1974–81; Vice-Pres., 1981–91; Vice-Pres. Emeritus, 1991. County Comr, Girl Guides, Dunbartonshire, 1958–68. DL Dunbartonshire,

1973. Officer, Order of Orange Nassau, 1947. *Address:* Dalnair House, Croftamie, Drymen G63 0EZ.
Died 23 Dec. 1999.

DENT, Sir Robin (John), KCVO 1992; a Managing Director, Baring Brothers & Co. Ltd, 1967–86; Director, Barings plc, 1985–89; *b* 25 June 1929; *s* of late Rear-Adm. John Dent, CB, OBE and Nancy Alys Mary, *d* of Mortimer Brutton Ford, Exmouth; *m* 1952, Hon. Ann Camilla Denison-Pender, *d* of 2nd Baron Pender, CBE; two *d. Educ:* Marlborough. Bank of England, 1949–51; joined M. Samuel & Co. Ltd, 1951: Dir, 1963–65; Dir, Hill Samuel & Co. Ltd, 1965–67; Chm., Mase Westpac Ltd, 1989–93; Dir (London Board), Commercial Banking Co. of Sydney Ltd, 1964–82. Member, London Adv. Cttee, Hong Kong & Shanghai Banking Corp., 1974–81; Dir, City of London Trust PLC, 1977–97. Mem., Deposit Protection Bd, 1982–85; Dep. Chm., Export Guarantees Adv. Council, 1983–85; Chm., Executive Cttee, British Bankers' Assoc., 1984–85; Comr, Public Works Loan Bd, 1987–97 (Chm., 1990–97). Member Council: Cancer Research Campaign, 1967–95; King Edward's Hosp. Fund for London, 1974– (Treas., 1974–92); Special Trustee, St Thomas' Hosp., 1988–97; Chm., Florence Nightingale Mus. Trust, 1993–. OStJ 1996. *Address:* 44 Smith Street, SW3 4EP. *T:* (020) 7352 1234. *Club:* White's.
Died 14 April 1999.

DENT, Ronald Henry; Chairman, Cape Industries Ltd, 1962–79; *b* 9 Feb. 1913; *s* of late Henry Francis Dent, MA, and Emma Bradley; *m* 1939, Olive May, *d* of late George Wilby, FCA; one *s* one *d. Educ:* Portsmouth Grammar Sch. Chartered accountant, 1936. Served War, 1939–45: UK, France, India; War Office, 1942–45. Joined Cape Industries, 1947; Man. Dir, 1957–71. Cancer Research Campaign: Mem. Council, 1965, Vice-Chm. 1975–83; Chm., Finance Cttee, 1969–75; Chm., Exec. Cttee, 1975–83, Dep Chm., Finance Cttee, Union Internationale contre le Cancer, Geneva, 1978–90; Dir, Internat. Cancer Foundn, 1978–90. British Inst. of Management: Fellow 1965; Mem. Council, 1968–77; Mem., Bd of Fellows, 1971–77; Chm. Finance Cttee, and Vice-Chm. of Inst., 1972–76. Mem. Council, UK S Africa Trade Assoc., 1969–80. FRSA. *Recreations:* golf, gardening. *Address:* Badgers Copse, Birtley Green, Bramley, Surrey GU5 0LE. *T:* (01483) 893649. *Club:* St George's Hill Golf. *Died 26 April 1993.*

DEOL, Prof. Malkiat Singh, PhD, DSc; Professor of Genetics, University College London, 1981–93, then Emeritus; *b* 1 May 1928; *s* of Santa Singh and Dilip Kaur; *m* 1955, Johanna Stolze; *m* 1990, Luise del Torto. *Educ:* Delhi Univ. (MSc); Univ. of London (PhD, DSc). Res. Assistant, UCL, 1954–55; Res. Fellow, Sloane-Kettering Inst., NY, 1955–56; Res. Associate, Columbia Univ., NY, 1956–57; Scientific Staff, MRC, 1957–69; Reader in Genetics, UCL, 1969–81. *Publications:* pubns on genetics of hearing, pigmentation and mosaicism. *Recreations:* reading, walking. *Address:* c/o Department of Genetics and Biometry, University College London, Gower Street, WC1E 6BT. *T:* (020) 7387 7050.
Died 12 June 1999.

de PURY, David; Co-Founder and Chairman, de Pury, Pictet, Turrettini & Co. Ltd, since 1996; *b* 4 Dec. 1943; *s* of Jean Jacques de Pury and Marguerite de Pury (*née* Miescher); *m* 1991, Maria Eugenia Echeverria. *Educ:* Geneva Univ. (law degree). Attorney; Mem., Geneva Bar. Swiss Diplomatic Service, 1970–91: served in Washington, Mission to EC in Brussels, The Hague and Berne; Ambassador Plenipotentiary and Delegate of Swiss Govt for Trade Agreements, 1986–91; Chm., OECD Trade Cttee, 1989–91; Gov. for Switzerland, Inter-American Develt Bank, 1987–88. Co-Chm., ABB Asea Brown Boveri Gp, 1992–96; Chairman: Brown Boveri Ltd,

1992–96; EIC Electricity Investment Co., 1997–; Le Temps daily newspaper, 1998–; Electrowatt Engineering; Director: Ciba-Geigy, 1992–96; UNOTEC, 1992–97; Nestlé, 1993–; Gpe Schneider (Paris), 1997–; Jaakko Pöyry Gp (Helsinki); Zurich Financial Services Gp. Member, European Advisory Board: Schroders; Air Products. Member: Eur. Roundtable of Industrialists, 1994–96; Council, World Economic Forum; Exec. Cttee, Geneva Grad. Inst. for Internat. Studies, 1993–. Trustee, Internat. Crisis Gp, 1997–. Vice Chm., Internat. Fest. of Music, Lucerne. *Publications:* numerous articles in Swiss and internat. papers and jls. *Recreations:* ski-ing, tennis, music. *Address:* de Pury, Pictet, Turrettini & Co., Postfach 8242, 8050 Zurich, Switzerland. *T:* (1) 3183401, *Fax:* (1) 3183411. *Died 26 Dec. 2000.*

DE ST JORRE, Danielle Marie-Madeleine J.; *see* Jorre De St Jorre.

de STE CROIX, Geoffrey Ernest Maurice, DLitt; FBA 1972; Fellow and Tutor in Ancient History, New College, Oxford, 1953–77, then Emeritus Fellow (Hon. Fellow, 1985); *b* 8 Feb. 1910; *s* of Ernest Henry de Ste Croix and Florence Annie (*née* Macgowan); *m* 1st, 1932, Lucile (marr. diss. 1959); (one *d* decd); 2nd, 1959, Margaret Knight; two *s. Educ:* Clifton Coll. (to 1925); University Coll. London (1946–50; BA 1st cl. Hons History, 1949); MA Oxon, 1953; DLitt Oxon, 1978. Solicitor, 1931. Served War, RAF, 1940–46. Asst Lectr in Ancient Economic History, London Sch. of Economics, and Part-time Lectr in Ancient History, Birkbeck Coll., London, 1950–53. Vis. Prof., Univ. of Amsterdam, 1978. Lectures included: J. H. Gray, Cambridge Univ., 1972–73; Gregynog, UCW, Aberystwyth, 1986; Townsend, Cornell Univ., 1988; gave many other lectures in Europe and N America. *Publications:* The Origins of the Peloponnesian War, 1972; The Class Struggle in the Ancient Greek World, from the Archaic Age to the Arab Conquests, 1981 (Isaac Deutscher Meml Prize, 1982; Spanish edn 1988, Greek edn 1997); contributions to: Studies in the History of Accounting, 1956; The Crucible of Christianity, 1969; Studies in Ancient Society, 1974; Debits, Credits, Finance and Profits, 1974; articles and reviews in various learned jls. *Recreation:* listening to music. *Address:* Evenlode, Stonesfield Lane, Charlbury, Oxford OX7 3ER. *T:* (01608) 810453. *Died 5 Feb. 2000.*

DESCH, Stephen Conway; QC 1980; a Recorder of the Crown Court, since 1979; *b* 17 Nov. 1939; *o s* of Harold Ernest Desch and Gwendolen Lucy Desch; *m* 1973, Julia Beatrice Little; two *d. Educ:* Dauntsey's Sch.; Magdalen Coll., Oxford (BCL, MA); Northwestern Univ., Chicago. Called to the Bar, Gray's Inn, 1962, Bencher, 1990; joined Midland Circuit, 1964. Lectr in Law, Magdalen Coll., Oxford, 1963–65. *Publication:* Legal Notes to H. E. Desch, Structural Surveying, 1970, 2nd edn (with Stephen Mika), 1988. *Recreations:* country pursuits, farming, mountain walking. *Address:* 2 Crown Office Row, Temple, EC4Y 7HJ. *T:* 0171–353 9337.
Died 31 Aug. 1996.

de THIER, Baron Jacques; Grand Officer, Order of Léopold II, Belgium; Commander, Order of Léopold and Order of the Crown, Belgium; Civic Cross (1914–18); Hon. GCVO; Director, Compagnie Financière et de Gestion pour l'Etranger (Cometra), Brussels, 1966–73; Counsellor, Cometra Oil Company, 1974–86; *b* Heusy, Belgium, 15 Sept. 1900; created Baron, 1975; *m* 1946, Mariette Negroponte (*d* 1973); three step *s. Educ:* University of Liège (Doctor of Laws 1922). Mem. of Bar (Liège and Verviers), 1923–29; attached to Prime Minister's Cabinet, Brussels, 1929–32; entered Diplomatic Service, 1930; Attaché, Belgian Legation, Berlin, 1933; Chargé d'Affaires in Athens, 1935, Teheran, 1936; First Sec., Berlin, 1937–38; First Sec., then Counsellor,

Washington, 1938–44; Chargé d'Affaires, Madrid, 1944–46; Asst to Dir-Gen., Polit. Dept, Min. of Foreign Affairs, Brussels, 1947, then Asst Head of Belgian Mission in Berlin; Consul-Gen. for Belgium, NY, 1948–55; Pres., Soc. of Foreign Consuls in New York, 1954; Belgian Ambassador: to Mexico, 1955–58; in Ottawa, 1958–61; Mem. Belgian Delegns to Gen. Assemblies of UN, 1956, 1957, 1959 and 1960; Belg. Rep. to Security Council, Sept. 1960; Belgian Ambassador to UK, 1961–65, and concurrently Belgian Perm. Rep. to Council of WEU, 1961–65. Hon. Chairman: Soc. Belgo-Allemande; Belgian Nat. Cttee, United World Colls. Holder of foreign decorations. *Publications:* Un diplomate au vingtième siècle, 1991; articles in La Revue Générale, Brussels: Dans l'Iran d'autrefois, 1979; Souvenirs d'un diplomate belge, Washington, 1938–44, 1981; Pourquoi l'Espagne de Franco n'a pas livré Degrelle, 1983. *Recreation:* golf. *Address:* 38 avenue des Klauwaerts, 1050 Brussels, Belgium. *Clubs:* Anglo-Belgian; Cercle Royal Gaulois, Cercle du Parc, Royal Golf de Belgique (Brussels).

Died 21 Oct. 1996.

DEUTSCH, André, CBE 1989; President, André Deutsch Ltd, 1989–91 (Chairman and Managing Director, 1951–84; Joint Chairman and Joint Managing Director, 1984–87; Joint Chairman, 1987–89); Director, Libra, Budapest, since 1991; Chairman, Aurum Press Ltd, since 1992; *b* 15 Nov. 1917; *s* of late Bruno Deutsch and Maria Deutsch (*née* Havas); unmarried. *Educ:* Budapest; Vienna; Zürich. First job in publishing, with Nicholson & Watson, 1942; started publishing independently under imprint of Allan Wingate (Publishers) Ltd, 1945; started André Deutsch Limited, 1951. Founded: African Universities Press, Lagos, Nigeria, 1962; East Africa Publishing House, Nairobi, Kenya, 1964. *Recreations:* travel preferably by train, publishing, talking, reading. *Address:* 5 Selwood Terrace, SW7 3QN. *Clubs:* Garrick, Groucho.

Died 11 April 2000.

DEVON, 17th Earl of, *cr* 1553; **Charles Christopher Courtenay;** Bt 1644; Lieutenant (W/Captain) Coldstream Guards (Regular Army Reserve of Officers); *b* 13 July 1916; *o* surv. *s* of 16th Earl of Devon and Marguerite (*d* 1950), *d* of late John Silva; *S* father, 1935; *m* 1939, (Sybil) Venetia, Countess of Cottenham, *d* of Captain J. V. Taylor; one *s* one *d. Educ:* Winchester; RMC, Sandhurst. Served War of 1939–45 (despatches). *Recreations:* shooting, fishing. *Heir: s* Lord Courtenay, *b* 5 May 1942. *Address:* Stables House, Powderham, Exeter EX6 8JQ. *T:* (01626) 890253.

Died 19 Nov. 1996.

DEW, Leslie Robert; Member, Bermuda Insurance Advisory Committee, 1979–93; President and Managing Director, Britamco Ltd, 1977–84; President, Insco Ltd, Bermuda (Gulf Oil Corporation Insurance Subsidiaries), 1980–84 (Executive Vice President-Underwriter, 1977–80); Chairman, 1971–77 and formerly Non-Marine Underwriter, Roy J. M. Merrett Syndicates; *b* 11 April 1914; *er s* of Robert Thomas Dew, RHA and Ellen Dora Frampton; *m* 1st, 1939, Vera Doreen Wills (marr. diss. 1956); 2nd, 1956, Patricia Landsberg (*née* Hyde); one *s. Educ:* privately. Underwriting Member of Lloyd's, 1950–; Mem. Cttee of Lloyd's, 1969–72, 1974–77; Dep. Chm. of Lloyd's, 1971, 1975, 1977; Mem. Cttee, Lloyd's Non-Marine Assoc., 1957–77 (Dep. Chm. 1963 and 1965, Chm. 1966); Chm., Lloyd's Common Market Working Gp, 1971–77; Dep. Chm., British Insurers' European Cttee, 1972–77. Binney Award for Civilian Bravery, 1975. *Recreations:* music, reading. *Club:* Metropolitan (NY).

Died 12 July 1996.

DEWAR, Rt Hon. Donald (Campbell); PC 1996; MP (Lab) Glasgow Anniesland, since 1997 (Glasgow, Garscadden, April 1978–1997); Member (Lab) Glasgow Anniesland, and First Minister of the Scottish Executive,

Scottish Parliament, since 1999; *b* 21 Aug. 1937; *s* of late Dr Alasdair Dewar, Glasgow; *m* 1964, Alison McNair (marr. diss. 1973); one *s* one *d. Educ:* Glasgow Acad.; Glasgow Univ. (MA, LLB). Admitted solicitor, 1963. Formerly Consultant, Ross Harper & Murphy, Glasgow. MP (Lab) South Aberdeen, 1966–70; PPS to Pres. of Bd of Trade, 1967; front bench spokesman on Scottish Affairs, 1981–92, on Social Security, 1992–95; Opposition Chief Whip, 1995–97; Mem., Shadow Cabinet, 1984–97; Sec. of State for Scotland, 1997–99. Chm., Select Cttee on Scottish Affairs, 1979–81. *Address:* House of Commons, SW1A 0AA.

Died 11 Oct. 2000.

DEWAR, George Duncan Hamilton; chartered accountant; Partner, Peat, Marwick, Mitchell & Co., Glasgow, 1949–81; *b* 11 Sept. 1916; *s* of George Readman Dewar and Elizabeth Garrioch Sinclair Hamilton; *m* 1940, Elizabeth Lawson Potts Lawrie; one *s* one *d. Educ:* High Sch. of Glasgow. Mem. Inst. Chartered Accountants of Scotland (admitted, 1940; Mem. Council, 1960–65; Vice-Pres., 1969–70; Pres., 1970–71). Mem., Scottish Tourist Bd, 1977–80. *Recreation:* golf. *Address:* Flat 28, Muirfield Court, 20 Muirend Road, Glasgow G44 3QP. *T:* (0141) 637 5683. *Club:* Western (Glasgow).

Died 9 Sept. 1998.

DEWAR, Prof. Michael James Steuart, DPhil; FRS 1960; Robert A. Welch Professor of Chemistry, University of Texas, 1963–90; Graduate Research Professor, University of Florida, since 1990; *b* 24 Sept. 1918; *s* of Francis D. Dewar, ICS, and Nan B. Keith; *m* 1944, Mary Williamson (*d* 1994); two *s. Educ:* Winchester Coll. (First Scholar); Balliol Coll., Oxford (Brackenbury, Frazer and Gibbs Scholar; DPhil 1942; MA 1943; Hon. Fellow, 1974). ICI Fellow in Chemistry, Oxford, 1945; Courtaulds Ltd, Fundamental Research Laboratory, 1945–51; Prof. of Chemistry and Head of Dept of Chemistry at Queen Mary Coll., University of London, 1951–59 (Hon. Fellow, 1993); Prof. of Chemistry, University of Chicago, 1959–63. Visiting Professor: Yale Univ., USA, 1957; Arthur D. Little, MIT, 1966; Maurice S. Kharasch, Univ. of Chicago, 1971; Firth, Sheffield, 1972; Dist. Bicentennial, Univ. of Utah, 1976; Pahlavi, Iran, 1977. Hon. Sec. Chemical Soc., 1957–59. Lectures: Reilly, Notre Dame Univ., USA, 1951; Tilden, Chem. Soc., 1954; Falk-Plaut, Columbia Univ., 1963; Daines Memorial, Univ. of Kansas, 1963; Glidden Company, Western Reserve Univ., 1964; Marchon Visiting, Univ. of Newcastle upon Tyne, 1966; Glidden Company, Kent State Univ., 1967; Gnehm, Eidgenössische Technische Hochschule, Zurich, 1968; Barton, Univ. of Oklahoma, 1969; (first) Kahlbaum, Univ. of Basel, 1970; (first) Benjamin Rush, Univ. of Pennsylvania, 1971; Venable, Univ. of N Carolina, 1971; Foster, State Univ. of NY at Buffalo, 1973; Robinson, Chem. Soc., 1974; Sprague, Univ. of Wisconsin, 1974; Bircher, Vanderbilt Univ., 1976; Faraday, Northern Illinois Univ., 1977; Priestley, Pennsylvania State Univ., 1980; J. Clarence Karcher, Univ. of Oklahoma, 1984; Res. Scholar Lectr, Drew Univ., 1984; (first) Charles O. A. Coulson, Univ. of Georgia, 1988. Fellow, Amer. Acad. of Arts and Sciences, 1966; Mem., Nat. Acad. of Sciences, 1983. Harrison Howe Award of Amer. Chem. Soc., 1961; (first) G. W. Wheland Meml Medal, Univ. of Chicago, 1976; Evans Award, Ohio State Univ., 1977; South West Regional Award, Amer. Chem. Soc., 1978; Davy Medal, Royal Soc., 1982; James Flack Norris Award, Amer. Chem. Soc., 1984; William H. Nichols Award, Amer. Chem. Soc., 1986; Auburn Kosolapoff Award, Amer. Chem. Soc., 1988; Tetrahedron Prize, 1989; World Assoc. of Theoretical Organic Chemistry Medal, 1989; Chemical Pioneer Award, Amer. Inst. of Chemists, 1990; Award for Computers in Chemistry, Amer. Chem. Soc., 1994. *Publications:* The Electronic Theory of Organic Chemistry, 1949;

Hyperconjugation, 1962; Introduction to Modern Chemistry, 1965; The Molecular Orbital Theory of Organic Chemistry, 1969; Computer Compilation of Molecular Weights and Percentage Compositions, 1970; The PMO Theory of Organic Chemistry, 1975; papers in scientific journals. *Address:* 10520 Northwest 36th Lane, Gainesville, FL 32606-5075, USA. *T:* (904) 3322050, *Fax:* (904) 3322055.   *Died 10 Oct. 1997.*

DEWDNEY, Duncan Alexander Cox, CBE 1968; Director, The Coverdale Organisation, since 1973; *b* 22 Oct. 1911; *o s* of late Claude Felix Dewdney and Annie Ross Cox; *m* 1935, Ann (*d* 1993), *d* of Walter Riley and Emily Sterratt; two *d. Educ:* Bromgrove Sch., Worcs; University of Birmingham (BSc Hons; Cadman Medallist). Served War of 1939–45; RAF, 1940–45 (Wing Comdr); Air Staff appts, Head RE8, Min. of Home Security (R&D Dept). British Petroleum Co., 1932–36; International Assoc. (Pet. Ind.) Ltd, 1936–40; Research Man., Esso Development Co., 1945–51; joined Esso Petroleum Co., 1951; Dir, 1957; Man. Dir, 1963–67; Vice-Chm., 1968; seconded to NBPI as Jt Dep. Chm., 1965–66, part-time Mem. Bd, 1967–69. Exec. Dir, Rio Tinto Zinc Corporation, 1968–72; Chairman: Irish Refining Co. Ltd, 1958–65; Anglesey Aluminium, 1968–71; RTZ Britain, 1969–72; RTZ Development Enterprises, 1970–72; Dir, Esso Chemicals SA, 1964. Chairman: National Economic Develt Cttee for the Mechanical Engrg Industry, 1964–68; Welsh Industrial Develt Bd, 1972–75; Underwater Training Centre, 1977–79; Dep. Chm., Manpower Services Commn, 1974–77. Legion of Merit, 1945. *Address:* Salters, Harestock, Winchester, Hants SO22 5JP. *T:* (01962) 852034. *Club:* Travellers'.   *Died 11 Feb. 1999.*

DE WOLF, Vice-Adm. Harry George, CBE 1946; DSO 1944, DSC 1944; *b* 26 June 1903; *s* of late Henry George De Wolf, Bedford, NS; *m* 1931, Gwendolen Fowle (*d* 1998), *d* of Thomas St George Gilbert, Somerset, Bermuda; one *s* (one *d* decd). Grad Royal Naval Coll. of Canada, 1921. Served War of 1939–45 (commanded HMCS St Laurent, 1939–40, HMCS Haida, 1943–44); Asst Chief of Naval Staff, Canada, 1944–47; Sen. Canadian Naval Officer Afloat, 1947–48; Flag Officer, Pacific Coast, 1948–50; Vice-Chief of Naval Staff, 1950–52; Chm. of Canadian Joint Staff, Washington, 1953–55; Chief of Naval Staff, Canada, 1956–60, retired. Hon. DScMil: Royal Military College of Canada, 1966; Royal Roads Mil. Coll., 1980. *Address:* Apt 804, 402 Mackay Street, Ottawa, ON K1M 2C4, Canada.   *Died 2000.*

DEWS, Peter; theatre and TV director; *b* 26 Sept. 1929; *er s* of John Dews and Edna (*née* Bloomfield); *m* 1960, Ann Rhodes. *Educ:* Queen Elizabeth Grammar Sch., Wakefield; University Coll., Oxford (MA). Asst Master, Holgate and District Grammar Sch., Barnsley, 1952–53; BBC Midland Region Drama Producer (Radio and TV), 1953–63; Dir, Ravinia Shakespeare Festival, Chicago, 1963–64; Artistic Director: Birmingham Repertory Theatre, 1966–72; Chichester Fest. Theatre, 1978–80. Directed: TV: An Age of Kings, 1960 (SFTA Award 1960); The Spread of the Eagle, 1963; theatre: As You Like It, Vaudeville, 1967; Hadrian VII, Mermaid, 1968, Haymarket and NY, 1969 (Tony Award 1969), Edmonton, 1987; Antony and Cleopatra, Chichester, 1969; Vivat! Vivat Regina!, Chichester, 1970, Piccadilly and NY, 1972; The Alchemist, Chichester, 1970; Crown Matrimonial, Haymarket, 1972, NY 1973; The Director of the Opera, Chichester, 1973; The Waltz of the Toreadors, Haymarket, 1974; King John, Stratford, Ont, 1974; The Pleasure of His Company, Toronto, 1974; Coriolanus, Tel Aviv, 1975; Othello, Chichester, 1975; Equus, Vancouver, 1975; Number Thirteen Rue de l'Amour, Phœnix, 1976; The Circle, Chichester, transf. to Haymarket, 1976; The Pleasure of His Company, Phœnix, 1976; Man and

Superman, Don Juan in Hell, When We Are Married, Ottawa, 1977, Julius Caesar, Chichester, 1977; A Sleep of Prisoners, Chichester Cathedral, 1978; Julius Caesar, A Sleep of Prisoners, Hong Kong Festival, 1979; The Devil's Disciple, The Importance of Being Earnest, Chichester, 1979; Terra Nova, Much Ado About Nothing, Chichester, 1980; Plenty, Toronto, 1981; The Taming of the Shrew, The Comedy of Errors, Stratford, Ont, 1981; Cards on the Table, Vaudeville, 1981; 56 Duncan Terrace, Edmonton, A Midsummer Night's Dream, Plymouth, and Terra Nova, Durban, 1982; Pierewaaien, Arnhem, 1983; Time and the Conways, Chichester, 1983; On The Razzle, Durban, 1983; Romeo and Juliet, Stratford, Ont, and Measure for Measure, Tel Aviv, 1984; Waiting for Godot, and Galileo, Scottish Theatre Co., 1985; King Lear, tour, 1986; An Inspector Calls, Clwyd and Westminster, 1987, tour, 1988; She Stoops to Conquer, tour, 1987. Hon. DLitt: Bradford, 1988; De Paul Univ., Chicago, 1990. *Address:* c/o Larry Dalzell Associates Ltd, 91 Regent Street, W1R 7TB.
                              Died 25 Aug. 1997.

DEXTER, Harold; organist; Professor, Guildhall School of Music and Drama (Head of General Musicianship Department, 1962–85); Organist, St Botolph's, Aldgate, 1969–94; *b* 7 Oct. 1920; *s* of F. H. and E. Dexter; *m* 1942, Faith Grainger; one *d. Educ:* Wyggeston Grammar Sch., Leicester; Corpus Christi Coll., Cambridge, 1939–41 and 1946 (Organ Scholar, 1939; John Stewart of Rannoch Scholar, 1940; BA, MusB 1942; MA 1946). ARCO 1938; FRCO 1940; ARCM 1941; RCO Choirmaster's Diploma; John Brook Prize, 1946; ADCM 1948. Royal Navy and RNVR, 1941–46. Organist, Louth Parish Church and Music-Master, King Edward VI Grammar Sch., Louth, 1947–49; Organist, Holy Trinity, Leamington Spa, 1949–56; Music Master, Bablake Sch., Coventry, 1952–56; Master of the Music, Southwark Cathedral, 1956–68. FGSM 1962, FRSCM 1964 (Hon. diplomas). *Address:* 29 Allington Court, Outwood Common Road, Billericay, Essex CM11 2JR. *T:* (01277) 652042.
                              Died 27 June 2000.

DIAMAND, Peter, Hon. CBE 1972; Artistic Adviser, Orchestre de Paris, since 1976; *b* Berlin, 8 June 1913; Austrian parents; became Netherlands citizen; *m* 1st, 1948, Maria Curcio, pianist (marr. diss. 1971); 2nd, Sylvia Rosenberg, violinist (marr. diss. 1977); one *s. Educ:* Schiller-Realgymnasium, Berlin; Berlin Univ. Studied law and journalism. Left Germany, 1933; became Private Sec. to Artur Schnabel, pianist; Personal Asst to Dir of Netherlands Opera, Amsterdam, 1946, subsequently Artistic Adviser until 1965; Gen. Manager of Holland Festival, 1948–65; Dir, Edinburgh Internat. Festival, 1965–78; Artistic Advr, Teatro alla Scala, Milan, 1977–78; Dir and Gen. Manager, RPO, 1978–81. Mem. Board of Netherlands Chamber Orchestra, 1955–77. Hon. LLD Edinburgh, 1972. Knight, Order of Oranje Nassau, Holland, 1959; Grosses Ehrenzeichen fuer Verdienste, Austria, 1964; Medal of Merit, Czechoslovakia, 1966; Commander Italian Republic, 1973; Commandeur, Ordre des Arts et des Lettres, France, 1996. *Address:* 28 Eton Court, Eton Avenue, NW3 3HJ. *T:* (0171) 586 1203.
                              Died 16 Jan. 1998.

DICK, Air Vice-Marshal (Alan) David, CB 1978; CBE 1968; AFC 1957; FRAeS 1975; *b* 7 Jan. 1924; *s* of late Brig. Alan MacDonald Dick, CBE, IMS (retd), and Muriel Angela Dick; *m* 1951, Ann Napier Jeffcoat, *d* of late Col A. C. Jeffcoat, CB, CMG, DSO; two *s* two *d. Educ:* Fettes; Aitchison Coll., Lahore; King's Coll., Cambridge (MA). Joined RAF, 1942; SE Asia Command, 1943–45; Fighter Comd, 1945–46; Central Flying Sch., 1950–53; Empire Test Pilots Sch., 1953; Test Pilot, A&AEE, 1954–57; Fighter Comd, 1957–60; RAF Staff Coll., 1960–63; OC 207 Sqdn, Bomber Comd, 1963–64; Supt of Flying,

A&AEE, 1964–68; Strike Comd, 1968–69; IDC 1970; MoD Air Staff, 1971–74; Comdt, A&AEE, 1974–75; Dep. Controller Aircraft/C, MoD (PE), 1975–78. Sec., British Assoc. of Occupational Therapists, 1979–84. *Recreations:* photography, walking, bird watching. *Club:* Royal Air Force. *Died 3 Aug. 1999.*

DICK, Prof. George (Williamson Auchinvole), MD, DSc (Edinburgh); FRCPE, FRCP, FRCPath, FIBMS; Emeritus Professor of Pathology, University of London; *b* 14 Aug. 1914; *s* of Rev. David Auchinvole Dick and Blanche Hay Spence; *m* 1941, Brenda Marian Cook; two *s* two *d. Educ:* Royal High Sch., Edinburgh; Univ. of Edinburgh; The Johns Hopkins Univ., Baltimore, Md, USA. BSc 1939 (1st Cl. Hons Path.); Vans Dunlop Scholar; Buchanan Medal; MD (Gold Medal) 1949; MPH Johns Hopkins. Asst Pathologist, Royal Infirmary, Edinburgh, 1939–40; Pathologist, RAMC, 1940–46: OC Medical Div. (Lt-Col) (E African Comd), 1945; Pathologist, Colonial Med. Res. Service, 1946–51; Rockefeller Foundn Fellow (Internat. Health Div.), Rockefeller Inst., New York and Johns Hopkins Univ., 1947–48; Res. Fellow, Sch. of Hygiene and Public Health, Johns Hopkins Univ., Baltimore, Md, 1949–50; Scientific Staff, MRC, 1951–54; Prof. of Microbiology, QUB, 1955–65; Dir, Bland-Sutton Inst. and Sch. of Pathology, Middlesex Hosp. Med. Sch., Univ. of London, 1966–73; Bland-Sutton Prof. of Pathology, Univ. of London, 1966–73; Asst Dir, BPMF, and Postgraduate Dean, SW Thames RHA, 1973–81; Prof. of Pathology, Univ. of London, and Hon. Lectr and Hon. Consultant, Inst. of Child Health, 1973–81. Examnr, Med. Schools in UK, Dublin, Nairobi, Kampala, Riyadh, Jeddah; Assessor, HNC and CMS, S London Coll. Member: Mid Downs Health Authority, W Sussex, 1981–84; Jt Bd of Clinical Nursing Studies, 1982–85; Chm., DHSS/Regl Librarians Jt Wking Party. President: Inst. of Med. Laboratory Technology, 1966–76; Inst. of Medical Lab. Technicians, 1970–75; Rowhook Med. Soc., 1975–85. Treasurer, RCPath, 1973–78; Member: RSM; BMA; Internat. Epidemiol. Soc.; Path. Soc. GB and Ireland; Soc. of Scholars, Johns Hopkins Univ., 1979; Alpha Chapter, Delta Omega Hon. Soc., USA, 1981. Hon. FLA. Freeman, City of London, 1981; Liveryman, Worshipful Co. of Apothecaries, 1981. Singapore Gold Medal, Edinburgh Univ., 1952 and 1958; Laurence Biedl Prize for Rehabilitation, 1958; Sims Woodhead Medal, 1975; Outstanding Alumnus in Public Health award, Johns Hopkins Univ., 1986; Hero of Public Health, Johns Hopkins Univ. Sch. of Hygiene and Public Health, 1992. *Publications:* Immunisation, 1978, re-issued as Practical Immunisation, 1986; Immunology of Infectious Diseases, 1979; Health on Holiday and other Travels, 1982; papers on yellow fever, Uganda S, Zika and other arbor viruses, Mengovirus, Marburgvirus, poliomyelitis, hepatitis (MHV), EHA (rabies) virus; smallpox, poliomyelitis, whooping cough and combined vaccines, vaccine reactions, immunisation policies, subacute sclerosing panencephalitis; multiple sclerosis, travel, etc. *Address:* Waterland, Rowhook, Horsham RH12 3PX. *T:* (01403) 790549. *Died 3 July 1997.*

DICK, John Kenneth, CBE 1972; FCA, FRSA; Director, N. M. Rothschild & Sons Ltd, 1978–90; *b* 5 April 1913; *s* of late John Dick and Beatrice May Dick (*née* Chitty); *m* 1942, Pamela Madge, 3rd *d* of late Maurice Salmon and Katie Salmon (*née* Joseph); two *s* (and one *s* decd). *Educ:* Sedbergh. Qual. with Mann Judd & Co., Chartered Accountants, 1936; Partner, Mann Judd & Co., 1947; Mitchell Cotts Group Ltd: Jt Man. Dir, 1957; Sole Man. Dir, 1959–78; Dep. Chm., 1964; Chm., 1966–78; Chm., Hume Holdings Ltd, 1975–80. Mem., Commonwealth Develt Corp., 1967–80; Gov., City of London Soc.; Member: British Nat. Export Cttee, 1968–71; Covent Gdn Mkt Authority, 1976–82; Chm., Cttee for Middle East

Trade, 1968–71; Pres., Middle East Assoc., 1976–81 (a Vice-Pres., 1970–76). *Recreation:* golf. *Address:* Overbye, Church Street, Cobham, Surrey KT11 3EG. *T:* (office) (01932) 867770; (home) (01932) 864393. *Club:* Caledonian. *Died 16 March 1997.*

DICKINS, Basil Gordon, CBE 1952 (OBE 1945); BSc, ARCS, DIC, PhD; Deputy Controller of Guided Weapons, Ministry of Technology, 1966–68; *b* 1 July 1908; *s* of late Basil Dickins; *m* 1st, 1935, Molly Aileen (*d* 1969), *d* of late H. Walters Reburn; 2nd, 1971, Edith, *widow* of Warren Parkinson. *Educ:* Royal Coll. of Science, London. Royal Aircraft Establishment, 1932; Air Min., 1936, later Min. of Aircraft Production; Head of Operational Research Section, HQ Bomber Command, 1941; Asst Scientific Adviser, Air Ministry, 1945; Dir of Tech. Personnel Administration, Min. of Supply, 1948; Dep. Scientific Adviser to Air Ministry, 1952; Dir of Guided Weapons Research and Development, Min. of Supply, 1956; Dir-Gen. of Atomic Weapons, Min. of Supply, 1959; Dir-Gen. of Guided Weapons, Ministry of Aviation, 1962. *Publications:* papers in Proc. Royal Society and Reports and Memoranda of Aeronautical Research Council. *Address:* 5 Batisse de la Mielle, Route de la Haule, St Brelade, Jersey. *Died 10 Aug. 1996.*

DICKSON, Rt Hon. Brian; *see* Dickson, Rt Hon. R. G. B.

DICKSON, Eileen Wadham, (Mrs C. F. Dickson); *b* 16 March 1908; *d* of John Edward Latton, Librarian to Inner Temple, and Ethel Letitia Baker; *m* 1931, Charles Frederick Dickson, OBE (*d* 1994). *Educ:* Convent of the Sacred Heart, Roehampton; Bruges, Belgium. Served War of 1939–45 with WVS and on Executive Council of Stage Door Canteen. Joined Harper's Bazaar, 1949; Fashion Editor, 1951; Editor, 1953–65. *Recreations:* theatre, reading, racing, gardens. *Died 17 Aug. 1997.*

DICKSON, Murray Graeme, CMG 1961; *b* 19 July 1911; *s* of Norman and Anne Dickson. *Educ:* Rugby; New Coll., Oxford. Prison Service (Borstals), 1935–40; served War of 1939–45, in Force 136; entered Colonial Service, 1947; Education Officer, Sarawak, 1947, Deputy Dir of Education, 1952, Dir of Education, 1955–66; retd. Unesco adviser on educl planning to Govt of Lesotho, 1967–68. *Publications:* Understanding Kant's Critique of Pure Reason, 1986; Tales from Herodotus, 1989; The Best of Thucydides, 1991; trans. Froissart, Conflict and Chivalry in the Fourteenth Century, 1992. *Address:* 1 Hauteville Court Gardens, Stamford Brook Avenue, W6 0YF. *Died 2 Feb. 1997.*

DICKSON, Rt Hon. (Robert George) Brian, CC 1991; PC (Can.) 1984; Chief Justice of Canada, 1984–90; *b* 25 May 1916; *s* of Thomas and Sarah Elizabeth Dickson (*née* Gibson); *m* 1943, Barbara Melville, *d* of Henry E. Sellers; three *s* one *d. Educ:* Regina Collegiate Institute; University of Manitoba; Manitoba Law School. LLB 1938 (Gold Medal). Served with Royal Canadian Artillery, 1940–45 (wounded, despatches); Hon. Col, 30th Field Regt, Royal Canadian Artillery, retd. Called to the Bar of Manitoba, 1940; practised law with Aikins, MacAulay & Co., 1945–63; Lectr, Manitoba Law Sch., 1948–54; QC (Can.) 1953; appointed to: Court of Queen's Bench, Manitoba, 1963; Manitoba Court of Appeal, 1967; Supreme Court of Canada, 1973. Chancellor of Diocese of Rupert's Land, 1960–71. Life Bencher, Law Soc. of Manitoba. Hon. Pres., Conf. of Defense Assoc.; Hon. Mem., Advocacy Resources Centre for the Handicapped. Hon. Bencher, Lincoln's Inn, 1984. Hon. Prof., Manitoba Univ., 1985 (Chm. Bd of Govs, 1971–73); Hon. Fellow, Amer. Coll. of Trial Lawyers, 1985. Hon. degrees: St John's Coll.; Law Soc. of Upper Canada; Universities: Manitoba, Saskatchewan, Ottawa, Queen's, Dalhousie, York, Laurentian, British Columbia, Toronto, Yeshiva, McGill,

Carleton, Mount Allison, Windsor, Winnipeg, Brock, Western Ontario, Victoria. KStJ 1985. Churchill Soc. Award, 1990; Royal Bank Award, 1992. Order of the Buffalo Hunt, Manitoba, 1961. Order of Ste Agathe (San Marino), 1991; Comdr, Nat. Order of Merit (France), 1994. *Recreations:* riding, swimming. *Address:* 360 Berry Side Road, RR # 1, Dunrobin, ON K0A 1T0, Canada. *Club:* Rideau (Ottawa). *Died 17 Oct. 1998.*

DIGBY, (Kenelm) Simon (Digby) Wingfield, TD 1946; DL; MA; *b* 13 Feb. 1910; *s* of late Col F. J. B. D. Wingfield Digby, DSO and Gwendolen Marjory, *d* of G. Hamilton Fletcher; *m* 1936, Kathleen Elizabeth, *d* of late Hon. Mr Justice Courtney Kingstone, Toronto, Canada; one *s* one *d. Educ:* Harrow Sch.; Trinity Coll., Cambridge. Delegate to International Studies Conference, 1934. Called to the Bar, Inner Temple. Served in Army (TA), 1939–45 in UK and NW Europe: Major 1943; GSO II 1944. Prospective Conservative Candidate for West Dorset, 1937–41; MP (U) West Dorset, 1941–Feb. 1974; a Conservative Whip, 1948–51; Civil Lord of the Admiralty, 1951–57. Member: Coastal Pollution Select Cttee, 1966–68; Select Cttee on Procedure; Public Accounts Cttee. Mem. of Empire Parly Delegn to East Africa, 1948 and Inter-Parliamentary Union Delegation to Chile, 1962. Pres., Wessex Young Conservatives, 1947–50; Sec., Conservative Social Services Cttee, 1947; Chairman: Conservative Forestry Sub-Cttee, 1959–67; Shipping and Shipbuilding Cttee, 1964–74. Delegate (C), Council of Europe Assembly and Assembly of WEU, 1968–74 (Leader, 1972–74). Pres., Soc. of Dorset Men, 1972–85. DL Dorset, 1953. Order of Leopold and Order of White Lion. Medal of Council of Europe Assembly, 1974. *Recreations:* fishing, bloodstock breeding. *Address:* Sherborne Castle, Sherborne, Dorset DT9 5NR. *T:* (01747) 822650, (office) (01935) 813182; Coleshill House, Coleshill, near Birmingham. *Club:* Carlton.
Died 22 March 1998.

DIGBY, Ven. Stephen Basil W.; *see* Wingfield-Digby.

DILKE, Sir John Fisher Wentworth, 5th Bt *cr* 1862, of Sloane Street; *b* 8 May 1906; *e s* of Sir Fisher Wentworth Dilke, 4th Bt, and Ethel Clifford (*d* 1959); *S* father, 1944; *m* 1st, 1934, Sheila (marr. diss. 1949), *d* of late Sir William Seeds, KCMG; two *s*; 2nd, 1951, Iris Evelyn, *d* of late Ernest Clark. *Educ:* Winchester; New Coll., Oxford. Foreign Office, 1929; Editorial Staff, The Times, 1936; rejoined Foreign Service, 1939; political corresp., COI, 1945; BBC External Service, 1950. *Heir: s* Charles John Wentworth Dilke, *b* 21 Feb. 1937. *Address:* Ludpits, Etchingham, Sussex TN19 7DB. *Died 28 June 1998.*

DIMSON, Gladys Felicia, (Mrs S. B. Dimson), CBE 1976; Member of Greater London Council for Battersea North, 1973–85 (for Haringey, 1964–67, Wandsworth, 1970–73); Member, Inner London Education Authority, 1970–85; *b* 23 July 1917; *o d* of late I. Sieve, BA; *m* 1936, Dr S. B. Dimson (*d* 1991), *e s* of late Rev. Z. Dimson; one *d. Educ:* Laurel Bank Sch., Glasgow; Glasgow Univ.; London Sch. of Economics. Voluntary social worker, mainly in E London, 1950–63. Co-opted Mem., Children's Cttee, LCC, 1958–65; Chm., gp of LCC Children's Homes and of a voluntary Hostel for Girls; Educn Counsellor, Marriage Guidance Council. Member: Home Office Advisory Cttee on Juvenile Delinquency, 1963–65 (Chm. Sub-Cttee on Transition from Sch. to Work); a Youth Employment Cttee, 1960; Hendon Gp Hosp. Management Cttee, 1965–70; Exec., Greater London Labour Party, 1964–74; Toynbee Housing Soc., 1967–(Chm., 1976–87); Council, Toynbee Hall, 1983–90; Bd of Governors, Nat. Hosp. for Nervous Diseases, 1976–79; Board of Management, Shelter, 1976–89 (Trustee, Shelter Housing Aid Centre); London Local Adv. Cttee, IBA, 1979–83; Hampstead DHA, 1981–84; Trustee, Sutton Housing

Trust, 1982–90; Chm., East London Housing Assoc., 1979–94. Formerly Vice-Chm., GLC Ambulance Cttee; GLC Housing Committee: Mem. (co-opted), 1968–70; Labour Spokesman, 1970–73, 1977–81; Chm., 1973–75, 1981–82. Contested (Lab) Hendon South, Gen. Election, 1970. Mem., Nat. and London Councils of Nat. Fedn of Housing Assocs, 1980–83. Co-Pres., Nat-amat UK (Internat. Orgn of Working Women and Volunteers), 1994–. FRSA 1977. *Recreations:* walking in the country, lazing in the sun, reading (incl. thrillers), theatre, watching TV. *Died 13 March 1999.*

DINGWALL, John James, OBE 1964; HM Inspector of Constabulary for Scotland, 1966–70; *b* 2 Sept. 1907; *s* of late James Dingwall, Bannockburn, Stirling; *m* 1932, Jane Anne (*d* 1980), *d* of late James K. Halliday, Falkirk; two *d. Educ:* Bridge of Allan and Stirling. Stirlingshire Constabulary, 1927–49; Stirling and Clackmannan Police Force, 1949–55; seconded to Directing Staff, Scottish Police Coll., 1953–55; Chief Constable of Angus, 1955–66. *Recreations:* angling, shooting, golf. *Address:* Tigh Na Muirn, 4 Victoria Street, Monifieth DD5 4HL.
Died 16 Nov. 1996.

DIONISOTTI-CASALONE, Carlo, FBA 1972; Professor of Italian, Bedford College (formerly Bedford College for Women), University of London, 1949–70, then Emeritus; *b* 9 June 1908; *s* of Eugenio Dionisotti-Casalone and Carla Cattaneo; *m* 1942, Maria Luisa Pinna-Pintor; three *d* (and one *d* decd). *Educ:* Turin, Italy. Dottore in lettere, Univ. of Turin, 1929; MA Oxon, 1947. Libero Docente di Letteratura Italiana, Univ. of Turin, 1937; Asst di Letteratura Italiana, Univ. of Rome, 1943; Italian Lectr, Univ. of Oxford, 1947. *Publications:* Indici del giornale storico della letteratura italiana (Turin), 1945; Guidiccioni-orazione ai nobili di Lucca (Rome), 1946; Bembo Savorgnan, Carteggio d'amore (Florence), 1950; Oxford Book of Italian Verse, revised edn 1952; Bembo, Prose e Rime (Turin), 1960; Geografia e storia della letter. ital. (Turin), 1967; Gli Umanisti e il Volgare (Florence), 1968; Machiavellerie (Turin), 1980; Appunti sui moderni (Bologna), 1988; Ricordo di A. Momigliano (Bologna), 1989; Natalino Sapegno dalla Torino di Gobetti alla cattedra romana (Turin), 1994; Appunti su arti e lettere (Milan), 1995; Aldo Manuzio umanista e editore (Milan), 1995. *Address:* 44 West Heath Drive, NW11 7QH.
Died 22 Feb. 1998.

DIPLOCK, Prof. Anthony Tytherleigh; Professor, Division of Biomolecular Science, and President, International Antioxidant Research Centre, Guy's, King's College and St Thomas' Hospitals' Medical and Dental School; *b* 24 July 1935; *s* of Bernard and Elsie Diplock; *m* 1st, 1957, Elisabeth Anne Price (marr. diss. 1979); one *s* one *d*; 2nd, 1980, Lynn Christine Richards; one *s. Educ:* Univ. of Bristol (BSc Physiol/Chemistry); PhD (Biochem.) London; DSc London 1976. Mem., then Hd, Biochem. Res. Dept, Vitamins Ltd, Tadworth, subseq. Beecham Res. Labs, 1956–67; Sen. Lectr, then Reader in Biochem., Royal Free Hosp. Med. Sch., Univ. of London, 1967–77; Guy's Hosp. Med. Sch., subseq. UMDS of Guy's and St Thomas' Hosps, then Guy's, King's Coll. and St Thomas' Hosps Med. and Dental School: Prof., 1977–; Chm., Div. of Biochem., later Div. of Biochem. and Mol. Biol., 1984–99; Co-Dir, Free Radical Res. Gp, 1991–96; Pres., Internat. Antioxidant Res. Centre, 1996–. University of London: Mem., Senate, 1980–94; Mem. Ct, 1989–94; Mem. Council, 1994–96; Dean, Faculty of Medicine, 1986–91; Chm., Academic Council Med. Cttee, 1984–91; Mem., numerous Univ. of London cttees and wkg parties, 1978–. Res. Prog. Manager and Advr, MAFF Initiatives in Food Prog., 1994–; Scientific Dir, Assured British Meat, 1998–. Chairman: EU ILSI Theme Gp on Defence Against Reactive Oxidative Species, 1995–; EU ILSI Drafting Gp on Functional Food Sci., 1997–99. Member, Council: BPMF, 1988–91; Hunterian Inst., RCS, 1989–92; Royal Free Hosp. Sch. of Medicine, 1989–95; Roedean Sch., 1989–; Mem., Council of Govs, 1987–, Chm., Academic Bd, 1991–95, UMDS; Advr, ACU, 1987–91; Mem., Commonwealth Scholarships Commn, 1991–97. Hon. Prof. of Biochem., Xi'an Med. Univ., People's Republic of China, 1985–. Evian Health Award, 1986; Caroline Walker Award for Science, 1993. *Publications:* Fat-Soluble Vitamins, 1985; (ed with L. J. Machlin) Vitamin E Biochemistry and Health Implications, 1990; (jtly) Techniques in Free Radical Research, 1991; (solely or jtly) over 230 pubns on fat-soluble vitamins, trace elements, antioxidant nutrients in human health, nutritional prevention of cancer and cardiovascular disease. *Recreations:* renovating an old cottage, sailing, the ships of Nelson's navy, music, building long-case clocks, dogs. *Address:* International Antioxidant Research Centre, Hodgkin Building, Guy's, King's College and St Thomas' Hospitals' Medical and Dental School, Guy's Hospital, SE1 9RT. *T:* (020) 7955 4521/2, *Fax:* (020) 7403 7195. *Club:* Athenæum. *Died 4 Feb. 2000.*

DISNEY, Harold Vernon, CBE 1956; Manager, Engineering Division, Reactor Group, UK Atomic Energy Authority, 1969–72, retired; *b* 2 July 1907; *s* of Henry Disney and Julia Vernon; *m* 1936, Lucy Quinton; two *d. Educ:* Hallcroft Higher Standard Sch., Ilkeston; Nottingham University Coll. Internat. Combustion, 1931–35; ICI (Alkali), 1935–46; on loan to Min. of Supply (RFF's), 1941–46; Dept of Atomic Energy, 1946–54; UKAEA: Asst Dir, Defence Projects, Industrial Gp, 1954; Dir of Engineering, Industrial Gp, 1958; Man. Dir, Engineering Gp, Risley, 1962. FIMechE 1947. *Recreation:* gardening. *Address:* Barrowmore Village Nursing Home, Great Barrow, Chester CH3 7JA.
Died 5 May 1998.

DIVERRES, Prof. Armel Hugh; Professor of French and Head of Department of Romance Studies, University College of Swansea, 1974–81, then Emeritus; *b* Liverpool, 4 Sept. 1914; *o s* of late Paul Diverres and Elizabeth (*née* Jones); *m* 1945, Ann Dilys, *d* of late James and Enid Williams; one *s* two *d. Educ:* Swansea Grammar Sch.; University Coll., Swansea; Univ. of Rennes; Sorbonne, Paris. MA (Wales), LèsL (Rennes), Docteur de l'Université de Paris. Fellow of Univ. of Wales, 1938–40; served in RA and Intelligence Corps, 1940–46, Captain. Asst Lectr in French, 1946–49, Lectr, 1949–54, Univ. of Manchester; Sen. Lectr in French, 1954–57, Carnegie Prof., 1958–74, Dean, Faculty of Arts, 1967–70, Univ. of Aberdeen. Governor: Nat. Mus. of Wales, 1978–81; Centre for Information on Language Teaching and Res., 1977–82; Aberdeen Coll. of Education, 1971–74. Member: CNAA Lang. Board, 1965–78, Cttee for Res., 1975–82, Humanities Bd, 1978–81; Welsh Jt Educn Cttee, 1975–81. Pres., British Br., Internat. Arthurian Soc., 1978–80, Internat. Pres., 1979–81; Pres., Soc. for French Studies, 1976–78. Officier des Palmes Académiques, 1971; Chevalier de l'Ordre National du Mérite, 1986. *Publications:* Voyage en Béarn by Froissart (ed), 1953; La Chronique métrique attribuée à Geffroy de Paris (ed), 1956; Chatterton by A. de Vigny (ed), 1967; articles and reviews in learned journals. *Recreation:* hill walking. *Address:* 23 Whiteshell Drive, Langland, Swansea, W Glamorgan SA3 4SY. *T:* (01792) 360322.
Died 27 May 1998.

DIXEY, Paul Arthur Groser; Chairman of Lloyd's, 1973, 1974 (Deputy Chairman, 1967, 1969, 1972); *b* 13 April 1915; *e s* of late Neville Dixey, JP (Chairman of Lloyd's, 1931, 1934 and 1936), and Marguerite (*née* Groser); *m* 1939, Mary Margaret Baring, JP (*d* 1996), 2nd *d* of late Geoffrey Garrod; four *s* one *d. Educ:* Stowe; Trinity Coll.,

Cambridge. Elected an Underwriting Mem. of Lloyd's, 1938. Served War of 1939–45, Royal Artillery. Member: London Insce market delegn to Indonesia, 1958; Cttee, Lloyd's Underwriters' Assoc., 1962–74; Cttee, Salvage Assoc., 1962–74; Cttee, Lloyd's, 1964–70, 1972–75; Gen. Cttee, Lloyd's Register of Shipping, 1964–90; Chm., Salvage Assoc., 1964–65. Chairman: Paul Dixey Underwriting Agencies Ltd, 1973–76; Pieri Underwriting Agencies Ltd, 1976–94; Director, Merrett Dixey Syndicates Ltd, 1976–78. Mem. Council, Morley Coll., 1952–62; Chm. Governors, Vinehall Sch., 1966–73. Leader, Barn Boys' Club, 1949–61. Mem., Dunmow RDC, 1958–64. Chm., Essex Hunt Cttee, 1981–. *Recreations:* riding, fly-fishing. *Address:* Little Easton Spring, Dunmow, Essex CM6 2JB. *T:* (01371) 872840.
Died 19 Aug. 1998.

DIXON, Jack Shawcross, OBE 1969; HM Diplomatic Service, retired 1976; *b* 8 March 1918; *s* of Herbert Dixon and Helen (*née* Woollacott); *m* 1941, Ida Hewkin; one *d. Educ:* Oldham Hulme Grammar Sch.; London Sch. of Economics (BScEcon). Served in Royal Welch Fusiliers and RAOC attached Indian Army, 1940–46. Colonial Office, 1948; entered HM Foreign (subseq. Diplomatic) Service, 1949; FO, 1949; HM Political Agency, Kuwait, 1950; Rep. of Polit. Agent, Mina al Ahmadi, 1951; FO, 1952; 1st Sec., Singapore, 1956; HM Consul, Barcelona, 1959; FO, 1962; 1st Sec., Rome, 1966; FCO, 1971; Head of Treaty and Nationality Dept, FCO, 1973–76. *Publications:* contribs to Jl of Imperial and Commonwealth History, Indica Jaipurensia. *Recreation:* art-historical research (India). *Address:* 26 Brook Court, 47 Meads Road, Eastbourne, E Sussex BN20 7PY.
Died 14 Feb. 1997.

DIXON, Margaret Rumer Haynes; *see* Godden, Rumer.

DIXON, Stanley; Chairman, Midland-Yorkshire Tar Distillers Ltd, 1968–71; *b* 12 Aug. 1900; *m* 1936, Ella Margaret Hogg; two *s. Educ:* Leeds Grammar Sch.; Queen's Coll., Oxford. Articled to Leather & Veale, Chartered Accountants in Leeds, 1924–27; Manager, Leather & Veale (later Peat, Marwick, Mitchell & Co.), Leeds, 1927–35; Sec., Midland Tar Distillers Ltd, 1935–66; Dir, Midland Tar Distillers Ltd (later Midland-Yorkshire Holdings Ltd), 1943–71. Pres., Inst. of Chartered Accountants in England and Wales, 1968–69. Hon. DSocSc Birmingham, 1972. *Publications:* The Case for Marginal Costing, 1967; The Art of Chairing a Meeting, 1975. *Recreations:* Church affairs, gardening and music. *Address:* 83 Norton Road, Stourbridge, West Midlands DY8 2TB. *T:* (01384) 395672.
Died 8 Sept. 2000.

DIXON, Group Captain William Michael, CBE 1972; DSO 1943; DFC 1941; AFC 1958; Bursar, Summer Fields School, Oxford, 1975–86; *b* 29 July 1920; *s* of late William Michael Dixon; *m* 1st, 1944, Mary Margaret (*d* 1957), *d* of late William Alexander Spence, MC, MM; three *s*; 2nd, 1988, Eileen Margaret Collinson, *d* of late Claud Henry Tucker, OBE. Served War of 1939–45, Bomber Comd; Air Staff, Rhodesian Air Trng Gp, 1946–49; psa 1949; comd No 2 (Bomber) Sqdn RAAF, 1952–55; comd No 192 Sqdn RAF, 1955–58; jssc 1958; comd RAF Feltwell, 1961–63; Sen. Officer Admin No 1 (Bomber) Gp, 1963–66; Sen. Personnel SO HQ Air Support Comd, 1966–68; DCAS, Royal Malaysian Air Force, 1968–71; Dir of Aircraft Projects (RAF), MoD, 1972–75; ADC to the Queen, 1968–73. *Recreation:* natural history. *Address:* Little Orchard, Brecon View, Bleadon, Weston-super-Mare BS24 9NF. *T:* (01934) 812437.
Died 20 Aug. 1999.

DOBB, Erlam Stanley, CB 1963; TD; *b* 16 Aug. 1910; *s* of Arthur Erlam Dobb, Old Colwyn, Denbighshire; *m* 1937,

Margaret Williams; no *c. Educ:* Ruthin; University Coll. of N Wales. Chartered Surveyor and Land Agent, Anglesey, Denbigh and Merioneth, 1930–35; Asst Land Comr to Dir, Agricultural Land Service, MAFF, 1935–70; a Dep. Dir-Gen., Agricl Develt and Adv. Service, MAFF, 1971–73, Dir-Gen., 1973–75. Mem., ARC, 1973–75; Vice-Chm., Adv. Council for Agriculture and Horticulture in England and Wales, 1974–75. Trustee, T. P. Price Charity, Markshall Estate, Essex, 1971–84 (Chm. Trustees, 1971–83). Governor, Royal Agricultural College, 1960–75. Royal Welch Fusiliers (TA), 1938–46, Major. FRICS; FRAgS. *Publications:* professional contributions to journals of learned societies. *Recreations:* golf, gardening. *Address:* Churchgate, Westerham, Kent TN16 1AS. *T:* Westerham (01959) 62294. *Clubs:* Farmers'; Crowborough Beacon Golf, Limpsfield Chart Golf.

Died 13 Feb. 1996.

DOBBING, Prof. John, DSc; FRCP, FRCPath; Professor of Child Growth and Development, Department of Child Health, University of Manchester, and Honorary Consultant, United Manchester Hospitals, 1968–84, then Professor Emeritus; *b* 14 Aug. 1922; *s* of Alfred Herbert Dobbing and May Gwendoline (*née* Cattell); *m* Dr Jean Sands. *Educ:* Bootham Sch., York; St Mary's Hosp., London (BSc 1st cl. hons, MB, BS); DSc Manchester, 1981. FRCPath 1976; FRCP 1981. Lectr in Path. and Gull Student, Guy's Hosp., 1954–61; Scn. Lectr in Physiol., London Hosp., 1961–64; Sen. Lectr, Inst. of Child Health, London, and Hon. Consultant, Hosp. for Sick Children, Gt Ormond Street, 1964–68. Hon. FRCPCH 1997. *Publications:* Applied Neurochemistry, 1968; (ed with J. A. Davis) Scientific Foundations of Paediatrics, 1974, 2nd edn 1981; Maternal Nutrition in Pregnancy: eating for two?, 1981; Prevention of Spina Bifida, 1983; Lipids, Learning and the Brain: fats in infant formulas, 1993; Developing Brain and Behaviour: the role of lipids in infant formula, 1997; pubns on undernutrition and developing brain in scientific literature. *Recreations:* writing, travel, France and the French. *Address:* Higher Cliff Farm, Birch Vale, High Peak SK22 1DL. *T:* (01663) 743220.

Died 2 May 1999.

DOBEREINER, Peter Arthur Bertram; golf correspondent, The Observer, 1965–90; *b* 3 Nov. 1925; *s* of Major Arthur Dobereiner and Dorothy (*née* Hassall); *m* 1951, Betty Evelyn Jacob; two *s* two *d. Educ:* King's College, Taunton; Lincoln College, Oxford. RNVR 1942. Asst Manager, Parry & Co. (Madras), 1946; various newspaper appts, 1949–: East Essex Gazette, Oxford Times, News Chronicle, Daily Express, Daily Mail, The Guardian. Hon. Mem., Amer. Soc. of Golf Course Architects. Screen Writers Guild Award (jtly) (That Was the Week That Was), 1962; MacGregor writing awards, 1977, 1981; Donald Ross award, 1985; Irish Golf Fellowship Award, 1987. *Publications:* The Game With a Hole In It, 1970, 3rd edn 1973; The Glorious World of Golf, 1973, 3rd edn 1975; Stroke, Hole or Match?, 1976; Golf Rules Explained, 1980, 8th edn 1992; For the Love of Golf, 1981; Tony Jacklin's Golf Secrets, 1982; Down the Nineteenth Fairway, 1982; The World of Golf, 1982; (ed) The Golfers, 1982; The Book of Golf Disasters, 1983; The Fifty Greatest Post-War Golfers, 1985; Arnold Palmer's Complete Book of Putting, 1986; Preferred Lies, 1987; Golf à la Carte, 1990; Maestro, 1992. *Recreation:* golf. *Address:* Chelsfield Hill House, Pratts Bottom, Orpington, Kent BR6 7SL. *T:* Farnborough (Kent) (01689) 853849. *Clubs:* West Kent Golf; Pine Valley Golf; Hon. Ballybunion (Ireland).

Died 2 Aug. 1996.

DOBREE, John Hatherley, FRCS; Consulting Ophthalmic Surgeon, St Bartholomew's Hospital (Consultant, 1956); Honorary Ophthalmic Surgeon, North Middlesex Hospital (Senior Ophthalmic Surgeon, 1947); *b* 25 April 1914; *s* of Hatherley Moor Dobree, OBE, and Muriel Dobree (*née* Hope); *m* 1941, Evelyn Maud Smyth; two *s. Educ:* Victoria Coll., Jersey; St Bartholomew's Hosp. MS London 1947, FRCS 1950. House Physician, Metropolitan Hosp., 1938–39; House Surgeon, Western Ophthal. Hosp., 1940; served in RAMC, 1940–46, in MEF, as RMO and Ophthalmic Specialist; Chief Asst, Eye Dept, St Bartholomew's Hosp., 1946–51. FRSocMed (Past Sec., Sect. of Ophthalmology); Vice-Pres. and Past Hon. Sec. Ophthalmological Soc. of UK; Dep. Master, Oxford Ophth. Congress, 1976. *Publications:* The Retina, vol. x, in Sir Stewart Duke-Elder's System of Ophthalmology, 1967; (with E. S. Perkins) Differential Diagnosis of Fundus Conditions, 1971; (with E. Boulter) Blindness and Visual Handicap, the Facts, 1982; Soldiers of the Company, 1988. *Recreations:* archaeology, walking. *Address:* The Rosery, Great Bealings, Woodbridge, Suffolk IP13 6NW. *Club:* Army and Navy.

Died 7 June 1999.

DODDS, James Pickering, CB 1954; Under-Secretary, Department of Health and Social Security, 1968–73; *b* 7 Feb. 1913; *s* of James Thompson and Elizabeth Fingland Dodds; *m* 1942, Ethel Mary Gill (*d* 1987); two *d. Educ:* Queen Elizabeth's Grammar Sch., Darlington; Jesus Coll., Cambridge. Entered Ministry of Health, 1935; Nuffield Home Civil Service Travelling Fellowship, 1950; Under-Sec., 1951; Dir of Establishments and Orgn, 1965–68. *Address:* 17 Herne Road, Oundle, Peterborough PE8 4BS.

Died 26 Aug. 1996.

DOIG, Very Rev. Dr Andrew Beveridge; General Secretary, National Bible Society of Scotland, 1972–82; Moderator, General Assembly of the Church of Scotland, 1981–82; *b* 18 Sept. 1914; *s* of George and Hannah Doig; *m* 1st, 1940, Nan Carruthers (*d* 1947); one *d*; 2nd, 1950, Barbara Young; one *s* one *d. Educ:* Hyndland Secondary Sch., Glasgow; Glasgow Univ. (MA, BD; Hon. DD 1974); Union Theol Seminary, New York (STM). Ordained, 1938; Church of Scotland Missionary to Nyasaland, 1939–63; service included: Dist Missionary and Sec. of Mission Council; Sen. Army Chaplain, E Africa Comd, 1941–45; Mem., Nyasaland Legislative Council, 1946–53, Mem., Adv. Cttee on African Educn, and Coll. Council, Univ. of Rhodesia and Nyasaland; Regional Sec., Nyasaland and N Rhodesia; seconded to represent African interests in Fed. Parlt, Rhodesias and Nyasaland, 1953–58; Gen. Sec., Synod of Ch. of Central Africa (Presbyterian), 1958–63; Minister, St John's and King's Park, Dalkeith, Scotland, 1963–72. *Address:* The Eildons, Moulin, Pitlochry PH16 5EW. *T:* (01796) 472892.

Died 21 Dec. 1997.

DOIG, Peter Muir; *b* 27 Sept. 1911; *m* 1938, Emily Scott; two *s. Educ:* Blackness Sch., Dundee. Served RAF, 1941–46. Sales Supervisor with T. D. Duncan Ltd, Bakers, Dundee, until 1963. Mem., TGWU; joined Labour Party, 1930; Mem. of Dundee Town Council, 1953–63, Hon. Treasurer, 1959–63. Contested (Lab) S Aberdeen, 1959; MP (Lab) Dundee West, Nov. 1963–1979. *Recreation:* chess. *Address:* 2 Westwater Place, Wormit, Newport-on-Tay, Fife DD6 8NS.

Died 31 Oct. 1996.

DOLCI, Danilo; Coordinator, Centro Studi e Iniziative, since 1958 (Founder); *b* Sesana, Trieste, 28 June 1924; *s* of Enrico Dolci and Mely Kontely; *m* 1952, Vincenzina Mangano; two step *s* three step *d. Educ:* University of Rome; University of Milan. Came to Sicily to work for improvement of social conditions, 1952; arrested and tried for non-violent "reverse strike" to find work for unemployed, 1958. Mem. Internat. Council of War Resisters' International, 1963. Hon. DPhil Berne, 1968; Hon. DScEd Bologna, 1996. Lenin Peace Prize, 1958; Gold Medal, Accademia Nazionale dei Lincei, 1969; Sonning Prize, 1971; Etna Taormina Poetry Prize, 1975;

Viareggio Internat. Prize, 1979. *Publications:* Banditi a Partinico, 1955; Inchiesta a Palermo, 1956; Spreco, 1960; Racconti siciliani, 1963; Verso un mondo nuovo, 1964 (trans. A New World in the Making, 1965); Chi Gioca Solo, 1966; Chissà se i pesci piangono (documentazione di un'esperienza educativa), 1973; Non esiste il silenzio, 1974; Esperienze e riflessioni, 1974; Creatura di creature, 1983; Palpitare di nessi, 1985; The World is One Creature, 1986; Se gli occhi fioriscono, 1990; Nessi fra esperiènza, etica e politica, 1993; Gente semplice, 1993; Comunicare, legge della vita, 1993; La comunicazione di massa non esiste, 1995; La struttura maieutica e l'evolverci, 1996. *Address:* Centro Studi, Largo Scalia 5, Partinico 90047 (Palermo), Italy. *T:* (91) 8781905.

Died 30 Dec. 1997.

DOLMETSCH, Carl Frederick, CBE 1954; Director of Haslemere Festival since 1940; specialist and authority on early music and instruments; recording artist in England and America; *b* 23 Aug. 1911; *s* of Arnold Dolmetsch and Mabel Johnston; *m* 1937, Mary Douglas (*née* Ferguson) (marr. diss. 1961; she *d* 1996); one *s* two *d* (and one *s* decd); *m* 1997, Greta Matthews. *Educ:* privately. Began studying music with Arnold Dolmetsch at age of 4; first performed in public at 7; first concert tour at 8; first broadcast on violin and viol, 1925, at 14 years of age; virtuoso recorder-player at 15. Toured and broadcast in America, 1935 and 1936; recorder recitals, Wigmore Hall, Feb. and Nov. 1939, and annually from 1946; toured and broadcast on radio and TV in Holland, 1946; Italy and Switzerland, 1947; Sweden, 1949; New Zealand, 1953; France, 1956; America, 1957; Switzerland, Austria, Germany, Holland, 1958; Belgium, America, 1959; Sweden, Austria, Germany, 1960; Australia, 1965; Colombia, 1966; France, Sweden, 1967; Alaska, Canada and Italy, 1969; Japan, 1974; Denmark, 1983; Colombia, 1984; Italy, 1985; France, 1991; America (yearly), 1961–81. Frequent broadcasts in this country and abroad. Chm. and Man. Dir, Arnold Dolmetsch Ltd, 1963 78; Chm., Dolmetsch Musical Instruments, 1982–. Musical Dir of Soc. of Recorder Players, 1937–; Musical Dir, Dolmetsch Internat. Summer School, 1970–; Mem. Incorporated Soc. of Musicians; Mem. Art Workers' Guild, 1953 (Master, 1988); Patron Early Music Soc., University of Sydney. Hon. Fellow of Trinity Coll. of Music, 1950. Hon. DLitt University of Exeter, 1960. Hon. Fellow London Coll. of Music, 1963. *Publications:* Recorder Tutors, 1957, 1962, 1970, 1977; edited and arranged numerous publications of 16th-, 17th- and 18th-century music; contrib. to many music jls. *Recreations:* ornithology, natural history. *Address:* Jesses, Haslemere, Surrey GU27 2BS. *T:* (01428) 643818.

Died 11 July 1997.

DONALDSON OF KINGSBRIDGE, Baron *cr* 1967 (Life Peer), of Kingsbridge, co. Buckingham; **John George Stuart Donaldson,** OBE 1943; retired farmer; *b* 9 Oct. 1907; *s* of Rev. S. A. Donaldson, Master of Magdalene Coll., Cambridge, and Lady Albinia Donaldson (*née* Hobart-Hampden) (*sister* of 7th Earl of Buckinghamshire); *m* 1935, Frances Annesley Lonsdale (*d* 1994), writer, *d* of Frederick Lonsdale; one *s* two *d. Educ:* Eton; Trinity Coll., Cambridge. Pioneer Health Centre, Peckham, 1935–38; Road Transport, 1938–39; Royal Engineers, 1939–45. Farmed in Glos, and later Bucks. Member: Glos Agric. Exec. Cttee, 1953–60; SE Regional Planning Council, 1966–69. Parly Under-Sec. of State, NI Office, 1974–76; Minister for the Arts, DES, 1976–79. Joined: SDP, 1981; Soc & Lib Dem, 1987, then Lib Dem. Hon. Secretary: Nat. Assoc. Discharged Prisoners Aid Socs, 1961; All Party Penal Affairs Gp, 1981; Chairman: Nat. Assoc. for the Care and Resettlement of Offenders, 1966–74; Bd of Visitors, HM Prison, Grendon, 1963–69; Consumer Council, 1968–71; EDC for Hotel and Catering

Industry, 1972–74; Nat. Cttee, Family Service Units, 1968–74; Cttee of Enquiry into conditions of service for young servicemen, 1969; Assoc. of Arts Instns, 1980–83; Confedn of Art and Design Assocs, 1982–84; British Fedn of Zoos, 1970–74; Pres., RSPB, 1975–80. Director: Royal Opera House, Covent Garden, 1958–74; Sadler's Wells, 1963–74; British Sugar Corp., 1966–74. *Recreations:* music in general, opera in particular. *Address:* 17 Edna Street, SW11 3DP. *Club:* Brooks's.

Died 8 March 1998.

DONALDSON, David Abercrombie, RSA 1962 (ARSA 1951); RP 1964; RGI 1977; painter; Head of Painting School, Glasgow School of Art, 1967–81; Her Majesty's Painter and Limner in Scotland, since 1977; *b* 29 June 1916; *s* of Robert Abercrombie Donaldson and Margaret Cranston; *m* 1st, 1942, Kathleen Boyd Maxwell; one *s*; 2nd, 1949, Maria Krystyna Mora-Szorc; two *d. Educ:* Coatbridge Sec. Sch.; Glasgow Sch. of Art. Travelling Scholarship, 1938. Joined Staff of Glasgow Sch. of Art, 1940. Paintings in private collections in America, Canada, Australia, South Africa and Europe and public collections in Scotland. Sitters include: The Queen, 1968; Sir Hector Hetherington; Dame Jean Roberts; Sir John Dunbar; Lord Binning; Rev. Lord McLeod; Mrs Winifred Ewing; Miss Joan Dickson; Earl of Haddo; Sir Samuel Curran; Roger Ellis; Sir Norman Macfarlane; Rt Hon. Margaret Thatcher; Dr Steven Watson; Rt Hon. David Steel; Sir Alwyn Williams. Hon. LLD Strathclyde, 1971; Hon. DLitt Glasgow, 1988. *Recreations:* music, cooking. *Address:* 5 Cleveden Drive, Glasgow G12 0SU. *T:* 0141–334 1029; 7 Chelsea Manor Studios, Flood Street, SW3 5SR. *T:* 0171–352 1932; St Roman de Malegarde, 84290 Vaucluse en Provence, France. *T:* 90289265. *Club:* Art (Glasgow).

Died 22 Aug. 1996.

DONKIN, Air Cdre Peter Langloh, CBE 1946; DSO 1944; retired; *b* 19 June 1913; *s* of Frederick Langloh and Phyllis Donkin; *m* 1941, Elizabeth Marjorie Cox (*d* 1998); two *d. Educ:* Sherborne; RAF Coll., Cranwell. Commissioned RAF, 1933; No 16 Sqdn, 1933–38; British Mission in Poland, 1939; CO 225 Sqdn, 1940; CO 239 Sqdn, 1941–42; CO 35 Wing, 1943–44; Sch. Land Air Warfare, 1945; HQ, RAF Levant, 1946; RCAF Staff Coll., 1948–49; Exchange USAF, 1950; CO, RAF Chivenor, 1951–53; Air Attaché, Moscow, 1954–57; Asst Chief of Staff, HQ Allied Air Forces, Central Europe, 1957–58; idc, 1959; AOC, RAF, Hong Kong, 1960–62. *Recreations:* shooting, yachting. *Address:* 71 Hill Street, Orange, NSW 2800, Australia. *Club:* Carlton. *Died 12 July 2000.*

DONOVAN, Terence Daniel, FRPS, FBIPP; photographer; film director, since 1957; *b* 14 Sept. 1936; *s* of Daniel Donovan and Constance Donovan (*née* Wright); *m* 1st, 1961, Janet Cohen (marr. diss.); one *s*; 2nd, 1970, Diana St Felix Dare; one *s* one *d.* FRPS 1968; FBIPP (FIIP 1968). Photography: worked for Vogue, Harpers & Queen, Elle, and Marie Claire; exhibn, Albemarle Gall., 1990. Films: directed TV commercials, 1967–; dir. feature film, Yellow Dog, 1972; also produced plays for CBS, documentaries for LWT, and pop promos. Trustee, Arts Foundn, 1991–. FRSA. *Publications:* Glances, 1983; Fighting Judo, 1985; *posthumous publication:* Terence Donovan: The Photographs, 2000. *Recreations:* judo (black belt), photography, painting abstract expressionism. *Address:* 47/48 New Bond Street, W1Y 9HA. *T:* (0171) 491 4477. *Clubs:* Victory Service Men's; Budokwai Judo. *Died 22 Nov. 1996.*

DORMAN, Lt-Col Sir Charles (Geoffrey), 3rd Bt *cr* 1923, of Nunthorpe, co. York; MC 1942; *b* 18 Sept. 1920; *o s* of Sir Bedford Lockwood Dorman, 2nd Bt, CBE and Lady (Constance Phelps) Dorman (*née* Hay) (*d* 1946); *S* father, 1956; *m* 1954, Elizabeth Ann (marr. diss. 1972; she *d* 1993), *d* of late George Gilmour Gilmour-White, OBE;

one *d. Educ:* Rugby Sch., Brasenose Coll., Oxford (MA). Commissioned, 1941; served with 3rd The King's Own Hussars at Alamein (MC) and in Italian Campaign; commissioned to 13th/18th Royal Hussars (QMO), 1947; GSO1, 1961–70; retired. *Recreation:* gliding. *Heir: cousin* Philip Henry Keppel Dorman [*b* 19 May 1954; *m* 1982, Myriam Jeanne Georgette, *d* of late René Bay; one *d*]. *Address:* La Plénelière, St Pierre-du-Chemin, La Châtaigneraie, Vendée, France.

Died 2 Sept. 1996.

DOUGHERTY, Maj.-Gen. Sir Ivan Noel, Kt 1968; CBE 1946; DSO 1941 (bar, 1943); ED; *b* Leadville, NSW, 6 April 1907; *m* 1936, Emily Phyllis Lofts; two *s* two *d* (and one *d* decd). *Educ:* Leadville Primary Sch.; Mudgee High Sch.; Sydney Teachers' Coll.; Sydney Univ. (BEc). NSW Education Department: Asst Teacher, 1928–32; Dep. Headmaster, 1933–39; Headmaster, 1946–47; Dist Inspector of Schs, 1948–53; Staff Inspector 1953–55. Commissioned Sydney Univ. Regt, 1927. Capt. 1931; Unattached List, 1932–34; transf. to 33/41 Bn, 1934; Major, 1938; command, 33rd Bn, 1938; Lt-Col 1939; served War of 1939–45 (DSO and Bar, CBE, despatches thrice); Australian Imperial Force, Second-in-Command, 2/2 Inf. Bn, 1939–40; commanded 2/4 Inf. Bn, Libya, Greece, Crete campaigns, 1940–42; Brig. 1942; commanded 23 Bde, 1942; commanded 21 Bde, South-West Pacific, 1942–45; R of O, 1946–47; commanded 8th Bde, Aust. Mil. Forces, 1948–52; Maj.-Gen., 1952; commanded 2nd Div., 1952–54; Citizen Military Forces Member, Australian Mil. Bd, 1954–57; R of O, 1957–64; Retired List, 1964. Hon. ADC to Governor-Gen. of Australia, 1949–52; Hon. Col, Australian Cadet Corps, Eastern Command, 1964–70; Representative Hon. Col, Australian Cadet Corps, 1967–70. Dir of Civil Defence for NSW, 1955–73. Mem. Council, Nat. Roads and Motorists' Assoc., 1969–79. Mcm. Senate, 1954–74, Dep. Chancellor, 1958–66, Hon. LLD 1976, Univ of Sydney. *Address:* 4 Leumeah Street, Cronulla, NSW 2230, Australia. *T:* (2) 95235465. *Died 4 March 1998.*

DOUGHTY, George Henry; General Secretary, Technical and Supervisory Section, Amalgamated Union of Engineering Workers, 1971–74, retired; Member, Central Arbitration Committee, 1976–85; *b* 17 May 1911; British; *m* 1941, Mildred Dawson; two *s. Educ:* Handsworth Tech. Sch.; Aston Technical Coll. Draughtsman; trained at General Electric Co., Birmingham, 1927–32; employed as Design Draughtsman: English Electric, Stafford 1932–33; GEC, Birmingham, 1934–46; with Draughtsmen's & Allied Technician's Assoc., 1946–71, General Secretary, 1952–71. Member: Gen. Council of TUC, 1968–74; Independent Review Cttee, 1976–89; Chm., EDC for Electrical Engrg, 1974–82. Mem., Royal Commn on Distribution of Income and Wealth, 1974–78. Industrial Relns Advr, SIAD, 1977–88. *Publications:* various technical and Trade Union publications. *Recreation:* photography. *Died 25 July 1998.*

DOUGLAS, Prof. Alexander Stuart; Regius Professor of Medicine, University of Aberdeen, 1970–85, then Emeritus; Senior Research Fellow, Department of Medicine, Aberdeen Royal Infirmary, since 1992; *b* 2 Oct. 1921; *s* of late Dr R. Douglas, MOH for Moray and Nairn; *m* 1954, Christine McClymont Stewart; one *s* one *d. Educ:* Elgin Academy, Morayshire. Mil. Service, RAMC, 1945–48 (despatches 1947). Research Fellow, Radcliffe Infirmary, Oxford, and Postgrad. Med. Sch., London, 1951–53; Lectr, Sen. Lectr and Reader in Medicine, Univ. Dept of Med., Royal Infirmary, Glasgow, 1953–64; Hon. Consultant status, 1957; Prof. of Med., Univ. of Glasgow, 1964–70; secondment to Univ. of East Africa with hon. academic rank of Prof., 1965; Hon. Consultant Physician in Administrative Charge of wards, Royal Infirmary,

Glasgow, 1968–70. Leverhulme Sen. Res. Fellow, 1990–92. *Publications:* scientific papers on haemostasis and thrombosis and seasonal variation in health and disease. *Recreation:* walking. *Address:* University Department of Medicine, Aberdeen Royal Infirmary, Foresterhill, Aberdeen AB25 2ZD. *T:* (01224) 681818 (ext. 53014). *Died 15 Nov. 1998.*

DOUGLAS, Sir (Edward) Sholto, Kt 1977; Solicitor of the Supreme Court of Queensland, since 1934; *b* 23 Dec. 1909; *s* of Hon. Edward Archibald Douglas (Hon. Mr Justice Douglas) and Annette Eileen Power; *m* 1939, Mary Constance Curr. *Educ:* St Ignatius Coll., Riverview, Sydney. Queensland Law Society Incorporated: Mem. Council, 1954–76; Actg Pres., 1960; Pres., 1962–64; Mem., Statutory Cttee, 1976–81. Member: Legal Assistance Cttee, Qld, 1965–80; Solicitors' Bd, 1969–75; Exec. Mem., Law Council of Aust., 1973–75. President: Taxpayers Assoc. of Qld, 1955–58; Federated Taxpayers of Aust., 1957–58; Mem. Adv. Cttee, Terminating and Permanent Building Socs, 1966–77. Pres., Qld Div., Nat. Heart Foundn, 1976–77 (Vice-Pres., 1966–75); Vice-Pres., RSPCA, 1965–86; Chm., Management Cttee, Currimbin Bird Sanctuary and Wildlife Reserve, 1978–80. *Recreations:* racing, gardening. *Address:* 81 Markwell Street, Hamilton, Brisbane, Qld 4007, Australia. *T:* (7) 32682759. *Clubs:* Queensland, Brisbane (Pres. 1965), Tattersalls, Royal Queensland Golf, Queensland Turf, Tattersalls Racing, Brisbane Amateur Turf (all Brisbane). *Died 17 Aug. 1997.*

DOUGLAS, Sir Robert (McCallum), Kt 1976; OBE 1956; President, Tilbury Douglas PLC, since 1991 (Director, 1930–88, Chairman, 1952–77, President, 1980–91, Robert M. Douglas Holdings); *b* 2 Feb. 1899; *s* of John Douglas and Eugenia McCallum; *m* 1927, Millicent Irene Tomkys Morgan (*d* 1980); one *s* one *d. Educ:* Terregles Sch.; Dumfries Academy. Served Army, 1916–19. Served 10 years with civil engineering contracting co., 1920–30; founded Douglas Group of Companies, 1930. Mem., MPBW Midland Regional Jt Adv. Cttee, 1940–46. Federation of Civil Engineering Contractors: Chm., Midland Section, 1942–43 and 1947–48; Chm. Council, 1948–49; Pres., 1958–60. Patron, Staffs Agric. Soc.; Pres., Burton Graduate Med. Centre, 1988–. Hon. DSc Aston, 1977. *Recreation:* farming. *Address:* Dunstall Hall, Barton-under-Needwood, Burton-on-Trent, Staffordshire DE13 8BE. *T:* (01283) 712471. *Club:* Caledonian. *Died 7 Dec. 1996.*

DOUGLAS, Prof. Ronald Walter, DSc; FInstP, FSGT; Professor of Glass Technology, University of Sheffield, 1955–75; *b* 28 March 1910; *s* of John H. P. and A. E. Douglas; *m* 1933, Edna Maud Cadle; two *s. Educ:* Latymer Upper Sch.; Sir John Cass Coll., London; DSc London. Mem., Research Staff, Research Laboratories of General Electric Company, 1927–55. Pres., Internat. Commn on Glass, 1972–75. *Publications:* (with S. Frank) A History of Glassmaking, 1972; many papers on the physics of glass and semiconductors. *Address:* Otter Close, Perrys Gardens, West Hill, Ottery St Mary, Devon EX11 1XA. *Died 14 Nov. 2000.*

DOUGLAS, Sir Sholto; *see* Douglas, Sir E. S.

DOUGLAS, Prof. William Wilton, MD; FRS 1983; Professor of Pharmacology, Yale University School of Medicine, New Haven, USA, 1968–94, then Professor Emeritus; *b* 15 Aug. 1922; *s* of Thomas Hall James Douglas and Catherine Dorward (*née* Wilton); *m* 1954, Jeannine Marie Henriette Dumoulin; two *s. Educ:* Glasgow Acad.; Univ. of Glasgow (MB, ChB 1946, MD 1949). Resident House Surgeon: Glasgow Western Infirm., 1946; Law Hosp., Carluke, 1947; Demonstr in Physiology, Univ. of Aberdeen, 1948; served RAMC, 1949–50: Chemical

Defence Res. Estab., Porton Down, Wilts (Major); Mem. Staff, National Inst. for Med. Res., Mill Hill, 1950–56; Prof. of Pharmacol., Albert Einstein Coll. of Medicine, New York, 1956–68. *Publications:* papers on cellular mechanisms of secretion and the critical function of calcium in stimulus-secretion coupling, in Jl of Physiol., Brit. Jl of Pharmacol., Nature, and Science. *Recreations:* yachting, skiing. *Address:* 76 Blake Road, Hamden, CT 06517, USA. *T:* (203) 7761800.   *Died 2 July 1998.*

DOUGLAS-MANN, Bruce Leslie Home; solicitor, in practice since 1954; Senior Partner, Douglas-Mann & Co.; *b* 23 June 1927; *s* of late Leslie John Douglas-Mann, MC and Alice Home Douglas-Mann; *m* 1955, Helen Tucker; one *s* one *d. Educ:* Upper Canada Coll., Toronto; Jesus Coll., Oxford. Leading Seaman, RN, 1945–48; Oxford, 1948–51. Admitted solicitor, 1954. Contested (Lab): St Albans, 1964; Maldon, 1966; MP North Kensington, 1970–74, Merton, Mitcham and Morden, 1974–May 1982, resigned (Lab 1970–81, Ind 1981, SDP Jan.-May 1982); contested: Merton, Mitcham and Morden (SDP), June 1982; Mitcham and Morden (SDP), 1983, (SDP/Alliance), 1987. Chairman: PLP Housing and Construction Gp, 1974–79; PLP Environment Gp, 1979–81 (Vice-Chm., 1972–79); Parly Select Cttee on Environment, 1979–82. Member: SDP Council, 1984–88; Steering Cttee, Yes to Unity, 1987–88; Mem., England Co-ordinating Cttee, SLD, 1988–89; Chm., Hammersmith SLD, 1988–89. Vice-Pres., Soc. of Lab. Lawyers, 1980–81 (Chm., 1974–80). Mem., Kensington or Kensington and Chelsea Borough Council, 1962–68. Trustee, Arts Council Trust for Special Funds, 1981–99 (Chm., 1981–97); Chm., Common Voice, 1990–92; Bd Mem., Shelter, 1974–99 (Chm., 1990–93; Chm., Exec. Cttee, 1987–90). *Publications:* pamphlets: (ed) The End of the Private Landlord, 1973; Accidents at Work—Compensation for All, 1974. *Address:* 33 Furnival Street, EC4A 1JQ. *T:* (020) 7405 7216.   *Died 27 July 2000.*

DOUGLAS-WITHERS, Maj.-Gen. John Keppel Ingold, CBE 1969; MC 1943; *b* 11 Dec. 1919; *s* of late Lt-Col H. H. Douglas-Withers, OBE, MC, FSA, and Mrs V. G. Douglas-Withers; *m* 1945, Sylvia Beatrice Dean, Croydon, Surrey; one *s* one *d. Educ:* Shrewsbury Sch.; Christ Church, Oxford. Diploma in French, Univ. of Poitiers, 1938; Associate of Inst. of Linguists, in French and German, 1939. Commissioned into RA, 1940; service in UK, Iraq, Western Desert, N Africa and Italy, 1940–45; Instr in Gunnery, Sch. of Artillery, Larkhill, 1945–47; service in Canal Zone, 1948–49; attended Staff Coll., Camberley, 1950; Staff appt in WO (Mil. Ops), 1951–53; service in The King's Troop, RHA, 1954–55; Instr, Staff Coll., Camberley, 1956–58; Battery Comdr, G Batt., Mercers Troop, RHA, 1959–60; Staff appt in WO (Mil. Sec. Dept), 1961; commanded 49 Field Regt in BAOR and Hong Kong, 1962–64; student at IDC, 1965; Comd 6 Inf. Bde in BAOR, 1966–67; Chief of Staff, 1st Brit. Corps, 1968–69; GOC SW District, 1970–71; Asst Chief of Personnel and Logistics, MoD, 1972–74; retired 1974. Col Comdt, RA, 1974–82. Asst Dir and Gp Personnel Man., Jardine Matheson & Co. Ltd, Hong Kong, 1974–80; Consultant, Matheson & Co. Ltd, London, 1980–94. MPIM (Hong Kong), 1976. *Recreations:* history, military music, gardening. *Address:* Lloyds Bank, 25 High Street, Shipston-on-Stour, Warwickshire CV36 4AJ. *Clubs:* East India, Devonshire, Sports and Public Schools, MCC.
                Died 3 Nov. 1997.

DOULTON, Alfred John Farre, CBE 1973 (OBE 1946); TD 1954; psc 1943; MA Oxon; Head of Statistical Team and Comptroller, Independent Schools Information Service, 1974–80, Consultant, 1980–81; *b* 9 July 1911; *s* of H. V. Doulton, Housemaster, Dulwich Coll., and Constance Jessie Farre, Dulwich; *m* 1940, Vera Daphne,

d of A. R. Wheatley, Esher; four *s* one *d. Educ:* Dulwich Coll.; Brasenose Coll., Oxford (Classical Scholar). Served War, 1940–46 (despatches twice): DAAG 11 Army Group, 1944; active service, Burma, Malaya, Java, 1945–46; DAQMG 4 Corps, AA&QMG 23 Indian Division, 1945–46. Burma Star, Far East and GS Medal with Java Clasp. Asst Master, Uppingham School, 1934–40; Head of Classics and Housemaster of The Lodge, Uppingham Sch., 1946; Headmaster, Highgate Sch., 1955–74. Vice-Chm., HMC, 1967 (Hon. Treasurer, 1964–74). Alderman, Haringey, 1968–71 (Vice-Chm. Educn Cttee). Mem., Governing Bodies Assoc., 1977–80. Vice-Chm. and Chm. Finance Cttee, Kelly Coll., 1974–86; Trustee, Uppingham Sch., 1966–85. Mem., Indep. Schools Careers Orgn Council, 1978–81. *Publications:* The Fighting Cock, 1951; Highgate School 1938–1944: the story of a wartime evacuation, 1976. *Recreations:* music, cricket, books, dinghy sailing, ornithology. *Address:* Field Cottage, Beadon Lane, Salcombe, Devon TQ8 8JS. *T:* Salcombe (01548) 842316. *Clubs:* Athenæum, MCC; Salcombe Yacht (Cdre, 1987–90).   *Died 14 Aug. 1996.*

DOW, (John) Christopher (Roderick), FBA 1982; Visiting Fellow, National Institute of Economic and Social Research, since 1984; *b* 25 Feb. 1916; *s* of Warrender Begernie and Amy Langdon Dow; *m* 1960, Clare Mary Keegan; one *s* three *d. Educ:* Bootham Sch., York; Brighton, Hove and Sussex Grammar Sch.; University College London (Fellow 1973). Economic Adviser, later Senior Economic Adviser, HM Treasury, 1945–54; on staff, and Dep. Dir, National Inst. for Economic and Social Research, 1954–62; HM Treasury, 1962–63; Asst Sec.-Gen., OECD, Paris, 1963–73; Exec. Dir, Bank of England, 1973–81; an Advr to the Governor of the Bank of England, 1981–84. *Publications:* The Management of the British Economy, 1945–1960, 1964; (jtly) Fiscal Policy for a Balanced Economy, 1968; (with I. D. Saville) A Critique of Monetary Policy: Theory and British Experience, 1988; Five Major Recessions: Britain & the world, 1920–95, 1998; various articles in learned jls. *Clubs:* Garrick, Reform.   *Died 1 Dec. 1998.*

DOWNES, Mollie Patricia P.; *see* Panter-Downes.

DOWNING, Charles; *see* Dowsett, C. J. F.

DOWNING, Henry Julian; HM Diplomatic Service, retired; *b* 22 March 1919; *o s* of Henry Julian Downing and Kate Avery; *m* 1951, Ruth Marguerite Ambler (*d* 1998). *Educ:* Boys' High Sch., Trowbridge; Hertford Coll., Oxford. Indian Civil Service (Madras), 1941–47; joined HM Foreign Service, 1947; 2nd Secretary, Madras and Dacca, 1947–50; Foreign Office, 1950–52; 1st Secretary (Commercial), Istanbul, 1952–56; Foreign Office, 1956–58; 1st Secretary and Head of Chancery, Kabul, 1958–62; Foreign Office, 1963–65; HM Consul-General, Lourenço Marques, 1965–69; Head of Claims Dept, 1969–71, of Migration and Visa Dept, 1971–73, FCO; Consul-Gen., Cape Town, 1973–77. *Recreations:* swimming, walking, bird watching. *Address:* 8b Greenaway Gardens, Hampstead, NW3 7DJ. *T:* (020) 7435 2593. *Club:* United Oxford & Cambridge University.   *Died 24 Nov. 1998.*

DOWSETT, Prof. Charles James Frank, MA, PhD Cantab; FBA 1977; Calouste Gulbenkian Professor of Armenian Studies, University of Oxford, 1965–91, then Emeritus Professor; Fellow of Pembroke College, Oxford, 1965–91, then Emeritus Fellow; *b* 2 Jan. 1924; *s* of late Charles Aspinall Dowsett and Louise (*née* Stokes); *m* 1949, Friedel (*d* 1984), *d* of Friedrich Lapuner, Kornberg, E Prussia. *Educ:* Owen's Sch.; St Catherine's Society, Oxford, 1942–43; Peterhouse, Cambridge (Thomas Parke Scholar), 1947–50 (Mod. and Mediaeval Languages Tripos, Part I, 1st Class Russian, 1st Class German, 1948,

Part II, Comparative Philology, 1st Class with distinction, 1949). Treasury Studentship in Foreign Languages and Cultures, 1949–54: Ecole Nationale des Langues Orientales Vivantes, Univ. de Paris, 1950–52 (diplôme d'arménien); Ecole des Langues Orientales Anciennes, Institut Catholique de Paris, 1950–53 (diplôme de géorgien). Lecturer in Armenian, School of Oriental and African Studies, University of London, 1954, Reader in Armenian, 1965. Vis. Prof., Univ. of Chicago, 1976. Member: Council, RAS, 1972–76; Philological Soc., 1973–77; Marjory Wardrop Fund for Georgian Studies, 1966–91. *Publications:* The History of the Caucasian Albanians by Movses Dasxuranci, 1961; The Penitential of David of Ganjak, 1961; (with J. Carswell) Kütahya Armenian Tiles, vol. 1, The Inscribed Tiles, 1972; Sayat-Nova, an 18th century troubadour, 1997; contributed: W. B. Henning Memorial Volume, 1970; Iran and Islam: Vladimir Minorsky Memorial Volume, 1971; Hayg Berberian Memorial Volume, 1986; articles in Bulletin of the School of Oriental and African Studies, Le Muséon, Revue des Etudes Arméniennes, Jl of Soc. for Armenian Studies, The Geographical Journal, Raft, etc; translations from Flemish (Felix Timmermans' Driekoningentryptiek, A Christmas Triptych, 1955, Ernest Claes' De Witte, Whitey, 1970); as Charles Downing (children's books): Russian Tales and Legends, 1956; Tales of the Hodja, 1964; Armenian Folktales and Fables, 1972. *Address:* 21 Hurst Rise Road, Cumnor Hill, Oxford OX2 9HE.
Died 8 Jan. 1998.

DOYLE, Air Comdt Dame Jean (Lena Annette) C.; *see* Conan Doyle.

D'OYLY, Sir Nigel Hadley Miller, 14th Bt *cr* 1663, of Shottisham, Norfolk; *b* 6 July 1914, *s* of Sir Hastings Hadley D'Oyly, 11th Bt, and Evelyn Maude, *d* of George Taverner Miller; *S* half-brother, 1986; *m* 1939, Dolores (*d* 1971), *d* of R. H. Gregory; one *s* two *d. Educ:* Radley; RMC Sandhurst. Formerly Major, Royal Scots; served War of 1939–45, Hong Kong, France and War Office. *Heir: s* Hadley Gregory D'Oyly [*b* 29 May 1956; *m* 1st, 1978, Margaret May Dent (marr. diss. 1982); 2nd, 1991, Annette Frances Elizabeth, *yr d* of Maj. Michael White; one *d*]. *Address:* 30 Delves House, Ringmer, Lewes, East Sussex BN8 5EW. *Died 1 May 2000.*

DRAKE, Sir (Arthur) Eric (Courtney), Kt 1970; CBE 1952; DL; *b* 29 Nov. 1910; *e s* of Dr A. W. Courtney Drake; *m* 1st, 1935, Rosemary Moore (marr. diss.); two *d*; 2nd, 1950, Margaret Elizabeth Wilson; two *s. Educ:* Shrewsbury; Pembroke Coll., Cambridge (MA; Hon. Fellow 1976). With The British Petroleum Co. Ltd, 1935–75, Chm., 1969–75; Dep. Chm., P&O Steam Navigation Co., 1976–81. Pres., Chamber of Shipping, 1964; Hon. Mem., General Council of British Shipping, 1975–; Member: Gen. Cttee, Lloyd's Register of Shipping, 1960–81, 1985–87; MoT Shipping Adv. Panel, 1962–64; Cttee on Invisible Exports, 1969–75; Bd of Governors, Pangbourne Nautical Coll., 1958–69; Court of Governors, London Sch. of Economics and Political Science, 1963–74; Governing Body of Shrewsbury Sch., 1969–83; Cttee of Management, RNLI, 1975–85; Life Mem., Court of City Univ., 1969; Pres., City and Guilds Insignia Award Assoc., 1971–75; Hon. Petroleum Adviser to British Army, 1971. Hon. Mem., Honourable Co. of Master Mariners, 1972; Elder Brother of Trinity House, 1975–. Vice Pres., Mary Rose Trust, 1984– (Chm., 1979–83). Freeman of City of London, 1974; one of HM Lieutenants, City of London. DL Hants, 1983. Hon. DSc Cranfield, 1971; Hon. Fellow, UMIST, 1974. Hambro British Businessman of the Year award, 1971; Cadman Meml Medal, Inst. of Petroleum, 1976. Comdr, Ordre de la Couronne, Belgium, 1969; Kt Grand Cross of Order of Merit, Italy, 1970; Officier, Légion d'Honneur, 1972; Order of Homayoun, Iran, 1974;

Comdr, Ordre de Leopold, Belgium, 1975. *Address:* Meadow Cottage, Cheriton, Alresford, Hants SO24 0PP. *T:* (01962) 771334. *Clubs:* London Rowing, Royal Cruising; Royal Yacht Squadron (Trustee); Leander.
Died 31 Oct. 1996.

DRAKE, Brig. Dame Jean Elizabeth R.; *see* Rivett-Drake.

DRAYCOTT, Douglas Patrick; QC 1965; MA; a Recorder, since 1972 (Recorder of Shrewsbury, 1966–71); *b* 23 Aug. 1918; *s* of George Draycott and Mary Ann Draycott (*née* Burke); *m* 1942, Elizabeth Victoria Hall (marr. diss. 1974); two *s* three *d; m* 1979, Margaret Jean Brunton (*née* Speed). *Educ:* Wolstanton Grammar Sch.; Oriel Coll., Oxford (MA). War Service: Royal Tank Regiment and General Staff, 1939–46. Barrister, Middle Temple, 1950, Bencher, 1972. Joined Oxford Circuit, 1950; Leader, Midland and Oxford Circuit, 1979–83. *Recreation:* cruising on inland waterways. *Address:* 4 King's Bench Walk, Temple, EC4Y 7DL. *T:* (0171) 353 3581; 11 Sir Harry's Road, Edgbaston, Birmingham B15 2UY. *T:* (0121) 440 1050; 5 Fountain Court, Steelhouse Lane, Birmingham, B4 6DR. *T:* (0121) 606 0500. *Died 1 Dec. 1997.*

DREW, Prof. George Charles, MA; London University Professor of Psychology, University College, 1958–79, then Professor Emeritus; Honorary Fellow, 1979; *b* 10 Dec. 1911; *e s* of George Frederick Drew; *m* 1936, Inez Annie, *d* of F. Hulbert Lewis; one *s* one *d. Educ:* St George's Sch., Bristol; Bristol, Cambridge and Harvard Univs. Viscount Haldane of Cloan Studentship, Cambridge, 1935–36; Rockefeller Fellowship, Harvard Univ., 1936–38; Rockefeller Research Fellowship, Cambridge, 1938–42; Psychological Adviser, Air Ministry, 1942–46; Lecturer in Psychology, University of Bristol, 1946–49, Reader, 1949–51, Prof. of Psychology, 1951–58; Dean of Science, UCL, 1973–76. Mem. Science Research Council, 1965–67. Vis. Prof., University of Calif, Berkeley, USA, 1967–68. C. S. Myers Lectr, 1973. Founder Mem., Exper. Psych. Soc., 1946 (Pres. 1950–51, 1959–60); Pres., British Psych. Soc., 1962–63; Pres. and Chm., Org. Cttee, 19th Internat. Congress of Psychology, 1969. *Publications:* articles on animal behaviour, learning, vision, and other psychological problems, in various British and American journals. *Died 19 Dec. 1997.*

DREW, Dame Jane (Beverley), DBE 1996; FRIBA; architect; Partner in firm of Fry Drew and Partners, since 1946; *b* 24 March 1911; *m* 1st, 1934, Jim Alliston (marr. diss.); one *d* (and one *d* decd); 2nd, 1942, Edwin Maxwell Fry, CBE, RA (*d* 1987). *Educ:* Croydon. Was in partnership with J. T. Alliston, 1934–39; independent practice, 1939–45; in partnership with Maxwell Fry, 1945–87. Asst Town Planning Adviser to Resident Minister, West African Colonies, 1944–45; Senior Architect to Capital project of Chandigarh, Punjab, India, 1951–54; Beamis Prof. Mass Inst. of Techn., Jan.-June 1961; Vis. Prof. of Architecture, Harvard, Feb-March 1970; Bicentennial Prof., Utah Univ., 1976. Completed work includes housing, hospitals, schools, and colleges in UK, West Africa, etc including Univs in Nigeria, Middle East and India; a section of Festival of Britain, 1951; town planning, housing and amenity buildings in Iran, W Africa and India. Past Pres., Architectural Association (1969). Hon. FAIA 1978; Hon. FNIA 1985; Hon. Fellow: Humberside Polytechnic, 1991; Yorks Br., RIBA, 1993; S African Inst. of Architects. Hon LLD Ibadan, 1966; DUniv Open, 1973; Hon. DLitt Newcastle, 1987; Hon. DArch Witwatersrand, 1994. *Publications:* (with Maxwell Fry) Architecture for Children, 1944; (with Maxwell Fry and Harry Ford) Village Housing in the Tropics, 1945; (Founder Editor, 1945) Architects' Year Book; (with Maxwell Fry) Architecture in the Humid Tropics; Tropical Architecture, 1956; (with Maxwell Fry) Architecture and the Environment, 1976. *Recreations:* reading, writing,

friends. *Address:* West Lodge, Cotherstone, Barnard Castle, Co. Durham DH12 9PF. *T:* Teesdale (01833) 650217. *Club:* Institute of Contemporary Arts.
Died 27 July 1996.

DRIVER, Christopher Prout; writer and broadcaster; Personal Page consultant, The Guardian, since 1994 (Personal Page Co-Editor, 1988–94); *b* 1 Dec. 1932; *s* of Dr Arthur Herbert Driver and Elsie Kathleen Driver (*née* Shepherd); *m* 1958, Margaret Elizabeth Perfect; three *d. Educ:* Dragon Sch., Oxford; Rugby Sch.; Christ Church, Oxford (MA). Friends Ambulance Unit Internat. Service, 1955–57; Reporter, Liverpool Daily Post, 1958–60; Reporter, 1960–64, Features Editor, 1964–68, Food and Drink Ed., 1984–88, The Guardian; Editor, Good Food Guide, 1969–82. Member: Christian Aid Bd, 1972–84; Highgate URC, 1962–. *Publications:* A Future for the Free Churches?, 1962; The Disarmers: a study in protest, 1964; The Exploding University, 1971; The British at Table 1940–1980, 1983; (publisher and co-ed) Shaftesbury, 1983; (jtly) Pepys at Table, 1984; Twelve Poems, 1985; Music for Love, 1994; Strokes (poems), 1996; (ed) John Evelyn, cook, 1996; (orchestration for wind and strings) Schubert's Grand Rondeau in A minor for piano, 1996; contribs on various topics to The Guardian and other serious jls. *Recreations:* cooking, playing violin and viola, avoiding cars, accumulating books. *Address:* 6 Church Road, Highgate, N6 4QT; The Guardian, 119 Faringdon Road, EC1R 3ER. *T:* (0171) 278 2332.
Died 18 Feb. 1997.

DRURY, Allen Stuart; author; *b* Houston, Texas, 2 Sept. 1918; *s* of Alden M. and Flora A. Drury. *Educ:* Stanford Univ. (BA). Served with US Army, 1942–43. Ed., The Tulare (Calif) Bee, 1939–41; county ed., The Bakersfield Californian, Bakersfield, Calif, 1941–42; United Press Senate Staff, Washington, DC, 1943–45; freelance correspondent, 1946; Nation Ed., Pathfinder Magazine, Washington, DC, 1947–53; National Staff, Washington Evening Star, 1953–54; Senate Staff, New York Times, 1954–59. Mem., National Council on the Arts (apptd by Pres. Reagan), 1982–88. Sigma Delta Chi Award for Editorial Writing, 1942. Hon. LitD Rollins Coll., Winter Park, Fla, 1961. *Publications:* Advise and Consent, 1959 (Pulitzer Prize for Fiction, 1960); A Shade of Difference, 1962; A Senate Journal, 1963; That Summer, 1965; Three Kids in a Cart, 1965; Capable of Honor, 1966; "A Very Strange Society", 1967; Preserve and Protect, 1968; The Throne of Saturn, 1971; Courage and Hesitation: inside the Nixon administration, 1972; Come Nineveh, Come Tyre, 1973; The Promise of Joy, 1975; A God Against the Gods, 1976; Return to Thebes, 1977; Anna Hastings, 1977; Mark Coffin, USS, 1978; Egypt: the eternal smile, 1980; The Hill of Summer, 1981; Decision, 1983; The Roads of Earth, 1984; Pentagon, 1986; Toward What Bright Glory?, 1990; Into What Far Harbor?, 1992; A Thing of State, 1995; *posthumous publication:* Public Men, 1999. *Address:* PO Box 941, Tiburon, CA 94920, USA. *Clubs:* Cosmos, University, National Press (Washington); Bohemian (San Francisco).
Died 2 Sept. 1998.

DUCHESNE, Brig. (Peter) Robin, OBE 1978; Secretary General, Royal Yachting Association, since 1986; *b* 25 Sept. 1936; *s* of late Herbert Walter Duchesne and Irene Duchesne (*née* Cox); *m* 1968, Jennifer Maclean Gouldsbury; one *s* one *d. Educ:* Colwyn Bay Grammar Sch.; RMA Sandhurst. Commissioned RA, 1956; Battery Comdr, 101 Airborne Div., USA, 1963–64; Instructor, RMA, 1965–67; RN Staff Coll., 1969; CO 49 Field Regt, RA, 1975–77; Directing Staff, Army Staff Coll., 1977–79; Comdr, Commonwealth Adv. Team, Ghana, 1979–81; CRA 1 Armd Div., 1981–83; Dep. Comdr and COS UNFICYP, 1984–86. Chm., Sail Trng Assoc., Internat.

(formerly Sail Trng Assoc., Tall Ships Races), 1996– (Vice-Chm., 1986–96); Mem. Council, Marine Conservation Soc., 1990– (Chm., 1993–97). FIMgt. *Recreations:* sailing, most sports, organising Tall Ships Races. *Address:* Lake Lodge, Churt, Farnham, Surrey GU10 2QB. *T:* (home) (01252) 793901, (office) (01703) 627420. *Clubs:* Royal Ocean Racing, Royal Thames Yacht. *Died 14 April 2000.*

DUCKWORTH, Sir Richard Dyce, 3rd Bt *cr* 1909, of Grosvenor Place, City of Westminster; *b* 30 Sept. 1918; *s* of Sir Edward Dyce Duckworth, 2nd Bt, and Cecil Gertrude, *y d* of Robert E. Leman; *S* father, 1945; *m* 1942, Violet Alison (*d* 1996), *d* of Lieut-Col G. B. Wauchope, DSO; two *s. Educ:* Marlborough Coll. Started business in 1937, retired 1969. *Recreations:* sailing, golf, squash, shooting. *Heir: s* Edward Richard Dyce Duckworth [*b* 13 July 1943; *m* 1976, Patricia, *o d* of Thomas Cahill; one *s* one *d*]. *Address:* Dunwood Cottage, Shootash, Romsey, Hants SO51 6GA. *T:* (01794) 513228.
Died 28 Dec. 1997.

DUDBRIDGE, Bryan James, CMG 1961; retired from HM Overseas Civil Service, 1961; Deputy Director, formerly Associate Director, British Council of Churches Department of Christian Aid, 1963–72; *b* 2 April 1912; *o s* of late W. Dudbridge, OBE, and Anne Jane Dudbridge; *m* 1943, Audrey Mary, *o d* of late Dr and Mrs Heywood, Newbury; two *s* one *d. Educ:* King's Coll. Sch., Wimbledon; Selwyn Coll., Cambridge. Appointed to Colonial Administrative Service as Cadet in Tanganyika, 1935; Asst Dist Officer, 1937; Dist Officer, 1947; Sen. Dist Officer, 1953; Actg Provincial Comr, Southern Province; Administrative Officer (Class IIA), 1955, and Actg Provincial Commissioner (Local Government); Provincial Commissioner, Western Province, 1957; Minister for Provincial Affairs, 1959–60, retd. *Publications:* contrib. Journal of African Administration, Tanganyika Notes and Records, and Avon and Gloucestershire Family History Socs. *Recreations:* family history, natural history, beagling, wildfowl. *Address:* Red Rock Bungalow, Elm Grove Road, Topsham, Exeter EX3 0EJ. *T:* (01392) 874468. *Club:* Royal Commonwealth Society. *Died 6 Sept. 1996.*

DUFF, Rt Hon. Sir (Arthur) Antony, GCMG 1980 (KCMG 1973; CMG 1964); CVO 1972; DSO 1944; DSC; PC 1980; Deputy Secretary, Cabinet Office, 1980–84; Director General, Security Service, 1985–87, retired; *b* 25 Feb. 1920; *s* of late Adm. Sir Arthur Allen Morison Duff, KCB and Margaret Grace Rawson; *m* 1944, Pauline Marion, *d* of Capt. R. H. Bevan, RN, and *widow* of Flt-Lieut J. A. Sword; one *s* two *d*, and one step *s. Educ:* RNC, Dartmouth. Served in RN, 1937–46. Mem., Foreign (subseq. Diplomatic) Service, 1946; 3rd Sec., Athens, 1946; 2nd Sec., 1948; 2nd Sec., Cairo, 1949; 1st Sec., 1952; transferred Foreign Office, Private Sec. to Minister of State, 1952; 1st Sec., Paris, 1954; Foreign Office, 1957; Bonn, 1960; Counsellor, 1962; British Ambassador to Nepal, 1964–65; Commonwealth Office, 1965–68; FCO, 1968–69; Dep. High Comr, Kuala Lumpur, 1969–72; High Comr, Nairobi, 1972–75; Dep. Under-Sec. of State, FCO, 1975–80. Dep. Governor, Southern Rhodesia, 1979–80. *Address:* c/o National Westminster Bank, 68 Palmerston Road, Southsea, Hants PO5 3PN. *Club:* Army and Navy. *Died 13 Aug. 2000.*

DUFF, Patrick Craigmile, CMG 1982; *b* 6 Jan. 1922; *o s* of late Archibald Craigmile Duff, ICS, and Helen Marion (*née* Phillips); *m* 1st, 1947, Pamela de Villeneuve Graham (*osp*); 2nd, 1950, Elizabeth Rachel, *d* of late Rt Rev. R. P. Crabbe (Bishop of Mombasa, 1936–53) and Margaret Crabbe; two *d. Educ:* Wellington Coll., Berks; New Coll., Oxford (MA 1946). War service, 1941–42. HMOCS, 1942–63: Tanganyika; Kenya; CRO, 1964–65;

ODM/ODA, 1966–74; Head, West Indian and Atlantic Dept, FCO, 1975–80; Head, British Develt for E Africa, FCO, 1980–82. *Recreations:* making music, fell walking, ball games. *Address:* 6 Christchurch Road, Winchester, Hants SO23 9SR. *T:* (01962) 865200. *Club:* Royal Commonwealth Society. *Died 31 March 2000.*

DUFF, Col Thomas Robert G.; *see* Gordon-Duff.

DUFFY, Peter Joseph Francis; QC 1997; *b* 25 Aug. 1954; *s* of Martin and Elizabeth Duffy; *m* 1980, Vivienne Joy Furneaux; three *d* (one *s* decd). *Educ:* Wimbledon Coll.; Gonville and Caius Coll., Cambridge (BA 1975; LLB 1977; MA 1979); Univ. of Brussels (licencié spécial en droit européen 1976). Called to the Bar, Lincoln's Inn, 1978; Mem., Law Faculty, 1979–89, Airey Neave Fellow, 1989–91, QMC; Mem., Supplementary Panel, Treasury Counsel (Common Law), 1994–97. Advr, Council of Europe (specialising in Central and Eastern Europe progs). Chm., Bar European Gp, 1998– (Vice Chm., 1996–98). Dir of Studies, Public International Law, Hague Acad., 1992; Sen. Vis. Res. Fellow, Centre of European Law, KCL, 1996–. Mem., Amnesty International, 1976– (Mem., Internat. Exec. Cttee, 1985–; Internat. Chm., 1989–91); Dir, Amnesty International (Charity) Ltd, 1990–. Ed., European Human Rights Reports, 1982–; European Law Columnist, Solicitor's Jl, 1992–. Hon. LLD Western State Univ., Calif. *Publications:* papers in learned jls. *Address:* Essex Court Chambers, 24 Lincoln's Inn Fields, WC2A 3ED. *T:* (020) 7813 8000. *Died 5 March 1999.*

DUGARD, Arthur Claude, CBE 1969; Chairman, Cooper & Roe Ltd, 1952–79, retired (Joint Managing Director until 1972); *b* 1 Dec. 1904; *s* of Arthur Thomas Turner Dugard, Nottingham; *m* 1931, Christine Mary Roe, Nottingham; two *s*. *Educ:* Oundle Sch., Northants. Joined Cooper & Roe Ltd, Knitwear manufacturers, 1923 (Dir, 1936; Man. Dir, 1947). President: Nottingham Hosiery Manufrs Assoc., 1952–53; Nat Hosiery Manufrs Fedn, 1959–61; Nottingham Chamber of Commerce, 1961–62. First Chm., CBI North Midland Regional Council, 1965–66; Chm. British Hosiery & Knitwear Export Gp, 1966–68; Mem. East Midlands Economic Planning Council, 1967–72. *Recreation:* golf. *Address:* 16 Hollies Drive, Edwalton, Nottingham NG12 4BZ. *T:* (0115) 923 3217. *Died 13 March 1996.*

DUGDALE, Peter Robin, CBE 1987; Managing Director, Guardian Royal Exchange plc, 1978–90; *b* 12 Feb. 1928; *s* of late Dr James Norman Dugdale and Lilian (*née* Dolman); *m* 1957, (Esmé) Cyraine, *d* of L. Norwood Brown; three *s*. *Educ:* Canford; Magdalen Coll., Oxford (MA). Joined Union Insurance Soc. of Canton, Hong Kong, 1949; merged with Guardian Assurance, London, 1960; Marine and Aviation Underwriter, Guardian Assurance, 1963–73; Pres., Guardian Insurance Company of Canada, 1973–76; Gen. Manager, 1976, Dir, 1977–91, Guardian Royal Exchange. Chairman: Trade Indemnity plc, 1980–93; Aviation and General Insurance Co. Ltd, 1982–84. Chairman: British Insurance Assoc., 1981–82; Assoc. of British Insurers, 1987–89. Master, Worshipful Co. of Insurers, 1989–90; Hon. Life Mem., Inst. of London Underwriters, 1985. Hon. Treas., GDBA, 1992–. Gov., Canford Sch., 1980– (Chm. Govs, 1995–). *Recreations:* military and naval history, flatcoated retrievers. *Address:* Cherry Copse, Broad Lane, Hambledon, Hants PO7 4QS. *T:* (01705) 632462. *Club:* Oriental.

Died 9 March 1998.

DUGGAN, Gordon Aldridge, CMG 1996; HM Diplomatic Service, retired; consultant; Director: (Europe), Singapore Technologies, since 1997; Marshall Cavendish, since 1997; *b* 12 Aug. 1937; *s* of late Joseph Nathan Duggan and Elizabeth Aldridge; *m* 1969, Erica Rose Anderssen; one *s* two *d*. *Educ:* Liverpool Collegiate Sch.; Lincoln

Coll., Oxford. BA, BPhil. FO, 1963–66; Canberra, 1966–69, FCO, 1969–72; Information Officer, Bonn, 1972–74; First Sec. and Head of Chancery, Jakarta, 1974–76; First Sec., Canberra, 1976–79; FCO, 1979–80; Commercial and Economic Counsellor, Lagos, 1981–84; Consul-Gen., Zürich, Dir of British Export Promotion in Switzerland, and Consul-Gen., Liechtenstein, 1985–88; Hd of Commercial Management and Exports Dept, FCO, 1988–89; (on secondment) Dir, Project Develt, NEI, 1989–90; High Comr, Singapore, 1991–97. Business Consultant (Europe), NOL/APL, 1997–. *Recreations:* armchair sport, jazz, theatre, walking, string quartets. *Address:* Lady Elisabeth Hall, Porthgwarra, St Levan, Penzance, Cornwall TR19 6JP. *Club:* United Oxford & Cambridge University. *Died 22 Oct. 1998.*

DUGGAN, Rt Rev. John Coote; an Hon. Assistant Bishop, Diocese in Europe, since 2000; *b* 7 April 1918; *s* of Rev. Charles Coote Whittaker Duggan, BD and Ella Thackeray Duggan (*née* Stritch); *m* 1948, Mary Elizabeth Davin; one *s* one *d* (and one *d* decd). *Educ:* High School, Dublin; Trinity Coll., Dublin (Schol.; Moderator (1st cl.) Men. and Moral Sci., 1940; Bernard Prize, Divinity Testimonium (2nd cl.); BA 1940; BD 1946). Deacon 1941, priest 1942; Curate Assistant: St Luke, Cork, 1941–43; Taney, Dublin, 1943–48; Hon. Clerical Vicar, Christ Church Cath., 1944–48; Incumbent: Portarlington Union, Kildare, 1948–55; St Paul, Glenageary, Dublin, 1955–69; Westport and Achill Union, Tuam, 1969–70; Archdeacon of Tuam, 1969–70; Bishop of Tuam, Killala and Achonry, 1970–85. Exam. Chaplain to Archbp of Dublin, 1958–69; Examiner in BD Degree, Univ. of Dublin, 1960–69. Editor, Irish Churchman's Almanack, 1958–69. *Publications:* A Short History of Glenageary Parish, 1968; A Century of Spanish Anglican Witness, 1995. *Recreation:* fishing. *Address:* 15 Beechwood Lawn, Rochestown Avenue, Dun Laoghaire, Co. Dublin. *Club:* Royal St George Yacht (Dun Laoghaire). *Died 20 July 2000.*

DUMBUTSHENA, Hon. Enoch; Chief Justice of Zimbabwe, 1984–90; Vice-President, International Commission of Jurists, since 1992 (Commissioner, since 1990); *b* 25 April 1920; *s* of late Job Matabasi Dumbutshena and Sarah Dumbutshena; *m* 1st, 1948, Alphosina (*née* Mahlangu) (marr. diss.; she *d* 1989); one *s* one *d*; 2nd, 1964, Miriam Masango (marr. diss.); one *s* two *d*; 3rd, 1997, Norah Ayamin. *Educ:* Univ. of South Africa (BA, BEd, UED). Called to the Bar, Gray's Inn, 1963, Hon. Bencher, 1989. Teacher, 1946–56; journalist, 1956–59; barrister, Southern Rhodesia, 1963–67; Zambia: founded Legal Aid Scheme, 1967–70; private practice, 1970–78; Zimbabwe: private practice, 1978–80; Judge of High Court, 1980; Judge President, 1983. Judge of Appeal, Transkei, 1991–93; Acting Judge of Appeal, Namibia, 1991–. Exec. Mem., Centre for the Independence of Judges and Lawyers. Member: Adv. Cttee of Interights, 1990–97; Commonwealth Human Rights Initiative Mission, Nigeria, 1995; UN Delegn to Scotland (with Prof. Henry Schermers), re trial of Lockerbie bombing suspects, 1997; also confs and colloquia. Pres., Forum Party, Zimbabwe, 1993–95. Chairman: Modus Publications; Art Printers Employees Trust, Harare. President: Boy Scouts; Zimbabwe Conservation Trust; Chairman: Moleli-Marshall Hartley Trust; Legal Resources Foundn Trust; Old Age Zimbabwe; Trustee: Omay Develt Trust, Harare; Ukubuyisa Trust, 2000–. Patron, Legal Resources Foundn. Governor: Arundel Sch., Harare, 1985–98; Moleli Secondary Sch. (Chm., Bd of Govs); Trustee: Chisipite Jun. Sch., Harare, 1985–91; Methodist Church of Zimbabwe, 1998– (Mem. Legal Cttee, Methodist Church, 1998–). Hon. DCL Oxford, 1990. *Publications:* Zimbabwe Tragedy, 1986; (contrib.) Toward Autonomous Development in Africa, 1999. *Recreations:* mountain climbing (average height), reading,

formerly tennis. *Address:* PO Box CH70, Chisipite, Harare, Zimbabwe. *T:* (4) 573972. *Club:* Harare.
Died 14 Dec. 2000.

DUNBAR, Charles, CB 1964; Director, Fighting Vehicles Research and Development Establishment, Ministry of Defence, 1960–67; *b* 12 Jan. 1907; *s* of John Dunbar, Barrow-in-Furness, Lancs; *m* 1933, Mary Alice (*née* Clarke), Barnes, SW; two *d. Educ:* Grammar Sch., Barrow-in-Furness; Manchester Univ. (MSc). National Physical Laboratory, Dept of Scientific and Industrial Research, 1929–43; Tank Armament Research Establishment, Min. of Supply, 1943–47; Fighting Vehicles Research and Development Establishments, 1947–67, retired. *Publications:* contribs to learned journals. *Recreations:* golf, fishing. *Address:* 3 Invereoch Court, Arrochar, Dunbartonshire G83 7AB. *Died 27 Aug. 1997.*

DUNBAR of Durn, Sir Drummond Cospatrick Ninian, 9th Bt *cr* 1698 (NS); MC 1943; Major Black Watch, retired; *b* 9 May 1917; *o s* of Sir George Alexander Drummond Dunbar, 8th Bt and Sophie Kathleen (*d* 1936), *d* of late J. Benson Kennedy; *S* father, 1949; *m* 1957, Sheila Barbara Mary, *d* of John B. de Fonblanque, London; one *s. Educ:* Radley Coll.; Worcester Coll., Oxford (BA 1938). Served War of 1939–45, Middle East, North Africa, Sicily, Normandy (wounded twice, MC); retired pay, 1958. *Heir: s* Robert Drummond Cospatrick Dunbar, Younger of Durn [*b* 17 June 1958; *m* 1994, Sarah, *yr d* of Robert Anthony Brooks; one *s* one *d*]. *Address:* Town Hill, Westmount, Jersey, Channel Islands JE2 3LP.
Died 12 June 2000.

DUNBAR of Hempriggs, Dame Maureen Daisy Helen, (Lady Dunbar of Hempriggs), Btss (8th in line) *cr* 1706 (NS); *b* 19 Aug. 1906; *d* of Courtenay Edward Moore and Janie King Moore (*née* Askins); assumed the name of Dunbar, in lieu of Blake, on claiming succession to the Hempriggs baronetcy after death of kinsman, Sir George Cospatrick Duff-Sutherland-Dunbar, 7th Bt, in 1963; claim established and title recognised by Lyon Court, 1965; *m* 1940, Leonard James Blake (*d* 1989); one *s* one *d. Educ:* Headington Sch.; Royal Coll. of Music. LRAM 1928. Music teacher at: Monmouth Sch. for Girls, 1930–33; Oxford High Sch., 1935–40; Malvern Coll., 1957–68. *Heir:* (to mother's Btcy) *s* Richard Francis Dunbar of Hempriggs, younger [*b* 8 Jan. 1945; assumed the name of Dunbar in lieu of Blake, 1965; *m* 1969, Elizabeth Margaret Jane Lister; two *d*]. *Address:* 51 Gloucester Street, Winchcombe, Cheltenham, Glos GL54 5LX. *T:* (01242) 602122. *Died 15 Feb. 1997.*

DUNBAR-NASMITH, Rear-Adm. David Arthur, CB 1969; DSC 1942; retired 1972; Vice Lord-Lieutenant, Morayshire, 1980–96; *b* 21 Feb. 1921; *e s* of late Admiral Sir Martin Dunbar-Nasmith, VC, KCB, KCMG, DL, and Justina Dunbar-Nasmith, CBE, DStJ; *m* 1951, Elizabeth Bowlby; two *s* two *d. Educ:* Lockers Park; RNC, Dartmouth. To sea as Midshipman, 1939; War Service, Atlantic and Mediterranean, in HM Ships Barham, Rodney, Kelvin and Petard; in command: HM Ships Haydon 1943, Peacock 1945–46, Moon 1946, Rowena 1946–48, Enard Bay 1951, Alert 1954–56, Berwick, and 5th Frigate Squadron, 1961–63; RN and Joint Service Staff Colls, 1948–49; Staff of Flag Officer 1st Cruiser Squadron, 1949–51; NATO HQ, SACLANT, 1952–54 and SACEUR, 1958–60; Dir of Defence Plans, Min. of Defence, 1963–65; Commodore, Amphibious Forces, 1966–67; Naval Secretary, 1967–70; Flag Officer, Scotland and N Ireland, 1970–72. Comdr 1951; Capt. 1958; Rear-Adm. 1967. Chm., Moray and Nairn Newspaper Co., 1982–91. Member: Highlands and Islands Develt Bd, 1972–83 (Dep. Chm., 1972–81; Chm., 1981–82); Countryside Commn for Scotland, 1972–76; British Waterways Bd, 1980–87; N of Scotland Hydro-

Electric Bd, 1982–85. Mem. Queen's Body Guard for Scotland (Royal Company of Archers), 1974–; Gentleman Usher of the Green Rod to the Order of the Thistle, 1979–97. DL Moray, 1974. *Recreations:* sailing, ski-ing, shooting. *Address:* Glen of Rothes, Rothes, Moray. *T:* (01340) 831216. *Clubs:* Royal Ocean Racing; New (Edinburgh). *Died 15 Sept. 1997.*

DUNCAN, Brian Arthur Cullum, CB 1972; CBE 1963 (MBE 1949); QC 1972; Judge Advocate General of the Forces, 1968–72; *b* 2 Feb. 1908; *yr s* of late Frank Hubert Duncan, LDS, RCS, and Edith Jane Duncan (*née* Cullum); *m* 1934, Irene Flora Templeman (*d* 1983), *o c* of late John Frederick Templeman and Flora Edith Templeman; two *s* two *d. Educ:* Queens' Coll., Cambridge (MA). Called to the Bar, Lincoln's Inn, 1931. Practised South Eastern Circuit, Central Criminal Court, North London Sessions, and Herts and Essex Sessions; commissioned RAF, April 1940; relinqd commn, 1950 (Wing Comdr); joined JAG's Dept, 1945; Dep. Judge Advocate Gen. (Army and RAF): Middle East, 1950–53; Germany, 1954–57; Far East, 1959–62; Vice Judge Advocate Gen., 1967–68. *Address:* Culverlands, Neville Park, Baltonsborough, Glastonbury, Som BA6 8PY. *Died 6 Jan. 1997.*

DUNCAN, Douglas John Stewart; Co-ordinator and Director of Psychotherapy and Mentoring Projects, Winchester Alliance for Mental Health, 1997–99; *b* 9 March 1945; *o s* of J. M. Duncan and Helen Stewart Collins; *m* 1972, Claire Isobel Callaghan (marr. diss. 1998; remarried 1999); four *s. Educ:* Aberdeen Univ. (LLB Hons 1966); Southampton Univ. (MA Contemporary Art and Theory, 1996); Peter Symond's Coll., Winchester (RSA Counselling Skills, 1996). Asst Lectr in Law, Univ. of Sheffield, 1966–68; Lectr, Scots Law, Univ. of Aberdeen, 1968–70; Lectr, Evidence, Univ. of Edinburgh, 1972–74; Advocate, 1972; practice at the Scottish Bar, 1972–75; Lord Advocate's Dept, 1975–92, Scottish Parly Counsel and Sen. Asst Legal Sec. to Lord Advocate, 1979–92; called to the Bar, Inner Temple, 1990; freelance legal/legislative draftsman, 1993–97. Developed Statlaw system for electronic origination and publication of legislation (with D. C. Macrae), 1983–84; Chm., Statute Law Database Group, 1986–90. Hon. Psychotherapist, Whittington Hosp., 1997–98. *Publications:* The Gestalt's Return: figure and ground in the paintings of Julian Schnabel, 1999; Permission to Abstain: psychotherapy in the treatment of addiction, 1999; professional articles. *Recreations:* painting, racing. *Address:* 86 Cromwell Road, Winchester, Hants SO22 4AE.
Died 29 Jan. 2000.

DUNCAN, Dr Kenneth Playfair, CB 1985; FRCP, FRCPE; Assistant Director (Biomedical Sciences), National Radiological Protection Board, 1985–88; *b* 27 Sept. 1924; *s* of late Dr J. H. Duncan, MA, BPhil, DD, and H. P. Duncan (*née* Ritchie); *m* 1950, Dr Gillian Crow, OBE, JP, MB, ChB; four *d. Educ:* Kilmarnock Acad.; Glasgow Acad.; Dundee High Sch.; St Andrews Univ. BSc, MB, ChB; DIH. FRCPE 1976; FFOM 1978; FRCP 1980. House Surg., Dundee Royal Infirmary, 1947; RAMC, 1948–50; gen. practice, Brighton, 1950–51; Area MO, British Rail, 1951–54; Chief Medical Officer: SW Gas Bd, 1954–58; UKAEA, 1958–69; Head of Health and Safety, BSC, 1969–75; Dir of Medical Services, HSE, 1975–82; Dep. Dir-Gen., HSE, 1982–84. External Examiner in Occupational Health, Univ. of Dundee, 1970–74; Examiner in Occupational Health, Soc. of Apothecaries, 1974–79. Vis. Prof., London Sch. of Hygiene and Tropical Medicine, 1977–82. Member: Industrial Health Adv. Cttee, Dept of Employment, 1960–74; MRC, 1975–83. Pres., Soc. of Occupational Medicine, 1970. *Publications:* contrib. medical and scientific jls on radiological protection and gen.

occupational health topics. *Recreation:* gardening. *Address:* Westfield, Steeple Aston, Oxon OX6 3SD. *T:* (01869) 340277.   *Died 26 June 1999.*

DUNCAN, Malcolm McGregor, OBE 1987; WS; Chief Executive, City of Edinburgh District Council, 1980–87; *b* 23 Jan. 1922; *s* of Rev. Reginald Duncan, BD, BLitt, and Clarice Ethel (*née* Hodgkinson); *m* 1954, Winifred Petrie (*née* Greenhorn); two *s* one *d*. *Educ:* George Watson's Coll., Edinburgh; Edinburgh Univ. (MA 1942; LLB 1948). Admitted Writer to the Signet, 1949. Served RAFVR, Flt Lieut, 1942–46. Edinburgh Corporation, 1952; Depute Town Clerk, 1971; Director of Administration, City of Edinburgh District Council, 1975–80. *Recreations:* playing golf, watching other sports, listening to music. *Address:* 52 Glendevon Place, Edinburgh EH12 5UJ. *T:* 0131–337 2869.
Died 3 July 1996.

DUNCAN MILLAR, Ian Alastair, CBE 1978; MC; DL; CEng, MICE; Member, Tay District Salmon Fisheries Board, 1962–80 and 1986–93; Member, Royal Company of Archers (Queen's Body Guard for Scotland), since 1956; *b* 22 Nov. 1914; *s* of late Sir James Duncan Millar and Lady Duncan Millar (*née* Forester Paton); *m* 1945, Louise Reid McCosh; two *s* two *d*. *Educ:* Gresham's Sch., Holt; Trinity Coll., Cambridge (MA). Served with Corps of Royal Engineers, 1940–45 (Major; wounded; despatches): 7th Armoured Div., N Africa and Normandy; 51 (Highland) Div., France and Germany. Contested Parly Elections (L): Banff, 1945; Kinross and W Perthshire, 1949 and 1963. Depute Chm., North of Scotland Hydro-Electric Bd, 1970–72 (Mem., 1957–72). Chm., United Auctions (Scotland) Ltd, 1967–74; Dir, Macdonald Fraser & Co. Ltd, Perth, 1961–85. Dir, Hill Farming Research Organisation, 1966–78; Chm., Consultative Cttee to Sec. of State for Scotland under 1976 Freshwater and Salmon Fisheries Act, 1981–86. Vice-Pres., Scottish Landowners Fedn, 1985–90. Mem, Ct, Dundee Univ., 1975–78. Perth CC, 1945–75: Chm. Planning Cttee, 1954–75; Convener, 1970–75; Chm. Jt CC of Perth and Kinross, 1970–75; Tayside Regional Council: Councillor and Chm., 1974–75; Convener, 1975–78. Fellow, Inst. of Fisheries Management, 1988. DL 1963, JP 1952, Perthshire. *Publications:* A Countryman's Cog, 1990; A Bit of Breadalbane, 1995. *Recreations:* studying and catching salmon, land management. *Address:* Reynock, Remony, Aberfeldy, Perthshire PH15 2HR. *T:* (01887) 830400. *Club:* Royal Perth Golfing Society.
Died 21 Aug. 1997.

DUNDONALD, James; *see* Lawlor, J. J.

DUNLEATH, 5th Baron *cr* 1892; **Michael Henry Mulholland;** Bt 1945; retired; *b* 15 Oct. 1915; *s* of Rt Hon. Sir Henry George Hill Mulholland, 1st Bt (3rd *s* of 2nd Baron Dunleath), and Sheelah (*d* 1982), *d* of Sir Douglas Brooke, 4th Bt; *S* to baronetcy of father, 1971; *S* to Barony of cousin, 1993; *m* 1st, 1942, Rosemary Ker (marr. diss. 1948); 2nd, 1949, Elizabeth (*d* 1989), *d* of Laurence B. Hyde; one *s*. *Educ:* Eton; Pembroke College, Cambridge (BA). Regular Army Commission, 1937, Oxford and Bucks Light Infantry; retired, 1951, with rank of Major. *Heir: s* Hon. Brian Henry Mulholland [*b* 25 Sept. 1950; *m* 1976, Mary Joana, *y d* of Major R. J. F. Whistler; two *s* one *d*]. *Address:* Storbrooke, Massey Avenue, Belfast BT4 2JT. *T:* (01232) 763394. *Clubs:* Light Infantry (Shrewsbury); Green Jackets (Winchester).
Died 3 May 1997.

DUNLEAVY, Philip, CBE 1983 (OBE 1978); JP; Leader, Cardiff City Council, 1974–76 and 1979–82; Lord Mayor of Cardiff, 1982–83; *b* 5 Oct. 1915; *s* of Michael and Bridget Dunleavy; *m* 1936, Valerie Partridge; two *s* two *d*. *Educ:* St Cuthbert's Sch., Cardiff. Served War, TA

(Sgt), 1939–46. Post Office, 1930–39 and 1946–75 (Executive Officer, 1960–75). Member: Cardiff City Council, 1962–83; South Glamorgan County Council, 1974–81. Hon. Freeman, City of Cardiff, 1993. JP 1960. *Recreations:* youth, conservation, local historical research, local govt political activity. *Address:* 35 Merches Gardens, Grangetown, Cardiff CF1 7RF.
Died 13 Jan. 1996.

DUNLOP, John; *b* 20 May 1910; *s* of Martin T. and Agnes Dunlop, Belfast; *m* 1st, 1936, Ruby Hunter; two *s* (and one *s* decd); 2nd, 1970, Joyce Campbell. *Educ:* primary sch. and techn. college. Apprentice multiple grocers, 1926; assumed management, 1934; acquired own business, 1944. Mem. (VULC), Mid-Ulster, NI Assembly, 1973–74. MP (UUUP) Mid-Ulster, 1974–83. Civil Defence Medal and ribbon 1945. *Recreations:* music, choral singing, amateur soccer. *Address:* Turnaface Road, Moneymore, Magherafelt, Co. Londonderry BT45 7YP. *T:* (016487) 48594.   *Died 10 March 1996.*

DUNLOP, Sir Thomas, 3rd Bt *cr* 1916, of Woodbourne, co. Renfrew; Partner, Thomas Dunlop & Sons, Ship and Insurance Brokers, Glasgow, 1938–86; *b* 11 April 1912; *s* of Sir Thomas Dunlop, 2nd Bt and Mary Elizabeth, *d* of William Beckett, solicitor, Glasgow; *S* father, 1963; *m* 1947, (Adda Mary) Alison, *d* of T. Arthur Smith, Lindsaylands, Biggar, Lanarks; one *s* one *d* (and one *d* decd). *Educ:* Shrewsbury; St John's Coll., Cambridge (BA). Chartered Accountant, 1939. Former Chm., Savings Bank of Glasgow. Mem. Cttee, Princess Louise Scottish Hosp., Erskine; Vice-Pres., Royal Alfred Seafarers' Soc. OStJ 1965. *Recreations:* shooting, fishing, golf. *Heir: s* Thomas Dunlop [*b* 22 April 1951; *m* 1984, Eileen, *er d* of A. H. Stevenson; one *s* one *d*]. *Address:* The Corrie, Kilmacolm, Renfrewshire PA13 4NY. *T:* (01505) 873239. *Club:* Western (Glasgow).   *Died 18 Aug. 1999.*

DUNLOP, Sir William (Norman Gough), Kt 1975; JP; retired 1990; *b* 9 April 1914; *s* of Norman Matthew Dunlop and Alice Ada Dunlop (*née* Gough); *m* 1940, Ruby Jean (*née* Archie); three *s* three *d*. *Educ:* Waitaki Boys' High Sch. Farmer in Canterbury, NZ; former Man. Dir, Dunlop Farms Ltd. President: Federated Farmers, NZ, 1973–74; Coopworth Sheep Soc., NZ, 1971–74; Member: Agriculture Adv. Council, NZ, 1970–74; Immigration Adv. Council, NZ, 1971–75; Transport Adv. Council, NZ, 1971–76; Dep. Chm., NZ Meat and Wool Board Electoral Coll., 1973. Director: Rural Bank & Finance Corp., NZ, 1974–81; New Zealand Light Leathers, 1973–80. Chm., Neurological Foundn (Canterbury), 1975–88; Trustee: Todd Foundn, 1973–81; Lincoln Coll. Foundn, 1977–88 (Chm. Bd). Anniv. Medal, NZ Animal Production Soc., 1991. Internat. Visitors Award, US Dept of State, 1971. JP 1972. *Recreations:* music, gardening. *Address:* 242 Main Road, Monks Bay, Christchurch 8, New Zealand. *T:* (8) 849056.   *Died 27 Sept. 1998.*

DUNN, Richard Johann, CBE 1995; Chairman, Digital Broadcasting Co. Ltd, since 1998; Adviser to the Football Association Premier League, since 1997; *b* 5 Sept. 1943; *s* of late Major Edward Cadwalader Dunn, MBE, TD, and of Gudlaug Johannesdóttir; *m* 1972, Virginia Gregory Gaynor, USA; two *s* one *d*. *Educ:* Forest Sch.; St John's Coll., Cambridge. Writer and Producer, Associated British Pathe, 1967–70; Exec. Producer, EMI Special Films Unit, 1970–72; Man. Dir, Swindon Viewpoint Ltd, cable community television service, 1972–76; EMI Film and Th. Corp., 1976–77; joined Thames Television, 1978: Dir of Prodn, 1981–85; Chief Exec., 1985–95; Man. Dir, Pearson Television Hldgs, 1993–95; Exec. Dir, News Internat. Television, 1995–97. Director: ITCA, subseq. ITV Assoc., 1985–92 (Chm., 1988–90); ITN, 1985–93 (Chm., 1991–93); ITV Publications, 1985–89. Chairman: Euston Films Ltd, 1985–91; Cosgrove Hall Productions,

1985–93; Thames Television Internat., 1985–95; Teddington Studios, 1992–95; Financial Times Television, 1993–95; UK Living, 1993–95; British Transport Advertising Ltd, 1994–95; Production Design Co., 1994–; Television Corp., 1996–98 (non-exec. Dir, 1998–); Jeremy Isaacs Productions Ltd, 1997–; St James's Investment Partnership Ltd, 1997–; Copyright Promotions Gp plc, 1998–; Magazine Channel Ltd, 1998–; Director: Thames Valley Broadcasting Plc, 1985–89; Starstream Ltd (The Children's Channel), 1986–90; Channel Four TV, 1988–91; UK Gold Television Ltd, 1992–95; Dorling Kindersley Hldgs, 1994–; Eur. Channel Management Ltd, 1995; News German Television Holding GmbH, 1995–; Globecast Northern Europe, 1997–. Director: Internat. Council of Nat. Acad. of Television Arts and Scis, NY, 1985– (Vice Chm., 1990–93); BARB, 1986–88; Société Européenne des Satellites, 1987–95; Association des Télévisions Commerciales en Europe, 1989–91. Vice Chm., Independent Broadcasting Telethon Trust, 1987–94. Vice Pres. and Fellow, RTS, 1988–. Chm., Film and Video Panel, GLAA, 1978–82; Pres., Battersea Arts Centre, 1989– (Chm., 1984–88). Internat. Emmy (Founders) Award, 1993. *Address:* Lovel Dene, Woodside, Windsor Forest, Berks SL4 2DP. *T:* (01344) 884968. *Clubs:* Garrick, Royal Automobile; Hawks (Cambridge).

Died 4 Aug. 1998.

DUNNACHIE, James Francis, (Jimmy); JP; *b* 17 Nov. 1930; *s* of William and Mary Dunnachie; *m* 1974, (Marion) Isobel Payne. Councillor, City of Glasgow Corp., 1972–74 (Chm., Clearance and Rehabilitation); District Councillor, City of Glasgow, 1974–77 (Chm., C and R Cttee); Councillor, Strathclyde Regional Council, 1978–87 (Vice-Chm., Social Work Cttee). MP (Lab) Glasgow, Pollok, 1987–97. An Opposition Whip, 1988–92, Scottish Whip, 1989–92. *Recreations:* gardening, reading, junior football. *Address:* 15 Loganswell Gardens, Glasgow G46 8HU. *T:* (0141) 638 9756. *Died 7 Sept. 1997.*

DUNNETT, Sir Alastair (MacTavish), Kt 1995; *b* 26 Dec. 1908; *s* of David Sinclair Dunnett and Isabella Crawford MacTavish; *m* 1946, Dorothy Halliday; two *s. Educ:* Overnewton Sch.; Hillhead High Sch., Glasgow. Commercial Bank of Scotland, Ltd, 1925; Co-founder of The Claymore Press, 1933–34; Glasgow Weekly Herald, 1935–36; The Bulletin, 1936–37; Daily Record, 1937–40; Chief Press Officer, Sec. of State for Scotland, 1940–46; Editor, Daily Record, 1946–55; Editor, The Scotsman, 1956–72; Man. Dir, The Scotsman Publications Ltd, 1962–70, Chm., 1970–74; Mem. Exec. Bd, The Thomson Organisation Ltd, 1974–78; Director: Scottish Television Ltd, 1975–79; Thomson Scottish Petroleum Ltd, 1979–87 (Chm., 1972–79). Smith-Mundt Scholarship to USA, 1951. Governor, Pitlochry Festival Theatre, 1958–84. Member: Scottish Tourist Board, 1956–69; Press Council, 1959–62; Council of Nat. Trust for Scotland, 1962–69; Council of Commonwealth Press Union, 1964–78; Edinburgh Univ. Court, 1964–66; Edinburgh Festival Council, 1967–80. Hon. Mem., Saltire Soc., 1991. FRSA 1987. Hon. LLD Strathclyde, 1978. *Publications:* Treasure at Sonnach, 1935; Heard Tell, 1946; Quest by Canoe, 1950, repr. 1967, as It's Too Late in the Year, repr. 1995, as The Canoe Boys; Highlands and Islands of Scotland, 1951; The Donaldson Line, 1952; The Land of Scotch, 1953; (as Alec Tavis) The Duke's Day, 1970; (ed) Alistair Maclean Introduces Scotland, 1972; No Thanks to the Duke, 1978; Among Friends (autobiog.), 1984; (with Dorothy Dunnett) The Scottish Highlands, 1988; End of Term, 1989; *plays:* The Original John Mackay, Glasgow Citizens, 1956; Fit to Print, Duke of York's, 1962. *Recreations:* sailing, riding, walking. *Address:* 87 Colinton Road, Edinburgh EH10 5DF. *T:* (0131) 337 2107. *Clubs:* Caledonian; Scottish Arts, New, Puffin's (Edinburgh).

Died 2 Sept. 1998.

DUNNETT, Sir (Ludovic) James, GCB 1969 (KCB 1960; CB 1957); CMG 1948; Permanent Under-Secretary of State, Ministry of Defence, 1966–74; *b* 12 Feb. 1914; *s* of late Sir James Dunnett, KCIE and Annie, *y d* of William Sangster; *m* 1st, 1944, Olga Adair (*d* 1980); no *c*; 2nd, 1984, Lady (Clarisse) Grover. *Educ:* Edinburgh Acad.; University Coll., Oxford. Entered Air Ministry, 1936; Private Sec. to Permanent Sec., 1937–44; transferred to Ministry of Civil Aviation, 1945; Under Sec., 1948; Under Sec., Min. of Supply, 1951, Deputy Sec., 1953; Deputy Sec., Min. of Transport, 1958; Permanent Secretary: Min. of Transport, 1959–62; Min. of Labour, 1962–66. Mem., SSRC, 1977–82. Visiting Fellow, Nuffield Coll., Oxford, 1964–72. Chm., Internat. Maritime Industries Forum, 1976–79; Pres., Inst. of Manpower Studies, 1977–80. Trustee, Charities Aid Foundn, 1974–88. *Recreation:* golf. *Address:* 85 Bedford Gardens, W8 7EQ. *T:* (0171) 727 5286. *Club:* Reform. *Died 30 Dec. 1997.*

DUNPHIE, Maj.-Gen. Sir Charles (Anderson Lane), Kt 1959; CB 1948; CBE 1942; DSO 1943; *b* 20 April 1902; *s* of late Sir Alfred Dunphie, KCVO, Rotherfield Greys, Oxon, and 2nd wife, Ethel Kate, *d* of Henry Hammond-Smith, surgeon, Stourbridge; *m* 1st, 1931, Eileen (*d* 1978), *d* of late Lt-Gen. Sir Walter Campbell, KCB, KCMG, DSO; one *s* one *d*; 2nd, 1981, Susan, *widow* of Col P. L. M. Wright. *Educ:* RN Colls Osborne and Dartmouth; RMA Woolwich. Commissioned into Royal Horse and RFA, 1921; served War of 1939–45 (wounded, despatches); Brig. RAC, 1941; Comdr 26 Armoured Bde, 1942–43; Dep. Dir RAC, War Office, 1943–45; Temp. Maj.-Gen., Dir Gen. Armoured Fighting Vehicles, 1945–48, retired; joined Vickers Ltd, 1948; Chm., 1962–67. One of HM's Honourable Corps of Gentlemen-at-Arms, 1952–62. US Legion of Merit (Commander); US Silver Star. *Address:* Roundhill, Wincanton, Somerset BA9 8HH. *Died 7 Jan. 1999.*

DUNROSSIL, 2nd Viscount *cr* 1959; **John William Morrison,** CMG 1981; JP; HM Diplomatic Service, retired; Lord-Lieutenant, Western Isles, since 1993 (Vice Lord-Lieutenant, 1992–93); *b* 22 May 1926; *e s* of William Shepherd Morrison, 1st Viscount Dunrossil, GCMG, MC, PC, QC; *S* father, 1961; *m* 1st, 1951, Mavis (marr. diss. 1969), *d* of A. Ll. Spencer-Payne, LRCP, MRCS, LDS; three *s* one *d*; 2nd, 1969, Diana Mary Cunliffe, *d* of C. M. Vise; two *d. Educ:* Fettes; Oriel Coll., Oxford (Hon. Fellow, 1994). Royal Air Force, 1945–48, Flt-Lieut (Pilot). Joined Commonwealth Relations Office, 1951; Asst Private Sec. to Sec. of State, 1952–54; Second Sec., Canberra, 1954–56; CRO, 1956–58; First Sec. and Acting Deputy High Commissioner, Dacca, East Pakistan, 1958–60; First Sec., Pretoria/Capetown, 1961–64; FO, 1964–68; seconded to Intergovernmental Maritime Consultative Orgn, 1968–70; Counsellor and Head of Chancery, Ottawa, 1970–74; Counsellor, Brussels, 1975–78; High Comr in Fiji, and High Comr (non-resident) to Republic of Nauru and to Tuvalu, 1978–82; High Comr, Bridgetown, Antigua, Barbuda, Dominica, Grenada, St Vincent and the Grenadines, and British Govt Rep. to WI Associated States, 1982–83; Governor and C-in-C, Bermuda, 1983–88. Chm., Bison Books Ltd, 1990–95; Dep. Chm., Bank of Bermuda (Luxembourg) SA, 1990–98; Mem. Bd, Internat. Registries Inc., 1996–. Chm., Bermuda Soc., London, 1989–99. JP Western Isles, 1994; DL Western Isles, 1990. Liveryman, Merchant Taylors' Co., 1984. KStJ. *Heir: s* Hon. Andrew William Reginald Morrison [*b* 15 Dec. 1953; *m* 1986, Carla Brundage; one *s* three *d*]. *Address:* Dunrossil House, Clachan Sands, by Lochmaddy, North Uist, Hebrides HS6 5AY. *T:* (01876) 500213. *Clubs:* Royal Air Force, Royal Commonwealth Society. *Died 22 March 2000.*

DUNSANY, 19th Baron of, *cr* 1439; **Randal Arthur Henry Plunkett;** Lieutenant-Colonel (retired) Indian Cavalry (Guides); *b* 25 Aug. 1906; *o s* of 18th Baron Dunsany, DL, LittD, and Beatrice, Lady Dunsany (*d* 1970); *S* father, 1957; *m* 1st, 1938, Mrs Vera Bryce (marr. diss. 1947, she *d* 1986), *d* of Señor G. De Sà Sottomaior, São Paulo, Brazil; one *s*; 2nd, 1947, Sheila Victoria Katrin, *o d* of Sir Henry Philipps, 2nd Bt and *widow* of Major John Frederick Foley, Baron de Rutzen, DL, JP, CC, Welsh Guards (killed in action, 1944); one *d*. *Educ:* Eton. Joined the 16th/5th Lancers (SR), 1926; transferred to the Indian Army, 1928, Guides Cavalry, Indian Armoured Corps; retired, 1947. *Heir: s* Hon. Edward John Carlos Plunkett [*b* 10 Sept. 1939; *m* 1982, Maria Alice Villela de Carvalho; two *s*]. *Address:* (seat) Dunsany Castle, Co. Meath, Ireland. *T:* (46) 25198. *Clubs:* Beefsteak, Cavalry and Guards; Kildare Street and University (Dublin).

Died 6 Feb. 1999.

DUNSTAN, Hon. Donald Allan, AC 1979; QC 1965; Restaurateur, Doric Table Restaurant, Norwood, South Australia, since 1995; *b* Suva, Fiji, 21 Sept. 1926; *s* of late Francis Vivian Dunstan, MBE, sometime Branch Manager, Morris Hedstrom Ltd, and Ida May Dunstan (*née* Hill); *m* 1st, 1949, Gretel Ellis (marr. diss.); two *s* one *d*; 2nd, 1976, Adele Koh (*d* 1978). *Educ:* Murray Bridge Infant and Primary Schs, SA; Suva Grammar Sch.; St Peter's Coll., Adelaide; St Mark's Coll., Univ. of Adelaide (LLB 1948). Admitted to S Australian Bar, 1948, to Fiji Bar, 1949; in practice: Fiji, 1949–50; Adelaide, 1951–. MHA (Labor) South Australia, for Norwood, 1953–79; Attorney-Gen., Minister for Social Welfare, for Aboriginal Affairs, 1965–67; Premier, Treasurer, Attorney-Gen. and Minister for Housing, 1967–68; Leader of Opposition, 1968–70; Premier, Treasurer, 1970–79; Minister for Develt and Mines, 1970–76, for Ethnic Affairs, 1976–79 Dir of Tourism, Victoria, 1982–83; Chm., Victorian Tourism Commn, 1983–86; Dep. Chm., Alpine Resorts Commn, 1983–86; Mem. Bd, Victorian Econ. Develt Corp., 1983–86. Nat. Pres., 1982–87, Chm., 1987–91, Australian Freedom from Hunger Campaign; Chm., Community Aid Abroad Freedom From Hunger, 1992–93. Adjunct Prof., Dept of Social Inquiry, Univ. of Adelaide, 1997–. President: Mus. of Chinese Aust. History, 1984–86; Movement for Democracy in Fiji, 1987–; Chairman: Chinatown Statutory Cttee, 1983–86; Mandela Foundn, 1987–93; Jam Factory Craft Workshops, 1990–94. Author and presenter, TV series, Australia: a personal view, 1981. DUniv Flinders, 1991. *Publications:* Don Dunstan's Cookbook, 1976; Don Dunstan's Australia, 1978; Felicia: the political memoirs of Don Dunstan, 1981; Australia: a personal view, 1981. *Address:* 15 Clara Street, Norwood, SA 5067, Australia.

Died 6 Feb. 1999.

DUNTZE, Sir Daniel (Evans), 8th Bt *cr* 1774, of Tiverton, Devon; graphics art consultant; *b* 4 April 1926; *s* of George Douglas Duntze (*d* 1946) and Mabel Lillian, *d* of Daniel Evans; *S* cousin, Sir John Alexander Duntze, 7th Bt, 1987; *m* 1954, Marietta Welsh; one *s* two *d*. *Educ:* Washington Univ. Sch. of Fine Arts, St Louis, Mo. Served in USAAF, World War II. *Heir: s* Daniel Evans Duntze, *b* 11 Aug. 1960.

His name did not appear on the Official Roll of the Baronetage.   *Died 1997.*

DURAS, Marguerite; French author and playwright; *b* Gia Dinh, Indochina, 4 April 1914; *d* of Henri Donnadieu and Marie (*née* Legrand); *m* 1st, 1939, Robert Anthelme (marr. diss. 1947); 2nd, 1947, Dionys Mascolo; one *s*. *Educ:* Lycée de Saigon; Faculté de droit de Paris; Ecole libre des sciences politiques. Sec., Colonies Ministry, 1935–41. *Screenplays:* also directed: Hiroshima, mon Amour, 1960; Jaune le soleil, 1971; India Song, 1973; Nathalie Granger, 1973; La femme du Gange, 1974; Aurélia Steiner, 1979;

L'homme assis dans le couloir, 1980, L'homme atlantique, 1981; Agatha et les lectures illimitées, 1981; Dialogue de Rome, 1982; Les Enfants, 1985; directed and appeared in Le Camion, 1977. Grand Prix du théâtre de l'Académie Française, 1983. *Publications:* Les Impudents, 1943; La vie tranquille, 1944; Un barrage contre la Pacifique, 1950; Le marin de Gibraltar, 1952; Les petits chevaux de Tarquinia, 1953; Des journées entières dans les arbres (short stories), 1954 (Prix Jean Cocteau) (adapted for stage, 1964); Le square, 1955; Moderato Cantabile, 1958; Les viaducs de la Seine-et-Oise, 1960; Dix heures et demi du soir en été, 1960 (filmed, 1967); L'après-midi de Monsieur Andesmas, 1962; Le ravissement de Lol V. Stein, 1964; L'amante anglaise, 1967; Détruire, dit-elle, 1969 (filmed, 1970 (also dir)); L'amour, 1972; L'été 80, 1980; Outside, 1981; La Maladie de la mort, 1983; L'amant, 1984 (Prix Goncourt; Ritz Paris Hemingway Award, 1986; filmed); La douleur (short stories), 1985; Les yeux bleus cheveux noirs, 1986; La Pute de la côte normande, 1986; Practicalities, 1990; Summer Rain, 1992; Yann Andrea Steiner, 1994; *plays:* Les eaux et les forêts, 1965; Théâtre I, le vice-consul, 1965; Théâtre II (5 plays), 1968; Susanna Andler, 1969; Yes, Peut-être, 1976; Abahn Sabana David, 1976; La Musica, 1976; Baxter Vera Baxter, 1977; L'Eden cinéma, 1977. *Address:* 5 rue le Benoît, 75006 Paris, France.   *Died 3 March 1996.*

DURBRIDGE, Francis Henry; playwright and author; *b* 25 Nov. 1912; *s* of late Francis and Gertrude Durbridge; *m* 1940, Norah Elizabeth Lawley; two *s*. *Educ:* Bradford Grammar Sch.; Wylde Green Coll.; Birmingham Univ. After period in stockbroker's office, began to write (as always intended); short stories and plays for BBC; many subseq. radio plays, including Promotion, 1933; created character of Paul Temple; entered television with The Broken Horseshoe, 1952 (the first adult television serial); other serials followed; Portrait of Alison, 1954; My Friend Charles, 1955; The Other Man, 1956; The Scarf, 1960; The World of Tim Frazer (Exec. Prod.), 1960–61, Melissa, 1962; Bat Out of Hell, 1964; Stupid Like a Fox, 1971; The Doll, 1976; Breakaway, 1980; the television serials were presented in many languages, and continue; novels, based on them, published in USA, Europe, etc. The European Broadcasting Union asked for a radio serial for an internat. market (La Boutique, 1967, broadcast in various countries); German, French and Italian productions, 1971–72. Films include two for Korda and Romulus, 1954–57. Stage plays: Suddenly at Home, 1971; The Gentle Hook, 1974; Murder With Love, 1976; House Guest, 1980; Nightcap, 1983; Murder Diary, 1986; A Touch of Fear, 1987; The Small Hours, 1989; Sweet Revenge, 1991; Fatal Encounter, 1996. *Publications:* include contribs to newspapers and magazines, at home and abroad. *Recreations:* family, reading, travel. *Address:* c/o Harvey Unna and Stephen Durbridge Ltd, 24 Pottery Lane, Holland Park, W11 4LZ.   *Died 11 April 1998.*

DUVAL, Sir (Charles) Gaëtan, Kt 1981; QC 1975; barrister; Deputy Prime Minister, 1983–88, and Minister of Employment and Tourism, 1986–88, Mauritius; Leader of the Opposition, 1973–76, 1982 and since 1996; *b* 9 Oct. 1930. *Educ:* Royal Coll., Curepipe; Faculty of Law, Univ. of Paris. Called to the Bar, Lincoln's Inn. Entered politics, 1958; Member: Town Council, Curepipe, 1960, re-elected 1963 (Chm., 1960–61, 1963–68); Legislative Council, Curepipe, 1960, re-elected, 1963; Municipal Council, Port Louis, 1969 (Mayor, 1969–71; Lord Mayor, 1971–74, 1981); Minister of Housing, 1964–65; Leader, Parti Mauritien Social Démocrate, 1966–; first MLA for Grand River NW and Port-Louis West, 1967; Minister of External Affairs, Tourism and Emigration, 1969–73; Minister of Justice, 1983–86. Comdr, Legion of Honour, France,

1973; Grand Officer, Order of the Lion, Senegal, 1973. *Address:* Chambers, Place Nelson Mandela, Port-Louis, Mauritius.   *Died 5 May 1996.*

DUXBURY, Air Marshal Sir (John) Barry, KCB 1986; CBE 1981 (MBE 1967); Director and Chief Executive, Society of British Aerospace Companies, since 1990; Secretary, Defence Industries Council, since 1990; *b* 23 Jan. 1934; *s* of Lloyd Duxbury and Hilda Robins; *m* 1954, Joan Leake; one *s. Educ:* Lancashire County Grammar Schs. Commnd 1954; served Maritime Sqdns, Aeroplane and Armament Exptl Estab., Canadian Forces Staff Coll., and Central Tactics and Trials Orgn, 1955–70; CO 201 Sqdn, 1971; PSO to CAS, 1971–74; CO RAF St Mawgan, 1976–77; Sec., Chiefs of Staff Cttee, 1978–80; RAF Dir, RCDS, 1982; Air Sec. (RAF), 1983–85; AOC No 18 Gp, RAF, and Comdr Maritime Air Eastern Atlantic and Channel, 1986–89, retd. ADC to the Queen, 1977. FRIN 1989; FRAeS 1992. *Recreations:* painting, photography. *Club:* Royal Air Force.   *Died 25 Jan. 1997.*

DYER, Simon, CBE 1995; MA; FCA; Director General, Automobile Association, since 1987; *b* 19 Oct. 1939; *s* of late Maj.-Gen. G. M. Dyer, CBE, DSO, and of Evelyn Dyer; *m* 1967, Louise Gay Walsh; two *d. Educ:* Ampleforth Coll.; Univ. of Paris; Univ. of Oxford (MA Jurisprudence). FCA 1978 (ACA 1967); FIMI 1992 (Vice-Pres., 1992–). Coopers and Lybrand, 1963–67; Automobile Association, 1967–: Dir, 1973; Asst Man. Dir, 1977; Man. Dir, 1983. Member: Exec. Cttee, British Road Fedn, 1987–92; Management Cttee, Alliance Internationale de Tourisme, 1987– (Pres., 1992–95); Council, Inst. of Advanced Motorists, 1989–; Council, CBI, 1989–. Trustee, Nat. Motor Mus., Beaulieu, 1992–. Gov., Queen Mary's Coll., Basingstoke, 1987–93. Freedom, City of London, 1984; Liveryman, Co. of Coachmakers and Coach Harness Makers, 1984– (Mem. Court, 1991–). CIMgt 1989. *Recreations:* gardening, tennis, ski-ing. *Address:* Norfolk House, Priestley Road, Basingstoke, Hants RG24 9NY. *Club:* Cavalry and Guards.   *Died 17 Feb. 1996.*

DYER-SMITH, Rear-Adm. John Edward, CBE 1972; Director-General Aircraft (Naval), Ministry of Defence, 1970–72, retired; *b* 17 Aug. 1918; *s* of Harold E. Dyer-Smith and Emily Sutton; *m* 1940, Kathleen Powell; four *s* one *d. Educ:* Devonport High Sch.; RNEC; Imperial Coll. of Science. Served War of 1939–45: Engineer Officer, HMS Prince of Wales, 1940–41; Asst Fleet Engr Officer, Eastern Fleet, 1942–43; HMS Illustrious, 1943; various MAP and Min. of Aviation appts, 1946–54; Head of Naval Air Dept, RAE, 1957–61; Dir of RN Aircraft/Helicopters, Min. of Aviation, 1961–64; Defence and Naval Attaché, Tokyo, 1965–67; Superintendent, RN Aircraft Yard, Belfast, 1968–70. *Recreations:* wood sculpting, piano, flute. *Address:* Ca'n Ranou, Cami de Barqueres-16, 07710 Sant Lluis, Menorca, Baleares. *T:* (9) 71150605.
Died 18 Dec. 1999.

DYSON, Rev. Anthony Oakley, DPhil; Samuel Ferguson Professor of Social and Pastoral Theology, Manchester University, 1980–97; Academic Director, Centre for Social Ethics and Policy, Manchester University, 1987–97; *b* 6 Oct. 1935; *s* of Henry Oakley Leslie Dyson and Lilian Dyson; *m* 1960, Edwina Anne Hammett; two *s. Educ:* William Hulme's Grammar Sch., Manchester; Univs of Cambridge (BA 1959, MA 1963) and Oxford (MA, BD 1964, DPhil 1968). 2nd Lieut, West Yorks Regt, 1954–56; Emmanuel Coll., Cambridge, 1956–59; Exeter Coll., Oxford and Ripon Hall, Oxford, 1959–61. Deacon 1961, priest 1962; Curate of Putney, Dio. Southwark, 1961–63; Chaplain of Ripon Hall, Oxford, 1963–69; Principal of Ripon Hall, 1969–74; Canon of St George's Chapel, Windsor Castle, 1974–77, Custodian, 1975–77; Lectr in Theology, Univ. of Kent, 1977–80. Vis. Prof., Univ. of Essex, 1992–93. Licensed to Officiate Dio. Oxford, 1965–75, Dio. Canterbury, 1978–80, Dio. Chester, 1980–, Dio. Manchester, 1980–. Examng Chaplain to Bishop of Carlisle; Select Preacher, Univ. of Oxford, 1971; University Preacher, Cambridge, 1985; Lectures: Hensley Henson, Univ. of Oxford, 1972–73; Pollock, Halifax, NS, 1973; Shann, Hong Kong, 1983. Associate Dir, Centre for the Study of Religion and Society, Canterbury, 1978–80. Hon. MA (Theol) Manchester, 1982. Editor: The Teilhard Review, 1966–72; The Modern Churchman, 1982–93. *Publications:* Existentialism, 1965; Who is Jesus Christ?, 1969; The Immortality of the Past, 1974; We Believe, 1977; (ed with J. Harris) Experiments on Embryos, 1990; Ethics and the New Reproductive Technologies, 1992; The Ethics of In-Vitro Fertilisation, 1994; (ed with J. Harris) Biotechnology and Ethics, 1994; *contributions to:* Evolution, Marxism and Christianity, 1967; What Kind of Revolution?, 1968; A Dictionary of Christian Theology, 1969, 2nd edn 1983; The Christian Marxist Dialogue, 1969; Teilhard Reassessed, 1970; Oxford Dictionary of the Christian Church, 2nd edn 1974; Education and Social Action, 1975; Ernst Troeltsch and the Future of Theology, 1976; The Language of the Church in Higher and Further Education, 1977; England and Germany: studies in theological diplomacy, 1981; The Nature of Religious Man, 1982; A New Dictionary of Christian Theology, 1983; The Church of England and Politics, 1986; A Dictionary of Pastoral Care, 1987; The British and their Religions, 1988; The Nuclear Weapons Debate: theological and ethical issues, 1989; The Ethics of IVF, 1995; Worship and Ethics, 1996; Dictionary of Ethics, Theology and Society, 1996; Encyclopedia of Protestantism, 1996; Changing Nature's Course, 1996; contrib. Theology, The Modern Churchman, Study Encounter, The Month, Contact, The Way, TLS, Bull. of John Rylands Library, Studia Theologica, Jl of Med. Ethics, etc. *Recreations:* literature, sport. *Address:* 33 Danesmoor Road, West Didsbury, Manchester M20 3JT. *T:* (0161) 434 5410.   *Died 19 Sept. 1998.*

E

EADIE, Douglas George Arnott, FRCS; Consulting Surgeon, The Royal London Hospital (Consultant Surgeon, 1969–87); Consultant Surgeon, King Edward VII Hospital, London, 1978–94; *b* 16 June 1931; *s* of Dr Herbert Arnott Eadie and Hannah Sophia (*née* Wingate); *m* 1957, Gillian Carlyon Coates; two *s* two *d. Educ:* Epsom Coll.; London Hosp. Med. Coll. (MB BS 1955; MS 1969). Jun. Specialist in Surgery and Captain RAMC, Far East Land Forces, 1957–60; Hugh Robertson Exchange Fellow, Presbyterian St Luke's Hosp., Chicago, 1962; Surgical Registrar, London Hosp., 1963–67. Cons. to Royal Masonic Hosp., 1980–82; Hon. Cons., Osborne House, IoW, 1980. Chm. of Council, Medical Protection Soc., 1976–83 (Mem. Council, 1974–96; Treasurer, 1986–90); Mem., Med. Adv. Cttee, Cromwell Hosp. (Chm., 1991–94). Examiner in Surgery: Soc. of Apothecaries of London, 1976–80; Univ. of London, 1976–84; Professional Linguistic Assessment Bd, 1992–94. Member: London Adv. Cttee, Barnardos, 1990; Court, Bradford Univ., 1991–94. Master, Soc. of Apothecaries, 1990–91 (Mem. Ct of Assts, 1980); rep. on GMC, 1983–88. FRSocMed 1956. *Publications:* contribs to med. jls on topics relating to vascular disease. *Recreations:* gardening, shooting. *Address:* Monks Lodge, Great Maplestead, Halstead, Essex CO9 2RN. *T:* (01787) 460440. *Club:* MCC. *Died 5 Dec. 2000.*

EAGERS, Derek; Under-Secretary, Department of Trade and Industry (formerly Department of Trade), 1975–84; *b* 13 Sept. 1924; *s* of late Horace Eagers and Florence (*née* Green); *m* 1953, Hazel Maureen Henson; two *s. Educ:* King Edward VII Sch., Sheffield; Brasenose Coll., Oxford. RNVR, 1943–47. Min. of Fuel and Power, 1949; UK Atomic Energy Authority, 1955–57; British Embassy, Washington, 1958–60; Principal Private Sec. to successive Ministers of Power, 1963–65; Petroleum Counsellor, Washington, 1966–68; Min. of Power (subseq. Min. of Technology, Dept of Trade and Industry), 1969; Dept of Industry, 1974. *Recreation:* concealing his true ignorance of cricket, gardening and railway history. *Address:* Bryniau Golau, Llangower, Bala, Gwynedd LL23 7BT. *T:* (01678) 520517. *Died 10 April 1998.*

EAST, Frederick Henry, CB 1976; FEng 1984; FIEE, FRAeS; Deputy Secretary, and Chief Weapon System Engineer (Polaris), Ministry of Defence, 1976–80, retired; *b* 15 Sept. 1919; *s* of Frederick Richard East; *m* 1st, 1942, Pauline Isabel Veale Horne (*d* 1972); 2nd, 1990, Christine Grace Veale Horne. *Educ:* Skinners' Company's Sch., Tunbridge Wells; University Coll., Exeter (Visc. St Cyres Schol., Tucker and Franklin Prize, 1939). BSc London, 1940; MInstP. Joined Research Dept, Min. of Aircraft Production, 1940; various appts in RAE, 1942–57; Asst Dir of Air Armament Research and Develt, Min. of Supply/Aviation, 1957–62; Head of Weapon Project Gp, RAE, 1962–67; Student, IDC, 1968; Asst Chief Scientific Adviser (Projects), MoD, 1969–70; Dir, Royal Armament Res. and Develt Establishment, 1971–75. Reader, C of E, 1969–; Mem., Candidates Cttee, ACCM, 1981–86. *Publications:* (contrib.) Application of Critical Path Techniques, 1968; official reports, and articles in jls. *Address:* The Folly, Mill Street, Prestbury, Cheltenham GL52 3BG. *T:* Cheltenham (01242) 230749. *Died 21 May 1996.*

EAST, William Gordon; Professor of Geography in the University of London at Birkbeck College, 1947–70, then Emeritus Professor; *b* 10 Nov. 1902; *s* of George Richard East and Jemima (*née* Nicoll); *m* 1934, Dorothea Small; two *s* two *d. Educ:* Sloane Sch., Chelsea; Peterhouse, Cambridge. Open scholarship in History, 1921, and research studentship, 1924, at Peterhouse; BA (Hons), Cambridge Univ. (History), 1924; MA 1928; Thirlwall Prizeman of Cambridge Univ., 1927. Asst in Historical Geography, London Sch. of Economics, 1927; temp. administrative officer in Ministry of Economic Warfare and Foreign Office, 1941–45; Reader in Geography in University of London, 1946. Visiting Professor: Univ. of Minnesota, 1952; Univ. of California, Los Angeles, 1959–60; Univ. of Michigan, 1966–67; Univ. of Wisconsin, 1969–70; Univ. of Saskatchewan, 1971. Myres Memorial Lectr, Oxford Univ., 1970–71. Mem., RGS Council, 1956–59 (Hon. Fellow, 1992); Pres., Inst. of British Geographers, 1959. Murchison Award, RGS, 1972. *Publications:* The Union of Moldavia and Wallachia, 1859, 1929, repr. 1973; An Historical Geography of Europe, 1935; The Geography Behind History, 1938; Mediterranean Problems, 1940; (ed jtly) The Changing Map of Asia, 1950, 1971; (jtly) The Spirit and Purpose of Geography, 1951; (ed jtly) The Changing World, 1956; (ed) The Caxton Atlas, 1960; (ed) Regions of The British Isles series, 1960; The Soviet Union, 1963, 2nd edn 1976; (jtly) Our Fragmented World, 1975; contributions to journals of geography, history and foreign affairs. *Address:* Wildwood, 17 Danes Way, Oxshott, Surrey KT22 0LU. *T:* (01372) 842351. *Died 27 Jan. 1998.*

ECCLES, 1st Viscount *cr* 1964, of Chute, co. Wilts; **David McAdam Eccles;** Baron 1962; CH 1984; KCVO 1953; PC 1951; *b* 18 Sept. 1904; *s* of late W. McAdam Eccles, FRCS and Anna Coralie, *d* of E. B. Anstie, JP; *m* 1st, 1928, Sybil (*d* 1977), *e d* of Viscount Dawson of Penn, GCVO, KCB, KCMG, PC; two *s* one *d;* 2nd, 1984, Mary, widow of Donald Hyde, Somerville, NJ. *Educ:* Winchester; New Coll., Oxford (MA). Joined Ministry of Economic Warfare, Sept. 1939; Economic Adviser to HM Ambassadors at Madrid and Lisbon, 1940–42; Ministry of Production, 1942–43. MP (C) Chippenham Div. of Wilts, 1943–62; Minister of Works, 1951–54; Minister of Education, 1954–57; Pres. of the Board of Trade, 1957–59; Minister of Education, 1959–62; Paymaster-General, with responsibility for the arts, 1970–73. Trustee, British Museum, 1963–, Chm. of Trustees, 1968–70; Chm., British Liby Bd, 1973–78. Dir, Courtaulds, 1962–70. Chm., Anglo-Hellenic League, 1967–70. Pres., World Crafts Council, 1974–78. Sen. Fellow, RCA. Hon. FRIBA; Hon. Fellow, Pierrepont Morgan Library. *Publications:* Half-Way to Faith, 1966; Life and Politics: a Moral Diagnosis, 1967; On Collecting, 1968; By Safe Hand: Letters of Sybil and David Eccles 1939–42, 1983. *Heir: s* Hon. John Dawson Eccles, CBE [*b* 20 April 1931; *m* 1955, Diana Catherine Sturge (later Baroness Eccles of Moulton); one *s* three *d*]. *Address:* Dean Farm, Chute, near Andover, Hants SP11 9ET. *T:* (01264) 730210; 6 Barton Street, SW1P 3NG. *T:* (020) 7222 1387. *Clubs:* Brooks's, Roxburghe; Knickerbocker, Grolier (New York); Nassau (Princeton). *Died 24 Feb. 1999.*

ECCLES, Sir John (Carew), AC 1990; Kt 1958; FRS 1941; FRSNZ; FAA; *b* 27 Jan. 1903; *s* of William James and Mary Eccles; *m* 1st, 1928, Irene Frances Miller (marr. diss. 1968); four *s* five *d;* 2nd, 1968, Helena Táboříková. *Educ:* Melbourne Univ.; Magdalen Coll., Oxford. Melbourne University: 1st class Hons MB, BS 1925;

Victorian Rhodes Scholar, 1925. Univ. of Oxford: Christopher Welch Scholar; 1st class Hons Natural Science (Physiology), 1927; MA 1929; DPhil 1929; Gotch Memorial Prize, 1927; Rolleston Memorial Prize, 1932. Junior Res. Fellow, Exeter Coll., Oxford, 1927–32; Staines Med. Fellow, Exeter Coll., 1932–34; Fellow and Tutor of Magdalen Coll., and Univ. Lectr in Physiology, 1934–37; Dir, Kanematsu Memorial Inst. of Pathology, Sydney, 1937–44; Prof. of Physiology: Univ. of Otago, Dunedin, NZ, 1944–51; ANU, Canberra, 1951–66; Mem., Inst. for Biomedical Res., Chicago, 1966–68; Dist. Prof. and Head of Res. Unit of Neurobiology, Health Sci. Faculty, State Univ. of NY at Buffalo, 1968–75, then Dist. Prof. Emeritus. Lectures: Waynflete, Magdalen Coll., Oxford, 1952; Herter, Johns Hopkins Univ., 1955; Ferrier, Royal Soc., 1959; Sherrington, Liverpool Univ., 1966; Patten, Indiana Univ., 1972; Pahlavi, Iran, 1976; Gifford, Edinburgh, 1978, 1979; Carroll, Georgetown, 1982; Idreos, Manchester Coll., Oxford, 1990. Pres., Australian Acad. of Science, 1957–61. Member: Pontifical Acad. of Science; Deutsche Akademie der Naturforscher Leopoldina. Foreign Hon. Member: Amer. Acad. of Arts and Sciences; Amer. Philosophical Soc.; Amer. Neurological Soc.; Accademia Nazionale dei Lincei. Hon. Life Mem., New York Acad. of Sciences, 1965; Foreign Associate, Nat. Acad. of Sciences; For. Mem., Max-Planck Soc. Hon. Fellow: Exeter Coll., Oxford, 1961; Magdalen Coll., Oxford, 1964; Amer. Coll. of Physicians, 1967. Hon. ScD Cantab; Hon. DSc: Oxon; Tasmania; British Columbia; Gustavus Adolphus Coll., Minnesota; Marquette Univ., Wisconsin; Loyola, Chicago; Yeshiva, NY; Fribourg; Georgetown, Washington DC; Hon. LLD Melbourne; Hon. MD: Charles Univ., Prague; Torino; Basel; Madrid, 1992; Hon. Dr Ulm, 1994. (Jointly) Nobel Prize for Medicine, 1963; Baly Medal, RCP, 1961; Royal Medal, Royal Soc., 1962; Cothenius Medal, Deutsche Akademie der Naturforscher Leopoldina, 1964; (first) Golden Medal, Charles Univ., Prague, 1993. Order of the Rising Sun, Gold and Silver Stars (Japan), 1987. *Publications:* (jtly) Reflex Activity of Spinal Cord, 1932; Neuro-physiological Basis of Mind, 1953; Physiology of Nerve Cells, 1957; Physiology of Synapses, 1964; (jtly) The Cerebellum as a Neuronal Machine, 1967; The Inhibitory Pathways of the Central Nervous System, 1969; Facing Reality, 1970; The Understanding of the Brain, 1973; (jtly) Molecular Neurobiology of the Mammalian Brain, 1977, 2nd edn 1987; (jtly) The Self and Its Brain, 1977; The Human Mystery, 1979; (jtly) Sherrington, his Life and Thought, 1979; The Human Psyche, 1980; (jtly) The Wonder of Being Human: our brain, our mind, 1984; Evolution of the Brain: creation of the self, 1989; (contrib.) Can Scientists Believe, 1991; How the Self Controls its Brain, 1993; papers in Proc. Royal Soc., Jl of Physiology, Jl of Neurophysiology, Experimental Brain Research. *Recreation:* European travel. *Address:* Ca' a la Gra', 6646 Contra, Ticino, Switzerland. *T:* 093–672931.

Died 2 May 1997.

ECKERSLEY, Thomas, OBE 1948; RDI 1963; AGI; graphic designer; Head of Department of Design, London College of Printing, 1958–76; *b* Sept. 1914; *s* of John Eckersley and Eunice Hilton; *m* 1st, Daisy Eckersley; two *s* (and one *s* decd); 2nd, 1966, Mary Kessell, painter. *Educ:* Salford Sch. of Art. Free-lance Graphic Designer for London Transport, Shell Mex, BBC, GPO, MOI, Unicef, CoID and other leading concerns from 1936. Work exhibited in Sweden, USA, Paris, Hamburg, Lausanne, Milan, Amsterdam; permanent collections of work in V&A Museum, Imperial War Museum, London Transport Museum, Nat. Gall. of Australia, Museum of Modern Art, USA, Library of Congress, USA and Die Neue Sammlung Staatliches Museum München; one-man exhibitions: Soc. of Artists and Designers, 1976; Camden

Arts Centre, British Arts Centre, Yale, 1980; Peel Park Gall., Salford, Edinburgh, 1981; Newcastle upon Tyne Polytechnic Gall., 1983; London Transport Museum, 1985; Maidstone Coll. of Art, 1985; Oxford Polytechnic, 1986; Emmerich Poster Museum, Germany, 1987. Mem. of Alliance Graphique Internationale; Hon. Fellow: Manchester Coll. of Art and Design; Humberside Coll. of Higher Educn, 1985; RCA, 1991. FSTD. Medal of CSD, 1990. *Publications:* contribs to Graphis, Gebrauchsgraphik, Form und Technik, Art and Industry, Print Design and Production, Penrose Annual; *relevant publication:* F. H. K. Henrion, Top Graphic Designers, 1983. *Recreation:* cricket. *Address:* 53 Belsize Park Gardens, NW3 4JL. *T:* (0171) 586 3586.

Died 1 Aug. 1997.

EDEL, (Joseph) Leon; Citizens Professor of English, University of Hawaii, 1970–78, then Emeritus; *b* 9 Sept. 1907; *e s* of Simon Edel and Fanny (*née* Malamud), Pittsburgh, Pa; *m* 1st, 1935, Bertha Cohen (marr. diss. 1950); 2nd, 1950, Roberta Roberts (marr. diss. 1979); 3rd, 1980, Marjorie Sinclair; no *c*. *Educ:* McGill Univ., Montreal (BA 1927, MA 1928); Univ. of Paris (Docteurès-Lettres 1932). Served with US Army in France and Germany, 1943–46: Bronze Star Medal (US), 1945; Chief of Information Control, News Agency, US Zone, 1946–47. Asst Prof., Sir George Williams Coll., Montreal, 1932–34; miscellaneous writing and journalism, 1934–43; Christian Gauss Seminar in Criticism, Princeton Univ., 1951–52; New York University: Vis. Prof., 1952–53; Associate Prof., 1953–55; Prof. of English, 1955–66; Henry James Prof. of English and American Letters, 1966–72. Guggenheim Fellow, 1936–38, 1965–66; Alexander Lectures, Toronto, 1956; Visiting Professor: Indiana, 1954; Hawaii, 1955, 1969, 1970; Harvard, 1959–60; Purdue, 1970; Centenary, Toronto, 1967; Vernon, in Biography, Dartmouth, 1977; Vis. Fellow, Humanities Res. Centre, Canberra, 1976. Westminster Abbey Address, Henry James Meml in Poets' Corner, 1976. Mem., Educnl Adv. Cttee, Guggenheim Foundn, 1968–80. Pres., US Center of PEN, 1957–59. Pres., Hawaii Literary Arts Council, 1978–79. Fellow, Amer. Acad. of Arts and Sciences, 1959; Bollingen Fellow, 1959–61. Member: Nat. Inst. of Arts and Letters, 1964– (Sec., 1965–67); Amer. Acad. of Arts and Letters, 1972; Council, Authors' Guild, 1965–68 (Pres., 1969–70); Soc. of Authors, 1968; Adv. Council, Amer. Trust for British Liby. FRSL 1970. Hon. Member: W. A. White Psychiatric Inst., 1966; Amer. Acad. Psychoanalysis, 1975; Hon. DLitt: McGill, 1963; Union Coll., Schenectady, 1963; Univ. of Saskatchewan, 1983; Hawaii Loa Coll., Honolulu, 1988. Nat. Inst. of Arts and Letters Award, 1959; US Nat. Book Award for nonfiction, 1963; Pulitzer Prize for biography, 1963; AAAL Gold Medal for biography, 1976; Hawaii Literary Arts Award, 1978; Nat. Arts Club Medal for Literature, 1981; Nat. Book Critics Circle Award (Biography), 1985. *Publications:* Henry James: les années dramatiques, 1932; The Prefaces of Henry James, 1932; James Joyce: The Last Journey, 1947; (with E. K. Brown) Willa Cather, 1953; The Life of Henry James: The Untried Years, 1953, The Conquest of London, 1962, The Middle Years, 1963, The Treacherous Years, 1969, The Master, 1972, rev. edn in 2 vols, 1978, rewritten, rev. into 1 vol., Henry James, a life, 1985; The Psychological Novel, 1955; Literary Biography, 1957; (with Dan H. Laurence) A Bibliography of Henry James, 1957; Thoreau, 1970; Bloomsbury: a House of Lions, 1979; Stuff of Sleep and Dreams (essays), 1982; Writing Lives: Principia Biographica, 1984; Some Memories of Edith Wharton, 1993; *edited:* The Complete Plays of Henry James, 1949, rev. edn 1991; Selected Letters of Henry James, 1956, 1987; (with Gordon N. Ray) James and H. G. Wells, Letters, 1958; The Complete Tales of Henry James, 12 vols, 1962–65; The Diary of

Alice James, 1964; Literary History and Literary Criticism, 1965; Henry James: Stories of the Supernatural, 1971; Harold Goddard Alphabet of the Imagination, 1975; Henry James Letters: vol. I, 1843–1875, 1975; vol. II, 1875–1883, 1980; vol. III, 1883–1895, 1981; vol. IV, 1895–1916, 1984; Edmund Wilson: The Twenties, 1975, The Thirties, 1980, The Forties, 1983, The Fifties, 1986; (with Mark Wilson) Henry James, Critical Essays, 1984 (two vols); (ed with Lyall H. Powers) The Complete Notebooks of Henry James, 1986; Memoir of Louis Rapkine, 1988. *Recreations:* music, swimming. *Address:* 3817 Lurline Drive, Honolulu, HI 96816, USA. *Club:* Century (New York).   *Died 5 Sept. 1997.*

EDGE, Maj.-Gen. Raymond Cyril Alexander, CB 1968; MBE 1945; FRICS 1949; FRGS; Director General, Ordnance Survey, 1965–69, retired; *b* 21 July 1912; *s* of Raymond Clive Edge and Mary (*née* Masters); *m* 1st, 1939, Margaret Patricia (*d* 1982), *d* of William Wallace McKee; one *s* one *d*; 2nd, 1983, Audrey Anne, *d* of Sir Lewis Richardson, 1st Bt, CBE, and *widow* of Jonathan Muers-Raby. *Educ:* Cheltenham Coll.; RMA; Caius Coll., Cambridge (BA). Commissioned in RE, 1932; served in India, Royal Bombay Sappers and Miners and Survey of India, 1936–39; War Service in India, Burma (despatches), and Malaya; Lt-Col 1951; Col 1954; Dir (Brig.) Ordnance Survey, 1961; Maj.-Gen. 1965. Col Comdt, RE, 1970–75 (Representative Col Comdt, 1974). Mem., Sec. of State for the Environment's Panel of Independent Inspectors, 1971–82. Chairman: Assoc. British Geodesists, 1963–65; Geodesy Sub-Cttee, Royal Soc., 1968–75; Field Survey Assoc., 1968–70. Pres., Section E, British Assoc., 1969. Member: Council, RGS, 1966–69; Council, RICS, 1966–72 (Vice-Pres. 1970–72); Land Surveyors Council (Chm, 1970–72). *Publications:* (contrib.) A History of the Ordnance Survey, 1980; various papers on geodetic subjects in Bulletin Géodesique and other publications. *Recreation:* music. *Address:* Crowcombe Court, Crowcombe, Taunton, Somerset, TA4 4AD.
                                    Died 30 Dec. 1999.

EDSBERG, John Christian; Director for Execution of the Budget, Directorate General for Budgets, European Commission, since 1986; *b* 10 Oct. 1938; *s* of Flight Lt Jørgen Palle Christian Edsberg and Olivia Alice Mary (*née* Gulland); *m* 1966, Rosalyn (*née* Padfield); two *s*. *Educ:* Westminster School; Brasenose College, Oxford (MA Hons Maths and Engrg Science). MICE. Civil engineer with Sir Alexander Gibb & Partners, 1961–66; Engineer and Contracts Manager, Soil Mechanics Ltd, 1966–67; Consultant and Senior Consultant, P. A. Management Consultants Ltd, 1967–74; Commission of the European Communities: Principal Administrator, 1974–81; Directorate Gen. for Transport, 1974–81; Directorate Gen. for Develt, 1981–82; Head of Div., Directorate Gen. for Financial Control, 1982–86. *Recreation:* architecture. *Address:* European Commission, 200 rue de la Loi, 1049 Brussels, Belgium. *T:* (2) 2955529; 46 Sydney Street, SW3 6PS. *T:* (020) 7351 0685.
                                    Died 10 June 1999.

EDWARDS, Charles Harold, FRCP; Dean of St Mary's Hospital Medical School, Paddington, 1973–79; *b* 1913; *m* 1959; one *s* two *d*. *Educ:* Blundell's Sch., Tiverton; Guy's Hosp. Med. Sch. MRCS 1937; LRCP 1937; MRCP 1946; FRCP 1961. Formerly: Resident Medical appts, Guy's Hosp.; Resident Med. Officer, Nat. Hosp., Queen Square; Neurological Registrar, St Mary's Hosp., Paddington; Consultant Physician, Dept Nervous Diseases, St Mary's Hosp., 1954–78; Consultant Neurologist: Royal Nat. Throat, Nose and Ear Hosp., 1955–78; King Edward VII Hosp., Windsor, 1952–78; Canadian Red Cross Meml Hosp., Taplow, 1952–78; Maidenhead Hosp., 1952–78. Co-ordinator, Special Progs, Wellcome Trust, 1979–85.

Mem., British Assoc. of Neurologists, 1952–; FRSocMed. *Publications:* Neurology of Ear, Nose and Throat, 1973; Neurological Section, in Synopsis of Otolaryngology, 1967; Scott-Brown, Diseases of Ear, Nose and Throat, 1971; contrib. Qly Jl Medicine, Lancet, etc. *Recreations:* words, gardening. *Address:* Cardinal House, The Green, Hampton Court, Surrey KT8 9BW. *T:* (0181) 979 6922. *Club:* Garrick.   *Died 1 Dec. 1996.*

EDWARDS, Sir Clive; *see* Edwards, Sir J. C. L.

EDWARDS, Prof. Edward George, PhD; BSc; FRSC; Vice-Chancellor and Principal, University of Bradford, 1966–78, Hon. Professor, since 1978 (Principal of Bradford Institute of Technology, 1957–66); *b* 18 Feb. 1914; *m* 1940, Kathleen Hewitt; two *s* two *d*. *Educ:* Cardiff High Sch.; University of South Wales; Cardiff Coll. of Technology. Lecturer in Chemistry, University of Nottingham, 1938–40; Research Chemist, ICI Ltd, 1940–45; Head of Dept of Chemistry and Applied Chemistry, Royal Technical Coll., Salford, 1945–54; Principal, Coll. of Technology, Liverpool, 1954–57. Hon. DTech Bradford, 1980; Fellow, University Coll., Cardiff, 1981. *Publications:* Higher Education for Everyone, 1982; various research papers in chemical jls; articles and papers on higher educn, technological innovation, university planning. *Recreations:* philosophy, music, walking, travel. *Address:* Corner Cottage, Westwood Drive, Ilkley, West Yorks LS29 9QX. *T:* Ilkley (01943) 607112.
                                    Died 21 Nov. 1996.

EDWARDS, Geoffrey Francis, CBE 1975 (OBE 1968; MBE 1956); TD; HM Diplomatic Service, retired; *b* 28 Sept. 1917; *s* of late Oliver and Frances Margaret Edwards, Langley, Bucks; *m* 1st, 1949, Joyce Black (*d* 1953); one *d*; 2nd, 1961, Johanna Elisabeth Franziska Taeger. *Educ:* Brighton Coll. Joined Pixley & Abell, Bullion Brokers, 1936; commissioned RA (TA), June 1939; served with 117 Fd Regt and 59 (Newfoundland) Heavy Regt RA in NW Europe, 1939–45; joined Control Commn for Germany, 1945; joined British Military Govt, Berlin, 1949; Economic Adviser, 1956; Consul-General, Berlin, 1966–75. Ernst Reuter Silver Plaque, Berlin, 1975. *Recreations:* gardening, fishing, golf. *Address:* Am Kurgarten 105, 53489 Sinzig-Bad Bodendorf, Germany. *T:* (2642) 44821.   *Died 29 April 1996.*

EDWARDS, Iorwerth Eiddon Stephen, CMG 1973; CBE 1968; MA, LittD; FSA; FBA 1962; Keeper of Egyptian Antiquities, British Museum, 1955–74; *b* 21 July 1909; *s* of late Edward Edwards, Orientalist, and Ellen Jane (*née* Higgs); *m* 1938, Elizabeth, *y d* of late Charles Edwards Lisle; one *d* (one *s* decd). *Educ:* Merchant Taylors'; Gonville and Caius Coll., Cambridge (Major Scholar; Merchant Taylors' Sch. Exhibitioner and John Stewart of Rannoch Univ. Scholar, Cambridge, 1928; 1st Cl. Oriental Languages Tripos (Arabic and Hebrew), Parts I and II, 1930–31; Mason Prize, Tyrwhitt Scholarship and Wright Studentship, 1932). FSA 1942. Entered Dept of Egyptian and Assyrian Antiquities, British Museum, 1934; seconded to Foreign Office; attached to British Embassies, Cairo and Baghdad, and to Secretariat, Jerusalem, 1942–45. Visiting Prof., Brown Univ., Providence, RI, USA, 1953–54. Glanville Meml Lectr, Cambridge Univ., 1980; Foreign Guest Lectr, Coll. de France, 1982. Pioneered and chose objects for Tutankhamun Exhibition, London, 1972; Consultant to Australian Govt, Gold of the Pharaohs Exhibn, 1988. Member, Unesco-Egyptian Min. of Culture Cttees for saving monuments of Philae, 1973–80, for planning Nat. Mus., Cairo, 1985, for re-organising Egyptian Mus. Cairo, 1985, for protection of monuments of Giza, 1990. Vice-Pres. Egypt Exploration Soc., 1962–88; Member: German Archæological Inst.; Austrian Archæol Inst.; Associate Mem., Inst. of Egypt; Mem., Cttee of Visitors of Metropolitan Museum of Art, NY;

Corresp. Mem., Fondation Egyptologique Reine Elisabeth, Brussels; Correspondant étranger de L'Institut, Académie des Inscriptions et Belles-Lettres, Paris; Hon. Life Mem., Austrian Acad. of Scis, 1996. T. E. Peet Prize, Liverpool Univ., 1947. *Publications:* Hieroglyphic Texts in the British Museum, Vol. VIII, 1939; The Pyramids of Egypt, 1947, 5th edn 1993; Hieratic Papyri in the British Museum, 4th Series (Oracular Amuletic Decrees of the Late New Kingdom), 1960; The Early Dynastic Period in Egypt, 1964; (ed jtly) The Cambridge Ancient History (3rd edn), vols I-III, 1970–91; Treasures of Tutankhamun (Catalogue of London exhibn), 1972; Treasures of Tutankhamun (Catalogue of US exhibn), 1976; Tutankhamun's Jewelry, 1976; Tutankhamun: his tomb and its treasures, 1976; articles in Journal of Egyptian Archæology and other scientific periodicals. *Recreations:* watching cricket, gardening. *Address:* Dragon House, The Bullring, Deddington, Oxon OX15 0TT. *T:* (01869) 338481. *Club:* Athenæum.   *Died 24 Sept. 1996.*

EDWARDS, Jane Elizabeth; *see* Hayward, J. E.

EDWARDS, John Basil, CBE 1972; JP; Chairman, Magistrates Association, 1976–79; *b* 15 Jan. 1909; *s* of Charles and Susan Edwards; *m* 1935, Molly Patricia Philips (*d* 1979); one *s* two *d*. *Educ:* King's Sch., Worcester; Wadham Coll., Oxford (BA Hons Jurisprudence, MA). Commnd Royal Warwickshire Regt (RE) TA, 1938. Admitted Solicitor, 1933. Worcester CC, 1936; Mayor of Worcester, 1947–49; Alderman, City of Worcester, 1948. JP Worcs, 1940; Chm., Worcester City Justices, 1951–79. Magistrates Association: Mem. Council, 1960; Chm., Worcestershire Br., 1960–66; Hon. Treasurer, 1968–70; Dep. Chm., 1970–76. Mem., James Cttee on Distribution of Criminal Business, 1973–75. Chm., Worcester Three Choirs Festival, 1947–72. Freeman, City of London. Liveryman: Haberdashers' Company; Distillers' Company. *Recreation:* gardening. *Address:* 21 Britannia Square, Worcester WR1 3DH. *T:* Worcester (01905) 29933.   *Died 10 Jan. 1996.*

EDWARDS, Sir (John) Clive (Leighton), 2nd Bt *cr* 1921, of Treforis, co. Glamorgan; *b* 11 Oct. 1916; *s* of Sir John Bryn Edwards, 1st Bt and Kathleen Ermyntrude (*d* 1975), *d* of late John Corfield, JP; *S* father, 1922. *Educ:* Winchester Coll. Volunteered and served in the Army, 1940–46. *Recreations:* motoring, gardening. *Heir:* none. *Address:* Milntown, Lezayre, Ramsey, Isle of Man IM7 2AB. *Clubs:* Royal Automobile (Hon. Mem.); Midland Automobile (Hon. Life Mem.), Bugatti Owners.
                                  Died 19 Feb. 1999 (ext).

EDWARDS, John Lionel; retired civil servant; *b* 29 Aug. 1915; *s* of Rev. Arthur Edwards and Constance Edwards; *m* 1948, Cecily Miller (*d* 1993); one *s* two *d*. *Educ:* Marlborough; Corpus Christi Coll., Oxford. Served War, Army, 1940–45. Entered Scottish Office, 1938; Ministry of Labour, 1945: Principal Private Sec. to Minister of Labour, 1956; Asst Sec., 1956; Sec., 1968–71; Under-Sec., Dept of Employment, 1971–75; Certification Officer for Trade Unions and Employers' Assocs, 1976–81. *Address:* Little Bedwyn, The Ridgway, Pyrford, Surrey GU22 8PN. *T:* (01932) 343459. *Club:* United Oxford & Cambridge University.
                                       Died 23 April 1999.

EDWARDS, Joseph Robert, CBE 1963; JP; Consultant, Canewdon Consultants plc, Southend-on-Sea, since 1989 (Chairman, 1986–89); Deputy Chairman, Theale Estates Ltd (formerly Martin Electrical Equipment (Theale) Ltd), since 1979; Director, Creative Industries Group Inc., Detroit, since 1985; *b* 5 July 1908; *y s* of late Walter Smith Edwards and Annie Edwards, Gt Yarmouth; *m* 1st, 1936, Frances Mabel Haddon Bourne (*d* 1975); three *s* one *d*; 2nd, 1976, Joan Constance Mary Tattersall. *Educ:* High

Sch., Great Yarmouth. Joined Austin Motor Co., Birmingham, 1928; Hercules factory, 1939; rejoined Austin Motor Co., 1941; Gen. Works Manager, 1951; Local Dir, 1953; Works Dir, 1954; Dir of Manufacturing, British Motor Corp., 1955; Managing Director: British Motor Corp., 1966–68; Pressed Steel/Fisher Ltd, 1956–67; Dep. Chm., Harland & Wolff Ltd, 1968–70, Chm. 1970; Dep. Chm., Associated Engrg, 1969–78; Dir, BPC Ltd, 1973–81; Vice-Chm., Lucas (Industries) Ltd, 1976–79; Chm., Penta Motors Ltd, Reading, 1978–87; Dir, CSE Aviation Ltd, 1973–87. Pres., Motor Industry Research Assoc. Mem., Commn on Industrial Relations to 1974. JP Oxford, 1964. Hon. MA Oxon, 1968. *Recreation:* golf. *Address:* Flat 16, Shoreacres, Banks Road, Sandbanks, Poole, Dorset BH13 7QH. *T:* (01202) 709315. *Club:* Royal Motor Yacht.   *Died 12 June 1997.*

EDWARDS, Dr Roger Snowden, CBE 1964; JP; Chairman, Gas Industry Training Board, 1965–74, retired; *b* 19 Dec. 1904; *s* of late Herbert George Edwards and Margaret Alice Edwards; *m* 1935, Eveline Brunton, MBE (*d* 1986); two *s* one *d*. *Educ:* Enfield Grammar Sch.; Imperial Coll. of Science. Junior Staff, Imperial Coll. of Science, 1925–28; Physicist, British Xylonite Co., 1928–29; Physicist, Boot Trade Research Association, 1929–39; Dir, Co-operative Wholesale Soc., 1939–49. Chairman: Council of Industrial Design, 1947–52 (Mem., 1944–47); NE Gas Board, 1949–66; Mem., Gas Council, 1966–70. JP Harrogate, 1960; Surrey, 1966. *Recreation:* golf. *Address:* 23 Manor Way, Letchworth, Herts SG6 3NL.
                                        Died 13 Aug. 1997.

EDWARDS, Vero Copner W.; *see* Wynne-Edwards.

EFFINGHAM, 6th Earl of, *cr* 1837; **Mowbray Henry Gordon Howard;** Baron Howard of Effingham 1554; *b* 29 Nov. 1905; *er s* of 5th Earl and Rosamond Margaret, *d* of late E. H. Hudson; *S* father, 1946; *m* 1st, 1938, Manci Maria Malvina Gertler (marr. diss. 1946); 2nd, 1952, Gladys Irene Kerry (marr. diss. 1971); 3rd, 1972, (Mabel) Suzanne Mingay Cragg, *d* of late Maurice Jules-Marie Le Pen, Paris, and *widow* of Wing Comdr Francis Talbot Cragg. *Educ:* Lancing. Served War 1939–45, RA and 3rd Maritime Regt. *Recreations:* shooting, fishing, philately. *Heir: n* Comdr David Peter Mowbray Algernon Howard, RN [*b* 29 April 1939; *m* 1st, 1964, Anne Mary Sayer (marr. diss. 1975); one *s*; 2nd, 1992, Mrs Elizabeth J. Turner]. *Address:* House of Lords, SW1A 0PW.
                                        Died 22 Feb. 1996.

EGELAND, Leif; *b* 19 Jan. 1903; *s* of late J. J. Egeland, Consul for Norway in Natal, and Ragnhild Konsmo; *m* 1942, Marguerite Doreen (*d* 1984), *d* of late W. J. de Zwaan, Waterkloof, Pretoria; one *d*. *Educ:* Durban High Sch.; Natal University Coll.; Oxford Univ. MA English Lang. and Literature, Natal Univ. Coll.; MA, Hons BA, Jurisprudence, BCL Oxon; Rhodes Scholar (Natal), Trinity Coll., Oxford, 1924–27; official Fellow in Law and Classics, Brasenose Coll., 1927–30 (Hon. Fellow, 1984); Harmsworth Scholar, Middle Temple, 1927–30; Barrister, Middle Temple, 1930, Hon. Bencher, 1948; Hon. LLD Cambridge, 1948. Admitted as Advocate of Supreme Court of S Africa, 1931; Vice-Consul for Norway, Natal, 1931–44; MP (House of Assembly) for Durban (Berea), 1933–38, for Zululand, 1940–43; SA Minister to Sweden, 1943, to Holland and Belgium, 1946. Served War of 1939–45, as AJAG, in UDF, 1940–43; Middle East with 6th Armoured Div. of UDF, 1943. SA Delegate to San Francisco Conf., 1945, to 1st Gen. Assembly of UN, London, 1946, to Final Assembly of League of Nations, 1946; SA delegate and Pres. of Commn on Italian Political and Territorial Questions at Peace Conf., Paris, 1946–47. High Comr in London for the Union of South Africa, 1948–50. Vice-Pres., Royal Commonwealth Soc., 1948–; Hon. Pres., South Africa Inst. of Internat. Affairs; Chm.,

Smuts Memorial Trust; Life Trustee, South Africa Foundn. Hon. Pres., SA Guide-dogs Assoc. for the Blind (Life Mem., 1994). LLD *hc* Univ. of Natal, 1990. FRSA 1948. Knight Commander with Star of St Olav (Norway), 1943; Knight Grand Cross of North Star (Sweden), 1946, Order of Meritorious Services (Class I) Gold (S Africa), 1987. *Publication:* (autobiog.) Bridges of Understanding, 1978. *Recreation:* bridge. *Address:* 41 The Guild, 213 Rivonia Road, Morningside, South Africa. *Clubs:* Rand, Inanda, South African International Lawn Tennis (Hon. Mem., 1950) (S Africa).   *Died 8 Feb. 1996.*

EGERTON, Sir John Alfred Roy, (Jack Egerton), Kt 1976; *b* Rockhampton, 11 March 1918; *s* of J. G. Egerton, Rockhampton; *m* 1940, Moya, *d* of W. Jones; one *s*. *Educ:* Rockhampton High Sch.; Mt Morgan High Sch.; Australian Admin. Staff Coll. A Union Exec. Officer, 1941–76; Federal Officer of Boilermakers' Union, 1951–66 (Vice-Pres. Fed. Council; rep. Union in China, 1956); Official, Metal Trades Fedn, 1951–67; Mem., ACTU Interstate Exec., 1969; former Pres., Qld Trades and Labor Council. Aust. Rep. ILO Congresses, Geneva, 1960, 1966, 1968, 1974; Qld Rep. to ACTU Congress and ALP Fed. Conf.; Pres., ALP Qld Exec., 1968–76 (Mem. Qld Central Exec., 1958); Mem., Fed. Exec. of ALP, 1970, Sen. Vice-Pres. 1972. Alderman and Dep. Mayor, Gold Coast City Council. Director: Qantas Airways Ltd, 1973–84; Mary Kathleen Uranium; SGIO Building Soc.; Beenleigh Rum. Member: Duke of Edinburgh Study Conf. Cttee, 1967–74; Griffith Univ. Council. *Recreations:* reading, Rugby League (Vice Pres. and Dir, Qld), golf, trotting. *Clubs:* NSW and Queensland League; Virginia Golf; Albion Park Trotting.   *Died 21 Dec. 1998.*

EGERTON, Sir Seymour (John Louis), GCVO 1977 (KCVO 1970); Director, Coutts & Co., Bankers, 1947–85 (Chairman, 1951–76); *b* 24 Sept. 1915; *s* of late Louis Egerton and Jane, *e d* of Rev. Lord Victor Seymour (4th *s* of 5th Marquess of Hertford); unmarried. *Educ:* Eton Served War of 1939–45, in Grenadier Guards. Governor, St George's Hosp., 1958–73. Treasurer, Boy Scouts' Assoc., 1953–64; Vice-Pres., Corporation of the Church House, 1954–81. Sheriff of Greater London, 1968. *Clubs:* Boodle's, Beefsteak, Pratt's.   *Died 26 May 1998.*

EGGLESTON, Prof. Harold Gordon; Professor Emeritus of Mathematics, London University; *b* 27 Nov. 1921; 2nd *s* of H. T. and E. M. Eggleston, Bents Green, Sheffield; *m* 1955, Elizabeth, *o d* of F. R. and C. A. W. Daglish, Beamish, County Durham; two *s* one *d*. *Educ:* High Storrs Grammar Sch., Sheffield; Trinity Coll., Cambridge. Lecturer and Senior Lecturer, University Coll. of Swansea, 1948–53; Lecturer, University of Cambridge, 1953–58; Prof. of Mathematics, University of London at Bedford Coll., 1958–66, at Royal Holloway Coll., 1966–81. *Publications:* Problems in Euclidean Space, 1957; Convexity, 1958; Elementary Real Analysis, 1962. *Address:* 22 Windsor Square, Exmouth, Devon EX8 1JY.   *Died 21 Aug. 1999.*

ELDER, David Renwick, MC 1940; CA; *b* 4 Jan. 1920; *s* of John Kidd Elder and Mary Kinnear Swanley; *m* 1947, Kathleen Frances Duncan; two *s* two *d*. *Educ:* Dundee High School. Served 1939–46, The Black Watch (RHR) and Sea Reconnaissance Unit (Major). Royal Dutch Shell Group, 1948–71; Ocean Transport & Trading Ltd, 1971–80 (Dep. Chm., 1975–80; Chm., Ocean Inchcape, 1974–80); Director: Letraset International Ltd, 1975; Capital & Counties Property Ltd, 1979; Whessoe Ltd, 1980. *Recreation:* golf. *Clubs:* Wentworth Golf (Virginia Water); Panmure Golf (Carnoustie).   *Died 19 Oct. 1996.*

ELDRIDGE, John Barron; Chairman, Matthews Wrightson Holdings Ltd, 1971–77; *b* 28 May 1919; *s* of

William John Eldridge and Jessie Winifred (*née* Bowditch); *m* 1940, Marjorie Potier; one *s* two *d*. *Educ:* Lancing Coll. FIA 1950. Dir, Matthews Wrightson Holdings Ltd, 1964. Croix de Guerre 1944. *Address:* Chantry Cottage, Linersh Wood, Bramley, Surrey GU5 0EE. *T:* (01483) 894930.   *Died 15 March 1998.*

ELEY, John L.; *see* Lloyd-Eley.

ELION, Prof. Gertrude Belle; Research Professor of Pharmacology and Medicine, Duke University, North Carolina, since 1983; *b* 23 Jan. 1918; *d* of Robert and Bertha Elion. *Educ:* Hunter Coll., New York (AB 1937); New York Univ. (MS 1941). Lab. Asst in Biochemistry, NY Hosp. Sch. of Nursing, 1937; Res. Asst in Organic Chem., Denver Chemical Manufg Co., NY, 1938–39; teacher, secondary schs, NYC, 1940–42; Food Analyst, Quaker Maid Co., 1942–43; Res. Asst in Organic Synthesis, Johnson and Johnson, 1943–44; Wellcome Research Laboratories: Biochemist, 1944–50; Sen. Res. Chemist, 1950–55; Asst to the Associate Res. Dir, 1955–63; Asst to Res. Dir (Chemotherapy), 1963–67; Head, Dept of Experimental Therapy, 1967–83; Scientist Emeritus, 1983–. Hon. Mem., Acad. of Pharmaceutical Sciences, 1983. Member: Nat. Acad. of Scis, 1990; Inst. of Medicine, 1991; Fellow, Amer. Acad. of Arts and Scis, 1991; For. Mem., Royal Soc., 1995. DStJ 1992. Hon. DSc: George Washington, 1969; Michigan, 1983; Hunter Coll. (CUNY), New York Univ., Polytechnic Univ., Brooklyn, NC State Univ., and Ohio State Univ., 1989; Univ. of NC/Chapel Hill, Russell Sage Coll., 1990; Duke, 1991; Columbia, McMaster and SUNY at Stony Brook, 1992, Washington Coll., S Florida, Wisconsin, E Carolina, 1993; Wake Forest, 1994; Philadelphia Coll. Pharmacy, Albany Coll. Pharmacy, Rensselaer Poly. Inst., 1996; Hon. DMS: Brown Univ., 1969; Utah State, 1994; Hon. MD Chieti, 1995; Hon. DHL Rochester Inst. Technology, 1996. Garvan Medal, Amer. Chemical Soc., 1968; President's Medal, 1970, Hall of Fame, 1973, Hunter Coll.; Distinguished NC Chemist Award, NC Inst. of Chemists, 1981; Judd Award, Sloan-Kettering Inst., 1983; (jtly) Cain Award, Amer. Assoc. for Cancer Res., 1984; NC Distinguished Chemist Award, NC Section, Amer. Chemical Soc., 1985; (jtly) Nobel Prize in Physiology or Medicine, 1988; Bertner Award, Univ. of Texas, 1989; Medal of Honor, Amer. Cancer Soc., 1990; City of Medicine Award, Durham, NC, 1990; (jtly) Discoverer's Award, Pharmaceutical Manufrs Assoc., 1990; Third Century Award, Foundn for a Creative America, 1990; Nat. Inventors Hall of Fame, 1991; Nat. Women's Hall of Fame, 1991; Nat. Medal of Science, 1991; Engrg and Sci. Hall of Fame, 1992; Ronald H. Brown Innovator Award, 1996; Dist. Alumnus Award, Amer. Assoc. State Colls and Univs, 1996; Lemelson/MIT Lifetime Achievement Award, 1997. *Publications:* contribs to scientific jls on chemistry, pharmacology and cancer research. *Recreations:* photography, travel, music. *Address:* 1 Banbury Lane, Chapel Hill, NC 27514, USA. *T:* (919) 9674102.   *Died 21 Feb. 1999.*

ELLIOT, James S.; *see* Scott Elliot.

ELLIOT-SMITH, Alan Guy, CBE 1957; *b* 30 June 1904; *s* of late F. Elliot-Smith; *m* 1939, Ruth Kittermaster; no *c*. *Educ:* Charterhouse; Oriel Coll., Oxford. Hons Mod. Lang. Sch., 1925. Asst Master, Harrow Sch., 1925–40; Headmaster, Cheltenham Coll., 1940–51; Head-master of Victoria Coll., Cairo, 1952–56; Representative in Nigeria of the West Africa Cttee, 1957–58; Headmaster, Markham Coll., Lima, Peru, 1960–63. Deleg. to Inst. of Pacific Relations Conf., Calif, 1936; lectured to German teachers on Education, 1947 and 1948; lectured to Service units in the Middle East, 1949. Mem., Harrow UDC, 1933–36.

Recreations: travel, reading. *Address:* 14 Rowsley Road, Eastbourne, Sussex BN20 7XS.

Died 10 Feb. 1997.

ELLIOTT, Air Vice-Marshal Robert D.; *see* Deacon Elliott.

ELLIOTT, William Rowcliffe, CB 1969; Senior Chief Inspector, Department of Education and Science, 1968–72, retired; *b* 10 April 1910; *s* of Thomas Herbert Elliott and Ada Elliott (*née* Rowcliffe); *m* 1937, Karin Tess, *d* of Ernest and Lilly Classen; one *s. Educ:* St Paul's Sch.; The Queen's Coll., Oxford. Schoolmaster, 1933–36; HM Inspector of Schools: in Leeds, 1936–39; in Leicestershire, 1940–44; in Liverpool, 1944–48; Staff Inspector: for Adult Education, 1948–55; for Secondary Modern Education, 1955–57; Chief Inspector for Educational Developments, 1957–59; for Secondary Educn, 1959–66; Dep. Sen. Chief Insp., DES, 1966–67. Pres., Section L, British Assoc., 1969; Mem., Oxfam Governing Council, 1974–80. Chm. of Governors, Friends' Sch., Saffron Walden, 1982–84. Governor of The Retreat, York, 1984–90. *Publications:* Monemvasia, The Gibraltar of Greece, 1971; Chest-tombs and 'tea caddies' by Cotswold and Severn, 1977. *Recreations:* village life, photography, gardenage. *Address:* Malthus Close, Farthinghoe, Brackley, Northants NN13 5NY. *T:* Banbury (01295) 710388. *Club:* Royal Over-Seas League.

Died 27 June 1996.

ELLIS, Humphry Francis, MBE 1945; writer; *b* 17 July 1907; 2nd *s* of late Dr John Constable Ellis, Metheringham, Lincs and Alice Marion Raven; *m* 1933, Barbara Pauline Hasseldine (*d* 1974); one *s* one *d. Educ:* Tonbridge Sch.; Magdalen Coll., Oxford (Demy; 1st cl. Hon. Mods 1928; 1st cl. Lit. Hum. 1930; MA). Asst Master, Marlborough Coll., 1930–31; Punch: contributor, 1931–68; editorial staff, 1933; Literary and Dep. Ed., 1949–53. Privilege Mem., RFU, 1952–. Served War of 1939–45 in RA (AA Command). *Publications:* So This is Science, 1932; The Papers of A. J. Wentworth, 1949; Why the Whistle Went (on the laws of Rugby Football), 1947; (co-ed) The Royal Artillery Commemoration Book, 1950; (ed) Manual of Rugby Union Football, 1952; Twenty Five Years Hard, 1960; Mediatrics, 1961; A. J. Wentworth, BA (Retd), 1962; The World of A. J. Wentworth, 1964 (re-issued as A. J. Wentworth, BA, 1980); Swansong of A. J. Wentworth, 1982; A Bee in the Kitchen, 1983; contribs to The New Yorker and Countryman. *Recreation:* fishing. *Address:* Hill Croft, Kingston St Mary, Taunton, Somerset TA2 8HT. *T:* (01823) 451264. *Clubs:* Garrick, MCC.

Died 8 Dec. 2000.

ELLIS, Sir John (Rogers), Kt 1980; MBE 1943; MA, MD; FRCP; Physician, 1951–81, Consulting Physician, since 1981, Royal London (formerly The London) Hospital; *b* 15 June 1916; 3rd *s* of late Frederick William Ellis, MD, FRCS; *m* 1942, Joan, *d* of late C. J. C. Davenport; two *s* two *d. Educ:* Oundle Sch.; Trinity Hall, Cambridge; London Hosp. Served RNVR, 1942–46, Mediterranean and Far East, Surg-Lieut. Gen. practice, Plymouth, 1946; Sen. Lectr, Med. Unit, London Hosp., 1948–51; Sub-Dean, London Hosp. Med. Coll., 1948–58, Vice-Dean, 1967–68, Dean, 1968–81, Fellow, 1986. Asst Registrar, RCP, 1957–61, Mem. Council 1969–72, Streatfield Schol., 1957; Physician to Prince of Wales Gen. Hosp., 1958–68; PMO (part-time), Min. of Health, 1964–68. Mem., City and E London AHA, 1974–81; Vice-Chm., Newham DHA, 1981–85. Vice-Chm., Med. Council on Alcoholism, 1983–94; Member: UGC's Med. Sub-cttee, 1959–69; WHO Expert Adv. Panel on Health Manpower, 1963–82; Jt Bd of Clinical Nursing Studies, 1969–74; formerly Member: Porritt (Med. Services) Cttee; Royal Commn on Med. Educn; UK Educn Cttee, RCN. Sec., Assoc. for Study of Med. Educn, 1956–71, Vice-Pres., 1971–; Pres.,

Medical Protection Soc., 1985–88. Lectures: Goulstonian, RCP, 1956; Wood-Jones, Univ. of Manchester, 1960; Porter, Univ. of Kansas, 1960; Sir Charles Hastings, BMA, 1964; Anders, Coll. of Physicians, Pa, 1965; Adams, RCSI, 1965; Shattuck, Massachusetts Med. Soc., 1969; Shorstein, 1979, 1985, Sprawson, 1980, 1985, London Hosp. Med. Coll.; Attlee Meml, Attlee Foundn, 1993; Visiting Lecturer: Assoc. of Amer. Med. Colls, 1957, 1960 and 1963; Ghana Acad. of Sciences, 1967. Former Examr in Med., Univs of Birmingham, Bristol, Cambridge, E Africa, London, Nairobi, Ireland, Newcastle upon Tyne, St Andrews. Corresp. Mem., Royal Flemish Acad. of Medicine; Hon. Member: Swedish Med. Soc.; AOA Honor Med. Soc., USA; Sect. of Med. Educn, RSocMed (former Pres.). Pres., Waltham Forest Sea Cadet Unit, 1977–; Chm., Graves Educnl Resources, 1982–94; Chairman of Governors: Inst. of Educn, London Univ., 1983–93; Woodford Co. High Sch. for Girls, 1992–; Member Bd of Governors, Atlantic Coll.; formerly Member Board of Governors: Inst. of Psychiatry; Bethlem Royal and Maudsley Hosps; London Hosp.; British Postgrad. Med. Fedn; Queen Mary Coll.; CARE for Mentally Handicapped. Pres., London Hosp. League of Friends, 1980–. Formerly Mem. Court, Univ. of Essex. Editor, British Jl of Medical Education, 1966–75. Hon. Fellow: QMC, 1985; London Hosp. Med. Coll., 1986; Inst. of Educn, Univ. of London, 1996. Hon. MD Uppsala, 1977. *Publications:* London Hospital Medical College 1785–1985, 1986; articles on medical education in medical and scientific journals. *Recreations:* painting, gardening. *Address:* Little Monkhams, Monkhams Lane, Woodford Green, Essex IG8 0NP. *T:* (0181) 504 2292.

Died 16 June 1998.

ELLIS, Maxwell (Philip), MD, MS; FRCS; retired; Dean of the Institute of Laryngology and Otology, University of London, 1965–71; Consulting Surgeon, Royal National Throat, Nose and Ear Hospital, 1937–71; Consulting Ear, Nose and Throat Surgeon, Central Middlesex Hospital, 1937–74; *b* 28 Feb. 1906; *s* of Louis Ellis; *m* 1st, 1935, Barbara Gertrude Chapman (*d* 1977); 2nd, 1979, Mrs Clarice Adler (*d* 1989). *Educ:* University Coll., London (Exhibitioner; Fellow 1975); University Coll. Hosp. (Bucknill Exhbnr). Liston and Alexander Bruce Gold Medals, Surgery and Pathology, UCH, 1927–29; MB, BS (London), Hons Medicine, 1930; MD 1931; FRCS 1932; MS 1937. Geoffrey Duveen Trav. Student, Univ. of London, 1934–36; Leslie Pearce Gould Trav. Schol., 1934, Perceval Alleyn Schol. (Surg. research), 1936, UCH; Lectr on Diseases of Ear, Nose and Throat, Univ. of London, 1952. Hunterian Prof., RCS, 1938. RAFVR, 1940–45 (Wing-Comdr). FRSM, also Mem. Council, Past Pres., Section of Otology; Trustee, Hon. Fellow and Mem. Council, Med. Soc. London (Hon. Sec. 1961–63; Pres., 1970–71); Hon. Member: Assoc. of Otolaryngologists of India; Salonika Soc. of Otolaryngology; Athens Soc. of Otolaryngology; Corresp. Mem., Société Française d'Oto-Rhino-Laryngologie; Hon. Corresp. Mem., Argentine Soc. of Otolaryngology. *Publications:* Modern Trends in Diseases of the Ear, Nose and Throat (ed and part author), 1954, 2nd edn 1971; Operative Surgery (Rob and Smith), Vol. 8 on Diseases of the Ear, Nose and Throat (ed and part author), 1958, 2nd edn 1969; Clinical Surgery (Rob and Smith), Vol. 11, Diseases of the Ear, Nose and Throat (cd and part author), 1966; Sections in Diseases of the Ear, Nose and Throat (ed Scott-Brown), 1952, new edns 1965, 1971; Sections in Cancer, Vol. 4 (ed Raven), 1958; Section in Modern Trends in Surgical Materials (ed Gillis), 1958; papers in various medical and scientific jls. *Recreations:* golf, gardening; formerly bridge, squash rackets. *Address:* 48 Townshend Road, NW8 6LE. *T:* (0171) 722 2252. *Clubs:* Royal Automobile; Sunningdale Golf.

Died 12 Dec. 1996.

ELLIS, Roger Henry, MA; FSA, FRHistS; Secretary, Royal Commission on Historical Manuscripts, 1957–72; *b* 9 June 1910; *e s* of late Francis Henry Ellis, Debdale Hall, Mansfield; *m* 1939, (Audrey) Honor (*d* 1993), *o d* of late H. Arthur Baker, DL; two *d. Educ:* Sedbergh (scholar); King's College, Cambridge (scholar, Augustus Austen Leigh Student). 1st Cl. Class. Tripos, Pts I and II. Asst Keeper, Public Record Office, 1934; Principal Asst Keeper, 1956. Served War of 1939–45: Private, 1939; Major, 5th Fusiliers, 1944; Monuments, Fine Arts and Archives Officer in Italy and Germany, 1944–45. Lectr in Archive Admin, Sch. of Librarianship and Archives, University Coll. London, 1947–57. Mem. London Council, British Inst. in Florence, 1947–55; Hon. Editor, British Records Assoc., and (first) Editor of Archives, 1947–57, Chm. Council, 1967–73, Vice-Pres., 1971–. Vice-Pres., Business Archives Council, 1958–; Member: Adv. Council on Export of Works of Art, 1964–72; Jt Records Cttee of Royal Soc. and Historical MSS Commn, 1968–76; ICA Cttee on Sigillography, 1962–77; Pres., Soc. of Archivists, 1964–73. Chm., Drafting Cttee, British Standard 5454 (The Storage and Exhibition of Archival Documents), 1967–76. A Manager, 1973–76, a Vice-Pres., 1975–76, Royal Instn. Corresp. Mem., Indian Historical Records Commn. *Publications:* The Principles of Archive Repair, 1951; (ed) Manual of Archive Administration by Sir Hilary Jenkinson, 2nd edn 1965; Manuscripts and Men (Royal Commn on Hist. MSS centenary exhibn cat.), 1969; Catalogue of Seals in the Public Record Office: Personal Seals, vol. I, 1978, vol. II, 1981, Monastic Seals, vol. I, 1986; Ode on St Crispin's Day (verse), 1979; (ed jtly) Select Writings of Sir Hilary Jenkinson, 1980; Walking Backwards (verse), 1986; opuscula and articles in British and foreign jls and compilations on care, study and use of archives and MSS. *Recreations:* poetry, travel, the arts. *Address:* 7 Straffan Lodge, Belsize Grove, NW3 4XE. *Club.* Athenæum   *Died 19 March 1998.*

ELLIS, Vivian, CBE 1984; Lieutenant-Commander RNVR; composer, author; President, Performing Right Society, since 1983 (Deputy President, 1975–83); *b* 1904; *s* of Harry Ellis and Maud Isaacson. *Educ:* Cheltenham Coll. (Musical Exhibition). Commenced his career as concert pianist after studying under Myra Hess; studied composition at the Royal Academy of Music; first song published when fifteen; his first work for the theatre was the composition of additional numbers for The Curate's Egg, 1922; contributed to The Little Revue and The Punch Bowl Revue, 1924; to Yoicks, Still Dancing, and Mercenary Mary, and composer of By the Way, 1925; to Just a Kiss, Kid Boots, Cochran's Revue, My Son John, Merely Molly and composer of Palladium Pleasures, 1926; to Blue Skies, The Girl Friend, and Clowns in Clover, 1927; to Charlot, 1928; and composer of Peg o' Mine, Will o' The Whispers, Vogues and Vanities, 1928; to A Yankee at the Court of King Arthur, The House that Jack Built, and (with Richard Myers) composer of Mister Cinders, 1929, new production, Fortune Theatre, 1983; part-composer of Cochran's 1930 Revue, and composer of Follow a Star and Little Tommy Tucker, 1930; part-composer of Stand Up and Sing, and Song of the Drum (with Herman Finck), and composer of Folly to be Wise, and Blue Roses, 1931; part-composer of Out of the Bottle, 1932; composer of Cochran's revue Streamline, 1934; Jill Darling, 1935; music and lyrics of Charlot Revue, The Town Talks, 1936; Hide and Seek, 1937; The Fleet's Lit Up, Running Riot, Under Your Hat, 1938; composer (to Sir A. P. Herbert's libretto) Cochran light operas: Big Ben, 1946; Bless the Bride, 1947 (new prodn, Exeter, 1985; Sadler's Wells, 1987); Tough at the Top, 1949; Water Gipsies, 1955; music and lyrics of And So To Bed, 1951; music for The Sleeping Prince, 1953; music and lyrics of Listen to the Wind, 1954; Half in Earnest (musical

adaptation of The Importance of Being Earnest), 1958; Spread a Little Happiness: a Celebration, King's Head, 1992; composer of popular songs, incl. Spread a Little Happiness, This is My Lovely Day, Ma Belle Marguerite, Other People's Babies and I'm on a See-Saw; many dance items; Coronation Scot; also music for the films Jack's the Boy, Water Gipsies, 1932; Falling for You, 1933; Public Nuisance No 1, 1935; Piccadilly Incident, 1946, etc. Hon. GSM, 1990. Ivor Novello Award for outstanding services to British music, 1973; Ivor Novello Award for Lifetime Achievement in British Music, 1983. Vivian Ellis Prize instituted by PRS in collab. with GSMD, to celebrate his 80th birthday. *Publications: novels:* Zelma; Faint Harmony; Day Out; Chicanery; *travel:* Ellis in Wonderland; *autobiography:* I'm on a See-Saw; *humour:* How to Make your Fortune on the Stock Exchange; How to Enjoy Your Operation; How to Bury Yourself in the Country; How to be a Man-about-Town; Good-Bye, Dollie; contrib: The Rise and Fall of the Matinée Idol; Top Hat and Tails: biography of Jack Buchanan; *for children:* Hilary's Tune; Hilary's Holidays; The Magic Baton; *song book:* Vivian Ellis: a composer's jubilee, 1982. *Recreations:* gardening, painting, operations. *Club.* Garrick.   *Died 19 June 1996.*

ELLISON, Prof. Arthur James, DSc(Eng); CEng, FIMechE, FIEE; Professor of Electrical and Electronic Engineering, and Head of Department, The City University, London, 1972–85, then Professor Emeritus; *b* 15 Jan. 1920; *s* of late Lawrence Joseph and Elsie Beatrice Ellison, Birmingham; *m* 1st, 1952, Marjorie Cresswell (*d* 1955); 2nd, 1963, Marian Elizabeth Gumbrell; one *s* one *d. Educ:* Solihull Sch., Warwicks; Birmingham Central Tech. Coll. (latterly Univ. of Aston); Northampton Polytechnic (latterly City Univ.), as ext. student of Univ. of London. BSc(Eng) (1st Cl. Hons); DSc(Eng) London. SMIEEE. Design Engr, Higgs Motors, Birmingham, 1938–43; Tech. Asst, RAE, 1943–46; Graduate apprentice with British Thomson-Houston Co, Rugby, 1946, Design Engr, 1947–58; Lectr, Queen Mary Coll. (Univ. of London), 1958–65, Sen. Lectr, 1965–72. Visiting Prof., MIT, USA, 1959; lecture tour of Latin Amer. for Brit. Council, 1968; Hon. Prof., Nat. Univ. of Engrg, Lima, Peru, 1968; numerous overseas lectures and conf. contribs. Ext. Examiner to many UK and overseas univs and polytechnics; Founder and Chm., biennial Internat. Conf. on Elec. Machines, 1974–84 (Pres. of Honour). Consultant to industrial cos and nationalised industry on elec. machines, noise and vibration problems; Director: Landspeed, 1975–99; Landspeed University Consultants, 1975–82; Landspeed International, 1975–83; Cotswold Research, 1983–99; Building Health Consultants, 1989–94. Pres., Soc. for Psychical Research, 1976–79, 1981–84; Chm., Theosophical Res. Centre, 1976–87. Member: Council, Scientific and Med. Network, 1973– (Vice-Pres., 1996–); Council, IEE, 1981–84; Bd, Eta Kappa Nu Assoc., USA, 1984–86 (Hon. Mem.); Trustee: Res. Council for Complementary Med., 1983–90; Psychosynthesis Educn Trust, 1996–. *Publications:* Electromechanical Energy Conversion, 1965, 2nd edn 1970; Generalized Electric Machines, 1967; Generalized Electric Machine Set Instruction Book (AEI), 1963, 2nd edn 1968; (jtly) Machinery Noise Measurement, 1985; The Reality of the Paranormal, 1988; (ed) Proc. Queen Mary Coll. Conf., The Teaching of Electric Machinery Theory, 1961; (ed jtly) Proc. Queen Mary Coll. Conf., Design of Electric Machines by Computer, 1969; contribs to: Psychism and the Unconscious Mind, 1968; Intelligence Came First, 1975; numerous papers in engrg and sci. jls on elec. machines, noise and vibration, future guided land transport (IEE premium, 1964); also papers in Jl Soc. for Psych. Res. *Recreations:* reading, meditation, psychical research, travel. *Address:* 10 Foxgrove Avenue,

Beckenham, Kent BR3 5BA. *T:* (020) 8402 3399; Department of Electrical Engineering, The City University, EC1V 0HB. *T:* (020) 7253 4399. *Club:* Athenæum.
Died 6 Sept. 2000.

ELLISON, His Honour John Harold, VRD 1948; a Circuit Judge, 1972–87; Chancellor of the Diocese of Salisbury, 1955–97, and of the Diocese of Norwich, 1955–98; *b* 20 March 1916; *s* of late Harold Thomas Ellison, MIMechE, and Frances Amy Ellison (subseq. Mrs Crossley Swithinbank), both of Woodspeen Grange, Newbury; *m* 1952, Margaret Dorothy Maud, *d* of late Maynard D. McFarlane, Sun City, Arizona; three *s* one *d. Educ:* Uppingham Sch.; King's Coll., Cambridge (MA). Called to the Bar, Lincoln's Inn, 1948. Res. Physicist, then Engr, Thos Firth & John Brown Ltd, Sheffield; Lieut, RE, TA (49th WR) Div., 1937–39; Officer in RNVR, 1939–51 (retd as Lt-Comdr): Gunnery Specialist, HMS Excellent, 1940; Sqdn Gunnery Officer, 8 Cruiser Sqdn, 1940–42; Naval Staff, Admty, 1942–44; Staff Officer (Ops) to Flag Officer, Western Mediterranean, 1944–45; practised at Common Law Bar, 1948–71. Pres., SW London Br., Magistrates' Assoc., 1974–87. Former Governor, Forres Sch. Trust, Swanage. FRAS. *Publications:* (ed) titles Allotments and Smallholdings, and Courts, in Halsbury's Law of England, 3rd edn, and Allotments and Smallholdings, 4th edn. *Recreations:* organs and music, sailing, ski-ing, shooting. *Address:* Goose Green House, Egham, Surrey TW20 8PE. *Clubs:* Army and Navy; Bar Yacht.
Died 29 Sept. 2000.

ELWES, Captain Jeremy Gervase Geoffrey Philip; Vice Lord-Lieutenant of Humberside, 1983–96; *b* 1 Sept. 1921; *s* of Rev. Rudolph, (Rolf), Elwes, OBE, MC; *m* 1955, Clare Mary Beveridge; four *s. Educ:* Avisford Sch.; Ampleforth Coll.; RMC Sandhurst. Joined Lincolnshire Regt, 1940; commissioned KRRC, 1941; served until 1946, S Africa, Middle East, 8th Army, Yugoslavia, Southern Albania (despatches), Dalmatia and Greece. Moulton Agricultural Coll., 1947; farmer, 1949–. Founder Dir, Linvend Ltd, 1960, later J. S. Linder Ltd; founder Dir, Universal Marine Ltd, 1965–71; founder, Elwes Enterprises, later Heavy Lift Co., Stanstead, 1970; founder Dir, Euro-Latin Aviation Ltd, 1975–88. Mem., BBC Northern Adv. Council, 1966–69; Vice-Chm., BBC Radio Humberside, 1970–73; founder Chm., Lincs and Humberside Arts and Heritage Assoc., 1964–69; Co-Founder, Mus. of Lincolnshire Life, 1969; Pres., Lincs Branch, CPRE, 1980–89 (Chm., 1959–80); Mem. Council, Vice-Pres. and Steward, Lincs Agric. Soc., 1964–; Mem., Lincs Branch Exec., CLA, 1966–69. Pres., Shrievalty Assoc. of GB (founder Chm., 1971–92); Joint Founder, Scarbank Trust Charity, 1978; Vice-Chm., Environmental Medicine Foundn, 1987–. Mem., Brigg and Scunthorpe Cons. Assoc. Exec. Cttee, 1948–73; Mem., Brigg RDC, 1957–73, Lindsey CC, 1961–71. Opened country park to the public, Conservation Year, 1970. High Sheriff, Lincs, 1969; DL Lincs 1970, Humberside 1975. Kt of SMO Malta, 1959. *Recreations:* the arts, countryside. *Address:* Elsham Hall, near Brigg DN20 0QZ. *T:* (01652) 688738.
Died 22 Feb. 1999.

ELYTIS, Odysseus; Order of the Phoenix, 1965; Grand Commander, Order of Honour, 1979; poet; *b* Crete, 2 Nov. 1911; *y c* of Panayiotis and Maria Alepoudelis. *Educ:* Athens Univ. (Law); Sorbonne (Lettres). First publication, 1940; Broadcasting and Programme Director, National Broadcasting Inst., 1945–47 and 1953–54; Mem. Administrative Board, Greek National Theatre, 1974–76. President, Admin. Board, Greek Broadcasting and Television, 1974. Hon. DLitt: Salonica, 1976; Sorbonne, 1980; Hon. DLit London, 1981. First National Prize in Poetry, 1960; Nobel Prize for Literature, 1979; Benson Silver Medal, RSL, 1981. Commander de la Légion

d'Honneur (France), 1989. *Publications:* Orientations, 1940; Sun the First, 1943; The Axion Esti, 1959; Six, but one remorses for the Sky, 1960; The Light Tree, 1971; The Monogram, 1972; Villa Natacha, 1973; The Painter Theophilos, 1973; The Open Book, 1974; The Second Writing, 1976; Maria Nefeli, 1978; Selected Poems, 1981; Three Poems, 1982; Journal of an Unseen April, 1984; Saphfo, 1984; The Little Mariner, 1985; Private Way, 1991. *Address:* Skoufa Street 23, Athens, Greece. *T:* (1) 3626458.
Died 18 March 1996.

EMMET, Dorothy Mary; Professor of Philosophy, University of Manchester, 1946–66, then Professor Emeritus; *b* 29 Sept. 1904; *d* of late Rev. C. W. Emmet, Fellow of University Coll., Oxford, and Gertrude Julia Emmet (*née* Weir). *Educ:* St Mary's Hall, Brighton; Lady Margaret Hall, Oxford. Classical Exhibitioner, 1923; Hon. Mods Class I, 1925; Lit. Hum. Class I, 1927; MA; Hon. Fellow; MA Cantab and Manchester. Tutor, Maesyrhaf Settlement, Rhondda Valley, 1927–28 and 1931–32; Commonwealth Fellow, Radcliffe Coll., Cambridge, Mass, USA, 1928–30; Research Fellow, Somerville Coll., Oxford, 1930–31; Lecturer in Philosophy, Armstrong Coll., Newcastle upon Tyne, 1932–38 (latterly Newcastle Univ.); Lecturer in Philosophy of Religion, University of Manchester, 1938–45, Reader in Philosophy, 1945–46. Dean of the Faculty of Arts, University of Manchester, 1962–64. Stanton Lecturer in Philosophy of Religion, University of Cambridge, 1950–53. Vis. Prof., Barnard Coll., Columbia Univ., New York, 1960–61. President Aristotelian Society, 1953–54. Fellow, Lucy Cavendish Coll., Cambridge, 1967, Emeritus Fellow, 1981. Hon. DLitt: Glasgow, 1974; Leicester, 1976; DUniv Open, 1997. *Publications:* Whitehead's Philosophy of Organism, 1932, 2nd edn 1982; Philosophy and Faith, 1936; The Nature of Metaphysical Thinking, 1945; Function, Purpose and Powers, 1958, 2nd edn 1972; Rules, Roles and Relations, 1966; (ed with Alasdair MacIntyre) Sociological Theory and Philosophical Analysis, 1970; The Moral Prism, 1979; The Effectiveness of Causes, 1984; The Passage of Nature, 1992; The Role of the Unrealisable, 1994; Philosophers and Friends, 1996; Outward Forms, Inner Springs, 1998; contributions to philosophical journals. *Recreation:* listening to music and talking books. *Address:* Hope Residential Home, Brooklands Avenue, Cambridge CB2 2BQ.
Died 20 Sept. 2000.

EMPSON, Adm. Sir (Leslie) Derek, GBE 1975; KCB 1973 (CB 1969); Commander-in-Chief Naval Home Command and Flag Officer Portsmouth Area, 1974–75; *b* 29 Oct. 1918; *s* of Frank Harold Empson and Madeleine Norah Empson (*née* Burge); *m* 1958, Diana Elizabeth Kelly; one *s* one *d. Educ:* Eastbourne Coll.; Clare Coll., Cambridge (Class. Exhibn). Athletics Blue, 1939; BA 1940. Joined Royal Navy for pilot duties, 1940; commd as Sub-Lieut (A) RNVR, 1940; flew as Fleet Air Arm pilot, 1940–45; perm. commn in RN, 1944; Naval Asst to First Sea Lord, 1957–59; Comd HMS Eagle, 1963–65; Imp. Def. Coll., 1966; Flag Officer, Aircraft Carriers, 1967–68; Asst Chief of Naval Staff (Operations and Air), 1968–69; Comdr, Far East Fleet, 1969–71; Second Sea Lord and Chief of Naval Personnel, 1971–74; Flag ADC to the Queen, 1974–75. Rear-Adm. of the UK, 1984–86; Vice-Adm. of the UK, 1986–88. Comdr 1952; Captain 1957; Rear-Adm. 1967; Vice-Adm. 1970; Adm. 1972. Chm., Roymark, 1985–92; Consultant: Thorn EMI, 1976–86; Warner Communications, 1987–88; Astra Hldgs, 1987–90. Chm. of Governors, Eastbourne Coll., 1972–88.
Died 20 Sept. 1997.

ENDERBY, Kenneth Albert; General Manager, Runcorn Development Corporation, 1978–81; *b* 7 Aug. 1920; *s* of Albert William Enderby and Frances Enderby; *m* 1946, Mary Florence; one *s* two *d. Educ:* Nottingham High Sch.;

London Univ. (BSc Econs). IPFA. Served War, Royal Corps of Signals (TA), 1939–46: BEF, MEF, CMF (mentioned in despatches, 1944); Captain. Local Government Finance: Nottingham, 1936–51; Buckingham, 1951–53; Chief Auditor, City of Sheffield, 1953–56; Dep. City Treasurer, Coventry, 1956–64; Chief Finance Officer, Runcorn Develt Corp., 1964–78. *Recreations:* gardening, camping, fresh air, zymology. *Address:* Four Winds, 2 Helmeth Road, Church Stretton, Salop SY6 7AS. *T:* (01694) 722328.

Died 17 Sept. 2000.

ENDERBY, Col Samuel, CVO 1977; DSO 1943; MC 1939; JP; *b* 15 Sept. 1907; *s* of Col Samuel Enderby and Mary Cuninghame; *m* 1936, Pamela, *e d* of Major Charles Beck Hornby, DSO; two *s* one *d. Educ:* Uppingham Sch.; RMC Sandhurst. Regular soldier, commissioned 5th Fusiliers, 1928; served War, 1939–46: MEF, CMF, comd 2/4th KOYLI and 2/5 Leicester Regt; Commandant, Sch. of Infantry: ACRE, 1945–46; Netheravon, 1947–48; comd, 7th Bn Royal Northumberland Fusiliers, 1949; retd 1949. JP 1956; High Sheriff of Northumberland, 1968. Mem., Hon. Corps of Gentlemen at Arms, 1954–77, Standard Bearer, 1976–77. *Address:* The Riding, Hexham, Northumberland NE46 4PF.   *Died 20 Dec. 1996.*

ENGLISH, Sir Cyril (Rupert), Kt 1972; retired; Director-General, City and Guilds of London Institute, 1968–76; *b* 19 April 1913; *s* of William James and Edith English; *m* 1936, Eva Moore; two *s. Educ:* Northgate Sch., Ipswich. BScEng Ext. London, 1934. Technical teacher, 1935–39. Served Royal Navy, 1939–46, Lieut-Commander (E). HM Inspector of Schools, 1946–55; Staff Inspector (Engineering), 1955–58; Chief Inspector of Further Education, in connection with Industry and Commerce, 1958–65; Senior Chief Inspector, Dept of Education and Science, 1965–67, Member, Anglo-American Productivity Team, 1951; attended Commonwealth Education Conferences, Delhi, 1962, Ottawa, 1964. Chairman: British Assoc. for Commercial and Industrial Educn, 1970–71, 1971–72; RAF Educn Adv. Cttee; Member: Services Colleges Cttee, 1965–66; Adv. Bd, RAF Coll., Cranwell; Academic Adv. Council, Royal Defence Acad.; Bd of Dirs, Industrial Training Service; Central Training Council; CTC Gen. Policy Cttee; Nat. Adv. Council for Educn in Industry and Commerce; Council for Tech. Educn and Training for Overseas Countries (Bd Mem., Chm. Educn Cttee); Reg. Adv. Council for Technol. Educn (London and Home Counties); Schools Science and Technology Cttee; Educn Cttee, IMechE; Associated Examining Bd; Cttee of Inquiry into Training of Teachers (James Cttee); Standing Conf. on Schs' Science and Technology; Cttee on Regular Officer Training (Army). Vice-Pres., Soc. Electronic and Radio Technicians, 1972–74, Pres., 1975. Governor, Imperial Coll. FIMechE; FIProdE; FIMarE. Hon. Fellow, Inst. of Road Transport Engrs, 1971. Hon. Fellow, Manchester Polytechnic, 1976. Hon. DTech Brunel, 1970; Hon. DSc Loughborough, 1973; DUniv Open, 1974. *Address:* 12 Pineheath Road, High Kelling, Holt, Norfolk NR25 6QF.

Died 11 May 1997.

ENGLISH, Sir David, Kt 1982; Editor in Chief, since 1989, and Chairman, since 1992, Associated Newspapers (Joint Deputy Chairman, 1989–92; Vice-Chairman, Associated Newspapers Group, 1986–88); Chairman, ITN, since 1997; *b* 26 May 1931; *m* 1954, Irene Mainwood; one *s* two *d. Educ:* Bournemouth Sch. Daily Mirror, 1951–53; Feature Editor, Daily Sketch, 1956; Foreign Correspondent: Sunday Dispatch, 1959; Daily Express, 1960; Washington Correspondent, Express, 1961–63; Chief American Correspondent, Express, 1963–65; Foreign Editor, Express, 1965–67; Associate Editor, Express, 1967–69; Editor: Daily Sketch, 1969–71; Daily

Mail, 1971–92; Mail on Sunday, 1982. Chairman: Teletext UK, 1993–; Channel One TV, 1993–. Member: Bd, Assoc. of British Editors, 1985–; Press Complaints Commn, 1993– (Chm., Editors' Code Cttee, 1993–). Pres., CPU, 1994–. *Publication:* Divided They Stand (a British view of the 1968 American Presidential Election), 1969. *Recreations:* reading, ski-ing, boating. *Address:* Northcliffe House, 2 Derry Street, W8 5TT. *T:* (0171) 938 6000. *Clubs:* Reform, London Press; Ski of Great Britain.
  Created a Baron (Life Peer), Queen's Birthday Honours List, 13 June 1998.   *Died 10 June 1998.*

ENGLISH, Rev. Donald, CBE 1996; Methodist Minister; Moderator, Free Church Federal Council, 1986–87; President of the Methodist Conference, 1978–79 and 1990–91; *b* 20 July 1930; *s* of Robert and Ena Forster English; *m* 1962, Bertha Forster Ludlow (*d* 1997); two *s. Educ:* Consett Grammar Sch.; University Coll., Leicester; Wesley House, Cambridge. BA London; DipEd Leicester; MA Cantab. Education Officer, RAF, 1953–55; Travelling Sec., Inter-Varsity Fellowship, 1955–58; Asst Tutor, Wesley Coll., Headingley, 1960–62; ordained into Methodist Ministry, 1962; New Testament Tutor, Trinity Coll., Umuahia, E Nigeria, 1962–66; Circuit Minister, Cullercoats, Northumberland, 1966–72; Tutor in Historical Theology, Hartley Victoria Coll., Manchester (Lord Rank Chair), 1972–73; Tutor in Practical Theol. and Methodism, Wesley Coll., Bristol (Lord Rank Chair), 1973–82; Gen. Sec., Div. of Home Mission, Methodist Ch., 1982–95. Chm., World Methodist Council Exec. Cttee, 1991–96; Hon. Pres., World Methodist Council. Hon. DD: Asbury, USA, 1979; Newcastle; DUniv Surrey, 1990; Hon. DLitt Leicester, 1994. *Publications:* Evangelism and Worship, 1971; God in the Gallery, 1975; Christian Discipleship, 1977; Windows on the Passion, 1978; From Wesley's Chair. Presidential Addresses, 1979; Why Believe in Jesus?: evangelistic reflections for Lent, 1986; Evangelistic Counselling, 1987; Evangelism Now, 1987; The Meaning of the Warmed Heart, 1988; Everything in Christ, 1988; The Message of Mark, 1992; (ed) Windows on Salvation, 1994; Into the 21st Century, 1995; An Evangelical Theology of Preaching, 1996. *Recreations:* gardening, reading. *Address:* 6 Tothill, Shipton-under-Wychwood, Oxon OX7 6BX. *T:* (01993) 830877.

Died 28 Aug. 1998.

ENRICI, Most Rev. Domenico, JCD; former Apostolic Nuncio; *b* 9 April 1909; *s* of late Domenico Enrici and Maria Dalmasso Enrici. *Educ:* Diocesan Seminary, Cuneo; Pontifical Gregorian Univ. and Pontifical Ecclesiastical Academy, Rome. Ordained, 1933; parochial work in Dio. Cuneo, 1933–35; served at various Apostolic Nunciatures and Delegations: Ireland, 1938–45; Egypt, 1946–48; Palestine and Jordan, 1948–53; Formosa, Free China, 1953–55; apptd Titular Archbp of Ancusa, 1955; Apostolic Internuncio to Indonesia, 1955–58; Apostolic Nuncio to Haiti and Apostolic Delegate to West Indies, 1958–60; Apostolic Internuncio to Japan, 1960–62; Apostolic Delegate to Australia, New Zealand and Oceania, 1962–69; Apostolic Delegate to GB and Gibraltar, 1969–73; Pro-Pres., Pontifical Ecclesiastical Acad., 1974–75; Delegate for Pontifical Representations, 1973–79; retired, 1979. Commander, Order of the Nile (Egypt), 1948; Order of the Sacred Treasure, 1st class (Japan), 1962; Assistant to the Pontifical Throne, Vatican City, 1979. *Publication:* Mistero e Luce (Mystery and Light), 1984. *Address:* Via Senatore Toselli 8, 12100 Cuneo, Italy.

Died 3 Dec. 1997.

EREAUT, Sir (Herbert) Frank (Cobbold), Kt 1976; Bailiff of Jersey, 1975–85; Judge of the Court of Appeal of Guernsey, 1976–89; *b* 6 May 1919; *s* of Herbert Parker Ereaut and May Julia Cobbold; *m* 1942, Kathleen FitzGibbon; one *d. Educ:* Tormore Sch., Upper Deal,

Kent; Cranleigh Sch., Surrey; Exeter Coll., Oxford. BA 1946, MA 1966. RASC, 1940–46: N Africa, Italy and NW Europe; Captain. Called to Bar, Inner Temple, 1947; Solicitor-General, Jersey, 1958–62, Attorney-General, 1962–69; Dep. Bailiff of Jersey, 1969–74. Chm., TSB Foundn for CI, 1986–90; Director: Standard Chartered Bank (CI), 1986–90; Standard Chartered Offshore, 1990–93. KStJ 1983 (CStJ 1978). *Recreations:* music, gardening, travel. *Address:* Les Cypres, St John, Jersey, Channel Islands JE3 4DQ. *T:* (01534) 22317.

Died 12 Sept. 1998.

ERROLL OF HALE, 1st Baron *cr* 1964, of Kilmun, co. Argyll; **Frederick James Erroll;** PC 1960; FIEE, FIMechE; Baron Erroll of Kilmun (Life Peer), 1999; Chairman, Bowater Corporation, 1973–84; *b* 27 May 1914; *s* of George Murison Erroll, engineer, and Kathleen Donovan Edington, both of Glasgow and London; *m* 1950, Elizabeth, *o d* of R. Sowton Barrow, Exmouth, Devon. *Educ:* Oundle Sch.; Trinity Coll., Cambridge (MA). Engineering apprenticeship, 1931–32; Cambridge Univ., 1932–35; Engineer at Metropolitan-Vickers Electrical Co. Ltd, Manchester, 1936–38; commissioned into 4th County of London Yeomanry (Sharpshooters), TA, 1939; technical appointments in connection with Tank Construction and Testing, 1940–43; service in India and Burma, 1944–45; Col 1945. MP (C) Altrincham and Sale, 1945–64. A Dir of Engineering and Mining Companies until 1955; Parly Sec., Min. of Supply, 1955–56; Parly Sec., BoT, 1956–58; Economic Sec. to the Treasury, 1958–59; Minister of State, BoT, 1959–61; Pres., BoT, 1961–63; Minister of Power, 1963–64. Mem., H of L Select Cttee on Science and Technology, 1985–91. Pres., Consolidated Gold Fields, 1982–89 (Chm., 1976–82); Chairman: Whessoe plc, 1970–87 (Consultant, 1987–90); ASEA Ltd, 1965–84; Fläkt Ltd, 1971–85; Gen. Advr, ASEA, Sweden, 1965–86. Member: Council, Inst. of Directors, 1949–55 and 1965–87 (Chm. Council, 1973–76, Pres., 1976–84, Chancellor, 1984–87); NEDC, 1962–63. President: Hispanic and Luso-Brazilian Councils, 1969–73; British Export Houses Assoc., 1969–72; British Exec. Service Overseas, 1972–85; UK South Africa Trade Assoc., 1979–84; World Travel Market, 1986–96; Vice-President: London Chamber of Commerce, 1969– (Pres., 1966–69); Inst. of Marketing, 1983–92; Automobile Assoc., 1986– (Chm., 1974–86). Dep. Chm., Decimal Currency Board, 1966–71; Chm., Cttee on Liquor Licensing, 1971–72; Pres., Electrical Research Assoc., 1971–74. Trustee, Westminster Abbey Trust, 1978–86. FRSA 1971. *Heir:* none. *Address:* House of Lords, SW1A 0PW. *Club:* Carlton. *Died 14 Sept. 2000 (ext).*

ESSAME, Enid Mary, MA; Headmistress of Queenswood School, 1943–71; *b* Sheffield, 5 Dec. 1906; 2nd *d* of Oliver Essame. *Educ:* Wyggeston Grammar Sch., Leicester; Girls' High Sch., Newark; Newnham Coll., Cambridge (Hist. Tripos, 1928; MA); King's Coll., University of London (Cert Ed 1929); AM in Education, American Univ., Washington, DC, USA, 1935. Mary Ewart Travelling Scholar, Newnham Coll., 1934–35; Asst Headmistress, Queenswood Sch., 1935–43. British Council lecturer, India and Pakistan, 1953, Nigeria, 1961. Hon. Sec., Assoc. of Headmistresses of Boarding Schools (Pres. 1962–64); Chm., Assoc. of Ind. and Direct Grant Schools. Bd Mem., Schoolmistresses and Governesses Benevolent Instn, 1974; Hon. Adviser, Nat. Assoc. for Gifted Children, 1974. Governor: Chorleywood Coll. for Girls with Little or No Sight, 1962; St Helen's Sch., Northwood; Channing Sch., Highgate; Trustee, Stormont Sch., Potters Bar. Mem., Overseas Grants Cttee, Help the Aged, 1981. JP Herts, 1952–76. *Address:* 4 Elmroyd Avenue, Potters Bar, Herts EN6 2ED. *T:* (01707) 653255. *Clubs:* Royal Over-Seas League, Arts Theatre.

Died 19 Dec. 1999.

ESSEN, Louis, OBE 1959; DSc, PhD; FRS 1960; retired; *b* 6 Sept. 1908; *s* of Fred Essen and Ada (*née* Edson); *m* 1937, Joan Margery Greenhalgh; four *d. Educ:* High Pavement Sch., Nottingham; London Univ. (Ext.). BSc 1928, PhD 1941, DSc 1948, London. Joined the National Physical Laboratory, 1929; Senior Principal Scientific Officer, 1956–60; Deputy Chief Scientific Officer, 1960–72. Charles Vernon Boys Prize, Phys. Soc. 1957; Tompion Gold Medal, Clockmakers' Company, 1957; Wolfe Award, 1959; A. S. Popov Gold Medal, USSR Acad. of Sciences, 1959. Hon. FUMIST, 1971. *Publications:* Velocity of Light and Radio Waves, 1969; The Special Theory of Relativity, 1971; scientific papers. *Recreations:* walking, gardening, music. *Address:* High Hallgarth, 41 Durleston Park Drive, Great Bookham, Surrey KT23 4AJ. *T:* (01372) 454103.

Died 24 Aug. 1997.

EUSTACE, Sir (Joseph) Lambert, GCMG 1985; GCVO 1985; Governor-General, St Vincent and the Grenadines, 1985–89; *b* 28 Feb. 1908; *s* of Reynold Lambert Eustace and Beatrice Alexandrine Eustace (*née* St Hilaire); *m* 1945, Faustina Eileen Gatherer; one *s* one *d* (and one *d* decd). *Educ:* St Vincent Grammar School. Founded Intermediate High Sch., 1926; teacher of English, Maths and French, latterly at St Vincent Grammar Sch., 1926–52; Manager, St Vincent Cotton Ginnery, 1952–59; Manager of own factory (oil, soap and feeds), 1959–66; MP South Leeward, 1966–71; Speaker, House of Assembly, 1972–74. Deleg. to overseas confs, 1957–74. *Recreations:* reading, gardening, woodwork. *Address:* c/o Government House, Montrose, St Vincent and the Grenadines, West Indies. *Died 2 Nov. 1996.*

EVANS, Ven. (David) Eifion; Archdeacon of Cardigan, 1967–79; *b* 22 Jan, 1911; *e s* of John Morris and Sarah Pryse Evans, Borth, Cards; *m* 1st, 1941, Iris Elizabeth Gravelle (*d* 1973); one *s*; 2nd, 1979, Madeleine Kirby. *Educ:* Ardwyn, Aberystwyth; UCW, Aberystwyth (BA 1932; MA 1951); St Michael's Coll., Llandaff. Deacon, 1934; priest, 1935; Curate: Llanfihangel-ar-Arth, 1934–36; Llanbadarn Fawr, 1936–40; Chaplain to the Forces, 1940–45; Vicar, Llandeloy with Llanrheithan, 1945–48; Penrhyncoch, 1948, with Elerch, 1952–57; St Michael, Aberystwyth, 1957–67; Rural Dean, Llanbadarn Fawr, 1957–67; Chaplain, Anglican Students, 1966–67; Canon of St David's Cathedral (Caerfai), 1963–67; Chaplain, Earl of Lisburne, 1967–69; Vicar: Llanafan with Llanwnnws, 1967–69; Newcastle Emlyn, 1969–79. Member: Governing Body of Church in Wales, 1956–79; Representative Body of Church in Wales, 1967–79; Court of Governors, and Council, UCW, Aberystwyth, 1958–69; Sub-Visitor, St David's University Coll., Lampeter, 1972–79. *Publications:* Influence of Tractarianism in Wales, 1952 (Welsh Nat. Eisteddfod, Aberystwyth, Special Prize); contributions to: Llên Cymru Yn Y Bedwaredd Ganrif Ar Bymtheg, 1968; Jl of Hist. Soc. of Church in Wales and other Welsh Church periodicals. *Recreations:* soccer, athletics, reading. *Address:* 31 Bryncastell, Bow Street, Ceredigion SY24 5DE. *T:* (01970) 828747. *Died 23 May 1997.*

EVANS, Rt Rev. Edward Lewis, BD, MTh; *b* 11 Dec. 1904; *s* of Edward Foley Evans and Mary (*née* Walker). *Educ:* St Anselm's, Croydon; Tonbridge Sch.; Bishops' Coll., Cheshunt. BD London 1935, MTh 1938. Deacon, 1937; priest 1938; Curate of St Mary's, Prittlewell, Essex, 1937–39; Warden of St Peter's Theological Coll., Jamaica, 1940–49; Rector, Kingston Parish Church, Jamaica, 1949–52; Rector of Woodford and Craigton, 1952–57; Archdeacon of Surrey, Jamaica, 1950–57; Bishop Suffragan of Kingston, 1957–60; Bishop of Barbados, 1960–71. *Publications:* A History of the Diocese of Jamaica, 1977; Legends of West Indian Saints, 1984.

Address: Terry's Cross, Woodmancote, Henfield, Sussex BN5 9SX. *Died 30 Dec. 1996.*

EVANS, Ven. Eifion; *see* Evans, Ven. D. E.

EVANS, Very Rev. Eric; *see* Evans, Very Rev. T. E.

EVANS, Frederick Anthony, CVO 1973; General Secretary, The Duke of Edinburgh's Award Scheme, 1959–72, Adviser for the Handicapped, 1972–84; *b* 17 Nov. 1907; *s* of Herbert Anthony Evans, mining engineer, and Pauline (*née* Allen); *m* 1934, Nancy (*née* Meakin); two *s* one *d. Educ:* Charterhouse; Corpus Christi Coll., Cambridge. Manager, Doondu Coffee Plantation, Kenya, 1927–31; Colonial Service, 1934; Asst District Officer, Nigeria, 1935–39; Provincial Commissioner and Asst Colonial Sec., Gambia, 1940–47; Colonial Sec., Nassau, Bahamas, 1947–51, Acting Governor, 1950; Permanent Sec., Gold Coast (later Ghana), 1951–57. Dir, Anglo-Gambian Archæological Expedition, 1965–66. *Publications:* The State Apartments at Buckingham Palace, 1985; St James's Palace, 1991. *Recreation:* gardening. *Address:* Bellsfield, South Ridge, Odiham, Hants RG25 1NG. *Club:* Royal Commonwealth Society. *Died 11 May 1999.*

EVANS, Godfrey; *see* Evans, T. G.

EVANS, Hywel Eifion, CB 1974; Welsh Secretary, Ministry of Agriculture, Fisheries and Food, 1968–75; *b* 24 Jan. 1910; *s* of late Gruffydd Thomas and Winnifred Evans, Felin Rhydhir, Pwllheli, Caernarvonshire; *m* 1st, 1939, Mary Elizabeth (*d* 1977), *d* of late Richard and Hannah Jones, Gilfach, Glanywydden, Llandudno; one *s* one *d*, 2nd, 1978, Mrs Mair Lloyd Jones (*d* 1991), *d* of late David Lloyd and Amelia Davies, Ceinfan, Narbeth, Dyfed. *Educ:* Pwllheli Grammar Sch., University Coll. of North Wales, Bangor. BSc (Hons) (Agric.). Research Asst, Dept of Agricultural Economics, UCW, Aberystwyth, 1934–40; Dist and Dep. Exec. Officer, Leicester War Agricl Exec Cttee, 1940–46; County Advisory Officer: Radnor AEC, 1946–47; Carmarthen AEC, 1947–57; Dep. Regional Dir, Nat. Agric Advisory Service for Wales, 1957–59, Regional Dir, 1959–66; Dep. Dir, Nat. Agricl Adv. Service (London), 1967–68. FRAgS 1972. *Publications:* articles on agricultural, economic and sociological topics in Welsh Jl of Agriculture, Agriculture, and other jls. *Recreations:* idling, fishing, shooting. *Address:* No 2 Edge Hill, Lleyn Street, Pwllheli, Gwynedd LL53 5SN. *Club:* Farmers'. *Died 6 Sept. 1997.*

EVANS, James Donald; Special Correspondent, Westminster Press Ltd, 1983–86; Acting Editor, UK Press Gazette, 1986; freelance columnist, The Citizen, Gloucester, since 1987; *b* 12 Nov. 1926; *yr s* of Arthur Evans and Isabella McKinnon Evans; *m* 1946, Freda Bristow; two *s* three *d. Educ:* Royal Grammar Sch., High Wycombe. Jun. Reporter, Bucks Free Press, 1943–45; Army, 1945–48; Chief Reporter, Maidenhead Advertiser, 1948–50; Northern Echo: District Chief Reporter, 1950–60; Industrial Corresp., 1961–65; Industrial Editor, 1965–66; Editor and Editor-in-Chief, 1966–82; Dir, North of England Newspapers, 1971–82. *Recreations:* driving, reading. *Address:* 11 Onslow Road, Newent, Glos GL18 1TL. *T:* (01531) 822001. *Club:* Presscala. *Died 25 July 1997.*

EVANS, Col J(ames) Ellis, CBE 1973 (OBE 1952); TD 1947; JP; Lord-Lieutenant of Clwyd, 1979–85; *b* 6 Aug. 1910; *s* of James William Evans and Eleanor Evans, MBE, JP; unmarried. *Educ:* Epworth Coll., Rhyl. Chartered Accountant (FCA). Joined TA, 1937; served War of 1939–45, RA: France, 1940; N Africa, 1941–44; Italy, 1944–45; comd 384 Light Regt RA (RWF), TA, 1947–52; Dep. CRA, 53 (Welsh) Div., 1953–57; Chm. Denbigh and Flint TA Assoc., 1961–68; Chm., Wales and Mon TA&VRA, 1971–74 (Vice-Chm., 1968–71); Pres., Wales TA&VRA, 1981–85. Mem., Prestatyn UDC, 1939–74 (Chm. 1947); Mayor, Prestatyn Town Council, 1974–75. Clwyd, formerly Flintshire: JP 1951; DL 1953; High Sheriff, 1970–71; Vice-Lieut, 1970–74, Vice Lord-Lieut, 1977–79. Chm., North Wales Police Authority, 1976–78. *Recreations:* lawn tennis (played for Wales and Lancashire, 1936–48), gardening. *Address:* Trafford Mount, 3 Cambrian Drive, Prestatyn, Clwyd LL19 9RL. *T:* (01745) 854119. *Club:* City (Chester). *Died 19 Feb. 1998.*

EVANS, Ven. John Mascal; Archdeacon of Surrey, 1968–80; *b* 17 May 1915; *s* of Rev. Edward Foley Evans and Mary Evans; *m* 1941, Mary Elizabeth (*née* Rathbone); three *s* two *d. Educ:* St John's Sch., Leatherhead; Brasenose Coll., Oxford; Wells Theological Coll. Asst Curate, St Martin's, Epsom, 1938; Perpetual Curate, Stoneleigh, Epsom, 1942, All Saints, Fleet, 1952; Vicar, St Mary, Walton-on-Thames, 1960–68; Hon. Canon of Guildford, 1963–80, Canon Emeritus, 1980–; Mem. of Ridgeway Team Ministry, Dio. Salisbury, 1980–84. Member: General Synod of C of E, 1977–80; C of E Pensions Bd, 1977–85; Council of Cremation Soc., 1969–80. *Address:* 6 Gracey Court, Woodland Road, Broadclyst, Exeter EX5 3LP. *Died 29 Feb. 1996.*

EVANS, Simon John; His Honour Judge Simon Evans; a Circuit Judge, since 1991; *b* 18 Jan. 1937; *s* of late Drs Thomas and Enid Evans; *m* 1968, Heather Wendy Champion; one *s* one *d. Educ:* Diocesan Coll., Cape Town. Apprentice motor mechanic, Lusaka, Northern Rhodesia, 1954; GCE student, Guildford, 1955–56; Bar student, London, 1956–59; called to the Bar, Middle Temple, 1959; barrister, Temple, 1959–91; a Recorder, South Eastern Circuit, 1989–91; Resident Judge, Isleworth Crown Court, 1997. *Recreations:* Balinese cats, French studies, English footpaths. *Address:* c/o Isleworth Crown Court, 36 Ridgeway Road, Isleworth, Middx TW7 5LP. *T:* (020) 8568 8811. *Died 13 May 1999.*

EVANS, Very Rev. (Thomas) Eric, KCVO 1996; Dean of St Paul's, since 1988; *b* 1 Feb. 1928; *s* of late Eric John Rhys Evans and Florence May Rogers; *m* 1957, Linda Kathleen Budge; two *d. Educ:* St David's Coll., Lampeter (BA); St Cathcrine's Coll., Oxford (MA); St Stephen's House, Oxford. Ordained, 1954; Curate, Margate Parish Church, 1954–58; Sen. Curate, St Peter's, Bournemouth, 1958–62; first Dir, Bournemouth Samaritans; Diocesan Youth Chaplain, dio. Gloucester, 1962–69; Residentiary Canon of Gloucester Cathedral, 1969–88; Archdeacon of Cheltenham, 1975–88. Wing Chaplain, ATC, 1963–69; Hon. Chaplain: Gloucester Coll. of Educn, 1968–75; Gloucestershire Constabulary, 1977–88. Chm., Glos Trng Cttee, 1967–69; Proctor in Convocation and Mem. Gen. Synod of C of E, 1970–95; a Church Comr, 1978–95 (Mem., Bd of Governors, 1978–95, Assets Cttee, 1985–88). Canon Missioner, dio. Gloucester, 1969–75; Chairman: House of Clergy, dio. Gloucester, 1979–82; Bd of Social Responsibility, dio. Gloucester, 1982–83; Glos Assoc. for Mental Health, 1983–85; Glos Diocesan Adv. Cttee, 1984–88. Mem. Exec. Cttee, 1975–88, Chm., 1981–88, Council for Places of Worship, subseq. Council for the Care of Churches. Dean, Order of St Michael and St George, 1988–; Dean, Order of the British Empire, 1988–; Chaplain to Guild of Freemen of City of London, 1988–; ChStJ 1988, Sub-Prelate, 1991. Dir, Ecclesiastical Insurance Office Ltd, 1979–. Mem. Council, Cheltenham Ladies' College, 1982–93. Freeman, City of London, 1988; Liveryman: Gardeners' Co., 1993–; Merchant Taylors' Co., 1996–. Hon. DD City, 1993. *Recreation:* travel, esp. Middle East. *Address:* The Deanery, 9 Amen Court, EC4M 7BU. *Clubs:* Carlton; Downhill Only (Wengen). *Died 17 Aug. 1996.*

EVANS, (Thomas) Godfrey, CBE 1960; public relations officer; *b* Finchley, 18 Aug. 1920; *s* of A. G. L. Evans; *m*; one *s*; *m* Jean Tritton; *m* 1973, Angela Peart; one *d*. *Educ:* Kent Coll., Canterbury. Joined Kent County Staff at age of 16; first kept wicket for England in Test *v* India, 1946; first overseas Test tour, Australia and New Zealand, 1946–47; also played in Test matches in W Indies and S Africa; played in 91 Test matches (world record 1959); dismissed 218 batsmen in Test cricket from behind the stumps, 88 more than Oldfield, the previous record-holder, and retained the record until 1976; the first wicket-keeper to have dismissed more than 200 victims and scored over 2000 runs in Test cricket; held world record for not conceding a bye while 1,054 runs were scored in a Test series (Australia, 1946); holder of: record for longest Test innings without scoring (95 minutes *v* Australia, Adelaide, 1947); (with Charles Barnett) record for fastest score before lunch in a Test match (98 *v* India, Lord's, 1952); in making 47 in 29 minutes was three runs off the fastest 50 in Test cricket (*v* Australia, Old Trafford, 1956); first Englishman to tour Australia with MCC four times after War of 1939–45. *Publications:* Behind the Stumps, 1951; Action in Cricket, 1956; The Gloves Are Off, 1960; Wicket Keepers of the World, 1984. *Recreations:* real tennis, golf, squash. *Address:* Commerce House, 57b High Street South, Rushden, Northants NN10 0RA. *Club:* MCC (Hon. Life Mem.). *Died 3 May 1999.*

EVERARD, Maj.-Gen. Sir Christopher Earle W.; *see* Welby-Everard.

EVEREST, David Anthony, PhD; FRSC; Research Associate, UK Centre for Economic and Environmental Development, since 1987; Editor, Energy and Environment, since 1989; *b* 18 Sept. 1926; *s* of George Charles and Ada Bertha Everest; *m* 1956, Audrey Pauline (*née* Sheldrick); three *s*. *Educ:* John Lyon Sch., Harrow; University Coll. London (Bsc, PhD). Lecturer in Chemistry, Battersea Polytechnic, 1949–56; Sen. Scientific Officer, 1956–58, PSO, 1958–64, Nat. Chemical Lab.; SPSO, 1964–70, DCSO, 1970–77, NPL; DCSO, RTP Div., Dept of Industry, 1977–79; Chief Scientist, Environmental Protection Gp, 1979–86, and Dir of Sci. Res. Policy, 1983–86, DoE. Vis. Res. Fellow, UEA, 1986–92. *Publications:* Chemistry of Beryllium, 1962; section on Beryllium in Comprehensive Inorganic Chemistry, 1972; The Greenhouse Effect: issues for policy makers, 1988; The Provision of Expert Advice to Government on Environmental Matters: the role of advisory committees, 1990; (contrib.) Science and Technology in the UK, 1991; (contrib.) Environmental Dilemmas: ethics and decisions, 1993; (contrib.) What Risk?: science, politics and public health, 1997; papers in Inorganic Chemistry, Extractive Metallurgy and Material Science. *Recreations:* astronomy, reading. *Address:* Beech Boles, Quarry Wood Road, Cookham Dean, Berks SL6 9UA. *T:* (01628) 487390. *Died 26 July 1998.*

EWER, Prof. Tom Keightley, OBE 1978; PhD; MRCVS; Professor of Animal Husbandry, Bristol University, 1961–77, then Emeritus; retired; *b* 21 Sept. 1911; *s* of William Edward Frederick Ewer and Maria Louisa Keightley; *m* 1st, 1937, Iva Rosalind Biddle; three *s*; 2nd, 1959, Margaret June Fischer; three *d*, and one step *s* two step *d*. *Educ:* Fowey Grammar Sch.; Sydney Univ. (BVSc); Cambridge Univ. (PhD); HDA. Veterinary research with NZ Govt, 1938–45; Senior Lecturer, Univ. of NZ, 1945–47; Wellcome Research Fellow, University of Cambridge, 1947–50; Prof. of Animal Husbandry, University of Queensland, 1950–61; Prof. of Animal Resources, King Faisal Univ., Saudi Arabia, 1978–80. *Publications:* Practical Animal Husbandry, 1982; contrib. to scientific publications, on animal nutrition and veterinary education. *Recreation:* music. *Address:* Oakridge, Winscombe, Avon BS25 1LZ. *T:* (01934) 843279. *Died 3 Oct. 1997.*

EWING; *see* Orr-Ewing.

EWING, Vice-Adm. Sir (Robert) Alastair, KBE 1962; CB 1959; DSC 1942; *b* 10 April 1909; *s* of Major Ian Ewing and Muriel Adèle Child; *m* 1st, 1940, Diana Smeed (*d* 1980), *d* of Major Harry Archer, DSO; one *s*; 2nd, 1984, Anne, *d* of Captain C. G. Chichester, DSO, RN and *widow* of Comdr Henry Wilkin. *Educ:* Royal Naval Coll., Dartmouth. In command of Destroyers during War of 1939–45; NATO Standing Group Staff, 1950–51; Imperial Defence Coll., 1952; in command of HMS Vanguard, 1953–54; Dir of Naval Staff Coll., Greenwich, 1954–56; Naval Sec. to First Lord of the Admiralty, 1956–58; Flag Officer Flotillas (Mediterranean), 1958–60; Adm. Commanding Reserves and Inspector of Recruiting, 1960–62; retd list, 1962. *Address:* 1 Garden Court, Sutton Manor, Sutton Scotney, Winchester, Hants SO21 3JX. *T:* (01962) 761351. *Clubs:* Army and Navy; Royal Yacht Squadron (Naval Mem.). *Died 19 May 1997.*

EXTON, Rodney Noel; JP; Editor, Johansens Hotel Guides, since 1993; *b* 28 Dec. 1927; *s* of Noel Exton and Winifred (*née* Stokes); *m* 1st, 1961, Pamela Sinclair (*née* Hardie) (marr. diss. 1989); two step *s* two step *d*; 2nd, 1995, Agnes Szent-Ivanyi (*née* Pongracz); one *d*. *Educ:* Clifton Coll.; Lincoln Coll., Oxford (MA Mod. Langs); Corpus Christi Coll., Cambridge (PGCE). FInstD. Served Royal Hampshire Regt, 1946–48. Asst Master, Eton, 1951–52; Internat. Research Fund Schol. to USA, 1952; Asst Master, Mill Hill Sch., 1953–63; Royal Commonwealth Schol. to Australia, 1959–60; Headmaster, Reed's Sch., 1964–77; Walter Hines Page Schol. to USA, 1971; Dir, ISCO, 1978–88. Vice-Chm., British Atlantic Educn Cttee, 1972–78; Chm., Exec. Cttee, GAP, 1982–87. Man. Dir, Exton Hotels Co. Ltd, 1966–80; Chm., Kandic Ltd, 1972–82; Dep. Chm., Johansens Ltd, 1989–93; Dir, Purbeck Properties Ltd, 1986–88. Dir, Vocational Guidance Assoc., 1988–90. Fellow, Atlantic Council of UK, 1993. Gov., Clifton Coll., 1986–; Vice-Pres., Reed's Sch., 1991–. Pres., Flycatchers CC, 1989–. Hampshire County Cricket XI, 1946. JP Surrey, 1968. *Publications:* Industrial Cadets, 1972; Trouble With The Rules, 1987. *Address:* 43 Temple Road, Kew Gardens, Surrey TW9 2EB. *T:* (020) 8940 0305. *Clubs:* MCC; Vincent's (Oxford); Royal Mid-Surrey Golf. *Died 22 Dec. 1999.*

EYRE, Sir Graham (Newman), Kt 1989; QC 1970; a Recorder, 1975–99; Justice of Appeal for British Indian Ocean Territory, since 1992; *b* 9 Jan. 1931; *s* of Newman Eyre; *m* 1954, Jean Dalrymple Walker; one *s* three *d*. *Educ:* Marlborough Coll.; Trinity Coll., Cambridge (BA 1953, LLB 1954, MA 1958). Council of Legal Educn Prizewinner, 1954. Called to the Bar, Middle Temple, 1954, Harmsworth Law Schol., 1955, Bencher, 1979; Mem., Lincoln's Inn, 1971; Head of Chambers, 1981. Inspector, The London Airports Inquiries, 1981–84. *Publications:* Rating Law and Valuation, 1963; contrib. Jl Planning Law. *Address:* Greyholme House, Bascombe Road, Churston Ferrers, Brixham TQ5 0JW. *Club:* Athenæum. *Died 14 Nov. 1999.*

EYSENCK, Prof. Hans Jürgen, PhD, DSc; Professor of Psychology, University of London, Institute of Psychiatry, 1955–83, Professor Emeritus, since 1983; Director, Psychological Department, Maudsley Hospital, 1946–83; *b* 4 March 1916; *s* of Eduard Anton and Ruth Eysenck; *m* 1st, 1938, Margaret Malcolm Davies (decd); one *s*; 2nd, 1950, Sybil Bianca Giuletta Rostal; three *s* one *d*. *Educ:* school in Germany, France and England; Univ. of London. BA 1938, PhD 1940, DSc 1964. Senior Research

Psychologist, Mill Hill Emergency Hosp., 1942–46; Reader in Psychology, Univ. of London (Inst. of Psychiatry), 1950–54. Visiting Prof., Univ. of Pennsylvania, 1949–50; Visiting Prof., Univ. of California, Berkeley, 1954. Pres., Internat. Soc. for Study of Individual Differences, 1983–85. Dist. Scientist Award, Amer. Psychol Assoc., 1988. *Publications:* Dimensions of Personality, 1947; The Scientific Study of Personality, 1952; The Structure of Human Personality, 1953; Uses and Abuses of Psychology, 1953; The Psychology of Politics, 1954; Sense and Nonsense in Psychology, 1957; Dynamics of Anxiety and Hysteria, 1957; Perceptual Processes and Mental Illness, 1957; (ed) Handbook of Abnormal Psychology, 1960, 2nd edn, 1972; (ed) Behaviour Therapy and the Neuroses, 1960; (ed) Experiments in Personality, 1960; (ed) Experiments with Drugs, 1963; (ed) Experiments in Behaviour Therapy, 1964; (ed) Experiments in Motivation, 1964; Crime and Personality, 1964; Causes and Cures of Neurosis, 1965; Fact and Fiction in Psychology, 1965; Smoking, Health and Personality, 1965; The Biological Basis of Personality, 1968; Personality Structure and Measurement, 1969; Race, Intelligence and Education, 1971; (ed) Readings in Introversion-Extraversion, 3 vols, 1971; Psychology is about People, 1972; (ed) Lexikon der Psychologie, 3 vols, 1972; The Measurement of Intelligence, 1973; The Inequality of Man, 1973; (ed jtly) The Experimental Study of Freudian Theories, 1973; (ed jtly) Encyclopaedia of Psychology, 1973; (with Glenn Wilson) Know Your Own Personality, 1975; (ed) Case Studies in Behaviour Therapy, 1976; Sex and Personality, 1976; (with S. B. G. Eysenck)

Psychoticism as a Dimension of Personality 1976; You and Neurosis, 1977; Die Zukunft der Psychologie, 1977; (with D. K. B. Nias) Sex, Violence and the Media, 1978; The Structure and Measurement of Intelligence, 1979; (with Glenn Wilson) The Psychology of Sex, 1979; The Causes and Effects of Smoking, 1980; (with M. W. Eysenck) Mindwatching, 1981; (ed) A Model for Personality, 1981; (with J. Kamin) Intelligence: the battle for the mind, 1981 (US as The Intelligence Controversy, 1981); (with D. K. B. Nias) Astrology: Science or Superstition?, 1982; Personality, Genetics and Behaviour, 1982; (ed) A Model for Intelligence, 1982; (with Carl Sargent) Explaining the Unexplained, 1982; I Do: your guide to happy marriage, 1983; (with Carl Sargent) Know your own psi-Q, 1984; (with M. W. Eysenck) Personality and Individual Differences, 1985; Decline and Fall of the Freudian Empire, 1985; (with L. Eaves and N. Martin) Genes, Culture and Personality, 1989; (with G. Gudjousson) Causes and Cures of Criminality, 1989; Rebel with a Cause (autobiog.), 1990; Smoking, Personality and Stress: environmental factors in the prevention of cancer and coronary heart disease, 1991; Genius: the natural history of creativity, 1995; Editor-in-Chief: Behaviour Research and Therapy, 1963–78; Personality and Individual Differences, 1980–; (ed) International Monographs of Experimental Psychology; some 1,000 articles in British, American, German, Spanish and French Jls of Psychology. *Recreations:* walking, tennis, chess, detective stories, squash. *Address:* 10 Dorchester Drive, SE24 0DQ.   *Died 4 Sept. 1997.*

F

FAIRBANKS, Douglas Elton, Jr, Hon. KBE 1949; DSC 1944; Captain, USNR, retired; actor, writer, producer, company director; Chairman: Fairtel, Inc. (US), 1946; Fairbanks Co. Inc., 1946; Douglas Fairbanks Ltd, 1952–58; formerly Chairman, Dougfair Corp.; *b* New York City, 9 Dec. 1909; *s* of Douglas Elton Fairbanks, Denver, Colorado, and Anna Beth Sully, Providence, RI; *m* 1st, 1929, Lucille Le Sueur, (Joan Crawford) (marr. diss. 1933); 2nd, 1939, Mary Lee Epling (*d* 1988), Keystone, W Virginia; three *d*; 3rd, 1991, Vera Shelton. *Educ:* Bovée Sch., Knickerbocker Greys, Collegiate Mil. Sch., NY; Pasadena Polytechnic, Harvard Mil. Sch., Los Angeles; tutored privately in London and Paris. Studied painting and sculpture, Paris, 1922–24; began career as film actor, 1923, on stage 1926; began writing, professionally, 1928, articles, fiction and essays on public affairs, etc, 1936–; organised own producing company, UK, 1935. Vice-Pres. Franco-British War Relief and National Vice-Pres. Cttee "Defend America by Aiding the Allies", 1939–40; Presidential Envoy, Special Mission to Latin America, 1940–41; one-time Consultant to Office of the Presidency (Washington, DC); Lieut (jG), USNR, 1941; promoted through grades to Capt., 1954. National Chm., Co-operative American Relief Everywhere Cttee, 1947–50; Nat. Chm., Amer. Relief for Korea, 1950–54; Nat. Vice-Pres. Amer. Assoc. for the UN, 1946–60; Mem., Council on Foreign Relations (NY); US Naval Mem., US Mil. Delegn, SEATO Conf., 1971. Pres. Brit.-Amer. Alumni Assoc., 1950; Bd Gov., English-Speaking Union of the US, 1949–60; Trustee, Edwina Mountbatten Trust; Mem., Bd of Dirs, Mountbatten Meml Trust (US); Mem. Bd of Dirs, Amer. Friends of RSC and RSC Trust; Dir, Shakespeare Globe Theatre; Mem. Council, American Museum in Brit.; a Governor and Exec. Cllr, Royal Shakespeare Theatre; Governor: United World Colleges, 1951; Ditchley Foundation; Co-Chm., US Capitol Bicentenary 1776–1976; Guild of St Bride's Church, Fleet Street, EC; Mem., Bd of Dirs, Pilgrims Soc. of US, 1985–. Director or Special Consultant: Norlantic Development; Boltons Trading; Alcoa Inc.; Scripto Pens Ltd (US and UK), 1952–73; Golden Cycle and subsidiaries, 1965–73; Rambagh Palace Hotel, Ltd (Jaipur, India); Cavalcade Film Co. Ltd (UK), etc. Vis. Fellow, St Cross Coll., Oxford; MA Oxon; Senior Churchill Fellow, Westminster Coll., Fulton, Mo; Hon. DFA Westminster Coll., Fulton, Mo, USA; Hon. LLD Univ. of Denver, Colo. Silver Star Medal (US); Legion of Merit ("Valor" clasp) (US), Special Naval Commendation (US), KJStJ 1950 (Hon. Dep. Chancellor, Amer. Friends, Order of St John), etc; Officer Legion of Honour (France); Croix de Guerre with Palm (France); Knight Comdr Order of George I (Greece); Knight Grand Officer, Order del Merito (Chile); Grand Officer, Order of Merit (Italy); Comdr Order of Orange Nassau (Neth.); Officer of: Orders of Crown (Belg.), of Star of Italy, Cross of Mil. Valour (Italy), Southern Cross (Brazil); Grand Comdr Order of Merit (West Germany); Murmansk Convoys Campaign (USSR); Hon. Citizen and National Medal of Korea, etc. *Films included:* Stella Dallas; Little Caesar; Outward Bound; Morning Glory; Catherine the Great; The Amateur Gentleman; The Prisoner of Zenda; Gunga Din; The Corsican Brothers; Sinbad the Sailor; The Exile; The Fighting O'Flynn; State Secret; The Young in Heart; Having Wonderful Time; The Rage of Paris; The Joy of Living; L'Athlète Malgré Lui (French); A Woman of Affairs; That Lady in Ermine; Stephen Steps Out; The Barker; Chances; The Life of Jimmy Dolan; Mimi; Angels Over Broadway. *Plays included:* Young Woodley; Romeo and Juliet; The Jest; Man in Possession; The Winding Journey; Moonlight is Silver; My Fair Lady; The Pleasure of his Company; The Secretary Bird; Present Laughter; Sleuth; The Youngest; The Dummy; Towards the Light; produced over 160 TV plays, acted in over 50; also recordings etc. *Publications: autobiography:* The Salad Days, 1988; A Hell of a War, 1993; short stories, poems, articles, to periodicals; *relevant publications:* Knight Errant, by Brian Connell; The Fairbanks Album, by Richard Schickel. *Recreations:* collecting rare books, swimming, travel. *Address:* The Beekman, 575 Park Avenue #608, New York, NY 10021, USA; (office) Inverness Corporation, 545 Madison Avenue, New York, NY 10022, USA. *Clubs:* Garrick, White's, Naval and Military; Brook, Knickerbocker, Century (NY); Metropolitan (Washington, DC); Racquet (Chicago); (Hon. Mem.) Myopia Hunt (Hamilton, Mass).

Died 7 May 2000.

FAIRCLOUGH, Wilfred, RE, RWS, ARCA; Assistant Director, Kingston Polytechnic, and Head of the Division of Design, 1970–72, retired; Principal of Kingston College of Art, Surrey, 1962–70; *b* 13 June 1907; *s* of Herbert Fairclough and Edith Amy Milton; *m* 1936, Joan Cryer; one *s* one *d. Educ:* Royal College of Art, London, 1931–34 (Diploma 1933); British Sch. at Rome, Italy, 1934–37; Rome Scholar in Engraving, 1934–37. Army and Royal Air Force, 1942–46. Rome Scholarships, Faculty of Engraving, 1951 (Chm., 1964–73); Leverhulme Research Award, 1961. RE 1946 (ARE 1934); RWS 1968 (ARWS 1961). Chairman: Assoc. of Art Instns, 1965–66; Assessors, Vocational Courses of Surrey CC. *Work in public and private collections: paintings:* Min. of Supply; Min. of Works; Surrey CC; Scottish Modern Art Assoc.; Beaumont Coll.; *drawings:* British Museum; V&A Museum; Arts Council; Contemporary Art Soc.; Wye Coll., London Univ.; English Electric Co.; Art Galls at Blackburn, Kingston-upon-Thames, Worthing; Graves Art Gall., Sheffield; Atkinson Art Gall., Southport; *prints:* British Museum, V&A Museum; Ashmolean Museum, Oxford; Contemporary Art Soc.; British Sch. at Rome; South London Art Gall.; Stoke Educn Authority; Wye Coll., London Univ.; Gottenburg Museum; Print Collectors Club. *Publications:* The Etchings of Wilfrid Fairclough, 1990; work reproduced: Recording Britain; Londoners' England; Royal Academy Illustrated; Studio; Fine Prints of the Year; Print Collectors Quarterly; illustrated article, Leisure Painter, 1969; paintings, drawings and prints. *Address:* 12 Manorgate Road, Kingston-upon-Thames, Surrey KT2 7AL.

Died 8 Jan. 1996.

FAIRGRIEVE, Sir (Thomas) Russell, Kt 1981; CBE 1974; TD 1959; JP; *b* 3 May 1924; *s* of late Alexander Fairgrieve, OBE, MC, JP, and Myrna Margaret Fairgrieve; *m* 1954, Millie Mitchell; one *s* three *d. Educ:* St Mary's Sch., Melrose; Sedbergh School; Scottish Coll. of Textiles. Major 8th Gurkha Rifles (Indian Army), 1946; Major KOSB, 1956–72. Man. Dir, Laidlaw & Fairgrieve Ltd, 1958; Director: Joseph Dawson (Holdings) Ltd, 1961–72; William Baird and Co. PLC, 1975–79, 1982; Bain Dawes (Scotland) Ltd, 1985; Bain Clarkson Ltd; Chm., Quality Guaranteed PLC. Formerly: Chairman: Hall Advertising; Aberdeen Construction Group PLC; Dir, Hall & Tawse Group Ltd. Indust. consultant on exec. selection, textile problems and marketing. Selkirk County and Galashiels

Town Councillor, 1949–59. MP (C) Aberdeenshire West, Feb. 1974–1983; Parly Under Sec. of State, Scottish Office, 1979–81. Formerly Mem., Council of Europe. Pres., Scottish Conservative Assoc., 1965, Vice-Chm., 1971; Chm., Conservative Party in Scotland, 1975–80. JP Selkirkshire, 1962. *Recreation:* golf. *Address:* Pankalan, Boleside, Galashiels, Selkirk TD1 3NX. *T:* (01896) 2278. *Clubs:* Carlton; New (Edinburgh); Royal and Ancient (St Andrews).   *Died 17 Feb. 1999.*

FAIRLIE-CUNINGHAME, Sir William Henry, 16th Bt *cr* 1630, of Robertland, Ayrshire; *b* 1 Oct. 1930; *s* of Sir William Alan Fairlie-Cuninghame, 15th Bt, MC, and Irene Alice (*d* 1970), *d* of Henry Margrave Terry; *S* father, 1981; *m* 1972, Janet Menzies, *d* of late Roy Menzies Saddington; one *s. Heir: s* (William) Robert (Henry) Fairlie-Cuninghame, *b* 19 July 1974. *Address:* 29A Orinoco Street, Pymble, NSW 2073, Australia.
Died 4 Jan. 1999.

FAITHFULL, Baroness *cr* 1975 (Life Peer), of Wolvercote, Oxfordshire; **Lucy Faithfull,** OBE 1972; *b* 26 Dec. 1910; *d* of Lieut Sydney Leigh Faithfull, RE (killed 1916) and late Elizabeth Adie Faithfull (*née* Algie); unmarried. *Educ:* Talbot Heath Sch. (formerly Bournemouth High Sch.). Social Science Dipl., Birmingham Univ., 1933; Family case work training (Charity Welfare Organisation, later Family Welfare Assoc.), 1936, and Cert. in Child Care, 1969. Club Leader and Sub-Warden, Birmingham Settlement, 1932–35; Asst Organiser, Child Care, LCC Education Dept, 1935–40, Regional Welfare Officer (Evacuation Scheme), Min. of Health, 1940–48; Inspector in Children's Br., Home Office, 1948–58; Oxford City Council: Children's Officer, 1958–70; Director of Social Services, 1970–74; retired, 1974. Chm., All Party Parly Gp for Children. Pres., Nat. Children's Bureau, 1984–; Vice President: Barnardo's, 1989–; Nat. Assoc. of Voluntary Hostels, 1978–; Chm., Faithfull Foundation dealing with child sexual abuse; Mem., Nursery and Family Care Assoc. Hon. Mem. Council, NSPCC, 1989–; Hon. Fellow BPA; Hon. FRCPsych. Chm. Council, Caldecott Community Kent Sch. for Distracted and Deliquent Children, 1975; Gov., Bessel Leigh Sch. for children experiencing emotional behavioural difficulties; Trustee, Gracewell Inst., Birmingham; Patron, Nat. Mediation and Conciliation Council. Hon. MA Oxford, 1974; Hon. DLitt Warwick, 1978. *Recreations:* friends, travel, garden. *Address:* 303 Woodstock Road, Oxford OX2 7NY. *T:* Oxford (01865) 55389.   *Died 13 March 1996.*

FALCON, Norman Leslie, FRS 1960; *b* 29 May 1904; 2nd *s* of late Thomas Adolphus Falcon, MA, RBA and Julia, *d* of E. Schwabe, Didsbury, Manchester; *m* 1938, Dorothy Muriel, 2nd *d* of late F. G. Freeman, HM Consular Service; two *s* one *d. Educ:* Exeter Sch.; Trinity Coll., Cambridge (Sen. Exhibitioner 1925; Natural Science Tripos Pt I 1925, 1st cl., Part II 1927, 1st cl.; MA Cantab). Joined Anglo-Persian Oil Company as geologist, 1927; geological exploration in Persia, UK and elsewhere, 1927–40; served War of 1939–45, Intelligence Corps, 1940–45; rejoined Anglo-Iranian Oil Company as Geologist on Head Office staff, 1945; Chief Geologist, 1955–65, Geological Adviser, 1965–72, British Petroleum Co Ltd. Geological Soc. of London: Mem. Council, 1954–58, 1967–71; Foreign Sec. 1967–70; Murchison Medal, 1963; Hon. Mem. 1988; Royal Geographical Society: Mem. Council, 1966–69; Vice-Pres. 1973; Founder's Medal, 1973. Mem., NERC, 1968–71. FGS, FRGS 1927; FInstPet 1959. Hon. Mem., American Assoc. Petroleum Geologists, 1973. Bronze Star Medal (USA), 1945. *Publications:* geological papers. *Recreations:* outdoor pursuits. *Address:* 2 Mansell Close, Church Hanborough, Witney, Oxon OX8 8AU.
Died 31 May 1996.

FALK, Sir Roger (Salis), Kt 1969; OBE (mil.) 1945; FIMC; CIMgt; Vice President, Sadler's Wells Foundation and Trust, since 1986 (Chairman, 1976–86); *b* 22 June 1910; *s* of Lionel David Falk; *m* 1938, Margaret Helen (*née* Stroud) (*d* 1958); one *s* two *d. Educ:* Haileybury (Life Governor, 1971; Council Mem., 1978–92); Geneva Univ. Gen. Manager's Office, Rhodesia Railways, Bulawayo, 1931; D. J. Keymer & Co: Manager in Bombay and Calcutta, 1932–35; Dir, 1935–49; Managing Dir, 1945–49; Vice-Chm., 1950; formerly: Dir, P-E International Ltd (Chm., 1973–76); Chm., London Bd, Provincial Insurance Co. Ltd. Shoreditch Borough Council, 1937–45. Dir-Gen. British Export Trade Research Organisation (BETRO) from 1949 until disbandment. Chairman: Furniture Development Council, 1963–82; Central Council for Agric. and Hort. Cooperation, 1967–75; British European Associated Publishers, 1976–79; Action for Dysphasic Adults (ADA), 1982–85 (Vice-Pres., 1985–); Dep. Chm., Gaming Bd, 1978–81; Member: Council of Industrial Design, 1958–67; Monopolies and Mergers Commn, 1965–80; Council, RSA, 1968–74; Council, Imp. Soc. of Knights Bachelor, 1979–; Pres., Design and Industries Assoc., 1971–72. Served War of 1939–45, RAFVR; Wing-Comdr, 1942. Hon. DLitt City Univ. *Publication:* The Business of Management, 1961, 5th rev. edn 1976. *Recreations:* writing, music, reading, theatre. *Address:* 603 Beatty House, Dolphin Square, SW1V 3PL. *T:* (0171) 828 3752. *Clubs:* Garrick, MCC.
Died 15 Jan. 1997.

FALKINER, Sir Edmond (Charles), 9th Bt *cr* 1778, of Annemount, Cork; proprietor, Huckaback, Old & New Linen & Lace, Monmouth, Gwent; *b* 24 June 1938; *s* of Sir Terence Edmond Patrick Falkiner, 8th Bt and Mildred Katherine (*d* 1989), *y d* of Sir John Cotterell, 4th Bt; *S* father, 1987; *m* 1st, 1960, Janet Iris (marr. diss. 1987), *d* of Arthur E. B. Darby; two *s*; 2nd, 1997, Diana Jean, *d* of Percy A. Childs. *Educ:* Downside. CQSW. Various jobs, 1956–60, Home Office Probation Training Course, 1968; Probation Officer, 1969–95; Hon. Chm., Drugcare (St Albans), 1986–94. *Recreations:* jazz, and playing a variety of saxophones. *Heir: s* Benjamin Simon Patrick Falkiner, *b* 16 Jan. 1962. *Address:* Arch Cottage, Goodrich, Herefordshire HR9 6HY. *T:* (01600) 890735.
Died 20 Sept. 1997.

FALKUS, Hugh Edward Lance; naturalist, independent writer, film director, broadcaster; latterly engaged in teaching salmon fishing and speycasting, and writing autobiography; *b* 15 May 1917; *s* of James Everest Falkus and Alice Musgrove; *m* 1st, 1939, Doris Walter (marr. diss. 1947); one *s* one *d* (and two *s* decd); 2nd, Diana Vaughan (*d* 1952); 3rd, 1952, Lady Margaret Vane-Tempest-Stewart (marr. diss. 1958), 2nd *d* of 7th Marquess of Londonderry; 4th, 1957, Kathleen Armstrong. Served War of 1939–45 (Fighter Pilot). Films include: Drake's England, 1950; Shark Island, 1952; TV films include: Salmo—the Leaper; (with Niko Tinbergen) Signals for Survival (Italia Prize, 1969; Amer. Blue Ribbon, New York Film Fest., 1971); Highland Story; The Gull Watchers; The Signreaders; The Beachcombers; The Riddle of the Rook (Venice Film Festival, 1972); Tender Trap (Certificate of Merit, BAAS, 1975); Self-Portrait of a Happy Man. Cherry Kearton Medal and Award, RGS, 1982. *Publications:* Sea Trout Fishing, 1962, 2nd edn 1975, revised 2nd edn 1981; The Stolen Years, 1965, 2nd edn 1979; (with Niko Tinbergen) Signals for Survival, 1970; (with Fred Buller) Freshwater Fishing, 1975, 9th edn 1987; (jtly) Successful Angling, 1977; Nature Detective, 1978, 2nd edn 1987; (with Joan Kerr) From Sydney Cove to Duntroon, 1982; Master of Cape Horn, 1982; Salmon Fishing, 1984; The Sea Trout, 1987; Speycasting: a new technique, 1994. *Recreations:* fishing, shooting, sailing, oil painting. *Address:* Cragg Cottage, near Ravenglass, Cumbria CA18 1RT. *T:* Ravenglass (01229) 717247. *Died 30 March 1996.*

FANSHAWE, Captain Thomas Evelyn, CBE 1971; DSC 1943; RN retired; Captain of the Sea Cadet Corps, 1972–81; *b* 29 Sept. 1918; *s* of Rev. Richard Evelyn Fanshawe and Mrs Isobel Fanshawe (*née* Prosser Hale); *m* 1944, Joan Margaret Moxon; one *s* two *d. Educ:* Dover Coll.; Nautical Coll., Pangbourne. Served 1939–45 in destroyers and frigates and comdg HMS Clover (DSC, despatches 1943 and 1944); HM Ships Ocean, Constance and Phoenix, 1945–51; command HM Ships: Zest and Obedient, 1951–54; Loch Insh, 1955–57; Temeraire, 1957–59; Tyne, 1959–61; NATO Defence Coll. and Liaison Officer with C-in-C Southern Europe, 1961–64; comd HMS Plymouth and Captain (D) 29th Escort Sqdn, 1964–66; Sen. Naval Officer Persian Gulf and Comdr Naval Forces Gulf, 1966–68 (Cdre); Sen. British Naval Officer and Naval Attaché, S Africa (Cdre), 1969–71; ADC to the Queen, 1970–71; retd 1971. Comdr 1955; Captain 1961. *Recreations:* gardening, golf, general interest in sport. *Address:* Freshwater House, Stroud, Petersfield, Hants GU32 3PN. *T:* (01730) 62430. *Club:* Royal Navy of 1765 and 1785.

Died 9 May 2000.

FARMER, Prof. Edward Desmond; Louis Cohen Professor of Dental Surgery, 1957–82, Director of Post-Graduate Dental Studies, 1972–77, Dean of the Faculty of Medicine, 1977–82, and Pro-Vice-Chancellor, 1967–70, University of Liverpool; *b* 15 April 1917; *s* of late S. R. and L. M. Farmer; *m* 1942, Mary Elwood Little; one *s* two *d. Educ:* Newcastle-under-Lyme High Sch.; Univ. of Liverpool (1936–41; MDS 1951); Queens' Coll., Cambridge (1948–50; MA 1955). FDSRCS 1952; FRCPath 1968; Hon. FRCR 1981. RNVR, Surgeon Lieut (D), 1942–45. Lectr in Parodontal Diseases, Univ. of Liverpool, 1950–57; Nuffield Fellow, 1948–50. Hon. Cons. Dent. Surg. to Bd of Governors of United Liverpool Hosps and Liverpool AHA (Teaching), formerly Liverpool Regional Hosp. Bd. Member Council: Brit. Soc. of Periodontology, 1954–59 (Pres. 1957–58); Odontol Sect., RSM, 1965–68 (Pres., 1983–84). Member: Central Cttee and Exec., Hosp. Dental Service, 1964–76; Negotiating Cttee of Central Cttee for Hosp. Medical Services, 1968–76; Bd of Govs, United Liverpool Hosps, 1968–71; UGC Dental Sect., 1968–77; Conf. and Exec., Dental Post-Grad. Deans, 1972–77; Cttee of Dental Teachers and Res. Workers Gp, BDA, 1974–79; Liverpool AHA(T) (and Chm., Regional Dental Cttee), 1975–77; RHA, 1977–82; Faculty of Dental Surgery, RCS, 1974–82; Dental Cttee of Medical Defence Union; Council, Medical Insurance Agency; Exec., Teaching Hospitals Assoc.; Chm., Commn of Dental Educn, Fédn Dentaire Internat., 1977–79 (Vice-Chm., 1974–77); Alternate, Dental Adv. Cttee to EEC, 1980–83; Vice-Chm., NW Cancer Research Fund, 1987–97 (Mem. Exec. Cttee, 1982–97); President: NW Br., BDA, 1967–68; Hospitals' Gp, BDA, 1972–73; Assoc. for Dental Educn in Europe, 1976–78; British Soc. of Oral Medicine, 1982–83. Chairman: Merseyside Conf. for Overseas Students, 1983–88; Age Concern, Liverpool, 1984–94; Member: Council, Liverpool Queen Victoria Dist Nursing Assoc., 1987–94; Exec. Cttee, Age Concern England, 1988–92. *Publications:* (with F. E. Lawton) Stones' Oral and Dental Diseases, 5th edn 1966; papers in Proceedings Royal Society Med., Jl of Gen. Microbiology, Brit. Med. Jl, Dental Practitioner, Internat. Dental Jl. *Recreations:* golf, gardening, painting, enjoyment of the countryside. *Address:* Brookville, 44 Dawstone Road, Heswall, Wirral CH60 0BS. *T:* (0151) 342 3179. *Clubs:* Athenæum (Liverpool); Royal Liverpool Golf; Caldy Golf.

Died 7 Oct. 1999.

FARMER, Sir (Lovedin) George (Thomas), Kt 1968; FCA, JDipMA; Coordinator, Rover and Triumph, 1972–73; Chairman: Rover Co. Ltd, 1963–73; Zenith Carburettor Co. Ltd, 1973–77; Deputy Chairman, British Leyland Motor Corporation, 1971–73; *b* 13 May 1908; *s* of Lovedin George Farmer, Droitwich Spa; *m* 1st, 1938, Editha Mary Fisher (*d* 1980); no *c*; 2nd, 1980, Muriel Gwendoline Mercer Pinfold. *Educ:* Oxford High Sch. 2nd Vice-Chm. and Mem. Adv. Cttee, Metalurgica de Santa Ana, Madrid, 1963–74; Director: Empresa Nacional de Automcamiones, 1968–73; ATV Network Ltd, 1968–75; Rea Brothers (Isle of Man) Ltd, 1976–88; Aero Designs (Isle of Man) Ltd, 1979–89. President: Birmingham Chamber of Commerce, 1960–61; Motor and Cycle Trades Benevolent Fund, 1962; SMMT, 1962–64 (Dep. Pres., 1964–65; Chm., Exec. Cttee, 1968–72); Fellowship of Motor Industry, 1965; Member: Midland Regl Bd for Industry, 1961–65; Midland Industrial Adv. Council, 1962; Engrg Adv. Council, 1962–66; Export Council for Europe, 1963; Iron and Steel Bd, 1964–66; Engrg ITB, 1964–66; EDC for Motor Industry, 1967; Past Member: Advisory Council, ECGD (Board of Trade); UK Committee of Federation of Commonwealth and British Chambers of Commerce; Vice-Pres., Inst. of Motor Industry, 1964; Vice-Chm., ABCC, 1964; Past Vice-Pres., West Midlands Engineering Employers' Assoc.; Governor, Chm. Finance Cttee, Dep. Chm. Executive Council (Chm., 1966–75), Royal Shakespeare Theatre; Pres., Loft Theatre, Leamington Spa. Pro-Chancellor, Birmingham Univ., 1966–75; Hon. LLD Birmingham, 1975; Hon. MA. Past Pres., Automobile Golfing Soc. Mem., Worshipful Co. of Coach and Coach Harness Makers. *Recreations:* theatre, golf, fishing. *Address:* Longridge, The Chase, Ballakillowey, Colby, Isle of Man. *T:* (01624) 832603. *Club:* Royal and Ancient (St Andrews). *Died 11 Nov. 1996.*

FARNDALE, Gen. Sir Martin (Baker), KCB 1983 (CB 1980); Defence Adviser, Deloitte Touche (formerly Touche Ross), since 1988; Chairman, Royal Artillery Museums Ltd , since 1996; *b* Alberta, Canada, 6 Jan. 1929; *s* of late Alfred Farndale and Margaret Louise Baker; *m* 1955, Margaret Anne Buckingham; one *s. Educ:* Yorebridge Grammar Sch., Yorks. Joined Indian Army, 1946; RMA, Sandhurst, 1947; commnd RA, 1948; Egypt, 1949; 1st RHA, 1950–54 (Germany from 1952); HQ 7 Armoured Div., 1954–57; Staff College, 1959; HQ 17 Gurkha Div., Malaya, 1960–62; MoD, 1962–64; comd Chestnut Troop 1st RHA, Germany and Aden, 1964–66; Instructor, Staff Coll., 1966–69; comd 1st RHA, UK, N Ire., Germany, 1969–71; MoD, 1971–73; comd 7th Armoured Bde, 1973–75; Dir, Public Relations (Army), 1976–78; Dir of Mil. Ops, MoD (Army), 1978–80; Comdr 2nd Armoured Div., BAOR, 1980–83; Comdr 1st (British) Corps, BAOR, 1983–85; C-in-C, BAOR, and Comdr, Northern Army Gp, 1985–87; retired, 1988. Dir and Sen. Defence Advr, Short Bros, 1988–97. Master Gunner, St James's Park, 1988–96. Colonel Commandant: Army Air Corps, 1980–88; RA, 1982–; RHA, 1988–. Hon. Colonel: 3rd Bn Yorkshire Volunteers TA, 1983–90; 1st RHA, 1983–90. Chm., RUSI, 1989–93. Consultant, Westland Helicopters, 1989–95. Chairman: RA Historical Affairs Cttee, 1988–95; English Heritage Battlefields Adv. Panel, 1993–; Vice-Pres., Royal Patriotic Fund Corp., 1989–92; Pres., RA Council of NI, 1988–. Patron, Air Observation Post Offices Assoc., 1990–. *Publications:* The History of the Royal Regiment of Artillery: France 1914–18, 1987, Forgotten Fronts and the Home Base 1914–18, 1989, The Years of Defeat 1939–41, 1996, The Far East 1939–46, 2000; articles for British Army Rev. and Jl RA. *Recreations:* military history, gardening. *Address:* c/o

Lloyds TSB, Cox's and King's Branch, 7 Pall Mall, SW1Y 5NA. *Club:* East India, Devonshire, Sports and Public Schools. *Died 10 May 2000.*

FARR, Sir John (Arnold), Kt 1984; Member of Lloyd's; *b* 25 Sept. 1922; *er s* of late Capt. John Farr, JP, and Mrs M. A. Farr, JP; *m* 1960, Susan Ann, *d* of Sir Leonard Milburn, 3rd Bt, and of Joan, Lady Milburn, Guyzance Hall, Acklington, Northumberland; two *s. Educ:* Harrow. RN, 1940–46 serving in Mediterranean and S Atlantic; Lieut-Comdr RNVR. Executive Dir, Home Brewery and Apollo Productions Ltd, 1950–55. Contested Ilkeston, 1955; MP (C) Harborough, 1959–92. Sec., Cons. Parly Agric. Cttee, 1970–74, Vice-Chm., 1979–83; Sec., Parly Conservation Cttee, 1972–92. Member: Exec. Cttee, UK Branch CPA, 1972–74; UK Delegn to WEU and Council of Europe, 1973–78 (Vice-Chm., Cttee on Agric.); Chairman: Anglo-Irish Parly Gp, 1977–80; Parly Knitwear Ind. Gp, 1980–92; British-Zimbabwe Parly Gp, 1980–91; British-Korea Parly Gp, 1983–91. Vice-Pres., Shooting Sports Trust, 1972–86; Chm., British Shooting Sports Council, 1977–86. *Recreations:* cricket, shooting. *Address:* Shortwood House, Lamport, Northants NN6 9HN. *T:* (01604) 686260; 11 Vincent Square, Westminster, SW1P 2LX. *Clubs:* Boodle's, Carlton. *Died 25 Oct. 1997.*

FARRANDS, Dr John Law, AO 1990; CB 1982; CEng; FTS; FInstP, FAIP; FIEAust; consultant to companies and government, since 1982; *b* 11 March 1921; *s* of Harold Rawlings Farrands and Hilda Elizabeth (*née* Bray); *m* 1946, Jessica (*née* Ferguson); three *s* one *d* (and one *s* decd). *Educ:* Melbourne Univ. (BSc), London Univ. (PhD); Imperial Coll. of Science and Technol. (DIC, CEng). FTS 1976; FInstP 1957; FAIP 1962; FIEAust 1987. Served RAEME, AIF, 1941 (Captain). Scientific Adviser to Mil. Bd, 1957; Chief Supt, Aeronautical Res. Labs, 1967; Chief Def. Scientist, 1971; Permanent Head, Dept of Science and Environment, later Dept of Science and Technol., 1977–82. Chairman: Aust. Inst. of Marine Science, 1982–90; R&D Bd, Overseas Telecommunications Commn, 1983–89. Leader, Aust. Delegn to UNCSTD, 1980. Cllr, Nat. Energy Res., Develt and Demonstration Council, 1978–83. Director: Interscan Australia, 1980–84; Quest Investment, 1986–91; SCIRAD, 1987–. Hon. DSc Melbourne, 1994. *Publications:* (jtly) Changing Disease Patterns and Human Behaviour, 1981; Don't Panic, PANIC!, 1993; articles in scientific and engrg jls. *Recreations:* fishing, music. *Address:* 20 The Boulevard, Glen Waverley, Vic 3150, Australia. *T:* (3) 98028195. *Died 14 July 1996.*

FARRELL, M. J.; *see* Keane, M. N.

FARRER, Margaret Irene, OBE 1970; Chairman of Central Midwives Board, 1973–79 (Member, 1952); *b* 23 Feb. 1914; *e d* of Alfred and Emblyn Farrer. *Educ:* Poltimore Coll., Exeter; UCH London. SRN, SCM, DN (London), MTD, RST. Midwifery Tutor, General Lying-in Hosp., 1942–49; Matron: St Mary's Hosp., Croydon, 1949–56; Forest Gate Hosp., 1956–71; Chief Nursing Officer, Thames Gp, 1971–74. Member: Central Health Services Council, 1963–74; NE Metropolitan Regional Hosp. Bd, 1969–74; NE Thames Regional Health Authority, 1973–76; Editorial Bd, Midwife and Health Visitor; Hon. Treas., Royal Coll. of Midwives, 1967–76. *Recreations:* gardening, walking. *Address:* Coombe Brook, Dawlish, South Devon EX7 0QN. *T:* (01626) 863323. *Died 25 July 1997.*

FASELLA, Prof. Paolo Maria; Professor, University of Rome Tor Vergata, since 1995; *b* 16 Dec. 1930; *s* of Felice Fasella and Margherita Parazzoli; *m* 1957, Sheila Hauck Dionisi; four *d. Educ:* Univ. of Rome. PhD Biolog. Chem. and Applied Biochem. Asst, then Associate Prof. in Biol Chem., Univ. of Rome, 1959–65; Associate, then Prof. in

Biochem., Univ. of Parma, 1965–71; Prof. of Biol Chem., Univ. of Rome, 1971–81; Dir-Gen. for Science, R&D, CEC, 1981–95; Dir-Gen. for Res., Min. for Univs and Scientific and Technological Res., Rome, 1997–98. Res. Associate, 1961–62, Vis. Scientist (part-time), 1963–64, MIT; Vis. Prof., Dept. of Chem., Cornell Univ., 1966. Mem., Cttee of Nine Experts for Res. Policies estabd by Italian govt, 1999. Member: Accademia Nazionale delle Scienze, detta dei XL; EMBO; Internat. Foundn for Artificial Intelligence, Tokyo; NY Acad. of Scis; Scientific Council, UNESCO; Internat. Council, Scientific Union Cttees for Central and Eastern Europe. MAE. Pres., Sincrotrone Trieste. Hon. Fellow: Inst. of Biology, 1990; Belgian Royal Acad. of Medicine, 1990. Hon. DSc NUI, 1990. Europe and Medicine Prize, Inst des Scis de la Santé, Paris, 1993. *Publications:* numerous papers on protein structure and functions, biological catalysis, biotechnology; articles on sci. res. policy and bioethics. *Address:* Università di Roma Tor Vergata, Dipartimento di Medicina Sperimentale e Scienze Biochimiche, Via di Tor Vergata 135, 00133 Roma, Italy.

Died 11 June 1999.

FATCHETT, Rt Hon. Derek (John); PC 1998; MP (Lab) Leeds Central, since 1983; Minister of State, Foreign and Commonwealth Office, since 1997; *b* 22 Aug. 1945; *s* of late Herbert and of Irene Fatchett; *m* 1969, Anita Bridgens (*née* Oakes); two *s. Educ:* Monks Road Primary School; Lincoln School; Birmingham University (LLB); LSE (MSc). Research Officer, LSE, 1968–70; Research Fellow, University College, Cardiff, 1970–71; Lectr in Industrial Relations, Univ. of Leeds, 1971–83. Labour Whip, 1986–87; Opposition spokesman on education (secondary and tertiary), 1987, on education and training, 1988–92; Opposition front bench spokesman on trade and industry, 1992–94, on defence, 1994–95, on foreign affairs, 1995–97. Dep. Campaigns Co-ordinator, 1987 92. *Publications:* (jtly) Workers Participation in Management, 1972; (jtly) Worker Participation: industrial control and performance, 1974; (jtly) The Worker Directors, 1976; Trade Unions and Politics in the 1980s: the political fund ballots, 1987; articles in learned jls. *Recreations:* cricket, reading, theatre. *Address:* House of Commons, SW1A 0AA. *Died 9 May 1999.*

FAULDS, Andrew Matthew William; *b* 1 March 1923; *s* of late Rev. Matthew Faulds, MA, and Doris Faulds; *m* 1945, Bunty Whitfield; one *d. Educ:* George Watson's, Edinburgh; King Edward VI Grammar Sch., Louth; Daniel Stewart's, Edinburgh; High Sch., Stirling; Glasgow Univ. Three seasons with Shakespeare Memorial Co., Stratford-upon-Avon; three yrs with BBC Repertory Co.: Jet Morgan in Journey into Space (BBC). Appeared in 37 films; many TV and radio performances; performed in 27 of Shakespeare's plays. MP (Lab) Smethwick, 1966–74, Warley East, 1974–97. Parliamentary Private Secretary: to Minister of State for Aviation, Min. of Technology, 1967–68; to Postmaster General, 1968–69; Opposition spokesman for the Arts, 1970–73, 1979–82. Founder, and Chm., British Br., Parly Assoc. for Euro-Arab Cooperation, 1974–97; Co-Chm., All-Party Parly Heritage Gp, 1974–97; H of C Works of Art Cttee, 1970–97; Member: British Delegn to Council of Europe and WEU, 1975–80, and 1987–97; Exec. Cttee, GB China Centre, 1976–97; Exec. Cttee, IPU (British Section), 1983–97; Exec. Cttee, Franco–British Council, 1978–88. *Recreations:* opera, collecting mediaeval pottery. *Address:* 18 Old Town, Stratford-upon-Avon, Warwicks CV37 6BG. *T:* (01789) 267993. *Club:* Arts. *Died 31 May 2000.*

FAULKNER, (Charles) Hugh (Branston), OBE 1980; Co-founder with wife, and Hon. Director, Persistent Virus Disease Research Foundation, since 1992; Director, Help the Aged, from formation, 1961–83; *b* Lutterworth, 8 June

1916; *s* of Frank and Ethel Faulkner; *m* 1954, Anne Carlton Milner; one *s* one *d*. *Educ:* Lutterworth Grammar Sch. FCIS. Educn Administration, City of Leicester, 1936–46; Organising Sec., Fellowship of Reconciliation, 1946–54; business and charity career from 1954. Hon. Dir and later Dir, Voluntary and Christian Service, 1954–79; a Director: Helpage International Ltd, 1966–83; Help the Aged Housing Appeal, 1975–83; Dir, Asthma Res. Council and Asthma Soc., 1983–88. Christian peace delegate to USSR, 1952, followed by lecture tour in USA, 1953, on internat. relations; deleg. and speaker, UN World Assembly on Ageing, Vienna, 1982. Mem., Exec. Cttee, Council for Music in Hospitals, 1983–96. Trustee: World in Need Trust; Lester Trust; Andrews Pension Trust; Voluntary and Christian Service; Nat. Asthma Training Centre; Advr, Elderly Accommodation Counsel. *Recreations:* music, gardening. *Address:* Longfield, 4 One Tree Lane, Beaconsfield, Bucks HP9 2BU. *T:* (01494) 674769. *Club:* National Liberal.

Died 6 April 1997.

FAULKS, His Honour Peter Ronald, MC 1943; a Circuit Judge, 1980–90; *b* 24 Dec. 1917; *s* of late M. J. Faulks and A. M. Faulks (*née* Ginner); *m* 1949, Pamela Brenda, *d* of Peter Lawless; two *s*. *Educ:* Tonbridge; Sidney Sussex Coll., Cambridge (MA). Served War of 1939–45, Duke of Wellington's Regt, Dunkirk, N Africa, Anzio, etc; Major 1943; wounded 3 times. Admitted a solicitor, 1949. A Recorder of the Crown Court, 1972–80; Dep. Chm., Agricultural Land Tribunal (SE England), 1972–80. Pres., Berks, Bucks and Oxon Law Soc., 1976–77. *Recreation:* country life. *Address:* Downs Cottage, Westbrook, Boxford, Newbury, Berks RG20 8DJ. *T:* (01488) 605382. *Clubs:* MCC, Farmers'.

Died 15 Feb. 1998.

FAWCETT, Colin; QC 1970; *b* 22 Nov. 1923; *s* of late Frank Fawcett, Penrith; *m* 1952, Elizabeth Anne Dickson; one *s* one *d*. *Educ:* Sedbergh. Commnd Border Regt, 1943. Called to Bar, Inner Temple, 1952, Bencher, 1978. Mem., Criminal Injuries Compensation Bd, 1983–95. *Recreations:* fishing, music. *Address:* 6 Hubert Day Close, Beaconsfield, Bucks HP9 1TL. *T:* Beaconsfield (01494) 670755.

Died 29 Aug. 1996.

FEAVER, Rt Rev. Douglas Russell; *b* 22 May 1914; *s* of late Ernest Henry Feaver, Bristol; *m* 1st, 1939, Katharine (*d* 1987), *d* of late Rev. W. T. Stubbs; one *s* two *d*; 2nd, 1988, Mary Frances Clare Harvey. *Educ:* Bristol Grammar School; Keble College, Oxford (Scholar; 1st cl. Hons. Mod. History, 1935; 1st Cl. Hons. Theology, 1937; Liddon Student, 1935–37; MA); Wells Theological College. Deacon 1938, priest 1939, St Albans; Curate, St Albans Abbey, 1938–42; Chaplain, RAFVR, 1942–46; Canon and Sub-Dean of St Albans, 1946–58; Chaplain to St Albans School, 1946–58; Proctor in Convocation, 1951–58; Examining Chaplain to Bp of St Albans, 1948–58, to Bp of Portsmouth, 1960–72; Vicar of St Mary's, Nottingham and Rural Dean of Nottingham, 1958–72; Hon. Canon of Southwell, 1958–72, Treasurer, 1959–69; Proctor in Convocation for Southwell, 1970–72; Bishop of Peterborough, 1972–84. Chairman of Trent House Boys' Probation Hostel, 1967–72; Governor of Nottingham Bluecoat School, 1958–72. *Address:* 6 Mill Lane, Bruton, Somerset BA10 0AT.

Died 9 Nov. 1997.

FEHR, Basil Henry Frank, CBE 1979; Life President, Frank Fehr & Co. Ltd UK, 1992; Chairman, Fehr Bros (Industries) Inc., Saugerties, USA, 1992; *b* 11 July 1912; *s* of Frank E. Fehr, CBE and Jane (*née* Poulter); *m* 1st, 1936, Jane Marner (*née* Tallent) (marr. diss. 1951); two *s* one *d*; 2nd, 1951, Greta Constance (*née* Bremner) (marr. diss. 1971); one *d*, and one step *d*; 3rd, 1974, Anne Norma (*née* Cadman); one *d*. *Educ:* Rugby Sch.; Neûchatel Ecole de Commerce, Switzerland. Served War, 1939–45: HAC,

later Instr, Gunnery Sch. of Anti-Aircraft, RA; retd Major. Joined father in family firm, Frank Fehr & Co., 1934; Partner, 1936; Governing Dir, Frank Fehr & Co. London, 1948; Pres., 1949, Chm., 1979–92, Fehr Bros (Manufactures) New York, later Fehr Bros Inc. New York; Chm. and Man. Dir, Frank Fehr & Co. Ltd London and group of cos, 1957–91; Dir, Colyer Fehr Hldgs Pty, Sydney, 1976 (Chm. 1984–89). Chairman: Cocoa Assoc. of London, 1952; London Commodity Exchange, 1954; London Oil and Tallow Trades Assoc., 1955; Copra Assoc. of London, 1957; Inc. Oilseed Assoc., 1958; United Assocs Ltd, 1959. Elected to Baltic Exchange, 1936; Director: Baltic Mercantile and Shipping Exchange, 1963–69 and 1970–77 (Vice Chm. 1973–75; Chm. 1975–77; Hon. Mem. 1991). Jurat of Liberty of Romney Marsh, 1979. *Recreations:* sports generally, farming. *Address:* Slodden Farm, Dymchurch, Romney Marsh, Kent TN29 0LW. *T:* (01303) 872241. *Clubs:* City Livery, Aldgate Ward, MCC, Royal Automobile, Ski of Great Britain; West Kent Cricket; Littlestone Golf.

Died 18 Oct. 1999.

FEIBUSCH, Hans Nathan; painter, mural painter, lithographer, sculptor, writer; *b* 15 Aug. 1898; *s* of Dr Carl Feibusch and Marianne Ickelheimer; *m* 1935, Sidonie (*d* 1963), *e d* of D. Gestetner. *Educ:* Frankfurt a/M and Munich Univs. Studied at the Berlin Academy, at Paris Art Schs, in Florence and Rome; received German State award and grant in 1931. Pictures in German Public Galleries; work banned and destroyed by Nazis in 1933; thereafter lived in London; large mural paintings in churches: St Wilfred's, Brighton; St Elizabeth's, Eastbourne; St Martin's, Dagenham; St John's, Waterloo Road, SE1; St Ethelburga's, Bishopsgate; St Alban's, Holborn; Chichester Cathedral; Chichester Palace; parish churches, Egham, Goring, Wellingborough, Welling, Preston, Plumstead, Eltham, Portsmouth, Bexley Heath, Wembley, Merton, Southwark, Harrow, Exeter, Battersea, Rotherhithe, Plymouth, Coventry, Christchurch Priory, Bournemouth, Christ Church, St Laurence, Sydney, Portmeirion, Bath; West London Synagogue; Town Hall, Dudley; Civic Centre, Newport, Mon (designs bought by V&A for Newport Mus., 1991); statues: St John the Baptist, St John's Wood Church; Christ, Ely Cathedral; Risen Christ, St Alban's, Holborn; posthumous portrait of Bishop Bell, Bonhoeffer Church, Forest Hill, 1994; acquisition by Tate Gall. of 1939 (painting), 1996; painting bought by Tate Gall., 1998. 80th birthday exhibn by GLC, Holland Park, 1978; 6 one-man exhibns, incl. Berlin 1980; retrospective exhibn 1925–85, Historisches Museum, Frankfurt, 1986; retrospective exhibitions: Frankfurt, 1987, 1988; Brighton Polytechnic, 1988; Pallant Gall., Chichester, and tour, 1995. Much portrait and figure sculpture, 1975–. Dr of Letters, Lambeth, 1985. German Cross of Merit, 1967, Grand Cross of Merit, 1989. *Publications:* Mural Painting, 1946; The Revelation of Saint John, 1946. *Recreations:* music, poetry. *Address:* 30 Wadham Gardens, NW3 3DP. *T:* (0171) 586 1456, (studio) (0171) 286 7420.

Died 18 July 1998.

FELL, Sir Anthony, Kt 1982; *b* 18 May 1914; *s* of Comdr David Mark Fell, RN; *m* 1938, June Warwick; one *s* one *d*. *Educ:* Bedford Grammar Sch.; New Zealand. Contested (C) Brigg, 1948, South Hammersmith, 1949 and 1950. MP (C) Yarmouth, Norfolk, 1951–66 and 1970–83. *Address:* 11 Denny Street, SE11 4UX.

Died 20 March 1998.

FENBY, Eric William, OBE 1962; Professor of Harmony, Royal Academy of Music, 1964–77; *b* 22 April 1906; *s* of late Herbert Henry and Ada Fenby; *m* 1944, Rowena Clara Teresa Marshall; one *s* one *d*. *Educ:* Municipal Sch., Scarborough; privately. Amanuensis to Frederick Delius, 1928–34; Mus. Advr, Boosey & Hawkes, 1936–39; début as composer, BBC Promenade Concerts, 1942. Captain, RAEC Sch. of Educn, Cuerdon Hall, 1942–45. Mus. Dir, N Riding Coll. of Educn, 1948–62. Artistic Dir, Delius Centenary Festival, 1962; Pres. Delius Soc., 1964–; Chm., Composers' Guild of Great Britain, 1968, Mem. Council, 1970. Visiting Prof. of Music and Composer in Residence, Jacksonville Univ., Fla, USA, 1968. Mem. Cttee of Management, Royal Philharmonic Soc., 1972. FRCM 1985; Hon. FTCL 1986; Hon. Member: RAM, 1965; Royal Philharmonic Soc., 1984; Hon. DMus Jacksonville, 1978; Hon. DLitt Warwick, 1978; Hon. DLitt Bradford, 1978. *Publications:* Delius as I Knew Him, 1936, rev. edn 1966, a further rev. edn 1981, packaged with own recordings of all works dictated to him by Delius, known as The Fenby Legacy; Menuhin's House of Music, 1969; Delius, 1971. *Recreations:* walking, chess. *Address:* 1 Raincliffe Court, Stepney Road, Scarborough, N Yorks YO12 5BT. *T:* (01723) 372988. *Club:* Royal Academy of Music. *Died 18 Feb. 1997.*

FERGUSON DAVIE, Sir Antony (Francis), 6th Bt *cr* 1847, of Creedy, Devonshire; *b* 23 March 1952; *s* of Rev. Sir (Arthur) Patrick Ferguson Davie, 5th Bt, TD, and Iris Dawn (*d* 1992), *d* of Captain Michael Francis Buller; *S* father, 1988. *Educ:* Stanbridge Earls Sch.; London University. BA (History). Writer. *Recreations:* art, travel. *Heir: cousin* John Ferguson Davie [*b* 1 May 1906; *m* 1942, Joan Zoe (*d* 1987), *d* of late Raymond Hoole; two *s*]. *Died 19 May 1997.*

FERGUSON DAVIE, Sir John, 7th Bt *cr* 1847, of Creedy, Devonshire; *b* 1 May 1906; *s* of Edward Cruger Ferguson Davie (*d* 1948), 4th *s* of 3rd Bt, and Blanche Keturah (*d* 1959), *d* of William Wyndham Hasler, Aldingbourne; *S* cousin, 1997; *m* 1942, (Joan) Zoë (Charlotte) (*d* 1987), *d* of Raymond Hoole, Vancouver, BC; two *s*. *Educ:* Winchester Coll. Brunner Mond & Co. (later ICI), 1924–64. *Recreations:* golf, bridge, squash. *Heir: s* Michael Ferguson Davie [*b* 10 Jan. 1944; *m* 1968, (Margaret) Jean Macbeth (marr. diss. 1992); one *s* decd]. *Address:* Coutts & Co., 1 Cadogan Place, SW1X 9PX. *Died 8 Jan. 2000.*

FERNANDES, Most Rev. Angelo Innocent; Archbishop of Delhi (RC), 1967–90, then Emeritus; President, International Catholic Education Organisation, 1990–94; *b* 28 July 1913; *s* of late John Ligorio and Evelyn Sabina Fernandes. *Educ:* St Patrick's, Karachi; St Joseph's Seminary, Mangalore; Papal University, Kandy, Ceylon (STL). Ordained priest, 1937; Secretary to Archbishop Roberts of Bombay, 1943–47; Administrator of Holy Name Cathedral, Bombay, 1947–59; Coadjutor Archbishop of Delhi, 1959–67; Sec. Gen., Catholic Bishops' Conf. of India, 1960–72 (Chm., Justice and Peace Commn, 1968–76, 1986–90). Pres., World Conf. of Religion for Peace, 1970–84, then Emeritus. Member: Vatican Secretariat for Non-Believers, 1966–71; Vatican Justice and Peace Acad., 1966–76; Secretariat of Synod of Bishops, 1971–74, 1980–83; Office of Human Develt of Fedn of Asian Bishops' Confs, 1973–78 (Chm., Exec. Cttee for Ecumenism and Inter-Religious Affairs, Asia, 1985–89). Founder Mem., Planetary Citizens, 1972. Hon. DD Vatican, 1959. *Publications:* Apostolic Endeavour, 1962; Religion, Development and Peace, 1971; Religion and the Quality of Life, 1974; Religion and a New World Order, 1976; Towards Peace with Justice, 1981; God's Rule and Man's Role, 1982 (Gandhi Meml Lect.); Summons to Dialogue, 1983; The Christian Way Today, 1987; As you Pray, so you Live, 1992; Building Bridges: the missing dimension in education, 1993; Experience of Dialogue, 1994; Vatican Two Revisited, 1997; Spirituality and Social Justice: pathway to peace, 2000; articles in Clergy Monthly, Vidyajyoti, World Justice, Religion and Society, Social Action, Reality, etc. *Recreations:* music,

especially classical, wide travel on the occasion of numerous meetings in many countries of the world. *Address:* Archbishop's House, Ashok Place, New Delhi 110001, India. *T:* (11) 3343457, 3362058, *Fax:* (11) 3746575. *Died 30 Jan. 2000.*

FERNYHOUGH, Ven. Bernard; Archdeacon of Oakham, 1977–99, then Emeritus; non-residentiary Canon of Peterborough Cathedral, 1974–77 and 1989–99 (Canon Residentiary, 1977–89); Priest-in-charge, Empingham and Exton with Horn and Whitwell, 1995–99; *b* 2 Sept. 1932; *s* of Edward and Edith Fernyhough; *m* 1957, Freda Malkin; one *s* one *d*. *Educ:* Wolstanton Grammar Sch.; Saint David's Coll., Lampeter (BA 1953). Precentor, Trinidad Cathedral, 1955–61; Rector of Stoke Bruerne with Grafton Regis and Alderton, 1961–67; Vicar of Ravensthorpe with East Haddon and Holdenby, 1967–77; Rural Dean: Preston, 1965–67; Haddon, 1968–70; Brixworth, 1971–77. *Address:* 3 Bullfinch Close, Oakham LE15 6BS. *T:* (01572) 756918. *Died 19 Feb. 2000.*

FERRALL, Sir Raymond (Alfred), Kt 1982; CBE 1969; retired; *b* 27 May 1906; *s* of Alfred C. Ferrall and Edith M. Ferrall; *m* 1st, 1931, Lorna (decd), *d* of P. M. Findlay; two *s* two *d*; 2nd, 1988, Sallie Sinclair Barnett. *Educ:* Launceston C of E Grammar Sch. Chairman: Launceston Bank for Savings, 1976–82; Tasmanian Colls of Advanced Educn, 1977–81; Launceston C of E Grammar Sch. Bd, 1956–73; Master Warden, Port of Launceston Authority, 1960–80. Captain, Tasmanian Cricket team, 1934; Vice Captain, Tasmanian Amateur Football team, 1932. Freeman, City of Launceston, 1981. Hon. DLitt Tasmania, 1999. Silver Jubilee Medal, 1977. *Publications:* Partly Personal, 1976; Idylls of the Mayor, 1978; Notable Tasmanians, 1980; The Age of Chiselry, 1981; The Story of the Port of Launceston, 1984; A Proud Heritage, 1985. *Recreations:* writing, print collecting, sailing. *Address:* Elphin House, 3 Olive Street, Launceston, Tas 7250, Australia. *T:* (3) 63317122. *Clubs:* Launceston, Northern, Tamar Yacht (Tasmania). *Died 1 June 2000.*

FERRIS; *see* Grant-Ferris, family name of Baron Harvington.

FEUILLÈRE, Edwige Caroline; Commandeur de la Légion d'Honneur; Commandeur des Arts et des Lettres; French actress; *b* 29 Oct. 1907; *d* of Guy Cunati, architect, and Cécile (*née* Kœnig); *m* 1929, Pierre Feuillère, actor (marr. diss.; he *d* 1945). *Educ:* Lycée de Dijon; Conservatoire National de Paris. *Plays included:* La Dame aux camélias, 1940–42, 1952–53; Sodome et Gomorrhe, 1943; L'Aigle a deux têtes, 1946; Partage de midi, 1948; Pour Lucrèce, La Parisienne, Phèdre, Lucy Crown, Constance, Rodogune, 1964; La Folle de Chaillot, 1965–66; Delicate Balance; Sweet Bird of Youth; Le bâteau pour Lipaïa, 1971; Leocadia, 1984–85; (with Jean Marais) La Maison du Lac, 1986. *Films included:* L'Idiot, 1946; L'Aigle a deux têtes, 1947; Olivia, 1950; Le Blé en herbe, 1952; En cas de malheur, 1958; La vie à deux, 1958; Les amours célèbres, 1961; Le crime ne paye pas, 1962; La chair de l'orchidée, 1975. *Television series:* Cinema, 1988. *Publications:* Les Feux de la Mémoire, 1977; Moi, La Clairon: biographie romancée de Mlle Clairon, 1984. *Address:* c/o Joëlle Bonnet, Agents Associés, 201 rue du Faubourg-Saint-Honoré, 75008 Paris, France. *Died 13 Nov. 1998.*

FFORDE, John Standish; official historian, Bank of England, 1984–92; *b* 16 Nov. 1921; 4th *s* of late Francis Creswell Fforde, Raughlan, Lurgan, Co. Armagh, and Cicely Creswell; *m* 1951, Marya, *d* of late Joseph Retinger; three *s* one *d*. *Educ:* Rossall Sch.; Christ Church, Oxford (1st cl. Hons PPE). Served RAF, 1940–46. Prime Minister's Statistical Branch, 1951–53; Fellow, Nuffield Coll., Oxford, 1953–56; entered Bank of England, 1957;

Dep. Chief, Central Banking Information Dept, 1959–64; Adviser to the Governors, 1964–66; Chief Cashier, 1966–70; Exec. Dir (Home Finance), 1970–82; Advr to the Governors, 1982–84. Chm., Jt Mission Hosp. Equipment Bd Ltd, subseq. Echo Internat. Health Services, 1985–93 (Dir, 1979–85); Director: Mercantile House Hldgs, 1984–87; Halifax BS, 1984–92; CL-Alexanders Laing and Cruickshank, subseq. Credit Lyonnais Capital Markets, 1987–91. *Publications:* The Federal Reserve System, 1945–49, 1953; An International Trade in Managerial Skills, 1957; The Bank of England and Public Policy 1941–1958, 1992. *Recreations:* travel, walking.
Died 10 April 2000.

FIDDES, James Raffan; QC (Scot.) 1965; Sheriff of South Strathclyde, Dumfries and Galloway at Hamilton, 1977–88; *b* 1 Feb. 1919; *er s* of late Sir James Raffan Fiddes, CBE and Constance Mary Dann Gibb; *m* 1st, 1954, Edith Margaret (*d* 1979), 2nd *d* of late Charles E. Lippe, KC; 2nd, 1985, Jiřina (marr. diss. 1991), *d* of late Jan Kuchař, Brno, Czechoslovakia. *Educ:* Aberdeen Grammar Sch.; Glasgow Univ. (MA 1942; LLB 1948); Balliol Coll., Oxford (BA 1944). Advocate, 1948. *Address:* 23 South Learmonth Gardens, Edinburgh EH4 1EZ. *T:* (0131) 332 1431. *Club:* Scottish Arts (Edinburgh).
Died 12 Oct. 1997.

FIENNES, Sir John Saye Wingfield T. W.; *see* Twisleton-Wykeham-Fiennes.

FIGGESS, Sir John (George), KBE 1969 (OBE 1949); CMG 1960; a Director of Christie, Manson and Woods Ltd, 1973–82; *b* 15 Nov. 1909; *e s* of Percival Watts Figgess and Leonora (*née* McCanlis); *m* 1948, Alette, *d* of Dr P. J. A. Idenburg, The Hague; two *d. Educ:* Whitgift Sch. In business in Japan, 1933–38; commissioned, Intelligence Corps, 1939; Staff Coll., 1941; served with Intelligence Corps, India/Burma Theatre, 1942–45; attached to UK Liaison Mission, Japan, 1945; Asst Mil. Adviser (Lt-Col), UK Liaison Mission, Tokyo, 1947–52; GSO1, War Office (MI Directorate), 1953–56; Military Attaché, Tokyo, 1956–61; Information Counsellor, Tokyo, 1961–68; Comr Gen. for Britain, World Exposition, Osaka, Japan, 1968–70. Mem., Expert Adv. Council, Percival David Foundn of Chinese Art, 1984–90; Pres., Oriental Ceramic Soc., 1987–90. Gold and Silver Star, Order of the Sacred Treasure, Japan, 1986. *Publications:* (with Fujio Koyama) Two Thousand Years of Oriental Ceramics, 1960; The Heritage of Japanese Ceramics, 1973; contrib. to Oriental Art, Far Eastern Ceramic Bulletin, etc. *Address:* The Manor House, Burghfield, Berks RG30 3TG. *Club:* Army and Navy.
Died 20 March 1997.

FILON, Sidney Philip Lawrence, TD; Librarian and Secretary to the Trustees, National Central Library, 1958–71, retired; *b* 20 Sept. 1905; *s* of late Prof. L. N. G. Filon, FRS and Anne Godet; *m* 1st, 1939, Doris Schelling; one *d;* 2nd, 1959, Liselotte Florstedt; one *d. Educ:* Whitgift Sch.; University Coll., London (BSc). Sch. of Librarianship, University Coll., London, 1929–30; FLA 1931. National Central Library, 1930–39; Military service, 1939–45; Dep. Librarian, National Central Library, 1946–58. Mem., Library Advisory Council (England), 1966–71. *Publication:* The National Central Library: an experiment in library cooperation, 1977. *Address:* 107 Littleheath Road, Selsdon, Surrey CR2 7SL.
Died 19 Oct. 1996.

FINGERHUT, John Hyman; consultant to the pharmaceutical and allied industries; *b* 2 Nov. 1910; *s* of late Abraham Fingerhut and Emily (*née* Rowe); *m* 1950, Beatrice Leigh, FCA; two *s* two *d. Educ:* Manchester Grammar Sch.; Manchester Univ. FBOA 1931; Hon. FRPharmS (Hon. FPS 1971). Pharmaceutical Chemist,

1932. Served with RAC and Infantry, France, Mauritius and E Africa, 1942–46; commnd Royal Pioneer Corps, transf. to Queen's Royal Regt (seconded King's African Rifles); demobilised as Captain. Merck Sharp & Dohme Ltd: medical rep., 1937–42; Sales Man., 1946; Dep. Man. Dir, 1957; Man. Dir, 1963; Chm., 1967–72; Consultant, 1972–77; Regional Dir, Merck Sharp & Dohme International, 1967–72; Chm., Thomas Morson & Son Ltd, 1967–72. Mem., Assoc. of British Pharm. Industry's Working Party on Resale Price Maintenance, 1970. Associate: Bracken Kelner and Associates Ltd, 1976; Key Pharmaceutical Appointments, 1978–88. Admin. Staff Coll., Henley, 1960. Mem., New Southgate Group Hosp. Management Cttee, 1972–74. Associate Mem., Faculty of Homœopathy, 1974. *Recreations:* music, reading, gardening, washing up. *Address:* 76 Green Lane, Edgware, Mddx HA8 7QA. *T:* (0181) 958 6163.
Died 29 Sept. 1996.

FINNEY, Jarlath John; His Honour Judge Finney; a Circuit Judge, since 1986; *b* Hale, Cheshire, 1 July 1930; *s* of late Victor Harold Finney, MA, sometime MP for Hexham, and Aileen Rose Finney (*née* Gallagher); *m* 1957, Daisy Emöke, *y d* of late Dr Matyas Veszy, formerly of Budapest; two *s* two *d. Educ:* Wimbledon College; Gray's Inn. Served, 2nd Lieut, 8th Royal Tank Regt, 1953–55 (Lieut 1955). Called to Bar, Gray's Inn, 1953; Member, SE Circuit, 1955–86; Member, Panel of Counsel for HM Customs and Excise before VAT Tribunals, 1973–86; a Recorder of the Crown Court, 1980–86. FLS 1990. *Publications:* Gaming, Lotteries, Fundraising and the Law, 1982; (jtly) Sales Promotion Law, 1986; articles. *Recreations:* wild flowers, books, walking in the country, pottering about looking things up. *Address:* The Crown Court, Lordship Lane, Wood Green, N22 5LF. *T:* (020) 8881 1400. *Club:* Wig and Pen.
Died 27 Aug. 1999.

FINSBERG, Baron *cr* 1992 (Life Peer), of Hampstead in the London Borough of Camden; **Geoffrey Finsberg,** Kt 1984; MBE 1959; JP; Deputy Chairman, Commission for New Towns, since 1992; *b* 13 June 1926; *o s* of late Montefiore Finsberg, MC, and May Finsberg (*née* Grossman); *m* 1st, 1969, Pamela Benbow Hill (*d* 1989); 2nd, 1990, (Yvonne) Elizabeth Sarch (*née* Wright). *Educ:* City of London Sch. National Chm., Young Conservatives, 1954–57; Mem., Exec. Cttee, Nat. Union of Cons. and Unionist Assocs, 1953–79 (Mem. Exec. Cttee, 1949–79, Pres., 1986–89, Gtr London Area); Chm., Gtr London Area Cons. Local Govt Cttee, 1972–75; a Vice-Chm., Conservative Party Organisation, 1975–79 and 1983–87. Borough Councillor: Hampstead, 1949–65; Camden, 1964–74 (Leader, 1968–70). MP (C) Hampstead, 1970–83, Hampstead and Highgate, 1983–92. Opposition spokesman on Greater London, 1974–79; Parly Under Sec. of State, DoE, 1979–81, DHSS, 1981–83. Mem. Exec., 1922 Cttee, 1974–75; Member, Select Cttee on Expenditure, 1970–79; Mem., Parly Assembly of Council of Europe (Pres., 1991–92), and of WEU, 1983–, delegn leader, 1987–. Controller of Personnel and Chief Industrial Relations Adviser, Great Universal Stores, 1968–79; Dep. Chm., South East Reg. Bd, TSB, 1986–89 (Mem., 1983–86). Vice-Pres., Assoc. of Municipal Corporations, 1971–74 (Dep. Chm., 1969–71); Member: Post Office Users Nat. Council, 1970–77; Council, CBI, 1968–79 (Chm., Post Office Panel). Jt Nat. Hon. Sec., CCJ, 1995– (Jt Nat. Treas., 1993–95). FIPD (FIPM 1975). Patron, Maccabi Assoc. of GB; Trustee, Marie Curie Cancer Foundn, 1993–. Governor, UCS. JP Inner London, 1962. Order of Merit, (Austria), 1989; Comdr, Order of Isabella the Catholic (Spain), 1990. *Recreations:* bridge, reading. *Address:* 18 Fairfax Road, NW6 4HA. *T:* (0171) 586 9979.
Died 7 Oct. 1996.

FISH, Sir Hugh, Kt 1989; CBE 1984 (OBE 1971); Chairman, National Environment Research Council, 1984–88 (Member, 1976–84); independent consultant on environmental management; *b* 6 Jan. 1923; *s* of Leonard Mark and Millicent Fish; *m* 1943, Nancy, *o d* of William and Louise Asquith; one *s* one *d* (and one *s* decd). *Educ:* Rothwell Grammar Sch.; Leeds Univ. (BSc). War Service, 1942–46, RNVR (Lieut). Chemist, W Riding Rivers Bd, 1949–52; Pollution and Fisheries Inspector, Essex River Bd, 1952–65; River Conservator, Essex River Authy, 1965–69; Chief Purification Officer, Thames Conservancy, 1969–74; Thames Water Authority: Dir of Scientific Services, 1974–78; Chief Exec., 1978–84; Mem., 1983–85. Chm., Water Engineering Ltd, 1988–91. Member: Central Adv. Water Cttee, 1970–72; OGDEN Cttee on Water Authority Management and Structure, 1973; Management Bd, BNSC, 1984–88; Nat. Rivers Authority, 1989–91 (Mem. Adv. Cttee, 1988–89). Pres., Inst. of Fisheries Management, 1987–. Member Council: IWES, 1975–85 (Pres. 1984); Freshwater Biol Assoc., 1972–74. Vis. Prof., Univ. of Hertfordshire, 1994–. FRSC, FIWEM. *Publications:* Principles of Water Quality Management, 1973; contribs to various jls on natural science of water. *Recreations:* gardening, water sports, inventions, theatre. *Address:* Red Roofs, Shefford Woodlands, Hungerford, Berks RG17 7AJ. *T:* (01488) 648369. *Died 27 May 1999.*

FISHER, Doris Gwenllian; *b* 22 March 1907; *d* of Gathorne John Fisher, Pontypool. *Educ:* Farringtons, Chislehurst; Royal Holloway Coll., University of London (BA Hons English 1929, French 1931), Sorbonne. Senior English Mistress, Maidenhead County Grammar Sch., 1934–39; Second Mistress, Dover County Grammar Sch., 1945; Headmistress of Farringtons, Chislehurst, Kent, 1946–57, retired; Lecturer at Westminster Training Coll, 1957–59; Lecturer at Avery Hill Training Coll., 1959–62. *Address:* 9 The Ridgeway, Newport, Gwent NP9 5AF *Died 17 June 1998.*

FISHER, Francis George Robson, MA; Deputy Secretary, Headmasters' Conference and Secondary Heads' Association, 1982–86; *b* 9 April 1921; *s* of late John Henry Fisher and Hannah Clayton Fisher; *m* 1965, Sheila Vernon Dunsire, *o d* of late D. Dunsire and Mrs H. E. Butt; one *s. Educ:* Liverpool Coll. (Schol.); Worcester Coll., Oxford (Classical Exhibitioner; MA). Served War of 1939–45: Capt. in Ayrshire Yeomanry, North Africa and Italy, 1942–45. Kingswood Sch., Bath, 1948–59, Housemaster and Sen. English Master, 1950–59; Schoolmaster Fellow, Balliol Coll., Oxford, 1958; Headmaster, Bryanston Sch., 1959–74; Chief Master, King Edward's Sch., Birmingham, and Head Master, Schs of King Edward VI in Birmingham, 1974–82. Chairman: HMC Direct Grant Sub-Cttee, 1979–80; HMC Assisted Places Sub-Cttee, 1981. Life Governor, Liverpool Coll., 1969; Governor: Harrow Sch., 1982–87; Bromsgrove Sch., 1985–95; Kelly Coll., Tavistock, 1985–; Trustee, Robert Owen Foundn, 1992– (Vice-Chm. Trustees, 1994; Chm. Trustees, 1995–97). *Recreations:* music, reading, sailing. *Address:* Craig Cottage, Lower Street, Dittisham, S Devon TQ6 0HY. *T:* (01803) 722309. *Club:* East India, Devonshire, Sports and Public Schools. *Died 26 Jan. 2000.*

FISHER, James Neil; Partner, Theodore Goddard & Co., Solicitors, 1951–83, Senior Partner, 1980–83; *b* 27 May 1917; *s* of Henry John Fisher and Ethel Marie Fisher; *m* 1953, Elizabeth Mary Preston, *d* of late Rt Rev. Arthur Llewelyn Preston, Bishop Suffragan of Woolwich, and Mrs Nancy Preston; one *s* two *d. Educ:* Harrow Sch.; Balliol Coll., Oxford (MA). Served War, Royal Signals, 1940–46 (Major 1945; despatches). Admitted solicitor, 1949. Hon. Organizer, Legal Advice Centre, Toynbee

Hall, 1983–93. Chm., Rochester DAC for the Care of Churches, 1984–90. *Recreations:* the piano, walking, sight-seeing. *Address:* Ridge Lea, Oak Avenue, Sevenoaks, Kent TN13 1PR. *Died 8 Jan. 1997.*

FISHER, John Mortimer, CMG 1962; HM Diplomatic Service, retired; *b* 20 May 1915; *yr s* of late Capt. Mortimer Fisher (W Yorks Regt) and Mrs M. S. Fisher (*née* Bailey); *m* 1949, Helen Bridget Emily Caillard (*d* 1993); two *s. Educ:* Wellington; Trinity Coll., Cambridge. Entered Consular (subseq. Diplomatic) Service, 1937; Probationer Vice-Consul, Bangkok, 1938; served at Casablanca, 1942, Naples, 1944; 1st Sec. in Foreign Office, 1946, Mexico City, 1949; Detroit, Mich, USA, 1952; Counsellor in charge of British Information Services, Bonn, 1955; an Inspector in HM Foreign Service, 1959; Counsellor and Consul-Gen. at Bangkok, 1962; Consul-General, Düsseldorf, 1966–70; part-time Course Dir (Eur. Trng), Civil Service Coll., 1971–85. *Address:* 36 Franklin Place, Chichester, W Sussex PO19 1BL. *T:* (01243) 531832. *Died 11 Sept. 1999.*

FISHER, Sir Nigel (Thomas Loveridge), Kt 1974; MC 1945; MA (Cambridge); *b* 14 July 1913; *s* of late Comdr Sir Thomas Fisher, KBE, Royal Navy and Lady Shakespeare; step *s* of Rt Hon. Sir Geoffrey Shakespeare, 1st Bt; *m* 1st, 1935, Lady Gloria Vaughan (marr. diss. 1952; she *m* 2nd, Ronald Philip Flower, OBE), *e d* of 7th Earl of Lisburne; one *s* one *d*; 2nd, 1956, Patricia (*d* 1995), *o d* of late Lieut-Col Sir Walter Smiles, CIE, DSO, DL, MP. *Educ:* Eton; Trinity Coll., Cambridge. Served War of 1939–45; volunteered Welsh Guards and commissioned as 2nd Lieut 1939; Hook of Holland, Boulogne, 1940 (despatches); Capt., 1940, Major, 1944; N West Europe, 1945 (wounded, MC). Mem., National Executive Cttee of Conservative Party, 1945–47 and 1973–83. Contested Chislehurst (N Kent), 1945. MP (C): Herts, Hitchin, 1950–55; Surbiton, 1955–74; Kingston-upon-Thames, Surbiton, 1974–83. Parly Private Sec. to Minister of Food, 1951–54, to Home Sec., 1954–57; Parly Under-Sec. of State for the Colonies, July 1962–Oct. 1963; Parly Under-Sec. of State for Commonwealth Relations and for the Colonies, 1963–64; Opposition Spokesman for Commonwealth Affairs, 1964–66. Mem. British Parly Delegn to Sweden, 1950, W Indies 1955, Malta 1966, Canada 1966, Uganda 1967, special mission to St Kitts, Anguilla, 1967. Treasurer, CPA, 1966–68 (Vice-Chm., 1975–76; Treasurer, 1977–79, Dep. Chm., 1979–83, UK Branch). Mem. Exec., 1922 Cttee, 1960–62, 1969–83; Pres., British Caribbean Assoc. Freedom of Kingston-upon-Thames, 1983. *Publications:* Iain Macleod, 1973; The Tory Leaders, 1977; Harold Macmillan, 1982. *Recreation:* reading. *Address:* 45 Exeter House, Putney Heath, SW15 3SX. *Clubs:* Boodle's, MCC. *Died 9 Oct. 1996.*

FISHER, Sylvia Gwendoline Victoria, AM 1994; formerly Principal Soprano, Royal Opera House, London; *b* 18 April 1910; *d* of John Fisher and Margaret Fisher (*née* Frawley); *m* 1954, Ubaldo Gardini (marr. diss.). *Educ:* St Joseph's Coll., Kilmore, Australia; Conservatorium of Music, Melbourne. Won "Sun" Aria Competition, Melbourne, 1936; International Celebrity Concert in Australia, 1947; tour of Australia, 1955. Operatic Debut in Cadmus and Hermione, 1932; Covent Garden Debut in Fidelio (Leonora), 1948; appeared in: Rome (Sieglinde), 1952; Cagliari (Isolde), 1954; Bologna (Gutrune), 1955; Covent Garden (Brunnhilde), 1956; Frankfurt Opera House (in Der Rosenkavalier), 1957, etc. *Recreations:* gardening, rare books on singing. *Address:* 25 Tintern Avenue, Toorak, Vic 3142, Australia. *Died 25 Aug. 1996.*

FitzGERALD, Brig. Gerald Loftus, CBE 1956; DSO 1945; *b* 5 May 1907; *s* of late Col D. C. V. FitzGerald, MC,

Nairobi Kenya; *m* 1937, Mary Stuart, *d* of late Charles E. Mills, Holbrook, Suffolk; one *s* one *d*. *Educ:* Wellington Coll.; Royal Military Academy, Woolwich. Commissioned 2nd Lieut RA, 1926; Regimental duty UK and overseas, 1926–39; staff and regimental duty in UK and NW Europe during War of 1939–45; British Mil. Mission to Greece, 1946–48; Chief Instructor, Officer Cadet Sch., 1949–50; British Joint Services Mission, Washington, USA, 1951–52; Comdr Trng Bde, RA, 1953–55; Dep. Dir, War Office, 1956–58; retired pay, 1959. OStJ 1982. Order of Leopold (with Palm), Belgium, 1944; Croix de Guerre (with Palm), 1944. *Recreations:* field sports, travel. *Club:* Army and Navy.
Died 23 Jan. 1999.

FITZGERALD, Penelope Mary, (Mrs Desmond Fitzgerald); writer; *b* 17 Dec. 1916; *d* of Edmund George Valpy Knox (formerly Editor of Punch), and Christina (*née* Hicks); *m* 1941, Desmond Fitzgerald, MC; one *s* two *d*. *Educ:* Wycombe Abbey; Somerville Coll., Oxford (BA). *Publications:* Edward Burne-Jones, 1975; The Knox Brothers, 1977; Charlotte Mew and her Friends, 1984 (Rose Mary Crawshay Prize, 1985); *fiction:* The Golden Child, 1977; The Bookshop, 1978; Offshore, 1979 (Booker Prize); Human Voices, 1980; At Freddie's, 1982; (ed) William Morris's unpublished Novel on Blue Paper, 1982; Innocence, 1986; The Beginning of Spring, 1988; The Gate of Angels, 1990; The Blue Flower, 1995 (US Book Critics' Circle Award, 1997); *posthumous publication:* The Means of Escape (short stories), 2000. *Recreations:* listening, talking, watching grandchildren. *Address:* c/o Harper Collins, 77 Fulham Palace Road, W6 8JB.
Died 28 April 2000.

FITZHERBERT-BROCKHOLES, Michael John, OBE 1989; JP; Vice Lord-Lieutenant of Lancashire, 1977–95; Constable of Lancaster Castle, since 1995; *b* 12 June 1920; *s* of John William Fitzherbert-Brockholes and Hon. Eileen Agnes, *d* of 4th Baron De Freyne; *m* 1950, Mary Edith Moore; four *s*. *Educ:* The Oratory Sch.; New Coll., Oxford. Scots Guards, 1940–46. Mem., Lancs CC, 1968–89; Chm., Educn Cttee, 1977–81. JP 1960, DL 1975, Lancs. KSG 1978. *Recreation:* gardening. *Address:* Claughton Hall, Garstang, near Preston, Lancs PR3 0PN. *T:* (01995) 640286.
Died 6 Jan. 1998.

FitzPATRICK, Air Cdre David Beatty, CB 1970; OBE 1953; AFC 1949 and Bar, 1958; *b* 31 Jan. 1920; *s* of late Comdr D. T. FitzPatrick, RN and Beatrice Anne Ward; *m* 1941, Kathleen Mary Miles (decd); one *d*. *Educ:* Kenilworth Coll., Exeter; Midhurst. Commnd RAF, 1938; served War of 1939–45, Atlantic, Mediterranean and Far East theatres; comd No 209 Sqdn (Far East), 1944; (GD Pilot) Sqdn flying duty, 1945–52; cfs, pfc and Guided Weapons Specialist, RAF Henlow, 1952–57; Guided Weapons (Trials) Project Officer, Min. of Supply, 1957–59; Base Comdr Christmas Island, 1959–60 (British Nuclear Trials); NATO Def. Coll., and jssc, 1960–61; Dep. Dir (Ops) Air Staff, 1961–64; comd RAF Akrotiri and Nicosia, 1964–66; Dir of (Q) RAF, MoD, 1966–69; attached NBPI for special duty, 1969; Dir, Guided Weapons (Trials and Ranges), Min. of Technology, 1969–72; Dir, Guided Weapons Trials, MoD (PE), 1972–74; retd RAF, 1975; Head, teaching dept of indep. sch., 1975–85, retd. FIMgt (FBIM 1970); FRMetS 1984; MRAeS 1971. *Recreations:* swimming (Life Vice-Pres., Royal Air Force Swimming Assoc.), deep-sea fishing, cricket. *Address:* Whistledown, 38 Courts Mount Road, Haslemere, Surrey GU27 2PP. *T:* (01428) 644589.
Died 19 April 1997.

FLEET, Kenneth George; journalist; *b* 12 Sept. 1929; *s* of late Fred Major Fleet and Elizabeth Doris Fleet; *m* 1953, (Alice) Brenda, *d* of late Captain H. R. Wilkinson, RD, RNR and Mrs Kathleen Mary Wilkinson; three *s* one *d*.

Educ: Calday Grange Grammar Sch., Cheshire; LSE (BScEcons). Jl of Commerce, Liverpool, 1950–52; Sunday Times, 1955–56; Dep. City Editor, Birmingham Post, 1956–58; Dep. Financial Editor, Guardian, 1958–63; Dep. City Editor, Daily Telegraph, 1963; City Editor, Sunday Telegraph, 1963–66; City Editor, Daily Telegraph, 1966–77; Editor, Business News, Sunday Times, 1977–78; City Editor, Sunday Express, 1978–82; City Editor-in-Chief, Express Newspapers plc, 1982–83; Exec. Ed. (Finance and Industry), The Times, 1983–87. Dir, TVS Entertainment plc, 1990–93. Dir, Young Vic, 1976–83; Chm., Chichester Fest. Theatre, 1985–93 (Dir, 1984–97). Wincott Award, 1974. *Publication:* The Influence of the Financial Press, 1983. *Recreations:* theatre, books, sport. *Address:* The Senate House, Canonbury Lane, N1 2AS. *T:* (020) 7226 7950. *Clubs:* MCC, Lord's Taverners; Piltdown Golf.
Died 21 Aug. 2000.

FLETCHER, Leslie; General Manager (Chief Executive Officer), Williams Deacon's Bank Ltd, 1964–70, Director, 1966–70, retired; *b* 30 Jan. 1906; *s* of late Edward Henry and Edith Howard Fletcher; *m* 1934, Helen, *d* of Frank Turton; one *s* one *d*. *Educ:* City Grammar Sch., Chester; Manchester Univ. (BA Com). Entered Williams Deacon's Bank Ltd, 1922; Asst Gen. Man., 1957; Dep. Gen. Man., 1961. Fellow and Mem. Council, Inst. of Bankers. *Recreations:* lawn tennis, golf. *Address:* Axon View, 13 Honey Lane, Burley, near Ringwood, Hants BH24 4EN. *T:* (01425) 403723.
Died 12 Dec. 1998.

FLETCHER, Paul Thomas, CBE 1959; FEng; Deputy President, British Standards Institution, 1982–89 (Chairman, 1979–82); Consulting Engineer: NNC Ltd, since 1977; BGE Co., Tokyo, since 1986; *b* 30 Sept. 1912; *s* of Stephen Baldwin Fletcher and Jessie Carrie; *m* 1941, Mary Elizabeth King; three *s*. *Educ:* Nicholson Inst., Stornaway, Isle of Lewis; Maidstone Grammar Sch.; Medway Techn. Coll. BSc(Eng); FEng 1978; FICE, FIMechE (Hon. FIMechE 1989), FIEE. Served 3–year apprenticeship with E. A. Gardner & Sons Ltd, Maidstone, remaining for 7 years; joined Min. of Works, 1939, initially in Test Br. of Engrg Div., later with responsibility for variety of engrg services in public bldgs and Govt factories and for plant and equipment for Govt civilian and service res. estabts; Chief Mech. and Elec. Engr, 1951; on formation of UKAEA in 1954, became Dep. Dir of Engrg in Industrial Gp, later Engrg Dir and Dep. Man. Dir; Dir, United Power Co., 1961; Man. Dir, GEC (Process Engrg) Ltd, 1965; Man. Dir, 1971–76, Dep. Chm., 1976–84, Atomic Power Constructions Ltd. Chm., Pressure Vessels Quality Assurance Bd, 1977–84. President: IMechE, 1975–76; ITEME, 1979–81, 1985–88; IMechIE, 1994–96. *Publications:* papers to IMechE. *Recreations:* photography, motoring. *Address:* 26 Foxgrove Avenue, Beckenham, Kent BR3 5BA. *T:* (0181) 650 5563.
Died 27 July 1998.

FLETCHER, Air Chief Marshal Sir Peter Carteret, KCB 1968 (CB 1965); OBE 1945; DFC 1943; AFC 1952; FRAeS; aerospace consultant, since 1983; Director, Corporate Strategy and Planning, British Aerospace, 1977–82, retired; Director, Airbus Industry Supervisory Board, 1979–82; *b* 7 Oct. 1916; *s* of F. T. W. Fletcher, Oxford (sometime tobacco farmer, Southern Rhodesia); and Dora Clulee, New Zealand; *m* 1940, Marjorie Isobel Kotze; two *d*. *Educ:* St George's Coll., Southern Rhodesia; Rhodes Univ., S Africa. Joined Southern Rhodesian Law Dept, 1937. Served War of 1939–45: Southern Rhodesia Air Force, 1939; transf. to RAF, 1941; commanded 135 and 258 Fighter Sqdns and RAF Station Belvedere; Directing Staffs at: RAF Staff Coll., 1945–46; Jt Services Staff Coll., 1946–48; Imp. Defence Coll., 1956–58; Mem. Jt Planning Staff, 1951–53; comdg RAF Abingdon, 1958–60; Dep. Dir Jt Planning Staff, 1960–61; Dir of Opl

Requirements (B), Air Min., 1961–63; Asst Chief of Air Staff (Policy and Plans), 1964–66; AOC, No 38 Group, Transport Command, 1966–67; VCAS, 1967–70; Controller of Aircraft, Min. of Aviation Supply (formerly Min. of Technology), 1970–71; Air Systems Controller, Defence Procurement Executive, MoD, 1971–73; Dir, Hawker Siddeley Aviation Ltd, 1974–77. FRAeS 1986. *Recreations:* books, travel. *Address:* 85A Campden Hill Court, Holland Street, Kensington, W8 7HW. *T:* (020) 7937 1982. *Died 2 Jan. 1999.*

FLOWER, Desmond John Newman, MC 1944; Chairman, Cassell & Co. Ltd, 1958–71; President, Cassell Australia Ltd, 1965–71; Editorial Consultant, Sheldon Press, 1973–85; *b* London, 25 Aug. 1907; *o s* of late Sir Newman Flower and 1st wife, Evelyne, *e d* of Thomas Readwin, Wells, Norfolk; *m* 1st, 1931, Margaret Cameron Coss (marr. diss. 1952); one *s*; 2nd, 1952, Anne Elizabeth Smith (marr. diss. 1972); one *s* two *d*; 3rd, 1987, Sophie Rombeyko. *Educ:* Lancing; King's Coll., Cambridge. Entered Cassell & Co. 1930; Dir, 1931; Literary Dir, 1938; Dep.-Chm., 1952; Chm. Cassell & Co. (Holdings) Ltd, 1958–70. Served War of 1939–45 (despatches, MC); commissioned 1941, 5 Bn Argyll and Sutherland Highlanders, later 91 (A and SH) A/T Regt. Chm., the Folio Society, 1960–71; Liveryman, Stationers' Co. Président des Comités d'Alliance Française en Grande Bretagne, 1963–72. Officier de la Légion d'Honneur, 1972 (Chevalier 1950). DLitt *(hc)* University of Caen, 1957. *Publications:* (founder and editor with A. J. A. Symons) Book Collector's quarterly, 1930–34; (ed) Complete Poetical Works of Ernest Christopher Dowson, 1934; (compiled with Francis Meynell and A. J. A. Symons) The Nonesuch Century, 1936; (with A. N. L. Munby) English Poetical Autographs, 1938; The Pursuit of Poetry, 1939; Voltaire's England, 1950; History of 5 Battalion Argyll and Sutherland Highlanders, 1950; (with James Reeves) The War, 1939–1945, 1960; (with Henry Maas) The Letters of Ernest Dowson, 1967; New Letters of Ernest Dowson, 1984; Fellows in Foolscap (memoirs), 1991; numerous translations, inc. Saint Simon, Voltaire, Maupassant, Morand. *Recreation:* book collecting. *Address:* 26 Grovedale Road, N19 3EQ. *T:* (0171) 281 0080. *Clubs:* Roxburghe; Royal and Ancient (St Andrews). *Died 7 Jan. 1997.*

FLOYD, John Anthony; Chairman: Christie Manson & Woods Ltd, 1974–85; Christie's International Ltd, 1976–88; *b* 12 May 1923; *s* of Lt-Col Arthur Bowen Floyd, DSO, OBE and Iris Clare, *d* of D. Turner Belding, East Dereham, Norfolk, and *widow* of Capt. A. Stewart Ritchie, MC, Black Watch; *m* 1948, Margaret Louise Rosselli; two *d*. *Educ:* Eton. Served King's Royal Rifle Corps, 1941–46. Joined Christie's, 1947; Partner, 1954. *Address:* Ecchinswell House, Newbury, Berks RG15 8AU. *Clubs:* Boodle's, White's, MCC. *Died 20 Feb. 1998.*

FLOYER, Prof. Michael Antony, MD; FRCP; Professor of Medicine, The London Hospital Medical College, University of London, 1974–86, then Professor Emeritus; Consulting Physician, The Royal London Hospital, since 1986; *b* 28 April 1920; *s* of Comdr William Antony Floyer, RN and Alice Rosalie Floyer (*née* Whitehead); *m* 1946, Lily Louise Frances Burns; two *s* one *d*. *Educ:* Sherborne Sch.; Trinity Hall, Cambridge (MA; MB, BChir; MD 1952); The London Hosp. Med. Coll. FRCP 1963. RAF Medical Service, Sqdn Leader, RAF Hosps, Karachi and Cawnpore, 1946–48. The London Hospital: House Officer, 1944–45; Registrar in Medicine, 1945–46; Hon. Registrar, 1948–51; Hon. Sen. Registrar, 1951–58; Hon. Consultant Physician, 1958–86; Consultant i/c Emergency and Accident Dept, 1975–86; The London Hospital Medical College: Lectr in Medicine, 1948–51;

Sen. Lectr, 1951–67; Asst Dir, Medical Unit, 1953–86; Reader in Medicine, 1967–74; Acting Dean, 1982–83; Dean, 1983–86; Fellow, 1988; seconded to Nairobi Univ., Kenya, as Prof. of Medicine, 1973–75. Oliver-Sharpey Prize, RCP, 1980. *Publications:* chapters in books and papers in scientific jls on the aetiology and mechanism of hypertension and on the physiology of the interstitial fluid space. *Recreations:* wild places and wild things. *Address:* Flat 40, Free Trade Wharf, 340 The Highway, E1 9ET. *T:* (020) 7702 7577; c/o The London Hospital Medical College, E1 2AD. *T:* (020) 7377 7602. *Died 17 Feb. 2000.*

FLUTE, Prof. Peter Thomas, TD 1970; MD; FRCP, FRCPath; Postgraduate Medical Dean, South West Thames Regional Health Authority and Assistant Director, British Postgraduate Medical Federation, 1985–93; *b* 12 Aug. 1928; *s* of Rev. Richard Prickett Flute and Katie Flute (*née* Click); *m* 1951, Ann Elizabeth Harbroe, *d* of late G. John Wright; two *s* two *d*. *Educ:* Southend High Sch.; King's College London; KCH Med. Sch. (Ware Prize; MB, BS; MD 1960). MRCS; FRCPath 1974; FRCP 1979. KCH, 1951–52; RAMC, 1952–54; Demonstrator in Pathology, KCH Med. Sch., 1955–56; Elmore Res. Student, Dept of Medicine, Cambridge, 1957–58; Lectr, 1958–62, Sen. Lectr, 1962–68, Reader, 1968–72, Dept of Haematology, KCH Med. Sch.; Hon. Consultant in Haematology, KCH, 1966–72; Prof. of Haematology, St George's Hosp. Med. Sch. and Hon. Consultant, St George's Hosp., 1972–85. RAMC T&AVR: Pathologist, 24 Gen. Hosp., 1955–58, 308 Gen. Hosp., 1958–67; OC 380 Blood Supply Unit, 1967–73, Hon. Col, 1977–82; Hon. Consultant to the Army in Haematology, 1977–87. Mem., Mid-Downs DHA, 1984–90. Royal College of Pathologists: Mem. Council, 1981–84; Exec. Cttee, 1982–84; SW Thames Regional Adviser in Postgraduate Educn, 1975–85; Royal College of Physicians: Mem., Cttee of Haematology, 1981–87; Jt Cttee on Higher Med. Training; Mem., Specialist Adv. Cttee on Haematology, 1977–83; Sec., 1978–83; British Society for Haematology. Mem., 1960–; Cttee, 1975–87; Associate Sec., 1977–81; Sec., 1981–83; Pres., 1985–86; Section of Pathology, Royal Society of Medicine: Mem. Council, 1964–68; Sec., 1972–76; Pres., 1978. Mem., Editorial Bd, British Jl of Haematology, 1971–81. *Publications:* chapters and contribs on thrombosis and blood diseases to med. and sci. jls. *Recreations:* mountain walking, reading. *Address:* 17 Church Lane, East Grinstead, West Sussex RH19 3AZ. *T:* (01342) 326288. *Died 19 Jan. 1999.*

FOLEY, Rt Rev. Brian Charles; Bishop of Lancaster, (RC), 1962–85; *b* Ilford, 25 May 1910. *Educ:* St Cuthbert's Coll., Ushaw; English College and Gregorian Univ., Rome (PhL 1934, STL 1938). Priest, 1937; Assistant Priest, Shoeburyness; subseq. Assistant Priest, Romford; Parish Priest, Holy Redeemer, Harold Hill, and Holy Cross, Harlow; Canon of Brentwood Diocese, 1959. President: Catholic Record Society, 1964–80; Catholic Archive Soc., 1979–. Hon. DLitt Lancaster, 1993. *Publications:* Some People of the Penal Times, 1991; Some Other People of the Penal Tinal Times, 1992; The Story of the Jubilee Years 1300–1975, 1998. *Address:* Nazareth House, Ashton Road, Lancaster LA1 5AQ. *T:* (01524) 382748. *Died 23 Dec. 1999.*

FOOT, Baron *cr* 1967 (Life Peer), of Buckland Monachorum, co. Devon; **John Mackintosh Foot;** Chairman, United Kingdom Immigrants Advisory Service, 1970–78 (President, 1978–84); *b* 17 Feb. 1909; 3rd *s* of late Rt Hon. Isaac Foot, PC and Eva Mackintosh; *m* 1936, Anne, *d* of Dr Clifford Bailey Farr, Bryn Mawr, Pa; one *s* one *d*. *Educ:* Forres Sch., Swanage; Bembridge Sch., IoW; Balliol Coll., Oxford (BA (2nd cl. hons Jurisprudence), 1931). Pres., Oxford Union, 1931; Pres., OU Liberal Club,

1931. Admitted Solicitor, 1934. Served in Army, 1939–45 (Hon. Major); jsc 1944. Partner, Foot & Bowden, solicitors, Plymouth, 1934–95 (Sen. Partner, 1960–95). Contested (L): Basingstoke, 1934 and 1935; Bodmin, 1945 and 1950. Member: Dartmoor National Park Cttee, 1963–74; Commn on the Constitution, 1969–73; President: Dartmoor Preservation Assoc., 1976–94; Commons, Open Spaces and Footpaths Preservation Soc., 1976–82. Chm. Council, Justice, 1984–89. *Recreations:* chess, crosswords, defending Dartmoor. *Address:* Yew Tree, Crapstone, Yelverton, Devon PL20 7PJ. *T:* (01822) 853417.
Died 11 Oct. 1999.

FOOTMAN, Charles Worthington Fowden, CMG 1952; *b* 3 Sept. 1905; *s* of Rev. William Llewellyn and Mary Elizabeth Footman; *m* 1947, Joyce Marcelle Law; one *s* two *d. Educ:* Rossall Sch.; Keble Coll., Oxford. Colonial Administrative Service, Zanzibar, 1930; seconded to East African Governors' Conference, 1942; seconded to Colonial Office, 1943–46; Financial Sec., Nyasaland, 1947; Chief Sec., Nyasaland, 1951–60; retired from HM Overseas Civil Service, 1960; Chm., Public Service Commissions, Tanganyika and Zanzibar, 1960–61; Commonwealth Relations Office, 1962–64; Min. of Overseas Development, 1964–70.
Died 27 March 1996.

FORBES, Ian, QPM 1966; Deputy Assistant Commissioner, Metropolitan Police and National Co-ordinator, Regional Crime Squads (England and Wales), 1970–72, retired; *b* 30 March 1914; *y s* of John and Betsy Forbes, Auchlossan, Lumphanan, Aberdeenshire; *m* 1941, Lilian Edith Miller, Edgware, Mddx; two *s. Educ:* Lumphanan School, Aberdeenshire. Joined Metropolitan Police, 1939; served in East End, Central London Flying Squad, New Scotland Yard; Detective Superintendent, 1964; served on New Scotland Yard Murder Squad, 1966–69; Commander, No 9 Regional Crime Squad (London area), 1969. *Publication:* Squadman (autobiog.), 1973. *Died 13 Aug. 1996.*

FORBES-LEITH of Fyvie, Sir Andrew (George), 3rd Bt *cr* 1923, of Jessfield, co. Midlothian; landed proprietor; *b* 20 Oct. 1929; *s* of Sir (Robert) Ian (Algernon) Forbes-Leith of Fyvie, 2nd Bt, KT, MBE, and Ruth Avis (*d* 1973), *d* of Edward George Barnett; *S* father, 1973; *m* 1962, Jane Kate (*d* 1969), *d* of late David McCall-McCowan; two *s* two *d. Heir: s* George Ian David Forbes-Leith [*b* 26 May 1967; *m* 1995, Camilla Frances, *e d* of Philip Ely, Crawley, Hants; one *s* one *d*]. *Address:* Dunachton, Kingussie, Inverness-shire PH21 1LY. *T:* (01540) 651226. *Club:* Royal Northern (Aberdeen). *Died 4 Nov. 2000.*

FORD, Prof. Boris, MA; Emeritus Professor, University of Bristol; freelance editor and writer; *b* 1 July 1917; *s* of late Brig. G. N. Ford, CB, DSO; *m* 1st, 1950, Noreen Auty (*née* Collins); one *s* three *d*; 2nd, 1977, Enid, (Inge), Inglis. *Educ:* Gresham's Sch., Holt, Norfolk; Downing Coll., Cambridge. Army Education, finally OC Middle East School of Artistic Studies, 1940–46; Chief Ed. and finally Dir, Bureau of Current Affairs, 1946–51; Information Officer, Technical Assistance Bd, UN (NY and Geneva), 1951–53; Sec., Nat. Enquiry into Liberalising Technical Educn, 1953–55; Editor: Journal of Education, 1955–58; Universities Quarterly: Culture, Education and Society, 1955–86; first Head of Sch. Broadcasting, Associated-Rediffusion, 1957–58; Educn Sec., Cambridge Univ. Press, 1958–60; Prof. of Education and Dir of the Inst. of Education, Univ. of Sheffield, 1960–63; Prof. of Education, Univ. of Sussex, 1963–73; Dean, Sch. of Cultural and Community Studies, 1963–71; Chm., Educn Area, 1971–73; Prof. of Educn, Univ. of Bristol, 1973–82. Chm., Nat. Assoc. for the Teaching of English, 1963–65; Educational Dir, Pictorial Knowledge, 1968–71. *Publications:* Discussion Method, 1949; Teachers' Handbook to Human Rights, 1950; (ed) Pelican

Guide to English Literature, 7 vols, 1954–61; Liberal Education in a Technical Age, 1955; (ed) Young Readers: Young Writers, 1960; Changing Relationships between Universities and Teachers' Colleges, 1975; (ed) New Pelican Guide to English Literature, 11 vols, 1982–88; Collaboration and Commitment, 1984; (ed) Cambridge Guide to the Arts in Britain, 9 vols, 1988–91 (paperback edn as Cambridge Cultural History of Britain, 9 vols, 1992); (ed) Benjamin Britten's Poets, 1994; (ed) Arts, Culture and Society in the Western World, vol. I, 1997. *Recreations:* music, living. *Address:* 35 Alma Vale Road, Clifton, Bristol BS8 2HL. *Died 19 May 1998.*

FORD, Sir Brinsley; *see* Ford, Sir R. B.

FORD, Charles Edmund, DSc; FRS 1965; FLS, FZS, FIBiol; Member of Medical Research Council's External Staff, Sir William Dunn School of Pathology, Oxford, 1971–78, retired; *b* 24 Oct. 1912; *s* of late Charles Ford and Ethel Eubornia Ford (*née* Fawcett); *m* 1940, Jean Ella Dowling; four *s. Educ:* Slough Grammar Sch.; King's Coll., University of London (DSc). Lieut Royal Artillery, 1942–43. Demonstrator, Dept of Botany, King's Coll., University of London, 1936–38; Geneticist, Rubber Research Scheme, Ceylon, 1938–41 and 1944–45; PSO Dept of Atomic Energy, Min. of Supply, at Chalk River Laboratories, Ont, Canada, 1946–49; Head of Cytogenetics Section, MRC, Radiobiology Unit, Harwell, 1949–71. *Publications:* papers on cytogenetics in scientific journals. *Recreations:* travel, friends. *Address:* 156 Oxford Road, Abingdon, Oxon OX14 2AF. *T:* (01235) 520001.
Died 7 Jan. 1999.

FORD, Rev. Preb. Douglas William C.; *see* Cleverley Ford.

FORD, Sir (Richard) Brinsley, Kt 1984; CBE 1978; FSA; Member of National Art-Collections Fund, since 1927 (Member: Executive Committee 1960–88 (Vice-Chairman, 1974–75, Chairman 1975–80); Advisory Panel, since 1988); *b* 10 June 1908; *e s* of late Capt. Richard Ford, Rifle Brigade, and Rosamund, *d* of Sir John Ramsden, 5th Bt; *g g s* of Richard Ford (1796–1858) who wrote the Handbook for Spain; *m* 1937, Joan, *d* of late Capt. Geoffrey Vyvyan; two *s* one *d. Educ:* Eton; Trinity Coll., Oxford. Joined TA, 1939; served for one year as Troop Sergeant Major, RA; commissioned 1941, and transferred to Intelligence Corps (Major 1945). Selected works for Arts Council Festival of Britain and Coronation Exhibitions; Jt Hon. Adviser on Paintings to Nat. Trust, 1980–95 (Chm., Nat. Trust Foundn for Art Cttee, 1986–90); a Trustee of the National Gallery, 1954–61; Trustee, Watts Gall., Compton, 1955–95 (Chm., 1974–84). Owner of the Ford Collection of Richard Wilsons. Dir, Burlington Magazine, 1952–86, Trustee, 1988–. Member: Soc. of Dilettanti, 1952– (Sec., 1972–88); Georgian Gp, from foundn, 1937–. Member: Council, Byam Shaw Sch., 1957–73; Exec. Cttee, City and Guilds of London Art Sch., 1976–94. President: St Marylebone Soc., 1974–77; Walpole Soc., 1986–98; Vice-Pres., Anglo-Spanish Soc. Patron, Attingham Summer Sch. Trust, 1984–. Founder, Richard Ford Award, Royal Acad., 1976; Brinsley Ford Archive given to Paul Mellon Centre, 1988 (Dictionary of British Travellers in Italy 1701–1800, ed J. Ingamells, 1997). Hon. Fellow, Royal Acad., 1981; Companion, NEAC, 1988. Hon. Fellow, Ateneo Veneto, 1988; Corresponding Member: Hispanic Soc. of Amer., 1963; Royal Acad. of San Fernando, Madrid, 1980. Hon. LLD Exeter, 1990. Order of Isabel la Católica of Spain, First Class A, 1986; Officer, Belgian Order of Leopold II, 1945; US Bronze Star, 1946; Médaille d'Argent de la Reconnaissance Française, 1947. *Publications:* The Drawings of Richard Wilson, 1951; The Walpole Society, the Ford Collection, 2 vols, 1998; contributor to the Burlington Magazine and Apollo. *Address:* 14 Wyndham

Place, Bryanston Square, W1H 1AQ. *T:* (020) 7723 0826. *Club:* Brooks's. *Died 4 May 1999.*

FORD, Rev. Wilfred Franklin, CMG 1974; *b* 9 Jan. 1920; *s* of Harold Franklin Ford and Sarah Elizabeth Ford; *m* 1st, 1942, Joan Mary Holland (*d* 1981); three *d*; 2nd, 1982, Hilda Mary Astley. *Educ:* Auckland Univ., NZ (BA); Trinity Theological Coll., NZ. Served War, NZ Army, 1942–44. Entered Methodist Ministry, 1945; Dir, Christian Educn, Methodist Church of NZ, 1956–68; President: Methodist Church of NZ, 1971; NZ Marriage Guidance Council, 1981–84. *Publications:* contribs to NZ and internat. jls, on Christian educn. *Recreations:* gardening, reading, bowls. *Address:* 40B Nigel Road, Browns Bay, Auckland 1310, New Zealand.
Died 12 Oct. 1999.

FORREST, Geoffrey; consultant chartered surveyor; *b* 31 Oct. 1909; *er s* of late George Forrest, CA, Rossie Lodge, Inverness; *m* 1st, 1951, Marjorie Ridehalgh (marr. diss. 1974); two *s*; 2nd, 1974, Joyce Grey. *Educ:* Marlborough Coll. Chartered Surveyor. Served War of 1939–45, in Lovat Scouts. Joined Forestry Commn, 1946; Chief Land Agent for Forestry Commn in Wales, 1958–64; Chief Land Agent for Forestry Commn in Scotland, 1964–65; Sen. Officer of Forestry Commn in Scotland, 1965–69. Scottish Partner, Knight, Frank & Rutley, 1973–76. *Publications:* papers on land use and estate management in professional jls. *Recreations:* fishing, shooting, lawn tennis. *Address:* Harelaw, Lilliesleaf, Melrose TD6 9JW.
Died 22 Oct. 1997.

FORREST, Cdre Geoffrey Cornish; Master of P & O vessel Arcadia from her completion in Jan. 1954 until Oct. 1956; Commodore P & O Fleet, 1955–56; *b* 1898; *s* of late William Forrest, an Examiner of Masters and Mates; *m* 1941, Monica Clemens. *Educ:* Thames Nautical Training Coll. (the Worcester) *Recreations:* photography, chess, bridge. *Died 21 April 1996.*

FORREST, Prof. (William) George (Grieve); Wykeham Professor of Ancient History, Oxford University, 1977–92, then Emeritus; Fellow of New College, Oxford, 1977–92, then Emeritus; *b* 24 Sept. 1925; *s* of late William and of Ina Forrest; *m* 1956, Margaret Elizabeth Mary Hall; two *d*. *Educ:* University College Sch., Hampstead; New Coll., Oxford (MA). Served RAF, 1943–47; New Coll., Oxford, 1947–51; Fellow, Wadham Coll., Oxford, 1951–76, then Emeritus. Visiting Professor: Trinity and University Colls, Toronto, 1961; Yale, 1968; Vis. Fellow, British Sch. at Athens, 1986; Fellow, Parmiter's Sch., Garston, 1991. Hon. DPhil Athens, 1991. *Publications:* Emergence of Greek Democracy, 1966; History of Sparta, 1968, 3rd edn 1995; articles in classical and archaeological periodicals. *Address:* 9 Fyfield Road, Oxford OX2 6QE. *T:* (01865) 556187. *Died 14 Oct. 1997.*

FORSBERG, (Charles) Gerald, OBE 1955; Commander RN, retired; author; Assistant Director of Marine Services, Ministry of Defence (Navy Department), 1972–75 (Deputy Director, 1958–72); *b* Vancouver, 18 June 1912; *s* of Charles G. Forsberg and Nellie (*née* Wallman); *m* 1952, Joyce Whewell Hogarth (*d* 1987), *d* of Dr F. W. Hogarth; one *s* one *d*. *Educ:* Polytechnic School; Training Ship Mercury; Sir John Cass Coll. Merchant Navy: Cadet to Chief Officer, 1928–38; qual. Master Mariner; transf. RN, 1938; Norwegian campaign, 1940; Malta Convoys, Matapan, Tobruk, Crete, etc, 1940–42; comd HMS Vega as Convoy Escort Comdr, 1943–45 (despatches); comd HMS Mameluke and HMS Chaplet, 1945–49; comd Salvage Sqdn off Elba in recovery of crashed Comet aircraft in 100 fathoms, 1954. Swam Channel (England-France) in record time, 1957; first person to swim Lough Neagh and Loch Lomond, 1959; British long-distance champion, 1957–58–59; swam Bristol Channel in record time, 1964; many long-distance championships and records, 1951–; BLDSA Veteran Swimmer of the Year, 1992. Younger Brother of Trinity House, 1958; Civil Service, 1962. President: Channel Swimming Assoc., 1963–; British Long Distance Swimming Assoc., 1982–83. Master of Navy Lodge, 1966; Liveryman, Hon. Co. of Master Mariners. Freeman, City of London, 1968. Hon. Life Mem., Scottish Amateur Swimming Assoc., 1988; Hon. Life Vice Pres., RN Amateur Swimming Assoc., 1998. Elected to Internat. Marathon Swimming Hall of Fame, 1971; The Observer newspaper's Sports Nut of the Year, 1982; Harold Fern Award, for outstanding contribn to swimming nationally and internationally, English Amateur Swimming Assoc., 1997; elected Honor Pioneer Open Water Contributor, Internat. Swimming Hall of Fame, 1998. *Publications:* Long Distance Swimming, 1957; First Strokes in Swimming, 1961; Modern Long Distance Swimming, 1963; Salvage from the Sea, 1977, new edn 1992; Pocket Book for Seamen, 1981; Navy Chapter: first 50 years of life, 1993; many short stories, articles, papers, and book reviews for general periodicals, technical jls and encyclopædia; regular monthly contribs to Nautical Magazine. *Recreations:* motoring, Association football affairs, books. *Address:* c/o Barclays Bank PLC, 19 Euston Road, Morecambe, Lancs LA4 5DE. *Clubs:* Victory Services; Otter Swimming.
Died 24 Oct. 2000.

FORSTER, His Honour Donald Murray; a Circuit Judge, 1984–90; *b* 18 June 1929; *s* of late John Cameron Forster and Maisie Constance Forster. *Educ:* Hollylea Sch., Liverpool; Merton House Sch., Penmaenmawr; Wrekin Coll., Wellington, Shropshire; St Edmund Hall, Oxford (Honour Sch. of Jurisprudence, 2nd Cl. Hons). Called to the Bar, Gray's Inn, 1953; Head of Chambers, 1968; a Recorder of the Crown Court, 1978–83. *Recreation:* sport. *Address:* Flat 8, Sutcliffe House, Edmund Castle, Corby Hill, Carlisle, Cumbria CA4 8QD. *Clubs:* Liverpool Ramblers Association Football (Vice-Pres.); Liverpool Racquet; Mersey Bowmen Lawn Tennis (Liverpool).
Died 12 Oct. 2000.

FORSTER, Brig. Eric Brown, MBE 1952; General Manager, Potato Marketing Board, 1970–82; *b* 19 May 1917; *s* of late Frank and Agnes Forster; *m* 1943, Margaret Bessie Letitia, *d* of late Lt-Col Arthur Wood, MBE and Edith Wood; one *s* two *d*. *Educ:* Queen Elizabeth Grammar Sch., Hexham. Commnd from RASC ranks into RAPC, 1941; Dir of Cost and Management Accounting (Army Dept), 1967–68. *Recreations:* philately, gardening. *Address:* Therncroft, Malt Kiln Lane, Appleton Roebuck, York YO5 7DT. *T:* (01904) 744393. *Club:* MCC.
Died 18 April 1997.

FORSTER, Prof. Leonard Wilson, FBA 1976; Schröder Professor of German, University of Cambridge, 1961–79; Fellow of Selwyn College, Cambridge, 1937–50 and since 1961, *b* 30 March 1913; *o s* of Edward James Forster, merchant, and Linda Charlotte (*née* Rogers), St John's Wood, NW8; *m* 1939, Jeanne Marie Louise, *e d* of Dr Charles Otto Billeter, Basel; one *s* two *d*. *Educ:* Marlborough Coll.; Trinity Hall, Cambridge (Thomas Carlyle Student, 1934–35; MA 1938; LittD 1976; Hon. Fellow 1989; Bonn Univ.; Basel Univ. (Dr phil. 1938). English Lektor: Univ. of Leipzig, 1934; Univ. of Königsberg, 1935–36; Univ. of Basel, 1936–38; Faculty Asst Lectr, Cambridge, and Lectr, Selwyn Coll., 1937; Naval Staff Admiralty, 1939–41; Foreign Office, 1941–45; Lt-Comdr RNVR (Special), 1945–46; Univ. Lectr in German, Cambridge, 1947–50; Dean and Asst Tutor, Selwyn Coll., Cambridge, 1946–50; Prof. of German, UCL, 1950–61. Pres., Internat. Assoc. for Germanic Studies (IVG), 1970–75. Corresponding Member: Deutsche Akademie für Sprache und Dichtung, 1957;

Royal Belgian Academy of Dutch Language and Literature, 1973; Member: Maatschappij der Nederlandse Letterkunde, Leiden, 1966; Royal Netherlands Acad. of Sciences and Letters, 1968. Visiting Professor: Univ. of Toronto, 1957; Univ. of Heidelberg, 1964, 1980; McGill Univ., 1967–68; Univ. of Otago, 1968; Univ. of Utrecht, 1976; Univ. of Kiel, 1980–81; Univ. of Basel, 1985–86. Sen. Consultant: Folger Shakespeare Liby, Washington, 1975; Herzog August Bibliothek, Wolfenbüttel, 1976–83. Co-Editor: German Life and Letters; Daphnis. Hon. DLitt: Leiden, 1975; Bath, 1979; Strasbourg, 1980; Heidelberg, 1986. Gold Medal, Goethe-Institut, Munich, 1966; Friedrich Gundolf-Preis für Germanistik im Ausland, 1981; J. A. Comenius Medal, Czechoslovak Republic, 1992. Grosses Verdienstkreuz (Germany), 1976. *Publications:* G. R. Weckherlin, zur Kenntnis seines Lebens in England, 1944; Conrad Celtis, 1948; German Poetry, 1944–48, 1949; The Temper of Seventeenth Century German Literature, 1952; Penguin Book of German Verse, 1957; Poetry of Significant Nonsense, 1962; Lipsius, Von der Bestendigkeit, 1965; Die Niederlande und die Anfänge der deutschen Barocklyrik, 1967; Janus Gruter's English Years, 1967; The Icy Fire, 1969; The Poet's Tongues: Multilingualism in Literature, 1971; Kleine Schriften zur deutschen Literatur im 17 Jahrhundert, 1977; Literaturwissenschaft als Flucht vor der Literatur?, 1978; Iter Bohemicum, 1980; The Man Who Wanted to Know Everything, 1981; Christian Morgenstern, Sämtliche Galgenlieder, 1985; Christoffel van Sichem in Basel und der frühe deutsche Alexandriner, 1986; articles in British and foreign jls. *Recreation:* foreign travel. *Address:* 1 Amhurst Court, Grange Road, Cambridge CB3 9BH. *T:* (01223) 562472; Selwyn College, Cambridge. *Died 18 April 1997.*

FORSTER, Sir Oliver (Grantham), KCMG 1983 (CMG 1976); LVO 1961; HM Diplomatic Service, retired; *b* 2 Sept. 1925; 2nd *s* of Norman Milward Forster and Olive Christina Forster (*née* Cockrell); *m* 1953, Beryl Myfanwy Evans; two *d. Educ:* Hurstpierpoint; King's Coll., Cambridge. Served in RAF, 1944–48. Joined Commonwealth Relations Office, 1951; Private Sec. to Parly Under-Sec., 1953–54; Second Sec., Karachi, 1954–56; Principal, CRO, 1956–59; First Sec., Madras, 1959–62; First Sec., Washington, 1962–65; Private Sec. to Sec. of State for Commonwealth Relations, 1965–67; Counsellor, Manila, 1967–70; Counsellor, New Delhi, 1970–75, Minister, 1975; Asst Under-Sec. of State and Dep. Chief Clerk, FCO, 1975–79; Ambassador to Pakistan, 1979–84. HQA 1984. Chm., Royal Commonwealth Soc. and Commonwealth Trust, 1992–96. *Address:* 71 Raglan Road, Reigate, Surrey RH2 0HP. *Clubs:* United Oxford & Cambridge University, Royal Commonwealth Society.
Died 3 Nov. 1999.

FORSTER, Sir William (Edward Stanley), Kt 1982; AE 1953; Judge of the Federal Court of Australia, 1977–89; *b* 15 June 1921; *s* of F. B. Forster; *m* 1950, Johanna B., *d* of Brig. A. M. Forbes; one *s* two *d. Educ:* St Peter's Coll., Adelaide; Adelaide Univ. (Stowe Prize; David Murray Scholar; LLB). Served RAAF, 1940–46. Private legal practice, 1950–59; Magistrate, Adelaide Police Court, 1959–61; Master, Supreme Court of SA, and Dist Registrar, High Court of Aust., 1966–71 (Dep. Master, and Dep. Dist Registrar, 1961–66); Sen. Judge, 1971, Chief Judge, 1977, Chief Justice, 1979–85, Supreme Court of NT. Chancellor, dio. of NT, 1975–85. Adelaide University: Lectr in Criminal Law, 1957–58; Lectr in Law of Procedure, 1967–71; Mem., Standing Cttee of Senate, 1967–71. President: NT Div., Australian Red Cross, 1973–85; Aboriginal Theatre Foundn, 1972–75; Chairman: Museum and Art Galls Bd, NT, 1974–85; NT Parole Bd, 1976–85. *Address:* 169 Stephen Terrace,

Walkerville, SA 5081, Australia. *Clubs:* Adelaide (Adelaide); Darwin Golf. *Died 31 Jan. 1997.*

FORSYTHE, Clifford; MP (UU) Antrim South, since 1983, resigned seat Dec. 1985 in protest against Anglo-Irish Agreement; re-elected Jan. 1986; Member, Antrim South, Northern Ireland Assembly, 1982–86; plumbing and heating contractor; *b* 24 Aug. 1929; *s* of Robert Forsythe. *Educ:* Glengormley public elementary sch. Formerly professional football player, Linfield and Derry City. Mem., Newtownabbey Borough Council, 1981–85; Mayor, 1983. Dep. Chm., DHSS Cttee, NI Assembly, 1982–86; UU Parly spokesman on transport, communications and local govt, 1992–97, on social security and transport, 1997–. Exec. Mem., Ulster Unionist Council, 1980–83; Chm., S Antrim Official Unionist Assoc., 1981–83. Mem., Select Cttee on Social Security, 1991–97, on Envmt, Transport and Regl Affairs, 1997–. Fellow, Industry and Parlt Trust, 1986. Chm., Glengormley Br., NI Chest, Heart and Stroke Assoc., 1987. *Recreations:* church choir, football, running. *Address:* House of Commons, SW1A 0AA. *Died 27 April 2000.*

FOSTER, John Robert; National Organiser, Amalgamated Union of Engineering Workers, 1962–81, retired; *b* 30 Jan. 1916; *s* of George Foster and Amelia Ann (*née* Elkington); *m* 1938, Catherine Georgina (*née* Webb); one *s* one *d. Educ:* London County Council. Apprentice toolmaker, 1931–36; toolmaker, 1936–47; Kingston District Sec. (full-time official), AEU, 1947–62. In Guyana for ILO, 1982. Lectr on industrial relns and trade union educn, WEA, 1981. Mem., Industrial Tribunals (England and Wales), 1984–86. Mem., Engrg Industry Trng Bd, 1974–80; Vice-Chm., Electricity Supply Industry Trng Cttee, 1967–81; Mem., Adv. Council on Energy Conservation, 1978–82. Mem., Soc. of Industrial Tutors, 1981–. MRI 1978. *Recreations:* music, photography, angling, 17th Century English Revolution. *Address:* 10 Grosvenor Gardens, Kingston-upon-Thames KT2 5BE.
Died 24 June 1999.

FOSTER, Rev. Canon John William, BEM 1946; Dean of Guernsey, 1978–88; Rector of St Peter Port, Guernsey, 1978–88; Canon Emeritus of Winchester Cathedral since 1988; *b* 5 Aug. 1921; *m* 1943, Nancy Margaret Allen (*d* 1992); one *s. Educ:* St Aidan's Coll., Birkenhead. Served Leicestershire Yeomanry, 1939–46; Chaplain, Hong Kong Defence Force, 1958; Reserve of Officers, Hong Kong Defence Force, 1967–73. Deacon 1954, priest 1955; Curate of Loughborough, 1954–57; Chaplain, St John's Cathedral, Hong Kong, 1957–60; Precentor, 1960–63; Dean of Hong Kong, 1963–73; Hon. Canon, St John's Cathedral, Hong Kong, 1973; Vicar of Lythe, dio. York, 1973–78; Hon. Canon of Winchester, 1979–88. *Address:* 14 Lightfoots Avenue, Scarborough, N Yorks YO12 5NS. *T:* (01723) 379012. *Died 7 March 2000.*

FOSTER-BROWN, Rear-Adm. Roy Stephenson, CB 1958; Royal Navy, retired; *b* 16 Jan. 1904; *s* of Robert Allen Brown and Agnes Wilfreda Stephenson; *m* 1933, Joan Wentworth Foster; two *s. Educ:* RNC, Osborne and Dartmouth. Specialised in Submarines, 1924–28; specialised in Signals, 1930; Fleet Signal Officer, Home Fleet, 1939–40; Staff Signal Officer, Western Approaches, 1940–44; Comdr HMS Ajax, 1944–46; Capt., 1946; Capt. Sixth Frigate Sqdn, 1951; Dir Signal Div., Admiralty, 1952–53; Capt. HMS Ceylon, 1954; Rear-Adm. 1955; Flag Officer, Gibraltar, 1956–59; retd 1959. Hon. Comdt, Girls Nautical Trng Corps, 1961–. Master, Armourers' and Braziers' Co., 1964–65, 1974–75. *Recreations:* sailing, shooting, golf, tennis. *Address:* 13 Ravenscroft Road, Henley on Thames, Oxon RG9 2DH. *Club:* Army and Navy. *Died 8 Jan. 1999.*

FOWLER, Henry Hamill; investment banker; Limited Partner, Goldman Sachs & Co., New York; *b* 5 Sept. 1908; *s* of Mack Johnson Fowler and Bertha Browning Fowler; *m* 1938, Trudye Pamela Hathcote; two *d* (one *s* decd). *Educ:* Roanoke Coll., Salem, Va; Yale Law Sch. Counsel, Tennessee Valley Authority, 1934–38, Asst Gen. Counsel, 1939; Special Asst to Attorney-Gen. as Chief Counsel to Sub-Cttee, Senate Cttee, Educn and Labor, 1939–40; Special Counsel, Fed. Power Commn, 1941; Asst Gen. Counsel, Office of Production Management, 1941, War Production Board, 1942–44; Econ. Adviser, US Mission Econ. Affairs, London, 1944; Special Asst to Administrator, For. Econ. Administration, 1945; Dep. Administrator, National Production Authority, 1951, Administrator, 1952; Administrator, Defense Prodn Administration, 1952–53; Dir Office of Defense Mobilization, Mem. Nat. Security Council, 1952–53; Under-Sec. of the Treasury, 1961–64; Secretary of the US Treasury, 1965–68. Sen. Mem. of Fowler, Leva, Hawes & Symington, Washington, 1946–51, 1953–61, 1964–65; Gen. Partner, Goldman Sachs & Co., 1969–80; Chm., Goldman Sachs Internat. Corp., 1969–84. Chairman: Roanoke Coll., 1974–81; Atlantic Council of the US, 1972–77; Inst. of Internat. Educn, 1973–78; US Treasury Adv. Cttee on Reform of Internat. Monetary System, 1973–84; Cttee to Fight Inflation, 1981–89; Bretton Woods Cttee, 1985–89; Co-Chairman: Cttee on Present Danger, 1976–88; Citizens Network for Foreign Affairs, 1988. Trustee: Lyndon B. Johnson Foundn; Franklin D. Roosevelt Four Freedoms Foundn; Carnegie Endowment for Peace, 1972–78; Alfred Sloan Foundn, 1970–80. Hon. Degrees: Roanoke Coll., 1961; Wesleyan Univ., 1966, Univ. of William and Mary, 1966. *Recreation:* bridge. *Address:* 209 South Fairfax Street, Alexandria, VA 22314, USA, 85 Broad Street, New York, NY 10004, USA. *Clubs:* Links, River (NYC); Metropolitan (Washington), Bohemian (San Francisco). *Died 3 Jan. 2000.*

FOWLER, Prof. Peter Howard, DSc; FRS 1964; private consultant in the application of physics to industry; Royal Society Research Professor in Physics, University of Bristol, 1964–88, then Emeritus; *b* 27 Feb. 1923; *s* of Sir Ralph Howard Fowler, FRS, and Eileen, *o c* of 1st and last Baron Rutherford; *m* 1949, Rosemary Hempson (*née* Brown); three *d*. *Educ:* Winchester Coll.; Bristol Univ. BSc 1948, DSc 1958. Flying Officer in RAF, 1942–46 as a Radar Technical Officer. Asst Lectr in Physics, 1948, Lectr, 1951, Reader, 1961, Bristol Univ. Visiting Prof., Univ. of Minnesota, 1956–57. Rutherford Meml Lectr, Royal Soc., 1971. Chairman: Jt Cttee on Radiol Protection, MRC, 1983–92; Neutron Facilities Review Panel, SERC, 1989; Mem., Meteorol Cttee, 1983–94. Governor: King's Sch., Bruton, 1982–; Jawaharlal Nehru Meml Trust, 1985–; Rutherford Foundn, 1991–. Chm., Herschel House Trust, 1989–. Hughes Medal, Royal Soc., 1974. *Publications:* (with Prof. C. F. Powell and Dr D. H. Perkins) The Study of Elementary Particles by the Photographic Method, 1959; (with Dr V. M. Clapham) Solid State Nuclear Track Detectors, 1981; (with Dr B. Foster) Forty Years of Particle Physics, 1988. *Recreations:* gardening, meteorology. *Address:* 320 Canford Lane, Westbury on Trym, Bristol BS9 3PL.
Died 8 Nov. 1996.

FOWLER, Ronald Frederick, CBE 1950; *b* 21 April 1910; *e s* of late Charles Frederick Fowler and Amy Beatrice (*née* Hollyoak); *m* 1937, Brenda Kathleen Smith. *Educ:* Bancroft's Sch.; LSE, University of London; Universities of Lille and Brussels. BCom (hons) London, 1931. Sir Ernest Cassel Travelling Scholar, 1929–30; Asst, later Lectr in Commerce, LSE, 1932–40; Central Statistical Office, 1940–50; Dir of Statistics and Under-Sec., Min. of Labour, 1950–68; Dir of Statistical Res., Dept of Employment, 1968–72. Consultant, Prices Div., Statistics Canada, Ottawa, 1971–72; Statistical Consultant, Prices Commn, 1973–77. *Publications:* The Depreciation of Capital, 1934; The Duration of Unemployment, 1968; Some Problems of Index Number Construction, 1970; Further Problems of Index Number Construction, 1973; articles in British and US economic and statistical jls. *Address:* 10 Silverdale Road, Petts Wood, Kent BR5 1NJ. *Club:* Reform. *Died 5 Jan. 1997.*

FOX, Sir (Henry) Murray, GBE 1974; FRICS; *b* 7 June 1912; *s* of late Sir Sidney Fox and Molly Button; *m* 1941, Helen Isabella Margaret (*d* 1986), *d* of late J. B. Crichton; one *s* two *d*. *Educ:* Malvern; Emmanuel Coll., Cambridge (MA). Joined Hallett, Fox & White, 1935, subseq. Sen. Partner; co. later merged with Chesterton & Son. Chairman: Trehaven Trust Group, 1963; City of London Sinfonia, 1978–91; Pres., City & Metropolitan Building Society, 1985–91 (Dir, 1972–85; Chm., 1976–85); Managing Trustee, Municipal Mutual Insurance Ltd, 1977–91. Dir, Toye, Kenning & Spencer Ltd, 1976–91. Governor: Christ's Hosp., 1966–82; Bridewell Royal Hosp., 1966 (Vice-Pres. 1976–82); Trustee, Morden Coll., 1976. Court of Common Council, 1963–82; Past Master: Wheelwrights' Co.; Coopers' Co.; Alderman, Ward of Bread Street, 1966–82; Sheriff, City of London, 1971–72; Lord Mayor of London, 1974–75; one of HM Lieutenants, City of London, 1976–83. *Recreation:* reading. *Address:* 5 Audley Court, 32–34 Hill Street, W1X 7FT. *Clubs:* City of London, City Livery (Pres., 1966–67).
Died 9 Nov. 1999.

FOX, Rt Rev. Langton Douglas, DD; retired Bishop of Menevia; *b* 21 Feb. 1917; *s* of Claude Douglas Fox and Ethel Helen (*née* Cox). *Educ:* Mark Cross, Wonersh and Maynooth. BA 1938; DD 1945. Priest 1942; Lectr, St John's Seminary, Wonersh, 1942–55; Mem., Catholic Missionary Soc., 1955–59; Parish Priest, Chichester, 1959–65; Auxiliary Bishop of Menevia, 1965–72; Bishop of Menevia, 1972–81. *Address:* Nazareth House, Hillbury Road, Wrexham, Clwyd LL13 7EU.
Died 26 July 1997.

FOX, Sir Murray; *see* Fox, Sir H. M.

FOXTON, Maj.-Gen. Edwin Frederick, CB 1969; OBE 1959; MA; Fellow and Domestic Bursar, Emmanuel College, Cambridge, 1969–79; *b* 28 Feb. 1914; *y s* of F. Foxton and T. Wilson; unmarried. *Educ:* Worksop Coll.; St Edmund Hall, Oxford. Commissioned from General List TA, 1937; served: India, 1939–42; Middle East, 1942–45; India, 1945–47 (Chief Educn Officer, Southern Comd, India); War Office, 1948–52; Chief Instructor, Army Sch. of Educn, 1952–55; Dist Educn Officer, HQ Northumbrian District, 1955–57; War Office, 1957–60; Commandant, Army Sch. of Educn, 1961–63; War Office, 1963–65; Chief Educn Officer, FARELF, 1965; Dir of Army Educn, 1965–69. *Address:* South Close, North Dalton, Driffield, East Yorks YO25 9XA.
Died 23 Dec. 1996.

FOYLE, Christina Agnes Lilian, (Mrs Ronald Batty); Managing Director, W. & G. Foyle Ltd; *b* 30 Jan. 1911; *d* of late William Alfred Foyle and Christina Tulloch; *m* 1938, Ronald Batty (*d* 1994). *Educ:* Aux Villas Unspunnen, Wilderswil, Switzerland. Began Foyle's Literary Luncheons, 1930, where book lovers have been able to see and hear great personalities. Member: Ct, Univ. of Essex; Council, RSA, 1963–69; Chm. East Anglian Region, RSA, 1978; Pres. Chelmsford District, Nat. Trust, 1979. DUniv Essex, 1975. *Publications:* So Much Wisdom, 1984; articles in various books and journals. *Recreations:* bird-watching, gardening, playing the piano. *Address:* Beeleigh Abbey, Maldon, Essex CM9 6LL.
Died 8 June 1999.

FOZARD, Prof. John William, OBE 1981; FRS 1987; FEng 1984; FRAeS, FAIAA; consultant, writer, teacher; *b* 16 Jan. 1928; *s* of John Fozard and Eleanor Paulkitt; *m* 1st, 1951, Mary (marr. diss. 1985), *d* of Regtl Sgt-Major C. B. Ward, VC, KOYLI; two *s*; 2nd, 1985, Gloria Ditmars Stanchfield Roberts, *widow* of Alan Roberts, Alexandria, Va, USA. *Educ:* Univ. of London (1st Cl. Hons BScEng 1948); Coll. of Aeronautics, Cranfield (DCAe with distinction 1950). FIMechE 1971; FRAeS 1964; FAIAA 1981. Hawker Aircraft Ltd: Design Engr, 1950; Head of Proj. Office, 1960; Hawker Siddeley Aviation: Chief Designer, Harrier, 1963–78; Exec. Dir, 1971; Marketing Dir, Kingston Brough Div., BAe, 1978–84; Divl Dir, Special Projects, Mil. Aircraft Div., BAe, 1984–87, retd 1989. Visiting Professor: Sch. of Mechanical, Aeronautical and Production Engrg, Kingston Polytech., 1982–87; Aircraft Design, RMCS, Shrivenham, 1986–87; Lindbergh Prof. of Aerospace Hist., Nat. Air and Space Mus., Smithsonian Instn, Washington, 1988; Vis. Lectr, Univ. of Michigan, 1989; Lectures: 1st J. D. North Meml, RAeS Wolverhampton Br., 1969, and 16th, 1985; 23rd R. J. Mitchell Meml, RAeS Southampton Br., 1976; 32nd Barnwell Meml, RAeS Bristol Br., 1982; 2nd Lindbergh Meml, Nat. Air & Space Museum, Smithsonian Instn, 1978, 12th Lindbergh Meml, 1988; Friday Evening Discourse, Royal Instn, 1986; 9th Sir Sydney Camm Meml, RAeS, 1987; Sir Izaac Newton series to young people around UK, IMechE, 1979–80; over 200 learned soc. lectures in UK, USA, Europe, Australia, China, 1965–. Vice Pres., 1980–85, Pres.-elect, 1985–86, Pres., 1986–87, RAeS. Hon. DSc: Strathclyde, 1983; Cranfield, 1996. Simms Gold Medal, Soc. of Engrs, 1971; British Silver Medal for Aeronautics, 1977; James Clayton Prize, IMechE, 1983; Mullard Award (with R. S. Hooper), Royal Soc., 1983. *Publications:* (ed) Sydney Camm and the Hurricane, 1991; papers in aeronautical jls and in specialist press, 1954–. *Recreations:* music, engineering history. *Address:* 306 North Columbus Street, Alexandria, VA 22314–2414, USA. *T:* (703) 5495142.
Died 17 July 1996.

FRANCE, Sir Arnold William, GCB 1972 (KCB 1965; CB 1957); retired; *b* 20 April 1911; *s* of late W. E. France; *m* 1940, Frances Margaret Linton, *d* of late Dr C. J. L. Palmer; four *d. Educ:* Bishop's Stortford Coll. District Bank, Ltd, 1929–40; served War of 1939–45, Army, 1940–43; Deputy Economic and Financial Adviser to Minister of State in Middle East, 1943; HM Treasury, 1945; Asst Sec., 1948; Under Sec., 1952; Third Sec., 1960; Ministry of Health: Dep. Sec., 1963–64; Permanent Sec., 1964–68; Chm., Bd of Inland Revenue, 1968–73. Director: Pilkington Bros, 1973–81; Tube Investments, 1973–81; Rank Organisation, 1973–83. Chm., Central Bd of Finance, C of E, 1973–78. Chm., Bd of Management, Lingfield Hosp. Sch., 1973–81. *Address:* Thornton Cottage, Lingfield, Surrey RH7 6BS. *T:* (01342) 832278. *Club:* Reform. *Died 2 Jan. 1998.*

FRANCE, Sir Joseph (Nathaniel), KCMG 1996; CBE 1976; General Secretary, St Kitts-Nevis Trades and Labour Union, since 1940; *b* 16 Sept. 1907; *s* of Thomas and Mary France. *Educ:* Combermere Govt Sch., Nevis. Sec., St Kitts-Nevis Labour Party, 1938–93; MP (Lab) West Basseterre, St Kitts-Nevis, 1946–89. *Address:* St Johnston Avenue, Basseterre, St Christopher, West Indies.
Died 21 May 1997.

FRANCIS, William Lancelot, CBE 1961; *b* 16 Sept. 1906; *s* of G. J. Francis and Ethel, *d* of L. G. Reed, Durham; *m* 1st, 1937, Ursula Mary Matthew (*d* 1966); two *s* three *d*; 2nd, 1968, Margaret Morris (*d* 1978). *Educ:* Latymer Upper Sch., Hammersmith; King's Coll., Cambridge. MA, PhD. DSIR Sen. Research Award, Cambridge, 1931–33; Rockefeller Foundn Fellowship in Experimental Zoology,

Rockefeller Institute, New York, 1933–34; Science Master, Repton Sch., 1935–40; Radar research and administration in Ministries of Supply and Aircraft Production (TRE Malvern), 1940–45; Dept of Scientific and Industrial Res. Headquarters, 1945–65; Secretary, Science Research Council, 1965–72; Consultant, Civil Service Dept, 1972–75. Member: Nat. Electronics Council, 1965–72; CERN, 1966–70; Advisory Councils: R&D, Fuel and Power, 1966–72; Iron and Steel, 1966–72. Mem. Council, Oxfam, 1975–83. *Publications:* papers on physical chemistry and experimental zoology in scientific jls, 1931–37. *Recreations:* gardening, travel. *Address:* 269 Sheen Lane, SW14 8RN. *T:* (0181) 876 3029. *Club:* Athenæum. *Died 11 March 1996.*

FRANCKLIN, Comdr (Mavourn Baldwin) Philip, DSC 1940; JP; RN; Lord-Lieutenant of Nottinghamshire, 1972–83 (Vice-Lieutenant, 1968–72); *b* 15 Jan. 1913; *s* of Captain Philip Francklin, MVO, RN (killed in action, 1914); *m* 1949, Xenia Alexandra, *d* of Alexander Davidson, Kilpedder, Co. Wicklow; two *s* one *d* (and one *s* decd). *Educ:* RNC Dartmouth. Joined RN, 1926; served War of 1939–45: Norway, N and S Atlantic, Indian Ocean (despatches twice); Asst to 5th Sea Lord, 1947–49; Comdr 1950; Korean War, 1950–51; Asst Naval Attaché, Paris, 1952–53. DL 1963, JP 1958, Notts; High Sheriff of Notts, 1965. KStJ 1973. Croix de Guerre (France). *Address:* Gonalston Hall, Nottingham NG14 7JA. *T:* (0115) 966 3635. *Club:* Boodle's. *Died 25 Sept. 1999.*

FRANK, Sir (Frederick) Charles, Kt 1977; OBE 1946; DPhil; FRS 1954; Henry Overton Wills Professor of Physics and Director of the H. H. Wills Physics Laboratory, University of Bristol, 1969–76 (Professor in Physics, 1954–69); then Emeritus Professor; *b* 6 March 1911; *e s* of Frederick and Medora Frank; *m* 1940, Maia Maita Asché, *y d* of late Prof. B. M. Asché; no *c. Educ:* Thetford Grammar Sch.; Ipswich Sch.; Lincoln Coll., Oxford. BA, BSc Oxon, 1933; DPhil Oxon, 1937; Hon. Fellow, Lincoln Coll., 1968. Research: Dyson Perrins Laboratory and Engineering Laboratory, Oxford, 1933–36; Kaiser Wilhelm Institut für Physik, Berlin, 1936–38; Colloid Science Laboratory, Cambridge, 1939–40; Scientific Civil Service (temp.), 1940–46: Chemical Defence Research Establishment, 1940, Air Ministry, 1940–46; research, H. H. Wills Physical Laboratory, Bristol Univ., 1946–; Research Fellow in Theoretical Physics, 1948; Reader in Physics, 1951–54. Vis. Prof., Univ. of California, San Diego, Inst. of Geophysics and Planetary Physics, and Dept of Physics, 1964–65; Raman Prof., Raman Res. Inst., Bangalore, 1979–80. A Vice-Pres., Royal Society, 1967–69. Foreign Associate: US Nat. Acad. of Engineering, 1980; Royal Soc. of S Africa, 1986; US Nat. Acad. of Sci., 1987. Hon. FIP 1978; Hon. FIASc 1984; Hon. Fellow, Bristol Univ., 1986. Hon. DSc: Ghent, 1955; Bath, 1974; TCD, 1978; Warwick, 1981; Leeds, 1992; DUniv Surrey, 1977; Docteur *hc* Univ. de Paris-Sud, 1986. Holweck Prize, French Physical Soc., 1963; Crystal Growth Award, Amer. Assoc. for Crystal Growth, 1978; Royal Medal, Royal Soc., 1979; Grigori Aminoff Gold Medal, Royal Swedish Acad. of Sciences, 1981; Guthrie Medal and Prize, Inst. of Physics, 1982; Robert Mehl Award, Amer. Metallurgical Soc., 1987; Von Hippel Award, Amer. Materials Res. Soc., 1988; Copley Medal, Royal Soc., 1994. *Publications:* (ed and introd) Operation Epsilon: the Farm Hall transcripts, 1993; articles in various learned journals, mostly dealing either with dielectrics or the physics of solids, in particular crystal dislocations, crystal growth, mechanical properties of polymers and mechanics of the earth's crust. *Address:* Orchard Cottage, Grove Road, Coombe Dingle, Bristol BS9 2RL. *T:* (0117) 968 1708. *Club:* Athenæum.
Died 5 April 1998.

FRANKEL, Prof. Herbert; see Frankel, Prof. S. H.

FRANKEL, Sir Otto (Herzberg), Kt 1966; DSc, DAgr; FRS 1953; FRSNZ; FAA; *b* 4 Nov. 1900; *s* of Dr L. Herzberg Frankel, Vienna; *m* 1st, 1925, Mathilde Donsbach (marr. diss. 1936); 2nd, 1939, Margaret Anderson. *Educ:* Vienna; Berlin (DAgr); Cambridge; DSc NZ. Plant Geneticist, 1929–42, and Chief Executive Officer, 1942–49, Wheat Research Institute, NZ; Dir, Crop Research Division, Dept of Scientific and Industrial Research, New Zealand, 1949–51; Chief, Division of Plant Industry, CSIRO, Australia, 1951–62; Member of Executive, CSIRO, Melbourne, 1962–66. Hon. Mem., Japan Academy, 1983; For. Associate, US Nat. Acad. of Scis, 1988. *Publications:* (ed jtly) Genetic Resources in Plants: their exploration and conservation, 1970; (ed jtly) Crop Genetic Resources for Today and Tomorrow, 1975, (with M. E. Soulé) Conservation and Evolution, 1981; (ed jtly) The Use of Plant Genetic Resources, 1989; (with A. H. D. Brown and J. J. Burdon) The Conservation of Plant Biodiversity, 1995; numerous articles in British, NZ and Australian scientific journals. *Address:* 4 Cobby Street, Campbell, Canberra, ACT 2612, Australia. *T:* (2) 62479460.   *Died 21 Nov. 1998.*

FRANKEL, Prof. (Sally) Herbert, MA Rand, PhD London, DScEcon London, MA Oxon; Emeritus Professor in the Economics of Underdeveloped Countries, University of Oxford, and Emeritus Fellow, Nuffield College, Oxford (Professor, and Professorial Fellow, 1946–71); *b* 22 Nov. 1903; *e s* of Jacob Frankel; *m* 1928, Ilse Jeanette Frankel (decd); one *s* one *d*. *Educ:* St John's Coll., Johannesburg; University of the Witwatersrand; London Sch. of Economics. Prof. of Economics, University of Witwatersrand, Johannesburg, 1931–46. Responsible for calculations of National Income of S Africa for the Treasury, 1941–48; Jt Editor of South African Journal of Economics from its inception to 1946; Mem. of Union of South Africa Treasury Advisory Council on Economic and Financial Policy, 1941–45; Mem. of Union of South Africa Miners' Phthisis Commission, 1941–42; Commissioner appointed by Govts of Southern and Northern Rhodesia and the Bechuanaland Protectorate to report upon Rhodesia Railways Ltd, 1942–43; Chm. Commission of Enquiry into Mining Industry of Southern Rhodesia, 1945; Mem. East Africa Royal Commission, 1953–55; Consultant Adviser, Urban African Affairs Commn, Govt of S Rhodesia, 1957–58. Vis. Prof. of Econs, Univ. of Virginia, until 1974. Mem., Mont Pellerin Soc., 1950–. Chm., Bd of Governors, Oxford Centre for Postgrad. Hebrew Studies, 1983–89. Hon. DScEcon Rhodes Univ., 1969; Hon. DLitt Rand Univ., 1970. *Publications:* Co-operation and Competition in the Marketing of Maize in South Africa, 1926; The Railway Policy of South Africa, 1928; Coming of Age: Studies in South African Citizenship and Politics (with Mr J. H. Hofmeyr and others), 1930; Capital Investment in Africa: its Course and Effects, 1938; The Economic Impact on Underdeveloped Societies: Essays on International Investment and Social Change, 1953; Investment and the Return to Equity Capital in the South African Gold Mining Industry 1887–1965: an International Comparison, 1967; Gold and International Equity Investment (Hobart Paper 45), 1969; Money: two philosophies, the conflict of trust and authority, 1977; Money and Liberty, 1980; An Economist's Testimony: the autobiography of S. Herbert Frankel, 1992. *Recreation:* gardening. *Address:* 62 Cutteslowe House, Park Close, Oxford OX2 8NP. *T:* (01865) 514748. *Club:* Reform.

Died 11 Dec. 1996.

FRANKHAM, Very Rev. Harold Edward; Provost of Southwark, 1970–82, then Provost Emeritus; *b* 6 April 1911; *s* of Edward and Minnie Frankham; *m* 1942,

Margaret Jean Annear; one *s* two *d* (and one *s* decd). *Educ:* London Coll. of Divinity (LCD). Ordained, 1941; Curate: Luton, 1941–44; Holy Trinity, Brompton, 1944–46; Vicar of Addiscombe, 1946–52; Rector of Middleton, Lancs, 1952–61; Vicar of Luton, 1961–70. Hon. Canon of St Albans, 1967–70. Exec. Sec., Archbishops' Council on Evangelism, 1965–73. *Recreations:* music, travel. *Address:* 3 Harnleigh Green, 80 Harnham Road, Salisbury SP2 8JN. *T:* Salisbury (01722) 321846.   *Died 17 Jan. 1996.*

FRANKLIN, Sir Eric (Alexander), Kt 1954; CBE 1952; *b* 3 July 1910; *s* of late William John Franklin; *m* 1936, Joy Stella, *d* of late George Oakes Lucas, Cambridge. *Educ:* The English Sch., Maymyo; Emmanuel Coll., Cambridge. Appointed to ICS in 1935 and posted to Burma; Subdivisional Officer, 1936–39; Deputy Registrar, High Court of Judicature at Rangoon, 1939–40; District and Sessions Judge, Arakan, 1941–42; Deputy Sec. to Government of Burma at Simla, 1942–45; Registrar, High Court of Judicature at Rangoon, 1946–47; retired prematurely from ICS, 1948; appointed on contract as Deputy Sec. to Government of Pakistan. Cabinet Secretariat, 1949; Joint Sec., Cabinet Secretariat, 1952; Establishment Officer and Head of Central Organisation and Methods Office, 1953–55; Establishment Sec. to Government of Pakistan, 1956–57; Chm. Sudan Government Commission on terms of service, 1958–59; Civil Service Adviser to Government of Hashemite Kingdom of Jordan, 1960–63; acting Resident Representative, UN Technical Assistance Board, Jordan, 1961; Senior UN Administrative Adviser to Government of Nepal, 1964–66. Chm., Cambridgeshire Soc. for the Blind, 1969–74, Vice-Pres., 1974–93. El Kawkab el Urdoni (Star of Jordan), 1963. *Recreations:* reading, music. *Address:* 18 Cavendish Avenue, Cambridge CB1 4US.   *Died 8 July 1996.*

FRANKLIN, Rt Rev. William Alfred, OBE 1964; Assistant Bishop (full time), Diocese of Peterborough, and Hon. Canon of the Cathedral, 1978–86, Canon Emeritus since 1986; *b* 16 July 1916; *s* of George Amos and Mary Anne Catherine Franklin; *m* 1945, Winifred Agnes Franklin (*née* Jarvis); one *s* one *d*. *Educ:* schools in London; Kelham Theol Coll. Deacon 1940, priest 1941, London; Curate, St John on Bethnal Green, Chaplain ATC and Univ. Settlements, 1941–43; Curate of St John's, Palmers Green, and Chm. for area Interdenominational Youth Activities, 1943–45; Asst Chaplain, St Saviour's, Belgrano, Buenos Aires, Argentina and teaching duties at Green's School, Buenos Aires, 1945–48; Rector of Holy Trinity, Lomas de Zamora, Buenos Aires, Domestic Chaplain to Bishop in Argentina, Sec. Dio. Bd of Missions, and Chaplain St Alban's Coll., Lomas, 1948–58; Rector, Canon and Sub-Dean of Anglican Cathedral, Santiago, Chaplain Grange School and Founder and Chm. Ecumenical Gp in Chile, 1958–65; Rector of St Alban's, Bogotá, Colombia, 1965–71; Archdeacon of Diocese, 1966–71; consecrated Bishop of Diocese, 1972; resigned, 1978, allowing a national to be elected. Hon. Asst Bishop of Canterbury, 1987–92. Founder and Editor of Revista Anglicana, official magazine of Arensa (Assoc. of Anglican Dioceses in North of S America). *Recreations:* fishing, tennis, cricket. *Address:* 26c The Beach, Walmer, near Deal, Kent CT14 7AJ. *T:* (01304) 361807. *Club:* Anglo-American (Bogotá, Colombia).   *Died 11 Feb. 1998.*

FRASER OF KILMORACK, Baron *cr* 1974 (Life Peer), of Rubislaw, Aberdeen; **Richard Michael Fraser,** Kt 1962; CBE 1955 (MBE mil. 1945); *b* 28 Oct. 1915; *yr s* of late Dr Thomas Fraser, CBE, DSO, TD, DL, LLD, Aberdeen and Maria-Theresia Kayser, Hanover; *m* 1944, Elizabeth Chloë, *er d* of late Brig. C. A. F. Drummond, OBE and Muriel Kyrle Ottley; one *s* (and one *s* decd).

Educ: Aberdeen Grammar Sch.; Fettes; King's Coll., Cambridge. Begg Exhibition, 1934; James Essay Prize, 1935; BA Hons History, 1937; MA 1945. Served War of 1939–45 (RA); 2nd Lieut 1939; War Gunnery Staff Course, 1940; Capt., Feb. 1941; Major, June 1941; Lieut-Col (GSO1), 1945. Joined Conservative Research Dept, 1946; Head of Home Affairs Sect., 1950–51, Jt Dir, 1951–59, Dir, 1959–64, Chm., 1970–74; Exec. Dep. Chm., Cons. Party Orgn, 1964–75; Dep. Chm., Conservative Party's Adv. Cttee on Policy, 1970–75 (Sec., 1951–64); Sec. to the Conservative Leader's Consultative Cttee (Shadow Cabinet), 1964–70 and 1974–75. Director: Glaxo Holdings plc, and subsid. cos, 1975–85; Glaxo Enterprises Inc., USA, 1983–86; Whiteaway Laidlaw Bank Ltd, 1981–94. Smith-Mundt Fellowship, USA, 1952. Mem. Council, Imperial Soc. of Knights Bachelor, 1971–94. President: Old Fettesian Assoc., 1977–80; London Old Fettesian Assoc., 1992–94. *Publications:* (contrib.) Ruling Performance: British governments from Attlee to Thatcher, 1987; contribs to political and hist. jls. *Recreations:* reading, music, opera, ballet, travel; collecting and recollecting. *Address:* 18 Drayton Court, SW10 9RH. *T:* 0171–370 1543. *Clubs:* Carlton, St Stephen's Constitutional (Hon. Mem.), Coningsby (Hon. Mem., Pres., 1988–95). *Died 1 July 1996.*

FRASER, Donald Blake, FRCS, FRCOG; Gynæcologist and Obstetrician, St Bartholomew's Hospital, 1946–75; retired 1978; *b* 9 June 1910; *o s* of Dr Thomas B. Fraser, Hatfield Point, NB, Canada; *m* 1939, Betsy, *d* of late Sir James Henderson, KBE; one *s* one *d*. *Educ:* University of New Brunswick; Christ Church, Oxford. Rhodes Scholar, 1930; BA 1st Cl. Hons 1932, BM, BCh Oxon 1936; MRCS, LRCP, LMCC 1936; FRCS 1939; MRCOG 1940, FRCOG 1952. Former Examiner: Central Midwives Bd; Universities of Oxford and London; Conjoint Bd; Royal College of Obstetricians and Gynæcologists. *Publications:* (joint) Midwifery (textbook), 1956; articles in medical journals. *Recreation:* philately. *Address:* 13 Stanton Crest, 7 Hale Street, Townsville, Qld 4810, Australia.
Died 2 June 1998.

FRASER, Sir Ian, Kt 1963; DSO 1943; OBE 1940; DL; FRSE; FRCS, FRCSI, FACS; Consulting Surgeon, Belfast; Senior Surgeon: Royal Victoria Hospital, Belfast, 1955–66; Royal Belfast Hospital for Sick Children, 1955–66; Director: Provincial Bank of Ireland; Allied Irish Bank; *b* 9 Feb. 1901; *s* of Robert Moore Fraser, BA, MD, Belfast; *m* 1931, Eleanor Margaret Mitchell (*d* 1992); one *s* one *d* (and one *s* decd). *Educ:* Royal Academical Institution, Belfast; Queen's Univ., Belfast. MB, BCh 1st Cl. Hons 1923; MD 1932; MCh 1927; Coulter Schol.; McQuitty Schol. FRCSI 1926 (1st place in Ire.); FRCS 1927; FACS 1945. Served War: (overseas) 1940–45: in W Africa, N Africa, Sicily, Italy (OBE, DSO, Salerno); invasion of France, India; Officer in charge of Penicillin in Research Team, N Africa; Brig, 1945. RSO, St Helens, Lancs, 1926–27; Surgeon: Royal Belfast Hosp. for Sick Children, 1927–55; Royal Victoria Hosp., Belfast, 1928–55, and former Asst Prof. of Surgery. Hon. Colonel (TA): No 204 Gen. Hosp., 1961–71; No 4 Field Amb., 1948–71; Surgeon in Ordinary to the Governor of Northern Ireland; Hon. Cons. Surg. to the Army in NI; Chm., Police Authority, Royal Ulster Constabulary, 1970–76; Mem. Adv. Council, Ulster Defence Regt. President: RCSI, 1956–57; Assoc. of Surgeons GB and Ireland, 1957; BMA, 1962–63; Irish Med. Graduates Assoc., London; Queen's Univ. Assoc., London; Services Club, QUB; Ulster Med. Soc. President: Ulster Surgical Club; Queen's Univ. Assoc., Belfast; Chm of Convocation and Mem. Senate QUB. Visiting Lecturer: Leicester, Birmingham, Edinburgh, Bradford, London, Sheffield, Dublin, Cheltenham, Rochester, New York, Copenhagen, Glasgow, Manchester, Middlesex Hosp., Bristol, Barnsley,

etc; Delegate to various assocs abroad. John Snow Oration, 1967; Downpatrick Hosp. Bi-Centenary Oration, 1967; Bishop Jeremy Taylor Lecture, 1970; Maj.-Gen. Philip Mitchiner Lecture, 1971; Robert Campbell Orator, 1973; David Torrens Lectr, NUU, 1981; Thos Vicary Lecture, RCS, 1983. Visiting Examiner in Surgery: Liverpool, Cambridge, and Manchester Univs; NUI; Apothecaries' Hall, Dublin; TCD; RCSI; RCS of Glasgow. Councillor, RCSI; Mem. and Trustee, James IV Assoc. of Surgeons; Mem., Health Educn Cttee, Min. of Health, London; FRSE 1938; Fellow: BMA; Royal Soc. Med. Lond.; Royal Irish Acad. of Med.; Hon. FRCPGlas 1972; Hon. FRCSE; Hon. FRCPI 1977; Hon. Fellow: Brit. Assoc. of Paediatric Surgeons; Ulster Med. Soc., 1977; Foreign Mem., L'Académie de Chirurgie, Paris; Hon. Mem., Danish Assoc. of Surgery, Copenhagen; Mem., Internat. Soc. of Surgeons. Hon. Life Governor, Royal Victoria Hosp., Belfast; Governor for GB, Amer. Coll. Surgeons. Hon. DSc: Oxon, 1963; New Univ. of Ulster, 1977; Hon. LLD QUB, 1992. GCStJ 1974 (KStJ 1940); Mem., Chapter General, London, and Knight Commander of Commandery of Ards, Ulster, Order of St John. DL Belfast, 1955. Gold Medal: Ulster Hosp. for Women and Children; Royal Belfast Hosp. for Sick Children. Commander: Ordre de la Couronne (Belgium) 1963; Order of Orange-Nassau (Netherlands), 1969; Ordre des Palmes Académiques (France), 1970; Chevalier de la Legion d'Honneur (France), 1981. *Publications:* Blood, Sweat and Cheers (autobiog.), 1989; various monographs on surgical subjects. *Recreations:* golf; formerly hockey and Rugby. *Address:* (residence) 19 Upper Malone Road, Belfast BT9 6TE. *T:* (028) 9066 8235. *Died 11 May 1999.*

FRASER, Very Rev. Dr Ian Watson, CMG 1973; Minister of St Stephen's Presbyterian Church, Lower Hutt, Wellington, NZ, 1961–73, retired; *b* 23 Oct. 1907; *s* of Malcolm Fraser (*b* Inverness; 1st NZ Govt Statistician) and Caroline (*née* Watson; *b* Napier, NZ); *m* 1932, Alexa Church Stewart; one *s* two *d*. *Educ:* Scots Coll., Wellington, NZ; Victoria Univ. of Wellington (MA Hons); Theol Hall, Dunedin; BD (Melb.); Univ. of Edinburgh; Univ. of Bonn, Germany; Union Theol Seminary, NY (STM, ThD). Minister: St Andrew's Presbyterian Church, Levin, 1933–39; Presbyterian Ch., Wyndham, 1939–42; Chaplain, St Andrew's Coll., Christchurch, 1942–48; Minister, St John's Pres. Ch., Papatoetoe, Auckland, 1948–61. Moderator, Presbyterian Church of NZ, 1968–69. Chm., Nansen Home Cttee, Presbyterian Support Services, 1984–86 (Chm., NZ Refugee Homes Bd, administering Nansen Home, 1962–84). Refugee Award of Nat. Council of Churches, 1970. Compiled biographical register of ministers in Presbyterian Church of NZ, 1840–1990. *Publications:* Understandest Thou? (introd. to NT), 1946; Understanding the Old Testament, 1958; The Story of Nansen Home, 1984; various booklets. *Recreations:* beekeeping, music, reading. *Address:* 19A Bloomfield Terrace, Lower Hutt 6301, Wellington, New Zealand. *T:* Wellington (4) 5697269.

Died 25 June 1996.

FRASER, Prof. Sir James (David), 2nd Bt *cr* 1943, of Tain, co. Ross; Postgraduate Dean, Faculty of Medicine, University of Edinburgh, 1981–89; retired; *b* 19 July 1924; *o s* of Sir John Fraser, 1st Bt, KCVO, MC, and Agnes Govane Herald (*d* 1983), The Manse, Duns, Berwickshire; *S* father, 1947; *m* 1951, Maureen, *d* of Rev. John Reay, MC, Bingham Rectory, Nottingham; two *s*. *Educ:* Edinburgh Academy; Magdalen Coll., Oxford (BA); Edinburgh Univ. (MB, ChB; ChM 1961). FRCSE 1953; FRCS 1973; FRCPE 1980; FRCSI 1984; FRACS 1984. RAMC (Major), 1948–51. Senior Lectr in Clinical Surgery, Univ. of Edinburgh and Hon. Cons. Surgeon, Royal Infirmary, Edinburgh, 1951–70; Prof. of Surgery, Univ. of Southampton, 1970–80, and Hon. Cons. Surgeon,

Southampton Univ. Hospital Gp, 1970–80. Pres., RCSEd, 1982–85. *Recreations:* golf, swimming. *Heir: s* Iain Michael Fraser [*b* 27 June 1951; *m* 1982, Sherylle (marr. diss. 1991), *d* of Keith Gillespie, New Zealand; one *s* one *d*]. *Address:* 2 Lennox Street, Edinburgh EH4 1QA.
Died 8 Jan. 1997.

FRASER, Ronald Petrie, CB 1972; Secretary, Scottish Home and Health Department, 1972–77; *b* 2 June 1917; *yr s* of late T. Petrie Fraser, Elgin; *m* 1962, Ruth Wright Anderson, Edinburgh; one *d. Educ:* Daniel Stewart's Coll., Edinburgh; University of Edinburgh; The Queen's Coll., Oxford. Joined Dept of Health for Scotland for work on emergency hosp. service, 1940; Asst Private Sec. to Sec. of State for Scotland, 1944; Cabinet Office, 1947; Sec., Scottish Hosp. Endowments Commn, 1950; Asst Sec., Dept of Health for Scotland, 1954; Asst Sec., Scottish Education Dept, 1961; Under-Sec., 1963; Under-Sec., 1968–71, Dep. Sec., 1971, Min. of Agriculture, Fisheries and Food. Chief Counting Officer for Scotland Act Referendum, 1979. *Recreations:* walking, music. *Address:* 40A Lygon Road, Edinburgh EH16 5QA. *T:* (0131) 667 8298. *Club:* New (Edinburgh).   *Died 2 Aug. 1998.*

FREEDMAN, Louis, CBE 1978; Proprietor, Cliveden Stud; *b* 5 Feb. 1917; 4th *s* of Sampson and Leah Freedman; *m* 1st, 1944, Cara Kathlyn Abrahamson (marr. diss.); one *s* one *d*; 2nd, 1960, Valerie Clarke; one *s. Educ:* University College School. FSVA. TA, RE, 1938; commnd RA, 1943; Devonshire Regt, 1944. Director: Land Securities Investment Trust, 1958–77; GRA Gp, then Wembley PLC, 1985–94. Mem., Race Relations Bd, 1968–77. Chm., Nat. Assoc. Property Owners, 1971–72; Pres., Racehorse Owners Assoc., 1972–74. Vice-Chm., NE Thames RHA, 1975–79; Chairman: Camden and Islington AHA, 1979–82; City and Hackney DHA, 1982–84. Governor: Royal Hosp. of St Bartholomew the Great, 1971–74; St Bartholomew's Hosp. Med. Coll., 1974–96 (Chm. Special Trustees, 1988–92). Owned and bred: Polygamy, winner of the Oaks, 1974; Reference Point, winner of the Derby, King George VI and Queen Elizabeth Stakes, and the St Leger, 1987. *Recreation:* gardening. *Address:* Cliveden Stud House, Taplow, Maidenhead, Berks SL6 0HL. *Clubs:* Garrick; Jockey (Newmarket) (Deputy Senior Steward, 1981–83).   *Died 21 Dec. 1998.*

FREEMAN, Sir Ralph, Kt 1970; CVO 1964; CBE 1952 (MBE (mil.) 1945); FEng 1976; FICE, FASCE, FWeldI; retired consulting engineer; Senior Partner, Freeman, Fox & Partners, 1963–79, (Partner, 1947–79); *b* 3 Feb. 1911; *s* of late Sir Ralph Freeman and Mary (*née* Lines); *m* 1939, Joan Elizabeth, *er d* of late Col J. G. Rose, DSO, VD, FRIC, Wynberg, Cape, S Africa; one *s* one *d* (and one *s* decd). *Educ:* Uppingham Sch.; Worcester Coll., Oxford (MA; Hon. Fellow, 1980). Construction Engineer: Dorman Long & Co., S Africa, Rhodesia and Denmark, 1932–36 and 1937–39; Braithwaite & Co., 1936–37; on staff of Freeman, Fox & Partners, 1939–46, Admty and other war work; served RE, Exp. Bridging Estabt (later seconded as bridging adviser to CE 21 Army Gp HQ, NW Europe campaign, 1943–45; Temp. Major, 1945). Consulting Engr for Sandringham Estate, 1949–76. Past Pres., Instn of Civil Engrs (Mem. Council, 1951–55 and 1957–61; Vice-Pres., 1962–66; Pres., 1966–67); Mem. Emeritus, Smeatonian Soc. of Civil Engrs, 1984 (Mem., 1960; Pres., 1978). Member: Governing Body, SE London Techn. Coll., 1952–58; Nat. Cons. Council to Min. of Works, 1952–56; Bd of Governors, Westminster Hosp., 1963–69; Council, Worcester Coll. Soc., 1964–87; Adv. Council on Scientific Res. and Develt (MoD), 1966–69; Defence Scientific Adv. Council, 1969–72; Royal Fine Art Commn, 1968–85; Council, Assoc. of Consulting Engrs, 1969–72, 1973–77, Chm., 1975–76; Governing Body, Imp. Coll. of Science and Technology, 1975–83; Chm., Limpsfield

Common Local Management Cttee, 1957–82 (Chm. NT Local Mgt Cttee, 1972–82). Pres., Welding Inst., 1975–77. Col, Engr and Rly Staff Corps RE (T&AVR), 1963–76, Col comdg 1970–74. Hon. Mem., Instn Royal Engrs, 1971; Hon. FIMcchE 1971; Hon. Fellow, Zimbabwe (formerly Rhodesian) Instn of Engrs, 1969; FRSA. DUniv Surrey, 1978. Kt, Order of Orange Nassau (Netherlands), 1945. *Publications:* several papers in Proc. ICE and other professional jls. *Recreations:* wood and metal work, letter writing. *Address:* Ballards Shaw, Ballards Lane, Limpsfield, Oxted, Surrey RH8 0SN. *T:* (01883) 723284. *Clubs:* Army and Navy; Leander (Henley-on-Thames).
Died 24 Aug. 1998.

FREEMAN, His Honour Richard Gavin; a Circuit Judge (formerly County Court Judge), 1968–83; *b* 18 Oct. 1910; *s* of John Freeman, MD, and Violet Alice Leslie Hadden, *m* 1937, Marjorie Pear; one *s* two *d*; *m* 1961, Winifred Ann Bell. *Educ:* Charterhouse; Hertford Coll., Oxford. Called to Bar, Gray's Inn, 1947. Deputy Chairman, Warwick Quarter Sessions, 1963–71. Hon. Major, RA. *Recreations:* cricket, gardening. *Address:* 10 Rees Street, N1 7AR. *Club:* Streatley Cricket.
Died 15 May 1997.

FREER, Charles Edward Jesse; DL; *b* 4 March 1901; *s* of late Canon S. Thorold Winckley, FSA and Elizabeth (*née* Freer); changed name to Freer by Deed Poll, 1922; *m* 1st, 1927, Violet Muriel (*d* 1944), *d* of H. P. Gae, CBE, Leicester; two *s* two *d*; 2nd, 1945, Cynthia Lilian, *d* of Leonard R. Braithwaite, FRCS, Leeds; two *d. Educ:* Radley Coll. Solicitor, 1924. Served RA (TA) in France, 1940; DJAG in Iceland, 1941–42; at SHAEF, 1943–44, Lt-Col. Chm., Leicestershire QS, 1949–71. Chm. Leicester Diocesan Board of Finance, 1946–56; Chm. Mental Health Tribunal, Sheffield Regional Board, 1961–73; a Chm. of Industrial Tribunals, 1966–73. DL 1946, JP 1946–71, Leics. *Recreations:* reading, walking. *Address:* Elmstead Lodge, 3 Elmstead Road, Canford Cliffs, Poole, Dorset BH13 7EY. *T:* (01202) 709490. *Clubs:* East India, Devonshire, Sports and Public Schools; Parkstone Yacht.
Died 10 April 1998.

FRENCH, Leslie Richard; actor; *b* Kent, 23 April 1904; *s* of Robert Gilbert French and Jetty Sands Leahy; unmarried. *Educ:* London Coll. of Choristers. Began stage work, 1914; early Shakespearean training with Sir Philip Ben Greet; parts included Hansel in Hansel and Gretel, Bert in Derby Day; Shakespearean parts included Puck, Ariel, Feste, Costard, etc; The Spirit in Comus; played Feste in the ballet Twelfth Night with the International Ballet at His Majesty's Theatre; Lord Fancourt Babberly in Charley's Aunt, Christmas 1943; produced Much Ado About Nothing and The Tempest for OUDS; Everyman as a ballet for the International Ballet Co., Lyric Theatre, 1943; Comus for the International Ballet, London Coliseum, 1946; other productions included: Charles and Mary, Cheltenham Festival, 1948; The Servant of Two Masters; Aladdin (Widow Twanky); Mother Goose (Mother Goose); She Stoops to Conquer (Tony Lumpkin), Edinburgh Festival, 1949; pantomime, Cinderella, 1950; The Dish Ran Away, Whitehall, 1950; Midsummer Night's Dream (Puck), Open Air Theatre during Cheltenham Festival; Open Air Theatre, Regent's Park, 1951; pantomime, Nottingham, 1951–52; The Ghost Train, Huddersfield, 1952; Pisanio in Cymbeline, Attendant Spirit in Comus, Open Air Theatre, 1952; Dyrkin in Out of the Whirlwind, Westminster Abbey, 1953; Open Air Theatre, Cape Town: The Taming of the Shrew, 1956; Midsummer Night's Dream, 1957; As You Like It (Touchstone), 1958; Johannesburg: The Tempest, 1956; Hamlet, 1957; Shakespearean seasons in Cape Town, 1959, 1960, 1961, 1962, 1963, 1966, 1969; The Tempest, E. Oppenheimer Theatre, OFS, 1968; The Tell Tale Heart,

1969; An Evening with Shakespeare (tour), 1969; Twelfth Night, Port Elizabeth, 1970; The Way of the World, S Africa, 1970; Co-dir, Open Air Theatre, Regent's Park, 1958; prod Twelfth Night (in Great Hall of Hampton Ct Palace), 1965; Le Streghe (for Visconti), 1966; toured USA, 1969–70 and 1970–71: one man Shakespearean recitals, and Shylock in Merchant of Venice; The Chaplain in The Lady's not for Burning, Chichester Festival, 1972; toured USA, 1973; recitals and prod Twelfth Night; The Tempest, Cape Town, 1973; As You Like It, Port Elizabeth, 1973; Shakespeare (one-man show), Cape Town, Port Elizabeth, 1991; prod Love's Labour's Lost, Maynardville Open Air Theatre, 1991; Caroline, Yvonne Arnaud Theatre; directed: Saturday Sunday Monday, Nat. Arts Council, S Africa, 1976; Romeo and Juliet, Cape Town, 1980; numerous appearances on TV, incl.: Villette (serial), 1970; The Singing Detective, 1986; The Book Liberator, 1988. *Films:* Orders to Kill (M Lafitte), 1957; The Scapegoat (M Lacoste), 1958; The Singer not the Song (Father Gomez); The Leopard (Chevalley), 1963; The Witches, 1966; Happy Ever After, 1966; Joseph of Coppertino, 1966; Death in Venice (dir, Visconti), 1970. First Exhibition of Paintings—oil and water colour, Parsons Gall. Presented with Key to City of Cape Town, Jan. 1963. Gold Medals: Port Elizabeth Shakespeare Society, 1973; 1820 Settlers, 1978; Grahamstown Festival, 1977; Hon. Life Mem., Mark Twain Soc., USA, 1976 (all in recognition of his contribution to art and culture in the theatre in England and overseas). Royal Corps of Signals, 1942. *Recreations:* gardening, painting. *Address:* 11 Chesterfield Road, Ewell West, Surrey KT19 9QR. *T:* (020) 8393 1333. *Club:* Garrick.

Died 21 Jan. 1999.

FRENCH, Neville Arthur Irwin, CMG 1976; LVO 1968; HM Diplomatic Service, retired; *b* Kenya, 28 April 1920; *s* of late Major Ernest French and Alice Irwin (*née* Powell); *m* 1945, Joyce Ethel, *d* of late Henry Robert Greene, Buenos Aires and Montevideo; one *s* two *d. Educ:* London Sch. of Economics (BSc (Econ)). Fleet Auxiliary and Special Duties, Min. of War Transport, 1939–45. Colonial Admin. Service, Tanganyika, 1948, later HMOCS; District Comr, 1949–61; Principal Asst Sec. (External Affairs), Prime Minister's Office, Dar es Salaam, 1961; retd from HMOCS, 1962; Central African Office, 1963–64; 1st Sec., British High Commn, Salisbury, 1964–66; Head of Chancery, British Embassy, Rio de Janeiro, 1966–69; Asst Head of Western Organisations Dept, FCO, 1970–72; Counsellor, and Chargé d'Affaires, Havana, 1972–75; Governor and C-in-C, Falkland Islands, and High Comr, British Antarctic Territory, 1975–77; Dep. High Comr, Madras, 1977–80. Mem., LSE Club. Comdr, Order of Rio Branco (Brazil), 1968. *Recreations:* sailing, books. *Address:* c/o Barclays Bank, 84 High Street, Bideford, Devon EX39 2AL. *Clubs:* Commonwealth Trust; Madras. *Died 21 April 1996.*

FRIEND, His Honour (Archibald) Gordon; a Circuit Judge, 1972–84, retired; *b* 6 July 1912; *m* 1940, Patricia Margaret Smith (*d* 1993); no *c. Educ:* Dulwich Coll.; Keble Coll., Oxford (MA). Called to the Bar, Inner Temple, 1933. Served War of 1939–45: enlisted RA, Feb. 1940, commnd Nov. 1940; on staff of JAG MEF and PAIFORCE, 1941–44 (Major); released 1945. Dep. Chm., Herts Quarter Sessions, 1963–71, Inner London, later Middx, QS, 1965–71; Inner London Crown Court, 1972–74; Knightsbridge Crown Court, 1974–84. *Recreation:* gardening. *Address:* Amesbury Abbey, Amesbury, Wilts SP4 7EX. *Died 25 April 1997.*

FRITH, Donald Alfred, OBE 1980; MA; Secretary, Headmasters' Conference, and General Secretary, Secondary Heads' Association, 1979–83; *b* 13 May 1918; *yr s* of late Charles Henry Frith and Mabel (*née* Whiting);

m 1941, Mary Webster Tyler (*d* 1989), *yr d* of late Raymond Tyler and Rosina Mary (*née* Wiles); four *s* one *d. Educ:* Whitgift Sch. (schol.); Christ's Coll., Cambridge (schol.; MA 1944). Served War, 1940–46; commnd RASC; served in Middle East, Italy and at WO. Deme Warden, University College Sch., 1946–52; Headmaster, Richmond Sch., Yorks, 1953–59; Headmaster, Archbishop Holgate's Grammar Sch., York, 1959–78. Asst Dir, Centre for Study of Comprehensive Schs, 1983–88; Chm., N Yorks Forum for Vol. Orgns, 1983–91; Dir, N Yorks TEC, 1990–93. Chm., School Curriculum (formerly Schools Council) Industry Project, 1979–86. Additional Mem., N Yorks CC Educn Cttee, 1973–77. Chm., York Community Council, 1971–79. JP York, 1966–79. *Publication:* (gen. ed.) School Management in Practice, 1985. *Recreations:* music, gardening, reading.

Died 23 March 2000.

FROST, Hon. Sir (Thomas) Sydney, Kt 1975; Chief Justice of Papua New Guinea, 1975–78, retired; *b* 13 Feb. 1916; *s* of late Thomas Frost, Redfern, NSW; *m* 1943, Dorothy Gertrude (*née* Kelly) (*d* 1990); two *s* one *d. Educ:* Univ. of Melbourne (Alexander Rushall Meml Scholarship; LLM). Served 2nd AIF, 1941–45. Barrister, Victoria, 1945–64; QC 1961; Judge of the County Court of Victoria, 1964; Judge of Supreme Court of Papua New Guinea, 1964–75. Chairman: Aust. Govt Inquiry into Whales and Whaling, 1978; Royal Commn of Inquiry into Housing Commn Land Purchases and Valuation Matters, Vic, 1979–81; Bd of Accident Inquiry into causes of crash of Beechcraft Super King Air, Sydney, 21 Feb. 1980, 1982. Pres., Medical Services Review Tribunal, 1979–84.

Died 20 April 1997.

FRY, Peter George Robin Plantagenet S.; *see* Somerset Fry.

FRY, Hon. Sir William Gordon, Kt 1980; JP; President, Legislative Council of Victoria, Australia, 1976–79; *b* 12 June 1909; *s* of A. G. Fry, Ballarat; *m* 1936, Lilian G., *d* of A. W. Macrae; four *s. Educ:* Ballarat High School; Melbourne Univ. Served War of 1939–45, 2nd AIF (Lt-Col, despatches). Education Dept of Victoria for 40 years; Headmaster of various schools, including Cheltenham East, Windsor, Cheltenham Heights. Councillor, City of Moorabbin; Mayor, 1968; MLC (Lib) for Higinbotham, Vic, 1967–79. Past Chm., Parly Select Cttee, Road Safety. Vice-Pres., Victoria League; Mem., RSL. Formerly Dep. Chm., World Bowls. Life Governor: Melbourne and Dist Ambulance Soc.; Royal Women's Hosp.; Royal Melbourne Hosp.; Gen. Management Cttee, Royal Victoria Eye and Ear Hosp.; Management Bd, Cheltenham-Mordialloc Hosp. (18 years service); Committee Member: Melbourne Family Care Orgn; Richmond Foundn; Legacy Australia; Brighton Tech. Coll. JP Melbourne, 1968. *Recreations:* lawn bowls, golf, swimming. *Address:* 139 Atherton Road, Oakleigh, Victoria 3166, Australia. *Clubs:* West Brighton; Royal Commonwealth Society (Victoria); Returned Services League (Cheltenham-Moorabbin).

Died 29 Sept. 2000.

FRYER, David Richard, OBE 1994; Secretary-General, Royal Town Planning Institute, since 1976; *b* 16 May 1936; *s* of Ernest William Fryer and Gladys Edith Battey; *m* 1961, Carole Elizabeth Hayes; one *s* two *d. Educ:* Chesterfield Sch.; New Coll., Oxford (MA, BCL). LMRTPI. Admitted solicitor, 1961. Articled Clerk and Asst Solicitor, Chesterfield Bor. Council, 1958–61; Associate Lawyer, Messrs Jones, Day, Cockley & Reavis, Cleveland, Ohio, 1961–63; Asst Solicitor, N Riding CC, 1963–65; Sen. Asst Solicitor, Bucks CC, 1966–69; Dep. Sec., RICS, 1970–75. Sec., Brit. Chapter, Internat. Real Estate Fedn, 1970–75; Pres., Internat. Fedn for Housing and Planning, 1992– (Mem., Bureau and Council, 1976–); Dep. Pres., 1984–92); Sec.-Gen., European Council of

Town Planners, 1987–. Member: Exec. Cttee and Council, Public Works Congress and Exhibn Council Ltd, 1976–90; Exec. Cttee, Nat. Council for Social Service, 1976–79 (Chm., Planning and Environment Gp); Council and Standards Cttee, Nat. House-Bldg Council, 1976–95; Exec. Cttee, Commonwealth Assoc. of Planners, 1984–88. FRSA 1981. *Recreations:* international affairs, architecture, the countryside. *Address:* Stairways, Portway Road, Hartwell, Aylesbury, Bucks HP17 8RP. *T:* Aylesbury (01296) 748538. *Club:* East India.

Died 27 Feb. 1996.

FUCHS, Sir Vivian (Ernest), Kt 1958; PhD; FRS 1974; Director of the British Antarctic Survey, 1958–73; Leader, Commonwealth Trans-Antarctic Expedition, 1955–58; *b* 11 Feb. 1908; *s* of late Ernest Fuchs, Farnham, Surrey, and Violet Anne Fuchs (*née* Watson); *m* 1st, 1933, Joyce (*d* 1990), 2nd *d* of late John Connell; one *s* one *d* (and one *d* decd); 2nd, 1991, Mrs Eleanor Honnywill. *Educ:* Brighton Coll.; St John's Coll., Cambridge (MA; PhD 1936; Hon. Fellow, 1983). Geologist with: Cambridge East Greenland Expedn, 1929; Cambridge Expedn to E African Lakes, 1930–31; E African Archæological Expedn, 1931–32; Leader, Lake Rudolf Rift Valley Expedn, 1933–34; Royal Geog. Society Cuthbert Peek Grant, 1936; Leader, Lake Rukwa Expedn, 1937–38, 2nd Lieut Cambs Regt, TA, 1939; served in W Africa, 1942–43; Staff Coll., Camberley, 1943; served NW Europe (despatches), 1944–46; demobilized (Major), 1946; Leader Falkland Islands Dependencies Survey (Antarctica), 1947–50; Dir, Falkland Is Dependencies Scientific Bureau, 1950–55. President: Internat. Glaciological Soc., 1963–66; British Assoc. for Advancement of Science, 1972; Mem. Council, RGS, 1958–61, Vice-Pres. 1961–64, Pres., 1982–84, Hon. Vice-Pres., 1985–. Founder's Gold Medal, Royal Geog. Soc., 1951; Silver Medal, RSA, 1952; Polar Medal, 1953, and Clasp, 1958; Special Gold Medal, Royal Geog. Soc., 1958; Gold Medal, Royal Scottish Geog. Society, 1958; Gold Medal, Geog. Society (Paris), 1958; Richthofen Medal (Berlin), 1958; Kirchenpauer Medal (Hamburg), 1958; Plancius Medal (Amsterdam), 1959; Egede Medal (Copenhagen), 1959; Hubbard Medal, Nat. Geog. Soc. (Washington), 1959; Explorers Club Medal (New York), 1959; Geog. Soc. (Chicago) Gold Medal, 1959; Geol Soc. of London Prestwich Medal, 1960. Hon. Fellow, Wolfson (formerly University Coll.), Cambridge, 1970. Hon. LLD Edinburgh, 1958; Hon. DSc: Durham, 1958; Cantab, 1959; Leicester, 1972; Hon. ScD Swansea, 1971; Hon. LLD Birmingham, 1974. *Publications:* The Crossing of Antarctica (with Sir Edmund Hillary), 1958; Antarctic Adventure, 1959; (ed) Forces of Nature, 1977; Of Ice and Men, 1982; (ed) The Physical World (Oxford Illustrated Encyclopedia), 1985; A Time to Speak (autobiog.), 1990; geographical and geological reports and papers in scientific jls. *Recreation:* gardening. *Address:* 106 Barton Road, Cambridge CB3 9LH. *T:* (01223) 359238. *Club:* Athenæum.					*Died 11 Nov. 1999.*

FUKUI, Prof. Dr Kenichi; Order of Culture, Person of Cultural Merits (Japan), 1981; Grand Cordon, Order of the Rising Sun (Japan), 1988; Director, Institute for Fundamental Chemistry, Kyoto, Japan, since 1988; *b* 4 Oct. 1918; *s* of Ryokichi Fukui and Chie Fukui (*née* Sugizawa); *m* 1947, Tomoe Horie; one *s* one *d. Educ:* Kyoto Imperial Univ. (AB Engrg, PhD Engrg). Lecturer, 1943–45, Asst Professor, 1945–51, Professor, 1951–82, Kyoto University; Pres., Kyoto Inst. of Technology, 1982–88. Member: European Acad. of Arts, Sciences and Humanities, 1981–; Japan Acad., 1983–; Pontifical Acad. of Sciences, 1985–. Foreign Associate, Nat. Acad. of Sciences, Washington, 1981–; Foreign Hon. Mem., Amer. Acad. of Arts and Sciences, 1983–; Foreign Mem., Royal Soc., 1989. Hon. DSc Wales, 1992. Nobel Prize in

Chemistry (jtly), 1981. *Address:* 23 Kitashirakawahirai-cho, Sakyo-ku, Kyoto 606, Japan. *T:* (075) 7815785.

Died 9 Jan. 1998.

FULCHER, Derick Harold, DSC 1944; Assistant Under-Secretary of State, Department of Health and Social Security, 1969–70; *b* 4 Nov. 1917; *s* of late Percy Frederick Fulcher and Gertrude Lilian Fulcher; *m* 1943, Florence Ellen May Anderson; one *s* one *d. Educ:* St Olave's Grammar School. Served in Royal Navy, 1940–46 (Lieut, RNVR). Entered Civil Service (War Office), 1936; Asst Principal, Ministry of National Insurance, 1947; Principal, 1950; Admin. Staff Coll., Henley, 1952; Asst Sec. 1959; seconded to HM Treasury, 1957–59; served on an ILO mission in Trinidad and Tobago, 1967–69. Interviewer for CS Commn, 1971–79. UK Delegate to and Chairman: NATO Management Survey Cttee, 1970–71; Council of Europe Management Survey Cttee, 1971–72. Chm., Supplementary Benefit Appeal Tribunals, 1971–75; Head of UK res. project in W Europe into social security provision for disablement, 1971–72; Res. Consultant, Office of Manpower Econs, 1972–73; served on technical aid mission to Indonesia, 1973; ILO Res. Consultant on Social Security, 1973–80; Consultant to: EEC Statistical Office, 1974; Govt of Thailand on Social Security, 1978–79 and 1981. Fellow, Inst. for European Health Services Research, Leuven Univ., Belgium, 1974. *Publications:* Medical Care Systems, 1974; Social Security for the Unemployed, 1976. *Recreations:* walking, photography, travel. *Address:* 100 Downs Road, Coulsdon, Surrey CR5 1AF. *T:* (01737) 554231. *Club:* Civil Service.					*Died 27 Aug. 1999.*

FULLER, Major Sir John (William Fleetwood), 3rd Bt *cr* 1910, of Neston Park, Corsham, Wiltshire; Major, The Life Guards, retired; *b* 18 Dec. 1936; *s* of Major Sir John Gerard Henry Fleetwood Fuller, 2nd Bt, and Fiona, Countess of Normanton, (*d* 1985), *d* of 4th Marquess Camden, OCVO, 9 Father, 1981, *m* 1960, Lorna Marian, *o d* of F. R. Kemp-Potter, Findon, Sussex; three *s. Heir: s* James Henry Fleetwood Fuller, *b* 1 Nov. 1970. *Address:* Neston Park, Corsham, Wilts SN13 9TG.

Died 3 April 1998.

FULTHORPE, Henry Joseph, FRINA; RCNC; General Manager, HM Dockyard, Portsmouth (Deputy Director of Naval Construction), 1967–75; *b* Portsmouth, 2 July 1916; *s* of Joseph Henry and Clarissa Fulthorpe; *m* 1939, Bette May Forshew; two *s* one *d. Educ:* Royal Naval Coll., Greenwich. Ship Design and Production, Admiralty, London and Bath, 1939–43; Principal (Ship) Overseer, Vickers, Barrow-in-Furness, 1943–46; Dep. Manager, HM Dockyard, Malta, 1946–49; Sec., Radiological Defence Panel, 1949–52; Staff Constr, first British atom bomb, Montebello Is, 1952–53; Constr i/c Minesweeper Design, Admty, Bath, 1953–54; Chief Constr, Maintenance, Bath, 1954–56; Dep. Manager, HM Dockyard, Portsmouth, 1956–58; Chief Constructor: HM Dockyard, Singapore, 1958–61; Dockyard Dept, Bath, 1961–63; Asst Dir of Naval Construction, Bath, 1963–64; Production Manager, HM Dockyard, Chatham, 1964–67; Manager, Constructive Dept, HM Dockyard, Portsmouth, 1967. *Address:* Apt 70, Holmbush Court, Queens Crescent, Southsea PO5 3HY. *T:* (023) 9275 0427.					*Died 31 Jan. 1999.*

FURLONG, Hon. Robert Stafford, MBE (mil.) 1945; Chief Justice of Newfoundland, 1959–79; *b* 9 Dec. 1904; *o s* of Martin Williams Furlong, KC, and Mary Furlong (*née* McGrath). *Educ:* St Bonaventure's Coll., St John's, Newfoundland. Called to the Newfoundland Bar, 1926; appointed KC 1944. Temp. Actg Lt-Comdr (S) RNVR. OStJ 1937; Knight of St Gregory 1958. *Recreations:* golf, motoring. *Address:* 8 Winter Avenue, St John's,

Newfoundland, Canada. *T:* (709) 7267228. *Clubs:* Bally Haly Golf and Country, Crow's Nest (St John's).

Died 9 Feb. 1996.

FURNIVAL JONES, Sir (Edward) Martin, Kt 1967; CBE 1957; *b* 7 May 1912; *s* of Edward Furnival Jones, FCA; *m* 1955, Elizabeth Margaret, *d* of Bartholomew Snowball, BSc, AMIEE; one *d. Educ:* Highgate Sch.; Gonville and Caius Coll., Cambridge (exhibitioner). MA 1938. Admitted a Solicitor, 1937. Served War of 1939–45: General Staff Officer at Supreme Headquarters, Allied Expeditionary Force, and War Office (despatches, American Bronze Star Medal). Head of MI5, 1965–72. Chm. of Bd, Frensham Heights, 1973–76 (Pres. 1977–95). *Recreation:* birdwatching.   *Died 1 March 1997.*

FUSSEY, Dr David Eric; Vice-Chancellor, University of Greenwich, since 1993; *b* 5 Sept. 1943; *s* of Frank Eric Fussey and Edna May Rowntree; *m* 1966, Beryl Kathleen Taylor; two *s. Educ:* Hymers College, Hull; Corpus Christi Coll., Cambridge (MA Mech. Scis); Univ. of Warwick (PhD Eng Sci.). CEng, FIMechE; FInstE; ARCM. Research Officer, CEGB Marchwood Engrg Labs, 1964–69; Lectr in Mech. Engrg, Univ. of Nottingham, 1969–78; Prof. and Head of Mech. Engrg, Univ. of Technology, PNG, 1978–82; Prof. and Head of Mech. Engrg, then Dean of Technology, Plymouth Poly., 1982–89; Dep. Dir, Coventry Poly., later Univ., 1989–93. Former appts with IMechE, CNAA and other professional orgns; Engineering Council: Mem. Council, 1990–96; Chm., Standing Cttee for Engrg Profession, 1994–95; Science and Engineering Research Council: Mem., Engrg and Technol. Bd, 1992–94; Chm., Educn and Trng Cttee, 1992–94. Mem., Jt Inf. Systems Cttee, 1993–96; Commonwealth Scholarships Comr, 1995–; Mem. Bd, HEFCE, 1996–. Mem. Council, Kent Opera, 1996–. Trustee, Greenwich Millennium Trust, 1996–. *Publications:* papers in magnetohydrodynamics, heat transfer, combustion and combustion-generated pollution. *Recreations:* choral and keyboard music, walking. *Address:* Maritime Greenwich University Campus, Greenwich, SE10 9NN.   *Died 16 March 2000.*

G

GABLE, Christopher Michael, CBE 1996; dancer, choreographer, actor; Artistic Director: Central School of Ballet, since 1982 (also Founder); Northern Ballet Theatre, since 1987; *b* 13 March 1940; *m* Carole Needham; one *s* one *d*. *Educ:* Sadler's Wells Ballet Sch. Former ballet dancer with Sadler's Wells Opera and Theatre Ballets, Covent Garden Opera Ballet and Royal Ballet; danced all the major classical rôles, partnered all the company ballerinas of his day and also created many rôles incl. Romeo in MacMillan's Romeo and Juliet, 1965. *Choreographed:* Coppélia, 1988; Romeo and Juliet; Don Quixote, 1988; Swan Lake, 1992; *directed:* Giselle (Manchester Evening News Award, Best Dance Prodn of Year), 1990; Romeo and Juliet (Dance and Dancers mag., Dance Prodn of Year), 1991; A Christmas Carol, 1992; Dracula, 1996; The Hunchback of Notre Dame, 1998; *directed and choreographed:* Cinderella, 1993; Swan Lake, 1994; Don Quixote, 1996; *films* included: (as actor): Women in Love, 1969; The Music Lovers, 1971; The Boy Friend, 1972; The Slipper and the Rose, 1976; The Rainbow, 1989; *theatre* included: (as actor): Time and the Conways, 1973; The Last of Mrs Cheyney, Chichester, 1980; A Midsummer Night's Dream, RSC; The Misanthrope, Royal Exchange, Manchester, 1981. *Address:* Northern Ballet Theatre, West Park Centre, Spen Lane, Leeds LS16 5BE; Central School of Ballet, 10 Herbal Hill, Clerkenwell Road, EC1R 5EJ.
Died 23 Oct. 1998.

GAINHAM, Sarah, (Rachel Ames); author; *b* 1 Oct. 1922; *d* of Tom Stainer and May Genevieve Gainham; *m* 1st, 1947, Antony Terry (marr. diss. 1964; he *d* 1992); 2nd, 1964, Kenneth Ames (*d* 1975). *Educ:* Newbury High Sch. for Girls; afterwards largely self educated. From 1947 onwards, travelled extensively in Central and E Europe; Central Europe Correspondent of The Spectator, 1956–66. FRSL 1984. *Publications:* Time Right Deadly, 1956; Cold Dark Night, 1957; The Mythmaker, 1957; Stone Roses, 1959; Silent Hostage, 1960; Night Falls on the City, 1967 (Book Soc. Choice and US Book of Month Club); A Place in the Country, 1968; Takeover Bid, 1970; Private Worlds, 1971; Maculan's Daughter, 1973; To the Opera Ball, 1975; The Habsburg Twilight, 1979; The Tiger, Life, 1983; A Discursive Essay on the Presentation of Recent History in England, 1999; contrib. to Encounter, Atlantic Monthly, BBC, etc. *Recreations:* theatre, opera, European history. *Address:* altes Forsthaus, Schlosspark, 2404 Petronell, Austria.
Died 24 Nov. 1999.

GAIRY, Rt Hon. Sir Eric Matthew, Kt 1977; PC 1977; Prime Minister of Grenada, 1974–79; also Minister of External Affairs, Planning and Development Lands and Tourism, Information Service, Public Relations and Natural Resources, 1974–79; *b* 18 Feb. 1922; *m* 1949, Cynthia Clyne; two *d*. Formerly: schoolteacher, Grenada; clerk, Trinidad. Founder and Leader, Grenada United Labour Party, 1950–. Member of Legislative Council, 1951–52 and 1954–55; Minister of Trade and Production, 1956–57; Chief Minister and Minister of Finance until 1962; Premier, 1967–74; independence of Grenada, 1974.
Died 23 Aug. 1997.

GAJE GHALE, VC 1943; Subedar 2/5 Royal Gurkha Rifles Field Force; *b* 1 July 1922; *s* of Bikram Ghale; *m* 1st, 1939, Dhansuba; no *c*; four *s* four *d* (and one *d* decd) from 2nd marriage. *Educ:* IA 2nd class certificate of education. Enlisted as a Recruit Boy 2nd Bn 5th Royal Gurkha Rifles

FF, Feb. 1935; transferred to the ranks, Aug. 1935; Naik, 1941; Acting Havildar, May 1942; War Subst. Havildar, Nov. 1942; Bn Havildar Major, June 1943; Jemadar, Aug. 1943. Waziristan operations, 1936–37 (medal with clasp); Burma, 1942–43 (1939–45 Star, VC). *Recreations:* football, basketball, badminton, draughts.
Died 28 March 2000.

GALE, Hon. George Alexander, CC 1977; Chief Justice of Ontario, 1967–76; Vice-Chairman, Ontario Law Reform Commission, 1977–81; *b* 24 June 1906; *s* of late Robert Henry and Elma Gertrude Gale; *m* 1934, Hilda Georgina Daly; three *s*. *Educ:* Prince of Wales High Sch., Vancouver; Toronto Univ. (BA); Osgoode Hall Law Sch., Toronto. Called to Ontario Bar, 1932; Partner, Mason, Foulds, Davidson & Gale, 1944; KC (Can.) 1945; Justice, Supreme Court of Ontario, 1946; Justice, Court of Appeal, Ontario, 1963; Chief Justice of High Court of Justice for Ontario, 1964. Formerly Chm. Judicial Council for Provincial Judges; Chm., Cttee on Rules of Practice for Ontario (Mem. 1941–76); former Mem. Canadian Bar Assoc. (formerly Mem. Council); Hon. Mem., Georgia Bar Assoc.; formerly Hon. Lectr, Osgoode Law Sch.; formerly Mem. Exec. Cttee, Canadian Judicial Council. Mem., Ontario Adv. Cttee on Confederation; formerly Chm., Ontario Rhodes Scholarship Selection Cttee; Hon. Mem., Canadian Corps of Commissionaires, 1977. Mem. Bd of Governors: Wycliffe Coll., Toronto Univ.; Ecumenical Foundn of Canada; formerly, Upper Canada Coll., Toronto. Mem. Delta Kappa Epsilon, Phi Delta Phi (Hon.). Anglican; Warden, St John's, York Mills, for 5 years. Hon. Pres., Ontario Curling Assoc. Hon. LLD: McMaster, 1968; York (Toronto), 1969; Windsor, 1980. *Publication:* (ed with Holmested) Practice and Procedure in Ontario, 6th edn. *Recreations:* golf, photography. *Clubs:* Lawyers, (Hon. Mem.) York (Toronto); Toronto Curling, Chippewa Golf.
Died 25 July 1997.

GALLIE, Prof. (Walter) Bryce; Professor of Political Science, and Fellow of Peterhouse, Cambridge University, 1967–78, Professor Emeritus, 1978, Emeritus Fellow 1982; *b* 5 Oct. 1912; 3rd *s* of Walter S. Gallie, structural engineer; *m* 1940, Menna Humphreys (*d* 1990); one *s* one *d*. *Educ:* Sedbergh Sch.; Balliol Coll., Oxford (Classical Exhibitioner). BA (1st Cl. PPE), 1934, BLitt 1937, MA Oxon, 1947. University College of Swansea: Asst Lectr, Philosophy, 1935; Lectr, 1938; Sen. Lectr, 1948; Prof. of Philosophy, University Coll. of North Staffordshire 1950; Prof. of Logic and Metaphysics, Queen's Univ., Belfast, 1954–67. Visiting Prof., New York Univ., 1962–63; Lectures: Lewis Fry Meml, Bristol Univ., 1964; Wiles, QUB, 1976; J. R. Jones Meml, UC Swansea, 1983; E. H. Carr Meml, UC Aberystwyth, 1987. Pres., Aristotelian Soc., 1970–71. Hon. Professorial Fellow, Univ. of Wales, 1980. Served War, 1940–45, ending with rank of Major; Croix de Guerre 1945. *Publications:* An English School, 1949; Peirce and Pragmatism, 1952; Free Will and Determinism Yet Again (Inaugural Lecture), 1957; A New University: A. D. Lindsay and the Keele Experiment, 1960; Philosophy and the Historical Understanding, 1964; Philosophers of Peace and War, 1978; Understanding War, 1990; articles in Mind, Aristotelian Soc. Proc., Philosophy, Political Studies, etc. *Recreations:* travelling, reading. *Address:* Cilhendre, Upper Saint Mary Street, Newport, Dyfed SA42 0PS. *T:* (01239) 820574.
Died 31 Aug. 1998.

GALLIERS-PRATT, Anthony Malcolm, CBE 1977; *b* 31 Jan. 1926; *s* of George Kenneth and Phyllis Galliers-Pratt; *m* 1950, Angela, *d* of Sir Charles Cayzer, 3rd Bt, and of Lady Cayzer, OBE; three *s. Educ:* Eton. Entered F. Pratt Engineering Corp. Ltd, 1949; Dir, 1951; subseq. Man. Dir and Chm., to 1981. *Recreations:* yachting, shooting. *Address:* Can Savella, Savella 13, Palma 07001, Mallorca. *Died 20 Feb. 1998.*

GAMES, Abram, OBE 1958; RDI 1959; graphic designer; *b* 29 July 1914; *s* of Joseph and Sarah Games; *m* 1945, Marianne Salfeld (*d* 1988); one *s* two *d. Educ:* Grocers' Company Sch., Hackney Downs. Studio, 1932–36; freelance designer, 1936–40; Infantry, 1940–41; War Office Poster Designer, 1941–46; freelance, 1946–; Lecturer Royal College of Art, 1947–53. Postage Stamps for Great Britain and Israel, Festival of Britain, BBC Television, Queen's Award to Industry Emblems. One-man shows of graphic design: London and UK, New York, Los Angeles, Chicago, Brussels, Stockholm, Jerusalem, Tel Aviv, São Paulo; Rep. GB at Museum of Modern Art, New York. Hon. FRCA 1992. Hon. DLitt Staffordshire Univ., 1994. First prizes, Poster Competitions: Helsinki, 1957; Lisbon, 1959; New York, 1960; Stockholm, 1962; Barcelona, 1964; Design Medal, Soc. of Industrial Artists, 1960; Silver Medal, Royal Society of Arts, 1962; first prize, Internat. Philatelic Competition, Italy, 1976; President's Award, Design and Art Direction, 1991. Inventor of Imagic Copying Processes. *Publication:* Over my Shoulder, 1960. *Recreations:* painting, carpentry. *Address:* 41 The Vale, NW11 8SE. *T:* 0181–458 2811. *Died 27 Aug. 1996.*

GAMMELL, James Gilbert Sydney, MBE 1944; CA; *b* 4 March 1920; *e s* of Lt-Gen. Sir James A. H. Gammell, KCB, DSO, MC and 1st wife, Gertrude, *e d* of Gilbert W. Don; *m* 1944, Susan Patricia Bowring Toms, *d* of late Edward Bowring Toms; five *s* one *d. Educ:* Winchester Coll. Chartered Accountant, 1949. Served War, Major Grenadier Guards, 1939–46: France, 1940 and 1944, Russia, 1945. Chm., Ivory & Sime, 1975–85. *Recreation:* farming. *Address:* Foxhall, Kirkliston, West Lothian EH29 9ER. *T:* (0131) 333 3275. *Club:* New (Edinburgh). *Died 19 April 1999.*

GARDINER, Patrick Lancaster, FBA 1985; Fellow and Tutor in Philosophy, Magdalen College, Oxford, 1958–89, then Emeritus Fellow; *b* 17 March 1922; *s* of Clive and Lilian Gardiner; *m* 1955, Kathleen Susan Booth; two *d. Educ:* Westminster School; Christ Church, Oxford (MA). Army service (Captain), 1942–45. Lectr, Wadham College, Oxford, 1949–52; Fellow, St Antony's College, Oxford, 1952–58. Vis. Prof., Columbia Univ., NY, 1955. *Publications:* The Nature of Historical Explanation, 1952; (ed) Theories of History, 1959; Schopenhauer, 1963, 2nd edn 1972, reissued 1997; (ed) Nineteenth Century Philosophy, 1969; (ed) The Philosophy of History, 1974; Kierkegaard, 1988; articles in philosophical and literary jls, anthologies. *Address:* The Dower House, Wytham, Oxford OX2 8QA. *T:* (01865) 242205. *Died 24 June 1997.*

GARDINER-SCOTT, Rev. William, OBE 1974; MA; Emeritus Minister of Scots Memorial Church and Hospice, Jerusalem; *b* 23 Feb. 1906; *o s* of late William Gardiner Scott, Portsoy, Banffshire; *m* 1953, Darinka Milo, *d* of late Milo Glogovac, Oakland, Calif; one *d. Educ:* Grange School, Bo'ness, West Lothian; Edinburgh University and New College, Edinburgh. In catering business, 1926–30; graduated in Arts, Edin., 1934; Theological Travel Scholarship to Palestine, 1936; travelled as ship's steward to America and India, 1936; ordained to Ministry of Church of Scotland, 1939; Sub-Warden 1939, Deputy Warden 1940, New College Settlement, Edinburgh; enlisted as Army Chaplain, 1941; served in Egypt,

1942–44 and developed community centre at RA Depot, Cairo and initiated publication of weekly Scots newspaper, The Clachan Crack; founded Montgomery House, Alexandria, as community centre for all ranks of allied troops, 1943; served in Palestine as Church of Scotland Chaplain for Galilee and district, 1944–46; Senior Chaplain at Scottish Command, 1946–47; Warden of Student Movement House, London, 1947–49; Chaplain at Victoria University Coll., Wellington, NZ, 1950–54; locum tenens St John's West Church, Leith, 1955; Minister of Church of Scotland, Jerusalem, 1955–60 and 1966–73; Parish of Abernethy, 1960–66. ChStJ. Distinguished Citizen of Jerusalem. *Recreations:* travel, gardening, cooking, walking. *Address:* Scots Memorial Church and Hospice, PO Box 8619, Jerusalem, Israel. *Died 27 May 1998.*

GARDNER, Sir Douglas Bruce B.; *see* Bruce-Gardner.

GARDNER, Ralph Bennett, MM 1944; Under Secretary (Legal), Treasury Solicitor's Department, 1976–82, retired; *b* 7 May 1919; *s* of late Ralph Wilson Gardner and Elizabeth Emma (*née* Nevitt-Bennett); *m* 1950, Patricia Joan Ward (*née* Bartlett); one *s* one *d. Educ:* Worksop Coll. Served War, 1939–46, RA. Admitted a solicitor, 1947; Solicitor, private practice, Chester, 1947–48; Legal Asst, Treasury Solicitor's Dept, 1948; Sen. Legal Asst, 1957; Asst Treas. Solicitor, 1972. Lord of the Manor of Shotwick, County of Chester (by inheritance, 1964). *Recreations:* gardening, local history. *Address:* Wychen, St Mary's Road, Leatherhead, Surrey KT22 8HB. *T:* (01372) 373161. *Club:* East India, Devonshire, Sports and Public Schools. *Died 25 Aug. 1997.*

GARDNER, Robert Dickson Robertson, CBE 1978; Secretary, Greater Glasgow Health Board, 1974–85, retired; *b* 9 May 1924; *s* of Robert Gardner and Isabella McAlonan; *m* 1950, Ada Stewart; two *s* one *d.* Dep. Sec., 1962–66, Sec., 1966–74, Western Regional Hospital Board, Scotland. *Recreations:* swimming, Scottish country dancing, reading. *Address:* 3 Williamwood Drive, Glasgow G44 3TA. *T:* (0141) 637 8070. *Died 16 March 1998.*

GARDNER, William Maving; designer, craftsman and writer; *b* 25 May 1914; *s* of Robert Haswell Gardner, MIMarE and Lucy (*née* Maving); *m* 1940, Joan Margaret Pollard (*d* 1982); two *s* one *d.* Trained at Royal College of Art, 1935–39 (ARCA 1938; Design Sch. Trav. Schol., Scandinavia, 1939). FCSD (FSIA 1964). Served Army, 1939–45 (Major, GS Camouflage). Mem., Royal Mint Panel of Artists, 1938–. Vis. Lectr, Central Sch. of Arts and Crafts, 1959–62, Cambridgeshire Coll. of Art and Technology, 1959–62, Hampstead Garden Suburb Inst., 1959–73; Examr in craft subjects Associated Examg Bd, City and Guilds of London Inst., 1957–60; External Examr in Lettering, City & Guilds of London Art Sch., 1987–90; served Typography Jury of RSA, Ind. Design Bursary Scheme. Leverhulme Res. Fellow, 1969–70. Vis. Prof. and Fine Art Program Lectr, Colorado State Univ., 1963; Churchill Meml Trav. Fellow, 1966–67 (USA, Polynesia, NZ, Australia, Nepal). Hon. Mem., RNS, NZ, 1966. FRSA 1955; FSNAD 1991. Work exhib. Fort Collins and Denver, Colo, 1963, Monotype House, London, 1965, Portsmouth Coll. of Art, 1965, Hammond Mus., NY, 1970; (with family) Rye Art Gall., 1977. Awarded the Queen's Silver Jubilee Medal, 1977. *Works included:* HM Privy Council Seal 1955, HM Greater and Lesser Royal Signets 1955, Seal of HM Dependencies 1955; seals for BMA, 1957, RSA, 1966, Univ. of Aston, Birmingham, 1966; *coinage designs and models:* for Jordan 1950, UK 1953, Cyprus 1955 and 1963, Algeria 1964, New Zealand 1967, Guyana 1967, Dominican Republic 1969, UNFAO (Ceylon 1968, Cyprus 1970, Guyana 1970), Falkland Islands 1974, UK 20p coin 1982; *medallic work:* included King's Medal for

Courage in the Cause of Freedom, Britannia Commemorative Soc. Shakespeare Medal 1967, Churchill Meml Trust's Foundn Medal 1969, Nat. Commemorative Soc. Audubon Medal 1970, Internat. Iron and Steel Inst. Medal 1971, Inst. of Metals Kroll Medal 1972, and thirty-six medallic engravings depicting the history of the Royal Arms, completed 1974; participant in series of Commonwealth Silver Jubilee crown pieces, 1977; *calligraphy:* included Rolls of Honour for House of Commons 1949, LTE 1954, Household Brigade, Life Guards, Royal Horse Guards, Grenadier, Coldstream, Scots, Irish and Welsh Foot Guards, completed 1956, Warrants of Appointment by Queen Elizabeth the Queen Mother as Lord Warden of the Cinque Ports, 1979, Royal Marines Corps Book of Remembrance, MSS for Canterbury Cath., Eton Coll. 1990, RSA 1991 and elsewhere; *work in other media* for Postmaster Gen. (Jersey definitive stamp 1958), Royal Soc. (Tercentenary stained glass window, 1960), King's College, London, 1971, City of London, 1972; and for univs, schools, presses, libraries, also privately. *Publications:* Chapter VIII of The Calligrapher's Handbook, 1956; Calligraphy for A Wordsworth Treasury, 1978; Alphabet at Work, 1982; New Calligraphy on an Old Theme, 1984; William Gardner's Book of Calligraphy, 1988. *Recreation:* books, books and more books. *Address:* Hollingrove Old Chapel, Brightling, near Robertsbridge, East Sussex TN32 5HU.
Died 28 Dec. 2000.

GARFIELD, Leon, FRSL; author; *b* 14 July 1921; *s* of David and Rose Garfield; *m* 1949, Vivien Dolores Alcock; one *d. Educ:* Brighton Grammar Sch. Served War, RAMC, 1941–46: attained and held rank of Private. Worked in NHS (biochemistry), until 1969; full-time author, 1969–. FRSL 1985. Guardian Award, 1967; Dutch Silver Griffel, 1973 and 1974; Prix de la Fondation de France, 1984; Swedish Golden Cat, 1985, Golden Phoenix (USA), 1987. *Publications:* Jack Holborn, 1964; Devil-in-the-Fog, 1966; Smith, 1967; Black Jack, 1968 (filmed 1979); Mister Corbett's Ghost and Other Stories, 1969; The Boy and the Monkey, 1969; The Drummer Boy, 1970; The Strange Affair of Adelaide Harris, 1971; The Ghost Downstairs, 1972; The Captain's Watch, 1972; Lucifer Wilkins, 1973; Baker's Dozen, 1973; The Sound of Coaches, 1974; The Prisoners of September, 1975; The Pleasure Garden, 1976; The Booklovers, 1976; The House of Hanover, 1976; The Lamplighter's Funeral, 1976; Mirror, Mirror, 1976; Moss and Blister, 1976; The Cloak, 1976; The Valentine, 1977; Labour in Vain, 1977; The Fool, 1977; Rosy Starling, 1977; The Dumb Cake, 1977; Tom Titmarsh's Devil, 1977; The Filthy Beast, 1977; The Enemy, 1977; The Confidence Man, 1978; Bostock & Harris, 1978; John Diamond, 1980 (Whitbread Book of the Year Award, 1980); Mystery of Edwin Drood (completion), 1980; Fair's Fair, 1981; The House of Cards, 1982; King Nimrod's Tower, 1982; The Apprentices, 1982; The Writing on the Wall, 1983; The King in the Garden, 1984; The Wedding Ghost, 1984; Guilt and Gingerbread, 1984; Shakespeare Stories, 1985; The December Rose, 1986; Blewcoat Boy, 1988; The Saracen Maid, 1991; The Animated Shakespeare, 1992; Shakespeare Stories II, 1994; Sabre-Tooth Sandwich, 1994; with Edward Blishen: The God Beneath the Sea, 1970 (Carnegie Medal, 1970); The Golden Shadow, 1973; with David Proctor: Child O'War, 1972. *Recreations:* collecting pictures and Staffordshire china. *Address:* c/o John Johnson (Authors' Agent) Ltd, Clerkenwell House, 45/47 Clerkenwell Green, EC1R 0HT. *T:* 0171–251 0125. *Club:* PEN.
Died 2 June 1996.

GARLAND, (Frederick) Peter (Collison), CVO 1969; QPM 1965; *b* 4 Sept. 1912; *s* of late Percy Frederick Garland, Southsea, Hants; *m* 1945, Gwendolen Mary, *d* of late Henry James Powell, Putney; three *d. Educ:* Bradfield

Coll. Joined Metropolitan Police, 1934. Served in RAF (Air Crew), 1941–45. Asst Chief Constable of Norfolk, 1952–56, Chief Constable, 1956–75. CStJ 1961. *Address:* Hilton Park Care Centre, Newmarket Suite, Room 18–19, Bottisham, Cambridge CB5 9BX. *Died 2 Nov. 2000.*

GARLICK, Prof. (George Frederick) John, BSc, PhD, DSc; FInstP; *b* 21 Feb. 1919; *s* of George Robert Henry Garlick and Martha Elizabeth (*née* Davies); *m* 1943, Dorothy Mabel Bowsher; one *d; m* 1977, Harriet Herta Forster. *Educ:* Wednesbury High Sch.; Univ. of Birmingham (BSc 1940; PhD 1943; DSc 1955). War service: Scientific Officer (Radar Research). In charge Luminescence Laboratory, Birmingham Univ., 1946–56 (Research Physicist, 1946–49, Lecturer in Physics, 1949–56); Prof. of Physics, Univ. of Hull, 1956–78; Research Prof., Univ. of Southern California, LA, 1978–79; private scientific consultant, 1979–89. FInstP 1949. Jubilee Medal, 1977. *Publications:* Luminescent Materials, 1949; numerous papers in learned scientific journals. *Recreation:* music (organ). *Address:* 267 South Beloit Avenue, Los Angeles, CA 90049, USA.
Died 28 Feb. 1997.

GARNETT, (William) John (Poulton Maxwell), CBE 1970; MA; lecturer on leadership and communication; *b* 6 Aug. 1921; *s* of Dr Maxwell Garnett, CBE, and Margaret Lucy Poulton; *m* 1st, 1943, Barbara Rutherford-Smith (marr. diss.); two *s* two *d*; 2nd, 1986, Julia Cleverdon, CBE; two *d. Educ:* Rugby Sch.; Kent Sch., USA; Trinity Coll., Cambridge. Royal Navy, 1941–46 (commnd, 1942). ICI Ltd, 1947–62; Dir, Industrial Soc., 1962–86; Chm., W Lambeth HA, 1986–90. Dep. Chm. UNA, 1954–56. Mem., Ct of inquiry into miners' strike, 1972; Arbitrator, Lorry Drivers' Strike, 1979. Mem., Royal Dockyard Policy Bd. Chm., Churches Council on Gambling, 1965–71. DUniv Essex, 1977, Hon. DTech Loughborough, 1978; Hon. LLD CNAA, 1980. *Publications:* The Manager's Responsibility for Communication, 1964; The Work Challenge, 1973, 1985. *Recreation:* timber construction. *Address:* 8 Alwyne Road, Canonbury, N1 2HH. *Club:* Leander (Henley). *Died 14 Aug. 1997.*

GARNSEY, Rt Rev. David Arthur; *b* 31 July 1909; *s* of Canon Arthur Henry Garnsey and Bertha Edith Frances Garnsey (*née* Benn); *m* 1934, Evangeline Eleanor Wood; two *s* two *d. Educ:* Trinity and Sydney Grammar Schs; St Paul's Coll., University of Sydney (BA (1st cl. Latin and Greek) 1930); New Coll., Oxford (NSW Rhodes Scholar, 1931; BA (2nd cl. Lit. Hum.) 1933, 2nd cl. Theol. 1934, MA 1937); Ripon Hall, Oxford, 1933. Travelling Sec., Australian SCM, 1930–31; deacon, 1934; priest, 1935; Curate, St Mary the Virgin (University Church), and Inter-Collegiate Sec. of SCM, Oxford, 1934–38; St Saviour's Cathedral, Goulburn, NSW, 1938–41; Rector of Young, NSW, 1941–45; Gen. Sec. Australian SCM, 1945–48; Exam. Chap. to Bp of Goulburn, 1939–45, 1948–58; Head Master Canberra Grammar Sch., 1948–58; Canon of St Saviour's Cathedral, Goulburn, 1949–58; Bishop of Gippsland, 1959–74. Pres., Australian Council of Churches, 1970–73. Chm., Bd of Delegates, Aust. Coll. of Theology, 1971–77; Hon. ThD Australian Coll. of Theology, 1955. Coronation Medal, 1953. *Publications:* A. H. Garnsey: a man for truth and freedom, 1985; Songs from a Dry Land (comments on the psalms), 1994; booklets for study. *Recreation:* reading. *Address:* 27/2 Berwick Street, Camberwell, Vic 3124, Australia. *T:* (3) 98822114. *Died 14 July 1996.*

GARSON, Greer, Hon. CBE 1993; actress; *b* Northern Ireland, 29 Sept. 1908; *d* of George Garson and Nina Sophia Greer; *m* 1st, Edward A. Snelson (later Sir E. A. A. Snelson, KBE); 2nd, 1943, Richard Ney (marr. diss.); 3rd, 1949, Col E. E. Fogelson (*d* 1987), Texas. *Educ:* London and Grenoble Univs. BA Hons London.

Birmingham Repertory Theatre, 1932 and 1933; London Theatre debut, Whitehall, 1935; lead roles in 13 London plays; entered films in 1939; *films include:* Goodbye Mr Chips, 1939; Pride and Prejudice, 1940; When Ladies Meet, Blossoms in the Dust, 1941; Mrs Miniver (Academy Award), Random Harvest, 1942; Madame Curie, 1943; Mrs Parkington, 1944; Valley of Decision, 1945; That Forsyte Woman, 1949; The Law and the Lady, 1951; Julius Caesar, 1953; Her Twelve Men, 1954; Strange Lady in Town, 1955; Sunrise at Campobello (Golden Globe award), 1960; The Singing Nun, 1966; The Happiest Millionaire, 1967; *stage appearances include:* Auntie Mame, Tonight at 8.30, Captain Brassbound's Conversion; appeared in pioneer British TV, on American TV. Hon. DHum, Rollins Coll., Florida, 1950; Hon. Dr in Communication Arts, Coll. of Santa Fe, 1970; Hon. DLitt Ulster, 1977; winner of many internat. awards. Later interests included The Greer Garson Theatre and Fogelson Library Center, Coll. of Santa Fe; Mem. Bd, Dallas Theater Center; Adjunct Prof. in Drama, Southern Methodist Univ., Dallas; Mem., State Commn on the arts in Texas and New Mexico; Principal Founding Donor: Fogelson Forum, Dallas Presbyterian Hosp.; Garson Communications Center, Coll. of Santa Fe; Fogelson Pavilion, Meyerson Symphony Center, Dallas; Fogelson Fountain, Dallas Arboretum; Greer Garson Theatre, Southern Methodist Univ., Dallas. Hon. Alumna, St John's Coll., Santa Fe. Operated Forked Lightning Ranch, Pecos, New Mexico, where Pecos Nat. Monument and Visitors Centre located (with Col E. E. Fogelson, received Conservation Service Award, US Dept of Interior, 1981, for this and other civic projects); also involved in breeding and racing thoroughbred horses (stable included Ack Ack, horse of the year, 1971). *Recreations:* nature study, music, primitive art. *Died 6 April 1996.*

GASSMAN, Lewis; JP; a Recorder of the Crown Court, 1972–83; *b* 28 Oct. 1910; 2nd *s* of late Isaac and Dora Gassman; *m* 1940, Betty Henrietta, *o c* of late H. Jerrold and Mrs A. F. Annenberg; one *d*. Admitted Solicitor, 1933. Borough of Barnes: Councillor and Chm. of Cttees, 1933–41. Contested (Lab): Richmond, Surrey, 1935; Hastings, 1945. War of 1939–45: Army service, Capt. RAOC. JP Surrey, 1948, also SW London; Chm., Mortlake Magistrates, 1953–56 and 1961–71; a Dep. Chm. of Surrey Quarter Sessions, 1968–71; Chm. of Magistrates, Richmond-upon-Thames, 1971–74. Consultant in law firm of Kershaw, Gassman & Matthews. *Recreations:* music, painting, walking. *Address:* 21 Castelnau, Barnes, SW13 9RP. *T:* (0181) 748 7172. *Club:* Reform.
Died 30 June 1998.

GAULT, Charles Alexander, CBE 1959 (OBE 1947); retired from HM Foreign Service, 1959; *b* 15 June 1908; *o s* of Robert Gault, Belfast, and Sophia Ranken Clark; *m* 1947, Madge, *d* of late William Walter Adams, Blundellsands; no *c. Educ:* Harrow; Magdalene Coll., Cambridge. Entered Levant Consular Service, 1931; served in Egypt, Persia, Saudi Arabia, at Foreign Office, India (on secondment to Commonwealth Relations Office), Libya, Israel, Bahrain (HM Political Agent, 1954–59). *Address:* 19 Queens Court, Queens Road, Cheltenham, Glos GL50 2LU. *Died 28 Aug. 1996.*

GAUSDEN, Ronald, CB 1982; nuclear consultant; *b* 15 June 1921; *s* of Jesse Charles William Gausden and Annie Gausden (*née* Durrant); *m* 1st, 1943, Florence May (*née* Ayres) (*d* 1987); two *s* two *d*; 2nd, 1988, Joan Betty (*née* Simcock). *Educ:* Varndean Grammar Sch., Brighton; Brighton Techn. Coll. and Borough Polytechnic. CEng, FIEE. RN Sci. Service, 1943–47; AERE, Harwell, 1947–50; UKAEA Windscale Works, Cumbria: Instrument Engr, 1950–53; Asst Gp Man., 1953–55; Gp Man., 1955–60; Nuclear Installations Inspectorate:

Principal Inspector, 1960–63; Asst Chief Inspector, 1963–73; Dep. Chief Inspector, 1973–75; Chief Inspector, 1976–81; Dir, Hazardous Installations Gp, HSE, 1978–81. *Publications:* contrib. Brit. Nuclear Energy Soc. and Inst. Nuclear Engrs. *Recreations:* golf, fishing. *Address:* Granary Cottage, Itchingfield, near Horsham, W Sussex RH13 7NU. *T:* (01403) 790646. *Died 31 Dec. 1997.*

GAVIN, Maj.-Gen. James Merricks Lewis, CB 1967; CBE 1963 (OBE 1953); *b* Antofagasta, Chile, 28 July 1911; *s* of Joseph Merricks Gavin; *m* 1942, Barbara Anne Elizabeth (*d* 1994), *d* of Group Capt. C. G. Murray, CBE; one *s* two *d. Educ:* Uppingham Sch.; Royal Military Academy; Trinity Coll., Cambridge. 2nd Lieut Royal Engineers, 1931; Mem. Mt Everest Expedn, 1936; Instructor, Royal Military Academy, 1938; Capt. 1939; served War of 1939–45 in Far East, Middle East, Italy, France, including special operations; Brit. Jt Services Mission, Washington, 1948–51; Commanding Officer, 1951–53; Col Staff Coll., Camberley, 1953–55; BAOR, 1956–58; Comdt (Brig.) Intelligence Centre, Maresfield, 1958–61; Maj.-Gen. 1964; Asst Chief of Staff (Intelligence), SHAPE, 1964–67. Technical Dir, BSI, 1967–76. Col Comdt, RE, 1968–73. *Recreations:* mountaineering, sailing, ski-ing. *Address:* Maysleith, Milland, near Liphook, Hants GU30 7JN. *Clubs:* Alpine, Royal Cruising, Royal Ocean Racing; Royal Yacht Squadron (Cowes). *Died 21 Aug. 2000.*

GAYRE of Gayre and Nigg, Robert, ERD; Lieutenant-Colonel (late Reserve of Officers); ethnologist and armorist; Editor: The Armorial, 1959–74; The Mankind Quarterly, 1960–78 (Hon. Editor in Chief, since 1979), etc; Director of several companies; *b* 6 Aug. 1907; *s* of Robert Gayre of Gayre and Nigg, and Clara Hull; *m* 1933, Nina Mary (*d* 1983), *d* of Rev. Louis Thomas Terry, MA and Margaret Nina Hill; one *s. Educ:* University of Edinburgh (MA); Exeter Coll., Oxford. BEF France, 1939; Staff Officer Airborne HQ, 1942; Educnl Adviser, Allied Mil. Govt, Italy, 1943–44; Dir of Educn, Allied Control Commn for Italy, 1944; Chief of Educn and Religious Affairs, German Planning Unit, SHAEF, 1944. Prof. of Anthropology and Head of Dept of Anthropo-geography, University of Saugor, India, 1954–56; Falkland Pursuivant Extraord., 1958; Consultore pro lingua Anglica, Coll. of Heralds, Rome, 1954–; Chamberlain to the Prince of Lippe, 1958–; Grand Bailiff and Comr-Gen. of the English Tongue, Order of St Lazarus of Jerusalem, 1961–69; Grand Referendary, 1969–73; Grand Comdr and Grand Almoner, 1973–; Vicar-Gen., 1985–; Sec.-Gen., VIth Internat. Congress of Genealogy, Edinburgh, 1962. Chm., The Seventeen Forty-Five Association, 1964–80. President: Scottish Rhodesia Soc., to 1968; Aberdeenshire and Banffshire Friends of Rhodesia Assoc., 1969; St Andrew Soc. of Malta, 1968; Ethnological Soc. of Malta; Life Pres., Heraldic Soc. of Malta, 1970; Hon. Pres., Sicilian Anthropological Soc. Sec.-Gen., Internat. Orders' Commn (Chm., 1978–); Mem. Council, Internat. Inst. of Ethnology and Eugenics, New York. Mem. Cttee of Honour: Inst. Politicos, Madrid; Cercle Internat. Généalogique, Paris; Mem. Nat. Acad. Sci. of India; Fellow: Collegio Araldico, Rome; Nat. Soc., Naples; Peloritana Acad., Messina; Pontaniana Acad., Naples; Royal Academy, Palermo; F Ist Ital di Geneal. e Arald., Rome; FRSH; MInstBE. Hon. or corr. mem. of heraldic and other socs of many countries. Grand Cross of Merit, SMO Malta, 1963 (Kt Comdr. 1957). Held knighthoods in international and foreign orders, hon. doctorates from Italian Univs, and heraldic societies' medals, etc. Hon. Lt-Col, ADC to Governor, Georgia, USA, 1969–; Hon. Lt-Col, ADC, State Militia, Alabama; Hon. Lt-Col, Canadian Arctic Air Force. Hon. Citizen, Commune of Gurro, Italy. *Publications:* Teuton and Slav on the Polish Frontier, 1944; Italy in Transition, 1946; Wassail! In Mazers of

Mead, 1948, new edn, USA, 1986; The Heraldry of the Knights of St John, 1956; Heraldic Standards and other Ensigns, 1959; The Nature of Arms, 1961; Heraldic Cadency, 1961, Gayre's Booke, 4 vols 1948–59; The Armorial Who is Who, 1961–62, 1963–65, 1966–69, 1970–75, 1976–78, 1979–80; Who is Who in Clan Gayre, 1962; A Case for Monarchy, 1962; Roll of Scottish Arms: Pt I Vol. I, 1964, Pt I Vol. II, 1969; Ethnological Elements of Africa, 1966; More Ethnological Elements of Africa, 1972; The Origin of the Zimbabwean Civilisation, 1972; Miscellaneous Racial Studies, 2 vols, 1972; The Knightly Twilight, 1973; Syro-Mesopotamian Ethnology, 1973; Aspects of British and Continental Heraldry, 1974; The Lost Clan, 1974; The Mackays of the Rhinns of Islay, 1979; Minard Castle, 1980; Minard Castle Collection of Pipe Music, 1986; An Autobiography, 1987; The Power Beyond, 1989; contribs to Mankind Quarterly, Encyc. Brit., etc. *Recreation:* reading. *Address:* Minard Castle, Minard, Argyll PA32 8YB. *Club:* Royal Highland Yacht.

Died 10 Feb. 1996.

GEAR, William, DA (Edinburgh) 1936; RA 1995; RBSA 1966; painter; Head of Department of Fine Art, Birmingham Polytechnic (formerly Birmingham College of Art and Design), 1964–75; Member London Group, 1953; *b* Methil, Fife, 2 Aug. 1915; *s* of Porteous Gordon Gear; *m* 1949, Charlotte Chertok (*d* 1988); two *s*. *Educ:* Buckhaven High Sch.; Edinburgh Coll. of Art; Edinburgh Univ.; Moray House Training Coll.; Edinburgh Coll. of Art. Post-grad schol., 1936–37; Travelling schol., 1937–38; Académie Fernand Leger, Paris, 1937; study in France, Italy, Balkans; Moray House Trg Coll., 1938–39. War Service with Royal Corps of Signals, 1940–46, in Middle East, Italy and Germany. Staff Officer, Monuments, Fine Arts and Archives Br., CCG, 1946–47; worked in Paris, 1947–50; Curator, Towner Art Gallery, Eastbourne, 1958–64. Guest Lecturer, Nat. Gall. of Victoria, Melbourne, and University of Western Australia, 1966. Chairman: Fine Art Panel, Nat. Council for Diplomas in Art and Design, 1972; Fine Art Bd, CNAA, 1974. One-man exhibitions: in various European cities, N and S America, Japan, etc, 1944–; Gimpel Fils Gall., London, 1948–; S London Art Gall. (retrospective), 1954; Edinburgh Fest., 1966; (retrospective) Arts Council, N Ireland, 1969; (retrospective) Scottish Arts Council, 1969; Univ. of Sussex, 1964–75; RBSA, 1976 (retrospective); Talbot Rice Art Centre, Univ. of Edinburgh, and Ikon Gall., Birmingham (retrospective), 1982; Kirkcaldy Art Gall., 1985; Netherbow Art Centre, Edinburgh, 1985; Redfern Gall., London, 1987, 1989, 1992, 1996; Galerie 1900–2000, Paris, 1988; Karl & Faber, Munich, 1988–89; Galerie Gabriele von Loeper, Hamburg, 1989, 1992; England & Co., London, 1989; Kunsthandel Leeman, Amsterdam, 1990, 1992; Galerie Doris Wullkopf, Darmstadt, 1992; Art Fair, Cologne, 1992; Emscote Lawn, Warwick, 1994; City Art Gall., Birmingham, Scottish Arts Club, 1995. Group exhibitions: with COBRA: Malmö, 1986; Taipeh, Stockholm, 1987; Odense, Oslo, Amsterdam, 1988; Munich, 1989; Berlin, 1990; Liège, 1993; Santiago, Buenos Aires, 1994; Neunenhaus, Antwerp, Amstelveen, 1995; others: Portrait of the Artist, Tate Gall., 1989; 4 Abstract Artists, Redfern Gall., 1989; Scottish Art since 1900, Scottish Nat. Gall. of Modern Art, 1989, Barbican Art Centre, 1990; Scotland's Pictures, Edinburgh Fest., 1990; Avant–Garde British Printmaking 1914–1960, BM, 1990; The Line of Tradition, Edinburgh Fest., 1993; works shown in many exhibitions of contemporary art, also at Royal Acad., 1960, 1961, 1967, 1968, 1995 and 1996, and RSA 1986. Awarded £500 Purchase prize, Fest. of Britain, 1951; David Cargill Award, Royal Glasgow Inst., 1967; Lorne Fellowship, 1976; Herbert Baker Scholarship, Royal Acad. of Arts, 1995. FIAL 1960; FRSA 1971. DUniv Central England,

1994. *Works in permanent collections:* Tate Gall.; Arts Council; Brit. Council; Contemp. Art Soc.; Scottish National Gall. of Modern Art; Scottish Arts Council; British Museum; Victoria & Albert Museum; Laing Art Gall., Newcastle; Nat. Gall. of Canada; Bishop Suter Art Gall., NZ; Art Gall., Toronto; City Art Gall., Toledo, Ohio; Museum of Art, Tel Aviv; New Coll., Oxford; Cincinnati Art Gall., Ohio; Nat. Gall. of NSW; Bishop Otter Coll., Chichester; City Art Gall., Manchester; Albright Art Gall., Buffalo, NY; Musée des Beaux Arts, Liège; Inst. of Contemp. Art, Lima, Peru; Towner Art Gall., Eastbourne; Brighton Art Gall.; Pembroke Coll., Cambridge; Chelsea Coll. of Physical Educn; Southampton Art Gall.; Univ. of Glasgow; Arts Council of Northern Ireland; Whitworth Art Gall., Manchester; Univ. of Birmingham; City Museum and Art Gall., Birmingham; Museum of Art, Fort Lauderdale, Fla; Nat. Gall. of Aust.; Karel van Stuÿvenberg Collection, Caracas, Venezuela; Birmingham Polytech.; City Art Centre, Edinburgh; Kirkcaldy Art Gall.; Strathclyde Regl Council; Hereford Liby & Mus.; Dept of Educn, Manchester; Rye Art Gall.; Peir Gall., Orkney; Mus. of Modern Art, Amstelveen; Aberdeen, Dundee and Glasgow Art Galleries, and in numerous private collections in GB, USA, Canada, Italy, France, etc. Furnishing textiles designed for various firms. *Recreations:* cricket, music, travel. *Address:* 46 George Road, Edgbaston, Birmingham B15 1PL. *Died 27 Feb. 1997.*

GEDDES, Sir (Anthony) Reay (Mackay), KBE 1968 (OBE 1943); President, Charities Aid Foundation, 1991–93 (Chairman, 1985–90); *b* 7 May 1912; *s* of late Rt Hon. Sir Eric Geddes, GCB, GBE, PC and Gwendolen, *d* of Rev. A. Stokes; *m* 1938, Imogen (*d* 1997), *d* of late Captain Hay Matthey, Brixham; two *s* three *d*. *Educ:* Rugby; Cambridge. Bank of England, 1932–35; Dunlop Rubber Company Ltd, 1935, Dir 1947, Chm. 1968–78; Dep. Chm., Midland Bank, 1978–84 (Dir, 1967–84). Director: Shell Transport and Trading Co., 1968–82; Rank Orgn, 1975–84. Pres., Soc. of Motor Manufacturers and Traders, 1958–59; Part-time Mem., UKAEA, 1960–65; Mem. Nat. Economic Develt Council, 1962–65; Chm., Shipbuilding Inquiry Cttee, 1965–66. Pres., Internat. Chamber of Commerce, 1980. Hon. DSc Aston, 1967; Hon LLD Leicester, 1969; Hon. DTech Loughborough, 1970. *Address:* 49 Eaton Place, SW1X 8DE.

Died 19 Feb. 1998.

GEE, Prof. Geoffrey, CBE 1958; FRS 1951; Sir Samuel Hall Professor of Chemistry, University of Manchester, 1955–77, then Emeritus Professor; *b* 6 June 1910; *s* of Thomas and Mary Ann Gee; *m* 1934, Marion (*née* Bowden); one *s* two *d*. *Educ:* New Mills Grammar Sch.; Univ. of Manchester (BSc 1931; MSc 1932); Fitzwilliam Coll., Cambridge (PhD 1936; ScD 1947). ICI (Dyestuffs Group), Research Chemist, 1933–38; British Rubber Producers' Research Association: Research Chemist, 1938–47; Dir, 1947–53; University of Manchester: Prof. of Physical Chemistry, 1953–55; Pro-Vice-Chancellor, 1966–68, 1972–77 (full-time, 1975–77). Pres., Faraday Soc., 1969 and 1970. Hon. Fellow, Manchester Polytechnic, 1979. Hon. DSc Manchester, 1983. *Publications:* numerous scientific papers in Transactions of the Faraday Soc., and other journals. *Recreation:* latterly interested in relation between science and theology. *Address:* 8 Holmfield Drive, Cheadle Hulme, Cheshire SK8 7DT. *T:* (0161) 485 3713.

Died 13 Dec. 1996.

GEE, Timothy Hugh; HM Diplomatic Service, retired; Consultant, The Entertainment Corporation, 1988–90; *b* 12 Nov. 1936; *s* of Arthur William Gee and Edith (*née* Ingham); *m* 1964, Gillian Eve St Johnston (marr. diss. 1988); two *s* one *d*. *Educ:* Berkhamsted; Trinity Coll.,

Oxford. 2 Lieut 3rd Regt RHA, 1959–61. Joined British Council, 1961; New Delhi, 1962–66; entered HM Diplomatic Service, 1966; FO, 1966–68; Brussels, 1968–72; FCO, 1972–74; Kuala Lumpur, 1974–79; Counsellor, on secondment to NI Office, 1979–81; Consul-General, Istanbul, 1981–85; Head of Cultural Relations Dept, FCO, 1985–87. *Address:* Charterhouse, EC1M 6AN. *Club:* Travellers. *Died 25 Dec. 1998.*

GELL, Dr Alfred Antony Francis, FBA 1995; Reader in Anthropology, London School of Economics, since 1979; *b* 12 June 1945; *s* of Prof. P. G. H. Gell, FRS and Albinia Susan Roope Gordon; *m* 1974, Simeran Man Singh; one *s. Educ:* Bryanston Sch.; Trinity Coll., Cambridge (MA 1967); London Sch. of Economics (PhD 1973). Lecturer in Anthropology: Univ. of Sussex, 1972–74; ANU, 1974–79. Anthropological fieldwork in West Sepik, New Guinea, and Bastar district, Madhya Pradesh, India. *Publications:* Metamorphosis of the Cassowaries, 1975; The Anthropology of Time, 1992; Wrapping in Images, 1993. *Recreations:* sketching, music. *Address:* Department of Anthropology, London School of Economics, Houghton Street, Aldwych, WC2 2AE. *T:* (0171) 955 7202.
Died 28 Jan. 1997.

GEORGE, Rev. (Alfred) Raymond, MA; Warden, John Wesley's Chapel, Bristol, 1982–95; *b* 26 Nov. 1912; *s* of A. H. and G. M. George. *Educ:* Crypt Sch., Gloucester; Balliol Coll., Oxford (1st cl. Hon. Classical Mods, 1st cl. Lit. Hum., BA 1935, MA 1938, BD 1955); Wesley House, Cambridge (1st cl. Theol Tripos, Pt I Sect. B, BA 1937, MA 1962); Marburg University. Asst Tutor, Handsworth Coll., Birmingham, 1938–40; ordained as Methodist minister, 1940; Asst Tutor, Hartley-Victoria Coll., Manchester, 1940–42; Circuit Minister, Manchester, 1942–46; Tutor, Wesley Coll., Headingley, Leeds, 1946–67, Principal, 1961–67; Associate Lectr, Leeds Univ., 1946–67, Actg Head, Theol. Dept, 1967–68; Principal, Richmond Coll., London Univ., 1968–72; Tutor, Wesley College, Bristol, 1972–81. Select Preacher, Cambridge, 1963. Member, World Council of Churches Commn on Faith and Order, 1961–75; Pres. of Methodist Conf., 1975–76; Moderator, Free Church Federal Council, 1979–80; Chm., Jt Liturgical Group, 1984–89. *Publications:* Communion with God in the New Testament, 1953; chapter in vol. I, A History of the Methodist Church in Great Britain, 1965, ed (jtly), vol. II, 1978, and contrib. chapter, ed (jtly), vol. III, 1983; jt Editor of series: Ecumenical Studies in Worship; also articles in jls. *Address:* 40 Knole Lane, Bristol BS10 6SS. *T:* (0117) 950 3698. *Died 22 June 1998.*

GERRARD, Prof. Alfred Horace; Professor of Sculpture in the University of London at University College Slade School of Fine Art, 1948–68, then Emeritus; *b* 7 May 1899; *m* 1st, 1933, Katherine Leigh-Pemberton (*d* 1970); 2nd, 1972, Nancy Sinclair (*d* 1995); 3rd, 1995, Karen Sinclair. *Educ:* Hartford County Council Sch.; Manchester Sch. of Art; Slade Sch. of Fine Art, University Coll., London. Head of Dept of Sculpture, Slade Sch., UCL, 1925–48; temp. Head, Slade Sch. of Fine Art, 1948–49. Served European War, 1914–18, Cameron Highlanders, 1916–17; RFC, 1917–19; War of 1939–45, Staff Captain, War Office, attached Royal Engineers, 1939–43; war artist, 1944–45. RBS Silver Medal, 1960. Fellow, University Coll. London, 1969. *Recreation:* gardening. *Address:* Dairy House, Leyswood, Groombridge, Tunbridge Wells, Kent TN3 9PH. *T:* (01892) 864268.
Died 13 June 1998.

GHALE, Subedar Gaje; *see* Gaje Ghale.

GIBBON, Gen. Sir John (Houghton), GCB 1977 (KCB 1972; CB 1970); OBE 1945 (MBE 1944); Master-General of the Ordnance, 1974–77; ADC (General) to the Queen,

1976–77; *b* 21 Sept. 1917; *er s* of Brigadier J. H. Gibbon, DSO, The Manor House, Little Stretton, Salop, and Jessie Willoughby, 2nd *d* of Brabazon Campbell, Warwick; *m* 1951, Brigid Rosamund, *d* of late Dr D. A. Bannerman, OBE, ScD, FRSE, and Muriel, *d* of T. R. Morgan; one *s. Educ:* Eton; Trinity Coll., Cambridge. Commissioned into Royal Artillery, 1939; served with 2nd Regt RHA: France, 1939–40; Western Desert, 1940–41; Greece, 1941; on staff of HQ 30 Corps; Western Desert, 1941–43; Sicily, 1943; GSO 1, RA, HQ 21 Army Gp, 1944–45; 6 Airborne Div., Palestine, 1946–47; Instructor and Chief Instructor, RMA Sandhurst, 1947–51; GSO 2, War Office, 1951–53; Battery Comdr, 1953–54; AQMG, War Office, 1955–58; CO Field Regt, BAOR, 1959–60; Bde Comdr, Cyprus, 1962; Dir of Defence Plans, Min. of Def., 1962–64; Sec., Chiefs of Staff Cttee, and Dir, Defence Operations Staff, 1966–69; Dir, Army Staff Duties, MoD, 1969–71; Vice-Chief of the Defence Staff, 1972–74. Col Comdt, RA, 1972–82. Chm., Regular Forces Employment Assoc., 1982–85 (Vice-Chm., 1977–82). *Recreations:* rowing, fishing. *Address:* Beech House, Northbrook Close, Winchester, Hants SO23 0JR. *T:* (01962) 866155. *Clubs:* Naval and Military; Leander. *Died 7 May 1997.*

GIBBS, Dame Molly (Peel), (Hon. Lady Gibbs), DBE 1969; *b* 13 July 1912; 2nd *d* of John Peel Nelson; *m* 1934, Rt Hon. Sir Humphrey Vicary Gibbs, GCVO, KCMG, OBE, PC (*d* 1990), *s* of 1st Baron Hunsdon of Hunsdon; five *s. Educ:* Girls' High School, Barnato Park, Johannesburg. *Address:* 22 Dornie Road, Pomona, PO Borrowdale, Harare, Zimbabwe. *T:* Harare (4) 883281; 6 The Square, High Street, Leigh, Kent TN11 8RJ.
Died 20 March 1997.

GIBSON, Rev. (Sir) David Ackroyd, (4th Bt *cr* 1926 of Great Warley, co. Essex, but does not use the title); Catholic priest; retired; *b* 18 July 1922; *s* of Sir Ackroyd Herbert Gibson, 3rd Bt and Maud Lilian, *d* of E. C. Arnold, FRCS; *S* father, 1975. Founder of Societas Navigatorum Catholica, 1954. *Publications:* A Series of Circles (autobiog.); Battle in the Irish Sea: the life and death of HMS Manners. *Address:* St Therese's Court, 138 Raglan Road, Devonport, Plymouth PL1 4NQ.
Died 16 July 1997 (ext).

GIBSON, Vice-Adm. Sir Donald Cameron Ernest Forbes, KCB 1968 (CB 1965); DSC 1941; JP; *b* 17 March 1916; *s* of late Capt. W. L. D. Gibson, Queen's Own Cameron Highlanders, and Elizabeth Gibson; *m* 1939, Marjorie Alice (*d* 1996), *d* of H. C. Harding, Horley, Surrey; one *s. Educ:* Woodbridge Sch., Suffolk. Cadet, Brit. India Steam Navigation Co. and Midshipman, Royal Naval Reserve, 1933–37; transf. to Royal Navy, 1937; specialised as Pilot, 1938; served War of 1939–45: HMS Glorious, Ark Royal, Formidable, Audacity; trng Pilots in USA; Empire Central Flying Sch., 1942; Chief Flying Instr, Advanced Flying Sch., 1946–47; HMS Illustrious, 1947–48; Air Gp Comdr, HMS Theseus, 1948–49; Comdr (Air), RNAS Culdrose, 1950–52; RN Staff Course, 1952–53; Comdr (Air) HMS Indomitable and Glory, 1953–54; Capt. RNAS Brawdy, 1954–56, HMS Dainty, 1956–58; Dep. Dir Air Warfare, 1958–60; Canadian Nat. Defence Coll., 1960–61; Capt., HMS Ark Royal, 1961–63; Rear-Adm. 1963; Flag Officer: Aircraft Carriers, 1963–64; Naval Flying Trng, 1964–65; Naval Air Comd, 1965–68; Vice-Adm. 1967. Dir, HMS Belfast Trust, 1971–72; Mem., Gen. Cttee, Devon Community Housing Soc. Ltd, 1983–. JP Barnstaple, 1973. *Publications:* Haul Taut and Belay (autobiog.), 1992; A Celebration of God's Creation, 1997. *Recreation:* painting. *Address:* Lympstone House Nursing Home, Strawberry Hill, Lympstone, Exmouth, Devon EX8 5JZ. *T:* (01395) 222839. *Died 22 Nov. 2000.*

GIBSON, Joseph David, CBE 1979; Ambassador of Fiji to Japan, 1984–87, retired; *b* 26 Jan. 1928; *s* of late Charles

Ivan Gibson and Mamao Lavenia Gibson; *m* Emily Susan Bentley; three *s* two *d*. *Educ:* Levuka Public Sch., Suva; Marist Brothers Secondary Sch.; Auckland Univ., NZ (BA); Auckland Teachers' Coll. (Teachers' Cert.). Asst Teacher, Suva Boys' Grammar Sch., 1952–57; Principal, Suva Educnl Inst., 1957; Principal, Queen Victoria School, Fiji, 1961–62 (Asst Teacher, 1958–59; Sen. Master, 1959; 1st Asst, 1960); Sec. Sch. Inspector, Fiji Educn Dept, 1964–65; Asst Dir of Educn, 1966–69; Dep. Dir of Educn, 1970; Dir of Educn and Permanent Sec. for Educn, 1971–74; Dep. High Comr, London, 1974–76, High Comr, 1976–81; High Comr, New Zealand, 1981–83. Represented Fiji at: Dirs of Educn Conferences, Western Samoa and Pago Pago, 1968, Honolulu, 1970; Commonwealth Ministers of Educn Meeting, Canberra, 1971; Head of Fiji Delegn, Commonwealth Ministers of Educn Meeting, Jamaica, 1974. Member: Fiji Broadcasting Commn, 1971–73; Univ. Council, Univ. of South Pacific, 1971–74. *Recreations:* golf, fishing; represented Auckland and Suva, Fiji, in hockey. *Address:* 15 Naimawi Street, Lami, Suva, Fiji.   *Died 5 July 1992.*

GIBSON, Major William David; Director, W. J. Tatem Ltd, since 1957 (Chairman, 1974–96); *b* 26 Feb. 1925; *s* of late G. C. Gibson, OBE, Landwade Hall, Exning, Newmarket, Suffolk; *m* 1st, 1959, Charlotte Henrietta (*d* 1973), *d* of N. S. Pryor; three *s* one *d*; 2nd, 1975, Jane Marion, *d* of late Col L. I. Hassell, DSO, MC. *Educ:* St Peter's Court; Harrow; Trinity Coll., Cambridge. Commissioned into Welsh Guards, July 1945; retired as Major, 1957. Dir, West of England Ship Owners Mutual Protection & Indemnity Assoc., 1959–86; Chairman: Atlantic Shipping and Trading Co., 1969–77; Internat. Shipowners Investment Co., SA Luxembourg, 1978–83; Waverley Components and Products, 1990–95; Dir, Tatem Ltd (formerly Tatem Industries Ltd), 1990– (Chm., 1990–95). National Hunt Cttee, Oct. 1959– (Sen. Steward, 1966); Jockey Club, 1966– (Dep. Sen. Steward, 1969–71); Tattersalls Cttee, 1963–69 (Chm., 1967–69). Master, Worshipful Co. of Farriers, 1979. *Recreations:* racing (won 4 Grand Military Gold Cups, 1950–52 and 1956), collecting, sailing. *Address:* Bishopswood Grange, Bishopswood, near Ross-on-Wye, Herefordshire HR9 5QX. *T:* (01594) 860444. *Clubs:* Cavalry and Guards; Royal Yacht Squadron.   *Died 3 March 1998.*

GIELGUD, Sir (Arthur) John, OM 1996; CH 1977; Kt 1953; actor; *b* 14 April 1904; *s* of late Frank Gielgud and Kate Terry Lewis; unmarried. *Educ:* Westminster. First appearance on stage at Old Vic, 1921; among parts played were Lewis Dodd in Constant Nymph, Inigo Jollifant in The Good Companions, Richard II in Richard of Bordeaux, Hamlet, Romeo, Valentine in Love for Love, Ernest Worthing in The Importance of Being Earnest, Macbeth and King Lear; directed Macbeth, Piccadilly, 1942; Raskolnikoff in Crime and Punishment, Jason in The Medea, New York, 1947; Eustace in The Return of the Prodigal, Globe, 1948; directed The Heiress, Haymarket, 1949; directed, and played Thomas Mendip, The Lady's not for Burning, Globe, 1949; Shakespeare Festival, Stratford-on-Avon, 1950: Angelo in Measure for Measure, Cassius in Julius Caesar, Benedick in Much Ado About Nothing, the name part in King Lear; directed Much Ado About Nothing and King Lear; Shakespeare season at Phoenix, 1951–52: Leontes in The Winter's Tale, 1951; directed Much Ado About Nothing and played Benedick, 1952; season at Lyric, Hammersmith, 1953: directed Richard II and The Way of the World (played Mirabel); played Jaffeir in Venice Preserved; directed A Day by the Sea, and played Julian Anson, Haymarket, Nov. 1953–1954; also directed Charley's Aunt, New Theatre, Dec. 1953, and directed The Cherry Orchard, Lyric, May, 1954; directed Twelfth Night, Stratford, 1955; played in King Lear, and Much Ado About Nothing (also produced)

Shakespeare Memorial Theatre Company (London, provinces and continental tour), 1955; directed The Chalk Garden, Haymarket, 1956; produced (with Noel Coward) Nude with Violin, and played Sebastien, Globe, 1956–57; produced The Trojans, Covent Garden, 1957; played Prospero, Stratford, and Drury Lane, 1957; played James Callifer in The Potting Shed, Globe, and Wolsey in Henry VIII, Old Vic, 1958; directed Variation on A Theme, 1958; produced The Complaisant Lover, Globe, 1959; (Shakespeare's) Ages of Man, Queen's, 1959 (recital, based on Shakespeare anthology of G. Rylands), previous recitals at Edinburgh Fest. and in US, also subseq. in US, at Haymarket, 1960, tour of Australia and NZ, 1963–64, Gothenburg, Copenhagen, Warsaw, Helsinki, Leningrad, Moscow and Dublin, 1964; produced Much Ado About Nothing, at Cambridge, Mass, Festival, and subseq. in New York, 1959; prod Five Finger Exercise, Comedy, 1958, NY, 1959; acted in The Last Joke, Phœnix, 1960; prod Britten's A Midsummer Night's Dream, Royal Opera House, 1961; prod Big Fish Little Fish, New York, 1961; prod Dazzling Prospect, Globe, 1961; took part of Othello, Stratford-on-Avon Season, 1961, also of Gaieff in The Cherry Orchard, Aldwych, 1962; produced The School for Scandal, Haymarket, 1962, USA tour and New York (and played Joseph Surface), 1962–63; dir. The Ides of March, and played Julius Caesar, Haymarket, 1963; dir. Hamlet, Canada and USA, 1964; Julian in Tiny Alice, New York, 1965; played and directed Ivanov, Phœnix, 1965, United States and Canada, 1966; played Orgon in Tartuffe, Nat. Theatre, 1967; directed Halfway up the Tree, Queen's, 1967; played Oedipus in Oedipus, Nat. Theatre, 1968; produced Don Giovanni, Coliseum, 1968; played Headmaster in 40 Years On, Apollo, 1968; played Sir Gideon in The Battle of Shrivings, Lyric, 1970; Home, Royal Court, 1970, NY 1971 (Evening Standard Best Actor award and Tony award, NY, 1971); dir. All Over, NY, 1971; Caesar and Cleopatra, Chichester Festival, 1971; Veterans, Royal Ct, 1972; dir. Private Lives, Queen's, 1972; dir. The Constant Wife, Albery, 1973; played Prospero, Nat. Theatre, 1974; Bingo, Royal Court, 1974; dir. The Gay Lord Quex, Albery, 1975; No Man's Land, Nat. Theatre, 1975, Toronto, Washington, NY, 1977; Julius Caesar, Volpone, Nat. Theatre, 1977; Half-Life, NT and Duke of York's, 1977; The Best of Friends, Apollo, 1988; *films included:* (GB and US) The Good Companions, 1932; The Secret Agent, 1937; The Prime Minister (Disraeli), 1940; Julius Caesar (Cassius), 1952; Richard III (Duke of Clarence), 1955; The Barretts of Wimpole Street (Mr Moulton Barrett), St Joan (Warwick), 1957; Becket (Louis VII), 1964; The Loved One, 1965; Chimes at Midnight, 1966; Mister Sebastian, 1967; The Charge of the Light Brigade, Shoes of the Fisherman, Oh What a Lovely War!, 1968; Julius Caesar, 1970; Eagle in a Cage, Lost Horizon, 1973; 11 Harrowhouse, Gold, Murder on the Orient Express, 1974; Aces High, 1976; Providence, Joseph Andrews, Portrait of a Young Man, Caligula, 1977; The Human Factor, The Elephant Man, 1979; The Conductor, Murder by Decree, Sphinx, Chariots of Fire, The Formula, Arthur (Oscar, 1982), 1980; Lion of the Desert, 1981; Priest of Love, 1982; Wagner, Invitation to the Wedding, Scandalous, The Wicked Lady, 1983; Camille, 1984; The Shooting Party, Plenty, 1985; Leave All Fair; The Whistle Blower, 1987; Arthur on the Rocks, Getting Things Right, Loser Takes All, 1988; Prospero's Books, Shining Through, Power of One, 1991. Appearances on *television* included: The Mayfly and the Frog, 1966; Great Acting, Dorian Gray, 1967; In Good King Charles's Golden Days, 1970; Parson's Pleasure, 1980; Richard Wagner, Brideshead Revisited, 1981; Inside the Third Reich, Neck, The Scarlet and the Black, 1983; presenter of Six Centuries of Verse, 1984; Time After Time, Marco Polo, Oedipus the King, 1986; War and Remembrance, The Canterville Ghost, 1987; Summer's

Lease, 1989; Summer Day's Dream, 1994. President: Shakespeare Reading Soc., 1958–; RADA, 1977–89 (Hon. Fellow, 1989). Fellow, BAFTA, 1992. Special award for services to theatre, Laurence Olivier Awards, 1985. Hon. LLD St Andrews, 1950; Hon. DLitt: Oxon, 1953; London, 1977; Hon. Dr Brandeis Univ. Companion, Legion of Honour, 1960. *Publications:* Early Stages, 1938; Stage Directions, 1963; Distinguished Company, 1972; (jtly) An Actor and His Time (autobiog.), 1979; Backward Glances, 1989; Shakespeare—Hit or Miss, 1991; Notes from the Gods, 1994. *Recreations:* music, painting. *Clubs:* Garrick, Arts; Players' (New York). *Died 21 May 2000.*

GIGGALL, Rt Rev. George Kenneth, OBE 1961; Assistant Bishop, diocese of Blackburn, since 1982; *b* 15 April 1914; *s* of Arthur William and Matilda Hannah Giggall; unmarried. *Educ:* Manchester Central High Sch.; Univ. of Manchester; St Chad's Coll., Univ. of Durham. BA, DipTheol. Deacon, 1939; priest, 1940. Curate of St Alban's Cheetwood, dio. Manchester, 1939–41, St Elisabeth's Reddish, 1941–45; Chaplain, RN, 1945; HMS Braganza, 1945; 34th Amphibious Support Regt, RM, 1945–46; Chaplain, Sch. of Combined Ops, 1946–47; HMS: Norfolk, 1947–49; Ocean, 1949–50; Flotilla Comd Mediterranean and HMS Phoenicia, 1950–52; HMS Campania for Operation Hurricane, 1952; BRNC Dartmouth, 1952–53; HMS: Centaur, 1953–56; Ceylon, 1956–58; Fisgard, 1958–60; Royal Arthur, and Lectr RAF Chaplains' Sch., 1960–63; HMS: Eagle, 1963–65; Drake, 1965–69; QHC, 1967–69; Dean of Gibraltar and Officiating Chaplain, HMS Rooke and Flag Officer, Gibraltar, 1969–73; Bishop of St Helena, 1973–79; Chaplain of San Remo with Bordighera, Italy, and Auxiliary Bishop, dio. of Gibraltar, 1979–81. *Recreation:* music. *Address:* Fosbrooke House, 8 Clifton Drive, Lytham, Lancs FY8 5RQ. *T:* (01253) 735683. *Clubs:* Royal Commonwealth Society; Exiles (Ascension Island). *Died 23 Sept. 1999.*

GILBERT, Hugh Campbell; Chairman: Camden and Islington Family Health Service Authority, 1989–92; Price & Pierce Group Limited, 1973–87 (Chief Executive Officer, 1969–87); *b* 25 March 1926; *s* of Hugh Gilbert and Nessie Campbell; *m* 1956, Beti Gwenllian, *d* of Prof. Henry Lewis, CBE. *Educ:* John Neilson High Sch.; Univ. of Glasgow (MA 1st Cl. Hons Pol Econ.). Mil. Service in Scots Gds, then in Argyll and Sutherland Highlanders, Europe and ME, 1944–48; Territorial Service with 5/6 Argyll and Sutherland Highlanders (Captain), 1948–53. Imperial Chemical Industries, 1951–53; PA Management Consultants Ltd, 1953–62; Dir, Blyth, Greene, Jourdain & Co. Ltd, 1962–81; Dir, Tozer, Kemsley & Millbourn (Holdings) Ltd, 1971–83. Hon. Professorial Fellow, UCNW, Bangor, 1975–79. *Recreations:* racing, opera, travel. *Address:* 59 Wynnstay Gardens, W8 6UU. *T:* (0171) 937 3134. *Clubs:* Caledonian, MCC.
Died 28 April 1998.

GILBERT, Prof. John Cannon; Professor of Economics in the University of Sheffield, 1957–73, then Emeritus; Dean of Faculty of Economic and Social Studies, 1959–62; *b* 28 Sept. 1908; *s* of James and Elizabeth Louisa Gilbert; *m* 1938, Elizabeth Hadley Crook; two *s. Educ:* Bancroft's Sch.; London Sch. of Economics and Political Science, University of London (BCom Hons 1929). Sir Ernest Cassel Travelling Schol., Handels-Hochschule, Berlin, 1927–28. Asst on teaching staff, LSE, 1929–31; Lecturer in Economics, Sch. of Economics, Dundee, 1931–41; Ministry of Supply, 1941–45; Lecturer in Economics, University of Manchester, 1945–48; Senior Lecturer in Economics, University of Sheffield, 1948–56, Reader, 1956–57. Mem. Editorial Bd, Bulletin of Economic Research, 1949–73. *Publications:* A History of Investment Trusts in Dundee, 1873–1938, 1939; Keynes's Impact on Monetary Economics, 1982; articles in Economica, Review of Economic Studies, etc. *Recreation:* reading. *Address:* 81 High Storrs Drive, Ecclesall, Sheffield S11 7LN. *T:* (0114) 266 3544. *Died 26 Feb. 2000.*

GILBERT, Thomas Ian J.; *see* Johnson-Gilbert.

GILL, David Ian; television producer; *b* 9 June 1928; *s* of Cecil and Iona Gill; *m* 1953, Pauline Wadsworth; two *d. Educ:* Belmont Abbey, Hereford. Dancer with Sadler's Wells Theatre Ballet, 1948–55; joined film-cutting rooms, Associated-Rediffusion TV, 1955; produced Stations of the Cross (mime), BBC, 1957; Film Editor, This Week, Rediffusion TV, 1957–68 (also documentaries); Technical Advisor and Editor, Dave Clark Special, 1968; directed for Thames Television: This Week, 1969–73; Till I End My Song (documentary), 1970; Destination America (documentary series), 1975; with Kevin Brownlow: co-wrote and produced: Hollywood, 1980; Unknown Chaplin, 1983; Buster Keaton: a hard act to follow, 1987; Harold Lloyd: the Third Genius, 1990; D. W. Griffith: Father of Film (3 part documentary), 1993; Cinema Europe: the other Hollywood, 1995; co-produced: Live Cinema; Thames Silents/Channel 4 Silents, 1980–; British Cinema: Personal View, 1986. *Recreations:* cinema, theatre, music, planting trees. *Address:* Photoplay Productions, 21 Princess Road, NW1 8JR. *Died 28 Sept. 1997.*

GILLARD, Francis George, CBE 1961 (OBE 1946); public broadcasting interests in USA, since 1970; *b* 1 Dec. 1908; *s* of late Francis Henry Gillard and Emily Jane Gillard, Stockleigh Lodge, Exford; unmarried. *Educ:* Wellington Sch., Som; St Luke's Coll., Exeter (BSc London). Schoolmaster, 1932–41; freelance broadcaster, 1936; joined BBC as Talks Producer, 1941; BBC War Correspondent, 1941; BBC Head of West Regional Programmes, 1945–55; Chief Asst to Dir of Sound Broadcasting with Controller rank, 1955–56; Controller, West Region, BBC, 1956–63; Dir, Radio, subseq. Man. Dir, and Dir Regions, BBC, 1963–70, retired. Distinguished Fellow, Corp. for Public Broadcasting, Washington, 1970–73. Mem. Council, Educational Foundn for Visual Aids, 1970–87 (Chm., 1977–86). Mem. Finance Cttee, Exeter Univ., 1968–86; Governor, Wellington Sch., Somerset, 1961–91 (Chm., 1974–80). FRSA 1971. Hon. LLD Exeter, 1987. Hon. Citizen, Creully, Normandy, 1995. *Address:* Trevor House, Poole, Wellington, Somerset TA21 9HN. *T:* (01823) 662890.
Died 21 Oct. 1998.

GILLIES, (Maurice) Gordon, TD and Bar 1948; QC (Scot.) 1958; Sheriff Principal of South Strathclyde, Dumfries and Galloway, 1982–88; *b* 17 Oct. 1916; *s* of James Brown Gillies, Advocate in Aberdeen, and Rhoda Ledingham; *m* 1954, Anne Bethea McCall-Smith. *Educ:* Aberdeen Grammar Sch.; Merchiston Castle; Edinburgh Univ. Advocate, 1946; Advocate Depute, 1953–58; Sheriff of Lanarkshire, later S Strathclyde, Dumfries and Galloway, 1958–82. *Recreation:* golf. *Address:* The Coach House, Broadgait, Gullane, East Lothian EH31 2DH. *T:* (01620) 842857. *Clubs:* New (Edinburgh); Hon. Company of Edinburgh Golfers. *Died 19 Jan. 1997.*

GILLINGHAM, Michael John, CBE 1997; FSA; Chairman, Advisory Board for Redundant Churches, 1989–99 (Member, 1979–99); *b* 26 June 1933; *s* of John Morey Gillingham and Marion Gillingham. *Educ:* Yeovil School; Corpus Christi College, Cambridge (MA, LLB). Director, John Sparks Ltd, 1976–91. Member: London Diocesan Adv. Cttee for Care of Churches, 1965–; Organs Adv. Cttee, Council for Care of Churches, 1967–91; Westminster Abbey Fabric Commn (formerly Westminster Abbey Architectural Adv. Panel), 1990–; Chichester Cathedral Fabric Cttee, 1990–93; Chm., British Inst. of Organ Studies, 1976–83; Organ Consultant: St Michael,

Framlingham, 1968; St James, Clerkenwell, 1978; Peterborough Cathedral, 1980; Chichester Cathedral, 1986; St Andrew, Holborn, 1989; St Matthew, Westminster, 1989; for restoration of organ-case, Gloucester Cathedral, 1971; and other historic organs in London and elsewhere. Trustee, Fitzwilliam Mus. Trust, 1990–. Hon. RCO 1986. *Publications:* articles on organ-cases, organ history, Chinese art. *Recreation:* looking at buildings and works of art. *Address:* 4 Fournier Street, Spitalfields, E1 6QE. *T:* (020) 7377 1576. *Club:* Athenæum. *Died 22 Oct. 1999.*

GILLINGHAM, Rev. Canon Peter Llewellyn, LVO 1955; MA 1949; Chaplain to the Queen, 1952–84; Hon. Canon of Chichester Cathedral (Wisborough Prebendary), 1969–77, Canon Emeritus since 1977; *b* 3 May 1914; *s* of late Rev. Canon Frank Hay Gillingham and 1st wife, Mary Ryder, 2nd *d* of Rev. E. W. Matthews; *m* 1947, Diana, *d* of Lt-Gen. Sir Alexander Hood, GBE, KCB, KCVO; two *s* two *d*. *Educ:* Cheam; Marlborough; Oriel Coll., Oxford. Deacon 1937, priest 1938; Curate, Tonbridge Parish Church, 1937–40; Curate-in-Charge, St George's Church, Oakdale, Poole, 1940–43; served War of 1939–45, Chaplain, RNVR, 1943–46; Chaplain, Blundell's Sch., Tiverton, 1946–49; Hon. Chaplain to King George VI, 1949–52; Chaplain to Royal Chapel of All Saints, Windsor Great Park, 1949–55; Vicar of St Mildred's, Addiscombe, 1955; Vicar of St Mary the Virgin, Horsham, 1960–77; Rural Dean of Horsham, 1974–77; Asst Chaplain, Sherborne Girls' Sch., 1977–79, Chaplain and Librarian, 1979–82. *Recreations:* golf, sailing. *Address:* Maplestead Cottage, Leiston Road, Aldeburgh, Suffolk IP15 5QD. *T:* Aldeburgh (0172845) 2739. *Died 4 April 1996.*

GILLIS, His Honour Bernard Benjamin; QC 1954, MA Cantab; a Circuit Judge (Additional Judge, Central Criminal Court), 1964–80; *b* 10 Aug. 1905; *m* Jessica; one *s*. *Educ:* Downing Coll., Cambridge (Hon. Fellow, 1976). Squadron Leader, RAF, 1940–45. Called to the Bar, Lincoln's Inn, 1927, Bencher 1960, Treasurer 1976; North Eastern Circuit and Central Criminal Court. Comr, Central Criminal Court, 1959; Commissioner of Assize: Lancaster, 1960; Chelmsford, 1961; Bodmin, 1963; Recorder of Bradford, 1958–64. *Address:* 3 Adelaide Crescent, Hove, E Sussex BN3 2JD. *Club:* Royal Air Force. *Died 5 May 1996.*

GILLMORE OF THAMESFIELD, Baron *cr* 1996 (Life Peer), of Putney in the London Borough of Wandsworth; **David Howe Gillmore,** GCMG 1994 (KCMG 1990; CMG 1982); HM Diplomatic Service, retired; Vice-Chairman, Vickers plc, since 1997 (Director, since 1995); Director, Prudential Corporation, since 1995; *b* 16 Aug. 1934; *s* of Air Vice-Marshal A. D. Gillmore, CB, CBE and Kathleen Victoria Morris; *m* 1964, Lucile Morin; two *s*. *Educ:* Trent Coll.; King's Coll., Cambridge (MA). Reuters Ltd, 1958–60; Asst to Dir-Gen., Polypapier, SA, Paris, 1960–65; teacher, ILEA, 1965–69; HM Diplomatic Service, 1970; Foreign and Commonwealth Office, 1970–72; First Sec., Moscow, 1972–75; Counsellor, UK Delegn, Vienna, 1975–78; Head of Defence Dept, FCO, 1979–81; Asst Under Sec. of State, FCO, 1981–83; High Comr in Malaysia, 1983–86; Dep. Under-Sec. of State, FCO, 1986–90; Visiting Fellow: Harvard Univ., 1990–91; WEU Inst., Paris, 1990–91; Perm. Under-Sec. of State, FCO, and Head of Diplomatic Service, 1991–94. Sen. Advr, BZW Ltd, 1995–97. Mem., Select Cttee on public service, H of L, 1996–97. Chm., LAPADA, 1995–. Governor: Ditchley Foundn, 1992– (Chm. Council, 1996–); Birkbeck Coll., 1994– (Dep. Chm., 1997–); ESU, 1997–. *Publication:* A Way From Exile (novel), 1967. *Recreations:* books, music, exercise. *Address:* c/o House

of Lords, SW1A 0PW. *Clubs:* Brooks's, Royal Automobile, Special Forces. *Died 20 March 1999.*

GILLMORE, Air Vice-Marshal Alan David, CB 1955; CBE 1944; Royal Air Force (retired); *b* 17 Oct. 1905; *s* of late Rev. David Sandeman Gillmore and Allis Emily Widmer; *m* 1931, Kathleen Victoria Morris; three *s*. *Educ:* St Dunstan's Sch., Burnham-on-Sea; King's Sch., Ely. RAF Cadet Coll., Cranwell, Lincs, 1923–25; Commission in RAF, 1925; 13 Sqdn, 1925–27; 208 Sqdn (Egypt), 1927–29; Instr, Sch. of Air Pilotage, 1931–33; Officer i/c Navigation Flight, 1934–35; 202 Flying Boat Sqdn (Malta), 1935–36; HQ no 6 (Aux.) Gp, 1936–39; RN Staff Coll., 1939; Future Ops Planning Staff, 1940–41; Dep. Dir, Overseas Orgn (Air Min.), 1940–41; Instr, RAF Staff Coll., 1942; OC RAF Station Wick, 1943–44; Dir, Maritime Ops (Air Min.), 1944–45; AOC RAF W Africa, 1945–46; Dir of Postings (Air Min.), 1946–47; IDC, 1948; AOC 64 Gp, 1949–51; Commandant RAF Staff Coll., Bracknell, 1951–53; SASO, FEAF, 1953–56; SASO, Home Command, 1956–59; retired 1959. *Address:* 23 Swallowfield Park, Swallowfield, Reading, Berks RG7 1TG. *Club:* Royal Air Force. *Died 27 May 1996.*

GILROY BEVAN, David; *see* Bevan.

GLADWYN, 1st Baron *cr* 1960, of Bramfield, co. Suffolk; **Hubert Miles Gladwyn Jebb,** GCMG 1954 (KCMG 1949; CMG 1942); GCVO 1957; CB 1947; Grand Croix de la Légion d'Honneur, 1957; Deputy Leader of Liberal Party in House of Lords, and Liberal Spokesman on foreign affairs and defence, 1965–88; *b* 25 April 1900; *s* of late Sydney Jebb, Firbeck Hall, Yorks, and Rose Eleanor, 3rd *d* of Maj.-Gen. Hugh Chichester, RA; *m* 1929, Cynthia (*d* 1990), *d* of Sir Saxton Noble, 3rd Bt; one *s* two *d*. *Educ:* Eton; Magdalen Coll., Oxon. 1st in History, Oxford, 1922. Entered Diplomatic Service, 1924; served in Tehran, Rome, and Foreign Office; Private Sec. to Parliamentary Under-Sec. of State, 1929–31, Private Sec. to Permanent Under-Sec. of State, 1937–40; appointed to Ministry of Economic Warfare with temp. rank of Asst Under-Sec., Aug. 1940; Acting Counsellor in Foreign Office, 1941; Head of Reconstruction Dept, 1942; Counsellor, 1943, in that capacity attended the Conferences of Quebec, Cairo, Tehran, Dunbarton Oaks, Yalta, San Francisco and Potsdam; Executive Sec. of Preparatory Commission of the United Nations, Aug. 1945, with temp. rank of Minister; Acting Sec.-Gen. of UN, Feb. 1946; Deputy to Foreign Sec. on Conference of Foreign Ministers, March 1946; Assistant Under-Sec. of State and United Nations Adviser, 1946–47; UK rep. on Brussels Treaty Permanent Commission with personal rank of Ambassador, April 1948; Dep. Under-Sec., 1949–50; Permanent Representative of the UK to the United Nations, 1950–54; Ambassador to France, 1954–60, retired. Mem., European Parlt, 1973–76 (Vice Pres., Political Cttee); contested (L) Suffolk, European Parlt, 1979. Pres., European Movement; former Pres., Atlantic Treaty Assoc.; Chm., Campaign for European Political Community; Mem., Parly Delegns to Council of Europe and WEU Assemblies, 1966–73. Hon. DCL: Oxford; Syracuse, NY, 1954; Essex, 1974; Hon. Fellow Magdalen Coll., Oxford. *Publications:* Is Tension Necessary?, 1959; Peaceful Co-existence, 1962; The European Idea, 1966; Half-way to 1984, 1967; De Gaulle's Europe, or, Why the General says No, 1969; Europe after de Gaulle, 1970; The Memoirs of Lord Gladwyn, 1972. *Recreations:* gardening, cooking. *Heir:* *s* Hon. Miles Alvery Gladwyn Jebb, *b* 3 March 1930. *Address:* Bramfield Hall, Halesworth, Suffolk IP19 9HX. *T:* (01986) 784241. *Died 24 Oct. 1996.*

GLANUSK, 4th Baron *cr* 1899; **David Russell Bailey;** Bt 1852; Lieutenant-Commander, Royal Navy (retired); *b* 19 Nov. 1917; *o s* of late Hon. Herbert Crawshay Bailey (4th *s* of 1st Baron Glanusk) and Kathleen Mary, *d* of Sir Shirley Harris Salt, 3rd Bt; *S* cousin, 1948; *m* 1941, Lorna Dorothy (*d* 1997), *o d* of late Capt. E. C. H. N. Andrews, MBE, RA; one *s* one *d. Educ:* Orley Farm Sch., Harrow; Eton. RN, 1935–51. Managing Dir, Wandel & Goltermann (UK) Ltd, 1966–81; Chm., W&G Instruments Ltd, 1981–87. *Heir: s* Hon. Christopher Russell Bailey [*b* 18 March 1942; *m* 1974, Frances, *d* of Air Chief Marshal Sir Douglas Lowe, GCB, DFC, AFC; one *s* one *d*]. *Address:* Po Anglada Camarasa 87–2B, 07470 Puerto Pollensa, Mallorca, Spain. *T:* (71) 865209.

Died 28 June 1997.

GLASSPOLE, Most Hon. Sir Florizel (Augustus), ON 1973; GCMG 1981; GCVO 1983; CD 1970; Governor-General of Jamaica, 1973–91; *b* Kingston, Jamaica, 25 Sept. 1909; *s* of late Rev. Theophilus A. Glasspole (Methodist minister) and Florence (*née* Baxter); *m* 1934, Ina Josephine Kinlocke (*d* 1999); one *d. Educ:* Central British Elementary Sch.; Wolmer's Sch.; Ruskin Coll., Oxford. British TUC Schol., 1946–47. Accountant (practising), 1932–44. General Secretary: Jamaica United Clerks Assoc., 1937–48; Jamaica TUC, 1939–52, resigned; Water Commn and Allied Workers Assoc., 1941–48; Municipal and Parochial Gen. Workers Union, 1945–47; First Gen. Sec., Nat. Workers Union, 1952–55; President: Jamaica Printers & Allied Workers Union, 1942–48; Gen. Hosp. and Allied Workers Union, 1944–47; Mental Hosp. Workers Union, 1944–47; Machado Employees Union, 1945–52; etc. Workers rep. on Govt Bds, etc, 1942–53. Vice-Pres., PNP (Founding Mem., 1938); MHR (PNP) for Kingston Eastern and Port Royal, 1944–73; Sec., PNP Parly Gp, 1944–73, resigned; Minister of Labour, Jamaica, 1955–57; Leader, House of Representatives, 1957–62, 1972–73; Minister of Educn, 1957–62, 1972–73; a Rep. for Jamaica, on Standing Fedn Cttee, West Indies Federation, 1953–58; Mem. House of Reps Cttee which prepared Independence of Jamaica Constitution, 1961; Mem. Delegn to London which completed Constitution document, 1962. Mem. Bd of Governors, Inst. of Jamaica, 1944–57; Mem., Kingston Sch. Bd, 1944. Hon. LLD Univ. of the West Indies, 1982. Order of Andres Bello, 1st cl. (Venezuela), 1973; Order of the Liberator (Venezuela), 1978. *Recreations:* gardening, sports, reading. *Address:* 6 Millsborough Crescent, Kingston 6, Jamaica. *Died 25 Nov. 2000.*

GLEDHILL, David Anthony, CBE 1992; JP; Chairman: John Swire & Sons (HK), 1988–92; Swire Pacific, 1988–92; Modern Terminals, 1981–94 (Director, 1973–81); Deputy Chairman, Cathay Pacific Airways, 1988–92 (Director, 1974–92); *b* 16 Oct. 1934; *s* of Arnold Grosland Gledhill and Marjorie Yates Johnson; *m* 1968, Kyoko Takeuchi. *Educ:* Ellesmere College, Shropshire; Sidney Sussex College, Cambridge. Joined John Swire and Sons (HK), 1958; served Hong Kong, Osaka, Yokohama, Tokyo; Manager, China Navigation Co., Hong Kong, 1963–65; Shipping Manager, John Swire & Sons (Japan), 1966–73; Dir, John Swire & Sons (HK), 1973–92, Dep. Chm., 1984–88; Dir, Swire Pacific, 1973–92, Dep. Chm., 1984–88; Chairman: Swire Properties Ltd, 1984–92; Swire Pacific Offshore Services, 1975–88; Dir, Swire Pacific Offshore Hldgs Ltd, 1990–; Director: Hongkong & Shanghai Banking Corp., 1988–92; Lee Gardens Internat. Hotels, 1988–92; Mass Transit Railway Corp., 1990–98; Hysan Development Co., 1990–98; China Investment & Develt Fund, 1992–98; Peregrine Internat. Hldgs, 1993–98; Fleming Chinese Investment Trust, 1996–98; Member: IBM World Trade Asia/Pacific Bd, 1989–93; IBM Asia Pacific and Greater China Bd, 1993–99; Advisory Board: PA Management Consultants, 1993–98; Textron Internat., 1996–98; Supervisory Bd, KLM Royal Dutch Airlines, 1995–99. Advr, Employers' Fedn of Hong Kong, 1991– (Council Mem., 1988–92;

Chm., 1989–91); Member: Bd and Exec. Cttee, Community Chest of Hong Kong, 1988–92; Consultative Cttee for Basic Law, 1988–92; Aviation Adv. Bd, 1988–92; Airport Authy, Hong Kong, 1990–98; Securities and Futures Commn, 1990–93; Council, Hong Kong Gen. Chamber of Commerce, 1988–92; Trustee and Council Mem., Business & Professionals Fedn Bd, 1990–. Chm., Hong Kong Sports Develt Bd, 1992–96. Mem. Council, 1994–98, and Finance Cttee, 1987–92 and 1994–98, Univ. of Hong Kong. JP Hong Kong, 1988. *Recreations:* swimming, sailing, fishing. *Address:* c/o Modern Terminals Ltd, Berth One, Kwai Chung, New Territories, Hong Kong. *T:* 21153530, *Fax:* 21154918; 29 The Little Boltons, SW10 9LL. *Fax:* (020) 7244 9857. *Clubs:* Royal Over-Seas League, Sloane; Phyllis Court (Henley); Hong Kong, Shek O Country, Hong Kong Country, China (Hong Kong), Hong Kong Jockey.

Died 9 Dec. 1999.

GLEN, Archibald; solicitor; *b* 3 July 1909; *m* 1938, Phyllis Mary; one *s* two *d. Educ:* Melville Coll., Edinburgh. Admitted Solicitor, 1932. Town Clerk: Burnley, Lancs, 1940–45; Southend-on-Sea, 1945–71. President: Soc. of City and Borough Clerks of the Peace, 1960; Soc. of Town Clerks, 1963–64; Assoc. of Town Clerks of British Commonwealth, 1963–64, etc. Lay Member, Press Council, 1969–75; Mem., Local Govt Staff Commn for England, 1972–76. Hon. Freeman, Southend-on-Sea, 1971. *Recreations:* golf, swimming. *Address:* Harbour House, 2 Drummochy, Lower Largo, Fife KY8 6BZ. *T:* Lundin Links (01333) 320724.

Died 24 May 1996.

GLENDEVON, 1st Baron *cr* 1964, of Midhope, Co. Linlithgow; **John Adrian Hope,** ERD 1988; PC 1959; Director and Deputy Chairman, Ciba-Geigy (UK) Ltd (formerly Geigy (UK) Ltd), 1971–78 (Chairman, 1967–71); Director: ITT (UK) Ltd; Colonial Mutual Life Assurance Society Ltd, 1952–54, 1962–82; British Electric Traction Omnibus Services Ltd, 1947–52, 1962–82; *b* 7 April 1912; *yr* twin *s* of 2nd Marquess of Linlithgow, KG, KT, GCSI, GCIE, OBE, TD, PC, and Doreen Maud, CI, 2nd *d* of Rt Hon. Sir Frederick Milner, 7th Bt; *m* 1948, Elizabeth Mary, *d* of late (William) Somerset Maugham, CH; two *s. Educ:* Eton; Christ Church, Oxford (MA 1936). Served War of 1939–45 (Scots Guards) at Narvik, Salerno and Anzio (despatches twice); psc†. MP (C) Northern Midlothian and Peebles, 1945–50, Pentlands Div. of Edinburgh, 1950–64; (Joint) Parliamentary Under-Sec. of State for Foreign Affairs, 1954–56; Parliamentary Under-Sec. of State for Commonwealth Relations, 1956–57; Jt Parly Under-Sec. of State for Scotland, 1957–59; Minister of Works, 1959–62. Mem., Departmental Cttee to examine operation of Section 2 of Official Secrets Act, 1971. Chairman: Royal Commonwealth Society, 1963–66; Historic Buildings Council for England, 1973–75. Fellow of Eton, 1956–67. FRSA 1962. *Publication:* The Viceroy at Bay, 1971. *Heir: s* Hon. Julian John Somerset Hope, *b* 6 March 1950. *Address:* Mount Lodge, Mount Row, St Peter Port, Guernsey, Channel Islands.

Died 18 Jan. 1996.

GLENDINNING, James Garland, OBE 1973; Chairman, Masterpack Ltd, since 1981; *b* 27 April 1919; *er s* of late George M. Glendinning and Isabella Green; *m* 1st, 1943, Margaret Donald (*d* 1980); one *d*; 2nd, 1980, Mrs Anne Ruth Law. *Educ:* Boroughmuir Sch., Edinburgh; Military Coll. of Science. Mil. Service, 1939–46: 2nd Bn London Scottish and REME in UK and NW Europe. HM Inspector of Taxes, 1946–50; various appts with Shell Petroleum Co. Ltd, 1950–58; Dir Anglo Egyptian Oilfields Ltd in Egypt, 1959–61; Gen. Manager in Borneo and East Java for Shell Indonesia, 1961–64; Head of Industrial Studies (Diversification) in Shell Internat. Petroleum Co. Ltd,

London, 1964–67; various Shell appts in Japan, 1967–72, incl.: Vice-President: Shell Sekiyu KK; Shell Kosan KK; Dir, various Shell/Showa and Shell/Mitsubishi jt venture cos. Chm., British Chamber of Commerce in Japan, 1970–72; Mem., London Transport Exec., 1972–80; Chairman: London Transport Pension Fund Trustees Ltd, 1974–80; North American Property Unit Trust, 1975–80; Director: Industrial and Commercial Property Unit Trust, 1977–81; The Fine Art Society plc, 1972–89; Man. Dir, Gestam International Realty Ltd, 1981–83. Exec. Sec., Japan Soc., 1985–93. FCIT 1973; FRSA 1977. *Address:* 20 Albion Street, W2 2AS. *Clubs:* Caledonian, Oriental.
Died 18 Nov. 1998.

GLENISTER, Prof. Tony William Alphonse, CBE (mil.) 1979; TD; Professor Emeritus, University of London (Professor of Anatomy, at Charing Cross Hospital Medical School, 1970–84, at Charing Cross and Westminster Medical School, 1984–89); Dean, Charing Cross Hospital Medical School, 1976–84, Charing Cross and Westminster Medical School, 1984–89; *b* 19 Dec. 1923; *o s* of late Dudley Stuart Glenister and Maria (*née* Leytens); *m* 1948, Monique Marguerite (*d* 1996), *o d* of late Emile and Marguerite de Wilde; four *s. Educ:* Eastbourne Coll.; St Bartholomew's Hosp. Med. Coll. MRCS, LRCP 1947; MB, BS 1948, PhD 1955, DSc 1963, London. House appts, St Bartholomew's Hosp. and St Andrew's Hosp., Dollis Hill, 1947–48; served in RAMC, 1948–50; Lectr and Reader in Anatomy, Charing Cross Hosp. Med. Sch., 1950–57; Internat. Project Embryological Res., Hubrecht Lab., Utrecht, 1954; Prof. of Embryology, Univ. of London, 1967–70; Vice-Dean, Charing Cross Hosp. Med. Sch., 1966–69, 1971–76; Hon. Cons. in Clin. Anatomy and Genetics to Charing Cross Gp of Hosps, 1972–89. Apothecaries' Soc. Lectr in History of Medicine, 1971–89; Arnott Demonstrator, RCS, 1972, 1986; Pres., Anatomical Soc. GB and Ireland, 1979–81 (Sec., 1974–76). Brig. late RAMC, TA (TD, TA 1963 and TAVR 1978); ADMS 44 (Home Counties) Div. TA, 1964–67; CO 217 (London) Gen. Hosp. RAMC (V), 1968–72; QHP 1971–73; Hon. Col 220 (1st Home Counties) Field Amb. RAMC (V), 1973–78; TAVR Advr to DGAMS, 1976–79; Hon. Col 217 (London) Gen. Hosp. RAMC (V), 1981–86. Member: Ealing, Hammersmith and Hounslow AHA (T), 1976–82; Hammersmith and Fulham DHA, 1982–83; North West Thames RHA, 1983–88; GMC, 1979–93; GDC, 1983–93; sometime Examiner: Univs of Cambridge, Liverpool, London, St Andrews, Singapore, NUI, Chinese Univ., Hong Kong; RCS; RCSE; RCPGlas. Trustee: Tablet Trust; RAMC Charitable Fund, 1984–98. Master, Soc. of Apothecaries of London, 1991–92; Freeman, City of London. OStJ 1967; KLJ 1993 (OLJ 1989). *Publications:* (with J. R. W. Ross) Anatomy and Physiology for Nurses, 1965, 3rd edn 1980; (contrib.) A Companion to Medical Studies, ed Passmore, 1963, 2nd edn 1976; (contrib.) Methods in Mammalian Embryology, ed Daniel, 1971; (contrib.) Textbook of Human Anatomy, ed Hamilton, 1976; papers and articles mainly on prenatal development. *Recreations:* the countryside, sketching, history. *Club:* Army and Navy.
Died 1 May 1998.

GLOCK, Sir William (Frederick), Kt 1970; CBE 1964; Controller of Music, BBC, 1959–72; *b* London, 3 May 1908; *s* of William George Glock; *m* 1st, 1944, Clemency (marr. diss. 1951), *d* of Swinburne Hale; (one *d* decd); 2nd, 1952, Anne Geoffroy-Dechaume. *Educ:* Christ's Hospital; Caius Coll., Cambridge. Studied pianoforte under Artur Schnabel. Served in RAF, 1941–46. Joined The Observer, 1934, chief music critic, 1939–45; Dir, Summer Sch. of Music, Bryanston, 1948–52, Dartington Hall, 1953–79; Editor: music magazine, The Score, 1949–61; Eulenburg books on music, 1973–86; Music Critic, New Statesman, 1958–59; Artistic Dir, Bath Fest., 1975–84. Adjudicated at Canadian music festivals, 1951;

lectured on music throughout England and Canada; planned major series of progs for South Bank: Haydn, 1990–91; Bach Cantatas, 1992; Mozart, 1998–99. Chm., London Orchestral Concerts Bd, 1975–86; Member: Bd of Dirs, Royal Opera House, 1968–73; Arts Council, 1972–75; South Bank Bd, 1986–91. Pres., Bath Fest. Soc., 1991. Hon. Mem., Royal Philharmonic Soc., 1971. Hon. DMus: Nottingham Univ., 1968; Plymouth Univ., 1993; DUniv York, 1972; Hon. DLitt Bath, 1984. Albert Medal, RSA, 1971. *Publication:* Notes in Advance (autobiog.), 1991. *Address:* Vine House, Brightwell cum Sotwell, Wallingford, Oxon OX10 0RT. *T:* (01491) 837144.
Died 28 June 2000.

GLOVER, Gen. Sir James (Malcolm), KCB 1981; MBE 1964; DL; Chairman: Royal Armouries International plc, since 1993; Merlin Communications (International), since 1997; *b* 25 March 1929; *s* of Maj.-Gen. Malcolm Glover, CB, OBE and Jean Catherine Ogilvy (*née* Will); *m* 1958, Janet Diones De Pree; one *s* one *d. Educ:* Wellington College; RMA, Sandhurst. Commissioned, 1949; RHA, 1950–54; Instructor RMA Sandhurst, 1955–56; transferred to Rifle Brigade, 1956; Brigade Major, 48 Gurkha Inf. Bde, 1960–62; Directing Staff, Staff Coll., 1966–68; CO, 3rd Bn Royal Green Jackets, 1970–71; Col General Staff, Min. of Defence, 1972–73; Comdr 19 Airportable Bde, 1974–75; Brigadier General Staff (Intelligence), Min. of Defence, 1977–78; Commander Land Forces N Ireland, 1979–80; Dep. Chief of Defence Staff (Intelligence) and Mem., Jt Intelligence Cttee, 1981–83; Vice Chief of General Staff, and Mem., Army Bd, 1983–85; C-in-C, UKLF, 1985–87. Served in W Germany, Malaya, Singapore, Hong Kong, Cyprus and N Ireland. Colonel Commandant: RMP, 1981–86; RGJ, 1984–88. Dir, British Petroleum plc, 1987–99; Mem. Adv. Bd, Business Training Systems, 1996–. Trustee, Rainbow Trust, 1997–. DL Hants, 1997. *Recreations:* reading biographies, shooting, mountain walking. *Address:* c/o Lloyds TSB, Cox's & King's Branch, 7 Pall Mall, SW1Y 5NA. *Club:* Boodle's.
Died 4 June 2000.

GLYN, Sir Alan, Kt 1990; ERD; *b* 26 Sept. 1918; *s* of John Paul Glyn, late Royal Horse Guards (Blues), Barrister-at-Law, Middle Temple, and Margaret Johnston, Edinburgh; *m* 1962, Lady Rosula Caroline Windsor Clive, OStJ, *y d* of 2nd Earl of Plymouth, PC, GCStJ (*d* 1943), St Fagan's, Cardiff, S Wales; two *d. Educ:* Westminster; Caius Coll., Cambridge; St Bartholomew's and St George's Hosps. BA (Hons) Cantab 1939; qualified medical practitioner, 1948. Served War of 1939–45: Far East, 1942–46; psc 1945; Bde Major, 1946; re-employed Captain, Royal Horse Guards (ER), retired 1967 (Hon. Major, 1967); attached French Foreign Legion, by special permission of French Govt, 1960. Called to Bar, Middle Temple, 1955. Co-opted Mem. LCC Education Cttee, 1956–58. MP (C) Clapham Div. of Wandsworth, 1959–64, Windsor, 1970–74, Windsor and Maidenhead, 1974–92. Member: Chelsea Borough Council, 1959–62; No 1 Divisional Health Cttee (London), 1959–61; Inner London Local Med. Cttee, 1967–92; Governing Body, Brit. Postgrad. Med. Fedn, 1967–82; Greater London Cent. Valuation Panel, 1967–91; Bd of Governors, Nat. Heart and Chest Hosps Special Health Authy, 1982–90. Former Governor, Henry Thornton and Aristotle Schs; Manager, Macaulay C of E Sch., Richard Atkins, Henry Cavendish, Telfescot, Glenbrook and Boneville Primary Schs in Clapham. One of Earl Marshal's Green Staff Officers at Investiture of HRH Prince of Wales, Caernarvon, 1969. Freeman, Worshipful Soc. of the Art and Mystery of Apothecaries of the City of London, 1961. Joined freedom fighters in Hungary during Hungarian Revolution, 1956; Pro-Hungaria Medal of SMO Malta, 1959; War correspondent, Vietnam, 1967. *Publications:* Let's Think Again, 1965; Witness to Viet Nam (the containment of communism in

South East Asia), 1968. *Address:* 17 Cadogan Place, Belgrave Square, SW1X 9SA. *T:* (0171) 235 2957. *Clubs:* Carlton, Pratt's, Royal Over-Seas League, Special Services. *Died 4 May 1998.*

GLYN, Sir Anthony (Geoffrey Leo Simon), 2nd Bt *cr* 1927, of Berbice, British Guiana; author; *b* 13 March 1922; *s* of Sir Edward Rae Davson, 1st Bt, KCMG and Margot, OBE (*d* 1966), *er d* of late Clayton Glyn and Mrs Elinor Glyn; *S* father, 1937; assumed by deed poll, 1957, the surname of Glyn in lieu of his patronymic, and the additional forename of Anthony; *m* 1946, Susan Eleanor, barrister-at-law, 1950, *er d* of Sir Rhys Rhys-Williams, 1st Bt, DSO, QC, and Dame Juliet Rhys-Williams, DBE; one *d* (and one *d* decd). *Educ:* Eton. Joined Welsh Guards, 1941; served Guards Armoured Div., 1942–45; Staff Captain, 1945. Vermeil Medal, City of Paris, 1985. *Publications:* Romanza, 1953; The Jungle of Eden, 1954; Elinor Glyn, a biography, 1955 (Book Society Non-Fiction Choice); The Ram in the Thicket, 1957 (Dollar Book Club Choice); I Can Take it All, 1959 (Book Society Choice; trans. Spanish, Swedish, Finnish); Kick Turn, 1963; The Terminal, 1965; The Seine, 1966; The Dragon Variation, 1969; The Blood of a Britishman, 1970 (US edn, The British; trans. French, Spanish, Japanese); The Companion Guide to Paris, 1985 (trans. Dutch). *Recreations:* ski-ing, chess. *Heir: b* Christopher Michael Edward Davson, ACA, late Capt. Welsh Guards [*b* 26 May 1927; *m* 1962, Evelyn Mary (marr. diss. 1971), *o d* of late James Wardrop; one *s*; 2nd, 1975, Kate, *d* of late Ludovic Foster, Greatham Manor, Pulborough]. *Address:* Marina Baie des Anges, Ducal Apt. U-03, 06270 Villeneuve Loubet, Alpes Maritimes, France. *T:* 493736752. *Club:* Pratt's. *Died 20 Jan. 1998.*

GOAD, Sir (Edward) Colin (Viner), KCMG 1974; Director, International Registries Inc., since 1980; *b* 21 Dec. 1914; *s* of Maurice George Viner Goad and Caroline (*née* Masters); *m* 1939, Joan Olive Bradley (*d* 1980); one *s*. *Educ:* Cirencester Grammar Sch.; Gonville and Caius Coll., Cambridge (Scholar, BA). Ministry of Transport: Asst Principal, 1937; Principal, 1942; Asst Sec., 1948; Imperial Defence Coll., 1953; Under-Sec., 1963; Dep. Sec.-Gen., 1963–68, Sec.-Gen., 1968–73, Inter-Govtl Maritime Consultative Orgn. *Address:* The Paddock, Ampney Crucis, Glos GL7 5RY. *T:* (01285) 851353. *Died 15 March 1998.*

GODBER, Geoffrey Chapman, CBE 1961; DL; Chief Executive, West Sussex County Council, 1974–75, retired (Clerk of the Peace and Clerk to the Council, 1966–74); Clerk to the Lieutenancy of West Sussex, 1974–76 (Sussex, 1968–74); *b* 22 Sept. 1912; *s* of late Isaac Godber, Willington Manor, near Bedford; *m* 1937, Norah Enid (*née* Finney); three *s*. *Educ:* Bedford Sch. LLB (London) 1935; Solicitor, 1936. Deputy Clerk of the Peace, Northants, 1938–44; Clerk of the Peace, Clerk of the County Council and Clerk of the Lieutenancy, Salop, 1944–66; Hon. Sec., Soc. of Clerks of the Peace of Counties, 1953–61 (Chm., 1961–64); Chm., Assoc. of County Chief Executives, 1974–75. Member: Probation Adv. and Trng Bd, 1949–55; Child Care Adv. Council, 1953–56; Cttee of Inquiry into Inland Waterways, 1956–58; Redevelopment Adv. Cttee, Inland Waterways, 1959–62; Waterways Sub-Commn, Brit. Transport, 1959–62; Central Adv. Water Cttee, 1961–70; Minister of Health's Long Term Study Group, 1965–69; W Midlands Economic Planning Council, 1965–66; SE Economic Planning Council, 1969–75; CS Adv. Council, 1971–78; British Waterways Bd, 1975–81; Chichester Harbour Conservancy, 1975–78; Shoreham Port Authority, 1976–82 (Dep. Chm., 1978–82); Chm., 1975–82, Pres., 1988–90, Open Air Museum, Weald and Downland. DL W Sussex, 1975. Hon. Freeman, Chichester Harbour,

1994. *Recreation:* sailing. *Address:* Pricklows, Singleton, Chichester, West Sussex PO18 0HA. *T:* (01243) 811238. *Died 13 April 1999.*

GODDEN, Ven. Max Leon; Archdeacon of Lewes and Hastings, 1975–88 (of Lewes, 1972–75); *b* 25 Nov. 1923; *s* of Richard George Nobel and Lucy Godden; *m* 1945, Anne, *d* of Kenneth and Edith Hucklebridge; four *d*. *Educ:* Sir Andrew Judd Sch., Tonbridge; Worcester Coll., Oxford (MA 1950). Served RAFVR, 1940–47 (despatches). Deacon, 1952; priest, 1953; Assistant Curate: Cuckfield, 1952–53; Brighton, 1953–57; Vicar of Hangleton, 1957–62; Vicar of Glynde, Firle and Beddingham, 1962–82. *Recreations:* life in a country parish, the garden. *Address:* 14 Oak Close, Chichester, W Sussex PO19 3AJ. *T:* (01243) 531344. *Died 1 March 2000.*

GODDEN, Rumer, (Margaret Rumer Haynes-Dixon), OBE 1993; writer, playwright, poet; *b* 10 Dec. 1907; *d* of late Arthur Leigh Godden, Lydd House, Aldington, Kent, and Katherine Norah Hingley; *m* 1934, Laurence Sinclair Foster (marr. diss. 1948; he *d* 1977), Calcutta; two *d*; *m* 1949, James Haynes-Dixon, OBE (*d* 1973). *Educ:* abroad and Moira House, Eastbourne. *Publications: novels:* Chinese Puzzle, 1935; Lady and Unicorn, 1937; Black Narcissus (novel and play), 1938 (filmed 1946); Gypsy Gypsy, 1940; Breakfast with the Nikolides, 1941; Fugue in Time (novel and play), 1945; The River, 1946 (filmed 1950); Candle for St Jude, 1948; A Breath of Air, 1950; Kingfishers Catch Fire, 1953; An Episode of Sparrows, 1955 (filmed 1957); The Greengage Summer, 1958 (filmed 1961); China Court, 1961; The Battle of the Villa Florita, 1963 (filmed 1964); (with Jon Godden) Two Under the Indian Sun, 1966; In This House of Brede, 1969; (with Jon Godden) Shiva's Pigeons, 1972; The Peacock Spring, 1975 (filmed 1995); Five for Sorrow, Ten for Joy, 1979; The Dark Horse, 1981; Thursday's Children, 1984; Coromandel Sea Change, 1991; Pippa Passes, 1994; Cromartie *v* The God Shiva Acting Through The Government of India, 1997; *biography:* Rungli-Rungliot, 1943; Hans Christian Andersen, 1955; The Tale of the Tales, 1971; Gulbadan Begum: portrait of a Rose Princess at the Mughal Court, 1980; *poetry:* In Noah's Ark, 1949; Book of Spiritual Poetry, 1996; Anthology of Poetry, 1996; *short stories:* Mooltiki, 1957; Swan and Turtles, 1968; (with Jon Godden) Indian Dust, 1989; *non-fiction:* (compiled) The Raphael Bible, 1970; *autobiography:* A Time to Dance, No Time to Weep, 1987; A House with Four Rooms, 1989; *children's books:* The Doll's House, 1949; The Mousewife, 1951; Impunity Jane, 1954; Fairy Doll, 1956; Mouse House, 1958; The Story of Holly and Ivy, 1958; Candy Floss, 1960; Miss Happiness and Miss Flower, 1961; Little Plum, 1962; Home is the Sailor, 1964; The Kitchen Madonna, 1967; Operation Sippacik, 1969; The Old Woman Who Lived in a Vinegar Bottle, 1972; The Diddakoi, 1972 (Whitbread Award); The Dragon of Og, 1981; Four Dolls, 1983; Fu-Dog, 1989; A Kindle of Kittens, 1991; Listen to the Nightingale, 1992; Great Grandfather's House, 1992; Premlata and the Festival of Lights, 1996; The Little Chair, 1996; published internationally (11 languages); *relevant publication:* Rumer Godden: a storyteller's life, by Anne Chisholm, 1998. *Address:* Macmillan & Co., 25 Eccleston Place, SW1W 9NF. *Died 8 Nov. 1998.*

GOLD, Sir Joseph, Kt 1980; Senior Consultant, International Monetary Fund, since 1979; *b* 12 July 1912; *m* 1939, Ruth Schechter; one *s* two *d*. *Educ:* Univ. of London (LLB 1935, LLM 1936); Harvard Univ. (SJD). Asst Lectr, University Coll., London, 1937–39; British Mission, Washington, DC, 1942–46; joined IMF, 1946; General Counsel and Dir, Legal Dept, 1960–79. Hon. LLD Southern Methodist Univ., 1985. Silver Medal, Columbia Univ., 1982; Theberge Medal in Internat. Law,

Amer. Bar Assoc., 1989. *Publications:* The Fund Agreement in the Courts, vol. I 1962, vol. II 1982, vol. III 1986; The Stand-by Arrangements of the IMF, 1970; Voting and Decisions in the IMF, 1972; Membership and Nonmembership in the IMF, 1974; Los Acuerdos de Derechos de Giro del Fondo Monetario Internacional, 1976; Legal and Institutional Aspects of the International Monetary System, vol I 1979, vol II 1984; Aspectos Legales de La Reforma Monetario Internacional, 1979; Exchange Rates in International Law and Organisation, 1988; Legal Effects of Fluctuating Exchange Rates, 1990; Interpretation: The IMF and International Law, 1996; numerous pamphlets and articles on internat. and nat. monetary law in many countries; *festschrift:* The Fund Agreement in the Courts, Vol. IV, 1989. *Recreations:* collecting first editions 20th century English and American poetry, assemblages of found objects, gardening, defence of English language. *Address:* 7020 Braeburn Place, Bethesda, MD 20817, USA. *T:* (301) 2293278.
Died 22 Feb. 2000.

GOLDBY, Prof. Frank; Professor of Anatomy, London University, St Mary's Hospital Medical School, 1945–70, then Emeritus; *b* Enfield, Middx, 25 May 1903; *s* of Frank and Ellen Maud Goldby; *m* 1932, Helen Rosa Tomlin; five *s* one *d. Educ:* Mercers' School, Holborn; Gonville and Caius College, Cambridge; King's College Hospital. MRCS, LRCP 1926; MRCP 1928; MD (Cambridge), 1936; FRCP 1963. Resident appointments King's Coll. Hospital, 1926–28; Asst Clinical Pathologist, King's College Hospital, 1929–30; Senior Demonstrator in Anatomy, University College, London, 1931; Lecturer in charge of Anatomy Dept, Hong Kong, 1932–33; Lecturer in Anatomy, University of Cambridge and Fellow of Queens' College, 1934–37; Prof. of Anatomy, Univ. of Adelaide, 1937–45. *Publications:* papers on embryology and on the pathology and comparative anatomy of the nervous system *Address:* 1 St Mark's Court, Barton Road, Cambridge CB3 9LE. *Died 20 Oct. 1997.*

GOLDING, Dame (Cecilie) Monica, DBE 1958; RRC 1950 (ARRC 1940); *b* 6 Aug. 1902; *o d* of Ben Johnson and Clara (*née* Beames); *m* 1961, Brig. Rev. Harry Golding, CBE (*d* 1969). *Educ:* Croydon Secondary Sch. Professional training: Royal Surrey County Hospital, Guildford, 1922–25; Louise Margaret Hosp., Aldershot and Queen Victoria's Institute of District Nursing. Joined Army Nursing Services, 1925; India, 1929–34; France, 1939–40; Middle East, 1940–43 and 1948–49; Southern Comd, 1943–44 and 1950–52; WO, 1945–46; India and SE Asia, 1946–48; Far East, 1952–55; Eastern Comd, 1955–56; Matron-in-Chief and Dir of Army Nursing Services, 1956–60, retired (with rank of Brig.), 1960. QHNS 1956–60; Col Commandant, Queen Alexandra's Royal Army Nursing Corps, 1961–66. OStJ 1955. *Recreations:* motoring, amateur bird watching, nature study. *Address:* Retired Nurses' Home, Riverside Avenue, Bournemouth, Dorset BH7 7EE. *T:* (01202) 396418.
Died 6 June 1997.

GOLDING, John; General Secretary, National Communications Union, 1986–88; *b* Birmingham, 9 March 1931; *s* of Peter John Golding; *m* 1st, 1958, Thelma Gwillym (marr. diss); one *s* (and one *s* decd); 2nd, 1980, Llinos Lewis, sometime MP. *Educ:* Chester Grammar Sch.; London Univ.; Keele Univ. BA History, Politics, Economics, 1956. Asst Res. Officer, 1960–64, Education Officer, 1964–69, Political and Parly Officer, 1969–86, Post Office Engineering Union. MP (Lab) Newcastle-under-Lyme, 1969–86; PPS to Minister of State, Min. of Technology, Feb.-June 1970; Opposition Whip, 1970–74; a Lord Comr, HM Treasury, Feb.-Oct. 1974; Parly Under-Sec. of State, Dept of Employment, 1976–79. Chm., Select Cttee on Employment, 1979–82; former Mem. Select

Cttee on Nationalised Industries. Mem., NEC, Lab. Party, 1978–83; Chm., Lab. Party Home Policy Cttee, 1982–83. Governor: University Coll. Hosp., 1970–74; Ruskin Coll., 1970–. *Publications:* co-author Fabian Pamphlets: Productivity Bargaining; Trade Unions—on to 1980. *Address:* 6 Lancaster Avenue, Newcastle-under-Lyme, Staffs ST5 1DR; 31 Westminster Mansions, Great Smith Street, SW1P 3BP. *Died 20 Jan. 1999.*

GOLDING, Hon. Sir John (Simon Rawson), Kt 1986; OJ 1980; CD 1974; OBE 1959; Princess Alice Professor of Orthopaedic Surgery, University of the West Indies, 1965, then Professor Emeritus; *b* 15 April 1921; *s* of Mark and Louise Golding; *m* 1961, Alice Patricia Levy; one *s* one *d. Educ:* Marlborough College; Cambridge Univ. MA, MB BChir. FRCS 1948. Middlesex Hosp., 1941–46 and 1948–52; RAMC, 1946–48; Royal Nat. Orthop. Hosp., 1952–53; Univ. of the West Indies, 1953–. ABC Travelling Fellow, Amer., British and Canadian Orthopaedic Assoc., 1956; Hunterian Prof., RCS, 1956; Nuffield Fellow, 1961–62. Hon. LLD Univ. of Toronto, 1984. *Publications:* The Ascent to Mona, 1994; papers in Jl of Bone and Joint Surgery, West Indian Med. Jl, etc. *Recreations:* sailing, walking, bridge. *Address:* 2A Bamboo Avenue, Kingston 6, Jamaica, WI. *Died 23 March 1996.*

GOLDING, Dame Monica; *see* Golding, Dame C. M.

GOLDSMITH, Sir James (Michael), Kt 1976; Member for France, European Parliament, since 1994; Chief Executive, Goldsmith Foundation, since 1991; *b* 26 Feb. 1933; *s* of late Frank Goldsmith, OBE, TD and Marcelle Mouiller; *m* 1st, 1954, Maria Isabel Patino (*d* 1954); one *d*; 2nd, Ginette Lery; one *s* one *d*, 3rd, 1978, Lady Annabel Vane Tempest Stewart, *d* of 8th Marquess of Londonderry; two *s* one *d. Educ:* Eton College. Founder of a number of industrial, commercial and financial enterprises; retired from active business, 1990. Hon. Pres., l'Europe des Nations parly gp, EP, 1997– (Pres., 1994–97); Founder, Referendum Party. Contested (Referendum) Putney, 1997. Chevalier, Légion d'Honneur, 1978. *Publications:* Counterculture, vol. I, 1985, vol. II, 1987, vol. III, 1990, vol. IV, 1991, vol. V, 1993; Pour la Révolution Permanente, 1986; Le Piège, 1993 (The Trap, 1994); The Response, 1995. *Address:* Ham Gate, Richmond, Surrey; Casa La Loma, Costa Cuixmala, Jalisco, Mexico. *Clubs:* Brooks's; Travellers' (Paris). *Died 19 July 1997.*

GOLDSWORTHY, Ian Francis; QC 1992; a Recorder of the Crown Court, 1991–99; *b* 7 July 1943; *s* of Francis Charles and Mary Goldsworthy; *m* 1974, Lindsay Mary Steel; three *d. Educ:* Clifton Coll.; University Coll., Oxford. Called to the Bar, Inner Temple, 1968. *Recreations:* Master of Ratte-hounds, antiques, music.
Died 9 June 2000.

GOLDWATER, Barry M(orris); US Senator from Arizona, 1953–64 and 1969–87; *b* Phoenix, Arizona, 1 Jan. 1909; *s* of late Baron Goldwater and Josephine Williams; *m* 1st, 1934, Margaret Johnson (*d* 1985); two *s* two *d*; 2nd, 1992, Susan McMurray Wechsler. *Educ:* Staunton Mil. Acad., Virginia; University of Arizona. 2nd Lieut, Army Reserve, 1930; transferred to USAAF, 1941; served as ferry-command and fighter pilot instructor, Asia, 1941–45 (Lieut-Col); Chief of Staff, Arizona Nat. Guard, 1945–52 (Col); Maj.-Gen., USAF Reserves. Joined Goldwater's Inc., 1929 (Pres., 1937–53). City Councilman, Phoenix, 1949–52; Republican Candidate for the Presidency of the USA, 1964. Chm., Senate Armed Services Cttee, 1985–87; Member: Advisory Cttee on Indian Affairs, Dept of Interior, 1948–50; Commerce, Science and Transportation Cttee; Small Business Cttee. Vice-Chairman: Amer. Graduate Sch. of Internat. Management; Bd of Regents, Smithsonian Institution; Member: Heard Museum; Museum of Northern Arizona;

St Joseph's Hosp.; Veterans of Foreign Wars; American Legion; Royal Photographic Society, etc. US Junior Chamber of Commerce Award, 1937; Man of the Year, Phoenix, 1949; Medal of Freedom, 1986. 33° Mason. *Publications:* Arizona Portraits (2 vols), 1940; Journey Down the River of Canyons, 1940; Speeches of Henry Ashurst: the Conscience of a Conservative, 1960; Why Not Victory?, 1962; Where I Stand, 1964; The Face of Arizona, 1964; People and Places, 1967; The Conscience of the Majority, 1970; Delightful Journey, 1970; The Coming Breakpoint, 1976; Barry Goldwater and the Southwest, 1976; With No Apologies, 1979; (with J. Casserly) Goldwater (autobiog.), 1988. *Address:* PO Box 1601, Scottsdale, AZ 85252, USA.
Died 29 May 1998.

GOLIGHER, Prof. John Cedric, ChM; FRCS; Professor and Chairman, Department of Surgery, Leeds University, 1954–77, then Emeritus; Emeritus Consultant, St Mark's Hospital for Diseases of the Rectum and Colon (Consulting Surgeon, 1954–95); *b* Londonderry, N Ireland, 13 March 1912; *s* of John Hunter Goligher; *m* 1952, Gwenllian Nancy, *d* of Norman R. Williams, Melbourne, Aust.; one *s* two *d*. *Educ:* Foyle Coll., Londonderry; Edinburgh Univ. MB, ChB 1934; ChM 1948, Edinburgh; FRCS, FRCSE 1938. Junior hosp. appts mainly in Edinburgh area; Res. Surg. Officer, St Mark's Hosp., London; served War 1940–46, RAMC, as Surgical Specialist, Major and Lt-Col; then Surgical Registrar, St Mary's Hosp., London; Surg., St Mary's Hosp., and St Mark's Hosp. for Diseases of the Rectum and Colon, 1947–54. Mem. Council, RCS, 1968–80. FRSocMed (Past Pres., Section of Proctology); Fellow, Assoc. Surgeons of Gt Brit. and Ire. (Past Pres.); Mem. Brit. Soc. of Gastroenterology (Past Pres.). Hon. FACS 1974; Hon. FRCSI 1977; Hon. FRACS 1978; Hon. FRSocMed 1986; Hon. Fellow: Brasilian Coll. of Surgeons; Amer. Surg. Assoc.; Amer. Soc. of Colon and Rectal Surgeons; Soc. for Surgery of the Alimentary Tract; British Soc. of Coloproctology; Internat. Soc. of Univ. Colon and Rectal Surgeons. Corresp. Mem., German Surgical Soc.; Hon. Mem., French, Swiss and Austrian Surg. Socs. Many vis. professorships and named lectures in UK, Europe, N and S America, ME, FE and the Antipodes. Hon. MD: Göteborg, 1976; Belfast, 1981; Uruguay, 1983; Hon. DSc Leeds, 1980. Liston Award, RCSE, 1977; Lister Award, RCS, 1981. *Publications:* Surgery of the Anus, Rectum and Colon, 1961, 5th edn 1984; numerous contribs to books and med. journals, dealing mainly with gastric and colorectal surgery. *Recreations:* reading, tennis, music, gastronomy and oenology, travel. *Address:* Ladywood, Northgate Lane, Linton, Wetherby, West Yorks LS22 4HP.
Died 18 Jan. 1998.

GOOCH, Sir (Richard) John Sherlock, 12th Bt *cr* 1746, of Benacre Hall, Suffolk; JP; *b* 22 March 1930; *s* of Sir Robert Eric Sherlock Gooch, 11th Bt, KCVO, DSO and Katharine Clervaux (*d* 1974), *d* of late Maj.-Gen. Sir Edward Walter Clervaux Chaytor, KCMG, KCVO, CB; *S* father, 1978. *Educ:* Eton. Captain, The Life Guards; retired, 1963. JP Suffolk, 1970. *Heir: b* Major Timothy Robert Sherlock Gooch, MBE [*b* 7 Dec. 1934; *m* 1963, Susan Barbara Christie, *o d* of late Maj.-Gen. Kenneth Christie Cooper, CB, DSO, OBE; two *d*]. *Address:* Benacre Hall, Beccles, Suffolk NR34 7LJ. *T:* (01502) 740333.
Died 19 April 1999.

GOODCHILD, Rt Rev. Ronald Cedric Osbourne; an Hon. Assistant Bishop, Diocese of Exeter, since 1983; *b* 17 Oct. 1910; *s* of Sydney Osbourne and Dido May Goodchild; *m* 1947, Jean Helen Mary (*née* Ross); one *s* four *d*. *Educ:* St John's School, Leatherhead; Trinity Coll., Cambridge (Monk Schol.; 2nd Cl. Hist. Tripos Parts I and II, 1931; Dealtry Exhibn 1932; 3rd Class Theol. Tripos,

1932); Bishops' Coll., Cheshunt. Asst Master, Bickley Hall Sch., Kent, 1932–34; ordained deacon, 1934, priest, 1935; Curate, Ealing Parish Church, 1934–37; Chaplain: Oakham Sch., 1937–42; RAFVR, 1942–46 (despatches); Warden St Michael's House, Hamburg, 1946–49; Gen. Sec., SCM in Schools, 1949–53; Rector of St Helen's Bishopsgate with St Martin Outwich, 1951–53; Vicar of Horsham, Sussex, 1953–59; Surrogate and Rural Dean of Horsham, 1954–59; Archdeacon of Northampton and Rector of Ecton, 1959–64; Bishop Suffragan of Kensington, 1964–80. Examiner, Religious Knowledge, Southern Univs Jt Bd, 1954–58; Examining Chaplain to Bishop of Peterborough, 1959. Chairman, Christian Aid Dept, British Council of Churches, 1964–74. Mem. of General Synod of C of E, 1974–80. *Publication:* Daily Prayer at Oakham School, 1938. *Recreations:* cabinet making, walking. *Address:* Mead, Welcombe, near Bideford, N Devon EX39 6HQ. *Club:* Royal Air Force.
Died 28 Dec. 1998.

GOODENOUGH, Cecilia Phyllis, MA, STh, DD; *b* 9 Sept. 1905; *d* of late Adm. Sir William Goodenough, GCB, MVO and Hon. (Henrietta) Margaret Stanley (OBE 1919), *e d* of 4th Baron Sheffield and Stanley of Alderley. *Educ:* Rochester Grammar Sch.; Liverpool Coll., Huyton; St Hugh's Coll., Oxford. LCC Care Cttee Sec., 1927–30; Sunday Sch. and Evangelistic work, Diocese of Caledonia, Fort St John, BC, Canada, 1931–36; Head of Talbot Settlement, 14 Bromley Hill, Bromley, Kent, 1937–45; Asst to Diocesan Missioner, Diocese of Southwark, 1954–72. *Address:* 115 Camberwell Grove, Camberwell, SE5 8JH. *T:* (0171) 701 0093.[ws*Died 4 April 1998.*

GOODENOUGH, Sir Richard (Edmund), 2nd Bt *cr* 1943, of Broadwell and Filkins, co. Oxford; *b* 9 June 1925; *e s* of Sir William (Macnamara) Goodenough, 1st Bt, and Dorothea (Louisa) (*d* 1987), *er d* of late Ven. Hon. Kenneth Francis Gibbs, DD (*s* of 1st Baron Aldenham); *S* father, 1951; *m* 1951, Jane, *d* of late H. S. P. McLernon and of Mrs McLernon, Gisborne, NZ; one *s* two *d*. *Educ:* Eton Coll.; Christ Church, Oxford. Military service, 1943–45, invalided. Christ Church, Oxford, 1945–47. *Heir: s* William McLernon Goodenough [*b* 5 Aug. 1954; *m* 1982, Louise Elizabeth, *d* of Captain Michael Ortmans, MVO, RN and Julia Ortmans; one *s* two *d*].
Died 13 Dec. 1996.

GOODFELLOW, Mark Aubrey; HM Diplomatic Service, retired; Ambassador to Gabon, 1986–90; *b* 7 April 1931; *y s* of Alfred Edward Goodfellow and Lucy Emily (*née* Potter); *m* 1964, Madelyn Susan Scammell; one *s* one *d*. *Educ:* Preston Manor County Grammar Sch. Served RAF, 1949–51. Joined HM Foreign (subseq. Diplomatic) Service, 1949; FO, 1951–54; British Mil. Govt, Berlin, 1954–56; Second Sec., Khartoum, 1956–59; FO, 1959–63; Second Sec., Yaoundé, 1963–66; Asst Comr, later Trade Comr, Hong Kong, 1966–71; FCO, 1971–74; First Sec., Ankara, 1974–78; Consul, Atlanta, 1978–82; Counsellor: Washington (Hong Kong Commercial Affairs), 1982–84; Lagos (Econ. and Comm.), 1984–86. *Recreations:* travelling, photography, visiting historic sites and buildings, gardening.
Died 27 Feb. 1999.

GOODISON, Robin Reynolds, CB 1964; consultant; Deputy Chairman, 1972–77, Acting Chairman, Jan.-March 1972, Civil Aviation Authority; *b* 13 Aug. 1912; *s* of Arthur Leathley Goodison; *m* 1936, Betty Lydia, *d* of Comdr L. Robinson, OBE, Royal Navy (retired); three *d*. *Educ:* Finchley Grammar Sch.; University Coll., London Univ. (MA). Joined Ministry of Labour, 1935; transferred to Ministry of Transport, 1936; Principal, 1940; Asst Sec., 1946; Imperial Defence Coll., 1950; Under-Sec., Ministry of Transport and Civil Aviation, 1957, Ministry of Aviation, 1959, Board of Trade, 1966; Second Sec., BoT, 1969–70; Dep. Sec., DTI, 1970–72. Assessor, Heathrow

Terminal Inquiry, 1978–79; Specialist Adviser, House of Lords Select Cttee, 1979–80, 1984–85. *Recreation:* sailing. *Address:* 37 Coldharbour Lane, Bushey, Herts WD2 3NU. *T:* (0181) 950 1911.   *Died 1 Feb. 1998.*

GOODMAN, Maj.-Gen. David; *see* Goodman, Maj.-Gen. J. D. W.

GOODMAN, Howard; *see* Goodman, R. H.

GOODMAN, Maj.-Gen. (John) David (Whitlock), CB 1987; Director and defence advisor to ML Holdings plc, 1989–97; *b* 20 May 1932; *s* of late Brig. Eric Whitlock Goodman, DSO, MC and Norah Dorothy Goodman (*née* Stacpoole); *m* 1957, Valerie-Ann McDonald; one *s* two *d. Educ:* Wellington Coll.; RMA Sandhurst. Commnd RA, 1952; served in UK and Northern Ireland, BAOR, Aden and Hong Kong; Staff Coll., 1962; Battery Comdr, 3rd Regt Royal Horse Artillery, 1966–69; Jt Services Staff Coll., Latimer, 1970; BMRA 2nd Div., 1970–72; Instr, Staff Coll. Camberley and Sudan, 1972–73; CO 26 Field Regt, RA, 1973–76; Comdt, Royal Sch. of Artillery, 1977–79; Royal Coll. of Defence Studies, 1980; Asst Military Secretary, MoD, 1981–82; Dir, Army Air Corps, 1983–87. Hon. Colonel: 26 Field Regt RA, 1985–92; 3 Regt, AAC, 1987–93; 266 (Glos Volunteer Artillery) Observation Post Batt. RA (Vol.), 1990–93. Mem., Regtl Cttee, AAC, 1991–99. Chm. Trustees, Mus. of Army Flying, 1992–99; Trustee, Kelly Holdsworth Artillery Trust, 1990–; Chm. of Govs, Avenue Primary Sch., Warminster, 1998–. Chm., Sutton Veny Parish Council, 1992–97. *Recreations:* the countryside, water colour painting, roses. *Address:* c/o Lloyds TSB, 37 Market Place, Warminster, Wilts BA12 9BD.
          Died 29 Sept. 2000.

GOODMAN, (Robert) Howard, ARIBA; Partner, MPA Health Planners, since 1988; *b* 29 March 1928; *s* of Robert Barnard Goodman and Phyllis Goodman; *m* 1955, Doris Richardson; two *s. Educ:* St George Grammar Sch., Bristol; Northern Polytechnic, London. DipArch (Hons). Articled pupil, 1944–47; Arch. Asst to City of Bristol, 1947–49; Asst Architect to SW Regional Hosp. Bd, 1949–54: design of various hosp. projects in SW England; with various private architects, 1954–60; design of several hosps in UK, Africa and India; Ministry, later Department, of Health: Main Grade Arch., 1960; Sen. Grade, 1961; Principal Arch., 1963; Asst Chief Arch., 1966; Chief Arch., 1971–78; Dir of Develt, 1978–85; Dir, Health Bldg, 1986–88. Councillor (Lab) Reigate and Banstead BC, 1989–93. Member: Constr. and Housing Res. Adv. Council, 1977–88; BRE Adv. Council, 1977–88; Council of Centre on Environment for the Handicapped, 1978–94; E Surrey CHC, 1992–. Research and develt into health planning, systems building and computer aided design. Hon. FICW 1984; Hon. FBID 1985; Hon. FIHopsE 1988. *Publications:* contribs to: Hospitals Handbook, 1960; Hospital Design, 1963; Hospital Traffic and Supply Problems, 1968; Portfolio for Health, 1971; Technology of the Eighties, 1972; Industrialised Hospital Building, 1972; CAD Systems, 1976; various articles in architectural, medical and general press. *Recreations:* eating, drinking, talking. *Address:* Ion House, 44 Nutley Lane, Reigate, Surrey RH2 9HS.   *Died 22 April 1999.*

GOODRIDGE, Hon. Noel Herbert Alan; Chief Justice of Court of Appeal and of Newfoundland, 1986–96; *b* 18 Dec. 1930; *s* of William Prout Goodridge and Freda Dorothy (*née* Hayward); *m* 1956, Isabelle (*née* Galway); three *s* one *d. Educ:* Bishop Field Coll.; King's Collegiate Sch., Windsor, NS; Bishop's College Sch., Lennoxville, PQ; Dalhousie Univ., Halifax, NS (BA, LLB). Practised law, 1953–75; QC (Newfoundland), 1972; originally with Hunt, Emerson, Stirling and Higgins, later Stirling, Ryan and Goodridge; at time of leaving practice, a sen. partner;

Puisne Judge, Trial Div. of Supreme Ct of Newfoundland, 1975; Puisne Judge, Ct Martial Appeal Ct, 1981–. Canadian Bar Association: Mem., 1956–; Mem. Nat. Exec., 1975–76; Pres., Nfld Br., 1973–75. Bencher, Law Soc. of Nfld, 1970–75, Sec., 1973–75; Member: Judicial Council estabd under the Provincial Ct Act, 1974–76; Canadian Judicial Council, 1986–96; Canadian Judges Conf., 1976–. Exec. positions with Jun. Ch. of Commerce, 1954–57, and Nfld BoT, 1962–64. Vice-Chm., Gen. Hosp. Corp., 1970–75; Chm., St John's Transportation Commn, 1971–75; Mem., Newfoundland Assoc. for the Help of Retarded Children, 1960–62. Life Mem., Assoc. of Kinsmen Clubs of Canada. *Recreations:* golf, tennis, walking, bridge, ski-ing. *Address:* Supreme Court of Newfoundland, Court of Appeal, PO Box 937, St John's, Newfoundland A1C 5M3, Canada. *T:* (709) 7290066.
          Died 12 Dec. 1997.

GOODWIN, Prof. Richard Murphey; Professor of Economic Science, Siena University, 1980–88, then Emeritus; *b* 24 Feb. 1913; *s* of William Murphey Goodwin and Mary Florea Goodwin; *m* 1937, Jacqueline Wynmalen; no *c. Educ:* Harvard Univ. (AB, PhD); Oxford Univ. (BA, BLitt). Harvard University: Instructor in Econs, 1939–42; Instructor in Physics, 1942–45; Asst Prof. of Econs, 1945–51; University of Cambridge: Lectr in Econs, 1951–69; Reader in Economics, 1969–80; Fellow of Peterhouse, 1956–80 (Emeritus Fellow, 1982). *Publications:* Elementary Economics from the Higher Standpoint, 1970; Essays in Economic Dynamics, 1982; Essays in Linear Economic Structures, 1983; (with I. F. Punzo) The Dynamics of a Capitalist Economy, 1987; Essays in Nonlinear Economic Dynamics, 1988; Chaotic Economic Dynamics, 1990; contrib. Econ. Jl, Econometrica, Review of Econs and Statistics. *Recreations:* painting, walking. *Address:* Dorvin's, Ashdon, Saffron Walden, Essex CB10 2HP. *T:* Ashdon (01799) 584302.   *Died 6 Aug. 1996.*

GOOLD, Baron *cr* 1987 (Life Peer), of Waterfoot in the District of Eastwood; **James Duncan Goold,** Kt 1983; CA; Lord-Lieutenant of Renfrewshire, since 1994; Chairman, Mactaggart & Mickel Ltd, since 1993 (Director, since 1965); *b* 28 May 1934; *s* of John Goold and Janet Agnes Kirkland; *m* 1959, Sheena Paton (*d* 1992); two *s* one *d. Educ:* Belmont House; Glasgow Acad. CA 1958. W. E. C. Reid & Co., Accts, NZ, 1958–60; Price Waterhouse & Co., Accts, Aust., 1960; Sec., Mactaggart & Mickel Ltd, 1961–65. Director: American Trust plc, 1984–; Edinburgh Oil & Gas PLC, 1986–. President: Scottish Bldg Contractors Assoc., 1971; Scottish Bldg Employers Fedn, 1977; Chm., CBI Scotland, 1981–83. Scottish Conservative Party: Hon. Treas., 1981–83; Chm., 1983–90; Hon. Pres., Eastwood Cons. Assoc., 1978–95. Chm., Royal Scottish Orch., 1991–93. Pres., Accord Hospice, Paisley, 1994–. Chm. Court, Univ. of Strathclyde, 1993–. Hon. Gov., Glasgow Acad., 1994 (Gov., 1982–89). Hon. Col, 71 (Scottish) Engr Regt, 1995–. DL Renfrewshire, 1985. FRSA 1987; Hon. FCIOB 1979; Hon. FFB 1983. DUniv Strathclyde, 1994. *Recreations:* gardening, the open air, golf. *Address:* Sandyknowe, Waterfoot, Clarkston, Glasgow G76 8RN. *T:* (0141) 644 2764. *Clubs:* Carlton; Royal Scottish Automobile (Glasgow); Royal Troon Golf (Troon).
          Died 27 July 1997.

GOOLD, Sir George (Leonard), 7th Bt *cr* 1801, of Old Court, Cork; retired engineer; *b* 26 Aug. 1923; *s* of Sir George Ignatius Goold, 6th Bt, and Rhoda, *d* of Albert Benn, SA; *S* father, 1967; *m* 1945, Joy Cecelia, *d* of William Cutler, Melbourne; one *s* four *d. Educ:* Port Pirie, S Australia. *Heir: s* George William Goold [*b* 25 March 1950; *m* 1973, Julie Ann, *d* of Leonard Crack; two *s*].

Address: Oldcourt 11, 60 Canterbury Road, Victor Harbor, SA 5211, Australia. *T:* (8) 85522872.

Died 31 Aug. 1997.

GORDON, Sir Alexander John, (Sir Alex), Kt 1988; CBE 1974 (OBE 1967); RIBA; architect; Consultant, Alex Gordon Partnership, since 1983; *b* 25 Feb. 1917; *s* of John Tullis Gordon and Euphemia Baxter Simpson Gordon. *Educ:* Swansea Grammar Sch.; Welsh Sch. of Architecture (Diploma with Special Distinction). ARIBA 1949; FRIBA 1962; FSIAD 1975. Served RE, 1940–46. Partnership with T. Alwyn Lloyd, 1948–60; Sen. Partner, Alex Gordon and Partners, 1960–82. Member: Welsh Arts Council, 1959–73 (Vice-Chm. 1969–73); Central Housing Adv. Cttee, 1959–71; Exec. Bd, BSI, 1971–74 (Chm., Codes of Practice Cttee for Building, 1965–77); UGC Planning, Architecture and Building Studies Sub-Cttee, 1971–74; UGC Technology Sub-Cttee, 1974–79; NAB UGC Review Gp in Architecture, 1983–84; Construction and Housing Res. Adv. Council, 1971–79; ARCUK, 1968–71; Design Council, 1973–77; Council, Architectural Heritage Year (and Welsh Cttee), 1973–76; Royal Fine Art Commn, 1973–91; RCA Visiting Cttee, 1973–82; Council for Sci. and Soc., 1973 (Vice-Chm., 1982); Bldg Res. Estab. Adv. Council (Chm., 1975–83); Adv. Cttee, York Centre for Continuing Educn, 1975–80; Construction Industry Continuing Professional Devlt Gp (Chm. 1981–86); Standing Cttee on Structural Safety, 1976–87; British Council Wales Cttee, 1976–87 (Chm., 1980–87, and Mem. Bd British Council); Pres., Comité de Liaison des Architectes du Marché Commun, 1974–75. Trustee, Civic Trust Board for Wales, 1965. Pres., Building Centre Trust, 1976–87. Life Mem., Court, UWIST (Mem. Council, 1980–85, Vice-Pres., 1982–85); Vis. Prof., Sch. of Environmental Studies, UCL, 1969, Mem. Bd of Studies, 1970–83, Governor, 1974–77, Centre for Environmental Studies. Vis. Fellow, Clare Hall, Cambridge Univ., 1983. Associate, RICS, 1986. Royal Institute of British Architects: Chm., Bd of Educn, 1968–70; Pres., 1971–73; Chm., European Affairs Cttee, 1973–80; Chm., Coordinating Cttee for Project Inf., 1979–87. Regl Dir, Nationwide Bldg Soc., 1972 (Chm., Welsh Bd, 1986–89); Mem., Cardiff Bay Devlt Corp., 1987–90. Extraord. Hon. Mem., Bund Deutscher Architekten, 1980; Hon. Mem., Soc. Mexican Architects, 1972; Hon. Corresp. Mem., Fedn of Danish Architects, 1976; Hon. FRAIC; Hon. FAIA 1974; Hon. FCIBSE 1975; Hon. FISE 1980. Hon. LLD Univ. of Wales, 1972. *Publications:* periodic contribs to professional jls. *Recreations:* ski-ing, the visual arts. *Address:* River Cottage, Llanblethian, near Cowbridge, S Glam CF7 7JL. *Died 23 July 1999.*

GORDON, Aubrey Abraham; a Recorder of the Crown Court, 1978–97; *b* 26 July 1925; *s* of Isaac and Fanny Gordon; *m* 1949, Reeva R. Cohen; one *s* twin *d. Educ:* Bede Collegiate Boys' Sch., Sunderland; King's Coll., Durham Univ., Newcastle upon Tyne (LLB 1945). Admitted solicitor, 1947. President: Houghton le Spring Chamber of Trade, 1955; Hetton le Hole Rotary Club, 1967; Sunderland Law Soc., 1976; NE Joel Intract Meml Home, 1990–93; Chairman: Houghton Round Table, 1959; Sunderland Victim Support Scheme, 1978–80; Sunderland Guild of Help, 1984–92. *Recreations:* local communal and religious interests, photography. *Address:* 1 Acer Court, Sunderland SR2 7EJ. *T:* (0191) 565 8993. *Died 11 Sept. 2000.*

GORDON, Maj.-Gen. Desmond Spencer, CB 1961; CBE 1952; DSO 1943; JP; DL; Commissioner-in-Chief, St John Ambulance Brigade, 1973–78; *b* 25 Dec. 1911; *s* of late Harold Easty Gordon and Gwendoline (*née* Blackett); *m* 1940, Sybil Mary Thompson; one *s* one *d. Educ:* Haileybury Coll.; RMC Sandhurst. Commissioned into Green Howards, 1932; India, 1933–38; Adjutant,

Regimental Depot, 1938–40; War of 1939–45 (despatches 1944): Norway with Green Howards, 1940; Bde Major, 69 Inf. Bde, 1941–42; Student Staff Coll., Quetta, 1942; Comd 1/7 Queens, 1943; Comd 151 (Durham) Inf. Bde, 146 Inf. Bde, 131 Lorried Inf. Bde, 1944–46; Col GS HQ BAOR, 1946–49; Student Joint Service Staff Coll., 1949; GSO1 Inf. Directorate, War Office, 1950; Dep. Dir Inf., War Office, 1951–52; Comd 16 Indep. Para. Bde Gp, 1952–55; Asst Comd RMA Sandhurst, 1956–57; Student, Imperial Defence Coll., 1958; DA&QMG HQ I (BR) Corps, 1959; GOC 4th Division, 1959–61; Chief Army Instructor, Imperial Defence Coll., 1962–64; Asst Chief of Defence Staff (G), 1964–66. Col The Green Howards, 1965–74. JP Hants, 1966; DL Hants, 1980. KStJ 1973 (CStJ 1972). Knight Commander, Order of Orange Nassau with swords (Holland), 1947. *Recreations:* fishing, gardening. *Address:* Southfields, Greywell, Basingstoke, Hants RG25 1BZ. *T:* (01256) 702088. *Club:* Army and Navy. *Died 4 Nov. 1997.*

GORDON, Peter Macie, CMG 1964; *b* 4 June 1919; *o s* of late Herbert and Gladys Gordon (*née* Simpson); *m* 1945, Marianne, *er d* of Dr Paul Meerwein, Basle; two *d. Educ:* Cotham Sch., Bristol; University Coll., Exeter; Merton Coll., Oxford. Served War, 1940–46; commissioned Argyll and Sutherland Highlanders, 1941; Campaign in North-West Europe, 1944–45 (despatches). Entered Colonial Administrative Service as District Officer, 1946; Senior District Commissioner, 1957; Asst Sec., Ministry of Agriculture, 1958; Under-Sec., 1960; Permanent Sec., Ministry of Agriculture and Animal Husbandry, Kenya, 1961; retired, 1964; Asst Sec., Univ. of Exeter, 1964–70. Supervisor, Zimbabwe-Rhodesia Elections, 1980; Mem., Commonwealth Observer Gp, Uganda Elections, 1980. *Address:* Old Poplars Farm House, Chipping Campden, Glos GL55 6EG. *Died 8 April 2000.*

GORDON, Lt-Col William Howat Leslie, CBE 1957 (MBE 1941); MC 1944; Adviser on overseas business to firms, to Ministry of Overseas Development, 1971–75, and to International Finance Corporation; *b* 8 April 1914; *o s* of late Frank Leslie Gordon, ISE, FICE; *m* 1944, Margot Lumb; one *s* three *d. Educ:* Rugby; RMA Woolwich. Commnd Royal Signals, 1934; Palestine, Africa, Italy, NW Europe; 1 Armoured, 1 Airborne Divs (despatches); Instructor, Staff Coll., Camberley, 1947–49. Chief Executive, The Uganda Co. Ltd, 1949–60; John Holt & Co. (Liverpool) Ltd and Lonrho Exports Ltd, 1960–71; Chm., Rickmansworth Water Co., 1986–88. MLC Uganda, 1952–57. Chm., St John Council, Bucks, 1974–82; KStJ. *Address:* La Feuilleraie, Ponson Soubiran, Mirande 32300, Le Gers, France. *Died 5 Dec. 1997.*

GORDON-DUFF, Col Thomas Robert, MC 1945; JP; Lord-Lieutenant of Banffshire, 1964–87; Convener of County Council, 1962–70; *b* 1911; *er s* of Lachlan Gordon-Duff (killed in action, 1914); *m* 1946, Jean (*d* 1981), *d* of late Leslie G. Moir, Bicester; one *s. Educ:* Eton; RMC, Sandhurst. Entered Army, 2nd Lieut, Rifle Brigade, 1932; served War of 1939–45 (MC); retired, 1947. Lt-Col 5/6 Bn Gordon Highlanders (TA), 1947, retiring as Col. DL 1948, JP 1959, Vice-Lieut 1961, Banffshire. *Address:* Drummuir, Keith, Banffshire AB55 3JE. *T:* (01542) 810300. *Club:* Army and Navy.

Died 4 May 1997.

GORE-BOOTH, Sir Angus (Josslyn), 8th Bt *cr* 1760 (Ire.), of Artarman, Sligo; *b* 25 June 1920; *s* of Sir Josslyn Augustus Richard Gore-Booth, 6th Bt and Mary Sibell (*d* 1968), *d* of Rev. S. L'Estrange-Malone; *S* brother, 1987; *m* 1948, Hon. Rosemary Myra Vane (marr. diss. 1954), *o d* of 10th Baron Barnard; one *s* one *d. Educ:* Radley; Worcester Coll., Oxford. Served War of 1939–45, Captain Irish Guards. *Heir:* *s* Josslyn Henry Robert Gore-Booth [*b* 5 Oct. 1950; *m* 1980, Jane Mary, *o d* of Rt Hon. Sir

Roualeyn Hovell-Thurlow-Cumming-Bruce, PC; two *d*].
Address: Lissadell, Sligo, Irish Republic. *T:* Sligo (71)
63150.   *Died 26 Jan. 1996.*

GORING, Marius, CBE 1991; FRSL; actor, manager,
director; *b* Newport, IoW, 23 May 1912; *s* of Dr Charles
Buckman Goring, MD, BSc, criminologist, and Katie
Winifred (Macdonald), pianist; *m* 1st, 1931, Mary
Westwood Steel (marr. diss.); one *d*; 2nd, 1941, Lucie
Mannheim (*d* 1976); 3rd, 1977, Prudence FitzGerald.
Educ: Perse Sch., Cambridge; Universities of Frankfurt,
Munich, Vienna, and Paris; studied for stage under
Harcourt Williams and at Old Vic dramatic school,
1929–32. First stage appearance in Crossings, Amateur
Dramatic Club, Cambridge, 1925; first professional
appearance in Jean Sterling Mackinlay's matinées,
Rudolph Steiner Hall, 1927; toured in France and Germany
with English Classical Players, 1931; stage managed two
seasons at Old Vic and Sadler's Wells, playing Romeo,
Macbeth, Epihodov and other rôles, 1932–34; first West
End appearance as Hugh Voysey, Shaftesbury, 1934;
toured France, Belgium, and Holland with Compagnie des
Quinze (acting in French), also Hamlet, Old Vic, Noah,
New, Hangman, Duke of York's, Sowers of the Hills,
Westminster, 1934–35; Mary Tudor, Playhouse, The
Happy Hypocrite, His Majesty's, Girl Unknown, New,
Wild Duck, Westminster, 1936; rôles in Witch of
Edmonton, Hamlet, Twelfth Night and Henry V at Old
Vic, Satyr, Shaftesbury, 1937; The Last Straw, Comedy,
Surprise Item, Ambassadors, The White Guard, Phoenix,
1938; in management at Duke of York's, 1939: dir, Nora
(A Doll's House); Lady Fanny; first player in Hamlet,
Lyceum and Elsinore; Pip in Great Expectations (produced
with George Devine and Alec Guinness at Rudolph
Steiner, first theatre to re-open after war closure); dir (with
G. Devine) The Tempest (also played Ariel), Old Vic;
toured British zone of Germany, 1947 (in German);
Rosmersholm, Too True to be Good, Cherry Orchard,
Marriage, at Arts Theatre; Daphne Laureola, Berlin
(playing in German), 1949; One Hundred Thousand
Pounds, Berlin, 1950; The Madwoman of Chaillot, St
James's, 1951; Richard III, Antony and Cleopatra, Taming
of the Shrew, King Lear, Stratford-upon-Avon, 1953;
Marriage, Wuppertal, 1954; toured France, Holland,
Finland, and India with own company of English
comedians, 1957–58; Tonight at 8.30 (in German), Berlin
Fest., 1960; Measure for Measure, Stratford-upon-Avon,
1962; A Penny for a Song, Aldwych, 1962; Ménage à
Trois, Lyric, 1963; The Poker Session, Dublin and Globe,
1964; The Apple Cart, Cambridge, 1965; The Bells, Derby
Playhouse and Midlands tour, 1966–67, and Vaudeville,
1968; The Demonstration, Nottingham, 1969; Sleuth, St
Martin's, 1970–73; The Wisest Fool, Guildford and tour,
1975; Habeas Corpus, Liverpool Playhouse, 1976, 1981;
The Concert, Theatre Royal York, 1977; Habeas Corpus,
Lyceum, Edinburgh, 1979; Zaïde, Old Vic, 1982; Lloyd
George Knew my Father, nat. tour, 1982; Peer Gynt,
Nottingham, 1982; Dame of Sark, nat. tour, 1983; The
Winslow Boy, nat. tour, 1984; I Have Been Here Before,
nat. tour, 1985; God in Mystery plays in Canterbury
Cathedral, 1986; The Applecart, Haymarket, 1986;
Beyond Reasonable Doubt, Queen's, 1988; Towards Zero,
Churchill Theatre, Bromley and nat. tour, 1989; Sunsets
and Glories, Playhouse, Leeds, 1990. Co-founder, London
Theatre Studio with Michel St Denis and George Devine.
Films included: Rembrandt; The Case of the Frightened
Lady, 1940; A Matter of Life and Death, 1946; The Red
Shoes, 1948; Odette, 1950; So Little Time, 1951; Pandora
and the Flying Dutchman, 1952; The Barefoot Contessa,
1955; Ill Met by Moonlight, 1956; The Inspector, 1961;
La Fille en Robe bleue, 1980; Loser Takes All, 1988.
Radio: broadcaster and writer of radio scripts; first
performance, Bulldog Drummond; Hitler in the Shadow

of the Swastika (first BBC war programme), 1939; for
BBC Third Programme, The Divine Comedy, Browning
Monologues, Henry Reed's Leopardi, Streets of Pompeii,
Tennyson's Maud, 1959; *television:* first appearance in
Tchekov's The Bear, 1938; exec. producer and played
lead in Adventures of the Scarlet Pimpernel (series), 1955;
The Expert (series), 1968–70, 1974; Fall of Eagles
Hindenburg (series), 1977; Edward and Mrs Simpson
(series), 1978; The Old Men at the Zoo (series), 1983;
Gnostics (series), 1987; War at Woburn, 1987;
autobiographical documentary, 1987. FRSL 1976.
Founder Mem., British Equity, 1929; Vice-Pres. British
Actors' Equity Assoc., 1963–65 and 1975–82. Served in
Queen's Royal Regiment, 1940; lent to Foreign Office,
1941–45; supervisor of BBC productions broadcast to
Germany under name of Charles Richardson. *Recreations:*
skating, riding. *Address:* c/o Film Rights Ltd, 483
Southbank House, Black Prince Road, Albert
Embankment, SE1 7SJ. *T:* (020) 7735 8171. *Club:*
Garrick.   *Died 30 Sept. 1998.*

GORMAN, John Peter; QC 1974; a Recorder of the Crown
Court, since 1972; *b* 29 June 1927; *er s* of James S.
Gorman, Edinburgh; *m* 1st, 1955, Avril Mary (*née*
Penfold); one *s* three *d*; 2nd, 1979, Patricia (*née* Myatt).
Educ: Stonyhurst Coll.; Balliol Coll., Oxford (MA).
Served with RA, 1945–48. Called to Bar, Inner Temple,
1953, Bencher 1983; Midland and Oxford Circuit. Dep.
Chm. 1969, Chm. 1972–79, Agricultural Lands Tribunal
(E Midlands); Dep. Chm., Northants QS, 1970–71. *Club:*
Reform.   *Died 23 Aug. 1996.*

GOSS, Very Rev. Thomas Ashworth; Dean of Jersey,
Rector of St Helier, and Hon. Canon of Winchester,
1971–85; Canon Emeritus, Winchester, since 1985; *b* 27
July 1912; *s* of George Woolnough Goss and Maud M.
(*née* Savage); *m* 1946, Frances Violet Patience Frampton
(*d* 1991); one *s* one *d*. *Educ:* Shardlow Hall; Aldenham
Sch.; St Andrews Univ. (MA). Deacon, 1937; priest, 1938;
Curate of Frodingham, 1937–41; Chaplain, RAFVR,
1941–47 (POW Japan, 1942–45); Vicar of Sutton-le-
Marsh, 1947–51; Chaplain, RAF, 1951–67; QHC,
1966–67; Rector of St Saviour, Jersey, 1967–71.
Recreations: gardening, theatricals. *Address:* Les Pignons,
Mont de la Rosière, St Saviour, Jersey JE2 7WD. *Clubs:*
Royal Air Force; Victoria (Jersey).
                                          Died 10 Dec. 1997.

GOUDIE, Hon. William Henry, MC 1944; Executive
Director and Deputy Chairman, Law Reform Commission
of Tasmania, 1974–81; *b* 21 Aug. 1916; *s* of Henry and
Florence Goudie; *m* 1948, Mourilyan Isobel Munro (*d*
1981); two *s*. *Educ:* Bristol Grammar School. Solicitor
(England), 1938; called to the Bar, Gray's Inn, 1952. War
service, 1939–45, London Scottish Regt and Som LI;
JAG's Dept, 1945–48; Prosecutor, Dep. JA, Officer i/c
branches Italy, Greece, Austria; Officer i/c Legal Section
War Crimes Gp, SE Europe; Sen. Resident Magistrate,
Acting Judge, Kenya, 1948–63; Puisne Judge, Aden,
1963–66; Puisne Judge, Uganda (Contract), 1967–71;
Puisne Judge, Fiji (Contract), 1971–73. Editor, Kenya and
Aden Law Reports. *Address:* 24 Nimala Street, Rosny,
Hobart, Tas 7018, Australia.   *Died 1 Aug. 2000.*

GOUGH, Cecil Ernest Freeman, CMG 1956; Director and
Secretary, 1974–78, Assistant Director-General, 1978–80,
Acting Director-General, 1980–81, British Property
Federation; *b* 29 Oct. 1911; *s* of Ernest John Gough; *m*
1938, Gwendolen Lily Miriam Longman; one *s* one *d*.
Educ: Southend High Sch.; London Sch. of Economics
(School of Economics Scholar in Law, 1932; LLB (Hons)
1934). Asst Examiner, Estate Duty Office, Board of Inland
Revenue, 1930; Air Ministry, 1938; Principal, 1944;
Ministry of Defence, 1947; Asst Sec., 1949; on loan to
Foreign Office, as Counsellor, United Kingdom Delegation

to NATO, Paris, 1952–56; Chm., NATO Infrastructure Cttee, 1952–53; First Chm., Standing Armaments Cttee, Western European Union, 1955; returned Ministry of Defence, 1956; Under-Sec., 1958; Under-Sec. at the Admiralty, 1962–64; Asst Under-Sec. of State, Min. of Defence, 1964–68. Man. Dir, Airwork (Overseas) Ltd, 1968–71; Dir, Airwork Services Ltd and Air Holdings Ltd, 1968–73; Sec., Associated Owners of City Properties, 1975–77. Medal of Freedom (USAF), 1946; Coronation Medal, 1953. *Recreations:* cookery, gardening, reading, travel. *Address:* 23 Howbridge Road, Witham, Essex CM8 1BY. *T:* (01376) 518969. *Clubs:* Naval and Military, Civil Service. *Died 8 Dec. 1998.*

GOUGH, Rt Rev. Hugh Rowlands, CMG 1965; OBE (mil.) 1945; TD 1950; Archbishop of Sydney and Primate of Australia, also Metropolitan of New South Wales, 1959–66; retired; *b* 19 Sept. 1905; *o s* of late Rev. Charles Massey Gough, Rector of St Ebbe's, Oxford; *m* 1929, Hon. Madeline Elizabeth, *d* of 12th Baron Kinnaird, KT, KBE; one *d. Educ:* Weymouth Coll.; Trinity Coll., Cambridge (BA 1927; MA 1931); London Coll. Divinity. Deacon, 1928; priest, 1929; Curate of St Mary, Islington, 1928–31; Perpetual Curate of St Paul, Walcot, Bath, 1931–34; Vicar of St James, Carlisle, 1934–39; Chaplain to High Sheriff of Cumberland, 1937; CF (TA), 1937–45; Chaplain to 4th Bn The Border Regt, 1937–39; Vicar of St Matthew, Bayswater 1939–46; Chaplain to 1st Bn London Rifle Bde, 1939–43; served Western Desert and Tunisia (wounded); Senior Chap. to 1st Armd Div., Tunisia, 1943; DACG 10 Corps, Italy, 1943–45 (despatches); DACG, North Midland Dist, 1945; Hon. Chaplain to the Forces (2nd cl.) 1945; Vicar of Islington, Rural Dean of Islington, 1946–48; Preb. St Paul's Cathedral, 1948; Suffragan Bishop of Barking, 1948–59; Archdeacon of West Ham, 1948–58; Rector of Freshford, dio. of Bath and Wells, 1967–72; Vicar of Limpley Stoke, 1970–72. Chaplain and Sub-Prelate, Order of St John of Jerusalem, 1959–72. Formerly Member Council: London Coll. of Divinity, Clifton Theol. Coll. (Chm.), Haileybury Coll., Monkton Combe Sch., St Lawrence Coll. (Ramsgate), Chigwell Sch., Stowe Sch., Kingham Hill Trust. Golden Lectr, Haberdashers' Co., 1953 and 1955. Pres. Conference, Educational Assoc., 1956. Mem., Essex County Education Cttee, 1949–59; DL Essex, 1952–59. DD Lambeth; Hon. DD Wycliffe Coll., Toronto; Hon. ThD, Aust. *Address:* Forge House, Over Wallop, Stockbridge, Hants SO20 8HT. *T:* (01264) 781315. *Club:* National. *Died 13 Nov. 1997.*

GOULDING, Sir (Ernest) Irvine, Kt 1971; Judge of the High Court of Justice, Chancery Division, 1971–85; *b* 1 May 1910; *s* of late Dr Ernest Goulding; *m* 1935, Gladys (*d* 1981), *d* of late Engr Rear-Adm. Marrack Sennett; one *s* one *d. Educ:* Merchant Taylors' Sch., London; St Catharine's Coll., Cambridge (Hon. Fellow, 1971). Served as Instructor Officer, Royal Navy, 1931–36 and 1939–45. Called to the Bar, Inner Temple, 1936; QC 1961; Bencher, Lincoln's Inn, 1966, Treasurer, 1983. Pres., Internat. Law Assoc., British branch, 1972–81, Hon. Pres., 1983–88. President: Omar Khayyám Club, 1988–89; Selden Soc., 1988–91. *Address:* Penshurst, Wych Hill Way, Woking, Surrey GU22 0AE. *T:* (01483) 761012. *Club:* Travellers. *Died 13 Jan. 2000.*

GOW, Sir (Leonard) Maxwell H.; *see* Harper Gow.

GOW, Very Rev. William Connell; Dean of Moray, Ross and Caithness, 1960–77, retired; Canon of St Andrew's Cathedral, Inverness, 1953–77, Hon. Canon, since 1977; Rector of St James', Dingwall, 1940–77; *b* 6 Jan. 1909; *s* of Alexander Gow, Errol, Perthshire; *m* 1938, Edith Mary (decd), *d* of John William Jarvis, Scarborough; two *s. Educ:* Edinburgh Theological Coll.; Durham Univ. (LTh). Deacon, 1936; priest, 1937; Curate St Mary Magdalene's,

Dundee, 1936–39. Awarded Frihetsmedalje (by King Haakon), Norway, 1947. *Recreations:* fishing, bridge. *Address:* 14 Mackenzie Place, Maryburgh, Ross-shire IV7 8DY. *T:* (01349) 61832. *Died 4 Oct. 1996.*

GOWER, Jim; *see* Gower, L. C. B.

GOWER, Laurence Cecil Bartlett, (Jim), MBE 1945; FBA 1965; solicitor; Professor Emeritus, Southampton University; *b* 29 Dec. 1913; *s* of Henry Lawrence Gower; *m* 1939, Helen Margaret Shepperson, *d* of George Francis Birch; two *s* one *d. Educ:* Lindisfarne Coll.; University Coll., London. LLB 1933; LLM 1934. Admitted Solicitor, 1937. Served War of 1939–45, with RA and RAOC. Sir Ernest Cassel Prof. of Commercial Law in University of London, 1948–62; Adviser on Legal Educn in Africa to Brit. Inst. of Internat. and Comparative Law and Adviser to Nigerian Council of Legal Educn, 1962–65; Prof. and Dean of Faculty of Law of Univ. of Lagos, 1962–65; Law Comr, 1965–71; Vice-Chancellor, Univ. of Southampton, 1971–79. Visiting Prof., Law Sch. of Harvard Univ., 1954–55; Holmes Lectr, Harvard Univ., 1966. Comr on Company Law Amendment in Ghana, 1958; Member: Jenkins Cttee on Company Law Amendment, 1959–62; Denning Cttee on Legal Education for Students from Africa, 1960; Ormrod Cttee on Legal Education, 1967–71; Royal Commn on the Press, 1975–77. Trustee, British Museum, 1968–83. For. Hon. Mem., Amer. Acad. of Arts and Scis, 1986; Lee Kuan Yew Distinguished Visitor, Nat. Univ. of Singapore, 1987. Fellow of University Coll., London; Hon. Fellow: LSE, 1970; Portsmouth Polytech., 1981; Hon. LLD: York Univ., Ont; Edinburgh Univ.; Dalhousie Univ.; Warwick Univ.; QUB; Southampton Univ.; Bristol Univ.; London Univ.; Hon. DLitt Hong Kong. Hon. QC 1991. *Publications:* Principles of Modern Company Law, 1954, 5th edn 1992; Independent Africa: the Challenge to the Legal Profession, 1967; Review of Investor Protection, Part 1, 1984, Part 2, 1985; numerous articles in legal periodicals. *Recreation:* travel. *Address:* 26 Willow Road, Hampstead, NW3 1TL. *T:* (0171) 435 2507. *Died 25 Dec. 1997.*

GOWING, Prof. Margaret Mary, CBE 1981; FRS 1988; FBA 1975; FRHistS; Professor of the History of Science, University of Oxford, and Fellow of Linacre College, 1973–86; *b* 26 April 1921; *d* of Ronald and Mabel Elliott; *m* 1944, Donald J. G. Gowing (*d* 1969); two *s. Educ:* Christ's Hospital; London Sch. of Economics (BSc(Econ); Hon. Fellow, 1988). Bd of Trade, 1941–45; Historical Section, Cabinet Office, 1945–59; Historian and Archivist, UK Atomic Energy Authority, 1959–66; Reader in Contemporary History, Univ. of Kent, 1966–72. Member: Cttee on Deptl Records (Grigg Cttee), 1952–54; Adv. Council on Public Records, 1974–82; BBC Archives Adv. Cttee, 1976–79; Public Records Inquiry (Wilson Cttee), 1978–80; Trustee: Nat. Portrait Gall., 1978–92; Imperial War Mus., 1986–87. Hon. Dir, Contemporary Scientific Archives Centre, 1973–86. Foundation Mem., Academia Europaea, 1988. Lectures: Royal Society Wilkins, 1976; Enid Muir, Newcastle, 1976; Bernal, Birkbeck, 1977; Rede, Cambridge, 1978; Herbert Spencer, Oxford, 1982; CEGB, Southampton, 1987. Hon. DLitt: Leeds, 1976; Leicester, 1982; Hon. DSc: Manchester, 1985; Bath, 1987. *Publications:* (with Sir K. Hancock) British War Economy, 1949; (with E. L. Hargreaves) Civil Industry and Trade, 1952; Britain and Atomic Energy, 1964; Dossier Secret des Relations Atomiques, 1965; Independence and Deterrence: vol. I, Policy Making, vol. II, Policy Execution, 1974; Reflections on Atomic Energy History, 1978; (with Lorna Arnold) The Atomic Bomb, 1979; various articles and reviews. *Address:* Linacre College, Oxford OX1 3JA. *Died 7 Nov. 1998.*

GOYDER, George Armin, CBE 1976; Managing Director, British International Paper Ltd, 1935–71; *b* 22 June 1908;

s of late William Goyder and Lili Julia Kellersberger, Baden, Switzerland; *m* 1937, Rosemary, 4th *d* of Prof. R. C. Bosanquet, Rock, Northumberland; five *s* three *d. Educ:* Mill Hill Sch.; London Sch. of Economics; abroad. The Geographical Magazine, 1935–58; Gen. Man., Newsprint Supply Co., 1940–47 (responsible for procurement, supply and rationing of newsprint to British Press). Mem., Gen. Synod of C of E (formerly Church Assembly), 1948–75; Chm., Liberal Party Standing Cttee on Industrial Partnership, 1966. Vice-Pres., Centre for Internat. Briefing, Farnham Castle, 1978– (Founding Mem., 1962; Chm., 1969–77); co-Founder and Trustee, William Blake Trust, 1949–82; Governor: Mill Hill Sch., 1943–69; Monkton Combe Sch., 1957–78; Trustee and Hon. Fellow, St Peter's Coll., Oxford; Mem. Council, Wycliffe Hall, 1950–79; Founder Mem. and Hon. Sec., British-North American Cttee, 1960–72. Chm., Suffolk Preservation Soc., 1983–85. *Publications:* The Future of Private Enterprise, 1951, 1954; The Responsible Company, 1961; The People's Church, 1966; The Responsible Worker, 1975; The Just Enterprise, 1987; (with Rosemary Goyder) Signs of Grace, 1994. *Recreations:* music, old books, theology. *Address:* Mansel Hall, Long Melford, Sudbury, Suffolk CO10 9JB. *Club:* Reform.   *Died 19 Jan. 1997.*

GRAAFF, Sir de Villiers, 2nd Bt *cr* 1911, of Cape Town; MBE 1946; barrister; advocate; MP for Hottentots Holland in Union Parliament, 1948–58, for Rondebosch, Cape Town, 1958–77; *b* 8 Dec. 1913; *s* of Sir David Pieter de Villiers Graaff, 1st Bt and Eileen (*d* 1950), *d* of Rev. Dr J. P. Van Heerden, Cape Town; *S* father, 1931; *m* 1939, Helena Le Roux, *d* of F. C. M. Voigt, Provincial Sec. of Cape Province; two *s* one *d. Educ:* Cape Town Univ. (BA 1932), Magdalen Coll., Oxford (BA 1935; BCL 1936; MA 1944), Called to the Bar, Inner Temple, 1937; Advocate of Supreme Court of S Africa, 1938. Served War of 1939–45 (prisoner, MBE). Leader, United Party, S Africa, 1956–77, formerly Leader of Official Opposition. Hon. Col, Cape Garrison Artillery, 1980. Hon. LLD Rhodes, 1969; Hon. DLit South Africa, 1989. Decoration for Meritorious Service (RSA), 1979. *Publication:* Div looks back (autobiog.), 1993. *Heir: s* David de Villiers Graaff [*b* 3 May 1940; *m* Sally Williams; three *s* one *d*]. *Address:* De Grendel, Private Bag, GPO, Capetown, South Africa. *Club:* Civil Service (Cape Town).

Died 4 Oct. 1999.

GRADE, Baron *cr* 1976 (Life Peer), of Elstree, county Hertfordshire; **Lew Grade,** Kt 1969; Chairman, The Grade Co., since 1985; Chairman for Life, ITC Entertainment Group, since 1995 (Chairman and Managing Director, 1958–82); *b* 25 Dec. 1906; *s* of late Isaac and Olga Winogradsky; *m* 1942, Kathleen Sheila Moody; one *s. Educ:* Rochelle Street Sch. Joint Managing Dir of Lew and Leslie Grade Ltd, until Sept. 1955; Chm. and Chief Exec., Associated Communications Corp. Ltd, 1973–82; Pres., ATV Network Ltd, 1977–82; Chairman: Bentray Investments Ltd, 1979–82; ACC Enterprises Inc., 1973–82; Stoll Moss Theatres Ltd, 1969–82; Chm. and Chief Exec., Embassy Communications Internat. Ltd, 1982–85; Dir, Supervisory Bd, Euro Disney SCA, Paris, 1988–. Vice Pres., British Olympic Assoc. Mem., Royal Naval Film Corp. Fellow, BAFTA, 1979. Comdr Grand Cross, Order of Malta, 1969; KCSS 1979. Commander, Order of Merit: Italy, 1974; Tunisia, 1976. *Publication:* (autobiog.) Still Dancing, 1987. *Address:* 34 Grosvenor Street, W1X 9FG.   *Died 13 Dec. 1998.*

GRAHAM, Prof. Alastair, DSc; FRS 1979; Professor of Zoology, University of Reading, 1952–72, then Emeritus Professor; *b* 6 Nov. 1906; *m* Gwynneth (decd); two *s*; *m* Beth. *Educ:* Edinburgh Univ. (MA, BSc); London Univ. (DSc). Lectr, Birkbeck Coll., London Univ., until 1952. Pres., Malacological Soc. of London, 1954–57 (Ed., Jl of

Molluscan Studies, 1969–86). Fellow, Zoological Soc., 1939 (Frink Medal, 1976); Gold Medal, Linnaean Soc., 1968. *Publications:* British Prosobranch Molluscs (jtly), 1962, rev. edn 1994; Molluscs: prosobranch and pyramidellid gastropods, 1988. *Address:* 207 Wokingham Road, Reading, Berks RG6 2DT. *T:* (0118) 926 4154.

Died 12 Dec. 2000.

GRAHAM, Sir Charles (Spencer Richard), 6th Bt *cr* 1783, of Netherby, Cumberland; Lord-Lieutenant of Cumbria, 1983–94; *b* 16 July 1919; *s* of Sir (Frederick) Fergus Graham, 5th Bt, KBE, and Mary Spencer Revell, CBE (*d* 1985), *d* of late Maj.-Gen. Raymond Reade, CB, CMG; *S* father, 1978; *m* 1944, Isabel Susan Anne, *d* of late Major R. L. Surtees, OBE; two *s* one *d. Educ:* Eton. Served with Scots Guards, 1940–50, NW Europe (despatches) and Malaya. President, Country Landowners' Assoc., 1971–73. Mem., Nat. Water Council, 1973–83. Master, Worshipful Co. of Farmers, 1982–83. High Sheriff 1955, DL 1971, Cumbria (formerly Cumberland). KStJ 1984. *Heir: s* James Fergus Surtees Graham [*b* 29 July 1946; *m* 1975, Serena Jane, *yr d* of Ronald Frank Kershaw; one *s* two *d*]. *Address:* Crofthead, Longtown, Cumbria CA6 5PA. *T:* (01228) 791231. *Clubs:* Brooks's, Pratt's.

Died 11 July 1997.

GRAHAM, Gordon, CBE 1980; PPRIBA; consultant architect; Director, Foster Associates Ltd, 1984–89; *b* Carlisle, 4 June 1920; *s* of late Stanley Bouch Graham and Isabel Hetherington; *m* 1946, Enid Pennington; three *d. Educ:* Creighton Sch.; Nottingham Sch. of Architecture. DipArch, RIBA, 1949; RIBA Arthur Cates Prizeman, 1949; travelling schol., S and Central America, 1953. Served Royal Artillery, N Africa, Italy and NW Europe, 1940–46. Sen. Lectr, Nottingham Sch. of Architecture, 1949–61; Sen. Partner, Architects Design Gp, 1958–84. Pres., Nottingham, Derby and Lincoln Soc. of Architects, 1965–66; Royal Institute of British Architects: Chm., E Midlands Region, 1967–69; Mem. Council, 1967–73 and 1974; Vice-Pres., 1969–71; Hon. Sec., 1971–72 and 1975–76; Sen. Vice-Pres., 1976; Pres., 1977–79. Mem., Building EDC, 1978–83. Hon. FRAIC 1978. Hon. MA Nottingham, 1979. *Recreations:* Rugby football, architecture. *Club:* Reform.   *Died 21 Sept. 1997.*

GRAHAM, Kathleen Mary, CBE 1958 (MBE 1945); HM Diplomatic Service, retired; *b* 14 Aug. 1903; *d* of late Col R. B. Graham, CBE, and Mrs M. G. Graham, London; unmarried. *Educ:* Cheltenham Ladies' Coll.; Univ. of London (Courtauld Inst. of Art). Courtauld Inst., Dept of Technology War-time Laboratory, 1940–41; Political Warfare Executive, 1942–45; entered HM Foreign Service, 1945; served in FO, 1946–49; Consul (Information) at San Francisco, Calif, 1949–53; served in FO, 1953–55; made Counsellor in HM Foreign Service in 1955 and appointed Dep. Consul-Gen. in New York, 1955–59; HM Consul-Gen. at Amsterdam, 1960–63; in FO, 1964–69, retired. Exec. Dir, 1970–73, a Governor, 1973–80, ESU. *Recreations:* music, history of art.

Died 12 March 2000.

GRAHAM-BRYCE, Dame Isabel, DBE 1968; Chairman: Oxford Regional Hospital Board, 1963–72; National Nursing Staff Committee, 1967–75; National Staff Committee, 1969–75; Consultant, British Transport Hotels, 1979–81 (Board Member, 1962–79); Vice-President, Princess Christian College, Manchester, since 1953; *b* 30 April 1902; *d* of late Prof. James Lorrain Smith, FRS; *m* 1934, Alexander Graham-Bryce, FRCS (*d* 1968); two *s. Educ:* St Leonards Sch., St Andrews; Edinburgh Univ. (MA). Investigator, Industrial Fatigue Research Board, 1926–27; HM Inspector of Factories, 1928–34; Centre Organiser, WVS, Manchester, 1938–39; Dir of Organization, Ontario Div., Canadian WVS, 1941–42; Tech. Adviser, American WVS, 1942–43; Res.

Fellow Fatigue Lab. Harvard Univ., 1943–44; Nat. Council of Women: Chm., Manchester Br., 1947–50; Vice-Chm., Education Cttee, 1950–51; Mem., Oxford Assoc., 1987–. JP and Mem. Juvenile Court Panel, Manchester City, 1949–55; Vice-Chairman: Assoc. of HMCs, 1953–55; Bd of Visitors, Grendon Prison, 1962–67. Member: Nurses and Midwives Whitley Council, 1953–57; General Nursing Council, 1956–61; Bd of Governors, Eastman Dental Hosp., 1957–63; Maternity and Midwifery Standing Cttee, 1957–72; Public Health Insp., Education Bd, 1958–64; Independent Television Authority, 1960–65 (Chm., General Advisory Council, 1964–65); Bd, ATV Network Ltd, 1968–72; Ancillary Dental Workers Cttee, 1956–68; Experimental Scheme for Dental Auxiliaries, 1958–69. Pres., Goring and Dist Day Centre for the Elderly, 1980–89; Vice Pres., League of Friends, Radcliffe Infirmary, Oxford, 1993– (Pres., 1988–93); Pres., Oxford Br., Motor Neurone Disease Assoc.; Friend, City of Oxford Orch. Life Mem., British Fedn Univ. Women; Mem., Oxford Br., Edinburgh Graduates; Hon. Member: Oxford Br., Zonta International; Edinburgh Univ. Club of Oxford. *Publications:* (joint) reports on research into industrial psychological problems. *Address:* 1 Quinton House, 98 Woodstock Road, Oxford OX2 7NE.
Died 29 April 1997.

GRANT, Alistair; *see* Grant, D. A. A.

GRANT, Allan Wallace, OBE 1974; MC 1941; TD 1947; President, Ecclesiastical Insurance Office Ltd, 1981–87 (Managing Director, 1971–77; Chairman, 1975–81); retired; *b* 2 Feb. 1911; *s* of late Henry Grant and Rose Margaret Sheppard; *m* 1st, 1939, Kathleen Rachel Bamford (marr. diss. 1990); one *d*; 2nd, 1990, Mary Wyles. *Educ:* Dulwich Coll. LLB Hons (London). FCII. Called to Bar, Gray's Inn, 1948. Eccles. Insurance Office, 1929; Chief Officer, 1952; Dir, 1966. Served War of 1939–45: Major, 2 i/c 3rd Co. of London Yeomanry (Sharpshooters), N Africa, Sicily, Italy, NW Europe. Pres., Sharpshooters Assoc. President: Insurance Inst. of London, 1966–67; Chartered Insce Inst., 1970–71; Insce Charities, 1973–74; Insce Orchestral Soc., 1973–74; Chairman: Insce Industry Training Council, 1973–75; Clergy Orphan Corp., 1967–80 (Vice-Pres., 1980); Coll. of All Saints, Tottenham, 1967–76; Allchurches Trust Ltd, 1975–85; Governor: St Edmund's Sch., Canterbury, 1967; St Margaret's Sch., Bushey, 1967; Mem., Policyholders Protection Bd, 1975–81; Treasurer: Historic Churches Preservation Trust, 1977–85; Soc. for Advancing Christian Faith, 1977–87. Master, Coopers' Co., 1984–85; Asst, Insurers' Co., 1979–86. Hon. DCanL Lexington, 1975. *Recreations:* golf, travel. *Address:* 5 Queens Court, Queens Road, Richmond, Surrey TW10 6LA. *T:* (0181) 940 2626. *Clubs:* City Livery; Richmond Golf (Captain 1977).
Died 17 Aug. 1997.

GRANT, Bernard Alexander Montgomery; MP (Lab) Tottenham, since 1987; *b* 17 Feb. 1944; *s* of Eric and late Lily Grant; *m* 1975, Yvonne (marr. diss.); three *s*; *m* 1998, Sharon (*née* Lawrence). *Educ:* St Stanislaus College, Georgetown, Guyana; Tottenham Technical College. Analyst, Demerara Bauxite Co., Guyana, 1961–63; Clerk, British Rail, 1963–65; Telephonist, Internat. Telephones, GPO, 1969–78; Area Officer, NUPE, 1978–83; Develt Worker, Black Trade Unionists Solidarity Movement, 1983–84; Local Govt Officer, London Borough of Newham, 1985–87. Councillor, London Borough of Haringey, 1978–88 (Council Leader, 1985–87). Mem., Select Cttee on Internat. Develt, 1997–. Chairman: All-Party Gp on Race and Community, 1995–; British Caribbean Parly Gp, 1997–; Vice-Chm., PLP Gp on Culture, Media and Sport, 1997–. Chm. and Founder Mem., Parly Black Caucus, 1988; Chm., Campaign Gp of Labour MPs, 1990–92; Mem., NEC, Anti-Apartheid

Movement, 1989–91; Chairman: Standing Conf. on Race Equality in Europe, 1990–; African Reparations Movement (UK), 1993–. Mem., Gp of Eminent Persons on Reparations for Africa, OAU, 1994–. Chm. Bd, Global Trade Centre, 1995–. Chm., Internat. Centre for Performing Arts, 1998–. Editor, Black Parliamentarian Magazine, 1990–92. Mem. Ct, Middlesex Univ., 1996–. Hon. LLD Pace Univ., NY, 1993. *Recreations:* cooking, cricket. *Address:* House of Commons, SW1A 0AA; *e-mail:* 100627.463@compuserve.com.
Died 8 April 2000.

GRANT, His Honour Derek Aldwin, DSO 1944; QC 1962; a Circuit Judge (formerly an Additional Judge of the Central Criminal Court), 1969–84; *b* 22 Jan. 1915; *s* of late Charles Frederick Grant, CSI, ICS; *m* 1954, Phoebe Louise Wavell-Paxton; one *s* three *d*. *Educ:* Winchester Coll.; Oriel Coll., Oxford. Served in RAF, 1940–46 (King's Commendation, DSO). Called to the Bar, 1938; Master of the Bench, Inner Temple, 1969. Deputy Chairman, East Sussex County Sessions, 1962–71; Recorder of Salisbury, 1962–67, and of Portsmouth, 1967–69. *Address:* Carters Lodge, Handcross, West Sussex RH17 6AA.
Died 29 Aug. 2000.

GRANT, Prof. (Duncan) Alistair (Antoine), RBA, RE, ARCA; Professor of Printmaking, 1984–90, Head of Printmaking Department, 1970–90, Royal College of Art; Professor Emeritus, 1990; *b* London, 3 June 1925; *s* of Duncan and Germaine Grant; *m* 1st, 1949, Phyllis Fricker (*d* 1988); one *d*; 2nd, 1991, Joan Strickland (*d* 1995). *Educ:* Froebel, Whitehill, Glasgow; Birmingham Sch. of Art; Royal Coll. of Art. Joined staff of RCA, 1955. *One Man Shows* at the following galleries: Zwemmer; Piccadilly; AIA; Ashgate; Bear Lane, Oxford; Midland Group, Nottingham; Balclutha; Ware, London; 46, Edinburgh; Editions Alecto; Redfern; Scottish; Le Touquet Museum, France. *Works in the collections of:* V&A Museum; Tate Gallery; Min. of Works; DoE; LCC (later GLC); Arts Council; Carlisle Art Gall.; Ferens Art Gall., Hull; The King of Sweden; Dallas Museum; Dallas Art Gall.; Cincinnati; Boston; Museum of Modern Art, New York; Public Library, NY; Chicago Art Inst.; Lessing J. Rosenwald Collection; Beaverbrook Foundn, Fredericton, NB; Vancouver Art Gall.; Victoria Art Gall; Tel Aviv Museum; Cairo Art Gall.; Nat. Gall. of S Australia; Nat. Museum of Stockholm; IBM; Mobil Oil; Unilever; BP International; BM; Hunterian Mus., Glasgow; Le Touquet Mus., France. *Group Exhibitions* in Bahamas, Canada, Europe, S America, USA and UK. FRSA. Awarded Silver Medal, Internat. Festival of Youth, Moscow, 1957. *Address:* 13 Redcliffe Gardens, SW10 9BG. *T:* (0171) 352 4312.
Died 12 April 1997.

GRANT, Edward; Lord Mayor, City of Manchester, May 1972–73; *b* 10 Aug. 1915; *s* of Edward and Ada Grant; *m* 1942, Winifred Mitchell. *Educ:* Moston Lane Sch.; Manchester High Sch. of Commerce. City Councillor, Manchester, 1950–84 (Alderman, 1970–74). Hosp. Administrator, Manchester AHA (T) North Dist (formerly NE Manchester HMC), 1948–75, retired. *Recreations:* swimming, reading, gardening. *Address:* 4 Hudson Court, Sherwell Road, Blackley, Manchester M9 8DJ. *T:* (0161) 720 8312.
Died 2 Jan. 1997.

GRANT, James Shaw, CBE 1968 (OBE 1956); Member, Highlands and Islands Development Board, 1970–82; *b* 22 May 1910; *s* of William Grant and Johanna Morison Grant, Stornoway; *m* 1951, Catherine Mary Stewart (*d* 1988); no *c*. *Educ:* Nicolson Inst.; Glasgow Univ. Editor, Stornoway Gazette, 1932–63; Mem., Crofters' Commn, 1955–63, Chm., 1963–78. Dir, Grampian Television, 1969–80. Mem. Scottish Adv. Cttee, British Council, 1972–94. Governor, Pitlochry Festival Theatre, 1954–84, Chairman, 1971–83; Chm., Harris Tweed Assoc. Ltd,

1972–84. Mem. Council, Nat. Trust for Scotland, 1979–84. FRAgS 1973; FRSE 1982. Hon. LLD Aberdeen, 1979. *Publications:* Highland Villages, 1977; Their Children Will See, 1979; The Hub of My Universe, 1983; Surprise Island, 1983; The Gaelic Vikings, 1984; Stornoway and the Lews, 1985; Discovering Lewis and Harris, 1987; Enchanted Island, 1989; A Shilling for your Scowl, 1992; Morrison of The Bounty, 1997; several plays. *Recreations:* golf, photography. *Address:* Ardgrianach, Inshes, Inverness IV2 5BQ. *T:* (01463) 231476. *Club:* Royal Over-Seas League. *Died 28 July 1999.*

GRANT, Rear-Adm. John, CB 1960; DSO 1942; *b* 13 Oct. 1908; *s* of late Maj.-Gen. Sir Philip Grant, KCB, CMG, and Annette, *d* of John Coventry, JP, Burgate Manor, Fordingbridge; *m* 1935, Ruth Hayward Slade; two *s* two *d. Educ:* St Anthony's, Eastbourne; RN Colls, Dartmouth and Greenwich. Midshipman, HMS Queen Elizabeth, 1926; Sub-Lieut, HMS Revenge, 1930; Lieut, HMS Kent, China Station, 1932; specialised in anti-submarine warfare, 1933–39; Staff Officer Convoys, Rosyth, 1940; in comd HMS Beverley, 1941–42 (DSO); Trng Comdr, HMS Osprey, 1942, and subseq. in HMS Western Isles; in comd HMS Philante, 1943; Trng Comdr, HMS Osprey, 1944; in comd HMS Opportune, Fame and Crispin, 1945–47; Joint Staff Coll., 1947; Executive Officer, HMS Vernon; Capt. 1949; Dep. Dir Torpedo Anti-Submarine and Mine Warfare Div., Naval Staff, Admiralty, 1949–51; in comd HMS Cleopatra, 1952–53; Imperial Defence Coll., 1954; in comd HMS Vernon, 1955–57; on staff of Chief of Defence Staff, Min. of Defence, 1957–59; Rear-Adm., 1959; Flag Officer Commanding Reserve Fleet (HMS Vanguard), 1959–60; retired list, 1961; Rank Organisation, 1961–65; Director, Conference of the Electronics Industry, 1965–71. *Address:* 9 Rivermead Court, Ranelagh Gardens, SW6 3RT. *Died 29 Feb. 1996.*

GRANT, John Douglas; writer, media and public affairs consultant; Chairman, South East Radio Ltd, since 1995; *b* 16 Oct. 1932; *s* of M. de Burgh Grant; *m* 1955, Patricia Julia Ann; two *s* one *d. Educ:* Stationers' Company's Sch., Hornsey. Reporter on various provincial newspapers until 1955; Daily Express, 1955–70 (Chief Industrial Correspondent, 1967–70). Head of Communications, EETPU, 1984–89; Mem., Radio Authy, 1990–95. Contested: (Lab) Beckenham, 1966; (SDP) Islington N, 1983; (SDP/Alliance) Carshalton and Wallington, 1987. MP Islington East, 1970–74, Islington Central, 1974–83 (Lab, 1970–81, SDP, 1981–83). Opposition Front Bench spokesman for policy on broadcasting and the press, 1973–74, on employment, 1979–81; Parly Sec., CSD, March–Oct. 1974; Parliamentary Under-Secretary of State: ODM, 1974–76; Dept of Employment, 1976–79; SDP employment spokesman, 1981–83; SDP industry spokesman, 1982–83. Chm., Bromley Constituency Labour Party, 1966–70. Chm., Labour and Industrial Correspondents' Group, 1967. *Publications:* Member of Parliament, 1974; Blood Brothers, 1992; articles in national newspapers and periodicals. *Recreations:* tennis, golf, barbershop singing, watching soccer. *Address:* Branscombe, Upper Street, Kingsdown, near Deal, Kent CT14 8BJ. *T:* (01304) 363991.

Died 29 Sept. 2000.

GRANT, Prof. Peter John, PhD; MIMechE, FINucE; FInstP; Professor of Nuclear Power, Imperial College of Science, Technology and Medicine, 1966–91, then Emeritus; Deputy Vice-Chancellor, University of London, 1990–92; *b* London, 2 July 1926; *s* of Herbert James Grant; *m* Audrey, *d* of Joseph Whitham; one *s. Educ:* Merchant Taylors' Sch.; Sidney Sussex Coll., Cambridge. BA 1947, MA, PhD 1951. Research in Nuclear Physics at Cavendish Laboratory, 1947–50; Lectr in Natural Philosophy, Univ. of Glasgow, 1950–55; Chief Physicist,

Atomic Energy Div., GEC Ltd, 1956–59; Reader in Engineering Science, Imperial Coll. of Science and Technology, 1959–66; Mem. Governing Body, Imperial Coll., 1985–89; London University: Dean of Engrg, 1984–86; Chm. of Academic Council, 1986–89; Mem. Court, 1988–93. Mem., Adv. Cttee on Safety of Nuclear Installation, 1983–94. Pres., Instn of Nuclear Engrs, 1994–96. Gov., Hampton Sch., 1984–96. *Publications:* Elementary Reactor Physics, 1966; Nuclear Science, 1971; papers on radioactivity, nuclear reactions, physics of nuclear reactors. *Address:* 49 Manor Road South, Esher, Surrey KT10 0QA. *Died 13 July 1999.*

GRANT-FERRIS, family name of **Baron Harvington.**

GRANT-SUTTIE, Sir (George) Philip; see Suttie.

GRANVILLE, 5th Earl *cr* 1833; **Granville James Leveson Gower,** MC 1945; Viscount Granville, 1815; Baron Leveson, 1833; Major Coldstream Guards (Supplementary Reserve); Lord-Lieutenant, Islands Area of the Western Isles, 1983–93 (Vice Lord-Lieutenant, 1976–83); *b* 6 Dec. 1918; *s* of 4th Earl Granville, KG, KCVO, CB, DSO, and Countess Granville, GCVO; *S* father, 1953; *m* 1958, Doon Aileen, *d* of late Hon. Brinsley Plunket and of Mrs V. Stux-Rybar, Luttrellstown Castle, Co. Dublin; two *s* one *d. Educ:* Eton. Served throughout War, 1939–45, Tunisia and Italy (twice wounded, despatches, MC). DL Inverness, 1974. *Heir: s* Lord Leveson, *b* 10 Sept. 1959. *Address:* 51 Lyall Mews, SW1X 8DJ. *T:* (0171) 235 5114; Callernish, Sollas, North Uist, Outer Hebrides, Inverness-shire PA51 3JH. *Died 31 Oct. 1996.*

GRANVILLE OF EYE, Baron *cr* 1967 (Life Peer), of Eye, co. Suffolk; **Edgar Louis Granville;** *b* Reading, 12 Feb. 1898; *s* of Reginald and Margaret Granville; *m* 1943, Elizabeth *d* of late Rev. W. C. Hunter; one *d. Educ:* High Wycombe, London and Australia. Served War of 1914–18 as officer in AIF, Gallipoli, Egypt and France; Capt. RA, 1939–40. MP (L.) Eye Div. of Suffolk, 1929–51, Hon. Sec., Liberal Agricultural Group, House of Commons, 1929–31; Hon. Sec. Foreign Affairs Group, Vice-Pres. National League of Young Liberals; Chm., Young Liberals Manifesto Group; Parliamentary Private Sec. to Sir Herbert Samuel, first National Government, 1931; Parliamentary Private Sec. to Sir John Simon, National Government, 1931–36; Mem. of Inter-Departmental Cttee for the World Economic Conference, 1933. Sat in House of Lords as an Independent. *Recreations:* cricket, football, ski-ing. *Address:* 112 Charlton Lane, Cheltenham, Glos GL53 9EA. *Died 14 Feb. 1998.*

GRAPPELLI, Stéphane; musician; *b* 26 Jan. 1908; *s* of Prof. Ernest Grappelli and Anna Grappelli (*née* Hanocke); one *d.* Placed in orphanage, 1911; 6 months training in dance with Isadora Duncan, 1914; orphanage to 1918; learnt to play violin together with father; studied for short period at Paris Conservatoire; musical accompanist for silent films, 1923–25; played at social functions, incl. Ambassadeurs Club, 1927–29; joined Grégor and Grégorians, Nice, 1929 (piano and violin, later saxophone and accordion); returned to Paris, 1931; played several instruments at La Croix du Sud, informally with Django Reinhardt, later founding Quintette de Hot Club de France; specialized in jazz improvisations; numerous recordings, 1935–39; spent war years, 1939–45, in London; teamed occasionally with Reinhardt, 1946–53; clubs in London and Paris (incl. Paris Hilton house band, 1967–71); concerts and recordings with fellow musicians, incl. Jean-Luc Ponty, George Shearing, Diz Disley, Oscar Peterson, Baden Powell, Barney Kessel, Earl Hines, Teddy Wilson, Martial Solal, Michel Legrand, Benny Goodman, Subramaniam, Yehudi Menuhin, Yo-Yo Ma, Juillard String Quartet; US début, Newport Jazz Festival, 1969, début Carnegie Hall, 1974. Had homes in Paris and

Cannes. Lifetime Achievement Grammy Award, 1997. Commandeur, Légion d'honneur, 1997; Commandeur, Ordre Nat. du Mérite; Commandeur des Arts et des Lettres; Médaille de Vermeil, Paris. *Address:* 87 rue de Dunkerque, 75009 Paris, France.   *Died 1 Dec. 1997.*

GRATTAN-COOPER, Rear Adm. Sidney, CB 1966; OBE 1946; *b* 3 Dec. 1911; *s* of Sidney Cooper; *m* 1940, Felicity Joan Pitt; two *s. Educ:* privately. Entered RN 1936; served in war of 1939–45; Chief of Staff Flag Officer (Air) Home, 1957–59; Staff of Supreme Allied Comdr Atlantic (NATO), 1961–63; Dep. Controller (Aircraft) RN, Min. of Aviation, 1964–66; retired 1966. *Recreations:* golf, swimming. *Address:* Hursley, Rodwell Road, St James, 7945, S Africa. *Club:* Army and Navy.
Died 24 Oct. 1999.

GRATWICK, John, OBE 1979; Chairman, Empire Stores Group plc (formerly Empire Stores (Bradford)), 1978–90 (Director, 1973–90); Director, New Law Publishing Co. plc, since 1993; *b* 23 April 1918; *s* of Percival John and Kathleen Mary Gratwick; *m* 1944, Ellen Violet Wright; two *s* two *d. Educ:* Cranbrook Sch., Kent; Imperial Coll., Univ. of London. Asst Production Manager, Armstrong Siddeley, 1941–45; Director, Urwick, Orr & Partners Ltd, 1959, Man. Dir, 1968, Vice-Chm., 1971. Chm., EDC for the Clothing Industry, 1985–90 (Mem., 1967–85); Member: Monopolies and Mergers Commn, 1969–76; CAA, 1972–74. Chm., Management Consultants Assoc., 1971–72. University of London: Member: Careers Adv. Bd, 1962–78; Senate, 1967–94; Court, 1987–94; Governor, Cranbrook Sch., Kent, 1972–85. Mem., Bd of Finance, dio. of Guildford, 1989–. Trustee, Foundn for Business Responsibilities. Liveryman, Worshipful Co. of Glovers (Master, 1993–94). *Recreations:* golf, sailing, photography, philately. *Address:* Silver Howe, Nuns Walk, Virginia Water, Surrey GU25 4RT. *T:* (01344) 843121. *Clubs:* City Livery; Wentworth (Surrey).
Died 12 March 1997.

GRAVE, Walter Wyatt, CMG 1958; PhD; Master, 1966–71, Hon. Fellow, since 1971, Fitzwilliam College, Cambridge; *b* 16 Oct. 1901; *o s* of late Walter and Annie Grave; *m* 1932, Kathleen Margaret, *d* of late Stewart Macpherson; two *d. Educ:* King Edward VII Sch., King's Lynn; Emmanuel Coll., Cambridge (Scholar; MA; PhD 1928). Fellow of Emmanuel Coll., 1926–66, 1972–; Tutor, 1936–40; University Lecturer in Spanish, 1936–40; Registrary of Cambridge Univ., 1943–52; Principal of the University Coll. of the West Indies, Jamaica, 1953–58; Censor of Fitzwilliam House, Cambridge, 1959–66. Temporary Administrative Officer, Ministry of Labour and National Service, 1940–43. Hon. LLD: Cantab, 1953; McMaster. *Publication:* Fitzwilliam College Cambridge 1869–1969, 1983. *Address:* 125A Long Road, Cambridge CB2 2HE. *T:* (01223) 845310.
Died 20 May 1999.

GRAY, Alexander Stuart, FRIBA; Consultant to Watkins, Gray, Woodgate International, 1968–75, retired; *b* 15 July 1905; *s* of Alexander and Mary Gray; *m* 1932, Avis (*d* 1980), *d* of John Radmore, Truro; one *s* two *d. Educ:* Mill Hill Sch. Articled to R. S. Balgarnie Wyld, ARIBA; studied at Central Sch. of Arts and Crafts; Royal Academy Schools (Bronze Medal, 1928; Silver Medal and Travelling Studentship, 1932; Gold Medal and Edward Stott Trav. Studentship (Italy), 1933); Brit. Instn Schol., 1929. Lectr on Arch. subjects at Central Sch. of Arts and Crafts, Brixton Sch. of Bldg, and Hammersmith Sch. of Bldg, 1936–39; Lectr on Hosp. Planning at King Edward VII Hosp. Fund Colleges, 1950. In partnership with W. H. Watkins won architectural comp. for new St George's Hosp., Hyde Park Corner, London (partnership 1939–68); before retirement Architect with partners to: Radcliffe Infirmary, Oxford, United Bristol Hospitals, Royal Free

Hospital, Guy's Hospital, London Hospital, Eastman Dental Hospital, St Mary's, Manchester, and other hosps in London and the provinces; also in West Indies, where they were responsible for banks, and commercial buildings as well; hospitals for Comptroller of Development and Welfare in BWI, 1941–46; rebuilding of centre of Georgetown, British Guiana, after the fire of 1945, including new GPO, Telecommunications Building, etc; in Nigeria, University Coll. Hosp., Ibadan, and other works; also in Qatar (Persian Gulf), etc. *Publications:* Edwardian Architecture: a biographical dictionary, 1985; (jtly) Fanlights, 1990; (jtly) Hampstead Garden Suburb, 1992; various papers read at confs on Hosp. Planning with special ref. to designing for the tropics, and contrib. Tech. Jls. *Address:* 1 Temple Fortune Hill, NW11 7XL. *T:* (0181) 458 5741. *Clubs:* Arts, Old Millhillians.
Died 20 Feb. 1998.

GRAY, Andrew Aitken, MC 1945; Chairman, Wellcome Foundation Ltd, 1971–77; *b* 11 Jan. 1912; *s* of John Gray and Margaret Eckford Gray (*née* Crozier); *m* 1st, 1939, Eileen Mary Haines (*d* 1980); three *s;* 2nd, 1984, Jess, *widow* of C. M. Carr. *Educ:* Wyggeston School, Leicester; Christ Church, Oxford. Served Royal Engineers, 1939–46 (MC, despatches). Unilever Ltd, 1935–52; Dir, Wellcome Foundation Ltd, 1954, Dep. Chm., 1967; Chm. and Man. Dir, Cooper, McDougall & Robertson, 1963–70. Chm., Herts AHA, 1974–77. Comdr, Orden del Mérito Agricola; Comdr, Order of Merit, Italy. *Recreations:* fishing, gardening, theatre. *Address:* Rainhill Spring, Stoney Lane, Bovingdon, Herts HP3 0DP. *T:* (01442) 833277. *Club:* East India, Devonshire, Sports and Public Schools.
Died 28 July 1997.

GRAY, Charles Horace, MD (London), DSc; FRCP, FRSC, FRCPath; Emeritus Professor of Chemical Pathology in the University of London (Professor, at King's College Hospital Medical School, 1948–76); Consulting Chemical Pathologist, King's College Hospital District, 1976–81 (Consultant, 1938–76); *b* 30 June 1911; *s* of Charles H. Gray and Ethel Hider, Erith, Kent; *m* 1938, (Florence) Jessie Widdup, ARCA, *d* of Frank Widdup, JP, Barnoldswick, Yorks; two *s. Educ:* Imperial Coll. and University Coll., London (Fellow, UCL, 1979); University Coll. Hospital Medical Sch. Demonstrator in Biochemistry, University Coll., London, 1931–36; Bayliss-Starling Scholar in Physiology and Biochemistry, 1932–33; Visiting Teacher in Biochemistry, Chelsea Polytechnic, 1933–36; Demonstrator and Lecturer in Physiology, University Coll., 1935–36; Graham Scholar in Pathology, UCH Medical Sch., 1936–38; Pathologist in Charge Sector Biochemical Laboratory, Sector 9, Emergency Health Service, 1939–44. Hon. Consultant, Miles Laboratories Ltd, 1953–76. Acting Head, Dept of Chem. Pathol., Hosp. for Sick Children, Gt Ormond St, Jan.-Dec. 1979. Vis. Prof., Div. of Clinical Chem., MRC Clinical Res. Centre, Harrow, 1976–83. Member: Clinical Res. Bd of Med. Res. Council, 1964–68; Arthritis and Rheumatism Council Res. Cttee, 1960–68 (Chm., 1963–66); Chairman: MCB Exams Cttee, 1971–73; Steroid Reference Collection and Radioactive Steroid Synthesis Steering Cttee, MRC, 1973–76; Regional Scientific Cttee, SE Thames RHA, 1974–76 (Mem. Regional Research Cttee, 1974–82). Sec., Soc. for Endocrinology, 1950–53; Chm. Cttee of Management, Jl of Endocrinology Ltd, 1970–74; Member: Cttee of Management, Inst. of Psychiatry, 1966–73; Council, and Chm., Specialist Adv. Cttee in Chemical Pathology, RCPath, 1972–75; Assoc. of Clinical Biochemists, 1961 (Pres. 1969–71, Emeritus Mem., 1980–). Mem. Livery, Worshipful Soc. of Apothecaries, 1951–. Mem., Editorial Bd, Biochemical Jl, 1955–60. *Publications:* The Bile Pigments, 1953; Clinical Chemical Pathology, 1953, 10th edn (jtly), 1985; The Bile Pigments in Health and Disease,

1961; (ed) Laboratory Handbook of Toxic Agents; (ed jtly) Hormones in Blood, 1961, 3rd edn vols 1–3, 1979, vols 4–5, 1983; (ed jtly) High Pressure Liquid Chromatography in Clinical Chemistry, 1976; contributions to medical and scientific journals. *Recreations:* music, travel. *Address:* Barn Cottage, Linden Road, Leatherhead, Surrey KT22 7JF. *T:* (01372) 372415; 34 Cleaver Square, SE11 4EA. *T:* (0171) 735 9652. *Clubs:* Athenæum, Royal Over-Seas League.

Died 15 Aug. 1997.

GRAY, David, CBE 1977 (OBE 1964); QPM 1960; HM Chief Inspector of Constabulary for Scotland, 1970–79; retired; *b* 18 Nov. 1914; *s* of William Gray and Janet Borland Gray; *m* 1st, 1944, Mary Stewart Scott (*d* 1985); two *d*; 2nd, 1989, Laura Margaret Mackinnon. *Educ:* Preston Grammar Sch. Chief Constable: Greenock, 1955–58; Stirling and Clackmannan, 1958–69. Hon. Sec., Chief Constables' (Scotland) Assoc., 1958–69. English-Speaking Union Thyne Scholar, 1969. *Recreations:* fishing, shooting, golf. *Address:* Ganavan, The Bay, Strachur, Argyll PA27 8DE. *T:* (01369) 860466.

Died 28 Dec. 1999.

GRAY, Dr Edward George, FRS 1976; Head of the Laboratory of Ultrastructure, National Institute for Medical Research, Mill Hill, 1977–83; *b* 11 Jan. 1924; *s* of Will and Charlotte Gray; *m* 1953, May Eine Kyllikki Rautiainen; two *s*. *Educ:* University Coll. of Wales, Aberystwyth (BSc, PhD). Anatomy Department, University College, London: Lectr, 1958, Reader, 1962; Prof. of Cytology, 1968–77. *Recreations:* violin playing, water colouring, gardening. *Address:* 58 New Park Road, Newgate Street, Hertford SG13 8RF *T:* (01707) 872891.

Died 14 Aug. 1999.

GRAY, Rear-Adm. Gordon Thomas Seccombe, CB 1964; DSC 1940; *b* 20 Dec. 1911; *s* of late Rev. Thomas Seccombe Gray and Edith Gray; *m* 1939, Sonia Moore-Gwyn; one *s* (one *d* decd). *Educ:* Nautical Coll., Pangbourne. Entered RN, 1929; Sub-Lieut and Lieut, Mediterranean Fleet, 1934–36, ashore Arab revolt in Palestine (despatches); 1st Lieut, HMS Stork, 1939, Norwegian campaign (despatches, DSC); Comd HMS Badsworth, 1942–43 (despatches); Comd HMS Lamerton, 1943–45 (despatches); after the War comd destroyers Consort, Contest and St Kitts; JSSC, 1948; Comdr 1949; Directing Staff, RN Staff Coll., Greenwich, 1950; Exec. Officer, cruiser HMS Glasgow, 1951–53; Capt. 1953; Naval Deputy to UK Nat. Military Representative at SHAPE; Capt. of 5th Frigate Sqdn, and Comd HMS Wakeful and HMS Torquay, 1956–59; Asst Chief of Staff to C-in-C Eastern Atlantic Command, 1959–61; in comd of Naval Air Anti-Submarine Sch. at Portland and Chief Staff Officer to Flag Officer Sea Trng, 1961–62; Senior Naval Instructor, Imperial Defence Coll., 1963–65, retd. *Recreation:* yachting. *Address:* c/o Lloyds Bank, Liphook, Hants GU30 7AE. *Died 12 June 1997.*

GRAY, Harold James, CMG 1956; Director, Legal Affairs, Confederation of British Industry, 1965–72; *b* 17 Oct. 1907; 2nd *s* of late John William Gray and Amelia Frances (*née* Miller); *m* 1928, Katherine Gray (*née* Starling) (*d* 1985); one *d*. *Educ:* Alleyn's Sch.; Dover County Sch.; Queen Mary Coll., London (MSc, LLB); Gray's Inn; Harvard University, USA (MPA). MInstP, CPhys; FRSA. Customs and Excise Dept, 1927; Asst Examiner, Patent Office, 1930, Examiner, 1935; Industries and Manufactures Dept, Board of Trade, 1938; Ministry of Supply, 1939; Asst Sec., Min. of Supply, 1942; transf. to Bd of Trade, 1946; Commercial Relations and Exports Dept, Board of Trade, 1950; Under-Sec., 1954; UK Senior Trade Comr and Economic and Commercial Adviser to High Comr in Australia, 1954–58; UK Senior Trade Comr and Economic Adviser to the High Comr in Union of South Africa, 1958–60; Dir, Nat. Assoc. of British Manufacturers, 1961–65. Commonwealth Fund Fellowship, 1949–50. Formerly Chm., NUMAS (Management Services) Ltd. *Publications:* Electricity in the Service of Man, 1949; Economic Survey of Australia, 1955; Dictionary of Physics, 1958; (jtly) New Dictionary of Physics, 1975. *Recreations:* golf, swimming, riding. *Address:* Copper Beeches, 58 Tudor Avenue, Maidstone, Kent ME14 5HJ. *Died 6 Aug. 1998.*

GRAY, Rev. Prof. John; Professor of Hebrew, University of Aberdeen, 1962–80, then Professor Emeritus; *b* 9 June 1913; *s* of James Telfer Gray; *m* Janet J. Gibson; five *c*. *Educ:* Kelso High Sch.; Edinburgh Univ. (MA, BD, PhD). Colonial Chaplain and Chaplain to Palestine Police, 1939–41; Minister of the Church of Scotland, Kilmory, Isle of Arran, 1942–47; Lectr in Semitic Languages and Literatures, Manchester Univ., 1947–53; Lectr in Hebrew and Biblical Criticism, University of Aberdeen, 1953–62. Mem., Soc. for Old Testament Study. Hon. DD St Andrews, 1977. *Publications:* The Krt Text in the Literature of Ras Shamra, 1955, 2nd edn 1964; The Legacy of Canaan, 1957, 2nd edn 1965; Archæology and the Old Testament World, 1962; The Canaanites, 1964; Kings I and II: a Commentary, 1964, 3rd edn 1977; Joshua, Judges and Ruth, 1967, 3rd edn 1986; A History of Jerusalem, 1969; Near Eastern Mythology, 1969, 2nd edn 1982; The Biblical Doctrine of the Reign of God, 1979; contribs to various Bible Dictionaries, memorial volumes and learned journals. *Recreations:* beekeeping, gardening, trout-fishing. *Address:* Tanlaw Cottage, Hendersyde, Kelso, Roxburgh TD5 7ST. *T:* (01573) 24374. *Died 1 April 2000.*

GRAY, Vice Adm. Sir John (Michael Dudgeon), KBE 1967 (OBE 1950); CB 1964; *b* Dublin, 13 June 1913; *s* of Col Arthur Claypon Horner Gray, OBE and Dorothy Margery, *d* of Rev. Canon Denham; British, *m* 1939, Margaret Helen Purvis (*d* 1994); one *s* one *d*. *Educ:* RNC, Dartmouth. HMS Nelson, 1931; Midshipman, HMS Enterprise, 1932–33; Sub-Lieut, HMS Devonshire, 1934; specialised in Gunnery, 1938; served War of 1939–45: HMS Hermes; HMS Spartan; with US in Anzio; 8th Army in Italy; French Army in France (despatches); HMS Duke of York, 1945, Comdr 1947; Naval Adviser, UK Mission, Japan, 1947–50 (OBE Korean War); HMS Swiftsure, 1950, Capt. 1952; HMS Lynx, 1956; HMS Victorious, 1961; Rear Adm. 1962; Dir-Gen. of Naval Trng, Min. of Def., 1964–65 (Admiralty, 1962–64); Vice Adm. 1965; C-in-C, S Atlantic and S America Station, 1965–67. Sec., 1973–91, Consultant, 1991–92, Oriental Ceramic Soc. *Recreations:* squash, tennis, athletics (represented RN in 220 and 440 yds). *Club:* Naval and Military. *Died 3 Feb. 1998.*

GRAY, Rt Rev. Joseph, DCL; Bishop of Shrewsbury, (RC), 1980–95, then Emeritus; *b* 20 Oct. 1919; *s* of Terence Gray and Mary Gray (*née* Alwill). *Educ:* Patrick's Coll., Cavan, Eire; St Mary's Seminary, Oscott, Birmingham; Dunboyne House, St Patrick's Coll., Maynooth, Eire (Licentiate in Canon Law, 1950); Pontifical Univ. of St Thomas Aquinas, Rome (DCL 1960). Priest, 1943; Asst Priest, Sacred Heart, Aston, Birmingham, 1943–48; Sec. to Archbp of Birmingham, 1950–55; Parish Priest, St Michael's, Birmingham, 1955–69; Diocesan Chancellor, Birmingham, 1951–69; Vicar-Gen., Birmingham, 1960–69; Papal Chamberlain, 1960; Domestic Prelate, 1966; Episcopal Ordination, Cathedral of Christ the King, Liverpool, Feb. 1969; Titular Bishop of Mercia and Auxiliary Bishop of Liverpool, 1969–80. Pres., Liturgy Commn of Bishops' Conf. of England and Wales, 1976–84; Chm., Commn for Religious Life, 1984–95.

Recreations: music, reading, travel. *Address:* Nazareth House, Manor Hill, Birkenhead L43 1UG. *T:* (0151) 653 3600. *Died 7 May 1999.*

GRAY, Milner Connorton, CBE 1963; RDI 1937; FCSD; AGI; FInstPack; Founder Partner and Senior Consultant, Design Research Unit; Past Master: Faculty of Royal Designers for Industry; Art Workers' Guild; Past President, Society of Industrial Artists and Designers (later Chartered Society of Designers); *b* 8 Oct. 1899; *s* of late Archibald Campbell Gray and Katherine May Hart, Eynsford, Kent; *m* 1934, Gnade Osborne-Pratt; no *c. Educ:* studied painting and design, Goldsmiths' Coll. Sch. of Art, London Univ. Senior Partner in Industrial Design Partnership, 1934–40; Principal, Sir John Cass Coll. of Art, 1937–40; on Visiting Staff: Goldsmiths' Coll. Sch. of Art, London Univ., 1930–40; Chelsea Sch. of Art, 1934–37; Royal Coll. of Art, 1940. Head of Exhibitions Branch, Ministry of Information, 1940–41, and Adviser on Exhibitions, 1941–44. Founder Mem., Soc. of Industrial Artists, 1930, Hon. Sec., 1932–40, Pres., 1943–48 and 1968; Member of Council: Design and Industries Assoc., 1935–38; RSA, 1959–65; Artists Gen. Benevolent Instn, 1959 (Vice Pres., 1986); Adviser to BBC "Looking at Things" Schs Broadcasts, 1949–55. Member: Min. of Education Nat. Adv. Cttee on Art Examinations, 1949–52; Nat. Adv. Council on Art Education, 1959–69; Royal Mint Adv. Cttee, 1952–86. Mem. Council, RCA, 1963–67, Mem. Court 1967, Senior Fellow, 1971. British Pres., Alliance Graphique Internationale, 1963–71. Consultant Designer: BR Bd for BR Corporate Design Prog., 1963–67; (jointly) to Orient Line, SS Oriana, 1957–61; Ilford Ltd, 1946–66; Internat. Distillers and Vintners, 1954–69; Watney Mann Group, 1956–70; British Aluminium Co., 1965–72; ICI, 1966–70; Min. of Technology, 1970. Governor: Central Sch. of Art and Design, 1944–46; Hornsey Coll. of Art and Design, 1959–65. Hon. Fellow, Soc. of Typographic Designers, 1979. Hon. DesRCA, 1963, Hon. Dr RCA, 1979; Hon. DA Manchester, 1964. Freeman City of London, 1987. Served in 19th London Regt, and Royal Engineers, attached Camouflage Sch., 1917–19; admitted HAC, 1923. Gold Medal, Soc. of Ind. Artists and Designers, 1955. *Publications:* The Practice of Design (jtly), 1946; Package Design, 1955; (jtly) Lettering for Architects and Designers, 1962; articles, lectures and broadcasts on various aspects of design. *Address:* Felix Hall, Kelvedon, Essex CO5 9DG. *T:* (01376) 570485. *Club:* Arts. *Died 29 Sept. 1997.*

GRAY, Robert Michael Ker; QC 1983; QC (NI) 1984; a Recorder, since 1985; *b* 29 Aug. 1938; *y s* of late Brig. Walter Ker Gray, DSO and of Violet Lascelles, Checkendon, Oxfordshire. *Educ:* Radley (Scholar); Humboldt Gymnasium, Düsseldorf (Exchange Scholar); Balliol College, Oxford (Scholar; MA 1963); St John's College, Cambridge (LLM (LLB 1967), Russian Tripos 1968). Articled to Sir Anthony Lousada, Messrs Stephenson, Harwood and Tatham; Solicitor, 1962; called to the Bar, Lincoln's Inn (Bencher, 1991), Gray's Inn, and Inner Temple, 1969, King's Inns, Dublin, 1989; MacMahon Studentship, St John's College, Cambridge, 1969–73. European Office, UN, Geneva, 1962–64; Dept of Slavonic Studies, Cambridge, 1964. A Dep. High Court Judge, Family Div., 1983–, Chancery Div., 1993–, QBD, 1994–. Chancellor, dio. of Southwark, 1990–. Mem., Gen. Council of the Bar, 1972–74; Mem., Senate of the Bar, 1974–79, 1980–87 (Chm., Young Barristers, 1978–79); Examr, Bar Finals, 1970–79. Gen. Comr of Income Tax, 1992–; a Legal Assessor, GMC and GDC, 1995–. Chm., Harrison Homes (formerly Homes for the Aged Poor), 1980–; Sec., London Friends of St George's Cathedral, Cape Town, 1983–; Mem., Cttee, Nat. Aural Gp, 1988–; Trustee, Holy Cross Centre Trust, 1988–. Freeman, City of London, 1994. *Recreations:* walking, swimming.

Address: 2 Mitre Court Buildings, Temple, EC4Y 7BX. *T:* 0171–583 1380. *Clubs:* Garrick, Royal Automobile; Budleigh Salterton; Pangbourne Working Men's; Stewards (Henley-on-Thames); Hampshire CC; City and Civil Service (Cape Town). *Died 23 May 1996.*

GRAY, Sir William (Stevenson), Kt 1974; JP; DL; solicitor and notary public; Lord Provost, City of Glasgow and Lord Lieutenant, County of the City of Glasgow, 1972–75; *b* 3 May 1928; *o s* of William Stevenson Gray and Mary Johnstone Dickson; *m* 1958, Mary Rodger; one *s* one d. *Educ:* Hillhead High Sch.; Glasgow Univ. Admitted solicitor, 1958; notary public, 1960. Chairman: Scottish Special Housing Assoc., 1966–72; WPHT Scotland Ltd (formerly World of Property Housing Trust Scottish Housing Assoc. Ltd), 1974–99; Irvine New Town Develt Corp., 1974–76; Scotland W Industrial Promotion Gp, 1972–75; Scottish Develt Agency, 1975–79; The Oil Club, 1975–; Barrell Selection Ltd, 1987–99; Gap Housing Assoc. Ltd, 1988–97; Gap Housing Assoc. (Ownership) Ltd, 1988–99; Norcity Homes plc, 1988–95; Norcity II plc, 1990–97; Clan FM Ltd, 1987–; Clan Homes plc, 1988–99; Manchester Village Homes plc, 1989–97; Norhomes plc, 1989–97; First & Second Tax Homes plc, 1990–97; Third & Fourth Tax Homes plc, 1990–98; Home Partners Plus 01 & 02 Plc, 1991–95; Peppa Plc, 1992–; Paragon Protected Growth plc, 1993–; Norcity III and IV plc (Glasgow Student Village Cos), 1993–99; Adv. Bd, Norcity Residential Unit Trust, 1995–. Member: Exec., Scottish Council (Develt and Industry), 1971–75; Scottish Econ. Council, 1975–83; Lower Clyde Water Bd, 1971–72; Clyde Port Authority, 1972–75; Adv. Council for Energy Conservation, 1974–84; Convention of Royal Burghs, 1971–75; Central Adv. Cttee on JPs, 1975–97; Glasgow Adv. Cttee on JPs, 1975–97; Third Eye Centre Ltd, Glasgow, 1984–90 (Chm., 1975–84); Hodgson Martin Ltd Adv. Bd, 1988–94. Chairman: Glasgow Independent Hosp. Ltd (Ross Hall Hosp.), 1982–89; Clyde Tourist Assoc., 1972–75; Res. Trust for Inst. of Neurol Scis, 1978–94. Member: Nat. Trust for Scotland, 1971–72; Scottish Opera Bd, 1971–72; Scottish Nat. Orch. Soc., 1972–75; Vice-President: Glasgow Citizens' Theatre, 1975– (Mem., Bd of Dirs, 1970–75); Strathclyde Theatre Gp, 1975–86; Charles Rennie Mackintosh Soc., 1974–; Scottish Assoc. for Care and Resettlement of Offenders, 1982–86 (Chm., 1975–82); Governor, Glasgow Sch. of Art, 1961–75; Patron: Scottish Youth Theatre, 1978–86; Scottish Pakistani Soc., 1984–. Member: Court, Glasgow Univ., 1972–75; Council, Strathclyde Univ. Business Sch., 1978–88. FRSA 1991. Hon. LLD: Strathclyde, 1974; Glasgow, 1980. Mem., Glasgow Corp., 1958–75 (Chm., Property Management Cttee, 1964–67); Treasurer, City of Glasgow, 1971–72. JP City of Glasgow, 1961–64, Co. of City of Glasgow 1965; DL Co. of City of Glasgow, 1971, City of Glasgow 1976. *Recreations:* sailing, theatre. *Address:* 13 Royal Terrace, Glasgow G3 7NY. *T:* (0141) 332 1330, *Fax:* (0141) 332 2809.

Died 9 July 2000.

GRAYSON, Prof. Cecil, CBE 1992; MA; FBA 1979; Serena Professor of Italian Studies in the University of Oxford, and Fellow of Magdalen College, 1958–87 (Emeritus Fellow, 1987); *b* 5 Feb. 1920; *s* of John M. Grayson and Dora Hartley; *m* 1947, Margaret Jordan; one *s* three d. *Educ:* Batley Grammar Sch.; St Edmund Hall, Oxford (Hon. Fellow, 1986). First Class Hons (Mod. Langs), 1947. Army service (UK and India), 1940–46 (Major). Univ. Lectr in Italian, Oxford, 1948; Lectr at St Edmund Hall, Oxford, 1948; Lectr at New Coll., Oxford, 1954. Barlow Lecturer, University Coll., London, 1963; Resident Fellow, Newberry Library, Chicago, 1965; Visiting Professor: Yale Univ., 1966; Berkeley, Calif, 1969, 1973; UCLA, 1980, 1984, 1989, 1994; Perth, WA, 1973, 1980; Cape Town, 1980, 1983; NY Univ., 1992–93.

Pres., Modern Humanities Res. Assoc., 1988. Corresp. Fellow, Commissione per i Testi di Lingua, Bologna, 1957; Mem., Accademia Letteraria Ital. dell' Arcadia, 1958; Corresp. Member: Accademia della Crusca, 1960; Accademia delle Scienze, Bologna, 1964; Accademia dei Lincei, 1967; Istituto Veneto di Scienze, Lettere ed Arti, 1977. Hon. Citizen, Mantua, 1998. Premio Internazionale Galileo (storia della lingua italiana), 1974; Serena Medal for Italian Studies, British Academy, 1976. Comdr, Order of Merit, Italy, 1975. *Publications:* Early Italian Texts (with Prof. C. Dionisotti), 1949; Opuscoli inediti di L. B. Alberti, 1954; Alberti and the Tempio Malatestiano, 1957; Vincenzo Calmeta, Prose e Lettere edite e inedite, 1959; A Renaissance Controversy: Latin or Italian?, 1960; L. B. Alberti, Opere volgari, I, 1960, II, 1966, III, 1973; L. B. Alberti e la prima grammatica volgare, 1964; (ed) Selected Works of Guicciardini, 1964; Cinque saggi su Dante, 1972; (ed and trans.) L. B. Alberti, De pictura, De statua, 1972; (ed) The World of Dante, 1980; (ed jtly) Piero della Francesca, *Libellus de quinque corporibus regularibus*, 1995; (trans.) Roberto Ridolfi, The Life of Savonarola, 1959, The Life of Machiavelli, 1963, The Life of Guicciardini, 1967; articles in Bibliofilia, Burlington Mag., English Misc., Giorn. Stor. d. Lett. Ital., Ital. Studies, Lettere Italiane, Lingua Nostra, Rassegna d. Lett. Ital., Rinascimento, The Year's Work in Mod. Languages. *Recreation:* music. *Address:* 11 Norham Road, Oxford OX2 6SF. *T:* (01865) 557045. *Died 29 April 1998.*

GREEN, Prof. Albert Edward, PhD, ScD; FRS 1958; Sedleian Professor of Natural Philosophy, University of Oxford, 1968–77, then Emeritus Professor; Supernumerary Fellow, The Queen's College, Oxford, since 1977 (Fellow, 1968–77); *b* 11 Nov. 1912; *m* 1939, Gwendoline May Rudston. *Educ:* Jesus Coll., Cambridge (Scholar; PhD 1937; MA 1938; ScD 1943). Fellow, Jesus Coll., Cambridge, 1936–39; Lecturer in Mathematics, Durham Colla, University of Durham, 1939–48; Prof. of Applied Mathematics, University of Newcastle upon Tyne, 1948–68. Hon. DSc: Durham, 1969; NUI, 1977; Hon. LLD Glasgow, 1975. Timoshenko Medal, ASME, 1974; Theodore von Karmen Medal, ASCE, 1983. *Address:* 25 Ritchie Court, 380 Banbury Road, Oxford OX2 7PW. *Died 12 Aug. 1999.*

GREEN, Benny; free-lance writer; *b* 9 Dec. 1927; *s* of David Green and Fanny Trayer; *m* 1962, Antoinette Kanal; three *s* one *d. Educ:* Clipstone Street Junior Mixed; subsequently uneducated at St Marylebone Grammar Sch. Mem., West Central Jewish Lads Club (now extinct). Saxophonist, 1947–60 (Most Promising New Jazz Musician, 1953); Jazz Critic, Observer, 1958–77; Literary Critic, Spectator, 1970–80; Film Critic, Punch, 1972–77, TV Critic, 1977–87; frequent radio and TV appearances, 1955–. Artistic Dir, New Shakespeare Co., 1973–; Mem., BBC Archives Cttee, 1976. Book and lyrics, Boots with Strawberry Jam, Nottingham Playhouse, 1968; revised libretto, Showboat, Adelphi Theatre, London, 1972; co-deviser: Cole, Mermaid, 1974; Oh, Mr Porter, Mermaid, 1977; lyrics, Bashville, Open Air Theatre, 1983–84; lyrics, Valentine's Day, Chichester Fest. Theatre, 1992, Globe Theatre, 1993. Sony Radio Award for best popular music series, 1984. *Publications:* The Reluctant Art, 1962; Blame it on my Youth, 1967; 58 Minutes to London, 1969; Drums in my Ears, 1973; I've Lost my little Willie, 1976; Swingtime in Tottenham, 1976; (ed) Cricket Addict's Archive, 1977; Shaw's Champions, 1978; Fred Astaire, 1979; (ed) Wisden Anthology, vol. I 1864–1900, 1979, vol. II 1900–1940, 1980, vol. III 1940–1963, 1982, vol. IV 1963–1982, 1983; P. G. Wodehouse: a literary biography, 1981; Wisden Book of Obituaries, 1986; (ed) The Last Empires, 1986; (ed) The Lord's Companion, 1987; (ed) A Hymn to Him, 1987; A History of Cricket, 1988; Let's Face the Music, 1989; (ed) The Wisden Papers

1888–1946, 1989; The Concise Wisden: an illustrated anthology of 125 years, 1990. *Recreation:* cricket. *Address:* c/o New Shakespeare Company, Regent's Park, NW1; c/o BBC, Broadcasting House, Portland Place, W1A 1AA. *Died 22 June 1998.*

GREEN, Sir (Edward) Stephen (Lycett), 4th Bt *cr* 1886, of Wakefield, Yorkshire and Ken Hill, Norfolk; CBE 1964; JP; Chairman, East Anglian Regional Hospital Board, 1959–74; *b* 18 April 1910; *s* of Sir E. A. Lycett Green, 3rd Bt, and Elizabeth Williams; *S* father, 1941; *m* 1935, Constance Mary, *d* of late Ven. H. S. Radcliffe; one *d. Educ:* Eton; Magdalene Coll., Cambridge. Called to Bar, Lincoln's Inn, 1933. Served War of 1939–45 (Major, RA). CC 1946–49, JP 1946, DL 1963–88, High Sheriff 1973, Norfolk; Dep. Chairman Norfolk QS, 1948–71. Chairman: King's Lynn Hospital Management Cttee, 1948–59; Assoc. of Hosp. Management Cttees, 1956–58; Cttee of Inquiry into Recruitment, Training and Promotion of Administrative and Clerical Staff in Hospital Service, 1962–63; Docking RDC, 1950–57. *Recreations:* shooting, watching TV, reading. *Heir: b* Lt-Col Simon Lycett Green, TD, Yorks Dragoons Yeomanry [*b* 11 July 1912; *m* 1st, 1935, Gladys (marr. diss. 1971; she *d* 1980), *d* of late Arthur Ranicar, JP, Springfield, Wigan; one *d*; 2nd, 1971, Mary, *d* of late George Ramsden]. *Address:* Ken Hill, Snettisham, King's Lynn PE31 7PG. *TA:* Snettisham, Norfolk. *T:* Heacham (01485) 570001. *Clubs:* White's, Pratt's; Norfolk (Norwich); Allsorts (Norfolk). *Died 13 May 1996.*

GREEN, John Dennis Fowler; *b* 9 May 1909; *s* of late Capt. Henry and Amy Gertrude Green, Chedworth, Glos; *m* 1946, Diana Judith, JP (*d* 1996), *y d* of late Lt-Col H. C. Elwes, DSO, MVO, Colesbourne, Glos. *Educ:* Cheltenham Coll.; Peterhouse, Cambridge. President of the Cambridge Union. Called to Bar, Inner Temple, 1933 (Entrance Scholar). BBC, 1934–62 (Controller, Talks Div., 1956–61); established agricultural broadcasting, 1935. Special Agric. Mission to Aust. and NZ (MAFF), 1945–47; Pres. National Pig Breeders Assoc., 1955–56; Chm., Agricultural Adv. Council, 1963–68; Exec. Mem., Land Settlement Assoc., 1965–80. Council for the Protection of Rural England: Mem., Nat. Exec., 1967–80; Pres., Glos. Br., 1985–98 (Chm., 1964–85). Dep. Pres., 1983–84, Trustee, 1984–99, RASE (FRASE 1990; Gold Medal, 1997); Fellow, Royal Agricl Soc. of the Commonwealth, 1991. Chm., Cirencester and Tewkesbury Conservative Assoc., 1964–78. *Publications:* Mr Baldwin: A Study in Post War Conservatism, 1933; articles and broadcasts on historical and agricultural subjects. *Recreations:* livestock breeding, forestry, shooting. *Address:* The Manor, Chedworth, Cheltenham GL54 4AA. *T:* (01285) 720233. *Clubs:* Oriental, Farmers'. *Died 25 March 2000.*

GREEN, Julian Hartridge; American and French writer; *b* Paris, France, 6 Sept. 1900; *s* of Edward M. Green and Mary Adelaide Hartridge; one adopted *s. Educ:* Lycée Janson, Paris; Univ. of Virginia. Mem., Académie Française, 1971–96. Member: Raven Club, 1922; Phi Beta Kappa, 1948; Jefferson Alumni Soc., 1972. *Publications: fiction:* The Apprentice Psychiatrist, 1920; Le voyageur sur la terre, 1924, new enl. edn 1979; Mont-Cinère, 1926; Adrienne Mesurat, 1927; Les clés de la mort, 1928; Léviathan, 1929; L'autre sommeil, 1930; Epaves, 1932; Le visionnaire, 1934; Minuit, 1936; Varouna, 1940; Si j'étais vous ...., 1947; Moira, 1950; Le malfaiteur, 1956, new enl. edn 1974; Chaque homme dans sa nuit, 1960; L'autre, 1971; La nuit des fantômes, 1976; Le Mauvais Lieu, 1977; Histoires de Vertige, 1984; Les Pays Lointains, 1987; Les Etoiles du Sud, 1989; Merveilles & Démons (trans. of Lord Dunsany's Tales), 1991; Ralph et la quatrième dimension, 1991; Dixie, 1995; *plays:* Sud,

1953; L'ennemi, 1954; L'ombre, 1956; Demain n'existe pas, 1979; L'automate, 1980; L'étudiant roux, 1993; *autobiography and journals:* Memories of Happy Days, 1942; Jeunes Années: i, Partir avant le jour, 1963; ii, Mille chemins ouverts, 1964; iii, Terre lointaine, 1966; iv, Jeunesse, 1974; Ce qu'il faut d'amour à l'homme, 1978; On est si sérieux quand on a 19 ans, Journal 1919–24, 1993; Journal: i, Les années faciles, 1928–34, 1938; ii, Derniers beaux jours, 1935–39, 1939; La fin d'un monde: Juin 1940, 1992; iii, Devant la porte sombre, 1940–43, 1946; iv, L'œil de l'ouragan, 1943–45, 1949; v, Le revenant, 1946–50, 1952; vi, Le miroir intérieur, 1950–54, 1955; vii, Le bel aujourd'hui, 1955–58, 1958; viii, Vers l'invisible, 1958–66, 1967; ix, Ce qui reste de jour, 1967–72, 1972; x, La bouteille à la mer, 1972–76, 1976; xi, La Terre est si belle, 1976–78, 1982; xii, La lumière du monde, 1978–81, 1983; xiii, L'arc-en-ciel, 1981–84, 1988; xiv, L'expatrié, 1984–90, 1990; xv, L'avenir n'est à personne, 1990–92, 1993; xvi, Pourquoi suis-je moi, 1993–96, 1996; Dans la gueule du temps (illust. jl), 1979; Journal du Voyageur (illust. jl), 1985; Œuvres complètes (La Pléiade), vol. I, 1972; vols II and III, 1973; vols IV and V, 1974; vol. VI, 1990; vol. VII, 1994; vol. VIII, 1998; Album de la Pléiade, 1998; *history:* Suite Anglaise, 1925; Frère François, 1983; *essays:* Pamphlet contre les catholiques de France, 1924; Liberté Chérie, 1974; Qui sommes-nous?, 1971; Une grande amitié: correspondance avec Jacques Maritain, 1982; Paris, 1983; *bilingual essays:* Le Langage et son double, 1985; L'homme et son ombre, 1991; Les statues parlent, 1991; The Apprentice Writer, 1992; *poem:* Dionysos et la chasse aventureuse, 1994. *Address:* Editions de la Pléiade, 5 rue Sébastien-Bottin, 75007 Paris, France. *Died 13 Aug. 1998.*

GREEN, Sir Peter (James Frederick), Kt 1982; Chairman, Janson Green Holdings Ltd, 1986–89 (Chairman, Janson Green Ltd, 1966–86); Chairman, Lloyd's, 1980, 1981, 1982, 1983; *b* 28 July 1924; *s* of J. E. Green and M. B. Holford; *m* 1st, 1950, A. P. Ryan (*d* 1985); 2nd, 1986, Jennifer Whitehead. *Educ:* Harrow Sch.; Christ Church, Oxford. Lloyd's: Underwriter, 1947; Mem. Cttee, 1974–77; Dep. Chm., 1979; Gold Medal, 1983. *Recreations:* shooting, fishing, sailing, farming. *Clubs:* City of London, Royal Ocean Racing, Pratt's; Royal Yacht Squadron (Cowes); Cruising of America (New York); Mount Royal (Montreal). *Died 27 July 1996.*

GREEN, Sam, CBE 1960; Chairman: Dula (ISMA) Ltd, since 1969; Green & Associates Ltd, since 1970; Spear Bros Ltd, since 1970; Vice Chairman, Royal British Legion Poppy Factory, Richmond (Director since 1964); Director, Royal British Legion Industries, since 1967; *b* Oldham, Lancs, 6 Feb. 1907; *s* of Fred Green; *m* 1942, Dr Lilly (*née* Pollak); one *d.* *Educ:* Manchester Coll. of Technology. Apprentice, Platt Bros, Oldham, 1920–34; Designer and Development Engr, British Northrop Automatic Loom Co., Blackburn, 1934–39 (invented 4-colour loom); Chief Engr, Betts & Co., London, 1939–42; Works Manager, Morphy-Richards Ltd, St Mary Cray, Kent, 1942–44; General Works Manager, Holoplast Ltd, New Hythe, near Maidstone, 1944–47; Industrial Adviser, Industrial and Commercial Finance Corp., London, 1947–52; Managing Dir of Remploy Ltd, 1952–64; Chm. and Man. Dir, Ralli Bros (Industries) Ltd, 1964–69; Chm., Industrial Advisers to the Blind, 1964–74; Director: J. E. Lesser Group Ltd, 1969–74; New Day Holdings Ltd, 1972–74. Chm., Inst. of Patentees and Inventors, 1975 (Vice-Chm., 1961); Vice Pres., Internat. Fedn of Inventors' Assocs, 1984–. FRSA 1962. CEng; FIEE. Gold Medal, World Intellectual Property Orgn, 1984. *Recreations:* reading, gardening, cycling, walking, golf. *Address:* Holly Lodge, 39 Westmoreland Road,

Bromley, Kent BR2 0TF. *T:* 0181–460 3306. *Clubs:* Reform, Directors', Pickwick (oldest Bicycle Club).
Died 21 Jan. 1996.

GREEN, Sir Stephen; *see* Green, Sir E. S. L.

GREENBAUM, Prof. Sidney; Director of the Survey of English Usage, since 1983, and Research Professor, since 1995, University College London; *b* 31 Dec. 1929; *s* of Lewis and Nelly Greenbaum. *Educ:* Univ. of London (BA Hons and MA Hebrew and Aramaic; Postgrad. Cert. in Educn; BA Hons English; PhD Mod. English Grammar). Teacher at London primary sch., 1954–57; Head of English Dept at London grammar sch., 1957–64; Research asst, Survey of English Usage, UCL, 1965–68; Vis. Asst Prof., English Dept, Univ. of Oregon, 1968–69; Associate Prof., English Dept, Univ. of Wisconsin-Milwaukee, 1969–72; Vis. Prof., English Dept, Hebrew Univ., Jerusalem, 1972–73; Prof., English Dept, Univ. of Wisconsin-Milwaukee, 1972–83; University College London: Quain Prof. of English Lang. and Lit., 1983–90; Dean of the Faculty of Arts, 1988–90; Vis. Prof., English Dept, 1990–95; Dean, Faculty of Arts, London University, 1986–88. Hon. DH Wisconsin-Milwaukee, 1989. Editor of series: (with C. Cooper) Written Communication Annual, 1984–91; Studies in English Language, 1987–. *Publications:* Studies in English Adverbial Usage, 1969; Verb-Intensifier Collocations in English: an experimental approach, 1970; (with R. Quirk) Elicitation Experiments in English: linguistic studies in use and attitude, 1970; (jtly) A Grammar of Contemporary English, 1972; (with R. Quirk) A University Grammar of English (Amer. edn A Concise Grammar of Contemporary English), 1973; Acceptability in Language, 1977; (jtly) Studies in English Linguistics: for Randolph Quirk, 1980; The English Language Today, 1985; (jtly) A Comprehensive Grammar of the English Language, 1985; (with C. Cooper) Studying Writing: linguistic approaches, 1986; (with J. Whitcut) rev. edn of Gower's Complete Plain Words, 1986; Good English and the Grammarian, 1988; (with J. Whitcut) Longman Guide to English Usage, 1988; A College Grammar of English, 1989; (with R. Quirk) A Student's Grammar of the English Language, 1990; An Introduction to English Grammar, 1991; (associate editor and contrib.) The Oxford Companion to the English Language, 1992; The Oxford English Grammar, 1996; Comparing English Worldwide: the international corpus of English, 1996; numerous articles in learned jls. *Address:* Department of English, University College London, Gower Street, WC1E 6BT. *T:* 0171–387 7050. *Club:* Reform.
Died 28 May 1996.

GREENBOROUGH, Sir John Hedley, KBE 1979 (CBE 1975); Chairman, Newarthill, 1980–93; Deputy Chairman: Bowater Industries (formerly Bowater Corporation), 1984–87 (Director, since 1979); Lloyds Bank, 1985–92 (Director, since 1980); *b* 7 July 1922; *s* of William Greenborough and Elizabeth Marie Greenborough (*née* Wilson); *m* 1951, Gerta Ebel; one step *s.* *Educ:* Wandsworth School. War service: Pilot, RAF, later Fleet Air Arm, 1942–45; graduated Pensacola; Naval Aviator, USN, 1944. Joined Asiatic Petroleum Co., London, 1939; served with Shell Oil, Calif, 1946–47; Shell Brazil Ltd, 1948–57; Commercial Dir, later Exec. Vice-Pres., Shell Argentina Ltd, Buenos Aires, 1960–66; Area Coordinator, East and Australasia, Shell Internat., London, 1967–68; Man. Dir (Marketing), Shell-Mex and BP Ltd, 1969–71, Man. Dir and Chief Exec., 1971–75; Chm., UK Oil Pipelines Ltd, 1971–77; Dep. Chm., 1976–80, Man. Dir, 1976–78, Shell UK Ltd. Director: Laporte Industries (Hldgs), 1983–86; Hogg Robinson, subseq. Hogg Gp, 1980–91. President of Confederation of British Industry, 1978–80 (Mem. Council, 1971–). Chairman: UK Oil Ind. Emergency Cttee, 1971–80; UK Petroleum Ind. Adv.

Cttee, 1971–77; Member: British Productivity Council, 1969–72; Clean Air Council, 1971–75; Bd of Fellows, BIM, 1973–78 (Chm., 1976–78); NEDC, 1977–80; Vice-Chairman: British Chamber of Commerce in Argentina, 1962–66; British Road Fedn, 1969–75. President: Nat. Soc. for Clean Air, 1973–75; Incorporated Soc. of British Advertisers (ISBA), 1976–78; Inst. of Petroleum, 1976–78; Nat. Council for Voluntary Orgns, 1980–86; Strategic Planning Soc., 1986–. Chm., Review Body for Nursing and Midwifery Staff and Professions Allied to Medicine, 1983–86. Fellow, Inst. Petroleum; CIMgt; FCIM (Vice-Pres., 1982–91); Hon. Fellow, UMDS, 1995. Mem., Management Bd, Adam Smith Inst., 1989–. Governor, Ashridge Management Coll., 1972– (Chm., 1977–92; Pres., 1992–); Chm. Governing Council, UMDS of Guy's and St Thomas' Hosps, 1982–89. Liveryman, Co. of Distillers, 1975. Freeman, City of London. Hon. LLD Birmingham, 1983. *Recreations:* golf, travel, music. *Clubs:* Carlton, MCC; Royal and Ancient Golf; Royal Wimbledon Golf.   *Died 3 July 1998.*

GREENHILL OF HARROW, Baron *cr* 1974 (Life Peer), of the Royal Borough of Kensington and Chelsea; **Denis Arthur Greenhill,** GCMG 1972 (KCMG 1967; CMG 1960); OBE (mil.) 1941; HM Government Director, British Petroleum Co. Ltd, 1973–78; Member, Security Commission, 1973–82; *b* 7 Nov. 1913; *s* of James and Susie Greenhill, Loughton; *m* 1941, Angela McCulloch; one *s* (and one *s* decd). *Educ:* Bishop's Stortford Coll.; Christ Church, Oxford (Hon. Student 1977). Served War of 1939–45 (despatches twice): Royal Engineers; in Egypt, N Africa, Italy, India and SE Asia; demobilised with rank of Col. Entered Foreign Service, 1946; served: Sofia, 1947–49; Washington, 1949–52, Foreign Office, 1952–54; Imperial Defence Coll., 1954; UK Delegation to NATO, Paris, 1955–57; Singapore, 1957–59; Counsellor, 1959–62; Minister, Washington DC, 1962–64; Asst Under-Sec. of State, FO, 1964–66; Dep. Under-Sec. of State, FO, 1966–69; Perm. Under-Sec. of State, FCO, and Head of the Diplomatic Service, 1969–73. Director: S. G. Warburg & Co., 1974–87 (Adviser, 1987–95); Clerical Medical and General Assce Soc., 1974–86; Wellcome Foundn Ltd, 1974–85; BAT Industries Ltd, 1974–83; Hawker Siddeley Group, 1974–84; Leyland International, 1977–82; Mem., Internat. Adv. Cttee, First Chicago Ltd, 1976–81. A Governor of the BBC, 1973–78. Mem., several H of L Select Cttees on European Communities, 1985–. Governor, BUPA, 1978–84, Dep. Chm., 1979–84. President: Royal Soc. for Asian Affairs, 1976–84; Anglo-Finnish Soc., 1981–84. Chm., KCH Med. Sch. Council, 1977–83; Fellow, King's Coll., London, 1984. Trustee, Rayne Foundn, 1974; Governor, Wellington Coll., 1974–83; Chm. of Governors, SOAS, 1978–85. Grand Cross, Order of the Finnish Lion, 1984. *Publication:* More By Accident (memoirs), 1992. *Address:* 25 Hamilton House, Vicarage Gate, W8 4HI. *T:* (020) 7937 8362. *Club:* Travellers.   *Died 8 Nov. 2000.*

GREENING, Wilfrid Peter, FRCS; Consultant Surgeon to Royal Marsden Hospital, 1952–79; Consulting Surgeon, Charing Cross Hospital, since 1975; *b* 16 May 1914; *s* of Rev. W. Greening and M. M. Waller, Saxlingham, Norfolk; *m* 1st, 1939, Hilary Berryman (marr. diss. 1961); one *d*; 2nd, 1962, Susan Ann Clair Huber (marr. diss. 1977); 3rd, 1978, Touba Ghazinoor. *Educ:* St Edmund's Sch., Canterbury; King's Coll. London; Charing Cross Hospital Medical Sch. MRCS, LRCP 1937; FRCS 1939. Houseman and Surgical Registrar, Charing Cross Hosp., 1938. Served War of 1939–45 (despatches); Wing Comdr i/c Surgical Div., RAFVR, 1943. Surgical Registrar, Gordon Hospital, 1946; Consultant Surgeon: Woolwich Hospital, 1948; Bromley and District Hospital, 1947–66. Lecturer in Surgery to Charing Cross Hospital Medical School.

Publications: contributions to medical literature. *Recreations:* fishing, golf. *Club:* Garrick.
                    Died 20 June 1999.

GREENWOOD, 2nd Viscount *cr* 1937, of Holbourne, co. London; **David Henry Hamar Greenwood;** Baron 1929; Bt 1915; *b* 30 Oct. 1914; *e s* of 1st Viscount Greenwood, PC, KC, and Margery, DBE (*d* 1968), 2nd *d* of Rev. Walter Spencer; *S* father, 1948; unmarried. *Educ:* privately and at Bowers Gifford. Agriculture and farming. *Heir: b* Hon. Michael George Hamar Greenwood, *b* 5 May 1923. *Recreations:* shooting, reading.
                    Died 30 July 1998.

GREGORY, Michael Anthony, OBE 1990; freelance journalist and author; Chief Legal Adviser, Country Landowners' Association, 1977–90; *b* 8 June 1925; *s* of late Wallace James Ignatius Gregory, FRIBA, FRICS, AMIMechE, and Dorothy Gregory; *m* 1951, Patricia Ann, *d* of late Frank and Gwendoline Hodges; three *s* four *d* (and one *d* decd). *Educ:* Douai Sch.; University Coll. London (LLB). Served RAF, Air Navigator, 1943–47. Called to the Bar, Middle Temple, 1952; practised at Bar, 1952–60; Legal Dept, Country Landowners' Assoc., 1960–90. Trustee, CLA Charitable Trust, 1980–. Member: BSI Cttee on Installation of Pipelines in Land, 1965–83; Thames Water Authority (later NRA (Thames), then Environment Agency) Reg. Fisheries Adv. Cttee, 1974–; Inland Waterways Amenity Adv. Council, 1982–92; Council, John Eastwood Water Protection Trust, 1984–95. Hon. Legal Advr, Nat. Anglers' Council, 1968–91; Pres., Basingstoke Canal Angling Assoc., 1991–97; Member Council: Salmon and Trout Assoc., 1980–90; Anglers' Co-op. Assoc., 1980–. Founder Mem., Agricl Law Assoc., 1975. Hon. Sec., Soc. of Our Lady of Good Counsel, 1953–58; Mem., Management Cttee, Bourne Trust (formerly Catholic Social Services for Prisoners), 1952–93 (Chm., 1960–71 and 1974–85; Hon. Sec., 1953–60); Pres., Douai Soc., 1984–86. Chairman: Internat. Help for Children, Fleet and Dist Br., 1967–77; Fleet United Bowling Club, 1992–95; Mcm. Cttee, 1981–, and Trustee, 1987–, Fedn for Promotion of Horticulture for Disabled People. Papal medal *pro ecclesia et pontifice,* 1988. *Publications:* Angling and the Law, 1967, 2nd edn 1974, supp. 1976; Organisational Possibilities in Farming, 1968; (with C. Townsend) Joint Enterprises in Farming, 1968, 2nd edn 1973; title, Pipelines, for Encyclopaedia of Forms and Precedents, 1970; (with Richard Seymour) All for Fishing, 1970; (contrib.) Walmsley's Rural Estate Management, 6th edn 1978; (with G. R. Williams) Farm Partnerships, 1979; (with Margaret Parrish) Essential Law for Landowners and Farmers, 1980, 3rd edn (with Angela Sydenham), 1990; (with Richard Stratton and G. R. Williams) Share Farming, 1983, 2nd edn 1985; (contrib.) Agriculture, Conservation and Land Use, ed Howarth and Rodgers, 1992; Conservation Law in the Countryside, 1994; numerous articles, booklets, short stories. *Recreations:* fishing, ball and saloon games, music, playing saxophones. *Address:* Beam Ends, Dipley Common, Hartley Wintney, Hook, Hampshire RG27 8JS. *T:* (01252) 842559, *Fax:* (01252) 845698.
                    Died 8 Feb. 1999.

GREGORY, Roland Charles Leslie Gregory, (Roy), CBE 1973; QC 1982; *b* 16 Jan. 1916; *s* of Charles James Alfred and Lilian Eugenie Gregory; *m* 1st, 1949, Olive Elizabeth (*d* 1973), *d* of late Andrew Gay; one *s*; 2nd, 1974, Charlotte, *d* of late Lt-Col Peter Goddard, MBE. *Educ:* Strand Sch.; London Univ. (LLB Hons). Served in Army, 1941–42. Called to Bar, Gray's Inn, 1950. First entered Civil Service, 1933; Head of Civil Procedure Br., Lord Chancellor's Office, 1966–79, retired; Consultant, 1979–82. Secretary: Austin Jones Cttee on County Court Procedure, 1947–49; Evershed Cttee on Supreme Court

Practice and Procedure, 1949–53; County Court Rule Cttee, 1962–79; Matrimonial Causes Rule Cttee, 1967–79; Asst Sec., Supreme Court Rule Cttee, 1968–79; Chm., Working Party on Revision of County Court Rules, 1979–81; Mem., Expert Cttees of Council of Europe, 1978–82. *Publications:* County Court Manual, 1st edn 1946 to 4th edn 1962; co-editor, County Court Practice, annually, 1950–; contribs to legal publications on civil procedure. *Recreations:* music, travel. *Address:* 36 Howard Avenue, Ewell, Surrey KT17 2QJ. *T:* (0181) 393 8933. *Died 4 July 1997.*

GREGSON, William Derek Hadfield, CBE 1970; DL; company director; Deputy Chairman, British Airports Authority, 1975–85; *b* 27 Jan. 1920; *s* of William Gregson; *m* 1944, Rosalind Helen Reeves (*d* 1994); three *s* one *d.* *Educ:* King William's Coll., IoM; Alpine Coll., Villars; Faraday House Engrg College. DFH, CEng, FIEE, CIMgt, FIIM. Served with RAF, NW Europe, 1941–45 (Sqdn Ldr); Techn. Sales Man., Ferranti Ltd, Edinburgh, 1946–51, London Man., 1951–59; Asst Gen. Man., Ferranti (Scotland) Ltd, 1959–83; Director: Ferranti EI, New York, 1969–83; Ferranti Hldgs, 1983–85. Director: British Telecom Scotland (formerly Scottish Telecommunications Bd), 1977–85; Anderson Strathclyde plc, 1978–86; Brammer plc, 1983–88; East of Scotland Industrial Investments plc, 1980; Consultant to ICI, 1984–88. Chm., Scottish Gen. Practitioners Res. Support Unit, 1971–79; Dep. Chm., Scottish Council (Develt and Industry), 1982–88 (Dir, 1974–88); Member Council: Electronic Engrg Assoc., 1959–83 (Pres. 1963–64); Soc. of British Aerospace Companies, 1966–83 (Chm. Equipment Gp Cttee, 1967); BIM, 1975–80. British Electrical and Allied Manufacturers' Association: Chm. Industrial Control and Electronics Bd, 1964; Mem. Council, 1970; Chm., Measurement, Control and Automation Conference Bd, 1973; Dep. Pres., 1982–83; Pres., 1983–85. Member: BIM Adv. Bd for Scotland, 1969–85 (Chm., 1970–75); Electronics EDC, 1965–75; Bd of Livingston New Town, 1968–76; Jt BIM/NEDO Prof. Management Adv. Cttee on Indust. Strategy, 1976–78; Management Assoc. of SE Scotland, 1977 (Chm., 1980–81); Scottish Econ. Planning Council, 1965–71; Machine Tool Expert Cttee, 1969–70; Scottish Design Council, 1974–81; Design Council, 1980–85; CBI (Mem.), Scottish Council, 1977–81); Bd, BSI, 1985–87; Edinburgh Chamber of Commerce, 1975–83. Commissioner, Northern Lighthouse Bd, 1975–90 (Chm., 1979). Dir, Scottish Nat. Orch., 1977–85 (Vice-Chm., 1981–84; Chm., 1984–85). DL City of Edinburgh, 1984. FRSA. *Recreations:* reading, cabinet-making, automation in the home. *Address:* Murrayfield House, 66 Murrayfield Avenue, Edinburgh EH12 6AY. *T:* (0131) 337 3858. *Clubs:* Royal Air Force; New (Edinburgh). *Died 15 Dec. 1998.*

GREIG of Eccles, James Dennis, CMG 1967; *b* 14 July 1926; *o s* of late Dennis George Greig of Eccles and Florence Aileen Marjoribanks; *m* 1st, 1952, Pamela Marguerite Stock (marr. diss. 1960); one *s* one *d*; 2nd, 1960 (marr. diss. 1967); one *s*; 3rd, 1968, Paula Mary Sterling. *Educ:* Winchester Coll.; Clare Coll., Cambridge; London Sch. of Economics. Military Service (Lieut, The Black Watch, seconded to Nigeria Regt), 1944–47. HM Overseas Civil Service: Administrative Officer, Northern Nigeria, 1949–55; Fedn of Nigeria, 1955–59; Dep. Financial Sec. (Economics), Mauritius, 1960–64; Financial Secretary, Mauritius, 1964–67; retired voluntarily on Mauritius achieving internal self-government, 1967; with Booker Bros (Liverpool) Ltd, 1967–68; Head of Africa and Middle East Bureau, IPPF, 1968–76; Dir, Population Bureau, ODA, 1976–80; retired. *Recreations:* rough shooting, bowls, gardening, national hunt racing. *Address:* 6 Beverley Close, Barnes, SW13 0EH. *T:* (020) 8876

5354; The Braw Bothy, Eccles, Kelso, Roxburghshire TD5 7QS. *T:* (01890) 840544. *Clubs:* Hurlingham, Annabel's. *Died 15 May 2000.*

GRENYER, Herbert Charles, FRICS; Vice-President, London Rent Assessment Panel, 1973–79; Deputy Chief Valuer, Board of Inland Revenue, 1968–73; *b* 22 Jan. 1913; *s* of Harry John Grenyer and Daisy Elizabeth (*née* De Maid); *m* 1940, Jean Gladwell Francis; one *s* one *d.* *Educ:* Beckenham Grammar Sch. Joined Valuation Office, 1938; Dist Valuer, Cardiff, 1948; Suptg Valuer, 1959; Asst Chief Valuer, 1964. *Recreations:* golf, gardening, listening to music. *Address:* Old Rickford, Worplesdon, Surrey GU3 3PJ. *T:* Worplesdon (01483) 232173. *Died 4 May 1996.*

GRESWELL, Air Cdre Jeaffreson Herbert, CB 1967; CBE 1962 (OBE 1946); DSO 1944; DFC 1942; RAF, retired; *b* 28 July 1916; *s* of William Territt Greswell; *m* 1939, Gwyneth Alice Hayes; one *s* two *d* (and one *d* decd). *Educ:* Repton. Joined RAF, 1935, Pilot; served War of 1939–45: in Coastal Command, Anti-Submarine No 217 Sqdn, 1937–41; No 172 Sqdn, 1942; OC No 179 Sqdn, Gibraltar, 1943–44; Air Liaison Officer, Pacific Fleet, 1946–47; Staff of Joint Anti-Submarine Sch., 1949–52; Staff of Flying Coll., Manby, 1952–54; Planning Staff, Min. of Defence, 1954–57; OC, RAF Station Kinloss, 1957–59; Plans HQ, Coastal Comd, 1959–61; Standing Group Rep. to NATO Council, Paris, 1961–64; Commandant, Royal Observer Corps, 1964–68. Sqdn Ldr 1941; Wing Comdr 1942; Gp Capt. 1955; Air Cdre 1961. *Recreation:* croquet. *Address:* Red Cedars, Oddley Lane, Saunderton, Princes Risborough, Bucks HP27 9NQ. *Died 19 Nov. 2000.*

GREY OF CODNOR, 5th Baron *cr* 1397 (in abeyance 1496–1989); **Charles Legh Shuldham Cornwall-Legh,** CBE 1977 (OBE 1971); AE 1946; DL; *b* 10 Feb. 1903; *er s* of late Charles Henry George Cornwall Legh, High Legh Hall, Cheshire, and Geraldine Maud, *d* of Lt-Col Arthur James Shuldham, Royal Inniskilling Fusiliers; *S* to barony on termination of abeyance, 1989; *m* 1930, Dorothy (*d* 1993), *er d* of late J. W. Scott, Seal, Sevenoaks; one *s* two *d.* Served 1939–45 with AAF and RAF. JP Cheshire, 1938–73; High Sheriff, 1939; DL, 1949; CC, 1949–77 (Shadow Chm., 1973; Chm., 1974–76; Hon. Alderman, 1977). Chm., Cheshire Police Authority, 1957–74. *Heir:* *s* Hon. Richard Henry Cornwall-Legh [*b* 14 May 1936; *m* 1974, Joanna Storm, *y d* of Sir Kenelm Cayley, 10th Bt; three *s* one *d*]. *Address:* High Legh House, Knutsford, Cheshire WA16 0QR. *T:* (01925) 752303. *Clubs:* Carlton, MCC. *Died 23 Dec. 1996.*

GREY OF NAUNTON, Baron *cr* 1968 (Life Peer), of Naunton, co. Gloucester; **Ralph Francis Alnwick Grey,** GCMG 1964 (KCMG 1959; CMG 1955); GCVO 1973 (KCVO 1956); OBE 1951; Chancellor, University of Ulster, 1984–93 (New University of Ulster, 1980–84); Lord Prior of the Order of St John, 1988–91; *b* 15 April 1910; *o s* of late Francis Arthur Grey and Mary Wilkie Grey (*née* Spence); *m* 1944, Esmé, DStJ (*d* 1996), *d* of late A. V. and Florence Burcher, Remuera, Auckland, NZ, and *widow* of Pilot Officer Kenneth Kirkcaldie, RAFVR; two *s* one *d.* *Educ:* Scots Coll.; Wellington Coll., NZ; Auckland University Coll. (LLB); Pembroke Coll., Cambridge. Barrister and Solicitor of Supreme Court of New Zealand, 1932; Associate to Hon. Mr Justice Smith, 1932–36; Probationer, Colonial Administrative Service, 1936; Administrative Service, Nigeria: Cadet, 1937; Asst Financial Sec., 1949; Administrative Officer, Class I, 1951; Development Sec., 1952; Sec. to Governor-Gen. and Council of Ministers, 1954; Chief Sec. of the Federation, 1955–57; Dep. Gov.-Gen., 1957–59; Gov. and C-in-C, British Guiana, 1959–64; Governor and C-in-C of The Bahamas, 1964–68, and of the Turks and Caicos

Islands, 1965–68; Governor of N Ireland, 1968–73. Dep. Chm., Commonwealth Development Corp., 1973–79; Chm. 1979–80. Pres., Chartered Inst. of Secretaries, NI, 1970; Hon. Life Mem., NI Chamber of Commerce and Industry, 1970; Hon. Pres., Lisburn Chamber of Commerce, 1972–. Mem., Bristol Regional Bd, Lloyds Bank Ltd, 1973–81. Grand Pres., Royal Over-Seas League, 1993 (Pres., 1981–93; Chm. Central Council, 1976–81); President: Scout Council, NI, 1968–93; Britain–Nigeria Assoc., 1983–89; Overseas Service Pensioners' Assoc., 1983–97. Mem. Council, Cheltenham Ladies' College, 1975–87. Hon. Bencher: Inn of Court of N Ireland, 1970; Gray's Inn, 1991. Hon. Freeman: City of Belfast, 1972; Lisburn, 1975; Freeman, City of London, 1980. Hon. LLD: QUB, 1971; NUI, 1985; Hon. DLitt NUU, 1980; Hon. DSc Ulster, 1985. GCStJ (Bailiff of Egle, 1975–87; Chancellor of the Order, 1987–88); Kt Comdr, Commandery of Ards, 1968–76. GC Merito Melitense, 1989. *Recreation:* golf. *Address:* Overbrook, Naunton, near Cheltenham, Glos GL54 3AX. *T:* (01451) 850263. *Club:* Travellers.   *Died 17 Oct. 1999.*

GRIDLEY, 2nd Baron *cr* 1955; **Arnold Hudson Gridley;** *b* 26 May 1906; *er* surv. *s* of 1st Baron Gridley, KBE, Culwood, Lye Green, Chesham, Bucks, and Mabel, *d* of Oliver Hudson, Fakenham, Norfolk; *S* father, 1965; *m* 1948, Edna Lesley, *d* of late Richard Wheen, Shanghai, China; one *s* three *d*. *Educ:* Oundle. Colonial Civil Service, Malaya, 1928–57; interned during Japanese occupation in Changi Gaol, Singapore, 1941–45; returned to duty, 1946; Dep.-Comptroller of Customs and Excise, Malaya, 1956, retired 1957. Mem. Council and Exec. Cttee, Overseas Service Pensioners Assoc., 1961; Govt Trustee, Far East (POW and Internee) Fund, 1971–94; with Parly Delegn to BAOR, 1976; visited and toured Rhodesia during Lancaster House Conf., speaking to local civil servants on the future of their pensions, 1979; special duty in Singapore and Malaya (incl. commemoration of those who gave their lives, 1941–45), during visit of HRH the Duke of Kent, 1985. Dir, New Homes Bldg Soc., 1963 (incorp. into Britannia Bldg Soc., 1970); Chm., Centralised Audio Systems Ltd, 1971–86, Life Pres., 1987. Mem., Somerset CC Rating Appeals Tribunal, 1970–73; Political Adviser to Peoples' Trust for Endangered Species, 1979–88. Pres., Gillingham (Dorset) Civic Trust, 1992–. Chm., Board of Governors, Hall Sch., Bratton Seymour, Som, 1970–76. *Heir: s* Hon. Richard David Arnold Gridley [*b* 22 Aug. 1956; *m* 1983, Suzanne Elizabeth Ripper; one *s* one *d*]. *Address:* Coneygore, Stoke Trister, Wincanton, Somerset BA9 9PG. *T:* Wincanton (01963) 32209. *Club:* Royal Over-Seas League.   *Died 15 June 1996.*

GRIER, Patrick Arthur, OBE 1963; HM Diplomatic Service, retired; *b* 2 Dec. 1918; *s* of late Very Rev. R. M. Grier, Provost of St Ninian's Cath., Perth, and Mrs E. M. Grier; *m* 1946, Anna Fraembs, *y d* of Hüttendirektor H. Fraembs, Rasselstein, Neuwied, Germany; one *d*. *Educ:* Lancing; King's Coll., Cambridge (MA 1946). Served War of 1939–45 with RA and Indian Mountain Artillery, NW Frontier of India and Burma (Major). Kreis Resident Officer of Mönchen-Gladbach, 1946–47; Colonial Administrative Service, N Nigeria, 1947, later HMOCS; Clerk to Exec. Council, Kaduna, 1953–55; W African Inter-territorial Secretariat, Accra, 1955–57; Principal Asst Sec. to Governor of N Nigeria, 1957–59; Dep. Sec. to Premier, 1959–63; retired from HMOCS, 1963; CRO, 1963–64; First Sec., Canberra, 1964–66; Head of Chancery, Port of Spain, 1966–69; Dep. UK Permanent Rep. to Council of Europe, Strasbourg, 1969–74; Counsellor and Head of Chancery, Berne, 1974–78. *Recreations:* tennis, ski-ing. *Address:* Buffalo Cottage, Wootton, New Milton, Hants BH25 5TT. *T:* (01425) 618398. *Club:* Royal Commonwealth Society.
                                    Died 30 June 1999.

GRIEVE, William Percival, (W. Percy Grieve); QC 1962; a Recorder, 1972–87 (Recorder of Northampton, 1965–71); *b* 25 March 1915; *o s* of 2nd Lieut W. P. Grieve, the Middlesex Regt (killed in action, Ypres, Feb. 1915), Rockcliffe, Dalbeattie, and Dorothy Marie Hartley (she *m* 2nd, 1925, Dr W. Cunningham, Monkseaton); *m* 1949, Evelyn Raymonde Louise (*d* 1991), *y d* of late Comdt Hubert Mijouain, Paris, and of Liliane, *e d* of late Sir George Roberts, 1st and last Bt; one *s* (and one *s* one *d* decd). *Educ:* privately; Trinity Hall, Cambridge (Exhibitioner, 1933); Lord Kitchener Nat. Memorial Schol., 1934; MA 1940. Called to Bar, Middle Temple, 1938 (Harmsworth Law Schol., 1937); Bencher, 1969; Master Reader, 1985; called to the Hong Kong Bar, 1960. Commissioned the Middlesex Regt, 1939; Liaison Officer, French Mil. Censorship, Paris, 1939–40; Min. of Information, 1940–41; HQ Fighting France, 1941–43; Staff Capt. and Exec. Officer, SHAEF Mission to Luxembourg, 1944; Major and GSO2 Brit. Mil. Mission to Luxembourg, 1945; DAAG, BAOR, 1946. Joined Midland Circuit, 1939; Asst Recorder of Leicester, 1956–65; Dep. Chm., Co. of Lincoln (Parts of Holland) QS, 1962–71. Mem. Mental Health Review Tribunal, Sheffield Region, 1960–64. Served on Gen. Council of the Bar. Contested (C) Lincoln, March 1962; MP (C) Solihull Div., Warks, 1964–83. Member: House of Commons Select Cttees on Race Relations and Immigration, 1968–70, on Members' Interests, 1979–83; UK Delegn, Council of Europe (Chm., Legal Affairs Cttee) and WEU (Chm. Procedure Cttee), 1969–83; Hon. Vice-Pres., Franco-British Parly Relations Cttee, 1975–83 (Chm., 1970–75); Chm., Luxembourg Soc., 1975; Chm., Parly Anglo Benelux Group, 1979–83; Hon. Associate: Council of Europe, 1989; WEU, 1990. Pres., Hammersmith and Fulham Cons. Assoc., 1995– (Fulham Cons. Assoc., 1982–95). Member: Council, Officers' Assoc., 1969–88; Council of Justice, 1971–; Council, Franco-British Soc., 1970; Council, Alliance Française, 1974–86. Officier avec Couronne, Order of Adolphe of Nassau; Chevalier, Order of Couronne de Chêne and Croix de Guerre avec Palmes (Luxembourg), 1945–46; Bronze Star (USA), 1945; Chevalier de la Légion d'Honneur, 1974; Commandeur de l'Ordre de Mérite (Luxembourg), 1976; Officier de l'ordre de la Couronne (Belgium), 1980; Silver Medal, Council of Europe, 1983; Commandeur de l'Ordre de la Couronne de Chêne (Luxembourg), 1990. *Recreations:* swimming, travel, the theatre. *Address:* 32 Gunterstone Road, W14 9BU. *T:* (0171) 603 0376. *Clubs:* Carlton, Hurlingham, Special Forces.
                                    Died 22 Aug. 1998.

GRIFFIN, Adm. Sir Anthony (Templer Frederick Griffith), GCB 1975 (KCB 1971; CB 1967); President, Royal Institution of Naval Architects, 1981–84; Chairman, British Shipbuilders, 1977–80 (Chairman-designate, Dec. 1975); *b* Peshawar, 24 Nov. 1920; *s* of late Col F. M. G. Griffin, MC, and B. A. B. Griffin (*née* Down); *m* 1943, Rosemary Ann Hickling; two *s* one *d*. *Educ:* RN Coll., Dartmouth. Joined RN, 1934; to sea as Midshipman, 1939; War Service in E Indies, Mediterranean, Atlantic, N Russia and Far East; specialised in navigation, 1944; Staff Coll., 1952; Imp. Defence Coll., 1963; comd HMS Ark Royal, 1964–65; Naval Secretary, 1966; Asst Chief of Naval Staff (Warfare), 1966–68; Flag Officer, Second-in-Command, Far East Fleet, 1968–69; Flag Officer, Plymouth, Comdr Central Sub Area, Eastern Atlantic, and Comdr Plymouth Sub Area, Channel, 1969–71; Adm. Supt Devonport, 1970–71; Controller of the Navy, 1971–75. Rear-Adm. of the UK, 1986–88; Vice-Adm., 1988–90. Comdr 1951; Capt. 1956; Rear-Adm. 1966; Vice-Adm. 1968; Adm., 1971. Vice-Pres., Wellington College, 1980–90; Chm., British Maritime League, 1982–87. Hon. FRINA 1984. *Recreation:* sailing. *Address:*

Moat Cottage, The Drive, Bosham, West Sussex PO18 8JG. *T:* (01243) 573373. *Clubs:* Army and Navy, Pratt's.
Died 16 Oct. 1996.

GRIFFIN, Col Edgar Allen, CMG 1965; OBE (mil.) 1943; ED 1945; Regional Director, Northern Region (Arras, France), Commonwealth War Graves Commission, 1969–72; *b* 18 Jan. 1907; 3rd *s* of Gerald Francis and Isabella Margaret Griffin; *m* 1936, Alethea Mary Byrne; two *s* two *d.* Asst Adjt and QMG, 3 Aust. Div., 1942–44; 5 Aust. Div., 1944–45; Grad., Sen. Wing, Aust. Mil. Staff Coll., 1944; Asst Adjt Gen. (Dir of PoWs and internees), Army HQ, Melbourne; retired from AMF, 1947; Australian Govt Nominee to Staff of War Graves Commn, 1947; Chief Admin. Officer, Eastern Dist (Cairo), 1947–54; UK Dist (London), 1954–58; Regional Dir, Southern Region (Rome), 1958–69. Chairman: Anglo-Amer. Hosp. Benevolent Fund, 1958–75; Commonwealth Club, Rome, 1968–69; Govs, English Sch., Rome, 1970–75. *Address:* 9 Arley Close, Plas Newton, Chester CH2 1NW.
Died 14 Sept. 1996.

GRIFFITHS, His Honour Bruce Fletcher; QC 1970; a Circuit Judge, 1972–86; *b* 28 April 1924; *s* of Edward Griffiths and Nancy Olga (*née* Fuell); *m* 1952, Mary Kirkhouse Jenkins, *y d* of late His Honour George Kirkhouse Jenkins, QC; two *s* one *d. Educ:* Whitchurch Grammar Sch., Cardiff; King's Coll., London. LLB (Hons) London, 1951 (Jelf Medallist); Cert. Theol. St David's UC, 1988. RAF, 1942–47. Chm., Local Appeals Tribunal (Cardiff), Min. of Social Security, 1964–70; an Asst Recorder of Cardiff, Swansea and Merthyr Tydfil, 1966–71; Vice-Chm., Mental Health Review Tribunal for Wales, 1968–72; Dep. Chm., Glamorgan QS, 1971; Comr of Assize, Royal Cts of Justice, London, 1971. Mem., Parole Bd, 1983–85. Chancellor, Dio. of Monmouth, 1977–92; President of Provincial Court, and Mem. Governing Body (Panel of Chairmen), Church in Wales, 1979–92. Chm., Welsh Sculpture Trust; former Mem., Welsh Arts Council, and Chm., Art Cttee; Chm., Contemp. Art Soc. for Wales, 1987–92 (Purchaser, 1975–76; Vice-Chm., 1977–87). *Address:* 15 Heol Don, Whitchurch, Cardiff CF4 2AR. *T:* (029) 2062 5001; 15 Carrer Alaró, Es Traves, Port de Soller, Mallorca, Spain. *T:* (71) 63380. *Clubs:* Naval and Military; Cardiff and County (Cardiff).
Died 17 Jan. 1999.

GRISEWOOD, Harman Joseph Gerard, CBE 1960; Chief Assistant to the Director-General, BBC, 1955–64, retired; *b* 8 Feb. 1906; *e s* of late Lieut-Col Harman Grisewood and Lucille Cardozo; *m* 1940, Clotilde Margaret Bailey; one *d. Educ:* Ampleforth Coll., York; Worcester Coll., Oxford. BBC Repertory Co., 1929–33; Announcer, 1933–36; Asst to Programme Organiser, 1936–39; Asst Dir Programme Planning, 1939–41; Asst Controller, European Div., 1941–45; Actg Controller, European Div., 1945–46; Dir of Talks, 1946–47; Planner, Third Programme, 1947–48; Controller of the Third Programme, BBC, 1948–52; Dir of the Spoken Word, BBC, 1952–55. Member: Younger Cttee on Privacy, 1970–72; Lord Chancellor's Cttee on Defamation, 1971; Res. Officer, Royal Commn on Civil Liberty, 1973–75. Vice-President: European Broadcasting Union, 1953–54; Royal Literary Fund. Chm., The Latin Mass Soc., 1969. King Christian X Freedom Medal, 1946. Mcm. Hon. Soc. of Cymmrodorion, 1956. Knight of Grace and Devotion, SMO Malta, 1960. *Publications:* Broadcasting and Society, 1949; The Recess (novel), 1963; The Last Cab on the Rank (novel), 1964; David Jones: Welsh National Lecture, 1966; One Thing at a Time (autobiog.), 1968; The Painted Kipper, 1970; Stratagem, 1987. *Address:* The Old School House, Castle Hill, Eye, Suffolk IP23 7AP.
Died 8 Jan. 1997.

GRONHAUG, Arnold Conrad; *b* 26 March 1921; *s* of James Gronhaug, MBE, and Beatrice May Gronhaug; *m* 1945, Patricia Grace Smith (*d* 1998); two *d. Educ:* Barry Grammar Sch.; Cardiff Technical Coll. CEng, FIEE; Hon. FCIBSE. Electrical Officer, RNVR, 1941–46. Air Ministry Works Directorate, 1946–63: Area Mech. and Elec. Engr, AMWD Malaya, 1951–52; Air Min. Headquarters, 1952–60; Dep. Chief Engr, AMWD, RAF Germany, 1960–63; Sen. Mech. and Elec. Engr, Portsmouth Area MPBW, 1963–67; Jt Services Staff Coll., 1964–65; Suptg Engr, MPBW, 1967–71; Dir Defence Works (Overseas), MPBW, 1971–73; Dir of Social and Research Services, DoE, 1973–75; Under Sec., and Dir of Engrg Services Develt, 1975–76; Dir of Mechanical and Electrical Engineering Services, 1976–81. Member: Engrg Council Nominations Cttee, 1983–96; IEE Membership Cttee, 1975–82 (Chm., 1979–82); CIBSE Qualifications Bd, 1981–87; IEE Memship Advr, Surrey, 1984–90. Freeman: City of London, 1979; Liveryman, Engineers' Co., 1984. *Recreations:* music, photography. *Address:* 6 Pine Hill, Epsom, Surrey KT18 7BG. *T:* (01372) 721888.
Died 8 Feb. 1999.

GROUNDS, Stanley Paterson, CBE 1968; Charity Commissioner, 1960–69; *b* 25 Oct. 1904; 2nd *s* of late Thomas Grounds and Olivia Henrietta (*née* Anear), Melbourne, Australia; *m* 1932, Freda Mary Gale Ransford (*d* 1994); twin *s* and *d. Educ:* Melbourne High Sch.; Queen's Coll., Melbourne Univ. (1st Cl. hons, MA). Called to the Bar, Middle Temple, 1933. Served Royal Air Force, 1940–45 (Squadron Leader). With Melbourne Herald, 1926–28; British Empire Producers' Organisation, London, 1928–33; at Chancery Bar, 1934–40; Asst Charity Commissioner, 1946–58; Sec., Charity Commission, 1958–60. *Publications:* contrib. Encyclopædia of Forms and Precedents, Encyclopædia of Court Forms (on Charities), Halsbury's Laws of England, 3rd edn (on Charities); articles in law jls. *Recreation:* keeping in touch. *Address:* St Helena, 19 Bell Road, Haslemere, Surrey GU27 3DQ. *T:* (01428) 651230.
Died 20 Jan. 1999.

GRUNFELD, Henry; Senior Adviser, Warburg Dillon Read (formerly SBC Warburg), since 1995; *b* 1 June 1904; *s* of Max Grunfeld and Rosa Grunfeld (*née* Haendler); *m* 1931, Berta Lotte Oliven (*d* 1993); one *s* (one *d* decd). Chairman, 1969–74, President, 1974–87, S. G. Warburg & Co. Ltd; Pres., S. G. Warburg Gp plc, 1987–95. *Address:* 1 Finsbury Avenue, EC2M 2PP. *T:* (020) 7567 8000.
Died 10 June 1999.

GRYN, Rabbi Hugo Gabriel, CBE 1992; Senior Rabbi, West London Synagogue, since 1964; *b* 25 June 1930; adopted British nationality, 1993; *s* of Bella and Geza Gryn; *m* 1957, Jacqueline Selby; one *s* three *d. Educ:* Univs of Cambridge, London and Cincinnati (BA, MA); Hebrew Union Coll., Cincinnati (BHL, MHL, DHL). Ordained rabbi, 1957; Rabbi, Jewish Religious Union, Bombay, 1957–60; Exec. Dir, World Union for Progressive Judaism, 1960–62; Senior Exec., American Jewish Jt Distrib. Cttee, 1962–64; Vice-Pres. and Lectr, Leo Baeck Coll., 1964–. Chairman: European Bd, World Union for Progressive Judaism, 1980–91; Standing Cttee for Interfaith Dialogue in Educn, 1972–; Joint Chairman: Interfaith Network (UK), 1987–94; London Rainbow Group, 1975–91; Pres., Reform Synagogues of GB, 1990–; Mem., numerous educnl and Jewish organisations. Hon. DD Hebrew Union Coll., 1982; DD London, 1995. *Publications:* Forms of Prayer, 1977; contribs to publications of Standing Conf. on Interfaith Dialogue in Educn, British Jl of Religious Educn, Jl of Central Conf. of Amer. Rabbis, Jewish Chronicle. *Recreations:*

swimming, travel, biblical archaeology. *Address:* 33 Seymour Place, W1H 6AT. *T:* 0171–723 4404.
Died 18 Aug. 1996.

GUDJONSSON, Halldór; *see* Laxness, H. K.

GUEST; *see* Haden-Guest.

GUEST, Douglas Albert, CVO 1975; FRCM, Hon. RAM, FRCO, FRSCM; Organist Emeritus, Westminster Abbey, since 1981; *b* 9 May 1916; 2nd *s* of late Harold Guest, Henley-on-Thames, Oxon; *m* 1941, Peggie Florentia, *d* of late Thomas Falconer, FRIBA, Amberley, Gloucestershire; two *d. Educ:* Reading Sch.; Royal College of Music, London; King's Coll., Cambridge (MusB, MA); MA Oxon. Organ Scholar, King's Coll., Cambridge, 1935–39; John Stewart of Rannoch Scholar in Sacred Music, Cambridge Univ., 1936–39. Served War of 1939–45, Major (Battery Comdr), Royal Artillery (HAC) (despatches, Normandy, 1944); gazetted Hon. Major, RA, April 1945. Dir of Music, Uppingham Sch., 1945–50; Organist and Master of the Choristers, Salisbury Cathedral, 1950–57; Conductor of Salisbury Musical Soc., 1950–57; Dir of Music, St Mary's Sch., Calne, 1950–57; Master of the Choristers and Organist, Worcester Cathedral, 1957–63; Conductor Worcester Festival Chorus and Three Choirs Festival, 1957–63; Organist and Master of the Choristers, Westminster Abbey, 1963–81. Examiner, Associated Bd of Royal Schs of Music, 1948–81; Prof., RCM, 1963–81. First Vice-Pres., National Youth Orchestra of Great Britain, 1984– (Chm. Council, 1953–84); Member Council: RCO, 1966; Musicians' Benevolent Fund, 1968. Hon. Mem., Royal Soc. of Musicians, 1963 . MusD Lambeth. *Recreations:* fly-fishing, golf. *Address:* The Gables, Minchinhampton, Glos GL6 9JE. *T:* Brimscombe 883191. *Club:* Flyfishers'. *Died 18 Nov. 1996.*

GUEST, Eric Ronald; Metropolitan Magistrate (West London), 1946–68; Barrister-at-law; *b* 7 June 1904; *s* of late William Guest; *m* 1932, Sybil Blakelock; one *d. Educ:* Berkhamsted Sch.; Oriel Coll., Oxford, BA 1925 (1st Class Hons Sch. of Jurisprudence); BCL 1926. Called to Bar, Inner Temple, 1927; practised in London and on Oxford Circuit; Recorder of Worcester, 1941–46. Served as Sqdn Leader with RAFVR, 1940–45.
Died 5 July 1997.

GUEST, Henry Alan, MBE 1990; Director, Rhodes Foods Ltd, since 1980 (Chairman, 1980–95); *b* 29 Feb. 1920; *m* 1947, Helen Mary Price; one *s* one *d. Educ:* Lindisfarne College. FHCIMA. War Service, 1940–46, France, India, Malaya; Captain RA. Supplies Manager, J. Lyons & Co. Ltd, Catering Div., 1955; Rank Organisation, Theatre Division: Dep. Controller, Catering, 1963; Controller, 1965; Group Catering Adviser, Associated British Foods, 1966; Chief Exec., Civil Service Catering Organisation, 1972–80. Mem. Royal Instn of Great Britain. *Publications:* papers on marketing and organisation in techn. jls and financial press. *Recreation:* swimming. *Address:* 14 Pensford Avenue, Kew, Surrey TW9 4HP.
Died 12 Nov. 1999.

GUEST, Trevor George; a District Judge (formerly Registrar of the Principal Registry), Family Division of the High Court of Justice, 1972–93; barrister; *b* 30 Jan. 1928; *m* 1951, Patricia Mary (*née* Morrison) (*d* 1983); two *d*; *m* 1988, Diane Constance (*née* Platts). *Educ:* Denstone Coll., Uttoxeter, Staffs; Birmingham Univ. (LLB Hons). Called to the Bar, Middle Temple, 1953. *Recreations:* dogs, Church affairs, gardening. *Address:* The Old Rectory, Purleigh, Essex CM3 6QH. *T:* (01621) 828375.
Died 5 Aug. 1999.

GUILFORD, 9th Earl of, *cr* 1752; **Edward Francis North;** DL; Baron Guilford 1683; *b* 22 Sept. 1933; *s* of Major Lord North (*d* 1940) and Joan Louise (she *m* 2nd, 1947, Charles Harman Hunt, and *d* 1993), *er d* of late Sir Merrik Burrell, 7th Bt, CBE; *S* grandfather, 1949; *m* 1956, Osyth Vere Napier (*d* 1992), *d* of Cyril Napier Leeston Smith; one *s. Educ:* Eton. FRSA 1976. DL Kent, 1976. *Heir: s* Lord North, *b* 9 March 1971. *Address:* Waldershare Park, Dover, Kent CT15 5BA. *T:* (01304) 820244.
Died 26 March 1999.

GUILLY, Rt Rev. Richard Lester, OBE 1945; SJ; *b* 6 July 1905; *s* of late Richard Guilly. *Educ:* Stonyhurst Coll.; Campion Hall, Oxford (Hons Mod. Hist.; BA, MA); Heythrop Coll. Entered Soc. of Jesus, 1924; Asst Master, Beaumont Coll., 1933–35; ordained 1938; served War of 1939–45, Chaplain to the Forces: BEF (France), 1939–40; CF 3rd Cl. 1940; Senior RC Chaplain, N Ireland, 1 Corps District, AA Comd, 2nd Army, 1940–45 (OBE, despatches); Superior of Soc. of Jesus in British Guiana and Barbados, 1946–54; Titular Bishop of Adraa and Vicar Apostolic of British Guiana and Barbados, 1954–56; Bishop of Georgetown, 1956–72; Parish Priest in Barbados, 1972–77 and 1981–93; Apostolic Administrator, Archdiocese of Castries, 1977–81. Dir, Caritas Antilles. *Publications:* various articles on Church history, Christian Social Doctrine and Church in Guyana. *Address:* Cathedral Presbytery, PO Box 97, Castries, St Lucia, West Indies. *Died 7 June 1996.*

GUINNESS, Sir Alec, CH 1994; Kt 1959; CBE 1955; actor; *b* Marylebone, 2 April 1914; *m* 1938, Merula Salaman; one *s. Educ:* Pembroke Lodge, Southbourne; Roborough, Eastbourne. On leaving school went into Arks Publicity, Advertising Agents, as copywriter; first professional appearance walking on in Libel at King's Theatre, Hammersmith, 1933; played Hamlet in modern dress, Old Vic, 1938; toured the Continent, 1939; served War of 1939–45: joined Royal Navy as a rating, 1941; commissioned 1942; rejoined Old Vic, 1946–47. Fellow, BAFTA, 1989. Hon. DFA Boston Coll., 1962; Hon. DLitt Oxon, 1977; Hon. LittD Cantab, 1991. Special Oscar, for contribution to film, 1979; Olivier Award for Services to the Theatre, SWET, 1989; Evening Standard Film Award for lifetime achievement, 1995. *Films included:* Great Expectations, 1946; Oliver Twist, 1949; Kind Hearts and Coronets, 1949; The Lavender Hill Mob, 1951; The Man in the White Suit, 1951; The Bridge on the River Kwai (Oscar for best actor of the year), 1957; Lawrence of Arabia, 1962; Star Wars, 1977; A Passage to India, 1984; Little Dorrit, 1987; A Handful of Dust, 1988. *Plays included:* The Cocktail Party, NY, 1950; Hamlet, 1951; Richard III, All's Well That Ends Well, 1953; Dylan, NY (Antoinette Perry Award), 1964; A Voyage Round My Father, 1971; Habeas Corpus, 1973; Yahoo, 1976; The Old Country, 1977; A Walk in the Woods, 1989; *television:* Tinker, Tailor, Soldier, Spy, 1979 (BAFTA Award, 1980); Smiley's People, 1981–82 (BAFTA Award, 1983); Tales from Hollywood, 1991; A Foreign Field, 1993; Eskimo Day, 1995. *Publications:* Blessings in Disguise (memoirs), 1985; My Name Escapes Me: the diary of a retiring actor, 1996; A Positively Final Appearance: a journal 1996–98, 1999. *Address:* c/o McReddie, 91 Regent Street, W1R 7TB. *Died 5 Aug. 2000.*

GULLIVER, James Gerald, CVO 1996; FRSE; Chairman, James Gulliver Associates Ltd, since 1977; *b* 17 Aug. 1930; *s* of William Frederick and Mary Gulliver; *m* 1st, 1958, Margaret Joan (*née* Cormack) (marr. diss.); three *s* two *d*; 2nd, 1977, Joanne (*née* Sims) (marr. diss.); 3rd, 1985, Marjorie H. Moncrieff (marr. diss. 1991); 4th, 1993, Melanie (*née* Crossley). *Educ:* Campbeltown Grammar Sch.; Univ of Glasgow; Georgia Inst. of Technol., USA. MICE. Royal Navy (Short Service Commn), 1956–59; Dir, Concrete (Scotland) Ltd, 1960–61; Management Consultant, Urwick, Orr & Partners Ltd, 1961–65; Man.

Dir, 1965–72, Chm., 1967–72, Fine Fare (Holdings) Ltd; Dir, Associated British Foods Ltd, 1967–72; Founder and Chm., James Gulliver Associates Ltd, subseq. Argyll Gp PLC, 1977–88; Chairman: Argyll Foods PLC, 1980–88; Broad Street Gp, 1987–90; Lowndes Queensway, 1988–90; non-executive Chairman: Select Country Hotels, 1986–89; Waverley Cameron, 1987–90; Jackson's of Bourne End, 1988–89; City Gate Estates, 1988–90; Ancasta Marine Hldgs, 1988–91. Vis. Prof., Glasgow Univ., 1985–. Mem. Council, Inst. of Directors, 1972–92; Vice-Pres., Marketing Soc. Chm., Prime Minister's Enquiry into Beef Prices, 1983; Member: Scottish Economic Council, 1985–93; Governing Council, Scottish Business in the Community, 1983–; Dir, Scottish Investment Trust, 1986–; Chm., Scottish Business Gp, 1988–92. Vice-Pres., Manchester United FC, 1984–. FRSE 1990; FInstD; FRSA; FIMgt. Freedom and Livery, Worshipful Co. of Gardeners. DUniv Glasgow, 1989. Guardian Young Businessman of the Year, 1972. *Recreations:* ski-ing, sailing, music, motoring. *Address:* 22 Godfrey Street, SW3 3TA.
Died 12 Sept. 1996.

GUMMER, Ellis Norman, CBE 1974 (OBE 1960); Assistant Director-General (Administration), British Council, 1972–75; *b* 18 June 1915; *o s* of late Robert Henry Gummer, engineer, and Mabel Thorpe, Beckenham, Kent; *m* 1949, Dorothy Paton Shepherd; one *s* (and one *s* decd). *Educ:* St Dunstan's Coll.; St Catherine's Society, Oxford (BLitt, MA). Library service: Nottingham Univ., 1939; Queen's Coll., Oxford, 1940–42; served War of 1939–45, Admty, 1942–45; British Council: East Europe Dept, 1945–50; Personnel Dept, 1950–52; Student Welfare Dept, 1952–59; Literature Group, 1959–61; Controller, Arts and Science Div., 1961–66; Controller, Finance Div., 1966–71. *Publication:* Dickens' Works in Germany, 1940. *Recreations:* books, topography, archaeology. *Address:* 9 Campden Street, W8 7EP. *T:* (020) 7727 4823.
Died 1 Nov. 1999.

GÜMRÜKÇÜOGLU, Rahmi Kamil, Hon. GCVO 1988; Co-Chairman, Euro Turkish Corporation, since 1990; *b* 18 May 1927; *m* Elçin; one *s* one *d*. *Educ:* Haydar Pasha Lycée, Istanbul; Faculty of Political Sciences, Ankara Univ. Master's degree in Pol Economy and Govt, Harvard Univ. Second Secretary, 1952–55, First Sec., 1955, Turkish Embassy, London; Head of Section dealing with Internat. Economic Affairs, Min. of Foreign Affairs, Ankara, 1958–60; Counsellor, Turkish Embassy, Cairo, 1960–63; Dep. Director General, Dept of Internat. Economic Affairs, Ankara, 1963–65; Head of Special Bureau dealing with Economic Co-operation between Turkey and the Soviet Union, 1965–67; Dir Gen., Dept of Internat. Economic Affairs, 1967–71; Turkish Ambassador: to Council of Europe, Strasbourg, 1971–75; to Iran, 1975–78; Sen. Advr to Min. of Foreign Affairs, 1978; Pres., Defence Industry Co-ordination Board, Ankara, 1978–79; Dep. Sec. Gen. for Economic Affairs, Min. of Foreign Affairs, 1979–81; Amb. to UK, 1981–88; Inspector, Min. of Foreign Affairs, 1989–90; Dep. Ldr for For. Affairs, Democratic Center Party, 1990–92. Actg Chm., Taturos Co., 1992–; Board Member: Turkish Airlines, 1992–; Degere Enterprises, 1992–; Kent Bank, 1992–; Petro-Chemical Industries, 1993–. *Publications:* various articles and booklets on foreign investment, questions of economic develt, Soviet economic develt, economic integration amongst developing countries. *Address:* Köybasi Caddesi 191, Yeniköy, Istanbul, Turkey.
Died 1 April 1998.

GUNN, (Alan) Richard, CBE 1991; High Commissioner for Eastern Caribbean States in London, 1987–94; *b* 19 Jan. 1936; *s* of Alan Leslie Gunn and Violet Gunn; *m* 1962, Flora Beryl (*née* Richardson); one *s* two *d*. *Educ:* Boys' Grammar Sch., St Vincent; Portsmouth College of Architecture; Regent Street Polytechnic, London. Marketing Dir, Hazells Ltd, St Vincent, 1968–74; Chm./ Man. Dir, Property Investments Ltd, St Vincent, 1974–87. Director: Vincentian Newspaper Ltd, 1970–; Caribbean Assoc. of Industry and Commerce, 1985–87; Chairman: St Vincent Chamber of Commerce, 1984–85; Nat. Shipping Corp., St Vincent, 1987; Nat. Broadcasting Corp., 1986–87; Sec.-Gen., Caribbean Assoc. of Industry and Commerce/EEC 'Europe-Caribbean Contact II', 1987. *Recreations:* yachting, fishing, reading. *Address:* Fairhall, PO Box 126, St Vincent and the Grenadines. *Clubs:* Royal Over-Seas League, Royal Commonwealth Society; St Vincent Yacht.
Died 6 April 1998.

H

HAAVELMO, Prof. Trygve Magnus; Norwegian economist; Professor of Economics, University of Oslo, since 1948; *b* 13 Dec. 1911; *s* of Halvor Haavelmo and Jenny Eugenie (*née* Gundersen). *Educ:* Oslo Univ. (Dr.phil 1946). Res. Asst, Cowles Commn, Univ. of Chicago, 1946–47. Leading pioneer in modern econometrics (quantitative economics). Pres., Econometric Soc., 1957. Member: Amer. Econ. Assoc.; Amer. Acad. of Arts and Letters. Nobel Prize for Economics, 1989. *Publications included:* Study in the Theory of Economic Evolution, 1954; Investment Decision, 1960. *Address:* Department of Economics, University of Oslo, POB 1095 Blindern, 0317 Oslo 3, Norway. *Died 28 July 1999.*

HACAULT, Most Rev. Antoine, STD; Archbishop of St Boniface, (RC), since 1974; *b* Bruxelles, Manitoba, 17 Jan. 1926. *Educ:* Sainte-Marie Elem. Sch., Bruxelles; St Boniface Coll. (BA 1947); St Boniface Major Seminary; Angelicum Univ., Rome (STD 1954). Priest, 1951; Prof. of Theology, St Boniface Major Seminary, 1954–64; Auxiliary Bishop of St Boniface and Titular Bishop of Media, 1964; also Rector, St Boniface College, 1967–69; Bishop Coadjutor of St Boniface, 1972–74. Member: Vatican Secretariat for Non-Believers, 1973–83; Vatican Secretariat for promoting Christian Unity, 1976–89; Pastoral Team, Canadian Catholic Conf. of Bishops, 1973–77 and 1983–87; Admin. Bd, St Boniface Gen. Hosp., 1981–; Gen. Bd of Canadian Council of Churches, 1986–. President: Canadian Episcopal Commn for Ecumenism, 1974–87; Inter-Church Cttee, 1982–85; Western Catholic Conf., 1988–92. *Address:* Archbishop's Residence, 151 avenue de la Cathédrale, St Boniface, MB R2II 0H6, Canada. *T:* (204) 2379851.

Died 13 April 2000.

HACKETT, Prof. Brian; Professor of Landscape Architecture, University of Newcastle upon Tyne, 1967–77, then Emeritus Professor; *b* 3 Nov. 1911; *s* of Henry and Ida Adeline Mary Hackett; *m* 1st, 1942, Frederica Claire Grundy (*d* 1979); one *s* two *d*; 2nd, 1980, Dr Elizabeth Ratcliff. *Educ:* Grammar Sch., Burton-on-Trent; Birmingham Sch. of Architecture; Sch. of Planning for Regional Development, London. MA Dunelm; RIBA, MRTPI. Professional experience, 1930–40; Flt-Lt, RAFVR, 1941–45; Lectr, Sch. of Planning for Regional Develt, London, 1945–47; Univ. of Durham: Lectr in Town and Country Planning, 1947; Lectr in Landscape Architecture, 1948, Sen. Lectr, 1949–59; Vis. Prof. of Landscape Architecture, Univ. of Illinois, 1960–61; Reader in Landscape Arch., Univ. of Newcastle upon Tyne, 1962–66. Member: N England Regl Adv. Cttee, Forestry Commn, 1983–90; Water Space Amenity Commn, 1973–80. Chairman: Northumberland and Newcastle Soc., 1968–77; Northumbria Historic Churches Trust, 1987–94. Pres., Inst. of Landscape Architects, 1967–68; Hon. Vice Pres., Landscape Inst., 1991; Hon. Corresp. Mem., Amer. Soc. of Landscape Architects, 1962. European Prize for Nature Conservation and Landscape Develt, 1975. *Publications:* Man, Society and Environment, 1950; (jtly) Landscape Techniques, 1967; Landscape Planning, 1971; Steep Slopes Landscape, 1971; (jtly) Landscape Reclamation, 1971–72; (jtly) Landscape Reclamation Practice, 1977; Planting Design, 1979; Landscape Conservation, 1980; numerous papers in internat. jls. *Recreation:* musical performance. *Address:*

27 Larkspur Terrace, Jesmond, Newcastle upon Tyne NE2 2DT. *T:* (0191) 281 0747. *Club:* Royal Commonwealth Society. *Died 22 March 1998.*

HACKETT, Prof. Cecil Arthur, DUP; Professor of French, University of Southampton, 1952–70, then Professor Emeritus; *b* 19 Jan. 1908; *s* of Henry Hackett and Alice Setchell; *m* 1942, (Mary) Hazel Armstrong. *Educ:* King's Norton Grammar Sch., Birmingham; University of Birmingham; Emmanuel Coll., Cambridge (Scholar and Prizeman; MA; Hon. Fellow, 1988). Served War of 1939–45: enlisted 1/8th Bn Middlesex Regt, 1939. Assistant d'Anglais, Lycée Louis-le-Grand, Paris, 1934–36; Lecturer in French and English, Borough Road Coll., Isleworth, 1936–39; Education Representative, British Council, Paris, 1945–46; Lecturer in French, University of Glasgow, 1947–52. Hon. DLitt Southampton, 1984. Prix de Littérature Française, Inst de France, 1994. Chevalier de la Légion d'Honneur, 1958. *Publications:* Le Lyrisme de Rimbaud, 1938; Rimbaud l'Enfant, 1948; An Anthology of Modern French Poetry, 1952, 4th edn 1976; Rimbaud, 1957; Autour de Rimbaud, 1967; (ed and introd) New French Poetry: an anthology, 1973; Rimbaud, a critical introduction, 1981; Rimbaud, Œuvres Poétiques, a critical edition, 1986; The Writer and his other Self, 1995; contributions to English and French Reviews. *Address:* Shawford Close, Shawford, Winchester, Hants SO21 2BL. *T:* (01962) 713506.

Died 27 April 2000.

HACKETT, Gen. Sir John Winthrop, GCB 1967 (KCB 1962; CB 1958); CBE 1953 (MBE 1938); DSO 1942 and Bar 1945; MC 1941; DL; BLitt, MA Oxon; FRSL 1982; Principal of King's College, London, 1968–75; *b* 5 Nov. 1910; *s* of Hon. Sir John Winthrop Hackett, KCMG, LLD, Perth, WA, and Deborah, *d* of Frederick Slade Drake–Brockman, Perth; *m* 1942, Margaret, *d* of Joseph Frena, Graz, Austria, and *widow* of Friedrich Grossman; (one *d* decd), and two adopted step *d*. *Educ:* Geelong Grammar Sch., Australia; New Coll., Oxford, Hon. Fellow 1972. Regular Army, commissioned 8th King's Royal Irish Hussars, 1931; Palestine, 1936 (despatches); seconded to Transjordan Frontier Force, 1937–41 (despatches twice); Syria, 1941 (wounded); Sec. Commn of Control, Syria and Lebanon; GSO2 9th Army; Western Desert, 1942 (wounded); GSO1 Raiding Forces GHQ, MELF; Comdr 4th Parachute Brigade, 1943; Italy, 1943 (despatches); Arnhem, 1944 (wounded); BGS (1) Austria, 1946–47; Comdr Transjordan Frontier Force, 1947–48; Sen. Army Instr, RNC, Greenwich, 1950; idc 1951; DQMG, BAOR, 1952; Comdr 20th Armoured Bde, 1954; GOC 7th Armoured Div., 1956–58; Comdt, Royal Mil. Coll. of Science, 1958–61; GOC-in-C, Northern Ireland Command, 1961–63; Dep. Chief of Imperial Gen. Staff, 1963–64; Dep. Chief of the Gen. Staff, Ministry of Defence, 1964–66; Comdr-in-Chief, British Army of the Rhine, and Comdr Northern Army Gp in NATO, 1966–68. ADC (Gen.), 1967–68. Col Commandant, REME, 1961–66; Hon. Colonel: 10th Bn The Parachute Regt, TA, 1965–67; 10th Volunteer Bn, The Parachute Regt, 1967–73; Oxford Univ. Officers Training Corps, 1967–78; Col, Queen's Royal Irish Hussars, 1969–75. Mem., Lord Chancellor's Cttee on Reform of Law of Contempt, 1971–74; Mem., Disciplinary Tribunal, Inns of Court and Bar, 1972–83. Vis. Prof. in Classics, KCL, 1977. Lectures: Lees Knowles, Cambridge, 1961; Basil Henriques Meml, 1970; Harmon Meml, USAF Acad., 1970; Jubilee,

Imperial Coll., 1979. President: UK Classical Assoc., 1971; English Assoc., 1973. Hon. Liveryman, Worshipful Company of Dyers, 1975; Freeman of City of London, 1976. DL Glos 1982. Hon. LLD: Queen's Univ. Belfast; Perth, WA, 1963; Exeter, 1977; Buckingham, 1987. FKC, 1968; Hon. Fellow St George's Coll., University of Western Australia, 1965. Chesney Gold Medal, RUSI, 1985. *Publications:* I Was a Stranger, 1977; (jtly) The Third World War, 1978; (jtly) The Untold Story, 1982; The Profession of Arms, 1983; (ed) Warfare in the Ancient World, 1989; articles and reviews. *Recreations:* fishing, wine, music; the pursuit of exactitude, called by some pedantry. *Address:* Coberley Mill, Cheltenham, Glos GL53 9NH. *T:* (01242) 870207. *Clubs:* Cavalry and Guards, Carlton, United Oxford & Cambridge University, White's. *Died 9 Sept. 1997.*

HADDON-CAVE, Sir (Charles) Philip, KBE 1980; CMG 1973; Director, Kleinwort Benson Group, 1986–95; Chairman, Fleming Overseas Investment Trust, 1988–95 (Director, 1986–95); *b* 6 July 1925; *s* of Francis Macnamara Haddon-Cave; *m* 1948, Elizabeth Alice May Simpson; two *s* one *d. Educ:* Univ. of Tasmania; King's Coll., Cambridge. Entered Colonial Administrative Service, 1952: East Africa High Commn, 1952; Kenya, 1953–62; Seychelles, 1961–62; Hong Kong, 1962–85; Financial Secretary, 1971–81, Chief Sec., 1981–85, Hong Kong. *Publication:* (with D. M. Hocking) Air Transport in Australia, 1951. *Address:* The Old Farmhouse, Nethercote Road, Tackley, Oxon OX5 3AW. *Clubs:* Oriental; Hong Kong, Hong Kong Golf. *Died 27 Sept. 1999.*

HADEN, William Demmery, TD; MA; Headmaster, Royal Grammar School, Newcastle upon Tyne, 1960–72, retired; *b* 14 March 1909; *s* of Rev. William Henry and Gertrude Haden, Little Aston; *m* 1939, Elizabeth Marjorie (decd), *d* of R. S. Tewson, Chorley Wood; one *s* one *d* (and one *d* decd). *Educ:* Nottingham High Sch.; Wadham Coll., Oxford (2nd Class Lit. Hum.; MA 1934). Headmaster, Mercers' Sch., 1946–59. War Service, 1940–45: served as Battery Comdr RA with Fourteenth Army in Burma Campaign (despatches twice); Administrative Commandant, Hmawbi Area, S Burma District, 1945. *Recreations:* games, gardening, listening to music. *Died 2 April 1999.*

HADEN-GUEST, 4th Baron *cr* 1950, of Saling, Essex; **Peter Haden Haden-Guest;** *b* 29 Aug. 1913; *s* of 1st Baron Haden-Guest, MC and Muriel Carmel (*d* 1943), *d* of Colonel Albert Goldsmid, MVO; *S* half-brother, 1987; *m* 1945, Jean, *d* of late Dr Albert George Hindes, NY; two *s* one *d. Educ:* City of London School; New Coll., Oxford (MA). Editorial and theatrical work, 1934–42; served War of 1939–45, Lieut RCNVR; UN official 1946–72. Took seat in House of Lords as cross-bencher, 1989. *Recreations:* grand-children, walking, reading, theatre. *Heir: s* Hon. Christopher Haden-Guest [*b* 5 Feb. 1948; *m* 1984, Jamie Lee, *d* of Tony Curtis and Janet Leigh; one *d*]. *Address:* 198 Old Stone Highway, East Hampton, NY 11937, USA. *Died 8 April 1996.*

HADFIELD, (Ellis) Charles (Raymond), CMG 1954; *b* 5 Aug. 1909; *s* of Alexander Charles Hadfield, Transvaal Colony Magistracy; *m* 1945, Alice Mary Miller (*d* 1989), *d* of Lt-Col Henry Smyth, DSO; one *s* one *d* (and one *s* decd). *Educ:* Blundell's Sch.; St Edmund Hall, Oxford. Joined Oxford University Press, 1936; Dir of Publications, Central Office of Information, 1946–48; Controller (Overseas), 1948–62. Dir, David and Charles (Publishers) Ltd, 1960–64. Mem., British Waterways Bd, 1962–66. *Publications:* The Young Collector's Handbook (with C. Hamilton Ellis), 1940; Civilian Fire Fighter, 1941; (with Alexander d'Agapayeff) Maps, 1942; (with Frank Eyre) The Fire Service Today, 1944; (with Frank Eyre) English

Rivers and Canals, 1945; (with J. E. MacColl) Pilot Guide to Political London, 1945; (with J. E. MacColl) British Local Government, 1948; (as Charles Alexander) The Church's Year, 1950; British Canals, 1950, 8th edn 1994; The Canals of Southern England, 1955; Introducing Canals, 1955; The Canals of South Wales and the Border, 1960; (with John Norris) Waterways to Stratford, 1962; Canals of the World, 1964; Canals and Waterways, 1966; (with Alice Mary Hadfield) The Cotswolds, 1966; The Canals of the East Midlands, 1966; The Canals of the West Midlands, 1966; The Canals of South West England, 1967; Atmospheric Railways, 1967; (with Michael Streat) Holiday Cruising on Inland Waterways, 1968; The Canal Age, 1968; The Canals of South and South East England, 1969; (with Gordon Biddle) The Canals of North West England, 1970; The Canals of Yorkshire and North East England, 1972; Introducing Inland Waterways, 1973; (with Alice Mary Hadfield) Introducing the Cotswolds, 1976; Waterways Sights to See, 1976; Inland Waterways, 1978; (with A. W. Skempton) William Jessop, Engineer, 1979; (with Alice Mary Hadfield) Afloat in America, 1979; World Canals, 1986; Thomas Telford's Temptation, 1993; *festschrift:* Canals: a new look; studies in honour of Charles Hadfield (ed M. Baldwin and A. Burton), 1984. *Recreations:* writing, exploring canals. *Address:* 13 Meadow Way, South Cerney, Cirencester, Glos GL7 6HY. *T:* Cirencester (01285) 860422.
Died 6 Aug. 1996.

HADFIELD, John Charles Heywood; author; Proprietor, The Cupid Press, since 1949; Director, Rainbird Publishing Group, 1965–82; *b* 16 June 1907; 2nd *s* of H. G. Hadfield, Birmingham; *m* 1st, 1931, (Phyllis) Anna McMullen (*d* 1973); (one *s* decd); 2nd, 1975, Joy Westendarp. *Educ:* Bradfield. Editor, J. M. Dent & Sons, Ltd, 1935–42; Books Officer for British Council in the Middle East, 1942–44; Dir of the National Book League, 1944–50; Organiser, Festival of Britain Exhibition of Books, 1951; Editor, The Saturday Book, 1952–73. *Publications:* The Christmas Companion, 1939; Georgian Love Songs, 1949; Restoration Love Songs, 1950; A Book of Beauty, 1952, rev. edn 1976; A Book of Delights, 1954, rev. edn 1977; Elizabethan Love Songs, 1955; A Book of Britain, 1956; A Book of Love, 1958, rev. edn 1978; Love on a Branch Line, 1959; A Book of Pleasures, 1960; (with Miles Hadfield) The Twelve Days of Christmas, 1961; A Book of Joy, 1962; (with Miles Hadfield) Gardens of Delight, 1964; A Chamber of Horrors, 1965; (ed) The Shell Guide to England, 1970, rev. edn 1981; (ed) Cowardy Custard, 1973; (ed) The Shell Book of English Villages, 1980; (ed) Everyman's Book of English Love Poems, 1980; The Best of The Saturday Book, 1981; Every Picture Tells a Story, 1985; Victorian Delights, 1987. *Recreations:* books, pictures, gardens. *Address:* 2 Quay Street, Woodbridge, Suffolk IP12 1BX. *T:* (01394) 387414. *Club:* Savile.
Died 10 Oct. 1999.

HADLEY, Sir Leonard Albert, Kt 1975; JP; Union Secretary, Wellington, NZ, retired 1984; *b* Wellington, 8 Sept. 1911; *s* of Albert A. Hadley, JP and Ethel Emily (*née* Armstrong); *m* 1st, 1939, Jean Lyell (*d* 1965), *d* of E. S. Innes; one *s* one *d*; 2nd, 1978, Amelia Townsend (*d* 1993). Mem., Nat. Exec., NZ Fedn of Labour, 1946–76; Dir, Reserve Bank of NZ, 1959–85; Mem., Bd of Trustees since formation, 1964–87, Pres., 1976–79, Wellington Trustee Savings Bank. Relieving Mem., Industrial Commn and Industrial Court, 1974 (Arbitration Court, 1960–84); Mem., Waterfront Industry Tribunal, 1981–83. Member: NZ Immigration Adv. Council; Industrial Relations Council, 1953–75; Periodic Detention Work Centre Adv. Cttee (Juvenile), and Adult Centre, 1962–84 (both since formation); Absolute Liability Enquiry Cttee, 1963; Govt Cttees to review Exempted Goods, 1959 and 1962. Union Representative: NZ Fedn of Labour Delegns to ILO,

Geneva, 1949 and 1966; Internat. Confedn of Free Trade Unions Inaugural Conf., 1949; Social Security Conf., Moscow, 1971; SE Asian Trade Union Conf., Tokyo, 1973; OECD Conf., Paris, 1974. Member: Terawhiti Licensing Trust, 1975–80; Witako Regl Prison Adv. Cttee, 1983–88. Life Member: Vogelmorn Tennis Club, 1961; Wellington Working Men's Club and Literary Inst., 1979; NZ Plumbers' Union, 1978; Wellington Clerical Union, 1983. Patron, Vogelmorn Bowling Club, 1982–. Awarded Smith-Mundt Ldr Study Grant in USA, 1953. JP 1967. *Recreations:* reading, music, outdoor bowls, Rugby, tennis, sport generally. *Address:* (private) 3 Cheesman Street, Brooklyn, Wellington, New Zealand.
Died 10 Nov. 1997.

HAFFNER, Albert Edward, PhD; Chairman, North Eastern Gas Board, 1971–72 (Deputy Chairman, 1966–71); *b* 17 Feb. 1907; 4th *s* of late George Christian and Caroline Haffner, Holme, near Burnley, Lancs; *m* 1934, Elizabeth Ellen Crossley (*d* 1989), Cheadle Heath, Stockport; one *s* one *d*. *Educ:* Burnley Grammar Sch.; Royal College of Science; Imperial Coll., London; Technische Hochschule, Karlsruhe. BSc (1st Cl. Hons), ARCS, PhD, DIC, London. Burnley Gas Works, 1924–26; Gas Light & Coke Co, 1932–56; Research Chemist and North Thames Gas Bd; Gp Engr, Chief Engineer and later Bd Member, Southern Gas Bd, 1956–66. Past Pres., Instn Gas Engineers (Centenary Pres., 1962–63); Past Vice-Pres., Internat. Gas Union. CEng, MIChemE. *Publications:* contributor to Proc. Royal Soc., Jl Instn Gas Engrs, Instn Chem. Engrs, Inst. of Fuel, New Scientist; papers presented to Canadian Gas Assoc., French Chem. Soc., Japanese Gas Industry and at IGU Confs in USA, USSR and Germany, etc. *Recreations;* photography, travel, gardening, cabinet-making. *Address:* Burnthwaite, Iwerne Courtney, near Blandford Forum, Dorset DT11 8QL. *T:* Child Okeford (01258) 860749. *Club:* New Cavendish.
Died 20 Jan. 1996.

HAGGART, Rt Rev. Alastair Iain Macdonald; *b* 10 Oct. 1915; *s* of Alexander Macdonald Haggart and Jessie Mackay; *m* 1st, 1945, Margaret Agnes Trundle (*d* 1979); two *d*; 2nd, 1983, Mary Elizabeth Scholes, OBE, SRN. *Educ:* Hatfield Coll. (Exhibnr); Durham Univ. (Exhibnr); Edinburgh Theol College. LTh 1941; BA 1942; MA 1945. Deacon, 1941, priest 1942. Curate: St Mary's Cath., Glasgow, 1941–45; St Mary's, Hendon, 1945–48; Precentor, St Ninian's Cath., Perth, 1948–51; Rector, St Oswald's, King's Park, Glasgow, 1951, and Acting Priest-in-Charge, St Martin's, Glasgow, 1953–58; Synod Clerk of Glasgow Dio. and Canon of St Mary's Cath., Glasgow, 1958–59; Provost, St Paul's Cathedral, Dundee, 1959–71; Principal and Pantonian Prof., Episcopal Theological Coll., Edinburgh, 1971–75; Canon, St Mary's Cathedral, Edinburgh, 1971–75; Bishop of Edinburgh, 1975–85; Primus of the Episcopal Church in Scotland, 1977–85. Exam. Chap. to Bp of Brechin, 1964. Hon. LLD Dundee, 1970. *Recreations:* walking, reading, listening to music, asking questions. *Address:* 14/2 St Margaret's Place, Edinburgh EH9 1AY. *T:* (0131) 446 9052.
Died 11 Jan. 1998.

HAIGH, Clifford; Editor, The Friend, 1966–73; *b* 5 Feb. 1906; *yr s* of Leonard and Isabel Haigh, Bradford, Yorks; *m* 1st, 1934, Dora Winifred Fowler (*d* 1959); one *s* one *d*; 2nd, 1970, (Grace) Elizabeth Cross. Editorial Staff: Yorkshire Observer, 1924–27; Birmingham Post, 1928–46; the Times, 1947–61; Assistant Editor, The Friend, 1961–65. *Recreation:* walking. *Address:* 4 Chichester Road, Sandgate, Kent CT20 3BN. *T:* (01303) 248212.
Died 7 Feb. 1999.

HALE, Prof. Sir John (Rigby), Kt 1984; FBA 1977; Professor of Italian History, 1981–83, and Professor of Italian, 1985–88, University College London, then

Professor Emeritus; Public Orator, University of London, 1981–83; *b* 17 Sept. 1923; *s* of E. R. S. Hale, MD, FRCP, and Hilda Birks; *m* 1st, 1952, Rosalind Williams; one *s* two *d*; 2nd, 1965, Sheila Haynes MacIvor; one *s*. *Educ:* Neville Holt Preparatory Sch.; Eastbourne Coll.; Jesus Coll., Oxford. BA first cl. hons Mod. Hist., 1948; MA Oxon, 1950; DLitt Oxon, 1986. Served War, Radio Operator in Merchant Service, 1942–45. Commonwealth Fellow, Johns Hopkins and Harvard Univs, 1948–49; Fellow and Tutor in Modern History, Jesus Coll., Oxford, 1949–64, Hon. Fellow, 1986; Prof. of History, Univ. of Warwick, 1964–69. Editor, Oxford Magazine, 1958–59. Visiting Prof., Cornell Univ., 1959–60; Vis. Fellow, Harvard Centre for Renaissance Studies, I Tatti, 1963; Vis. Prof., Univ. of California, Berkeley, 1969–70; Fellowship, Folger Shakespeare Library, Washington, 1970; Fellow, Davis Center, Univ. of Princeton, 1982; Mem., Princeton Inst. for Adv. Study, 1984–85. Chm. of Trustees, Nat. Gallery, 1974–80 (Trustee, 1973–80); Trustee: V&A Museum, 1984–88 (Chm., Theatre Museum Cttee, 1984–87); BM, 1985–92; Member: Royal Mint Adv. Cttee, 1979–92; Museums and Galleries Commn, 1983–93 (Chm., Working Party on Museum Professional Trng and Career Structure, report pubd 1987); Royal Commn for Exhibn of 1851, 1983–88. Chairman: British Soc. for Renaissance Studies, 1973–76; Advisory Cttee, Govt Art Collection, 1983–92; Pres., British Assoc. of Friends of Museums, 1988–94. FSA 1962; FRHistS 1968; FRSA 1974; FRSL 1998. Socio Straniero: Accademia Arcadia, 1972; Ateneo Veneto, 1987; Accademia dei Lincei, 1993. Academicus ex Classe (Bronze Plaque Award), Accademia Medicea, 1980; Commendatore, Ordine al Merito della Repubblica Italiana, 1981; Premio Bolla (services to Venice), 1982; Serena Medal, British Acad., 1986. *Publications:* England and the Italian Renaissance, 1954, 3rd edn 1996; The Italian Journal of Samuel Rogers, 1956; Machiavelli and Renaissance Italy, 1961; (trans. and ed) The Literary Works of Machiavelli, 1961, (ed) Certain Discourses Military by Sir John Smythe, 1964; The Evolution of British Historiography, 1964; (co-ed) Europe in the Late Middle Ages, 1965; Renaissance Exploration, 1968; Renaissance Europe 1480–1520, 1971; (ed) Renaissance Venice, 1973; Italian Renaissance Painting, 1977; Florence and the Medici: the pattern of control, 1977; Renaissance Fortification: art or engineering?, 1978; The Travel Journal of Antonio de Beatis, 1979; (ed) A Concise Encyclopaedia of the Italian Renaissance, 1981; Renaissance War Studies, 1983; (with M. E. Mallett) The Military Organisation of a Renaissance State: Venice *c* 1400–1617, 1984; War and Society in Renaissance Europe 1450–1620, 1985 (Edmund Gardner Prize, London Univ., 1983–87), 2nd edn 1998; Artists and Warfare in the Renaissance, 1990; The Civilisation of Europe in the Renaissance, 1993 (RSL Award; Time-Life Silver Pen Award); contributor: New Cambridge Modern History, vols 1, 2, 3; The History of the King's Works, vol. 4; Past and Present; Studi Veneziani, Italian Studies, etc. *Recreation:* Venice. *Address:* 26 Montpelier Row, Twickenham, Middx TW1 2NQ. *T:* (020) 8892 9636.
Died 12 Aug. 1999.

HALE, Kathleen, (Mrs Douglas McClean), OBE 1976; artist; illustrator and author of books for children; *b* 24 May 1898; *d* of Charles Edward Hale and Ethel Alice Aylmer Hughes; *m* 1926, Dr Douglas McClean (*d* 1967); two *s*. *Educ:* Manchester High Sch. for Girls; Manchester Sch. of Art; Art Dept (scholar) of University Coll., Reading; Central Sch. of Art; East Anglian Sch. of Painting and Drawing. Exhibited paintings at: New English Art Club, Whitechapel Art Gallery, London Group, Grosvenor Galleries, Vermont Gallery, Warwick Public Library Gallery, Gallery Edward Harvane, New Grafton Gallery, Parkin Gallery, Gekoski Gallery, Uppingham Gallery (also lino-cuts *et al*); metal groups and pictures at: Lefèvre Galleries; Leicester Galleries; Oxford Arts Council, Arts Centre; Mural for South Bank (Festival) Schs Section, 1951; Orlando Ballet for Festival Gardens, 1951; contrib. ballet exhibn and exhibited Orlando Ballet costume and scenery designs, V&A Museum. TV and radio programmes included Kaleidoscope and Desert Island Discs. *Publications:* The Orlando The Marmalade Cat Series, 1938–: Camping Holiday; Trip Abroad; Buys a Farm; Becomes a Doctor; Silver Wedding; Keeps a Dog; A Seaside Holiday; The Frisky Housewife; Evening Out; Home Life; Invisible Pyjamas; The Judge; Zoo; Magic Carpet; Country Peep-Show; Buys a Cottage; and The Three Graces; Goes to the Moon; and the Water Cats; Henrietta, the Faithful Hen, 1946; Puss-in-Boots Peep-Show, 1950; Manda, 1952; Henrietta's Magic Egg, 1973; A Slender Reputation (autobiog.), 1994. *Recreation:* painting. *Address:* c/o Frederick Warne & Co., Penguin Books Ltd, 27 Wrights Lane, W8 5TZ.

Died 26 Jan. 2000.

HALEY, Prof. Kenneth Harold Dobson, FBA 1987; Professor of Modern History, Sheffield University, 1962–82, then Emeritus Professor; *b* 19 April 1920; *s* of Alfred Harold Dobson Haley and Winifred Hetty Haley (*née* Beal); *m* 1948, Iris (*née* Houghton); one *s* two *d*. *Educ:* Huddersfield College; Balliol College, Oxford (MA, BLitt). University of Sheffield: Asst Lectr in Modern History, 1947, later Lectr, Sen. Lectr and Prof.; Dean, Faculty of Arts, 1979–81. Member: Anglo-Netherlands Mixed Cultural Commn, 1976–82; William and Mary Tercentenary Trust, 1985–89. Hon. Vice-Pres., Historical Assoc., 1994–. *Publications:* William of Orange and the English Opposition 1672–1674, 1953, repr. 1975; The First Earl of Shaftesbury, 1968; The Dutch in the Seventeenth Century, 1972 (Dutch trans. 1979); Politics in the Reign of Charles II, 1985; An English Diplomat in the Low Countries: Sir William Temple and John de Witt 1665–1672, 1986; The British and the Dutch, 1988; articles in historical jls. *Recreation:* computer chess. *Address:* 15 Haugh Lane, Sheffield S11 9SA. *T:* (0114) 236 1316. *Died 2 July 1997.*

HALFORD, Maj.-Gen. Michael Charles Kirkpatrick, DSO 1946; OBE 1957 (MBE 1944); DL; *b* 28 Oct. 1914; *s* of Lt-Col M. F. Halford, OBE, and Violet Halford (*née* Kirkpatrick); *m* 1945, Pamela Joy (*née* Wright); two *s* (and one *s* decd). *Educ:* Wellington Coll.; Trinity Coll., Cambridge. Commissioned Royal Guernsey Militia, 1932; 2nd Lieut York and Lancaster Regt, 1935; served Egypt and Palestine, 1936; France 1940; N Africa, Italy, France and Germany; comd Hallamshire Bn, York and Lancaster Regt, 1945, 1st Bn, 1954; GSO1 (Intelligence), Hong Kong, 1953; Asst Army Instr, Imperial Defence Coll., 1957; comd 147 Inf. Bde (TA), 1960; COS HQ Western Comd, 1963; GOC 43 (Wessex) Div./District, 1964–67; retd, 1967. Representative Col The York and Lancaster Regt, 1966–79. DL Hants, 1975. *Recreations:* fishing, golf. *Died 4 Jan. 1999.*

HALFORD-MacLEOD, Aubrey Seymour, CMG 1958; CVO 1965; HM Diplomatic Service, retired; *b* 15 Dec. 1914; *o s* of late Joseph and Clara Halford; changed name by deed poll from Halford to Halford-MacLeod, 1964; *m* 1939, Giovanna Mary (*d* 1999), *o d* of late W. H. Durst; three *s* one *d*. *Educ:* King Edward's Sch., Birmingham; Magdalen Coll., Oxford. Entered HM Diplomatic (subseq. Foreign, then again Diplomatic) Service as Third Sec., 1937; Bagdad, 1939; Second Sec., 1942; transferred to Office of Minister Resident in N Africa, 1943; First Sec., 1943; British Mem. of Secretariat of Advisory Council for Italy, 1944; British High Commission in Italy, 1944; Asst Political Adviser to Allied Commission in Italy, Sept. 1944, Political Adviser, 1945; transferred to HM Foreign Office, 1946, Principal Private Sec. to Permanent Under-Sec.; Dep. Exec. Sec. to Preparatory Commission for Council of Europe, May 1949, and promoted Counsellor; Dep. Sec. Gen. of the Council of Europe, 1949–52; Counsellor, HM Embassy, Tokyo, 1953–55; in charge of HM Legation, Seoul, 1954; Counsellor at HM Embassy in Libya, 1955–57; Political Agent at Kuwait, 1957–59; Consul-Gen., Munich, 1959–65; Ambassador to Iceland, 1966–70. Foreign Affairs Adviser, Scottish Council (Develt and Ind.), 1971–78. Dir, Scottish Opera, 1971–78. Pres., Scottish Soc. for Northern Studies, 1973–76. Vice-Pres., Clan MacLeod Soc. of Scotland, 1976–79. *Publication:* (with G. M. Halford) The Kabuki Handbook, 1956. *Recreations:* fishing, shooting, ornithology. *Address:* Mulag House, Ardvourlie, N Harris HS3 3AB. *T:* (01859) 502054. *Died 21 Aug. 2000.*

HALL, Sir Arnold (Alexander), Kt 1954; FRS 1953; FREng; Chairman, Hawker Siddeley Group plc, 1967–86 (Director, 1955; Executive Chairman, 1967–84); *b* 23 April 1915; *s* of Robert Alexander Hall; *m* 1st, 1946, Dione (decd), *d* of Rev. J. A. Sykes, Derby; three *d*; 2nd, 1986, Iola Nealon. *Educ:* Clare Coll., Cambridge (Rex Moir Prize in Engineering, John Bernard Seely Prize in Aeronautics, Ricardo Prize in Thermodynamics; MA; Hon. Fellow, 1966). Res. Fellow in Aeronautics, Company of Armourers and Brasiers (held at University of Cambridge), 1936–38; Principal Scientific Officer, Royal Aircraft Establishment, Farnborough, Hants, 1938–45; Zaharoff Prof. of Aviation, University of London, and Head of Dept of Aeronautics, Imperial Coll. of Science and Technology, 1945–51; Dir of the Royal Aircraft Establishment, Farnborough, 1951–55; Managing Director: Bristol Siddeley Engines, 1959–63; Hawker Siddeley Gp plc, 1963–81 (Vice-Chm., 1963–67); former Chairman: Hawker Siddeley Diesels Ltd; Hawker Siddeley Electric Ltd; Hawker Siddeley Canada Inc.; Hawker Siddeley Rail Ltd. Pres., Royal Aeronautical Society, 1958–59; Dep. Pres., BEAMA, 1966–67, Pres., 1967–68; Vice-Pres., Engineering Employers' Fedn, 1968–80, 1984–86; President: Locomotive and Allied Manufacturers Assoc. of GB, 1968–69, 1969–70; SBAC, 1972–73. Member: Advisory Council on Scientific Policy, 1962–64; Air Registration Board, 1963–73; Electricity Supply Research Council, 1963–72; Advisory Council on Technology (Min. of Technology), 1964–67; Defence Industries Council, 1969–77; Industrial Develt Adv. Bd, 1973–75; Dep. Chm., Engineering Industries Council, 1975–86. Chm., Fasco Industries Inc., 1980–81; Director: Lloyds Bank, 1966–85; Lloyds Bank UK Management Ltd, 1979–84; Phoenix Assurance, 1969–85; ICI, 1970–85; Onan Corp., 1976–80; Rolls-Royce Ltd, 1983–88; Royal Ordnance, 1984–86. Pro-Chancellor, Warwick Univ., 1965–70; Chancellor, Loughborough Univ. of Technology, 1980–89. Chm. Bd of Trustees, Science Museum, 1983–85. Freeman, City of London, 1988. Fellow, Imperial Coll. of Science and Technology, 1963–; FREng (Founder Fellow, Fellowship of Engineering, 1976; Vice-Pres., 1977); For. Associate, US Nat. Acad. of Engrg, 1976–. Hon. ACGI; Hon. FRAeS 1965; Hon. FAIAA; Hon. MIMechE 1968; Hon. FIEE 1975. Hon. DTech Loughborough, 1976; Hon. DSc: London, 1980; Cambridge, 1986. Gold Medal, RAeS, 1962; Hambro Award (Business Man of the Year), 1975; Gold Medal, BIM, 1981; Albert Medal, RSA, 1983. *Address:* Wakehams, Boveney Road, Dorney, near Windsor, Berks SL4 6QD. *Died 9 Jan. 2000.*

HALL, Dame Catherine (Mary), DBE 1982 (CBE 1967); FRCN; General Secretary, Royal College of Nursing of the United Kingdom, 1957–82; *b* 19 Dec. 1922; *d* of late Robert Hall, OBE and Florence Irene Hall (*née* Turner). *Educ:* Hunmanby Hall Sch. for Girls, Filey, Yorks. Gen. Infirmary, Leeds: nursing trng, 1941–44 (SRN); Ward

Sister, 1945–47; sen nursing appts, 1949–53; midwifery trng, Leeds and Rotherham, 1948 (SCM); travelling fellowship, US and Canada, 1950–51; student in nursing administration, Royal College of Nursing, 1953–54; Asst Matron, Middlesex Hosp., London, 1954–56. Part-time Member: CIR, 1971–74; British Railways Regional Bd for London and the South East, 1975–77; Mem. GMC, 1979–89; Chm., UK Central Council for Nursing, Midwifery and Health Visiting, 1980–85. Hon. Mem., Florida Nurses Assoc., 1973. FRCN 1976. OStJ 1977. Hon. DLitt City, 1975. *Address:* Barnsfield, Barnsfield Lane, Buckfastleigh, Devon TQ11 0NP. *T:* Buckfastleigh (01364) 642504.   *Died 26 Aug. 1996.*

HALL, Prof. David Oakley, PhD; Professor of Biology, King's College London, since 1974; *b* 14 Nov. 1935; *s* of Charles Edward Hall and Ethel Marion Oakley; *m* 1981, Peta Jacqueline Smyth; two *d. Educ:* Kearsney Coll., S Africa (matric. 1952); Univ. of Natal, SA (BSc 1957); Univ. of California, Berkeley (PhD 1962). Fellow, Johns Hopkins Med. Sch., Baltimore, USA (Post-doctoral Fellow, 1963–64); Lectr, 1964–68, Reader, 1968–74, KCL. Vis. Sen. Res. Scientist, Princeton Univ., 1990–91. Chm., UK SCOPE Cttee, Royal Soc., 1994–99 (Mem. Cttee, 1999–); Treas., SCOPE (Paris), 1998–. Linneborn Biomass Prize, 1998. *Publications:* Photosynthesis, 1972, 6th edn 1998; Biomass, 1987; Plants as Solar Collectors, 1983; numerous articles in jls on photosynthesis, biomass for energy, bioproductivity, biotechnology, and climate change. *Recreations:* swimming, reading, theatre. *Address:* King's College London, Campden Hill Road, W8 7AH. *T:* (020) 7333 4317. *Club:* Athenæum.
                                    Died 22 Aug. 1999.

HALL, Air Marshal Sir Donald (Percy), KCB 1984 (CB 1981); CBE 1975; AFC 1963; Deputy Chairman, GEC-Marconi, 1990–95; *b* 11 Nov. 1930; *s* of William Reckerby Hall and Elsie Hall; *m* 1953, Joyce (*née* Warburton); two *d. Educ:* Hull Grammar Sch. Royal Air Force Coll., 1949; flying appts until 1963; staff and command appointments, 1964–86, including: OC, No 111 Sqdn, Empire Test Pilots Sch., and RAF Akrotiri; AOC No 11 Gp; ACAS (Operational Requirements); AOC No 38 Gp; Dep. Chief of the Defence Staff, 1983–86. Chm., Marconi Defence Systems, 1987–89. *Recreations:* walking, swimming, planting trees. *Address:* c/o Lloyds Bank, Cox's and King's Branch, 7 Pall Mall, SW1Y 5NA. *Clubs:* Royal Air Force; Colonels.   *Died 12 Jan. 1999.*

HALL, Francis Woodall; HM Diplomatic Service, retired; *b* 10 May 1918; *s* of Francis Hall and Florence Adelaide Woodall; *m* 1951, Phyllis Anne Amelia Andrews; one *s* one *d. Educ:* Taunton School. Inland Revenue, 1936–40; Admty (Alexandria, Port Said, Haifa, Freetown), 1940–46; FO, 1946; Bahrain and Baghdad, 1949; Vice-Consul, Malaga, 1950; FO, 1952; 2nd Sec., Cairo, 1955; Consul: Madrid, 1957; Zagreb, 1960; FO, 1962; Consul, Stockholm, 1964; Head of Mombasa Office of British High Commn to Kenya, 1969; Consul-Gen., Alexandria, 1971–78, retd. Hon. Consul, Seville, 1979–83. *Recreations:* music, walking. *Address:* Ed. Torre de la Roca, Piso 1002, 29620 Torremolinos, Málaga, Spain. *T:* (95) 2389590.   *Died 15 May 2000.*

HALL, His Honour (Harold) George; a Circuit Judge, 1975–91; *b* 20 Sept. 1920; *s* of late Albert Hall and Violet Maud Hall (*née* Etherington); *m* 1950, Patricia Delaney; four *s* one *d. Educ:* Archbishop Holgate's Grammar Sch., York. RAF, 1940–46 (Flt-Lt). Called to Bar, Middle Temple, 1958; practised NE Circuit; Dep. Chm., WR Yorks QS, 1970; a Recorder, 1972–75.
                                    Died 17 Jan. 1996.

HALL, Vernon Frederick, CVO 1960; Anæsthetist, King's College Hospital, 1931–69, retired; *b* 25 Aug. 1904; *s* of

Cecil S. and M. M. Hall; *m* 1935, C. Marcia Cavell; one *s* two *d. Educ:* Haberdashers' Sch.; King's Coll. Hosp., London. MRCS, LRCP 1927; DA 1938; FFARCS 1948. Served War of 1939–45 in Army (Emergency Commission), 1942–46; Consultant Anæsthetist, India Command (Local Brig.), 1945. Dean, King's Coll. Hosp. Medical Sch., 1951–65; Chm., London Univ. Bd of Advanced Med. Studies, 1952–62; former Member: Senate, Univ. of London; Faculty of Medicine, Univ. of London. FKC 1958; Hon. FFARCS 1975. *Publications:* History of King's College Hospital Dental School, 1973; A Scrapbook of Snowdonia, 1982; (jtly) The Story of King's College Hospital and its Medical School 1839–1990, part II, 1991; chapters on anaesthesia in Rose & Carless, Surgery, etc. *Recreations:* riding, walking, reading, music. *Address:* 164A Kingshall Road, Beckenham, Kent BR3 1LN.   *Died 19 Aug. 1998.*

HALL, Brig. Sir William (Henry), KBE 1979 (CBE 1962); Kt 1968; DSO 1942; ED; Comptroller of Stores, State Electricity Commission of Victoria, 1956–70; *b* 5 Jan. 1906; *s* of William Henry Hall, Edinburgh, Scotland; *m* 1930, Irene Mary, *d* of William Hayes; one *s* four *d. Educ:* Morgan Acad., Dundee; Melbourne Univ. Joined Staff of State Electricity Commn of Vic, 1924. Enlisted AIF, 1939: Capt. Royal Aust. Artillery, Palestine, Egypt; Syria, Papua, New Guinea, 1941 (Major); Aust. Dir of Armaments at AHQ, 1942 (Lt-Col); Dir of Armament at AHQ, 1945 (Col); CRA 3 Div. Artillery CMF, 1955–59 (Brig.). Col Comdt, RAA Southern Comd, 1967–72. Director: Royal Humane Society of Vic; Multiple Sclerosis Soc.; Chairman: War Widows and Widowed Mothers' Trust; RSL War Veterans' Trust; State Pres. Victorian Br., RSL, 1964–74 (Chm. Trustees); Nat. Pres., Aust. RSL, 1974–78; Aust. Councillor, World Veterans' Foundn; Patron: Aust.-Free China Economic Assoc.; Royal Artillery Assoc., Carry On, and Blinded Soldiers Assoc., Vic; Trustee, Victorian Overseas Foundn. Associate Fellow, Aust. Inst. Management, Mem., Inst. of Purchasing and Supply (London). *Recreation:* golf. *Address:* Rosemont, 112 Kooyong Road, Caulfield, Vic 3162, Australia; Montrose, Flinders, Vic 3929. *Clubs:* Naval and Military (Melbourne); Melbourne Cricket, Flinders Golf.
                                    Died 10 Sept. 1998.

HALLADAY, Eric, MA; Principal, St Chad's College, University of Durham, 1991–94; *b* 9 July 1930; *s* of Rev. A. R. Halladay and Helena Renton; *m* 1956, Margaret Baister; one *s* two *d. Educ:* Durham Sch.; St John's Coll., Cambridge (BA 1953; MA 1957); Ripon Hall, Oxford. National Service, commnd 5th Regt, RHA, 1948–50. Exeter Sch., 1954–60, Sen. History Master, 1956–60; Sen. Lectr in History, RMA, Sandhurst, 1960–64; Grey College, University of Durham: Sen. Tutor, and part-time Lectr in History, 1964–80; Vice-Master, 1967–80; Master, 1980–89; Rector, 1989–91; Rector, St Aidan's Coll., Univ. of Durham, 1990–91. Chm., Northumbrian Univs Military Educn Cttee, 1981–94; Mem. Exec. Cttee, Council of Military Educn Cttees of Univs of UK, 1982–87. Mem., TA&VRA, N of England, 1980–96; Sec., Durham City Div., SSAFA, 1977–89; Trng Officer, Northumberland Br., SSAFA, 1996–. Chm., Durham Regatta, 1982–88; Steward, Henley Royal Regatta, 1993; Mem. Rowing Cttee, Rowing Mus., Henley-on-Thames, 1995–. *Publications:* The Building of Modern Africa (with D. D. Rooney), 1966, 2nd edn 1968; The Emergent Continent: Africa in the Nineteenth Century, 1972; Rowing in England—a Social History, 1990. *Recreations:* gardening, rowing. *Address:* The Coign, Corbridge, Northumberland NE45 5LE. *T:* (01434) 632838. *Club:* Leander (Henley-on-Thames).   *Died 19 July 1997.*

HALLETT, Prof. (George Edward) Maurice, MDS; Child Dental Health Professor, University of Newcastle upon

Tyne (formerly King's College, University of Durham), 1951–77, then Emeritus; Dean, Sutherland Dental School, 1960–77, and Hospital, 1970–77; retired; *b* 30 July 1912; *s* of Edward Henry and Berthe Hallett; *m* 1936, Annetta Eva Grant Napier (decd); three *d*. *Educ:* Birkenhead Institute; Liverpool Univ. (LDS, Gilmour Medal and other prizes). HDD RCSE 1939; FDS RCS 1948; MDS Durham, 1952; DOrthRCS, 1954; FDSRCSE 1960; FFDRCSI 1964. House Surgeon, Liverpool Dental Hosp., 1934–35; School Dental Officer, Doncaster CB, 1935–36, Notts, 1936–40; served War, 1940–46: Army Dental Corps, Major, despatches; University of Durham: Lecturer in Children's Dentistry, 1946, Reader, 1948; Lectr in Orthodontics, 1946. Examiner in Dental subjects: Universities of Dundee, Durham, Edinburgh and Glasgow; RCS, 1954–77; Consultant, United Teaching Hosps, Newcastle upon Tyne; Head of Dept of Child Dental Health, Dental Hosp., Newcastle upon Tyne, 1948. Mem. Dental Council, RCSE; Past President: Société Française d'Orthopedie Dento-Faciale; European Orthodontic Soc. (also former Editor; Hon. Life Mem.); North of England Odontological Soc.; Brit. Soc. for the study of Orthodontics (Hon. Life Mem.); Newcastle Medico-Legal Soc.; former Mem., Newcastle RHB; former Mem., Newcastle AHA (T). Hon. Life Mem., British Dental Assoc. Past Pres., British Med. Pilots' Assoc. Hon. FDSRCPSGlas 1979. Silver Medal, Ville de Paris, 1980. *Publications:* contribs to scientific and dental jls. *Recreations:* dilettantism in the glyptic arts, flying. *Address:* 63 Runnymede Road, Darras Hall, Ponteland, Newcastle upon Tyne NE20 9HJ. *T:* (01661) 822646. *Club:* Newcastle Aero.
Died 11 Sept. 1998.

HALLINAN, Sir (Adrian) Lincoln, Kt 1971; DL; Barrister-at-law; Stipendiary Magistrate, South Glamorgan (Cardiff), 1976–93; a Recorder of the Crown Court, 1972–82; *b* 13 Nov. 1922; *e s* of late Sir Charles Hallinan, CBE and Theresa Doris Hallinan, JP (*née* Holman); *m* 1955, Mary Parry Evans; two *s* two *d*. *Educ:* Downside. Lieut, Rifle Bde, 1942–47; TA, 1950–52 (Captain). Called to Bar, Lincoln's Inn, 1950; Wales and Chester Circuit. A Legal Mem., Mental Health Review Tribunal for Wales, 1966–76; Chm., Med. Appeals Tribunal, 1970–76. Cardiff CC, 1949–74 (serving on several educational and cultural cttees); Alderman, 1961–74; Lord Mayor of Cardiff, 1969–70. Chm., Cardiff Educn Cttee, 1961–63 and 1965–70. Contested (C) Aberdare, 1946, Cardiff West, 1951, 1959. Chm., Governing Body, Cardiff Coll. of Art, and Cardiff Coll. of Music and Drama, 1961–73; first Chm., Nat. Court of Governors, Welsh Coll. of Music and Drama, 1970. Chm., Commemorative Collectors Soc.; Patron, S Wales Gp, Victorian Soc.; Founder and Chm., Cardiff 2000–Cardiff Civic Trust, 1964–73, 1st Pres. 1973; Chm., Cardiff-Nantes Fellowship, 1961–68. DL Glamorgan, 1969. OStJ 1969. Chevalier, Ordre des Palmes Académiques, 1965; Chevalier de la Légion d'Honneur, 1973. *Publications:* British Commemoratives, 1996; Royal Commemoratives, 1997. *Recreations:* music, the arts. *Address:* Cotham Lodge, Newport, Pembrokeshire SA42 0TD. *Died 2 Nov. 1997.*

HALLIWELL, Brian; VAT Consultant, KPMG (formerly Peat, Marwick, Mitchell & Co.), since 1985; *b* 17 Dec. 1930; *s* of late Norman and Emma Halliwell; *m* 1957, Agnes Lee. *Educ:* Preston Grammar Sch. DMS 1968. Joined HM Customs and Excise as Clerical Officer, 1947; Principal, 1969; Asst Sec., 1973; Dep. Accountant General, 1976; Accountant and Comptroller Gen., 1980–85; Hd of VAT Services, Peat, Marwick, Mitchell & Co., subseq. KPMG Peat Marwick McLintock, 1989–93. FIMgt. *Recreations:* chess, reading, sport. *Address:* Waverlee, Great Heads Road, Grange-over-Sands, Cumbria LA11 7EA. *T:* (015395) 34335. *Died 14 May 1999.*

HALPIN, Kathleen Mary, CBE 1953 (OBE 1941); Chief Administrator, Regions, Women's Royal Voluntary Service (formerly Women's Voluntary Services), 1945–73; *b* 19 Nov. 1903; *d* of James Francis Halpin, ISO, Forest Hill; unmarried. *Educ:* Sydenham High Sch. (GPDST). Organising Sec., Women's Gas Council, 1935, and represented Gas Industry at International Management Congress, Washington, USA, 1938, Sweden, 1947. Appointed Chief of Metropolitan Dept, WVS, 1939; lent to Min. of Health and went to Washington as UK representative on Standing Technical Cttee on Welfare, UNRRA. Comr, Trainer, and Camp Adviser, Girl Guides Assoc., 1924–48; Comdt, BRCS, 1937–39; Mem. Council, London Hostels Assoc., 1941–91. Chm. Women's Gas Fedn, 1945–49, Pres., 1949–60. A Governor of St Bartholomew's Hospital, 1948–73. Chm., Soroptimist (London) Housing Assoc., 1963–89; President Fedn of Soroptomist Clubs of Gt Britain and Ireland, 1959–60; Vice-Pres., Fawcett Soc., 1978– (Chm., 1967–71); Trustee, Women's Service Trust, 1964–89. OStJ. *Recreations:* motoring, reading, theatre. *Address:* 3 Chagford House, Chagford Street, NW1 6EG. *T:* (020) 7262 6226.
Died 4 Jan. 1999.

HALSBURY, 3rd Earl of, *cr* 1898; **John Anthony Hardinge Giffard,** FRS 1969; FREng; Baron Halsbury 1885; Viscount Tiverton 1898; Chancellor of Brunel University, 1966–97; *b* 4 June 1908; *o s* of 2nd Earl of Halsbury and Esmé Stewart (*d* 1973), *d* of late James Stewart Wallace; *S* father, 1943; *m* 1st, 1930, Ismay Catherine (marr. diss. 1936), *er d* of late Lord Ninian Crichton-Stuart and Hon. Ismay, *o d* of 14th Viscount Gormanston (she *m* 2nd, Capt. Archibald Maule Ramsay); one *s*; 2nd, 1936, Elizabeth Adeline Faith (*d* 1983), *o d* of late Major Harry Crewe Godley, DSO, Northamptonshire Regt and Mrs Godley, Claremont Lodge, Cheltenham; two *d*. *Educ:* Eton; BSc (1st Cl. Hons Chem. and Maths) London (External), 1935. FRIC 1947, Hon. FRSC 1983; FInstP 1946; CEng, FREng (FEng 1976); FIProdE 1956, Hon. FIProdE 1979. Employed by Lever Bros, 1935–42; Brown-Firth Res. Labs, 1942–47; Dir of Res., Decca Record Co., 1947–49; Man. Dir, Nat. Research Development Corporation, 1949–59; Consultant and Director: Joseph Lucas Industries, 1959–74; Distillers Co. Ltd, 1959–78; Head-Wrightson Ltd, 1959–78. External Examiner, OECD, on mission to Japan, 1965. Chairman: Science Museum Advisory Council, 1951–65; Cttee on Decimal Currency, 1961–63; Cttee of Management, Inst. of Cancer Research, Royal Marsden Hosp., 1962–77; Review Body on Doctors' and Dentists' Pay, 1971–74; Deptl Cttee of Enquiry into pay of Nurses, Midwives, Speech Therapists and Professions Supplementary to Medicine, 1974–75; Meteorological Cttee, 1970–82; President: Institution of Production Engineers, 1957–59; Royal Inst. of Philosophy, 1961–90; Parly and Scientific Cttee, 1963–66; Instn of Nuclear Engineers, 1963–65; Nat. Inst. of Industrial Psychol., 1963–75; Machine Tool Industry Res. Assoc., 1964–77; Coll. of Speech Therapists, 1983–87; Nat. Council for Christian Standards in Society, 1986–. Chm., Atlas Computing Lab., 1965–69; Member: Adv. Council to Cttee of Privy Council for Scientific and Industrial Research, 1949–54; SRC, 1965–69; Computer Bd for Univs and Research Councils, 1966–69; Decimal Currency Bd, 1966–71; Nationalised Transport Advisory Council, 1963–67; Standing Commn on Museums and Galleries, 1960–76; MRC, 1973–77; Cttee of Managers, Royal Institution, 1976–79. Governor: BBC, 1960–62; LSE, 1959–90; UMIST, 1966 (Mem. Council, Manchester Coll. of Sci. and Technol., 1956–65). Hon. FICE 1975; Hon. ARCVS 1984; Hon. FIBiol 1989. Hon. DTech Brunel Univ., 1966; DUniv Essex, 1968. *Heir: s* Adam Edward Giffard [*b* 3 June 1934; *m* 1976, Joanna Elizabeth, *d* of late Frederick Harry Cole; two *d*]. *Address:* 4 Campden

House, 29 Sheffield Terrace, W8 7NE. *T:* (020) 7727 3125. *Clubs:* Athenæum, Royal Automobile (Steward, 1966–98). *Died 14 Jan. 2000.*

HAM, Prof. James Milton, OC 1980; ScD; FIEEE; President, Canadian Academy of Engineering, 1990–91; President, 1978–83, then Emeritus, and Professor Emeritus, University of Toronto; *b* 21 Sept. 1920; *s* of James Arthur Ham and Harriet Boomer Gandier; *m* 1955, Mary Caroline, *d* of Albert William Augustine; one *s* two *d. Educ:* Runnymede Coll. Inst., Toronto, 1936–39; Univ. of Toronto (BASc 1943); MIT (SM, ScD). Served with RCNVR as Elect. Lt, 1944–45. Lectr and Housemaster, Univ. of Toronto, 1945–46; Massachusetts Institute of Technology: Res. Associate, 1949–51; Res. Fellow in Electronics, 1950; Asst Prof. of Elect. Engrg, 1951–52; University of Toronto: Associate Prof., 1952–59; Prof., 1959–88; Prof. of Science, Technology and Public Policy, 1983–88; Fellow, New Coll., 1963; Head, Dept of Elect. Engrg, 1964–66; Dean, Fac. of Applied Science and Engrg, 1966–73; Chm., Research Bd, 1974–76; Dean, Sch. of Graduate Studies, 1976–78. Vis. Scientist, Cambridge Univ. and USSR, 1960–61. Dir, Shell Canada, 1981–91. Mem., Nat. Res. Council, 1969–74 (Chm., Associate Cttee on Automatic Control, 1959–65); Governor, Ont. Res. Foundn, 1971–86; Chairman: Cttee on Engrg Educn of World Fedn of Engrg Orgns, 1970; Res. and Technol. Review Bd, Noranda Inc., 1985; Industrial Disease Standards Panel, Ont, 1986–88. Member: Assoc. Prof. Engrs, Ont, 1943–; Internat. Fedn Automatic Control (Exec. Council), 1966–72; Fellow: Engrg Inst. Canada; Canadian Academy of Engrg, 1987. Hon. DèsScA Montreal, 1973; Hon. DSc: Queen's, 1974; New Brunswick, 1979; McGill, 1979; McMaster, 1980; Guelph, 1992; Hon. LLD: Manitoba, 1980; Hanyang (Korea), 1981; Concordia Univ., 1983; Hon. DEng: Tech. Univ. of Nova Scotia, 1980; Memorial Univ., 1981; Toronto, 1991; Hon. DSacLet Wycliffe Coll., 1983. British Assoc. for Advancement of Science Medal, 1943; Centennial Medal, 1967, Engrg Medal, 1974, Gold Medal, 1984, Assoc. Professional Engrs, Ontario; Engrg Alumni Medal, 1973; McNaughton Medal, IEEE, 1977; Sir John Kennedy Medal, Engrg Inst. Canada, 1983. Silver Jubilee Medal, 1977; Order of Ontario, 1989; Confederation Medal, 1992. *Publications:* Scientific Basis of Electrical Engineering (with G. R. Slemon), 1961; Report of Royal Commission on Health and Safety of Workers in Mines, 1976; papers for scientific jls on automatic control. *Recreations:* sailing, fractals, photography. *Address:* 135 Glencairn Avenue, Toronto, Ontario M4R 1N1, Canada.
Died 16 Sept. 1997.

HAMILL, Sir Patrick, Kt 1984; QPM 1979; Chief Constable, Strathclyde Police, 1977–85; *b* 29 April 1930; *s* of Hugh Hamill and Elizabeth McGowan; *m* 1954, Nell Gillespie; four *s* one *d. Educ:* St Patrick's High Sch., Dumbarton; Open Univ. (BA). Joined Dunbartonshire Constabulary, 1950; transf. to City of Glasgow Police, 1972; apptd Assistant Chief Constable: Glasgow, 1974; Strathclyde Police, 1975; attended Royal Coll. of Defence Studies Course, 1976. Association of Chief Police Officers (Scotland): Rep. to Interpol, 1977–81; Pres., 1982–83; Hon. Sec., 1983–85. Chm., Management Bd, St Margaret's Hospice, Clydebank, 1986–99; Member Board of Governors: Scottish Police Coll., 1977–85; St Aloysius' Coll., Glasgow, 1983–90 (Vice-Chm., 1986–90); St Andrew's Coll. of Educn, Bearsden, 1987–88; Mem., Gen. Convocation, Univ. of Strathclyde, 1984–87. OStJ 1978. *Recreations:* walking, reading history, golf.
Died 25 Feb. 2000.

HAMILTON, Graeme Montagu, TD; QC 1978; a Recorder, 1974–99; *b* 1 June 1934; *s* of late Leslie Montagu Hamilton and Joan Elizabeth (*née* Moxey; she

m 1946, Sir Richard Burbidge, 3rd Bt, CBE); *m* 1978, Mrs Deirdre Lynn. *Educ:* Eton; Magdalene Coll., Cambridge (MA). National Service, 4/7 Royal Dragoon Guards, 1953–55. Called to the Bar, Gray's Inn, 1959, Bencher, 1987; Mem., Senate of Inns of Court and Bar, 1975–78. Mem., Criminal Injuries Compensation Bd, 1987–2000. Gen. Comr of Income Tax, 1989–. Chm., Disciplinary Appeal Cttee, ICAEW, 1998–2000. TA City of London Yeomanry, Inns of Court and City Yeomanry, 1955–70. *Recreations:* sailing, shooting, gardening. *Address:* 2 Crown Office Row, Temple, EC4Y 7HJ. *Clubs:* Cavalry and Guards, Royal Thames Yacht, Royal Automobile; Hong Kong Jockey. *Died 18 July 2000.*

HAMILTON, Iain Ellis, FRAM; composer; pianist; Mary Duke Biddle Professor of Music, Duke University, North Carolina, USA, 1962–78 (Chairman of the Department, 1966); *b* Glasgow, 6 June 1922; *s* of James and Catherine Hamilton. *Educ:* Mill Hill; Royal Academy of Music (Scholar, 1947–51; FRAM 1960); BMus London Univ., 1951. Engineer (Handley Page Ltd), 1939–46. Lecturer at Morley Coll., 1952–58; Lecturer, London Univ., 1956–60. Prizes and awards included: Prize of Royal Philharmonic Society, 1951; Prize of Koussevitsky Foundation, USA, 1951; Butterworth Award, 1954; Arnold Bax Gold Medal, 1956; Ralph Vaughan Williams Award, Composers' Guild of GB, 1975. Chm. Composers' Guild, 1958; Chm. ICA Music Cttee, 1958–60. *Works: orchestral works:* Symphonies; Sinfonia for two orchestras (Edinburgh Festival Commission); Concertos, for piano, clarinet, organ, violin and harp; Symphonic Variations for string orchestra; Overture, Bartholomew Fair; Overture, 1912; Ecossaise; Scottish Dances; 5 Love Songs for tenor and orchestra; Jubilee; Arias for small orchestra; Vers Apollinaire, for orch.; Epitaph for this World and Time: 3 choruses and 2 organs; Vespers, for chorus, 2 pianos, harp and percussion; Voyage for horn and orchestra; Alastor; Amphion for violin and orchestra; Commedia; St Mark Passion, for 4 soloists, chorus and orchestra; Cleopatra, for soprano and orchestra; Prometheus, for soloists, chorus and orch.; La Mort de Phèdre, for mezzo-soprano and orch.; BBC Commissions: The Bermudas, for baritone, chorus and orch.; Concerto for jazz trumpet and orch.; Cantos; Circus; The Transit of Jupiter; Bulgaria–Invocation: Evocation; *chamber works included:* four String Quartets; String Octet; Sonatas for piano, viola, clarinet, flute and oboe; Sonata for chamber orchestra; Flute Quartet; Clarinet Quintet; 3 Nocturnes for clarinet and piano; 5 Scenes for trumpet and piano; Sextet; Sonatas and Variants for 10 winds; Antigone for Winds; Octet for Winds; Dialogues for soprano and 5 instruments; Sextet for Strings; *solo piano:* Nocturnes with Cadenzas; *solo organ:* Threnos; Aubade and Paraphrase; *opera:* Agamemnon; Royal Hunt of the Sun; Pharsalia; The Catiline Conspiracy; Tamburlaine; Anna Karenina; Lancelot; Raleigh's Dream; The Tragedy of Macbeth; London's Fair; On The Eve; 4 Border Songs, The Fray of Suport, a Requiem and a Mass for unaccompanied voices; Clerk Saunders (ballet); music for theatre and films. Hon. DMus Glasgow, 1970. *Publications:* articles for many journals. *Address:* Flat 4, 85 Cornwall Gardens, SW7 4XY. *Died 21 July 2000.*

HAMILTON, Prof. James; Professor of Physics, Nordic Institute for Theoretical Atomic Physics, 1964–86; *b* 29 Jan. 1918; *s* of Joseph Hamilton, Killybegs, Co. Donegal and Jessie Mackay, Keiss, Caithness; *m* 1945, Glen, *d* of Charles Dobbs, London; one *s* one *d* (and one *s* decd). *Educ:* Royal Academical Institution, Belfast; Queen's Univ., Belfast; Institute for Advanced Study, Dublin, 1941–43; Manchester Univ. Scientific Officer (Ops Research), Admiralty, London, and South East Asia Command, 1943–45; ICI Fellow, Manchester Univ., 1945–48; Lectr in Theoretical Physics, Manchester Univ.,

1948–49; University Lectr in Mathematics, Cambridge Univ., 1950–60. Fellow of Christ's Coll., Cambridge, 1953–60; Research Associate in Nuclear Physics, Cornell Univ., NY, 1957–58; Prof. of Physics, University Coll., London, 1960–64. Donegall Lectr, TCD, 1969. Dir, Nordita, 1984–85. Foreign Mem., Royal Danish Acad., 1967. Dr *hc* Trondheim, 1982; DrPhil *hc* Lund, 1986. *Publications:* The Theory of Elementary Particles, 1959; (with B. Tromborg) Partial Wave Amplitudes and Resonance Poles, 1972; Aharonov-Bohm and other Cyclic Phenomena, 1997; Admty report (1944), on first use of radar in marine navigation, Normandy; papers and articles on interaction of radiation with atoms, elementary particle physics, causality, and related topics. *Address:* 4 Almoners Avenue, Cambridge CB1 4PA. *T:* (01223) 244175.
Died 6 July 2000.

HAMILTON, Hon. Liam; *see* Hamilton, Hon. W.

HAMILTON, Sir Michael Aubrey, Kt 1983; *b* 5 July 1918; *s* of Rt Rev. E. K. C. Hamilton, KCVO and Jessie, *d* of Sir Walter Cassels; *m* 1947, Lavinia, 3rd *d* of Col Sir Charles Ponsonby, 1st Bt, TD; one *s* three *d. Educ:* Radley; UC, Oxford. Served War of 1939–45, with 1st Bn, Coldstream Guards. MP (C): Wellingborough Div. Northants, 1959–64; Salisbury, Feb. 1965–1983; Asst Govt Whip, 1961–62; a Lord Comr of the Treasury, 1962–64; PPS to Sec. of State for Foreign and Commonwealth Affairs, 1982–83. Former Director: Army & Navy Stores; Hops Marketing Board; Royal Exchange Assurance. UK Representative: UN Gen. Assembly, 1970; US Bicentennial Celebrations, 1976. *Address:* Lordington House, Chichester, Sussex PO18 9DX. *T:* (01243) 371717.
Died 3 July 2000.

HAMILTON, Hon. William, (Liam); Chief Justice of Ireland, 1994–2000; *b* 1928. *Educ:* Mitchelstown Christian Brothers' Sch.; King's Inns Sch. of Law, Dublin; Law Sch., University Coll., Dublin. Civil Servant, Central Office of High Court, 1946–51; called to the Bar, King's Inns, Dublin, 1956; private practice at Irish Bar, 1957; QC 1972; Judge of High Court of Ireland, 1974, Pres. of High Court, 1985–94. Mem., Irish Labour Party, 1956–74, contested local elections, 1960. KJStJ 1981. *Address:* c/o The Supreme Court, The Four Courts, Dublin 7, Ireland.
Died 29 Nov. 2000.

HAMILTON, Prof. William Donald, FRS 1980; Royal Society Research Professor, Department of Zoology, and Fellow of New College, Oxford University, since 1984; *b* 1 Aug. 1936; *s* of Archibald Milne Hamilton and Bettina Matraves Hamilton (*née* Collier); *m* 1967, Christine Ann Friess; three *d. Educ:* Tonbridge Sch.; St John's Coll., Cambridge (BA); London Univ. (PhD). Lecturer in Genetics, Imperial Coll., London Univ., 1964–77; Prof. of Evolutionary Biology, Mus. of Zoology and Div. of Biol Scis, Michigan Univ., 1978–84. For. Mem., American Acad. of Arts and Sciences, 1978; Member: Royal Soc. of Scis of Uppsala, 1987; Brazilian Acad. of Scis, 1993; Acad. of Finland, 1997. Darwin Medal, Royal Soc., 1988; Linnean Medal for Zoology, Linnean Soc. of London, 1989; Frink Medal for Zoology, Zoological Soc. of London, 1991; Wander Prize, Bern Univ., 1992; Crafoord Prize and Medal, Swedish Acad. of Scis, 1993; Kyoto Prize, Inamori Foundn, 1993; Fyssen Prize, Fyssen Foundn, 1996. *Publications:* Narrow Roads of Gene Land (Collected Papers Vol. 1, 1996); contribs to Jl of Theoretical Biology, Science, Nature, Amer. Naturalist. *Address:* Department of Zoology, South Parks Road, Oxford OX1 3PS. *Died 7 March 2000.*

HAMILTON, William Winter; *b* 26 June 1917; *m* 1st, 1944, Jean Cullow (*d* 1968); one *s* one *d*; 2nd, 1982, Mrs Margaret Cogle. *Educ:* Washington Grammar Sch., Co. Durham; Sheffield Univ. (BA, DipEd). Joined Lab. Party,

1936; contested: W Fife, 1945; S Hams, 1987. MP (Lab): Fife W, 1950–74, Fife Central, 1974–87. Chairman, H of C Estimates Cttee, 1964–70; Vice-Chm., Parly Labour Party, 1966–70. Mem., European Parlt, 1975–79; Vice-Chm., Rules and Procedure Cttee, 1979–79 (Chm., 1975–76). Served War of 1939–45, Middle East, Capt. *Publications:* My Queen and I, 1975; Blood on the Walls: memoirs of an anti-Royalist, 1992.
Died 23 Jan. 2000.

HAMILTON-JONES, Maj.-Gen. John, CBE 1977; Consultant, Cubic Defense Systems, since 1992; *b* 6 May 1926; *s* of late George and Lillian Hamilton-Jones; *m* 1st, 1952, Penelope Ann Marion Derry (*d* 1993); three *d*; 2nd, 1993, Frances Helen Arnold; one step *d. Educ:* Cranbrook Sch.; Edinburgh Univ.; Technical Staff Coll. US Army Guided Missile Grad., 1957. Commnd RA, 1945; Indian Artillery, 1945–47; Regtl Service, Far East/ME, 1947–60; Jt Services Staff Coll., 1966; comd a regt, 1966–69; DS RMCS, 1970–72; MoD Dir, 1975–78 (Brig.); Pres., Ordnance Bd, 1980–81 (Maj.-Gen.). Pres., Army Advance Class, 1981–83; Vice-Pres., Internat. Marketing, Gen. Defense Corp. of Pennsylvania, 1986–88 (Dir, 1984–86). CEng; FRAeS; FInstD 1987; MIERE; FBIM (MBIM 1979). CommanInternet. Internat. Marketing, Internat. eur. Assoc. Franco-Britannique, 1979. *Recreations:* rowing, Rugby, squash, music, hi-fi. *Address:* c/o Lloyds Bank, Cox's & King's Branch, PO Box 1190, 7 Pall Mall, SW1Y 5NA. *Died 9 Sept. 1997.*

HAMMETT, Sir Clifford (James), Kt 1969; Regional Legal Adviser with British Development Division in the Caribbean, 1975–92; *b* 8 June 1917; *s* of late Frederick John and Louisa Maria Hammett; *m* 1946, Olive Beryl Applebee; four *s* one *d. Educ:* Woodbridge. Admitted Solicitor, 1939; called to the Bar, Middle Temple, 1948. Indian Army, 1st Punjab Regt, 1940, North Africa, 1941; captured at Singapore, 1942 (despatches); POW on Siam Railway, 1942–45. Magistrate, Nigeria, 1946–52; transferred to Fiji, 1952; Senior Magistrate, 1954; Puisne Judge, 1955; conjointly Chief Justice, Tonga, 1956–68; Chief Justice, Fiji, 1967–72; Actg Governor Gen. of Fiji, 1971. *Recreation:* gardening. *Address:* The Bury, High Street, Henham, Bishop's Stortford, Herts CM22 6AR. *Club:* Naval and Military. *Died 28 June 1999.*

HAMMETT, Harold George; Deputy High Commissioner, Peshawar, 1964–66; *b* 2 Aug. 1906; 2nd *s* of Arthur Henry Hammett; *m* 1st, 1936, Daphne Margaret Vowler; one *s*; 2nd, 1947, Natalie Moira Sherratt; one *s* one *d. Educ:* St Olave's; Clare Coll., Cambridge. Malayan Civil Service, 1928–57; retired from post of Resident Commissioner, Malacca, on Malayan Independence, 1957; Commonwealth Office (formerly CRO), 1958–66. *Recreations:* woodwork, gardening. *Address:* Wiltons, 22 East Cliff Road, Dawlish, Devon EX7 0DJ. *T:* (01626) 862114. *Died 7 Dec. 1999.*

HAMMOND, Catherine Elizabeth, CBE 1950; Colonel, Women's Royal Army Corps, retired; *b* 22 Dec. 1909; *d* of late Frank Ernest Rauleigh Eddolls and Elsie Eddolls (*née* Cooper); *m*; one *s* one *d*; *m* 1949, Aldwyn Hammond, racehorse trainer (marr. diss. 1954). *Educ:* Lassington House, Highworth, Wilts; Chesterville Sch., Cirencester, Glos. Joined ATS (TA) (FANY), 1938; Private, 7th Wilts MT Co., 1939; 2nd Subaltern 1940; Capt., 1942; Major, Commanding Devon Bn, 1942; Lt-Col, Asst Dir ATS Oxford, 1943; Col, Dep. Dir ATS (later WRAC), Eastern Command, 1947–50. Hon. Col 54 (East Anglia) Div./Dist WRAC/TA, 1964–67. Chm., WRAC Assoc., 1966–70, Life Vice-Pres., 1971. Chm., Highworth and District Br., RNLI, 1970–; President: Royal British Legion, Highworth (Women's Section), 1977–84; Highworth Amateur Dramatic Soc., 1982–86. Deputy Mayor, Highworth Town Council, 1978, Mayor, 1979–81, 1984–85. SSStJ 1986. *Recreations:* hockey (Army (women), 1947–48), all games, racing. *Address:* Red Down, Highworth, Wilts SN6 7SH. *T:* (01793) 762331.

Died 25 Oct. 1999.

HAMMOND, Dame Joan (Hood), DBE 1974 (CBE 1963; OBE 1953); CMG 1972; Australian operatic, concert, oratorio, and recital singer; *b* 24 May 1912; *d* of late Samuel Hood Hammond and Hilda May Blandford. *Educ:* Presbyterian Ladies Coll., Pymble, Sydney, Australia. Student of violin and singing at Sydney Conservatorium of Music. Formerly Sports writer, Daily Telegraph, Sydney. Played with Sydney Philharmonic Orchestra for three years; commenced public appearances (singing) in Sydney, 1929; studied in Europe, 1936; made operatic debut, Vienna, 1939; London debut in Messiah, 1938. World Tours: British Isles, USA, Canada, Australasia, Malaya, India, E and S Africa, Europe, Scandinavia, Russia, etc. Guest Artist: Royal Opera House, Covent Garden; Carl Rosa; Sadler's Wells; Vienna Staatsoper; Bolshoi, Moscow; Marinsky, Leningrad; Riga, Latvia; New York City Centre; Australian Elizabethan Theatre Trust; Netherlands Opera; Barcelona Liceo. Operatic roles: Aida, Madame Butterfly, Tosca, Salome, Otello, Thais, Faust, Don Carlos, Eugene Onegin, Invisible City of Kitej, La Traviata, Il Trovatore, La Bohème, Pique Dame, Manon, Manon Lescaut, La Forza del Destino, Fidelio, Simone Boccanegra, Turandot, Tannhauser, Lohengrin, Damnation of Faust, Martha, Pagliacci, Der Freischutz, Oberon, Magic Flute, Dido and Aeneas; World Premieres: Trojan Women, Wat Tyler, Yerma; British Premiere, Rusalka. HMV Recording artist. Head of Vocal Studies, 1975–89, Vocal Consultant, 1990–93, Victorian College of the Arts; Vocal Consultant, Faculty of Music, Univ. of Melbourne, 1993. Volunteer Ambulance Driver, London, War of 1939–45. Sir Charles Santley Award, Worshipful Co. of Musicians, 1970; Lifetime Achievement Award, Green Room Awards Assoc., 1988; Lifetime Achievement Award for Excellence in Recording, Australasian Sound Recordings Assoc., 1994. Hon. Life Member, Australian Opera Victoria State Opera. Hon. MusD Western Australia, 1979. Coronation Medal, 1953. *Publication:* A Voice, A Life, 1970. *Recreations:* golf (won first junior Golf Championship of NSW, 1930 and 1931; NSW Ladies' Golf Union State Title, 1932, 1934, 1935; runner-up Australian Open Championship, 1933; Mem. first Ladies' Golf Union team of Australia to compete against GB, 1935) (runner-up NSW State Squash Championship, 1934), yachting, swimming, tennis, writing, reading. *Address:* PO Box 267, South Yarra, Vic 3141, Australia. *Died 26 Nov. 1996.*

HAMMOND INNES, Ralph, (Hammond Innes), CBE 1978; author and traveller; *b* 15 July 1913; *s* of late William Hammond and Dora Beatrice Innes; *m* 1937, Dorothy Mary Lang (*d* 1989). Staff of Financial News, 1934–40. Served Artillery, 1940–46. Member: various cttees, Soc. of Authors, sailing foundns; Vice President: Assoc. of Sea Training Orgns; World Ship Trust. Hon. DLitt Bristol, 1985. Works regularly translated into numerous languages; many book club and paperback edns throughout the world. *Publications include:* Wreckers Must Breathe, 1940; The Trojan Horse, 1940; Attack Alarm, 1941; Dead and Alive, 1946; The Lonely Skier, 1947; The Killer Mine, 1947; Maddon's Rock, 1948; The Blue Ice, 1948; The White South (Book Society Choice), 1949; The Angry Mountain, 1950; Air Bridge, 1951; Campbell's Kingdom (Book Society Choice), 1952; The Strange Land, 1954; The Mary Deare (chosen by Literary Guild of America, Book Soc. Choice), 1956; The Land God Gave to Cain, 1958; Harvest of Journeys (Book Soc. Choice), 1959; The Doomed Oasis (chosen by Literary Guild of America, Book Soc. Choice), 1960; Atlantic Fury (Book Society Choice), 1962; Scandinavia, 1963; The Strode Venturer, 1965; Sea and Islands (Book Society

Choice), 1967; The Conquistadors (Book of the Month and Literary Guild), 1969; Levkas Man, 1971; Golden Soak, 1973; North Star, 1974; The Big Footprints, 1977; The Last Voyage (Cook), 1978; Solomons Seal, 1980; The Black Tide, 1982; High Stand, 1985; Hammond Innes' East Anglia, 1986; Medusa, 1988; Isvik, 1991; Target Antarctica, 1993; Delta Connection, 1996; *films:* Snowbound, Hell Below Zero, Campbell's Kingdom, The Wreck of the Mary Deare; *TV:* Explorers (Cook), 1975; Golden Soak, 1979; Levkas Man, 1981. *Recreations:* cruising and ocean racing, forestry. *Address:* Ayres End, Kersey, Suffolk IP7 6EB. *T:* (01473) 823294. *Clubs:* Garrick, Royal Ocean Racing, Royal Cruising; Royal Yacht Squadron. *Died 10 June 1998.*

HAMPSON, Prof. Elwyn Lloyd, MDS; FDSRCS; Professor of Restorative Dentistry, University of Sheffield, 1960–81, then Emeritus; Hon. Consultant Dental Surgeon to Sheffield Area Health Authority, since 1981; *b* 31 Jan. 1916; *s* of John and Mary Hampson; *m* 1940, Anne Cottrell; one *s* one *d*. *Educ:* Calday Grange Grammar Sch., W Kirby, Cheshire; Univ. of Liverpool. BDS with 1st Class Hons 1939; HDD RCSE 1944; FDSRCS 1949; MDS 1954; FDSRCSE 1964. House surg., Liverpool Dental Hosp., 1939; Royal Army Dental Corps, 1941–45; Lecturer in Operative Dental Surgery, Edinburgh Dental Sch., 1945–47; Lecturer and later Senior Lecturer in Operative Dental Surgery, 1947–60, Dean of Sch. of Clinical Dentistry, 1968–72, Univ. of Sheffield. Mem., GDC, 1968–73. *Publications:* Hampson's Textbook of Operative Dental Surgery, 1961, 4th edn 1980; many papers in scientific jls. *Recreations:* water colour painting, golf. *Address:* 19 Wealstone Court, Chester CH2 1HA. *Died 18 May 1998.*

HANCOCK, Air Marshal Sir Valston Eldridge, KBE 1962 (CBE 1953; OBE 1942); CB 1958; DFC 1945; grazier; *b* 31 May 1907; *s* of R. J. Hancock, Perth, W Australia; *m* 1932, Joan E. G., *d* of Col A. G. Butler, DSO VD; two *s* one *d*. *Educ:* Hale Sch., Perth; RMC, Duntroon; psa; idc. Joined Royal Military College, Duntroon, 1925; transferred RAAF, 1929; Dir of Plans, 1940–41; commanded 71 (Beaufort) Wing, New Guinea, 1945; Commandant RAAF Academy, 1947–49; Deputy Chief of Air Staff, 1951–53; Air Mem. for Personnel, Air Board, 1953–54; Head of Australian Joint Services Staff, UK, 1955–57; Extra Gentleman Usher to the Royal Household, 1955–57; AOC 224 Group, RAF, Malaya, 1957–59; Air Officer Commanding Operational Command, 1959–61; Chief of Air Staff, Royal Australian Air Force, 1961–65. Commissioner-Gen., Australian Exhibit Organization, Expo 1967. Foundation Chm., Australian Defence Assoc., 1975–81, Life Patron, 1982. Life Mem., Royal Commonwealth Soc. (WA) (Pres., 1976–81). *Recreations:* literature, sport. *Address:* 445/31 Williams Road, Nedlands, WA 6099, Australia. *Club:* Weld (Perth). *Died 29 Sept. 1998.*

HANDS, David Richard Granville; QC 1988; *b* 23 Dec. 1943; *s* of late Leonard Frederick Horace Hands and Nancye Wilkes (*née* Kenyon); *m* 1982, Penelope Ann Jervis. *Educ:* Radley. Called to the Bar, Inner Temple, 1965. *Recreations:* gardening, trees, looking after dogs and cats. *Address:* 4 Breams Buildings, Temple, EC4A 1AQ. *T:* (020) 7353 5835. *Club:* Travellers. *Died 10 Dec. 2000.*

HANFF, Helene; writer and broadcaster; *b* 15 April 1916; *d* of Arthur and Miriam Levy Hanff. *Educ:* none beyond secondary sch. Won a playwriting fellowship from The Theatre Guild, 1939; wrote: unproduced plays through '40s; dramatic TV scripts in '50s; American history books for children in '60s; books in '70s and '80s. Monthly radio broadcasts, Woman's Hour, BBC, 1978–85. *Publications:* Underfoot in Show Business, 1961, repr. 1980; 84 Charing

Cross Road, 1970; Duchess of Bloomsbury Street, 1973; Apple of My Eye, 1978; Q's Legacy, 1985; Letter from New York, 1992 (BBC scripts); Helene Hanff Omnibus, 1995. *Recreations:* classical music lover, (Mets) baseball fan; also addicted to Guardian (Weekly) crossword puzzles. *Address:* 305 East 72nd Street, New York, NY 10021, USA. *T:* (212) 8794952.
Died 9 April 1997.

HANHAM, Leonard Edward; HM Diplomatic Service, retired; Consul-General, Amsterdam, 1978–80; *b* 23 April 1921; *m* 1945, Joyce Wrenn; two *s* two *d*. Served War, RN, 1939–48. Foreign Office, 1948; Vice-Consul: Rouen, 1949; Basra, 1950; Ponta Delgada, 1952; Foreign Office, 1955; 1st Secretary and Consul: Rangoon, 1957; Tegucigalpa, 1961; Foreign Office, 1963; Consul: Durban, 1965; Medan, 1969; FCO, 1972; Counsellor and Consul-Gen., Lisbon, 1975–78. *Address:* 26 First Avenue, Gillingham, Kent ME7 2LG. *Died 7 Sept. 1998.*

HANKEY, 2nd Baron *cr* 1939, of The Chart, Surrey; **Robert Maurice Alers Hankey,** KCMG 1955 (CMG 1947); KCVO 1956; *D* 4 July 1905; *s* of 1st Baron Hankey, GCB, GCMG, GCVO, PC, FRS, and Adeline (*d* 1979), *d* of A. de Smidt; *S* father, 1963; *m* 1st, 1930, Frances Bevyl Stuart-Menteth (*d* 1957); two *s* two *d*; 2nd, 1962, Joanna Riddall Wright (*d* 1991), *d* of late Rev. James Johnstone Wright; 3rd, 1992, Mrs Stephanie Langley, *yr d* of late Brig. Percy Paulet King. *Educ:* Rugby Sch.; New Coll., Oxford. Diplomatic Service, 1927; served Berlin, Paris, London, Warsaw, Bucharest, Cairo, Teheran, Madrid, Budapest; HM Ambassador at Stockholm, 1954–60; Permanent UK Delegate to OEEC and OECD, and Chm., Economic Policy Cttee, 1960–65. Vice-Pres., European Inst. of Business Administration, Fontainebleau, 1966–82. Dir, Alliance Bldg Soc., 1970–83. Member: Internat. Council of United World Colleges, 1966–78; Council, Internat. Baccalaureat Foundn, Geneva, 1967–76. Pres., Anglo-Swedish Soc., 1969–75. Grand Cross of Order of the North Star (Sweden), 1954. *Recreations:* reading, tennis, ski-ing, music. *Heir: s* Hon. Donald Robin Alers Hankey [*b* 12 June 1938; *m* 1st, 1963, Margaretha (marr. diss. 1974), *yr d* of H. Thorndahl, Copenhagen; 2nd, 1974, Eileen Désirée (marr. diss. 1994), *yr d* of late Maj.-Gen. Stuart Battye, CB; two *d*; 3rd, 1994, June, *d* of late Dr Leonard Taboroff.]. *Address:* Hethe House, Cowden, Edenbridge, Kent TN8 7DZ. *T:* (01342) 850538.
Died 28 Oct. 1996.

HANKEY, Hon. Henry Arthur Alers, CMG 1960; CVO 1959; HM Diplomatic Service, retired; *b* 1 Sept. 1914; *y s* of 1st Baron Hankey, GCB, GCMG, GCVO, PC, FRS and Adeline, *d* of A. de Smidt, formerly Surveyor Gen. of Cape Colony; *m* 1941, Vronwy Mary Fisher (*d* 1998); three *s* one *d*. *Educ:* Rugby Sch.; New Coll., Oxford. Entered HM Diplomatic Service, 1937; Third Sec., HM Embassy, Paris, 1939; Second Sec., Madrid, 1942; First Sec., Rome, 1946; Consul, San Francisco, 1950; First Sec., Santiago, 1953; promoted Counsellor and apptd Head of American Dept, Foreign Office, 1956; Counsellor, HM Embassy, Beirut, 1962–66; Ambassador, Panama, 1966–69; Asst Under-Sec. of State, FCO, 1969–74. Director: Lloyds Bank International, 1975–80; Antofagasta (Chile) & Bolivia Railway Co. Ltd, 1975–82. Sec., British North American Cttee, 1981–85. *Publications:* Archaeology: artifacts and artifiction, 1985; More Artifacts and Artifiction, 1996. *Recreations:* ski-ing, tennis, music, painting. *Address:* Llandaff Barn, 11 Thames Street, Eynsham, Witney OX8 1HF. *T:* (01865) 884028. *Died 27 Aug. 1999.*

HANNING, Hugh Peter James; Vice-President, Atlantic Council of the United Kingdom, since 1991; Chairman, Fontmell Group on Disaster Relief, since 1990; *b* 5 Feb. 1925; *s* of John Rowland Hanning and Valentine Mary

(*née* Bradshaw); *m* 1954, Caragh McClure Williams; one *s*. *Educ:* Winchester Coll. (Schol.); University Coll., Oxford (BA Hons 1949). Served War, RNVR (rocketships). Leader-writer, Westminster Press, 1951–60; Defence Corresp., ITN, 1961; Consultant, IISS, 1964–70; Defence Corresp., Observer, 1963–; Defence Consultant, Guardian, 1967–69. Advr to MoD, NATO and US Govt. Dep. Dir, RUSI, 1967–70. Dir, Brit. Atlantic Cttee, 1975–82. Founder Member: ITDG, 1967; Internat. Peace Acad., NY, 1970. Mission to Biafra with Leonard Cheshire, 1969. Internat. Sec., C of E, 1972–80. Lectures to Chatham Hse, RUSI, IISS and sen. officers courses. *Publications:* Bow Group pamphlets on the UN, 1963–64; The Peaceful Uses of Military Forces, 1968; NATO: our guarantee of peace, 1985; Peace: the plain man's guide, 1988; Five Wars, One Cause, 1996; reports for Fontmell Gp on military and disaster relief. *Recreations:* piano, golf, painting, Weltverbesserungswahn. *Address:* 18 Montpelier Row, Blackheath, SE3 0RL. *T:* (020) 8852 4101. *Club:* Army and Navy. *Died 5 May 2000.*

HANSON, Sir Anthony (Leslie Oswald), 4th Bt *cr* 1887, of Bryanston Square, co. Middlesex; *b* 27 Nov. 1934; *s* of Sir Gerald Stanhope Hanson, 2nd Bt, and 3rd wife, Flora Liebe (*d* 1956), *e d* of late Lieut-Col W. A. R. Blennerhassett; *S* half-brother, 1951; *m* 1964, Denise Jane, (Tuppence), *e d* of Richard Rolph; one *d*. *Educ:* Hawtrey's; Gordonstoun, Elgin, Morayshire; St Luke's College, Exeter Univ. (BEd Hons 1974). Career in Royal Navy until 1955; farming, 1956–67; teacher, 1974–83; took very early retirement due to severe road accident; Conservation Officer, MSC, 1984. Supported by wife who teaches at St Luke's, Teignmouth. Member: Greenpeace; Amnesty International. *Recreations:* sailing, talking. *Heir:* none. *Address:* Woodland Cottage, Woodland, Ashburton, Devon TQ13 7HJ. *T:* Ashburton (01364) 652711.
Died 14 March 1996 (ext).

HANSON, Sir (Charles) John, 3rd Bt *cr* 1918, of Fowey, Cornwall; *b* 28 Feb. 1919; *o s* of Major Sir Charles Edwin Bourne Hanson, 2nd Bt, and Violet Sybil (*d* 1966), 3rd *d* of late John B. Johnstone, Coombe Cottage, Kingston Hill, Surrey; *S* father, 1958; *m* 1st, 1944, Patricia Helen (marr. diss. 1968), *o c* of late Adm. Sir (Eric James) Patrick Brind, GBE, KCB; one *s* one *d*; 2nd, 1968, Mrs Helen Yorke, *d* of late Charles Ormonde Trew. *Educ:* Eton; Clare Coll., Cambridge. Late Captain, The Duke of Cornwall's Light Infantry; served War of 1939–45. *Heir: s* Charles Rupert Patrick Hanson [*b* 25 June 1945; *m* 1977, Wanda, *d* of Don Arturo Larrain, Santiago, Chile; one *s*]. *Address:* Gunn House, Shelfanger, near Diss, Norfolk IP22 2DP. *T:* Diss (01379) 643207. *Clubs:* Army and Navy, MCC. *Died 30 March 1996.*

HANWORTH, 2nd Viscount *cr* 1936, of Hanworth, co. Middlesex; **David Bertram Pollock,** CEng, MIMechE, FIEE, FRPS, FIQA; Bt 1922; Baron 1926; Lieutenant-Colonel Royal Engineers, retired; Barrister-at-Law (Inner Temple), 1958; *b* 1 Aug. 1916; *s* of Charles Thomas Anderson Pollock (killed in action, 1918), and Alice Joyce Becher; *S* grandfather, 1936; *m* 1940, Isolda Rosamond, DL, FSA, *yr d* of Geoffrey Parker, Cairo; two *s* one *d*. *Educ:* Wellington Coll.; Trinity Coll., Cambridge (Mechanical Science Tripos, 1939). Joined Social Democratic Party, 1981, Soc & Lib Dem, 1989; latterly independent. *Publications:* Amateur Carbro Colour Prints, 1950; Amateur Dye Transfer Colour Prints, 1956. *Heir: s* Hon. David Stephen Geoffrey Pollock [*b* 16 Feb. 1946; *m* 1968, Elizabeth Liberty, *e d* of Lawrence Vambe, MBE; two *d*]. *Address:* Quoin Cottage, Shamley Green, Guildford, Surrey GU5 0UJ. *Died 31 Aug. 1996.*

HAPPOLD, Prof. Sir Edmund (Frank Ley), Kt 1994; RDI 1983; FEng 1983; Professor of Building Engineering, University of Bath, since 1976; Senior Partner, Buro

Happold, consulting engineers, since 1976; *b* 8 Nov. 1930; *s* of late Prof. Frank Charles Happold, PhD, DSc and A. Margaret M. Smith, MA; *m* 1967, Evelyn Claire Matthews, MSc; two *s*. *Educ:* Leeds Grammar Sch.; Bootham Sch., York; Leeds Univ. BSc, FICE, FIStructE, FCIOB, FIEHK. Site Engineer, Sir Robert McAlpine & Sons, 1952–54; Engineer, Ove Arup & Partners, 1956–58, Severud Elstad & Kruger, NY, 1958–60; Senior Engineer, then Associate, later Exec. Partner, Ove Arup & Partners, 1960–76; assisted Tom Hancock in winning 2nd prize, Houses of Parlt competition, 1972; won jtly with 4 others Centre Pompidou, Plateau Beaubourg competition, 1971; won jtly with 2 others Vauxhall Cross competition, 1982; jtly with 4 others won High Wycombe Cultural Centre Competition, 1987; won, with Sir Norman Foster, competition for Faisal Foundn Complex, Saudi Arabia, 1994. Chm., Construction Industry Council, 1988–91. Institution of Structural Engineers: Mem. Council, 1974–77, 1979–93; Chm., Educn Cttee, 1979–82; Vice-Pres., 1982–86; Pres., 1986–87; Guthrie Brown Medal, 1970; Oscar Faber Medal, 1974, 1977; Henry Adams Award, 1976; Gold Medal, 1992; Mem., Standing Cttee on Structural Safety, 1976–86; International Association of Bridge and Structural Engineers: Mem., Nat. Council, 1977–; Mem., Internat. Tech. Cttee, 1978–83; Chm., Commn V, 1978–83. Member: Board, Property Services Agency, 1979–81, Adv. Bd, 1981–86; Design Council, 1988–94; Building Regulations Adv. Cttee, 1988–. Master, RDI, 1991–93; Vice-Pres., RSA, 1991–. Chm., Theatre Royal, Bath, 1988–94. Murray Leslie Medal, CIOB, 1982. Sen. FRCA 1993; Hon. FRIBA 1983; Hon. FCIBSE 1988; Hon. FBIAT 1991; Hon. FASI 1991; Hon. FABE 1994. Hon. DSc City Univ., 1988; Hon. DEng Braunschweig, 1995. *Publications:* papers in learned journals. *Recreations:* engineering, family activities. *Address:* 4 Widcombe Terrace, Bath, Avon BA2 6AJ. *T:* Bath (01225) 337510; Flat 18, 32 Grosvenor Street, W1X 9FF. *Club:* Athenæum.   *Died 12 Jan. 1996.*

HARBOTTLE, Brig. Michael Neale, OBE 1959; PhD; Director, Centre for International Peacebuilding, since 1983; *b* 7 Feb. 1917; *s* of Thomas Benfield Cecil and Kathleen Millicent Harbottle; *m* 1st, 1940, Alison Jean Humfress; one *s* one *d*; 2nd, 1972, Eirwen Helen Simonds. *Educ:* Marlborough Coll.; Royal Military Coll., Sandhurst; Open Internat. Univ. for Complementary Medicine, Sri Lanka (PhD 1993). Commissioned Oxfordshire and Buckinghamshire Light Infantry, 1937 (despatches 1944); commanded 1st Royal Green Jackets, 1959–62; Security Commander, Aden, 1962–64; Comd 129 Inf. Bde, TA, 1964–66; Chief of Staff, UN Peacekeeping Force Cyprus, 1966–68; retired, 1968. Vice-Pres., Internat. Peace Academy, 1971–73, Consultant, 1973–; Vis. Sen. Lectr (Peace Studies), Bradford Univ., 1974–79; Vice-Pres., UNA (UK), 1974–; Cons., United World College of Atlantic, 1974–81; Member: Management Cttee, Council for Educn in World Citizenship, 1978–89; Generals (Retd) for Peace and Disarmament, 1981–90; Internat. Council, Inst. of Conflict Analysis and Resolution, USA, 1992–; Educn Planning Dir, British Council for Aid to Refugees (Vietnamese Sec.), 1979–80; Gen. Sec., World Disarmament Campaign, 1980–82; Co-ordinator, Worldwide Consultative Assoc. of Retd Generals and Admirals, 1991–. Cons./Advr, Internat. Inst. for Peaceful Change. FRSA. *Publications:* The Impartial Soldier, 1970; The Blue Berets, 1971, 2nd edn 1975; (jtly) The Thin Blue Line: International Peacekeeping and its Future, 1974; The Knaves of Diamonds, 1976; (collator) Peacekeeper's Handbook, 1978; (jtly) 10 Questions Answered, 1983; (jtly) Reflections on Security in the Nuclear Age, 1988; What is Proper Soldiering, 1991; New Roles for the Military, 1995; contributor to: Unofficial Diplomats, 1977 (USA); The Arab-Israel Conflict,

Readings and Documents, 1977 (USA). *Recreations:* cricket, golf, crossword puzzles. *Address:* 9 West Street, Chipping Norton, Oxon OX7 5LH. *T:* (01608) 642335.
                                  Died 30 April 1997.

HARDEN, Major James Richard Edwards, DSO 1945; OBE 1983; MC 1944; farmer; *b* 12 Dec. 1916; *s* of late Major J. E. Harden, DL, JP, Royal Irish Fusiliers, and L. G. C. Harden; *m* 1948, Ursula Joyce, *y d* of G. M. Strutt, Newhouse, Terling, Chelmsford, Essex; one *s* two *d*. *Educ:* Oriel House, St Asaph; Bedford Sch.; Sandhurst. Commissioned into Royal Tank Regt, 1937; retired on agricultural release, 1947. MP (UU) for County Armagh, 1948–54. JP County Armagh, 1956, Cærnarvonshire, later Gwynedd, 1971–82; DL, Co. Armagh, 1946, Cærnarvonshire, later Gwynedd, 1968; High Sheriff, Cærnarvonshire, 1971–72. *Recreations:* shooting, fishing. *Address:* Hendy, Nanhoran, Pwllheli, Gwynedd LL53 8DL. *T:* (01758) 730432.   *Died 22 Oct. 2000.*

HARDERS, Sir Clarence Waldemar, Kt 1977; OBE 1969; Partner and Consultant, Freehill, Hollingdale and Page, Canberra, ACT, 1980–92; *b* Murtoa, 1 March 1915; *s* of E. W. Harders, Dimboola, Vic; *m* 1947, Gladys, *d* of E. Treasure; one *s* two *d*. *Educ:* Concordia Coll., Unley, S Australia; Adelaide Univ. (LLB). Joined Dept of the Attorney-General, 1947; Dep. Sec., 1965–70; Sec., 1970–79; Legal Adviser, Dept of Foreign Affairs, 1979–80. *Address:* 43 Stonehaven Crescent, Deakin, ACT 2600, Australia. *Clubs:* Commonwealth, National Press, Canberra Bowling (Canberra); Royal Canberra Golf.
                                  Died 22 Feb. 1997.

HARDIE, Ven. Archibald George; Archdeacon of West Cumberland and Hon. Canon of Carlisle Cathedral, 1971–79; also Vicar of Haile, 1970–79; *b* 19 Dec. 1908; *s* of late Most Rev. William George Hardie, formerly Archbishop of the West Indies, and Alice Annie Hardie; *m* 1936, Rosalie Sheelagh Hamilton (*née* Jacob) (*d* 1995); three *s* one *d*. *Educ:* St Lawrence Coll., Ramsgate; Trinity Coll., Cambridge (MA); Westcott House, Cambridge. Hockey Blue, Cambridge, 1931–32. Deacon 1934, priest 1935; Curate of All Hallows, Lombard St, EC, and London Sec. of Student Christian Movement, 1934–36; Chaplain, Repton Sch., 1936–38; Vicar of St Alban, Golders Green, London, NW11, 1938–44; OCF; Rector of Hexham Abbey, 1944–63; Vicar and Rural Dean of Halifax, 1963–71, and Hon. Canon of Wakefield Cathedral. *Recreations:* tilling the soil, chewing the cud. *Address:* Westcliffe, Pondicherry, Rothbury, Northumberland NE65 7YP.   *Died 28 Feb. 1997.*

HARDIE, Sir Charles (Edgar Mathewes), Kt 1970; CBE 1963 (OBE 1943); chartered accountant; Partner in Dixon, Wilson, 1934–81, Senior Partner, 1975–81; *b* 10 March 1910; *s* of Dr C. F. Hardie and Mrs R. F. Hardie (*née* Moore), Barnet, Herts; *m* 1st, 1937, Dorothy Jean (*née* Hobson) (*d* 1965); one *s* three *d*; 2nd, 1966, Mrs Angela Richli (marr. diss. 1975), *widow* of Raymond Paul Richli; 3rd, 1975, Rosemary Margaret Harwood. *Educ:* Aldenham Sch. Qualified as Chartered Accountant, 1932; practised in London, 1934–81. War Service, 1939–45, Col (GS). Chairman: BOAC, 1969–70 (Dir, 1964–70); Metropolitan Estate & Property Corp., 1964–71; White Fish Authority, 1967–73; Fitch Lovell plc, 1970–77; Director: British American and General Trust plc, 1961–85; British Printing Corp. plc, 1965–82 (Chm., 1969–76); Royal Bank of Canada, 1969–81; Mann Egerton & Co. Ltd, 1959–80; Forte plc (formerly Trusthouse Forte plc), 1970–96 (Dep. Chm., 1983–93); Hill Samuel Group plc, 1970–77; William Cook Ltd, 1953–93; Dep. Chm., NAAFI, 1953–72; Mem., BEA Board, 1968–70. Mem. Council, Inst. of Directors, 1966–80 (Hon. Life Fellow, 1991). Liveryman, Fishmongers' Co., 1968. Hon. Admiral, Texas Navy, 1987. Legion of Merit, USA, 1944. *Recreation:*

bridge. *Address:* Pitt House, 25 New Street, Henley-on-Thames, Oxon RG9 2BP. *T:* (01491) 577944.
Died 20 Feb. 1998.

HARDIE, Colin Graham; Official Fellow and Tutor in Classics, Magdalen College, Oxford, 1936–73; Public Orator of Oxford University, 1967–73; *b* 16 Feb. 1906; 3rd *s* of William Ross Hardie, Fellow of Balliol Coll. and Prof. of Humanity in Edinburgh Univ., and Isabella Watt Stevenson; *m* 1940, Christian Viola Mary Lucas; two *s. Educ:* Edinburgh Acad.; Balliol Coll., Oxford (Warner Exhibitioner and Hon. Scholar). 1st class Classical Moderations, 1926, and Lit.Hum. 1928; BA; MA 1931; Craven Scholar, 1925; Ireland Scholar, 1925; Hertford Scholar, 1926; Gaisford Prize for Greek Prose, 1927. Junior Research Fellow, Balliol Coll., Oxford, 1928–29, Fellow and Classical Tutor, 1930–33; Dir of the British Sch. at Rome, 1933–36. Hon. Prof. of Ancient Lit., RA, 1971–90. *Publications:* Vitae Vergilianae antiquae, 1954; papers on Virgil and Dante. *Recreation:* gardening. *Address:* Rackham Cottage, Greatham Lane, Pulborough, Sussex RH20 2ES. *T:* (01798) 873170.
Died 17 Oct. 1998.

HARDING, Sir Christopher (George Francis), Kt 1991; Chairman: Legal & General Group plc, since 1994 (Director, since 1993); United Utilities plc, since 1998 (Deputy Chairman, 1997); Vice Chairman, Hanson Transport Group, since 1991 (Managing Director, 1974–85); *b* 17 Oct. 1939; *s* of Frank Harding and Phyllis Rachel Pledger (*née* Wise); *m* 1st, 1963, Susan Lilian Berry (marr. diss. 1977); one *s* one *d*; 2nd, 1978, Françoise Marie Baile de Laperrière (*née* Grouillé) (marr. diss. 1988); 3rd, 1994, Anne Skelley; one *d. Educ:* Merchant Taylors' School; Corpus Christi College, Oxford (MA Hons). Imperial Chemical Industries, 1961–69; Hanson PLC, 1969–97, non-exec. Dir, 1979–97; Dir, 1984–92, Chm., 1986–92, British Nuclear Fuels plc; Chm. and Dir, BET plc, 1992–96. Director: ProShare (UK), 1992–93; English China Clays, 1992–94; Slough Estates, 1992–94; Newarthill, 1992– (Chm., 1993–); Marconi (formerly General Electric Co.), 1992–; Post Office Bd, 1993–98; The Energy Group, 1996–97. Council Member: CBI, 1986–97; Business in the Community, 1986–92; Member: Adv. Bd, Univ. of Bradford Management Centre, 1981–93; Exec. Cttee, British Energy Assoc., 1986– (Chm., 1989–92); UK–Japan 2000 Gp, 1987– (Dir, 1995–); Court, UMIST, 1987–92; Adv. Bd, Prince's Youth Business Trust, 1988– (Chm., 1994–99); Science & Industry Cttee, BAAS, 1989–93; NACETT, 1993–96; Commn on Public Policy & British Business, 1995–97. Dir, 1992–98, Mem. UK Nat. Council, 1998–, Foyer Fedn for Youth. Chm., Supporters of Nuclear Energy, 1998–. Pres., NW Chambers of Commerce Assoc., 1998–. FRSA 1987; CIMgt (CBIM 1988). Freeman, City of London, 1965; Member, 1965, Liveryman, 1986, Merchant Taylors' Co. Hon. Fellow: Huddersfield Univ. (formerly Poly.), 1990; Linacre Coll., Oxford, 1993; Hon. FCGI 1990; Hon. FIChemE 1992; Hon. FINucE 1992. Hon. PhD Anglia Poly. Univ., 1998. *Recreations:* theatre, music, travel, tennis, pocillovy. *Address:* United Utilities plc, 55 Grosvenor Street, W1X 9DA. *T:* (020) 7307 0300, *Fax:* (020) 7307 0310. *Club:* Brooks's.
Died 13 Dec. 1999.

HARDING, Hugh Alastair, CMG 1958; Under-Secretary, Department of Education and Science, 1967–77; *b* 4 May 1917; 2nd *s* of late Roland Charles Harding, Norton-le-Moors, Staffordshire; *m* 1943, Florence Esnouf; one *s* one *d. Educ:* Rugby; Trinity Coll., Cambridge. Colonial Office, 1939; Asst Sec., 1950; Asst Sec., Treasury, 1961; Under-Sec., Treasury, 1962–64; Minister, UK Delegation to OECD, 1964–67. Served War of 1939–45, Army (Captain

RA). *Address:* c/o National Westminster Bank, Fountain Place, Burslem, Stoke-on-Trent, Staffs ST6 3QA.
Died 25 July 2000.

HARDING, John Philip, PhD; Keeper of Zoology, British Museum (Natural History), 1954–71, retired; *b* 12 Nov. 1911; *s* of Philip William and Eleanor Harding, Rondebosch, Cape Town; *m* 1937, Sidnie Manton, PhD, ScD, FRS (*d* 1979); one *s* one *d. Educ:* Torquay; University Coll., Exeter; University of Cincinnati; King's Coll., Cambridge. Ministry of Agriculture and Fisheries, 1936–37; British Museum (Natural History), 1937–71. Vis. Prof., Westfield Coll., Univ. of London, 1971–77. *Publications:* scientific papers on crustacea. *Recreations:* photomicrography, mechanical devices, handicap aids. *Address:* Lydfords, High Street, East Hoathly, E Sussex BN6 6DR. *Died 14 July 1998.*

HARDING, Peter Thomas; Director General, Petroleum Engineering Division, Department of Energy, 1989–91; *b* 5 Dec. 1930; *s* of late James Alfred Harding and Catherine Frances Harding; *m* 1954, Joyce Holmes; two *s* two *d. Educ:* Ealing Grammar School. Exec. Officer, Min. of Supply, 1949; Principal, Min. of Technology, 1967; Asst Sec., DTI, 1973, Dept of Energy, 1974, Under Sec., 1989. *Recreations:* music, watching cricket, gardening. *Address:* Pookwell, Ridgway, Pyrford, Woking, Surrey GU22 8PW. *T:* (01932) 346766. *Died 4 May 1998.*

HARDING, Air Vice-Marshal Ross Philip, CBE 1968; Royal Air Force, retired; *b* 22 Jan. 1921; *s* of P. J. Harding, Salisbury; *m* 1948, Laurie Joy Gardner; three *s. Educ:* Bishop Wordsworth Sch., Salisbury; St Edmund Hall, Oxford (MA). No 41 Sqdn Fighter Comd and 2 TAF, 1943–45 (despatches); RAF Staff Coll., Andover, 1951; Air Min. (ACAS Ops), 1952–54; CO No 96 Sqdn, Germany, 1955–58; Directing Staff, RAF Staff Coll., Andover, 1958–60; CO Oxford Univ. Air Sqdn, 1960–62; Dep. Chief, British Mil. Mission, Berlin, 1963–65; CO RAF Valley, 1965–68; Senior Directing Staff (Air), Jt Services Staff Coll., 1968–69; Defence and Air Attaché, Moscow, 1970–72; Dir of Personal Services 1, MoD (Air), 1973; Senior RAF Member, RCDS, 1974–76. Hd of Airwork Services Ltd, Oman, 1976–78. Chm., MoD Selection Bd, 1979–96. Specialist Advr to H of C Defence Cttee, 1979–84. *Recreations:* ski-ing, shooting. *Address:* Tally-Ho, 8 Hadrian's Close, Lower Bemerton, Salisbury, Wilts SP2 9NN. *Club:* Royal Air Force.
Died 29 Nov. 1998.

HARDINGE OF PENSHURST, 3rd Baron *cr* 1910; **George Edward Charles Hardinge;** *b* 31 Oct. 1921; *o s* of 2nd Baron Hardinge of Penshurst, GCB, GCVO, MC, PC, and Helen Mary Cecil (*d* 1979); *S* father, 1960; *m* 1st, 1944, Janet Christine Goschen (marr. diss. 1962; she *d* 1970), *d* of late Lt-Col F. C. C. Balfour, CIE, CVO, CBE, MC; three *s*; 2nd, 1966, Margaret Trezise; one *s*, and one adopted step *s. Educ:* Eton; Royal Naval College, Dartmouth. RN, 1940–47; subsequently in publishing. Sen. Editor: Collins; Longmans; Macmillan (London) Ltd, 1968–86 (also dir); Founder and Editor, Winter's Crime series. Founder Mem., Booker Prize for Fiction. *Publication:* An Incompleat Angler, 1976. *Recreations:* reading, fishing, bridge. *Heir: s* Hon. Julian Alexander Hardinge, *b* 23 Aug. 1945. *Address:* Bracken Hill, 10 Penland Road, Bexhill-on-Sea, East Sussex TN40 2JG. *T:* (01424) 211866. *Club:* Brooks's.
Died 14 July 1997.

HARDMAN, James Arthur, MBE 1968; HM Diplomatic Service, retired; *b* 12 Sept. 1929; *er s* of late James Sidney Hardman and Rachel Hardman; *m* 1953, Enid Mary Hunter; two *s. Educ:* Manchester Grammar Sch.; Manchester Univ. (BA Hons 1950). FCIS (FCCS 1964). Served in Intelligence Corps, 1951–53; Admiralty,

1953–54; HM Foreign Service, 1954; served: Tehran, 1955; FO, 2nd Sec., 1960; Bonn, 2nd, later 1st, Sec. (Comm.), 1962; Atlanta, Consul, 1967; New York, Consul (Comm.), 1970; FCO, Dep. Dir Diplomatic Service Language Centre, 1972; Consul-Gen., Strasbourg, 1975–79; Consul (Commercial), Düsseldorf, 1979–83; FCO, 1983–85; First Sec. (Commercial), Algiers, 1985–88. Mem., Secretariat, Internat. Primary Aluminium Inst., 1988–94. *Address:* Gulestan, Apers Avenue, Westfield, Woking, Surrey GU22 9NB. *Club:* Civil Service.   *Died 13 March 1996.*

HARDY, Sir Rupert (John), 4th Bt *cr* 1876, of Dunstall Hall, co. Stafford; Lieutenant-Colonel Life Guards, retired; *b* 24 Oct. 1902; *s* of 3rd Bt and Violet Agnes Evelyn (*d* 1972), *d* of Hon. Sir Edward Chandos Leigh, KCB, KC; *S* father, 1953; *m* 1930, Hon. Diana Joan Allsopp, *er d* of 3rd Baron Hindlip; one *s* one *d. Educ:* Eton; Trinity Hall, Cambridge (BA 1925). Joined The Life Guards, 1925; Major, 1940; retired, 1948, and rejoined as RARO, 1952; Lieut-Col comdg Household Cavalry Regt, 1952–56; ceased to belong to R of O, Dec. 1956; granted hon. rank of Lieut-Col. *Recreations:* hunting, shooting. *Heir: s* Richard Charles Chandos Hardy [*b* 6 Feb. 1945; *m* 1972, Venetia, *d* of Simon Wingfield Digby, TD; four *d*]. *Address:* Gullivers Lodge, Guilsborough, Northampton NN6 8RB. *Club:* Turf.   *Died 22 March 1997.*

HARDY-ROBERTS, Brig. Sir Geoffrey (Paul), KCVO 1972; CB 1945; CBE 1944 (OBE 1941); JP; DL; Master of HM's Household, 1967–73; Extra Equerry to the Queen, since 1967; Secretary-Superintendent of Middlesex Hospital, 1946–67; *b* 16 May 1907; *s* of A. W. Roberts; *m* 1945, Eldred (*d* 1987), *widow of* Col J. R. Macdonell, DSO. *Educ:* Eton, RMC Sandhurst. Regular Commission, 9th Lancers, 1926–37; served War of 1939–45 (OBE, CBE, CB). Mem., West Sussex AHA, 1974–82; Dep. Chm., King Edward VII Hospital, Midhurst, 1972–82. JP 1960, DL 1964, West Sussex (formerly Sussex); High Sheriff, Sussex, 1965. Officer, Legion of Merit, 1945. *Address: c/o* Bury Gate House, Pulborough, West Sussex RH20 1HA.   *Died 9 April 1997.*

HARE, Sir Philip (Leigh), 6th Bt *cr* 1818, of Stow Hall, Norfolk; antique dealer, since 1969; *b* 13 Oct. 1922; *s* of Captain Edward Philip Leigh Hare (*d* 1954) (*y s* of Sir Thomas Hare, 2nd Bt), and his 3rd wife, Lady Kathleen Florence Mary Hare (*d* 1971), *d* of 9th Earl of Harrington; *S* cousin, 1993; *m* 1950, Anne Lisle, *d* of Major Geoffrey Nicholson, CBE, MC; one *s* one *d* (twins). *Educ:* private crammers; RAC Cirencester. Military service, 1941–46 (Trooper, 7th Queen's Own Hussars). Farming, 1947–69. *Recreations:* gardening, field sports, furniture and picture restoration. *Heir: s* Nicholas Patrick Hare [*b* 27 Aug. 1955; *m* 1982, Caroline Keith, *d* of T. P. K. Allan; two *s*]. *Address:* The Nettings, Hook Norton, near Banbury, Oxon OX15 5NP. *T:* (01608) 737964. *Club:* Universal Skint.
                                                    Died 5 July 2000.

HARKNESS, Lt-Col Hon. Douglas Scott, OC 1978; GM 1943; ED 1944; PC (Can.) 1957; Minister of National Defence, Canada, 1960–63; *b* 29 March 1903; *s* of William Keefer Harkness and Janet Douglas Harkness (*née* Scott); *m* 1932, Frances Elisabeth, *d* of James Blair McMillan, Charlottetown and Calgary; (one *s* decd). *Educ:* Central Collegiate, Calgary; University of Alberta (BA). Served overseas in War (Italy and NW Europe), 1940–45; Major and Lt-Col, Royal Canadian Artillery; with Reserve Army, CO 41st Anti-Tank Regt (SP), Royal Canadian Artillery. MP (Calgary E) gen. elecs, 1945, 1949; re-elected: (Calgary N) gen. elecs, 1953, 1957, 1958, 1962, 1963, 1965, (Calgary Centre) 1968, retired 1972; Minister for Northern Affairs and Nat. Resources and Actg Minister of Agric., June 1957; Minister of Agric., Aug. 1957; relinquished portfolios of Northern Affairs and Nat.

Resources, Aug. 1957, of Agriculture, Oct. 1960. Mem. Alta Military Institute. Hon. LLD Calgary, 1975. *Address:* 716 Imperial Way SW, Calgary, AB T2S 1N7, Canada. *T:* (403) 2430825. *Clubs:* Ranchmen's, Calgary Petroleum (Calgary).   *Died 2 May 1999.*

HARMAR-NICHOLLS, Baron *cr* 1974 (Life Peer), of Peterborough, Cambridgeshire; **Harmar Harmar-Nicholls;** JP; Bt 1960; Member (C) Greater Manchester South, European Parliament, 1979–84; *b* 1 Nov. 1912; 3rd *s* of Charles E. C. Nicholls and Sarah Anne Nicholls, Walsall; assumed by deed poll surname of Harmar-Nicholls, 1974; *m* 1940, Dorothy Elsie, *e d* of James Edwards, Tipton; two *d. Educ:* Dorsett Road Sch., Darlaston; Queen Mary's Grammar Sch., Walsall. Called to the Bar, Middle Temple, 1941. Chairman: Nicholls and Hennessy (Hotels) Ltd; Malvern Festival Theatre Trust Ltd; Radio Luxembourg (London) Ltd, 1983– (Dir, 1963–); Dir, J. & H. Nicholls & Co., Paints, etc, 1945–. Mem. of Syndicate at Lloyd's. Mem. Darlaston UDC at age of 26 (Chm., 1949–50); County Magistrate, 1946. Vice-Chm. W Midland Fedn, Junior Imperial League, 1937; contested (C): Nelson and Colne, 1945; Preston by-election, 1946; MP (C) Peterborough Div. of Northants, 1950–Sept. 1974; PPS to Asst Postmaster-Gen., 1951–April 1955; Parliamentary Secretary: Min. of Agriculture, Fisheries and Food, April 1955–Jan. 1957; Min. of Works, 1957–60; Mem. Conservative Housing Cttee; Sec. of Parly Road Safety Cttee (Conservative); Jt Sec. All party Parly Group Empire Migration; Mem. Govt Overseas Settlement Board on migration to Commonwealth. War of 1939–45: volunteered as sapper, commnd Royal Engineers, served India and Burma. *Recreations:* gardening, reading, walking, theatre. *Heir* (to baronetcy): none. *Address:* Abbeylands, Weston, Stafford ST18 0HX. *T:* (01889) 270252. *Clubs:* St Stephen's Constitutional; (Pres.) Unionist, City and Counties (Peterborough); Conservative (Darlaston); Unionist (Walsall).   *Died 15 Sept. 2000 (Btcy ext).*

HARMER, Michael Hedley, FRCS; Consulting Surgeon, Royal Marsden Hospital and Paddington Green Children's Hospital (St Mary's Hospital); *b* 6 July 1912; *y s* of late Douglas Harmer, MC, FRCS, and May (*née* Hedley); *m* 1939, Bridget Jean, *d* of late James Higgs-Walker, MA, and Muriel Jessie, *e d* of Rev. Harold Smith; one *s* one *d. Educ:* Marlborough; King's Coll., Cambridge (BA 1934; MA, MB, BChir 1939); St Bartholomew's Hosp., London. Surgical Specialist, RAFVR, 1943–46. Bellman, Snark Club, Cambridge, 1934–. Freeman of Norwich by Patrimony, 1935; Freeman, City of London, 1936. *Publications:* A Handbook of Surgery, 1951; Aids to Surgery, 1962; (ed jtly) Rose and Carless's Manual of Surgery, 19th edn 1959; The Forgotten Hospital, 1982; Look Back in Happiness, 1992; papers on the surgery and classification of malignant disease. *Recreations:* music, the country. *Address:* Perrot Wood, Graffham, Petworth, Sussex GU28 0NZ. *T:* (01798) 867307.
                                                Died 11 Nov. 1998.

HARNIMAN, John Phillip, OBE 1984; Director, British Council (Counsellor, Cultural Affairs), Canada, 1992–96; *b* 7 May 1939; *s* of William Thomas Harniman and Maud Kate Florence (*née* Dyrenfurth); *m* 1961, Avryl (*née* Hartley); one *s* one *d. Educ:* Leyton County High School; Culham College, Oxon (DipEd); London University (BA Hons); Université de la Sorbonne. William Morris School, Walthamstow, 1960–62; Ecole Normale Supérieure de Saint-Cloud, 1962–67; British Council: Algeria, 1967–70; Specialist Careers Officer, Personnel, 1970–73; Head, Overseas Careers, Personnel, 1973–76; Representative, Singapore, 1976–81; Cultural Attaché, Romania, 1981–84; Rep. and Cultural Counsellor, Belgium and Luxembourg, 1984–87; Asst Controller, Personnel Div., 1987–92. Hon.

Sec., Suffolk Preservation Soc., 1997–. FRSA. *Recreations:* reading, singing with Kirbye Consort and Bury St Edmunds Bach Choir, letter-writing, cats. *Address:* Shilling Orchard, Shilling Street, Lavenham, Suffolk CO10 9RH; *e-mail:* johnharniman@classic.msn.com.

Died 18 Sept. 1999.

HARPER, Alan Henry; Managing Director, Jackson Son & Co. (London), 1989; *b* 27 Jan. 1943; *s* of Frank Dennis Luker and Patricia May (*née* Harper); took mother's surname at birth; *m* 1965, Nicol Susan Reid; three *d. Educ:* Southend Grammar Sch. General office, Louis Dreyfus and Co., London, 1958–62; worked in: jute industry, Louis Dreyfus and Co., Calcutta, 1963; animal feeds, India, 1964, and grain trade, London, 1965–73, European Grain & Shipping Ltd, commodity futures, Coley & Harper Ltd, 1974–89. Dir, Baltic Exchange Ltd, 1982–87 and 1989–94 (Chm., 1994–96). *Recreations:* dinghy sailing, tennis. *Address:* Hillersdon, Hervines Road, Amersham, Bucks HP6 5HS. *T:* (01494) 724861.

Died 26 March 1997.

HARPER, Alfred Alexander, MA, MD; Professor of Physiology, University of Newcastle upon Tyne, 1963–72; *b* 19 June 1907; *er s* of James and Elizabeth Harper. *Educ:* Aberdeen Grammar Sch.; Aberdeen Univ. Lecturer in Physiology, University of Leeds, 1935–36; Demonstrator in Physiology, St Thomas' Hosp., London, 1936–39; Lectr, later Reader, in Human Physiology, Univ. of Manchester, 1939–49; Prof. of Physiology, Univ. of Durham, 1949–63. *Publications:* papers in Jl of Physiology mostly on physiology of digestion. *Address:* Wellburn House, Benwell Lane, Newcastle upon Tyne NE15 6LX. *T:* (0191) 274 8178. *Died 18 Nov. 1996.*

HARPER GOW, Sir (Leonard) Maxwell, Kt 1985; MBE 1944; CIMgt; Director, 1952–87, Chairman, 1964–81, Vice-Chairman, 1981–87, Christian Salvesen PLC; *b* 13 June 1918; *s* of late Leonard Harper Gow and Eleanor Amalie (*née* Salvesen); *m* 1944, Lillan Margaret Kiaer; two *s* one *d. Educ:* Cargilfield; Rugby; Corpus Christi Coll., Cambridge Univ. (BA). CIMgt (FBIM 1976). Served War, 1939–46: Major RA 1st Commando Bde. 3 seasons with Antarctic Whaling Fleet, 1946–47, 1948–49 and 1952–53. Director: Scottish Widows' Fund and Life Assurance Soc., 1964–85 (Chm., 1972–75); Royal Bank of Scotland plc, 1965–87; Royal Bank of Scotland Group plc, 1978–87; DFM Holdings Ltd, 1985–89 (Chm., 1985–89); Radio Forth Ltd, 1973–89 (Chm., 1977–87). Member Council: Inst. of Directors, 1983–88; Scottish Council of Develt and Industry, 1972– (Vice Pres., 1985–88; elected Founder Fellow, 1987). Member, Queen's Body Guard for Scotland, the Royal Co. of Archers. Liveryman, Royal Co. of Shipwrights. Hon. Consul for Norway in Edinburgh/Leith, 1949–88. Comdr, Order of St Olav, Norway. *Recreations:* hill farming, fishing. *Address:* Eventyr, Lyars Road, Longniddry, East Lothian EH32 0PT. *T:* Longniddry (01875) 52142. *Club:* New (Edinburgh). *Died 1 Jan. 1996.*

HARPHAM, Sir William, KBE 1966 (OBE 1948); CMG 1953; HM Diplomatic Service, retired; Director, Great Britain-East Europe Centre, 1967–80; *b* 3 Dec. 1906; *o s* of W. Harpham and N. Harpham (*née* Stout); *m* 1943, Isabelle Marie Sophie Droz; one *s* one *d. Educ:* Wintringham Secondary Sch., Grimsby; Christ's Coll., Cambridge. Entered Dept of Overseas Trade, 1929; transferred to Embassy, Brussels, 1931, Rome, 1934; Private Sec. to Parliamentary Sec. for Overseas Trade, 1936; seconded to League of Nations, 1937; Dept of Overseas Trade, 1939; served: Cairo, 1940–44; Beirut, 1944–47; appointed Counsellor (Commercial) at Berne, 1947; Head of Gen. Dept, Foreign Office, 1950–53; Dep. to UK Delegate to OEEC, 1953–56; Minister, British Embassy, Tokyo, 1956–59; Minister (Economic), Paris,

1959–63; Ambassador to Bulgaria, 1964–66; retd 1967. Order of Madara Horseman, Bulgaria, 1969; Order of Stara Planina, Bulgaria, 1976. *Address:* 9 Kings Keep, Putney Hill, SW15 6RA. *T:* (020) 8788 1383. *Club:* Royal Automobile. *Died 5 June 1999.*

HARRIMAN, Pamela Beryl; Ambassador of the United States of America to France, since 1993; *b* 20 March 1920; *e d* of 11th Baron Digby, KG, DSO, MC, TD and Hon. Pamela Bruce, OBE, *y d* of 2nd Baron Aberdare; *m* 1st, 1939, Hon. Randolph Frederick Edward Spencer Churchill, MBE (marr. diss 1946; he *d* 1968); one *s*; 2nd, 1960, Leland Hayward (*d* 1971); 3rd, 1971, William Averell Harriman (*d* 1986). *Educ:* Downham Sch., Suffolk; Sorbonne. Mem., Democratic Nat. Cttee, 1988–93; Chm., Qly Policy Issues Forum, Democratic Govs Assoc., 1990–92; Nat. Co-Chm., Clinton-Gore campaign, 1990–92. Mem., Council on Foreign Relns; former Vice-Chm., Atlantic Council. Formerly: Vice-Pres., ESU of US; Trustee: Rockefeller Univ. Winston Churchill Foundn of US; Mem., Trustees Council, Nat. Gall. of Art; Hon. Trustee and Hon. Mem., Exec. Cttee, Brookings Instn. Former Member: Adv. Council, W. Averell Harriman Inst., Columbia Univ.; Bd of Dirs, Franklin and Eleanor Roosevelt Inst. Hon. LLD: Columbia; Coll. of William and Mary. *Address:* American Embassy, 2 avenue Gabriel, 75382 Paris, France. *T:* 143122755.

Died 5 Feb. 1997.

HARRIS, 7th Baron *cr* 1815, of Seringapatam and Mysore, E Indies and of Belmont, Kent; **Derek Marshall Harris;** *b* 23 July 1916; *s* of Major Thomas Guy Marriott Harris, OBE (*d* 1955), *ggs* of 1st Baron, and Beryl (*d* 1960), *d* of Frederick Alexander Wilson; *S* cousin, 1995; *m* 1st, 1938, Laura Cecilia (marr. diss. 1968), *e d* of Major Edmund Thomas William McCausland; one *s* one *d*; 2nd, 1987, Mrs Pauline Elisabeth Skinner (*née* Giles). Major, The Duke of Wellington's Regt, retired. *Heir: s* Hon. Anthony Harris [*b* 8 March 1942; *m* 1966, Anstice, *d* of Alfred Winter; two *d*]. *Address:* The Orchard, Loders, Bridport, Dorset. *Died 30 June 1996.* *This entry did not appear in Who's Who.*

HARRIS, Prof. Sir Alan (James), Kt 1980; CBE 1968; FREng, FICE, FIStructE; Senior Partner, Harris & Sutherland, Consulting Engineers, 1955–81, consultant since 1981; Professor of Concrete Structures, Imperial College, London, 1973–81, then Emeritus; *b* 8 July 1916; *s* of Walter Herbert Harris and Ethel Roach, Plymouth; *m* 1948, Marie Thérèse, *d* of Prof. Paul Delcourt, Paris; two *s. Educ:* Owen's Sch., Islington; Northampton Polytechnic (London Univ. BScEng). Local Government engineer, 1933–40; served Royal Engineers (Mulberry, Rhine Bridges) (despatches), 1940–46; with Eugène Freyssinet in Paris studying prestressing, 1946–49; Director, Prestressed Concrete Co. Ltd, 1949–55; in private practice, 1955–81. Member: Council, Agrément Board, 1968–81; Engrg Council, 1981–84; part-time Board Mem., Property Services Agency, 1974–78; Pres., Hydraulics Research Station, 1989– (Chm., 1982–89). President, Instn of Structural Engineers, 1978–79 (Gold Medal, 1984). Trustee, Imperial War Museum, 1983–90. FREng (FEng 1979); FCGI 1995. Hon. DSc: City, 1982; Aston, 1982; Exeter, 1984. Croix de Guerre (France); 1945; Ordre du Mérite (France), 1975. *Publications:* numerous papers in learned jls. *Recreation:* sailing. *Address:* 128 Ashley Gardens, Thirleby Road, SW1P 1HL. *T:* (020) 7834 6924. *Died 26 Dec. 2000.*

HARRIS, Sir Anthony (Travers Kyrle), 2nd Bt *cr* 1953, of Chepping Wycombe, Bucks; retired; *b* 18 March 1918; *s* of Marshal of the RAF Sir Arthur Travers Harris, 1st Bt, GCB, OBE, AFC, and Barbara Kyrle, *d* of Lt-Col E. W. K. Money, 85th KSLI; *S* father, 1984. *Educ:* Oundle. Served European War, 1939–45 with Queen Victoria's

Rifles and Wiltshire Regt; Auxiliary Units, 1941; ADC to GOC-in-C Eastern Command, 1944. Reader for MGM, 1951–52; subsequently work with antiques and objets d'art. *Recreations:* music, horology. *Heir:* none. *Address:* 33 Cheyne Court, Flood Street, SW3 5TR.
Died 6 Sept. 1996 (ext).

HARRIS, Sir Charles Herbert S.; *see* Stuart-Harris.

HARRIS, Dame Diana R.; *see* Reader Harris.

HARRIS, Rev. Donald Bertram; Vicar of St Paul's, Knightsbridge, 1955–78; *b* 4 Aug. 1904; unmarried. *Educ:* King's Coll. Choir Sch., Cambridge; Haileybury Coll.; King's Coll., Cambridge; Cuddesdon Coll., Oxford. Chorister, King's Coll. Choir, 1915–19; Choral Scholar, King's Coll., Cambridge, 1923–26; BA 1925; MA 1929. Ordained deacon, 1927; priest, 1928; Curate of Chesterfield Parish Church, 1927–31; St Mary the Less, Cambridge, 1931–36; Chaplain of King's Coll., Cambridge, 1932–33; Examg Chaplain to Bishop of Wakefield, 1932–36; Rector of Great Greenford, Middx, 1936–45; Archdeacon of Bedford 1946–55, and Rector of St Mary's Bedford, 1945–55. Life Governor, Haileybury and Imperial Service Coll., 1946. Pres., Assoc. for Promoting Retreats, 1968–71. *Address:* 105 Marsham Court, Marsham Street, SW1P 4LA. *T:* 0171–828 1132. *Club:* Royal Thames Yacht. *Died 20 Jan. 1996.*

HARRIS, Dr Edmund Leslie, CB 1981; FRCP, FRCPE, FFPHM, FFPM; Director of Medical Services, Disablement Services Authority, 1988–91, retired; *b* 11 April 1928; *s* of late M. H. and S. Harris; *m* 1959, Robina Semple (*née* Potter). *Educ:* Univ. of Witwatersrand. MB, BCh 1952; MRCPE 1959, FRCPE 1971; MRCP 1959, FRCP 1975; MFCM 1978; FFPHM (FFCM 1980); FFPM 1989. Gen. practice, Benoni, S Africa, 1954; various NHS posts, 1955–61; Medical Dir, pharmaceutical industry, 1962–68; SMO, DHSS, 1969–72; PMO, Cttee on Safety of Medicines and Medicines Commn, 1973; SPMO, Under-Sec., and Head of Medicines Div., DHSS, 1974–77; Dep. Chief Med. Officer, Dept of Health (formerly DHSS), 1977–89. Examiner for Dip. Pharm. Med., Royal Colls of Physicians, 1976–84. Chairman: Assoc. of Med. Advisers in Pharmaceutical Industry, 1966; Adv. Cttee on Nat. Blood Transfusion Service, 1980–89; Expert Gp on Viral Haemorrhagic Fevers, 1984–89; Adv. Cttee, NHS Drugs, 1985–89. Member: Nat. Biol. Bd, 1975–77; Bd, Public Health Lab. Service, 1977–91; Central Blood Products Authority, 1982–85; Adviser to WHO, 1970–90. Rep. Governor, Imperial Cancer Res. Fund, 1977–89. Mem., Court of Govs and Bd of Management, LSHTM, 1986–89. *Publications:* various, mainly on aspects of clinical pharmacology and control of medicines. *Recreations:* walking, photography. *Address:* 5 Ashcroft Court, 10 Oaklands Road, Bromley, Kent BR1 3TX. *T:* (020) 8460 3665. *Died 29 Sept. 1998.*

HARRIS, Geoffrey Herbert; Member, Transport Users' Consultative Committee for London, 1961–77 (Chairman, 1972–77, Deputy Chairman, 1971–72); Chairman, London Transport Passengers' Committee, 1972–74; *b* 31 Jan. 1914; *s* of late W. Leonard Harris and Sybil M. Harris; *m* 1945, Eve J. Orton; two *d. Educ:* Colchester Royal Grammar School. FCIS. Commercial Union Gp of Cos, 1932–37; Shell Gp of Cos, 1937–73: Manager Office Administration, London, 1963–73. Royal Artillery, 1937–45. *Recreations:* music, architecture, travel. *Address:* Fyfield Cottage, West Street, Marlow, Bucks SL7 2BU. *T:* (01628) 472550. *Club:* Phyllis Court (Henley-on-Thames). *Died 18 Feb. 1998.*

HARRIS, Lt-Gen. Sir Ian (Cecil), KBE 1967 (CBE 1958); CB 1962; DSO 1945; Chairman, 1977–79, President, 1984–88, Irish Bloodstock Breeders Association; *b* 7 July 1910; *y s* of late J. W. A. Harris, Victor Stud, Golden,

Tipperary; *m* 1945, Anne-Marie Desmotreux; one *s* (and one *s* decd). *Educ:* Portora Royal Sch., Enniskillen, Northern Ireland; RMC, Sandhurst. 2nd Lieut Royal Ulster Rifles, 1930; served War of 1939–45, NW Frontier of India, 1939 (despatches); comd 2nd Bn Royal Ulster Rifles, 1943–45; GSO1, 25 Ind. Div. and 7 Div. in Burma and Malaya, 1945–46 (despatches), India and Pakistan, 1946–47; AQMG Scottish Comd, 1949–51; comd 6th Bn Royal Ulster Rifles (TA), 1951–52; Chief of Staff, Northern Ireland, 1952–54; Comdr 1 Federal Infantry Bde, Malaya, 1954–57 (despatches); Dep. Dir of Staff Duties (A), WO, 1957–60; GOC Singapore Base District, 1960–62; Chief of Staff, Contingencies Planning, Supreme HQ, Allied Powers, Europe, 1963–66; GOC-in-C, then GOC, N Ireland, 1966–69. Colonel: Royal Ulster Rifles, 1962–68; Royal Irish Rangers, 1968–72. Chm., British Support Cttee for Meml Museum of Caen, 1988. Hon. Citizen of Caen, 1984. *Address:* 24 Belgrave Square, Monkstown, Co. Dublin, Ireland. *T:* (1) 2807312. *Club:* Army and Navy. *Died 12 March 1999.*

HARRIS, Margaret Frances, OBE 1975; Co-Director, Motley Theatre Design Course, Drury Lane, since 1993; *b* 28 May 1904; *d* of late William Birkbeck Harris and Kathleen Marion Carey. *Educ:* Downe House. In partnership with Elizabeth Montgomery and Sophie Devine as firm of Motley, 1931–; founder, and Dir until 1993, Theatre Design Course, at RNT Studio, Almeida, Riverside Studios, ENO, and Sadler's Wells. Designed many productions in London and New York of drama, opera and ballet: first notable production, Richard of Bordeaux, for John Gielgud, 1932; sets and costumes for: Prokofiev's War and Peace, Coliseum, 1972; (with Elizabeth Montgomery) Unknown Soldier and His Wife, New London, 1973; A Family and a Fortune, 1975; Tosca, English Nat Opera, 1976; Paul Bunyan, English Music Theatre, 1976; The Consul, Coliseum, 1978. Olivier Special Award, 1997; RSA award for services to industrial design, 1997. *Publications:* Designing and Making Costume, by Motley, 1965; Theatre Props, by Motley, 1976; *relevant publication:* Design by Motley, by Michael Mullin, 1996. *Address:* 36 Rocks Lane, Barnes, SW13 0DA. *T:* (020) 8878 3705; Motley Theatre Design Course, 67 Drury Lane, WC2B 5SP. *Died 10 May 2000.*

HARRIS, Nigel John; General Secretary, Engineering Section, since 1995, and Member, Executive Council, since 1980, Amalgamated Engineering and Electrical Union; *b* 20 March 1943; *s* of Frederick and Irene Harris; *m* 1964, Cynthia; two *s. Educ:* C of E Sch., Dawley, Shropshire; Pool Hill Sec. Modern. Worked at Kemberton Colliery to 1962; ironfounding, John Maddocks & Co., 1963–65; Union representative, Glynwed Foundries, 1965–80; full time Officer, 1980, rep. foundry workers for AEW and on health and safety matters; Nat. Sec., Foundry Sect., AEU, then AEEU, 1980–95; Pro-tem. Pres., AEEU, Feb.–Nov. 1995. Member: Exec. Cttee, CSEU, 1985–; NEC, Lab. Party, 1991–. Former Editor, The Foundry Worker. Mem., Royal British Legion. *Recreations:* swimming, driving. *Address:* 18 Merlin Avenue, Knutsford, Cheshire WA16 8HJ. *T:* (01565) 652094.
Died 5 Aug. 1996.

HARRIS, Hon. Walter Edward, PC (Can.); QC (Can.); DCL; *b* 14 Jan. 1904; *s* of Melvin Harris and Helen (*née* Carruthers); *m* 1933, Grace Elma Morrison; one *s* two *d. Educ:* Osgoode Hall, Toronto; DCL Acadia, 1955. Served War of 1939–45. First elected to House of Commons, Canada, 1940 (re-elected 1945, 1949, 1953); MP (Canada) until 1957. Parliamentary Asst to Sec of State for External Affairs, 1947; Parly Asst to Prime Minister, 1948; Minister of Citizenship and Immigration, 1950; of Finance,

1954–57. Mem. of the firm of Harris, Willis, Barristers, Markdale. *Address:* Markdale, ON N0C 1H0, Canada.
Died 10 Jan. 1999.

HARRIS, William Barclay; QC 1961; *b* 25 Nov. 1911; *s* of W. Cecil Harris, Moatlands, E Grinstead, Sussex; *m* 1937, Elizabeth, 2nd *d* of Capt. Sir Clive Milnes-Coates, 2nd Bt, and Lady Celia Milnes-Coates, JP, 2nd *d* of 1st and last Marquess of Crewe, KG; one *s* two *d. Educ:* Harrow; Trinity Coll., Cambridge (MA). Served 1940–45: with Coldstream Guards, N Africa, Italy, Germany (despatches), Major. Barrister, Inner Temple, 1937 (Bencher, 1991). Chm., Rowton Hotels, 1965–83. A Church Commissioner, 1966–82 (Chm., Redundant Churches Cttee, 1972–82; Mem., Bd of Governors, 1972–82). Pres., Georgian Group, 1990– (Chm., 1985–90). Liveryman, Worshipful Co. of Merchant Taylors. *Address:* Moatlands, East Grinstead, West Sussex RH19 4LL. *T:* (01342) 810228; 29 Barkston Gardens, SW5 0ER. *T:* (020) 7373 8793. *Clubs:* Athenæum, MCC, Brooks's, Nikaean. *Died 4 Feb. 2000.*

HARRISON, Prof. Charles Victor; retired; Professor of Pathology, University of Ife, Nigeria, 1972–75; *b* Newport, Mon, 1907; *s* of Charles Henry Harrison, LDS, and Violet Harrison (*née* Witchell); *m* 1937, Olga Beatrice Cochrane; one *s* one *d. Educ:* Dean Close Sch., Cheltenham; University Coll., Cardiff; University Coll. Hosp., London. MB, BCh, BSc (Wales), 1929; MB, BS (London), 1929; MD (London), 1937; FRCPath 1965; FRCP 1967. Demonstrator in Pathology, Welsh National School of Medicine, 1930; Asst Morbid Anatomist, British Postgraduate Medical Sch., 1935; Senior Lecturer, Liverpool Univ., 1939; Reader in Morbid Anatomy, Postgraduate Medical Sch. of London, 1946; Prof., Royal Postgrad. Med. Sch., Univ. of London, 1955–72. Hon. DSc Wales, 1972. Willie Seager Gold Medal in Pathology, 1927. *Publications:* (ed) Recent Advances in Pathology, 1973; various scientific papers in Jl of Pathology and Bacteriology, British Heart Journal, Jl Clin. Pathology, etc. *Recreations:* carpentry, gardening. *Address:* 8 Wattleton Road, Beaconsfield, Bucks HP9 1TS. *T:* (01494) 672046. *Died 24 Oct. 1996.*

HARRISON, Douglas Creese, DSc London, PhD Cantab; CChem; Professor of Biochemistry, Queen's University, Belfast, 1935–67, then Professor Emeritus; *b* 29 April 1901; *s* of Lovell and Lillian E. Harrison, MBE, JP; *m* 1926, Sylva Thurlow, MA, PhD Philadelphia, USA; one *s. Educ:* Highgate Sch.; King's Coll., London; Emmanuel Coll., Cambridge. MRSC. Keddey Fletcher-Warr Research Studentship, 1925–28; Lecturer at Sheffield Univ., 1926–35. Hon. DSc Belfast, 1987. *Publications:* various papers in the Biochemical Journal, Proc. Royal Society, Lancet, etc. *Address:* 4 Broomhill Park Central, Belfast BT9 5JD. *T:* (01232) 665685.
Died 12 April 1997.

HARRISON, John H.; *see* Heslop-Harrison.

HARRISON, Prof. Sir Richard (John), Kt 1984; MD, DSc; FRS 1973; Professor of Anatomy, Cambridge University, 1968–82, then Emeritus; Fellow of Downing College, Cambridge, 1968–82, Hon. Fellow, 1982; *b* 8 Oct. 1920; *er s* of late Geoffrey Arthur Harrison, MD, and Theodora Beatrice Mary West; *m* 1st, 1943, Joanna Gillies (marr. diss. 1967); two *s* one *d*; 2nd, 1967, Barbara Fuller (*d* 1988); 3rd, 1990, Gianetta Drake, *d* of late Capt. C. K. Lloyd, CBE, RN retd and Phyllis Lloyd. *Educ:* Oundle; Gonville and Caius Coll., Cambridge (Scholar; MB, BChir, 1944; MA 1946; MD 1954); St Bartholomew's Hosp. Medical Coll.; DSc Glasgow 1948. LRCP, MRCS, 1944. House Surgeon, St Bartholomew's Hosp., 1944; Demonstrator in Anatomy, St Bartholomew's Hosp. Medical Coll., 1944; Lectr in Anatomy, Glasgow Univ.,

1946; Sen. Lectr, 1947, and Reader in Anatomy, 1950, Charing Cross Hosp. Medical Sch. (Symington Prize for research in Anatomy); Reader in charge of Anatomy Dept, London Hosp. Medical Coll., 1951–54; Prof. of Anatomy, University of London, at London Hosp. Medical Coll., 1954–68; Fullerian Prof. of Physiology, Royal Institution, 1961–67. Wooldridge Lectr, BVA, 1983. Chairman: Farm Animal Welfare Adv. Cttee, MAFF, 1974–79; Farm Animal Welfare Council, 1979–88. President: European Assoc. for Aquatic Mammals, 1974–76; Anat. Soc. of GB and Ireland, 1978–79. XIIth Internat. Congress of Anatomists, London, 1985; Internat. Fedn of Assocs of Anatomists, 1985–87. A Trustee, British Museum (Natural History), 1978–88 (Chm. Trustees, 1984–88); Member Council: Royal Soc., 1981–82; Zool. Soc., 1974–78, 1980–83; Nat. Trust, 1984–85; Internat. Monachus Cttee, Ministère de l'Environnement, Paris, 1987–90. Hon. Member: American Assoc. of Anatomists; Società Italiana Anatomia; Soc. Marine Mammalogy. *Publications:* Man the Peculiar Animal, 1958; (with J. E. King) Marine Mammals, 1965, 2nd edn 1979; Reproduction and Man, 1967; (with W. Montagna) Man, 2nd edn 1972; Functional Anatomy of Marine Mammals, vol. I, 1972, vol. II, 1974, vol. III, 1977; (with S. H. Ridgway) Handbook of Marine Mammals, vols I and II, 1981, vol. III, 1985, vol. IV, 1989, vol. V, 1994, vol. VI, 1999; (with M. M. Bryden): Research on Dolphins, 1986; Whales, Dolphins and Porpoises, 1988; numerous papers on embryology, comparative and human anatomy. *Recreations:* marine biology, painting. *Address:* Milestone House, 58A High Street, Barkway, Royston, Herts SG8 8EE. *T:* (01763) 848974. *Died 17 Oct. 1999.*

HARRISON, Theophilus George, OBE 1971; JP; Member, Greater Manchester Council, 1973–77 (Chairman, 1973–74 and 1974–75, Deputy Chairman, 1975–76); General Secretary, National Association of Powerloom Overlookers, 1947–76, then Life Member; Member Executive, General Union of Associations of Loom Overlookers, 1947–76, then Life Member (President, 1964–66); *b* 30 Jan. 1907; *s* of Alfred and Emma Harrison; *m* 1935, Clarissa Plevin; one *s* one *d*. Swinton and Pendlebury Borough Council: Mem., 1941–56; Alderman, 1956–74; Mayor, 1954–55; Chairman: Housing Cttee; Highways and Lighting Cttee; Mem., Div. Planning Cttee; Lancs CC: Mem. Educn Cttee, 1946–74 (Vice-Chm. 1951–53, Chm. 1953–74); Chm., Road Safety Cttee; Vice-Chairman: Public Health and Housing Cttee; Greater Manchester Transport Cons. Cttee; Pres., Lancs Non-County Boroughs Assoc., 1960–62; Chairman: Swinton and Pendlebury Youth Employment Cttee; Youth Adv. Cttee and Youth Centres; Mem., Div. Exec., Educn Cttee; Member: Gen. Council, Lancs and Merseyside Ind. Develt Corp.; N Counties Textile Trades Fedn Central Board; Life Member: Salford Trades Council (formerly Mem., Swinton and Pendlebury Trades Council); Swinton Labour Club. Member: Manchester Reg. Hosp. Bd, 1961–74; Mental Health Review Tribunals, 1961–70; W Manchester HMC, 1957–74 (Chm. 1963–74); Wrightington HMC, 1957–74; Salford Community Health Council, 1973–83 (former Vice-Chm. and Chm., Develt Cttee); Assoc. of Community Health Councils, 1973–83 (former Vice-Chm., NW Region). Hon. Vice-Pres., Greater Manchester Council for Voluntary Service. Past Chm. or Mem. many other county or local organizations and cttees. Former Pres., SE Lancs and Cheshire Accident Prevention Fedn; Dir, RoSPA. Freeman of Swinton and Pendlebury, 1973 (later Salford BC). JP 1949. *Recreations:* reading, Rugby League football (spectator); much of his political and public activities. *Died Nov. 1996.*

HARRISON-CHURCH, Prof. Ronald James; Professor of Geography, University of London, at London School of Economics, 1964–77; *b* 26 July 1915; *s* of late James

Walter Church and Jessie May Church; *m* 1944, Dorothy Violet, *d* of late Robert Colchester Harrison and Rose Harrison; one *s* one *d*. *Educ:* Westminster City Sch.; Universities of London and Paris. BSc (Econ) 1936, PhD 1943, London. London School of Economics and Political Science: Asst Lectr, 1944–47; Lectr, 1947–58; Reader, 1958–64. Consultant to UN Economic Commn for Africa on large-scale irrigation schemes, 1962. Geographical Dir, Trans-African Hovercraft Expedition, 1969. Visiting Professor: University of Wisconsin, 1956; Indiana Univ., 1965; Tel Aviv and Haifa Univs, 1972–73. Lectured in many other univs in Brazil, US, Canada, West Africa, Belgium, France, Germany, Poland and Sweden. Member: French Embassy Scholarships Cttee, 1946–68; British Cttee. Coll. of Europe, 1951–72; Cttee for Staff Fulbright Awards, US-UK Educnl Commn, 1958–61 and 1972–75; Cttee, British Fulbright Schols Assoc., 1981–83; Africa Field Cttee, Oxfam, 1974–80. Chm., Firbank Housing Soc., 1977–83. Hon. Vice-Pres., Royal Afr. Soc., 1992– (Vice-Pres., 1977–92; Mem. Council, 1973–92; Mem., Speakers and Publics Cttee, 1972–85). Hon. Mem., Société Géographique de Liège, 1977. Back Award, RGS, 1957; Regl Conf. IGU Award, 1978. *Publications:* Modern Colonization, 1951; West Africa, 1957, 8th edn 1980; Environment and Policies in West Africa, 1963, 2nd edn 1976; (jtly) Africa and the Islands, 1964, 4th edn 1979; (jtly) An Advanced Geography of Northern and Western Europe, 1967, 3rd edn 1980; Looking at France, 1970, rev. repr. 1976, French edn 1969, US edn 1970, Spanish edn 1973; contribs to Geograph. Jl, W Africa, etc. *Recreations:* lecturing on cruises, private travel, wine. *Address:* 40 Handside Lane, Welwyn Garden City, Herts AL8 6SJ. *T:* (01707) 323293.

Died 30 Nov. 1998.

HARSANYI, Prof. John Charles, PhD; Professor of Business Administration and Economics, University of California, Berkeley, 1964–90, then Emeritus; *b* 29 May 1920; *s* of Charles and Alice Harsanyi; *m* 1951, Anne Klauber; one *s*. *Educ:* Univ of Budapest, Hungary (Dr Phil 1947); Sydney Univ., Australia (MA 1953); Stanford Univ. (PhD 1959). Asst, Univ. of Budapest, 1947–48; Lectr in Econs, Univ. of Qld, 1954–56; Sen. Fellow, ANU, 1959–61; Prof. of Econs, Wayne State Univ., 1961–63. Hon. DSc: Northwestern, 1989; Veszprem, 1995; Hon. Dr Buenos Aires, 1995; Hon. DEconScs Budapest, 1995; Hon. DSc Econs Sydney, 1995; Hon. DEc: Caen, 1996; Beijing, 1997. (Jtly) Nobel Prize in Econs, 1994. *Publications:* Essays on Ethics, Social Behaviour and Scientific Explanation, 1976; Rational Behaviour and Bargaining Equilibrium in Games and Social Situations, 1977; Papers in Game Theory, 1982; (with R. Selten) A General Theory of Equilibrium Selection in Games, 1988; numerous articles in learned jls. *Address:* Haas School of Business, University of California, Berkeley, CA 94720–1900, USA. *T:* (510) 6425588.

Died 9 Aug. 2000.

HARSCH, Joseph Close, Hon. CBE 1965; writer; *b* Toledo, Ohio, 25 May 1905; *s* of Paul Arthur Harsch and Leila Katherine Close; *m* 1st, 1932, Anne Elizabeth Wood (*d* 1997); three *s*; 2nd, 1998, Edna Raemer. *Educ:* Williams Coll., Williamstown, Mass (MA); Corpus Christi Coll., Cambridge (MA). Joined staff Christian Science Monitor, 1929; Washington corresp., then foreign corresp.; Asst Dir, Intergovt Cttee, London, 1939; Monitor Corresp. in Berlin, 1940, SW Pacific area, 1941 and 1942; began radio broadcasting, 1943; Senior European Correspondent, NBC, 1957–65; Diplomatic Correspondent, NBC, 1965–67; Commentator, American Broadcasting Co., 1967–71; Chief Editorial Writer, Christian Science Monitor, 1971–74. Edward Weintal award for writing on foreign affairs, 1979. *Publications:* Pattern of Conquest, 1941; The Curtain Isn't Iron, 1950; At the Hinge of

History, 1993. *Address:* PO Box 457, Jamestown, RI 02835, USA. *Clubs:* Garrick; Metropolitan, Cosmos (Washington, DC); Century (New York); St Botolph (Boston). *Died 3 June 1998.*

HART, Anthony Bernard, PhD; Co-Chairman, World Disarmament Campaign, since 1986; Head of Chemistry Division, Research Division of Central Electricity Generating Board, 1976–82; *b* 7 July 1917; *s* of late Oliver and Jessie Hart; *m* 1946, Judith Ridehalgh (later Baroness Hart of South Lanark, DBE, PC) (*d* 1991); two *s*. *Educ:* Enfield Grammar Sch.; Queen Mary Coll., London. BSc, PhD; CEng, CChem, FRSC, FInstE. RN Cordite Factories, 1940–46; RN Scientific Service, 1946–50; Lectr in Physical Chem., Royal Coll. of Sci. and Technol., Glasgow (latterly Strathclyde Univ.), 1950–60; Res. Div., CEGB, 1960–82. Exec. Mem., later Chm., Glasgow Trades Council, 1952–60; Nat. Exec. Mem., AUT, 1954–59. Mem., Barnes BC, 1962–64; Mem. and Leader of Opposition, Richmond upon Thames Council, 1964–68 and 1971–74; Chm., Richmond upon Thames Local Govt Cttee, 1968–77; Mem. (Lab) for Hornsey, GLC, 1981–86 (Chm., F & GP Cttee, 1981–82; Dep. Chief Whip, 1983–86). *Publications:* (with G. J. Womack) Fuel Cells, 1967; (with A. J. B. Cutler) Deposition and Corrosion in Gas Turbines, 1973; contribs to scientific jls. *Recreation:* campaigning for peace and socialism. *Address:* 3 Ennerdale Road, Kew, Richmond, Surrey TW9 3PG. *T:* (020) 8948 1989. *Died 12 June 1999.*

HART, George Vaughan; retired; Consultant, Law Reform Division, Department of Justice, Dublin, 1972–92; *b* 9 Sept. 1911; *e s* of George Vaughan Hart and Maude (*née* Curran); *m* 1949, Norah Marie, *d* of Major D. L. J. Babington; one *s* one *d*. *Educ:* Rossall; Corpus Christi Coll., Oxford. Called to Bar, Middle Temple, 1937. Served Royal Irish Fusiliers, 1940–45. Emerel Home Office as Legal Asst, 1946; Principal Asst Legal Advr, 1967–72. Sec., Criminal Law Revision Cttee, 1959–72. *Recreations:* walking, bird-watching. *Address:* 1 Mount Salus, Knocknacree Road, Dalkey, Co. Dublin. *T:* Dublin 2850420. *Clubs:* Athenæum; Kildare Street and University (Dublin). *Died 29 Jan. 1996.*

HART, Captain Raymond, CBE 1963; DSO 1945; DSC 1941, Bar 1943; Royal Navy, retired; *b* 24 June 1913; *o s* of late H. H. Hart, Bassett, Southampton; *m* 1945, Margaret Evanson, *o d* of Capt. S. B. Duffin, Danesfort, Belfast; two *s* one *d*. *Educ:* Oakmount Preparatory Sch.; King Edward VI Sch, Southampton. Joined Merchant Navy, 1929; joined Royal Navy, 1937; HMS Hasty, 2nd Destroyer Flotilla, 1939–42; in command: HMS Vidette, 1942–44 (despatches); HMS Havelock, 1944; Sen. Officer, 21st Escort Gp, 1944–45; served in HMS Vanguard during Royal Tour of S Africa, 1947; RN Staff Course, 1949–52; in command, HMS Relentless, 1952–53; Joint Services Staff Course, 1953–54; Staff C-in-C Allied Forces Mediterranean, as Liaison Officer to C-in-C Allied Forces Southern Europe, HQ Naples, Italy, 1954–56; in command, HMS Undine, and Capt. 6th Frigate Sqdn, 1957–58; Cdre Naval Drafting, 1960–62; retd from RN, 1963; Nautical Advr, British & Commonwealth Shipping Co., 1963–72; Fleet Manager, Cayzer, Irvine & Co. Ltd, 1972–76 (Dir, 1966–76); Director: Union-Castle Mail Steamship Co. Ltd; Clan Line Steamers Ltd, 1964–76; British & Commonwealth Shipping Co. Ltd, 1966–76. Vice President: Seamen's Hosp. Soc., 1983; Marine Soc., 1989. FNI 1966; FRIN 1970. Officer Order of Merit of Republic of Italy, 1958. *Died 6 Aug. 1999.*

HART, Maj.-Gen. Trevor Stuart, CB 1982; FFPHM; Hospital and Medical Director, National Guard King Khalid Hospital, Jeddah, 1983–84; *b* 19 Feb. 1926; *s* of R. J. Hart and C. G. Hart (*née* Blyfield); *m* 1954, Patricia G. Lloyd (decd); two *s* one *d*. *Educ:* Dulwich Coll.; Guy's

Hosp. MB, BS London, 1950. MRCS, LRCP 1950; FFPHM (FFCM 1979); DPH, DTM&H. DDMS HQ 1 (BR) Corps, 1975–78; Director of Medical Services: UKLF, 1978–81; BAOR, 1981–83. QHP 1978–83. Col Comdt, RAMC, 1984–90. Mem., Wessex RHA, 1984–88. OStJ 1973. *Recreations:* gardening, growing orchids (more leaves than blooms). *Address:* c/o Barclays Bank plc, Moorgate Group of Branches, 128 Moorgate, EC2M 6SX. *Died 7 Oct. 2000.*

HART-DAVIS, Sir Rupert (Charles), Kt 1967; author, editor and former publisher; Director of Rupert Hart-Davis, Ltd, Publishers, 1946–68; Vice-President, Committee of the London Library, since 1971 (Chairman 1957–69); *b* 28 Aug. 1907; *o s* of Richard Vaughan Hart-Davis and Sybil Mary Cooper, *er sister* of 1st Viscount Norwich; *m* 1st, 1929, Peggy Ashcroft (later Dame Peggy Ashcroft) (marr. diss. 1932; she *d* 1991); 2nd, 1933, Catherine Comfort Borden-Turner (marr. diss.), *d* of Mary Borden and George Douglas Turner; two *s* one *d*; 3rd, 1964, Winifred Ruth (*d* 1967), *d* of C. H. Ware, Bromyard, and *widow* of Oliver Simon; 4th, 1968, June (*née* Clifford), *widow* of David Williams. *Educ:* Eton; Balliol Coll., Oxford. Student at Old Vic, 1927–28; actor at Lyric Theatre, Hammersmith, 1928–29; office boy at William Heinemann Ltd, 1929–31; Manager of Book Soc., 1932; Dir of Jonathan Cape Ltd, 1933–40; founded Rupert Hart-Davis Ltd, 1946. Served in Coldstream Guards, 1940–45. Hon. DLitt: Reading, 1964; Durham, 1981. *Publications:* Hugh Walpole: a biography, 1952; The Arms of Time: a memoir, 1979; The Power of Chance: a table of memory, 1991; Praise from the Past: tributes to writers, 1996; Halfway to Heaven: concluding memoirs of a literary life, 1998; *edited:* The Essential Neville Cardus, 1949; E. V. Lucas: Cricket all his Life, 1950; George Moore: Letters to Lady Cunard, 1957; The Letters of Oscar Wilde, 1962; Max Beerbohm: Letters to Reggie Turner, 1964; Max Beerbohm: More Theatres, 1969; Max Beerbohm: Last Theatres, 1970; Max Beerbohm: A Peep into the Past, 1972; A Catalogue of the Caricatures of Max Beerbohm, 1972; The Autobiography of Arthur Ransome, 1976; William Plomer: Electric Delights, 1978; The Lyttelton Hart-Davis Letters, vol. I, 1978, vol. II, 1979, vol. III, 1981, vol. IV, 1982, vol. V, 1983, vol. VI, 1984; Selected Letters of Oscar Wilde, 1979; Two Men of Letters, 1979; Siegfried Sassoon Diaries: 1920–1922, 1981, 1915–1918, 1983, 1923–25, 1985; The War Poems of Siegfried Sassoon, 1983; A Beggar in Purple: commonplace book, 1983; More Letters of Oscar Wilde, 1985; Siegfried Sassoon: Letters to Max Beerbohm, 1986; Letters of Max Beerbohm 1892–1956, 1989. *Recreations:* reading, book-collecting, watching cricket. *Address:* The Old Rectory, Marske-in-Swaledale, Richmond, N Yorks DL11 7NA. *Died 8 Dec. 1999.*

HARTLEY, Brian Joseph, CMG 1950; OBE 1945 (MBE 1934); *b* 1907; *s* of late John Joseph Hartley, Tring, Herts; *m* 1951, Doreen Mary, *d* of Col R. G. Sanders; three *s* one *d*. *Educ:* Loughborough; Midland Agricultural Coll.; Wadham Coll., Oxford; Imperial Coll. of Tropical Agriculture, Trinidad. Entered Colonial Service; Agricultural Officer, Tanganyika, 1929; Aden Protectorate: Agricultural Officer, 1938; Asst Comdt, Govt Guards Auxiliaries (Camel Corps, Subeihi), 1940; Agricultural Adviser, 1944; Dir of Agriculture, 1946–54; retd 1954; Chief, FAO mission in Iraq, 1955; Mem., Tanganyika Agricultural Corporation, 1956–62; Trustee, Tanganyika Nat. Parks, 1957–64; Mem., Ngorongoro Conservation Authority Advisory Board, 1963–64. UN (Special Fund) Consultant Team Leader, Kafue Basin Survey, N Rhodesia, 1960; Team Leader, Livestock Develt Survey, Somalia, 1966; Chief Livestock Adviser, FAO, Somalia, 1967–70; Project Manager, UNSF Survey of Northern Rangelands Project, Somalia, 1970–72;

Consultant, FAO-IBRD Project, Anatolia, Turkey, 1972–73; Consultant, ODA, Wadi Rima and Montane Plains, Yemen Arab Republic, 1975; Consultant, 1973–76, Technical Manager, 1976–79, World Bank Nomadic Rangelands Project, Ethiopia; Consultant: Oxfam Karamoja Relief Prog. in Uganda, 1980; Oxfam E Africa, 1981–85; Oxfam Red Sea Province, Relief Project, Sudan, Jan.–Feb. 1988. Estabd Tanganyika Camel Co., 1987. Consultant: Food and Agricl Res. Management; Africa Camel Project, Oman, 1989. *Publications:* Camels in the Horn of Africa, 1979; (contrib.) The Camelid, 1985; scientific report, Camelus dromedarius in N Tanzania, 1987 (following the introduction of camels to Tanzania by the author). *Address:* Box 337, Malindi, Kenya. *Died 5 June 1996.*

HARTLEY, Air Marshal Sir Christopher (Harold), KCB 1963 (CB 1961); CBE 1957 (OBE 1949); DFC 1945; AFC 1944; *b* 31 Jan. 1913; *s* of late Brig.-Gen. Sir Harold Hartley, GCVO, CH, CBE, MC, FRS and Gertrude, *e d* of Arthur Lionel Smith, Master of Balliol Coll., Oxford; *m* 1st, 1937, Anne Sitwell (marr. diss., 1943); 2nd, 1944, Margaret Watson (*d* 1989); two *s*. *Educ:* Eton; Balliol Coll., Oxford (Williams Exhibnr; BA); King's Coll., Cambridge. Zoologist on Oxford Univ. expeditions: to Sarawak, 1932; Spitsbergen, 1933; Greenland, 1937. Asst Master at Eton Coll., 1937–39. Joined RAFVR, 1938; served War of 1939–45: 604 Sqdn, 256 Sqdn, Fighter Interception Unit, Central Fighter Establishment; Permanent Commission, 1945; AOC 12 Group, Fighter Command, 1959; ACAS (Operational Requirements), Air Min., 1961; DCAS, 1963–66; Controller of Aircraft, Min. of Aviation and Min. of Technology, 1966–70, retired. Dep. Chm., British Hovercraft Corporation, 1979 (Chm., 1974–78); Dir, Westland Aircraft Ltd, 1971–83. *Recreation:* fishing. *Address:* c/o Barclays Bank, PO Box 36, Bank Plain, Norwich NR2 4SP. *Club:* Travellers'. *Died 29 July 1998.*

HARTLEY, Sir Frank, Kt 1977; CBE 1970; PhD London; CChem, FRPharmS, FRSC; Vice-Chancellor, University of London, 1976–78; Dean of the School of Pharmacy, University of London, 1962–76; *b* 5 Jan. 1911; *s* of late Robinson King Hartley and Mary Hartley (*née* Holt); *m* 1937, Lydia May England (*d* 1996); two *s*. *Educ:* Municipal Secondary (later Grammar) Sch., Nelson, Lancs; Sch. of Pharmacy (Fellow, 1977), University Coll. (Fellow, 1972), and Birkbeck Coll. (Fellow, 1970), University of London. Jacob Bell Schol., 1930, Silver Medallist in Pharmaceutics, Pharmaceut. Chem. and Pharmacognosy, 1932; 1st cl. hons BSc (Chem.), University of London, 1936; PhD 1941. Pharmacy apprenticeship with J. Hayhurst, MPS, Nelson, Lancs, 1927–30; Pharmaceutical Chemist, 1932, Demonstrator and Lectr, 1932–40, at Sch. of Pharmacy; Chief Chemist, Organon Laboratories Ltd, 1940–43; Sec., Therapeutic Research Corp., 1943–46; Sec., Gen. Penicillin Cttee (Min. of Supply), 1943–46; Dir of Research and Sci. Services, The British Drug Houses, Ltd, 1946–62. Chm. Brit. Pharmaceut. Conf., 1957, and of Sci. Adv. Cttee of Pharmaceut. Soc. of Great Britain, 1964–66; Mem. Council, 1955–58, 1961–64, Vice-Pres., 1958–60, 1964–65, 1967–69, Pres., 1965–67, of Royal Institute of Chemistry; Hon. Treasurer, 1956–61, Chm. 1964–68 of Chem. Council; Mem. 1953–80, Vice-Chm. 1963–68, Chm. 1970–80, of British Pharmacopoeia Commn (Mem., Nomenclature Cttee, 1946), and a UK Deleg., 1964–80, to European Pharmacopoeia Commn; Mem., 1970–84, Vice-Chm., 1977–84, Medicines Commn; Member: Poisons Bd (Home Office), 1958–66; Cttee on Safety of Drugs (Min. of Health), 1963–70; Cttee on Prevention of Microbiol Contamination of Medicinal Products, 1972–73; Nat. Biological Standards Bd, 1975–83; Cttee of Enquiry on Contaminated Infusion Fluids, 1972; NW Thames

RHA Univ. Liaison Cttee, 1984–89; Chairman: Bd of Studies in Pharmacy, Univ. of London, 1964–68; Pharmacy Bd, CNAA, 1965–77; Collegiate Council, 1969–73; Panel on Grading of Chief Pharmacists in Teaching Hosps, 1972–74, Qualified Person Adv. Cttee, 1979, DHSS; Comrs for Lambeth, Southwark and Lewisham Health Area, 1979–80; Pharmacy Working Gp, Nat. Adv. Bd for Higher Educn, Local Authorities, 1982–84; Health Care Sci. Adv. Cttee, Council of Science and Technol. Insts, 1982–86; Working Gp on Cardiothoracic Surgery Options, 1986–87; Member: Academic Council, 1969–73; British Council for Prevention of Blindness, 1975– (Chm., 1988–95). Co-opted Mem. Senate, 1968–76, 1978–88, ex officio Mem., 1976–78, Senate Mem. of Court, 1970–76, 1978–88, ex officio Mem., 1976–78, Dep. Vice-Chancellor, 1973–76, University of London; Member Council: St Thomas's Hosp. Medical Sch., University of London, 1968–80; Royal Free Hosp. Med. Sch., 1970–88; Mem., Consultative Bd of Regents, Univ. of Qatar, 1978–; Member Bd of Governors: Royal Free Hosp. Gp, 1970–74; Kingston Polytechnic, 1970–75; British Postgrad. Med. Fedn, London Univ., 1972–89; Royal Postgrad. Med. Sch., 1972–91 (Vice-Chm., 1989–91); Inst. of Basic Med. Sci, 1973–86, subseq. Hunterian Inst., RCS, 1986–91. Chm., Consortium of Charing Cross and Westminster Med. Schs, London Univ., 1981–84. Lectures: Sir William Pope Meml, RSA, 1962; Wilkinson, Inst. of Dental Surg., 1978; Astor, Middlesex Hosp. Med. Sch., 1980; Bernal, Birkbeck Coll., 1982; Association, Hosp. Physicists Assoc., 1986. Hon. FRCP 1979; Hon. FRCS 1980 (Mem. Finance Bd, RCS, 1985–91); Hon. FRSC 1981; Hon. Fellow: Hosp. Physicists Assoc., 1986; Imperial Coll. of Science, Technol. and Medicine, 1990. Liveryman, Worshipful Soc. of Apothecaries of London, 1958. Freeman, City of London, 1959. Hon. DSc Warwick, 1978; Hon. LLD: Strathclyde, 1980; London, 1987. Charter Gold Medal, Pharm. Soc. of GB, 1974. *Publications:* papers on chem. and pharmaceut. research in *Quarterly Jl of Pharmacy, Jl of Pharmacy and Pharmacology and Jl of Chem. Soc.;* reviews and articles in sci. and tech. jls. *Recreations:* reading, watching sport. *Address:* 16 Town Thorns, Easenhall, Rugby, Warwickshire CV23 0JE. *T:* (01788) 833483.　　　　　　　　　　　*Died 26 Jan. 1997.*

HARTLING, Poul; Grand Cross of Dannebrog; United Nations High Commissioner for Refugees, 1978–85; Member of Folketing, Denmark, 1957–60 and 1964–78; *b* 14 Aug. 1914; *s* of Mads Hartling and Mathilde (*née* Nielsen); *m* 1940, Elsebeth Kirkemann; three *s* one *d*. *Educ:* Univ. of Copenhagen (Master of Divinity 1939). Curate, Frederiksberg Church, 1941–45; Chaplain, St Luke Foundn, 1945–50; Principal, Zahle's Teachers' Trng Coll., 1950–68. Chm., Liberal Party Parly Group, 1965–68; Mem., Nordic Council, 1964–68 (Pres., 1966–68); Minister of Foreign Affairs, 1968–71; Prime Minister, 1973–75; Chm., Liberal Party, 1964–78. Secretary: Christian Academic Soc., 1934–35; Christian Movement of Sen. Secondary Students, 1939–43. Dr *hc* Valparaiso Univ., Indiana, 1981. Grand-Croix: l'Ordre de la Couronne, Belgique; l'Ordre de Mennlik II, Ethiopie; Grosskreuz des Verdienstordens der Bundesrep., Deutschland; Royal Order of St Olav, Norway; Falcon of Iceland; Merit of Luxembourg; Yugoslovenske Zvezde. *Publications:* Sursum Corda, 1942; Growth of Church Idea in the Missionary Field, 1945; (ed) Church, School, Culture, 1963; The Danish Church, 1964, 2nd edn 1967; From 17 Years in Danish Politics, 1974; Autobiography vol. I, 1980, vol. II, 1981, vol. III, 1983, vol. IV, 1985; Erik Eriksen (biog.), 1990. *Recreation:* music. *Address:* Breelteparken 1, Bolig 402, 2970 Hørsholm, Denmark.
　　　　　　　　　　　　　　　　　Died 30 April 2000.

HARTOPP, Sir John Edmund Cradock-, 9th Bt *cr* 1796, of Freathby, Leicestershire; TD; *b* 8 April 1912; *s* of late Francis Gerald Cradock-Hartopp (*g s* of 3rd Bt), Barbrook, Chatsworth, Bakewell, Derbyshire, and Elizabeth Ada Mary (*née* Stuart); *S* kinsman, Sir George Francis Fleetwood Cradock-Hartopp, 8th Bt, 1949; *m* 1953, Prudence, 2nd *d* of Sir Frederick Leith-Ross, GCMG, KCB; three *d*. *Educ:* Summer Fields, Oxford; Uppingham Sch. Travelled in United States of America before joining at age of 18, Staff of Research Laboratories, Messrs Thos Firth & John Brown Ltd, Steel Makers, Sheffield, 1930; travelled in India and the Far East, 1948–49; Dir, Firth Brown Tools Ltd, 1961–76. War of 1939–45 (despatches twice); joined TA and served with Royal Engineers in UK; Norway, 1940; North Africa (1st Army), 1943; Italy, 1943–45; released, 1945, with rank of Major. Member Council: Machine Tool Research Assoc., 1965–70; Machine Tool Trades Assoc., 1970–73. *Recreations:* golf (semi-finalist English Golf Champ., 1935, first reserve, England *v* France, 1935), cricket, tennis, motoring. *Heir: cousin* Lt-Comdr Kenneth Alston Cradock-Hartopp, MBE, DSC, RN [*b* 26 Feb. 1918; *m* 1942, Gwendolyn Amy Lilian Upton; one *d*]. *Address:* The Cottage, 27 Wool Road, Wimbledon Common, SW20 0HN. *Clubs:* East India, MCC; Royal and Ancient (St Andrews).
　　　　　　　　　　　　　　　　　Died 7 Aug. 1996.

HARTOPP, Lt-Comdr Sir Kenneth Alston C.; *see* Cradock-Hartopp.

HARTWELL, Benjamin James, OBE 1959; Clerk to Southport Borough Justices, 1943–73; *b* Southport, 24 June 1908; *s* of late Joseph Hartwell, Bucks, and Margaret Ann Hartwell; *m* 1937, Mary (*née* Binns) (*d* 1986), Southport; one *s* one *d*. *Educ:* Kirkcudbright Acad.; King George V Sch., Southport; London Univ. (LLM). Admitted a Solicitor of the Supreme Court, 1936; Hon. Sec. Justices' Clerks' Soc., 1947–59; Pres. Lancs and Cheshire Dist of Boys' Brigade, 1950–63. Chm, Congregational Union of England and Wales, 1959–60 (Chm. Council, 1952–58). Member: Central Cttee, World Council of Churches, 1954–61; Home Secretary's Advisory Council on the Treatment of Offenders, 1955–63. *Address:* Willow Cottage, New Road, Pamber Green, Tadley, Hants RG26 3AG.　　　　　　　　　　*Died 18 Jan. 1999.*

HARVEY, Benjamin Hyde, OBE 1968; FCA; General Manager, Harlow Development Corporation, 1955–73; *b* 29 Sept. 1908; *s* of Benjamin Harvey and Elizabeth (*née* Hyde); *m* 1938, Heather Frances Broom; one *d*. *Educ:* Stationers' Company's Sch. IPFA; DPA. Local Govt, 1924–40; Treas., Borough of Leyton, 1940–47; Comptroller, Harlow Develt Corp., 1947–55. Hon. LLD Newfoundland, 1985. *Publication:* (jtly) Harlow: the story of a new town, 1980. *Recreations:* books, sport. *Address:* Brick House, Broxted, Essex CM6 2BU. *T:* (01279) 850233.　　　　　　　　　　　*Died 7 Nov. 1999.*

HARVEY, Colin Stanley, MBE 1964; TD 1962; DL; a Recorder, Western Circuit, 1975–96; a Solicitor of the Supreme Court; *b* 22 Oct. 1924; *s* of Harold Stanley and Lilian May Harvey; *m* 1949, Marion Elizabeth (*née* Walker); one *s* one *d*. *Educ:* Bristol Grammar Sch.; University Coll., Oxford (BA). Served 1939–45 War in Queen's Regt and RA, India, Burma, Malaya, Java. In private practice as a solicitor. Bt Lt-Col TAVR, 1973. DL Bristol (Avon), 1977). *Recreations:* TAVR, riding, beagling. *Address:* 12 Southfield Road, Westbury-on-Trym, Bristol BS9 3BH. *T:* (0117) 962 0404. *Clubs:* Royal Commonwealth Society; Clifton (Bristol); Royal Western Yacht (Plymouth).　　　　　*Died 12 May 2000.*

HARVEY-JAMIESON, Lt-Col Harvey Morro, OBE 1969; TD; DL; WS; Member, Queen's Body Guard for Scotland (Royal Company of Archers), since 1934; *b* 9

Dec. 1908; s of late Major Alexander Harvey Morro Jamieson, OBE, RGA, advocate, Edinburgh, and Isobel, d of late Maj.-Gen. Sir Robert Murdoch Smith, KCMG; assumed additional surname of Harvey, with authority of Lord Lyon King of Arms, 1958; m 1936, Frances, o c of late Col J. Y. H. Ridout, DSO; three s. Educ: Merchiston Castle Preparatory Sch.; Edinburgh Acad.; RMC Sandhurst (Prize Cadetship); Edinburgh Univ. (BL). Commissioned 1st Bn KOSB, 1928; Capt. RARO, 1938; Major, 1939, to raise 291 HAA Battery RA (TA); served War of 1939–45, Belgium, Holland and Germany, RA and Staff, Lt-Col, 1942; Comd 3rd Edinburgh Royal Scots HG Bn, 1954–57. Secretary and Legal Adviser, Co. of Merchants of City of Edinburgh, 1946–71; former Mem., Cttee on Conveyancing Legislation and Practice (apptd by Sec. of State for Scotland, 1964). Mem. Council, Cockburn Assoc. (Edinburgh Civic Trust), 1958–78; Hon. Manager, Edinburgh and Borders Trustee Savings Bank, 1957–78. Chairman, Scottish Committee: HMC; Assocs of Governing Bodies of Boys' and Girls' Public Schs, 1966–71. DL County of the City of Edinburgh, 1968–84. France and Germany Star; General Service and Home Defence Medals; Jubilee Medals, 1935 and 1977; Coronation Medals, 1937 and 1953. Publications: The Historic Month of June, 1953; contrib. to Juridical Review, Scots Law Times and Yachting Monthly. Address: 20 Dean Terrace, Edinburgh EH4 1NL. T: (0131) 332 4589. Clubs: Royal Forth Yacht (Granton); Army Sailing Association. Died 30 Jan. 1999.

HARVINGTON, Baron cr 1974 (Life Peer), of Nantwich, in the County Palatine of Chester; **Robert Grant Grant-Ferris**, Kt 1969; AE 1942; PC 1971; b 30 Dec. 1907; s of late Robert Francis Ferris, MB, ChB; m 1930, Florence (d 1996), d of Major W. Brennan De Vine, MC; one s one d. Educ: Douai Sch., Woolhampton. Called to Bar, Inner Temple, 1937; joined RAuxAF, 1933, 605 (County of Warwick) Fighter Sqdn; Flight Comdr 1939–40; Wing Comdr, 1941. Contested (C) Wigan, 1935, North St Pancras, 1945, Central Wandsworth, 1950, 1951. MP (C) North St Pancras, 1937–45; MP (C) Nantwich, Cheshire, 1955–Feb. 1974; PPS to Minister of Town and Country Planning (Rt Hon. W. S. Morrison, KC, MP), 1944–45; Temp. Chm. House of Commons and Chairman of Cttees, 1962–70; Chm. of Ways and Means and the Dep. Speaker, House of Commons, 1970–74. Chm., Bd of Management, Hosp. of St John and St Elizabeth, 1963–70. Pres. Southdown Sheep Soc. of England, 1950–52, 1959–60, 1973; Pres. Nat. Sheep Breeders' Assoc., 1956–58; a Vice-Pres. Smithfield Club, 1964, Pres. 1970. Mem., Broderers' Co., 1987–. Mem. Council, Imperial Soc. of Knights Bachelor, 1973–. Knight Grand Cross of Magistral Grace, 1949, with Riband, 1985, the Sovereign and Military Order of Malta, Grand Cross of Merit with Star of same Order, 1953; Comdr, Order of Leopold II (Belgium), 1964. Recreations: formerly hunting, golf, yachting (sometime Hon. Admiral, House of Commons Yacht Club; captained his yacht over 100,000 miles of European coasts and waterways, 1960–). Address: 6 Batisse de la Mielle, St Aubin, Jersey, Channel Islands JE3 8BA. T: (01534) 32326. Clubs: Carlton, MCC, Royal Thames Yacht; Royal Yacht Squadron (Cowes); Royal and Ancient Golf (St Andrews).
Died 1 Jan. 1997.

HASELDINE, (Charles) Norman; public relations consultant, retired; b 25 March 1922; s of Charles Edward Haseldine and Lily White; m 1946, Georgette Elise Michelle Bernard; four s. Educ: Nether Edge Grammar Sch., Sheffield. Education Officer, Doncaster Co-operative Soc., 1947–57; PRO, Sheffield & Ecclesall Co-op. Soc., 1957–70. MP (Lab and Co-op) Bradford West, 1966–70; PPS to Minister of Power, 1968–69; PPS to Pres. Bd of Trade, 1969–70; Mem. Select Cttee on Nationalised Inds,

1969–70. Recreation: classical music. Address: 115 Psalter Lane, Sheffield S11 8YR.
Died 16 Oct. 1998.

HASKELL, Francis James Herbert, FBA 1971; Professor of Art History, Oxford University, 1967–95, then Professor Emeritus; Fellow of Trinity College, Oxford, 1967–95, Hon. Fellow, 1995; b 7 April 1928; s of late Arnold Haskell, CBE, and Vera Saitzoff; m 1965, Larissa Salmina. Educ: Eton Coll.; King's Coll., Cambridge. Junior Library Clerk, House of Commons, 1953–54; Fellow of King's Coll., Cambridge, 1954–67, Hon. Fellow, 1987; Librarian of Fine Arts Faculty, Cambridge Univ., 1962–67. Mem., British Sch. at Rome, 1971–74. A Trustee, Wallace Collection, 1976–. Mem. Exec. Cttee, Nat. Art Collections Fund, 1976–. Foreign Hon. Mem., Amer. Acad. of Arts and Scis, 1979; Corresp. Mem., Accad. Pontaniana, Naples, 1982; Foreign Mem., Ateneo Veneto, 1986. Hon. DLitt Nottingham Trent. Serena medal for Italian studies, British Acad., 1985. Publications: trans., Venturi, Roots of Revolution, 1960; Patrons and Painters: a study of the relations between Art and Society in the Age of the Baroque, 1963, 2nd edn 1980 (trans. Italian, Spanish, French and Portuguese); Géricault (The Masters), 1966; An Italian Patron of French Neo-Classic Art, 1972; (ed jtly) The Artist and Writer in France, 1975; Rediscoveries in Art, 1976, 2nd edn 1980 (trans. Italian and French) (Mitchell Prize for Art History, 1977; Prix de l'Essai Vasari, 1987); L'arte e il linguaggio delta politica (Florence), 1977; (with Nicholas Penny) Taste and the Antique, 1981, 2nd edn 1982 (trans. Italian, French and Spanish); Past and Present in Art and Taste: selected essays, 1987 (trans. Italian, French and German); Painful Birth of the Art Book, 1988; History and Its Images, 1993 (trans. French, German, Spanish and Italian); articles in Burlington Mag., Jl Warburg Inst., etc; reviews in NY Review of Books, etc. Recreation: foreign travel. Address: Trinity College, Oxford OX1 3BH.
Died 18 Jan. 2000.

HASLAM, Hon. Sir Alec (Leslie), Kt 1974; Judge of the Supreme Court of New Zealand, 1957–76, Senior Puisne Judge, 1973–76; b 10 Feb. 1904; s of Charles Nelson Haslam and Adeline Elsie Haslam; m 1933, Kathleen Valerie Tennent (d 1985); two s two d. Educ: Waitaki Boys' High Sch.; Canterbury UC; Oriel Coll., Oxford. Rhodes Scholar 1927; 1st cl. hons LLM NZ; DPhil, BCL Oxon. Served with 10th Reinf. 2 NZEF, ME and Italy, 1943–46. Barrister and Solicitor, 1925; in private practice, 1936–57. Lectr in Law, Canterbury Univ., 1936–50 (except while overseas). Chm. Council of Legal Educn, 1962–75 (Mem. 1952); Mem., Rhodes Scholarship Selection Cttee, 1936–74; NZ Sec. to Rhodes Scholarships, 1961–74; Mem., Scholarships (Univ. Grants) Cttee, 1962–80; Pres., Canterbury District Law Soc., 1952–53; Vice-Pres., NZ Law Soc., 1954–57; Mem., NZ Univ. Senate, 1956–61; Sen. Teaching Fellow, Univ. of Canterbury, 1977–81. Mem., Waimairi County Council, 1950–56. Hon. LLD Canterbury, 1973. Publication: Law Relating to Trade Combinations, 1931. Recreations: reading; formerly athletics (rep. Canterbury Univ. and Oriel Coll.), rowing (rep. Oriel Coll.). Address: 22 Brackendale Place, Burnside, Christchurch 4, NZ. T: (3) 588589.
Died 23 April 1997.

HASLEGRAVE, Herbert Leslie, WhSch (Sen.); PhD; CEng, FIMechE, FIEE; FIMgt; Vice-Chancellor, Loughborough University of Technology, 1966–67; b 16 May 1902; s of late George Herbert Haslegrave and Annie (née Tottey), Wakefield; m 1938, Agnes Mary (decd), er d of Leo Sweeney, Bradford; one d. Educ: Wakefield Grammar Sch.; Bradford Technical Coll.; Trinity Hall, Cambridge (Scholar; Rex Moir Prizeman, John Bernard Seeley Prizeman, Ricardo Prizeman, 1928; 1st Cl.

Mechanical Sciences Tripos, 1928; MA); MSc (Eng); PhD London. English Electric Co. Ltd: engineering apprentice, 1918–23; Asst Designer, Stafford, 1928–30; Lecturer: Wolverhampton and Staffs Technical Coll., 1931; Bradford Technical Coll., 1931–35; Head of Continuative Education Dept, Loughborough Coll., 1935–38; Principal: St Helens Municipal Technical Coll., 1938–43; Barnsley Mining and Technical Coll., 1943–46; Leicester Coll. of Technology, 1947–53; Loughborough Coll. of Technology, 1953–66. Bernard Price Lectr, SA Inst. of Electrical Engrs, 1971. Member: Productivity Team on Training of Supervisors, visiting USA, 1951; Delegation on Education and Training of Engineers visiting USSR, 1956; Council, IMechE, 1965–66; Council, IEE, 1956–58. Chairman: Council, Assoc. of Technical Institutions, 1963–64; Cttee on Technician Courses and Examinations, 1967–69; Pres., Whitworth Soc., 1972–73. FRSA. Hon. FIMGTechE. Hon. DTech Loughborough Univ. of Technology. *Publications:* chapter in Management, Labour and Community; various pubns on engineering, education and management in proceedings of professional engineering bodies and educational press. *Recreations:* motoring, swimming, music.   *Died 19 Sept. 1999.*

HASLEGRAVE, Neville Crompton; Town Clerk, 1965–74, and Chief Executive Officer, 1969–74, Leeds; solicitor; *b* 2 Aug. 1914; *o s* of late Joe Haslegrave, Clerk of Council, and Olive May Haslegrave; *m* 1943, Vera May, *o d* of late Waldemar Julius Pedersen, MBE, and Eva Pedersen; two *d. Educ:* Exeter Cathedral Choristers School; Leeds Univ. Asst Examr, Estate Duty Office, Bd of Inland Revenue, 1940–44; Asst Solicitor, Co. Borough of Leeds, 1944–46; Chief Prosecuting Solicitor, Leeds, 1946–51; Principal Asst Solicitor, Leeds, 1951–60; Dep. Town Clerk, Leeds, 1960–65. Pres., Leeds Law Soc., 1972–73. Mem., IBA Adv. Council, 1969–73. *Recreations:* cricket, music, walking. *Address:* 37 West Court, Roundhay, Leeds LS8 2JP.   *Died 1 Sept. 1998.*

HASSAN, Hon. Sir Joshua (Abraham), GBE 1988 (CBE 1957); KCMG 1986; Kt 1963; LVO 1954; QC (Gibraltar) 1961; JP; Chief Minister of Gibraltar, 1964–69, and 1972–87; *b* 1915; *s* of late Abraham M. Hassan, Gibraltar; *m* 1945, Daniela (marr. diss. 1969), *d* of late José Salazar; two *d; m* 1969, Marcelle, *d* of late Joseph Bensimon; two *d. Educ:* Line Wall Coll., Gibraltar. Called to Bar, Middle Temple, 1939; Hon. Bencher, 1983. HM Deputy Coroner, Gibraltar, 1941–64; Mayor of Gibraltar, 1945–50 and 1953–69; Mem. Executive Council, Chief Mem. Legislative Council, Gibraltar, 1950–64; Leader of the Opposition, Gibraltar House of Assembly, 1969–72. Chm., Gibraltar Bar Council, 1992–95. Chairman: Cttee of Management, Gibraltar Museum, 1952–65; Gibraltar Govt Lottery Cttee, 1955–70; Central Planning Commn, 1947–70. Freeman, City of Gibraltar, 1996. Hon. LLD Hull, 1985. *Address:* 11/18 Europa Road, Gibraltar. *T:* 77295. *Clubs:* United Oxford & Cambridge University; Royal Gibraltar Yacht.   *Died 1 July 1997.*

HAVILAND, Denis William Garstin Latimer, CB 1957; FIIM; Director, Organised Office Designs Ltd, 1972; *b* 15 Aug. 1910; *s* of late William Alexander Haviland and Edyth Louise Latimer. *Educ:* Rugby Sch.; St John's Coll., Cambridge (MA, exam. of AMInstT); idc. LMS Rly, 1934–39; Army, RE (Col), 1940–46; Prin., Control Office for Germany and Austria, 1946; Asst Sec., 1947; transf. FO (GS), 1947; seconded to IDC, 1950; transf. Min. of Supply, 1951; Under Sec., 1953; Dep. Sec., 1959; transf. Min. of Aviation, 1959; Deputy Sec., 1959–64; Chm., Preparatory Commn European Launcher Develt Organisation, 1962–64; Jt Man. Dir and Dep. Chm., 1964, Chm. and Man. Dir, 1965–69, Staveley Industries Ltd; Dir, Short Bros Ltd, 1964–81; consultant. Mem. Council, BIM, 1967–83 (Vice-Chm., 1973–74; Chm., Professional

Standards Cttee, 1975–82). Member: Management Studies Bd, CNAA, 1974–79; Business and Management Cttee and Academic Cttee, CNAA, 1979–83; Ct, Cranfield Inst. of Technology, 1970–83. Chairman: Confedn of Healing Organisations, 1981–90; Holistic Cancer Council, 1984–86; Mem., Council, and Exec. Cttee, British Complementary Medicine Assoc., 1990–98. CIMgt; FRSA. Verulam Gold Medal, BIM, 1984. *Address:* 113 Hampstead Way, NW11 1JN. *T:* (020) 8455 2638.
                                               Died 30 May 2000.

HAWKES, Jacquetta, OBE 1952; author and archaeologist; *b* 5 Aug. 1910; *yr d* of Sir Frederick Gowland Hopkins, OM and Jessie Anne Stephens; *m* 1st, 1933, Christopher Hawkes, FBA (marr. diss. 1953; he *d* 1992); one *s*; 2nd, 1953, J. B. Priestley, OM (*d* 1984). *Educ:* Perse Sch.; Newnham Coll., Cambridge. MA; Associate, Newnham Coll., 1951. FSA 1940. Research and excavation in Great Britain, Eire, France and Palestine, 1931–40; Asst Principal, Post-War Reconstruction Secretariat, 1941–43; Ministry of Education, becoming established Principal and Sec. of UK National Commn for UNESCO, 1943–49; retired from Civil Service to write, 1949. John Danz Vis. Prof., Univ. of Washington, 1971. Vice-Pres. Council for Brit. Archæology, 1949–52; Governor, Brit. Film Inst., 1950–55. Archæological adviser, Festival of Britain, 1949–51. Mem., UNESCO Culture Advisory Cttee, 1966–79. Pres., Warwicks CPRE, 1989–. Life Trustee, Shakespeare Birthplace Trust, 1985. Hon. DLitt Warwick, 1986. *Publications:* Archæology of Jersey, 1939; Prehistoric Britain (with Christopher Hawkes), 1944; Early Britain, 1945; Symbols and Speculations (poems), 1948; A Land, 1951 (£100 Kemsley Award); Guide to Prehistoric and Roman Monuments in England and Wales, 1951; (with J. B. Priestley) Dragon's Mouth (play), 1952; Fables, 1953; Man on Earth, 1954; Journey Down a Rainbow (with J. B. Priestley), 1955; Providence Island, 1959; Man and the Sun, 1962; Unesco History of Mankind, Vol. I, Part 1, 1963; The World of the Past, 1963; King of the Two Lands, 1966; The Dawn of the Gods, 1968; The First Great Civilizations, 1973; (ed) Atlas of Ancient Archaeology, 1975; The Atlas of Early Man, 1976; A Quest of Love, 1980; Mortimer Wheeler: Adventurer in Archaeology, 1982; Shell Guide to British Archæology, 1986; contrib. learned jls and national periodicals. *Recreation:* natural history. *Address:* Littlecote, Leysbourne, Chipping Campden, Glos GL55 6HL.
                                            Died 18 March 1996.

HAWKINS, (Alexander) Desmond, OBE 1963; BBC Controller, South and West, 1967–69; *b* 20 Oct. 1908; *m* Barbara (*née* Skidmore) (decd); two *s* two *d.* Novelist, critic and broadcaster, 1935–45; Literary Editor of New English Weekly and Purpose Quarterly; Fiction Chronicler of The Criterion; Features Producer, BBC West Region, 1946; Head of Programmes, 1955; founded BBC Natural History Unit, 1957. FRSL 1977. Hon. LLD Bristol, 1974. Silver Medal, RSPB, 1959; Imperial Tobacco Radio Award for best dramatisation, 1976 and 1978; Wildscreen Panda award for outstanding achievement, 1998. *Publications:* Poetry and Prose of John Donne, 1938; Hawk among the Sparrows, 1939; Stories, Essays and Poems of D. H. Lawrence, 1939; Lighter than Day, 1940; War Report, 1946, 2nd edn (as BBC War Report), 1985, 3rd edn 1994; Sedgemoor and Avalon, 1954; The BBC Naturalist, 1957; Hardy the Novelist, 1965; Wild Life in the New Forest, 1972; Avalon and Sedgemoor, 1973; Hardy, Novelist and Poet, 1976; preface to Richard Jefferies' Wild Life in a Southern County, 1978; Cranborne Chase, 1980; Concerning Agnes, 1982; Hardy's Wessex, 1983; (ed and introd) Wake Smart's Chronicle of Cranborne, 1983; The Tess Opera, 1984; (introd) Thomas Hardy's Collected Short Stories, 1988; When I Was (autobiog.), 1989; Hardy at Home, 1989; Thomas Hardy:

his life and landscape, 1990; Wessex: an anthology, 1991; (ed and introd) William Chafin, Anecdotes and History of Cranborne Chase, 1991; Shelley's First Love, 1992; The Grove Diaries, 1995; Dorset Bedside Book, 1996; Discover Dorset, 1998; Pilfold, 1998. *Address:* 2 Stanton Close, Blandford Forum, Dorset DT11 7RT. *T:* (01258) 454954. *Clubs:* BBC, Royal Over-Seas League.

Died 6 May 1999.

HAWKINS, Sir Arthur (Ernest), Kt 1976; CEng, FIMechE, FIEE, FInstE; Chairman, 1972–77, Member, 1970–77, Central Electricity Generating Board; *b* 10 June 1913; *s* of Rev. H. R. and Louisa Hawkins; *m* 1939, Laura Judith Tallent Draper; one *s* two *d. Educ:* The Grammar Sch., Gt Yarmouth; City of Norwich Technical Coll. BScEng. Served (prior to nationalisation) with Gt Yarmouth Electricity Dept, Central Electricity Bd and Islington Electricity Dept (Dep. Engr and Gen. Manager); Croydon Dist Manager of SE Elec. Bd, 1948; joined Brit. Electricity Authority as Chief Asst Engr in System Operation Br., 1951; Personal Engrg Asst to Chief Engr, 1954; with the CEGB from its formation in 1957, at first as System Planning Engr and then as Chief Ops Engr, 1959–64; Midlands Regional Dir, 1964–70. Mem., Nuclear Power Adv. Bd, 1973. Chm., F International Ltd, 1978–79. *Publications:* contrib. Jl of Management Studies; various papers to technical instns. *Recreations:* walking, swimming. *Address:* 19 North End House, Fitzjames Avenue, W14 0RS. *Club:* Hurlingham.

Died 13 Jan. 1999.

HAWKINS, Desmond; *see* Hawkins, A. D.

HAWKINS, Frank Ernest; Chairman, 1959–73, and Managing Director, 1956–73, International Stores Ltd, Mitre Square, EC3, retired; *b* 12 Aug. 1904; 2nd *s* of late George William and Sophie Hawkins; *m* 1933, Muriel, *d* of late Joseph and Isabella Sinclair; two *s* one *d. Educ:* Leyton County High Sch. Joined staff of International Stores Ltd as boy clerk, 1919; Asst Sec., 1934; Sec., 1935; Director, 1949; Managing Dir, 1956; Vice-Chm., 1958; Chairman, 1959.   *Died 24 July 1996.*

HAWKINS, Sir Howard Caesar, 8th Bt *cr* 1778, of Kelston, Somersetshire; *b* 17 Nov. 1956; *e s* of Sir Humphry Hawkins, 7th Bt and of Anita, *d* of C. H. Funkey, Johannesburg; *S* father, 1993. *Educ:* Hilton Coll.; S African Air Force, 1975. *Heir: b* Richard Caesar Hawkins, *b* 29 Dec. 1958.   *Died 2 April 1999.*

HAWORTH, Lionel, OBE 1958; RDI 1976; FRS 1971; FREng; Senior Partner, Lionel Haworth and Associates; *b* 4 Aug. 1912; *s* of John Bertram Haworth and Anna Sophia Ackerman; *m* 1956, Joan Irene Bradbury; one *s* one *d. Educ:* Rondebosch Boys' High Sch.; Univ. of Cape Town. Cape Town Corp.'s Gold Medal and schol. tenable abroad. BSc (Eng); FIMechE; FRAeS. Graduate Apprentice, Associated Equipment Co., 1934; Rolls-Royce Ltd, Derby: Designer, 1936; Asst Chief Designer, 1944; Dep. Chief Designer, 1951; Chief Designer (Civil Engines), 1954; Chief Engr (Prop. Turbines), 1962; Bristol Siddeley Engines Ltd: Chief Design Consultant, 1963; Chief Designer, 1964; Dir of Design, Aero Div., 1965; Dir of Design, Aero Div., Rolls-Royce Ltd, 1968–77. FREng (Founder Fellow, Fellowship of Engineering, 1976). British Gold Medal for Aeronautics, 1971. *Recreation:* sailing. *Address:* 10 Hazelwood Road, Sneyd Park, Bristol BS9 1PX. *T:* (0117) 968 3032.

Died 12 April 2000.

HAY, John Albert; Managing Director, Walport Group, 1968–84; *b* 24 Nov. 1919; *er s* of Alderman J. E. Hay; *m* 1st, 1947, Beryl Joan (marr. diss. 1973), *o d* of Comdr H. C. Found, RN (retired); one *s* one *d*; 2nd, 1974, Janet May, *y d* of A. C. Spruce. *Educ:* Brighton, Hove and Sussex Grammar Sch. Solicitor, admitted May 1945.

Chairman: Brighton and Hove Young Conservatives, 1945–47; Sussex Federation of Young Conservatives, 1945–47; Young Conservative and Unionist Central Cttee, 1947–49. MP (C) Henley, Oxon, 1950–Feb. 1974; PPS to Pres. of BoT, 1951–56; Parly Sec., MoT, 1959–63; Civil Lord of the Admiralty, 1963–64; Parly Under-Sec. of State for Defence for the Royal Navy, April-Oct. 1964. Chm., Conservative Party Housing and Local Govt Cttee, 1956–59; formerly Vice-Pres. Urban District Councils Assoc.; Hon. Sec. UK Council of the European Movement, 1965–66; Mem. of Exec. Cttee, Nat. Union of Conservative and Unionist Assoc., 1947–49 and 1950–51; Member: British Delegn, Congress of Europe, 1948 and 1973; UK Delegns, Council of Europe and Western European Union, 1956–59; Chm., British Section, Council of European Municipalities, 1971–76, Vice-Chm., 1976–77, Pres., 1977–81, Vice-Pres., 1981–87. Formerly Dir, London Municipal Soc. Served War of 1939–45, in RNVR; temp. Sub-Lieut, RNVR, 1940–44; temp. Lieut, RNVR, 1944; invalided 1944. *Recreations:* writing, music, historical study. *Address:* 1134 Hillside, West Vancouver, BC V7S 2G4, Canada. *T:* (604) 9251623.

Died 27 Jan. 1998.

HAY, Maj.-Gen. Robert Arthur, CB 1970; MBE 1946; Australian Army Officer, retired 1977; *b* 9 April 1920; *s* of Eric Alexander Hay and Vera Eileen Hay (*née* Whitehead); *m* 1944, Endrée Patricia, *d* of Sir Patrick (Silvesta) McGovern; two *s* one *d* (and one *s* decd). *Educ:* Brighton Grammar Sch., Melbourne, Victoria; RMC Duntroon, ACT (graduated Dec. 1939); Australian Staff Coll., 1944; USA Staff Coll., Fort Leavenworth, 1944. Lt-Col, 1945; Col, 1955; Col GS HQ Eastern Comd; Military Attaché, Washington, DC, 1956; Dir Administrative Planning, AHQ, 1959; Defence Representative, Singapore and Malaya, 1962; Brig., 1964; IDC London, 1965; Dir Military Ops and Plans, AHQ, 1966; Maj.-Gen., 1967; Dep. Chief of the General Staff, AHQ; Comdr, Australian Forces, Vietnam, 1969; Comdr, First Australian Div., 1970; Chief, Mil. Planning Office, SEATO, 1971–73; Comdt, Royal Military Coll., Duntroon, 1973–77. Sec., Australian Council of Professions, 1978–86; Exec. Officer, Australian Centre for Publications acquired for Develt, 1982–87. Pres., Veterans Tennis Assoc. of Australia, 1981–92. *Recreations:* tennis, golf. *Address:* Unit 6, Kingston Tower, 9 Jardine Street, Kingston, ACT 2604, Australia. *Clubs:* Melbourne Cricket; Commonwealth, Royal Canberra Golf (Canberra); Tanglin (Singapore).

Died 28 Jan. 1998.

HAYBALL, Frederick Ronald, CMG 1969; *b* 23 April 1914; *s* of late Frederick Reuben Hayball and Rebecca Hayball; *m* 1938, Lavinia Violet Palmer; one *s* one *d. Educ:* Alleyn's Sch., Dulwich. Accountant, Myers, Gondouin & Co. Ltd, 1932–39; Flying Officer, RAF, 1939–45; Foreign and Commonwealth Office, 1945–69 (Counsellor, retired); Asst Sec., Longman Gp Ltd, 1969–81. *Recreations:* cricket, angling, motoring, bowls. *Address:* 50 Theydon Park Road, Theydon Bois, Essex CM16 7LP. *T:* Theydon Bois (01992) 812195.

Died 26 Jan. 1996.

HAYCRAFT, John Stacpoole, CBE 1982; Director General, International House (formerly English International), 1975–90 (Consultant, 1990–91); *b* 11 Dec. 1926; *s* of late Major W. C. S. Haycraft and Olive Haycraft; *m* 1953, Brita Elisabeth Langenfelt; two *s* one *d. Educ:* Wellington Coll.; Jesus Coll., Oxford (Open Exhibnr; MA). ESU Fellowship, Yale Univ., 1951–52. Founder and Dir, Academia Britanica, Córdoba, 1953; Founder and Principal: International Language Centre, London, 1960; International Teacher Trng Inst., 1963; Founder and Director: International House, London, 1964–90; International House, Rome, 1967–68; Director:

International House, Paris, 1971–72; Soros English Lang. Prog., 1991–94; Founder: English Teaching Theatre, 1970; English Language Schools in Tinnisoara and Kiev, 1992, Vilnius and Tallinn, 1993. Mem., English Teaching Adv. Cttee, British Council, 1974–80. *Publications:* Babel in Spain, 1958, 2nd edn 1958; Getting on in English, 1964, 7th edn 1982 (trans. 9 langs); Babel in London, 1965; George and Elvira, 1970; Choosing Your English, 1972, 8th edn 1982; Action, 1977; Introduction to English Language Teaching, 1978; Think, Then Speak, 1984; Italian Labyrinth, 1985; In Search of the French Revolution, 1989; contrib. Guardian, Independent, The Times, Observer (Spanish correspondent, 1958–59), Modern English Teacher, etc. *Recreations:* swimming, chess, cinema, theatre, history, travel. *Address:* 79 Lee Road, SE3 9EN. *T:* 0181–852 5495. *Club:* Canning.
Died 23 May 1996.

HAYDON, Sir Walter Robert, (Sir Robin), KCMG 1980 (CMG 1970); HM Diplomatic Service, retired; *b* 29 May 1920; *s* of Walter Haydon and Evelyn Louise Thom; *m* 1943, Joan Elizabeth Tewson (*d* 1988); one *d* (and one *s* one *d* decd). *Educ:* Dover Grammar Sch. Served in Army in France, India and Burma, 1939–46. Entered Foreign Service, 1946; served at London, Berne, Turin, Sofia, Bangkok, Khartoum, UK Mission to UN (New York), Washington; FO spokesman and Head of News Dept, FCO, 1967–71; High Comr, Malaŵi, 1971–73; Chief Press Sec., 10 Downing Street, 1973–74; High Comr, Malta, 1974–76; Ambassador to Republic of Ireland, 1976–80. Dir of Gp Public Affairs, Imperial Gp, 1981–84; Dir, Imperial Tobacco Ltd, 1984–87. Member: Reviewing Cttee on Export of Works of Art, 1984–87; Tobacco Adv. Council, 1984–88. Governor: ESU, 1980–86, 1987–93; Dover Grammar Sch., 1982–89. *Recreation:* walking. *Address:* c/o Lloyds TSB, Cox's & King's Branch, 7 Pall Mall, SW1Y 5NA. *Clubs:* Travellers, Special Forces.
Died 1 Dec. 1999.

HAYES, Sir Claude (James), KCMG 1974 (CMG 1969); MA, MLitt; Chairman, Crown Agents for Oversea Governments and Administrations, 1968–74; *b* 23 March 1912; *er s* of late J. B. F. Hayes, West Hoathly, Sussex; *m* 1940, Joan McCarthy (*d* 1984), *yr d* of Edward McCarthy Fitt, Civil Engineer; two *s* one *d. Educ:* Ardingly Coll.; St Edmund Hall, Oxford (Scholar); Sorbonne; New Coll., Oxford (Sen. Scholar). Heath Harrison Travelling Scholarship; Zaharoff Travelling Fellowship; Paget Toynbee Prize; MA, MLitt. Captain RASC 1st Inf. Div. BEF, 1939; Major 1940, Combined Ops; Lieut-Col, 1942–45 (N Africa, Sicily, Italy, NW Europe). Asst Dir of Examinations, Civil Service Commn, 1938; Dep. Dir of Examinations, Civil Service Commn, 1945; Dir and Comr, 1949, also Sec., 1955; Nuffield Foundn Fellowship, 1953–54, toured Commonwealth studying public service recruitment and management; Asst Sec., HM Treasury, 1957; British Govt Mem., Cttee on Dissolution of Central African Fedn, 1963; Under-Sec., HM Treasury, 1964–65; Prin. Finance Officer, Min. of Overseas Development, 1965–68. *Recreations:* music, unaided gardening, antique furniture, 18th century bourgeois chattels, getting value for money from shops. *Address:* Prinkham, Chiddingstone Hoath, Kent TN8 7DN. *T:* (01342) 850335.
Died 20 Nov. 1996.

HAYES, Vice-Adm. Sir John (Osler Chattock), KCB 1967 (CB 1964); OBE 1945; Lord-Lieutenant of Ross and Cromarty, Skye and Lochalsh, 1977–88; *b* 9 May 1913; *er s* of late Major L. C. Hayes, RAMC and Mrs Hayes; *m* 1939, Hon. Rosalind Mary Finlay, *o d* of 2nd and last Viscount Finlay of Nairn; two *s* one *d. Educ:* RN Coll., Dartmouth. Entered RN, 1927; served War of 1939–45: Atlantic, HMS Repulse, Singapore, Russian Convoys, Malta; Naval Sec., 1962–64; Flag Officer: Flotillas, Home

Fleet, 1964–66; Scotland and NI, 1966–68; retd. Comdr 1948; Capt. 1953; Rear-Adm. 1962; Vice-Adm. 1965. Chm., Cromarty Firth Port Authority, 1974–77. Pres., Scottish Council, King George's Fund for Sailors, 1968–78. King Gustav V of Sweden Jubilee Medal, 1948. *Publication:* Face the Music: a sailor's story, 1991. *Recreations:* walking, music, writing. *Address:* Wemyss House, Nigg, by Tain, Ross and Cromarty IV19 1QW. *T:* (01862) 851212.
Died 7 Sept. 1998.

HAYES, Walter Leopold Arthur, CBE 1980; Director, since 1990, and Life President, 1994, Aston Martin Lagonda Ltd (Executive Chairman, 1991–94); *b* 12 April 1924; *s* of Walter and Hilda Hayes; *m* 1949, Elizabeth (*née* Holland); two *s* one *d. Educ:* Hampton Grammar Sch.; Royal Air Force. Editor, Sunday Dispatch, 1956; Associate Editor, Daily Mail, 1959; Dir, 1965–89, Vice Pres., 1977–89, Ford Motor Co.; Vice Pres., 1968, Vice Chm., 1984–89, Ford of Europe Inc.; Director: Ford Werke A.G., 1963–70; Ford Advanced Vehicles Ltd, 1963–70; Dagenham Motors Ltd, 1994–; Vice-Pres., Public Affairs, Ford Motor Co. in the United States, 1980–84. Chairman: Stowe Gardens Appeal, Nat. Trust, 1990–; Aston Martin Heritage Trust, 1998–; Dir, Grand Prix Mechanics Trust, 1991–; Trustee: Nat. Motor Mus. Trust, 1964–; Churches Conservation Trust (formerly Redundant Churches Fund), 1991–99 (Chm., 1998–99). Gov., William L. Clements Library, Univ. of Michigan, 1996–. *Publications:* Angelica: a story for children, 1968; The Afternoon Cat and Other Poems, 1976; Henry: a memoir of Henry Ford II, 1990; The Captain from Nantucket, 1996. *Recreations:* old books, cricket. *Address:* Battlecrease Hall, Russell Road, Shepperton TW17 8JW. *Clubs:* Brooks's, Royal Automobile, MCC.
Died 26 Dec. 2000.

HAYNES, David Francis, (Frank); JP; *b* London, March 1926; *m* 1948, Vera Lancaster; one *s* two *d. Educ:* secondary schs in London. Fireman, Southern Railway, then coalminer. Member: Notts CC, 1965–81; Mansfield DC; Chm., Central Notts Community Health Council. MP (Lab) Ashfield, 1979–92. Mem., NUM. *Address:* 44 Palmerston Street, Westwood, Jacksdale, Nottingham NG16 5JA.
Died 11 Sept. 1998.

HAYNES, Prof. Robert Hall, OC 1990; PhD; FRSC 1982; President, Royal Society of Canada, 1995–97; *b* 27 Aug. 1931; *s* of James Wilson Haynes and Lillian (*née* Hall); *m* 1st, 1954, Joanne May (marr. diss. 1965); three *s*; 2nd, 1966, Prof. Jane Banfield. *Educ:* Univ. of Western Ontario (BSc 1953; PhD 1957). British Empire Cancer Campaign Fellow, Physics Dept, St Bartholomew's Hosp. Med. Coll., 1957–58; Asst Prof. of Biophysics, Univ. of Chicago, 1958–64; Associate Prof. of Biophysics, Univ. of Calif, Berkeley, 1964–68; York University, Toronto: Prof. of Biol., 1968–86; Chm., 1968–73; Distinguished Res. Prof., 1986–92, then Emeritus. Visiting Professor: USSR Acad. of Scis, 1972 and 1978; Japan Soc. for Promotion of Sci., Kyoto Univ., 1979; Chinese Acad. of Scis, Beijing, 1980; Fudan Univ., Shanghai, 1981. British Council Exchange Visitor, Univ. of Oxford, 1973; Vis. Fellow, Dept of Molecular Biophysics, Yale Univ., 1974–75; Fellow, Wissenschaftskolleg zu Berlin, 1988–89. Member: Nat. Res. Council (Sub-cttee on Radiobiol.), US Nat. Acad. of Scis, 1963–73; Governing Bd, NRCC, 1975–81; Tech. Adv. Cttee on Nuclear Fuel Waste Mgt Prog., Atomic Energy of Canada Ltd, 1979–83; Council and Exec. Cttee, Canadian Inst. for Advanced Res., 1982–87. Mem., Governor Gen.'s Adv. Council on Appts to Order of Canada, 1995–97. Pres., 16th Internat. Congress of Genetics, Toronto, 1988; Hon. Vice Pres., 18th Internat. Congress of Genetics, Beijing, 1998. FAAAS 1984. Foreign Member: Third World Acad. of Scis, 1990; Pakistan Acad. of Scis, 1994. Hon. DSc:

Manitoba, 1995; Western Ontario, 1997. EMS Award, Envmtl Mutagen Soc. of N America, 1984; Gold Medal, Biol Council of Canada, 1984; Flavelle Medal, RSC, 1988; Genetics Society of Canada: Presidential Citation, 1989; Award of Excellence, 1993. *Publications:* (with P. C. Hanawalt) The Molecular Basis of Life, 1968 (trans. Portuguese and Spanish 1971, Japanese 1972); (with W. Kaufmann) The Excitement and Fascination of Science: reflections by eminent scientists, Vol. 4, 1995; numerous res. papers and reviews on radiation microbiol., DNA repair and mutagenesis, and planetary bioengrg. *Recreation:* antiquarian book collecting in science and philosophy. *Address:* Biology Department, York University, Toronto, Ont M3J 1P3, Canada. *Fax:* (416) 6508002; 15 Queen Mary's Drive, Toronto, Ont M8X 1S1, Canada. *Fax:* (416) 2330413; *e-mail:* haynes@science.yorku.ca.   *Died 22 Dec. 1998.*

HAYNES-DIXON, Margaret Rumer; *see* Godden, Rumer.

HAYWARD, Maj.-Gen. George Victor, CEng, FICE, FIMechE; *b* 21 June 1918; *e s* of late G. H. Hayward; *m* 1953, Gay Benson, *d* of late H. B. Goulding, MB, BCh, FRCSI; one *s* one *d. Educ:* Blundells; Birmingham Univ. (BSc). War of 1939–45: commissioned, 1940; transf. to REME, 1942; GSO1 REME Training Centre, 1958; Comdr, REME 2nd Div., 1960; Asst Mil. Sec., War Office, 1962; Col, RARDE, Fort Halstead, 1963; CO, 38 Central Workshop, 1965; Dep. Comdt, Technical Group, REME, 1966; Comdt, REME Training Centre, 1969; Comdt, Technical Gp, REME, 1971–73; Planning Inspector, DoE, 1973–88. Col Comdt, REME, 1973–78. *Recreations:* sailing, ski-ing, shooting. *Address:* Chart Cottage, Chartwell, Westerham, Kent TN16 1PT. *T:* (01732) 866253. *Club:* Army and Navy.

Died 7 Jan. 1999.

HAYWARD, Jane Elizabeth; Her Honour Judge Hayward; a Circuit Judge, since 1998; *b* 31 Aug. 1946; *d* of Joseph and Diana Hayward; *m* 1967 (marr. diss. 1981); one *s* one *d. Educ:* Marlborough Grammar Sch.; University Coll. of Wales, Aberystwyth (LLB 2nd Cl. (1) Hons, 1967). Called to the Bar, Gray's Inn, 1968; Wales and Chester Circuit, in practice at the Bar, 1970–91; Stipendiary Magistrate, Greater Manchester, 1991–98; a Recorder, 1996–98. *Recreations:* tennis, theatre, ballet, travel. *Address:* Warrington Combined Court Centre, Legh Street, Warrington WA1 1UR.

Died 14 July 2000.

HAYWARD, Ronald George, CBE 1970; General Secretary of the Labour Party, 1972–82; *b* 27 June 1917; *s* of F. Hayward, small-holder, Oxon; *m* 1943, Phyllis Olive (*née* Allen); three *d. Educ:* Bloxham C of E Sch.; RAF Technical Schools, Halton, Cosford, Locking. Apprenticed Cabinet-maker, 1933–36. NCO, RAF: Technical Training Instructor, 1940–45. Labour Party: Secretary-Agent: Banbury Constituency, 1945–47; Rochester and Chatham Constituency, 1947–50; Asst Regional Organiser, 1950–59; Regional Organiser, 1959–69; National Agent, 1969–72. *Address:* 37 Sutherland Drive, Birch Hill Bank, Birchington, Kent CT7 9XD.   *Died 22 March 1996.*

HAZELL, Sir (Eric) Quinton, Kt 1995; CBE 1978 (MBE 1961); DL; Director, Foreign and Colonial Investment Trust, 1978–90; *b* 14 Dec. 1920; *s* of late Thomas Arthur Hazell and Ada Kathleen Hazell; *m* 1942, Morwenna Parry-Jones; one *s. Educ:* Manchester Grammar School. FIMI 1964. Management Trainee, Braid Bros Ltd, Colwyn Bay, 1936–39; Royal Artillery, 1939–46; formed Quinton Hazell Ltd, 1946, Chm., 1946–73; Chairman: Edward Jones (Contractors) Ltd, 1973–74; Supra Group plc, 1973–82 (Pres., 1983–85); Humberside Electronic Controls, 1987–89; Aerospace Engineering PLC, 1987–90

(Dir, 1986–90). Chm., W Midlands Econ. Planning Council, 1971–77. Mem., Welsh Adv. Cttee for Civil Aviation, 1961–67; Director: Wales Gas Bd, 1961–65; Phoenix Assce Co., 1965–85; Winterbottom Energy Trust, 1978–82; Hawker-Siddeley Gp, 1979–91; Banro Industries plc, 1985–89; British Law Executor and Trustee Co., 1986–87; Wagon Industries plc, 1989–; Non-Exec. Chm., F&C Enterprise Trust plc, 1981–86; Dep. Chm., Warwickshire Private Hosp., Leamington Spa, 1981–94; Chm., WPH Charitable Trust, 1994–; Governor, Lord Leycester Hosp., Warwick, 1971–. Member Council: UC Bangor, 1966–68; Univ. of Birmingham. Freeman, City of London, 1960; Liveryman, Coachmakers' and Coach Harness Makers' Co., 1960. DL Warwicks, 1982. *Recreations:* antiques, horology. *Address:* Avon Tor, Barford Hill, Barford, Warwick CV35 8BZ. *T:* Barford (01926) 624061.   *Died 24 June 1996.*

HAZLEWOOD, Rt Rev. John, SSC; Bishop of Ballarat, 1975–93; *b* 19 May 1924; *s* of George Harold Egerton Hazlewood and Anne Winnifred Edeson; *m* 1961, Dr Shirley Shevill (*d* 1995); one *s* (and one *s* decd). *Educ:* Nelson Coll., New Zealand; King's Coll., Cambridge (BA 1948, MA 1952); Cuddesdon Coll., Oxford. Deacon 1949; priest 1950, Southwark; Asst Curate: SS Michael and All Angels, Camberwell, 1949–50, 1953–55; St Jude, Randwick, Sydney, 1950–51; Holy Trinity, Dubbo, NSW, 1951–53; Vice-Principal, St Francis Coll., Brisbane, 1955–60; Asst Lectr in Ecclesiastical History, Univ. of Queensland, 1959–60; Dean of Rockhampton, Qld, 1960–68; Dean of Perth, WA, 1968–75. Chaplain to Victorian Br., Order of St Lazarus of Jerusalem, 1984–. Mem., Australian Anglican Nat. Doctrine Commn, 1978–89. Mem., Soc. of Holy Cross (SSC), 1985–. *Recreations:* travelling, music, gardening, reading, theatre, art. *Address:* 6 Eagle Court, Ballarat, Vic 3350, Australia. *Clubs:* Melbourne, Royal Automobile of Victoria (Melbourne).   *Died 4 Sept. 1998.*

HEADLY, Derek, CMG 1957; lately Malayan Civil Service; Midlands Secretary, Independent Schools Careers Organisation, 1966–77; *b* 1908; *s* of L. C. Headly, The House-on-the-Hill, Woodhouse Eaves, Leics; *m* 1946, Joyce Catherine (marr. diss. 1975), *d* of C. F. Freeman; one *s* one *d. Educ:* Repton Sch.; Corpus Christi Coll., Cambridge (BA). Military Service, 1944–46, Lieut-Col, Special Ops Exec., Force 136 (despatches), and British Mil. Admin. Malayan CS, 1931; served Trengganu, Muar, Pekan etc; seconded to Palestine Mandate, 1938–44; Resident N Borneo, 1949–53; British Adviser, Kelantan, 1953–57. Dir, Vipan & Headly Ltd, 1957–66. Mem. Melton and Belvoir RDC, 1958–67. Officer (Brother) Order of St John. *Publication:* From Learning to Earning (Independent Schools Careers Organisation Careers Guide), 1977. *Recreations:* hill walking, gardening. *Address:* 5 Goosenford, Cheddon Fitzpaine, Taunton TA2 8LJ. *T:* (01823) 413981. *Club:* Special Forces.

Died 11 March 1998.

HEANEY, Henry Joseph, OBE 1996; FRSE; FLA; University Librarian and Keeper of the Hunterian Books and Manuscripts, Glasgow, 1978–98; *b* 2 Jan. 1935; *s* of late Michael Heaney and Sarah (*née* Fox); *m* 1976, Mary Elizabeth Moloney. *Educ:* Abbey Grammar Sch., Newry; Queen's Univ. of Belfast (MA). FLA 1967; FRSE 1992. Asst Librarian, QUB, 1959–62; Libr., Magee University Coll., Londonderry, 1962–67; Dep. Libr., New Univ. of Ulster, 1967–69; Asst Sec., Standing Conf. of National and Univ. Libraries, 1969–72; Librarian: QUB, 1972–74; University Coll., Dublin, 1975–78. Hon. Sen. Res. Fellow, Univ. of Glasgow, 1998–. Member: Adv. Cttee on Public Liby Service, NI, 1965; Standing Cttee, Univ. Libraries Sect., IFLA, 1985–91; British Liby Bd, 1989–95; Jt Funding Councils' Libraries Review Gp, 1992–93; Chm.,

Consortium of Univ. Res. Libraries, 1995–97. Dir, Co. of Biologists, 1993–98. Chm., NI Branch, Liby Assoc., 1966, 1973; Pres., Scottish Liby Assoc., 1990. Trustee: Nat. Liby of Scotland, 1980–91; Nat. Manuscripts Conservation Trust, 1990–95. FRSA 1996. *Publications:* (ed) IFLA Annual, 1971; (ed) World Guide to Abbreviations of Organisations, 8th edn, 1988 to 10th edn, 1993; (ed) A Scottish Whig in Ireland 1835–38: the Irish journals of Robert Graham of Redgorton, 1999. *Address:* 1 Coalway Avenue, Wolverhampton WV3 7LT. *T:* (01902) 342375; *e-mail:* hheaney@clanrye.u-net.uk.
Died 13 Sept. 1999.

HEAP, Sir Desmond, Kt 1970; LLM; PPRTPI; solicitor; *b* 17 Sept. 1907; *o s* of William Heap, architect, Burnley, Lancs, and Minnie Heap; *m* 1945, Adelene Mai, *o d* of Frederick Lacey, Harrogate, and Mrs F. N. Hornby; one *s* two *d. Educ:* The Grammar Sch., Burnley; Victoria University of Manchester (LLB Hons 1929; LLM 1936); admitted Solicitor, 1933; Hons Final Law Examination. Lecturer in the Law of Town and Country Planning and Housing, Leeds Sch. of Architecture, 1935–47; Prosecuting Solicitor, 1935–38 and Chief Asst Solicitor for City of Leeds, 1938–40; Dep. Town Clerk of Leeds, 1940–47; Comptroller and City Solicitor to the Corporation of London, 1947–73. Consultant: Coward Chance, London, 1974–87; Hammond Suddards, Leeds and Bradford, 1974–91; Sugden & Spencer, Bradford, 1974–94. Pres., Law Soc., 1972–73 (Mem. Council, 1954–78, Chm. Law Reform Cttee, 1955–60, and Chm., Town Planning Cttee, 1964–70). Legal Mem., RTPI (formerly TPI), 1935–, Mem. of Council, 1947–77, Pres., 1955–56; Mem. of Editorial Board of Journal of Planning and Environment Law, 1948–; Mem. of Colonial Office Housing and Town Planning Adv. Panel, 1953–65; Mem., Council on Tribunals, 1971–77; Vice-Pres., Statute Law Soc., 1982–94. Dep. Pres., City of London Branch, British Red Cross Soc., 1956–76. Chm. of Governors, Hurstpierpoint Coll., 1975–82. Senior Past Master, Worshipful Company of Solicitors (Hon. Associate, 1987); Liveryman of Worshipful Company of Carpenters (Hon. Mem. of Ct, 1993); Hon. Mem., Court of Worshipful Co. of Chartered Surveyors. ARICS 1953 (Mem. Council, 1957–84); FRSA (Mem. Council, 1974–78). Hon. Member: Amer. Bar Foundn, 1971–; Hawaii Chapter, Phi Beta Kappa; Hon. Fellow, Inc. Soc. of Valuers and Auctioneers, 1979–. Hon. LLD Manchester, 1973. Gold Medal, RTPI, 1983; Gold Medal, Lincoln Inst. of Land Policy, Cambridge, Mass, 1983. *Publications:* Planning Law for Town and Country, 1937; Planning and the Law of Interim Development, 1944; The Town and Country Planning Act 1944, 1945; An Outline of Planning Law, 1943 to 1945, 1945; The New Towns Act 1946, 1947; Introducing the Town and Country Planning Act 1947, 1947; Encyclopædia of Planning, Compulsory Purchase and Compensation, Vol. 1, 1949; An Outline of Planning Law, 1949, 11th edn 1996; Heap on the Town and Country Planning Act 1954, 1955; Encyclopædia of Planning Law and Practice, 6 vols, 1960; Introducing the Land Commission Act 1967, 1967; Encyclopædia of Betterment Levy, 1967; The New Town Planning Procedures, 1969; How to Control Land Development, 1974, 2nd edn 1981; The Land and the Development; or, the Turmoil and the Torment (Hamlyn Lectures), 1975; Lectures on tape: The Community Land Act, 1975; The Marvellous Years: pages from a scrapbook, 1993; articles in legal jls. *Recreations:* formerly swimming, pedal biking, stage and theatre; now, taking things gently and observing the injunction to "consider the lilies of the field" because, though they neither toil nor spin, Solomon in *all* his glory "was not arrayed like one of these". *Clubs:* Athenæum, City Livery, Guildhall.
Died 27 June 1998.

HEATH, Andrew; HM Diplomatic Service; Deputy High Commissioner to New Zealand, since 1993; *b* 17 April 1953; *s* of Eric Loveland Heath and Marjorie Irene Heath (*née* Pollard); *m* 1982, Christina Friday; two *s. Educ:* Christ's Hospital; Corpus Christi Coll., Cambridge (BA Hons 1975). FCO 1975; language trng, 1976; MECAS, 1977–78; Amman, 1978–81; on loan to Cabinet Office, 1981–83; FCO, 1983–85; Kuwait, 1985–88; Washington, 1988–92; FCO, 1992–93. *Recreations:* reading, squash. *Address:* c/o Foreign and Commonwealth Office, SW1A 2AH.
Died 25 Feb. 1996.

HEATH, Air Marshal Sir Maurice (Lionel), KBE 1962 (OBE 1946); CB 1957; CVO 1978; DL; Gentleman Usher to the Queen, 1966–79, Extra Gentleman Usher to the Queen since 1979; *b* 12 Aug. 1909; *s* of Lionel Heath, artist and Principal of the Mayo Sch. of Arts, Lahore, India; *m* 1st, 1938, Kathleen Mary (*d* 1988), *d* of Boaler Gibson, Bourne, Lincs; one *s* one *d*; 2nd, 1989, Lisa (*d* 1996), *widow* of Col J. M. B. Cooke, MC. *Educ:* Sutton Valence Sch.; Cranwell. Commissioned RAF, 1929; service with Nos 16 and 28 Squadrons; Specialist Armament duties, 1933–42; Chief Instructor, No 1 Air Armament Sch., 1942; Station Commander, Metheringham, No 5 Group, Bomber Comd, 1944 (despatches); Dep. to Dir-Gen. of Armament, Air Min., 1946–48; CO Central Gunnery Sch., 1948–49; Sen. Air Liaison Officer, Wellington, NZ, 1950–52; CO Bomber Comd Bombing Sch., 1952–53; idc, 1954; Dir of Plans, Air Min., 1955; Deputy Air Secretary, Air Ministry, 1955–57; Commander, British Forces, Arabian Peninsula, 1957–59; Commandant, RAF Staff Coll., 1959–61; Chief of Staff, HQ Allied Air Forces Central Europe, 1962–65, retd. Dir, Boyd and Boyd, Estate Agents, 1971–76; Private Agent, Henderson Financial Management, 1980–89. Chief Hon. Steward, Westminster Abbey, 1965–74. Appeal Dir, Voluntary Res. Trust, King's Coll. Hosp. and Med. Sch., 1977–79, Appeal Consultant, 1979–84; Pres., Storrington Br., RAFA, 1966–84, Life Vice Pres., 1984. DL West Sussex, 1977. *Recreation:* keeping in touch with family and friends.
Died 9 July 1998.

HEATH, Oscar Victor Sayer, DSc (London); FRS 1960; Professor of Horticulture, University of Reading, 1958–69, then Emeritus; *b* 26 July 1903; *s* of late Sir (Henry) Frank Heath, GBE, KCB, and Frances Elaine (*née* Sayer); *m* 1930, Sarah Margery, (*d* 1984), *d* of Stephen Bumstead, Guestling, Hastings; two *s* one *d. Educ:* Imperial Coll., London (Forbes Medallist; Fellow, 1973). Asst Demonstrator in Botany, Imperial Coll., 1925–26; Empire Cotton Growing Corp. Sen. Studentship, Imperial Coll. of Tropical Agriculture, Trinidad, 1926–27; Plant Physiologist, Empire Cotton Growing Corp., Cotton Experiment Station, Barberton, S Africa, 1927–36; Research Student, Imperial Coll., London, 1936–39; Leverhulme Research Fellow, 1937–39; Research Asst, 1939–40, and Mem. of Staff, Research Inst. of Plant Physiology of Imperial Coll., Rothamsted, 1940–46, London, 1946–58; Sen. Principal Scientific Officer, 1948–58; Special Lectr in Plant Physiology, Imperial Coll., 1946–58. Dir, ARC Unit of Flower Crop Physiology, 1962–70; Mem. ARC, 1965–70; Leverhulme Emeritus Res. Fellow, 1970–72. *Publications:* chapters on physiology of leaf stomata in Encyclopædia of Plant Physiology (ed Ruhland), 1959, in Plant Physiology: a Treatise (ed Steward), 1959, and (with T. A. Mansfield) in Physiology of Plant Growth (ed Wilkins), 1969; The Physiological Aspects of Photosynthesis, 1969 (trans. German, 1972, Russian, 1972); Investigation by Experiment, 1970 (trans. Spanish, 1977, Portuguese, 1981); Stomata, 1975, 2nd edn 1981; papers in scientific jls. *Address:* 10 St Peter's Grove, W6 9AZ. *T:* (0181) 748 0471.
Died 16 June 1997.

HEATHCOAT AMORY, Lady; *see* Wethered, J.

HEATON, Rev. Eric William; Dean of Christ Church, Oxford, 1979–91; Pro-Vice-Chancellor, Oxford University, 1984–91; *b* 15 Oct. 1920; *s* of late Robert William Heaton and Ella Mabel Heaton (*née* Brear); *m* 1951, Rachel Mary, *d* of late Rev. Charles Harold Dodd, CH, FBA; two *s* two *d. Educ:* Ermysted's, Skipton; (Exhibnr) Christ's Coll., Cambridge (MA). English Tripos, Part I; Theological Tripos, Part I (First Class). Deacon, 1944; priest, 1945; Curate of St Oswald's, Durham, 1944–45; Staff Sec., Student Christian Movement in University of Durham, 1944–45; Chaplain, Gonville and Caius Coll., Cambridge, 1945–46, Dean and Fellow, 1946–53, Tutor, 1951–53; Bishop of Derby's Chaplain in University of Cambridge, 1946–53; Canon Residentiary, 1953–60, and Chancellor, 1956–60, Salisbury Cathedral; Tutor in Theology, Official Fellow and Chaplain, 1960–74, Senior Tutor, 1967–73, St John's College, Oxford; Dean of Durham, 1974–79. Chm. Council, Headington Sch., Oxford, 1968–74; Chm. Governors, High Sch., Durham, 1975–79. Moderator, Gen. Ordination Exam., 1971–81. Examining Chaplain to: Archbishop of York, 1951–56; Bishop of Portsmouth, 1947–74; Bishop of Salisbury, 1949–64; Bishop of Norwich, 1960–71; Bishop of Wakefield, 1961–74; Bishop of Rochester, 1962–74. Select Preacher: Cambridge University, 1948, 1958; Oxford Univ., 1958–59, 1967, 1971. Hon. Lectr, Univ. of Durham, 1975–79. Hon. Fellow, Champlain Coll., Univ. of Trent, Ont, Canada, 1973; Hon. Fellow: St John's Coll., Oxford, 1979; Christ's Coll., Cambridge, 1983; Hon. Student, Christ Church, Oxford, 1991. DD Lambeth, 1991. Cavaliere Ufficiale, Order of Merit (Italy), 1991. *Publications:* His Servants the Prophets, 1949 (revised and enlarged Pelican edn, The Old Testament Prophets, 1958, 2nd rev. edn, 1977); The Book of Daniel, 1956; Everyday Life in Old Testament Times, 1956; Commentary on the Sunday Lessons, 1959; The Hebrew Kingdoms, 1968; Solomon's New Men, 1974; The School Tradition of the Old Testament (Bampton Lectures), 1994; For Questioning Christians, 1996; A Short Introduction to the Old Testament Prophets, 1996; articles in Jl of Theological Studies, Expository Times, etc. *Address:* Tree Cottage, Elsfield, Oxford OX3 9UH. *T:* Oxford (01865) 351604.   *Died 24 Aug. 1996.*

HEENAN, Maurice, CMG 1966; QC (Hong Kong) 1962; The General Counsel, United Nations Relief and Works Agency for Palestine Refugees in the Near East, 1973–77; *b* NZ, 8 Oct. 1912; 2nd *s* of late David Donnoghue Heenan and Anne Frame; *m* 1951, Klara Gabriela Stephanie, (Claire), 2nd *d* of late Emil Ciho and Irene Rotbauer, Trencin, Bratislava, Czechoslovakia; two *d. Educ:* Canterbury Coll., University of New Zealand (LLB). Law Professional; Solicitor, 1937, and Barrister, 1946, of Supreme Court of New Zealand; practised law in NZ, 1937–40; War of 1939–45: Major, 2nd NZEF; active service Western Desert, Libya, Cyrenaica and Italy, 1940–45 (despatches); Crown Counsel, Palestine, 1946–48; Solicitor-Gen., Hong Kong, 1961; Attorney-Gen., Hong Kong, and *ex officio* MEC and MLC, Hong Kong, 1961–66; Dep.-Dir, Gen. Legal Div., Office of Legal Affairs, Offices of the Sec.-Gen., UN, NY, 1966–73. *Recreations:* Rugby football, tennis, squash, ski-ing, golf. *Address:* Plane Trees, West Road, New Canaan, CT 06840, USA. *T:* (203) 9668677. *Clubs:* Hong Kong; Country (New Canaan).   *Died 26 Sept. 2000.*

HEES, Hon. George Harris, PC (Can.) 1957; OC (Can.) 1989; Ambassador-at-Large, Canada, since 1988; *b* Toronto, 17 June 1910; *s* of Harris Lincoln Hees, Toronto, and Mabel Good, New York; *m* 1934, Mabel, *d* of late Hon. E. A. Dunlop; three *d. Educ:* Trinity Coll. Sch., Port Hope, Ont; RMC, Kingston, Ont; University of Toronto;

Cambridge Univ. Served War of 1939–45: Royal Canadian Artillery, 1941–44; 3rd Anti-Tank Regt, Royal Canadian Artillery; Bde Major, 5th Infantry Bde, Holland (wounded); retd as Major. Contested (Prog. C) Spadina Riding, 1945; MP (Prog. C): Toronto–Broadview, May 1950–1963; Prince Edward–Hastings Riding, subseq. Northumberland, Ont, Nov. 1965–88; Minister of Transport, Canada, 1957–60; Minister of Trade and Commerce, 1960–63; Minister of Veterans Affairs, 1984–88. Pres., Montreal and Canadian Stock Exchanges, 1964–65. Formerly Dir and Executive with George H. Hees Son & Co., Toronto; Dir, Expo 67. Hon. LLD Waterloo UC (later Sir Wilfrid Laurier Univ.), 1961; Hon. DMilSc Royal Mil. Coll., Kingston, Ont, 1988. *Recreations:* reading, ski-ing, swimming, golf, tennis, riding, bridge; formerly boxing. *Clubs:* Toronto Golf, Toronto Badminton and Racquet (Toronto); Royal Ottawa Golf.   *Died 11 June 1996.*

HELY, Air Cdre Arthur Hubert McMath, CB 1962; OBE 1945; Air Commodore Operations, HQ Maintenance Command, 1961–64, retired; *b* 16 Feb. 1909; *s* of Hamilton McMath Hely, OBE, RD and Lubie Thrine Hely (*née* Jörgensen); *m* 1935, Laura Mary Sullivan, 6th *d* of Serjeant A. M. Sullivan, QC; two *s* two *d. Educ:* Truro Sch.; Mt Albert GS, Auckland, NZ; Auckland University. Joined Royal Air Force, 1934; Staff Coll., 1942; HQ SACSEA, 1944, 1945; Joint Chiefs of Staff, Australia, 1946–48; Joint Services Staff Coll., 1948; Group Capt. 1950; HQ Fighter Command, 1953–56; HQ Far East Air Force, 1956, 1958; ADC to HM the Queen, 1957–59; Air Ministry (acting Air Commodore), 1958; Air Commodore, 1959. *Recreations:* golf, painting. *Address:* 5 Brewer's Yard, Storrington, West Sussex RH20 4DN. *Club:* West Sussex Golf.   *Died 21 March 1996.*

HENDERSON OF BROMPTON, Baron *cr* 1984 (Life Peer), of Brompton in the Royal Borough of Kensington and Chelsea and of Brough in the County of Cumbria; **Peter Gordon Henderson,** KCB 1975; Clerk of the Parliaments, 1974–83; *b* 16 Sept. 1922; *s* of James Alexander Leo Henderson; *m* 1950, Susan Mary Dartford; two *s* two *d. Educ:* Stowe Sch.; Magdalen Coll., Oxford. Served War, Scots Guards, 1942–44. Clerk, House of Lords, 1954–60; seconded to HM Treasury as Sec. to Leader and Chief Whip, House of Lords, 1960–63; Reading Clerk and Clerk of Public Bills, 1964–74; Clerk Asst, 1974. Mem., Cttee on Preparation of Legislation, 1973–74. Pres., Progress, 1991–; Vice-President: Nat. Assoc. of Motor Projects, 1991–; New Bridge. Patron, John Hunt Award Trust, 1999– (Chm., 1990–99).
                              Died 13 Jan. 2000.

HENDERSON, Ven. Edward Chance, ALCD; Archdeacon of Pontefract, 1968–81, then Archdeacon Emeritus; *b* 15 Oct. 1916; *s* of William Edward and Mary Anne Henderson; *m* 1942, Vera Massie Pattison; two *s* three *d. Educ:* Heaton Grammar Sch.; London University (BD 1939). Deacon 1939, priest 1940; Asst Curate, St Stephen, Newcastle upon Tyne, 1939–42; Organising Sec., CPAS, 1942–45; Vicar of St Mary of Bethany, Leeds, 1945–51; Priest i/c: Armley Hall, Leeds, 1948–51; St John, New Wortley, Leeds, 1949–51; Vicar of: All Souls, Halifax, 1951–59; Dewsbury, 1959–68; Darrington with Wentbridge, 1968–75. Examining Chaplain to Bishop of Wakefield, 1972–81. *Address:* 12 Park Lane, Balne, Goole, North Humberside DN14 0EP. *T:* (01405) 861934.   *Died 24 Sept. 1997.*

HENDERSON, Rt Rev. George Kennedy Buchanan, MBE 1974; JP; Bishop of Argyll and the Isles, 1977–92; Primus of the Episcopal Church in Scotland, 1990–92; *b* 5 Dec. 1921; *s* of George Buchanan Henderson and Anna Kennedy Butters; *m* 1950, Isobel Fergusson Bowman. *Educ:* Oban High School; University of Durham (BA,

LTh). Deacon 1943, priest 1945; Assistant Curate, Christ Church, Glasgow, 1943–48; Priest in Charge, St Bride's, Nether Lochaber, 1948–50; Chaplain to Bishop of Argyll and The Isles, 1948–50; Rector, St Andrew's, Fort William, 1950–77; Canon, St John's Cathedral, Oban, 1960; Synod Clerk, 1964–73; Dean of Argyll and The Isles, 1973–77. JP of Inverness-shire, 1963; Hon. Sheriff, 1971–; Provost of Fort William, 1962–75; Hon. Burgess of Fort William, 1973. *Address:* Benvoulin, Achnalea, Onich, by Fort William PH33 6SA. *T:* (01855) 821240.
Died 26 Sept. 1996.

HENDERSON, Robert Alistair; Chairman: Kleinwort, Benson, Lonsdale plc, 1978–88; Kleinwort Development Fund PLC (formerly Cross Investment Trust Ltd), 1969–91; Merchants Trust PLC, 1985–94; Deputy Chairman, Cadbury Schweppes plc, 1983–92 (Director, 1977–92); *b* 4 Nov. 1917; *s* of Robert Evelyn Henderson and Beatrice Janet Elsie Henderson; *m* 1947, Bridget Elizabeth, *d* of late Col J. G. Lowther, CBE, DSO, MC, TD, and Hon. Lilah White, *er d* of 3rd Baron Annaly; one *s* one *d* (and one *s* decd). *Educ:* Eton; Magdalene Coll., Cambridge (BA Hons in History). Served War: 60th Rifles, 1940–45, Captain. Jessel Toynbee & Co. Ltd, 1945–48; Borneo Co. Ltd, 1948–51 (Dir, 1956–66; then, on merger, Dir, Inchcape, 1966–87); Robert Benson, Lonsdale & Co. Ltd, 1951 (Dir, 1957); Dir, Kleinwort, Benson Ltd, 1961 (on merger of Robert Benson, Lonsdale & Co. Ltd with Kleinwort Sons & Co.; Vice-Chm., 1970–71, Dep. Chm., 1971–75, Chm., 1975–83). Dir, 1958–81, Pres., 1974–79, Equitable Life Assurance Soc.; Dir, 1981–89, Dep. Chm., 1985–89, British Airways; Chm., MT Oil & Gas, 1985–87. *Recreations:* gardening, shooting, fishing. *Address:* 7 Royal Avenue, Chelsea, SW3 4QE; North Ecchinswell Farm, Ecchinswell, near Newbury, Berks RG15 8UJ. *T:* (01635) 268244. *Clubs:* White's, Brooks's.
Died 25 Nov. 1999.

HENDERSON, Roy Galbraith, CBE 1970; FRAM; retired baritone and teacher of singing (private); Professor of Singing, Royal Academy of Music, London, 1940–74; *b* Edinburgh, 4 July 1899; *er s* of late Rev. Dr Alexander Roy Henderson, formerly Principal of Paton Congregational Coll., Nottingham, and Jean Boyd Galbraith; *m* 1926, Bertha Collin Smyth (*d* 1985); one *s* one *d* (and one *d* decd). *Educ:* Nottingham High Sch.; Royal Academy of Music, London (Worshipful Company of Musicians Medal). Debut as baritone singer, Queen's Hall, London, 1925; sang at all leading Festivals in England, and Internat. Festival for contemporary music, Amsterdam, 1933; recitals at first two Edinburgh Festivals, 1947 and 1948; principal parts in all Glyndebourne Opera festivals, 1934–40, associated chiefly with works of Delius, Elgar and Vaughan Williams, and sang many first performances of contemp. music; retired from concert platform, 1952, to devote his whole time to teaching (among his pupils was Kathleen Ferrier). Conductor, Huddersfield Glee and Madrigal Soc., 1932–39; Founder and Conductor, Nottingham Oriana Choir, 1937–52; Conductor of Bournemouth Municipal Choir, 1942–53. Adjudicator at International Concours, Geneva, 1952, and Triennially, 1956–65. Mem. of the Jury of the International Muziekstad s'Hertogenbosch, Holland, 1955–62, 1965, and Barcelona, 1965. Master classes in singing: Royal Conservatory of Music, Toronto, 1956; Toonkunst Conservatorium, Rotterdam, 1957, 1958; s'Hertogenbosch, 1967. Awarded the Sir Charles Santley memorial by Worshipful Company of Musicians for distinguished services to the art of singing, 1958. *Publications:* contributed to: Kathleen Ferrier, ed Neville Cardus, 1954; Opera Annual, 1958; The Voice, ed Sir Keith Falkner, 1983. *Recreations:* watching cricket,

television, radio, reading. *Address:* Ivor Newton House, 10 Edward Road, Bromley BR1 3NQ. *T:* (020) 8460 9150.
Died 16 March 2000.

HENDERSON, Sir William (MacGregor), Kt 1976; FRS 1976; FRSE 1977; President, Zoological Society of London, 1984–89; *b* 17 July 1913; *s* of late William Simpson Henderson and Catherine Alice Marcus Berry; *m* 1941, Alys Beryl Goodridge; four *s*. *Educ:* George Watson's Coll., Edinburgh; Royal (Dick) Veterinary Coll., Edinburgh (MRCVS); Univ. of Edinburgh (BSc, DSc). FRCVS, by election, 1973; FIBiol. Assistant, Dept of Medicine, Royal (Dick) Veterinary Coll., Edinburgh, 1936–38; Member Scientific Staff, Animal Virus Research Inst., Pirbright, 1939–56, Dep. Dir, 1955–56; Director, Pan American Foot-and-Mouth Disease Center, Rio de Janeiro, 1957–65; Head, Dept of Microbiology, ARC Inst. for Research on Animal Diseases, Compton, 1966–67, Director, 1967–72; Sec., ARC, 1972–78. Visiting Prof., Univ. of Reading, 1970–72. Chm., Genetic Manipulation Adv. Gp, 1979–81. Mem., Science Council, 1980–82, Bd Mem., 1982–84, Celltech Ltd; Bd Mem., Wellcome Biotechnology Ltd, 1983–89; Chm., Woodstock Breeding Services, 1988–89. Pres., Royal Assoc. of British Dairy Farmers, 1985–87. Hon. FRASE 1979. Corresponding Member: Argentine Assoc. of Microbiology, 1959; Argentine Soc. of Veterinary Medicine, 1965; Foreign Mem., Argentine National Acad. of Agronomy and Veterinary Science, 1980; Hon. Mem., Brasilian Soc. of Veterinary Medicine, 1965; Hon. DVMS Edinburgh, 1974; Hon. DVSc Liverpool, 1977; Hon. DSc Bristol, 1985; DUniv Stirling, 1989. Dalrymple-Champneys Award, 1974; Massey-Ferguson National Award, 1980; Underwood-Prescott Award, 1981. Orden de Mayo (Argentina), 1962. *Publications:* Quantitative Study of Foot-and-Mouth Disease Virus, 1949; Man's Use of Animals, 1981; British Agricultural Research and the Agricultural Research Council, 1981; A Man of the Country, 1994; contribs to scientific jls principally on foot-and-mouth disease. *Recreation:* gardening. *Address:* Culvers, Croft Road, Goring-on-Thames, Reading RG8 9ES. *Club:* Athenæum.
Died 29 Nov. 2000.

HENDERSON, William Ross, CBE 1988; TD 1972, clasps 1978, 1984; Conservative Central Office Regional Director, Western Region (formerly Conservative Central Office Agent, Western Area), 1989–97; *b* 15 Sept. 1936; *s* of Major William Ross Henderson and Jean Elizabeth Doxford Henderson; *m* 1969, Valerie Helen Thomas; one *s* one *d*. *Educ:* Argyle House School, Sunderland. Agent and Secretary, Newcastle upon Tyne West Cons. Assoc., 1961–68; Dep. Central Office Agent, Greater London Area, 1968–76; Cons. Party Training Officer, 1976–80; Central Office Agent, East of England Area, 1980–84; Dir, Scottish Cons. and Unionist Central Office, 1984–87. Cross of Merit, Gold Class, Poland, 1972. KLJ 1985. *Recreations:* gardening, reading. *Address:* Barratt's, Clyst Hydon, Cullompton, Devon EX15 2NQ. *Club:* St Stephen's Constitutional.
Died 25 Oct. 1998.

HENLEY, Rear-Adm. Sir Joseph (Charles Cameron), KCVO 1963; CB 1962; *b* 24 April 1909; *e s* of Vice-Adm. J. C. W. Henley, CB and Esmé Gordon, *y d* of Col Aylmer Spicer Cameron, VC, CB, 72nd Highlanders; *m* 1st, 1934, Daphne Ruth (marr. diss. 1965), *d* of late A. A. H. Wykeham, Pitt Place, Brighstone, IW; one *s* three *d*; 2nd, 1966, Patricia Sharp (MBE 1952) (*d* 1997), *d* of late Roy Eastman, Alberta, Canada. *Educ:* Sherborne. Joined Royal Navy, 1927; served War of 1939–45, in HMS Birmingham and King George V; Capt., 1951; in command HMS Defender, 1954–55; Naval Attaché; Washington (as Commodore), 1956–57; Dir, Royal Naval Staff Coll., 1958; Chief of Staff, Mediterranean Station, 1959–61, as Commodore; Rear-Adm. 1960; Flag Officer, Royal Yachts

and Extra Naval Equerry to the Queen, 1962–65; retd 1965. *Clubs:* Royal Yacht Squadron; Royal Sydney Golf.
Died 16 June 1999.

HENNELL, Rev. Canon Michael Murray; Residentiary Canon, Manchester Cathedral, 1970–84, Canon Emeritus, since 1984; *b* 11 Sept. 1918; *s* of Charles Murray and Jessie Hennell; *m* 1950, Peggy Glendinning; four *s. Educ:* Bishops Stortford Coll. (Prep.); Royal Masonic Sch.; St Edmund Hall and Wycliffe Hall, Oxford. MA Oxon and, by incorporation, MA Cantab. Deacon 1942, priest 1943; Assistant Curate: St Stephen's With St Bartholomew's, Islington, N1, 1942–44; All Saints, Queensbury, Middx, 1944–48; Tutor, Ridley Hall, Cambridge, 1948–51; St Aidan's Coll., Birkenhead: Sen. Tutor, 1951; Vice-Principal, 1952–59; Principal, 1959–63; Principal, Ridley Hall, Cambridge, 1964–70. *Publications:* John Venn and the Clapham Sect, 1958; Sons of the Prophets, 1979; (ed and contrib.) Charles Simeon, 1759–1836, 1959; The Deans and Canons of Manchester Cathedral 1840–1948, 1989; contribs to: The Anglican Synthesis, 1964; Popular Belief and Practice, 1972; A Dictionary of Christian Spirituality, 1983; The Study of Spirituality, 1986; The Blackwell Dictionary of Evangelical Biography, 1994. *Address:* 53 Cleveley Road, Meols, Wirral, Merseyside L47 8XN. *Died 1 Aug. 1996.*

HENRI, Adrian Maurice; President, Liverpool Academy of Arts, 1972–81; *b* Birkenhead, 10 April 1932; *s* of Arthur Maurice Henri and Emma Johnson; *m* 1959, Joyce Wilson (marr. diss. 1974; she *d* 1987). *Educ:* St Asaph Grammar Sch., N Wales; Dept of Fine Art, King's Coll., Newcastle upon Tyne, 1951–55 (Hons BA Fine Art (Dunelm) 1955). Worked for ten seasons in Rhyl fairground, later as a scenic-artist and secondary school teacher; taught at Manchester then Liverpool Colls of Art, 1961–67. Led the poetry/rock group, Liverpool Scene, 1967–70; thereafter freelance poet/painter/singer/ songwriter/lecturer. Tour of USA, 1973; Bicentennial Poetry Tour of USA, 1976; exchange tour of Canada, 1980. Pres., Merseyside Arts Assoc., 1978–80; Writer-in-Residence: Tattenhall Centre, Cheshire, 1980–82; Liverpool Univ., 1989. Hon. Prof., Liverpool John Moores Univ. Hon. DLitt Liverpool, 1990; Hon. Dr Liverpool John Moores. *Exhibitions:* included: Biennale della Giovane Pintura, Milan, 1968; Pen as Pencil, Brussels, 1973; John Moores Liverpool Exhibns, 1962, 1965, 1967, 1974, 1978, 1980, 1989, 1993; Peter Moores Project, Real Life, Liverpool, 1977; Art and the Sea, 1980–81; Hedgerow mural, 1980, Summer Terrace mural, 1983. Royal Liverpool Hosp. John Moores Liverpool £2000 prize, 1972. *Major One-Man Shows:* ICA, London, 1968; ArtNet, London, 1975; Williamson Art Gall., Birkenhead, 1975; Retrospective 1960–76, Wolverhampton City Art Gall., 1976; Demarco Gall., Edinburgh, 1978; Touring Retrospective, The Art of Adrian Henri, South Hill Park and elsewhere, 1986–87; Hanover Gall., Liverpool, 1987; Library Centre, Skelmersdale, 1989; Poetry Soc., 1990; Acorn Gall., Liverpool, 1992; Storey Inst., Lancaster, 1994; Merkmal Gall., Liverpool, 1994; Whitford Fine Art, London, 1997; Liverpool Univ., 1998; Galerie Zander, Cologne, 1998; Retrospective, Walker Art Gall., Liverpool, 2000. Lowlands Away (oratorio, music by Richard Gordon-Smith), perf. 1996 and 2000. Various recordings. *Publications:* Tonight at Noon, 1968; City, 1969; Autobiography, 1971; (with Nell Dunn) I Want (novel), 1972 (play, 1983); World of Art Series: Environments and Happenings, 1974; The Best of Henri, 1975; City Hedges 1970–76, 1977; From The Loveless Motel, poems 1976–79, 1980; Penny Arcade, poems 1978–82, 1983; Collected Poems, 1986; Wish You Were Here (poems), 1990; Not Fade Away (poems), 1994; *for children:* Eric, the Punk Cat, 1982; The Phantom Lollipop-Lady (poems), 1986; Eric and Frankie in Las Vegas, 1987;

Rhinestone Rhino (poems), 1989; The Postman's Palace, 1990; Dinner with the Spratts (poems), 1993; The World's Your Lobster, 1998; Robocat (poems), 1998; *for teenagers:* Box (poems), 1990; The Wakefield Mysteries (playscript), 1991; *anthologies:* The Oxford Book of Twentieth Century Verse, 1973; The Liverpool Scene (ed Edward Lucie-Smith), 1967; Penguin Modern Poets No 10: The Mersey Sound, 1967, rev. and enlarged edn 1974, rev. edn 1983; British Poetry since 1945 (ed Edward Lucie-Smith), 1970; New Volume, 1983; Liverpool Accents: seven poets and a city, 1996; *plays:* I Wonder, a Guillaume Apollinaire Show (with Mike Kustow), 1968; The Wakefield Mysteries, 1988; (jtly) Fears and Miseries of the Third Term, 1989; *TV plays:* Yesterday's Girl, 1973; The Husband, the Wife and the Stranger, 1986. *Recreations:* watching Liverpool FC, visiting Shropshire and Normandy, old movies, SF, Gothic and crime novels. *Address:* 21 Mount Street, Liverpool L1 9HD. *T:* (0151) 709 6682; (literary agent) Rogers, Coleridge and White Ltd, 20 Powis Mews, W11 1JN. *Clubs:* Chelsea Arts; Private Chauffeurs' (Liverpool). *Died 20 Dec. 2000.*

HENRY, Sir Denis (Aynsley), Kt 1975; OBE 1962; QC (Grenada) 1968; barrister; Senior Partner, Henry, Henry & Bristol, St George's, Grenada, WI; *b* 3 Feb. 1917; *s* of Ferdinand H. Henry and Agatha May Henry; *m* 1966, Kathleen Carol (*née* Sheppard); two *s* three *d. Educ:* Grenada Boys' Secondary Sch.; King's Coll., London (LLB Hons). Called to the Bar, Inner Temple (Certif. of Honour), 1939, then in practice at Bar, Grenada. Served three terms as nominated MLC, Grenada, 1952–65; Sen. nominated Mem. Exec. Council, 1956–65; Senator in First Parlt of Associated State of Grenada, 1966–67. Mem. Council, Univ. of West Indies, 1956–68. Pres. and Dir, Windward Islands Banana Growers Assoc., 1957–75; Pres., Commonwealth Banana Exporters Assoc., 1973–75; Chairman: Grenada Banana Co-operative Soc., 1953–75; Grenada Cocoa Assoc., 1973–75. Vice-Pres., Commonwealth Caribbean Society for the Blind, 1972–75; Mem. Exec., West India Cttee, London, 1972–75. *Recreations:* golf, swimming, tennis. *Clubs:* Royal Commonwealth Society; Grenada Golf, Richmond Hill Tennis (Grenada). *Died 5 April 2000.*

HENRY, Sir James Holmes, 2nd Bt *cr* 1923, of Cahore, co. Londonderry; CMG 1960; MC 1944; TD 1950; QC (Tanganyika) 1953, (Cyprus) 1957; Chairman, Foreign Compensation Commission, 1977–83 (Commissioner, 1960–77); *b* 22 Sept. 1911; *er s* of Rt Hon. Sir Denis Stanislaus Henry, 1st Bt, (first Lord Chief Justice of Northern Ireland), Cahore, Draperstown, Co. Londonderry, and Violet (*d* 1966), 3rd *d* of late Rt Hon. Hugh Holmes, Court of Appeal, Ireland; *S* father, 1925; *m* 1st, 1941, S. M. Blackwell (marriage terminated by divorce and rescript of Holy Office in Rome); 2nd, 1949, Christina Hilary, *e d* of late Sir Hugh Holmes, KBE, CMG, MC, QC (formerly Mixed Courts, Egypt), and widow of Lieut-Commander Christopher H. Wells, RN; three *d. Educ:* Mount St Mary's Coll., Chesterfield; Downside Sch.; University College, London (BA (Hons) Classics (1st Class), University Scholarships). Called to Bar, Inner Temple, 1934; practised, London, 1934–39. Served War of 1939–45, London Irish Rifles (wounded). Crown Counsel, Tanganyika, 1946; Legal Draftsman, 1949; Jt Comr, Revised Edn of Laws of Tanganyika (1947–49), 1950; Solicitor-General, Tanganyika, 1952; Attorney-General, Cyprus, 1956–60. *Heir: nephew* Patrick Denis Henry, *b* 20 Dec. 1957. *Address:* Kandy Lodge, 18 Ormond Avenue, Hampton on Thames, Middx TW12 2RU. *Club:* Travellers'. *Died 19 Feb. 1997.*

HENRY, William Robert, CBE 1979; Chairman: Coats Patons Ltd, 1975–81; Scottish Amicable Life Assurance Society, 1981–84; *b* 30 April 1915; *s* of William Henry and Sarah (*née* Lindsay); *m* 1947, Esther Macfayden; two *s* one *d. Educ:* Govan High Sch.; London Univ. Entered Company's service, 1934; Head of Financial Dept, 1953; Asst Accountant, 1957; Dir, J. & P. Coats Ltd (Parent Co.), 1966; Dep. Chm., Coats Patons Ltd, 1970. FIMgt (FBIM 1976). *Recreations:* golf, gardening. *Address:* Hawkstone Lodge, Ascog, Isle of Bute, Scotland PA20 9EU.   *Died 16 Feb. 1996.*

HEPBURN, Surg. Rear-Adm. Nicol Sinclair, CB 1971; CBE 1968; *b* 2 Feb. 1913; *s* of late John Primrose and Susan Hepburn, Edinburgh; *m* 1939, Dorothy Blackwood (*d* 1989); two *s. Educ:* Broughton; Edinburgh Univ. MB, ChB 1935; DPH London, 1948; DIH London, 1952. Barrister-at-law, Gray's Inn, 1956. Joined RN, 1935; served during war in Atlantic and Pacific Stations; Senior Medical Officer, HM Dockyard: Plymouth, 1952; Portsmouth, 1955; Naval Medical Officer of Health: Portsmouth, 1959; Malta, 1962; Surg. Cdre and Dep. Med. Dir-Gen., 1966; Surg. Rear-Adm. 1969; MO i/c RN Hosp., Haslar, 1969–72; retd. MO, DHSS, 1972–80. *Address:* Mallows, 10 Chilbolton Avenue, Winchester, Hants SO22 5HD.   *Died 7 May 2000.*

HEPPER, Anthony Evelyn, CEng, FIMechE; CIMgt; Chairman, Hyde Sails Ltd, since 1984; *b* 16 Jan. 1923; *s* of Lt-Col J. E. Hepper; *m* 1970, Jonquil Francisca Kinloch-Jones. *Educ:* Wellington Coll., Berks. Royal Engrs, 1942–47 (retd as Hon. Major); Courtaulds Ltd, 1947–53; Cape Asbestos Co. Ltd, 1953–57; Thomas Tilling Ltd, 1957–68 (Dir from 1963 until secondment); seconded as Industrial Adviser, DEA, 1966–67, and Mem., SIB, 1967; Chairman: Upper Clyde Shipbuilders Ltd, 1968–71; Henry Sykes Ltd, 1972–81; Richardsons Westgarth plc, 1982–85; Lamont & Partners plc, 1986–90; Director: Cape plc, 1968–94; Cardinal Investment Trust plc, 1982–84; General Investors Trustees plc, 1982–84; F. & Pacific Investment Trust PLC, 1984–87. *Recreation:* golf. *Address:* 70 Eaton Place, SW1X 8AT. *T:* (020) 7235 7518. *Club:* Boodle's.
                                                Died 16 July 1999.

HEPPLESTON, Prof. Alfred Gordon; Professor of Pathology, University of Durham, 1960–63, of Newcastle upon Tyne, 1963–77, then Emeritus Professor; *b* 29 Aug. 1915; *s* of Alfred Heppleston, Headmaster, and Edith (*née* Clough); *m* 1942, Eleanor Rix Tebbutt; two *s. Educ:* Manchester Grammar Sch. Chief Asst, Professorial Medical Unit, University of Manchester; Asst Lecturer in Pathology, Welsh Nat. Sch. of Medicine, Univ. of Wales, 1944–47; Dorothy Temple Cross Research Fellow, Univ. of Pennsylvania, 1947–48; Sen. Lectr in Pathology, Univ. of Wales, 1948–60. *Publications:* on pathological topics, largely in reference to pulmonary disorders. *Recreations:* ornithology, cricket, music. *Address:* Bridgeford Gate, Bellingham, Hexham, Northumberland NE48 2HT. *T:* (01434) 220431.   *Died 27 Jan. 1998.*

HERBISON, Rt Hon. Margaret McCrorie, PC 1964; Lord High Commissioner to the General Assembly of the Church of Scotland, 1970–71; *b* 11 March 1907; *d* of John Herbison, Shotts. *Educ:* Dykehead Public Sch., Shotts; Bellshill Acad.; Glasgow Univ. Teacher of English and History in Glasgow schs; MP (Lab) North Lanark, 1945–70; Jt Parly Under-Sec. of State, Scottish Office, 1950–51; Minister of Pensions and National Insurance, Oct. 1964–Aug. 1966, of Social Security, 1966–67. Chm., Select Cttee on Overseas Aid, 1969. Member National Executive Cttee, Labour Party; Chm. Labour Party, 1957. Mem., Royal Commn on Standards of Conduct in Public Life, 1974. Scotswoman of the Year, 1970. Hon. LLD Glasgow, 1970. *Recreations:* reading, gardening. *Address:* 4 Mornay Way, Shotts, Lanarkshire ML7 4EG. *T:* (01501) 822223.   *Died 29 Dec. 1996.*

HERFORD, Geoffrey Vernon Brooke, CBE 1956 (OBE 1946); FIBiol; Director of Pest Infestation Research, Agricultural Research Council, 1940–68, retired; *b* 18 Nov. 1905; *s* of late Henry J. R. Herford, Hampstead; *m* 1933, Evelyn Cicely (*d* 1969), *d* of W. G. Lambert. *Educ:* Gresham's School, Holt; Magdalen College, Oxford (BA); Minnesota University (MSc). *Address:* Horsfall House, Windmill Road, Minchinhampton, Glos GL6 9EY.
                                                Died 2 Feb. 2000.

HERMAN, Josef, OBE 1980; RA 1990; painter; *b* 3 Jan. 1911; *m* 1942, Catriona MacLeod (marr. diss. 1955); *m* 1955, Eleanor Ettlinger; one *s* (one *d* decd). *Educ:* Warsaw. First exhibition, Warsaw, 1932; left for Belgium, 1938; arrived in Britain, June 1940; lived in: Glasgow, 1940–43; Ystradgynlais (mining village, Wales), 1944–53. Exhibitions included: Glasgow, 1942; Edinburgh, 1942; London, 1943; Roland, Browse and Delbanco Gallery, 1946–76; British Council; Arts Council; (retrospective) Whitechapel Art Gallery, 1956; (retrospective) Camden Arts Centre, 1980; New Grafton Gall., 1996, 1998; Flowers East Gall., 1998; contrib. to British Mining exhibn, Science Museum, 1983. Work in permanent collections: Arts Council; British Council; British Museum; National Museum, Cardiff; Contemporary Art Society, National Museum Bezalel, Jerusalem; National Gallery, Johannesburg; Tate Gallery, London; Victoria and Albert Museum, London; National Gallery, Melbourne; National Gallery, Ottawa; National Gallery, Wellington, etc. Gold Medal, Royal National Eisteddfod, Llanelly, 1962; Contemporary Art Society prize, 1952 and 1953; prize, John Moore Exhibition, 1956; Trust House Award, 1962. *Publications:* Related Twilights (autobiog.), 1975; Reflections on Drawing, 1985; Notes from a Welsh Diary, 1988; Song of the Migrant Bird (prints), 1999; *relevant publication:* Josef Herman: a working life, by Nini Herman, 1997. *Address:* 120 Edith Road, W14 9AP.
                                                Died 19 Feb. 2000.

HERNIMAN, Ven. Ronald George; Archdeacon of Barnstaple 1970–88; *b* 18 April 1923; *s* of George Egerton and Rose Herniman; *m* 1949, Grace Jordan-Jones; one *s* two *d. Educ:* Geneva; Bideford, Devon; Birkbeck Coll., London Univ., 1948–51 (BA); Oak Hill Theological Coll., 1951–53. Tutor, Oak Hill Coll., 1953–54; deacon 1954, priest 1955; Asst Curate, Christ Church, Cockfosters, 1954–56; Dir of Philosophical Studies, Oak Hill, 1956–61; Rector of Exe Valley Group of Churches (Washfield, Stoodleigh, Withleigh, Calverleigh Oakford, Morebath, Rackenford, Loxbeare and Templeton), 1961–72; Rector of Shirwell with Loxhore, 1972–82. Served RAF, 1941–46. *Recreations:* sailing, making and mending things. *Address:* Castleland House, Oakfordbridge, Tiverton, Devon EX16 9JA.   *Died 22 Jan. 1998.*

HERON, Patrick, CBE 1977; painter; *b* 30 Jan. 1920; *e s* of late T. M. and Eulalie Heron; *m* 1945, Delia Reiss (*d* 1979); two *d. Educ:* St Ives, Cornwall; Welwyn Garden City; St Georges Sch., Harpenden; Slade Sch. of Fine Art. Art criticism in: New English Weekly, 1945–47; New Statesman and Nation, 1947–50 (Art Critic); London correspondent, Arts (NY), 1955–58. John Power Lectr, Sydney Univ., 1973; Doty Prof., Univ. of Texas at Austin, 1978. Trustee, Tate Gall., 1980–87. *One-man exhibitions:* Redfern Gallery, London, 1947, 1948, 1950, 1951, 1954, 1956, 1958; Waddington Galleries, London, 1959, 1960, 1963, 1964, 1965, 1967, 1968, 1970 (canvases), 1970 (prints), 1973, 1975, 1977, 1979, 1983, 1987; Bertha Schaefer Gallery, NY, 1960, 1962, 1965; Galerie Charles Lienhard, Zürich, 1963; Traverse Theatre Gallery, Edinburgh, 1965; São Paulo Bienal VIII, 1965 (Silver Medal) (exhibn toured S Amer., 1966); Harrogate Festival, 1970; Rudy Komon Gall., Sydney, 1970; Waddington Fine Arts, Montreal, 1970; Whitechapel Gallery, 1972;

Bonython Art Gall., Sydney, 1973; Rutland Gall., London, 1975; Galerie le Balcon des Arts, Paris, 1977; *retrospective exhibitions:* Wakefield City Art Gallery, Leeds, Hull, Nottingham, 1952; Richard Demarco Gallery, Edinburgh, 1967; Kunstnernes Hus, Oslo, 1967; Museum of Modern Art, Oxford, 1968; Univ. of Texas at Austin Art Mus., 1978 (69 works); Oriel Gallery, Cardiff, 1979; Barbican Art Gall., 1985; Tate Gallery, 1998. Twelve paintings shown at São Paulo Bienal II, Brazil, 1953–54; paintings exhibited: Carnegie International, Pittsburgh, 1961; British Art Today, San Francisco, Dallas, Santa Barbara, 1962–63; Painting and Sculpture of a Decade, 1954–64, Tate Gallery, 1964; British Painting and Sculpture, 1960–70, National Gallery of Art, Washington DC; British Painting 1952–1977, RA, 1977; Color en la Pintura Británica (tour of S Amer.), 1977–78; exhibited in group and British Council exhibitions in many countries; *works owned by:* Tate Gallery; Arts Council; British Council; V&A Museum; British Museum; Gulbenkian Foundation; Leeds City Art Gallery; Stuyvesant Foundation; National Portrait Gallery; Broadcasting House; Wakefield City Art Gallery; Manchester City Art Gallery; Contemporary Art Society; Oldham Art Gallery; CEMA, N Ireland; Abbot Hall Art Gallery, Kendal; The Art Gallery, Aberdeen; National Gallery of Wales, Cardiff; Art Gall. of Ont, Toronto; Scottish Nat. Portrait Gall.; Scottish Nat. Gall. of Modern Art; Univ. of Galway; Eliot Coll., Univ. of Kent; Montreal Museum of Fine Art; Vancouver Art Gallery; Toledo Museum of Art, Ohio; Smith College Museum of Art, Mass; Brooklyn Museum, NY; Albright-Knox Art Gallery, Buffalo, NY; Univ. of Michigan Museum of Art; Univ. of Texas at Austin Art Museum; Museum of Art, Carnegie Inst., Pittsburgh; Yale Center for British Art, New Haven, Conn; Stuyvesant Foundn, Holland; Boymans Museum, Rotterdam; Musée d'Art Contemporain, Montreal; Western Australian Art Gallery, Perth; Art Gall. of NSW, Sydney; Pembroke, Merton and Nuffield Colleges, Oxford; Bristol City Art Gall.; Exeter Art Gallery; Exeter Univ. (Cornwall House); Plymouth City Art Gallery; Power Collection, Sydney; London Art Gall., London, Ont; Hatton Art Gall., Newcastle Univ.; Southampton Art Gall.; Norwich Art Gall.; also represented in Fitzwilliam Museum, Cambridge, and in municipal collections at Glasgow, Reading and Sheffield. Hon. FRIBA 1991. Hon. DLitt: Exeter, 1982; Kent, 1986; Hon. Dr RCA, 1987. Awarded Grand Prize by international jury, John Moores' 2nd Liverpool Exhibition, 1959. *Publications:* Vlaminck: Paintings, 1900–1945, 1947; The Changing Forms of Art, 1955; Ivon Hitchens, 1955; Braque, 1958; The Shape of Colour, 1973; Paintings by Patrick Heron 1965–1977, 1978; The Colour of Colour, 1978; Patrick Heron, 1988; contrib. The Guardian, Studio International, etc. *Address:* Eagles Nest, Zennor, near St Ives, Cornwall TR26 3BP. *T:* (01736) 796921; 12 Edith Mansions, Edith Grove, SW10 0NN. *T:* (020) 7352 1787.

Died 20 March 1999.

HERRIDGE, Geoffrey Howard, CMG 1962; Chairman, Iraq Petroleum Co. Ltd and Associated Companies, 1965–70, retired (Managing Director, 1957–63; Deputy Chairman, 1963–65); *b* 22 Feb. 1904; 3rd *s* of late Edward Herridge, Eckington, Worcestershire; *m* 1935, Dorothy Elvira Tod; two *s* two *d. Educ:* Crypt Sch., Gloucester; St John's Coll., Cambridge. Joined Turkish Petroleum Co. Ltd (later Iraq Petroleum Co. Ltd), Iraq, 1926; served in Iraq, Jordan, Palestine, 1926–47; General Manager in the Middle East, Iraq Petroleum Co. and Associated Companies, 1947–51; Executive Director, 1953–57. Member of London Cttee, Ottoman Bank, 1964–79. Chairman, Petroleum Industry Training Board, 1967–70. *Address:* Flint, Sidlesham Common, Chichester, West Sussex PO20 7PY. *Club:* Oriental.

Died 21 March 1997.

HERRON, Henry, CBE 1975; Procurator-Fiscal, Glasgow, 1965–76, retired; Deputy Chairman of Traffic Commissioners and Licensing Authority for Scottish Traffic Area, 1978–81; *b* 6 May 1911; *s* of William and Jessie Herron; *m* 1942, Dr Christina Aitkenhead Crawford; one *s* two *d. Educ:* Hamilton Academy; Glasgow Univ. (MA, LLB). Solicitor. Depute Procurator-Fiscal, Glasgow, 1946; Procurator-Fiscal, Banff, 1946–51; Asst Procurator-Fiscal, Glasgow, 1951–55; Procurator-Fiscal, Paisley, 1955–65. *Recreations:* gardening, jurisprudence, criminology. *Address:* 51 Craw Road, Paisley PA2 6AE. *T:* (0141) 889 3091. *Died 17 Nov. 1996.*

HERSHEY, Dr Alfred Day; Director, Genetics Research Unit, Carnegie Institution of Washington, 1962–74, retired; *b* 4 Dec. 1908; *s* of Robert D. Hershey and Alma (*née* Wilbur); *m* 1945, Harriet Davidson; one *s. Educ:* Michigan State Coll. (later Univ.). BS 1930; PhD 1934. Asst Bacteriologist, Washington Univ. Sch. of Medicine, St Louis Missouri, 1934–36; Instructor, 1936–38; Asst Prof., 1938–42; Assoc. Prof., 1942–50; Staff Mem., Dept of Genetics (later Genetics Research Unit), Carnegie Instn of Washington, 1950–62. Albert Lasker Award, Amer. Public Health Assoc., 1958; Kimber Genetics Award, Nat. Acad. Sci., US, 1965. Hon. DSc Chicago, 1967; Hon. Dr Med. Science Michigan State, 1970. Nobel Prize for Physiology or Medicine (jtly), 1969. *Publications:* numerous articles in scientific jls or books. *Address:* RD Box 1640, Moores Hill Road, Syosset, NY 11791–9641, USA. *T:* (516) 6926855. *Died 22 May 1997.*

HERTFORD, 8th Marquess of, *cr* 1793; **Hugh Edward Conway Seymour;** DL; Baron Conway of Ragley 1703; Baron Conway of Killultagh 1712; Earl of Hertford, Viscount Beauchamp 1750; Earl of Yarmouth 1793; formerly Lieutenant Grenadier Guards; *b* 29 March 1930; *s* of late Brig.-General Lord Henry Charles Seymour, DSO (2nd *s* of 6th Marquess) and Lady Helen Frances Grosvenor (*d* 1970), *d* of 1st Duke of Westminster; *S* uncle, 1940; *m* 1956, Comtesse Louise de Caraman Chimay, *o d* of late Lt-Col Prince Alphonse de Chimay, TD; one *s* three *d. Educ:* Eton. Chm., Hertford Public Relations Ltd, 1962–73. DL Warwicks, 1959. Chief interests were estate management (Diploma, Royal Agricultural Coll., Cirencester, 1956) and fox hunting. *Heir: s* Earl of Yarmouth [*b* 6 July 1958; *m* 1990, Beatriz, *d* of Jorge Karam; two *s* one *d*]. *Address:* North Wing, Ragley Hall, Alcester, Warwickshire B49 5NJ. *T:* (01789) 762455/762090. *Clubs:* White's, Pratt's, Turf.

Died 22 Dec. 1997.

HERWARTH von BITTENFELD, Hans Heinrich; Grand Cross (2nd Class), Order of Merit, Federal Republic of Germany, 1963; Hon. GCVO 1958; State Secretary, Foreign Office, Bonn, 1969, retired; *b* Berlin, 14 July 1904; *s* of Hans Richard Herwarth von Bittenfeld and Ilse Herwarth von Bittenfeld (*née* von Tiedemann); *m* 1935, Elisabeth Freiin von Redwitz; one *d. Educ:* Universities of Berlin, Breslau and Munich (Law and Nat. Econ.). Entered Auswärtiges Amt, Berlin, 1927; Attaché, Paris, 1930; Second Secretary and Personal Secretary to Ambassador, Moscow, 1931–39; Military Service, 1939–45; Oberregierungsrat, Regierungsdirektor, Bavarian State Chancellery, 1945–49; Ministerialdirigent and Chief of Protocol, Federal Government, 1950, Minister Plenipotentiary, 1952; German Ambassador to Court of St James's, 1955–61; State Secretary and Chief of German Federal Presidential Office, 1961–65; German Ambassador to Republic of Italy, 1965–69. Pres., Commn for Reform of German Diplomatic Service, 1969–71. Chm., Supervisory Council, Unilever, Germany, 1969–77. Chm., Venice Cttee, German Unesco Commn; Pres., Internat. Adv. Cttee for Venice. Pres., Goethe Institut, Munich, 1971–77. Cavaliere di San Marco, 1989; Hon.

Citizen, Augsburg Univ., 1989. *Publications:* Against Two Evils: memoirs of a diplomat-soldier during the Third Reich, 1981 (German edn, Zwischen Hitler und Stalin, 1982); Von Adenauer zu Brandt, 1990. *Recreation:* antiques. *Address:* Schloss, 96328 Küps, Germany. *T:* (9264) 7174. *Died 21 Aug. 1999.*

HERZBERG, Hon. Gerhard, CC (Can.) 1968; PC (Can.) 1992; FRS 1951; FRSC 1939; Director, Division of Pure Physics, 1949–69, Distinguished Research Scientist, 1969–95, National Research Council of Canada, then Distinguished Research Scientist Emeritus; *b* Hamburg, Germany, 25 Dec. 1904; *s* of late Albin and Ella Herzberg; *m* 1st, 1929, Luise (*née* Oettinger) (*d* 1971); one *s* one *d*; 2nd, 1972, Monika (*née* Tenthoff). *Educ:* Inst. of Technology, Darmstadt, Germany; Univ. of Göttingen, Germany; Univ. of Bristol, England. Lecturer, Darmstadt Inst. of Technology, 1930; Research Professor, Univ. of Saskatchewan, 1935; Prof. of Spectroscopy, Yerkes Observatory, Univ. of Chicago, 1945; Principal Research Officer, National Research Council of Canada, 1948. President: Canadian Association of Physicists, 1956; RSC, 1966; Vice-Pres., International Union of Pure and Applied Physics, 1957–63. University Medal, Univ. of Liège, Belgium, 1950; Henry Marshall Tory Medal, RSC, 1953; Joy Kissen Mookerjee Gold Medal of Indian Association for Cultivation of Science, 1954 (awarded 1957); Gold Medal of Canadian Association Phys., 1957; Bakerian Lecture, Royal Society, 1960; Faraday Lecture and Medal, Chem. Soc., 1970; Nobel Prize for Chemistry, 1971; Royal Medal, Royal Soc., 1971. Hon. Fellow: Indian Academy of Science, 1954; Indian Physical Society, 1957; Chemical Society of London, 1968. Hon. Member: Hungarian Academy of Sciences, 1964; Optical Society of America, 1968; Royal Irish Acad., 1970; Japan Acad., 1976; Chem. Soc. of Japan, 1978; Hon. Foreign Member, American Academy Arts and Sciences, 1965; Foreign Associate, National Academy of Sciences, US, 1968; Foreign Mem. (Physics), Royal Swedish Acad. of Sciences, 1981 Numerous hon. degrees, including Hon. ScD Cantab, 1972. *Publications:* Atomic Spectra and Atomic Structure, 1937, 2nd edn 1944; Molecular Spectra and Molecular Structure: I, Spectra of Diatomic Molecules, 1939, 2nd edn 1950; II, Infra-red and Raman Spectra of Polyatomic Molecules, 1945; III, Electronic Spectra and Electronic Structure of Polyatomic Molecules, 1966; (with K. P. Huber) IV, Constants of Diatomic Molecules, 1979; The Spectra and Structures of Simple Free Radicals. an introduction to Molecular Spectroscopy, 1971; original research on atomic and molecular spectra published in various scientific journals. *Address:* National Research Council, Ottawa, ON K1A 0R6, Canada. *T:* (613) 9900917; 190 Lakeway Drive, Rockcliffe Park, Ottawa, ON K1L 5B3, Canada. *T:* (613) 7464126. *Died 3 March 1999.*

HERZOG, (Vivian) Chaim, Hon. KBE 1970; President of Israel, 1983–93; *b* Ireland, 17 Sept. 1918; *s* of Rabbi Isaac Halevy Herzog, first Chief Rabbi of Israel and formerly of Ireland, and Sarah Herzog (*née* Hillman); *m* 1947, Aura (*née* Ambache); three *s* one *d. Educ:* Univ. of London (LLB). Called to the Bar, Lincoln's Inn, 1942 (Hon. Bencher, 1987); Advocate, Israel Bar. Immigrated to Palestine, 1935; Army service: Jerusalem, 1936–38; British Army, war of 1939–45; RMC; served 2nd Army, NW Europe; Israel Defence Forces: Defence Attaché, USA, 1950–54; Dir of Mil. Intell., 1948–50 and 1959–62; Comdr, Jerusalem Brigade, 1954–57; Chief of Staff, Southern Comd, 1957–59; retired 1962 (Maj.-Gen.); 1st Mil. Governor, W Bank and Jerusalem, 1967; Ambassador and Perm. Rep. to UN, 1975–78; Mem. Tenth Knesset, 1981–83. Director, 1962–83: Israel Aircraft Industries; Industrial Development Bank of Israel; Israel Discount Bank; Man. Dir, G. U. S. Industries, 1962–72; Senior

Partner, Herzog, Fox and Neeman, 1972–83. President: Variety Club of Israel, 1967–72; ORT Israel, 1968–83; World ORT Union, 1980–83. Hon. Fellow, UCL, 1986. Hon. degrees from home and overseas univs. *Publications:* Israel's Finest Hour, 1967; Days of Awe, 1973; (ed) Judaism, Law and Ethics, 1974; The War of Atonement, 1975; Who Stands Accused?, 1978; (with Mordechai Gichon) Battles of the Bible, 1978; The Arab–Israeli Wars, 1982; Heroes of Israel, 1990; Living History, 1996. *Recreations:* sailing, flying light aircraft, golf. *Address:* Beit Ammot Mishpat, 8 King Saul Boulevard, Tel Aviv 64733, Israel. *Died 17 April 1997.*

HESLOP-HARRISON, Prof. John, MSc, PhD, DSc; FRS 1970; FRSE, MRIA, FRSA, FLS; Royal Society Research Professor, University College of Wales, Aberystwyth, 1977–85; *b* 10 Feb. 1920; *s* of late Prof. J. W. Heslop-Harrison, FRS and Christian Watson, *d* of Capt. John Watson Henderson, Leith; *m* 1950, Yolande Massey; one *s. Educ:* Grammar School, Chester-le-Street; King's Coll. (University of Durham), Newcastle upon Tyne. MSc (Dunelm), PhD (Belfast), DSc (Dunelm). Army service, 1941–45. Lecturer in Agricultural Botany, King's Coll., Univ. of Durham, 1945–46; Lecturer in Botany: Queen's Univ., Belfast, 1946–50; UCL, 1950–53; Reader in Taxonomy, UCL, 1953–54; Prof. of Botany, Queen's Univ., Belfast, 1954–60; Mason Prof. of Botany, Univ. of Birmingham, 1960–67; Prof. of Botany, Inst. of Plant Develt, Univ. of Wisconsin, 1967–71; Dir, Royal Botanic Gardens, Kew, 1971–76. Visiting Professor: (Brittingham), Univ. of Wisconsin, 1965; US Dept of Agriculture Institute of Forest Genetics, Rhinelander, Wis, 1968; Univ. of Massachusetts, Amherst, Mass, 1976–77, 1978–79; lectures: Sigma Xi, Geneva, NY, 1969; William Wright Smith, Edinburgh, 1972; George Bidder, Soc. Exptl Biol., Leeds, 1973; Ghosh, Univ. of Calcutta, 1973; Kennedy Orton Meml, UCW, Bangor, 1974; Croonian, Royal Society, 1974; Amos Meml, E Malling, 1975; Holden Univ. of Nottingham, 1976; Dewley, Glasshouse Crops Res. Inst., 1978; Hooker, Linnean Soc., 1979; Bateson, John Innes Inst., 1979; Waller Meml, Univ. of Ohio, 1980; Blackman, Univ. of Oxford, 1980. Mem., ARC, 1977–82; Vice-President: Botanical Soc. of British Isles, 1972; Linnean Soc., 1973; President: Inst. of Biology, 1974–75; Sect. K, British Assoc. for Advancement of Science, 1974. Editor, Annals of Botany, 1961–67. Corresp. Mem., Royal Netherlands Botanical Soc., 1968; For. Fellow, Indian Nat. Sci. Acad., 1974; For. Associate, National Acad. of Sciences, USA, 1983; Mem., German Acad. of Science, 1975; For. Mem., American Botanical Soc., 1976; For. Hon. Mem., Amer. Acad. Arts and Scis, 1982; For. Mem., Acad. Royale de Belgique (Sci. Div.), 1985. Hon. DSc: Belfast, 1971; Bath, 1982; Edinburgh, 1984; Hull, 1986. Trail-Crisp Award, Linnean Soc., 1967; Univ. of Liège Medal, 1967; Erdtman Internat. Medal for Palynology, 1971; Cooke Award, Amer. Acad. of Allergy, 1974; Darwin Medal, Royal Soc., 1983; Keith Medal, RSE, 1984; Navashin Medal, Komarov Inst., USSR Acad., 1991; Linnean Medal for Botany, Linnean Soc., 1996; Royal Medal, Royal Soc., 1996. *Publications:* New Concepts in Flowering Plant Taxonomy, 1953; papers and monographs on botanical and cell physiological subjects in various British and foreign journals. *Recreations:* hill walking, photography, painting. *Address:* The Pleasaunce, 137 Bargates, Leominster, Herefordshire HR6 8QS. *T:* (01568) 611566; Institute of Grassland and Environmental Research, Plas Gogerddan, near Aberystwyth SY23 3EB. *Died 7 May 1998.*

HESS, Ellen Elizabeth, NDH; Administrator, Studley College Trust, 1970–80; Principal, Studley College, Warwickshire, 1956–69; *b* 28 Dec. 1908; *d* of Charles Michael Joseph Hess and Fanny Thompson Hess (*née* Alder). *Educ:* Grammar School for Girls, Dalston; Royal

Botanic Society, Regent's Park. Lecturer in Horticulture, Swanley Horticultural College for Women, 1934–39; Agricultural Secretary, National Federation of Women's Institutes, 1939–46; Ellen Eddy Shaw Fellowship, Brooklyn Botanic Gardens, New York, USA, 1946–47; School of Horticulture, Ambler, Pa, USA, 1947–48; HM Inspector of Schools (Agriculture and Further Education), 1948–56. Veitch Meml Medal, RHS, 1967. *Recreations:* travel, photography, walking. *Address:* Royal Bay Retirement Hotel, 86 Aldwick Road, Bognor Regis PO21 2PE. *Died 17 July 1996.*

HETHERINGTON, (Hector) Alastair; journalist; Research Professor in Media Studies, Stirling University, 1982–87, then Emeritus; Editor, Manchester Guardian, later The Guardian, 1956–75; *b* Llanishen, Glamorganshire, 31 Oct. 1919; *yr s* of late Sir Hector Hetherington and Lady (Mary Ethel Alison) Hetherington; *m* 1st, 1957, Miranda (marr. diss. 1978), *d* of late Prof. R. A. C. Oliver; two *s* two *d*; 2nd, 1979, Sheila Janet Cameron, *widow* of Hamish Cameron; one step *s* two step *d*. *Educ:* Gresham's Sch., Holt; Corpus Christi Coll., Oxford (Hon. Fellow, 1971). Royal Armoured Corps, 1940–46. Editorial staff, The Glasgow Herald, 1946–50; joined Manchester Guardian, 1950: Asst Editor and Foreign Editor, 1953–56; Director: Guardian and Manchester Evening News Ltd, 1956–75; Guardian Newspapers Ltd, 1967–75; Controller, BBC Scotland, 1975–78; Manager, BBC Highland, 1979–80. Member, Royal Commission on the Police, 1960–62. Vis. Fellow, Nuffield Coll., Oxford, 1973–79. Trustee, Scott Trust, 1970–89 (Chm., 1984–89). Dr *hc* Univ. of Lille 3, 1989. Journalist of the Year, Nat. Press awards, 1970; Special Award, Bank of Scotland Press awards, 1992. *Publications:* Guardian Years, 1981; News, Newspapers and Television, 1985; News in the Regions, 1989; Highlands and Islands: a generation of progress, 1990; Cameras in the Commons, 1990; BBC Scotland 1975–80, 1992; A Walker's Guide to Arran, 1994. *Recreations:* hill walking, golf. *Address:* 38 Chalton Road, Bridge of Allan, Stirling FK9 4EF. *T:* (01786) 833316. *Club:* Athenæum. *Died 3 Oct. 1999.*

HEWITT, Rev. Canon George Henry Gordon; Residentiary Canon, Chelmsford Cathedral, 1964–78, Canon Emeritus since 1978; *b* 30 May 1912; *s* of Rev. G. H. Hewitt; *m* 1942, Joan Ellen Howden; two *s* one *d*. *Educ:* Trent Coll.; Brasenose Coll., Oxford; Wycliffe Hall, Oxford. Deacon 1936, priest 1937; Asst Curate, St Clement, Leeds, 1936–39; Chaplain, Ridley Hall, Cambridge, 1939–41; Asst Curate, Leeds Parish Church, 1941–43; Religious Book Editor, Lutterworth Press, 1943–52; Diocesan Education Sec., Sheffield, 1952–58; Residentiary Canon, Sheffield Cathedral, 1953–58; Vicar of St Andrew, Oxford, 1958–64. Chaplain to the Queen, 1969–82. *Publications:* Let the People Read, 1949; The Problems of Success: a history of the Church Missionary Society, 1910–1942, vol. I, 1971, vol. II, 1977. *Address:* Flat Eleven, Ellesborough Manor, near Aylesbury, Bucks HP17 0XF. *Died 16 June 1998.*

HEY, James Stanley, MBE 1945; DSc; FRS 1978; Research Scientist at Royal Radar Establishment, 1952–69, Chief Scientific Officer, 1966–69; *b* 3 May 1909; *s* of William Rennie Hey and Barbara Elizabeth Hey (*née* Matthews); *m* 1934, Edna Heywood (*d* 1998). *Educ:* Rydal Sch.; Manchester Univ. (BSc (Physics), 1930; MSc (X-ray Crystallography), 1931; DSc (Radio Astronomy and Radar Research), 1950). Army Operational Research Group, 1940–52 (Head of Estab., 1949–52). Hon. DSc: Birmingham, 1975; Kent, 1977. Eddington Medal, RAS, 1959. *Publications:* The Radio Universe, 1971, rev. 3rd edn 1983; The Evolution of Radio Astronomy, 1973; The Secret Man (autobiog.), 1992; research papers in scientific

jls (RAS, Royal Society, Phys Soc., Philosophical Magazine, Nature, Lancet, Jl Tissue Viabil.), including pioneering papers in radio astronomy. *Address:* 4 Shortlands Close, Eastbourne, East Sussex BN22 0JE. *Died 27 Feb. 2000.*

HEYMAN, Allan; QC 1969; *b* 27 Feb. 1921; *e s* of late Erik Heyman and Rita Heyman (*née* Meyer); *m* 1958, Anne Marie (*née* Castenschiold); one *d. Educ:* Stenhus Kostskole, Denmark; Univ. of Copenhagen (Master of Law 1947). Called to Bar, Middle Temple, 1951, Bencher, 1975, Treasurer, 1992; retired 1995. Mem., London Court of Internat. Arbitration, 1992. UN Observer, Yugoslav War Crime Trial, Copenhagen, 1994. Pres., Internat. Lawn Tennis Fedn, 1971–74, Hon. Life Vice-Pres., 1979. Kt Comdr, Royal Order of Dannebrog (Denmark). *Recreations:* shooting, reading, music. *Address:* Marshland House, Sudbourne, Woodbridge, Suffolk IP12 2HA. *Clubs:* Naval and Military, Shikar; All England Lawn Tennis and Croquet. *Died 6 Sept. 1998.*

HEYMAN, Sir Horace (William), Kt 1976; CEng, FIEE; Chairman, English Industrial Estates Corporation, 1970–77; Hotelplan International AG: Member, Supervisory Board, Zurich, 1955–84; Director: UK Group, 1965–86; Ingham Travel, 1965–77; *b* 13 March 1912; *m* 1st, 1939; one *s* one *d*; 2nd, 1966, Dorothy Forster Atkinson. *Educ:* Ackworth (Soc. of Friends) Sch.; Technische Hochschule, Darmstadt; Birmingham Univ. BSc Hons, electrical engrg, 1936. Electricars Ltd, 1936–40; Metropolitan Vickers Ltd, Sheffield, 1940–45; Smith's Electric Vehicles Ltd and Subsids, 1945–64 (Man. Dir, 1949–64); Co-Founder, Sevcon Engineering Ltd, 1960; Vice-Pres., Battronic Corp., Philadelphia, 1960–64. Export Marketing Adviser for Northern Region, BoT, 1969–70; Consultant: DoI Invest in Britain Bureau, 1977–79; Elmwood Sensors Ltd, 1977–86; Thermal Quarz Schmelz GmbH, 1983–86; Chm., Newcastle Polytechnic Products Ltd, 1983–86. Newcastle Polytechnic: Governor, 1974–86; Vice-Chm., 1983–86; Hon. Fellow, 1985. Mem. Council, Soc. of Motor Manufrs and Traders, 1949–64 (Man. Cttee, 1952–64); Chm., Electric Vehicle Assoc. of Gt Britain, 1953–55. Witness at US Senate hearings on air and water pollution, 1967. Chairman: N Region Energy Conservation Group, 1973–77; NEDO Working Party on House Bldg Performance, 1976–79. Pres., Northumbria Tourist Bd, 1983–86. FIEE 1952; FRSA 1969. *Address:* 20 Whitburn Hall, Whitburn, Sunderland SR6 7JQ. *Died 4 Sept. 1998.*

HICKLIN, Denis Raymond, OBE 1969; Partner, Middle Greadow Dairy Farm, Lanlivery, Cornwall, since 1986; *b* 15 April 1918; *s* of Joseph Herbert and Florence May Hicklin; *m* 1949, Joyce Grisdale Smith; two *s. Educ:* Merchant Taylors' Sch. Served War, 1939–46, RA (Major; despatches). John Dickinson, 1936–48; St Anne's Board Mill Co. Ltd, 1948–78 (Chm. and Man. Dir, 1966–78). Pt-time Mem., Forestry Commn, 1978–81. *Recreations:* gardening, golf. *Address:* 1 Bumpers Batch, Midford Road, Bath BA2 5SQ. *T:* (01225) 833123. *Died 8 April 1998.*

HICKMAN, His Honour Michael Ranulf; a Circuit Judge, 1974–93; *b* 2 Oct. 1922; *s* of John Owen Hickman and Nancy Viola Hickman (*née* Barlow); *m* 1943, Diana Richardson; one *s* one *d. Educ:* Wellington; Trinity Hall, Cambridge (2nd cl. Hons in Law). Served War, RAFVR, 1940–46. Cambridge Univ., 1946–48; called to Bar, Middle Temple, 1949. Actg Dep. Chm., Hertfordshire QS, 1965–72; a Recorder of Crown Court, 1972–74. *Recreations:* shooting, fishing, gun dog training. *Address:* The Acorn, Bovingdon, Herts HP3 0NA. *T:* (01442) 832226. *Died 3 Sept. 1999.*

HICKS, David Nightingale; interior decorator, author, garden and jewellery designer; Director, David Hicks Ltd, since 1960; *b* 25 March 1929; 3rd surv. *s* of late Herbert Hicks (stockbroker and twice past Master Salters' Company) and Iris Elsie Hicks (*née* Platten); *m* 1960, Lady Pamela Carmen Louise Mountbatten, *yr d* of Admiral of the Fleet 1st Earl Mountbatten of Burma, KG, GCB, OM, GCSI, GCIE, GCVO, DSO, PC, FRS; one *s* two *d*. *Educ:* Charterhouse; Central School of Arts and Crafts, London. Interiors for: Helena Rubinstein; QE2; HRH the Prince of Wales; Govt of NSW; British Steel Corp.; Aeroflot Offices; Marquess of Londonderry; Library in British Embassy, Washington; Royal Yacht for HM King Fahd. Designer of gardens, jewellery, fabrics, carpets, furniture, etc. Master, Salters' Co., 1977–78. FRSA. CoID (later Design Council) design award, 1970. *Publications:* David Hicks on Decoration, 1966; David Hicks on Living—with taste, 1968; David Hicks on Bathrooms, 1970; David Hicks on Decoration—with fabrics, 1971; David Hicks on Decoration—5, 1972; David Hicks Book of Flower Arranging, 1976; David Hicks Living with Design, 1979; David Hicks Garden Design, 1982; David Hicks Style and Design, 1988; Cotswold Gardens, 1996; My Kind of Garden, 1998. *Recreations:* gardening, preservation. *Address:* Albany, Piccadilly, W1V 9RP. *T:* (0171) 734 3183, *Fax:* (0171) 437 3454.
Died 29 March 1998.

HIGGINS, Alec Wilfred, MBE 1944; MC 1940; TD 1945; Deputy Chairman of Lloyd's, 1975, 1976, 1980 and 1981; Chairman: Higgins, Brasier & Co. Ltd (formerly Higgins & Doble Ltd), 1962–88; M. J. Marchant Underwriting Ltd, 1982–88; *b* 1 Nov. 1914; *s* of late Frederick Gladstone Higgins and Beatrice Louisa Scriven; *m* 1939, Denise May Philcox; two *s* one *d*. *Educ:* Merton Court Sch., Sidcup; Sutton Valence Sch. Joined Woods & Maslen Ltd, 1937, Chm., 1963 80. Underwriting Mem. of Lloyd's, 1948 (Mcm. Cttee, 1967–73, 1975–77, 1980–83); Mem. Cttee, Lloyd's Insce Brokers Assoc., 1960–63 and 1965 66 (Dep. Chm. 1965, Chm. 1966); Mem., Gen. Cttee, Lloyd's Register of Shipping, 1978–81; Chm., Insce Section, London Chamber of Commerce, 1963–64; Vice-Pres., Insce Inst. of London, 1967; Member: Council, Chartered Insce Inst., 1972–80; Insce Industry Trng Council, 1969; Export Guarantee Adv. Council, 1977–83 (Dep. Chm., 1982–83). Mem., Court of Assistants, Insurers' Co., 1980, Master 1984. Councillor, Chislehurst and Sidcup UDC, 1962–65 (Vice-Chm. of Council, 1964); Alderman, London Borough of Bexley, 1968–78; JP Bexley, 1967–84; DL Greater London, 1973, Representative DL, Havering, 1978–89. *Recreation:* swimming. *Address:* Farthings, Beaulieu Road, Cooden, E Sussex TN39 3AD. *T:* (01424) 842659. *Clubs:* City of London, Royal Automobile. *Died 5 Sept. 1997.*

HIGGINS, Sir Christopher (Thomas), Kt 1977; Chairman, Peterborough Development Corporation, 1968–81; *b* 14 Jan. 1914; *s* of late Thomas Higgins and Florence Maud Higgins; *m* 1936, Constance Joan Beck; one *s* one *d*. *Educ:* West Kensington Central Sch.; London Univ. Executive with Granada Group Ltd, 1939–68. Served War of 1939–45: with RA, 1940–46. Member: Acton Borough Council, 1945–65; GLC, 1964–67; Hemel Hempstead Develt Corp., 1947–52; Bracknell Develt Corp., 1965–68. Chm., North Thames Gas Consumers' Council, 1969–79. *Recreations:* reading, gardening, walking, watching most sports. *Address:* 2 North Lodge, Bicester House, Kings End, Bicester, Oxon OX6 7HZ. *Died 29 April 1998.*

HIGHGATE, Sir James (Brown), Kt 1994; CBE 1981; Consultant to Miller Beckett & Jackson, Solicitors, Glasgow, since 1985; *b* 18 June 1920; *s* of William Highgate and Margaret H. C. Highgate (*née* Brown). *Educ:* High Sch. of Glasgow; Glasgow Univ. (MA 1941;

LLB 1949). Served War, 1941–45, RA; Royal Indian 8th Rajput Regt, 1945–47, demobilised as Maj. RA. Partner, Brownlie Watson & Beckett, Solicitors, Glasgow, 1951–75, Sen. Partner, 1975–85. General Comr of Income Tax, 1969– (Chm., Glasgow N Div., 1981–95). Scottish Conservative and Unionist Association: Jt Hon. Sec., 1973–86; Pres., 1987–89; Hon. Pres., Motherwell N Cons. Assoc. Mem., Strathclyde Adv. Bd, Salvation Army, 1970–. Gov., High Sch. of Glasgow, 1981–90. Elder, Park Church of Scotland, Uddingston, 1947– (Chm., Bd of Mgt, 1960–96). *Recreations:* golf, travel. *Address:* c/o Messrs Miller Beckett & Jackson, Solicitors, 190 St Vincent Street, Glasgow G2 5SP; Broomlands, 121 Kylepark Drive, Uddingston, Glasgow G71 7DD. *T:* (01698) 813377. *Club:* Royal Over-Seas League.
Died 16 March 1997.

HILDYARD, Sir David (Henry Thoroton), KCMG 1975 (CMG 1966); DFC 1943; HM Diplomatic Service, retired; *b* 4 May 1916; *s* of late His Honour G. M. T. Hildyard, QC, and Sybil, *d* of H. W. Hamilton Hoare; *m* 1947, Millicent (*née* Baron), *widow* of Wing Commander R. M. Longmore, OBE; one *s* one *d*. *Educ:* Eton; Christ Church, Oxford. Served with RAF, 1940–46. Entered HM Foreign (subseq. Diplomatic) Service, 1948; Montevideo, 1950; Madrid, 1953; FO, 1957; Counsellor, Mexico City, 1960–65; Head of Economic Relations Dept, FO, 1965–68; Minister and Alternate UK Rep. to UN, 1968–70; Ambassador to Chile, 1970–73; Ambassador and Permanent UK Rep. to UN and other International Organisations, Geneva, 1973–76; Head, UK Delegn to CSCE, 1974–75. *Address:* 97 Onslow Square, SW7 3LU. *Clubs:* Brooks's, Reform, Hurlingham.
Died 5 April 1997.

HILL, (Arthur) Derek, CBE 1997; artist, writer, and organiser of exhibitions; *b* Bassett, Hampshire, 6 Dec. 1916; *s* of A. J. L. Hill and Grace Lilian Mercer. *Educ:* Marlborough Coll. Designed sets and dresses for Covent Garden and Sadler's Wells. *One-man exhibitions:* Nicholson Gall., London, 1943; Leicester Galls, London, 1947, 1950, 1953 and 1956; represented in exhibns, Europe and USA, 1957–; exhibns in New York, 1966 and 1969; *retrospective exhibitions:* Whitechapel Gall., London, 1961; Arts Council of NI, Belfast, 1970; Municipal Gall., Dublin, 1971; portraits, Marlborough Fine Arts, London, 1978; King's Lynn Fest., 1986; *organised exhibitions:* 1934–: Dégas Exhibn for Edinburgh Fest. and Tate Gall., London, 1952; Landseer exhibn (with John Woodward) at Royal Academy, 1961, etc. *Pictures owned by:* Tate Gall.; Nat. Gall. of Canada; Arts Council; Fogg Museum, Harvard; Nat. Portrait Gall. of Denmark; Liechtenstein Gall., Vaduz; National Gall. of Ireland and Municipal Gall. of Dublin; Ulster Mus., Belfast; Walker Gall., Liverpool; City Art Galleries of Southampton, Birmingham, Bradford, Coventry, Carlisle, Sheffield, etc. FRGS. Hon. DLit TCD, 1990. Hon. Irish Citizen, 1999. *Publications:* (with Prof. Oleg Grabar) Islamic Architecture and Its Decoration, 1965; (with L. Golvin) Islamic Architecture in North Africa, 1976; articles in Illustrated London News, Apollo, Burlington Magazine, etc; *relevant publication:* Derek Hill: an appreciation, by the Earl of Gowrie, 1987. *Recreations:* gardening, travelling. *Died 30 July 2000.*

HILL, Prof. Dorothy, AC 1993; CBE 1971; FRS 1965; FAA 1956; Research Professor of Geology, University of Queensland, 1959–72, then Emeritus Professor; President, Professorial Board, 1971–72, Member of Senate, 1976–77; *b* 10 Sept. 1907; *d* of R. S. Hill, Brisbane; unmarried. *Educ:* Brisbane Girls' Grammar Sch.; Univs of Queensland and Cambridge. BSc Qld, 1928, 1st Cl. Hons in Geol. and Univ. Gold Medal; PhD Cantab, 1932; DSc Qld, 1942. Foundn Trav. Fellowship of Univ. of Queensland held at

Newnham Coll., Cambridge, 1930–32; Old Students' Res. Fellowship, Newnham Coll., Cambridge, 1932–35; Sen. Studentship (Exhibn of 1851) held at Cambridge, 1935–37; Council for Sci. and Indust. Res. Fellowship, held at Univ. of Queensland, 1937–42; Women's Royal Aust. Naval Service, Second Off., 1942–45 (RAN Ops Staff); Univ. of Queensland: Lectr in Geol., 1946–56, Reader, 1956–59. Hon. Editor, Geol Soc. of Aust., 1958–64; Mem. Council, Australian Acad. of Science, 1968–70, Pres. 1970; Pres., Geol Soc. of Aust., 1973–75. Foreign and Commonwealth Mem., Geol Soc. London, 1967; Hon. Fellow, Geol Soc. of America, 1971. Hon. LLD Queensland, 1974. Lyell Medal, Geol Soc. of London, 1964; Clarke Medal, Royal Society of NSW, 1966; Mueller Medal, ANZAAS, 1967; W. R. Browne Medal, Geol Soc. of Australia, 1980; ANZAAS Medal, 1983. *Publications:* numerous, in geology and palæontology jls on fossil corals, archæocyatha, brachiopods, reef sediments and Australian geology and stratigraphy. *Recreations:* travel, reading. *Address:* 66 Sisley Street, St Lucia, Brisbane, Qld 4067, Australia.   *Died 23 April 1997.*

HILL, Col (Edward) Roderick, DSO 1944; JP; Lord-Lieutenant of Gwent, 1974–79 (HM Lieutenant for Monmouthshire, 1965–74); Patron, Chepstow Race Course Co. Ltd (Director, 1958–83; Chairman, 1964–81); *b* 1904; *s* of late Capt. Roderick Tickell Hill; *m* 1934, Rachel (*d* 1983), *e d* of Ellis Hicks Beach, Witcombe Park, Glos; one *s* one *d. Educ:* Winchester; Magdalen Coll., Oxford. Gazetted to Coldstream Guards, 1926; served War of 1939–45, with Regt (despatches, DSO); commanded 5th Bn and 1st Bn Coldstream Guards and Guards Training Bn; comd Regt, 1949–52. JP Co. Monmouth; High Sheriff of Monmouthshire, 1956; DL Monmouthshire, 1957; Vice-Lieut, 1963–65. Chm. of the Curre Hunt, 1959–65. Pres., Royal Welsh Agricl Soc., 1970–71. Chm. Governors, Monmouth Sch. and Monmouth Sch. for Girls, 1961–66. Chm. Chepstow RDC, 1962–63. Hon. Col, 104 Light AD Regt RA (V), 1967–69. Pres., TA&VRA for Wales and Monmouthshire, 1971–74. Freeman and Liveryman, Haberdashers' Co., 1969. Officer, Order of Orange-Nassau (with swords) (Netherlands), 1946. KStJ 1972. *Publication:* (with the Earl of Rosse) The Story of the Guards Armoured Division, 1941–1945, 1956. *Address:* Manor Farm Cottage, Stanford in the Vale, Faringdon, Oxfordshire SN7 8NN. *Club:* Cavalry and Guards.

Died 21 Nov. 1998.

HILL, Dame Elizabeth (Mary), DBE 1976; Emeritus Professor of Slavonic Studies, Cambridge; *b* 24 Oct. 1900; *d* of Frederick Hill and Louise de Miller; *m* 1984, Stojan J. Veljković (marr. diss. 1996). *Educ:* University and King's Colls, London Univ. BA London 1924, PhD London 1928; MA Cantab 1937. War of 1939–45: Slavonic specialist, Min. of Information. University Lecturer in Slavonic, 1936–48; Prof. of Slavonic Studies, Univ. of Cambridge, 1948–68; Andrew Mellon Prof. of Slavic Languages and Literatures, Pittsburgh Univ., 1968–70. Fellow of University Coll., London; Fellow, Girton Coll., Cambridge; Hon. Fellow, SSEES, Univ. of London, 1990. Hon. LittD East Anglia, 1978. *Address:* 10 Croft Gardens, Cambridge CB3 9LD.

Died 17 Dec. 1996.

HILL, Gladys, MA, MD; FRCS, FRCOG; Obstetrician and Gynæcologist, Royal Free Hospital, 1940–59, retired; *b* 28 Sept. 1894; *d* of late Arthur Griffiths Hill and Caroline Sutton Hill. *Educ:* Cheltenham Ladies' Coll.; Somerville Coll., Oxford (MA); Royal Free Hosp. Med. Sch. MB, BS London, 1923; MD London, 1925; FRCS 1936; FRCOG 1943. *Publications:* contribs to medical journals. *Recreations:* architecture, amateur dramatics, reading.

Address: The Manor Nursing Home, Haydon Close, Bishops Hull, Taunton TA1 5HF.   *Died 11 Jan. 1998.*

HILL, Ivan Conrad, CBE 1960; Chairman, Industrial Coal Consumers Council, 1965, retired; *b* 22 Jan. 1906; *s* of Wilfred Lawson Hill and Annie Jane (*née* England); *m* 1st, 1931, Alexandrina Ewart (marr. diss. 1962); four *d*; 2nd, 1963, Sheila Houghton. *Educ:* Oakham Sch.; St John's Coll., Cambridge (Exhibitioner and Open Scholar; 1st cl. Hons Law Tripos 1928). Apptd Jt Man. Dir, Kelsall & Kemp Ltd, 1933. Chairman: Wool Industries Research Assoc., 1950–53; British Rayon Research Assoc., 1956–61; Mem. Monopolies and Restrictive Practices Commn, and Monopolies Commn, 1951–63. Chairman: Samuel Courtauld & Co. Ltd, 1962–66; Illingworth Morris & Co. Ltd, 1976–80; Convoy Woollen Co. Ltd, 1984–90. Liveryman, Weavers' Company, 1938. *Recreations:* travel, architecture, sport. *Address:* Crystal Spring, 120c Duchy Road, Harrogate, N Yorks HG1 2HE.

Died 10 May 1998.

HILL, Sir James; see Hill, Sir S. J. A.

HILL, Col Roderick; see Hill, Col E. R.

HILL, Sir (Stanley) James (Allen), Kt 1996; company director; *b* 21 Dec. 1926; *s* of James and Florence Cynthia Hill; *m* 1958, Ruby Susan Evelyn Ralph, CBE; two *s* three *d. Educ:* Regents Park Sch., Southampton; Southampton Univ.; North Wales Naval Training Coll. Former Pilot. Mem., Southampton City Council, 1966–70, 1976–79, 1979–97; Chm. of Housing, 1967–70, 1976–79; Mem. Cttee, Southampton Conservative and Ratepayers Fedn. MP (C) Southampton Test, 1970–Oct. 1974 and 1979–97; contested (C) same seat, Oct. 1974, 1997. Mem., Speaker's Panel of Chairmen, 1990–97. Secretary: Cons. Parly Cttee on Housing and Construction, 1971–73; Cons. Industry Cttee, 1979–81; Member, Select Committee: on European Legislation, 1979–84; on Transport, 1993–97; on Procedure, 1993–97; Chm., Cons. Cttee on Housing Improvement, 1985–97; Chm., Constitutional Affairs Cons. Backbench Cttee, 1993–97. Vice Chm., 1988–92, Chm., 1992–97, All Party Anglo-Sri Lanka Gp; Vice Chm., All Party Anglo-Singapore Gp, 1992–97; Mem., British Delegn to European Parlt, Strasbourg, and Chm., Regional Policy and Transport Cttee, 1973–75; Member: Hon. Cttee for Europe Day, Council of Europe, 1973–75; Scientific, Technol and Aerospace Cttee, Western European Defence, 1979–89; Political and Legal Affairs Cttee, Council of Europe, 1984–89, 1994–95; Govt Whip to Council of Europe and WEU, 1980–89. Pres., Motor Schools Assoc., 1980–85; Mem. Council, IAM, 1982–89. *Recreations:* private aviation, farming. *Address:* Gunsfield Lodge, Melchet Park, Plaitford, near Romsey, Hants SO51 6ES. *Club:* St Stephen's Constitutional.

Died 16 Feb. 1999.

HILLABY, John; writer, naturalist and traveller; *b* 24 July 1917; *er s* of late Albert Ewart Hillaby, Pontefract, and Mabel Colyer; *m* 1st, 1940, Eleanor Riley (marr. diss.), Leeds; two *d*; 2nd, 1966, Thelma Gordon (*d* 1972), child analyst, London and Montreal; 3rd, 1981, Kathleen Burton, Easingwold, Yorks. *Educ:* Leeds; Woodhouse Grove, Yorkshire. Served War, RA, 1939–44. Local journalism up to 1939; magazine contributor and broadcaster, 1944–; Zoological Corresp., Manchester Guardian, 1949; European science writer, New York Times, 1951; biological consultant, New Scientist, 1953. Formerly a dir, Universities Fedn for Animal Welfare; Founder Pres., Backpackers Club. Travelled on foot through parts of boreal Canada, Appalachian Trail, USA, Congo; traversed Ituri Forest and Mountains of the Moon (Ruwenzori), Sudan, Tanzania; three months foot safari with camels to Lake Rudolf, Kenya, and walked from Lands End to John o'Groats, from The Hague to Nice via the Alps, from

Provence to Tuscany, from Lake District to London, and from Athens to Mt Olympus via the Pindos mountains. Woodward Lectr, Yale, 1973. Radio and TV series include: Men of the North, Expedition South, Alpine Venture, Hillaby Walks, Globetrotter, etc. FZS (scientific). Hon. DLitt City, 1993. *Publications:* Within The Streams, 1949; Nature and Man, 1960; Journey to the Jade Sea, 1964; Journey through Britain, 1968; Journey through Europe, 1972; Journey through Love, 1976; Journey Home, 1983; John Hillaby's Yorkshire: the moors and dales, 1986; John Hillaby's London, 1987; Journey to the Gods, 1991; Hillaby's World, 1992. *Recreations:* talking, reading, music, walking; observing peculiarities of man, beast, fowl and flora. *Club:* Savage.

Died 19 Oct. 1996.

HILLARD, His Honour Richard Arthur Loraine, MBE 1946; a Circuit Judge (formerly a County Court Judge), 1956–72; *b* 1906; *e s* of Frederick Arthur Hillard, Puriton Manor, Bridgwater, Som; *m* 1st, 1936, Nancy Alford (*d* 1964), *d* of Dr Alford Andrews, Cambridge; one *s* one *d*; 2nd, 1969, Monica Constance (*d* 1996), *er d* of John Healey Carus, Darwen, and *widow* of Paul Hillard; one step *s* one step *d. Educ:* Worcester Royal Grammar Sch.; Christ Church, Oxford. Barrister, Gray's Inn, 1931; South-Eastern circuit. Served, 1940–45: Military Dept, Judge Advocate General's Office, 1941–45, Lt-Col 1945. Asst Reader and Lecturer, Council of Legal Education, 1945–55. Chm. Agricultural Land Tribunal, South Eastern Province, 1955. *Recreation:* gardening. *Address:* Oakchurch House, Staunton-on-Wye, Hereford HR4 7NE. *T:* (01981) 500345. *Club:* United Oxford & Cambridge University. *Died 2 Nov. 1996.*

HILLIS, Arthur Henry Macnamara, CMG 1961; Comptroller General, National Debt Office, 1961–68; *b* 29 Dec. 1905; *s* of late John David Hillis, FRCS, Dublin; *m* 1936, Mary Francis (*d* 1990), no *c. Educ:* Trinity Coll., Dublin. Called to Bar, Inner Temple, 1931. HM Treasury, 1941; Harkness Fund Fellow, USA, 1930–31; Minister (Treasury Adviser), UK Permanent Mission to United Nations, 1958–61; Under-Sec., Treasury, 1961. Mem., Internat. CS Commn (UN), 1974–81. *Address:* 2 Hare Court, Temple, EC4Y 7BH. *T:* (0171) 353 3443. *Club:* Athenæum. *Died 16 Sept. 1997.*

HILLMAN, Ellis Simon; consultant on city infrastructures; Principal Lecturer in Environmental Studies, University of East London (formerly North East London Polytechnic, then Polytechnic of East London), since 1972 (Head of International Office, 1981–84); *b* 17 Nov. 1928; *s* of David and Annie Hillman; *m* 1967, Louise; one *s. Educ:* University Coll. Sch.; Chelsea Coll. of Science and Technol. (BSc). Served RAF, 1947–49. Scientific Technical Officer: Soil Mechanics Ltd; NCB Field Investigation Group; Architectural Assoc.; Organiser of Conference NELP/British Telecom on Rewiring Britain—Technical Challenge of Cable TV; Chm., London Subterranean Survey Assoc., 1968–. Elected to LCC, 1958; GLC Cllr, 1964–81; Councillor (Lab), Colindale, 1986–; Mayor, London Borough of Barnet, 1994–95. Chairman: GLC Arts and Recreation Cttee, 1973–77; AMA Arts and Recreation Cttee, 1974–78; Further and Higher Educn Sub-Cttee, ILEA, 1977–81 (Bldgs Section, 1970–73); London Br. ACFHE, 1987–88 (Vice Chm., 1986–87); Vice-Chm., ILEA, 1980–81. Member: Lee Conservancy Catchment Bd, 1966–67; Lee Valley Reg. Park Authority, 1973–81; Sports Council, 1975–81; TWA, 1975–78; Water Space Amenity Commn, 1977–80; Inland Waterways Amenity Adv. Council, 1977–80; ARCUK Bd of Educn, 1973–82, 1986–94; Exec. Cttee, Field Studies Council, 1962–70; Exec. Cttee, Greater London Arts Assoc., 1973–77, 1982–86; Adv. Bd, NFT, 1973–78; Council, Science Fiction Foundn, 1986–; Sen. Vice-Pres.,

Hackney Soc., 1987– (Vice-Pres., 1984–87). Invited Member: Green Alliance, 1984–; Soc. of Educn Consultants, 1994–. Founder and Hon. Pres., Lewis Carroll Soc., 1969–. Consultant, London the Underground City Exhibn, 1992–93. Founding Gov., Museum of London, 1973– (Mem., Archaeol. Cttee, 1982–92); Chm. Governors, Hackney Coll., 1974–82, 1985–; Governor: Imperial Coll. of Science and Technol., later Imperial Coll. of Science, Technol. and Medicine, 1969–91, and Queen Mary Coll., 1973–82, Univ. of London; Coombe Lodge Staff Further Educn Coll., 1978–82; Hendon Coll., 1986–93; London Festival Ballet, 1973–77. Trustee, Contemporary Dance Trust, 1981–. Chm., Colson Trust and Mem. Editl Bd, Colson News: Two Way Numbers, 1984–. Guest Editor, The Built Environment (one edn), 1984. FRSA 1979. *Publications:* Essays in Local Government Enterprise, 1964–67; (ed) Towards a Wider Use, 1976; Novellae on the Scroll of Esther, 1982; (ed) Space for the Living or Space for the Dead, 1977; (jtly) London Under London, 1985; contrib. Underground Services, Architects Jl, Arch. Design, Municipal Rev., Municipal Jl, Structural Survey and the Environmentalist. *Recreations:* walking, gardening, allotment cultivation, classical music, reading, writing poetry. *Address:* 29 Haslemere Avenue, NW4 2PU. *T:* 0181–202 7792.

Died 21 Jan. 1996.

HILTON, William Samuel; Director General, Federation of Master Builders, 1987–91 (National Director, 1970–87); Managing Director: Trade Press (FMB) Ltd, 1972–91; National Register of Warranted Builders Ltd, 1980–91; *b* 21 March 1926; *m* 1st, 1948, Agnes Aitken Orr (marr. diss. 1985); three *s*; 2nd, 1986, Betty Ann Penfold. *Educ:* Kyleshill, Saltcoats; Ardrossan Academy. Railway fireman until 1949; Labour Party Agent to Rt Hon. David Kirkwood, later 1st Baron Kirkwood, 1949–52; Research and Education Officer for Building Trade Operatives, 1952–66. MP (Lab and Co-op) Bethnal Green, 1966–Feb. 1974. Director: Trade Debt Recovery Services Ltd, 1986–92; Construction Industry Services Ltd, 1986–92; Anglo-European Developments (GB) Ltd, 1995–; Griffin Construction Co. Ltd, 1996–97; Stephen Lonsdale Ltd, 1997–; Viking Europe Ltd, 1997–. Member: Agrément Bd for Building Industry, 1965–66; EDC for Building Industry, 1964–66; Construction ITB, 1985–91; Employers' Sec., Building and Allied Trades Jt Industrial Council, 1979–91. Editor, Builders Standard, 1954–66. *Publications:* Building by Direct Labour, 1954; Foes to Tyranny, 1964; Industrial Relations in Construction, 1968; The Plug Dropper, 1986; The Wee Spartans, 1998; Speakers Are Born?, 1999. *Address:* Pilgrim Cottage, 18 Court Hill, Coulsdon, Surrey CR5 3NQ.

Died 12 June 1999.

HINSLEY, Prof. Sir (Francis) Harry, Kt 1985; OBE 1946; FBA 1981; Master of St John's College, Cambridge, 1979–89 (Fellow, 1944–79; President, 1975–79); *b* 26 Nov. 1918; *s* of Thomas Henry and Emma Hinsley; *m* 1946, Hilary Brett, *d* of H. F. B. and Helena Brett-Smith, Oxford; two *s* one *d. Educ:* Queen Mary's Grammar Sch., Walsall; St John's Coll., Cambridge. HM Foreign Office, war service, 1939–46. University of Cambridge: Research Fellow, St John's Coll., 1944–50, Tutor, 1956–63; University Lectr in History, 1949–65; Reader in the History of International Relations, 1965–69; Prof., History of Internat. Relations, 1969–83; Vice-Chancellor, 1981–83; Chm., Faculty Bd of History, 1970–72; Lees-Knowles Lectr on Military Science, Trinity Coll., 1970–71. Lectures: Cecil Green, Univ. of BC, 1976; Sir Douglas Robb, Univ. of Auckland, and Yencken Meml, ANU, 1980; Martin Wight Meml, Univ. of Sussex, 1981; Lindsay Meml, Univ. of Keele, 1985; Chancellor's, Univ. of Witwatersrand, 1985; Earl Grey Meml, Univ. of Newcastle upon Tyne, 1985; Chettiar Meml, Univ. of Madras, 1988;

Harmon Meml, USAF Acad., Colorado, 1988; Liddell Hart, KCL, 1992; Montague Burton, Univ. of Nottingham, 1992. UK Rep., Provisional Academic Cttee for European Univ. Inst., 1973–75. Trustee, BM, 1984–89. Hon. Fellow: TCD, 1981; Darwin Coll., Cambridge, 1987. Hon. DLitt Witwatersrand, 1985; Hon. DMilSci Royal Roads Mil. Coll., Canada, 1987. Editor, The Historical Jl, 1960–71. *Publications:* Command of the Sea, 1950; Hitler's Strategy, 1951; (ed) New Cambridge Modern History, Vol. XI, 1962; Power and the Pursuit of Peace, 1963; Sovereignty, 1966, 2nd edn 1986; Nationalism and the International System, 1973; (ed) British Foreign Policy under Sir Edward Grey, 1977; (jtly) British Intelligence in the Second World War, vol. 1, 1979, vol. 2, 1981, vol. 3 (Pt 1), 1984, (Pt 2), 1988, vol. 4, 1990, abridged edn 1993; (ed) Codebreakers: the inside story of Bletchley Park, 1993. *Address:* St John's College, Cambridge CB2 1TP. *T:* (01223) 355075. *Died 16 Feb. 1998.*

HINTON, Nicholas John, CBE 1985; President, International Crisis Group, since 1995; *b* 15 March 1942; *s* of late Rev. Canon Hinton and Mrs J. P. Hinton; *m* 1971, Deborah Mary Vivian; one *d. Educ:* Marlborough Coll., Wiltshire; Selwyn Coll., Cambridge (MA). Asst Dir, Northorpe Hall Trust, 1965–68; Nat. Assoc. for Care and Resettlement of Offenders, 1968–77, Dir, 1973–77; Dir, NCVO (formerly Nat. Council of Social Service), 1977–84; Dir-Gen., SCF, 1985–94. Member: Central Council for Educn and Trng in Social Work, 1974–79; Stonham Housing Assoc., 1976–79; Cttee of Inquiry into UK Prison Services, 1978–79; Exec Cttees, Councils of Social Service, NI, Scotland and Wales, 1977–84; Exec. Cttee, Business in the Community, 1982–88; Parole System Review, 1987–88; Member Council: VSO, 1981–86; Industrial Soc., 1987–; RSA, 1988–94; Atlantic Coll., 1994–. Trustee, Charities Aid Foundn, 1977–84. Dir, Edington Music Festival, 1965–70. Contested (SDP-Liberal Alliance) Somerton and Frome, 1983. FRSA 1981. *Recreation:* music. *Address:* 22 Westmoreland Place, SW1V 4AE. *T:* (0171) 828 3965.
Died 20 Jan. 1997.

HIRST, Prof. John Malcolm, DSC 1945; PhD; FRS 1970; FIBiol; consultant on aerobiology and international agriculture; Director, Long Ashton Research Station, and Professor of Agricultural and Horticultural Science, Bristol University, 1975–84, then Professor Emeritus; *b* 20 April 1921; *s* of Maurice Herbert Hirst and Olive Mary (*née* Pank); *m* 1957, Barbara Mary Stokes; two *d. Educ:* Solihull Sch.; Reading University (BSc Hons Agric. Bot. 1950); PhD London, 1955. Royal Navy (Coastal Forces), 1941–46. Rothamsted Exper. Stn, Harpenden, 1950–75, Hd of Plant Pathology Dept, 1967–75. Vice-Chm. Tech. Adv. Cttee, Consultative Gp, Internat. Agricl Research, 1981–82; Chm., Scientific Adv. Bd, Twyford Plant Labs. Pres., British Aerobiology Fedn, 1990–93. Jakob Eriksson Gold Medal (Internat. Botanical Congress), 1959; Research Medal, RASE, 1970. *Publications:* papers in scientific jls mainly in Trans British Mycological Soc., Annals of Applied Biology, Jl of General Microbiology. *Address:* The Cottage, Butcombe, Bristol BS18 6XQ. *T:* (01275) 472880. *Died 30 Dec. 1997.*

HIRST, Prof. Rodney Julian; Professor of Logic and Rhetoric, University of Glasgow, 1961–81, then Emeritus; *b* 28 July 1920; *s* of Rev. William Hirst and Elsie Hirst; *m* 1st, 1942, Jessica (*d* 1978), *y d* of Charles Alfred Podmore; two *d*; 2nd, 1985, Mary, *widow* of John Patrick. *Educ:* Leeds Grammar Sch.; Magdalen Coll., Oxford. Demy, 1938–47; 1st Cl. Hons Classical Mods, 1940; First Class Hons Lit. Hum., 1947; MA. War Service, 1940–45, mainly as REME Officer (Radar) at home and in Italy. Lectr in Logic and Metaphysics, St Andrews Univ., 1948; Glasgow University: Lectr, 1949, Sen. Lectr, 1959, in Logic; Dean

of Arts, 1971–73; Senate Assessor on Univ. Court, 1973–78; Vice-Principal, 1976–79. *Publications:* Problems of Perception, 1959; (co-author) Human Senses and Perception, 1964; Perception and the External World, 1965; Philosophy: an outline for the intending student, 1968; contribs to Encyclopedia of Philosophy and philosophical journals. *Address:* 26 Riverside Court, Netherlee, Glasgow G44 3PH. *T:* (0141) 637 9433.
Died 14 Jan. 1999.

HISCOCKS, Prof. (Charles) Richard, MA, DPhil; Professor of International Relations, University of Sussex, 1964–72, then Emeritus; *b* 1 June 1907; *y s* of F. W. Hiscocks; unmarried. *Educ:* Highgate Sch.; St Edmund Hall, Oxford; Berlin University (DPhil 1935). Asst Master, Trinity Coll. Sch., Port Hope, Ont, 1929–32; Bradfield Coll., 1936–39; Marlborough Coll., 1939–40. Served with Royal Marines, 1940–45, Lieut-Col; seconded to army for mil. govt duties in Germany, 1945; Brit. Council Rep. in Austria, 1946–49, S India, 1949–50; Prof. of Pol Sci. and Internat. Relations, Univ. of Manitoba, 1950–64. UK Mem., UN Sub-Commn for Prevention of Discrimination and Protection of Minorities, 1953–62. Pres., Winnipeg Art Gall., 1959–60. Vis. Fellow, Princeton Univ., 1970–71; Fellow, Adlai Stevenson Inst. of Internat. Affairs, Chicago, 1971–72. Vice-Pres., UNA 1977. *Publications:* The Rebirth of Austria, 1953; Democracy in Western Germany, 1957; (jtly) The Shaping of Post-war Germany, 1960; Poland: Bridge for the Abyss?, 1963; Germany Revived, 1966; The Security Council: a study in adolescence, 1973. *Recreations:* music, art, gardening. *Address:* Dickers, Hunworth, Melton Constable, Norfolk NR24 2AA. *T:* (01263) 712503. *Club:* Garrick. *Died 2 July 1998.*

HISS, Alger; commercial printing, 1959–80 (manufacturing, 1957–59); lecturer, 1970–80; retired; *b* 11 Nov. 1904; *s* of Charles Alger Hiss and Mary L. Hughes; *m* 1st, 1929, Priscilla Fansler Hobson (*d* 1984); one *s*; 2nd, Isabel; one step *s. Educ:* Johns Hopkins Univ. (AB 1926, Hon. LLD 1947); Harvard Univ. (LLB 1929). Mem., Massachusetts Bar. Sec. and law clerk to Supreme Court Justice Holmes, 1929–30; law practice, 1930–33; asst to gen. counsel and asst gen. counsel, Agricultural Adjustment Admin, 1933–35; legal asst, special Senate cttee investigating munitions industry, 1934–35; special attorney, US Dept of Justice, 1935–36; asst to Asst Sec. of State, 1936; asst to Adviser on Political Relations, 1939; special asst to Dir, Office of Far Eastern Affairs, 1944; special asst to Dir, Office of Special Political Affairs, May 1944; Dep. Dir, Nov. 1944, Dir, 1945; accompanied Pres. Roosevelt and Sec. of State Stettinius to Malta and Yalta Conferences, Feb. 1945; exec. sec., Dumbarton Oaks Conversations, Aug.-Oct. 1944; Sec.-Gen., United Nations Conference on International Organization, San Francisco, 1945; Principal Adviser to US Delegation, Gen. Assembly of United Nations, London, 1946; elected Pres. and Trustee of Carnegie Endowment for Internat. Peace, Dec. 1946 (Pres. until 1949). Mem., Alpha Delta Phi, Phi Beta Kappa. *Publications:* The Myth of Yalta, 1955; In the Court of Public Opinion, 1957, new edn 1972; Holmes-Laski Letters (abridged edn), 1963; Recollections of a Life, 1988. *Address:* 303 East 83 Street, New York, NY 10028, USA. *Died 15 Nov. 1996.*

HITCHIN, Prof. Aylwin Drakeford, CBE 1970; Boyd Professor of Dental Surgery, Director of Dental Studies, University of Dundee (formerly University of St Andrews), 1947–77, Professor Emeritus, 1978; Dean of Dundee Dental Hospital, 1947–73; Dental Consultant, Dundee Royal Infirmary, 1947–77; Civil Consultant Dental Surgeon to Royal Navy, 1957–77; *b* 31 Dec. 1907; *s* of Alfred Leonard Hitchin, FRPS, and Ruth Drakeford; *m* 1942, Alice Stella Michie; one *s* one *d. Educ:* Rutherford College, Newcastle upon Tyne; Durham University Coll.

of Medicine, LDS (Dunelm) 1931, BDS 1932, MDS 1935, DDSc 1957; FDSRCSE 1951; FFDRCSI 1964; FDSRCPSGlas 1967. Asst Hon. Dental Surgeon and Demonstrator of Dental Surgery, Newcastle upon Tyne Dental Hosp., 1932–36; Private Dental Practice, Newcastle upon Tyne, 1932–46 (except for 6 yrs with AD Corps during War of 1939–45; Dental Surgical Specialist, Scottish Command, 1943–45, with rank of Major). Chairman: Dental Educn Advisory Council, 1951–52; Dental Hosp. Assoc., 1959–60; Dental Cttee, Scot. Post-Grad. Med. Council, 1969–79; Member: Dental Cttee of MRC, 1966–72; Advisory Cttee on Medical Research (Scotland), 1967–71; Dental Adv. Cttee, Scottish Health Services Council, 1952–57, 1968–74; Jt Cttee on Higher Training in Dentistry, 1969–74; East Scotland Regional Hosp. Bd, 1948–52; Dental Sub Cttee, UGC, 1969–73; Nominated Mem., Gen. Dent. Council, 1956–74; Convener, Dental Council, RCSE, 1971–74; External Examiner Dental Subjects, Universities, Durham, Edinburgh, Queen's, Belfast, Dublin, Manchester, Liverpool, Birmingham, Leeds, Newcastle, Bristol, Wales, RCS in Ireland; Examiner, LDS, FDSRCSE, FFDRCSI and FDSRCPSGlas. William Guy Meml Lectr, RCSE, 1972; Founders and Benefactors Lectr, Univ. of Newcastle upon Tyne Dental Sch., 1973. President: Oral Surgery Club, 1956–57; Christian Dental Fellowship, 1966–69; Brit. Soc. Dental Radiology, 1961–63; Royal Odonto-Chir. Soc. of Scotland, 1969–70; Pres., Inter-Varsity Fellowship, 1966–67; Foundation Fellow of the British Assoc. of Oral Surgeons; Hon. Mem., Swedish Dental Soc. Dr Odont. (*hc*) Lund, 1977; Hon. FDSRCPSGlas 1979. *Publications:* contribs to dental periodical literature. *Address:* Coniston, Prieston Road, Bridge of Weir, Renfrewshire PA11 3AJ. *T:* (01505) 614936.
Died 1 Oct. 1996.

HITCHINGS, Dr George Herbert; Scientist Emeritus, Burroughs Wellcome Co., then Glaxo Wellcome, since 1975; Director, The Burroughs Wellcome Fund, 1971–94 (President, 1971–90); *b* 18 April 1905; *s* of George Hitchings and Lillian B. (*née* Matthews); *m* 1st, 1933, Beverly Reimer (*d* 1985); one *s* one *d*; 2nd, 1989, Joyce Shaver. *Educ:* Univ. of Washington (BS *cum laude* Chem. 1927; MS 1928); PhD Biochem. Harvard, 1933. Teaching Fellow, Univ. of Washington, 1926–28; Harvard University: Teaching Fellow, 1928–34; Instructor and Tutor, 1932–36; Res. Fellow, 1934–36; Associate, 1936–39; Sen. Instructor, Western Reserve Univ., 1939–42; Burroughs Wellcome Co.: Biochemist, 1942–46; Chief Biochemist, 1946–55; Associate Res. Dir, 1955–63; Res. Dir (Chemotherapy Div.), 1963–67; Vice-Pres. in charge of Res., 1967–75; Dir, 1968–77. Prof. of Pharmacology, Brown Univ., 1968–80; Adjunct Prof. of Pharmacology and Adjunct Prof. of Experimental Medicine, Duke Univ., 1970–85; Staff, Dept of Medicine, Roger Williams Gen. Hosp., Brown Univ., 1970–80; Adjunct Prof. of Pharmacology, Univ. of N Carolina at Chapel Hill, 1972–85; Vis. Prof. of Clinical Pharmacology, Chuang-Ang Univ., Seoul, 1974–77; Vis. Lectr, Pakistan, Iran, Japan, India, Republic of S Africa. Mem., US and internat scientific bodies, incl. Royal Soc., RSocMed, RSC. Hon. degrees from univs in US, UK and Italy. Numerous medals and awards; (jtly) Nobel Prize in Physiology or Medicine, 1988; Albert Schweitzer Internat. Prize for Medicine, 1989. Member, Editorial Boards: Molecular Pharmacology, 1967; Biochemical Pharmacology, 1967; Research Communications in Chemical Pathology and Pharmacology, 1969; Life Sciences, 1978. *Publications:* contribs to learned jls on chemotherapy, antimetabolites, organic chemistry of heterocycles, nucleic acids, antitumor, antimalarial and antibacterial drugs. *Address:* 1 Carolina Meadows, Apt 102, Chapel Hill, NC 27514, USA. *T:* (home) (919) 9335023.
Died 27 Feb. 1998.

HIVES, 2nd Baron *cr* 1950, of Duffield, co. Derby; **John Warwick Hives,** CBE 1989; *b* 26 Nov. 1913; *s* of 1st Baron Hives, CH, MBE and Gertrude Ethel (*d* 1961), *d* of John Warwick; *S* father, 1965; *m* 1st, 1937, Olwen Protheroe Llewellin (*d* 1972); no *c*; 2nd, 1972, Gladys Mary Seals. *Educ:* Manor School, Mickleover, Derby. *Recreation:* shooting. *Heir: nephew* Matthew Peter Hives, *b* 25 May 1971. *Address:* Langdale House, Sutton-on-the-Hill, Derby DE6 5JA. *Club:* Farmers'.
Died 8 Oct. 1997.

HOBLER, Air Vice-Marshal John Forde, CB 1958; CBE 1943; *b* Rockhampton, Qld, Australia, 26 Sept. 1907; *s* of late L. E. Hobler, Rockhampton; *m* 1939, Dorothy Evelyn Diana Haines, Wilsford, Wilts; one *s* one *d* (and one *s* decd). *Educ:* Rockhampton, Qld. Served whole of War of 1939–45 in Bomber Command; commanded RAF Lossiemouth; Palestine, 1945; Staff Coll., 1946–48; Air Ministry, 1948–50; Comd Habbaniya, Iraq, 1950–52; HQ Flying Trg Comd, 1952–54; Air Ministry, 1954–56; AO i/c Administration, Middle East Air Force, 1956–58; Air Officer Commanding No 25 Gp, 1958–61; Air Officer i/c Administration, Far East Air Force, 1961–63, retd. Mem., RAF Escaping Soc.; Founder Mem., Central Queensland Aero Club, 1929–. FRGS. *Address:* Unit P8, The Domain Country Club, 74 Wardoo Street, Ashmore, Qld 4214, Australia. *Club:* United Services (Brisbane).
Died 13 Jan. 1996.

HOBSON, Valerie Babette Louise, (Mrs John Profumo); film and stage actress; *b* Larne, Ireland, 14 April 1917; *d* of Comdr R. G. Hobson, RN, and Violette Hamilton-Willoughby; *m* 1st, 1939, Sir Anthony James Allan Havelock-Allan, Bt (marr. diss. 1952); one *s* (and one *s* decd); 2nd, 1954, John Dennis Profumo; one *s*. *Educ:* St Augustine's Priory, London, Royal Academy of Dramatic Art. Was trained from early age to become ballet dancer; first stage appearance at Drury Lane in Ball at the Savoy, aged 15; The King and I, Drury Lane, 1953; first film, Badgers Green; went to Hollywood and appeared in Werewolf of London, Bride of Frankenstein, The Mystery of Edwin Drood, etc; at 18 returned to England. Films included: The Drum, This Man is News, This Man in Paris, The Spy in Black, Q Planes, Silent Battle, Contraband, Unpublished Story, Atlantic Ferry, The Adventures of Tartu, The Years Between, Great Expectations, Blanche Fury, The Small Voice, Kind Hearts and Coronets, Train of Events, Interrupted Journey, The Rocking Horse Winner, The Card, Who Goes There?, Meet Me Tonight, The Voice of Merrill, Background, Knave of Hearts. *Recreations:* listening to music, writing, reading, painting.
Died 13 Nov. 1998.

HOCKER, Dr Alexander; Grosses Verdienstkreuz mit Stern des Verdienstordens der Bundesrepublik Deutschland, 1973; Director-General, European Space Research Organisation, 1971–74; *m* 1940, Liselotte Schulze; five *s* one *d*. *Educ:* Univs of Innsbruck, Hamburg and Leipzig. Asst, Law Faculty, Leipzig Univ.; County Court Judge; Officer, Advanced Scientific Study Div., Min. of Educn, Hannover, 1947–49; Dep. of Sec.-Gen. of German Res. Assoc. (Deutsche Forschungsgemeinschaft), 1949–56; Ministerialrat and Ministerialdirigent (responsible for res., trng and sci. exchanges), Fed. Min. for Atomic Energy, 1956–61; Mem. Directorate, Nuclear Res. Centre (Kernforschungsanlage) Jülich, 1961–69; Sci. Adviser to Foundn Volkswagenwerk, 1969–71. German Deleg. to CERN, Geneva, 1952–61 (Chm. of Finance Cttee, 1960–61); Chm. of Legal, Admin. and Financial Working Gp of Preparatory Commn, Eur. Space Res., 1961–63; Chm. of Council, ESRO, 1965–67 (Vice-Chm.

1964); Member: German Commn for Space Res., 1964–71; Kuratorium Max-Planck-Institut für Physik und Astrophysik, 1968–71; Max-Plank-Institut für Plasmaphysik, 1971–80, Hon. Member 1980–. *Publication:* (jtly) Taschenbuch für Atomfragen, 1968. *Address:* Bad Godesberg, Augustastrasse 63, 53173 Bonn, Germany. *T:* (228) 363961. *Died 7 Aug. 1996.*

HOCKING, Frederick Denison Maurice; formerly Cornwall County Pathologist; Consulting Biologist and Toxicologist, Devon River Board; late Consulting Pathologist, South-Western Regional Hospital Board; *b* 28 Feb. 1899; *o s* of late Rev. Almund Trevosso Hocking and Gertrude Vernon Mary, *o d* of J. Parkinson; *m* 1st, 1927, Amy Gladys (*d* 1956), *y d* of A. T. Coucher; two *d*; 2nd, 1957, Kathleen (*d* 1996), *e d* of Dr G. P. O'Donnell. *Educ:* High Sch., Leytonstone; City and Guilds of London Coll., Finsbury; Middlesex Hospital Medical Sch. MB, BS, BSc, MSc London; MRCS, LRCP, CChem, FRSC, FCS, FRMS, MIBiol, FRSH. RN Experimental and Antigas Station, 1917–18; Asst Laboratory Dir to the Clinical Research Assoc.; formerly: Acting Director Public Health Laboratory Service, Cornwall, and other hospitals in Cornwall; Chemical Pathologist, Biochemist, and Assistant Pathologist, Westminster Hospital; Lecturer in General and Clinical Pathology, Westminster Hospital Medical School, University of London. Associate of the City and Guilds of London Tech. Coll., Finsbury; Member: Pathological Soc. of Great Britain and Ireland; Association of Clinical Pathologists (Councillor, 1944–46); Society of Public Analysts; Medico-Legal Society; Brit. Assoc. in Forensic Medicine; former Mem. Court, Univ. of Exeter (representing Royal Institute of Chemistry); Pres. South-Western Branch, British Medical Association, 1946; Chm. South-Western Branch, RIC, 1955–57; Mem. Council, RIC, 1959–62, 1965–68. Mem. Brit. Acad. of Forensic Sciences; Mem. Soc. for Forensic Science. *Publications:* The Employment of Uranium in the Treatment of Malignant New Growths, British Empire Cancer Campaign International Conference, London, 1928; Disseminated Sclerosis (with Sir James Purves-Stewart), 1930; Seaside Accidents, 1958; Delayed Death due to Suicidal Hanging, 1961; Hanging and Manual Strangulation, 1966; Christmas Eve Crime in Falmouth (Murder in the West Country), 1975; The Porthole Murder: Gay Gibson (Facets of Crime), 1975; Bodies and Crimes: a pathologist speaks, 1993; numerous scientific papers in medical journals, etc. *Recreations:* hotels, good food, wine, conversation. *Address:* Strathaven, Carlyon Bay, Cornwall. *Clubs:* National Liberal (Associate Mem.), English-Speaking Union. *Died 4 April 1996.*

HODGART, Prof. Matthew John Caldwell; Professor of English, Concordia University, Montreal, 1970–76; *b* 1 Sept. 1916; *s* of late Matthew Hodgart, MC (Major RE), and Katherine Barbour Caldwell (*née* Gardner); *m* 1st, 1940, Betty Joyce Henstridge (*d* 1948); one *s* one *d*; 2nd, 1949, Margaret Patricia Elliott; one adopted *d*. *Educ:* Rugby Sch. (Scholar); Pembroke Coll., Cambridge (Scholar; BA 1938, MA 1945). Jebb Studentship, Cambridge, 1938–39. Served War, 1939–45: Argyll and Sutherland Highlanders and in Intelligence (mentioned in despatches). Cambridge University: Asst Lectr in English, 1945–49; Lectr in English, and Fellow of Pembroke Coll., 1949–64; Prof. of English, Sussex Univ., 1964–70. Vis. Professor: Cornell Univ., 1961–62 and 1969; Univ. of Calif, Los Angeles, 1977–78; Stanford Univ., 1979; La Trobe Univ., Australia, 1979–80; Hinckley Prof., Johns Hopkins Univ., 1982. Chevalier de la Légion d'honneur, and Croix de guerre, 1945. *Publications:* The Ballads, 1950; (with Prof. M. Worthington) Song in the Work of James Joyce, 1959; Samuel Johnson, 1962; (ed) Horace Walpole, Memoirs, 1963; (ed) Faber Book of Ballads, 1965; Satire, 1969 (trans. various languages); A New

Voyage (fiction), 1969; James Joyce, Student Guide, 1978; *posthumous publication:* (with Prof. R. Bauerle) Joyce's Grand Operoar: Opera in Finnegans Wake, 1996; contrib. Rev. of English Studies, and TLS. *Recreations:* travel, music, computers. *Address:* 13 Montpelier Villas, Brighton BN1 3DG. *T:* Brighton (01273) 326993.
Died 3 April 1996.

HODGE, Alexander Mitchell, GC 1940; VRD; DL; WS; Captain RNVR, retired; Member of firm of Cowan & Stewart, WS, Edinburgh, 1946–84; Director, Standard Life Assurance Co., 1965–87 (Chairman, 1977–82); *b* 23 June 1916; *y s* of James Mackenzie Hodge, Blairgowrie, Perthshire; *m* 1944, Pauline Hester Winsome, *o d* of William John Hill, Bristol; one *s* two *d*. *Educ:* Fettes Coll.; Edinburgh Univ. (MA 1936, LLB 1938). Joined RNVR, 1938; served with Royal Navy, 1939–45 (despatches, GC); Comdr RNVR, 1949, Capt. RNVR, 1953; CO of the Forth Div. RNVR, 1953–57. Chm., Edinburgh Dist Sea Cadet Cttee, 1959–63; Chm., Lady Haig's Poppy Factory, 1961–67; Mem. Council, Earl Haig Fund (Scotland), 1963–67; Chm., Livingston New Town Licensing Planning Cttee, 1963–69; Dir, Edinburgh Western Gen. Hosp. Assoc. of Friends, 1962 (Chm., 1962–68); Trustee and Member Cttee of Management: Royal Victoria Hosp. Tuberculosis Trust, 1964–87 (Pres., 1970–87); Royal Edinburgh Inst. for Sailors, Soldiers and Airmen, 1964–71; Chm. General Comrs of Income Tax, Edinburgh South Div., 1967–85; Pres., Edinburgh Chamber of Commerce, 1968–70; Chm., The Cruden Foundn, 1983–92 (Dir, 1969–72, 1973–83). Governor, Fettes Coll., 1970–75; Mem. Court, Heriot-Watt Univ., 1982–88. DL Edinburgh, 1972. *Address:* Springbank, Barnton, Edinburgh EH4 6DJ. *T:* (0131) 339 3054. *Clubs:* Royal Automobile; New (Edinburgh). *Died 4 Jan. 1997.*

HODGINS, Ven. Michael Minden; Archdeacon of Hackney, 1951–71; Secretary of London Diocesan Fund, 1946–74; *b* 26 Aug. 1912; *yr s* of late Major R. Hodgins, Indian Army, and Margaret Hodgins (*née* Wilson); unmarried. *Educ:* Wellington; Cuddesdon Theological Coll. Deacon, 1939; priest, 1940; Curate, S Barnabas, Northolt Park, 1939; Asst Secretary, London Diocesan Fund, 1943. MA Lambeth, 1960. *Address:* 5 Up, The Quadrangle, Morden College, Blackheath, SE3 0PW. *T:* (0181) 858 4762. *Died 11 May 1998.*

HODGKIN, Sir Alan (Lloyd), OM 1973; KBE 1972; ScD; FRS 1948; Master of Trinity College, Cambridge, 1978–84 (Fellow, 1936–78 and since 1984); Chancellor, University of Leicester, 1971–84; *b* 5 Feb. 1914; *s* of G. L. Hodgkin and M. F. Wilson; *m* 1944, Marion de Kay, *d* of late F. P. Rous; one *s* three *d*. *Educ:* Gresham's Sch., Holt; Trinity Coll., Cambridge (MA, ScD). Scientific Officer working on Radar for Air Ministry and Min. of Aircraft Production, 1939–45. Lecturer and then Asst Dir of Research at Cambridge, 1945–52; Foulerton Research Prof., Royal Soc., 1952–69; John Humphrey Plummer Prof. of Biophysics, Univ. of Cambridge, 1970–81. Pres., Royal Society, 1970–75; Pres., Marine Biological Assoc., 1966–76. Foreign Member: Royal Danish Acad. of Sciences, 1964; Amer. Acad. of Arts and Sciences, 1962; Amer. Philosophical Soc.; Royal Swedish Acad. of Sciences; Member: Physiological Soc.; Leopoldina Acad., 1964; Hon. Mem., Royal Irish Acad., 1974; Hon. For. Mem., USSR Acad. of Scis, 1976; For. Assoc., Nat. Acad. of Scis, USA, 1974. Fellow, Imperial Coll. London, 1972; Hon. FRSE 1974; Hon. Fellow: Indian National Science Acad., 1972; Girton Coll., Cambridge, 1979; Pharmaceutical Soc. Hon. MD: Berne, 1956; Louvain, 1958; Hon. DSc: Sheffield, 1963; Newcastle upon Tyne, 1965; E Anglia, 1966; Manchester, 1971; Leicester, 1971; London, 1971; Newfoundland, 1973; Wales, 1973; Rockefeller Univ., 1974; Bristol, 1976; Oxford, 1977;

Hon. LLD: Aberdeen, 1973; Salamanca, 1984; Pisa, 1987; Cambridge, 1991. Baly Medal, RCP, 1955; Royal Medal of Royal Society, 1958; Nobel Prize for Medicine (jtly), 1963; Copley Medal of Royal Society, 1965. Lord Crook Medal, 1983; Helmerich Prize, Retina Res. Foundn, USA, 1988. *Publications:* The Conduction of the Nervous Impulse, 1963; Chance and Design, 1992; (contrib.) History of Neuroscience in Autobiography, 1996; scientific papers dealing with the nature of nervous conduction, muscle and vision, Jl Physiology, etc. *Recreations:* travel, ornithology, fishing. *Address:* Physiological Laboratory, Downing Street, Cambridge CB2 3EG; 18 Panton Street, Cambridge CB2 1HP. *T:* (01223) 352707.

Died 20 Dec. 1998.

HODGKINSON, Terence William Ivan, CBE 1958; Trustee, The Burlington Magazine, since 1986 (Editor, 1978–81; Member, Editorial Board, 1978–86); *b* 7 Oct. 1913; *s* of late Ivan Tattersall Hodgkinson, Wells, Som, and Kathryn Van Vleck Townsend, New York (who *m* 2nd, 1929, Sir Gilbert Upcott, KCB); unmarried. *Educ:* Oundle Sch.; Magdalen Coll., Oxford. Served War of 1939–45: Major, Gen. Staff, 1943. Joined staff of Victoria and Albert Museum (Dept of Architecture and Sculpture), 1946; Asst to the Dir, 1948–62; Secretary to the Advisory Council, 1951–67; Keeper, Dept of Architecture and Sculpture, 1967–74; Dir, Wallace Collection, 1974–78. Member: Exec. Cttee, Nat. Art Collections Fund, 1975–88; Museums and Galleries Commn, 1981–88 (Vice-Chm., 1987–88). *Publications:* (jtly) Catalogue of Sculpture in the Frick Collection, New York, 1970; Catalogue of Sculpture at Waddesdon Manor, 1970; articles in Burlington Magazine, Bulletin and Yearbook of the Victoria and Albert Museum and for Walpole Society. *Recreation:* music. *Address:* 9 The Grove, N6 6JU.

Died 4 Oct. 1999.

HODGSON, (Arthur) Brian, CMG 1962; Consultant, League of Red Cross Societies, 1982–92; *b* 24 Aug. 1916; *s* of late Major Arthur H. F. Hodgson, Westfields, Iffley, Oxford, and Isabel, *d* of late W. H. Kidston, Rosebank, Helensburgh; *m* 1945, Anne Patricia Halse, *d* of late Lt-Col Edward Marlborough Ley, DSO, KRRC and Marjorie (*née* Broadbridge); two *s* two *d.* *Educ:* Edinburgh Academy; Eton Coll.; Oriel Coll., Oxford; Trinity Coll., Cambridge. Colonial Civil Service, Tanganyika Administration, 1939–62, retiring as Principal Sec. and Dir of Establishments. British Red Cross Society: Sec., 1964; Dep. Dir-Gen., 1966–70; Dir-Gen., 1970–75; Counsellor, 1975–91. Steward, Henley Royal Regatta, 1970. FRGS 1991. Henry Dunant Medal, Internat. Red Cross, 1993. *Recreations:* rowing, gardening, messing about in boats. *Address:* Chandlers, Furners Green, near Uckfield, Sussex TN22 3RH. *T:* (01825) 790310. *Clubs:* Naval; Leander (Henley-on-Thames).

Died 2 Oct. 1999.

HODGSON, James, CBE 1984; Vice-Chairman, British Telecom, 1983–85; Chairman, Printing Equipment Economic Development Committee, 1986–88; *b* 14 Oct. 1925; *s* of late Frederick and Lucy Hodgson; *m* 1951, Patricia (*née* Reed); *m* (Brenda) Dawn (*née* Giles). *Educ:* Exeter Sch.; St John's Coll., Cambridge. Entered GPO, 1950; Private Sec. to Asst PMG, 1952–55 and to Dir Gen. GPO, 1955–56; seconded to Cabinet Office, 1961–63; Head of Telephone Operating Div. of GPO Headquarters, 1965–67; Dir, later Sen. Dir, PO Internat. Telecommunications, 1969–81; Man. Dir, British Telecom Internat., 1981–83. Dir (non-exec.), Cable and Wireless Ltd, 1970–78. FRSA 1984. *Recreations:* travel, archaeology. *Address:* 2 Park Place, Bath BA1 2TY.

Died 25 May 1999.

HODGSON, John Bury; Special Commissioner of Income Tax, 1970–78; *b* 17 March 1912; *s* of Charles Hodgson and Dorothy Hope Hodgson; *m* 1948, Helen Sibyl Uvedale Beaumont. *Educ:* Derbyshire Grammar Sch.; Manchester Univ. Solicitor, 1942; Asst Solicitor of Inland Revenue, 1956–70. *Publications:* (contrib.) Halsbury's Laws of England; (Consulting Editor) Sergeant on Stamp Duties. *Recreations:* sailing, beekeeping. *Address:* Five Thorns Cottage, North Weirs, Brockenhurst, Hants SO42 7QA. *T:* (01590) 22653. *Clubs:* various yacht.

Died 24 March 2000.

HODGSON, Prof. Phyllis; Professor of English Language and Mediæval Literature, Bedford College, University of London, 1955–72, retired; *b* 27 June 1909; *d* of late Herbert Henry Hodgson, MA, BSc, PhD, FRIC and Annie, *e d* of T. W. Procter, Bradford. *Educ:* Bolling Grammar Sch. for Girls, Bradford; Bedford Coll., University of London (BA); Lady Margaret Hall, Oxford (Sen. Schol.; BLitt, DPhil); MA Cantab. Tutor of St Mary's Coll., Durham Univ., 1936–38; Jex-Blake Fellow, Girton Coll., Cambridge, 1938–40; Lecturer in English Language (part-time), Queen Mary Coll., University of London, and Lecturer in English, Homerton Coll., Cambridge, 1940–42; Lecturer in English Language and Mediæval Literature, Bedford Coll., University of London, 1942–49; Reader in English Language in the University of London, 1949–55. External examiner for Reading Univ., 1955–57, 1961–63. Mem. Council of Early English Text Soc., 1959–79; Chm., Bd of Studies in English, 1964–66. Sir Israel Gollancz Prize, British Academy, 1971. *Publications:* The Cloud of Unknowing (EETS), 1944, 1958; Deonise Hid Divinite (EETS), 1955, 1958, 1973; The Franklin's Tale, 1960; The Orcherd of Syon and the English Mystical Tradition (Proc. Brit. Acad. 1964), 1965; The Orcherd of Syon (EETS), 1966; Three 14th Century English Mystics, 1967; The General Prologue to the Canterbury Tales, 1969; The Cloud of Unknowing and Related Treatises (Analecta Cartusiana), 1982; articles in Review of English Studies, Modern Language Review, Contemporary Review, etc. *Recreations:* music, walking, travel.

Died 3 June 2000.

HODSON, Henry Vincent; Provost of Ditchley (Director, Ditchley Foundation), 1961–71; *b* 12 May 1906; *er s* of late Prof. T. C. Hodson and Kathleen, 4th *d* of Henry Manly, FIA; *m* 1933, Margaret Elizabeth Honey, Sydney; four *s*. *Educ:* Gresham's Sch.; Balliol Coll., Oxford. Fellow of All Souls Coll., Oxford, 1928–35; Staff of Economic Advisory Council, 1930–31; Asst Editor of the Round Table, 1931–34, Editor, 1934–39; Director, Empire Div., Ministry of Information, 1939–41; Reforms Commissioner, Govt of India, 1941–42; Principal Asst Sec., and later Head of Non-Munitions Div., Min. of Production, 1942–45; Asst Editor, Sunday Times, 1946–50, Editor, 1950–61. Sole Partner, Hodson Consultants, 1971–. Editor, 1973–88, Chm. Adv. Bd, 1988–, Annual Register (of world events); Consultant Editor, The International Foundation Directory, 1974–89. Past Master, Mercers' Co. *Publications:* Economics of a Changing World, 1933; Slump and Recovery, 1929–37, 1938; The British Commonwealth and the Future, 1939; Twentieth Century Empire, 1948; Problems in Anglo-American Relations, 1963; The Great Divide: Britain-India-Pakistan, 1969 (reissued 1985); The Diseconomics of Growth, 1972. *Address:* Flat 1, 105 Lexham Gardens, W8 6JN. *T:* (020) 7373 2859.

Died 27 March 1999.

HOFFMAN, Michael Richard, FEng 1989; Chairman, Building Research Establishment Ltd, since 1997; *b* 31 Oct. 1939; *s* of Sydney William Hoffman and Ethel Margaret Hoffman (*née* Hill); *m* 1st, 1963, Margaret Edith Tregaskes (marr. diss. 1978); one *d*; 2nd, 1982, Helen Judith Peters. *Educ:* Hitchin Grammar Sch.; Univ. of Bristol (BScEng Hons). Eur Ing; FIMechE, FIEE. Rolls

Royce, 1961; AE Ltd, 1973; Perkins Engines Group: Managing Director, 1976; Chairman, 1977; Massey Ferguson Ltd: Vice President, 1980; President, Farm Machinery Div., 1981; Chief Exec. and Man. Dir, Babcock Internat., 1983–87; Deputy Chairman: Airship Industries, 1988–90 (Chief Exec., 1987–88); Cosworth Engrg Ltd, 1988–91; Thames Water plc (formerly Thames Water Authority), 1992–96 (Chief Exec., 1989–96); Director: Anite Group (formerly Cray Electronics), 1990–; PowerGen, 1993–; Hornby plc, 1997–; Chm., International Plastic Technologies, 1997–. Mem. Bd of Management, Naval Manning Agency, 1996–. Pres., IProdE, 1987–88 (Vice Pres., 1985–87); Vice-Pres., EEF, 1985–87. Pres., Water Services Assoc. of England and Wales, 1996; Dir, WaterAid, 1995–96. Chm., UK S African Trade Assoc., 1987; Member: Technology Requirements Bd, 1985–88; Monopolies and Mergers Commn, 1988–94; BOTB, 1986–89; Engrg Council, 1991–95. Chm. Council, Brunel Univ., 1991–97 (Mem., 1984–). Freeman, City of London, 1984; Liveryman, Engineers' Co., 1984. *Recreations:* Real tennis, shooting, sailing. *Address:* 43 De Vere Gardens, W8 5AW. *T:* (0171) 581 4612. *Clubs:* Reform, Royal Automobile, MCC, Royal Thames Yacht.

Died 17 April 1998.

HOFFMEISTER, Maj.-Gen. Bertram Meryl, OC 1982; CB 1945; CBE 1944; DSO 1943; ED; *b* 15 May 1907; *s* of Louis George Hoffmeister and Flora Elizabeth Rodway; *m* 1935, Donalda Strauss; one *s* one *d. Educ:* Public Schs, Vancouver. Previous to war of 1939–45 employed by H. R. MacMillan Export Co. Ltd, Vancouver, BC. 1st Lieut Seaforth Highlanders of Canada, 1927; Capt. 1934; Major 1939 and given command of a rifle Co.; served with Seaforth Highlanders in England as Co. Comdr, 1939–40; returned to Canada, 1942, to attend Canadian Junior War Staff Course; given Command of Seaforth Highlanders of Canada and commanded this Bn in assault on Sicily in July 1943 (DSO); Brig., Oct. 1943 and assumed command 2 Canadian Infantry Brigade (Bar to DSO, battle of Ortona); Maj.-Gen. and commanded 5 Cdn Armoured Div., March 1944; operations on Hitler Line, May-June 1944 (2nd Bar to DSO, CBE); in NW Europe until conclusion of hostilities (CB); GOC Canadian Army Pacific Force, 1945. Gen. Manager, Canadian White Pine Co. Ltd, and MacMillan Industries Ltd (Plywood Div.), 1945–47; H. R. MacMillan Export Co. Ltd: Gen. Mgr Prod., 1947–49 and Vice-Pres. Prod., 1949; Pres., 1949–51; MacMillan & Bloedel Ltd: Pres. 1951–56; Chm. Bd, 1956–57. Agent-Gen. for British Columbia, 1958–61. Pres., Council of the Forest Industries of BC, Vancouver, 1961–71. Chm., Nature Trust of BC (formerly Nat. Second Century Fund of BC), 1971–92. *Recreations:* Rugby, rowing, shooting, skiing. *Address:* 1501–2240 Bellevue Avenue, West Vancouver, BC V7V 1C7, Canada. *Clubs:* Vancouver, Capilano Golf and Country, Vancouver Rowing (Vancouver). *Died 4 Dec. 1999.*

HOGG, Sir Edward William L.; *see* Lindsay-Hogg.

HOGG, Sir John (Nicholson), Kt 1963; TD 1946; Deputy Chairman: Williams & Glyn's Bank Ltd, 1970–83; Gallaher Ltd, 1964–78; Chairman, Banque Française de Crédit International Ltd, 1972–83; *b* 4 Oct. 1912; *o s* of late Sir Malcolm Hogg and Lorna Beaman; *m* 1948, Barbara Mary Elisabeth (*d* 1998), *yr d* of Capt. Arden Franklyn, Shedfield, Southampton and *widow* of Viscount Garmoyle (*d* of wounds, 1942); one *s* one *d. Educ:* Eton; Balliol Coll., Oxford. Joined Glyn, Mills and Co., 1934. Served War of 1939–45, with KRRC in Greece, Crete, Western Desert, Tunisia, NW Europe. Rejoined Glyn, Mills and Co. 1945, a Man. Dir, 1950–70, Dep. Chm. 1963–68, Chm. 1968–70; Director: Royal Bank of Scotland Gp Ltd, 1969–82; Prudential Corp. Ltd, 1964–85. Chm., Export Credits Guarantee Department's Adv.

Council, 1962–67. Chm., Abu Dhabi Investment Bd, 1967–75. Fellow of Eton Coll., 1951–70. Mem. of Commonwealth War Graves Commission, 1958–64; a Trustee, Imperial War Graves Endowment Fund, 1965–87. Sheriff County of London, 1960. Hon. Treasurer, Inst. of Child Health, 1974–87 (Hon. Fellow 1987). *Recreations:* cricket, tennis, fishing. *Address:* The Red House, Shedfield, Southampton SO32 2HN. *T:* (01329) 832121. *Club:* Brooks's. *Died 12 April 1999.*

HOLDEN, Basil Munroe; Rector, Glasgow Academy, 1959–75, retired; *b* 10 Nov. 1913; *m* 1951, Jean Watters; two *s* two *d. Educ:* Queen Elizabeth's Grammar Sch., Blackburn; King's Coll., Cambridge (Foundation Scholar). BA 1935, Maths Tripos (Wrangler), MA 1939. Instructor Lieut RN, 1940. Mathematical Master, Highgate Sch., 1937; Head of Mathematical Dept, Oundle Sch., 1947; Housemaster, Oundle Sch., 1956. *Address:* Orchard House, Blennerhasset, Carlisle, Cumbria CA5 3QX. *T:* (01697) 320735. *Died 24 May 1998.*

HOLDEN, Sir David (Charles Beresford), KBE 1972; CB 1963; ERD 1954; *b* 26 July 1915; *s* of Oswald Addenbrooke Holden and Ella Mary Beresford; *m* 1948, Elizabeth Jean Odling; one *s* one *d. Educ:* Rossall Sch.; King's Coll., Cambridge. Northern Ireland Civil Service, 1937–76: Permanent Sec., Dept of Finance, NI, and Head of NI Civil Service, 1970–76; Dir, Ulster Office, 1976–77. Royal Artillery, 1939–46. *Address:* Falcons, Wilsford Cum Lake, Amesbury, Salisbury SP4 7BL. *T:* (01980) 622493. *Died 31 Aug. 1998.*

HOLDERNESS, Sir Richard William, 3rd Bt *cr* 1920, of Tadworth, Surrey; Partner, Whiteheads, Estate Agents and Surveyors, 1967–86; retired; *b* 30 Nov. 1927; *s* of Sir Ernest William Elsmie Holderness, 2nd Bt, CBE, and Emily Carlton (*d* 1950), *y d* of late Frederick McQuade, Sydney, NSW; *S* father, 1968; *m* 1953, Pamela, *d* of late Eric Chapman, CBE; two *s* one *d. Educ:* Dauntsey's Sch.; Corpus Christi Coll., Oxford. ARICS 1976. *Recreations:* golf, gardening, travel. *Heir: s* Martin William Holderness, CA [*b* 24 May 1957; *m* 1984, Elizabeth, BSc, DipHV, *d* of Dr William and Dr Maureen Thornton, Belfast; one *s* one *d*]. *Address:* 1 Tollhouse Close, Chichester, W Sussex PO19 1SE. *Club:* West Sussex Golf.

Died 30 May 1998.

HOLDSWORTH, Lt-Comdr (Arthur) John (Arundell), CVO 1980; OBE 1962; RN; an Extra Gentleman Usher to the Queen, since 1985 (Gentleman Usher, 1967–85); Vice Lord-Lieutenant for Devon, 1982–90; *b* 31 March 1915; *s* of Captain F. J. C. Holdsworth, JP, DL, Totnes, and M. W. Holdsworth (*née* Arundell); *m* 1940, Barbara Lucy Ussher (*d* 1996), *d* of Col and Mrs W. M. Acton; one *s* one *d. Educ:* Stanmore Park Prep. Sch.; Royal Naval Coll., Dartmouth. Entered RN, 1928; served War at sea (despatches); Asst Naval Attaché Warsaw, 1947–49; BJSM Washington, 1950–51; Naval Staff, Germany, 1954–56; Flag Lieut to Bd of Admiralty, 1956–65; retired 1965. Steward, Newton Abbot Race Course, 1967–85; Dep. Pres., Devon Br., BRCS, 1971–85 (Patron, 1985–); Chm., Silver Jubilee Trust Council, Devon, 1978–85. DL 1973, High Sheriff, 1976–77, Devon. *Address:* Holbeam Mill, Ogwell, Newton Abbot, Devon TQ12 6LX. *T:* (01626) 365547. *Died 12 June 1999.*

HOLFORD, Surg. Rear-Adm. John Morley, CB 1965; OBE 1954; Senior Principal Medical Officer, Department of Health and Social Security, 1973–74, retired; *b* 10 Jan. 1909; *o s* of late Rev. W. J. Holford and Amy Finnemore Lello; *m* 1935, Monica Peregrine (*d* 1986), *d* of late Preb. P. S. G. Propert; two *s. Educ:* Kingswood, Bath; Trinity Hall, Cambridge. MA, MB Cantab; FRCP. Joined RN 1935; War service in HMS Nelson, 1940–42; RN Hosp. Plymouth, 1942–44; Consultant in Medicine to RN,

1954–66; Surgeon Capt., 1957; Surgeon Rear-Adm. 1963; Medical Officer in Charge, RN Hosp. Haslar, 1963–66; retired, 1966. MO, Min. of Health, 1966, SMO, 1967, SPMO, 1973. Gilbert Blanc Medal, 1956; F. E. Williams Prize in Geriatric Medicine, RCP, 1972. CStJ 1964. *Publications:* articles in medical journals. *Recreations:* chess (jt champion of South Africa, 1946), bridge. *Address:* c/o Lloyds Bank, 84 Park Lane, W1Y 4BX. *Club:* Army and Navy.　　　　　　　　*Died 4 Nov. 1997.*

HOLGATE, Hon. Harold Norman, AO 1994; Manager, Tasmanian Branch, Australian Tourism Council, since 1994; *b* 5 Dec. 1933; *s* of late H. W. Holgate; *m* 1963, Rosalind, *d* of E. C. Wesley; two *s* two *d*. *Educ:* Maitland (NSW) High Sch.; Univ. of Tasmania (BA). Journalist: Sydney Morning Herald, 1952–55; Melbourne Herald, 1955–62; Political Journalist, Dep. Chief of Staff, Launceston Examiner, 1963–66; Public Relns Manager, Tasmanian Directorate of Industrial Development, 1966–70; Exec. Producer, ABC TV Public Affairs Programme, This Day Tonight, Hobart, 1970–73; Press Sec. to Dep. Prime Minister and Minister for Defence, Govt of Australia, Mr Lance Barnard, 1973–74; MHA (Lab) for Bass, Tasmania, 1974–92; Speaker of House of Assembly, 1975–76; Minister (Government of Tasmania): for Housing and Construction, and Minister assisting the Dep. Premier, 1976–77; for Education, Recreation and the Arts, and for Racing and Gaming, 1977–79; for Education, Recreation and the Arts, and for Police and Emergency Services, 1979–80; for Education, for Police and Emergency Services, and for Racing and Gaming, 1980–81; for Police and Emergency Services, for Local Govt, for the Environment, for Water Resources, and for Racing and Gaming, 1981; Premier of Tasmania, Treasurer and Minister for Racing and Gaming, 1981–82; Dep. Leader of the Opposition, Tasmanian House of Assembly, 1982–86; Chm., Tasmanian Party Labor Party, 1986–89; Minister for Tourism, Sport and Recreation, 1989–92, for Roads and Transport, 1990, and for Parks, Wildlife and Heritage, 1991–92. *Recreations:* horse racing, music, reading, swimming. *Address:* RSD 3670, Hillwood, Tasmania 7252, Australia. *T:* (3) 63948208.
　　　　　　　　　　　　　　Died 16 March 1997.

HOLLAMBY, Edward Ernest, OBE 1970, FRIBA, FRTPI, FCSD; Chief Architect and Planner to London Docklands Development Corporation, 1981–85, retired; architectural consultant; *b* 8 Jan. 1921; *s* of late Edward Thomas Hollamby and Ethel May (*née* Kingdom); *m* 1941, Doris Isabel Parker; one *s* two *d*. *Educ:* School of Arts and Crafts, Hammersmith; University Coll. London. DipTP London. Served RM Engrs, 1941–46. Architect, Miners' Welfare Commn, 1947–49; Sen. Architect, LCC, 1949–62; Borough Architect, Lambeth, 1963–65, Bor. Architect and Town Planning Officer, 1965–69, Dir of Architecture, Planning and Develt, 1969–81. Works, 1957–, included: Christopher Wren and N Hammersmith Sec. Schs; Brandon Estate, Southwark; housing at Elephant and Castle; study for Erith Township, Kent (prototype study for Thamesmead); pioneered conservation, LCC Brixton Town Centre Develt Plan; housing schemes, Lambeth, 1965–, included: Lambeth Towers; Central Hill, Norwood; Stockwell; Brixton; Clapham; Tulse Hill and Vauxhall; also conservation and historic bldgs restoration, parks and open spaces, sheltered housing, old people's homes, health centres, doctors' gp practices, community centres, commercial and civic offices; Area rehabil. and renewal schemes, Clapham Manor and Kennington; Norwood Liby and Nettlefold Hall; schs for mentally retarded, Clapham and Kennington; rehabil. centre for disabled, Clapham; recreation centre, Brixton; study, Civic Centre, Brixton; holiday hotel for severely disabled, Netley, near Southampton; Girls' Secure Unit, Croydon, 1978; scheme for village development, Shirley Oaks, Croydon, 1979;

Isle of Dogs Urban Design Guide, 1982; develt strategies for Limehouse, Surrey and Greenland Docks, Bermondsey and Wapping, 1982–83; refurbishment of exterior and landscape, St George's in the East, 1983; Royal Docks Develt Strategy, 1984; overall layout, Western Dock, Wapping; Chm., Design Gp, Docklands Light Railway, 1982–84. Assessor, numerous architectural competitions and award schemes. Lectured on architecture and environmental planning; numerous radio and TV appearances. Mem. Council, 1961–70, Hon. Treas., 1967–70, RIBA. Vice-Pres., London Forum of Amenity and Civic Socs, 1991–; Member: Historic Buildings Council, 1972–82; London Adv. Cttee, English Heritage, 1986–90; Founder Member: William Morris Soc.; Bexley Civic Soc. Mem., Univ. of Greenwich Assembly, 1997–. FRSA. Hon. ALI. Hon. DDes Greenwich, 1996. Numerous design and Civic Trust awards. *Publications:* (with Raphaele Gorjux) La Red House, 1983; Docklands Heritage: conservation and regeneration in Docklands, 1987; Red House, Bexleyheath by Philip Webb: the home of William Morris, 1991; contrib. architectural and town planning jls. *Recreations:* travel, classical music, opera, gardening. *Address:* Red House, Red House Lane, Upton, Bexleyheath, Kent DA6 8JF. *T:* (020) 8303 8808. *Club:* Arts.　　　　　　　　　*Died 29 Dec. 1999.*

HOLLAND, Brian Arthur; Solicitor to the Post Office, 1981–93; postal law consultant, since 1994; *b* 14 June 1935; *s* of late George Leigh Holland and Hilda Holland, MBE; *m* 1964, Sally Edwards; one *s* one *d*. *Educ:* Manchester Grammar Sch.; Manchester Univ. (LLB Hons). Admitted Solicitor, 1961. Joined Solicitor's Dept, GPO, 1961; Solicitor's Office, Post Office: Head of Civil Litigation Div., 1977–79; Dir, Litigation and Prosecution Dept, 1979–81. *Publication:* (contrib.) Halsbury's Laws of England, 4th edn, vol. 36. *Recreations:* photography, studying railways, sketching, gardening. *Address:* 23 Grasmere Road, Purley, Surrey CR8 1DY. *T:* (020) 8660 0479.　　　　　　　　　　　*Died 21 Sept. 1999.*

HOLLAND, David George, CMG 1975; Chief Adviser, Bank of England, 1980–85; *b* 31 May 1925; *s* of late Francis George Holland and Mabel Ellen Holland; *m* 1954, Marian Elizabeth Rowles; two *s* one *d*. *Educ:* Taunton Sch.; Wadham Coll., Oxford. Inst. of Economics and Statistics, Oxford, 1949–63; Internat. Bank for Reconstruction and Development, Washington, DC, 1963–65; Min. of Overseas Development, 1965–67; Chief Economic Adviser, FCO, 1967–75; Dep. Chief, Economic Intelligence and Overseas Depts, Bank of England, 1975–80; Exec. Dir, 1986–90, consultant, 1990–93, The Group of Thirty; Chm., Securities Standards Adv. Bd, 1993–94. *Address:* Coombe Cottage, Missenden Road, Butlers Cross, Aylesbury, Bucks HP17 0UP.
　　　　　　　　　　　　　　Died 25 July 1996.

HOLLAND, Sir Guy (Hope), 3rd Bt *cr* 1917, of Westwell Manor, co. Oxford; farmer; art dealer; *b* 19 July 1918; *s* of Sir Reginald Sothern Holland, 1st Bt and Stretta Aimée Holland (*née* Price) (*d* 1949); *S* brother, 1981; *m* 1945, Joan Marianne Street, *d* of late Captain Herbert Edmund Street, XXth Hussars, and Evelyn (who later *m* Adm. Sir Francis Tottenham, KCB, CBE); two *d*. *Educ:* privately and Christ Church, Oxford. Served War of 1939–45 (wounded); Captain, Royal Scots Greys; ADC to Gen. Sir Andrew Thorne, 1944. *Heir:* none. *Address:* Sheepbridge Barn, Eastleach, Cirencester, Gloucestershire GL7 3PS. *T:* (01367) 850296. *Clubs:* Boodle's, Pratt's.
　　　　　　　　　　　　　Died 2 Sept. 1997 (ext).

HOLLAND, Rt Rev. Thomas, DSC 1944; DD (Gregorian); retired Bishop of Salford; *b* 11 June 1908; *s* of John Holland and Mary (*née* Fletcher). *Educ:* Upholland; Valladolid Univ. (PhD 1929); Rome (DD Gregorian, 1936). Ordained priest, 1933. Taught theology: Spain,

1936–41; Lisbon, 1941–43; Chaplain, RN, 1943–46; Port Chaplain, Bombay, 1946–48; CMS, 1948–56; Secretary to Apostolic Delegate, 1956–60; Coadjutor Bp of Portsmouth, 1960–64; RC Bishop of Salford, 1964–83; Apostolic Administrator, 1983–84. Privy Chamberlain to the Pope, 1958. Member of Vatican Secretariat for Promoting Christian Unity, 1961–73, for Unbelievers, 1965–73; Mem., Vatican Synod, 1974. Mem., Jt Working Gp, RC Ch and WCC, 1965–74 (Co-Chm., 1972–74). Hon. DLitt Salford, 1980. *Publications:* Great Cross, 1958; For Better and For Worse (autobiog.), 1989. *Address:* Nazareth House, Scholes Lane, Prestwich, Manchester M25 8AP. *Died 30 Sept. 1999.*

HOLLENDEN, 3rd Baron *cr* 1912, of Leigh, Kent; **Gordon Hope Hope-Morley;** I. & R. Morley Ltd, 1933–67, retired as Chairman; *b* 8 Jan. 1914; *s* of Hon. Claude Hope-Morley (*d* 1968) (*yr s* of 1st Baron) and Lady Dorothy Edith Isabel (*d* 1972), *d* of 7th Earl of Buckinghamshire; *S* uncle, 1977; *m* 1945, Sonja Sundt, Norway; three *s*. *Educ:* Eton. War medals of 1939–45; King Haakon of Norway Liberation medal. *Heir: s* Hon. Ian Hampden Hope-Morley [*b* 23 Oct. 1946; *m* 1st, 1972, Beatrice Saulnier (marr. diss. 1985), *d* of Baron Pierre d'Anchald, Paris; one *s* one *d*; 2nd, 1988, Caroline Ash; two *s*]. *Address:* Hall Place, Leigh, Tonbridge, Kent TN11 8HH. *T:* (01732) 832255. *Clubs:* Brooks's, MCC.
Died 12 April 1999.

HOLLINGS, Rev. Michael Richard, MBE 1993; MC 1943; Parish Priest, St Mary of the Angels, Bayswater, since 1978; Dean of North Kensington, since 1980; *b* 30 Dec. 1921; *s* of Lieut-Commander Richard Eustace Hollings, RN, and Agnes Mary (*née* Hamilton-Dalrymple). *Educ:* Beaumont Coll.; St Catherine's Society, Oxford (MA). St Catherine's, 1939; Sandhurst, 1941. Served War of 1939–45 (despatches): commnd Coldstream Guards, 1941; served N Africa, Italy, Palestine, 1942–45; Major. Trained at Beda Coll., Rome, 1946–50. Ordained Rome, 1950; Asst Priest, St Patrick's, Soho Square, W1, 1950–54; Chaplain, Westminster Cathedral, 1954–58; Asst Chaplain, London Univ., 1958–59; Chaplain to Roman Catholics at Oxford Univ., 1959–70; Parish Priest, St Anselm's, Southall, Middx, 1970–78. Religious Adviser: ATV, 1958–59; Rediffusion, 1959–68; Thames Television, 1968; Advr, Prison Christian Fellowship, 1983–. Member: Nat. Catholic Radio and TV Commn, 1968; Westminster Diocesan Schools Commn, 1970–; Southall Chamber of Commerce, 1971–78; Oxford and Cambridge Catholic Educn Bd, 1971–78; Executive, Council of Christians and Jews, 1971–79, 1984–; Lay Mem., Press Council, 1969–75; Nat. Conf. of Priests Standing Cttee, 1974–76; Rampton Cttee, 1979–81; Swann Cttee, 1981–84; Exec., Ealing Community Relations Council, 1973–76; Exec., Notting Hill Social Council, 1980–; Chairman: N Kensington Action Group, 1980–81; W London Family Service Unit, 1984–; Portobello Trust, 1988–. Mem. Bd, Christian Aid, 1984–87. Chaplain: to Sovereign Military Order of Malta, 1957; to Nat. Council of Lay Apostolate, 1970–74; to Catholic Inst. of Internat. Relations, 1971–80. Chm., Bd of Govs, Sion-Manning Sch., 1991–; Gov., St Charles Catholic Sixth Form Coll., 1990–93. *Publications:* Hey, You!, 1955; Purple Times, 1957; Chaplaincraft, 1963; The One Who Listens, 1971; The Pastoral Care of Homosexuals, 1971; It's Me, O Lord, 1972; Day by Day, 1972; The Shade of His Hand, 1973; Restoring the Streets, 1974; I Will Be There, 1975; You Must Be Joking, Lord, 1975; The Catholic Prayer Book, 1976; Alive to Death, 1976; Living Priesthood, 1977; His People's Way of Talking, 1978; As Was His Custom, 1979; St Thérèse of Lisieux, 1981; Hearts not Garments, 1982; Chaplet of Mary, 1982; Path to Contemplation, 1983; Go In Peace, 1984; Christ Died at Notting Hill, 1985; Athirst for God,

1985; Prayers before and after Bereavement, 1986; By Love Alone, 1986; Prayers for the Depressed, 1986; You Are Not Alone, 1988; Dying to Live, 1990; Thoughts of Peace, 1991; Love Heals, 1993; Reflections through the Church's Year: Year A, 1995; contrib. Tablet, Clergy Review, Life of the Spirit, The Universe. *Recreations:* reading, walking, people. *Address:* St Mary of the Angels, Moorhouse Road, Bayswater, W2 5DJ. *T:* (0171) 229 0487. *Died 21 Feb. 1997.*

HOLLIS, Prof. (James) Martin, FBA 1990; Professor of Philosophy, University of East Anglia, since 1982; *b* 14 March 1938; *s* of Hugh Marcus Noel Hollis and Ruth Margaret Hollis; *m* 1965, Patricia Lesley Wells (later Baroness Hollis of Heigham); two *s*. *Educ:* Winchester Coll.; New Coll., Oxford (BA 1961; MA 1964). Harkness Commonwealth Fund Fellow, Berkeley and Harvard, 1961; FCO, 1964; Extraordinary Lectr, New Coll., Oxford, 1964; Lectr, Balliol Coll., Oxford, 1965; University of East Anglia: Lectr, 1967; Sen. Lectr, 1972; Pro-Vice-Chancellor, 1992–95. Dist. Visitor and Lectr, Univs of British Columbia, 1980; Kingston, 1982, Bayreuth, 1988; Wake Forest, 1995; Munich, 1996. Pres., Aristotelian Soc., 1986. Mem. Council, Univ. of Bayreuth, 1989–; Gov., Eaton (City of Norwich Sch.) Sch., 1972–75. JP Norwich, 1972–82. Editor, Ratio, 1980–87. *Publications:* The Light of Reason, 1971; (with E. J. Nell) Rational Economic Man, 1975; Models of Man, 1977; (with F. Hahn) Philosophy and Economic Theory, 1979; (with S. Lukes) Rationality and Relativism, 1982; Invitation to Philosophy, 1985; The Cunning of Reason, 1988; (with S. Smith) Explaining and Understanding International Relations, 1990; Rationalität und soziales Verstehen, 1991; The Philosophy of Social Science, 1994; Reason in Action, 1996. *Recreation:* puzzles. *Address:* School of Economic and Social Studies, University of East Anglia, Norwich NR4 7TJ. *T:* (01603) 456161.
Died 27 Feb. 1998.

HOLLOWAY, Derrick Robert Le Blond; Registrar of the Family Division, Principal Registry, 1966–83; retired; *b* 29 May 1917; *s* of Robert Fabyan Le Blond and Mary Beatrice Holloway; *m* 1942, Muriel Victoria Bower; one *s*. *Educ:* Brentwood; Univ. of London (LLB Hons). Principal Probate Registry, 1937. Served War of 1939–45: DCLI, RASC, Claims Commn. Sec., Cttee on Law of Intestate Succession, 1951; Sec., Cttee on Ancient Probate Records, 1953; Asst Sec., Royal Commn on Marriage and Divorce, 1952–56; Acting Registrar, Probate, Divorce and Admiralty Div., 1965. Gp Chm. (Amersham), Civil Service Retirement Fellowship, 1985; Chm., S Bucks Br., CS Retirement Fellowship, 1990. *Publications:* (ed jtly) Latey on Divorce, 14th edn 1952; (ed) Proving a Will, 2nd edn 1952; (ed) Obtaining Letters of Administration, 1954; Divorce Forms and Precedents, 1959; Probate Handbook (later Holloway's Probate Handbook), 1961, 7th edn 1984, (Consultant Editor) 8th edn 1987; Phillips' Probate Practice, 6th edn 1963; (contrib.) Butterworths' Costs, 4th edn 1971; Acting in Person: how to obtain an undefended divorce, 1977. *Recreations:* marriage, gardening, foreign travel, music, photography. *Address:* 1 Chiltern Manor Park, Great Missenden, Bucks HP16 9BL.
Died 16 Sept. 1997.

HOLLOWAY, Prof. John, DPhil, DLitt, LittD; Professor of Modern English, University of Cambridge, 1972–82 (Reader, 1966–72); Fellow of Queens' College, Cambridge, 1955–82, Life Fellow, 1982; *b* 1 Aug. 1920; *s* of George Holloway and Evelyn Astbury; *m* 1946, Audrey Gooding; one *s* one *d; m* 1978, Joan Black. *Educ:* County Sch., Beckenham, Kent; New Coll., Oxford (Open History Scholar; 1st class Modern Greats, 1941; MA, DPhil 1947); DLitt Aberdeen, 1954; MA Cambridge; LittD Cambridge, 1969. Served War of 1939–45, commnd

RA, 1942; subsequently seconded to Intelligence. Temporary Lecturer in Philosophy, New Coll., Oxford, 1945; Fellow of All Souls Coll., Oxford, 1946–60; John Locke Scholar, 1947; University Lecturer in English: Aberdeen, 1949–54; Cambridge, 1954–66; Sec., 1954–56, Librarian, 1964–66, Chm., 1970, 1971, English Faculty. FRSL 1956. Lecture Tours: Ceylon, India, Pakistan, 1958; Middle East, 1965; France, 1970; Tunisia, 1972; Hong Kong, NZ, Fiji, 1984; Kyoto, 1986; India, 1988; California, 1989; Visiting appointments: Byron Professor, University of Athens, 1961–63; Alexander White Professor, Chicago, 1965; Hinkley Prof., Johns Hopkins Univ., 1972; Virginia Lectr, Charlottesville, 1979; Berg Prof., New York Univ., 1987. *Publications:* Language and Intelligence, 1951; The Victorian Sage, 1953; (ed) Poems of the Mid-Century, 1957; The Charted Mirror (essays), 1960; (ed) Selections from Shelley, 1960; Shakespeare's Tragedies, 1961; The Colours of Clarity (essays), 1964; The Lion Hunt, 1964; Widening Horizons in English Verse, 1966; A London Childhood, 1966; Blake, The Lyric Poetry, 1968; The Establishment of English, 1972; (ed with J. Black) Later English Broadside Ballads, vol. I, 1975, vol. II, 1979; The Proud Knowledge, 1977; Narrative and Structure, 1979; The Slumber of Apollo, 1983; (ed) The Oxford Book of Local Verses, 1987; *verse:* The Minute, 1956; The Fugue, 1960; The Landfallers, 1962; Wood and Windfall, 1965; New Poems, 1970; Planet of Winds, 1977; Civitatula—Cambridge, the little city, 1994; contributions to journals. *Recreation:* enjoyment. *Address:* Queens' College, Cambridge CB3 9ET.

Died 29 Aug. 1999.

HOLLOWAY, Maj.-Gen. Robin Hugh Ferguson, CB 1976; CBE 1974; *b* Hawera, 22 May 1922; *s* of late Hugh Ferguson Holloway and Phyllis Myrtle Holloway; *m* 1947, Margaret Jewell, *d* of late E. G. Munk, Temple Cloud, Somerset; one *s* two *d*. *Educ:* Hawera Technical High Sch.; RMC, Duntroon, Australia. Commnd NZ Staff Corps, 1942; served in 2nd NZEF, Solomon Is, Italy and Japan, 1943–47; qual. Air Observation Post Pilot, 1948–49; Staff Coll., Camberley, 1952; Jt Services Staff Coll., Latimer, 1958; Dir of Mil. Intelligence, 1959–61; Dep. Adjt Gen., 1962–63; Head, NZ Defence Liaison Staff, Singapore and Malaysia, 1964–65; ACDS, 1967–68; IDC, 1969; Comdr Northern Mil. Dist, and Comdr 1st Inf. Bde Gp, 1970; DCGS, 1971–73; CGS, 1973–76; R of O, 1977; Dir of Civil Defence, NZ, 1977–83. Referee, Small Claims Tribunal: Lower Hutt, 1982–91; Wellington, 1985–91. Pres., Scout Assoc. of NZ, 1979–89; Dep. Chief Scout, 1979–89. *Recreations:* gardening, walking, bowls. *Address:* 435 Te Moana Road, Waikanae, New Zealand. *T:* (4) 2934089. *Club:* Wellington (NZ).

Died 7 June 1998.

HOLMES, John Wentworth, MBE 1983; Chief Agent, Liberal Party, and Deputy Head, Party Headquarters, 1974–86; *b* 14 Jan. 1925; *s* of Arthur and Annie Holmes; *m* 1969, Sonia Pratt; four *d*. *Educ:* Caverswall Church Sch.; Longton Sch. of Commerce; N Staffs Technical Coll. (crash course in war-time). Foxwell Colliery Co., 1941–47, NCB 1947–51; Labour Agent, Rugby and Meriden, 1951–62; Liberal Agent, Leicester, 1963–65; Regional Sec., Liberal Party, Home Counties Region, 1965–74. Member: National Exec., Liberal Party, 1986–88; Council, Liberal Party, 1986–88. Mem., North Staffs District and Midland Area Council, NUM, 1947–50; formerly Mem., Warwickshire CC; Dir, Rugby Co-operative Soc. Ltd and its subsidiary interests, 1952–70 (Pres. and Chm., Bd of Dirs, 1964–70). *Recreations:* gardening, cooking. *Address:* Windles, Sea Road, Winchelsea Beach, Winchelsea, East Sussex TN36 4LB. *T:* (01797) 222068. *Died 17 Oct. 1998.*

HOLMES, Sir Maurice (Andrew), Kt 1969; barrister-at-law; *b* 28 July 1911; *o s* of Rev. A. T. Holmes and Ellen Holmes; *m* 1935, Joyce Esther, *d* of late E. C. Hicks, JP, CC; no *c. Educ:* Felsted Sch., Essex. Served with RASC, 1941–45 (Major, despatches). Called to Bar, Gray's Inn, 1948. Practised at Bar, 1950–55; Director, 1955–60, Chairman, 1960–65, The Tilling Association Ltd; Chairman, London Transport Board, 1965–69; Circuit Administrator, South Eastern Circuit, 1970–74. *Recreations:* golf, music. *Address:* The Limes, Felsted, near Dunmow, Essex CM6 3HB. *T:* (01371) 820352. *Club:* Forty. *Died 21 Dec. 1997.*

HOLT, Christopher Robert Vesey, CVO 1976; VRD 1952; Member of London Stock Exchange, 1938–82; *b* 17 Oct. 1915; *s* of late Vice-Adm. R. V. Holt, CB, DSO, MVO, and Evelyn Constance Holt; *m* 1945, (Margaret) Jane (Venetia), *d* of late Sir Michael Albert James Malcolm, 10th Bt; one *s* one *d. Educ:* Eton. Partner, James Capel & Co., Stockbrokers, 1938, Sen. Partner, 1968–70, Chm. (on firm becoming a company), 1970–75, Dir, 1975–76. Served RNVR, War of 1939–45, mostly in destroyers; retd with rank of Lieut-Comdr, 1957. Mem. Council, King George's Fund for Sailors, 1983–87; Treas., Hants Wildlife Trust, 1984–89. Mem., Armed Forces Art Soc. and other art socs. *Recreations:* painting, wildlife. *Address:* Westbury Manor, West Meon, Petersfield, Hants GU32 1ND. *Clubs:* Boodle's, Lansdowne.

Died 11 Nov. 1997.

HOME, John Gavin M.; *see* Milne Home.

HONIG, His Honour Frederick; a Circuit Judge (formerly a County Court Judge), 1968–86; *b* 22 March 1912; 2nd *s* of late Leopold Honig; *m* 1940, Joan, *o d* of late Arthur Burkart. *Educ:* Berlin Univ.; Heidelberg Univ. (LLD (Hons) 1934) Barrister, Middle Temple, 1937. War service, 1940–47: Capt., JAG's Dept; Judge Advocate in civilian capacity, 1947–48; subseq. practised at Bar. *Publications:* (jtly) Cartel Law of the European Economic Community, 1963; contribs to Internat. Law Reports (ed Lauterpacht) and legal jls, incl. Amer. Jl of Internat. Law, Internat. and Comparative Law Quarterly, Law Jl, Propriété Industrielle, etc. *Recreations:* foreign languages, country walking. *Address:* Lamb Building, Temple, EC4Y 7AS. *T:* (020) 7353 1612. *Died 23 Jan. 2000.*

HOOD, 7th Viscount *cr* 1796, of Whitley, co. Warwick; **Alexander Lambert Hood;** Bt 1778; Baron (Ire.) 1782, (GB) 1795; Chairman, Petrofina (UK) Ltd, 1982–87 (Director, 1958–87); *b* 11 March 1914; *s* of Rear-Adm. Hon. Sir Horace Hood, KCB, DSO, MVO (*d* 1916) (3rd *s* of 4th Viscount) and Ellen Floyd (*d* 1950), *d* of A. E. Touzalin; *S* brother, 1981; *m* 1957, Diana Maud (CVO 1957), *d* of late Hon. G. W. Lyttelton; three *s. Educ:* RN Coll., Dartmouth; Trinity Coll., Cambridge; Harvard Business Sch. RNVR, 1939–45. Director: J. Henry Schroder Wagg & Co., 1957–75; George Wimpey, 1957–90; Tanks Consolidated Investments PLC, 1971–84 (Chm., 1976–83); Benguela Railway Co., 1979–84; Union Minière, 1973–84; Abbott Laboratories Inc., 1971–83; Abbott Laboratories Ltd, 1964–85. Part-time Mem., British Waterways Bd, 1963–73. *Heir: s* Hon. Henry Lyttelton Alexander Hood [*b* 16 March 1958; *m* 1991, Flora, *yr d* of Comdr M. B. Casement; three *s* one *d* (incl. twin *s* and *d*)]. *Address:* 67 Chelsea Square, SW3 6LE. *T:* (020) 7352 4952; Loders Court, Bridport, Dorset DT6 3RZ. *T:* (01308) 422983. *Club:* Brooks's.

Died 2 Oct. 1999.

HOOK, Rt Rev. Ross Sydney, MC 1945; *b* 19 Feb. 1917; *o s* of late Sydney Frank and Laura Harriet Hook; *m* 1948, Ruth Leslie, *d* of late Rev. Herman Masterman Biddell and Violet Marjorie Biddell; one *s* one *d. Educ:* Christ's Hosp.; Peterhouse, Cambridge (MA); Ridley Hall,

Cambridge. Deacon 1941, priest 1942; Asst Curate, Milton, Hants, 1941–43; Chaplain, RNVR (Royal Marine Commandos), 1943–46; Chaplain, Ridley Hall, Cambridge, 1946–48; Rector, Chorlton-cum-Hardy, Manchester, 1948–52; Rector and Rural Dean, Chelsea, 1952–61; Chaplain: Chelsea Hosp. for Women, 1954–61; St Luke's Hosp., Chelsea, 1957–61; Residentiary Canon of Rochester and Precentor, 1961–65; Treasurer, 1965; Diocesan Dir of Post Ordination Training, 1961–65; Bishop Suffragan of Grantham, 1965–72; Prebendary of Brampton (Lincoln Cathedral), 1966–72; Dean of Stamford, 1971–72; Bishop of Bradford, 1972–80; Chief of Staff to Archbishop of Canterbury, 1980–84. Examining Chaplain to Bishop of Rochester, 1961–65, to Bishop of Lincoln, 1966–72. Select Preacher, Univ. of Cambridge, 1948. Chm., Inspections Cttee, Central Advisory Council for the Ministry, 1966–71 (Sec., 1960–66). Hon. DLitt Bradford, 1981. *Recreation:* cricket. *Address:* 23A White Cliff Mill Street, Blandford, Dorset DT11 7BQ.
Died 26 June 1996.

HOOLE, Alan Norman, CMG 1997; OBE 1991; Consultant on UK Overseas Territories, since 1998; *b* 25 April 1942; *s* of Walter Norman and Elsie Hoole; *m* 1st, 1962, Pauline Claire Bettison (marr. diss.); one *s* one *d*; 2nd, 1982, Delia Rose Clingham. *Educ:* Chesterfield Grammar Sch.; Lady Manners Grammar Sch., Bakewell; Sheffield Univ.; Coll. of Law, London. Admitted as Solicitor, 1964 (S. H. Clay Prize, Law. Soc., 1963). Partner, Blakesley & Rooth, Solicitors, Chesterfield, 1965–78; Attorney General: St Helena, 1978–83; Anguilla, 1983–85; Chief Sec., Turks and Caicos Is, 1986–88; Attorney Gen., Anguilla, 1989–90; Dep. Gov., Anguilla, 1990–91; Gov. and C-in-C, St Helena and its Dependencies, 1991–95; Gov., Anguilla, 1995–97. *Recreations:* fishing, tennis. *Address:* 79 Postern Close, York YO23 1JF. *Club:* Royal Commonwealth Society.
Died 8 May 2000.

HOOLE, Sir Arthur (Hugh), Kt 1985; Consultant, Tuck & Mann, Epsom, since 1989 (Partner, 1951–88); *b* 14 Jan. 1924; *s* of Hugh Francis and Gladys Emily Hoole; *m* 1945, Eleanor Mary Hobbs; two *s* two *d*. *Educ:* Sutton County School; Emmanuel College, Cambridge (MA, LLM). Served RAFVR, 1943–46. Admitted solicitor, 1951. Mem. Council, Law Society, 1969–87 (Vice-Pres., 1983–84; Pres., 1984–85); Governor, College of Law, 1976–93 (Chm., 1983–90); Member: Adv. Cttee on Legal Educn, 1977–90; Common Professional Examination Bd, 1977–81 (Chm., 1978–81); Criminal Injuries Compensation Bd, 1985–. Governor: St John's Sch., Leatherhead, 1987–94; Sutton GS for Boys (formerly Sutton Manor High Sch.), 1987–. *Recreations:* cricket, books, music. *Address:* Yew Tree House, St Nicholas Hill, Leatherhead, Surrey KT22 8NE. *T:* (01372) 373208. *Club:* Royal Automobile.
Died 17 March 1998.

HOOVER, Herbert William, Jr; President, 1954–66, and Chairman of the Board, 1959–66, The Hoover Company, North Canton, Ohio; *b* 23 April 1918; *s* of late Herbert William Hoover and Grace Hoover (*née* Steele); *m* 1941, Carl Maitland Good; one *s* one *d. Educ:* Choate Sch., Wallingford, Conn; Rollins Coll. (AB). Served in US Army, 1943–45. Offices held with Hoover Co.: Exec. Sales, 1941; Dir Public Relations, 1945; Asst Vice-Pres., 1948; Vice-Pres. Field Sales, 1952; Exec. Vice-Pres., 1953; The Hoover Co. Ltd, Canada: Pres., 1954; Dir, 1952; Hoover Ltd, England: Dir, 1954; Chm., 1956; Hoover Inc., Panama: Dir and Pres., 1955; Hoover (America Latina) SA, Panama: Dir and Pres., 1955; Hoover Mexicana, Mexico: Dir and Pres., 1955; Hoover Industrial y Comercial SA, Colombia: Dir and Pres., 1960; Hoover Worldwide Corp., NY City: Pres. and Chm., 1960; S. A. Hoover, France: Dir, 1965. Past Regional Vice-Chm., US Cttee for the UN. Dir, Miami Heart Inst.; Mem.,

Bd of Trustees, Univ. of Miami. Hon. LLD Mount Union Coll., 1959. Chevalier Légion d'Honneur, France, 1965. *Address:* 20 Indian Creek Island, Surfside, FL 33154–2904, USA.
Died 19 May 1997.

HOPE, Sir (Charles) Peter, KCMG 1972 (CMG 1956); TD 1945; HM Diplomatic Service, retired; Ambassador to Mexico, 1968–72; *b* 29 May 1912; *s* of G. L. N. Hope and H. M. V. Riddell, Weetwood, Mayfield, Sussex; *m* 1936, H. M. Turner, *d* of late G. L. Turner, company director; two *s* (and one *s* decd). *Educ:* Oratory Sch., Reading; London and Cambridge Univs. BSc (Hons); ACGI. Asst, War Office, 1938; RA, TA, 1939; served until 1946 (TD); transferred to Foreign Office and posted HM Embassy, Paris, as Temp. First Sec., 1946; transferred to United Nations Dept, Foreign Office, 1950; to HM Embassy, Bonn, as Counsellor, 1953; Foreign Office Spokesman (Head of News Dept, Foreign Office), 1956–59; Minister, HM Embassy, Madrid, 1959–62; Consul-General, Houston, USA, 1963–64; Minister and Alternate UK Rep. to UN, 1965–68. Mem., Acad. of International Law. Pres., British Assoc. of Sovereign Military Order of Malta, 1983–89; KStJ 1984. Grand Cross: Order of the Aztec Eagle (Mexico), 1972; Order of St George and St Constantine (Greece), 1981; Order of Malta, 1984; Grand Officer, Order of Merito Militense, 1975. *Recreations:* shooting, fishing. *Address:* Guillard's Oak House, Midhurst, W Sussex GU29 9JZ. *Club:* White's.
Died 12 March 1999.

HOPE, Laurence Frank, OBE 1968; HM Diplomatic Service, retired; HM Consul General, Seattle, 1975–76; *b* 18 May 1918; *y s* of late Samuel Vaughan Trevylian Hope and Ellen Edith Hope (*née* Cooler); *m* 1940, Doris Phyllis Rosa Hulbert; one *s* one *d. Educ:* County GS, Lewes. Served War, 1939–46: reached rank of Major, in British Army (12th (2nd City of London Regt) Royal Fusiliers, TA and York and Lancaster Regt); Indian Army (7th Rajput Regt); Mil. Govt of Germany (Economic Div.). Bd of Trade, London, 1946–47; Asst Brit. Trade Comr, Pretoria, 1947–51; Cape Town, 1951–53; Bd of Trade, London, 1953–56; British Trade Comr, Sydney, 1956–60; Canberra, 1960–61; Lahore, 1961–63; Singapore, 1964; transferred to HM Diplomatic Service; Head of Commercial Section, High Commn, Singapore, 1965–68; Counsellor (Economic and Commercial), Lagos, 1969–72; HM Consul-Gen., Gothenburg, 1972–75. *Recreations:* oil painting, reading. *Address:* 22 Cranford Avenue, Exmouth, Devon EX8 2HU.
Died 28 April 1997.

HOPE, Sir Peter; *see* Hope, Sir C. P.

HOPE-JONES, Ronald Christopher, CMG 1969; HM Diplomatic Service, retired; *b* 5 July 1920; *s* of William Hope-Jones and Winifred Coggin; *m* 1944, Pamela Hawker; two *s* one *d. Educ:* Eton (scholar); King's Coll., Cambridge (scholar). Served with HM Forces, 1940–45. 3rd Sec., Foreign Office, 1946, Paris, 1947; 2nd Sec., Beirut, 1949; 1st Sec., FO, 1952; Head of Chancery and Consul, Quito, 1955; Commercial Sec., Budapest, 1959; Head of Chancery, 1960; FO, 1961, Counsellor, 1963; UK Rep. to Internat. Atomic Energy Agency, Vienna, 1964–67; FCO, 1967; Head of Disarmament Dept, 1967–70; Head of N African Dept, 1970–71; Counsellor, Brasilia, 1972–73; Ambassador in La Paz, 1973–77. *Address:* Wellfield House, Mill Lane, Headley, Bordon, Hants GU35 0PD. *T:* (01420) 472793.
Died 18 Feb. 2000.

HOPKIN, Sir David (Armand), Kt 1987; Chief Metropolitan Stipendiary Magistrate, 1982–92; *b* 10 Jan. 1922; *s* of Daniel and Edmée Hopkin; *m* 1948, Doris Evelyn (*née* Whitaker); one *s* three *d. Educ:* St Paul's Sch., W Kensington; University Coll., Aberystwyth; Corpus Christi Coll., Cambridge (BA). Called to the Bar,

Gray's Inn, 1949. Served in Army, 1942–47, Hon. Major, 1947. Member of Staff of Director of Public Prosecutions, 1950–70; Metropolitan Stipendiary Magistrate, 1970–92. Pres., British Boxing Board of Control, 1991– (Chm., 1983–96). *Recreations:* fencing, tennis. *Address:* 8 Crane Grove, N7 8LE. *T:* (0171) 607 0349.
Died 21 Aug. 1997.

HOPKINS, Dr Anthony Philip, MD; FRCP, FFPHM, FACP; Director, Research Unit, Royal College of Physicians, since 1988; Consultant Neurologist, St Bartholomew's Hospital, since 1972; *b* 15 Oct. 1937; *s* of Gerald Hopkins and Barbara Isobel Hopkins; *m* 1965, Elizabeth Ann Wood; three *s. Educ:* Sherborne Sch.; Guy's Hospital Med. Sch. MD London. FRCP 1976; FACP 1991; FFPHM 1991. Postgraduate work: Hammersmith and National Hosps, 1961–69; Salpêtrière Hosp., Paris, 1962–63; Mayo Clinic, Rochester, Minn, 1970. St Bartholomew's Hospital: Cons. Neurologist, 1972–76; Physician-in-charge, Dept of Neurological Scis, 1976–88. Res. into experimental pathology, headache, epilepsy, and into the evaluation of the effectiveness and quality of med. care. *Publications:* Epilepsy, 1987, 2nd edn 1995; Measuring the quality of medical care, 1990; Clinical Neurology: a modern approach, 1993; contribs to sci. and med. literature. *Recreations:* walking, sailing, dining. *Address:* Research Unit, Royal College of Physicians, 11 St Andrews Place, NW1 4LE; 149 Harley Street, W1N 2DE. *T:* (0171) 935 4444. *Club:* Garrick.
Died 6 March 1997.

HOPKINS, John Richard; writer; *b* 27 Jan. 1931; *m* 1st, Prudence Knight (marr. diss.); one *d* (one *s* decd); 2nd, Shirley Knight; one *d*, and one step *d. Plays:* This Story of Yours, Royal Court, 1968; Long Wharf Theatre, 1981, Hampstead Theatre, 1987; Find Your Way Home, Open Space, 1970, NY, 1974; Economic Necessity, Haymarket Theatre, Leicester, 1973; Next of Kin, Nat. Theatre, 1974; Losing Time, Manhattan Theatre Club, 1979, Deutsches Schauspielhaus, 1984; Valedictorian, Williston-Northampton Sch., 1982; Absent Forever, Great Lakes Theatre Festival, 1987; *TV* includes: That Quiet Earth; Walk into the Dark; Some Distant Shadow; The Greeks and their Gifts, 1966; Talking to a Stranger (quartet), 1968; A Story to Frighten the Children, 1976; Fathers and Families (sextet), 1977; Codename Kyril, 1987; (with John Le Carré) Smiley's People (series), 1982; Hiroshima, 1995 (Humanitas Prize, Penn Literary Prize); scripts for Z-Cars (series); adaptations of classic novels; *film scripts:* The Offence, 1973; Murder by Decree, 1979; The Holcroft Covenant, 1985. *Publications:* Talking to a Stranger: four television plays, 1969; This Story of Yours, 1969; Find Your Way Home, 1971; Losing Time, 1982.
Died 23 July 1998.

HOPPER, Prof. Frederick Ernest, FDSRCS, FFDRCSI; Professor of Dental Surgery and Dean of the School of Dentistry, University of Leeds, 1959–85, then Professor Emeritus; Consultant Dental Surgeon, Leeds Area Health Authority, 1959–85; Chairman, Board of Faculty of Medicine, University of Leeds, 1975–78; *b* 22 Nov. 1919; *s* of Frederick Ernest Hopper, MPS and Margaret Ann Carlyle; *m* 1949, Gudrun Eik-Nes, LDSRCS, *d* of Prost Knut Eik-Nes and Nina Eik-Nes, Trondheim, Norway; three *s. Educ:* Dame Allan's Sch., Newcastle upon Tyne; King's Coll., University of Durham. BDS (with dist.) 1943; FDSRCS 1948; MDS 1958. House Surg., Newcastle upon Tyne Dental Hosp. and Royal Dental Hospital, 1943–44; served in EMS in Maxillo-Facial Centres at E Grinstead and Shotley Bridge, 1944–46; successively Lecturer, 1946, and Sen. Lecturer, 1956, in Periodontal Diseases, King's Coll., University of Durham, Lecturer in Dental Pharmacology and Therapeutics, 1947–59; Dental Surgeon in charge Parodontal Dept, Newcastle upon Tyne

Dental Hosp., and Sen. Dental Surg., Plastic and Jaw Unit, Shotley Bridge, 1946–59; Cons. Dent. Surg., United Newcastle Hosps, 1955–59. Examiner in Dental subjects, Univs of Durham, Edinburgh, St Andrews, Bristol, Liverpool. Hon. Treas., Brit. Soc. of Periodontology, 1949–53, Pres. 1954. Pres., British Soc. for Oral Medicine, 1986. Member: General Dental Council, 1959–85 (Chm., Educn Cttee, 1980–85); Brit. Dental Assoc., 1943–; Internat. Dental Fedn, 1948–. GDC Visitor, 1986–87, to Medical Univ. of Southern Africa and to Univs of Pretoria, Stellenbosch, Western Cape, the Witwatersrand, Otago, Hong Kong and Singapore. *Publications:* contribs to med. and dental jls. *Recreations:* photography (still and ciné), golf. *Address:* 23 Ancaster Road, Leeds LS16 5HH. *Club:* Alwoodley Golf (Leeds).
Died 5 Dec. 1997.

HORAN, Rt Rev. Forbes Trevor; Bishop Suffragan of Tewkesbury, 1960–73; *b* 22 May 1905; *s* of Rev. Frederick Seymour Horan and Mary Katherine Horan; *m* 1st, 1939, Veronica (*d* 1983), *d* of Rt Rev. J. N. Bateman-Champain, sometime Bishop of Knaresborough; two *s* two *d*; 2nd, 1988, Elizabeth Lyona Lancaster, Cheltenham. *Educ:* Sherborne; Trinity Hall, Cambridge. RMC Sandhurst, 1924–25; Oxford and Bucks Lt Infantry, Lieutenant, 1925–29; Trinity Hall, Cambridge, 1929–32; Westcott House, Cambridge, 1932–33; ordained deacon 1933, priest 1934; Curate, St Luke's, Newcastle upon Tyne, 1933–35; Curate, St George's, Jesmond, Newcastle upon Tyne, 1935–37; Priest-in-charge, St Peter's, Balkwell, 1937–40; RNVR, 1940–45; Vicar of St Chad's, Shrewsbury, 1945–52; Vicar of Huddersfield Parish Church, 1952–60. *Recreations:* listening to the Third Programme on the radio, bicycling in order to maintain some semblance of independence, cooking, housekeeping. *Address:* 3 Silverthorn Close, Shurdington Road, Cheltenham, Glos GL53 0JL. *T:* Cheltenham (01242) 527313.
Died 11 May 1996.

HORDER, 2nd Baron *cr* 1933, of Ashford in the County of Southampton; **Thomas Mervyn Horder;** Bt 1923; *b* 8 Dec. 1910; *s* of 1st Baron Horder, GCVO, MD, FRCP, and Geraldine Rose (*d* 1954), *o d* of Arthur Doggett, Newnham Manor, Herts; *S* father, 1955; *m* 1946, Mary Ross (marr. diss. 1957), *d* of Dr W. S. McDougall, Wallington, Surrey. *Educ:* Winchester; Trinity Coll., Cambridge. BA 1932; MA 1937. Served War of 1939–45: HQ, RAF Fighter Comd, 1940–42 (despatches); Air HQ, India, 1942–44; Headquarters, South-East Asia Command, 1944–45; United Kingdom Liaison Mission, Tokyo, 1945–46. Chairman, Gerald Duckworth & Co. Ltd, 1948–70. *Publications:* The Little Genius, 1966; (ed) Ronald Firbank: memoirs and critiques, 1977; On Their Own: shipwrecks & survivals, 1988; *music:* (ed) The Orange Carol Book, 1962; Six Betjeman Songs, 1967; A Shropshire Lad (songs), 1980; (ed) The Easter Carol Book, 1982; Seven Shakespeare Songs, 1988; Black Diamonds (six Dorothy Parker songs), 1990; Five Burns Songs, 1996; Dorset Delight, 1996; Five Causley Sea Songs, 1997; Four Causley Songs, 1997. *Recreations:* music, idling. *Heir:* none. *Address:* 4 Hamilton Close, NW8 8QY.
Died 30 June 1997 (ext).

HORNE, Prof. Michael Rex, OBE 1981; PhD, ScD; FRS 1981; FREng, FICE, FIStructE; Professor of Civil Engineering, University of Manchester, 1960–83 (Beyer Professor, 1978–83); *b* 29 Dec. 1921; *s* of late Rev. Ernest Horne, Leicester; *m* 1947, Molly, *d* of late Mark Hewett, Royston, Herts; two *s* two *d. Educ:* Boston (Lincs) Grammar Sch.; Leeds Grammar Sch.; St John's Coll., Cambridge (MA 1945; PhD 1950; ScD 1956); MSc Manchester. John Winbolt Prize for Research, Cambridge Univ., 1944. Asst Engineer, River Great Ouse Catchment Bd, 1941–45; Scientific Officer, British Welding Research Assoc., 1945–51; Asst Dir of Research in Engineering,

1951–56, Lectr in Engineering, 1957–60, Fellow of St John's Coll., 1957–60, Univ. of Cambridge. Royal Soc. Vis. Prof., Univ. of Hong Kong, 1986. Chm., NW Branch, 1969–70, Pres., 1980–81, IStructE; Pres., Section G, BAAS, 1981–82; Mem., Merrison Cttee on Box Girders, 1970–73; Chm., Review for Govt of Public Utility Streetworks Act, 1984. Hon. DSc Salford, 1981. Diploma, 1971, Bronze Medal, 1973, Gold Medal, 1986, IStructE; Telford Premiums, 1956, 1966, 1978, Baker Medal, 1977, ICE. *Publications:* (with J. F. Baker and J. Heyman) The Steel Skeleton, 1956; (with W. F. Merchant) The Stability of Frames, 1965; The Plastic Theory of Structures, 1971; (with L. J. Morris) Plastic Design of Low Rise Frames, 1981; contribs on structures, strength of materials and particulate theory of soils to learned journals. *Recreations:* theatre-going, watching and understanding people. *Address:* 19 Park Road, Hale, Altrincham, Cheshire WA15 9NW. *Died 6 Jan. 2000.*

HORNER, Arthur William, CMG 1964; TD and clasp 1946; *b* 22 June 1909; *s* of Francis Moore and Edith Horner; *m* 1938, Patricia Denise (*née* Campbell) (*d* 1996); two *s* one *d. Educ:* Hardenwick; Felsted. Marine insurance, 1926–39; served War, 1939–46, Rifle Brigade; Lt-Col; psc; farming in Kenya, 1948–50; Colonial Administrative Service (later HM Overseas Civil Service), Kenya, 1950–64; Commissioner of Lands, 1955–61; Permanent Sec., 1961–64; Dir of Independence Celebrations, 1963; Principal, ODM, 1964–73; seconded Diplomatic Service, 1968–70; retired 1973. *Address:* Oquassa, Western Road, Hawkhurst, Cranbrook, Kent TN18 4BW. *T:* (01580) 754997. *Died 24 Oct. 1999.*

HORNER, John; *b* 5 Nov. 1911; *s* of Ernest Charles and Emily Horner; *m* 1936, Patricia (*d* 1994), *d* of Geoffrey and Alice Palmer; two *d. Educ:* elementary sch. and Sir George Monoux Grammar Sch., Walthamstow. Apprenticed Merchant Navy, 1927; Second Mate's Certificate, 1932. Joined London Fire Brigade, 1933; Gen. Sec. Fire Brigades Union, 1939–64; MP (Lab) Oldbury and Halesowen, 1964–70. Mem. Select Cttee on Nationalised Industries. *Publication:* Studies in Industrial Democracy, 1974. *Recreations:* gardening, reading history. *Address:* c/o Barclays Bank, Ross-on-Wye, Herefordshire. *Died 11 Feb. 1997.*

HORSEFIELD, John Keith, CB 1957; Historian, International Monetary Fund, 1966–69; *b* 14 Oct. 1901; *s* of Rev. Canon F. J. Horsefield, Bristol; *m* 1934, Lucy G. G. Florance. *Educ:* Monkton Combe Sch.; University of Bristol (MA 1948); London Sch. of Economics. Lecturer, LSE, 1939; Min. of Aircraft Production, 1940; International Monetary Fund, 1947; Under-Sec., Min. of Supply, 1951; Dep. Asst Sec.-Gen. for Economics and Finance, NATO, 1952; Supply and Development Officer, Iron and Steel Bd, 1954; Dir of Finance and Accounts, Gen. Post Office, 1955–60; Chief Editor, International Monetary Fund, 1960–66. Hon. Treas., Carisbrooke Castle Museum, 1971–92. Hon. DSc Bristol. *Publications:* The Real Cost of the War, 1940; British Monetary Experiments, 1650–1710, 1960; The International Monetary Fund, 1945–1965, 1970; articles in Economica, etc. *Address:* 60 Clatterford Road, Carisbrooke, Newport, Isle of Wight PO30 1PA. *T:* (01983) 523675.

Died 25 March 1997.

HORSFORD, Alan Arthur; Group Chief Executive, Royal Insurance plc, 1985–89; *b* 31 May 1927; *s* of Arthur Henry Horsford and Winifred Horsford; *m* 1957, Enid Maureen Baker; one *s* one *d. Educ:* Holt School; Liverpool University (BA). FCII. Secretary, Royal Insurance Co. Ltd, 1970–72; Dep. General Manager, 1972–74, General Manager, 1974–79, Royal Insurance Canada; General Manager and Director, 1979–83, Dep. Chief Gen. Manager, 1983–84, Royal Insurance plc. Dep. Chm.,

Assoc. of British Insurers, 1985–88. *Recreations:* theatre, music, cycling, golf. *Address:* 17 Darnhills, Watford Road, Radlett, Herts WD7 8LQ. *Died 28 Nov. 1999.*

HORWOOD, Hon. Owen Pieter Faure, DMS; President, Council of Governors, Development Bank of Southern Africa, 1983–93; Chancellor, University of Durban-Westville, 1973–88; *b* 6 Dec. 1916; *e s* of late Stanley Ebden Horwood and Anna Johanna Horwood (*née* Faure); *m* 1946, Helen Mary Watt; one *s* one *d. Educ:* Boys' High Sch., Paarl, CP; University of Cape Town (BCom). South African Air Force, 1940–42. Associate Prof. of Commerce, University of Cape Town, 1954–55; Prof. of Economics, University Coll. of Rhodesia and Nyasaland, 1956–57; Univ. of Natal: William Hudson Prof. of Economics, 1957–65; Dir of University's Natal Regional Survey; Principal and Vice-Chancellor, 1966–70. Mem., 1970–80, Leader, 1978–80, South African Senate; Minister of Indian Affairs and Tourism, 1972–74; Minister of Economic Affairs, 1974–75; Minister of Finance, 1975–84. Financial Adviser to Govt of Lesotho, 1966–72. Past Chairman: Nedbank Gp; Cape Wine and Distillers Ltd; Nedbank Ltd; Finansbank Ltd; UAL Merchant Bank Ltd; Past Director: South African Mutual Life Assurance Soc.; Rembrandt Group; South African Permanent Building Soc.; Macsteel Group; TNT Express International; Dir, Bank of Taiwan (SA) Ltd. Patron, S Africa Sports Assoc. for Physically Disabled. Vis. Prof., Duke Univ., USA, 1960–61. Hon. DCom: Port Elizabeth, 1980; Stellenbosch, 1983; Hon. Scriptural degree, Israel Torah Res. Inst. and Adelphi Univ., 1980; Hon. DEcon Rand Afrikaans, 1981. Order of the Brilliant Star (Republic of China), 1982. *Publications:* (jtly) Economic Systems of the Commonwealth, 1962; contribs to SA Jl of Economics, SA Bankers' Jl, Economica (London), Optima, etc. *Recreations:* cricket, gardening, sailing. *Address:* 19 Paradyskloof Villas, Stellenbosch, 7600, South Africa. *Clubs:* Durban (Durban); Pretoria Country; Western Province Cricket; Cape Town Cricket (Captain, 1943–48). *Died 13 Sept. 1998.*

HOSIER, John, CBE 1984; Director and Member of Council, Hong Kong Academy for Performing Arts, 1989–93 (Fellow, 1993); *b* 18 Nov. 1928; *s* of Harry J. W. Hosier and Constance (*née* Richmond); *m* Biddy Baxter, BBC producer. *Educ:* Preston Manor Sch.; St John's Coll., Cambridge (MA 1954). Taught in Ankara, Turkey, 1951–53; Music Producer, BBC Radio for schools, 1953–59; seconded to ABC, Sydney, to advise on educational music programmes, 1959–60; Music Producer, subseq. Sen. and Exec. Producer, BBC TV, pioneering first regular music broadcasts to schools, 1960–73; ILEA Staff Inspector for music, and Dir of Centre for Young Musicians, 1973–76; Principal, Guildhall Sch. of Music and Drama, 1978–89. Vice-Chm., Kent Opera, 1985–87; Founder Mem. and Vice-Chm., UK Council for Music Educn and Training, 1975–81; Dir, Early Music Centre, 1994–; Chairman: Music Panel, Caird Scholarship Trust, 1995–; Performing Arts Panel, HEFCE, 1998–; Member: Gulbenkian Enquiry into training musicians, 1978; Music Panel, British Council, 1984–88; Music Panel, GLAA, 1984–86; Council of Management, Royal Philharmonic Soc., 1982–89; Cttee, Hong Kong Philharmonic Orch., 1990–93; Conservatoires Adv. Gp, HEFCE, 1993–97; Board, Trinity Coll. of Music, 1993–97; Governing Body, Chetham's Sch., 1983–88; Pres., ISM, 1998–99. Trustee, Kathleen Ferrier Meml Scholarship Fund, 1994–. FRSA 1976; FGSM 1978; Hon. RAM 1980; FRCM 1981; FRNCM 1985; Hon. FTCL 1986. Mem. Court, Musicians' Co., 1993–. Hon. DMus City, 1986. *Compositions:* music for: Cambridge revivals of Parnassus, 1949, and Humorous Lovers, 1951; Something's Burning, Mermaid, 1974; many radio and TV productions. *Publications:* The Orchestra, 1961, rev. edn 1977; various books, songs and arrangements for children; contribs on music to educnl jls.

Address: 5 Royal Crescent, Brighton BN2 1AL. *Clubs:* City Livery; Hong Kong. *Died 28 March 2000.*

HOUGH, Richard Alexander; writer; *b* 15 May 1922; *s* of late George and Margaret May Hough; *m* 1st, 1943, Helen Charlotte (marr. diss.), *o d* of Dr Henry Woodyatt; four *d*; 2nd, 1980, Judy Taylor, writer and publisher. *Educ:* Frensham Heights. Served War, RAF Pilot, Fighter Command, home and overseas, 1941–46. Publisher, 1947–70: Bodley Head until 1955; Hamish Hamilton as Dir and Man. Dir, Hamish Hamilton Children's Books Ltd, 1955–70. Contributed to: Guardian; Observer; Washington Post; NY Times; Encounter; History Today; New Yorker. Mem. Council, 1970–73, 1975–84, Vice-Pres., 1977–82, Navy Records Society. Chm., Auxiliary Hospitals Cttee, King Edward's Hospital Fund, 1975–80 (Mem. Council, 1975–86). *Publications:* The Fleet that had to Die, 1958; Admirals in Collision, 1959; The Potemkin Mutiny, 1960; The Hunting of Force Z, 1963; Dreadnought, 1964; The Big Battleship, 1966; First Sea Lord: an authorised life of Admiral Lord Fisher, 1969; The Pursuit of Admiral von Spee, 1969; The Blind Horn's Hate, 1971; Captain Bligh and Mr Christian, 1972 (Daily Express Best Book of the Sea Award) (filmed as The Bounty, 1984); Louis and Victoria: the first Mountbattens, 1974; One Boy's War: per astra ad ardua, 1975; (ed) Advice to a Grand-daughter (Queen Victoria's letters), 1975; The Great Admirals, 1977; The Murder of Captain James Cook, 1979; Man o' War, 1979; Nelson, 1980; Mountbatten: Hero of Our Time, 1980; Edwina: Countess Mountbatten of Burma, 1983; The Great War at Sea 1914–1918, 1983; Former Naval Person: Churchill and the Wars at Sea, 1985; The Longest Battle, 1986; The Ace of Clubs: a history of the Garrick, 1986; Born Royal, 1988; (with Denis Richards) The Battle of Britain: the jubilee history, 1989; Winston and Clementine: the triumph of the Churchills, 1990; Bless our Ship: Mountbatten and HMS Kelly, 1991; Other Days Around Me: a memoir, 1992; Edward & Alexandra: their private and public lives, 1992; Captain James Cook: a biography, 1994; Victoria and Albert, 1996; Sister Agnes: the history of King Edward VII's Hospital, 1998; Naval Battles of the Twentieth Century, 1999; *novels:* Angels One Five, 1978; The Fight of the Few, 1979; The Fight to the Finish, 1979; Buller's Guns, 1981; Razor Eyes, 1981; Buller's Dreadnought, 1982; Buller's Victory, 1984; The Raging Sky, 1989; numerous books on motoring history; also books for children under *pseudonym* Bruce Carter. *Address:* 31 Meadowbank, Primrose Hill, NW3 3AY. *T:* (020) 7722 5663, *Fax:* (020) 7722 7750. *Clubs:* Garrick, MCC. *Died 7 Oct. 1999.*

HOUGHTON OF SOWERBY, Baron *cr* 1974 (Life Peer), of Sowerby, W Yorks; **Arthur Leslie Noel Douglas Houghton,** CH 1967; PC 1964; *b* 11 Aug. 1898; *s* of John and Martha Houghton, Long Eaton, Derbyshire; *m* 1939, Vera Travis (CBE 1986); no *c.* Civil Service Rifles, 1916–19; 1st 60th Rifles, 1919–20. Inland Revenue, 1915–22; Sec., Inland Revenue Staff Fedn, 1922–60. Mem. Gen. Council, TUC, 1952–60; Chm., Staff Side, Civil Service National Whitley Council, 1956–58. Broadcaster in "Can I Help You?" Programme, BBC, 1941–64. Alderman LCC, 1947–49. MP (Lab) Sowerby, WR Yorks, March 1949–Feb. 1974; Chm. Public Accounts Cttee, 1963–64; Chancellor of the Duchy of Lancaster, 1964–66; Minister Without Portfolio, 1966–67. Chm., Parly Lab. Party, 1967–70, Nov. 1970–1974. Chairman: British Parly Gp, Population and Develt, 1978–84; House of Lords Industry Study Gp, 1979–87. Member: Commn on the Constitution, 1969–73; Royal Commn on Standards of Conduct in Public Life, 1974–75. Chairman: Commonwealth Scholarships Commn, 1967–68; Young Volunteer Force Foundation, 1967–70 (Jt Vice-Chm. 1970–71); Teachers' Pay Inquiry, 1974; Cttee on aid to Political Parties, 1975–76; Cttee on Security of Cabinet Papers, 1976; Cttee for Reform of Animal Experimentation, 1977; Vice-Pres., RSPCA, 1978–82. *Publication:* Paying for the Social Services, 2nd edn 1968. *Address:* 110 Marsham Court, SW1P 4LA. *T:* 0171–834 0602; Becks Cottage, Whitehill Lane, Bletchingley, Surrey RH1 4QS. *T:* Godstone (01883) 743340. *Club:* Reform. *Died 2 May 1996.*

HOUGHTON, Rt Rev. Michael Alan; Bishop Suffragan of Ebbsfleet, since 1998; Episcopal Visitor for the Province of Canterbury, since 1998; Assistant Bishop in Bath and Wells, since 1999; *b* 14 June 1949; *s* of Edwin Wilfred Houghton and Esther Houghton; *m* 1970, Diana Knights; one *s* one *d. Educ:* Univ. of Lancaster (BA History); Univ. of Durham (PGCE 1971); Chichester Theol Coll. (BTh Soton 1983). British Railways, 1971–73; schoolteacher, Hayward Lever Sch., Bolton, and Royal Sch., Wolverhampton, 1973–74; Schoolteacher Missionary, St Agnes, Teyateyaneng, Lesotho, 1975–77; ordained deacon, 1980, priest, 1981; Asst Curate, All Hallows, Wellingborough, 1980–84; Parish Priest, Jamestown, St Helena, 1984–89; Tutor, Coll. of the Ascension, Birmingham, 1990; Vicar, St Peter, Folkestone, 1990–98. *Publications:* SSM at TY: a history of the Society of the Sacred Mission at St Agnes, Teyateyaneng, 1976; The Indian Christians of St Thomas, 1996; contrib. to New Directions, and Faith. *Recreations:* running, cricket, bellringing, cycling, walking, railways, psephology. *Address:* 8 Goldney Avenue, Clifton, Bristol BS8 4RA. *T:* (0117) 973 1752, *Fax:* (0117) 973 1762. *Club:* Executive (Royal Naval Assoc., Folkestone). *Died 18 Dec. 1999.*

HOUSEMAN, Alexander Randolph, CBE 1984; FEng 1980; FIMechE, FIEE; Deputy Chairman, British Rail Engineering Ltd, since 1985 (Director, since 1979), *b* 9 May 1920; *e s* of Captain Alexander William Houseman and Elizabeth Maud (*née* Randolph); *m* 1942, Betty Edith Norrington; one *d. Educ:* Stockport Grammar School and College. FIMC, CIMgt. Apprenticed Crossley Motors, 1936–40; Production Engineer: Ford Motor Co. (Aero Engines) Ltd, 1940–43; Saunders-Roe Ltd, 1943–48, General Works Manager, 1948–54; Consultant, Director, Man. Dir and Dep. Chm., P-E International Ltd, 1954–81; Dir, P-E Consulting Gp Ltd, 1968–85; Chm., W. Canning Ltd, 1975–80; Dir, Record Ridgway Ltd, 1978–81. Chm., NEDO EDC for Gauge and Tool Industry, 1979–85; Institution of Production Engineers: Chm., Technical Policy Bd, 1978–82; Vice-Pres., 1982–83; Pres., 1983–84. Member: Industrial Adv. Panels of Fellowship of Engineering, 1980–82; Council, Inst. of Management Consultants, 1984–85; Inst. of Directors; Life Member: Soc. of Manufg Engrs, USA, 1985; Inst. of Industrial Engrs, USA, 1985. Distinguished Engrg Management Award, Nat. Soc. of Professional Engrs, USA, 1983; Distinguished Achievements Award, LA Council of Engrs and Scientists, 1984; Nuffield Award, 1984. *Publications:* articles to learned jls and technical and management press on manufacturing technology and management. *Recreations:* DIY, sailing, photography, walking. *Address:* 11 Kings Avenue, Ealing, W5 2SJ. *T:* (0181) 997 3936. *Clubs:* Caledonian; Royal Anglesey Yacht (Beaumaris). *Died 23 Feb. 1997.*

HOVELL-THURLOW-CUMMING-BRUCE, Rt Hon. Sir (James) Roualeyn; *see* Cumming-Bruce.

HOWARD DE WALDEN, 9th Baron *cr* 1597, **AND SEAFORD,** 5th Baron *cr* 1826; **John Osmael Scott-Ellis,** TD; *b* 27 Nov. 1912; *s* of 8th Baron and Margherita (CBE 1920) (*d* 1974), *d* of late Charles van Raalte, Brownsea Island, Dorset; *S* father, 1946; *m* 1st, 1934, Countess Irene Harrach (*d* 1975), *y d* of Count Hans Albrecht Harrach; four *d*; 2nd, 1978, Gillian Viscountess

Mountgarret. *Educ:* Eton; Magdalene Coll., Cambridge (BA 1934, MA). Member of the Jockey Club (Senior Steward, 1957, 1964, 1976). *Heir:* (to Barony of Howard de Walden) four co-heiresses; (to Barony of Seaford) *cousin* Colin Humphrey Felton Ellis [*b* 19 April 1946; *m* 1971, Susan Magill; two *s* two *d*]. *Address:* Avington Manor, Hungerford, Berks RG17 0UL. *T:* (01488) 658229; Flat K, 90 Eaton Square, SW1W 9AG. *T:* (020) 7235 7127. *Clubs:* Turf, White's.   *Died 9 July 1999.*

HOWARD OF PENRITH, 2nd Baron *cr* 1930, of Gowbarrow, co. Cumberland; **Francis Philip Howard;** DL; Captain, late Royal Artillery; *b* 5 Oct. 1905; *s* of 1st Baron Howard of Penrith and Lady Isabella Giustiniani-Bandini (*d* 1963), *d* of Prince Giustiniani-Bandini, 8th Earl of Newburgh; *S* father, 1939; *m* 1944, Anne, *d* of John Beaumont Hotham and *widow* of Anthony Bazley; four *s. Educ:* Downside; Trinity Coll., Cambridge (BA); Harvard Univ. Called to the Bar, Middle Temple, 1931. Served in War, 1939–42 (wounded). DL County of Glos, 1960. *Heir: s* Hon. Philip Esme Howard [*b* 1 May 1945; *m* 1969, Sarah, *d* of late Barclay Walker and of Mrs Walker, Perthshire; two *s* two *d*]. *Address:* Dean Farm, Coln St Aldwyns, Glos GL7 5AX.

Died 13 Nov. 1999.

HOWARD, Alexander Edward, CBE 1972; Lecturer in Education, London University Centre for Teachers, 1977–81; *b* 2 Aug. 1909; *o s* of Alexander Watson Howard and Gertrude Nellie Howard; *m* 1937, Phyllis Ada Adams; no *c. Educ:* Swindon Coll.; University Coll. and Westminster Coll., London Univ. BSc (London) 1930; Pt I, BSc (Econ.) 1934. Flt-Lieut, RAF, 1940–46. Asst Master, Sanford Boys' Sch., Swindon, 1931–34; Lectr in Maths, Wandsworth Tech. Coll., 1935–40; Maths Master, Wilson's Grammar Sch., 1946–48; Headmaster: Northfleet Sch. for Boys, Kent, 1948–51; Borough-Beaufoy Sch., London, 1951–54; Forest Hill Sch., London, 1955–63; Wandsworth Sch., 1963–74; Co-ordinating Officer, Teaching Practice Organisation, London Univ. Inst. of Educn, 1975–77. Member: Naval Educn Adv. Cttee, 1966–80; Army Educational Adv. Bd, 1957–74; Academic Council, RMA, 1970–75. FRSA 1970. Hon. Mem., CGLI, 1979. Member: Wandsworth Rotary; Sanderstead and Riddlesdown Probus. *Publications:* The Secondary Technical School in England, 1955; Longman Mathematics Stages 1–5, 1962–67, new Metric edns, 1970–71; Teaching Mathematics, 1968; articles in Times Educational Supplement, The Teacher, Technology, Inside the Comprehensive Sch. *Recreations:* music, cricket, travel. *Address:* 19 Downsway, Sanderstead, Surrey CR2 0JB. *T:* (020) 8657 3399.   *Died 13 June 1999.*

HOWARD, Dame Christian; *see* Howard, Dame R. C.

HOWARD, Dr James Griffiths, FRS 1984; Programme Director, The Wellcome Trust, 1986–90, retired; *b* 25 Sept. 1927; *s* of late Joseph Griffiths Howard and Kathleen Mildred Howard; *m* 1951, Opal St Clair (*née* Echalaz); two *d* (one *s* decd). *Educ:* Middlesex Hosp. Med. Sch., Univ. of London (MB, BS 1950; PhD 1957; MD 1960). Public Health Lab. Service, 1951–53; Jun. Specialist in Pathology, RAMC, 1953–55; Res. Fellow, Wright-Fleming Inst., St Mary's Hosp., 1955–58; Edinburgh University: Immunologist (Lectr, Sen. Lectr and Reader), Dept of Surgical Science, 1958–66; Reader and Head of Immunobiology Section, Dept of Zoology, 1966–69; Wellcome Research Laboratories: Head, Experimental Immunobiology Dept, 1969–74; Head, Exp. Biology Div., 1974–83; Dir, Biomedical Res., 1984–85. *Publications:* some 130 scientific articles, reviews and chapters in books, pre-dominantly on immunology. *Recreations:* fine arts, music, cooking, hill walking. *Address:* Sarnesfield Grange, Sarnesfield, Herefordshire HR4 8RG. *T:* (01544) 318302.

Died 6 Oct. 1998.

HOWARD, John James, CBE 1985; Chief General Manager, Royal Insurance plc, 1980–84; *b* 9 March 1923; *s* of late Sir Henry Howard, KCIE, CSI, and Lady (Mabel Rosa) Howard; *m* 1949, Julia Tupholme Mann; one *s* one *d* (and one *d* decd). *Educ:* Rugby Sch.; Trinity Hall, Cambridge (MA). Pilot, RAFVR, 1942–46 (Flt Lieut). Royal Insurance Company Ltd: Financial Secretary, 1964–69; General Manager, 1970–80; Director, 1970–84. Chm., British Insurance Assoc., 1983–84 (Dep. Chm., 1981–83). Chm., YWCA Central Club, 1986–90. *Recreations:* golf, competitive bridge, gardening, grandchildren. *Address:* Highfields, High Barn Road, Effingham, Surrey KT24 5PX.   *Died 4 Jan. 2000.*

HOWARD, Dame (Rosemary) Christian, DBE 1986; *b* 5 Sept. 1916; *d* of Hon. Geoffrey Howard, *s* of 9th Earl of Carlisle, and Hon. Christian, *d* of 3rd Baron Methuen. *Educ:* Westbourne House, Folkestone; Villa Malatesta, Florence; Ozannes, Paris; and privately. STh Lambeth 1943; MA Lambeth 1979. Divinity Teacher, Chichester High Sch. for Girls, 1943–45; Licensed Lay Worker, Dio. York, 1947–; Sec., Bd of Women's Work, 1947–72; Sec., Lay Ministry, 1972–79; retired 1980. Deleg. to WCC Assemblies, 1961 and 1968; Member: Faith and Order Commn, WCC, 1961–75; BCC, 1974–87; Church Assembly, 1960–70, General Synod, 1970–85; Churches' Council for Covenanting, 1978–82. *Publications:* The Ordination of Women to Priesthood, 1972, Supplement 1978, Further Report 1984; Praise and Thanksgiving, 1972; contribs to Ecumenical Review, Year Book of Social Policy, Crucible, New Directions, Chrysalis. *Recreations:* woodwork, gardening, foreign travel. *Address:* Coneysthorpe, York YO60 7DD. *T:* (01653) 648264.   *Died 22 April 1999.*

HOWARD-JOHNSTON,   Rear-Adm.   Clarence Dinsmore, CB 1955; DSO 1942; DSC 1940; *b* 13 Oct. 1903; *s* of late John Howard-Johnston and of Comtesse Pierre du Brevil de St Germain; *m* 1st, 1928, Esmé Fitzgibbon (marr. diss. 1940); (one *s* decd); 2nd, 1941, Lady Alexandra Henrietta Louis Haig (marr. diss. 1954), *d* of 1st Earl Haig; two *s* one *d*; 3rd, 1955, Paulette, *d* of late Paul Helleu. *Educ:* Royal Naval Colls Osborne and Dartmouth. Midshipman, 1921; Commander, 1937; Dir of Studies, Greek Naval War Coll., Athens, 1938–40; Naval staff, anti-submarine Warfare Div., Admlty, 1940; detached to set up anti-sub. trng, Quiberon, 1940; i/c ops for destruction port facilities St Malo, evacuation British troops St Malo and Jersey (despatches); anti-sub. ops, Norwegian fjords, evacuation troops and wounded, Molde and Andalsnes (DSC); in comd anti-sub. escort group, N Atlantic, 1941–42; escorted 1,229 ships (DSO for sinking U651); staff, Battle of Atlantic Comd, Liverpool, 1942–43; Captain, 1943; Dir, Anti-U-boat Div., Admlty, 1943–45, anti-sub. specialist; PM's Cabinet U-boat meetings; in Comd, HMS Bermuda, British Pacific Fleet and occupation of Japan forces, 1946–47; Naval Attaché, Paris, 1947–50; Naval ADC to the Queen, 1952; Rear-Adm., 1953; Chief of Staff to Flag Officer, Central Europe, 1953–55, retired, 1955. Inventor of simple hydraulic mechanisms; commended by Lords Comrs of the Admiralty for invention and develt of anti-submarine training devices including Johnston Mobile A/S target, 1937. Participated in and prepared maritime historical programmes on French TV, 1967–81. Order of Phœnix (Greece), 1940; Legion of Merit (USA), 1945. *Recreations:* fishing, pisiculture, hill-walking, gardening. *Address:* 45 Rue Emile Ménier, 75116 Paris, France; Le Coteau, Chambre d'Amour, 64600 Anglet, France. *Clubs:* White's, Naval and Military; (Naval Member) Royal Yacht Squadron; Jockey (Paris).

Died 26 Jan. 1996.

HOWAT, Prof. Henry Taylor, CBE 1971; MD, FRCP, FRCPE; Professor of Gastroenterology, University of

Manchester, 1972–76, then Emeritus; Physician, Manchester Royal Infirmary, 1948–76; *b* 16 May 1911; *s* of late Adam Howat, MA, and Henrietta Howat, Pittenweem, Fife; *m* 1940, Rosaline, *o d* of late Miles Green, Auckland, NZ; two *s* one *d*. *Educ:* Cameron Public Sch. and Madras Coll., St Andrews; Univ. of St Andrews (MB, ChB 1933; MD with Hons and Univ. Gold Medal 1960); MSc Manchester. MRCP 1937, FRCP 1948; MRCPE 1961, FRCPE 1965. Resident MO, Manchester Royal Infirmary, 1938–40. Served War, MEF and BLA; RMO, Physician Specialist, Officer in charge of Med. Div., Mil. Hosps, 1940–46; temp. Lt-Col, RAMC. University of Manchester: Asst Lectr in Applied Physiology, 1946–48; Lectr in Med., 1948–69 (Chm., Faculty of Med., 1968–72); Reader, 1969–72; Physician, Ancoats Hosp., Manchester, 1946–62. United Manchester Hospitals, 1948–76: Chm., Med. Exec. Cttee, 1968–73; Mem., Bd of Governors, 1966–74. President: European Pancreatic Club, 1965; British Soc. of Gastroenterology, 1968–69; Assoc. of Physicians of GB and Ireland, 1975–76; Manchester Med. Soc., 1975–76; Pancreatic Soc. of GB and Ireland, 1978–79. Hon. MD Univ. of Louvain, Belgium, 1945. Manchester Man of the Year, 1973. Medallist, J. E. Purkyně Czechoslovak Med. Soc., 1968; Diploma and Medallion of Hungarian Gastroenterol Soc., 1988. *Publications:* (ed) The Exocrine Pancreas, 1979; articles on gastrointestinal physiology and disease. *Recreation:* golf. *Address:* 3 Brookdale Rise, Hilton Road, Bramhall, Cheshire SK7 3AG. *T:* (0161) 439 2853; 40 High Street, Pittenweem, Fife KY10 2PL. *T:* (01333) 311325. *Club:* Royal and Ancient Golf (St Andrews).
                                                                     Died 29 Oct. 1998.

HOWE, Allen; Circuit Administrator, Wales and Chester Circuit, 1974–82; Chairman, Medical Appeals Tribunal for Wales, 1982–92; *b* 6 June 1918; *s* of late Frank Howe and Dora Howe, Monk Bretton, Yorks; *m* 1952, Katherine, *d* of late Griffith and Catherine Davies, Pontypridd; two *d*. *Educ:* Holgate Grammar Sch., Barnsley. Called to Bar, Middle Temple, 1953. Served with E Yorks Regt and RWAFF, 1939–46, France, Africa, India and Burma (Major). HM Colonial Admin. Service, Gold Coast, 1946–55 (Sen. Dist Comr); Judicial Adviser, Ashanti, 1954–55; practised Wales and Chester Circuit, 1955–59; Legal Dept, Welsh Bd of Health, 1959–65; Legal Dept, Welsh Office, 1965–74. *Recreations:* golf, gardening, walking. *Address:* 2 Orchard Drive, Whitchurch, Cardiff CF4 2AE. *T:* (01222) 626626. *Clubs:* Cardiff and County; Radyr Golf.
                                                                     Died 5 April 1998.

HOWELL, Baron *cr* 1992 (Life Peer), of Aston Manor in the City of Birmingham; **Denis Herbert Howell;** PC 1976; *b* 4 Sept. 1923; *s* of Herbert and Bertha A. Howell; *m* 1955, Brenda Marjorie, *d* of Stephen and Ruth Willson, Birmingham; two *s* one *d* (and one *s* decd). *Educ:* Gower Street Sch.; Handsworth Grammar Sch., Birmingham. Mem., Birmingham City Council, 1946–56; served Catering Establishment, General Purposes, Health and Watch Cttees, Clitt. Catering Cttee, 1952–55; Health (Gen. Purposes) Sub-Cttee for setting up of first smokeless zones; Hon. Sec. Birmingham City Council Labour Group, 1950–55. MP (Lab): All Saints Div., Birmingham, 1955–Sept. 1959; Birmingham, Small Heath, March 1961–1992. Jt Parly Under-Sec. of State, Dept of Educn and Science (with responsibility for sport), 1964–69; Minister of State, Min. of Housing and Local Govt (with responsibility for sport), 1969–70; Opposition spokesman for Local Govt and Sport, 1970–74; Minister of State, DoE (responsible for environment, water resources and sport), 1974–79; Opposition spokesman on Environment (Environment and Services, Water Resources, Sport, Recreation and Countryside), 1979–83, on Home Affairs, 1983–84; Opposition front bench spokesman on the Environment (specializing in Sport), 1984–92. Opposition

Defence spokesman, H of L, 1993–97. Mem., Labour Party NEC, 1982–83. Pres., Labour Movement for Europe, 1995 (Chm., 1979–95); Vice Pres., European Movt, 1979–. Chairman: Sports Council, 1965–70; Youth Service Develt Council, 1964–69 (report: Youth and Community Work in the 70's); Central Council of Physical Recreation, 1973–74 (Vice Pres., 1985); Cttee of Enquiry into Sponsorship of Sport, 1981–83 (report: The Howell Report on Sports Sponsorship); Severn Trent Water Trust, 1997–; Member: Dudley Road Hosp. Group Management Cttee, 1948–64; Albemarle Cttee on the Youth Service; Management Cttee, City of Birmingham Symphony Orchestra, 1950–55; Pres., Canoldir Choir, 1980–. Governor, Handsworth Grammar Sch., 1948–56. Chairman: Birmingham Assoc. of Youth Clubs, 1963–64; Birmingham Settlement, 1963–64. St Peter's Urban Village Trust, 1985–; President: Birmingham Olympic Council, 1985–86; Middlesex Wanderers FC, 1993–; Midland Club Cricket Conf., 1993–94; Council of Cricket Socs, 1993–; Vice-President: Warwicks CCC, 1986–; Birchfield Harriers, 1987–; Aston Villa FC, 1994–. Pres., Assoc. of Professional, Exec. Clerical and Computer Staffs (APEX) (formerly CAWU), 1971–83. FIPR 1987 (MIPR 1961). Football League Referee, 1956–70. Hon. Freeman, City of Birmingham, 1991. Hon. LLD Birmingham, 1993. Silver Medal, Olympic Order, 1981. Midlander of the Year Award, 1987. *Publications:* Soccer Refereeing, 1968; Made in Birmingham (autobiog.), 1990. *Recreations:* sport, theatre, music. *Address:* 33 Moor Green Lane, Moseley, Birmingham B13 8NE. *Clubs:* Reform, MCC; Warwickshire County Cricket (Birmingham).
                                                                     Died 19 April 1998.

HOWELLS, Dr Gwyn, CB 1979; MD; FRCP, FRACP; Director-General and Permanent Head, Federal Department of Health, Canberra, Australia, 1973–83; Chairman, Cochlear Pty Ltd, Sydney, 1984–95; Director, Nucleus Ltd, Sydney, 1984–95; *b* 13 May 1918; *s* of Albert Henry and Ruth Winifred Howells; *m* 1942, Simone Maufe; two *s* two *d*. *Educ:* University College Sch., London; St Bartholomew's Hosp., Univ. of London (MB BS 1942, MD 1950). MRCS 1941; FRCP 1974 (MRCP 1950, LRCP 1941); FRACP 1971 (MRACP 1967). Cons. Phys., Thoracic Annexe, Toowoomba, Qld, Aust.; Chest Phys., Toowoomba Gen. Hosp., Qld, 1957–66; Federal Dept of Health, Canberra: First Asst Director-General, 1966–73; Dep. Dir-Gen., Feb.-Sept. 1973. Chairman, Nat. Health and Med. Res. Council, 1973–83; Director of Quarantine for Australia, 1973–83. *Publications:* several articles in Lancet, BMJ, Aust. Med. Jl and other specialist jls. *Recreation:* reading. *Address:* 1 Boake Place, Garran, ACT 2605, Australia. *T:* (2) 62812575. *Club:* Commonwealth.
                                                                     Died 26 July 1997.

HOWLETT, Jack, CBE 1969; PhD; FSS, FBCS, FIMA; Consultant to International Computers Ltd, since 1975 and Editor, ICL Technical Journal, since 1978; Managing Editor, Journal of Information Technology for Development, since 1985; *b* 30 Aug. 1912; *s* of William Howlett and Lydia Ellen Howlett; *m* 1939, Joan Marjorie Simmons; four *s* one *d*. *Educ:* Stand Grammar Sch., Manchester; Manchester Univ. (PhD); MA Oxon. Mathematician, LMS Railway, 1935–40 and 1946–48; mathematical work in various wartime research estabts, 1940–46; Head of Computer Group, Atomic Energy Research Estabt, Harwell, 1948–61; Dir, Atlas Computer Lab., Chilton, Didcot, Berks, 1961–75 (under SRC, 1965–75). Chm., Nat. Cttee on Computer Networks, 1976–78. Fellow by special election, St Cross Coll., Oxford, 1966. Hon. Sec., British Cttee of Honour for Celebration of 1300th Anniversary of Foundn of Bulgarian State, 1980–82; 1300th Anniversary Medal of Bulgarian State, 1982. *Publications:* reviews and gen. papers on numerical mathematics and computation; translations of

French books on computational subjects. *Recreations:* hill walking, music. *Address:* 20B Bradmore Road, Oxford OX2 6QP. *T:* (01865) 52893. *Clubs:* New Arts, Savile.
Died 5 May 1999.

HOWSE, Lt-Comdr (Humphrey) Derek, MBE 1954; DSC 1945; FSA, FRIN, FRAS; RN retired; Caird Research Fellow, National Maritime Museum, 1982–86; *b* Weymouth, 10 Oct. 1919; *s* of late Captain Humphrey F. Howse, RN and Rose Chicheliana (*née* Thornton); *m* 1946, Elizabeth de Warrenne Waller; three *s* one *d*. *Educ:* RN Coll., Dartmouth. FRIN 1976; FRAS 1967; FSA 1986. Midshipman, RN, 1937–39; Sub-Lt 1939, Lieut 1941; war service in HMS Boadicea, Sardonyx, Garth, Inconstant, Rinaldo, 1939–45; specialized in navigation, 1944, in aircraft direction, 1947 (despatches 3 times 1943–45); Lt-Comdr 1949; HMS Newcastle, Korean War, 1952–54, Inshore Flotilla, 1954–56; retd 1958. Atomic Energy Div., Gen. Electric Co., 1958–61; Associated Industrial Consultants, 1961–62; Continental Oil Co., 1962–63; Asst Keeper, Dept of Navigation and Astronomy, National Maritime Museum, 1963; Head of Astronomy, 1969; Dep. Keeper and Head of Navigation and Astronomy, 1976; Keeper, 1979–82. Clark Library Vis. Prof., UCLA, 1983–84. Member Council: IUHPS (Pres., Scientific Instrument Commn, 1977–82); British Astronomical Assoc., 1980–88 (Pres., 1980–82); Antiquarian Horological Soc., 1976–82; Royal Astronomical Soc., 1982–83; Royal Inst. of Navigation, 1982–83 (Gold Medal, 1998); Soc. for Nautical Research, 1982–86 (Vice-Pres., 1992–98); Hakluyt Soc., 1984–88; Scientific Instrument Soc., 1987–90. Liveryman, Clockmakers' Co., 1981. *Publications:* Clocks and Watches of Captain James Cook, 1969; The Tompion Clocks at Greenwich, 1970; (with M. Sanderson) The Sea Chart, 1973; Greenwich Observatory: the buildings and instruments, 1975; Francis Place and the Early History of Greenwich Observatory, 1975; Greenwich Time and the Discovery of the Longitude, 1980, 2nd edn as Greenwich Time and the Longitude, 1997; Nevil Maskelyne: the seaman's astronomer, 1989; (ed) Background to Discovery, 1990; (with N. J. W. Thrower) A Buccaneer's Atlas, 1992; Radar at Sea, 1993; papers to Mariners' Mirror, L'Astronomie, Antiquarian Horology, Jl of Navigation and Jl of British Astronomical Assoc. *Recreations:* reading, writing, sticking in photos, pottering in the vegetable beds. *Address:* 12 Barnfield Road, Riverhead, Sevenoaks, Kent TN13 2AY. *T:* (01732) 454366.
Died 26 July 1998.

HOY, Rev. (Augustine) David (Joseph), SJ; Superior, St John's, Beaumont, since 1984; *b* 1 March 1913; *s* of Augustine Hilary Hoy and Caroline Lovelace. *Educ:* Mount St Mary's Coll. Entered Society of Jesus, 1931. Senior English Master, Wimbledon Coll., 1947, Asst Head Master, 1957–59; Rector of St Robert Bellarmine, Heythrop, Chipping Norton, 1959–64; Rector of Stonyhurst College, 1964–71 and 1980–84; Superior of Farm St Church, 1972–75. *Recreation:* walking. *Address:* St John's, Beaumont, Old Windsor, Berks SL4 2JN.
Died 16 March 1997.

HOYES, Thomas, PhD; FRICS; Member, Lands Tribunal, since 1989; *b* 19 Nov. 1935; *s* of late Fred Hoyes and Margaret Elizabeth (*née* Hoyes); *m* 1960, Amy Joan (*née* Wood); two *d*. *Educ:* Queen Elizabeth's Grammar Sch., Alford, Lincs; Downing Coll., Cambridge (BA 1956; MA 1960; PhD 1963). FRICS 1969 (ARICS 1964). Partner, Hallam Brackett, Chartered Surveyors, Nottingham, 1963–83; Prof. of Land Management, Univ. of Reading, 1983–88 (Head of Dept, 1986–88). Royal Institution of Chartered Surveyors: Mem., Gen. Council, 1982–85; Pres., Planning and Develt Div., 1983–84. President: Cambridge Univ. Land Soc., 1973; Land Inst., 1991;

Mem., Rating Surveyors Assoc., 1968–. Governor, Nottingham High Sch. for Girls (GPDST), 1976–82. Hon. FSVA 1996. Hon. DSc De Montfort, 1997. *Publications:* The Practice of Valuation, 1979; articles and papers in Estates Gazette, Chartered Surveyor Weekly, and Jl of Planning and Environment Law. *Recreations:* gardening, adapting houses. *Address:* (office) 48–49 Chancery Lane, WC2A 1JR. *T:* (0171) 936 7200. *Club:* Farmers'.
Died 5 April 1997.

HUDDIE, Sir David (Patrick), Kt 1968; FEng 1981; retired; *b* 12 March 1916; *s* of James and Catherine Huddie; *m* 1941, Wilhelmina Betty Booth; three *s*. *Educ:* Mountjoy Sch., Dublin; Trinity Coll., Dublin. FIQA 1980; FIMechE 1974. Aero Engine Division, Rolls-Royce Ltd: Asst Chief Designer, 1947; Chief Development Engineer, 1953; Commercial Dir, 1959; General Manager, 1962; Dir, Rolls-Royce Ltd, 1961; Man. Dir, Aero Engine Div., 1965; Chm. Rolls-Royce Aero Engines Inc., 1969–70; Senior Res. Fellow, Imperial Coll., London, 1971–80, Hon. Fellow, 1981. Hon. DSc Dublin, 1968. *Recreations:* gardening, music, archaeology. *Address:* The Croft, Butts Road, Bakewell, Derbyshire DE45 1EB. *T:* (01629) 813330.
Died 14 May 1998.

HUDDLESTON, Most Rev. (Ernest Urban) Trevor, KCMG 1998; CR; DD; Chairman, International Defence and Aid Fund for Southern Africa, since 1983; *b* 15 June 1913; *s* of late Capt. Sir Ernest Huddleston, CIE, CBE and 1st wife, Elsie, *d* of John Barlow-Smith, Buenos Aires; unmarried. *Educ:* Lancing; Christ Church, Oxford (BA 2nd class Hon. Mod. Hist. 1934; MA 1937; Hon. Student, 1993); Wells Theological College. Deacon, 1936; priest, 1937; joined Community of the Resurrection; professed, 1941. Apptd Priest-in-charge Sophiatown and Orlando Anglican Missions, diocese Johannesburg, Nov. 1943; Provincial in S Africa, CR, 1949–55; Guardian of Novices, CR, Mirfield, 1956–58; Prior of the London House, Community of the Resurrection, 1958–60; Bishop of Masasi, 1960–68; Bishop Suffragan of Stepney, 1968–78; Bishop of Mauritius, 1978–83; Archbishop of the Indian Ocean, 1978–83. Provost, Selly Oak Colls, 1983–. President: Anti-Apartheid Movement, 1981–94 (Vice-Pres., 1969–81); Nat. Peace Council, 1983–; IVS, 1984–. Trustee, Runnymede Trust, 1972–90. Fellow, Queen Mary and Westfield Coll., London Univ., 1990. Hon. DD: Aberdeen, 1956; City, 1987; Exeter, 1992; Oxford, 1993; Birmingham, 1993; Whittier Coll., Calif, 1994; Dundee, 1994; Hon. DLitt: Lancaster, 1972; Warwick, 1988; CNAA, 1989; City of London Polytechnic, 1989; Hon. DHL Denison Univ., USA, 1989; Hon. LLD: Leeds, 1991; Natal Univ., S Africa, 1995. Indira Gandhi Meml Prize, 1995. *Publications:* Naught for Your Comfort, 1956; The True and Living God, 1966; God's World, 1966; I Believe: reflections on the Apostles Creed, 1986; Return to South Africa, 1991. *Recreation:* listening to music. *Address:* House of the Resurrection, Mirfield, W Yorks WF14 0BN.
Died 20 April 1998.

HUDSON, Sir Havelock (Henry Trevor), Kt 1977; Lloyd's Underwriter 1952–88; Chairman of Lloyd's, 1975, 1976 and 1977 (Deputy Chairman, 1968, 1971, 1973); *b* 4 Jan. 1919; *er s* of late Savile E. Hudson and Dorothy Hudson (*née* Cheetham); *m* 1st, 1944, Elizabeth (marr. diss. 1956), *d* of Brig. W. Home; two *s*; 2nd, 1957, Cathleen Blanche Lily (*d* 1994), *d* of 6th Earl of St Germans; one *s* one *d*. *Educ:* Rugby. Merchant Service, 1937–38. Served War of 1939–45: Royal Hampshire Regt (Major), 1939–42; 9 Parachute Bn, 1942–44. Member: Cttee, Lloyd's Underwriters Assoc., 1963; Cttee of Lloyd's, 1965–68, 1970–73, 1975–78; Exec. Bd, Lloyd's Register of Shipping, 1967–78. Dir, Ellerman Lines Ltd, 1979–84. Vice-Pres., Chartered Insurance Inst., 1973–76, Dep. Pres., 1976–77; Chairman: Arvon Foundn, 1973–85;

Oxford Artificial Kidney and Transplant Unit, 1976–90; Pres., City of London Outward Bound Assoc., 1979–88; Member, Board of Governors: Pangbourne Coll., 1976–88; Bradfield Coll., 1978–88. Lloyd's Gold Medal, 1977. *Recreation:* shooting. *Address:* The Old Rectory, Stanford Dingley, Reading, Berkshire RG7 6LX. *T:* (01734) 744346. *Club:* Boodle's.   *Died 14 Nov. 1996.*

HUDSON, Lt-Gen. Sir Peter, KCB 1977; CBE 1970 (MBE 1965); DL; Lieutenant of the Tower of London, 1986–89; *b* 14 Sept. 1923; *s* of Captain William Hudson, late The Rifle Bde, and Ivy (*née* Brown); *m* 1949, Susan Anne Knollys; one *d*, and one adopted *s* one adopted *d*. *Educ:* Wellingborough; Jesus Coll., Cambridge. Commnd into The Rifle Bde, 1944; psc 1954; comd company in Mau Mau and Malayan campaigns, 1955–57; jssc 1963; comd 3rd Bn The Royal Green Jackets, 1966–67; Regimental Col The Royal Green Jackets, 1968; Comdr 39 Infantry Bde, 1968–70; IDC 1971; GOC Eastern Dist, 1973–74; Chief of Staff, Allied Forces Northern Europe, 1975–77; Dep. C-in-C, UKLF, 1977–80; Inspector-Gen., T&AVR, 1978–80. Col Comdt, The Light Div., 1977–80; Hon. Colonel: Southampton Univ. OTC, 1980–85; 5 (Volunteer) Bn, The Royal Green Jackets, TA, 1985–93. Mem., Gen. Adv. Council, BBC, 1981–85. Mem., Rifle Bde Club and Assoc. (Chm., 1979–85); Trustee, Rifle Bde Museum (Chm., Trustees, 1979–85); Chairman: Green Jacket Club, 1979–85; Council, TA&VRA, 1981–90; Pres., Reserve Forces Assoc., 1985–91. Vice Chm., St John Fellowship, 1994–. Governor: Royal Sch., Bath, 1976–96 (Chm., 1981–88); Bradfield Coll., 1983–94. Mem., Frilsham Parish Council, 1988–96. Freeman of City of London, 1965. DL Berks, 1984. FIMgt. KStJ (Sec.-Gen., Order of St John, 1981–88; Mem. Council, Royal Berks, 1988–). *Recreations:* travel, fishing, most games. *Address:* Little Orchard, Frilsham, Berks RG18 9XB. *Clubs:* I Zingari; Green Jackets; Free Foresters.   *Died 8 Aug. 2000.*

HUDSON-WILLIAMS, Prof. Harri Llwyd; Professor of Greek in the University of Newcastle upon Tyne (formerly King's College, Newcastle upon Tyne, University of Durham), 1952–76 and Head of Department of Classics, 1969–76; then Emeritus Professor; *b* 16 Feb. 1911; *yr s* of late Prof. Thomas Hudson-Williams and Gwladys, *d* of W. Prichard Williams, Cae'r Onnen, Bangor; *m* 1946, Joan, *er d* of late Lt-Col H. F. T. Fisher; two adopted *d*. *Educ:* University College of North Wales; King's Coll., Cambridge (Browne Medallist; Charles Oldham Scholar; MA); Munich University. Asst Lectr in Greek, Liverpool Univ., 1937–40; Intelligence Corps, 1940–41; Foreign Office, 1941–45; Lectr in Greek, Liverpool Univ., 1945–50; Reader in Greek, King's Coll., Newcastle upon Tyne, 1950–52; Dean of the Faculty of Arts, Univ. of Newcastle upon Tyne, 1963–66. *Publications:* contribs to various classical jls, etc. *Recreation:* gardening. *Address:* The Pound, Mill Street, Islip, Oxon OX5 2SZ. *T:* (01865) 375893.   *Died 14 Dec. 1998.*

HUGGINS, Prof. Charles Brenton; Professor Emeritus, Ben May Institute and Department of Surgery, University of Chicago, since 1969; William B. Ogden Distinguished Service Professor since 1962; *b* Halifax, Canada, 22 Sept. 1901; *s* of Charles Edward Huggins and Bessie Huggins (*née* Spencer); citizen of USA by naturalization, 1933; *m* 1927, Margaret Wellman; one *s* one *d*. *Educ:* Acadia Univ. (BA 1920); Harvard (MD 1924). University of Michigan: Interne in Surgery, 1924–26; Instructor in Surgery, 1926–27; Univ. of Chicago, 1927–: Instructor in Surgery, 1927–29; Asst Prof., 1929–33; Assoc. Prof., 1933–36; Prof. of Surgery, 1936–69; Dir, Ben May Laboratory for Cancer Research, 1951–69. Chancellor, Acadia Univ., 1972–79. Alpha Omega Alpha, 1942; Mem. Nat. Acad. of Sciences, 1949; Mem. Amer. Philosophical Soc., 1962. Sigillum Magnum, Bologna Univ., 1964; Hon. Prof.,

Madrid Univ., 1956; Hon. FRSocMed 1956; Hon. FRCSE 1958; Hon. FRCS 1959; Hon. FACS 1963; Hon. FRSE 1983. Hon. MSc Yale, 1947; Hon. DSc: Acadia, 1946; Washington Univ., St Louis, 1950; Leeds Univ., 1953; Turin Univ., 1957; Trinity Coll., Hartford, Conn, 1965; Wales, 1967; Univ. of California, Berkeley, 1968; Univ. of Michigan, 1968; Medical Coll. of Ohio, 1973; Gustavus Adolphus Coll., 1975; Wilmington Coll. of Ohio, 1980; Univ. of Louisville, 1980; Hon. LLD: Aberdeen Univ., 1966; York Univ., Toronto, 1968; Hon. DPS George Washington Univ., 1967. Gave many memorial lectures and won numerous gold medals, prizes and awards for his work on urology and cancer research, including Nobel Prize for Medicine (jtly), 1966. Held foreign orders. *Publications:* Experimental Leukemia and Mammary Cancer: Induction, Prevention, Cure, 1979; over 275 articles. *Address:* Ben May Institute, University of Chicago, 5841 South Maryland Avenue, Chicago, IL 60637, USA.   *Died 12 Jan. 1997.*

HUGHES, Baron *cr* 1961 (Life Peer), of Hawkhill, co. of City of Dundee; **William Hughes,** CBE 1956 (OBE 1942); PC 1970; DL; company director; *b* 22 Jan. 1911; *e s* of late Joseph and Margaret Hughes; *m* 1951, Christian Clacher (*d* 1994), *o c* of late James and Sophia Gordon; two *d*. *Educ:* Balfour Street Public Sch., Dundee; Dundee Technical Coll. ARP Controller, Dundee, 1939–43; Armed Forces, 1943–46: commissioned RAOC, 1944; demobilised as Capt., 1946. Mem., Dundee Town Council, 1933–36 and 1937–61; Hon. City Treasurer, Dundee, 1946–47; Chairman, Eastern Regional Hospital Board, Scotland, 1948–60; Lord Provost of Dundee and HM Lieut of County of City of Dundee, 1954–60. Contested (Lab) E Perthshire, 1945 and 1950. Jt Parly Under-Sec. of State for Scotland, 1964–69; Minister of State for Scotland, 1969–70, 1974–75. Mem., Council of Europe and WEU, 1976–87. Member: Cttee on Civil Juries, 1958–59; Cttee to Enquire into Registration of Title to Land in Scotland, 1960–62; North of Scotland Hydro-Electric Bd, 1957–64; Scottish Transport Council, 1960–64; Chairman: Glenrothes Develt Corp., 1960–64; East Kilbride Develt Corp., 1975–82; Royal Commn on Legal Services in Scotland, 1976–80. Member: Court, St Andrews Univ., 1954–63; Council, Queen's Coll., Dundee, 1954–63. Hon. LLD St Andrews, 1960. JP County and City of Dundee, 1943–76; DL Dundee, 1960. Chevalier, Légion d'Honneur, 1958. *Recreation:* gardening. *Address:* The Stables, Ross, Comrie, Perthshire PH6 2JU. *T:* (01764) 70557.   *Died 31 Dec. 1999.*

HUGHES, Edward James, (Ted), OM 1998; OBE 1977; author; Poet Laureate, since 1984; *b* 17 Aug. 1930; *s* of William Henry Hughes and Edith Farrar Hughes; *m* 1st, 1956, Sylvia Plath (*d* 1963); one *s* one *d*; (one *d* decd by Assia Wevill); 2nd, 1970, Carol Orchard. *Educ:* Pembroke Coll., Cambridge (Hon. Fellow, 1986). Author of Orghast (performed at 5th Festival of Arts of Shiraz, Persepolis, 1971). Awards: first prize, Guinness Poetry Awards, 1958; John Simon Guggenheim Fellow, 1959–60; Somerset Maugham Award, 1960; Premio Internazionale Taormina, 1973; The Queen's Medal for Poetry, 1974. *Publications:* verse: The Hawk in the Rain, 1957 (First Publication Award, NY); Lupercal, 1960 (Hawthornden Prize, 1961); Recklings, 1966; The Burning of the Brothel, 1966; Scapegoats and Rabies, 1967; Animal Poems, 1967; Wodwo, 1967 (City of Florence Internat. Poetry Prize, 1969); Poetry in the Making, 1967 (US as Poetry Is, 1970); Five Autumn Songs for Children's Voices, 1968; Crow, 1970; A Few Crows, 1970; Crow Wakes, 1970; Shakespeare's Poem, 1971; (with R. Fainlight and Alan Sillitoe) Poems, 1971; Eat Crow, 1971; Prometheus on His Crag, 1973; Spring Summer Autumn Winter, 1974; (with illustrations by Leonard Baskin) Cave Birds, 1975; Season Songs, 1976; Earth-Moon, 1976; (introd and trans.

jtly) János Pilinsky, Selected Poems, 1976; Gaudete, 1977; Orts, 1978; Moortown Elegies, 1978; (introd. and trans. jtly) Yehuda Amichai, Amen, 1978; Adam and the Sacred Nine, 1979; Remains of Elmet, 1979; Moortown, 1979 (Heinemann Bequest, RSL, 1980); (contrib.) Michael Morpurgo, All Around the Year, 1979; Selected Poems 1957–1981, 1982; River, 1983; Flowers and Insects, 1987; Wolfwatching, 1989; Moortown Diary, 1989; Rain-charm for the Duchy, 1992; New Selected Poems 1957–1994, 1995; Tales from Ovid, 1997 (W. H. Smith Lit. Award, Whitbread Book of the Year); Birthday Letters, 1998 (Forward Poetry Prize for Best Collection; T. S. Eliot Prize for Poetry; Whitbread Book of the Year); *libretti:* The Demon of Adachigahara, 1969; The Story of Vasco, 1974; *stage:* adaptation of Seneca's Oedipus, 1969 (perf. NT, 1968); The Coming of the Kings (4 plays for children), 1970 (US as The Tiger's Bones, 1974); (trans.) Wedekind, Spring Awakening, 1995; (trans.) Lorca, Blood Wedding, 1996; (trans.) Euripides, Alcestis, 1998; *prose:* Shakespeare and the Goddess of Complete Being, 1992; Winter Pollen, 1994; Difficulties of a Bridegroom, 1995; *for children: verse:* Meet My Folks!, 1961; The Earth-Owl and Other Moon People, 1963 (reissued as Moon Whales, 1988); Moon-Bells and other poems (Signal Award), 1978; Under the North Star (Signal Award), 1981; *verse story:* Nessie, The Mannerless Monster, 1964 (US as Nessie the Monster, 1974); *stories:* How the Whale Became, 1963; The Iron Man, 1968 (US as The Iron Giant); What is the Truth, 1984 (Guardian Children's Fiction Award, 1985); Ffangs the Vampire Bat and the Kiss of Truth, 1986; Tales of the Early World, 1988; The Iron Woman, 1993; The Dreamfighter, 1995; Collected Animal Poems, 1995; *edited:* (jtly) Five American Poets, 1963; (with introd.) Selected Poems of Keith Douglas, 1964; A Choice of Emily Dickinson's Verse, 1968; A Choice of Shakespeare's Verse, 1971 (US as With Fairest Flowers while Summer Lasts); (with introd.) Sylvia Plath, Johnny Panic and the Bible of Dreams, 1977; Henry Williamson—A Tribute, 1979; Sylvia Plath, Collected Poems, 1981; (with Seamus Heaney) The Rattle Bag, 1982; (with introd.) A Choice of Coleridge's Verse, 1996; (with Seamus Heaney) The School Bag, 1997; By Heart: 101 poems to remember, 1997. *Address:* c/o Faber and Faber Ltd, 3 Queen Square, WC1N 3AU.
Died 28 Oct. 1998.

HUGHES, Prof. Sir Edward (Stuart Reginald), Kt 1977; CBE 1971; Chairman and Professor, Department of Surgery, Monash University, Alfred Hospital, 1973–84, then Emeritus Professor of Surgery; *b* 4 July 1919; *s* of Reginald Hawkins Hughes and Annie Grace Langford; *m* 1944, Alison Clare Lelean; two *s* two *d*. *Educ:* Melbourne C of E Grammar Sch.; Univ. of Melbourne. MB, BS 1943; MD 1945; MS 1946; FRCS 1946 (Hon. FRCS 1985); FRACS 1950. Resident Medical Officer, 1943–45, Asst Surgeon, 1950–53, Surgeon, 1954–74, Royal Melbourne Hosp.; Surgeon, Alfred Hosp., 1973–84. Consultant Surgeon to Australian Army, 1976–82. Royal Australasian College of Surgeons: Mem. Council, 1967–78; Chm. Exec. Cttee, 1971–78; Sen. Vice-Pres., 1974–84; Pres., 1975–78. First Dir, Menzies Foundn for Health, Fitness and Physical Achievement, 1979–. Cabrini Surgical Lectures, 1989. Fellow, Queen's Coll., Melbourne, 1955. Hon. FACS, Hon. FRCSCan, Hon. FRCSE, Hon. FRCSI; Hon. FPCS 1977. Hon. LLD Monash, 1985. Sir Hugh Devine Medal, RACS, 1977. *Publications:* Surgery of the Anal Canal and Rectum, 1957; All about an Ileostomy, 1966, 3rd edn 1971; All about a Colostomy, 1970, 2nd edn 1977; Ano-Rectal Surgery, 1972; Colo-Rectal Surgery, 1983; Rectal Cancer, 1989. *Recreations:* tennis, racing. *Address:* 308A Glenferrie Road, Malvern, Vic 3144, Australia. *T:* (3) 98227688. *Clubs:* Melbourne,

Melbourne Cricket, Victoria Racing, Victoria Amateur Turf (Melbourne). *Died 16 Oct. 1998.*

HUGHES, George; Chairman and Chief Executive, Hughes Technology Ltd, since 1984; *b* 4 May 1937; *s* of Peter and Ann Hughes; *m* 1963, Janet; two *s*. *Educ:* Liverpool Collegiate (Sen. City Scholar; Open State Schol. with 3 distinctions); Gonville and Caius Coll., Cambridge (Open Scholar; MA Hons 1st Cl. German Mod. Lang. Tripos); Harvard Business Sch. (MBA 1968). Ski instructor, 1959; lead in J. Arthur Rank film, Holiday with Pay, 1959–60; banking, Paris, 1960; IBM, London, 1960–69 (Strategy Develt Man., 1968–69; IBM European Salesman of the Year, Rome, 1965); merchant banking, London, 1969–70; Vice-Chm., Chief Exec. and Gp Man. Dir, Duple Gp Ltd, 1970–71; Chairman and Chief Executive: Hughes International, 1970–83; Willowbrook International, 1970–83; Willowbrook World Wide, 1971–83; Hampton Court Farms (formerly Castle Hughes Gp), 1975–87; Hughes Truck and Bus, 1976–84. Mem., Mensa, 1961. Chm., Derbys CCC, 1976–77; Mem., TCCB, 1976–77. *Publications:* The Effective Use of Computers, 1968; Military and Business Strategy, 1968; many papers on technical and management topics. *Recreations:* perception of visual patterns in thinking, creativity and innovation, historic buildings, Renoir, soccer, tennis, cricket. *Address:* Xanadu, Matthews Green, Wokingham RG41 1JU; Château de Beauchamps, Sarthe, France. *Clubs:* MCC, Carlton, Annabel's. *Died 31 Oct. 1998.*

HUGHES, Air Marshal Sir (Sidney Weetman) Rochford, KCB 1967 (CB 1964); CBE 1955 (OBE 1942); AFC 1947; *b* 25 Oct. 1914; *s* of late Capt. H. R. Hughes, Master Mariner, and Mrs Hughes (*née* Brigham), Auckland, NZ; *m* 1942, Elizabeth, *d* of A. Duncum, Colombo, Ceylon; one *d*. *Educ:* Waitaki Boys' High School; Oamaru, NZ. Editorial Staff, NZ Herald, 1933–37; RNZAF, 1937–38; RAF, Far East and Middle East, 1939–44 (despatches; Greek DFC); Chief Ops, USAF All Weather Centre, 1948–49; Air Min. and CO Farnborough, 1950–54; Imperial Defence Coll., 1955; CO RAF Jever, Germany, 1956–59; Air Mem. and Chm., Defence Res. Policy Staff, MoD, 1959–61; Air Officer Commanding No 19 Group, 1962–64; Dep. Controller Aircraft (RAF), Ministry of Aviation, 1964–66; Air Comdr, Far East Air Force, 1966–69, retd 1969. Air Adviser, Civil and Military, to Govt of Singapore, 1969–72; Commissioner, Northland Harbour Bd, NZ, 1974. Chm., Mazda Motors NZ, 1972–87; Director: NZ Steel, 1973–84; General Accident, 1975–84; Reserve Bank NZ, 1974–77; Whangarei Engrg Co., 1975–83; Lees Industries, 1976–84; First City Finance Corp., 1981–87. Patron, Taupo Brevet Club. Livery, GAPAN. *Recreations:* motoring, fishing. *Address:* 24 Scenic Heights, Acacia Bay, Taupo, New Zealand. *Club:* Royal NZ Yacht Squadron. *Died 17 Sept. 1996.*

HUGHES, Ted; *see* Hughes, E. J.

HUGHES, Maj.-Gen. William Dillon, CB 1960; CBE 1953; MD; FRCPI; Commandant, Royal Army Medical College, 1957–60; *b* 23 Dec. 1900; *s* of R. Hughes, JP; *m* 1929, Kathleen Linda Thomas (*d* 1976); one *s*; *m* 1982, Jennifer Stedall (*d* 1996). *Educ:* Campbell Coll., Belfast; Queen's Univ., Belfast. MB, BCh, BAO 1923; MD 1937; FRCPI 1953; DTM&H. Lieut, RAMC, 1928; Officer i/c Medical Div. 64 and 42 Gen. Hosps, MEF, 1940–42; Officer i/c Medical Div. 105 Gen. Hosp., BAOR, 1944–46; Sen. MO, Belsen, 1945; Consulting Physician, Far East Land Forces, 1950–53; ADMS, Aldershot Dist, 1954; Prof. in Tropical Medicine and Consulting Physician, Royal Army Med. Coll., 1955–56. Col Comdt RAMC, 1961–65. QHP 1957. Vice-Pres., Royal Society of Tropical Medicine and Hygiene, 1959–60. Mitchiner Medal, RCS, 1960. *Died 13 Dec. 1999.*

HUGO, Lt-Col Sir John (Mandeville), KCVO 1969 (CVO 1959); OBE 1947; Gentleman Usher to the Queen, 1952–69, an Extra Gentleman Usher since 1969; *b* 1 July 1899; *s* of R. M. Hugo; *m* 1952, Joan Winifred, *d* of late D. W. Hill; two *d. Educ:* Marlborough Coll.; RMA, Woolwich, Commissioned RA, 1917; transf. to Indian Cavalry, 1925; Military Sec. to Governor of Bengal, 1938–40; rejoined 7th Light Cavalry, 1940; Military Sec. to Governor of Bengal, 1946–47; Asst Ceremonial Sec., Commonwealth Relations Office, 1948–52; Ceremonial and Protocol Sec. to the Queen, 1952–69. *Address:* Hilltop House, Vines Cross, Heathfield, East Sussex TN21 9EN. *T:* (01435) 812562. *Died 21 July 2000.*

HULSE, Sir (Hamilton) Westrow, 9th Bt *cr* 1739, of Lincoln's Inn Fields; Barrister-at-Law; *b* 20 June 1909; *o s* of Sir Hamilton Hulse, 8th Bt, and Estelle (*d* 1933) *d* of late William Lorillard Campbell, of New York, USA; *S* father, 1931; *m* 1st, 1932, Philippa Mabel (marr. diss. 1937), *y d* of late A. J. Taylor, Strensham Court, Worcs; two *s*; 2nd, 1938, Amber (*d* 1940), *o d* of late Captain Herbert Stanley Orr Wilson, RHA, Rockfield Park, Mon; 3rd, 1945, Dorothy (marr. diss. 1954), *o d* of William Durran and *widow* of James A. M. Hamilton; 4th, 1954, Elizabeth, *d* of late Col George Redesdale Brooker Spain, CMG, TD, FSA. *Educ:* Eton; Christ Church, Oxford. Called to the Bar, Inner Temple, 1932. Wing Comdr RAFVR, served 1940–45 (despatches). *Heir: s* Edward Jeremy Westrow Hulse [*b* 22 Nov. 1932; *m* 1957, Verity Ann, *d* of William Pilkington, Ivy Well, St John, Jersey; one *s* one *d*]. *Address:* Breamore, Hants SP6 2BU. *TA:* Breamore. *T:* Downton (01725) 512773. *Clubs:* Carlton; Leander. *Died 10 April 1996.*

HUME, His Eminence Cardinal (George) Basil, OM 1999; Archbishop of Westminster, (RC), since 1976; *b* 2 March 1923; *s* of Sir William Hume, CMG, FRCP and Marie Elisabeth, *e d* of Col Tisseyre. *Educ:* Ampleforth Coll.; St Benet's Hall, Oxford; Fribourg Univ., Switzerland Ordained priest 1950. Ampleforth College: Senior Modern Language Master, 1952–63; Housemaster, 1955–63; Prof. of Dogmatic Theology, 1955–63; Magister Scholarum of the English Benedictine Congregation, 1957–63; Abbot of Ampleforth, 1963–76. Cardinal, 1976. President: RC Bishops' Conf. of England and Wales, 1979–; Council of European Bishops' Confs, 1978–87; (jtly) Churches Together in England, 1990–; CCJ; Member: Congregation for Eastern Churches, 1994–; Congregation for the Sacraments and Divine Worship; Congregation for Religious and Secular Institutes; Pontifical Council for the Promotion of Christian Unity; Pontifical Council for Pastoral Assistance to Health Care Workers. Hon. Bencher, Inner Temple, 1976. Hon. Freeman: Newcastle upon Tyne, 1980; London, 1980; Skinners' Co, 1994. Hon. DD: Cantab, 1979; Newcastle upon Tyne, 1979; London, 1980; Oxon, 1981; York, 1982; Kent, 1983; Durham, 1987; Collegio S Anselmo, Rome, 1987; Hull, 1989; Keele, 1990; Hon. DHL: Manhattan Coll., NY, 1980; Catholic Univ. of America, 1980; Hon. LLD Newcastle upon Tyne Polytechnic, 1992; DUniv Surrey, 1992. *Publications:* Searching for God, 1977; In Praise of Benedict, 1981; To Be a Pilgrim, 1984; Towards a Civilisation of Love, 1988; Light in the Lord, 1991; Remaking Europe: the gospel in a divided continent, 1994; Footprints of the Northern Saints, 1996; The Mystery of Love, 1996; Basil in Blunderland, 1997; The Mystery of the Cross, 1998. *Address:* Archbishop's House, Westminster, SW1P 1QJ. *Club:* Athenæum. *Died 17 June 1999.*

HUMPHREYS, Sir Myles; see Humphreys, Sir R. E. M.

HUMPHREYS, Sir Olliver (William), Kt 1968; CBE 1957; BSc; FInstP, CEng, FIEE, FRAeS; *b* 4 Sept. 1902; *s* of late Rev. J. Willis Humphreys, Bath; *m* 1st, 1933, Muriel Mary Hawkins (*d* 1985); 2nd, 1993, Dr P. E. R. Read, AM. *Educ:* Caterham Sch.; University Coll., London. Joined staff GEC Research Labs, 1925, Dir, 1949–61; Director 1953, Vice-Chm., 1963–67, GEC Ltd; Chm. all GEC Electronics and Telecommunications subsidiaries, 1961–66 and GEC (Research) Ltd, 1961–67. Mem. Bd, Inst. Physics, 1951–60 (Pres., 1956–58); Mem. Council, IEE, 1952–55 (Vice-Pres., 1959–63; Pres., 1964–65); Faraday Lectr, 1953–54. Mem., BoT Cttee on Organisation and Constitution of BSI, 1949–50; Chm., BSI Telecommunications Industry Standards Cttee, 1951–63 (Mem. Gen. Council, 1953–56; Mem. Exec. Cttee, 1953–60); Chm., Internat. Special Cttee on Radio Interference (CISPR), 1953–61; Chm., Electrical Res. Assoc., 1958–61; Chm., DSIR Radio Res. Bd, 1954–62; Pres., Electronic Engrg Assoc., 1962–64; Founder Chm., Conf. of Electronics Industry, 1963–67; Mem., Nat. ERC, 1963–67. Fellow UCL, 1963. Sen. Freeman, Worshipful Co. of Makers of Playing Cards. *Publications:* various technical and scientific papers in proceedings of learned societies. *Recreations:* travel, walking, reading. *Address:* c/o Gledhurst Manor, West Cliff Road, Bournemouth BH4 8BB. *Died 3 Nov. 1996.*

HUMPHREYS, Sir (Raymond Evelyn) Myles, Kt 1977; JP; DL; Chairman: Northern Ireland Railways Co. Ltd, 1967–90; Northern Ireland Transport Holding Company, 1988–93 (Director, 1968–74); *b* 24 March 1925; *s* of Raymond and May Humphreys; *m* 1st, 1963, Joan Tate (*d* 1979); two *s*; 2nd, 1987, Sheila Clements-McFarland. *Educ:* Skegoniel Primary Sch.; Londonderry High Sch.; Belfast Royal Acad. Research Engineer: NI Road Transport Bd, 1946–48; Ulster Transport Authy, 1948–55; Transport Manager, Nestle's Food Products (NI) Ltd, 1955–59; Director: Walter Alexander (Belfast) Ltd, 1959–92; Quick Service Stations Ltd, 1971–85; Bowring Martin Ltd, 1978–88; Abbey National plc (formerly Abbey National Bldg Soc.), 1981–91 (Chm., NI Adv. Bd, 1981–92); NI Railways Leasing, 1986–90; Belfast Harbour Pension Fund Ltd, 1987–88; NI Railways Travel Ltd, 1988–90. Chm., Belfast Marathon Ltd, 1981–85. Mem., Belfast City Council, 1964–81; Chairman: Belfast Corp. Housing Cttee, 1966–69; City Council Planning Cttee, 1973–75; City Council Town Planning and Environmental Health Cttee, 1973–75; Finance and Gen. Purposes Cttee, 1978–80; High Sheriff of Belfast, 1969; Dep. Lord Mayor, 1970; Lord Mayor, 1975–77. Chm., NI Police Authy, 1976–86; Member: Bd, Ulster Transport Authy, 1966–69; Nat. Planning and Town Planning Council, 1970–81 (Chm., 1976–77); NI Tourist Bd, 1973–80; NI Housing Exec., 1975–78; Chm., Ulster Tourist Develt Assoc., 1968–78; Belfast Harbour Comr, 1979–88. Member: May Cttee of Inquiry into UK Prison Services, 1978–79; Lord Chancellor's Cttee, 1985–95. Past Chairman: Bd of Visitors, HM Prison, Belfast; Bd of Management, Dunlambert Secondary Sch. Past Pres., Belfast Junior Chamber of Commerce; Mem. Exec., NI Chamber of Commerce and Industry (Pres., 1982); NI Rep., Motability Internat.; Senator, Junior Chamber Internat.; Pres., Belfast Br., BIM, 1983–96. Member: TA&VRA for NI, 1980; Council, Queen's Silver Jubilee Appeal. Pres., NI Polio Fellowship, 1977–. Pres., City of Belfast Youth Orch., 1980; Dir, Ulster Orch. Soc., 1980–82; Trustee, Ulster Folk & Transport Mus., 1976–81; Pres., Belfast Transport Officials Club, 1996–; Vice Pres., Railway Preservation Soc. of Ire., 1994–; Patron, Model Engineers Soc., 1974–. Mem. Senate, QUB, 1975–77; Mem. Court, Ulster Univ., 1984–. District Transport Officer, St John Ambulance Brigade, 1946–66. Freeman of City of London, 1976. JP 1969; DL Belfast, 1983. FCIT. OStJ. *Address:* Mylestone, 23 Massey Avenue, Belfast BT4 2JT. *T:* (028) 9076 1166. *Club:* Ulster Reform (Belfast). *Died 21 Feb. 1998.*

HUMPHREYS, Prof. Robert Arthur, OBE 1946; PhD; Director, Institute of Latin-American Studies, University of London, 1965–74; Professor of Latin-American History in University of London, 1948–74, then Emeritus; *b* 6 June 1907; *s* of late Robert Humphreys and Helen Marion Bavin, Lincoln; *m* 1946, Elisabeth (*d* 1990), *er d* of late Sir Bernard Pares, KBE, DCL. *Educ:* Lincoln Sch.; Peterhouse, Cambridge (Scholar; MA, PhD). Commonwealth Fund Fellow, Univ. of Michigan, 1930–32; Asst Lectr in American History, UCL, 1932, Lectr 1935; Reader in American History in Univ. of London, 1942–48; Prof. of Latin-American History, UCL, 1948–70. Research Dept, FO, 1939–45. Mem., UGC Cttee on Latin American Studies, 1962–64; Chairman: Cttee on Library Resources, Univ. of London, 1969–71; Management Cttee, Inst of Archæology, 1975–80; Mem. Adv. Cttee, British Library Reference Div., 1975–79. Governor, SOAS, 1965–80, Hon. Fellow 1981. Pres., RHistS, 1964–68 (Hon. Vice-Pres., 1968). Lectures: Enid Muir Meml, Univ. of Newcastle upon Tyne, 1962; Creighton, Univ. of London, 1964; Raleigh, Brit. Acad., 1965. Corresponding Member: Hispanic Soc. of America; Argentine Acad. of History; Instituto Histórico e Geográfico Brasileiro; Academia Chilena de la Historia; Sociedad Chilena de Historia y Geografia; Instituto Ecuatoriano de Ciencias Naturales; Sociedad Peruana de Historia; Instituto Histórico y Geográfico del Uruguay; Academia Nacional de la Historia, Venezuela. Hon. DLitt: Newcastle, 1966; Nottingham, 1972; Hon. LittD Liverpool, 1972; DUniv Essex, 1973. Comdr, Order of Rio Branco, Brazil, 1972. Machado de Assis Medal, Academia Brasileira de Letras, 1974. *Publications:* British Consular Reports on the Trade and Politics of Latin America, 1940; The Evolution of Modern Latin America, 1946; Liberation in South America, 1806–1827, 1952; Latin American History: a Guide to the Literature in English, 1958; The Diplomatic History of British Honduras, 1638–1901, 1961; (with G. S. Graham) The Navy and South America, 1807–1823 (Navy Records Soc.), 1962; (with J. Lynch) The Origins of the Latin American Revolutions, 1808–1826, 1965; Tradition and Revolt in Latin America and other Essays, 1969; The Detached Recollections of General D. F. O'Leary, 1969; The Royal Historical Society, 1868–1968, 1969; Robert Southey and his History of Brazil, 1978; Latin American Studies in Great Britain (autobiog.), 1978; Latin America and the Second World War, vol. I, 1939–1942, 1981, vol. II, 1942–1945, 1982; Elisabeth Humphreys, 1904–1990: a memoir, 1992; co-edited: (with A. D. Momigliano) Byzantine Studies and Other Essays by N. H. Baynes, 1955; (with Elisabeth Humphreys) The Historian's Business and Other Essays by Richard Pares, 1961; contrib. to The New Cambridge Modern History, vols VIII, IX and X. *Address:* 5 St James's Close, Prince Albert Road, NW8 7LG. *T:* (020) 7722 3628.

Died 2 May 1999.

HUNN, Sir Jack (Kent), Kt 1976; CMG 1964; LLM; Secretary of Defence, New Zealand, 1963–66, retired; *b* 24 Aug. 1906; *s* of Frederic John Hunn and Annie (*née* Peterson); *m* 1st, 1932, Dorothy Murray (decd); two *s*; 2nd, 1985, Mabel Duncan. *Educ:* Wairarapa Coll.; Auckland Univ. Public Trust Office, 1924–46; Actg Sec. of Justice, 1950; Public Service Comr, 1954–61; Actg Sec. of Internal Affairs and Dir of Civil Defence, 1959; Sec. for Maori Affairs and Maori Trustee, 1960–63. Reviewed Cook Islands Public Service, 1949 and 1954; Mem. NZ delegn to Duke of Edinburgh's Conf., 1956; Mem. UN Salary Review Cttee, 1956; reviewed organisation of South Pacific Commn, Noumea and Sydney, 1957, and of SEATO, Bangkok, 1959. Chairman: Wildlife Commission of Inquiry, 1968; Fire Safety Inquiry, 1969; Fire Service Council, 1973; Fire Service Commn,

1974; Electricity Distribution Enquiry, 1987. *Publications:* Hunn Report on Maori Affairs, 1960; Not Only Affairs Of State, 1982. *Address:* 40 Wren Street, Waikanae, New Zealand. *Died 14 June 1997.*

HUNT, Baron *cr* 1966 (Life Peer), of Llanfairwaterdine, co. Salop; **Henry Cecil John Hunt,** KG 1979; Kt 1953; CBE 1945; DSO 1944; *b* 22 June 1910; *s* of late Capt. C. E. Hunt, MC, IA, and E. H. Hunt (*née* Crookshank); *m* 1936, Joy Mowbray-Green; four *d. Educ:* Marlborough Coll.; RMC, Sandhurst. Commissioned King's Royal Rifle Corps, 1930; seconded to Indian Police, 1934–35 and 1938–40 (Indian Police Medal, 1940); War of 1939–45: Comd 11th Bn KRRC, 1944; Comd 11th Indian Inf. Bde, 1944–46; Staff Coll., 1946; GSO 1, Jt Planning Staffs, MELF, 1946–48; Joint Services Staff Coll., 1949; Western Europe C's-in-C Cttee, 1950–51; Allied Land Forces, Central Europe, 1951–52; Col Gen. Staff, HQ I (British) Corps, 1952; Asst Comdt, Staff Coll., 1953–55; Comdr 168 Inf. Bde, TA, 1955–56; retired, 1956; Hon. Brigadier. Dir, Duke of Edinburgh's Award Scheme, 1956–66. Rector, Aberdeen Univ., 1963–66. Personal Adviser to Prime Minister during Nigerian Civil War, 1968–70. Chairman: Parole Bd for England and Wales, 1967–74; Adv. Cttee on Police in N Ireland, 1969; President: Nat. Assoc. of Youth Clubs, 1954–70; Council for Volunteers Overseas, 1968–74; Nat. Assoc. of Probation Officers, 1974–80; Rainer Foundn, 1971–85; Council for Nat. Parks, 1980–86; Nat. Assoc. for Outdoor Educn, 1991–93; Mem., Royal Commn on the Press, 1974–77. Joined Social Democratic Party, 1981, Social and Liberal Democrats, 1988. Leader, British Expedition to Mount Everest, 1952–53. President: Alpine Club, 1956–58; Climbers' Club, 1963–66; British Mountaineering Council, 1965–68; Britain and Nepal Soc., 1960–75; National Ski Fedn, 1968–72; RGS, 1977–80 (Hon. Mem., 1984). Hon. DCL Durham, 1954; Hon. LLD: Aberdeen, 1954; London, 1954; City, 1976; Leeds, 1979; Hon. DSc Sheffield, 1989. Order 1st Class Gurkha Right Hand, 1953; Indian Everest Medal, 1953; Hubbard Medal (US), 1954; Founder's Medal, RGS, 1954; Lawrence Memorial Medal, RCAS, 1954; King Albert I Meml Medal for Mountaineering, 1994. *Publications:* The Ascent of Everest, 1953; Our Everest Adventure, 1954; (with C. Brasher) The Red Snows, 1959; Life is Meeting, 1978; (ed) My Favourite Mountaineering Stories, 1978; In Search of Adventure, 1989. *Recreation:* mountain activities. *Address:* Highway Cottage, Aston, Henley-on-Thames RG9 3DE. *Clubs:* Alpine, Ski Club of Great Britain. *Died 8 Nov. 1998.*

HUNT, Sir David (Wathen Stather), KCMG 1963 (CMG 1959); OBE 1943; HM Diplomatic Service, retired; Director: Observer Newspapers, 1982–94; Trigraph Ltd, since 1988; *b* 25 Sept. 1913; *s* of late Canon B. P. W. Stather Hunt, DD, and Elizabeth Milner; *m* 1st, 1948, Pamela Muriel Medawar (marr. diss. 1967); two *s*; 2nd, 1968, Iro Myrianthousis. *Educ:* St Lawrence Coll.; Wadham Coll., Oxford (1st Class Hon. Mods. 1934; 1st Class Lit. Hum. 1936; Thomas Whitcombe Greene Prize, 1936; Diploma in Classical Archæology, 1937). Served 1st Bn Welch Regt and General Staff in Middle East, Balkans, North Africa, Sicily, Italy, 1940–46 (despatches 3 times, OBE, US Bronze Star); GSO1 18th Army Group, 1943; 15th Army Group, 1943–45; Col General Staff, Allied Force HQ, 1945–46; attached staff Governor-General Canada, 1946–47; released and granted hon. rank of Colonel, 1947. Fellow of Magdalen Coll., Oxford, 1937–47; Principal, Dominions Office, 1947; 1st Secretary, Pretoria, 1948–49; Private Secretary to Prime Minister (Mr Attlee), 1950–51, (Mr Churchill) 1951–52; Asst Secretary, 1952; Deputy High Commissioner for UK, Lahore, 1954–56; Head of Central African Dept, Commonwealth Relations Office, 1956–59; Asst Under

Secretary of State, Commonwealth Relations Office, 1959–60; accompanied the Prime Minister as an Adviser, on African tour, Jan.-Feb. 1960; Dep. High Comr for the UK in Lagos, Fedn of Nigeria, 1960–62; High Commissioner: in Uganda, 1962–65; in Cyprus, 1965–67; in Nigeria, 1967–69; Ambassador to Brazil, 1969–73. Dep. Chm., Exim Credit Management and Consultants, 1974–77, Consultant, 1978–82. Chm., Bd of Governors, Commonwealth Inst., 1974–84. Mem. Appts Commn, Press Council, 1977–82. Montague Burton Vis. Prof. of Internat. Relations, Univ. of Edinburgh, 1980. President: Classical Assoc., 1981–82; Soc. for Promotion of Hellenic Studies, 1986–90. Chm., Attlee Foundn, 1995–96. FSA 1984. Corresp. Mem., Brazilian Acad. of Arts, 1972. BBC TV Mastermind, 1977 and Mastermind of Masterminds, 1982. Hon. DHum Ball State Univ., 1991. US Bronze Star 1945; Grand Cross, Order of the Southern Cross, Brazil, 1985. *Publications:* A Don at War, 1966, 2nd edn 1990; On the Spot, 1975; Footprints in Cyprus, 1982, rev. edn 1990; (ed and trans.) Gothic Art and the Renaissance in Cyprus, by Camille Enlart, 1987; (ed with Iro Hunt) Caterina Cornaro: Queen of Cyprus, 1989; articles in Annual of British School of Archæology at Athens, Journal of Hellenic Studies, and Slavonic Rev.; Editor, The Times Yearbook of World Affairs, 1978–81. *Recreations:* reading, writing, roses. *Address:* Old Place, Lindfield, West Sussex RH16 2HU. *T:* (01444) 482298. *Clubs:* Athenæum, Beefsteak; Pen Clube do Brasil.

Died 30 July 1998.

HUNT, Kevan, MVO 1998; independent consultant, since 1995; Corporation Member and Employee Relations Director, British Coal Corporation, 1991–95; *b* Seaham Harbour, Co. Durham, 13 Oct. 1937; *s* of late Martin Hunt and of Mary Patilla (formerly Hunt, *née* Lavery); *m* 1958, Valerie Anne Scattergood; two *s*. *Educ:* William Rhodes Sch., Chesterfield; Chesterfield Coll. of Technology; Extramural Studies Dept, Sheffield Univ.; Derby and Dist Coll. of Art. National Coal Board, later British Coal: Mining Technician (Electrical), 1955–68; Personnel Manager, 1969–74; Industrial Relations Br. Head, 1974–76; Area IR Officer (S Notts), 1976–82; HQ IR Dir (Nat.), 1982–84; IR Dep. Dir-Gen. (Nat.), 1984–85; Head of IR, 1985–88; Exec. Dir, 1988–91; Chairman: British Coal Enterprise, 1993–96; Internat. Mining Consultants Gp Holdings, 1993–95; Centris Coal Benefits Ltd, 1994–95. Chm., Nationalised Industry's Personnel Panel. Dist Councillor, 1964–76; Chm., Alfreton UDC, 1970–71; Leader, Amber Valley Dist Council, 1973–76. Chairman: Youth Enterprise Services International, 1994; PYBT Notts, 1996. CIMgt; FIPM; FInstD; FRSA; MIMinE. *Publications:* papers in personnel, training and industrial relations field. *Recreations:* travel, walking, reading. *Address:* Craigside, 168 Greenhill Lane, Riddings, Alfreton, Derbys DE55 4EX.

Died 17 March 1999.

HUNT, Sir Peter (John), Kt 1995; FRICS; Chairman and Managing Director, Land Securities PLC, since 1987 (Managing Director, since 1978); *b* 1 July 1933; *s* of Prof. Herbert James Hunt and Sheila Jessamine Hunt; *m* 1955, Madeleine Meier; one *s*. *Educ:* Bedford Sch.; College of Estate Management (BScEstMan; Hon Fellow, 1995). Borrett and Borrett, 1956–60; Chamberlain Gp, 1960–64; Land Securities Gp, 1964–. Chm., Central London Housing Trust, 1981–92 (Mem. Mgt Cttee, 1973–92); Member: Covent Garden Market Authority, 1975–; Council, British Property Fedn, 1978– (Pres., 1990–91); Council, British Council for Offices, 1990–. Trustee, Architecture Foundn, 1992–. *Recreations:* boating, tennis. *Address:* 37 Devonshire Mews West, W1N 1FQ.

Died 8 Dec. 1997.

HUNT, Richard Henry; Chief Registrar of the High Court of Justice in Bankruptcy, 1980–84, retired; *b* 19 Jan. 1912; *s* of late Francis John and Lucy Edwyna Louise Hunt; *m* 1947, Peggy Ashworth Richardson; two *s*. *Educ:* Marlborough Coll.; Queen's Coll., Oxford. Called to Bar, 1936; Bencher, Middle Temple, 1964. Served with RA, 1939–45: Western Desert, Greece and Crete campaigns (POW, Crete, 1941). Registrar of the High Court of Justice in Bankruptcy, 1966–80. *Recreations:* foreign travel, languages.

Died 29 Sept. 1998.

HUNT, Roger; His Honour Judge Hunt; a Circuit Judge, since 1986; *b* 15 Jan. 1935; *s* of late Richard Henry Hunt and Monica Hunt; *m* 1963, Barbara Ann Eccles; two *d*. *Educ:* Giggleswick Sch.; Pembroke Coll., Oxford (MA). Commnd Royal Signals, 1955; served Germany, HQ 4th Guards Bde, 1956; TA 49th Inf. Div., Signal Regt, 1956–63. Called to the Bar, Lincoln's Inn, 1960; joined NE Circuit, 1961; a Recorder, 1978–86. *Recreations:* golf, gardening. *Club:* Moortown Golf.

Died 26 April 1999.

HUNT, Roland Charles Colin, CMG 1965; HM Diplomatic Service, retired; Director, British National Committee, International Chamber of Commerce, 1973–76; *b* 19 March 1916; *s* of Colin and Dorothea Hunt, Oxford; *m* 1939, Pauline (*d* 1989), 2nd *d* of late Dr J. C. Maxwell Garnett, CBE; three *s* two *d*. *Educ:* Rugby Sch. (scholar); The Queen's Coll., Oxford (scholar). Entered Indian Civil Service, 1938; served in various districts in Madras as Sub-Collector, 1941–45; Joint Sec. and Sec., Board of Revenue (Civil Supplies), Madras, 1946–47; joined Commonwealth Relations Office, 1948; served on staff of United Kingdom High Commissioner in Pakistan (Karachi), 1948–50; Mem. UK Delegation to African Defence Facilities Conference, Nairobi, 1951; served in Office of UK High Comr in S Africa, 1952–55; Asst Sec., 1955; attached to Office of High Comr for Fedn of Malaya, Kuala Lumpur, 1956; Dep. High Commissioner for the UK in the Federation of Malaya, Kuala Lumpur, 1957–59; Imperial Defence Coll., 1960; Asst Sec., Commonwealth Relations Office, 1961; British Dep. High Comr in Pakistan, 1962–65; British High Commissioner in Uganda, 1965–67; Asst Under-Sec. of State, CO and FCO, 1967–70; High Comr, Trinidad and Tobago, 1970–73. *Publication:* (ed jtly) The District Officer in India, 1930–1947, 1980. *Recreations:* ball-games, piano-playing.

Died 24 March 1999.

HUNTER, (Adam) Kenneth (Fisher), CBE 1990; formerly Sheriff of North Strathclyde at Paisley, retired; *b* 1920; *o s* of late Thomas C. Hunter, MBE, AMIEE, and Elizabeth Hunter; *m* 1949, Joan Stella Hiscock, MB, ChB; one *s* two *d*. *Educ:* Dunfermline High Sch.; St Andrews Univ. (MA Hons); Edinburgh Univ. (LLB). Admitted to Faculty of Advocates, 1946; Chm. of the Supreme Court Legal Aid Cttee of the Law Society of Scotland, 1949–53; Standing Junior Counsel to HM Commissioners of Customs and Excise, 1950–53; Sheriff-Substitute, later Sheriff, of Renfrew and Argyll (subseq. N Strathclyde) at Paisley, 1953–90. *Recreations:* photography, music, philately. *Address:* Ravenswood, Bridge of Weir, Renfrewshire PA11 3AN. *T:* Bridge of Weir (01505) 612017.

Died 11 April 1996.

HUNTER, Sir Alexander (Albert), KBE 1976; Representative, Pecten Belize Company, since 1983; Speaker of the House of Representatives of Belize, 1974–79; *b* Belize, British Honduras, 21 May 1920; *s* of Alexander J. Hunter, KSG, and Laura Hunter (*née* Reyes); *m* 1947, Araceli Marin Sanchez, Alajuela, Costa Rica; one *s* two *d*. *Educ:* St John's Coll. (Jesuit), Belize City; Regis Coll. (Jesuit), Denver, Colo; Queen's Univ., Kingston, Ont. Served War, NCO, Radar Br., RCAF, 1941–45: active service in UK, Azores, Gibraltar, with 220 Sqdn

Coastal Comd, RAF. In Accounting Dept, United Fruit Co., Costa Rica, 1940–41 and 1945–47; joined staff of James Brodie & Co. Ltd, as Accountant, 1947; Company Sec., 1948; Dir 1952–61; Consultant: James Brodie & Co. Ltd, 1975–83; Anschutz Overseas Corp., Denver, Colo, 1975–82; Chm., Belize Airways Ltd, 1978–80. MLA (PUP), Fort George Div., 1961; Minister of Natural Resources, Commerce and Industry, March 1961; MHR (PUP), Fort George, under new Constitution, 1965; Minister of Natural Resources and Trade, 1965–69; Minister of Trade and Industry, 1969–74; Mem., Constitutional Ministerial External Affairs Cttee, 1965–74. Represented Belize: Bd of Governors, Caribbean Develt Bank, 1969–74; Council of Ministers, CARIFTA, 1971–73; Council of Ministers, Caribbean Economic Community, 1973–74; acted as Dep. Governor, Aug.–Sept. 1975, and as Dep. Premier on several occasions, 1969–74. Hon. Consul of El Salvador, 1951–78; official observer to Salvadoran Elections, 1982 and 1984. People's United Party: Treasurer and Mem. Central Party Council, 1961–74; Mem. Exec. Cttee, 1961–74; Chm. Fort George Div., 1961–74. Former Vice-Pres., Belize Chamber of Commerce; Member: Property Valuation Appeal Bd, 1960; Citrus Industry Investigation Cttee, 1960. Member: West India Cttee; Nat. Geographic Soc.; Belize Ex-Servicemen's League. 1939–45 Star; Atlantic Star; Defence of Britain medal; Canadian Service medal and bar; British War medal. *Recreations:* target shooting, hunting, light and heavy tackle salt-water fishing. *Address:* 6 St Matthew Street, Caribbean Shores, PO Box 505, Belize City, Belize. *T:* (2) 44482.

Died 27 Aug. 1996.

HUNTER, Kenneth; *see* Hunter, A. K. F.

HUNTER-TOD, Air Marshal Sir John (Hunter), KBE 1971 (OBE 1957); CB 1969; Head of Engineer Branch and Director-General of Engineering, Royal Air Force, 1970–73, retired; *b* 21 April 1917; *s* of late Hunter Finlay Tod, FRCS and Yvonne Grace, *e d* of Stanley Rendall, Aix-les-Bains, France; *m* 1959, Anne, *d* of late Thomas Chaffer Howard; one *s*. *Educ:* Marlborough; Trinity Coll., Cambridge (MA). CEng; DCAe 1948. Commissioned, 1940; Fighter Command and Middle East, 1939–45; Group Capt. 1958; Air Cdre 1963; Dir, Guided Weapons (Air), Min. of Aviation, 1962–65; AO Engrg, RAF Germany, 1965–67; AOC No 24 Group, RAF, 1967–70; Air Vice-Marshal, 1968; Air Marshal, 1971. Hon. DSc Cranfield Inst. of Technol., 1974. *Address:* 21 Ridge Hill, Dartmouth, S Devon TQ6 9PE. *T:* (01803) 833130. *Club:* Royal Air Force. *Died 11 May 2000.*

HUNTING, (Lindsay) Clive; Chairman: Hunting plc, 1974–91; Battle of Britain Memorial Ltd, since 1995 (Director, 1993–95); *b* 22 Dec. 1925; *s* of late Gerald Lindsay Hunting and Ruth (*née* Pyman); *m* 1952, Shelagh (*née* Hill Lowe); one *d* (one *s* decd). *Educ:* Loretto; Trinity Hall, Cambridge (MA). Royal Navy, 1944–47; Cambridge, 1947–50; joined Hunting Group, 1950: Dir, 1952; Vice-Chm., 1962; Chm., 1975. Chm., Field Aviation Ltd, 1970–94. President: British Independent Air Transport Assoc., 1960–62; Fédn Internationale de Transporte Aérien Privée, 1961–63; Air Educn and Recreation Organisation, 1970–90; SBAC, 1985–86 (Treas., 1988–); Chm., Air League, 1968–71; Mem. Council, Cranfield Inst. of Technol., 1989–. Master, Coachmakers' and Coach Harness Makers' Co., 1983–84. CIMgt (CBIM 1980); CRAeS 1983. Nile Gold Medal for Aerospace Educn, 1982. *Recreations:* yachting, fishing. *Address:* April Cottage, Alderbourne Lane, Fulmer, Bucks SL3 6JB. *T:* (01753) 662300, *Fax:* (01753) 663978. *Clubs:* Royal Yacht Squadron, Royal London Yacht (Cdre, 1989) (Cowes). *Died 25 July 2000.*

HURST, Dr Robert, CBE 1973; GM 1944; FRSC; retired; *b* Nelson, NZ, 3 Jan. 1915; *s* of late Percy Cecil Hurst and Margery Hurst; *m* 1946, Rachael Jeanette (*née* Marsh); three *s*. *Educ:* Nelson Coll.; Canterbury Coll., NZ (MSc); Cambridge Univ. (PhD). FRIC 1977. Experimental Officer, Min. of Supply, engaged in research in bomb disposal and mine detection, 1940–45. Group Leader Transuranic Elements Group, AERE, Harwell, 1948–55; Project Leader, Homogeneous Aqueous Reactor Project, AERE, Harwell, 1956–57; Chief Chemist, Research and Development Branch, Industrial Group UKAEA, 1957–58; Director, Dounreay Experimental Reactor Establishment, UKAEA, 1958–63; Dir of Res., British Ship Res. Assoc., 1963–76. *Publication:* (ed) Progress in Nuclear Engineering, Series IV (Technology and Engineering), 1957. *Recreation:* gardening. *Address:* 15 Elms Avenue, Parkstone, Poole, Dorset BH14 8EE.

Died 15 May 1996.

HUSSEIN bin Talal; King of Jordan; *b* 14 Nov. 1935; *s* of late King Talal (*d* 1972) and Queen Zein (*d* 1994); *S* father, 1952; *m* 1st, 1955, Sherifa Dina Abdul Hamid, (Princess Dina) (marr. diss. 1957); one *d*; 2nd, 1961, Antoinette Gardiner, (Princess Muna) (marr. diss. 1972); two *s* twin *d*; 3rd, 1972, Alia Baha Eddin Toukan, (Queen Alia) (*d* 1977); one *s* one *d*; 4th, 1978, Lisa Hallaby, (Queen Noor); two *s* two *d*. *Educ:* Victoria Coll., Alexandria; Harrow; RMA, Sandhurst. Held many foreign decorations. *Publications:* Uneasy Lies the Head, 1962; My War with Israel, 1969; Mon Metier de Roi, 1975. *Recreations:* water sports, karate, flying, driving, fencing, photography, ham radio. *Address:* Royal Hashemite Court, Amman, Jordan. *Died 7 Feb. 1999.*

HUTCHINGS, Andrew William Seymour, CBE 1973; General Secretary, Assistant Masters Association, 1939–78, Joint General Secretary, Assistant Masters and Mistresses Association, Sept-Dec. 1978; Vice-President, National Foundation for Educational Research in England and Wales, since 1983 (Chairman, 1973–83); *b* 3 Dec. 1907; *o s* of William Percy and Mellony Elizabeth Louisa Hutchings; unmarried. *Educ:* Cotham Sch., Bristol; St Catharine's Coll., Cambridge (MA). Asst Master: Downside Sch., 1929–30; Methodist Coll., Belfast, 1930–34; Holt Sch., Liverpool, 1934–36; Asst Sec., Asst Masters Assoc., 1936–39. Hon. Sec., Jt Cttee of Four Secondary Assocs, 1939–78; Sec.-Gen. 1954–65, Pres. 1965–71 and 1972–73, Internat. Fedn of Secondary Teachers; Member: Exec. Cttee, World Confedn of Organisations of Teaching Profession, 1954–80; Secondary Schs Examination Council, and subseq. of Schools Council, 1939–78; Norwood Cttee on Curriculum and Examinations in Secondary Schs, 1941–43; Chm., Teachers' Panel, Burnham Primary and Secondary Cttee, 1965–78; Vice-Pres., Associated Examining Bd, 1994– (Chm., 1992–94); Vice-Chm., 1982–92; Chm., Exec. Cttee, 1979–92). FEIS 1963; FCP 1975. *Publications:* educnl and professional articles and memoranda for Asst Masters Assoc. *Address:* Lower Eastacott House, Umberleigh, North Devon EX37 9AJ. *T:* (01769) 540486. *Club:* Kennel. *Died 30 Oct. 1996.*

HUTCHINS, Captain Ronald Edward, CBE 1961; DSC 1943; RN; *b* 7 Jan. 1912; *s* of Edward Albert Hutchins and Florence Ada (*née* Sharman); *m* 1937, Irene (*née* Wood) (*d* 1996); two *s*. *Educ:* St John's (elem. sch.), Hammersmith; TS Mercury, Hamble, Hants (C. B. Fry); RN Coll., Greenwich. Royal Navy, 1928–61, service in submarines, then Exec. Br. specialising in gunnery; Computer Industry, 1961–79: Manager and Company Dir, ICL and some of its UK subsids, and associated engrg cos. *Recreations:* walking, gardening. *Address:* 11 Virginia Beeches, Callow Hill, Virginia Water, Surrey GU25 4LT. *Died 23 June 1998.*

HUTCHISON, Sir Peter, 2nd Bt *cr* 1939, of Thurle, Streatley, co. Berks; *b* 27 Sept. 1907; *er s* of Sir Robert Hutchison, 1st Bt, MD, CM, and Lady (Laetitia Norah) Hutchison; *S* father, 1960; *m* 1949, Mary-Grace (*née* Seymour); two *s* two *d. Educ:* Marlborough; Lincoln Coll., Oxford (MA). Admitted as a Solicitor, 1933. Dep.-Clerk of the Peace and of the CC, E Suffolk, 1947–71, Clerk of the Peace, 1971. Mem., Suffolk Coastal DC, 1973–83. Chm. of Governors, Orwell Park Prep. Sch., 1975–85. *Recreations:* gardening, reading. *Heir: s* Robert Hutchison [*b* 25 May 1954; *m* 1987, Anne Margaret, *er d* of Sir Michael Thomas, 11th Bt; two *s*]. *Address:* Melton Mead, near Woodbridge, Suffolk IP12 1PF. *T:* (01394) 382746.   *Died 16 Jan. 1998.*

HUTCHISON, Sidney Charles, CVO 1977 (LVO 1967); Hon. Archivist, Royal Academy of Arts, since 1982; *b* 26 March 1912; *s* of late Henry Hutchison; *m* 1937, Nancy Arnold Brindley (*d* 1985); no *c. Educ:* Holloway Sch., London; London Univ. (Dip. in Hist. of Art, with Dist.). Joined staff of Royal Academy, 1929. Served War of 1939–45: Royal Navy, rising to Lt-Comdr (S), RNVR. Librarian of Royal Academy, 1949–68, also Sec. of Loan Exhibitions, 1955–68; Sec., Royal Academy, 1968–82, Hon. Mem. (Antiquary), 1992–. Secretary: E. A. Abbey Meml Trust Fund for Mural Painting, 1960–87; Incorporated E. A. Abbey Scholarships Fund, 1965–92; E. Vincent Harris Fund for Mural Decoration, 1970–87; British Institution Fund, 1968–82; Chantrey Trustees, 1968–82; Richard Ford Award Fund, 1977–82. Lectr in the History of Art, for Extra-Mural Dept of Univ. of London, 1957–67. Gen. Comm of Tax, 1972–87. Governor, Holloway Sch., 1969–81. Trustee, Chantrey Bequest, 1982–; Pres., Southgate Soc. of Arts, 1983–. Organist and Choirmaster of St Matthew's, Westminster, 1933–37. Associate Mem., ICOM, 1964. FRSA 1950; FSA 1955; FMA 1962; Fellow, Assoc. of Art Historians, 1974. Officer, Order of Polonia Restituta (Poland), 1971; Chevalier, Order of the Crown (Belgium), 1972; Grand Decoration of Honour (silver) (Austria), 1972; Cavaliere Ufficiale, Al Merito della Repubblica Italiana, 1980. *Publications:* The Homes of the Royal Academy, 1956; The History of the Royal Academy, 1768–1968, 1968, enl. and updated, 1768–1986, 1986; articles for Walpole Society, Museums Jl, Encyclopædia Britannica, DNB, Apollo, etc. *Recreations:* music, travel. *Address:* 60 Belmont Close, Mount Pleasant, Cockfosters, Barnet, Herts EN4 9LT. *T:* (020) 8449 9821. *Clubs:* Athenæum, Arts.   *Died 22 April 2000.*

HUTCHISON, Thomas Oliver, FRSE; Director, since 1985, Deputy Chairman, 1992–98, Cadbury Schweppes; *b* 3 Jan. 1931; *s* of late James Hutchison and Thomasina Oliver; *m* 1955, Frances Mary Ada Butterworth; three *s. Educ:* Hawick High Sch.; Univ. of St Andrews (BSc Hons First Cl. Natural Philosophy). Joined ICI General Chemicals Division, 1954; key prodn, technical and commercial appts on general chemicals side of the Company's business until apptd Head of ICI's Policy Groups Dept, London, 1974; Dep. Chm., ICI Plastics Div., 1977–79; Chairman: ICI Petrochemicals and Plastics Div., 1981–85; Phillips-Imperial Petroleum, 1982–85; Dir, ICI plc, 1985–91. Dir, 1985–97, Dep. Gov., 1991–97, Bank of Scotland; Director: Océ Finance Ltd, 1977–79; ICI Australia, 1985–91; ICI Impkemix Investments Pty, 1985–91; Enterprise Oil, 1987–90; Hammerson plc, 1991–; AMP Asset Management, 1991–; Bank of Wales, 1993–96. Mem. Council, British Plastics Fedn, 1977–80; Pres., Assoc. of Plastics Manufacturers in Europe, 1980–82; Mem., Cttee of Dirs and Associate, Corporate Assembly Membership, CEFIC, 1986–91. FRSE 1991. *Recreations:* golf, opera, music. *Address:* Cadbury

Schweppes plc, 25 Berkeley Square, W1X 6HT. *Clubs:* Athenæum, Royal Automobile.
                                        Died 6 June 1998.

HUTCHISON, Prof. William McPhee; Personal Professor in Parasitology, University of Strathclyde, 1971–89, then Emeritus; *b* 2 July 1924; *s* of William Hutchison and Ann McPhee; *m* 1963, Ella Duncan McLaughland; two *s. Educ:* Eastwood High Sch.; Glasgow Univ. BSc, PhD, DSc; FLS, FIBiol, CBiol; FRSE. Glasgow Univ. Fencing Blue, 1949; Ford Epée Cup; Glasgow Univ. Fencing Champion, 1950 (McLure Foil Trophy, 1950). Strathclyde University: Asst Lectr, 1952; Lectr, 1953; Sen. Lectr, 1969. Engaged in res. on toxoplasma and toxoplasmosis; discoverer of life cycle of Toxoplasma, 1968–70. Robert Koch Medal, 1970. *Publications:* contrib. Trans Royal Soc. Trop. Med. and Hygiene, Ann. Tropical Med., Parasitology, BMJ. *Recreations:* general microscopy, academic heraldry, collection of zoological specimens. *Address:* 597 Kilmarnock Road, Newlands, Glasgow G43 2TH. *T:* (0141) 637 4882.   *Died 28 Dec. 1998.*

HUXLEY, Elspeth Josceline, (Mrs Gervas Huxley), CBE 1962; JP; *b* 23 July 1907; *d* of Major Josceline Grant, Njoro, Kenya; *m* 1931, Gervas Huxley (*d* 1971); one *s. Educ:* European Sch., Nairobi, Kenya; Reading Univ. (Diploma in Agriculture); Cornell Univ., USA. Asst Press Officer to Empire Marketing Board, London, 1929–32; subsequently travelled in America, Africa and elsewhere. Mem. BBC Gen. Advisory Council, 1952–59; UK Independent Mem., Monckton Advisory Commission on Central Africa, 1959. *Publications:* White Man's Country: Lord Delamere and the Making of Kenya, 2 vols, 1935; Murder at Government House (detective story), 1937, repr. 1987; Murder on Safari (detective story), 1938, repr. 1982; The African Poison Murders, 1939, repr. 1988; Red Strangers (novel), 1939; Atlantic Ordeal, 1943; (with Margery Perham) Race and Politics in Kenya, 1944; The Walled City (novel), 1948; The Sorcerer's Apprentice (travel), 1948; I Don't Mind If I Do (light novel), 1951; Four Guineas (travel), 1952; A Thing to Love, 1954; The Red Rock Wilderness, 1957; The Flame Trees of Thika, 1959 (filmed, 1981); A New Earth, 1960; The Mottled Lizard, 1962; The Merry Hippo, 1963; Forks and Hope, 1964; A Man from Nowhere, 1964; Back Street New Worlds, 1965; Brave New Victuals, 1965; Their Shining Eldorado: a Journey through Australia, 1967; Love Among the Daughters, 1968; The Challenge of Africa, 1971; Livingstone and his African Journeys, 1974; Florence Nightingale, 1975; Gallipot Eyes, 1976; Scott of the Antarctic, 1977; Nellie: letters from Africa, 1980; Whipsnade: captive breeding for survival, 1981; The Prince Buys the Manor, 1982; (with Hugo van Lawick) Last Days in Eden, 1984; Out in the Midday Sun: My Kenya, 1985; Nine Faces of Kenya (anthology), 1990; Peter Scott: painter and naturalist, 1993. *Recreations:* resting, gossip. *Address:* Green End, Oaksey, near Malmesbury, Wilts SN16 9TL. *TA:* Oaksey, Malmesbury. *T:* (01666) 577252.   *Died 10 Jan. 1997.*

HUYGHE, René Louis; Grand Officier de la Légion d'Honneur; Member of the Académie Française since 1960; Hon. Professor of Psychology of Plastic Arts, Collège de France (Professor, 1950–76); Hon. Head Keeper, Musée du Louvre; Director, Museum Jacquemart-André, Paris, since 1974; *b* Arras, Pas-de-Calais, France, 3 May 1906; *s* of Louis Huyghe and Marie (*née* Delvoye); *m* 1950, Lydie Bouthet; one *s* one *d. Educ:* Sorbonne; École du Louvre, Paris. Attached to Musée du Louvre, 1927; Asst Keeper, 1930; Head Keeper, Départment des Peintures, Dessins, Chalcographie, 1937. Mem., Conseil Artistique de la Réunion des Musées Nationaux, 1952 (Vice-Pres. 1964, Pres. 1975–89); Pres. Assoc. Internationale du Film d'Art, 1958. Held foreign decorations. Praemium Erasmianum, The Hague, 1966. *Publications:* Histoire de l'Art contemporain: La Peinture, 1935; Cézanne 1936 and 1961; Les Contemporains, 1939 (2nd edn 1949); Vermeer, 1948; Watteau, 1950; various works on Gauguin, 1951, 1952, 1959; Dialogue avec le visible, 1955 (trans. Eng.); L'Art et l'homme, Vol. I, 1957, Vol. II, 1958, Vol. III, 1961 (trans. Eng.); Van Gogh, 1959; Merveilles de la France, 1960; L'Art et l'Ame, 1960 (trans. Eng.); La peinture française aux XVIIe et XVIIIe Siècles, 1962; Delacroix ou le combat solitaire, 1963, 2nd edn 1990 (trans. Eng.); Puissances de l'Image, 1965; Sens et Destin de l'Art, 1967; L'Art et le monde moderne, Vol. I, 1970, Vol. II, 1971; Formes et Forces, 1971; La Relève du réel, 1974; La Relève de l'imaginaire, 1976; Ce que je crois, 1976; De l'Art à la Philosophie, 1980; (with D. Ikeda) La Nuit appelle l'Aurore, 1980; Les Signes du Temps et l'Art moderne, 1985; (with M. Brion) Se perdre dans Venise, 1987; Psychologie de l'Art, 1991. *Address:* 3 rue Corneille, Paris 75006, France. *Club:* Union Interalliée (Paris).   *Died 7 Feb. 1997.*

HYATALI, Sir Isaac (Emanuel), Kt 1973; TC 1974; barrister and attorney-at-law; Chief Justice and President, Court of Appeal, Trinidad and Tobago, 1972–83; Legal Consultant to law firm of Hyatali and Co.; Chairman, Elections and Boundaries Commission, since 1983; *b* 21 Nov. 1917; *s* of late Joseph and Esther Hyatali; *m* 1943, Audrey Monica Joseph; two *s* one *d. Educ:* Naparima Coll., San Fernando; Gray's Inn and Council of Legal Education, London. Called to the Bar, Gray's Inn, 1947. Private practice at the Bar, 1947–59; Trinidad and Tobago: Judge, Supreme Court, 1959–62; Justice of Appeal, 1962–72; Pres., Industrial Court, 1965–72; Justice of Appeal, Seychelles Republic, 1983–86. Chairman: Arima Rent Assessment Bd, 1953–59; Agricultural Rent Bd (Eastern Counties), 1953–59; Agricultural Wages Council, 1958–59; Oil and Water Bd, 1959–62; Constitution Commn, 1987–90. Arbitrator and Umpire, ICAO,

1981–86. Chm., Amer. Life and Gen. Insce Co. (Trinidad) Ltd, 1983–91 (Hon. Chm., 1991–94); Chm., Ansa McAl Foundn, 1992– (amalgamation of Ansa Foundn (Chm., 1987) and McEneaney-Alston Foundn (Chm., 1989)). Trinidad and Tobago Editor of West Indian Law Reports, 1961–65. Mem., World Assoc. of Judges; Hon. Mem., World Peace through Law Center. Chm., St Ann's Hosp. Commn of Enquiry, 1992–93. Hon. LLD Univ. of WI, 1996. *Recreations:* reading, social work. *Address:* (chambers) 44 Edward Street, Port of Spain, Trinidad and Tobago. *T:* (62) 34007; Elections and Boundaries Commission, 134–138 Frederick Street, Port of Spain. *T:* (62) 38320; (home) 8 Pomme Rose Avenue, Cascade, St Anns, Republic of Trinidad and Tobago.

Died 2 Dec. 2000.

HYMAN, Joe; *b* 14 Oct. 1921; *yr s* of late Solomon and Hannah Hyman; *m* 1st, 1948, Corinne I. Abrahams (marr. diss.); one *s* one *d;* 2nd, 1963, Simone Duke; one *s* one *d. Educ:* North Manchester Grammar Sch. In textiles, 1939–80; Founder, Viyella International, and Chm., 1961–69; Chm., John Crowther Gp, 1971–80. Trustee, Pestalozzi Children's Village Trust, 1967–; Governor, LSE. FRSA 1968; FIMgt. CompTI. *Recreations:* music, golf, gardening. *Address:* 59 Kingston House North, Prince's Gate, SW7 1LN. *Club:* MCC.

Died 6 July 1999.

HYSLOP, James Telfer, OBE 1968; HM Diplomatic Service, retired; Consul General, Detroit, 1971–76; *b* 21 Sept. 1916; *s* of Mr and Mrs John J. Hyslop; *m* 1942, Jane Elizabeth Owers (*d* 1995); one *s* one *d. Educ:* Queen Elizabeth's Grammar Sch., Hexham. Royal Navy, 1939–46. Entered Diplomatic Service, 1948; served at: Baltimore, 1948; Valparaíso, 1951; Amman, 1954; Tegucigalpa, 1958; San Francisco, 1961; Johannesburg, 1964; Bogotá, 1968. *Recreations:* reading, music. *Address:* 12 Quay Walls, Berwick-on-Tweed TD15 1HB. *T:* (01289) 305197.   *Died 11 Sept. 1997.*

I

IBBOTSON, Lancelot William Cripps, CBE 1971 (MBE 1948); General Manager of Southern Region, British Railways, and Chairman, Southern Railway Board, 1968–72; *b* 10 Feb. 1909; *s* of William Ibbotson, FRCS and Dora Ibbotson (*née* Chapman), London; *m* 1st, 1931, Joan Marguerite Jeffcock (*d* 1989); one *s* one *d*; 2nd, 1990, Rhoda Margot Beck. *Educ:* Radley Coll. Traffic Apprentice, LNER, 1927; Chief Clerk to Dist Supt, Newcastle, 1939; Asst Dist Supt, York, 1942; Dist Supt, Darlington, 1945; Asst to Operating Supt, Western Region, 1950; Asst Gen. Man., Western Region, 1959; Chief Operating Officer, British Railways, 1963; Gen. Man., Western Region, BR, and Chm., Western Railway Board, 1966–68. Gen. Man., A. Pearce, Partners & Assoc., 1975–79; Dir, Flameless Furnaces Ltd, 1976–84. *Recreations:* foreign travel, photography. *Address:* 60 Carlton Hill, St John's Wood, NW8 0ET. *T:* (0171) 624 7853. *Died 6 Feb. 1998.*

ILIFFE, 2nd Baron *cr* 1933, of Yattendon; **Edward Langton Iliffe;** Vice-Chairman of the Birmingham Post and Mail Ltd, 1957–74; Chairman: Coventry Evening Telegraph, 1957–75; Cambridge News, 1959–75; *b* 25 Jan. 1908; *er s* of 1st Baron Iliffe, GBE, and Charlotte Gilding (*d* 1972); *S* father, 1960; *m* 1938, Renée, *er d* of René Mcrandon du Plessis, Mauritius. *Educ:* Sherborne; France; Clare Coll., Cambridge. Served, 1940–46, with RAFVR (despatches). Trustee, Shakespeare's Birthplace; Mem. Council, Univ. of Warwick, 1965–71; Past Pres., Internat. Lawn Tennis Club of Gt Britain. High Sheriff of Berks, 1957. Hon. Freeman, City of Coventry. *Heir: n* Robert Peter Richard Iliffe [*b* 22 Nov. 1944; *m* 1966, Rosemary Anne Skipwith; three *s* one *d* (incl. twin *s* and *d*)]. *Address:* Basildon Park, Lower Basildon, near Reading, Berks RG8 9NR. *T:* Pangbourne (01734) 844409. *Clubs:* Brooks's, Carlton; Royal Yacht Squadron. *Died 15 Feb. 1996.*

ILIFFE, Barrie John; Controller, Arts Division, The British Council, 1983–85; *b* 9 Jan. 1925; *s* of Edward Roy Iliffe; *m* 1959, Caroline Fairfax-Jones; three *d*. *Educ:* Westcliff High Sch.; University College London. Concerts Manager, Liverpool Philharmonic Orchestra, 1951–55; Orchestral Manager, Philharmonia Orch., 1955–56; Manager, Cape Town Orch., 1956–58; Concerts Manager, Philharmonia Orch., 1958–60; Manager, London Mozart Players, 1961–63; General Manager, New Philharmonia Orch., 1964–65; British Council: Head of Music, 1966–77; Director, Music Dept, 1977–83; Dep. Controller, Arts Div., 1981–83. Sec., William and Mary Tercentenary Trust, 1985–86; Asst to Chm., John Lewis Partnership, 1988–90. Royal Philharmonic Society: Mem., Hon. Council of Management, 1987–94; Hon. Co-Treasurer, 1989–93; Hon. Sec., 1993–94. Trustee, Eric Thompson Charitable Trust for Organists and Organ Music, 1993–. *Recreation:* inland waterways. *Address:* 29 Murray Mews, NW1 9RH. *T:* (0171) 485 5154. *Died 19 Aug. 1997.*

INGRAM, Dame Kathleen Annie; *see* Raven, Dame K.

INNES, Hammond; *see* Hammond Innes, Ralph.

INNISS, Sir Clifford (de Lisle), Kt 1961; retired; Judge of the Court of Appeal of Belize, 1974–81; Chairman, Integrity Commission, National Assembly of Belize, 1981–87; Member, Belize Advisory Council, Feb.–Oct. 1985; *b* Barbados, 26 Oct. 1910; *e s* of late Archibald de Lisle Inniss and Lelia Emmaline, *e d* of Elverton Richard Springer. *Educ:* Harrison Coll., Barbados; Queen's Coll., Oxford (BA Hons Jurisprudence, BCL). Called to the Bar, Middle Temple, 1935; QC (Tanganyika) 1950, (Trinidad and Tobago) 1953. Practised at Bar, Barbados; subseq. Legal Draughtsman and Clerk to Attorney-Gen., Barbados, 1938; Asst to Attorney General and Legal Draughtsman, 1941; Judge of Bridgetown Petty Debt Court, 1946; Legal Draughtsman, Tanganyika, 1947; Solicitor Gen., Tanganyika, 1949; Attorney-Gen., Trinidad and Tobago, 1953; Chief Justice, British Honduras, later Belize, 1957–72; Judge of the Courts of Appeal of Bermuda, the Bahamas, and the Turks and Caicos Is, 1974–75. *Recreations:* music, gardening, tennis. *Address:* 11/13 Oriole Avenue, Belmopan, Belize. *Clubs:* Barbados Yacht; Kenya Kongonis (Hon. Mem.). *Died 21 Dec. 1998.*

IONESCU, Prof. George Ghita; Professor of Government, University of Manchester, 1970–80, then Emeritus; Editor, Government and Opposition, since 1965; *b* 21 March 1913; *s* of Alexandre Ionescu and Hélène Sipsom; *m* 1950, Valence Ramsay de Bois Maclaren (*d* 1996). *Educ:* Univ. of Bucharest (Lic. in Law and Polit. Sci.). Gen. Sec., Romanian Commn of Armistice with Allied Forces, 1944–45; Counsellor, Romanian Embassy, Ankara, 1945–47; Gen. Sec., Romanian Nat. Cttee, NY, 1955–58; Dir, Radio Free Europe, 1958–63; Nuffield Fellow, LSE, 1963–68. Chm., 1975–94, Hon Life Chm. 1994, Res. Cttee, Internat. Pol Sci. Assoc.; Life Vice-Pres., British Pol Sci. Assoc., 1994. Hon. MA(Econ) Manchester; Dr *hc* Univ. of Bucharest, 1992. *Publications:* Communism in Romania, 1965; The Politics of the Eastern European Communist States, 1966; (jtly) Opposition, 1967; (jtly) Populism, 1970; (ed) Between Sovereignty and Integration, 1973; Centripetal Politics, 1975; The Political Thought of Saint-Simon, 1976; (ed) The European Alternatives, 1979; Politics and the Pursuit of Happiness, 1984; Leadership in an Independent World, 1991. *Recreations:* music, bridge, racing. *Address:* 36 Sandileigh Avenue, Manchester M20 3LW. *T:* 0161–445 7726. *Club:* Athenæum. *Died 28 June 1996.*

IRELAND, Frank Edward, CChem, FRSC; FREng; FIChemE; SFInstE; consultant in air pollution control, retired; HM Chief Alkali and Clean Air Inspector, 1964–78; *b* 7 Oct. 1913; *s* of William Edward Ireland and Bertha Naylor; *m* 1941, Edna Clare Meredith; one *s* three *d*. *Educ:* Liverpool Univ. (BSc). CChem, FRSC (FRIC 1945); FIChemE 1950; SFInstE 1956; FREng (Founder FEng 1976). Plant Superintendent, Orrs Zinc White Works, Widnes, Imperial Smelting Corp. Ltd, 1935–51; Prodn Manager, Durham Chemicals Ltd, Birtley, Co. Durham, 1951–53; Alkali Inspector based on Sheffield, 1953–58; Dep. Chief Alkali Inspector, 1958–64. Visited many countries, *eg* Mexico, Malaysia, India, ME, Africa, Australia and most of Europe, as consultant on behalf of UN, ODA and foreign govts. Pres., Inst. of Fuel, 1974–75; Vice Pres., Instn of Chem. Engrs, 1969–72. Freeman 1983, Liveryman, 1986, Engineers' Co. George E. Davis Gold Medal, Instn of Chem. Engrs, 1969. *Publications:* Annual Alkali Reports, 1964–77; contrib. Jl of IChemE; papers to nat. and internat. organisations. *Recreations:* golf, gardening. *Address:* 59 Lanchester Road, Highgate, N6 4SX. *T:* (020) 8883 6060. *Died 29 June 2000.*

IREMONGER, Thomas Lascelles Isa Shandon Valiant; *b* 14 March 1916; *o s* of Lt-Col H. E. W. Iremonger, DSO, Royal Marine Artillery, and Julia St Mary Shandon, *d* of Col John Quarry, Royal Berks Regiment; *m* Lucille Iremonger, MA Oxon, FRSL (*d* 1989), author and broadcaster; one *d. Educ:* Oriel Coll., Oxford (MA; Rear-Cdre Oxford Univ. Yacht Club, 1937–38). HM Overseas Service (Western Pacific, Gilbert & Ellice Islands Colony and Colony of Fiji), 1938–46; RNVR (Lieut), 1942–46. MP (C) Ilford North, Feb. 1954–Feb. 1974, Redbridge, Ilford North, Feb.-Sept. 1974; PPS to Fitzroy Maclean, CBE, MP (later Sir Fitzroy Maclean of Dunconnel, 1st Bt, KT), when Under-Sec. of State for War, 1954–57. Contested (C Ind. Democrat) Redbridge, Ilford N, March 1978 and (C, independently), 1979. Mem., Royal Commn on the Penal System, 1964–66. *Publications:* Disturbers of the Peace, 1962; Money, Politics and You, 1963. *Address:* Milbourne Manor, near Malmesbury, Wilts SN16 9JA; La Voûte, Montignac-le-Coq, 16390 St Séverin, France. *Died 13 May 1998.*

IRENS, Alfred Norman, CBE 1969; Chairman: South Western Electricity Board, 1956–73; British Approvals Board for Telecommunications, 1982–84; *b* 28 Feb. 1911; *s* of Max Henry and Guinevere Emily Irens; *m* 1934, Joan Elizabeth, *d* of John Knight, FRIBA, Worsley, Manchester; two *s. Educ:* Blundell's Sch., Tiverton; Faraday House, London. College apprentice, Metropolitan Vickers, Ltd, Manchester; subsequently with General Electric Co., Ltd, until joining Bristol Aeroplane Co., Ltd, 1939, becoming Chief Electrical Engineer, 1943; Consulting Engineer to Govt and other organisations, 1945–56. Part-time Mem., SW Electricity Bd, 1948–56. Past Chm. IEE Utilization Section and IEE Western Sub-Centre; Chairman: British Electrical Development Assoc., 1962–63; SW Economic Planning Council, 1968–71; BEAB for Household Equipment, 1974–84. Chm., Bristol Waterworks Co., 1975–81 (Dir, 1967–81); Dir, Avon Rubber Co. Ltd, 1973–81. JP Long Ashton, Som, 1960–66. Hon. MSc Bristol, 1957. *Recreations:* general outdoor activities. *Address:* Crete Hill House, Cote House Lane, Bristol BS9 3UW. *T:* Bristol (0117) 962 2419.

Died 14 May 1996.

IRVINE, Surg. Captain Gerard Sutherland, CBE 1970; RN retired; Medical Officer, Department of Health and Social Security, 1971–78; *b* 19 June 1913; *s* of Major Gerard Byrom Corrie Irvine and Maud Andrée (*née* Wylde); *m* 1939, Phyllis Lucy Lawrie (*d* 1988); one *s. Educ:* Imperial Service Coll., Windsor; Epsom Coll.; University Coll. and Hosp., London. MB, BS 1937; DLO 1940; MRCS, LRCP 1937; FRCS 1967. Jenks Meml Schol. 1932; Liston Gold Medal for Surgery 1936. Surg. Sub-Lt RNVR 1935, Surg. Lt RNVR 1937; Surg Lt RN 1939; Surg. Lt-Comdr 1944; Surg. Comdr 1953; Surg. Capt. 1963. Served War of 1939–45 (1939–45 Star, Atlantic Star with Bar for France and Germany, Burma Star, Defence Medal, Victory Medal); subseq. service: Ceylon, 1946; Haslar, 1947–49 and 1957–60; Malta, 1953–56; HMS: Maidstone (Submarine Depot Ship), 1949–51; Osprey (Torpedo and Anti Submarine Trng Sch.), 1951–53; Collingwood, 1956–57; Lion, 1960–62; Vernon (Torpedo Sch.), 1962–63; Sen. Cons. in ENT, 1953–70; Adviser in ENT to Med. Dir-Gen. (Navy), 1966–70; Sen. MO i/c Surgical Div., RN Hosp. Haslar, 1966–70; QHS 1969–70; retd 1970. Member: BMA 1938; Sections of Otology and Laryngology, RSM, 1948–77 (FRSocMed 1948–77); British Assoc. of Otolaryngologists, 1945–71 (Council, 1958–70); S Western Laryngological Assoc., 1951–71; Hearing Sub-Cttee of RN Personnel Res. Cttee, 1947–70; Otological Sub-Cttee of RAF Flying Personnel Res. Cttee, 1963–70. OStJ 1969. *Publications:* numerous articles in various medical jls. *Recreations:* gardening, philately, do-it-

yourself. *Address:* 9 Alvara Road, Alverstoke, Gosport PO12 2HY. *T:* (01705) 580342.

Died 9 Aug. 1997.

IRVINE, Maj.-Gen. John, OBE 1955; Director of Medical Services, British Army of the Rhine, 1973–75; *b* 31 May 1914; *s* of late John Irvine and Jessie Irvine (*née* McKinnon); *m* 1941, Mary McNicol, *d* of late Andrew Brown Cossar, Glasgow; one *d. Educ:* Glasgow High Sch.; Glasgow Univ. MB, ChB 1940. MFCM 1973. Commnd into RAMC, 1940; served War of 1939–45 (despatches and Act of Gallantry, 1944): Egypt, Greece, Crete, Western Desert, 1941–43; Sicily, Italy and Yugoslavia, 1943–45; served with British Troops, Austria, 1947–49; Korea, 1953–54 (OBE); Malaya, 1954–56 (despatches); Germany, 1958–61; Ghana, 1961; Germany, 1962–64; DDMS, HQ BAOR, 1968–69; DDMS, 1st British Corps, 1969–71; Dep. Dir-Gen., AMS, 1971–73. QHS 1972–75. OStJ 1971. *Recreations:* tennis, ski-ing. *Address:* Greenlawns, 11 Manor Road, Aldershot, Hants GU11 3DG. *Died 17 July 1997.*

IRVINE, Sir Robin (Orlando Hamilton), Kt 1989; FRCP, FRACP; Vice-Chancellor, University of Otago, Dunedin, New Zealand, 1973–93, Emeritus Professor 1994; *b* 15 Sept. 1929; *s* of late Claude Turner Irvine; *m* 1957, Elizabeth Mary, *d* of late Herbert Gray Corbett; one *s* two *d. Educ:* Wanganui Collegiate Sch.; Univ. of Otago. Otago University Med. Sch., 1948–53; MB, ChB 1953; MD (NZ), 1958; FRACP 1965; FRCP 1973. House Phys., Auckland Hosp., 1954; Dept of Medicine, Univ. of Otago: Research Asst (Emily Johnston Res. Schol.), 1955; Asst Lectr and Registrar, 1956–57; Leverhulme Research Scholar, Middlesex Hosp., London, 1958; Registrar, Postgraduate Medical Sch., London, 1959–60; Isaacs Medical Research Fellow, Auckland Hosp., 1960–61; Med. Tutor and Med. Specialist, Auckland Hosp., 1962–63; Lectr, Sen. Lectr in Med., Univ. of Otago, 1963–67, Associate Prof., 1968; Clinical Dean and Personal Professor, Univ. of Otago Medical Sch., 1969–72. Girdlers' Co. Senior Vis. Res. Fellowship, Green Coll., Oxford, 1986–87. Consultant, Asian Development Bank, 1974–; Dir, Dunedin City Hldgs, 1993–; Chm. Bd of Dirs, Mercy Hospital Dunedin Ltd, 1994–. Member: Selwyn Coll. Bd, 1966–; Pharmacology and Therapeutic Cttee, Min. of Health, 1967–73; Otago Hosp. Bd, 1969–88; Med. Educn Cttee of Med. Council of NZ, 1969–73; Cent. Educn Cttee, NZ Med. Assoc., 1970–73; Social Council of Nat. Devell Council of NZ, 1971–74; Cttee on Nursing Educn, Min. of Educn, 1972; Social Develt Council, 1974–79; Commn for the Future, 1976–80; NZ Planning Council, 1977–82; Otago Polytech. Council, 1973–87; Dunedin Teachers Coll. Council, 1973–90; NZ Adv. Cttee, Nuffield Foundn, 1973–81; NZ Rhodes Scholarships Selection Cttee, 1976–81; Lottery Health Res. Distn Cttee, 1985–91; Hon. Adv. Bd, Royal NZ Plunket Soc., 1980–93; Council, Dunedin Coll. of Educn, 1991–92; Chairman: Otago Med. Res. Foundn, 1975–81; Ministerial working party on novel genetic techniques, 1977; NZ Vice-Chancellors' Cttee, 1979–80, 1992; Council, ACU, 1991–92 (Mem., 1979–80, 1991–93); Ross Dependency Res. Cttee, 1993–; Bd, Internat. Centre of Antarctic Information and Research, 1994–; Chm., Interim Estab. Bd, NZ Antarctic Inst., 1996. Convenor, Med. Educn Mission to Univ. of S Pacific, 1971. Dir, Otago Develt Corp., 1982–85; Dir, 1991–, and Dep. Chm., Inst. of Envmtl Science and Res. (formerly Envmtl Health and Forensic Sci.). Trustee: McMillan Trust, 1973–93 (Chm., 1977–86, 1990–93; Mem., Investment Adv. Cttee, 1994–); Rowheath Trust, 1973–93; NZ Red Cross Foundn, 1988–; NZ Educn and Scholarship Trust, 1990–. Nat. Liby of NZ, 1992–; Antarctic Heritage Trust, 1993–. Hon. ADC 1969, and Hon. Physician 1970, to the Governor-General, Sir Arthur Porritt. Hon. Mem., Australian Soc. of Nephrology.

Dr *hc* Edinburgh, 1976; Hon LLD Otago, 1993. FRSA 1980; FNZIM 1984. Silver Jubilee Medal, 1977. *Publications:* various papers on high blood pressure, renal med. and medical educn. *Recreations:* computing, walking, reading, music, travel. *Address:* 950 George Street, Dunedin, New Zealand. *T:* (03) 4021023. *Club:* Fernhill (Dunedin). *Died 29 Sept. 1996.*

IRVING, Prof. John; Freeland Professor of Natural Philosophy (Theoretical Physics), University of Strathclyde, Glasgow, 1961–84; retired; *b* 22 Dec. 1920; *s* of John Irving and Margaret Kent Aird; *m* 1948, Monica Cecilia Clarke; two *s. Educ:* St John's Grammar Sch.; Hamilton Academy; Glasgow Univ. MA (1st Class Hons in Maths and Nat. Phil.), Glasgow Univ., 1940; PhD (Mathematical Physics), Birmingham Univ., 1951. FInstP 1980. Lectr, Stow Coll., Glasgow, 1944–45; Lectr in Maths, Univ. of St Andrews, 1945–46; Lectr in Mathematical Physics, University of Birmingham, 1946–49; Nuffield Research Fellow (Nat. Phil.), University of Glasgow, 1949–51; Sen. Lectr in Applied Maths, University of Southampton, 1951–59; Prof. of Theoretical Physics and Head of Dept of Applied Mathematics and Theor. Physics University of Cape Town, 1959–61. Dean of Sch. of Mathematics and Physics, Strathclyde Univ., 1964–69. *Publications:* Mathematics in Physics and Engineering, 1959 (New York); contrib. to Proc. Physical Soc., Philosophical Magazine, Physical Review. *Recreations:* gardening, computing. *Address:* 12 Lomond Road, Wemyss Bay, Renfrewshire PA18 6BD. *Died 10 Sept. 1996.*

IRWIN, John Conran; Keeper, Indian Section, Victoria and Albert Museum, 1959–78, with extended responsibility for new Oriental Department, 1970–78; *b* 5 Aug. 1917; *s* of late John Williamson Irwin; *m* 1947, Helen Hermione Scott (*née* Fletcher) (separated 1982), *d* of late Herbert Bristowe Fletcher; three *s. Educ:* Canford Sch., Wimborne, Dorset. Temp. commission, Gordon Highlanders, 1939. Private Sec to Gov. of Bengal, 1942–45; Asst Keeper, Victoria and Albert Museum, 1946. Exec. Sec., Royal Academy Winter Exhibition of Indian Art, 1947–48; UNESCO Expert on museum planning: on mission to Indonesia, 1956, to Malaya, 1962. British Acad. Travelling Fellowship, 1974–75; Leverhulme Res. Fellow, 1978–80; Sen. Fellow, Center for Advanced Study in the Visual Arts, Nat. Gall. of Art, Washington, DC, 1983–84; Vis. Prof., Univ. of Michigan, 1986. Working with research grants from Leverhulme Trust and British Acad., 1978–84. Lectures: Birdwood Meml, 1972; Tagore Meml, 1973; Lowell Inst., Boston, Mass, 1974; guest lectr, Collège de France, 1976. Pres., Res. into Lost Knowledge Orgn, 1960; Hon. Pres., Indian Circle, SOAS, 1990. FRSA 1972; FRAS 1946; FRAI 1977; FSA 1978. *Publications:* Jamini Roy, 1944; Indian art (section on sculpture), 1947; The Art of India and Pakistan (sections on bronzes and textiles), 1951; Shawls, 1955; Origins of Chintz, 1970; (with M. Hall) Indian Painted and Printed Fabrics, 1972; Indian Embroideries, 1974; articles in Encyclopædia Britannica, Chambers's Encyclopædia, Enciclopedia Italiana (2nd Supplement), Jl of Royal Asiatic Soc., Burlington Magazine, Artibus Asiae etc. *Recreations:* music, walking. *Died 23 Jan. 1997.*

ISAAC, Alfred James; Director of Home Regional Services, Property Services Agency, Department of the Environment, 1971–75; *b* 1 Aug. 1919; *s* of Alfred Jabez Isaac and Alice Marie Isaac; *m* 1943, Beryl Marjorie Rist (*d* 1995); one *s* two *d. Educ:* Maidenhead Grammar Sch. Served War, RAFVR, Flt Lt (pilot), Coastal Command, 1941–46. Post Office Engineering Dept, 1936–49; Asst Principal, Min. of Works, 1949; Regional Dir, Southern Region, 1960–67; Dir of Professional Staff Management, 1967. Business Coordinator, Danbury Drilling Ltd, 1977–78; Chm. (part-time), Recruitment Bds, CS Commn, 1978–87. Vice-Chm., Bigbury Parish Council, 1987–91 (part-time Clerk, 1981–83). *Recreations:* 9 grandchildren, amateur radio. *Address:* Wave Crest, Marine Drive, Bigbury on Sea, Kingsbridge, Devon TQ7 4AS. *T:* (01548) 810387. *Club:* Civil Service. *Died 11 Oct. 1997.*

ISAACS, Sir Kendal (George Lamon), KCMG 1993; CBE 1970; QC (Bahamas) 1968; Member (FNM), Bahamas House of Assembly, 1972–76 and 1982–92; *b* 23 July 1925; *s* of Edward Adolphus and Julia Isaacs; *m* Patricia Eleanor Fountain. *Educ:* Queens' Coll., Cambridge (MA, LLB). Called to the Bar, Middle Temple and Bahamas, 1950; Stipendiary and Circuit Magistrate, Bahamas, 1952; Solicitor General, 1955; Attorney General, 1963; Acting Chief Justice, 1959; Acting Judge, Supreme Court, 1964–65, 1977–78; private practice, 1965; Mem., Senate, 1965; Vice-Pres., Senate, 1968–71. *Recreations:* tennis, golf, travel. *Address:* Sandyport, PO Box N1372, Nassau, Bahamas. *Clubs:* Gym Tennis; Cable Beach Golf. *Died 25 May 1996.*

ISAACSON, Richard; QC 1997; *b* 7 Sept. 1950; *o s* of S. H. Isaacson, MPS and Laura Isaacson (*née* Taylor). *Educ:* Liverpool Coll.; Liverpool Univ. (LLB Hons 1971; Pres., Law Faculty, 1970–71). Called to the Bar, Middle Temple, 1972 (Winston Churchill Pupillage Scholar); Standing Counsel, Northern Circuit, to HM Customs and Excise, 1994–97; Asst Recorder, 1995–. Liverpool City Councillor (Dingle Ward), 1986–90. Contested Garston Div. of Liverpool, 1987. *Recreations:* the arts, the turf. *Address:* Exchange Chambers, Pearl Assurance House, Derby Square, Liverpool L2 9XX. *T:* (0151) 236 7767. *Died 16 April 1998.*

J

JACKSON, Brig. (Alexander) Cosby (Fishburn), CVO 1957; CBE 1954 (OBE 1943); *b* 4 Dec. 1903; *s* of late Col S. C. F. Jackson, CMG, DSO, and Lucy B. Jackson (*née* Drake); *m* 1934, Margaret Hastings Hervey (*d* 1984), Montclair, NJ, USA; one *s* (and one *s* decd). *Educ:* Yardley Court, Tonbridge; Haileybury Coll.; RMC Sandhurst. 2nd Lieut, Royal Hants Regt, 1923; Brig. 1944; employed RWAFF, 1927–33; served in Middle East, 1940–45 (despatches twice, OBE); Dep. Dir of Quartering, War Office, 1945–48; Comdr Northern Area, Kenya, 1948–51; Comdr Caribbean Area, 1951–54; HBM Military Attaché, Paris, 1954–58. ADC to the Queen, 1955–58. Order of Kutuzov 2nd Class, USSR, 1944; Comdr Legion of Honour, France, 1957. *Publications:* Rose Croix: a history of the Ancient and Accepted Rite for England and Wales, 1981; English Masonic Exposures 1760–1769, 1986; A Glossary of the Craft and Holy Royal Arch Rituals of Freemasonry, 1992. *Address:* Glenwhern, Golf Lane, Grouville, Jersey JE3 9BD.

Died 3 Jan. 2000.

JACKSON, Air Chief Marshal Sir Brendan (James), GCB 1992 (KCB 1987); Air Member for Supply and Organisation, Ministry of Defence, 1988–93, retired; *b* 23 Aug. 1935; *m* 1959, Shirley Ann Norris; one *s* one *d*. *Educ:* Chichester High Sch. for Boys; London Univ. (BA Modern Japanese); qualified Interpreter. Joined RAF, 1956; flew Meteors, Canberras, Victors, B-52s; Sqdn Leader, 1965; RAF Staff Coll., 1966; PSO to C of S, HQ 2nd ATAF, 1969; Wing Comdr, 1972; US Armed Forces Staff Coll., 1972; PSO to CAS, 1974; Group Captain, 1977; Dir of Air Staff Plans, Dept of ACAS (Policy), MoD, 1980; Air Cdre, 1981; Air Vice-Marshal, 1984; ACOS (Policy), SHAPE, 1984; Air Marshal, 1986; COS and Dep. C-in-C, RAF Strike Comd, 1986–88; Air Chief Marshal, 1990. *Recreations:* reading, writing on defence, gardening, golf, ski-ing. *Club:* Royal Air Force.

Died 19 Nov. 1998.

JACKSON, Brig. Cosby; *see* Jackson, Brig. A. C. F.

JACKSON, Gerald Breck; *b* 28 June 1916; *o s* of Gerald Breck Jackson and Mary Jackson, Paterson, NJ; *m* 1940, Brenda Mary, *o d* of William and Mary Titshall; one *s*. *Educ:* various schs in USA; Canford Sch., Dorset; Faraday House Engrg Coll. Graduate Trainee, Central Electricity Bd, 1938. HM Forces, RE, 1939–43. Various appts in HV transmission with CEB and BEA, 1943–55; Overhead Line Design Engr, BEA, 1955–61; Asst Regional Dir, CEGB, 1961–64; Chief Ops Engr, CEGB, 1964–66; Regional Dir, NW Region, CEGB, 1966–68; Dir Engineering, English Electric Co. Ltd, 1968–69; Sen. Exec., Thomas Tilling Ltd, and Dir subsid. cos, 1969–71; Man. Dir, John Mowlem & Co. Ltd, 1971–72; Man. Dir, NCB (Ancillaries) Ltd, 1972–78. DFH, CEng, FIEE. *Publications:* Network for the Nation, 1960; Power Controlled, 1966. *Recreations:* photography, pen-and-ink drawing. *Address:* Larchwood, 1A Lansdowne Square, Tunbridge Wells, Kent TN1 2NF.

Died 1 Dec. 2000.

JACKSON, (Gordon) Noel, CMG 1962; MBE 1945; HM Diplomatic Service, retired; Ambassador to Ecuador, 1967–70; *b* 25 Dec. 1913; *m* 1959, Mary April Nettlefold, *er d* of late Frederick John Nettlefold and of Mrs Albert Coates; one *s* two *d*. Indian Political Service until 1947; then HM Foreign Service; Political Officer, Sharjah, 1947; transf. to Kuwait, Persian Gulf, 1949; transf. to Foreign Office, 1950; Consul, St Louis, USA, 1953; Foreign Service Officer, Grade 6, 1955; Consul-General: Basra, 1955–57; Lourenço Marques, 1957–60; Benghazi, 1960–63; Ambassador to Kuwait, 1963–67. *Publications:* Effective Horsemanship (for Dressage, Hunting, Three-day Events, Polo), 1967; (with W. Steinkraus) The Encyclopædia of the Horse, 1973. *Address:* Lowbarrow House, Leafield, Witney, Oxfordshire OX8 5NH. *T:* (01993) 878443. *Club:* Travellers.

Died 13 Sept. 1999.

JACKSON, Raymond Allen, (JAK); Cartoonist, Evening Standard, since 1952; *b* 11 March 1927; *s* of Maurice Jackson and Mary Ann Murphy; *m* 1957, Claudie Sidone Grenier; one *s* two *d*. *Educ:* Lyulph Stanley Central; Willesden School of Art (NDD). Army, 1945–48. General artist, Link House Publishing, 1950–51; Keymers Advertising Agency, 1951–52; Evening Standard, 1952–. *Publications:* JAK Annual, 1969–. *Recreations:* golf, walking. *Club:* Special Forces.

Died 27 July 1997.

JACKSON, Gen. Sir William (Godfrey Fothergill), GBE 1975 (OBE 1958); KCB 1971; MC 1940, and Bar, 1943; Military Historian, Cabinet Office, 1977–78 and 1982–87; Governor and Commander-in-Chief, Gibraltar, 1978–82; *b* 28 Aug. 1917; *s* of late Col A. Jackson, RAMC, Yanwath, Cumberland, and E. M. Jackson (*née* Fothergill), Brownber, Westmorland; *m* 1946, Joan Mary Buesden; one *s* one *d*. *Educ:* Shrewsbury; RMA, Woolwich (King's Medal, 1937); King's Coll., Cambridge (BA 1939). Commnd into Royal Engineers, 1937; served War of 1939–45: Norwegian Campaign, 1940; Tunisia, 1942–43; Sicily and Italy, 1943–44; Far East, 1945; GSO1, HQ Allied Land Forces SE Asia, 1945–48; Instructor, Staff Coll., Camberley, 1948–50; Instructor, RMA, Sandhurst, 1951–53; AA&QMG (War Plans), War Office, during Suez ops, 1956; Comdr, Gurkha Engrs, 1958–60; Col GS, Minley Div. of Staff Coll., Camberley, 1961–62; Dep. Dir of Staff Duties, War Office, 1962–64; Imp. Def. Coll., 1965; Dir, Chief of Defence Staff's Unison Planning Staff, 1966–68; Asst Chief of General Staff (Operational Requirements), MoD, 1968–70; GOC-in-C, Northern Command, 1970–72; QMG, 1973–76. Colonel Commandant: RE, 1971–81; Gurkha Engrs, 1971–76; RAOC, 1973–78; Hon. Col, Engineer and Rly Staff Corps, RE, TAVR, 1977–83; ADC (Gen.) to the Queen, 1974–76. Kermit Roosevelt Lectr, USA, 1975. Chm., Friends of Gibraltar's Heritage, 1990–94. Reviewer of mil. books, The Times, 1987–93. *Publications:* Attack in the West, 1953; Seven Roads to Moscow, 1957; The Battle for Italy, 1967; Battle for Rome, 1969; Alexander of Tunis as Military Commander, 1971; The North African Campaigns, 1975; Overlord: Normandy 1944, 1978; (ed jtly) The Mediterranean and the Middle East (British Official History, vol. VI), Pt 1, 1984, Pt 2, 1987, Pt 3, 1988; Withdrawal From Empire, 1986; The Alternative Third World War 1985–2035, 1987; The Rock of the Gibraltarians, 1988; British Defence Dilemmas, 1990; The Chiefs, 1992; The Governor's Cat, 1992; The Pomp of Yesterday, 1995; Fortress to Democracy, 1995; Britain's Triumph and Decline in the Middle East, 1996; contribs to Royal United Service Instn Jl (gold medals for prize essays, 1950 and 1966). *Recreations:* fishing, writing, gardening.

Died 12 March 1999.

JACKSON, William Unsworth, CBE 1985; DL; Chief Executive, Kent County Council, 1974–86; *b* 9 Feb. 1926; *s* of William Jackson and Margaret Esplen Jackson (*née* Sunderland); *m* 1952, Valerie Annette (*née* Llewellyn); one *s* one *d*. *Educ:* Alsop High Sch., Liverpool. Solicitor. Entered local govt service, Town Clerk's Office, Liverpool, 1942; Dep. County Clerk, Kent, 1970. Pres., Soc. of Local Authority Chief Execs, 1985–86 (Hon. Sec., 1980–84). Adjudicator on political restrictions in local govt in England and Wales, 1989–. Trustee, Charities Aid Foundn, 1986–96. Gov., Henley Management Coll., 1983–86. DL Kent, 1992. *Address:* 34 Yardley Park Road, Tonbridge, Kent TN9 1NF. *T:* (01732) 351078. *Club:* Royal Over-Seas League. *Died 2 Aug. 1999.*

JACOB, Sir Isaac Hai, (Sir Jack), Kt 1979; QC 1976; Senior Master of the Supreme Court, Queen's Bench Division, and Queen's Remembrancer, 1975–80; Director, Institute of Advanced Legal Studies, University of London, 1986–88; *b* 5 June 1908; 3rd *s* of late Jacob Isaiah and Aziza Jacob; *m* 1940, Rose Mary Jenkins (*née* Samwell) (*d* 1995); two *s*. *Educ:* Shanghai Public Sch. for Boys; London Sch. of Economics; University Coll., London (LLB (1st class Hons); Joseph Hume Scholar in Jurisprudence, 1928 and 1930; Fellow, 1966). Arden Scholar, Gray's Inn, 1930; Cecil Peace Prizeman, 1930. Called to the Bar, Gray's Inn, 1930; Hon. Bencher, 1978; Mem., Senate of Inns of Court and the Bar, 1975–78. Served in ranks from 1940 until commissioned in RAOC, 1942; Staff Capt., War Office (Ord. I), 1943–45. Master, Supreme Court, Queen's Bench Div., 1957–80. Prescribed Officer for Election Petitions, 1975–80. Hon. Lectr in Law, UCL, 1959–74; teaching LLM subject, Principles of Civil Litigation, 1959–87; Hon. Lectr in Legal Ethics, Birmingam Univ., 1969–72; Hon. Visiting Lecturer: Imperial Coll. of Science and Technology, 1963–64; Birmingham Univ., 1964–65; Bedford Coll., 1969–71; European Univ. Institute, Florence, 1978; Visiting Professor: Sydney Univ., 1971; Osgoode Hall Law Sch., York Univ., Toronto, 1971; of English Law, UCL, 1974–87; Polytechnic of Central London, 1981–83. Member: Lord Chancellor's (Pearson) Cttee on Funds in Court, 1958–59; Working Party on the Revision of the Rules of the Supreme Court, 1960–65; (Payne) Cttee on Enforcement of Judgment Debts, 1965–69; (Winn) Cttee on Personal Injuries Litigation, 1966–68; (Kerr) Working Party on Foreign Judgments, 1976–80; Chm., Working Party on Form of the Writ of Summons and Appearance, 1977. Mem., Fourth Anglo-Amer. Legal Exchange on Trial of Civil Actions, 1973. Vice-President: Industrial Law Soc., 1968–; Selden Soc., 1978–84 (Mem. Council, 1976–78, 1985); Inst. of Legal Executives, 1978–; Mansfield Law Club, City of London Polytechnic, 1965–; Governor, Polytechnic of Central London, 1968–88; Member, Committee of Management: Inst. of Judicial Admin, 1968; Brit. Inst. of Internat. and Comparative Law, 1965; Law Adv. Cttee of Associated Examining Bd, 1964–84; Friends of Hebrew Univ., Jerusalem, 1965–85; Mem. Council, Justice; Mem. Gen. Cttee, Bar Assoc. of Commerce, Finance and Industry, 1981–85; Life Mem., Assoc. of Law Teachers, 1985 (Vice Pres., 1965–78; Pres., 1978–85). Pres., Univ. of London Law Students' Soc., 1930; Chm., Univ. of London Jewish Students Union, 1931; Chm., Bentham Club, UCL, 1964–84, Pres. 1985, Vice Pres. 1986–. Hon. Member: SPTL, 1981; Council of Justice, 1988; Internat. Assoc. of Procedural Law, 1985; Inst of Internat. and Comparative Law, 1998. Hon. Freeman, City of London, 1976. Mem., Broderers' Co., 1977. FCIArb 1984. Hon. Fellow, Univ. of Westminster (formerly Polytechnic of Central London), 1988. Hon. LLD: Birmingham, 1978; London, 1981; Staffordshire, 1994; Dr Jur *hc* Würzburg, Bavaria, 1982. Chief Adv. Editor, Atkin's Court Forms, 1984– (Adv. Editor, 1962–83); Editor, Annual Practice, 1961–66; General Editor: Supreme Court Practice, 1967–; Civil Justice Quarterly, 1982–; Adv. Editor, Internat. Encyclopedia of Comparative Law (Civil Procedure vol.), 1968–; Consultant Editor, Malaysian Court Practice, 1995. *Publications:* Law relating to Rent Restrictions, 1933, 1938; Law relating to Hire Purchase, 1938; (ed jtly) Bullen and Leake, Precedents of Pleadings, 11th edn 1959; (ed) Bullen, Leake and Jacob, Precedents of Pleadings, 12th edn 1975, 13th edn (with Iain Goldrein) 1990; chapter on Civil Procedure, including Courts and Evidence, in Annual Survey of Commonwealth Law, 1965–77; Chitty and Jacob's Queen's Bench Forms, 19th edn 1965, to 21st edn 1986; The Reform of Civil Procedural Law and Other Essays in Civil Procedure, 1982; The Fabric of English Civil Justice (Hamlyn Lectures), 1986; (gen. ed.) Private International Litigation, 1988; (ed jtly) Trends in Enforcement of Non-Money Judgments and Orders, 1988; (with Ian Goldrein) Pleadings: principles and practice, 1990; Halsbury's Laws of England, 4th edition: Discovery, Vol. 13, 1975; (jtly) Execution, Vol. 17, 1976; Practice and Procedure, Vol. 37, 1982; Atkin's Court Forms: Compromise and Settlement, Vol. 12, 1990; Default, Vol. 14, 1991; Discontinuance, and Discovery, Vol. 15, 1990; Interim Orders, and Interlocutory Proceedings (QBD), Vol. 22, 1991; Issues, and Judgments (QBD), Vol. 23, 1991; References and Inquiries, Vol. 33, 1989; Service of Process, Vol. 35, 1991; Stay of Proceedings, and Third Party Procedure, Vol. 37, 1990; Transfer and Consolidation, Vol. 39, 1991; Writs of Summons, Vol. 41, 1991; *festschrift:* International Perspectives on Civil Justice, ed Prof. I. R. Scott, 1990. *Recreation:* painting. *Address:* The Bushey House Beaumont, High Street, Bushey, Herts WD2 1BJ. *T:* (020) 8421 8844.

Died 26 Dec. 2000.

JACOBS, Prof. Arthur David; musicologist and critic; Member of Editorial Board, Opera, since 1961, *b* 14 June 1922; *s* of late Alexander S. and Estelle Jacobs; *m* 1953, Betty Upton Hughes; two *s*. *Educ:* Manchester Grammar Sch.; Merton Coll., Oxford (MA). Music Critic: Daily Express, 1947–52; Jewish Chronicle, 1963–75; critic, Hi-Fi News and Record Review (formerly Audio and Record Review), 1964–89; record reviewer, Sunday Times, 1968–89. Professor, RAM, 1964–79; Hd of Music Dept, Huddersfield Polytechnic, 1979–84, created Prof. 1984. Founder and Editor, British Music Yearbook (formerly Music Yearbook), 1971–79, Adv. Editor, 1979–83. Leverhulme Res. Fellow in Music, 1977–78; Leverhulme Emeritus Res. Fellow, 1991–93. Vis. Fellow, Wolfson Coll., Oxford, 1979, 1984–85, 1991–92; Centennial Lectr, Univ. of Illinois, 1967; Vis. Professor: Univ. of Victoria, BC, 1968; Univ. of California at Santa Barbara, 1969; Temple Univ., Philadelphia, 1970, 1971; UCLA, 1973; Univ. of Western Ontario, 1974; McMaster Univ., 1975, 1983; Univ. of Queensland, 1985. Hon. RAM 1969. *Publications:* Music Lover's Anthology, 1948; Gilbert and Sullivan, 1951; A New Dictionary of Music, 1958 (also Spanish, Portuguese, Danish and Swedish edns), new edn, as The New Penguin Dictionary of Music, 1978, 5th edn, as The Penguin Dictionary of Music, 1991, 6th edn 1996; Choral Music, 1963 (also Spanish and Japanese edns); Libretto of opera One Man Show by Nicholas Maw, 1964; (with Stanley Sadie) Pan Book of Opera, 1966, expanded edn 1984 (US edns, Great Operas in Synopsis, The Limelight Book of Opera); A Short History of Western Music, 1972 (also Italian edn); (ed) Music Education Handbook, 1976; Arthur Sullivan: a Victorian musician, 1984, 2nd edn 1992; The Pan Book of Orchestral Music, 1987; Penguin Dictionary of Musical Performers, 1990; Henry J. Wood: Maker of the Proms, 1994; many opera translations incl. Berg's Lulu (first US perf. of complete work, Santa Fe, New Mexico, 1979); contributions to: A

History of Song, 1960; Grove's Dictionary of Music and Musicians, 1980; Shakespeare and the Victorian Stage, 1986; The New Grove Dictionary of Opera, 1992; TLS, Musical Times, foreign jls, etc. *Recreations:* puns, swimming, walking, theatre. *Address:* 7 Southdale Road, Oxford OX2 7SE. *T:* and *Fax:* Oxford (01865) 515240. *Club:* Commonwealth Trust. *Died 13 Dec. 1996.*

JACOBS, Sir (James) Piers, KBE 1989 (OBE 1981); JP; Vice Chairman and Director, China Light and Power Company, Ltd, since 1992; Chairman, Sir Elly Kadoorie & Sons Ltd, since 1995; *b* 27 May 1933; *s* of Selwyn and Dorothy Jacobs; *m* 1964, Josephine Lee; one *d. Educ:* St Paul's Sch. Solicitor (Hons), England and Wales, 1955; Solicitor, Hong Kong, 1976. Hong Kong: Registrar General, 1976; Sec. for Economic Services, 1982; Financial Sec., 1986–91; Mem., Exec. and Legislative Councils, 1986–91. JP Hong Kong, 1992. *Recreations:* walking, swimming, reading. *Address:* St George's Building, 24th Floor, 2 Ice House Street, Hong Kong. *Clubs:* Oriental; Hong Kong, Royal Hong Kong Jockey (Hong Kong). *Died 23 Sept. 1999.*

JACOBSEN, Frithjof Halfdan; Norwegian Ambassador, retired; *b* 14 Jan. 1914; *m* 1941, Elsa Tidemand Anderson; one *s* two *d. Educ:* Univ. of Oslo (Law). Entered Norwegian Foreign Service, 1938; Legation, Paris, 1938–40; Norwegian Foreign Ministry, London, 1940–45; held posts in Moscow, London, Oslo, 1945–55; Director-Gen., Political Affairs, Oslo, 1955–59; Ambassador to: Canada, 1959–61; Moscow, 1961–66; Under-Sec. of State, Oslo, 1966–70; Ambassador to Moscow, 1970–75; Ambassador to the Court of St James's and to Ireland, 1975–82. *Address:* Schwachsgate 4, Oslo 3, Norway. *Died 16 March 1999.*

JAFFÉ, (Andrew) Michael, CBE 1989; LittD; Director, Fitzwilliam Museum, Cambridge, 1973–90, then Emeritus; Professor of the History of Western Art, 1973–90, then Emeritus; Fellow of King's College, Cambridge, since 1952; *b* 3 June 1923; *s* of Arthur Daniel Jaffé, OBE, and Marie Marguerite Strauss; *m* 1964, Patricia Anne Milne-Henderson; two *s* two *d. Educ:* Eton Coll.; King's Coll., Cambridge (MA; LittD 1980); Courtauld Inst. of Art. Lt-Comdr, RNVR, retd. Commonwealth Fund Fellow, Harvard and New York Univ., 1951–53; Asst Lectr in Fine Arts, Cambridge, 1956; Prof. of Renaissance Art, Washington Univ., St Louis, 1960–61; Vis. Prof., Harvard Univ., Summer 1961; Lectr in Fine Arts, Cambridge, 1961; Reader in History of Western Art, Cambridge, 1968; Head of Dept of History of Art, Cambridge, 1970–73; a Syndic, Fitzwilliam Museum, 1971–73. Mem., Adv. Council, V&A Museum, 1971–76. Organiser: (for Nat. Gall. of Canada) of Jordaens Exhibn, Ottawa, 1968–69; (for BM) of Old Master Drawings from Chatsworth, 1993. Vis. Prof., Harvard Univ., 1968–69. Hon. Mem., Amer. Acad. of Arts and Scis, 1990. FRSA 1969. Officier, Ordre de Léopold (Belgium), 1980; Officier, Ordre des Arts et des Lettres (France), 1989. *Publications:* Van Dyck's Antwerp Sketchbook, 1966; Rubens, 1967; Jordaens, 1968; Rubens and Italy, 1977; Rubens: catalogo completo, 1989; (ed) The Devonshire Collection of Italian Drawings, 4 vols, 1994; articles and reviews (art historical) in European and N American jls, etc. *Recreation:* viticulture. *Address:* King's College, Cambridge CB2 1ST. *Clubs:* Brooks's, Turf, Beefsteak. *Died 13 July 1997.*

JAGAN, Cheddi, DDS; Guyanese politician; President, Co-operative Republic of Guyana, since 1992; *b* 22 March 1918; *m* 1943, Janet Rosenberg; one *s* one *d. Educ:* Howard Univ.; YMCA Coll., Chicago (BSc); Northwestern Univ. (DDS). Member of Legislative Council, British Guiana, 1947–53; Leader of the House and Minister of Agriculture, Lands and Mines, May-Oct.

1953; Chief Minister and Minister of Trade and Industry, 1957–61; (first) Premier, British Guiana, and Minister of Development and Planning, 1961–64; Leader of Opposition in Nat. Assembly, 1964–92. Hon. Pres., Guyana Agricl and General Workers' Union; Pres., Guyana Peace Council. Order of Friendship, USSR, 1978. *Publications:* Forbidden Freedom, 1954; Anatomy of Poverty, 1964; The West on Trial, 1966; Caribbean Revolution, 1979; The Caribbean—Whose Backyard?, 1984. *Recreations:* swimming, tennis. *Address:* Office of the President, Vlissengen Road, Georgetown, Guyana. *Died 6 March 1997.*

JAK; *see* Jackson, R. A.

JAKOBOVITS, Baron *cr* 1988 (Life Peer), of Regent's Park in Greater London; **Immanuel Jakobovits,** Kt 1981; Chief Rabbi of the United Hebrew Congregations of the British Commonwealth of Nations, 1967–91; *b* 8 Feb. 1921; *s* of Rabbi Dr Julius Jakobovits and Paula (*née* Wreschner); *m* 1949, Amelie Munk; two *s* four *d. Educ:* London Univ. (BA; PhD 1955; Fellow, UCL, 1984–; Hon. Fellow, QMC, 1987); Jews' Coll. and Yeshivah Etz Chaim, London. Diploma, 1944; Associate of Jews' Coll. Minister: Brondesbury Synagogue, 1941–44; SE London Synagogue, 1944–47; Great Synagogue, London, 1947–49; Chief Rabbi of Ireland, 1949–58; Rabbi of Fifth Avenue Synagogue, New York, 1958–67. Hon. DD Yeshiva Univ., NY, 1975; Hon. DLitt City, 1986; DD Lambeth, 1987; Hon. DD Wales, 1993. Templeton Prize for Progress in Religion, 1991. *Publications:* Jewish Medical Ethics, NY 1959, 4th edn 1975; Jewish Law Faces Modern Problems, NY 1965; Journal of a Rabbi, 1967 (NY 1966); The Timely and the Timeless, 1977; If Only My People … Zionism in My Life, 1984; (ed) Centenary Edition of the Authorised Daily Prayer-Book, 1990; Dear Chief Rabbi: from the correspondence of Chief Rabbi Immanuel Jakobovits on matters of Jewish law, ethics and contemporary issues, 1980–1990, 1995; contrib. learned and popular jls in America, England and Israel. *Address:* Jews' College, 44a Albert Road, NW4 2SJ. *Died 31 Oct. 1999.*

JALLAND, His Honour William Herbert Wainwright; a Circuit Judge, Manchester, 1975–88 (sitting in Crown Court, Manchester, and County Courts, Manchester and Salford); *b* 21 Dec. 1922; *o s* of Arthur Edgar Jalland, JP, QC and Elizabeth Hewitt Jalland; *m* 1945, Helen Monica (BEM 1984), *o d* of John and Edith Wyatt; one *s* one *d. Educ:* Manchester Grammar Sch.; Manchester Univ. (LLB 1949). Served War of 1939–45, HM Forces at home and abroad, 1941–46: Captain, King's Own Royal Regt, attached 8th Bn Durham LI. Called to the Bar, Gray's Inn, 1950; practised Northern Circuit; part-time Dep. Coroner, City of Salford, 1955–65; part-time Dep. Recorder, Burnley, 1962–70; part-time Dep. Chm., Lancs County Sessions, 1970–71; Recorder, 1972; a Circuit Judge, Liverpool and Merseyside, 1972–75. JP Lancs, 1970–88; Liaison Judge at Magistrates' Courts, Rochdale, Middleton and Heywood, 1974–86. Vice-Pres., Old Mancunians' Assoc., 1979–; Pres., Styal Sports and Social Club, 1979–88. *Recreations:* hillwalking, gardening, photography. *Address:* c/o Circuit Administrator, Northern Circuit, 15 Quay Street, Manchester M60 9FD. *Died 9 Aug. 2000.*

JAMES, Air Vice-Marshal Edgar, CBE 1966; DFC 1945; AFC 1948 (Bar 1959); FRAeS; aviation consultant, retired; *b* 19 Oct. 1915; *s* of Richard George James and Gertrude (*née* Barnes); *m* 1941, Josephine M. Steel; two *s. Educ:* Neath Grammar School. Joined RAF, 1939; commnd; flying instr duties, Canada, until 1944; opl service with Nos 305 and 107 Sqdns, 1944–45; Empire Flying Sch. and Fighter Comd Ops Staff, until Staff Coll., 1950; Ops Requirements, Air Min., 1951–53; 2nd TAF Germany,

1953–56; comd No 68 Night Fighter Squadron, 1954–56; CFE, 1956–58; HQ Fighter Comd Staff, 1958–59; Asst Comdt, CFS, 1959–61; CO, RAF Leeming, 1961–62; Dir Ops Requirements 1, Min. of Def. (Air Force Dept), 1962–66; Comdr British Forces, Zambia, Feb.-Sept. 1966; Dep. Controller of Equipment, Min. of Technology, 1966–69. Wing Comdr 1953; Gp Capt. 1959; Air Cdre 1963; Air Vice-Marshal 1967. FRAeS 1971. QCVSA 1943, 1944, 1956. *Recreation:* sailing. *Address:* Lowmead, Traine Paddock, Modbury, Devon PL21 ORN. *T:* Modbury (01548) 830492. *Clubs:* Royal Air Force; Royal Western Yacht (Plymouth).   *Died 22 Aug. 1996.*

JAMES, Georgina Giselle; Member, since 1996, Deputy Chairwoman, 1997, Equal Opportunities Commission; Managing Director, De Ritter Ltd, since 1980; *b* 6 July 1951; *d* of late Leonard James and Georgina De Ritter; *m* 1973, Neil Kirk (marr. diss. 1994) (decd); *m* 1999, David Martin Burgess. *Educ:* Ursuline Convent High Sch., Essex; Exeter Univ. (BA English). Film prodn and distribution, 1972–77; joined family retailing co., De Ritter Ltd, 1977; concurrently Mem., Audio-Visual Partnership, 1978–89; journalist in business and trade jls, 1980–96. Pres., Chelmsford Chamber of Commerce, 1981–83; Mem. Bd, Nat. Chamber of Trade, 1986–89 (Chm., 1989–91); merged with British Chamber of Commerce, 1992: Retail Pres., 1992–96; Hon. Pres., Essex Chamber of Commerce, 1997–. Dep. Chm., British Retail Consortium, 1991–96. UK Rep., EU Commerce and Distribn Cttee, 1994–98. Mem., Business Link Adv. Bd, DTI, 1996–; Dir, Business Link Essex, 1996–98; Mem. Bd, Essex TEC, 1998–. Non-exec. Dir, Essex and Suffolk Water, 1997–. Gov., Anglia Polytechnic Univ., 1995–. *Recreations:* books, friends, basking in France. *Address:* Georgina De Ritter, The Village, Felsted, Essex CM6 3DJ, *T:* (01371) 820442.   *Died 11 Feb. 2000.*

JAMES, Henry Leonard, CB 1980; communications consultant and retirement counsellor, since 1997; Consultant, Tolley Publishing, since 1987; Director, Pielle & Co. Ltd (PR Consultants), since 1989; *b* 12 Dec. 1919; *o s* of late Leonard Mark James and Alice Esther James; *m* 1949, Sylvia Mary Bickell (*d* 1989). *Educ:* King Edward VI Sch., Birmingham. Entered Civil Service in Min. of Health, 1938; Founder Editor, The Window, Min. of Nat. Insce, 1948–51; Dramatic Critic and London Corresp. of Birmingham News, 1947–51; Press Officer, Min. of Pensions and Nat. Insce, 1951–55; Head of Films, Radio and Television, Admty, 1955–61; Head of Publicity, Min. of Educn, 1961–63; Chief Press Officer, Min. of Educn, 1963–64; Dep. Public Relations Adviser to Prime Minister, 1964; Dep. Press Sec. to Prime Minister, 1964–68; Chief Information Officer, Min. of Housing and Local Govt, 1969–70; Press Sec. to Prime Minister, 1970–71; Dir of Information, DoE, 1971–74; Dir-Gen., COI, 1974–78; Chief Press Sec. to the Prime Minister, 1979; Public Relations Advr to Main Bd, Vickers Ltd, 1978–80; Dir-Gen., Nat. Assoc. of Pension Funds, 1981–86; Dir-Gen., European Fedn for Retirement Provision, 1982–86; Associate Dir, Godwins Ltd, 1987–97. Vice-Pres., Retirement Trust, 1992–. Member: Pub. Cttee, Internat. Year of the Child, 1979; Council, RSPCA, 1980–84; BOTB, 1980–83. Alumni Guest Lectr, Gustavus Adolphus Coll., Minnesota, 1977. FCAM 1980 (Dep. Chm., 1979–84; Vice-Pres., 1984–). FRSA. FIPR (Hon. Fellow, 1998; Pres., 1979; President's Medal, 1976). *Recreation:* visual arts. *Address:* 17 Beaumont Avenue, Richmond, Surrey TW9 2HE. *T:* (020) 8940 9229.
                    Died 10 Nov. 1998.

JAMES, John, CBE 1981; Founder and Chairman: John James Group of Companies Ltd, Bristol, 1961–79; Broadmead Group of Companies, 1946–60; Dawn Estates Ltd, since 1945; *b* 25 July 1906; *m* 1st (marr. diss.); two *d*

(and one *s* one *d* decd); 2nd, Margaret Theodosia Parkes (*d* 1991). *Educ:* Merchant Venturers, Bristol. Chm. Bd of Trustees: Dawn James Charitable Foundn, 1965–; John James Bristol Foundn (formerly Bristol Charitable Foundn), 1983–. Hon. LLD Bristol, 1983. *Recreations:* chess, swimming. *Address:* 7 Clyde Road, Redland, Bristol BS6 6RG.*T:* Bristol (0117) 923 9444.
                    Died 31 Jan. 1996.

JAMES, Sir Robert Vidal R.; *see* Rhodes James.

JAMES, Thomas Geraint Illtyd, FRCS; Hon. Surgeon, Central Middlesex Hospital; late Teacher of Surgery, Middlesex Hospital, and Hon. Surgical Tutor, Royal College of Surgeons of England; *b* 12 July 1900; *s* of late Evan Thomas and Elizabeth James, Barry; *m* 1932, Dorothy Marguerite, *o d* of late David John, Cardiff; two *s. Educ:* Barry, Glam; University Coll., Cardiff; Welsh National Sch. of Medicine; St Mary's Hosp., London; Guy's Hosp., London. BSc Wales, 1921, Alfred Sheen Prize in Anat. and Physiol.; MRCS, LRCP 1924; MB, ChB 1925, Maclean Medal and Prize in Obst. and Gynæcol.; FRCSE 1927; FRCS 1928; MCh Wales, 1932; FRSocMed; Fellow Association of Surgeons of Great Britain and Ireland. Formerly: House phys., House surg. and Resident Surgical Officer, Cardiff Royal Infirmary; Clinical Asst St Mark's, St Peter's and Guy's Hosps, London; Asst to Neurosurg. Dept, London Hosp.; Mem., Management Cttee, Leavesden Gp of Hosps. Erasmus Wilson Lectr, RCS, 1972. Mem., Internat. Soc. for Surgery. Corr. Mem. Spanish-Portuguese Soc. of Neurosurgery. Mem. Soc. of Apothecaries; Freeman of City of London. Formerly: Assoc. Examr University of London, Mem. and Chm., Court of Examiners RCS; Examr in Surgery, University of Liverpool. *Publications:* in various jls on surg. and neurosurg. subjects. *Recreations:* literature, travelling. *Address:* 1 Freeland Road, W5 3HR. *T:* (0181) 992 2430.   *Died 21 Dec. 1996.*

JAMESON, Air Cdre Patrick Geraint, CB 1959; DSO 1943; DFC 1940 (and Bar 1942); psa; Royal Air Force, retired, 1960; *b* Wellington, NZ, 10 Nov. 1912; *s* of Robert Delvin Jameson, Balbriggan, Ireland, and Katherine Lenora Jameson (*née* Dick), Dunedin, NZ; *m* 1941, Hilda Nellie Haiselden Webster, *d* of B. F. Webster, Lower Hutt, NZ; one *s* one *d*. *Educ:* Hutt Valley High Sch., New Zealand. Commissioned in RAF, 1936; 46 Squadron, 1936–40; War of 1939–45 (despatches 5 times, DFC and Bar, DSO); one of 37 survivors of sinking of HM Aircraft Carrier Glorious by enemy action in Arctic Ocean, 1940); commanded 266 Squadron, 1940–41; Wing Commander Flying, Wittering, 1941–42; Wing Commander (Flying), Norwegian Wing, North Weald, 1942–43; Group Capt. Plans, HQ No II Group, 1943–44; 122 Wing in France, Belgium, Holland, Germany and Denmark, 1944–46; Staff Coll., Haifa, 1946; Air Ministry, 1946–48; CFE, West Raynham, 1949–52; Wunsdorf (2nd TAF), 1952–54; SASO, HQ No II Group, 1954–56; SASO HQ RAF Germany (2nd TAF) 1956–59; Task Force Comdr, Operation Grapple, Christmas Is., 1959–60. Norwegian War Cross, 1943; Netherlands Order of Orange Nassau, 1945; American Silver Star, 1945. *Recreations:* fishing, shooting, sailing, golf. *Address:* 70 Wai-Iti Crescent, Lower Hutt, New Zealand. *Clubs:* Royal Air Force; Hutt Golf.   *Died 1 Oct. 1996.*

JAMIESON, Lt-Col Harvey Morro H.; *see* Harvey-Jamieson.

JAMIESON, John Kenneth; Chairman of Board and Chief Executive Officer, Exxon Corporation (formerly Standard Oil Co. (NJ)), 1969–75; *b* Canada, 28 Aug. 1910; *s* of John Locke and Kate Herron Jamieson; US citizen, 1964; *m* 1937, Ethel May Burns (*d* 1999); one *s* one *d*. *Educ:* Univ. of Alberta; Massachusetts Inst. of Technology (BS).

Northwest Stellarene Co. of Alberta, 1932; British American Oil Co., 1934; Manager, Moose Jaw Refinery; served War of 1939–45 in Oil Controller's Dept of Canadian Govt; subseq. Manager, Manufrg Dept, British American Oil Co.; joined Imperial Oil Co., 1948: Head of Engrg and Develt Div., Sarnia Refinery, 1949; Asst Gen. Man. of Manufrg Dept, 1950; on loan to Canadian Dept of Defence Production, 1951; Dir, Imperial Oil, 1952, Vice-Pres. 1953; Pres. and Dir, International Petroleum Co., 1959; Vice-Pres., Dir and Mem. Exec. Cttee, Exxon Co., USA (formerly Humble Oil & Refining Co.), 1961, Exec. Vice-Pres. 1962, Pres. 1963–64; Exec. Vice-Pres. and Dir, 1964–65, Pres., 1965–69, Standard Oil Co. (NJ). *Address:* Kellogg Tower, 601 Jefferson, Suite 975, Houston, TX 77002, USA. *Clubs:* Ramada, Houston Country (Houston); Ristigouche Salmon (Matapedia, Quebec). *Died 26 Sept. 1999.*

JAMISON, James Hardie, OBE 1974; chartered accountant; Partner, Coopers & Lybrand, Chartered Accountants, 1939–78, retired; *b* 29 Nov. 1913; *s* of late W. I. Jamison; *m* 1940, Mary Louise, *d* of late W. R. Richardson; two *s* one *d. Educ:* Sydney Church of England Grammar Sch. Chm., Commn of Inquiry into Efficiency and Admin of Hosps, 1979–80. Mem., Nat. Council, Aust. Inst. of Chartered Accountants, 1969–77, Vice Pres., 1973–75, Pres., 1975–76. *Recreation:* sailing. *Address:* 16 Tivoli Street, Mosman, NSW 2088, Australia. *Clubs:* Australasian Pioneers' (Pres. 1970–72), Australian, Royal Sydney Yacht Squadron (Sydney).

Died 7 Jan. 1996.

JANSEN, Peter Johan, Hon. CBE 1998; Chairman, Caradon (formerly MB-Caradon), since 1998 (Group Chief Executive, 1989–98; Deputy Chairman, 1994–98); *b* 13 Feb. 1940; *s* of Eric Jansen and Elizabeth (*née* Keesman); *m* 1963, Françoise Marie-Paule; three *s. Educ:* Parktown Boys' High School, Johannesburg. Internat. Marketing Exec., Pfizer Corp., 1959–65; Marketing Dir, Bristol Myers, 1966–69; Partner, Urwick Orr & Partners, 1969–72; Senior Partner, Lee, Jansen & Partners, 1972–77; Redland plc: Divl Man. Dir, 1977–80; Director, 1981–85; led management buy-out and subseq. flotation, Caradon plc; Dep. Chm. and Chief Exec., 1985–89. Dir, Burmah Castrol plc, 1993–; Non-exec. Dir, Southern Africa Investors Ltd, 1995–; Chm. Supervisory Bd, Nutreco Holding BV, 1995–. Pres., Nat. Council of Bldg Material Producers, 1994–96; Mem. Council, CBI, 1992–96. Chm. Adv. Bd, 1994–, and Trustee, 1996–, Construction Industry Relief & Assistance for the Single Homeless. Gov., St George's Coll., Weybridge, 1990–; Chm. Bd of Advrs, St Edmund Hall, Oxford, 1995–. CIMgt; FCIM; FRSA. *Recreations:* golf, opera, theatre. *Address:* Caradon House, 24 Queens Road, Weybridge, Surrey KT13 9UX. *T:* (01932) 850850. *Died 19 June 1998.*

JARDINE PATERSON, Sir John (Valentine), Kt 1967; *b* 14 Feb. 1920; *y s* of late Robert Jardine Paterson, Balgray, Lockerbie, Dumfriesshire; *m* 1953, Priscilla Mignon, *d* of late Sir Kenneth Nicolson, MC; one *s* three *d. Educ:* Eton Coll.; Jesus Coll., Cambridge. Emergency commn, The Black Watch, RHR, 1939. Director: Jardine Henderson Ltd, Calcutta, 1952–67 (Chm. 1963–67); McLeod Russel PLC, 1967–84 (Chm., 1979–83). Chm., Indian Jute Mills Assoc., 1963; Pres., Bengal Chamber of Commerce and Industry and Associated Chambers of Commerce of India, 1966. *Address:* Norton Bavant Manor, Warminster, Wilts BA12 7BB. *T:* (01985) 840378. *Club:* Oriental.

Died 12 March 2000.

JAY, Baron *cr* 1987 (Life Peer), of Battersea in Greater London; **Douglas Patrick Thomas Jay;** PC 1951; *b* 23 March 1907; *s* of Edward Aubrey Hastings Jay and Isobel Violet Jay; *m* 1st, 1933, Margaret Christian (marr. diss. 1972), *e d* of late J. C. Maxwell Garnett, CBE, ScD; two *s*

twin *d*; 2nd, 1972, Mary Lavinia Thomas, *d* of Hugh Lewis Thomas. *Educ:* Winchester Coll.; New Coll., Oxford (Scholar). First Class, Litteræ Humaniores. Fellow of All Souls' Coll., Oxford, 1930–37, and 1968–; on the staff of The Times, 1929–33, and The Economist, 1933–37; City Editor of the Daily Herald, 1937–40; Asst Sec., Ministry of Supply, 1940–43; Principal Asst Sec., BoT, 1943–45; Personal Asst to Prime Minister, 1945–46. MP (Lab) Battersea N, July 1946–1974, Wandsworth, Battersea N, 1974–83; Economic Sec. to Treasury, 1947–50; Financial Sec. to Treasury, 1950–51; President, BoT, 1964–67. Chairman: Common Market Safeguards Campaign, 1970–77; London Motorway Action Group, 1968–80. Director: Courtaulds Ltd, 1967–70; Trades Union Unit Trust, 1967–79; Flag Investment Co., 1968–71. *Publications:* The Socialist Case, 1937; Who is to Pay for the War and the Peace, 1941; Socialism in the New Society, 1962; After the Common Market, 1968; Change and Fortune, 1980; Sterling: a plea for moderation, 1985. *Address:* Causeway Cottage, Minster Lovell, Oxon OX8 5RN. *T:* Witney (01993) 775235.

Died 6 March 1996.

JAYES, Percy Harris, MB, BS; FRCS; Plastic Surgeon: St Bartholomew's Hospital, London, 1952–73; Queen Victoria Hospital, East Grinstead, 1948–73; Consultant in Plastic Surgery to the Royal Air Force, 1960; Consultant Plastic Surgeon, King Edward VII Hospital for Officers, 1966–85; *b* 26 June 1915; *s* of Thomas Harris Jayes; *m* 1945, Kathleen Mary Harrington (*d* 1963); two *s* one *d*; *m* 1964, Aileen Mary McLaughlin; one *s* one *d. Educ:* Merchant Taylors' Sch.; St Bartholomew's Hosp. Resid. Plastic Surg., EMS Plastic Unit, East Grinstead, 1940–48; Surgeon in Charge, UNRRA Plastic Unit, Belgrade, 1946. Mem. Council, Brit. Assoc. Plastic Surgeons, 1954–64 (Pres., Assoc., 1960). *Publications:* contrib. British Journal of Plastic Surgery, Annals of Royal College of Surgeons and other journals. *Recreation:* tennis. *Address:* Pierpoint House, 110 High Street, Lindfield, West Sussex RH16 2HS. *T:* (01444) 483906. *Died 17 Jan. 1997.*

JAYEWARDENE, Junius Richard; President of Sri Lanka, 1978–88; *b* Colombo, 17 Sept. 1906; *s* of Mr Justice E. W. Jayewardene, KC and A. H. Jayewardene; *m* 1935, Elina B. Rupesinghe; one *s. Educ:* Royal Coll., Colombo; Ceylon University Coll.; Ceylon Law Coll. Sworn Advocate of Supreme Court of Ceylon, 1932. Ceylon National Congress, later United National Party, 1938–89: Hon. Sec., 1940–47; Hon. Treasurer, 1946–48, 1957–58; Vice-Pres., 1954–56, 1958–72; Sec., 1972–73; Pres., 1973–88. Member: Colombo Municipal Council, 1940–43; State Council, 1943–47; House of Representatives, 1947–56, 1960–77 (Leader, 1953–56); Minister of: Agriculture and Food, 1953–56; Finance, 1947–52, 1952–53, 1960; Chief Opposition Whip, 1960–65; Minister of State and Parly Sec. to Prime Minister, Minister of Defence and External Affairs, and Chief Govt Whip, 1965–70; Leader of the Opposition, House of Representatives, 1970–72, Nat. State Assembly, 1972–77; Prime Minister, and Minister of Planning and Economic Affairs, 1977; Minister of: Defence, and Plan Implementation, 1977–88; Power and Energy, 1981–88; Higher Education, Janatha Estates Develt and State Plantations. Was a co-author of Colombo Plan, 1950; leader of delegations to many UN and Commonwealth conferences; Governor, World Bank and IMF, 1947–52. *Publications:* Some Sermons of Buddha, 1940; Buddhist Essays; In Council (speeches), 1946; Buddhism and Marxism, 1950, 3rd edn 1957; Golden Threads, 1986; Selected Speeches. *Address:* 66 Ward Place, Colombo 7, Sri Lanka. *T:* 692332, 695028.

Died 1 Nov. 1996.

JEELOF, Gerrit, Hon. CBE 1981; Member, Board of Directors, Philips Electronics NV, since 1990; *b* 13 May 1927; *m* 1951, Jantje Aleida Plinsinga (*d* 1992); two *d*. *Educ:* Dutch Trng Inst. for Foreign Trade, Nijenrode. Philips Industries: Eindhoven, Holland, 1950–53; Spain and S America, 1953–65; Eindhoven, Holland, 1965–70; Varese, Italy, 1970–76; Chm. and Man. Dir, Philips Industries UK, 1976–80; Exec. Vice-Pres., 1981–86, Vice-Chm., 1986–90, Philips Industries Eindhoven. Chm., European Chamber of Commerce in USA, 1990–; Director: VNU Publishing, Haarlem, 1985–; ROBECO Investment Fund, Rotterdam, 1988–; Centraal Beheer Insce, Naarden, 1990–; Cabot Corp., Boston, 1990–. Chm., Bd of Trustees, Univ. for Business Administration Nijenrode, Breukelen, 1983–. Commendatore del Ordine al Merito della Repubblica Italiana, 1974; Officer, Order of Oranje-Nassau (Netherlands), 1985. *Recreations:* sailing, golf. *Address:* Apt 3F, Long Island Apartements, Le Zoute, Zwinlaan 11, 8300 Knokke-Heist, Belgium. *T:* 50610085. *Clubs:* Royal Ocean Racing; Royal Yacht Squadron; Koninklijke Nederlandsche Zeil-en Roeivereeniging (Holland). *Died 1 May 1996.*

JEFFS, Group Captain (George) James (Horatio), CVO 1960 (LVO 1943); OBE 1950; *b* 27 Jan. 1900; *s* of late James Thomas Jeffs, Chilvers Coton, Warwicks; *m* 1921, Phyllis Rosina (*née* Bell); two *s* one *d*. *Educ:* Kedleston Sch., Derby. Served European War: RNAS, 1916–18; RAF, 1918–19; Air Ministry, 1919–23; Croydon Airport, 1923–34; Heston Airport, 1934–37; Air Ministry, 1937–39; served War of 1939–45, RAF: Aircrew Mem. of flights of HM King George VI and Sir Winston Churchill; Fighter, Ferry, and Transport Commands, Group Captain, UK Delegate to Civil Aviation Conf., Chicago, 1944; Ministry of Transport and Civil Aviation, 1945; Nat. Air Traffic Control Officers' Licence No 1; Airport Commandant, Prestwick, 1950–57; Airport Commandant, London-Heathrow Airport, 1957–60. Pioneered the opening and early functioning of all the major civil airports in the UK; for many years responsible for safe functioning of air traffic control in UK. Legion of Merit, USA, 1944. Liveryman, GAPAN. *Address:* Pixham Firs Cottage, Pixham Lane, Dorking, Surrey RH4 1PH. *T:* Dorking (01306) 884084. *Club:* Naval and Military.
Died 14 May 1996.

JEHANGIR, Sir Hirji, 3rd Bt *cr* 1908; *b* 1 Nov. 1915; 2nd *s* of Sir Cowasjee Jehangir, 2nd Bt, GBE, KCIE, and Hilla, MBE, *d* of late Hormarji Wadia, Lowji Castle, Bombay; *S* father, 1962; *m* 1952, Jinoo, *d* of K. H. Cama; two *s*. *Educ:* St Xavier Sch., Bombay; Magdalene Coll., Cambridge. Chairman: Jehangir Art Gallery, Bombay; Parsi Public School Soc.; Cowasji Jehangir Charitable Trust. *Heir: s* Jehangir [*b* 23 Nov. 1953; *m* 1988, Jasmine, *d* of Bejan Billimoria; one *s* one *d*]. *Address:* Readymoney House, 49 Nepean Sea Road, Bombay 400036, India; 24 Kensington Court Gardens, Kensington Court Place, W8 5QF. *T:* (020) 7937 9587. *Clubs:* Royal Over-Seas League, English Speaking Union; Willingdon (Bombay).
Died 2000.

JELLICOE, Sir Geoffrey (Alan), Kt 1979; CBE 1961; RA 1991; FRIBA (DistTP); PPILA; FRTPI; formerly Senior Partner of Jellicoe & Coleridge, Architects; *b* London, 8 Oct. 1900; *s* of George Edward Jellicoe; *m* 1936, Ursula (*d* 1986), *d* of late Sir Bernard Pares, KBE, DCL. *Educ:* Cheltenham Coll.; Architectural Association. Bernard Webb Student at British School at Rome; RIBA Neale Bursar. Principal, Arch. Assoc. Schs, 1939–41. Arch. Cons. to N Rhodesian Govt, 1947–52. Pres., Inst. of Landscape Architects, 1939–49; Hon. Pres. Internat. Fed. of Landscape Architects; Mem. Royal Fine Art Commission, 1954–68; former Trustee of the Tate Gallery; Hon. Corr. Mem. American, Italian and Venezuelan Societies of Landscape Architects. Gardens for: Sandringham; Royal Lodge, Windsor; Ditchley Park; RHS central area, Wisley; Chequers; Horsted Place, Sussex; Hartwell House, Aylesbury; Shute House, Wilts; Tidcombe Manor, Wilts; St Paul's Walden, Herts; Delta Works, W Bromwich; Hilton Hotel, Stratford-upon-Avon; Dewlish House, Dorchester; The Grange, Winchester; Sutton Place, Surrey; Barnwell Manor, Northants; Giza, Egypt; Denbies, Surrey; Historica Park, Atlanta, Ga; historical gardens for Moody Foundn, Galveston, Texas, USA, 1984; Town Plans for: Guildford, Wellington (Salop), Hemel Hempstead New Town; housing for Basildon, Scunthorpe, LCC; Plymouth Civic Centre; Chertsey Civic Centre; Cheltenham Sports Centre; GLC Comprehensive Sch., Dalston; Durley Park, Keynsham; Grantham Crematorium and Swimming Pool; comprehensive plans for central area, Gloucester, and for Tollcross, Edinburgh; civic landscapes for Modena, Brescia, Asolo and Turin, Italy; Kennedy Memorial, Runnymede; Plans for Sark, Isles of Scilly, and Bridgefoot, Stratford-upon-Avon. Medal of Amer. Soc. of Landscape Architects, 1981; Medal of Landscape Inst., 1985; VMH 1994; Royal VMH 1995. *Publications:* Italian Gardens of the Renaissance (joint), 1925, rev. edn 1986; (with J. C. Shepherd) Gardens and Design, 1927; Baroque Gardens of Austria, 1931; Studies in Landscape Design, Vol. I 1959, Vol. II 1966, Vol. III 1970; Motopia, 1961; (with Susan Jellicoe) Water, 1971; The Landscape of Man, 1975, rev. edn 1987; The Guelph Lectures on Landscape Design, 1983; (ed with Susan Jellicoe, Patrick Goode and Michael Lancaster) The Oxford Companion to Gardens, 1986; The Moody Historical Gardens, 1989; The Landscape of Civilisation, 1989; Writings, vol. 1, 1993. *Address:* c/o Colway Manor, Lyme Regis, Dorset DT7 3HD. *Died 17 July 1996.*

JENKINS, (David) Clive; Joint General Secretary, Manufacturing, Science and Finance, 1988–89, then General Secretary Emeritus (Joint General Secretary, 1968–70, General Secretary, 1970–88, Association of Scientific, Technical and Managerial Staffs); Member of the General Council of the TUC, 1974–89 (Chairman, 1987–88); *b* 2 May 1926; *s* of David Samuel Jenkins and Miriam Harris Jenkins (*née* Hughes); *m* 1955, Jean Lynn (marr. diss. 1963); *m* 1963, Moira McGregor Hilley (marr. diss. 1989); one *s* one *d*. *Educ:* Port Talbot Central Boys' Sch.; Port Talbot County Sch.; Swansea Techn. Coll. (evenings). Started work in metallurgical test house, 1940; furnace shift supervisor, 1942; i/c of laboratory, 1943; tinplate night shift foreman, 1945; Branch Sec. and Area Treas., AScW, 1946; Asst Midlands Divisional Officer, ASSET, 1947; Transport Industrial Officer, 1949; Nat. Officer, 1954; Gen. Sec., ASSET, 1961–68. Woodrow Wilson Fellow, 1968; Australian Commonwealth Fellow, 1989. Metrop. Borough Councillor, 1954–60 (Chm. Staff Cttee, St Pancras Borough Council); Chm., Nat. Jt Council for Civil Air Transport, 1967–68; Member: NRDC, 1974–80; Bullock Cttee on Industrial Democracy, 1975; Wilson Cttee to Review the Functioning of Financial Institutions, 1977–80; BNOC, 1979–82; BOTB, 1980–83; NEDC, 1983–89; Commn of Inquiry into Labour Party, 1979 (Chm., Finance Panel, 1979); TUC-Labour Party Liaison Cttee, 1980–89; Council, ACAS, 1986–89; Chairman: TUC Educnl Trust, 1979; Roosevelt Meml Trust, 1979–89; Friends of the Earth Trust, 1984–86; Trustee, Nat. Heritage Meml Fund, 1980–88; Governor, Sadler's Wells Foundn, 1985–88. Editor, Trade Union Affairs, 1961–63; sometime columnist, Tribune, Daily Mirror, Daily Record. *Publications:* Power at the Top, 1959; Power Behind the Screen, 1961; (with J. E. Mortimer) British Trade Unions Today, 1965; (with J. E. Mortimer) The Kind of Laws the Unions Ought to Want, 1968; with B. D. Sherman: Computers and the Unions,

1977; Collective Bargaining: what you always wanted to know about trade unions and never dared ask, 1977; The Collapse of Work, 1979; The Rebellious Salariat: white collar unionism, 1979; The Leisure Shock, 1981; All Against the Collar (autobiog.), 1990. *Recreations:* working with the Green movements, keeping an eye on multinational exploiters and Fairy Penguins.

Died 22 Sept. 1999.

JENKINS, Prof. Harold, DLitt; FBA 1989; Professor Emeritus, University of Edinburgh; *b* 19 July 1909; *s* of Henry and Mildred Jenkins, Shenley, Bucks; *m* 1939, Gladys Puddifoot (*d* 1984); no *c. Educ:* Wolverton Grammar Sch.; University Coll., London (MA; Fellow, 1991); DLitt Witwatersrand. George Smith Studentship, 1930; Quain Student, University Coll., London, 1930–35; William Noble Fellow, University of Liverpool, 1935–36; Lecturer in English, University of the Witwatersrand, South Africa, 1936–45; Lecturer in English, 1945–46, Reader in English, 1946–54, UCL; Prof. of English, University of London (Westfield Coll.), 1954–67; Regius Prof. of Rhetoric and English Lit., Edinburgh Univ., 1967–71. Visiting Professor: Duke Univ., USA, 1957–58; Univ. of Oslo, 1974. Pres., Malone Soc., 1989– (Mem. Council, 1955–89). FRSL 1999. Hon. LittD Iona Coll., New Rochelle, NY, 1983. Shakespeare Prize, FVS Foundn, Hamburg, 1986. Jt Gen. Editor, Arden Shakespeare, 1958–82. *Publications:* The Life and Work of Henry Chettle, 1934; Edward Benlowes, 1952; The Structural Problem in Shakespeare's Henry IV, 1956; The Catastrophe in Shakespearean Tragedy, 1968; John Dover Wilson (British Acad. memoir), 1973; (ed) Hamlet (Arden edn), 1982; articles in Modern Language Review, Review of English Studies, The Library, Shakespeare Survey, Studies in Bibliography, etc. *Address:* 22 North Crescent, Finchley, N3 3LL. *Club:* Athenæum.

Died 4 Jan. 2000.

JENKINS, Sir Owain (Trevor), Kt 1958; *b* 20 Feb. 1907; 5th *s* of Sir John Lewis Jenkins, KCSI, ICS and Florence Mildred, *d* of Sir Arthur Trevor, KCSI; *m* 1940, Sybil Léonie, *y d* of late Maj.-Gen. Lionel Herbert, CB, CVO. *Educ:* Charterhouse; Balliol Coll., Oxford. Employed by Balmer Lawrie & Co. Ltd, Calcutta, 1929; Indian Army, 1940–44; Man. Dir, Balmer Lawrie, 1948–58. Pres. of the Bengal Chamber of Commerce and Industry and Pres. of the Associated Chambers of Commerce of India, 1956–57. Formerly Director: Singapore Traction Co.; Calcutta Electric Supply Corp.; Macleod Russel PLC; retd 1982. Mem., Econ. Survey Mission to Basutoland, Bechuanaland Protectorate and Swaziland, 1959. *Publications:* (with Rumer Godden) The Dark Horse, 1981; (with Rumer Godden) The Valiant Chatti-Maker, 1983; Merchant Prince (memoirs), 1987. *Address:* Boles House, East Street, Petworth, West Sussex GU28 0AB. *Club:* Oriental. *Died 5 June 1996.*

JENKINS, Very Rev. Thomas Edward; *b* 14 Aug. 1902; *s* of late David Jenkins, Canon of St David's Cathedral and Vicar of Abergwili, and Florence Helena Jenkins; *m* 1928, Annie Laura (*d* 1976), *d* of late David Henry, Penygroes, Carms; one *s. Educ:* Llandyssul Grammar Sch.; St David's Coll., Lampeter; Wycliffe Hall, Oxford. St David's Coll., Lampeter, BA 1922, BD 1932, Powys Exhibitioner, 1924; Welsh Church Scholar, 1921. Ordained, 1925; Curate of Llanelly, 1925–34; Rector of Begelly, 1934–38; Vicar: Christ Church, Llanelly, 1938–46; Lampeter, 1946–55 (Rural Dean, 1949–54); Canon, St David's Cathedral, 1951–57; Vicar of Cardigan, 1955–57; Dean of St David's, 1957–72. *Address:* Brynderwen, Capel Dewi Road, Llangunnor, Carmarthen. *Died 28 Aug. 1996.*

JENKINS, Vivian Evan, MBE 1945; Director of Social Services, Cardiff City Council, 1971–74, retired; *b* 12 Sept. 1918; *s* of late Arthur Evan Jenkins and Mrs Blodwen Jenkins; *m* 1946, Megan Myfanwy Evans; one *s* one *d. Educ:* UC Cardiff (BA). Dipl. Social Science. Army, 1940; commnd Royal Signals, 1943; served with 6th Airborne Div. as parachutist, Europe, Far East and Middle East, 1943–46 (Lieut). Child Care Officer, Glamorgan CC, 1949; Asst Children's Officer, 1951; Mem. Home Office Children's Dept Inspectorate, 1952. *Recreations:* Rugby football (former Captain of Univ. XV and Pontypridd RFC; awarded two Wales Rugby caps as schoolboy, 1933 and 1937), cricket, golf. *Address:* 24 Windsor Road, Radyr, Cardiff CF4 8BQ. *T:* (01222) 842485. *Club:* Radyr Golf. *Died 19 April 1997.*

JERSEY, 9th Earl of, *cr* 1697; **George Francis Child Villiers;** Viscount Grandison of Limerick (Ire.), 1620; Viscount Villiers of Dartford and Baron Villiers of Hoo, 1691; *b* 15 Feb. 1910; *e s* of 8th Earl of Jersey and Lady Cynthia Almina Constance Mary Needham (who *m* 2nd, 1925, W. R. Slessor (*d* 1945); she died 1947), *o d* of 3rd Earl of Kilmorey; *S* father, 1923; *m* 1st, 1932, Patricia Kenneth (marr. diss. 1937; she *m* 2nd, 1937, Robin Filmer Wilson, who *d* 1944; 3rd, 1953, Col Peter Laycock, who *d* 1977; 4th, 1987, Roderick More O'Ferrall, who *d* 1990), *o d* of Kenneth Richards, Cootamundra, NSW, and Eileen Mary (who *m* later Sir Stephenson Kent, KCB); one *d*; 2nd, 1937, Virginia (marr. diss. 1946), *d* of James Cherrill, USA; 3rd, 1947, Bianca Maria Adriana Luciana, *er d* of late Enrico Mottironi, Turin, Italy; one *d* (two *s* decd). *Heir: g s* George Francis William Child Villiers, Viscount Villiers, *b* 5 Feb. 1976. *Address:* Radier Manor, Le Chemin du Radier, Grouville, Jersey, Channel Islands JE3 9DR. *T:* (01534) 853102. *Died 9 Aug. 1998.*

JERVIS, Charles Elliott, OBE 1966; Editor-in-Chief, Press Association, 1954–65; *b* Liverpool, 7 Nov. 1907; *y s* of late J. H. Jervis, Liverpool; *m* 1931, Ethel Braithwaite (*d* 1979), Kendal, Westmorland; one *d.* Editorial Asst, Liverpool Express, 1921–23; Reporter, Westmorland Gazette, 1923–28; Dramatic Critic and Asst Editor, Croydon Times, 1928–37; Sub-Editor, Press Assoc., 1937–47, Asst Editor, 1947–54. Pres., Guild of British Newspaper Editors, 1964–65; Mem. of the Press Council, 1960–65. *Address:* The Old Vicarage, Allithwaite, Grange-over-Sands, Cumbria LA11 7QN.

Died 19 March 1999.

JESSEL, Dame Penelope, DBE 1987; International Officer, Liberal Party, 1985–88; *b* 2 Jan. 1920; *d* of Sir Basil Blackwell and late Marion Christine, *d* of John Soans; *m* 1940, Robert George Jessel (*d* 1954); two *s. Educ:* Dragon Sch., Oxford; St Leonard's, St Andrews, Fife; Somerville Coll., Oxford (MA). On staff of Oxford House, London, 1940–41; ATS, 1941–43; Lecturer: William Temple Coll., 1956–62; Plater Coll., Oxford, 1968–84. President: Women's Liberal Fedn, 1970–72; Oxford Civic Soc.; Convenor of Trustees, John Stuart Mill Inst. *Publication:* Owen of Uppingham, 1965. *Recreations:* looking at old churches, music, gardening, looking at gardens. *Address:* The Cottage, The Green, Cassington, Oxford OX8 1DW. *T:* (01865) 881322. *Club:* National Liberal.

Died 2 Dec. 1996.

JEWELL, Prof. Peter Arundel, PhD; CBiol, FIBiol; Mary Marshall and Arthur Walton Professor of Physiology of Reproduction, University of Cambridge, 1977–92, then Professor Emeritus; Fellow of St John's College, Cambridge, since 1977; *b* 16 June 1925; *s* of Percy Arundel Jewell and Ivy Dorothea Enness; *m* 1958, Juliet Clutton-Brock; three *d. Educ:* Wandsworth Sch.; Reading Univ. (BScAgr); Cambridge Univ. (BA, MA, PhD). Lectr, Royal Veterinary Coll., 1950–60; Research Fellow, Zoological Soc. of London, 1960–66; Prof. of Biological Sciences, Univ. of Nigeria, 1966–67; Sen. Lectr and Dir of Conservation Course, University Coll. London, 1967–72; Prof. of Zoology, Royal Holloway Coll.,

1972–77. Pres., Mammal Soc., 1991 93; Vice-Pres., Rare Breeds Survival Trust, 1991–. *Publications:* The Experimental Earthwork on Overton Down, Wiltshire, 1960; Island Survivors: the Ecology of the Soay Sheep of St Kilda, 1974; Management of Locally Abundant Wild Mammals, 1981; scientific papers in Jl Animal Ecology, Jl Physiology, Jl Zoology, Ark, etc. *Recreations:* emulating Cornish ancestors, drinking real ale, watching wild animals, saving rare breeds, life drawing, pottery, archaeology, Japanese. *Address:* St John's College, Cambridge CB2 1TP. *Died 23 May 1998.*

JOCELYN, Prof. Henry David, PhD; FBA 1982; Hulme Professor of Latin, University of Manchester, 1973–96, then Professor Emeritus; *b* 22 Aug. 1933; *s* of late John Daniel Jocelyn and Phyllis Irene Burton; *m* 1958, Margaret Jill, *d* of Bert James Morton and Dulcie Marie Adams; two *s*. *Educ:* Canterbury Boys' High Sch.; Univ. of Sydney (BA); St John's Coll., Univ. of Cambridge (MA, PhD). Teaching Fellow in Latin, Univ. of Sydney, 1955; Cooper Travelling Scholar in Classics, 1955–57; Scholar in Classics, British Sch. at Rome, 1957–59; University of Sydney: Lectr in Latin, 1960–64; Sen. Lectr in Latin, 1964–66; Reader in Latin, 1966–70; Prof. of Latin, 1970–73. Visiting Lectr in Classics, Yale Univ., 1967; Vis. Fellow, ANU, 1979; British Acad. Leverhulme Vis. Prof., *Thesaurus Linguae Latinae*, Munich, 1983; Vis. Lectr in Classics, Univ. of Cape Town, 1985; Visiting Professor: Univ. of Fribourg, 1990; Univ. of Catania, 1994; Cornell Univ., 1995. Corresp. Fellow, Accademia Properziana del Subasio, 1985. FAHA 1970. Member: Editorial Bd, Cambridge Classical Texts and Commentaries, 1982–97; Adv. Bd, *Res Publica Litterarum*, 1992–; Scientific Cttee, *Sileno*, 1994–; Internat. Commn, *Thesaurus Linguae Latinae*, 1994–. Hon. DLitt Sydney, 1995. *Publications:* The Tragedies of Ennius, 1967, corr. reprint 1969; (with B. P. Sotchell) Regimer de Graat on the Human Reproductive Organs, 1972; Philology and Education, 1988; (cd jtly) Studies in Latin Literature and its Tradition, 1989; (ed jtly) F. R. D. Goodyear: papers on Latin Literature, 1992; (ed) Tria Lustra: papers in honour of J. Pinsent, 1993; (ed) Aspects of Nineteenth-Century British Classical Scholarship, 1996; papers on Greek and Latin subjects in various collective vols and periodicals. *Address:* The Bent House, 56–60 Lyne Road, Kidlington, Oxfordshire OX5 1AD. *T:* (01865) 842754. *Died 22 Oct. 2000.*

JOEL, Hon. Sir Asher (Alexander), KBE 1974 (OBE 1956); AO 1986; Kt 1971; Member of Legislative Council of New South Wales, 1957–78; company director and public relations consultant; *b* 4 May 1912; *s* of Harry and Phoebe Joel, London and Sydney; *m* 1st, 1937 (marr. diss. 1948); two *s*; 2nd, 1949, Sybil, *d* of Frederick Mitchell Jacobs; one *s* one *d. Educ:* Enmore Public Sch.; Cleveland Street High Sch., Sydney. Served War of 1939–45: AIF, 1942, transf. RAN; Lieut RANVR, 1943; RAN PRO staff Gen. MacArthur, 1944–45, New Guinea, Halmaheras, Philippines. Nat. Pres., Anzac Meml Forest in Israel. Chairman: Asher Joel Media Gp; Carpentaria Newspapers Pty Ltd. Mem., Sydney Cttee (Hon. Dir, 1956–64); Hon. Dir and Organiser, Pageant of Nationhood (State welcome to the Queen), 1963; Exec. Mem., Citizens Welcoming Cttee visit Pres. Johnson, 1966; Chm., Citizens Cttee Captain Cook Bi-Centenary Celebrations, 1970; Dep. Chm., Citizens Welcoming Cttee visit Pope Paul VI to Australia, 1970; Chm., Sydney Opera Hse Official Opening Citizens Cttee, 1972; Dep. Chm., Aust. Govt Adv. Commn on US Bi-Centenary Celebrations, 1976; Mem., Nat. Australia Day Cttee, Royal North Shore Hosp. of Sydney, 1959–81; Mem., Sydney Opera Hse Trust, 1969–79; Chm., Sydney Entertainment Centre, 1979–84. Chm. Emeritus, Organising Cttee 1988 Public Relations World Congress, 1985–88; Member: Adv.

Council 31st IAA World Advertising Congress, 1984–88; Australia–US Coral Sea Commemorative Council, 1992. Life Mem., RSL, 1992. Gov., Sir David Martin Foundn, 1990–94 (Life Fellow, 1994). Fellow: Advertising Inst. of Aust. (Federal Patron); Public Relations Inst. of Aust.; FAIM; Foundn FAICD; FInstD; FRSA; Hon. Mem., Royal Australian Historical Soc., 1970. Hon. Fellow, Internat. Coll. of Dentists, 1975. Hon. DLitt Macquarie, 1988. Torch of Learning Award, Hebrew Univ. of Jerusalem, 1978; Tel Aviv Univ. Presidential Citation, 1992; Archbishop of Sydney Citation, 1992. KSS 1994. US Bronze Star, 1943; Ancient Order of Sikatuna (Philippines), 1975; Kt Comdr, Order of Rizal (Philippines), 1978. *Publications:* Without Chains Free (novel), 1977; Australian Protocol and Procedures, 1982, 2nd edn 1988. *Recreations:* fishing, gardening, reading, writing. *Address:* 120 Clarence Street, Sydney, NSW 2000, Australia. *Clubs:* American, Journalists, Australasian Pioneers, Royal Agricultural Society (Sydney); Royal Sydney Yacht Squadron.
Died 9 Nov. 1998.

JOHN, Sir Rupert (Godfrey), Kt 1971; Governor of St Vincent, 1970–76; Director, St Vincent Building and Loan Association, since 1977; Consultant to UNITAR, since 1978; *b* 19 May 1916; 2nd *s* of late Donelley John; *m* 1937, Hepsy (*d* 1988), *d* of late Samuel Norris; three *s* one *d* (and one *s* decd). *Educ:* St Vincent Grammar Sch.; Univ. of London (BA, DipEd); New York University. Called to the Bar, Gray's Inn, 1952. First Asst Master, St Kitts/Nevis Grammar Sch., 1944; Asst Master, St Vincent Grammar Sch., 1944–52; private practice at Bar of St Vincent, 1952–58; Magistrate, Grenada, 1958–60; Actg Attorney-General, Grenada, 1960–62; Human Rights Officer, UN, 1962–69; Mcm. Internat. Team of Observers, Nigeria, 1969–70; Senior Human Rights Officer, 1970. Attended numerous Internat. seminars and confs as officer of UN. President: Assoc. of Sen. Citizens of St Vincent and the Grenadines, 1981–; Caribbean Inst. for Promotion of Human Rights, 1987–88 (Human Rights Award, 1988). Mem., Barclays Bank Internat. Ltd Policy Adv. Cttee (St Vincent), 1977–86. Mem. Editorial Adv. Bd, Jl of Third World Legal Studies, 1981–. KStJ 1971. *Publications:* St Vincent and its Constitution, 1971; Pioneers in Nation-Building in a Caribbean Mini-State, 1979; Racism and its Elimination, 1980; papers in various jls. *Recreations:* cricket, walking, swimming. *Address:* PO Box 677, Cane Garden, St Vincent, West Indies. *T:* 61500. *Club:* Commonwealth Trust. *Died 25 Dec. 1996.*

JOHNSON, Alan C.; *see* Campbell-Johnson.

JOHNSON, Carol Alfred, CBE 1951; *b* 1903; *m* 1940, Edna Alice Cann. Admitted a Solicitor, 1933 (Hons); practised City of London; Hon. Solicitor to Housing Assocs in Southwark and Fulham; Asst Town Clerk, Borough of Southall, 1940–43; Secretary of the Parliamentary Labour Party, 1943 59. Alderman, Lambeth Borough Council, 1937–49 (sometime Leader). MP (Lab) Lewisham S, Sept. 1959–Feb. 1974; served on Chairman's Panel, presiding over cttees and occasionally the House; sometime Chm., History of Parliament Trust and Anglo-Italian Parly Cttee; Mem., Parly delegations to Nigeria, Persia (Iran), the Cameroons and India. Served on Council of Europe; many years Jt Hon. Sec., British Council of European Movement, latterly Vice-Pres., Lab. Cttee for Europe. Sometime Hon. Sec., Friends of Africa and later Treasurer, Fabian Colonial Bureau; original Mem., Local Govt Adv. Panel, Colonial Office; Member: Fabian delegn to Czechoslovakia, 1946; British Council Lecture Tour to Finland, 1946. Exec. Mem., Commons (later Open Spaces) Soc. (formerly Chm.); Mem., Standing Cttee on Nat. Parks (later Council for Nat. Parks). Trustee, William Morris Soc.; Mem. Exec. Cttee, British-Italian

Soc.; Life Governor, British Inst., Florence (Gov., 1965–86). Comdr, Italian Order of Merit. *Address:* Grosvenor Park, Brookfield Road, Bexhill-on-Sea, Sussex TN40 1NY. *Died 30 July 2000.*

JOHNSON, Prof. David Hugh Nevil; Professor of International Law, Sydney University, 1976–85, then Emeritus; *b* 4 Jan. 1920; 2nd *s* of James Johnson and Gladys Mary (*née* Knight); *m* 1952, Evelyn Joan Fletcher. *Educ:* Winchester Coll.; Trinity Coll., Cambridge (MA, LLB); Columbia Univ., New York; Sydney Univ. (MA 1965). Served Royal Corps of Signals, 1940–46. Called to the Bar, Lincoln's Inn, 1950. Asst Legal Adviser, Foreign Office, 1950–53; Reader in Internat. Law, 1953–59, in Internat. and Air Law, 1959–60, Prof., 1960–75, Dean of Faculty of Laws, 1968–72, Univ. of London. Sen. Legal Officer, Office of Legal Affairs, UN, 1956–57. Registrar, Court of Arbitration, Argentine-Chile Frontier Case, 1965–68. *Publications:* Rights in Air Space, 1965; articles in legal jls, particularly Internat. and Comparative Law Qly and British Year Book of Internat. Law. *Address:* 1 Flannel Flower Fairway, Shoal Bay, NSW 2315, Australia. *Died 12 Sept. 1999.*

JOHNSON, David John, CMG 1995; CVO 1994; HM Diplomatic Service, retired; *b* 2 March 1938; *s* of Herbert John Victor Johnson and Mildred Frances (*née* Boyd); *m* 1976, Kathleen Johanna Hicks; three *d. Educ:* Harvey Grammar Sch., Folkestone. Served RAF, 1957–59. Entered FO, 1959; Third Sec., Moscow, 1962; Third, later Second Sec., Dakar, 1965; Second Secretary: Ulan Bator, 1969; UK Mission to UN, Geneva, 1969; First Secretary: UK Mission to negotiations on mutual reduction of forces and armaments and associated measures, Vienna, 1973; Moscow, 1975; FCO, 1978; Counsellor, NATO Defence Coll., Rome, 1982; seconded to NATO Internat. Secretariat, Brussels, 1982; Counsellor and Head of Chancery, Islamabad, 1985–90; Head, CSCE Unit, FCO, 1990–92; High Comr to Guyana and Ambassador to Suriname, 1993–98; Head, OSCE Mission to Latvia, 1998–99. *Recreations:* marquetry, music, reading. *Address:* The Old Stables, Llandegley, Llandrindod Wells, Powys LD1 5UD. *Died 23 Dec. 2000.*

JOHNSON, Rt Hon. Sir David Powell C.; *see* Croom-Johnson.

JOHNSON, Howard Sydney; solicitor; Senior Partner, Howard Johnson & McQue, 1933–83; *b* 25 Dec. 1910; *s* of Sydney Thomas Johnson; *m* 1st; (one *s* decd); 2nd, 1939, Betty Frankiss (decd), actress. *Educ:* Brighton; Highgate. Served War of 1939–45, Africa; invalided out as Major. Joined TA before the war. Mem. of Brighton Town Council, 1945–50. MP (C) Kemptown Div. of Brighton, 1950–Sept. 1959. Director: Alliance Bldg Soc., 1960–83; Alliance & Leicester (Isle of Man) Ltd, 1992–96. *Publication:* (contrib.) Against Hunting, ed Patrick Moore, 1965. *Address:* Ballakinnag Cottage, Smeale, Andreas, Isle of Man IM7 3ED. *T:* (01624) 880712. *Died 13 Sept. 2000.*

JOHNSON, Patrick, OBE 1945; MA; *b* 24 May 1904; 2nd *s* of A. F. W. Johnson, JP, and F. E. L. Cocking; unmarried. *Educ:* RN Colls, Osborne and Dartmouth; Tonbridge Sch.; Magdalen Coll., Oxford. Fellow and Lecturer in Natural Science, Magdalen Coll., Oxford, 1928–47 (Dean, 1934–38, Vice-Pres., 1946–47); Flying Officer, RAFO, 1929–34; commissioned in RA (TA), 1938; served War of 1939–45, in Middle East and NW Europe, Lt-Col, Asst Dir of Scientific Research, 21st Army Group and comdg No 2 operational research section; Dir of Studies, RAF Coll., Cranwell, 1947–52; Dean of Inst. of Armament Studies, India, 1952–55; Scientific Adviser to the Army Council, 1955–58; Asst Scientific Adviser, SHAPE, 1958–62; Head of Experimental Develt Unit, Educnl

Foundn for Visual Aids, 1962–70. *Recreations:* rowing (rowed against Cambridge, 1927), sailing, shooting. *Address:* 5 Linley Court, Rouse Gardens, SE21 8AQ. *Club:* Leander (Henley-on-Thames).

Died 29 Oct. 1996.

JOHNSON, Sir Ronald (Ernest Charles), Kt 1970; CB 1962; JP; *b* 3 May 1913; *o c* of Ernest and Amelia Johnson; *m* 1938, Elizabeth Gladys Nuttall; two *s* (and one *s* decd). *Educ:* Portsmouth Grammar Sch.; St John's Coll., Cambridge. Entered Scottish Office, 1935; Sec., Scottish Home and Health Dept, 1963–72; Sec. of Commissions for Scotland, 1972–78. Chm., Civil Service Savings Cttee for Scotland, 1963–78; Chm., Scottish Hosp. Centre, 1964–72. Member: Scottish Records Adv. Council, 1975–81; Cttee on Admin of Sheriffdoms, 1981–82; Chm., Fire Service Res. and Training Trust, 1976–89. Served RNVR on intelligence staff of C-in-C, Eastern Fleet, 1944–45. President: Edinburgh Bach Soc., 1973–86; Edinburgh Soc. of Organists, 1980–82. JP Edinburgh, 1972. *Publications:* articles in religious and musical jls. *Address:* 14 Eglinton Crescent, Edinburgh EH12 5DD. *T:* (0131) 337 7733.

Died 8 March 1996.

JOHNSON-GILBERT, Thomas Ian; Joint Senior Partner, Clifford Chance, Solicitors, 1987–89; *b* 2 June 1923; *s* of Sir Ian Johnson-Gilbert, CBE, LLD and late Rosalind Bell-Hughes (Lady Johnson-Gilbert); *m* 1950, Gillian June Pool; one *s* one *d. Educ:* Edinburgh Academy; Rugby School; Trinity College, Oxford (1942 and 1946–47) (Open Classical Scholarship; MA). RAFVR, 1943–46. Admitted solicitor, 1950; Coward Chance, 1950–87 (Partner, 1954, Senior Partner, 1980–87). Mem. Council, Law Society, 1970–88. *Recreations:* reading, arts, travel, spectator sport. *Clubs:* Athenæum, Garrick, MCC.

Died 4 Nov. 1998.

JOHNSTON, Rear-Adm. Clarence Dinsmore H.; *see* Howard-Johnston.

JOHNSTON, Kenneth Robert Hope; QC 1953; *b* 18 June 1905; *e s* of Dr J. A. H. Johnston, Headmaster of Highgate Sch., 1908–36, and Kate Winsome Gammon; *m* 1937, Dr Priscilla Bright Clark (*d* 1993), *d* of Roger and Sarah Clark, Street, Somerset; one *s* three *d. Educ:* Rugby Sch.; Sidney Sussex Coll., Cambridge Univ.; Harvard Univ., USA. Called to the Bar, Gray's Inn, 1933; Bencher, 1958. RAFVR, 1939–45. *Address:* 28 Leigh Road, Street, Somerset BA16 0HB. *T:* (01458) 443559. *Club:* MCC.

Died 23 March 1998.

JOHNSTONE, Air Vice-Marshal Alexander Vallance Riddell, CB 1966; DFC 1940; AE; Air Officer Scotland and Northern Ireland, Air Officer Commanding No 18 Group, and Maritime Air Commander Northern Atlantic (NATO), 1965–68; *b* 2 June 1916; *s* of late Alexander Lang Johnstone and Daisy Riddell; *m* 1940, Margaret Croll; one *s* two *d. Educ:* Kelvinside Academy, Glasgow. 602 (City of Glasgow) Sqdn, AAF, 1934–41; CO RAF Haifa, 1942; Spitfire Wing, Malta, 1942–43 (despatches, 1942); RAF Staff Coll., 1943; OC Fairwood Common, 1943–44; HQ AEAF, 1944; Air Attaché Dublin, 1946–48; OC RAF Ballykelly, 1951–52; OC Air/Sea Warfare Develt Unit, 1952–54; SASO HQ No 12 Gp, 1954–55; Founder and First CAS Royal Malayan Air Force, 1957; OC Middleton St George, 1958–60; idc, 1961; Dir of Personnel, Air Min., 1962–64; Comdr, Air Forces, Borneo, 1964–65. Vice-Chm. Council, TA&VRA, 1969–79. DL Glasgow, 1971–94. Johan Mengku Negara (Malaya), 1958. *Publications:* One Man's War (television series), 1964; Where No Angels Dwell, 1969; Enemy in the Sky, 1976; Adventure in the Sky, 1978; Spitfire into War, 1986; Diary of an Aviator, 1993. *Recreations:* golf, sailing.

Address: 36 Castle Brooks, Framlingham, Suffolk IP13 9SE. *Club:* Royal Air Force. *Died 13 Dec. 2000.*

JONES; *see* Lloyd-Jones.

JONES; *see* Morris-Jones.

JONES, Alan Payan P.; *see* Pryce-Jones.

JONES, Maj.-Gen. Anthony George Clifford, CB 1978; MC 1945; President, Regular Commissions Board, 1975–78; *b* 20 May 1923; *s* of late Col R. C. Jones, OBE, and M. D. Jones; *m* Kathleen Mary, *d* of Comdr J. N. Benbow, OBE, RN; two *d. Educ:* St Paul's School; Trinity Hall, Cambridge. Commissioned RE, 1942; service included: Troop Comdr, Guards Armd Div., Nijmegen, 1945 (MC 1945; despatches, 1947); Indian Sappers and Miners; Staff Coll., 1954; Bde Major, 63 Gurkha Inf. Bde, 1955 (despatches, 1957); jssc; OC 25 Corps Engineer Regt, 1965–67; Comdr, RE Trng Bde, 1968–72; Head of Ops Staff, Northern Army Group, 1972–74; Dep. Comdr SE District, 1974–75. Hon. Col, RE Volunteers (Sponsored Units), 1978–86. *Club:* Army and Navy.
Died 11 July 1999.

JONES, Barri; *see* Jones, G. D. B.

JONES, Brian Leslie; Judge of the High Court of Justice, Hong Kong, 1981–94; *b* 19 Oct. 1930; *s* of late William Leslie Jones and Gladys Gertrude Jones; *m* 1966, Yukiko Hirokane; one *s* two *d. Educ:* Bromsgrove Sch.; Birmingham Univ. Admitted Solicitor, 1956; called as Barrister and Solicitor, Supreme Court, Victoria, Australia, 1968. Solicitor, private practice, England, 1956–64; Asst Registrar, Supreme Court, Hong Kong, 1964–68; Legal Officer, Attorney General's Dept, Canberra, 1968–69; Asst Registrar, Hong Kong, 1969–74; District Judge, Hong Kong, 1974–81. Comr, Supreme Ct of Brunei, 1982, 1985, 1990. Chm., Standing Cttee on Company Law Reform, Hong Kong, 1991–94. *Recreations:* squash, chess, walking, reading. *Address:* 3 Mitchell Gardens, Slinfold, W Sussex RH13 7TY. *Club:* Hong Kong.
Died 12 July 1999.

JONES, Prof. David Morgan; Professor of Classics in the University of London (Westfield College), 1953–80; *b* 9 April 1915; *m* 1965, Irene M. Glanville. *Educ:* Whitgift Sch.; Exeter Coll., Oxford (Scholar; MA). 1st Class, Classical Hon. Mods, 1936; 1st Class, Lit. Hum. 1938; Derby Scholar, 1938; Oxford Diploma in Comparative Philology, 1940. Junior Research Fellow, Exeter Coll., Oxford, 1938–40; Lecturer in Classics, University Coll. of North Wales, 1940–48; Reader in Classics in the University of London (Birkbeck Coll.), 1949–53. *Publications:* papers and reviews in classical and linguistic journals. *Address:* Kemyell Vean, 3 Laregan Hill, Penzance TR18 4NY. *T:* (01736) 363389.
Died 9 Jan. 2000.

JONES, His Honour Edward; *see* Jones, His Honour J. E.

JONES, Emlyn Bartley, MBE 1975; Director General, The Sports Council, 1978–83; sport and leisure consultant, since 1983; *b* 9 Dec. 1920; *s* of Ernest Jones and Sarah Bartley; *m* 1944, (Constance) Inez Jones; one *d. Educ:* Alun Grammar School, Mold, Clwyd; Bangor Normal Coll.; Loughborough Coll. of Physical Education. Diploma Loughborough Coll. (Hons). Flight Lieut, RAF, 1941–46; Teacher, Flint Secondary Modern Sch., 1946; Technical Representative, CCPR, N Wales, 1947–51; Technical Adviser, CCPR, 1951–62; Dir, Crystal Palace Nat. Sports Centre, 1962–78. Television commentator, 1955–. Pres., British Inst. of Sports Admin (formerly British Assoc. of Nat. Sports Administrators), 1984–97; Vice-Pres., NABC, 1989–. FIMgt (FBIM 1984). *Publications:* Learning Lawn Tennis, 1958; Sport in Space: the implications of cable and satellite television, 1984. *Recreations:* golf, ski-ing,

travel, conversation, reading. *Address:* Chwarae Teg, 1B Allison Grove, Dulwich Common, SE21 7ER. *T:* (020) 8693 7528. *Club:* Royal Air Force.
Died 19 June 1999.

JONES, Sir Emrys; *see* Jones, Sir W. E.

JONES, Eryl O.; *see* Owen-Jones, J. E.

JONES, Sir Francis A.; *see* Avery Jones.

JONES, Prof. F(rank) Llewellyn-, CBE 1965; MA, DPhil, DSc Oxon; Hon. LLD; Principal, University College of Swansea, 1965–74 (Vice-Principal, 1954–56 and 1960–62; Acting Principal, 1959–60); Professor Emeritus, since 1974; *b* 30 Sept. 1907; *er s* of Alfred Morgan Jones, JP, Penrhiwceiber, Glamorgan; *m* 1st, 1938, Eileen (*d* 1982), *d* of E. T. Davies, Swansea; one *s* (one *d* decd); 2nd, 1983, Mrs Gwendolen Thomas, Rhossili. *Educ:* West Monmouth Sch.; Merton Coll., Oxford. Science Exhibnr 1925; 1st Cl. Nat. Sci. physics, BA 1929; Research Scholar, Merton Coll., 1929; DPhil, MA 1931; Senior Demy, Magdalen Coll., 1931; DSc 1955. Demonstrator in Wykeham Dept of Physics, Oxford, 1929–32; Lecturer in Physics, University Coll. of Swansea, 1932–40; Senior Scientific Officer, Royal Aircraft Establishment, 1940–45; Prof. of Physics, Univ. of Wales, and Head of Dept of Physics, University Coll. of Swansea, 1945–65. Vice-Chancellor, Univ. of Wales, 1969–71. Member: Radio Research Board, DSIR, 1951–54; Standing Conference on Telecommunications Research, DSIR, 1952–55; Sen. Consultant in Plasma Physics, Radio and Space Research Station of SRC, 1964–65. Member: Board of Institute of Physics, 1947–50; Council of Physical Society, 1951–58 (Vice-Pres., 1954–59). Visiting Prof. to Univs in Australia, 1956; Supernumerary Fellow, Jesus Coll., Oxford, 1965–66, 1969–70; Hon. Professorial Res Fellow, Univ. of Wales, 1974–; Leverhulme Emeritus Fellow, 1977–79; Fellow, UC of Swansea, 1990. Regional Scientific Adviser for Home Defence, Wales, 1952–59, Sen. and Chief Reg. Sci. Adv., 1959–77; Pres., Royal Institution of South Wales, 1957–60; Mem. of Council for Wales and Mon, 1959–63, 1963–66; Dir (Part-time), S Wales Gp, BSC, 1968–70; Chm., Central Adv. Council for Education (Wales), 1961–64. Vice-Pres., Hon. Soc. of Cymmrodorian, 1982. Hon. LLD Wales, 1975. C. V. Boys' Prizeman, Physical Soc., 1960; Inaugural Ragnar Holm Scientific Achievement Award, 6th Internat. Conf. on Electric Contact Phenomena, Chicago, 1972. *Publications:* Fundamental Processes of Electrical Contact Phenomena, 1953; The Physics of Electrical Contacts, 1957; Ionization and Breakdown in Gases, 1957, 2nd edn 1966; The Glow Discharge, 1966; Ionization, Avalanches and Breakdown, 1966; papers in scientific jls on ionization and discharge physics. *Recreation:* industrial archaeology. *Address:* Brynheulog, 24 Sketty Park Road, Swansea SA2 9AS. *T:* (01792) 202344. *Club:* Athenæum.
Died 3 Feb. 1997.

JONES, Prof. (Geraint Dyfed) Barri, DPhil; FSA; Professor of Archaeology, University of Manchester, since 1972; *b* 4 April 1936; *s* of Emlyn Jones and Phyllis Margaret Jones; *m* 1st, 1969, Victoria Ann Sanderson (marr. diss. 1983); one *s* one *d*; 2nd, 1983, Brigitte Ann Bowland Barrett (marr. diss. 1998); one *d. Educ:* Royal Grammar Sch., High Wycombe; Jesus Coll., Oxford (BA; DPhil 1963); British Sch. at Rome (Rome Schol.). FSA 1966. University of Manchester: Lectr, 1964–71; Head: Dept of Hist., 1973–76; Dept of Archaeol., 1981–93 and 1995–96. Sen. Res. Fellow, British Sch. at Rome, 1980. Co-Dir, UNESCO Libyan Valleys Survey, 1979–89. Member: Royal Commn for Ancient and Historic Monuments in Wales, 1988–; Ancient Monuments Adv. Cttee, English Heritage, 1984–88. Sec., 1974–77, Trustee, 1980–, Rescue Trust for Brit. Archaeol.; Vice-Pres.,

Council for Brit. Archaeol., 1984–87. Chm., Soc. for Libyan Studies, 1984–88. Editor: Popular Archaeol., 1981–86; Archaeol. Today, 1987–88; Minerva, 1990–92. *Publications:* Roman Manchester, 1974; Past Imperfect, 1984; (with N. J. Higham) The Carvetii, 1985; Neolithic Apulia, 1987; Roman Lancaster, 1989; (jtly) Farming the Desert, 2 vols, 1996; (with D. J. Mattingly) An Atlas of Roman Britain, 1990, 2nd edn 1992; Edge of Empire, 1996. *Recreations:* hill-walking, flying and photography in light aircraft, watching Rugby. *Address:* Department of Art History and Archaeology, University of Manchester, Manchester M13 9PL. *T:* (0161) 275 3017.
Died 16 July 1999.

JONES, Geraint Iwan, FRAM; *b* 16 May 1917; *s* of Rev. Evan Jones, Porth, Glam; *m* 1st, 1940, M. A. Kemp; one *d*; 2nd, 1949, Winifred Roberts. *Educ:* Caterham Sch.; Royal Academy of Music (Sterndale Bennett Scholar). FRAM 1954. National Gallery Concerts, 1940–44; played complete organ works of Bach in 16 recitals in London, 1946; Musical Dir of Mermaid Theatre performances of Purcell's Dido and Aeneas with Kirsten Flagstad, 1951–53; formed Geraint Jones Singers and Orchestra, 1951, with whom many broadcasts, and series of 12 Bach concerts, Royal Festival Hall, 1955; series of all Mozart's piano concertos (with Stephen Kovacevich), Queen Elizabeth Hall, 1969–70. Frequent European engagements, 1947–, and regular US and Canadian tours, 1948–. Musical Director: Lake District Festival, 1960–78; Kirckman Concert Soc., 1963–; Artistic Director: Salisbury Festival, 1973–77; Manchester Internat. Festival, 1977–87. Prof., RAM, 1961–88. As consultant, designed many organs, incl. RNCM, St Andrew's Univ., RAM, Acad. for Performing Arts, Hong Kong, and Tsim Sha Tsni Culture Centre, Hong Kong. Recordings as organist and conductor; Promenade Concerts; also concerts and recordings as harpsichordist, including sonatas with violinist wife, Winifred Roberts. Grand Prix du Disque, 1959 and 1966. *Publications:* translations: Clicquot's Théorie Pratique de la facture de l'orgue, 1985; Davy's Les Grandes Orgues de L'Abbatiale St Etienne de Caen, 1985. *Recreations:* photography, architecture, antiques, reading. *Address:* The Long House, Arkley Lane, Barnet Road, Arkley, Herts EN5 3JR.   *Died 3 May 1998.*

JONES, Gerallt; *see* Jones, R. G.

JONES, Sir Gordon (Pearce), Kt 1990; Chairman: Yorkshire Water, 1983–96; Water Authorities Association, 1986–89; *b* 17 Feb. 1927; *s* of Alun Pearce Jones and Miriam Jones; *m* 1951, Gloria Stuart Melville; twin *s* (one *d* decd). *Educ:* Univ. of Wales (BSc Hons Chemistry). Royal Navy, 1947. British Iron & Steel Research Assoc., 1951; Esso Petroleum Co., 1961; English Steel Corp., 1964; Managing Director: Rotherham Tinsley Steels, 1970; Firth Vickers, 1974; Chm., Hickson Internat., 1991–94; Dir, T. W. Ward plc, 1979–83. Mem., President's Adv. Cttee, CBI, 1987–89. Mem., Adv. Cttee on Business and the Envmt, 1993–96. Mem. Court of Governors, Univ. of Leeds, 1992–96. CIMgt 1990; FRSA 1994. Hon. FIWEM 1990. Hon. Fellow, UC, Swansea, 1991. Hon. DSc Bradford, 1992. *Recreations:* gardening, music, opera, travel, railway history. *Address:* 10 Heneage Drive, West Cross, near Swansea SA3 5BR. *T:* (01792) 405148. *Club:* Naval and Military.   *Died 31 Jan. 1999.*

JONES, Griffith Winston Guthrie, QC 1963; a Recorder, 1972–74 (Recorder of Bolton, 1968–71); *b* 24 Sept. 1914; second *s* of Rowland Guthrie Jones, Dolgellau, Merioneth; *m* 1st, 1959, Anna Maria McCarthy (*d* 1969); 2nd, 1978, Janet, widow of Commodore Henry Owen L'Estrange, DSC. *Educ:* Bootham Sch., York; University of Wales; St John's Coll., Cambridge. Called to the Bar, Gray's Inn, 1939. Dep. Chm., Cumberland QS, 1963–71. War service in Royal Artillery, 1940–46. *Publication:* The Wynnes of

Sligo and Leitrim, 1995. *Recreation:* gardening. *Address:* Culleenamore, Sligo, Ireland.   *Died 4 Aug. 1996.*

JONES, Prof. Gwyn, CBE 1965; Professor of English Language and Literature, University College, Cardiff, 1965–75, Fellow, 1980; *b* 24 May 1907; *s* of George Henry Jones and Lily Florence (*née* Nethercott); *m* 1st, 1928, Alice (*née* Rees) (*d* 1979); 2nd, 1979, Mair (*née* Sivell), widow of Thomas Jones. *Educ:* Tredegar Grammar School; University of Wales. Schoolmaster, 1929–35; Lecturer, University Coll. of S Wales and Monmouthshire, 1935–40; Prof. of Eng. Language and Lit., University Coll. of Wales, Aberystwyth, 1940–64, Fellow, 1987. Ida Beam Vis. Prof., Iowa Univ., 1982. Dir of Penmark Press, 1939–. Mem. of various learned societies; Pres. of Viking Soc. for Northern Research, 1950–52 (Hon. Life Mem., 1979); Mem. of Arts Council and Chm. of Welsh Cttee of Arts Council, 1957–67. Gwyn Jones Annual Lecture established 1978. Hon. DLitt: Wales, 1977; Nottingham, 1978; Southampton, 1983. Fellow, Institut Internat. des Arts et des Lettres, 1960. Christian Gauss Award, 1973; Cymmrodorion Medal, 1991. Hon. Freeman of Islwyn, 1988. Commander's Cross, Order of the Falcon (Iceland), 1987 (Knight, 1963). *Publications: novels:* Richard Savage, 1935; Times Like These, 1936, repr. 1979; Garland of Bays, 1938; The Green Island, 1946; The Flowers Beneath the Scythe, 1952; The Walk Home, 1962; *short stories:* The Buttercup Field, 1945; The Still Waters, 1948; Shepherd's Hey, 1953; Selected Short Stories, 1974; *non-fiction:* A Prospect of Wales, 1948; Welsh Legends and Folk-Tales, 1955; Scandinavian Legends and Folk-Tales, 1956; The Norse Atlantic Saga, 1964, new edn 1986; A History of the Vikings, 1968, rev. and enlarged edn 1984; Kings, Beasts and Heroes, 1972; Being and Belonging (BBC Wales Annual Radio Lecture), 1977; Background to Dylan Thomas and Other Explorations, 1992; *translations:* The Vatnsdalers' Saga, 1942; (with Thomas Jones) The Mabinogion, 1948; Egil's Saga, 1960; Eirik the Red, 1961; *edited:* Welsh Review, 1939–48; Welsh Short Stories, 1956; (with I. Ff. Elis) Twenty-Five Welsh Short Stories, 1971; The Oxford Book of Welsh Verse in English, 1977; Fountains of Praise, 1983; contrib. to numerous learned and literary journals. *Address:* Castle Cottage, Sea View Place, Aberystwyth, Dyfed SY23 1DZ.   *Died 6 Dec. 1999.*

JONES, Sir Harry (Ernest), Kt 1971; CBE 1955; Agent in Great Britain for Northern Ireland, 1970–76; *b* 1 Aug. 1911; *s* of H. C. O. Jones, Peterborough; *m* 1935, Phyllis Eva Dixon (*d* 1987); one *s* one *d. Educ:* Stamford Sch.; St John's Coll., Cambridge. Entered Northern Ireland Civil Service, 1934; Ministry of Commerce: Principal Officer, 1940; Asst Sec. 1942; Perm. Sec. 1955; Industrial Development Adviser to Ministry of Commerce, 1969. *Recreation:* fishing. *Address:* 51 Station Road, Nassington, Peterborough PE8 6QB. *T:* (01780) 782675.
Died 4 Feb. 1998.

JONES, Hywel Glyn; independent economic and marketing consultant; Partner, Hywel Jones and Associates, economic consultants, since 1985; *b* 1 July 1948; *s* of late Thomas Glyndwr Jones and Anne Dorothy Jones (*née* Williams); *m* 1970, Julia Claire (*née* Davies). *Educ:* Trinity College, Cambridge (Open Scholar, Sen. Scholar, Res. Scholar; MA Hons Econ 1st cl.; Wrenbury Scholarship in Political Economy). Lectr in Economics, Univ. of Warwick, 1971–73; Univ. Lectr in Economics of the Firm, Fellow of Linacre Coll., and Lectr, Worcester Coll., Oxford, 1973–77; Henley Centre for Forecasting: Dir of Internat. Forecasting, 1977–81; Dir and Chief Exec., 1981–85. *Publications:* Second Abstract of British Historical Statistics (jtly), 1971; An Introduction to Modern Theories of Economic Growth, 1975, trans. Spanish and Japanese; Full Circle into the Future?: Britain into the 21st Century, 1984. *Recreations:* conversation, travel, military history, walking.

Died 29 Dec. 1999.

JONES, Prof. Ian C.; *see* Chester Jones.

JONES, Ivor R.; *see* Roberts-Jones.

JONES, His Honour (John) Edward; a Circuit Judge (formerly County Court Judge), 1969–84; *b* 23 Dec. 1914; *s* of Thomas Robert Jones, Liverpool; *m* 1945, Katherine Elizabeth Edwards, SRN, *d* of Ezekiel Richard Edwards, Liverpool; one *s* one *d*. *Educ:* Sefton Park Council Sch.; Liverpool Institute High School. ACIS 1939–70; BCom London, 1942; LLB London, 1945. Called to Bar, Gray's Inn, 1945; Member of Northern Circuit, 1946; Dep. Chm., Lancs QS, 1966–69. Dep. Chm., Workmen's Compensation (Supplementation) and Pneumoconiosis and Byssinosis Benefit Boards, 1968–69. Director: Chatham Building Soc., 1955–59; Welsh Calvinistic Methodist Assurance Trust, 1953–59. Vice-Pres., Merseyside Br., Magistrates' Assoc., 1974–84. Pres., Liverpool Welsh Choral Union, 1987– (Vice Pres., 1973–87); Member: Liverpool Welsh XXV Soc., 1946–; Cymmrodorion Soc., 1961–; Life Member: Welsh National Eisteddfod Court; Gorsedd of Bards (as Ioan Maesgrug), 1987. Governor: Aigburth Vale Comprehensive Sch., 1976–85; Calderstones Community Comprehensive Sch., 1985–88. Pres., Merseyside Branch, British Red Cross Soc., 1980–88 (Mem. Nat. Council, 1983–86). Chm., World Friendship, 1990–. Exec. Cttee, Liverpool Free Church Federal Council, 1988– (Pres., 1992–94); Welsh Presbyterian Church: Deacon, 1947; Liverpool Presbytery Moderator, 1971, 1997. JP Lancs, 1966. *Address:* 45 Sinclair Drive, Liverpool L18 0HW. *Club:* Athenæum (Liverpool).

Died 28 June 1998.

JONES, Air Vice Marshal John Ernest A.; *see* Allen Jones.

JONES, Maj.-Gen. John H.; *see* Hamilton-Jones.

JONES, Sir John (Lewis), KCB 1983; CMG 1972; *b* 17 Feb. 1923; *m* 1948, Daphne Nora (*née* Redman) (*d* 1988). *Educ:* Christ's College, Cambridge (MA). Royal Artillery, 1942–46; Sudan Government, 1947–55; Security Service, 1955–85: Dep. Dir-Gen., 1976–81; Dir-Gen., 1981–85. *Recreation:* golf. *Club:* United Oxford & Cambridge University.

Died 9 March 1998.

JONES, Sir Martin F.; *see* Furnival Jones.

JONES, Dr Michael Barry; HM Chief Inspector of Mines, Health and Safety Executive, 1986–92; *b* 28 April 1932; *s* of Mynorydd Jones and Dorothy Anne Jones; *m* 1957, Josephine Maura (*née* Dryden); two *d*. *Educ:* Alsop High Sch., Liverpool; Leeds Univ. (BSc; PhD 1956). CEng, FIMinE 1959. Trainee, NCB, 1956; Underofficial, Whitwick Colliery, 1959; Undermanager, Rawdon, Ellistown and Donisthorpe Collieries, 1961; HM Inspector of Mines and Quarries, Lancs, 1965; HM Dist Inspector of Mines and Quarries, Yorks, 1974; HM Sen. Dist Inspector, Scotland, 1980; HM Dep. Chief Inspector, 1982. *Publications:* author and co-author of papers in The Mining Engineer. *Recreation:* growing and showing sweet peas. *Address:* The Old Farm, Christleton, Chester CH3 7AS. *T:* (01244) 336204.

Died 8 Oct. 1996.

JONES, Norman Stewart C.; *see* Carey Jones.

JONES, Sir Philip; *see* Jones, Sir T. P.

JONES, Philip Mark, CBE 1986 (OBE 1977); musician; pioneer of chamber music for brass ensembles; Chairman, Musicians Benevolent Fund, since 1995; *b* 12 March 1928; *s* of John and Mabel Jones; *m* 1956, Ursula Strebi. *Educ:* Royal College of Music (FRCM 1983 (ARCM 1947)). Principal Trumpet with all major orchestras in London, 1949–72; Founder and Dir, Philip Jones Brass Ensemble, 1951–86; Head of Dept of Wind and Percussion, Royal Northern Coll. of Music, Manchester, 1975–77; Head of Wind and Percussion Dept, GSMD, 1983–88; Principal, Trinity Coll. of Music, London, 1988–94. Member: Arts Council of GB, 1984–88; Royal Soc. of Musicians of GB. Over 50 gramophone records. Gov., Chetham's Sch., Manchester, 1988–94. FRNCM 1977; FGSM 1984. Hon. FTCL 1988; Hon. FRAM 1991. FRSA. Freeman, City of London, 1988. Grand Prix du Disque, 1977; Composers Guild Award, 1979; Cobbett Medal, Musicians' Co., 1986; Cesare Bendinelli Award, Verona, 1993. *Publications:* Joint Editor, Just Brass series (for Chester Music London), 1975–89. *Recreations:* history, ski-ing, mountain walking. *Address:* 14 Hamilton Terrace, NW8 9UG. *T:* (020) 7286 9155.

Died 17 Jan. 2000.

JONES, Reginald Victor, CH 1994; CB 1946; CBE 1942; FRS 1965; Professor of Natural Philosophy, University of Aberdeen, 1946–81, then Emeritus; *b* 29 Sept. 1911; *s* of Harold Victor and Alice Margaret Jones; *m* 1940, Vera (*d* 1992), *d* of late Charles and Amelia Cain; one *s* one *d* (and one *d* decd). *Educ:* Alleyn's Sch.; Wadham Coll., Oxford (Exhibitioner; MA, DPhil 1934; Hon. Fellow, 1968); Balliol Coll., Oxford (Skynner Senior Student in Astronomy, 1934–36; Hon. Fellow 1981). Air Ministry: Scientific Officer, 1936 (seconded to Admiralty, 1938–39); Air Staff, 1939; Asst Dir of Intelligence, 1941, Dir, 1946; Dir of Scientific Intelligence, MoD, 1952–53; Mem., Carriers Panel, 1962–63; Chm., Air Defence Working Party, 1963–64; Scientific Adv. Council, War Office, 1963–66. Chairman: Infra-Red Cttee, Mins of Supply and Aviation, 1950–64; British Transport Commn Res. Adv. Council, 1954–55; Safety in Mines Res. Advisory Bd, 1956–60 (Mem., 1950–56); Electronics Res. Council, Mins of Aviation and Technol., 1964–70. Royal Society: Chm., Paul Fund Cttee, 1962–84; a Vice-Pres., 1971–72; Jt Editor, Notes and Records of the Royal Society, 1969–89; Chairman: Inst. of Physics Cttee on Univ. Physics, 1961–63; British Nat. Cttee for History of Science, Medicine and Technol., 1970–78 (Chm., Org. Cttee, Internat. Congress, 1977); President: Crabtree Foundation, 1958; Sect. A, British Assoc., 1971. Also a mem., various cttees on electronics, scientific res., measurement, defence and educn. Rapporteur, European Convention on Human Rights, 1970. Companion, Operational Res. Soc., 1983. Governor, Dulwich Coll., 1965–79; Life Governor, Haileybury Coll., 1978. Vis. Prof., Univ. of Colorado, 1982; Visitor, RMCS, 1983. Hon. Member: Manchester Lit. and Phil. Soc., 1981; American Soc. for Precision Engrg, 1990. Hon. Fellow: College of Preceptors, 1978; IERE, 1982; Inst. of Measurement and Control, 1984; British Horological Inst., 1985. Hon. Freeman, Clockmakers' Co., 1984. Hon. DSc: Strathclyde, 1969; Kent, 1980; Westminster Coll. Missouri, 1992; Aberdeen, 1996; DUniv: York, 1976; Open, 1978; Surrey, 1979; Hon. LLD Bristol, 1979. Bailie of Benachie, 1980. US Medal of Freedom with Silver Palm, 1946; US Medal for Merit, 1947; BOIMA Prize, Inst. of Physics, 1934; Duddell Medal, Physical Soc., 1960; Parsons Medal, 1967; Hartley Medal, Inst. of Measurement and Control, 1972; Mexican Min. of Telecommunications Medal, 1973; Rutherford Medal, USSR, 1977; R. G. Mitchell Medal, 1979; Old Crows Medal, 1980; R. V. Jones Intelligence Award, CIA, 1993. Hon. Mem., US Air Force, 1982; Hon. Mayor, San Antonio, Texas, 1983. *Publications:* Most Secret War (USA, as The Wizard War; France as La Guerre Ultra Secrète), 1978; Future Conflict and New Technology, 1981; Some Thoughts on 'Star Wars', 1985; Instruments and Experiences, 1988; Reflections on Intelligence, 1989; lectures and papers on scientific subjects, defence, educn,

engrg, history of science and policy. *Address:* 8 Queens Terrace, Aberdeen AB10 1XL. *T:* (01224) 648184. *Clubs:* Athenæum, Special Forces; Royal Northern (Aberdeen).
Died 17 Dec. 1997.

JONES, (Robert) Gerallt, OBE 1996; writer; Warden of Gregynog Hall, University of Wales, 1989–95; *b* 11 Sept. 1934; *s* of Rev. R. E. Jones and Elizabeth Jones, Nefyn, Wales; *m* 1962, Susan Lloyd Griffith; two *s* one *d. Educ:* Denstone; University of Wales (University Student Pres., 1956–57). Sen. English Master, Sir Thomas Jones Sch., Amlwch, 1957–60; Lectr in Educn, University Coll., Aberystwyth, 1961–65; Prin., Mandeville Teachers' Coll., Jamaica, 1965–67; Warden and Headmaster, Llandovery Coll., 1967–76; Fellow in Creative Writing, Univ. of Wales, 1976–77; Sen. Tutor, Extra-Mural Dept, UCW, Aberystwyth, 1979–89. Consultant, Drama, Film and TV Dept, Univ. of Wales, Aberystwyth, 1996–. Director: Sgrîn 82, 1981–83; S4C, 1991–. Chm., Wales Film Council, 1992; Mem., Welsh Books Council, 1989–. Member: Gov. Body, Church in Wales, 1959–; Welsh Acad. (Yr Academi Gymreig), 1959– (Vice-Chm., 1981; Chm., 1982–87); Broadcasting Council for Wales; Welsh Arts Council (Chm., Film Cttee, 1989–); Univ. Council, Aberystwyth. FRSA. Editor: Impact (the Church in Wales quarterly); Taliesin, 1987–. Nat. Eisteddfod Prose Medal, 1977, 1979; Hugh McDiarmid Trophy, 1987; Welsh Arts Council Poetry Prize, 1990. *Publications: poetry:* Ymysg Y Drain, 1959; Cwlwm, 1962; Jamaican Landscape, 1969; Cysgodion, 1973; (ed) Poetry of Wales 1930–1970, 1975; Dyfal Gerddwyr y Maes, 1981; Cerddi 1955–89, 1989 (Poetry Prize, Welsh Arts Council, 1989); *novels:* Y Foel Fawr, 1960; Naddig Gwyn, 1963; Triptych, 1978; Cafflogion, 1979; *short stories:* Gwared Y Gwirion, 1966; *criticism:* Yn Frawd i'r Eos, 1962; (ed) Fy Nghymru, 1962; The Welsh Literary Revival, 1966; T. S. Eliot, 1981; Dathlu, 1985; Seicoleg Cardota, 1989; The Writer's Craft, 1992; *autobiography:* Jamaica, Y Flwyddyn Gyntaf, 1974; Bardsey, 1976; Jamaican Interlude, 1977; Murmur Llawer Man, 1980; *travel:* Teithiau Gerallt, 1978; Pererindota, 1978; *drama:* Tair Drama, 1988. *Recreations:* cricket, journalism. *Address:* Leri Dale, Dolybont, Borth, Aberystwyth, Wales SY24 5LX.
Died 9 Jan. 1999.

JONES, Ronald Christopher H.; *see* Hope-Jones.

JONES, Brig. Ronald M.; *see* Montague-Jones.

JONES, Air Cdre Shirley Ann, CBE 1990; Director, Women's Royal Air Force, 1986–89; *d* of late Wilfred Esmond Jones, FRICS, and Louise May Betty Jones (*née* Dutton). *Educ:* Micklefield Sch., Seaford, Sussex; Open Univ. (BA 1992). Joined Royal Air Force, 1962; commnd 1962; served UK and Libya, 1962–71; Netherlands and UK, 1971–74; sc 1975; served UK, 1975–82; Dep. Dir, 1982–86. ADC 1986–89. *Recreations:* golf, music, gardening, cookery. *Club:* Royal Air Force.
Died 16 July 1997.

JONES, S(tuart) Lloyd; *b* 26 Aug. 1917; *s* of Hugh and Edna Lloyd Jones, Liverpool; *m* 1942, Pamela Mary Hamilton-Williams (decd), Heswall; one *s* three *d. Educ:* Rydal Sch.; Univ. of Liverpool. Solicitor, 1940. Dep. Town Clerk, Nottingham, 1950–53; Town Clerk of Plymouth, 1953–70; Chief Exec. Officer and Town Clerk of Cardiff, 1970–74; Chm., Welsh Health Technical Services Orgn, 1973–76. Chief Counting Officer, Welsh Referendum, 1979. US State Dept Foreign Leader Scholarship, 1962. One of Advisers to Minister of Housing and Local Govt on Amalgamation of London Boroughs, 1962; Indep. Inspector, extension of Stevenage New Town, 1964; Member: Adv. Cttee on Urban Transport Manpower, 1967–69; Cttee on Public Participation in Planning, 1969; PM's Cttee on Local Govt Rules of

Conduct, 1973–74. Pres., Soc. of Town Clerks, 1972. Chm. of Governors, Plymouth Polytechnic, 1982–87 (Hon. Fellow, 1987). Distinguished Services Award, Internat. City Management Assoc., 1976. *Recreations:* gardening, bookbinding. *Address:* High Dolphin, Dittisham, near Dartmouth, Devon TQ6 0HR. *T:* (01803) 722224. *Club:* Royal Western Yacht Club of England (Plymouth). *Died 17 April 1998.*

JONES, Sir (Thomas) Philip, Kt 1986; CB 1978; Chairman: Total Oil Marine plc, 1990–98; Total Oil Holdings, 1991–98; *b* 13 July 1931; *s* of William Ernest Jones and Mary Elizabeth Jones; *m* 1955, Mary Phillips (*d* 2000); two *s. Educ:* Cowbridge Grammar Sch.; Jesus Coll., Oxford (MA; Hon. Fellow, 1990). 2nd Lieut, Royal Artillery, 1953–55. Asst Principal, Min. of Supply, 1955; Principal, Min. of Aviation, 1959; on loan to HM Treasury, 1964–66; Principal Private Sec. to Minister of Aviation, 1966–67; Asst Sec., Min. of Technology, subseq. Min. of Aviation Supply, 1967–71; Under Secretary, DTI, 1971; Under Sec., 1974, Dep. Sec., 1976–83, Dept of Energy; Chm., Electricity Council, 1983–90. Dir, Ivo Energy Ltd, 1990–97. Member: BNOC, 1980–82; BOTB, 1985–88; Chairman: Nationalized Industries' Chairmen's Gp, 1986–87; HEFCW, 1996– (Mem., 1992–96). Pres., Oil Industries Club, 1995–96. Gov., Henley Management Coll., 1986–. Curator, Oxford Univ. Chest, 1992–. Freeman, City of London, 1986. CIMgt (CBIM 1983); CompIEE 1987; FInstPet 1990. FRSA 1987. Hon. DEng Heriot-Watt, 1993; Hon. DTech Brunel, 1998. Comdr, Order of the Lion (Finland), 1997. *Recreations:* walking, reading, watching Rugby football. *Address:* 62 Tachbrook Street, SW1V 2NA. *Club:* Travellers.
Died 19 July 2000.

JONES, Timothy Fraser; Vice Lord-Lieutenant of East Sussex, since 1992; *b* 15 July 1931; *o s* of Lionel Herbert Jones, DFC and Mary Jones; *m* 1955, Mary Cobbold Nicolle; one *s* two *d. Educ:* Shrewsbury Sch.; St John's Coll., Cambridge (MA). Nat. Service, commnd 1st Bn Rifle Bde, 1950–51; London Rifle Bde Rangers, 1951–54. Buckmaster & Moore, 1954–57; Akroyd & Smithers, 1957, Jt Chm., 1981–86; Dir, S. G. Warburg Group, 1985–88. Trustee, Chichester Cathedral, 1988–92; Mem., Regl Cttee, NT for Kent and E Sussex, 1991–. High Sheriff, 1987–88, DL 1989, E Sussex. *Recreations:* travel, gardening, wine. *Address:* The Old Rectory, Berwick, Polegate, East Sussex BN26 6SR. *T:* Eastbourne (01323) 870523; 11 Ropers Orchard, Danvers Street, SW3 5AX. *T:* 0171–352 6539. *Clubs:* White's, Brooks's, Beefsteak.
Died 6 July 1996.

JONES, Sir (William) Emrys, Kt 1971; Principal, Royal Agricultural College, Cirencester, 1973–78; *b* 6 July 1915; *s* of late William Jones and Mary Ann (*née* Morgan); *m* 1938, Megan Ann Morgan (marr. diss. 1966); three *s*; *m* 1967, Gwyneth George. *Educ:* Llandovery Grammar Sch.; University Coll. of Wales, Aberystwyth (BSc). Agricultural Instr, Gloucester CC, 1940–46; Provincial Grassland Adv. Officer, NAAS, Bristol, 1946–50; County Agricultural Officer, Gloucester, 1950–54; Dep. Dir, 1954–57, Dir 1957–59, NAAS, Wales; Sen. Advisory Officer, NAAS, 1959–61, Dir, 1961–66; Chief Agricl Advr, NAAS, then Dir-Gen., Agricultural Develt and Adv. Service, MAFF, 1967–73. Mem., Adv. Council for Agriculture and Horticulture in England and Wales, 1973–79. Independent Chm., Nat. Cattle Breeders' Assoc., 1976–79. Dir, North and East Midlands Reg. Bd, Lloyds Bank, 1978–86. Hon. LLD Wales, 1973; Hon. DSc Bath, 1975. *Recreations:* golf, shooting. *Address:* 18 St Mary's Park, Louth, Lincs LN11 0EF. *T:* (01507) 602043. *Club:* Farmers'. *Died 29 June 2000.*

JONES, Hon. Sir William Lloyd M.; *see* Mars-Jones.

JONZEN, Karin, FRBS; sculptor; *b* London (Swedish parents), 22 Dec. 1914; *d* of U. Löwenadler and G. Munck av Fulkila; *m* 1944, Basil Jonzen (marr. diss.; he *d* 1967); one *s*; *m* 1972, Åke Sucksdorff (*d* 1992). Studied Slade Sch., 1933; Slade Dipl. and Scholarship, 1937; studied Royal Academy, Stockholm, 1939. Lectr, Camden Arts Centre, 1968–72; extra mural lectures in art appreciation, London Univ., 1965–71. Prix de Rome, 1939; Mem. Accad. delle Arte e Lavore, Parma, Italy, 1980 (Gold Medal, 1980); Diploma of Merit, Università delle Arti, Parma, 1982; Gold Medal, Internat. Parliament for Safety and Peace, USA, 1983; Silver Medal, RBS, 1983. *Works in municipal museums and art galleries:* Tate Gall., Bradford, Brighton, Glasgow, Southend, Liverpool, Melbourne, Andrew White Museum, Cornell Univ., USA; *works commissioned by:* Arts Council (reclining figure in terracotta), 1950; Festival of Britain for sports pavilion (standing figure), 1950; Modern Schs in Leics and Hertford, 1953 and Cardiff, 1954 (animals and figures in terracotta and stone); Selwyn Coll. Chapel, Cambridge (over-life size ascension group, bronze), 1956; St Michael's Church, Golders Green (carving on exterior), 1959; Arts Council (life size bronze mother and child for a housing estate in Lewisham), 1959; Guildford Cathedral (carving on exterior), 1961; WHO HQ, New Delhi (life size bronze torso), 1963 (gift of British Govt); St Mary le Bow, Cheapside (Madonna and child), 1969; City of London Corp. for London Wall site (life size bronze figure), 1971; Guildhall Forecourt (over-life size bronze group), 1972; Sadler's Wells Theatre (bronze of Dame Ninette de Valois, a gift from the sculptor), 1974; Swedish Church, Marylebone (three-quarter life size Pietà, bronze resin), 1975; Action Research (annual trophy), 1979; Cadogan Estate (figure of young girl for Sloane Gardens), 1981; St Mary and St Margaret Church, South Harting, Hants (Madonna and child), 1985; St Saviour's Church, Warwick Ave (Madonna and child), 1986; Nat. Portrait Gall. (over-life size bronze of Lord Constantine), 1989; St Anne and St Mary Church, Lewes (St Anne and St Mary gp), 1990; *works exhibited by invitation:* Battersea Park open air exhibns, 1948–51; Tate Gall., 1952 (Four Seasons), 1954 (Religious Art), and 1957–59; City of London Festival, 1968; (one man exhibn) Fieldbourne Gall., London, 1974, 1990 (mainly portraits); Poole Wills Gall., NY, 1983; Royal Festival Hall: purchases by Arts Council, 1992, sculptures for 1951 Festival of Britain, 1996; Messum Gall., 1995; *portrait busts include:* Sir Alan Herbert, Lord Constantine (purchased by Nat. Portrait Gall.), Dame Ninette de Valois, Sir Hugh Casson, Donald Trelford, Sir Monty Finniston, Samuel Pepys (over-life size bronze, Seething Lane, EC3), Max von Sydow, Yuki, Paul Scofield. *Publication:* Karin Jonzen Sculpture (autobiog.), introd. Carel Weight, foreword by Edward Lucie-Smith, 1994; *relevant publication:* Karin Jonzen: sculptor, introd. Carel Weight, foreword by Norman St John-Stevas, 1976. *Recreations:* music, travel. *Address:* The Studio, 6A Gunter Grove, SW10 0UJ.
Died 29 Jan. 1998.

JOPE, Prof. Edward Martyn, FBA 1965; FSA 1946; MRIA 1973; Professor of Archæology, The Queen's University of Belfast, 1963–81, then Emeritus; Visiting Professor in Archaeological Sciences, University of Bradford, 1974–81, Honorary Visiting Professor, since 1982; *b* 28 Dec. 1915; *s* of Edward Mallet Jope and Frances Margaret (*née* Chapman); *m* 1941, Margaret Halliday; no *c. Educ:* Whitgift Sch., Croydon; Kingswood Sch., Bath; Oriel Coll., Oxford (Open Schol., Chemistry, 1935). Staff of Royal Commission on Ancient Monuments (Wales), 1938; Biochemist, Nuffield and MRC Grants, 1940; Queen's Univ., Belfast: Lectr in Archæology, 1949; Reader, 1954. Member: Ancient Monuments Adv. Council (NI), 1950; Royal Commission on Ancient Monuments

(Wales), 1963–86; Sci.-based Archaeology Cttee, SRC, 1976–82; Ancient Monuments Bd (England), 1980–84; Pres. Section H, British Assoc., 1965. Rhys Res. Fellow and Vis. Sen. Res. Fellow, Jesus Coll., Oxford, 1977–78. Lectures: Munro, Edinburgh, 1953; O'Donnell, Oxford, 1968; Rhŷs, British Acad., 1987; Davies, Belfast, 1992. Hon. DSc Bradford, 1980. *Publications:* Early Celtic Art in the British Isles, 1977; (ed) Studies in Building History, 1961; (ed and contrib.) Archaeological Survey of Co. Down, 1966; papers in Biochem. Jl, Proc. RSocMed, Phil. Trans Royal Soc., Spectrochemica Acta, Trans Faraday Soc., Proc. Prehistoric Soc., Antiquaries' Jl, Medieval Archæology, Oxoniensia, Ulster Jl of Archæology, Proc. Soc. of Antiquaries of Scotland, etc. *Recreations:* music, travel. *Address:* 1 Chalfont Road, Oxford OX2 6TL. *T:* (01865) 59024.
Died 14 Nov. 1996.

JORDAN, David Harold, CMG 1975; MBE 1962; *b* Sunderland, 27 Oct. 1924; *er s* of late H. G. Jordan, OBE, and Gwendolyn (*née* Rees); *m* 1st, 1951, Lorna Mary Holland (marr. diss.), *er d* of late W. R. Harvey; three *s* one *d*; 2nd, 1971, Penelope Amanda, *d* of late Lt-Col B. L. J. Davy, OBE, TD; one *d. Educ:* Roundhay Sch., Leeds; Berkhamsted; Magdalen Coll., Oxford (1st Cl. Chinese; MA 1956). 9th Gurkha Rifles, Indian Army, 1943–47. HMOCS (Hong Kong), 1951–79: Chinese Language Sch., Univ. of Hong Kong, 1951–52; Asst Sec. for Chinese Affairs, 1952–55; Colonial Secretariat, 1956–68: Asst Sec., 1956–60; jssc 1960; Defence Sec., 1961–66; Dep. Dir, Commerce and Industry, 1968–70; Dep. Economic Sec., 1970–71; Dep. Financial Sec., 1971–72; Dir of Commerce and Industry, later Trade, Industry and Customs, and MLC, Hong Kong, 1972–79. *Address:* The Lower Farm, Drayton Parslow, Milton Keynes, Bucks MK17 0JS. *T:* (01296) 720688. *Clubs:* Hong Kong, Hong Kong Jockey.
Died 1 Aug. 1998.

JORDAN, Douglas Arthur, CMG 1977; Senior Partner, Douglas Jordan Consultants, since 1991; *b* 28 Sept. 1918; *s* of late Arthur and Elizabeth Jordan; *m* 1st, 1940, Violet Nancy (*née* Houston); one *d*; 2nd, 1970, Constance Dorothy (*née* Wallis) (*d* 1996). *Educ:* East Ham Grammar Sch., London. HM Customs and Excise: Officer, 1938; Surveyor, 1953; Inspector, 1960; Asst Collector, Manchester and London, 1962–68; Sen. Inspector, 1968–69; Chief Investigation Officer, 1969–77; Dep. Comr, 1977–79, Comr of Customs and Controls, 1979, Trade, Industry and Customs Dept, Hong Kong (Comr of Customs and Excise, Customs and Excise Dept, 1982–84); Special Anti-Piracy Advr, SE Asia, 1984, Customs and Anti-Piracy Consultant, 1985–90, Internat. Fedn of Phonogram and Videogram Producers. Freeman, City of London, 1964. *Recreations:* golf, music. *Address:* 10 Crouchmans Close, Sydenham Hill, SE26 6ST. *T:* (020) 8670 9638. *Clubs:* Wig and Pen, Royal Commonwealth Society; Dulwich and Sydenham Golf.
Died 22 March 1999.

JORDAN-MOSS, Norman, CB 1972; CMG 1965; Director, Crown Financial Management, 1984–90; *b* 5 Feb. 1920; *o s* of Arthur Moss and Ellen Jordan Round; *m* 1st, Eleri (marr. diss.); 2nd, Dorothy (marr. diss.); 3rd, 1965, Kathleen Lusmore (*d* 1974); one adopted *s* one adopted *d*; 4th, 1976, Philippa Rands (*d* 1993); one step *d. Educ:* Manchester Grammar Sch.; St John's Coll., Cambridge (MA). Ministry of Economic Warfare, 1940–44; HM Treasury, 1944–71; Asst Representative of HM Treas. in Middle East, 1945–48; Principal, 1948; First Sec. (Econ.), Belgrade, 1952–55; Financial Counsellor, Washington, 1956–60; Counsellor, UK Permanent Delegation to OECD, Paris, 1963–66; Asst Sec., 1956–68, Under-Sec., 1968–71, HM Treasury; Dep. Under-Sec. of State, DHSS, 1971–76; Dep. Sec., HM Treasury, 1976–80. Consultant, Hambros Bank, 1981–84; Dir, 1928 Investment Trust,

1981–84. *Publication:* Don't Kill the Cuckoos, 1991. *Recreations:* music, theatre. *Address:* Milton Way, Westcott, Dorking, Surrey RH4 3PZ. *Club:* Travellers'.
Died 27 May 1998.

JORRE DE ST JORRE, Danielle Marie-Madeleine; Secretary of State, since 1986 and Minister of the Environment, Economic Planning and External Relations, since 1992, Republic of Seychelles (Minister for Planning and External Relations, 1989); *b* 30 Sept. 1941; *d* of Henri Jorre De St Jorre and Alice Corgat; *m* 1965 (marr. diss. 1983); one *s* one *d*. *Educ:* Univ. of Edinburgh (MA 1965); Inst. of Education, Univ. of London (PGCE 1966); Univ. of York (BPhil 1972). French Teacher, Streatham Hill and Clapham High Sch. (GPDST), 1967–69; French and English Teacher, and Hd of French Dept, Seychelles Coll., 1969–71; Principal, Teacher Training College, Seychelles, 1974–76; Principal Educn Officer, Min. of Educn, Seychelles, 1976–77; Principal Secretary: Min. of Foreign Affairs, Tourism and Aviation, 1977–79; Min. of Education and Information, 1980–82; Dept of External Relations and Co-operation, Min. of Planning and External Relations: Principal Sec., External Relns, 1982–83; Principal Sec., Planning and External Relns, 1983–86; High Comr for Seychelles in UK, concurrently Ambassador to France, Canada, Cuba, Federal Republic of Germany, Greece and USSR, 1983–85. Mem. or Head of delegn at numerous overseas meetings and conferences. Mem. Exec. Cttee, Seychelles People's Progressive Front, 1991–. Gov. for Seychelles, Bd of Governors, World Bank and African Develt Bank, 1984–; Chairperson: Seychelles Nat. Printing Co., 1977–82; Nat. Bookshop, 1977–82; Nat. Consultancy Services, 1983–88; Seychelles Hotels Ltd, 1986–91; Nat. Monument Bd, 1987–88; Develt Bank of Seychelles, 1988–91; Dir, Internat. Centre for Ocean Develt, 1987–. Vice-President: Comité International des Etudes Créoles, 1984–; E African Reg., Adv. Cttee on Protection of the Sea, 1994–; Pres., Bannzil Kreyol, 1986–. *Publications:* Apprenons la nouvelle orthographe, 1978; Dictionnaire Créole Seychellois-français, 1982; (jtly) Lexique des Spécificités de la Langue Française aux Seychelles, 1989. *Address:* Ministry of Foreign Affairs, Planning and Environment, PO Box 656, Victoria, Mahé, Republic of Seychelles.   *Died 25 Feb. 1997.*

JOSEPHS, Wilfred; composer; *b* 24 July 1927; *s* of Philip Josephs and Rachel (*née* Block); *m* 1956, Valerie Wisbey; two *d*. *Educ:* Rutherford Coll. Boys' Sch.; Univ. of Durham at Newcastle (later Newcastle Univ.) (BDS Dunelm). Qual. dentistry, 1951. Army service, 1951–53. Guildhall Sch. of Music (scholar in composition, prizes), 1954; Leverhulme Scholar to study musical composition in Paris with Maître Max Deutsch, 1958–59; abandoned dentistry completely and thereafter a full-time composer, writing many concert works (incl. choral and orchestral works and 12 symphonies), many film and television scores and themes, incl. music for: The Great War, I, Claudius, Disraeli, Cider with Rosie, All Creatures Great and Small, Sister Dora, Swallows and Amazons, The Brontë Series, The Somerset Maugham Series, Horizon, Chéri, A Place in Europe, The Inventing of America, The Norman Conquests, The Ghosts of Motley Hall, The House of Bernardo Alba, The Hunchback of Notre Dame, The Voyage of Charles Darwin, Enemy at the Door, People Like Us, Black Sun, The Uncanny, The Atom Spies, Churchill and the Generals, Pride and Prejudice, Strangled, A Walk in the Dark, Gift of Tongues, Miss Morison's Ghosts, The Human Race, Weekend Theatre, The Moles, The Home Front, The Making of Britain, Courts Martial series, A Married Man, The Gay Lord Quex, Pope John Paul II, Martin's Day, Mata Hari, Drummonds, Return of the Antelope, Art of the Western World, Horizon (Wasting the Alps; The Company of Ants and Bees; Red Star in Orbit); television opera, The

Appointment; one-act opera, Pathelin; children's operas: Through the Looking-glass and What Alice Found There; Alice in Wonderland; children's musical, King of the Coast (Guardian/Arts Council Prize, 1969); Equus, the ballet (best ballet award, USA, 1980); Rebecca, 3–act opera, 1981–83; Cyrano de Bergerac, 3–act ballet, 1990–91. Vis. Prof. of Comp. and Composer-in-Residence at Univ. of Wisconsin-Milwaukee, 1970, at Roosevelt Univ., Chicago, 1972; Dist. Vis. Prof., Ohio State Univ., 1992; Music Consultant, London Internat. Film Sch., 1988–. Member: Council, RPS; BAFTA; RSM; ISM; Composers' Guild of GB; Assoc. of Professional Composers; Producers' Assoc. Hon. DMus Newcastle, 1978. Harriet Cohen Commonwealth Medal (for 1st quartet) and prizes; First Prize, La Scala, Milan, for Requiem, 1963. *Publications:* Requiem, Symphonies 1–12, various sonatas, quartets, concertos etc. *Recreations:* writing music, swimming, reading, opera, theatre, films. *Address:* Flat 3, 156 Haverstock Hill, NW3 2AT. *T:* and *Fax:* (0171) 722 6889.   *Died 18 Nov. 1997.*

JOUGHIN, Sir Michael, Kt 1991; CBE 1971; JP; Chairman, Scottish Hydro-Electric plc (formerly North of Scotland Hydro-Electric Board), 1983–93; farmer, 1952–90; *b* 26 April 1926; *s* of John Clague Joughin and May Joughin; *m* 1st, 1948, Lesley Roy Petrie; one *s* one *d*; 2nd, 1981, Anne Hutchison. *Educ:* Kelly Coll., Tavistock. Lieut, Royal Marines, 1944–52; RM pilot with Fleet Air Arm, 1946–49. Pres., NFU of Scotland, 1964–66. Chm. of Governors: N of Scotland Coll. of Agriculture, 1969–72; Blairmore Prep. Sch., 1966–72; Chairman: N of Scotland Grassland Soc., 1970–71; Elgin Market Green Auction Co., 1969–70; Scottish Agricl Develt Council, 1971–80; N of Scotland Milk Marketing Bd, 1974–83. Governor: Rowett Research Inst., 1968–74; Scottish Plant Breeding Inst., 1969–74; Animal Diseases Research Assoc., Moredun Inst., 1969–74; Member: Intervention Bd for Agric. Produce, 1972–76; Econ. Develt Council for Agriculture, 1967–70; Agric. Marketing Develt Exec. Cttee, 1965–68; Scottish Constitutional Cttee, 1969–70; British Farm Produce Council, 1965–66. Mem. Aberdeen Bd, 1988–91, East of Scotland Bd, 1991–95, Bank of Scotland. Contested (C) Highland and Islands, European Parly Elections, 1979. FRAgS 1975. CIMgt (CBIM 1988; FBIM 1979). JP Moray, 1965; DL Moray, 1974–80. *Recreation:* sailing. *Address:* Elderslie, Findhorn, Moray IV30 3TN. *T:* Findhorn (01309) 690277. *Clubs:* New (Edinburgh); Royal Naval Sailing Assoc., Royal Marines Sailing, Royal Findhorn Yacht, Goldfish.
Died 11 April 1996.

JUKES, John Andrew, CB 1968; *b* 19 May 1917; *s* of Captain A. M. Jukes, MD, IMS, and Mrs Gertrude E. Jukes (*née* King); *m* 1943, Muriel Child; two *s* two *d*. *Educ:* Shrewsbury Sch.; St John's Coll., Cambridge; London Sch. of Economics. MA in Physics Cambridge, BSc (Econ.) London. Cavendish Laboratory, Cambridge, 1939; Radar and Operational Research, 1939–46; Research Dept, LMS Railway, 1946–48; Economic Adviser, Cabinet Office and Treasury, 1948–54; British Embassy, Washington, DC, 1949–51; Economic Adviser to UK Atomic Energy Authority, 1954–64 and Principal Economics and Programming Office, UKAEA, 1957–64; Dep. Dir Gen., DEA, 1964; Dep. Under-Sec. of State, Dept of Economic Affairs, 1967; Dir Gen., Research and Economic Planning, MoT, 1969–70; Dir Gen., Economics and Resources, DoE, 1970–72; Dep. Sec. (Environmental Protection), DoE, 1972–74; Chm., Steering Gp on Water Authority Econ. and Financial Objectives, 1973–74; Dir-Gen., Highways, DoE, 1974–76, Dept of Transport, 1976–77. Mem., CEGB, 1977–80. Mem., Merton and Sutton DHA, 1986–90. Alliance (SDP) Councillor, London Borough of Sutton, 1986–90 (Chm., Finance Sub-Cttee, 1986–90). Rep. Sutton SDP on Council for Social

Democracy, 1982–86; Pres., Sutton Lib Dems, 1990–93. *Recreations:* gardening, travelling, sometime orienteer and Himalayan trekker. *Address:* 38 Albion Road, Sutton, Surrey SM2 5TF. *T:* (0181) 642 5018.

Died 12 Dec. 1997.

JUNOR, Sir John (Donald Brown), Kt 1980; Editor, Sunday Express, 1954–86; *b* 15 Jan. 1919; *s* of Alexander Junor, Black Isle, Ross and Cromarty; *m* 1942, Pamela Mary Welsh; one *s* one *d*. *Educ:* Glasgow Univ. (MA Hons English). Lieut (A) RNVR, 1939–45. Contested (L) Kincardine and West Aberdeen, 1945, East Edinburgh, 1948, Dundee West, 1951. Asst Editor, Daily Express, 1951–53; Dep. Editor, Evening Standard, 1953–54; Director: Beaverbrook (later Express) Newspapers, 1960–86; Fleet Hldgs, 1981–85. Columnist: Sunday Express, 1973–89; Mail on Sunday, 1990–. Hon. LLD New Brunswick, 1973. *Publications:* The Best of JJ, 1981; Listening for a Midnight Tram (memoirs), 1990. *Recreations:* golf, tennis. *Address:* c/o Associated Newspapers, Northcliffe House, 2 Derry Street, W8 5AT. *Clubs:* Royal and Ancient; Walton Heath.

Died 3 May 1997.

K

KAHAN, Barbara Joan, OBE 1990; Vice President, National Children's Bureau, since 1994 (Chair, 1985–94); consultant in child care, since 1988; *b* 18 March 1920; *d* of Alfred George Langridge and Emily Kathleen (*née* Bromley); *m* 1955, Dr Vladimir Leon Kahan (*d* 1981). *Educ:* Newnham Coll., Cambridge (MA); LSE (Post-grad. Dip. in Social Sci.). HMI of Factories, 1943–48; Children's Officer, 1948–70; Dep. Chief Inspector, Children's Dept, Home Office, 1970–71, DHSS, 1971–80. Mem., Finer Cttee on One Parent Families, 1969–73; Dir, Gatsby Project, 1980–91; Professional Advr to H of C Select Cttee on Social Services, 1983–90; jtly with A. Levy, QC, investigation into Staffordshire "Pindown" abuse, 1990–91. Chair, Wagner Develt Children's Gp, 1990–93. Pres., Assoc. of Children's Officers, 1964; Hon. Mem., Assoc. of Dirs of Social Services, 1983. Life Fellow, Nat. Inst. for Social Work, 1997. MUniv Open, 1987; Hon. LLD Victoria, BC, 1994. *Publications:* (with G. Banner) Residential Task in Child Care, 1968; Growing Up in Care: ten people talking, 1979; (with G. Banner and D. Lane) Staff: finding them, choosing them, keeping them, 1986; (ed) Child Care Research, Policy and Practice, 1989; (with A. Levy) The Pindown Experience and the Protection of Children, 1991; Growing up in Groups, 1994. *Recreations:* reading, writing, music. *Address:* Hampton House, The Green, Cassington, Witney, Oxon OX8 1DW. *T:* (01865) 881265, *Fax:* (01865) 880986. *Club:* Reform.
Died 6 Aug. 2000.

KAHN, Prof. Franz Daniel, DPhil; FRS 1993; Professor of Astronomy, University of Manchester, 1966–93, then Emeritus; *b* 13 May 1926; *s* of Siegfried and Grete Kahn; *m* 1951, Carla Copeland (*d* 1981); two *s* two *d. Educ:* St Paul's Sch.; Queen's and Balliol Colls, Oxford Univ. MA, DPhil (Oxon) 1950. University of Manchester: Asst Lectr in Mathematics, 1949–52; Turner Newall Fellow, 1952–55; Lectr in Astronomy, 1955–58; Sen. Lectr, 1958–62; Reader, 1962–66. Jt Winner, Prize Essay Comp. on Star Formation, German Soc. of Scientists and Physicians, 1958. Asteroid Kahnia named by Internat. Astronomical Union, 1991. *Publications:* (with H. P. Palmer) Quasars, 1966; scientific papers in Monthly Notices, Astronomy and Astrophysics and other astronomical jls. *Recreations:* food and drink, with special interest in processes involving fermentation, *eg* baking bread and visiting distilleries. *Address:* 27 Ballbrook Avenue, Manchester M20 3JG. *T:* (0161) 445 3648.
Died 8 Feb. 1998.

KALISHER, Michael David Lionel; QC 1984; a Recorder, since 1985; *b* 24 Feb. 1941; *s* of Samuel and Rose Kalisher; *m* 1967, Helen (*née* McCandless); one *s* two *d. Educ:* Hove County Grammar Sch.; Bristol Univ. (LLB Hons 1962). Articled as solicitor to Gates & Co., Sussex, 1962–64; admitted as solicitor, 1965; practised as solicitor in London with Avery Midgen & Co., 1965–69, Partner from 1966; called to the Bar, Inner Temple, 1970, Bencher, 1989; practised first from 9 King's Bench Walk, until 1976; then at 1 Hare Court, Temple. Chm., Criminal Bar Assoc., 1991–93; Mem., Bar Council, 1994–. Member: Crown Court Rules Cttee, 1989–; Lord Chancellor's Efficiency Commn, 1989–. *Recreations:* tennis, reading. *Address:* 1 Hare Court, Temple, EC4Y 7BE. *Clubs:* Athenæum; Roehampton.
Died 19 Sept. 1996.

KANE, Jack, OBE 1969; DL; JP; Hon. Vice President, Age Concern, Scotland, since 1987 (Chairman, 1983–86); Lord Provost of the City of Edinburgh and Lord Lieutenant of the County of the City of Edinburgh, 1972–75; *b* 1 April 1911; *m* 1940, Anne Murphy; one *s* two *d. Educ:* Bathgate Academy. Served War, 1940–46. Librarian, 1936–55. Pres., SE of Scotland Dist, Workers' Educnl Assoc., 1983– (Sec., 1955–76). Chm., Board of Trustees for Nat. Galls of Scotland, 1975–80; Mem., South of Scotland Electricity Bd, 1975–81, Chm., Consultative Council, 1977–81. JP Edinburgh, 1945; DL City of Edinburgh, 1976. Dr *hc* Edinburgh, 1976. Grand Officer, Order of the Oaken Crown (Luxembourg), 1972; Grand Cross of Merit (W Germany). *Recreations:* reading, walking. *Address:* 42 Palmerston Place, Edinburgh EH12 5BJ. *Club:* Newcraighall Miners' Welfare Inst.
Died 10 Oct. 1999.

KANTOROWICH, Prof. Roy Herman, BArch (Witwatersrand), MA (Manchester); RIBA, FRTPI; Professor of Town and Country Planning, 1961–84, Professor Emeritus, since 1984, Dean of the Faculty of Arts, 1975–76 and Director of Wolfson Design Unit, 1981–84, University of Manchester; *b* Johannesburg, 24 Nov. 1916; *s* of George Kantorowich and Deborah (*née* Baranov); *m* 1943, Petronella Sophie Wissema (violinist, as Nella Wissema); one *s* two *d. Educ:* King Edward VII Sch., Johannesburg; University of Witwatersrand. BArch 1939; ARIBA 1940; MTPI 1965 (AMTPI 1946). Post-grad. studies in Housing and Planning, MIT and Columbia Univ., 1939–41; Planning Officer: Vanderbijl Park New Town, 1942–45; directing Cape Town Foreshore Scheme, 1945–48; private practice in Cape Town, in architecture and town planning, 1948–61. Pres., S African Inst. Town and Regional Planners, 1960. Formerly Town Planning Consultant to Cape Provincial Admin, and for many cities and towns in S Africa incl. Durban, Pretoria and Port Elizabeth; Cons. for New Town of Ashkelon, Israel, 1950–56. Member: NW Econ. Planning Council, 1965–79; Council (Chm., Educn Cttee), RTPI, 1965–70; Planning Cttee, SSRC, 1969–73; Construction and Environment Bd, and Chm., Town Planning Panel, CNAA, 1971–75; Natal Building Soc. Fellowship, 1980. Buildings include: Civic Centre, Welkom, OFS; Baxter Hall, University of Cape Town; Sea Point Telephone Exchange (Cape Province Inst. of Architects Bronze Medal Award); Architecture and Planning Building, Univ. of Manchester. FRSA 1972. *Publications:* Cape Town Foreshore Plan, 1948; (with Lord Holford) Durban 1985, a plan for central Durban in its Regional Setting, 1968; Three Perspectives on planning for the 'eighties, 1981; contribs to SA Arch. Record, Jl RTPI and other professional jls. *Recreations:* music, tennis. *Address:* 4 Old Dry Lane, Brigstock, Kettering, Northants NN14 3HY. *T:* (01536) 373154.
Died 23 Nov. 1996.

KARAMANLIS, Konstantinos; President of Greece, 1980–85 and 1990–95; *b* 8 March 1907; *m* Amalia Kanelopoulos (marr. diss.). *Educ:* Univ. of Athens. Lawyer, 1932; MP, 1935–67, 1974–80 (Deputy for Serres, Populist Party, 1935; founded National Radical Union Party, 1955; reformed as New Democracy Party, 1974). Minister of: Labour, 1946; Transport, 1947; Social Welfare, 1948–50; Nat. Defence, 1950–52; Public Works, 1952–54; Communications and Public Works, 1954–55; Prime Minister, 1955–63; self-imposed exile in France, 1963–74; Leader of New Democracy Party and Prime Minister, 1974–80. Gold Medal, Onassis Foundn, 1981;

Gold Medal, European Parlt. *Address:* c/o Office of the President, Athens, Greece.   *Died 23 April 1998.*

KARK, Mrs Evelyn Florence, (Lucie Clayton); Director; *b* 5 Dec. 1928; *d* of Emily and William Gordine; *m* 1956, (Arthur) Leslie Kark; one *s* one *d. Educ:* privately and inconspicuously. Asst to Editor, Courier Magazine, 1950; became Head of model school and agency (assuming name of Lucie Clayton), 1952; founded Lucie Clayton Sch. of Fashion Design and Dressmaking, 1961, and Lucie Clayton Secretarial College, 1966. *Publications* (as Lucie Clayton): The World of Modelling, 1968; Modelling and Beauty Care, 1985. *Recreations:* talking, tapestry, cooking. *Address:* 9 Clareville Grove, SW7 5AU. *T:* (0171) 373 2621; Roche House, Burford, Oxfordshire OX18 4LS. *T:* (01993) 823007.   *Died 8 March 1997.*

KARMEL, His Honour Alexander David; QC 1954; an Additional Judge, Central Criminal Court, later a Circuit Judge, 1968–79; *b* 16 May 1904; *s* of Elias Karmel and Adeline (*née* Freedman); *m* 1937, Mary, *d* of Newman Lipton, and *widow* of Arthur Lee; one *s. Educ:* Newcastle upon Tyne Royal Grammar Sch. Barrister-at-law, Middle Temple, 1932; Bencher, 1962; Leader of Northern Circuit, 1966; Comr of Assize, Stafford, summer 1967; Recorder of Bolton, 1962–68. Mem., Bar Council, 1950–53, 1961–64. *Recreations:* croquet, golf. *Club:* Hurlingham.   *Died 27 Sept. 1998.*

KARN, Prof. Valerie Ann; Professor of Housing Studies, University of Manchester, since 1994 (Chair, School of Social Policy, 1995–97); *b* 17 May 1939; *d* of Arthur and Winnifred Karn; one *d; m* 1989, Prof. Constantine Solomonides. *Educ:* Newquay County Grammar School; Lady Margaret Hall, Oxford (BA Geography); Univ. of the Punjab, Lahore (Commonwealth scholar); Graduate Sch. of Design, Harvard Univ.; PhD Birmingham (Urban Studies). Res. Officer, ODI, 1963; Res. Fellow, Inst. of Social and Economic Res., Univ. of York, 1964–66; Res. Associate, Lectr, Sen. Lectr, Centre for Urban and Regional Studies, Univ. of Birmingham, 1966–84; Prof. of Envmtl Health and Housing, Univ. of Salford, 1984–94; Co-Dir, Salford Centre for Housing Studies, 1986–94. Res. Officer, Central Housing Adv. Cttee, Sub-Cttee on Housing Management, 1967–69; Chair, Hulme Study, 1989–91; Member: Housing Services Adv. Gp, 1976–79; Inquiry into British Housing, 1984–86 and 1990–91; Inquiry into Glasgow's Housing, 1985–86; ESRC Social Affairs Cttee, 1985–87; Co-ordinating Cttee, Eur. Network for Housing Res., 1994–; Adv. Panel, Housing Assoc. Tenants Ombudsman Service, 1994–97. Special Comr, CRE, 1987–89. BAAS Lister Lectr, 1979; Vis. Fellow, Urban Inst., Washington DC, 1979–80. MCIH. Gov., Peabody Trust, 1993–. *Publications:* Retiring to the Seaside, 1977 (Oddfellows Social Concern Book Prize); *jointly:* Housing in Retirement, 1973; (ed) The Consumers' Experience of Housing, 1980; Home-ownership in the Inner City, Salvation or Despair, 1985; Race, Class, and Public Housing, 1987; Comparing Housing Systems Performance and Housing Policy in the United States and Britain, 1992; Neighbour Disputes: responses by social landlords, 1993; New Homes in the 1990s, 1994; Choosing Your Home, 1995; The Settlement of Refugees in Britain, 1995; Housing Quality: a practical guide for tenants and their representatives, 1995; Home Owners and Clearance, 1996; Small Voices, Big Issues, 1996; Tenants' Complaints and the Reform of Housing Management, 1997; Ethnicity in the 1991 Census: Vol. 4, Ethnic Differences in Employment, Education and Housing, 1997; Tradition, Change and Diversity, 1999; *chapters in:* The Future of Council Housing, 1982; Family Matters, 1983; Ethnic Pluralism and Public Policy, 1983; Between Centre and Locality, 1986; Low Cost Home Ownership, 1986; The Housing Crisis, 1986; The Property Owning

Democracy, 1987; Urban Housing Segregation of Minorities in Western Europe and the United States, 1991; Implementing Housing Policy, 1992; Directions in Housing Policy, 1997; The Politics of Race Relations, 1997; res. reports and articles in jls. *Recreations:* gardening, house renovations. *Address:* 4 Harricroft Farm Cottages, Smithills Dean Road, Bolton BL1 7NS. *T:* (01204) 300203.   *Died 8 June 1999.*

KARP, David; novelist; *b* New York City, 5 May 1922; *s* of Abraham Karp and Rebecca Levin; *m* 1st, 1944, Lillian Klass (*d* 1987); two *s;* 2nd, 1988, Claire Leighton. *Educ:* College of The City of New York. US Army, 1943–46, S Pacific, Japan; College, 1946–48; Continuity Dir, Station WNYC, New York, 1948–49; free-lance motion picture-television writer and motion picture producer, 1949–; Pres., Leda Productions Inc., 1968–; Mem. Editorial Bd, Television Quarterly, 1966–71, 1972–77. Pres., Television-Radio Branch, Writers Guild of America West, 1969–71; Member: Council, Writers Guild of America, 1966–73; Bd of Trustees, Producer-Writers Guild of America Pension Plan, 1968– (Chm., 1978, 1988, 1996; Sec., 1987, 1995); Bd of Trustees, Writers Guild-Industry Health Fund, 1973– (Chm., 1980, 1988, 1996; Sec., 1987, 1995). Guggenheim Fellow, 1956–57. *Publications:* One, 1953; The Day of the Monkey, 1955; All Honorable Men, 1956; Leave Me Alone, 1957; The Sleepwalkers, 1960; (with Murray D. Lincoln) Vice-President in Charge of Revolution, 1960; The Last Believers, 1964; short stories in Saturday Evening Post, Collier's, Esquire, Argosy, The American, etc; articles and reviews in NY Times, Los Angeles Times, Saturday Review, Nation, etc. *Recreations:* photography, reading. *Address:* 300 East 56th Street #3C, New York, NY 10022, USA. *Club:* PEN (New York).   *Died 11 Sept. 1999.*

KASTNER, Prof. Leslie James, MA, ScD Cantab; FIMechE; Professor of Mechanical Engineering, King's College, University of London, 1955 76, then Emeritus, Dean of Faculty of Engineering, University of London, 1974–76; *b* 10 Dec. 1911; *o s* of late Professor Leon E. Kastner, sometime Prof. of French Language and Literature, University of Manchester, and Elsie E. Kastner; *m* 1958, Joyce, *o d* of Lt-Col Edward Lillingston, DSO, Belstone, Devon. *Educ:* Dreghorn Castle Sch.; Colinton, Midlothian; Highgate Sch.; Clare Coll., Cambridge (Mechanical Science Tripos). Apprenticeship with Davies and Metcalfe, Ltd, Locomotive Engineers, of Romiley, Stockport, 1930–31 and 1934–36; Development Engineer, 1936–38; Osborne Reynolds Research Fellowship, University of Manchester, 1938; Lectr in Engineering, University of Manchester, 1941–46; Senior Lectr, 1946–48; Prof. of Engineering, University Coll. of Swansea, University of Wales, 1948–55. Mem. of Council, Institution of Mechanical Engineers, 1954. FKC 1974. Graduates' Prize, IMechE, 1939; Herbert Ackroyd Stuart Prize, 1943; Dugald Clerk Prize, 1956. *Publications:* various research papers in applied thermodynamics and fluid flow. *Address:* 37 St Anne's Road, Eastbourne BN21 2HP.   *Died 30 Oct. 1996.*

KATO, Tadao, Hon. KBE 1988; 1st Class Order of Sacred Treasure, 1988; Counsellor, Suntory, Long-Term Credit Bank, since 1980; *b* 13 May 1916; *m* 1946, Yoko; two *s. Educ:* Tokyo Univ.; Cambridge Univ. Joined Japanese Diplomatic Service 1939; Singapore, 1952; London, 1953; Counsellor, Economic Affairs Bureau, Min. of Foreign Affairs, 1956–69; Counsellor, Washington, 1959–63 (Vis. Fellow, Harvard, 1959–60); Dep. Dir, Econ. Affairs Bureau, Min. of Foreign Affairs, 1963–66, Dir, 1966–67; Ambassador to OECD, 1967–70, to Mexico, 1970–74, to UK, 1975–79. Advisor: NI Development Bd, 1981–; Hotel Okura; Nitto Kogyo Enterprise. Vice-Pres., Japan British Soc., 1988– (Chm., 1981–88); Mem., UK-Japan 2000 Gp,

1988– (Japanese Chm., 1985–88). 1st Class Order of Aztec Star, Mexico, 1972. *Recreations:* golf, goh. *Address:* 3–10–22, Shimo-Ochiai, Shinjuku-Ku, Tokyo, Japan. *Clubs:* Tokyo (Tokyo); Oxfordshire Golf (Hon. Mem., 1993); Royal Co. Down Golf; Koganei Golf, Abiko Golf, Karuizawa Golf, Hamano Golf (Chm., 1984–), Mito Golf (Chm., 1988–), Shinyo Golf (Chm., 1989–) (Japan); Green Academy Country (Chm., 1985–) (Fukushima).
Died 11 Jan. 1996.

KAY, Brian Wilfrid; Consultant, Culham College Institute, 1989–95 (Senior Research Fellow, 1982–89); *b* 30 July 1921; *s* of Wilfrid and Jessie Kay; *m* 1st, 1947, Dorothea Sheppard Lawson (*d* 1993); two *d*; 2nd, 1994, Anthea Grace Barrett. *Educ:* King's Sch., Chester; University Coll., Oxford (exhibnr). Classics Master, Birkenhead Sch., 1947–59; Head of Classics, Liverpool Collegiate Sch., 1959–64; HM Inspector of Schs (Wales), 1964–71; Staff Inspector, Classics, Secondary Educn, 1971–74; Head of Assessment of Performance Unit, DES, 1974–77; Chief Inspector, Res. and Planning, DES, 1977–79; Chief Inspector, Teacher Trng and Res., DES, 1979–81, retired. Co-ordinator, Hulme Project, Dept Educnl Studies, Oxford Univ., 1982–87. *Recreations:* gardening, music, architecture. *Address:* Pond Cottage, Botolph Claydon, Buckingham MK18 2NG. *T:* (01296) 713477.
Died 30 Oct. 1997.

KAYE, Sir David Alexander Gordon, 4th Bt *cr* 1923, of Huddersfield, co. York; *b* 26 July 1919; *s* of Sir Henry Gordon Kaye, 2nd Bt and Winifred (*d* 1971), *d* of Walter H. Scales, Verwood, Bradford; *S* brother, 1983; *m* 1st, 1942, Elizabeth (marr. diss. 1950), *o d* of Captain Malcolm Hurtley; 2nd, 1955, Adelle, *d* of Denis Thomas, Brisbane, Queensland; two *s* four *d*. *Educ:* Stowe; Trinity Coll., Cambridge (BA). MRCS, LRCP 1943. *Heir: s* Paul Henry Gordon Kaye [*b* 19 Feb. 1958; *m* 1984, Sally Ann Louise Grützner]. *Died 23 June 1994.*

KAYE, Col Douglas Robert Beaumont, DSO 1942 (Bar 1945); JP; DL; *b* 18 Nov. 1909; *s* of late Robert Walter Kaye, JP, Great Glenn Manor, Leics; *m* 1946, Florence Audrey Emma, *d* of late Henry Archibald Bellville, Tedstone Court, Bromyard, Herefordshire; one *s* one *d*. *Educ:* Harrow. 2nd Lieut Leicestershire Yeo., 1928; 2nd Lieut 10th Royal Hussars, 1931; served War of 1939–45: Jerusalem, 1939–41; Cairo and HQ 30 Corps, 1941–42; Lieut-Col comdg 10th Royal Hussars, Africa and Italy, 1943–46 (despatches twice; wounded); Bde Major, 30 Lowland Armd Bde (TA), 1947–49; Lieut-Col comdg 16th/5th Queen's Royal Lancers, 1949–51; AA&QMG 56 London Armd Div. (TA), 1952–54; Col Comdt and Chief Instructor, Gunnery Sch., RAC Centre, 1954–56; retd 1956. Master of Newmarket and Thurlow Foxhounds, 1957–59. DL 1963, JP 1961, High Sheriff 1971, Cambridgeshire and Isle of Ely. Newmarket RDC, 1958–74 (Chm., 1972–74), E Cambridgeshire DC, 1974–84. *Recreations:* hunting, shooting. *Address:* Brinkley Hall, near Newmarket, Suffolk CB8 0SB. *T:* Stetchworth (01638) 507202. *Club:* Cavalry and Guards.
Died 21 Feb. 1996.

KAYE, Sir Emmanuel, Kt 1974; CBE 1967; Founder and Chairman: The Kaye Organisation Ltd, 1966–89; Kaye Enterprises Ltd, since 1989; Thrombosis Research Institute, since 1990; *b* 29 Nov. 1914; *m* 1946, Elizabeth Cutler; one *s* two *d*. *Educ:* Richmond Hill Sch.; Twickenham Technical Coll. Founded jtly with J. R. Sharp (*d* 1965), J. E. Shay Ltd, Precision Gauge, Tool and Instrument Makers, and took over Lansing Bagnall & Co. of Isleworth, 1943; then founded Lansing Bagnall Ltd, 1943–89; transf. to Basingstoke, 1949 (from being smallest manufr of electric lift trucks, became largest in Europe). Royal Warrant as supplier of Industrial Trucks to Royal Household, 1971; Queen's Awards for Export

Achievement in 1969, 1970, 1971, 1979, 1980 and only co. to win Queen's Awards for both Export Achievement and Technological Innovation, 1972; Design Council Awards, 1974, 1980; winners of Gold and other Continental Awards. Chairmanships included: Elvetham Hall Ltd, 1965–98; Lansing GmbH, Germany, 1966–91; Pool & Sons (Hartley Wintney) Ltd, 1967–90; Kaye Steel Stockholders, 1978–95; Kaye Office Supplies Ltd, 1983–89; Hart Ventures, 1989–; Pres., Lansing Linde Ltd, 1989–. Founded Unquoted Companies' Gp, 1968. Confederation of British Industry: Member: Taxation Cttee, 1970–77; Wealth Tax Panel, 1974–77; President's Cttee, 1976–85; Council, 1976–89; Econ. and Financial Policy Cttee, 1985–92. Member: Council of Industry for Management Educn, 1970–87; Export Credit Guarantees Adv. Council, 1971–74; Inflation Accounting Cttee, 1974–75; Queen's Award Review Cttee, 1975; Reviewing Cttee on Export of Works of Art, 1977–80. Visiting Fellow, Univ. of Lancaster, 1970–87. Governor: Girls' High Sch., Basingstoke, 1955–70; Queen Mary's Coll., Basingstoke, 1971–75. Trustee, Glyndebourne, 1977–84. Chairman: Thrombosis Research Trust, 1985– (Vice Chm., 1981–85); Vice President: Natural Medicines Soc., 1986–; Nat. Pure Water Assoc., 1988–; Patron, British Homœopathic Assoc., 1987–. Fellow, Psionic Medical Soc., 1977–. Liveryman, Farriers' Co., 1953; Freeman, City of London, 1954. FIMgt (FBIM 1975); FRSA 1978. Hon. Mem., Emmanuel Coll., Cambridge, 1994. *Recreations:* chess, music, walking. *Club:* Brooks's.
Died 28 Feb. 1999.

KAYLL, Wing Comdr Joseph Robert, DSO 1940; OBE 1946; DFC 1940; DL; JP; *b* 12 April 1914; *s* of late J. P. Kayll, MBE, The Elms, Sunderland; *m* 1940, Annette Lindsay Nisbet; two *s*. *Educ:* Aysgarth; Stowe. Timber trader; joined 607 Sqdn AAF, 1934; mobilised, Sept. 1939; Commanding Officer 615 Squadron, 1940; prisoner, 1941; OC 607 Sqdn AAF, 1946. DL Durham, 1956; JP Sunderland, 1962. Mem., Wear Boating Assoc. *Recreation:* yachting. *Address:* Hillside House, Hillside, Sunderland, Tyne and Wear SR3 1YN. *T:* (0191) 528 3282. *Club:* Sunderland Yacht.
Died 3 March 2000.

KEAN, Arnold Wilfred Geoffrey, CBE 1977; Secretary and Legal Adviser, Civil Aviation Authority, 1972–79; *b* 29 Sept. 1914; *s* of Martin Kean; *m* 1939, Sonja Irene, *d* of Josef Andersson, Copenhagen; two *d*. *Educ:* Blackpool Grammar Sch.; Queens' Coll., Cambridge (Schol.; 1st cl. 1st div. Law Tripos, Pts I and II; Pres., Cambridge Union, 1935; Wallenberg (Scandinavian) Prize). Commonwealth Fund Fellow, Harvard Law Sch., 1936–38; Yarborough-Anderson Schol., Inner Temple; called to the Bar (studentship, certif. of honour, 1939). Wartime service on legal staff of British Purchasing Commn and UK Treas. Delegn in N America. HM Treasury Solicitor's Dept, 1945; Prin. Asst Solicitor, 1964–72. Mem., Legal Cttee, ICAO, 1954–92 (Chm., 1978–83); Hon. Pres., UN Administrative Tribunal (Mem., 1980–92; Vice-Pres., 1982–88; Pres., 1988–89). Visiting Lecturer: Univ. of Auckland, NZ, 1980; Univ. of Sydney, NSW, 1982; UCL, 1983–88 (Hon. Fellow). Air Law Editor, Jl of Business Law, 1970–94. Edward Warner award, ICAO, 1993. King Christian X Liberation Medal (Denmark), 1945. *Publications:* (ed) Essays in Air Law, 1982; articles in legal periodicals. *Recreations:* music, stamps, gardening. *Address:* Tall Trees, South Hill Avenue, Harrow HA1 3NU. *T:* (020) 8422 5791. *Died 18 Jan. 2000.*

KEANE, Mary Nesta, (Molly), (Mrs Robert Keane); (*nom de plume* **M. J. Farrell**); *b* 20 July 1904; *d* of Walter Clarmont Skrine and Agnes Shakespeare Higginson; *m* 1938, Robert Lumley Keane (*d* 1946); two *d*. *Educ:* privately. Author of plays: (with John Perry) Spring

Meeting (play perf. Ambassadors Theatre and New York, 1938); Ducks and Drakes (play perf. Apollo Theatre, 1941); Guardian Angel (play perf. Gate Theatre, Dublin, 1944); Treasure Hunt (play perf. Apollo Theatre, 1949); Dazzling Prospects. *Publications: as M. J. Farrell:* The Knight of Cheerful Countenance; This Angel Knight; Young Entry; Taking Chances; Mad Puppettstown; Conversation Piece; Devoted Ladies, 1934; Full House, 1935; The Rising Tide, 1937; Two Days in Aragon, 1941; Loving Without Tears, 1951; Treasure Hunt, 1952; *as Molly Keane:* Good Behaviour, 1978 (televised 1983); Time After Time, 1983 (televised 1986); Nursery Cooking, 1985; Loving and Giving, 1988. *Address:* Dysert, Ardmore, Co. Waterford, Ireland. *TA:* Ardmore. *T:* Youghal (24) 4225. *Clubs:* Lansdowne, Groucho.
Died 22 April 1996.

KEATINGE, Sir Edgar (Mayne), Kt 1960; CBE 1954; *b* Bombay, 3 Feb. 1905; *s* of late Gerald Francis Keatinge, CIE and Marion, *d* of J. S. Cotton; *m* 1930, Katharine Lucile Burrell (*d* 1990); one *s* one *d. Educ:* Rugby Sch.; School of Agriculture, S Africa. Diploma in Agriculture, 1925, S African Dept of Agriculture, 1926–29. Served War of 1939–45 with RA, resigned with rank of Lieut-Col: West African Frontier Force, 1941–43; Commandant Sch. of Artillery, West Africa, 1942–43. CC West Suffolk, 1933–45. Parliamentary Candidate, Isle of Ely, 1938–44; MP (C) Bury St Edmunds, 1944–45. Chm. Wessex Area Nat. Union of Conservative Assocs, 1950–53; Mem. Panel, Land Tribunal, SW Area. Director: St Madeleine Sugar Co., 1944–62; Caromi Ltd, 1962–66. Governor, Sherborne Sch., 1951–74. Mem. Council, Royal African Soc., 1970–80. JP Wilts, 1946. *Recreations:* travel, shooting. *Address:* Rose Cottage, Teffont, Salisbury, Wilts SP3 5RG. *T:* (01722) 716224. *Clubs:* Carlton, Boodle's.
Died 7 Aug. 1998.

KEAY, Ronald William John, CBE 1977 (OBE 1966); DPhil; Executive Secretary, The Royal Society, 1977–85; *b* 20 May 1920; *s* of Harold John Keay and Marion Lucy (*née* Flick); *m* 1944, Joan Mary Walden; one *s* two *d. Educ:* King's College Sch., Wimbledon; St John's Coll., Oxford (BSc, MA, DPhil). Colonial Forest Service, Nigeria, 1942–62; seconded to Royal Botanic Gardens, Kew, 1951–57; Dir, Federal Dept of Forest Research, Nigeria, 1960–62; Dep. Exec. Sec., The Royal Society, 1962–77. Leverhulme Emeritus Fellow, 1987–88; Vis. Prof., Univ. of Essex, 1991–93. Pres., Science Assoc. of Nigeria, 1961–62; Vice-President: Linnean Soc., 1965–67, 1971–73, 1974–76 (Treas., 1989–95); Nigerian Field Soc., 1987– (Chm., UK Br., 1985–91); President: African Studies Assoc., 1971–72; Inst. of Biology, 1988–90. Chm., Finance Cttee, Internat. Biological Programme, 1964–74; Treasurer, Scientific Cttee for Problems of the Environment, 1976–77; Scientific Advr, Earthwatch Europe, 1991–97; Member: Lawes Agricl Trust Cttee, 1978–90; RHS Review Cttee, 1984–85 (Chm., RHS Liby Rev. Cttee, 1988–89); Council, Roehampton Inst. of Higher Educn, 1986–89; Council, British Initiative Against Avoidable Disablement (IMPACT Foundn), 1985–92. Church Warden, St Martin-in-the-Fields, 1981–87. Hon. FIBiol 1985; Hon. FRHS 1986. *Publications:* Flora of West Tropical Africa, Vol. 1, pt 1 1954, pt 2 1958; Nigerian Trees, pt 1 1960, pt 2 1964, rev. edn as Trees of Nigeria, 1989; papers on tropical African plant ecology and taxonomy, and science policy. *Recreations:* gardening, walking, natural history. *Address:* 38 Birch Grove, Cobham, Surrey KT11 2HR. *T:* (01932) 865677. *Club:* Athenæum.
Died 7 April 1998.

KEELING, Surg. Rear-Adm. John, CBE 1978; Director of Medical Policy and Plans, Ministry of Defence, 1980–83; Chairman, NATO Joint Civil/Military Medical Group, 1981–83; *b* 28 Oct. 1921; *s* of John and Grace

Keeling; *m* 1948, Olwen Anne Dix; one *s* (and one *s* decd). *Educ:* Queen Elizabeth's Sch., Hartlebury; Birmingham Univ. MRCS, LRCP; MFOM. Entered RN as Surg. Lieut, 1946; served with Fleet Air Arm, 1947–75: Pres., Central Air Med. Bd, 1954–56 and 1960–63; SMO, HMS Albion, 1956–57, HMS Victorious, 1965–67, and several Royal Naval Air Stns; Staff MO to Flag Officer Sea Trng, 1970–73; Dir of Environmental Medicine and Dep. MO i/c Inst. of Naval Medicine, 1975–77; Dep. Med. Dir-Gen. (Naval), 1977–80. Surg. Captain 1970, Surg. Cdre 1977, Surg. Rear-Adm. 1980. QHP, 1977–83. Member: Fleet Air Arm Officers' Assoc., 1973–; Soc. of Occupational Medicine, 1976–. Membership Sec., Herefordshire Nature Trust, 1988–. *Recreations:* computer programming, music. *Address:* Merlin Cottage, Brockhampton, Hereford HR1 4TQ. *T:* and *Fax:* (01989) 740649; *e-mail:* j.kccling@cwcom.net.
Died 20 June 2000.

KEITH-LUCAS, Prof. Bryan, CBE 1983; Professor of Government, University of Kent at Canterbury, 1965–77, then Emeritus (Master of Darwin College, 1970–74); *b* 1 Aug. 1912; *y s* of late Keith Lucas, ScD, FRS, and Alys (*née* Hubbard); *m* 1946, Mary Hardwicke (MBE 1982; Sheriff of Canterbury, 1971); one *s* two *d. Educ:* Gresham's Sch., Holt; Pembroke Coll., Cambridge. MA Cantab 1937, MA Oxon 1948; DLitt Kent, 1980. Solicitor, 1937. Served 1939–45 in Buffs and Sherwood Foresters, N Africa and Italy (Major, despatches); DAAG Cyprus, 1945–46. Asst Solicitor: Kensington Council, 1938–46; Nottingham, 1946–48; Sen. Lectr in Local Govt, Oxford, 1948–65; Faculty Fellow of Nuffield Coll., 1950–65, Domestic Bursar, 1957–65. Leverhulme Emeritus Fellow, 1983. Part-time Asst Master, King's Sch., Canterbury, 1978–83. Chairman: Commn on Electoral System, Sierra Leone, 1954; Commn on local govt elections, Mauritius, 1955–56. Member: Roberts Cttee on Public Libraries, 1957–59; Commn on Administration of Lagos, 1963; Mallaby Cttee on Staffing of Local Govt, 1964–67, Local Govt Commn for England, 1965–66; Royal Commn on Elections in Fiji, 1975. Vice-Chm., Hansard Soc., 1976–80. Chairman: Nat. Assoc. of Parish Councils, 1964–70 (Vice-Pres., 1970–; Pres., Kent Assoc., 1972–81); Canterbury Soc., 1972–75; President: Kent Fedn of Amenity Socs, 1976–81; Wye Historical Soc., 1986–. City Councillor, Oxford, 1950–65. Hon. Fellow, Inst. of Local Govt Studies, Birmingham Univ., 1973. *Publications:* The English Local Government Franchise, 1952; The Mayor, Aldermen and Councillors, 1961; English Local Government in the 19th and 20th Centuries, 1977; (with P. G. Richards) A History of Local Government in the 20th Century, 1978; The Unreformed Local Government System, 1980; Parish Affairs, 1986; (with Dr G. M. Ditchfield) A Kentish Parson, 1991; (with K. P. Poole) Parish Government 1894–1994, 1994; Wye in the Eighteenth Century, 1995; various articles on local govt. *Address:* 7 Church Street, Wye, Kent TN25 5BN. *T:* (01233) 812621. *Club:* National Liberal.
Died 7 Nov. 1996.

KEITH-LUCAS, Prof. David, CBE 1973; MA; FEng, FIMechE, Hon. FRAeS; Chairman, Airworthiness Requirements Board, 1972–82; *b* 25 March 1911; *s* of late Keith Lucas, ScD, FRS, and Alys (*née* Hubbard); *m* 1st, 1942, Dorothy De Bauduy Robertson (*d* 1979); two *s* one *d*; 2nd, 1981, Phyllis Marion Everard (*née* Whurr). *Educ:* Gresham's Sch., Holt; Gonville and Caius Coll., Cambridge. BA (Mech. Sci. Tripos, 2nd Class Hons) 1933; MA 1956; FRAeS 1948, Hon. FRAeS 1979; FIMechE 1949; FAIAA 1973, Hon. FAIAA 1974; FEng 1978. Apprenticed 1933–35, design team 1935–39, C. A. Parsons & Co. Ltd; Chief Aerodynamicist, Short Bros Ltd, 1940–49; Short Bros & Harland Ltd: Chief Designer, 1949–58; Technical Dir, 1958–64; Dir of Research, 1964–65; Dir, John Brown & Co., 1970–77; Cranfield

Inst. of Technology: Prof. of Aircraft Design, 1965–72; Pro-Vice-Chancellor, 1970–73; Prof. of Aeronautics and Chm. College of Aeronautics, 1972–76, then Emeritus Prof. Member: Senate, Queen's Univ., Belfast, 1955–65; Council, Air Registration Board, 1967–72; Commn on Third London Airport, 1968–70; Civil Aviation Authority, 1972–80. President: RAeS, 1968; Engrg Section, British Assoc. for the Advancement of Science, 1972. Hon. DSc: Queen's Univ., Belfast, 1968; Cranfield Inst. of Technology, 1975. Gold Medal, RAeS, 1975. *Publications:* The Shape of Wings to Come, 1952; The Challenge of Vertical Take-Off (lects IMechE), 1961–62; The Role of Jet Lift (lect. RAeS), 1962; Design Council report on design educn; papers on aircraft design, vertical take-off, engrg economics, in engrg jls. *Recreation:* small boats. *Address:* Manor Close, Emberton, Olney, Bucks MK46 5BX. *T:* (01234) 711552.

Died 6 April 1997.

KEKWICK, Prof. Ralph Ambrose, FRS 1966; Professor of Biophysics, University of London, 1966–71, then Emeritus; Member Staff, Lister Institute, 1940–71 (Head, Division of Biophysics, 1943–71); *b* 11 Nov. 1908; 2nd *s* of late Oliver A. and Mary Kekwick; *m* 1st, 1933, Barbara (*d* 1973), 3rd *d* of W. S. Stone, DD, New York; one *d*; 2nd, 1974, Dr Margaret Mackay (*d* 1982), *er d* of J. G. Mackay, MB, BS, Adelaide, Australia. *Educ:* Leyton County High Sch.; University Coll., London (BSc 1928; MSc 1936; DSc 1941; Fellow, 1971). Bayliss-Starling Scholar, University Coll. London, 1930–31; Commonwealth Fund Fellow, New York and Princeton Univs, 1931–33; Lectr in Biochemistry University Coll. London, 1933–37; Rockefeller Fellow, University of Uppsala, Sweden, 1935; MRC Fellow, Lister Inst., 1937–40; Reader in Chemical Biophysics, University of London, 1954–66. Vice-Chm., Swinburne-Woodford Assoc. for Welfare of Blind, 1982–94. Oliver Memorial Award for Blood Transfusion, 1957. *Publications:* (with M. E. Mackay) Separation of protein fractions from human plasma (MRC Special Report), 1954; papers on physical biochemistry and hæmatology, mostly in Biochemical Jl and Brit. Jl of Hæmatology. *Recreations:* music, gardening, bird watching. *Address:* 31 Woodside Road, Woodford Wells, Essex IG8 0TW. *T:* (020) 8504 4264.

Died 17 Jan. 2000.

KELLAND, Gilbert James, CBE 1978; QPM 1975; Assistant Commissioner (Crime), Metropolitan Police, 1977–84, retired; *b* 17 March 1924; *m* 1950, Edith Ellen Marshall; two *d*. *Educ:* Georgeham Church Sch.; Braunton Secondary Modern Sch.; National Police Coll. Served RN, Fleet Air Arm, 1942–46. Metropolitan Police, 1946–84: Police Coll. Jun. Comd (Insp.) Course, 1955, Sen. Comd Course, 1964; Chm., London Dist of Supts' Assoc. of England & Wales and Mem. Police Council of GB and of Police Adv. Bd, 1966–69; Pres., Supts' Assoc. of England & Wales, 1968; Ford (Dagenham Trust) Fellowship studying Fed. Law Enforcement in USA, 1969; Hon. Sec., London Reg. Assoc. of Chief Police Officers, 1971–77; Brit. rep., INTERPOL, 1977–84, and Mem. Exec. Cttee, 1978–81. Stated Cases: Kelland *v* de Frietas, 1961 and Kelland *v* Raymond, 1964. Member: Parole Bd, 1986–89; AAA Cttee of Enquiry into Drug Abuse, 1988. Chairman: Met. Pol. Athletic Club, 1964–84; UK Pol. Athletic Assoc. and Met. Pol. Athletic Assoc., 1977–84; Life Vice Pres., Pol. AA, and Hon. Life Mem., Met. Pol. AA, 1984. Freeman, City of London, 1983. *Publication:* Crime in London, 1986, 1987. *Recreations:* following athletics, walking, gardening, reading. *Address:* c/o Metropolitan Police Athletic Association, Wellington House, 67 Buckingham Gate, SW1E 6BE.

Died 30 Aug. 1997.

KELLER, Prof. Andrew, FRS 1972; Research Professor in Polymer Science, Department of Physics, University of Bristol, 1969–91, then Professor Emeritus; *b* 22 Aug. 1925; *s* of Imre Keller and Margit Klein; *m* 1951, Eva Bulhack (*d* 1997); one *s* one *d*. *Educ:* Budapest Univ. (BSc); Bristol Univ. (PhD). FInstP. Techn. Officer, ICI Ltd, Manchester, 1948–55; Bristol University: Min. of Supply res. appt, 1955–57; Res. Asst, 1957–63; Lectr, 1963–65; Reader, 1965–69. MAE 1994. High Polymer Prize, Amer. Phys. Soc., 1964; Swinburne Award, Plastics Inst., 1974; Max Born Medal, Inst. Physics and Deutsche Physik Gesellschaft, 1983; Rumford Medal, Royal Soc., 1994; Medal, Collège de France, 1994. *Publications:* numerous papers in Jl Polymer Science, Progress Reports in Physics, Proc. Royal Soc., Macromol. Chem., etc. *Recreations:* outdoor sports, mountain walking, ski-ing, travel, reading, opera, concerts. *Address:* 41 Westbury Road, Bristol BS9 3AU. *T:* (0117) 962 9767.

Died 7 Feb. 1999.

KELLER, René Jacques; Ambassador of Switzerland to Austria, 1976–79, retired; *b* 19 May 1914; *s* of Jacques Keller and Marie (*née* Geiser); *m* 1942, Marion (*née* Werder); one *s* two *d*. *Educ:* Geneva; Trinity Coll., Cambridge. Vice-Consul, Prague, 1941–45; 2nd Sec. of Legation, The Hague, 1947–50; 1st Sec., London, 1950–54; Head of News Dept, Berne, 1954–56; 1st Counsellor, Swiss Embassy, Paris, 1957–60; Ambassador to Ghana, Guinea, Liberia, Mali and Togo, 1960–62; Ambassador to Turkey, 1962–65; Head of Perm. Mission of Switzerland to Office of UN and Internat. Organisations, Geneva, 1966–68; Ambassador of Switzerland to UK, 1968–71; Head of Direction for International Organisation, Foreign Ministry of Switzerland, 1971–75. *Address:* 1 Promenade du Pin, 1204 Geneva, Switzerland.

Died 19 May 1997.

KELLY, Rev. Dr John Norman Davidson, FBA 1965; Principal of St Edmund Hall, Oxford, 1951–79, Honorary Fellow 1979; Vice-Chancellor, Oxford University, Sept.-Oct. 1966 (Pro-Vice-Chancellor, 1964–66, 1972–79); *b* 13 April 1909; *s* of John and Ann Davidson Kelly. *Educ:* privately; Glasgow Univ.; The Queen's Coll., Oxford (Ferguson Scholar; Hertford Scholar; 1st Cl. Hon. Mods, Greats and Theology; Hon. Fellow, 1963); St Stephen's House; DD Oxon 1951. Deacon, 1934; priest, 1935; Curate, St Lawrence's, Northampton, 1934; St Edmund Hall, Oxford: Chaplain, 1935; Vice-Principal and Trustee, 1937; Dean of Degrees, 1982–89; Oxford University: Speaker's Lectr in Biblical Studies, 1945–48; Lecturer in Patristic Studies, 1948–76. Select Preacher: Oxford, 1944–46, 1959, 1961, 1962; Cambridge, 1953; Chm. Cttee of Second Internat. Conf. on Patristic Studies, Oxford, 1955; Proctor in Convocation of Canterbury representing Oxford University, 1958–64; Chm. Archbishop's Commn on Roman Catholic Relations, 1964–68; accompanied Archbishop of Canterbury on his visit to Pope Paul VI, 1966; Mem., Academic Council, Ecumenical Theological Inst., Jerusalem, 1966–. In the War of 1939–45 did part-time work at Chatham House and collaborated in organizing the Oxford Leave Courses for United States, Allied, and Dominions Forces. Canon of Chichester and Prebendary of Wightring, 1948, Highleigh, 1964–93. Took lead in obtaining Royal Charter, new statutes and full collegiate status for St Edmund Hall, 1957. Mem. Governing Body: Royal Holloway Coll., London, 1959–69; King's Sch., Canterbury. Lectures: Paddock, General Theological Seminary, NY, 1963; Birkbeck, Cambridge, 1973; Hensley Henson, Oxford, 1979–80. Hon. DD: Glasgow, 1958; Wales, 1971. *Publications:* Early Christian Creeds, 1950, 3rd edn 1972; Rufinus, a Commentary on the Apostles' Creed, 1955; Early Christian Doctrines, 1958, 5th edn 1977; The Pastoral Epistles, 1963; The Athanasian Creed, 1964; The Epistles of Peter

and of Jude, 1969; Aspects of the Passion, 1970; Jerome, 1975; The Oxford Dictionary of Popes, 1986; St Edmund Hall: almost seven hundred years, 1989; Golden Mouth, 1995. *Recreations:* videos of films, chatting with young people. *Address:* 7 Crick Road, Oxford OX2 6QJ. *T:* (01865) 512907. *Clubs:* Athenæum; Vincent's (Oxford).
Died 31 March 1997.

KELLY, Sir William Theodore, (Sir Theo), Kt 1966; OBE 1958; JP; Chairman, Woolworths Ltd, Australia, 1963–80 (Managing Director, 1945–71), and its subsidiary and associated companies; Chairman: Woolworths (NZ) Ltd, 1963–79; Woolworths Properties Limited, 1963–80; retired 1980; *b* 27 June 1907; *s* of William Thomas Kelly and Lily Elizabeth (*née* Neely); *m* 1944, Nancy Margaret, *d* of W. E. Williams, NZ; two *s* two *d. Educ:* Sydney, NSW. War of 1939–45; RAAF, 1942–44, Wing Comdr. Chm., RAAF Canteen Services Bd, 1944–59. General Manager, 1932–45, Man. Dir, 1945–71, Woolworths Ltd (NZ) (Dir, 1934). Mem. Board, Reserve Bank of Australia, 1961–75; Dep. Chm., Australian Mutual Provident Soc., 1972–79 (Dir, 1967–79); Chm., Aust. Mutual Provident Fire and Gen. Insurance Pty Ltd, 1967–79. Life Governor, Royal Life Saving Soc.; Trustee, National Parks and Wildlife Foundn, 1969–. Mem. Board, Royal North Shore Hosp., 1969–77. Fellow, Univ. of Sydney Senate, 1968–75. JP NSW, 1946. *Recreations:* golf, boating. *Address:* 8/73 Yarranabbe Road, Darling Point, Sydney, NSW 2027, Australia. *Clubs:* Rotary, 18ft Sailing, White City Tennis (Sydney).
Died 19 Oct. 1998.

KEMBALL, Prof. Charles, CBE 1991; MA, ScD Cantab; FRS 1965; MRIA; FRSE; Professor of Chemistry, Edinburgh University, 1966–83 (Dean of the Faculty of Science, 1975–78; Fellow, 1983–88, Hon. Fellow, 1988–96; *b* 27 March 1923; *s* of late Charles Henry and Janet Kemball; *m* 1956, Kathleen Purvis, *o d* of late Dr and Mrs W. S. Lynd, Alsager, Cheshire; one *s* two *d. Educ:* Edinburgh Academy; Trinity Coll., Cambridge (Sen. Schol.). First Class Hons in Natural Sciences Tripos, Pt I, 1942, Pt II, 1943. Employed by Ministry of Aircraft Production in Dept of Colloid Science, University of Cambridge, 1943–46; Commonwealth Fund Fellow, Princeton Univ., 1946–47; Fellow of Trinity Coll., Cambridge, 1946–54 (Junior Bursar, 1949–51; Asst Lectr, 1951–54); Univ. Demonstrator in Physical Chemistry, 1951–54; Professor of Physical Chemistry, Queen's Univ., Belfast, 1954–66 (Dean of the Faculty of Science, 1957–60; Vice-Pres., 1962–65). President: RIC, 1974–76 (Vice-Pres., 1959–61); British Assoc. Section B (Chem.), 1976–77; RSE, 1988–91 (Vice-Pres., 1971–74, 1982–85); Vice-Pres., Faraday Soc., 1970–73; Chm., Publications Bd, Chem. Soc./RSC, 1973–81. Governor, East of Scotland Coll. of Agriculture, 1977–84. Hon. DSc: Heriot-Watt, 1980; QUB, 1983. Meldola Medal, Royal Inst. of Chemistry, 1951; Corday-Morgan Medal, 1958, Tilden Lectr, 1960, Surface and Colloid Chem. Award, 1972, Chemical Soc.; Ipatieff Prize, American Chemical Soc., 1962; Gunning Victoria Jubilee Prize, RSE, 1981; Award for Service to RSC, 1985. *Publications:* contributions to various scientific jls. *Recreations:* walking, gardening, genealogy. *Address:* 24 Main Street, Tyninghame, Dunbar, East Lothian EH42 1XL. *T:* (01620) 860710. *Clubs:* English-Speaking Union; New (Edinburgh).
Died 4 Sept. 1998.

KEMMER, Prof. Nicholas, DrPhil; FRS 1956; FRSE 1954; Tait Professor of Mathematical Physics, University of Edinburgh, 1953–79, then Professor Emeritus; *b* St Petersburg, 7 Dec. 1911; *o s* of late Nicholas P. Kemmer and Barbara Kemmer (*née* Stutzer; later Mrs Barbara Classen); *m* 1947, Margaret, *o d* of late George Wragg and Nellie (who *m* 2nd, C. Rodway); two *s* one *d. Educ:* Bismarckschule, Hannover; Universities of Göttingen and

Zürich. DrPhil Zürich, 1935; MA Cantab. Imperial College, London: Beit Scientific Research Fellow, 1936–38; Demonstrator, 1938; Fellow 1971. Mem. of UK Govt Atomic Energy Research teams in Cambridge and Montreal, 1940–46; University Lecturer in Mathematics, Cambridge, 1946–53 (Stokes Lecturer, 1950–53). Hon. FInstP 1988. Hughes Medal, Royal Society, 1966; J. Robert Oppenheimer Meml Prize, Univ. of Miami, 1975; Max Planck Medal, German Physical Soc., 1983; Gunning Victoria Jubilee Prize, RSE, 1985. *Publications:* The Theory of Space, Time and Gravitation, 1959 (trans. from the Russian of V. Fock, 1955); What is Relativity?, 1960 (trans from the Russian, What is the Theory of Relativity?, by Prof. L. D. Landau and Prof. G. B. Rumer, 1959); Vector Analysis, 1977; papers in scientific jls on theory of nuclear forces and elementary particles. *Address:* 35 Salisbury Road, Edinburgh EH16 5AA. *T:* (0131) 667 2893.
Died 21 Oct. 1998.

KEMP, Rear-Adm. Cuthbert Francis, CB 1967; Chief Service Manager, Westland Helicopters, 1968–69; *b* 15 Sept. 1913; *s* of A. E. Kemp, Willingdon; *m* 1947, Margaret Law, *d* of L. S. Law, New York; two *s. Educ:* Victoria Coll., Jersey. Joined RN, 1931; RNEC, 1936; served in HMS Ajax and Hood; Pilot, 1939; served War of 1939–45: carriers and air stations at home and abroad; Naval Staff, Washington, 1945–47; Fleet Engr Officer, E Indies, 1950–52; qual. Staff Coll., 1956; Admty, 1957–59; qual. Canadian Nat. Defence Coll., 1962; Supt RN Aircraft Yard, Belfast, 1962–65; ADC 1965; Rear-Adm., Engineering, Staff of Flag Officer, Naval Air Command, 1965, retd 1967. *Recreations:* cricket, gardening, shooting. *Address:* Beech House, Marston Magna, Som BA22 8DQ. *T:* (01935) 850563. *Club:* Army and Navy.
Died 27 Oct. 1999.

KEMP, Oliver, CMG 1969; OBE 1960; HM Diplomatic Service, retired 1970; *b* 12 Sept. 1916; *s* of Walter Kemp; *m* 1940, Henrietta Taylor, two *s. Educ:* Wakefield Grammar Sch.; Queen's Coll., Oxford. MA Oxon (Lit. Hum.), 1939. Served in HM Forces, 1939–45. Apptd Officer in HM Foreign Service, 1945; served in Moscow, Egypt, Indonesia, Yemen, Laos, Mongolia and Foreign Office; HM Chargé d'Affaires in Yemen, 1957–58; First Secretary and Head of Chancery in Laos, 1958–60; Ambassador to Togo (and Consul-General), 1962–64; Deputy Head of the United Kingdom Delegation to the European Communities, Luxembourg, 1964–67; Ambassador to Mongolia, 1967–68; FCO, 1968–70 and 1971–73 (European affairs). Dir, BSC Office, Brussels, 1973–81. *Recreations:* music, reading, gardening. *Address:* 16 The Oval, Scarborough, N Yorks YO11 3AP. *T:* (01723) 373354.
Died 2 Nov. 1996.

KEMPSTER, Hon. Michael Edmund Ivor, CBE 1993; a Justice of Appeal, Court of Appeal, Bermuda, since 1993; a Justice of Appeal, 1984–93, Vice-President, 1993, of the Supreme Court of Hong Kong (a Judge of the Supreme Court, 1982–84); *b* 21 June 1923; *s* of late Rev. Ivor T. Kempster, DSO; *m* 1949, Sheila, *d* of late Dr T. Chalmers, K-i-H, Inverness; two *s* two *d. Educ:* Mill Hill Sch.; Brasenose Coll., Oxford (Scholar, MA, BCL). Royal Signals, 1943–46; commissioned in India, served 14th Army. Called to Bar, Inner Temple, 1949; Profumo Prize; Bencher 1977. QC 1969; a Recorder of the Crown Court, 1972–81. Mem., Govt Cttee on Privacy, 1971. Comr, Supreme Court of Brunei, 1983–97; apptd to report to Gov. of Hong Kong on an incident in a Vietnamese Detention Centre, 1992; Comr to report to Gov. of Hong Kong on Witness Protection, 1993; Comr, Royal Court of Jersey, 1995–96. Chm., Court of Governors, Mill Hill School, 1979–86. FCIArb, 1982. *Recreations:* fishing, hare-hunting, travel. *Address:* 5 King's Bench Walk, Temple, EC4Y 7DN; Knapp House, Gillingham, Dorset

SP8 4NQ. *Clubs:* Travellers, Pilgrims; Hong Kong (Hong Kong). *Died 28 May 1998.*

KEMSLEY, 2nd Viscount *cr* 1945, of Dropmore, co. Bucks; **Geoffrey Lionel Berry;** DL; Bt 1928; Baron Kemsley 1936; *b* 29 June 1909; *e s* of 1st Viscount Kemsley, GBE and Mary Lilian (*d* 1928), *d* of Horace George Holmes; *S* father, 1968; *m* 1933, Lady Helen Hay, DStJ, *e d* of 11th Marquess of Tweeddale; four *d. Educ:* Marlborough; Magdalen Coll., Oxford. Served War of 1939–45: Capt. Grenadier Guards; invalided out of Army, 1942. MP (C) Buckingham Div. of Bucks, 1943–45. Dep. Chm., Kemsley Newspapers Ltd, 1938–59. Chm., St Andrew's Hospital, Northampton, 1973–84; Pres., Assoc. of Independent Hospitals, 1976–83. Mem. Chapter General, Order of St John; KStJ. Master of Spectacle Makers' Co., 1949–51, 1959–61. CC Northants, 1964–70. High Sheriff of Leicestershire, 1967, DL 1972. FRSA. *Heir: nephew* Richard Gomer Berry [*b* 17 April 1951; *m* 1981, Tana-Marie, *e d* of Clive Lester]. *Address:* Field House, Thorpe Lubenham, Market Harborough, Leics LE16 9TR. *T:* (01858) 462816. *Clubs:* Pratt's, Royal Over-Seas League. *Died 28 Feb. 1999.*

KENDALL, Prof. Henry Way, PhD; J. A. Stratton Professor of Physics, Massachusetts Institute of Technology, since 1991; *b* Boston, 9 Dec. 1926; *s* of Henry Kendall and Evelyn Way. *Educ:* Amherst Coll. (BA Maths 1950; Hon. ScD 1975); MIT (PhD Nuclear and Atomic Physics 1954). Nat. Sci. Foundn Postdoctoral Fellow, Brookhaven Nat. Lab. and MIT, 1954–56; Res. Associate, Lectr, Asst Prof., Physics Dept, Stanford Univ., 1956–61; Prof. of Physics, Physics Dept, MIT, 1967–91. Consultant: Dept of Defense, as Mem. Jason Gp, Inst. for Defense Analysis, 1960–71; classified Dept of Defense project, 1966–70; Dir and Founding Mem., Union for Concerned Scientists, 1969–, Chm., 1973–. Member: Jason Div., Inst. Defense Analysis, 1960–73; Subcttee on Nuclear Constants, Nat. Acad. Scis, 1961; Scientific Adv. Panel, Defense Communications Planning Gp, US Dept of Defense, 1966–70; Port of NY Authy Steering and Rev. Cttee NAS-PONYA Jamaica Bay Study, Nat. Acad. Scis, 1970–71; Energy Study Planning Cttee, APS, 1973–76; Public Participation Panel, Congressional Office of Technology Assessment, 1977; Director: Bulletin of Atomic Scientists, 1975–84; Arms Control Assoc., 1979–. Fellow: Amer. Acad. of Arts and Scis, 1982; APS, 1985; AAAS, 1988; Nat. Acad. Scis, 1992. Public Service Award, Fedn Amer. Scientists, 1976; (jtly) Leo Szilard Award, APS, 1981; Bertrand Russell Soc. Award, 1982; (jtly) W. K. H. Panofsky Prize, APS, 1989; (jtly) Nobel Prize in Physics, 1990; Envmtl Leadership Award, Tufts Univ., Lincoln Filene Center, 1991. *Publications:* (jtly) Nuclear Fuel Cycle: a survey of the public health environmental and national security effects of nuclear power, 1975; (with S. Nadis) Strategies: toward a solar future, 1980; (with S. Nadis and D. Ford) The Freeze, 1982; (jtly) Fallacy of Star Wars, 1985; (jtly) Crisis Stability and Nuclear War, 1988; numerous articles on nuclear power, nuclear safety and effects of nuclear war in Nuclear News, Environment, Trial, Bull. Atomic Scientists, Think, Scientific American, etc. *Address:* Room 24–514, Laboratory for Nuclear Sciences, Massachusetts Institute of Technology, Cambridge, MA 02139, USA. *Died 15 Feb. 1999.*

KENDALL, William Leslie, CBE 1983; Secretary General, Council of Civil Service Unions (formerly Civil Service National Whitley Council, Staff Side), 1976–83; *b* 10 March 1923; *m* 1943, Irene Canham; one *s* one *d.* Clerk, S Shields Insurance Cttee, 1937–41. RAF, 1941–46. Entered Civil Service, 1947; Civil Service Clerical Association: Asst Sec., 1952; Dep. Gen. Sec., 1963; Gen. Sec., CPSA (formerly CSCA), 1967–76. Sec., Civil Service Alliance, 1967; Governor, Ruskin Coll., 1967–76.

Member: CS Nat. Whitley Council (Chm. Staff Side, 1973–75); Advisory Council, Civil Service Coll., 1976–83; Civil Service Pay Bd, 1978–81; Vice Pres., Civil Service Council Further Educn, 1978–83. Member: Employment Appeal Tribunal, 1976–87; CS Appeal Bd, 1985–93; ACAS Indep. Panel on Teachers' Dispute, 1986–87. Dir, Civil Service Building Soc., 1980–87; Mem., Management Cttee, CS Housing Assoc., 1984–87; Trustee, CS Benevolent Fund, 1987–93. *Recreations:* reading, music, pottering. *Address:* 38 The Glade, Shirley, Croydon CR0 7QD. *T:* (020) 8654 8612.

Died 5 March 2000.

KENDREW, Sir John (Cowdery), Kt 1974; CBE 1963; ScD; FRS 1960; President of St John's College, Oxford, 1981–87, Hon. Fellow, since 1987; *b* 24 March 1917; *s* of late Wilfrid George Kendrew, MA, and Evelyn May Graham Sandberg. *Educ:* Dragon Sch., Oxford; Clifton Coll., Bristol; Trinity Coll., Cambridge (Hon. Fellow, 1972). Scholar of Trinity Coll., Cambridge, 1936; BA 1939; MA 1943; PhD 1949; ScD 1962. Min. of Aircraft Production, 1940–45; Hon. Wing Comdr, RAF, 1944. Fellow, Peterhouse, Cambridge, 1947–75 (Hon. Fellow, 1975); Dep. Chm., MRC Lab. for Molecular Biology, Cambridge, 1946–75; Dir Gen., European Molecular Biology Lab., 1975–82. Reader at Davy-Faraday Laboratory at Royal Instn, London, 1954–68. Mem., Council for Scientific Policy, 1965–72 (Dep. Chm., 1970–72); Sec.-Gen., European Molecular Biology Conf., 1970–74. Chm., Defence Scientific Adv. Council, 1971–74; Pres., British Assoc. for Advancement of Science, 1973–74; Trustee, British Museum, 1974–79. President: Internat. Union for Pure and Applied Biophysics, 1969–72; Confedn of Science and Technology Orgns for Develt, 1981–85; Sec. Gen, ICSU, 1974–80, first Vice-Pres., 1982–83, Pres., 1983–88, Past Pres., 1988–90; Trustee, Internat. Foundn for Science, 1975–78; Mem. Council, UN Univ., 1980–86, (Chm., 1983–85); Chm., Bd of Governors, Joint Research Centre, EEC, 1985–92. Hon. MRIA 1981; Hon. Member: American Soc. of Biological Chemists, 1962; British Biophysical Soc.; Chilean Acad. of Scis, 1992; Foreign Hon. Mem., Amer. Acad. of Arts and Sciences, 1964; Leopoldina Academy, 1965; Foreign Assoc., Amer. Nat. Acad. of Sciences, 1972; Hon. Fellow: Inst. of Biology, 1966; Weizmann Inst., 1970; Corresp. Mem., Heidelberg Acad. of Scis, 1978; Foreign Mem., Bulgarian Acad. of Scis, 1979; Foreign Fellow, Indian Nat. Science Acad., 1989. Lectures: Herbert Spencer, Univ. of Oxford, 1965; Crookshank, Faculty of Radiologists, 1967; Procter, Internat. Soc. of Leather Chemists, 1969; Fison Meml, Guy's Hosp., 1971; Mgr de Brún, Univ. Coll. of Galway, 1979; Saha Meml, Univ. of Calcutta, 1980. Hon. Prof., Univ. of Heidelberg, 1982. Hon. DSc: Univ. of Reading, 1968; Univ. of Keele, 1968; Exeter, 1982; Univ. of Buckingham, 1983; DUniv Stirling, 1974; Dr *honoris causa:* Pécs, Hungary, 1975; Madrid, 1987; Siena, 1991; Santiago, 1992. (Jointly) Nobel Prize for Chemistry, 1962; Royal Medal of Royal Society, 1965; William Procter Prize, Sigma xi, 1988. Order of Madara Horseman, 1st degree, Bulgaria, 1980. Editor in Chief, Jl of Molecular Biology, 1959–87. *Publications:* The Thread of Life, 1966; (Ed. in Chief) The Encyclopedia of Molecular Biology, 1994; scientific papers in Proceedings of Royal Society, etc. *Address:* The Old Guildhall, 4 Church Lane, Linton, Cambridge CB1 6JX. *T:* (01223) 891545. *Club:* Athenæum. *Died 23 Aug. 1997.*

KENNARD, Sir George Arnold Ford, 3rd Bt *cr* 1891, of Fernhill, co. Southampton; *b* 27 April 1915; *s* of Sir Coleridge Kennard, 1st Bt and his first wife, Dorothy Katharine, *o c* of Sir George Head, KCSI, KCMG; *S* brother, 1967; *m* 1st, 1940, Cecilia Violet Cokayne Maunsel (marr. diss. 1958); one *d*; 2nd, 1958, Jesse Rudd

Miskin (marr. diss. 1974), *d* of Hugh Wyllie; 3rd, 1985, Nichola (marr. diss. 1992), *o d* of late Peter Carew, Tiverton; 4th, 1992, Georgina Phillips, *er d* of Sir Harold Wernher, 3rd Bt, GCVO, TD. *Educ:* Eton. Commissioned 4th Queen's Own Hussars, 1939; served War of 1939–45 (despatches twice), Egypt, Greece (POW Greece); comd Regt, 1955–58; retired, 1958. Joined Cement Marketing Co., 1967, becoming Midland Representative; retired 1979. *Recreations:* hunting, shooting, fishing. *Publication:* Loopy (autobiog.), 1990. *Heir:* none. *Address:* 13 Burton Court, Franklin's Row, SW3 4TA. *Club:* Cavalry and Guards.   *Died 13 Dec. 1999 (ext).*

KENNEDY, David Matthew; American banker; formerly Special Representative of the First Presidency of The Church of Jesus Christ of Latter-day Saints; *b* Randolph, Utah, 21 July 1905; *s* of George Kennedy and Katherine Kennedy (*née* Johnson); *m* 1925, Lenora Bingham; four *d. Educ:* Weber Coll., Ogden, Utah (AB); George Washington Univ., Washington, DC (MA, LLB); Stonier Grad. Sch. of Banking, Rutgers Univ. (grad.). Special Asst to Chm. of Bd, Federal Reserve System, 1930–46; Vice-Pres. in charge of bond dept, Continental Illinois Bank and Trust Co., Chicago, 1946–53, full Vice-Pres., 1951, Pres., 1956–58, Chm. Bd and Chief Exec. Officer, 1959 (temp. resigned, Oct. 1953–Dec. 1954, to act as special Asst to Sec. of Treas., in Republican Admin.); after return to Continental Illinois Bank, still advised Treasury (also under Democrat Admin). Appointed by President Kennedy as incorporator and dir of Communication Satellite Corp.; Chm. of Commn (apptd by President Johnson) to improve drafting of Federal budget, 1967; Chm of Cttee (apptd by Mayor of Chicago) for Economic and Cultural Devel of Chicago, 1967. Again in Govt, when nominated to Nixon Cabinet, Dec. 1968; Secretary of the Treasury, 1969–70; Ambassador-at-large, USA, and Mem. President Nixon's Cabinet, 1970–73, US Ambassador to NATO, 1972. Director or Past Director of many corporations and companies including: Internat. Harvester Corp.; Abbott Laboratories; Swift & Co.; Pullman Co.; Nauvoo Restoration Inc.; Member of numerous organizations; Trustee: Univ. of Chicago; George Washington Univ.; Brookings Instn, etc. Held hon. doctorates. *Address:* 3793 Parkview Drive, Salt Lake City, UT 84124, USA. *Clubs:* Union League, Commercial Executives (Chicago); Old Elm Country (Fort Sheridan, Ill); Glenview Country, etc.   *Died 1 May 1996.*

KENNEDY, Horas Tristram, OBE 1966; HM Diplomatic Service, retired; *b* 29 May 1917; *s* of George Lawrence Kennedy and Mary Dow; *m* 1953, Maureen Beatrice Jeanne Holmes (formerly Stevens) (*d* 1976); three *d* (one *s* decd). *Educ:* Oundle; King's Coll., Cambridge. History and Mod Langs, MA. Entered HM Consular Service, 1939; Vice-Consul, Valparaiso, Chile, 1939–46; Foreign Office, 1946–48; 1st Secretary: Belgrade, 1949–52; Buenos Aires, 1952–56; Berne, 1956–61; Santiago de Chile, 1961–67; Commercial Counsellor, Warsaw, 1967–70; Consul-Gen., Barcelona, 1971–73. *Recreations:* country walking, painting, carpentry. *Address:* Borea Farm, Nancledra, Penzance, Cornwall TR20 8AY. *T:* (01736) 62722.   *Died 6 March 1997.*

KENNEDY, Kevin; Chairman, Text Systems Ltd, 1996–99; *b* 1 May 1937; *s* of John and Catherine Kennedy; *m* 1962, Ann Larkin; three *s. Educ:* Our Lady's High Sch., Motherwell. Dir and Gen. Man., Honeywell Information Systems Ltd, 1983–86; Group Man. Dir, Philips, 1986–89; Chm. and Sen. Man. Dir, Philips Information Systems, 1989–91; Chm. and Man. Dir, Philips Electronics and Associated Industries, 1991–93; Chm. and Chief Exec., Domestic Appliances and Personal Care Div., and Mem., Gp Management Cttee, 1993–96, Advr, Bd of Mgt, 1996–97, Philips Electronics NV. CIMgt; FInstD.

Freeman, City of London, 1988. *Recreations:* golf, music, classic cars. *Address:* 28 Holt Mansions, 96 Wyatt Drive, SW13 8AJ.   *Died 12 Sept. 2000.*

KENNY, Arthur William, CBE 1977; CChem, FRSC; Director in the Directorate General of Environmental Protection of the Department of the Environment, 1974–79; *b* 31 May 1918; *s* of Ernest James Kenny and Gladys Margaret Kenny; *m* 1947, Olive Edna West; one *s* two *d. Educ:* Canton High Sch., Cardiff; Jesus Coll., Oxford (schol.); BA 1st Cl. Hons Natural Sci., MA, BSc). Min. of Supply, 1941; Min. of Health, 1950; Min. of Housing and Local Govt, 1951; DoE, 1971. *Publications:* papers on disposal of radioactive and toxic wastes and on quality of drinking water. *Address:* 134 Manor Green Road, Epsom, Surrey KT19 8LL. *T:* (01372) 724850.   *Died 5 Oct. 1998.*

KENNY, Douglas Timothy, PhD; psychologist, educator; President and Vice Chancellor, University of British Columbia, 1975–83, President Emeritus, since 1989; *b* Victoria, BC, 20 Oct. 1923; *s* of John Ernest Kenny and Margaret Julia (*née* Collins); *m* 1st, 1950, Lucille Rabowski (decd); one *s* one *d*; 2nd, 1976, Margaret Lindsay Little. *Educ:* Victoria Coll.; Univ. of British Columbia (BA 1945, MA 1947); Univ. of Washington (PhD 1952). University of British Columbia: Lectr, 1950–54; Asst Prof., 1954–57; Associate Prof., 1957–64; Prof., 1965; Pres., Faculty Assoc., 1961–62; Head, Dept of Psychology, 1965–69; Acting Dean, Faculty of Arts, 1969–70, Dean, 1970–75; Hon. Pres., Alumni Assoc., 1975–83. Vis. Associate Prof., Harvard Univ., 1963–65. Member, Internat. Assoc. of Univ. Presidents, 1975–83; Social Science and Humanities Res. Council, 1978–83; BC Res. Council, 1975; Canada Council, 1975–78; Monterey Inst. of Internat. Studies, 1980–83; Discovery Foundn, BC, 1979–83; Amer. Psychol Assoc.; Amer. Psychol Soc.; Bd of Trustees, Vancouver Gen. Hosp., 1976–78; Bd of Governors, Arts, Sciences and Technol. Centre, Vancouver, 1980 (Founder Mem.); President: BC Psychol Assoc., 1951–52; Vancouver Inst., 1973–75 (Hon. Pres., 1975–83). Hon. Patron, Internat. Foundn of Learning, 1983–. Hon. LLD Univ. of BC, 1983. Park O. Davidson Meml Award for outstanding contribn to develt of psychol., 1984. Silver Jubilee Medal, 1977. *Publications:* articles in professional jls. *Address:* 401–2128 West 43rd Avenue, Vancouver, BC V6M 2E1, Canada. *Clubs:* Vancouver, University, Faculty (Vancouver).   *Died 4 June 1996.*

KENNY, Michael, RA 1986 (ARA 1976); FRBS 1992; RWA 1998; sculptor; Principal, City and Guilds of London Art School, since 1995; *b* 10 June 1941; *s* of James Kenny and Helen (*née* Gordon); *m* 1968, Rosemary Flood (marr. diss. 1988); one *s* one *d*, and one step *d*; *m* Angela Helen (*née* Smith) (marr. diss. 1992); *m* 1993, Susan (*née* Rowland). *Educ:* St Francis Xavier's Coll., Liverpool; Liverpool Coll. of Art, Slade Sch. of Fine Art (DFA London). Works in public collections of: Arts Council; V&A; British Council; British Museum; Borough of Camden; Contemporary Arts Soc.; Tate Gall.; Leicestershire Education Cttee; North West Arts Assoc.; Wilhelm Lehmbruck Museum, Duisburg; Staatsgalerie, Stuttgart; Unilever Collection, London; Hara Mus. of Contemporary Tokyo; Leeds City Art Gall.; Hat Hill Sculpture Foundn, Goodwood; Walker Art Gall.; Dulwich Gall.; Nat. Gall., Bucharest; public works sited at: Lumsden, Aberdeenshire; Addenbrooke's Hosp., Cambridge; Le Parc de la Courneuve, St Denis, Paris; Yokohama Business Park, Yokohama; Prittlewell Sch., Southend, 1994; P&O Liner Oriana, 1995; Nene Coll., Northampton, 1997; Central Park, Gothenburg, Sweden, 1998; public commissioned work: Muraoka-cho, Japan, 1992; London Docklands, 1993; works in private collections in England, Europe, Japan and America. Numerous one-man and mixed exhibitions in GB, Europe, S America, Canada, Japan, Australia and USA. Chairman, Faculty of Sculpture, British School at Rome, 1982–87; Hd of Fine Art Dept, later Dir of Fine Art Studies, Goldsmiths' Coll., Univ. of London, 1983–88. Treas. and Trustee, Royal Acad., 1995–. *Relevant publications:* Contemporary Artists, 1977, 4th edn 1996; Contemporary British Artists, 1979; British Art in 20th Century, 1991; Peter Davies, Michael Kenny (monograph), 1997; exhibition catalogues. *Recreations:* ornithology, physics, cosmology. *Address:* 71 Stepney Green, E1 3LE. *Club:* Chelsea Arts. *Died 28 Dec. 1999.*

KENT, Arthur William, CMG 1966; OBE 1950; Chairman, United Transport Overseas Ltd, 1980–82 (Deputy Chairman, 1978–80; Joint Managing Director, 1977–80); Managing Director, United Transport Co., 1980–82; *b* 22 March 1913; *s* of Howard and Eliza Kent; *m* 1st, 1944, Doris Jane (*née* Crowe) (marr. diss. 1958); one *s* one *d*; 2nd, 1958, Mary (*née* Martin). Deputy City Treasurer, Nairobi, 1946–48, City Treasurer, 1948–65; Chief Executive: United Transport Overseas Ltd, Nairobi, 1966–69; Transport Holdings of Zambia Ltd, 1969–71; United Transport Holdings (Pty) Ltd, Johannesburg, 1971–76; Dir of a number of cos owned by United Transport Overseas Ltd and other BET cos. IPFA; FCA; FCIT. *Address:* Muthaiga, Beechwood Road, Combe Down, Bath, Avon BA2 5JS. *T:* (01225) 834940. *Died 7 Sept. 1998.*

KENT, Sir Harold Simcox, GCB 1963 (KCB 1954; CB 1946); QC 1973; Commissary to Dean and Chapter of St Paul's Cathedral, since 1976; *b* 11 Nov. 1903; *s* of late P. H. B. Kent, OBE, MC and Anna Mary, *y d* of Rev. Henry Kingdon Simcox, formerly Rector of Ewelme, Oxfordshire; *m* 1930, Zillah Lloyd (*d* 1987); one *s* (one *d* decd). *Educ:* Rugby School; Merton Coll., Oxford. Barrister-at-law, Inner Temple, 1928; Parliamentary Counsel to the Treasury, 1940–53; HM Procurator-General and Treasury Solicitor, 1953–63; Solicitor to Vassall Tribunal, 1963; Mem., Security Commn, 1965–71; Standing Counsel to Church Assembly and General Synod, 1964–72; Vicar-General of the Province of Canterbury, 1971–76; Dean of the Arches Court of Canterbury and Auditor of the Chancery Court of York, 1972–76. Mem., Departmental Cttee to examine operation of Section 2 of Official Secrets Act, 1911, 1971–72. DCL Lambeth, 1977. *Publication:* In On the Act, 1979. *Address:* Alderley, Calf Lane, Chipping Campden, Glos GL55 6JQ. *T:* (01386) 840421. *Club:* United Oxford & Cambridge University. *Died 4 Dec. 1998.*

KENT, John Philip Cozens, PhD; FSA; FMA; FBA 1986; Keeper, Department of Coins and Medals, British Museum, 1983–90; *b* 28 Sept. 1928; *s* of late John Cozens Kent, DCM and Lucy Ella Kent; *m* 1961, Patricia Eleanor Bunford; one *s* one *d*. *Educ:* Minchenden County Grammar Sch.; University Coll. London (BA 1949; PhD 1951). FSA 1961; FMA 1988. Nat. Service, 1951–53. Asst Keeper, 1953, Dep. Keeper, 1974, Dept of Coins and Medals, BM. Hon. Lectr in Numismatics, Birmingham Univ., 1993–99. President: British Assoc. of Numismatic Socs, 1974–78; Royal Numismatic Soc., 1984–89; London and Middlesex Archaeological Soc., 1985–88. Member: Instituto de Sintra, 1986; Internat. Numismatic Commn, 1986–91 (Hon. Mem., 1991). Medallist: RNS, 1990; Amer. Numismatic Soc., 1994; Derek Allen Prize, British Acad., 1996. *Publications:* (jtly) Late Roman Bronze Coinage, 1960; (with K. S. Painter) Wealth of the Roman World, 1977; Roman Coins, 1978; 2000 Years of British Coins and Medals, 1978 (Lhotka Meml Prize, RNS); (ed) Roman Imperial Coinage: vol. VIII, the family of Constantine I 337–364, 1981; vol. X, the divided Empire

and the fall of the western parts 395–491, 1994; A Selection of Byzantine Coins in the Barber Institute of Fine Arts, 1985; (ed with M. R. Mays) Catalogue of the Celtic Coins in the British Museum, vol. I, 1987, vol. II, 1990; contribs to Festschriften, congress procs, and Numismatic Chronicle, British Numismatic Jl etc. *Recreations:* local history and archaeology, early (mediaeval) music, railway history and model railways, monumental brasses. *Address:* 16 Newmans Way, Hadley Wood, Barnet, Herts EN4 0LR. *T:* (020) 8449 8072. *Died 22 Oct. 2000.*

KENT, Ronald Clive, CB 1965; Deputy Under-Secretary of State, Ministry of Defence, 1967–76; *b* 3 Aug. 1916; *s* of Dr Hugh Braund Kent and Margaret Mary Kent; *m* 1965, Mary Moyles Havell; one step *d* (one step *s* decd). *Educ:* Rugby Sch.; Brasenose Coll. Air Ministry, 1939; Royal Artillery, 1940–45; Air Ministry, 1945–58; Asst Under-Sec. of State, Air Min., 1958–63, MoD, 1963–67. Dir (Admin), ICE, 1976–79, Consultant and Council Sec., 1980–85. *Address:* 21 Heathside Court, Tadworth Street, Tadworth, Surrey KT20 5RY. *Died 9 Jan. 2000.*

KENT, Brig. Sidney Harcourt, OBE 1944; *b* 22 April 1915; *s* of Major Geoffrey Harcourt Kent, Hindhead; *m* 1945, Nina Ruth, *d* of Gen. Sir Geoffry Scoones, KCB, KBE, CSI, DSO, MC; one *s* one *d*. *Educ:* Wellington Coll.; RMC Sandhurst. 2nd Lieut KOYLI, 1935; Lt-Col 1944; Brig. 1944; GSO1 Eighth Army, 1944; BGS Allied Land Forces, SE Asia, 1944. Comd 128 Inf. Bde (TA), 1960–63. Manager and Sec., Turf Board, 1965; Gen. Manager, 1969, Chief Executive, 1973–76, The Jockey Club; Racing Adviser, Royal Horse Soc., Iran, 1978; Consultant Steward, Jamaica Racing Commn, 1984–86; Dir of Racing, 1989–91, Racing consultant, 1991–92, Macau Jockey Club. *Recreations:* farming, travel. *Address:* The Old Vicarage, Kingsey, Aylesbury, Bucks HP17 8LT. *T:* (01844) 291411. *Died 15 Aug. 1999.*

KENWORTHY, Cecil; Registrar of Family Division (formerly Probate and Divorce Division), High Court of Justice, 1968–83; *b* 22 Jan. 1918; *s* of John T. and Lucy Kenworthy; *m* 1944, Beryl Joan Willis; no *c*. *Educ:* Manchester and Bristol Grammar Schools. Entered Principal Probate Registry, 1936. *Publications:* (co-ed) supplements to Rayden on Divorce, 1967, 1968; (co-ed) Tolstoy on Divorce, 7th edn 1971. *Address:* Gable Lodge, 2 Zetland Road, Malvern, Worcs WR14 2JJ. *Died 28 Feb. 2000.*

KENYON, Prof. John Philipps, FBA 1981; Joyce and Elizabeth Hall Distinguished Professor in Early Modern British History, University of Kansas, 1987–94, then Professor Emeritus; *b* 18 June 1927; *s* of William Houston Kenyon and Edna Grace Philipps; *m* 1962, Angela Jane Ewert (*née* Venables); one *s* two *d*. *Educ:* King Edward VII Sch., Sheffield; Univ. of Sheffield (BA 1948; Hon. LittD 1980); Christ's Coll., Cambridge (PhD). Fellow of Christ's Coll., Cambridge, 1954–62; Lectr in Hist., Cambridge, 1955–62; Junior Proctor, Cambridge, 1961–62; G. F. Grant Prof. of History, Univ. of Hull, 1962–81; Prof. of Modern History, Univ. of St Andrews, 1981–87. Visiting Prof., Columbia Univ., New York, 1959–60; John U. Nef Lectr, Univ. of Chicago, 1972; Ford's Lectr in English Hist., Oxford, 1975–76; Andrew W. Mellon Fellow, Huntington Library, Calif, 1985. *Publications:* Robert Spencer Earl of Sunderland, 1958; The Stuarts, 1958, 2nd edn 1970; The Stuart Constitution, 1966, 2nd edn 1986; The Popish Plot, 1972; Revolution Principles, 1977, 2nd edn 1990; Stuart England, 1978, 2nd edn 1985; The History Men, 1983, 2nd edn 1993; The Civil Wars of England, 1988; contribs to various learned jls. *Recreation:* bridge. *Address:* Breck House, Church

Lane, Mattishall Burgh, Dereham, Norfolk NR20 3QZ. *T:* Mattishall (01362) 858364. *Died 6 Jan. 1996.*

KEOHANE, Dr Kevin William, CBE 1976; Rector, Roehampton Institute of Higher Education, 1976–88, Hon. Fellow, 1988; *b* 28 Feb. 1923; *s* of William Patrick and Mabel Margaret Keohane; *m* 1949, Mary Margaret (Patricia) Ashford; one *s* three *d*. *Educ:* Borden Grammar Sch., Sittingbourne, Kent; Univ. of Bristol (BSc; PhD). FInstP. War service, RAF, Radar Br, Flt Lt. Research appts and Lectr in Anatomy, Univ. of Bristol, 1947–59; Chelsea College, London: Reader in Biophysics, 1959; Prof. of Physics and Head of Dept of Physics, 1965; Prof. of Science Educn and Dir, Centre for Science Educn, 1967–76; Vice-Principal, 1966–76. Royal Society Leverhulme Prof., Fed. Univ. of Bahia, Brazil, 1971; Visiting Professor: Chelsea College, 1977–82; KCL, 1989; Vis. Prof. of Science Educn, KCL, 1990–. Member: Academic Adv. Cttee, Open Univ., 1970–81 (Chm., 1978–81); Court, Univ. of Bristol, 1968–76; Court, 1982–92, Council, 1988–92, Univ. of Surrey; Court, Brunel Univ., 1993–; University of London: Member: Academic Council, 1974–76; Extra-Mural Council, 1974–76; School Examinations Council, 1975–76. Dir, Nuffield Foundn Science Projects, 1966–79; Chairman: DES Study Gp on Cert. of Extended Educn, 1978 79; Education Cttee, Commonwealth Inst., 1978–85; Nuffield-Chelsea Curriculum Trust, 1979–; Southwark Archdiocesan Educn Cttee, 1989–; Vice Chm., Internat. Adv. Panel for Provincial Univs in China, 1986–92; Member: Nat. Programme Cttee for Computers in Educn, 1974–78; Royal Society/Inst. of Physics Educn Cttee, 1970–73; SSRC Educn Bd, 1971–74, BBC Further Educn Adv. Cttee, 1972–75; TEAC, RAF, 1977–79; Gen. Optical Council, 1979 84; Bd of Educn, Royal Coll. of Nursing, 1980–84; National Adv. Bd for Higher Educn, 1983–86; Froebel Council, 1992–95; Merton Educn Authy, 1986–90; Richmond, Twickenham and Rochampton DHA, 1987 90. Dir, Taylor & Francis, Scientific Pubns, 1972– (Vice-Chm., 1978–93). Manager, Royal Instn, 1972–75. Mem. Delegacy, Goldsmiths' Coll., 1974–76; Chairman of Governors: Garnett Coll., 1974–78; St Francis Xavier VIth Form Coll., 1985–95; Governor: Philippa Fawcett and Digby Stuart Colls, 1973–76; Ursuline Convent Sch., Wimbledon, 1967–; Heythrop Coll., Univ. of London, 1977–86; Wimbledon Coll., 1982–; Commonwealth Inst., 1977–85; W London Inst. of Higher Educn, 1990–94. Numerous overseas consultancies and visiting professorships; Academic Mem., British Assoc. of Science Writers, 1971–94; Editor, Jl of Physics Educn, 1966–69; Mem., Editorial Bd, Jl Curriculum Studies, and Studies in Sci. Educn. DUniv Surrey, 1987. Bragg Medal, Inst. of Physics, 1991. KCSG 1994 (KSG 1983). *Recreations:* Rugby (spectator), railways, bee-keeping. *Address:* 3 Thetford Road, New Malden, Surrey KT3 5DN. *T:* 0181–942 6861. *Club:* Athenæum.

Died 13 April 1996.

KERLE, Rt Rev. Ronald Clive; Rector of St Swithun's, Pymble, Diocese of Sydney, 1976–82; *b* 28 Dec. 1915; *s* of William Alfred Ronald Kerle and Isabel Ada (*née* Turner); *m* 1940, Helen Marshall Jackson; one *s* one *d*. *Educ:* Univ. of Sydney (BA 1942); Moore Theological Coll., Sydney; Sydney ACT (ThL 1937). Deacon, 1939; priest, 1940; Curate: St Paul's, Sydney, 1939; St Anne, Ryde, 1939–41; Rector: Kangaroo Valley, 1941–43; St Stephen, Port Kembla, 1943–47; Chaplain, AIF, 1945–47; Gen. Sec., NSW Branch, Church Missionary Society, 1947–54; Rector of Summer Hill, 1954–56; Archdeacon of Cumberland, 1954–60; Bishop Co-adjutor of Sydney, 1956–65; Bishop of Armidale, 1965–76. *Address:* Gowrie Retirement Village, 10 Edward Street, Gordon, NSW 2072, Australia. *Died 5 April 1997.*

KERR, Desmond Moore, OBE 1970; HM Diplomatic Service, retired; *b* 23 Jan. 1930; *s* of late Robert John Kerr and Mary Elizabeth Kerr; *m* 1956, Evelyn Patricia South; one *s* two *d*. *Educ:* Methodist Coll., Belfast; Queen's Univ., Belfast (BA Hons Classics and Ancient History). CRO, 1952; British High Commn, Karachi, 1956–59, Lagos, 1959–62; Second Sec., 1960; Commonwealth Office, 1962–66; First Sec., 1965; Dep. British Govt Rep., West Indies Associated States, 1966–70; FCO, 1970–76; Dep. High Comr, Dacca, 1976–79; High Comr, Swaziland, 1979–83; Head of Claims Dept, FCO, 1983–87. Mem. Exec. Council, CS Pensioners' Alliance, 1991–96 (Vice-Chm., 1996–98). *Address:* c/o Foreign and Commonwealth Office, SW1A 2AH.

Died 27 Sept. 1998.

KERR, Donald Frederick, CVO 1961; OBE 1960; Manager, Government Press Centre, Foreign and Commonwealth Office, 1976–77, retired; *b* 20 April 1915; *s* of Dr David Kerr, Cheshire; *m* 1942, Elizabeth Hayward (*d* 1978); two *s* one *d*. *Educ:* Sydney High Sch.; University of Sydney (BEcon). Served RAF (Navigator), SEAC, 1942–46. Deputy Director: British Information Services, New Delhi, 1947–53; UK Information Service, Ottawa, 1953–55; UK Information Service, Toronto, 1955–56; Dir, UK Information Service in Canada, Ottawa, 1956–59; Dir, British Information Services in India, New Delhi, 1959–63; Controller (Overseas), COI, 1963–76; on secondment, Dir of Information, Commonwealth Secretariat, 1969–70. *Recreation:* surviving. *Address:* 4 Southdown House, 11 Lansdowne Road, Wimbledon, SW20 8AN. *Died 9 Oct. 1997.*

KERSHAW, Prof. William Edgar, CMG 1971; VRD; Professor of Biology, University of Salford, 1966–76, then Emeritus Professor; *b* 9 Feb. 1911, *m* 1st, 1941, Mary Alexa Clayton Cowell, MD (marr. diss.); one *s* one *d*; 2nd, 1961, Lois Freeland. *Educ:* Stand Grammar Sch., Manchester; Manchester University. MB, ChB 1935; MRCS, LRCP 1936; DTM&H 1946; MD 1949; DSc 1956. FIBiol; FIFM. Surgeon Captain, RNR. Formerly: Demonstrator in Morbid Anatomy, Manchester Univ.; Leverhulme Senior Lectr in Med. Parasitology, Liverpool Sch. of Trop. Med. and Liverpool Univ.; Walter Myers and Everett Dutton Prof. of Parasitology and Entomology, Liverpool Univ., 1958–66. Hon. Lectr, Dept of Bacteriology, Univ. of Manchester, 1977–96. Scientific Advisor: Ribble Fisheries Assoc.; Humane Res. Trust; formerly Advr in Tropical Medicine, Manchester AHA; Hon. MO, Manchester, Salford and Liverpool Univs Naval Units; formerly: Cons. in Parasitology, WHO; Cons. to UN Envmt Prog., SE Asia; Chm., Tsetse Fly and Trypanosomiasis Cttee, ODM; Mem., Tropical Medicine Res. Bd, MRC (Chm., Helminthiasis Cttee). Vice-Pres., RSTM&H (Chalmers Meml Gold Medal, 1955); Hon. Fellow, British Soc. of Parasitology. Non-exec. Chm., Mayor's Boatyard, Tarlton. Vice-Chm., W Lancs Victims Support; Mem., Dunkirk Veterans' Assoc. Hon. Freeman, City of Rangoon, 1961. *Recreation:* work. *Address:* Mill Farm, Hesketh Bank, Preston PR4 6RA. *T:* (01772) 814299. *Clubs:* East India, Naval.

Died 20 March 1998.

KERSS, William; Chief Executive, National Grid Company plc, 1990–94; *b* 8 March 1931; *s* of William Kerss and Josephine Kerss (*née* Rankin); *m* 1959, Amy Murrey; two *d*. *Educ:* Durham Univ. (BSc Hons Elec. Eng). Student apprentice, NE Electricity Bd, 1948–53; power stations, research, planning and ops, transmission system design, system ops, CEGB, 1957–77; management appts, CEGB, 1963–77; Chief Engineer, SE Electricity Bd, 1977–83; Dep. Chm., S Wales Electricity Bd, 1983–88. Chm., Cegelec Controls plc, 1994–. *Recreations:* golf, gardening.

Address: Veddw Farm, Devauden, Gwent NP6 6PH. *T:* (01291) 650321. *Died 18 Dec. 1997.*

KESTELMAN, Morris, RA 1996; RWA 1976; *b* 5 Oct. 1905; *s* of Joseph and Sarah Kestelman; *m* 1935, Dorothy Mary Creagh (decd); one *d. Educ:* Central Sch. of Art and Design; Royal Coll. of Art. Part-time teaching, 1929–: various London schs of art, 1930–51; Head of Fine Art, CSAD, 1951–71. Designer of theatre décor: Old Vic Seasons, 1944–47; Sadler's Wells Opera; designs and paintings for two pavilions, Fest. of Britain, 1951. Mem., London Gp, 1948–. *Address:* 74B Belsize Park Gardens, NW3 4NG. *T:* (0171) 722 0569. *Club:* Chelsea Arts. *Died 15 June 1998.*

KETTLE, Roy Henry Richard; Group Deputy Chairman, Evered Bardon plc, 1991; retired 1993; *b* 2 May 1924; *s* of Arthur Charles Edwin and Emily Grace Kettle; *m* 1956, Jean Croudace; one *s* three *d. Educ:* Wolverhampton Grammar School. Tarmac Roadstone Ltd: Accountancy Asst, 1947; Management Acct, 1960; Chief Management Acct, 1964; Dir of Admin, 1967; Man. Dir, 1976; Tarmac plc: Dir, 1977; Gp Man. Dir, 1982–86, retd. Chm., CI Gp plc (formerly Cooper Industries), 1985–89; Dir, Evered Hldgs, subseq. Evered Bardon, 1985–91; Chief Exec., Evered Hldgs, 1989–91; Dir, London and Northern Gp, 1987–91. Mem., Black Country Develt Corp., 1987–92. *Recreations:* walking, gardening. *Address:* Hilbre, Watling Street South, Church Stretton, Shropshire SY6 7BG. *T:* Church Stretton (01694) 722445. *Died 14 June 1996.*

KEYS, Sir (Alexander George) William, AC 1988; Kt 1980; OBE 1969; MC 1951; Director, Australian Overseas Resources (formerly Australian Overseas Mining), since 1978; Chairman, Now Financial Services Pty Ltd; *b* 2 Feb. 1923; *s* of John Alexander Binnie Keys and Irene Daisy Keys; *m* 1950, Dulcie Beryl (*née* Stinton); three *d. Educ:* Hurlstone Agricultural High Sch. Nuffield Schol., 1956; Churchill Fellow, 1969. National Sec., 1961–78, National Pres., 1978–88, RSL (Life Member); Nat. President, Korea and SE Asia Forces Assoc. of Australia, 1964–90; World Pres., Internat. Fedn of Korean War Veterans Assoc., 1978–; Member: Fed. Govt adv. cttees; Council, Aust. War Memorial, 1975–94. Korean Order of National Security Merit, 1980. *Publication:* Flowers In Winter, 1995. *Address:* Glenlee, Post Office Box 455, Queanbeyan, NSW 2620, Australia. *T:* (home) (2) 62975440; (office) (2) 62844240. *Clubs:* Commonwealth, National Press (Canberra); Returned Services League (Queanbeyan). *Died 3 May 2000.*

KIDMAN, Thomas Walter, ERD 1954; Regional Administrator, East Anglian Regional Health Authority, 1973–75, retired; *b* 28 Aug. 1915; *s* of Walter James Kidman and Elizabeth Alice Kidman (*née* Littlejohns); *m* 1939, Lilian Rose Souton (*d* 1988); one *s* two *d. Educ:* Cambridge Central Sch.; Cambs Techn. Coll. FHSM, 1972–88. War service, 1939–46: Warrant Officer, RAMC, BEF France, 1940; Major, Suffolk Regt, seconded Corps of Mil. Police, MEF Egypt and Palestine, 1943–46; served in TA/AER, 1939–67. Local Govt Officer, Health and Educn, Cambridgeshire CC, 1930–48; East Anglian Regional Hospital Board: Admin. Officer, 1948; Asst Sec., 1952; Dep. Sec., 1957; Sec. of Bd, 1972. Mem., NHS Advisory Service, 1976–83; Chm., Cambs Mental Welfare Assoc., 1977–86. *Recreations:* photography, walking, gardening, swimming. *Address:* Alwoodley, 225 Arbury Road, Cambridge CB4 2JJ. *T:* Cambridge (01223) 357384. *Died 29 Feb. 1996.*

KILÉNYI, Edward A.; Adjunct Professor of Music, Florida State University, since 1982 (Professor of Music, 1953–82); *b* 7 May 1911; *s* of Edward Kilényi and Ethel Frater; *m* 1945, Kathleen Mary Jones (*d* 1986); two *d.*

Educ: Budapest; from childhood studied piano with Ernö Dohnányi; theory and conducting, Royal Academy of Music. First concert tour with Dohnányi (Schubert Centenary Festivals), 1928; concert tours, recitals, and soloist with Principal Symphony Orchestras, 1930–39, in Holland, Germany, Hungary, Roumania, France, Scandinavia, North Africa, Portugal, Belgium; English debut, 1935, with Sir Thomas Beecham in Liverpool, Manchester, London; tours, 1940–42, and 1946–, US, Canada, Cuba. Pathé, Columbia and Remington records internationally distributed; original Pathé recordings re-issued on CD, 1995. Hon. Mem., Franz Liszt Soc., Hungary, 1987. Liszt Commemorative Medal awarded by Hungarian Govt, 1986; named Florida Ambassador of the Arts by Sec. of State for Florida, 1990. Served War of 1939–45, Capt. US Army, European theatre of operations. *Address:* 2206 Ellicott Drive, Tallahassee, FL 32312, USA. *Died 6 Jan. 2000.*

KILLANIN, 3rd Baron *cr* 1900, of Galway, co. Galway; **Michael Morris,** MBE 1945; TD 1945; Bt 1885; author, film producer; President, International Olympic Committee, 1972–80, then Honorary Life President; *b* 30 July 1914; *o s* of late Lt-Col Hon. George Henry Morris, Irish Guards (2nd *s* of 1st Baron), and Dora Maryan (who *m* 2nd, 1918, Lt-Col Gerard Tharp, Rifle Brigade (*d* 1934)), *d* of late James Wesley Hall, Mount Morgan and Melbourne, Australia; *S* uncle, 1927; *m* 1945, Mary Sheila Cathcart (MBE 1946), *o d* of late Rev. Canon Douglas L. C. Dunlop, MA, Kilcummin, Galway; three *s* one *d. Educ:* Eton; Sorbonne, Paris; Magdalene Coll., Cambridge (BA 1935; MA 1939). Formerly on Editorial Staff, Daily Express; Daily Mail, 1935–39; Special Daily Mail War Correspondent, Japanese-Chinese War, 1937–38; Political Columnist, Sunday Dispatch, 1938–39. Served War of 1939–45 (MBE, TD), KRRC (Queen's Westminsters); Brigade Maj. 30 Armd Bde, 1943–45. Past Director: Chubb (Ireland) Ltd (Chm.); Northern Telecom (Ireland) Ltd (Chm.); Gallahers (Dublin) Ltd (Chm.); Irish Shell Ltd; Hibernian Life Association Ltd (Chm.); Ulster Investment Bank (Chm.); Lombard & Ulster Banking Ireland Ltd (Chm.); Dir, Syntex Ireland Ltd. International Olympic Committee: Mem., 1952; Mem., Exec. Bd, 1967; Vice-Pres., 1968–72; President: Olympic Council of Ireland, 1950–73; Incorporated Sales Managers' Association (Ireland), 1955–58; Galway Chamber of Commerce, 1952–53; Chm. of the Dublin Theatre Festival, 1958–70. Mem., Irish Govt Commn on Film Industry, 1957; Chairman: Irish Govt Commn on Thoroughbred Horse Breeding, 1982; Nat. Heritage Council, 1988–. Member: Council, Irish Red Cross Soc., 1947–72; Cttee, RNLI (a Life Vice-Pres.); Cultural Adv. Cttee to Minister for External Affairs, 1947–72; Nat. Monuments of Ireland Advisory Council, 1947–80 (Chm., 1961–65); RIA, 1952; Irish Nat. Sports Council, 1970–72; Irish Turf Club (Steward 1971–73, 1981–83); Irish National Hunt Steeplechase Cttee; first President, Irish Club, London, 1947–65; Hon. Life Mem., Royal Dublin Soc., 1982; Trustee, Irish Sailors and Soldiers Land Trust, 1955. Fellow, Irish Management Inst., 1987. Hon. LLD NUI, 1975; Hon. DLitt New Univ. of Ulster, 1977. Mem., French Acad. of Sport, 1974. Knight of Honour and Devotion, SMO, Malta, 1943; Comdr, Order of Olympic Merit (Finland), 1952; Star of Solidarity 1st Class (Italy), 1957; Comdr, Order of the Grimaldis (Monaco), 1961; Medal, Miroslav Tyrš (Czechoslovakia), 1970; Commander, Order of Merit (German Federal Republic), 1972; Star of the Sacred Treasure (Japan), 1972; Order of the Madara Rider (Bulgaria), 1973; Grand Officer, Order of Merit of Rep. of Italy, 1973; Grand Cross, Order of Civil Merit (Spain), 1976; Grand Officer, Order of Republic (Tunis), 1976; Grand Officer, Order of the Phoenix of Greece, 1976; Commander, Order of Sports

Merit (Ivory Coast), 1977; Chevalier, Order of Duarte Sanchez y Mella (Dominican Rep.), 1977; Commander's Order of Merit with Star (Poland), 1979; Comdr, Legion of Honour (France), 1980; Olympic Order of Merit (gold), 1980; Yugo Slav Flag with ribbon, 1984; Commander, Order of Merit (Congo), 1978; decorations from Austria, Brazil, China, Columbia, USSR etc. *Films:* The Quiet Man (with John Ford); The Rising of the Moon; Gideon's Day; Young Cassidy; Playboy of the Western World; Alfred the Great; Connemara and its Pony (scriptwriter). *Publications:* Four Days (ed and contrib.), 1938; Sir Godfrey Kneller, 1947; (with Prof. M. V. Duignan) Shell Guide to Ireland, 1975; (ed with J. Rodda) The Olympic Games, 1976; (with J. Rodda) Olympic Games Moscow-Lake Placid, 1979; My Olympic Years (autobiog.), 1983; (ed with J. Rodda) Olympic Games—Los Angeles and Sarajevo, 1984; My Ireland, 1987; contribs to British, Amer. and Eur. Press. *Heir: s* Hon. (George) Redmond (Fitzpatrick) Morris, film producer [*b* 26 Jan. 1947; *m* 1972, Pauline, *o d* of late Geoffrey Horton, Dublin; one *s* one *d*]. *Address:* 9 Lower Mount Pleasant Avenue, Dublin 6. *T:* (1) 4972114; St Annins, Spiddal, County Galway. *T:* (91) 83103. *Clubs:* Garrick; Stephen's Green (Dublin); County (Galway). *Died 25 April 1999.*

KILLEARN, 2nd Baron *cr* 1943, of Killearn, co. Stirling; **Graham Curtis Lampson;** Bt 1866; *b* 28 Oct. 1919; *er s* of 1st Baron Killearn, GCMG, CB, MVO, PC, and Rachel Mary Hele Phipps (*d* 1930), *d* of W. W. Phipps; *S* father as 2nd Baron, 1964, and kinsman as 4th Bt, 1971; *m* 1946, Nadine Marie Cathryn, *o d* of late Vice-Adm. Cecil Horace Pilcher, DSO; two *d*. *Educ:* Eton Coll.; Magdalen Coll., Oxford (MA). Served war of 1939–45, Scots Guards (Major): served ME and N Africa with 2nd Bn, and Italy on staff of HQs 5th US and 8th British Armies, and 15th Allied Army Gp. US Bronze Star. *Heir: half-b* Hon. Victor Miles George Aldous Lampson, Captain RARO, Scots Guards [*b* 9 Sept. 1941; *m* 1971, Melita Amaryllis Pamela Astrid, *d* of Rear-Adm. Sir Morgan Morgan-Giles, DSO, OBE; two *s* two *d*]. *Address:* 58 Melton Court, Old Brompton Road, SW7 3JJ. *T:* 0171–584 7700.
Died 27 July 1996.

KILLICK, Paul Victor St John, OBE 1969; HM Diplomatic Service, retired; Ambassador to the Dominican Republic, 1972–75; *b* 8 Jan. 1916; *s* of C. St John Killick and Beatrice (*née* Simpson); *m* 1947, Sylva Augusta Leva; one *s* two *d*. *Educ:* St Paul's School. Served with Army, N Africa and Italy, 1939–46 (despatches 1944). Diplomatic Service: Singapore, 1946–47; Tokyo, 1947–49; Katmandu, 1950–53; FO, 1953–55; Oslo, 1955–58; San Francisco, 1958–60; Djakarta, 1960–61; Rome, 1962–66; Pretoria/Cape Town, 1966–70; Tangier, 1971–72. *Recreations:* walking, gardening.
Died 26 June 1998.

KILROY, Dame Alix Hester Marie; *see* Meynell, Dame A. H. M.

KINAHAN, Sir Robert (George Caldwell), (Sir Robin), Kt 1961; ERD 1946; JP; Lord-Lieutenant, County Borough of Belfast, 1985–91 (Vice Lord-Lieutenant, 1976–85); *b* 24 Sept. 1916; *s* of Henry Kinahan, Lowwood, Belfast; *m* 1950, Coralie I., *d* of late Capt. C. de Burgh, DSO, RN; two *s* three *d*. *Educ:* Stowe Sch., Buckingham. Vintners' Scholar (London), 1937. Served Royal Artillery, 1939–45, Capt. Chairman: Inglis & Co. Ltd, 1962–82; E. T. Green Ltd, 1964–82; Ulster Bank Ltd, 1970–82 (Dir, 1963–85); Director: Bass Ireland, 1958–78; Gallaher Ltd, 1967–82; NI Bd, Eagle Star, 1970–81; Nat. Westminster Bank, 1973–82; Abbey Life, 1981–87; STC, 1984–87; Abbeyfield Belfast Soc., 1983–; Cheshire House (NI), 1983–87. Mem., NI Adv. Commn, 1972–73. MP (NI) Clifton, 1958–59. Councillor, Belfast Corporation, 1948; Lord Mayor of Belfast, 1959–61. JP Co. Antrim, 1950,

DL 1962; High Sheriff: Belfast, 1956; Co. Antrim, 1969. Hon. LLD Belfast, 1962. *Publication:* autobiography, 1996. *Recreations:* gardening, family life. *Address:* Castle Upton, Templepatrick, Co. Antrim BT39 0BE. *T:* (018494) 32466.
Died 2 May 1997.

KINCH, Anthony Alec, CBE 1987; counsellor for European Community affairs; Member, since 1988, Hon. Leader, since 1993, Speakers Panel, Commission of the European Communities; *b* 13 Dec. 1926; *s* of late Edward Alec Kinch, OBE, former Polit. Adviser, Iraq Petroleum Co. Ltd, and Catherine Teresa Kinch (*née* Cassidy); *m* 1st, 1952, Barbara Patricia (*née* Paton Walsh) (*d* 1992); four *s* one *d* (and one *d* decd); 2nd, 1995, Barbara (*née* Cook), widow of James Mortimer. *Educ:* Ampleforth; Christ Church, Oxford (MA). Practised at Bar, 1951–57; Contracts Manager, Electronics Div., Plessey Co. Ltd, 1957–60; Legal Adviser and Insce Consultant, R. & H. Green and Silley Weir Ltd, 1960–66; Dir, Fedn of Bakers, 1966–73; Head of Foodstuffs Div., Commn of EEC, 1973–82; Head of Div. for Project Ops, European Regl Develt Fund ops, EEC, 1982–86. Chm., Brussels Area, SDP, 1981–84; Vice Chm., SDP Europe, 1989; Mem., Council for Social Democracy, 1982–90. Contested (SDP) Kent E, 1984, London SE, 1989, European Parly elecns. Chef de Division Honoraire, EEC, 1987. *Recreation:* living. *Address:* 36 Greenways, Beckenham, Kent BR3 3NG. *T:* (020) 8658 2298, *Fax:* (020) 8663 0737; *e-mail:* akinchie@compuserve.com. *Died 25 Oct. 1999.*

KING, Albert Leslie, MBE 1945; *b* 28 Aug. 1911; *s* of late William John King and Elizabeth Mary Amelia King; *m* 1938, Constance Eileen Stroud (*d* 1989); two *d*. *Educ:* University Coll. Sch., Hampstead. Joined Territorial Army, 1939; Major, RA, 1944. Joined Shell-Mex and BP Statistical Dept, 1928; Manager, Secretariat, Petroleum Board, 1947; Manager, Trade Relations Dept, Shell-Mex and BP Ltd, 1948; General Manager: Administration, 1954; Sales, 1957; Operations, 1961; apptd Dir, 1962, Managing Dir, 1963–66. Dep. Dir-Gen., BIM, 1966–68. Barrister (called to the Bar 1980). FCCA; FSS; CIMgt; Hon. JDipMA. *Club:* Saracens.
Died 7 July 1999.

KING, Very Rev. Edward Laurie; Dean of Cape Town, 1958–88, Dean Emeritus since 1988; *b* 30 Jan. 1920; *s* of William Henry and Norah Alice King; *m* 1950, Helen Stuart Mathers, MB, BCh, MMed; one *s* three *d*. *Educ:* King's Coll., Taunton; University of Wales (BA). Deacon, 1945; priest, 1946, Monmouth; Associate in Theology (S Africa). Curate of Risca, 1945–48; Diocese of Johannesburg, 1948–50; Rector of Robertson, Cape, 1950–53; Rector of Stellenbosch, 1953–58. Hon. DTh Western Cape, 1997. *Publications:* A Good Place to Be, 1997; Distant Music, 1998. *Recreations:* cricket, reading. *Address:* 30 6th Avenue, Rondebosch East, Western Cape, 7700, South Africa. *T:* (21) 6868204. *Club:* City and Civil Service. *Died 4 Aug. 1998.*

KING, Gen. Sir Frank (Douglas), GCB 1976 (KCB 1972; CB 1971); MBE 1953; Director, 1978–92: Kilton Properties; Springthorpe Property Co.; *b* 9 March 1919; *s* of Arthur King, farmer, and Kate Eliza (*née* Sheard), Brightwell, Berks; *m* 1947, Joy Emily Ellen Taylor-Lane; one *s* two *d*. *Educ:* Wallingford Grammar Sch. Joined Army, 1939; commnd into Royal Fusiliers, 1940; Parachute Regt, 1943; dropped Arnhem, Sept. 1944; Royal Military College of Science (ptsc), 1946; Staff Coll., Camberley (psc), 1950; comd 2 Parachute Bn, Middle East, 1960–62; comd 11 Infantry Bde Gp, Germany, 1963–64; Military Adviser (Overseas Equipment), 1965–66; Dir, Land/Air Warfare, MoD, 1967–68; Dir, Military Assistance Overseas, MoD, 1968–69; Comdt, RMCS, 1969–71; GOC-in-C, Army Strategic Comd, 1971–72; Dep. C-in-C UK Land Forces, 1972–73; GOC and Dir of Ops, N Ireland, 1973–75; Comdr, Northern Army Gp, and C-in-C BAOR, 1976–78; ADC Gen. to the Queen, 1977–78. Col Comdt, Army Air Corps, 1974–79. Mil. Advr, Short Bros Ltd, 1979–85; Chairman: Assets Protection Internat. Ltd, 1981–86; John Taylor Trust, 1978–88; Director: Control Risks Ltd, 1979–86; Plaza Fish, 1978–91; Director 1978–88: John Taylor Ltd; John Taylor (Worksop); Leicester Frozen Foods. Trustee, Airborne Forces Security Trust, 1981–; Mem. Council, Air League, 1982–90; Dir, Airborne Forces Charitable Trust, 1988–; Pres., Arnhem Veterans Club, 1988–. Kermit Roosevelt Lectr, 1977. *Recreation:* gardening. *Address:* c/o Royal Bank of Scotland, Columbia House, 69 Aldwych, WC2B 4JJ. *Died 30 March 1998.*

KING, Frederick Ernest, DPhil, DSc, PhD; FRS 1954; Scientific Adviser to British Petroleum Co. Ltd, 1959–71, retired; *b* 2 May 1905; *er s* of late Frederick and Elizabeth King, Bexhill, Sussex; *m* 1st, 1928, Rose Ellen Holyoak (marr. diss. 1969; she *d* 1988); two *s* two *d*; 2nd, Dorothea Marcia Molone Haines. *Educ:* Bancroft's Sch.; University of London; Oriel Coll., Oxford. MA, DPhil, DSc Oxon; PhD London. Ramsay Memorial Fellow, 1930–31; Demonstrator, Dyson Perrins Laboratory, 1931–34; University Lecturer and Demonstrator in Chemistry, Oxford Univ., 1934–48, and sometime Lecturer in Organic Chemistry, Magdalen Coll. and Balliol Coll.; Sir Jesse Boot Prof. of Chemistry, University of Nottingham, 1948–55; Dir in charge of research, British Celanese Ltd, 1955–59. Fellow, Queen Mary Coll., London, 1955. Tilden Lectr, Chem. Soc., 1948. *Publications:* scientific papers mainly in Jl of Chem. Soc. *Recreation:* gardening. *Address:* 9 Saffrons Court, Compton Place Road, Eastbourne, East Sussex BN21 1DX.

Died 14 Aug. 1999.

KING, Prof. James Lawrence; Regius Professor of Engineering, 1968–83, University Fellow, 1983–87, Edinburgh University; *b* 14 Feb. 1922; *s* of Lawrence Aubrey King and Wilhelmina Young McLeish; *m* 1951, Pamela Mary Ward Hitchcock; one *s* one *d. Educ:* Latymer Upper Sch.; Jesus Coll., Cambridge; Imperial Coll., London. Min. of Defence (Navy), 1942–68. *Recreation:* gardening. *Address:* 16 Lyne Park, West Linton, Peeblesshire EH46 7HP. *T:* (01968) 660038.

Died 5 April 2000.

KING, Prof. (John) Oliver (Letts), FRCVS; FIBiol; Professor of Animal Husbandry, University of Liverpool, 1969–82, then Emeritus; *b* 21 Dec. 1914; *s* of Richard Oliver King and Helen Mary (*née* Letts); *m* 1942, Helen Marion Gudgin (decd); one *s* one *d. Educ:* Berkhamsted Grammar Sch.; Royal Veterinary Coll. (MRCVS); Univ. of Reading (BScAgric); Univ. of Liverpool (MVSc, PhD); FRCVS 1969. Assistant in veterinary practice, 1937; Ho. Surg., Royal Veterinary Coll., 1938; Lectr in Animal Husbandry, 1941, Sen. Lectr 1948, Reader 1961, Univ. of Liverpool. Mem. Council, British Veterinary Assoc., 1953–68; Chairman: British Council Agric. and Vet. Adv. Panel, 1978–84; Council, UFAW, 1987–90 (a Vice-Pres., 1990–95); Member: Medicines Commn, 1969–71; Horserace Anti-Doping Cttee, 1973–86, Horserace Scientific Adv. Cttee, 1986–89; Farm Animal Welfare Council, 1979–84; a Vice-President: N of England Zoological Soc., 1987–99 (Chm. Council, 1972–86); BVA Animal Welfare Foundn, 1989–; President: Assoc. of Veterinary Teachers and Research Workers, 1961; Lancashire Veterinary Assoc., 1967; British Veterinary Zoological Soc., 1971–74; Royal Coll. of Veterinary Surgeons, 1980. Dalrymple-Champneys Cup, 1976; Bledisloe Vet. Award, 1983. *Publications:* Veterinary Dietetics, 1961; An Introduction to Animal Husbandry, 1978; papers on animal husbandry in various scientific pubns. *Recreation:* gardening. *Address:* 6 Ashtree Farm

Court, Willaston, Neston CH64 2XL. *T:* (0151) 327 4850. *Club:* Athenæum. *Died 11 Dec. 2000.*

KING, Ralph Malcolm MacDonald, OBE 1968; Colonial Service, retired; *b* 8 Feb. 1911; *s* of Dr James Malcolm King and Mrs Norah King; *m* 1948, Rita Elizabeth Herring; two *s* one *d. Educ:* Tonbridge Sch. Solicitor (Hons) 1934; called to Bar, Gray's Inn, 1950; disbarred at his own request and restored to Roll of Solicitors, April 1961. Asst to Johnson, Stokes and Master, Solicitors, Hong Kong, 1936–41. Commissioned Middx Regt, 1941; prisoner of war, 1941–45; demobilised, 1946. Colonial Legal Service, 1947; Legal Officer, Somaliland, 1947; Crown Counsel, Somaliland, 1950; Solicitor-General, Nyasaland, 1953; Attorney-General, Nyasaland, 1957–61. Legal Draftsman to Government of Northern Nigeria, 1963–67, and to Northern States of Nigeria, 1967–73; Dir, Legislative Drafting Courses, Commonwealth Secretariat, Jamaica, 1974–75; Trinidad, 1976, and Barbados, 1977. *Recreations:* watching cricket, walking. *Address:* 36 Mill View Close, Woodbridge, Suffolk IP12 4HR. *T:* (01394) 385417. *Died 15 March 1997.*

KING, Sir Richard (Brian Meredith), KCB 1976 (CB 1969); MC 1944; Trustee, Simon Population Trust, since 1985; Director, Rural Investment Overseas, since 1987; *b* 2 Aug. 1920; *s* of late Bernard and Dorothy King; *m* 1944, Blanche Phyllis Roberts; two *s* one *d. Educ:* King's Coll. Sch., Wimbledon. Air Ministry, 1939; Min. of Aircraft Prodn, 1940; Army, 1940–46: Major, N Irish Horse; N African and Italian campaigns (MC, Cassino); Min. of Supply, 1946; Asst Principal, Ministry of Works, 1948, Principal, 1949; Asst Regional Dir (Leeds), 1949–52; seconded HM Treas., 1953–54; Prin. Priv. Sec. to Minister of Works, 1956–57; Asst Sec., 1957; seconded Cabinet Off., 1958 (Sec. of Commonwealth Educn. Conf., Oxford, 1959; Constitutional Conferences: Kenya, 1960; N Rhodesia, Nyasaland and Fed. Review, 1960; WI Fedn, 1961); Dept of Tech. Co-op., on its formation, 1961; Min. of Overseas Develt, on its formation, 1964: Under-Sec., 1964; Dep. Sec., 1968; Permanent Sec., 1973–76; Exec. Sec., IMF/World Bank Develt Cttee, 1976–80; Senior Advr to S. G. Warburg & Co. Ltd, 1980–85. *Publications:* The Planning of the British Aid Programme, 1971; Criteria for Europe's Development Policy to the Third World, 1974. *Recreations:* music, lawn tennis, gardening, doing-it-himself. *Address:* Woodlands Farm House, Woodlands Lane, Stoke D'Abernon, Cobham, Surrey KT11 3PY. *T:* (01372) 843491. *Club:* All England Lawn Tennis.

Died 5 Oct. 1998.

KING, Air Vice-Marshal Walter MacIan, CB 1961; CBE 1957; retired, 1967; *b* 10 March 1910; *s* of Alexander King, MB, ChB, DPH, and Hughberta Blannin King (*née* Pearson); *m* 1946, Anne Clare Hicks (*d* 1991); two *s. Educ:* St Mary's Coll., Castries, St Lucia, BWI; Blundell's Sch., Tiverton, Devon. Aircraft Engineering (Messers Westland Aircraft Ltd, Handley-Page Ltd, Saunders-Roe Ltd), 1927–33; joined Royal Air Force, 1934; Overseas Service: No 8 Sqdn, Aden, 1935–37; South-East Asia, 1945–47; Middle East (Egypt and Cyprus), 1955–57; Directing Staff, RAF Staff Coll., 1957–58; Comdt, No 16 MU, Stafford, 1958–60; Dir of Equipment (B), Air Ministry, 1961–64; Air Cdre Ops (Supply), HQ's Maintenance Comd, during 1964; SASO, RAF Maintenance Command, 1964–67. Student: RAF Staff Coll., 1944; Joint Services Staff Coll., 1947; IDC, 1954. Joined Hooker Craigmyle & Co. Ltd, 1967; Gen. Manager, Hooker Craigmyle (Scotland) Ltd, 1969–72; Dir, Craigmyle & Co. (Scotland) Ltd, 1972–76. *Recreations:* reading, making small models. *Address:* 24 Arthur's Avenue, Harrogate HG2 0DX.

Died 24 Jan. 1999.

KINGS NORTON, Baron *cr* 1965 (Life Peer), of Wotton Underwood in the co. of Buckinghamshire; **Harold Roxbee Cox,** Kt 1953; PhD, DIC; FEng 1976; FIMechE; Chairman: Landspeed Ltd, since 1975; Cotswold Research Ltd, since 1978; President: Campden and Chorleywood Food Research Association (formerly Campden Food Preservation Research Association), since 1961; British Balloon Museum and Library, since 1980; Chancellor, Cranfield University (formerly Cranfield Institute of Technology), 1969–97; *b* 6 June 1902; *s* of late William John Roxbee Cox, Birmingham, and Amelia Stern; *m* 1st, 1927, Marjorie (*d* 1980), *e d* of late E. E. Withers, Northwood; two *s*; 2nd, 1982, Joan Ruth Pascoe, *d* of late W. G. Pack, Torquay. *Educ:* Kings Norton Grammar Sch.; Imperial Coll. of Science and Technology (Schol.). Engineer on construction of Airship R101, 1924–29; Chief Technical Officer, Royal Airship Works, 1931; investigations in wing flutter and stability of structures, RAE, 1931–35; Lectr in Aircraft Structures, Imperial Coll., 1932–38; Principal Scientific Officer. Aerodynamics Dept, RAE, 1935–36; Head of Air Defence Dept, RAE, 1936–38; Chief Technical Officer, Air Registration Board, 1938–39; Supt of Scientific Research, RAE, 1939–40; Dep. Dir of Scientific Research, Ministry of Aircraft Production, 1940–43; Dir of Special Projects Ministry of Aircraft Production, 1943–44; Chm. and Man. Dir, Power Jets (Research and Development) Ltd, 1944–46; Dir National Gas Turbine Establishment, 1946–48; Chief Scientist, Min. of Fuel and Power, 1948–54. Chairman: Metal Box Co., 1961–67 (Dir, 1957–67; Dep. Chm., 1959 60); Berger Jenson & Nicholson Ltd, 1967 75; Applied Photophysics, 1974 81; Withers Estates, 1976–81; Director: Ricardo & Co. (Engrs) 1927 Ltd, 1965–77; Dowty Rotol, 1968–75; British Printing Corp., 1968–77; Hoechst UK, 1970–75. Chm. Gas Turbine Collaboration Cttee, 1941–44, 1946–48; Mem. Aeronautical Research Council, 1944–48, 1958–60; Chairman: Council for Scientific and Industrial Research, 1961–65; Council for National Academic Awards, 1964–71; Air Registration Bd, 1966–72; President: Royal Aeronautical Soc., 1947–49; Royal Instn, 1969–76. Fellow of Imperial Coll. of Science and Technology, 1960; FCGI 1976; Hon. FIFST 1992; Hon. FRAeS. Membre Correspondant, Faculté Polytechnique de Mons, 1946–. R38 Memorial Prize, 1928; Busk Memorial Prize, 1934; Wilbur Wright Lecturer, 1940; Wright Brothers Lecturer (USA), 1945; Hawksley Lecturer, 1951; James Clayton Prize, 1952; Thornton Lectr, 1954; Parsons Memorial Lectr, 1955; Handley Page Memorial Lectr, 1969. Freeman, City of London, 1987; Liveryman, GAPAN, 1987. Hon. DSc: Birmingham, 1954; Cranfield Inst. of Technology, 1970; Warwick, 1986; Hon. DTech Brunel, 1966; Hon. LLD CNΛΛ, 1969. Bronze Medal, Univ. of Louvain, 1946; Medal of Freedom with Silver Palm, USA, 1947. *Publications:* numerous papers on theory of structures, wing flutter, gas turbines, civil aviation and airships. *Address:* Westcote House, Chipping Campden, Glos GL55 6AG. *T:* (01386) 840440. *Club:* Athenæum.
Died 21 Dec. 1997.

KINGSLEY, Sir Patrick (Graham Toler), KCVO 1962 (CVO 1950); Secretary and Keeper of the Records of the Duchy of Cornwall, 1954–72 (Assistant Secretary, 1930–54); *b* 1908; *s* of late Gerald Kingsley; *m* 1947, Priscilla Rosemary, *o d* of late Capt. Archibald A. Lovett Cameron, RN; three *s* (one *d* decd). *Educ:* Winchester; New Coll., Oxford. OUCC, 1928–30 (Capt. 1930), OUAFC, 1927 and 1929. Served War of 1939–45 with Queen's Royal Regt. *Address:* West Hill Farm, West Knoyle, Warminster, Wilts BA12 6AL.
Died 24 Aug. 1999.

KINNAIRD, 13th Lord *cr* 1682, of Inchture; **Graham Charles Kinnaird;** Baron Kinnaird of Rossie (UK), 1860;

Flying Officer RAFVR; *b* 15 Sept. 1912; *e s* of 12th Lord Kinnaird, KT, KBE, and Frances Victoria (*d* 1960), *y d* of late T. H. Clifton, Lytham Hall, Lancs; *S* father, 1972; *m* 1st, 1938, Nadia (who obtained a decree of divorce, 1940), *o c* of H. A. Fortington, OBE, Isle of Jethou, Channel Islands; 2nd, 1940, Diana, *yr d* of R. S. Copeman, Roydon Hall, Diss, Norfolk; four *d* (one *s* decd). *Educ:* Eton. Demobilised RAF, 1945. *Heir:* none. *Address:* The Garden House, Rossie Estate, Inchture, Perthshire; Durham House, Durham Place, SW3 4ET. *Clubs:* Brooks's, Pratt's.
Died 27 Feb. 1997 (ext).

KINNEAR, Nigel Alexander, FRCSI; Surgeon to Federated Dublin Voluntary Hospitals until 1974, retired; *b* 3 April 1907; *s* of James and Margaret Kinnear; *m* 1947, Frances Gardner; one *d. Educ:* Mill Hill Sch.; Trinity Coll., Dublin (MA, MB). Surgeon to Adelaide Hosp., Dublin, 1936; Regius Prof. of Surgery, TCD, 1967–72. President: RCSI, 1961; Royal Academy of Medicine of Ireland, 1968 (Hon. Fellow, 1983); James IV Surgical Assoc. Hon. FRCSGlas. *Publications:* articles in surgical jls. *Recreations:* salmon fishing, gardening. *Address:* Mount Tabor Care Centre and Nursing Home, 1 Newgrove Avenue, Sandymount, Dublin 4. *Club:* Kildare Street and University (Dublin).
Died 19 July 2000.

KIRK, Grayson Louis, Hon. KBE 1955; President Emeritus, Columbia University; *b* 12 Oct. 1903; *s* of Traine Caldwell Kirk and Nora Eichelberger; *m* 1925, Marion Louise Sands, one *s. Educ:* Miami Univ. (AB), Clark Univ. (AM); Ecole Libre des Sciences Politiques, Paris, 1928–29; PhD University of Wisconsin, 1930. Prof. of History, Lamar Coll., Beaumont, Tex, 1925–27; Social Science Research Council Fellowship (chiefly spent at London Sch. of Economics), 1936–37; Instructor in Political Science, 1929–30, Asst Prof., 1930–36, Associate Prof., 1936–38, Prof., 1938–40, University of Wisconsin; Associate Prof. of Government, Columbia Univ., 1940–43; Head, Security Section, Div. of Political Studies, US Dept of State, 1942–43; Research Associate, Yale Inst. of Internat. Studies, 1943–44; Prof. of Government, Columbia Univ., 1943–47; Prof. of Internat Relations, Acting Dir of Sch. of Internat. Affairs, and Dir of European Inst., 1947–49; appointed Provost in Nov. 1949, and also Vice-Pres. in July 1950, Columbia Univ.; became Acting Head of Columbia in President Eisenhower's absence on leave, March 1951; Pres. and Trustee of Columbia Univ., 1953–68; Bryce Prof. of History of Internat. Relations, Columbia, 1959–72, Emeritus Prof., 1972. Mem. US Deleg'n Staff, Dumbarton Oaks, 1944; Exec. Officer, Third Commn, San Francisco Conf., 1945. Trustee Emeritus, The Asia Foundation; Trustee: American Philosophical Soc.; Pilgrims of the US (Vice-Pres.); Council on Foreign Relations; Λmer. Λcad. of Λrts and Sciences; Λmer. Soc. of French Legion of Honour. Hon. LLD: Miami, 1950; Waynesburg Coll., Brown Univ., Union Coll., 1951; Puerto Rico, Clark, Princeton, New York, Wisconsin, Columbia, Jewish Theol Seminary of America, 1953; Syracuse, Williams Coll., Pennsylvania, Harvard, Washington, St Louis, Central Univ., Caracas, Univ. of the Andes, Merida, Venezuela, Univ. of Zulia, Maracaibo, Venezuela, Univ. of Delhi, India, Thamasset Univ., Bangkok, 1954; Johns Hopkins Univ., Baltimore, Amherst, 1956; Dartmouth Coll., Northwestern Univ., 1958; Tennessee, 1960; St Lawrence, 1963; Denver, Notre Dame, Bates Coll., 1964; Waseda (Japan), Michigan, 1965; Sussex, 1966; Hon. LHD N Dakota, 1958; Hon. PhD Bologna, 1951; Dr of Civil Law King's Coll., Halifax, Nova Scotia, 1958. Associate KStJ 1959. Comdr, Order of Orange-Nassau, 1952; Grand Officer, Order of Merit of the Republic, Italy, 1956; Medal of the Order of Taj, Iran, 1961; Grand Cross, Order of George I (Greece), 1965; Order of the Sacred Treasure, 1st Class (Japan), 1965; Comdr, Ordre des Palmes Académiques (France), 1966;

Grand Officier, Légion d'Honneur, France, 1973. *Publications:* Philippine Independence, 1936; Contemporary International Politics (with W. R. Sharp), 1940; (with R. P. Stebbins) War and National Policy, Syllabus, 1941; The Study of International Relations in American Colleges and Universities, 1947. *Address:* 28 Sunnybrook Road, Bronxville, NY 10708, USA. *T:* (914) 7930808. *Died 21 Nov. 1997.*

KIRK, Dame (Lucy) Ruth, DBE 1975; *m* 1941, Norman Eric Kirk (later, Rt Hon. Norman Kirk, PC, Prime Minister of New Zealand; *d* 1974); three *s* two *d*. Former Patron, SPUC. Awarded title, Dame of the Order of the British Empire, for public services. *Address:* Flat 1, 8(A) Ansonby Street, Avonhead, Christchurch, S Island, New Zealand. *Died 20 March 2000.*

KIRKLAND, (Joseph) Lane; President, American Federation of Labor—Congress of Industrial Organizations, 1979–95, then Emeritus; *b* Camden, SC, 12 March 1922; *s* of Randolph Withers Kirkland and Louise Richardson; *m* 1st, 1944, Edith Draper Hollyday (marr. diss. 1972); five *d*; 2nd, 1973, Irena Neumann. *Educ:* US Merchant Marine Academy, Kings Point, NY (grad. 1942); Georgetown Univ. Sch. of Foreign Service (BS 1948). Deck officer, various merchant ships, 1942–46; master mariner; Staff Scientist, US Navy Hydrographic Office, 1946–48; Staff Representative, AFL-CIO, 1948–58; Research and Educn Dir, Internat. Union of Operating Engrs, 1958–60; Exec. Asst to President, AFL-CIO, 1960–69; Sec.-Treasurer, AFL-CIO, 1969–79. Member: Blue Ribbon Defense Panel, 1969–70; Commn on CIA Activities within the US, 1975; Commn on Foundns and Private Philanthropy, 1969–70; Gen. Adv. Cttee on Arms Control and Disarmament, 1974–78; Nat. Commn on Productivity, 1971–74; Presidential Commn on Financial Structure and Regulation, 1970–72; President's Maritime Adv. Cttee, 1964–66; President's Missile Sites Labor Commn (Alternate), 1961–67; Commn on Exec., Legislative and Judicial Salaries; Cttee on Selection of Fed. Judicial Officers; President's Commn on Social Security, 1982–83; Bipartisan Commn on Central America, 1983–84; Bd for Internat. Broadcasting; Polish American Enterprise Fund (Dir, 1990); Nat. Endowment for Democracy, 1983–93. Dir, Amer. Arbitration Assoc. Mem., Internat. Org. of Masters, Mates and Pilots. Presidential Citizen's Medal; Distinguished Public Service Medal, Dept of Defense; Presidential Medal of Freedom; Distinguished Service Medal, Dept of Transportation. Comdr, Order of Merit (Poland); Order of Merit (Hungary); Order of Francisco de Miranda (Venezuela). *Recreation:* archaeology. *Address:* (office) George Meany Center for Labor Studies, 1000 New Hampshire Avenue, Silver Spring, MD 20903, USA. *T:* (301) 4315444. *Died 14 Aug. 1999.*

KIRKWOOD, Prof. Kenneth; Rhodes Professor of Race Relations, University of Oxford, 1954–86, Professor Emeritus, since 1986; Fellow of St Antony's College, 1954–86, Emeritus Fellow, since 1986, and Sub-Warden, 1968–71; *b* Benoni, Transvaal, 1919; *s* of late Thomas Dorman Kirkwood and Lily Alexander (*née* Bewley); *m* 1942, Deborah Burton, *d* of late Burton Ireland Collings and Emily Frances Collings (*née* Loram); three *s* three *d*. BA, BSc Rand; MA Oxon 1954. Captain, South African Engineer Corps, War of 1939–45; served in East Africa, North Africa and Italy (despatches). Lecturer, University of the Witwatersrand, 1947; Lecturer, University of Natal, 1948–51; Fellowship, University of London (Inst. of Commonwealth Studies), 1952; Carnegie Travelling Fellowship, USA, 1953; Senior Research Officer, Inst. of Colonial Studies, Oxford Univ., 1953; Organiser of Institute for Social Research, University of Natal, 1954. Chm. Regional Cttee, S African Inst. of Race Relations in

Natal, 1954; UK Rep. SA Inst. of Race Relations, 1955–86. Investigation on behalf UNESCO into trends in race relations in British Non-Self-Governing Territories of Africa, 1958; Visiting Prof. of Race Relations (UNESCO), University Coll. of Rhodesia and Nyasaland, 1964; composed memorandum on meaning, and procedure for further study of 'racial discrimination,' for UN Div. of Human Rights, 1966–67; Mem., Africa Educational Trust, Oxfam, etc, 1955. Chm., UK Standing Cttee on University Studies of Africa, 1975–78; Chm. of Trustees, Oxford Project for Peace Studies, 1983; Hon. Pres., Oxford Br., UNA, 1986. UK Official Observer, Rhodesian Elections, March 1980. *Publications:* The Proposed Federation of the Central African Territories, 1952; (contrib.) Lord Hailey's An African Survey, rev. edn 1957; (ed) St Antony's Papers: African Affairs, number 1, 1961, number 2, 1963, number 3, 1969; (contrib.) Vol. VIII, Cambridge History of the British Empire, 2nd edn 1963; (ed with E. E. Sabben-Clare and D. J. Bradley) Health in Tropical Africa during the Colonial Period, 1980; (ed and contrib.) Biosocial Aspects of Ethnic Minorities, 1983; Peace within States, Ethnic, Cultural and Racial Issues (lecture), 1989; booklets and articles on race relations and internat. affairs; *relevant publication:* Ethnicity, Empire and Race Relations: essays in honour of Kenneth Kirkwood, ed Anthony Kirk-Greene and John Stone, 1986. *Address:* St Antony's College, Oxford; 233 Woodstock Road, Oxford OX2 7AD. *T:* (01865) 515867. *Died 16 Oct. 1997.*

KIRSTEIN, Lincoln Edward; Founder, 1934, former Director, latterly President Emeritus, School of American Ballet; General Director, New York City Ballet, until 1989; *b* Rochester, NY, 4 May 1907; *s* of Louis E. Kirstein and Rose Stein; *m* 1941, Fidelma Cadmus; no *c*. *Educ:* Harvard Coll.; BS 1930. Edited Hound & Horn, 1927–34; founded and directed American Ballet Caravan, 1936–41; Third US Army (Arts, Monuments and Archives Section), 1943–45. Editor, The Dance Index, 1941–47. Benjamin Franklin Medal, RSA, 1981; Governor's Arts Award, NY State, 1984; US Presidential Medal of Freedom, 1984; Nat. Medal of Arts, 1985; Municipal Art Soc. Award, 1985. *Publications:* Flesh is Heir, 1932, repr. 1975; Dance, A Short History of Theatrical Dancing, 1935; Blast at Ballet, 1938; Ballet Alphabet, 1940; Drawings of Pavel Tchelitchew, 1947; Elie Nadelman Drawings, 1949; The Dry Points of Elie Nadelman, 1952; What Ballet is About, 1959; Three Pamphlets Collected, 1967; The Hampton Institute Album, 1968; Movement and Metaphor: four centuries of ballet, 1970; Lay This Laurel, 1974; Nijinsky, Dancing, 1975; Ballet: bias and belief, 1983; Quarry: a collection in lieu of memoirs, 1986; Mosaic (memoirs), 1994; *verse:* Rhymes of a PFC (Private First Class), 1964; The Poems of Lincoln Kirstein, 1987; *monographs:* Gaston Lachaise, 1935; Walker Evans, 1938; Latin American Art, 1942; American Battle Art, 1945; Henri Cartier-Bresson, 1946; Dr William Rimmer, 1946; Elie Nadelman, 1948; Pavel Tchelitchew, 1964; W. Eugene Smith, 1970; George Tooker, 1983; Paul Cadmus, 1983; *edited:* The Classic Dance, Technique and Terminology, 1951; William Shakespeare: A Catalogue of the Works of Art in the American Shakespeare Festival Theater, 1964; Elie Nadelman, 1973; New York City Ballet, 1973; Thirty Years: the New York City Ballet, 1978; A. Hyatt Mayor: collected writings, 1983. *Address:* School of American Ballet, 144 West 66th Street, New York, NY 10023–6547, USA. *T:* 8770600. *Died 5 Jan. 1996.*

KIRTON, Col Hugh, TD 1952; Vice Lord-Lieutenant, County Durham, 1978–87; *b* Plawsworth, Co. Durham, 7 Aug. 1910; 2nd *s* of late Hugh Kirton and Margaretta Kirton (*née* Darling). *Educ:* Durham Sch. Chartered Accountant, 1933. Army Service: commnd in Tyne Electrical Engrs (TA), 1937; RE (TA), 1937–40; RA (TA),

1940–45 and 1951–56, Lt Col 1945; Dep. Comdr, 31AA Bde (TA), 1959–61, Col 1959; Hon. Col 439 (Tyne) Light AD Regt RA (TA), 1961–67. With Procter & Gamble Ltd, Newcastle upon Tyne, 1934–70, Dir, 1963–70; retired 1970. Mem., North Regional Health Authority, 1973–76; General Comr of Taxes (Newcastle upon Tyne), 1965–85. Mem. Council, Inst. of Chartered Accountants in England and Wales, 1966–70; Pres., Northern Soc. of Chartered Accountants, 1968–69. Mem., St John Council for Co. Durham, 1970, Chm., 1974–86. DL: Northumberland, 1961; Durham, 1974; High Sheriff Co. Durham, 1973–74. KStJ 1983. *Recreations:* golf, gardening. *Address:* Ovington, Plawsworth, Chester-le-Street, Co. Durham DH2 3LE. *T:* (0191) 3710261. *Clubs:* Northern Counties (Newcastle upon Tyne); Brancepeth Castle Golf (Captain, 1969–71).   *Died 5 Dec. 1997.*

KIRWAN, Sir (Archibald) Laurence (Patrick), KCMG 1972 (CMG 1958); TD; Hon. Vice-President, Royal Geographical Society, since 1981 (Director and Secretary, 1945–75); *b* 13 May 1907; 2nd *s* of Patrick Kirwan, Cregg, County Galway, Ireland, and Mabel Norton; *m* 1st, 1932, Joan Chetwynd (marr. diss. 1945) (*d* 1989); one *d*; 2nd, 1949, Stella Mary Monck (*d* 1997). *Educ:* Wimbledon Coll.; Merton Coll., Oxford. Asst Dir of the Archaeological Survey of Nubia, Egyptian Dept of Antiquities, 1929–34; Field Dir, Oxford Univ. Expeditions to Sudan, 1934–37; Tweedie Fellowship in Archæology and Anthropology, Edinburgh Univ., 1937–39; Boston and Philadelphia Museums, 1937; exploratory journeys, Eastern Sudan and Aden Protectorate, 1938–39. TARO Capt., Intell. Corps, 1939; Major, 1941; Lieut-Col 1943; Joint Staffs, Offices of Cabinet and Ministry of Defence, 1942–45; Hon. Lt-Col, 1957. Editor, Geographical Journal, 1945–78. Pres., Brit. Inst. in Eastern Africa, 1961–81, Hon. Life Pres. and Hon. Mem., 1981. Pres. (Section E), British Assoc. for the Advancement of Science, 1961–62; Member: Court of Arbitration, Argentine-Chile Frontier (Queen's Award) Case, 1965–68 (Leader, Field Mission, 1966); Sec. of State for Transport's Adv. Cttee on Landscape Treatment of Trunk Roads and Motorways, 1968–81 (Dep. Chm., 1970–80); UN Register of fact-finding experts, 1968–81. Mem. Court, Exeter Univ., 1969–80; a Governor, Imperial Coll. of Science and Technology, 1962–81; British Academy/Leverhulme Vis. Prof., Cairo, 1976; Mortimer Wheeler Lectr, Brit. Acad., 1977. Hon. Pres., Sudan Archaeol Res. Soc., 1992. Fellow: University Coll. London; Imperial College of Science and Technology; Hon. Fellow: SOAS; Amer. Geographical Soc.; Hon. Member: Geographical Societies of Paris, Vienna, Washington; Royal Inst. of Navigation; Institut d'Egypte; Internat. Soc. for Nubian Studies (Patron). Founder's Medal, RGS, 1975. Knight Cross of the Order of St Olav, Norway; Silver Jubilee Medal, 1977. *Publications:* (with W. B. Emery) Excavations and Survey between Wadi-es-Sebua and Adindan, 1935; (with W. B. Emery) Royal Tombs of Ballana and Qustal, 1938; Oxford University Excavations at Firka, 1938; The White Road (polar exploration), 1959; papers on archæology, historical and political geography, exploration, in scientific and other publications. *Recreation:* travel. *Address:* c/o Royal Geographical Society, SW7 2AR. *Club:* Geographical.
Died 16 April 1999.

KISSIN, Baron *cr* 1974 (Life Peer), of Camden in Greater London; **Harry Kissin;** Life President: Guinness Peat Group plc, 1979; Lewis & Peat Holdings Ltd, 1987; Director of public and private companies in the City of London, since 1934; *b* 23 Aug. 1912; *s* of Israel Kissin and Reusi Kissin (*née* Model), both of Russian nationality; *m* 1935, Ruth Deborah Samuel, London; one *s* one *d*. *Educ:* Danzig and Switzerland. Dr of Law, Basle. Swiss lawyer until 1933. Chairman: Lewis & Peat Ltd, 1961–72; Guinness Peat Group, 1973–79; Lewis & Peat Holdings

Ltd, 1982–87; Linfood Holdings, 1974–81; Esperanza International Services plc, 1970–83; Director: Transcontinental Services NV, 1982–86; Tycon SPA Venice, 1975–95. Dir, Royal Opera Hse, Covent Gdn, 1973 84; Mem., Royal Opera House Trust, 1974–87 (Chm., 1974–80). Chm. Council, ICA, 1968–75. Governor: Bezalel Acad. of Arts and Design, 1975–87; Hebrew Univ. of Jerusalem, 1980. FRSA. Comdr, Ordem Nacional do Cruzeiro do Sul (Brazil), 1977; Chevalier, Légion d'honneur, 1981; Bulgarian Commemorative Medal (1300 Years Bulgaria Medal), 1982. *Address:* c/o House of Lords, SW1A 0PW. *Clubs:* Reform, East India, Devonshire, Sports and Public Schools.
Died 22 Nov. 1997.

KITCHING, Maj.-Gen. George, CBE 1945; DSO 1943; Canadian Military Forces, retired; President, Duke of Edinburgh's Award in Canada, 1967–70, President, British Columbia and Yukon Division, 1979–82; *b* 19 Sept. 1910; *s* of George Charlesworth Kitching and Florence Dagmar (*née* Rowe); *m* 1946, Audrey Calhoun (*d* 1997); one *s* (one *d* decd). *Educ:* Cranleigh; Royal Military College. 2nd Lieut Glos Regt, 1930, resigned, 1938; served War of 1939–45 with Royal Canadian Regt and Loyal Edmonton Regt, in Sicily, Italy and North-West Europe; commanding Canadian Infantry Brigade, 1943; actg Maj.-Gen. comdg an armoured div., 1944 (DSO, despatches 1945, CBE); subseq. Vice-Chief of General Staff at Army Headquarters, Ottawa; Chairman of the Canadian Joint Staff in London, 1958–62; GOC Central Command, Canada, 1962–65, retd. Col Comdt of Infantry, 1974–78. Comr, Ont Pavilion, EXPO 70, Osaka, Japan, 1970; Chief Comr, Liquor Control Bd of Ont, 1970–76. Chm. and Patron, Gurkha Welfare Appeal (Canada), 1974; Patron: United World Colls, 1970 (Exec. Dir, Canadian Nat. Cttee, 1968–70); Sir Edmund Hillary Foundn (Canada), 1976; Old Fort York, Toronto, 1975. Lord of the Manor of Bluntisham, Cambs. Commander: Order of Orange Nassau (Netherlands); Military Order of Italy; Order of Merit (US). *Publication:* Mud and Green Fields (autobiog.), 1986. *Address:* 3434 Bonair Place, Victoria, BC V8P 4V4, Canada.   *Died 15 June 1999.*

KITCHING, John Alwyne, OBE 1947; ScD (Cambridge); PhD (London); FRS 1960; Professor of Biology, University of East Anglia, 1963–74, then Emeritus Professor; Dean of School of Biological Sciences, 1967–70; Leverhulme Fellowship, 1974; *b* 24 Oct. 1908; *s* of John Nainby Kitching; *m* 1933, Evelyn Mary Oliver; one *s* three *d*. *Educ:* Cheltenham Coll.; Trinity Coll., Cambridge. BA 1930, MA 1934, ScD 1956; PhD London. Lecturer: Birkbeck Coll., London, 1931; Edinburgh Univ., 1936; Bristol Univ., 1937; Rockefeller Fellow, Princeton Univ., 1938; Research in aviation-medical problems under Canadian Nat. Research Council, 1939–45; Reader in Zoology, University of Bristol, 1948–63. Hon. DSc NUI, 1983. *Publications:* contrib. Jl of Experimental Biol., Jl of Ecology, Jl of Animal Ecology, etc. *Recreations:* travel, gardening. *Address:* Oakwood House, Old Watton Road, Colney, Norwich NR4 7TP. *T:* Norwich (01603) 250101.
Died 1 April 1996.

KITSON, Alexander Harper, JP; Chairman, Lothian Region Transport Board, since 1990 (Director, since 1986); *b* 21 Oct. 1921; *m* 1942, Ann Brown McLeod (*d* 1997); two *d. Educ:* Kirknewton Sch., Midlothian, Scotland. Lorry Driver, 1935–45; Trade Union official, 1945–86: Gen. Sec., Scottish Commercial Motormen's Union, 1959–71; Dep. Gen. Sec., TGWU, 1980–86; Chm., Scottish TUC (Treas., 1974–81). Mem., Freight Integration Council, 1969–78. Mem. Nat. Exec. Cttee of Labour Party, 1968–86; Chm., Labour Party, 1980–81. Mem., War on Want Council, 1986–90. Member: Lothian Health Challenge Cttee, 1988–; Corstorphine Community

Council, Edinburgh, 1989. Chm., Heart of Midlothian FC, 1993–94 (Chm., 500 fundraising Club, 1992–94). Fellow, Scottish Council of Develt and Industry, 1986. *Address:* 47 Craigs Crescent, Edinburgh EH12 8HU.

Died 2 Aug. 1997.

KITSON, Prof. Michael William Lely; Director of Studies, Paul Mellon Centre for Studies in British Art, 1986–92; *b* 30 Jan. 1926; *s* of Rev. Bernard Meredyth Kitson and Helen May (*née* Lely); *m* 1950, Annabella Leslie Cloudsley (separated 1971); two *s. Educ:* Gresham's School; King's Coll., Cambridge (BA 1950; MA 1953); Courtauld Inst. of Art, Univ. of London. Served Army, 1945–48; commnd RE, 1946 and attached SIME, Egypt. Asst Lectr in History of Art, Slade Sch. of Art, 1952–54; Courtauld Institute of Art: Lectr, 1955–67; Reader, 1967–78; Prof., 1978–85; Dep. Dir, 1980–85; Fellow, 1985. Adjunct Prof., Yale Univ., 1986–92. Vice-Chm., Turner Soc., 1984–93. Chm., Courtauld Assoc. of Former Students, 1992–98. *Publications:* J. M. W. Turner, 1964; The Age of Baroque, 1966; Claude Lorrain: Landscape with the Nymph Egeria (Charlton Lecture), 1968; The Art of Claude Lorrain (exhibn catalogue), 1969; The Complete Paintings of Caravaggio, 1969; Rembrandt, 1969, 3rd rev. edn 1992; Turner Watercolours from the Collection of Stephen Courtauld, 1974; Claude Lorrain: Liber Veritatis, 1978; (with Gabriele Finaldi) Discovering the Italian Baroque: the Denis Mahon collection, 1997; *edited exhibition catalogues:* La Peinture romantique anglaise et les préraphaélites, 1972; Salvator Rosa, 1973; British Painting 1600–1800, 1977; Zwei Jahrhunderte Englische Malerei, 1979; contrib. Burlington Magazine, Jl of Warburg and Courtauld Insts, Walpole Soc., Turner Studies, etc. *Address:* 72 Halton Road, N1 2AD. *T:* (0171) 359 6757. *Died 7 Aug. 1998.*

KLEINDIENST, Richard Gordon; attorney; *b* 5 Aug. 1923; *s* of Alfred R. Kleindienst and Gladys Love, Massachusetts; *m* 1948, Margaret Dunbar; two *s* two *d. Educ:* Harvard Coll. (Phi Beta Kappa, *magna cum laude*); Harvard Law Sch. Associate and Partner of Jennings, Strouss, Salmon & Trask, Phoenix, Arizona, 1950–57; Sen. Partner of Shimmel, Hill, Kleindienst & Bishop, 1958–69; Dep. Attorney-Gen. of the US, 1969–72; Actg Attorney-Gen. of the US, Feb.–June 1972; Attorney-Gen. of the US, 1972–73, resigned 1973; private practice of law, Washington DC, 1973–75. Pres., Federal Bar Assoc., US, 1972– (Pres. elect, 1971–72). Hon. Dr of Laws, Susquehanna Univ., 1973. *Publication:* Justice: the memoirs of Attorney General Richard G. Kleindienst, 1985. *Recreations:* golf, chess, classical music, art. *Address:* 3103 W Crest View, Prescott, AZ 86305, USA. *Died 3 Feb. 2000.*

KNIGHT, Sir Allan (Walton), Kt 1970; CMG 1960; FTS; Commissioner, The Hydro-Electric Commission, Tasmania, 1946–77; Chief Commissioner, Tasman Bridge Restoration Commission, 1975–80; *b* 26 Feb. 1910; *s* of late Mr and Mrs G. W. Knight, Lindisfarne, Tasmania; *m* 1936, Margaret Janet Buchanan; two *s* one *d. Educ:* Hobart Technical Coll.; University of Tasmania. Diploma of Applied Science, 1929; BSc 1932; ME 1935; BCom 1946. Chief Engineer, Public Works Dept, Tasmania, 1937–46. Member: Australian Univs Commn, 1966–74; Council, Tasmanian Coll. of Advanced Education, 1968–75. Peter Nicol Russell Medal, Instn of Engrs of Australia, 1963; William Kernot Medal, Univ. of Melbourne, 1963; Wilfred Chapman Award, Inst. of Welding, Australia, 1974; John Storey Medal, Inst. of Management, Australia, 1975. Hon. FIEAust. Hon. DEng Tasmania, 1980. *Recreation:* royal tennis. *Address:* 64 Waimea Avenue, Sandy Bay, Hobart, Tasmania 7005, Australia. *T:* (3) 62251498. *Club:* Tasmanian (Hobart). *Died 14 May 1998.*

KNIGHT, Geoffrey Egerton, CBE 1970; Chairman, Fenchurch Insurance Group Ltd, 1980–92 (Executive Vice-Chairman, 1975–80); *b* 25 Feb. 1921; *s* of Arthur Egerton Knight and Florence Gladys Knight (*née* Clarke); *m* 1947, Evelyn Bugle; two *d. Educ:* Stubbington House; Brighton Coll. Royal Marines, 1939–46. Joined Bristol Aeroplane Co. Ltd, 1953; Dir, Bristol Aircraft Ltd, 1956; Dir, BAC Ltd, 1964–77, Vice Chm., 1972–76. Director: Guinness Peat Group, later GPG plc, 1976–89 (Jt Dep. Chm., 1987–89; Chm., 1989); GPA Gp, 1977–93; Trafalgar House PLC, 1980–91. *Publication:* Concorde: the inside story, 1976. *Address:* 33 Smith Terrace, SW3 4DH. *T:* (0171) 352 5391. *Clubs:* Boodle's, White's. *Died 31 March 1997.*

KNIGHT, Nora; *see* Swinburne Johnson, Elinore.

KNIGHT, Richard James; JP; MA; *b* 19 July 1915; *s* of Richard William Knight; *m* 1953, Hilary Marian, *d* of Rev. F. W. Argyle; two *s* one *d. Educ:* Dulwich Coll. (Scholar); Trinity Coll., Cambridge (Scholar; 1st class Hons Classical Tripos Pt I, 1936, Part II, 1937); BA Open Univ., 1988. Served War of 1939–45 in Gordon Highlanders, Capt. Asst Master, Fettes Coll., Edinburgh, 1938–39; Asst Master and Housemaster, Marlborough Coll., 1945–56; Headmaster of Oundle Sch., 1956–68, of Monkton Combe Sch., 1968–78. Reader, Dio. Bath and Wells. JP Northants, 1960, Bath, 1970, Avon, 1974. Hon. Liveryman, Grocers' Co., 1989. *Recreations:* cricket and other games. *Address:* 123 Midford Road, Bath BA2 5RX. *T:* (01225) 832276. *Died 8 Sept. 2000.*

KNIGHT, William Arnold, CMG 1966; OBE 1954; Controller and Auditor-General of Uganda, 1962–68, retired; *b* 14 June 1915; *e s* of late William Knight, Llanfairfechan, and Clara Knight; *m* 1939, Bronwen Parry; one *s* one *d. Educ:* Friars' Sch., Bangor; University Coll. of North Wales (BA Hons). Entered Colonial Audit Dept as an Asst Auditor, 1938; service in Kenya, 1938–46; Mauritius, 1946–49; Sierra Leone, 1949–52; British Guiana, 1952–57; Uganda, 1957–68; Commissioner, inquiry into economy and efficiency, Uganda, 1969–70. *Recreations:* fishing, gardening. *Address:* Neopardy Mills, near Crediton, Devon EX17 5EP. *T:* Crediton (01363) 772513. *Club:* East India. *Died 10 June 1996.*

KNIGHTS, Lionel Charles, MA, PhD; King Edward VII Professor of English Literature, University of Cambridge, 1965–73, then Emeritus Professor; Fellow, Queens' College, Cambridge, 1965–73; *b* 15 May 1906; *s* of C. E. and Lois M. Knights; *m* 1936, Elizabeth M. Barnes; one *s* one *d. Educ:* grammar schs; Selwyn Coll. (Hon. Fellow, 1974), and Christ's Coll., Cambridge Univ. Charles Oldham Shakespeare Scholar, 1928; Members' Prize, 1929. Lecturer in English Literature, Manchester Univ., 1933–34, 1935–47; Prof. of English Lit., Univ. of Sheffield, 1947–52; Winterstoke Prof. of English, Bristol Univ., 1953–64. Fellow, Kenyon Sch. of Letters, 1950; Andrew Mellon Vis. Prof., Univ. of Pittsburgh, 1961–62 and 1966; Mrs W. Beckman Vis. Prof., Berkeley, 1970. Mem. of editorial board of Scrutiny, a Quarterly Review, 1932–53. For. Hon. Mem., Amer. Acad. of Arts and Sciences, 1981. Docteur (*hc*) de l'Univ. de Bordeaux, 1964; Hon. DUniv York, 1969; Hon. DLitt: Manchester, 1974; Sheffield, 1978; Warwick, 1979; Bristol, 1984. *Publications:* Drama and Society in the Age of Jonson, 1937; Explorations: Essays in Literary Criticism, 1946; Shakespeare's Politics (Shakespeare Lecture, British Academy), 1957; Some Shakespearean Themes, 1959; An Approach to Hamlet, 1960; (ed with Basil Cottle) Metaphor and Symbol, 1961; Further Explorations, 1965; Public Voices: literature and politics (Clark Lectures), 1971; Explorations 3, 1976; Hamlet and other Shakespeare

Essays, 1979; Selected Essays in Criticism, 1981. *Address:* 11 Summerville, Durham DH1 4QH.
Died 8 March 1997.

KNILL, Sir John Kenelm Stuart, 4th Bt *cr* 1893, of The Grove, Blackheath, Kent; *b* 8 April 1913; *s* of Sir John Stuart Knill, 3rd Bt and Lucy Emmeline (*d* 1952), *o d* of Captain Thomas Willis, MN, FRGS; *S* father, 1973; *m* 1951, Violette Maud Florence Martin Barnes (*d* 1983); two *s. Educ:* St Gregory's School, Downside. Served as Lieut, RNVR, 1940–45 (Atlantic Star, Italy, France and Germany Stars). Industrial management trainee, 1945–48; canal transport operator, 1948–54; pig farmer, 1954–63; civil servant, MoD, 1963–77. President: Avon Transport 2000; Commercial Narrowboat Operators' Assoc.; Vice-President: Cotswold Canals (formerly Thames Severn Canal) Trust; Hereford and Gloucester Canal Trust; Founder and Pres., Assoc. of Canal Enterprises, 1982; Member: Great Western Soc.; Inland Waterways Assoc. *Recreations:* canal and railway restoration, scouting. *Heir: s* Thomas John Pugin Bartholomew Knill [*b* 24 Aug. 1952; *m* 1977, Kathleen Muszynski]. *Address:* 11 St Nicholas Court, Bathampton, Somerset BA2 6UZ. *T:* (01225) 463603. *Club:* Victory Services.
Died 15 April 1998.

KNOTT, Sir John Laurence, AC 1981; Kt 1971; CBE 1960; *b* 6 July 1910; *s* of J. Knott, Kyneton, Victoria; *m* 1935, Jean R., *d* of C. W. Milnes; three *s* one *d. Educ:* Cobram State Sch.; Melbourne Univ. (Dip Com). Private Sec. to Minister for Trade Treaties, 1935–38; Sec., Aust. Delegn, Eastern Gp Supply Council, New Delhi, 1940; Exec. Officer, Secondary Industries Commn, 1943–45; Mem. Jt War Production Cttee; Dir, Defence Prodn Planning Br., Dept of Supply, 1950–52; Sec., Dept of Defence Prodn, 1957–58; Mem., Aust. Defence Mission to US, 1957; Sec., Dept of Supply, Melb., 1959–65; Dep. High Comr for Australia, London, 1966–68; Dir-Gen., Australian PO, 1968–72. Leader, Aust. Mission to Eur. Launcher Develt Orgn Conferences: London, 1961; Paris, 1965, 1966; Rome, 1967; Vice-Pres. Council, Eur. Launcher Develt Orgn, 1967–69. Mem. Council, Melbourne Univ., 1973–76. Pres., ESU (Victoria); Chm., Epworth Hosp. Foundn; Chm., Salvation Army Red Shield Appeal, 1982–87. Freeman, City of London. AASA, FCIS, AFAIM, LCA; idc. *Recreations:* bowls (Vice-Pres., Royal Victorian Bowling Assoc., 1957–58; Chm., World Bowls (1980) Ltd), golf, gardening. *Address:* 3 Fenwick Street, Kew, Vic 3101, Australia. *T:* (3) 98537777. *Clubs:* Melbourne, West Brighton (Melbourne).
Died 8 March 1999.

KNOWELDEN, Prof. John, CBE 1983; JP; MD; FRCP, FFCM, DPH; Professor of Community Medicine (formerly of Preventive Medicine and Public Health), University of Sheffield, 1960–84, retired; *b* 19 April 1919; *s* of Clarence Arthur Knowelden; *m* 1946, Mary Sweet; two *s. Educ:* Colfe's Grammar Sch., Lewisham; St George's Hosp. Med. Sch.; London Sch. of Hygiene and Trop. Med.; Johns Hopkins Sch. of Public Health, Baltimore. Surg. Lt, RNVR, 1942–46. Rockefeller Fellowship in Preventive Med., 1947–49; Lectr in Med. Statistics and Mem., MRC Statistical Research Unit, 1949–60. Academic Registrar, FCM, 1977–83. Civil Consultant in Community Medicine to Royal Navy, 1977–84. Editor, Brit. Jl of Preventive and Social Medicine, 1959–69 and 1973–76. Formerly Hon. Sec., Sect. of Epidemiology, Royal Society Medicine and Chm., Soc. for Social Medicine; Mem., WHO Expert Advisory Panel on Health Statistics. *Publications:* (with Ian Taylor) Principles of Epidemiology, 2nd edn 1964; papers on clinical and prophylactic trials and epidemiological topics. *Recreations:* photography,

gardening. *Address:* 69 Esplanade, Scarborough, N Yorks YO11 2UZ. *T:* (01723) 374502.
Died 23 July 1997.

KNOX, Rev. Canon Ian Carroll; Canon Residentiary of Wakefield Cathedral, 1989–97, then Canon Emeritus; Adult Education Officer, 1989–97, and Director of Ecumenical Affairs, 1994–97, Diocese of Wakefield; Chaplain to the Queen, since 1996; *b* 29 March 1932; *m* 1958, Sheila Thacker; two *s* (one *d* decd). *Educ:* Queen Elizabeth Grammar Sch., Wakefield; St John's Coll., Durham (BA 1954; DipTh 1955). Ordained deacon, 1955, priest, 1956; Assistant Curate: Illingworth, 1955–58; Lightcliffe, 1958–60; Vicar: St Matthew, Rastrick, 1960–77; Huddersfield, 1977–89; Rural Dean of Huddersfield, 1977–89; Diocesan Dir of Educn, 1989–96, Chm., Diocesan Cttee for Parish Educn, 1996–97, Wakefield. Hon. Canon, Wakefield, 1976–89. Mem., Gen. Synod of C of E, 1980–85, 1987–90 and 1991–95. *Recreations:* walking, gardening, sailing, ornithology, meeting people. *Address:* 12 Inglemere Gardens, Arnside, Cumbria LA5 0BX. *T:* (01524) 762404.
Died 5 Dec. 1997.

KNOX, Robert, MD, FRCP, FRCPath; Emeritus Professor of Bacteriology, University of London (Professor of Bacteriology, Guy's Hospital Medical School, 1949–69); *b* 29 May 1904; *s* of Dr Robert Knox, radiologist; *m* 1936, Bessie Lynda Crust (*d* 1998); three *d. Educ:* Highgate; Balliol Coll., Oxford (Classical Scholar; 1st Class Hon. Mods 1924, 2nd Class Lit. Hum. 1926; BA 1927; MA 1945); St Bartholomew's Hosp. (MB, BS London, 1932; MD 1934); MA Cambridge, 1935. MRCS 1932; LRCP 1932, MRCP 1934, FRCP 1953; FRCPath (FCPath 1964). House Physician and Chief Asst, St Bartholomew's Hosp , 1932–35; Demonstrator in Pathology, University of Cambridge, 1935–37; Mem. of Scientific Staff, Imperial Cancer Research Fund, 1937–39; Dir of Public Health Laboratories (Med. Research Council) at Stamford, 1939, Leicester 1940, and Oxford, 1945. Fellow, Royal Soc. of Medicine; Member: Pathological Soc.; Soc. of Gen. Microbiology; Assoc. of Clinical Pathologists. *Publications:* on bacteriological subjects in medical and scientific journals. *Recreations:* coxed Oxford Univ., 1925; golf. *Address:* Five Pines, The Marld, Ashtead, Surrey KT21 1RQ. *T:* (01372) 275102.
Died 23 Aug. 2000.

KNUDSEN, Semon Emil; retired; Chairman and Chief Executive, White Motor Corporation, 1971–80; *b* 2 Oct. 1912; *o s* of William S. and Clara Euler Knudsen; *m* 1938, Florence Anne McConnell; one *s* three *d. Educ:* Dartmouth Coll.; Mass Inst. of Technology. Joined General Motors, 1939; series of supervisory posts; Gen. Man., Detroit Diesel Div., 1955; Gen. Man., Pontiac Motor Div., 1956; Gen. Man., Chevrolet Motor Div., 1961; Dir of General Motors and Gp Vice-Pres. i/c of all Canadian and overseas activities, 1965; Exec. Vice-Pres. with added responsibility for domestic non-automotive divs, 1966, also defense activities, 1967; resigned from Gen. Motors Corp., 1968; Pres., Ford Motor Co., 1968–69. Mem., MIT Corp. Mem. Bd of Dirs, Boys Clubs of Amer.; Trustee, Oakland (Mich) Univ. Foundn and Cleveland Clinic Fund. *Recreations:* golf, tennis, deepsea fishing, hunting. *Address:* 1965 N Woodward Avenue, Bloomfield Hills, MI 48304–2238, USA. *Clubs:* Detroit Athletic (Detroit); Bloomfield Hills Country (Mich); Everglades, Bath & Tennis (Fla).
Died 6 July 1998.

KOECHLIN-SMYTHE, Patricia Rosemary, OBE 1956; President, 1983–86, Vice-President, since 1987, British Show Jumping Association; Member of British Show Jumping Team, 1947–64; *b* 22 Nov. 1928; *d* of late Capt. Eric Hamilton Smythe, MC, Légion d'Honneur, and Frances Monica Smythe (*née* Curtoys); *m* 1963, Samuel

Koechlin (*d* 1985), Switzerland; two *d. Educ:* St Michael's Sch., Cirencester; Talbot Heath, Bournemouth. Show Jumping: first went abroad with British Team, 1947; Leading Show Jumper of the Year, 1949, 1958 (with T. Edgar), and 1962; European Ladies' Championship: Spa, 1957; Deauville, 1961; Madrid, 1962; Hickstead, 1963; Harringay: BSJA Spurs, 1949, 1951, 1952, 1954 (Victor Ludorum Championship), 1953 and 1954; Harringay Spurs, 1953; Grand Prix, Brussels, 1949, 1952 and 1956. Ladies' record for high jump (2 m. 10 cm.) Paris, 1950; won in Madrid, 1951. White City: 1951 (Country Life Cup); 1953 (Selby Cup). Was Leading Rider and won Prix du Champion, Paris, 1952; Leading Rider, etc, Marseilles, 1953; Individual Championship, etc, Harrisburg, Penn, USA, 1953; Pres. of Mexico Championship, New York, 1953; Toronto (in team winning Nations Cup), 1953; Lisbon (won 2 events), Grand Prix, Madrid, and Championship, Vichy, 1954; Grand Prix de Paris and 3 other events, 1954; Bruxelles Puissance and new ladies' record for high jump (2m. 24 cm.), Leading Rider of Show, 1954; BHS Medal of Honour, Algiers Puissance and Grand Prix, 4 events in Paris, 4 events at White City including the Championship, 1955; Grand Prix and Leading Rider of Show and 4 other events, Brussels, 1956; Grand Prix Militaire and Puissance, Lucerne; Mem. British Equestrian Olympic Team, Stockholm (Show Jumping Bronze Medal), 1956; IHS National Championship, White City; Leading Rider and other events, Palermo, 1956; won 2 Puissance events, Paris, 1957; BSJA, 1957; Ladies' National Championship in 1954–59 and 1961 and 1962 (8 times); Daily Mail Cup, White City, 1955, 1957, 1960, 1962; Mem. winning British Team, White City: 1952, 1953, 1956, 1957; Amazon Prize, Aachen, 1958; Queen's Cup, Royal Internat. Horse Show, White City, 1958; Preis von Parsenn, Davos, 1957, 1958, 1959; Championship Cup, Brussels Internat. Horse Show, 1958; Lisbon Grand Prix, 1959; Olympic Trial, British Timken Show, and Prix de la Banque de Bruxelles at Brussels, 1959. Lucerne Grand Prix; Prince Hal Stakes, Country Life and Riding Cup, White City; Pembroke Stakes, Horse Show Cttee Cup, and Leading Rider, Dublin (all in 1960). Mem. British Olympic Team in Rome, 1960. Copenhagen Grand Prix; Amazon Prize, Aachen; John Player Trophy, White City; St Gall Ladies Championship (all in 1961); Saddle of Honour and Loriners' Cup, White City, 1962; British Jumping Derby, Hickstead, 1962. Member: Internat. Council, WWF; Nat. Council, WWF UK; Bd, Earthwatch Europe; Achievement Bd, ICBP. Hon. Freeman, Worshipful Co. of Farriers, 1955; Freeman of the City of London, 1956; Hon. Freeman, Worshipful Company of Loriners, 1962; Yeoman, Worshipful Company of Saddlers, 1963. *Publications:* (as Pat Smythe): Jump for Joy: Pat Smythe's Story, 1954; Pat Smythe's Book of Horses, 1955; One Jump Ahead, 1956; Jacqueline rides for a Fall, 1957; Three Jays against the Clock, 1957; Three Jays on Holiday, 1958; Three Jays go to Town, 1959; Horses and Places, 1959; Three Jays over the Border, 1960; Three Jays go to Rome, 1960; Three Jays Lend a Hand, 1961; Jumping Round the World, 1962; Florian's Farmyard, 1962; Flanagan My Friend, 1963; Bred to Jump, 1965; Show Jumping, 1967; (with Fiona Hughes) A Pony for Pleasure, 1969; A Swiss Adventure, 1970; (with Fiona Hughes) Pony Problems, 1971; A Spanish Adventure, 1971; A Cotswold Adventure, 1972; Leaping Life's Fences, 1992. *Recreations:* swimming, music, sailing, all sports, languages. *Address:* Sudgrove House, Miserden, near Stroud, Glos GL6 7JD. *T:* Cirencester (01285) 821360. *Died 27 Feb. 1996.*

KOHLER, Irene; pianist; Professor, Trinity College of Music, London, 1952–79; *b* London, 7 April 1912; *m* 1950, Dr Harry Waters, medical practitioner. *Educ:* Royal College of Music. Studied with Arthur Benjamin; Challen Medal, Danreuther Prize, etc; travelling scholarship to Vienna; studied there with Edward Steuermann and Egon Wellesz. BMus; Hon. FTCL, GRSM, LRAM, ARCM. First professional engagement, Bournemouth, 1933, resulting in engagement by BBC; played at first night of 40th Promenade Season, 1934; first foreign tour (recitals and broadcasts), Holland, 1938; during War of 1939–45 gave concerts for the Forces in this country and toured France and Belgium, also India and Burma, under auspices of ENSA; subsequently played in many countries of Europe and made tours. Eugene Goossens selected her for first European performance of his Phantasy Concerto; broadcast 1st performance of Sonata by Gunilla Lowenstein, Stockholm. She gave 3 concerts at the Festival Hall in Festival of Britain Year, 1951. Canadian American Tour, 1953; World Tour, 1955–56; African Tour, 1958; 2nd African Tour, 1959; Bulgarian Tour, 1959; 2nd World Tour, 1962; Czechoslovakian Tour, 1963; Scandinavian Tour, 1970; Far and Middle East Tour, 1972; recitals and master classes, Japan, 1979, 1981; Polish Tour, 1980. Film appearances include: Train of Events, Odette, Secret People, Lease of Life, and a documentary for the Ministry of Information. *Address:* 28 Castelnau, SW13 9RU. *T:* 0181–748 5512.
Died 23 April 1996.

KOHNSTAM, George, PhD; Principal of the Graduate Society, University of Durham, 1981–86 (Deputy Principal, 1972–81); Reader in Physical Chemistry, University of Durham, 1962–86; *b* 25 Dec. 1920; *s* of Emil and Margaret Kohnstam; *m* 1953, Patricia Elizabeth, *d* of Rev. A. W. G. Duffield and Margaret Duffield; one *s* three *d. Educ:* Royal Grammar Sch., High Wycombe; University Coll. London (BSc 1940, PhD 1948). Tuffnel Scholar, Univ. of London, 1940 (postponed); applied chemical res., 1941–45; Temp. Asst Lectr in Chemistry, UCL, 1948–50; Lectr in Phys. Chem., Univ. of Durham, 1950–59, Sen. Lectr, 1959–62. *Publications:* papers and review articles in chemical jls. *Recreations:* dinghy sailing, gardening, bridge, travel. *Address:* 67 Hallgarth Street, Durham City DH1 3AY. *T:* (0191) 3842018.
Died 21 June 1997.

KÖRNER, Prof. Stephan, JurDr, PhD; FBA 1967; Professor of Philosophy, Bristol University, 1952–79, and Yale University, 1970–84; *b* Ostrava, Czechoslovakia, 26 Sept. 1913; *o s* of Emil Körner and Erna (*née* Maier); *m* 1944, Edith Laner, CBE, BSc, LLD, JP (*d* 18 Aug. 2000); one *s* one *d. Educ:* Classical Gymnasium; Charles' Univ., Prague (JurDr); Trinity Hall, Cambridge (PhD; Hon. Fellow, 1991). Army Service, 1936–39, 1943–46. University of Bristol: Lectr in Philosophy, 1946; Dean, Faculty of Arts, 1965–66; Pro-Vice-Chancellor, 1968–71; Hon. Fellow, 1987. Visiting Professor of Philosophy: Brown Univ., 1957; Yale Univ., 1960; Texas Univ., 1964; Indiana Univ., 1967; Graz Univ., 1980–86 (Hon. Prof., 1982). President: Brit. Soc. for Philosophy of Science, 1965; Aristotelian Soc., 1967; Internat. Union of History and Philosophy of Science, 1969; Mind Assoc., 1973. Editor, Ratio, 1961–80. Hon. DLitt Belfast, 1981; Hon. Phil. Dr Graz, 1984. *Publications:* Kant, 1955; Conceptual Thinking, 1955; (ed) Observation and Interpretation, 1957; The Philosophy of Mathematics, 1960; Experience and Theory, 1966; Kant's Conception of Freedom (British Acad. Lecture), 1967; What is Philosophy?, 1969; Categorial Frameworks, 1970; Abstraction in Science and Morals (Eddington Meml Lecture), 1971; (ed) Practical Reason, 1974; (ed) Explanation, 1976; Experience and Conduct, 1976; Metaphysics: its structure and function, 1984; contribs to philosophical periodicals. *Recreation:* walking. *Address:* 10 Belgrave Road, Bristol BS8 2AB.
Died 18 Aug. 2000.

KOSTERLITZ, Hans Walter, MD, PhD, DSc; FRCPE 1981; FRS 1978; FRSE 1951; Director, Unit for Research on Addictive Drugs, University of Aberdeen, since 1973; *b* 27 April 1903; *s* of Bernhard and Selma Kosterlitz; *m* 1937, Johanna Maria Katherina Gresshöner; one *s*. *Educ:* Univs of Heidelberg, Freiburg and Berlin. MD Berlin 1929; PhD 1936, DSc 1944, Hon. LLD 1979, Aberdeen. Assistant, 1st Medical Dept, Univ. of Berlin, 1928–33; University of Aberdeen: Research Worker in Physiology, 1934–36; Asst and Carnegie Teaching Fellow, 1936–39; Lectr, 1939–45; Sen. Lectr, 1945–55; Reader in Physiology, 1955–68; Prof. of Pharmacology and Chm., 1968–73. Visiting Lecturer: in Pharmacology, Harvard Med. Sch., 1953–54; in Biology, Brown Univ., 1953; Vis. Prof. of Pharmacology, Harvard Med. Sch., 1977; Lectures: J. Y. Dent Meml, 1970; Otto Krayer, 1977; Scheele, 1977; Gen. Session, Fedn Amer. Socs for Experimental Biol., 1978; Sutcliffe Kerr, 1978; Charnock Bradley Meml, 1979; Arnold H. Maloney, 1979; Lister, 1980; Lita Annenberg Hazen, 1980; Lilly, 1980; Sherrington Meml, RSocMed, 1982; N. J. Giarman Meml, Yale Univ. Sch. of Med., 1982; Third Transatlantic, Endocrine Soc., 1982; Lorenzini, Milan, 1982; Sherrington, Univ. of Liverpool, 1989. Foreign Associate, National Acad. of Sciences, USA, 1985. Dr *hc* Liège, 1978; Hon. DSc St Andrews, 1982; Hon. LLD Dundee, 1988. Schmiedeberg Plakette, German Pharmacol Soc., 1976; Pacesetter Award, US Nat. Inst. on Drug Abuse, 1977; Nathan B. Eddy Award, US Cttee on Problems of Drug Dependence, 1978; (jtly) Albert Lasker Prize, 1978; Baly Medal, RCP, 1979; Royal Medal, 1979, Wellcome Foundn Prize, 1982, Royal Soc.; Makdougall-Brisbane Medal, RSE, 1980; Thudichum Medal, Biochem. Soc., 1980; Feldberg Foundn Prize, 1981; Harvey Prize, Technion, 1981; Prof. Lucien Dautrebande Prize, 1982; Wellcome Gold Medal, British Pharmacol Soc., 1987; Cameron Prize, Univ. of Edinburgh, 1988. *Publications:* (joint editor): Agonist and Antagonist Actions of Narcotic Analgesic Drugs, 1972; The Opiate Narcotics, 1975; Opiates and Endogenous Opioid Peptides, 1976; Pain and Society, 1980; Neuroactive Peptides, 1980; Opioids 1 and 2, 1993; articles in Nature, Jl of Physiol., Brit. Jl of Pharmacol. *Recreations:* music, walking, travelling. *Address:* Unit for Research on Addictive Drugs, University of Aberdeen, Aberdeen AB9 1AS. *T:* (01224) 273000; 16 Glendee Terrace, Cults, Aberdeen AB1 9HX. *T:* (01224) 867366. *Club:* Lansdowne.   *Died 26 Oct. 1996.*

KRUSIN, Sir Stanley (Marks), Kt 1973; CB 1963; Second Parliamentary Counsel, 1970–73; *b* 8 June 1908; *m* 1st, 1937 (wife *d* 1972); one *s* one *d*; 2nd, 1976 (wife *d* 1988). *Educ:* St Paul's Sch.; Balliol Coll., Oxford. Called to the Bar, Middle Temple, 1932. Served RAFVR, Wing Comdr, 1944. Dep. Sec., British Tabulating Machine Co. Ltd, 1945–47; entered Parliamentary Counsel Office, 1947; Parliamentary Counsel, 1953–69. *Address:* 5 Coleridge Walk, NW11 6AT. *T:* (0181) 458 1340. *Club:* Royal Air Force.   *Died 28 April 1998.*

KUBELIK, Rafael; conductor and composer; Chief Conductor of Bayerischer Rundfunk, München, 1961–79; *b* Bychory, 29 June 1914; *s* of Jan Kubelik, violinist, and Marianne (*née* Szell); *m* 1942, Ludmila Bertlova (*d* 1961), violinist; one *s*; *m* 1963, Elsie Morison, soprano. *Educ:* Prague Conservatoire. Conductor, Czech Philharmonic Society, Prague, 1936–39; Musical Director of Opera, Brno, Czechoslovakia, 1939–41; Musical Dir, Czech Philharmonic Orchestra, 1941–48; Musical Dir, Chicago Symphony Orchestra, 1950–53; Musical Dir of the Covent Garden Opera Company, 1955–58; Music Dir, Metropolitan Opera, New York, 1973–74. *Compositions* include: 2 symphonies with chorus; a third symphony (in one movement); Orphikon, symphony for orch.; Sequences for orch.; symphonic Peripeteia for organ and orch.;

Invocation for tenor solo, boys' choir and orch.; 6 string quartets; 1 cantata; Cantata Without Words, for chorus and orch.; Inventions and Interludes, for children's chorus, oboes and trumpets; Children Ballades, after Czech national poems, for soprano solo and string sextet; Concerto in Modo Classico, for violin and strings; Trio Concertante, for piano, violin and cello; *operas:* Veronika; Daybreak; Cornelia Faroli; (after Hans Christian Anderson) Emperor's New Clothes; Flowers of Little Ida; *requiems:* Pro Memoria Patris; Pro Memoria Uxoris; Libera Nos; Quattro Forme per Archi; songs; piano and violin music. Hon. RAM; Hon. Member: Bavarian Acad. of Fine Arts; Royal Swedish Acad. of Music; Italian Assoc. Anton Bruckner; Royal Philharmonic Soc. Hon. Dr Amer. Conservatory of Music, Chicago; Hon. Dr Karls-Univ., Prague. Karl Amadeus Hartmann Gold Medal; Gold Medal, City of Munich; Gustav Mahler Gold Medal, Gustav Mahler Soc., Vienna; Carl Nielsen Gold Medal, Copenhagen; Medal of City of Amsterdam; Mahler Medal, Bruckner Soc. of Amer.; Hans von Bülow Medal, Berlin Phil. Orch.; Gold Medal, City of Lucerne; Medal of Dutch Bruckner Soc.; Gold Medal, Royal Philharmonic Soc.; Grand Prix Nat. du Disque, Paris; Czechoslovak Soc. of Arts and Scis, Washington; Golden Book of the Jewish Nat. Fund; Golden Key, City of Cleveland. Hon. Citizen: Prague; Brno. Grosses Bundesverdienstkreuz (FRG); Bavarian Order of Merit; Chevalier, Order of the Dannebrog (Denmark); Comtur Istrucao Publica (Portugal); Commandeur de l'ordre des Arts et des Lettres (France); Thomas G. Masaryk Order, 1 (Czech and Slovak Fed. Republic), 1991. *Address:* 6047 Kastanienbaum, Haus im Sand, Switzerland.   *Died 11 Aug. 1996.*

KUBRICK, Stanley; producer, director, script writer; *b* 26 July 1928; *s* of Dr Jacques L. Kubrick and Gertrude Kubrick; *m* 1958, Suzanne Christiane Harlan; three *d*. *Educ:* William Howard Taft High Sch.; City Coll. of City of New York. Joined Look Magazine, 1946; at age of 21 made documentary, Day of the Fight; made short for RKO, Flying Padre. *Feature films:* Fear and Desire, 1953 (at age of 24); Killer's Kiss, 1954; The Killing, 1956; Paths of Glory, 1957; Spartacus, 1960; Lolita, 1962; Dr Strangelove or How I Learned to Stop Worrying and Love the Bomb, 1964; 2001: A Space Odyssey, 1968; A Clockwork Orange, 1971; Barry Lyndon, 1975; The Shining, 1978; Full Metal Jacket, 1987; Eyes Wide Shut, 1999. *Recreations:* literature, music, public affairs. *Address:* c/o Loeb & Loeb, 10100 Santa Monica Boulevard, Suite 2200, Los Angeles, CA 90067, USA.   *Died 7 March 1999.*

KUENSSBERG, Ekkehard von, CBE 1969; FRCGP, FRCOG, FRCPEd; President, Royal College of General Practitioners, 1976–79; *b* 17 Dec. 1913; *s* of Prof. Eberhard von Kuenssberg; *m* 1941, Dr Constance Ferrar Hardy; two *s* two *d*. *Educ:* Schloss Schule, Salem; Univs of Innsbruck, Heidelberg and Edinburgh (MB, ChB Edin. 1939). FRCGP 1967; FRCOG (*aeg*) 1981; FRCPEd 1981. Gen. practice, Edinburgh. RAMC, 1944–46 (Lt-Col, DADMS E Africa Comd). Mem., Safety of Drugs Cttee, 1964–71; Chm., Gen. Med. Services Cttee, Scotland; Member: Gen. Med. Services Cttee, UK, 1960–68; Lothian Area Health Bd, 1974–80. Royal College of General Practitioners: Chm. Council, 1970–73; Hon. Treas., Research Foundn Bd, 1960–77; Mackenzie Lectr, 1970; Wolfson Travelling Prof., 1974. Member: Council, Queen's Nursing Inst., 1972–76; Court, Edinburgh Univ., 1971–79. Foundation Council Award, RCGP, 1967; Hippocrates Medal, SIMG, 1974. FRSocMed. *Publications:* The Team in General Practice, 1966; An Opportunity to Learn, 1977. *Recreations:* music, history. *Address:* Hilton Lodge, Court Street, Haddington, East Lothian EH41 3AF. *T:* (01620) 822529.   *Died 27 Dec. 2000.*

KUNERALP, Zeki, Hon. GCVO 1971; *b* Istanbul, 5 Oct. 1914; *s* of Ali Kemal and Sabiha, *d* of Mustafa Zeki Pasha; *m* 1943, Necla Ozdilci (*d* 1978); two *s. Educ:* Univ. of Berne. DrIuris 1938. Entered Diplomatic Service, 1940: served Bucharest, Prague, Paris, Nato Delegn and at Min. of Foreign Affairs, Ankara; Asst Sec.-Gen. 1957; Sec.-Gen. 1960; Ambassador to Berne, 1960, to Court of St James's, 1964–66; Sec.-Gen. at Min. of Foreign Affairs, Ankara, 1966–69; Ambassador to Court of St James's, 1969–72, to Spain, 1972–79, retired. Mem., Hon. Soc. of Knights of the Round Table. Held German, Greek, Italian, Papal, Jordanian, Iranian and National Chinese orders. *Publication:* Sadece Diplomat (memoirs), 1981. *Recreations:* reading, ballet. *Address:* Fenerbahçe Cadessi 85/B, D4, Kiziltoprak, Istanbul 81030, Turkey.
Died 26 July 1998.

KURONGKU, Most Rev. Sir Peter, KBE 1986; DD; Archbishop of Port Moresby, (RC), since 1981; *b* 1930; *s* of Adam Mapa and Eve Kawa. *Educ:* Holy Spirit Seminary, Bomana. Ordained priest, 1966; consecrated Bishop, 1978. *Address:* PO Box 1032, Boroko, NCD 111, Papua New Guinea. *T:* (office) 3251192, *Fax:* 3256731.
Died 11 June 1996.

KUROSAWA, Akira; Japanese film director; *b* 23 March 1910; *m* 1945, Yoko Yaguchi (*d* 1985); one *s* one *d. Educ:* Keika Middle School. Assistant Director, Toho Film Co., 1936. Mem. Jury, Internat. Film Fest. of India, 1977. Directed first film, Sanshiro Sugata, 1943; *films include:* Sanshiro Sugata; The Most Beautiful, 1944; Sanshiro Sugata II, 1945; They Who Step on the Tiger's Tail, 1945; No Regret for our Youth, 1946; One Wonderful Sunday, 1947; Drunken Angel, 1948; The Quiet Duel, 1949; Stray Dog, 1949; Scandal, 1950; Rashomon (1st prize, Venice Film Fest.), 1950; The Idiot, 1951; Ikuru, 1952; Seven Samurai, 1954; Record of a Living Being, 1955; The Throne of Blood, 1957; The Lower Depths, 1957; The Hidden Fortress, 1958; The Bad Sleep Well, 1960; Yojimbo, 1961; Sanjuro, 1962; High and Low, 1963; Red Beard, 1965; Dodes'kaden, 1970; Dersu Uzala (Oscar award), 1975; Kagemusha (Golden Palm Award, Cannes Film Festival), 1980; Ran, 1985; Dreams, 1990; Rhapsody in August, 1991. *Publication:* Something like an Autobiography (trans. Audie Bock), 1984.
Died 6 Sept. 1998.

KURTI, Prof. Nicholas, CBE 1973; FRS 1956; DrPhil; FInstP; Emeritus Professor of Physics, University of Oxford; Vice-President, Royal Society, 1965–67; *b* 14 May 1908; *s* of late Károly Kürti and Margit Pintér, Budapest; *m* 1946, Georgiana, (Giana), *d* of late Brig.-Gen. and Mrs C. T. Shipley; two *d. Educ:* Minta-Gymnasium, Budapest; University of Paris (Licence ès sci. phys.); University of Berlin (DrPhil); MA Oxon. Asst, Techn. Hochschule, Breslau, 1931–33; Research Position, Clarendon Laboratory, Oxford, 1933–40; UK Atomic Bomb Project, 1940–45; University Demonstrator in Physics, Oxford, 1945–60; Reader in Physics, Oxford, 1960–67; Prof. of Physics, Oxford, 1967–75; Senior Research Fellow, Brasenose Coll., Oxford, 1947–67, Professorial Fellow, 1967–75, then Emeritus Fellow. Buell G. Gallagher Visiting Prof., City Coll., New York, 1963; Vis. Prof., Univ. of Calif, Berkeley, 1964; Dist. Vis. Prof., Amherst Coll., 1979. Lectures: May, Inst. of Metals, 1963; Kelvin, IEE, 1971; Larmor, Queen's Univ., Belfast, 1975; James Scott (also Prize), RSE, 1976; Cherwell-Simon, Oxford Univ., 1977; Tyndall, Inst. of Physics, Royal Dublin Soc., 1980. Member: Electricity Supply Research Council, 1960–79; Advisory Cttee for Scientific and Technical Information, 1966–68; Comité de Direction, Service Nat. des Champs Intenses, CNRS, 1973–75; Comité, Problèmes Socio-économique de l'Energie, CNRS, 1975–78; Chairman: Adv. Cttee for Research on Measurement and Standards, DTI, 1969–73; Jt Cttee on Scientific and Technol Records, Royal Soc./Royal Commn on Historical MSS, 1970–76 (Mem., 1966–70). Member: Council, Royal Soc., 1964–67; Council, Soc. Française de Physique, 1957–60, 1970–73; Council, Inst. of Physics and Physical Soc., 1969–73; Treasurer, CODATA (Cttee on data for sci. and technol., ICSU), 1973–80; Chm., Cttee of Management, Science Policy Foundn, 1970–75. Governor: College of Aeronautics, Cranfield, 1953–69; British Nutrition Foundn, 1986–97. Editor-in-Chief, Europhysics Letters, 1985–89. Emeritus Mem., Acad. Europaea, 1990; Foreign Hon. Mem., Amer. Acad. Arts and Sciences, 1968; Hon. Member: Hungarian Acad. of Sciences, 1970; Société Française de Physique, 1974; Fachverband deutscher Köche, 1978; European Physical Soc., 1989; Hungarian Physical Soc., 1993; Foreign Member: Finnish Acad. of Sciences and Letters, 1974; Akad. der Wissenschaften der DDR, 1976–92. Holweck Prize, British and French Physical Socs, 1955; Fritz London Award, 1957; Hughes Medal, Royal Soc., 1969. Chevalier de la Légion d'Honneur, 1976; Hungarian Order of the Star, 1988; Hungarian Order of Merit, 1996. *Publications:* (jtly) Low Temperature Physics, 1952; (ed jtly) Experimental Cryophysics, 1961; (ed with Giana Kurti) But the Crackling is Superb, 1988; papers on cryophysics, magnetism, energy and culinary physics; articles in the New Chambers's Encyclopædia. *Recreations:* cooking, enjoying its results and judiciously applying physics to the noble art of cookery. *Address:* 38 Blandford Avenue, Oxford OX2 8DZ. *T:* (01865) 556176; Clarendon Laboratory, Parks Road, Oxford OX1 3PU. *T:* (01865) 282192, *Fax:* (01865) 272400. *Club:* Athenæum.
Died 24 Nov. 1998.

L

LABOUCHERE, Sir George (Peter), GBE 1964; KCMG 1955 (CMG 1951); HM Diplomatic Service, retired; *b* 2 Dec. 1905; *s* of late F. A. Labouchere; *m* 1943, Rachel Katharine (*d* 1996), *d* of Hon. Eustace Hamilton-Russell. *Educ:* Charterhouse Sch.; Sorbonne, Paris. Entered Diplomatic Service, 1929; served in Madrid, Cairo, Rio de Janeiro, Stockholm, Nanking, Buenos Aires; UK Deputy-Commissioner for Austria, 1951–53; HM Minister, Hungary, 1953–55; Ambassador to Belgium, 1955–60; Ambassador to Spain, 1960–66. Mem., Dilettanti Society; FRSA. *Recreations:* shooting, fishing, Chinese ceramics, contemporary painting and sculpture. *Address:* Dudmaston, Bridgnorth, Salop WV15 6QN. *Clubs:* Brooks's, Pratt's, Beefsteak, White's.
Died 14 June 1999.

LACEY, Ven. Clifford George; Archdeacon of Lewisham, 1985–89, then Emeritus; *b* 1 April 1921; *s* of Edward and Annie Elizabeth Lacey; *m* 1944, Sylvia Lilian George; one *s* two *d*. *Educ:* King's College London (AKC); St Boniface Coll., Warminster. RAFVR, 1941–46. Deacon 1950, priest 1951; Curate: St Hilda, Crofton Park, 1950–53; Kingston-upon-Thames, 1953–56; Vicar: St James, Merton, 1956–66; Eltham, 1966–79 (Sub-dean, 1970–79); Borough Dean of Greenwich, 1979–85; Bp of Norwich's Officer for retired clergy and widows, 1991–. Hon Canon of Southwark, 1974–. *Recreation:* photography. *Address:* 31 Kerridges, East Harling, Norwich NR16 2QA. *T:* (01953) 718458.
Died 16 Feb. 1997.

LACEY, Frank; Director, Metrication Board, 1976–79, retired; *b* 4 Feb. 1919; *s* of Frank Krauter and Maud Krauter (*née* Lacey); *m* 1944, Maggie Tyrrell Boyes, 2nd *d* of late Sydney Boyes; one *s* one *d*. *Educ:* St Ignatius Coll., N7. Served War, 1939–46, RAFVR. Tax Officer, Inland Revenue, 1936; joined Board of Trade, 1946; Regional Dir, E Region, 1967–70; Counsellor (Commercial), UK Mission, Geneva, 1973–76. *Recreation:* wood turning. *Address:* Alma Cottage, Whistley Green, Hurst, Berks RG10 0EH. *T:* Twyford (01734) 340880. *Died 31 Jan. 1996.*

LACHS, His Honour Henry Lazarus; a Circuit Judge, 1979–99; *b* 31 Dec. 1927; *s* of Samuel and Mania Lachs; *m* 1959, Edith Bergel; four *d*. *Educ:* Liverpool Institute High Sch.; Pembroke Coll., Cambridge (MA, LLB). Called to the Bar, Middle Temple, 1951. A Recorder, 1972–79. Chm., Merseyside Mental Health Review Tribunal, 1968–79. *Address:* 41 Menlove Gardens West, Liverpool L18 2ET. *T:* (0151) 722 5936.
Died 1 Jan. 2000.

LACY, Sir Hugh Maurice Pierce, 3rd Bt *cr* 1921, of Ampton, co. Suffolk; *b* 3 Sept 1943; *s* of Sir Maurice John Pierce Lacy, 2nd Bt, and his 2nd wife, Nansi Jean, *d* of late Myrddin Evans, Bangor, Caernarvonshire; *S* father, 1965; *m* 1968, Deanna, *d* of Howard Bailey. *Educ:* Aiglon Coll., Switzerland. *Heir: b* Patrick Bryan Finucane Lacy [*b* 18 April 1948; *m* 1971, Phyllis Victoria, *d* of E. P. H. James; one *s* one *d*]. *Died 5 Dec. 1998.*

LAITHWAITE, Prof. Eric Roberts; Professor of Heavy Electrical Engineering, Imperial College of Science and Technology, London, 1964–86, then Emeritus; *b* 14 June 1921; *s* of Herbert Laithwaite and Florence (*née* Roberts); *m* 1951, Sheila Margaret Gooddie; two *s* two *d*. *Educ:* Kirkham Grammar Sch.; Regent Street Polytechnic; Manchester Univ. (BSc 1949; MSc 1950; PhD 1957; DSc 1964). RAF, 1941–46 (at RAE Farnborough, 1943–46). Manchester University: Asst Lectr, 1950–53; Lectr, 1953–58; Sen. Lectr, 1958–64. Prof. of Royal Instn, 1967–76; Vis. Prof., Univ. of Sussex, 1990–. President: Assoc. for Science Educn, 1970; SEE, 1991–. FIC 1990. Hon. FIEE 1993. S. G. Brown Award and Medal of Royal Society, 1966; Nikola Tesla Award, IEEE, 1986; Man of Achievement Award, IEE, 1992; Eureka Lillehammer Award, Eur. Council of Ministers, 1995; Electrical Rev. Special Award, 1995. *Publications:* Propulsion without Wheels, 1966; Induction Machines for Special Purposes, 1966; The Engineer in Wonderland, 1967; Linear Electric Motors, 1971; Exciting Electrical Machines, 1974; (with A. Watson and P. E. S. Whalley) The Dictionary of Butterflies and Moths, 1975; (ed) Transport without Wheels, 1977; (with M. W. Thring) How to Invent, 1977; Engineer through the Looking-Glass, 1980; (with L. L. Freris) Electric Energy: its Generation, Transmission and Use, 1980; Invitation to Engineering, 1984; A History of Linear Electric Motors, 1987; An Inventor in the Garden of Eden, 1994; many papers in Proc. IEE (7 premiums) and other learned jls. *Recreations:* entomology, gardening. *Address:* Department of Electrical Engineering, Imperial College, SW7 2BT. *T:* (0171) 589 5111. *Club:* Athenæum. *Died 27 Nov. 1997.*

LAMB, Sir Albert, (Sir Larry), Kt 1980; Editor, Daily Express, 1983–86; Chairman, Larry Lamb Associates, since 1986; *b* Fitzwilliam, Yorks, 15 July 1929; *m* Joan Mary Denise Grogan; two *s* one *d*. *Educ:* Rastrick Grammar Sch. Worked as journalist on Brighouse Echo, Shields Gazette, Newcastle Journal, London Evening Standard; Sub-Editor, Daily Mirror; Editor: (Manchester) Daily Mail, 1968–69; The Sun, 1969–72, 1975–81; Dir, 1970–81, Editorial Dir, 1971–81, News International Ltd; Dep. Chm., News Group, 1979–81; Dir, The News Corporation (Australia) Ltd, 1980–81; Dep. Chm. and Editor-in-Chief, Western Mail Ltd, Perth, Australia, 1981–82; Editor-in-Chief, The Australian, 1982–83. *Publication:* Sunrise, 1989. *Recreations:* fell-walking, cricket, fishing. *Address:* 42 Malvern Court, Onslow Square, SW7 3HY. *Club:* Royal Automobile.
Died 18 May 2000.

LAMB, Harold Norman, CBE 1978; Regional Administrator, South East Thames Regional Health Authority, 1973–81; *b* 21 July 1922; *s* of Harold Alexander and Amelia Lamb; *m* 1946, Joyce Marian Hawkyard; one *s* one *d*. *Educ:* Saltley Grammar School. FHA. Served War, RAF, 1941–46. House Governor, Birmingham Gen. Hosp., 1958; Dep. Sec., United Birmingham Hosps. and House Governor, Queen Elizabeth Hosp., 1961; Sec., SE Metrop. RHB, 1968. Mem. Exec. Council, Royal Inst. of Public Admin., 1970–78. *Recreations:* golf, music. *Address:* 40 Windmill Way, Reigate, Surrey RH2 0JA. *T:* (01737) 221846. *Club:* Walton Heath Golf.
Died 23 April 1998.

LAMB, Sir Larry; see Lamb, Sir Albert.

LAMBERT, 3rd Viscount *cr* 1945, of South Molton, co. Devon; **Michael John Lambert;** *b* 29 Sept. 1912; *s* of 1st Viscount Lambert, PC and Barbara (*d* 1963), *d* of George Stavers; *S* brother, 1989; *m* 1939, Florence Dolores, *d* of Nicholas Lechmere Cunningham Macaskie, QC; three *d*. *Educ:* Harrow; New College, Oxford (MA). *Heir:* none.

Address: Casanuova di Barontoli, 53010 S Rocco a Pilli, Siena, Italy. *Died 22 Oct. 1999 (ext).*

LAMBERT, Eric Thomas Drummond, CMG 1969; OBE 1946; KPM 1943; retired, 1968; *b* 3 Nov. 1909; *s* of late Septimus Drummond Lambert. *Educ:* Royal Sch., Dungannon; Trinity Coll., Dublin, 1928–29. Indian (Imperial) Police, 1929–47: Political Officer for Brahmaputra-Chindwin Survey, 1935–36, and Tirap Frontier Tract, 1942; District Comr, Naga Hills, 1938; commnd General, Chinese Armed Forces, to find and evacuate Chinese Vth Army from Burma to Assam, India, June-Aug. 1942; Chief Civil Liaison Officer XIVth Army, 1944; FCO, 1947–68, with service in SE Asia, W Africa, S America, Nepal, Afghanistan. Pres., Republic of Ireland Br., Burma Star Assoc. Trustee, Nat. Library of Ireland, retired 1991. Corresp. Mem., Acad. of History, Venezuela. Chinese Armed Forces Distinguished Service, 1st Order, 1st class, 1942; Cruz Militar, Venezuela, 1983; Orden del Libertador, Venezuela, 1996. *Publications:* Assam (with Alban Ali), 1943; Carabobo 1821, 1974; Voluntarios Britanicos y Irlandeses en la Gesta Bolivariana, 1982; articles in jls of RGS and Royal Siam Soc., Man in India, The Irish Sword. *Recreations:* historical research, lecturing a bit, golf just done with. *Club:* Stephen's Green (Dublin). *Died 20 Nov. 1996.*

LAMBERT, Prof. Thomas Howard; Professor, 1967–91, and Kennedy Professor, 1983–91, then Emeritus, Department of Mechanical Engineering, University College London; *b* 28 Feb. 1926; *s* of Henry Thomas Lambert and Kate Lambert; *m*; three *s. Educ:* Emanuel Sch.; Univ. of London (BSc (Eng), PhD). FIMechE. D. Napier & Sons: Graduate Apprentice, 1946–48; Develt Engr, 1948–51; University College London: Lectr, 1951–63; Sen. Lectr, 1963–65; Reader, 1965–67; Head of Mech. Engrg Dept, 1977–89; Hon. Fellow, 1991. Hon. RCNC. *Publications:* numerous articles in learned jls, principally in stress analysis, medical engrg and automatic control. *Recreations:* gardening, sailing, practical engineering. *Address:* Department of Mechanical Engineering, University College London, Gower Street, WC1E 6BT. *T:* (0171) 387 7050.

Died 10 Jan. 1997.

LAMERTON, Leonard Frederick, PhD, DSc; FInstP; Director, Institute of Cancer Research, London, 1977–80; Professor of Biophysics as Applied to Medicine, University of London, 1960–80; *b* 1 July 1915; *s* of Alfred Lamerton and Florence (*née* Mason); *m* 1965, Morag MacLeod. *Educ:* King Edward VI Sch., Southampton; University Coll., Southampton (PhD, DSc London). Staff member, Royal Cancer Hosp. and Inst. of Cancer Research, 1938–41 and 1946–80, Dean of the Inst., 1967–77; seconded to United Nations as a Scientific Sec. of first UN Conf. on Peaceful Uses of Atomic Energy, 1955. President: British Inst. of Radiology, 1957–58; Hosp. Physicists Assoc., 1961; Member: Bd of Governors, Royal Marsden Hosp., 1955–80; Bd of Governors, 1978–82, and Cttee of Management, 1978–82, Cardiothoracic Hosp. and Inst. Hon. FRCPath 1972. Roentgen Award, 1950, Barclay Medal, 1961, British Inst. of Radiology. *Publications:* various papers on medical physics, radiation hazard, cell kinetics, experimental cancer therapy. *Recreations:* music, study of the development of Man. *Address:* 10 Burgh Mount, Banstead, Surrey SM7 1ER. *T:* (01737) 353697. *Died 19 Sept. 1999.*

LAMPARD, Martin Robert; *b* 21 Feb. 1926; *s* of late Austin Hugo Lampard and Edith Gertrude Lampard (formerly White); *m* 1957, Felice MacLean; three *d. Educ:* Radley College, Oxford; Christ Church, Oxford (MA). Served RNVR. Admitted solicitor, 1952; joined Ashurst Morris Crisp & Co., 1954, Partner, 1957, Sen. Partner, 1974–86. Formerly Dir, Allied Lyons plc; dir of other

companies. *Address:* Tiffany, 3 Wentworth Road, Aldeburgh, Suffolk IP15 5BB. *T:* (01728) 454078. *Clubs:* Royal Ocean Racing; Royal Yacht Squadron.

Died 25 April 2000.

LANCASTER, Dame Jean, DBE 1963 (OBE 1958); Director, Women's Royal Naval Service, 1961–64; *b* 11 Aug. 1909; *d* of late Richard C. Davies; *m* 1967, Roy Cavander Lancaster (*d* 1981). *Educ:* Merchant Taylors' Sch., Crosby, Lancashire. Joined WRNS, 1939. *Address:* Warren Park Nursing Home, Warren Road, Blundellsands, Liverpool L23 6US. *Died 29 Aug. 1996.*

LANE, Sir David (William Stennis Stuart), Kt 1983; *b* 24 Sept. 1922; *s* of Hubert Samuel Lane, MC; *m* 1955, Lesley Anne Mary Clauson; two *s. Educ:* Eton; Trinity Coll., Cambridge; Yale Univ. Served War of 1939–45 (Royal Navy). Called to the Bar, Middle Temple, 1955. British Iron and Steel Federation, 1948 (Sec., 1956); Shell International Petroleum Co., 1959–67. Chm., N Kensington Cons. Assoc., 1961–62. Contested (C) Lambeth (Vauxhall), 1964, Cambridge, 1966; MP (C) Cambridge, Sept. 1967–Nov. 1976; PPS to Sec. of State for Employment, 1970–72; Parly Under-Sec. of State, Home Office, 1972–74. Chairman: Commn for Racial Equality, 1977–82; NAYC, 1982–87. *Recreations:* walking, golf, travel. *Address:* 5 Spinney Drive, Great Shelford, Cambridge CB2 5LY. *Club:* MCC.

Died 16 Nov. 1998.

LANESBOROUGH, 9th Earl of, *cr* 1756; **Denis Anthony Brian Butler,** TD; DL; Baron of Newtown-Butler, 1715; Viscount Lanesborough, 1728; Major, Leicestershire Yeomanry (RA); *b* 28 Oct. 1918; *er s* of 8th Earl of Lanesborough and 2nd wife, Grace Lilian (*d* 1983), *d* of late Sir Anthony Abdy, 3rd Bt; *S* father, 1950; *m* 1st, 1939, Bettyne Ione (marr. diss. 1950), *d* of late Sir Lindsay Everard; one *d* (and one *d* decd); 2nd, 1995, (Patricia) Julia, *d* of late F. W. Meston, MC. *Educ:* Stowe. Leicestershire Yeomanry; Lieutenant, 1939; Major, RAC, TA, 1945. Member: Nat. Gas Consumers' Council, 1973–78; Trent RHA, 1974–82 (Vice-Chm., 1978–82). Chm., Loughborough and District Housing Assoc., 1978–85. Chm., 1953–64, Pres., 1964–86, Guide Dogs for the Blind Assoc. DL 1962, JP 1967, Leicester. *Heir:* none. *Address:* Allerly, Gattonside, Melrose, Roxburghshire TD6 9LT. *T:* (01896) 823482.

Died 21 Dec. 1998 (ext).

LANG, Henry George, ONZ 1989; CB 1977; Secretary to the Treasury, New Zealand, 1968–77; *b* 3 March 1919; *s* of Robert and Anna Lang; *m* 1942, Octavia Gwendolin (*née* Turton); one *s* three *d* (and one *d* decd). *Educ:* Victoria Univ., Wellington. DPA, BA, BCom. Private enterprise, 1939–44; RNZAF, 1944–46; NZ government service: various economic appointments, 1946–55; Economic Advisor to High Comr in London, 1955–58; Treasury, 1958–77. Vis. Prof. of Economics, Victoria Univ. of Wellington, 1977–82; consultant and company dir, 1982–96. Dir, NZ Press Council, 1984–96. Hon. LLD Victoria Univ., Wellington, 1984. *Publications:* (with J. V. T. Baker) Economic Policy and National Income, in, NZ Official Year Book, 1950; articles in learned journals. *Recreations:* skiing, swimming, reading. *Address:* 81 Hatton Street, Wellington, NZ. *T:* (0) 4768788. *Club:* Wellington (Wellington, NZ). *Died 16 April 1997.*

LANGRISHE, Sir Hercules (Ralph Hume), 7th Bt *cr* 1777, of Knocktopher Abbey, Kilkenny; *b* 17 May 1927; *s* of Sir Terence Hume Langrishe, 6th Bt, and Joan Stuart (*d* 1976), *d* of late Major Ralph Stuart Grigg; *S* father, 1973; *m* 1955, Hon. Grania Sybil Enid Wingfield, *d* of 9th Viscount Powerscourt; one *s* three *d. Educ:* Summer Fields, St Leonards; Eton. 2nd Lieut, 9th Queen's Royal

Lancers, 1947; Lieut, 1948; retd 1953. *Recreations:* shooting, fishing. *Heir:* s James Hercules Langrishe [b 3 March 1957; m 1985, Gemma, d of Patrick O'Daly; one s one d]. *Address:* Arlonstown, Dunsany, Co. Meath. *T:* (46) 25243. *Club:* Kildare Street and University (Dublin).
Died 25 May 1998.

LANGTON, Sir Henry Algernon; *see* Calley, Sir H. A.

LANSDOWNE, 8th Marquess of, cr 1784 (GB); George John Charles Mercer Nairne Petty-Fitzmaurice; PC 1964; 29th Baron of Kerry and Lixnaw, 1181; Viscount Clanmaurice and Earl of Kerry, 1722; Baron Dunkeron and Viscount Fitzmaurice, 1751; Earl of Shelburne, 1753; Baron Wycombe (GB), 1760; Viscount Calne and Calston and Earl of Wycombe (GB), 1784; b 27 Nov. 1912; o s of Major Lord Charles George Francis Mercer Nairne, MVO (killed in action, 1914) (2nd s of 5th Marquess), and Lady Violet Mary Elliot (she m 2nd, 1916, 1st Baron Astor of Hever), d of 4th Earl of Minto; S cousin, 1944; m 1st, 1938, Barbara, (d 1965), d of Harold Stuart Chase, Santa Barbara; two s one d (and one d decd); 2nd, 1969, Mrs Polly Carnegie (marr. diss. 1978), d of 1st Viscount Eccles, CH, KCVO, PC; 3rd, 1978, Gillian Ann (d 1982), d of Alured Morgan; 4th, 1995, Hon. Mrs John Astor. *Educ:* Eton; Christ Church, Oxford. Served War of 1939–45, Capt. Royal Scots Greys 1940, formerly 2nd Lieut Scottish Horse (TA); Major 1944; served with Free French Forces (Croix de Guerre, Légion D'Honneur); Private Sec. to HM Ambassador in Paris (Rt Hon. A. Duff Cooper), 1944–45. Lord-in-Waiting to the Queen, 1957–58; Joint Parliamentary Under-Sec. of State, Foreign Office, 1958–62; Minister of State for Colonial Affairs, 1962–64, and for Commonwealth Relations, 1963–64. Chm., Inter-Governmental Cttee on Malaysia, 1962. Mem. Royal Company of Archers (Queen's Body Guard for Scotland). JP Perthshire, 1950; DL Wilts, 1952–73. Patron of two livings. Sec. Junior Unionist League for E Scotland, 1939; Chm., Victoria League in Scotland, 1952–56; Chm., Franco-British Soc., 1972–83; Pres., Franco-Scottish Soc. President: Officers' Families Fund, 1946–89; Royal Surgical Aid Soc., 1985–. Prime Warden, Fishmongers' Company, 1967–68. Comdr, Légion d'Honneur, 1979. *Heir:* s Earl of Shelburne, b 21 Feb. 1941. *Address:* Meikleour House, Perthshire PH2 6EA. *Clubs:* Turf; New (Edinburgh).
Died 25 Aug. 1999.

LARGE, Prof. John Barry; Professor of Applied Acoustics, University of Southampton, 1969–93, then Emeritus; Group Chief Executive, University of Southampton Holdings Ltd, since 1989; b 10 Oct. 1930; s of Thomas and Ada Large; m 1958, Barbara Alicia Nelson; two s. *Educ:* Queen Mary Coll., London Univ. (BScEng Hons); Purdue Univ., USA (MS). Group Engr, EMI Ltd, Feltham, Middx, 1954–56; Sen. Systems Engr, Link Aviation, Binghampton, NY, USA, 1956–58; Chief Aircraft Noise Unit, Boeing Co., Seattle, USA, 1958–69; Southampton University: Dir, Inst. of Sound and Vibration Res., 1978–82; Dean, Faculty of Engrg and Applied Sci., 1982–86; Dir of Industrial Affairs, 1986–92. Chm., Chilworth Centre Ltd; Chief Exec., Chilworth Manor Ltd; Chairman: Southern Reg. Chambers of Commerce; Solent Maritime; Director: Hants TEC; Hampshire Technol. Centre; Southampton Chamber of Commerce (Pres., 1992–94); Business Link Hampshire, 1996–. Mem., Noise Adv. Council, 1976–80; Chm., Co-ordinating Cttee, BCAR-N (Noise), Air Registration Bd, 1973–; Pres., Assoc. Noise Consultants, 1985–94. Member: Southern Regl Council, CBI, 1993–; CBI SME Council. Hon. Dep. Chief Scientific Officer, Defence Res. Estabt, 1974–. Corresp. Mem., Inst. Noise Control Engrg, USA, 1985–. *Publications:* contrib. (regarding aircraft noise, etc) to: Commn of European Communities, Eur 5398e, 1975; Proceedings of Internoise conferences, including Miami,

1980, San Francisco, 1982, Edinburgh, 1983, Hawaii, 1984, Hong Kong, 1985; The Development of Criteria for Environmental Noise Control (Proc. Royal Instn, vol. 52), 1979; Congress of Acoustics, 1983. *Recreations:* skiing, gardening. *Address:* Chinook, Southdown Road, Shawford, Hants. *T:* (01962) 712307.
Died 15 Jan. 1998.

LARKIN, (John) Cuthbert, MA; Headmaster, Wyggeston School, Leicester, 1947–69, retired; b 15 Oct. 1906; s of J. W. Larkin; m 1933, Sylvia Elizabeth Pilsbury (d 1991); one s three d. *Educ:* King Edward VI Sch., Nuneaton; Downing Coll., Cambridge. Assistant Master, Shrewsbury Sch., 1928–45; Headmaster, Chesterfield Grammar Sch., 1946–47. *Recreations:* cricket, gardening. *Address:* The Old Farm, Hungarton, Leics LE7 9JR. *T:* (0116) 259 5228.
Died 8 May 1998.

LARMOUR, Sir Edward Noel, (Sir Nick), KCMG 1977 (CMG 1966); HM Diplomatic Service, retired; b 25 Dec. 1916; s of Edward and Maud Larmour, Belfast, N Ireland; m 1946, Nancy, 2nd d of Thomas Bill; one s two d. *Educ:* Royal Belfast Academical Institution (Kitchener Scholar); Trinity Coll., Dublin (Scholar; 1st Class Hons and University Studentship in Classics, 1939); Sydney Univ., NSW. Royal Inniskilling Fusiliers, 1940; Burma Civil Service, 1942; Indian Army, 1942–46 (Major); Dep. Secretary to Governor of Burma, 1947; Commonwealth Relations Office, 1948; served in New Zealand, Singapore, Australia and Nigeria, 1950–68; Asst Under-Secretary of State, 1964; Dep. Chief of Administration, FCO, 1968–70; High Comr, Jamaica, and non-resident Ambassador, Haiti, 1970–73; Asst Under Sec. of State, FCO, 1973–75; High Comr (non-resident) for New Hebrides, 1973–76; Dep. Under Sec. of State, FCO, 1975–76. Mem., Price Commn, 1977–80; Chm., Bermuda Constituency Boundaries Commn, 1979. *Recreations:* cricket, golf, music. *Address:* 68 Wood Vale, N10 3DN. *T:* (020) 8444 9744. *Club:* Royal Commonwealth Society.
Died 21 Aug. 1999.

LASCELLES, Maj.-Gen. Henry Anthony, CB 1967; CBE 1962 (OBE 1945); DSO 1944; Director-General, Winston Churchill Memorial Trust, 1967–80; b 10 Jan. 1912; s of Edward Lascelles and Leila Kennett-Barrington; m 1941, Ethne Hyde Ussher Charles. *Educ:* Winchester; Oriel Coll., Oxford (MA). Served War of 1939–45: Egypt, North Africa, Sicily and Italy, rising to second in command of an armoured brigade; Instructor, Staff Coll., Camberley, 1947–49; GSO 1, HQ 7th Armoured Div., BAOR, 1949–52; Comdg Officer 6th Royal Tank Regt, BAOR, 1952–55; Instructor, NATO Defence Coll., 1955–56; Brigadier Royal Armoured Corps HQ 2nd Infantry Div., BAOR, 1956–57; National Defence Coll., Canada, 1958–59; BGS Military Operations, War Office, 1959–62; Chief of Staff, HQ Northern Ireland Command, 1962–63; Maj.-Gen., General Staff, Far East Land Forces, 1963–66. Pres., British Water Ski Fedn, 1980–. *Recreations:* squash, tennis, golf, music, gardening. *Address:* Manor Farm Cottage, Hedgerley Green, Bucks SL2 3XJ. *T:* (01753) 883582. *Club:* Naval and Military.
Died 13 July 2000.

LASOK, Prof. Dominik; QC 1982; PhD, LLD; Professor of European Law, 1973–86, and Director of Centre for European Legal Studies, 1972–86, University of Exeter; b 4 Jan. 1921; s of late Alojzy Lasok and Albina (*née* Przybyla); m 1952, Sheila May Corrigan; one s three d (and one s decd). *Educ:* secondary educn in Poland and Switzerland; Fribourg Univ. (Lic. en Droit); Univ. of Durham (LLM); Univ. of London (PhD, LLD); Universitas Polonorum in Exteris (Dr Juris). Called to the Bar, Middle Temple, 1954. Served Polish Army, Poland, France and Italy, 1939–46 (British, French and Polish mil. decorations). Industry, 1948–51; commerce, 1954–58;

academic career, 1958–: Prof. of Law, Univ. of Exeter, 1968. Visiting Professor: William and Mary, Williamsburg, Va, 1966–67 and 1977; McGill, Montreal, 1976–77; Rennes, 1980–81; Fribourg, 1984; Coll. d'Europe, Bruges, 1984–86; Aix-Marseille, 1985; Marmara, Istanbul, 1987–94; Chukyo, Nagoya, 1990; Surugadi, Hanno-shi, 1990; Poznan, 1994–97; Kraków, 1995–97. Dhc: Aix/Marseille, 1987; Istanbul, 1996; Poznan, 1997. Officier dans l'Ordre des Palmes Académiques (France), 1983; Officer, Cross of Merit (Poland), 1996. Publications: Polish Family Law, 1968; (jtly, also ed) Polish Civil Law, 4 vols, 1973–75; (with J. W. Bridge) Law and Institutions of the European Communities, 1973, 6th edn 1994; The Law of the Economy in the European Communities, 1980; (jtly, also ed) Les Communautés Européennes en Fonctionnement, 1981; Customs Law of the European Communities, 1983, 3rd edn 1997; Professions and Services in the European Community, 1986; (with P. A. Stone) Conflict of Laws in the European Community, 1987; (contrib.) Halsbury's Laws of England, 5th edn 1991; Turkey and the European Community, 1992; Zarys Prawa Unii Europejskiej, 1995; Prawo Gospodarcza Unii Europejskiej, 1997; over 170 articles in British and foreign legal jls. Address: Reed, Barley Lane, Exeter EX4 1TA. T: (01392) 72582.
Died 11 April 2000.

LATEY, Rt Hon. Sir John (Brinsmead), Kt 1965; MBE (mil.) 1943; PC 1986; Judge of the High Court of Justice, Family Division (formerly Probate, Divorce and Admiralty Division), 1965–89; b 7 March 1914; s of late William Latey, CBE, QC, and Anne Emily, d of late Horace G. Brinsmead; m 1938, Betty Margaret (née Beresford); one s one d. Educ: Westminster; Christ Church, Oxford (Hon. Sch. Jurispr.; MA). Called to the Bar, Middle Temple, 1936, Master, 1964; QC 1957. Served in Army during War, 1939–45, mainly in MEF (Lt-Col 1944). Mem., General Council of the Bar, 1952–56, 1957–61 and 1964–65 (Hon. Treasurer, 1959–61). Chairman, Lord Chancellor's Cttee on Age of Majority, 1965–67. Dep. Chairman, Oxfordshire QS, 1966. Publications: (Asst Ed.) Latey on Divorce, 14th edn 1952; Halsbury's Laws of England (Conflict of Laws: Husband and Wife), 1956. Recreations: golf, bridge, chess. Address: 1 Adderbury Park, Adderbury, near Banbury, Oxon OX17 3EN. T: (01295) 810208. Club: United Oxford & Cambridge University.
Died 24 April 1999.

LATTER, Leslie William; Director General, Merseyside Passenger Transport Executive, 1977–86; b 4 Nov. 1921; s of William Richard and Clara Maud Latter; m 1948, Pamela Jean Marsh (d 1996); (one s decd). Educ: Beckenham Grammar Sch., Kent. IPFA, FCIT. Served Royal Air Force, 1940–46. London County Council, 1947–62; Chief Asst, Beckenham Borough Council, 1962–64; Asst Borough Treasurer, Bromley, 1964–68; Dep. Borough Treasurer, Greenwich, 1968–74; Dir of Finance and Administration, Merseyside PTE, 1974–77. Recreations: gardening, music.
Died 24 April 1998.

LATTO, Dr Douglas; private medical practice; Chairman, British Safety Council, 1971–97 (Vice-Chairman, 1968–71); b Dundee, Scotland, 13 Dec. 1913; s of late David Latto, Town Clerk of Dundee, and Christina Latto; m 1945, Dr Edith Monica Druitt (d 1990); one s three d. Educ: Dundee High Sch.; St Andrews Univ. (MB, ChB 1939). DObstRCOG 1944, MRCOG 1949, FRCOG 1989. During War: Ho. Surg., Dundee Royal Infirmary, 1939; Ho. Phys., Cornelia and East Dorset Hosp., Poole, 1940; Resident Obstetrician and Gynaecologist, Derbyshire Hosp. for Women, Derby, 1940; Res. Surgical Officer, Hereford Gen. Hosp., 1941; Res. Obst. and Gynaec., East End Maternity Hosp., London, 1942; Res. Obst. and

Gynaec., City of London Maternity Hosp., 1943; Res. Surgical Officer, Birmingham Accident Hosp., 1944; Casualty Officer, Paddington Gen. Hosp., London, 1944; Asst Obst. and Gynaec., Mayday Hosp., Croydon, 1945; Res. Obst. and Gynaec., Southlands Hosp., Shoreham-by-Sea, Sussex, 1946–49; Asst, Nuffield Dept of Obstetrics and Gynaecology, Radcliffe Infirmary, Oxford, 1949–51. Member: BMA; Council, Soil Assoc.; Chm., Plantmilk Soc.; Vice-President: International Vegetarian Union; GB Philatelic Soc., 1986–. Governor, Internat. Inst. of Safety Management. Freeman, City of London, 1988; Liveryman, Worshipful Co. of Apothecaries. Mem., Order of the Cross. FRSocMed; FRPSL 1975. Estabd right to arms, 1995. Silver Jubilee Medal, 1977; Sword of Honour, British Safety Council, 1985. Publications: Smoking and Lung Cancer: a report to all Members of Parliament for the British Safety Council, 1969; contribs to BMJ, Proc. Royal Soc. Med., Philatelic Jl, etc. Recreations: squash, travelling, gardening, philately (Internat. Stamp Exhibns: Large Gold Medal, London, 1970; Gold Medal, Brussels, 1972, Munich, 1973, Basle, 1974; Large Gold Medal, Paris, 1975; Copenhagen, 1976 (and Prix d'Honneur), London, 1980 (and GB Philatelic Soc. Award), Vienna, 1981). Address: Lethnot Lodge, 4 Derby Road, Caversham, Reading, Berks RG4 5EZ. T: (0118) 947 2282. Clubs: Royal Automobile, Rolls-Royce Enthusiasts' (Paulersbury).
Died 26 Dec. 1999.

LAVIN, Mary, (Mrs M. MacDonald Scott); writer; b East Walpole, Mass, USA, 11 June 1912; m 1st, 1942, William Walsh (d 1954), MA, NUI; three d; 2nd, 1969, Michael MacDonald Scott (d 1990), MA, MSc. Educ: National Univ. of Ireland, Dublin (Graduate, MA; Hon DLitt 1968). Member: Irish Academy of Letters (President, 1971); Aosdána, 1992. Guggenheim Fellow 1959, 1962 and 1972. Katherine Mansfield Prize, 1961; Ella Lynam Cabot Award, 1971; Eire Soc. Gold Medal, Boston, 1974; Arts Award, Royal Meath Assoc., 1975; Gregory Medal, Dublin, 1975; Amer. Irish Foundn Literary Award, 1979; Allied Irish Bank Award, 1981; Irish Arts Council Award, 1993. Personality of the Year, Royal Meath Assoc., 1976. Publications: Tales from Bective Bridge (short stories, awarded James Tait Black Memorial Prize), 1942; The Long Ago (short stories), 1944; The House in Clewe Street (novel), 1945, repr. 1987; At Sally Gap, 1946 (Boston); The Becker Wives, 1946; Mary O'Grady (novel), 1950, repr. 1986; Patriot Son (short stories), 1956; A Single Lady (short stories); A Likely Story (short novel), 1957; Selected Stories, 1959 (New York); The Great Wave (short stories), 1961; The Stories of Mary Lavin, 1964, vol. II, 1973, vol. III, 1985; In the Middle of the Fields (short stories), 1966; Happiness (short stories), 1969; Collected Stories, 1971; A Memory and other Stories, 1972; The Second Best Children in the World, 1972; The Shrine and other stories, 1976; A Family Likeness, 1985; In a Café and other stories, 1995. Address: Apt 5 Gilford Pines, Gilford Road, Sandymount, Dublin 4, Ireland. T: 2692402.
Died 25 March 1996.

LAW, Graham Couper, RSA 1995 (ARSA 1980); RIBA, FRIAS; Consultant, Law and Dunbar-Nasmith, Architects (Partner, 1957–89); b 28 Sept. 1923; s of William Ramsay Law and Eliza Templeton Hammond Couper; m 1951, Isobel Evelyn Alexander Drysdale; one s three d. Educ: Merchiston Castle Sch.; King's Coll., Cambridge (Exhibn and Book Prize; MA). ARIBA 1951 (Dist. in Thesis). Royal Engineers, QVO Madras Sappers and Miners, 1941–46. Member: Council, Edinburgh Arch. Assoc., 1964–69; RIAS, 1965–67 (Mem., Investigation Cttee, 1979–85); Architects' Registration Council, 1967–75; ARCUK Professional Purposes Cttee, 1967–75. Chm., Workshop and Artists' Studio Provision Scotland Ltd, 1977–81. Theatre designs include: Eden Court, Inverness; Festival Theatre, Pitlochry; exhibitions include: Epstein,

Shakespeare, Scottish Treasures, Barbara Hepworth.
Publication: Greek Thomson, 1954. *Recreations:* music,
particularly opera, reading, painting. *Address:* Easter
Society, Hopetoun, South Queensferry EH30 9SL. *T:*
0131–331 1268. *Club:* New (Edinburgh).
Died 13 Sept. 1996.

LAWLOR, Prof. John James, DLitt; FSA; Professor of
English Language and Literature, University of Keele,
1950–80, then Emeritus; *b* 5 Jan. 1918; *o s* of Albert John
Lawlor, Chief Armourer, RN, and Teresa Anne Clare
Lawlor, Plymouth; *m* 1st, 1941, Thelma Joan Weeks,
singer (marr. diss. 1979); one *s* three *d*; 2nd, 1984, Kimie
Imura, Prof. Meisei Univ., Tokyo. *Educ:* Ryder's;
Magdalen Coll., Oxford (BA Hons English Cl. I, 1939;
MA); DLitt. Service in Devonshire Regt, 1940–45; Asst
Chief Instructor, 163 Artists' Rifles OCTU, 1943–44;
CMF, 1944–45; Allied Mil. Govt, Austria. Sen. Mackinnon
Scholar, Magdalen Coll., Oxford, 1946; Sen. Demy, 1947;
Lectr in English, Brasenose and Trinity Colls, Oxford,
1947–50; University Lectr in Eng. Lit., Oxford, 1949–50.
Fellow of Folger Shakespeare Library, Washington, DC,
1962. Toured Australian and NZ Univs and visited Japan,
1964; Ziskind Visiting Prof., Brandeis Univ., Mass, 1966;
Visiting Professor: Univ. of Hawaii, 1972; Univ. of
Maryland, 1981–82; Univ. of Arizona, 1983–84. Sec.-
Gen. and Treasurer, Internat. Assoc. of University Profs
of English, 1971–95; Contrib. Mem. Medieval Academy
of America. Gov., Oswestry Sch.; Pres., N Staffs Drama
Assoc.; Mem. Western Area Cttee, Brit. Drama League;
Vice-Pres., The Navy League. *Publications:* The Tragic
Sense in Shakespeare, 1960; Piers Plowman, an Essay in
Criticism, 1962; (with Rosemary Sisson) The Chester
Mystery Plays, perf. Chester, 1962; The Vision of Piers
Plowman, commnd, Malvern, 1964; (ed) Patterns of Love
and Courtesy, 1966; (with W. H. Auden) To Nevill Coghill
from Friends, 1966; Chaucer, 1968; (ed) The New
University, 1968; (ed) Higher Education: patterns of
change in the seventies, 1972; Elysium Revisited, 1978:
(as James Dundonald). Letters to a Vice-Chancellor, 1962;
La Vita Nuova, 1976; C. S. Lewis: memories and
reflections, 1998; articles on medieval and modern
literature in various journals and symposia. *Recreations:*
travel, book-collecting, any sort of sea-faring. *Address:*
Penwithian, Higher Fore Street, Marazion, Cornwall TR17
0BQ. *T:* (01736) 711180; 2-45-13 Misawa, Hinoshi,
Tokyo 191, Japan. *T:* (425) 944177. *Clubs:* Athenæum;
Royal Fleet (Devonport). *Died 31 May 1999.*

LAWRENCE, Sir Guy Kempton, Kt 1976; DSO 1943;
OBE 1945; DFC 1941; retired; Chairman, Eggs Authority,
1978–81; *b* 5 Nov. 1914; *s* of Albert Edward and Bianca
Lawrence; *m* 1947, Marcia Virginia Powell; two *s* one *d*.
Educ: Marlborough Coll. RAFO, 1934–45; War of
1939–45: Bomber Pilot (48 sorties), Sqdn Comdr, 78
Sqdn, Gp Captain Trng, HQ Bomber Command (DFC
DSO, despatches, OBE). Contested (L) Colne Valley,
1945. Man. Dir, Chartair Ltd-Airtech Ltd, 1945–48;
Chairman: Glacier Foods Ltd, 1948–75; Findus (UK) Ltd,
1967–75; Deputy Chairman: J. Lyons & Co. Ltd, 1950–75;
Spillers French Holdings Ltd, 1972–75; Vice-Chm., DCA
Food Industries Inc., 1973–75; Dir, Eagle Aircraft
Services, 1977–81. Chm., Food and Drink Industries
Council, 1973–77. Member of Stock Exchange, London,
1937–45. British Ski Team, 1937–38. FIMgt; FIGD.
Recreations: farming, carpentry, squash, tennis. *Address:*
Courtlands, Kier Park, Ascot, Berks SL5 7DS. *T:* (01344)
621074. *Club:* Royal Air Force.
Died 30 Nov. 2000.

LAWRENCE, Sir John (Waldemar), 6th Bt *cr* 1858, of
Lucknow; OBE 1945; freelance writer; Editor of Frontier,
1957–75; *b* 27 May 1907; *s* of Sir Alexander Waldemar
Lawrence, 4th Bt, and Anne Elizabeth Le Poer (*née*

Wynne); *S* brother, Sir Henry Eustace Waldemar
Lawrence, 1967; *m* 1st, 1948, Jacynth Mary (*née* Ellerton)
(*d* 1987); no *c*; 2nd, 1988, Audrey Viola, *widow* of John
Woodiwiss. *Educ:* Eton; New Coll., Oxford (MA, Lit.
Hum.). Personal Asst to Dir of German Jewish Aid Cttee,
1938–39; with BBC as European Intelligence Officer and
European Services Organiser, 1939–42; Press Attaché,
HM Embassy, USSR, 1942–45; became freelance writer,
1946. Pres., Keston Inst. (formerly Centre for Study of
Religion and Communism), 1984– (Chm., 1969–83);
Chm., GB USSR Assoc., 1970–85. Officer, Order of
Orange Nassau (Netherlands), 1950. *Publications:* Life in
Russia, 1947; Russia in the Making, 1957; A History of
Russia, 1960, 7th edn 1993; The Hard Facts of Unity,
1961; Russia (Methuen's Outlines), 1965; Soviet Russia,
1967; Russians Observed, 1969; Take Hold of Change,
1976; The Journals of Honoria Lawrence, 1980; The
Hammer and the Cross, 1986; Lawrence of Lucknow,
1990. *Recreations:* travelling, reading in ten languages.
Heir: nephew Henry Peter Lawrence [*b* 2 April 1952; *m*
1979, Penny Maureen Nunan (marr. diss. 1993); one *s* one
d]. *Address:* 36A Norham Road, Oxford OX2 6QD. *T:*
(01865) 311983; 1 Naishes Cottages, Northstoke, Bath
BA1 9AT. *Club:* Athenæum. *Died 30 Dec. 1999.*

LAWRENCE, William Robert, QPM 1991; Chief
Constable, South Wales Police (formerly Constabulary),
since 1989; *b* 21 Sept. 1942; *s* of William Thomas and
Norah Lawrence; *m* 1965, Kathleen Ann Lawrence; one *s*
one *d*. *Educ:* Maesydderwen Grammar Sch. BA Open
Univ., 1988. Joined Mid Wales, then Dyfed Powys
Constabulary, 1961; Sergeant, 1970; Inspector, 1972;
Chief Inspector, 1973; transf. to W Mercia as Supt, 1978;
Chief Supt, 1982; Asst Chief Constable 1983, Dep. Chief
Constable 1985, Staffordshire Police. SBStJ 1986.
Recreations: golf, fly fishing, Rugby, amateur boxing.
Address: Chief Constable's Office, South Wales Police,
Police Headquarters, Bridgend, Mid Glamorgan CF31
3SU. *T:* Bridgend (01656) 655555.
Died 21 May 1996.

LAWS, Courtney Alexander Henriques, OBE 1987; OD
1978; Director, Brixton Neighbourhood Community
Association, since 1971; *b* Morant Bay, St Thomas,
Jamaica, 16 June 1934; *s* of Ezekiel Laws and Agatha
Laws; *m* 1955, Wilhel, (Rubie), Brown, JP; one *s* two *d*.
Educ: Morant Bay Elem. Sch.; Jones Pen and Rollington
Town Elem. Sch.; Lincoln Coll.; Nat. Coll. for Youth
Workers, Leicester; Cranfield Coll., Bedford. Rep., Works
Cttee, Peak Freans Biscuit Co., 1960–69; Shop Steward,
TGWU, 1960–70. Member: Lambeth Council for
Community Relations, 1964–; Consortium of Ethnic
Minorities, Lambeth, 1978–; W Indian Standing Conf.,
1959–; Campaign against Racial Discrimination, 1960–;
NCCI, 1960–; Commn for Racial Equality, 1977–80;
Central Cttee, British Caribbean Assoc. (Exec. Mem.),
1960–; Assoc. of Jamaicans (Founder Mem.), 1965;
Geneva and Somerleyton Community Assoc., 1966–;
Consultative Cttee, ILEA, Lambeth, 1975–; Consultative
Council, City and E London Coll., 1975–; South Eastern
Gas Consumers' Council, 1980–; Governor, Brixton Coll.
of Further and Higher Educn, 1970–; Member: W Indian
Sen. Citizens' Assoc. (Pres.), 1973–; St John's Interracial
Club, 1958–; Brixton United Cricket Club, 1968– (Pres.);
Brixton Domino Club (Chm.); Oasis Sports and Social
Club, 1969–. Medal of Appreciation, Prime Minister of
Jamaica, 1987; Community of Brixton Award, 1987.
Recreations: reading, music. *Address:* 71 Atlantic Road,
SW9 8PU. *T:* 0171–274 0011.
Died 22 July 1996.

LAWS, John William, CBE 1982; FRCP, FRCR; formerly
consultant diagnostic radiologist; Director of Radiology,
King's College Hospital, and Director of Radiological

Studies, King's College Hospital Medical School, 1967–86; *b* 25 Oct. 1921; *s* of Robert Montgomery Laws and Lucy Ibbotson; *m* 1st, 1945, Dr Pamela King, MRCS, LRCP (*d* 1985); one *s* one *d*; 2nd, 1986, Dr Diana Brinkley (*née* Rawlence), FRCR. *Educ:* The Leys Sch., Cambridge; Sheffield Univ. Med. Sch. MB ChB 1944; DMRD 1952; MRCP 1951; FRCR (FFR 1955); FRCP 1967. Nat. Service, 1947–49 (Captain RAMC). House Physician and House Surg., Royal Hosp., Sheffield, 1944–45; Res. Surgical Officer, Salisbury Gen. Infirmary, 1945–47; Med. Registrar, 1949–51, Radiology Registrar and Sen. Registrar, 1951–55, United Sheffield Hosps; Consultant Radiologist, Dep. Dir, Hammersmith Hosp., and Hon. Lectr, RPMS, 1955–67. Consultant Civilian Advr to Army, 1976–86; Med. Dir, King's Centre for Assessment of Radiol Equipment, 1979–86. Chm., Radiol Equipment Sub-Cttee, DHSS, 1972–81; Member: Central Adv. Cttee on Hosp. Med. Records, DHSS, 1969–74; Radiol Adv. Cttee, DHSS, 1972–86; Consultant Advr in Radiol., DHSS, 1982–86. Chm., British Delegn, XV Internat. Congress of Radiol., 1981. Royal College (formerly Faculty) of Radiologists: Mem. Fellowship Bd, 1966–71; Hon. Sec., 1974–75; Registrar, 1975–76; Warden of Fellowship, 1976–80; Pres., 1980–83; Knox Lectr, 1984. Mem. Council, RCS, 1981–84. Vis Prof. and Lectr at academic instns and congresses worldwide. Member Editorial Board: Clin. Radiol., 1960–63; Gut, 1970–74; Gastrointestinal Radiol., 1975–85; Asst, later Hon., Editor, British Jl of Radiol., 1961–71. Hon. FACR 1973; Hon. FFR RCSI 1975; Hon. FRACR 1979. Barclay Prize, British Inst. of Radiol., 1964. *Publications:* numerous papers and pubns on various aspects of clinical radiology, particularly gastrointestinal and hepatic radiology and the radiology of pulmonary disease, in medical journals and books. *Recreations:* listening to music, sculpting. *Address:* 5 Frank Dixon Way, Dulwich, SE21 7BB. *T:* (0181) 693 4815. *Died 20 March 1999.*

LAWSON, Hugh McDowall, BScEng London; CEng, FICE; Director of Leisure Services, Nottingham City Council, 1973–76; *b* Leeds, 13 Feb. 1912; *s* of late John Lawson, Pharmaceutical Chemist; *m* 1st, 1937, Dorothy (*d* 1982), *d* of late Rev. T. H. Mallinson, BA; two *s*; 2nd, 1988, Eva (*d* 1991), *d* of late Prof. David Holde, Berlin, and *widow* of Richard Koch. *Educ:* Nottingham High Sch.; University Coll., Nottingham. Served in Royal Engineers, 1940–44. MP (Common Wealth) Skipton Div. of Yorks, 1944–45. Contested: (Common Wealth) Harrow West Div., 1945; (Lab) Rushcliffe Div., 1950; (Lab) King's Lynn Div., 1955. Dep. City Engr, Nottingham, 1948–73. Mem. Council, ICE, 1972–75. *Address:* Flat 1, 127 Melton Road, West Bridgford, Nottingham NG2 6FG. *T:* (0115) 945 2886. *Died 23 March 1997.*

LAWSON, Air Vice-Marshal Ian Douglas Napier, CB 1965; CBE 1961; DFC 1941, Bar 1943; AE 1945; Royal Air Force, retired; *b* 11 Nov. 1917; *y s* of late J. L. Lawson and Ethel Mary Lawson (*née* Ludgate); *m* 1945, Dorothy Joyce Graham Nash; one *s* one *d*. *Educ:* Brondesbury Coll.; Polytechnic, Regent Street. Aircraft industry, 1934–39; joined RAFVR, 1938; served War of 1939–45 (despatches thrice): Bomber Comd, 1940–41; Middle East Comd, 1941–45; Permanent Commission, 1945; Bomber Comd, 1945–46; Staff Coll., 1946; Air Ministry, 1946–49; Transport Comd, 1949–50; Middle East Comd, 1950–52; JSSC, 1953; Ministry of Defence, 1953–56; Flying Coll., Manby, 1956–57; Transport Comd, 1957–62; Air Forces Middle East, 1962–64; Commandant, RAF Coll., Cranwell, 1964–67; Asst Chief Adviser (Personnel and Logistics), MoD, 1967–69; joined BAC, 1969, Chief Sales Exec., Weybridge, Bristol Div., 1974–79; Gen. Marketing Manager (civil), BAe, 1979–81; non-exec. Dir, Glos Air (Holdings) Ltd, 1981–82. FIMgt (FBIM 1974). US Legion of Merit. *Recreations:* gardening, motor sport. *Address:*

The Dower Cottage, Bewley Lane, Lacock, Wilts SN15 2PG. *T:* (01249) 730307. *Club:* Royal Air Force. *Died 22 Jan. 1998.*

LAWSON, Hon. Sir Neil, Kt 1971; Judge of High Court of Justice, Queen's Bench Division, 1971–83; *b* 8 April 1908; *s* of late Robb Lawson and Edith Marion Lawson (*née* Usherwood); *m* 1933, Gweneth Clare (*née* Wilby); one *s* one *d*. Called to Bar, Inner Temple, 1929; QC 1955; Recorder of Folkestone, 1962–71; a Law Commissioner, 1965–71. RAFVR, 1940–45. Hon. Fellow, LSE, 1974. Foreign decorations: DK (Dato' Peduka Kerubat), 1959; DSNB, 1962; PSMB, 1969. *Recreations:* literature, music, the country. *Address:* 30a Heath Drive, Hampstead, NW3 7SB. *Died 26 Jan. 1996.*

LAWTON, Alistair; *see* Lawton, J. A.

LAWTON, Prof. Sir Frank (Ewart), Kt 1981; DDS; FDSRCS; Professor of Operative Dental Surgery, University of Liverpool, 1956–80, then Emeritus Professor; *b* 23 Oct. 1915; *s* of Hubert Ralph Lawton and Agnes Elizabeth (*née* Heath); *m* 1943, Muriel Leonora Bacon; one *s* one *d*. *Educ:* Univ. of Liverpool (BDS 1937); Northwestern Univ., Chicago (DDS 1948). FDSRCS 1948. Lectr, 1939, and Dir of Dental Educn, 1957–80, Univ. of Liverpool. President: BDA, 1973–74; GDC, 1979–89. Editor, Internat. Dental Jl, 1963–81. Hon. DDSc Newcastle, 1981; Hon. DDS Birmingham, 1982; Hon. DSc Manchester, 1984. *Publications:* (ed with Ed Farmer) Stones Oral and Dental Diseases, 1966; contrib. scientific and prof. jls. *Recreation:* music. *Address:* Newcroft, Castle Bolton, Leyburn, N Yorks DL8 4EX. *T:* (01969) 622802. *Died 19 Feb. 2000.*

LAWTON, (John) Alistair, CBE 1981; DL; with Sea Properties Ltd, since 1955; *b* 1 Oct. 1929; *s* of Richard Geoffrey Lawton and Emma Lawton; *m* 1952, Iris Lilian Barthorpe; one *s* two *d*. *Educ:* Crewkerne Sch., Somerset. Southern Rhodesia Govt, 1946–55. Member: Deal Borough Council, 1956–74 (Mayor, 1966–68); Kent County Council, 1966–89 (Chm., 1977–79; Chm., Educn Cttee, 1973–77); Chairman: Kent Police Authority, 1987–89; SE Kent HA, 1988–94; S Kent Community Healthcare NHS Trust, 1994–. Comr, Manpower Services Commn, 1983–85. Treas., Kent CCC, 1988–92. Mem. Council and Court, Univ. of Kent at Canterbury, 1974–. DL Kent, 1983. Hon. DCL Kent, 1982. *Recreations:* cricket, Rugby (non-participating latterly). *Address:* The Sett, 1 Badgers Rise, Walmer, Deal, Kent CT14 7QW. *T:* (01304) 375060. *Died 13 Aug. 2000.*

LAXNESS, Halldór Kiljan; Icelandic writer; *b* 23 April 1902; *s* of Gudjon Helgason and Sigridur Halldorsdottir, Iceland; one *d*; *m* 1st, 1930, Ingibjörg Einarsdottir (marr. diss.); one *s*; 2nd, 1945, Audur Sveinsdottir; two *d*. Hon. PhD: Aabo Univ., 1968; Eberhard-Karls Univ., Tübingen, 1982; Hon. DLitt Univ. of Iceland, 1972; Hon. Dr Edinburgh Univ., 1977. Nobel Prize for Literature, 1955; Nexö Prize for Literature, 1955; Sonning Prize, 1969. *Publications* include over 50 titles (originally published in Icelandic, trans. into over 40 langs): *novels:* Barn náttúrunnar, 1919; Undir Helgahnúk (Under the Holy Mountain), 1924; Vefarinn mikli frá Kasmir (The Great Weaver from Kashmir), 1927; Salka Valka, 1934 (first published as Þú vínviður hreini, 1931, and Fuglinn í fjörunni, 1932; filmed, 1954); Sjálfstætt fólk (Independent People), 2 vols, 1934–35; Ljós heimsins, 1937, Höll sumarlandsins, 1938, Hús skáldsins, 1939, Fegurð himinsins, 1940 (these four republished as Heimsljos (The Light of the World), 2 vols, 1955); Íslandsklukkan, 1943, Hið ljósa man, 1944, Eldur í Kaupinhafn, 1946 (these three republished as Íslandsklukkan (Iceland's Bell), 1957); Atómstöðin (The Atom Station), 1948; Gerpla (Happy Warriors), 1952; Brekkukotsannáll (Fish Can

Sing), 1957 (filmed, 1973); Paradísarheimt (Paradise Reclaimed), 1960; Kristnihald undir Jökli (Christianity at Glacier), 1968 (filmed, 1989); Innansveitarkronika, 1970; Guðsgjafathula, 1972; *autobiography:* Skáldatími, 1963; Íslendíngaspjall, 1967; Í túninu heima, 1975; Úngur eg var, 1976; Sjömeistarasagan, 1978; Grikklandsárið, 1980; Dagar hjá múnkum, 1987; collections of short stories, essays, poems and plays; translations into Icelandic include: Farewell to Arms, and A Moveable Feast, by Ernest Hemingway; Candide by Voltaire. *Address:* Gljúfrasteinn, 270 Mosfellsbær, Iceland; Vaka-Helgafell, Síðumúli 6, 108 Reykjavík, Iceland.

Died 8 Feb. 1998.

LAYDEN, Sir John, Kt 1988; JP; miner; Councillor, Rotherham Metropolitan Borough Council, 1974–96 (Leader, 1974–96); *b* 16 Jan. 1926; *m* 1949, Dorothy Brenda McLean; two *s.* Joined Labour Party, 1944. Elected to Maltby UDC, 1953 (Chm., 1959–60 and 1970–71). Chm., S Yorks Police Authy, 1985–96. Chm., Assoc. of Metropolitan Authorities, 1984–91; Vice-Chm., British Section, IULA/CEM, 1974–96; Mem., Bd of Trustees, Municipal Mutual Insurance Co., 1983–. Freeman, City of London, 1988. JP Rotherham Borough, 1965. Hon. Citizen of Indianapolis, 1985. *Recreations:* music, sport (particularly football). *Address:* 9 Lilac Grove, Maltby, Rotherham, South Yorkshire S66 8BX. *T:* Rotherham (01709) 812481. *Died 28 May 1996.*

LAYE, Evelyn, CBE 1973; actress, singer; *b* London, 10 July 1900; *o d* of Gilbert Laye and Evelyn Froud; *m* 1st, 1926, Sonnie Hale (marr. diss. 1931); 2nd, 1934, Frank Lawton (*d* 1969). *Educ:* Folkestone; Brighton. Made first appearance on stage, Theatre Royal, Brighton, 1915, in Mr Wu; first London appearance in The Beauty Spot, Gaiety, 1918; first big success in title-role of The Merry Widow, Daly's, 1923; subsequently starred in London in Madame Pompadour, Daly's, 1923; The Dollar Princess, Daly's, 1925; Cleopatra, Daly's, 1925; Betty in Mayfair, Adelphi, 1925, Merely Molly, Adelphi, 1926; Princess Charming, Palace, 1927; Lilac Time, Daly's, 1927; Blue Eyes, Piccadilly, 1928; The New Moon, Drury Lane, 1929; Bitter Sweet, His Majesty's, 1930; Helen!, Adelphi, 1932; Give Me A Ring, Hippodrome, 1933; Paganini, Lyceum, 1937; Lights Up, Savoy, 1940; The Belle of New York, Coliseum, 1942; Sunny River, Piccadilly, 1943; Cinderella, His Majesty's, 1943; Three Waltzes, Prince's, 1945; Cinderella, Palladium, 1948; Two Dozen Red Roses, Lyric, 1949; Peter Pan, Scala, 1953; Wedding in Paris, Hippodrome, 1954–56; Silver Wedding, Cambridge, 1957; The Amorous Prawn, Saville/Piccadilly, 1959–62; Never Too Late, Prince of Wales, 1964; The Circle, Savoy, 1965; Strike A Light!, Piccadilly, 1966; Let's All Go Down the Strand, Phoenix, 1967; Charlie Girl, Adelphi, 1969; Phil the Fluter, Palace, 1969; No Sex, Please-We're British, Strand, 1971–73; A Little Night Music (revival), Exeter, 1979, 1981, on tour, 1979, Nottingham, 1980–81, 1982; one woman show, 1983; Babes in the Wood, Chichester, 1984, Richmond, 1985; A Glamorous Night with Evelyn Laye and Friends, tour and London Palladium, 1992. First New York appearance in Bitter Sweet, Ziegfeld Theatre, 1929; subsequently on Broadway in Sweet Aloes, Booth, 1936; Between the Devil, Majestic, 1937. Film début in silent production, The Luck of the Navy, 1927; films include: One Heavenly Night (Hollywood), 1932; Waltz Time, 1933; Princess Charming, 1934; Evensong, 1935; The Night is Young (Hollywood), 1936; Make Mine A Million, 1959; Theatre of Death, 1967; Within and Without, 1969; Say Hello to Yesterday, 1971. Numerous broadcasts and television appearances incl. rôles in Dizzy, Tales of the Unexpected, The Gay Lord Quex, 1983; My Family and Other Animals, 1987. *Publication:* Boo, to my Friends (autobiog.), 1958.

Address: c/o Mary-Jane Burcher, Flat 6, Oak House, 6 Carlton Drive, Putney, SW15 2BZ.

Died 17 Feb. 1996.

LAYFIELD, Sir Frank (Henry Burland Willoughby), Kt 1976; QC 1967; *b* Toronto, 9 Aug. 1921; *s* of late H. D. Layfield; *m* 1965, Irene Patricia, *d* of late Captain J. D. Harvey, RN (retired); one *s* one *d. Educ:* Sevenoaks Sch. Army, 1940–46. Joined HAC as Private, 1953, Lt, 1955, Capt., 1959, Major, 1964. Called to the Bar, Gray's Inn, 1954, Bencher, 1974; a Recorder, 1979–82. Chairman: Inquiry into Greater London Development Plan, 1970–73; Tribunal for the Protection of St Paul's Cathedral, 1971; Cttee of Inquiry into Local Government Finance, 1974–76; Inspector, Inquiry into Sizewell B Nuclear Power Station, 1983–85; Mem., Sec. of State's Housing Finance Policy Review Gp, 1975–77; Gen. Comr of Taxes, 1975–96; Counsel to Univ. of Oxford, 1971–. First Chm., Statute Law Soc., 1968; Pres., ACC, 1985–97. Chm., Inst. of Envmtl Assessment, 1991–. Trustee, Prince's Youth Business Trust, 1985–89. Mem. Court, Pewterers' Co., 1982– (Master, 1993–94). ARICS, 1977; Hon. FSVA 1978; Hon. Fellow, Coll. of Estate Management, 1982; Hon. FLI (Hon. FILA 1989). Gold Medal, Lincoln Inst. of Land Policy, 1984. *Publications:* (with A. E. Telling) Planning Applications, Appeals and Inquiries, 1953; (with A. E. Telling) Applications for Planning Payments, 1955; Engineering Contracts, 1956. *Recreations:* walking, tennis. *Address:* Flat 15, 9 Manson Place, SW7 5LT. *T:* and *Fax:* (020) 7584 5401. *Club:* Garrick.

Died 2 Feb. 2000.

LEACH, Norman, CMG 1964; Under-Secretary, Foreign and Commonwealth Office (Overseas Development Administration), 1970–72; *b* 8 March 1912; *s* of W. M. Leach. *Educ:* Ermysted's Grammar Sch., Skipton in Craven, Yorks; St Catharine's Coll., Cambridge (Scholar). 1st Class Hons, Pts I and II English Tripos, 1933 and 1934; Charles Oldham Shakespeare Schol., 1933. Asst Principal, Inland Revenue Dept, 1935; Under-Secretary: Ministry of Pensions and National Insurance, 1958–61; Dept of Technical Co-operation, 1961–64; ODM, 1964–70. *Address:* Low Bank, 81 Gargrave Road, Skipton in Craven, North Yorks BD23 1QN. *T:* (01756) 793719.

Died 27 Nov. 1996.

LEACH, Sir Ronald (George), GBE 1976 (CBE 1944); Kt 1970; FCA; Chairman: Standard Chartered Bank(CI), since 1980; Standard Chartered Trust (CI) Ltd, since 1980; *b* 21 Aug. 1907; *s* of William T. Leach, 14 Furze Croft, Hove; *m* 1st, 1933, Betty Dene Corbett; one *s* one *d*; 2nd, Margaret Alice (*d* 1994), *d* of H. W. Binns and formerly wife of Sir Humphrey Sherston-Baker, 6th Bt. *Educ:* Alleyn's. Dep. Financial Sec. to Ministry of Food, Sept. 1939–June 1946. Sen. Partner in firm of Peat, Marwick, Mitchell & Co., Chartered Accountants, 1966–77; Dir, Samuel Montagu & Co., 1977–80. Director: Internat. Investment Trust of Jersey, 1980–93; Ann Street Brewery, 1981–; Barrington Management (CI), 1984–87; Berkeley Australian Develt Capital, 1985–90; Govett American Endeavour Fund Ltd. Member: Cttee on Coastal Flooding, 1953; Inquiry into Shipping, 1967–70; National Theatre Board, 1972–79; Chairman: Consumer Cttee for GB (Agricultural Marketing Acts, 1931–49), 1958–67; Accounting Standards Steering Cttee, 1970–76. Pres. Inst. of Chartered Accountants in England and Wales, 1969–70. Hon. LLD Lancaster, 1977. *Publication:* (with Prof. Edward Stamp) British Accounting Standards: the first ten years, 1981. *Address:* La Rosière, St Saviour, Jersey, CI. *T:* Jersey (01534) 77039 or 78427.

Died 26 Aug. 1996.

LEADBITTER, Edward; *b* 18 June 1919; *s* of Edward Leadbitter, Easington, Durham; *m* 1940, Phyllis Irene Mellin, Bristol; one *s* one *d. Educ:* State schs; Teachers'

Training Coll. Served War, 1939–45, with RA; commissioned 1943; War Office Instructor in Gunnery. Became a teacher. Joined Labour Party, 1938; Pres., Hartlepools Labour Party, 1958–62. Mem., West Hartlepool Borough Council, 1954–67 (sometime Mem., Town Planning, Finance, Housing, Industrial Develt, and Educn Cttees). MP (Lab) The Hartlepools, 1964–92. Member: Estimates Cttee, 1966–69; Select Cttee on Science and Technology, 1970–80; Select Cttee on Energy, 1980–92; Chairmen's Panel, House of Commons, 1980–92; Chm., Anglo-Tunisian Parly Group, 1974–92. Sponsored Children's Homes Registration Bill, 1982. Mem. NUPE, 1963–. Organizer of Exhibition on History of Labour Movement, l956. Pres., Hartlepool Football Club, 1983–. First Hon. Freeman, Co. Borough of Hartlepool, 1981; Freeman of City of London, 1986. *Address:* 32 Brimston Close, Hartlepool, Cleveland TS26 0QA. *T:* (01429) 263404. *Died 23 Dec. 1996.*

LEAKEY, Maj.-Gen. (Arundell) Rea, CB 1967; DSO 1945; MC 1941 (Bar 1942); General Officer Commanding British and Maltese Troops in Malta and Libya, 1967–68; *b* 30 Dec. 1915; *s* of Arundell Gray Leakey; parents British; *m* 1st, 1949, Muriel Irene Le Poer Trench (marr. diss. 1984); two *s*; 2nd, 1994, Joan Morant. *Educ:* Weymouth Coll.; Royal Military Coll., Sandhurst. Command of 5th Royal Tank Regt, 1944; Instructor at Staff Coll., Camberley, 1951–52; Comdr, 1st Arab Legion Armoured Car Regt, 1954–56; Instructor (Col), Staff Coll., Camberley, 1958–60; Comdr, 7th Armoured Brigade, 1961–63; Dir-Gen. of Fighting Vehicles, 1964–66; declared redundant, 1968. Dir and Sec., Wolfson Foundn, 1968–80; fund raiser for St Swithun's Girls' Sch., Winchester, 1980–82. Mem., Houghton Br., Royal British Legion, 1984–96. Czechoslovakian Military Cross, 1944. *Publication:* Leakey's Luck, ed G. Forty, 1999. *Recreations:* gardening, enjoying retirement. *Address:* Ladymead Cottage, Houghton, Stockbridge, Hants SO20 6LU. *T:* (01794) 388396. *Club:* Victory Services.
Died 6 Oct. 1999.

LEAKEY, Prof. Felix William; author; *b* 29 June 1922; *s* of Hugh Leakey and Kathleen Leakey (*née* March); *m* 1947, Daphne Joan Sleep (*née* Salter); one *s* two *d. Educ:* St Christopher Sch., Letchworth; Queen Mary Coll., London. BA, PhD (London). Asst Lectr, then Lectr in French, Univ. of Sheffield, 1948–54; University of Glasgow: Lectr in French, 1954–64; Sen. Lectr, 1964–68; Reader, 1968–70; Prof. of French, Univ. of Reading, 1970–73; Prof. of French Lang. and Lit., Bedford Coll., London, 1973–84 (Head of Department, 1973–79 and 1982–84). Carnegie Research Fellow, 1961–62; Leverhulme Research Fellow, 1971–72. Association of University Professors of French: Hon. Sec., 1972–73; Jt Hon. Sec., 1973–75; Vice-Chm., 1975–76; Chm., 1976–77. Public performances as poetry speaker: Baudelaire's Les Fleurs du Mal, French Inst., London, 1984, and Glasgow Univ., 1985; bilingual recital, Chants/Songs, univ. centres in Britain, France and W Germany, 1976–84. *Publications:* Baudelaire and Nature, 1969; (ed jtly) The French Renaissance and its Heritage: essays presented to Alan Boase, 1968; Sound and Sense in French Poetry (Inaugural Lecture, with readings on disc), 1975; (ed jtly) Samuel Beckett, Drunken Boat, 1977; Baudelaire: Love Poems (videotape), 1989; Baudelaire: Selected Poems from Les Fleurs du Mal (audiotape), 1989; Baudelaire: collected essays 1953–1988, 1990; Baudelaire: Les Fleurs du Mal, 1992; (trans. into English verse) Selected Poems from Baudelaire's Les Fleurs du Mal, 1994, 2nd edn 1997; contribs to: French Studies; MLR, Rev. d'hist. litt. de la France; Rev. de litt. comparée; Rev. des sciences humaines; Etudes baudelairiennes; etc. *Recreations:* poetry, art, music, especially opera.
Died 7 Dec. 1999.

LEAKEY, Mary Douglas, FBA 1973; FRAI; former Director, Olduvai Gorge Excavations; *b* 6 Feb. 1913; *d* of Erskine Edward Nicol and Cecilia Marion Frere; *m* 1936, Louis Seymour Bazett Leakey, FBA (*d* 1972); three *s. Educ:* privately. Hon. Mem., American Assoc. for Arts and Sciences, 1979–; Foreign Associate, Amer. Nat. Acad. of Science, 1987; For. Mem., Royal Swedish Acad. of Scis., 1978. Hon. FSA. (With S. B. Leakey) Prestwich Medal, Geological Soc., and Hubbard Medal, Nat. Geographic Soc.; Gold Medal, Soc. of Women Geographers, USA; Linneus Gold Medal, Royal Swedish Acad., 1978. Elizabeth Blackwell Award, Mary Washington Coll., 1980; Bradford Washburn Award, Boston, 1980. Hon. DSc: Witwatersrand, 1968; Western Michigan, 1980; Chicago, 1981; Cambridge, 1982; Emory, 1988; Massachusetts, Amherst, 1988; Brown, 1990; Columbia, 1991; Hon. DSSc Yale, 1976; Hon. DLitt Oxford, 1981. *Publications:* Olduvai Gorge: vol. 3, Excavation in Beds I and II, 1971; vol. 5, Excavations in Beds III, IV and the Masek Beds, 1994; Africa's Vanishing Art: the rock paintings of Tanzania, 1983; Disclosing the Past (autobiog.), 1984; various papers in Nature and other scientific jls. *Recreations:* reading, game watching. *Address:* Box 15028, Nairobi, Kenya.
Died 9 Dec. 1996.

LEAKEY, Maj. Gen. Rea; *see* Leakey, Maj. Gen. A. R.

LEAROYD, Wing Comdr Roderick Alastair Brook, VC 1940; RAF; *b* 5 Feb. 1913; *s* of late Major Reginald Brook Learoyd, HLI and Marjorie Scott Boadle. *Educ:* Wellington Coll. Commnd RAF, 1936; served War, 1939–45. With British Motor Corp. until retirement. *Address:* 12 Fittleworth Garden, Rustington, W Sussex BN16 3EW. *Died 24 Jan. 1996.*

LEATHART, Air Cdre James Anthony, CB 1960; DSO 1940; *b* 5 Jan. 1915; *s* of P. W. Leathart, BSc, MD, ENT specialist, Liverpool; *m* 1939, E. L. Radcliffe, Birkenhead; two *s* one *d. Educ:* St Edward's, Oxford; Liverpool Univ. Joined Auxiliary Air Force (610 County of Chester Squadron), 1936; transferred RAF, 1937; CO 54 Sqn, Battle of Britain, 1940; Air HQ (Ops Requirements), ME; OC No 89 (Night Fighter) Sqn, ME (one Night Fighter victory over Western Desert); Chief of Staff Headquarters, 12 Group, RAF, 1959–61; Dir of Operational Requirements, Air Ministry, 1961–62, retd. *Recreations:* fly-fishing, motoring, ornithology, gardening. *Address:* Wortley Farmhouse, Wotton-under-Edge, Glos GL12 7QP. *T:* (01453) 842312. *Died 17 Nov. 1998.*

LEATHERS, 2nd Viscount, *cr* 1954, of Purfleet, co. Essex; **Frederick Alan Leathers;** Baron Leathers, 1941; *b* 4 April 1908; *er s* of 1st Viscount Leathers, CH, PC, LLD, and Emily Ethel Baxter; *S* father, 1965; *m* 1st, 1940, Elspeth Graeme (marr. diss. 1983; she *d* 1985), *yr d* of late Sir Thomas (Alexander) Stewart; two *s* two *d*; 2nd, 1983, Mrs Lorna M. Barnett. *Educ:* Brighton Coll.; Emmanuel Coll., Cambridge (MA (hons) in Economics). Mem. of Baltic Exchange. Director: Wm Cory & Son Ltd, 1929–72 (Chm.); Cory Mann George Ltd, 1941–72 (Chm.); Cory Ship Towage Ltd, 1941–72 (Chm.); Smit & Cory International Port Towage Ltd, 1970–72 (Chm.); Hull Blyth & Co. Ltd, 1949–72 (Chm.); Rea Ltd, 1941–72 (Chm.); St Denis Shipping Co. Ltd, 1957–72 (Chm.); Laporte Industries Ltd, 1959–71; Laporte Industries (Holdings) Ltd, 1959–71; Tunnel Cement Ltd, 1960–74; Guardian Cement Co. Ltd, 1963–71; New Zealand Cement Holdings Ltd, 1963–71; National Westminster Bank, Outer London Region, 1968–78. Member: Court of Worshipful Company of Shipwrights; Court of Watermen's and Lightermen's Company; Fellow Institute of Chartered Shipbrokers; MInstPet. *Heir: s* Hon. Christopher Graeme Leathers [*b* 31 Aug. 1941; *m* 1964, Maria Philomena, *yr d* of Michael Merriman, Charlestown,

Co. Mayo; one *s* one *d*]. *Address:* Park House, Chiddingfold, Surrey GU8 4TS. *T:* Wormley (01428) 683222. *Club:* Royal Automobile.
Died 21 Jan. 1996.

LEAVEY, John Anthony, (Tony); *b* 3 March 1915; *s* of George Edwin Leavey and Marion Louise Warnock; *m* 1952, Lesley Doreen, *d* of Rt Hon. Sir Benjamin Ormerod. *Educ:* Mill Hill Sch.; Trinity Hall, Cambridge (BA). Served War, 1939–46; 5th Royal Inniskilling Dragoon Guards. MP (C) Heywood and Royton Div. of Lancashire, 1955–64. PPS to Minister of Defence, 1956–57, to Chancellor of Exchequer, 1959–60. Chairman: Wilson (Connolly) Hldgs, 1966–82 (Dir, 1966–85); Robert Moss, 1981–82 (Dir, 1981–86); Edward Barber & Co., 1982–88; Director: Smith & Nephew, 1948–80 (Dep. Chm., 1962–72); BIA, 1976–85; Fläkt, 1976–85; CSE Aviation, 1986–88. Panel Mem., SE London Indust. Tribunal, 1978–84. Mem. Council, Outward Bound Trust, 1974–92; Trustee, Kurt Hahn Trust, 1987–92. *Recreation:* fishing. *Address:* 30 Pembroke Gardens Close, W8 6HR. *Club:* Army and Navy. *Died 9 July 1999.*

LEDWIDGE, Sir (William) Bernard (John), KCMG 1974 (CMG 1964); HM Diplomatic Service, retired; writer; Chairman, United Kingdom Committee for UNICEF, 1976–89; *b* 9 Nov. 1915; *s* of late Charles Ledwidge and Eileen O'Sullivan; *m* 1st, 1948, Anne Kingsley (marr. diss. 1970); one *s* one *d*; 2nd, 1970, Flora Groult. *Educ:* Cardinal Vaughan Sch.; King's Coll., Cambridge; Princeton Univ., USA. Commonwealth Fund Fellow, 1937–39. Served War of 1939–45: RA, 1940; Indian Army, 1941–45. Private Secretary to Permanent Under-Secretary, India Office, 1946; Secretary, Frontier Areas Cttee of Enquiry, Burma, 1947; Foreign Office, 1947–49; British Consul, St Louis, USA, 1949–52; First Secretary, British Embassy, Kabul, 1952–56; Political Adviser British Military Govt, Berlin, 1956–61; Foreign Office, 1961–65; Minister, Paris, 1965–69; Ambassador to Finland, 1969–72; Ambassador to Israel, 1972–75. Mem., Police Complaints Bd, 1977–82. *Publications:* Frontiers (novel), 1979; (jtly) Nouvelles de la Famille (short stories), 1980; De Gaulle, 1982; De Gaulle et les Américains, 1984; Sappho, La première voix de femme, 1987. *Recreation:* drinking and talking. *Address:* 54 rue de Bourgogne, 75007 Paris, France. *T:* 247058026; 19 Queen's Gate Terrace, SW7 5PR. *T:* (0171) 584 4132. *Clubs:* Travellers', MCC. *Died 20 Feb. 1998.*

LEE, His Honour John (Thomas Cyril); Circuit Judge (attached Midland Oxford Circuit), 1972–93; *b* 14 Jan. 1927; *s* of late Dorothy Lee; *m* 1956, Beryl Lee (*née* Haden); one *s* three *d*. *Educ:* Holly Lodge Grammar Sch., Staffs; Emmanual Coll., Cambridge (MA, LLB). Called to the Bar, Gray's Inn, 1952; practised, Oxford Circuit, 1952–72. Chairman various Tribunals. *Recreation:* golf. *Address:* The Red House, Upper Colwall, Malvern, Worcs WR13 6PX. *T:* Colwall (01684) 540645. *Clubs:* Union and County (Worcester); Worcester Golf and Country. *Died 30 Sept. 1999.*

LEE, Laurie, MBE 1952; FRSL; poet and author; *b* 1914; *s* of Reg Lee; *m* 1950, Catherine Francesca Polge; one *d*. *Educ:* Slad Village Sch.; Stroud Central Sch. Travelled Mediterranean, 1935–39; GPO Film Unit, 1939–40; Crown Film Unit, 1941–43; Publications Editor, Ministry of Information, 1944–46; Green Park Film Unit, 1946–47; Caption Writer-in-Chief, Festival of Britain, 1950–51. Freeman of City of London, 1982. Hon. DLitt Cheltenham and Gloucester Coll. of Higher Educn, 1992. *Publications:* The Sun My Monument (poems), 1944; Land at War (HMSO), 1945; (with Ralph Keene) A Film in Cyprus, 1947; The Bloom of Candles (poems), 1947; The Voyage of Magellan, 1948; My Many-Coated Man (poems), 1955; A Rose for Winter, 1955; Pocket Poets (selection), 1960;

The Firstborn, 1964; I Can't Stay Long, 1975; Selected Poems, 1983; Two Women, 1983; *autobiography:* Cider With Rosie, 1959; As I Walked Out One Midsummer Morning, 1969; A Moment of War, 1991 (trilogy reprinted as Red Sky At Sunrise, 1992). *Recreations:* indoor sports, music, travel. *Address:* 9/40 Elm Park Gardens, SW10 9NZ. *T:* (0171) 352 2197. *Clubs:* Chelsea Arts, Garrick.
Died 13 May 1997.

LEE, Malcolm Kenneth; QC 1983; **His Honour Judge Malcolm Lee;** a Circuit Judge, and Designated Circuit Mercantile Judge in the Mercantile Court in Birmingham, since 1993; *b* 2 Jan. 1943; 2nd *s* of late Thomas Marston Lee, solicitor, Birmingham, and Fiona Margaret Lee, JP (*née* Mackenzie); *m* 1970, Phyllis Anne Brunton Speed, *er d* of Andrew Watson Speed, Worcs; three *s* three *d* (and one *d* decd). *Educ:* King Edward's Sch., Birmingham (Foundation Schol.); Worcester Coll., Oxford (Schol.; MA Class. Hon. Mods and Lit.Hum.). Assistant Master: Marlborough Coll., 1965; King Edward's Sch., Birmingham, 1966; Major Schol., Inner Temple, 1967; called to the Bar, Inner Temple, 1967; practised on Midland Circuit, 1968–71, Midland and Oxford Circuit, 1972–93; a Recorder, 1980–93. Dep. Chm., Agricl Land Tribunal, E Midland Area, 1979–82, Midland Area, 1982–94; Chm., Agricl Land Tribunal, Midland and Oxford Circuit, 1979–83. *Recreations:* squash, tennis, walking, reading. *Address:* The Priory Courts, 33 Bull Street, Birmingham B4 6DS. *T:* (0121) 681 3134. *Clubs:* Edgbaston Priory (Birmingham); Beechwood Lawn Tennis (Coventry). *Died 29 Aug. 1999.*

LEE, Sir William (Allison), Kt 1975; OBE 1945; TD 1948; DL; Chairman, Northern Regional Health Authority, 1973–78; *b* 31 May 1907; *s* of Samuel Percy and Florence Ada Lee, Darlington; *m* 1st, 1933, Elsa Norah (*d* 1966), *d* of late Thomas Hanning, Darlington; 2nd, 1967, Mollie Clifford (*d* 1989), *d* of late Sir Cuthbert Whiteside, Knysna, S Africa; no *c*. *Educ:* Queen Elizabeth Grammar Sch., Darlington. Insurance Branch Manager, retd. Served Royal Signals, 1935–53; Dep. Comdr, 151 Inf. Bde (TA), 1953–58; County Comdt, Durham ACF, 1962–70. Mem., Darlington RDC, 1949–61, Chm. 1957–60. Chairman: Winterton HMC, 1967–70 (Mem., 1954–70); Newcastle Reg. Hosp. Bd, 1973–74 (Mem., 1956–74). Pres., Darlington Div., SSAFA. DL County of Durham, 1965; High Sheriff, Durham, 1978. *Recreation:* gardening. *Address:* Whiteside, 23 Low Green, Gainford, Co. Durham DL2 3DS. *T:* Darlington (01325) 730564.
Died 17 Feb. 1996.

LEES-MILNE, James; *b* 6 Aug. 1908; *er s* of George Crompton Lees-Milne, Crompton Hall, Lancs and Wickhamford Manor, Worcs; *m* 1951, Alvilde (*d* 1994), *d* of late Lt-Gen. Sir Tom Molesworth Bridges, KCB, KCMG, DSO and formerly wife of 3rd Viscount Chaplin; no *c*. *Educ:* Eton Coll.; Magdalen Coll., Oxford. Private Sec. to 1st Baron Lloyd, 1931–35; on staff, Reuters, 1935–36; on staff, National Trust, 1936–66; Adviser on Historic Buildings to National Trust, 1951–66. 2nd Lieut Irish Guards, 1940–41 (invalided). FRSL 1957; FSA 1974. *Publications:* The National Trust (ed), 1945; The Age of Adam, 1947; National Trust Guide: Buildings, 1948; Tudor Renaissance, 1951; The Age of Inigo Jones, 1953; Roman Mornings, 1956 (Heinemann Award, 1956); Baroque in Italy, 1959; Baroque in Spain and Portugal, 1960; Earls of Creation, 1962; Worcestershire: A Shell Guide, 1964; St Peter's, 1967; English Country Houses: Baroque 1685–1714, 1970; Another Self, 1970; Heretics in Love, 1973; Ancestral Voices, 1975; William Beckford, 1976; Prophesying Peace, 1977; Round the Clock, 1978; Harold Nicolson, vol. I, 1980, vol. II, 1981 (Heinemann Award, RSL, 1982); (with David Ford) Images of Bath,

1982; The Country House (anthology), 1982; Caves of Ice, 1983; The Last Stuarts, 1983; Midway on the Waves, 1985; The Enigmatic Edwardian, 1986; Some Cotswold Country Houses, 1987; Venetian Evenings, 1988; The Fool of Love, 1990; The Bachelor Duke, 1991; People and Places, 1992; A Mingled Measure: diaries 1953–1972, 1994; Fourteen Friends, 1996; Ancient as the Hills: diaries 1973–1974, 1997; *posthumous publications:* Through Wood and Dale: diaries 1975–1978, 1998; Deep Romantic Chasm: diaries 1979–1981, 2000. *Address:* Essex House, Badminton, Avon GL9 1DD. *T:* (01454) 218288. *Club:* Brooks's.   *Died 28 Dec. 1997.*

LEGG, Allan Aubrey R.; *see* Rowan-Legg.

LEIGH, (Archibald) Denis, MD; FRCP; Consultant Physician, Bethlem Royal and Maudsley Hospitals, 1949–80, then Emeritus; Secretary-General, World Psychiatric Association, 1966–78; Hon. Consultant in Psychiatry to the British Army, 1969–80; Lecturer, Institute of Psychiatry; *b* 11 Oct. 1915; *o s* of Archibald Leigh and Rose Rushworth; *m* 1941, Pamela Parish; two *s* three *d. Educ:* Hulme Grammar Sch.; Manchester Univ.; University of Budapest. Manchester City Schol. in Medicine, 1932; BSc 1936; MB, ChB (1st class hons) 1939; Dauntesey Med. Sen. Schol., Prof. Tom Jones Exhibitioner in Anatomy; Sidney Renshaw Jun. Prize in Physiol.; Turner Med. Prize; John Henry Agnew Prize; Stephen Lewis Prize; Prize in Midwifery; MRCP 1941; MD (Manchester), 1947; FRCP 1955. RAMC, 1940–45 (Lt-Col); Adviser in Neurology, Eastern Army, India. 1st Assistant, Dept of Neurology, London Hospital; Nuffield Fellow, 1947–48; Clinical Fellow, Harvard Univ., 1948; Recognised Clinical Teacher, London Univ. Founder, European Society of Psychosomatic Research; Editor-in-Chief and Founder, Journal of Psychosomatic Res.; Editorial Bd, Japanese Journal of Psychosomatic Medicine, Medicina Psychosomatica, Psychosomatic Medicine, Behaviour Therapy; Examiner in Psychological Med., Edinburgh Univ., 1958–65; Beattie Smith Lectr, Melbourne Univ., 1967. Governor, Bethlem Royal and Maudsley Hospitals, 1956–62; President Sect. of Psychiatry, Royal Society Med., 1967–68. Hon. Member: Deutschen Gesellschaft für Psychiatrie und Nervenheilkunde; Italian Psychosomatic Soc.; Assoc. Brasileira de Psiquiatria; Sociedad Argentina de Medicina Psicosomática; Polish Psychiatric Assoc.; Corresp. Mem., Pavlovian Soc. of N America; Hon. Corresp. Mem., Aust. Acad. of Forensic Scis; Hon Fellow: Swedish Soc. of Med. Scis; Soc. Colombiana de Psiquiatría; Soviet Soc. of Neurologists and Psychiatrists; Czechoslovak Psychiatric Soc.; Finnish Psychiatric Soc.; Distinguished Fellow: Amer. Psychiatric Assoc.; Hong Kong Psychiatric Assoc. *Publications:* Chertok, Psychosomatic Method in Painless Childbirth (trans.), 1959; The Historical Development of British Psychiatry, Vol. I, 1961; Bronchial Asthma, 1967; A Concise Encyclopaedia of Psychiatry, 1977; chapters in various books; papers on neurology, psychiatry, history of psychiatry and psychosomatic medicine. *Recreations:* fishing, collecting. *Address:* 152 Harley Street, W1N 1HH. *T:* (0171) 935 8868; The Grange, Otford, Kent TN14 5PL. *T:* (01959) 523427.

Died 20 April 1998.

LEIGH-PEMBERTON, John, AFC 1945; artist painter; *b* 18 Oct. 1911; *s* of Cyril Leigh-Pemberton and Mary Evelyn Megaw; *m* 1948, Doreen Beatrice Townshend-Webster (*d* 1992). *Educ:* Eton. Studied Art, London, 1928–31. Past Member Royal Institute of Painters in Oils and other Societies. Served 1940–45 with RAF as Flying Instructor. Series of pictures for Coldstream Guards, 1950; Festival Almanack, 1951, for Messrs Whitbread; Royal Progress, 1953, for Shell Mex & BP Ltd. Works in public and private collections, UK and America; decorations for

ships: City of York, City of Exeter, Britannic, Caledonia, Corfu, Carthage, Kenya, Uganda. Many series of paintings, chiefly of natural history subjects, for Midland Bank Ltd. *Publications:* A Book of Garden Flowers, 1960; A Book of Butterflies, Moths and other Insects, 1963; British Wildlife, Rarities and Introductions, 1966; Garden Birds, 1967; Sea and Estuary Birds, 1967; Heath and Woodland Birds, 1968; Vanishing Wild Animals of the World, 1968; Pond and River Birds, 1969; African Mammals, 1969; Australian Mammals, 1970; North American Mammals, 1970; Birds of Prey, 1970; European Mammals, 1971; Asian Mammals, 1971; South American Mammals, 1972; Sea and Air Mammals, 1972; Wild Life in Britain, 1972; Disappearing Mammals, 1973; Ducks and Swans, 1973; Lions and Tigers, 1974; Baby Animals, 1974; Song Birds, 1974; Leaves, 1974; Big Animals, 1975; Apes and Monkeys, 1975; Reptiles, 1976; Seals and Whales, 1976; Butterflies and Moths, 1978; Hedges, 1979; Birds of Britain and Northern Europe, 1979; Bears and Pandas, 1979. *Address:* 5 Roehampton Gate, Roehampton, SW15 5JR. *T:* (0181) 876 3332.   *Died 10 May 1997.*

LEIGHTON OF ST MELLONS, 2nd Baron *cr* 1962; **John Leighton Seager;** Bt 1952; *b* 11 Jan. 1922; *er s* of 1st Baron Leighton of St Mellons, CBE, JP, and Marjorie (*d* 1992), *d* of William Henry Gimson, Breconshire; *S* father, 1963; *m* 1st, 1953, Elizabeth Rosita (*d* 1979), *o d* of late Henry Hopgood, Cardiff; two *s* one *d* (and one *d* decd); 2nd, 1982, Ruth Elizabeth Hopwood. *Educ:* Caldicott Sch.; The Leys Sch., Cambridge. Formerly Partner, Probity Industrial Maintenance Services. Past Chm., Bristol Channel Shipowners Assoc. *Heir: s* Hon. Robert William Henry Leighton Seager, *b* 28 Sept. 1955. *Address:* 24 Clwyd, Northcliffe, Penarth CF64 1DZ.

Died 28 April 1998.

LEITCH, William Andrew, CB 1963; Law Reform Consultant, Government of Northern Ireland, 1973–78; Examiner of Statutory Rules, Northern Ireland Assembly, 1974–78, retired; *b* 16 July 1915; *e s* of Andrew Leitch, MD, DPH, Castlederg, Co. Tyrone, and May, *d* of W. H. Todd, JP, Fyfin, Strabane, Co. Tyrone; *m* 1939, Edna Margaret, *d* of David McIlvennan, Solicitor, Belfast; one *s* two *d. Educ:* Methodist Coll., Belfast; Queen's Univ., Belfast; London Univ. (LLB). Admitted Solicitor, NI, 1937; Asst Solicitors Dept, Ministry of Finance, NI, 1937–43; Asst Parly Draftsman, 1944–56; First Parly Draftsman, 1956–74. Hon. LLM Queen's Univ., Belfast, 1967. *Publications:* A Handbook on the Administration of Estates Act (NI) 1955, 1957; (jtly) A Commentary on the Interpretation Act (Northern Ireland) 1954, 1955; articles in various legal publications. *Recreations:* fishing, golf, reading. *Address:* 53 Kensington Road, Belfast BT5 6NL. *T:* (028) 9079 4784.   *Died 11 Dec. 1999.*

LEITH, Sir Andrew George F.; *see* Forbes-Leith.

LEITHEAD, James Douglas; *b* 4 Oct. 1911; *s* of late William Leithead, Berwick-on-Tweed; *m* 1936, Alice (*d* 1989), *d* of late Thomas Wylie, Stirling, Scotland; one *s. Educ:* Bradford Grammar Sch. ACA 1932; FCA 1960; Accountant, 1927–32. Chartered Accountant, 1932–39; Lecturer, Bradford Technical Coll., 1934–39; Secretarial Assistant, Midland (Amalgamated) District (Coal Mines) Scheme, 1939–42; Ministry of Supply, 1942–45; BoT, 1945–64, HM Diplomatic Service, 1965–68 (British Trade Commissioner: Australia, 1950–63; New Zealand, 1963–67); BoT, later DTI, 1968–72, retired. Vice-Pres., W Australian Branch of Royal Commonwealth Soc., 1957–63. *Recreation:* chess. *Address:* 48 Eaton Road, Appleton, Oxon OX13 5JH.   *Died 13 Dec. 1998.*

LE MASURIER, Sir Robert (Hugh), Kt 1966; DSC 1942; Bailiff of Jersey, 1962–74; *b* 29 Dec. 1913; *s* of William Smythe Le Masurier and Mabel Harriet Briard; *m* 1941,

Helen Sophia Sheringham, one s two d. Educ: Victoria Coll., Jersey; Pembroke Coll., Oxford. MA 1935; BCL 1936. Sub-Lieut RNVR, 1939; Lieut RNVR, 1943; Lieut-Commander RNVR, 1944. Solicitor-General, Jersey, 1955; Attorney-General, Jersey, 1958. *Recreations:* sailing, carpentry. *Address:* Flat 8, Oaklands, Mont de la Rosière, St Saviour, Jersey JE2 7XL. *T:* Jersey (01534) 865234. *Clubs:* St Helier Yacht, United (Jersey).

Died 30 July 1996.

LEMMON, David Hector; writer; *b* 4 April 1931; *s* of Frederick Robert Lemmon and Sophie Elizabeth Lemmon (*née* Beadle); *m* 1958, (Jean) Valerie Fletcher; two *s.* *Educ:* Southgate Grammar Sch.; Coll. of St Mark and St John, Chelsea. Teacher's Cert., 1953; BA Hons London 1968. ACP 1968. Shell Mex & BP Co., 1947–49; RAF, 1949–51; Master: Bound's Green Sch., 1953–57; Ankara Coll., Turkey, 1957–60 (Dir, Amer. Little Theatre, 1958–59); Head of English: Kingsbury High Sch., Warwicks, 1960–63; Torells Girls Sch., Thurrock, 1963–68; Nicholas Sch., Basildon, 1968–73 (and Dir of Studies, 1973–83); full-time writer, 1983–. English Speaking Board: Mem., 1964–; Examnr, 1967–; Fellow, 1997; Examnr, Advanced Level Theatre Studies Practical, 1980–93. Pres., Old Commoners CC. Mem. Editl Bd, Cricket World, 1991–92. FRSA 1998. (Jtly) J. M. Kilburn Meml Award, Cricket Writer of the Year, 1994. *Publications:* Summer of Success, 1980; Great One-Day Cricket Matches, 1982, new edn 1984; Tich Freeman, 1982; Wisden Book of Cricket Quotations, 1, 1982, 2, 1990; The Book of One-Day Internationals, 1983; Johnny Won't Hit Today, 1983; The Great Wicket-Keepers, 1984; Percy Chapman, 1985; Ken McEwan, 1985; (with Ted Dexter) A Walk to the Wicket, 1984; (ed) Cricket Heroes, 1984; (with Ken Kelly) Cricket Reflections, 1985; Cricket Mercenaries, 1987; (with Mike Marshall) The Official History of Essex CCC, 1987; The Crisis of Captaincy, 1988; One-Day Cricket, 1988; The Official History of Middlesex CCC, 1988, of Worcestershire CCC, 1989, of Surrey CCC, 1989; (with Chris Cowdrey) Know Your Sport—Cricket, 1989; British Theatre Yearbook, 1989, 2nd edn 1990, then Benson and Hedges British Theatre Yearbook, 1992; Len Hutton, a Pictorial Biography, 1990; Cricket's Champion Counties, 1991; The Cricketing Greigs, 1991; The Guinness Book of Test Cricket Captains, 1992; For Love of the Game, 1993; The Book of Essex Cricketers, 1994; A Vision Achieved: a history of the Hampshire schools, 1996; Changing Seasons: English cricket since the Second World War, 1997; Arsenal in the Blood, 1998; Pelham Cricket Year, then Benson and Hedges Cricket Year, annually 1979–. *Recreations:* work—theatre, Arsenal FC and sport; music, literature, art, people, entertaining. *Address:* 26 Leigh Road, Leigh-on-Sea, Essex SS9 1LD. *T:* (01702) 479640. *Clubs:* MCC, Cricket Writers'; Essex County Cricket.

Died 25 Oct. 1998.

LENNON, Prof. (George) Gordon; retired gynæcologist; Professor Emeritus, University of Western Australia, Perth, 1974; *b* 7 Oct. 1911; *s* of late J. Lennon; *m* 1940, Barbara Brynhild (*née* Buckle); two *s.* *Educ:* Aberdeen Academy; Aberdeen Univ. MB, ChB Aberdeen, 1934; MRCOG 1939; FRCOG 1952; MMSA 1943; ChM (Hons) Aberdeen, 1945. Served War of 1939–45, Sqdn-Ldr in charge of Surgical Div., RAFVR, 1942–46. Served in hospital posts in Aberdeen, Glasgow, London, Birmingham; First Asst, Nuffield Dept of Obstetrics and Gynæcology, Radcliffe Infirmary (University of Oxford), 1946–51; Prof. of Obstetrics and Gynæcology, Univ. of Bristol, 1951–67; Dean, Faculty of Med., Univ. of WA, Perth, 1967–74. Visiting Professor: Iraq and Turkey, 1956; South Africa and Uganda, 1958; Iran, 1965. *Publications:* Diagnosis in Clinical Obstetrics; articles in British Medical Journal, Proceedings of the Royal Society of Medicine,

Journal of Obstetrics and Gynæcology of the British Empire, etc. *Recreation:* golf. *Address:* 3 Brouncker House, Canon's Court, Church Street, Melksham, Wilts SN12 6UR. *T:* (01225) 700291.

Died 2 April 1996.

LEONTIEF, Prof. Wassily; Economist, New York University, since 1975 (Founder, 1978, Director, 1978–85, Institute for Economic Analysis; Member of Research Staff, since 1986); *b* Leningrad, Russia, 5 Aug. 1906; *s* of Wassily Leontief and Eugenia Leontief (*née* Bekker); *m* 1932, Estelle Helena Marks; one *d.* *Educ:* Univ. of Leningrad (Learned Economist, 1925; MA); Univ. of Berlin (PhD 1928). Research Associate, Inst. of World Econs, Univ. of Kiel, Germany, 1927–28; Economic Adviser to Chinese Govt, Nanking, 1928–29; Res. Associate, Nat. Bureau of Econ. Res., NY, 1931; Harvard University: Instr, Economics, 1932–33; Asst Prof., 1933–39; Associate Prof., 1939–46; Prof. of Econs, 1946–53; Henry Lee Prof. of Pol Econs, 1953–75; Sen. Fellow, Soc. of Fellows, 1956–75 (Chm., 1965–75); Dir, Harvard Economic Research Project, 1948–72; Guggenheim Fellow, 1940, 1950. General Consultant: US Dept of Labor, 1941–47 and 1961–65; US Dept of Commerce, 1966–82; Office of Technology Assessment, 1980–; Econ. Consultant, Russian Econs Sub-Div., Office of Strategic Services, 1943–45; Consultant: UN Sec.-Gen.'s Consultative Gp of Econ. and Social Consequences of Disarmament, 1961–62; UN Develt Prog., 1980–; Mem., Exec. Bd, Science Adv. Council, Environmental Protection Agency, 1975–80. President: Amer. Econ. Assoc., 1970; Sect. F, BAAS, 1976; Mem., Nat. Acad. of Sciences, 1974; FAAAS 1977; Foreign Mem., USSR Acad. of Sciences, 1988; Mem., Soc. of the Optimate, Italian Cultural Inst., NY, 1989; Corresp. Mem., Institut de France, 1968; Corresp. FBA, 1970; Hon. MRIA 1976. Dr *hc:* Brussels, 1962; York, 1967; Louvain, 1971; Paris (Sorbonne), 1972; Pennsylvania, 1976; Lancaster, 1976; Toulouse, Louisville, Vermont, Long Island, 1980; Karl Marx Univ., Budapest, 1981; Adelphi Coll., 1988; Cordoba, 1990; Hon. DHL Rensselaer Polytechnic Inst., 1988. Nobel Prize in Economic Science, 1973; Takemi Meml Award, Inst. of Seizon and Life Scis, Japan, 1991. Order of the Cherubim, Univ. of Pisa, 1953. Officier, Légion d'Honneur, 1968; Order of the Rising Sun, Japan, 1984; Commandeur des Arts et des Lettres, France, 1985. *Publications:* The Structure of the American Economy 1919–29, 1941, 2nd edn 1953; Studies in the Structure of the American Economy, 1953; Input-Output Economics, 1966, 2nd edn 1986; Essays in Economics, vol. I 1966, vol. II 1977; The Future of the World Economy, 1977; (with F. Duchin) Military Spending: facts and figures, worldwide implications and future outlook, 1983; (jtly) The Future of Non-Fuel Minerals in the US and World Economy, 1983; (with F. Duchin) The Impact of Automation on Workers, 1986; contribs to learned jls. *Recreation:* fly fishing. *Address:* Institute for Economic Analysis, 269 Mercer Street, 2nd floor, New York, NY 10003, USA.

Died 5 Feb. 1999.

LESLIE, Prof. Frank Matthews; JP; DSc, PhD; FRS 1995; FRSE; Professor of Mathematics, Strathclyde University, since 1982; *b* 8 March 1935; *s* of late William Ogilvy Leslie and Catherine Pitkethly Leslie (*née* Matthews); *m* 1965, Ellen Leitch Reoch; one *s* one *d.* *Educ:* Queen's Coll., Dundee, Univ. of St Andrews (BSc; DSc 1995); Manchester Univ. (PhD 1961). FRSE 1980. Asst Lectr in Maths, Manchester Univ., 1959–61; Res. Associate in Maths, MIT, 1961–62; Lectr in Maths, Newcastle Univ., 1962–68; Strathclyde University: Sen. Lectr, 1968–71; Reader, 1971–79; Personal Prof., 1979–82. Vis. Asst Prof. in Mechanics, Johns Hopkins Univ., 1966–67. Chm., Brit. Liquid Crystal Soc., 1987–91. JP Bearsden and Milngavie, 1984. Annual Award, Brit. Soc. Rheology, 1982; Mem.,

Johns Hopkins Soc. Scholars, 1980; Sykes Gold Medal, St Andrews Univ., 1996; G. W. Gray Medal, British Liquid Crystal Soc., 1997. *Publications:* res. papers in scientific jls mostly on theory of liquid crystals. *Recreations:* golf, hill-walking, gardening. *Address:* Department of Mathematics, Strathclyde University, Livingstone Tower, Richmond Street, Glasgow G1 1XH. *T:* (0141) 548 3655. *Died 15 June 2000.*

LESTOR OF ECCLES, Baroness *cr* 1997 (Life Peer), of Tooting Bec, in the London Borough of Wandsworth; **Joan Lestor;** freelance lecturer; *b* Vancouver, British Columbia, Canada, 13 Nov. 1931; *d* of late Charles and Ettie Lestor; one *s* one *d* (both adopted). *Educ:* Blaenavon Secondary Sch., Monmouth; William Morris Secondary Sch., Walthamstow; London Univ. (Diploma in Sociology). Nursery sch. teacher, 1959–66. Member: Wandsworth Borough Council, 1958–68; LCC, 1962–64; Exec. Cttee of the London Labour Party, 1962–65; Nat. Exec., Labour Party, 1967–82 (Chm., 1977–78) and 1987–97; Chm., Internat. Cttee, Labour Party, 1978–97. Contested (Lab) Lewisham W, 1964; MP (Lab) Eton and Slough, 1966–83; contested (Lab) Slough, 1983; MP (Lab) Eccles, 1987–97. Parliamentary Under-Secretary of State: Dept of Educn and Science, Oct. 1969–June 1970; FCO, 1974–75; DES, 1975–76; resigned from Labour Govt on cuts policy, 1976; frontbench spokesperson on overseas aid and develt co-operation, 1988–89, on children's affairs, young offenders and race relations, 1989–92, on children and the family, 1993–94, on overseas develt, 1994–96. Chairman: Council, Nat. Soc. of Children's Nurseries, 1969–70; UK Branch, Defence for Children International; Dir, Trade Unions Child Care Project, 1986–87. Co-Chm., Jt Cttee against Racialism, 1978–; Mem., CND Nat. Council, 1983–. *Recreations:* theatre, reading, playing with children and animals. *Address:* House of Lords, SW1A 0PW.
Died 27 March 1998.

L'ETANG, Hugh Joseph Charles James; medical editor and writer; *b* 23 Nov. 1917; *s* of Dr J. G. L'Etang and Frances L'Etang; *m* 1951, Cecily Margaret Tinker, MD, MRCP; one *s* one *d*. *Educ:* Haileybury Coll.; St John's Coll., Oxford; St Bartholomew's Hosp.; Harvard Sch. of Public Health. BA 1939, BM, BCh 1942, DIH 1952. War Service, 1943–46, RMO 5th Bn Royal Berks Regt; TA from 1947, RAMC; Lt-Col 1953–56. Medical Adviser: North Thames Gas Bd, 1948–56; British European Airways, 1956–58; John Wyeth & Brother Ltd, 1958–69; Asst and Dep. Editor, The Practitioner, 1969–72, Editor 1973–82. Hira S. Chouké Lectr, Coll. of Physicians of Philadelphia, 1972 (Hon. Fellow, 1985); Henry Cohen Hist. of Medicine Lectr, Univ. of Liverpool, 1986. Member: RUSI; IISS; Military Commentators' Circle; Amer. Civil War Round Table, London. Consultant Editor: The Physician, 1983–91; Travel Medicine International, 1996– (Editor, 1983–95); Editor-in-Chief: RSM International Congress and Symposium Series, 1983–89; RSM Round Table Series, 1989–; Section Editor, Jl of Med. Biography, 1992–. *Publications:* The Pathology of Leadership, 1969; Fit to Lead?, 1980; (ed) Regulation and Restraint in Contemporary Medicine in the UK and USA, 1983; (Consultant Editor) Fontana Dictionary of Modern Thought, 1988; (Specialist Corresp.) Chronicle of the 20th Century, 1988; (ed) Health Care Provision under Financial Constraint: a decade of change, 1990; Ailing Leaders in Power 1914–1994, 1995; articles in Practitioner, Jl RAMC, Jl RUSI, Army Qly, Brassey's Annual, Navy Internat., NATO's Fifteen Nations, Politics and the Life Sciences, Dictionary of Literary Biography Yearbook 1994. *Recreation:* medical aspects of military and foreign affairs. *Address:* 27 Sispara Gardens, West Hill Road, SW18 1LG. *T:* (0181) 870 3836. *Club:* United Oxford & Cambridge University. *Died 25 Nov. 1996.*

LE TOCQ, Eric George, CMG 1975; HM Diplomatic Service, retired; British Government Representative in the West Indies Associated States, 1975–78; *b* 20 April 1918; *s* of Eugene Charles Le Tocq; *m* 1946, Betty Esdaile; two *s* one *d*. *Educ:* Elizabeth Coll., Guernsey; Exeter Coll., Oxford (MA). Served War of 1939–45: commissioned in Royal Engineers, 1939; North Africa, 1942–43; Italy, 1943; Austria and Greece; Major. Taught Modern Languages and Mathematics at Monmouth Sch., 1946–48; Assistant Principal, Commonwealth Relations Office, 1948; Karachi, 1948–50; Principal, 1950; Dublin, 1953–55; Accra, 1957–59; Assistant Secretary, 1962; Adviser on Commonwealth and External Affairs, Entebbe, 1962; Deputy High Commissioner, Uganda, 1962–64; Counsellor, British High Commission, Canberra, 1964–67; Head of E African Dept, FCO, 1968–71; High Comr in Swaziland, 1972–75. *Address:* Forest Edge, May Lane, Pilley, Hants SO41 5QR. *Died 30 Aug. 1996.*

LETTS, Charles Trevor; Underwriting Member of Lloyd's, since 1944; Deputy Chairman of Lloyd's, 1966 (entered Lloyd's, 1924; Member, 1941; Committee, 1964–67); *b* 2 July 1905; *o s* of late Charles Hubert and Gertrude Letts; *m* 1942, Mary R. (Judy), *o d* of late Sir Stanley and Lady (Hilda) Woodwark; two *s* one *d*. *Educ:* Marlborough Coll. Served RNVR, Lieut-Commander, 1940–45. Member: Cttee, Lloyd's Underwriters' Assoc., 1960–70 (Chairman, 1963–64); Council, Lloyd's Register of Shipping, 1964–77 (Chairman, Yacht Sub-Cttee, 1967–75); Salvage Association, 1963–70. Dir, Greig Fester (Agencies) Ltd, 1980–85. *Recreations:* sailing, golf. *Address:* Bearwood, Holtye, Edenbridge, Kent TN8 7EG. *T:* Cowden (01342) 850472. *Club:* Royal Ocean Racing.
Died 12 April 1996.

LEUPENA, Sir Tupua, GCMG 1986; MBE 1977; Governor General of Tuvalu, 1986–90; *b* 2 Aug. 1922; *s* of Leupena Vaisua, Vaitupu, and Tolotea Vaisua (*née* Tavita), Niutao; *m* 1947, Annie Nitz, Vaitupu; four *s* three *d* (and one *s* decd). *Educ:* Ellice Is Govt Sch., Vaitupu; King George V Secondary Sch., Tarawa, Gilbert Is (later Republic of Kiribati). Clerk, Gilbert and Ellice Is Colony, 1941; Sgt, GEIC Labour Corps, 1944; Clerk 1945, Chief Clerk 1953, Resident Comr's Office; transf. to Dist Admin as Asst Admin Officer, 1957, frequently serving in Gilbert Is and Ellice Is Dists, 1958–64 and 1967–69; District Commissioner: Phoenix Is Dist, 1965–66; Ocean Is, 1970–72; Dist Officer, Ellice Is District, 1973–75; acted as Sec. to Govt on Separation of Tuvalu from Kiribati in 1976 and retired from service same year; re-employed on contract as Sec. Reserved Subjects in Queen's Comr's Office, 1977; Speaker of Tuvalu Parlt, 1978; Man., Vaitupu's Private Commercial Enterprise, 1979–81; Chm., Tuvalu's Public Service Commn, 1982–86. *Recreations:* fishing, gardening, cricket, football. *Address:* Vaiaku, Funafuti Island, Tuvalu. *T:* 714.
Died 24 Nov. 1996.

LEUTWILER, Fritz, PhD; Chairman, Leutwiler & Partners Ltd, Zürich, since 1992; *b* 30 July 1924; *m* 1951, Andrée Cottier; one *s* one *d*. *Educ:* Univ. of Zürich (PhD 1948). Sec., Assoc. for a Sound Currency, 1948–52; Swiss National Bank, Zürich: Econ. Scientist, 1952–59; Manager, 1959–66; Dep. Gen. Man., 1966–68; Mem., Governing Bd, and Head, Dept III, 1968–74; Chm., Governing Bd, and Head, Dept I, 1974–84; Chm. and Pres., BIS, Basle, 1982–84; Chm., Bd of Dirs, BBC Brown, Boveri Ltd, Baden, 1985–92; Co-Chm., Bd of Dirs, ABB Asea Brown Boveri Ltd, Zürich, 1988–92. Hon. Dr: Berne, 1978; Zürich, 1983; Lausanne, 1984. *Recreations:* golf; collector of rare books (Helvetica, Economica). *Address:* Zumikon, Switzerland. *Club:* Golf and Country (Zumikon). *Died 27 May 1997.*

LEVERHULME, 3rd Viscount *cr* 1922, of the Western Isles, in the cos of Inverness and Ross and Cromarty; **Philip William Bryce Lever,** KG 1988; TD; Baron 1917; Bt 1911; Major, Cheshire Yeomanry; Lord-Lieutenant of City and County of Chester, 1949–90; Advisory Director of Unilever Ltd; Chancellor of Liverpool University, 1980–94; *b* 1 July 1915; *s* of 2nd Viscount Leverhulme and Marion, *d* of late Bryce Smith, Manchester; *S* father, 1949; *m* 1937, Margaret Ann (*d* 1973), *o c* of John Moon, Tiverton; three *d. Educ:* Eton; Trinity Coll., Cambridge. Hon. Air Commodore: 663 Air OP Squadron, RAuxAF; 610 (County of Chester) Squadron, RAuxAF; Dep. Hon. Col, Cheshire Yeomanry, T&AVR, 1971–72, Hon. Col, 1972–81; Hon. Col, The Queen's Own Yeomanry, 1979–81. Pres. Council, Liverpool Univ., 1957–63, Sen. Pro-Chancellor, 1963–66. Mem., National Hunt Cttee, 1961 (Steward, 1965–68); Deputy Senior Steward, Jockey Club, 1970–73, Senior Steward, 1973–76. Mem. Council of King George's Jubilee Trust; Chairman, Exec. Cttee, Animal Health Trust, 1964. Hon. FRCS 1970; Hon. ARCVS 1975. Hon. LLD Liverpool, 1967. KStJ. *Recreations:* shooting, fishing. *Heir:* none. *Address:* Thornton Manor, Thornton Hough, Wirral, Merseyside L63 1JB; Badanloch, Kinbrace, Sutherland KW11 6UE; Flat 6, Kingston House East, Prince's Gate, Kensington, SW7 1LJ. *Clubs:* Boodle's, Jockey.
Died 4 July 2000 (ext).

LEVERSEDGE, Leslie Frank, CMG 1955; MA Cantab; Economic Secretary to Northern Rhodesia Government, 1956–60, retired; *b* 29 May 1904; *s* of F. E. Leversedge, UP, India; *m* 1945, Eileen Melegueta Spencer Payne; two *s* three *d. Educ:* St Paul's Sch., Darjeeling, India; St Peter's Sch., York; St John's Coll., Cambridge. Called to the Bar, Inner Temple, 1933. Cadet in Colonial Administrative Service, Northern Rhodesia, Dec. 1926; District Officer, Dec. 1928; Provincial Commissioner, Jan. 1947; Senior Provincial Commissioner, Dec. 1948; Development Secretary to Northern Rhodesia Government, 1951–56. MLC 1951, MEC 1951, Northern Rhodesia. British Council Local Correspondent for Kent, 1963–75. FRSA 1973. *Recreations:* walking, overseas travelling. *Address:* 24 Ashley Brake, West Hill, Ottery St Mary, Devon EX11 1TW. *T:* (01404) 813956. *Died 12 June 1996.*

LEVESQUE, Most Rev. Louis, ThD; Archbishop Emeritus of Rimouski, since 1973; *b* 27 May 1908; *s* of Philippe Levesque and Catherine Levesque (*née* Beaulieu). *Educ:* Laval Univ. Priest, 1932; Bishop of Hearst, Ontario, 1952–64; Archbishop of Rimouski, 1967–73. Chm., Canadian Cath. Conf., 1965–67; Mem. Congregation Bishops, Rome, 1968–73. *Address:* 300 avenue du Rosaire, Rimouski, QC G5L 3E3, Canada.
Died 12 March 1998.

LEVI, Prof. Edward Hirsch; Glen A. Lloyd Distinguished Service Professor, University of Chicago, 1977–84, then Emeritus; *b* 26 June 1911; *s* of Gerson B. Levi and Elsa B. Levi (*née* Hirsch); *m* 1946, Kate Sulzberger; three *s. Educ:* Univ. of Chicago; Yale Univ. Law Sch. Mem. of Bar, US Supreme Ct, Ill, 1945–. University of Chicago: Asst Prof. of Law, 1936–40; Prof. of Law, 1945–75; Dean of the Law School, 1950–62; Provost, 1962–68; President, 1968–75, then Emeritus; Hon Trustee, 1975. Herman Phleger Vis. Prof., Stanford Law Soc., 1978. Special Asst to Attorney-Gen., Washington, DC, 1940–45; 1st Asst, War Div., Dept of Justice, 1943; 1st Asst, Anti-trust Div., 1944–45; Chm., Interdeptl Cttee on Monopolies and Cartels, 1944; Counsel, Subcttee on Monopoly Power Judiciary Cttee, 81st Congress, 1950; Attorney-Gen. of US, 1975–77. Chm., Council on Educn in Professional Responsibility, 1965–69; Member: Nat. Council on Legal Clinics, 1960–76; White House Task Force on Educn, 1966–67; President's Task Force on Priorities in Higher Educn, 1969–70; White House Central Gp in Domestic Affairs, 1964; Citizens Commn on Graduate Medical Educn, 1963–66; Sloan Commn on Cable Communications, 1970–71; Nat. Commn on Productivity, 1970–75; Commn on Foundations and Private Philanthropy, 1969–70; Martin Luther King, Jr, Federal Holiday Commn, 1985–86; Council on Legal Educn for Prof. Responsibility, 1968–74; Res. Adv. Bd, Commn Econ. Develt, 1951–54; Bd Dirs, SSRC, 1959–62; Nat. Commn on Productivity, 1970–75; Nat. Council on the Humanities, 1974–75. Dir Emeritus, MacArthur Foundn, 1984 (Dir, 1979–84); Mem. Council, Amer. Law Inst., 1965; Trustee: Internat. Legal Center; Museum of Science and Industry, 1971–75; Russell Sage Foundn, 1971–75; Aspen Inst. for Humanist Studies, 1970–75, 1977–79; Univ. Chicago, 1966; Woodrow Wilson Nat. Fellowship Foundn, 1972–75, 1977–79; Inst. Psycho-analysis, Chicago, 1961–75; Skadden Fellowship Foundn, 1988–94; Member Board of Trustees: Nat. Humanities Center, 1978 (Chm., 1979–83); The Aerospace Corp., 1978–80 (Life Trustee, 1989); William Benton Foundn, 1980–92; Hon. Trustee, Inst. of Internat. Educn. Public Dir, Chicago Bd of Trade, 1977–80; Mem. Bd of Dirs, Continental Illinois Holding Corp., 1985. Salzburg Seminar in Amer. Studies, 1980; Mem. Bd of Overseers, Univ. of Pennsylvania Law Sch., 1978–82; Mem. Bd of Governors, Univ. of Calif Humanities Res. Inst., 1988–91. Pres., Amer. Acad. of Arts and Scis, 1986–89. Fellow: Amer. Bar Foundn; Amer. Acad. Arts and Scis; Amer. Philos. Soc. (Vice-Pres., 1991–94); Chubb Fellow, Yale, 1977. Member: Amer. Judicature Soc.; Amer., Ill and Chicago Bar Assocs. Member, Editorial Board: Jl Legal Educn, 1956–68; Encyclopaedia Britannica, 1968–75. Hon. degrees: LHD: Hebrew Union Coll.; Loyola Univ.; DePaul Univ.; Kenyon Coll.; Univ. of Chicago; Bard Coll.; Beloit Coll.; LLD: Univ. of Michigan, Univ. of California at Santa Cruz; Univ. of Iowa; Jewish Theological Seminary of America; Brandeis Univ.; Lake Forest Coll.; Univ. of Rochester; Univ. of Toronto; Yale Univ.; Notre Dame; Denison Univ.; Nebraska Univ. Law Sch.; Univ. of Miami; Boston Coll.; Ben N. Cardozo Sch. of Law, Yeshiva Univ., NYC; Columbia Univ.; Dropsie Univ., Pa; Univ. of Pa Law Sch.; Brigham Young Univ.; Duke Univ.; Ripon Coll.; Georgetown Univ.; Claremont Univ. Center and Grad. Sch.; Indiana Univ.; DCL NY Univ. Chicago Bar Assoc. Centennial Award, 1975; Distinguished Citizen Award, Ill St Andrews Soc., 1976; Herbert H. Lehman Ethics Medal, Jewish Theol Seminary, 1976; Learned Hand Medal, Fedn Bar Council, NYC, 1976; Wallace Award, Amer.-Scottish Foundn, 1976; Morris J. Kaplun Meml Prize, Dropsie, 1976; Laureate of Lincoln, Acad. of Illinois, 1976; Fed. Bar Assoc. Award, 1977; Fordham Stein Prize, Fordham, 1977; Citation of Merit, Yale, 1977; Louis Dembitz Brandeis Award, 1978; Award of Honor, Illinois Bar Assoc, 1990; Dist. Service Award, Illinois Bar Foundn, 1990; Constitutional Rights Award, Constitutional Rights Foundn, 1992. Order of Coif; Phi Beta Kappa. Legion of Honour (France). *Publications:* (ed with Roscoe Steffen) Elements of the Law, 1936; (ed with James W. Moore) Gilbert's Collier on Bankruptcy, 1936; Introduction to Legal Reasoning, 1949; Four Talks on Legal Education, 1952; Point of View, 1969; The Crisis in the Nature of Law, 1969. *Address:* (office) 1116 East 59th Street, Chicago, IL 60637, USA. *T:* (312) 7028588; (home) 4950 Chicago Beach Drive, Chicago, IL 60615. *Clubs:* Quadrangle, Columbia Yacht, Mid-America (Chicago); Chicago (DC). *Died 7 March 2000.*

LEVI, Peter Chad Tigar, FSA; FRSL; Professor of Poetry, University of Oxford, 1984–89; Fellow of St Catherine's College, Oxford, 1977–91, Emeritus Fellow, since 1993; *b* 16 May 1931; *s* of Herbert Simon Levi and Edith Mary Tigar; *m* 1977, Deirdre, *o d* of Hon. Dennis Craig, MBE, and *widow* of Cyril Connolly, CBE, CLit. *Educ:* Beaumont; Oxford Univ. (MA). FSA 1976; FRSL 1985. Society of Jesus, 1948–77: priest, 1964; resigned priesthood, 1977. Tutor and Lectr in Classics, Campion Hall, Oxford, 1965–77; student, Brit. Sch. of Archaeol., Athens, 1965–68; Lectr in Classics, Christ Church, Oxford, 1979–82. The Times Archaeol Correspondent, 1977–78. Mem., Kingman Cttee on English, 1987–88. Pres., Virgil Soc., 1993–95; Corresp. Mem., Soc. of Greek Writers, 1983. Television films: Ruined Abbeys, 1966; Foxes have holes, 1967; Seven black years, 1975; presenter of TV series, Art, Faith and Vision, 1989. *Publications: poetry:* The Gravel Ponds, 1960; Water, Rock and Sand, 1962; The Shearwaters, 1965; Fresh Water, Sea Water, 1966; Ruined Abbeys, 1968; Pancakes for the Queen of Babylon, 1968; Life is a Platform, 1971; Death is a Pulpit, 1971; Collected Poems, 1976; Five Ages, 1978; Private Ground, 1981; The Echoing Green, 1983; Shakespeare's Birthday, 1985; Shadow and Bone, 1989; Goodbye to the Art of Poetry, 1989; (with Alan Powers) The Marches, 1989; Rags of Time, 1994; Reed Music, 1997; *edited:* The Penguin Book of English Christian Verse, 1985; New Verses by Shakespeare, 1988; *prose:* Beaumont, 1961; ʾΟ τόνος τῆς φωνῆς τοῦ Σεφέρη (Mr Seferis' Tone of Voice), 1970; The Lightgarden of the Angel King, 1973; The English Bible (1534–1859), 1974; In Memory of David Jones, 1975; John Clare and Thomas Hardy, 1975; The Noise made by Poems, 1976; The Hill of Kronos, 1980; Atlas of the Greek World, 1980; The Flutes of Autumn, 1983; (ed) Johnson and Boswell, Western Islands, 1984; The Lamentation of the Dead, 1984; A History of Greek Literature, 1985; The Frontiers of Paradise: a study of monks and monasteries, 1987; Life and Times of Shakespeare, 1988; To the Goat (novella), 1988; Boris Pasternak, 1990; The Art of Poetry (lectures), 1991; Life of Lord Tennyson, 1993; Edward Lear, 1994; A Bottle in the Shade, 1996; Eden Renewed: the public and private life of John Milton, 1996; Horace: a life, 1997; Virgil: his life and times, 1998; *thrillers:* The Head in the Soup, 1979; Grave Witness, 1985; Knit One, Drop One, 1987; (with Cyril Connolly) Shade Those Laurels, 1990; *translations:* Yevtushenko, 1962; Pausanias, 1971; Pavlopoulos, The Cellar, 1976; The Psalms, 1976; Marko the Prince (Serbo-Croat heroic verse), 1983; Papadiamantis, The Murderess, 1983; The Holy Gospel of John, a New Translation, 1985; Revelation, 1992. *Recreations:* elderly. *Address:* Prospect Cottage, The Green, Frampton on Severn, Glos GL2 7DY.

Died 1 Feb. 2000.

LEVIN, Richard, OBE 1952; RDI 1971; photographer, since 1975; *b* 31 Dec. 1910; *s* of Henry Levin and Margaret Sanders; *m* 1st, 1932, Evelyn Alexander; two *d;* 2nd, 1960, Patricia Foy, Producer, BBC TV. *Educ:* Clayesmore; Slade, UC London. Assistant Art Director, Gaumont British, 1928; private practice; graphic and industrial designer working for BBC, C. C. Wakefield Ltd, Bakelite Ltd, LEB, etc, 1931–39; Camouflage Officer, Air Ministry, 1940; MOI Exhibn Div.; Designer, British Army Exhibns, UK and Paris, 1943; private practice, 1946; Designer, Festival of Britain, Land Travelling Exhibn, 1951; Head of Design, BBC Television, 1953–71. FSIAD 1955. Silver Medal, RTS, 1972; Judge's Award, RTS Design Awards, 1992. *Publications:* Television by Design, 1960; Design for Television (BBC lunch-time lecture), 1968. *Recreation:* fishing. *Address:* Sandells House, West Amesbury, Wilts SP4 7BH. *T:* (01980) 623857.

Died 2 July 2000.

LEVY, Sir Ewart Maurice, 2nd Bt *cr* 1913, of Humberstone Hall, co. Leicester; *b* 10 May 1897; *o s* of Sir Maurice Levy, 1st Bt and Elise Ray, *d* of M. Zossenheim, Leeds and Harrogate; *S* father, 1933; *m* 1932, Hylda (*d* 1970), *e d* of late Sir Albert Levy; one *d. Educ:* Harrow. Served,

1940–45, Royal Pioneer Corps, Lieut-Colonel, 1944; BLA, 1944–45 (despatches). High Sheriff of Leicestershire, 1937; JP Co. Leicester. *Heir:* none. *Address:* Welland House, Weston-by-Welland, Market Harborough, Leicestershire LE16 8HS. *Club:* Reform.

Died 11 April 1996 (ext).

LEVY, George Joseph, MBE 1992; Chairman, H. Blairman & Sons Ltd, since 1965; *b* 21 May 1927; *s* of Percy and Maude Levy; *m* 1952, Wendy Yetta Blairman; one *s* three *d. Educ:* Oundle Sch. Joined H. Blairman & Sons Ltd (Antique Dealers), 1950, Dir, 1955. Pres., British Antique Dealers Assoc., 1974–76. Chairman: Grosvenor House Antiques Fair, 1978–79; Somerset Hse Art Treasures Exhibn, 1979; Burlington Hse Fair, 1980–82; Friends of the Iveagh Bequest, Kenwood, 1978–; London Historic House Museums Liaison Gp, English Heritage, 1985–96; Trustee, Jewish Museum, London, 1996– (Mem. Council, 1980–95). FRSA 1993. *Recreations:* theatre, visiting museums, photography. *Address:* Apartment 4, 6 Aldford Street, W1Y 5PS. *T:* 0171–495 1730.

Died 1 Sept. 1996.

LEWIN, Baron *cr* 1982 (Life Peer), of Greenwich in Greater London; **Admiral of the Fleet Terence Thornton Lewin,** KG 1983; GCB 1976 (KCB 1973); LVO 1958; DSC 1942; Chief of the Defence Staff, 1979–82; *b* Dover, 19 Nov. 1920; *s* of E. H. Lewin; *m* 1944, Jane Branch-Evans; two *s* one *d. Educ:* The Judd Sch., Tonbridge. Joined RN, 1939; War Service in Home and Mediterranean Fleets in HMS Valiant, HMS Ashanti in Malta Convoys, N Russian Convoys, invasion N Africa and Channel (despatches); comd HMS Corunna, 1955–56; Comdr HM Yacht Britannia, 1957–58; Captain (F) Dartmouth Training Squadron and HM Ships Urchin and Tenby, 1961–63; Director, Naval Tactical and Weapons Policy Division, MoD, 1964–65; comd HMS Hermes, 1966–67; Asst Chief of Naval Staff (Policy), 1968–69; Flag Officer, Second-in-Comd, Far East Fleet, 1969–70; Vice-Chief of the Naval Staff, 1971–73; C-in-C Fleet, 1973–75; C-in-C Naval Home Command, 1975–77; Chief of Naval Staff and First Sea Lord, 1977–79. Flag ADC to the Queen, 1975–77; First and Principal ADC to the Queen, 1977–79. Life Col Comdt, RM, 1995. Mem. Council, White Ensign Assoc. Ltd, 1982– (Chm. Council and Assoc., 1983–87); Chm., Trustees, National Maritime Museum, 1987–95 (Trustee, 1981–95; Dep. Chm., 1986–87); Mem., Museums and Galleries Commn, 1983–87; President: Shipwrecked Fishermen and Mariners' Royal Benevolent Soc., 1984–95; British Schools Exploring Soc., 1985–; George Cross Island Assoc., 1988–; Soc. for Nautical Res., 1989–. Elder Brother of Trinity House, 1975. Freeman and Liveryman, Stationers' and Newspaper Makers' Co., 1996; Hon. Freeman: Skinners' Co., 1976; Shipwrights' Co., 1978. Hon. DSc City, 1977; Hon. DLitt Greenwich, 1993. *Address:* House of Lords, SW1A 0PW.

Died 23 Jan. 1999.

LEWIS, Arthur William John; ex-Trade Union Official (National Union of General and Municipal Workers); *b* 21 Feb. 1917; *s* of late J. Lewis; *m* 1940, Lucy Ethel Clack; one *d. Educ:* Elementary Sch.; Borough Polytechnic. Shop steward of his Dept of City of London Corporation at 17; Vice-Chairman of Trade Union branch (City of London NUGMW) at 18; full-time London district official, NUGMW, 1938–48; Member of London Trades Council and Holborn City Trades Council, various joint industrial councils, Government cttees, etc; Member: ASTMS; APEX; GMWU. MP (Lab): West Ham, Upton, 1945–50; W Ham N, 1950–74; Newham NW, 1974–83; contested (Ind. Lab) Newham NW, 1983. Mem., Expenditure Cttee. Formerly Member Exec. Cttee, London Labour Party; Chairman, Eastern Regional Group of Labour MPs, 1950–83; Member, Eastern Regional Council of Labour

Party and Exec. Cttee of that body, 1950–83. Served in the Army. *Recreations:* swimming, motoring, boxing, general athletics. *Died 25 June 1998.*

LEWIS, His Honour Bernard; a Circuit Judge (formerly a County Court Judge), 1966–80; *b* 1 Feb. 1905; 3rd *s* of late Solomon and Jeannette Lewis, London; *m* 1934, Harriette, *d* of late I. A. Waine, Dublin, London and Nice; one *s. Educ:* Trinity Hall, Cambridge (MA). Called to the Bar, Lincoln's Inn, 1929. Mem., SE Circuit. Hon. Mem., Central Criminal Court Bar Mess. *Recreations:* revolver shooting, bricklaying. *Address:* Trevelyan House, Arlington Road, Twickenham, Middx TW1 2AS. *T:* (020) 8892 1841. *Clubs:* Reform, Aula; Cambridge Society.
Died 28 Oct. 1999.

LEWIS, Cecil Arthur, MC; author; *b* Birkenhead, 29 March 1898; *m* 1921, Evdekia Dmitrievna Horvath (marr. diss. 1940), Peking; one *s* one *d*; *m* 1942, Olga Burnett (marr. diss. 1950); no *c*; *m* 1960, Frances Lowe. *Educ:* Dulwich Coll.; University Coll. Sch.; Oundle. Royal Flying Corps, 1915 (MC, despatches twice); Manager Civil Aviation, Vickers, Ltd, 1919; Flying Instructor to Chinese Government, Peking, 1920, 1921; one of four founders of BBC, Chm. of Programme Board, 1922–26; varied literary activities: stage, screen (first two adaptations of Bernard Shaw's plays to screen, 1930–32), and television plays (Nativity, Crucifixion and Patience of Job, 1956–59) and production connected therewith. RAF, 1939–45. Sheep farming, South Africa, 1947–50. United Nations Secretariat, New York, radio and television, 1953–55; Commercial television, London, 1955–56; Daily Mail, 1956–66; retd. Compiled and presented, Between Ourselves (radio play), 1991. *Publications:* Broadcasting From Within, 1924; The Unknown Warrior, trans. from French of Paul Raynal, 1928; Sagittarius Rising (autobiog.), 1936, 5th edn 1993; The Trumpet is Mine, 1938; Challenge to the Night, 1938; (ed) Self Portrait: Letters and Journals of the late Charles Ricketts, RA, 1939 (filmed for TV, 1979); Pathfinders, 1943, rev. edn 1986; Yesterday's Evening, 1946; Farewell to Wings, 1964; Turn Right for Corfu, 1972; Never Look Back (autobiog.), 1974 (filmed for TV, 1978); A Way to Be, 1977; Gemini to Joburg, 1984; The Gospel According to Judas, 1989; The Dark Sands of Shambala, 1990; Sagittarius Surviving, 1991; (Introd.) Wind, Sand and Stars by Antoine De St Exupéry, 1991; All My Yesterdays (autobiog.), 1993; A Wish to Be, 1994. *Died 27 Jan. 1997.*

LEWIS, Very Rev. (David) Gareth; Dean of Monmouth, 1990–96; *b* 13 Aug. 1931; *s* of Mordecai Lewis and Bronwen May Lewis (*née* Evans). *Educ:* Cyfarthfa Grammar Sch., Merthyr Tydfil; Bangor Coll., Univ. of Wales (BA); Oriel Coll., Oxford (MA); St Michael's Coll., Llandaff. Deacon 1960, priest 1961; Curate of Neath, 1960–63; Vice-Principal, Salisbury Theol Coll., 1963–69; Dean of Belize, 1969–78; Vicar of St Mark, Newport, 1978–82; Canon Residentiary of Monmouth, 1982–90. Clerical Sec., Church in Wales Governing Body, 1986–96; Chairman: Provincial Stewardship Council, 1985–87; Provincial Evangelism and Adult Educn Council, 1987–95. Mem., BCC, 1985–90. *Publication:* The History of St John's Cathedral, Belize, 1976. *Recreations:* swimming, travelling. *Address:* 7A The Cathedral Green, Llandâf, Cardiff CF5 2EB. *T:* (01222) 560520.
Died 27 May 1997.

LEWIS, Maj.-Gen. John Michael Hardwicke, CBE 1970 (OBE 1955); *b* 5 April 1919; *s* of late Brig. Sir Clinton Lewis, OBE, and Lilian Eyre (*née* Wace); *m* 1943, Barbara Dorothy (*née* Wright); three *s. Educ:* Oundle; RMA, Woolwich. Commissioned, 2nd Lieut, RE, 1939; served War: 18 Div. and Special Force (Chindits), Far East, 1940–45; Staff Coll., Camberley, 1949; CRE, Gibraltar, 1959–61; Instr, JSSC, 1961–63; IDC, 1966; Asst Chief of

Staff (Ops), HQ Northern Army Gp, 1967–69; BGS (Intell.), MoD, 1970–72; ACOS (Intelligence), SHAPE, 1972–75. *Publications:* Michiel Marieschi: Venetian artist, 1967; J. F. Lewis, RA (1805–1876): a monograph, 1978; The Lewis Family—Art and Travel: a family history, 1992. *Recreations:* English water-colours, Swiss painters, picture framing. *Address:* Bedford's Farm, Frimley Green, Surrey GU16 6HE. *T:* (01252) 835188.
Died 6 March 1999.

LEWIS, Sir Kenneth, Kt 1983; DL; *b* 1 July 1916; *s* of William and Agnes Lewis, Jarrow; *m* 1948, Jane (*d* 1991), *d* of Samuel Pearson, Adderstone Mains, Belford, Northumberland; one *s* one *d. Educ:* Jarrow; Edinburgh Univ. Served War of 1939–45: RAF, 1941–46; Flt Lt. CC Middx, 1949–51; Mem., NW Metropolitan Hosp. Management Cttee, 1949–62. Contested (C) Newton-le-Willows, 1945 and 1950, Ashton-under-Lyne, 1951. MP (C): Rutland and Stamford, 1959–83; Stamford and Spalding, 1983–87. Chm., Cons. Back Bench Labour Cttee, 1962–64. DL Rutland, 1973. *Recreations:* music, travel. *Address:* Redlands, Preston, Oakham, Rutland LE15 9NW. *T:* (01572) 737320. *Clubs:* Carlton, Royal Air Force. *Died 2 July 1997.*

LEWIS, Prof. Leonard John, CMG 1969; Professor of Education, with special reference to Education in Tropical Areas, in the University of London, 1958–73, then Emeritus; *b* 28 Aug. 1909; of Welsh-English parentage; *s* of Thomas James Lewis and Rhoda Lewis (*née* Gardiner); *m* 1940, Nora Brisdon (marr. diss. 1976); one *s* (and one *s* decd; *m* 1982, Gwenda Black (decd). *Educ:* Lewis Sch., Pengam; University Coll. of South Wales and Monmouth (BSc); University of London Institute of Education (DipEd). Lecturer, St Andrew's Coll., Oyo, Nigeria, 1935–36; Headmaster, CMS Grammar Sch., Lagos, Nigeria, 1936–41; Education Sec., CMS Yoruba Mission, 1941–44; Lectr, University of London Institute of Education, 1944–48; Editorial staff, Oxford Univ. Press, 1948–49; Prof. of Educn and Dir of Institute of Educn, University Coll. of Ghana, 1949–58. Principal and Vice-Chancellor, Univ. of Zimbabwe, 1980–81; Vice-Chancellor, PNG Univ. of Technology, 1982–83. Nuffield Visiting Prof., University of Ibadan, 1966. Hon. Professorial Fellow, University Coll., Cardiff, 1973; Hon. FCP 1974. Coronation Medal, 1953; Zimbabwe Independence Medal, 1980. *Publications:* Equipping Africa, 1948; Henry Carr (memoir), 1948; Education Policy and Practice in British Tropical Areas, 1954; (ed and contrib.) Perspectives in Mass Education and Community Development, 1957; Days of Learning, 1961; Education and Political Independence in Africa, 1962; Schools, Society and Progress in Nigeria, 1965; (with A. J. Loveridge) The Management of Education, 1965. *Address:* 3 Ashley Close, Winscombe, Avon BS25 1BD. *T:* (01934) 844342. *Died 23 Oct. 1999.*

LIARDET, Maj.-Gen. Henry Maughan, CB 1960; CBE 1945 (OBE 1942); DSO 1945; DL; *b* 27 Oct. 1906; *s* of late Maj.-Gen. Sir Claude Liardet, KBE, CB, DSO, TD, DL, and Dorothy, *y d* of A. R. Hopper, MD; *m* 1st, 1933, Joan Sefton (*d* 1991), *d* of Major G. S. Constable, MC, JP; three *s*; 2nd, 1994, Mrs Barbara Corcoran. *Educ:* Bedford School. 1st Commission for Territorial Army, 1924, Royal Artillery; Regular Commission, Royal Tank Corps, 1927; service UK, India, Egypt, 1927–38; Staff Coll., Camberley, 1939; War of 1939–45: War Office, 1939–41; active service in Egypt, N Africa, Italy, 1941–45; General Staff appointments, command of 6th RTR, 1942–44; GSO1, 10th Armoured Div., Alamein; Comdr, 1st Armoured Replacement Gp, 1944; 2nd in Comd, 25th Tank Brigade (later Assault Brigade), 1944–45; Commander: 25th Armoured Engr Brigade, April–Sept. 1945 (despatches twice); Detachment, 1st Armoured Div.,

Palestine, 1947; Brig., RAC, MELF, 1947–49; Comdr, 8th RTR, 1949–50; Dep. Dir, Manpower Planning, War Office, 1950–52; Comdr, 23 Armd Bde, 1953–54; idc, 1955; Chief of Staff, British Joint Services Mission (Army Staff), Washington, DC, 1956–58; ADC to the Queen, 1956–58; Director-General of Fighting Vehicles, WO, 1958–61; Deputy Master-General of the Ordnance, War Office, 1961–64, retired. Colonel Comdt, Royal Tank Regt, 1961–67. Dir, British Sailors' Soc., 1961–78; Chm., SS&AFA W Sussex Cttee, 1966–85. DL, Sussex, 1964–74, W Sussex 1974–. W Sussex CC, 1964–74; Alderman, 1970–74. Pres. Sussex Council, Royal British Legion, 1975–81. *Recreations:* shooting, gardening. *Address:* 44 Martlets Court, Arundel, West Sussex BN18 9NZ. *T:* Arundel (01903) 882533. *Clubs:* Army and Navy; Sussex. *Died 8 Feb. 1996.*

LICHINE, Tatiana, (Mme David Lichine); *see* Riabouchinska, T.

LICHTENSTEIN, Roy; American painter and sculptor; *b* 27 Oct. 1923; *s* of Milton Lichtenstein and Beatrice (*née* Werner); *m* 1st, 1949, Isabel Wilson (marr. diss.); two *s*; 2nd, 1968, Dorothy Herzka. *Educ:* Art Students League, NY; Ohio State Univ. (BFA 1946; MFA 1949). Cartographical draughtsman, US Army, 1943–46; Instructor, Fine Arts Dept, Ohio State Univ., 1946–51; product designer for various cos, Cleveland, 1951–57; Asst Prof., Fine Arts Dept, NY State Univ., 1957–60, Rutgers Univ., 1960–63. Mem., Amer. Acad. and Inst. of Arts and Letters, 1979. Hon. RA 1994. Hon. degrees in Fine Arts. Skowhegan Medal for Painting, 1977. Created outside wall for Circarama of NY State Pavilion, NY World's Fair, 1963; large painting for Expo '67, Montreal, 1967; brushstroke murals for Düsseldorf Univ. Med. Centre, 1970; public sculpture, Mermaid, for Theater of Performing Arts, Miami, 1979; Brushstrokes in Flight, Port Columbus Airport, Columbus, Ohio, 1984; Mural with Blue Brushstrokes, Equitable Life Tower, NY, 1985; Coups de Pinceau, Caisse des Dépôts et Consignations, Paris, 1988; Tel Aviv Mural, Tel Aviv Mus. of Art, 1989; worked in Pop Art and other themes derived from comic strip techniques. One-man shows included: Carlebach Gall., NY, 1951; Leo Castelli Gall., NY, 1962, 1963, 1965, 1967, 1971–75, 1977, 1979, 1981, 1983, 1985, 1986, 1987; Galerie Illeana Sonnabend, Paris, 1963, 1965, 1970, 1975; Venice Biennale, 1966; Pasadena Art Museum, 1967; Walker Art Center, Minneapolis, 1967, 1986; Stedelijk Museum, Amsterdam, 1967; Tate Gall., London, 1968; Guggenheim Museum, NY, 1969; Nelson Gall., Kansas City, 1969; Museum of Contemporary Art, Chicago, 1970; Centre Nat. d'Art Contemporain, Paris, 1975, travelling to Berlin; Seattle Art Museum, 1976; Inst. of Contemp. Art, Boston, 1979; Portland Center for Visual Arts, 1980; St Louis Art Museum, 1981; Fundación Juan March, Madrid, 1982; Seibu Mus., Takanawa, 1983; Mus. of Modern Art, NY, 1987, travelling to Amsterdam and Tel Aviv, 1987, to Frankfurt, Oxford and Washington, 1988; group shows included: Nat. Collection of Fine Art, Washington, 1966; Venice Biennale, 1966; 36th Biennial Exhibn of Contemp. Amer. Painting, Corcoran Gall., Washington, DC, 1979; Nat. Mus. of Amer. Art, Smithsonian Instn, Washington, 1984; retrospectives: Guggenheim Mus., NY, and Tate Gall., Liverpool, 1993. Represented in permanent collections: Albright Knox Gall., Buffalo; Chicago Art Inst.; Corcoran Gall. of Art, Washington; Hirschorn Mus. and Sculpture Garden, Washington; Liby of Congress, Washington; Ludwig Mus., Cologne; Mus. of Modern Art, NY; Nat. Gall. of Art, Washington; Norton Simon Mus., Pasedena; San Francisco Mus. of Modern Art; Seibu Art Mus., Tokyo; Smithsonian Instn, Washington; Stedelijk Mus.,

Amsterdam; Tate Gall.; V&A Mus.; Walker Art Center, Minneapolis; Whitney Mus. of Amer. Art, NY; Yale Univ. *Died 29 Sept. 1997.*

LICKLEY, Sir Robert (Lang), Kt 1984; CBE 1973; FRSE; FEng 1977; FRAeS; FIEE; consultant; *b* Dundee, 19 Jan. 1912; *m* Doris May; one *s* one d. *Educ:* Dundee High Sch.; Edinburgh Univ.; Imperial Coll. (Fellow, 1973). BSc; DIC; FCGI 1976. Formerly: Professor of Aircraft Design, College of Aeronautics, Cranfield; Managing Director, Fairey Aviation Ltd; Hawker Siddeley Aviation Ltd, 1960–76 (Asst Man. Dir, 1965–76); Head, Rolls Royce Support Staff, NEB, 1976–79. President: IMechE, 1971; IProdE, 1981–82. FRSE 1977. Hon. FIMechE 1982; Hon. MIED. Hon. DSc: Edinburgh, 1973; Strathclyde, 1987. *Address:* Moorlands, Midway, Walton-on-Thames, Surrey KT12 3HY. *Died 7 July 1998.*

LIDDELL, Dr Donald Woollven, FRCP 1964; FRCPsych; Head of Department of Psychological Medicine, King's College Hospital, 1961–79; *b* 31 Dec. 1917; *m* 1954, Emily (*née* Horsfall) (marr. diss. 1977); one *s* one d. *Educ:* Aldenham Sch.; London Hospital. MRCP 1941. Neurological training as RMO, The National Hospital, Queen Square, 1942–45; Psychiatric training, Edinburgh and Maudsley Hospital. Medical Superintendent, St Francis Hospital, Haywards Heath, 1957–61; retired as Physician to Bethlem and Maudsley Hosps, 1968. Examr to RCP and RCPsych. Founder FRCPsych, 1971. *Publications:* contrib. Journal of Mental Science, Journal of Neurology, Psychiatry and Neuro-surgery, American Journal of Mental Diseases, Journal of Social Psychology. *Address:* 8 Newmarket Street, Usk, Gwent NP5 1AT. *Died 29 Jan. 1996.*

LIDDERDALE, Sir David (William Shuckburgh), KCB 1975 (CB 1963); TD; Clerk of the House of Commons, 1974–76; *b* 30 Sept. 1910; *s* of late Edward Wadsworth and Florence Amy Lidderdale; *m* 1943, Lola, *d* of late Rev. Thomas Alexander Beckett, Tubbercurry and Ballinew; one *s*. *Educ:* Winchester; King's Coll., Cambridge (MA). Served War of 1939–45, The Rifle Brigade (TA); active service, N Africa and Italy. House of Commons: Assistant Clerk, 1934; Senior Clerk, 1946; Fourth Clerk at the Table, 1953; Second Clerk Assistant, 1959; Clerk Assistant, 1962. Association of Secretaries-General of Parliaments (Inter-Parliamentary Union): Jt Sec., 1946–54; Mem., 1954–76; Vice-Pres., 1973–76; Hon. Vice-Pres., 1976. *Publications:* The Parliament of France, 1951; (with Lord Campion) European Parliamentary Procedure, 1953; (ed) Erskine May's Parliamentary Practice, 19th edn, 1976. *Recreation:* walking. *Address:* 46 Cheyne Walk, SW3 5LP. *Club:* Travellers'. *Died 16 Dec. 1998.*

LIGHTHILL, Sir (Michael) James, Kt 1971; FRS 1953; FRAeS; Provost of University College London, 1979–89; Hon. Fellow, 1982, Hon. Research Fellow, 1989; *b* 23 Jan. 1924; *s* of E. B. Lighthill and Marjorie (*née* Holmes); *m* 1945, Nancy Alice Dumaresq; one *s* four d. *Educ:* Winchester Coll.; Trinity Coll., Cambridge (Hon. Fellow, 1986). Aerodynamics Division, National Physical Laboratory, 1943–45; Fellow, Trinity Coll., Cambridge, 1945–49; Sen. Lectr in Maths, Univ. of Manchester, 1946–50; Beyer Prof. of Applied Mathematics, Univ. of Manchester, 1950–59; Dir, RAE, Farnborough, 1959–64; Royal Soc. Res. Prof., Imperial Coll., 1964–69; Lucasian Prof. of Mathematics, Univ. of Cambridge, 1969–79. Chairman: Academic Adv. Cttee, Univ. of Surrey, 1964; ICSU Special Cttee on Natural Disaster Reduction, 1990–95; Member: Adv. Council on Technology, 1964; NERC, 1965–70; Shipbuilding Inquiry Cttee, 1965; (part-time) Post Office Bd, 1972–74. First Pres., Inst. of Mathematics and its Applications, 1964–66; a Sec. and Vice-Pres., Royal Soc., 1965–69; President: Internat.

Commn on Mathematical Instruction, 1971–74; Internat. Union of Theoretical and Applied Mechanics, 1984–88. FRAeS 1961, Hon. FRAeS 1990; FIC 1991; Hon. Fellow, American Inst. of Aeronautics and Astronautics, 1961. Foreign Member: American Academy of Arts and Sciences, 1958; American Philosophical Soc., 1970; US Nat. Acad. of Sciences, 1976; US Nat. Acad. of Engineering, 1977; Russian Acad. of Scis, 1994; Associate Mem., French Acad. of Sciences, 1976. Hon. DSc: Liverpool, 1961; Leicester, 1965; Strathclyde, 1966; Essex, Princeton, 1967; East Anglia, Manchester, 1968; Bath, St Andrews, Surrey, 1969; Cranfield, 1974; Paris, Aachen, 1975; Rensselaer, 1980; Leeds, 1983; Brown, Southern California, 1984; Lisbon, 1986; Rehovot, 1987; London, 1993; Compiègne, Kiev, 1994; St Petersburg, Tallahassee, 1996. Royal Medal, Royal Society, 1964; Gold Medal, Royal Aeronautical Society, 1965; Harvey Prize for Science and Technol., Israeli Inst. of Technol., 1981; Gold Medal, Inst. of Maths and Its Applications, 1982; Ludwig-Prandtl-Ring, 1984. Comdr Order of Léopold (Belgium), 1963. *Publications:* Introduction to Fourier Analysis and Generalised Functions, 1958; Mathematical Biofluiddynamics, 1975; Newer Uses of Mathematics, 1977; Waves in Fluids, 1978; An Informal Introduction to Theoretical Fluid Mechanics, 1986; Collected Scientific Papers, 1996; articles in Royal Soc. Proc. and Trans, Qly Jl of Mechanics and Applied Maths, Philosophical Magazine, Jl of Aeronautical Scis, Qly Jl of Maths, Aeronautical Qly, Communications on Pure and Applied Maths, Proc. Cambridge Philosophical Soc., Jl of Fluid Mechanics, Reports and Memoranda of ARC; contrib. to Modern Developments in Fluid Dynamics: High Speed Flow; High Speed Aerodynamics and Jet Propulsion; Surveys in Mechanics; Laminar Boundary Layers; Twentieth Century Physics. *Recreations:* music, swimming. *Address:* Department of Mathematics, University College London, Gower Street, WC1E 6BT. *Club:* Athenæum. *Died 17 July 1998.*

LIGHTMAN, Harold; QC 1955; *b* 8 April 1906; *s* of Louis Lightman, Leeds; *m* 1936, Gwendoline Joan, *d* of David Ostrer, London; three *s*. *Educ:* City of Leeds Sch.; privately. Accountant, 1927–29. Barrister, Lincoln's Inn, 1932; Bencher. Home Guard, 1940–45. Defence Medal, 1946. Liveryman, Company of Glovers, 1960. *Publication:* (ed) 40th edn, Gore Browne, Company Law and Emergency War Legislation, 1945. *Recreation:* reading. *Address:* 4 Stone Buildings, Lincoln's Inn, WC2A 3XT. *T:* (0171) 242 3840. *Club:* Royal Automobile. *Died 27 Sept. 1998.*

LILLICRAP, Harry George, CBE 1976; Chairman, Cable and Wireless, 1972–76; *b* 29 June 1913; *s* of late Herbert Percy Lillicrap; *m* 1938, Kathleen Mary Charnock; two *s*. *Educ:* Erith County Sch.; University College London (BSc (Eng) 1934). Post Office Telecommunications, 1936–72: Sen. Dir Planning, Sen. Dir Customer Services, 1967–72. Dir, Telephone Rentals Ltd, 1976–84. *Address:* Lower Flat, Leysters, Highfield Road, East Grinstead, West Sussex RH19 2DX. *T:* (01342) 325811. *Died 30 July 2000.*

LILLY, Prof. Malcolm Douglas, FRS 1991; FEng 1982; Professor of Biochemical Engineering, University College London, since 1979; *b* 9 Aug. 1936; *s* of Charles Victor Lilly and Amy Gardiner; *m* 1959, Sheila Elizabeth Stuart; two *s*. *Educ:* St Olave's Grammar Sch.; University College London (BSc, PhD, DSc). FIChemE, FIBiotech. University College London: Lecturer in Biochemical Engrg, 1963–72; Reader in Enzyme Technology, 1972–79; Dir, Centre for Biochem. Engrg and Biotechnol., 1982–89; Chm., Advanced Centre for Biochemical Engrg, 1991–96; Vice-Dean, Faculty of Engrg, 1987; Fellow, 1988. Director, Whatman Biochemicals, 1968–71. Vis. Prof.,

Univ. of Pennsylvania, 1969; Vis. Engrg Fellow, Merck & Co., USA, 1987. Hon. Mem., Internat. Orgn for Biotechnology and Bioengineering, 1996– (Chm, 1972–80; Past Chm., 1980–95); Dir, Internat. Inst. of Biotechnology, 1989–95; Member: Council, Soc. for Gen. Microbiol., 1979–83; Research Cttee, British Gas, 1982–94; Bd of Management and Executive Cttee, Inst. for Biotechnological Studies, 1983–89; Bd, PHLS, 1988–94; Biotechnology Jt Adv. Bd, 1992–94; AFRC Engrg Res. Bd, 1992–94. Hartley Lecture, Royal Soc., 1988; Danckwerts Lecture, IChemE, 1993. Food, Pharmaceutical and Bioengrg Award, Amer. Inst. of Chem. Engrs, 1976; Enzyme Engrg Award, Engrg Foundn, 1993. *Publications:* (jtly) Fermentation and Enzyme Technology, 1979; (jtly) OECD Report, Biotechnology: international trends and perspectives, 1982; numerous papers on biochemical engrg, fermentation and biotransformation. *Recreations:* knotting, advanced motoring (IAM Observer), volunteer countryside ranger. *Address:* 8 Tower Road, Orpington, Kent BR6 0SQ. *T:* (01689) 821762. *Died 18 May 1998.*

LIMANN, Dr Hilla, Hon. GCMG 1981; President of Ghana, 1979–81; *b* 1934; *m*; five *c*. *Educ:* Lawra Primary Boarding Sch.; Tamale Middle Boarding Sch.; Govt Teacher Trng Coll.; London Sch. of Economics (Hon. Fellow, 1982), Sorbonne; Univ. of London; Faculty of Law and Econ. Sciences, Univ. of Paris. BSc(Econ.) 1960; BA Hons (Hist.), 1964; PhD (Polit. Sci. and Law), 1965. Teacher, 1952–55; examiner for Civil Service grad. entry, W African Exams Council. Councillor, Tumu Dist Council, 1952 (Chm., 1953–55); contested (Indep.) Constituency, Party Elec., 1954. Head of Chancery and Official Sec., Ghana Embassy, Lomé, Togo, 1968–77; Mem., Constitutional Commn on 1969 Constitution for Ghana; Mem. Govt Delegns for opening of borders of Ghana with the Ivory Coast/Upper Volta; Mem./Sec. to Ghana delegns, OAU and Non-aligned States, Confs of ILO, WHO, Internat. Atomic Energy Agency. Leader, People's National Party. *Died 23 Jan. 1998.*

LINCOLN, F(redman) Ashe; QC 1947; Captain RNVR; a Recorder, 1972–79 (Recorder of Gravesend, 1967–71); Master of the Moots, 1955–64, and 1968–70; *b* 30 Oct. 1907; *s* of Reuben and Fanny Lincoln; *m* 1933, Sybil Eileen Cohen; one *s* one *d*. *Educ:* Hoe Grammar Sch., Plymouth; Haberdashers' Aske's Sch.; Exeter Coll., Oxford (MA, BCL). Called to the Bar, Inner Temple, 1929; Master, 1955. Joined RNVSR, 1937; served in Royal Navy (RNVR), 1939–46: Admiralty, 1940–42; in parties to render mines safe, May 1940; rendered safe first type G magnetic mine (King's Commendation for bravery); Mediterranean, 1943, with commandos in Sicily and Italy at Salerno landings, 1943; Scine Bay (D-day) Landings, 1944; assault crossing of Rhine, March 1945 (despatches twice). Dep. World Pres., Internat. Assoc. of Jewish Lawyers and Jurists, 1973–. Renter Warden of Worshipful Company of Plaisterers, 1946–47, Master, 1949–50; Freeman and Liveryman of City of London. Contested general election 1945 (C) Harrow East Div. (Middx). Chm. Administrative Law Cttee of Inns of Court Conservative Association, 1951; Mem. Exec., Gen. Council of the Bar, 1957–61. Associate MNI, 1976; Pres., RNR Officers' Club, 1981–; Member: Council, British Maritime League, 1983–92; Exec., London Flotilla, 1984– (Vice-Pres., 1994–). Mem., RNSA. Pres., Royal Masonic Hosp., 1993–; Chm., London Devonian Assoc., 1965–85, Pres., 1985–; Nat. Chm., Maritime Volunteer Service, 1994–. Trustee: British Maritime Charitable Fund, 1983; Associated Marine and Related Charities (Trng, Educn and Safety), 1985–91. GCStJ 1992 (KStJ 1980). *Publications:* The Starra, 1939; Secret Naval Investigator, 1961; Odyssey of a Jewish Sailor, 1995. *Recreation:* yachting. *Address:* 9 King's Bench Walk, Temple, EC4Y

7DX. *T:* (0171) 353 7202. *Clubs:* Athenæum, Royal Automobile, MCC, Naval; Royal Corinthian Yacht (Burnham-on-Crouch and Cowes); Bar Yacht; RNVR Yacht. *Died 19 Oct. 1998.*

LINDSAY, Hon. James Louis; *b* 16 Dec. 1906; *yr s* of 27th Earl of Crawford and Balcarres and Constance, *y d* of Sir Henry Pelly, 3rd Bt, MP; *m* 1933, Bronwen Mary, *d* of 8th Baron Howard de Walden; three *s* one *d. Educ:* Eton; Magdalen Coll., Oxford. Served 1939–45 War, Major KRRC. Contested (C) Bristol South-East, 1950 and 1951; MP (C) N Devon, 1955–Sept. 1959.
Died 27 Aug. 1997.

LINDSAY, John Vliet; Of Counsel, Mudge Rose Guthrie Alexander & Ferdon, New York City, 1991–95; *b* 24 Nov. 1921; *s* of George Nelson and Eleanor (Vliet) Lindsay; *m* 1949, Mary Harrison; one *s* three *d. Educ:* St Paul's Sch., Concord, NH; Yale Univ. (BA 1944; LLB 1948). Lieut, US Navy, 1943–46. Admitted to: NY Bar, 1949; Fed. Bar, Southern Dist NY, 1950; US Supreme Court, 1955; DC Bar, 1957. Mem., law firm of Webster & Sheffield, NYC, 1949–55, 1957–61, 1974–91 (Presiding Partner, 1989–91). Exec. Asst to US Attorney Gen., 1955–57; Mem., 86th-89th Congresses, 17th Dist, NY, 1959–66. Mayor of NYC, 1965–73 (elected as Republican-Liberal, Nov. 1965, re-elected as Liberal-Independent, Nov. 1969). Bd Mem. Emeritus, Lincoln Center for Performing Arts; Chm. Emeritus, Bd of Dirs, Lincoln Center Theatre Co. Hon. LLD: Williams Coll., 1968; Harvard, 1969. *Publications:* Journey into Politics, 1967; The City, 1970; The Edge, 1976. *Address:* 14 Outerbridge Circle, Hilton Head Island, SC 29926, USA. *Died 19 Dec. 2000.*

LINDSAY-HOGG, Sir Edward William, 4th Bt *cr* 1905; of Rotherfield Hall, Sussex; Hereditary Cavaliere d'Italia; dramatist and scriptwriter; *b* 23 May 1910; *s* of William Lindsay Lindsay-Hogg (*d* 1918) (1st *s* of 1st Bt) and Nora Cicely (*d* 1929), *d* of John James Barrow; *S* nephew, 1988; *m* 1st, 1936, Geraldine (marr. diss. 1946), *d* of E. M. Fitzgerald; one *s*; 2nd, 1957, Kathleen Mary, *d* of James Cooney and *widow* of Captain Maurice Cadell, MC. *Educ:* Eton. Former racehorse trainer and amateur jockey when living at the Curragh. *Publications:* contrib. to literary periodicals, mainly in Ireland. *Recreations:* gardening, reading, walking. *Heir: s* Michael Edward Lindsay-Hogg [*b* 5 May 1940; *m* 1967, Lucy Mary (marr. diss. 1971), *o d* of Donald Davies]. *Club:* Stephen's Green (Dublin).
Died 18 June 1999.

LINDT, Auguste Rudolph, LLD; retired as Swiss Ambassador; *b* Berne, Switzerland, 5 Aug. 1905; *m* Susan Margaret (*née* Dunsterville) (marr. diss.; she *d* 1994); one *s* two *d*. Studied law at Universities of Geneva and Berne. Special correspondent of several European newspapers in Manchuria, Liberia, Palestine, Jordan, the Persian Gulf, Tunisia, Roumania and Finland, 1932–40; served in Swiss Army, 1940–45; Special delegate of International Cttee of the Red Cross at Berlin, 1945–46; Counsellor, and Press Attaché, 1946, Swiss Legation in London; Switzerland's Permanent Observer to the United Nations, 1953–56, Minister plenipotentiary, 1954; appointments connected with work of the United Nations: Chairman Exec. Board of UNICEF, 1953 and 1954; President, UN Opium Conference, 1953; Head of Swiss Delegation to Conference on Statute of International Atomic Energy Agency, held in New York, 1956; United Nations High Commissioner for Refugees (elected by acclamation), 1956–60; Swiss Ambassador to USA, 1960–63; Delegate, Swiss Fed. Council for Technical Co-operation, 1963–66; Swiss Amassador to Soviet Union and Mongolia, 1966–69, on leave as International Red Cross Comr-Gen. for Nigeria-Biafra relief operation, 1968–69; Swiss Ambassador to India and Nepal, 1969–70. Adviser to Pres. of Republic of Rwanda, 1972–75. Pres., Internat. Union

for Child Welfare, Geneva, 1971–77. Hon. Dr Univ. of Geneva, 1960; Hon. Dr, Coll. of Wilmington, Ohio, 1961. *Publications:* Special Correspondent with Bandits and Generals in Manchuria, 1933; Generäle hungern nie: Geschichte einer Hilfsaktion in Afrika, 1983; Die Schweiz: das kleine Staehelschwein, 1992. *Address:* Jolimontstrasse 2, 3006 Bern, Switzerland. *Died 14 April 2000.*

LINKLATER, Nelson Valdemar, CBE 1974 (OBE 1967); Drama Director, Arts Council of Great Britain, 1970–77; *b* 15 Aug. 1918; *s* of Captain Arthur David Linklater and Elsie May Linklater; *m* 1944, Margaret Lilian Boissard; two *s. Educ:* Imperial Service Coll.; RADA. RNVR, 1939–46 (final rank Lieut (S)). Professional theatre as actor and business manager, 1937–39. Documentary Films Manager, Army Kinema Corp., 1946–48; Arts Council of Great Britain: Asst Regional Dir (Nottingham), 1948–52; Asst and Dep. Drama Dir (London), 1952–70. Mem., Southern Arts Gen. Council and Exec. Cttee, 1978–89. Chm., CPRE, Wallingford Area Cttee, 1977–80. Member: Bd, Anvil Productions (Oxford Playhouse), 1977–88; Trent Polytechnic Theatre Design Adv. Cttee, 1980–83; Develt Panel, Cheek by Jowl Theatre Co., 1988–93. Mem., London Inst. Formation Cttee, 1985; Governor: Central Sch. of Art and Design, London, 1978–87; Wyvern Arts Trust (Swindon), 1978–91; Theatre Design Trust, 1988–91; Trustee, Arts Council Trust for Special Funds, 1981–97. *Publication:* (contrib.) The State and the Arts, 1980. *Recreations:* painting, reading, gardening. *Address:* 1 Church Close, East Hagbourne, Oxon OX11 9LP. *T:* (01235) 813340. *Died 19 Oct. 1997.*

LINKS, Mary, (Mrs J. G. Links); *see* Lutyens, M.

LINNETT, Dr Michael Joseph, OBE 1975; FRCGP; Apothecary to the Prince and Princess of Wales, 1983–90; general medical practitioner, 1957–90, retired; *b* 14 July 1926; *s* of late Joseph Linnett and of Dora Alice (*née* Eabry); *m* 1950, Marianne Patricia, *d* of Aubrey Dibdin, CIE; two *d* (one *s* decd). *Educ:* Wyggeston Grammar School for Boys, Leicester; St Bartholomew's Hosp. Med. Coll., London (MB BS 1949; Wix Prize Essay 1947). FRCGP 1970 (MRCGP 1957). House Physician, 1949, Demonstrator in Pharmacology, 1954, Jun. Registrar, 1955, St Bartholomew's Hosp., London; Ho. Phys., Evelina Children's Hosp., 1950; RAF Medical Br., Sqdn Ldr, 1950–54. Chm. Council, RCGP, 1976–79; Member: Cttee on Safety of Medicines, 1970–75; Medicines Commn, 1976–92 (Vice-Chm., 1984–92); Med. Adv. Panel, IBA, 1979–92; Pres., Chelsea Clinical Soc., 1987–88; Governor: National Hosp. for Nervous Diseases, 1974–82; Sutton's Hosp., Charterhouse, 1985–95. Freeman, City of London, 1980; Chm., Livery Cttee, Worshipful Soc. of Apothecaries, 1982–84, Mem., Ct of Assts, 1985–92, Asst Emeritus, 1992. Chm., Editorial Bd, Prescribers' Jl, 1973–74. FRSocMed 1958. *Publications:* chapter, People with Epilepsy—the Burden of Epilepsy, in A Textbook of Epilepsy, ed Laidlaw & Richens, 1976; chapter, Ethics in General Practice, in Doctors' Decisions—Ethical Conflicts in Medical Practice, ed Dunstan and Shinebourne, 1989; contrib. BMJ (jtly) Drug Treatment of Intractable Pain, 1960. *Recreations:* music, grandchildren, reading. *Address:* Oxford Beaumont, 2 Woodland Walk, Bayworth Lane, Boar's Hill, Oxford OX1 5DE. *T:* (01685) 736502.
Died 6 Dec. 1996.

LIPFRIEND, His Honour Alan; Circuit Judge, 1974–91; *b* 6 Oct. 1916; 2nd *s* of I. and S. Lipfriend; *m* 1948, Adèle Burke (*d* 1986); one *s. Educ:* Central Foundation Sch., London; Queen Mary Coll., London (BSc(Eng) (Hons) 1938; Pres. Union Soc., 1938–39; Fellow, 1987). Design Staff, Hawker Aircraft Ltd, 1939–48. Called to Bar, Middle Temple, 1948; Pres., Appeal Tribunal, under Wireless and Telegraphy Act, 1949, 1971–73; Mem.

Parole Bd, 1978–81. A Governor, Queen Mary Coll., Univ. of London, 1981–89; Trustee and Gov., Central Foundation School for Boys, 1985–. *Recreations:* theatre, all sport. *Address:* 27 Edmunds Walk, N2 0HU. *T:* 0181–883 4420. *Club:* Royal Automobile.
Died 12 March 1996.

LISLE, 7th Baron *cr* 1758 (Ire.), of Mount North, co. Cork; **John Nicholas Horace Lysaght;** *b* 10 Aug. 1903; *s* of Hon. Horace G. Lysaght (*d* 1918), *o s* of 6th Baron Lisle, and Alice Elizabeth, *d* of Sir John Wrixon Becher, 3rd Bt; *S* grandfather, 1919; *m* 1st, 1928, Vivienne Brew (marr. diss. 1939; she *d* 1948); 2nd, 1939, Mary Helen Purgold, Shropshire. *Heir: nephew* Patrick James Lysaght [*b* 1 May 1931; *m* 1957, Mrs Mary Louise Shaw-Stewart (marr. diss.); two *s* one *d*]. *Address:* The Chestnuts, Barge Farm, Taplow, Bucks SL6 0AE. *Died 29 Dec. 1997.*

LISTER, Dame Unity (Viola), DBE 1972 (OBE 1958); Member of Executive, European Union of Women, since 1971 (Vice-Chairman, 1963–69); Member: European Movement, since 1970; Conservative Group for Europe, since 1970; *b* 19 June 1913; *d* of Dr A. S. Webley; *m* 1940, Samuel William Lister (*d* 1995). *Educ:* St Helen's, Blackheath; Sorbonne Univ. of Paris. Member: LCC, 1949–65 (Dep. Chm., 1963–64); GLC, 1965–83. Chairman: Women's Nat. Advisory Cttee, 1966–69; Nat. Union of Conservative and Unionist Assocs, 1970–71 (Mem. Exec.); Mem., Inner London Adv. Cttee on Appt of Magistrates, 1966–92. Vice-Chm., Horniman Museums (Chm., 1967–70); Governor: Royal Marsden Hosp., 1952–80; various schools and colleges. *Recreations:* languages, travel, music, gardening, theatre, museums, reading, walking. *Address:* 32 The Court Yard, Eltham, SE9 5QE. *T:* (0181) 850 7038. *Club:* St Stephen's Constitutional. *Died 15 Dec. 1998.*

LISTON, James Malcolm, CMG 1958; Chief Medical Adviser, Foreign and Commonwealth Office, Overseas Development Administration, 1970–71; *b* 27 Aug. 1909; *s* of James Liston, Glasgow; *m* 1935, Isobel Prentice Meiklem, Edinburgh; one *s* one *d*. *Educ:* Glasgow High Sch.; Glasgow Univ. MB, ChB Glasgow, 1932; DTM&H Eng., 1939; DPH University of London, 1947; FRCPGlas 1963. Medical Officer, Kenya, 1935; Director of Medical and Health Services, Sarawak, 1947–52; Deputy Director of Medical Services, Hong Kong, 1952–55; Director of Medical Services, Tanganyika, 1955–59; Permanent Secretary to Ministry of Health, Tanganyika, 1959–60; Deputy Chief Medical Officer: Colonial Office, 1960–61; Dept of Tech. Co-op., 1961–62; Chief Medical Adviser, Dept of Tech. Co-op., 1962–64; Medical Adviser, Min. of Overseas Develt, 1964–70. *Address:* 6A Western Terrace, Murrayfield, Edinburgh EH12 5QF. *T:* 0131–337 4236.
Died 1 Jan. 1996.

LISTOWEL, 5th Earl of, *cr* 1822 (Ire.); **William Francis Hare,** GCMG 1957; PC 1946; Baron Ennismore (Ire.), 1800; Viscount Ennismore and Listowel (Ire.), 1816; Baron Hare (UK), 1869; Chairman of Committees, House of Lords, 1965–76; *b* 28 Sept. 1906; *e s* of 4th Earl of Listowel and Hon. Freda Vanden-Bempde-Johnstone (*d* 1968), *y d* of 2nd Baron Derwent; *S* father, 1931; *m* 1st, 1933, Judith (marr. diss. 1945), *o d* of R. de Marffy-Mantuano, Budapest; one *d*; 2nd, 1958, Stephanie Sandra Yvonne Wise (marr. diss. 1963), Toronto; one *d*; 3rd, 1963, Mrs Pamela Read; two *s* one *d*. *Educ:* Eton; Balliol Coll., Oxford. PhD London Univ. Lieut, Intelligence Corps. Member (Lab) LCC for East Lewisham, 1937–46, for Battersea North, 1952–57. Whip of Labour Party in House of Lords, 1941–44; Parliamentary Under-Secretary of State, India Office, and Deputy Leader, House of Lords, 1944–45; Postmaster-General, 1945–47; Secretary of State for India, April-Aug. 1947; for Burma, 1947–Jan. 1948; Minister of State for Colonial Affairs, 1948–50; Joint

Parliamentary Secretary, Ministry of Agriculture and Fisheries, 1950–51; Governor-General of Ghana, 1957–60. Jt Patron, British Tunisian Soc.; Jt Pres., Anti-Slavery Soc. for Protection of Human Rights; Vice-Pres., European-Atlantic Gp. *Publications:* The Values of Life, 1931; A Critical History of Modern Æsthetics, 1933 (2nd edn, as Modern Æsthetics: an Historical Introduction, 1967). *Heir: s* Viscount Ennismore, *b* 28 June 1964. *Address:* 10 Downshire Hill, NW3 1NR.
Died 12 March 1997.

LITCHFIELD, Jack Watson, FRCP; Consulting Physician, St Mary's Hospital, since 1972 (Physician, 1946–72 and Physician i/c Cardiac Department, 1947–72); *b* 7 May 1909; *s* of H. L. Litchfield, Ipswich; *m* 1941, Nan (*d* 1984), *d* of A. H. Hatherly, Shanghai; two *s* one *d*. *Educ:* Ipswich Sch.; Oriel Coll., Oxford (Scholar; Theodore Williams Schol. in Physiology, 1929, in Pathology, 1931; Radcliffe Schol. in Pharmacology, 1932; BA (2nd class hons) 1930; BM, BCh 1933); St Mary's Hosp. Med. Sch. (University Schol, 1931). MRCP 1936; FRCP 1947. Medical Registrar: St Mary's Hospital, 1936; Brompton Hospital, 1938; Physician, King Edward Memorial Hosp., W13, 1947–69. Served in RAMC in N Africa, Italy, etc (despatches); Lt-Col i/c Medical Div. *Publications:* papers on various subjects in medical journals. *Recreations:* gardening, conservation. *Address:* 2 Pound Cottages, The Green, Long Melford, Sudbury, Suffolk CO10 9DX. *T:* (01787) 312730. *Died 4 Feb. 2000.*

LITTLE, John Eric Russell, OBE 1961 (MBE 1943); HM Diplomatic Service, retired; *b* 29 Aug. 1913; *s* of William Little and Beatrice Little (*née* Biffen); *m* 1945, Christine Holt; one *s* one *d*. *Educ:* Strand Sch. Served in FO, 1930–40, and in Army, 1940–41; transferred to Minister of State's Office, Cairo, 1941, and seconded to Treasury; returned to FO and appointed to British Middle East Office, 1946; transferred to FO, 1948; Consul, Milan, 1950 (acting Consul-General, 1951, 1952); Bahrain as Asst Political Agent, 1952 (acting Political Agent, 1953, 1954, 1955); 1st Secretary, Paris, 1956; Asst Finance Officer, Foreign Office, 1958; HM Consul-General: Basra, 1962–65; Salonika, 1965–70; Counsellor, British Embassy, Brussels, 1970–72. *Recreations:* walking, reading, music. *Died 5 April 1998.*

LITTLEJOHN COOK, George Steveni; HM Diplomatic Service, retired; *b* 29 Oct. 1919; *s* of late William Littlejohn Cook, OBE, and Xenia Steveni, BEM; *m* 1st, 1949, Marguerite Teresa Bonnaud; one *d*; 2nd, 1964, Thereza Nunes Campos; one *s*. *Educ:* Wellington Coll.; Trinity Hall, Cambridge. Served with 2nd Bn Cameronians (Scottish Rifles), 1939–46, rank of Capt.; POW Germany; Political Intelligence Dept, Foreign Office, 1945–46. Entered Foreign Service, 1946; Third Secretary, Foreign Office, 1946–47; Second Secretary, Stockholm, 1947–49; Santiago, Chile, 1949–52; First Secretary, 1950; Foreign Office, 1952–53; Chargé d'Affaires, Phnom-Penh, 1953–55; Berne, 1956–58; Director of British Information Service in Brazil, 1959–64; Head of Information Depts, FO, later FCO, 1964–69; Counsellor and Consul-General, Bangkok, 1969–71. Underwriting Mem. of Lloyd's, 1957–. *Recreations:* painting, sailing, ski-ing. *Address:* Quinta da Madrugada, Apartado 30, 8600 Lagos, Algarve, Portugal. *Clubs:* Brooks's, Royal Automobile.
Died 20 June 1998.

LITTLER, (William) Brian, CB 1959; PhD; *b* 8 May 1908; *s* of William Littler, Tarporley, Cheshire; *m* 1937, Pearl Davies (*d* 1990), Wrexham; three *d*. *Educ:* Grove Park, Wrexham; Manchester Univ. (BSc (1st Class), Chemistry, 1929; MSc 1930; PhD 1932; Beyer Fellow, 1930–31). Joined Res. Dept, Woolwich, 1933; loaned by Min. of Supply to Defence Res. Bd, Canada; Chief Supt, Cdn Armament Research and Develt Establishment, Valcartier,

Quebec, 1947–49; Supt of Propellants Research, Explosives Research and Develt Estab., Waltham Abbey, 1949–50; in industry (Glaxo Laboratories Ltd, Ulverston), 1950–52; Dir of Ordnance Factories (Explosives), Min. of Supply, 1952–55; Principal Dir of Scientific Research (Defence), Ministry of Supply, 1955–56; Dir-Gen. of Scientific Research (Munitions), Ministry of Supply, 1956–60; Dep. Chief Scientist, Min. of Defence (Army), 1960–65; Minister, and Head of Defence R&D Staff, British Embassy, Washington, DC, 1965–69; Chemist-in-Charge, Quality Assurance Directorate (Materials), Royal Ordnance Factory, Bridgwater, 1969–72. *Publications:* papers on flame and combustion in Proc. Royal Society and Jl Chem. Soc. *Recreations:* supporting Manchester United, following golf. *Address:* Gloucester House, Lansdowne Road, Sevenoaks, Kent TN13 3XU.
Died 8 April 1999.

LITTLEWOOD, James, CB 1973; Director of Savings, Department for National Savings, 1972–81; *b* Royton, Lancashire, 21 Oct. 1922; *s* of late Thomas and Sarah Littlewood; *m* 1950, Barbara Shaw; two *s* one *d. Educ:* Manchester Grammar Sch.; St John's Coll., Cambridge (Scholar, MA). Army (Captain), 1942–46. HM Treasury, 1947–67; Civil Service Selection Bd, 1951–52; Sec. to Cttee on Administrative Tribunals and Enquiries, 1955–57; Colombo Plan Conf. Secretariat, 1955 and 1959; Dept for Nat. Savings, 1967–81. *Recreations:* golf, bridge. *Address:* 3 Smugglers Lane South, Highcliffe, Christchurch, Dorset BH23 4NF.   *Died 14 Jan. 1998.*

LIVINGS, Henry; playwright; *b* 20 Sept. 1929; *m* 1957, Judith Francis Carter; one *s* one *d. Educ:* Park View Primary Sch.; Stand Grammar Sch.; Liverpool Univ. Served in RAF. Joined Puritex, Leicester; actor, with Century Mobile Th., Hinckley, Leics, 1954, Theatre Royal Leicester, then many Repertories; London début, Prisoner C in The Quare Fellow, Theatre Workshop, Stratford E, transf. West End, 1956. Plays as author included: Stop It Whoever You Are (first stage play), Arts, 1961; Big Soft Nellie, Century, 1961, also Theatre Royal, Stratford E; Nil Carborundum, Arts, 1962; Kelly's Eye, Royal Court, 1963; Eh?, RSC, Aldwych, 1964; The Little Mrs Foster Show, Liverpool Playhouse, 1966, Nottingham Playhouse, 1968; The Finest Family in the Land, Theatre Royal, Lincoln, 1970, Theatre Workshop, Stratford E, 1972. First TV play, 1961. *Publications:* contribs to Penguin New English Dramatists 5 and 6; Kelly's Eye and Other Plays, 1964; Eh?, 1965; Good Grief!, 1968; The Little Mrs Foster Show, 1969; Honour and Offer, 1969; Pongo Plays 1–6, 1971; This Jockey Drives Late Nights, 1972; The Ffinest Ffamily in the Land, 1973; Jonah, 1974; Six More Pongo Plays, 1975; That the Medals and the Baton be Put on View, 1975; Cinderella, 1976; Pennine Tales, 1983; Flying Eggs and Things, 1986; The Rough Side of the Boards, 1993; trans., Lorca, The Public, 1994. *Recreations:* dominoes, walking. *Address:* 49 Grains Road, Delph, Oldham, Lancs OL3 5DS. *T:* (01457) 770854. *Clubs:* Dobcross Band, Delph Band.   *Died 20 Feb. 1998.*

LLEWELLYN, Sir Henry Morton, (Sir Harry), 3rd Bt *cr* 1922, of Bwllfa, Aberdare, co. Glamorgan; Kt 1977; CBE 1953 (OBE (mil.) 1944); DL; late Warwickshire Yeomanry; President, Whitbread Wales Ltd, since 1972 (Chairman, 1958–72); Vice-Chairman, Civic Trust for Wales, since 1960; *b* 18 July 1911; 2nd *s* of Sir David Llewellyn, 1st Bt, and Magdalene (*d* 1966), *d* of Dr H. Hiley Harries, DD, Porthcawl; *S* brother, 1978; *m* 1944, Hon. Christine Saumarez (*d* 1998), 2nd *d* of 5th Baron de Saumarez; two *s* one *d. Educ:* Oundle; Trinity Coll., Cambridge (MA). Joined Warwickshire Yeo., Sept. 1939; Iraq-Syria Campaign, 1941; Middle East Staff Coll., Haifa, 1942; 8th Army from El Alamein to Tunis as GSO II Ops (Liaison) (despatches), 1942–43; Sicily, Italy (despatches),

1943; MA to Chief of Staff HQ 21 Army Gp, 1943; NW Europe GSO I Ops (Liaison), 1943–44; Hon. Lt Col. Member: Nat. Hunt Cttee, 1946– (Steward, 1948–50); The Jockey Club, 1969–. Jt Master Monmouthshire Hounds, 1952–57, 1963–65. Riding Ego, came 2nd in Grand National 'chase, 1936, 4th, 1937; Captain, winning Brit. Olympic Show-Jumping Team, Helsinki (riding Foxhunter), 1952; Chm., Brit. Show Jumping Assoc., 1967–69; Pres./Chm., British Equestrian Fedn, 1976–81; Pres., Royal Internat. Horse Show, 1989–91; Hon. Deleg., FEI, 1983. Chm., Welsh Sports Council, 1971–81; Mem., GB Sports Council, 1971–81. President: Inst. of Directors (Wales), 1963–65; Inst. of Marketing, Wales, 1965–67. Chairman: C. L. Clay & Co. Ltd (Coal Exporters), 1936–47; Wales Bd, Nationwide Building Soc., 1972–86; Eagle Star Assurance Co. (Wales Bd), 1963–81; formerly Director: Chepstow Racecourse Co. Ltd; North's Navigation Colliery Ltd; TWW Ltd; Rhigos Colliery Ltd; S Wales Regl Bd, Lloyds Bank, 1963–82. Member: Wales Tourist Board, 1969–75; WWF Council, 1986–; Pres., Royal Welsh Agricl Show, 1985. DL Monmouthshire, 1952, JP 1954–68, High Sheriff 1966. Royal Humane Soc. Medal for Life-saving, 1956; FEI Gold Medal, 1962. US Legion of Merit, 1945. *Publications:* Foxhunter in Pictures, 1952; Passports to Life, 1980. *Recreations:* hunting, all sports, wild life photography. *Heir: s* David St Vincent Llewellyn [*b* 2 April 1946; *m* 1980, Vanessa Mary Theresa (marr. diss. 1987), *y d* of Lt-Comdr Peregrine Hubbard, RN and Lady Miriam Hubbard; two *d*]. *Address:* Ty'r Nant, Llanarth, Raglan, Gwent NP5 2AR. *Clubs:* Cavalry and Guards; Shikar.
Died 15 Nov. 1999.

LLEWELLYN-JONES, Frank; *see* Jones, F. Ll.

LLEWELYN-DAVIES OF HASTOE, Baroness *cr* 1967 (Life Peer), of Hastoe, co. Hertford; **Patricia Llewelyn-Davies;** PC 1975; Principal Deputy Chairman of Committees and Chairman, Select Committee on European Communities, House of Lords, 1982–87; *b* 16 July 1915; *d* of Charles Percy Parry and Sarah Gertrude Parry (*née* Hamilton); *m* 1943, Richard Llewelyn-Davies (later Baron Llewelyn-Davies) (*d* 1981); three *d. Educ:* Liverpool Coll., Huyton; Girton Coll., Cambridge (Hon. Fellow, 1979). Civil Servant, 1940–51 (Min. of War Transp., FO, Air Min., CRO). Contested (Lab) Wolverhampton S-W, 1951, Wandsworth Cent., 1955, 1959. A Baroness-in-Waiting (Govt Whip), 1969–70; Dep. Opposition Chief Whip, House of Lords, 1972–73; Opposition Chief Whip, 1973–74, 1979–82; Captain of the Gentlemen at Arms (Govt Chief Whip), 1974–79. Hon. Sec., Lab. Parly Assoc., 1960–69. Chm., Women's National Cancer Control Campaign, 1972–75; Member: Bd of Govs, Hosp. for Sick Children, Gt Ormond Street, 1955–67 (Chm. Bd, 1967–69); Court, Univ. of Sussex, 1967–69. Dir, Africa Educnl Trust, 1960–69. Co-Chm., Women's Nat. Commn, 1976–79. *Address:* Flat 15, 9–11 Belsize Grove, NW3 4UU. *T:* (0171) 586 4060.   *Died 6 Nov. 1997.*

LLOYD, Charles William; JP; MA; Master, Dulwich College, 1967–75; *b* 23 Sept. 1915; *s* of late Charles Lloyd and Frances Ellen Lloyd, London; *m* 1939, Doris Ethel (decd), *d* of late David Baker, Eastbourne; one *s* one *d* (and one *d* decd). *Educ:* St Olave's Sch.; Emmanuel Coll., Cambridge (MA). War Service with RA, 1940–46 (despatches). Assistant Master: Buckhurst Hill Sch., 1938–40; Gresham's Sch., Holt, 1946–51; Headmaster, Hutton Grammar Sch., near Preston, 1951–63; Headmaster, Alleyn's Sch., London, 1963–66. Trustee, Nat. Maritime Museum, 1974–86. JP Inner London, 1970. *Recreations:* reading, travel, golf. *Address:* 5 The Grange, Harlow Oval, Harrogate, N Yorks HG2 0DS. *T:* (01423) 527618.   *Died 16 Feb. 1999.*

LLOYD, His Honour Denis Thelwall; a Circuit Judge, 1972–94; Senior Resident Judge, Knightsbridge Crown Court, 1988–94; *b* 3 Jan. 1924; *s* of late Col Glyn Lloyd, DSO, FRCVS, barrister, and Olga Victoria Lloyd (*née* Roberts); *m* 1st, 1950, Margaret Sheila (*d* 1976), *d* of Bernard Bushell, Wirral, Cheshire; one *s* two *d*; 2nd, 1983, Ann, *d* of John and Georgia Cunningham, Montana and Hawaii, USA. *Educ:* Wellington College. Enlisted KRRC, 1942; commnd KRRC, Dec. 1942; Central Mediterranean Force (Italy, S France, Greece), 1943–45; attached 1st York and Lancaster Regt and then joined Parachute Regt, 1944 (wounded); Palestine, 1945–46; GSO3 (ops) HQ British Troops Austria, 1946; Staff Captain British Mil. Mission to Czechoslovakia, 1947. Called to the Bar, Gray's Inn, 1949; joined NE Circuit, 1950; Asst Recorder, Leeds, 1961–67; Recorder of Pontefract, 1971; Dep. Chm., WR Yorks QS, 1968–71. Dep. Chm., Agricultural Land Tribunal, Yorks and Lancs, 1968–71; Legal Chm., Mental Health Review Tribunal, 1983–86. Contested (L): York, 1964; Hallam Div. of Sheffield, 1966. Czech War Cross, 1946. *Recreations:* gardening, travel. *Address:* Flat 5, 37 Cadogan Square, SW1X 0HU. *T:* (0171) 235 7439.
Died 14 Dec. 1998.

LLOYD, George Walter Selwyn; composer and conductor; *b* 28 June 1913; *s* of William Alexander Charles Lloyd and Constance Priestley Rawson; *m* 1937, Nancy Kathleen Juvet. *Educ:* privately, and with Albert Sammons for violin, Harry Farjeon for composition. Works composed and conducted: Symphony No 1, Bournemouth, 1933; Symphony No 2, Eastbourne, 1934; opera Iernin, Lyceum, London, 1935; Symphony No 3, BBC Symph. Orch., 1935; composed 2nd opera The Serf, perf. Convent Garden, 1938; during 1939–45 war served in Royal Marines Band aboard HMS Trinidad, severely shell-shocked 1942, whilst on Arctic convoy; composed opera John Scoman, 1st perf. Bristol, 1951; due to poor health lived in Dorset growing carnations and mushrooms, only composing intermittently; health improved; subseq. composed many more symphonies, concertos (Symphonies No 11 and 12 commissioned and recorded by Albany Symph. Orch, NY; first perf. of No 11, 1986, of No 12, 1990); numerous recordings. Hon. DMus Salford, 1992. *Compositions:* The Serf, 1948; John Socman, 1951; Piano Concerto No 1, 1964; Symphony No 8, 1977; Symphony No 5, 1979; Symphony No 7, 1979; Symphony No 6, 1980; Aubade, 1981; Symphony No 4, 1981; Symphony No 9, 1982; Symphony No 10, 1982; A Miniature Tryptich, 1982; Piano Concerto No 2, 1983; Piano Concerto No 4, 1984; Royal Parks, 1985; Diversion on a Bass Theme, 1986; Violin Concerto No 2, 1986; The Forest of Arden, 1988; Piano Concerto No 3, 1988; English Heritage, 1988; Lament, Air & Dance, 1989; Sonata, 1989; Vigil of Venus, 1989; Evening Song, 1991; Charade (suite), 1992; A Symphonic Mass, 1993; Floating Cloud, 1993; Dying Tree, 1994; King's Messenger, 1994; A Litany, 1996. *Recreation:* reading. *Address:* 199 Clarence Gate Gardens, Glentworth Street, NW1 6AU. *T:* (0171) 262 7969.
Died 3 July 1998.

LLOYD, Sir (John) Peter (Daniel), Kt 1971; Chancellor, University of Tasmania, 1982–85; *b* 30 Aug. 1915; *s* of late David John Lloyd; *m* 1947, Gwendolen, *d* of late William Nassau Molesworth; two *s* four *d*. *Educ:* Rossall Sch.; Brasenose Coll., Oxford (MA). Royal Artillery, 1940–46 (despatches, Order of Leopold, Belgian Croix de Guerre). Joined Cadbury Bros Ltd, Birmingham, 1937; served in UK and Australia; Dir, Cadbury Fry Pascall Australia Ltd, 1949, Chm., 1953–71. Member: Council, Univ. of Tasmania, 1957–85; Council, Australian Admin. Staff Coll., 1959–71; Board, Commonwealth Banking Corp., 1967–82; Board, Goliath Cement Holdings, 1969–88; Board, Australian Mutual Provident Society,

1970–88. Member: Australian Taxation Review Cttee, 1972–74; Cttee of Inquiry into Educn and Training, 1976–78. Hon. LLD Tasmania, 1986. *Address:* 90 Carrington Street, Macedon, Vic 3440, Australia. *Club:* Australian (Sydney).
Died 1 Sept. 1996.

LLOYD, Prof. Seton Howard Frederick, CBE 1958 (OBE 1949); FBA 1955; archæologist; Professor of Western Asiatic Archæology, University of London, 1962–69, then Emeritus; *b* 30 May 1902; *s* of John Eliot Howard Lloyd and Florence Louise Lloyd (*née* Armstrong); *m* 1944, Margery Ulrica Fitzwilliams Hyde (*d* 1987); two *s* one *d*. *Educ:* Uppingham; Architectural Assoc. ARIBA 1926. Asst to Sir Edwin Lutyens, PRA, 1926–28; excavated with Egypt Exploration Society, 1928–30; excavated in Iraq for University of Chicago Oriental Institute, 1930–37; excavated in Turkey for University of Liverpool, 1937–39; Technical Adviser, Government of Iraq; Directorate-General of Antiquities, 1939–49; Director British Institute of Archæology, Ankara, Turkey, 1949–61. FSA 1938 (Vice-Pres., 1965–69). Hon. MA (Edinburgh), 1960. Lawrence of Arabia Meml Medal, RCAS, 1971; Gertrude Bell Meml Medal, British Sch. of Archaeology in Iraq, 1979. *Publications:* Sennacherib's Aqueduct at Jerwan, 1935; Mesopotamia, 1936; The Gimilsin Temple, 1940; Presargonid Temples, 1942; Ruined Cities of Iraq, 1942; Twin Rivers, 1942; Foundations in the Dust, 1947, rev. edn 1980; Early Anatolia, 1956; Art of the Ancient Near East, 1961; Mounds of the Ancient Near East, 1963; Highland Peoples of Anatolia, 1967; Archaeology of Mesopotamia, 1978; The Interval, 1986; Ancient Turkey, 1989; Excavation Reports and many articles in journals. *Recreation:* mnemonics. *Address:* Woolstone Lodge, Faringdon, Oxon SN7 7QL. *T:* Uffington (0136782) 248. *Club:* Chelsea Arts.
Died 7 Jan. 1996.

LLOYD DAVIES, J(ohn) Robert, CMG 1953; *b* 24 March 1913; *o s* of late J. R. and Mrs Davies, Muswell Hill; *m* 1st, 1943, Margery (*née* McClelland) (*d* 1978) Nottingham; one *s* one *d*; 2nd, 1982, Grace, widow of Frederick Reynolds, Bethesda, Md, USA. *Educ:* Highgate Sch.; Oriel Coll., Oxford. Served War of 1939–45: Royal Navy; Lieut RNVR. Joined Min. of Labour, 1936; Dep. Labour Attaché, Washington, 1945–47; Asst Sec., Overseas Dept, 1947–56; Labour Attaché, Paris, 1956–60; Asst Sec., Dept of Employment, 1960–72; Labour Counsellor, Washington, 1972–73; Principal, Trng Services Agency, 1973–79. Part-time Teacher, Working Men's Coll., London, 1970–94. *Recreations:* key-board music, reading. *Address:* 59 Elm Park Court, Pinner, Middlesex HA5 3LL. *Club:* United Oxford & Cambridge University.
Died 12 Jan. 1999.

LLOYD DAVIES, Trevor Arthur, MD; FRCP; *b* 8 April 1909; *s* of Arthur Lloyd Davies and Grace Margret (*née* Bull); *m* 1936, Joan (*d* 1972), *d* of John Keily, Co. Dublin; one *d*; *m* 1975, Margaret, *d* of Halliday Gracey, Woodford. *Educ:* Woking County Sch.; St Thomas' Hospital, SE1. MRCS, LRCP 1932; MB, BS London (gold medal and hons in surgery, forensic med., obst. and gynæc.); MRCP 1933; MD London, 1934; FRCP 1952. Resident Asst Physician, St Thomas' Hospital, 1934–36; MO, Boots Pure Drug Co., 1937–53; Prof. of Social Medicine, University of Malaya, 1953–61; Senior Medical Inspector of Factories, Min. of Labour and Dept of Employment and Productivity, 1961–70; Chief Med. Adviser, Dept of Employment, 1970–73. QHP 1968–71. *Publications:* The Practice of Industrial Medicine, 1948, 2nd edn 1957; Respiratory Diseases in Foundrymen, 1971; Whither Occupational Medicine?, 1973; The Bible: medicine and myth, 1991; numerous papers on industrial and social medicine, in Lancet and Medical Journal of Malaya. *Recreations:* gardening, carpentry, bricklaying. *Address:*

The Old Bakery, High Street, Elmdon, Saffron Walden, Essex CB11 4NL. *Club:* Athenæum.

Died 1 May 1998.

LLOYD-ELEY, John; QC 1970; a Recorder of the Crown Court, 1972–95; *b* 23 April 1923; *s* of Edward John Eley; *m* 1946, Una Fraser Smith; two *s. Educ:* Xaverian Coll., Brighton; Exeter Coll., Oxford (MA). Served War, 1942–46, Lieut 50th Royal Tank Regt and 7th Hussars, N Africa, Sicily and Italy. Barrister, Middle Temple, 1951; South-Eastern Circuit; Mem., Bar Council, 1969. *Recreations:* farming, travel. *Address:* Luxfords Farm, East Grinstead. *T:* (01342) 321583.

Died 6 July 1998.

LLOYD-JONES, His Honour David Trevor, VRD 1958; a Circuit Judge, 1972–88; *b* 6 March 1917; *s* of Trevor and Ann Lloyd-Jones, Holywell, Flints; *m* 1st, 1942, Mary Violet (marr. diss.; she *d* 1980), *d* of Frederick Barnardo, CIE, CBE, MD, London; one *d;* 2nd, 1958, Anstice Elizabeth, MB, BChir (*d* 1981), *d* of William Henry Perkins, Whitchurch; one *s* one *d;* 3rd, 1984, Florence Mary, *d* of William Fairclough, MM, Wallasey. *Educ:* Holywell Grammar School. Banking, 1934–39 and 1946–50. Called to the Bar, Gray's Inn, 1951; practised Wales and Chester Circuit, 1952–71; Prosecuting Counsel to Post Office (Wales and Chester Circuit), 1961–66; Dep. Recorder, Chester and Birkenhead, 1964–70; Dep. Chm., Caerns QS, 1966–70, Chm, 1970–71; Legal Mem., Mental Health Appeal Tribunal (Wales Area), 1960–72; Dep. Chm., Agricultural Land Tribunal (Wales Area), 1968–72. JP Gwynedd, 1966–71. Served War of 1939–45, RNVR, Atlantic, Mediterranean and Pacific; Lt-Comdr, RNR, 1952–60, retd. *Recreations:* golf, music. *Address:* 29 Curzon Park North, Chester CH4 8AP. *T:* (01244) 675144. *Clubs:* Army and Navy; Royal Dornoch Golf.

Died 28 April 1998.

LLOYD-JONES, Robert; Director-General, Brick Development Association, 1984–94; *b* 30 Jan. 1931; *s* of Robert and Edith Lloyd-Jones; *m* 1958, Morny Baggs-Thompson (marr. diss. 1977); two *s* one *d. Educ:* Wrekin Coll.; Queens' Coll., Cambridge (MA Hons); Harvard Business School. Short Service Commission, RN, 1956; Shell International, 1959; BTR Industries Ltd, 1962; International Wool Secretariat, 1964; Schachenmayr, Germany, 1971; British Textile Employers Association, 1977–81; Dir-Gen., Retail Consortium, 1981–83. Chm., Nordic Country Gp, and Mem., European Trade Cttee, DTI, 1994–. Consultant: Corporate Marketing and Advertising Services Ltd, 1994–; EEF, 1996–; Millstream Internat., 1998–. Governor, Coll. for Distributive Trades, 1982–84; Founder Chm., Nat. Retail Trng Council, 1982–84. Trustee, Building Crafts and Conservation Trust, 1990–. Mem., BFI. Member: RN Golf Soc. (Match Sec.); China Golfing Soc. Friend of Royal Acad. and of Tate Gall. FRSA. Freeman, City of London, 1986; Liveryman, Co. of Tylers and Bricklayers, 1986. *Recreations:* golf, squash, tennis, music, chess, art, and the general pursuit of pleasure. *Address:* Mill Cottage, 10 High Street, Odiham, Hants RG29 1LG. *Clubs:* Lansdowne, Institute of Directors; Dormy House (Rye); Royal Birkdale Golf, Rye Golf, Formby Golf, Liphook Golf; Royal Ascot Squash, Royal Ascot Tennis, Odiham Tennis.

Died 22 May 1999.

LOCK, Lt-Comdr Sir (John) Duncan, Kt 1978; Royal Navy, retired; Chairman, Association of District Councils of England and Wales, 1974–79 (Member, 1974–93); *b* 5 Feb. 1918; *s* of Brig. Gen. F. R. E. Lock, DSO, and Mary Elizabeth Lock; *m* 1947, Alice Aileen Smith (*d* 1982); three *d. Educ:* Royal Naval Coll., Dartmouth. Served as regular officer in Royal Navy (retiring at his own request), 1931–58: specialised in navigation and navigated Battleships HMS King George V and Howe, the Cruiser

Superb, destroyers and minesweepers; served War of 1939–45: took part in Battle of Atlantic, Norwegian and N African campaigns, Pacific War, and Normandy and Anzio landings. Farmed family estate in Somerset, 1958–61; with Admty Compass Observatory as specialist in magnetic compasses, 1962–83. Member: Eton RDC, 1967–74; S Bucks Dist Council, 1973– (Chm., 1985–87). Chairman: Bucks Br., RDC Assoc., 1969–74; Assoc. of Dist Councils of England and Wales Council and Policy Cttee, 1974–79 (Chm. Bucks Br., 1974–91); Rep. Body for England, 1977–89; Local Authorities Management Services and Computer Cttee, 1981–86; Mem., Adv. Cttee on Local Govt Audit, 1979–82; British Rep., Conference of Local and Regl Authorities of Europe, 1979–94. Chm., Beaconsfield Constituency Conservative Assoc., 1972–75; Mem., S Bucks Housing Assoc., 1990– (Chm., 1990–91). *Recreations:* gardening, shooting. *Address:* Red Cottage, Ethorpe Close, Gerrards Cross, Bucks SL9 8PL. *T:* (01753) 882467.

Died 14 Jan. 1999.

LOCKE, John Howard, CB 1984; Chairman, National Examination Board in Occupational Safety and Health, 1986–92; *b* 26 Dec. 1923; *s* of Percy Locke and Josephine Locke (*née* Marshfield); *m* 1948, Eirene Sylvia Sykes; two *d. Educ:* Hymers Coll., Hull; Queen's Coll., Oxford. MIOSH. Ministry of Agriculture, Fisheries and Food, 1945–65; Under-Secretary: Cabinet Office, 1965–66; MoT, 1966–68; Dept of Employment and Productivity, 1968–71; Dep. Sec., Dept of Employment, 1971–74; Dir, Health and Safety Exec., 1975–83. *Address:* Box Trees, 8 Sea Road, East Preston, Sussex BN16 1JP. *T:* (01903) 785154.

Died 26 Sept. 1998.

LOCKLEY, Ronald Mathias; author and naturalist; *b* 8 Nov. 1903; *m* 1st, Doris Shellard (marr. diss.); one *d;* 2nd, Jill Stocker (marr. diss.); two *s;* 3rd, Jean St Lawrence (decd). *Educ:* Cardiff High Sch. Set up first bird observatory in UK, Skokholm, 1933. Hon. MSc Wales, 1977. *Publications:* Dream Island, 1930, rev. edn 1988; The Island Dwellers, 1932; Island Days, 1934; The Sea's a Thief, 1936; Birds of the Green Belt, 1936; I Know an Island, 1938; Early Morning Island, 1939; A Pot of Smoke, 1940; The Way to an Island, 1941; Shearwaters, 1942; Dream Island Days, 1943; Inland Farm, 1943; Islands Round Britain, 1945; Birds of the Sea, 1946; The Island Farmers, 1947; Letters from Skokholm, 1947; The Golden Year, 1948; The Cinnamon Bird, 1948; Birds of Pembrokeshire, 1949; The Charm of the Channel Islands, 1950; (with John Buxton) Island of Skomer, 1951; Travels with a Tent in Western Europe, 1953; Puffins, 1953; (with Rosemary Russell) Bird Ringing, 1953; The Seals and the Curragh, 1954; Gilbert White, 1954; (with James Fisher) Sea-Birds, 1954; Pembrokeshire, 1957; The Pan Book of Cage Birds, 1961; Britain in Colour, 1964; The Private Life of the Rabbit, 1964; Wales, 1966; Grey Seal, Common Seal, 1966; Animal Navigation, 1967; The Book of Bird-Watching, 1968; The Channel Islands, 1968, rev. edn as A Traveller's Guide to the Channel Islands, 1971; The Island, 1969; The Naturalist in Wales, 1970; Man Against Nature, 1970; Seal Woman, 1974; Ocean Wanderers, 1974; Orielton, 1977; Myself when Young, 1979; Whales, Dolphins & Porpoises, 1979; (with Noel Cusa) New Zealand Endangered Species, 1980; The House Above the Sea, 1980; (with Richard Adams) Voyage Through the Antarctic, 1982; Flight of the Storm Petrel, 1983; (with Geoff Moon) New Zealand's Birds, 1983; The Lodge above the Waterfall, 1987; (with Betty Brownlie) Secrets of Natural New Zealand, 1987; Birds and Islands: travels in wild places, 1991; (with Ann Mark) Dear Islandman, 1996; *edited:* Natural History of Selborne, by G. White, 1949, rev. edn 1976; Nature Lover's Anthology, 1951; The Bird-Lover's Bedside Book, 1958; *compiled:* In

Praise of Islands, 1957. *Address:* Te Puke County Lodge, No 1 Road, Te Puke, New Zealand.
Died 12 April 2000.

LODER, Sir Giles Rolls, 3rd Bt *cr* 1887, of Whittlebury, Northamptonshire, and of High Beeches, Slaugham, Sussex; DL; *b* 10 Nov. 1914; *o s* of late Capt. Robert Egerton Loder (*s* of 2nd Bt), and Muriel Rolls, *d* of J. Rolls-Hoare; *S* grandfather, 1920; *m* 1939, Marie, *o c* of Bertram Hanmer Bunbury Symons-Jeune; two *s*. *Educ:* Eton; Trinity Coll., Cambridge (MA). High Sheriff of Sussex, 1948–49; DL West Sussex, 1977. Vice-Pres., RHS, 1983–. VMH 1971. *Recreations:* sailing, horticulture. *Heir: s* Edmund Jeune Loder [*b* 26 June 1941; *m* 1st, 1966, Penelope Jane Forde (marr. diss. 1971); one *d*; 2nd, 1992, Susan Warren Pearl]. *Address:* Ockenden House, Cuckfield, Haywards Heath, West Sussex RH17 5LD; Leonardslee Gardens, Horsham, Sussex RH13 6PP. *Club:* Royal Yacht Squadron.
Died 24 Feb. 1999.

LODGE, Sir Thomas, Kt 1974; Consultant Radiologist, United Sheffield Hospitals, 1946–74, retired; Clinical Lecturer, Sheffield University, 1960–74; *b* 25 Nov. 1909; *s* of James Lodge and Margaret (*née* Lowery); *m* 1940, Aileen Corduff (*d* 1990); one *s* one *d*. *Educ:* Univ. of Sheffield. MB, ChB 1934, FFR 1945, FRCP 1967, FRCS 1967. Asst Radiologist: Sheffield Radium Centre, 1936; Manchester Royal Infirmary, 1937–38; 1st Asst in Radiology, United Sheffield Hosps, 1938–46. Cons. Adviser in Radiology, DHSS, 1965–74. Fellow, BMA, 1968; Hon. FRSocMed; Hon. FFR RCSI; Hon. FRACR 1963; Hon. FACR 1975; Hon. MSR 1975; Hon. Mem., British Inst. of Radiology, 1990. Twining Medal, 1945, Knox Lectr, 1962, Pres., 1963–66, Faculty of Radiologists. Gold Medal, RCR, 1986. Hon. Editor, Clinical Radiology, 1954–59. Hon. MD Sheffield, 1985. *Publications:* (ed) Recent Advances in Radiology, 3rd edn 1955, 4th edn 1964, (ed jtly) 5th edn 1975, 6th edn 1979, as Recent Advances in Radiology and Medical Imaging; articles in Brit. Jl Radiology, Clinical Radiology, etc. *Recreation:* gardening. *Address:* 46 Braemore Court, Kingsway, Hove, E Sussex BN3 4FG. *T:* (01273) 724371.
Died 16 Feb. 1997.

LOMAS, Kenneth; *b* 16 Nov. 1922, *s* of George Lomas and Rhoda Clayton; *m* 1945, Helen Wilson (*d* 1998); two *s* one *d*. *Educ:* Ashton-under-Lyne Elementary and Central Schs. Served with Royal Marines and RM Commando Gp, 1942–46 (Sergeant). Central Office, USDAW, 1937–55; Asst Regl Organiser, Manchester, Blood Transfusion Service, 1955–64. Resigned from NUPE, 1977; joined Apex, 1978. Consultant: 3M Co. (UK); Rothmans Internat. Contested: (Lab) Blackpool S, 1951; Macclesfield, 1955; MP (Lab) Huddersfield W, 1964–79. PPS to Minister of Technology, 1969–70. Mem., Select Cttees on Race Relations and Parly Comr for Admin, and Mr Speaker's Cttee on Election Law; Vice-Chm., All-Party Wool Textile Cttee. Mem., Political Cttees for Econ., Mil., Educn, Inf. and Cultural Affairs, N Atlantic Assembly. JP Cheshire, 1961, Kirlees, Huddersfield, 1972. *Recreations:* arguing, reading.
Died 15 July 2000.

LONG, Gerald; *b* 22 Aug. 1923; *o s* of Fred Harold Long and Sabina Long (*née* Walsh); *m* 1951, Anne Hamilton Walker; two *s* three *d*. *Educ:* St Peter's Sch., York; Emmanuel Coll., Cambridge. Army Service, 1943–47. Joined Reuters, 1948: served as Reuter correspondent in Germany, France and Turkey, 1950–60; Asst General Manager, 1960; Chief Exec., 1963–81 (Gen. Manager, 1963–73; Man. Dir, 1973–81); Man. Dir, Times Newspapers Ltd, 1981–82; Dep. Chm., News International plc, 1982–84. Chairman: Visnews Ltd, 1968–79; Exec. Cttee, Internat. Inst. of Communications Ltd, 1973–78.

Mem., Design Council, 1974–77; Council Mem., Journalists in Europe, 1974–95 (Exec. Dir, 1987–88). CBIM (FBIM 1978). Commander, Royal Order of the Phoenix, Greece, 1964; Grand Officer, Order of Merit, Italy, 1973; Commander, Order of the Lion of Finland, 1979; Chevalier de la Légion d'Honneur, France, 1979; Commander's Cross, Order of Merit, Federal Republic of Germany, 1983. *Recreation:* cooking. *Address:* 15 rue d'Aumale, BP5.09, 75421 Paris, France. *T:* 148746726; 15 rue W. K. Ferguson, 14400 St Martin-des-Entrees, France. *T:* 231924712.
Died 8 Nov. 1998.

LONG, Pamela Marjorie, (Mrs John Nichols); Metropolitan Stipendiary Magistrate, 1978–92; *b* 12 Sept. 1930; *d* of late John Holywell Long, AMICE, and Emily McNaughton; *m* 1966, Kenneth John Heastey Nichols (*d* 1996). *Educ:* Carlisle and County High School for Girls. Admitted Solicitor of Supreme Court, 1959; private practice, 1959–63; Solicitor's Dept, New Scotland Yard, 1963–77. Mem., Cttee of Magistrates for Inner London, 1984–90. *Recreations:* music, decorative arts, The Times crossword. *Address:* Flat 1, 36 Buckingham Gate, SW1E 6PB.
Died 13 Sept. 1999.

LONGDEN, Sir Gilbert (James Morley), Kt 1972; MBE 1944; *b* 16 April 1902; *e s* of late Lieut-Colonel James Morley Longden, Castle Eden, Co. Durham, and Kathleen, *d* of George Blacker Morgan, JP; unmarried. *Educ:* Haileybury; Emmanuel Coll., Cambridge (MA, LLB). Practised as solicitor, 1924–30; Secretary ICI (India) Ltd, 1930–37; travelled throughout Asia (Middle and Far East) and in North and South America; student at University of Paris, 1937; called up from AOER into DLI, 1940; served with 2nd and 36th Divisions in Burma campaigns (MBE (mil.)). Adopted Parliamentary Candidate for Morpeth, 1938; contested (C) Morpeth, 1945; MP (C) SW Herts, 1950–Feb. 1974. UK Representative to Council of Europe, 1953–54; United Kingdom Delegate to 12th and 13th Sessions of United Nations; Past Chairman: British Atlantic Cttee; Conservative Gp for Europe; Great Britain-East Europe Centre. Vice-Chm., British Council. *Publications:* A Conservative Philosophy, 1947; (jointly): One Nation, 1950; Change is our Ally, 1954; A Responsible Society, 1959; One Europe, 1969. *Recreations:* reading, writing, gardening. *Address:* 89 Cornwall Gardens, SW7 4AX. *T:* (0171) 584 5666. *Club:* Brooks's.
Died 16 Oct. 1997.

LONGDEN, Henry Alfred, FEng 1977; FICE, FIMinE; FGS; Director, Trafalgar House Investments Ltd, 1970–76; *b* 8 Sept. 1909; *s* of late Geoffrey Appleby Longden and Marjorie Mullins; *m* 1935, Ruth, *d* of Arthur Gilliat, Leeds; one *s* four *d*. *Educ:* Oundle; Birmingham Univ. (BSc Hons). Served in Glass Houghton and Pontefract Collieries, 1930; Asst Gen. Manager, Stanton Ironworks Co., 1935; Gen. Manager, Briggs Colliers Ltd, 1940; Director: Blackwell Colliery Co., 1940; Briggs Collieries Co., 1941; New Hucknell Colliery Co., 1941; Area Gen. Manager, 1947, and Production Dir, 1948, NE Div., NCB; Dir-Gen., Production, NCB, 1955; Chm., W Midlands Div., NCB, 1960; Chm. and Chief Exec., Cementation Co. Ltd, 1963–70 (Dep. Chm. and Chief Exec, 1961–63). President: Instn of Mining Engineers, 1958; Engineering Industries Assoc., 1965–71; Member: Engineering Industry Trng Bd, 1967–70; Confedn of British Industry, 1968. *Publication:* Cadman Memorial Lecture, 1958. *Recreations:* Rugby football, cricket, tennis, shooting, fishing, sailing. *Address:* Raeburn, Northdown Road, Woldingham, Surrey CR3 7BB. *T:* (01883) 852245.
Died 12 March 1997.

LONGRIGG, Roger Erskine; author; *b* 1 May 1929; *s* of Brig. Stephen Hemsley Longrigg, OBE and Florence Longrigg (*née* Anderson); *m* 1957, Jane Chichester; three *d*. *Educ:* Bryanston Sch.; Magdalen Coll., Oxford (BA

Hons Mod. Hist. 1952); Surrey Inst. of Art and Design (BA Hons Fine Art 1996). *Publications:* A High Pitched Buzz, 1956; Switchboard, 1957; Wrong Number, 1959; Daughters of Mulberry, 1961; The Paper Boats, 1963; The Artless Gambler, 1964; Love among the Bottles, 1967; The Sun on the Water, 1969; The Desperate Criminals, 1971; The History of Horse Racing, 1972; The Jevington System, 1973; Their Pleasing Sport, 1975; The Turf, 1975; The History of Foxhunting, 1975; The Babe in the Wood, 1976; The English Squire and his Sport, 1977; Bad Bet, 1982; also 38 books under pseudonyms Megan Barker, Grania Beckford, Laura Black, Ivor Drummond, Rosalind Erskine, Frank Parrish, Domini Taylor. *Recreation:* painting. *Address:* Orchard House, Crookham, Hants GU13 0SY. *T:* (01252) 850333. *Clubs:* Brooks's, Pratt's; Greenjackets.   *Died 26 Feb. 2000.*

LORANT, Stefan; *b* 22 Feb. 1901; US citizen, 1948; *m* 1st, Njura; one *s*; 3rd, 1963, Laurie Robertson (marr. diss. 1978); one *s* (and one *s* decd). *Educ:* Evangelical Gymnasium, Budapest; Academy of Economics, Budapest; Harvard Univ. (MA 1961). Editor: Das Magazin, Leipzig, 1925; Bilder Courier, Berlin, 1926; Chief Editor, Muenchner Illustrierte Presse, Munich, 1928–33; Editor, in England, Weekly Illustrated, 1934 (also creator); Founding editor and creator of Lilliput, Editor, 1937–40; creator and first editor of Picture Post, 1938–40. Hon. LLD Knox Coll., Galesburg, Ill, 1958; DHL *hc* Syracuse Univ., NY, 1985; Hon. Dr Univ. of Bradford, 1989. *Publications:* Wir vom Film, 1928, repr. 1986; I Was Hitler's Prisoner, 1935 (trans. of Ich war Hitlers Gefangener, German edn first pubd 1985); Chamberlain and the Beautiful Llama, 1940; Lincoln, His Life in Photographs, 1941; The New World, 1946, rev. edn 1965; F.D.R., a pictorial biography, 1950; The Presidency, a pictorial history of presidential elections from Washington to Truman, 1951; Lincoln: a picture story of his life, 1952, rev. and enl. edns 1957, 1969; The Life of Abraham Lincoln, 1954; The Life and Times of Theodore Roosevelt, 1959; Pittsburgh, the story of an American city, 1964, rev. and enl. edns 1975, 1980, 1988, 1996; The Glorious Burden: the American Presidency, 1968, rev. and enl. edn 1976; Sieg Heil: an illustrated history of Germany from Bismarck to Hitler, 1974 (German trans. 1976); Pete: the story of Peter F. Flaherty, 1978; My Years in England, fragments to an autobiography, 1995; Mark I Love You (a memorial to my son), 1995. *Address:* Farview, PO Box 803, Lenox, MA 01240, USA. *T:* (413) 6370666.

Died 14 Nov. 1997.

LOTT, Dr Bernard Maurice, OBE 1966; academic columnist; Research Fellow, University College London, since 1980; *b* 13 Aug. 1922; *s* of late William Lott and Margaret Lott (*née* Smith); *m* 1949, Helena, *d* of late Clarence Winkup; one *s* one *d* (and one *s* decd). *Educ:* Bancroft's Sch.; Keble Coll., Oxford (MA); Univ. of London (MA Distinction, PhD); Univ. of Edinburgh (Dip. in Applied Linguistics, Dist.). RN, 1942–46. Brit. Council Lectr in English, Ankara Univ. and Gazi Inst. of Educn, Turkey, 1949–55; Brit. Council Asst Rep., Finland, 1955–57; Prof. of English and Head of Dept, Univ. of Indonesia, 1958–61; Dir of Studies, Indian Central Inst. of English, 1961–66; Dep. Controller, Educn Div., Brit. Council, 1966–72; Controller, English Teaching Div., Brit. Council, 1972–75; Brit. Council Representative, Poland, 1975–77; English Language Teaching Develt Adviser, British Council, 1977–79; Course Tutor, Open Univ., 1979–86; Lectr in Applied Linguistics, Poly. of Central London, 1989–90. *Publications:* A Course in English Language and Literature, 1986; Gen. Editor, New Swan Shakespeare series, and edited: Macbeth, 1958, Twelfth Night, 1959, Merchant of Venice, 1962, Hamlet, 1968 (also Open Univ. edn 1970), King Lear, 1974, Much

Ado About Nothing, 1977; contribs on teaching of English as foreign lang. to Times Educnl Supp. and Eng. Lang. Teaching Jl. *Recreations:* local studies, music. *Address:* 8 Meadway, NW11 7JT. *T:* (0181) 455 0918.

Died 5 Dec. 1996.

LOUDON, John Hugo; Jonkheer (Netherlands title); Knight in the Order of the Netherlands Lion, 1953; Grand Officer, Order of Orange-Nassau, 1965; Hon. KBE 1960; *b* 27 June 1905; *s* of Jonkheer Hugo Loudon and Anna Petronella Alida Loudon (*née* van Marken); *m* 1st, 1931, Baroness Marie Cornelie van Tuyll van Serooskerken (*d* 1988); three *s* (and one *s* decd); 2nd, 1996, Charlotte van Simia. *Educ:* Netherlands Lyceum, The Hague; Utrecht Univ., Holland. Doctor of Law, 1929. Joined Royal Dutch/Shell Group of Cos, 1930; served in USA, 1932–38; Venezuela, 1938–47 (Gen. Man., 1944–47); Man. Dir, 1947–52, Pres., 1952–65, Chm., 1965–76, Royal Dutch Petroleum Co.; former Chm., Shell Oil Co. (New York); Vice-Chm. Bd, Royal Netherlands Blast-furnaces & Steelworks, NV, 1971–76; Director: Orion Bank Ltd, 1971–81; Chase Manhattan Corp., 1971–76; Estel NV Hoesch-Hoogovens, 1972–76; Russell Reynolds Assocs Inc., 1977–; Adv. Dir, Bd, Arrow Partners CV, NY, 1983–. Chairman: Internat. Adv. Cttee, Chase Manhattan Bank, 1965–77; Bd, Atlantic Inst., 1969–84; European Adv. Cttee, Ford Motor Co., 1976–83. Internat. Bd Mem., Institut Européen d'Administration des Affaires, 1971–; Mem., Rockefeller Univ. Council, NY, 1978–95; Mem. Bd Trustees, Ford Foundation, 1966–75; Internat. Pres., World Wildlife Fund, 1977–81. Officer, Légion d'Honneur (France); held other decorations. *Recreations:* golf, yachting. *Address:* Koekoeksduin, 5 Vogelenzangseweg, 2111 HP Aerdenhout, Netherlands. *T:* Haarlem 245924. *Clubs:* White's; Royal Yacht Squadron.

Died 4 Feb. 1996.

LOUDOUN, Maj.-Gen. Robert Beverley, CB 1973; OBE 1965; Director, Mental Health Foundation, 1977–90; *b* 8 July 1922; *s* of Robert and Margaret Loudoun; *m* 1950, Audrey, (Sue), Stevens; two *s. Educ:* University College Sch., Hampstead. Served War of 1939–45 (despatches): enlisted Royal Marines, 1940; commissioned, 1941; 43 Commando, Central Mediterranean, 1943–45; 45 Commando, Hong Kong, Malta and Palestine, 1945–48; Instructor, RNC Greenwich, 1950–52; Staff of C-in-C America and West Indies, 1953–55; RN Staff Coll., 1956; Adjt, 40 Commando, Malta and Cyprus, 1958–59; USMC Sch., Quantico, Virginia, 1959–60; MoD, 1960–62; Second-in-Command, 42 Commando, Singapore and Borneo, 1963–64; CO, 40 Commando, Far East, 1967–69; Brig., UK Commandos, Plymouth, 1969–71; Maj.-Gen. RM Training Gp, Portsmouth, 1971–75, retired. Representative Col Comdt, RM, 1983–84. Chairman: Jt Shooting Cttee for GB, 1977–82; British Southern Slav Soc. (formerly British Yugoslav Soc.), 1990–95. Freeman, City of London, 1979. *Address:* The Heathers, Bathampton Lane, Bathampton, Bath BA2 6SU.

Died 28 Dec. 1998.

LOUGH, Prof. John, FBA 1975; Professor of French, Durham Colleges, later University of Durham, 1952–78; *b* 19 Feb. 1913; *s* of Wilfrid Gordon and Mary Turnbull Lough, Newcastle upon Tyne; *m* 1939, Muriel Barker (*d* 1998); one *d. Educ:* Newcastle upon Tyne Royal Grammar Sch.; St John's Coll., Cambridge; Sorbonne. Major Schol., St John's Coll., 1931; BA, First Cl. Hons Parts I and II Mod. and Medieval Langs Tripos, 1934; Esmond Schol. at British Inst. in Paris, 1935; Jebb Studentship, Cambridge, 1936; PhD 1937, MA 1938, Cambridge. Asst, later Lectr, Univ. of Aberdeen, 1937; Lectr in French, Cambridge, 1946. Leverhulme Res. Fellow, 1973. Hon. Dr, Univ. of Clermont, 1967; Hon. DLitt Newcastle, 1972. Officier de l'Ordre National du Mérite (France), 1973.

Publications: Locke's Travels in France, 1953; (ed) Selected Philosophical Writings of Diderot, 1953; (ed) The Encyclopédie of Diderot and d'Alembert: selected articles, 1954; An Introduction to Seventeenth Century France, 1954; Paris Theatre Audiences in the 17th and 18th centuries, 1957; An Introduction to Eighteenth Century France, 1960; Essays on the Encyclopédie of Diderot and D'Alembert, 1968; The Encyclopédie in 18th Century England and other studies, 1970; The Encyclopédie, 1971; The Contributors to the Encyclopédie, 1973; (ed with J. Proust) Diderot: Œuvres complètes, vols V-VIII, 1977; (with M. Lough) An Introduction to Nineteenth Century France, 1978; Writer and Public in France, 1978; Seventeenth Century French Drama: the background, 1979; The Philosophes and Post-Revolutionary France, 1982; France Observed in the Seventeenth Century by British Travellers, 1985; France on the Eve of Revolution: observations by British travellers 1763–1788, 1987; (with E. Merson) John Graham Lough (1798–1876), a Northumbrian Sculptor, 1987; articles on French literature and ideas in 17th and 18th centuries in French and English learned jls. Address: Hallgarth Nursing Home, Hallgarth Street, Durham DH1 3AY. T: (0191) 384 8034.   Died 21 June 2000.

LOVAT, Sheriff Leonard Scott; Sheriff of South Strathclyde, Dumfries and Galloway at Hamilton, 1978–93; b 28 July 1926; s of late Charles Lovat and Alice (née Hunter); m 1960, Elinor Frances (decd), d of late J. A. McAlister and Mary McAlister; one s one d. Educ: St Aloysius Coll., Glasgow; Glasgow Univ. (BL 1947). Solicitor, 1948; in partnership, 1955–59. Asst to Prof. of Roman Law, Glasgow Univ., 1954–63; Cropwood Fellow, Inst. of Criminology, Univ. of Cambridge, 1971. Procurator Fiscal Depute, Glasgow, 1960; Sen. Asst Procurator Fiscal, Glasgow and Strathkelvin, 1976. Mem., CCJ (Mem., West of Scotland Cttee, 1990–93). Hon. Member: Aloysian Assoc.; Sheriffs' Soc. Publication: Climbers' Guide to Glencoe and Ardgour, 2 vols, 1959, 1963. Recreations: music, hill-walking, bird-watching. Address: 38 Kelvin Court, Glasgow G12 0AE. T: 0141-357 0031.   Died 21 April 1996.

LOVICK, Albert Ernest Fred; retired; Chairman, 1964–68, Director, 1950–68 and 1969–78, Co operative Insurance Society Ltd; Chairman, Cumbrian Co-operative Society Ltd, Carlisle, 1972–86; Director: CWS Ltd, 1949–78; Shoefayre Ltd, 1975–78; b 19 Feb. 1912; s of late Arthur Alfred Lovick and Mary Lovick (née Sharland); m 1934, Florence Ena Jewell; no c. Educ: Elementary Sch., Eastleigh, Hants; Peter Symonds, Winchester. Hearne & Partner, rating surveyors, 1928; Eastleigh Co-operative Society, 1929–33; Harwich, Dovercourt and Parkeston Co-op. Soc., 1933–35; Managing Secretary, Basingstoke Co-op. Soc., 1935–49. During War of 1939–45, government cttees. Member, Basingstoke Borough Council, 1946–49. Former Chm., Centratours Ltd. Member: Export Credits Guarantees Advisory Council, 1968–73; Bristol Rent Assessment Cttee, 1973; Bristol Rent Tribunal, 1973. Fellow, Co-operative Secretaries Assoc.; FCIS. Recreations: golf, gardening. Address: Coedway, Bristol Road, Stonehouse, Glos GL10 2BQ. T: (01453) 823167.   Died 14 March 1996.

LOWE, David Nicoll, OBE 1946; FRSE; Secretary, Carnegie United Kingdom Trust, 1954–70; b 9 Sept. 1909; s of George Black Lowe and Jane Nicoll, Arbroath, Angus; m 1939, Muriel Enid Bryer, CSP (d 1991); one s three d. Educ: Arbroath High Sch.; St Andrews Univ. (Kitchener Scholar). MA 1931; BSc (1st Class Hons Botany) 1934; President Union, 1933–34; President Students' Representative Council, 1934–35; Founder President, University Mountaineering Club. Asst Secretary British Assoc. for the Advancement of Science, 1935–40,

Secretary 1946–54. War Cabinet Secretariat, 1940–42 and 1945–46; Ministry of Production, 1942–45. Joint Hon. Secretary, Society of Visiting Scientists, 1952–54. Member Executive Committee: Scottish Council of Social Service, 1953–71; Nat. Trust for Scotland, 1971–81; Member, Countryside Commn for Scotland, 1968–78. Chairman: Scottish Congregational Coll., 1961–68; Pollock Meml Missionary Trust, 1973–84; Governor, Scottish Nat. Meml to David Livingstone, 1974–80. Contributor to Annual Register, 1947–59. Silver Jubilee Medal, 1977. Recreations: gardening, choral music, painting in watercolours. Address: 34 Strathearn Court, Crieff, Perthshire PH7 3DS.   Died 10 Aug. 1999.

LOWE, (John) Duncan, CB 1995; Sheriff of Glasgow and Strathkelvin, since 1997; b 18 May 1948; s of John Duncan Lowe and Davina Lowe (née Hunter); m 1971, Jacqueline Egan; two s. Educ: Hamilton Acad.; Glasgow Univ. (MA, LLB). Procurator Fiscal Depute, Kilmarnock, 1974–76; Legal Asst, later Sen. Legal Asst, Crown Office, 1976–78; Sen. Procurator Fiscal Depute, 1978–79, Asst Procurator Fiscal, 1979–83, Glasgow; Asst Solicitor, Crown Office, 1983–84; Dep. Crown Agent, 1984–88; Regl Procurator Fiscal, Edinburgh, 1988–91; Crown Agent for Scotland, 1991–96. Recreations: golf, fishing. Address: 1 Carlton Place, Glasgow G5 9DA.
                                            Died 7 Sept. 1998.

LOWE, John Eric Charles, LVO 1965; MBE 1937; HM Diplomatic Service, retired; b 11 Aug. 1907; 6th s of late John Frederick Lowe; m 1935, Gertrude, (Trudy) (née Maybury); one s two d. Educ: Burghley Road Sch., Highgate. Vice-Consul, Jibuti, 1930–37, Harar, 1940; Political Officer, Aden Protectorate, 1940; served in HM Forces, Somaliland and Ethiopia, 1941–46; Senior Asst, Foreign Office, 1947–49; Acting Consul, Suez, 1949; Vice Consul, Beira, 1950; Vice-Consul, Hamburg, 1951 and Frankfurt, 1953; 2nd Secretary, Helsinki, 1953; Political Agent's Representative, Min, Al Ahmadi (Kuwait), 1956; Vice-Consul, Leopoldville, 1959; Consul, Khartoum, 1962; Consul-General, Basra, 1965–67, retired. Order of the Two Niles (Sudan), 1965. Recreations: gardening, golf, sailing. Address: Dunnocks, Turners Green Lane, Wadhurst, E Sussex TN5 6TS. T: (01892) 784451.   Died 18 Dec. 1998.

LOWE, Robson; philatelist, publisher, editor, author, auctioneer; b 7 Jan. 1905; s of John Lowe and Gertrude Lee; m 1928, Winifred Marie Denne (d 1973); two d. Educ: Fulham Central Sch. Started own business, 1920; worked on PO Records, 1926; purchased control of Woods of Perth (Printers), 1964; formed Australian co., 1967; joined bd of Christie, Manson & Woods, 1968; formed Italian co., 1969 (founded Il Piccolo for Italian collectors). Chm., Expert Cttee of British Philatelic Assoc., 1941–61; Pres., British Philatelic Fedn, 1979–81; Co-founder, Postal History Soc., 1935; Founder: Soc. of Postal Historians, 1950; annual British Philatelic Exhibn, 1965. Mem. jury at internat. philatelic exhibns: first, Durban, 1928; Chm., Cape Town, 1979. Over 1,000 lectures. Took over Philatelic Jl of GB, 1958 (publisher); Editor, The Philatelist, 1934–74 (centenary, 1966), 1986–91. Publications: Philatelic Encyclopaedia (ed), 1935; Handstruck Stamps of the Empire, 1937, 4th edn 1941; Sperati and his Craft, 1953; British Postage Stamps, 1968; (jtly) St Vincent, 1971; Encyclopaedia of Empire Stamps: Europe, 1947, 2nd edn 1951; Africa, 1949; Asia, 1951; Australia, 1962; North America, 1973; Leeward Islands, 1991; monographs (US Military Mail, WWII etc); articles in philatelic pubns. Recreations: history, philately, study of forgers and forgery. Address: Robson Lowe, Premier House, Hinton Road, Bournemouth BH1 2EF. T: (01202) 299277. Clubs: East India; Collectors (New York).
                                            Died 19 Aug. 1997.

LOWENSTEIN, Prof. Otto Egon, DSc, PhD, DrPhil; FRS 1955; FRSE; Honorary Senior Research Fellow, Pharmacology Department (formerly at Neurocommunications Research Unit), Birmingham University Medical School, since 1976 (Leverhulme Emeritus Research Fellow, 1974–76); *b* 24 Oct. 1906; *s* of Julius Lowenstein and Mathilde Heusinger; *m* 1st, Elsa Barbara, *d* of R. Ritter; two *s*; 2nd, Gunilla Marika (*d* 1981), *d* of Prof. Gösta Dohlman; one step *s*; 3rd, Maureen Josephine, *d* of K. McKernan. *Educ:* Neues Realgymnasium, Munich; Munich Univ. (DrPhil); DSc Glasgow; PhD Birmingham. Asst, Munich Univ., 1931–33; Research Scholar, Birmingham Univ., 1933–37; Asst Lecturer, University College, Exeter, 1937–38; Senior Lecturer, Glasgow Univ., 1938–52; Mason Prof. of Zoology and Comparative Physiology, Birmingham Univ., 1952–74. President: Assoc. for the Study of Animal Behaviour, 1961–64; Section D, British Assoc., 1962; Institute of Biology, 1965–67; Member Council, Royal Society, 1968–69. *Publications:* revision of 6th edn of A Textbook of Zoology (Parker and Haswell), Vol. I; The Senses, 1966; papers in various learned journals on electrophysiology and ultrastructure of sense organs, esp. inner ear of vertebrates. *Recreations:* music, mountain walking, painting. *Address:* 22 Estria Road, Birmingham B15 2LQ. *T:* (0121) 440 2526.

Died 31 Jan. 1999.

LOWRY, Baron *cr* 1979 (Life Peer), of Crossgar in the County of Down; **Robert Lynd Erskine Lowry,** Kt 1971; PC 1974; PC (NI) 1971; a Lord of Appeal in Ordinary, 1988–94; *b* 30 Jan. 1919; *o s* of late Rt Hon. William Lowry (formerly Judge, High Court of Justice, NI), and Catherine Hughes Lowry, 3rd *d* of Rev. R. J. Lynd, DD; *m* 1st, 1945, Mary Audrey (*d* 1987), *o d* of John Martin, Belfast; three *d*; 2nd, 1994, Barbara Adamson Calvert, QC. *Educ:* Royal Belfast Academical Institution (Porter exhibnr, 1937); Jesus Coll., Cambridge (Hon. Fellow 1977). Entrance Exhibn (Classics); Scholar, 1939; 1st Class Classical Tripos, Part I, 1939, Part II 1940; MA 1944. Served HM Forces, 1940–46; enlisted Royal Inniskilling Fusiliers, 1940; Tunisia, 1942–43 with 38 Irish Inf. Bde; commissioned Royal Irish Fusiliers, 1941; Major, 1945; Hon. Colonel: 7th Bn Royal Irish Fusiliers, 1969–71 (5th Bn, 1967–68); 5th Bn Royal Irish Rangers, 1971–76. Called to the Bar of N Ireland, 1947; Bencher of the Inn of Court, 1955; Hon. Bencher, Middle Temple, 1973; Hon. Bencher, King's Inns, Dublin, 1973; QC (NI), 1956. Counsel to HM Attorney-General, 1948–56; Judge of the High Court of Justice (NI), 1964–71; Lord Chief Justice of N Ireland, 1971–88. Member Departmental Cttees on Charities, Legal Aid and Registration of Title; Dep. Chm., Boundaries Commn (NI) 1964–71; Chairman: Interim Boundary Commn (NI Constituencies), 1967; Permanent Boundary Commn, 1969–71; Dep. Chm., Lord Chancellor's Cttee on NI Supreme Court; Member, Jt Law Enforcement Commn, 1974; Chairman: N Ireland Constitutional Convention, 1975; Council of Legal Educn (NI), 1976–79. Chm., SJAI Exec., 1969–72; Member: Nat. Equestrian Fedn, 1969–78; Judicial Cttee, FEI, 1991– (Chm., 1995–); Internat. Showjumping Judge, 1973, Official Internat. Judge, 1987–93. Governor, Royal Belfast Academical Instn, 1956–71 (Pres., 1996–); Chm., Richmond Lodge Sch., 1956–77; Chm. Governing Bodies Assoc. (NI), 1965; Visitor, Univ. of Ulster, 1989–. Hon. LLD QUB, 1980; Hon. DLitt NUU, 1981. *Recreations:* golf (Pres., Royal Portrush GC, 1974–97); showjumping, cricket, Rugby. *Address:* House of Lords, SW1A 0PW; White Hill, Crossgar, Co. Down BT30 9HJ. *T:* (01396) 830397. *Clubs:* Army and Navy, MCC; Royal and Ancient (St Andrews); Royal Co. Down Golf, Malone Golf, Portmarnock Golf (Hon. Mem.); Royal Fowey Yacht.

Died 15 Jan. 1999.

LOXAM, John Gordon; Director of Veterinary Field Services, Ministry of Agriculture, Fisheries and Food, 1983–86, retired; *b* 26 April 1927; *s* of John Loxam and Mary Elizabeth Loxam (*née* Rigby); *m* 1950, Margaret Lorraine Smith; one *d* (one *s* decd). *Educ:* Lancaster Royal Grammar Sch.; Royal (Dick) Veterinary Coll., Edinburgh. MRCVS 1949 (Hon. FRCVS 1997). General veterinary practice: Marlborough, 1949–51; Carlisle, 1951–53; Vet. Officer, MAFF, Lincoln, 1953–63; Divisional Veterinary Officer: Tolworth, Surrey, 1963–66; Bury St Edmunds, 1966–71; Dep. Regl Vet. Officer, Leeds, 1971–76; Regl Vet. Officer, Tolworth, 1976–78; Asst Chief Vet. Officer, Tolworth, 1979–83. Hon. Sec., 1987–90, Pres., 1990–96, Vet. Benevolent Fund. Life Mem., BVA, 1993. Churchwarden, All Saints, Chelsworth, 1990–; Chm., Chelsworth Parish Meeting, 1992–94. *Recreations:* gardening, spectator sports, particularly Rugby football and equestrian events. *Address:* Riverside, Chelsworth, Ipswich, Suffolk IP7 7HU. *T:* (01449) 740619. *Club:* Farmers'.

Died 13 Dec. 2000.

LOYN, Prof. Henry Royston, DLitt; FSA, FRHistS; FBA 1979; Professor Emeritus, University of London; Professor of History, Westfield College, University of London, 1977–87 (Vice-Principal, 1980–86; Fellow, 1989); *b* 16 June 1922; *s* of late Henry George Loyn and Violet Monica Loyn; *m* 1950, Patricia Beatrice, *d* of late R. S. Haskew, OBE; three *s. Educ:* Cardiff High Sch.; University Coll., Cardiff (MA 1949, DLitt 1968). FRHistS 1958; FSA 1968. Department of History, University College, Cardiff: Asst Lectr, 1946; Lectr, 1949; Sen. Lectr, 1961; Reader, 1966; Prof. of Medieval Hist., 1969–77; Dean of Students, 1968–70 and 1975–76; Fellow, 1981; Hon. Prof., 1996–. President: Historical Assoc., 1976–79; Glam Hist. Soc., 1975–77; Cardiff Naturalists Soc., 1975–76; Soc. for Medieval Archaeol., 1983–86 (Vice-Pres., 1971–74); St Albans and Herts Architectural and Archaeol Soc., 1990–93; Vice-President: Soc. of Antiquaries, 1983–87; RHistS, 1983–86. Mem., Ancient Monuments Bd for England, 1982–84. W. N. Medlicott Medal for service to history, Historical Assoc., 1986. *Publications:* Anglo-Saxon England and the Norman Conquest, 1962, 2nd edn 1991; Norman Conquest, 1965; Norman Britain, 1966; Alfred The Great, 1967; A Wulfstan MS, Cotton, Nero Ai, 1971; (ed with H. Hearder) British Government and Administration, 1974; (with J. Percival) The Reign of Charlemagne, 1975; The Vikings in Britain, 1977, rev. edn 1995; (with Alan and Richard Sorrell) Medieval Britain, 1977; The Governance of England, vol. 1, 1984; (introd.) facsimile edn, Domesday Book, 1987; (ed) The Middle Ages: a concise encyclopaedia, 1989; The Making of the English Nation, 1991; Society and Peoples: studies in the history of England and Wales *c* 600–1200, 1992; The English Church *c* 940–1154, 2000; contribs to Eng. Hist. Rev., History, Antiquaries Jl, and Med. Archaeol. *Recreations:* natural history, gardening. *Address:* 4 Clinton Road, Penarth, Vale of Glam CF64 3JB. *Club:* Athenæum.

Died 9 Oct. 2000.

LUBBOCK, Christopher William Stuart; a Master of the Supreme Court (Queen's Bench Division), 1970–90; *b* 4 Jan. 1920; 2nd *s* of late Captain Rupert Egerton Lubbock, Royal Navy; *m* 1947, Hazel Gordon, *d* of late Gordon Chapman; one *s* one *d. Educ:* Charterhouse; Brasenose Coll., Oxford. Served 1939–46, RNVR. Called to the Bar, Inner Temple, 1947. *Address:* Great Horkesley, Essex.

Died 16 May 2000.

LUCAS; *see* Keith-Lucas.

LUCAS, Percy Belgrave, CBE 1981; DSO 1943 and Bar 1945; DFC 1942; Chairman: GRA Property Trust Ltd, 1965–75 (Managing Director, 1957–65); John Jacobs Golf

Consultants Ltd, 1978–91; John Jacobs Golf Associates Ltd, 1985–94; *b* Sandwich Bay, Kent, 2 Sept. 1915; *y s* of late Percy Montagu Lucas, Prince's, Sandwich, formerly of Filby House, Filby, Norfolk; *m* 1946, Jill Doreen, *d* of Lt-Col A. M. Addison, Ascot; two *s* (and one *s* decd). *Educ:* Stowe; Pembroke Coll., Cambridge. Editorial Staff, Express Newspapers, 1937–40. Joined RAFVR, 1939; commanded: 249 (Fighter) Sqdn, Battle of Malta, 1942; 616 (Fighter) Sqdn, 1943; Coltishall Wing, Fighter Command, 1943; 613 (Mosquito) Sqdn, 2 Gp, 2nd TAF, North-West Europe, 1944–45; Fighter Command, HQ Staff, 1942; Air Defence of Great Britain HQ Staff, 1944; demobilised with rank of Wing Comdr, 1946. Contested (C) West Fulham, 1945; MP (C) Brentford and Chiswick, 1950–59. Capt. Cambridge Univ. Golf team, 1937; Pres. Hawks Club, Cambridge, 1937; English International Golf team, 1936, 1948, 1949 (Capt. 1949); British Walker Cup team, 1936, 1947, 1949 (Capt. 1949); Capt., Walker Cup Society, 1986–88. Vice-President: Golf Foundation Ltd, 1983– (Mem. Council, 1966–83; Pres., 1963–66); Nat. Golf Clubs Advisory Assoc., 1969– (Pres., 1963–69); Assoc. of Golf Club Secretaries, 1974– (Pres., 1968–74). Member: General Advisory Council, BBC, 1962–67; Council, National Greyhound Racing Soc. of Great Britain, 1957–72; Policy Cttee, Nat. Greyhound Racing Club Ltd, 1972–77; AAA Cttee of Inquiry, 1967; Exec. Cttee, General Purposes and Finance Cttee; Central Council of Physical Recreation; Management Cttee, Crystal Palace Nat. Sports Centre, 1961–73; Sports Council, 1971–83 (Chm., Finance Cttee, 1978–82; Chm., Sports Trade Adv. Panel, 1972–83). Governor, Stowe Sch., 1964–79. Pres., Old Stoic Soc., 1979–81. Croix de Guerre avec Palme, 1945. *Publications:* Five Up (autobiography), 1978, 2nd edn 1991; The Sport of Prince's (reflections of a golfer), 1980; Flying Colours: the epic story of Douglas Bader, 1981, 2nd edn 1990; Wings of War: airmen of all nations tell their stories 1939–1945, 1983; Out of the Blue: the role of luck in air warfare 1917–66, 1985; John Jacobs' Impact on Golf: the man and his methods, 1987; Thanks for the Memory: unforgettable characters in air warfare 1939–1945, 1989; Malta—the thorn in Rommel's side, 1992; with Air Vice-Marshal J. E. Johnson: Glorious Summer: the story of the Battle of Britain, 1990; Courage in the Skies: great air battles from the Somme to Desert Storm, 1992; Winged Victory: the recollections of two Royal Air Force leaders, 1995. *Recreations:* golf, photography. *Address:* 11 Onslow Square, SW7 3NJ. *T:* (0171) 584 8373. *Clubs:* Naval and Military, Royal Air Force; Sandy Lodge Golf (Hon. Mem.); Walton Heath Golf (Hon. Mem.); Prince's Golf (Hon. Mem.); Royal West Norfolk Golf.   *Died 20 March 1998.*

LUCKHOO, Hon. Sir Edward Victor, Kt 1970; QC (Guyana) 1965; Order of Roraima (Guyana), 1979; attached to Luckhoo and Luckhoo, Guyana, 1949–66 and 1984–87; *b* Guyana (when British Guiana), 24 May 1912; *s* of late E. A. Luckhoo, OBE; *g s* of Moses Luckhoo, official interpreter to the Courts; *m* 1981, Maureen Moxlow, Batley, Yorks. *Educ:* New Amsterdam Scots Sch.; Queen's Coll., Guyana; St Catherine's Coll., Oxford (BA). Called to Bar, Middle Temple, 1936. Began career in magistracy as acting Magistrate, Essequibo District, 1943; Magistrate, 1944–47; Judge of Appeal, 1966; Chancellor and President of Court of Appeal, Guyana, 1968–76; Actg Governor-General, 1969–70; Actg Pres. of Guyana, Feb.–March, 1970; High Comr in India and Sri Lanka, 1970–78. Chairman: Customs Tariff Tribunal, 1954–56; Judicial Service Commn, 1966–75; Honours Adv. Council, 1970–76. Mem. Exec. Bd, UNESCO, 1983–87. *Address:* 43 Penn Drive, Liversedge, W Yorks WF15 8DB.   *Died 2 March 1998.*

LUCKHOO, Sir Lionel (Alfred), KCMG 1969; Kt 1966; CBE 1962; QC (Guyana) 1954; Judge of Supreme Court,

Guyana, 1980, retired; *b* 2 March 1914; 2nd *s* of late Edward Alfred Luckhoo, OBE, solicitor, and Evelyn Luckhoo; *g s* of Moses Luckhoo, official interpreter to the Courts; *m* 1st, Sheila Chamberlin (marr. diss. 1972); two *s* three *d*; 2nd, Jeannie. *Educ:* Queen's Coll., Georgetown, British Guiana; Middle Temple, London. MLC, 1949–51; Mem. State Council, 1952–53; Minister without Portfolio, 1954–57; Mem. Georgetown Town Council, 1950–64; Mayor, City of Georgetown, 1954, 1955, 1960, 1961 (Dep. Mayor three times); High Comr in UK, for Guyana, May 1966–1970; for Barbados, Nov. 1966–1970; Ambassador of Guyana and Barbados, to Paris, Bonn and The Hague, 1967–70. Pres., Manpower Citizens' Assoc., British Guiana, 1949–52, and of several Trade Unions; served on Commns of Enquiry, Public Cttees, Statutory Bodies, Legal Cttees, Drafting Cttees, Disciplinary Cttees, etc. Head of Luckhoo & Luckhoo, Legal Practitioners. Chm., Red Cross Soc., 1978. Pres., Guyana Olympic Assoc., 1974–79. Mem. of the Magic Circle. Listed in the Guinness Book of Records as the world's most successful advocate with 245 successful defences in murder cases. Travelled more than four million miles around the world speaking of Jesus. *Publications:* (jtly) The Fitzluck Theory of Breeding Racehorses, 1960; I Believe, 1968; God is Love, 1975; Life After Death, 1975; The Xmas Story, 1975; Sense of Values, 1975; Dear Atheist, 1977; Dear Boys and Girls, 1978; Dear Adults, 1979; God and Science, 1980; Dear Muslims, 1980; The Question Answered, 1984; The Verdict is Yours, 1985, (jtly) Destiny of Guilt, 1988; Silent Witness, 1990. *Recreation:* cricket. *Address:* Luckhoo Ministries, PO Box 815881, Dallas, TX 75381, USA.   *Died 12 Dec. 1997.*

LUKE, 2nd Baron *cr* 1929, of Pavenham, co. Bedford; **Ian St John Lawson Johnston,** KCVO 1976; TD; JP; DL; *b* 7 June 1905; *e s* of 1st Baron Luke, KBE and Hon. Edith Laura (*d* 1941), *d* of 16th Baron St John of Bletsoe; *S* father, 1943; *m* 1932, Barbara, *d* of Sir FitzRoy Hamilton Anstruther-Gough-Calthorpe, 1st Bt, four *s* one *d*. *Educ:* Eton; Trinity Coll., Cambridge (MA). Life President, Electrolux Ltd, 1978 (Chm., 1963–78); Chm., Gateway Building Society, 1978–86; Dir, Ashanti Goldfields Corporation Ltd and other companies; Chm., Bovril Ltd, 1943–70. One of HM Lieutenants, City of London, 1953–. Served War OC 9th Bn Beds and Herts Regt, 1940–43; Hon. Col 5th Bn Beds Regt, 1947–62. Chairman: Area Cttee for National Fitness in Herts and Beds, 1937–39; London Hospitals Street Collections Central Cttee, 1943–45; Beds TAA, 1943–46; Duke of Gloucester's Red Cross and St John Fund, 1943–46; Nat. Vice-Pres., Royal British Legion; Chm., National Playing Fields Assoc., 1950–76 (a Vice-Pres., 1977–); an Hon. Sec., Assoc. of British Chambers of Commerce, 1944–52; Mem. of Church Assembly (House of Laity), 1935; Lay Reader, St Alban's dio., 1933–; Mem., International Olympic Cttee, 1951–88, Hon. Mem., 1988–; President: Incorporated Sales Managers Assoc., 1953–56; Advertising Assoc., 1955–58; Outdoor Advertising Council, 1957; Operation Britain Organisation, 1957–62; London Chamber of Commerce, 1952–55; Inst. of Export, 1973–83; Chm. Governors, Queen Mary Coll., Univ. of London, 1963–82, Fellow, 1980. MFH Oakley Hunt, 1947–49. CC Beds, 1943–52; DL, JP Bedfordshire. *Heir: s* Hon. Arthur Charles St John Lawson Johnston, DL [*b* 13 Jan. 1933; *m* 1st, 1959, Silvia Maria (marr. diss. 1971), *yr d* of Don Honorio Roigt and Doña Dorothy Goodall de Roigt; one *s* two *d*; 2nd, 1971, Sarah, *d* of Richard Hearne; one *s*]. *Address:* Odell Castle, Odell, Beds MK43 7BB. *T:* Bedford (01234) 720240. *Club:* Carlton.
Died 25 May 1996.

LUTYENS, Mary, (Mrs J. G. Links), FRSL; writer since 1929; *b* 31 July 1908; *y d* of Sir Edwin Lutyens, OM,

KCIE, PRA, and late Lady Emily Lutyens, *d* of 1st Earl of Lytton; *m* 1st, 1930, Anthony Sewell (marr. diss. 1945; decd); one *d*; 2nd, 1945, J. G. Links, OBE (*d* 1997). *Educ:* Queen's Coll., London; Sydney, Australia. FRSL 1976. *Publications: fiction:* Forthcoming Marriages, 1933; Perchance to Dream, 1935; Rose and Thorn, 1936; Spider's Silk, 1939; Family Colouring, 1940; A Path of Gold, 1941; Together and Alone, 1942; So Near to Heaven, 1943; And Now There is You, 1953; Week-End at Hurtmore, 1954; The Lucian Legend, 1955; Meeting in Venice, 1956; Cleo, 1973; *for children:* Julie and the Narrow Valley, 1944; *autobiography:* To Be Young, 1959, repr. 1989; *edited:* Lady Lytton's Court Diary, 1961; (for Krishnamurti) Freedom from the Known, 1969; The Only Revolution, 1970; The Penguin Krishnamurti Reader, 1970; The Urgency of Change, 1971; (with Malcolm Warner) Rainy Days at Brig O'Turk, 1983; *biography:* Effie in Venice, 1965; Millais and the Ruskins, 1967; The Ruskins and the Grays, 1972; Krishnamurti: the years of awakening, 1975; The Lyttons in India, 1979; Edwin Lutyens, 1980, repr. 1991; Krishnamurti: the years of fulfilment, 1982; Krishnamurti: the open door, 1988; The Life and Death of Krishnamurti, 1990, repr. 1991; also numerous serials, afterwards published, under pseudonym of Esther Wyndham; contribs to TLS, Apollo, The Cornhill, The Walpole Soc. Jl. *Address:* 8 Elizabeth Close, Randolph Avenue, W9 1BN. *T:* (020) 7286 6674.

Died 9 April 1999.

LYNCH, Rev. Preb. Donald MacLeod, CBE 1972; *b* 2 July 1911; *s* of Herbert and Margaret Lynch; *m* 1st, 1941, Ailsa Leslie Leask (decd); three *s* one *d*; 2nd, 1963, Jean Wileman. *Educ:* City of London Sch.; Pembroke Coll., Cambridge (MA); Wycliffe Hall, Oxford. Deacon 1935, priest 1936; Curate, Christ Church, Chelsea, 1935; Tutor, Oak Hill Theological Coll., 1938; Curate, St Michael's, Stonebridge Park, 1940; Minister, All Saints, Queensbury, 1942; Vicar, St Luke's, Tunbridge Wells, 1950; Principal, Church Army Training Coll., 1953; Chief Sec., Church Army, 1960–76; Preb. of Twiford, St Paul's Cathedral, 1964–76, then Emeritus; Priest-in-Charge of Seal, St Lawrence, dio. of Rochester, 1974–85, also of Underriver, 1980–85; RD, Sevenoaks, 1979–84. Chaplain to the Queen, 1969–81. *Publications:* Action Stations, 1981; Chariots of the Gospel, 1982. *Recreation:* reading. *Address:* Flat 2, 20 Grassington Road, Eastbourne, Sussex BN20 7BJ. *T:* (01323) 720849.

Died 27 Nov. 2000.

LYNCH, John; *b* 15 Aug. 1917; *y s* of Daniel Lynch and Norah O'Donoghue; *m* 1946, Mairin O'Connor. *Educ:* Christian Brothers' Schools, N Monastery, Cork; University College, Cork; King's Inns, Dublin. Entered Civil Service (Dept of Justice), 1936; called to the Bar, 1945; resigned from Civil Service, became Mem. Munster Bar and commenced practice in Cork Circuit, 1945. Teachta Dala (TD) for Cork, Parlt of Ireland, 1948–81; Parly Sec. to Govt and to Minister for Lands, 1951–54; Minister for: Education, 1957–59; Industry and Commerce, 1959–65; Finance, 1965–66; Leader of Fianna Fáil, 1966–79; Taoiseach (Head of Government of Ireland), 1966–73 and 1977–79; Pres., European Council (EEC), July–Dec. 1979. Vice-Pres., Consultative Assembly of Council of Europe, 1958; Pres., Internat. Labour Conf., 1962. Alderman, Co. Borough of Cork, 1950–57; Mem. Cork Sanatoria Board and Cttee of Management, N Infirmary, Cork, 1950–51 and 1955–57; Mem. Cork Harbour Comrs, 1956–57. Freeman, City of Cork, 1980. Hon. LLD: Univ. of Dublin, 1967; Nat. Univ. of Ireland, 1969; Rhode Island Coll., USA, 1980; Limerick, 1995; Hon. DCL N Carolina, 1971. Grand Cross, Order of the Crown (Belgium), 1968. Robert Schumann Gold Medal, 1973; Mérite Européen Gold Medal, 1981. *Address:* 21 Garville Avenue, Rathgar, Dublin 6, Ireland.

Died 20 Oct. 1999.

LYNCH-ROBINSON, Sir Niall (Bryan), 3rd Bt *cr* 1920, of Foxrock, co. Dublin; DSC 1941; late Lieutenant RNVR; one time Chairman, Leo Burnett Ltd, 1969–78; *b* 24 Feb. 1918; *s* of Sir Christopher Henry Lynch-Robinson, 2nd Bt and Dorothy (*d* 1970), *d* of Henry Warren, Carrickmines, Co. Dublin; *S* father 1958; *m* 1940, Rosemary Seaton, *e d* of Mrs M. Seaton Eller; one *s* (one adopted *d* decd). *Educ:* Stowe. Sub-Lieut 1939, Lieut 1940, RNVR; served War of 1939–45 (DSC, Croix de Guerre). Mem. Exec. Cttee, Nat. Marriage Guidance Council, 1961–86. Chm. of Governors, Cranbourne Chase School, 1970–82. *Recreations:* fishing, gardening. *Heir: s* Dominick Christopher Lynch-Robinson [*b* 30 July 1948; *m* 1973, Victoria, *d* of Kenneth Weir; one *s* one *d*]. *Address:* Flat 25, Headbourne Worthy House, Headbourne Worthy, Winchester, Hants SO23 7JG.   *Died 3 June 1996.*

LYNE, Air Vice-Marshal Michael Dillon, CB 1968; AFC (two Bars); DL; *b* 23 March 1919; *s* of late Robert John Lyne, Winchester; *m* 1943, (Avril) Joy Buckley, OStJ, *d* of late Lt-Col Albert Buckley, CBE, DSO (and Bar); two *s* two *d*. *Educ:* Imperial Service Coll.; RAF Coll., Cranwell. Fighter Comd and Middle East, 1939–46; Comdg No 54 Fighter Squadron, 1946–48; led first jet fighter formation aerobatic display (Brussels), 1947; pilot of first jet flight from Europe to N America via N Pole, 1955; Comdg RAF Wildenrath, 1958–60; Air Attaché, Moscow, 1961–63; Commandant, Royal Air Force Coll., Cranwell, 1963–64; Air Officer Commanding No 23 Group, RAF Flying Training Command, 1965–67; Senior RAF Instructor, Imperial Defence Coll., 1968–69; Dir-Gen. Training, RAF, 1970–71; retired. Sec., Diocese of Lincoln, 1971–76. Vice Chm., Governing Body, Bishop Grosseteste Coll., 1976–86. Vice-Chm. (Air), TAVRA for East Midlands, 1977–84. Vice-President: RAF Gliding and Soaring Assoc.; RAF Motor Sport Assoc.; Old Cranwellian Assoc., 1982–96. Founder and first Chm., Lincs Microprocessor Soc., 1979–83; Mem. Council, British Computer Soc., 1980–83. President: Lincoln Branch, SCF, 1977–89; Grantham Constituency Liberal Assoc., 1979–88; Grantham Constituency Liberal Democrats, 1990–93; No 54 Squadron Assoc., 1981–94. DL Lincs, 1973. *Recreations:* writing, gardening. *Address:* Far End, Far Lane, Coleby, Lincoln LN5 0AH. *T:* (01522) 810468. *Club:* Royal Air Force.   *Died 21 Dec. 1997.*

LYTHGOE, Ian Gordon, CB 1975; company director, retired; *b* 30 Dec. 1914; *s* of John and Susan Lythgoe; *m* 1st, 1939, Marjory Elsie Fleming; three *s*; 2nd, 1971, Mary Margaret Pickard (CBE 1980). *Educ:* Southland Boys' High Sch., Invercargill; Victoria UC, Wellington (MCom Hons). FCA. Private Sec., Ministers of Finance, 1944–53; Asst Sec., Treasury, 1962; State Services Commission: Mem., 1964–66; Dep. Chm., 1967–70; Chm., 1971–74. NZ Society of Accountants: Mem. Council, 1966–76; Vice-Pres., 1973–74; Pres., 1974–75; Chm., Disciplinary Cttee, 1982–87 (Mem., 1979–87). Mem. Council, Central Inst. of Technology, 1977–86 (Vice-Chm., 1978–80; Chm., 1980–86). Member: Commn of Enquiry into Rescue and Fire Safety at Internat. Airports (NZ); Information Authority, 1982–88; Commn of Enquiry concerning Ian David Donaldson, 1983. Director: Fletcher Challenge Corp. Ltd (formerly Challenge Corp. Ltd), 1975–84; Philips Electrical Industries Ltd, 1975–87. *Recreations:* gardening, reading. *Address:* 9C/19 Cottleville Terrace, Wellington 6001, New Zealand. *Club:* Wellington (Wellington, NZ).

Died 16 Feb. 2000.

LYVEDEN, 6th Baron *cr* 1859, of Lyveden, co. Northampton; **Ronald Cecil Vernon;** retired; *b* 10 April 1915; *s* of 5th Baron Lyveden and Ruby (*née* Shanley) (*d* 1932); *S* father, 1973; *m* 1938, Queenie Constance, *d* of Howard Ardern; three *s. Educ:* Te Aroha College. *Heir: s* Hon. Jack Leslie Vernon [*b* 10 Nov. 1938; *m* 1961, Lynette June, *d* of William Herbert Lilley; one *s* two *d*]. *Address:* 20 Farmer Street, Te Aroha, New Zealand. *Club:* Returned Services Association (Te Aroha).

Died 12 Sept. 1999.

M

MABY, (Alfred) Cedric, CBE 1962; HM Diplomatic Service, retired; *b* 6 April 1915; 4th *s* of late Joseph Maby, Penrhos, Monmouthshire; *m* 1944, Anne-Charlotte, *d* of Envoyén Einar Modig, Stockholm; one *s* two *d. Educ:* Cheltenham; Keble Coll., Oxford. Joined HM Consular Service, 1939; served at Peking, 1939, Chungking, 1940, Tsingtao, 1941, Istanbul, 1943, Angora, 1944, Buenos Aires, 1946, Caracas, 1949, Singapore, 1954; Counsellor and Consul-General, Peking, 1957–59 (Chargé d' Affaires, 1957 and 1958); Deputy Consul-General, New York, 1959–62; Counsellor (Commercial), Vienna, 1962–64; Asst Sec., Min. of Overseas Development, 1964–67; Consul-General, Zürich and Liechtenstein, 1968–71; Dir, Trade Promotion for Switzerland, 1970–71. Member: Governing Body, Church in Wales, 1975–78; Church in Wales Adv. Commn on Church and Society, 1977–86. Fellow, Huguenot Soc. of GB and Ire., 1977. High Sheriff of Gwynedd, 1976. *Publications:* Dail Melyn o Tseina, 1983; Y Cocatŵ Coch, 1987; Looking Both Ways, 1995; contribs to Planet, Y Faner and other Welsh periodicals. *Address:* Cae Canol, Minffordd, Penrhyn-Deudraeth, Gwynedd LL48 6EN. *Died 28 Nov. 2000.*

McADAM, Sir Ian (William James), Kt 1966; OBE 1957; FRCS, FRCSE; *b* 15 Feb. 1917; *s* of W. J. McAdam and Alice Culverwell; *m* 1st, 1939, Hrothgarde Gibson (marr. diss. 1961); one *s* two *d*; 2nd, 1967, Lady (Pamela) Hunt (*née* Medawar). *Educ:* Plumtree Sch., S Rhodesia; Edinburgh Univ. MB, ChB 1940. FRCSE 1946, FRCS 1966. Cambridge Anatomy Sch., 1940; Dept of Surgery, Edinburgh, 1942; Wilkie Surgical Research Fellow, 1942; Clinical Tutor, Royal Infirmary, Edinburgh, 1942; Surgical Specialist, Uganda, 1946; Senior Consultant, Uganda, 1957; Prof. of Surgery, Makerere Univ., Univ. of E Africa, 1957–72, also Consultant Surgeon, Uganda Govt and Kenyatta Hosp., Kenya; Consultant to Nat. Insts of Health, Bethesda, Md, 1973–74. *Publications:* various papers in medical jls. *Recreations:* golf, gardening. *Address:* 16 Middleton Park, Middleton Stoney, Oxon OX6 8SQ. *Died 4 March 1999.*

MACADAM, Sir Peter, Kt 1981; Chairman: BAT Industries plc, 1976–82; Libra Bank, 1984–90; *b* 9 Sept. 1921; *s* of late Francis Macadam and Marjorie Mary Macadam (*née* Browne); *m* 1949, Ann Musson; three *d. Educ:* Buenos Aires, Argentina; Stonyhurst Coll., Lancs. Served as Officer in Queen's Bays, 1941–46. Joined BAT Gp tobacco co., Argentina, 1946; Chm. and Gen. Man., gp co., Argentina, 1955–58; PA in London to Dir resp. for Africa, 1959–60 (travelled widely in Africa); Chm., BAT Hong Kong, 1960–62; Mem. BAT Main Bd, 1963 (resp. at times for interest in S and Central Africa, S and Central America and Caribbean); Mem., Chm.'s Policy Cttee with overall resp. for tobacco interests and special interest, USA, Canada and Mexico, 1970; Chm., Tobacco Div. Bd and Dir, Gp HQ Bd, 1973; Vice-Chm., 1975. Dir, National Westminster Bank, 1978–84. Chm., British Nat. Cttee, ICC, 1978–85; Mem. Exec. Cttee, ICC, Paris, 1982–85. Pres., Hispanic and Luso Brazilian Council, 1982–87; Chm., Anglo-Argentine Soc., 1987–92. Hon. FBIM; FRSA 1975. *Recreations:* golf, shooting. *Address:* Layham Hall, Layham, near Hadleigh, Suffolk IP7 5LE. *T:* (01473) 822137. *Club:* Canning. *Died 28 June 1997.*

McADOO, Most Rev. Henry Robert, PhD, STD, DD; *b* 10 Jan. 1916; *s* of James Arthur and Susan McAdoo; *m* 1940, Lesley Dalziel Weir; one *s* two *d. Educ:* Cork Grammar School; Mountjoy School, Dublin. Deacon, 1939; priest, 1940; Curate of Holy Trinity Cathedral, Waterford, 1939–43; Incumbent of Castleventry with Ardfield, 1943–48 (with Kilmeen, 1947–48); Rector of Kilmocomogue, Diocese of Cork, 1948–52; Rural Dean of Glansalney West and Bere, 1948–52; Canon of Kilbrittain in Cork Cathedral, and Canon of Donoughmore in Cloyne Cathedral, 1949–52; Dean of Cork, 1952–62; Canon of St Patrick's Cathedral, Dublin, 1960–62; Bishop of Ossory, Ferns and Leighlin, 1962–77; Archbishop of Dublin and Primate of Ireland, 1977–85. Member, Anglican-Roman Catholic Preparatory Commission, 1967–68; Jt Chm., Anglican-Roman Catholic International Commission, 1969–81 (Canterbury Cross). Hon. Fellow, TCD, 1989. *Publications:* The Structure of Caroline Moral Theology, 1949; John Bramhall and Anglicanism, 1964; The Spirit of Anglicanism, 1965; Modern Eucharistic Agreement, 1973; Modern Ecumenical Documents on Ministry, 1975; Being an Anglican, 1977; Rome and the Anglicans, 1982; The Unity of Anglicanism: Catholic and Reformed, 1983; The Eucharistic Theology of Jeremy Taylor Today, 1989; Anglican Heritage: theology and spirituality, 1991; First of its Kind: Jeremy Taylor's life of Christ, 1994; (with K. Stevenson) The Mystery of the Eucharist in the Anglican Tradition, 1995; Anglicans and Tradition and the Ordination of Women, 1997; Jeremy Taylor: Anglican theologian, 1997; contribs to: Authority in the Anglican Communion, 1987; Christian Authority, 1988; The English Religious Tradition and the Genius of Anglicanism, 1992. *Address:* 2 The Paddocks, Dalkey, Co. Dublin. *Club:* Kildare Street and University (Dublin). *Died 10 Dec. 1998.*

MACARTHUR, Charles Ramsay; QC (Scot.) 1970; Sheriff of Tayside, Central and Fife, 1981–91; *b* 29 July 1922; *s* of late Alastair and Joan Macarthur; *m* 1973, Rosemary Valda Morgan (marr. diss. 1982), Edinburgh. *Educ:* Glasgow Univ. (MA, LLB). Served War of 1939–45: joined Royal Navy, 1942; demobilised as Lieut, RNVR, 1946. Solicitor, 1952–59; admitted Scottish Bar, 1960; Standing Junior Counsel, Highlands and Islands Development Board, 1968–70; Sheriff of the Lothians and Borders, 1974–76. *Recreations:* travel, talking. *Club:* New (Edinburgh). *Died 21 July 2000.*

MACARTNEY, Dr (William John) Allan; Member (SNP) North East Scotland, European Parliament, since 1994; Deputy Leader, Scottish National Party, since 1992; *b* Accra, Ghana, 17 Feb. 1941; *s* of Rev. William M. Macartney and late Jessie H. I. Macartney (*née* Low); *m* 1963, J. D. Anne Forsyth; two *s* one *d. Educ:* Elgin Acad., Moray; Univ. of Tübingen; Univ. of Marburg; Univ. of Edinburgh (MA; PhD 1978); Univ. of Glasgow (BLitt). Teacher, Eastern Nigeria, 1963–64; Lectr in Govt and Admin, Univ. of Botswana, Lesotho and Swaziland, 1966–74; Staff Tutor in Politics, Open Univ., 1975–94. SNP spokesman on foreign affairs, 1987–. Vice-Pres., EP Fisheries Cttee, 1997–; Mem., African, Caribbean, Pacific–EU Jt Assembly, 1994–. Rector, Univ. of Aberdeen, 1997–. *Publications:* Readings in Boleswa Government, 1971; The Referendum Experience, 1981; Islands of Europe, 1984; Self-determination in the Commonwealth, 1987; Scotland on the move, 1997. *Recreations:* music, languages, walking, vexillology.

Address: 70 Rosemount Place, Aberdeen AB25 2XJ. *T:* (01224) 623150, *Fax:* (01224) 623160.
Died 25 Aug. 1998.

MACAULAY, Janet Stewart Alison, MA; Headmistress of St Leonards and St Katharines Schools, St Andrews, 1956–70; *b* 20 Dec. 1909; 3rd *d* of late Rev. Prof. A. B. Macaulay, DD, Trinity Coll., Glasgow. *Educ:* Laurel Bank Sch., Glasgow; Glasgow Univ.; Somerville Coll., Oxford (BA 1932; BLitt 1934; MA 1936). Asst Mistress, Wycombe Abbey Sch., Bucks, 1933–36; Sutton High Sch. (GPDST), Sutton, Surrey, 1937–45; Headmistress, Blackheath High Sch. (GPDST), 1945–55. Hon. LLD St Andrews, 1977. *Address:* 3 Drummond Place, Edinburgh EH3 6PH. *Died 10 Dec. 2000.*

MacCAIG, Norman (Alexander), OBE 1979; MA; ARSA 1981; FRSL; FRSE; *b* 14 Nov. 1910; *s* of Robert McCaig and Joan MacLeod; *m* 1940, Isabel Munro (*d* 1990); one *s* one *d. Educ:* Edinburgh University. MA Hons Classics. FRSL 1965; FRSE 1983. Schoolteacher, 1932–67 and 1969–70; Fellow in Creative Writing, Univ. of Edinburgh, 1967–69; Lectr in English Studies, Univ. of Stirling, 1970–72, Reader in Poetry, 1972–77. Travelling Scholarship, Soc. of Authors, 1964; RSL Award (Heinemann Bequest), 1967; Cholmondeley Award, 1975; Scottish Arts Council Awards, 1954, 1966–67, 1970, 1971, 1978, 1980, 1986; Royal Bank of Scotland Saltire Award, 1985; Queen's Gold Medal for Poetry, 1986; Poetry Soc. Award, 1992. DUniv Stirling, 1981; Hon. DLitt Edinburgh, 1983; Hon. LLD Dundee, 1986. *Publications: poetry:* Far Cry, 1943; The Inward Eye, 1946; Riding Lights, 1955; The Sinai Sort, 1957; A Common Grace, 1960; A Round of Applause, 1962; Measures, 1965; Surroundings, 1966; Rings on a Tree, 1968; A Man in My Position, 1969; The White Bird, 1973; The World's Room, 1974; Tree of Strings, 1977; The Equal Skies, 1980; A World of Difference, 1983; Collected Poems, 1985; Voice-over, 1988; Collected Poems, a new edition, 1990; (ed) Honour'd Shade (anthology), 1959; (ed with Alexander Scott) Contemporary Scottish Verse (anthology), 1970. *Recreations:* fishing, music. *Address:* 7 Leamington Terrace, Edinburgh EH10 4JW. *T:* 0131–229 1809. *Club:* Scottish Arts (Edinburgh). *Died 23 Jan. 1996.*

McCARTHY, (Daniel) Donal John, CMG 1969; HM Diplomatic Service, retired; *b* 31 March 1922; *s* of Daniel and Kathleen McCarthy; *m* 1st, 1951, Rosanna Parbury (marr. diss.); three *s*; 2nd, Margaretha Luijke-Roskott. *Educ:* Holloway Sch.; London Univ. Served Royal Navy, 1942–46. Foreign Office, 1946; Middle East Centre for Arab Studies, 1947–48; 3rd and 2nd Sec., Brit. Embassy, Jedda, 1948–51; 2nd Sec., Political Div., Brit. Middle East Office, 1951–55; 1st Sec., FO, 1955–58; Asst Polit. Agent, Kuwait, 1958–60; Brit. High Commn, Ottawa, 1960–63; FO, 1963–64; Counsellor, Brit. High Commn, Aden, and Polit. Adviser to C-in-C Middle East, 1964–67; Head of Aden Dept, FO, 1967–68, of Arabian Dept, FCO, 1968–70; IDC, 1970–71; Minister (Economic and Social Affairs), UK Mission to UN, 1971–73; Ambassador to United Arab Emirates, 1973–77; FCO, 1978–79. *Recreations:* music, sailing, golf. *Address:* Church Farmhouse, Sudbourne, Suffolk IP12 2BP. *T:* (01394) 450443. *Clubs:* Travellers', Royal Automobile; Aldeburgh Golf.
Died 28 May 1997.

McCLEAN, Kathleen, (Mrs Douglas McClean); *see* Hale, K.

McCLURE, David, RSA 1971 (ARSA 1963); RSW 1965; RGI 1990; SSA 1951; painter and printmaker; *b* 20 Feb. 1926; *s* of Robert McClure, MM, and Margaret Helena McClure (*née* Evans); *m* 1st, 1950, Joyce Dixon Flanigan (*d* 1988); two *s* one *d*; 2nd, 1991, Angela Bradbury. *Educ:*

Queen's Park Sch., Glasgow; Glasgow Univ., 1943–44; (coal-miner, 1944–47); Edinburgh Univ., 1947–49; Edinburgh Coll. of Art, 1947–52 (DA). Travelled in Spain and Italy, 1952–53; on staff of Edinburgh Coll. of Art, 1953–55; one year painting in Italy and Sicily, 1956–57; Duncan of Jordanstone Coll. of Art, Dundee: Lectr, 1957–71; Sen. Lectr, 1971–83; Head of Drawing and Painting, 1983–85. *One man exhibitions:* Palermo, 1957; Edinburgh, 1957, 1961, 1962, 1966, 1969, 1989, 1994; Univ. of Birmingham, 1965; Thackeray Gall., London, 1978, 1986, 1991; retrospective exhibn, Dundee Art Galls, 1984; 14 Scottish Painters, London, 1964; Forty Years of Painting, Fine Art Soc., Glasgow, Edinburgh, 1988. *Work in public and private collections:* UK, USA, Canada, Italy. *Publication:* John Maxwell (monograph), 1976. *Recreations:* collecting Victorian china, gardening, the pianoforte, cooking. *Address:* 16 Strawberry Bank, Dundee, Scotland. *T:* (01382) 66959.
Died 20 Feb. 1998.

McCONNELL, Baron *cr* 1995 (Life Peer), of Lisburn in the County of Antrim; **Robert William Brian McConnell;** PC (NI) 1964; Social Security (formerly National Insurance) Commissioner, Northern Ireland, 1968–87; *b* 25 Nov. 1922; *s* of late Alfred E. McConnell, Belfast; *m* 1951, Sylvia Elizabeth Joyce Agnew; two *s* one *d. Educ:* Sedbergh Sch.; Queen's Univ., Belfast (BA, LLB). Called to the Bar of Northern Ireland, 1948. MP (U) for South Antrim, NI Parlt, 1951–68; Dep. Chm. of Ways and Means, NI Parlt, 1962; Parly Sec. to Min. of Health and Local Govt for N Ireland, 1963; Minister of Home Affairs for Northern Ireland, 1964–66; Minister of State, Min. of Develt, 1966–67; Leader of the House of Commons, NI, 1967–68. President: Industrial Court of NI, 1968–81; European Move in NI, 1992–95 (Vice-Chm., 1987–92). *Address:* 50A Glenavy Road, Knocknadona, Lisburn, Co Antrim, Northern Ireland BT28 3UT. *T:* (028) 9266 3432; House of Lords, SW1A 0PW. *Clubs:* Farmers'; Ulster Reform (Belfast). *Died 25 Oct. 2000.*

McCORMACK, Most Rev. John; Bishop of Meath (RC), 1968–90, then Emeritus; *b* 25 March 1921; *s* of Peter McCormack and Bridget Mulvany. *Educ:* St Finian's Coll., Mullingar; Maynooth Coll.; Lateran Univ., Rome. Priest, 1946. Ministered: Multyfarnham, 1950–52; St Loman's Hosp., 1952–58; Mullingar, 1958–68; Diocesan Sec., Meath, 1952–68. *Address:* Bishop's House, Dublin Road, Mullingar, Co. Westmeath, Ireland. *T:* Mullingar 48841/42038. *Died 25 Sept. 1996.*

McCORQUODALE, Dame Barbara; *see* Cartland, Dame M. B. H.

McCOWAN, Sir Hew Cargill, 3rd Bt *cr* 1934, of Dalwhat, Dumfries; *b* 26 July 1930; *s* of Sir David James Cargill McCowan, 2nd Bt and of Muriel Emma Annie, *d* of W. C. Willmott; *S* father, 1965. *Heir: b* David William Cargill McCowan [*b* 28 Feb. 1934; *m*; one *s* one *d*].
Died 12 March 1998.

McCRAE, Alister Geddes, CBE 1973; Chairman: Clyde Port Authority, 1966–77; British Ports Association, 1972–74; *b* 7 Aug. 1909; *s* of Alexander McCrae and Grace Flora Murdoch; *m* 1st, 1938, Margaret Montgomery Reid (*d* 1977); one *s*; 2nd, 1978, Norah Crawford Orr. *Educ:* Kelvinside Academy; High School of Glasgow. Joined: P. Henderson & Co., Shipowners, Glasgow, 1927; Irrawaddy Flotilla Co. Ltd (in Burma), 1933; served War: Middle East and Burma, 1941–45; Lt-Col, Royal Indian Engrs (despatches); Irrawaddy Flotilla Co. Ltd, 1946–48 (Dep. Gen. Manager, in Burma); re-joined P. Henderson & Co., as Partner, 1948; Sen. Partner and Man. Dir, British & Burmese Steam Navigation Co. Ltd, 1963; retd 1972. Member: Nat. Dock Labour Bd, 1953–57; UK Chamber of Shipping Council, 1954–65; Clyde Navigation Trust,

1962–65; British Transport Docks Bd, 1963–65; Nat. Ports Council, 1967–71; Scottish Economic Council, 1969–74; Aldington/Jones Commn on Docks, 1972; Chm., Clyde Estuary Develt Gp, 1968–71; Dir, Hunterston Develt Co. Ltd, 1970–74. Chm., Glasgow Old People's Welfare Assoc. (Age Concern), 1969–79; Founder Chm., Abbeyfield Killearn Soc., 1978–87. Freeman, City of London, 1959; Liveryman, Worshipful Co. of Shipwrights, 1959. FRSA. *Publications:* Irrawaddy Flotilla, 1978; (jtly) Tales of Burma, 1981; Pioneers in Burma, 1986, new edn as Scots in Burma, 1990. *Recreation:* reading the classic novelists. *Address:* Malin Court, Turnberry, Ayrshire KA26 9PB. *Died 6 Nov. 1996.*

McCRAITH, Col Patrick James Danvers, MC 1943; TD; DL; solicitor and notary public; *b* 21 June 1916; *s* of late Sir Douglas McCraith and Phyllis Marguerite, *d* of A. D'Ewes Lynam; *m* 1946, Hon. Philippa Mary Ellis, *yr d* of 1st and last Baron Robins, KBE, DSO, Rhodesia and Chelsea; one *s* one *d*. *Educ:* Harrow. 2nd Lieut, Sherwood Rangers Yeomanry, 1935; served War, 1939–45, N Africa and NW Europe (three times wounded); raised and commanded Yeomanry Patrol of Long Range Desert Group, 1940–41; commanded Sherwood Rangers Yeomanry, 1953–57; Bt Colonel, 1958. Hon. Col, B (Sherwood Rangers Yeomanry) Squadron, The Royal Yeomanry, 1968–79. High Sheriff of Nottinghamshire, 1963; DL Notts, 1965. *Address:* Cranfield House, Southwell, Notts NG25 0HQ. *T:* (01636) 812129. *Club:* Special Forces. *Died 13 June 1998.*

McCREA, Sir William (Hunter), Kt 1985; PhD, ScD; FRS 1952; FRSE, FRAS, MRIA; Research Professor of Theoretical Astronomy, University of Sussex, 1966–72, then Emeritus; *b* Dublin, 13 Dec. 1904; *er s* of late Robert Hunter McCrea; *m* 1933, Marian Nicol Core (*d* 1995), 2nd *d* of late Thomas Webster, JP, Burdiehouse, Edinburgh; one *s* two *d*. *Educ:* Chesterfield Grammar Sch.; Trinity Coll., Cambridge (Scholar; MA); University of Göttingen; PhD, ScD Cambridge; BSc London. Wrangler, Rayleigh Prizeman, Sheepshanks Exhibitioner, and Isaac Newton Student, Cambridge Univ.; Rouse Ball Travelling Student, and Rouse Ball Senior Student, Trinity Coll., Cambridge; Comyns Berkeley Bye-Fellow, Gonville and Caius Coll., Cambridge, 1952–53. Lecturer in Mathematics, Univ. of Edinburgh, 1930–32; Reader in Mathematics, Univ. of London, and Assistant Prof., Imperial Coll. of Science, 1932–36; Professor of Mathematics: Queen's Univ., Belfast, 1936–44; Royal Holloway Coll., Univ. of London, 1944–66 (Hon. Fellow, 1984). Temp. Prin. Experimental Officer, Admty, 1943–45; commnd RAFVR (Training Branch), 1941–45. Consulting Astronomer, Kitt Peak National Observatory, Arizona, 1965, 1975; Royal Society Exchange Visitor: to USSR, 1960, 1968; to Mexico, 1971; to Argentina, 1971, 1983; to India, 1976; to Egypt, 1981. Visiting Professor of Astronomy: Univ. of California, 1956; Case Inst. of Technology, 1964; Univ. of BC, Vancouver, 1975–76; For. Visiting Prof. of American Astronomical Soc. and Vis. Prof., Berkeley Astronomy Dept, 1967; first occupant, Chaire Georges Lemaître, Louvain Univ., 1969; Royal Soc. Leverhulme Vis. Prof. of Astronomy, Cairo Univ., 1973; Vis. Prof., Istanbul Univ., 1977, 1978; William Evans Vis. Prof., Otago Univ., 1979. Visiting Lecturer: Univ. of Liège, 1960; Technische Hochschule, Aachen, 1962; various universities in Greece and Turkey (British Council), 1971; York Univ., 1965; lectures: Harland, Univ. of Exeter, 1970; Larmor, QUB, 1970; Halley, Oxford, 1975; Milne, Oxford, 1985; R. H. Fowler Meml, Cambridge, 1989. Mem., Governing Board of School of Theoretical Physics, Dublin Institute for Advanced Studies, 1940–50; Governor: Royal Holloway Coll., 1946–49; Ottershaw Sch., 1947–52; Barclay Sch. for Partially Sighted Girls, 1949–66; Mem. Adv. Council, Chelsea Coll. of Aeronautical and Automobile

Engineering, 1958–86. Secretary of Section A of British Assoc., 1935–39, Section Pres. 1966; Pres., Mathematical Assoc., 1973–74 (Hon. Mem., 1985). Joint Editor of The Observatory, 1935–37. Pres., Royal Astronomical Soc., 1961–63 (Sec., 1946–49; Foreign Correspondent, 1968–71; Treasurer, 1976–79). Fellow, Imperial Coll., 1967–; Leverhulme Emeritus Fellow, 1973–75. Mem., Akademie Leopoldina, 1972–; Foreign Mem., Turin Acad. of Scis, 1990–. Freeman, City of London, 1988. Keith Prize, RSE, 1939–41; Gold Medal, RAS, 1976. Hon. DSc: National Univ., Ireland, 1954; QUB, 1970; Sussex, 1978; Dr *hc* National Univ., Cordoba, Argentina, 1971; Hon. ScD Dublin, 1972. *Publications:* Relativity Physics, 1935; Analytical Geometry of Three Dimensions, 1942; Physics of the Sun and Stars, 1950; trans. A. Unsöld's The New Cosmos, 1969; Royal Greenwich Observatory, 1975; (jtly) History of the Royal Astronomical Society 1920–1980, 1987; various papers and reviews in mathematical and astronomical journals. *Address:* 87 Houndean Rise, Lewes, East Sussex BN7 1EJ. *Died 25 April 1999.*

McCREERY, His Honour (Henry Edwin) Lewis; QC 1965; a Circuit Judge (formerly Judge of County Courts), 1971–90, retired; *b* 26 July 1920; *s* of late Rev. William John McCreery, BD, and Anne Cullen McCreery; *m* 1945, Margaret Elizabeth Booth (*d* 1990); two *d*. *Educ:* St Andrew's Coll., Dublin; Trinity Coll., Dublin. RAF, 1942–47. Called: Irish Bar, King's Inns, 1943; English Bar, Middle Temple, 1946 (Bencher, 1971). Dep. Chm., Quarter Sessions: Cornwall, 1966–71; Devon, 1967–71; Recorder of Salisbury, 1969–71. *Recreation:* gardening. *Address:* 110 Clare Park, Crondall, Farnham, Surrey GU10 5DT. *Died 19 Jan. 1998.*

McCRINDLE, Sir Robert (Arthur), Kt 1990; Public Affairs Consultant, Federation of Tour Operators, since 1994; *b* 19 Sept. 1929; *o s* of Thomas Arthur and Isabella McCrindle; *m* 1953, Myra Anderson; two *s*. *Educ:* Allen Glen's Coll., Glasgow. Vice-Chm., Sausmarez, Carey & Harris, Financial Consultants, 1972–75; Director: Langham Life Assurance Co. Ltd, 1972–76; Worldmark Travel Ltd, 1978–82; Hogg Robinson PLC, 1987–; M & G Assurance Gp, 1988–; London and Edinburgh Insurance Group, 1991–; Bradford and Bingley Bldg Soc., 1991–; Chairman: Cometco Ltd, Commodity Brokers, 1972–78; Citybond Storage, 1975–91. Consultant, British Caledonian Airways, 1984–88. Contested: Dundee (East), 1959; Thurrock, 1964; MP (C) Billericay, 1970–74; Brentwood and Ongar, 1974–92. PPS to Minister of State, Home Office, 1974; Chm., All-Party Parly Aviation Cttee, 1980–92; Mem., Transport Select Cttee, 1988–92. Mem., UK Delegn to N Atlantic Assembly, 1977–92 (Chm., Economic Cttee, 1980–84). Parliamentary Consultant: British Transport Police Fedn, 1974–92; British Insurance and Investment Brokers' Assoc., 1976–92; Guild of Business Travel Agents, 1975–78. Nat. Vice-Pres., Corp. of Mortgage Brokers, 1970–76. Fellow, Corp. of Insurance Brokers; ACII. *Address:* 26 Ashburnham Gardens, Upminster, Essex RM14 1XA. *T:* (01708) 227152. *Died 8 Oct 1998.*

McCUBBIN, Very Rev. David; Provost and Canon of Cumbrae Cathedral, 1987–94; *b* 2 Nov. 1929; *s* of late David McCubbin and Annie Robertson Cram (*née* Young). *Educ:* Finnart School; Greenock Academy; King's Coll., London (AKC 1954); St Boniface Coll., Warminster. National service, RAF, 1948–50. Deacon 1955, priest 1956; Curate: Christ Church, Frome, 1955–57; Glastonbury Parish Church, 1957–60; Rector: Holy Trinity, Dunoon, 1960–63; St Peter's, Kirkcaldy, 1963–70; Wallsend (and Surrogate), 1970–79; St John's, Aberdeen, 1979–81; St Bride's, Kelvinside, 1981–87; St Andrew's, Millport, 1987–94; Canon of St John's Cathedral, Oban, 1987–94; Synod Clerk, Diocese of Argyll and The Isles,

1988–95; Hon. Canon, Cathedral of the Holy Spirit, Cumbrae, 1994–. Chm., Prayer Book Soc., Scotland, 1988–91. *Recreations:* music, reading, walking. *Address:* 137 Marlborough Avenue, Glasgow G11 7JE. *T:* (0141) 357 1553.   *Died 6 Aug. 1999.*

MacDERMOT, Niall, CBE 1991 (OBE (mil.) 1944); QC 1963; barrister-at-law; Secretary-General, International Commission of Jurists, 1970–90; *b* 10 Sept. 1916; *s* of late Henry MacDermot, KC, Dublin; *m* 1940, Violet Denise Maxwell (marr. diss.); one *s*; *m* 1966, Ludmila Benvenuto. *Educ:* Rugby Sch.; Corpus Christi Coll., Cambridge; Balliol Coll., Oxford. Served in Intelligence Corps, 1939–46; GSO1 HQ 21 Army Group, 1944–45. Called to the Bar, Inner Temple, 1946, Bencher, 1970. MP (Lab) Lewisham North, Feb. 1957–1959, Derby North, April 1962–1970; Financial Sec., Treasury, 1964–67; Minister of State, Min. of Housing and Local Govt, 1967–68. Mem. Exec., London Labour Party, 1958–62. Dep. Chm., Beds QS, 1961–64, 1969–72; Recorder of Newark-on-Trent, 1963–64; a Recorder of the Crown Court, 1972–74. Hon. Treasurer, Justice, 1968–70. Member: Council, Internat. Inst. of Human Rights, Strasbourg, 1972–; Adv. Council, Interights, 1984–; Bd, Internat. Alert, 1985–; Pres., Special NGO Cttee on Human Rights, Geneva, 1973–86, Vice-Pres., 1986–. Founding Mem., Groupe de Bellerive, 1977–. Trustee of Tate Gall., 1969–76. *Address:* 34 avenue Weber, 1208 Geneva, Switzerland. *T:* (22) 354086.
                                   Died 22 Feb. 1996.

MacDONALD, Alistair Archibald; DL; Chairman, Social Security Appeal Tribunal, and Disability Appeal Tribunal, 1992–98; Sheriff of Grampian, Highland and Islands at Lerwick and Kirkwall, 1975–92, *b* 8 May 1927; *s* of James and Margaret MacDonald; *m* 1950, Jill Russell; one *s* one *d. Educ:* Broughton Sch.; Edinburgh Univ. (MA, LLB). Served in Army, 1945–48. Called to Scottish Bar, 1954. Formerly Sheriff Substitute, Caithness, Sutherland, Orkney and Zetland at Lerwick, 1961 and at Kirkwall, 1968. DL Shetland Islands, 1986. KHS 1988. *Address:* West Hall, Shetland Islands ZE1 0RN. *Club:* Royal Northern (Aberdeen).   *Died 15 July 1998.*

MACDONALD, Alistair Huistean; Deputy Secretary, Equipment Leasing Association, 1971–87, retired; *b* 18 May 1925; *m*; one *s* two *d. Educ:* Dulwich Coll.; Enfield Technical Coll.; Corpus Christi Coll., Cambridge. MP (Lab) Chislehurst, 1966–70. Councillor, Chislehurst and Sidcup UDC, 1958–62; Alderman, 1964–68, Councillor, 1971–90, London Borough of Bromley. *Address:* 1 Springbourne Court, The Avenue, Beckenham, Kent BR3 5ED. *T:* (0181) 658 6953.   *Died 6 Feb. 1999.*

MACDONALD, Angus Stewart, CBE 1985; DL; FRAgS; farmer; *b* 7 April 1935; *s* of Angus Macdonald and Mary Macdonald (*née* Anderson); *m* 1959, Janet Ann Somerville; three *s. Educ:* Conon Bridge School; Gordonstoun School. FRAgS 1982. Director: British Wool Marketing Board and Associated Cos, 1974–; Scottish English Welsh Wool Growers, 1974–95; Grampian Television, 1980–. Chairman: Dingwall Auction Mart (formerly Reith & Anderson (Tain & Dingwall) Ltd), 1991–; SCOTVEC, Sector Bd 1, 1989–93; Dingwall & UA Partnership Ltd. Chairman: RHAS, 1978–79 (Pres., 1995–96); Scottish Agricl Devett Council, 1980–86; Member: Highlands & Islands Enterprise (formerly Devett Bd), 1980–95; Panel of Agricl Arbiters, 1976–. Crown Estate Comr, 1990–. Mem. Queen's Body Guard for Scotland (Royal Co. of Archers), 1985–. Trustee: MacRobert Trust, 1982–; Moredun Animal Health Trust Fund, 1990–. Governor: Gordonstoun School (Chm., 1989–); Aberlour School, 1979–94. DL Ross and Cromarty, 1984. *Recreations:* field sports. *Address:*

Torgorm, Conon Bridge, Dingwall, Ross-shire IV7 8DN. *T:* Dingwall (01349) 61365. *Club:* Caledonian.
                                   Died 15 Jan. 1996.

McDONALD, Air Marshal Sir Arthur (William Baynes), KCB 1958 (CB 1949); AFC 1938; DL; CEng, FRAeS 1959; retired; *b* 14 June 1903; *s* of late Dr Will McDonald, OBE, Antigua, BWI; *m* 1928, Mary Julia Gray, Hindhead, Surrey; two *s* two *d. Educ:* Antigua Grammar Sch.; Epsom Coll.; Peterhouse, Cambridge (MA). Joined RAF, 1924; served in Singapore, 1933–35; in Air Ministry, 1939–40; Fighter Command, 1941; appointed Air Defence Commander, Ceylon, 1942; Air Officer Training, Air HQ, India, 1943–44; Air Officer Commanding No 106 Group, 1945–46; Comdt RAF Staff Coll., Bulstrode and later Andover, 1947–48; Student Imperial Defence Coll., 1949; OC Aeroplane and Armament Experimental Establishment, under the Ministry of Supply, 1950–52; Director-General of Manning, Air Ministry, 1952–55; Commander-in-Chief, Royal Pakistan Air Force, 1955–57; AOC-in-C, RAF Technical Training Comd, 1958–59; Air Mem. for Personnel, Air Council, 1959–61, retired 1962. DL Hampshire, 1965. *Recreations:* writing; formerly sailing (rep. Great Britain in Olympic Games, 1948), skiing. *Clubs:* Royal Air Force; Royal Lymington Yacht; RAF Sailing Association (Adm.).
                                   Died 26 July 1996.

McDONALD, Sir Duncan, Kt 1983; CBE 1976; BSc; FRSE; FEng 1980; CIMgt; SMIEE; Chairman, Northern Engineering Industries plc, 1980–86 (Group Managing Director, 1977–80; Chief Executive, 1980–83); *b* 20 Sept. 1921; *s* of Robert McDonald and Helen Orrick; *m* 1955, Jane Anne Guckian; three *s* one *d. Educ:* Inverkeithing Public Sch.; Dunfermline High Sch.; Edinburgh Univ. (BSc). Grad. App., BTH, Rugby, 1942 45; Transformer Design, Research and Devell, BTH, 1945–54, Bruce Peebles Industries Ltd: Chief Transformer Designer, 1954 59; Chief Engr, 1959; Dir and Chief Engr, 1960; Managing Dir, 1962; Chm. and Chief Exec. (and of A. Reyrolle & Co. Ltd); 1974; Reyrolle Parsons Ltd: Dir, 1973–77; Chief Exec., 1976–77. Director: Barclays Bank (Newcastle), 1980–86; Nat. Nuclear Corp., 1982–86; General Accident, 1983–92; Northern Rock (Scotland), 1986–; Adv. Dir, Barclays Bank (Scotland), 1986–91. Member: Scottish Council Devell and Industry, 1967 (Vice-Pres., 1984–90); Scottish Economic Council, 1975–87. Mem. Court, Heriot-Watt Univ., 1984–90. Pres. Watt Club, 1986–87. FH-WC 1962. Fellow, Scottish Council (Devell and Industry), 1987. FRSA 1965. Hon. FIEE 1984. Hon. DSc Heriot-Watt, 1982; Hon. DEng Newcastle, 1984. *Publications:* various papers to learned socs, nat. and internat. *Recreations:* fishing, golf. *Address:* Duncliffe, Kinellan Road, Edinburgh EH12 6ES. *T:* (0131) 337 4814.   *Died 23 Feb. 1997.*

MACDONALD, His Honour George Grant; a Circuit Judge, 1972–87; *b* 5 March 1921; *s* of late Patrick Macdonald, MB, ChB, MA and Charlotte Primrose (*née* Rintoul); *m* 1967, Mary Dolores (*née* Gerrish), widow of G. G. Taylor; no *c. Educ:* Kelly Coll., Tavistock; Bristol Univ. (LLB Hons). Served War of 1939–45, RN, 1941–46, in Western Approaches, and Mine Sweeping, RNVR. Called to the Bar, Gray's Inn, 1947; practised on Western Circuit, from Albion Chambers, Bristol; Dep. Chm., Dorset QS, apptd 1969; Temp. Recorder of Barnstaple, Dec. 1971. *Recreations:* sailing, bridge, chess. *Address:* 30 Melton Court, Lindsay Road, Poole, Dorset BH13 6BH. *T:* (01202) 757309.   *Died 19 April 2000.*

McDONALD, Graeme Patrick Daniel, OBE 1988; drama consultant; Head of Drama, Ardent Productions, 1994–96; *b* 30 July 1930; *s* of Daniel McDonald and Eileen (*née* McLean); unmarried. *Educ:* St Paul's Sch.; Jesus Coll., Cambridge. Entered TV, 1960; Dir, Granada TV, 1960–65;

BBC Television: Producer, 1966–76: prodns include Thirty Minute Theatre, 1966–67, Wednesday Play, 1967–70 and Play for Today, 1970–76; Head of Drama Series and Serials, 1977–81; Head of Drama Gp, 1981–83; Controller, BBC 2, 1983–87; Man. Dir, Anglia Films Ltd, 1988–94. *Address:* 13 Tryon Street, SW3 3LG.
Died 29 Sept. 1997.

MACDONALD, Prof. James Alexander, BSc (Agric.), PhD (Edinburgh), DSc (St Andrews); Professor of Botany, University of St Andrews, 1961–77, then Emeritus; *b* 17 June 1908; *s* of late James Alexander Macdonald and Jessie Mary Simpson; *m* 1935, Constance Mary Simmie (decd); one *d. Educ:* Inverness Royal Academy; Edinburgh Univ. Steven Scholarship in Agriculture, 1930; DSc with Sykes Gold Medal, 1947. Asst Lecturer in Botany, East of Scot. Coll. of Agriculture, 1932–35; St Andrews University: Lecturer in Botany, 1935–52; Senior Lecturer, 1952–60; Dean, Faculty of Science, 1967–69. Pres., Botanical Soc. of Edinburgh, 1955–57; FRSE 1940 (Council Mem., 1956–59; Vice-Pres., 1961–64). Fellow, Inst. Biology. Silver Jubilee Medal, 1977. *Publications:* Introduction to Mycology, 1951; scientific papers in Trans Brit. Mycol Soc., Annals Applied Biol., Mycologia, Proc. and Trans Bot. Soc. Edinburgh, Proc. and Trans Royal Soc. Edinburgh. *Recreations:* golf, fishing, philately. *Address:* 17 Hepburn Gardens, St Andrews, Fife KY16 9DF. *Club:* Royal and Ancient (St Andrews).
Died 26 April 1997.

MACDONALD, Air Cdre John Charles, CB 1964; CBE 1957; DFC 1940 (Bar 1942); AFC 1941; President, Abbeyfield (Weymouth) Society; *b* 25 Dec. 1910; *s* of late Robert Macdonald; *m* 1952, (Gladys) Joan (*d* 1996), *d* of John Hine, Beaminster, Dorset; two *s. Educ:* Berkhamsted Sch.; RAF Cadet Coll., Cranwell. Commissioned RAF, 1930; served War of 1939–45 in Bomber Command; POW Stalag Luft III, 1942–45, escaped April 1945; commanded RAF Akrotiri during Suez campaign; UK National Military Representative, SHAPE, 1959–61; Comdr RAF East Africa, 1961–64; Min. of Defence, 1964, retd. Chevalier, Légion d'Honneur, 1958; Croix de Guerre, 1958. *Recreations:* golf, sailing, shooting. *Address:* Woodbine Cottage, Osmington, Weymouth, Dorset DT3 6EX. *T:* (01305) 833259.   *Died 26 Sept. 2000.*

MacDONALD, Margaret; *see* Casson, M. MacD., (Lady Casson).

MACDONALD, Ronald John, CEng, MIMechE; Director-General, Royal Ordnance Factories/Production, 1974–79, retired; *b* 2 Nov. 1919; *s* of Ronald Macdonald and Sarah Jane Macdonald; *m* 1944, Joan Margaret Crew; two *s. Educ:* Enfield Grammar Sch.; Enfield Technical Coll. Army service, REME, in India, China and Hong Kong, 1943–47 (Major). Engrg apprenticeship at Royal Small Arms Factory, Enfield, 1936–40; Established Civil Servant, Royal Small Arms Factory, 1948; Royal Ordnance Factory, Radway Green, 1949; ROF Headquarters, Mottingham, 1953; ROF, Blackburn, 1960; Director: ROF, Birtley, Co. Durham, 1964; Ordnance Factories/Ammunition, 1972. *Address:* 72 Lincoln Park, Amersham, Bucks HP7 9HF. *T:* (01494) 727402. *Club:* Army and Navy.   *Died 30 Nov. 1999.*

MACDONALD, Rt Rev. Thomas Brian, OBE 1970; Coadjutor Bishop of Perth, Western Australia, 1964–79, retired; *b* 25 Jan. 1911; *s* of Thomas Joseph Macdonald, MD, and Alice Daisy Macdonald; *m* 1936, Audrey May Collins; three *d. Educ:* Mercers' Sch., Holborn, EC; Aust. Coll. of Theol. (LTh 1932). Deacon 1934, priest 1935, Diocese of Ballarat, Vic; Deacon in charge of All Saints, Ballarat, 1934; Priest in charge of Landsborough, 1935; Rector of Williams, Dio. of Bunbury, 1935–39; Rector of Manjimup, WA, 1939–40; Chaplain, Australian Imperial

Forces, 1940–44 (despatches); Rector of Christ Church, Claremont, Dio. of Perth, 1944–50; Chaplain of Collegiate Sch. of St Peter, Adelaide, S Australia, 1950–58; Dean of Perth, Western Australia, 1959–61; Archdeacon of Perth, 1961–63. Administrator, Diocese of Perth during 1963 and 1969. *Address:* 33 Thomas Street, Nedlands, WA 6009, Australia. *Club:* Weld (Perth).
Died 18 Sept. 1997.

MACDONALD, Air Vice-Marshal Thomas Conchar, CB 1962; AFC 1942; MD; retired; *b* 6 Aug. 1909; *s* of John Macdonald, MA, BSc, and Mary Jane Conchar; *m* 1937, Katharine Cairns Frew. *Educ:* Hermitage Sch.; Glasgow High Sch.; University of Glasgow. MB, ChB 1932; MD 1940; DPH (London) 1949. Joined RAF Medical Br., 1933; served in Iraq, Egypt and England, before 1939; War service included RAF Inst. of Aviation Med., Farnborough, as Asst to Consultant in Applied Physiology, 1939–41; USA and Canada, 1941–42; DPMO (Flying) Fighter Command, 1942–45; Far East, 1945–46 (despatches, AFC); post-war appts include: PMO 2nd TAF (Germany), 1951–53; Dir of Hygiene and Research, Air Min., 1953–56 (Chm. Aero-Medical Panel of Advisory Gp for Research and Develt (AGARD) of NATO); PMO, Bomber Command, 1956–58; PMO Middle East Air Force, 1958–61; PMO Technical Training Command, RAF, 1961–66. Air Vice-Marshal, 1961. QHP 1961–66; CStJ 1961. *Publications:* contributions to various med. jls. *Recreations:* sailing, fishing. *Address:* Wakeners Wood, Midhurst Road, Haslemere, Surrey GU27 2PT. *T:* Haslemere (01428) 643685. *Club:* Royal Air Force.
Died 8 Sept. 1996.

MacDONALD SCOTT, Mary, (Mrs Michael MacDonald Scott); *see* Lavin, M.

McDONAUGH, James, CBE 1970 (OBE 1965); retired 1973; reappointed 1973–75, Director North Europe Department, British Council; *b* 26 July 1912; *s* of late Edward McDonaugh and Christina, *d* of William Bissell; *m* 1944, Mary-Eithné Mitchell, *d* of James Vyvyan Mitchell; three *s* two *d. Educ:* Royal Grammar Sch., Worcester; St Edmund Hall, Oxford (Exhibitioner; MA). Asst Master, Ampleforth Coll., 1935–40; War Service, 1940–45; Lecturer, Graz and Innsbruck Univs, 1947–50; Asst Rep., British Council, Austria, 1950–54; Representative, Malta, 1954–58; Dep. Counsellor (Cultural), Bonn, 1958–59; Dep. Rep., Germany, 1958–61; Dir, Specialist Tours Dept, 1961–65; Asst Controller, Education Div., 1965; Rep., Germany, 1966–73. *Address:* Old Rectory Cottage, Whitestaunton, Chard, Somerset TA20 3DL.   *Died 17 Feb. 1998.*

MacDONELL OF GLENGARRY, Air Cdre (Aeneas Ranald) Donald, CB 1964; DFC 1940; Hereditary 22nd Chief of Glengarry and 12th Titular Lord MacDonell; *b* 15 Nov. 1913; *e s* of late (Æneas) Ranald MacDonell of Glengarry, CBE and Dora Edith, 2nd *d* of Dr H. W. Hartford, Christchurch; *m* 1st, 1940, Diana Dorothy (marr. diss. 1973) (*d* 1980), *yr d* of late Henry Keane, CBE; two *s* one *d*; 2nd, 1973, Lois Eirene Frances, *d* of Rev. Gerald Champion Streatfeild; one *s* one *d. Educ:* Hurstpierpoint Coll.; Royal Air Force Coll., Cranwell. No 54 Fighter Sqdn, 1934; Fleet Air Arm, 1935–37; Flying Instructor, 1938–39; Air Ministry, 1939–40; CO No 64 Fighter Sqdn, 1940–41; POW, 1941–45; Ministry of Defence, 1946–47; HQ Flying Training Command, 1947–49; Chief Flying Instructor, RAF Coll., Cranwell, 1949–51; Ministry of Defence, 1952–54; Senior RAF Instructor, Joint Services Staff Coll., 1954–56; Air Attaché, Moscow, 1956–58; Dir of Management and Work Study, Ministry of Defence, Air Force Dept, 1960–64, retd. Ops Res. Manager, CJB, 1964–67; Personnel Manager, CITB, 1967–73; Dept Head, Industrial Soc., 1973–76; Partner, John Courtis and Partners, 1976–80. Hon. Vice-Pres., Ross and Cromarty

Br., SSAFA, 1983–; Trustee: Clan Donald Lands Trust, 1973–; Finlaggan Trust, 1984–. MIMgt. *Recreations:* ciné photography, art, travel. *Address:* Elonbank, 23 Castle Street, Fortrose, Ross-shire IV10 8TH. *T:* (01381) 620121. *Club:* Royal Air Force. *Died 7 June 1999.*

McDOWELL, Sir Henry (McLorinan), KBE 1964 (CBE 1959); *b* Johannesburg, S Africa, 10 Dec. 1910; *s* of John McDowell and Margaret Elizabeth Bingham; *m* 1939, Norah (*d* 1995), *d* of Walter Slade Douthwaite; one *s* one *d. Educ:* Witwatersrand Univ.; Queen's Coll., Oxford; Yale Univ. Served War of 1939–45, 1 Bn Northern Rhodesia Regt, East Africa and South East Asia, 1940–44. Entered HM Colonial Service (Cadet, Northern Rhodesia), 1938; Clerk, Legislative and Executive Councils, 1945; Assistant Secretary, 1950; Deputy Financial Secretary, 1952. Imperial Defence Coll., 1948; seconded Colonial Office, 1949; Economic and Financial Working Party, in preparation for federation of Rhodesias and Nyasaland, 1953; Federal Treasury, 1954; Secretary, Ministry of Transport, 1955; Secretary, Federal Treasury, 1959–63. Chm., Zimbabwe Board, Barclays Bank Internat. Ltd, 1969–79; Chm. or Dir, other cos in Zimbabwe, 1964–79. Chancellor, Univ. of Rhodesia, 1971–81; Chm. or Mem., governing bodies, educational institutions, Zimbabwe, 1964–79. Hon. LLD Witwatersrand, 1971; Hon. DLitt Rhodesia, 1975. *Recreations:* walking, reading. *Address:* 128 Court Lane, SE21 7EA. *Club:* Harare (Zimbabwe).
Died 10 May 2000.

MacEWEN, Malcolm; journalist; *b* 24 Dec. 1911; *s* of late Sir Alexander MacEwen and Lady (Mary Beatrice) MacEwen; *m* 1st, 1937, Barbara Mary Stebbing, BSc (*d* 1944); (one *d* decd); 2nd, 1947, Mrs Ann Maitland Wheeler; one *d*, and two step *d. Educ:* Edinburgh Univ. (MA, LLB). Member (Lab) Ross and Cromarty CC, 1938–40. Wrote for Daily Worker, mainly as Parliamentary Correspondent, 1943–56; Asst Editor, Architects' Jl, 1956–60; Editor, RIBA Jl, 1964–71; RIBA: Head of Information Services, 1966–66; Publishing Services, 1966–70; Dir, Public Affairs, 1971–72. Leverhulme Res. Fellow, 1972–73; Research Fellow: UCL, 1977–84; Birkbeck Coll., 1985–88. Mem., Exmoor Nat. Park Cttee, 1973–81. Hon. Fellow, RIBA, 1974. *Publications:* Crisis in Architecture, 1974; (ed) Future Landscapes, 1976; (with A. M. MacEwen) National Parks—Cosmetics or Conservation?, 1982; (with G. Sinclair) New Life for the Hills, 1983; (jtly) Countryside Conflicts, 1986; (with A. M. MacEwen) Greenprints for the Countryside? the story of Britain's National Parks, 1987; The Greening of a Red, 1991. *Address:* Manor House, Wootton Courtenay, Somerset TA24 8RD. *T:* Timberscombe (01643) 841325.
Died 11 May 1996.

McFADZEAN, Baron *cr* 1966 (Life Peer), of Woldingham, co. Surrey; **William Hunter McFadzean,** KT 1976; Kt 1960; Director, Midland Bank, 1959–81 (Deputy Chairman, 1968–77); Hon. President, BICC plc, 1973 (Managing Director, 1954–61; Chairman, 1954–73); *b* Stranraer, 17 Dec. 1903; *s* of late Henry and Agnes McFadzean, Stranraer; *m* 1933, Eileen, *e d* of Arthur Gordon, Blundellsands, Lancs; one *s* one *d* (and one adopted *d* decd). *Educ:* Stranraer Academy and High Sch.; Glasgow Univ. Served articles with McLay, McAllister & McGibbon, Chartered Accountants, Glasgow, 1922–27; qualified as Chartered Accountant, 1927; with Chalmers Wade & Co., 1927–32; joined British Insulated Cables Ltd, as Accountant, 1932 (Financial Secretary, 1937; Exec. Manager, 1942); on amalgamation of British Insulated Cables Ltd and Callender's Cable & Construction Co. Ltd, in 1945, appointed to Board of British Insulated Callender's Cables Ltd as Exec. Director (Dep. Chairman, 1947; Chief Exec. Director, 1950), retd 1973; Chairman:

Standard Broadcasting Corp. (UK) Ltd, 1972–79 (Hon. Pres., 1979–83); Home Oil (UK) Ltd, 1972–78; Scurry-Rainbow (UK) Ltd, 1974–78; Deputy Chairman: RTZ/BICC Aluminium Holdings Ltd, 1967–73; National Nuclear Corp., 1973–80; Canada Life Unit Trust Managers Ltd (Chm., 1971–82); Director: Anglesey Aluminium Ltd, 1968–73; Midland Bank Executor and Trustee Co., 1959–67; English Electric Co., 1966–68; Steel Co. of Wales Ltd, 1966–67; Canadian Imperial Bank of Commerce, 1967–74; Canada Life Assurance Co., 1969–79; Canada Life Assurance Co. of GB, 1971–84 (Dep. Chm., 1971–84); Home Oil Co. Ltd, 1972–77; Standard Broadcasting Corp. Ltd, 1976–79. Pres. FBI, 1959–61. Chairman: Council of Industrial Fedns of EFTA, 1960–63; (Founder) Export Council for Europe, 1960–64 (Hon. Pres. 1964–71); Commonwealth Export Council, 1964–66; British Nat. Export Council, 1964–66 (Pres. 1966–68); President: Brit. Electrical Power Convention, 1961–62; Brit. Nuclear Forum, 1964–66; Coal Trade Benevolent Assoc., 1967–68; Electrical and Electronics Industries Benevolent Assoc., 1968–69. Vice-President: Middle East Assoc., 1965; City of London Soc., 1965–72; British/Swedish Chamber of Commerce, 1963–74. Member: Inst. of Directors, 1954–76 (Council, 1954–74); Min. of Labour Adv. Bd on Resettlement of Ex-Regulars, 1957–60; Bd of Trade Adv. Council on ME Trade, 1958–60; MoT Shipping Adv. Panel, 1962–64; Ct of British Shippers' Council, 1964–74 (Pres., 1968–71); Council, Foreign Bondholders, 1968–74; Anglo-Danish Soc., 1965–75 (Chm., 1969–75; Hon. Pres., 1975); Adv. Cttee, Queen's Award for Industry, 1965–67 (Chm., Review Cttee, 1970). CompIEE 1956. JDipMA 1965. Commander Order of Dannebrog (Denmark), 1964; Grand Commander, 1974; Grande Oficial da Ordem do Infante Dom Henrique (Portugal), 1972. *Address:* 16 Lansdown Crescent, Bath, Avon BA1 5EX. *T:* Bath (01225) 335487. *Died 14 Jan. 1996.*

McFARLANE, Prof. James Walter, Professor of European Literature, University of East Anglia, 1964–82, then Emeritus; *b* 12 Dec. 1920; *s* of James and Florence McFarlane; *m* 1944, Lillie Kathleen Crouch; two *s* one *d. Educ:* Bede Grammar Sch., Sunderland; St Catherine's Society, Univ. of Oxford (MA, BLitt 1948). Oxford Soccer blue, 1947. War Service, Intell. Corps, 1941–46 (Major). Lectr and Sen. Lectr, Dept of German and Scandinavian Studies, King's Coll., Univ. of Durham, later Univ. of Newcastle upon Tyne, 1947–63; University of East Anglia: Founding Dean of European Studies, 1964–68; Public Orator, 1964–68, 1974–75, 1978–79; Pro-Vice-Chancellor, 1968–71; Professorial Fellow, 1982–86. Vis. Prof., Univ. of Auckland, NZ, 1967; Herbert F. Johnson Vis. Res. Prof., Inst. for Res. in Humanities, Univ. of Wisconsin-Madison, 1983–84. Mem., BBC Gen. Adv. Council, 1970–75; Chm., East Anglia Regional Adv. Council, 1970–75; Chm., Hunworth Crafts Trust, 1973–77; Mem. Exec., Eastern Arts Assoc., 1977 82. Founder Trustee, Norwich Puppet Theatre, 1979; Chm., The Wells Centre, Norfolk, 1981–88. Editor-at-large, Scandinavica: an International Journal of Scandinavian Studies, 1991– (Editor, 1975–90); Man. Editor, Norvik Press, 1985–. Leverhulme Faculty Fellow in European Studies, 1971–72; Brit. Acad. Wolfson Fellow. Fellow, Det Norske Videnskaps-Akademie, Oslo, 1977; Corresp. Mem., Svenska Litteratursällskapet i Finland, Helsinki, 1977; Foreign Member: Royal Norwegian Soc. of Sciences and Letters, 1982; Royal Danish Acad. of Sciences and Letters, 1983. Hon. Mem., Phi Beta Kappa, 1984. Hon. DLitt: Loughborough, 1990; Sunderland, 1995. Commander's Cross, Royal Norwegian Order of St Olav, 1975. *Publications:* Ibsen and the Temper of Norwegian Literature, 1960; Discussions of Ibsen, 1962; Henrik Ibsen, 1970; (with Malcolm Bradbury) Modernism: European

Literature 1890–1930, 1976; Ibsen and Meaning, 1989; (ed. and trans.) The Oxford Ibsen, 1960–77: vol. 1, Early Plays, 1970; vol. 2, The Vikings at Helgeland, Love's Comedy, The Pretenders, 1962; vol. 3, Brand, Peer Gynt, 1972; vol. 4, The League of Youth, Emperor and Galilean, 1963; vol. 5, Pillars of Society, A Doll's House, Ghosts, 1961; vol. 6, An Enemy of the People, The Wild Duck, Rosmersholm, 1960; vol. 7, The Lady from the Sea, Hedda Gabler, The Master Builder, 1966; vol. 8, Little Eyolf, John Gabriel Borkman, When We Dead Awaken, 1977; (ed. and trans. with Janet Garton) Slaves of Love and other Norwegian short stories, 1982; (ed with Harald Næss) Knut Hamsun's Letters, vol. 1, 1990, vol. 2, 1998; (ed and contrib.) The Cambridge Companion to Henrik Ibsen, 1994; *translations:* Hamsun's Pan, 1955; Hamsun's Wayfarers, 1980; Obstfelder's A Priest's Diary, 1988; *festschrift:* (ed J. Garton) Facets of European Modernism: essays in honour of James McFarlane, 1985. *Recreation:* cyber-adventuring. *Address:* The Croft, Stody, Melton Constable, Norfolk NR24 2EE. *T:* (01263) 860505.
Died 9 Aug. 1999.

McGLASHAN, Prof. Maxwell Len, FRSC; Professor of Chemistry and Head of the Department of Chemistry, University College London, 1974–89, then Professor Emeritus; Hon. Research Fellow, since 1989; *b* 1 April 1924; *s* of late Leonard Day McGlashan and Margaret Cordelia McGlashan; *m* 1947, Susan Jane, *d* of late Col H. E. Crosse, MC, OBE, and Mrs D. Crosse, Patoka Station, Hawkes Bay, NZ. *Educ:* Greymouth, NZ; Canterbury Univ. Coll., Christchurch, NZ; Univ. of Reading. MSc (NZ) 1946, PhD (Reading) 1951, DSc (Reading) 1962. Asst Lectr, 1946–48, Lectr, 1948–53, Sen. Lectr, 1953, in Chemistry, at Canterbury Univ. Coll., Christchurch, NZ; Sims Empire Scholar, 1949–52; Lectr in Chem., Univ. of Reading, 1954–61; Reader in Chem., Univ. of Reading, 1962–64; Prof. of Physical Chem., Univ. of Exeter, 1964–74 (Dean, Faculty of Science, 1973–74). Mem., 1963–65, Vice-Chm., 1965–67, Chm., 1967–71, Commn on Physicochemical Symbols, Terminology, and Units; Chairman: Interdivl Cttee on Nomenclature and Symbols, Internat. Union of Pure and Applied Chem., 1971–76; Technical Cttee (Quantities, Units, Symbols, and Conversion Factors), ISO, 1996–; Member: Royal Society Symbols Cttee, 1963–88; BSI's Tech. Cttee on physical quantities and units, 1963– (Chm., 1978–96); Council, Faraday Soc., 1965–67; Metrication Bd, 1969–80; Comité Consultatif des Unités (Metre Convention), 1969–; Council, Chem. Soc., 1970–73; SRC Chem. Cttee, 1974–76; Data Compilation Cttee, 1974–77; Res. Cttee, British Gas Corp., 1979–90; Trustee, Ramsay Meml Fellowships Trust, 1982–96 (Chm. Adv. Council, 1975–89). Editor, Jl of Chemical Thermodynamics, 1969–95. Hon. Fellow, UCL, 1991. *Publications:* Physicochemical Quantities and Units, 1968 (Royal Inst. of Chem.), 2nd edn 1971; Chemical Thermodynamics, 1979; papers on chemical thermodynamics and statistical mechanics in Proc. Royal Soc., Trans Faraday Soc., Jl Chem. Thermodynamics, etc. *Recreations:* climbing in the Alps, gardening, the theatre. *Address:* Patoka, Fairwarp, Uckfield, E Sussex TN22 3DT. *T:* (01825) 712172. *Club:* Athenæum.
Died 18 July 1997.

MACGOUGAN, John; General Secretary, National Union of Tailors and Garment Workers, 1969–79; *b* 21 Aug. 1913; *m* 1941, Lizzie Faulkner; three *s* one *d. Educ:* various Northern Ireland schs; Technical Sch.; Correspondence courses. Accountancy profession, 1930–45; Irish Officer, NUTGW, in charge of all Irish affairs, 1945–69. Contested (Irish Labour) N Ireland Parly Elections, Oldpark 1938, Falls Div. 1951; Westminster Parly Election, South Down 1950. Member: Belfast Corporation, 1949–58; Executive, Irish TUC, 1950–69 (Pres. 1957–58 and 1963–64); TUC Gen. Council,

1970–79; MSC, 1977–79; Central Arbitration Cttee, 1977–83; Economic and Social Cttee, EEC, 1978–80. Irish and UK Rep., ILO, 1962–85. *Recreations:* proletarian pastimes. *Address:* 96 Whalley Drive, Bletchley, Milton Keynes, Bucks MK3 6HU. *T:* (01908) 372174.
Died 12 Dec. 1998.

McGREGOR OF DURRIS, Baron *cr* 1978 (Life Peer), of Hampstead in co. of Greater London; **Oliver Ross McGregor;** Chairman, Press Complaints Commission, 1991–94; Professor of Social Institutions in the University of London, 1964–85; Head of Department of Sociology, at Bedford College, 1964–77; Joint Director, Rowntree Legal Research Unit, 1966–84; *b* 25 Aug. 1921; *s* of late William McGregor and Anne Olivia Ross; *m* 1944, Nellie Weate; three *s. Educ:* Worksop Coll.; University of Aberdeen; London School of Economics (Hon. Fellow 1977). Temp. civil servant, War Office and Ministry of Agriculture, 1940–44; Asst Lecturer and Lecturer in Economic History, University of Hull, 1945–47; Lecturer, Bedford Coll., London, 1947–60; Reader in University of London, 1960–64; Simon Senior Research Fellow, University of Manchester, 1959–60. Fellow of Wolfson Coll., Oxford, 1972–75; Dir, Centre for Socio-Legal Studies, Univ. of Oxford, 1972–75. Member: Cttee on Enforcement of Judgment Debts, 1965; Cttee on Statutory Maintenance Limits, 1966; Cttee on Land Use (Recreation and Leisure), 1967; National Parks Commission, 1966–68; Independent Television Authority's General Advisory Council, 1967–73; Countryside Commission, 1968–80; Legal Aid Adv. Cttee, 1969–78; Cttee on One-Parent Families, 1969–74; Chairman: Royal Commn on Press, 1975–77 (Mem., 1974); Advertising Standards Authy, 1980–90; Forest Philharmonic Soc., 1975–96. President: Nat. Council for One Parent Families, 1975–91; Nat. Assoc. of Citizens' Advice Bureaux, 1981–86. Chm., Reuters Founders Share Co., 1987– (Independent Trustee, 1984–). Hon. Mem., Fédération Internationale des Editeurs de Journaux, 1992. Lectures: Fawcett Meml, Bedford Coll., 1966; James Seth Meml, Edinburgh Univ., 1968; Hobhouse Meml, LSE, 1971; Maccabaean in Jurisprudence, British Acad., 1973; Hamlyn, Univ. of Kent, 1979; Eleanor Rathbone Meml, Durham Univ., 1979; Ian Gulland, Goldsmiths' Coll., 1980; 150th Anniversary of Univ. of London, LSE, 1986; Tom Olsen, St Bride's Church, 1991; Harold W. Andersen, Nat. Press Club, Washington, 1995. Hon. LLD Bristol, 1986. *Publications:* Divorce in England, 1957; (ed) Lord Ernle, English Farming Past and Present, 6th edn 1960; (jtly) Separated Spouses, 1970; Social History and Law Reform, 1981; various papers in British Journal of Sociology and other journals. *Address:* Far End, Wyldes Close, NW11 7JB. *T:* (0181) 458 2856, *Fax:* (0181) 455 3309. *Club:* Garrick.
Died 10 Nov. 1997.

MacGREGOR, Geddes; *see* MacGregor, J. G.

McGREGOR, Ian Alexander, FRCS, FRCSGlas; Director, West of Scotland Regional Plastic and Oral Surgery Unit, 1980–86; *b* 6 June 1921; *s* of late Walker McGregor and Mary Duncan (*née* Thompson); *m* 1st, 1950, Christeen Isabel Mackay (decd); three *s*; 2nd, 1970, Frances Mary Vint. *Educ:* North Kelvinside Secondary Sch.; Glasgow Univ. (MB, ChB 1944; ChM 1972). FRCS 1950, FRFPSG 1951, FRCSGlas; Hon. FRACS 1977; Hon. FRCSI 1984; Hon. FRCSE 1985; Hon. FACS 1986. Served RAMC, 1945–48. Consultant Surgeon, Glasgow Royal Infirmary, 1957–59; Consultant Plastic Surgeon, Greater Glasgow Health Bd, 1959–80. Visitor, 1982–84, Pres., 1984–86, RCPSGlas. Hon. DSc Glasgow, 1986. *Publications:* Fundamental Techniques of Plastic Surgery, 1960, 9th edn (with A. D. McGregor) 1995; (with W. H. Reid) Plastic Surgery for Nurses, 1966; (with Frances M. McGregor) Cancer of the Face and Mouth, 1986; scientific papers to surgical jls on reconstructive aspects of plastic surgery. *Recreations:* music, literature, golf. *Address:* 7 Ledcameroch Road, Bearsden, Glasgow G61 4AB. *T:* (0141) 942 3419.   *Died 13 April 1998.*

MacGREGOR, Sir Ian (Kinloch), Kt 1986; Partner, McFarland, Dewey & Co., New York, since 1991; *b* 21 Sept. 1912; *m* Sibyl Spencer (*d* 1996); one *s* one *d*. *Educ:* George Watson's Coll., Edinburgh; Hillhead High Sch., Glasgow; Univ. of Glasgow. BSc (1st cl. Hons); Royal Coll. of Science and Technol. (later Univ. of Strathclyde) (Dip. with distinction). Pres. and Chief Exec., 1966, Chm., 1969–77, Amax Inc. (Hon. Chm., 1977–82); Deputy Chairman, BL Ltd, 1977–80; Chm. and Chief Exec., BSC, 1980–83; Chm., NCB, 1983–86. Chm., Alumax, 1973–82; non-exec. Dir, Lazard Brothers & Co., 1986–90. President of the International Chamber of Commerce, Paris, 1978. Hon. degrees from Univs. of Glasgow (LLD), Strathclyde (LLD), Denver (LLD), Montana State (DEng), Rochester (LLD), Colorado Sch. of Mines (DEng), Wyoming (LLD), and Tri-State Coll., Indiana (DSc). Jackling Medal, Amer. Inst. of Mining and Metallurgical Engrs; John Fritz Gold Medal, Amer. Inst. of Mining, Metallurgical and Petroleum Engrs, 1981; Bessemer Gold Medal, Metals Soc., London, 1983. Chevalier, Légion d'Honneur, 1972. *Publication:* The Enemies Within, 1986. *Address:* 21 Mount Wyndham Drive, Hamilton Parish, CR 04, Bermuda.
                                                    Died 13 April 1998.

MacGREGOR, Prof. (John) Geddes, DèsL, DPhil, DD; FRSL 1948; Distinguished Professor of Philosophy, University of Southern California, 1966–75, then Emeritus; Dean of Graduate School of Religion, 1960–66; Canon Theologian of St Paul's Cathedral, Los Angeles, 1968–74; *b* 13 Nov. 1909; *o s* of late Thomas and Blanche Geddes MacGregor, Angus; US citizen, 1957; *m* 1941, Elizabeth (*d* 1994), *e d* of late Archibald McAllister, Edinburgh; one *s* one *d*. *Educ:* Univ. of Edinburgh (BD 1939; LLB 1943); Queen's Coll., Oxford (DPhil 1945); Sorbonne (DèsL); Univ. of Heidelberg; BD, DD Oxon Ordained Minister, Ch of Scotland, 1939; Senior Assistant to Dean of Chapel Royal in Scotland, at St Giles' Cathedral, Edinburgh, 1939–41; served in Civil Defence, War of 1939–45; Minister, Trinity Church, Glasgow, S1, 1941–49; Assistant to Prof. of Logic and Metaphysics, Edinburgh Univ., 1947–49; first holder of Rufus Jones Chair of Philosophy and Religion, Bryn Mawr, USA, 1949–60. Ordained deacon and priest, Episcopal Ch, USA, 1968. Examiner: Swarthmore Coll., USA, 1950, 1953, 1955–57; Hebrew Union Coll., USA, 1959, 1961; Visiting Professor: Univ. of British Columbia, 1963, 1966, 1973; Hebrew Union Coll., 1964–65; Univ. of Santa Clara, 1968; World Campus Afloat (Orient, 1974; Mediterranean, 1975); McGill Univ., Montreal, 1976; Inst. for Shipboard Educn (round-the-world-voyage), 1977; Univ. of Iowa, 1979; Univ. of Saskatchewan, 1979; Visiting Fellow: Dept of Religious Studies, Yale Univ., 1967–68; Coll. of Preachers, Washington Nat. Cathedral, 1991; occasional lectr at many US and Canadian univs (Birks, Montreal, 1976; Warren, Dubuque, 1979; Arnett, Kansas, 1982; Fairchild, Miss, 1982); Vis. Lectr, Rikkyo Univ., Tokyo, 1981; Guest Lectr, Univ. Complutense, Madrid, 1992. Program Speaker, Parliament of the World's Religions, 1993. Dir, Amer. Friends of the Univ. of Edinburgh, 1983–86; Hon. Fellow, Emporia State Univ., Kansas, 1982. Diplomate, Internat. Soc. for Philosophical Enquiry, 1986. Special Preacher: St Paul's Cathedral, London, 1969; Westminster Abbey, 1970. Regent, American-Scottish Foundation, Inc., NY; Hon. Chaplain and Historian, St Andrew's Soc. of LA, 1981 (Pres., 1987–88); Hon. Canon of San Diego, California, 1987. Hon. LHD Hebrew Union, 1978. Hon. Phi Kappa Phi, 1972 (Distinguished Award, 1982). Hon. Assoc., Order of Agape and Reconciliation, 1988. California Literature

Award (Gold Medal, non-fiction), 1964; Medallist, Nat. Soc. of the Sons of the American Revolution, 1989; Distinguished Emeritus Award, Univ. of Southern California, 1993. *Publications:* Aesthetic Experience in Religion, 1947; Christian Doubt, 1951; Les Frontières de la Morale et de la Religion, 1952; From a Christian Ghetto, 1954; The Vatican Revolution, 1957; The Tichborne Impostor, 1957; The Thundering Scot, 1957; Corpus Christi, 1959; Introduction to Religious Philosophy, 1959; The Bible in the Making, 1959; The Coming Reformation, 1960; The Hemlock and the Cross, 1963; God Beyond Doubt, 1966; A Literary History of the Bible, 1968; The Sense of Absence, 1968; So Help Me God, 1970; Philosophical Issues in Religious Thought, 1973; The Rhythm of God, 1974; He Who Lets Us Be, 1975, rev. edn 1987; Reincarnation in Christianity, 1978 (trans. German as vol. I, Reinkarnation und Karma im Christentum, 1985); Gnosis, 1979; Scotland Forever Home, 1980, rev. edn 1984; The Nicene Creed, 1981; Reincarnation as a Christian Hope, 1982; The Gospels as a Mandala of Wisdom, 1982; The Christening of Karma, 1984 (trans. German as vol. II, Reinkarnation und Karma im Christentum, 1986); Apostles Extraordinary, 1986; (ed) Immortality and Human Destiny, 1986; Angels: ministers of grace, 1988; Dictionary of Religion and Philosophy, 1989; Scotland: an intimate portrait, 1990; Images of Afterlife: beliefs from antiquity to modern times, 1992 (trans. French as Enquête sur l'existence de la réincarnation, 1995). *Recreations:* manual labour; latterly oftener reading, music. *Address:* 876 Victoria Avenue, Los Angeles, CA 90005–3751, USA. *T:* (213) 9384826. *Clubs:* Athenæum, English-Speaking Union, Royal Commonwealth Society; Union Society (Oxford); Automobile (Los Angeles).   *Died 9 Oct. 1998.*

MACGREGOR, His Honour John Roy; a Circuit Judge, 1974–87; Honorary Recorder of Margate, 1972–79; *b* Brooklyn, NY, 9 Sept. 1913; 4th *s* of Charles George McGregor, Jamaica and New York. *Educ:* Bedford School. Called to the Bar, Gray's Inn, 1939; Inner Temple (*ad eundem*), 1968; Holker Sen. Scholar, Gray's Inn, 1947. Served in Royal Artillery, 1939–46; RA (TA) and Special Air Service (TA), 1950–61. Dep. Chm., Cambridgeshire and Isle of Ely QS, 1967–71; a Recorder, 1972–74. Legal Assessor to Gen. Optical Council, 1972–74. *Address:* Nether Gaulrig, Yardley Hastings, Northampton NN7 1HD. *T:* (01604) 696861. *Club:* Special Forces.
                                                    Died 31 Oct. 1997.

MacGUIGAN, Hon. Mark Rudolph; PC (Can.) 1980; PhD, JSD; **Hon. Mr Justice MacGuigan;** Judge, Federal Court of Appeal, Canada, since 1984; *b* 17 Feb. 1931; *s* of Hon. Mark R. MacGuigan and Agnes V. Trainor; *m* 1961, Maryellen Symons; two *s* one *d*; *m* 1987, Judge Patricia Dougherty, Oklahoma Ct of Appeals. *Educ:* Queen Square Sch.; Prince of Wales (Jun.) Coll.; St Dunstan's Univ., Charlottetown (BA *summa cum laude*); Univ. of Toronto (MA, PhD); Osgoode Hall Law Sch. (LLB); Columbia Univ. (LLM, JSD). Admitted to Law Soc. of Upper Canada, 1958. Asst Prof. of Law, 1960–63, and Associate Prof. of Law, 1963–66, Univ. of Toronto; Prof. of Law, Osgoode Hall Law Sch., 1966–67; Dean, Faculty of Law, Univ. of Windsor, 1967–68. MP for Windsor–Walkerville, Ont, 1968–84; Parliamentary Secretary: to Minister of Manpower and Immigration, 1972–74; to Minister of Labour, 1974–75; Opposition Critic of Solicitor Gen., 1979–80; Sec. of State for External Affairs, 1980–82; Minister of Justice, 1982–84. Chairman: House of Commons Special Cttee on Statutory Instruments, 1968–69; Standing Cttee on Justice and Legal Affairs, 1975–79; Sub-Cttee on Penitentiary System in Canada, 1976–77; Co-Chairman, Special Jt Cttee on Constitution of Canada, 1970–72 and 1978. Hon. LLD: Univ. of PEI, 1971; St Thomas Univ., 1981; Law Soc. of Upper Canada,

1983; Univ. of Windsor, Ont, 1983; Univ. of York, Ont, 1996. *Publications:* Cases and Materials on Creditors' Rights, 2nd edn 1967; Jurisprudence: readings and cases, 2nd edn 1966; Abortion, Conscience and Democracy, 1994. *Recreations:* running, tennis, skiing, swimming. *Address:* 23 Linden Terrace, Ottawa, ON K1S 1Z1, Canada. *Club:* Cercle Universitaire (Ottawa).
Died 12 Jan. 1998.

McGURK, Colin Thomas, OBE 1971 (MBE 1963); HM Diplomatic Service, retired; *b* 9 July 1922; *m* 1946, Ella Taylor; (one *s* decd). *Educ:* St Mary's Coll., Middlesbrough. Served in Army, 1942–45. HM Foreign (subseq. Diplomatic) Service; served in British Embassies, Cairo, Addis Ababa, Ankara; 3rd Sec., HM Legation, Sofia, 1953–55; 2nd Sec. (Commercial), Athens, 1956–58; FO, 1958–62; HM Consul, Stanleyville, 1962; 1st Sec., Yaoundé, Brussels and Kuwait, 1962–70; Commercial Counsellor, Kuwait, 1971–72; Commercial Inspector, FCO, 1972–75; Counsellor (Economic and Commercial), New Delhi, 1975–77 and Canberra, 1977–81. Member: Burnham Art Club, 1993–; Nat. Acrylic Painters Assoc, 1993–. *Recreations:* computer programming, painting, sailing. *Address:* 113 High Street, Burnham-on-Crouch, Essex CM0 8AH. *T:* (01621) 782467. *Club:* Royal Burnham Yacht.
Died 28 Aug. 2000.

McGURK, Prof. Harry, PhD; FBPsS; Director, Australian Institute of Family Studies, since 1994; *b* 23 Feb. 1936; *s* of Harry McGurk and Katherine (*née* Gallagher); *m* 1961, Elizabeth Lockhart Hannah (marr. diss. 1995); one *d.* *Educ:* Univ. of Glasgow (Dip of Qualification in Social Work, 1961); Univ. of Strathclyde (BA 1968; PhD 1971). CPsychol 1987; FBPsS 1980. Probation Officer, Edinburgh, 1961–63; Relief Manager, Educn Authy of E Nigeria, 1963–64; Vis. Res. Fellow, Educnl Testing Service, Princeton, 1971–72; Lectr, New School for Social Research, NY, 1971–72; University of Surrey: Lectr in Psychology, 1972–76; Sen. Lectr, 1976–86; Prof. of Develtl Psychology, 1986–90; Dir, Thomas Coram Res. Univ., Inst. of Educn, London Univ., 1990–94. FRSocMed 1994. *Publications:* Growing and Changing: a primer of developmental psychology, 1975; Ecological Factors in Human Development, 1976; Issues in Childhood Social Development: contemporary perspectives, 1992; numerous papers and other pubns. *Recreations:* music, theatre, cycling, tennis, hill climbing. *Address:* 7 Saxonwood Court, South Frankston, Vic 3199, Australia.
Died 17 April 1998.

McHARDY, Rev. Prof. William Duff, CBE 1990; Regius Professor of Hebrew, Oxford University, and Student of Christ Church, 1960–78; *b* 26 May 1911; *o s* of late W. D. McHardy, Cullen, Banffshire; *m* 1941, Vera (*d* 1984), *y d* of late T. Kemp, York; one *d.* *Educ:* Fordyce Academy; Aberdeen Univ. (MA, BD); Edinburgh Univ. (MA); St John's Coll., Oxford (DPhil 1943). Research Fellow in Syriac, Selly Oak Colleges, Birmingham, 1942; Lecturer in Aramaic and Syriac, University of Oxford, 1945; ordained Minister, Ch of Scotland, 1947; Samuel Davidson Professor of Old Testament Studies in the University of London, 1948–60. Examiner, Universities of Aberdeen, Cambridge, Durham, Edinburgh, Leeds, London, Oxford and University Colleges of the Gold Coast/Ghana and Ibadan. Hon. Curator of Mingana Collection of Oriental Manuscripts, 1947. Grinfield Lecturer on the Septuagint, Oxford, 1959–61. Dep. Dir, 1968, Jt Dir, 1971, New English Bible; Dir, Revised English Bible, 1973–90. Burgess, Royal Burgh of Cullen, 1975. Hon. DD Aberdeen, 1958. Hon. Fellow, Selly Oak Colleges, 1980. *Publications:* articles in journals. *Address:* 2 Ogilvie Park, Cullen, Banffshire AB56 2XZ. *T:* (01542) 841008.
Died 9 April 2000.

MACHIN, Arnold, OBE 1965; RA 1956 (ARA 1947); FRBS 1955; sculptor; Master of Sculpture, Royal Academy School, 1958–67; Tutor, Royal College of Art, 1951–58; *b* 30 Sept. 1911; *s* of William James Machin, Stoke-on-Trent; *m* 1949, Patricia, *d* of late Lt-Col Henry Newton; one *s.* *Educ:* Stoke School of Art; Derby School of Art; Royal College of Art. Silver Medal and Travelling Scholarship for Sculpture, 1940. Two works in terracotta, St John the Baptist and The Annunciation, purchased by Tate Gallery, 1943; Spring terracotta purchased by President and Council of Royal Academy under terms of Chantrey Bequest, 1947; designed: new coin effigy, 1964, 1967 (decimal coinage); definitive issue of postage stamp, 1967; Silver Wedding commemorative crown, 1972; commemorative Silver Jubilee crown, 1977. *Recreations:* music, garden design. *Address:* 4 Avenue Studios, Sydney Close, SW3 6HW; Garmelow Manor, near Eccleshall, Staffordshire ST21 6HL.
Died 9 March 1999.

McILVENNA, Maj.-Gen. John Antony, CB 1980; Director of Army Legal Services, 1978–80, retired; *b* 10 Dec. 1919; *s* of Joseph Henry McIlvenna and Dorothy (*née* Brown); *m* Dr Hildegard Paula Gertrud Overlack; one *s* one *d.* *Educ:* Royal Grammar School, Newcastle upon Tyne; Hymers Coll., Hull; Durham Univ. LLB 1940; admitted Solicitor, 1947. Private, KOYLI; 2nd Lieut, DLI, 1941; despatches 1945; Captain, Army Legal Services, 1950; served in Hong Kong, Aden, Egypt, Libya and BAOR; Maj.-Gen. and Dir, newly formed Army Legal Corps, 1978. Chm. and Dir, United Services Catholic Assoc., 1979–81, Vice-Pres., 1981–. *Recreations:* swimming, music, history. *Address:* Westfield, Biddenden, Kent TN27 8BB. *Club:* Army and Navy.
Died 18 Dec. 1997.

McINTOSH, Sir Malcolm (Kenneth), AC 1998; Kt 1996; CPEng; FTSE, FRAeS, FIEAust; Chief Executive, Commonwealth Scientific and Industrial Research Organisation, since 1996; *b* Melbourne, 14 Dec. 1945; *s* of Kenneth Stuart McIntosh and Valerie McIntosh (*née* MacKenzie); *m* 1971, Margaret Beatrice (*née* Stevens); three *s* one *d.* *Educ:* Telopea Park; Australian National Univ. (BSc Hons, PhD Physics). Research Scientist, Aust. Weapons Res. Estabt, 1970–72; Aust. Army, 1972–74 (Major); Aust. Economic Ministries, 1974–82; Australian Department of Defence, 1982–90: Chief of Defence Production, 1987; Dep. Sec., Acquisition and Logistics, 1988; Sec., Aust. Dept of Industry, Technology and Commerce, 1990; Chief of Defence Procurement, MoD, UK, 1991–96. FRAeS 1995; CPEng, FIEAust 1996; FTSE 1997. US Distinguished Public Service Medal, 1996. *Address:* CSIRO, Limestone Avenue, Canberra, ACT 2600, Australia. *Fax:* (6) 2766628.
Died 7 Feb. 2000.

McINTYRE, Robert Douglas; JP; Hon. Consultant, Stirling Royal Infirmary (Consultant Chest Physician, Stirlingshire and Clackmannan, 1951–79); Member, Stirling and Clackmannan Hospital Board, 1964–74; *b* 15 Dec. 1913; 3rd *s* of Rev. John E. McIntyre and Catherine, *d* of Rev. William Morison, DD; *m* 1954, Letitia, *d* of Alexander Macleod; one *s.* *Educ:* Hamilton Acad.; Daniel Stewart's Coll.; University of Edinburgh (MB, ChB); DPH Glasgow. MP (Scottish Nationalist), Motherwell and Wishaw, April-July 1945; contested (SNP): Motherwell, 1950; Perth and E Perthshire, 1951, 1955, 1959, 1964; W Stirlingshire, 1966, 1970; Stirling, Falkirk and Grangemouth, by-election 1971, Feb. and Oct. 1974. Chm., 1948–56, Pres., 1958–80, Scottish National Party. Mem., Stirling Town Council (Hon. Treas., 1958–64; Provost, 1967–75); Chancellor's Assessor, Stirling Univ. Court, 1979. Fellow, Scottish Council, 1987. Freeman, Royal Burgh of Stirling, 1975. DUniv Stirling, 1976. JP Co. Stirling. *Publications:* numerous articles on Scottish, political and medical subjects, including regular contribs to the Scots

Independent, *Recreation:* yachting. *Address:* 8 Gladstone Place, Stirling FK8 2NN. *T:* (01786) 73456. *Clubs:* Scottish Arts (Edinburgh); Stirling and County.
Died 2 Feb. 1998.

McKAIG, Adm. Sir (John) Rae, KCB 1973; CBE 1966; *b* 24 April 1922; *s* of late Sir John McKaig, KCB, DSO, and Lady (Annie Wright) McKaig (*née* Lee); *m* 1945, Barbara Dawn, *d* of Dr F. K. Marriott, MC, Yoxford, Suffolk; two *s* one *d*. *Educ:* Loretto Sch. Joined RN as Special Entry Cadet, 1939; served in cruisers and destroyers in Home and Mediterranean Waters, 1940–43; in Amphibious Force S at invasion of Normandy, 1944; in coastal forces until 1945; qual. in Communications, 1945; Commander, 1952; Captain, 1959; served as Dep. to Chief Polaris Exec., 1963–66; comd HM Signal Sch., 1966–68; Rear-Adm., 1968; Asst Chief of Naval Staff (Operational Requirements), 1968–70; Vice-Adm., 1970; Flag Officer, Plymouth, and Port Admiral, Devonport, 1970–73; Adm., 1973; UK Mil. Rep. to NATO, 1973–75. Chm. and Chief Exec., Gray Mackenzie & Co., 1983–86; Dir, Inchcape plc, 1981–86. Mem., Royal Patriotic Fund Corp., 1978–. Dir, ALVA, 1989–92. *Recreations:* offshore sailing, shooting, fishing. *Clubs:* Army and Navy, Royal Ocean Racing. *Died 7 Jan. 1996.*

MACKAY, Alastair, CMG 1966; *b* 27 Sept. 1911; *s* of late Alexander Mackay; *m* 1st, 1939, Janetta Brown Ramsay (*d* 1973); one *s* one *d*; 2nd, 1975, Edith Whicher. *Educ:* George Heriot's Sch.; Edinburgh Univ.; Berlin Univ. Entered HM Treasury, 1940; Member, UK Treasury and Supply Delegation, Washington, 1951–54; seconded to Foreign Service Inspectorate, 1957–59; Financial Adviser to the British High Commissioner in India, 1963–66; Under-Sec., HM Treasury, 1967–71; Financial and Development Sec., Gibraltar, 1971–75. *Recreation:* the garden. *Address:* 12 The Park Close, Eastbourne, East Sussex BN20 8AG. *Died 13 Feb. 1999.*

McKAY, Maj.-Gen. Alexander Matthew, CB 1975; FEng 1984; Secretary, Institution of Mechanical Engineers, 1976–87; *b* 14 Feb. 1921; *s* of Colin and Anne McKay; *m* 1949, Betty Margaret Lee; one *s* one *d* (and one *d* decd). *Educ:* Esplanade House Sch.; RN Dockyard Sch.; Portsmouth Polytechnic. FIEE, FIMechE; psc, sm; MASME. Served War of 1939–45; Palestine, 1945–48 (despatches); Malaya, 1954–56; with 16th Indep Para. Bde Gp and 6th Airborne Div.; Staff Coll., Quetta, 1954; staff appts include GSO2, DAA&QMG, DAQMG, AQMG; Dir, Elect. and Mech. Engrg, Army, 1972–75; Col Comdt, REME, 1974–80. 2nd Lieut, 1943; Lieut 1944; Captain 1944; Major 1947; Lt-Col 1960; Col 1966; Brigadier 1968; Maj.-Gen. 1972. Gen. Sec., IChemE, 1975–76; Mem. Council, IEE, 1973–76. Clayton Lectr, IMechE, 1975. Chm., Stocklake Hldgs 1976–87; Vice-Chm., Mechanical Engrg Publications Ltd, 1976–87. Pres. and Chm., Winchester Div., SSAFA, 1988–; Pres., Itchen Valley Br., RBL, 1996–. FRSE 1985. Freeman, City of London, 1984; Liveryman, Engineers' Co., 1984–88. *Publications:* papers in Proceedings IMechE and REME Institution. *Recreations:* fly fishing, gardening, restoring antique furniture. *Address:* Church Cottage, Martyr Worthy, near Winchester, Hants SO21 1DY.
Died 28 March 1999.

MACKAY, A(rthur) Stewart, ROI 1949; Teacher, Hammersmith College of Art, 1960–68, retired; *b* 25 Feb. 1909; British. *Educ:* Wilson's Grammar Sch.; Regent Street Polytechnic School of Art. Art Master, Regent Street Polytechnic School of Art, 1936, Assistant Lecturer, 1936–60. Served War of 1939–45: enlisted Army, Jan. 1942; released with rank of Captain, 1946. Exhibitor: RA (44 pictures exhibited); Paris Salon; ROI; RBA; Leicester Galleries; Imperial War Museum; Royal Scottish Academy; New York. *Publications:* How to Make Lino

Cuts, 1935; articles for Artist and Kent Life, 1953, 1963. *Recreations:* reading, writing, archaeology. *Address:* 4 Dog Kennel Hill, East Dulwich, SE22 8AA.
Died 6 May 1998.

McKAY, Very Rev. Frederick; *see* McKay, Very Rev. J. F.

MACKAY, Sir (George Patrick) Gordon, Kt 1966; CBE 1962; Director, World Bank, 1975–78; Member, Board of Crown Agents, 1980–82; *b* 12 Nov. 1914; *s* of Rev. Adam Mackay and Katie Forrest (*née* Lawrence); *m* 1954, Margaret Esmé Martin; one *s* two *d*. *Educ:* Gordon Sch., Huntly; Aberdeen Univ. Joined Kenya and Uganda Railways and Harbours (later East African Railways and Harbours), 1938; Chief Asst to Gen. Manager, 1948; Chief Operating Supt, 1954; Dep. General Manager, 1960; General Manager, 1961–64; with World Bank, 1965–78. FCIT (MInstT 1961). OStJ 1964. *Recreation:* golf. *Address:* Well Cottage, Sandhills, Brook, Surrey GU8 5UP. *T:* (01428) 682549. *Club:* Nairobi (Kenya).
Died 16 March 1998.

McKAY, Very Rev. (James) Frederick, AC 1998; CMG 1972; OBE 1964 (MBE 1953); Associate Minister, St Stephen's Uniting (formerly Presbyterian) Church, Sydney, 1974–80; Chairman, Uniting Church Negotiators, NSW, 1976–80; recognised as a foundation minister of Uniting Church in Australia at time of Union, 1977; *b* 15 April 1907; *s* of J. McKay, Northern Ireland; mother, Australian; *m* 1938, Margaret Mary Robertson; one *s* three *d*. *Educ:* Thornburgh Coll., Charters Towers, Qld; Emmanuel Coll., Brisbane, Qld (MA, BD, Univ. of Queensland). Ordained Minister, Presbyterian Church of Australia, 1935; Patrol Padre, Australian Inland Mission, working with Rev. Dr John Flynn (Flynn of the Inland), 1935–41; Chaplain, RAAF, 1941–46; Command Chaplain, Middle East, 1943–45; Minister, Toowong Parish, Qld, 1946–50; Superintendent (succeeding Flynn of the Inland), Aust. Inland Mission, 1951–74, Archivist, 1974–85. Moderator, Presbyterian Church of NSW, 1965; Moderator-Gen., Presbyterian Church of Australia, 1970–73. Editor, Frontier News, 1951–74. Hon. LLD Queensland, 1992. Vocational Award, Sydney Rotary, 1972. *Publication:* Traeger, the Pedal Radio Genius, 1995. *Address:* Hawkesbury Village, Chapel Street, Richmond, NSW 2753, Australia. *T:* (2) 45784561. *Club:* Australian (Sydney). *Died 31 March 2000.*

MACKAY, John; Headmaster, Bristol Grammar School, 1960–75; *b* 23 June 1914; *s* of William Mackay, Nottingham, and Eliza Mackay; *m* 1952, Margaret Ogilvie (*d* 1996); two *s* two *d*. *Educ:* Mundella Grammar Sch., Nottingham; University of Nottingham (BA London (External) 1st Class Hons (English), 1935; Cambridge Teacher's Certificate, 1936); Merton Coll., Oxford, 1946–48; DPhil Oxon, 1953. Served War of 1939–45, in Royal Navy, 1940–46. On staff of SCM, 1936–38; English Lecturer, St John's Coll., York, 1938–40; English Master, Merchant Taylors' School, Crosby, Liverpool, 1948–54; Second Master, Cheltenham Coll., 1954–60. Chm., HMC, 1970, Treasurer, 1974–75. *Recreations:* literature, gardening, cricket, arguing, senile reminiscence. *Address:* The Old Post Office, Tormarton, Badminton, S Glos GL9 1HU. *T:* (01454) 218243. *Club:* East India, Devonshire, Sports and Public Schools. *Died 8 Oct. 1999.*

McKAY, Margaret; Public Relations consultant; *b* Jan. 1911; *née* McCarthy; *m*; one *d*. *Educ:* Elementary. Member of Co-operative Society, 1928–; joined Labour Party 1932. Held administrative posts with Civil Service Clerical Association and Transport and General Workers' Union; Chief woman officer, TUC, 1951–62. MP (Lab) Clapham, 1964–70. Commander, Order of the Cedar (Lebanon). World Culture Award, Accademia Italia, 1984. *Publications:* Generation in Revolt (pen name Margaret

McCarthy), 1953; Women in Trade Union History (TUC), 1954; Arab Voices from the Past; Electronic Arabia, 1974; The Chainless Mind, 1974; Timeless Arabia, 1978; Strangers in Palestine, 1982; Gulf Saga, 1982; Eve's Daring Daughters, 1985; Boadicea's Daughters; Middle Eastern Legacy, 1992. *Address:* PO Box 668, Abu Dhabi, Union of Arab Emirates. *Died 1 March 1996.*

MacKEIGAN, Hon. Ian Malcolm; Supernumerary Justice of Appeal Division of Supreme Court of Nova Scotia, 1985–90 (Chief Justice of Nova Scotia and Chief Justice of Appeal Division of Supreme Court of Nova Scotia, 1973–85); *b* 11 April 1915; *s* of Rev. Dr J. A. MacKeigan and Mabel (*née* McAvity); *m* 1942, Jean Catherine Geddes; two *s* one *d. Educ:* Univs of Saskatchewan, Dalhousie and Toronto. BA (Great Distinction) 1934, MA 1935, LLB 1938, Dalhousie; MA Toronto, 1939. Member of Nova Scotia and Prince Edward Island Bars; QC (Nova Scotia) 1954. Dep. Enforcement Administrator, Wartime Prices and Trade Bd, Ottawa, 1942–46; Dep. Comr, Combines Investigation Commn, Ottawa, 1946–50; Partner, MacKeigan, Cox, Downie & Mitchell and predecessor firms, Halifax, NS, 1950–73. Chm., Atlantic Develt Bd, 1963–69; Dir, Gulf Oil (Canada) Ltd, 1968–73; Dir, John Labatt Ltd, 1971–73. Hon. LLD Dalhousie, 1975. Centennial Medal, 1967; Silver Jubilee Medal, 1977. *Publications:* articles in Can. Bar Review and Can. Jl Polit. Sci. and Econs. *Recreations:* fishing, golf. *Address:* 833 Marlborough Avenue, Halifax, NS B3H 3G7, Canada. *T:* (902) 4291043. *Clubs:* Halifax, Saraguay, Ashburn Golf (Halifax). *Died 1 May 1996.*

McKELVEY, Air Cdre John Wesley, CB 1969; MBE 1944; CEng, MRAeS; RAF, retired; *b* 25 June 1914; *s* of late Captain John Wesley McKelvey, Enfield, Middx; *m* 1938, Eileen Amy Carter, *d* of John Charles Carter, Enfield; two *s. Educ:* George Spicer Sch., Enfield. RAF Aircraft Apprentice, 1929; commnd 1941 (Engrg Branch); served War of 1939–45, Egypt, Syria, Iraq and Bomber Comd (despatches, 1943); Group Captain 1960; Dep. Dir Intelligence (Tech.), Air Min., 1962–64; Dir of Aircraft and Asst Attaché, Defence Research and Development, British Embassy, Washington, 1964–66; Air Officer Wales and CO, RAF St Athan, 1966–69, retd. RAF Benevolent Fund: Sec. (Appeals), 1971–77; Legacies and Trusts Officer, 1977–79. *Recreations:* bowls, gardening, photography. *Address:* 19 Greensome Drive, Ferndown, Dorset BH22 8BE. *T:* (01202) 894464. *Club:* Royal Air Force. *Died 22 May 2000.*

MACKENZIE, Major Colin Dalzell, MBE 1945; MC 1940; Vice Lord-Lieutenant of Inverness, 1986–94; *b* 23 March 1919; *s* of Lt-Col (Douglas William) Alexander Dalziel Mackenzie, CVO, DSO, DL and Patience Elizabeth, *e d* of R. B. Hoare, Eaton Place, SW; *m* 1947, Lady Anne FitzRoy, *d* of 10th Duke of Grafton; one *s* three *d* (and one *s* decd). *Educ:* Eton; RMC Sandhurst. Page of Honour to King George V, 1932–36; joined Seaforth Highlanders, 1939; ADC to Viceroy of India, 1945–46, Dep. Mil. Sec. to Viceroy, 1946–47; retired Seaforth Highlanders, 1949. Mem., Queen's Body Guard for Scotland, Royal Company of Archers, 1959–. Mem., Inverness-shire County Council, 1949–51. *Address:* Farr House, Inverness IV2 6XB. *T:* (01808) 521202. *Clubs:* Turf, Pratt's; New (Edinburgh). *Died 1 Oct. 1999.*

McKENZIE, Prof. Donald Francis, FBA 1986; Professor of Bibliography and Textual Criticism, University of Oxford, 1989–96, then Emeritus; Professorial Fellow, Pembroke College, Oxford, 1986–96, then Supernumerary Fellow; *b* 5 June 1931; *s* of Leslie Alwyn Olson McKenzie and Millicent McKenzie; *m* 1951, Dora Mary Haigh; one *s*; *m* 1994, Christine Yvonne Ferdinand. *Educ:* Victoria UC, Wellington, NZ (BA 1954; DipJourn 1955; MA 1957); Corpus Christi Coll., Cambridge (PhD 1961); MA,

DPhil Oxford, 1986. Public servant, NZ PO, 1949–56; various teaching positions, Victoria UC and Victoria Univ. of Wellington, 1956–69; Prof. of Eng. Lang. and Lit., Victoria Univ. of Wellington, 1969–87, then Emeritus; Reader in Textual Criticism, Oxford Univ., 1986–89. Fellow, Corpus Christi Coll., Cambridge, 1960–66; Sandars Reader in Bibliography, Cambridge, 1975–76; Lyell Reader in Bibliography, Oxford Univ., 1987–88. Panizzi Lectr, British Liby, 1985; Clark Lectr, Cambridge, 1997. Founder-manager, Wai-te-ata Press, 1961–86. Pres., Bibliographical Soc., 1982–83 (Gold Medal, 1990); Hon. Member: Bibliographical Soc. of America, 1986; Cambridge Bibliographical Soc., 1988. Corresp. FBA 1980; Hon. Fellow, Australian Acad. of Humanities, 1988. Hon. LittD Victoria Univ. of Wellington, NZ, 1997. Mark Fitch Gold Medal for Bibliography, 1988; Walford Award, LA, 1994. *Publications:* (ed) Stationers' Company Apprentices 1605–1800, 3 vols, 1961–78; The Cambridge University Press 1696–1712: a bibliographical study, 1966; (ed with J. C. Ross) A Ledger of Charles Ackers, 1968; (ed) Robert Tailor, The Hogge hath lost his Pearl, 1972; Oral Culture, Literacy and Print in early New Zealand, 1985; Bibliography and the Sociology of Texts, 1986; contribs to bibliographical jls. *Address:* 20 Bardwell Court, Bardwell Road, Oxford OX2 6SX. *T:* (01865) 558962. *Died 22 March 1999.*

MACKENZIE, Vice-Adm. Sir Hugh (Stirling), KCB 1966 (CB 1963); DSO 1942 and Bar 1943; DSC 1945; *b* 3 July 1913; 3rd *s* of Dr and Mrs T. C. Mackenzie, Inverness; *m* 1946, Helen Maureen, *er d* of Major J. E. M. Bradish-Ellames; one *s* two *d. Educ:* Cargilfield Sch.; Royal Naval Coll., Dartmouth. Joined Royal Naval Coll., 1927; qualified in Submarines, 1935; served throughout War of 1939–45 in Submarines, comdg HMS Thrasher, 1941–43; HMS Tantalus, 1943–45; Comdr 1946; Capt. 1951; Rear-Adm. 1961; Flag Officer, Submarines, 1961–63; Chief Polaris Executive, 1963–68; Vice-Adm. 1964; retired 1968. Chm., Navy League, 1969–74; Dir, Atlantic Salmon Research Trust Ltd, 1969–79 (renamed Atlantic Salmon Trust, 1979), Chm., 1979–83, Vice Pres., 1984–. Hon. Freeman, Borough of Shoreditch, 1942. CIMgt. *Publication:* The Sword of Damocles (memoirs), 1996. *Recreation:* the country. *Address:* Sylvan Lodge, Puttenham, near Guildford, Surrey GU3 1BB. *Club:* Naval and Military. *Died 8 Oct. 1996.*

MacKENZIE, James Sargent Porteous, OBE 1963; *b* 18 June 1916; *s* of late Roderick and Daisy W. MacKenzie; *m* 1944, Flora Paterson; three *s. Educ:* Portree High Sch.; Edinburgh Univ. (MA Hons 1939); Glasgow Univ. (Dip. Social Studies 1947). War Service, 1939–45: Captain RA (Combined Ops, Burma and Normandy). Scottish HQ, Min. of Labour, 1947–56; Labour Advr, UK High Commn, New Delhi, 1956–62 (First Sec., 1956, Counsellor, 1959); Ministry of Labour: Asst Controller, Scottish HQ, 1962–65; Dep. Controller, Yorks and Humberside Regional Office, 1965–67; Principal Dep. Controller, Scottish HQ, Dept of Employment, 1967–72; Asst Sec., 1970; Counsellor (Labour) British Embassy, Bonn, 1972–77, retired. Exec. Mem., Church of Scotland Cttee on Church and Nation, 1977–83. *Address:* 11 Baberton Park, Juniper Green, Edinburgh EH14 5DW.
Died 6 Dec. 2000.

MACKENZIE of Mornish, Captain John Hugh Munro; President, SEET plc, since 1997; *b* 29 Aug. 1925; *s* of Lt-Col John Munro Mackenzie of Mornish, DSO, JP, Mil. Kt of Windsor, Henry VIII Gateway, Windsor Castle, and Mrs E. H. M. Mackenzie (*née* Taaffe); *m* 1951, Eileen Louise Agate, *d* of Alexander Shanks, OBE, MC, and Mrs Shanks; three *s* one *d* (and two *s* decd). *Educ:* Edinburgh Acad.; Loretto Sch.; Trinity Coll., Oxford (MA Hons); Hague Acad. of Internat. Law; Inns of Court Law Schs;

McGill Univ., Montreal. Served Army, 1945–49: Captain, The Royal Scots (Royal Regt); war service, Europe; 1st KOSB, A Company, 9th Brigade, 3rd Inf. Div. (despatches, certs of gallantry); Far East HQ Allied Land Forces SE Asia and HQ Ceylon Army Comd, Staff Captain, Mil. Sec's Branch; HM Guard of Honour, Balmoral, 1946; HQ 3rd Auto Aircraft Div., 1946–47 (GSO III). Harmsworth Law Scholar, Middle Temple, 1950; called to the Bar, Middle Temple, 1950. Trainee, United Dominions Trust Ltd; Legal Asst, Estates Dept, ICI Ltd, 1951; Hudson's Bay Scholar, 1952–53; Buyer, Crop and misc. products, ICI Ltd, 1953–54; Co. Sec. and Legal Advisor, Trubenised (GB) Ltd and Associated Cos, 1955–56; Gp Develt Officer, Aspro-Nicholas Ltd, 1956–57; PA to Man. Dir, Knitmaster Holdings, 1957; formed: Grampian Holdings Ltd (Manager and Sec.), 1958, Man. Dir, 1960; London and Northern Gp Ltd (Dep. Chm. and Man. Dir), 1962, Chm., 1967–87; Tace plc (Chm., 1967–91); Scottish, English and European Textiles, later SEET plc, 1969 (Chm., 1969–97). Chairman: Pauling plc, 1976–87; Goring Kerr plc, 1983–91. Eight Queen's Awards for Export won by Group Cos. FRSA, CIMgt. *Recreations:* opera, bridge, shooting, fishing, all field sports. *Address:* Mortlake House, Vicarage Road, SW14 8RU; Scaliscro Lodge, Isle of Lewis, Outer Hebrides PA86 9EL; Shellwood Manor, Leigh, Surrey RH2 8NX. *Clubs:* New, Royal Scots (Edinburgh). *Died 1 May 2000.*

MacKENZIE, Kenneth William Stewart, CMG 1958; CVO 1975; FRAI; Colonial Administrative Service, retired; *b* 30 July 1915; *s* of late W. S. MacKenzie and E. MacKenzie (*née* Johnson); *m* 1939, Kathleen Joyce Ingram; one *s* one *d. Educ:* Whitcliffe Mount Grammar Sch., Cleckheaton; Downing Coll., Cambridge (1st Cl. Hist. Tripos, Part I, 1935; Class II, Div. I, 1936; 1st Cl. Arch. and Anthrop. Tripos, Section A, 1937; BA 1936, MA 1962). Cadet, Colonial Administrative Service, Basutoland, 1938; Asst Sec., Mauritius, 1944; Administrative Officer, Kenya, 1948; Asst Financial Sec., Kenya, 1950; seconded to HM Treasury, 1951–53; Dep. Sec., 1954 and Permanent Sec., 1955, Treasury, Kenya; Minister for Finance and Development and Financial Sec., Kenya, 1959–62. MLC Kenya, 1955–62; MLA East Africa, 1959–62; retired, 1963 to facilitate constitutional change; re-employed as Principal, Colonial Office, 1963; Principal, HM Treasury, 1966–70; Asst Sec., DoE, 1970–75; Dir of Studies, RIPA (Overseas Unit), 1976–90. *Publication:* pamphlet, How Basutoland is Governed, 1944. *Recreations:* reading, gardening. *Address:* Beaumont, 28 Greenhurst Lane, Oxted, Surrey RH8 0LB. *T:* (01883) 713848. *Clubs:* Royal Over-Seas League; Achilles; Nairobi (Nairobi). *Died 15 Oct. 1999.*

MACKENZIE, Prof. William James Millar, CBE 1963; FBA 1968; Professor of Politics, Glasgow University, 1966–74, then Emeritus; *b* 8 April 1909; *s* of Laurence Millar Mackenzie, WS, Edinburgh; *m* 1943, Pamela Muriel Malyon; one *s* four *d. Educ:* Edinburgh Academy; Balliol Coll., Oxford; (Ireland Schol. 1929; MA); Edinburgh Univ. (LLB). Fellow of Magdalen Coll., Oxford, 1933–48, Emeritus Fellow, 1990; Temp. Civil Servant, Air Ministry, 1939–44; Official War Historian, SOE, 1945–48. Faculty Fellow, Nuffield Coll., 1948; Lecturer in Politics, Oxford Univ., 1948; Prof. of Government, Manchester Univ., 1949–66, Glasgow Univ., 1966–74; Special Comr, for Constitutional Development, Tanganyika, 1952; Co-opted Mem., Manchester City Educn Cttee, 1953–64; apptd Mem., British Wool Marketing Board, 1954–66; Mem. Royal Commn on Local Govt in Greater London, 1957; Constitutional Adviser, Kenya, 1959; Vice-Chm., Bridges Cttee on Training in Public Administration for Overseas Countries, 1962; Member: Maud Cttee on Management in Local Govt, 1964–66; Cttee on Remuneration of Ministers and

Members of Parliament, 1963–64; North-West Regional Economic Planning Council, 1965–66; SSRC, 1965–69; Parry Cttee on University Libraries, 1964–67; Chm., Children's Panel Adv. Cttee, Glasgow City, 1973–75. Hon. LLD: Dundee, 1968; Lancaster, 1970; Manchester, 1975; Hon. DLitt Warwick, 1972; Hon. DSc (Econ) Hull, 1981; DUniv Open Univ., 1984. *Publications:* (in part) British Government since 1918, 1950; (jtly) Central Administration in Great Britain, 1957; Free Elections, 1958; (ed with Prof. K. Robinson) Five Elections in Africa, 1959; Politics and Social Science, 1967; (jtly) Social Work in Scotland, 1969; Power, Violence, Decision, 1975; Explorations in Government, 1975; Political Identity, 1977; Biological Ideas in Politics, 1978; Power and Responsibility in Health Care, 1979. *Address:* 12 Kirklee Circus, Glasgow G12 0TW.

Died 22 Aug. 1996.

MACKENZIE-STUART, Baron *cr* 1988 (Life Peer), of Dean in the District of the City of Edinburgh; **Alexander John Mackenzie Stuart;** President of the Court of Justice, European Communities at Luxembourg, 1984–88 (Judge of the Court of Justice, 1972–84); a Senator of the College of Justice in Scotland, 1972; *b* 18 Nov. 1924; *s* of late Prof. A. Mackenzie Stuart, KC, and Amy Margaret Dean, Aberdeen; *m* 1952, Anne Burtholme Millar, *d* of late J. S. L. Millar, WS, Edinburgh; four *d. Educ:* Fettes Coll., Edinburgh (Open Schol.); Sidney Sussex Coll., Cambridge (Schol. 1949; 1st cl. Pt II Law Tripos; BA 1949; Hon. Fellow, 1977); Edinburgh Univ. (LLB (dist.) 1951). Royal Engineers (Temp. Capt. 1946), 1942–47. Admitted Faculty of Advocates, 1951; QC (Scot.) 1963; Keeper of the Advocates Library, 1970–72. Standing Junior Counsel: to Scottish Home Dept, 1956–57; to Inland Revenue in Scotland, 1957–63; Sheriff-Principal of Aberdeen, Kincardine and Banff, 1971–72. President: British Acad. of Experts, 1989–92; European Movement (Scotland), 1991. Governor, Fettes College, 1962–72. Hon. Bencher: Middle Temple, 1978; King's Inns, Dublin, 1984; Hon. Mem., SPTL, 1982. FCIArb 1990; FRSE 1991. Hon. Prof., Collège d'Europe, Bruges, 1974–77. DUniv Stirling, 1973; Hon. LLD: Exeter, 1978; Edinburgh, 1978; Glasgow, 1981; Aberdeen, 1983; Cambridge, 1987; Birmingham, 1988. Prix Bech for services to Europe, 1989. Grand Croix, Ordre Grand-Ducal de la Couronne de Chêne (Luxembourg), 1988. *Publications:* Hamlyn Lectures: The European Communities and the Rule of Law, 1977; A French King at Holyrood, 1995; articles in legal publications. *Recreation:* collecting. *Address:* 7 Randolph Cliff, Edinburgh EH3 7TZ; Le Garidel, Gravières, 07140 Les Vans, Ardèche, France. *Clubs:* Athenæum; New (Edinburgh); Golf Club du Grand Guérin (Villefort). *Died 1 April 2000.*

MACKIE, Sir Maitland, Kt 1982; CBE 1965; JP; farmer since 1932; *b* 16 Feb. 1912; *s* of late Dr Maitland Mackie, OBE and Mary (*née* Yull); *m* 1st, 1935, Isobel Ross (*d* 1960); two *s* four *d*: 2nd, 1963, Martha Pauline Turner (*d* 1993). *Educ:* Aberdeen Grammar Sch.; Aberdeen Univ. (BScAgric). FEIS 1972; FRAgSS 1974; FInstM. County Councillor, Aberdeenshire, 1951–75 (Convener 1967–75); Chm., NE Develt Authority, 1969–75; Chairman: Jt Adv. Cttee, Scottish Farm Bldgs Investigation Unit, 1963–75; Aberdeen Milk Marketing Bd, 1965–82; Peterhead Bay Management Co., 1975–86; Hanover (Scotland) Housing Assoc., 1981–86. Member: Agric. Sub-Cttee, UGC, 1965–75; Bd, Scottish Council for Development and Industry, 1975–82 (Chm., Oil Policy Cttee, 1975–82); Clayson Cttee on Drink Laws in Scotland. Chm., Aberdeen Cable Services, 1983–87; Director: Scottish Telecommunications, 1969–85; Aberdeen Petroleum plc, 1980–. Governor: N of Scotland Coll. of Agriculture, 1968–82 (Vice-Chm., 1974–78); Rowett Inst., 1973–82. Fellow, Scottish Council Develt and Industry, 1986.

Burgess of Guild, Aberdeen, 1978. JP 1956; Lord-Lieut, Aberdeenshire, 1975–87. KStJ 1977. Hon. LLD Aberdeen, 1977. *Publication:* A Lucky Chap, 1993. *Recreation:* travel. *Address:* The Stables, Westertown, Rothienorman, Aberdeenshire. *T:* Rothienorman (01651) 671392. *Clubs:* Farmers'; Royal Northern (Aberdeen).

Died 18 June 1996.

MacKINLAY, Sir Bruce, Kt 1978; CBE 1970; company director; *b* 4 Oct. 1912; *s* of Daniel Robertson MacKinlay and Alice Victoria Rice; *m* 1943, Erica Ruth Fleming; two *s. Educ:* Scotch Coll. Served War, AASC, 1940–45 (Lieut). Dir, J. Gadsden Australia Ltd, 1954–77. President: WA Chamber of Manufactures, 1958–61; Confedn of WA Industry, 1976–78; WA Employers' Fedn, 1974–75; Fremantle Rotary Club, 1956; Vice-Pres., Associated Chambers of Manufactures of Aust., 1960. Chairman: WA Inst. of Dirs, 1975–77; WA Div., National Packaging Assoc., 1967–69; WA Finance Cttee for the Duke of Edinburgh's Third Commonwealth Study Conf., 1967–68; Mem., Commonwealth Manufg Industries Adv. Council, 1962–70. Leader: Aust. Trade Mission, E Africa, 1968; WA Trade Mission, Italy, 1970; Employers' Rep., Internat. Labour Conf., 1977; Comr, State Electricity Commn, 1961–74. University of Western Australia: Mem. Senate, 1970–84; Chm., Master of Business Admin Appeal, 1973. Life Governor, Scotch Coll. Council (Chm., 1969–74); Chm. Nat. Council, Keep Australia Beautiful, 1984–86 (Mem. 1967–, Chm. 1981–86, WA Council); Councillor: Organising Council of Commonwealth and Empire Games, 1962; Aust. Council on Population and Ethnic Affairs, 1981–83. Pres., Most Excellent Order of the British Empire, WA Div., 1983–90. *Recreations:* swimming, gardening. *Address:* 9B Melville Street, Claremont, WA 6010, Australia. *T:* (9) 93832220. *Clubs:* Weld (Perth); WACA, Claremont Football (WA).

Died 23 Sept. 1999.

McKINNEY, Judith, (Mrs J. P. McKinney); *see* Wright, J.

McKINNON, Maj.-Gen. Walter Sneddon, CB 1966; CBE 1961 (OBE 1947); *b* 8 July 1910; *s* of Charles McKinnon and Janet Robertson McKinnon (*née* Sneddon); *m* 1937, Anna Bloomfield Plimmer; four *s* one *d. Educ:* Otago Boys High Sch., Dunedin, NZ; Otago Univ. (BSc). Commissioned in NZ Army, 1935; various military courses, including Staff Coll., Camberley, England; served War of 1939–45: Pacific, Italy (Lt-Col; despatches), Japan (occupation) (OBE); Brigadier, 1953; subsequent appointments: Comdr, Southern Mil. Dist (NZ), 1953; Head, NZ Joint Mil. Mission, Washington, DC, 1954–57; Comdr, Northern Military District, 1957–58; Adjutant-General, 1958–63; Quartermaster-General, 1963–65, Maj.-Gen. 1965; Chief of the General Staff, NZ Army, 1965–67; retired, 1967. Chairman: NZ Broadcasting Corp., 1969–74; Everton Trust Bd, Victoria Univ., 1969–73. Member: Taupo Borough Council, 1977–80; Tongariro United Council, 1979–80. Pres., Taupo Regional Museum and Art Centre, 1975–79; Mem., Social Develt Council, New Zealand, 1976–79. *Recreations:* golf, fishing, gardening. *Address:* 27/19 Liston Avenue, Taupo, New Zealand. *Clubs:* Wellesley (Wellington); Taupo Golf.

Died 20 May 1998.

MACKNIGHT, Dame Ella (Annie Noble), DBE 1969; Consultant Emeritus (Obstetrician and Gynaecologist), Queen Victoria Hospital, Melbourne, 1964–77; *b* 7 Aug. 1904; 4th *d* of Dr Conway Macknight. *Educ:* Toorak Coll., Melbourne; Univ. of Melbourne, resident student, Janet Clarke Hall. MB, BS 1928; MD Melbourne, 1931; Dip. in Gyn. and Obst. Melbourne, 1936; MRCOG 1951; FRCOG 1958; FRACS 1971; FAGO 1973; FRACOG (FAustCOG 1978); FAMA, 1976. Hon. Obstetrician and Gynaecologist, Queen Victoria Hosp., Melbourne,

1935–64; Pres., Queen Victoria Hosp., Melbourne, 1971–77 (Vice-Pres., 1965–71). Hon. Sec., 1963–67, Vice-Pres., 1967–70, Pres., 1970–72, Australian Council, RCOG. Mem. of Exec., and Chm. of Blood Transfusion Cttee, Vic Div., Red Cross Soc., 1964–70. Fellow, Asia and Oceania Fedn, 1993. Hon. MD Monash, 1972. *Recreation:* golf. *Address:* 8/16 Wooriguleen Road, Toorak, Vic 3142, Australia. *Clubs:* Lyceum (Melbourne); Royal Melbourne Golf.

Died 1 April 1997.

MACKWORTH, Comdr Sir David Arthur Geoffrey, 9th Bt *cr* 1776, of The Gnoll, Glamorganshire; Royal Navy, retired; *b* 13 July 1912; *o s* of late Vice-Admiral Geoffrey Mackworth, CMG, DSO, and Noel Mabel, *d* of late William I. Langford; *S* uncle, 1952; *m* 1st, 1941, Mary Alice (marr. diss. 1972; she *d* 1993), *d* of Thomas Henry Grylls; one *s*; 2nd, 1973, Beryl Joan, 3rd *d* of late Pembroke Henry Cockayn Cross and of Jeanie Cross, and formerly wife of late Ernest Henry Sparkes. *Educ:* Farnborough Sch., Hants; RNC Dartmouth. Joined RN, 1926; served HMS Eagle, HMS Suffolk, 1939–45; Naval Adviser to Director of Guided Weapon Research and Development, Ministry of Supply, 1945–49; Commander, 1948; retired, 1956. MRIN. *Recreations:* sailing, cruising. *Heir: s* Digby John Mackworth, pilot, British Airways [*b* 2 Nov. 1945; *m* 1971, Antoinette Francesca, *d* of Henry James McKenna, Ilford, Essex; one *d*]. *Address:* 36 Wittering Road, Hayling Island, Hants PO11 9SP. *Clubs:* Royal Ocean Racing; Royal Naval Sailing Association; Royal Yacht Squadron (Cowes).

Died 8 Feb. 1998.

MACKWORTH-YOUNG, Sir Robert Christopher, (Sir Robin), GCVO 1985 (KCVO 1975; CVO 1968; MVO 1961); Librarian Emeritus to HM the Queen; *b* 12 Feb. 1920; *s* of late Gerard Mackworth-Young, CIE and Natalie, *d* of Rt Hon. Sir Walter Hely-Hutchinson, GCMG, PC; *m* 1953, Rosemarie, *d* of W. C. R. Aue, Menton, France; one *s. Educ:* Eton (King's Schol.); King's Coll., Cambridge. Pres., Cambridge Union Soc., 1948. Served in RAF, 1939–46. HM Foreign Service, 1948–55; Deputy Librarian, Windsor Castle, 1955–58; Librarian, Windsor Castle, and Asst Keeper of the Queen's Archives, 1958–85. Mem. Bd, British Library, 1984–90. FSA; Hon. FLA. *Recreations:* music, electronics, ski-ing. *Club:* Roxburghe.

Died 5 Dec. 2000.

McLACHLAN, Angus Henry; journalist; *b* 29 March 1908; *s* of James H. and Mabel McLachlan; unmarried. *Educ:* Scotch Coll., Melbourne; University of Melbourne. Melbourne Herald, 1928–36; joined Sydney Morning Herald, 1936; News Editor, 1937–49; General Manager, John Fairfax & Sons Ltd (publishers of Sydney Morning Herald, Australian Financial Review), 1949–64, Dir, 1965–80 (Man. Dir, 1965–70). Jt Man. Dir, Australian Associated Press Pty Ltd, 1965–82 (Chairman, 1958–59, 1964–65, 1975–77); Director: Reuters Ltd, London, 1966–71 (Trustee, 1979–84, Chm. 1980–84); Amalgamated Television Services Pty Ltd, 1955–85; Macquarie Broadcasting Holdings Ltd, 1966–80; David Syme & Co. Ltd, Publishers of The Age, 1970–79; Federal Capital Press Ltd, Publishers of Canberra Times, 1970–79. Mem. Council, Library of NSW, 1966–75 (Dep. Pres., 1974–75); Mem., Library Council of NSW, 1975–78; Member, Sydney University Extension Board, 1960–75. *Address:* Box 5303, GPO, Sydney, NSW 2001, Australia. *Clubs:* Australian, Union (Sydney); Royal Sydney Yacht Squadron.

Died 10 Aug. 1996.

McLACHLAN, Peter John, OBE 1983; DL; Company Secretary, Bryson House, since 1998 (General Secretary, Belfast Voluntary Welfare Society, later Director, then Chief Executive, 1980–97); Director: North City Training Ltd, since 1989 (Chairman, since 1996); Lagan Watersports Ltd, since 1994; Partnership Care (West), since 1995; *b* 21 Aug. 1936; *s* of Rev. Dr Herbert John McLachlan and Joan Dorothy McLachlan (*née* Hall); *m* 1965, Gillian Mavis Lowe (marr. diss. 1992); two *d. Educ:* Magdalen College Sch., Oxford; Queen's Coll., Oxford (schol.; BA Lit.Hum.; MA). Administrative trainee, Min. of Finance, NICS, 1959–62; Administrator, NYO of GB, 1962–65 and 1966–69; Personal Asst to Chm., IPC, 1965–66; Cons. Res. Dept, 1970–72; Exec. Dir, Watney & Powell Ltd, 1972–73; Mem. (Unionist) S Antrim, NI Assembly, 1973–75; Gen. Manager, S. H. Watterson Engineering, 1975–77; Jt Man. Dir, Ulster Metalspinners Ltd, 1976–77; Projects Manager, Peace By Peace Ltd, 1977–79; Sec., Peace People Charitable Trust, 1977–79; Chm., Community of The Peace People, 1978–80. Mem., MRC, 1995–. Founder Chairman: NI Fedn of Housing Assocs, 1976–78; Belfast Improved Houses Ltd, 1975–81 (Dir, 1975–97); Lisnagarvey Housing Assoc., 1977–91; Dismas House, 1983–87 (Cttee Mem., 1983–89); Chm., NI Peace Forum, 1980–82; Vice-Chm., NI Hospice Ltd, 1981–90; Member: Minister's Adv. Cttee on Community Work, NI, 1982–84; Central Personal Social Services Adv. Cttee, 1984–88; Eastern Health and Social Services Bd, NI, 1991–94; Administrative Council: Royal Jubilee Trusts, 1975–81; NI Projects Trust, 1977–88; Trustee: Buttle Trust, 1987–; Anchor Trust, 1987–90; Victoria Homes Trust, 1988–99; Chm., Cecil King Meml Foundn, 1990–. Founder, NI Fedn Victims Support Schemes (Hon. Sec., 1982–96; Chm., 1996–98); Mem. Council, Victim Support UK, 1987–94 and 1998–99 (Vice Chm., 1988–90). Mem., Bd of Visitors, HM Prison Maghaberry, 1986–91. Dir, Belfast Community Radio Ltd, 1989–98 (Chm., 1992–98); Chairman: Belfast Br., Carers Nat. Assoc., 1992–96; Forum for Community Work Educn, 1992–94; Belfast Hills Regl Park Cttee, 1994–99; Mem., Adv. Council, Belfast Common Purpose, 1992–98; Dir, Community Network Ltd; Cttee Mem., Belfast Civic Trust. Member: Corrymeela Community, 1975–97; Cttee, Fellowship of Reconciliation, 1982–98 (Chm., 1992–98); Cttee, Thanksgiving Square, Belfast, 1998– (Chm., 1995–97). Mem., Internat. Advisory Cttee, Eisenhower Exchange Fellowships Foundn, Philadelphia, 1991–. DL Belfast, 1992. Salzburg Seminar Alumnus, 1979; UK Eisenhower Fellow, 1986. *Recreations:* keyboard playing, poetry. *Address:* 44 Salisbury Street, Belfast BT7 1AH. *T:* (028) 9032 5099. *Club:* Royal Commonwealth Society.   *Died 4 Aug. 1999.*

McLAUGHLAN, Rear-Adm. Ian David, CB 1970; DSC 1941 and Bar, 1953; Admiral Commanding Reserves and Director General, Naval Recruiting, 1970–72, retired; *b* 2 May 1919; *s* of Richard John and Margaret McLaughlan; *m* 1942, Charity Pomeroy Simonds; two *d. Educ:* St Paul's Sch. Entered Navy, 1937; served in destroyers, 1940–45 (despatches three times); comd HMS: Flint Castle, 1948–50; Concord, 1950–52; jssc 1952; Armed Forces Staff Coll., Norfolk, Va, 1953; HMS Jupiter, 1953–55; comd HMS: Chieftain, 1955; Chevron, 1955–56 (despatches); Staff of C-in-C, Portsmouth, 1957–59; Asst Dir of Plans, Admty, 1959–61; Capt. (F), 2nd Frigate Sqdn, 1961–62; idc 1963; Dir, Naval Ops and Trade, 1964–66; comd HMS Hampshire, 1966–67; Chief of Staff to Comdr Far East Fleet, 1967–70. Comdr 1951; Capt. 1958; Rear-Adm. 1968. Commendador d'Aviz (Portugal), 1956. *Recreation:* gardening. *Address:* The Five Gables, Mayfield, East Sussex TN20 6TZ. *T:* Mayfield (01435) 872218.   *Died 18 Sept. 1996.*

McLAUGHLIN, (Florence) Patricia (Alice), OBE 1975; *b* 23 June 1916; *o d* of late Canon F. B. Aldwell; *m* 1937, Henry (decd), *o s* of late Major W. McLaughlin, of McLaughlin & Harvey Ltd, London, Belfast and Dublin; one *s* one *d* (and one *d* decd). *Educ:* Ashleigh House, Belfast; Trinity Coll., Dublin. MP (UU) Belfast West, 1955–64; Hon. Sec., Parly Home Safety Cttee, 1956–64;

Deleg. to Council of Europe and WEU, 1959–64. Past Chm., Unionist Soc.; Past Vice-Chm., Women's National Advisory Cttee of Cons. Party; Former Nat. Advisor on Women's Affairs to European Movement. Active in voluntary and consumer work for many years; Chairman: Steering Gp on Food Freshness, 1973–75; Housewife's Trust; Former Mem., Exec. Cttee, BSI. Vice-Pres., Royal Society for Prevention of Accidents, 1962–85. *Recreations:* talking, travelling. *Address:* 10 the Dower House, Headbourne Worthy, Winchester, Hants SO23 7JG.   *Died 7 Jan. 1997.*

MacLEAN, Hon. Angus; *see* MacLean, Hon. J. A.

MACLEAN of Dunconnel, Sir Fitzroy Hew, 1st Bt *cr* 1957, of Strachur and Glensluain, co. Argyll; KT 1993; CBE (mil.) 1944; 15th Hereditary Keeper and Captain of Dunconnel; *b* 11 March 1911; *s* of Major Charles Maclean, DSO, OBE and Frances Elaine Gladys, *d* of Lt-Comdr George Royle, RN; *m* 1946, Hon. Veronica Nell Fraser, 2nd *d* of 16th Lord Lovat, KT, and *widow* of Lieut Alan Phipps, RN; two *s. Educ:* Eton; Cambridge. 3rd Sec., Foreign Office, 1933; transferred to Paris, 1934, and to Moscow, 1937; 2nd Sec., 1938; transferred to Foreign Office, 1939; resigned from Diplomatic Service, and enlisted as private in Cameron Highlanders; 2nd Lieut Aug. 1941; joined 1st Special Air Service Regt, Jan. 1942; Capt. Sept. 1942; Lt-Col 1943; Brig. Comdg British Military Mission to Jugoslav partisans, 1943–45. MP (C) Lancaster, 1941–59, Bute and N Ayrshire, 1959–Feb. 1974; Parly Under-Sec. of State for War and Financial Sec. War Office, Oct. 1954–Jan. 1957. Member: UK Delegn to North Atlantic Assembly, 1962–74 (Chm., Mil. Cttee, 1964–74); Council of Europe and WEU, 1972–74. Hon. Col, 23rd SAS Regt, 1984–88. Lees Knowles Lecturer, Cambridge, 1953. Hon. LLD: Glasgow 1969; Dalhousie 1971; Dundee, 1981; Hon. DLitt Acadia, 1970. French Croix de Guerre with Palm, 1943; Order of Kutusov, 1944; Order of Partisan Star (First Class) (Yugoslavia), 1945; Order of Merit (Yugoslavia), 1969; Order of the Yusoslav Star with Ribbon, 1981. *Publications:* Eastern Approaches, 1949; Disputed Barricade, 1957; A Person from England, 1958; Back to Bokhara, 1959; Jugoslavia, 1969; A Concise History of Scotland, 1970; The Battle of Neretva, 1970; To the Back of Beyond, 1974; To Caucasus, 1976; Take Nine Spies, 1978; Holy Russia, 1979; Tito, 1980; The Isles of the Sea, 1985; Portrait of the Soviet Union, 1988; Bonnie Prince Charlie, 1988; All The Russias, 1992; Highlanders, 1995. *Heir: s* Charles Maclean, yr of Dunconnel [*b* 31 Oct. 1946; *m* 1986, Deborah, *d* of Lawrence Young; three *d*]. *Address:* Strachur House, Argyll PA27 8BX. *T:* Strachur (0136986) 242. *Clubs:* White's, Pratt's; Puffin's, New (Edinburgh).   *Died 15 June 1996.*

McLEAN, Sir Francis (Charles), Kt 1967; CBE 1953 (MBE 1945); *b* 6 Nov. 1904; *s* of Michael McLean; *m* 1930, Dorothy Mabel Blackstaffe; one *s* one *d. Educ:* University of Birmingham (BSc). Chief Engineer, Psychological Warfare Division, SHAEF, 1943–45. Dep. Chief Engineer, BBC, 1952–60; Dep. Dir of Engineering, BBC, 1960–63; Director, Engineering, BBC, 1963–68. Dir, Oxley Developments Ltd, 1961–. Chairman: BSI Telecommunications Industry Standards Cttee, 1960–77; Royal Commn on FM Broadcasting in Australia, 1974. Pres., Newbury Dist Field Club. FIEE. *Publications:* contrib. Journal of IEE. *Address:* Greenwood Copse, Tile Barn, Woolton Hill, Newbury, Berks RG15 9XE. *T:* (01635) 253583.   *Died 19 Dec. 1998.*

McLEAN, John Alexander Lowry, QC 1974; Principal Secretary to Lord Chief Justice (formerly Permanent Secretary, Supreme Court of Northern Ireland) and Clerk of the Crown for Northern Ireland, 1966–93; *b* 21 Feb. 1921; *o s* of John McLean and Phoebe Jane (*née* Bowditch);

m 1950, Diana Elisabeth Campbell (*d* 1986), *e d* of S. B. Boyd Campbell, MC, MD, FRCP, and Mary Isabel Ayre, St John's, Newfoundland; one *s* two *d*. *Educ:* Methodist Coll., Belfast; Queen's University, Belfast. Served Intell. Corps, 1943–47. Called to Bar of Northern Ireland, 1949. Asst Sec., NI Supreme Court, and Private Sec. to Lord Chief Justice of NI, 1956–66; Under Treas., Hon. Soc. of Inn of Court of NI, 1966; Clerk of Restrictive Practices Court in NI, 1957. Member: Jt Working Party on Enforcement of Judgments of NI Courts, 1963–65; Lord Chancellor's Cttee on NI Supreme Court, 1966–69; Lord Chancellor's Foreign Judgments Working Party, 1974–81. Mem. and Chm., Wages Councils (NI), 1950–94. *Publications:* contrib. legal periodicals. *Recreations:* not golf. *Address:* 24 Marlborough Park South, Belfast BT9 6HR. *T:* (01232) 667330; Lifeboat Cottage, Cloughey, Co. Down BT22 1HS. *T:* (01247) 771313. *Club:* Royal Commonwealth Society.   *Died 27 April 1997.*

MacLEAN, Hon. (John) Angus, PC (Can.) 1957; OC 1992; DFC 1942; CD; Premier of Prince Edward Island, 1979–81; *b* 15 May 1914; *s* of late George A. MacLean; *m* 1952, Gwendolyn Esther M. Burwash; two *s* two *d*. *Educ:* Mount Allison Academy; Summerside High Sch.; Univ. of British Columbia; Mount Allison Univ. BSc. Served War of 1939–45, RCAF: commanded Test and Development Estabt, 1943–45; Missing and Enquiry Unit, Europe, 1945–47, Wing Comdr (despatches). First elected to House of Commons by by-election, June 1951, re-elected 1953, 1957, 1958, 1962, 1963, 1965, 1968, 1972, 1974; Minister of Fisheries in the Diefenbaker Cabinet, 1957–63; elected Leader of PC Party of PEI, 1976; first elected to PEI Legislature at by-election, 1976, re-elected 1978 and 1979. PEI's Comr to EXPO '86. Member: PEI Energy Commn, 1984–87; Sen. Adv. Bd, Maritime Provinces Educn Foundn, 1983–86; Nat. Mus. of Natural Scis, Nat. Museums of Canada, 1985–88. Member: Royal Air Forces Escaping Soc. (Canadian Br.); RCAF Assoc. Hon. LLD: Mount Allison Univ., 1958; Univ. of PEI, 1985. OStJ 1982. *Publication:* Making it Home (memoirs), 1998. *Recreations:* genealogical research, bird watching. *Address:* Lewes, RR3, Belle River, PEI COA 1B0, Canada. *T:* (902) 9622235. *Clubs:* United Services, Charlottetown, Masonic Lodge, AF and AM, Royal Canadian Legion, Charlottetown Chamber of Commerce, Canadian (PEI).   *Died 16 Feb. 2000.*

MACLEAN, Sir Robert (Alexander), KBE 1973; Kt 1955; DL; Honorary President, Stoddard Holdings Ltd; *b* 11 April 1908; *s* of Andrew Johnston Maclean, JP, Cambuslang, Lanarkshire, and Mary Jane Cameron; *m* 1938, Vivienne Neville Bourke (*d* 1992), *d* of Captain Bertram Walter Bourke, JP, Heathfield, Co. Mayo; two *s* two *d*. *Educ:* High Sch. of Glasgow. JDipMA. President: Glasgow Chamber of Commerce, 1956–58; Association British Chambers of Commerce, 1966–68; Chairman: Council of Scottish Chambers of Commerce, 1960–62; Scottish Cttee, Council of Industrial Design, 1949–58 (Mem., CoID, 1948–58); Council of Management, Scottish Industries Exhibns, 1949, 1954 and 1959; Scottish Exports Cttee, 1966–70; Scottish Industrial Estates Corp., 1955–72 (Mem., 1946–72); Pres., British Industrial Exhibn, Moscow, 1966; Vice-Chm., Scottish Bd for Industry, 1952–60; Member: Pigs and Bacon Marketing Commn, 1955–56; BNEC, 1966–70; Scottish Aerodromes Bd, 1950–61; Export Council for Europe, 1960–64; BoT Trade Exhbns Adv. Cttee, 1961–65; Nat. Freight Corp., 1969–72; Regional Controller (Scotland): Board of Trade, 1944–46; Factory and Storage Premises, 1941–44. Director: Scottish Union & Nat. Insce Co., 1965–68; Scottish Adv. Bd, Norwich Union Insce Gp, 1965–81. Vice-Pres., Scottish Council (Develt and Industry), 1955–82. Trustee, Clyde Navigational Trust, 1956–58; Pres., Scottish Youth Clubs, 1959–68. DL Renfrewshire, 1970. CStJ 1975. FRSA;

CIMgt. Hon. LLD Glasgow, 1970. *Recreations:* golf, fishing. *Address:* South Branchal Farm, Bridge of Weir, Renfrewshire PA11 3SJ. *Clubs:* Carlton; Western (Glasgow).   *Died 8 Feb. 1999.*

MacLEHOSE OF BEOCH, Baron *cr* 1982 (Life Peer), of Maybole in the District of Kyle and Carrick, and of Victoria in Hong Kong; **Crawford Murray MacLehose,** KT 1983; GBE 1976 (MBE 1946); KCMG 1971 (CMG 1964); KCVO 1975; DL; HM Diplomatic Service, retired; *b* 16 Oct. 1917; *s* of Hamish A. MacLehose and Margaret Bruce Black; *m* 1947, Margaret Noël Dunlop; two *d*. *Educ:* Rugby; Balliol Coll., Oxford. Served War of 1939–45, Lieut, RNVR. Joined Colonial Service, Malaya, 1939; joined Foreign Service, 1947; Acting Consul, 1947, Acting Consul-General, 1948, Hankow; promoted First Secretary, 1949; transferred to Foreign Office, 1950; First Secretary (Commercial), and Consul, Prague, 1951; seconded to Commonwealth Relations Office, for service at Wellington, 1954; returned to Foreign Office and transferred to Paris, 1956; promoted Counsellor, 1959; seconded to Colonial Office and transferred to Hong Kong as Political Adviser, 1959–62; Hd, Far Eastern Dept, Foreign Office, 1963–65; Principal Private Secretary to Secretary of State for Foreign Affairs, 1965–67; Ambassador: to Vietnam, 1967–69; to Denmark, 1969–71; Governor and C-in-C, Hong Kong, 1971–82. Dir, Nat. Westminster Bank, 1982–88. Chairman: Scottish Trust for the Physically Disabled, 1982–90; Margaret Blackwood Housing Assoc., 1982–90. Pres., GB-China Centre, 1982–93. Chm. Govs, SOAS, Univ. of London, 1985–90 (Hon. Fellow, 1983). DL Ayr and Arran, 1983. Hon. LLD: York, 1983; Strathclyde, 1984; Hong Kong, 1992. KStJ 1972. *Recreations:* farming, reading. *Address:* Beoch, Maybole, Ayrshire KA19 8EN. *Club:* Athenæum.
                          Died 27 May 2000.

MacLELLAN, Prof. George Douglas Stephen, PhD; CEng; FIMechE, FIEE; Professor and Head of Department of Engineering, University of Leicester, 1965–88, then Emeritus Professor; *b* Glasgow, 1 Nov. 1922; *e s* of late Alexander Stephen MacLellan and Anne MacLellan (*née* Mackinlay). *Educ:* Rugby Sch.; Pembroke Coll., Cambridge. Mech. Sci. Tripos, 1942; MA, PhD. Dept of Colloid Science, Cambridge, and Callenders Cable and Construction Co. Ltd, 1942–44; Fellow, Pembroke Coll., Cambridge, 1944–59; Vickers-Armstrong Ltd, Newcastle upon Tyne, 1944–46; University Demonstrator and Lecturer in Engineering, Cambridge, 1947–59; Rankine Professor of Mechanical Engineering (Mechanics and Mechanism), University of Glasgow, 1959–65. Commonwealth Fund Fellow, MIT, 1948–49; Visiting Professor: Michigan State University, 1958; MIT, 1962; Nanyang Technological Inst., then Nanyang Technolog. Univ., Singapore, 1986, 1989–93; Nat. Univ. of Singapore, 1988–89. Member: CNAA, 1970–80; Engrg Bd, SRC, 1971–74; Vis. Cttee, RCA, 1973–82; Council, IMechE, 1974–76; Nominations Cttee, Engrg Council, 1984–95; Council, Inst. of Measurement and Control, 1993–96 (Pres., Soc. of Instrument Technol., 1964–65). Mem. Council, Loughborough Univ. of Technology, 1979–91; Chm., Engrg Professors' Conference, 1983–85. Pres., Pembroke Coll. Cambridge Soc., 1993. Hon. FInstMC 1995. Hon. DEd CNAA, 1992. *Publications:* contribs to mech. and elec. jls. *Address:* 6 Southmeads Close, Leicester LE2 2LT. *T:* (0116) 271 5402. *Clubs:* Athenæum; Leander.   *Died 27 Jan. 1999.*

MacLENNAN, Maj.-Gen. Alastair, OBE 1945; Curator, Royal Army Medical Corps Historical Museum, Mytchett, Hants, 1969–77; *b* 16 Feb. 1912; *s* of Col Farquhar MacLennan, DSO; *m* 1940, Constance Anne Cook (*d* 2000); two *s* one *d*. *Educ:* Aberdeen Grammar Sch.; University of Aberdeen (MB, ChB). Commissioned Lieut,

RAMC, 1934; Captain, 1935; Major, 1942; Lt-Col, 1942; Colonel, 1952; Brigadier, 1964; Maj.-Gen., 1967; retired 1969. Appointments held included regimental, staff and Ministry of Defence in UK, Malta, NW Europe, India, Malaya, Korea, Egypt and Germany; ADGMS (Army), Min. of Defence, 1957–61; DDMS, HQ, BAOR, 1961–64; Inspector Army Medical Services, 1964–66; Deputy Director of Medical Services: 1 (BR) Corps, 1966–67; HQ Eastern Command, 1967–68; Dep. Dir-Gen., Army Med. Services, MoD, 1968–69; QHP, 1968–69. Col Comdt, RAMC, 1971–76. US Bronze Star Medal, 1952. OStJ 1966. *Publications:* papers on history of military firearms and on Highland Regiments in North America 1756–1783. *Recreations:* bird-watching, military history, collecting antique military firearms and swords, vintage motor-cars. *Address:* Gable House, Chequers Lane, North Crawley, Bucks MK16 9LJ. *T:* (01234) 391700.

Died 29 July 2000.

McLENNAN, Sir Ian (Munro), KCMG 1979; KBE 1963 (CBE 1956); President, Australian Academy of Technological Sciences, 1976–83, The Foundation President, 1983; *b* 30 Nov. 1909; *s* of R. B. and C. O. McLennan; *m* 1937, Dora H. (decd), *d* of J. H. Robertson; two *s* two *d. Educ:* Scotch Coll., Melbourne; Melbourne Univ. Cadet engineer, Broken Hill Pty Co. Ltd, 1933; Asst Manager, Newcastle Steelworks of BHP Co. Ltd, 1943; Asst Gen. Man., BHP Co. Ltd, 1947; Gen. Man., 1950; Sen. Gen. Man., 1956; Chief Gen. Man., 1959; Man. Dir, 1967–71; Chm., 1971–77; Chairman: BHP-GKN Hldgs Ltd, 1970–78; Tubemakers of Australia Ltd, 1973–79; Australia and New Zealand Banking Group Ltd, and Australia and New Zealand Group Hldgs Ltd, 1977–82; Interscan Australia Pty Ltd, 1978–84; Bank of Adelaide, 1979–80; Henry Jones IXL Ltd, 1981; Elders IXL Ltd, 1981–85; Dir, ICI Australia Ltd, 1976–79. Chairman: Defence (Industrial) Cttee, 1956–75; Ian Clunies Ross Meml Foundn; Australian Mineral Development Laboratories, 1959–67 (Mem. Council, 1959–77); Dep. Chm., Immigration Planning Council, 1949–67. Former Dir, International Iron and Steel Inst.; Pres., Australia-Japan Business Co-operation Cttee, 1977–85; Member: Internat. Council, Morgan Guaranty Trust Co. of NY, 1973–79; Australian Mining Industry Council, 1967–77; Australasian Inst. of Mining and Metallurgy (Pres., 1951, 1957 and 1972); Australian Mineral Industries Research Assoc. Ltd, 1958–77; General Motors Australian Adv. Council, 1978–82; Adv. Council, CSIRO, 1979–82. Chm., Queen Elizabeth II Jubilee Trust for Young Australians, 1978–81. For. Associate, Nat. Acad. of Engrg (USA), 1978; For. Mem., Fellowship of Engrg, UK, 1986. FIAM 1978; FAA 1980. Hon. DEng: Melbourne, 1968; Newcastle, 1968; Hon. DSc Wollongong, 1978; Hon. LLD Melbourne, 1988. *Recreations:* golf, gardening. *Address:* Apt 3, 112–120 Walsh Street, South Yarra, Victoria 3141, Australia. *Clubs:* Melbourne, Athenæum, Australian (Melbourne); Royal Melbourne Golf; Melbourne Cricket. *Died 25 Oct. 1998.*

MACLEOD OF BORVE, Baroness *cr* 1971 (Life Peer), of Borve, Isle of Lewis; **Evelyn Hester Macleod;** JP; DL; *b* 19 Feb. 1915; *d* of Rev. Gervase Vanneck Blois (*d* 1961), and Hon. Hester Murray Pakington (*d* 1973), *y d* of 3rd Baron Hampton; *m* 1st, 1937, Mervyn Charles Mason (killed by enemy action, 1940); 2nd, 1941, Rt Hon. Iain Norman Macleod, MP (*d* 1970), *e s* of late Norman A. Macleod, MD, Scaliscro, Isle of Lewis; one *s* one *d.* Chm., 1973–85, Pres., 1985–90, Nat. Association of the Leagues of Hospital Friends; first Chm., Nat. Gas Consumers' Council, 1972–77; Member: IBA (formerly ITA), 1972–75; Energy Commn, 1977–78; Metrication Bd, 1978–80. Co-Founder, Crisis at Christmas, 1967; Pres., Nat. Assoc. of Widows, 1976–. Governor, Queenswood Sch., 1978–85. JP Middlesex, 1955; DL Greater London,

1977. Hon. DSocSc Middlesex, 1998. *Recreation:* my family. *Address:* House of Lords, SW1A 0PW; Luckings Farm, Coleshill, Amersham, Bucks HP7 0LS.

Died 17 Nov. 1999.

MacLEOD, Aubrey Seymour H.; *see* Halford-MacLeod.

MACLEOD-SMITH, Alastair Macleod, CMG 1956; *b* 30 June 1916; *s* of late R. A. Smith, MIEE, and Mrs I. Macleod-Smith (*née* Kellner); *m* 1945, Ann (*née* Circuitt); one *s* one *d. Educ:* The Wells House, Malvern Wells, Worcs; Ellesmere Coll., Salop; The Queen's Coll., Oxford (BA 1938). Entered HM Oversea Service as administrative cadet, Nigeria, 1939; Asst Dist Officer, 1942, Dist Officer, Nigeria, 1949; seconded to Windward Islands as Financial and Economic Adviser, 1949–52; Financial Sec., Western Pacific High Commission, 1952–57; Financial Sec., Sierra Leone, 1957–61. Dir, Selection Trust Ltd, 1967–80; Consultant, National Westminster Bank, 1981–83. *Address:* Roughetts Lodge, Coldharbour Lane, Hildenborough, Kent TN11 9JX.

Died 30 Dec. 1999.

McMANUS, Dermot Aloysius; Agent-General for Queensland in London, since 1996; *b* 25 Oct. 1944; *s* of Thomas Paul McManus and Kathleen Mary McManus (*née* Freney); *m* 1970, Phillipa Lorraine Channon; one *s* two *d. Educ:* St Joseph's Coll., Brisbane; Univ. of Queensland (BEcon). Advertising and journalism, Brisbane and London, 1962–70; Australian Federal Govt Trade Ministry, 1970–89: postings included: Geneva, 1973–77; Riyadh, 1981–83; Nairobi, 1983–86; Rome, 1987–89; Dir, Internat. Trade, Qld State Govt, Brisbane, 1989–95. *Recreations:* music, touring, reading. *Address:* Queensland House, 392 Strand, WC2R 0LZ. *T:* (020) 7836 1333. *Died 3 Oct. 2000.*

MacMANUS, His Honour John Leslie Edward, TD 1945; QC 1970; a Circuit Judge (formerly a Judge of County Courts), 1971–90, retired; *b* 7 April 1920; *o s* of F. H. MacManus and H. S. MacManus (*née* Colton); *m* 1942, Gertrude Mary Frances, (Trudy), Koppenhagen; two *d. Educ:* Eastbourne College. Served 1939–45 with RA: Middle East, Italy, Crete, Yugoslavia; Captain 1942; Major 1945. Called to Bar, Middle Temple, 1947. Dep. Chm., East Sussex QS, 1964–71. *Recreations:* gardening, travel. *Address:* The Old Rectory, Twincham, Haywards Heath, West Sussex RH17 5NR. *T:* (01444) 881221.

Died 25 April 1998.

McMASTER, Gordon James; MP (Lab and Co-op) Paisley South, since Nov. 1990; *b* 13 Feb. 1960; *s* of William McMaster, retired Parks Superintendent and Alison McMaster (*née* Maxwell), clerkess. *Educ:* Cochrane Castle Primary Sch.; Johnstone High Sch.; Woodburn House FE Centre (City and Guilds in Horticulture); West of Scotland Agricl Coll. (OND Hort.); Jordanhill Coll. of Education (Cert. in Further Educn.) Apprentice gardner, Renfrew DC, 1976–77; full time student, 1977–78 and 1979–80; trainee hort. technician, Renfrew DC, 1978–79; Craftsman Gardener, Renfrew DC, 1980; Lectr in Hort., Langside Coll., 1980–86, Sen. Lectr, 1986–88; Co-ordinator, Growing Concern Initiative, Strathclyde, 1988–90. Member: Johnstone Community Council 1980–84 (Chm., 1982–84); Renfrew DC, 1984–91 (Dep. Leader, 1987–88; Leader, 1988–90). Opposition spokesman on disabled people's rights, 1995–97; Scottish opposition whip, 1992–94; Asst to Dep. Chief Opposition Whip, 1994–95; Sec., All-Party Disablement Gp, 1992–94. *Recreations:* reading, gardening, computers. *Address:* 47 Hagg Crescent, Johnstone PA5 8TB. *T:* (01505) 336259; House of Commons, SW1A 0AA. *T:* (0171) 219 5104. *Club:* United Services (Johnstone). *Died 28 July 1997.*

McMINNIES, John Gordon, OBE 1965; HM Diplomatic Service, retired 1977; *b* 1 Oct. 1919; *s* of late William

Gordon McMinnies and Joyce Millicent McMinnies; *m* 1947, Mary (*née* Jackson) (*d* 1978), novelist. *Educ:* Bilton Grange; Rugby Sch.; Austria (language trng). Reporter: Western Mail, 1938; Reuters, 1939. Served War, Army, 1940–46: comd R Troop, RHA; retd, Major. HM Diplomatic Service (Athens, Warsaw, Bologna, Malaysia, Cyprus, Nairobi, Lusaka, New Delhi), 1946–77; retd, Counsellor. *Recreations:* crazy paving, crosswords, cricketology, the sea. *Address:* 14 rue de la Corderie, 34300 Agde, France. *T:* 467214438.

Died 16 Sept. 1998.

MACNAGHTEN, Robin Donnelly, MA; Headmaster of Sherborne, 1974–88; *b* 3 Aug. 1927; 2nd *s* of Sir Henry Pelham Wentworth Macnaghten and Lady (Frances) Macnaghten; *m* 1961, Petronella, *er d* of late Lt-Col A. T. Card and Mrs Card; two *s* one *d. Educ:* Eton (Schol.); King's Coll., Cambridge (Schol.; 1st cl. Class. Tripos Pt I, 1947; 1st cl. with dist. Pt II, 1948; Browne Medallist; MA 1954). Travelled in Italy and Turkey, 1949. Asst, Mackinnon Mackenzie & Co., Bombay, 1949–54; Asst Master, Eton Coll., 1954, and Housemaster, 1965. Hon. Sec. and Treas., 1970–74, Pres., 1991–92, OEA; Pres., Old Shirburnian Soc., 1984–85. Governor: Sandroyd Sch., 1986–98; Dauntsey's Sch., 1988–98; Chairman of Governors: Hall Sch., Wincanton, 1978–; Forres at Sandle Manor (formerly Forres) Sch., 1991–96 (Gov., 1974–88). *Publication:* trans. Vita Romana (by U. E. Paoli), 1963. *Recreations:* numismatics (FRNS), walking, gardening. *Address:* Prospect House, Tisbury, Wilts SP3 6QQ. *T:* (01747) 870355. *Club:* Western India Turf (Bombay).

Died 23 April 1999.

McNEICE, Sir (Thomas) Percy (Fergus), Kt 1956; CMG 1953; OBE 1947; *b* 16 Aug. 1901; *s* of late Canon W. G. McNeice, MA, and Mary Masterson; *m* 1947, Yuen Peng Loke, *d* of late Dr Loke Yew, CMG, LLD; one *s* one *d. Educ:* Bradford Grammar Sch.; Keble Coll., Oxford (MA). Malayan Civil Service, 1925; Captain, Straits Settlements Volunteer Force (Prisoner of War, 1942–45). MLC, Singapore, 1949; MEC 1949; President of the City Council, Singapore, 1949–56, retired. FZS. *Recreations:* bird watching, walking, swimming. *Address:* 12 Jalan Sampurna, Singapore 268 280. *Club:* Royal Commonwealth Society.

Died 8 Feb. 1998.

McNEILL, (Gordon) Keith; Editor, Woman's Own, since 1990; *b* 6 Aug. 1953; *s* of Gordon Francis McNeill and Vera McNeill; *m* 1983, Ruth Brotherhood; one *s. Educ:* Slough Grammar School. Features Editor, Chat Magazine, 1985; London Evening News, 1988; Deputy Editor, Woman's Own, 1988. *Recreations:* walking, Bournemouth AFC, modern art, historical architecture. *Address:* Woman's Own, King's Reach Tower, Stamford Street, SE1 9LS. *T:* (0171) 261 5500.

Died 11 May 1998.

McNEILL, Maj.-Gen. John Malcolm, CB 1963; CBE 1959 (MBE 1942); *b* 22 Feb. 1909; *s* of Brig.-Gen. Angus McNeill, CB, CBE, DSO, TD, Seaforth Highlanders, and Lilian, *d* of Maj.-Gen. Sir Harry Barron, KCVO; *m* 1939, Barbara, *d* of Colonel C. H. Marsh, DSO, Spilsby, Lincs; two *d. Educ:* Imperial Service Coll., Windsor; RMA, Woolwich. 2nd Lieut, RA, 1929; served Western Desert, Sicily, Italy, NW Europe and Burma, 1939–45; commanded 1st Regt RHA, 1948–51; Student Imperial Defence Coll., 1952; Dep. Secretary, Chiefs of Staff Cttee, Ministry of Defence, 1953–55; Comdr RA 2nd Div. 1955–58; Comdt School of Artillery, 1958–60; Commander, British Army Staff, and Military Attaché, Washington, DC, 1960–63; Col Comdt RA, 1964–74. Principal Staff Officer to Sec. of State for Commonwealth Relations, 1964–69. ADC to the Queen, 1958–60. *Address:* Hole's Barn, Pilton, Shepton Mallet, Som BA4 4DF. *T:*

Pilton (01749) 890212. *Clubs:* Army and Navy, English-Speaking Union.

Died 25 May 1996.

McNEILL, Keith; *see* McNeill, G. K.

MACOUN, Michael John, CMG 1964; OBE 1961; QPM 1954; Overseas Police Adviser, and Inspector-General of Police, Dependent Territories, Foreign and Commonwealth Office, 1967–79, retired; Police Training Adviser, Ministry of Overseas Development, 1967–79; *b* 27 Nov. 1914; *o s* of late John Horatio Macoun, Comr of Chinese Maritime Customs; *m* 1940, Geraldine Mabel, *o d* of late Brig.-Gen. G. C. Sladen, CB, CMG, DSO, MC; two *s. Educ:* Stowe Sch., Buckingham; Univ. of Oxford (MA); Munich Univ. (Diploma in German Language and Literature). At Metropolitan Police Coll., 1938; Tanganyika Police, 1939–42, 1945–58; War Service, 1943–44; Inspector-Gen. of Police, Uganda, 1959–64; Directing Staff, Police Coll., Bramshill, 1965; Commonwealth Office, 1966. Lecture tour: of USA, under auspices of British Information Services, 1964; of Eastern Canada, for Assoc. of Canadian Clubs, 1966; Vis. Lectr, Police Coll., Bramshill, 1980–86. Rep. of Sec. of State, Police Appointments Bd, Hong Kong Govt, 1980–86. Non-exec. Dir, Control Risks Gp, 1983–86. Colonial Police Medal, 1951; OStJ 1959. *Publication:* Wrong Place, Right Time (autobiog.), 1996. *Recreations:* travel, walking. *Address:* Furzedown, Rowledge, near Farnham, Surrey GU10 4EB. *T:* (01252) 793196. *Clubs:* Royal Commonwealth Society; County (Guildford).

Died 25 March 1997.

MACPHERSON, Sheriff Alexander Calderwood; a Sheriff of South Strathclyde, Dumfries and Galloway, at Hamilton, since 1978; *b* 14 June 1939; *s* of Alexander and Jean Macpherson; *m* 1963, Christine Isobel Hutchison (marr. diss. 1985); two *s; m* 1984, Eileen Mary Joyce or Gray; *m* 1990, Marian Claire Hall. *Educ:* Glasgow Academy; Glasgow Univ. (MA 1959, LLB 1962). Qualified as solicitor, 1962; private practice, 1962–78; part-time Assistantship in Private Law at Glasgow Univ., 1962–69; Partner in West, Anderson & Co., Solicitors, Glasgow, 1968–78; Lectr in Evidence and Procedure at Strathclyde Univ., 1969–78. *Recreations:* piping (especially Piobaireachd), psychotherapy, reading. *Address:* Sheriff Court, Hamilton, Lanarks ML3 6AA. *Clubs:* Glasgow Highland, Glasgow Art, Royal Scottish Automobile (Glasgow); Royal Scottish Pipers' Society (Edinburgh).

Died 11 March 1999.

MACPHERSON, Fiona Mary, (Mrs Adrian Bailey); Editor-in-chief, Affluent Magazine group, since 2000; *b* 2 Sept. 1940; *d* of late John Macpherson and Winifred Macpherson (*née* Armitage); *m* 1st, 1967, J. Douglas Findlay (marr. diss. 1974); 2nd, 1975, Adrian Bailey; one *s* one *d. Educ:* Inverness Royal Acad.; St Andrews Univ. (MA Hons). Sub-editor: D. C. Thomson, Dundee, 1962–63; IPC Magazines, 1963–64; Arts Editor, Queen magazine, 1965–70; Dep. Editor, Harpers & Queen, 1970–75; freelance editor, contract publishing for Dept of Employment, Robinsons Baby Foods, Boots the Chemist, and Tea Council, 1976–93; Ed., Harpers & Queen, 1994–2000. *Recreations:* fiction, cinema, plants, Scotland. *Address:* c/o National Magazine Co., 72 Broadwick Street, W1V 2BP. *T:* (020) 7439 5480. *Club:* Soho House.

Died 28 Nov. 2000.

MACPHERSON, Roderick Ewen; Fellow, King's College, Cambridge, since 1942; Registrary, University of Cambridge, 1969–83; *b* 17 July 1916; *s* of Ewen Macpherson, Chief Charity Commissioner, and Dorothy Mildred Hensley; *m* 1941, Sheila Joan Hooper, *d* of H. P. Hooper; two *s* two *d. Educ:* Eton College; King's College, Cambridge (Math. Tripos, Part II, Wrangler; Math. Tripos, Part III, Distinction; Smith's Prizeman, 1940). Served

RAFVR, 1940–46, Navigator (Radio). Cambridge University: Third Bursar, 1947–50, Second Bursar, 1950–51, First Bursar, 1951–62, King's Coll.; University Treasurer, 1962–69; Member: Council of the Senate, 1957–62; Financial Board, 1955–62. Cambridge City Council, 1958–74, Hon. Councillor, 1974–. *Recreations:* gardening, hill-walking. *Address:* 11 St Peter's Close, Lugwardine, Hereford HR1 4AT. *T:* (01432) 850996.
Died 21 Jan. 2000.

McQUEEN, Maj.-Gen. Keith John; *b* 17 June 1923; *s* of late Robert Harvey McQueen and Gladys McQueen (*née* Edwards); *m* 1959, Henrietta Mary (*d* 1992), *y d* of Lt-Col Sir Charles Wickham, KCMG, KBE, DSO. *Educ:* Quiristers Sch.; Winchester Coll.; King Edward VI Sch., Southampton. psc, psc†. Enlisted RA 1942; commissioned RA, India, 1944; served India, Burma, Thailand, Malaya (Mountain Artillery), 1944–46; Combined Ops, Malta, Palestine, Hong Kong, Korea, 1947–50; RHA, BAOR, 1951–53; Instructor, RMA Sandhurst, 1954; sc 1955; 1 (BR) Corps, BAOR, 1956–58; L (Néry) Battery, Malaysia, 1958–61; 20 Armd Bde Gp, BAOR, 1961–63; DS RMCS, 1964–65; 5 Regt RA, BAOR, 1965–67; Asst Mil. Sec., MoD, 1967–68; CRA 3 Div. (UK Mobile Force), 1968–71; rcds 1972; Comdt, Royal Sch. of Artillery, 1973–74; GOC NW Dist, 1974–77, retired. Man. Dir, EML Ltd (Lopex Gp), 1977–80; Dep. Chm., Gencor (UK) Ltd, 1980–86. Col Comdt, RA, 1978–83; Hon. Colonel: Royal Sch. of Artillery, 1985–93; 14 Regt RA, 1985–95. *Recreations:* shooting, fishing, gardening. *Address:* 1 New Court, Sutton Manor, Sutton Scotney, Winchester, Hants SO21 3JX. *T:* (01962) 761045. *Club:* Naval and Military.
Died 2 June 2000.

MacQUITTY, James Lloyd, OBE 1983; QC (NI) 1960; Chairman, Ulster Television Ltd, 1977–83; *b* 2 Nov. 1912; *s* of James MacQuitty and Henrietta Jane (*née* Little); *m* 1941, Irene Frances McDowell (*d* 1999). *Educ:* Campbell Coll. and Methodist Coll., Belfast; St Catherine's Coll., Oxford (MA); Trinity Hall, Cambridge (MA, LLM). Vice-Pres., Cambridge Univ. Conservative Assoc., 1936. HG Instructor, 1940–43; HAA, 1943–44. Called to English Bar, 1938, to NI Bar, 1941. Chairman: Compensation Appeals Tribunal; Compensation Tribunal for Loss of Employment through Civil Unrest (discontinued); Wages Councils in NI, 1951–89; Arbitrator under the Industrial Courts Act 1919, 1958–78; Mem., Industrial Injuries Adv. Council, 1960–86. Before reorganisation in 1973 of Local Govt in NI, was Chm. of Jt Adv. Bds for Local Authorities' Services, Municipal Clerks, Rural Dist Clerks and County Chief Educn Officers and County Surveyors. Vice-Chm., Management Cttee, Glenlola Collegiate Sch., 1964–75; Chm., Trustees of Ulster Folk and Transport Museum, 1976–85 (Vice-Chm., 1969–76). Hon. LLD QUB, 1987. Freeman, City of London, 1967. *Recreations:* swimming, sailing. *Address:* 10 Braemar Park, Bangor, Co. Down, Northern Ireland BT20 5HZ. *T:* (028) 9145 4420. *Clubs:* Carlton; Royal Ulster Yacht.
Died 26 Aug. 1999.

MacRAE, Prof. Donald Gunn; Martin White Professor of Sociology, University of London, 1978–87, then Emeritus; *b* 20 April 1921; *o s* of Donald MacRae and Elizabeth Maud Gunn; *m* 1st, 1948, Helen Grace McHardy (marr. diss. 1966; she *d* 1995); two *d*; 2nd, 1987, Mrs Jean Ridyard; one *s* one *d*. *Educ:* various schools in Scotland; Glasgow High Sch.; Glasgow Univ.; Balliol Coll., Oxford. MA Glasgow, 1942; BA 1945, MA 1949, Oxon. Asst Lectr, LSE, 1945; Univ. Lectr in Sociology, Oxford, 1949; Reader in Sociology, London Univ., 1954; Prof. of Sociology: UC Gold Coast, 1956; Univ. of California, Berkeley, 1959; Univ. of London, 1961–87. Fellow, Center for Advanced Studies in Behavioral Sciences, Stanford, 1967. Vis. Prof., Univ. of the Witwatersrand, 1975; Senior Member, Keynes Coll., Darwin Coll., Univ.

of Kent at Canterbury. Member: Council, CNAA (Chm. Cttee for Arts and Social Studies, to 1978); Archbp of Canterbury's Gp on Divorce Law, 1964–66; Gaitskell Commn of Inquiry into Advertising, 1962–66; Internat. Council on the Future of the University, 1973–82. Editor, British Jl of Sociology, from formation to 1965; Mem., Editl Adv. Cttees, Encyclopædia Britannica, 1968–. *Publications:* Ideology and Society, 1960; (ed) The World of J. B. Priestley, 1967; (ed with introdn) The Man Versus the State, by Herbert Spencer, 1969; Ages and Stages, 1973; Max Weber, 1974. *Recreations:* talking, music, walking. *Address:* Norfolk House, 44 High Street, Sandwich, Kent CT13 9EG. *Club:* Athenæum.
Died 23 Dec. 1997.

MACRAE, Col Sir Robert (Andrew Alexander Scarth), KCVO 1990; MBE 1953; JP; Lord-Lieutenant of Orkney, 1972–90 (Vice-Lieutenant, 1967–72); farmer; *b* 14 April 1915; *s* of late Robert Scarth Farquhar Macrae, CIE, CBE, Grindelay House, Orphir, Orkney and Beatrix Reid, *d* of Andrew McGeoch, Glasgow; *m* 1945, Violet Maud (*d* 1997), *d* of late Walter Scott MacLellan; two *s*. *Educ:* Lancing; RMC Sandhurst. 2nd Lieut Seaforth Highlanders, 1935; Col 1963; retd 1968. Active Service: NW Europe, 1940–45 (despatches, 1945); Korea, 1952–53; E Africa, 1953–54. Member: Orkney CC, 1970–74; Orkney Islands Council, 1974–78; Vice Chairman: Orkney Hospital Bd, 1971–74; Orkney Health Bd, 1974–79. Hon. Sheriff, Grampian, Highlands and Islands, 1972. DL, Co. of Orkney, 1946; JP Orkney, 1975. Freedom of Orkney, 1990. *Recreations:* sailing, fishing. *Address:* Grindelay House, Orkney KW17 2RD. *T:* (01856) 811228. *Clubs:* Army and Navy; New, Puffin's (Edinburgh).
Died 15 Nov. 1999.

MADDEN, Rear-Adm. Colin Duncan, CB 1966; CBE 1964; LVO 1954, DSC 1940 and Bar, 1944; Registrar and Secretary, Order of the Bath, 1979–85; *b* 19 Aug. 1915; *s* of late Archibald Maclean Madden, CMG, and Cecilia Catherine Moor; *m* 1943, Agnes Margaret, *d* of late H. K. Newcombe, OBE, Canada and London, and Eleanor Clare; two *d*. *Educ:* RNC, Dartmouth. During War of 1939–45, took part in blocking Ijmuiden harbour and Dutch evacuation; Navigating Officer of 7th Mine Sweeping Flotilla; HMS Arethusa; Assault Group J1 for invasion of Europe, and HMS Norfolk; thence HMS Triumph; Commander, 1950; Comd HMS Crossbow, 1952; staff of Flag Officer Royal Yachts, SS Gothic and Comdr (N) HM Yacht Britannia, for Royal Commonwealth Tour, 1953–54; Captain, Naval Attaché, Rome; Captain D 7 in HMS Trafalgar; IDC; Comd HMS Albion, 1962; Rear-Admiral, 1965; Senior Naval Member Directing Staff, Imperial Defence Coll., 1965–67; retired, 1967. Dir, Nat. Trade Develt Assoc., 1967–69. Gentleman Usher of the Scarlet Rod to the Order of the Bath, 1968–79. Dir Gen., Brewers' Soc., 1969–80. *Recreations:* sailing, gardening, fishing, tapestry. *Clubs:* Army and Navy; Royal Naval Sailing Association.
Died 1 July 2000.

MADDISON, Vincent Albert, CMG 1961; TD 1953; *b* 10 Aug. 1915; *s* of late Vincent Maddison; *m* 1954, Jennifer Christian, (Judy), Bernard; two *s* one *d*. *Educ:* Wellingborough Sch.; Downing Coll., Cambridge (MA). Served War of 1939–45: Ethiopian and Burma Campaigns. Colonial Administrative Service, 1939; District Officer, Kenya, 1947; seconded to Secretariat, 1948; Director, Trade and Supplies, 1953; Secretary, 1954, Perm. Secretary, 1957–63, Min. of Commerce and Industry; retired from Kenya Government, 1963; Chairman: East African Power and Lighting Co. Ltd, 1965–70; Tana River Development Co. Ltd, 1965–70; The Kenya Power Co. Ltd 1965–70; Director: Nyali Ltd, 1966–70; Kisauni Ltd, 1966–70; East African Trust and Investment Co. Ltd, 1966–70; East African Engineering Consultants, 1966–70;

Recreations: ski-ing, gardening, sailing. *Address:* The Hayloft, 2 Lower Woodhouse, Shobdon, Leominster, Herefordshire HR6 9NL. *T:* (01568) 708688. *Club:* Muthaiga Country (Kenya).   *Died 21 Dec. 1998.*

MADGE, Charles Henry; *b* 10 Oct. 1912; *s* of Lieut-Colonel C. A. Madge and Barbara (*née* Hylton Foster); *m* 1st, Kathleen Raine, FRSL (marr. diss.); one *s* one *d*; 2nd, Inez Pearn (*d* 1976); one *s* one *d*; 3rd, Evelyn Brown (*d* 1984). *Educ:* Winchester Coll. (Scholar); Magdalene Coll., Cambridge (Scholar). Reporter on Daily Mirror, 1935–36; founded Mass-Observation, 1937; directed survey of working-class saving and spending for National Institute of Economic and Social Research, 1940–42; Research staff of PEP, 1943; Director, Pilot Press, 1944; Social Development Officer, New Town of Stevenage, 1947; Prof. of Sociology, Univ. of Birmingham, 1950–70. Mission to Thailand on UN Technical Assistance, 1953–54; UNESCO Missions to India, 1957–58, to South-East Asia, 1959 and 1960 and Leader of Mission to Ghana for UN Economic Commission for Africa, 1963. *Publications:* The Disappearing Castle (poems), 1937; part-author of Britain by Mass-Observation, 1938, and other books connected with this organisation; The Father Found (poems), 1941; War-time Pattern of Saving and Spending, 1943; (ed) Pilot Papers: Social Essays and Documents, 1945–47; Society in the Mind, 1964; (with Barbara Weinberger) Art Students Observed, 1973; (with Peter Willmott) Inner City Poverty in Paris and London, 1981; (ed with Mary-Lou Jennings) Pandaemonium, by Humphrey Jennings, 1985; (with Tom Harrisson) Britain by Mass-Observation, 1986; (with Humphrey Jennings) May the Twelfth, 1987; Of Love, Time and Places (poems), 1994; contributions to Economic Journal, Town Planning Review, Human Relations, etc. *Address:* 28 Lynmouth Road, N2 9LS.   *Died 17 Jan. 1996.*

MADIGAN, Sir Russel (Tullie), Kt 1981; OBE 1970; Chairman: Remproc Ltd, since 1991; AUSI Limited, 1994–97; *b* 22 Nov. 1920; *s* of Dr Cecil T. Madigan and Wynnis K. Wollaston; *m* 1st, 1942, Margaret Symons (decd); four *s* one *d*; 2nd, 1981, Satsuko Tamura (decd). *Educ:* Univ. of Adelaide (BScEng 1941, BE 1946, ME 1954, LLB 1960). FSASM 1941; FTS. Joined Zinc Corp., 1946; Gowrie Schol. in Canada and USA, 1947–49; Underground Manager, Zinc Corp., NBHC Ltd, 1956–59; CRA Ltd (Conzinc Rio Tinto of Australia Ltd): Gen. Manager, Gen. Mining Div., 1960–64; Dir, 1968–87; Dep. Chm., 1978–87; Hamersley Iron: Man. Dir, 1965–71; Chm., 1971–81. Chairman: Blair Athol Coal Pty, 1971–80; Interstate Oil, 1972–81; Hamersley Hldgs, 1971–81; APV Asia Pacific, 1983–87; Muswellbrook Energy & Minerals, 1987–90; Director: Nat. Commercial Union, 1969–90; Rio Tinto Zinc Corp., 1971–85; Comalco, 1976–82; APV Hldgs, 1983–87. Pres., Aust. Inst. of Internat. Affairs, 1984–89; Chairman: Aust.-Japan Foundn, 1977–81; Aust. Mineral Foundn, 1984–88; Aust. Pacific Econ. Co-operation Cttee, 1986–92; Member: Export Develt Council, 1970–86; Consultative Cttee on Relations with Japan, 1977–82; Life Mem., Pacific Basin Econ. Council, 1982; Councillor: Australasian Inst. of Mining and Metallurgy, 1958–87 (Pres., 1980); Aust. Acad. of Technological Scis and Engrg, 1978–89 (Treas., 1985–89). *Recreations:* flying, farming. *Address:* 99 Spring Street, Melbourne, Vic 3000, Australia. *Clubs:* Athenæum, Melbourne (Melbourne); Royal Melbourne Golf.
                                                Died 19 July 1999.

MAGILL, Air Vice-Marshal Graham Reese, CB 1966; CBE 1962 (OBE 1945); DFC 1941 and Bar, 1943; *b* 23 Jan. 1915; *s* of late Robert Wilson Magill and Frances Elizabeth Magill, Te Aroha, NZ; *m* 1942, Blanche Marie Colson (*d* 1991); two *s*. *Educ:* Te Aroha High Sch.; Hamilton Technical Coll., NZ. Joined Royal Air Force,

1936; served War of 1939–45, Sudan and Eritrea (despatches 1941), Egypt, UK, NW Europe; subsequently, UK, Egypt, France; Director of Operations (Bomber and Reconnaissance), Air Ministry, 1959–62; Commandant, RAF College of Air Warfare, Manby, Lincs, 1963–64; Director-General of Organisation (RAF), Ministry of Defence, 1964–67; AOC, 25 Group, RAF, 1967–68; AOC 22 Group, RAF, 1968–69; retd 1970. *Address:* c/o Holmhurst, The Common, Vale of Glamorgan CF64 4DL. *Club:* Royal Air Force.   *Died 1 Dec. 1998.*

MAHOMED, Ismail; Hon. Mr Justice Mahomed; Chief Justice of South Africa, since 1997; Chairman, Law Commission of South Africa, since 1996; *b* 25 July 1931; *s* of Hajee Mahomed and Khatoon Mahomed (*née* Suliman); *m* 1956, Hawa Bava. *Educ:* Univ. of Witwatersrand (BA Hons 1954; LLB 1957). Advocate, Johannesburg Bar, 1957–91; SC 1974; called to the Bar, Gray's Inn, 1984; acting Judge, Botswana High Court, 1978; Judge, Court of Appeal, Swaziland, 1979–89; Pres. and Judge, Court of Appeal, Lesotho, 1982–86; Judge, Supreme Court of South Africa, 1991–93; Chief Justice of Namibia, 1992–97; Dep. Pres., Constitutional Ct of S Africa, 1995–96. Hon. Prof. of Law, Univ. of Witwatersrand, 1989–97. Hon. LLD: Pennsylvania, 1992; Delhi, 1993; Natal, 1995; Nat. Univ. of India, 1997; Pretoria, 1998. Human Rights Award, Indicator newspaper, Johannesburg, 1990; Black Lawyers' Human Rights Award, 1995; Duma Nokwe Prize on Human Rights, 1997; Achiever of the Year Award, Rotary Club of Johannesburg, 1997; Paul Harris Award, 1998; Maulana Azad Meml Lecture Award, 1998. *Publications:* articles on jurisprudence in legal jls. *Recreations:* political philosophy, religious studies, cricket (spectator). *Address:* Box 13434, Laudium 0037, South Africa. *T:* (12) 374 3863.   *Died 17 June 2000.*

MAHONY, Francis Joseph, CB 1980; OBE 1972; President, Repatriation Review Tribunal, Australia, 1979–84; *b* 15 March 1915; *s* of Cornelius J. Mahony and Angela M. Heagney; *m* 1939, Mary K. Sexton; seven *s* one *d*. *Educ:* De La Salle Coll., Armidale; Sydney Univ. (LLB 1940). Served War, CMF and AIF, 1942–44. Called to the Bar, Supreme Court of NSW, 1940; Commonwealth Crown Solicitor's Office, 1941; admitted Practitioner, High Ct of Australia, 1950; admitted Solicitor, Supreme Ct of NSW, 1952; Dep. Commonwealth Crown Solicitor, NSW, 1963–70; Dep. Sec., Attorney-Gen.'s Dept, Canberra, 1970–79; Dir-Gen., Australian Security Intelligence Orgn, 1975–76. Leader, Aust. Delegn to Diplomatic Conf. on Humanitarian Law Applicable in Armed Conflicts, 1974–77. Chairman: Criminology Res. Council, 1972–79; Bd of Management, Aust. Inst. of Criminology, 1973–79; Mem. UN Cttee, Crime Prevention and Control, 1980–83. *Recreation:* golf. *Address:* 92 Cliff Avenue, Northbridge, NSW 2063, Australia. *T:* (2) 99587853. *Club:* Northbridge Golf.

                                                Died 22 Jan. 2000.

MAILLART, Ella Kini; traveller; *b* 20 Feb. 1903; Swiss father and Danish mother; unmarried. *Educ:* Geneva; and also while teaching French at two schools in England. Took to the seas at 20, cruising with 3 ton Perlette, 10 ton Bonita, 45 ton Atalante—all these manned by girls; then 120 ton Volunteer, 125 ton Insoumise; in Mediterranean, Biscay, Channel; sailed for Switzerland, Olympic Games, Paris, 1924, single-handed competition; hockey for Switzerland as captain in 1931; skied for Switzerland in the Internat. Ski Fedn races in 1931–34; went to Russia for 6 months, 1930; travelled in Russian Turkestan for 6 months 1932; went to Manchoukuo for Petit Parisien, 1934; returned overland accompanied by Peter Fleming, via Koko Nor; travelled overland to Iran and Afghanistan in 1937 and 1939, in South India, 1940–45, Nepal, 1951,

Everest Base Camp, 1965. FRGS; Member: Royal Soc. for Asian Affairs; Club des Explorateurs, Paris; Hon. Mem., GB-China Centre. Sir Percy Sykes Medal. *Publications:* Parmi la Jeunesse Russe, 1932; Des Monts Célestes aux Sables Rouges, 1934 (in English as Turkestan Solo, 1934, repr. 1985); Oasis Interdites, 1937 (in English as Forbidden Journey, 1937, repr. 1983); Gipsy Afloat, 1942; Cruises and Caravans, 1942; The Cruel Way, 1947, repr. 1986; Ti-Puss, 1952; The Land of the Sherpas, 1955; La Vie Immédiate, 1991; Photo Album. *Recreations:* skiing, gardening. *Address:* 10 Avenue G. Vallette, 1206 Geneva, Switzerland. *T:* (22) 3464657; Atchala, Chandolin sur Sierre, Switzerland. *Clubs:* Kandahar, (Hon.) Ski Club of Great Britain; (Hon.) Alpine.

Died 27 March 1997.

MAINI, Sir Amar (Nath), Kt 1957; CBE 1953 (OBE 1948); *b* Nairobi, 31 July 1911; *e s* of late Nauhria Ram Maini, Nairobi, Kenya, and Ludhiana, Punjab, India; *m* 1935, Ram Saheli Mehra (*d* 1982), Ludhiana; two *s. Educ:* Govt Indian Sch., Nairobi; London Sch. of Economics (BCom Hons 1932). Barrister-at-law, Middle Temple, 1933. Advocate of High Court of Kenya, and of High Court of Uganda. From 1939, in Uganda; associated with family cotton business of Nauhria Ram & Sons (Uganda) Ltd. Actg MLC Kenya, and Mem., Nairobi Municipal Council, 1933–39; first Mayor of Kampala, Uganda, 1950–55; MLC, 1944–61, MEC 1952–61, Uganda; MLA Central E Africa, 1948–61 (Speaker, 1961–67); Minister for Corporations and Regl Communications, Uganda, 1955–58; Minister of Commerce and Industry, Uganda, 1958–61. Formerly: Mem. Kampala Township Authority; Chm., Kampala Municipal Council; Dep. Chm., Uganda Electricity Board; Member: Uganda Development Corporation; Lint Marketing Board; Civil Defence Bd; Asian Manpower Cttee; Transport Bd; Supplies Bd; Immigration Advisory Bd, Advisory Bd of Health; Railway Advisory Council; Advisory Bd of Commerce; Rent Restriction Bd; Makerere Coll. Assembly, etc; Past Pres. Central Council of Indian Assocs in Uganda; Indian Assoc., Kampala; served on Cttees of Cotton Association; formerly Member: Development Council, Uganda; E African Postal Advisory Bd; E African Transport Adv. Council; E African Air Adv. Council, etc. Mem., E African Common Market Tribunal, 1967–69. Dep. Chm. Kenya Broadcasting Corp., 1962–63. *Recreations:* walking, listening. *Address:* 55 Vicarage Road, East Sheen, SW14 8RY. *T:* (020) 8878 1497. *Clubs:* Reform; Nairobi.

Died 17 Aug. 1999.

MAIS, Hon. Sir (Robert) Hugh, Kt 1971; Judge of the High Court of Justice, Queen's Bench Division, 1971–82; *b* 14 Sept. 1907; *s* of late Robert Stanley Oliver Mais, Chobham, Surrey; *m* 1938, Catherine (*d* 1987), *d* of J. P. Pattinson, and *widow* of C. E. Kessler; one *s*, and two step *s* (one step *d* decd). *Educ:* Shrewsbury Sch.; Wadham Coll., Oxford (MA 1948; Hon. Fellow, 1971). Called to the Bar, Inner Temple, 1930, Bencher, 1971; Mem. of Northern Circuit. Chancellor of the Diocese of: Manchester, 1948–71; Carlisle, 1950–71; Sheffield, 1950–71; Judge of County Courts: Circuit No 37 (West London), 1958–60; Circuit No 42 (Marylebone), 1960–71. Dep. Chm., Berkshire QS, 1964–71; Commissioner of Assize: SE Circuit, 1964, 1967; Oxford Circuit, 1968, 1969; NE Circuit, 1971. Mem., Winn Cttee on Personal Injuries Litigation. Served as Wing Comdr, RAF, 1940–44. *Recreations:* fishing, golf. *Address:* Ripton, Streatley-on-Thames, Berks RG8 9LE. *T:* Goring (01491) 872397.

Died 14 Feb. 1996.

MAJOR, Kathleen, FBA 1977; Professor (part-time) of History, University of Nottingham, 1966–71; Principal of St Hilda's College, Oxford, 1955–65; *b* 10 April 1906; *er d* of late George Major and Gertrude Blow. *Educ:* various private schools; St Hilda's College, Oxford (Honour School of Modern History, 1928; BLitt 1931; Hon. Fellow, 1965). Librarian, St Hilda's College, 1931; Archivist to the Bishop of Lincoln, 1936; Lecturer, 1945, subsequently Reader in Diplomatic in the University of Oxford, until 1955. Hon. Secretary, Lincoln Record Society, 1935–56 and 1965–74, Hon. Gen. Editor, 1935–75. Member, Academic Planning Board for the University of Lancaster, 1962, and of Academic Advisory Cttee, 1964–70. Trustee of the Oxford Preservation Trust, 1961–65; Pres., Lincoln Civic Trust, 1980–84; a Vice-Pres., RHistS, 1967–71, Hon. Vice-Pres., 1981–. Hon. DLitt Nottingham, 1961. *Publications:* (ed jtly with Rev. Canon C. W. Foster) Registrum Antiquissimum of the Cathedral Church of Lincoln, vol. IV, 1938, (sole editor) vols V–X, 1940–73; *Acta Stephani Langton,* 1950; The D'Oyrys of South Lincolnshire, Norfolk and Holderness, 1984; (with S. R. Jones and J. Varley) A Survey of Ancient Houses in Lincoln, Fascicule I, Minster Yard I, 1984, Fascicule II, Minster Yard II, 1987, Fascicule III, Minster Yard III, 1990, Fascicule IV, The Bail of Lincoln, 1996; articles in English Hist. Review, Journal of Ecclesiastical Hist., etc. *Recreation:* reading. *Address:* 21 Queensway, Lincoln LN2 4AJ.

Died 19 Dec. 2000.

MAJURY, Maj.-Gen. James Herbert Samuel, CB 1974; MBE 1961; Senior Steward, National Greyhound Racing Club, 1976–88; *b* 26 June 1921; *s* of Rev. Dr M. Majury, BA, DD, and Florence (*née* Stuart), Antrim, N Ireland; *m* 1948, Jeanetta Ann (*née* Le Fleming); two *s. Educ:* Royal Academical Institution, Belfast; Trinity College, Dublin. Royal Ulster Rifles, 1940; attached 15 Punjab Regt, 1942; seconded South Waziristan Scouts, 1943–47; Korean War, 1950 (Royal Ulster Rifles); Prisoner of War, Korea, 1950–53 (despatches 1954); Parachute Regiment, 1957–61; Comd Royal Irish Fusiliers, 1961–62; Comd 2nd Infantry Bde, 1965–67; GOC West Midland District, 1970–73, idc 1968. Col Comdt, The King's Division, 1971–75; Col The Royal Irish Rangers, 1972–77; Hon. Col, 2nd Bn Mercian Volunteers, 1975–79. President: SSAFA for E Sussex, 1986–92; Indian Army Assoc., 1987–92. *Recreations:* golf, racing. *Address:* c/o Ulster Bank, 8 Market Square, Antrim BT41 4AT. *Club:* Naval and Military (Chm., 1983–88).

Died 4 Sept. 1996.

MAKINS, Sir Paul (Vivian), 4th Bt *cr* 1903, of Rotherfield Court, Henley-on-Thames, co. Oxford; company director, 1962–73; *b* 12 Nov. 1913; *yr s* of Sir Paul Makins, 2nd Bt, and Gladys Marie (*d* 1919), *d* of William Vivian, Queen's Gate, London; *S* brother, 1969; *m* 1945, Maisie (*d* 1986), *d* of Major Oswald Pedley and *widow* of Major C. L. J. Bowen, Irish Guards; no *c. Educ:* Eton Coll.; Trinity Coll., Cambridge (MA). Commissioned in Welsh Guards, 1935; served War of 1939–45: France, 1940; Italy, 1944–45; retd as Major, 1952. Dir and Sec., Vitalba Co. Ltd (Gibraltar), 1962–73; Dir, Compañia Rentistica SA (Tangier), 1967–73. Kt of Magistral Grace, SMO Malta, 1955. JP Gibraltar, 1964–70. *Heir:* none. *Address:* Casas Cortijo 135, 11310 Sotogrande, Provincia de Cadiz, Spain. *Clubs:* Cavalry and Guards, Pratt's.

Died 17 Dec. 1999 (ext).

MALCOLM, Dugald, CMG 1966; CVO 1964; TD 1945; HM Diplomatic Service, retired; Minister to the Holy See, 1975–77; *b* 22 Dec. 1917; 2nd *s* of late Maj.-Gen. Sir Neill Malcolm, KCB, DSO, and Lady (Angela) Malcolm; *m* 1st, 1957, Patricia Anne Gilbert-Lodge (*d* 1976), *widow* of Captain Peter Atkinson-Clark; one *d*, and one step *d*; 2nd, 1989, Margaret Roy Anderson, *d* of Rev. R. P. R. Anderson. *Educ:* Eton; New Coll., Oxford. Served Argyll and Sutherland Highlanders, 1939–45; discharged wounded. Appointed Foreign Office, 1945; served Lima, Bonn, Seoul; HM Vice-Marshal of the Diplomatic Corps,

1957–65; Ambassador: to Luxembourg, 1966–70; to Panama, 1970–74. Member Queen's Body Guard for Scotland (Royal Company of Archers). *Address:* 3 South Cuil, Duror of Appin, Argyll PA38 4DA. *T:* (01631) 740234. *Clubs:* Boodle's, Brooks's.

Died 16 Feb. 2000.

MALCOLM, George John, CBE 1965; musician; *b* London, 28 Feb. 1917; *o s* of George Hope Malcolm, Edinburgh, and Johanna Malcolm (*née* Brosnahan). *Educ:* Wimbledon Coll.; Balliol Coll., Oxford (Scholar; MA, BMus; Hon. Fellow, 1966); Royal College of Music (Scholar). Served in RAFVR, 1940–46. Master of the Cathedral Music, Westminster Cathedral, 1947–59, training a famous boys' choir; later mainly known as harpsichordist, pianist and conductor (making frequent concert tours). Hon. RAM 1961; FRCM 1974; Hon. FRCO 1987. Hon. DMus Sheffield, 1978. Papal Knight of the Order of St Gregory the Great, 1970. *Address:* 99 Wimbledon Hill Road, SW19 7QT.

Died 10 Oct. 1997.

MALCOLM, (William) Gerald, CB 1976; MBE 1943; Member, Planning Appeals Commission (NI), 1978–83; Permanent Secretary, Department of the Environment for Northern Ireland, 1974–76; *b* Stirling, 19 Dec. 1916; *s* of late John and Jane M. Malcolm; *m* 1949, Margaret Cashel. *Educ:* High Sch. of Stirling; Glasgow Univ. (MA Hons French and German, 1945); London Univ. (BA 1945). Served War, Army, 1939–46: RASC and Intelligence Corps; Major, 1944; Africa and Italy Stars, 1939–45. Min. of Home Affairs for NI, Asst Principal, 1948; Min. of Agriculture for NI: Principal, 1956; Asst Sec., 1962; Sen. Asst Sec., 1966; Dep. Sec., 1970. *Recreations:* angling, swimming, ornithology, nature.

Died 10 Dec. 1996.

MALDEN, Air Vice Marshal (Francis) David (Stephen) S.; *see* Scott-Malden.

MALE, Peter John Ellison, CMG 1967; MC 1945; HM Diplomatic Service, retired; Ambassador to Czechoslovakia, 1977–80; *b* 22 Aug. 1920; *s* of late H. J. G. Male and Mrs E. A. Male; *m* 1947, Patricia Janet Payne; five *s* two *d. Educ:* Merchant Taylors' Sch.; Emmanuel Coll., Cambridge. HM Forces, 1940–45. HM Foreign Service (later HM Diplomatic Service), 1946; served in: Damascus, 1947–49; Wahnerheide, 1949–53; London, 1953–55; Guatemala City, 1955–57; Washington, 1957–60; London, 1960–62; Oslo, 1962–66; Bonn, 1966–70; New Delhi, 1970–74; Asst Under-Sec. of State, FCO, 1974–77. *Recreations:* gadgets, gardening. *Address:* Swinley Edge, Coronation Road, Ascot, Berks SL5 9LG. *Club:* United Oxford & Cambridge University.

Died 11 Feb. 1996.

MALLETT, Ven. Peter, CB 1978; AKC; Chaplain-General to the Forces, 1974–80; Managing Director, Inter-Church Travel, 1981–86; *b* 1925; *s* of Edwin and Beatrice Mallett; *m* 1958, Joan Margaret Bremer; one *s* two *d. Educ:* King's Coll., London; St Boniface Coll., Warminster, Wilts. Deacon, 1951, priest, 1952. Curate, St Oswald's, Norbury, S London, 1951–54; joined Royal Army Chaplains' Dept (CF), 1954, and served overseas in Far East, Aden, Germany (despatches, Malaya, 1957); Senior Chaplain of Aden Brigade, and at RMA, Sandhurst; Dep. Asst Chaplain-General, Berlin, 1968, in N Ireland, 1972; Asst Chaplain-General, BAOR, 1973. QHC 1973. Canon, dio. of Europe, 1982. Hon. Chaplain: RA Assoc., 1985–; RTR, 1987–; Queen's Regt/Princess of Wales Royal Regt, 1991–. OStJ 1976. FRGS 1987. Hon. DLitt Geneva Theol Coll., 1976. *Address:* Hawthorne Cottage, Hampstead Lane, Yalding, Kent ME18 6HJ. *T:* Maidstone (01622) 812607. *Clubs:* Army and Navy, Naval and Military (Hon.).

Died 5 June 1996.

MALLIN, Rev. Canon Stewart Adam Thomson, CSG; Minister, St Paul's, Strathnairn, since 1991; *b* 12 Aug. 1924; *s* of George Garner Mallin and Elizabeth Thomson. *Educ:* Lasswade Secondary School; Coates Hall Theological Coll., Edinburgh. Deacon 1961, priest 1962; Curate, St Andrew's Cathedral, Inverness, 1961–64; Itinerant Priest, Diocese of Moray, Ross and Caithness, 1964–68; Priest-in-Charge of St Peter and the Holy Rood, Thurso, and St John's, Wick, 1968–77; Rector, St James, Dingwall and St Anne's, Strathpeffer, 1977–91; Dean of Moray, Ross and Caithness, 1983–91. Member of CSG, 1968–; Canon of St Andrew's Cathedral, Inverness, 1974. Hon. Chaplain, British Legion. Associate, Order of the Holy Cross (USA). OStJ 1995 (SBStJ 1992). *Recreations:* amateur drama, amateur opera. *Address:* St Paul's Parsonage, Croachy, Strathnairn, Inverness IV2 6UB. *Club:* Rotary (Thurso, then Dingwall; Pres., Dingwall, 1985–86).

Died 21 Jan. 2000.

MALLORIE, Air Vice-Marshal Paul Richard, CB 1979; AFC 1947; military command and control systems consultant; *b* 8 March 1923; *s* of late Rev. W. T. Mallorie and Margaret Mallorie; *m* 1951, Ursula Joyce Greig; three *s* one *d. Educ:* King's Sch., Canterbury. Flying Instructor, 1945; India and Middle East, 1946–49; Air Ministry, 1951–53; Staff Coll., 1954; No 139 Sqdn, 1955–57; JSSC, 1960; UK Mil. Advisers' Rep., SEATO, Bangkok, 1963–66; OC RAF Wittering, 1967–68; IDC, 1969; Min. of Defence, 1974–76; Asst Chief of Staff (Info. Systems), SHAPE, 1976–79; retd, 1980. Res. Fellow, NATO, 1981–82. *Recreations:* gardening, computers. *Address:* c/o Barclays Bank, Framlingham, Woodbridge, Suffolk IP13 9AW. *Club:* Royal Air Force.

Died 22 April 1999.

MALMESBURY, 6th Earl of, *cr* 1800; **William James Harris,** TD 1944 (2 Clasps); JP; DL; Baron Malmesbury 1788; Viscount FitzHarris 1800; Official Verderer of the New Forest, 1966–74; Lord-Lieutenant and Custos Rotulorum of Hampshire, 1973–82; *b* 18 Nov. 1907; *o s* of 5th Earl of Malmesbury and Hon. Dorothy Gough-Calthorpe (*d* 1973), CBE (DGStJ, Order of Mercy, with bar), *y d* of 6th Baron Calthorpe; *S* father, 1950; *m* 1st, 1932, Hon. Diana Carleton (*d* 1990), *e d* of 6th Baron Dorchester, OBE; one *s* two *d*; 2nd, 1991, Margaret Fleetwood (*née* Campbell-Preston), OBE (*d* 1994), *widow* of Raymond Baring; two step *s* one step *d*; 3rd, 1996, Mrs Bridget Hawkings, MA Cantab (*d* 1999). *Educ:* Eton; Trinity Coll., Cambridge (MA). Vice-Pres. of the Cambridge Univ. Conservative Association, 1929; Professional Associate of Surveyors Institution, 1937. Personal Liaison Officer to Min. of Agric., SE Region, 1958–64; Mem., Agric. and Forestry Cttee, RICS, 1953–69; Chairman: Hants Agric. Exec. Cttee, 1959–67; Cttee which produced White Paper on the Growing Demand for Water, 1961. Dir, Mid-Southern Water Co., 1961–78. Pres., New Forest 9th Centenary Trust, 1987– (Chm., 1977–87). Chairman: Hants Br., Country Landowners Assoc., 1954–56; T&AFA, Hants and IoW, 1960–68; first Chm., Eastern Wessex TA&VRA, 1968–70 (Vice-Pres., 1973–78; Pres., 1978–80); Hon. Col, 65th (M) Signal Regt, Royal Signals (TA), 1959–66; Hon. Col, 2nd Bn The Wessex Regt (V), 1970–73; served Royal Hampshire Regt (TA). Mem. Basingstoke RDC, 1946–52; County Councillor, Hants CC, 1952. Vice-Lt, Co. Southampton, 1960–73; DL Hants, 1955 and 1983. Master, Worshipful Co. of Skinners, 1952–53. KStJ 1973. Coronation Medal, 1937, 1953; Silver Jubilee Medal, 1977. *Heir: s* Viscount FitzHarris [*b* 19 June 1946; *m* 1969, Sally Ann, *yr d* of Sir Richard Newton Rycroft, 7th Bt; three *s* two *d*]. *Address:* The Ford, Greywell, Hook, Hants RG29 1BS. *T:* (01256) 703223. *Club:* Royal Yacht Squadron (Vice-Cdre, 1971–77).

Died 11 Nov. 2000.

MALONE, Hon. Sir Denis (Eustace Gilbert), Kt 1977; Chief Justice of the Cayman Islands, 1990–93; b 24 Nov. 1922; s of Sir Clement Malone, OBE, QC, and Lady (Ethel Louise) Malone; m 1963, Diana (née Traynor). Educ: St Kitts-Nevis Grammar Sch.; Wycliffe Coll., Stonehouse, Glos; Lincoln Coll., Oxford (BA). Called to the Bar, Middle Temple, 1950. Royal Air Force, Bomber Comd, 1942–46. Attorney-General's Chambers, Barbados, WI, 1953–61, Solicitor-Gen., 1958–61; Puisne Judge: Belize, 1961–65; Trinidad and Tobago, 1966–74; Chief Justice of Belize, 1974–79; Puisne Judge, Bahamas, 1979–89. Recreations: tennis, swimming, walking, bridge, reading. Address: 21B Carefree Apartments, PO Box N-4811, Nassau, Bahamas, West Indies.

Died 23 Feb. 2000.

MALOTT, Deane Waldo; President, Cornell University, Ithaca, NY, 1951–63, President Emeritus, 1963; Consultant, Association of American Colleges, 1963–70; b 10 July 1898; s of Michael Harvey Malott and Edith Gray Johnson; m 1925, Eleanor Sisson Thrum; one s two d. Educ: Univ. of Kansas (AB); Harvard Univ. (MBA). Asst Dean, Harvard Business Sch., 1923–29, Assoc. Prof. of Business, 1933–39; Vice-Pres., Hawaiian Pineapple Co., Honolulu, 1929–33; Chancellor, Univ. of Kansas, 1939–51. Educational Advisor, Ops Analysis Div., US Army Air Corps, 1943–45; Mcm., Business Council, Washington, DC, 1944. Trustee: Corning Museum of Glass, 1952–73; Teagle Foundation, 1952–85; William Allen White Foundation, 1952–; Kansas Univ. Endowment Assoc., 1962–; Nat. (formerly Pacific) Tropical Botanical Garden, 1964–; Mem. Bd, Univ. of Kansas Alumni Assoc., 1974–; Director: General Mills, Inc., 1948–70; Citizens Bank, Abilene, Kans, 1944–73; Pitney-Bowes, Inc., 1951–71; First Nat. Bank, Ithaca, NY, 1951–83; Owens-Corning Fiberglas Corp., 1951–72; Lane Bryant, Inc., 1963–77; Servomation Corp., 1963–74 Mem., Adv Bd, Security Northstar Bank, 1983–. Hon. LLD: Washburn Univ., 1941; Bryant Coll., 1951; Hamilton Coll., 1951; Univ. of California, 1954; Univ. of Liberia, 1962; Univ. of New Hampshire, 1963; Emory Univ., 1963; Juniata Coll., 1965; Hon. DCS Univ. of Pittsburgh, 1957; Hon. DHL Long Island Univ., 1967. Held foreign orders. Publications: (with Philip Cabot) Problems in Public Utility Management, 1927; (with J. C. Baker) Introduction to Corporate Finance, 1936; (with J. C. Baker and W. D. Kennedy) On Going into Business, 1936; Problems in Agricultural Marketing, 1938; (with B. F. Martin) The Agricultural Industries, 1939; Agriculture—the Great Dilemma (an essay in Business and Modern Society), 1951. Address: 322 Wait Avenue, Cornell University, Ithaca, NY 14850, USA. Clubs: University, Cornell (New York); Bohemian (San Francisco).

Died 11 Sept. 1996.

MALTBY, John Newcombe, CBE 1988; Chairman: Harrisons & Crosfield plc, 1991–94 (Director, 1987–94); Dover Harbour Board, 1989–96; b 10 July 1928; s of Air Vice-Marshal Sir Paul Maltby, KCVO, KBE, CB, DSO, AFC, DL and Winifred Russell Paterson; m 1956, Lady Sylvia Veronica Anthea Harris, d of 6th Earl of Malmesbury, TD; one s two d. Educ: Wellington Coll.; Clare Coll., Cambridge (MA Mech. Scis). Shell Internat. Petrolem, 1951–69; Founder and Man. Dir, Panocean Shipping & Terminals, 1969–75; Man. Dir, Panocean-Anco Ltd, 1975–79; The Burmah Oil plc: Dir, 1980–82; Dep. Chm., 1982–83; Gp Chief Exec., 1982–88; Chm., 1983–90. Director: J. Bibby and Sons plc, 1984–87; DRG plc, 1987–89. Mem., 1988–93, Chm., 1990–93, UKAEA. Chm., British Ports Fedn, 1992 (Dep. Chm., 1990–92). Recreations: history, gardening, sailing. Address: The Coach House, Greywell Hill, Hook, Hants RG29 1DG. Clubs: Brooks's; Royal Yacht Squadron.

Died 13 Sept. 1998.

MANKOWITZ, (Cyril) Wolf; author; Honorary Consul to the Republic of Panama in Dublin, 1971; b 7 Nov. 1924; s of Solomon and Rebecca Mankowitz; m 1944, Ann Margaret Seligmann; three s (and one s decd). Educ: East Ham Grammar Sch.; Downing Coll., Cambridge (MA, English Tripos). Served World War II, as volunteer coal miner and in Army. Play and film producer: with Oscar Lewenstein, 1955–60; independently, 1960–70; with Laurence Harvey, 1970–72. Adjunct Prof. of English, Univ. of New Mexico, Albuquerque, 1982–86 (Adjunct Prof. of Theatre Arts, 1987–88). Exhibitions (collages): Davis Gall., Dublin, 1990; Grosvenor Gall., London, 1994. Soc. of Authors Award, for poetry, 1946; Cork Film Fest. Internat. Critics Prize, 1972, Grand Prize, 1973. Plays include: The Bespoke Overcoat, 1953 (filmed, 1955; Venice Film Fest. Prize, BAFTA Award, and Academy Award for best screenplay); The Boychick, 1954; The Mighty Hunter, 1956; The Last of the Cheesecake, 1956; (with Julian More) Expresso Bongo, 1958 (filmed, 1959); (with Beverley Cross) Belle, or The Ballad of Dr Crippen, 1961; Pickwick, 1963; Passion Flower Hotel (musical), 1965; Stand and Deliver, 1972; Samson and Delilah, 1978; The Irish Hebrew Lesson, 1978; screenplays include: (some jtly): Make Me an Offer, 1954; A Kid for Two Farthings, 1955; The Millionairess, 1960; The Long and The Short and The Tall, 1961; The Day the Earth Caught Fire, 1961 (BAFTA Best Screenplay); The Waltz of the Toreadors, 1962; Where The Spies Are, 1965; Casino Royale, 1967; The Assassination Bureau, 1969; Bloomfield, 1970; Black Beauty, 1971; Treasure Island, 1972; The Hebrew Lesson (also dir.), 1972; The Hireling, 1973 (Grand Prix, Cannes); (documentary) Almonds and Raisins (a treatment of Yiddish films, 1929–39), 1984; television series: Dickens of London, 1976. Publications: novels: Make Me An Offer, 1952 (televised, 1952); A Kid for Two Farthings, 1953; Laugh Till You Cry, 1955 (USA); My Old Man's a Dustman, 1956; Cockatrice, 1963; The Biggest Pig in Barbados, 1965; Raspberry Reich, 1979; [cb-2]; [cb0]Abracadabra!, 1980; The Devil in Texas, 1984; Gioconda, 1987; The Magic Cabinet of Professor Smucker, 1988; Exquisite Cadaver, 1990; A Night with Casanova, 1991; short stories: The Mendelman Fire and Other Stories, 1957; Expresso Bongo: a Wolf Mankowitz Reader, 1961; The Blue Arabian Nights, 1973; The Day of the Women and The Night of the Men (fables), 1977; biography: Dickens of London, 1976; The Extraordinary Mr Poe, 1978; Mazeppa, 1982; poetry: XII Poems, 1971; plays: The Bespoke Overcoat and Other Plays, 1955; Five One-Act Plays, 1955; Expresso Bongo, 1960; The Samson Riddle, 1972; miscellaneous: The Portland Vase and the Wedgwood Copies, 1952; Wedgwood, 1953, rev. edn 1980; Majollika and Company (for childen), 1955; ABC of Show Business, 1956; (with R. G. Haggar) A Concise Encyclopedia of English Pottery and Porcelain, 1957; The Penguin Wolf Mankowitz, 1967. Recreations: sleeping or making collage. Address: The Bridge House, Ahakista, Durrus, near Bantry, Co. Cork, Ireland.

Died 20 May 1998.

MANLEY, Rt Hon. Michael Norman, PC 1989; Prime Minister of Jamaica, 1972–80, and 1989–92; President, People's National Party, Jamaica, 1969–92 (Member, Executive, 1952–92); b St Andrew, Jamaica, 10 Dec. 1924; s of late Rt Excellent Norman W. Manley, QC, and Edna Manley (née Swithenbank); m 1972, Beverly Anderson (marr. diss. 1990); one s one d, and one s two d by previous marriages; m 1992, Glynne Ewart. Educ: Jamaica Coll.; London Sch. of Economics (BSc Econ Hons). Began as freelance journalist, working with BBC, 1950–51; returned to Jamaica, Dec. 1951, as Associate Editor of Public Opinion, 1952–53; Sugar Supervisor, Nat. Workers' Union, 1953–54; Island Supervisor and First Vice-Pres., 1955–72; Mem. Senate, 1962–67; MP for Central Kingston, Jamaica, 1967–92; Leader of the Opposition, 1969–72, and 1980–89. Held various posts in Labour cttees and in Trade Union affairs; organised strike in sugar industry, 1959, which led to Goldenberg Commn of Inquiry; Pres., Nat. Workers Union, 1984–89. Vice-Pres., Socialist Internat., 1978. Hon. Doctor of Laws Morehouse Coll., Atlanta, 1973. UN Special Award for contrib. to struggle against apartheid, 1978; Joliot Curie Medal, World Peace Council, 1979. Order of the Liberator, Venezuela, 1973; Order of Mexican Eagle, 1975; Order of Jose Marti, Cuba, 1975. *Publications:* The Politics of Change, 1974; A Voice at the Workplace, 1976; The Search for Solutions, 1977; Jamaica: Struggle in the Periphery, 1982; A History of West Indies Cricket, 1988; The Poverty of Nations, 1991. *Recreations:* sports, music, gardening, reading. *Address:* 89 Old Hope Road, Kingston 6, Jamaica. *Died 7 March 1997.*

MANN, Bruce Leslie Home D.; *see* Douglas-Mann.

MANN, Rt Hon. Sir Michael, Kt 1982; PC 1988; a Lord Justice of Appeal, 1988–95; *b* 9 Dec. 1930; *s* of late Adrian Bernard Mann, CBE and of Mary Louise (*née* Keen); *m* 1st, 1957, Jean Marjorie (*née* Bennett), MRCVS (marr. diss. 1988); two *s*; 2nd, 1989, Audrey Edith Umpleby. *Educ:* Whitgift; King's Coll., London (LLB, PhD; FKC 1984). Called to Bar, Gray's Inn, 1953 (Bencher 1980; Master of the Estate, 1993; Chm., Management Cttee 1994). Practised, 1955–82; Junior Counsel to the Land Commn (Common Law), 1967–71; QC 1972; a Recorder of the Crown Court, 1979–82; a Judge of the High Court of Justice, QBD, 1982–88. Asst Lectr 1954–57, Lectr 1957–64, in Law, LSE; part-time Legal Asst, FO, 1954–56. Inspector, Vale of Belvoir Coal Inquiry, 1979–80. Pres., Administrative Law Bar Assoc., 1993. *Publications:* (ed jtly) Dicey, Conflict of Laws, 7th edn 1957, Dicey and Morris, Conflict of Laws, 8th edn 1967 to 10th edn 1980. *Died 14 June 1998.*

MANN, Rt Rev. Peter Woodley, CBE 1994; Bishop of Dunedin, 1976–90; *b* 25 July 1924; *s* of Edgar Allen and Bessie May Mann; *m* 1955, Anne Victoria Norman; three *d. Educ:* Prince Alfred Coll., Adelaide; St John's Coll., Auckland (Fellow); Univ. of London (BD). Deacon, Dio. Waiapu, 1953; priest, 1954; Curate: Waiapu Cathedral, 1953–55; Rotorua, 1955–56; Vicar: Porangahau, 1956–61; Dannevirke, 1961–66; Vicar of Blenheim and Archdeacon of Marlborough, 1966–71; Vicar of St Mary's and Archdeacon of Timaru, 1971–75; Vicar of St James', Lower Hutt, 1975–76. *Recreations:* bowls, walking, gardening. *Address:* 182 Maitland Street, Dunedin, New Zealand. *T:* (3) 4775245. *Died 24 Aug. 1999.*

MANNING, Thomas Henry, OC 1974; zoologist, retired; *b* 22 Dec. 1911; *s* of Thomas E. and Dorothy (*née* Randall) Manning, Shrublands, Dallington, Northampton; *m* 1938, Ella Wallace Jackson. *Educ:* Harrow; Cambridge. Winter journey across Lapland, 1932–33; survey and zoological work on Southampton Island, 1933–35; Leader, Brit. Canadian-Arctic Expedn, 1936–41; Royal Canadian Navy, 1941–45; Geodetic Service of Canada, 1945–47; Leader Geographical Bureau Expedition to Prince Charles Is. (Foxe Basin), 1949; zoological and geographical work in James Bay, 1950; Leader, Defence Research Board Expeditions: Beaufort Sea, 1951; Banks Island, 1952, 1953; Nat. Mus. Canada Expedition, King William Island, Adelaide Peninsula, 1957, Prince of Wales Island, 1958. Hon. LLD McMaster, 1979. Bruce Medal (Royal Society of Edinburgh, RPS, RSGS), 1944; Patron's Gold Medal, RGS, 1948; Massey Medal, Royal Canadian Geographical Soc., 1977. Guggenheim Fellow, 1959. *Publications:* The Birds of North Western Ungava, 1949; Birds of the West James Bay and Southern Hudson Bay Coasts, 1952; Birds of Banks Island, 1956; Mammals of Banks Island, 1958; A Biological Investigation of Prince of Wales Island,

1961; articles in The Auk, Journal Mamm., Geog. Journal, Canadian Geog. Jl, Canadian Field-Naturalist, Arctic, Nat. Mus. Can. Bull., Canadian Jl of Zool., Syllogeus. *Recreations:* shooting, book-binding, cabinet-making, gardening. *Address:* RR4, Merrickville, ON K0G 1N0, Canada. *T:* (613) 2694940. *Died 8 Nov. 1998.*

MANT, Prof. (Arthur) Keith, MD; FRCP, FRCPath; Emeritus Professor of Forensic Medicine, University of London, since 1984; *b* 11 Sept. 1919; *s* of George Arthur Mant and Elsie Muriel (*née* Slark); *m* 1947, Heather Smith, BA (*d* 1989); two *s* one *d. Educ:* Denstone Coll., Staffs; St Mary's Hosp., Paddington. MB BS London, 1949, MD 1950; MRCS, LRCP 1943; FRCPath 1967; MRCP 1977, FRCP 1982. Dept of Obst. and Gynæc., St Mary's Hosp., 1943; RAMC, i/c Path. Section, War Crimes Gp, 1945–48 (Major); Registrar (ex-service), Med. Unit, St Mary's Hosp., 1948–49; Department of Forensic Medicine, Guy's Hospital, University of London: Research Fellow, 1949–55; Lectr, 1955–66; Reader in Forensic Med., 1966–74; Prof. of Forensic Med., 1974–84; Head of Dept, 1972–84. Sen. Lectr in Forensic Med., 1965, Hon. Consultant in Forensic Med., 1967–84, KCH. WHO Consultant, Sri Lanka, 1982, 1984 and 1987. Visiting Lectr in Med. Jurisprudence and Toxicology, St Mary's Hosp., 1955–84; British Council Lectr, India, 1979; Visiting Professor: Univ. of Jordan, 1985; Nihon Univ., Japan, 1985. Lectures: Niels Dungal Meml, Reykjavik, 1979; J. B. Firth Meml, London, 1981; W. D. L. Fernando Meml, Sri Lanka, 1982; Douglas Kerr Meml, London, 1985. Examiner in Forensic Medicine: NUI, 1960; St Andrews Univ., 1967; Dundee Univ., 1968; RCPath, 1971; Soc. of Apothecaries, 1971; Univ. of Riyadh, Saudi Arabia, 1976; Univ. of Garyounis, Libya, 1976; Univ. of Tripoli, 1979. A. D. Williams Distinguished Scholar Fellowship, Univ. Med. Coll. of Virginia, 1963 and 1968. President: Internat. Assoc. in Accident and Traffic Med., 1972–83 (Pres. Emeritus); British Acad. of Forensic Sci., 1975–76; Forensic Sci. Soc., 1963–65; British Assoc. in Forensic Med., 1970–71; Vice-Pres., Medico-Legal Soc. Nat. correspondent for GB, Internat. Acad. of Legal and Social Med.; Mem., Amer. Acad. of Forensic Sci.; Corresp. For. Mem., Soc. de Méd. Légale; Hon. Member: Brazilian Assoc. for Traffic Med.; Soc. de Méd. Légale, Belgium. Member, Editorial Board: Internat. Reference Org. in Forensic Med. (INFORM), 1971–; Amer. Jl of Forensic Medicine and Pathology, 1980–; Hon. Editor, Jl of Traffic Medicine, 1989–; formerly English Editor, Zeitschrift für Rechtsmedizin; Internat. Editorial Bd, Excerpta Medica (Forensic Sci. abstracts). Fellow: Indian Acad. of Forensic Sci.; Indian Assoc. in Forensic Medicine; Swedish Soc. of Med. Scis. Hon. DMJ(Path), Soc. of Apothecaries, 1979. *Publications:* Forensic Medicine: observation and interpretation, 1960; Modern Trends in Forensic Medicine, Series 3, 1973; (ed) Taylor's Principles and Practice of Medical Jurisprudence, 13th edn 1984; contribs to med. and sci. literature. *Recreations:* fishing, orchid culture. *Address:* 29 Ashley Drive, Walton-on-Thames, Surrey KT12 1JT. *T:* (01932) 225005.

Died 12 Oct. 2000.

MARA, Prof. Timothy Nicholas; professional artist; Professor of Printmaking, Royal College of Art, since 1990; *b* 27 Sept. 1948; *s* of Timothy Anthony Mara and Angela Mara; *m* 1970, Belinda Julie Reeves; two *d. Educ:* St Joseph's Coll., London; Epsom and Ewell Sch. of Art; Wolverhampton Polytechnic (DipAD 1st Class Hons); Royal Coll. of Art (MA). Lectr in Fine Art, Nat. Coll. of Art and Design, Dublin, 1977; Lectr in Printmaking, Brighton Polytechnic, 1978; Principal Lectr in Printmaking, Chelsea Sch. of Art, 1980–90. Curator, The Spirit of the Staircase, V&A, 1996–97. Gallery Artist with Flowers East and founder mem., Wildman Corner Studio, London, 1989–; solo exhibitions, 1976–: ICA; Project

Arts Centre, Dublin; Thumb Gallery; David Hendriks Gallery, Dublin; Angela Flowers Gallery; Flowers East; Glasgow Print Studio Gallery; numerous group exhibns, UK and overseas; work in collections: Tate Gallery; V&A; BBC; Brooklyn Museum; NY Public Library; UCLA; Arts Council; British Council; commercial bodies. Hon. DArts Wolverhampton, 1997. 11th Norwegian Internat. Triennale Prize, 1995. *Publication:* Thames and Hudson Technical Manual of Screenprinting, 1978. *Recreations:* tennis, reading. *Address:* Royal College of Art, Kensington Gore, SW7 2EU. *T:* (0171) 584 5020. *Club:* Chelsea Arts.   *Died 12 Aug. 1997.*

MARAJ, Prof. James Ajodhya; Special Adviser, University of South Africa, since 1997; Consultant, Confederation of Open Learning Agencies, South Africa, since 1997; *b* 28 Sept. 1930; *s* of Ramgoolam and Popo Maraj; *m* 1951, Etress (*née* Ouditt); two *s* two *d*. *Educ:* St Mary's Coll. and Govt Teachers' Coll., Trinidad; Univ. of Birmingham (BA, PhD). FRICS 1981. Teacher, lectr, 1947–60; Sen. Lectr, 1965–70, Head, Inst. of Educn, 1968–70, Univ. of the WI; Dir, Educn Div., Commonwealth Secretariat, 1970–72; Commonwealth Asst Sec.-Gen., 1973–75; Vice-Chancellor, Univ. of S Pacific, 1975–82 (Hon. Prof. of Educn, 1978); Sen. Evaluation Officer, The World Bank, 1982–84; High Comr for Fiji in Australia, Malaysia and Singapore, 1985–86; Perm. Sec., Prime Minister's Office, Min. of Foreign Affairs, and Civil Aviation, Fiji, 1986–88; High Comr to India, 1986–87; Pres. and Chief Exec. Officer, Commonwealth of Learning, 1989–95; Exec. Dir, Tertiary Educn Commn, Mauritius, 1995–97. External examr, educn adviser and consultant to several countries; Chm. or Sec. nat. or internat. commns. Hon. Prof., Univ. of Mauritius, 1991; Adjunct Professor: Univ. of Vic, Canada, 1990; Simon Fraser Univ., 1991; Griffith Univ., Australia, 1996; Vis. Prof., Higher Educn Mgt, Univ. of Bath, 1997. Hon. DLitt: Loughborough, 1980; Andhra Pradesh Univ., 1990; Indira Gandhi Nat. Open Univ., 1994; Hon. LLD Hull, 1993; Sri Lanka Open Univ., 1993; West Indies, 1995; Hon. DEd South Africa, 1996; DU South Pacific, 1983. Gold Medal of Merit, Trinidad and Tobago, 1974; Pacific Person of the Year, Fiji Times, 1978; Dist. Scholar's Award, British Council, 1979. Chevalier de la Légion d'Honneur, France, 1982. *Publications:* miscellaneous research papers. *Recreations:* sport (cricket, squash, horse-racing), poetry, music. *Address:* c/o Vice Chancellor's Office, University of South Africa, Pretoria 0001, South Africa. *Clubs:* Athenæum, Royal Commonwealth Society, Royal Over-Seas League.
                                            Died 3 April 1999.

MARCHANT, Catherine; *see* Cookson, Dame C.

MARCHANT, (Edgar) Vernon; retired; *b* 7 Dec. 1915; *s* of E. C. Marchant; *m* 1945, Joyce Allen Storey; one *s* two *d*. *Educ:* Marlborough Coll.; Lincoln Coll., Oxford. Engr, Bahrain Petroleum Co., 1938; various technical and scientific posts in Min. of Aircraft Production, Min. of Supply and RAE, 1940–51; Principal, Min. of Supply, 1951; Principal, BoT, 1955; Asst Sec., BoT, 1959; Asst Registrar of Restrictive Trading Agreements, 1964; Asst Sec., Dept of Economic Affairs, 1966; Nat. Board for Prices and Incomes: Asst Sec., 1967–68; Under-Sec., 1968–71; Under-Sec., DTI, 1971–75. Dir, Paddington Building Soc., 1977–87. Mem., CS Appeal Bd, 1976–84. *Recreations:* gardening, messing about in boats. *Address:* 87 New Forest Drive, Brockenhurst, Hants SO42 7QT. *Clubs:* Royal Southampton Yacht; Cruising Association.
                                            Died 18 Aug. 1997.

MARCUS, Frank Ulrich; playwright; *b* Breslau, Germany, 30 June 1928; *s* of late Frederick and Gertie Marcus; *m* 1951, Jacqueline (*née* Sylvester) (*d* 1993); one *s* two *d*. *Educ:* Bunce Court Sch., Kent (evac. to Shropshire during war); St Martin's Sch. of Art, London. Actor, dir, scenic

designer, Unity Theatre, Kensington (later Internat. Theatre Gp). Theatre Critic, Sunday Telegraph, 1968–78. *Stage plays:* Minuet for Stuffed Birds, 1950; The Man Who Bought a Battlefield, 1963; The Formation Dancers, 1964; The Killing of Sister George, 1965 (3 'Best Play of the Year' Awards: Evening Standard, Plays and Players, Variety); Cleo, 1965; Studies of the Nude, 1967; Mrs Mouse, Are You Within?, 1968; The Window, 1969; Notes on a Love Affair, 1972; Blank Pages, 1972; Carol's Christmas, 1973; Beauty and the Beast, 1975; Portrait of the Artist (mime scenario), 1977; Blind Date, 1977; The Ballad of Wilfred the Second, 1978; The Merman of Orford (mime scenario), 1978; *television plays:* A Temporary Typist, 1966; The Glove Puppet, 1968; *radio plays:* The Hospital Visitor, 1980; The Beverley Brooch, 1981; The Row over La Ronde, 1982; *translations:* Schnitzler's Reigen, 1952 (as La Ronde, TV, 1982); Liebelei (TV), 1954; Anatol, 1976; Molnar's The Guardsman, 1978 (first perf., 1969); Kaiser's From Morning Till Midnight, 1979; Hauptmann's The Weavers, 1980. *Publications:* The Formation Dancers, 1964; The Killing of Sister George, 1965; The Window, 1968; Mrs Mouse, Are You Within?, 1969; Notes on a Love Affair, 1972; Blank Pages, 1973; Beauty and the Beast, 1977; Blind Date, 1977; *translations:* Molnar, The Guardsman, 1978; Hauptmann, The Weavers, 1980; Schnitzler, La Ronde, and Anatol, 1982; contribs to: Behind the Scenes, 1972; Those Germans, 1973; On Theater, 1974 (US), etc; also to London Magazine, Plays and Players, Dramatists' Quarterly (US), New York Times, etc. *Recreation:* observing. *Address:* 79 Griffiths Road, SW19 1ST. *T:* 0181-542 4728; c/o Casarotto Ramsay Ltd, 60–66 Wardour Street, W1V 3HP.   *Died 5 Aug. 1996.*

MARDEN, John Louis, CBE 1976; JP; former Chairman, Wheelock, Marden & Co. Ltd; *b* Woodford, Essex, 12 Feb. 1919; *s* of late George Ernest Marden; *m* 1947, Anne Harris; one *s* three *d*. *Educ:* Gresham Sch., Norfolk; Trinity Hall, Cambridge (MA). Served War, as Captain 4th Regt RHA, in N Africa, France and Germany, 1940–46. Joined Wheelock, Marden & Co. Ltd, as trainee (secretarial and shipping, then insurance side of business), 1946; Dir of company, 1952, Chm., 1959. Chm., Hong Kong Shipowners' Assoc., 1978–79. JP Hong Kong, 1964. *Recreations:* solely sedentary and cerebral. *Address:* 14 Shek O, Hong Kong.   *Died 18 March 1999.*

MARGADALE, 1st Baron *cr* 1964, of Islay, Co. Argyll; **John Granville Morrison,** TD; JP; DL; Lord-Lieutenant of Wiltshire, 1969–81; Member Royal Company of Archers (Queen's Body Guard for Scotland); *b* 16 Dec. 1906; *s* of late Hugh Morrison and Lady Sophia Castalia Mary Leveson-Gower, 2nd *d* of 2nd Earl Granville; *m* 1928, Hon. Margaret Esther Lucie Smith (*d* 1980), 2nd *d* of 2nd Viscount Hambleden; two *s* one *d* (and one *s* decd). *Educ:* Eton; Magdalene Coll., Cambridge. Served 1939–45 with Royal Wilts Yeomanry; in MEF, 1939–42. MP (C) Salisbury Division of Wilts, 1942–64; Chairman, Conservative Members' (1922) Cttee, 1955–64. Yeomanry Comdt and Chm., Yeomanry Assoc., 1965–71; Hon. Col, The Royal Wiltshire Yeomanry Sqdn, 1965–71; Hon. Col, The Royal Yeomanry, 1965–71; Dep. Hon. Col, The Wessex Yeomanry, 1971–. JP 1936, High Sheriff, 1938, DL 1950, Wilts. MFH S and W Wilts Foxhounds, 1932–65. KstJ 1972. *Heir:* *s* Hon. James Ian Morrison [*b* 17 July 1930; *m* 1952, Clare Barclay; two *s* one *d*]. *Address:* Fonthill House, Tisbury, Salisbury, Wilts SP3 5SA. *T:* Tisbury (01747) 870202. *Clubs:* Turf, Jockey, White's.   *Died 25 May 1996.*

MARKS OF BROUGHTON, 2nd Baron *cr* 1961, of Sunningdale in the Royal Co. of Berks; **Michael Marks;** *b* 27 Aug. 1920; *o s* of 1st Baron and Miriam (*d* 1971), *d* of Ephraim Sieff; *S* father, 1964; *m* 1st, 1949, Ann

Catherine (marr. diss. 1958), *d* of Major Richard Pinto, MC; one *s* two *d*; 2nd, 1960, Hélène (marr. diss. 1965), *d* of Gustav Fischer; 3rd, 1976, Toshiko Shimura (marr diss. 1985); 4th, 1988, Liying Zhang (marr. diss.); 5th, 1994, Marina Collins (*née* Sakalis). *Heir: s* Hon. Simon Richard Marks [*b* 3 May 1950; *m* 1982, Marion, *o d* of Peter F. Norton; one *s* three *d*]. *Died 9 Sept. 1998.*

MARPLES, Brian John; Emeritus Professor of Zoology, University of Otago, NZ; *b* 31 March 1907; 2nd *s* of George and Anne Marples; *m* 1931, Mary Joyce Ransford; two *s. Educ:* St Bees Sch.; Exeter Coll., Oxford. Lecturer in Zoology, Univ. of Manchester, 1929–35; Lecturer in Zoology, Univ. of Bristol, 1935–37; Prof. of Zoology, Univ. of Otago, NZ, 1937–67. *Publications:* Freshwater Life in New Zealand, 1962; various technical zoological and archaeological papers. *Address:* 1 Vanbrugh Close, Old Woodstock, Oxon OX20 1YB.

Died 4 Oct. 1997.

MARRIOTT, John Miles; Non-Executive Director, Phillips & Drew Fund Management Ltd, 1986–95; *b* 11 Oct. 1935; *s* of James Marriott and May Lavinia (*née* Goodband); *m* 1967, Josephine Anne (*née* Shepherd). *Educ:* High Pavement Grammar Sch., Nottingham. CIPFA 1962; MBCS 1970. E Midlands Electricity Bd, Nottingham (incl. 2 yrs National Service in RAF), 1952–60; Morley Bor. Council, 1960–62; Wolverhampton County Bor. Council, 1962–67; Asst Bor. Treasurer, Torbay Co. Bor. Council, 1967–70; Dep. Bor. Treas., 1970–72, Bor. Treas., 1972–73, Ipswich Co. Bor. Council; Dir of Finance, Bolton Metrop. Bor. Council, 1973–78; County Treasurer, Greater Manchester Council, 1978–86; Principal, Grant Thornton, Chartered Accountants, 1986–90. Non-Exec. Dir, Wigan and Bolton (formerly Bolton) HA, 1992–96. Gov., Bolton Inst. of Higher Educn, 1993–. *Publications:* papers in prof. jls. *Recreations:* golf, reading, bird watching, motoring. *Address:* 12 Martinsclough, Lostock, Bolton BL6 4PF. *T:* (01204) 847444.

Died 2 Nov. 1997.

MARS-JONES, Hon. Sir William (Lloyd), Kt 1969; MBE 1945; a Judge of the High Court of Justice, Queen's Bench Division, 1969–90; *b* 4 Sept. 1915; *s* of Henry and Jane Mars Jones, Llansannan, Denbighshire; *m* 1947, Sheila Mary Felicity Cobon (*d* 1998); three *s. Educ:* Denbigh County Sch.; UCW, Aberystwyth (LLB Hons); St John's Coll., Cambridge (BA). Entrance Schol., Gray's Inn, 1936; Pres. Students' Rep. Council and Central Students' Rep. Council, UCW, 1936–37; MacMahon Studentship, 1939. Barrister-at-Law, Gray's Inn, 1941, Bencher, 1964, Treas., 1982; QC 1957. War of 1939–45, RNVR (MBE); Lt-Comdr RNVR 1945. Contested W Denbigh Parly Div., 1945. Joined Wales and Chester Circuit, 1947, Presiding Judge, 1971–75; Recorder of: Birkenhead, 1959–65; Swansea, 1965–68; Cardiff, 1968–69; Dep. Chm., Denbighshire Quarter Sessions, 1962–68; Comr of Assize, Denbigh and Mold Summer Assize, 1965. Member: Bar Council, 1962; Home Office Inquiry into allegations against Metropolitan Police Officers, 1964; Home Secretary's Adv. Council on Penal System, 1966–68. President: N Wales Arts Assoc., 1976–; UCNW, Bangor, 1983–95; UCW Old Students' Assoc., 1987–88; London Welsh Trust, 1989–95. Hon. LLD UCW, Aberystwyth, 1973. *Recreations:* singing, acting, guitar. *Clubs:* Garrick, Royal Naval Reserve. *Died 10 Jan. 1999.*

MARSDEN, Arthur Whitcombe, MSc, DIC; ARCS; formerly Education Officer/Technical Editor, Animal Production and Health Division, Food and Agriculture Organization of the United Nations, Rome, 1964–73; *b* Buxton, Derbyshire, 14 June 1911; *o s* of late Hubert Marsden and Margaret Augusta Bidwell; *m* 1st, 1940, Ailsa Anderson (*d* 1992), *yr d* of late William Anderson McKellar, physician, and Jessie Reid Macfarlane, Glasgow

and Chester-le-Street, Co. Durham; one *s* two *d*; 2nd, 1994, Dr Peggy B. Houghton (*née* Taylor). *Educ:* St Paul's; Imperial Coll. (Royal College of Science), London. BSc Special, ARCS 1933; MSc, DIC 1940. Research in agricultural chemistry at Imperial Coll., 1933–36; research asst, 1936; demonstrator, 1937; Asst Lecturer, 1939; Lecturer, 1946; Dept Head, Seale-Hayne Agricultural Coll., Newton Abbot, 1946–48; dir of research to grain companies in Aberdeen, 1948–49; Dir of Commonwealth Bureau of Dairy Science and Technology, Shinfield, Reading, 1950–57; Organising Secretary: 15th International Dairy Congress, London, 1957–60; 2nd World Congress of Man-made Fibres, 1960–63. Hon. Sec., Agriculture Group, Soc. of Chem. Industry, 1947–52, Chm., 1954–56; Organising Cttee of 2nd International Congress of Crop Protection, London, 1949; delegate on OEEC Technical Assistance Mission in USA and Canada, 1951; toured research centres in Pakistan, India, Australia, NZ and USA, Oct. 1954–Feb. 1955. Temp. Instr Lieut RN, 1942; HMS Diomede, 1943; HMS King Alfred, 1944; RN Coll., Greenwich, and HMS Superb, 1945. *Publications:* papers in scientific journals. *Recreations:* gardening, travel, music, philately, making model ships. *Address:* 5 Deepdale Close, Penylan, Cardiff CF2 5LR. *T:* (01222) 483719. *Died 22 April 1997.*

MARSDEN, Prof. (Charles) David, DSc; FRCP; FRS 1983; Professor of Clinical Neurology, since 1987, Director, MRC Human Movement and Balance Unit, since 1988, Dean, since 1995, Institute of Neurology and National Hospitals for Neurology and Neurosurgery (formerly for Nervous Diseases), Queen Square; *b* 15 April 1938; *s* of Charles Moustaka Marsden, CBE and Una Maud Marsden; *m* 1961, Jill Slaney Bullock (marr. diss.); one *s* three *d* (and one *s* decd); *m* 1979, Jennifer Sandom (marr. diss.); three *d. Educ:* Cheltenham Coll.; St Thomas's Hosp. Med. Sch. (MSc 1960; MB, BS 1963). FRCP 1975 (MRCP 1965); MRCPsych 1978. Sen. House Physician, National Hosp. for Nervous Diseases, 1968–70; Institute of Psychiatry and King's College Hospital, London: Sen. Lectr in Neurol., 1970–72; Prof. of Neurol., 1972–87. Mem., MRC, 1988–91. Mem. Council, Royal Soc., 1991–94. Founder FMedSci 1998. *Publications:* papers on human movement disorders, motor physiology, and basal ganglia pharmacology. *Recreation:* the human brain. *Address:* Institute of Neurology, National Hospital for Neurology and Neurosurgery, Queen Square, WC1N 3BG. *Club:* Athenæum. *Died 29 Sept. 1998.*

MARSDEN, Sir Nigel (John Denton), 3rd Bt *cr* 1924, of Grimsby, co. Lincoln; gardener since 1983; *b* 26 May 1940; *s* of Sir John Denton Marsden, 2nd Bt and of Hope, *yr d* of late G. E. Llewelyn; *S* father, 1985; *m* 1961, Diana Jean, *d* of Air Marshal Sir Patrick Hunter Dunn, KBE, CB, DFC; three *d. Educ:* Ampleforth College, York. Vice-Chairman and Managing Director of family business, Consolidated Fisheries Ltd, of Grimsby, 1973 until 1982, when Company ceased trading and was sold. *Recreations:* walking, shooting, family. *Heir: b* Simon Neville Llewelyn Marsden [*b* 1 Dec. 1948; *m* 1st, 1970, Catherine Thérèsa (marr. diss. 1978), *d* of late Brig. James Charles Windsor-Lewis, DSO, MC; 2nd, 1984, Caroline, *y d* of John Stanton, Houghton St Giles, Norfolk; one *d*]. *Address:* The Homestead, 1 Grimsby Road, Waltham, Grimsby, South Humberside DN37 0PS. *T:* (01472) 822166.

Died 16 Nov. 1997.

MARSH, Ven. Bazil Roland, BA; Archdeacon of Northampton, Non-Residentiary Canon of Peterborough, and Rector of St Peter's, Northampton, 1964–91, then Archdeacon Emeritus; *b* Three Hills, Alta, Canada, 11 Aug. 1921; *s* of late Ven. Wilfred Carter Marsh and Mary Jean (*née* Stott), Devil's Lake, North Dakota, USA; *m* 1946, Audrey Joan, *d* of late Owen George Oyler, farmer,

Brookmans Park, Hatfield, and Alma Lillian Oyler; three s one d. *Educ:* State schs in USA and Swindon, Wilts; Leeds Univ.; Coll. of the Resurrection, Mirfield, Yorks. Deacon 1944, priest 1945; Curate of: St Mary the Virgin, Cheshunt, Herts, 1944–46; St John Baptist, Coventry, 1946–47; St Giles-in-Reading, Berks, 1947–51; Rector of St Peter's, Townsville, Qld, Australia, 1951–56; Vicar of St Mary the Virgin, Far Cotton, Northampton, 1956–64. MLitt Lambeth, 1990. *Address:* 12 Parkway, Northampton NN3 3BS. *T:* (01604) 406644.

Died 23 May 1997.

MARSHALL OF GORING, Baron *cr* 1985 (Life Peer), of South Stoke in the County of Oxfordshire; **Walter Charles Marshall,** Kt 1982; CBE 1973; FRS 1971; Ambassador to World Association of Nuclear Operators, since 1993 (Chairman, 1989–93); *b* 5 March 1932; *s* of late Frank Marshall and Amy (*née* Pearson); *m* 1955, Ann Vivienne Sheppard; one *s* one *d. Educ:* Birmingham Univ. Scientific Officer, AERE, Harwell, 1954–57; Research Physicist: University of California, 1957–58; Harvard Univ., 1958–59; AERE, Harwell: Group Leader, Solid State Theory, 1959–60; Head of Theoretical Physics Div., 1960–66; Dep. Dir, 1966–68; Dir, 1966–75; Chief Scientist, Dept of Energy, 1974–77; United Kingdom Atomic Energy Authority: Dir, Research Gp, 1969–75; Mem., 1972–82; Dep. Chm., 1975–81; Chm., 1981–82; Chm., CEGB, 1982–89. Member: NRDC, 1969–75; NEDC, 1984–86; Chairman: Adv. Council on R&D for Fuel and Power, 1974–77; Offshore Energy Technology Bd, 1975–77. Adviser: Lloyd's nuclear insurance syndicate, 1991–; Inst. of Nuclear Safety System Inc., KANSAI Electric Power Co., Japan, 1992–. Pres., Assoc. of Science Educn, 1987. Editor, Oxford Internat. Series of Monographs on Physics, 1966–. Freeman, City of London, 1984. Fellow, Royal Swedish Acad. of Engrg Scis, 1977; For. Associate, Nat. Acad. of Engineering, USA Hon, FWeldI, 1987; Hon. Fellow, St Hugh's Coll., Oxford, 1983; Hon. DSc Salford, 1977. Maxwell Medal, 1964; Glazebrook Medal, 1975. Henry De Wolf Smyth Nuclear Statesman Award, USA, 1985; Internat. Award, Canadian Nuclear Assoc., 1991. *Publications:* Thermal Neutron Scattering, 1971; Nuclear Power Technology, 1984; research papers on magnetism, neutron scattering and solid state theory. *Recreations:* gardening, origami, physics. *Address:* Bridleway House, Goring-on-Thames, Oxon RG8 0HS. *T:* Goring-on-Thames (01491) 875017, *Fax:* (01491) 875009. *Died 20 Feb. 1996.*

MARSHALL, Fredda, (Mrs Herbert Marshall); *see* Brilliant, F.

MARSHALL, Martin John, CMG 1967; HM Diplomatic Service, retired; *b* 21 March 1914; *s* of late Harry Edmund Marshall and Kate Ann (*née* Bishop); *m* 1938, Olive Emily Alice, *d* of Thomas and Olive King; two *d. Educ:* Westminster City Sch.; London Sch. of Economics, University of London. Called to Bar, Gray's Inn, 1947 (Lee Prizeman). Customs and Excise Officer, 1935–39; Technical Officer, Min. of Aircraft Prodn, 1940–46; Principal, Min. of Supply, 1947–50; Trade Commissioner: Montreal, 1950–52; Atlantic Provinces, 1953; Alberta, 1954–57; Principal Trade Commissioner: Montreal, 1957–60; Calcutta (for Eastern India), 1961–63; Dep. High Comr, Sydney, 1963–67; Consul-General, Cleveland, Ohio, 1968–71; Dep. High Comr, Bombay, 1971–74. Dir, Finance/Administration, Royal Assoc. for Disability and Rehabilitation, 1977–79. *Recreation:* golf. *Address:* 8 Sunnyside Place, SW19 4SJ. *T:* (0181) 946 5570. *Club:* Royal Wimbledon Golf. *Died 19 March 1998.*

MARSHALL, Norman Bertram, MA, ScD; FRS 1970; Professor and Head of Department of Zoology and Comparative Physiology, Queen Mary College, University

of London, 1972–77, then Professor Emeritus; *b* 5 Feb. 1915; *s* of Arthur Harold and Ruby Eva Marshall; *m* 1944, Olga Stonehouse; one *s* three *d. Educ:* Cambridgeshire High Sch.; Downing Coll., Cambridge. Plankton Biologist, Dept of Oceanography, UC Hull, 1937–41; Army (mostly involved in operational research), 1941–44; seconded from Army for Service in Operation Tabarin to Antarctic, 1944–46; British Museum (Natural History): Marine fishes, 1947–72; Sen. Principal Scientific Officer, 1962–72. In charge of Manihine Expedns to Red Sea, 1948–50; Senior Biologist, Te Vega Expedn, 1966–67. Polar Medal (Silver), 1948; Rosenstiel Gold Medal for distinguished services to marine science; Senior Queen's Fellow in Marine Science, Aust., 1982. *Publications:* Aspects of Deep Sea Biology, 1954; The Life of Fishes, 1965; Explorations in the Life of Fishes, 1970; Ocean Life, 1971; Developments in Deep Sea Biology, 1979; various papers in learned jls. *Recreations:* music, fishing, golf. *Address:* 5 St John's Close, Great Chesterford, Saffron Walden, Essex CB10 1PB. *T:* Saffron Walden (01799) 531347. *Died 13 Feb. 1996.*

MARSHALL, Sir Robert (Braithwaite), KCB 1971 (CB 1968); MBE 1945; Chairman, National Water Council, 1978–82; *b* 10 Jan. 1920; *s* of Alexander Halford Marshall and Edith Mary Marshall (*née* Lockyer); *m* 1945, Diana Elizabeth Westlake; one *s* three *d. Educ:* Sherborne Sch.; Corpus Christi Coll., Cambridge (Mod. Langs, Pt I, 1938–39; Economics Pts I and II, 1945–47; BA). Foreign Office temp. appointment, 1939–45. Entered Home Civil Service, 1947; Ministry of Works, 1947–50; Private Sec. to Sec., Cabinet Office, 1950–53; Min. of Works, 1953–62; Min. of Aviation, 1962–66; Min. of Power, 1966–69; Min. of Technology, 1969–70; Under-Sec., 1964; Dep. Sec., 1966; Second Perm. Sec., 1970; Secretary (Industry), DTI, 1970–73; Second Permanent Sec., DoE, 1973–78. Chm., Can Ltd, 1985–86. Founder and first Chm., then a Vice-Pres., Wateraid. Mem. and Vice Chm. Council, Surrey Univ., 1975–87; Chm. Governors, W Surrey Coll. of Art, 1985–89. Coronation Medal, 1953. *Recreations:* travel, gardening, music, arts. *Address:* 1 Shatcombe, Uploders, Bridport, Dorset DT6 4NR. *T:* (01308) 485348. *Died 25 Dec. 2000.*

MARSLAND, Prof. Edward Abson, BDS, PhD; FDSRCS, FRCPath; Vice-Chancellor and Principal, University of Birmingham, 1981–86; Professor of Oral Pathology, University of Birmingham, 1964–81, Emeritus since 1986; *b* Coventry, 18 May 1923; *s* of T. Marsland; *m* 1957, Jose, *d* of J. H. Evans; one *s* two *d. Educ:* King Edward's Sch. and Univ. of Birmingham. House Surgeon, Gen. and Dental Hosps, Birmingham, 1946; Birmingham University: Research Fellow, 1948–50; Lectr in Dental Pathology, 1950–58; Sen. Lectr, 1958–64; Pro-Vice-Chancellor, 1977–79; Vice-Principal, 1979–81; Dir, Birmingham Dental Sch., 1969–74. Chairman: Co-ord. Cttee for Welfare of Handicapped, Birmingham, 1972–81; W Midlands Council for Disabled People, 1977–83 (Pres., 1985–); Midlands Council for Preparatory Trng of Disabled, 1987–89 (Vice-Chm., 1976–87); Regional Council, Sense in the Midlands, 1990–; Member: W Midlands RHA, 1984–87 (Chm., Rehabilitation Cttee, 1987–93); Disablement Services Authority, 1987–91. Pres., Blue Coat Sch., Birmingham, 1984–; Hon. Vice-Pres., Ironbridge Museum Trust, 1986; Chairman: Council, Edgbaston C of E Coll. for Girls, 1988–91 (Mem. Council, 1984–88); Council of Management, St Mary's Hospice, 1990– (Mem. Council, 1987–90). Trustee: Selly Oak Colls, 1987– (Hon. Fellow, 1986); Sense in the Midlands Foundn, 1987–93; Royal Orthopaedic Hospital Trust, Birmingham, 1990–; Midland Assoc. for Spina Bifida and Hydrocephalus, 1990–. Hon. LLD Birmingham, 1987; DUniv Open, 1987. Gold Medal, Birmingham Civic Soc., 1988. *Publications:* An Atlas of Dental Histology, 1957;

A Colour Atlas of Oral Histopathology, 1975; scientific papers in various jls; articles on disability. *Recreations:* work for disabled people, gardening, motoring, photography. *Address:* 9 Bryony Road, Selly Oak, Birmingham B29 4BY. *T:* 0121–608 1285.
Died 9 Feb. 1996.

MARTELL, Vice-Adm. Sir Hugh (Colenso), KBE 1966 (CBE 1957); CB 1963; *b* 6 May 1912; *s* of late Engineer Capt. A. A. G. Martell, DSO, RN (Retd) and Mrs S. Martell; *m* 1st, 1941, Marguerite Isabelle (marr. diss. 1983), *d* of late Sir Dymoke White, 2nd Bt; five *s* one *d*; 2nd, Margaret, *d* of late Major A. R. Glover; two *s* six *d*. *Educ:* Edinburgh Academy; RNC Dartmouth. Royal Navy, 1926–67, retired; served War, 1940–45 (despatches): Gunnery Officer in HMS Berwick and HMS Illustrious; Naval Adviser to Dir Air Armament Research and Development, Min. of Supply, 1952–54; Capt. (F) 7 and in Comd HMS Bigbury Bay, 1954–55; Overall Operational Comdr, Nuclear Tests, in Monte Bello Is as Cdre, 1956; IDC, 1957; Capt., HMS Excellent, 1958; ADC, 1958; Dir of Tactical and Weapons Policy, Admiralty and Naval Mem. Defence Research Policy Staff, Min. of Defence, 1959–62; Admiral Commanding Reserves and Dir-Gen. of Naval Recruiting (as Rear-Adm.), 1962–65; Chief of Allied Staff, Mediterranean, Aegean and Black Sea (as Vice-Adm.), 1965–67. Life Mem., RNSA. *Recreation:* sailing. *Club:* Naval (Hon. Life Mem.).
Died 25 Dec. 1998.

MARTIN, Charlie; *see* Martin, J. C.

MARTIN, Frederick Royal, CEng, FICE, FIStructE; Under-Secretary, Department of the Environment and Director, Defence Services II, Property Services Agency, 1975–79, retired; *b* 10 Oct. 1919; *e s* of late Frederick Martin and Lois Martin (*née* Royal); *m* 1946, Elsie Winifred Parkes (*d* 1984); one *s* three *d*. *Educ:* Dudley Grammar Sch.; Univ. of Birmingham (BSc Hons). Asst Engr, Birmingham, Tame and Rea Dist Drainage Bd, 1940; entered Air Min. Directorate-Gen. of Works, as Engrg Asst, 1941; Asst Civil Engr: Heathrow, Cardington, London, 1944–48; Civil Engr: Cambridge, Iraq, Jordan, Persian Gulf, London, 1948–54; Sqdn Leader, RAF, 1949–52; Sen. CE, London, 1954–58; Suptg CE, London, also Chief Engr, Aden, Aden Protectorate, Persian Gulf and E Africa, 1958–62; Suptg CE, Exeter, 1962–64; Area Officer, Bournemouth, Min. of Public Bldg and Works, 1964–66; Suptg CE, Directorate of Civil Engrg Develt, 1966–70; Asst Dir, 1970–72; Dir of Directorate of Social and Research Services, Property Services Agency, 1972; Chief Engineer, Maplin Develt Authority, 1973–74. Crampton Prize, ICE, 1946. *Publications:* various papers and articles to Instn Civil Engrs, etc, on airfield pavements. *Recreations:* looking at medieval building, reading, gardening. *Address:* 25 East Avenue, Bournemouth, Dorset BH3 7BS. *T:* (01202) 555858.
Died 7 Dec. 1997.

MARTIN, John Christopher, (Charlie), CBE 1989; Deputy Chief Scientific Officer (Special Merit), United Kingdom Atomic Energy Authority, 1974–86; *b* 21 Sept. 1926; *s* of late Percy Martin and Marjorie Etta Caselton. *Educ:* Edward Alleyn's Sch.; King's Coll., London (BSc Hons Physics 1946). MoS, Fort Halstead, 1947; Woolwich Arsenal, 1950; UKAEA/MoD, AWRE, Aldermaston, 1952–89. EMP Fellow, 1988. USA Defense Nuclear Agency Exceptional Public Service Gold Medal, 1977; (first) Erwin Marx Award in Pulse Power Technology, 3rd Internat. Meeting on Pulsed Power, 1981. *Publications:* contribs to learned jls. *Recreations:* friends, food, snorkling, science fiction and fact (not always distinguishable). *Died 23 March 1999.*

MARTIN, John Francis Ryde, CMG 1993; HM Diplomatic Service; *b* 8 Feb. 1943; *s* of Frank George Martin and Phyllis Mary Wixcey; *m* 1st, 1966, Hélène Raymonde Henriette Pyronnet (marr. diss. 1984); two *s*; 2nd, 1985, Kathleen Marie White; one *s*. *Educ:* Bedford School; Brasenose College, Oxford (MA); Bologna Center, Johns Hopkins Univ. FCO, 1966; Buenos Aires, 1968–70; Athens, 1970–74; Private Sec. to Minister of State, FCO, 1976–78; Nicosia, 1978–81; Asst Sec., Internat. Telecommunications, DTI, 1983–84; Counsellor: Lagos, 1984–88; (Econ. and Social), UKMIS to UN, 1988–93; High Comr, Republic of Malaŵi, 1993–98. *Recreations:* travel, collecting, bibliomania. *Address:* c/o Foreign and Commonwealth Office, SW1A 2AH. *Club:* Travellers'.
Died 5 Jan. 1999.

MARTIN, Sir (John) Leslie, Kt 1957; RA 1986; PhD; FRIBA; Professor of Architecture, University of Cambridge, 1956–72, Emeritus Professor, 1973; Fellow, Jesus College, Cambridge, 1956–73, Hon. Fellow 1973, Emeritus Fellow, 1976; *b* 17 Aug. 1908; *s* of late Robert Martin, FRIBA; *m* 1934, Sadie Speight, MA, ARIBA (*d* 1992); one *s* one *d*. *Educ:* Manchester Univ. Sch. of Architecture (MA, PhD); MA Cantab; MA Oxon. Asst Lectr, Manchester Univ. Sch. of Architecture, 1930–34; Head of Sch. of Architecture, Hull, 1934–39; Principal Asst Architect, LMS Railway, 1939–48; Dep. Architect, LCC, 1948–53; Architect to the LCC, 1953–56. Slade Prof. of Fine Art, Oxford, 1965–66; Ferens Prof. of Fine Art, Hull, 1967–68; William Henry Bishop Vis. Prof. of Architecture, Univ. of Yale, 1973–74; Lethaby Prof., RCA, 1981. Lectures: Gropius, Harvard, 1966; Cordingley, Manchester, 1968; Kenneth Kassler, Princeton, 1974; annual, Soc. Arch. Historians, 1976; Townsend, UCL, 1976; Convocation, Leicester, 1978. Scheme concept for Royal Festival Hall, 1948–51, and design for its final completion; buildings included: work in Cambridge and for Univs of Cambridge, Oxford, Leicester and Hull; Gall. of Modern Art, Gulbenkian Foundn, Lisbon; scheme design, Royal Concert Hall, Glasgow, and RSAMD, Glasgow (Hon. FRSAMD). Mem. Council, RIBA, 1952–58 (Vice-Pres., 1955–57); Mem., Royal Fine Art Commn, 1958–72. Hon. Fellow, Humberside Coll. of Educn. Hon. LittD Cantab; Hon. LLD: Leicester, Hull, Manchester; DUniv Essex. RIBA Recognised Schs Silver Medallist, 1929; Soane Medallist, 1930; London Architecture Bronze Medallist, 1954; RIBA Distinction in Town Planning, 1956; Civic Trust Award, Oxford, 1967; Commend., Cambridge, 1972; Concrete Soc. Award, Oxford, 1972; Royal Gold Medal for Architecture, RIBA, 1973; RIBA Trustees Medal, 1991; Architects' Jl Centenary Award, 1995. Hon. Mem., Assoc. of Finnish Architects; Accademico corrispondente, National Acad. of S Luca, Rome. Comdr, Order of Santiago da Espada (Portugal). *Publications:* (ed jtly) Circle, 1937, repr. 1971; (in collab. with wife) The Flat Book, 1939; Whitehall: a Plan for a National and Government Centre, 1965; The Framework of Planning (Inaugural Lecture) Hull, 1967; (ed jtly) Cambridge Urban and Architectural Studies, Vol. I: Urban Space and Structure, 1972; Building and Ideas (1933–83) from the Studio of Leslie Martin, 1983; The Work of Leslie Martin: papers and selected articles; *relevant publication:* Architecture, Education and Research, ed P. Carolin and T. Dannatt, 1996. *Address:* The Barns, Church Street, Great Shelford, Cambridge CB2 5EL. *T:* (01223) 842399.
Died 28 July 2000.

MARTIN, Prof. John Powell; Professor Emeritus, University of Southampton; Visiting Professor, Department of Social Policy and Social Work, Manchester University, since 1992; *b* 22 Dec. 1925; *s* of Bernard and Grace Martin; *m* 1st, 1951, Sheila Feather (marr. diss. 1981); three *s*; 2nd, 1983, Joan Higgins. *Educ:* Leighton

Park Sch., Reading; Univ. of Reading (BA); London Sch. of Economics and Political Science (Certif. in Social Admin, PhD); Univ. of Cambridge (MA). Lectr, London Sch. of Economics, 1953–59; Asst Dir of Research, Inst. of Criminology, Univ. of Cambridge, 1960–66; Fellow, King's Coll., Cambridge, 1964–67, Prof. of Sociology and Social Admin, later of Social Policy, 1967–89, Res. Prof., 1989–92, Univ. of Southampton. Hill Foundn Vis. Prof., Univ. of Minnesota, 1973; Vis. Fellow, Yale Law Sch., 1974. Mem., Jellicoe Cttee on Boards of Visitors of Penal Instns, 1974–75. *Publications:* Social Aspects of Prescribing, 1957; Offenders as Employees, 1962; The Police: a study in manpower (with Gail Wilson), 1969; The Social Consequences of Conviction (with Douglas Webster), 1971; (ed) Violence and the Family, 1978; (jtly) The Future of the Prison System, 1980; Hospitals in Trouble, 1984; (with J. B. Coker) Licensed to Live, 1985; (with Douglas Webster) Probation Motor Projects in England and Wales, 1994; articles in: Lancet, British Jl of Criminology, British Jl of Sociology, International Review of Criminal Policy, etc. *Recreations:* sailing, photography, do-it-yourself. *Address:* 3 Gordon Place, Manchester M20 3LD. *Club:* Lymington Town Sailing.
Died 17 Aug. 1997.

MARTIN, Sir Leslie; see Martin, Sir J. L.

MARTIN, Patrick William, TD; JP; MA; Headmaster of Warwick School, 1962–77; *b* 20 June 1916; *e s* of Alan Pattinson Martin, Bowness-on-Windermere, Westmorland; *m* 1st, 1939, Gwendoline Elsie Helme (*d* 1987), MA, St Hilda's Coll., Oxford; two *d*; 2nd, 1989, Eileen Muriel Beattie, JP. *Educ:* Windermere Grammar Sch.; Balliol Coll., Oxford (2nd cl. hons in Modern History, 1937). Commissioned in TA, 1938; served War of 1939–45, on active service with Royal Artillery; Staff College, Quetta; GSO 2, and 1 HQ RA 14th Army in Burma (despatches), British Mil. Mission to Belgium, 1946. Asst Master, Abingdon Sch., Berks, 1938–40; schoolmaster, 1946–49; Asst Dir of Educn, Brighton, 1950–52; Headmaster: Chipping Norton Grammar Sch., 1952–57; Lincoln Sch., 1958–62. Chm., Midland Div., Headmasters' Conf., 1972; Pres., Headmasters' Assoc., 1976; Treasurer, Warwick Univ., 1983–89. CC Warwickshire, 1977–85 (Leader, 1981–83). JP Warwicks, 1966; Dep. Chm., Warwick Petty Sessions. *Publications:* History of Heart of England Building Society, 1981; articles in educational and other periodicals. *Recreations:* books, music, foreign countries and people, being alone in the countryside. *Address:* 80 High Street, Kenilworth, Warwicks CV8 1LZ. *T:* (01926) 854140.
Died 17 Nov. 2000.

MARTIN, Peter Lewis, CBE 1980; building services engineer, retired; *b* 22 Sept. 1918; *s* of George Lewis and Madeleine Mary Martin; *m* 1949, Elizabeth Grace, *d* of John David Melling; two *d*. *Educ:* Wyggeston Boys Sch., Leicester; Kibworth Beauchamp Grammar Sch.; Leicester Coll. of Art and Technology; Borough Polytechnic. CEng; MConsE. Apprenticed to engrg contractor, 1934–39. Served War, 1940–46, RAF Engrg Branch. Joined consulting engrg practice of Dr Oscar Faber, 1947; Partner, 1961–83; Consultant, 1983–85. Pres., IHVE, 1971–72; Chairman: Heating and Ventilating Res. Assoc., 1967–69; Assoc. of Consulting Engrs, 1983–84; Member: Cttee for Application of Computers to the Construction Industry, 1970–72; Technical Data on Fuel Cttee, World Energy Conf., 1971–77; Construction and Housing Res. Adv. Council, 1975–77; Building Services Bd, CNAA, 1975–80; Engrg Council, 1982–86. Vis. Prof., Univ. of Strathclyde, 1974–85; Hon. DSc Strathclyde, 1985. Governor, Herts Coll. of Building, 1970–74. Master, Plumbers' Co., 1979–80; Freeman: Fanmakers' Co.; Engineers' Co. Silver Medal, 1956, Bronze Medal, 1968,

Gold Medal, 1976, IHVE. *Publications:* (jtly) Heating and Air Conditioning of Buildings, by Faber and Kell, 5th edn 1971 to 8th edn 1995; contribs to engrg jls and confs. *Recreation:* avoiding gardening. *Address:* Quietways, Lower Bodham, Holt, Norfolk NR25 6PS. *T:* (01263) 712591. *Club:* Lansdowne.
Died 22 Dec. 1998.

MARTIN, William McChesney, Jr; Chairman, Board of Governors, Federal Reserve System, 1951–70; *b* St Louis, Mo, 17 Dec. 1906; *s* of William McChesney Martin and Rebecca (*née* Woods); *m* 1942, Cynthia Davis; one *s* two *d*. *Educ:* Yale Univ. (BA 1928); Benton Coll. of Law, St Louis, 1931. Graduate student (part time), Columbia Univ., 1931–37. Served in Bank Examination Dept of Federal Reserve Bank of St Louis, 1928–29; Head of Statistics Dept, A. G. Edwards & Sons, St Louis, 1929–31, Partner, 1931–38. Mem., New York Stock Exch., 1931–38; Gov., 1935–38; Chm. Cttee on Constitution, 1937–38; Sec. Conway Cttee to reorganize the Exchange, 1937–38; Chm. Bd and Pres. pro tem. May-June 1938; Pres. 1938–41. Asst Exec., President's Soviet Protocol Cttee and Munitions Assignments Board, Wash., DC, 1942; appointed Mem. Export-Import Bank, 1945; Chm. and Pres., 1946–49 (as Chm. of Federal Reserve Board, served on National Advisory Council on Internat. Monetary and Financial Problems). Asst Sec. of the Treasury, 1949–51; US Exec. Dir, IBRD, 1949–52. Dir of several corporations. Trustee: Berry Schs, Atlanta, Ga; Johns Hopkins Univ., Baltimore; Nat. Geographic Soc. Held numerous hon. degrees from univs in USA and Canada. Drafted, Selective Service Act, private, US Army, 1941; Sergeant, GHQ Army War Coll., 1941; commnd 1st Lieut, Inf., Feb. 1942; Captain Aug. 1942; Major, 1943; Lt-Col 1944; Col 1945. Legion of Merit, 1945. *Recreations:* tennis, squash. *Address:* 2861 Woodland Drive, NW, Washington, DC 20008, USA. *Clubs:* West Side Tennis, Yale; Metropolitan, Alibi (Washington); Chevy Chase (Md).
Died 27 July 1998.

MARTINEAU, Rt Rev. Robert Arnold Schürhoff; Bishop of Blackburn, 1972–81; *b* 22 Aug. 1913; *s* of late Prof. C. E. Martineau, MA, MCom, FCA, and Mrs Martineau, Birmingham; *m* 1941, Elinor Gertrude Ap-Thomas; one *s* two *d*. *Educ:* King Edward's Sch., Birmingham; Trinity Hall, Cambridge (MA); Westcott House, Cambridge (Tyson Medal for Astronomy, 1935). Deacon 1938, priest 1939; Curate, Melksham, 1938–41; Chaplain: RAFVR, 1941–46; RAuxAF, 1947–52; Vicar: Ovenden, Halifax, 1946–52; Allerton, Liverpool, 1952–66; St Christopher, San Lorenzo, Calif, 1961–62; Bishop Suffragan of Huntingdon, 1966–72; Residentiary Canon of Ely, 1966–72. Hon. Canon of Liverpool, 1961–66; Rural Dean of Childwall, 1964–66. Proctor in Convocation, 1964–66. First Jt Chm., C of E Bd of Educn and Nat. Soc. for Promoting Religious Educn, 1973–79; Chm., Central Readers Bd, C of E, 1971–76. *Publications:* The Church in Germany in Prayer (ed jtly), 1937; Rhodesian Wild Flowers, 1953; The Office and Work of a Reader, 1970; The Office and Work of a Priest, 1972; Moments that Matter, 1976; Preaching through the Christian Year, 1977; Truths that Endure, 1977; Travelling with Christ, 1981. *Recreations:* gardening, swimming. *Address:* Gwenallt, Park Street, Denbigh, Clwyd LL16 3DB.
Died 28 June 1999.

MARX, Enid Crystal Dorothy, RDI 1944; painter and designer; *b* London, 20 Oct. 1902; *y d* of Robert J. Marx. *Educ:* Roedean Sch.; Central Sch. of Arts and Crafts; Royal College of Art Painting Sch. Designing and printing handblock printed textiles, 1925–39; wood engraving and autolithography pattern papers, book jackets, book illustration and decorations, trademarks, etc; designed moquettes and posters for LPTB; industrial designing for printed and woven furnishing fabrics, wallpapers, ceramics, plastics. Fellow, 1982, Senior Fellow, 1987, RCA; FRSA, FSIAD; original Mem. National Register of Industrial Designers of Central Institute of Art and Design. Mem. of Bd of Trade design panel on utility furniture. Designed postage stamps: ½d-2d for first issue Elizabeth II; Christmas 1976 issue. Exhibited in USA and Europe; various works purchased by Victoria and Albert Museum, Musée des Arts Décoratifs, Boston Museum, Scottish Arts Council, Sheffield Art Gall., etc. Mem. Society of Wood Engravers. Lectured on textiles and folk art. *Publications:* (jtly) English Popular and Traditional Art, 1947; (with Margaret Lambert) English Popular Art, 1951, 2nd edn 1988; articles and broadcasts on aspects of industrial design in various countries; author and illustrator of twelve books for children. *Recreations:* study of popular art in different countries, gardening. *Address:* The Studio, 39 Thornhill Road, Barnsbury Square, N1 1JS. *T:* (0171) 607 2286. *Died 18 May 1998.*

MASON, Arthur Malcolm; Director, Reckitt & Colman Ltd, 1958–79 (Chairman, 1970–77); *b* 19 Dec. 1915; British parents; *m* 1938, Mary Hall (*d* 1981); one *s* (one *d* decd). *Educ:* Linton House, London; Blundells School. Trainee, Unilever Ltd, 1934–38; Chiswick Products Ltd: Asst Sales Man., 1938; Sales and Advertising Man., 1939; Dir, 1943; Chm., 1957; Reckitt & Colman Holdings Ltd: Assoc. Dir, 1957; Dir, 1958; Vice-Chm., 1965–70. FInstD. OStJ 1975. *Recreations:* sailing, sea fishing, gardening. *Clubs:* Seaview Yacht, Brading Haven Yacht.
Died 1 Oct. 1998.

MASON, Vice-Adm. Dennis Howard, CB 1967; CVO 1978; *b* 7 Feb. 1916; *s* of Wilfred Howard Mason, Broadwater, Ipswich, and Gladys (Mouse) Mason (*née* Teague), Trevenson, Cornwall; *m* 1940, Patricia D. M. (*née* Hood); three *d. Educ:* Royal Naval Coll., Dartmouth. Served War of 1939–45, Coastal Forces, Frigates and Destroyers; Comdr 1951; Captain 1956; Senior Naval Officer, Northern Ireland, 1961–63; Dir RN Tactical Sch., 1964–65; Rear-Adm. 1965; Chief of Staff to Commander, Far East Fleet, 1965–67; Vice-Adm. 1968; Comdt, Jt Services Staff Coll., 1968–70, retired 1970. ADC 1964. With Paper and Paper Products Industry Training Bd, 1971–72; Warden, St George's House, Windsor Castle, 1972–77. Mem., East Hants DC, 1979–87. *Recreations:* fishing, gardening. *Address:* Church Cottage, East Meon, Hants GU32 1NJ. *T:* East Meon (01730) 823466.
Died 11 July 1996.

MASON, Philip, CIE 1946; OBE 1942; writer; *b* 19 March 1906; *s* of Dr H. A. Mason, Duffield, Derbs; *m* 1935, Eileen Mary, *d* of Courtenay Hayes, Charmouth, Dorset; two *s* two *d. Educ:* Sedbergh; Balliol Coll., Oxford. 1st Cl. Hons Philosophy, Politics and Economics, 1927; MA 1952; DLitt 1972. Indian Civil Service: Asst Magistrate, United Provinces, 1928–33; Under-Sec., Government of India, War Dept, 1933–36; Dep. Commissioner, Garhwal, 1936–39; Dep. Sec. Govt of India, Defence Co-ordination and War Depts, 1939–42; Sec. Chiefs of Staff Cttee, India, and Head of Conf. Secretariat, SE Asia Command, 1942–44; represented War Dept in Central Assembly, 1946; Joint Sec. to Government of India, War Dept, 1944–47; Tutor and Governor to the Princes, Hyderabad, 1947; retd from ICS, 1947. Mem. Commn of Enquiry to examine problems of Minorities in Nigeria, 1957. Dir of Studies in Race Relations, Chatham House, 1952–58; Dir, Inst. of Race Relations, 1958–69. Chairman: National Cttee for Commonwealth Immigrants, 1964–65; Exec. Cttee, UK Council for Overseas Student Affairs, 1969–75; Trustees, S African Church Develt Trust, 1976–83 (Pres., 1983–88). Hon. Fellow, Sch. of Oriental and African Studies, 1970; Hon. DSc Bristol, 1971. Received into Catholic Church, 1978. *Publications:* (as Philip Woodruff): Call the Next Witness, 1945; The Wild Sweet Witch, 1947; Whatever Dies, 1948; The Sword of Northumbria, 1948; The Island of Chamba, 1950; Hernshaw Castle, 1950; Colonel of Dragoons, 1951; The Founders, 1953; The Guardians, 1954; (as Philip Mason): Racial Tension, 1954; Christianity and Race, 1956; The Birth of a Dilemma, 1958; Year of Decision, 1960; (ed) Man, Race and Darwin, 1960; Common Sense about Race, 1961; Prospero's Magic, 1962; (ed) India and Ceylon: Unity and Diversity, 1967; Patterns of Dominance, 1970; Race Relations, 1970; How People Differ, 1971; A Matter of Honour, 1974; Kipling: The Glass The Shadow and The Fire, 1975; The Dove in Harness, 1976; A Shaft of Sunlight, 1978; Skinner of Skinner's Horse, 1979; The English Gentleman, 1982; A Thread of Silk, 1984; The Men who Ruled India (abridged from The Founders, and The Guardians), 1985; Since I Last Wrote, 1996. *Recreation:* living. *Address:* 97 Glebe Road, Cambridge CB1 4TE. *T:* (01223) 213569.
Died 25 Jan. 1999.

MASON, Richard; author; *b* 16 May 1919. *Educ:* Bryanston School. *Publications: novels:* The Wind Cannot Read, 1947; The Shadow and the Peak, 1949; The World of Suzie Wong, 1957; The Fever Tree, 1962. *Address:* c/o A. M. Heath & Co. Ltd, 79 St Martin's Lane, WC2N 4AA.
Died 13 Oct. 1997.

MASON, Rev. Canon Richard John; Archdeacon of Tonbridge, 1977–95; Minister of St Luke's, Sevenoaks, 1983–95; *b* 26 April 1929; *s* of Vice-Adm. Sir Frank Mason, KCB and late Dora Margaret Mason; *m* 1972, Susan Eileen Nunnerley. *Educ:* Shrewsbury School. Newspaper journalist, 1949–55; Lincoln Theological College, 1955–58; deacon 1958, priest 1959; Asst Curate, Bishop's Hatfield, Herts, 1958–64; Domestic Chaplain to Bishop of London, 1964–69; Vicar of Riverhead with Dunton Green, Kent, 1969–73; Vicar of Edenbridge, 1973–83, also Priest in Charge of Crockham Hill, 1981–83. Canon Emeritus, Rochester Cathedral, 1995. *Address:* 61 Nelson Road, Ipswich, Suffolk IP4 4DU. *T:* (01473) 726350.
Died 6 Oct. 1997.

MASSEY, Daniel Raymond; actor; *b* London, 10 Oct. 1933; *s* of late Raymond Massey and Adrianne Allen; *m* 1st, 1961, Adrienne Corri (marr. diss. 1968); no *c*; one *s*; 2nd, 1975, Penelope Alice Wilton (marr. diss. 1984); one *d*; 3rd, Lindy Wilton. *Educ:* Eton; King's Coll., Cambridge. Connaught Theatre, Worthing, 1956–57. *Plays:* The Happiest Millionaire, Cambridge, 1957; Living for Pleasure, Garrick, 1958; Make Me an Offer (musical), New, 1959; The School for Scandal, Haymarket, 1962; The Three Musketeers, and A Subject of Scandal and Concern, Nottingham, 1962; She Loves Me (musical), NY, 1963; Julius Caesar, Royal Court, 1964; A Month in the Country, and Samson Agonistes, Guildford, 1965; Barefoot in the Park, Piccadilly, 1965; The Rivals, Haymarket, 1966; The Importance of Being Earnest, Haymarket, 1967; Spoiled, Glasgow, 1970; Abelard and Heloise, Wyndham's, 1970; Three Sisters, and Trelawny of The Wells, 1971; Becket, Guildford, 1972; Popkiss, Globe, 1972; Gigi, NY, 1973; Bloomsbury, Phoenix, 1974; The Gay Lord Quex, Albery, 1975; Othello, Nottingham, 1976; Rosmersholm, Haymarket, 1977; Don Juan comes back from the War, Betrayal, Nat. Theatre, 1978; The Philanderer, Nat. Theatre, 1979; Appearances, May Fair, 1980; Man and Superman, The Mayor of Zalamea, The Hypochondriac, Nat. Theatre, 1981; The Time of Your Life, Twelfth Night, Measure for Measure, RSC, 1983; Breaking the Silence, Waste, RSC, 1984; Follies, Shaftesbury, 1987; The Doll's House, Haymarket, Leicester, 1989; Heartbreak House, Haymarket, 1992; Love's Labour's Lost, RSC, 1993; The Devil's Disciple, NT, 1994; Taking Sides, Minerva, Chichester, transf. Criterion, 1995, NY, 1996. *Films* include: Girls at Sea,

1957; Upstairs and Downstairs; The Entertainer; The Queen's Guard, 1960; Go to Blazes, 1962; Moll Flanders, 1966; Star, 1968 (Best Supporting Actor, Hollywood Golden Globe Award, 1968); The Incredible Sarah, 1977; The Cat and the Canary, 1978; Escape to Victory, 1981; Stalin, 1992. *TV:* serials: Roads to Freedom, 1970; The Golden Bowl, 1972; Good Behaviour, 1982; Intimate Contact, 1987; GBH, 1991; numerous plays. Actor of the Year, SWET Award, 1981; Stage Actor of the Year, Variety Club of GB, and (jtly) Actor of the Year, London Critics' Circle, 1995. *Recreations:* golf, classical music, reading, travel. *Address:* c/o Wim Hance, London Management Ltd, 2 Noel Street, W1V 3RB.
                                                      Died 25 March 1998.

MASTEL, Royston John, CVO 1977; CBE 1969; Assistant Commissioner (Administration and Operations), Metropolitan Police, 1972–76; *b* 30 May 1917; *s* of late John Mastel and Rose Mastel (*née* Gorton); *m* 1940, Anne Kathleen Johnson; two *s*. *Educ:* Tottenham Grammar School. Joined Metropolitan Police as Constable, 1937; Pilot, RAF, 1941–45; Metropolitan Police: Sergeant 1946; Inspector 1951; Supt 1955; Comdr, No 2 District, 1966; subseq. Dep. Asst Comr, Head of Management Services Dept and D Dept (Personnel); Asst Comr (Personnel and Training), 1972. OStJ 1976. *Recreations:* Rugby football, golf. *Address:* The Retreat, Nottage, Porthcawl CF36 3RU.   *Died 7 April 1998.*

MASTERS, Rt Rev. Brian John; Area Bishop of Edmonton, since 1984; *b* 17 Oct. 1932; *s* of late Stanley William and Grace Hannah Masters; unmarried. *Educ:* Collyers School, Horsham; Queens' Coll., Cambridge (MA 1955); Cuddesdon Theological Coll. Lloyd's broker, 1955–62. Deacon 1964, priest 1965; Asst Curate, S Dunstan and All Saints, Stepney, 1964–69; Vicar, Holy Trinity with S Mary, Hoxton, N1, 1969–82; Bishop Suffragan of Fulham, 1982–84. Chm. Exec. Cttee, Church Union, 1984–88. *Recreation:* theatre. *Address:* 1 Regent's Park Terrace, NW1 7EE. *T:* (0171) 267 4455, *Fax:* (0171) 267 4404. *Club:* United Oxford & Cambridge University.
                                                      Died 23 Sept. 1998.

MATHER, Sir William (Loris), Kt 1968; CVO 1986; OBE 1957; MC 1945; TD and 2 clasps 1949; CEng; Vice Lord-Lieutenant of Cheshire, 1975–90; *b* 17 Aug. 1913; *s* of Loris Emerson Mather, CBE and Leila, *d* of John S. Morley; *m* 1937, Eleanor, *d* of Prof. R. H. George, Providence, RI, USA; two *s* two *d*. *Educ:* Oundle; Trinity Coll., Cambridge (MA Engrg and Law, 1939). Commissioned Cheshire Yeomanry, 1935; served War of 1939–45: Palestine, Lebanon, Syria, Iraq, Iran, Western Desert, Italy, Belgium, Holland, Germany (wounded twice, MC); Instructor, Staff Coll., Camberley, 2nd i/c 1st RTR, and GSO1, 1944–45. Chm., Mather & Platt Ltd, 1960–78; Divisional Dir, BSC, 1968–73; Chairman: CompAir Ltd, 1978–83 (Dir, 1973–83); Neolith Chemicals Ltd, 1983–88; Advanced Manufacturing Technology Group, 1985–88. Director: District Bank, 1960–84; National Westminster Bank, 1970–84 (Chm., Northern Bd, 1972–84); Manchester Ship Canal Co. Ltd, 1970–84; Wormold Internat. Ltd, 1975–78; Imperial Continental Gas Assoc. Ltd, 1980–84. Chairman: NW Regional Economic Planning Council, 1968–75; Inst. of Directors, 1979–82 (Manchester Inst. of Dirs, 1967–72); British Pump Manufrs Assoc., 1970–73; President: Manchester Chamber of Commerce, 1964–66 (Emeritus Dir, 1978–89); Manchester Guardian Soc. for Protection of Trade, 1971–85; British Mech. Engrg Confedn, 1975–78; Civic Trust for the NW, 1979–91 (Chm., 1961–78); Vice Pres., Assoc. of British Chambers of Commerce, 1979–85; Pres., Mech. Engrg Council, 1978–80; Member: Council of Industrial Design, 1960–71; Engineering Industries Council, 1976–80; Council, Duchy of Lancaster, 1977–85.

Member Court: Manchester Univ., 1956–94; Salford Univ., 1968–86; Royal College of Art, 1967–85; Mem. Council, Manchester Business Sch., 1964–85; Governor: Manchester University Inst. of Science and Technology (Pres., 1976–85; Hon. Fellow, 1986); Manchester Grammar Sch., 1965–80; Feoffee, Chetham's Hosp. Sch., 1961–91; President: Manchester YMCA, 1982–91 (Chm., 1953–82); Greater Manchester East County Scout Council, 1978–94. Hon. Fellow, Manchester Coll. of Art and Design, 1967; Hon. DEng: Liverpool, 1980; UMIST, 1997; Hon. LLD Manchester, 1983. Comdr, Cheshire Yeomanry, 1954–57; Col and Dep. Comdr, 23 Armoured Bde, TA, 1957–60; ADC to the Queen, 1961–66. CIMgt; FRSA. DL City and County of Chester, 1963; High Sheriff of Cheshire, 1969–70. KLJ 1988. *Recreations:* field sports, golf, swimming. *Address:* Whirley Hall, Macclesfield, Cheshire SK10 4RN. *T:* (01625) 422077. *Club:* Leander (Henley-on-Thames).   *Died 19 Dec. 1998.*

MATHEW, Theobald David; Windsor Herald of Arms, 1978–97; *b* 7 April 1942; *s* of Robert Mathew (solicitor), London and West Mersea, Essex, and Joan Alison, *d* of Sir George Young, 4th Bt, MVO, Formosa. *Educ:* Downside; Balliol Coll., Oxford (MA). Green Staff Officer at Investiture of HRH the Prince of Wales, 1969; Rouge Dragon Pursuivant of Arms, 1970; Dep. Treasurer, Coll. of Arms, 1978–82. OStJ 1986. *Recreations:* cricket, sailing. *Address:* Kings Hard, Coast Road, West Mersea, Essex. *Clubs:* Athenæum, MCC; Middlesex CC; Royal Harwich Yacht.   *Died 24 Dec. 1998.*

MATHIESON, William Allan Cunningham, CB 1970; CMG 1955; MBE 1945; consultant to international organisations; *b* 22 Feb. 1916; *e s* of Rev. William Miller Mathieson, BD, and Elizabeth Cunningham Mathieson (*née* Reid); *m* 1946, Elizabeth Frances, *y d* of late Henry Morrell Carr, RA, two *s*. *Educ:* High Sch. of Dundee; Edinburgh Univ.; King's Coll., Cambridge. Joined Colonial Office, 1939; served War, 1940–45: Royal Artillery in UK, France and Germany (Major, despatches); rejoined Colonial Office, 1945; Middle East Dept, 1945–48; Private Sec. to Minister of State, 1948–49; Asst Sec., Colonial Office, 1949; Counsellor (Colonial Affairs), UK Delegn to UN, New York, 1951–54; Head of East African Department, CO, 1955–58; Minister of Education, Labour and Lands, Kenya, 1958–60; Asst Sec., Dept of Technical Co-operation, 1961–64; Under-Sec., 1964–68; Dep. Sec., 1968–75, Min. of Overseas Development; Consultant, UN Develt Prog., 1976–81. Chm., Executive Council, Commonwealth Agricultural Bureaux, 1963; Member: Exec. Bd, Unesco, 1968–74; Bd of Trustees, Internat. Centre for Maize and Wheat Improvement (Mexico), 1976–86; Council, ODI, 1977–90; Council, Commonwealth Soc. for the Deaf, 1979–94; Bd of Management, LSHTM, 1981–84; Bd of Governors, Internat. Centre for Insect Physiol. and Ecol., Nairobi, 1985–90; Chm., Bd of Trustees, Internat. Service for Nat. Agr. Res., 1980–84. Hon. Fellow, Queen Elizabeth House, Oxford, 1973; Foreign Fellow, African Acad. of Scis, 1989. FRSA. *Recreations:* photography, travel. *Address:* 13 Sydney House, Woodstock Road, W4 1DP.
                                                      Died 12 Feb. 1999.

MATTHEW, Prof. (Henry) Colin (Gray), DPhil; FBA 1991; Editor, New Dictionary of National Biography, since 1992; Professor of Modern History, Oxford, since 1992; Fellow and Tutor in Modern History, St Hugh's College, Oxford, since 1978; *b* 15 Jan. 1941; *s* of late Henry Johnston Scott and of Joyce Mary Matthew; *m* 1966, Sue Ann (*née* Curry); two *s* one *d*. *Educ:* Edinburgh Acad.; Sedbergh Sch.; Christ Church, Oxford (MA, DPhil); Makerere Coll., Univ. of E Africa (DipEd). Education Officer, Grade IIA, Tanzanian Civil Service, 1963–66; Lectr in Gladstone Studies, 1970–94, Student, 1976–78,

Christ Church, Oxford. Literary Dir, RHistS, 1985–89. Vice-Pres., British Acad., 1998–; Mem., Royal Commn on Histl Manuscripts, 1998–; Trustee, Nat. Portrait Gall., 1998–. Editor, The Gladstone Diaries, 1972–94. *Publications:* The Liberal Imperialists, 1973; (ed) The Gladstone Diaries: vols 3 and 4 (with M. R. D. Foot), 1974; vols 5 and 6, 1978; vols 7 and 8, 1982; vol. 9, 1986; vols 10 and 11, 1990; vols 12, 13 and 14 (Wheatley Medal, Soc. of Indexers), 1994; Gladstone 1809–1874, 1986; Gladstone 1875–1898, 1995 (Wolfson History Prize, 1995); Gladstone 1809–1898, 1997; (ed with Jane Garnett) Religion and Revival since 1700, 1993; contributor to: Studies in Church History, vol. xv, Oxford Illustrated History of Britain, 1984, and learned jls. *Recreations:* fishing, bag-pipe playing, second-hand book buying. *Address:* 107 Southmoor Road, Oxford OX2 6RE. *T:* (01865) 267808/557959. *Died 29 Oct. 1999.*

MATTHEWS, David Napier, CBE 1976 (OBE 1945); MA, MD, MCh (Cambridge); FRCS; Hon. FDSRCS; retired; Consulting Plastic Surgeon, University College Hospital and Hospital for Sick Children; Civilian Consultant in Plastic Surgery to the Royal Navy since 1954; *b* 7 July 1911; *m* 1940, Betty Eileen Bailey Davies; two *s* one *d.* *Educ:* Leys Sch., Cambridge; Queens' Coll., Cambridge; Charing Cross Hosp. Qualified as doctor, 1935. Surgical Registrar, Westminster Hospital, until 1940; Surgeon Plastic Unit, East Grinstead, 1939–41; Surgical Specialist, RAFVR, 1941–46; Consulting Practice as Surgeon 1946–80; Plastic Surgeon: UCH and Hosp. for Sick Children, 1946–76; Royal Nat. Orthopædic Hosp., 1947–54; King Edward's Hosp. for Officers, 1972–80. Adviser in Plastic Surgery, DHSS, 1962–77. Hunterian Professor, RCS, 1941, 1944, 1976; President: British Assoc. of Plastic Surgeons, 1954 and 1971; Plastic Section, RSM, 1970–71; Sec., Harveian Soc. of London, 1951, Vice-Pres., 1954, Pres., 1962; Gen. Sec. Internat. Confederation for Plastic Surgery, 1959; Pres., Chelsea Clinical Soc., 1962. *Publications:* Surgery of Repair, 1943, 2nd edn 1946; (ed) Recent Advances in the Surgery of Trauma, 1963; chapters in surgical books; contrib. to Lancet, BMJ and Post Graduate Jl etc. *Recreation:* fishing. *Address:* River Walk, Shooters Hill, Pangbourne, Reading RG8 7DU. *T:* (0118) 984 4476. *Died 25 Aug. 1997.*

MATTHEWS, Dr Drummond Hoyle, VRD 1967; FRS 1974; Senior Research Associate, Scientific Director, British Institutions Reflection Profiling Syndicate, at the University of Cambridge, 1982–90; Fellow, Wolfson College, Cambridge, 1980–90; *b* 5 Feb. 1931; *s* of late Captain C. B. and Mrs E. M. Matthews; *m* 1st, 1963, (Elizabeth) Rachel McMullen (marr. diss. 1980); one *s* one *d*; 2nd, 1987, Sandie Adam. *Educ:* Bryanston Sch.; King's Coll., Cambridge. BA 1954, MA 1959, PhD 1962. RNVR, 1949–51, retd 1967. Geologist, Falkland Islands Dependencies Survey, 1955–57; returned to Cambridge Univ. (BP student), 1958; Research Fellow, King's Coll., 1960; Sen. Asst in Research, Dept of Geophysics, 1960; Asst Dir of Research, 1966; Reader in Marine Geology, 1971. Balzan Prize (jtly), 1982. *Publications:* papers on marine geophysics in jls and books. *Recreations:* walking, sailing. *Address:* 9 Carlton Mews, Wells, Somerset BA5 1SG. *Clubs:* Antarctic, Cruising Association. *Died 20 July 1997.*

MATTHEWS, Gordon Richards, CBE 1974; FCA; *b* 16 Dec. 1908; *m* 1st, 1934, Ruth Hillyard Brooks (*d* 1980), *d* of Sir David Brooks, GBE; one *s* one *d* (and one *d* decd); 2nd, 1982, Freda E. Evans (*née* Ledger). *Educ:* Repton Sch. Chartered Accountant, 1932. Contested (U) Deritend, Birmingham, 1945, and Yardley, Birmingham, 1950; MP (C) Meriden Division of Warwicks, 1959–64; PPS to the Postmaster-General, 1960–64. Hon. Treas., Deritend

Unionist Assoc., 1937–45; Hon. Sec., Birmingham Unionist Association, 1948–53; Pres., West Midlands Cons. Council, 1983–85 (Dep. Chm., 1967–70; Chm., 1970–73). Pres. City of Birmingham Friendly Soc., 1957–64; Mem. Board of Management, Linen and Woollen Drapers Institution and Cottage Homes, 1950–65 (Pres. of Appeal, 1954–55); Chm. of Exec. Cttee, Birmingham Area of YMCA, 1951–59; Mem., Nat. Council and Nat. Exec. Cttee, YMCA, 1968–71; Chm., Finance Cttee, YWCA, Birmingham Area, 1965–72. Chm., Oxfordshire Br., CPRE, 1978–81. FRSA 1986. *Recreations:* fly-fishing, foreign travel. *Address:* 12 Cherry Orchard Close, Chipping Campden, Glos GL55 6DH. *T:* (01386) 840626. *Died 4 Feb. 2000.*

MATTHEWS, Pamela Winifred, (Mrs Peter Matthews); Principal, Westfield College (University of London), 1962–65; *b* 4 Dec. 1914; *d* of Lt-Col C. C. Saunders-O'Mahony; *m* 1938, H. P. S. Matthews (*d* 1958); one *s* one *d.* *Educ:* St Paul's Girls' Sch.; London Sch. of Economics (BSc (Econ)). Royal Institute of International Affairs, 1938–39; Foreign Office, 1939–40; The Economist Newspaper, 1940–43; Foreign Office, 1943–45; Reuters, 1945–61; Nat. Inst. for Social Work Trng, 1961–62. Independent Mem., Advertising Standards Authority, 1964–65; Industrial Tribunal rep. for CAB, 1974–89. Mem., RIIA, 1990. Governor: Northwood Coll., Middlesex, 1962–89; Cardinal Manning Boys' RC School, 1980–91. *Publications:* diplomatic correspondence for Reuters. *Recreations:* travel, theatre. *Address:* Alan Morkill House, 88 St Mark's Road, W10 6BY. *Died 12 Nov. 1999.*

MATTHEWS, Richard Bonnar, CBE 1971; QPM 1965; Chief Constable, Warwickshire, 1964–76 (Warwickshire and Coventry, 1969–74); *b* 18 Dec. 1915; *er s* of late Charles Richard Matthews, Worthing; *m* 1943, Joan, *d* of late Basil Worsley, Henstridge, Som; two *d.* *Educ:* Stowe School. Served War of 1939–45, Lieut, RNVR. Joined Metropolitan Police, 1936; Asst Chief Constable, E Sussex, 1954–56; Chief Constable of Cornwall and Isles of Scilly, 1956–64. Chm., Traffic Cttee, Assoc. of Chief Police Officers, 1973–76. Mem., Williams Cttee on Obscenity and Film Censorship, 1977–79; Chm., CS selection bds, 1979–85. Founder, Adv. Cttee on Beach Life Saving for Cornwall, 1959. Pres., Old Stoic Soc., 1986. *Recreations:* ski-ing, fishing, gardening. *Address:* Smoke Acre, Great Bedwyn, Marlborough, Wilts SN8 3LP. *T:* (01672) 870584. *Club:* Naval. *Died 26 Aug. 1997.*

MATTHEWS, Sir Stanley (John), Kt 1965; CBE 1957; President, Stoke City Football Club, since 1990; *b* Hanley, Stoke-on-Trent, 1 Feb. 1915; *s* of late Jack Matthews, Seymour Street, Hanley; *m* 1st, 1935, Elizabeth Hall Vallance (marr. diss. 1975); one *s* one *d*; 2nd, 1975, Gertrud, (Mila), Winterova (*d* 1999). *Educ:* Wellington Sch., Hanley. Professional footballer: played in first Football League match, 1931; first played for England, 1934, and fifty-five times subsequently; Stoke City FC, 1932–47; Blackpool FC, 1947–61 (FA Cup, 1953); Stoke City FC, 1961–65. Freedom of Stoke-on-Trent, 1963. FIFA Gold Merit Award, 1992. *Publications:* The Stanley Matthews Story, 1960; The Way It Was: my autobiography, 2000. *Recreations:* golf, tennis. *Address:* Stoke City Football Club, Victoria Ground, Stoke-on-Trent ST4 4EG. *Club:* National Sporting. *Died 23 Feb. 2000.*

MAUND, Rt Rev. John Arthur Arrowsmith, CBE 1975; MC 1946; Hon. Assistant Bishop, Worcester, 1983–93; *b* 1909; *s* of late Arthur Arrowsmith and Dorothy Jane Maund, Worcester; *m* 1948, Catherine Mary Maurice (decd), Bromley, Kent; no *c.* *Educ:* Worcester Cathedral King's Sch.; Leeds Univ. (BA 1931); Mirfield Theological

Coll. Deacon 1933, priest 1934; Assistant Priest: All Saints and St Laurence, Evesham, Worcs, 1933–36; All Saints, Blackheath, London, 1936–38; Pretoria Native Mission, Pretoria, South Africa, 1938–40; CF 1940–46 (despatches, 1942); Asst Priest, Pretoria Native Mission, in charge Lady Selborne, Pretoria, 1946–50; Bishop of Lesotho, 1950–76 (diocese known as Basutoland, 1950–66); Chaplain to Hengrave Community and Hon. Asst Bishop, St Edmundsbury and Ipswich, 1977–83; Chaplain to Beauchamp Community, Malvern, 1983–89. Fellow, Royal Commonwealth Society. *Recreations:* gardening, bridge, the daily newspaper. *Address:* Flat 1, Warden's Lodge, The Quadrangle, Newland, Malvern, Worcs WR13 5AX. *T:* (01684) 568072.

Died 9 July 1998.

MAXWELL of Ardwell, Col Frederick Gordon, CBE 1967; TD; FCIT; *b* 2 May 1905, *s* of late Lt-Col Alexander Gordon Maxwell, OBE, Hon. Corps of Gentlemen-at-Arms; *m* 1st, 1935, Barbara Margaret (marr. diss. 1964) (decd), *d* of late Edward Williams Hedley, MBE, MD, Thursley, Surrey; two *s* (one *d* decd); 2nd, 1965, True Hamilton Exley, *d* of Francis George Hamilton, Old Blundells Cottage, Tiverton, Devon. *Educ:* Eton. Joined London Transport, 1924; Operating Manager (Railways), London Transport, 1947–70, retired 1971; Protocol and Conference Dept, FCO, 1971–88. OC 2nd Bn The London Scottish, 1939–42; GSO1, 52nd (Lowland) Div., 1943–44, served in Holland and Germany (despatches); GSO1, Allied Land Forces SE Asia, 1945; OC 1st Bn The London Scottish, 1947–50; Mem., Co. of London T&AFA, 1947–68; Lt-Col RE (T&AVR, IV), 1956–70; Regimental Col, The London Scottish, 1969–73. DL, Co. of London 1962; DL, Greater London, 1966–81. OStJ 1969. *Address:* 41 Cheyne Court, Cheyne Place, SW3 5TS. *T:* (0171) 352 9801. *Clubs:* Naval and Military, Highland Brigade.

Died 23 June 1997.

MAXWELL, Rear-Adm. Thomas Heron, CB 1967; DSC 1942; idc, jssc, psc; Director General of Naval Training, Ministry of Defence, 1965–67; retired, 1967; *b* 10 April 1912; *s* of late H. G. Maxwell; *m* 1947, Maeve McKinley; two *s* two *d. Educ:* Campbell Coll., Belfast; Royal Naval Engineering Coll. Cadet, 1930; Commander, 1946; Captain, 1956; Rear-Adm., 1965. *Address:* Tokenbury, Shaft Road, Bath, Avon BA2 7HP.

Died 15 March 1997.

MAY, Rt Hon. Sir John (Douglas), Kt 1972; PC 1982; a Lord Justice of Appeal, 1982–89; *b* 28 June 1923; *s* of late Mr and Mrs E. A. G. May, Shanghai and Chelsea; *m* 1958, Mary, *er d* of Sir Owen Morshead, GCVO, KCB, DSO, MC, and Paquita, *d* of J. G. Hagemeyer; two *s* one *d. Educ:* Clifton Coll. (Scholar); Balliol Coll., Oxford (Schol.). Lieut (SpSc) RNVR, 1944–46. Barrister-at-Law, Inner Temple, 1947 (Schol.), Master of the Bench, 1972; QC 1965; Recorder of Maidstone, 1971; Leader, SE Circuit, 1971; Presiding Judge, Midland and Oxford Circuit, 1973–77; a Judge of the High Ct, Queen's Bench Division, 1972–82; a Judge of the Employment Appeal Tribunal, 1978–82. Member: Parole Bd, 1977–80 (Vice-Chm., 1980); Royal Commn on Criminal Justice, 1991–93; Chairman: Inquiry into UK Prison Services, 1978–79; University Comrs, 1989–95; Guildford and Woolwich Inquiry, 1989–94. Treas., Inner Temple, 1993. Clifton College: Mem. Council, 1980–93; Pres., 1987–93. *Address:* Lindens, Sturminster Newton, Dorset DT10 1BU. *T:* (01258) 473321. *Club:* Vincent's (Oxford).

Died 15 Jan. 1997.

MAY, Sir Kenneth Spencer, Kt 1980; CBE 1976; Director: Advertiser Newspapers Ltd, Adelaide, since 1988; The News Corporation Ltd, 1979–89; *b* 10 Dec. 1914; *s* of late O. and N. May; *m* 1943, Betty C. Scott; one *s* one *d. Educ:* Woodville High School. Editorial staff, News, 1930;

political writer, 1946–59; Asst Manager, News, Adelaide, 1959–64, Manager, 1964–69; Dir, News Ltd, 1969–86; Man. Dir, News Ltd, Aust., 1977–80; Chm., Mirror Newspapers Ltd and Nationwide News Pty Ltd, 1969–80; Director: Independent Newspapers Ltd, Wellington, NZ, 1971–84; Santos Ltd, 1980–83. *Address:* 26 Waterfall Terrace, Burnside, SA 5066, Australia.

Died 22 May 2000.

MAY, Paul, CBE 1970; retired 1970; *b* 12 July 1907; *s* of William Charles May and Katharine Edith May; *m* 1st, 1933, Dorothy Ida Makower (*d* 1961); two *s* one *d*; 2nd, 1969, Frances Maud Douglas (*née* Tarver); two step *s. Educ:* Westminster; Christ Church, Oxford (MA). United Africa Co. Ltd, 1930–32; John Lewis Partnership, 1932–40; Min. of Aircraft Production, 1940–45; John Lewis Partnership, 1945–70 (Dep. Chm., 1955–70). Mem. Exec. Cttee, Land Settlement Assoc. Ltd, 1962–71. *Recreations:* walking, reading, etc. *Address:* Chesterford, Whittingham, Northumberland NE66 4UP. *T:* Whittingham (01665) 574642.

Died 19 Feb. 1996.

MAYHEW, Baron *cr* 1981 (Life Peer), of Wimbledon in Greater London; **Christopher Paget Mayhew;** *b* 12 June 1915; *e s* of Sir Basil Mayhew, KBE and Dorothea Mary, *d* of Stephen Paget, FRCS; *m* 1949, Cicely Elizabeth Ludlam; two *s* two *d. Educ:* Haileybury Coll. (Scholar); Christ Church, Oxford (Open Exhibitioner, MA). Junior George Webb-Medley Scholar (Economics), 1937; Pres., Union Soc., 1937. Gunner Surrey Yeomanry RA; BEF, Sept. 1939–May 1940; served with BNAF and CMF; BLA 1944 (despatches); Major, 1944. MP (Lab) S Norfolk, 1945–50; MP (Lab) Woolwich East, later Greenwich, Woolwich East, June 1951–July 1974; PPS to Lord Pres. of the Council, 1945–46; Parly Under-Sec. of State for Foreign Affairs, 1946–50; Minister of Defence (RN), 1964, resigned 1966; left Lab. Party, joined Lib. Party, 1974; MP (L) Greenwich, Woolwich East, July–Sept 1974; contested (L): Bath, Oct. 1974 and 1979; Surrey, for European Parlt, 1979, London SW, for European Parlt, Sept. 1979. Vice-Chm., Liberal Action Gp for Electoral Reform, 1974–80. Lib Dem (formerly Liberal Party) Spokesman on Defence, 1980–. President: Parly Assoc. for Euro-Arab Co-operation, 1980– (former Chm.); ANAF Foundn, 1992 (former Chm.); Middle East International (Publishers) Ltd, 1992– (former Chm.); former Chm., MIND (Nat. Assoc. for Mental Health). Chm., Liverpool Victoria Staff Pensions Trustee Cos, 1976–95. *Publications:* Planned Investment—The Case for a National Investment Board, 1939; Socialist Economic Policy, 1946; "Those in Favour . . ." (television play), 1951; Dear Viewer . . ., 1953; Men Seeking God, 1955; Commercial Television: What is to be done?, 1959; Coexistence Plus, 1962; Britain's Role Tomorrow, 1967; Party Games, 1969; (jtly) Europe: the case for going in, 1971; (jtly) Publish It Not . . .: the Middle East cover-up, 1975; The Disillusioned Voter's Guide to Electoral Reform, 1976; Time To Explain: an autobiography, 1987. *Recreations:* music, golf. *Address:* 39 Wool Road, Wimbledon, SW20 0HN.

Died 7 Jan. 1997.

MAYNARD, Joan; *see* Maynard, V. J.

MAYNARD, Air Chief Marshal Sir Nigel (Martin), KCB 1973 (CB 1971); CBE 1963; DFC 1942; AFC 1946; *b* 28 Aug. 1921; *s* of late Air Vice-Marshal F. H. M. Maynard, CB, AFC, and of Irene (*née* Pim); *m* 1946, Daphne, *d* of late G R. P. Llewellyn, Baglan Hall, Abergavenny; one *s* one *d. Educ:* Aldenham; RAF Coll., Cranwell. Coastal Comd, UK, Mediterranean, W Africa, 1940–43; Flt-Lieut 1942; Sqdn-Ldr 1944; Mediterranean and Middle East, 1944; Transport Comd, 1945–49; comd 242 Sqdn on Berlin Air Lift; Air Staff, Air Min., 1949–51; Wing Comdr 1952; psa 1952; Staff Officer to Inspector Gen., 1953–54;

Bomber Comd, 1954–57; jssc 1957; Gp Capt. 1957; SASO 25 Gp, 1958–59; CO, RAF Changi, 1960–62; Gp Capt. Ops, Transport Comd, 1963–64; Air Cdre 1965; Dir of Defence Plans (Air), 1965; Dir of Defence Plans and Chm. Defence Planning Staff, 1966; idc 1967; Air Vice-Marshal, 1968; Commandant, RAF Staff College, Bracknell, 1968–70; Commander, Far East Air Force, 1970–71; Air Marshal, 1972; Dep. C-in-C, Strike Command, 1972–73; C-in-C RAF Germany, and Comdr, 2nd Allied Tactical Air Force, 1973–76; Air Chief Marshal 1976; C-in-C, RAF Strike Command, and C-in-C, UK Air Forces, 1976–77. ADC to the Queen, 1961–65. *Address:* Manor House, Piddington, Bicester, Oxon OX6 0QB. *T:* (01844) 238270. *Clubs:* Naval and Military, Royal Air Force, MCC. *Died 18 June 1998.*

MAYNARD, (Vera) Joan; JP; *b* 5 July 1921; *d* of late Mathew Maynard, farmer. Mem. Labour Party Nat. Exec. Cttee, 1972–82, 1983–87; Sec., Yorks Area, Agricl and Allied Workers National Trade Group TGWU (formerly Nat. Union of Agricl and Allied Workers), 1956–78 (Nat. Vice Pres., 1966–72, sponsored as MP by the Union). MP (Lab) Sheffield, Brightside, Oct. 1974–1987. Mem., Parly Select Cttee on Agriculture, 1975–87; Vice-Chm., Labour Party, 1980–81. Chair, Campaign Gp of Lab. MPs, 1979–87. Former Parish Rural Dist and County Councillor, N Yorks. JP Thirsk, 1950. *Address:* Lansbury House, 76 Front Street, Sowerby, Thirsk, N Yorks YO7 1JF. *T:* (01845) 522355. *Died 27 March 1998.*

MEADOWS, Robert; company director, motor trade; Lord Mayor of Liverpool, 1972–73; *b* 28 June 1902; *m* 1st, 1926, Ivy L. Jenkinson (*d* 1963); three *s*; 2nd, 1967, Nora E. Bullen. *Educ:* locally and Bootle Technical Coll. Engineering, 1917–21. Liverpool: City Councillor, Fairfield Ward, 1945; City Alderman, Princes Park Ward, 1961–74. Pres., Exec. Cttee, Broadgreen Conservative Assoc. *Recreations:* motor vehicle development, property improvement, landscape gardening. *Died 24 Aug. 1998.*

MEATH, 14th Earl of, *cr* 1627; **Anthony Windham Normand Brabazon;** Baron Ardee (Ire.) 1616; Baron Chaworth (UK) 1831; late Major Grenadier Guards; *b* 3 Nov. 1910; *o s* of 13th Earl of Meath, CB, CBE and Lady Aileen Wyndham-Quin (*d* 1962), *d* of 4th Earl of Dunraven; *S* father, 1949; *m* 1940, Elizabeth Mary, *d* of late Capt. Geoffrey Bowlby, Royal Horse Guards, and Hon. Mrs Geoffrey Bowlby, CVO; two *s* two *d. Educ:* Eton; RMC Sandhurst. Joined Grenadier Guards, 1930; ADC to Governor of Bengal, 1936; Capt., 1938; served War of 1939–45, Grenadier Guards (wounded, Italy, 1943); Major, 1941; retired, 1946. *Heir: s* Lord Ardee, *b* 11 May 1941. *Address:* Killruddery, Bray, Co. Wicklow, Ireland. *Died 19 Dec. 1998.*

MEECHIE, Brig. Helen Guild, CBE 1986; Deputy Director General, Personal Services, Ministry of Defence, 1990–91, retired; *b* 19 Jan. 1938; *d* of John Strachan and Robina Guild Meechie. *Educ:* Morgan Academy, Dundee; St Andrew's University (MA). Commissioned 1960; served in UK, Cyprus and Hong Kong, 1961–76, in UK and Germany, 1977–82; Dir, WRAC, 1982–86; Mem., RCDS, 1987; Dir, Army Service Conditions, MoD, 1988–90. Hon. ADC to the Queen, 1982–86; ADC to the Queen, 1986. Hon. Col, Tayforth Univs OTC, 1986–91; Dep. Col Comdt, AGC, 1993–. Mem. Council, Union Jack Club, 1989–91. Gov., Royal Soldiers' Daughters' Sch., 1984–91. Vice Pres., WRAC Assoc., 1997–. Freeman, City of London, 1983. CIMgt (CBIM 1986). Hon. LLD Dundee, 1986. *Recreations:* golf, gardening, travel. *Address:* 28 London Road, Amesbury, Salisbury, Wilts SP4 7DY. *Died 24 Aug. 2000.*

MEEK, Charles Innes, CMG 1961; Chief Executive, 1962–81, Chairman, 1973–81, White Fish Authority, retired; *b* 27 June 1920; *er s* of late Dr C. K. Meek and Helen Marjorie, *e d* of Lt-Col C. H. Innes Hopkins; *m* 1947, Nona Corry Hurford; two *s* one *d. Educ:* King's Sch., Canterbury; Magdalen Coll., Oxford (Demyship 1939; MA 1947). Served in Army, 1940–41; District Officer, Tanganyika, 1941; Principal Asst Sec., Tanganyika, 1958; Permanent Sec., Chief Secretary's Office, 1959; Permanent Sec. to Prime Minister, Sec. to Cabinet, 1960; Government Dir, Williamson Diamonds; Head of the Civil Service, Tanganyika, 1961–62, retd. FRSA 1969. *Publications:* occasional articles in Journal of African Administration, etc. *Recreations:* travel, Spectator crossword, gardening. *Address:* Mariteau Cottage, German Street, Winchelsea, E Sussex TN36 4ES. *T:* (01797) 226408. *Club:* Royal Over-Seas League. *Died 4 Nov. 1999.*

MEGAW, Rt Hon. Sir John, Kt 1961; CBE 1956; TD 1951; PC 1969; a Lord Justice of Appeal, 1969–80; *b* 16 Sept. 1909; 2nd *s* of late Robert Dick Megaw (formerly Judge, High Court of Justice, NI), Belfast; *m* 1938, Eleanor Grace Chapman; one *s* two *d. Educ:* Royal Academical Institution, Belfast; St John's Coll., Cambridge Univ. (Open Schol. in classics; Hon. Fellow, 1967); Harvard Univ. Law Sch. (Choate Fellowship). Served War, 1939–45; Col, RA. Barrister-at-Law, Gray's Inn, 1934 (Certificate of Honour, Bar Final exam.); Bencher, 1958; Treasurer, 1976; QC 1953; QC (NI) 1954; Recorder of Middlesbrough, 1957–61; Judge of the High Court of Justice, Queen's Bench Div., 1961–69; Pres., Restrictive Practices Court, 1962–68. Chm., Cttee of Inquiry into Civil Service Pay, 1981–82. Visitor: New Univ. of Ulster, 1976; Univ. of Ulster, 1984–89. Hon. LLD Queen's Univ., Belfast, 1968; Hon. DSc Ulster, 1990. Legion of Merit (US), 1946. Played Rugby football for Ireland, 1934, 1938. *Died 27 Dec. 1997.*

MEINERTZHAGEN, Sir Peter, Kt 1980; CMG 1966; General Manager, Commonwealth Development Corporation, 1973–85; Director, Booker Tate Ltd, 1989–95; *b* 24 March 1920; *y s* of late Louis Ernest Meinertzhagen, Theberton House, Leiston, Suffolk and Gwynnedd, *d* of Sir William Llewellyn, PRA; *m* 1949, Dido Pretty; one *s* one *d. Educ:* Eton. Served Royal Fusiliers, 1940–46 (Croix de Guerre, France, 1944). Alfred Booth & Co., 1946–57; Colonial (later Commonwealth) Development Corporation, 1958–85. Member: Council, London Chamber of Commerce, 1968–69; Council, Overseas Develt Inst., 1979–85. Hon. Vice-Pres., Royal African Soc., 1998. *Address:* Mead House, Ramsbury, Wilts SN8 2QP. *T:* (01672) 520715. *Club:* Muthaiga Country (Nairobi). *Died 12 Nov. 1999.*

MELLERSH, Air Vice-Marshal Francis Richard Lee, CB 1977; DFC 1943 and Bar 1944; Air Officer Flying and Officer Training, HQ Training Command, 1974–77; *b* 30 July 1922; *s* of Air Vice-Marshal Sir Francis Mellersh, KBE, AFC and Mary Margaret Lee; *m* 1st, Joan (*d* 1988), widow of Eric Greenwood; two *s*; 2nd, 1967, Elisabeth Nathalie Komaroff; one *d. Educ:* Winchester House Sch.; Imperial Service College. Joined RAFVR, 1940; Nos 29, 600 and 96 Sqdns, 1941–45; various staff and flying appts, 1946–57; Dirg Staff, RAF Staff Coll., 1957–59; Staff of Chief of Defence Staff, 1959–61; Dep. Dir Ops (F), 1961–63; OC RAF West Raynham, 1965–67; Chief Current Plans, SHAPE, 1967–68; RCDS 1969; SASO, RAF Germany, 1970–72; ACDS (Ops), 1972–74. *Address:* Rother Lea, Lossenham Lane, Newenden, Kent TN18 5QD. *Club:* Royal Air Force. *Died 19 Dec. 1996.*

MELLING, Cecil Thomas, CBE 1955; MScTech, CEng, Hon. FIEE, FIMechE, Sen. FInstE, CIMgt; *b* Wigan, 12 Dec. 1899; *s* of William and Emma Melling; *m* 1929,

Ursula Thorburn Thorburn (decd); two *s* one *d* (and one *s* and one *d* decd). *Educ:* Manchester Central High Sch.; College of Technology, University of Manchester. 2nd Lieut RE, 1918. Metropolitan Vickers Electrical Co. Ltd, 1920–34; Yorkshire Electric Power Co., 1934–35; Edmundson's Electricity Corporation Ltd, 1935–43; Borough Electrical Engineer, Luton, 1943–48; Chm., Eastern Electricity Board, 1948–57. Member: British Electricity Authority, 1952–53 and 1957; Electricity Council, 1957–61 (a Dep. Chm., 1961–65); Clean Air Council, 1961–64; Adv. Cttee on R&D, 1961–64. Chm. Utilization Sect., Institution of Electrical Engineers, 1949–50; Vice-Pres., IEE, 1957–62, Pres., 1962–63; Chm. of Council, British Electrical Development Association, 1951–52; Founder-Chm. 1945, and Pres. 1947, Luton Electrical Soc.; Pres. Ipswich & District Electrical Assoc., 1948–57; Chm. of Council, British Electrical and Allied Industries Research Assoc., 1953–55; Pres. Assoc. of Supervising Electrical Engineers, 1952–54; Chm., British Nat. Cttee for Electro-Heat, 1958–68; Mem. Council, BIM, 1961–78; Vice-Pres. Internat. Union for Electro-Heat, 1964–68, Pres., 1968–72; Pres., Manchester Technol. Assoc., 1967; Pres., British Electrotechnical Approvals Bd, 1974–84 (Chm., 1964–73); Chm., Electricity Supply Industry Trng Bd, 1965–68; Vice-Pres., Union of Internat. Engineering Organisations, 1969–75; Pres., Soc. of Retired Chartered Engrs in SE Kent, 1988– (Founder Chm., 1982–84). *Publications:* Light in the East, 1987; Memories of an Edwardian Childhood, 1993 (family circulation); contribs to Proc. Engineering Instns and Confs. *Address:* Durham Suite, The Grand, Folkestone CT20 2LR. *Club:* Athenæum.

Died 10 July 1998.

MELLISH, Baron *cr* 1985 (Life Peer), of Bermondsey in Greater London; **Robert Joseph Mellish;** PC 1967; *b* 3 March 1913; *s* of John Mellish, Deptford, SE8; *m* 1938, Anne Elizabeth, *d* of George Warner; four *s* (and one *s* decd). Served War of 1939–45, Captain RE, SEAC. Official, TGWU, 1938–46. MP (Lab 1946–82, Ind. 1982) Bermondsey, Rotherhithe 1946–50, Bermondsey 1950–74, Southwark, Bermondsey 1974–82. PPS to Minister of Supply, 1950–51, to Minister of Pensions, 1951; Jt Parly Sec., Min. of Housing, 1964–67; Minister of Public Building and Works, 1967–69; Parly Sec. to Treasury and Govt Chief Whip, 1969–70 and 1974–76; Opposition Chief Whip, 1970–74. Chm., London Regional Lab. Party, 1956–77. Dep. Chm., LDDC, 1981–85. *Address:* House of Lords, SW1A 0PW.

Died 9 May 1998.

MELLON, Paul, Hon. KBE 1974; Hon. RA 1978; Hon. Trustee, National Gallery of Art, Washington, DC, since 1985 (Trustee, 1945–85; President, 1963–79; Chairman of Trustees, 1979–85); *b* 11 June 1907; *s* of late Andrew William Mellon and Nora McMullen Mellon; *m* 1st, 1935, Mary Conover (*d* 1946); one *s* one *d*; 2nd, 1948, Rachel Lambert. *Educ:* Choate Sch., Wallingford, Conn; Yale Univ.; Univ. of Cambridge (BA 1931; MA 1938; Hon. LLD 1983). Trustee: Andrew W. Mellon Foundn (successor to merged Old Dominion and Avalon Foundns), 1969–85 (Hon. Trustee, 1985–); Virginia Mus. of Fine Arts, Richmond, Va, 1938–68, 1969–79. Fellow, Amer. Acad. of Arts and Scis, 1992; Member: Amer. Philosophical Soc., Philadelphia, 1971; Grolier Soc.; Soc. of Dilettanti; Roxburghe Club. Hon. Citizen, University of Vienna, 1965. Yale Medal, 1953; Horace Marden Albright Scenic Preservation Medal, 1957; Distinguished Service to Arts Award, Nat. Inst. Arts and Letters, 1962; Benjamin Franklin Medal, 1965, Benjamin Franklin Fellow, 1969, Royal Society of Arts; Alumni Seal Prize Award, Choate Sch., 1966; Skowhegan Gertrude Vanderbilt Whitney Award, 1972; Nat. Medal of Arts, USA, 1985; Medal in Architecture, Thomas Jefferson

Meml Foundn, 1989; Hadrian Award, World Monuments Fund, 1989; Benjamin Franklin Award, Amer. Philosophical Soc., 1989; Medal for Distinguished Philanthropy, Amer. Assoc. of Museums, 1993; Nat. Humanities Medal, 1997. Hon. FRIBA 1978; Hon. FBA 1994. Hon. DLitt Oxford Univ., 1961; Hon. LLD Carnegie Inst. of Tech., 1967; Hon. DHL Yale, 1967; Hon. DVM London, 1991. *Publication:* (with John Baskett) Reflections in a Silver Spoon: a memoir, 1992. *Recreations:* fox-hunting, thoroughbred breeding and racing, sailing, swimming. *Address:* (office) 1140 Connecticut Avenue, NW, Suite 1201, Washington, DC 20036, USA; (home) Oak Spring, 8554 Oak Spring Road, Upperville, VA 20184. *Clubs:* Buck's; Travellers (Paris); Jockey, Knickerbocker, Links, Racquet and Tennis, River, Yale (New York); Metropolitan, 1925 F Street (Washington). *Died 2 Feb. 1999.*

MELLOR, Brig. James Frederick McLean, CBE 1964 (OBE 1945); Norfolk County Commandant, Army Cadet Force, 1969–72; *b* 6 June 1912; *s* of late Col A. J. Mellor, RM, Kingsland, Hereford; *m* 1942, Margaret Ashley (*d* 1987), *d* of Major F. A. Phillips, DSO, Holmer, Hereford; one *s* one *d*. *Educ:* Radley Coll.; Faraday House. C. A. Parsons, 1933; Yorkshire Electric Power, 1935; commnd in Regular Army as Ordnance Mechanical Engr, 1936; France, Belgium, Dunkirk, 1940; Burma, Malaya, HQ, SEAC, 1944–47 (despatches, 1945); Brig. AQ Northern Comd, 1961–64; Dir of Technical Trng and Inspector of Boys' Trng (Army), MoD, 1966–69; ADC to the Queen, 1963–69. Various appts in engineering and technical educn. Chm., IMechE Eastern Branch, 1971–72. DFH, FIMechE, FIEE. *Address:* Pinewood, Saxlingham Road, Blakeney, Holt, Norfolk NR25 7PB. *T:* (01263) 740990. *Clubs:* Naval and Military, Royal Automobile; Norfolk (Norwich). *Died 24 April 1997.*

MELVILLE, Sir Harry (Work), KCB 1958; PhD, DSc, FRS 1941; FRSC; Principal, Queen Mary College, University of London, 1967–76; *b* 27 April 1908; *s* of Thomas and Esther Burnett Melville; *m* 1942, Janet Marian, *d* of late Hugh Porteous and Sarah Cameron; two *d*. *Educ:* George Heriot's Sch., Edinburgh; Edinburgh Univ. (Carnegie Res. Scholar; PhD, DSc); Trinity Coll., Cambridge (1851 Exhibitioner; PhD); MSc Birmingham. Fellow of Trinity College, Cambridge, 1933–44. Asst Dir, Colloid Science Laboratory, Cambridge, 1938–40; Prof. of Chemistry, Univ. of Aberdeen, 1940–48; Scientific Adviser to Chief Superintendent Chemical Defence, Min. of Supply, 1940–43; Superintendent, Radar Res. Station, 1943–45; Mason Prof. of Chemistry, Univ. of Birmingham, 1948–56. Chief Scientific Adviser for Civil Defence, Midlands Region, 1952–56; Member: Min. of Aviation Scientific Adv. Council, 1949–51; Adv. Council, Dept of Scientific and Industrial Res., 1946–51; Res. Council, British Electricity Authority, 1949–56; Royal Commn on Univ. Educn in Dundee, 1951–52; Res. Council, DSIR, 1961–65; London Electricity Bd, 1968–75; Nuclear Safety Adv. Cttee, DTI, 1972; Cttee of Managers, Royal Institution, 1976; Sec. to Cttee of the Privy Council for Scientific and Industrial Research, 1956–65; Chairman: SRC, 1965–67; Adv. Council on Research and Develt, DTI, 1970–74. Mem., Parly and Scientific Cttee, 1971–75. Pres., Plastics Inst., 1970–75. Bakerian Lecture, Royal Soc., 1956. Hon. LLD Aberdeen; Hon. DCL Kent; Hon. DSc: Exeter; Birmingham; Liverpool; Leeds; Heriot-Watt; Essex; Hon. DTech Bradford. Meldola Medal, Inst. of Chemistry, 1936; Davy Medal, Royal Society, 1955; Colwyn Medal, Instn of the Rubber Industry. *Publications:* papers in Proceedings of Royal Society, etc. *Address:* Norwood, Dodds Lane, Chalfont St Giles, Bucks HP8 4EL. *T:* (01494) 872222. *Died 14 June 2000.*

MELVIN, John Turcan, TD and star; MA; *b* 19 March 1916; *m* 1951, Elizabeth Ann Parry-Jones; one *s* three *d*. *Educ:* Stowe Sch.; Trinity Coll., Cambridge (MA); Berlin Univ. (Schol.). Served with Dorset Regt, 1939–46. Asst Master, Sherborne Sch., 1938, Housemaster, 1950; Headmaster, Kelly Coll., 1959–72; Hd of German Dept, Foster's Sch., 1972–75; Sixth Form Tutor, Sherborne Sch., 1975–82. Gov., Hall Sch. Trust, Wincanton. *Recreations:* walking, reading, tennis, dramatics. *Address:* Culverhayes Lodge, Sherborne, Dorset DT9 3BY. *Club:* English-Speaking Union. *Died 13 Sept. 1999.*

MENDE, Dr Erich; Member of the Bundestag, German Federal Republic, 1949–80; *b* 28 Oct. 1916; *m* 1st, Ruth Mautschke (marr. diss.); one *s*; 2nd, 1948, Margot (*née* Hattje); two *s* one *d*. *Educ:* Humane Coll., Gross-Strehlitz; Universities of Cologne and Bonn (Dr jur). Military service in Infantry Regt 84, Gleiwitz; served War of 1939–45, Comdr of a Regt (wounded twice, prisoner of war); Major, 1944. Co-founder of FDP (Free Democratic Party), 1945, Mem. Exec. Cttee, British Zone, 1947; Parliamentary Group of FDP: Whip, and Mem. Exec. Cttee, 1950–53; Dep. Chm., 1953; Chm., 1957; Chm. of FDP, 1960–68; Vice-Chancellor and Minister for All-German Affairs, Federal Republic of Germany, 1963–66. Joined CDU, 1970 (Mem., Hessen, 1970). *Publications:* autobiography: Das verdammte Gewissen 1921–1945, 1982; Die neue Freiheit 1945–1961, 1984; Von Wende zu Wende 1962–1982, 1986. *Address:* Am Stadtwald 62, 53177 Bonn, Germany. *Died 6 May 1998.*

MENDOZA, Maurice, CVO 1982; MSM 1946; heritage consultant; Under Secretary, Ancient Monuments and Historic Buildings, Department of the Environment, 1978–81; *b* 1 May 1921; *e s* of Daniel and Rachel Mendoza; *m* 1949, Phyllis Kriger. *Educ:* Sir Henry Raine's Foundation; Dip. Sociology, London. Clerical Officer, HM Office of Works, 1938; served Royal Signals and Cheshire Yeo., 1941–46 (Sgt); Mil. Mission to Belgium, 1944–46; Organisation Officer, Treasury, 1956–61; Principal, MPBW, 1963; Asst Sec., 1968; DoE, 1970; Under-Sec., 1973; Dir of Manpower and Management Services, DoE and later, also Dept of Transport, 1974–78. Chairman: Friends of the Ridgeway, 1982–94; Common Land Forum, 1984–86; Sec., British Architectural Library Review Gp, 1987–88. Hon. Mem., 10th Battalion Transportation Corps, US Army, 1977. *Recreations:* theatre, walking, photography. *Address:* 45 Grange Grove, Canonbury, N1 2NP. *Clubs:* Athenæum, Civil Service. *Died 11 Oct. 2000.*

MENNEER, Stephen Snow, CB 1967; retired, 1970, as Assistant Under-Secretary of State, Department of Health and Social Security; *b* 6 March 1910; *s* of Sydney Charles Menneer, LLD, and Minnie Elizabeth Menneer; *m* 1935, Margaret Longstaff Smith (*d* 1976); one *s* one *d*. *Educ:* Rugby Sch.; Oriel Coll., Oxford. Min. of Information, 1939; Min. of National Insurance, 1948; Under-Sec., Min. of Pensions and Nat. Insurance, then Min. of Social Security, 1961. *Address:* Wester Ground, Chittlehamholt, Umberleigh, N Devon EX37 9NU. *Died 16 Jan. 1996.*

MENSFORTH, Sir Eric, Kt 1962; CBE 1945; DL; FREng, FIMechE, FRAeS; Hon. FIEE; Vice Lord-Lieutenant, South Yorkshire, 1974–81; President, Westland Aircraft Ltd, 1979–85 (Director, 1968–83; Managing Director, 1938–45; Vice-Chairman, 1945–53, 1968–71; Chairman, 1953–68); Director, John Brown & Co. Ltd, 1948–83 (Deputy Chairman, 1959–78); *b* 17 May 1906; 2nd *s* of late Sir Holberry Mensforth, KCB, CBE and Alice Maud, 3rd *d* of William Jennings, Rossington, Yorks; *m* 1934, Betty (*d* 1996), *d* of late Rev. Picton W. Francis; three *d*. *Educ:* Altrincham County High Sch.; University Coll. Sch.; King's Coll., Cambridge (Price Exhibn; 1st class

Mechanical Sciences tripos; MA). Engineering work at Woolwich Arsenal, Mather & Platt Ltd, Bolckow Vaughan Ltd, Kloecknerwerke A. G., Dorman Long Ltd, English Electric Ltd (Founder, Domestic Appliance Div., 1931), Markham & Co. Ltd, T. Firth & John Brown Ltd, Firth Brown Tools Ltd, Wickman Ltd, Boddy Industries Ltd, Rhodesian Alloys Ltd (Founder, 1949), Normalair Ltd; Chief Production Adviser to: Chief Executive, Ministry of Aircraft Production, 1943–45; first Naval Dragonfly helicopter, 1950; 100 KW Orkney Windmill, 1951; Surform, 1956; London Battersea Heliport, 1959; SRN3 Hovercraft ascent of Lachine Rapids, 1963. Master Cutler, Sheffield, 1965–66. Chairman: EDC for Electronics Industry, 1968–70; Cttee on Quality Assurance, 1968–70; Council of Engineering Instns, 1969–72. Member: British Productivity Council, 1964–69; Royal Ordnance Factories Bd, 1968–72; Council, RGS, 1968–70; Smeatonian Soc. of Civil Engrs, 1966–77; Treasurer, BAAS, 1970–75; Pres., IProdE, 1967–69; a founder Vice-Pres., Fellowship of Engineering, 1977. President: Helicopter Assoc. of GB, 1953–55; S Yorks Scouts' Assoc., 1969–76; CPRE (Sheffield and Peak District Branch), 1975–86. Chm. Governing Body, Sheffield Polytechnic, 1969–75; Hon. Fellow, Sheffield City Polytechnic. Hon. DEng Sheffield 1967; Hon. DSc Southampton, 1970. Freeman, Coachmakers' and Coach-Harness Makers' Co., 1950. DL S (formerly WR) Yorks, 1971. *Publications:* Air Frame Production, 1947 (Instn Prize, IMechE); Future of the Aeroplane (Cantor Lectures), 1959; Production of Helicopters and Hovercraft (Lord Sempill Lecture, IProdE), 1964; Future of Rotorcraft and Hovercraft (Cierva Meml Lecture, RAeS), 1967; Extracts from the Records of the Cutlers' Company, 1972; Family Engineers, 1981; Clogs to Clogs, 1991. *Address:* 42 Oakmead Green, Woodcote Side, Surrey KT18 7JS. *T:* (01372) 742313. *Clubs:* Alpine, Royal Automobile.

Died 20 Feb. 2000.

MENUHIN, Baron *cr* 1993 (Life Peer), of Stoke d'Abernon in the County of Surrey; **Yehudi Menuhin,** OM 1987; KBE 1965; violinist, conductor; *b* New York, 22 April 1916; adopted British nationality, 1985; *s* of late Moshe and Marutha Menuhin; *m* 1938, Nola Ruby (marr. diss.), *d* of George Nicholas, Melbourne, Australia; one *s* one *d*; *m* 1947, Diana Rosamond, *d* of late G. L. E. Gould and Lady Harcourt, (Evelyn Suart); two *s*. *Educ:* private tutors; studied music under Sigmund Anker and Louis Persinger, in San Francisco; Georges Enesco, Rumania and Paris; Adolph Busch, Switzerland. Made début with orchestra, San Francisco, aged 7, Paris, aged 10, New York, 11, Berlin, 13; thereafter played with most of world's orchestras and conductors; introduced among contemp. works Sonata for unaccompanied Violin, by Béla Bartók (composed for Yehudi Menuhin, 1944), as well as works by William Walton, Ben-Haim, Georges Enesco, Pizzetti, Ernest Bloch, etc; during War of 1939–45 devoted larger part of his time to concerts for US and Allied armed forces and benefit concerts for Red Cross, etc (500 concerts); series of concerts in Moscow (by invitation), 1945; seven visits to Israel, 1950–; first tour of Japan, 1951; first tour of India (invitation of Prime Minister), 1952; largely responsible for cultural exchange programme between US and Russia, 1955, and for bringing Indian music and musicians to West. Initiated his own annual music festival in Gstaad, Switzerland, 1957–96, and in Bath, 1959–68; Jt Artistic Dir, Windsor Festival, 1969–72; Founder, Live Music Now, 1977. Founded Yehudi Menuhin Sch. of Music, Stoke d'Abernon, Surrey, 1963; Founder/Pres., Internat. Menuhin Music Acad., Gstaad, 1976; President: Trinity Coll. of Music, 1971; Young Musicians' Symphony Orch., 1989–; Hallé Orch., 1992–; Associate Conductor and Pres., Royal Philharmonic Orch., 1982–; Principal Guest Conductor: English String Orch., 1988–;

Warsaw Sinfonia, 1982–. Good Will Ambassador, UNESCO, 1992. Mem., Comité d'Honneur Service Européen d'Information Ministerielle et Parlementaire, 1987; Hon. Fellow: St Catharine's Coll., Cambridge, 1970; Fitzwilliam Coll., Cambridge, 1991; Hon. DMus: Oxford, 1962; Cambridge, 1970; Sorbonne, 1976; Toronto, 1984; Virginia Commonwealth Univ., 1987; Hartford, Conn, 1987; Santa Clara, Calif, 1988; Hon. Dr Gakushuin, Tokyo, 1988, and 10 other degrees from Brit. Univs. Freedom of the City of Edinburgh, 1965; City of Bath, 1966. He recorded for several companies, both as soloist and as Conductor of Menuhin Festival Orch., with which he toured USA, Australia, NZ and Europe; appeared regularly on American and British Television. Gold Medal, Royal Philharmonic Soc., 1962; Jawaharlal Nehru Award for International Understanding, 1970; Sonning Music Prize, Denmark, 1972; Handel Medal, NY; City of Jerusalem Medal; Peace Prize, Börsenverein des Deutschen Buchhandels, 1979; Albert Medal, RSA, 1981; Una Vita Nella Musica, Omaggio a Venezia, 1983; Grande Plaque du Bimillenaire de Paris, 1984; Ernst von Siemens Prize, 1984; Moses-Mendelssohn-Preis des Landes Berlin; Internat. Soc. of Performing Arts Administrators Award, 1987; Brahms Medal, City of Hamburg, 1987; Preis der Stiftung für Freiheit und Menschenrechte, Bern, 1987; Golden Viotti Prize, Vercelli, Italy, 1987; Diploma Magistrale, Italy, 1987; Buber-Rosenzweig Medal, Ges. für Christlich-Jüdische Zusammenarbeit, 1989; Epée d'Academicien, Académie des Beaux Arts, 1988; Wolf Foundn Prize, 1991. Decorations included: Grand Officier de la Légion d'Honneur, 1986; Commander: Order of Arts and Letters (France); Order of Leopold (Belgium); Order of Orange-Nassau (Netherlands); Grand Officer, Order of Merit of the Republic (Italy), 1987; Officer, Ordre de la Couronne (Belgium); Kt Comdr, Order of Merit (FRG); Royal Order of the Phœnix (Greece); Grand Cross, Order of Merit (FRG); Hon. Citizen of Switzerland, 1970. *Films:* Stage Door Canteen; Magic Bow; The Way of Light (biog.). *Publications:* The Violin: six lessons by Yehudi Menuhin, 1971; Theme and Variations, 1972; Violin and Viola, 1976; Sir Edward Elgar: My Musical Grandfather (essay), 1976; Unfinished Journey (autobiog.), 1977, 2nd edn 1996; The Music of Man, 1980 (also TV series); (with Christopher Hope) The King, the Cat and the Fiddle, (children's book), 1983; Life Class, 1986; *relevant publications:* Yehudi Menuhin, The Story of the Man and the Musician, by Robert Magidoff, 1956 (USA); Conversations with Menuhin, by Robin Daniels, 1979. *Address:* SYM Music Company Ltd, PO Box 6160, SW1W 0XJ. *Clubs:* Athenæum, Garrick.
Died 12 March 1999.

MENZIES, Sir Peter (Thomson), Kt 1972; Director: National Westminster Bank Ltd, 1968–82; Commercial Union Assurance Co. Ltd, 1962–82; *b* 15 April 1912; *s* of late John C. Menzies and Helen S. Aikman; *m* 1st, 1938, Mary McPherson Alexander (*d* 1992), *d* of late John T. Menzies and Agnes Anderson; one *s* one *d*; 2nd, 1994, Muriel, *d* of late Harold McKee Langton and Ethel Miles. *Educ:* Musselburgh Grammar Sch.; University of Edinburgh. MA 1st Class Hons Math. and Natural Philosophy, 1934. Inland Revenue Dept, 1933–39; Treasurer's Dept, Imperial Chemical Industries Ltd, 1939–56 (Asst Treas. 1947, Dep. Treas. 1952); Director: Imperial Chemical Industries Ltd, 1956–72 (Dep. Chm., 1967–72); Imperial Metal Industries Ltd, 1962–72 (Chm., 1964–72). Part-time Mem., CEGB, 1960–72; Mem., Review Body on Doctors' and Dentists' Remuneration, 1971–83; Chairman: Electricity Council, 1972–77; London Exec. Cttee, Scottish Council (Develt and Industry), 1977–82. A Vice-Pres., Siol na Meinnrich; Pres., UNIPEDE, 1973–76; Vice-Pres. and Gen. Treas., BAAS, 1982–86. FInstP; CompIEE. *Address:* 9 Fern

Grove, Welwyn Garden City, Herts AL8 7ND. *T:* (01707) 327234. *Club:* Caledonian.   *Died 13 Dec. 1998.*

MERCER, John Charles Kenneth; a Recorder of the Crown Court, 1975–82; *b* 17 Sept. 1917; *s* of late Charles Wilfred Mercer and Cecil Maud Mercer; *m* 1944, Barbara Joan, *d* of late Arnold Sydney Whitehead, CB, CBE, and Maud Ethel Whitehead; one *s* (one *d* decd). *Educ:* Ellesmere Coll.; Law Sch., Swansea University Coll. (LLB). Solicitor. War Service, 1940–45, Captain RA. Partner, Douglas-Jones & Mercer, 1946–88, then Consultant. Mem., Royal Commn on Criminal Procedure, 1978–81; Mem., SW Wales River Authority, 1960–74. *Recreations:* fishing, shooting, golf, watching sport. *Address:* 334 Gower Road, Killay, Swansea, West Glamorgan SA2 7AE. *T:* (01792) 202931. *Club:* Clyne Golf (Swansea).   *Died 22 April 1999.*

MERCHANT, Rev. Prof. William Moelwyn, FRSL; writer and sculptor; *b* 5 June 1913; *s* of late William Selwyn and Elizabeth Ann Merchant, Port Talbot, Glamorgan; *m* 1938, Maria Eluned Hughes, Llanelly; one *s* one *d*. *Educ:* Port Talbot Grammar Sch.; (Exhibnr) University Coll., Cardiff. BA, 1st Cl. English hons 1933; 2nd Cl. 1st div. Hist., 1934; MA 1950; DLitt 1960; Hon. Fellow, University Coll., Cardiff, 1981. Hist. Master, Carmarthen Grammar Sch., 1935; English Master, Newport High Sch., 1936; English Lectr, Caerleon Trg Coll., 1937; University Coll. Cardiff: Lectr in Eng. Lang. and Lit., 1939; Sen. Lectr, 1950; Reader, 1961; Prof. of English, Univ. of Exeter, 1961–74; Ordained to Anglican Orders, 1940, priest 1941; Examining Chaplain to the Bishop of Salisbury; Canon of Salisbury Cathedral, 1967–73, Canon Emeritus, 1973 (Chancellor, 1967–71); Vicar of Llanddewi Brefi, dio. St Davids, 1974–78; Hon. Lectr, All Saints Church, Leamington Spa, 1979. Fellow, Folger Shakespeare Library, Washington, DC, and Fulbright Fellow, 1957; Woodward Lectr, Yale Univ., 1957; Dupont Lectr, Sewanee Univ., Tenn, 1963; Willett Prof. of English and Theology, Univ. of Chicago, 1971; Hon. Prof. of Drama, UC Aberystwyth, 1985–87; Lyttelton Lectr, Eton Coll., 1983. Founded Rougemont Press, 1970 (with Ted Hughes, Eric Cleave and Paul Merchant). Welsh Cttee of Arts Council of GB, 1960 and 1975–; Council, Llandaff Festival, 1958–61. Mem., Archbishops' Commn on Faculty Jurisdiction, 1979–. Founded Llanddewi Brefi Arts Fest., 1975. Mem., Welsh Acad., 1991. FRSL 1976; Hon. Fellow, University Coll. of Wales, Aberystwyth, 1975. Hon. Mem., Old Etonian Assoc., 1990. Hon. HLD Wittenberg Univ., Ohio, 1973. Consultant and scriptwriter on film, The Bible, Rome, 1960–64. *Publications:* Wordsworth's Guide to the Lakes (illus. John Piper), 1952 (US 1953); Reynard Library Wordsworth, 1955 (US 1955); Shakespeare and the Artist, 1959; Creed and Drama, 1965; (ed) Merchant of Venice, 1967; (ed) Marlowe's Edward the Second, 1967; Comedy, 1972; Tree of Life (libretto, music by Alun Hoddinott), 1972; Breaking the Code (poems), 1975; (ed) Essays and Studies, 1977; No Dark Glass (poems), 1979; R. S. Thomas, a critical evaluation, 1979 (US 1990); Confrontation of Angels (poems), 1986; Jeshua (novel), 1987 (US 1991); Fire from the Heights (novel), 1989 (US 1991); A Bundle of Papyrus (novel), 1989; Fragments of a Life (autobiog.), 1990 (Welsh Arts Council Literary Award, 1991); Inherit the Land (short stories), 1992; Triple Heritage (novel), 1994; Preaching the Word, 1994; The Boy Hasid and Other Tales, 1995; articles in Times Literary Supplement, Warburg Jl, Shakespeare Survey, Shakespeare Quarterly, Shakespeare Jahrbuch, Encyc. Britannica, etc. *Recreations:* theatre, typography, sculpting (thirty one-man exhibns at Exeter, Cardiff, Swansea, Plymouth, Southampton, Aberystwyth, Glasgow, Stirling, Birmingham, London, 1971–89). *Address:* 32A Willes

Road, Leamington Spa, Warwicks CV31 1BN. *T:* (01926) 314253.   *Died 22 April 1997.*

MERMAGEN, Air Cdre Herbert Waldemar, CB 1960; CBE 1945 (OBE 1941); AFC 1940; retired, 1960; Director, Sharps, Pixley Ltd (Bullion Brokers), 1962–77; *b* 1 Feb. 1912; *s* of late L. W. R. Mermagen, Southsea; *m* 1937, Rosemary, *d* of late Major Mainwaring Williams, DSO and Mrs Tristram Fox, Cheltenham; two *s. Educ:* Brighton Coll., Sussex. Joined RAF, 1930; 43 (F) Sqdn, 1931–34; Instructor CFS, 1936–38; Squadron Leader, 1938; served War of 1939–45 in Fighter Command, UK, Middle East, France and Germany (SHAEF); AOC British Air Command, Berlin, 1945–46; Sen. RAF Liaison Officer, UK Services Liaison Staff, Australia, 1948–50; AOC, RAF Ceylon, 1955–57; Air Officer i/c Administration, Headquarters, RAF Transport Command, 1958–60. Air Commodore, 1955. Comdr Legion of Merit (USA), 1946; Medal for Distinguished Services (USSR), 1945; Chevalier, Légion d'Honneur (France) 1951. *Recreations:* Rugby (RAF (colours), Sussex, Richmond), golf, gardening. *Address:* Allandale, Vicarage Street, Painswick, Glos GL6 6XS. *Club:* Royal Air Force.
Died 10 Jan. 1998.

MERRIMAN, Dr Basil Mandeville; *b* 28 March 1911; *s* of Thomas Henry Merriman and Ida, *d* of Mandeville Blackwood Phillips; *m* 1938, Yvonne Flavelle (marr. diss. 1968; she *d* 1974); one *s. Educ:* Colet Court Prep. Sch.; St Paul's School; St Bartholomew's Hospital Med. Coll. MRCS, LRCP 1934. House appointments, St Bartholomew's Hosp., 1934–36; post graduate studies, Berlin, Vienna, Prague, 1936–38; Medical Adviser, British Drug Houses, 1938; Med. Dir, Carter Foundn, 1956; Consultant, Home Office Prison Department, 1963. *Publications:* contribs to medical and social jls on drug action and drug addiction and their relationship to crime, also various related aspects of social anthropology. *Recreation:* travel of all forms, particularly Asiatic (journeys mainly in Arab Asia, Central Asiatic region, and Japan).   *Died 22 Oct. 1999.*

MERRIMAN, James Henry Herbert, CB 1969; OBE 1961; MSc; MInstP, FEng 1977; FIEE, FIEEIE; Chairman, National Computing Centre, 1977–83; Member for Technology, Post Office Corporation, 1969–76; *b* 1 Jan. 1915; *s* of Thomas P. Merriman, AMINA and A. Margaretta Jenkins; *m* 1942, Joan B. Frost; twin *s* one *d. Educ:* King's Coll. Sch., Wimbledon; King's Coll., University of London. BSc (Hons) 1935; MSc (Thesis) 1936. Entered GPO Engrg Dept (Research), 1936; Officer i/c Castleton Radio Stn, 1940; Asst Staff Engr, Radio Br., 1951; Imp. Def. Coll., 1954; Dep. Dir, Organisation and Methods, HM Treasury, 1956; GPO: Dep. Engr-in-Chief, 1965; Sen. Dir Engrg, 1967. Chairman: NEDO Sector Working Party on Office Machinery, 1979–83; NEDO Information Technology Cttee, 1980–83 (Mem. NEDO Electronics EDC, 1980–83); SERC/DoI/Industry Project Universe Steering Cttee, 1981–83; Home Office Radio Spectrum Review Cttee, 1982–83. Vis. Prof. of Electronic Science and Telecommunications, Strathclyde Univ., 1969–79. Chm., Inspec, 1975–79; Dir, Infoline, 1976–80; Member: Nat. Electronics Council, 1969–76; Computer Bd for Univ. and Res. Councils, 1976–81; Exec. Bd, BSI, 1981–85 (Chm. Council for Inf. Systems); Science Museum Adv. Council, 1976–81; Council, Spurgeon's Coll., 1972–87. Mem. Council, IEE, 1965–80 (Chm. Electronics Div. Bd, 1968; Vice-Pres., 1969–72, Dep. Pres., 1972; Pres., 1974–75; Hon. FIEE 1981; Faraday Lectr, 1969–70); Governor, Imperial College, Univ. of London, 1971–83. Royal Instn Discourse, 1971. FKC 1972. Mem., Hon. Soc. of Cymmrodorion, 1979–89. Hon. DSc Strathclyde, 1974. *Publications:* contribs to scientific

and professional jls on telecommunications and inf. technology subjects. *Recreations:* walking, music, cactus growing.   *Died 15 Sept. 1997.*

MERTON, Patrick Anthony, MD; FRCP; FRS 1979; Professor of Human Physiology, University of Cambridge, 1984–88; Fellow of Trinity College, Cambridge, since 1962; *b* 8 Oct. 1920; *s* of late Gerald Merton, MC, PhD, FRAS and Mary Elizabeth (*née* Crowley); *m* 1951, Anna Gabriel, *d* of Foster Garfield Howe; one *s* three *d. Educ:* The Leys; Beaumont; Trinity Coll., Cambridge (MB 1946; MD 1982); St Thomas' Hosp. FRCP 1991. On staff of MRC's Neurol. Res. Unit, National Hosp., Queen Sq., 1946–57; Nobel Inst. for Neurophysiology, Stockholm, 1952–54; Lectr, 1957–77, Reader, 1977–84, Univ. of Cambridge; Hon. Consultant in Clin. Neurophysiol., Nat. Hosp., Queen Sq., 1979–; Hon. Sen. Res. Fellow, Royal Postgrad. Med. Sch., 1981–82. *Publications:* scientific papers. *Address:* Trinity College, Cambridge CB2 1TQ.
Died 13 June 2000.

METCALFE, Air Cdre Joan, CB 1981; RRC 1976; Director of Royal Air Force Nursing Services, and Matron in Chief, Princess Mary's Royal Air Force Nursing Service, 1978–81; *b* 8 Jan. 1923; *d* of late W. and S. H. Metcalfe. *Educ:* West Leeds High Sch. for Girls; Leeds Coll. of Commerce. St James's Hosp., Leeds, 1943–47 (SRN); St James's Hosp. and Redcourt Hostel, Leeds, 1947–48 (SCM); PMRAFNS, 1948: served in RAF Hospitals in Egypt, Iraq, Libya, Cyprus, Germany, Singapore, and UK; Sen. Matron, 1970; Principal Matron, 1973. QHNS 1978–81. OStJ 1977. *Recreations:* classical music, theatre, needlework, gardening, non-fiction literature. *Address:* Flat 8, Homewood Court, Badgers Walk, Chorleywood, Herts WD3 5GB. . *T:* (01923) 336213. *Club:* Royal Air Force.   *Died 18 May 2000.*

MEYER, Michael Leverson; free-lance writer, since 1950; *b* London, 11 June 1921; 3rd and *y s* of Percy Barrington Meyer and Eleanor Rachel Meyer (*née* Benjamin); unmarried; one *d* by Maria Rossman. *Educ:* Wellington Coll.; Christ Church, Oxford (MA). Operational Res. Section, Bomber Comd HQ, 1942–45; Lectr in English Lit., Uppsala Univ., 1947–50. Visiting Professor of Drama: Dartmouth Coll., USA, 1978; Univ. of Colorado, 1986; Colorado Coll., 1988; Hofstra Univ., 1989; UCLA, 1991. Mem. Editorial Adv. Bd, Good Food Guide, 1958–72. FRSL. Gold Medal, Swedish Academy, 1964. Knight Commander, Polar Star (1st class) (Sweden), 1977; Order of Merit (Norway), 1995. *Publications:* (ed with Sidney Keyes, and contrib.) Eight Oxford Poets, 1941; (ed) Collected Poems of Sidney Keyes, 1945, rev. edn 1989; (ed) The Minos of Crete, by Sidney Keyes, 1948; The End of the Corridor (novel), 1951; The Ortolan (play), 1967; Henrik Ibsen (3 vols): The Making of a Dramatist, 1967, The Farewell to Poetry, 1971, The Top of a Cold Mountain, 1971 (Whitbread Biography Prize, 1971); Lunatic and Lover (play), 1981; (ed) Summer Days, 1981; Ibsen on File, 1985; Strindberg: a biography, 1985; File on Strindberg, 1986; Not Prince Hamlet (memoirs; US edn as Words through a Window Pane), 1989; The Odd Women (play, after the novel by George Gissing), 1993; *translated:* The Long Ships, by Frans G. Bengtsson, 1954; Ibsen: Brand, The Lady from the Sea, John Gabriel Borkman, When We Dead Awaken, 1960; The Master Builder, Little Eyolf, 1961; Ghosts, The Wild Duck, Hedda Gabler, 1962; Peer Gynt, An Enemy of the People, The Pillars of Society, 1963; The Pretenders, 1964; A Doll's House, 1965; Rosmersholm, 1966; Emperor and Galilean, 1986; Strindberg: The Father, Miss Julie, Creditors, The Stronger, Playing with Fire, Erik the Fourteenth, Storm, The Ghost Sonata, 1964; A Dream Play, 1973; To Damascus, Easter, The Dance of Death, The Virgin Bride, 1975; Master Olof, 1991; Road to

Auschwitz: fragments of a life, by Hedi Fried, 1990; Three Danish Comedies, by Ludvig Holberg and J. L. Heiberg, 1999. *Recreations:* eating, sleeping. *Address:* 3 Highbury Place, N5 1QZ. *T:* (020) 7226 3050, *Fax:* (020) 7226 4273. *Clubs:* Savile, Garrick, MCC.

Died 3 Aug. 2000.

MEYNELL, Dame Alix (Hester Marie), (Lady Meynell), DBE 1949; *b* 2 Feb. 1903; *d* of late Surgeon Commander L. Kilroy, RN, and Hester Kilroy; *m* 1946, Sir Francis Meynell, RDI (*d* 1975); no *c. Educ:* Malvern Girls' Coll.; Somerville Coll., Oxford. Joined Civil Service, Board of Trade, 1925; seconded to the Monopolies and Restrictive Practices Commission as Sec., 1949–52; Under-Sec., Board of Trade, 1946–55; resigned from the Civil Service, 1955. Called to the Bar, Lincoln's Inn, 1956. Man. Dir, Nonesuch Press Ltd, 1976–86. Member: SE Gas Board, 1956–69 (Chm. Cons. Council, 1956–63); Harlow New Town Corp., 1956–65; Performing Right Tribunal, 1956–65; Cttees of Investigation for England, Scotland and Great Britain under Agricultural Marketing Acts, 1956–65; Monopolies Commn, 1965–68; Cosford RDC, 1970–74. *Publications:* Public Servant, Private Woman (autobiog.), 1988; What Grandmother Said (biog.), 1998. *Recreations:* family bridge, entertaining my friends and being entertained. *Address:* Lion House, Lavenham, Sudbury, Suffolk CO10 9PR. *T:* (01787) 247526.

Died 31 Aug. 1999.

MICHELIN, Reginald Townend, CMG 1957; CVO 1953; OBE 1952; General Manager: Agualta Vale Estates, Jamaica, 1958–64; Jamaica Tourist Board, 1964–73; *b* 31 Dec. 1903; *s* of V. A. Michelin, planter, Jamaica; *m* 1940, Nina Gladys Faulkner, Iffley, Oxford; one *s* one *d. Educ:* Exeter Sch., England. Sub-Inspector, Police, Jamaica, 1924; Inspector, Police, Leeward Islands, 1928; Asst Commissioner of Police, Nigeria, 1930; Comr of Police, Barbados, 1949; Commissioner of Police, Jamaica, 1953–58, retd. *Address:* Box 267, Montego Bay, Jamaica, West Indies. *Died 22 Sept. 1998.*

MICHENER, James Albert; author; *b* New York City, 3 Feb. 1907; parents unknown; raised by Mabel Michener (*née* Haddock); *m* 1st, 1935, Patti Koon (marr. diss. 1948); 2nd, 1948, Vange Nord (marr. diss. 1955); 3rd, 1955, Mari Yoriko Sabusawa (*d* 1994); no *c. Educ:* Swarthmore Coll., Pennsylvania; St Andrews Univ., Scotland; Harvard Coll., Mass. Teacher, George Sch., Pa, 1933–36; Prof., Colorado State Coll. of Educn, 1936–41; Visiting Prof., Harvard, 1940–41; Associate Editor, Macmillan Co., 1941–49. Member: Adv. Cttee on the Arts, US State Dept, 1957; Adv. Cttee, US Information Agency, 1970–76; Cttee to reorganise US Inf. Service, 1976; US Postal Service Adv. Cttee, 1978–87; NASA Adv. Council, 1979–83; US Internat. Broadcasting Bd, 1983–89. Sec., Pennsylvania Constitutional Convention, 1968. Served with USNR on active duty in South Pacific, 1942–45. Hon. DHL, LLD, LittD, DSc and DHum, from numerous univs. US Medal of Freedom, 1977. *Publications:* Unit in the Social Studies, 1940; (ed) Future of Social Studies, for National Education Association, 1940; Tales of the South Pacific (Pulitzer prize for fiction), 1947 (Rodgers and Hammerstein musical, as South Pacific, 1949); The Fires of Spring, 1949; Return to Paradise, 1951; The Voice of Asia, 1951; The Bridges at Toko-ri, 1953; Sayonara, 1954; Floating World, 1955; The Bridge at Andau, 1957; (with A. Grove Day) Rascals in Paradise, 1957; Selected Writings, 1957; The Hokusai Sketchbook, 1958; Japanese Prints, 1959; Hawaii, 1959; Report of the County Chairman, 1961; Caravans, 1964; The Source, 1965; Iberia, 1968; Presidential Lottery, 1969; America *vs* America, 1969; The Quality of Life, 1970; Kent State, 1971; The Drifters, 1971; Centennial, 1974; Sports in America, 1976; Chesapeake, 1978; The Covenant, 1980;

Space, 1982 (televised, 1987); Poland, 1983; Texas, 1985; Legacy, 1987; Alaska, 1988; Journey, 1988; Caribbean, 1989; (with John Kings) Six Days in Havana, 1989; The Novel, 1991; The Eagle and the Raven, 1990; Pilgrimage, 1990; The World is My Home, 1992; Mexico, 1992; My Lost Mexico, 1992; James A. Michener's Writer's Handbook, 1992; Creatures of the Kingdom, 1993; Literary Reflections, 1993; Recessional, 1994; Miracle in Seville, 1995. *Address:* Texas Center for Writers, PCL 3.102, University of Texas, Austin, TX 78713, USA.

Died 16 Oct. 1997.

MIDDLETON, Sir George (Humphrey), KCMG 1958 (CMG 1950); HM Diplomatic Service, retired; *b* 21 Jan. 1910; *e s* of George Close Middleton and Susan Sophie (*née* Harley, subsequently Elphinstone); *m* 1st, 1934, Elizabeth Rosalie, (Tina), Okeden-Pockley, Qld, Australia; 2nd, (Marie Elisabeth Camille) Françoise Sarthou, Bordeaux; one *s*, and one step *s* one step *d. Educ:* St Lawrence Coll., Ramsgate; Magdalen Coll., Oxford. Entered Consular Service, 1933, Vice-Consul, Buenos Aires; transferred to Asunción, 1934, with local rank of 3rd Sec. in Diplomatic Service; in charge of Legation, 1935; transferred to New York, 1936; to Lemberg (Lwów), 1939; local rank of Consul; in charge of Vice-Consulate at Cluj, 1939–40; appointed to Genoa, 1940, to Madeira, 1940, to Foreign Office, 1943; 2nd Sec. at Washington, 1944; 1st Sec. 1945; transferred to FO, 1947; Counsellor, 1949; Counsellor, British Embassy, Tehran, 1951; acted as Chargé d'Affaires, 1951 and 1952 (when diplomatic relations severed); Dep. High Comr for UK, in Delhi, 1953–56; British Ambassador at Beirut, 1956–58; Political Resident in the Persian Gulf, 1958–61; British Ambassador to: Argentina, 1961–64; United Arab Republic, 1964–66. Mem. *Ad hoc* Cttee for UN Finances, 1966. Consultant, Industrial Reorganisation Corporation, 1967–68; Chm., Mondial Expatriate Services Ltd, 1988–91; Director: Overseas Medical Supplies Ltd; Britarge Ltd; Decor France Ltd; Chm., Exec. Cttee, British Road Fedn, 1972; Chief Executive, British Industry Roads Campaign, 1969–76. Past Chairman: Bahrain Soc.; Anglo-Peruvian Soc.; British Moroccan Soc. FRSA. Comdr, Order of Merit, Peru, 1974; Chevalier, National Order of the Cedar, Lebanon, 1988. *Recreations:* gardening, talking. *Address:* 1 Carlyle Square, SW3 6EX. *T:* (0171) 352 2962. *Club:* Travellers'. *Died 12 Feb. 1998.*

MIDDLETON, Sir Lawrence (Monck), 10th Bt *cr* 1662, of Belsay Castle, Northumberland; *b* 23 Oct. 1912; *s* of Lt Hugh Jeffery Middleton, RN (*d* 1914); 3rd *s* of Sir Arthur Middleton, 7th Bt, and Mary Katharine Middleton, OBE (*d* 1949); *S* brother, 1993; *m* 1984, Primrose Westcombe. *Educ:* Eton Coll.; Edinburgh Univ. (BSc Forestry). Forestry Commn, 1939–45. *Recreations:* mountaineering, birdwatching, gardening. *Heir:* none. *Address:* Estate Office, Belsay Castle, Newcastle upon Tyne NE20 0DY.

Died 16 March 1999 (ext).

MIDDLETON, Ronald George, DSC 1945; solicitor; *b* 31 July 1913; *o s* of late Sir George Middleton and Edith, *d* of William Cornes, Sodylt; *m* 1959, Sybil Summerscale (*d* 1976); no *c. Educ:* Whitgift Middle Sch.; University Coll., London. Solicitor, 1936. RNVR, 1939–47 (Lt-Comdr); Radar Officer HMS Queen Elizabeth, 1944–45; Fleet Radar Officer, Indian Ocean, 1945. Partner, Coward, Chance & Co., 1949, Senior Partner, 1972–80. Part-time Mem., NBPI, 1965–68. *Recreation:* sailing. *Address:* Flat 18, 76 Jermyn Street, SW1Y 6NP. *T:* (020) 7839 7993. *Clubs:* Reform, Garrick, Royal Ocean Racing.

Died 31 March 1999.

MIDGLEY, Eric Atkinson, CMG 1965; MBE 1945; HM Diplomatic Service, retired; *b* 25 March 1913; *s* of Charles Ewart Midgley, Keighley, Yorks; *m* 1937, Catherine Gaminara; two *d. Educ:* Christ's Hosp.; Merton Coll.,

Oxford. Indian Civil Service, 1937–47; Trade Commissioner at Delhi, 1947–57; Board of Trade, 1957–60; Commercial Counsellor at The Hague, 1960–63; Minister (Economic) in India, 1963–67; Minister (Commercial), Washington, 1967–70; Ambassador to Switzerland, 1970–73. *Recreation:* sailing. *Address:* 4 Monmouth Court, Church Lane, Lymington, Hants SO41 3RB. *Club:* Royal Lymington Yacht.

Died 23 April 2000.

MILBURN, Very Rev. Robert Leslie Pollington, FSA; *b* 28 July 1907; *er s* of late George Leslie and Elizabeth Esther Milburn; *m* 1944, Margery Kathleen Mary (*d* 1993), *d* of Rev. Francis Graham Harvie; one *d* (one *s* decd). *Educ:* Oundle; Sidney Sussex Coll., Cambridge (MA); New Coll., Oxford. Deacon 1934, priest 1935. Asst Master, Eton Coll., 1930–32; Worcester College, Oxford: Fellow and Chaplain, 1934–57; Tutor, 1945–57; Jun. Bursar, 1936–46; Estates Bursar, 1946–57; Hon. Fellow, 1978; University of Oxford: Select Preacher, 1942–44; University Lectr in Church History, 1947–57; Bampton Lectr, 1952. Examining Chaplain to Bishop of St Edmundsbury and Ipswich, 1941–53, to Bishop of Southwark, 1950–57, to Bishop of Oxford, 1952–57; Dean of Worcester, 1957–68, then Emeritus; Master of the Temple, 1968–80. Mem. of Oxford City Council, 1941–47. A Trustee, Wallace Collection, 1970–76. *Publications:* Saints and their Emblems in English Churches, 1949; Early Christian Interpretations of History, 1954; Early Christian Art and Architecture, 1988; articles in Journal of Theological Studies and Church Quarterly Review. *Address:* Highwell House, Bromyard, Herefordshire HR7 4DG. *Died 14 Feb. 2000.*

MILES, Geoffrey, OBE 1970; HM Diplomatic Service, retired; Consul-General, Perth, Western Australia, 1980–82; *b* 25 Oct. 1922; *s* of late Donald Frank Miles and Honorine Miles (*née* Lambert); *m* 1946, Mary Rozel Cottle (*d* 1989); one *s* one *d*. *Educ:* Eltham College. Joined Home Civil Service (Min. of Shipping), 1939; War service as pilot in RAF, 1941–46 (commnd, 1945); Min. of Transport, 1946–50; British Embassy, Washington, 1951; Sec., Copper-Zinc-Lead Cttee, Internat. Materials Conf., Washington 1952–53; BoT, 1953–55; Asst Trade Comr, Perth, 1955–59; Second Sec., Ottawa, 1960–63; First Sec., Salisbury, Southern Rhodesia, 1963–66, Dublin, 1967–71; Trade Comr (later Consul) and Head of Post, Edmonton, 1971–75, Consul-Gen., 1976–78; Consul-Gen., Philadelphia, 1979–80. *Recreations:* music, golf, amateur radio. *Address:* Farthings, Appledram Lane, Chichester, W Sussex PO20 7PE. *Clubs:* Royal Air Force; British Officers (Philadelphia); Goodwood Golf.

Died 19 Jan. 2000.

MILFORD, 3rd Baron *cr* 1939, of Llanstephan, co. Radnor; **Hugo John Laurence Philipps;** Bt 1919; farmer and forester; *b* 27 Aug. 1929; *o s* of 2nd Baron Milford and his 1st wife, Rosamond Nina Lehmann, CBE (*d* 1990); *S* father, 1993; *m* 1st, 1951, Margaret Heathcote (marr. diss. 1958); one *d*; 2nd, 1959, Hon. Mary Makins (marr. diss. 1984), *e d* of 1st Baron Sherfield, GCB, GCMG, FRS; three *s* one *d*; 3rd, 1989, Felicity Ballantyne. *Educ:* Eton; King's Coll., Cambridge. Lloyd's, 1951–86. High Sheriff, Powys, 1976–77. *Recreations:* fishing, reading, motoring in Europe, watching 1st class cricket. *Heir: s* Hon. Guy Wogan Philipps [*b* 25 July 1961; *m* 1996, Alice Sherwood; one *s*]. *Address:* Llanstephan House, Llanstephan, Brecon, Powys LD3 0YR. *T:* (01982) 560693. *Clubs:* Boodle's, Pratt's, MCC. *Died 4 Dec. 1999.*

MILKOMANE, George Alexis Milkomanovich; *see* Sava, G.

MILLAR, Ian Alastair D.; *see* Duncan Millar.

MILLAR, Sir Ronald (Graeme), Kt 1980; playwright, screenwriter and political writer; Deputy Chairman, Theatre Royal Haymarket, since 1977; *b* 12 Nov. 1919; *s* of late Ronald Hugh Millar and Dorothy Ethel Dacre Millar (*née* Hill). *Educ:* Charterhouse; King's Coll., Cambridge. Served as Sub-Lt, RNVR, 1940–43 (invalided out). Began in the Theatre as an actor; first stage appearance, London, Swinging the Gate, Ambassadors', 1940, subseq. in Mr Bolfry, The Sacred Flame, Murder on the Nile, Jenny Jones, (own play) Zero Hour, 1944; Ealing Studios, 1946–48, worked on Frieda, Train of Events, etc; screenwriter, Hollywood, 1948–54: So Evil My Love, The Miniver Story, Scaramouche, Rose-Marie, The Unknown Man, Never Let Me Go, Betrayed. Plays produced in London: Frieda, 1946; Champagne for Delilah, 1948; Waiting for Gillian, 1954; The Bride and the Bachelor, 1956; The More the Merrier, 1960; The Bride Comes Back, 1960; The Affair (from C. P. Snow novel), 1961; The New Men (from C. P. Snow), 1962; The Masters (from C. P. Snow), 1963; (book and lyrics) Robert and Elizabeth (musical), 1964; Number 10, 1967; Abelard and Heloise, 1970; The Case in Question (from C. P. Snow), 1975; A Coat of Varnish (from C. P. Snow), 1982. *Publication:* A View from the Wings (autobiog.), 1993. *Recreations:* all kinds of music, all kinds of people. *Address:* 7 Sheffield Terrace, W8 7NG. *T:* (0171) 727 8361. *Clubs:* Brooks's, Dramatists'.

Died 16 April 1998.

MILLAR, Prof. William Malcolm, CBE 1971; MD; Crombie-Ross Professor of Mental Health, University of Aberdeen, 1949–77; *b* 20 April 1913; *s* of Rev. Gavin Millar, BD, Logiealmond, Perthshire, and Margaret Malcolm, Stanley, Perthshire; *m* 1st, 1941, Catherine McAuslin Rankin; two *s* four *d*; 2nd, 1981, Maria Helen Ramsay. *Educ:* George Heriot's Sch., Edinburgh; Edinburgh Univ. MB, ChB (Edinburgh) 1936; MD (Edinburgh) 1939; Dip. Psych. (Edinburgh) 1939; MRCPE 1958; FRCPE 1962. Asst Physician, Royal Edinburgh Hospital for Mental Disorders, 1937–39; served 1939–46 (Lieut, Captain, Major), Specialist in Psychiatry, RAMC; Senior Lecturer, Dept of Mental Health, Aberdeen Univ., 1946–49; Dean, Faculty of Medicine, Aberdeen Univ., 1965–68. Member: MRC, 1960–64; Mental Welfare Commn for Scotland, 1964–78. FBPsS 1946. *Publications:* contributions to various learned journals. *Recreations:* golf, chess, gardening. *Address:* 35 Beechgrove Avenue, Aberdeen AB2 4HE.

Died 24 Jan. 1996.

MILLARD, Raymond Spencer, CMG 1967; PhD; FICE; FIHT; retired; *b* 5 June 1920; *s* of Arthur and Ellen Millard, Ashbourne, Derbs; *m* 1st, 1945, Irene Guy (marr. diss.); one *s* one *d*; 2nd, 1977, Sheila Taylor (*née* Akerman). *Educ:* Queen Elizabeth Grammar Sch., Ashbourne; University Coll., London (BSc (Eng)). Site Engr, R. M. Douglas, Contractors, 1941–42; Road Research Laboratory, 1943–74: Hd of Tropical Section, 1955–65; Dep. Dir, 1965–74; Partner, Peter Fraenkel & Partners, Asia, 1974–76; Highway Engrg Advisor, World Bank, 1976–82; Dir of Technical Affairs, British Aggregate Construction Inds, 1983–87. *Publications:* Road Building in the Tropics, 1993; technical papers on highway engineering. *Recreations:* bonsai culture, painting. *Address:* Drapers Cottage, 93 High Street, Odiham, Hook, Hants RG29 1LB.

Died 1 June 1997.

MILLER, Alexander Ronald, CBE 1970; President, Motherwell Bridge Holdings Ltd, since 1989 (Managing Director, 1958–85; Chairman, 1958–88); *b* 7 Nov. 1915; *s* of Thomas Ronald Miller and Elise Hay. *Educ:* Craigflower; Malvern Coll.; Royal Coll. of Science and Technology. Royal Engineers (Major) and Royal Bombay

Sappers and Miners, 1940–46. Member: Scottish Council, CBI (formerly FBI), 1955–82 (Chm., 1963–65); Council, CBI, 1982–; Design Council (formerly CoID), 1965–71 (Chm. Scottish Cttee, 1965–67); Scottish Economic Planning Council, 1965–71 (Chm., Industrial Cttee, 1967–71); British Railways (Scottish) Board, 1966–70; British Rail Design Panel, 1966–82; Gen. Convocation, Univ. of Strathclyde, 1967–; Steering Cttee, W Central Scotland Plan, 1970–75; Lanarkshire Area Health Bd, 1973–85 (Chm., 1973–77); Oil Develt Council for Scotland, 1973–78; Instn of Royal Engineers; BIM Adv. Bd for Scotland, 1974–89; Coll. Council, Bell Coll. of Technology, Hamilton, 1976–89; Lloyd's Register of Shipping Scottish Cttee, 1977–89, Gen. Cttee, 1982–; Lloyd's Register Quality Assce Ltd, 1984–89; Incorporation of Hammermen, Merchants' House of Glasgow. Chm., Management Cttee, Scottish Health Servs Common Servs Agency, 1977–83. Pres., Lanarkshire (formerly Hamilton and Other Districts) Br., Forces Help Soc. and Lord Roberts Workshops, 1979–90. A Burgess of the City of Glasgow. DUniv Stirling, 1986. FRSA; AIMechE; CIMgt. *Address:* Lairfad, Auldhouse, by East Kilbride, Lanarks. *T:* East Kilbride (013552) 63275. *Clubs:* Directors; Royal Scottish Automobile, Western (Glasgow). *Died 20 June 1996.*

MILLER, Maj.-Gen. David Edwin, CB 1986; CBE 1980 (OBE 1973); MC 1967; JP; Chief of Staff Live Oak, SHAPE, 1984–86, retired; *b* 17 Aug. 1931; *s* of late Leonard and Beatrice Miller; *m* 1958, Mary Lamley Fisher; two *s. Educ:* Loughton Sch., Essex; Royal Military Academy, Sandhurst. psc, jssc, ndc. Commissioned, Border Regt, 1951; Comd 1st Bn King's Own Royal Border Regt, 1971–73; Instructor, National Defence Coll., 1973–76; Colonel GS MoD, 1976–78; Comd Ulster Defence Regt, 1978–80; Dep. Chief of Staff Headquarters DAOR, 1980 83. Colonel, King's Own Royal Border Regt, 1981–88. JP Barnstaple, 1989. *Recreations:* wine, clocks, forestry. *Club:* Army and Navy. *Died 6 Oct. 1996.*

MILLER, Donald C.; *see* Crichton-Miller.

MILLER, Sir Douglas; *see* Miller, Sir I. D.

MILLER, Sir Douglas (Sinclair), KCVO 1972; CBE 1956 (OBE 1948); HM Overseas Colonial Service, retired, *b* 30 July 1906; *s* of Albert Edward Miller, Hove; British parentage; *m* 1933, Valerie Madeleine Carter (*d* 1995); one *d. Educ:* Westminster Sch.; Merton Coll., Oxford. HM Overseas Colonial Service, 1930–61: Supt of Native Educn, N Rhodesia, 1930–45; Director of Education: Basutoland, 1945–48; Nyasaland, 1948–52; Uganda, 1952–58; Kenya, 1958–59; Dir of Educn and Permanent Sec., Min. of Educn, Kenya, 1959 60; Temp. Minister of Educn, Kenya, 1960–61; Sec., King George's Jubilee Trust, 1961–71; Develt Adviser, Duke of Edinburgh's Award Scheme, 1971–85. *Address:* The Lodge, 70 Grand Avenue, Worthing, Sussex. *T:* Worthing (01903) 501195. *Clubs:* Commonwealth Trust; Kampala (Uganda). *Died 11 July 1996.*

MILLER, Edward, FBA 1981; Master, Fitzwilliam College, Cambridge, 1971–81 (Hon. Fellow, 1981); *b* Acklington, Northumberland, 16 July 1915; *e s* of Edward and Mary Lee Miller; *m* 1941, Fanny Zara Salingar; one *s. Educ:* King Edward VI's Grammar Sch., Morpeth; St John's Coll., Cambridge (Exhibnr, Schol.; BA 1937; MA 1945; Hon. Fellow, 1974). Nat. Service, 1940–45 in Durham Light Inf., RAC and Control Commn for Germany; Major. St John's College, Cambridge: Strathcona Res. Student, 1937–39; Fellow, 1939–65; Dir of Studies in History, 1946–55; Tutor, 1951–57; Asst Lectr in History, 1946–50 and Lectr, 1950–65, University of Cambridge; Warden of Madingley Hall, Cambridge, 1961–65; Prof. of Medieval

Hist., Sheffield Univ., 1965–71. FRHistS; Chm., Victoria Co. Histories Cttee of Inst. Hist. Research, 1972–79; Dep. Chm., Cttee to review Local Hist., 1978–79; Mem., St Albans Res. Cttee. Chm., Editorial Bd, History of Parliament Trust, 1975–89. Hon. LittD Sheffield, 1972. *Publications:* The Abbey and Bishopric of Ely, 1951; Portrait of a College, 1961; (ed jtly) Cambridge Economic History of Europe, vol. iii, 1963, vol. ii, 2nd edn, 1987; Historical Studies of the English Parliament, 2 vols, 1970; (jtly) Medieval England: rural society and economic change, 1978; (ed) Agrarian History of England and Wales, vol. iii, 1991; (jtly) Medieval England: towns, commerce and crafts, 1995; articles in Victoria County Histories of Cambridgeshire and York, Agrarian History of England and Wales, vol. ii, English Hist. Rev., Econ. History Rev., Trans Royal Historical Society, Past and Present, etc. *Recreations:* with advancing years watching any form of sport, especially Rugby and cricket. *Address:* 36 Almoners Avenue, Cambridge CB1 8PA. *T:* (01223) 246794. *Died 21 Dec. 2000.*

MILLER, Air Chief Marshal Frank Robert, CC 1972; CBE 1946; CD; retired from military service, 1966; Director, United Aircraft of Canada Ltd, 1967–76; *b* Kamloops, BC, April 1908; *m* Dorothy Virginia Minor, Galveston, Texas. *Educ:* Alberta Univ. (BSc, Civil Engrg). Joined RCAF, 1931; served War of 1939–45: commanded Air Navigation Schs at Rivers, Man, and Penfield Ridge, NB, and Gen. Reconnaisance Sch., Summerside, PEI; subseq. Dir of Trng Plans and Requirements and Dir of Trng, Air Force HQ; service overseas with Can. Bomber Gp as Station Comdr, later Base Comdr, 1944; Tiger Force, 1945 (despatches); Chief SO (later AOC), Air Material Comd, 1945; US Nat. War Coll., 1948; Air Mem. Ops and Trng, Air Force HQ, 1949; Vice Chief of Air Staff, 1951; Vice Air Deputy, SHAPE HQ, Paris, 1954; Dep. Minister, Dept of Nat. Defence, 1955; Chm., Chiefs of Staff, 1960; first Pres., NATO Mil. Cttee, 1963–64; Chief of Defence Staff, Canada, 1964–66. Air Chief Marshal, 1961. Hon. LLD Alta, 1965; Hon. DScMil RMC Canada, 1968. *Recreations:* golf, fishing. *Address:* 1654 Brandywine Drive, Charlottesville, VA 22901, USA. *Died 14 Oct. 1997.*

MILLER, Sir (Ian) Douglas, Kt 1961; FRCS; FRACS; Hon. Consulting Neurosurgeon, since 1960 (Hon. Neurosurgeon, 1948), St Vincent's Hospital, Sydney, and Repatriation General Hospital (Chairman of Board, 1966–76, Dean of Clinical School, 1931–64, St Vincent's Hospital); *b* Melbourne, 20 July 1900; *s* of Joseph John Miller; *m* 1939, Phyllis Laidley Mort; three *s* two *d. Educ:* Xavier Coll., Melbourne; University of Sydney. MB, ChM Sydney 1924; FRCS 1928; FRACS 1931. Hon. Asst Surgeon, St Vincent's Hosp., Sydney, 1929; Lectr in Surgical Anat., Univ. Sydney, 1930; Hon. Surg., Maternity Hosp. Sydney, 1934; Hon. Surg., St Vincent's Hosp., 1939; Major AIF, Surgical Specialist, 1940; Lt-Col (Surgical CO), 102 AGH, 1942; o/c Neurosurgical Centre, AIF. Chairman: Community Systems Foundn of Aust., 1965–72; Foundn of Forensic Scis, Aust. President: RACS, 1957–59 (Mem. Ct of Examrs, 1946; Mem. Council, 1947); Asian Australasian Soc. of Neurological Surgeons, 1964–67. Chairman: Editorial Cttee, ANZ Jl of Surgery, 1958–73; Editorial Bd, Modern Medicine in Australia, 1970–. Hon. FRCSE 1980. Hon. AM 1964, Hon. LittD 1974, Singapore; Hon. MD Sydney, 1979. *Publications:* A Surgeon's Story, 1985; Earlier Days, 1970; contrib. Med. Jl of Aust., 1956, 1960. *Recreation:* agriculture. *Address:* 170 Kurraba Road, Sydney, NSW 2089, Australia. *T:* 9092415. *Club:* Australian (Sydney). *Died 3 Jan. 1996.*

MILLER, Prof. Merton Howard, PhD; Professor of Banking and Finance, Graduate School of Business,

University of Chicago, 1961–96, then Emeritus; *b* 16 May 1923; *s* of Joel L. Miller and Sylvia F. Miller (*née* Starr); *m* 1st, Eleanor (*d* 1969); three *d*; 2nd, Katherine. *Educ:* Harvard Univ.; Johns Hopkins Univ. Asst Lectr, LSE, 1952; Asst Prof. and Associate Prof., Graduate Sch. of Indust. Admin, Carnegie Inst. of Technology, Pittsburgh, 1958–61. Nobel Prize for Economics (jtly), 1990. *Publications* include: Theory of Finance, 1972; Macroeconomics, 1974; Financial Innovations and Market Volatility, 1991; Merton Miller on Derivatives, 1997. *Address:* University of Chicago Graduate School of Business, 1101 East 58th Street, Chicago, IL 60637, USA. *Died 3 June 2000.*

MILLER, Rev. Canon Paul William; Canon Residentiary of Derby Cathedral, 1966–83, Canon Emeritus since 1983; Chaplain to the Queen, 1981–88; *b* 8 Oct. 1918; *s* of F. W. Miller, Barnet. *Educ:* Haileybury; Birmingham Univ. (Dip. Theology). Served in ranks with Sherwood Foresters, 1939–45; POW of Japanese, 1942–45; despatches 1946. Deacon, 1949; Curate: of Staveley, Derbyshire, 1949–52; of Matlock, Derbyshire, 1952–55; Vicar of Codnor, Derbyshire, 1955–61; Novice, Community of the Resurrection, Mirfield, 1961–63; Priest-in-charge, Buxton, 1963–64; Chaplain, Derby Cathedral, 1964–66. *Recreations:* painting, travel. *Address:* 15 Forester Street, Derby DE1 1PP. *T:* (01332) 344773.

Died 18 Oct. 2000.

MILLER, Peter Francis Nigel, RIBA, FCSD; Surveyor to the Fabric of Ely Cathedral, 1974–94, then Emeritus; *b* 8 May 1924; *s* of late Francis Gerald Miller, writer (as Ambrose Heath) and Dorothy Emily (*née* Leftwich); *m* 1950, Sheila Gillian Branthwayt, RI, ARCA, FCSD (*née* Stratton) (marr. diss. 1984); one *s* two *d*. *Educ:* King's Sch., Canterbury; Sch. of Architecture, Coll. of Art, Canterbury. ARIBA 1952, FRIBA 1968; MSIA 1956, FSIA 1968. Served army, 1942–47, NI, NW Europe, Austria, Italy and India; commnd Duke of Cornwall's LI, 1943. Private practice: Peter Miller and Sheila Stratton, 1954; Miller and Tritton, 1956; Purcell Miller and Tritton, 1965; Sen. Partner, Purcell Miller Tritton and Partners, Architects, Surveyors and Design Consultants, 1973–88, Consultant, 1988–94. Vice-Pres., SIAD, 1976. *Recreation:* salmon and trout fishing. *Address:* The Old Foundry House, Letheringsett, Holt, Norfolk NR25 7JL. *T:* (01263) 712329; The Studio, Thornage Watermill, Holt, Norfolk NR25 7QN. *T:* (01263) 711339. *Club:* Norfolk (Norwich). *Died 12 June 1997.*

MILLER, Sir Stephen (James Hamilton), KCVO 1979; MD; FRCS; Consulting Ophthalmic Surgeon, retired 1986; Hospitaller, St John Ophthalmic Hospital, Jerusalem, 1980–90; Surgeon-Oculist: to the Queen, 1974–80; to HM Household, 1965–74; Ophthalmic Surgeon: St George's Hospital, 1951–80; National Hospital, Queen Square, 1955–78; King Edward VII Hospital for Officers, 1965–80; Surgeon, Moorfields Eye Hospital, 1954–80; Recognised Teacher in Ophthalmology, St George's Medical School and Institute of Ophthalmology, University of London, retired; *b* 19 July 1915; *e s* of late Stephen Charles Miller and Isobel Hamilton; *m* 1949, Heather P. Motion; three *s*. *Educ:* Arbroath High Sch.; Aberdeen Univ. House Physician and Surgeon, Royal Infirmary, Hull, 1937–39. Surgeon Lieut-Comdr RNVR, 1939–46 (Naval Ophthalmic Specialist, RN Aux. Hosp., Kilmacolm and RN Hosp., Malta). Resident Surgical Officer, Glasgow Eye Infirmary, 1946; Registrar and Chief Clinical Asst, Moorfields Eye Hosp., 1947–50; Registrar St George's Hosp., 1949–51; Research Associate, Institute of Ophthalmology, 1949–80. Ophthalmic Surgeon, Royal Scottish Corp.; Advr in Ophthalmol., BUPA; Civilian Consultant in Ophthalmol. to RN and MoD, 1971–80, Emeritus, 1980. Mem., Med.

Commn for Accident Prevention. FRSocMed (Hon. Mem., Sect. of Ophthalmol.); Fellow Faculty of Ophthalmology; Editor, British Journal of Ophthalmology, 1973–83; Mem. Editorial Bd, Ophthalmic Literature; Ophthalmological Soc. of UK; Oxford Ophthalmological Congress (Master, 1969–70); Examiner in Ophthalmology: for Royal Colls and Brit. Orthoptic Bd; RCS and RCSE. Mem. Exec. Cttee, London Clinic, 1975–85; Governor, Moorfields Eye Hosp., 1961–67 and 1974–77. Chm., TFC Frost Charitable Trust (formerly Frost Foundn Charity), 1966–; Vice-Pres., Iris Fund, 1987–; Trustee, Guide Dogs for the Blind, 1981–91. Hon. FRCOphth (Hon. FCOphth 1989). Hon. Mem., Amer. Acad. of Ophthalmology. Freeman, City of London; Liveryman, Soc. of Apothecaries. Doyne Medal, 1972; Montgomery Medal, 1974. GCStJ 1987 (KStJ 1978). *Publications:* Modern Trends in Ophthalmology, 1973; Operative Surgery, 1976; Parsons' Diseases of the Eye, 16th edn 1978, to 18th edn 1990; Clinical Ophthalmology for the Post-Graduate, 1987; articles in BMJ, Brit. Jl of Ophthalmology, Ophthalmic Literature. *Recreations:* golf, fishing. *Address:* Sherma Cottage, Pond Road, Woking GU22 0JT. *T:* Woking (01483) 762287. *Clubs:* Caledonian; Woking Golf.

Died 12 April 1996.

MILLER, Stewart Crichton, CBE 1990; FRS 1996; FREng, FIMechE, FRAeS; FRSE; Director, 1985–96, Director, Engineering & Technology, 1993–96, Rolls-Royce plc; *b* 2 July 1934; *s* of William Young Crichton Miller and Grace Margaret Miller (*née* Finlay); *m* 1960, Catherine Proudfoot (*née* McCourtie); two *s* two *d*. *Educ:* Kirkcaldy High Sch.; Univ. of Edinburgh (BSc). FRAeS 1986; FREng (FEng 1987); FIMechE 1987; FRSE 1996. Rolls-Royce plc, 1954–96: training, 1954–56; technol. appts, 1956–76; Chief Engr, RB211-535, 1977–84; Dir of Engrg, 1985–90; Man. Dir, Aerospace Gp, 1991–92. Member: EPSRC, 1994–98; SHEFC, 1997–. Chm. Council, Loughborough Univ., 1995–; Mem. Court, Univ. of Strathclyde, 1997–. Foreign Associate Mem., Académie Nationale de l'Air et de l'Espace, France, 1996. Hon. DTech Loughborough, 1992; Hon. DEng: Birmingham, 1996; UMIST, 1997. British Gold Medal, RAeS, 1988; Faraday Medal, IEE, 1996; James Clayton Prize, IMechE, 1997. *Publications:* many papers to professional bodies on engrg and technol. *Recreations:* family, music, walking. *Address:* Mid Balchandy, by Pitlochry, Perthshire PH16 5JT. *T:* (01796) 482616. *Died 7 Aug. 1999.*

MILLIGAN, Wyndham Macbeth Moir, MBE 1945; TD 1947; Principal of Wolsey Hall, Oxford, 1968–80, retired; *b* 21 Dec. 1907; *s* of Dr W. Anstruther Milligan, MD, London, W1; *m* 1941, Helen Penelope Eirene Cassavetti, London, W1; three *s* two *d*. *Educ:* Sherborne; Caius Coll., Cambridge (Christopher James Student, 1931; 1st Cl. Classical Tripos, Parts 1 and 2). Asst Master, 1932, House Master, 1946, Eton Coll.; Warden, Radley Coll., 1954–68. Served 1939–45, with Scots Guards, in NW Europe (Major). Former Chm., N Berks Area Youth Cttee. Governor: St Mary's Sch., Wantage (Chm.); Reed's Sch., Cobham; Lay Chm., Vale of White Horse Deanery Synod; Mem., Administrative Council, King George's Jubilee Trust. FRSA 1968. *Recreations:* gardening, sketching. *Address:* Church Hill House, Stalbridge, Sturminster Newton, Dorset DT10 2LR. *T:* (01963) 362815.

Died 20 Nov. 1999.

MILLING, Air Marshal Sir Denis C.; *see* Crowley-Milling.

MILLS, Edward David William, CBE 1959; FRIBA; architect and design consultant in private practice since 1937; Senior Partner, Edward D. Mills & Partners, Architects, London, since 1956; *b* 19 March 1915; *s* of Edward Ernest Mills; *m* 1939, Elsie May Bryant; one *s* one *d*. *Educ:* Ensham Sch.; Polytechnic Sch. of

Architecture, ARIBA 1937, FRIBA 1946; FCSD (FSIAD 1975). Mem. of RIBA Council, 1954–62 and 1964–69; Chm. RIBA Bd of Architectural Education, 1960–62 (Vice-Chm., 1958–60). RIBA Alfred Bossom Research Fellow, 1953; Churchill Fellow, 1969. Mem., Uganda Soc. of Architects. Chm., Faculty Architecture, British School at Rome; Patron, Soc. of Architectural Illustrators. Architect for British Industries Pavilion, Brussels Internat. Exhibn, 1958; works include: St Andrews Cathedral, Mbale, Uganda; Nat. Exhibn Centre, Birmingham; Birmingham Internat. Arena; churches, schools, industrial buildings, research centres, flats and houses in Great Britain and overseas. Hon. DLitt Univ. of Greenwich, 1993. *Publications:* The Modern Factory, 1951; Architects Details, Vols 1–6, 1952–61; The New Architecture in Great Britain, 1953; The Modern Church, 1956; Factory Building, 1967; The Changing Workplace, 1971; (ed) Planning, 5 vols, 9th edn 1972, 10th edn (combined Golden Jubilee vol.), 1985; The National Exhibition Centre, 1976; Building Maintenance and Preservation, 1980, 2nd edn 1994; Design for Holidays and Tourism, 1983; contribs to RIBA journal, Architectural Review, etc. *Recreations:* photography, foreign travel. *Address:* The Studio, Gate House Farm, Newchapel, Lingfield, Surrey RH7 6LF. *T:* (01342) 832241.

Died 23 Jan. 1998.

MILLS, Iain Campbell; MP (C) Meriden, since 1979; *b* 21 April 1940; *s* of John Steel Mills and Margaret Leitch; *m* 1971, Gaynor Lynne Jeffries. *Educ:* Prince Edward Sch., Salisbury, Rhodesia. Dunlop Rhodesia Ltd, 1961–64; Dunlop Ltd, UK, 1964–79 (latterly Marketing Planning Manager). Parly Private Secretary: to Minister of State for Industry, 1981–82; to Sec. of State for Employment, 1982–83; to Sec. of State for Trade and Industry, 1983–85; to Chancellor of Duchy of Lancaster, 1985–87. Mem., Select Cttee on Educn and Employment (formerly on Employment), 1989; Jt Chm., All Party Motor Industry Gp, 1992–; Chm., Community Trade Mark Cttee, 1984–; Vice-Chm., Transport Safety Cttee, 1984–. *Address:* House of Commons, SW1A 0AA.

Died 16 Jan. 1997.

MILLS, Ivor; writer and broadcaster; corporate affairs and media consultant; *b* 7 Dec. 1929; *e s* of John Mills and Matilda (*née* Breen); *m* 1956, Muriel (marr. diss. 1987), *o d* of Wilson and Muriel Hay; one *s* one *d*. *Educ:* High sch.; Stranmillis Coll.; Queen's Univ., Belfast. Radio and television journalist, and freelance writer, Ulster TV, 1959, and Southern TV, 1963; freelance writer/editor/producer/presenter, contrib. to BBC World Service and Home Radio Networks, and ITV Regions, 1964; joined ITN as reporter, 1963; newscaster, 1967–78; Head of Public Affairs, Post Office, 1978–81; Head of Public Affairs and Dep. Dir, Corporate Relns, British Telecommunications plc, 1981–88. *Recreations:* art, music, theatre, tennis, food, wine. *Address:* 46B Glenhurst Avenue, Parliament Hill, NW5 1PS.

Died 30 May 1996.

MILLS, John Robert, CEng, FIEE; CPhys, MInstP; Under Secretary and Deputy Director (Systems) Royal Signals and Radar Establishment, Ministry of Defence, 1976–77, retired; *b* 12 Nov. 1916; *s* of Robert Edward Mills and Constance H. Mills; *m* 1950, Pauline Phelps; two *s*. *Educ:* Kingston Grammar Sch., Kingston-upon-Thames; King's Coll., London (BSc 1939). MInstP; FIEE 1971. Air Ministry Research Estab., Dundee, 1939; RAE Farnborough, 1940–42; TRE, later RRE, Malvern, 1942–60; Supt (Offensive), Airborne Radar, RRE, 1954–60; Asst Dir, Electronics R&D (Civil Aviation), Min. of Aviation, 1960–61; Head of Radio Dept, RAE Farnborough, 1961–65; Electronics Div., Min. of Technology, 1965–67; Dir, Signals R&D Establishment,

Christchurch, 1967–76. *Publications:* (jtly) Radar article in Encyclopædia Britannica; various papers in journals. *Address:* Meadowbank, Holly Green, Upton-upon-Severn, Worcester WR8 0PG. *Died 6 May 1998.*

MILLS, Leonard Sidney, CB 1970; Deputy Director General (2), Highways, Department of the Environment, 1970–74; *b* 20 Aug. 1914; *s* of late Albert Edward Mills; *m* 1940, (Kathleen) Joyce Cannicott; two *s*. *Educ:* Devonport High Sch.; London Sch. of Economics; Birkbeck Coll., University of London. Entered Exchequer and Audit Dept, 1933; transferred to Min. of Civil Aviation, 1946; Asst Sec., 1950; Ministry of Transport: Under-Sec., 1959; Chief of Highway Administration, 1968–70. Commonwealth Fund Fellow, 1953–54. *Recreations:* walking, croquet, gardening. *Address:* Pine Rise, 7A Bedlands Lane, Budleigh Salterton, Devon EX9 6QH. *Died 17 March 2000.*

MILMAN, Lt-Col Sir Derek, 9th Bt *cr* 1800, of Levaton-in-Woodland, Devonshire; MC 1941; *b* 23 June 1918; *s* of Brig.-Gen. Sir Lionel Charles Patrick Milman, 7th Bt, CMG and Marjorie Aletta (*d* 1980), *d* of Col A. H. Clark-Kennedy; *S* brother, 1990; *m* 1942, Margaret Christine Whitehouse; two *s*. *Educ:* Bedford School; Sandhurst. Commnd Unattached List IA, 1938; joined 3/2nd Punjab Regt, 1939; served War of 1939–45, Eritrea (MC, despatches), N Africa, Burma; with Pakistan Army, 1947–50; joined 1st Bn Beds and Herts Regt, 1950; Instructor, RMA Sandhurst, 1957; comd 5th Beds TA, 1959–61; retired, 1963. Instructor, Civil Defence Staff Coll., 1963–68; London Business School, 1970–83. *Recreation:* bird watching. *Heir: s* David Patrick Milman [*b* 24 Aug. 1945; *m* 1969, Christina Hunt; one *s* one *d*].

Died 12 May 1999.

MILNE, Denys Gordon, (Tiny), CBE 1982; *b* 12 Jan. 1926; *s* of late Dr George Gordon Milne and of Margaret (*née* Campbell); *m* 1951, Doreen Letitia; two *s* one *d*. *Educ:* Epsom Coll.; Brasenose Coll., Oxford (MA Hons Mod. History). Pilot Officer, RAF Regt, RAFVR, 1944–47. Colonial Admin. Service, Northern Nigeria, 1951–55; British Petroleum Company, 1955–81, retired as Man. Dir and Chief Exec., BP Oil Ltd; Dir, Business in the Community, 1981–84. Director: Silkolene Lubricants Plc, 1981–91; Fluor Daniel Ltd (formerly Fluor (GB)), 1981–90; The Weir Group Plc, 1983–92. Member: Scottish Economic Council, 1978–81; Adv. Cttee on Energy Conservation, 1980–81. President: UK Petroleum Industry Assoc., 1980–81; Inst. of Petroleum, 1978–80. Chm., Horder Centre for Arthritis, 1983–96. Trustee, Nat. Motor Mus., 1979–89. Chm. Council, Epsom Coll., 1990–95. Trustee and Dep. Chm., Centre for Southern African Studies, York Univ., 1990–95. Mem., Court of Assistants, Tallow Chandlers' Co., 1986– (Master, 1993–94). *Recreations:* gardening, cruising. *Address:* Westbury, Old Lane, St Johns, Crowborough, East Sussex TN6 1RX. *T:* (01892) 652634. *Club:* Royal Air Force.

Died 9 Feb. 2000.

MILNE, Maj.-Gen. Douglas Graeme; retired; Civilian Medical Officer, Ministry of Defence, 1979–84; Deputy Director General Army Medical Services, 1975–78; *b* 19 May 1919; *s* of George Milne and Mary Panton; *m* 1944, Jean Millicent Gove; one *d*. *Educ:* Robert Gordon's Coll.; Aberdeen Univ. MB, ChB, FFCM, DPH. Commnd into RAMC, 1943; service in W Africa, Malta, Egypt, BAOR, Singapore; Dir of Army Health and Research, 1973–75. QHS 1974–78. Col Comdt, RAMC, 1979–84. OStJ 1976. *Recreations:* gardening, reading. *Address:* 17 Stonehill Road, SW14 8RR. *Died 6 May 1996.*

MILNE, James L.; *see* Lees-Milne.

MILNE, Maurice, CB 1976; FEng 1980; Deputy Director General of Highways, Department of the Environment,

1970–76; retired; *b* 22 July 1916; *s* of James Daniel Milne, stonemason, and Isabella Robertson Milne; *m* 1947, Margaret Elizabeth Stewart Monro; (one *d* decd). *Educ:* Robert Gordon's Coll., Aberdeen; Aberdeen University (BScEng 1st cl. Hons). FICE, FIStructE, FIHT, FRTPI. Chief Asst, D. A. Donald & Wishart, Cons. Engrs, Glasgow, 1947–48; Sen. Engr and Chief Engr, Crawley Develt Corp., 1948–59; Engr, Weir Wood Water Board, 1953–57; County Engr and Surveyor, W Sussex CC, 1960–68; Dir, S Eastern Road Construction Unit, MoT, 1968–70. Chairman: Downland Housing Soc. Ltd, 1978–83; London and SE Region Anchor Housing Assoc., 1982–88. Trustee: Humane Research Trust, 1983– (Dep. Chm., 1992–94); Rees Jeffreys Road Fund, 1976–. (Chm., 1990–93). Hon. Sec., County Surveyors' Soc., 1963–67; Pres., Instn Highway Engineers, 1974–75; Mem. Council, ICE, 1967–71 and 1972–75; Pres., Perm. Internat. Assoc. of Road Congresses, 1977–84 (Hon. Pres., 1988–). *Publications:* contributions to Jl Instn of Civil, Municipal and Highway Engrs. *Recreations:* gardening, painting, photography. *Address:* 24 Ferndale Road, Summersdale, Chichester, West Sussex PO19 4QJ. *T:* (01243) 528002.
Died 17 June 1998.

MILNE, Norman; Sheriff of North Strathclyde at Campbeltown and Oban, 1975–81, retired; *b* 31 Dec. 1915; *s* of William Milne and Jessie Ferguson; *m* 1947, Phyllis Christina Philip Rollo; no *c. Educ:* Logie Central Sch., Dundee. Solicitor, 1939. Army, 1939–46: active service in Madagascar, Sicily, Italy, and Germany (despatches). Procurator Fiscal Depute: Perth, 1946–51; Edinburgh, 1951–55; Senior Depute Fiscal, Glasgow, 1955–58; Procurator Fiscal: Banff, 1959–64; Kirkcaldy, 1964–65; Paisley, 1965–71; Edinburgh, 1971–75. *Recreation:* music. *Address:* The Anchorage, Machrihanish, Argyll PA28 6PT.
Died 24 Aug. 2000.

MILNE HOME, John Gavin, TD; FRICS; Lord-Lieutenant of Dumfries and Galloway, 1988–91 (Vice-Lord-Lieutenant, 1983–88); *b* 20 Oct. 1916; *s* of Sir John Hepburn Milne Home and Lady (Mary Adelaide) Milne Home; *m* 1942, Rosemary Elwes; two *s* one *d. Educ:* Wellington College; Trinity College, Cambridge (BA Estate Management). Served with King's Own Scottish Borderers (4th Bn), 1939–45 (TA, 1938–49). Factor for Buccleuch Estates Ltd and Duke of Buccleuch on part of Scottish estates, 1949–74. Mem., Dumfries County Council, 1949–75. DL Dumfries, 1970. *Recreations:* fishing, shooting. *Address:* Kirkside of Middleholm, Lockerbie, Dumfriesshire DG11 3JW. *T:* (01576) 300204.
Died 29 June 2000.

MILNE-WATSON, Sir Michael, 3rd Bt *cr* 1937, of Ashley, Longbredy, co. Dorset; Kt 1969; CBE 1953; *b* 16 Feb. 1910; *yr s* of Sir David Milne-Watson, 1st Bt, and Olga Cecily (*d* 1952), *d* of Rev. George Herbert; *S* brother, 1982; *m* 1940, Mary Lisette (*d* 1993), *d* of late H. C. Bagnall, Auckland, New Zealand; one *s. Educ:* Eton; Balliol Coll., Oxford (MA). Served War of 1939–45: RNVR, 1943–45. Joined Gas Light & Coke Co., 1933; Managing Dir, 1945; Governor, 1946–49; Chairman: North Thames Gas Board, 1949–64; Richard Thomas & Baldwins Ltd, 1964–67; The William Press Group of Companies, 1969–74; a Dep. Chm., BSC, 1967–69 (Mem. Organizing Cttee, 1966–67); Mem., Iron and Steel Adv. Cttee, 1967–69. Director: Industrial and Commercial Finance Corp. Ltd, 1963–80; Commercial Union Assurance Co. Ltd, 1968–81; Finance for Industry Ltd, 1974–80; Finance Corp. for Industry Ltd, 1974–80; Rose Thomson Young (Underwriting) Ltd, 1982–87. President: Soc. of British Gas Industries Guild, 1970–71; Pipeline Industries Guild, 1971–72. Vice-Pres., BUPA, 1981– (Chm., 1976–81). Liveryman, Grocers' Co., 1947.

Governor, Council, Reading Univ., 1971–82 (Pres., 1975–80). *Heir: s* Andrew Michael Milne-Watson [*b* 10 Nov. 1944; *m* 1st, 1970, Beverley Jane Gabrielle (marr. diss. 1981), *e d* of Philip Cotton, Majorca; one *s* one *d*; 2nd, 1983, Gisella Tisdall; one *s*]. *Address:* The Stables, Oakfield, Mortimer, Berks RG7 3AJ. *T:* (01189) 832200. *Clubs:* Athenæum, MCC; Leander.
Died 27 April 1999.

MILOSLAVSKY, Dimitry T.; *see* Tolstoy, Dimitry.

MINCHINTON, Prof. Walter Edward; Professor of Economic History, University of Exeter, 1964–86 (Head of Department, 1964–84), then Emeritus; *b* 29 April 1921; *s* of late Walter Edward and Annie Border Minchinton; *m* 1945, Marjorie Sargood; two *s* two *d. Educ:* Queen Elizabeth's Hosp., Bristol; LSE, Univ. of London. 1st cl. hons BSc (Econ). FRHistS. War Service, RAOC, REME, Royal Signals (Lieut), 1942–45. UC Swansea: Asst Lectr, 1948–50; Lectr, 1950–59; Sen. Lectr, 1959–64. Rockefeller Research Fellow, 1959–60; Fellow, John Carter Brown Liby, Providence, RI, 1993. Visiting Professor: Fourah Bay Coll., Sierra Leone, 1965; La Trobe Univ., Australia, 1981–82. Chairman: Confedn for Advancement of State Educn, 1964–67; Devon History Soc., 1967–86; Exeter Industrial Arch. Gp, 1967–92; SW Maritime History Soc., 1984–87 (Pres., 1987–); British Agricultural History Soc., 1968–71 (Mem. Council, 1952–86); Export Research Group, 1971–72; Exeter Educn Cttee, 1972; Devon Historic Buildings Trust, 1980–86 (Mem. Council, 1967–). Vice-President: Assoc. for the History of the Northern Seas, 1989– (Pres., 1982–89); Internat. Commn for Maritime History, 1968–80 (Mem. Council, 1985–90; Mem. Council, British Cttee, 1974–); Council Member: Economic History Soc., 1955–66; Soc. for Nautical Research, 1969–72, 1978–81. Alexander Prize, RHistS, 1953. General Editor: Exeter Papers in Economic History, 1964–86; British Records Relating to America in Microform, 1962–89. *Publications:* The British Tinplate Industry: a history, 1957; (ed) The Trade of Bristol in the Eighteenth Century, 1957; (ed) Politics and the Port of Bristol in the Eighteenth Century, 1963; Industrial Archaeology in Devon, 1968; (ed) Essays in Agrarian History, 1968; (ed) Industrial South Wales 1750–1914, essays in Welsh economic history, 1969; (ed) Mercantilism, System or Expediency?, 1969; The Growth of English Overseas Trade in the Seventeenth and Eighteenth Centuries, 1969; Wage Regulation in Pre-industrial England, 1972; Devon at Work, 1974; Windmills of Devon, 1977; (with Peter Harper) American Papers in the House of Lords Record Office: a guide, 1983; A Limekiln Miscellany: the South-West and South Wales, 1984; (with Celia King and Peter Waite) Virginia Slave-Trade Statistics 1698–1775, 1984; A Guide to Industrial Archaeological Sites in Britain, 1984; Devon's Industrial Past: a guide, 1986; Life to the City: an illustrated history of Exeter's water supply from the Romans to the present day, 1987; (ed) Britain and the Northern Seas: some essays, 1988; (ed) The Northern Seas: politics, economics and culture: eight essays, 1989; (ed) People of the Northern Seas, 1992; articles in Econ. History Review, Explorations in Entrepreneurial History, Mariner's Mirror, Trans RHistS, etc. *Recreations:* walking, music, industrial archaeology. *Address:* 60 Rosebarn Lane, Exeter EX4 5DG. *T:* Exeter (01392) 277602.
Died 25 Aug. 1996.

MINNITT, Robert John, CMG 1955; *b* 2 April 1913; *s* of Charles Frederick Minnitt and Winifred May Minnitt (*née* Buddle); *m* 1st, 1943, Peggy Christine Sharp (*d* 1973); one *s* two *d*; 2nd, 1975, Hon. Primrose Keighley Muncaster (*d* 2000), 3rd *d* of 1st Baron Riverdale, GBE, and *widow* of Claude Muncaster. *Educ:* Marlborough Coll.; Trinity Coll., Cambridge. Appointed to Colonial Administrative

Service, Hong Kong, 1935; Chief Sec., Western Pacific High Commission, 1952–58, retired. Furniture designer and craftsman, 1960–66; temp. Civil Servant, CO, 1966; FCO, 1968–69. *Address:* Little Denmans, East Street, Petworth, W Sussex GU28 0AB. *T:* (01798) 343081.
Died 26 Aug. 2000.

MIRALLES MOYA, Enric; architect, in partnership with Benedetta Tagliabue, since 1992; *b* 12 Feb. 1955; *s* of Jose Miralles Ruiz and Pilar Moya Lazaro; *m* 1st, Carme Pinos (marr. diss.); 2nd, 1992, Benedetta Tagliabue; one *s* one *d* (twins). *Educ:* Escuela Técnica Superior de Arquitectura, Barcelona (PhD 1983). Architect, 1979–; Prof. of Planning, 1985; Professor of Architecture: Stadelschule, Frankfurt, 1990–95; Escuela Técnica Superior de Arquitectura, Barcelona, 1995–. Commissions included: Archery Range, Barcelona (City of Barcelona Prize, 1992), 1992; Huesca Sports Hall, 1993 (Golden Lion, Venice Bienale, 1996); school, Morella (Nat. Architect. Prize), 1993; Parliament of Scotland building, Edinburgh. *Publications:* Enric Miralles: mixed talks, 1995; contrib. to professional jls. *Address:* Pasaje de la Paz Pau, 10 bis Pral, 08002 Barcelona, Spain. *T:* (93) 4125342, *Fax:* (93) 4123718. *Club:* Circulo del Liceo (Barcelona).
Died 3 July 2000.

MIRON, Wilfrid Lyonel, CBE 1969 (OBE 1945; MBE 1944); TD 1950; JP; DL; Regional Chairman (Midlands), National Coal Board, 1967–76 and Regional Chairman (South Wales), 1969–76; National Coal Board Member (with Regional responsibilities), 1971–76; *b* 27 Jan. 1913; *s* of late Solman Miron and Minnie Pearl Miron; *m* 1958, Doreen (*née* Hill) (*d* 1992); no *c. Educ:* Llanelli Grammar Sch. Admitted Solicitor, 1934; private practice and Legal Adviser to Shipley Collieries and associated companies. TA Commn, Sherwood Foresters, 1939; served War of 1939–45; Home Forces, 1939; France and Dunkirk, 1940, IO 139 Inf. Bde, 1940–41; GSO3 Aldershot Dist, 1941–42; Staff Coll., Quetta, 1942 (sc); DAAG 17 India Div., 1943–44, and AA&QMG 17 India Div., 1944–45, Chin Hills, Imphal, Burma (despatches, 1944). E Midlands Division, National Coal Board: Sec. and Legal Adviser, 1946–51; Dep. Chm., 1951–60; Chm., 1960–67. Pres., Midland Dist Miners' Fatal Accident Relief Soc., 1970–97. Chairman: E Mids Regional Planning Council, 1976–79 (Mem., 1965–76); (part-time), Industrial Tribunals, 1976–85. Freeman (by redemption), City of London; Master, Pattenmakers' Company, 1979–80. Hon. Lt-Col. JP Notts, 1964 (Chairman: Nottingham PSD, 1982–83; Notts Magistrates' Cts Cttee, 1981–83); DL Notts, 1970. FRSA 1965–86. OStJ 1961. Hon. Fellow, Trent Polytechnic, 1980. *Publications:* Bitter Sweet Seventeen, 1946; articles and papers in mining and other jls. *Recreations:* cricket, music, reading, crosswords. *Address:* Briar Croft, School Lane, Halam, Newark, Notts NG22 8AD. *T:* (01636) 812446. *Clubs:* Army and Navy, MCC; XL; Nottingham and Notts United Services (Pres., 1992–) (Nottingham).
Died 1 Jan. 2000.

MITCHELL, Lt-Col Colin Campbell; former soldier and politician; Chairman, The HALO Trust, since 1987; *b* 17 Nov. 1925; *o s* of Colin Mitchell, MC, and Janet Bowie Gilmour; *m* 1956, Jean Hamilton Susan Phillips; two *s* one *d. Educ:* Whitgift Sch. British Army, 1943; commissioned Argyll and Sutherland Highlanders, 1944, serving in Italy (wounded); Palestine, 1945–48 (wounded); Korea, 1950–51; Cyprus, 1958–59; Borneo, 1964 (brevet Lt-Col); Aden, 1967 (despatches). Staff appts as ADC to GOC-in-C Scottish Command; Directorate of Mil. Ops (MO4), WO; qualified Camberley Staff Coll., 1955; subsequently: GSO2, 51st Highland Div. (TA) Bde Major, King's African Rifles, and GSO1 Staff of Chief of Defence Staff at MoD; retired at own request, 1968; subseq. Special Correspondent, Vietnam. MP (C) W

Aberdeenshire, 1970–Feb. 1974 (did not seek re-election); PPS to Sec. of State for Scotland, 1972–73. Mem., Select Cttee on Armed Services, 1970–71. Specialist Consultant: Rhodesia, 1975–79; Mexico, 1980; Afghanistan, 1983; Nicaragua, 1985; Pakistan NWFP, 1986; Eritrea, 1987; Cambodia, 1990. Mem., UNHCR Mission to Cambodia, 1991, Mozambique, Angola and Transcaucasus, 1994–96. Freedom of City of London, 1979. *Publication:* Having Been A Soldier, 1969. *Address:* c/o Coutts & Co., 440 Strand, WC2R 0QS.
Died 20 July 1996.

MITCHELL, Constance, (Mrs Eric Mitchell); *see* Shacklock, C.

MITCHELL, George Francis, (Frank), FRS 1973; MRIA; environmental historian; *b* 15 Oct. 1912; *s* of late David William Mitchell and late Frances Elizabeth Kirby; *m* 1940, Lucy Margaret Gwynn (*d* 1987); two *d. Educ:* High Sch., Dublin; Trinity Coll., Dublin (MA, MSc; FTCD 1945). Joined staff of Trinity Coll., Dublin, 1934; Professor of Quaternary Studies, 1965–79. Pro-Chancellor, Univ. of Dublin, 1985–88. Pres., Internat. Union for Quaternary Research, 1969–73. MRIA 1939, PRIA 1976–79. HRHA 1981; Pres., An Taisce, 1991–93; Hon. Life Mem., RDS, 1981; Hon. Member: Prehistoric Soc., 1983; Quaternary Res. Assoc., 1983; Internat. Assoc. for Quaternary Res., 1985; Hon. FRSE 1984. DSc (*hc*): Queen's Univ., Belfast, 1976; NUI, 1977; fil.D (*hc*) Uppsala, 1977. *Publications:* The Irish Landscape, 1976; Treasures of Early Irish Art, 1977; Shell Guide to Reading the Irish Landscape, 1986; Archaeology and Environment in Early Dublin, 1987; Man and Environment on Valencia Island, Co. Kerry, 1989; The Way that I Followed, 1990; Where has Ireland come from?, 1994; (jtly) The Great Bog of Ardee, 1995; (jtly) Reading the Irish Landscape, 1997. *Address:* Gardener's Cottage, Townley Hall, Drogheda, Co. Louth, Republic of Ireland. *T:* (41) 34615.
Died 25 Nov. 1997.

MITCHELL, Robert, OBE 1984; Chairman and Managing Director, R. Mitchell & Co. (Eng) Ltd, 1959–81; Councillor, Greater London Council, 1964–86; *b* 14 Dec. 1913; *s* of Robert Mitchell and Lizzie Mitchell (*née* Snowdon); *m* 1946, Reinholda Thorretta L. C. Kettlitz; two *s*, and one step *s. Educ:* West Ham Secondary Sch.; St John's Coll., Cambridge (MA Hons NatSci). Councillor, Wanstead and Woodford Council, 1958–65, Dep. Mayor, 1960–61. Chairman: GLC, 1971–72; Fire Brigade and Ambulance Cttees, 1967–71; Nat. Jt Negotiating Cttee for Local Authority Fire Brigades, 1970–71; Covent Gdn Jt Develt Cttee, 1972–73; Professional and Gen. Services Cttee, 1977–79; Greater London Jt Supply Bd, 1977–79. Member: CBI Cttee on State Intervention in Private Industry, 1976–78; London and SE Reg. Council, 1969–79; Smaller Firms Council, 1977–79; Policy Cttee, AMA, 1978–79. Wanstead and Woodford Conservative Association: Vice-Chm., 1961–65; Chm., 1965–68; Vice-Pres., 1968–; contested (C) West Ham South, 1964 and 1966. Represented: Cambridge Univ., swimming and water polo, 1932–35 (Captain, 1935); England and Gt Britain, water polo, 1934–48, incl. Olympic Games, 1936 and 1948; Gt Britain, swimming and water polo, World Univ. Games, 1933, 1935; Rest of World *v* Champions, water polo, Univ. Games, 1935; Captain, 1946–49, Pres., 1955–56, Plaistow United Swimming Club; London Rep., Cambridge Univ. Swimming Club, 1953–75. Mem. Cttee, Crystal Palace Nat. Sports Centre, 1965–88. Chm., London Ecology Centre Ltd, 1986–88; Gov., London Ecology Centre Trust, 1985–88; Verderer, Epping Forest, 1976–; Mem., Lea Valley Regl Park Auth., 1982–85. Liveryman, Worshipful Co. of Gardeners, 1975–. Governor, Chigwell Sch., 1966–96 (Vice-Chm., 1968–88). Grand Officer, Order of Orange Nassau (Holland), 1972; Order of Star (Afghanistan), 1971; Order of Rising Sun (Japan), 1971.

Publications: Bob Mitchell's Epping Forest Companion, 1991; newspaper and magazine articles mainly on countryside and political subjects. *Recreation:* planting trees, then sitting watching them grow. *Address:* Hatchwood House, Nursery Road, Loughton, Essex IG10 4EF. *T:* (0181) 508 9135; Little Brigg, Bessingham, Norfolk NR11 7JR. *Clubs:* Carlton; Hawks (Cambridge).
Died 12 Nov. 1996.

MITCHELL, Hon. Dame Roma (Flinders), AC 1991; DBE 1982 (CBE 1971); CVO 2000; Governor of South Australia, 1991–96; Senior Puisne Judge, Supreme Court of South Australia, 1979–83 (Judge of Supreme Court, 1965–83); *b* 2 Oct. 1913; *d* of Harold Flinders Mitchell and Maude Imelda Victoria (*née* Wickham). *Educ:* St Aloysius Coll., Adelaide; Univ. of Adelaide (LLB 1934). Admitted as Practitioner, Supreme Court of SA, 1934; QC 1962 (first woman QC in Australia). Sen. Dep. Chancellor, 1972–83, Chancellor, 1983–90, Univ. of Adelaide. Chairman: Parole Bd of SA, 1974–81; Criminal Law Reform Cttee of SA, 1971–81; Human Rights Commn of Australia, 1981–86; State Heritage Cttee of SA, 1978–81; SA Council on Child Protection, 1988–90; Adv. Bd on the Ageing, SA, 1996–; National President: Winston Churchill Meml Trust, 1988–91 (Dep. Chm., 1975–84; Nat. Chm., 1984–88); Australian Assoc. of Ryder-Cheshire Foundn, 1979–91. Member: Council for Order of Australia, 1980–90; Bd of Governors, Adelaide Festival of Arts, 1981–84. Boyer Lectr, ABC, 1975. Hon. FRACP 1992. DUniv Adelaide, 1985; Hon. LLD: Queensland, 1992; Flinders Univ. of S Australia, 1993; Univ. of S Australia, 1994. Medal, Instn of Engrs, 1994. Comdr, Légion d'Honneur (France), 1997. *Recreations:* theatre, music, art, swimming, walking. *Address:* PO Box 7030, Hutt Street, Adelaide, SA 5000, Australia. *T:* and *Fax:* (8) 82324273. *Clubs:* Queen Adelaide, Lyceum (Adelaide).
Died 5 March 2000.

MITCHELL, Dame Wendy, DBE 1992 (OBE 1986); Hon. Vice President, National Union of Conservative and Unionist Associations, since 1995 (Vice-Chairman, 1990–93; President, 1993–94); *b* 14 Sept. 1932; *d* of Guy Francis Dell and Sophia Dell; *m* 1963, Anthony John Mitchell; one *s* one *d. Educ:* Heathfield House High Sch., Cardiff. Cardiff Royal Infirmary (SRN); St David's Hosp. and Queen's Inst., Cardiff (SCM). Mem., SE Thames RHA, 1986–94, S Thames RHA, 1994–96; Dep. Chm., Women's Nationwide Cancer Control Campaign, 1986–97; Chm., Gen. Medicine Service Standards Wkg Gp, Health Services Accreditation, 1994–. Councillor, London Borough of Greenwich, 1974–94; Chairman: W Woolwich (Eltham) Cons. Assoc., 1974–77 (Pres., 1988–91); Greater London Area Cons. Women's Cttee, 1983–86; Cons. Women's Nat. Cttee, 1987–90; Dep. Chm., Greater London Area Cons. Exec., 1987. Chairman: Skill Swap Adv. Cttee, 1994–; Membership Cttee, Executive Gold Club (Hldgs) Ltd, 1996–. FRSocMed; FRSA. *Recreations:* reading, learning to be a silversmith. *T:* (01424) 775914. *Died 3 July 1999.*

MITCHISON, Naomi Margaret, (Lady Mitchison), CBE 1985; *b* Edinburgh, 1 Nov. 1897; *d* of late John Scott Haldane, CH, FRS, and Kathleen Trotter; *m* 1916, Gilbert Richard Mitchison, later Baron Mitchison (*d* 1970), CBE, QC; three *s* two *d* (and one *s* one *d* decd). *Educ:* Dragon Sch., Oxford; home student, Oxford. Argyll CC, 1945–65, on and off; Highland and Island Advisory Panel, 1947–65; Highlands and Islands Develt Consult. Council, 1966–76. Tribal Mother to Bakgatla, Botswana, 1963–. DUniv: Stirling, 1976; Dundee, 1985; DLitt Strathclyde, 1983. Hon. Fellow: St Anne's Coll., Oxford, 1980; Wolfson Coll., Oxford, 1983. Officier d'Académie Française, 1924. *Publications:* The Conquered, 1923; When the Bough Breaks, 1924; Cloud Cuckoo Land, 1925; The Laburnum

Branch, 1926; Black Sparta, 1928; Anna Comnena, 1928; Nix-Nought-Nothing, 1928; Barbarian Stories, 1929; The Hostages, 1930; Comments on Birth Control, 1930; The Corn King and the Spring Queen, 1931; The Price of Freedom (with L. E. Gielgud), 1931; Boys and Girls and Gods, 1931; The Powers of Light, 1932; (ed) An Outline for Boys and Girls, 1932; The Delicate Fire, 1933; Vienna Diary, 1934; The Home, 1934; We Have Been Warned, 1935; Beyond this Limit, 1935; The Fourth Pig, 1936; Socrates (with R. H. S. Crossman), 1937; An End and a Beginning, 1937; The Moral Basis of Politics, 1938; The Kingdom of Heaven, 1939; As It was in the Beginning (with L. E. Gielgud), 1939; The Blood of the Martyrs, 1939; (ed) Re-educating Scotland, 1944; The Bull Calves, 1947; Men and Herring (with D. Macintosh), 1949; The Big House, 1950; Spindrift (play, with D. Macintosh), Citizens' Theatre, Glasgow, 1951; Lobsters on the Agenda, 1952; Travel Light, 1952; The Swan's Road, 1954; Graeme and the Dragon, 1954; The Land the Ravens Found, 1955; To the Chapel Perilous, 1955; Little Boxes, 1956; Behold your King, 1957; The Far Harbour, 1957; Five Men and a Swan, 1958; Other People's Worlds, 1958; Judy and Lakshmi, 1959; The Rib of the Green Umbrella, 1960; The Young Alexander, 1960; Karensgaard, 1961; The Young Alfred the Great, 1962; Memoirs of a Space Woman, 1962; (ed) What the Human Race is Up To, 1962; The Fairy who Couldn't Tell a Lie, 1963; When we Become Men, 1965; Ketse and the Chief, 1965; Return to the Fairy Hill, 1966; Friends and Enemies, 1966; The Big Surprise, 1967; African Heroes, 1968; Don't Look Back, 1969; The Family at Ditlabeng, 1969; The Africans: a history, 1970; Sun and Moon, 1970; Cleopatra's People, 1972; A Danish Teapot, 1973; Sunrise Tomorrow, 1973; Small Talk: memoirs of an Edwardian childhood (autobiog.), 1973; A Life for Africa, 1973; Oil for the Highlands?, 1974; All Change Here (autobiog.), 1975; Solution Three, 1975; Snake!, 1976; The Two Magicians, 1979; The Cleansing of the Knife, 1979; You May Well Ask (autobiog.), 1979; Images of Africa, 1980; The Vegetable War, 1980; Mucking Around, 1980; What Do You Think Yourself? (Scottish stories), 1982; Not By Bread Alone, 1983; Among You Taking Notes, 1985; Beyond this Limit (short stories), 1986; Early in Orcadia, 1987; A Girl Must Live, 1990; Sea-Green Ribbons, 1991; The Oathtakers, 1991. *Recreation:* surviving so far. *Address:* Carradale House, Carradale, Campbeltown, Scotland PA28 6QQ. *Died 11 Jan. 1999.*

MITFORD, Jessica Lucy, (Mrs Jessica Treuhaft); author; *b* 11 Sept. 1917; *d* of 2nd Baron Redesdale and Sydney, *er d* of Thomas Gibson Bowles, formerly MP King's Lynn; US citizen, 1944; *m* 1st, 1937, Esmond Marcus David Romilly (*d* 1941); one *d* (and one *d* decd); 2nd, 1943, Robert Edward Treuhaft; one *s* (and one *s* decd). Distinguished Prof., San José State Univ., Calif, 1973–74. *Publications:* (as Jessica Mitford): Hons and Rebels, 1960; The American Way of Death, 1963; The Trial of Dr Spock, 1969; Kind and Usual Punishment, 1974; The American Prison Business, 1975; A Fine Old Conflict, 1977; The Making of a Muckraker, 1979; Faces of Philip: a memoir of Philip Toynbee, 1984; Grace had an English Heart: the story of Grace Darling, heroine and Victorian superstar, 1988; The American Way of Birth, 1992. *Address:* 6411 Regent Street, Oakland, CA 94618, USA.
Died 23 July 1996.

MITTERRAND, François Maurice Marie; Grand Croix de l'Ordre National de la Légion d'Honneur; Grand Croix de l'Ordre National du Mérite; Croix de Guerre (1939–45); President of the French Republic, 1981–95; advocate; *b* Jarnac, Charente, 26 Oct. 1916; *s* of Joseph Mitterrand and Yvonne (*née* Lorrain); *m* 1944, Danielle Gouze; two *s. Educ:* Coll. Saint-Paul, Angoulême; Facultés de droit et des lettres, Univ. of Paris. Licencié en droit, Lic. ès lettres;

Dip. d'études supérieures de droit public. Served War, 1939–40 (prisoner, escaped; Rosette de la Résistance); missions to London and to Algiers, 1943; Sec.-Gen., Organisation for Prisoners of War, War Victims and Refugees, 1944–46; Chm., UDSR, 1951–52. Deputy from Nièvre, 1946–58 and 1962–81; Minister for Ex-Servicemen, 1947–48; Sec. of State for Information, attached Prime Minister's Office, 1948–49; Minister for Overseas Territories, 1950–51; Minister of State, Jan.-Feb. 1952 and March 1952–July 1953; Deleg. to Council of Europe, July-Sept. 1953; Minister of the Interior, June 1954–Feb. 1955; Minister of State, 1956–57; Senator, 1959–62; Candidate for Presidency of France, 1965, 1974. Pres., Fedn of Democratic and Socialist Left, 1965–68; First Sec., Socialist Party, 1971–81. Vice-Pres., Socialist International, 1972–81. Pres., Conseil général de la Nièvre, 1964–81. *Publications:* Aux frontières de l'Union française, 1953; Présence française et abandon, 1957; La Chine au défi, 1961; Le Coup d'Etat permanent, 1964; Ma part de vérité, 1969; Un socialisme du possible, 1970; La rose au poing, 1973; La paille et le grain, 1975; Politique 1, 1977; L'Abeille et l'architecte, 1978; Ici et maintenant, 1980; Politique 2, 1981; Reflexions sur la politique extérieure de la France, 1986; numerous contribs to the Press. *Recreation:* golf. *Address:* 22 rue de Bièvre, 75005 Paris, France.   *Died 8 Jan. 1996.*

MITTON, Rev. Dr Charles Leslie, BA; MTh; PhD; Principal of Handsworth College, Birmingham, 1955–70 (Tutor, 1951–55); *b* 13 Feb. 1907; *s* of Rev. Charles W. Mitton, Bradford, Yorks; *m* 1937, Margaret J. Ramage; one *s* one *d. Educ:* Kingswood Sch., Bath; Manchester Univ.; Didsbury Coll., Manchester. Asst Tutor at Wesley Coll., Headingley, 1930–33; Minister in Methodist Church at: Dunbar, 1933–36; Keighley, 1936 39; Scunthorpe, 1939–45; Nottingham, 1945–51; Tutor in New Testament Studies at Handsworth Coll., Birmingham, 1951–70. Editor of Expository Times, 1965–76. Hon. DD Aberdeen, 1964. *Publications:* The Epistle to the Ephesians: Authorship, Origin and Purpose, 1951; Pauline Corpus of Letters, 1954; Preachers' Commentary on St Mark's Gospel, 1956; The Good News, 1961; The Epistle of James, 1966; Jesus: the fact behind the faith, 1974; The Epistle to the Ephesians: a commentary, 1976; Your Kingdom Come, 1978. *Recreations:* Rugby football, Association football, cricket, tennis. *Address:* 14 Cranbrook Road, Handsworth, Birmingham B21 8PJ. *T:* (0121) 554 7892.   *Died 7 March 1998.*

MOERAN, Edward Warner; *b* 27 Nov. 1903; *s* of E. J. Moeran; *m* Pymonie (*née* Fincham); one *d*; *m* 1938, Nadine Marie, Countess de Normanville; two *s* one *d. Educ:* Christ's Coll., Finchley; University of London. Solicitor. MP (Lab) South Beds, 1950 51. Pres., W London Law Soc., 1971–72. Chm., Solicitors' Ecology Gp, 1972–74. *Publications:* Practical Conveyancing, 1949; Invitation to Conveyancing, 1962; Practical Legal Aid, 1970; (jtly) Social Welfare Law, 1977; Legal Aid Summary, 1978; Introduction to Conveyancing, 1979.
                                     Died 12 Dec. 1997.

MOIR, Sir Ernest Ian Royds, 3rd Bt *cr* 1916; *b* 9 June 1925; *o s* of Sir Arrol Moir, 2nd Bt, and Dorothy Blanche, *d* of Admiral Sir Percy Royds, CB, CMG; *S* father, 1957; *m* 1954, Margaret Hanham Carter; three *s. Educ:* Rugby; Gonville and Caius Coll., Cambridge (BA 1949). Served War of 1939–45 in Royal Engineers. *Heir: s* Christopher Ernest Moir [*b* 22 May 1955; *m* 1983, Mrs Vanessa Kirtikar, *yr d* of V. A. Crosby; twin *s*, and one step *d*].
                                     Died 5 Aug. 1998.

MOIR CAREY, David Macbeth; *see* Carey.

MOKAMA, Hon. Moleleki Didwell, BA (Rhodes), LLM (Harvard), LLM (London); **Hon. Mr Justice Mokama;**

Advocate of the Supreme Court of Botswana; Chief Justice of Botswana, since 1992; *b* 2 Feb. 1933; *e s* of Mokama Moleleki and Baipoledi Moleleki, Maunatlala, Botswana; *m* 1962, Kgopodiso Vivien Robi; one *s. Educ:* Moeng; Fort Hare; London Univ. Called to the Bar, Inner Temple, 1962; Crown Counsel to Botswana Govt, 1963–66; High Comr for Botswana in London, 1966–69; Botswana Ambassador Extraordinary and Plenipotentiary: to France, 1967–69; to Germany, 1967–69; to Sweden, 1968–69; to Denmark, 1968–69; Attorney-Gen. of Botswana, 1969–91. Comr (1 of 11), African Commn on Human and People's Rights. Hon. Mem., American Soc. of International Law, 1965. *Recreations:* swimming, shooting, hunting. *Address:* Chief Justice's Chambers, Private Bag 1, Lobatse, Botswana. *Fax:* 332317, *Telex:* 2758 Court BD.
                                     Died 5 July 1997.

MOLESWORTH, 11th Viscount, *cr* 1716 (Ireland); **Richard Gosset Molesworth;** Baron Philipstown, 1716; *b* 31 Oct. 1907; *s* of 10th Viscount Molesworth and Elizabeth Gladys Langworthy (*d* 1974); *S* father, 1961; *m* 1958, Anne Florence Womersley, MA (*d* 1983); two *s. Educ:* Lancing Coll.; private tutors. Farmed for many years. Freeman, City of London, 1978. Served War, in RAF, 1941–44 (Middle East, 1941–43). *Recreations:* foreign travel, music. *Heir: s* Hon. Robert Bysse Kelham Molesworth [*b* 4 June 1959. *Educ:* Sussex Univ. (BA Hons)].   *Died 15 Oct. 1997.*

MOLESWORTH-ST AUBYN, Lt-Col Sir (John) Arscott, 15th Bt *cr* 1689, of Pencarrow; MBE 1963; DL; *b* 15 Dec. 1926; *s* of Sir John Molesworth-St Aubyn, 14th Bt, CBE, and Celia Marjorie (*d* 1965), *d* of Lt-Col Valentine Vivian, CMG, DSO, MVO; *S* father, 1985; *m* 1957, Iona Audrey Armatrude, *d* of late Adm. Sir Francis Loftus Tottenham, KCB, CBE; two *s* one *d. Educ:* Eton. 2nd Lieut KRRC 1946; Captain 1954; psc 1959; Major 1961; jssc 1964; served Malaya and Borneo, 1961–63 and 1965; Royal Green Jackets, 1966; Lt-Col 1967; retd 1969. County Comr, Scouts, Cornwall, 1969–79. Mem., Cornwall River Authority, 1969–74; Chairman: West Local Land Drainage Cttee, SW Water Authority, 1974–89; West Local Flood Alleviation Cttee, Nat. Rivers Authority, SW Region, 1989–92; Devon Exec. Cttee, 1975–77, and Cornwall Exec. Cttee, 1987–89, CLA. Wessex Region, Historic Houses Assoc., 1981–83. Pres., Royal Cornwall Agricl Assoc., 1976; Mem. Council, Devon County Agricl Assoc., 1979–82; JP Devon, 1971–84; DL Cornwall, 1971; High Sheriff Cornwall, 1975. *Recreations:* shooting, ornithology. *Heir: s* William Molesworth-St Aubyn [*b* 23 Nov. 1958; *m* 1988, Carolyn, *er d* of William Tozier; one *s* one *d*]. *Address:* Pencarrow, Bodmin, Cornwall PL30 3AG. *Clubs:* Army and Navy; Cornish 1768.
                                     Died 22 April 1998.

MONCRIEFF, William S.; *see* Scott-Moncrieff.

MONDAY, Horace Reginald, CBE 1967 (OBE 1958); JP; *b* 26 Nov. 1907; *s* of late James Thomas Monday, Gambia Civil Servant, and Rachel Ruth Davis; *m* 1932, Wilhelmina Roberta Juanita, *d* of late William Robertson Job Roberts, a Gambian businessman; one *s. Educ:* Methodist Mission Schools, Banjul, The Gambia; correspondence course with (the then) London Sch. of Accountancy. Clerk, 1925–48; Asst Acct, Treasury, 1948–52; Acct and Storekeeper, Marine Dept, 1953–54; Acct-Gen., The Gambia Govt, 1954–65; Chm., Gambia Public Service Commn, 1965–68; High Comr for The Gambia in the UK and NI, 1968–71. MP Banjul Central, 1977–82. Chairman: Management Cttee, Banjul City Council, 1971–79; Gambia Utilities Corp., 1972–76; Dir, Gambia Currency Bd, 1964–68. Governor, Gambia High Sch., 1964–68; Pres., Gambia Red Cross Soc., 1967–68. JP 1944. Comdr, National Order of Republic of Senegal, 1968. *Address:* Rachelville, 24 Clarkson Street, Banjul, The Gambia. *T:* 27511.

Died 5 Sept. 1996.

MONOD, Prof. Théodore André, DèsSc; Grand Officier de la Légion d'Honneur, 1997 (Officier, 1958; Commandeur, 1989); Professor Emeritus at National Museum of Natural History, Paris (Assistant 1922, Professor, 1942–73); *b* 9 April 1902; *s* of Rev. Wilfred Monod and Dorina (*née* Monod); *m* 1930, Olga Pickova; two *s* one *d. Educ:* Sorbonne (Paris). Docteur ès sciences, 1926. Sec.-Gen. (later Dir) of l'Institut Français d'Afrique Noire, 1938–65; Prof., Univ. of Dakar, 1957–59; Doyen, Science Faculty, Dakar, 1957–58. Mem. de l'Institut (Académie des Sciences), 1963; Member: Acad. des Sciences d'Outre-Mer, 1949; Académie de Marine, 1957; Corresp. Mem., Académie des Sciences de Lisbonne and Académie Royale des Sciences d'Outre-Mer. Dr *hc* Köln, 1965, Neuchâtel, 1968. Gold Medallist, Royal Geographical Soc., 1960; Gold Medallist, Amer. Geographical Soc., 1961; Haile Sellassie Award for African Research, 1967; Grande Médaille d'Or, Société pour l'Encouragement au Progrès, 1991; Lauréat, Prix Marguerite Yourcenar, 1991. Comdr, Ordre du Christ, 1953; Commandeur, Mérite Saharien, 1962; Officier de l'Ordre des Palmes Académiques, 1966, etc. *Publications:* Méharées, Explorations au vrai Sahara, 1937, 3rd edn 1989; L'Hippopotame et le philosophe, 1942; Bathyfolages, 1954, 2nd edn 1991; (ed) Pastoralism in Tropical Africa, 1976; L'Emeraude des Garamantes, Souvenirs d'un Saharien, 1984; Sahara, désert magique, 1986; Déserts, 1988; Mémoires d'un Naturaliste Voyageur, 1990; (with Brigitte Zanda) Le Fer de Dieu: histoire de la météorite de Chinguetti, 1992; many scientific papers in learned jls. *Address:* 14 quai d'Orléans, 75004 Paris, France. *T:* 43267950; Muséum national d'Histoire naturelle, 43 rue Cuvier, 75005 Paris, France. *T:* 40793750. *Died 22 Nov. 2000.*

MONTAGU, Prof. (Montague Francis) Ashley; *b* 28 June 1905; *o c* of Charles Ehrenberg and Mary Montagu; US citizen, 1940; *m* 1931, Helen Marjorie Peakes; one *s* two *d. Educ:* Central Foundation Sch., London; University College London; Univ. of Florence; Columbia Univ. (PhD 1937). Research Worker, Brit. Mus. (Natural Hist.), 1926; Curator, Physical Anthropology, Wellcome Hist. Mus., London, 1929; Asst Prof. of Anatomy, NY Univ., 1931–38; Dir, Div. of Child Growth and Develt, NY Univ., 1931–38; Associate Prof. of Anat., Hahnemann Med. Coll. and Hosp., Philadelphia, 1938–49; Prof. and Head of Dept of Anthropology, Rutgers Univ., 1949–55; Dir of Research, NJ Cttee on Growth and Develt, 1951–55. Chm., Anisfield-Wolf Award Cttee on Race Relations, 1950–96 (drafted Statement on Race, for Unesco, 1950). Vis. Lectr, Harvard Univ., 1945; Regent's Prof., Univ. of Calif, Santa Barbara, 1961; Lectr, Princeton Univ., 1978–83, and Dir, Inst. Natural Philosophy, 1979–85. Fellow, Stevenson Hall, Princeton Univ., 1978–. Produced, directed and financed film, One World or None, 1946. Hon. DSc: Grinnell Coll., Iowa, 1967; Univ. of N Carolina, 1987; Hon. DLitt Ursinus Coll., Pa, 1972. Distinguished Service Award, Amer. Anthropological Assoc., 1984; Phi Beta Kappa Distinguished Service Award, 1985; Distinguished Service Award, Nat. Assoc. of Parents and Professionals for Safe Alternatives in Childbirth, 1986; Distinguished Service Award, Rollo May Center for Humanistic Studies, 1991; Distinguished Service Award, Pre and Perinatal Psychology Assoc. of America, 1993; Lifetime Achievement and Charles Darwin Award, Amer. Assoc. of Physical Anthropologists, 1994. Eponymous annual award by US Common Bond Inst. and Harmony Inst. of Russia, instituted 1995. *Publications:* Coming Into Being Among the Australian Aborigines, 1937, 2nd edn 1974; Man's Most Dangerous Myth: the Fallacy of Race, 1942,

6th edn 1997; Edward Tyson, MD, FRS (1650–1708): and the Rise of Human and Comparative Anatomy in England, 1943; Introduction to Physical Anthropology, 1945, 3rd edn 1960; Adolescent Sterility, 1946; On Being Human, 1950, 2nd edn 1970; Statement on Race, 1951, 3rd edn 1972; On Being Intelligent, 1951, 3rd edn 1972; Darwin, Competition, and Cooperation, 1952; The Natural Superiority of Women, 1953, 4th edn 1992; Immortality, 1955; The Direction of Human Development, 1955, 2nd edn 1970; The Biosocial Nature of Man, 1956; Anthropology and Human Nature, 1957; Man: His First Million Years, 1957, 2nd edn 1969; The Reproductive Development of the Female, 1957, 3rd edn 1979; Education and Human Relations, 1958; The Cultured Man, 1958; Human Heredity, 1959, 2nd edn 1963; (with E. B. Steen) Anatomy and Physiology, 2 vols, 1959, 2nd edn 1984; A Handbook of Anthropometry, 1960; Man in Process, 1961; The Humanization of Man, 1962; Prenatal Influences, 1962; Race, Science and Humanity, 1963; (with John Lilly) The Dolphin in History, 1963; The Science of Man, 1964; Life Before Birth, 1964, 2nd edn 1978; The Human Revolution, 1965; The Idea of Race, 1965; (with C. Loring Brace) Man's Evolution, 1965; Up the Ivy, 1966; The American Way of Life, 1967; The Anatomy of Swearing, 1967; (with E. Darling) The Prevalence of Nonsense, 1967; (with Floyd Matson) The Human Dialogue, 1967; Man Observed, 1968; Man: His First Two Million Years, 1969; Sex, Man and Society, 1969; (with E. Darling) The Ignorance of Certainty, 1970; (with M. Levitan) Textbook of Human Genetics, 1971, 2nd edn 1977; Immortality, Religion and Morals, 1971; Touching: the human significance of the skin, 1971, 3rd edn 1986; The Elephant Man, 1971, 3rd edn 1996; (with S. S. Snyder) Man and the Computer, 1972; The Nature of Human Aggression, 1976; (with C. L. Brace) Human Evolution, 1977; (with F. Matson) The Human Connection, 1979; Growing Young, 1981, 2nd edn 1989; (with F. Matson) The Dehumanization of Man, 1983; What We Know About Race, 1985; Humanity Speaking to Humankind, 1986; Living and Loving, 1986; The Peace of the World, 1986; The World of Humanity, 1988; Coming into Being, 1988; *edited:* Studies and Essays in the History of Science and Learning; The Meaning of Love, 1953; Toynbee and History, 1956; Genetic Mechanisms in Human Disease, 1961; Atlas of Human Anatomy, 1961; Culture and the Evolution of Man, 1962; International Pictorial Treasury of Knowledge, 6 vols, 1962–63; The Concept of Race, 1967; The Concept of the Primitive, 1967; Culture: Man's Adaptive Dimension, 1968; Man and Aggression, 1968; The Origin and Evolution of Man, 1973; The Endangered Environment, 1973; Culture and Human Development, 1974; The Practice of Love, 1974; Frontiers of Anthropology, 1974; Race and IQ, 1975, 2nd edn 1996; Learning Non-Aggression, 1978; Sociobiology Examined, 1980; Science and Creationism, 1983. *Recreations:* book collecting, gardening. *Address:* 321 Cherry Hill Road, Princeton, NJ 08540, USA. *T:* (609) 9243756.

Died 26 Nov. 1999.

MONTAGUE OF OXFORD, Baron *cr* 1997 (Life Peer), of Oxford in the co. of Oxfordshire; **Michael Jacob Montague,** CBE 1970; Chairman: Superframe plc, since 1995; Acorn Assets Ltd; *b* 10 March 1932; *s* of David Elias Montague and Eleanor Stagg. *Educ:* High Wycombe Royal Grammar Sch.; Magdalen Coll. Sch., Oxford. Founded Gatehill Beco Ltd, 1958 (sold to Valor Co., 1962); Man. Dir, 1963, Chm., 1965–91, Yale and Valor plc. Non-executive Director: Pleasurama PLC, 1985–88; Jarvis Hotels Ltd, 1990–; Williams Hldgs plc, 1991–92. Chairman: English Tourist Bd, 1979–84; Nat. Consumer Council, 1984–87; Member: BTA, 1979–84; Ordnance Survey Advisory Bd, 1983–85; Millennium Commn,

1994–97. Pres., BAIE, 1983–85; Chairman: Asia Cttee, BNEC, 1968–71; Henley Festival Ltd, 1992–94. Pres., Econ. and Industrial Res. Soc., 1990–; Vice-Pres., Royal Albert Hall, 1992–94 (Mem. Council, 1985–). *Address:* House of Lords, SW1A 0PW. *Died 5 Nov. 1999.*

MONTAGUE-JONES, Brig. Ronald, CBE 1944 (MBE 1941); jssc; psc; *b* 10 Dec. 1909; *yr s* of late Edgar Montague Jones (formerly Headmaster of St Albans Sch., Herts), and Emmeline Mary Yates; *m* 1st, 1937, Denise Marguerite (marr. diss.), *y d* of late General Sir Hubert Gough, GCB, GCMG, KCVO; one *s*; 2nd, 1945, Barbara Elizabeth Margaret, *d* of Bruce Gibbon; 3rd, 1955, Pamela, *d* of late Lieut-Col Hastings Roy Harington, 8th Gurkha Rifles, and Hon. Mrs Harington; one *s. Educ:* St Albans; RMA, Woolwich; St John's Coll., Cambridge (BA 1933, MA 1937). 2nd Lieut RE 1930; Temp. Brig. 1943; Bt Lt-Col 1952; Brig. 1958. Egypt, 1935; Palestine, 1936–39 (despatches twice); War of 1939–45 (MBE, CBE, US Bronze Star, Africa Star, 1939–45 Star, Italy Star, Burma Star, General Service Medal with Clasps Palestine, SE Asia and Malaya). CC Dorset, for Swanage, 1964–85. Br. Pres., Royal British Legion. *Address:* 10 Battlemead, Swanage, Dorset BH19 1PH. *T:* Swanage (01929) 423186. *Died 18 Aug. 1996.*

MONTGOMERY, Group Captain George Rodgers, CBE 1946; DL; RAF (retired); Secretary, Norfolk Naturalists' Trust, 1963–75; Hon. Appeal Secretary, and Member of the Court, University of East Anglia, since 1966; *b* 31 May 1910; *s* of late John Montgomery, Belfast; *m* 1st, 1932, Margaret McHarry Heslip (*d* 1981), *d* of late William J. Heslip, Belfast; two *s*; 2nd, 1982, Margaret Stephanie (*née* Reynolds), *widow* of Colin Vanner Hedworth Foulkes. *Educ:* Royal Academy, Belfast. Commnd in RAF, 1928; served in UK and ME, 1928–38; War of 1939–45: Bomber Comd, NI, Air Min. and ME; served UK, Japan and W Europe, 1946–58: Comdr RAF Wilmslow, 1946–47; Air Adviser to UK Polit. Rep. in Japan, and Civil Air Attaché, Tokyo, 1948–49; Chief Instr RAF Officers' Advanced Trg Sch., 1950; Comdt RAF Sch. of Admin, Bircham Newton, 1951–52; Comdr RAF Hednesford, 1953–54; Dep. Dir of Orgn (Estabts) Air Min. and Chm. RAF Western European Estabts Cttee, Germany, 1955–57; retd 1958. On retirement, Organising Sec. Friends of Norwich Cathedral, 1959–62; Appeal Sec., Univ. of East Anglia, 1961–66; Hon. Vice-President: Norfolk Naturalists' Trust, 1979–; Broads Soc., 1983–; Mem., Great Bustard Trust Council, 1972–. DL Norfolk, 1979. *Recreations:* river cruising, gardening. *Address:* 24 Cathedral Close, Norwich, Norfolk NR1 4DZ. *T:* (01603) 628024. *Clubs:* Royal Air Force; Norfolk (Norwich). *Died 8 Feb. 1997.*

MOODY, Helen Wills; *see* Roark, H. W.

MOORE, Antony Ross, CMG 1965; HM Diplomatic Service, retired; *b* 30 May 1918; *o s* of late Arthur Moore and Eileen Maillet; *m* 1st, 1941, Philippa Weigall (marr. diss.); two *d*; 2nd, 1963, Georgina Mary Galbraith; one *s. Educ:* Rugby; King's Coll., Cambridge. Served in Friends Ambulance Unit, 1939–40; HM Forces, 1940–46. Apptd Mem., Foreign (subseq. Diplomatic) Service, 1946; transf. to Rome, 1947; FO, 1949; 1st Sec., 1950; transf. to Tel Aviv, 1952; acted as Chargé d'Affaires, 1953, 1954; apptd Consul, Sept. 1953; FO, 1955; UK Perm. Delegn to UN, NY, 1957; Counsellor and transf. to IDC, 1961; FO, 1962–64; Internat. Fellow, Center for Internat. Affairs, Harvard Univ., 1964–65; Regional Information Officer, Middle East, British Embassy, Beirut, 1965–67; Head of Eastern Dept, FO, 1967; retd, 1968. Dir, Iranian Selection Trust, 1969–72. *Address:* Touchbridge, Boarstall, Aylesbury, Bucks HP18 9UJ. *T:* (01844) 238247. *Died 3 Nov. 2000.*

MOORE, Brian; novelist; *b* 25 Aug. 1921; *s* of James Bernard Moore, FRCS, Northern Ireland, and Eileen McFadden; *m* 1st, 1952, Jacqueline Scully (marr. diss.); one *s*; 2nd, 1966, Jean Denney. Guggenheim Fellowship (USA), 1959; Canada Council Senior Fellowship (Canada), 1960; Scottish Arts Council Internat. Fellowship, 1983. National Institute of Arts and Letters (USA) Fiction Award 1960. *Publications: novels:* The Lonely Passion of Judith Hearne, 1955 (filmed, 1989); The Feast of Lupercal, 1956; The Luck of Ginger Coffey (Governor-Gen. of Canada's Award for Fiction), 1960 (filmed, 1963); An Answer from Limbo, 1962; The Emperor of Ice-Cream, 1965; I am Mary Dunne, 1968; Fergus, 1970; Catholics, 1972 (W. H. Smith Literary Award, 1973); The Great Victorian Collection (James Tait Black Meml Award; Governor Gen. of Canada's Award for Fiction), 1975; The Doctor's Wife, 1976; The Mangan Inheritance, 1979; The Temptation of Eileen Hughes, 1981; Cold Heaven, 1983 (filmed, 1990); Black Robe, 1985 (Heinemann Award, RSL, 1986; filmed 1991); The Colour of Blood (Sunday Express Book of the Year Award), 1987; Lies of Silence, 1990; No Other Life, 1993; The Statement, 1995; The Magician's Wife, 1997; *non-fiction:* Canada (with Editors of Life), 1964; The Revolution Script, 1972. *Address:* c/o Curtis Brown Ltd, 10 Astor Place, New York, NY 10003, USA.
 Died 11 Jan. 1999.

MOORE, Rt Rev. Edward Francis Butler, DD; Bishop of Kilmore and Elphin and Ardagh, 1959–81; *b* 30 Jan. 1906; *s* of Rev. W. R. R. Moore; *m* 1932, Frances Olivia Scott; two *s* two *d. Educ:* Trinity Coll., Dublin (MA, PhD, DD). Deacon, 1930; priest, 1931; Curate, Bray, 1930–32; Hon. Clerical Vicar, Christ Church Cathedral, Dublin, 1931–35; Curate, Clontarf, 1932–34; Incumbent, Castledermot with Kinneagh, 1934–40; Greystones, Diocese of Glendalough, 1940–49; Chaplain to Duke of Leinster, 1934–40; Rural Dean, Delgany 1950–59; Canon of Christ Church, Dublin, 1951–57; Archdeacon of Glendalough, 1957–59. *Recreations:* tennis, golf, fishing. *Address:* Drumlona, Sea Road, Kilcoole, Co. Wicklow, Ireland. *Club:* Royal Dublin Society (Dublin). *Died 13 Dec. 1997.*

MOORE, Maj.-Gen. Frederick David, CB 1955; CBE 1954; *b* 27 Nov. 1902; *s* of Sir Frederick W. Moore and Phyllis, *d* of Robert Paul, Broomhill, Co. Dublin; *m* 1932, Anna Morrell Hamilton (*d* 1974), *d* of Col T. H. M. Clarke, CMG, DSO; one *s. Educ:* Wellington Coll.; RMA Woolwich. Commnd in RFA, 1923; served War of 1939–45: BEF 1940, 5th Regt RHA; BLA, 1944–45, CO 5th Regt RHA and CRA 53rd (W) Div.; GOC 5th AA Group, 1953–55; retd, 1956. DL Beds, 1958, Vice-Lieutenant, 1964–70. Officer Order of Crown (Belgian); Croix de Guerre (Belgian), 1940, with palm, 1945. *Recreations:* country pursuits. *Address:* Riverview, Bunclody, Co. Wexford, Ireland. *T:* (54) 77184. *Club:* Army and Navy. *Died 14 Sept. 1997.*

MOORE, Prof. Geoffrey Herbert; Professor of American Literature and Head of the Department of American Studies, University of Hull, 1962–82, then Professor Emeritus; *b* 10 June 1920; *e s* of late Herbert Jonathan Moore, Norwich; *m* 1947, Pamela Marguerite (marr. diss. 1962; she *d* 1998), *d* of Bertram Munn, Twickenham; one *s* one *d. Educ:* Mitcham Grammar Sch.; Emmanuel Coll., Cambridge; Univ. of Paris. 1st Cl. English Tripos, Cambridge, 1946; MA 1951. War Service (Air Ministry and RAF), 1939–43. Instr in English, Univ. of Wisconsin, 1947–49; Vis. Prof. of English, Univs of Kansas City and New Mexico, 1948, 1949; Asst Prof. of English, Tulane Univ., 1949–51; Vis. Prof. of English, Univ. of Southern California and Claremont Coll., 1950; Extra Mural Lectr, London and Cambridge Univs, 1951–52; Editor and Producer, BBC Television Talks, 1952–54; Rose Morgan

Prof., Univ. of Kansas, 1954–55; Lectr in Amer. Lit., Manchester Univ., 1955–59; Vis. Lectr, Univs of Mainz, Göttingen and Frankfurt, 1959; Rockefeller Fellow, Harvard Univ., 1959–60; Sen. Lectr in Amer. Lit., Manchester Univ., 1960–62; Dean, Faculty of Arts, Univ. of Hull, 1967–69. Visiting Professor: Univs of Montpellier, Aix-en-Provence and Nice, 1967, 1971; Univs of Frankfurt, Heidelberg, Mainz, Saarbrücken, Tübingen, 1967, 1968; Univs of Perpignan, Turin, Florence, Pisa, Rome, New Delhi, Hyderabad, Madras, Bombay, Calcutta, 1971; York Univ., Toronto, 1969–70; Univ. of Tunis, 1970, 1971; Harvard, 1971; Univs of Düsseldorf, Heidelberg, Freiburg, Mainz, 1972; Univs of Teheran, Shiraz, Isfahan, Mashad, 1978; Univs of Berlin, Bremen, Osnabrück, 1981; Univs of Münster, Duisburg, Bonn, Düsseldorf, Aachen, 1982; Univ. of Göttingen, 1983; Tällberg, Sweden, 1984; Univs of Madrid, Bilbao, Barcelona, 1985; Univs of Warsaw, Lodz, Katowice, Cracow, 1992; Univs of Athens and Thessaloniki, 1993; Fellow, Sch. of Letters, Indiana Univ., 1970; Research Fellow: Univ. of California at San Diego, 1974; Rockefeller Centre, Bellagio, 1979. Mem. Cttee, British Assoc. for Amer. Studies, 1957–60. Sen. Scholar Award, Amer. Council of Learned Socs, 1965. Editor and Founder, The Bridge (Cambridge lit. mag.), 1946; reviewer, Financial Times, 1976–; Gen. Editor of Henry James for Penguin Classics, 1981–. *Publications:* Voyage to Chivalry (under pseud.), 1947; Poetry from Cambridge in Wartime, 1947; The Penguin Book of Modern American Verse, 1954; (ed) 58 Short Stories by O. Henry, 1956; Poetry Today, 1958; American Literature and the American Imagination, 1964; American Literature, 1964; The Penguin Book of American Verse, 1977, 2nd edn 1983; *edited:* Portrait of a Lady, 1984; Roderick Hudson, 1986; Daisy Miller, 1986; Selected Poems of Emily Dickinson, 1986; Selected Poems of Robert Frost, 1986; Selected Poems of Walt Whitman, 1987; Selected Poems of Edgar Allan Poe, 1988; Selected Poems of Longfellow, 1989; Selected Poems of Thomas Hardy, 1990; Selected Poems of John Keats, 1991; Selected Poems of Rudyard Kipling, 1992; Selected Poems of William Wordsworth, 1992; Selected Poems of Gerard Manley Hopkins, 1993; Selected Poems of Tennyson, 1994; articles in TLS, Amer. Mercury, BBC Quarterly, Kenyon Review, Review of English Lit., The Year's Work in English Studies, Jl of American Studies, Studi Americani and other scholarly and literary jls. *Recreations:* swimming, driving. *Club:* Savile.   *Died 5 Feb. 1999.*

MOORE, His Honour George Edgar; HM First Deemster and Clerk of the Rolls, Isle of Man, 1969–74; *b* 13 July 1907; *er s* of Ramsey Bignall Moore, OBE, formerly HM Attorney-General for Isle of Man, and Agnes Cannell Moore; *m* 1937, Joan Mary Kissack; one *s* one *d*. *Educ:* Rydal School. Served in RAF, 1940–45 (Sqdn Ldr). Admitted to Manx Bar, 1930; Attorney-General for Isle of Man, 1957–63; HM Second Deemster, 1963–69. MLC; Chairman: IoM Criminal Injuries Compensation Tribunal, 1967–69; IoM Income Tax Appeal Comrs, 1969–74; Tynwald Common Market Select Cttee, 1970–74; Mem., Exec. Council Manx Museum and Nat. Trust, 1970–74; Chm. of Directors: Commercial Bank of Wales (IoM) Ltd, 1975–84; Securicor (IoM) Ltd, 1975–83; Trustee, Manx Blind Welfare Soc.; Pres., Isle of Man Badminton Assoc., 1953–72; Hon. County Representative of Royal Air Force Benevolent Assoc., 1948–72. *Address:* Brookdale, 8 Cronkbourne Road, Douglas, Isle of Man. *Club:* Ellan Vannin (IoM).   *Died 8 April 1996.*

MOORE, Gordon Charles; Chief Executive, City of Bradford Metropolitan Council, 1974–86, retired; *b* 23 July 1928; *s* of John Edward and Jessie Hamilton Moore; *m* 1956, Ursula Rawle; one *s* two *d*. *Educ:* Uppingham; St Catharine's Coll., Cambridge (MA, LLM). Solicitor. Legal

Asst, Cambs CC, 1955–56; Asst Solicitor: Worcester CB, 1956–58; Bath CB, 1958–60; Sen. Asst Solicitor: Bath CB, 1960–63; Croydon CB, 1963–65; Asst Town Clerk, Croydon LB, 1965; Dep. Town Clerk, Bradford CB, 1965–68, Town Clerk, 1968–74. FRSA; CIMgt. Hon. DLitt Bradford, 1986. Silver Jubilee Medal, 1977. *Recreations:* music, railways, supporting Yorkshire County Cricket. *Address:* 22 Fern Hill Road, Shipley, W Yorks BD18 4SL. *T:* (01274) 585606.
Died 18 Jan. 1998.

MOORE, Hon. Sir John (Cochrane), AC 1986; Kt 1976; President, Australian Conciliation and Arbitration Commission, 1973–85; *b* 5 Nov. 1915; *s* of E. W. and L. G. Moore; *m* 1st, 1946, Julia Fay (*d* 1986), *d* of Brig. G. Drake-Brockman; two *s* two *d*; 2nd, 1988, Freda Beryl. *Educ:* N Sydney Boys' High Sch.; Univ. of Sydney (BA, LLB). Private, AIF, 1940; R of O Hon. Captain 1945. Admitted NSW Bar, 1940; Dept of External Affairs, 1945; 2nd Sec., Aust. Mission to UN, 1946; practice, NSW Bar, 1947–59; Dep. Pres., Commonwealth Conciliation and Arbitration Commn, 1959–72, Actg Pres. 1972–73. Chm. (Pres.), Aust. Council of Nat. Trusts, 1969–82; President: Nat. Trust of Aust. (NSW), 1966–69; Ind. Relations Soc. of NSW, 1972–73; Ind. Relations Soc. of Aust., 1973–74. Pres., NSW Br., Scout Assoc. of Aust., 1978–82. Hon. Vis. Prof., Univ. of NSW, 1987; Hon. Res. Associate, Univ. of Sydney, 1987. *Recreations:* swimming, reading. *Address:* 2 Lindfield Manor, 1 Bent Street, Lindfield, NSW 2070, Australia.   *Died 30 Aug. 1998.*

MOORE, Very Rev. Peter Clement, OBE 1993; Dean of St Albans, 1973–93, then Dean Emeritus; *b* 4 June 1924; *s* of Rev. G. G. Moore and Vera (*née* Mylrea); *m* 1965, Mary Claire (*d* 1993), *o d* of P. A. M. Malcolm and Celia (*née* Oldham); one *s* one *d*. *Educ:* Cheltenham Coll.; Christ Church, Oxford (MA; DPhil 1954); Cuddesdon Coll., Oxford. Deacon 1947, priest 1948; Minor Canon of Canterbury Cathedral and Asst Master, Cathedral Choir School, 1947–49; Curate of Bladon with Woodstock, 1949–51; Chaplain, New Coll., Oxford, 1949–51; Vicar of Alfrick with Lulsley, 1952–59; Hurd Librarian to Bishop of Worcester, 1953–62; Vicar of Pershore with Pinvin and Wick, 1959–67; Rural Dean of Pershore, 1965–67; Canon Residentiary of Ely Cathedral, 1967–73, Vice-Dean, 1971–73. Select Preacher, Oxford Univ., 1986–87. Member: Archbishops' Liturgical Commission, 1968–76; General Synod, 1978–85; Governing Body, SPCK. Past Master, Worshipful Co. of Glaziers and Painters of Glass. Mem., Woodard Corp. Trustee, Historic Churches Preservation Trust. FSA. OStJ 1987. *Publications:* Tomorrow is Too Late, 1970; Man, Woman and Priesthood, 1978; Footholds in the Faith, 1980; Crown in Glory, 1982; Bishops: but what kind?, 1982; In Vitro Veritas, 1985; The Synod of Westminster, 1985; Sharing the Glory, 1990. *Recreations:* gardening, music, fishing, barrel organs. *Address:* Amesbury Abbey, Amesbury, Wilts. *Club:* United Oxford & Cambridge University.
Died 16 June 2000.

MOORE, Robert, CBE 1973; Commissioner for Local Administration in Scotland, 1975–78; *b* 2 Nov. 1915; *m* 1940, Jean Laird Dick (*d* 1995); two *s*. *Educ:* Dalziel High Sch., Motherwell; Glasgow Univ. (BL). Admitted solicitor, 1939. Town Clerk, Port Glasgow, 1943–48; Secretary, Eastern Regional Hosp. Bd, 1948–60; Principal Officer: Scottish Hosp. Administrative Staffs Cttee, 1960–74; Manpower Div., Scottish Health Service, 1974–75. Lectr in Administrative Law, St Andrews Univ., 1960–65; External Examr in Administrative Law, Glasgow Univ., 1967–71. Mem., Scottish Cttee, Council on Tribunals, 1964–82. *Address:* 20/35 Craiglea Place, Edinburgh EH10 5QD. *T:* (0131) 447 5493.   *Died 4 April 1998.*

MORAY, Edward Bruce D.; *see* Dawson-Moray.

MORCOM, Rev. Canon Anthony John; b 24 July 1916; s of late Dr Alfred Farr Morcom and Sylvia Millicent Morcom (née Birchenough); m 1st, 1955, Pamela Cappel Bain (d 1963); 2nd, 1965, Richenda, widow of Frederick Williams. Educ: Repton; Clare Coll., Cambridge; Cuddesdon Coll. Deacon 1939, priest 1940, Curate: St Mary Magdalene, Paddington, 1939 42; St Mary the Virgin, Pimlico, 1942–47; Domestic Chaplain to the Bishop of London, 1947–55; Archdeacon of Middx, 1953–66; Vicar of St Cyprian's, Clarence Gate, 1955–66; Vicar of St Mary the Less, Cambridge, 1966–73; Rural Dean of Cambridge, 1971–73; Residentiary Canon, 1974–84, Vice-Dean, 1981–84, Ely Cathedral. Recreation: travel. Address: 33 Porson Road, Cambridge CB2 2ET. T: (01223) 362352. Clubs: United Oxford & Cambridge University, MCC.   Died 2 Dec. 1997.

MORCOM, John Brian; a Social Security Commissioner, since 1981; a Child Support Commissioner, since 1993; b 31 May 1925; s of Albert John Morcom and Alice Maud Morcom (née Jones), Carmarthen; m 1st, 1958, Valerie Lostie de Kerhor Rivington (d 1960); one s; 2nd, 1965, Sheila Myfanwy Adams-Lewis (d 1986); one d. Educ: Queen Elizabeth Grammar Sch., Carmarthen; Balliol Coll., Oxford (State schol., 1943; MA). Bevin Ballottee, Oakdale Colliery, 1944; Medical Orderly, RAMC, Talgarth Mil. Mental Hosp. and BMH Suez, 1944–47. Called to the Bar, Inner Temple, 1952, Lincoln's Inn, 1955; Wales and Chester Circuit, 1954–81. Publications: Estate Duty Saving, 1959, 5th edn 1972; (jtly) Capital Transfer Tax, 1976, 2nd edn 1978. Recreations: Welsh genealogy, forestry. Address: Social Security Commission, Harp House, 83–86 Farringdon Street, EC1A 4DH. Clubs: Royal Commonwealth Society, London Welsh Association.   Died 29 Jan. 1997.

MORCOS-ASAAD, Prof. Fikry Naguib; Professor of Architecture, Department of Architecture and Building Science, University of Strathclyde, 1970–85, Professor Emeritus since 1986; b 27 Sept. 1930; s of Naguib and Marie A. Morcos-Asaad; m 1958, Sarah Ann (née Gribben); three s. Educ: Cairo Univ. (BArch); Georgia Inst. of Techn. (MArch); MIT (SM); IIT (PhD). FRIAS Lectr in Architecture, Fac. of Engrg, Cairo Univ., 1952–54 and 1958–63; Dir of Structural Studies, Sch. of Arch., Univ. of Liverpool, 1963–70. Design Critic and Vis. Prof. in Arch. Engrg, Calif State Polytechnic Univ., 1969, 1970 and 1973; Vis. Prof. of Architecture, Assuit Univ., Egypt, 1980; Vis. Prof. of Architecture, 1985, of Architecture and Res., 1986–89, Univ. of Jordan, Amman. Research into: culture and arch.; housing design in hot, dry climates; prefabricated multi-storey housing in developing countries. Comr, Royal Fine Art Commn for Scotland, 1972–86; formerly Mem. Educn Cttee, Architects Registration Council of UK; former Member Council: Glasgow Inst. of Architects; Royal Incorp. of Architects in Scotland; Mem. Council, Glasgow Coll. of Building and Printing. Mem., Rotary International. Publications: Circular Forms in Architecture, 1955; High Density Concretes for Radiation Shielding, 1956; Structural Parameters in Multi-Storey Buildings under Dynamic Loading, 1956; The Egyptian Village, 1956; Architectural Construction, vol. 1 1960, vol. 2 1961; Plastic Design in Steel, 1975; Large-span Structures, 1976; Brickwork: some pertinent points, 1978; Design and Building for a Tropical Environment, 1978; Structural Systems in Architectural Configuration, 1987; Understanding Architectural Structure, 1988; various papers on structural form in architecture and on socio-cultural considerations in urban design. Recreations: renovation of antique clocks, gardening, reading, travelling. Address: Staneacre House, Townhead Street, Hamilton ML3 7BP. T: (01698) 420644. Clubs: Rotary, Burns, Hamilton Civic Society (Hamilton).   Died 8 June 1998.

MORGAN, Ellis, CMG 1961; HM Diplomatic Service, retired; b 26 Dec. 1916; s of late Ben Morgan and Mary Morgan, The Grove, Three Crosses, Gower, S Wales, m 1st, 1948, Molly Darby (marr. dlss.); three d; 2nd, 1975, Mary, d of late Slade Baker Stallard-Penoyre; one s twin d (one decd). Educ: Bishop Gore Grammar Sch., Swansea. Dep. Librarian, County Borough of Swansea, 1937–39. Commissioned Royal Artillery, 1941; served War of 1939–45, in India, Burma, Malaya, 1943–47. Entered Foreign (subseq. Diplomatic) Service, 1948; 3rd Sec., 1948–50, 2nd Sec., 1951–53, subseq. 1st Sec., British Embassy, Rangoon; 1st Sec., British Embassy, Bangkok, 1954–55; 1st Sec., Office of Commissioner-Gen., Singapore, 1957–60; Student at Imperial Defence Coll., 1961; Counsellor: UK High Commission, New Delhi, 1964; FO, later FCO, 1966–73; Political and Economic Adviser, Commercial Union Assurance, 1973–79. Club: Farmers'.   Died 29 Oct. 1998.

MORGAN, John Lewis, OBE 1981; Member (C) Test Valley Borough Council, since 1974; b 12 May 1919; s of Charles Lewis Morgan and Elsie Winifred (née Smith); m 1943, Grace Barnes; one s three d. Educ: St Paul's Sch. Member: Wherwell Parish Council, 1947– (Chm., 1962–); Andover RDC, 1950–74 (Vice-Chm., 1960–72; Chm., 1972–74; Chm. of Finance, 1956–74); Hampshire CC, 1956–66; Mayor of Test Valley, 1977–78 and 1978–79. Mem., Assoc. of Dist Councils, 1974–97 (Chm., 1984–87, Vice-Chm., 1983–84; Chm. of Housing and Environmental Health, 1979–83); President: IULA/CEMR (British Sections), 1984–98 (Chm., 1980–84); CLRAE, Strasbourg, 1987–90 (Mem., 1975–; Vice-Pres., 1984–87; Pres., 1987–90; 1st Vice-Pres., 1990–94; Chm., Environment and Town Planning Cttee, 1983–85); Chm., Eur. Affairs Cttee, IULA, The Hague, 1981–86; Vice Chm., CEMR Paris, 1981–87; Chm., Consultative Cttee, CEMR/IULA, Brussels, 1986–94. Church lay reader. Recreations: keen supporter of Southampton Football Club, avid gardener. Address: Dancing Ledge, Wherwell, Andover, Hants SP11 7JS. T: (01264) 860296, Died 7 Jan. 2000.

MORGAN, Rt Hon. William (James); PC (NI) 1961; Member (UUUC) for North Belfast, Northern Ireland Constitutional Convention, 1975–76; b 17 July 1914; m 1942, Dorothy; two s one d. Retired company director. MP, Oldpark Div. of Belfast, 1949–58, Clifton Div. of Belfast, 1959–69, NI Parlt; Minister: of Health and Local Government, Northern Ireland, 1961–64; of Labour and National Insurance, 1964; of Health and Social Services, 1965–69. Address: 6 Demesne Grove, Holywood, Co. Down, N Ireland BT18 9NQ. T: (01232) 423925.
                                        Died 12 May 1999.

MORITA, Akio, Hon. KBE 1992; Hon. Chairman, Sony Corporation, since 1994 (Chairman, 1976–94); b Nagoya, Japan, 26 Jan. 1921; s of Shuko Morita and S. Kyuzaemon; m 1950, Yoshiko Kamei; two s one d. educ: Osaka Imperial Univ. (BSc Physics). Sony corporation, Tokyo (formerly Tokyo Tsushin Kogyo K. K); co-founder, 1946; Man. Dir. 1047–55; Sen. Man. dir, 1955–56; Exec. Vice-Pres., 1959–71; Pres., 1971–76; Chief Executive Officer, 1976–93; Sony Corporation of America: Pres., 1960–66, Chm., 1966–72; Chm. Finance Cttee, 1972–74; Chm. Exec. Cttee, 1974–77; Chm. Finance Cttee, 1977–81; Chm., Exec. Cttee, 1981–94. Dir, IBM World Trade Americas/Far East Corp., 1972–77; Mem., Internat. Council, Morgan Guaranty Trust Co. chm., Cttee on Internat. Industrial Co-operation, Keidanren (Japan Fedn of Economic Organizations), 1981–94; Vice-Chm., Bd of councillors, Keidanren, 1992–94 (Chm., Council for better Corporate Citizenship). Albert Medal, RSA 1982. Officier de la Légion d'Honneur, France, 1984; Commander's Cross, Order of Merit, FRG. Publications: Gakureki

Muyooron (Never Mind Education Records), 1966; Shin Jitsuryoku (A New Merit System), 1969; Made in Japan: Akio Morita and the Sony Corporation (autobiog.), 1987; (jtly) A Japan That Can Say No, 1989. *Recreations:* music, golf, tennis. *Address:* Sony Corporation, 6–7–35 Kitashinagawa, Shinagawa-ku, Tokyo 141, Japan. *T:* (3) 54482111. *Died 3 Oct. 1999.*

MORLEY, Cecil Denis, CBE 1967; Secretary General, The Stock Exchange, London, 1965–71; retired; *b* 20 May 1911; *s* of Cornelius Cecil Morley and Mildred Irene Hutchinson; *m* 1936, Lily Florence Younge (*d* 1992); one *s. Educ:* Clifton; Trinity Coll., Cambridge. Solicitor, 1935. Asst Sec., Share & Loan Dept, Stock Exchange, 1936; Sec. to Council of Stock Exchange, 1949. Served War of 1939–45, Major RA (TA). *Recreations:* travel, gardening. *Address:* The Dower House, Headbourne Worthy, Winchester, Hants SO23 7JG. *T:* (01962) 886065. *Died 14 Feb. 1999.*

MORLEY, Eric Douglas; Chairman, Miss World Ltd; joined Mecca Ltd, 1946, Chairman on leaving, 1978; Director, Grand Metropolitan Group, 1970–78; *b* 26 Sept. 1918; *s* of William Joseph Morley and Bertha Emily Menzies; orphaned age 11; *m* 1958, Julia Evelyn Pritchard; four *s* (one *d* decd). *Educ:* grammar sch.; Army. Training ship, Exmouth, 1930–34; Royal Fusiliers Band Boy, 1934; left Army, 1945 (Captain). Creator: Come Dancing, 1949 (world's longest-running TV series); Miss World, 1951 (world's greatest beauty pageant with TV audience of over 2·5 billion in 155 countries in 1997, a world record for any such pageant); introduced commercial bingo to UK, 1961. President: Outward Bound Trust; Variety Clubs Internat., 1977–79 (world's greatest children's charity); with wife, Julia, has raised over £100 million for charity worldwide. Freeman and Liveryman, City of London. Contested (C) Dulwich, Oct. 1974 and 1979 (reduced majority of the then Attorney-Gen. from 7,500 to 122). Liveryman, Marketors' Co. *Publications:* Miss World Story, 1967; 50 Years of Miss World and Come Dancing (autobiog.). *Recreations:* London Marathon for charity, French horn. *Club:* MCC. *Died 9 Nov. 2000.*

MORO, Peter, CBE 1977; FRIBA; architect; *b* 27 May 1911; *s* of Prof. Ernst Moro and Grete Hönigswald; *m* 1940, Anne Vanneck (marr. diss. 1984); three *d. Educ:* Stuttgart, Berlin and Zürich. Swiss Dip. Architecture, 1936; FRIBA 1948; FSIAD 1957. Practice with Tecton, 1937–39; Mem. Exec. Cttee, Mars Gp, 1938; Lectr, Sch. of Arch., Regent Street Polytechnic, 1941–47; LCC Associated Architect, Royal Festival Hall (later listed), 1948–51; Peter Moro Partnership, 1952–86; Tutor, Architectural Assoc., 1954–55. External Examiner: Strathclyde Univ., 1973, 1975; Manchester Univ., 1977, 1981; Visiting Critic: Thames Polytechnic; Bath Univ.; Oxford Polytechnic; Sheffield Univ.; QUB. Architect: Fairlawn Sch., LCC, 1957; own house, 1957 (listed 1988); Nottingham Playhouse, 1964 (listed 1994); alterations, Royal Opera House, Covent Garden, 1964; Birstall Sch., Leics, 1964; housing schemes, GLC and Southwark, 1967–80; theatre, Hull Univ., the Gulbenkian Centre, 1970; additions and alterations, Bristol Old Vic, 1972; theatre, New Univ. of Ulster, 1976; Plymouth Theatre Royal, 1982; Taliesin Theatre, UC Swansea, 1984; theatre planning consultants, Hong Kong Acad. for Performing Arts, 1983–85. Sen. Pres., Assoc. of British Theatre Technicians (Founder Mem.); Member: Council, RIBA, 1967–73; Housing the Arts Cttee, Arts Council of GB, 1975–78. Governor, Ravensbourne Coll. of Art and Design, 1976–87. Lectured in UK, Finland, Norway, Germany and Holland. Bronze Medal, RIBA, 1964; 4 Civic Trust Awards and Commendations; Heritage Award, 1975; Concrete Award, 1983. *Publications:* contribs to technical jls in UK, Germany, France, Italy, Portugal and

Japan. *Recreation:* tennis. *Address:* 20 Blackheath Park, SE3 9RP. *T:* (0181) 852 0250. *Died 10 Oct. 1998.*

MORPURGO, Prof. Jack Eric; Professor of American Literature, University of Leeds, 1969–83, then Emeritus; author; *b* 26 April 1918; *s* of late Mark Morpurgo, Islington; *m* 1946, Catherine Noel Kippe (*d* 1993), *d* of late Prof. Emile Cammaerts; three *s* one *d. Educ:* Christ's Hosp.; Univ. of New Brunswick; Coll. of William and Mary, USA (BA; Hon. Fellow, 1949); Durham Univ. Enlisted RA, 1939; served as regimental and staff officer in India, Middle East, Greece and Italy; GSO 2, Public Relations Directorate, War Office. Editorial Staff, Penguin Books, 1946–49; Editor, Penguin Parade; General Editor, Pelican Histories, 1949–67; Asst Dir, Nuffield Foundation, 1950–54; Dir-Gen., Nat. Book League, 1955–69, Dep. Chm., 1969–71, Vice-Pres., 1971–87. Prof. of American Studies, Univ. of Geneva, 1968–70; Visiting Professor: Michigan State Univ., 1950; Free Univ., Berlin, 1958; George Washington Univ., 1970; Vanderbilt Univ., 1981; Scholar-in-residence: Rockefeller Res. Center, Italy, 1974; Coll. of Idaho, 1986; Vis. Fellow, ANU, 1975, 1977; lectured in USA, Canada, Germany, India, Burma, etc. Dir of Unesco Seminar on Production of Reading Materials, Rangoon, 1957, Madras, 1959. Almoner, Christ's Hospital (Dep. Chm., 1980–84); Chm., Working Pty on Medical Libraries; Dir, William and Mary Historical Project, 1970–76. Director: Sexton Press Ltd, 1984–; P. and M. Youngman Carter Ltd, 1985–. Phi Beta Kappa, 1948. Hon. LitD Maine, 1961; Hon. DLitt Elmira, 1966; Hon. DHL William and Mary, 1970; Hon. DHum Idaho, 1984; Hon. DA Rocky Mountain Coll., Montana, 1995. Yorkshire Post Special Literary Award, 1980. *Publications:* American Excursion, 1949; Charles Lamb and Elia, 1949, rev. edn 1993; (contrib.) The Impact of America, 1951; (with Russel B. Nye) History of The United States, 1955; The Road to Athens, 1963; (with Martin Hürlimann) Venice, 1964; Barnes Wallis, 1972; Treason at West Point, 1975; Their Majesties Royall Colledge, 1976; Allen Lane: King Penguin, 1979; Verses Humorous and Post-Humorous, 1981; (with G. A. T. Allan) Christ's Hospital, 1984; Master of None: an autobiography, 1990; Christ's Hospital: an introductory history, 1991; *edited:* Leigh Hunt: Autobiography, 1949; E. J. Trelawny: Last Days of Shelley and Byron, 1952; (with Edmund Blunden) The Christ's Hospital Book, 1952; Poems of John Keats, 1953, rev. edn 1985; (with Kenneth Pelmear) Rugby Football: an Anthology, 1958; Cobbett: Journal of a Year's Residence in the United States of America, 1964; Cooper: The Spy, 1968; Cobbett's America, 1985; Margery Allingham: The Return of Mr Campion, 1989; In Honour of Edmund Blunden, 1997. *Recreations:* watching Rugby football, music. *Address:* 12 Laurence Mews, Askew Road, W12 9AT. *Clubs:* Army and Navy, Pilgrims. *Died 2 Oct. 2000.*

MORRELL, James George; Founder Director, Henley Centre for Forecasting, 1974–79; author and business forecaster; *b* 1923; *s* of late Frederick Morrell and Violet (*née* Smart); *m* 1st, 1944, Elizabeth Bristow (marr. diss. 1970); one *s* two *d*; 2nd, 1972, Margaret Helen Nickolls. *Educ:* Christ's Hospital; Ruskin Coll., Oxford; Wadham Coll., Oxford (BA 1953; MA). Served RAF, 1941–46. Ford Motor Co., 1955; Phillips & Drew, 1957; Econ. Advr, Charterhouse Group, 1964–95; founded James Morrell & Associates, 1967. Consultant to OECD, 1985–87. Visiting Professor, Univ. of Bradford, 1970–73; Associate Fellow, Oxford Centre for Management Studies, 1981–84. *Publications:* Business Forecasting for Finance and Industry, 1969; Business Decisions and the Role of Forecasting, 1972; Inflation and Business Management, 1974; 2002: Britain plus 25, 1977; The Regeneration of British Industry, 1979; Britain through the 1980s, 1980;

The Future of the Dollar and the World Reserve System, 1981; Employment in Tourism, 1982, 2nd edn 1985; Business Forecasts for the UK Economy, annually, 1982–99; Business Forecasts for the Housing Market, annually, 1985–99; The Impact of Tourism on London, 1985; Business Forecasts for the Motor Trades, annually, 1986–97; The Productivity Performance Index, 1989; Business Forecasts for the Commercial Property Market, 1994, 2nd edn 1996; A Short Guide to the 21st Century, 1999. *Recreations:* Samuel Pepys, stock market. *Address:* 81 Speed House, Barbican, EC2Y 8AU. *Club:* Middlesex CC. *Died 29 Sept. 2000.*

MORRELL, Rt Rev. James Herbert Lloyd; Canon and Prebend of Heathfield in Chichester Cathedral, 1959–82, Canon Emeritus since 1982; Provost of Lancing (Southern Division Woodard Schools), 1961–82; *b* 12 Aug. 1907; *s* of George Henry and Helen Adela Morrell. *Educ:* Dulwich Coll.; King's Coll., London; Ely Theological Coll. Deacon, 1931; priest, 1932; Curate of St Alphage, Hendon, 1931–35; Curate of St Michael and All Angels, Brighton, 1935–39; Bishop of Chichester's Chaplain for men, 1939–41; Lecturer for The Church of England Moral Welfare Council, 1941–44; Vicar of Roffey, 1944–46; Archdeacon of Lewes, 1946–59; Bishop Suffragan of Lewes, 1959–77; Asst Bishop, Diocese of Chichester, 1978–85. Fellow of King's Coll., London, 1960. *Publications:* Four Words (broadcast talks to the Forces), 1941; The Heart of a Priest, 1958; A Priest's Notebook of Prayer, 1961; The Catholic Faith Today, 1964. *Recreations:* walking, photography. *Address:* 83 Davigdor Road, Hove BN3 1RA. *T:* Brighton (01273) 733971.
Died 28 March 1996.

MORRIS, Denis Edward, OBE 1958; Head, and ultimately Controller of Light Programme, BBC, 1960–67; *b* 29 June 1907; *s* of Philip and Edith Morris; *m* 1st, 1931, Angela Moore (marr. diss. 1942); (one *s* decd); 2nd, 1943, Catharine Garrett (*née* Anderton); one *s. Educ:* Tonbridge Sch. BBC Talks Producer, 1936; BBC Midland Public Relations Officer, 1938; BBC Empire Public Relations Officer, 1939; MOI Dir, Midland Region, 1940–42; BBC Midland Regional Programme Dir, 1943–48; Head of Midland Regional Programmes, 1948–60. Wine Correspondent, Daily Telegraph, 1967–87. Leicester City Council, 1933–36; Chm., Findon Parish Council, 1971–74; Chm., Lord Mayor of Birmingham's War Relief Fund Publicity and Appeals Cttee, 1942–48; Pres., Shoreham Cons. Assoc., 1976–79 and 1983–86 (Chm., 1971–75). Member: Hosp. Management Cttee, St Francis Hosp. and Lady Chichester Hosp., 1966–71; Exec. Cttee, Nat. Cricket Assoc., 1969–74 (Chm., Public Relations Standing Cttee, 1969–72); Dep. Chm., Lord's Taverners' Council, 1963–65 (Mem., 1962–67); Public Relations Advisor to MCC and the Counties, 1967–68; Mem., Public Relations and Promotion Sub-Cttee, TCCB, 1968–75. *Publications:* Poultry-Keeping for Profit, 1949; The French Vineyards, 1958; A Guide to the Pleasures of Wine-Drinking, 1972; ABC of Wine, 1977. *Recreations:* bridge, drinking wine. *Clubs:* MCC; Incogniti CC, Sussex Martlets CC, Gentlemen of Leicestershire CC; Blackheath Rugby, Sussex Rugby Football. *Died 8 March 1999.*

MORRIS, Edward Allan, CMG 1967; OBE 1961; *b* 8 Sept. 1910; *s* of late John and Edith Morris, Twickenham; *m* 1937, Phyllis, *d* of late Francis and Mary Guise, Twickenham; one *d* (one *s* decd). *Educ:* Hampton Grammar Sch.; Univ. of London (BCom). RAFVR, 1942–46; Sqdn Leader (King's Commendation, 1946). Entered Crown Agents' Office, 1928; Asst Head of Dept, 1956; Head of Dept, 1958; Asst Crown Agent, 1964; Crown Agent for Oversea Governments and Administrations, 1968–71. *Recreations:* cricket, Rugby Union football, church bells and change-ringing,

preserving the riverside area of Twickenham. *Address:* 56 Lebanon Park, Twickenham, Mddx TW1 3DQ. *T:* (0181) 241 3447. *Clubs:* Royal Air Force, MCC, Corona; Harlequin Football. *Died 24 April 1997.*

MORRIS, Air Cdre Edward James, CB 1966; CBE 1959; DSO 1942; DFC 1944; Royal Air Force, retired; *b* 6 April 1915; *s* of late D. G. Morris and Mrs E. Morris, Bulawayo, Southern Rhodesia; *m* 1945, Alison Joan, *d* of Sir Charles Henderson, KBE; two *s. Educ:* Michaelhouse, Natal, S Africa. Commnd, 1937; Fighter Comd, 1938–41; Desert Air Force, 1941–45; Staff Coll., 1945–46; BAFO Germany, 1946–49; Old Sarum, 1949–52; Caledonian Sector, Fighter Command, 1952–53; RAF Flying Coll., 1953–54; Exchange Posting with USAF, Florida, 1954–56; SASO HQ 12 Group, 1956–58; OC Wattisham, 1958–59; HQ Fighter Command, 1959–60; Air Ministry, 1960–64; Chief of Staff, Headquarters Middle East Command, 1964–66; AOC Air Cadets, and Comdt Air Training Corps, 1966–68. American DFC 1945. *Address:* 300 Amberfield, Private Bag X010, Howick 3290, South Africa. *Died 13 Jan. 1999.*

MORRIS, (James) Peter; public affairs analyst; *b* 17 Sept. 1926; *s* of Frank Morris and Annie Mary (*née* Collindridge); *m* 1st, Peggy Giles (marr. diss.); 2nd, Margaret Law. *Educ:* Barnsley Holgate Grammar Sch.; Manchester Univ. (BA, Teaching Dip.). CAM Dip 1976; MIPR 1965, FIPR 1990; AMInstR 1980; Fellow, Soc. of Assoc. Execs, 1985 (Pres., 1992–93). Served RAF, 1945–48; Research Dept, Labour Party, 1952–59; Govt Information Services, 1960–73; Dir of Information, GLC, 1973–77; Sec. Gen., Nat. Cold Storage Fedn, later Cold Storage and Distribn Fedn, 1977–90. Sen. Treas. and Mem. Travel Bd, NUS, 1952–56; Borough Councillor, Hackney, 1956–59; Member: Nat. Exec., IPCS, 1964–73; Council for Social Democracy, 1984–90; Council, CBI, 1989–90. Vice-Pres., Techl Cttee, European Refrigerated Warehouses Assoc., 1985–90. Consultant, Europ. Assoc. of Addiction Treatment Providers, later Europ. Assoc. for Treatment of Addiction, 1992–. Trustee, Addiction Recovery Foundn, 1995–. Dir, Westminster Gardens Ltd, 1998–; Chairman: Charlotte Street Assoc., 1990–96; Holborn Police Gp, 1991–96. Trustee, Whitechapel Art Gall. and Theatre Workshop, 1956–59. *Publications:* Road Safety: a Study of Cost Benefit in Public Service Advertising, 1972; Legitimate Lobbying, 1997. *Recreations:* painting, writing, cricket. *Address:* 71 Westminster Gardens, Marsham Street, SW1P 4JG. *T:* (0171) 834 2098. *Clubs:* MCC, Reform.
Died 15 Aug. 1998.

MORRIS, Nigel Godfrey, CMG 1955; LVO 1966; QPM 1954; *b* 11 Nov. 1908; 2nd *s* of late Lt-Col G. M. Morris, 2/8th Gurkha Rifles and Mrs Morris; *m* 1st, 1941, Mrs G. E. Baughan, widow (*d* 1982), *e d* of late J. C. Sidebottom; one *d*, and one step *d*; 2nd, 1984, Mrs M. C. Berkeley-Owen (*née* Mullally). *Educ:* Wellington Coll. Asst Superintendent SS Police, 1928; Chinese language course, Amoy, China, 1929; Asst Supt of Police, Singapore CID, 1931; Special Branch, 1935; Asst Supt of Police, Town Penang, 1939; interned by Japanese, 1942; repatriated to UK, 1945; Asst Dir, Malayan Security Service, 1946; Dir, Special Branch, Singapore, 1948; Dep. Commissioner, CID, Singapore, 1950, Comr, 1952; Deputy Inspector-General of Colonial Police, Colonial Office, 1957–63; Commissioner of Police, Bahamas, 1963–68, retired. Colonial Police Medal, 1949. *Address:* 119 Cranmer Court, SW3 3HE. *T:* (0171) 584 9875. *Club:* Phyllis Court (Henley). *Died 6 Oct. 1996.*

MORRIS, Peter; *see* Morris, J. P.

MORRIS, Sir Robert (Byng), 10th Bt *cr* 1806, of Clasemont, Glamorganshire; *b* 25 Feb. 1913; *s* of Percy

Byng Morris (*d* 1957) (*g s* of 2nd Bt), and Ethel Maud (*d* 1923), *d* of William Morley Glascott, Melbourne; *S* cousin, 1982; *m* 1947, Christina Kathleen, *d* of Archibald Field, Toddington, Glos; one *s* three *d*. *Heir:* s Allan Lindsay Morris [*b* 27 Nov. 1961; *m* 1986, Cheronne, *e d* of Dale Whitford, Truro, Cornwall; two *s* one *d*]. *Address:* Norton Creek Stables (RR5), St Chrysostome, QC J0S 1R0, Canada. *Died 21 Jan. 1999.*

MORRIS, Air Vice-Marshal Ronald James Arthur, CB 1974; retired; *b* 27 Nov. 1915; *s* of late Dr James Arthur Morris, Ladybank, Fife; *m* 1945, Mary Kerr Mitchell (decd); one *s* two *d*; *m* Myra. *Educ:* Madras Coll., St Andrews; St Andrews Univ. MB, ChB 1939; DPH Edinburgh, 1953; MFCM 1972. Commnd RAF, 1939; served on Fighter Comd Stns, 1940–41; India and Burma Campaign, 1941–45; HQ Techn. Trng Comd, 1946–48; SMO, HQ Air Forces Western Europe, 1948–50; Sen. Trng Officer and Comdt Med. Trng Estabt, 1950–52; Exchange Officer, Sch. of Aviation Medicine (USAF), 1955–56; Dept MA7, Air Min., 1956–60; OC RAF Chessington, 1960–61; OC RAF Hosp. Wroughton, 1961–63; PMO, Signals Comd, 1963–65; Dep. PMO, Far East Air Forces, 1965–69; PMO, Maintenance Comd, 1969–70; Dep. Dir Gen. Med. Services (RAF), 1971–73; PMO, RAF Strike Comd, 1974–75. QHS, 1971–75. CStJ 1974. *Recreations:* golf, fishing. *Address:* 2 Cairnsden Gardens, St Andrews, Fife KY16 8SQ. *T:* (01334) 475326. *Died 10 June 2000.*

MORRIS, Most Rev. Thomas, DD; Archbishop of Cashel and Emly, (RC), 1960–88, now Emeritus; *b* Killenaule, Co. Tipperary, 16 Oct. 1914; *s* of James Morris and Johanna (*née* Carrigan). *Educ:* Christian Brothers Schs, Thurles; Maynooth Coll. Ordained priest, Maynooth, 1939; studied, Dunboyne Institute, 1939–41. (DD). Professor of Theology, St Patrick's Coll., Thurles, 1942–Dec. 1959, Vice-Pres., 1957–60; appointed Archbishop, 1959; consecrated, 1960; retired, 1988. *Recreation:* reading. *Address:* The Green, Holy Cross, Thurles, Co. Tipperary, Ireland. *T:* (01504) 43209. *Died 16 Jan. 1997.*

MORRIS, Timothy Denis, CBE 1994; DL; Director, Yattendon Investment Trust PLC, since 1985; Chairman: Herts & Essex Newspapers Ltd, since 1989; Burton Daily Mail Ltd, since 1991 (Director, since 1983); Cambridge Newspapers Ltd, since 1993 (Director, 1970–77 and since 1985); Staffordshire Newsletter Ltd, since 1994; *b* 15 Feb. 1935; *s* of D. E. Morris, OBE, and Angela (*née* Moore, later Mrs P. H. Skey); *m* 1959, Caroline Wynn; one *s* one *d*. *Educ:* Tonbridge Sch.; Pembroke Coll., Cambridge (MA). Dir, The Birmingham Post & Mail Ltd, 1967–90 (Chm., 1982–90); Man. Dir, Coventry Newspapers Ltd, 1970–77 (Dir, 1985–90; Chm., 1988–90); Chairman: Packet Newspapers (Cornwall) Ltd, 1986–94; West of England Newspapers Ltd, 1990–94; Director: Press Association Ltd, 1980–87 (Chm., 1985–86); South Hams Newspapers Ltd, 1985–94 (Chm., 1985–86); Reuters Founders Share Co. Ltd, 1987–; Midland Newspapers Ltd, 1988–90; Coventry Building Soc., 1991–; Heart of England Radio Ltd, 1993–. Dir, W Midlands RHA, 1990–93. Chairman: Birmingham Civic Soc., 1979–83; Birmingham Hippodrome Theatre Trust, 1990– (Dir, 1980–); Director: Royal Opera House Ballet Bd, 1990–; Birmingham Royal Ballet, 1993–; Gov., Royal Ballet, 1992–. President: W Midlands Newspaper Soc., 1975–76; Newspaper Soc., 1984–85; Coventry Chamber of Commerce, 1976–77. County Comr, Warwickshire Scouts, 1974–77. DL West Midlands, 1975. *Recreations:* golf, philately. *Address:* c/o Yattendon Investment Trust PLC, 1 Waterloo Street, Birmingham B2 5PG. *Club:* Naval. *Died 17 Feb. 1996.*

MORRIS, Walter Frederick, ACII; HM Diplomatic Service, retired; *b* 15 Oct. 1914; *s* of late Captain Frederick James Morris and Elsie Eleanor (*née* Williams); *m* 1945, Marjorie Vaughan, *o d* of late Thomas Vaughan Phillips and Eleanor Mirren (*née* Jones); one *s* one *d*. *Educ:* Cardiff High Sch.; University Coll., Cardiff (Law Prizeman); LLB London. Admitted Solicitor, 1936; legal practice, 1936–39; served RA (TA), 1939–45: GHQ Home Forces (Intelligence); WO Sch. of Military Administration; Certificate of Merit, Western Comd; GSO1 (Lt-Col), HQ 21st Army Gp, BLA (later BAOR); commanded Legal Aid Organisation, which provided legal assistance to all British Army and RAF personnel in Europe; legal practice (and Hon. District Army Welfare Officer), 1945–47; entered Administrative Home Civil Service, 1947; Min. of Social Security, 1947–68 (Prin. Dep. Chief Insce Off., Asst Sec.); Admin. Staff Coll., Henley, 1953; on loan to Export Credits Guarantee Dept, 1955–57; Manchester Business Sch., 1968; transf. to HM Diplomatic Service, 1968; HM Consul-Gen., Cairo, 1968–70; ME Centre for Arab Studies, Shemlan, Lebanon, 1969; Head of Claims Dept, FCO, 1970–72; Dep. High Comr, later Consul-Gen., Lahore, 1972–73; retired from HM Diplomatic Service and re-entered legal practice, 1973; Founder, 1973, Senior Partner, 1973–82 and Consultant, 1982–92, Morris, Scott & Co., Solicitors, Highcliffe, Christchurch, Dorset. Mem., Law Soc. FIMgt. Liveryman, Solicitors' Co. *Recreations:* travel, computers. *Address:* 19463 Ravines Court, Fort Myers, FL 33903, USA. *T:* (941) 7312262. *Clubs:* Civil Service; Pine Lakes Golf (Florida); Punjab (Lahore). *Died 26 Jan. 1999.*

MORRIS-JONES, His Honour Ifor Henry; QC 1969; a Circuit Judge, 1977–92; *b* 5 March 1922; *s* of late Rev. Prof. and Mrs D. Morris-Jones; *m* 1950, (Anne) Diana, *d* of late S. E. Ferris, OBE, Blundellsands; one *s* two *d*. *Educ:* Taunton Sch.; Sidney Sussex Coll., Cambridge. Called to the Bar, Lincoln's Inn, 1947. Joined Northern Circuit, 1947; Assistant Recorder, Carlisle, 1962; Dep. Chm., Cumberland Sessions, 1969–72; a Recorder, 1972–76. Mem., Bar Council, 1972. *Recreation:* golf. *Club:* Artists' (Liverpool). *Died 23 Oct. 1999.*

MORRIS-JONES, Prof. Wyndraeth Humphreys; Emeritus Professor of University of London; *b* 1 Aug. 1918; *s* of late William James Jones, Carmarthen, and Annie Mary Jones (*née* Morris); *m* 1953, Graziella Bianca Genre; one *s* two *d*. *Educ:* University Coll. Sch., Hampstead; London Sch. of Economics (BSc(Econ.) First Class, 1938; Leverhulme Research Grant, 1939; Hon. Fellow, 1980); Christ's Coll., Cambridge (Research Schol., 1940). Indian Army, 1941–46 (Lt-Col, Public Relations Directorate, 1944); Constitutional Adviser to Viceroy of India, 1947; Lecturer in Political Science, London Sch. of Economics, 1946–55; Prof. of Political Theory and Instns, Univ. of Durham, 1955–65; Prof. of Commonwealth Affairs and Dir, Inst. of Commonwealth Studies, Univ. of London, 1966–83. Leverhulme Emeritus Fellow, 1984–87. Rockefeller Travel Grants, 1954, 1960 and 1967. Vis. Prof. of Commonwealth Hist. and Instns, Indian Sch. of Internat. Studies, New Delhi, 1960; Visiting Professor: Univ. of Chicago, 1962; Univ. of California, Berkeley, 1964–65. Editor, Jl of Commonwealth and Comparative Politics (formerly Commonwealth Polit. Studies), 1964–80. *Publications:* Parliament in India, 1957; Government and Politics of India, 1964, 4th edn 1987; (with Biplab Dasgupta) Patterns and Trends in Indian Politics, 1976; Politics Mainly Indian, 1978; articles in Polit. Studies, Asian Survey, Modern Asian Studies, etc. *Address:* 95 Ridgway, SW19 4SX. *Died 22 Sept. 1999.*

MORRISON, 2nd Baron *cr* 1945, of Tottenham; **Dennis Morrison;** Manufacturing Executive with The Metal Box

Co. Ltd, 1957–72, retired; *b* 21 June 1914; *e* and *o* surv. *s* of 1st Baron Morrison, PC, and Grace, *d* of late Thomas Glossop; *S* father, 1953; *m* 1940, Florence Alice Helena (marr. diss. 1958), *d* of late Augustus Hennes, Tottenham; *m* 1959, Joan (marr. diss. 1975), *d* of late W. R. Meech. *Educ:* Tottenham County Sch. Employed by The Metal Box Co. Ltd on research work, 1937–51; Quality Controller, 1952–57. Lord Lieutenant's Representative for Tottenham, 1955–. FSS 1953–57. Vice-Pres., Acton Chamber of Commerce, 1972 (Mem., Exec. Cttee, 1962). Hon. President: Robert Browning Settlement, 1967–; 5th Acton Scout Group, 1969. *Recreation:* gardening. *Heir:* none. *Address:* 7 Ullswater Avenue, Felixstowe, Suffolk IP11 9SD. *T:* (01394) 77405.

Died 29 Oct. 1997 (ext).

MORRISON, Air Vice-Marshal Ian Gordon, CB 1965; CBE 1957 (OBE 1946); RNZAF (retired); *b* 16 March 1914; *s* of W. G. Morrison; *m* 1938, Dorothy, *d* of W. H. Franks; one *s* two *d*. *Educ:* Christchurch Boys' High Sch., NZ. RAF 1935; RNZAF 1939; No 75 Sqdn, UK, 1939; Comd RNZAF, Omaka, 1941; Comd RNZAF, Gisborne, 1942; SASO, Islands Gp, 1943; Comd No 3 BR Sqdn Pacific, 1944–45; jssc, UK, 1950; Comd RNZAF, Ohakea, 1952; Air Mem. for Supply, 1954; idc, 1958; AOC, RNZAF, HQ London, 1959–60; Air Mem. for Personnel, 1961–62; Chief of the Air Staff, Royal New Zealand Air Force, 1962–66. Develt Dir, A. S. Cornish Gp, 1970–80; Dep. Chm., Wm Scollay & Co., 1980–85. Nat. Pres., Scout Assoc. of NZ, 1967–79. *Recreations:* golf, angling. *Address:* 11 Mayfair Village, Oteha Valley Road, Browns Bay, Auckland, New Zealand. *T:* (9) 4789986. *Clubs:* Wellington (Pres., 1978–82), Wellington Golf (both in NZ). *Died 5 Sept. 1997.*

MORRISON, John Sinclair, CBE 1991; President, Wolfson College (formerly University College), Cambridge, 1966–80; *b* 15 June 1913; *s* of Sinclair Morrison (and *g s* of William Morrison, NY and Stagbury, Chipstead, Surrey) and Maria Elsie, *d* of William Lamaison, Salmons, Kenley, Surrey; *m* 1942, Elizabeth Helen, *d* of S. W. Sulman, Bexhill, Sussex; three *s* two *d*. *Educ:* Charterhouse; Trinity Coll., Cambridge. Fellow, Trinity College, Cambridge, 1937–45; Asst Lecturer, Manchester University, 1937–39; Editor of Cambridge Review, 1939–40, Ordinary Seaman (Volunteer), 1940–41, in service of British Council, Cairo, Zagazig, Baghdad, 1941–42; British Council Rep. in Palestine and Transjordan, 1942–45; Prof. of Greek and Head of Dept of Classics and Ancient History at the Durham Colls of Univ. of Durham, 1945–50; Fellow, Tutor and Senior Tutor of Trinity Coll., Cambridge, 1950–60; Vice-Master and Sen. Tutor of Churchill Coll., Cambridge, 1960–65, then Hon. Fellow. Leverhulme Fellow, 1965. Mellon Prof., 1976–77, Kenan Prof., 1981–82, Reed Coll., Oregon, USA; Leverhulme Emeritus Fellow, 1984–85. Member: Sierra Leone Educn Commission, 1954; Annan Cttee on Teaching of Russian, 1961; Hale Cttee on University Teaching Methods, 1961; Schools Council, 1965–67; Jt Working Party on 6th Form Curriculum and Examinations, 1968–72; Governing Bodies Assoc., 1965. Governor: Bradfield Coll., 1963–83; Wellington Coll., 1963–83; Charterhouse Sch., 1970–93. Jt Editor, Classical Review, 1968–75. Trustee, National Maritime Museum, 1975–82; Chm., Trireme Trust, 1984–96. Pres. Jerusalem Rotary Club, 1945. Hon. FBA 1988. Hon. DLitt Davidson Coll., N Carolina, 1987. Caird Medal, Nat. Maritime Mus., 1991. *Publications:* (with R. T. Williams) Greek Oared Ships, 1968; Long Ships and Round Ships, 1980; (with J. F. Coates) The Athenian Trireme, 1986; (with J. F. Coates) Greek and Roman Oared Warships, 1996. *Address:* Granhams, Granhams Road, Great Shelford, Cambridge CB2 5JX. *T:* (01223) 843158. *Died 25 Oct. 2000.*

MORROCCO, Alberto, OBE 1993; RSA 1963 (ARSA 1952); RSW 1965; RP 1977; RGI; Head of School of Painting, Duncan of Jordanstone College of Art, Dundee, 1950–82; *b* 14 Dec. 1917; *m* 1941, Vera Cockburn Mercer; two *s* one *d*. *Educ:* Gray's Sch. of Art, Aberdeen. Carnegie Schol., 1937; Brough Schol., 1938. In the Army, 1940–46. Guthrie Award, 1943; San Vito Prize, Rome, 1959. Pictures in: Scottish Modern Arts Coll.; Contemporary Arts Soc.; Scottish Arts Council Coll.; Hull, Aberdeen, Glasgow, Perth, Dundee and Edinburgh City Art Galleries and Scottish Gall. of Modern Art. Mem., Royal Fine Art Commn for Scotland, 1978–88. Mem., Arts and Crafts in Architecture Panel, Saltire Soc., 1983–. Hon. LLD Dundee, 1980; DUniv Stirling, 1987. *Recreations:* travel, swimming, eating. *Address:* Binrock, 456 Perth Road, Dundee DD2 1NG. *T:* (01382) 69319. *Club:* Scottish Arts. *Died 10 March 1998.*

MORT, Rt Rev. John Ernest Llewelyn, CBE 1965; Assistant Bishop, Diocese of Leicester, since 1972; *b* 13 April 1915; *s* of late Trevor Ll. Mort, JP, and Ethel Mary Mort; *m* 1953, Barbara Gifford. *Educ:* Malvern Coll.; St Catharine's Coll., Cambridge (BA Hist. Tripos 1938; MA 1942); Westcott House, Cambridge. Deacon 1940, priest 1941; Asst Curate, Dudley, 1940–44; Worcester Diocesan Youth Organiser, 1944–48; Private Chaplain to Bishop of Worcester, 1943–52; Vicar of St John in Bedwardine, Worcester, 1948–52; Bishop of N Nigeria, 1952–69; Canon Residentiary and Treasurer of Leicester Cathedral, 1970–88. Hon. LLD Ahmadu Bello Univ., 1970. *Address:* 271 Forest Road, Old Woodhouse, Loughborough, Leics LE12 8TZ. *Died 30 July 1997.*

MORTIMER, Gerald James, CBE 1979 (MBE (mil.) 1944); DL; FIng 1977; Councillor, Surrey County Council, 1973–93 (Chairman, Policy Committee, 1986–90); *b* 2 Sept. 1918; *s* of late Rev. Fernley Mortimer and Grace Mortimer (*née* Whiting); *m* 1st, 1942, Connie (*née* Dodd) (*d* 1989); two *s* two *d*; 2nd, 1990, Theresa Ella Walker. *Educ:* Caterham Sch.; Royal School of Mines, London Univ. (BSc (mining engrg), ARSM). Served War, Major, RE, UK and NW Europe, 1939–46. Mining official on Witwatersrand gold mines, S Africa, and in E Africa, 1946–55; Consolidated Gold Fields Ltd: Management staff, London, 1955–63; Exec. Dir, 1963–78; Dep. Chm., 1969–78; Gp Chief Exec., 1976–78; non. exec. Dir, 1978–80; Consultant, 1978–83; Dir, other Gp cos, 1957–79; in charge Goldsworthy iron ore project, W Australia, 1964–65; Exec. Chm., Amey Roadstone Corp. Ltd, 1967–75. President: Overseas Mining Assoc., 1972–73; Instn of Mining and Metallurgy, 1977–78; Inst. of Quarrying, 1980–81; Board Mem., 1978–83, Vice-Chm., 1981–82, Chm., 1982–83, CEI. Hon. Treas., Fellowship of Engrg, 1981–84. President: Old Caterhamians Assoc., 1970–71; RSM Assoc., 1976–77. Chm., E Surrey Cons. Assoc., 1980–82, Treasurer, 1982–83. Governor: Caterham Sch., 1965– (Vice-Chm., 1978–); Marden Lodge County Primary Sch., Surrey (Vice-Chm., 1973–81; Chm., 1981–). DL Surrey, 1990. FRSA; Hon. FIMM; Hon. FIQ. *Publication:* Never a Shot in Anger (autobiog.), 1993. *Recreations:* history, politics. *Address:* 40 Harestone Valley Road, Caterham, Surrey CR3 6HD. *T:* (01883) 344853.

Died 1 June 1997.

MORTIMER, Penelope Ruth, FRSL; writer; *b* 19 Sept. 1918; *d* of Rev. A. F. G. and Amy Caroline Fletcher; *m* 1st, 1937, Charles Dimont (marr. diss. 1949); two *d*; one *d* by Kenneth Harrison; one *d* by Randall Swingler; 2nd, 1949, John Clifford Mortimer (marr. diss. 1972); one *s* one *d*. *Educ:* Croydon High Sch.; New Sch., Streatham; Blencathra, Rhyl; Garden Sch., Lane End; St Elphin's Sch. for Daughters of Clergy; Central Educnl Bureau for Women; University Coll., London. *Screenplay:* Portrait of a Marriage, 1990. *Publications:* Johanna (as Penelope Dimont), 1947; A Villa in Summer, 1954; The Bright Prison, 1956; (with John Mortimer) With Love and Lizards, 1957; Daddy's Gone A-Hunting, 1958; Saturday Lunch with the Brownings, 1960; The Pumpkin Eater, 1962; My Friend Says It's Bulletproof, 1967; The Home, 1971; Long Distance, 1974; About Time (autobiog.), 1979 (Whitbread Prize); The Handyman, 1983; Queen Elizabeth: a life of the Queen Mother, 1986; About Time Too (autobiog.), 1993; Queen Mother: an alternative portrait of her life and times, 1995. *Address:* 19 St Gabriel's Road, NW2 4DS. *T:* (020) 8452 8551, *Fax:* (020) 8208 1946. *Died 19 Oct. 1999.*

MORTON, Rev. Arthur, CVO 1979; OBE 1961; Director, National Society for the Prevention of Cruelty to Children, 1954–79; *b* 29 June 1915; *s* of Arthur Morton and Kate Floyd Morton; *m* 1940, Medora Gertrude Harrison (*d* 1995); two *d*. *Educ:* Imperial Service Coll., Windsor; Jesus Coll., Cambridge (MA); Wycliffe Hall, Oxford (GOE). Deacon 1938, priest 1939; Curate, St Catherine's, Neasden, NW2, 1938–41; Chaplain, Missions to Seamen, Manchester, 1941–51; Asst Dir, NSPCC, 1951–54. Member, Adv. Council in Child Care and of Central Trng Council, 1956–71; frequent broadcasts on work of NSPCC. Mem., Glaziers' Co., 1976–. *Publication:* (with Anne Allen) This is Your Child: the story of the NSPCC, 1961. *Recreations:* golf, fishing, reading, gardening. *Address:* 25 Cottes Way, Hill Head, Fareham, Hants PO14 3NF. *T:* Stubbington (01329) 663511.

Died 25 March 1996.

MORTON, Air Cdre Crichton Charles, CBE 1945; Command Electronics Officer, HQ Bomber Command, 1962–66, retired; *b* 26 July 1912; *s* of late Charles Crichton Morton, Ramsey, IOM; *m* 1956, Diana Yvonne (*d* 1992), *d* of late Maj.-Gen. R. C. Priest, CB, RMS and *widow* of Group Captain N. D. Gilbart-Smith, RAF; no *c*. *Educ:* King William's Coll., IOM; RAF Coll., Cranwell. Various flying duties, 1932–36; RAF Officers Long Signals Course, Cranwell, 1936–37; signals duties, 1937–39; radar duties at HQ Fighter Comd, No 5 Signals Wing France, HQ 60 Signals Gp, Air HQ Iceland, HQ Air Comd SE Asia, 1939–45; Dir of Radar and Dep. Dir of Signals, Air Min., 1945–49; jssc Latimer, 1949–50; OC No 3 Radio Sch., RAF Compton Bassett, 1950–52; OC Communications Gp, Allied Air Forces Central Europe, 1952–55; Inspector of Radio Services, 1955–58; Dep. Chief Signals Office, HQ, SHAPE, 1958–60; Chm. of Brit. Jt Communications Electronics Board, Ministry of Defence, 1960–62. AMIEE 1955; AFRAeS 1965; MIERE 1965; CEng 1966. *Recreation:* researching Visigothic remains. *Address:* Apartamento 102, Torre Tramontana, Apartado 50, 17250 Playa de Aro, Gerona, Spain. *T:* (72) 817871.

Died 6 Nov. 1996.

MORTON, Prof. Frank, CBE 1976 (OBE 1968); DSc, PhD; FIChemE; Professor of Chemical Engineering, University of Manchester, 1956–73, then Professor Emeritus; a Pro-Vice-Chancellor, 1968–72; *b* Sheffield, 11 Aug. 1906; *s* of late Joseph Morton, Manchester; *m* 1936, Hilda May, *d* of John W. Seaston, Withington, Manchester; one *s*. *Educ:* Manchester Univ. (PhD 1936, DSc 1952); MSc Tech. Demonstrator in Chemical Technology, 1931–36; Research Chemist, Trinidad Leaseholds Ltd, 1936–40; Superintendent of Research and Development, Trinidad Leaseholds, Trinidad, 1940–45; Chief Chemist, Trinidad Leaseholds Ltd, UK, 1945–49; Prof. of Chemical Engineering, Univ. of Birmingham, 1949–56. Actg Principal, Manchester Coll. of Science and Technology, 1964–65; Dep. Principal, Univ. of Manchester Inst. of Science and Technology, 1966–71. Member: Council, Manchester Business Sch., 1964–72; Chemical and Allied Products Training Board, 1968–71;

European Fedn of Chemical Engineering, 1968–72. Pres., IChemE, 1963–64 (Hon. FIChemE 1983). Society of Chemical Industry: Vice-Pres., 1967–; Jubilee Memorial Lectr, 1967; Medal, 1969. Hon. Fellow, UMIST, 1978. *Publications:* report of Inquiry into the Safety of Natural Gas as a Fuel (Ministry of Technology), 1970; various papers on petroleum, organic chemistry, chemical engineering and allied subjects. *Recreation:* golf. *Address:* 47 Penrhyn Beach East, Llandudno, Gwynedd LL30 3RG. *T:* (01492) 548037. *Died 21 Jan. 1999.*

MORTON BOYD, John; *see* Boyd.

MOSS, Norman J.; *see* Jordan-Moss.

MOSS, Trevor Simpson, PhD, ScD; FInstP; Editor, Journal of Infra Red Physics and Technology, since 1961; *b* 28 Jan. 1921; *s* of William Moss and Florence Elizabeth (*née* Simpson); *m* 1948, Audrey (*née* Nelson). *Educ:* Alleynes, Uttoxeter; Downing Coll., Cambridge. MA, PhD, ScD Cantab. Research on radar, Royal Aircraft Establishment, 1941–43; research on radar and semiconductors, Telecommunications Research Estabt, 1943–53; RAE, 1953–78; Dep. Dir, Royal Signals and Radar Estabt, 1978–81. Mem., Lloyd's, 1979–. Various hon. commissions in RAF, 1942–45. Max Born Medal, German and British Physical Societies, 1975; Dennis Gabor award, Internat. Soc. of Optical Engrs, 1988. *Publications:* Photoconductivity, 1952; Optical Properties of Semiconductors, 1959; Semiconductor Optoelectronics, 1973; Handbook of Semiconductors, vol. I, Basic Properties of Semiconductors, 1980, 2nd edn (ed P. T. Landsberg) 1992, vol. II, Optical Properties of Semiconductors, 1980, 2nd edn (ed Balkanski) 1994, vol. III, Materials and Preparation, 1980, 2nd edn (ed Mahajari) 1994, vol. IV, Device Physics, 1980, 2nd edn (ed C. Hilsum) 1993; approx. 100 res. papers in internat. physics jls. *Address:* 2 Shelsley Meadow, Colwall, Malvern, Worcs WR13 6PX. *T:* Colwall (01684) 40079.

Died 23 March 1996.

MOSTYN, 5th Baron *cr* 1831, of Mostyn, co. Flint; **Roger Edward Lloyd Lloyd-Mostyn,** MC 1943; Bt 1778; *b* 17 April 1920; *e s* of 4th Baron Mostyn and Constance Mary, *o c* of W. H. Reynolds, Aldeburgh; *S* father, 1965; *m* 1943, Yvonne Margaret Stuart (marr. diss. 1957), *y d* of A. Stuart Johnson, Henshall Hall, Congleton, Cheshire; one *s* one *d*; 2nd, 1957, Mrs Sheila Edmondson Shaw, OBE, DL, *o c* of Major Reginald Fairweather, Stockwell Manor, Silverton, Devon, and of Mrs Fairweather, Yew Tree Cottage, Fordcombe, Kent. *Educ:* Eton; Royal Military College, Sandhurst. 2nd Lieut, 9th Queen's Royal Lancers, 1939; served War 1939–45, France, North Africa, and Italy (wounded, despatches, MC); Temp. Major, 1946. *Heir: s* Hon. Llewellyn Roger Lloyd Lloyd-Mostyn [*b* 26 Sept. 1948; *m* 1974, Denise Suzanne, *d* of Roger Duvanel; one *s* one *d*]. *Address:* Mostyn Hall, Mostyn, Clwyd, North Wales. *T:* (01745) 560222.

Died 6 June 2000.

MOTT, Sir Nevill (Francis), CH 1995; Kt 1962; MA Cantab; FRS 1936; Cavendish Professor of Physics, Cambridge University, 1954–71; Senior Research Fellow, Imperial College, London, 1971–73, Fellow, 1978; *b* 30 Sept. 1905; *s* of C. F. Mott, late Dir of Educn, Liverpool, and Lilian Mary Reynolds; *m* 1930, Ruth Horder; one *d* (and one *d* decd). *Educ:* Clifton Coll.; St John's Coll., Cambridge. Lecturer at Manchester Univ., 1929–30; Fellow and Lecturer, Gonville and Caius Coll., Cambridge, 1930–33; Melville Wills Prof. of Theoretical Physics in the Univ. of Bristol, 1933–48; Henry Overton Wills Prof. and Dir of the Henry Herbert Wills Physical Laboratories, Univ. of Bristol, 1948–54. Master of Gonville and Caius Coll., Univ. of Cambridge, 1959–66. Pres., International Union of Physics, 1951–57; Pres., Mod. Languages Assoc.,

1955; Pres., Physical Soc., 1956–58; Mem. Governing Board of Nat. Inst. for Research in Nuclear Science, 1957–60; Mem. Central Advisory Council for Education for England, 1956–59; Mem. Academic Planning Cttee and Council of University Coll. of Sussex; Chairman: Ministry of Education's Standing Cttee on Supply of Teachers, 1959–62; Nuffield Foundation's Cttee on Physics Education, 1961–73; Physics Education Cttee, Royal Society and Inst. of Physics, 1965–71. Chairman, Taylor & Francis, Scientific Publishers, 1970–75, Pres., 1976–86. Corr. Mem., Amer. Acad. of Arts and Sciences, 1954; Foreign Associate, Nat. Acad. of Sciences of USA, 1957; Hon. Member: Akademie der Naturforscher Leopoldina, 1964; Société Française de Physique, 1970; Inst. of Metals, Japan, 1975; Sociedad Real Española de Fisica y Quimica, 1980; European Physical Soc., 1985; Hon. Fellow: St John's Coll., Cambridge, 1971; UMIST, 1975; Darwin Coll., Cambridge, 1977; For. Fellow, Indian Nat. Science Acad., 1982. Hon. DSc: Louvain, Grenoble, Paris, Poitiers, Bristol, Ottawa, Liverpool, Reading, Sheffield, London, Warwick, Lancaster, Heriot-Watt, Oxon, East Anglia, Bordeaux, St Andrews, Essex, William and Mary, Stuttgart, Sussex, Marburg, Bar Ilan, Lille, Rome, Lisbon, Cambridge; Hon. Doctorate of Technology, Linköping, Sweden. Hon. FInstP 1972. Hughes Medal, 1941, Royal Medal, 1953, Copley Medal, 1972, Royal Society; Grande Médaille de la Société Française de Métallurgie, 1970; Copley Medal, 1972; Faraday Medal, IEE, 1973; (jtly) Nobel Prize for Physics, 1977. Chevalier, Ordre Nat. du Mérite, France, 1977. *Publications:* An Outline of Wave Mechanics, 1930; The Theory of Atomic Collisions (with H. S. W. Massey), 1933; The Theory of the Properties of Metals and Alloys (with H. Jones), 1936; Electronic Processes in Ionic Crystals (with R. W. Gurney), 1940; Wave Mechanics and its Applications (with I. N. Snedden), 1948; Elements of Wave Mechanics, 1952; Atomic Structure and the Strength of Metals, 1956; Electronic Processes in Non-Crystalline Materials (with E. A. Davis), 1971, 2nd edn 1979; Elementary Quantum Mechanics, 1972; Metal-Insulator Transitions, 1974, 2nd edn 1990; Conduction in Non-crystalline Materials, 1986, 2nd edn 1993; A Life in Science (autobiog.), 1986; (ed) Can Scientists Believe? some examples of the attitude of scientists to religion, 1991; (with A. Alexandrov) High Temperature Superconductors and other Superfluids, 1994; (with A. Alexandrov) Polarons & Bipolarons, 1995; various contribs to scientific periodicals about atomic physics, metals, semi-conductors, superconductors and photographic emulsions and glasses. *Recreation:* photography. *Address:* The Cavendish Laboratory, Madingley Road, Cambridge CB3 0HE; 63 Mount Pleasant, Aspley Guise, Milton Keynes MK17 8JX. *Club:* Athenæum. *Died 8 Aug. 1996.*

MOTTRAM, Maj.-Gen. John Frederick, CB 1983; LVO 1976; OBE 1969; Chief Executive, General Council of the Bar, 1987–94; *b* 9 June 1930; *s* of Frederick Mottram and Margaret Mottram (*née* Butcher); *m* 1956, Jennifer Thomas; one *s* one *d. Educ:* Enfield Central Sch.; Enfield Technical Coll. Joined RM, 1948; 42 Commando, Malaya, ME, 1951–54; Special Boat Squadron, 1955–56; HMS Loch Lomond, Persian Gulf, 1957–58; Adjutant, Commando Trng Centre, 1959–62; Student, Army Staff Coll., 1963; Staff of CGRM and RM Equerry to HRH The Duke of Edinburgh, 1964–65; Bde Major, 3 Commando Bde, Far East, 1966–68; Directing Staff, Army Staff Coll., 1969–71; CO, 40 Commando, NI and Plymouth, 1972–74 (mentioned in Despatches, 1973); Student, Naval War Coll., 1974; Jt Warfare Attaché, British Embassy, Washington DC, 1974–77; Col GS, DCGRM and RM ADC to HM The Queen, 1978–80; Maj.-Gen., 1980; Maj.-Gen. Training and Reserve Forces, RM, 1980–83, retd.

Dir Gen., Fertiliser Manufacturers Assoc., 1983–86. *Recreations:* fishing, watercolour painting. *Died 27 April 1998.*

MOUND, Trevor Ernest John, CVO 1986; OBE 1977; HM Diplomatic Service, retired; writer; Chairman, Ephew II Consultants, since 1991; *b* 27 July 1930; *e s* of late Harvey Mound and late Margaret Webb; *m* 1955, Patricia Kathleen de Burgh (marr. diss. 1972); two *s. Educ:* Royal Grammar Sch., Worcester; RMA Sandhurst; Univs of London and Hong Kong. Enlisted Coldstream Gds; 2nd Lieut, Worcs Regt (Malayan Campaign), 1951–54; Parachute Regt (ME), 1954–56; Adjutant, Airborne Forces, 1956–58; GSO 3, 16 Parachute Bde (ME), 1958–60; MoD, 1965–67; retired 1967; joined HM Diplomatic Service, 1967; First Secretary and Head of Chancery: Luxembourg, 1969–71; Calcutta, 1971–73; FCO, 1973–76; Beirut, 1976–77; Counsellor (Commercial), Peking, 1978–81; Counsellor (Econ.), Oslo, 1981–83; Counsellor (Hong Kong negotiations), FCO, 1984; Consul General: Shanghai, 1985–87; Marseilles Principality of Monaco, 1987–90. Mem., Bath Royal Lit. and Scientific Instn. *Recreation:* astericology (study of artefacts and life of Roman Gaul). *Address:* 8 Beaufort East, Bath BA1 6QD. *T:* (01225) 420657. *Died 22 March 1998.*

MOUNSEY, (John) Patrick (David), MD, FRCP; Provost, Welsh National School of Medicine, 1969–79, retired; *b* 1 Feb. 1914; *s* of late John Edward Mounsey and Christine Frances Trail Robertson; *m* 1947, Vera Madeline Sara King (*d* 1990); one *s* one *d. Educ:* Eton Coll.; King's Coll., Cambridge (MA); King's Coll. Hosp., London. MD Cantab 1950; FRCP 1962. Sherbrook Res. Fellow, Cardiac Dept, London Hosp., 1951; Royal Postgraduate Medical School: Lectr, 1960; Sen. Lectr and Sub-Dean, 1962; Cons. Cardiologist, Hammersmith Hosp., 1960; Dep Dir, British Postgrad. Med. Fedn, 1967. Member: GMC, 1970–79; GDC, 1973–79; Council, St David's University Coll., Lampeter, 1975–83; South Glamorgan AHA (T); British Cardiac Soc.; Assoc. of Physicians; Soc. of Physicians in Wales. Corresp. Mem., Australasian Cardiac Soc.; late Asst Ed., British Heart Jl. Hon. LLD Wales, 1980. *Publications:* articles on cardiology mainly in British Heart Jl. *Recreations:* painting, gardening, music. *Address:* Esk House, Coombe Terrace, Wotton-under-Edge, Glos GL12 7NA. *T:* (01453) 842792. *Club:* Athenæum. *Died 21 Feb. 1999.*

MOVERLEY, Rt Rev. Gerald, JCD; Bishop of Hallam (RC), since 1980; *b* 9 April 1922; *s* of William Joseph Moverley and Irene Mary Moverley (*née* Dewhirst). *Educ:* St Bede's Grammar Sch., Bradford; Ushaw Coll., Durham; Angelicum Univ., Rome. Priest, 1946; Sec. to Bishop Poskitt, Leeds, 1946–51; Angelicum Univ., 1951–54; Chancellor, Dio. Leeds, 1958–68; Domestic Prelate to HH Pope Paul VI, 1965; apptd Bishop, Dec. 1967; Titular Bishop of Tinisa in Proconsulari and Bishop Auxiliary of Leeds, 1968–80; translated the new diocese of Hallam, established May 1980. *Address:* Quarters, Carsick Hill Way, Sheffield S10 3LT. *T:* Sheffield (0114) 230 9101. *Died 14 Dec. 1996.*

MOYLAN, His Honour (John) David (FitzGerald); a Circuit Judge (formerly Judge of the County Courts), 1967–88; *b* 8 Oct. 1915; *s* of Sir John FitzGerald Moylan, CB, CBE, and late Lady (Ysolda Mary Nesta) Moylan (*née* FitzGerald); *m* 1946, Jean, *d* of late F. C. Marno-Edwards, Lavenham, Suffolk; one *s* two *d. Educ:* Charterhouse; Christ Church, Oxford. Served War of 1939–45, with Royal Marines. Called to the Bar, Inner Temple, 1946; practised on the Western Circuit. *Recreations:* travel, music. *Address:* Ufford Hall, Fressingfield, Diss, Norfolk IP21 5TA. *Died 23 Dec. 1996.*

MUELLER, Dame Anne Elisabeth, DCB 1988 (CB 1980); Second Permanent Secretary, HM Treasury, 1987–90; *b* 15 Oct. 1930; *d* of late Herbert Constantin Mueller and Phoebe Ann Beevers; *m* 1958, James Hugh Robertson (marr. diss. 1978). *Educ:* Wakefield Girls' High Sch.; Somerville Coll., Oxford (Hon. Fellow, 1984). Entered Min. of Labour and Nat. Service, 1953; served with Orgn for European Econ. Co-op., 1955–56; HM Treasury, 1962; Dept of Economic Affairs, 1964; Min. of Technology, 1969; DTI, 1970; Under-Sec., DTI, later DoI, 1972–77; Dep. Sec., DoI, later DTI, 1977–84; Second Perm. Sec., Cabinet Office (MPO), 1984–87. Director: EIB, 1978–84; STC plc, 1990–91; CARE Britain, 1990–99; Phonepoint Ltd, 1990–92; British Sky Broadcasting, 1991–2000; Sedgwick Lloyd's Underwriting Agents Ltd, 1992–95; CARE International, 1992–99 (Vice-Pres., 1992–96). Ind. Investigator, SIB, 1990–94; Member: Bd, Business in the Community, 1984–88; Rural Develt Commn, 1990–98; Nurses and Allied Professions Review Body, 1991–94; Vice Pres., Industrial Participation Assoc., 1986–90. Member Council: Inst. of Manpower Studies, 1981–95 (Vice-Pres., 1989–95); Templeton Coll., Oxford, 1985–95; Manchester Business Sch., 1985–92; Queen Mary and Westfield Coll., 1990–95; Trustee: Whitechapel Art Gall., 1985–95; Duke of Edinburgh's Study Confs, 1986–93; Res. Inst. for Consumer Affairs, 1991–; Chm., European Centre for Public Affairs, 1992–96. Ind. Gov., 1988–98, Chancellor, 1991–95, De Montfort Univ. (formerly Leicester Polytechnic). CIMgt (CBIM 1978); FRSA 1981; FIPM 1986. Hon. Fellow, QMW, 1997. Hon. DLitt: Warwick, 1985; CNAA, 1991; Hon. LLD Nottingham, 1993; DUniv De Montfort, 1995. *Address:* 46 Kensington Heights, Campden Hill Road, W8 7BD. *T:* (020) 7727 4780. *Died 8 July 2000.*

MUIR, Alec Andrew, CBE 1968; QPM 1961; DL; Chief Constable of Durham Constabulary, 1967–70; *b* 21 Aug. 1909; *s* of Dr Robert Douglas Muir, MD, and Edith Muir, The Limes, New Cross, SE14; *m* 1948, Hon. Helen Farr (*d* 1994), *er d* of Baron du Parcq, PC; one *s* one *d*, and one step *s* one step *d*. *Educ:* Christ's Hosp.; Wadham Coll., Oxford (MA). Receivers' Office, Metropolitan Police, 1933; Metropolitan Police Coll., 1934; Supt, 1948; Chief Constable, Durham Co. Constabulary, 1950. DL Co. Durham, 1964. OStJ 1957. *Address:* Beanlands Nursing Home, Crosshills, Keighley, W Yorks BD20 8PL. *Died 1 Aug. 1997.*

MUIR, Frank, CBE 1980; writer and broadcaster; *b* 5 Feb. 1920; *s* of Charles James Muir and Margaret Harding; *m* 1949, Polly McIrvine; one *s* one *d*. *Educ:* Chatham House, Ramsgate; Leyton County High Sch. Served RAF, 1940–46. Wrote radio comedy-series and compered TV progs, 1946. With Denis Norden, 1947–64; collaborated for 17 years writing comedy scripts, including: (for radio): Take it from Here, 1947–58; Bedtime with Braden, 1950–54; (for TV): And so to Bentley, 1956; Whack-O,! 1958–60; The Seven Faces of Jim, 1961, and other series with Jimmy Edwards; resident in TV and radio panel-games; collaborated in film scripts, television commercials, and revues (Prince of Wales, 1951; Adelphi, 1952); joint Advisors and Consultants to BBC Television Light Entertainment Dept, 1960–64; jointly received Screenwriters Guild Award for Best Contribution to Light Entertainment, 1961; together on panel-games My Word!, 1956–, and My Music, 1967–. Asst Head of BBC Light Entertainment Gp, 1964–67; Head of Entertainment, London Weekend Television, 1968–69, resigned 1969, and reverted to being self-unemployed; resumed TV series Call My Bluff, 1970; began radio series Frank Muir Goes Into . . ., 1971; The Frank Muir Version, 1976. Pres., Johnson Soc., Lichfield, 1975–76. Rector, Univ. of St Andrews, 1977–79. (With Simon Brett) Writers' Guild Award for Best Radio Feature Script, 1973; (with Denis Norden) Variety Club of GB Award for Best Radio Personality of 1977; Radio Personality of the Year, Radio Industries Club, 1977; Sony Gold Award, 1983. Hon. LLD St Andrews, 1978; Hon. DLitt Kent, 1982. *Publications:* (with Patrick Campbell) Call My Bluff, 1972; (with Denis Norden) You Can't Have Your Kayak and Heat It, 1973; (with Denis Norden) Upon My Word!, 1974; Christmas Customs and Traditions, 1975; The Frank Muir Book: an irreverant companion to social history, 1976; What-a-Mess, 1977; (with Denis Norden) Take My Word for It, 1978; (with Simon Brett) Frank Muir Goes Into ..., 1978; What-a-Mess the Good, 1978; (with Denis Norden) The Glums, 1979; (with Simon Brett) The Second Frank Muir Goes Into ..., 1979; Prince What-a-Mess, 1979; Super What-a-Mess, 1980; (with Simon Brett) The Third Frank Muir Goes Into ..., 1980; (with Simon Brett) Frank Muir on Children, 1980; (with Denis Norden) Oh, My Word!, 1980; What-a-Mess and the Cat-Next-Door, 1981; (with Simon Brett) The Fourth Frank Muir Goes Into ..., 1981; (with Polly Muir) The Big Dipper, 1981; A Book at Bathtime, 1982; What-a-Mess in Spring, What-a-Mess in Summer, What-a-Mess in Autumn, What-a-Mess in Winter, 1982; (with Simon Brett) The Book of Comedy Sketches, 1982; What-a-Mess at the Seaside, 1983; (with Denis Norden) The Complete and Utter "My Word!" Collection, 1983; What-a-Mess goes to School, 1984; What-a-Mess has Breakfast, 1986; What-a-Mess has Lunch, 1986; What-a-Mess has Tea, 1986; What-a-Mess has Supper, 1986; What-a-Mess goes on Television, 1989; (with Denis Norden) You Have "My Word'', 1989; The Oxford Book of Humorous Prose: from William Caxton to P. G. Wodehouse, a conducted tour, 1990; What-a-Mess and the Hairy Monster, 1990; Frank Muir Retells: Three Little Pigs, Jack and the Beanstalk, Goldilocks and the Three Bears, 1991; The Walpole Orange, 1993; A Kentish Lad (autobiog.), 1997. *Recreations:* book collecting, staring silently into space. *Address:* Anners, Thorpe, Egham, Surrey TW20 8UE. *T:* (01932) 562759. *Club:* Garrick. *Died 2 Jan. 1998.*

MUIR, Prof. Kenneth Arthur, FBA 1970; King Alfred Professor of English Literature, University of Liverpool, 1951–74, then Professor Emeritus; *b* 5 May 1907; *s* of Dr R. D. Muir; *m* 1936, Mary Ewen (*d* 1975); one *s* (one *d* decd). *Educ:* Epsom Coll.; St Edmund Hall, Oxford (Hon. Fellow, 1987). Lectr in English, St John's Coll., York, 1930–37; Lectr in English Literature, Leeds Univ., 1937–51; Liverpool University: Public Orator, 1961–65; Dean of the Faculty of Arts, 1958–61. Visiting Professor: Univ. of Pittsburgh, 1962–63; Univ. of Connecticut, 1973; Univ. of Pennsylvania, 1977. Editor, Shakespeare Survey, 1965–80; Hon. Vice-Pres., Internat. Shakespeare Assoc., 1996– (Chm., 1974–85; Vice-Pres., 1986); Pres., English Assoc., 1987. Leeds City Councillor, 1945–47, 1950–51; Chm. of Leeds Fabian Soc., 1941–46; Pres., Leeds Labour Party, 1951; Birkenhead Borough Councillor, 1954–57. FRSL 1978. Docteur de l'Université: de Rouen, 1967; de Dijon, 1976. *Publications:* The Nettle and the Flower, 1933; Jonah in the Whale, 1935; (with Sean O'Loughlin) The Voyage to Illyria, 1937; English Poetry, 1938; Collected Poems of Sir Thomas Wyatt, 1949; Arden edn Macbeth, 1951; King Lear, 1952; Elizabethan Lyrics, 1953; (ed) Wilkins' Painful Adventures of Pericles, 1953; John Milton, 1955; The Pelican Book of English Prose I, 1956; Shakespeare's Sources, 1957; (ed with F. P. Wilson) The Life and Death of Jack Straw, 1957; (ed) John Keats, 1958; Shakespeare and the Tragic Pattern, 1959; trans. Five Plays of Jean Racine, 1960; Shakespeare as Collaborator, 1960; (ed) Unpublished Poems by Sir Thomas Wyatt, 1961; Last Periods, 1961; (ed) U. Ellis-Fermor's Shakespeare the Dramatist, 1961; (ed) Richard II, 1963; Life and Letters of Sir Thomas Wyatt, 1963; Shakespeare: Hamlet, 1963; (ed) Shakespeare: The

Comedies, 1965; Introduction to Elizabethan Literature, 1967; (ed) Othello, 1968; (ed) The Winter's Tale, 1968; (ed with Patricia Thomson) Collected Poems of Sir Thomas Wyatt, 1969; The Comedy of Manners, 1970; (ed) The Rivals, 1970; (ed) Double Falsehood, 1970; (ed with S. Schoenbaum) A New Companion to Shakespeare Studies, 1971; Shakespeare's Tragic Sequence, 1972; Shakespeare the Professional, 1973; (ed) Essays and Studies, 1974; (ed) Three Plays of Thomas Middleton, 1975; The Singularity of Shakespeare, 1977; The Sources of Shakespeare's Plays, 1977; Shakespeare's Comic Sequence, 1979; Shakespeare's Sonnets, 1979; (trans.) Four Comedies of Calderón, 1980; (ed) U. Ellis-Fermor's Shakespeare's Drama, 1980; (ed with S. Wells) Aspects of the Problem Plays, 1982; (ed with M. Allen) Shakespeare's Plays in Quarto, 1982; (ed) Troilus and Cressida, 1982; (ed with S. Wells) Aspects of King Lear, 1982; (ed with J. Halio and D. Palmer) Shakespeare: man of the theater, 1983; Shakespeare's Didactic Art, 1984; (ed) King Lear: Critical Essays, 1984; (ed) Interpretations of Shakespeare, 1985; Shakespeare: contrasts and controversies, 1985; (trans. with A. L. Mackenzie) Three Comedies of Calderón, 1985; King Lear: a critical study, 1986; Antony and Cleopatra: a critical study, 1987; Negative Capability and the Art of the Dramatist, 1987; (trans. with A. L. Mackenzie) Calderón's La Cisma de Inglaterra, 1990. *Recreation:* theatre. *Address:* 6 Chetwynd Road, Oxton, Birkenhead, Merseyside L43 2JJ. *T:* (0151) 652 3301. *Died 30 Sept. 1996.*

MUIR BEDDALL, Hugh Richard; *see* Beddall.

MUIRHEAD, Sir David (Francis), KCMG 1976 (CMG 1964); CVO 1957; HM Diplomatic Service, retired; *b* 30 Dec. 1918; *s* of late David Muirhead, Kippen, Stirlingshire; *m* 1942, Hon. Elspeth Hope-Morley (*d* 1989), *d* of 2nd Baron Hollenden and Hon. Mary Gardner, *d* of 1st Baron Burghclere; two *s* one *d*. *Educ:* Cranbrook Sch. Commissioned into Rifles (Rifle Brigade), 1937; passed Officers Exam., RMC Sandhurst; apptd to Beds and Herts Regt, 1939; served War of 1939–45 in France, Belgium and SE Asia; Hon. Attaché, Brit. Embassy, Madrid, 1941; passed Foreign Service Exam., 1946; appointed to Foreign Office, 1947; La Paz, 1948; Buenos Aires, 1949; Brussels, 1950; Foreign Office, 1953; Washington, 1955; Foreign Office, 1959; Under-Sec., Foreign Office, 1966–67; HM Ambassador: Peru, 1967–70; Portugal, 1970–74; Belgium, 1974–78. Special Rep. of Sec. of State for Foreign and Commonwealth Affairs, 1979–94. Mem. Council, St Dunstan's, 1981–89; Comr, Commonwealth War Graves Commn, 1981–86. Grand Cross, Military Order of Christ (Portugal); Grand Cross, Order of Distinguished Service (Peru). *Address:* 16 Pitt Street, W8 4NY. *T:* (0171) 937 2443. *Club:* Travellers'. *Died 3 Feb. 1999.*

MULLAN, Charles Heron, CBE 1979; VRD 1950; DL; Resident Magistrate, 1960–82, retired; Lieutenant-Commander RNR; retired, 1951; *b* 17 Feb. 1912, *s* of Frederick Heron Mullan, DL, BA, solicitor, Newry, Co. Down, and Minnie Mullan, formerly of Stow Longa, Huntingdonshire; *m* 1940, Marcella Elizabeth Sharpe, *er d* of J. A. McCullagh, Ballycastle, Co. Antrim; one *s*. *Educ:* Castle Park, Dalkey, Co. Dublin; Rossall Sch., Fleetwood; Clare Coll., Cambridge. Hons Degree Law, Cambridge, 1934; MA 1939. Solicitor 1948. Joined Ulster Div. RNVR, 1936; called up for active service with Royal Navy, Aug. 1939; served throughout the war; HMS Rodney 1939–40; destroyers and escort vessels, Channel, North Sea, North Atlantic, etc, 1940–44 (with Royal Norwegian Navy, 1941–43); King Haakon VII War Decoration 1944. MP (UU) Co. Down, 1946–50, Westminster Parlt; contested S Down, 1945, for NI Parlt. Mem. Ulster Unionist Council, 1946–60. JP 1960; Chm., Belfast Juvenile Courts, 1964–79. Member: N Ireland

Section of British Delegn to 3rd UN Congress on Prevention of Crime and Treatment of Offenders, Stockholm, 1965; initial N Ireland Legal Aid Adv. Cttee, 1967–75; Mem. Exec. Cttee, British Juvenile Courts Soc., 1973–79; Vice-Pres., NI Juvenile Courts Assoc., 1980–93; NI Rep. to 9th Congress of Internat. Assoc. of Youth Magistrates, Oxford, 1974; Adviser, Internat. Assoc. of Youth Magistrates, 1974–82. Hon. Governor, South Down Hospitals Gp, 1965–73; Vice-Pres., Rossallian Club, 1974. DL Co. Down, 1974. *Recreations:* ornithology, walking, boating. *Address:* Casanbarra, Carrickmore Road, Ballycastle, Co. Antrim, Northern Ireland BT54 6QS. *T:* (012657) 62323. *Died 26 Oct. 1996.*

MULLINS, Leonard, CMG 1976; PhD, DSc; Director of Research, Malaysian Rubber Producers' Research Association, Brickendonbury, Hertford, 1962–83; *b* 21 May 1918; *s* of Robert and Eugenie Alice Mullins; *m* 1943, Freda Elaine Churchouse; two *d*. *Educ:* Eltham Coll.; University Coll., London; Inst. of Educn, London. BSc (Hons), Post Grad. Teacher's Diploma, PhD, DSc. CPhys; FInstP; FIM. Experimental Officer, Min. of Supply, 1940–44; Scientific Officer, finally Head of Physics Gp, Research Assoc. of British Rubber Manufrs, 1944–49; Malaysian (previously British) Rubber Producers' Research Assoc., 1950–83. Scientific Advr, UNIDO projects in China, Côte d'Ivoire, Malaysia, Vietnam, 1984–91. Pres., Plastics and Rubber Inst., 1981–83 (Chm., 1976–77; Vice-Pres., 1977–81); Chm., Adv. Cttee, Nat. Coll. of Rubber Technology, 1976–87; Vice-Pres., Rubber and Plastics Research Assoc., 1983–. Member: Court, Cranfield Inst. of Technology; Adv. Bd, Inst. of Technol., Loughborough Univ.; Council, Rubber and Plastics Res. Assoc. Discovered Mullins Effect, relating to elastic behaviour of rubber. Foundn Lectr, Instn of Rubber Industry, 1968; Moore Meml Lecture, Bradford Univ., 1982. Governor of local schools. Paul Harris Fellow, Rotary Internat., 1991. Colwyn Medal, IRI, 1966; Médaille de la Ville de Paris, 1968; Outstanding Service Award, PRI, 1985; Charles Goodyear Medal Award, Rubber Div., American Chem. Soc., 1986; Carl Dietrich Harries Medal, Deutsche Kautschuk Ges., 1988; Eminent Citizen's Medal, Ho Chi Minh City, 1988. Comdr, Order of Chivalry, JMN, 1975. *Publications:* numerous original scientific papers in field of rubber physics. *Address:* 32 Sherrardspark Road, Welwyn Garden City, Herts AL8 7JS. *T:* (01707) 323633. *Club:* Athenæum. *Died 19 Sept. 1997.*

MUNRO, Ian Arthur Hoyle, MB; FRCP; Editor of The Lancet, 1976–88; *b* 5 Nov. 1923; *o s* of Gordon Alexander and Muriel Rebecca Munro; *m* 1948, Olive Isabel, MRCS, LRCP, *o d* of Ernest and Isabella Jackson; three *s* two *d*. *Educ:* Huddersfield Coll.; Paston Sch., North Walsham; Royal Liberty Sch., Romford; Guy's Hosp. (MB 1946). FRCP 1984 (MRCP 1980). Served with RAMC, 1947–50. Joined staff of The Lancet, 1951, Dep. Editor, 1965–76. Regents' Lectr, UCLA, 1982. Pres., Physicians for Human Rights (UK), 1991–. *Recreations:* cricket, crosswords. *Address:* Oakwood, Bayley's Hill, Sevenoaks, Kent TN14 6HS. *T:* (01732) 454993. *Clubs:* Athenæum; Yorkshire CC. *Died 22 Jan. 1997.*

MUNRO, Sir Ian Talbot, 15th Bt *cr* 1634, of Foulis-Obsdale, Ross-shire; yacht consultant; *b* 28 Dec. 1929; *s* of Robert Hector Munro (*d* 1965) (*n* of 12th and 13th Bts) and Ethel Amy Edith, *d* of Harry Hudson; *S* cousin, Sir Arthur Herman Munro, 14th Bt, 1972. *Heir: cousin* Kenneth Arnold William Munro [*b* 26 June 1910; *m* 1935, Olive Freda, *d* of Francis Broome; one *s* one *d*]. *Address:* 22 rue d'Occitanie, 11120 Ginestas, Aude, France. *Died 15 Dec. 1996.*

MUNSTER, 7th Earl of, *cr* 1831; **Anthony Charles FitzClarence;** Viscount FitzClarence, Baron Tewkesbury, 1831; stained glass conservator for Chapel Studio,

Hertfordshire, 1983–90; *b* 21 March 1926; *s* of 6th Earl of Munster, and Monica Shiela Harrington (*d* 1958), *d* of Lt-Col Sir Henry Mulleneux Grayson, 1st Bt, KBE; *S* father, 1983; *m* 1st, 1949, Diane Delvigne (marr. diss. 1966); two *d*; 2nd, 1966, Pamela Hyde (marr. diss. 1979); one *d*; 3rd, 1979, Alexa Maxwell (*d* 1995); 4th, 1997, Halina Winska, MD, PhD; one step *d. Educ:* St Edward's School, Oxford; Central Sch. of Art, London. Served RN, 1942–47. Graphic Designer: Daily Mirror Newspapers, 1957–66; IPC Newspapers Division (Sun), 1966–69; freelance 1971–79; stained glass conservator for Burrell collection, 1979–83. MSIA 1960–69. FRSA 1987. *Recreations:* field sports, photography, computer design. *Heir:* none. *Club:* Carlton.   *Died 30 Dec. 2000 (ext).*

MURCHIE, His Honour John Ivor; DL; a Circuit Judge, 1974–99; *b* 4 June 1928; *s* of Captain Peter Archibald Murchie, OBE, RD, RNR; *m* 1953, Jenifer Rosalie Luard; one *s* two *d. Educ:* Edinburgh Academy; Rossall Sch.; Exeter Coll., Oxford (MA). Called to the Bar, Middle Temple, 1953; Harmsworth Scholarship, 1956. Dep. Chm., Berkshire QS, 1969–71; a Recorder of the Crown Court, 1972–74; Dep. Sen. Judge, Sovereign Base Areas, Cyprus (non-res.), 1987–. Mem., Criminal Cttee, Judicial Studies Bd, 1988–91. Chm. Council, Rossall Sch., 1979–94; Life Gov., 1994; Governor, Queen Anne's Sch., Caversham, 1991–99. DL Berks, 1994. *Recreations:* versifying and diversifying, taking photographs and awaiting developments.   *Died 29 April 1999.*

MURDOCH, Dame (Jean) Iris, (Dame Iris Bayley), DBE 1987 (CBE 1976); CLit 1987; novelist and philosopher; Fellow of St Anne's College, Oxford, since 1948, Hon. Fellow, 1963; *b* Dublin, 15 July 1919; *d* of Wills John Hughes Murdoch and Irene Alice Richardson; *m* 1956, John Oliver Bayley, FBA. *Educ:* Froebel Educational Inst., London; Badminton Sch., Bristol; Somerville Coll., Oxford (Lit. Hum. 1st Class 1942; Hon. Fellow, 1977). Asst Principal, Treasury, 1942–44; Administrative Officer with UNRRA, working in London, Belgium, Austria, 1944–46; Sarah Smithson studentship in philosophy, Newnham Coll., Cambridge, 1947–48; Lectr, RCA, 1963–67. Mem., Irish Academy, 1970; Hon. Member: Amer. Acad. of Arts and Letters, 1975; Amer. Acad. of Arts and Sciences, 1982. Hon. Fellow, Newnham Coll., Cambridge, 1986. Hon. DLitt Oxford, 1987; Hon. LittD Cambridge, 1993. Shakespeare Prize, FVS Foundn, Hamburg, 1988. *Publications:* Sartre, Romantic Rationalist, 1953; Under the Net, 1954; The Flight from the Enchanter, 1955; The Sandcastle, 1957; The Bell, 1958; A Severed Head, 1961 (play, Criterion, 1963); An Unofficial Rose, 1962; The Unicorn, 1963; The Italian Girl, 1964 (play, Criterion, 1967); The Red and the Green, 1965; The Time of The Angels, 1966; The Nice and The Good, 1968; Bruno's Dream, 1969; A Fairly Honourable Defeat, 1970; The Sovereignty of Good, 1970; An Accidental Man, 1971; The Black Prince, 1973 (James Tait Black Meml Prize; play, Aldwych, 1989); The Sacred and Profane Love Machine, 1974 (Whitbread Prize); A Word Child, 1975; Henry and Cato, 1976; The Fire and the Sun, 1977; The Sea, the Sea, 1978 (Booker Prize, 1978); Nuns and Soldiers, 1980; The Philosopher's Pupil, 1983; The Good Apprentice, 1985; Acastos, 1986; The Book and the Brotherhood, 1987; The Message to the Planet, 1989; Metaphysics as a Guide to Morals, 1992; The Green Knight, 1993; Jackson's Dilemma, 1995; Existentialists and Mystics, 1997; *plays:* The Servants and the Snow (Greenwich), 1970; The Three Arrows (Arts, Cambridge), 1972; Art and Eros (Nat. Theatre), 1980; *poems:* A Year of Birds, 1978; papers in Proc. Aristotelian Soc., etc. *Recreation:* learning languages.
Died 8 Feb. 1999.

MURLEY, Sir Reginald (Sydney), KBE 1979; TD 1946; FRCS; President, Royal College of Surgeons, 1977–80; *b* 2 Aug. 1916; *s* of Sydney Herbert Murley and Beatrice Maud Baylis; *m* 1947, Daphne, 2nd *d* of Ralph E. and Rowena Garrod; three *s* two *d*, and one step *d. Educ:* Dulwich Coll.; Univ. of London; St Bartholomew's Hosp. (MB, BS Hons 1939, MS 1948). MRCS, LRCP 1939; FRCS 1946. Served War, RAMC, 1939–45: ME, E Africa, N Africa, Sicily, Italy and NW Europe; regtl and fld ambulance MO; Surgical Specialist, No 1 and 2 Maxillo-Facial Units and Field Surg. Units; Major. St Bartholomew's Hospital: Jun. Scholarship, 1935; Sen. Schol., and Sir William Dunn Exhibn in Anat., Univ. of London, 1936; House Surg., 1939; Anat. Demonstrator, 1946; Surg. Chief Asst, 1946–49; Cattlin Res. Fellow and Mackenzie Mackinnon Res. Fellow, RCP and RCS, 1950–51; Surgeon: St Albans Hosp., 1947; Royal Northern Hosp., London, 1953; Hon. Consultant Surgeon, St Bartholomew's Hosp., 1979. Chm., Med. Council on Alcoholism, 1980–92. Royal Coll. of Surgeons: formerly Tutor and Reg. Adviser; Examiner, primary FRCS, 1966–72; Mem. Council, 1970–82; Hunterian Orator, 1981; Bradshaw Lectr, 1981; Mem. Ct of Patrons, 1981–; Trustee of Hunterian Mus., 1981– (Chm., 1988–96); Thomas Vicary Lectr, 1995. Vis. Prof., Cleveland Clinic, USA, 1979, 1982 and 1986. Mitchiner Lectr, RAMC, 1981 and 1993. FRSocMed, 1945–84 (Hon. Sec., Clinical Sect., 1958–60, Sect. of Surgery, 1964–66); Fellow, Assoc. of Surgeons of GB and Ireland. Member: Hunterian Soc. (former Mem. Council; Pres., 1970–71; Orator, 1978); Med. Soc. of London (former Mem. Council; Pres., 1982); Harveian Soc. (former Mem. Council; Pres., 1983); BMA (former Councillor); Exec. Cttee, Soc. Internat. de Chirurgie, 1979–83 (Vice-Pres., 1985–86; Hon. Mem., 1991); European and internat. cardiovascular socs., 1954–79; Adv. Council, The Social Affairs Unit, 1981–; Adv. Council, Health and Welfare Unit (formerly Health Unit), Inst. of Economic Affairs, 1986–. Hon. Vice-Pres., Nat. Stroke Campaign, 1985; Hon. Member: Brit. Assoc. of Plastic Surgs, 1983; Brit. Assoc. of Clinical Anatomists, 1983; Reading Pathological Soc., 1985; First Hon. Mem. and Medallist, Indep. Doctors' Forum, 1995. Pybus Lectr. and Medal, Newcastle, 1975; Sir Thomas & Lady Edith Dixon Meml Lect., Belfast, 1979, and sundry other eponymous lectures and orations; Hon. FRACS and Syme Orator, 1979; Hon. FCSSA 1979; Hon. FRCSI 1980; Hon. FDSRCS 1981; Hon. Fellow: Italian Soc. Surg., 1979; Polish Assoc. of Surgeons, 1983. President: Sir John Charnley Trust, 1983–; Alleyn Club, 1983; Fellowship for Freedom in Medicine 1972–86; Mem. Council, Freedom Assoc., 1982–; Patron: Med. Aid to Poland, 1984–; Jagiellonian Trust, 1984–; Sponsor, 1984, Trustee, 1986, Family & Youth Concern (The Responsible Soc.). Freeman, City of London, 1955; Hon. Freeman, Barbers' Co., 1986; Liveryman, Apothecaries' Co., 1955–. *Publications:* (contrib.) Financing Medical Care, 1962; Surgical Roots and Branches (autobiog.), 1990; (ed jtly) The Case Books of John Hunter, FRS, 1993; contrib. surg. textbooks; articles in med. literature on breast, thyroid and vascular diseases; articles on med. politics and econs. *Recreations:* gardening, music, reading history and economics. *Address:* (home) Cobden Hill House, 63 Cobden Hill, Radlett, Herts WD7 7JN. *T:* (01923) 856532; (office) Consulting Suite, Wellington Hospital, Wellington Place, NW8 9LE. *T:* (0171) 586 5959. *Clubs:* Royal Automobile; Fountain (St Bart's Hospital).
Died 2 Oct. 1997.

MURRAY, Sir Donald (Frederick), KCVO 1983; CMG 1973; DL; HM Diplomatic Service, retired; Channel Tunnel Complaints Commissioner, 1987–95; *b* 14 June 1924; *s* of A. T. Murray and F. M. Murray (*née* Byfield); *m* 1949, Marjorie Culverwell; three *s* one *d. Educ:* Colfe's

Grammar Sch.; King's Sch., Canterbury (King's and Entrance Schols); Worcester Coll., Oxford. Royal Marines, 1943–46 (41 (RM) Commando). Entered Foreign Office, 1948; Third Sec., Warsaw, 1948; FO 1951; Second Sec., Vienna, 1953; First Sec., Political Office, ME Forces, 1956; FO, 1957; First Sec. (Comm.), Stockholm, 1958; Head of Chancery, Saigon, 1962; FO 1964; Counsellor, 1965; Head of SE Asia Dept, 1966; Counsellor, Tehran, 1969–72; RCDS, 1973; Ambassador to Libya, 1974–76; Asst Under-Sec. of State, FCO, 1977–80; Ambassador to Sweden, 1980–84. Assessor Chm., CS Selection Bd, 1984–86. Director: Goodlass Wall and Co., 1985–90; Winsor and Newton, subseq. Col Art Fine Art and Graphics, 1991–95. Kent County Chm., SSAFA, 1985–90, Vice-Pres., 1991–96; Trustee, World Resource Foundn, 1986–96. DL Kent, 1992. Grand Cross, Order of North Star (Sweden), 1983. *Recreations:* gentle sports (Oxford v Cambridge cross-country, 1942; athletics, 1943; small-bore shooting, 1947), gardening, music. *Address:* Southridge, Church Square, Rye TN31 7HH.
Died 8 Jan. 1998.

MURRAY, Elisabeth; *see* Murray, K. M. E.

MURRAY, George Raymond B.; *see* Beasley-Murray.

MURRAY, (Katherine Maud) Elisabeth, FSA; Principal, Bishop Otter College, Chichester, 1948–70; *b* 3 Dec. 1909; *d* of Harold J. R. Murray (former HMI of Schools) and Kate M. Crosthwaite. *Educ:* Colchester County High Sch.; Somerville Coll., Oxford (BLitt 1933; MA). Tutor and Librarian, Ashburne Hall, Manchester, 1935–37; Mary Somerville Research Fellow, Somerville Coll., Oxford, 1937–38; Asst Tutor and Registrar, 1938–44, Domestic Bursar, 1942–44, and Junior Bursar, 1944–48, Girton Coll., Cambridge. Chairman of Council, Sussex Archæological Soc., 1964–77, Pres., 1977–80. Mem., Chichester District Council, 1973 87 (Chm. Planning Cttee, 1979–82; Vice-Chm., 1976–79). Hon. DLitt: Sussex, 1978; Coll. of Wooster, Ohio, 1979. Chichester Civic Award, 1993. *Publications:* The Constitutional History of the Cinque Ports, 1935; Register of Daniel Rough, Kent Record Soc., 1945; Caught in the Web of Words: James A. H. Murray and the Oxford English Dictionary, 1977 (Crashaw Prize, British Academy, 1979); articles in Sussex Notes and Queries, Transactions of the Royal Historical Society, Archæologia Cantiana, English Historical Review. *Recreations:* archæology, downland and nature conservation. *Address:* Upper Cranmore, Heyshott, Midhurst, West Sussex GU29 0DL. *T:* (01730) 812325.
Died 6 Feb. 1998.

MURRAY, Peter, CMG 1959; HM Diplomatic Service, retired; *b* 18 July 1915; *s* of Rear-Adm. H. P. W. G. Murray, DSO and Mabel C. (*née* Avens); *m* 1960, Evelyn Mary, (Mollie), Batchelor. *Educ:* Portsmouth Grammar Sch.; Merton Coll., Oxford. Burma Commission, 1937–49; served Burma RNVR, 1940–43, Civil Affairs Staff, Burma, 1944–45; joined Foreign Service, 1947; Ambassador to Cambodia, 1961–64; Ambassador to Ivory Coast, Upper Volta and Niger, 1970–72. *Died 25 June 2000.*

MUSCROFT, Harold Colin; barrister; *b* Leeds, 12 June 1924; *s* of Harold and Meta Catrina Muscroft; *m* 1958; three *d*. *Educ:* Dept of Navigation, Southampton Univ.; home; Exeter Coll., Oxford (MA). Volunteer, Royal Corps of Signals, 1942; commnd RA, 1943; served in India, Burma (wounded), Malay and Java; demobilised 1947 (Captain). Oxford, 1947–51. Called to the Bar, Inner Temple, 1953; called to Hong Kong Bar, 1982. Practised NE Circuit; a Recorder of the Crown Court, 1972–82. Huddersfield Town Councillor, 1958–59. *Recreation:* writing. *Address:* 11 Chelmsford Road, Harrogate, North Yorks HG1 5NA. *T:* (01423) 503344; Les Oliviers, 28 Boulevard Eugene-Tripet, 06400 Cannes, France.
Died 22 Jan. 1999.

MUSGRAVE, Dennis Charles, FICE; Director, British Water Industries Group, 1981–85; *b* 10 Feb. 1921; *s* of Frederick Charles Musgrave and Jane Elizabeth (*née* Gulliver); *m* 1942, Marjorie Cynthia (*née* Chaston); one *s*. *Educ:* privately. MIStructE, FIWES. Engineering Assistant: Howard Humphreys and Sons, Consulting Engrs; Coode and Partners, Cons. Engrs, 1938–45; Asst Port Engr, Lagos, Nigeria, 1945–47; Engrg Asst, Borough of Willesden, 1947–49; Agent, Ruddock and Meighan, Civil Engrg Contractors, 1949–56; Associate Partner, Sandford, Fawcett and Partners, Cons. Engrs, in Canada, 1956–63, in Westminster, 1963–66; Engineering Inspector, Min. of Housing and Local Govt, 1966, Sen. Inspector, 1971; Asst Dir, DoE, 1974; Under Sec. and Chief Water Engr, DoE, 1977–82. *Publications:* various technical papers. *Recreations:* music, literature. *Address:* Gaywoods, Ringshall Road, Little Gaddesden, near Berkhamstead, Herts HP4 1PE. *T:* (01442) 843501.
Died 3 Nov. 1999.

MUSGRAVE, Sir Richard James, 7th Bt *cr* 1782, of Tourin, Waterford; *b* 10 Feb. 1922; *s* of Sir Christopher Norman Musgrave, 6th Bt, OBE, and Kathleen (*d* 1967), 3rd *d* of late Robert Chapman, Co. Tyrone; *S* father, 1956; *m* 1958, Maria, *d* of late Col M. Cambanis, and Mrs Cambanis, Athens, Greece; two *s* four *d. Educ:* Stowe. Capt., The Poona Horse (17th Queen Victoria's Own Cavalry), 1940–45. *Recreation:* shooting. *Heir: s* Christopher John Shane Musgrave, *b* 23 Oct. 1959. *Address:* PO Box 82, Syros, Greece. *Club:* Kildare Street and University (Dublin). *Died 2 Dec. 2000.*

MUSGROVE, Prof. John, RIBA; Professor Emeritus, University of London; Haden Pilkington Professor of Environmental Design and Engineering, 1978–85 and Head of the Bartlett School of Architecture and Planning, 1980–85, University College London; *b* 20 June 1920; *s* of James Musgrove and Betsy (*née* Jones); *m* 1941, Gladys Mary Webb; three *s. Educ:* Univ. of Durham (King's Coll.) (BArch, 1st Cl. Hons). Asst to Baron Holford, RA, 1952–53; Research Architect, Nuffield Foundn, 1953–60; Sen. Lectr and Reader in Architecture, University Coll. London, 1960–70, Prof., 1970–78. Hon. Fellow, Inst. of Architects, Sri Lanka, 1972. *Publications:* (jtly) The Function and Design of Hospitals, 1955; (jtly) The Design of Research Laboratories, 1960; (ed) Sir Banister Fletcher's History of Architecture, 19th edn 1987; numerous articles and papers in Architects' Jl, RIBA Jl, and reviews. *Recreations:* painting in oils, gardening. *Address:* Netherby, 79 Green End Road, Boxmoor, Hemel Hempstead, Herts HP1 1QW. *Died 8 May 2000.*

MUSKIE, Edmund Sixtus; Secretary of State, USA, 1980–81; lawyer and politician; *b* Rumford, Maine, 28 March 1914; *s* of Stephen Muskie and Josephine Czarnecki; *m* 1948, Jane Frances Gray; two *s* three *d. Educ:* Bates Coll., Maine (AB); Cornell Law Sch., Ithaca, New York (LLB). Served War, Lieut USNR, 1942–45. Admitted to Bar: Massachusetts, 1939; Maine, 1940, and practised at Waterville, Maine, 1940 and 1945–55; Federal District Court, 1941. Mem., Maine House of Reps, 1947–51; Democratic Floor Leader, 1949–51; Dist Dir for Maine, Office of Price Stabilisation, 1951–52; City Solicitor, Waterville, Maine, 1954–55; Governor of State of Maine, 1955–59; US Senator from Maine, 1959–80; Senate Assistant Majority Whip, 1966–80; Chm., Senate Budget Cttee, 1974–80; Mem., Senate Foreign Relations Cttee, 1970–74, 1979–80; Former Chm., and Mem. *ex officio*, Democratic Senatorial Campaign Cttee; Chairman, Senate Sub-Cttees on: Environmental Pollution, Senate Environment and Public Wks Cttee; Intergovtl Relations,

Senate Governmental Affairs Cttee, 1959–78. Cand. for Vice-Presidency of US, 1968. Former Member: Special Cttee on Aging; Exec. Cttee, Nat. Governors' Conf.; Chm., Roosevelt Campobello Internat. Park Commn. Mem, Amer. Acad. of Arts and Sciences. Had numerous hon. doctorates. Phi Beta Kappa; Phi Alpha Delta. Presidential Medal of Freedom, 1981; Notre Dame Laetare Medal, 1981; Distinguished Service Award, Former Members of Congress Assoc., 1981. *Publication:* Journeys, 1972. *Address:* Chadbourne Parke, 1101 Vermont Avenue, NW, Washington, DC 20005, USA.
Died 26 March 1996.

MYERS, Dr David Milton, CMG 1974; Vice-Chancellor, La Trobe University, Melbourne, 1965–76; *b* 5 June 1911; *s* of W. H. Myers, Sydney; *m* 1st, 1937, Beverley A. H. (*d* 1993), *d* of Dr T. D. Delprat; three *s*; 2nd, 1994, Moyna Lien, *d* of Dr T. D. Delprat. *Educ:* Univ. of Sydney (BSc, BE, DScEng); Univ. of Oxford. FIEAust, FIEE, FInstP. 1st Chief of Div. of Electrotechnology, CSIR, 1939–49; P. N. Russell Prof. of Elec. Engrg, Univ. of Sydney, 1949–59; Dean, Faculty of Applied Science, and Prof. of Elec. Engrg, Univ. of British Columbia, 1960–65. Mem. Adv. Council, CSIRO, 1949–55; Mem., Nat. Res. Council of Canada, 1965; Chairman: Cttee on Overseas Professional Qualifications, 1969–84; Inquiry into Unemployment Benefits, for Aust. Govt, 1977; Cttee of Inquiry into fluoridation of Victorian water supplies, 1979–80; Consultative Council on Victorian Mental Health Act, 1981. Pres., Aust. Inst. of Engineers, 1958. Kernot Meml Medal, Melbourne Univ., 1974; P. N. Russell Meml Medal, Instn of Engrs, Aust., 1977. *Publications:* various research papers in sci. jls. *Recreations:* golf, tennis, music. *Address:* 23 Ethel Street, Balgowlah, NSW 2093, Australia. *T:* (2) 99485776. *Club:* Melbourne (Melbourne).   *Died 10 Nov. 1999.*

MYERS, Brig. Edmund Charles Wolf, CBE 1944; DSO 1943; CEng, MICE; *b* 12 Oct. 1906; *er s* of late Dr C. S. Myers, CBE, FRS and Edith (*née* Seligman); *m* 1943, Louisa (*d* 1995), *er d* of late Aldred Bickham Sweet-Escott; one *d*. *Educ:* Haileybury; Royal Military Academy, Woolwich; Caius Coll., Cambridge (BA 1929).

Commissioned into Royal Engineers, 1926; served Palestine, 1936 (despatches); War of 1939–45; Comdr, British Mil. Mission to Greek Resistance Forces, 1942–43; Middle East, including Balkans, until 1944 (African Star, Italy Star, DSO, CBE); North-West Europe, 1944–45 (France and Germany Star, Dutch Bronze Lion, Norwegian Liberty Medal); Far East, 1945; Korea, 1951–52 (despatches, American Legion of Merit); Army Instructor, RAF Staff Coll., Bracknell, 1952–55; Chief Engineer, British Troops in Egypt, 1955–56; Dep. Dir, Personnel Administration in the War Office, 1956–59; retired 1959. Chief Civil Engineer, Cleveland Bridge & Engineering Co. Ltd, 1959–64; Construction Manager, Power Gas Corp. Ltd, Davy-Ashmore Group, 1964–67. Regional Sec., British Field Sports Soc., 1968–71. *Publication:* Greek Entanglement, 1955. *Recreations:* horse training and riding, sailing, flying (1st Sec. RE Flying Club, 1934–35), fishing. *Address:* Newlands Nursing Care Centre, Evesham Road, Stow-on-the-Wold, Glos GL54 1EJ. *Clubs:* Army and Navy, Special Forces.
Died 6 Dec. 1997.

MYERS, Harry Eric; QC 1967; QC (Gibraltar) 1977; *b* 10 Jan. 1914; *s* of Harry Moss Myers and Alice Muriel Serjeant; *m* 1951, Lorna Babette Kitson (*née* Blackburn); no *c*. *Educ:* Bedford Sch. HAC, City of London, 1931. Admitted Solicitor of Supreme Court, 1936; called to Bar, Middle Temple, 1945. Prosecuting Counsel to Bd of Inland Revenue on SE Circuit, 1965. *Address:* 202 Beatty House, Dolphin Square, SW1V 3PH; 10 King's Bench Walk, Temple, EC4Y 7EB.   *Died Aug. 1996.*

MYERS, Sir Kenneth (Ben), Kt 1977; MBE 1944; FCA; Director, South British Insurance Co. Ltd, 1934–82 (Chairman, 1945–78); retired; *b* 5 March 1907; *s* of Hon. Sir Arthur Myers and Lady (Vera) Myers (*née* Levy); *m* 1933, Margaret Blair Pirie; one *s* two *d*. *Educ:* Marlborough Coll.; Gonville and Caius Coll., Cambridge (BA 1928). FCA 1933. Returned to NZ, 1933; served War with 2nd NZEF, ME and Italy, 1940–45. *Recreation:* looking after my family. *Address:* PO Box 112, Auckland 1, New Zealand. *Clubs:* Boodle's; Northern (Auckland).
Died 15 June 1998.

N

NABARRO, Sir John (David Nunes), Kt 1983; MD; FRCP; Consultant Physician, The Middlesex Hospital, London, 1954–81, then Emeritus Consultant Physician; Hon. Research Associate, Departments of Medicine and Biochemistry, University College and Middlesex School of Medicine (formerly Middlesex Hospital Medical School), since 1981; Director, Cobbold Laboratories, Middlesex Hospital Medical School, 1970–81; Hon. Consultant Physician, Royal Prince Alfred Hospital, Sidney, since 1959; *b* 21 Dec. 1915; *s* of David Nunes Nabarro and Florence Nora Nabarro (*née* Webster); *m* 1948, Joan Margaret Cockrell; two *s* two *d. Educ:* Oundle Sch.; University Coll., London (Howard Cluff Meml Prize 1935; Fellow, UCL, 1963); University Coll. Hosp. Med. Sch. (Magrath Schol., Atkinson Morley Schol., Atchison Schol., 1938); MD London 1946. Medical Specialist, OC Med. Div., RAMC, 1939–45: served in Iraq; 8th Army, Italy (Salerno Anzio); Middle East (despatches). University College Hospital: House Phys., 1939; Med. Registrar, 1945–47; Res. Asst Phys., 1948–49; First Asst, Med. Unit, UCH Med. Sch., 1950–54; WHO Travelling Fellowship, 1952. Hon. Cons. Endocrinologist to Army, 1965–81. Examiner in Medicine, Univs of Cambridge, London and Sheffield. Chm., Jt Consultants Cttee, 1979–84. Mem., Assoc. of Physicians of GB and Ire., 1952, Pres., Sect. of Endocrinology, RSM, 1968–70; Chm., Med. and Sci. Sects, 1975–77, Chm. Council, 1986–90, Brit. Diabetic Assoc. Royal College of Physicians: Mem. Council, 1954 55; Oliver Sharpey Lectr, 1960; Joseph Senior White Fellow, 1960; Examiner for MRCP, 1964–81; Procensor, 1973; Censor, 1974; Croonian Lectr, 1976; Sen. Censor and First Vice-Pres., 1977. William McIlwrath Guest Prof., Royal Prince Alfred Hosp., Sidney, 1959; John Mathison Shaw Lectr, RCPE, 1963; Guest Visitor, St Vincent's Hosp., Sidney, 1963; Guest Lectr, Postgrad. Cttee, Christchurch Hosps, NZ, 1973; Banting Meml Lectr, Brit. Diabetic Assoc., 1978; Best Meml Lectr, Toronto Diabetes Assoc., 1984. Hon. FRSocMed 1988. *Publications:* Biochemical Investigations in Diagnosis and Treatment, 1954, 3rd edn, 1962; papers on endocrinology and diabetes in med. jls. *Recreations:* gardening, postal history. *Address:* 33 Woodside Avenue, N12 8AT. *T:* (0181) 445 7925.
Died 28 April 1998.

NAILOR, Prof. Peter; Provost of Gresham College, since 1988; *b* 16 Dec. 1928; *o s* of Leslie Nailor and Lily Matilda (*née* Jones). *Educ:* Mercers' Sch.; Wadham Coll., Oxford (BA 1952, MA 1955). Home Civil Service, 1952; Asst Principal, Admiralty, 1952; First Lord's Representative on Admiralty Interview Bd, 1960–62; Polaris Executive, 1962–67; Asst Sec., MoD, 1967–69; Professor of Politics, Univ. of Lancaster, 1969–77; Prof. of Hist., 1977–88, Dean, 1982–84 and 1986–88, RNC, Greenwich. Visiting research appts and professorships in Canada, Australia and India. Member: Political Science Cttee, SSRC, 1975–81; FCO adv. panel on arms control and disarmament, 1975–88; MoD adv. panel on historical records, 1979–88; Chairman, British International Studies Assoc., 1983–86. *Publications:* (ed) The Soviet Union and the Third World, 1981; The Nassau Connection, 1988; Learning from Precedent in Whitehall, 1991; articles in learned jls, pamphlets. *Address:* Gresham College, Barnard's Inn Hall, Holborn EC1N 2HH.
Died 5 April 1996.

NAPIER, Rev. Michael Scott; Priest of the London Oratory, since 1959; *b* 15 Feb. 1929; *s* of Maj.-Gen. Charles Scott Napier, CB, CBE and Ada Kathleen Napier (*née* Douetil). *Educ:* Wellington Coll.; Trinity Hall, Cambridge (MA). Ordained priest, 1959; Superior of London Oratory, 1969–81, 1991–94; Visitor or Delegate of Holy See for Oratory of St Philip Neri, 1982–94. *Recreations:* art and architecture, history, travel. *Address:* The Oratory, SW7 2RP. *T:* 0171–589 4811. *Clubs:* Athenæum, Chelsea Arts.
Died 22 Aug. 1996.

NARAYAN, Rudy; Chairman and Director, Civil Rights UK, since 1994; *b* Guyana, 11 May 1938; *s* of Sase Narayan and Taijbertie (*née* Sawh); *m* 1970, Dr Naseem Akbar (marr. diss.); two *d*; *m* 1988, Saeeda Begum Asif. *Educ:* Lincoln's Inn. Came to UK, 1953; served HM Forces, BAOR and HQ MELF, 1958–65. Lincoln's Inn: Founder/1st Pres., Students Union, 1966; Chm. of Debates, and Captain of Cricket, 1967; called to the Bar, 1968. Vice-Chm., Lambeth Council for Community Relations, 1974; Founder Chm., Lambeth Law Centre; Councillor, Lambeth, 1974–76. Founder, Black Rights (UK); Legal Adviser: Caribbean Times, Asian Times, African Times (London). Formerly: Mem., Race Relations Bd; Legal Officer, W Indian Standing Conf.; Founder, Soc. of Black Lawyers (Pres., 1987 89). Contested (Ind) Vauxhall June 1989. *Publications:* Black Community on Trial, 1976; Black England, 1977; Barrister for the Defence, 1985; Black Silk, 1985; When Judges Conspire, 1989. *Recreations:* cricket, debating, theatre, ballet opera *Address:* (office) Justice House, 411A Brixton Road, SW9 7DG. *T:* (0171) 738 7375, (0171) 501 9394. *Club:* Wig and Pen.
Died 28 June 1998.

NASH, (Denis Frederic) Ellison, OBE 1982; AE 1943; FRCS; Consulting Surgeon, St Bartholomew's Hospital; *b* 10 Feb. 1913; *m* 1938, Joan Mary Andrew (*d* 1998); two *s* two *d. Educ:* Dulwich College; St Bartholomew's Medical College. MRCS, LRCP 1935; FRCS 1938. Served war of 1939–45, RAFVR, Wing-Comdr. Consultant Surgeon: St Bartholomew's Hosp., 1947–78; Chailey Heritage Hosp., 1952–78; Dean, St Bartholomew's Hospital Medical College, 1957–62; Special Trustee, St Bartholomew's Hosp., 1974–78; Regional Postgraduate Dean, and Asst Dir, British Postgraduate Medical Fedn, Univ. of London, 1948–74. Hunterian Professor, 1949 and 1956. Arris and Gale Lecturer, 1950. Special interest in the education and care of the physically handicapped; Hon. Medical Adviser: Shaftesbury Soc.; John Groom's Assoc. for Disabled. Senior Member, British Assoc. of Urological Surgeons. Senior Fellow, British Orthopædic Assoc.; Fellow, Assoc. of Surgeons of GB. Hon. Fellow, Med. Artists Assoc. *Publications:* The Principles and Practice of Surgery for Nurses and Allied Professions, 1955, 7th rev. edn 1980; scientific papers in medical journals particularly concerned with surgery of childhood. *Recreations:* photography, fuchsias. *Address:* Carleton Lodge, Marine Road, Deal, Kent CT14 7DN. *Club:* City of London Guild of Freemen.
Died 4 Aug. 2000.

NASMITH, Rear-Adm. David Arthur D.; *see* Dunbar-Nasmith.

NATHANS, Prof. Daniel; Professor of Molecular Biology and Genetics, The Johns Hopkins University School of Medicine, since 1980; Senior Investigator, Howard Hughes Medical Institute, since 1982; *b* 30 Oct. 1928; *s* of Samuel Nathans and Sarah Nathans (*née* Levitan); *m*

1956, Joanne Gomberg; three s. *Educ:* Univ. of Delaware, Newark (BS Chemistry); Washington Univ., St Louis, Mo (MD). Intern, 1954–55, and resident, 1957–59, in Medicine, Columbia-Presbyterian Medical Center, NYC; Clinical Associate, Nat. Cancer Inst., Bethesda, Md, 1955–57; Guest Investigator, Rockefeller Inst., NYC, 1959–62; Prof. of Microbiology, 1962 and Faculty Mem., Johns Hopkins Univ. Sch. of Medicine, Baltimore, Md, 1962–; Interim Pres., Johns Hopkins Univ., 1995. Mem., President's Council of Advrs on Science and Technol., 1990–93. US Nat. Acad. of Scis Award in Molecular Biology, 1976; Nobel Prize in Physiology or Medicine, 1978; US Nat. Medal of Sci., 1993. *Address:* 2227 Crest Road, Baltimore, MD 21209, USA.

Died 16 Nov. 1999.

NEILL, Prof. Derrick James, DFC 1943; Emeritus Professor of Prosthetic Dentistry, University of London; Sub-Dean of Dental Studies, Guy's Hospital Dental School, 1969–76; Consultant Dental Surgeon, Guy's Hospital, since 1960; *b* 14 March 1922; *s* of Jameson Leonard Neill, MBE, and Lynn (*née* Moyle); *m* 1st, 1952, Iris Jordan (*d* 1970); one *s* one *d*; 2nd, 1971, Catherine Mary Daughtry. *Educ:* East Sheen County Grammar Sch.; Guy's Hosp. Dental Sch., Univ. of London. LDSRCS 1952; FDSRCS 1955; MDS London, 1966. Served RAFVR, 1941–46, 150 Sqdn, Bomber Comd (Sqdn Ldr). Department of Dental Prosthetics, Guy's Hospital Dental School: Lectr, 1954; Sen. Lectr, 1959; Univ. Reader in Dental Prosthetics, 1967; Prof. of Prosthetic Dentistry, 1969. Council Member, Odontological Section, Royal Soc. of Medicine, 1966–73; Past Pres., British Soc. for Study of Prosthetic Dentistry. Mem. Council of Governors: Guy's Hosp. Med. Sch., 1980–82; United Med. Schs of Guy's and St Thomas's Hosps, 1982–87. Fellow, Internat. Coll. of Cranio-Mandibular Orthopedics, 1986. Mem. Editorial Bd, Internat. Jl of Prosthodontics. *Publications:* (jtly) Complete Dentures, 1968; Partial Denture Construction, 1976; Restoration of the Partially Dentate Mouth, 1984; numerous papers in dental jls. *Recreations:* golf, music. *Address:* Hurst, Clenches Farm Road, Kippington, Sevenoaks, Kent TN13 2LU. *T:* (01732) 452374. *Club:* Royal Automobile.

Died 7 July 2000.

NEILSON, Nigel Fraser, MC 1943; Chairman, Nigel F. Neilson, Public Relations (formerly Neilson McCarthy, then Neilson Associates), since 1962; *b* 12 Dec. 1919; *s* of Lt-Col W. Neilson, DSO, 4th Hussars and Maud Alice Francis Anson; *m* 1949, Pamela Catherine Georgina Sheppard (*d* 1989); one *s* one *d*. *Educ:* Hereworth Sch.; Christ's Coll., New Zealand; RADA. Inns of Court Regt; commnd Staffs Yeomanry, 1939; seconded Cavalry Regt, Transjordanian Frontier Force; served Syrian Campaign; returned Staffs Yeo., Seventh Armoured Div., GSO 111 Ops; served desert and Italy; Staff Coll., 1944; served in Germany, Holland and France; C of S, Bergen area, Norway; served with SAS and French SAS. On demobilisation worked in theatre, cabaret, films, London, USA and NZ; joined J. Walter Thompson, 1951; became personal rep. to Aristotle Onassis, 1955, later consultant to his daughter, Christina; founded Neilson McCarthy Internat. Public Relations Consultants in UK, USA, Australia, NZ and SE Asia, 1962. Past Pres., NZ Soc., 1978–79. Chevalier de la Légion d'Honneur, 1946; Croix de Guerre avec Palme, 1946. *Recreations:* riding, shooting, music, theatre. *Address:* c/o Coutts & Co., 1 Old Park Lane, W1Y 4BS. *Died 3 June 2000.*

NEILSON, Richard Alvin, CMG 1987; LVO 1968; HM Diplomatic Service, retired; High Commissioner to Trinidad and Tobago, 1994–96; *b* 9 July 1937; *s* of Robert and Ethel Neilson; *m* 1961, Olive Tyler; one *s*. *Educ:* Burnley Grammar Sch.; Leeds Univ. (BA Hons 1958, MA

1960). Fulbright Fellow, Univ. of Wisconsin, 1959–60; Asst Lectr, Univ. of Edinburgh, 1960–61; joined FO, 1961; Third (later Second) Sec., Kinshasa, 1963–65; Treasury Centre for Admin. Studies, 1965; Second (later First) Sec. (Information), Santiago, 1966–69; First Sec., Canberra, 1969–73; FCO, 1973–77; Counsellor, seconded to NI Office as Head of Political Affairs Div., 1977–79; Dep. High Comr, Lusaka, 1979–80, Acting High Comr, Nov. 1979–June 1980; Dep. Governor and Political Advr, Gibraltar, 1981–84; Head of Southern European Dept, FCO, 1984–86; Ambassador to Colombia, 1987–90; Ambassador to Chile, 1990–93. *Publications:* contribs to geomorphological literature. *Address:* Maynes Hill Farm, Hoggeston, Buckingham, Bucks MK18 3LG. *T:* (01296) 714837. *Clubs:* Royal Commonwealth Society; Middlesex CC. *Died 6 June 1997.*

NELSON, Air Cdre Eric Douglas Mackinlay, CB 1952; retired, 1963; *b* 2 Jan. 1912; *e s* of late Rear-Adm. R. D. Nelson, CBE, and Ethel Nelson (*née* MacKinlay); *m* 1939, Margaret Yvonne Taylor (*d* 1988); one *s* one *d*. *Educ:* Dover Coll.; RAF Coll., Cranwell. Commissioned RAF, 1932; served War of 1939–45 (despatches); CO 103 (HB) Sqdn Elsham Wolds, 1943–44; Group Capt., 1944; ADC to the Queen, 1953–57; Air Commodore, 1956; Commandant, RAF, Halton, 1956–58; Commandant, Royal Air Force Staff College, Andover, 1958–60; AOA Transport Command, 1960–61; Air Officer Commanding and Commandant, Royal Air Force College, Cranwell, 1961–63. DL Lincs, 1966. *Recreations:* sailing, beagling. *Address:* 23 The Link, Wellingore, Lincoln LN5 0BJ. *T:* (01522) 810604. *Club:* Royal Air Force.

Died 5 Dec. 1996.

NEMETZ, Hon. Nathaniel Theodore, CC 1989; Canada Medal 1967; Chief Justice of British Columbia and Administrator of the Province of British Columbia, 1979–88; *b* 8 Sept. 1913; *s* of Samuel Nemetz and Rebecca (*née* Birch); *m* 1935, Bel Newman (*d* 1991); one *s*. *Educ:* Univ. of British Columbia (BA 1st Cl. Hons History). Called to the Bar, BC, 1937; KC (Canada) 1950; Justice: Supreme Court of BC, 1963–68; Court of Appeal of BC, 1968–73; Chief Justice, Supreme Court of BC, 1973–78. Exec. Mem., Canadian Judicial Council, 1973–88 (Vice-Chm., 1985–88). Special counsel to: City of Vancouver, City of New Westminster and Municipality of Burnaby; Electrical Assoc.; BC Hosp. Assoc.; Public Utilities Commn of BC; Royal Commission on: Expropriation, 1961; Fishing, 1964; Election Regulations, 1965; Forest Industry, 1966. Chm., Educational Delegn to People's Republic of China, 1974; Advisor to Canadian Govt Delegn, ILO, Geneva, 1973. University of British Columbia: Mem. Senate and Bd of Govs, 1957–68 (Chm. Bd of Govs, 1965–68); Chancellor, 1972–75, now Chancellor Emeritus; Pres., Alumni Assoc., 1957; Hon. Mem., Faculty Assoc., 1972; Chancellor's Medal, 1988. Mem., Bd of Governors, Canadian Inst. for Advanced Legal Studies, Cambridge, England. Hon. Fellow, Hebrew Univ., Jerusalem, 1976. Hon. LLD: Notre Dame (Nelson), 1972; Simon Fraser, 1975; British Columbia, 1975; Victoria, 1976. Freeman, City of Vancouver, 1988. Hon. Consul, Singapore, 1989–. Silver Jubilee Medal, 1977; Medal of Yugoslav Flag with Ribbon, 1989. *Publications:* articles on: Swedish Labour Law and Practice, 1967; Judicial Administration and Judicial Independence, 1976; The Jury and the Citizen, 1985; The Concept of the Independence of the Judiciary, 1985. *Recreations:* reading, travelling. *Address:* 5688 Newton Wynd, Vancouver, BC V6T 1H5, Canada. *T:* (604) 2245383. *Clubs:* Vancouver (Life Mem.), University (Life Mem.; Pres., 1961–62), Faculty of University of British Columbia (Hon. Life Mem.) (Vancouver). *Died 21 Oct. 1997.*

NENDICK, David Alan Challoner, CBE 1990; Secretary for Monetary Affairs, Hong Kong Government, 1985–93; b 31 July 1932; s of late Cyril Arthur and Kathleen Nendick; m 1964, Miriam Louise Gibbons; one s two d. *Educ:* Haileybury College. National Service, commissioned RA, 1950–52. Bank of England, 1953–89 (seconded Bank of Mauritius, 1970–72 and Hong Kong Govt, 1985–89); Hong Kong Govt, 1989–93. Gov., Dean Close Sch., Cheltenham, 1979–. Mem., Investment Cttee, Newnham Coll., Cambridge, 1993–. *Recreations:* tennis, walking, watching cricket. *Address:* Hideaway House, 83 Cheap Street, Sherborne, Dorset DT9 3BA. *T:* (01935) 814023; 26 St Stephens Gardens, W2 5QX. *T:* (0171) 792 2940. *Clubs:* East India, Bankers'; Hong Kong Country, Hong Kong Overseas Bankers.
Died 6 June 1997.

NEUBERGER, Albert, CBE 1964; PhD (London), MD (Würzburg); FRCP; FRS 1951; FRSC; Professor of Chemical Pathology, St Mary's Hospital, University of London, 1955–73, then Emeritus Professor; b 15 April 1908; s of late Max and Bertha Neuberger; m 1943, Lilian Ida, d of late Edmond and Marguerite Dreyfus, London; four s (one d decd). *Educ:* Gymnasium, Würzburg; Univs of Würzburg and London. Beit Memorial Research Fellow, 1936–40; Research at the Biochemistry Department, Cambridge, 1939–42; Mem. of Scientific Staff, Medical Research Council, 1943; Adviser to GHQ, Delhi (Medical Directorate), 1945; William Julius Mickle Fellowship of Univ. of London, 1946–47; Head of Biochemistry Dept, Nat. Inst. for Medical Research, 1950–55; Principal of the Wright Fleming Institute of Microbiology, 1958–62. Visiting Lectr on Medicine, 1960, on Biol Chemistry, 1964, Harvard Univ., and Physician-in-Chief (pro tem.), Peter Bent Brigham Hosp., Boston; Merck, Sharp and Dohme Vis. Prof., Sch. of Medicine, Univ. of Washington, 1965; Royal Soc./Israel Acad. Vis. Res. Prof., 1969; Julius Schultz Vis. Prof., Univ. of Miami Sch. of Medicine, 1988. Mem. of Editorial Bd, Biochemical Jl, 1947–55, Chm., 1952–55; Associate Man. Editor, Biochimica et Biophysica Acta, 1968–81. Member: MRC, 1962–66; Council of Scientific Policy, 1968–69; ARC, 1969–79; Indep. Cttee on Smoking and Health, 1973–82; Sci. Adv. Cttee, Rank Prize Funds, 1974–86; Chm., Jt ARC/MRC Cttee on Food and Nutrition Res., 1971–73; Chairman: Governing Body, Lister Inst., 1971–88 (Mem., 1968–); Advisory Board, Beit Memorial Fellowships, 1967–73; Biochemical Soc., 1967–69 (Hon. Mem., Biochemical Soc., 1973); Dep. Chm., Bd of Governors, Hebrew Univ., Jerusalem. Pres., Assoc. of Clinical Biochemists, 1972–73; Hon. Pres., British Nutrition Foundn, 1982–86. For. Hon. Mem., Amer. Acad. Arts and Sciences, 1972. FRCPath 1964; FRCP 1966. Heberden Medal, 1959; Frederick Gowland Hopkins Medal, 1960; Kaplun Prize, 1973. Hon. LLD Aberdeen, 1967; Hon. PhD Jerusalem, 1968; Hon. DSc Hull, 1981. *Publications:* papers in Biochemical Jl, Proceedings of Royal Society and other learned journals. *Address:* 37 Eton Court, Eton Avenue, NW3 3HJ. *T:* 0171–586 5470. *Club:* Athenæum.
Died 14 Aug. 1996.

NEVILE, Sir Henry (Nicholas), KCVO 1992; Lord-Lieutenant of Lincolnshire, 1975–95; High Steward, Lincoln Cathedral, since 1985; b 13 March 1920; e s of late Charles Joseph Nevile, Wellingore, Lincoln and Muriel (née O'Conor), m 1944, Jean Rosita Mary (MBE 1984), d of Cyril James Winceslas Torr and Maude (née Walpole); two s three d. *Educ:* Ampleforth; Trinity Coll., Cambridge. Served war, Scots Guards, in NW Europe, 1940–46 (despatches). Member: Upper Witham IDB, 1952–83 (Chm., 1964–76); Lincs River Bd and Authy, 1962–82; Kesteven CC, 1964–72. Liveryman, Farmers' Co., 1975– (Master, 1991–92). JP 1950, DL 1962, High Sheriff, 1963, Lincolnshire. Hon. Col, Lincs ACF. Hon.

LLD Hull, 1994. KStJ. *Address:* Aubourn Hall, Lincoln LN5 9DZ. *T:* (01522) 788270. *Club:* Brooks's.
Died 20 Oct. 1996.

NEVILLE, (Eric) Graham; His Honour Judge Neville; a Circuit Judge, since 1980; b 12 Nov. 1933; s of late Frederick Thomas Neville and Doris Winifred (née Toye); m 1966, Jacqueline Catherine, d of late Major Francis Whalley and Alexandrina Whalley (née MacLeod). *Educ:* Kelly Coll.; Sidney Sussex Coll., Cambridge. Served Royal Air Force, General Duties. Called to the Bar, Middle Temple, 1958. A Recorder of the Crown Court, 1975–80. Hon. Air Cdre, No 3 Maritime HQ Unit, RAuxAF, 1995–. *Recreations:* sailing, fishing. *Address:* Exeter Crown Court, The Castle, Exeter EX4 3PS. *Club:* Royal Western Yacht (Plymouth).
Died 8 May 1999.

NEVILLE, Royce Robert; Agent-General for Tasmania, in London, 1971–78; Governing Director, Neville Constructions Pty Ltd, Burnie; b 5 Oct. 1914; s of R. P. Neville, Launceston, Tasmania; m 1941, Joan (decd), d of G. A. Scott; two s two d. *Educ:* Launceston Technical Coll. Served War, Sqdn Ldr (OC Flying, Chief Flying Instr, Gen Reconnaissance Sqdn), RAAF, 1941–45. OC Air Trg Corps, Burnie, 1947. Past President: Air Force Assoc., 1947; Tas. Apex, 1948; Tas. Master Builders' Assoc., 1965–67; Master Builders' Fedn of Aust., 1965–66; Comr of Oaths for Tasmania, 1971; Mem., Australia Soc., London; Life Mem., Tasmanian Master Builders' Assoc. FInstD, FRAIB, AFAIM, Fellow, Inst. of Dirs, Aust., 1971; MIEx 1973; FFB 1976; FIArb 1977. Freeman, City of London, 1975; Freeman, Guild of Air Pilots and Air Navigators, 1976. JP 1974. *Recreations:* boating, fishing, painting. *Address:* 57 Illabunda Drive, Malua Bay, NSW 2536, Australia. *Clubs:* Wig and Pen; Naval, Military and Air Force (Hobart).
Died 25 Oct. 1997.

NEVIN, His Honour (Thomas) Richard, TD 1949 (and Bar); JP; a Judge of County Courts, later a Circuit Judge, 1967–84 (retired as Senior Circuit Judge, North Eastern Circuit); a Deputy High Court Judge, 1974–84; b 9 Dec. 1916; e s of late Thomas Nevin, JP, and Phyllis (née Strickland), Ebchester Hall and Mirfield; m 1955, Brenda Micaela (marr. diss. 1979), e d of Dr B. C. Andrade-Thompson, MC, Scarborough; one s (and one s decd). *Educ:* Bilton Grange; Shrewsbury School; Leeds University (LLB 1939). 2nd Lieut, W Yorks Regt (Leeds Rifles) TA, 1935; served London Bombardment, India and Burma, 1939–46; Indian Artillery, Lt-Col 1944 (despatches), SEAC; DJAG, XII Army, 1945; Major, TARO, 1951. WR Special Constab., 1938–66. Articled Clerk to Sir Arthur M. Ramsden, Solicitor, 1935. Called to the Bar, Inner Temple, 1948; practised 19 years on NE Circuit (Junior, 1951); Law Lectr, Leeds Coll. of Commerce, 1949–51; Asst Recorder of Leeds, 1961–64; Recorder of Doncaster, 1964–67; Dep. Chm. Quarter Sessions, W Riding, 1965–71, E Riding, 1968–71, Yorkshire; Chm., Northern Agricultural Land Tribunal, 1963–67 (Dep. Chm., 1961–63); a special Divorce Comr, 1967–72; Mem., County Court Rule Cttee, 1974–80. Hon. Life Member, Council of HM Circuit Judges. Chm., Lord Chancellor's Adv. Cttee on JPs, Hull, 1968–74; apptd by Minister of Transport to conduct enquiries under Merchant Shipping Acts, 1986–89. Founder Chm., Leeds Family Mediation Service, 1979–84. Mem., Leeds Gp Hospital Management Cttee, 1965–67. Director, Bowishott Estates Ltd. Hon. Life Mem., Yorks Archæological Soc.; President, Yorks Numismatic Soc., 1968; Life Mem., Guild of Freemen of London; Vice-Pres. Leeds Univ. Law Graduates; Mem., Leeds Univ. Adv. Cttee on Law. FRNS; FRSA; FCIArb. Freeman of City of London. JP West Yorks, 1965. *Publications:* Hon. Editor, Yorkshire Numismatic Soc.; and various articles. *Recreations:*

coinage, our past, retirement, and rest. *Address:* The Court House, 1 Oxford Row, Leeds LS2 7DG; 11 King's Bench Walk, Temple, EC4Y 7EQ. *Died 24 Dec. 2000.*

NEWBIGIN, Rt Rev. (James Edward) Lesslie, CBE 1974; DD; Minister, United Reformed Church, Winson Green, 1980–88, retired; *b* 8 Dec. 1909; *s* of Edward Richmond Newbigin, Shipowner, Newcastle, and Annie Ellen Newbigin (*née* Affleck); *m* 1936, Helen Stewart, *d* of Rev. Robert Henderson; one *s* three *d. Educ:* Leighton Park Sch.; Queens' Coll., Cambridge; Westminster Coll., Cambridge. Intercollegiate Secretary, Student Christian Movement, Glasgow, 1931–33. Ordained by Presbytery of Edinburgh and appointed to Madras Mission of Church of Scotland, 1936; served as missionary in Chingleput and Kancheepuram, 1936–46; Bishop in Madura and Ramnad, Church of South India, 1947–59; Chm., Adv. Cttee on Main Theme for Second Assembly, WCC, 1954; Vice-Chairman, Commission on Faith and Order, 1956; Chm., 1958, Gen. Sec., 1959, Internat. Missionary Council; Associate General Secretary, WCC, 1961–65; Bishop in Madras, 1965–74; Lectr in Theology, Selly Oak Colls, Birmingham, 1974–79. Moderator, Gen. Assembly of URC, 1978. Hon. DD: Chicago Theological Seminary, 1954; St Andrews, 1958; Hamburg, 1960; Basel, 1965; Hull, 1975; Newcastle, 1981. *Publications:* Christian Freedom in the Modern World, 1937; The Reunion of the Church, 1948; South India Diary, 1951; The Household of God, 1953; Sin and Salvation, 1956; A Faith for This One World?, 1962; Honest Religion for Secular Man, 1966; The Finality of Christ, 1969; The Good Shepherd, 1977; The Open Secret, 1978; The Light has come, 1982; The Other Side of 1984, 1983; Unfinished Agenda, 1985; Foolishness to the Greeks, 1986; The Gospel in a Pluralist Society, 1989; Truth to Tell, 1991; Proper Confidence: faith, doubt and certainty in Christian discipleship, 1995. *Recreations:* music, walking. *Address:* 91 Stradella Road, SE24 9HL. *Died 30 Jan. 1998.*

NEWBOROUGH, 7th Baron *cr* 1776 (Ire.), of Bodvean; **Robert Charles Michael Vaughan Wynn,** DSC 1942; Bt 1742; *b* 24 April 1917; *er s* of 6th Baron Newborough, OBE, JP, DL, and Ruby Irene (*d* 1960), 3rd *d* of Edmund Wigley Severne, Thenford, Northamptonshire and Wallop, Shropshire; *S* father, 1965; *m* 1st, 1945, Rosamund Lavington Barbour (marr. diss. 1971); one *s* two *d*; 2nd, 1971, Jennifer, *y d* of late Captain C. C. A. Allen, RN, and Eirene Marjorie Allen (who *m* 1962, Adm. Sir Vaughan Morgan). *Educ:* Oundle. Served as 2nd Lieut, SR, 1935–39, with 9th Lancers, 5th Inniskilling Dragoon Guards, then as Lieut with 16th/5th Lancers after 6 months attachment with Royal Dragoon Guards; invalided out of Army, 1940; took command of vessel attached to Fleet Air Arm, 1940, as civilian, and took part in Dunkirk evacuation; then joined RNVR as Sub Lieut; later had command of MTB 74 and took part in St Nazaire raid, 1942 (wounded, despatches, DSC, POW, escaped from Colditz 1944). High Sheriff of Merionethshire, 1963. *Recreation:* yachting. *Heir: s* Hon. Robert Vaughan Wynn [*b* 11 Aug. 1949; *m* 1st, 1981, Sheila Christine (marr. diss. 1988), *d* of William A. Massey; one *d*; 2nd, 1988, Mrs Susan Elizabeth Hall, *d* of late Andrew Francis Lloyd]. *Address:* Rhug, Corwen, Clwyd, North Wales LL21 0EH. *T:* (01490) 412510. *Clubs:* Goat, Naval and Military. *Died 11 Oct. 1998.*

NEWBY, (Percy) Howard, CBE 1972; novelist; *b* 25 June 1918; *o s* of Percy Newby and Isabel Clutsam Newby (*née* Bryant); *m* 1945, Joan Thompson; two *d. Educ:* Hanley Castle Grammar Sch., Worcester; St Paul's Coll., Cheltenham. Served War of 1939–45, RAMC, 1939–42; BEF, France, 1939–40; MEF, 1941–42; seconded as Lecturer in English Literature, Fouad 1st University, Cairo, 1942–46. Joined BBC, 1949; Controller: Third

Programme, 1958–69; Radio Three, 1969–71; Dir of Programmes, Radio, 1971–75; Man. Dir, BBC Radio, 1975–78. Chm., English Stage Co., 1978–84. Atlantic Award, 1946; Somerset Maugham Prize, 1948; Yorkshire Post Fiction Award, 1968; Booker Prize, 1969 (first recipient). *Publications:* A Journey to the Interior, 1945; Agents and Witnesses, 1947; The Spirit of Jem, 1947; Mariner Dances, 1948; The Snow Pasture, 1949; The Loot Runners, 1949; Maria Edgeworth, 1950; The Young May Moon, 1950; The Novel, 1945–50, 1951; A Season in England, 1951; A Step to Silence, 1952; The Retreat, 1953; The Picnic at Sakkara, 1955; Revolution and Roses, 1957; Ten Miles from Anywhere, 1958; A Guest and his Going, 1959; The Barbary Light, 1962; One of the Founders, 1965; Something to Answer For, 1968; A Lot to Ask, 1973; Kith, 1977; (with F. Maroon) The Egypt Story, 1979; Warrior Pharaohs, 1980; Feelings Have Changed, 1981; Saladin in his Time, 1984; Leaning in the Wind, 1986; Coming in with the Tide, 1991; Something About Women, 1995. *Address:* Garsington House, Garsington, Oxford OX44 9AB. *T:* (01865) 361420.
Died 6 Sept. 1997.

NEWHOUSE, Ven. (Robert) John (Darrell); Archdeacon of Totnes and Canon Residentiary of Exeter Cathedral, 1966–76, then Archdeacon Emeritus and Canon Emeritus; Treasurer of Exeter Cathedral, 1970–76; *b* 11 May 1911; *s* of Rev. R. L. C. Newhouse; *m* 1938, Winifred (*née* Elton); two *s. Educ:* St Edward's Sch.; Worcester Coll., Oxford; Cuddesdon College. Ordained deacon 1936, priest 1937; Curate of: St John's, Peterborough, 1936–40; St Giles, Cambridge, 1940–46; Chaplain, RNVR, 1941–46; Rector of Ashwater, Devon, 1946–56; Rural Dean of Holsworthy, 1954–56; Vicar of Littleham-cum-Exmouth, 1956–66; Rural Dean of Aylesbeare, 1965–66. *Address:* Pound Cottage, Northlew, Okehampton, Devon EX20 3NN. *T:* (01409) 221532. *Died 27 Nov. 2000.*

NEWLEY, (George) Anthony; actor since 1946; author, composer; *b* 24 Sept. 1931; *m* 1956, Ann Lynn (marr. diss. 1963); *m* 1963, Joan Henrietta Collins (OBE 1997) (marr. diss. 1970); one *s* one *d*; *m* Dareth Rich (marr. diss. 1998); one *s* one *d. Educ:* Mandeville Street Sch., Clapton, E5. Appeared on West End stage in: Cranks, 1955; Stop the World, I Want to Get Off (co-author and co-composer with Leslie Bricusse), 1961–62, subseq. starred in New York production, 1962–63, new production, Lyric, 1989 (also co-dir); The Good Old Bad Old Days (co-author and co-composer with Leslie Bricusse), 1972; The Roar of the Greasepaint- the Smell of the Crowd (co-author and composer with Leslie Bricusse, star and director), New York, 1965; Chaplin, Los Angeles, 1983; Scrooge (3 tours), 1995–97. Acted in over 40 films; *films included:* Adventures of Dusty Bates; Oliver Twist; Up To His Neck; Cockleshell Heroes; High Flight; Idle on Parade; Jazz Boat; The Small World of Sammy Lee; Dr Doolittle; Sweet November; (wrote, produced and acted) Can Heironymus Merkin ever forget Mercy Humppe and find True Happiness?; (directed) Summertree, 1970; (score) Willy Wonka and the Chocolate Factory (Academy Award nomination, 1972); Quilp, 1974; It Seemed Like a Good Idea at the Time, 1974. *TV appearances included:* Anthony Newley Shows; The Strange World of Gurney Slade, 1960–61; Johnny Darling Show, 1962; Lucy in London, 1966; starred in leading night clubs and theatres in US; also a successful recording star. *Recreations:* photography, painting, fishing. *Address:* c/o Peter Charlesworth, 2nd Floor, 68 Old Brompton Road, SW7 3LQ.
Died 14 April 1999.

NEWMAN, Cyril Wilfred Francis; QC 1982; **His Honour Judge Newman;** a Judge of the Technology and Construction Court of the High Court, since 1998; *b* 2 July 1937; *s* of late Wilfred James Newman and Cecilia

Beatrice Lily Newman; *m* 1966, Winifred de Kok; two *s* one *d*. *Educ:* Sacred Heart Coll., Droitwich; Lewes County Grammar Sch. for Boys; Merton Coll., Oxford (BA 1959, MA 1964). President: OU Law Soc., 1959; OU Middle Temple Soc., 1959. Blackstone Entrance Scholar, Blackstone Pupillage Prize, and Harmsworth Major Scholar, Middle Temple, 1958–60; called to the Bar, Middle Temple, 1960; a Recorder, 1982–86; a Circuit Judge, 1986–94; an Official Referee, 1994–98. Asst Comr, Boundary Commn for England, 1976; Mem., Criminal Injuries Compensation Bd, 1985–86. Hon. Treasurer, Bar Yacht Club, 1973–88 (Rear-Cdre, 1985–86). Mem., Ashford Choral Soc., 1992–. *Recreations:* sailing, shooting, swimming, opera, church music. *Address:* Orlestone Grange, near Ashford, Kent TN26 2EB. *Club:* Bar Yacht. *Died 15 Jan. 2000.*

NEWMAN, Sir Jack, Kt 1977; CBE 1963; FCIT 1955; JP; Founder, 1938, President, 1981, Newman Group Ltd (formerly TNL), Nelson, New Zealand; *b* 3 July 1902; *s* of Thomas Newman and Christina Thomson; *m* 1926, Myrtle O. A. Thomas; four *d*. *Educ:* Nelson Coll. for Boys, NZ. Joined Newman Bros Ltd (family business), 1922; Manager, 1927; Managing Director, 1935. Past President and Life Member: NZ Cricket Council; NZ Travel Assoc.; NZ Passenger Transport Fedn; former Dir, Pacific Area Travel Assoc. Represented: NZ, at cricket, 1931–33; Nelson, Canterbury and Wellington, at cricket; Nelson, at Rugby football, golf, and lawn bowls. JP Nelson, 1950. *Recreation:* lawn bowls. *Clubs:* MCC; Wellesley (Wellington); Nelson (Nelson). *Died 23 Sept. 1996.*

NEWMAN, Sydney Cecil, OC 1981; film and television producer and executive; President, Sydney Newman Enterprises; *b* Toronto, 1 April 1917; *m* 1944, Margaret Elizabeth (*d* 1981), *d* of Rev. Duncan McRae, DD; three *d*. *Educ:* Ogden Public School and Central Technical School, Toronto. Painter, stage, industrial and interior designer; still and cinema photographer, 1935–41. National Film Board of Canada: joined under John Grierson as splicer-boy, 1941; Editor and Dir of Armed Forces training films and war information shorts, 1942; Exec. Producer in charge of all films for cinemas, including short films, newsreels, films for children and travel, 1947–52 (assigned to NBC in New York by Canadian govt, to report on American television techniques, 1949–50); TV Dir of Features and Outside Broadcasts, Canadian Broadcasting Corp., 1953; Superviser of Drama and Producer of General Motors Theatre, On Camera, Ford Theatre, Graphic, 1954; Superviser of Drama and Producer, Armchair Theatre, ABC Television, England, 1958–62 (devised The Avengers, 1961); Head of Drama Group, TV, BBC, 1963–67 (devised Dr Who, 1963, and Adam Adamant Lives!, 1966); Producer, Associated British Productions Ltd, Elstree, 1968–69; Special Advr to Chm. and Dir, Broadcast Programmes Branch, Canadian Radio and Television Commn, 1970; Canadian Govt Film Comr and Chm., Nat. Film Bd of Canada, 1970–75; Special Advr on Film to Sec. of State for Canada, 1975–77; Chief Creative Consultant, Canadian Film Develt Corp., 1978–84 (Dir, Montreal, 1970–75). Dir, Canadian Broadcasting Corp., 1972–75. Producer: Canada Carries On, 1945–52; over 300 documentaries, including: Suffer Little Children (UN), It's Fun to Sing (Venice Award), Ski Skill, After Prison What? (Canada Award); Stephen D, BBC TV, 1963; Weill and Brecht's The Rise and Fall of the City of Mahagonny, BBC TV, 1965; Pinter's The Tea Party, BBC TV, 1965; Britten's The Little Sweep, Channel 4, 1989; produced first plays by Arthur Hailey, incl. Flight into Danger, Course for Collision; commissioned and prod. first on-air plays of Alun Owen, Harold Pinter, Angus Wilson, Robert Muller, Peter Luke, and plays by Clive Exton, David Perry and Hugh Leonard.

Trustee, Nat. Arts Center, Ottawa, 1970–75; Gov., Canadian Conf. of the Arts; Member: New Western Film and TV Foundn; BAFTA; FRTS 1991; FRSA 1967; Fellow Soc. of Film and Television Arts, 1958. Ohio State Award for Religious Drama, 1956; Liberty Award, Best Drama Series, 1957; Desmond Davis Award, 1967, Soc. of Film and Television Arts; President's Award, 1969, and Zeta Award, 1970, Writers Guild of GB; Canadian Picture Pioneers Special Award, 1973; Special Recognition Award, SMPTE, 1975; TV Hall of Fame, RTS, 1996. Kt of Mark Twain, USA. *Address:* (office) 3 Nesbitt Drive, Toronto, Ont M4W 2G2, Canada. *Died 30 Oct. 1997.*

NEWNS, Sir (Alfred) Foley (Francis Polden), KCMG 1963 (CMG 1957); CVO 1961; *b* 30 Jan. 1909; *s* of late Rev. Alfred Newns, AKC; *m* 1st, 1936, Jean (*d* 1984), *d* of late A. H. Bateman, MB, BS; one *s* one *d*; 2nd, 1988, Beryl Wattles, BEd Cantab, MSc London, AMBDA. *Educ:* Christ's Hospital; St Catharine's College, Cambridge (MA). Colonial Administrative Service, Nigeria, 1932; served E Reg. and Colony: Enugu Secretariat, 1947; Lagos Secretariat, 1949; attached Cabinet Office, London, 1951; Resident, 1951; Secretary to Council of Ministers, 1951; Secretary to Governor-General and the Council of Ministers, Federation of Nigeria, 1955–59; Dep. Governor, Sierra Leone, 1960–61; Acting Gov. during 1960; Adviser to the Government of Sierra Leone after Independence, 1961–63; Sec. to Cabinet, Govt of the Bahamas, 1963–71. Consultant to several governments on internal political procedure. President: St Catharine's Coll. Soc., 1986–87 (Sec., 1976–85); Foxton Gardens Assoc., 1989–91 (Chm., 1973–89); Member: Cambridgeshire Wild Life Fundraising Cttee (formerly Trust Appeal), 1986–90; Cttee, UK Br., Nigerian Field Soc., 1983–90 (Life Mem., 1934); Life Member: Britain Nigeria Assoc.; Sierra Leone Soc., and other societies. Hon. Treasurer, Cambridge Specific Learning Disabilities Gp, 1986–; Hon. Auditor, Cambridge Decorative and Fine Arts Soc., 1984–98. FRSA 1969. *Publications:* various papers on Cabinet procedure and government machinery, circulated in Commonwealth. *Address:* 47 Barrow Road, Cambridge CB2 2AR. *T:* (01223) 356903. *Died 21 June 1998.*

NEWSON-SMITH, Sir John (Kenneth), 2nd Bt *cr* 1944; DL; *b* 9 Jan. 1911; *s* of Sir Frank Newson-Smith, 1st Bt and Dorothy (*d* 1955), *d* of late Sir Henry Tozer; *S* father, 1971; *m* 1st, 1945, Vera Margaret Allt (marr. diss. 1971); one *s* two *d*; 2nd, 1972, Anne (*d* 1987), *d* of late Harold Burns; 3rd, 1988, Sarah Ramsay, *d* of late R. A. W. Bicknell. *Educ:* Dover Coll.; Jesus Coll., Cambridge (MA). Joined Newson-Smith & Co, 1933, Partner 1938. Served War, Royal Navy, 1939–40; RNVR 1940–45. Rejoined Newson-Smith & Co., 1946 (which subseq. became Fielding Newson-Smith & Co.). Master of Turners' Co., 1969–70; Liveryman: Merchant Taylors' Co.; Spectaclemakers' Co. Court of Common Council, 1945–78; Deputy, Ward of Bassishaw, 1961–76. DL City of London, 1947. *Recreations:* travelling, gardening. *Heir:* *s* Peter Frank Graham Newson-Smith [*b* 8 May 1947; *m* 1974, Mrs Mary-Ann Owens, *o d* of Cyril C. Collins; one *s* one *d*]. *Address:* East End, 67 East Street, Warminster BA12 9BZ. *Clubs:* City Livery, Army and Navy, Sloane. *Died 11 Nov. 1997.*

NEWTON, Sir Gordon; *see* Newton, Sir L. G.

NEWTON, John David; a Recorder of the Crown Court, 1983–92; *b* 4 April 1921; *s* of late Giffard and Mary Newton; *m* 1942, Mary Bevan; one *s* one *d*. *Educ:* Berkhamsted School; University College London (LLB 1947). Served war of 1939–45 in Royal Artillery and Indian Army (Major). Called to the Bar, Middle Temple,

1948; Lectr in Law, University College, Hull, 1948–51; Lectr, then Senior Lectr in Law, Liverpool University, 1951–82. Dir, Liverpool Philharmonic Hall Trust, 1986–88. *Publications:* (ed) Halsbury's Laws of England, 4th edn 1982, Vol. 39, Rent Charges and Annuities; (ed jtly) Encyclopaedia of Forms and Precedents, 5th edn 1988, Vol. 33, Rent Charges and Annuities. *Recreations:* fishing, golf. *Address:* 58 Talbot Court, Prenton, Wirral CH43 6UG. *T:* (0151) 652 4675. *Clubs:* Athenæum (Liverpool); Royal Liverpool Golf.

Died 13 July 2000.

NEWTON, Sir (Leslie) Gordon, Kt 1966; Editor of The Financial Times, 1950–72, Director 1967–72; *b* 1907; *s* of John and Edith Newton; *m* 1935, Peggy Ellen Warren (*d* 1995); (one *s* decd). *Educ:* Blundell's School; Sidney Sussex College, Cambridge. Chm., LBC, 1974–77; Director: Trust Houses Forte Ltd, 1973–80; Mills & Allen (Internat.) Ltd, 1974–81. Hannen Swaffer Award for Journalist of the Year, 1966; Granada Television special award, 1970. *Address:* c/o 10 New Square, Lincoln's Inn, WC2A 3QG. *Died 31 Aug. 1998.*

NIARCHOS, Stavros Spyros; Grand Cross of Order of the Phœnix (Greece), 1957; Commander of Order of George I (Greece), 1954; Commander of Order of St George and St Constantine (Greece), 1964; Head of Niarchos Group of Shipping Companies which controlled over 5.75 million tons of shipping (operational and building); *b* 3 July 1909; *s* of late Spyros Niarchos and of Eugenie Niarchos; *m* 1st, 1930, Helen Sporides (marr. diss. 1930); 2nd, 1939, Melpomene Capparis (marr. diss. 1947); no *c*; 3rd, 1947, Eugenie Livanos (marr. diss. 1965; she *d* 1970); three *s* one *d*; 4th, 1965, Charlotte Ford (marr. diss. 1967); one *d*; 5th, 1971, Mrs Athina Livanos (*d* 1974). *Educ:* Univ. of Athens (Dr of Laws). On leaving Univ. joined family grain and shipping business; started independent shipping concern, 1939. Joined Royal Hellenic Navy Volunteer Reserve, 1941; served on destroyer engaged in North Atlantic convoy work (despatches); demobilised, 1945, with rank of Lieut-Comdr; returned to Shipping business; pioneered super-tankers. *Recreations:* yachting, ski-ing. *Address:* c/o Niarchos (London) Ltd, 41/43 Park Street, W1A 2JR. *T:* 0171–629 8400. *Clubs:* Athenian, Royal Yacht Club of Greece (both in Athens).

Died 15 April 1996.

NIBLOCK, Henry, (Pat), OBE 1972; HM Diplomatic Service, retired; HM Consul-General, Strasbourg, 1968–72; *b* 25 Nov. 1911; *s* of Joseph and Isabella Niblock, Belfast; *m* 1940, Barbara Mary Davies, *d* of late Captain R. W. Davies, Air Ministry; two *s*. Vice-Consul: Bremen, 1947–50; Bordeaux, 1951; Second Sec. (Commercial), Copenhagen, 1951–53; Consul, Frankfurt-on-Main, 1954–57; First Sec. and Consul, Monrovia, 1957–58; Consul, Houston, 1959–62; Chargé d'Affaires, Port-au-Prince, 1962–63; First Sec. and Consul, Brussels, 1964; Consul (Commercial), Cape Town, 1964–67. *Recreations:* walking, photography. *Address:* 10 Clifton House, 2 Park Avenue, Eastbourne, East Sussex BN22 9QN. *T:* (01323) 505695. *Club:* Civil Service.

Died 24 April 1996.

NICHOLAS, Sir Harry; *see* Nicholas, Sir H. R.

NICHOLAS, Prof. Herbert George, FBA 1969; Rhodes Professor of American History and Institutions, Oxford University, 1969–78; Fellow of New College, Oxford, 1951–78, Emeritus 1978–80, Honorary Fellow since 1980; Director, New College Development Fund, 1989–94; *b* 8 June 1911; *s* of late Rev. W. D. Nicholas. *Educ:* Mill Hill Sch.; New Coll., Oxford (MA 1938). Commonwealth Fund Fellow in Modern History, Yale, 1935–37; Exeter College, Oxford: Lectr, 1938; Fellow, 1946–51; Amer. Div., Min. of Information, and HM Embassy, Washington,

1941–46; Faculty Fellow, Nuffield Coll., Oxford, 1948–57; Nuffield Reader in the Comparative Study of Institutions, Oxford Univ., 1956–69. Chm., British Assoc. for American Studies, 1960–62; Vice-Pres., British Academy, 1975–76. Vis. Prof., Brookings Instn, Washington, 1960; Albert Shaw Lectr in Diplomatic History, Johns Hopkins, 1961; Vis. Fellow, Inst. of Advanced Studies, Princeton, 1964; Vis. Faculty Fellow, Inst. of Politics, Harvard, 1968. Hon. DCL Pittsburgh, 1968. *Publications:* The American Union, 1948; The British General Election of 1950, 1951; To the Hustings, 1956; The United Nations as a Political Institution, 1959, 5th edn 1975; (ed) Tocqueville's De la Démocratie en Amérique, 1961; Britain and the United States, 1963; The American Past and The American Present, 1971; The United States and Britain, 1975; The Nature of American Politics, 1980, 2nd edn 1986; (ed) Washington Despatches 1941–45, 1981; La Naturaleza de la Política Norteamericana, 1985; articles. *Recreations:* gardening, listening to music. *Address:* 2 Quarry Hollow, Headington, Oxford OX3 8JR. *T:* (01865) 63135. *Club:* Athenæum.

Died 3 July 1998.

NICHOLAS, Sir Herbert Richard, (Sir Harry), Kt 1970; OBE 1949; General Secretary of the Labour Party, 1968–72; *b* 13 March 1905; *s* of Richard Henry and Rosina Nicholas; *m* 1932, Rosina Grace Brown. *Educ:* Elementary sch., Avonmouth, Bristol; Evening Classes; Correspondence Courses. Clerk, Port of Bristol Authority, 1919–36; Transport and Gen. Workers Union: District Officer, Gloucester, 1936–38; Regional Officer, Bristol, 1938–40; National Officer, London: Commercial Road Transport Group, 1940–42; Chemical Section, 1942–44; Metal and Engineering Group, 1944–56; Asst Gen. Sec., 1956–68 (Acting Gen. Sec., Oct. 1964–July 1966). Mem., TUC General Council, 1964–67. Mem., Labour Party Nat. Exec. Cttee, 1956–64, 1967–68; Treasurer, Labour Party, 1960–64. *Publications:* occasional articles in press on industrial relations subjects. *Recreations:* Rugby football, fishing, reading, gardening. *Address:* 33 Madeira Road, Streatham, SW16 2DG. *T:* (0181) 769 7989.

Died 15 April 1997.

NICHOLLS; *see* Harmar-Nicholls.

NICHOLLS, Rear-Adm. (Francis) Brian (Price) B.; *see* Brayne-Nicholls.

NICHOLLS, Rt Rev. Vernon Sampson; Hon. Assistant Bishop of Coventry, since 1983; *b* 3 Sept. 1917; *s* of Ernest C. Nicholls, Truro, Cornwall; *m* 1943, Phyllis, *d* of Edwin Potter, Stratford-on-Avon; one *s* one *d*. *Educ:* Truro Sch.; Univ. of Durham; Clifton Theological Coll., Bristol. Deacon 1941, priest 1941; Curate: St Oswald Bedminster Down, Bristol, 1941–42; Liskeard, Cornwall, 1942–43; CF, 1944–46 (Hon. CF 1946); Vicar of Meopham, 1946–56; Rural Dean of Cobham, 1953–56; Vicar and Rural Dean of Walsall, and Chaplain to Walsall Gen. Hosp., 1956–67; Preb. of Curborough, Lichfield Cath., 1964–67; Archdeacon of Birmingham, 1967–74; Diocesan Planning Officer and Co-ordinating Officer for Christian Stewardship, 1967–74; Bishop of Sodor and Man, 1974–83; Dean of St German's Cathedral, Peel, 1974–83. Mem., Strood RDC, 1948–56; MLC, Tynwald, IoM, 1974–83; Member: IoM Bd of Educn, 1974–83; Bd of Social Security, 1974–81; IoM Health Services Bd, 1981–83; Founder Chm., IoM Council on Alcoholism, 1979. Mem., S Warwicks Drug Adv. Cttee, 1984–90. JP, IoM, 1974–83. Provincial Grand Master, Warwicks Province of Freemasons, 1985–92. *Recreations:* meeting people, motoring. *Address:* Apartment 18, Lucy's Mill, Mill Lane, Stratford-upon-Avon, Warwickshire CV37 6DE. *T:* Stratford-upon-Avon (01789) 294478.

Died 2 Feb. 1996.

NICHOLS, Clement Roy, CMG 1970; OBE 1956; Chairman, Alpha Spinning Mills Pty Ltd; *b* 4 Jan. 1909; *s* of C. J. Nichols, Melbourne; *m* 1933, Margareta, *d* of A. C. Pearse, Melbourne; one *s* one *d. Educ:* Scotch Coll., Melbourne. CText; ATI. Lifetime in wool worsted manufacturing. Past Pres., Wool Textile Mfrs of Australia; Vice-Pres., Internat. Wool Textile Organisation, 1970–75; President: Victorian Chamber of Mfrs, 1970–72, 1977–78; Associated Chambers of Mfrs of Australia, 1971–74. Mem., World Scouts' Cttee, 1959–65, 1967–73; Chm., Asia Pacific Region, 1962–64; Chief Comr, Scout Assoc., 1963–66; Chief Comr, Victorian Br., 1952–58; Nat. Chm., Scout Assoc. of Australia, 1973–79, Vice-Pres., 1979–88. *Address:* 82 Studley Park Road, Kew, Victoria 3101, Australia. *Clubs:* Australian (Melbourne); Rotary (Heidelberg). *Died 2 May 1996.*

NICHOLS, (Kenneth) John (Heastey); Metropolitan Stipendiary Magistrate, 1972–92; *b* 6 Sept. 1923; *s* of Sidney Kenneth Nichols, MC and Dorothy Jennie Heastey Richardson; *m* 1st, 1946, Audrey Heather Powell; one *d*; 2nd, 1966, Pamela Marjorie Long. *Educ:* Westminster School. Served War of 1939–45: 60th Rifles, 1941–43; Parachute Regt, NW Europe, SE Asia Comd, 1943–46 (Captain). Admitted Solicitor, 1949; Partner, Speechly, Mumford & Soames (Craig), 1949–69. Mem., Inner London Probation Service Cttee, 1975–91. Mem. Council of Law Soc., 1959–68. Pres., Newheels, 1980–86; Vice-Pres., David Isaacs Fund, 1982–86. *Recreations:* cricket, music. *Address:* Dolphin House, Porthgwarra, St Levan, Cornwall TR19 6JP; Flat 1, 36 Buckingham Gate, SW1E 6PB. *Club:* MCC. *Died 24 Jan. 1996.*

NICHOLS, Pamela Marjorie, (Mrs John Nichols); *see* Long, P. M.

NICHOLSON, Anthony Thomas Cuthbertson; a Recorder of the Crown Court, 1980–84; *b* 17 May 1929; *s* of Thomas and Emma Cuthbertson Nicholson, Stratford, E; *m* 1955, Sheila Rose, *er d* of Albert and Rose Pigrum, Laindon, Essex; two *s* one *d. Educ:* St Bonaventure's Grammar Sch., Forest Gate, E7. Journalist, 1944–62. Served Army, 1947–49, RAF, 1950–53. Called to the Bar, Gray's Inn, 1962. *Publications:* (play) Van Call, 1954; Esprit de Law, 1973. *Recreation:* wildfowling. *Address:* The Old Vicarage, Burnham Road, Southminster, Essex CM0 7ES. *Died 8 April 1999.*

NICHOLSON, Hon. Sir David (Eric), Kt 1972; Speaker of the Legislative Assembly of Queensland, 1960–72 (record term); MLA (CP) for Murrumba, 1950–72; *b* 26 May 1904; *s* of J. A. Nicholson; *m* 1934, Cecile F., *d* of M. E. Smith; two *s* two *d*. Company director. *Recreations:* bowls, swimming, gardening. *Address:* 232 Klingner Road, Kippa-Ring, Qld 4021, Australia. *Clubs:* Redcliffe Trotting (Life Mem.), Redcliffe Agricl, Horticultural and Industrial Soc. (Life Mem.); Caboolture, Returned Servicemen's (Life Mem.), Caboolture Bowls (Caboolture). *Died 13 Dec. 1997.*

NICHOLSON, (Edward) Rupert, FCA; Partner, Peat Marwick Mitchell & Co. (UK), 1949–77; *b* 17 Sept. 1909; *s* of late Alfred Edward Nicholson and Elise (*née* Dobson); *m* 1935, Mary Elley (*d* 1983); one *s* one *d. Educ:* Whitgift Sch., Croydon. Articled to father, 1928–33; joined Peat Marwick Mitchell & Co., 1933. Apptd Receiver, Rolls-Royce Ltd, 1971; Liquidator, Court Line Ltd, 1974. Chm., Techn. Adv. Cttee, Inst. Chartered Accountants, 1969–70; Mem., Post Office Review Cttee, 1976. Founder Chm., Croydon Business Venture, 1976 (Chm., 1978–91). Governor, Whitgift Foundn, 1976–94 (Chm., 1978–91; Gov. Emeritus, 1994–96). Master, Horners' Co., 1984–85. *Publications:* articles in learned jls. *Address:* Grey Wings, The Warren, Ashtead, Surrey KT21 2SL. *T:* (01372) 272655. *Club:* Caledonian. *Died 15 Dec. 2000.*

NICHOLSON, Lewis Frederick, (Nick), CB 1963; *b* 1 May 1918; *s* of Harold and May Nicholson; *m* 1947, Diana Rosalind Fear (*d* 1999); one *s* two *d. Educ:* Taunton Sch.; King's Coll., Cambridge. Research Laboratories of GEC, 1939; Royal Aircraft Establishment, 1939–59: Head of Aerodynamics Dept, RAE, 1953–59; Imperial Defence Coll., 1956; Director-General of Scientific Research (Air), Ministry of Aviation, 1959–63; Dep. Director (Air) Royal Aircraft Establishment, 1963–66; Chief Scientist, RAF, 1966–69; Vice Controller Aircraft, MoD (PE), 1969–78, retired. *Publications:* (jtly) Compressible Airflow-Tables; Compressible Airflow-Graphs; papers on aerodynamic subjects. *Address:* 18 Quay Courtyard, South Street, Manningtree, Essex CO11 1BA.
Died 28 Nov. 1999.

NICHOLSON, Nick; *see* Nicholson, L. F.

NICHOLSON, Rupert; *see* Nicholson, E. R.

NICKSON, Francis; solicitor, retired; Chief Executive and Town Clerk, London Borough of Camden, 1977–90; *b* 9 Sept. 1929; *s* of Francis and Kathleen Nickson; *m* 1957, Helena Towers (decd); *m* 1998, Christine M. Wares. *Educ:* Preston Catholic College; Liverpool Univ. (LLB). LMRTPI. Admitted Solicitor (Hons), 1953; Asst Solicitor, Newcastle-under-Lyme, 1953–56; Senior Asst Solicitor, Wood Green, 1956–60; Assistant Town Clerk, Enfield, 1960–71; Deputy Town Clerk, Camden, 1971–77. Hon. Clerk, Housing and Works Cttee, London Boroughs Assoc., 1979–84; Hon. Sec., London Boroughs Children's Regional Planning Cttee, 1977–90. Freeman, City of London, 1990. FRSA. *Recreations:* listening to music, travel, discovering French wines. *Address:* 14 Waggon Road, Hadley Wood, Barnet, Herts EN4 0HL. *T:* (0181) 449 9390. *Died 17 March 1999.*

NICOLSON, Sir David (Lancaster), Kt 1975; FEng 1977; company chairman and business consultant, retired; *b* 20 Sept. 1922; *s* of Charles Tupper Nicolson, consulting engineer, and Margaret Lancaster Nicolson; *m* 1st, 1943, Joan Eileen (*d* 1991), *d* of Major W. H. Griffiths, RA; one *s* two *d*; 2nd, 1992, Beryl, *widow* of Sir Gerald Thorley, TD, FRICS. *Educ:* Haileybury; Imperial Coll., London Univ. (BSc; Hon. Fellow 1971). FCGI, FIMechE, FIProdE; FIMgt; FRSA. Constructor Lt, Royal Corps Naval Constructors, 1942–45; served N Atlantic and Normandy, 1944 (despatches). Production Manager, Bucyrus-Erie Co., Milwaukee, 1950–52; Manager, later Dir, Production-Engineering Ltd, 1953–62; Chairman: P-E Consulting Gp, 1963–68; British Airways Board, 1971–75; BTR plc, 1969–84 (Dep. Chm., 1965–69, Dir, 1984); Rothmans International plc, 1975–84; Bulk Transport Ltd, 1984–89; German Securities Investment Trust, 1985–89; Lazard Leisure Fund, 1985–91; VSEL (Vickers Shipbuilding and Engineering), 1986–87; British Rail Engineering, 1987–89; Union Group, 1988–; DRG Ltd, 1989–; TACE PLC, 1991–93; Director: Delta Metal Co., 1967–79; Bank of Montreal, 1970–85; Richard Costain, 1970–78; MEPC, 1976–80; Todd Shipyards Corp., 1976–91; CIBA-Geigy (UK), 1978–90; GKN Plc, 1984–89; London & Scottish Marine Oil, 1983–92; Northern Telecom Ltd, 1987–92; Britannia Arrow Holdings plc, later Invesco MIM PLC, 1987–93; STC PLC, 1987–91; Dawnay Day & Co., 1988–; Brel Group Ltd, 1989–92; Southern Water plc, 1989–93; Churchill Leisure Internat., 1989–90; Strategic Hldgs SA, 1991–93. European Adviser, NY Stock Exchange, 1985–. Mem. (C) London Central, European Parlt, 1979–84. Mem. Council: CBI, 1972–90 (Chm., Environment Cttee, 1976–79); Inst. of Directors, 1971–76; Brit. Inst. of Management, 1964–69; Inst. of Production Engrs, 1966–68; City and Guilds of London Inst., 1968–76; Mem., SRC Engineering Bd, 1969–71; Chm. Management Consultants Assoc., 1964; Mem. Brit. Shipbuilding Mission to India, 1957; Chairman: Cttee for Hosiery and

Knitwear, NEDC, 1966–68; BNEC Cttee for Canada, 1967–71. Pres., ABCC, 1983–86. Chm., Amer. European Community Assoc., 1981–; Chm., European Movement, 1985–88. Mem. Council, Templeton Coll. (formerly Oxford Centre for Management Studies), 1982–94; Governor: Imperial Coll., London Univ., 1966–77; Cranleigh Sch., 1979–90; Pro-Chancellor, Surrey Univ., 1987–93. Lectured and broadcast on management subjects in UK, USA, Australia, etc. *Publications:* contribs to technical jls. *Recreation:* sailing. *Address:* Church House, Bale, near Fakenham, Norfolk NR21 0QR. *T:* Fakenham (01328) 878314. *Clubs:* Brooks's, Royal Thames Yacht; Norfolk (Norwich). *Died 19 July 1996.*

NIELD, Sir Basil Edward, Kt 1957; CBE 1956 (MBE 1943); DL; Judge of High Court of Justice, Queen's Bench Division, 1960–78; *b* 7 May 1903; *yr s* of late Charles Edwin Nield, JP, and Mrs F. E. L. Nield, MBE, Upton-by-Chester. *Educ:* Harrow Sch.; Magdalen Coll., Oxford (MA). Officers Emergency Reserve, 1938; served War of 1939–45: commnd Captain, 1940; GHQ MEF (Major), HQs E Africa Force, Palestine; Pres., Palestine Military Courts in Jerusalem; 9th Army, Beirut; HQs Eritrea and 8th Army; 1943: HQ Persia and Iraq; Asst Dep. Judge Advocate-Gen., ME (Lt-Col; despatches; MBE (mil.)); 21 Army Gp; HQ Lines of Communication, BLA, Normandy; HQ 2nd Army, Low Countries, Rhine; RARO until 1948. Called to Bar, Inner Temple, 1925, Master of the Bench, 1952, Reader, 1976, Treasurer, 1977; Northern Circuit, Chambers in Liverpool; KC 1945; Recorder of Salford, 1948–56; Recorder and first permanent Judge of Crown Court at Manchester, 1956–60; the only Judge to have presided at all sixty-one Assize towns in England and Wales before abolition of Assize system, 1972. Mem., Gen. Council of Bar, 1951. MP (C) City of Chester, 1940–56; sponsored as Private Member's Bill the Adoption of Children Act, 1949; Hon. Parly Chm., Dock and Harbour Authorities Assoc., 1944–50; Mem. Exec., 1922 Cttee; Mem., Special Cttee under Reorganisation Areas Measure for Province of York, 1944. Member: Magistrates' Rules Cttee, 1952–56; Legal Bd, Church Assembly, 1952–56; Home Secretary's Adv. Cttee on Treatment of Offenders, 1957. Chancellor, Diocese of Liverpool, 1948–56. Vice-President: Nat. Chamber of Trade, 1948–56; Graduate Teachers Assoc., 1950–56; Corp. of Secretaries, 1950; Assoc. of Managers of Approved Schools, 1956; Cheshire Soc. in London; Spastics Soc., Manchester. Chm., Chester Conservative Assoc., 1930–40. Member: Court, Liverpool Univ., 1948–56; Adv. Council, ESU, 1951; Oxford Soc.; Imperial Soc. of Knights Bachelor; Life Mem., Royal Soc. of St George. Governor, Harrow Sch., 1961–71. FAMS. DL County Palatine of Chester, 1962. Freeman, City of London, 1963. *Publication:* Farewell to the Assizes, 1972. *Address:* Osborne House, Isle of Wight PO32 6JY. *T:* (01983) 200056. *Clubs:* Carlton; City, Grosvenor (Chester). *Died 4 Dec. 1996.*

NIGHTINGALE, Edward Humphrey, CMG 1955; farmer in Kenya since 1954; *b* 19 Aug. 1904; *s* of Rev. Edward Charles Nightingale and Ada Mary Nightingale; *m* 1944, Evelyn Mary Ray; three *s* one *d. Educ:* Rugby Sch.; Emmanuel Coll., Cambridge. Joined Sudan Political Service, 1926; Dep. Civil Sec., Sudan Government, 1951–52; Gov., Equatoria Province, Sudan, 1952–54. Order of the Nile, 4th Class (Egypt), 1940. *Recreations:* carpentry, ornithology, photography. *Address:* Nunjoro Farm, PO Box 100, Naivasha, Kenya. *T:* (311) 21100. *Clubs:* Muthaiga Country (Nairobi); Naivasha Sports (Naivasha). *Died 14 June 1996.*

NIGHTINGALE of Cromarty, Michael David, OBE 1960; FSA; Laird Baron of Cromarty; Esquire Bedell, University of London, 1953–94; Chairman, Anglo-

Indonesian Corporation plc, 1971–96; *b* 6 Dec. 1927; *s* of late Victor Russell John Nightingale, Wormshill, Kent; *m* 1st, 1951, Antonia (marr. diss. 1956), *d* of Stephen Coleby Morland, Glastonbury; 2nd, 1956, Hilary Marion Olwen, *d* of late John Eric Jones, Swansea; two *s* three *d. Educ:* Winchester; Wye Coll. (BSc); Magdalen Coll., Oxford (BLitt 1952). Organised Exhibition from Kent Village Churches, Canterbury, 1951; Asst to Investment Manager, Anglo-Iranian Oil Co., 1951–53; Investment Adviser, Univ. of London, 1954–66; Advr, Kuwait Investment Bd, 1961–62; Dir, Charterhouse Japhet Ltd, 1965–70. Chm., Chillington Corp. plc, 1986–89. Secretary: Museums Assoc. (and Editor of Museums Jl), 1954–60; Museum Cttee, Carnegie UK Trust, 1954–60; Member: Advisory Council on Export of Works of Art, 1954–60; British Cttee of International Council of Museums, 1956–60; Canterbury Diocesan Advisory Cttee, 1964–79; Exec. Cttee, SE Arts Assoc., 1974–77; Area Archaeol. Adv. Cttee for SE England, 1975–79; Investment Cttee, Univs Superannuation Scheme, 1977–84; Mem. Bd, Commonwealth Develt Corp., 1985–92. Mem., Gen. Synod of C of E, 1979–85 (Panel of Chairmen, 1984–85). Member: Kent CC, 1973–77; Maidstone Borough Council, 1973– (Chm., Planning Cttee, 1973–77; Leader, 1976–77; Mayor, 1984–85). Vice-Pres., North Downs Soc.; Chairman: Cromarty Arts Trust, 1987–; Mid Kent Downs Adv. Gp, 1991–; Churches Cttee, Kent Archaeological Soc.; Wye Rural Mus. Trust, 1997–; Member: Council, Romney Marsh Historic Churches Trust; Council, Canterbury Archaeol Trust; Charles Darwin Trust, 1997–; Council, Bridge Wardens' Coll., 1997–. Dep. Steward, Royal Manor of Wye, 1954–; Asst, Rochester Bridge, 1985– (Warden, 1989–92); a Lord of the Level of Romney Marsh. *Publications:* articles on agrarian and museum subjects. *Address:* Wormshill Court, Sittingbourne, Kent ME9 0TS. *T:* (01622) 884235; Perceval House, 21 Dartmouth Row, Greenwich, SE10 8AW. *T:* (0181) 692 6033; Cromarty House, Ross and Cromarty IV11 8XS. *T:* (01381) 600265. *Died 2 Sept. 1998.*

NILSSON, Lars-Åke; Ambassador of Sweden to the Court of St James's, since 1995; *b* 23 May 1943; *s* of Hans and Olga Nilsson; *m* 1974, Charlotte Arnell. *Educ:* Univ. of Lund (MBA 1966). Joined Swedish Diplomatic Service, 1968: Attaché, Paris, 1969; Attaché and Second Sec., Tokyo, 1970–73; 2nd Sec., Washington, 1973–76; 1st Sec., Stockholm, 1976–79; Dep. Asst Under-Sec., Stockholm, 1979–80; Counsellor, London, 1980–84; Minister, Moscow, 1984–88; Ambassador to Czechoslovakia, 1988–91; Perm. Under-Sec., Stockholm, 1991–94. *Publications:* articles and booklets. *Recreations:* reading, talking, spectator sports, especially cricket and football. *Address:* Embassy of Sweden, 11 Montagu Place, W1H 2AL. *T:* (0171) 724 2101. *Clubs:* Travellers'; Sällskapet (Stockholm); Swedish Jockey. *Died 5 Nov. 1996.*

NIMMO, Derek Robert; actor, author and producer; *b* 19 Sept. 1930; *s* of Harry Nimmo and Marjorie Sudbury (*née* Hardy); *m* 1955, Patricia Sybil Ann Brown; two *s* one *d. Educ:* Quarry School, Liverpool. *Stage:* first appearance, Hippodrome, Bolton, as Ensign Blades in Quality Street, 1952; repertory and variety; Waltz of the Toreadors, Criterion, 1957; Duel of Angels, Apollo, 1958; How Say You?, Aldwych, 1959; The Amorous Prawn, Saville, 1959; The Irregular Verb to Love, Criterion, 1961; See How They Run, Vaudeville, 1964; Charlie Girl, Adelphi, 1965–71 and overseas, 1971–72; Babes in the Wood, Palladium, 1972; Why Not Stay for Breakfast?, Apollo, 1973–75, and overseas tours; Same Time Next Year, Prince of Wales, 1978; Shut Your Eyes and Think of England, Australia, 1979; See How They Run, Shaftesbury, 1984; A Friend Indeed, Shaftesbury, 1984; The Cabinet Minister, Albery, 1991–92; produced and appeared in numerous plays and countries for Intercontinental Entertainment, 1976–; *television: series included:* All Gas and Gaiters; Oh Brother; Oh Father; Sorry I'm Single; The Bed Sit Girl; My Honorable Mrs; The World of Wooster; Blandings Castle; Life Begins at Forty; Third Time Lucky; Hell's Bells; *interview series:* If it's Saturday it must be Nimmo; Just a Nimmo; numerous other appearances; *radio:* Just A Minute, 1968–; *films included:* Casino Royale; The Amorous Prawn; The Bargee; Joey Boy; A Talent for Loving; The Liquidator; Tamahine; One of our Dinosaurs is Missing. Freeman: City of London, 1991; Co. of World Traders, 1996. Hon. MA Leicester, 1996. RTS Silver Medal, 1970; Variety Club Show Business Personality of the Year, 1971. *Publications:* Derek Nimmo's Drinking Companion, 1979; Shaken and Stirred, 1984; (ed) Oh, Come On All Ye Faithful!, 1986; Not in Front of the Servants, 1987; Up Mount Everest Without a Paddle, 1988; As the Actress said to the Bishop, 1989; Wonderful Window Boxes, 1990; Table Talk, 1990; Memorable Dinners, 1991. *Recreations:* sailing, collecting English 17th and 18th century walnut furniture and Derby porcelain. *Address:* c/o Barry Burnett Ltd, 31 Coventry Street, W1V 8AS. *T:* (0171) 839 0202, *Fax:* (0171) 839 0438. *Clubs:* Garrick, Beefsteak; Lord's Taverners.   *Died 24 Feb. 1999.*

NIMMO, Hon. Sir John (Angus), Kt 1972; CBE 1970; Justice of the Federal Court of Australia, 1977–80; Justice of Australian Industrial Court, 1969–80; *b* 15 Jan. 1909; *s* of John James Nimmo and Grace Nimmo (*née* Mann); *m* 1st, 1935, Teanie Rose Galloway (*d* 1984); two *s*; 2nd, 1985, Maude Pearce. *Educ:* Univ. of Melbourne. Admitted to practise at Victorian Bar, 1933; QC (Vic.) 1957. Mem., Commonwealth Taxation Bd of Review No 2, 1947–54; Actg Supreme Court Justice, Victoria, 1963; Dep. Pres., Commonwealth Conciliation and Arbitration Commn, 1964–69, Chm., Health Insce Cttee of Enquiry, 1968–69. Dep. Pres., Trade Practices Tribunal, 1966–73, also a Justice of Supreme Courts of ACT and NT, 1966–74; on secondment as Chief Justice of Fiji, 1972–74. Royal Comr into future of Norfolk Is, 1975–76; Chm., Commonwealth Legal Aid Commn, 1978–79; Mem., Cttee on Overseas Professional Qualifications, 1978–82. OStJ 1945. *Recreations:* reading, walking. *Address:* 3/9 Dalsten Grove, Mount Eliza, Vic 3930, Australia. *T:* (3) 97877252.   *Died 7 July 1997.*

NIVEN, Margaret Graeme, ROI 1936; landscape and portrait painter; *b* Marlow, 1906; *yr d* of William Niven, JP, FSA, ARE, Marlow Place, Marlow, Bucks, and Eliza Mary Niven. *Educ:* Prior's Field, Godalming. Studied at Winchester Sch. of Art, Heatherley Sch. of Fine Art, and under Bernard Adams, RP, ROI; Mem. of National Soc. Painters, Sculptors, and Engravers, 1932. Exhibitor at Royal Academy and Royal Soc. of Portrait Painters. Works purchased by Bradford Art Gallery, The Ministry of Works, Homerton Coll., Cambridge, and Bedford Coll., London. Served with WRNS, 1940–45. *Address:* Broomhill, Sandhills, Wormley, near Godalming, Surrey GU8 5UF.   *Died 30 March 1997.*

NIXON, Rev. Sir Kenneth Michael John Basil, 4th Bt *cr* 1906, of Roebuck Grove, Milltown, co. Dublin and Merrion Square, City of Dublin; SJ; Teaching Member of the Jesuit Community at St George's College, Harare, 1954–93; *b* 22 Feb. 1919; *s* of Sir Christopher William Nixon, 2nd Bt, DSO, and Louise (*d* 1949), *d* of Robert Clery, JP, The Glebe, Athlacca, Limerick; *S* brother, 1978. *Educ:* Beaumont College; Heythrop College, Oxon. Catholic priest and member of the Society of Jesus; ordained, 1952. *Recreation:* cricket. *Heir:* nephew Simon Michael Christopher Nixon, *b* 20 June 1954. *Address:*

Canisius House, 37 Admiral Tait Road, Marlborough, Harare, Zimbabwe. *T:* (4) 300811.
Died 2 June 1997.

NOBES, Peter John, QPM 1986; Chief Constable, West Yorkshire Police, 1989–93; *b* 1 Oct. 1935; *s* of Cornelius James Nobes and Ivy Kathleen (*née* Eke); *m* 1955, Ruth Winifred Barnett; two *d. Educ:* Fakenham Modern Secondary Sch.; University Coll. London (Bramshill Scholarship; LLB 1968). Nat. Service, Royal Corps of Signals. W Suffolk (later Suffolk) Constabulary, 1956; Constable to Inspector, Newmarket, Brandon, Ipswich; Police Staff Coll., Bramshill, 1963–64 (Cert. with Dist.); University, 1965–68; Essex and Southend-on-Sea Jt Constabulary (later Essex Police), 1969; Chief Inspector to Chief Supt, Harlow, Basildon, Chelmsford; courses at Police Staff Coll., 1970, 1976; Asst Chief Constable, W Yorks Metropolitan Police, 1977 (management services, criminal investigation, complaints and discipline); Dep. Chief Constable, 1983; Chief Constable, N Yorks Police, 1985. *Publication:* A Policeman's Lot, 1973. *Recreations:* music, gardening, taking exercise.
Died 13 Oct. 1997.

NOBLE, Kenneth Albert, CBE 1975; Member, Price Commission, 1973–77 (Deputy Chairman, 1973–76); Director, 1954–73, Vice-Chairman, 1966–73, Co-operative Wholesale Society Ltd; Director of associated organisations and subsidiaries; *b* 7 May 1912; *s* of Percival Noble and Hester (*née* Oliver); *m* 1935, Mary Jane Geraghty; one *s* one *d.* Served War, 1940–46 (despatches); Major RASC. Chief Exec. Officer, Co-op. Soc., Irthlingborough, 1935–40, Wellingborough, 1947–54. Chm., Irthlingborough UDC, 1939–40; CC Northants, 1952–54. Member: CoID, 1957–65; Post Office Users Nat. Council, 1965–73; Monopolies Commn, 1969–73; London VAT Tribunals Panel, 1977–82. *Publications:* (jtly) Financial Management Handbook, 1977, 2nd edn 1980; contrib. specialist jls.   *Died 19 Jan. 1998.*

NONWEILER, Prof. Terence Reginald Forbes, PhD; CEng; Professor of Mathematics, Victoria University of Wellington, 1975–91, then Emeritus; *b* 8 Feb. 1925; *s* of Ernest James Nonweiler and Lilian Violet Amalie Nonweiler (*née* Holfert); *m* 1949, Patricia Hilda Frances (*née* Neame); four *s* two *d*; *m* Gwyn. *Educ:* Bethany Sch., Goudhurst, Kent; University of Manchester (BSc 1944, PhD 1960). Scientific Officer, Royal Aircraft Establishment, Farnborough, Hants, 1944–50; Scientific Officer, Scientific Advisor's Dept, Air Ministry, 1950–51; Senior Lecturer in Aerodynamics, College of Aeronautics, Cranfield, Beds, 1951–57; Senior Lecturer in Aeronautical Engineering, The Queen's Univ. of Belfast, 1957–61; Mechan Prof. of Aeronautics and Fluid Mechanics, Glasgow Univ., 1961–75. Consultant: to Admiralty, 1951; to Ministry of Aviation, 1959; to Ministry of Agriculture, 1966; to Wellington City Corp., 1977. Vis. Prof., Cranfield Inst. of Technology, 1991–93. Member, International Academy of Astronautics. *Publications:* Jets and Rockets, 1959; Computational Mathematics, 1984; numerous technical papers on aeronautics, space flight, and submarine motion. *Recreations:* acting, stage production. *Address:* 15 Tui Road, Raumati Beach 6450, New Zealand.   *Died 17 Dec. 1999.*

NORBURY, 6th Earl of, *cr* 1827 (Ire.); **Noel Terence Graham-Toler;** Baron Norwood 1797; Baron Norbury 1800; Viscount Glandine 1827; *b* 1 Jan. 1939; *s* of 5th Earl of Norbury and Margaret Greenhalgh (*d* 1984); *S* father, 1955; *m* 1965, Anne Mathew; one *s* one *d. Heir: s* Viscount Glandine, *b* 5 March 1967. *Address:* The Woodlands, Seer Green, Bucks HP9 2UL.
Died 11 Sept. 2000.

NORMAN, (Alexander) Vesey (Bethune); Inspector of the Wallace Collection's Armouries, 1977–94; *b* 10 Feb. 1930; *s* of Lt-Col A. M. B. Norman and Sheila M. Maxwell; *m* 1st, 1954, Catherine Margaret Barne (marr. diss. 1987); one *s*; 2nd, 1988, (Elizabeth) Anne Buddle. *Educ:* Alford Sch.; Trinity Coll., Glenalmond; London Univ. (BA Gen.). FSA; FSAScot. Asst Curator, Scottish United Services Museum, Edinburgh Castle, 1957; Hon. Curator of Arms and Armour, Abbotsford, 1957–63; Asst to Dir, Wallace Collection, 1963; Master of the Armouries, The Royal Armouries, HM Tower of London, 1977–88, retd. Vice-President: Church Monuments Soc., 1991– (Pres., 1986–91); NADFAS, 1984–89; Arms and Armour Soc., 1983– (Medal, 1988). Liveryman, Gunmakers' Co., 1981–. *Publications:* Arms & Armour, 1964 (also foreign edns); (with Don Pottinger) Warrior to Soldier 449–1660, 1966 (USA edn as A History of War and Weapons 449–1660, reprinted as English Weapons and Warfare 449–1660, 1979); Small Swords and Military Swords, 1967; The Medieval Soldier, 1971 (also USA); Arms and Armour in the Royal Scottish Museum, 1972; A Catalogue of Ceramics, Wallace Collection, Pt I, 1976; (with C. M. Barne) The Rapier and Small-Sword 1460–1820, 1980; Catalogue of European Arms and Armour, supplement, Wallace Collection, 1986; articles in learned jls. *Recreation:* study of arms and armour. *Address:* 15 Lansdowne Crescent, Edinburgh EH12 5EH.

Died 20 July 1998.

NORMAN, Sir Robert (Wentworth), Kt 1970; JP; *b* 10 April 1912; *s* of William Henry Norman and Minnie Esther Brown; *m* 1942, Grace Hebden, *d* of Sidney Percy Hebden; one *s* one *d*. *Educ:* Sydney Grammar Sch. Served Army, 1940–46: Captain, AIF. Joined Bank of New South Wales, 1928; Manager, Head Office, 1961; Dep. Gen. Manager, 1962; Chief Gen. Manager, 1964–77; Dir, 1977–84. Senator and Life Mem., Junior Chamber Internat. Life Mem., Sydney Adv. Bd, Salvation Army. FAIM. JP NSW, 1956. 3rd Order of the Rising Sun (Japan), 1983. *Recreations:* bowls, reading. *Address:* 26/16 Rosemont Avenue, Woollahra, NSW 2025, Australia. *T:* (2) 3631900. *Clubs:* Union, Royal Sydney Golf, Australian Jockey (Sydney). *Died 30 March 1997.*

NORMAN, Vesey; *see* Norman, A. V. B.

NORMAN, Willoughby Rollo; Hon. President, The Boots Co. Ltd, since 1972 (Chairman, 1961–72); Deputy Chairman, English China Clays Ltd; *b* 12 Oct. 1909; 2nd *s* of Major Rt Hon. Sir Henry Norman, 1st Bt; *m* 1st, 1934, Hon. Barbara Jacqueline Boot (marr. diss. 1973), *er d* of 2nd and last Baron Trent, KBE; one *s* two *d*; 2nd, 1973, Caroline Haskard, *d* of William Greville Worthington and Lady Diana Worthington. *Educ:* Eton; Magdalen Coll., Oxford. Served War of 1939–45, Major, Grenadier Guards. Director: National Westminster Bank (Chm. Eastern Region), 1963–79; Sheepbridge Engineering Ltd, 1979; Guardian Royal Exchange Assurance, 1961–79. Vice-Chairman Boots Pure Drug Co. Ltd, 1954–61. High Sheriff of Leicestershire, 1960. *Recreations:* shooting, farming, gardening. *Address:* The Grange, South Harting, Petersfield, Hants GU31 5NR; 28 Ranelagh House, Elystan Place, SW3 3LD. *T:* (0171) 584 9410. *Club:* White's.

Died 28 Oct. 1997.

NORMANTON, Sir Tom, Kt 1987; TD; BA (Com); past chairman of a group of companies; *b* 12 March 1917; *m* 1942, Annabel Bettine (*née* Yates); two *s* one *d*. *Educ:* Manchester Grammar Sch.; Manchester Univ. (BA (Com); Chm., Cons. Assoc., 1937–38; Vice-Pres. Students' Union, 1938). Joined family group of textile cos, 1938. Served War of 1939–45: Army (commnd TA 1937) Europe and N Africa; GS appts, GHQ BEF, HQ First and Eighth Armies; HQ 21 Army Gp (wounded, Calais, 1940; despatches, 1944); demob., rank Major, 1946. Chm.,

Rochdale YC, 1948; Mem. Rochdale CB Council, 1950–53; contested (C) Rochdale, 1959 and 1964. MP (C) Cheadle, 1970–87; opposition front bench spokesman on energy, 1975–79. Hon. Sec., Cons. Backbencher Industry Cttee, 1972–74; Mem., Expenditure Cttee, 1972–73. Contested (C) Cheshire E, European parly elecn, 1989. MEP (C) 1973–89 (elected for Cheshire E, 1979); Member: Cttee on Energy and Research, 1973–79 (Vice-Chm., 1976–79 and (as elected Member), 1979–89); Cttee on Economic and Monetary Affairs, 1973–79; Budgets Cttee, 1986–89; Pol Affairs Cttee, 1986–89; Jt Africa, Caribbean, Pacific States Standing Conf., 1975–79; spokesman on Competition Policy, 1975; Deleg. to US Congress, 1975–78; Mem., delegn to Turkey, 1987–89; Mem. European Cons. Gp, resp. Indust. Policy; special interests energy and defence; Chm., European All-Party Gp Friends with Israel, 1979–89; Vice-Pres., Pan European Union e V, 1980–92 (Hon. Treas., 1989–93). Mem. Supervisory Bd, European Inst. for Security; apptd Employer panel, NBPI, 1966–68; Member: Council, British Employers Confedn, 1959–64; Council, CBI, 1964–86 (Mem. Europe Cttee, 1964–86, and 1989–94, and Econ. Policy Cttee, 1964–70); Stockport Chamber of Commerce, 1970–87; Central Training Council, 1968–74; Exec., UK Automation Council, 1966–73 (Vice-Chm., 1970–73); Cotton and Allied Textiles Ind. Trng Bd, 1966–70; Exec. Council, British Textile Confederation, 1972–76; Mem. Cttee, 1955, Vice-Chm., 1969–71, Manchester Br. of Inst. of Dirs; Chm., European Textile Industries Cttee; President: British Textile Employers Assoc., 1970–71; Internat. Fedn of Cotton & Allied Textiles Industries, 1970– (Vice-Pres., 1972–76, Pres., 1976–78). Director: Industrial Training Services Ltd, 1972–92; N Reg. Bd, Commercial Union Assurance Ltd, 1974–86; Manchester Chamber of Commerce, 1970–89. Consultant, Midland Bank Gp, EEC, Brussels, 1979–91. Mem. Cttee, Anglo-Austrian Soc.; Patron, Assoc. for Free Russia. Manager, Lancashire Fusiliers Compassionate Fund, 1964; Trustee, Cotton Industry War Memorial Fund, 1965; Pres., New Forest Br., Normandy Veterans Assoc., 1990–; Chairman: British Sect., Confedn of European Ex-servicemen, 1986–90; Hampshire Remembers D-Day Ltd, 1992–96. Spoke French and German. AIMgt. *Recreations:* sailing, walking, gardening. *Address:* Nelson House, Nelson Place, Lymington, Hants SO41 3RT. *T:* (01590) 675095. *Clubs:* Beefsteak; St James's (Manchester); Royal Yacht Squadron; Royal Lymington Yacht.

Died 6 Aug. 1997.

NOSWORTHY, Harold George, CMG 1965; FCCA; FCA; *b* 15 March 1908; *m* 1941, Marjorie Anjelique; two *d*. *Educ:* Kingston Technical High Sch.; private tuition. Entered Jamaica Civil Service, 1929; 2nd class Clerk, 1938; Examiner of Accounts, 1943; Asst Commissioner, Income Tax, 1947; Asst Trade Administrator, 1950; Trade Administrator and Chairman Trade Control Board, 1953; Principal Asst Secretary, Ministry of Finance, 1955; Auditor-General, 1957–66; Dir, Internal Audit Service, UN, 1966–68. Coronation Medal, 1953; Jamaica Independence Medal, 1962. *Recreations:* reading, billiards, bridge, swimming. *Address:* 18 Hyperion Avenue, PO Box 127, Kingston 6, Jamaica. *T:* 9279889. *Club:* Kingston Cricket (Jamaica).

Died 20 April 1997.

NOTT, Charles Robert Harley, CMG 1959; OBE 1952; Secretary for Fijian Affairs, 1957–59; *b* 24 Oct. 1904; *e s* of late John Harley Nott, JP, Leominster, Herefordshire and late Mrs Nott, formerly of Bodenham Hall, Herefordshire; *m* 1935, Marion (*née* Macfarlane), Auckland, NZ; one *s* one *d*. *Educ:* Marlborough; Christ's Coll., Cambridge (MA). Colonial Administrative Service: Fiji, 1926; Administrative Officer (Grade II), 1938, (Grade I), 1945. Member of the Legislative Council, Fiji, 1950;

HBM's Agent and Consul, Tonga, 1954–57; MLC, MEC, retired, 1960. *Recreation:* trout fishing. *Address:* 5 Nigel Street, Havelock North, New Zealand.

Died 19 Sept. 1997.

NOTT, Kathleen Cecilia, FRSL; author, broadcaster, lecturer and journalist; *b* 19 Feb. 1905; *d* of Philip and Ellen Nott; *m* Christopher Bailey (marr. diss.). *Educ:* Mary Datchelor Sch., London; King's Coll., London; Somerville Coll., Oxford (Open Exhibn in English; BA Hons PPE). FRSL 1977. President: Progressive League, 1959–61; English PEN, 1974–75. Editor, PEN International (formerly Internat. PEN Bulletin of Selected Books), 1960–88. *Publications: poetry:* Landscapes and Departures, 1947; Poems from the North, 1956; Creatures and Emblems, 1960; Elegies and Other Poems, 1980; *novels:* Mile End, 1938; The Dry Deluge, 1947; Private Fires, 1960; An Elderly Retired Man, 1963; *criticism and philosophy:* The Emperor's Clothes, 1954; A Soul in the Quad, 1969; Philosophy and Human Nature, 1970; The Good Want Power, 1977; *general:* A Clean Well-lighted Place, 1961 (Sweden); contribs to collections of essays, and to periodicals. *Recreations:* playing the piano, gardening. *Address:* Wemyss Lodge Residential Home, Ermin Street, Stratton St Margaret, Swindon, Wilts SN3 4NX. *Clubs:* University Women's, PEN, Society of Authors. *Died 20 Feb. 1999.*

NOWELL-SMITH, Simon Harcourt, FSA; *b* 5 Jan. 1909; *s* of late Nowell Charles Smith, sometime Headmaster of Sherborne, and Cecil Violet, 3rd *d* of A. G. Vernon Harcourt; *m* 1st, 1938, Marion Sinclair (*d* 1977), *d* of late W. S. Crichton, Liverpool; two *s* one *d*; 2nd, 1986, Judith Adams, *d* of Frederick B. Adams. *Educ:* Sherborne; New Coll., Oxford (MA). Editorial Staff of The Times, 1932–44; Assistant Editor, Times Literary Supplement, 1937–39; attached to Intelligence Division, Naval Staff, 1940–45; Secretary and Librarian, The London Library, 1950–56; Secretary, Hospital Library Services Survey, 1958–59; President, Bibliographical Society, 1962–64, Lyell Reader in Bibliography, Oxford Univ., 1965–66. Pres., Oxford Bibliographical Soc., 1972–76. Trustee, Dove Cottage Trust, 1974–82. OStJ. *Publications:* Mark Rutherford, a bibliography, 1930; The Legend of the Master (Henry James), 1947; The House of Cassell, 1958; (ed) Edwardian England, 1964; Letters to Macmillan, 1967; International Copyright Law and the Publisher, 1968; Postscript to Autobiography of William Plomer, 1975. *Address:* St Luke's Nursing Home, 4 Latimer Road, Headington, Oxford OX3 7PF.

Died 28 March 1996.

NOYES, Ralph Norton; writer; *b* 9 June 1923; *s* of late Sidney Ralph Noyes and Nova (*née* Pearce); *m* 1948, Margaret Isaacs; two *s* one *d. Educ:* Haberdashers' Aske's Hampstead Sch.; London School of Economics (BScEcon). War service, RAF (aircrew), 1940–46. Air Ministry, 1949–63: Private Sec. to VCAS, 1950–52, and to CAS, 1953; Air Force Dept, 1964–69; idc 1966; Defence Secretariat, 1969–77: Asst Under-Sec. of State (Logistics), 1975–77; UK Rep., NATO Maintenance and Supply Org., 1975–77. Hon. Secretary: SPR, 1990–97 (Vice-Pres., 1997–); Centre for Crop Circle Studies, 1990–92. Member: Folklore Soc., 1987–; British UFO Res. Assoc., 1983–. *Publications:* A Secret Property, 1985; (ed) The Crop Circle Enigma, 1990; several short stories, articles, papers and broadcasts on speculative themes, in Punch, Country Life, Argosy, Fiction Magazine, BBC2, Jl of Soc. for Psych. Res., etc (several times reprinted in anthologies). *Recreations:* travel, research into anomalous topics. *Address:* 2 Bramerton Street, SW3 5JX. *T:* (0171) 351 6659. *Died 23 May 1998.*

NUNBURNHOLME, 4th Baron *cr* 1906; **Ben Charles Wilson;** Major, Royal Horse Guards, retired; *b* 16 July 1928; *s* of 3rd Baron Nunburnholme, and Lady Mary Thynne, *y d* of 5th Marquess of Bath, KG, PC, CB; *S* father, 1974; *m* 1958, Ines Dolores Jeanne (marr. diss.), *d* of Gerard Walravens, Brussels; four *d* (including twin *d*). *Educ:* Eton. *Heir: b* Hon. Charles Thomas Wilson [*b* 27 May 1935; *m* 1969, Linda Kay (marr. diss.), *d* of Cyril James Stephens; one *s* one *d*]. *Address:* c/o House of Lords, SW1A 0PW. *Died 28 July 1998.*

NUNBURNHOLME, 5th Baron *cr* 1906; **Charles Thomas Wilson;** *b* 27 May 1935; *s* of 3rd Baron Nunburnholme and Lady Mary Thynne (*d* 1974), *y d* of 5th Marquess of Bath, KG, CB, PC; *S* brother, 1998; *m* 1969, Linda Kay (marr. diss.), *d* of Cyril James Stephens; one *s* one *d*. *Educ:* Eton. A Page of Honour to HM King George VI, 1950–52. Mem., Stock Exchange, 1956–66. *Heir: s* Hon. Stephen Charles Wilson, *b* 29 Nov. 1973. *Club:* Hemswell Village. *Died 20 Nov. 2000.*

NUTTING, Rt Hon. Sir (Harold) Anthony, 3rd Bt *cr* 1902, of St Helens, Booterstown, co. Dublin; PC 1954; *b* 11 Jan. 1920; 3rd and *y s* of Sir Harold Stansmore Nutting, 2nd Bt, and Enid Hester Nina (*d* 1961), *d* of F. B. Homan-Mulock; *S* father, 1972; *m* 1st, 1941, Gillian Leonora (marr. diss. 1959), *d* of Edward J. Strutt, Hatfield Peverel, Essex; two *s* one *d*; 2nd, 1961, Anne Gunning (*d* 1990), *d* of Arnold Parker, Cuckfield, Sussex; 3rd, 1991, Margarita, *d* of Carlos Sanchez. *Educ:* Eton; Trinity College, Cambridge. Leics Yeo., 1939; invalided, 1940; in HM Foreign Service on special duties, 1940–45. MP (C) Melton Division of Leics, 1945–56, resigned. Parliamentary Under-Secretary of State for Foreign Affairs, 1951–54; Minister of State for Foreign Affairs, 1954–56, resigned. Leader, UK Delegn to UN General Assembly and to UN Disarmament Commn, 1954–56. Chairman: Young Conservative and Unionist Movement, 1946; National Union of Conservative and Unionist Associations, 1950; Conservative National Executive Cttee, 1951. *Publications:* I Saw for Myself, 1938; Disarmament, 1959; Europe Will Not Wait, 1960; Lawrence of Arabia, 1961; The Arabs, 1964; Gordon, Martyr and Misfit, 1966; No End of a Lesson, 1967; Scramble for Africa: the Great Trek to The Boer War, 1970; Nasser, 1972. *Recreation:* fishing. *Heir: s* John Grenfell Nutting [*b* 28 Aug. 1942; *m* 1974, Diane, Countess Beatty, *widow* of 2nd Earl Beatty, DSC; one *s* one *d*, and one step *s* one step *d*]. *Club:* Boodle's.

Died 24 Feb. 1999.

NUTTING, Prof. Jack, ScD, PhD; FEng 1981; FIM; Professor of Metallurgy, Houldsworth School of Applied Science, University of Leeds, 1960–89, now Emeritus; consultant metallurgist; *b* 8 June 1924; *o s* of Edgar and Ethel Nutting, Mirfield, Yorks; *m* 1st, 1950, Thelma Kippax (*d* 1994), *y d* of Tom and Florence Kippax, Morecambe, Lancs; one *s* two *d*; 2nd, 1995, D. K. Walters, *widow* of Cedric Walters. *Educ:* Mirfield Grammar School, Yorks; Univ. of Leeds (BSc 1945; PhD 1948); MA Cantab 1952; ScD Cantab 1967. Research at Cavendish Lab., Cambridge, 1948–49; Univ. Demonstrator, 1949–54, Univ. Lectr, 1954–60, Dept of Metallurgy, Cambridge Univ. Vis. Prof., Univ. of Barcelona, 1991–. President: Metals Soc., 1977–78; Instn of Metallurgists, 1980–81; Historical Metallurgy Soc., 1984–86. Hon. DSc: Acad. of Mining and Metallurgy, Cracow, 1969; Moratuwa Univ., Sri Lanka, 1981. Beilby medal and prize, 1961; Hadfield medal and prize, 1964; Institute of Metals Platinum Medal, 1988; Wilkinson Medal, 1989. *Publications:* numerous papers in Jls of Iron and Steel Inst., Inst. of Metals and Metals Soc. *Recreations:* foreign travel, mountain walking. *Address:* 19 Cliveden Mead, Maidenhead, Berks SL6 8HE. *T:* and *Fax:* (01628) 770065.

Died 8 July 1998.

NYERERE, Julius Kambarage; President, United Republic of Tanzania (formerly Tanganyika and Zanzibar), 1964–85; President, Tanganyika African National Union, 1954–77; *b* 13 April 1922; *s* of Chief Nyerere Burito; *m* 1953, Maria Magige; five *s* two *d. Educ:* Tabora Secondary School; Makerere University College; Edinburgh University (MA). Began as teacher; became President, African Association, Dar es Salaam, 1953; formed Tanganyika African National Union, left teaching and campaigned for Nationalist Movement, 1954; addressed Trusteeship Council, 1955, and Cttee of UN Gen. Assembly, 1956. MLC Tanganyika, July-Dec. 1957, resigned in protest; elected Mem. for E Prov. in first elections, 1958, for Dar es Salaam, 1960; Chief Minister, 1960; Prime Minister of Tanganyika, 1961–62; President, Tanganyika Republic, 1962–64. Chm., Chama cha Mapinduzi (The Revolutionary Party) (born of merger between mainland's TANU and Zanzibar Afro-Shiraz Party), 1977–90. Chm., OAU, 1984. First Chancellor, Univ. of East Africa, 1963–70; Chancellor: Univ. of Dar es Salaam, 1970–85; Sokoine Univ. of Agriculture, 1984–92. Chairman: South Commn, 1987–90; South Centre, 1990–. Holder of hon. degrees. *Publications:* Freedom and Unity—Uhuru Na Umoja, 1966; Freedom and Socialism—Uhuru na Ujamaa, 1969; Essays on Socialism, 1969; Freedom and Development, 1973; Swahili trans of Julius Caesar and The Merchant of Venice, 1969. *Address:* PO Box 71000, Dar es Salaam, United Republic of Tanzania; South Centre, Ch. du Champs d'Anier 17, Case postale 228, 1211 Geneva 19, Switzerland. *Died 14 Oct. 1999.*

O

OAKELEY, Mary, MA; Headmistress, St Felix School, Southwold, 1958–78; *b* 2 April 1913; *d* of Maj. Edward Francis Oakeley, S Lancs Regt, and Everilde Anne (*née* Beaumont); *sister* of Sir Atholl Oakeley, 7th Bt. *Educ:* St John's Sch., Bexhill-on-Sea; St Hilda's Coll., Oxford (BA Hons History 1935; MA 1939). Assistant Mistress: St James's, West Malvern, 1935–38; St George's, Ascot, 1938–39; Headmistress, Craighead Diocesan Sch., Timaru, NZ, 1940–55; Head of American Section, La Châtelainie, St Blaise, Switzerland, 1956–58. *Recreations:* gardening, embroidery. *Address:* 8 Newland Close, Eynsham, Witney, Oxon OX8 1LE. *T:* (01865) 880759. *Club:* Royal Over-Seas League.

Died 18 Dec. 1997.

OAKLEY, Wilfrid George, MD, FRCP; Hon. Consulting Physician, King's College Hospital, since 1971; Vice President, British Diabetic Association, since 1971; *b* 23 Aug. 1905; *s* of late Rev. Canon G. D. Oakley and Mrs Oakley; *m* 1931, Hermione Violet Wingate-Saul (*d* 1993); one *s. Educ:* Durham School; Gonville and Caius College, Cambridge; St Bartholomew's Hospital. Tancred studentship in Physic, Gonville and Caius Coll., 1923; Bentley Prize and Baly Research Schol., St Bart's Hosp., 1933; MD (Hon. Mention) Cantab 1934; FRCP 1942. Physician i/c Diabetic Dept, King's College Hosp., 1957–70. Examr, Cambridge and Glasgow Univs. Pres., Med. Soc., London, 1962; Mem. Assoc. of Physicians of Great Britain; Vice-Pres., British Diabetic Assoc., 1971. *Publications:* (jtly) Clinical Diabetes and Its Biochemical Basis, 1968; Diabetes and its Management, 1973, 3rd edn 1978; scientific articles and chapters on diabetes in various text-books. *Address:* 12 Courtmead Close, Burbage Road, SE24 9HW. *T:* (0171) 737 1920.

Died 25 Dec. 1998.

OATLEY, Sir Charles (William), Kt 1974; OBE 1956; MA; FRS 1969, FEng, FIEE, FIEEE; Professor of Electrical Engineering, University of Cambridge, 1960–71, then Emeritus; Fellow of Trinity College, Cambridge, since 1945; *b* 14 Feb. 1904; *s* of William Oatley and Ada May Dorrington; *m* 1930, (Dorothy) Enid West; two *s. Educ:* Bedford Modern Sch.; St John's Coll., Cambridge. Demonstrator, later lecturer, Dept of Physics, KCL, 1927–39; Min. of Supply, Radar Research and Development Establishment, 1939–45: Actg Supt in charge of scientific work, 1944–45; Lecturer, later Reader, Dept of Engineering, Cambridge Univ., 1945–60. Director, English Electric Valve Company, 1966–85. Member: Council, Inst. of Electrical Engineers, 1954–56, 1961–64 (Chm. of Radio Section, 1954–55); Council, Royal Society, 1970–72. FEng 1976. Hon. Fellow, Royal Microscopical Soc., 1970; FKC 1976; Foreign Associate, Nat. Acad. of Engineering, USA, 1979. Hon. DSc: Heriot-Watt, 1974; Bath, 1977; Hon. ScD Cambridge, 1990. Achievement Award, Worshipful Co. of Scientific Instrument Makers, 1966; Duddell Medal, Inst. of Physics and Physical Soc., 1969; Royal Medal, Royal Soc., 1969; Faraday Medal, IEE, 1970; Mullard Award, Royal Soc., 1973; James Alfred Ewing Medal, ICE, 1981; Distinguished Scientist Award, Electron Microscopy Soc. of America, 1984; Howard N. Potts Medal, Franklin Inst., 1989. *Publications:* Wireless Receivers, 1932; The Scanning Electron Microscope, 1972; Electric and Magnetic Fields, 1976; papers in scientific and technical

journals. *Recreation:* gardening. *Address:* 16 Porson Road, Cambridge CB2 2EU. *T:* Cambridge (01223) 356194.

Died 11 March 1996.

O'BRIEN, Oswald; Director, Workplace Advisory Service, Alcohol Concern (national charity), since 1986 (Director, Education Division, 1984–86); freelance lecturer, since 1983; *b* 6 April 1928; *s* of Thomas and Elizabeth O'Brien; *m* 1950, Freda Rosina Pascoe; one *s. Educ:* St Mary's Grammar Sch., Darlington; Fircroft Coll., Birmingham; Durham Univ. BA Hons Politics and Economics. Royal Navy, 1945–48; various posts in industry, 1948–59; College and University, 1959–63; Tutor, WEA, 1963–64; Staff Tutor, Durham Univ., 1964–78; Senior Industrial Relations Officer, Commn on Indust. Relations, 1970–72 (secondment); Dir of Studies and Vice-Principal, Co-operative Coll., 1978–83. Dept of Employment and ACAS Arbitrator in Shipbuilding, 1968–78; Indust. Relations Adviser to various statutory bodies, 1965–78; Chm., Soc. of Indust. Tutors, 1978–82. Mem., Durham CC, 1990–. MP (Lab) Darlington, March–June 1983; contested (Lab) Darlington, 1987. FIMgt. *Publications:* (jtly) Going Comprehensive, 1970; (jtly) Drink and Drugs at Work, 1988; various papers, reports and case studies. *Recreations:* reading, talking, opera. *Address:* 6 Hillclose Avenue, Darlington, Co. Durham DL3 8BH. *T:* (01325) 315540.

Died 10 March 1997.

O'BRIEN, Turlough Aubrey, CBE 1959; Public Relations Consultant, 1972–82; *b* 30 Sept. 1907; *er s* of late Lt-Col Aubrey John O'Brien, CIE, CBE; *m* 1945, Phyllis Mary (*d* 1986), twin *d* of late E. G. Tew; two *s* one *d. Educ:* Charterhouse; Christ Church, Oxford. Assistant to Director of Public Relations, Board of Trade, 1946–49; Public Relations Officer, Home Office, 1949–53; Post Office: PRO, 1953–64; Chief PRO, 1964–66; Director, Public Relations, 1966–68; Public Relations Manager, Bank of London and South America, 1968–72. President, Institute of Public Relations, 1965. *Recreation:* fishing. *Address:* Claremount, 11 Kiln Gardens, Hartley Wintney, Basingstoke, Hants RG27 8RG. *Club:* United Oxford & Cambridge University.

Died 7 Nov. 1997.

OCKRENT, Michael Robert; film and theatre director; *b* 18 June 1946; *s* of Charles Ockrent and Eve (*née* Edels); *m* 1975, Susan Pamela Carpenter (marr. diss.); one *s* one *d*; *m* 1995, Susan Stroman. *Educ:* Highgate Sch.; Edinburgh Univ. (BSc Hons Physics). Trainee dir, Perth Theatre, 1969–73; Artistic Dir, Traverse Theatre, Edinburgh, 1973–76; freelance dir, 1976–; *productions included:* Once a Catholic, Royal Court and Wyndham's, 1977; And a Nightingale Sang, Queen's, 1979; Educating Rita, RSC and Piccadilly, 1980 (Evening Standard Award, Best Play); Passion Play, RSC and Wyndham's, 1984 (Evening Standard Award, Best Comedy); Me and My Girl, 1986 (Olivier Award, Best Musical); Follies, Shaftesbury, 1987 (Olivier Award, Best Musical); Crazy For You, Prince Edward, 1993 (Olivier Award, Best Musical); Broadway productions: Me and My Girl, 1985; Once a Catholic, 1986; Atkinson at the Atkinson, 1986; Crazy For You, 1992 (Tony Award); A Christmas Carol, 1994–95; Big, 1996; King David, 1997; La Terrasse, 1999; *feature films and television:* Dancin' thru the Dark, 1990; Money For Nothing, 1993; Quest for Camelot, 1998. *Publication:* Running Down Broadway, 1992.

Recreations: tennis, swimming. *Address:* c/o Sara Randall, 265 Liverpool Road, N1 1LX. *T:* (020) 7609 5313.
Died 2 Dec. 1999.

O'CONNOR, Francis Brian, PhD; Director, Enviropower, since 1993; *b* 27 Dec. 1932; *s* of Francis Arthur and Marjorie O'Connor; *m* 1957, Dilys Mary Mathew-Jones (*d* 1995); one *s* one *d. Educ:* Quarry Bank High Sch., Liverpool; University Coll. of N Wales, Bangor (BSc, PhD). Univ. of Wales Res. Fellow, 1956–58; Lecturer in Zoology: TCD, 1958–60; UCL, 1960–67; Prof. of Soil Biology, Univ. of Aarhus, Denmark, 1968–69; Dir of Studies in Conservation, UCL, 1969–75; Nature Conservancy Council: Dep. Dir Gen., 1975–84; Dir (England), 1984–90; Dir of Policy, Planning and Services, 1990–91; Chief Officer, Jt Nature Conservation Cttee, 1991–92. *Publications:* numerous scientific. *Recreations:* boating, motoring, restoration of old houses. *Address:* Manor Farm Cottage, 52 Main Street, Ailsworth, Peterborough PE5 7AF. *T:* (01733) 380248.
Died 8 Feb. 2000.

ODLING, Maj.-Gen. William, CB 1963; OBE 1951; MC; DL; President, English-Speaking Union (Eastern Counties); Chairman: Roman River (Colchester) Conservation Zone; Friends of Essex Churches; Vice-Chairman of School, and Chairman of Hall, Fingringhoe; Treasurer/Secretary, Fingringhoe Ancient Charities; *b* 8 June 1909; *s* of late Major and Mrs W. A. Odling, Paxford, Campden, Glos; *m* 1939, Margaret Marshall (*née* Gardner); one *s* two *d. Educ:* Temple Grove; Wellington Coll.; RMA, Woolwich. Subaltern RHA and RA, chiefly in India until 1938; Captain, 1938; Major, 1946; Lieut-Colonel, 1951; Colonel, 1953; Brigadier 1957; Maj.-General, 1961; Adjutant, TA, 1939; CRA, Madagascar Force, 1942 (MC); GSO 1, RA, COSSAC, Planning Staff for Operation Overlord, 1943; NW Europe Campaign (despatches), 1944; GSO 1, War Office, 1945; GSO 1, Training, GHQ MELF, 1948; AQMG, MELF, 1950; AAG Colonel, War Office, 1953; CRA E Anglian Div., 1957; Brig. AQ, HQ E Comd, 1959; Maj.-Gen. i/c Admin, GHQ FELF, 1961–62; COS GHQ FELF, 1962–64. DL Essex, 1975. *Recreations:* sailing (Cdre, Atalanta (Yacht) Owners Assoc.), print collecting, gardening, brick building, economising. *Address:* Gun House, Fingringhoe, Colchester CO5 7AL. *T:* (01206) 735320. *Club:* Army and Navy.
Died 22 June 1997.

OFFALY, Earl of; Thomas FitzGerald; *b* 12 Jan. 1974; *s* of Marquess of Kildare and *g s* of 8th Duke of Leinster.
Died 9 May 1997.

OFFORD, (Albert) Cyril, DSc, PhD; FRS 1952; FRSE; Emeritus Professor of Mathematics, University of London; Professor, 1966–73; Hon. Fellow, 1978, London School of Economics and Political Science; *b* 9 June 1906; *s* of Albert Edwin and Hester Louise Offord; *m* 1945, Marguerite Yvonne Pickard (*d* 1998); one *d. Educ:* Hackney Downs School, London; University Coll. London (Fellow, 1969); St John's Coll., Cambridge; DSc London; PhD Cantab. Fellow of St John's Coll., Cambridge, 1937–40; Lectr, UC N Wales, Bangor, 1940–41; Lectr, King's Coll., Newcastle upon Tyne, 1941–45; Professor: King's College, Newcastle upon Tyne, 1945–48; Birkbeck Coll., Univ. of London, 1948–66. *Publications:* papers in various mathematical journals. *Recreation:* early, especially Renaissance, music. *Address:* Fairfield, 115 Banbury Road, Oxford OX2 6LA. *T:* (01865) 513703.
Died 4 June 2000.

OGDEN, Eric; *b* 23 Aug. 1923; *s* of Robert and Jane Lillian Ogden, Rhodes, Co. Lancaster; *m* 1945, Mary M. Patricia (*née* Aitken); one *s*; *m* Marjorie (*née* Smith); two *s*, two step *d. Educ:* Queen Elizabeth's Grammar School, Middleton, Lancs; Leigh Tech. Coll.; Wigan Mining and

Tech. Coll. Merchant Service, 1942–46. Textiles, 1946–52; NCB, 1952–64. Mem., Nat. Union of Mineworkers. Councillor, Borough of Middleton, 1958–65. NUM sponsored candidate, West Derby, Liverpool, 1962. MP (Lab 1964–81, SDP 1981–83) Liverpool, Derby W, 1964–83; contested (SDP) Liverpool, Derby W, 1983. Dir, Ogden's, Fotografica & Fulcrum Ltd. Mem., Royal Mail Stamps Adv. Cttee, 1971–92. Chairman: Falkland Islands Assoc., 1983–87; UK Falkland Islands Cttee, 1983–88 (Mem., 1982–90); Vice-Pres., Tristan da Cunha Assoc. FRGS 1987. *Recreations:* Central European and Balkan affairs, photography, motoring, heraldry, surviving. *Club:* Europe House.
Died 5 May 1997.

OGILVIE, Sir Alec (Drummond), Kt 1965; Chairman, Powell Duffryn Ltd, 1969–78 (Deputy Chairman, 1967–69); *b* 17 May 1913; *s* of late Sir George Drummond Ogilvie, KCIE, CSI; *m* 1945, Lesley Constance, *d* of E. B. Woollan; two *s. Educ:* Cheltenham College. Served War of 1939–45; 2/2nd Gurkha Rifles (Indian Army), 1940–45; Captain 1941; PoW, Singapore, 1942–45. Joined Andrew Yule & Co. Ltd, Calcutta, 1935, Man. Dir, 1956, and Chm., 1962–65. Director: Westinghouse Brake & Signal Co. Ltd, 1966–79; Lindustries Ltd, 1973–79; J. Lyons & Co. Ltd, 1977–78. Pres., Bengal Chamber of Commerce and Industry, 1964–65; Pres., Associated Chambers of Commerce and Industry of India, 1964–65. Member: Council, King Edward VII Hosp. for Officers, 1967–95 (Vice-Pres., 1979–95); Council, Cheltenham Coll., 1973–85 (Dep. Pres., 1983–85). *Recreations:* golf, walking. *Clubs:* Oriental, MCC; Bengal (Calcutta).
Died 13 Nov. 1997.

OGILVY, David Mackenzie, CBE 1967; Founder, Ogilvy and Mather, 1948, Chairman to 1973; Chairman, WPP Group, 1989–92; *b* 23 June 1911; *s* of Francis John Longley Ogilvy and Dorothy Fairfield; *m* 1st, 1939, Melinda Street (marr. diss. 1957); one *s*; 2nd, 1957, Anne Cabot (marr. diss.); 3rd, 1973, Herta Lans. *Educ:* Fettes College, Edinburgh; Christ Church, Oxford (Scholar). British Security Coordination, 1942–45. Dir, NY Philharmonic, 1957–67. Chm., Utd Negro Coll. Fund, 1968. Mem. of Honor, WWF. Dr of Letters (*hc*), Adelphi Univ., USA, 1977. Officier, l'Ordre des Arts et des Lettres (France), 1990. *Publications:* Confessions of an Advertising Man, 1963; Blood, Brains and Beer (autobiog.), 1978; Ogilvy On Advertising, 1983. *Recreation:* gardening. *Address:* Château de Touffou, 86300 Bonnes, France.
Died 21 July 1999.

OGSTON, Alexander George, MA, DSc; FRS 1955; President of Trinity College, Oxford, 1970–78, Hon. Fellow 1978; Fellow, 1937, and Bedford Lecturer, 1950, Balliol College; *b* 30 Jan. 1911; *s* of late Walter Henry Ogston and Josephine Elizabeth Ogston (*née* Carter); *m* 1934, Elizabeth Wicksteed; one *s* three *d. Educ:* Eton College (King's Scholar); Balliol College, Oxford. DPhil 1936, MA 1937, DSc 1970. Demonstrator, Balliol College, 1933; Freedom Research Fellow, London Hospital, 1935; Departmental Demonstrator (Biochemistry), 1938; University Demonstrator, Oxford, 1944; Reader in Biochemistry, University of Oxford, 1955–59; Prof. of Physical Biochemistry, John Curtin School of Medical Research, ANU, 1959–70, Prof. Emeritus, 1970. Vis. Fellow, Inst. for Cancer Research, Philadelphia, Nov. 1978–Jan. 1979 and March-June 1981; Silver Jubilee Vis. Fellow, University House, ANU, March-Aug. 1979. Chairman, Editorial Bd, Biochemical Journal, 1955–59 (Member of Board, 1951–55). Chm., Central Council, Selly Oak Colleges, Birmingham, 1980–84 (Vice-Chm., 1976–80). Fellow, Australian Acad. of Science, 1962; Hon. Fellow: Balliol Coll., Oxford, 1969; Univ. of York, 1980; Selly Oak Colls, 1984; Hon. Mem. American Soc.

of Biological Chemists, 1965. Hon. DMed Uppsala, 1977. Davy Medal, Royal Soc., 1986. *Publications:* scientific papers on physical chemistry and biochemistry. *Address:* 6 Dewsbury Terrace, York YO1 1HA.

Died 29 June 1996.

O'HALLORAN, Michael Joseph; Building and Construction Works Manager; *b* 20 Aug. 1933; *s* of Martin O'Halloran; British; *m* 1956, Stella Beatrice McDonald; three *d* (one *s* decd). *Educ:* Clohanes National School, Eire; self-educated. Railway worker, 1948–63; building works manager, 1963–69; returned to building industry, 1983. MP (Lab 1969–81, SDP 1981–82, Ind. Lab 1983) Islington N, Oct. 1969–1983; contested (Ind. Lab) Islington N, 1983. *Address:* 34 Sherwood Park Road, Sutton, Surrey SM1 2SG. *Died 29 Nov. 1999.*

O'HARA, Air Vice-Marshal Derek Ive, CB 1981; Manager, Birch Grove Estate, 1984–97; *b* 14 Feb. 1928; *s* of late William Edward O'Hara and Daisy Bathurst O'Hara (*née* Ive); *m* 1953, Angela Elizabeth (*née* Marchand); two *s* (one *d* decd). *Educ:* Ardingly Coll., Sussex; RAF Coll., Cranwell. Commnd RAF Coll., 1950; RAF Horsham St Faith and Tuddenham, 1950–54; Egypt, 1954–56; HQ Bomber Comd, 1956–59; Instructor, RAF Coll., 1959–61; RAF Staff Coll., Andover, 1961; Jt Planning HQ ME, Aden, 1962–64; OC Supply, RAF Finningley, 1964; Manchester Univ., 1965; OC Supply, 14 MU RAF Carlisle, 1966–68; Directing Staff, RAF Staff Coll., Andover, 1968–70; Comd of RAF Stafford, 1970–72; Dep. Dir, Supply Management, MoD Harrogate, 1972; RCDS, 1973; Air Commodore Supply and Movements, HQ Strike Comd, 1974–75; Dir, Engrg and Supply Policy, 1975–79; Dir Gen. of Supply, RAF, 1979–82. *Recreations:* sailing, fishing, gardening. *Club:* Royal Air Force.

Died 19 Oct. 1998.

OLAGBEGI II, The Olowo of Owo, (Sir Olateru), Kt 1960; Oba Alaiyeluwa, Olagbegi II, Olowo of Owo, since 1941; Minister of State, Western Region (now Western Provinces) of Nigeria, 1952; President of the House of Chiefs, Western Region (now Western Provinces), 1965; *b* 1910; *s* of Oba Alaiyeluwa, Olagbegi I, Olowo of Owo; married; many *s* and *d* (some decd). *Educ:* Owo Government School. A Teacher in 1934; Treasury Clerk in Owo Native Administration, 1935–41. Queen's Medal, 1957. *Recreations:* lawn tennis, squash racquets. *Address:* PO Box 1, Afin Oba Olowo, Owo, Western Provinces of Nigeria. *T:* Owo 1. *Died 1999.*

OLDFIELD, John Richard Anthony; *b* 5 July 1899; *s* of late Major H. E. Oldfield; *m* 1953, Jonnet Elizabeth, *d* of late Major H. M. Richards, DL, JP. *Educ:* Eton; Trinity College, Cambridge. Served in: Coldstream Guards, 1918–20; RN, 1939–45. MP (Lab) South-East Essex, 1929–31; Parliamentary Private Secretary to Sec. of State for Air, 1929–30. Member: LCC, 1931–58 (Vice-Chairman, 1953); CC (C) Kent, 1965–81. *Address:* Doddington Place, near Sittingbourne, Kent ME9 0BB.

Died 11 Dec. 1999.

OLDHAM, Rev. Canon Arthur Charles Godolphin; Canon Residentiary, Guildford Cathedral, 1961–71; *b* 5 April 1905; *s* of late Sidney Godolphin and Lilian Emma Oldham; *m* 1934, Ursula Finch Wigham Richardson (*d* 1984), *d* of late George and Isabel Richardson, Newcastle upon Tyne; one *s* two *d*. *Educ:* King's College School; King's College, London. Business, music and journalism to 1930. Ordained deacon 1933, priest 1934; Curate, Witley, Surrey, 1933–36; Vicar of Brockham Green, 1936–43; Rector of Merrow, 1943–50; Rural Dean of Guildford, 1949–50; Vicar of Godalming, 1950–62; Rural Dean of Godalming, 1957–62; Director of Ordination Training, and Bishop's Examining Chaplain, 1958–71; Hon. Canon of Guildford, 1959–61. *Recreations:* music,

sketching. *Address:* The Lawn, Holybourne, Alton, Hants GU34 4ER. *T:* (01420) 544293.

Died 2 March 1998.

OLIPHANT, Sir Marcus Laurence Elwin, (Sir Mark), AC 1977; KBE 1959; FRS 1937; FAA; FTSE; Governor of South Australia, 1971–76; *b* Adelaide, 8 Oct. 1901; *e s* of H. G. Oliphant; *m* 1925, Rosa Wilbraham (*d* 1987), Adelaide, S Australia; one *d*. *Educ:* Unley and Adelaide High Schools; University of Adelaide; Trinity Coll., Cambridge (1851 Exhibitioner, Overseas 1927, Senior 1929; PhD 1929). Messel Research Fellow of Royal Society, 1931; Fellow and Lecturer St John's Coll., Cambridge, 1934–37 (Hon. Fellow, 1952); Assistant Director of Research, Cavendish Laboratory, Cambridge, 1935; Poynting Professor of Physics, University of Birmingham, 1937–50; Dir, Research Sch. of Physical Sciences, ANU, Canberra, 1950–63; Prof. of Physics of Ionised Gases, Inst. of Advanced Studies, ANU, 1964–67, then Professor Emeritus. Pres., Aust. Acad. of Sciences, 1954–57. FAA 1954; FTSE (FTS 1976). Hon. DSc: Toronto, Belfast, Melbourne, Birmingham, New South Wales, ANU, Adelaide, Flinders; Hon. LLD St Andrews. KStJ 1972. *Publications:* Rutherford: recollections of the Cambridge days, 1972; various papers on electricity in gases, surface properties and nuclear physics. *Address:* 28 Carstensz Street, Griffith, ACT 2603, Australia. *Club:* Adelaide (Adelaide). *Died 14 July 2000.*

OLIVER, Dennis Stanley, CBE 1981; PhD; FEng, FIM, FInstP; Director, Pilkington Brothers plc, 1977–86, *b* 19 Sept. 1926; *s* of late James Thomas Oliver and Lilian Mabel Oliver (*née* Bunn); *m* 1st, 1952, Enid Jessie Newcombe (marr. diss. 1984); 2nd, 1988, Elizabeth Emery. *Educ:* Deacon's School, Peterborough; Birmingham Univ. BSc, PhD. Research Fellowship, Univ. of Bristol, 1949–52; Senior Scientific Officer, UKAEA, Culcheth, 1952–55; Head of Metallurgy Div., UKAEA, Dounreay, 1955–63; Chief R&D Officer, Richard Thomas & Baldwin Ltd, 1963–68; Group R&D Dir, Pilkington Brothers plc, 1968–77. Member: Board, British Technology Gp (Member: NEB, 1981–92; NRDC, 1981–92); Court and Council, Cranfield Inst. of Technology, 1976–88. Vis. Prof., Cranfield Inst. of Technology, 1984–88. Director: Anglo-American Venture Fund Ltd, 1980–84; Monotype Corp., 1985–90. Chm., Industrial Experience Projects Ltd, 1981–86; Pres., European Industrial Res. Management Assoc., 1977–81. Patron, Science and Technology Educn on Merseyside, 1982– (Pres., 1978–81); Governor: Liverpool Inst. of Higher Educn, 1979–85; Christ's and Notre Dame Coll., Liverpool, 1979–87; Royal Nat. Coll. for the Blind, 1981–85; Dir, L'Ecole Supérieure du Verre, Belgium, 1971–86; Governor, Community of St Helens Trust Ltd, 1978–86; Founder Trustee, Anfield Foundn, 1983–88. Gov., Sr Brigid's Sch., Denbigh. Freeman of City of London; Liveryman: Spectaclemakers' Co. (Court of Assts, 1985–88); Co. of Engrs, 1984. FIMgt. KSG 1980. *Publications:* The Use of Glass in Engineering, 1975; Glass for Construction Purposes, 1977; various publications on technical subjects and technology transfer. *Recreations:* music, poetry, cooking. *Address:* Castell Bach, Bodfari, Denbigh, Clwyd LL16 4HT. *T:* Bodfari (01754) 710354. *Died 31 July 1996.*

OLIVER, Group Captain John Oliver William, CB 1950; DSO 1940; DFC 1940; RAF retired; *b* 11 Oct. 1911; *e s* of William and Cicely Oliver; *m* 1st, 1935, Irene Oxberry (marr. diss. 1951); one *s* two *d*; 2nd, 1954, Christine Guthrie (marr. diss. 1960); 3rd, 1962, Anne Fraser Porteous; one *s* two *d* (incl. twin *s* and *d*). *Educ:* Christ's Hospital; Cranwell. Commissioned from Cranwell, General Duties Pilot Branch permanent commn, 1931; served 43 (F) Squadron and 55 (B) Squadron, Iraq;

qualified CFS; served War of 1939–45 (despatches thrice); commanded 85 (F) Squadron, 1940 (BEF, France, 1939–40); Fighter Command and Tactical Air Force; Wing Commander, 1940; Group Captain, 1942 (Trng Fighter Comd, and TAF Plans for Overlord); QS Camberley and Bracknell; Assistant Commandant, RAF Coll., Cranwell, 1948–50; SASO 2 Gp, Germany, CO Kabrit, Egypt, Gp Capt Ops Egypt, and SASO Iraq, 1951–58; ACOS Ops, Allied Forces Northern Europe, 1958–60; retired, 1961. Personnel Officer, ENV (Engineering) Ltd, 1961; Staff Institute Personnel Management, 1962; Personnel Manager, Humber Ltd, 1963; Manager, Training and Administrative Service, Rootes, Coventry, 1965; Senior Training Officer, Engineering Industry Training Board, 1968; Personnel and Trng Manager, Thorn Gp, 1970–76, retired. *Recreations:* painting, sailing.   *Died 4 Feb. 1997.*

OLIVER, Prof. Richard Alexander Cavaye; Professor of Education and Director of the Department of Education in the University of Manchester, 1938–70, then Emeritus; *b* 9 Jan. 1904; *s* of Charles Oliver and Elizabeth Smith; *m* 1929, Annabella Margaret White (*d* 1992), MA Edin, MA Oxon; one *s* one *d. Educ:* George Heriot's Sch.; University of Edinburgh; Stanford Univ., California, USA (Commonwealth Fund Fellowship, 1927–29). Research educational psychologist in Kenya, 1929–32; Asst Master, Abbotsholme Sch. and in Edinburgh, 1933–34; University Extension Lecturer, 1933–34; Asst Director of Education, Wilts Education Cttee, 1934–36; Dep. Secretary, Devon Education Cttee, 1936–38; University of Manchester: Dean, Faculty of Educn, 1938–48, 1962–65; Dir, School of Education, 1947–51; Dean, Faculty of Music, 1952–62, 1966–70; Pro Vice-Chancellor, 1953–57 and 1960–61; Presenter of Hon. Graduands, 1959–64, 1966. Member: Nat. Adv. Council on Training and Supply of Teachers, 1949–59; Northern Univs Jt Matriculation Bd, 1942–70 (Chm., 1952–55); Secondary School Examinations Council, 1958–64. FBPsS. Hon. Research Fellow, Princeton Univ., 1961. Hon. LLD Manchester, 1981. *Publications:* (jtly) The Educational Guidance of the School Child, 1936; Research in Education, 1946; The Content of Sixth Form General Studies, 1974; Joint Matriculation Board Occasional Publications; contrib. to East Africa Medical Journal, Africa, British Journal of Psychology, Yearbook of Education, Universities Quarterly, Research in Education, etc. *Recreations:* gardening, painting. *Address:* Waingap, Crook, Kendal, Cumbria LA8 9HT. *T:* (01539) 821277.

           Died 9 March 1998.

OLLIS, Prof. William David, PhD; FRS 1972; CChem; FRSC; Hon. Professor of Organic Chemistry, University of Birmingham, since 1991; *b* 22 Dec. 1924; *s* of Albert George and Beatrice Charlotte Ollis; *m* 1951, Sonia Dorothy Mary Weekes (marr. diss. 1974); two *d. Educ:* Cotham Grammar Sch., Bristol; University of Bristol (BSc, PhD). Assistant Lecturer in Organic Chemistry, 1946–49, Lecturer, 1949–62, Reader, 1962–63, University of Bristol; Prof. of Org. Chem., Univ. of Sheffield, 1963–90. Research Fellow, Harvard, 1952–53; Visiting Professor: UCLA, 1962; University of Texas, 1966; Universidade Federal Rural do Rio de Janeiro, Brasil, 1967–70 (Hon. Prof., 1969); Wesleyan Univ., Conn, 1970–71; Univ. of Sri Lanka, 1974; Univ. of Kuwait, 1986, 1990. Lectures: Robert Gnehm, 1965; Tilden, Chemical Soc., 1969; Peboc, 1982; Irvine, 1984; Syntex, 1985, Pedler, RSC, 1988. Consultant, MoD, 1952–76; Scientific Advr, Home Office, 1954–76; Member: Individual Merit Promotion Panel Scientific CS, 1971–90; Adv. Council for Misuse of Drugs, 1981–95. Founder-Chm., Phytochem. Soc., 1966–67; Chm., Publication Cttee, Chem. Soc., 1972–74; Pres., Organic Chem. Div., RSC, 1983–85. Organic Synthesis Medal, RSC, 1982.

FRSA. *Publications:* Recent Developments in the Chemistry of Natural Phenolic Compounds, 1961; Structure Determination in Organic Chemistry, 1973; (ed with Sir Derek Barton) Comprehensive Organic Chemistry, vols 1–6, 1979; (contrib.) Advances in Medicinal Phytochemistry, 1986; scientific papers mainly in Jl of Chemical Soc., Perkin Trans I, Tetrahedron. *Address:* c/o School of Chemistry, University of Birmingham, Edgbaston, Birmingham B15 2TT. *Club:* Athenæum.   *Died 13 June 1999.*

O'NEIL, Most Rev. Alexander Henry, DD; *b* 23 July 1907; *s* of Alexander O'Neil and Anna Henry; *m* 1931, Marguerite (*née* Roe); one *s. Educ:* Univ. of W Ontario (BA 1928; BD 1936; MA 1943; DD 1945); Huron Coll., London, Ont (LTh 1929). Deacon, 1929; priest, 1930; Principal, Huron Coll., London, Ont, 1941–52; Gen. Sec., British and Foreign Bible Soc. in Canada, 1952–57; Bishop of Fredericton, 1957–63; Archbishop of Fredericton and Metropolitan of the Province of Canada, 1963–71. Hon. DD: Univ. of W Ontario, 1945; Wycliffe Coll., Toronto, 1954; King's Coll., Halifax, 1958; Hon. LLD: W Ontario, 1962; St Thomas Univ., Fredericton, 1970; Hon. DCL Bishop's Univ., Lennoxville, 1964. *Address:* Apt 807 Grosvenor Gates, 1 Grosvenor Street, London, ON N6A 1Y2, Canada.

           Died 21 Oct. 1997.

O'NEIL, Hon. Sir Desmond (Henry), Kt 1980; Chairman: Western Australia Lotteries Commission, 1981–84; Western Australia Greyhound Racing Association, 1981–84; *b* 27 Sept. 1920; *s* of late Henry McLelland O'Neil and Lilian Francis O'Neil; *m* 1944, Nancy Jean Culver; two *d. Educ:* Aquinas Coll., Perth; Claremont Teachers Coll., WA. Served War, Australian Army, 1939–46: Captain, Aust. Corps of Signals. Educn Dept, WA, 1939–58. Mem., Legislative Assembly, WA, 1959–80; Govt Whip, 1962–65; Minister for Housing and Labour, 1965–71; Dep. Leader of Opposition, 1972–73; Minister for: Works and Housing, 1974–75; Works, Housing and the North-West, 1975–77; Dep. Premier, Chief Sec., Minister for Police and Traffic, Minister for Regional Admin and the NW, Western Australia, 1977–80. Col Comdt, Royal Aust. Corps of Signals 5 Mil. Dist, 1980–82. *Recreations:* power boating, fishing. *Address:* 42 Godwin Avenue, South Como, WA 6152, Australia. *T:* 3132526.   *Died 25 Sept. 1999.*

OPIE, Roger Gilbert, CBE 1976; Fellow and Lecturer in Economics, New College, Oxford, 1961–92, Emeritus Fellow, since 1992; *b* Adelaide, SA, 23 Feb. 1927; *o s* of late Frank Gilbert Opie and late Fanny Irene Grace Opie (*née* Tregoning); *m* 1955, Norma Mary, *o d* of late Norman and late Mary Canter; two *s* one *d. Educ:* Prince Alfred Coll., S Aust; Adelaide Univ. (BA 1st cl. Hons 1948; MA 1950); Christ Church and Nuffield Coll., Oxford (SA Rhodes Schol., 1951; Boulter Exhibnr, 1952; George Webb Medley Jun. Schol., 1952, Sen. Schol., 1953; PPE 1st Cl. 1953; Nuffield Coll. Studentship, 1954; BPhil 1954). Tutor and Lectr, Adelaide Univ., 1949–51; Asst Lectr and Lectr, LSE, 1954–61; Econ. Adviser, Econ. Section, HM Treasury, 1958–60; Asst Dir, HM Treasury Centre for Administrative Studies, 1964; Asst Dir, Planning Div., Dept of Economic Affairs, 1964–66; Advr, W. Pakistan Planning Commn, 1966; Economic Adviser to Chm., NBPI, 1967–70; Special Univ. Lectr in Econs, Oxford, 1970–75; Tutor and Sen. Tutor, Oxford Univ. Business Summer Sch., 1974–79. Visiting Professor: Brunel Univ., 1975–77; Univ. of Strathclyde, 1984–87. Member: Monopolies and Mergers Commn, 1968–81; Price Commn, 1977–80. Mem., ILO Mission to Ethiopia, 1982. City Councillor, Oxford, 1972–74; Oxford Dist Councillor, 1973–76. Presenter, TV series: Wealth of a Nation; History Today. Economic Correspondent, New

Statesman, 1967–71, 1974–76; Editor: The Bankers' Magazine, 1960–64; International Currency Review, 1970–71. *Publications:* co-author of a number of works in applied economics, including: Causes of Crime, 1956; Banking in Western Europe, 1962; Sanctions against South Africa, 1964; Economic Growth in Britain, 1966; Crisis in the Civil Service, 1968; Unfashionable Economics, 1970; The Labour Government's Economic Record 1964–70, 1972. *Recreations:* sailing, photography, hiding in Cornwall. *Address:* New College, Oxford OX1 3BN. *T:* (01865) 279555.　　　　　　*Died 22 Jan. 1998.*

OPPENHEIM, Tan Sri Sir Alexander, Kt 1961; OBE 1955; DSc, PhD; FRSE; Vice-Chancellor, University of Malaya, 1957–65 (Acting Vice-Chancellor, 1955); *b* 4 Feb. 1903; *o s* of late Rev. H. J. and Mrs F. Oppenheim; *m* 1st, 1930, Beatrice Templer (marr. diss. 1977; she *d* 1990), *y d* of Dr Otis B. Nesbit, Indiana, USA; one *d*; 2nd, 1982, Margaret Ng; two *s*. *Educ:* Manchester Grammar Sch.; Balliol Coll., Oxford (Scholar; Sen. Mathematical Schol., Oxf., 1926; MA 1952; DSc 1954); PhD Chicago 1930. Commonwealth Fund Fell., Chicago, 1927–30; Lectr, Edinburgh Univ., 1930–31; Prof. of Mathematics, 1931–42, 1945–49, Dep. Principal, 1947, 1949, Raffles Coll., Singapore; Prof. of Mathematics, 1949–57, Dean, Faculty of Arts, 1949, 1951, 1953, Univ. of Malaya. L/Bdr, Straits Vol. RA, POW (Singapore, Siam), 1942–45; Dean POW University, 1942. President: Malayan Mathematical Soc., 1951–55, 1957; Singapore Chess Club, 1956–60; Amer. Univs. Club, 1956. Chm. Bd of Management, Tropical Fish Culture Research Institute (Malacca), 1962; Member: Unesco-International Assoc. of Universities Study of Higher Education in Development of Countries of SE Asia, 1962, Academic Adv. Cttee, Univ. of Cape Coast, 1972. Visiting Professor: Univ. of Reading, in Dept of Mathematics, 1965–68; Univ. of Ghana, 1968–73; Univ. of Benin, Nigeria, 1973–77. FWA 1963; HMA 1964. Hon. degrees: DSc Hong Kong, 1961; LLD: Singapore, 1962; Leeds, 1966; DLitt Malaya, 1965. Alumni Medal, Univ. of Chicago Alumni Assoc., 1977. Panglima Mangku Negara (Fedn of Malaya), 1962. *Publications:* papers on mathematics in various periodicals. *Recreations:* chess, bridge. *Address:* Matson House, Remenham, Henley-on-Thames RG9 3HB. *T:* (01491) 572049. *Clubs:* Royal Over-Seas League; Selangor (Kuala Lumpur).　　　　*Died 13 Dec. 1997.*

OPPENHEIMER, Harry Frederick; Chairman: Anglo-American Corporation of South Africa Ltd, 1957–82 (Director, 1934–82); De Beers Consolidated Mines, Ltd, 1957–84 (Director, 1934–94); *b* Kimberley, S Africa, 28 Oct. 1908; *s* of late Sir Ernest Oppenheimer and his first wife, Mary Lina, *d* of Joseph Pollak; *m* 1943, Bridget, *d* of late Foster McCall; one *s* one *d*. *Educ:* Charterhouse; Christ Church, Oxford (MA; Hon. Student). Served 4th SA Armoured Car Regt, 1940–45. MP (SA) Kimberley City, 1948–58. Chancellor, Univ. of Cape Town, 1967–96. Hon. DEcon Natal, 1960; Hon. LLD: Witwatersrand, 1963; Leeds, 1965; Rhodes, 1965; Hon. DLitt Cape Town, 1985. IMM Gold Medal, 1965; Gold Medal, Amer. Inst. of Mining and Metallurgy, 1990. Decoration for Meritorious Service (S Africa), 1985. *Recreations:* horse breeding and racing. *Address:* Brenthurst, Federation Road, Parktown, Johannesburg 2193, South Africa; PO Box 61631, Marshalltown 2107, South Africa. *Clubs:* Brooks's, Roxburghe; Rand, Inanda (Johannesburg); Kimberley (SA); Harare (Zimbabwe).
　　　　　　　　　　　　　　Died 19 Aug. 2000.

OPPERMAN, Hon. Sir Hubert (Ferdinand), Kt 1968; OBE 1952; Australian High Commissioner in Malta, 1967–72; *b* 29 May 1904; *s* of A. Opperman; Australian; *m* 1928, Mavys Paterson Craig; one *s* (one *d* decd). *Educ:* Armadale, Vic; Bailieston, Vic. Served RAAF, 1940–45;

commissioned 1942. Commonwealth Public Service: PMG's Dept, 1918–20; Navigation Dept, Trade and Customs, 1920–22. Cyclist: Australian Road Champion, 1924, 1926, 1927, 1929; Winner French Bol d'Or, 1928, and Paris-Brest-Paris, 1931; holder, numerous world's track and road unpaced and motor paced cycling records. Director, Allied Bruce Small Pty Ltd, 1936–60. MHR for Corio, Vic, 1949–67; Mem. Australian Delegn to CPA Conf., Nairobi, 1954; Chief Govt Whip, 1955–60; Minister for Shipping and Transport, 1960–63; Minister for Immigration, 1963–66. Convenor, Commonwealth Jubilee Sporting Sub-Cttee, 1951; Nat. Patron, Aust. Sportsmen's Assoc., 1980–; Chm. Selection Cttee, Aust. Hall of Sporting Fame, 1985; Hon. Master of Sport, Confedn of Aust. Sport, 1984. Selected as one of 200 People Who Made Australia Great, Heritage 200, 1988. GCSJ 1980 (KSJ 1973); Bailiff Prior, Victoria, 1980–83; Bailiff, Aust. Grand Council, 1983–. Hon. Rotarian, St Kilda Rotary, 1984. Coronation Medal, 1953; Silver medal, 1971, Gold medal, 1991, of City of Paris; Medals of Brest, 1971, Verona, 1972; Médaille Mérite, French Cycling Fedn, 1978; Paul Harris Rotary Award, 1992. *Publication:* Pedals, Politics and People (autobiog.), 1977. *Recreations:* cycling, swimming. *Address:* Apt 243, Salford Park, 100 Harold Street, Wantirna, Vic 3152, Australia. *T:* 8014010. *Clubs:* USI, Air Force (Victoria); Naval and Military (Melbourne).　　　　　　*Died 18 April 1996.*

ORAM, Baron *cr* 1975 (Life Peer), of Brighton, co. of E Sussex; **Albert Edward Oram;** *b* 13 Aug. 1913; *s* of Henry and Ada Edith Oram; *m* 1956, Frances Joan, *d* of Charles and Dorothy Barber, Lewes; two *s*. *Educ:* Burgess Hill Elementary Sch.; Brighton Grammar Sch.; University of London (London School of Economics and Institute of Education). Formerly a teacher. Served War 1942–45; Royal Artillery, Normandy and Belgium. Research Officer, Co-operative Party, 1946–55. MP (Lab and Co-op) East Ham South, 1955–Feb. 1974; Parly Secretary, ODM, 1964–69; a Lord in Waiting (Govt Whip), 1976–78. Co-ordinator, Develt Programmes, Internat. Co-operative Alliance, 1971–73; Develt Administrator, Intermediate Technol. Develt Gp, 1974–76; Mem., Commonwealth Develt Corp., 1975–76; Chm., Co-op. Develt Agency, 1978–81. *Publication:* (with Nora Stettner) Changes in China, 1987. *Recreations:* country walking, cricket, chess. *Address:* 19 Ridgeside Avenue, Patcham, Brighton BN1 8WD. *T:* (01273) 505333.　　　　*Died 4 Sept. 1999.*

ORKNEY, 8th Earl of, *cr* 1696; **Cecil O'Bryen Fitz-Maurice;** Viscount of Kirkwall and Baron of Dechmont, 1696; *b* 3 July 1919; *s* of Douglas Frederick Harold FitzMaurice (*d* 1937; *g g s* of 5th Earl) and Dorothy Janette (who *m* 2nd, 1939, Commander E. T. Wiggins, DSC, RN), *d* of late Capt. Robert Dickie, RN; *S* kinsman, 1951; *m* 1953, Rose Katharine Durk (*d* 1995), *yr d* of late J. W. D. Silley, Brixham. Joined RASC, 1939; served in North Africa, Italy, France and Germany, 1939–46, and in Korea, 1950–51. *Heir:* kinsman Oliver Peter St John [*b* 27 Feb. 1938; *m* 1st, 1963, Mary Juliet (marr. diss. 1985), *d* of late W. G. Scott-Brown, CVO, MD, FRCS, FRCSE; one *s* three *d* (and one *d* decd); 2nd, 1985, Mrs Mary Barbara Huck, *d* of Dr David B. Albertson; one step *s* three step *d*]. *Address:* Ferndown, Dorset BH22 9JG.
　　　　　　　　　　　　　　Died 5 Feb. 1998.

ORLEBAR, Sir Michael Keith Orlebar S.; *see* Simpson-Orlebar.

ORMONDE, 7th Marquess of, *cr* 1825; **James Hubert Theobald Charles Butler,** MBE 1921; Earl of Ormonde, 1328; Viscount Thurles, 1525; Earl of Ossory, 1527; Baron Ormonde (UK), 1821; 31st Hereditary Chief Butler of Ireland; retired; *b* 19 April 1899; *s* of Lord Theobald Butler (4th *s* of 2nd Marquess) and Annabella Brydon (*d* 1943), *o d* of Rev. Cosmo Reid Gordon, DD; *S* cousin,

1971; *m* 1st, 1935, Nan Gilpin (*d* 1973); two *d*; 2nd, 1976, Elizabeth Liles (*d* 1980). *Educ:* Haileybury College; RMC Sandhurst. Commissioned Dec. 1917, King's Royal Rifle Corps; resigned commission, May 1926 (Lieut). Various business connections in USA. *Heir:* (to earldoms of Ormonde and Ossory) 17th Viscount Mountgarret. *Address:* King-Bruwaert House, 6101 South County Line Road, Burr Ridge, IL 60521, USA. *Club:* Naval and Military.   *Died 25 Oct. 1997.*

ORR, Jean Fergus Henderson; Director, Office of Manpower Economics, 1973–80; *b* 3 April 1920; *yr d* of late Peter Orr, OBE and Janet Muir Orr (*née* Henderson). *Educ:* privately; University Coll., London (BA; Fellow, 1982). Min. of Aircraft Prodn, temp. Asst Principal, 1942; Min. of Supply: Asst Principal, 1946; Principal, 1949; HM Treasury, 1954: Principal, Official Side Sec. to Civil Service Nat. Whitley Council negotiations on Report of Royal Commn on Civil Service, 1953–55; Asst Sec. 1961; on loan to Office of Manpower Econs as Sec. to Top Salaries Review Body, 1971. FZS 1996. *Publication:* (contrib.) Edward Boyle: his life by his friends, ed Ann Gold, 1991. *Recreations:* music, travel, natural history. *Address:* 21 Bathwick Hill, Bath, Somerset BA2 6EW. *T:* (01225) 463664. *Club:* United Oxford & Cambridge University.   *Died 17 April 1997.*

ORR-EWING, Baron *cr* 1971 (Life Peer), of Little Berkhamsted in the county of Hertfordshire; **Charles Ian Orr-Ewing,** OBE (mil.) 1945; Bt 1963; consultant and director of various companies; Chairman, Metrication Board, 1972–77; *b* 10 Feb. 1912; *s* of Archibald Ian Orr Ewing and Gertrude (*née* Runge); *m* 1939, Joan McMinnies; four *s. Educ:* Harrow; Trinity Coll., Oxford (MA (Physics)). Graduate apprentice, EMI, Hayes, 1934–37; BBC Television Service, 1938–39, 1946–49. Served RAFVR, 1939–46, N Africa, Italy, France and Germany, Wing Comdr, 1941; Chief Radar Officer, Air Staff, SHAEF, 1945 (despatches twice); BBC Television Outside Broadcasts Manager, 1946–48. MP (C) North Hendon, 1950–70; PPS to Sir Walter Monckton, Minister of Labour and National Service, 1951–55; Parliamentary Under-Secretary of State, for Air, Air Ministry, 1957–59; Parliamentary and Financial Secretary to Admiralty, 1959; Civil Lord of the Admiralty, 1959–63. Joint Secretary, Parliamentary Scientific Cttee, 1950; Vice-Pres., Parliamentary and Scientific Cttee, 1965–68; Vice-Chm., 1922 Cttee, 1966–70 (Secretary, 1956); Vice-Chairman, Defence Cttee, 1966–70. Dep. Chm., Assoc. of Cons. Peers, 1980–86. Mem., Royal Commn on Standards of Conduct in Public Life, 1975–76. Pres. and Chm. of Council, Electronic Engineering Assoc., 1969–70. Pres., Nat. Ski Fedn of GB, 1972–76. FIEE. *Publication:* (ed) A Celebration of Lords and Commons Cricket 1850–1988, 1989. *Recreations:* tennis, light-hearted cricket, ski-ing. *Heir* (to baronetcy only): *s* Hon. (Alistair) Simon Orr-Ewing [*b* 10 June 1940; *m* 1968, Victoria, *er d* of late Keith Cameron, Fifield House, Milton-under-Wychwood, Oxon; two *s* one *d*]. *Address:* House of Lords, SW1A 0AA. *Clubs:* Boodle's, MCC; All England Lawn Tennis; Vincent's (Oxford).   *Died 19 Aug. 1999.*

OSMAN, Louis, BA (Arch.); FRIBA; artist, architect, goldsmith, medallist; *b* 30 Jan. 1914; *s* of Charles Osman, Exeter; *m* 1940, Dilys Roberts, *d* of Richard Roberts, Rotherfield, Sussex; one *d. Educ:* Hele's School, Exeter; London University (Fellow, UCL, 1984–). Open exhibn at Bartlett School of Architecture, University Coll. London, 1931, and at Slade School; Donaldson Medallist of RIBA, 1935. With British Museum and British School of Archæology Expeditions to Syria, 1936, 1937; designed private and public buildings, 1937–39; served War of 1939–45, Major in Intelligence Corps: Combined Ops HQ and Special Air Service as specialist in Air Photography,

Beach Reconnaissance Cttee, prior to invasion of Europe; resumed practice in London, 1945; designed buildings, furniture, tapestries, glass, etc; work in Westminster Abbey, Lincoln, Ely, Exeter and Lichfield Cathedrals; Staunton Harold for National Trust; Bridge, Cavendish Square, with Jacob Epstein; Newnham Coll., Cambridge; factory buildings for Cambridge Instrument Co.; aluminium Big Top for Billy Smart's Circus; two villages on Dartmoor, etc; consultant architect to British Aluminium Co.; executed commissions as goldsmith and jeweller, 1956–; commissioned by De Beers for 1st Internat. Jewellery Exhibn, 1961; designed and made Prince of Wales' crown for investiture, 1969; British Bicentennial Gift to America housing Magna Carta, 1976. Verulam Medal for Metals Soc., 1975; EAHY Medal, 1975; Olympic Medal, 1976; works in art galleries, museums and private collections in GB, Europe, Canada, USA, S Africa, Australia, Japan, etc; one-man retrospective exhibn, Goldsmiths' Hall, 1971; exhibn, Lisbon, 1990. Mem. Exec. Cttee: The Georgian Group, 1952–56; City Music Soc., 1960–70. *Publications:* reviews and contributions to learned jls. *Recreation:* music. *Address:* Harpton Court, near New Radnor, Presteigne, Powys LD8 2RE. *T:* New Radnor (01544) 350380.   *Died 11 April 1996.*

OSMOND, Mervyn Victor, OBE 1978; Secretary, Council for the Protection of Rural England, 1966–77; *b* 2 July 1912; *s* of Albion Victor Osmond and Florence Isabel (*née* Edwards), Bristol; *m* 1940, Aimée Margaret Moir; one *d. Educ:* Clifton Coll. (Schol.); Exeter Coll., Oxford (Schol.; 1st cl. Hon. Class. Mods; 2nd cl. Lit. Hum.; 2nd cl. Jurisprudence; Poland Prizeman (Criminal Law), 1937; MA 1939). Called to Bar, Inner Temple, 1938; practising Barrister, Western Circuit, 1938–40. Joined Gloucestershire Regt, TA, 1931; served war of 1939–45; Royal Fusiliers; DAAG (Major) 352 L of C Sub-Area and 303 L of C Area (Calcutta). Asst Sec., 1946–63, Dep. Sec., 1963–66, CPRE. *Recreations:* reading, enjoying rural England. *Address:* Lynde House, 28 Cambridge Park, Twickenham TW1 2JB.   *Died 8 June 1998.*

OSMOND, Sir (Stanley) Paul, Kt 1980; CB 1966; *b* 13 May 1917; *o s* of late Stanley C. and Susan Osmond; *m* 1942, Olivia Sybil, JP, *yr d* of late Ernest E. Wells, JP, Kegworth, Leicestershire; two *s. Educ:* Bristol Grammar School; Jesus College, Oxford. Served War of 1939–45, in Army (Gloucestershire Regiment and staff), 1940–46. Home Civil Service, 1939–75: Ministry of Education, 1946–48; Private Secretary to Prime Minister, 1948–51; Admiralty, 1951, Asst Secretary, 1954; Under-Secretary, 1959; HM Treasury, 1962, Third Secretary, 1965; Deputy Secretary: Civil Service Dept, 1968–70; Office of the Lord Chancellor, 1970–72; DHSS, 1972–75. Sec. to the Church Commissioners, 1975–80. Member: Lord Chancellor's Cttee on Public Records, 1978–80; Adv. Council on Public Records, 1983–88. Royal Institution: a Manager, 1966–69, 1970–73; Hon. Treas., 1981–86; Vice-Pres., 1981–86, 1989–92; Mem. Council, 1989–92 (Chm., 1989–92). Chm., Nat. Marriage Guidance Council, 1982–88. Mem., Clergy Orphan Corp., 1980–92; Hon. Treasurer, Central London YMCA, 1982–85; Governor, Bristol Grammar Sch., 1972–93 (Vice-Chm., 1984–92); Chm., Lingfield Hosp. Sch., 1981–87. CIMgt (CBIM 1978). *Recreations:* theatre, travel. *Address:* 20 Beckenham Grove, Bromley, Kent BR2 0JU. *T:* (020) 8460 2026. *Club:* Athenæum.

Died 17 Jan. 2000.

OTTER, Air Vice-Marshal Victor Charles, CBE 1967 (OBE 1945); Air Officer Engineering, Air Support Command Royal Air Force, 1966–69, retired; *b* 9 Feb. 1914; *s* of Robert and Ada Annie Otter; *m* 1943, Iris Louise Dykes; no *c. Educ:* Weymouth Grammar School.

RAF Aircraft Apprentice, 1929–32; flying duties, 1935–37; commissioned Engr. Br., 1940; SO (Techn.) Controller Research and Development (MAP), 1942–47; Asst Air Attaché, Budapest, 1947–48; Officer Comdg Central Servicing Develt Establt, 1953–55; Chief Engrg Officer, Bomber Comd, 1956–59; OC No 32 Maintenance Unit, 1959–61; STSO Flying Trng Comd, 1961–63; Project Dir, P1154/P1127, 1963–66. CEng, FRAeS, psc. *Address:* Harpenden, 21 Keats Avenue, Littleover, Derby DE23 7EE. *T:* Derby (01332) 512048. *Club:* Royal Air Force.   *Died 5 May 1996.*

OULTON, Air Vice-Marshal Wilfrid Ewart, CB 1958; CBE 1953; DSO 1943; DFC 1943; CEng; FRIN; FIEE; Chairman, Medsales Executive Ltd, since 1982; *b* 27 July 1911; *s* of Llewellin Oulton, Monks Coppenhall, Cheshire; *m* 1st, 1935, Sarah (*d* 1990), *d* of Rev. E. Davies, Pitsea, Essex; three *s*; 2nd, 1991, Leticia Sara Malcolm. *Educ:* University Coll., Cardiff; Cranwell. Commissioned, 1931; Director, Joint Anti-Submarine School, 1946–48; Joint Services Staff College, 1948–50; Air Attaché, Buenos Aires, Montevideo, Asunción, 1950–53; idc 1954; Director of Operations, Air Ministry, 1954–56; commanded Joint Task Force "Grapple" for first British megaton weapon tests in the Pacific, 1956–58; Senior Air Staff Officer, RAF Coastal Command, HQ, 1958–60; retd. *Publications:* Christmas Island Cracker, 1987; Technocrat, 1995. *Recreations:* music, travel, grandchildren and great-grandchildren. *Address:* Farthings, Hollywood Lane, Lymington, Hants SO41 9HD. *T:* (01590) 673498. *Clubs:* Royal Air Force; Royal Lymington Yacht.
                                              Died 31 Oct. 1997.

OUTERIÑO, Felix C.; *see* Candela Outeriño.

OWEN, Maj.-Gen. Harry, CB 1972; Chairman, Medical Appeal Tribunal, 1972–84; *b* 17 July 1911; *s* of John Lewis Owen; *m* 1952, Maureen (*née* Summers), one *s* one *d. Educ:* University Coll., Bangor (BA Hons Philosophy, 1934). Solicitor of Supreme Court, 1939. Commissioned in Queen's Own Cameron Highlanders, 1940–43; joined Mil. Dept of Office of Judge Advocate General, 1943; served in: W Africa, 1945–46; Middle East, 1947–50; Austria, 1952–53; Dep. Dir of Army Legal Services: Far East, 1960–62; HQ, BAOR, 1962–67; Brig. Legal Staff, 1968–69; Maj.-Gen. 1969; Dir, Army Legal Services, 1969–71, retd. *Recreations:* philosophy, history of art, walking. *Address:* 7 The Chyne, South Park, Gerrards Cross, Bucks SL9 8HZ. *T:* (01753) 890701.
                                              Died 26 Oct. 1998.

OWEN, Prof. John Benjamin Brynmor, DSc, MSc; CEng; John William Hughes Professor of Civil Engineering, University of Liverpool, 1950–77, then Emeritus Professor; *b* 2 Sept. 1910; *s* of David Owen, (Degwyl), and Mary Alice Owen; *m* 1938, Beatrice Pearn (*née* Clark); two *d. Educ:* Universities of Oxford and Wales (DSc Oxon, MSc Wales). Drapers' Company Scholar, Page Prize and Medal, University College, Cardiff, 1928–31 (Fellow, 1981); Meyricke Scholar, Jesus Coll., Oxford, 1931–32; British Cotton Industry Research Association, 1933–35; Messrs A. V. Roe, Manchester, 1935–36; Royal Aircraft Establishment, Farnborough, 1936–48; Naval Construction Research Establishment, 1948–50. *Publications:* Light Structures, 1965; many contributions to learned journals on design of structures, helicopters and on investigation of aircraft accidents. *Address:* The University of Liverpool, PO Box 147, Liverpool L69 3BX. *T:* (0151) 709 6022.
                                              Died 7 April 1998.

OWEN, Maj.-Gen. John Ivor Headon, OBE 1963; *b* 22 Oct. 1922; *s* of Major William H. Owen; *m* 1948, (Margaret) Jean Hayes; three *d. Educ:* St Edmund's Sch., Canterbury. FBIM; psm, jssc, idc. Joined Royal Marines

(as Marine), 1942; temp. 2nd Lieut, 1942; 44 Commando RM, Far East, 1942–46; demobilised 1946 (Captain); Constable, Metropolitan Police, 1946–47; rejoined Royal Marines as Lieut, 1947; regimental service, 1948–55; Staff Coll., Camberley, 1956; Bde Major, HQ 3 Cdo Bde, 1959–62; Naval Plans, Admty/MoD, 1962–64; 42 Cdo RM, 1964–66; Instructor, Jt Services Staff Coll., 1966–67; CO 45 Cdo RM, 1967–68 (despatches); Col GS, Staff of CGRM, 1969–70; Royal Coll. of Defence Studies, 1971–72; Maj.-Gen., Commando Forces RM, Plymouth, 1972–73. Lt-Col 1966; Col 1970; Maj.-Gen. 1972; Col Comdt, RM, 1983–84, Rep. Col Comdt, 1985–86. UK Partnership Sec. to KMG Thomson McLintock, Chartered Accountants, 1974–87 (the British Mem. of KMG Klynveld Main Goerdeler, 1979 87). Editor, Current Mil. and Political Lit., 1983–91. Chm. Exec. Cttee, Bowles Outdoor Centre, 1984–98; a Vice Chm., Clergy Orphan Corp., 1995–97 (Treas. and Chm., 1980–95); Mem., Ct of Assistants, Corp. of Sons of the Clergy, 1981–98; Chairman of Governors: St Edmund's Sch., Canterbury, 1980–94; St Margaret's Sch., Bushey, 1980–; Chm. of Trustees, Royal Marines Mus., 1989–97. *Publications:* Brassey's Infantry Weapons of the World, 1975; contrib. Seaford House Papers, 1971; articles in Contemporary Review and the press. *Recreations:* woodworking, gardening. *Address:* c/o HSBC, 62 Hills Road, Cambridge CB2 1LA. *Club:* Army and Navy.
                                              Died 31 May 1999.

OWEN, Rear-Adm. Richard Arthur James, CB 1963; *b* 26 Aug. 1910; *s* of late Captain Leonard E. Owen, OBE, JP; *m* 1941, Jean Sophia (*née* Bluett); one *s* two *d. Educ:* Sevenoaks Sch. Joined RN, 1927; Commander (S) 1945; Captain, 1954; Rear-Admiral, 1961; Director-General, Personal Services, Admiralty, 1962–64; retired. *Address:* Oakridge, Mayfield Road, Fordingbridge, Hants SP6 1DU. *T:* (01425) 655984.   *Died 10 Oct. 1999.*

OWEN, Thomas Arfon; development and funding consultant; Director, Welsh Arts Council, 1984–93; *b* 7 June 1933; *s* of late Hywel Peris Owen and Jennie Owen; *m* 1955, Joy (*née* Phillips); three *s* one *d. Educ:* Ystalyfera Grammar School; Magdalen College, Oxford (MA); MA Wales. Deputy Registrar, 1959, Registrar 1967–84, UCW Aberystwyth. Chm., Mid-Wales Hosp. Management Cttee, 1972–74; Member: East Dyfed Health Authy, 1982–84; S Glam Health Authy, 1984–87 (Vice-Chm., 1986–87); Consumers' Cttee for GB, 1975–90; Vice-Chm., Coleg Harlech, 1984–98; Member Council: UWIST, 1987–88; Univ. of Wales, Cardiff (formerly Univ. of Wales Coll. of Cardiff), 1988–2000; Univ. of Wales, Aberystwyth (formerly UCW, Aberystwyth), 1991–2000; Univ. of Wales Coll. of Medicine, 1996–; Nat. Library of Wales, 1987– (Vice-Pres., 1992–). Vice-Pres., Llangollen Internat. Eisteddfod, 1984–93; Mem., Gorsedd of Bards, Royal National Eisteddfod, 1984–. Master, Welsh Livery Guild, 1997–98. FRSA 1991. High Sheriff, Dyfed, 1976–77. *Publications:* articles in educnl jls. *Recreations:* the arts, crossword puzzles. *Address:* Argoed, Clôs Glan yr Afon, Sketty, Swansea SA2 9GP. *T:* and *Fax:* (01792) 203049. *Club:* Cardiff and County (Cardiff).   *Died 2 Aug. 2000.*

OWEN-JONES, (John) Eryl, CBE 1969; JP; DL; Clerk of Caernarvonshire County Council, 1956–74, and Clerk of Lieutenancy; *b* 19 Jan. 1912; *s* of late John Owen-Jones, Hon. FTSC, Rhydwenfa, Old Colwyn; *m* 1944, Mabel Clara (decd), *d* of Grant McIlvride, Ajmer, Rajputana; one *s* one *d. Educ:* Portmadoc Grammar Sch.; University Coll. of Wales, Aberystwyth (LLB 1933); Gonville and Caius Coll., Cambridge (MA 1939). Admitted Solicitor, 1938. Served War, RAF Radar Operation Torch, N Africa, 1942; Sqdn Ldr, RAFVR, 1945; Legal Staff Officer, Judge Advocate General's Dept, Mediterranean. Asst Solicitor,

Chester Corp., 1939–41; Dep. Clerk, Caernarvonshire CC, 1946; Clerk of the Peace, Caernarvonshire, 1956–71. Formerly: Sec., N Wales Combined Probation and After-Care Cttee; Dep. Clerk, Snowdonia Jt Adv. Cttee; Clerk, Gwynedd Police Authority, 1956–67. Member: Central Council, Magistrates' Cts Cttees, 1980–82; Bd, Civic Trust for Wales, 1982–; Bd, Gwynedd Archaeological Trust Ltd, 1982–99; Chm., Caernarvon Civic Soc., 1980–89; Hon. Sec., Caernarvonshire Historical Soc.; Vice Pres., Gwynedd Magistrates' Assoc., 1992–. Mem., Gorsedd of Royal National Eisteddfod of Wales. FRSA 1987. DL Caernarvonshire, 1971; JP 1974, DL 1974, Gwynedd. *Publication:* Caernarvonshire—A Choice of Celebrities: a lecture, with pictorial mementos, 1993. *Recreations:* music, gardening, photography. *Address:* Rhiw Dafnau, Caernarfon, Gwynedd LL55 1LF. *T:* (01286) 673370. *Club:* National Liberal.

Died 2 Sept. 2000.

OWENS, Sir Robert (Arthur), KNZM 1997; CBE 1991; Founder President, Owens Group Ltd, since 1993 (Chairman, 1953–93); *b* Manchester, 26 Aug. 1921; *s* of Arthur Owens and Gertrude Annie Owens (*née* Burns); *m* 1950, Constance Joy Walker (marr. diss.); one *s* three *d*; *m* 1987, Maria Ximena Langevin. *Educ:* Manchester Grammar Sch. Served War of 1939–45, Marine Service; RN Transport Tanker, Mediterranean, 1942–44. Emigrated to NZ, 1946; started shipping and stevedoring business, Mount Maunganui & Tauranga Stevedores Ltd, 1953, which later also included numerous cos in areas of transport, containers, customs agencies, hire services, import/export, manufacturing of car components, etc. Led NZ Trade Mission to Chile, 1982. Chm., Air New Zealand, 1981–84; Director: Port of Tauranga Ltd, 1988; Compania Puerto Coronel Ltda, Chile; New Zealand Dredging and General Works Ltd. Mayor: Tauranga, 1968–77 (Mem., Tauranga CC, 1962–77); Mount Maunganui, 1971–74. Member: Gen. Stevedoring Council (Pres., 1994); Exec. Cttee, Municipal Assoc. of NZ, 1962–77; Pacific Basin Economic Council; Bay of Plenty Harbour Board, 1962–84 (Dep. Chm., 1977; Chm., 1981–84). Life Mem., Bay of Plenty Racing Club, 1988 (Pres., 1981–83; Cttee Mem., 1957–88); bred and raced trotting and galloping stock. Trustee, Owens Charitable Trust; Patron: Logistics Mgt Assoc. of NZ; Tauranga Highland Games; Turning Point Trust. Fellow, Inst. of Dirs, NZ, 1987. Univ. of Waikato Medal, 1995. Commemoration Medal (NZ), 1990; OM (Chile), 1994. *Address:* Owens Group Ltd, PO Box 1809, Auckland, New Zealand. *T:* 95251700, *Fax:* 95251689. *Clubs:* Auckland, Auckland Racing, Aviation Country (Patron) (Auckland); Tauranga (Tauranga); Prince of Wales (Santiago, Chile). *Died 5 Sept. 1999.*

OWO, The Olowo of; *see* Olagbegi II.

OXFORD, Sir Kenneth (Gordon), Kt 1988; CBE 1981; QPM 1976; DL; Chief Constable, Merseyside Police, 1976–89; Regional Director, Lloyds Bank plc, 1989–91; *b* Lambeth, 25 June 1924; *s* of late Ernest George Oxford and Gladys Violet (*née* Seaman); *m* 1954, Muriel (*née* Panton). *Educ:* Caldecot Sch., Lambeth. RAF, VR Bomber Comd, SEAC, 1942–47. Metropolitan Police, 1947–69, with final rank Det. Ch. Supt, following Intermed. Comd Course, 1966, Sen. Staff Course, 1968, The Police Coll., Bramshill; Asst Chief Constable (Crime), Northumberland Constabulary, 1969, Northumbria Police, 1974; Dep. Chief Constable, Merseyside Police, 1974–75. Member: Forensic Science Soc., 1970; Medico-Legal Soc., 1975; Chairman: Crime Cttee, Assoc. of Chief Police Officers of Eng., Wales and NI, 1977–83; Jt Standing Cttee on Police Use of Firearms, 1979–89; Anti-Terrorist Cttee, 1982–89; Rep., ICPO (Interpol), 1983–86; President: NW Police Benevolent Fund, 1978–89; Assoc. of Chief Police Officers of England, Wales and NI, 1982–83. Pres., Merseyside Br., BIM, 1983–93 (Chm., 1978–81; Vice-Chm., 1975–78); CIMgt (CBIM 1980). Merseyside County Dir, St John Ambulance Assoc., 1976–84 (County Vice Pres., 1985). Chm., Merseyside Community Trust, 1988–. Hon. Colonel: 156 (Liverpool and Greater Manchester) Transport Regt, RCT (Volunteers), 1989–93; 156 (NW) Transport Regt, RLC (V), 1993–95. Freeman, City of London, 1983. FRSA 1983. OStJ 1977. DL Merseyside, 1988. *Publications:* contrib. articles and papers to prof. papers on crime and kindred matters. *Recreations:* shooting, cricket, music, books, roses. *Address:* c/o Chief Constable's Office, PO Box 59, Liverpool L69 1JD. *Clubs:* Royal Commonwealth Society, Special Forces; Artists (Liverpool); Surrey CC, Lancashire CC, Rainford CC, Liverpool St Helens Rugby Union Football. *Died 23 Nov. 1998.*

P

PACKARD, Lt-Gen. Sir (Charles) Douglas, KBE 1957 (CBE 1945; OBE 1942); CB 1949; DSO 1943; General Officer Commanding-in-Chief Northern Ireland Command, 1958–61, retired; *b* 17 May 1903; *s* of late Capt. C. T. Packard, MC, Copdock, near Ipswich; *m* 1st, 1937, Marion Lochhead (*d* 1981); one *s* two *d*; 2nd, 1982, Mrs Patricia Miles Sharp. *Educ:* Winchester; Royal Military Academy, Woolwich. 2nd Lieut, RA, 1923; served War of 1939–45, in Middle East and Italy (despatches, OBE, DSO, CBE); Dep. Chief of Staff, 15th Army Group, 1944–45; Temp. Maj.-Gen. and Chief of Staff, Allied Commission for Austria (British Element), 1945–46; Director of Military Intelligence, WO, 1948–49; Commander British Military Mission in Greece, 1949–51; Chief of Staff, GHQ, MELF, 1951–53; Vice-Quarter-Master-General War Office, 1953–56; Military Adviser to the West African Governments, 1956–58; Lt-Gen. 1957. Col Comdt, RA, 1957–62. Officer Legion of Merit (USA). *Address:* Park Side, Lower Road, Ufford, Woodbridge, Suffolk IP13 6DL. *T:* (01394) 460418.
Died 20 Nov. 1999.

PACKARD, Vance (Oakley); author; *b* 22 May 1914, *s* of Philip and Mabel Packard; *m* 1938, Mamie Virginia Mathews; two *s* one *d*. *Educ:* Pennsylvania State Univ.; Columbia Univ. Reporter, The Boston Record, 1938; Feature Editor, The Associated Press, 1939–42; Editor and Staff writer, The American Magazine, 1942–56; Staff writer, Colliers, 1956. Distinguished Alumni Award, Pennsylvania State University, 1961; Outstanding Alumni Award, Columbia University Graduate School of Journalism, 1963. LittD Monmouth Coll., 1974. *Publications:* (books on social criticism): The Hidden Persuaders, 1957; The Status Seekers, 1959; The Waste Makers, 1960; The Pyramid Climbers, 1962; The Naked Society, 1964; The Sexual Wilderness, 1968; A Nation of Strangers, 1972; The People Shapers, 1977; Our Endangered Children, 1983; The Ultra Rich, 1989; numerous articles for The Atlantic Monthly. *Recreations:* reading, boating. *Address:* 236 RFD Chappy, Edgartown, MA, USA. *T:* (508) 6275305.
Died 12 Dec. 1996.

PADMORE, Sir Thomas, GCB 1965 (KCB 1953; CB 1947); MA; FCIT; *b* 23 April 1909; *e s* of Thomas William Padmore, Sheffield; *m* 1st, 1934, Alice (*d* 1963), *d* of Robert Alcock, Ormskirk; two *d* (one *s* decd); 2nd, 1964, Rosalind Culhane, LVO, OBE (*d* 1995). *Educ:* Central Sch., Sheffield; Queens' Coll., Cambridge (Foundation Scholar; Hon. Fellow, 1961). Secretaries' Office, Board of Inland Revenue, 1931–34; transferred to HM Treasury, 1934; Principal Private Secretary to Chancellor of Exchequer, 1943–45; Second Secretary, 1952–62; Permanent Sec., Min. of Transport, 1962–68. Dir, Laird Gp Ltd, 1970–79; Dep. Chm., Metropolitan Cammell Ltd, 1969–80. Chairman: Rehearsal Orchestra, 1961–71; Handel Opera Soc., 1963–86. Hon. Treas., Inst. of Cancer Res., 1973–81. *Address:* 39 Cholmeley Crescent, Highgate, N6 5EX. *T:* 0181–340 6587. *Club:* Reform.
Died 8 Feb. 1996.

PAFFORD, John Henry Pyle, MA, DLit (London); FSA; FLA; Goldsmiths' Librarian of the University of London, 1945–67; *b* 6 March 1900; *s* of John Pafford and Bessie (*née* Pyle); *m* 1941, Elizabeth Ford, *d* of R. Charles Ford and Margaret Harvey; one *d* (and one *d* decd). *Educ:* Trowbridge High Sch.; University Coll., London (Fellow,

1956). Library Asst, University College, London, 1923–25; Librarian, and Tutor, Selly Oak Colleges, 1925–31 (Hon. Fellow 1985); Sub-Librarian, National Central Library, 1931–45; Lecturer at University of London School of Librarianship, 1937–61. Library Adviser, Inter-Univ. Council for Higher Education Overseas, 1960–68. *Publications:* Bale's King Johan, 1931, and The Sodder'd Citizen, 1936 (Malone Society); Library Co-operation in Europe, 1935; Accounts of Parliamentary Garrisons of Great Chalfield and Malmesbury, 1645–46, 1940; Books and Army Education, 1946; W. P. Ker, A Bibliography, 1950; (ed) The Winter's Tale (Arden Shakespeare), 1963; Watts's Divine Songs for Children, 1971; L. Bryskett's Literary Works, 1972; (with E. R. Pafford) Employer and Employed, 1974; John Clavell, 1601–43: highwayman, author, lawyer, doctor, 1993. *Address:* Hillside, Allington Park, Bridport, Dorset DT6 5DD. *T:* Bridport (01308) 422829.
Died 11 March 1996.

PAIGE, Rear-Adm. Richard Collings, CB 1967; *b* 4 Oct. 1911; *s* of Herbert Collings Paige and Harriet Pering Paige; *m* 1937, Sheila Brambles Ward, *d* of late Dr Ernest Ward, Paignton; two *s*. *Educ:* Blundell's School, Tiverton; RNEC, Keyham. Joined Royal Navy, 1929; served in HMS Neptune, Curaçao, Maori, King George V, Superb, Eagle (despatches twice); Captain, 1957; Commanding Officer, RNEC, 1960–62; Commodore Supt, HM Naval Base, Singapore, 1963–65; Admiral Supt HM Dockyard, Portsmouth, 1966–68. Rear-Adm. 1965.
Died 9 Dec. 1998.

PAISLEY, Robert, OBE 1977; Life Vice-President, Liverpool Football Club, 1992 (Manager, 1974–83; Board Member, 1983–92; Team Consultant, 1985–87); *b* 23 Jan. 1919; *s* of Samuel and Emily Paisley; *m* 1946, Jessie Chandler; two *s* one *d*. *Educ:* Eppleton Sen. Mixed Sch., Tyne and Wear. Apprentice bricklayer, 1934; also Hetton Juniors Amateur FC, 1934–37; Bishop Auckland Amateur FC, 1937–39; signed as professional for Liverpool FC, 1939; Army Service, RA, 1939–46; Liverpool FC: 2nd Team Trainer, 1954–59; 1st Team Trainer, 1959–70; Asst Manager, 1970–74. Successes as manager: UEFA Cup, 1976; League Championship, 1976, 1977, 1979, 1980, 1982, 1983; European Cup, 1977, 1978, 1981; League Cup (later known as Milk Cup, then Littlewoods Cup), 1981, 1982, 1983. Manager of the Year Award, 1976, 1977, 1979, 1980, 1982, 1983; Special Merit Award, PFA Award, 1983. Hon. Fellow, Liverpool Polytechnic, 1988. Hon. MSc Liverpool, 1983. Freeman, City of Liverpool, 1983. *Publications:* Bob Paisley's Liverpool Scrap Book, 1979; Bob Paisley: an autobiography, 1983; Bob Paisley's Assessment of the 1986–1987 Liverpool Team, 1987; Fifty Golden Reds, 1990. *Recreations:* all types of sport.
Died 14 Feb. 1996.

PALMER, Gen. Sir (Charles) Patrick (Ralph), KCVO 1999; KBE 1987 (CBE 1982; OBE 1974); Constable and Governor of Windsor Castle, 1992–99; *b* 29 April 1933; *s* of late Charles Dudley Palmer and Catherine Anne (*née* Hughes-Buller); *m* 1st, 1960, Sonia Hardy Wigglesworth (*d* 1965); one *s*; 2nd, 1966, Joanna Grace Baines; two *d*. *Educ:* Marlborough Coll.; RMA Sandhurst. psc 1963. Commnd Argyll and Sutherland Highlanders, 1953; served British Guiana, Berlin, Suez Operation and Cyprus; Instructor, RMA Sandhurst, 1961–62; BM 153(H) Inf. Bde, 1964–65; 1 Argyll and Sutherland Highlanders,

Borneo, Singapore and Aden, 1965–68; MA to Dep. CDS (Intell.), MoD, 1968–70; Instructor, Staff Coll., 1970–72; reformed and commanded 1st Bn Argyll and Sutherland Highlanders, 1972–74; Chief of Staff to Comd British Forces Hong Kong, 1974–76; RCDS, 1977; Comd 7th Armoured Bde, 1977–78; Dep. Comd 1 Armoured Div., 1978–80; Comd British Mil. Adv. and Training Team, Zimbabwe, 1980–82; GOC NE Dist, 1982 and Comd 2nd Inf. Div., 1983; Comdt, Staff Coll., Camberley, 1984–86; Military Sec., 1986–89; C-in-C, AFNORTH, 1989–92. Col of the Argyll and Sutherland Highlanders, 1982–92; Captain of Tarbert Castle, 1982–92. President: Windsor Fest. Soc., 1992–; Royal Windsor Rose and Horticl Soc., 1992–. Patron: King Edward VII Hosp (Windsor) League of Friends, 1992–; E Berks Br., BLESMA, 1993–. CIMgt. *Recreations:* travel, outdoor interests. *Address:* c/o Royal Bank of Scotland, Comrie Branch, Comrie, Perthshire PH6 2DW. *Clubs:* Army and Navy; Highland Brigade (Pres., 1992–). *Died 23 Nov. 1999.*

PALMER, Charles William; Sheriff of Tayside, Central and Fife at Dunfermline, since 1992; *b* 17 Dec. 1945; *s* of Charles J. S. Palmer and Patricia Palmer; *m* 1969, Rosemary Ann Holt; one *s* two *d. Educ:* Inverness Royal Academy; Edinburgh University (LLB 1971). Prior to University, short stints in banking and Police Force; Partner, Allan McDougall & Co., SSC, 1975; temporary Sheriff, 1984; Sheriff of N Strathclyde at Dunoon and Dumbarton, 1986–92. *Recreations:* ski-ing, opera, photography, cycling, music. *Address:* East Wing, Logie House, Dunfermline KY12 8QN. *T:* (01383) 729455.
Died 29 March 2000.

PALMER, Gen. Sir Patrick; *see* Palmer, Gen. Sir C. P. R.

PANKHURST, Air Vice-Marshal Leonard Thomas, CB 1955; CBE 1944; *b* 26 Aug. 1902; *s* of late Thomas William Pankhurst, Teddington, Middlesex; *m* 1939, Ruth, *d* of late Alexander Phillips, Cromer, Norfolk; one *s* two *d. Educ:* Hampton Grammar School. Joined Royal Air Force, 1925; Group Captain, 1942; Air Commodore, 1947; Actg Air Vice-Marshal, 1954. Served War of 1939–45 (despatches, CBE): Directorate of War Organisation, Air Ministry, 1938–41; Coastal Command, 1941–42; Mediterranean Air Forces, 1942–45; Air Officer Commanding 44 Group Transport Command, 1945–46; Asst Comdt RAF Staff Coll., 1946; idc, 1947; Dir Staff Trg, Air Ministry, 1948–50; Air Officer Commanding RAF E Africa, 1950–52; Dir of Postings, Air Ministry, 1953–54; Director-General of Personnel (I), Air Ministry, 1954–57. *Address:* Earl's Eye House, 8 Sandy Lane, Chester CH3 5UL. *T:* (01244) 320993.
Died 2 Dec. 1996.

PANTER-DOWNES, Mollie Patricia, (Mrs Clare Robinson); London Correspondent, The New Yorker, 1939–87; *b* 25 Aug. 1906; *o c* of late Major Edward Panter-Downes, Royal Irish Regt, and Kathleen Cowley; *m* 1927, Clare, 3rd *s* of late Aubrey Robinson; two *d. Educ:* mostly private. Wrote novel, The Shoreless Sea, at age of 16 (published John Murray, 1924); wrote in various English and American publications. *Publications:* Letter from England, 1940; Watling Green (children's book), 1943; One Fine Day, 1947; (contrib.) The New Yorker Book of War Pieces, 1947; Ooty Preserved, 1967; At the Pines, 1971; London War Notes, 1972.
Died 22 Jan. 1997.

PANTIN, Most Rev. Anthony, CSSp; Archbishop of Port of Spain (RC), since 1968; *b* 27 Aug. 1929; *s* of Julian and Agnes Pantin, both of Trinidad. *Educ:* Sacred Heart Private Sch., Belmont Boys' Intermediate Sch., St Mary's Coll., Port of Spain; Seminary of Philosophy, Montreal; Holy Ghost Missionary Coll., Dublin. Ordained Dublin, 1955; Guadeloupe, French West Indies, 1956–59; Fatima

College, Port of Spain, 1959–64; Superior, St Mary's Coll., Port of Spain, 1965–68. Member: Vatican Secretariat for Christian Unity, 1971–83; Vatican Congregation for Evangelisation of Peoples, 1989–. Vice-Pres., Antilles Episcopal Conference, 1990–93 (Pres., 1979–84). Hon. FCP 1982. *Address:* Archbishop's House, 27 Maraval Road, Port of Spain, Trinidad. *T:* 6221103.
Died 12 March 2000.

PAPADOPOULOS, Achilles Symeon, CMG 1980; LVO 1972; MBE 1954; HM Diplomatic Service, retired; High Commissioner in the Bahamas, 1981–83; *b* 16 Aug. 1923; *s* of late Symeon and Polyxene Papadopoulos; *m* 1954, Joyce Martin (*née* Stark); one *s* two *d. Educ:* The English School, Nicosia, Cyprus. British Mil. Admin, Eritrea, 1943; HMOCS: Cyprus, 1953; Dar es Salaam, 1959; Malta, 1961; HM Diplomatic Service: Malta, 1965; Nairobi, 1965; FCO, 1968; Colombo, 1971; Washington, 1974; Havana, 1974; Ambassador to El Salvador, 1977–79, to Mozambique, 1979–80; attached UK Mission to UN, Sept.-Dec. 1980. *Recreations:* golf, bridge. *Address:* 14 Mill Close, Great Bookham, Leatherhead, Surrey KT23 3JX. *Died 29 July 1996.*

PAPANDREOU, Dr Andreas George; Prime Minister of Greece, 1981–89 and 1993–96; *b* 5 Feb. 1919; *s* of late George Papandreou and Sophia (*née* Mineiko); *m* 2nd, 1951, Margaret Chadd (marr. diss. 1989); three *s* one *d*; *m* 3rd, 1989, Mrs Dimitra Liani. *Educ:* Athens Univ. Law Sch.; Harvard, USA. Associate Professor: Univ. of Minnesota, 1947–50; Northwestern Univ., 1950–51; Professor: Univ. of Minnesota, 1951–55; Univ. of California, 1955–63; Dir, Centre of Econ. Res., Athens, 1961–64; Minister to Prime Minister, Greece, Feb.–Nov. 1964; Minister of Economic Co-ordination, 1965; Deputy for Ahaia, 1965–67; in prison, April–Dec. 1967; Founder and Chm., Pan-Hellenic Liberation Movement, 1968–74; Prof., Univ. of Stockholm, 1968–69; Prof. of Economics, York Univ., Canada, 1969–74; Founder and Pres., Panhellenic Socialist Movement, 1974–; Leader of the Opposition, 1977–81 and 1989–93; Minister of Defence, 1981–86. *Publications:* Economics as a Science, 1958; A Strategy for Greek Economic Development, 1962; Fundamentals of Model Construction in Microeconomics, 1962; The Greek Front, 1970; Man's Freedom, 1970; Democracy at Gunpoint, 1971; Paternalistic Capitalism, 1972; Project Selection for National Plans, 1974; Socialist Transformation, 1977. *Address:* c/o Office of the Prime Minister, Parliament Building, Athens, Greece.
Died 23 June 1996.

PARDOE, Dr Geoffrey Keith Charles, OBE 1988; PhD; FEng, FRAeS; FBIS; consultant, since 1993; Chairman: General Technology Systems Ltd, 1973–93 (Managing Director, 1973–88); General Technology Systems (Scandinavia) A/S, 1985–93; President: General Technology Systems SA, Belgium, since 1979; General Technology Systems Inc. (USA), since 1986; Director, International Academy of Science, since 1993; *b* 2 Nov. 1928; *s* of James Charles Pardoe and Ada Violet Pardoe; *m* 1953, Dorothy Patricia Gutteridge; one *s* one *d. Educ:* Wanstead County High Sch., London; London Univ. (BScEng Hons); Loughborough Coll. (DLC Hons Aeronautics; PhD (Astronautics) Loughborough Univ., 1984). FRAeS 1968; FEng 1988. Sen. Aerodynamicist, Armstrong Whitworth Ltd, 1949–51; Chief Aerodynamicist, Guided Weapons, De Havilland Props Ltd, 1951–56, Proj. Manager, Blue Streak, 1956–60; Hawker Siddeley Dynamics Ltd: Chief Engr, Weapons and Space Research, 1960–63; Chief Proj. Engr, Space Div., 1963–69; Sales Exec., 1969–73; Exec. Dir, British Space Develt Co. Ltd, 1960–74. Chm., Procogen Computer Systems Ltd, 1981–86; Man. Dir, 1985–87; Dep. Chm., 1987–93; Surrey Satellite Technology Ltd;

Director: Philip A. Lapp Ltd, Canada, 1973–; Gen. Technology Systems (Netherlands) BV, Den Haag, 1982–; Eurosat SA, Switzerland, 1971–83; Eurotech Develts Ltd, 1981–83; 3 DIS (Europe) Ltd, 1994–. Vice Pres., Eurospace (Paris), 1961–73; Pres., RAeS, 1984–85 (Vice-Pres., 1981–83). Dep. Chm., 1981–86, Chm., 1986–, Watt Cttee on Energy. Mem., Internat. Acad. of Astronautics, 1982. FRSA; FInstD. *Publications:* The Challenge of Space, 1964; Integration of Payload and Stages of Space Carrier Vehicles, 1964; Project Apollo: the way to the Moon, 1969, 2nd edn 1970; The Future for Space Technology, 1984; over 50 main pubns in learned society pubns and jls; about 100 articles; about 2,000 TV and radio interviews 1959–. *Recreations:* skiing, flying, badminton, photography, wind-surfing. *Address:* 23 Stewart Road, Harpenden, Herts AL5 4QE. *T:* Harpenden (01582) 460719. *Clubs:* Royal Air Force, Institute of Directors.   *Died 3 Jan. 1996.*

PARISH, Sir David Elmer W.; *see* Woodbine Parish.

PARKER, Clifford Frederick, MA, LLB Cantab; Bracton Professor of Law at the University of Exeter, 1957–85 (Deputy Vice-Chancellor, 1963–65, Public Orator, 1977–81); *b* 6 March 1920; *yr s* of late Frederick James Parker and Bertha Isabella (*née* Kemp), Cardiff; *m* 1945, Christine Alice (*née* Knowles); two *d. Educ:* Cardiff High Sch.; Gonville and Caius Coll., Cambridge. Royal Air Force, 1940–43. Solicitor of Supreme Court, 1947–94. Lecturer in Common Law, University of Birmingham, 1951–57; Senior Tutor and Asst Director of Legal Studies, Faculty of Law, University of Birmingham, 1956–57. Pres., Soc. of Public Teachers of Law, 1974–75. Chm., Exeter Area, Supplementary Benefit, later Social Security Appeal Tribunal, 1978–93. JP Devon, 1969–92. *Publications:* contrib. to legal periodicals. *Address:* Lynwood, Exton, Exeter EX3 0PR. *T:* Exeter (01392) 874051.   *Died 5 July 1996.*

PARKER, Rear-Adm. Douglas Granger, CB 1971, DSO 1945; DSC 1945; AFC 1952; Assistant Chief of Naval Staff (Operations and Air), 1969–71, retired; *b* 21 Nov. 1919; *s* of R. K. Parker; *m* 1953, Margaret Susan, *d* of late Col W. Cooper; one *s* one *d. Educ:* W Hartlepool Technical Coll. Joined Royal Navy, 1940; Command Fleet Air Arm Fighter Squadrons, 1948–51; commanded: HMS Cavendish, 1961–62; RN Air Station, Lossiemouth, 1965–67; HMS Hermes, 1967–69. Captain 1959; Rear-Adm. 1969. *Address:* High Meadow, Walhampton, Lymington, Hants. *T:* (01590) 673259. *Club:* Royal Lymington Yacht.   *Died 24 March 2000.*

PARKER, Ronald William, CBE 1959; JP; *b* 21 Aug. 1909; *s* of late Ernest Edward Parker, MBE, Accountant of Court, and Margaret Parker (*née* Henderson); *m* 1937, Phyllis Mary (*née* Sherren); two *s. Educ:* Royal High School, Edinburgh. Chartered Accountant, 1933. Secretary, later Dir, Weston Group of Companies, 1935; Asst Dir of Finance, Ministry of Fuel and Power, 1942; Partner, J. Aikman, Smith & Wells, CA, 1946; National Coal Board: Finance Dir, Scottish Division, 1947; Dep. Chm., North Western Division, 1954; Chm., Scottish Division, 1955–67; Regional Chm., Scottish Region, 1967–68; Chm., Scottish Gas Bd, 1968–72, Scottish Gas Reg., 1972–74. Chm., BEEC Tech. Assistance Mission to USA, 1950. Mem., Scottish Economic Council, 1972–73. Dir, Queensferry House Hosp., Edinburgh, 1976–94. Governor, Heriot-Watt Coll., Edinburgh, 1955–66. CIMgt (CBIM 1970). JP City and County of Edinburgh, 1972. *Recreation:* gardening. *Address:* Claremont, 3 South Lauder Road, Edinburgh EH9 2LL. *T:* (0131) 667 7666. *Club:* New (Edinburgh).   *Died 9 Oct. 1996.*

PARKINSON, Desmond John, OBE 1950; Under-Secretary, Agricultural Research Council, 1971–73; *b* 8

March 1913; *s* of late Frederick A. Parkinson, Rio de Janeiro; *m* 1st, 1940, Leonor Hughes (marr. diss. 1954); 2nd, 1955, Lorna Mary Britton (*née* Wood); no *c. Educ:* Hereford Cathedral Sch.; St John's Coll., Cambridge; Brasenose Coll., Oxford. BA Cantab 1935. Colonial Admin. Service, 1936–60 (Gold Coast, Colonial Office, British Guiana, Nigeria); UK MAFF, 1960–63; ARC, 1963–73. *Recreation:* gardening. *Address:* Glebe House, North Cadbury, Yeovil, Somerset BA22 7DW. *T:* North Cadbury (01963) 440181. *Club:* United Oxford & Cambridge University.   *Died 20 May 1996.*

PARKINSON, Thomas Harry, CBE 1972; DL; Town Clerk, 1960–72, Clerk of the Peace, 1970–72, Birmingham; *b* Bilston, 25 June 1907; *y s* of G. R. J. Parkinson; *m* 1936, Joan Catherine, *d* of C. J. Douglas-Osborn; two *s one d. Educ:* Bromsgrove; Birmingham University (LLB Hons 1929). Admitted Solicitor, 1930. RAF, 1939–45. Asst Solicitor, Birmingham Corp., 1936–49; Dep. Town Clerk, Birmingham, 1949–60. Pres., Birmingham Law Soc., 1969–70. Secretary: W Midlands Passenger Transport Authority, 1969–72; Nat. Exhibn Centre Ltd, 1972–78; Member: Water Services Staff Adv. Commn, 1973–78; W Midlands Rent Assessment Panel, 1972–78. Hon. Member: Birmingham Assoc. of Mech. Engrs; Inst. of Housing. DL Warwickshire, 1970. Hon. DSc Aston, 1972. *Recreations:* walking, sailing, gardening. *Address:* Three Springs Barn, Stanford Bishop, Bringsty, Worcester WR7 5UA. *T:* (01886) 884314.
                Died 4 June 1996.

PARRY, Robert; *b* 8 Jan. 1933; *s* of Robert and Sarah Parry (*née* Joyce); *m* 1956, Marie (*née* Hesdon) (*d* 1987). *Educ:* Bishop Goss RC School, Liverpool. Became a building trade worker. Full-time organizer for National Union of Public Employees, 1960–67; then sponsored Member, Transport and General Workers' Union. Member of Co-operative Party. Member, Liverpool City Council, 1963–74. MP (Lab): Liverpool Exchange, 1970–74; Liverpool, Scotland Exchange, 1974–83; Liverpool, Riverside, 1983–97. Chm., Merseyside Gp of Labour MPs, 1976–87. Mem., UK Delegn to Council of Europe Assembly and WEU, 1984–92. President: Assoc. for Democracy in Hong Kong, 1980; World League for Freedom and Democracy; Co-President: Internat. Cttee for Human Rights in S Korea, 1984; Internat. Cttee for Peaceful and Indep. Reunification of Korea, 1984; Founder Pres., Human Rights Internat., 1994–. Patron: UNA Hong Kong, 1977; Rotunda Boxing Club, 1975; KIND (Kids in Need and Distress); President: Liverpool and Dist Sunday Football League (largest in Europe), 1973–; Liverpool Transport Boxing and Sporting Club, 1982–. Special interests: human rights, peace and disarmament, civil liberties, foreign affairs, particularly Central and SE Asia, overseas aid and the third world.
                Died 9 March 2000.

PARSONS, Sir Anthony (Derrick), GCMG 1982 (KCMG 1975; CMG 1969); LVO 1965; MC 1945; HM Diplomatic Service, retired; Research Fellow, University of Exeter, since 1984 (Lecturer, 1984–87); *b* 9 Sept. 1922; *s* of late Col H. A. J. Parsons, MC; *m* 1948, Sheila Emily Baird; two *s two d. Educ:* King's Sch., Canterbury; Balliol Coll., Oxford (Hon. Fellow 1984). HM Forces, 1940–54; Asst Mil. Attaché, Baghdad, 1952–54; Foreign Office, 1954–55; HM Embassy: Ankara, 1955–59; Amman, 1959–60; Cairo, 1960–61; FO, 1961–64; HM Embassy, Khartoum, 1964–65; Political Agent, Bahrain, 1965–69; Counsellor, UK Mission to UN, NY, 1969–71; Under-Sec., FCO, 1971–74; Ambassador to Iran, 1974–79; FCO, 1979; UK Perm. Rep. to UN, 1979–82; Special Advr to PM on foreign affairs, 1982–83. Bd Mem., British Council, 1982–86. Order of the Two Niles (Sudan), 1965. *Publications:* The Pride and the Fall, 1984; They Say the

Lion, 1986; From Cold War to Hot Peace: UN interventions 1947–1994, 1995. *Recreations:* gardening, golf, tennis. *Address:* Highgrove, Ashburton, South Devon TQ13 7HD. *Club:* Royal Over-Seas League.

Died 12 Aug. 1996.

PARSONS, Kenneth Charles, CMG 1970; OBE 1962; HM Diplomatic Service, retired; Counsellor, Foreign and Commonwealth Office, 1972–80; *b* 9 Jan. 1921; *s* of William Stanley Parsons; *m* 1st, 1949, Monica (*née* Howell) (decd); two *d*; 2nd, 1977, Mary Woolhouse. *Educ:* Haverfordwest Grammar Sch.; Exeter Coll., Oxford (1st Class Hons Mod. Langs 1948). Served War of 1939–45: with Oxfordshire and Buckinghamshire LI, 1941–46. Joined Diplomatic Service, 1949; served FO, Moscow, Tokyo, Rangoon and Athens, 1951–72; FCO, 1972–77; Counsellor, with British Forces, Hong Kong, 1977–79. *Recreations:* rowing, swimming, walking. *Address:* 46 Lackford Road, Chipstead, Surrey CR5 3TA. *T:* (01737) 555051. *Club:* Carlton.

Died 2 April 1999.

PARSONS, Patricia, (Mrs J. D. Parsons); *see* Beer, P.

PASMORE, (Edwin John) Victor, CH 1981; CBE 1959; RA 1984; artist; *b* Chelsham, Surrey, 3 Dec. 1908; *s* of late E. S. Pasmore, MD; *m* 1940, Wendy Blood; one *s* one *d*. *Educ:* Harrow; attended evening classes, LCC Central School of Arts and Crafts. Local government service, LCC County Hall, 1927–37; joined the London Artists' Assoc., 1932–34, and the London Group, 1932–52; associated with the formation of the Euston Road School, 1937–39, and the first post-war exhibitions of abstract art, 1948–53; joined the Penwith Society, St Ives, 1951–53. Visiting teacher, LCC Camberwell School of Art, 1945–49; Central School of Arts and Crafts, 1949–53; Master of Painting, Durham University, 1954–61. Consultant urban and architectural designer, South West Area, Peterlee New Town, 1955–77. Trustee, Tate Gall., 1963–66. Hon. degrees from: Newcastle-upon-Tyne, 1967; Surrey, 1969; RCA; Warwick, 1985. *Retrospective exhibitions:* Venice Biennale, 1960; Musée des Arts Décoratifs, Paris, 1961; Stedelijk Museum, Amsterdam, 1961; Palais des Beaux Arts, Brussels, 1961; Louisiana Museum, Copenhagen, 1962; Kestner-Gesellschaft, Hanover, 1962; Kunsthalle, Berne, 1963; Tate Gallery, 1965; São Paolo Biennale, 1965; Cartwright Hall, Bradford, 1980; Royal Acad., London, 1980; Musée des Beaux Arts, Calais, 1985; Yale Center for British Art, USA, 1988; Phillips Mus., Washington, 1988; Center for Internat. Contemp. Art, NY, 1990; Serpentine Gall., 1991; Marlborough Galleries, London, Rome, NY, Zurich, Toronto and Tokyo; *retrospective graphic exhibitions:* Marlborough Gallery, Tate Gallery, Galleria 2RC, Rome, Milan, Lubjlana, Messina, Oslo, Osaka. Works represented in: Tate Gallery and other public collections in Gt Britain, Canada, Australia, Holland, Italy, Austria, Switzerland, France and the USA. Stage backcloth designs for Young Apollo, Royal Ballet, Covent Gdn, 1984. Carnegie Prize for painting, Pittsburgh International, 1964. Grand Prix d'Honneur, International Graphics Biennale, Lubjlana, 1977; Charles Wollaston Award, Royal Acad., 1983. *Publication:* Monograph and Catalogue Raisonnée, Vol. I 1980, Vol. II 1992. *Address:* Dar Gamri, Gudja, Malta; 12 St Germans Place, Blackheath, SE3 0NN. *Club:* Arts.

Died 23 Jan. 1998.

PASTON BROWN, Dame Beryl, DBE 1967; *b* 7 March 1909; *d* of Charles Paston Brown and Florence May (*née* Henson). *Educ:* Streatham Hill High School; Newnham Coll., Cambridge (MA); London Day Training College. Lecturer: Portsmouth Training Coll., 1933–37; Goldsmiths' Coll., Univ. of London, 1937–44 and 1946–51; Temp. Asst Lecturer, Newnham Coll., 1944–46; Principal of City of Leicester Training Coll., 1952–61;

Principal, Homerton College, Cambridge, 1961–71. Chairman, Assoc. of Teachers in Colleges and Depts of Educn, 1965–66. *Address:* 21 Keere Street, Lewes, East Sussex BN7 1TY. *T:* (01273) 473608.

Died 25 July 1997.

PATCHETT, Terry; MP (Lab) Barnsley East, since 1983; *b* 11 July 1940; *s* of Wilfred and Kathleen Patchett; *m* 1961, Glenys Veal; one *s* two *d*. *Educ:* State schools; Sheffield University (Economics and Politics). Miner; NUM Houghton Main Branch Delegate, 1966–83; Mem., Yorkshire Miners' Exec., 1976–83. Former Member: Appeals Tribunals; Community Health Council. Mem., Wombwell UDC, 1969–73. Mem., H of C Expenditure Cttee (Social Services Sub-Cttee), 1985–87. *Recreations:* walking, gardening, golf. *Address:* 71 Upperwood Road, Darfield, near Barnsley, S Yorks S73 9RQ. *T:* (01226) 757684. *Clubs:* Darfield Working Men's; Darfield Cricket.

Died 11 Oct. 1996.

PATERSON, Sir George (Mutlow), Kt 1959; OBE 1946; QC (Sierra Leone) 1950; Chairman, Industrial Tribunals, 1965–79; *b* 3 Dec. 1906; *s* of late Dr G. W. Paterson; *m* 1935, Audrey Anita, *d* of late Major C. C. B. Morris, CBE, MC; one *s* two *d*. *Educ:* Grenada Boys' School; St John's College, Cambridge. Called to the Bar, Inner Temple, 1933. Appointed to Nigerian Administrative Service, 1929; Magistrate, Nigeria, 1936; Crown Counsel, Tanganyika, 1938; War of 1939–45: served with the King's African Rifles, 1939 (wounded 1940); Occupied Enemy Territories Admin, 1941; Lieutenant-Colonel 1945; Solicitor-General, Tanganyika, 1946; Attorney-General, Sierra Leone, 1949, Ghana, 1954–57; Chief Justice of Northern Rhodesia, 1957–61, retired 1961; appointed to hold an inquiry into proposed amendments to the Potato Marketing Scheme, 1962; appointed Legal Chairman (part-time), Pensions Appeal Tribunals, 1962; appointed Chairman Industrial Tribunals, South Western Region, 1965. *Recreations:* shooting, gardening, genealogy. *Address:* St George's, Westbury, Sherborne, Dorset DT9 3RA. *T:* Sherborne (01935) 814003. *Club:* Bath and County (Bath). *Died 24 Jan. 1996.*

PATERSON, Jennifer Mary; television presenter, since 1996; food writer, since 1984; *b* 3 April 1928; *d* of Robert Edward Michael Paterson and Josephine Antonia Bartlett. *Educ:* Convent of the Assumption, Ramsgate. China, 1928–33. Asst Stage Manager, Windsor Repertory Theatre, 1944; Berlin, Portugal, Sicily, Benghazi, 1946–52; editor, Norman Kark Publications, 1953; sculptor's assistant, 1958; Candid Camera TV, 1960; Matron, Padworth Sch., 1964; language studies, 1966; Cook housekeeper, to Ugandan Legation, 1968, to Chm. of Spiller's, 1970; Cook, 1978, and Food Writer, 1984–, Spectator; presenter, TV Series: Two Fat Ladies, 1996; Food & Drink, 1997; Wish You Were Here, 1998. *Publications:* Feast Days, 1990; Two Fat Ladies, 1996; Jennifer's Diary (from The Oldie), 1997; Two Fat Ladies Ride Again, 1997; Jennifer Paterson's Seasonal Recipes, 1998. *Recreations:* swimming, music, reading, opera, partying, drinking, smoking. *Address:* 180A Ashley Gardens, SW1P 1PD. *T:* (020) 7828 9564.

Died 10 Aug. 1999.

PATERSON, John Mower Alexander, OBE 1985; JP; Vice Lord-Lieutenant of Buckinghamshire, 1984–97; *b* 9 Nov. 1920; *s* of Leslie Martin Paterson and Olive Harriette (*née* Mower); *m* 1st, 1944, Daisy Miriam Ballanger Marshall (*d* 1993); one *s* two *d*; 2nd, 1995, Jean Kennard (*née* Irving-Prior). *Educ:* Oundle; Queens' Coll., Cambridge (MA Hons). Served War, RE, 1941–46. Cincinnati Milling Machines, Birmingham, 1946–48; Dir, 1945–87, Chm., 1960–85, Bifurcated Engineering, later BETEC PLC, Aylesbury; Dir and Works Man., Bifurcated & Tubular Rivet Co. Ltd, Aylesbury, 1948–60; Chm.,

Rickmansworth Water Co., 1988–90 (Dir, 1984–90; Dep. Chm., 1986–88); Dir, Three Valleys Water Services plc, 1991–92. Member: Southern Regional Council, CBI, 1971–85 (Chm., 1974–76); Grand Council, CBI, 1971–84. Gen. Comr of Taxes, Aylesbury Div., 1959–95. Mem., Lloyd's, 1960–. Pres., Aylesbury Div., Cons. and Unionist Assoc., 1984–85; Chm., Bucks Council for Voluntary Youth Services, 1978–91 (Pres., 1992–); Member: Management Cttee, Waddesdon Manor (NT), 1980–; Governing Body, Aylesbury Coll. of Further Educn, 1961–88 (Chm., 1977–87); Governing Body, Aylesbury GS, 1974– (Chm., 1984–). JP 1962, High Sheriff 1978, DL 1982, Bucks. KStJ 1991 (Mem., Chapter-Gen., 1992–; Mem., 1980–, Chm., 1981–98, Council, Bucks Br.). *Recreations:* sailing, veteran cars, gardening. *Address:* Park Hill, Potter Row, Great Missenden, Bucks HP16 9LT. *T:* (01494) 862995. *Clubs:* Royal Ocean Racing; Royal Yacht Squadron (Cowes); Royal Lymington Yacht (Cdre, 1973–76); Veteran Car of Great Britain.
Died 15 Jan. 2000.

PATERSON, Sir John Valentine J.; *see* Jardine Paterson.

PATON, Sir (Thomas) Angus (Lyall), Kt 1973; CMG 1960; FRS 1969; FEng; consulting civil engineer, since 1984; *b* 10 May 1905; *s* of Thomas Lyall Paton and Janet (*née* Gibb); *m* 1932, Eleanor Joan Delmé-Murray (*d* 1964); two *s* two *d. Educ:* Cheltenham Coll.; University College, London (Fellow, 1952). Joined Sir Alexander Gibb & Partners as pupil, 1925; after experience in UK, Canada, Burma and Turkey on harbour works, hydro-electric projects and industrial development schemes, was taken into partnership, 1938; Senior Partner, 1955–77; Senior Consultant, 1977–84. Responsible for design and supervision of construction of many large industrial factories and for major hydro-electric and irrigation projects, including Owen Falls and Kariba Schemes, and for overall supervision of Indus Basin Project in W Pakistan; also for economic surveys in Middle East and Africa on behalf of Dominion and Foreign Governments. Member UK Trade Mission to: Arab States, 1953; Egypt, Sudan and Ethiopia, 1955. Mem. NERC, 1969–72. Pres. ICE, 1970–71; Chm., Council of Engineering Instns, 1973; Past Chairman Assoc. of Consulting Engineers; Past Pres., British Section, Soc. of Civil Engineers (France); a Vice-Pres., Royal Soc., 1977–78. FICE (Hon. FICE, 1975); FIStructE; Fellow Amer. Soc. of Civil Engineers; For. Associate, Nat. Acad. of Engineering, USA, 1979. Founder Fellow, Fellowship of Engineering, 1976; FRSA. Fellow, Imperial Coll., London, 1978. Hon. DSc: London, 1977; Bristol, 1981. *Publications:* Power from Water, 1960; technical articles on engineering subjects. *Address:* L'Epervier, Route Orange, St Brelade, Jersey JE3 8LW. *T:* (01534) 45619.
Died 7 April 1999.

PATRICK, (James) McIntosh, OBE 1997; ROI 1949; ARE; RSA 1957 (ARSA 1949); painter and etcher; *b* 4 Feb. 1907; *s* of Andrew G. Patrick and Helen Anderson; *m* 1933, Janet (*d* 1983), *d* of W. Arnot Watterston; one *s* one *d. Educ:* Morgan Academy, Dundee; Glasgow School of Art. Awarded Guthrie Award, RSA, 1935; painting, Winter in Angus, purchased under the terms of the Chantrey Bequest, 1935; paintings purchased for Scottish Nat. Gall. of Modern Art; Tate Gall.; National Gallery of South Africa, Cape Town; Art Gallery of South Australia; Scottish Contemp. Art Assoc.; and Municipal collections Manchester, Aberdeen, Hull, Dundee, Liverpool, Glasgow, Greenock, Perth, Southport, Newport (Mon), Arbroath, also for Lady Leverhulme Art Gallery, etc; etchings in British Museum and other print collections. 90th birthday tribute exhibns at Scottish Nat. Gall. and Dundee Art Gall., 1997. Served War of 1939–46, North Africa and Italy; Captain (General List). Fellow: Duncan of Jordanstone Coll. of Art, Dundee, 1987; Glasgow Sch.

of Art, 1994. Hon. LLD: Dundee, 1973; Abertay, 1995. *Recreations:* gardening, music. *Address:* c/o Fine Art Society, 148 New Bond Street, W1Y 0JT; 67 Magdalen Yard Road, Dundee DD2 1AL. *T:* (01382) 668561.
Died 7 April 1998.

PATRICK, John Bowman; Sheriff of North Strathclyde (formerly Renfrew and Argyll) at Greenock, 1968–83; *b* 29 Feb. 1916; *s* of late John Bowman Patrick, boot and shoe maker, Greenock, and Barbara Patrick (*née* James); *m* 1945, Sheina Struthers McCrea (*d* 1993); one *d. Educ:* Greenock Academy; Edinburgh Univ. (MA 1937); Glasgow Univ. (LLB 1946). Served War in Royal Navy, 1940–45; conscripted as Ordinary Seaman, finally Lieut RNVR. Admitted as a Solicitor in Scotland, 1947; admitted to Faculty of Advocates, 1956. Sheriff of Inverness, Moray, Nairn, Ross and Cromarty at Fort William and Portree (Skye), 1961–68. *Address:* 107 Springfield Road, Aberdeen AB15 7RT. *T:* (01224) 318979.
Died 14 Aug. 1999.

PATRICK, McIntosh; *see* Patrick, J. McI.

PATTEN, Prof. Thomas Diery, (Tom), CBE 1981; PhD; FEng 1986; FIMechE; FRSE; consultant; Chairman, Marine Technology Directorate Ltd, since 1992 (Director, since 1988); Professor and Head of Department of Mechanical Engineering, Heriot-Watt University, 1967–82, then Emeritus; *b* 1 Jan. 1926; *s* of late William Patten and Isabella (*née* Hall); *m* 1950, Jacqueline McLachlan (*née* Wright); one *s* two *d. Educ:* Leith Acad.; Edinburgh Univ. (BSc, PhD). CEng, FIMechE 1965, FRSE 1967. Captain REME, 1946–48: served Palestine and Greece. Barry Ostlere & Shepherd Ltd, Kirkcaldy, 1949; Asst Lectr, Lectr and Sen. Lectr, Dept of Engrg, Univ. of Edinburgh, 1950–67; Dir, Inst. of Offshore Engineering, Heriot-Watt Univ., 1972–79; Vice-Principal, Heriot Watt Univ., 1978–80, Acting Principal, 1980–81. Vis. Res. Fellow, McGill Univ., Canada, 1958. Researches in heat transfer, 1950–83; British and foreign patents for heat exchange and fluid separation devices. Man. Dir, Compact Heat Exchange Ltd, 1970–87; Chm., Envmt and Resource Technology Ltd, 1982–91; Director: Pict Petroleum, 1981–93; Melville Street Investments plc, 1983–95; New Darien Oil Trust plc, 1985–88; Seaboard Lloyd Ltd, 1986–87; Brown Brothers & Co. Ltd, 1986–88; Sealand Industries plc, 1987–94 (Chm., 1987–91); Benson Gp plc, 1991–96; Edinburgh Petroleum Services Ltd, 1992–. Member: Council, IMechE, 1971–73, 1975–88 and 1989–96 (Pres., 1991–92); Oil Develt Council for Scotland, 1973–78; SRC Marine Technol. Task Force, 1975–76; Design Council (Scottish Cttee), 1979–82; Offshore Technol. Bd, Dept of Energy, 1985–88; Co-ordinating Cttee on Marine Sci. and Technol., 1987–91; Supervisory Bd, NEL, 1989–91; Pres., Engrg Cttee on Oceanic Resources, 1987–90. Member Council: RSE, 1969–79 (Vice-Pres. RSE, 1976–79); Fellowship of Engrg, 1988–91; Pres., Soc. for Underwater Technol., 1985–87. Freeman, City of London, 1991, Liveryman, Engineers' Co., 1992. Hon. Fellow, Napier Univ. (formerly Poly.), 1992. Alick Buchanan-Smith Meml Award, 1997. Hon. DEng Heriot-Watt, 1987; Hon. DSc Edinburgh, 1992; Dr *hc* Univ. Politécnica de Madrid, 1993. *Publications:* technical and scientific papers in field of heat transfer in Proc. IMechE, and Internat. Heat Transfer Conf. Proc.; also papers on offshore engineering. *Recreations:* squash, music. *Address:* 67/7 Grange Loan, Edinburgh EH9 2EG. *T:* (0131) 662 1101. *Clubs:* Caledonian; New (Edinburgh).
Died 10 April 1999.

PATTERSON, Arthur, CMG 1951; Assistant Secretary, Department of Health and Social Security, 1968–71; *b* 24 June 1906; 2nd *s* of late Alexander and Margaret Patterson; *m* 1942, Hon. Mary Ann Stocks, *er d* of late J. L. Stocks and Baroness Stocks; two *s* one *d. Educ:* Methodist Coll.,

Belfast; Queen's Univ., Belfast; St John's Coll., Cambridge. Entered Ministry of Labour, 1929; Assistant Secretary, 1941; transferred to Ministry of National Insurance, 1945; lent to Cyprus, 1953; Malta, 1956; Jamaica, 1963; Kuwait, 1971. *Address:* 8 Searles Meadow, Dry Drayton, Cambs CB3 8BU. *T:* Crafts Hill (01954) 789911. *Died 7 March 1996.*

PATTERSON, Maj.-Gen. Arthur Gordon, CB 1969; DSO 1964; OBE 1961; MC 1945; Director of Army Training, 1969–72; retired; *b* 24 July 1917; *s* of late Arthur Abbey Patterson, Indian Civil Service; *m* 1949, Jean Mary Grant; two *s* one *d. Educ:* Tonbridge Sch.; RMC Sandhurst. Commnd, 1938; India and Burma, 1939–45; Staff Coll., Camberley, 1949; jssc 1955; CO 2nd 6th Queen Elizabeth's Own Gurkha Rifles, 1959–61; Comdr 99 Gurkha Inf. Brigade, 1962–64; idc 1965; GOC 17 Div. and Maj.-Gen., Bde of Gurkhas, 1965–69. Col, 6th Queen's Own Gurkha Rifles, 1969–73. *Address:* Burnt House, Benenden, Cranbrook, Kent TN17 4DT. *Club:* Naval and Military. *Died 27 May 1996.*

PATTERSON, Dr Colin, FRS 1993; FLS; Curator of Fossil Fishes, Natural History Museum (formerly British Museum (Natural History)), 1962–93, then Honorary Research Fellow, Department of Palaeontology; *b* 13 Oct. 1933; *o s* of late Maurice William Patterson and Norah Joan (*née* Elliott); *m* 1955, Rachel Caridwen, *e d* of late Ceri Richards, CBE, DLitt, FRCA and Frances Richards, ARCA; two *d. Educ:* Tonbridge Sch.; Imperial Coll. of Science and Technology (BSc 1957); University Coll. London (PhD 1961). ARCS 1957; FLS 1967. Commnd RE, 1952–54. Lectr in Biology, Guy's Hosp. Med. Sch., 1957–62. Research Associate in Ichthyology, Amer. Mus. of Natural History, NY, 1969–; Agassiz Vis. Lectr, Mus. of Comparative Zoology, Harvard Univ., 1970. Linnean Society: Zool Editor, 1978–82; Editorial Sec., 1982–85; Vice-Pres., 1981. Scientific Medal, Zool Soc. of London, 1972. *Publications:* (ed jtly) Interrelationships of Fishes, 1973; Evolution, 1978; (ed) Molecules and Morphology in Evolution, 1987; papers and monographs on living and fossil fishes, systematics, evolution, etc. *Recreations:* cinema, drink, walking. *Address:* The Natural History Museum, SW7 5BD. *T:* (0171) 938 8846; 22 Wyatt Drive, SW13 8AA. *Died 9 March 1998.*

PATTERSON, Hugh Foggan; Secretary, King's College London, 1977–83; *b* 8 Nov. 1924; *s* of late Sir John Robert Patterson, KBE, CMG, and Esther Margaret Patterson; *m* 1956, Joan Philippa Abdy Collins (*d* 1994); one *s* two *d. Educ:* Royal Grammar Sch., Newcastle upon Tyne; King's Coll., Cambridge (MA). Served War, Royal Artillery, 1943–47. HMOCS, Nigeria, 1950–61; Universities of: Birmingham, 1962–63; Warwick, 1964–69; London, 1969–83 (Clerk of the Senate, 1976–77). *Recreation:* music. *Died 21 Feb. 1999.*

PATTINSON, John Mellor, CBE 1943; *b* 21 April 1899; *s* of late J. P. Pattinson, JP, Mobberley, Cheshire; *m* 1927, Wilhelmina (*d* 1983), *d* of late W. J. Newth, Cheltenham; two *s. Educ:* Rugby Sch.; RMA; Jesus Coll., Cambridge (BA 1922; MA). RFA with BEF, 1918–19. Anglo-Iranian Oil Co., South Iran, 1922–45, General Manager, 1937–45. Director until 1969: British Petroleum Co. of Canada Ltd; Triad Oil Co. Ltd; BP Germany AG; Dep. Chm., 1960–65, and Man. Dir, 1952–65, British Petroleum Co. Ltd; Dir, Chartered Bank, 1965–73. *Died 1 Nov. 1999.*

PATTISON, Prof. Bruce; Professor of Education, University of London Institute of Education, 1948–76, then Emeritus; *b* 13 Nov. 1908; *s* of Matthew and Catherine Pattison; *m* 1937, Dorothy Graham (*d* 1979). *Educ:* Gateshead Grammar Sch.; King's Coll., Newcastle upon Tyne; Fitzwilliam House, Cambridge. Henry Mellish Sch., Nottingham, 1933–35; Hymers Coll., Hull, 1935–36;

Lecturer in English, University College, London, 1936–48 (Reader, 1948). Board of Trade, 1941–43; Ministry of Supply, 1943–45. *Publications:* Music and Poetry of the English Renaissance, 1948, 2nd edn 1970; Special Relations, 1984. *Address:* 62 The Vale, Coulsdon, Surrey CR5 2AW. *T:* (0181) 660 2991. *Clubs:* Athenæum, National Liberal. *Died 19 Nov. 1996.*

PAUL, Roderick Sayers, CBE 1997; Chief Executive, Severn Trent Water, later Severn Trent plc, 1988–95; *b* 22 April 1935; *s* of late Dr Robert Andrew Patrick Paul and Dr Margaret Louisa Paul; *m* 1965, Ann Broadway; one *s* one *d. Educ:* Wellington College; St Edmund Hall, Oxford (MA Jurisp.). FCA 1963. Glynwed plc, 1962; British Oxygen, 1969; British Oxygen, S Africa, 1977; Mitchell Cotts, 1984–88, Chief Exec., 1986–88. Director: Rugby Gp; Entrust Ltd, 1997–. Vice Chm., Water Aid. Mem., UK Round Table for Sustainable Develt. *Recreations:* model making, boating, golf. *Address:* Church Cottage, Lower Quinton, Stratford-upon-Avon CV37 8SH. *Died 19 Sept. 1998.*

PAYNTER, Air Cdre Noel Stephen, CB 1946; DL; retired; *b* 26 Dec. 1898; *s* of late Rev. Canon F. S. Paynter, sometime Rector of Springfield, Essex; *m* 1925, Barbara Grace Haagensen; one *s* one *d. Educ:* Haileybury; RMC, Sandhurst. Flying Brevet, 1917; France and Russia, 1918–19 (Order of St Anne, 3rd Class); North-West Frontier, 1919–21 and 1925–30; Malta, 1934; Directorate of Intelligence, Air Ministry, 1936–39; Chief Intelligence Officer, Middle East, 1939–42 (despatches); Chief Intelligence Officer, Bomber Command, 1942–45 (CB); Directorate of Intelligence, Air Ministry, 1946. Chm. Buckinghamshire Playing Fields Assoc., 1958–65; Chm. Bucks Army Cadet Force (TA), 1962–65. High Sheriff, Bucks, 1965; DL Buckinghamshire, 1963. *Address:* Lawn House, Edgcott, near Aylesbury, Bucks HP18 0TN. *T:* (01296) 770238. *Died 16 March 1998.*

PAZ, Octavio; Mexican author; poet; Director, Revista Vuelta; *b* Mexico City, 31 March 1914; *s* of Octavio Paz and Josefina Lozano; *m* Elena Garro (marr. diss.); *m* Marie José Tramini; one *d. Educ:* National Univ. of Mexico. Guggenheim Fellowship, USA, 1944. Founded and directed Mexican literary reviews: Barandal, 1931; Taller, 1938; El Hijo Pródigo, 1943; Editor, Plural, Mexico City, 1971–75. Sec., Mexican Embassy, Paris, 1946; New Delhi, 1952; Chargé d'Affaires *ad interim,* Japan, 1952; posted to Secretariat for External Affairs México, 1953–58; Extraordinary and Plenipotentiary Minister to Mexican Embassy, Paris, 1959–62; Ambassador to India, 1962–68; in Oct. 1968 resigned in protest at bloody students' repression in Tlatelolco. Vis. Prof. of Spanish American Lit., Univ. of Texas, Austin, and Pittsburgh Univ., 1968–70; Simon Bolivar Prof. of Latin-American Studies, Cambridge Univ., and Fellow, Churchill Coll., 1970–71; Charles Eliot Norton Prof. of Poetry, Harvard Univ., 1971–72. Prizes include: Internat. Poetry Grand Prix, 1963; Nat. Prize for Literature, Mexico, 1977; Jerusalem Prize, 1977; Critics' Prize, Spain, 1977; Golden Eagle, Nice, 1978; Ollin Yoliztli, Mexico, 1980; Cervantes, Spain, 1982; Neustadt Internat. Prize for Literature, US, 1982; T. S. Eliot Prize, Ingersoll Foundn, USA, 1987; Nobel Prize for Literature, 1990. *Publications: poetry:* Luna Silvestre, 1933; Bajo tu Clara Sombra y otras poemas sobre Espanã, 1937; Raiz del Hombre, 1937; Entre la Piedra y la Flor, 1941; A la Orilla del Mundo, 1942; Libertad bajo Palabra, 1949; Aguila o Sol?, 1951 (trans. as Eagle or Sun?, 1970); Semillas para un Himno, 1956; Piedra de Sol, 1957 (trans. as Sun Stone, 1960); La Estación Violenta, 1958; Libertad bajo Palabra (poetical works 1935–57), 1960; Salamandra (poetical works 1958–61), 1962; Viento Entero, 1965; Blanco, 1967; Discos Visuales, 1968; Ladera Este, 1969; La Centena,

1969; Topoemas, 1971; Renga, 1971; New Poetry of Mexico (anthol.), 1972; Pasado en Claro, 1975; Vuelta, 1976; Poemas 1935–1975, 1979; Arbol adentro, 1987; *in English:* Early Poems (1935–57), 1963; Configurations, 1971; A Draft of Shadows and Other Poems, 1979; Airborn/Hijos del Aire, 1981; Selected Poems, 1984; Collected Poems (1957–87), 1987; *prose:* El Laberinto de la soledad, 1950 (trans. as Labyrinth of Solitude, 1961); El Arco y la Lira, 1956 (trans. as The Bow and The Lyre, 1975); Las Peras del Olmo, 1957; Cuadrivio, 1965; Los Signos en Rotación, 1965; Piertas al campo, 1966; Corriente Alterna, 1967 (trans. as Alternating Current, 1972); Claude Lévi-Strauss o el Nuevo Festín de Esopo, 1967 (trans. as On Lévi-Strauss, 1970); Marcel Duchamp o El Castillo de la Pureza, 1968 (trans. as Marcel Duchamp or the Castle of Purity, 1970); Conjunciones y Disyunciones (essay), 1969 (trans. as Conjunctions and Disjunctions, 1974); Postdata, 1970 (trans. as The Other Mexico, 1972); El Mono Gramático, 1971 (trans. as The Monkey Grammarian, 1989); Las Cosas en su Sitio, 1971; Traducción: Literatura y Literalidad, 1971; El Signo y el Garabato, 1973; Los Hijos del Limo, 1974 (trans. as Children of the Mire, 1974); Marcel Duchamp: Apariencia Desnuda, 1978 (trans. as Marcel Duchamp: Appearance Stripped Bare, 1981); Xavier Villaurrutia en Persona y en Obra, 1978; El Ogro Filantrópico, 1979; In mediaciones, 1979; Sombras de Obra, 1983; Tiempo Nublado, 1983 (trans. as One Earth, Four or Five Worlds); Hombres en su siglo, 1984; Pasión Critica, 1985; On poets and others (essays on literature), 1986; Convergences, 1987; Sor Juana: her life and world, 1988; The Double Flame: essays on love and eroticism, 1996; In Light of India, 1997; *translation:* Versiones y Diversiones, 1974. *Address: c/o* Revista Vuelta, Presidente Canonza 210, Coyoacán, México 4000 DF, México. *Died 19 April 1998.*

PEACH, Denis Alan, CB 1985; Chief Charity Commissioner, 1982–88; *b* 10 Jan. 1928; *s* of late Richard Peach and Alice Ellen Peach; *m* 1957, Audrey Hazel Chamberlain. *Educ:* Selhurst Grammar Sch., Croydon. Home Office, 1946–82: Asst Principal, 1951; Private Sec. to Perm. Under Sec of State, 1956; Principal, 1957; Sec. to Anglo-Egyptian Resettlement Bd, 1957–58; Prison Commn, 1958–62; Asst Sec., 1967; Asst Under Sec. of State, 1974–82 (Prin. Finance Officer, 1974–80). *Recreations:* painting, gardening. *Address:* 10 Morkyns Walk, Alleyn Park, SE21 8BG. *T:* (020) 8670 5574. *Club:* Reform. *Died 8 Aug. 2000.*

PEARCE, Sir Eric (Herbert), Kt 1979; OBE 1970; Consultant to General Television Corporation, Channel Nine, Melbourne, Australia, since 1990 (Director of Community Affairs, 1979–90); *b* 5 March 1905; *s* of Herbert Clement Pearce and Louise Mary Pearce; *m* 1956, Betty Constance Ham (*d* 1987). *Educ:* Raynes Sch., Hants. Served War, FO RAAF, 1942–44. Studio Manager/Chief Announcer, Radio Stn 3DB, Melbourne, 1944–50; Gen. Man., Radio Stns 5KA-AO-RM, SA, 1950–55; Dir of Progs, major broadcasting network, Australia, 1955–56; Chief Announcer/Sen. Newsreader, General TV, Channel Nine, 1957–79. *Recreations:* walking, swimming, golf. *Address: c/o* General Television Corporation, Channel Nine, 22 Bendigo Street, Richmond, Vic 3121, Australia. *Clubs:* Athenæum, Toorak Services (Melbourne). *Died 12 April 1997.*

PEARCE, John Trevor Archdall, CMG 1964; *b* 7 May 1916; *s* of late Rev. W. T. L. A. Pearce, Seven Hills, NSW, Australia, and N. B. Pearce, Prahran, Victoria, Australia; *m* 1st, 1948, Isabel Bundey Rankine(*d* 1983), Hindmarsh Island, S Australia; no *c;* 2nd, 1984, Judith Burland Kingsley-Strack, Sydney, NSW. *Educ:* The King's Sch., Parramatta, Australia; Keble Coll., Oxford (MA). War Service: Kenya, Abyssinia, Ceylon, India,

Burma, 1940–46, Major RE. Tanganyika: District Officer, 1939; District Commissioner, 1950; Provincial Commissioner, 1959; Permanent Secretary (Admin), Office of the Vice-President, 1961; Chairman, Public Service Commn, Basutoland, 1963, Swaziland, 1965; Registrar, Papua and New Guinea Univ. of Technology, 1969–73. *Recreations:* golf, piano music, solitude, travel in remote places. *Address:* Clippings, 14 Golf Street, Buderim, Qld 4556, Australia.

Died 27 Feb. 2000.

PEARSALL, Phyllis Isobel, MBE 1986; FRGS; painter, water colourist, etcher, writer; Founder and Director, since 1936, and Chairman and Managing Director, since 1958, Geographers' A to Z Map Co. Ltd; Founder and Director, since 1966, and Chairman, since 1987, Geographers' Map Trust; *b* 25 Sept. 1906; *d* of Alexander Gross and Isobel (*née* Crowley); *m* 1926, Richard Montague Stack Pearsall (marr. diss. 1938). *Educ:* Roedean; Collège de Jeunes Filles, Fécamp; Sorbonne. One-man shows: continuously 1926–; Little Gall., Arundel, 1983– (1988 exhibn opened by Minister for the Arts); Sally Hunter Fine Art Gall., 1989, 1995; exhibn, New Ashgate Gall., Farnham, 1990. Work in V&A Mus. and Mus. of London. 50th Anniversary Exhibn of A to Z develt at RGS (opened by Speaker of the H of C), 1986. Designer of book jackets and Christmas cards. Hd of Sect., MOI, 1942–45. FRGS 1936. *Publications:* Castilian Ochre, 1934; Fleet Street, Tite Street, Queer Street, 1983; Only the Unexpected Happens, 1985; Women 1939–40, 1985; Women at War, 1990; From Bedsitter to Household Name: the personal story of A to Z Maps, 1990; An Artist's Pilgrimage in Business, 1993; short stories in Cornhill Mag, New Yorker. *Recreations:* cooking, opera, theatre. *Address:* Geographers' A to Z Map Co. Ltd, Fairfield Road, Borough Green, Sevenoaks, Kent TN15 8PP. *T:* Sevenoaks (01732) 781000. *Clubs:* Arts, University Women's. *Died 28 Aug. 1996.*

PEARSON, Brig. Alastair Stevenson, CB 1958; DSO; OBE 1953; MC; TD; farmer; Lord Lieutenant of Dunbartonshire, 1979–90; Keeper of Dumbarton Castle, since 1981; *b* 1 June 1915; *s* of Alexander Stevenson Pearson, Glasgow; *m* 1944, Mrs Joan Morgan Weld-Smith (decd); one *d,* and two step *d. Educ:* Kelvinside Acad.; Sedbergh. Co. Director, 1936–39; served War of 1939–45 (MC, DSO, and three Bars); embodied 6th Bn Highland LI, TA, 1939; transferred to Parachute Regt, 1941; Lt-Col 1942; CO 1st and 8th Para Bns, 1942–45; CO 15th (Scottish) Bn The Parachute Regt (TA), 1947–53; Dep. Comd 46 Parachute Bde (TA), 1953–59. Comd Scotland Army Cadet Force, Brigadier, 1967–81. ADC to the Queen, 1956–61. Hon. Col, 15th (Scottish) Bn The Parachute Regt (TA), 1963–77 and 1983–90. Hon. Sheriff, Dunbarton, 1991. DL Glasgow, 1951, Dunbartonshire, 1975. KStJ 1980. *Address:* Tullochan, Gartocharn, by Alexandria, Dunbartonshire G83 8ND. *T:* Gartocharn (01389) 830205. *Died 29 March 1996.*

PEARSON, Prof. James Douglas; Emeritus Professor of Bibliography, with reference to Asia and Africa, School of Oriental and African Studies, University of London (Professor, 1972–79); *b* 17 Dec. 1911; *m* 1st, Rose Betty Burden (marr. diss.); one *s;* 2nd, Hilda M. Wilkinson; three *s. Educ:* Cambridge Univ. (MA). Asst Under-librarian, Cambridge Univ. Library, 1939–50; Librarian, Sch. of Oriental and African Studies, Univ. of London, 1950–72. Hon. FLA 1976. Walford Award for services to bibliography, 1992. *Publications:* Index Islamicus, 1958–82; Oriental and Asian Bibliography, 1966; Oriental Manuscripts in Europe and North America, 1971; (ed jtly) Arab Islamic Bibliography, 1977; (ed) South Asia Bibliography, 1978; Creswell's Bibliography of the Architecture, Arts and Crafts of Islam, Supplement II,

1984; A Guide to Manuscripts and Documents in the British Isles relating to South and SE Asia, Vol. I, 1989, Vol. II, 1990; A Guide to Manuscripts and Documents in the British Isles relating to Africa, Vol. I, 1993, Vol. II, 1994. *Recreations:* natural history, travel. *Address:* 79 Highsett, Hills Road, Cambridge CB2 1NZ.

Died 1 Aug. 1997.

PEDDIE, Robert Allan; general management consultant since 1983; Chairman, Polymeters Response International Ltd, since 1992; *b* 27 Oct. 1921; *s* of Robert Allan Peddie and Elizabeth Elsie (*née* Sharp); *m* 1946, Ilene Ivy Sillcock (*d* 1990); one *d. Educ:* Nottingham Univ. (BSc Eng). Electricity Dept, Hull Corp., 1946; joined nationalised electricity supply industry, 1948, and held various appts; Supt, Bradwell Nuclear Power Stn, 1958; Asst Reg. Dir, NW Region, 1962; Dep. Reg. Dir, Mids Region, 1967; Dir-Gen., SE Region, 1970; Mem. CEGB, 1972–77; part-time Mem., UKAEA, 1972–77; Chm., S Eastern Electricity Bd, 1977–83. *Recreations:* swimming, golf, walking. *Address:* c/o PRI, Moorside Road, Winchester SO23 7RX. *T:* (01962) 840048. *Died 11 Nov. 1998.*

PEECH, Alan James; *b* 24 Aug. 1905; *s* of late Albert Orlando Peech; *m* 1948, Betty Leese; no *c. Educ:* Wellington College; Magdalen College, Oxford (BA). Former Dep. Chm., Steetley Co. Ltd, retd 1976; Pres., British Iron and Steel Fedn, Jan.-June 1967; Jt Man. Dir, United Steel Cos Ltd, 1962–67, Chm., 1962–71; a Dep. Chm., BSC, 1967–70; Man. Dir, Midland Gp BSC, 1967–70; Independent Chm., Cement Makers' Fedn, 1970–76. Governor, Wellington College, retd 1975. Hon. LLD Sheffield, 1966. *Recreations:* fishing, shooting. *Address:* High House, Blyth, Worksop, Notts S81 8HG. *T:* (01909) 591255. *Club:* MCC.

Died 11 Jan. 1997.

PEECH, Neil Malcolm; President, Steetley PLC, 1976–92 (Managing Director, 1935–68, Chairman, 1935–76); *b* 27 Jan. 1908; *s* of Albert Orlando Peech; *m* 1932, Margaret Josephine (*d* 1991), *d* of late R. C. Smallwood, CBE, Worplesdon, Surrey; one *s* one *d. Educ:* Wellington College; Magdalen College, Oxford. Developed the production of magnesia from seawater and dolomite, 1939. Underwriting Member of Lloyd's, 1950–69; Director, Sheepbridge Engineering Ltd, 1949–79, and Albright & Wilson Ltd, 1958–79. Chairman, Ministry of Power Solid Smokeless Fuel Committee, 1959. High Sheriff of Yorkshire, 1959. Consul for Sweden, 1974–76 (Vice Consul, 1949–74). Chevalier, Order of Vasa, Sweden, 1963. *Recreation:* fishing. *Address:* Park House, Firbeck, Worksop, Notts S81 8JW. *T:* (01909) 732494.

Died 10 June 1997.

PEEK, Sir Francis (Henry Grenville), 4th Bt *cr* 1874, of Rousden, Devon; *b* 16 Sept. 1915; *o s* of Sir Wilfred Peek, 3rd Bt, DSO and Edwine Warner (*d* 1959), *d* of late W. H. Thornburgh, St Louis, USA; *S* father, 1927; *m* 1st, 1942, Ann (marr. diss. 1949; she *d* 1968), *d* of late Captain Gordon Duff and *widow* of Sir Charles Mappin, 4th Bt (she *m* 1951, Sir William Rootes, later 1st Baron Rootes); 2nd, Marilyn (marr. diss. 1967; she *m* 1967, Sir Peter Quennell, CBE), *d* of Dr Norman Kerr, London and Bahamas; (one *s* decd); 3rd, Mrs Caroline Kirkwood, *d* of late Sir Robert Kirkwood, KCMG, OJ. *Educ:* Eton; Trinity College, Cambridge. ADC to Governor of Bahamas, 1938–39; served Irish Guards, 1939–46. *Heir: cousin* William Grenville Peek [*b* 15 Dec. 1919; *m* 1950, Lucy Jane, *d* of late Major Edward Dorrien-Smith, DSO; one *s* three *d*]. *Address:* Villa du Parc, 8 Avenue Jean de Noailles, Cannes 06400, France. *Club:* White's.

Died 19 June 1996.

PEELER, Joseph; Regional Director for the South-East Region, Departments of the Environment and Transport,

and Chairman of Regional Board, 1979–86, retired; *b* 22 April 1930; *s* of late Edward Francis Peeler and Marjorie Cynthia Peeler; *m* 1958, Diana Helen (*née* Wynne); three *s* one *d. Educ:* King Edward VI Grammar Sch., Stratford-on-Avon; Wimbledon Coll.; Jesus Coll., Oxford (Scholar, 1948; BA 1st Cl. Hons Modern History, 1951; MA 1955). RAF, 1951–53. Entered Civil Service (Min. of Transport and Civil Aviation), 1953; Private Sec. to Parly Sec., 1956–58; Principal, 1958; seconded to Home Office, 1964–66; Asst Sec., 1966; Under Sec., 1978. Chairman: Burford and Dist Soc., 1990–93, 1996– (Vice-Chm., 1993–96); Burford Guild of Arts, 1993–. *Recreations:* history, crosswords, bridge, walking. *Address:* Cocklands, Fulbrook, Burford, Oxon OX18 4BE. *T:* (01993) 822612.

Died 29 April 1997.

PEGLER, Alfred Ernest, OBE 1978; DL; Councillor: Crawley Borough Council, since 1956; West Sussex County Council, since 1959 (Leader, Labour Group, since 1977); *b* 18 Jan. 1924; *s* of Frank Walter James Pegler and Violet Maud Pegler; *m* 1944, E. E. McDonald; one *s* one *d. Educ:* Cork Street Sch., Peckham; Oliver Goldsmith Sch., Peckham. Engrg apprentice, 1938–42; served War, RAF Air Crew, 1942–46; toolmaker, 1946–62; Civil Service Engrg Inspector, 1963–81. Chm., Crawley Council, 1959 and 1966; Chm. Housing Cttee, 1971–77. Mem., Crawley Cttee, New Towns Commn, 1962–78 (Chm., 1974). Mayor, Crawley Borough Council, 1982–83, 1983–84. Mem., Sussex Police Authority, 1973–96. Contested (Lab): Horsham, 1959 and 1964; Gloucester, Feb. 1974. DL West Sussex, 1982. *Recreations:* gardening, politics. *Address:* 7 Priors Walk, Three Bridges, Crawley, West Sussex RH10 1NX. *T:* (01293) 827330. *Died 2 Sept. 1996.*

PELLING, Henry Mathison, FBA 1992; Fellow of St John's College, Cambridge, 1966–80 and since 1980 (*socius ejectus*); Supernumerary Fellow, Queen's College, Oxford, 1980; *b* 27 Aug. 1920; *s* of late D. L. Pelling, Prenton, Cheshire, and Mrs M. M. Pelling; unmarried. *Educ:* Birkenhead School; St John's Coll., Cambridge. Class. Tripos Part I, 1941; History Tripos Part II, 1947; MA 1945; PhD 1950; LittD 1975. Army service, 1941–45; commnd RE, 1942; served NW Europe campaign, 1944–45. Fellow, Queen's Coll., Oxford, 1949–65; Tutor, 1950–65; Dean, 1963–64; Asst Dir of Research (History), Cambridge Univ., 1966–76; Reader in Recent British History, Cambridge, 1976–80. Smith-Mundt Schol., University of Wisconsin, USA, 1953–54; Fellow, Woodrow Wilson Center, Washington, DC, 1983. Hon. DHL New Sch. for Social Res., New York, 1983. *Publications:* Origins of the Labour Party, 1954; Challenge of Socialism, 1954; America and the British Left, 1956; British Communist Party, 1958; (with Frank Bealey) Labour and Politics, 1958; American Labor, 1960; Modern Britain, 1885–1955, 1960; Short History of the Labour Party, 1961, 11th edn 1996; History of British Trade Unionism, 1963, 5th edn 1992; Social Geography of British Elections, 1967; Popular Politics and Society in Late Victorian Britain, 1968, 2nd edn 1979; Britain and the Second World War, 1970; Winston Churchill, 1974, 2nd edn 1989; The Labour Governments 1945–51, 1984; Britain and the Marshall Plan, 1988; Churchill's Peacetime Ministry, 1997; articles and reviews in learned journals. *Recreations:* theatre, films. *Address:* St John's College, Cambridge CB2 1TP. *T:* (01223) 338600. *Clubs:* National Liberal, Royal Commonwealth Society.

Died 14 Oct. 1997.

PEMBERTON, Rev. Desmond Valdo; Assistant National Superintendent, Wesleyan Church, 1990–92; a President, Churches Together in England, 1990–92; *b* 23 March 1927; *s* of Charles and Lilla Pemberton; *m* 1951, Inez Pauline Fieulleteau; six *s* four *d. Educ:* Dept of Education and Ministry, Wesleyan Church HQ, USA; Wolverhampton Univ. Clergyman, ordained 1969. Voluntary work for Church, 1958–66; Pastoral work, 1966–72; Dist Superintendent, Wesleyan Holiness Church, 1972–Aug. 1990 when Church adopted Nat. status. Distinguished Service Award, Wesleyan Church, 1983. *Publication:* contrib. Faith in The City of Birmingham, 1990. *Recreations:* walking, reading. *Address:* c/o Churches Together in England, Inter-Church House, 35–41 Lower Marsh, SE1 7RL. *T:* 0121–444 3883. *Died 10 Jan. 1996.*

PEMBERTON, John L.; *see* Leigh-Pemberton.

PENNELL, Rev. Canon (James Henry) Leslie, TD and Bar, 1949; Rector of Foxearth and Pentlow (Diocese of Chelmsford), 1965–72, and of Borley and Lyston (Diocese of Chelmsford), 1969–72; Hon. Canon, Inverness Cathedral, since 1965 (Provost, 1949–65); *b* 9 Feb. 1906; *s* of late J. H. L. Pennell and Elizabeth Esmé Gordon Steel; *m* 1939, Ursula Mary, *d* of Rev. A. E. Gledhill; twin *s* and *d*. *Educ:* Edinburgh Academy; Edinburgh University (BL); Edinburgh Theological College. Deacon 1929, priest 1930; Precentor, Inverness Cathedral, 1929–32; Rector, St Mary's, Dunblane, and Offic. Chaplain to Queen Victoria School, 1932–49; Officiating Chaplain, Cameron Barracks, 1939 64. TA, 1934; BEF, 1940; SCF, 1943; DACG, 34th Ind. Corps, 1945; SCF Corps Troops, Scottish Comd, 1946–50. *Recreations:* reading, travel. *Address:* The Croft, Hundon, Sudbury, Suffolk CO10 8EW. *T:* Hundon (01440) 786221.

Died 8 Feb. 1996.

PENNY, Joseph Noel Bailey; QC 1971; *b* 25 Dec. 1916; *s* of Joseph A. Penny, JP and Isabella Downie, JP; *m* 1st, 1947, Celia (*d* 1969), *d* of Mr and Mrs R. H. Roberts; three *s* one *d*; 2nd, 1972, Sara Margaret, *d* of Sir Arnold France, GCB; one *d*. *Educ:* Workbop College, Christ Church, Oxford (MA). Major, Royal Signals, 1939–46 (despatches). Called to the Bar, Gray's Inn, 1948. A Social Security (formerly Nat. Ins.) Comr, 1977–89. *Recreations:* wine and song, travel, amateur dramatics. *Address:* Fair Orchard, Camden Road, Lingfield, Surrey RH7 6AF. *T:* (01342) 832191. Died 28 Nov. 1998.

PENROSE, Prof. Edith Tilton; economic consultant; Professor, 1977–84, Associate Dean for Research and Development, 1982–84, Professor Emeritus, since 1984, Institut Européen d'Administration des Affaires, Fontainebleau; Professor of Economics (with reference to Asia), School of Oriental and African Studies, University of London, 1964–78, Professor Emeritus, since 1978; *b* 29 Nov. 1914; *d* of George Albert Tilton and Hazel Sparling Tilton; *m* 1st, 1934, David Burton Denhardt (*d* 1938); one *s*; 2nd, 1944, Ernest F. Penrose (*d* 1984); two *s* (and one *s* decd). *Educ:* Univ. of California, Berkeley (AB); Johns Hopkins Univ. (MA, PhD). Research Assoc., ILO, Geneva and Montreal, 1939–41; Special Asst, US Ambassador, London, 1941–46; US Delegn to UN, NY, 1946–47; research at Johns Hopkins Univ., 1948–50; Lectr and Res. Assoc., Johns Hopkins Univ., 1950–60; Vis. Fellow, Australian Nat. Univ., 1955–56; Assoc. Prof. of Econs, Univ. Baghdad, 1957–59; Reader in Econs, Univ. of London (LSE and SOAS), 1960–64; Head, Dept of Econs, SOAS, 1964–79. Associate Fellow, Oxford Centre of Management Studies, later Templeton College, Oxford, 1982–85; Visiting Professor: Univ. of Dar es Salaam, 1971–72; Univ. of Toronto, 1977; Hon. Vis. Fellow in Management Econs, Bradford Univ., 1989–95. Member: Sainsbury Cttee of Enquiry into Relationship of Pharmaceutical Industry with Nat. Health Service, 1965–67; SSRC, 1974–76 (Econ. Cttee, 1970–76, Chm., 1974–76); Medicines Commn, 1975–78; Dir, Commonwealth Develt Corp., 1975–78; Mem. Council, Royal Economic Soc., 1975–80; Governor, NIESR, 1974–.

Dr *hc:* Uppsala, 1984; Helsinki Sch. of Econs, 1991; Hon. DLitt Bradford, 1994; Hon. DPhil London Guildhall, 1996. Award: for distinguished contribs to literature of energy econs, Internat. Assoc. of Energy Economists, 1986; for outstanding contrib. to research, Acad. of Internat. Business, 1993. *Publications:* Food Control in Great Britain, 1940; Economics of the International Patent System, 1951; The Theory of the Growth of the Firm, 1959, new edn 1995; The Large International Firm in Developing Countries: the International Petroleum Industry, 1968; The Growth of Firms, Middle East Oil and Other Essays, 1971; (with E. F. Penrose) Iraq: international relations and national development, 1978; articles and contributions to books. *Recreations:* travel, theatre, gardening. *Address:* The Barn, 30A Station Road, Waterbeach, Cambridge CB5 9HT. *T:* (01223) 861618. *Club:* Commonwealth Trust. *Died 11 Oct. 1996.*

PENROSE, Maj.-Gen. (John) Hubert, OBE 1956; MC 1944; *b* 24 Oct. 1916; *e s* of late Brig. John Penrose, MC and Mrs M. C. Penrose (*née* Hendrick-Aylmer); *m* 1941, Pamela Elizabeth, *d* of late H. P. Lloyd, Neath, Glam; four *d. Educ:* Winchester Coll.; RMA Woolwich. 2nd Lieut, RA, 1936; war service in European Theatre, BEF, 1939–40, and BLA, 1944; subseq. service in India, Germany, Malaya and UK; idc 1964; Defence Adviser to British High Comr, New Delhi, 1968–71; retired 1972. *Publication:* (with Brigitte Mitchell) Letters from Bath, 1766–1767, by the Rev. John Penrose, 1983. *Address:* West Hoe House, Bishop's Waltham, Southampton SO32 1DT. *T:* (01489) 892363. *Died 30 March 2000.*

PENTECOST, David Henry; Business Excellence Assessor, British Quality Foundation, since 1996; *b* 17 March 1938; *s* of Walter Henry Pentecost and Emily Louisa Pentecost; *m* 1st, 1959, Maureen Monica Taylor (marr. diss. 1979); one *s* one *d*; 2nd, 1980, Ann Carol Ansell (*née* Hills); one *s* one *d. Educ:* Battersea Grammar Sch.; Wandsworth Sch.; King's Coll., London (LLB, AKC); BA (Hons) 1996, MA (Humanities) 1999, Open Univ. FCIPS. Called to the Bar, Gray's Inn, 1962. Post Office: Asst Principal, 1962; Asst Private Sec. to Postmaster General, 1969; Dep. Telephone Man., 1972; Dir, Major Systems Procurement, British Telecom, 1982, subseq. British Telecom Plc, 1984; Chief Procurement Officer, 1986–88, Gp Dir of Quality, 1988–90, British Telecom Plc. Exec. Dir, European Foundn for Quality Management, 1990–92; quality management consultant, 1992–96; Dir, Paragon Consulting Assocs, 1994–96. *Recreations:* walking, reading, fitness. *Address:* 47 Chilbolton Avenue, Winchester, Hants SO22 5HJ. *T:* (01962) 861329, *Fax:* (01962) 855713; *e-mail:* DavidPente@aol.com. *Died 24 Jan. 2000.*

PERCIVAL, Rt Hon. Sir (Walter) Ian, Kt 1979; PC 1983; QC 1963; *b* 11 May 1921; *s* of Eldon and Chrystine Percival; *m* 1942, Madeline Buckingham Cooke; one *s* one *d. Educ:* Latymer Upper School; St Catharine's College, Cambridge (MA). Served HM Forces, 1940–46: 2nd Bn the Buffs, N Africa and Burma; Major. Called to the Bar, Inner Temple, 1948, Bencher, 1970, Reader, 1989, Treas., 1990. Recorder of Deal, later of the Crown Court, 1971–. MP (C) Southport, 1959–87. Solicitor-General, 1979–83; Conservative Party Legal Committee: Sec., 1964–68; Vice-Chm., 1968–70; Chm., 1970–74 and 1983–87. Mem., Sidley & Austin, US and Internat. Attorneys at Law, 1984–92. Fellow, Inst. of Taxation (Chm., Parly Cttee, 1965–71); Mem., Royal Economic Soc.; FCIArb 1983. Pres., Masonic Trust for Girls and Boys, 1989–93. Sole Trustee, Bhopal Hosp. Trust, 1992–. Freeman, City of London, 1987; Master, Co. of Arbitrators, 1993–94. *Recreations:* golf, parachuting, windsurfing, tennis. *Address:* 2 Harcourt Buildings, Temple, EC4Y 9DB. *T:* (0171) 583 2939; (chambers) 5 Paper Buildings,

Temple, EC4Y 7HB. *T:* (0171) 583 9275; Oxenden, Stone-in-Oxney, near Tenterden, Kent TN30 7HD. *Clubs:* Carlton, City Livery; Rye Golf.

Died 4 April 1998.

PERDUE, Rt Rev. Richard Gordon; *b* 13 Feb. 1910; *s* of Richard Perdue; *m* 1943, Evelyn Ruth Curry, BA; two *d. Educ:* Trinity Coll., Dublin (BA 1931; MA and BD 1938). Deacon 1933, priest 1934, Dublin. Curate: of Drumcondra with N Strand, 1933–36; of Rathmines, 1936–40; Incumbent: of Castledermot with Kinneagh, 1940–43; of Roscrea, Diocese of Killaloe, 1943–54; Archdeacon of Killaloe and Kilfenora, 1951–54; Examining Chaplain to Bishop of Killaloe, 1951–54; Bishop of Killaloe, Kilfenora, Clonfert and Kilmacduagh, 1953–57; Bishop of Cork, Cloyne and Ross, 1957–78. *Address:* Hadlow RD4, Timaru, New Zealand. *Died 8 Aug. 1998.*

PEREGRINE, Gwilym Rhys; DL; Member: Independent Broadcasting Authority, 1982–89 (Chairman, Welsh Advisory Committee, 1982–89); Welsh Fourth Channel Authority, 1982–89; *b* 30 Oct. 1924; *s* of Rev. and Mrs T. J. Peregrine; *m* 1958, Gwyneth Rosemary Williams; one *s* one *d. Educ:* Caterham Sch., Surrey; Gwendraeth Valley Grammar Sch. Admitted Solicitor, 1949. Carmarthenshire County Council: Asst Solicitor, 1949–56; Dep. Clerk, 1956–72 (also Dep. Clerk of the Peace); Clerk and Chief Exec., 1972–74; Chief Exec., Dyfed CC, 1974–81. DL Dyfed, 1974. *Recreations:* golf, cricket, Rugby, music, reading. *Address:* 1 Newnham Crescent, Sketty, Swansea SA2 0RZ. *Clubs:* Fairwood Park Golf (Swansea); Glamorgan Cricket, Bronwydd Cricket.

Died 12 Nov. 1998.

PEREIRA, Arthur Leonard, FRCS; Consulting Ear, Nose and Throat Surgeon to St George's Hospital, London; *b* 10 March 1906; British; *m* 1973, Mrs Jane Wilson (*née* Lapworth). *Educ:* Merchant Taylors' School. MRCS, LRCP 1929; MB, BS London 1931; FRCS 1936. Otologist to: the Metropolitan Hospital, E8, 1941–47; St George's Hospital, 1946–71. *Died 3 Dec. 1999.*

PERKINS, Bernard James; Chairman, Harlow Development Corporation, 1972–79; *b* 25 Jan. 1928; *y s* of George and Rebecca Perkins; *m* 1956, Patricia (*née* Payne); three *d. Educ:* Strand School. Member: Lambeth Council, 1962–71 (Leader, 1968–71); Community Relations Commn, 1970–72; SE Econ. Planning Council, 1971–79; Alderman, GLC, 1971–73; Chm., GLC Housing Cttee, 1972–73. *Recreation:* social service. *Address:* 38 Cedar Close, Dulwich, SE21 8HX. *T:* 0181–761 8695.

Died 17 Sept. 1996.

PERKINS, Air Vice-Marshal Irwyn Morse, MBE 1957; Royal Air Force, retired; Medical Officer, 1981–85 and Hon. Consultant in Medical Computing, 1985–93, Royal Military College of Science; *b* 15 Dec. 1920; *s* of William Lewis Perkins and Gwenllian Perkins, Ystalyfera, Swansea; *m* 1948, Royce Villiers Thompson, *d* of William Stanley Thompson and Zöe Thompson, The Mountain, Tangier; one *s* one *d. Educ:* Pontardawe, Swansea; St Mary's Hospital, Paddington. MRCS, LRCP 1945; MFCM 1973. Commnd RAF, 1946; SMO: RAF Gibraltar, 1946–49; several flying stations in UK; DGMS Dept, MoD, 1955–57; RAF Laarbruch, Germany, 1958–61; RAF Khormaksar, Aden, 1964–66; DPMO, Bomber and Strike Commands, 1966–69; CO RAF Hospital, Ely, Cambs, 1969–72; PMO RAF Germany, 1972–75; CO Princess Mary's RAF Hospital, Halton, 1975–77; PMO, Support Comd, 1977–80. Hon. Surgeon to HM the Queen, 1975–80. *Publication:* (with Prof. R. W. Shephard) Shephard-Perkins Injury Classification, 1990. *Recreations:* study of archival medical records, woodworking, DIY. *Address:* 5 Redlands Close,

Highworth, Swindon, Wilts SN6 7SN. *T:* Swindon (01793) 765097. *Club:* Royal Air Force.

Died 14 July 1996.

PERKINS, James Alfred, PhD; Chairman and Chief Executive Officer, International Council for Educational Development, 1970–90, then Chairman Emeritus; *b* 11 Oct. 1911; *s* of H. Norman Perkins and Emily (*née* Taylor); *m* 1st, 1938, Jean Bredin (*d* 1970); two *s* three *d*; 2nd, 1971, Ruth B. Aall; one step *s* three step *d. Educ:* Swarthmore Coll., Pa (AB); Princeton Univ., NJ (MA, PhD). Instructor Polit. Sci., Princeton Univ., 1937–39; Asst Prof. and Asst Dir, Sch. of Public and Internat. Affairs, Princeton, 1939–41; Dir, Pulp and Paper Div., Office of Price Admin, 1941–43; Asst to Administrator, For. Econ. Admin, 1943–45; Vice-Pres. Swarthmore Coll., 1945–50; Exec. Associate, Carnegie Corp. of NY, 1950–51; Dep. Chm. (on leave) Res. and Develt Bd, Dept of Defense, 1951–52; Vice-Pres., Carnegie Corp. of NY, 1951–63; Pres., Cornell Univ., 1963–69. Carnegie Foundn for the Advancement of Teaching: Sec. 1954–55; Vice-Pres., 1955–63. Chm., Pres. Johnson's Gen. Adv. Cttee on Foreign Assistance Prog., 1965–68; Trustee: Rand Corp., 1961–71; United Negro Coll. Fund (Chm. of Bd), 1965–69; Educnl Testing Service, 1964–68; Dir Emeritus, Council on Foreign Relations; Mem. Gen. Adv. Cttee of US Arms Control and Disarmament Agency, 1963–66; Chm. NY Regents Adv. Cttee on Educational Leadership, 1963–67. Member: Bd of Directors, Chase Manhattan Bank, 1967–75; Stevenson Memorial Fund, 1966–69; Trustee, Aspen Inst., 1973–; Director: Overseas Develt Council, 1969–; Center for Inter-Amer. Relations, 1969–76; Inst. of Internat. Educn, 1981–87; Vice Chm., Acad. for Educnl Develt. Chm., President Carter's Commn on Foreign Language and Internat. Studies, 1978–79. Mem. Society of Friends, Swarthmore, Pa. Hon. LLD and Hon. LHD 32 colls and univs. *Publications:* The University in Transition, 1966; Higher Education: from Autonomy to Systems, 1972; The University as an Organization, 1973; contribs to Public Admin. Review, Amer. Polit. Sci. Review, Educational Record, etc. *Address:* 94 North Road, Princeton, NJ 08540, USA. *Clubs:* University (NYC); Nassau (Princeton). *Died 20 Aug. 1998.*

PERRING, Sir Ralph (Edgar), 1st Bt *cr* 1963, of Frensham Manor, Surrey; Kt 1960; Chairman, Perring Furnishings Ltd, 1948–81; *b* 23 March 1905; *yr s* of late Colonel Sir John Perring, DL, JP and Florence, *d* of Charles Higginson; *m* 1928, Ethel Mary, OStJ (*d* 1991), *o d* of late Henry T. Johnson, Putney; two *s* (and one *s* decd). *Educ:* University College Sch., London. Lieut, RA (TA), 1938–40, invalided. Member Court of Common Council (Ward of Cripplegate), 1948–51; Alderman of City of London (Langbourn Ward), 1951–75, one of HM Lieutenants of the City of London, and Sheriff, 1958–59; Lord Mayor of London, 1962–63. Chairman, Spitalfields Market Cttee, 1951–52; Member: LCC for Cities of London and Westminster, 1952–55; County of London Licensing Planning Cttee; New Guildford Cathedral Council; Consumer Advisory Council, BSI, 1955–59; Bd of Governors, ESU, 1976–81. Governor: St Bartholomew's Hospital, 1964–69; Imperial College of Science and Technology, 1964–67; Christ's Hospital; Vice-President, Royal Bridewell Hospital (King Edward's Sch., Witley, 1964–75); Trustee, Morden Coll., Blackheath, 1970–, Chm. 1979–95. Master Worshipful Co. of Tin Plate Workers, 1944–45; Master, Worshipful Co. of Painter-Stainers, 1977–78; Sen. Past Master and Founder Mem., Worshipful Co. of Furniture Makers; Mem. Court, Farmers' Co.; President Langbourn Ward Club, 1951–75. Vice-Chairman, BNEC Cttee for Exports to Canada, 1964–67, Chairman, 1968–70; Dir, Confederation Life Insurance Co. of Canada, 1969–81. FRSA 1975. JP County of London, 1943. KStJ. Grand Cross of Merit

(Republic of Germany), 1959; Order of Homayoun (Iran), 1959; Grand Officer, Order of Leopold (Belgium), 1963; Knight Commander, Royal Order of George I (Greece), 1963; Commander de la Valeur Camerounaise, 1963. *Heir: s* John Raymond Perring, TD [*b* 7 July 1931; *m* 1961, Ella Christine Pelham; two *s* two *d*]. *Address:* 15 Burghley House, Somerset Road, Wimbledon, SW19 5JB. *T:* (0181) 946 3433. *Clubs:* Royal Automobile (Senior Hundred), City Livery (President, 1951–52).
Died 28 June 1998.

PERRY, Charles Bruce; Professor of Medicine, University of Bristol, 1935–69, Emeritus since 1969; *b* 1903; *s* of Charles E. and Sarah Duthie Perry; *m* 1929, Mildred Bernice Harvey (*d* 1995); three *d*. *Educ:* Bristol Grammar Sch.; University of Bristol (MB, ChB 1926; MD 1928). FRCP 1936. Physician, Bristol Royal Hospital for Sick Children and Women, 1928; Physician, Winford Orthopædic Hospital, 1930; Asst Physician, Bristol General Hospital, 1933. Lectures: Long Fox Memorial, 1943; Bradshaw, RCP, 1944; Lumleian, RCP, 1969; Carey Coombs, Univ. of Bristol, 1969; Cyril Fernando Meml, Ceylon, 1971. Pro-Vice-Chancellor, University of Bristol, 1958–61 (Hon. Fellow, 1986). President Assoc. of Physicians of Great Britain and Ireland, 1961–62; Chairman, British Cardiac Society, 1961–62; Censor, RCP, 1962–64; Medical Mem., Pensions Appeals Tribunals, 1969–79; Trustee, Jenner Appeal, 1982–. Buckston Browne Prize, Harveian Society of London, 1929; Markham Skeritt Memorial Prize, 1931. *Publications:* Bacterial Endocarditis, 1936; The Bristol Royal Infirmary 1904–1974, 1981; The Voluntary Medical Institutions of Bristol, 1984; The Bristol Medical School, 1984; Edward Jenner, 1986, various papers in the Medical Press dealing with research in diseases of the heart. *Address:* Beechfield, 54 Grove Road, Coombe Dingle, Bristol BS9 2RR. *T:* Bristol (0117) 968 2713.
Died 12 March 1996.

PERRY, Ernest George; *b* 25 April 1908; British; *m* 1950, Edna Joyce Perks-Mankelow (*d* 1998); one *s*. *Educ:* LCC secondary school. Textiles, 1923–33; insurance, 1933–64. Member (Lab), Battersea Borough Council, 1934–65 (Mayor of Battersea, 1955–56); Alderman, London Borough of Wandsworth, 1964–72. MP (Lab) Battersea S, 1964–74, Wandsworth, Battersea S, 1974–79; Asst Govt Whip, 1968–69; Lord Commissioner, HM Treasury, 1969–70; an Opposition Whip, 1970–74; an Asst Govt Whip, 1974–75. Served with Royal Artillery, 1939–46: Indian Army and Indian Artillery (Troop Sgt); Far East, 1942–45. *Recreations:* local government, sport, reading.
Died 28 Dec. 1998.

PETERS, Kenneth Jamieson, CBE 1979; DL; FSAScot; Member, Peterhead Bay Authority Board, 1983–96 (Vice-Chairman, 1989–96); *b* 17 Jan. 1923; *s* of William Jamieson Peters and Edna Rosa Peters (*née* Hayman); *m* 1951, Arunda Merle Jane Jones. *Educ:* Aberdeen Grammar Sch.; Aberdeen Univ. Served War of 1939–45: last rank Captain/Adjutant, 2nd Bn King's Own Scottish Borderers. Editorial staff, Daily Record and Evening News Ltd, 1947–51; Assistant Editor: Evening Express, Aberdeen, 1951–52; Manchester Evening Chronicle, 1952–53; Editor: Evening Express, Aberdeen, 1953–56; The Press and Journal, Aberdeen, 1956–60; Dir, 1960–90, Man. Dir, 1960–80, Chm., 1980–81, Aberdeen Journals Ltd. Director: Highland Printers Ltd (Inverness), 1968–83; Aberdeen Assoc. of Social Service, 1973–78; Thomson Regional Newspapers, 1974–80; Thomson Scottish Petroleum Ltd, 1981–86; Thomson N Sea, 1981–88; Thomson Forestry Hldgs, 1982–88; Member: Scottish Reg. Bd, BR, 1982–92; Girobank, Scotland Bd, 1984–90. Pres., Scottish Daily Newspaper Soc., 1964–66 and 1974–76; Mem., Press Council, 1974–77; Pres., Publicity

Club of Aberdeen, 1972–81; Member: Scottish Adv. Cttee of British Council, 1967–84; Cttee, Films of Scotland, 1970–82; Chm., NE Cttee, 1982–88, Mem. Exec., 1982–88, Fellow, 1988, Scottish Council (Develt and Industry). FSAScot 1980; FIMgt (FBIM 1980); ACIT 1985; FRSA 1989. JP City of Aberdeen, 1961; DL City of Aberdeen, 1978. *Publications:* The Northern Lights, 1978; (ed) Great North Memories, vol. 1, 1978, vol. 2, 1981; Burgess of Guild, 1982. *Recreations:* cricket, Rugby football, walking. *Address:* 47 Abergeldie Road, Aberdeen AB10 6ED. *T:* (01224) 587647. *Clubs:* MCC; Royal Northern and University (Aberdeen).
Died 25 Sept. 2000.

PETIT, Sir Dinshaw Manockjee, 4th Bt *cr* 1890, of Petit Hall, Bombay; *b* 13 Aug. 1934; *s* of Sir Dinshaw Manockjee Petit, 3rd Bt and Sylla (*d* 1963), *d* of R. D. Tata; *S* father, 1983; *m* 1st, 1964, Nirmala Nanavatty (marr. diss. 1985); two *s*; 2nd, 1986, Elizabeth Maria Tinkelenberg. President: N. M. Petit Charities, 1983–; Sir D. M. Petit Charities, 1983–; F. D. Petit Sanatorium, 1983–; Persian Zoroastrian Amelioration Fund, 1983–; Petit Girls' Orphanage, 1983–; D. M. Petit Gymnasium, 1983–; J. N. Petit Institute, 1983–; Native Gen. Dispensary, 1983–; Trustee, Soc. for Prevention of Cruelty to Animals; Mem., Managing Cttee, B. D. Petit Parsi Gen. Hospital. Pres., Ripon Club, Bombay. *Heir: s* Jehangir Petit [*b* 21 Jan. 1965; *m* 1994, Laila Commissariat; one *s* one *d*]. *Address:* Petit Hall, 66 Nepean Sea Road, Bombay 400006, India.
Died 31 March 1998.

PETRIE, Joan Caroline, (Lady Bathurst); HM Diplomatic Service, retired 1972; *b* 2 Nov. 1920; *d* of late James Alexander Petrie, Barrister-at-law, and Adrienne Johanna (*née* van den Bergh); *m* 1968, Sir Maurice Edward Bathurst, CMG, CBE, QC; one step *s*. *Educ:* Wycombe Abbey Sch.; Newnham Coll., Cambridge (Mary Ewart Schol.). 1st cl. Med. and Mod. Langs Tripos, 1942, MA 1964. Entered HM Foreign Service, 1947: FO, 1947–48; 2nd Sec., The Hague, 1948–50; FO, 1950–54; 1st Sec., 1953; Bonn, 1954–58; FO (later FCO), 1958–71; Counsellor 1969; Head of European Communities Information Unit, FCO, 1969–71. Mem., UK Delegn to Colombo Plan Consultative Cttee, Jogjakarta, 1959. Adviser, British Group, Inter-Parly Union, 1962–68. Officer, Order of Leopold (Belgium), 1966. *Recreations:* music, genealogy, gardening. *Address:* Airlie, The Highlands, East Horsley, Surrey KT24 5BG. *T:* (01483) 283269. *Club:* United Oxford & Cambridge University.
Died 31 Jan. 1999.

PEYREFITTE, (Pierre-) Roger; French author; *b* 17 Aug. 1907; *o s* of Jean Peyrefitte, landowner, and Eugénie Jamme; unmarried. *Educ:* Collège St Benoit, Ardouane, Hérault (Lazarist); Collège du Caousou, Toulouse, Hte Garonne (Jesuit); Lycée de Foix, Ariège; Université de Toulouse; Ecole libre des Sciences Politiques, Paris. Bachelier de l'enseignement secondaire; Diplôme d'études supérieures de langue et de littérature française; Diplômé de l'Ecole libre des Sciences Politiques (major de la section diplomatique). Concours diplomatique, 1931; attached to Ministry of Foreign Affairs, 1931–33; Secretary, French Embassy, Athens, 1933–38; attached to Ministry of Foreign Affairs, 1938–40 and 1943–45. *Publications:* Du Vésuve à l'Etna, 1952; Chevaliers de Malte, 1957; La Coloquinte, 1971; Manouche, 1972; Un Musée de l'Amour, 1972; La Muse garçonnière (poems trans. from Greek), 1973; Catalogue de la collection de monnaies grecques et romaines de l'auteur, 1974; Tableaux de chasse, ou la vie extraordinaire de Fernand Legros, 1976; Propos secrets, 1977; La Jeunesse d'Alexandre, 1977; L'Enfant de coeur, 1978; Les Conquêtes d'Alexandre, 1980; Propos secrets 2, 1980; Alexandre le Grand, 1981; Henry de Montherlant-Roger Peyrefitte:

correspondence, 1983; Voltaire, sa Jeunesse et son Temps, 1985; L'Innominato, nouveaux propos secrets, 1989; Réflexion sur De Gaulle, 1992; Voltaire et Frédéric II, 1992; Retours en Sicile, 1996; *novels:* Les Amitiés particulières, 1944 (Prix Théophraste Renaudot, 1945); Mademoiselle de Murville, 1947; L'Oracle, 1948; Les Amours singulières, 1949; La Mort d'une mère, 1950; Les Ambassades, 1951; La Fin des Ambassades, 1953; Les Clés de Saint Pierre, 1955; Jeunes proies, 1956; L'Exilé de Capri, 1959; Les Fils de la lumière, 1962; La Nature du prince, 1963; Les juifs, 1965; Notre Amour, 1967; Les Américains, 1968; Des Français, 1970; Roy, 1979; L'Illustre écrivain, 1982; La Soutane rouge, 1983; *plays:* Le Prince des neiges, 1947; Le Spectateur nocturne, 1960; Les Ambassades (adaptation of A. P. Antoine), 1961. *Recreations:* travel, walks, collecting antiques. *Address:* 9 Avenue du Maréchal Maunoury, 75016 Paris, France.

Died 5 Nov. 2000.

PFLIMLIN, Pierre Eugène Jean; *b* 5 Feb. 1907; *s* of Jules Pflimlin and Léonie (*née* Schwartz); *m* 1939, Marie-Odile Heinrich (decd); one *s* two *d. Educ:* Mulhouse; University of Strasbourg. DenD 1932. Mem. for Bas-Rhin Dept, French Parliament (Nat. Assembly), 1945–67; Under Sec. of State, Ministries for Public Health and for Economics, 1946; Minister: of Agriculture, 1947–49 and 1950–51; of Trade and External Economic Relations, 1951–52; of State in charge of relations with Council of Europe, 1952; for Overseas Territories, 1952–53; of Finance and Economics, 1955–56 and 1957–58; Prime Minister, May-June 1958; Minister of State in de Gaulle Govt, 1958–59; Minister of State for Co-operation with Overseas Countries, 1962. Mem., Consultative Assembly of Council of Europe (President, 1963–66) and of European Parliament, 1959–67; European Parliament: Mem., 1979–89; Vice-Pres., 1979–84; Pres., 1984–87. Mayor, City of Strasbourg, 1959–83. *Publications:* Industry in Mulhouse, 1932; The Economic Structure of the Third Reich, 1938; Alsace: destiny and will, 1963; The Europe of the Communities, 1966; Mémoires d'un Européen de la IVe à la Ve République, 1991. *Address:* 24 avenue de la Paix, 67000 Strasbourg, France. *T:* 88373235.

Died 27 June 2000.

PHELPS, Charles Frederick, DPhil, DSc; educational consultant; Consultant to Rector on International Affairs, Imperial College of Science, Technology and Medicine, 1990–92; *b* 18 Jan. 1934; *s* of Seth Phelps and Rigmor Kaae; *m* 1960, Joanna Lingeman; one *s* one *d. Educ:* Bromsgrove Sch.; Oxford Univ. (MA, DPhil; DSc 1990). University of Bristol: Lectr in Chemical Physiology, 1960–63; Lectr in Biochemistry, 1963–70; Reader in Biochemistry, 1970–74; Prof. of Biochemistry, Univ. of Lancaster, 1974–80; Principal, Chelsea Coll., London, 1981–84; Pro-Rector (Internat. Affairs), Imperial Coll., 1984–89. Visiting Fellow, Univ. of Rome, 1968–69. Consultant, World Bank Educational Mission to China, 1980 and to Korea, 1982. Mem. Senate, 1980–84, Mem., F and GP Cttee, 1983–88, Chm., Univ. Trng Cttee, 1984–92, London Univ. Member: Cttee, Biochemical Soc., 1980–84; Cttee, British Biophysical Soc., 1974–84 (Chm., 1983–84); Research Cttee of Arthritis and Rheumatism Council, 1974–78. Trustee, America European Community Assoc. Trust, 1986–. Mem. Governing Body, Royal Postgraduate Med. Fedn, 1986–92; Mem. Council, Queen Elizabeth Coll., 1983–85; Governor: Furzedown Sch., 1980–85; King Edward Sch., Witley, 1984–; Mill Hill Sch., 1985–; Royal Grammar Sch., Guildford, 1989–99. FKC 1985. Editorial Board: Biochim. Biophys. Acta, 1976–80, 1983–84; Internat. Research Communications Systems Jl of Med. Scis, 1980–. *Publications:* numerous papers in medical and science jls. *Recreations:* enjoying things Italian, 17th Century science, landscape gardening. *Address:*

Brockhurst, The Green, Chiddingfold, Surrey GU8 4TU. *T:* (01428) 683092. *Club:* Athenæum.

Died 21 Jan. 2000.

PHILIP, John Robert, AO 1998; DSc; FRS 1974; FAA 1967; Fellow, Commonwealth Scientific and Industrial Research Organization, Australia, 1991–92, then Emeritus; *b* 18 Jan. 1927; *e s* of late Percival Norman Philip and Ruth (*née* Osborne), formerly of Ballarat and Maldon, Vic, Australia; *m* 1949, Frances Julia, *o d* of late E. Hilton Long; two *s* one *d. Educ:* Scotch Coll., Melbourne; Univ. of Melbourne (Queen's Coll.). BCE 1946, DSc 1960. Research Asst, Melb. Univ., 1947; Engr, Qld Irrig. Commn, 1948–51; Research Staff, CSIRO, 1951–; Sen. Prin. Res. Scientist, 1961–63; Chief Res. Scientist and Asst Chief, Div. of Plant Industry, 1963–71; Chief, Div. of Envmtl Mechanics, subseq. Centre for Envmtl Mechanics, 1971–80 and 1983–91; Associate Mem., CSIRO Exec., 1978; Dir, Inst. of Physical Scis, 1980–83. Visiting Scientist, Cambridge Univ., 1954–55; Res. Fellow, Calif. Inst. Techn., 1957–58; Vis. Prof., Univ. of Illinois, 1958 and 1961; Nuffield Foundn Fellow, Cambridge Univ., 1961–62; Res. Fellow, Harvard Univ., 1966–67; Vis. Prof., Univ. of Florida, 1969; Vinton-Hayes Fellow, Harvard Univ., 1972; Vis. Res. Fellow, Cornell Univ., 1979; Vis. Fellow Commoner, Trinity Coll., Cambridge, 1994. Mem. Council, Australian Acad. of Sci., 1972–78 (Biol. Sec., 1974–78); Pres. Section 1 (Physics), 1970, Pres. Sect. 8 (Maths), 1971, ANZAAS. FRMetS; Fellow: Amer. Geophys. Union, 1981; Amer. Soil Sci. Soc., 1992; Foreign Mem., All-Union (subseq. Russian) Acad. of Agricl Scis, 1991; For. Associate, NAE, USA, 1995. Hon. DEng Melbourne, 1983; Hon. DPh Agricl Univ. of Athens, 1991; Hon. DSc Guelph, 1995. Horton Award, 1957, Horton Medal, 1982, Amer. Geophys. Union; David Rivett Medal, 1966; Thomas Ranken Lyle Medal, 1981; Eminent Researcher Award, Aust. Water Res. Adv. Council, 1990; University Medal, Agricl Univ. of Athens, 1993; Internat. Hydrology Prize, UNESCO, WMO and Internat. Assoc. Hydrological Scis, 1995; Jaeger Medal, 1998. *Publications:* papers in scientific jls on soil and porous medium physics, fluid mechanics, hydrology, micrometeorology, mathematical and physical aspects of physiology and ecology. *Recreations:* reading, writing, architecture. *Address:* CSIRO Land and Water, GPO Box 1666, Canberra, ACT 2601, Australia. *T:* (2) 62465645; 42 Vasey Crescent, Campbell, ACT 2612, Australia. *T:* (2) 62478958.

Died 26 June 1999.

PHILIPPS, Hon. (Richard) Hanning, MBE 1945; JP; Hon. Major Welsh Guards; Lord-Lieutenant of Dyfed, 1974–79 (HM Lieutenant of Pembrokeshire, 1958–74); *b* 14 Feb. 1904; 2nd *s* of 1st Baron Milford and Ethel Georgina, *d* of Rev. Benjamin Speke, Ilminster, Som; *b* of 2nd Baron Milford; *m* 1930, Lady Marion Violet Dalrymple, FRAgS (*d* 1995), *d* of 12th Earl of Stair, KT, DSO; one *s* one *d. Educ:* Eton. Contested (Nat) Brecon and Radnor, 1939. Served War of 1939–45: NW Europe, 1944–45 (MBE). Vice-Lieutenant of Pembrokeshire, 1957. Hon. Colonel Pembroke Yeomanry, 1959. Chairman: Dun & Bradstreet Ltd, 1946–69; Milford Haven Conservancy Bd, 1963–75; Northern Securities Trust Ltd, 1950–80; Hon. Pres. (former Chm.) Schweppes Ltd; Dir, Picton Land and Investment Pty Ltd, W Australia; Trustee, Picton Castle Trust, Graham and Kathleen Sutherland Foundn. Pres., Order of St John, Pembrokeshire, 1958–. CStJ. *Recreations:* painting, forestry, gardening. *Address:* Picton Castle, Haverfordwest, Pembrokeshire, Dyfed SA62 4AS. *T:* (01437) 751201. *Club:* Boodle's.

Died 29 Jan. 1998.

PHILLIPS OF ELLESMERE, Baron *cr* 1994 (Life Peer), of Ellesmere in the County of Shropshire; **David Chilton**

Phillips, KBE 1989; Kt 1979; PhD; FRS 1967; FInstP; Professor of Molecular Biophysics, University of Oxford, and Fellow of Corpus Christi College, Oxford, 1966–90, then Emeritus Professor and Hon. Fellow; *b* 7 March 1924; *o s* of late Charles Harry Phillips and Edith Harriet Phillips (*née* Finney), Ellesmere, Shropshire; *m* 1960, Diana Kathleen (*née* Hutchinson); one *d. Educ:* Ellesmere C of E Schools; Oswestry Boys' High Sch.; UC, Cardiff (BSc, PhD Wales). Radar Officer, RNVR, 1944–47. UC, Cardiff, 1942–44 and 1947–51. Post-doctoral Fellow, National Research Council of Canada, 1951–53; Research Officer, National Research Laboratories, Ottawa, 1953–55; Research Worker, Davy Faraday Research Lab., Royal Institution, London, 1955–66. Fullerian (Vis.) Prof. of Physiology, Royal Institution, 1979–85, Christmas lectures, 1980. Chm., ABRC, 1983–93 (part-time, 1983–90); Mem., MRC, 1974–78; Royal Soc. Assessor, MRC, 1978–83; Member: ACARD, 1983–87; Technology Requirements Bd, 1985–88; ACOST, 1987–93; HEFCE, 1992–93. Mem., H of L Select Cttee on Science and Technol., 1995– (Chm., 1997–). Dir, Celltech Ltd, 1982–97; Chm., Finsbury Communications Ltd, 1992–97. UK Co-ordinator, Internat. Science Hall, Brussels Exhibition, 1958. Member, European Molecular Biology Organization (EMBO), 1964, Mem. Council, 1972–78; Royal Society: Vice-Pres., 1972–73, 1976–83; Biological Sec., 1976–83; Vice Pres., Foundn for Sci. and Technology, 1995–. Trustee, Wolfson Foundn, 1988–; Gov., De Montfort Univ., 1993–98; Mem. Council, John Innes Centre, 1994–96. Founder FMedSci 1998. Foreign Hon. Member: Amer. Academy of Arts and Sciences, 1968; Royal Swedish Acad. of Scis, 1989; Hon. Mem., Amer. Society of Biological Chemists, 1969 (Lecturer, 1965); For. Associate, Amer. Nat. Acad. of Science, 1985; Mem., Academia Europaea, 1989 (Vice-Pres., 1994–97). Lectures: Almroth Wright Meml, 1966; Plenary, Internat. Biochem. Congress, Tokyo, 1967, Hamburg, 1976, Internat. Crystallography Congress, Kyoto, 1972; Hassel, Oslo, 1968; Harvey, NY, 1971; Ramsden, Manchester, 1973; Edward Clark Lee, Chicago, 1978; A. L. Patterson, Philadelphia, 1979; W. H. Stein, NY, 1983; Bragg, Leeds and London, 1985; Chancellor's, Salford, 1988; Dunham, Harvard Med. Sch., 1989; Romanes, Edinburgh, 1990; Rutherford, Royal Soc. UK–Canada, 1990; Irvine, St Andrews, 1991; Krebs Lecture and Medal, FEBS, 1971; Feldberg Prize, 1968; CIBA Medal, Biochem. Soc., 1971; Royal Medal, Royal Society, 1975; (jtly) Prix Charles Léopold Mayer, French Académie des Sciences, 1979; (jtly) Wolf Prize for Chemistry, Wolf Foundn, Israel, 1987; Gregoric Aminoff Prize, Swedish Royal Acad., 1991; Actonian Prize, Royal Instn, 1991; President's Medal, Royal Acad. of Engrg, 1994. Hon. FRSE 1991; Hon. FRCP 1991. Hon. DSc: Leicester, 1974; Univ. of Wales, 1975; Chicago, 1978; Exeter, 1982; Warwick, 1982; Birmingham, 1987; Glasgow, 1990; Glamorgan, 1994; Bath, 1994; Sheffield, 1998; Hon. PhD Weizmann Inst. of Science, 1990; DUniv: Essex, 1983; Stirling, 1995. Member, Ed. Board, Journal of Molecular Biology, 1966–76. *Publications:* papers in Acta Cryst. and other journals. *Address:* 35 Addisland Court, Holland Villas Road, W14 8DA. *T:* (0171) 602 0738. *Club:* Athenæum.
Died 23 Feb. 1999.

PHILLIPS, Edwin William, MBE 1946; Chairman: Friends Provident Life Office, 1968–88; United Kingdom Provident Institution, 1986–88; Director, Lazard Bros & Co. Ltd, 1960–83; *b* 29 Jan. 1918; *s* of C. E. Phillips, Chiswick; *m* 1951, P. M. Matusch; two *s. Educ:* Latymer Upper Sch. Army, 1939–46; Major, Sherwood Rangers Yeomanry. Joined Edward de Stein & Co., Merchant Bankers, 1934, rejoined, 1946, Partner, 1954; merged into Lazard Bros & Co. Ltd, 1960. Director: British Rail Property Bd, 1970–87; Phoenix Assurance, 1975–85;

Woolwich Equitable Building Soc., 1977 (Vice-Chm., 1984–86; Sen. Vice-Chm., 1986–88); Chm., Higgs and Hill, 1975–82. *Recreation:* cricket. *Address:* Down House, Downsway, Merrow, Surrey GU1 2YA. *T:* (01483) 301196. *Club:* MCC.
Died 20 Jan. 1997.

PHILLIPS, John Fleetwood Stewart, CMG 1965; HM Diplomatic Service, retired; *b* 16 Dec. 1917; *e s* of late Major Herbert Stewart Phillips, 27th Light Cavalry, and Violet Gordon, *d* of late Sir Alexander Pinhey, KCSI; *m* 1948, Mary Gordon Shaw, MB, BS; two *s* two *d. Educ:* Brighton; Worcester Coll., Oxford (Open Exhibition in Classics, MA). Represented Univ. and County intermittently at Rugby football, 1938–39. Served with 1st Bn, Argyll and Sutherland Highlanders in N Africa and Crete (wounded and captured, 1941). Appointed to Sudan Political Service, 1945; served in Kordofan and Blue Nile Provinces; HM Diplomatic Service, 1955, served in Foreign Office; Oriental Secretary in Libya, 1957; Consul-General at Muscat, 1960–63; Counsellor, British Embassy, Amman, 1963–66; Imperial Defence Coll., 1967; Dep. High Comr, Cyprus, 1968; Ambassador to Southern Yemen, 1969–70, to Jordan, 1970–72, to Sudan, 1973–77. *Recreations:* gardening, feuding. *Address:* Southwood, Gordon Road, Horsham, Sussex RH12 2EF. *T:* (01403) 252894.
Died 8 May 1998.

PHILLIPS, John Francis, CBE 1977 (OBE 1957); QC 1981; arbitrator; Chairman: London Court of International Arbitration, 1984–87; Private Patients Plan (formerly Provident Association for Medical Care), 1977–84, then President (Vice-Chairman, 1972–77; Director, since 1958); *b* 1911; *e s* of late F. W. Phillips and Margaret (*née* Gillan); *m* 1937, Olive M. Royer; one *s* two *d. Educ:* Cardinal Vaughan Sch.; London Univ.; Trinity Hall, Cambridge. LLB (Hons) London; LLB (1st Cl. Hons), LLM Cantab. Barrister-at-law, Gray's Inn, 1944 Civil Servant (Lord Chancellor's Dept, Royal Courts of Justice), 1933–44; Parly Sec. and Asst Gen. Sec., Nat. Farmers' Union of England and Wales, 1945–57; Deleg. to Internat. Labour Conf., 1950–56; Institute of Chartered Secretaries and Administrators: Sec. and Chief Exec., 1957–76; Mem. Council, 1976–81; Pres., 1977. Member: Council, Chartered Inst. of Arbitrators, 1969–83 (Vice-Pres., 1974–76; Pres., 1976–77); Gen. Cttee, Bar Assoc. for Commerce, Finance and Industry, 1967–88 (Vice-Chm., 1976–78 and 1980–81; Chm., 1978–80; Vice-Pres., 1982–88; Hon. Mem., 1989–); Senate of the Inns of Court and the Bar; Bar Council; Cttees of Senate and Council, 1978–83; Council for Accreditation of Correspondence Colls, 1969–80 (Hon. Treas., 1969–74; Chm., 1975–80); Vice-Chm. and Mem., Business Educn Council, 1974–80; Chairman: Jt Cttee for Awards in Business Studies and Public Admin, 1968–75 (Mem. Jt Cttee for Awards, 1960–75); Pres., Associated Examining Bd, GCSE (formerly GCE), 1992– (Mem., 1958–; Vice-Chm., 1973–76; Chm., 1976–92). Mem., British Egg Marketing Bd, 1969–71; Dep. Chm., Eggs Authy, 1971–80; Mem., Deptl Cttee of Enquiry into Fowl Pest, 1971; Chm., Houghton Poultry Res. Station, 1976–82 (Gov., 1973–82). Governor: Christ's Hospital, 1957–; Crossways Trust, 1959–71 (Financial Advisor, 1966–71); Nuffield Nursing Homes Trust, 1975–81 (Vice-Pres., 1981–84); Mem. Council and Exec. Cttee, Animal Health Trust, 1976–95 (Hon. Fellow, 1995); FCIS 1958; FCIArb (FIArb 1966); CIMgt (Council, BIM, 1969–74); FRSA 1983. Hon. Mem. CGLI, 1992. Master, Co. of Chartered Secretaries and Administrators, 1978 and 1986–87; Founder Master, Worshipful Co. of Arbitrators, 1980–82; Master, Co. of Scriveners, 1982–83. CStJ 1995. Hon. DCL City Univ., 1985. *Publications:* (ed with Hunt) Heywood and Massey's Lunacy Practice, 1939; The Agriculture Act, 1947, 1948; Arbitration: Law, Practice and Precedents, 1988; many articles on aspects of law relating to land,

agriculture and arbitration. *Recreation:* travel. *Address:* 17 Ossulton Way, Hampstead Garden Suburb, N2 0DT. *T:* (0181) 455 8460; (office) Private Patients Plan, Phillips House, Tunbridge Wells, Kent TN1 2PL; (chambers) Verulam Chambers, Peer House, Verulam Street, Gray's Inn Road, WC1X 8LZ. *Clubs:* Athenæum, United Oxford & Cambridge University, City Livery.
Died 19 Feb. 1998.

PHIPPS, Alan Thomas; Director General Commercial, Ministry of Defence, since 1995; *b* 31 Jan. 1944; *s* of Henry Thomas Phipps and Margaret Lilian May Phipps (*née* Goodwin); *m* 1973, Diana Kirke; two *d. Educ:* William Ellis Sch., London. FCIPS 1997. Contracts Div., Min. of Aviation, 1963–71; Asst Private Sec. to Chief Exec., Procurement Exec., 1971–72; seconded to Marks and Spencer, 1972–74; Ministry of Defence: Civilian Mgt Div., 1974–76; Equipment Secretariat Fighting Vehicles, 1977–79; Asst Dir of Contracts, 1980–86; Dir of Contracts, Mil. Guided Weapons, 1986–89; Dir of Contracts Policy, 1989–91; Principal Dir, Navy and Nuclear Contracts, 1991–95. *Recreations:* opera, bowls, military history, Chelsea FC. *Address:* c/o Ministry of Defence, Maple 2B, Abbey Wood # 22, Bristol BS34 8JH. *T:* (0117) 913 2600.
Died 12 Jan. 1999.

PICK, Charles Samuel; Managing Director, Heinemann Group of Publishers, 1979–85; Founder, Charles Pick Consultancy, 1985; Consultant to Wilbur Smith; *b* 22 March 1917; *s* of Samuel and Ethel Pick; *m* 1938, Hilda Beryl Hobbs (*d* 1999); one *s* one *d. Educ:* Masonic School, Bushey. Served War, 1939–46; commnd RA, AA Command; apptd Staff Captain; served ALFSEA, India, Ceylon and Singapore. Started in publishing with Victor Gollancz, 1933; founder member, Michael Joseph Ltd, 1935; Jt Man. Dir, Michael Joseph Ltd, 1959, resigned, 1962; joined William Heinemann Ltd as Man. Dir, 1962; Director: Heinemann Group of Publishers, 1962; Pan Books, 1968–85; Chairman: Secker & Warburg, 1973–80; William Heinemann, 1973–80; William Heinemann, Australia and South Africa, 1973–80; William Heinemann International, 1979–85; Heinemann Educational Books International, 1979–85; Heinemann Inc., 1980–85; Heinemann Distribution Ltd, 1980–85; Chm. and Pres., Heinemann Holdings Inc., 1980–85. Mem. Council, Publishers' Assoc., 1980–83. *Recreations:* walking, reading, theatre. *Address:* Littlecot, 28 Compton Road, Lindfield, Sussex RH16 2JZ *T:* (01444) 482218; 3 Bryanston Place, W1H 7FN. *T:* (020) 7402 8043. *Clubs:* Savile, MCC.
Died 14 Jan. 2000.

PICKETT, Thomas, CBE 1972; retired,1986; Senior Regional Chairman, North West Area, Industrial Tribunals (England and Wales), 1975–85 (Chairman for Manchester, 1972); *b* 22 Nov. 1912; *s* of John Joseph Pickett and Caroline Pickett (*née* Brunt); *m* 1940, Winifred Irene Buckley (*d* 1993), *yr d* of late Benjamin Buckley; no *c. Educ:* Glossop Grammar School; London University (LLB). Called to the Bar, Lincoln's Inn, 1948. Served in Army, 1939–50, retiring with permanent rank of Major: Dep. Asst Dir of Army Legal Services, 1948; Dist Magistrate, Gold Coast, 1950; Resident Magistrate, Northern Rhodesia, 1955, Sen. Res. Magistrate, 1956, Acting Puisne Judge, 1960; Puisne Judge, High Courts of Northern Rhodesia, 1961–64, Zambia, 1964–69; Justice of Appeal, 1969–71, Acting Chief Justice, 1970, Judge President, Court of Appeal, 1971, Zambia. Chairman: Tribunal on Detainees, 1967; Electoral Commn (Supervisory); Delimitation Commn for Zambia, 1968; Referendum Commn, 1969; Local Govt Commn, 1970. *Recreations:* walking, swimming. *Address:* Bryn Awelon, Aber Place, Craigside, Llandudno LL30 3AR. *T:* (01492) 544244. *Clubs:* Royal Over-Seas League; Victoria (Llandudno).
Died 26 April 1997.

PICTON, Jacob Glyndwr, (Glyn), CBE 1972; Senior Lecturer in Industrial Economics, University of Birmingham, 1947–79; *b* Aberdare, Glam, 28 Feb. 1912; *s* of David Picton and Ellen (*née* Evans); *m* 1939, Rhiannon Mary James, (Merch Megan), LRAM, ARCM (*d* 1978); one *s* one *d. Educ:* Aberdare Boys' County Sch.; Birmingham Univ. (MCom). Chance Bros Ltd, 1933–47, Asst Sec. 1945–47. Pres., W Midland Rent Assessment Panel, 1965–72 (Chm. Cttee, 1973–81); Governor, United Birmingham Hosps, 1953–74; Chm., Children's Hosp., 1956–66; Teaching Hosps Rep. Professional and Techn., Whitley Council, 1955–61; Mem., Birmingham Regional Hosp. Bd, 1958–74 (Vice-Chm. 1971–74); Mem., NHS Nat. Staff Cttee, 1964–73 (Vice-Chm. 1968–73); Chm., Birmingham Hosp. Region Staff Cttee, 1964–74; Vice-Chm., W Mids RHA, 1973–79 (Mem., 1979–82); Vice-Chm., NHS Nat. Staff Cttee (Admin. and Clerical), 1973–82; NHS Nat. Assessor (Admin), 1973. Chm., Birmingham Industrial Therapy Assoc. Ltd, 1965–79 and W Bromwich Industrial Therapy Assoc. Ltd, 1969–79; Indep. Mem., Estate Agents Council, 1967–69; Chm. of Wages Councils, 1953–82; Dep. Chm., Commn of Inquiry concerning Sugar Confectionery and Food Preserving Wages Council, 1961; Chm., Commn of Inquiry concerning Licensed Residential Estabts and Restaurants Wages Council, 1963–64; sole Comr of Inquiry into S Wales Coalfield Dispute, 1965 (report published, 1965, introducing concept of constructive tension into industrial relns inspired by wife's analogy with the harp which produces harmony under tension); Dep. Chm., Commn of Inquiry concerning Industrial and Staff Canteens Wages Council, 1975; Independent Arbitrator, Lock Industry, 1976–81. Donated working papers: on Picton family to Nat. Liby of Wales; on academic and public service to Univ. of Birmingham. *Publications:* various articles and official reports. *Recreations:* music, gardening, Pembrokeshire history.
Died 28 Sept. 1998.

PIERCE, Francis William; Hughes Professor of Spanish, University of Sheffield, 1953–80, then Emeritus Professor; Dean of the Faculty of Arts, 1964–67; *b* 21 Sept. 1915; *s* of late Robert Pierce, JP and Catherine Ismay Pierce; *m* 1944, Mary Charlotte Una, *o d* of late Rev. J. C. Black, Asyut, Upper Egypt; two *s* (and one *s* decd). *Educ:* Royal Belfast Academical Institution; Queen's University, Belfast (BA 1st Cl. Hons, Spanish studies, 1938; MA 1939); MA *jure officii* Dublin, 1943. Postgrad. Schol., Columbia Univ., New York, 1938–39; Asst Lectr in Spanish, Univ. of Liverpool, 1939–40; Dep. to Prof. of Spanish, TCD, 1940–45; Hughes Lectr in Spanish, Univ. of Sheffield, 1946–53. Visiting Professor: Brown Univ., Providence, RI, 1968; Case Western Reserve Univ., Cleveland, Ohio, 1968. President: Anglo-Catalan Soc., 1955–57; Assoc. of Hispanists of GB and Ireland, 1971–73. Commander, Orden de Isabel la Católica (Spain), 1986. *Publications:* The Heroic Poem of the Spanish Golden Age: Selections, chosen with Introduction and Notes, 1947; Hispanic Studies: Review and Revision, 1954; (ed) Hispanic Studies in Honour of I. González Llubera, 1959; La poesía épica del siglo de oro, 1961 (Madrid), 2nd edn 1968; The Historie of Aravcana, transcribed with introd. and notes, 1964; (ed with C. A. Jones) Actas del Primer Congreso Internacional de Hispanistas, 1964; (ed) Two Cervantes Short Novels, 1970, 2nd edn 1976; (ed) La Cristiada by Diego de Hojeda, 1971; (ed) Luís de Camõcs: Os Lusíadas, 1973, 2nd edn 1981; Amadís de Gaula, 1976; Alonso de Ercilla y Zúñiga, 1984; (ed) Repertorio de Hispanistas de Gran Bretaña e Irlanda, 1984; Asociación Internacional de Hispanistas: fundación e historia, 1986; (ed A. Bernat) Narrativa española de los siglos XVI y XVII: cuatro lecciones, 1991; articles and reviews in Hispanic Review, Mod. Language Review, Bulletin of Hispanic Studies, Bulletin Hispanique,

Ocidente, Estudis Romànics, Quaderni Ibero-Americani. *Address:* 357 Fulwood Road, Sheffield S10 3BQ. *T:* (0114) 266 4239.   *Died 19 July 1999.*

PIERCE, Hugh Humphrey; *b* 13 Oct. 1931; *s* of Dr Gwilym Pierce, Abercynon, Glam; *m* 1958, Rachel Margaret Procter; two *s. Educ:* Clifton; King's Coll., Univ. of London. LLB Hons 1954; Pres. Faculty of Laws Soc.; Pres. Union. Called to Bar, Lincoln's Inn, 1955. Diploma Personnel Management, 1962; MIPM 1963. Army Service, 2nd Lieut Intell. Corps (Cyprus), 1955–57. Kodak Ltd, legal and personnel work, 1957–63; joined BBC, 1963, personnel and industrial relations; Admin. Officer, Local Radio, 1967–68; Local Radio Develt Manager, 1968–69; General Manager, Local Radio, 1970–74; Asst Controller, Staff Admin, 1974–78; Asst Controller, Employment Policy and Appts, 1978–80. Chm., First Framework Ltd, 1988–93; Member: Indep. Cttee for Supervision of Telephone Information Standards, 1987–93; Indep. Manpower Commn, Coll. of Occupational Therapists, 1988–89; Exec. Cttee, Howard League, 1979–90; Treas., Prisoners' Advice and Law Service, 1986–89; Member: Justice (produced report on Regina *v* Iain Hay Gordon 1953, 1959); Amnesty; Trustee: Community Develt Trust; Nat. Council for the Welfare of Prisoners Abroad. *Recreations:* chamber music, narrow boats. *Address:* 13 Southwood Hall, Muswell Hill Road, N6 5UF. *T:* (0181) 444 6001; Pant y Bryn, Llanwnog, Caersws, Powys SY17 5JG. *T:* (01686) 688229.   *Died 10 Sept. 1998.*

PIERCY, Hon. Penelope Katherine, CBE 1968; Under-Secretary, Ministry of Technology, 1965–68; *b* 15 April 1916; *d* of 1st Baron Piercy, CBE and 1st wife, Mary Louisa, OBE, *d* of Hon. Thomas Henry William Pelham, CB. *Educ:* St Paul's Girls' School; Somerville College, Oxford. War of 1939–45, various appointments, Military Intelligence. Foreign Office, 1945–47; Economist, Colonial Development Corp., 1948–54; Department of Scientific and Industrial Research, 1955–65 (Sen. Prin. Scientific Officer, 1960). *Address:* Charlton Cottage, Tarrant Rushton, Blandford Forum, Dorset DT11 8SD.
                                    Died 27 Dec. 1997.

PIERS, Sir Charles Robert Fitzmaurice, 10th Bt *cr* 1661, of Tristernagh Abbey, Westmeath; Lieutenant-Commander Royal Canadian Naval Volunteer Reserve; *b* 30 Aug. 1903; *s* of Sir Charles Piers, 9th Bt, and Hester Constance, (Stella) (*d* 1936), *e d* of late S. R. Brewis, Ibstone House, Ibstone; *S* father, 1945; *m* 1936, Ann Blanche Scott (*d* 1975), *o d* of late Capt. Thomas Ferguson (The Royal Highlanders); one *s* (one *d* decd). *Educ:* RN Colleges, Osborne and Dartmouth. Served European War, 1939–45. *Heir: s* James Desmond Piers [*b* 24 July 1947; *m* 1975, Sandra Mae Dixon; one *s* one *d*].
                                    Died 1 Jan. 1996.

PIGGOTT, Maj.-Gen. Francis James Claude, CB 1963; CBE 1961; DSO 1945; *b* Tokyo, Japan, 11 Oct. 1910; *s* of late Maj.-Gen. F. S. G. Piggott, CB, DSO and Jane, *d* of W. James Smith, Gibraltar and Algeciras; *m* 1940, Muriel Joan, *d* of late Wilfred E. Cottam, Rotherham, Yorks; one *s* one *d. Educ:* Cheltenham; RMC Sandhurst. 2nd Lieut The Queen's Royal Regt, 1931; Language Officer, Japan, 1935–37; Captain, 1939; served 1939–45 in France (despatches), New Zealand, India and Burma (DSO); in Japan, UK and Egypt (OBE and Bt Lt-Col), 1946–52; attended 1st Course, Joint Services Staff Coll., 1947; Lt-Col comdg 1st Bn The Queen's Royal Regt, 1952, BAOR and Malaya; Colonel, War Office, 1954; Comd 161 Infantry Bde (TA), 1956; Dep. Director of Military Intelligence, War Office (Brigadier), 1958; Major-General, 1961; Assistant Chief of Staff (Intelligence), SHAPE, 1961–64; retired, 1964; served in Civil Service (Security), 1965–75. Col, The Queen's Royal Surrey Regt, 1964–66; Dep. Col (Surrey) The Queen's Regt, 1967–69.

Recreations: cricket, foreign travel. *Address:* Meeting House Farm, Long Lane, Wrington, Avon BS18 7SP. *Clubs:* Army and Navy, Free Foresters.
                                    Died 21 July 1996.

PIGGOTT, Prof. Stuart, CBE 1972; FBA 1953; Abercromby Professor of Prehistoric Archæology, University of Edinburgh, 1946–77; *b* 28 May 1910; *s* of G. H. O. Piggott; *m* 1936, Cecily Margaret Preston (marr. diss. 1954). *Educ:* Churchers Coll., Petersfield; St John's Coll., Oxford (Hon. Fellow, 1979). On staff of Royal Commn on Ancient Monuments (Wales), 1929–34; Asst Dir of Avebury excavations, 1934–38; from 1939 in ranks and later as Intelligence Officer in Army in charge of military air photograph interpretation, South-East Asia; conducted archæological excavations in southern England and carried out research on European prehistory up to 1942; in India, 1942–45; studied Oriental prehistory; travelled in Europe and Asia. FRSE; FSA (Gold Medal, 1983); Fellow, UCL, 1985. Mem. German Archæolog. Inst., 1953; Hon. Mem. Royal Irish Acad., 1956; Foreign Hon. Member: American Academy of Arts and Sciences, 1960; Archæolog. Inst. of America, 1990. Trustee, British Museum, 1968–74. Hon. DLittHum Columbia, 1954; Hon. DLitt Edinburgh, 1984. Grahame Clark Medal, British Acad., 1993. *Publications:* Some Ancient Cities of India, 1946; Fire Among the Ruins, 1948; British Prehistory, 1949; William Stukeley: an XVIII Century Antiquary, 1950; Prehistoric India, 1950; A Picture Book of Ancient British Art (with G. E. Daniel), 1951; Neolithic Cultures of British Isles, 1954; Scotland before History, 1958; Approach to Archæology, 1959; (ed) The Dawn of Civilization, 1961; The West Kennet Long Barrow, 1962; Ancient Europe, 1965; Prehistoric Societies (with J. G. D. Clark), 1965; The Druids, 1968; Introduction to Camden's Britannia of 1695, 1971; (ed jtly) France Before the Romans, 1974; Ruins in a Landscape, 1977; Antiquity Depicted, 1978; (ed and contrib.) Agrarian History of England and Wales Ii, 1981; The Earliest Wheeled Transport, 1983; Ancient Britons and the Antiquarian Imagination, 1989; Wagon, Chariot and Carriage, 1992; numerous technical papers in archæological jls. *Recreation:* reading. *Address:* The Cottage, West Challow, Wantage, Oxon OX12 9TN.   *Died 23 Sept. 1996.*

PIGOT, His Honour Thomas Herbert; QC 1967; a Circuit Judge, 1972–90; Common Serjeant in the City of London, 1984–90; Senior Judge (non-resident), Sovereign Base Area, Cyprus, 1984–90 (Deputy Senior Judge, 1971–84); *b* 19 May 1921; *e s* of late Thomas Pigot and of Martha Ann Pigot; *m* 1950, Zena Marguerite, *yr d* of late Tom and Dorothy Gladys Wall; three *d. Educ:* Manchester Grammar Sch. (Schol.); Brasenose Coll., Oxford (Somerset Schol.). BA (1st cl. Hons Jurisprudence) 1941; MA 1946; BCL 1947. Commissioned Welch Regt, 1942; served N Africa with Royal Lincs Regt; wounded and taken prisoner, 1943; released, 1945. Called to Bar, Inner Temple, 1947, Bencher, 1985; practised in Liverpool on Northern Circuit until 1967. Mem., Bar Council, 1970. One of HM Comrs of Lieutenancy, City of London, 1984–90. Hon. Liveryman, Cutlers' Co. *Recreation:* golf. *Clubs:* Vincent's (Oxford); Huntercombe Golf.
                                    Died 10 Sept. 1998.

PIKE, Air Cdre James Maitland Nicholson, CB 1963; DSO 1942; DFC 1941; Royal Air Force, retired; with Ministry of Defence, 1969–78; *b* 8 Feb. 1916; *s* of late Frank Pike, Glendarary, Achill Island, Co. Mayo, Eire, and Daphne (*née* Kenyon Stow), Worcester; *m* 1st, 1942, Mary Bettina Dell (marr. diss. 1952); one *d*; 2nd, 1955, Amber Pauline Bettesworth Hellard (*d* 1971); one *s*, one step *d*; 3rd, 1972, Dorothy May Dawson (*née* Holland) (*d* 1994); one step *d. Educ:* Stowe; RAF Coll., Cranwell (Sword of Honour, King's Medal). Commnd 1937; War

Service: Aden, Middle East, UK (Coastal Command), Malta and Azores; Directing Staff, RAF Staff Coll., 1945–47; Group Capt. 1955; Comd RAF Station, St Mawgan and RAF Station, Kinloss, 1955–57; SASO, RAF Malta, 1958–60; Air Cdre 1961; AOC, RAF Gibraltar, 1961–62; Imperial Defence College, 1963; Air Cdre Intelligence (B), Ministry of Defence, 1964; Dir of Security, RAF, 1965–69. *Recreations:* shooting, fishing, gundog training. *Address:* The Hyde, 31 Brookside, Watlington, Oxford OX9 5AQ.

Died 23 March 1999.

PILE, Sir William (Dennis), GCB 1978 (KCB 1971; CB 1968); MBE 1944; Chairman, Board of Inland Revenue, 1976–79; *b* 1 Dec. 1919; *s* of James Edward Pile and Jean Elizabeth Pile; *m* 1st, 1939, Brenda Skinner (marr. diss. 1947); 2nd, 1948, Joan Marguerite Crafter; one *s* two *d. Educ:* Royal Masonic School; St Catharine's College, Cambridge. Served Border Regt, 1940–45. Ministry of Education, 1947–50, 1951–66; Cabinet Office, 1950; Asst Under-Sec. of State: Dept of Education and Science, 1962; Ministry of Health, 1966; Dep. Under-Sec. of State, Home Office, 1967–70; Director-General, Prison Service, 1969–70; Permanent Under-Sec. of State, DES, 1970–76. Director: Nationwide Building Soc., 1980–88; Distillers' Co. Ltd, 1980–85. *Address:* The Manor House, Riverhead, near Sevenoaks, Kent TN13 2AS. *T:* (01732) 54498. *Clubs:* United Oxford & Cambridge University; Hawks (Cambridge). *Died 26 Jan. 1997.*

PILKINGTON, Sir Antony (Richard), Kt 1990; DL; Chairman, Pilkington plc, 1980–95; *b* 20 June 1935; *s* of Arthur Cope Pilkington and Otilia Dolores Pilkington; *m* 1960, Alice Kirsty, *er d* of Sir Thomas Dundas, 7th Bt, MBE and Lady (Isabel) Dundas; three *s* one *d. Educ:* Ampleforth Coll.; Trinity Coll., Cambridge (MA History). Coldstream Guards, 1953–55. Joined Pilkington Brothers, 1959; Dir, 1973–95; Dep. Chm., 1979–80. Director: BSN Gervais Danone (France), 1975–80 (Mem., Internat. Consultative Cttee, 1982–94); GKN, 1982–91; National Westminster Bank, 1984–94; Libbey-Owens-Ford Co. (USA), 1984–89; ICI, 1991–98; Nortel Networks (formerly Northern Telecom), 1998–. Member: European Round Table, 1984–95; CBI President's Cttee, 1992–95. Chm., Community of St Helens Trust, 1978–96. Mem. Council, Liverpool Univ., 1977–79; Gov., Liverpool John Moores Univ., 1997–. Hon. LLD Liverpool, 1987. DL Merseyside, 1988; High Sheriff, Cheshire, 1996–97. *Recreations:* interesting motor cars, shooting, sailing, P. G. Wodehouse. *Address:* Pilkington plc, Prescot Road, St Helens WA10 3TT. *T:* (01744) 28882. *Clubs:* Pratt's, Boodle's, MCC. *Died 22 Sept. 2000.*

PILKINGTON, Lawrence Herbert Austin, CBE 1964; JP; Director, Pilkington Brothers Ltd, 1943–81; *b* 13 Oct. 1911; 2nd *s* of Richard Austin Pilkington and Hon. Hope, 2nd *d* of 1st Baron Cozens-Hardy; *m* 1936, Norah Holden (*d* 1992), Whitby, Ont, Canada; two *d. Educ:* Bromsgrove School; Magdalene College, Cambridge. Volunteer with Grenfell Mission, 1933–34. Joined Pilkington Brothers Limited, 1935. Chairman: Glass Delegacy, 1949–54; Glass Industry Research Assoc., 1954–58; British Coal Utilisation Research Assoc., 1963–68; Soc. of Acoustic Technology, 1963; Member: Building Research Board, 1958–62; Wilson Cttee on Noise, 1960–63; Adv. Council on R&D for Fuel and Power, 1973–75. President, Soc. of Glass Technology, 1960–64. JP Lancs, 1942. Hon. LLD Sheffield, 1956; Hon. DSc Salford, 1970. *Publications:* mainly on glass in various technical jls. *Recreations:* sailing, climbing, amateur radio, shooting. *Address:* Coppice End, Colborne Road, St Peter Port, Guernsey GY1 1EP. *Club:* Royal Dee Yacht.

Died 11 March 2000.

PILLAR, Adm. Sir William (Thomas), GBE 1983; KCB 1980; CEng, FIMechE; FIMarE; Lieutenant-Governor and Commander-in-Chief, Jersey, 1985–90; *b* 24 Feb. 1924; *s* of William and Lily Pillar; *m* 1946, Ursula, *d* of Arthur B. Ransley, MC; three *s* one *d. Educ:* Blundells Sch., Tiverton; RNEC. FIMechE 1969, FIMarE 1972. Entered RN, 1942; HMS Howe, HMS Ajax, 1944; HMS Illustrious, 1946–48; staff RNEC, 1948–51; HMS Alert, 1951–53; HM Dockyard, Gibraltar, 1954–57; HMS Corunna, 1957–59; BEO, HMS Lochinvar, 1959–61; staff of C-in-C, SASA, Cape Town, 1961–64; HMS Tiger, 1964–65; staff of Dir of Naval Officer Appts (Eng), 1965–67; sowc 1967; Naval Ship Prodn Overseer, Scotland and NI, 1967–69; IDC 1970; Asst Dir, DG Ships, 1971–73; Captain RNEC, 1973–75; Port Adm., Rosyth, 1976–77; Asst Chief of Fleet Support, 1977–79; Chief of Fleet Support (Mem., Admiralty Bd of Defence Council), 1979–81; Comdt, RCDS, 1982–83. Cdre, RNSA, 1980–83 (Life Vice Cdre, 1990). Mem. Council, RUSI, 1984–87 (Vice Chm., 1986–87). President: RN Modern Pentathlon Assoc., 1978–83; Square Rigger Club (Support of Trng Ship Royalist), 1988–97; RNVR Youth Sail Training Trust, 1993–; Forces Help Soc. and Lord Roberts Workshops, 1991–96. Chm., Zeals Parish Council, 1992–98. KStJ 1985. *Recreations:* reading, sorting paperwork, thinking of things he used to be able to do. *Address:* Selwood, Zeals Row, Zeals, Warminster, Wilts BA12 6PE. *Clubs:* Naval (Pres., 1991–97); Royal Yacht Squadron (Cowes), Royal Naval Sailing Association (Portsmouth). *Died 18 March 1999.*

PINDER, Ven. Charles; Archdeacon of Lambeth, 1986–88, then Archdeacon Emeritus; *b* 5 May 1921; *s* of Ernest and Gertrude Pinder; *m* 1943, Ethel, *d* of Albert and Emma Milke; four *d. Educ:* King's College London (AKC). Ordained deacon, 1950, priest 1951; Curate, St Saviour, Raynes Park, 1950–53; Vicar: All Saints, Hatcham Park, 1953–60; St Laurence, Catford, 1960–73; Sub-Dean of Lewisham, 1968–73; Borough Dean of Lambeth, 1973–86. Hon. Chaplain to Bishop of Southwark, 1963–80; Hon. Canon of Southwark, 1973–86. Member of Parole Board, 1976–80; Chm., Brixton Prison Bd of Visitors, 1983–86. *Recreations:* most outdoor sports and selective indoor games, listening to music. *Address:* 22 Somerstown, Chichester, West Sussex PO19 4AG. *T:* (01243) 779708.

Died 2 April 1999.

PINDLING, Rt Hon. Sir Lynden Oscar, KCMG 1983; PC 1976; Member, House of Assembly, Bahamas, 1956–97; Leader of the Opposition, 1992–97; *b* 22 March 1930; *s* of Arnold Franklin and Viola Pindling; *m* 1956, Marguerite McKenzie; two *s* two *d. Educ:* Western Senior Sch., Nassau Govt High Sch.; London Univ. (LLB 1952; LLD 1970; DHL 1978). Called to the Bar, Middle Temple, 1953. Practised as lawyer, 1952–67. Leader of Progressive Liberal Party, 1956; elected to Bahamas House of Assembly, 1956, re-elected 1962, 1967, 1968, 1972, 1977, 1982, 1987, 1992. Worked for human rights and self-determination in the Bahamas; Mem., several delegns to Colonial Office, 1956–66; took part in Constitutional Conf., May 1963; Leader of Opposition, 1964; Mem., Delegns to UN Special Cttee of Twenty-four, 1965, 1966; Premier of the Bahamas and Minister of Tourism and Development, 1967; led Bahamian Delegn to Constitutional Conf., London, 1968; to Independence Conf., 1972; Prime Minister and Minister of Econ. Affairs, 1969–92 (first Prime Minister, Commonwealth of the Bahamas, after Independence, 1973–92). Chm., Commonwealth Parly Assoc., 1968. *Recreations:* swimming, boating, travel. *Address:* Pindling & Co., PO Box N-8174, Nassau, Bahamas.

Died 26 Aug. 2000.

PINSENT, Roger Philip; HM Diplomatic Service, retired; *b* 30 Dec. 1916; *s* of late Sidney Hume Pinsent; *m* 1941, Suzanne Smalley; one *s* two *d. Educ:* Downside Sch.; Lausanne, London and Grenoble Univs. London Univ. French Scholar, 1938; BA Hons London, 1940. HM Forces, 1940–46; HM Diplomatic Service, May 1946; 1st Sec., HM Legation, Havana, 1948–50; HM Consul, Tangier, 1950–52; 1st Sec., HM Embassy, Madrid, 1952–53; FO, 1953–56; 1st Sec., Head of Chancery, HM Embassy, Lima, 1956–59 (Chargé d'Affaires, 1958, 1959); Dep. Head of UK Delegation to the European Communities, Luxembourg, 1959–63; HM Ambassador to Nicaragua, 1963–67; Counsellor (Commercial), Ankara, 1967–70; Consul-Gen., São Paulo, 1970–73. Mem., Inst. of Linguists, 1976–79. Mem., Stow Probus Club, 1974–. *Recreations:* music, study of oenology, photography, book-binding, golf. *Address:* Cranfield Cottage, Maugersbury, Stow-on-the-Wold, Glos GL54 1HR. *T:* (01451) 830992. *Clubs:* Broadway Golf; Stow on the Wold RFC. *Died 29 June 1997.*

PIRIE, Norman Wingate, FRS 1949; *b* 1 July 1907; *yr s* of late Sir George Pirie, RSA, painter, Torrance, Stirlingshire, and Jean S., *d* of John Wingate, manufacturer, Glasgow; *m* 1931, Antoinette Patey (*d* 1992); one *s*; one *d. Educ:* Emmanuel Coll., Cambridge. Demonstrator in Biochemical Laboratory, Cambridge, 1932–40; Virus Physiologist, 1940–46, Head of Biochemistry Dept, 1947–73, Rothamsted Experimental Station, Harpenden. Copley Medal, 1971; Rank Prize for Nutrition, 1976. *Publications:* Food Resources: conventional and novel, 1969, 2nd edn 1976; Leaf Protein and other aspects of fodder fractionation, 1978, 2nd edn as Leaf Protein and its by-products in human and animal nutrition, 1987; ed several works on world food supplies; scientific papers on various aspects of biochemistry but especially on separation and properties of macromolecules; articles on viruses, the origins of life, biochemical engineering, and the need for greatly extended research on food production and contraception. *Address:* Rothamsted Experimental Station, Harpenden, Herts AL5 2JQ. *T:* (01582) 763133. *Died 29 March 1997.*

PITBLADO, Sir David (Bruce), KCB 1967 (CB 1955); CVO 1953; *b* 18 Aug. 1912; *o s* of Robert Bruce and Mary Jane Pitblado; *m* 1941, Edith (*d* 1978), *yr d* of Captain J. T. and Mrs Rees Evans, Cardigan; one *s* one *d. Educ:* Strand Sch.; Emmanuel Coll., Cambridge (Hon. Fellow 1972); Middle Temple. Entered Dominions Office, 1935; Asst Private Secretary to Secretary of State, 1937–39; served in War Cabinet Office, 1942; transferred to Treasury, 1942; deleg. to UN Conf., San Francisco, 1945; Under-Secretary, Treasury, 1949; Principal Private Secretary to the Prime Minister (Mr Clement Attlee, Mr Winston Churchill, and Sir Anthony Eden), 1951–56; Vice Chm., Managing Bd, European Payments Union, 1958; Third Secretary, Treasury, 1960; Economic Minister and Head of Treasury Delegation, Washington, and Executive Dir for the UK, IMF and World Bank, 1961–63; Permanent Sec., Min. of Power, 1966–69; Permanent Sec. (Industry), Min. of Technology, 1969–70; Civil Service Dept, 1970–71; Comptroller and Auditor-General, 1971–76. Advr on non-exec. directorships, Inst. of Dirs, 1977–81. Chm., Davies's Educnl Trust, 1979–89. Member: Data Protection Cttee, 1976–78; Victoria County Histories Cttee, 1974–; Finance Cttee, RPMS, 1980–; Council, SSAFA, 1976–90 (Hon. Treasurer). Jt Editor, The Shetland Report, 1978. Companion Inst. of Fuel. *Address:* 23 Cadogan Street, SW3 2PP; Pengoitan, Borth, Dyfed SY24 5LN. *Club:* Athenæum. *Died 9 July 1997.*

PITCHFORTH, Harry; General Manager, Home Grown Cereals Authority, 1974–78, retired; *b* 17 Jan. 1917; *s* of John William Pitchforth and Alice Hollas; *m* 1941, Edna May Blakebrough; one *s* one *d. Educ:* Heath Sch., Halifax; Queen's Coll., Oxford. 1st class Hons, School of Modern History, Oxford, 1939. Served War, 1940–45, Captain, RASC, and later Education Officer, 5 Guards Brigade. Ministry of Food, 1945; Principal Private Secretary to Minister, Major G. Lloyd-George (later 1st Viscount Tenby), 1952–54; seconded to National Coal Board, 1955–58; Ministry of Agriculture, Fisheries and Food: Regional Controller, 1957–61; Director of Establishments and Organisation, 1961–65; Under-Sec., HM Treasury, 1965–67; Controller of HM Stationery Office and the Queen's Printer of Acts of Parliament, 1967–69; Chief Executive, Metropolitan Water Bd, 1969–74. *Recreations:* walking, music. *Address:* 93 George V Avenue, Pinner, Middx HA5 5SU. *T:* (0181) 863 1229. *Died 5 Oct. 1996.*

PLATT, Sir (Frank) Lindsey, 2nd Bt *cr* 1958; barrister; *b* 16 Jan. 1919; *s* of Sir Harry Platt, 1st Bt, MD, FRCS and Gertrude Sarah (*d* 1980), *d* of Richard Turney; *S* father, 1986; *m* 1951, Johanna Magdalena Elisabeth Laenger (*d* 1995); one *d* (and one *d* decd). *Educ:* Stowe; Magdalen Coll., Oxford. Called to the Bar, Inner Temple, 1954. *Heir:* none. *Died 11 Feb. 1998 (ext).*

PLATT, Hon. Sir Peter, 2nd Bt *cr* 1959, of Grindleford, co. Derby; AM 1999; Professor Emeritus, University of Sydney (Professor of Music, 1975–89); *b* 6 July 1924; *s* of Baron Platt (Life Peer), and Margaret Irene (*d* 1987), *d* of Arthur Charles Cannon; *S* to baronetcy of father, 1978; *m* 1948, Jean Halliday, *d* of late Charles Philip Brentnall, MC; one *s* two *d. Educ:* Abbotsholme School, Derbyshire; Magdalen Coll., Oxford (BMus 1950; BLitt 1952; MA 1954); Royal College of Music. FGSM 1973. Lectr and Sen. Lectr in Music, Univ. of Sydney, 1952–57; Professor of Music, Univ. of Otago, NZ, 1957–75. Served War in 1939–45 with RNVR (despatches). *Heir:* *s* Martin Philip Platt [*b* 9 March 1952; *m* 1971, Frances Corinne Moana, *d* of Trevor Samuel Conley; two *s* two *d*]. *Address:* 1 Ellison Place, Pymble, NSW 2073, Australia. *Died 3 Aug. 2000.*

PLATT, Sir Lindsey; see Platt, Sir F. L.

PLAYFAIR, Sir Edward (Wilder), KCB 1957 (CB 1949); *b* 17 May 1909; *s* of late Dr Ernest Playfair; *m* 1941, Dr Mary Lois Rae; three *d. Educ:* Eton; King's Coll., Cambridge (Hon. Fellow, 1986). Inland Revenue, 1931–34; HM Treasury, 1934–46 and 1947–56 (Control Office for Germany and Austria, 1946–47); Permanent Under-Secretary of State for War, 1956–59; Permanent Sec., Ministry of Defence, 1960–61. Chairman, International Computers and Tabulators Ltd, 1961–65; Director: National Westminster Bank Ltd, 1961–79; Glaxo Hldgs Ltd, 1961–79; Tunnel Holdings Ltd, 1966–80; Equity and Law Life Assce Soc. plc, 1968–83. Governor, Imperial Coll. of Science and Technology, 1958–83 (Fellow, 1972); College Cttee of UCL, 1961–77 (Hon. Fellow, UCL, 1969); Chm., National Gallery, 1972–74 (Trustee, 1967–74). Hon. FBCS. *Address:* 62 Coniger Road, Fulham, SW6 3TA. *T:* (0171) 736 3194. *Club:* Brooks's. *Died 21 March 1999.*

PLEETH, William, OBE 1989; FGSM, FRCM; Professor of 'Cello, Guildhall School of Music, 1948–78; *b* 12 Jan. 1916; *s* of John and Edith Pleeth; *m* 1944, Margaret Good; one *s* one *d. Educ:* London until 1929; Leipzig Conservatoire, 1930–32. Internat. concert 'cellist in duos, trios, string quartets and concertos incl. Amadeus Quartet, Melos Ensemble and Allegri Quartet (Jt Founder, 1952); début: Leipzig, 1931; London, 1933; broadcasting and recording, 1933–80; 'cello master classes in Europe, Canada, USA; frequent member, internat. music juries. *Publication:* Cello (Menuhin series), 1982. *Recreations:*

gardening, reading, researching into old English furniture. *Address:* 19 Holly Park, N3 3JB. *T:* (020) 8346 0277.
Died 6 April 1999.

PLENDERLEITH, Harold James, CBE 1959; MC 1918; PhD; FRSE; FBA 1973; FSA, FMA; Director, International Centre for the Study of the Preservation and Restoration of Cultural Property (created by UNESCO), 1959–71, then Emeritus; Vice-President, International Institute for the Conservation of Museum Objects, 1958 (President, 1965–67; Hon. Fellow 1971); *b* 19 Sept. 1898; *s* of Robert James Plenderleith, FEIS; *m* 1st, 1926, Elizabeth K. S. Smyth (*d* 1982); 2nd, 1988, Margaret MacLennan. *Educ:* Dundee Harris Acad.; St Andrews Univ. (BSc, PhD). Scientific Asst, Dept of Scientific and Indust. Res., attached to British Museum, Bloomsbury, 1924; Asst Keeper, British Museum, 1927; Keeper, Research Lab., British Museum, 1949–59. Mem., Hon. Scientific Adv. Cttee, Nat. Gallery, 1935–81 (Chm., 1944–58); Professor of Chemistry, Royal Academy of Arts, London, 1936–58. Hon. Treas. Internat. Inst. for Conservation of Museum Objects, 1950–58; Hon. Mem., Internat. Council of Museums; Hon. Chm., Scottish Soc. for Conservation and Restoration, 1984. Rhind Lecturer, Edinburgh, 1954. Gold Medal, Society of Antiquaries of London, 1964; Gold Medal, Univ. of Young Nam, Tae Gu, Korea, 1970; Bronze Medal, UNESCO, 1971; Conservation Service Award, US Dept of the Interior, 1976; ICCROM International Oscar, Rome, 1979. Hon. LLD St Andrews. *Publications:* The Preservation of Antiquities, 1934; The Conservation of Prints, Drawings and Manuscripts, 1937; The Preservation of Leather Bookbindings, 1946; The Conservation of Antiquities and Works of Art, 1956, 2nd edn, with A. E. A. Werner, 1971; papers on allied subjects and on technical examinations of museum specimens in museum and scientific journals. *Recreations:* art, music. *Address:* Riverside, 17 Rockfield Crescent, Dundee DD2 1JF. *T:* (01382) 641552. *Club:* Athenæum. *Died 2 Nov. 1997.*

PLIATZKY, Sir Leo, KCB 1977 (CB 1972); Civil Service, 1947–80; *b* 22 Aug. 1919; *s* of Nathan Pliatzky; *m* 1948, Marian Jean Elias (*d* 1979); one *s* one *d. Educ:* Manchester Grammar Sch.; City of London Sch.; Corpus Christi Coll., Oxford (Hon. Fellow, 1980). First Cl. Classical Honour Mods, 1939; First Cl. Philosophy, Politics and Economics, 1946. Served in RAOC and REME, 1940–45 (despatches). Research Sec., Fabian Soc., 1946–47; Min. of Food, 1947–50; HM Treasury, 1950–77: Under-Sec., 1967; Dep. Sec., 1971; Second Permanent Sec., 1976; Permanent Sec., Dept of Trade, 1977; retired 1979, retained for special duties, 1979–80. Mem., British Airways Bd, 1980–84 (non-exec. Dir, 1984–85); Director: Associated Communications Corporation Ltd, 1980–82; Central Independent Television plc, 1981–89; Ultramar plc, 1981–90. Chm., Industry Wkg Pty on Production of Television Commercials, 1986–89 (report published, 1987). Vis. Prof., City Univ., 1980–84; Associate Fellow, LSE, 1982–85; Sen. Res. Fellow, PSI, 1983–84. Trustee, History of Parliament Trust, 1982–, Treasurer 1983–94. Gov., Charles Dickens Primary Sch., 1996–97. Hon. DLitt Salford, 1986. *Publications:* Getting and Spending, 1982, rev. edn 1984; Paying and Choosing, 1985; The Treasury under Mrs Thatcher, 1989. *Address:* 27 River Court, Upper Ground, SE1 9PE. *T:* (020) 7928 3667. *Club:* Reform. *Died 4 May 1999.*

PLOWDEN, Lady; Bridget Horatia Plowden, DBE 1972; Chairman: Independent Broadcasting Authority, 1975–80; Training Commission (formerly Manpower Services Commission) Area Manpower Board, North London, 1983–88; *b* 5 May 1910; 2nd *d* of late Admiral Sir Herbert William Richmond, KCB, and Lady ((Florence) Elsa) Richmond (*née* Bell); *m* 1933, Edwin Noel Plowden, later

Baron Plowden, GBE, KCB; two *s* one *d* (and one *d* decd). *Educ:* Downe House. Dir, Trust Houses Forte Ltd, 1961–72. A Governor and Vice-Chm., BBC, 1970–75. Chairman: Mary Feilding Guild (formerly Working Ladies Guild), 1945–88 (Pres., 1992–) Professional Classes Aid Council, 1958–73 (Pres., 1973–86); Central Adv. Council for Educn (England), 1963–66; Metropolitan Architectural Consortium for Educn, 1968–79; Member: (Co-opted) Educn Cttee, ILEA, 1967–73 (Vice-Chm., ILEA Schs Sub-Cttee, 1967–70); Houghton Inquiry into Pay of Teachers, 1974; President: Relate (formerly Nat. Marriage Guidance Council), 1983–93; Adv. Cttee for Educn of Romany and other Travellers, 1983– (Chm., 1973–83); Voluntary Orgns Liaison Council for Under-Fives, 1985– (Founder and Chm., 1978); Pre-School Playgroups Assoc., 1972–82 (Vice-Pres., 1982–); Nat. Inst. of Continuing Adult Educn, 1981–88; Coll. of Preceptors, 1987–94 (Vice-Pres., 1983; Hon. Fellow, 1973); Harding House Assoc.; Delves House, 1961–88 (formerly Chm.). Member: Nat. Theatre Bd, 1976–88; Drake Fellowship, 1981–87; Fairbridge/Drake Soc., 1988–89. Chairman: Governors, Philippa Fawcett Coll. of Educn, 1967–76; Robert Montefiore Comprehensive Sch., 1968–78. Liveryman, Goldsmiths' Co., 1979. JP Inner London Area Juvenile Panel, 1962–71. FRTS 1980. Hon. LLD: Leicester, 1968; Reading, 1970; London, 1976; Hon. DLitt Loughborough, 1976; DUniv Open, 1974. *Address:* Martels Manor, Dunmow, Essex CM6 1NB. *T:* (01371) 872141. *Died 29 Sept. 2000.*

PLOWDEN, Anna Bridget, CBE 1997; Managing Director, Plowden & Smith Ltd, since 1985; *b* 18 June 1938; *d* of Baron Plowden, GBE, KCB, and Lady Plowden, DBE. *Educ:* New Hall, Chelmsford; Inst. of Archaeology, Univ. of London. Man. Dir, Anna Plowden Ltd, 1968–85; Dir, Recollections Ltd, 1986–93; Chm., Art Services Ltd, 1994–97. Chm., Conservation Cttee, Crafts Council, 1979–83. Mem., Conservation Adv. Cttee, Museums & Galleries Commn, 1987–97. Trustee: V&A Mus., 1990–; Edward James Foundn, West Dean, Sussex, 1990–; Queen Elizabeth Scholarship Trust, 1990–97; St Andrews Conservation Trust, Wells, 1987–96. Member: Adv. Cttee for Conservation and Restoration Dip. Course, C&G, 1994–; Council, Textile Conservation Centre, Hampton Court, 1989–. Royal Warrant Holders Association: Mem. Council, 1990–96; Vice-Pres., 1997–. FIIC 1970. *Publication:* (jtly) Looking After Antiques, 1987. *Address:* Plowden & Smith Ltd, 190 St Ann's Hill, SW18 2RT. *T:* (0181) 874 4005, *Fax:* (0181) 874 7248.
Died 21 Aug. 1997.

PLUMLEY, Rev. Prof. Jack Martin; Herbert Thompson Professor of Egyptology, 1957–77, and Fellow of Selwyn College, since 1957, University of Cambridge; Priest-in-Charge, Longstowe, Cambs, 1981–95; *b* 2 Sept. 1910; *e s* of Arthur Henry Plumley and Lily Plumley (*née* Martin); *m* 1st, 1938, Gwendolen Alice Darling (*d* 1984); three *s*; 2nd, 1986, Ursula Clara Dowle. *Educ:* Merchant Taylors' Sch., London; St John's Coll., Durham (BA, Univ. Hebrew Schol., MLitt); King's Coll., Cambridge (MA). Deacon 1933; priest 1934; curacies, 1933–41; Vicar of Christ Church, Hoxton, 1942–45, of St Paul's, Tottenham, 1945–47; Rector and Vicar of All Saints', Milton, Cambridge, 1948–57; Cambridge University: Associate Lectr in Coptic, 1949–57; Acting Dean, Pembroke Coll., 1981–82; Mem. Council of Senate, 1965–70. Stephen Glanville Meml Lectr, Fitzwilliam Mus., Cambridge, 1982. Dir of excavations on behalf of Egypt Exploration Soc. at Qasr Ibrim, Nubia, 1963, 1964, 1966, 1969, 1972, 1974, 1976; Chm., British Cttee of Internat. Critical Greek New Testament Project, 1963–87. Pres., Internat. Soc. for Nubian Studies, 1978–82, Patron, 1982–. FSA 1966; Fellow, Inst. of Coptic Studies, United Egyptian Repub., 1966; Corresp. Mem., German Inst. of Archaeology, 1966.

Recreations: music, rowing, photography, travel. *Address:* Selwyn College, Cambridge CB3 9DQ; 13 Lyndewode Road, Cambridge CB1 2HL. *T:* (01223) 350328.

Died 2 July 1999.

POCOCK, Kenneth Walter, (Peter), MBE 1993; *b* 20 June 1913; *s* of Walter Dunsdon Pocock and Emily Marion Pocock; *m* 1939, Anne Tidmarsh; one *s* one *d*. *Educ:* Canford School. United Dairies (London) Ltd, 1930; Armed Forces, 1942–46; Man. Dir, Edinburgh and Dumfriesshire Dairy Co. Ltd, 1946; Dir, United Dairies Ltd, 1948; Pres., Scottish Milk Trade Fedn, 1956–59; Dir, Unigate Ltd, 1959; Man. Dir, Unigate Ltd and United Dairies Ltd, 1963; Chm. of Milk Div., Unigate Ltd, 1968; Dep. Chm., Unigate Ltd, 1970–75. Life Pres., Unigate Long Service Corps (40 years), 1992 (Pres., 1971–92); Governor, Nat. Dairymen's Benevolent Instn, 1962– (Chm., 1977–81). *Recreations:* motoring, shooting, photography, gardening. *Address:* 4 Dorchester House, 29 Marsham Lane, Gerrards Cross, Bucks SL9 8HA. *T:* (01753) 889278. *Died 12 Nov. 2000.*

POLLARD, Maj.-Gen. (Charles) Barry; Chairman, Haig Homes, 1987–94; *b* 20 April 1927; *s* of Leonard Charles Pollard and Rose Constance (*née* Fletcher); *m* 1954, Mary Heyes; three *d*. *Educ:* Ardingly Coll.; Selwyn Coll., Cambridge. Commnd, Corps of RE, 1947; served in ME, Korea and UK, 1947–58; Student, Staff Coll., Camberley, 1958; GSO 2 (Trng), HQ Eastern Comd, 1959–61; Liaison Officer, Ecole du Genie, France, 1961–63; OC 5 Field Sqdn, 1963–65; JSSC, 1965; Mil. Asst to DCOS, Allied Forces Central Europe, 1966; GSO 1 MoD, 1967; GSO 1 (DS), Staff Coll., Camberley, 1968; CRE 3 Div., 1969–71; Col GS 3 Div., 1971–72; CCRE 1st British Corps, 1972–74; RCDS, 1975; Chief Engr, BAOR, 1976–79. Col Comdt, RE, 1982–87. National Dir, Trident Trust, 1980–84; Gen. Man., Sulent Business Fund, 1984–91. *Recreations:* sailing, golf. *Address:* Yateley, Coombe Road, Salisbury, Wilts SP2 8BT. *Died 18 Oct. 2000.*

POLLARD, Prof. Sidney; Professor of Economic History, University of Bielefeld, 1980–90, Emeritus Professor since 1990; *b* 21 April 1925; *s* of Moses and Leontine Pollak; *né* Siegfried Pollak; *m* 1st, 1949, Eileen Andrews (marr. diss.); two *s* one *d*; 2nd, 1982, Helen Trippett. *Educ:* London School of Economics. University of Sheffield: Knoop Fellow, 1950–52; Asst Lecturer, 1952–55; Lecturer, 1955–60; Senior Lecturer, 1960–63; Prof. of Economic History, 1963–80. Corresp. Fellow, British Acad., 1989. Hon. DLitt Sheffield, 1992. *Publications:* Three Centuries of Sheffield Steel, 1954; A History of Labour in Sheffield 1850–1939, 1959; The Development of the British Economy 1914–1950, 1962, 4th edn, 1914–1990, 1992; The Genesis of Modern Management, 1965; The Idea of Progress, 1968; (with D. W. Crossley) The Wealth of Britain, 1086–1966, 1968; (ed) The Gold Standard and Employment Policies between the Wars, 1970; (ed jtly) Aspects of Capital Investment in Great Britain, 1750–1850, 1971; (ed) The Trades Unions Commission: the Sheffield outrages, 1971; (ed with J. Salt) Robert Owen, prophet of the poor, 1971; (ed with C. Holmes) Documents of European Economic History, vol. 1, 1968, vols 2 and 3, 1972; The Economic Integration of Europe, 1815–1970, 1974; (ed with C. Holmes) Essays in the Economic and Social History of South Yorkshire, 1977; (with Paul Robertson) The British Shipbuilding Industry 1870–1914, 1979; Peaceful Conquest, 1981; The Wasting of the British Economy, 1982; (with C. H. Feinstein) Studies in Capital Formation in Great Britain, 1988; Britain's Prime and Britain's Decline, 1988; Wealth and Poverty, 1990; Typology of Industrialization Processes in the 19th Century, 1990; (ed with Karl Ditt) Von der Heimarbeit in die Fabrik, 1992; (ed with D. Ziegler)

Markt, Staat, Planung, 1992; Marginal Europe, 1997; articles in learned journals in field of economics, economic history and history. *Recreations:* walking, music. *Address:* 34 Bents Road, Sheffield S11 9RJ. *T:* (0114) 236 8543.

Died 22 Nov. 1998.

POLLOCK, Ellen Clara; actress and director; President, The Shaw Society; Professor at RADA and Webber Douglas School of Acting; *b* 29 June 1902; *m* 1st, 1929, Lt-Col L. F. Hancock, OBE, RE (*d* 1944); one *s*; 2nd, 1945, James Proudfoot (*d* 1971). *Educ:* St Mary's College, W2; Convent of The Blessed Sacrament, Brighton. First appeared, Everyman, 1920, as page in Romeo and Juliet; accompanied Lady Forbes-Robertson on her S African tour, and later visited Australia as Moscovitch's leading lady. West End successes include: Hit the Deck, Hippodrome, 1927; Her First Affaire, Kingsway, and Duke of York's, 1930; The Good Companions, Her Majesty's, 1931; Too True to be Good, New, 1933; Finished Abroad, Savoy, 1934; French Salad, Westminster and Royalty, 1934; The Dominant Sex, Shaftesbury and Aldwych, 1935; Open Air Theatre: Lysistrata; As You Like It; seasons of Shaw's plays: at Lyric, Hammersmith, 1944, and with Sir Donald Wolfit at King's, Hammersmith, 1953; three seasons of Grand Guignol plays at The Irving and Granville, Walham Green; Six Characters in Search of an Author, New Mayfair Theatre, 1963; Lady Frederick, Vaudeville and Duke of York's, 1969–70; Ambassador, Her Majesty's, 1971; Pygmalion, Albery, 1974; Tales from the Vienna Woods, Nat. Theatre, 1976; The Dark Lady of the Sonnets, Nat. Theatre, 1977; The Woman I Love, Churchill, 1979; Country Life, Lyric, Hammersmith, 1980; Harlequinade, and Playbill, Nat. Theatre, 1980. Acted in numerous films and TV, incl. Forsyte Saga, The Pallisers, World's End and The Nightingale Saga; also radio broadcasts. *Productions include:* Summer in December, Comedy Theatre, 1949, Miss Turner's Husband, St Martin's, 1949; The Third Visitor, Duke of York's, 1949; Shavings, St Martin's, 1951; Mrs Warren's Profession, Royal Court, 1956; A Matter of Choice, Arts, 1967. *Recreations:* motoring, antiques, cooking. *Address:* 9 Tedworth Square, SW3 4DU. *T:* (0171) 352 5082.

Died 29 March 1997.

POLLOCK, Martin Rivers, FRS 1962; Professor of Biology, University of Edinburgh, 1965–76, then Emeritus; *b* 10 Dec. 1914; *s* of Hamilton Rivers Pollock and Eveline Morton Pollock (*née* Bell); *m* 1st, 1941, Jean Ilsley Paradise (marr. diss.); two *s* two *d*; 2nd, 1979, Janet Frances Machen. *Educ:* Winchester Coll.; Trinity Coll., Cambridge (BA 1936; Sen. Schol., 1936; MB BCh 1940); University College Hospital, London. MRCS, LRCP 1939. House appointments at UCH and Brompton Hospital, 1940–41; Bacteriologist, Emergency Public Health Laboratory Service, 1941–45; seconded to work on infective hepatitis with MRC Unit, 1943–45; apppointment to scientific staff, Medical Research Council, under Sir Paul Fildes, FRS, 1945; Head of Division of Bacterial Physiology, Nat. Inst. for Medical Research, Mill Hill (MRC), 1949–65. *Publications:* (ed) Report of Conference on Common Denominators in Art and Science, 1983; articles in British Journal of Experimental Pathology, Biochemical Journal, Journal of General Microbiology, etc. *Recreations:* contemplating, planning but no longer undertaking various forms of mildly adventurous travel through deserts, painting. *Address:* Marsh Farm House, Margaret Marsh, Shaftesbury, Dorset SP7 0AZ. *T:* (01258) 820479.

Died 22 Dec. 1999.

POLUNIN, Nicholas, CBE 1976; MS, MA, DPhil, DSc; FLS; FRGS; Editor (founding), Environmental Conservation, 1974–95; Co-Editor, Environmental Challenges, since 1993; President and Chief Executive

Officer, The Foundation for Environmental Conservation, since 1975; President, World Council for the Biosphere, since 1984; *b* Hammonds Farm, Checkendon, Oxon, 26 June 1909; *e s* of late Vladimir Polunin and Elizabeth Violet (*née* Hart); *m* 1st, 1939, Helen Lovat Fraser (marr. diss. 1947; she *d* 1973); one *s*; 2nd, 1948, Helen Eugenie Campbell; two *s* one *d. Educ:* The Hall, Weybridge; Latymer Upper and privately; Oxford, Yale and Harvard Univs (MA, DPhil, DSc Oxon; MS Yale). Open Scholar of Christ Church, Oxford, 1928–32; First Class Hons Nat. Sci. Final Examination, Botany and Ecology; Goldsmiths' Senior Studentship for Research, 1932–33; Botanical Tutor in various Oxford Colls, 1932–47; Henry Fellowship at Pierson Coll., Yale Univ., USA, 1933–34 (Sigma Xi); Departmental Demonstrator in Botany, 1934–35, and Senior (Research) Scholar of New Coll., Oxford, 1934–36; Senior Research Award, 1935–38, Special Investigator, 1938, DSIR; Research Associate, Gray Herbarium, Harvard Univ., USA, 1936–37, and subseq. Foreign Research Associate; Fielding Curator and Keeper of the University Herbaria, Oxford, and Univ. Demonstrator and Lectr in Botany, 1939–47; Lectr and Sen. Res. Fellow, New Coll., Oxford; Oxford Univ. Botanical Moderator, 1941–45; Macdonald Prof. of Botany, McGill Univ., Canada, 1947–52 (Visiting Prof., 1946–47); Research Fellow, Harvard Univ., 1950–53; Lectr in Plant Science and Research Associate, Yale Univ., 1953–55; Project Dir, US Air Force, 1953–55, and Consultant to US Army Corps of Engineers; Prof. of Plant Ecology and Taxonomy, Head of Dept of Botany, and Dir of Univ. Herbarium, etc, Baghdad, Iraq, 1956–58 (revolution); Founding Prof. of Botany and Head of Dept, Faculty of Science (which he established as Dean), Univ. of Ife, Nigeria, 1962–66 (revolutions, etc). Rolleston Meml Prize, Oxford Univ., 1938; Leverhulme Res. Award, 1941–43; Arctic Inst. Res. Fellowship, 1946–48; Guggenheim Meml Fellowship, 1950–52. Haley Lectr, Acadia Univ., NS, 1950; Visiting Lectr and Adviser on Biology, Brandeis Univ., Waltham, Mass, 1953–54; Guest Prof., Univ. of Geneva, 1959–61 and 1975–76. FRHS; Fellow: AAAS, Arctic Inst. of N America. Vice Pres., Internat. Soc. of Naturalists. Member or Leader, numerous scientific expeditions from 1930, particularly in arctic or sub-arctic regions, including Spitsbergen (widely, including crossing alone), Lapland (3 times), Iceland, Greenland, Canadian Eastern Arctic (5 times, including confirmation of Spicer Islands in Foxe Basin north of Hudson Bay and discovery in 1946 of last major islands to be added to world map following their naming in 1949 as Prince Charles Is and Air Force Is), Labrador-Ungava (many times), Canadian Western Arctic (including Magnetic Pole), Alaska, summer and winter flights over geographical North Pole; subsequently in Middle East and West Africa. Ford Foundation Award, Scandinavia and USSR, 1966–67. International Botanical Congresses: VII (Stockholm, 1950); VIII (Paris, 1954); X (Edinburgh, 1964); XI (Seattle, 1969, symposium chm., etc); XII (Leningrad, 1975, Conservation Section 1st chm., etc); XIII (Sydney, 1981); International Congresses of Ecology: I (The Hague, 1974); II (Jerusalem, 1978); IV (Syracuse, NY, 1986, contrib. paper *in absentia* with E. P. Odum). International Conferences on Environmental Future, 1971–91: Chm., Internat. Steering Cttee, and Editor of Proceedings, 1st Conf. Finland, 1971; Secretary-General and Editor: 2nd Conf., Iceland, 1978, 3rd Conf., Edinburgh, 1987, 4th Conf., Budapest, 1990; Founding Chm. Foundn for Environmental Conservation, 1973 (consolidated and placed under Geneva cantonal and Swiss federal surveillance, 1975; Life Pres., 1975). Editor, International Industry, 1943–46; Convener and Gen. Ed., Envmtl Monographs and Symposia, 1979–88; Founding Editor: Biological Conservation, 1967–74; Plant Science Monographs, 1954–78; World Crops Books, 1954–69; Chm. Editl Bd, Cambridge Studies in Environmental

Policy; Member, Advisory Board: The Environmentalist, 1981–95; Environmental Awareness, 1989–, and other jls. Initiated annual Biosphere Day, 21 Sept. 1991. US Order of Polaris; Marie-Victorin Medal for services to Canadian botany; Ramdeo Medal for Environmental Scis, India, 1986; Internat. Sasakawa Environment Prize, 1987; Academia Sinica Medal, China, 1988; USSR Vernadsky Medal, 1988; Hungarian Acad. of Sciences' Founder's (Zéchenyi) Medal, 1990. Elected to Global 500 Roll of Honour, UN Envmt Programme, 1991. Officer, Order of Golden Ark (Netherlands), 1990. *Publications:* Russian Waters, 1931; The Isle of Auks, 1932; Botany of the Canadian Eastern Arctic: vol. I, Pteridophyta and Spermatophyta, 1940; (ed) vol. II, Thallophyta and Bryophyta, 1947; vol. III, Vegetation and Ecology, 1948; Arctic Unfolding, 1949; Circumpolar Arctic Flora, 1959; Introduction to Plant Geography, 1960 (subseq. Amer., Indonesian and other edns); Eléments de Géographie botanique, 1967; (ed) The Environmental Future, 1972; Growth Without Ecodisasters?, 1980; Ecosystem Theory and Application, 1986; (with Sir John Burnett) Maintenance of The Biosphere, 1990; Surviving With The Biosphere, 1993; (with Mohammad Nazim) Environmental Challenges, vol. I, 1993, vol. II, Population and Global Security, 1997; (ed) World Who Is Who and Does What in Environment & Conservation, 1997; papers chiefly on arctic and boreal flora, phytogeography, ecology, vegetation, aerobiology, and conservation; contrib. Encyclopædia Britannica, Encyclopedia of the Biological Scis, etc, and some 650 other scientific papers, editorials, reviews, etc, to various jls. *Recreations:* travel and scientific exploration, nature conservation, working towards establishing planetary econetwork of environmental/conservational watch-dogs, stock-markets. *Address:* 7 Chemin Taverney, 1218 Grand-Saconnex, Geneva, Switzerland. *Fax:* (22) 7982344; c/o New College, Oxford. *Clubs:* Reform (life); Harvard (life), Torrey Botanical (New York City); Canadian Field Naturalists' (Ottawa). *Died 8 Dec. 1997.*

PONSONBY, Myles Walter, CBE 1966; HM Diplomatic Service, retired; County Councillor, Idmiston Division, Wiltshire County Council, 1988–93; *b* 12 Sept. 1924; *s* of late Victor Coope Ponsonby, MC and Gladys Edith Ponsonby (*née* Walter); *m* 1951, Anne Veronica Theresa Maynard, *y d* of Brig. Francis Herbert Maynard, CB, DSO, MC, and Ethel Maynard (*née* Bates); one *s* two *d. Educ:* St Aubyn's, Rottingdean; Eton College. HM Forces (Captain, KRRC), 1942–49. Entered Foreign (subseq. Diplomatic) Service, 1951; served in: Egypt, 1951; Cyprus, 1952–53; Beirut, 1953–56; Djakarta, 1958–61; Nairobi, 1963–64; Hanoi (Consul-Gen.), 1964–65; FO, 1966–69; Rome, 1969–71; FCO, 1972–74; Ambassador to Mongolian People's Republic, 1974–77; FCO, 1977–80. *Recreation:* exploring the British Isles. *Address:* 6 Hyde House Gardens, Hyde Street, Winchester, Hants SO23 7EL. *Clubs:* Army and Navy, Travellers.

Died 1 Feb. 1999.

PONTECORVO, Guido, PhD, DrAgr; FRS 1955; FRSE; FLS; *b* Pisa, Italy, 29 Nov. 1907; *s* of Massimo Pontecorvo and Maria (*née* Maroni); *m* 1939, Leonore Freyenmuth (*d* 1986), Frauenfeld, Switzerland; one *d. Educ:* Univ. of Pisa (DrAgr 1928); Univ. of Edinburgh (PhD 1941). Ispettorato Agrario per la Toscana, Florence, 1931–38; Inst. of Animal Genetics, Univ. of Edinburgh, 1938–40 and 1944–45; Dept of Zoology, Univ. of Glasgow, 1941–44; Dept of Genetics, Univ. of Glasgow, 1945–68 (Prof. 1956–68); Hon. Dir, MRC Unit of Cell Genetics, 1966–68; Mem. Res. Staff, Imperial Cancer Res. Fund, 1968–75, Hon. Consultant Geneticist, 1975–80. Vis. Lectr, Washington State Univ., 1967; Royal Society, Leverhulme Overseas Vis. Prof., Inst. of Biophysics, Rio de Janeiro, 1969 and Dept of Biology, Pahlavi Univ., 1974; Sloane

Foundn Vis. Prof., Vermont, 1971; Visiting Professor: Albert Einstein Coll. Med., 1965, 1966; UCL, 1968–75; King's Coll., London, 1970–71; Biology Dept, Tehran Univ., 1975; Prof. Ospite Linceo, Scuola Normale Superiore, Pisa, 1976–81; Raman Prof., Indian Acad. of Scis, 1982–83. Lectures: Jesup, Columbia Univ., 1956; Messenger, Cornell Univ., 1957; Leeuwenhoek, Royal Soc., 1962; L. C. Dunn, NY Blood Center, 1976; J. Weigle Meml, CIT, 1984; Gandhi Meml, Raman Inst., 1983. Pres., Genetical Soc., 1964–66; Vice-Pres., Inst. of Biology, 1969–71. FRSE 1946; FLS 1971. Emeritus Mem., Academia Europaea, 1989; Foreign Hon. Member: Amer. Acad. Arts and Sciences, 1958; Danish Royal Acad. Sci. and Letters, 1966; Peruvian Soc. of Medical Genetics, 1969; Indian National Science Acad., 1983; Indian Acad. of Scis, 1984; Accademia dei XL, 1993; For. Associate, Nat. Acad. of Scis, USA, 1983. Hon. DSc: Leicester, 1968; Camerino, 1974; East Anglia, 1974; Hon. LLD Glasgow, 1978. Hansen Prize, Carlsberg Foundn, 1961; Darwin Medal, Royal Soc., 1978. Campano d'Oro, Pisa, 1979. *Publications:* Ricerche sull' economia montana dell' Appennino Toscano, 1933 (Florence); Trends in Genetic Analysis, 1958; Topics in Genetic Analysis, 1985; numerous papers on genetics and high mountain botany. *Recreation:* alpine plants photography. *Address:* 60 Thornhill Square, N1 1BE. *T:* (020) 7700 5320.
Died 25 Sept. 1999.

PONTIN, Sir Frederick William, (Sir Fred), Kt 1976; Founder: Pontin's Ltd, 1946, Pontinental Ltd, 1963; Chairman and Joint Managing Director of Pontin's Ltd, 1946–79 (Hon. President, since 1987), and Pontinental (HS) Ltd, 1972–79; Chairman, 1983–85, Deputy Chairman, 1985–87, Kunick Leisure; Chairman, Ponti's, 1988, retired; *b* 24 Oct. 1906; *m* 1st, 1929, Dorothy Beatrice Mortimer (*d* 1993); one *d*; 2nd, 1999, Joyce Hey. *Educ:* Sir George Monoux Grammar Sch., Walthamstow. Began career on London Stock Exchange, 1920; catering and welfare work for Admiralty, Orkney Is, 1939–46; acquired: Industrial Catering Bristol, 1946; Brean Sands Holiday Village, 1946. Chief Barker, Variety Club of GB (raising £1,000,000 for charity), 1968; Mem. Exec. Bd, Variety Club, 1968–, Pres. 1969–75, formed 15 regional centres of club; Companion Mem., Grand Order of Water Rats. Prescot Band. Life Mem., BRCS (Hon. Vice Pres., Dorset Branch). Freeman of Christchurch, Dorset. *Recreations:* racing (owner of Specify, winner of 1971 Grand National, and Cala Mesquida, winner of 1971 Schweppes Gold Trophy); connected with Walthamstow Avenue FC for many years prior to 1939–45 war; interested in all sporting activities. *Address:* Flat 127, 3 Whitehall Court, SW1A 2EL. *T:* (020) 7839 5251. *Clubs:* Farmers', Saints and Sinners, Variety of GB; Derby.
Died 30 Sept. 2000.

POOLEY, Frederick Bernard, CBE 1968; PPRIBA; Architect to Greater London Council, 1978–80, Controller of Planning and Transportation, 1974–80, and Superintending Architect of Metropolitan Buildings, 1978–80; *b* 18 April 1916; *s* of George Pooley and Elizabeth Pawley; *m* 1944, Hilda Olive Williams; three *d*. *Educ:* West Ham Grammar Sch. RIBA, FRICS, FRTPI, MIStructE, FCIArb. Served War, RE, 1940–45. Deputy Borough Architect and Planning Officer, County Borough of West Ham, 1949–51; Deputy City Architect and Planning Officer, Coventry, 1951–54; County Architect and Planning Officer, Bucks, 1954–74. Major projects included: public and sch. bldg programme; scheme for public acquisition of bldgs of arch. or hist. interest for preservation and resale; new methods for assembling and servicing land; early planning work for new Milton Keynes. Royal Institute of British Architects: Mem. Council, 1962; Treasurer, 1972; Pres., 1973–75. *Publications:* contribs on planning, transport and

architecture. *Address:* Long Ridge, Whiteleaf, Aylesbury, Bucks HP17 0LZ. *T:* (01844) 346151.
Died 11 March 1998.

POPE, Dudley Bernard Egerton; naval historian and author; *b* 29 Dec. 1925; *s* of late Sydney Broughton Pope and Alice Pope (*née* Meehan); *m* 1954, Kathleen Patricia Hall; one *d*. *Educ:* Ashford (Kent). Served War of 1939–45: Midshipman, MN, 1941–43 (wounded and invalided). The Evening News: naval and defence correspondent, 1944–57, Dep. Foreign Editor, 1957–59; resigned to take up full-time authorship, 1959. Counsellor, Navy Record Soc., 1964–68. Cruising trans-Atlantic and Caribbean in own yacht, doing naval historical research, 1965–87. Created: "Lt Ramage RN" series of historical novels covering life of naval officer in Nelson's day, 1965; series of novels portraying sea life of Yorke family, 1979. Hon. Mem., Mark Twain Soc., 1976. *Publications: non-fiction:* Flag 4, the Battle of Coastal Forces in the Mediterranean, 1954; The Battle of the River Plate, 1956, repr. 1987; 73 North, 1958; England Expects, 1959; At 12 Mr Byng was Shot, 1962, repr. 1987; The Black Ship, 1963; Guns, 1965; The Great Gamble, 1972; Harry Morgan's Way, 1977; Life in Nelson's Navy, 1981; The Devil Himself, 1987; *fiction: the Ramage series:* Ramage (Book Society Choice) 1965; Ramage and the Drum Beat (Book Society Alternative Choice), 1967; Ramage and the Freebooters (Book of the Month Club Alt. Choice), 1969; Governor Ramage, RN, 1973; Ramage's Prize, 1974; Ramage and the Guillotine, 1975; Ramage's Diamond, 1976; Ramage's Mutiny, 1977; Ramage and the Rebels, 1978; The Ramage Touch, 1979; Ramage's Signal, 1980; Ramage and the Renegades, 1981; Ramage's Devil, 1982; Ramage's Trial, 1984; Ramage's Challenge, 1985; Ramage at Trafalgar, 1986; Ramage and the Saracens, 1988; Ramage and the Dido, 1989; *the Yorke series:* Convoy (Book Club Associates' Choice), 1979; Buccaneer, 1981; Admiral, 1982; Decoy (World Book Club Choice), 1983; Galleon, 1986; Corsair, 1987. *Recreations:* ocean cruising, skin-diving. *Address:* c/o Campbell Thomson & McLaughlin, 1 King's Mews, WC1N 2JA.
Died 25 April 1997.

POPE, Vice-Adm. Sir (John) Ernle, KCB 1976; *b* 22 May 1921; *s* of Comdr R. K. C. Pope, DSO, OBE, RN retd, Homme House, Herefordshire; *m* 1st, 1945, Pamela Davies (marr. diss.); five *s*; 2nd, Bunnie Webber. *Educ:* RN Coll., Dartmouth. Royal Navy, 1935; served throughout War of 1939–45, in Destroyers; CO, HMS Decoy, 1962–64; Dir, Naval Equipment, 1964–66; CO, HMS Eagle, 1966–68; Flag Officer, Western Fleet Flotillas, 1969–71; C of S to C-in-C Western Fleet, 1971–74; Comdr, Allied Naval Forces, S Europe, 1974–76. Rear-Adm. 1969; Vice-Adm. 1972. Dep. Pres., Royal Naval Assoc. *Recreations:* sailing, shooting. *Address:* Homme House, Much Marcle, Herefordshire. *Club:* Army and Navy.
Died 21 May 1998.

POPHAM, Mervyn Reddaway, FBA 1988; FSA; Lecturer in Aegean Archaeology, Oxford University, and Fellow, Linacre College, Oxford, 1972–94, then Emeritus Fellow; *b* 14 July 1927; *s* of Richard and Lilly Popham. *Educ:* Exeter Sch.; Univ. of St Andrews (MA); Univ. of Oxford (DipArch). FSA 1960. Colonial Administrative Service, Cyprus, 1951–58 (Comr, Troodos Dist, 1955–56); Macmillan Student, 1961–63 and Asst Dir, 1963–70, British Sch. of Archaeology at Athens; Asst Prof., Univ. of Cincinnati, 1970–72. *Publications:* The Last Days of the Palace at Knossos, 1964; The Destruction of the Palace at Knossos, 1970; Lefkandi I: the iron age settlement and cemeteries, 1980; The Unexplored Mansion at Knossos, 1984; Lefkandi II, 1992–93; Lefkandi III (Plates), 1996; articles and excavation reports in learned jls. *Recreations:*

music, photography. *Address:* 110 Woodstock Road, Oxford OX2 7NF. *T:* (01865) 512605.
Died 24 Oct. 2000.

POPJÁK, George Joseph, DSc, MD; FRS 1961; FRSC; Professor of Biochemistry at University of California in Los Angeles, 1968–84, then Emeritus; *b* 5 May 1914; *s* of late George and Maria Popják, Szeged, Hungary; *m* 1941, Hasel Marjorie, *d* of Duncan and Mabel Hammond, Beckenham, Kent. *Educ:* Royal Hungarian Francis Joseph University, Szeged; MD; DSc London. Demonstrator at Department of Morbid Anatomy and Histology, University of Szeged, 1938–39; British Council Scholar, Postgraduate Med. School of London, 1939–41; Demonstrator in Pathology, Dept of Pathology, St Thomas's Hosp. Med. School, London, 1941–43; Beit Meml Fellow for medical research at St Thomas's Hosp. Med. School, London, 1943–47; Member scientific staff of Med. Research Council at Nat. Inst. for Med. Research, 1947–53; Director of Medical Research Council Experimental Radiopathology Research Unit, Hammersmith Hosp., 1953–62; Jt Dir, Chemical Enzymology Lab., Shell Res. Ltd, 1962–68; Assoc. Prof. in Molecular Sciences, Warwick Univ., 1965–68. Foreign Member, Royal (Flemish) Acad. of Science, Literature and Fine Arts, Belgium, 1955; Hon. Member: Amer. Soc. of Biological Chemists, 1968; Alpha-Omega-Alpha, 1970; Mem., Amer. Acad. of Arts and Sciences, 1971. CIBA Medal (with Dr J. W. Cornforth), Biochemical Soc., 1965 (first award); Stouffer Prize, 1967; Davy Medal, Royal Soc., 1968; Award in Lipid Chem., Amer. Oil Chem. Soc., 1977; Distinguished Scientific Achievement Award, Amer. Heart Assoc., 1978. *Publications:* Chemistry, Biochemistry and Isotopic Tracer Technique (Royal Inst. of Chemistry monograph), 1955; (jtly) Lipids, Chemistry, Biochemistry and Nutrition, 1986; articles on fat metabolism in Jl Path. Bact., Jl Physiol., Biochemical Jl, etc. *Recreations:* music, modelling, gardening. *Address:* Departments of Medicine and Biological Chemistry, University of California at Los Angeles, Center for the Health Sciences 47–123 CHS, Los Angeles, CA 90024–1679, USA.
Died 30 Dec. 1998.

PORTEOUS, Col Patrick Anthony, VC 1942; Royal Artillery, retired 1970; *b* 1 Jan. 1918; *s* of late Brig.-Gen. C. McL. Porteous, 9th Ghurkas, and Mrs Porteous, Fleet, Hampshire; *m* 1st, 1943, Lois Mary (*d* 1953), *d* of late Maj.-Gen. Sir H. E. Roome, KCIE; one *d* (one *s* decd); 2nd, 1955, Deirdre, *d* of late Eric King; three *d. Educ:* Wellington Coll.; Royal Military Acad., Woolwich. BEF France, Sept. 1939–May 1940, with 6th AA Regt, RA; No 4 Commando, Dec. 1940–Oct. 1944; Dieppe, Aug. 1942 (VC); BLA June–Sept. 1944; 1st Airborne Div., Dec. 1944–July 1945; 6th Airborne Div., 1945–46; Staff Coll., Camberley, 1946; 16 Airborne Div. TA, 1947–48; 33 Airborne Lt Regt, RA, 1948–49; No 1 Regular Commission Board, 1949; Instructor, RMA, Sandhurst, 1950–53; GHQ, Far East Land Forces, Singapore, 1953–55; 1st Singapore Regt, RA, 1955; 14 Field Regt, RA, 1956–58; RAF Staff Coll., 1958; AMS, HQ Southern Comd, 1959–60; Colonel Junior Leaders Regt, RA, 1960–63; Colonel, General Staff War Office, later Ministry of Defence, 1963–66; Comdr Rheindahlen Garrison, 1966–69. *Recreation:* sailing. *Address:* Christmas Cottage, Church Lane, Funtington, W Sussex PO18 9LQ. *T:* (01243) 575315. *Died 9 Oct. 2000.*

PORTER, Barry; *see* Porter, G. B.

PORTER, Dorothea Noelle Naomi, (Thea Porter); fashion designer; *b* 24 Dec. 1927; *d* of Rev. Dr M. S. Seale and Renée Seale; *m* 1953, Robert S. Porter (marr. diss. 1967); one *d. Educ:* Lycée français, Damascus; Fernhill Manor; Royal Holloway Coll., London Univ. Embassy wife, Beirut; fashion designer, 1967; interior and fabric designer.

Recreations: cooking, travelling, music, painting, collecting antique Islamic fabrics and objets, consulting clairvoyants. *Died 24 July 2000.*

PORTER, George Barrington, (Barry); MP (C) Wirral South, since 1983 (Bebington and Ellesmere Port, 1979–83); *b* 11 June 1939; *s* of Kenneth William Porter and Vera Porter; *m* 1965, Susan Carolyn James; two *s* three *d. Educ:* Birkenhead Sch.; University Coll., Oxford (BA Hons). Admitted solicitor, 1965. Councillor: Birkenhead County Bor. Council, 1967–74; Wirral Bor., 1975–79 (Chm., Housing Cttee, 1976–77, and Educn Cttee, 1977–79). Member: Select Cttee on Trade and Industry; All Party Parly Solicitors Gp; British-Irish Inter-Parly Body. *Recreations:* golf, Rugby Union football, watching cricket, real ale. *Address:* House of Commons, SW1A 0AA. *Clubs:* Royal Automobile; Oxton Conservative, Ellesmere Port Conservative; Birkenhead Park Football, Birkenhead Squash Racquets, Oxton Cricket. *Died 3 Nov. 1996.*

PORTER, Stanley; *see* Porter, W. S.

PORTER, Thea; *see* Porter, D. N. N.

PORTER, (Walter) Stanley, TD 1950; MA; Headmaster of Framlingham College, 1955–71; *b* 28 Sept. 1909; *s* of late Walter Porter, Rugby; *m* 1937, Doreen (*d* 1992), *o d* of B. Haynes, Rugby; one *d. Educ:* Rugby Sch.; Gonville and Caius Coll., Cambridge (MA). Assistant Master and Officer Commanding Training Corps, Trent Coll., 1933–36; Felsted Sch., 1936–43; Radley Coll., 1944–55. FRSA 1968. *Recreations:* travel, amateur dramatics; formerly Rugby football, hockey. *Address:* 28 Grove Court, Beech Way, Woodbridge, Suffolk IP12 4BW. *T:* (01394) 382340. *Died 6 July 2000.*

PORTLAND, 11th Earl of, *cr* 1689; **Henry Noel Bentinck;** Viscount Woodstock, Baron Cirencester, 1689; Count of the Holy Roman Empire; *b* 2 Oct. 1919; *s* of Capt. Count Robert Bentinck (*d* 1932) and Lady Norah Ida Emily Noel (*d* 1939), *d* of 3rd Earl of Gainsborough; *S* to Earldom of kinsman, 9th Duke of Portland, CMG, 1990; *m* 1st, 1940, Pauline (*d* 1967), *y d* of late Frederick William Mellowes; one *s* two *d*; 2nd, 1974, Jenifer, *d* of late Reginald Hopkins. *Heir: s* Viscount Woodstock [*b* 1 June 1953; *m* 1979, Judith Ann, *d* of John Robert Emerson; two *s*]. *Died 30 Jan. 1997.*

PORTMAN, 9th Viscount *cr* 1873; **Edward Henry Berkeley Portman;** Baron 1837; *b* 22 April 1934; *s* of late Hon. Michael Berkeley Portman (*d* 1959) (*yr s* of 7th Viscount), and June Charles (*d* 1947); *S* uncle, 1967; *m* 1st, 1956, Rosemary Farris (marr. diss. 1965); one *s* one *d*; 2nd, 1966, Penelope Allin; three *s* (and one *s* decd). *Educ:* Canford; Royal Agricultural College. Farmer. *Recreations:* shooting, fishing, music. *Heir: s* Hon. Christopher Edward Berkeley Portman [*b* 30 July 1958; *m* 1983, Caroline Steenson (marr. diss.); one *s*; *m* 1987, Patricia Martins Pim, *er d* of Senhor Bernardino Pim; two *s*]. *Address:* Clock Mill, Clifford, Herefordshire HR3 5HB. *T:* (01497) 831235. *Club:* White's.
Died 2 May 1999.

POST, Col Kenneth Graham, CBE 1945; TD; *b* 21 Jan. 1908; *s* of Donnell Post and Hon. Margaret Mary, *e d* of 1st Baron Muir-Mackenzie, GCB, PC, KC; *m* 1st, 1944, Stephanie Bonté Wood (marr. diss. 1963); one *s* two *d*; 2nd, 1963, Diane Allen; two *s. Educ:* Winchester; Magdalen Coll., Oxford. London Stock Exchange, 1929–37; 2nd Lieut, RA (TA) 1937; Norway, 1940; War Office, 1941–42; Ministry of Supply, 1943–44; Ministry of Works, 1945–47; Ministry of Housing, 1956–57; Ministry of Defence, 1957–59. Member, Corby New Town Development Corporation, 1955–62; Co-founder and Director, Civic Trust, 1957–63. *Address:* 3 Shepherds

Walk, Pembury Road, Tunbridge Wells, Kent TN2 3QR. *T:* (01892) 548560. *Club:* Pratt's.

Died 22 Feb. 1998.

POTTER, Arthur Kingscote, CMG 1957; CBE (mil.) 1946; *b* Dublin, 7 April 1905; *s* of late Richard Ellis Potter, Ridgewood, Almondsbury, Glos and Harriott Isabel Potter (*née* Kingscote), Kingscote, Glos; *m* 1950, Hilda, *d* of late W. A. Butterfield, OBE; one *d. Educ:* Charterhouse; New Coll., Oxford (BA). Entered Indian CS, 1928; posted to Burma; in charge of Pegu earthquake relief, 1930–31; District Comr, 1934; Controller of Finance ('reserved' subjects), 1937; Financial Adviser, Army in Burma, 1942 (despatches); Finance Secretary, Government of Burma (in Simla), 1942–43; Financial Adviser (Brigadier), 11th Army Group, 1943, and Allied Land Forces, South-East Asia, 1943–44; Chief Financial Officer (Brig.), Military Administration of Burma, 1944–47; HM Treasury Representative in India, Pakistan and Burma, 1947–50; Asst Secretary, HM Treasury, 1950–56; Counsellor, UK Delegation to NATO, Paris, 1956–65. *Address:* Lower House Barns, Bepton, Midhurst, W Sussex GU29 0JB.

Died 25 Feb. 1998.

POTTER, (Ronald) Jeremy; Director, Constable & Co. (Publishers), since 1980; *b* 25 April 1922; *s* of Alistair Richardson Potter and Mairi Chalmers (*née* Dick); *m* 1950, Margaret, *d* of Bernard Newman; one *s* one *d. Educ:* Clifton Coll.; Queen's Coll., Oxford (Neale Exhibnr, MA). Served War, Intell. Officer, Indian Army. Manager, subseq. Man. Dir, Dep. Chm., New Statesman, 1951–69; Man. Dir, Independent Television Publications Ltd, 1970–79; Chm., Independent Television Books Ltd, 1971–79; Chm., Hutchinson Ltd, 1982–84 (Dir, 1978–84; Dep. Chm., 1980–82); Director: Page and Moy (Holdings) plc, 1979–88; LWT (Holdings) plc, 1979–92. Pres., Periodical Publishers Assoc., 1978–79; Appeals Chm., Newsvendors' Benevolent Instn, 1979; Chairman: Twickenham Arts Council, 1967–68; Richard III Soc., 1971–89; Oxford Playhouse Trust, 1990–92. FRSA. Captain, Hampstead Hockey Club, 1954–57; World Amateur over 60s Champion, Real tennis, 1986–88. *Publications:* Good King Richard?, 1983; Pretenders, 1986; Independent Television in Britain, Vol. 3: Politics and Control 1968–80, 1989, Vol. 4: Companies and Programmes 1968–80, 1990; Tennis and Oxford, 1994; Headmaster: the life of John Percival, radical autocrat, 1998; *novels:* Hazard Chase, 1964; Death in Office, 1965; Foul Play, 1967; The Dance of Death, 1968; A Trail of Blood, 1970; Going West, 1972; Disgrace and Favour, 1975; Death in the Forest, 1977; The Primrose Hill Murder, 1992; The Mystery of the Campden Wonder, 1995. *Recreations:* reading, writing, Real tennis. *Address:* The Old Pottery, Larkins Lane, Headington, Oxford OX3 9DW. *Clubs:* Garrick, MCC, Puritans Hockey.

Died 15 Nov. 1997.

POTTER, Dr Timothy William, FSA; Keeper of Prehistoric and Romano-British Antiquities, British Museum, since 1995; *b* 6 July 1944; *yr s* of late Cedric Hardcastle Potter and Phyllis Potter (*née* Rendall); *m* 1985, Sandra Caroline Bailey; one *s* one *d. Educ:* March Grammar Sch.; Trinity Coll., Cambridge (Sen. Scholar; MA, PhD 1974). FSA 1980. Rome Scholar in Classical Studies, British Sch. at Rome, 1966–68; Vis. Prof. in Archaeology, Univ. of Calif, Santa Cruz, 1969–70; Ellaina Macnamara Meml Fellow, Rome, 1971–72; Sir James Knott Fellow, Univ. of Newcastle upon Tyne, 1972–73; Lectr in Archaeology, Lancaster Univ., 1973–78; British Museum: Asst Keeper, Dept of Prehistory and Roman Britain, 1978–89; Dep. Keeper, 1989–95. Mem., Faculty of Archaeol., Hist. and Letters, Brit. Sch. at Rome, 1975–79 and 1989–91 (Chm., 1991–96). Pres., Royal Archaeol. Inst., 1999–. Trustee, Roman Research Trust, 1998–. *Publications:* A Faliscan

Town in South Etruria: excavations at Narce, 1976; The Changing Landscape of South Etruria, 1979; Romans in North-West England: excavations at Ravenglass, Watercrook and Bowness on Solway, 1979; (with C. F. Potter) A Romano-British Village at Grandford, March, Cambs, 1982; Roman Britain, 1983, 2nd edn 1997; (with C. M. Johns) The Thetford Treasure, 1983; Roman Italy, 1987; (with S. D. Trow) Puckeridge-Braughing, Hertfordshire: the Ermine Street excavations, 1988; Una stipe votiva da Ponte di Nona, 1989; (with C. M. Johns) Roman Britain, 1992; (with N. Benseddik) Fouilles du Forum de Cherchel: rapport final, 1993; Towns in Late Antiquity, 1995; (with R. P. J. Jackson) Excavations at Stonea, Cambridgeshire, 1996; Excavations at the Mola di Monte Gelato, 1997. *Recreations:* listening to cricket commentary, drawing. *Address:* Summerfield, 6 Sydenham Avenue, SE26 6UH.

Died 11 Jan. 2000.

POTTINGER, (William) George; *b* 11 June 1916; *e s* of late Rev. William Pottinger, MA, Orkney, and Janet Woodcock; *m* 1946, Margaret Rutherfurd Clark McGregor; one *s. Educ:* George Watson's Coll., Edinburgh; High School of Glasgow; Edinburgh Univ.; Heidelberg; Queens' Coll., Cambridge (Major Scholar). Served War of 1939–45, RFA; France, N Africa, Italy (despatches), Lieut-Col RA. Entered Scottish Home Dept, as Assistant Principal, 1939; Principal, 1945; Private Secretary to successive Secretaries of State for Scotland, 1950–52; Asst Secretary, Scottish Home Dept, 1952; Secretary, Royal Commn on Scottish Affairs, 1952–54; Under-Secretary: Scottish Home Dept, 1959–62; Scottish Home and Health Dept, 1962–63; Scottish Development Dept, 1963–64; Scottish Office, 1964–68; Dept of Agriculture and Fisheries for Scotland, 1968–71; Secretary, Dept of Agriculture and Fisheries for Scotland, 1971. *Publications:* The Winning Counter, 1971, Mun held and the Honourable Company, 1972; St Moritz: an Alpine caprice, 1972; The Court of the Medici, 1977; The Secretaries of State for Scotland 1926–76, 1979; Whisky Sour, 1979; The Afghan Connection, 1983; Mayo, Disraeli's Viceroy, 1990; (with Sir Patrick Macrory) The Ten Rupee Jezail, 1993; Heirs of the Enlightenment, 1993; The Real Admirable Crichton, 1995; Sir Henry Pottinger: first Governor of Hong Kong, 1997; papers and reviews. *Recreations:* Real tennis, golf, fishing. *Address:* West Lodge, Balsham, Cambridge CB1 6EP. *T:* (01223) 892958. *Club:* Savile.

Died 15 Jan. 1998.

POTTS, Peter; JP; General Secretary, General Federation of Trade Unions, 1977–94; *b* 29 June 1935; *s* of late John Peter Potts and of Margaret (*née* Combs); *m* 1st, 1956, Mary Longden (*d* 1972); two *s* one *d*; 2nd, 1974, Angela Elouisc van Lieshout (*née* Liddelow); one step *s* one step *d. Educ:* Chorlton High Sch., Manchester; Ruskin Coll., Oxford; Oxford Univ. (Dip. in Econs and Pol Science). Served RAF, 1953–55. USDAW, 1951–65; Res. Officer, Union of Tailors and Garment Workers, 1965–74; National Officer, Clerical and Supervisory Staffs, 1974–77. Member: Clothing EDC, 1970–77 (Trade Union Advisor, 1966–70); Jt Textile Cttee, NEDO, 1970–77; Trade Union Unit Trust Investors Cttee, 1977–94 (Chm., 1984–94); Trade Union Res. Unit, 1975– (Chm., 1984–); Trade Union Internat. Res. and Educn Gp, 1979– (Chm., 1994–); Press Council, 1987–90; Governing Council, Ruskin Coll., 1977– (Mem. Exec. Cttee, 1977–; Vice-Chm., 1984–). JP N Beds, 1983. *Recreations:* do-it-yourself hobbies, art, listening to jazz. *Address:* 3 Tadmere, Two Mile Ash, Milton Keynes, Bucks MK8 8DG.

Died 30 Jan. 1996.

POUNCEY, Denys Duncan Rivers, FRCO; Organist and Master of the Choristers, Wells Cathedral, 1936–70; Conductor of Wells Cathedral Oratorio Chorus and

Orchestra, 1946–66; Hon. Diocesan Choirmaster, Bath and Wells Choral Association, 1946–70; *b* 23 Dec. 1906; *s* of late Rev. George Ernest Pouncey and Madeline Mary Roberts; *m* 1st, 1937, Evelyn Cottier (*d* 1981); 2nd, 1996, Edith Joan Hensley. *Educ:* Marlborough College; Queens' College, Cambridge (MusB, MA). Asst to Dr Cyril Rootham, Organist and Choirmaster of St John's Coll., Cambridge, 1928–34; Organist and Choirmaster, St Matthew's, Northampton, 1934–36; Founder Conductor of Northampton Bach Choir. *Address:* 4 Watery Lane, Minehead, Somerset TA24 5NZ.

Died 18 July 1999.

POWDITCH, Alan Cecil Robert, MC 1944; JP; District Administrator, NW District, Kensington and Chelsea and Westminster Area Health Authority, 1974–77, retired; *b* 14 April 1912; *s* of Cecil John and Annis Maudie Powditch; *m* 1942, Barbara Leggat (*d* 1992); one *s* one d. *Educ:* Mercers School. Entered Hospital Service, 1933; Accountant, St Mary's Hospital, W2, 1938. Served War of 1939–45, with 51st Royal Tank Regt, 1941–46. Dep. House Governor, St Mary's Hospital, 1947–50, Sec. to Bd of Governors, 1950–74. Mem., Nat. Staff Cttee (Min. of Health), 1964–72; Chm., Juvenile Panel, Gore Div., 1973–76. Mem. Council, Sue Ryder Foundn, 1977–85; Mem. Magistrates' Courts Cttee, 1979–81. JP Co. Middlesex 1965, Supp. List 1982. *Recreations:* golf; interested in gardening when necessary.

Died 15 Nov. 1997.

POWELL, Anthony Dymoke, CH 1988; CBE 1956; *b* 21 Dec. 1905; *o s* of late Lt-Col P. L. W. Powell, CBE, DSO and Maud M. Wells-Dymoke; *m* 1934, Lady Violet Pakenham, 3rd *d* of 5th Earl of Longford, KP; two *s*. *Educ:* Eton; Balliol College, Oxford (MA; Hon. Fellow, 1974). Served War of 1939–45, Welch Regt and Intelligence Corps, Major. A Trustee, National Portrait Gallery, 1962–76. Hon. Mem., Amer. Acad. of Arts and Letters, 1977; Hon. Fellow, Mod. Lang. Assoc. of Amer., 1981. Hon. DLitt: Sussex, 1971; Leicester, 1976; Kent, 1976; Oxon, 1980; Bristol, 1982; Wales, 1992; Bath, 1995. Hudson Review Bennett Prize, 1984; T. S. Eliot Prize for Creative Lit., Ingersoll Foundn, 1984. Orders of: the White Lion, (Czechoslovakia); the Oaken Crown and Croix de Guerre (Luxembourg); Leopold II (Belgium). *Publications:* Afternoon Men, 1931 (adapted for stage by Riccardo Aragno, perf. Arts Th. Club, 1963); Venusberg, 1932; From a View to a Death, 1933; Agents and Patients, 1936; What's become of Waring, 1939; John Aubrey and His Friends, 1948, rev. edn 1988; Selections from John Aubrey, 1949; A Dance to the Music of Time, 12 vol. sequence, 1951–75 (televised 1997): A Question of Upbringing, 1951; A Buyer's Market, 1952; The Acceptance World, 1955; At Lady Molly's, 1957 (James Tait Black Memorial Prize); Casanova's Chinese Restaurant, 1960; The Kindly Ones, 1962; The Valley of Bones, 1964; The Soldier's Art, 1966; The Military Philosophers, 1968; Books do Furnish a Room, 1971; Temporary Kings, 1973 (W. H. Smith Prize, 1974); Hearing Secret Harmonies, 1975; O, How The Wheel Becomes It!, 1983; The Fisher King, 1986; The Album of Anthony Powell's Dance to the Music of Time (ed V. Powell), 1987; Miscellaneous Verdicts (criticism), 1990; Under Review (criticism), 1992; *memoirs:* To Keep the Ball Rolling, 4 vols, 1976–82 (abridged one vol. edn 1983); Infants of the Spring, 1976; Messengers of Day, 1978; Faces In My Time, 1980; The Strangers All are Gone, 1982; Journals 1982–1986, 1995; Journals 1987–89, 1996; Journals 1990–1992, 1997; *plays:* The Garden God, 1971; The Rest I'll Whistle, 1971; *posthumous publication:* A Writer's Notebook, 2001. *Address:* The Chantry, near Frome, Somerset BA11 3LJ. *T:* (01373) 836314. *Clubs:* Travellers, Pratt's.

Died 28 March 2000.

POWELL, Rt Hon. Enoch; *see* Powell, Rt Hon. J. E.

POWELL, Geoffry Charles Hamilton; Founding Partner, Chamberlin, Powell & Bon, 1952–85, retired; Consultant, Chamberlin, Powell, Bon and Woods, 1985; *b* 7 Nov. 1920; *s* of late Col D. H. Powell and Violet (*née* Timins); *m* 1st, 1954, Philippa Cooper (marr. diss.); two *d* (one *s* decd); 2nd, 1971, Dorothy Louise Grenfell Williams (head, African Service, BBC) (*d* 1994); one *s*. *Educ:* Wellington College; AA School of Architecture. RIBA; AA Dipl. Asst to Frederick Gibberd, 1944, to Brian O'Rorke, 1946; teaching at Kingston School of Art (School of Architecture), 1949. Work included: Golden Lane Estate; expansion of Leeds Univ.; schools, houses, commercial buildings; Barbican. Member: Council, Architectural Assoc., 1969–75; SE Economic Planning Council, 1967–69. *Recreations:* travel, painting. *Address:* Glen Cottage, River Lane, Petersham, Surrey TW10 7AG. *T:* (020) 8940 6286.

Died 17 Dec. 1999.

POWELL, John Alfred, MA, DPhil; CEng, FIEE; FRSE; consultant; *b* 4 Nov. 1923; *s* of Algernon Powell and Constance Elsie (*née* Honour); *m* 1949, Zena Beatrice (*née* Steventon); one *s* one d. *Educ:* Bicester County Sch.; The Queen's Coll., Oxford. No 1 Sch. of Technical Trng, RAF Halton, 1940–42; The Queen's Coll., Oxford, 1945–48; DPhil, Clarendon Lab., Oxford, 1948–51. Post-Doctorate Research Fellowship, Nat. Research Council, Ottawa, Canada, 1952–54; Marconi Research Labs, 1954–57; Texas Instruments Ltd: joined, 1957; Gen. Manager, 1959; Man. Dir, 1963; Asst Vice-Pres., TI Inc. (US), 1968; EMI Ltd: Main Bd Dir, Group Tech. Dir, 1971; Dir, Commercial Electronics, 1972; Dep. Man. Dir, 1973; Gp Man. Dir, 1974–78; Vice Chm., 1978–79. Mem., Honeywell Adv. Council, 1978–82. Faraday Lectr, 1978–79. CBIM (FBIM 1974); FRSA 1975; SMIEE (US). Member: Electronic Components Bd, 1968–71; Court of Cranfield Coll. of Technology, 1968–72; Electronics Research Council, 1972–74; Cttee of Inquiry into Engrg Profession, 1977–80; Physical Scis Sub-Cttee, UGC, 1980–85. Hon. Mem., BIR, 1980. *Recreations:* arts, sports, the rural scene. *Address:* Kym House, 21 Buccleuch Road, Branksome Park, Poole, Dorset BH13 6LF.

Died 31 Dec. 1996.

POWELL, Rt Hon. (John) Enoch, MBE 1943; PC 1960; MA; *b* 16 June 1912; *s* of Albert Enoch Powell and Ellen Mary Breese; *m* 1952, Margaret Pamela, *d* of Lt-Col L. E. Wilson, IA; two d. *Educ:* King Edward's, Birmingham; Trinity College, Cambridge (Craven Scholar, 1931; First Chancellor's Classical Medallist; Porson Prizeman; Browne Medallist, 1932; BA; Craven Travelling Student, 1933; MA 1937). Dip. in Oriental and African Studies. Fellow of Trinity College, Cambridge, 1934–38; Professor of Greek in the University of Sydney, NSW, 1937–39. Pte and Lance Cpl Royal Warwickshire Regt, 1939–40; 2nd Lieut General List, 1940; Captain, General Staff, 1940–41; Major, General Staff, 1941; Lieut-Col, GS, 1942; Col, GS, 1944; Brig. 1944. MP: (C) Wolverhampton SW, 1950–Feb. 1974; (UU) Down South, Oct. 1974–1983, South Down, 1983–87 (resigned seat Dec. 1985 in protest against Anglo-Irish Agreement; re-elected Jan. 1986); contested (UU) South Down, 1987. Parly Sec., Ministry of Housing and Local Government, Dec. 1955–Jan. 1957; Financial Secretary to the Treasury, 1957–58; Minister of Health, July 1960–Oct. 1963. *Publications:* The Rendel Harris Papyri, 1936; First Poems, 1937; A Lexicon to Herodotus, 1938; The History of Herodotus, 1939; Casting-off, and other poems, 1939; Herodotus, Book VIII, 1939; Llyfr Blegywryd, 1942; Thucydidis Historia, 1942; Herodotus (trans.), 1949; (jtly) One Nation, 1950; Dancer's End and The Wedding Gift (poems), 1951; The Social Services, Needs and Means, 1952; Change is our Ally, 1954; Biography of a Nation (with Angus Maude),

1955, 2nd edn 1970; Great Parliamentary Occasions, 1960; Saving in a Free Society, 1960; A Nation not Afraid, 1965; Medicine and Politics, 1966, rev. edn 1976; The House of Lords in the Middle Ages (with Keith Wallis), 1968; Freedom and Reality, 1969; Common Market: the case against, 1971; Still to Decide, 1972; Common Market: renegotiate or come out, 1973; No Easy Answers, 1973; Wrestling with the Angel, 1977; Joseph Chamberlain, 1977; A Nation or No Nation (ed R. Ritchie), 1978; Enoch Powell on 1992 (ed R. Ritchie), 1989; Collected Poems, 1990; The Evolution of the Gospel, 1994; numerous political pamphlets. *Address:* 33 South Eaton Place, SW1W 9EN. *T:* (0171) 730 0988. *Club:* Athenæum.

Died 8 Feb. 1998.

POWELL, Lewis Franklin, Jr; Associate Justice of US Supreme Court, 1971–87, retired; *b* Suffolk, Va, USA, 19 Sept. 1907; *s* of Lewis Franklin Powell and Mary Lewis (*née* Gwathmey); *m* 1936, Josephine Pierce Rucker (*d* 1996); one *s* three *d. Educ:* McGuire's Univ. Sch., Richmond, Va; Washington and Lee Univ., Lexington, Va (BS *magnum cum laude*, LLB); Harvard Law Sch. (LLM). Admitted to practice, Bar of Virginia, 1931; subseq. practised law; partner in firm of Hunton, Williams, Gay, Powell and Gibson, in Richmond, 1938–71. Member: Nat. Commn on Law Enforcement and Admin of Justice, 1965–67; Blue Ribbon Defence Panel, 1969–70. Chairman or Dir of companies. Pres., Virginia State Bd of Educn; Past Chm. and Trustee, Colonial Williamsburg Foundn; Trustee, Washington and Lee Univ., etc. Mem., Amer. Bar Assoc. (Pres. 1964–65); Fellow, Amer. Bar Foundn (Pres. 1969–71); Pres. or Mem. various Bar Assocs and other legal and social instns; Hon. Bencher, Lincoln's Inn. Held several hon. degrees. Phi Beta Kappa. A Democrat. Served War, May 1942–Feb. 1946, USAAF, overseas, to rank Col; subseq. Col US Reserve. Legion of Merit and Bronze Star (US), also Croix de Guerre with Palms (France). *Publications:* contribs to legal periodicals, etc. *Address:* c/o Supreme Court Building, 1 First Street NE, Washington, DC 20543, USA. *Club:* University (NYC).

Died 25 Aug. 1998.

POWELL, Robert William; Headmaster of Sherborne, 1950–70; retired; *b* 29 Oct. 1909; *s* of late William Powell and Agnes Emma Powell; *m* 1938, Charity Rosamond Collard; one *s. Educ:* Bristol Grammar School; Christ Church, Oxford. Assistant Master, Repton, May-Dec. 1934; Assistant Master, Charterhouse, 1935; served War of 1939–45, 1940–45; Housemaster of Gownboys, Charterhouse, 1946–50. *Recreations:* fishing, music. *Address:* Manor Farm House, Child Okeford, near Blandford, Dorset DT11 8EE. *T:* (01258) 860648.

Died 23 April 1998.

POWELL, Victor George Edward; Senior Partner, Victor G. Powell Associates, Management Consultants, 1963–88; Professor of Management, ILO International Centre for Advanced Training, 1982–88; Director, Mosscare Housing Association Ltd, 1974–88; retired; *b* London, 1 Jan. 1929; *s* of George Richard Powell and Kate Hughes Powell, London; *m* 1956, Patricia Copeland Allen; three *s* one *d. Educ:* Beckenham Grammar Sch.; Univs of Durham and Manchester. BA 1st cl. hons Econs 1954, MA Econ. Studies 1957, Dunelm; PhD Manchester 1963. RN Engrg Apprentice, 1944–48. Central Work Study Dept, ICI, London, 1954–56; Chief Work Study Engr, Ind Coope Ltd, 1956–58; Lectr in Industrial Administration, Manchester Univ., 1959, Hon. Lectr 1959–63; Asst Gen. Manager, Louis C. Edwards & Sons Ltd, 1959–63; Chm., Food Production & Processing Ltd, 1971–74. Sen. Advr, 1976, Dir and Chief Advr, 1977–82, ILO. Gen. Sec., 1970–72, Dir, 1972–73, War on Want. MBIM 1957; Mem. Inst. Management Consultants, 1968. *Publications:* Economics of Plant Investment and Replacement

Decisions, 1964; Techniques for Improving Distribution Management, 1968; Warehousing, 1976; Improving the Performance of Public Enterprises, 1986; various articles. *Recreations:* music, walking. *Address:* Knowles House, Hollin Lane, Sutton, Macclesfield, Cheshire SK11 0HR. *T:* (01260) 252334. *Died 14 May 1997.*

POYNTON, Sir (Arthur) Hilton, GCMG 1964 (KCMG 1949; CMG 1946); *b* 20 April 1905; *y s* of late Arthur Blackburne Poynton, formerly Master of University College, Oxford, and Mary, *e d* of J. Y. Sargent, Fellow of Hertford College; *m* 1946, Elisabeth Joan, *d* of late Rev. Edmund Williams; two *s* one *d. Educ:* Marlborough Coll.; Brasenose Coll., Oxford (Hon. Fellow 1964). Entered Civil Service, Department of Scientific and Industrial Research, 1927; transferred to Colonial Office, 1929; Private Secretary to Minister of Supply and Minister of Production 1941–43; reverted to Colonial Office, 1943; Permanent Under-Secretary of State, CO, 1959–66. Mem. Governing Body, SPCK, 1967–72. Mem., Ct of Governors, London Sch. Hygiene and Tropical Med., 1965–77; Treas., Soc. Promotion Roman Studies, 1967–76; Dir, Overseas Branch, St John Ambulance, 1968–75. KStJ 1968. *Recreations:* music, travel. *Address:* Craigmillar, 47 Stanhope Road, Croydon CR0 5NS. *T:* 0181–688 3729.

Died 24 Feb. 1996.

PRATLEY, Clive William; Under Secretary, Lord Chancellor's Department, 1976–85; Circuit Administrator: Midland and Oxford Circuit, 1976–82; North-Eastern Circuit, 1982–85; a Reference Secretary (reserve panel), Monopolies and Mergers Commission, 1990–92; *b* 23 Jan. 1929; *s* of late F. W. Pratley and Minnie Pratley (*née* Hood); *m* 1962, Eva, *d* of late Nils and of Kerstin Kellgren, Stockholm; one *s* one *d. Educ:* RMA Sandhurst; and after retirement from Army, at Univs of Stockholm, 1961–62, and Hull, 1962–65 (LLB Hons). Commissioned into Royal Tank Regt, 1949; active list, 1949–61; Adjt, 2nd RTR, 1959–61; reserve list, 1961–79; Hon. Captain, 1979–. Entered Administrative Class of Home Civil Service as Principal, 1966; Lord Chancellor's Department: Sen. Principal, 1971; Asst Sec., 1974; Under Sec., 1976. *Recreations:* (before disablement) offshore and ocean sailing (RYA coastal skipper; Cape Horner, 1992), the countryside, badminton, music. *Address:* The Old Chapel, Aldfield, near Ripon, North Yorkshire HG4 3BE. *T:* Sawley (01765) 620277. *Died 16 March 1996.*

PRATT, Anthony Malcolm G.; *see* Galliers-Pratt.

PRATT, (Ewart) George, CVO 1986; Trustee, The Prince's Trust, 1976–94 (Chairman, 1978–86; Hon. Administrator, 1976–78); *b* 10 Oct. 1917; *s* of George William Pratt and Florence (*née* Redding); *m* 1948, Margaret Heath; two *s. Educ:* an independent sch.; London Sch. of Economics and Political Science (Dip. Social Sci. and Public Admin). Successively, probation officer, sen. probation officer, asst chief and, from 1970, dep. chief probation officer, Inner London Probation Service, 1949–81. Member numerous govtl, professional and charitable adv. gps, including: Cttee on the Voluntary Worker in the Social Services, 1966–69; Home Office Working Party on Community Service by Offenders, 1971–72; Social Responsibility Cttees of the Baptist Union and BCC, and Sec., a church-related housing assoc., 1964–81. Chm., Assoc. of Social Workers, 1959–70; Founder-Gov., Nat. Inst. for Social Work, 1961–71; Treas., BASW, 1970–73; Vice Pres., REACT. Elder, URC. Silver Jubilee Medal, 1977. *Publications:* essays and articles on issues relating to field of criminal justice and treatment of offenders. *Recreations:* music, theatre, travel. *Died 3 Aug. 1999.*

PRELOG, Prof. Dr Vladimir; Professor of Organic Chemistry, Swiss Federal Institute of Technology, 1950–76, retired; *b* 23 July 1906; *s* of Milan Prelog and

Maria Cettolo; *m* 1933, Kamila Vitek; one *s. Educ:* Inst. of Technology, Prague. Chemist, Prague, 1929–34; Lecturer and Professor, University of Zagreb, 1935–41; Privatdozent, Swiss Federal Inst. of Technology, Zürich, 1941, Associate Professor, 1947, Full Professor, 1950. Mem. Bd, CIBA-GEIGY Ltd, Basel, 1960–78. Vis. Prof. of Chemistry, Univ. of Cambridge, 1974. Mem., Deutsche Akademie der Naturforscher Leopoldina, Halle/Saale, 1963; Hon. Member: American Acad. of Arts and Sciences, 1960; Chem. Society, 1960; Nat. Acad. of Sciences, Washington, 1961; Royal Irish Acad., Dublin, 1971; Foreign Member: Royal Society, 1962; Acad. of Sciences, USSR, 1966; Acad. dei Lincei, Roma 1965; Istituto Lombardo, Milano, 1964; Royal Danish Acad. of Sciences, 1971; Amer. Philosophical Soc., Philadelphia, 1976; Acad. of Sciences, Paris, 1981; Mem., Pontifical Acad. of Sciences, 1986. Dr *hc* Universities of: Zagreb, 1954; Liverpool, 1963; Paris, 1963; Bruxelles, 1969; Weizmann Inst., Rehovot, 1985; Hon. DSc: Cambridge, 1969; Manchester, 1977; Inst. Quimico Sarria, Barcelona, 1978; Edvard Kardelj Univ. of Ljubljana, 1989; Univ. of Osijek, 1989; Prague Inst. of Chemical Technol., 1992; Univ. of Sarajevo. Davy Medal, Royal Society, 1967; A. W. Hofmann Medal, Gesell. deutscher Chem., 1967; Marcel Benoist Prize, 1965; Roger Adams Award, 1969; (jtly) Nobel Prize for Chemistry, 1975. Order of Rising Sun, Japan, 1977; Order of Yugoslav Star, 1977; Order of Yugoslav Banner with Golden Wreath, 1986. *Publications:* numerous scientific papers, mainly in Helvetica chimica acta. *Address:* (office) Laboratorium für organische Chemie, ETH-Zentrum, Universitätstrasse 16, 8092 Zürich, Switzerland; (homc) Bellariastrasse 33, 8002 Zürich. *T:* (1) 2021781. *Died 6 Jan. 1998.*

PRENDERGAST, (Christopher) Anthony, CBE 1981; DL; Chairman, Dolphin Square Trust Ltd, since 1967; Director General, Location of Industry Bureau Ltd, since 1983; *b* 4 May 1931; *s* of Maurice Prendergast, AINA, and Winifred Mary Prendergast, Falmouth; *m* 1959, Simone Ruth Laski (Dame S. R. Prendergast, DBE); one *s. Educ:* Falmouth Grammar School. Westminster City Council: Mem., 1959–90; Chairman: Housing Cttee, 1962–65; Health Cttee, 1965–68; Town Planning Cttee, 1972–75, 1976–78; Gen. Purposes Cttee, 1978–80; Management Services, 1981–83; Licensing Sub Cttee, 1983–90; Lord Mayor and Dep. High Steward of Westminster, 1968–69; High Sheriff of Greater London, 1980. Additional Mem., GLC (Covent Garden Cttee), 1971–75; Member: London Boroughs Trng Cttee, 1965–68; Docklands Develt Cttee, 1974; AMA Cttee, 1976–89; Nat Jt Council (Manual Workers), 1978–82, 1983–89; Conf. of Regl and Local Authorities of Europe, 1983–89. Chairman: Location of Offices Bureau, 1971–79; LACSAB, 1983–89; Joint Negotiating Cttee for Chief Execs of Local Authorities, 1984–89, for Chief Officers of Local Authorities, 1984–89; Gen. Purposes Cttee, London Boroughs Assoc., 1986–90. Mem., LEB, 1983–89; Dir, LE plc, 1990–94. Governor, Westminster Sch., 1974–. Master, Pattenmakers' Co., 1983–84. DL Greater London, 1988. FRSA 1984. *Recreations:* fishing, shooting, photography. *Address:* 52 Warwick Square, SW1V 2AJ. *T:* (0171) 821 7653. *Clubs:* Carlton, Irish, MCC. *Died 22 Jan. 1998.*

PRESSMAN, Claudette, (Mrs Joel J. Pressman); *see* Colbert, C.

PRESTON, Sir Peter (Sansome), KCB 1978 (CB 1973); Permanent Secretary, Overseas Development Administration, Foreign and Commonwealth Office (formerly Ministry of Overseas Development), 1976–82; *b* Nottingham, 18 Jan. 1922; *s* of Charles Guy Preston, solicitor; *m* 1951, Marjory Harrison; two *s* three *d. Educ:* Nottingham High School. War Service, RAF, 1942–46;

Board of Trade: Exec. Officer, 1947; Higher Exec. Off., 1950; Asst Principal, 1951; Principal, 1953; Trade Comr, New Delhi, 1959; Asst Sec., 1964; idc 1968; Under-Sec., BoT, later DTI, 1969–72; Dep. Sec., Dept of Trade, 1972–76. Mem., BOTB, 1975–76. Dir, Wellcome Internat. Trading Co. Ltd, 1985–92; Dep. Chm., CARE Britain, 1985–95. *Address:* 5 Greville Park Avenue, Ashtead, Surrey KT21 2QS. *T:* Ashtead (01372) 272099.
Died 9 Feb. 1996.

PRESTON, Prof. Reginald Dawson, FRS 1954; Professor of Plant Biophysics, 1953–73 and Head, Astbury Department of Biophysics, 1962–73, University of Leeds, then Professor Emeritus; *b* 21 July 1908; *s* of late Walter C. Preston, builder, and Eliza Preston; *m* 1935, Sarah J. Pollard (decd); two *d* (one *s* decd); *m* 1963, Dr Eva Frei. *Educ:* Leeds Univ. (BSc Hons Physics, Class I, 1929; PhD Botany, 1931; 1851 Exhibition Fellowship, 1932–35; DSc 1943); Cornell Univ., USA (Rockefeller Foundation Fellowship, 1935–36). CPhys; FInstP 1944. University of Leeds: Lecturer, Botany Dept, 1936–46; Sen. Lectr, 1946–49; Reader, 1949–53; Dean, Faculty of Science, 1955–58; Chm., Sch. of Biol Scis, 1970–73. Vis. Prof. of Botany, Imperial Coll., London, 1976–79. Mem. NY Acad. Sci., 1960. Hon. Mem., Internat. Assoc. of Wood Anatomists, 1981. FLS 1958; FIWSc 1960; FIAWS 1973. Anselme Payen Award, Amer. Chem. Soc., 1983; Dist. Service Medal, Leeds Phil. Lit. Soc., 1983. Editor: Proc. Leeds Phil. Soc. Sci. Sect., 1950–74; Advances in Botanical Research, 1968–77; Associate Editor, Jl Exp. Bot., 1950–77. *Publications:* Molecular Architecture of Plant Cell Walls, 1952; Physical Biology of Plant Cell Walls, 1974; about 180 articles in Proc. Royal Soc., Nature, Ann. Bot., Biochem. Biophys Acta, Jl Exp. Bot., etc. *Recreations:* walking, climbing, music. *Address:* 117 St Anne's Road, Leeds, West Yorks LS6 3NZ. *T:* (0113) 278 5248. *Died 3 May 2000.*

PRESTON of Ardchattan, Robert Modan Thorne C.; *see* Campbell-Preston.

PRESTON, Sir Ronald (Douglas Hildebrand), 7th Bt *cr* 1815, of Beeston St Lawrence, Norfolk; HM Diplomatic Service, retired; country landowner; journalist, retired; *b* 9 Oct. 1916; *s* of Sir Thomas Hildebrand Preston, 6th Bt, OBE, and Ella Henrietta (*d* 1989), *d* of F. von Schickendantz; *S* father, 1976; *m* 1st, 1954, Smilya Stefanovic (marr. diss. 1971); 2nd, 1972, Pauleen Jane, *d* of late Paul Lurcott. *Educ:* Westminster School; Trinity Coll., Cambridge (Hons History and Economics, MA); Ecole des Sciences Politiques, Paris. Served War, 1940–46, in Intelligence Corps, reaching rank of Major: Western Desert, Middle East, Italy, Austria, Allied Control Commn, Bulgaria. Reuter's Correspondent, Belgrade, Yugoslavia, 1948–53; The Times Correspondent: Vienna and E Europe, 1953–60; Tokyo and Far East, 1960–63; HM Diplomatic Service, 1963–76; retired, 1976. *Recreations:* shooting, tennis, picture frame making. *Heir: cousin* Philip Charles Henry Hulton Preston [*b* 31 Aug. 1946; *m* 1980, Kirsi Sylvi Annikk, *d* of late Eino Yrjö Pullinen; one *s* two *d*]. *Clubs:* Travellers; Norfolk (Norwich); Tokyo (Tokyo). *Died 4 April 1999.*

PREY, Hermann; baritone; *b* Berlin, 11 July 1929; *s* of Hermann Prey; *m* 1954, Barbara Pniok; one *s* two *d. Educ:* Humanistisches Gymnasium, Berlin; Staatliche Musikhochschule, Berlin. With State Opera, Wiesbaden, 1952; appearances in Germany, Vienna, (La Scala) Milan, (Metropolitan Opera) New York, Buenos Aires, San Francisco, Covent Garden, etc. Festivals include: Salzburg, Bayreuth, Edinburgh, Vienna, Tokyo, Aix-en-Provence, Perugia, Berlin. *Address:* 82152 Krailling vor München, Fichtenstrasse 14, Germany; c/o Kristian Lange, Ludwig

Behr Strasse 7, 82327 Tutzing, Germany; c/o Lies Askonas, 6 Henrietta Street, WC2E 8LA.
Died 23 July 1998.

PRICE, Sir (Charles) Keith (Napier) Rugge-, 9th Bt *cr* 1804, of Spring Grove, Richmond, Surrey; Supervisor, Management and Organisation Design, City of Edmonton, since 1989; *b* 7 Aug. 1936; *s* of Lt-Col Sir Charles James Napier Rugge-Price, 8th Bt, and Lady (Maeve Marguerite) Rugge-Price (*née* de la Peña) (*d* 1995); *S* father, 1966; *m* 1965, Jacqueline Mary (*née* Loranger); two *s. Educ:* Middleton College, Eire. 5th Regt Royal Horse Artillery, Germany and Wales, 1954–59. Actuarial Dept, William Mercers Ltd, Canada, 1959–60; Alexander and Alexander Services Ltd, Montreal, Canada, 1960–67; with Domtar Ltd, 1968–71; Manager, Tomenson Alexander Ltd, Toronto, 1971–76; Supervisor, Compensation, City of Edmonton, 1976–81, Sen. Management Consultant, 1982–89. *Heir: s* James Keith Peter Rugge-Price, *b* 8 April 1967. *Address:* 2 Lorne Crescent, St Albert, AB T8N 3R2, Canada. *Died 22 July 2000.*

PRICE, Very Rev. Hilary Martin Connop; Rector and Provost of Chelmsford, 1967–77, then Provost Emeritus; *b* 1912; *s* of late Rev. Connop Lewis Price and Shirley (*née* Lewis); *m* 1939, Dorothea (*née* Beaty-Pownall); one *s* two *d. Educ:* Cheltenham Coll.; Queens' Coll., Cambridge (MA); Ridley Hall, Cambridge. Deacon 1936, priest 1937; Asst Curate, St Peter's, Hersham, Surrey, 1936–40; Sen. Chaplain, Portsmouth Cathedral, 1940–41; Asst Curate, Holy Trinity, Cambridge, 1941–46; Chaplain, RAFVR, 1943–46; Vicar, St Gabriel's, Bishopwearmouth, 1946–56; Rector and Rural Dean, Newcastle-under Lyme, 1956–67. Prebendary of Lichfield, 1964–67. Proctor in Convocation: of York for Durham Dio., 1954–56; of Canterbury for Lichfield Dio., 1962–67. Mem., General Synod, 1970–75. *Address:* 98 St James Street, Shaftesbury, Dorset SP7 8HF. *T:* (01747) 852118.
Died 22 March 1998.

PRICE, Sir (James) Robert, KBE 1976; FAA 1959; Chairman of the Executive, Commonwealth Scientific and Industrial Research Organization, 1970–77; *b* 25 March 1912; *s* of Edgar James Price and Mary Katherine Price (*née* Hughes); *m* 1940, Joyce Ethel (*née* Brooke); one *s* two *d. Educ:* St Peter's Coll., Adelaide; Univ. of Adelaide (BSc Hons, MSc, DSc), Univ. of Oxford (DPhil). Head, Chemistry Section, John Innes Horticultural Inst., London, 1937–40; (UK) Min. of Supply, 1941–45; Council for Scientific and Industrial Research, later Commonwealth Scientific and Industrial Research Organization: Div. of Industrial Chemistry, 1945; Officer-in-Charge, Organic Chem. Section, 1960, Chief of Div. of Organic Chem., 1961–66; Mem. Executive, 1966–70. Pres., Royal Aust. Chemical Inst., 1963–64. *Publications:* numerous scientific papers in learned jls. *Recreation:* growing Australian native plants. *Address:* Yangoora, 2 Ocean View Avenue, Red Hill South, Victoria 3937, Australia. *Club:* Sciences (Melb.). *Died 8 March 1999.*

PRICE, Sir Leslie Victor, Kt 1976; OBE 1971; Chairman, Australian Wheat Board, 1977–86 (Member, 1971–86); *b* Toowoomba, Qld, 30 Oct. 1920; *s* of late H. V. L. Price; *m* Lorna Collins; one *s* two *d.* President: Queensland Graingrowers Assoc., 1966–77; Australian Wheatgrowers Fedn, 1970–72; Mem., Queensland State Wheat Bd, 1968–77. *Recreation:* clay target shooting. *Address:* 20 Muir Street, Richmond, Vic 3121, Australia. *Clubs:* Queensland (Brisbane); Melbourne (Melbourne).
Died 18 May 1996.

PRICE, Peter S.; *see* Stanley Price.

PRICE, Sir Robert; *see* Price, Sir J. R.

PRICE, William George; *b* 15 June 1934; *s* of George and Lillian Price; *m* 1963, Joy Thomas (marr. diss. 1978); two *s. Educ:* Forest of Dene Technical Coll.; Gloucester Technical Coll. Staff Journalist: Three Forest Newspapers, Cinderford, until 1959; Coventry Evening Telegraph, 1959–62; Birmingham Post & Mail, 1962–66. MP (Lab) Rugby, Warks, 1966–79; Parliamentary Private Secretary: to Sec. of State for Educn and Science, 1968–70; to Dep. Leader, Labour Party, 1972–74; Parliamentary Secretary: ODM, March-Oct. 1974; Privy Council Office, 1974–79. Contested (Lab): Rugby, 1979; Dudley W, 1983. Consultant, Nat. Fedn of Licensed Victuallers, 1979. *Recreation:* sport. *Address:* 53 West Heath Court, Northend Road, NW11 7RG. *Died 6 May 1999.*

PRIESTLEY, Prof. Charles Henry Brian, AO 1976; FAA 1954; FRS 1967; Professor of Meteorology, Monash University, Australia, 1978–80; *b* 8 July 1915; *s* of late T. G. Priestley; *m* 1946, Constance, *d* of H. Tweedy; one *s* two *d. Educ:* Mill Hill Sch.; St John's Coll., Cambridge (MA 1942, ScD 1953). Served in Meteorological Office, Air Ministry, 1939–46; subseq. with CSIRO, Australia; Chief of Div. of Meteorological Physics, 1946–71; Chm., Environmental Physics Res., 1971–78. David Syme Prize, University of Melbourne, 1956. Member Exec. Cttee, International Assoc. of Meteorology, 1954–60, Vice-Pres., 1967–75; Vice-Pres., Australian Acad. of Science, 1959–60; Mem., Adv. Cttee, World Meteorological Organisation, 1964–68 (Chm., 1967; Internat. Met. Orgn Prize, 1973). FRMetSoc (Hon. Life Fellow, 1978; Buchan Prize, 1950; Symons Medal, 1967); FInstP. Hon. Mem., Amer. Met. Soc., 1978 (Rossby Medal, 1975). Hon. DSc Monash, 1981. *Publications:* Turbulent Transfer in the Lower Atmosphere, 1959; about 60 papers in scientific journals. *Recreation:* golf. *Address:* Unit 7, 4 Fraser Street, Malvern, Vic 3144, Australia.
Died 18 May 1998.

PRIESTLEY, Jacquetta, (Mrs J. B. Priestley); *see* Hawkes, J.

PRIME, Prof. Henry Ashworth, CEng, FIEE; Professor of Electronic and Electrical Engineering, University of Birmingham, 1963–86, then Professor Emeritus; *b* 11 March 1921; *s* of late E. V. Prime and Elsie (*née* Ashworth); *m* 1943, Ella Stewart Reid; one *s* one *d. Educ:* N Manchester High Sch.; Manchester Univ. (MSc). CEng, FIEE 1964. Scientific Officer, Admiralty Signal and Radar Estab., 1942–46; Lectr, Univ. of Liverpool, 1946–50; Sen. Lectr, Univ. of Adelaide, 1950–55; Chief Electronic Engr and Manager, Control Div., Brush Elec. Engrg Co., 1955–63. Pro-Vice-Chancellor, Univ. of Birmingham, 1978–82. Visiting Professor: Univ. of Teheran, 1971; Univ. of Hanover, 1978; Univ. of Cape Town, 1984. Chm., IFAC Technical Cttee on Terminology, 1987–93. Member: CNAA Elec. Engrg Bd, 1970–74; Naval Educn Adv. Cttee, 1973–79 (Chm., 1978–79). Mem. Council, IEE, 1974–77, 1980–84, 1985–88; Chm., Computing and Control Divl Bd, IEE, 1982–83. *Publications:* (contrib.) Telecommunication Satellites, ed Gatland, 1964; Modern Concepts in Control Theory, 1970; papers in scientific jls on electrical discharges, microwave interaction with ionised gases, and control systems. *Address:* 2 Oakdene Drive, Birmingham B45 8LQ. *T:* (0121) 445 2545.
Died 9 Jan. 2000.

PRINGLE, John Martin Douglas; Editor, Sydney Morning Herald, 1952–57 and 1965–70; *b* 28 June 1912; *s* of late J. Douglas Pringle, Hawick, Scotland; *m* 1936, Celia (*d* 1997), *d* of E. A. Carroll; one *s* two *d. Educ:* Shrewsbury Sch.; Lincoln Coll., Oxford (First Class Literae Humaniores, 1934). Served War of 1939–45 with King's Own Scottish Borderers, 1940–44. Editorial Staff of Manchester Guardian, 1934–39, Assistant Editor, 1944–48; Special Writer on The Times, 1948–52; Deputy

Editor, The Observer, 1958–63; Managing Editor, Canberra Times, 1964–65. *Publications:* China Struggles for Unity, 1938; Australian Accent, 1958; Australian Painting Today, 1963; On Second Thoughts, 1971; Have Pen, Will Travel, 1973; The Last Shenachie, 1976; The Shorebirds of Australia, 1987. *Address:* 8/105A Darling Point Road, Darling Point, NSW 2027, Australia.
Died 4 Dec. 1999.

PRINGLE, Dr Robert William, OBE 1967; BSc, PhD; CPhys; FRSE; FRS(Can); President, Nuclear Enterprises Ltd, Edinburgh, since 1976; *b* 2 May 1920; *s* of late Robert Pringle and Lillias Dalgleish Hair; *m* 1948, Carol Stokes; three *s* one *d. Educ:* George Heriot's Sch., Edinburgh; Edinburgh Univ. (Vans Dunlop Scholar in Natural Philosophy). Lecturer, Natural Philosophy, Edinburgh, 1945; Associate Professor of Physics, Manitoba, 1949; Prof. and Chairman of Physics, Manitoba, 1953–56; Mem. Bd, Manitoba Cancer Inst., 1949–55; Chm. and Man. Dir, Nuclear Enterprises Ltd, 1956–76 (Queen's Award to Industry, 1966, 1979). Dir, N Sea Assets Ltd, 1977–78. Member: Scottish Council, CBI (Cttee), 1966–72; Scottish Univs Industry Liaison Cttee, 1968–75; Bd, Royal Observatory (Edinburgh), 1968–79; Council, SRC, 1972–76 (Member: Bd, Astronomy, Space and Radio, 1970–72; Bd, Nuclear Physics, 1972–76); Economic Council for Scotland, 1971–75; Bd, Scottish Sch. Business Studies, 1972–83. University of Edinburgh: Mem. Court, 1967–75; Mem., Finance Cttee, 1967–75; Mem. Bd, Centre for Indust. Liaison and Consultancy, 1968–84; Mem., Press Cttee, 1977–78. Trustee: Scottish Hospitals Endowments Res. Trust, 1976–88; Scottish Trust for the Physically Disabled, 1977–84. Hon. Adviser, Nat. Museum of Antiquities of Scotland, 1969–. FInstP 1948; Fellow, American Physical Soc., 1950; FRS(Can) 1955; FRSE 1964; Hon. Fellow, Royal Scottish Soc. Arts, 1972; CPhys 1985; Sen. Life Mem., IEEE, 1990. *Publications:* (with James Douglas) 20th Century Scottish Banknotes, Vol. II, 1986; papers on nuclear spectroscopy and nuclear geophysics in UK and US scientific journals. *Recreations:* golf, book-collecting, Rugby (Edinburgh, Edinburgh and Glasgow, Rest of Scotland, 1945–48; Pres., Manitoba RU, 1952–55; organiser, first Monte Carlo Internat. Rugby Sevens, 1987). *Address:* 27 avenue Princesse Grace, Monaco. *Clubs:* Athenæum; New (Edinburgh); Yacht Club de Monaco, Golf de Monte Carlo. *Died 10 June 1996.*

PRITCHARD, Hugh Wentworth, CBE 1969; Member of Council of Law Society, 1947–66; *b* 15 March 1903; *s* of late Sir Harry G. Pritchard and Amy Louisa Harriet Bayly; *m* 1934, Barbara Stableforth (*d* 1987); two *s. Educ:* Charterhouse; Balliol College, Oxford. Admitted a Solicitor, 1927; Partner in Sharpe Pritchard & Co., 1928–80. Pres. Soc. of Parliamentary Agents, 1952–55; Member: Statute Law Committee, 1954–81; Committee on Administrative Tribunals and Enquiries, 1955; Council on Tribunals, 1958–70. Lay Reader, 1947–95. Served War of 1939–45, in England, France, Belgium and Germany; joined 4th Queen's Royal Regt as a private; commissioned in RAOC, attaining rank of Lt-Col. *Address:* 128 Foxley Lane, Purley, Surrey CR8 3NE. *T:* (0181) 660 9029.
Died 20 Jan. 1999.

PRITCHETT, Sir Victor (Sawdon), CH 1993; Kt 1975; CBE 1968; CLit 1988; author and critic; *b* 16 Dec. 1900; *s* of Sawdon Pritchett and Beatrice Martin; *m* 1936, Dorothy, *d* of Richard Samuel Roberts, Welshpool, Montgomeryshire; one *s* one *d. Educ:* Alleyn's School. Christian Gauss Lectr, Princeton Univ., 1953; Beckman Prof., Univ. California, Berkeley, 1962; Writer-in-Residence, Smith Coll., Mass, 1966; Vanderbilt Univ., Tenn., 1981; Visiting Professor: Brandeis Univ., Mass; Columbia Univ.; Clark Lectr, 1969. Foreign Member:

Amer. Acad. and Inst., 1971; Amer. Acad. Arts and Sciences, 1971. Pres., Internat. PEN, 1974–76; Soc. of Authors, 1977–. Hon. LittD Leeds, 1972; Hon. DLitt: Columbia, 1978; Sussex, 1980; Harvard, 1985. *Publications:* Marching Spain, 1928, repr. 1988; Clare Drummer, 1929; The Spanish Virgin, 1930; Shirley Sanz, 1932; Nothing Like Leather, 1935; Dead Man Leading, 1937; You Make Your Own Life, 1938; In My Good Books, 1942; It May Never Happen, 1946; The Living Novel, 1946; Why Do I Write?, 1948; Mr Beluncle, 1951; Books in General, 1953; The Spanish Temper, 1954; Collected Stories, 1956; When My Girl Comes Home, 1961; London Perceived, 1962; The Key to My Heart, 1963; Foreign Faces, 1964; New York Proclaimed, 1965; The Working Novelist, 1965; Dublin: A Portrait, 1967; A Cab at the Door (autobiog.), 1968 (RSL Award); Blind Love, 1969; George Meredith and English Comedy, 1970; Midnight Oil (autobiog.), 1971; Balzac, 1973; The Camberwell Beauty, 1974; The Gentle Barbarian, 1977; Selected Stories, 1978; The Myth Makers, 1979; On the Edge of the Cliff, 1980; The Tale Bearers, 1980; (ed) The Oxford Book of Short Stories, 1981; (with Reynolds Stone) The Turn of the Years, 1982; Collected Stories, 1982; More Collected Stories, 1983; The Other Side of a Frontier, 1984; Man of Letters, 1985; Chekhov, 1988; A Careless Widow and Other Stories, 1989; At Home and Abroad, 1990; The Complete Short Stories, 1990; Lasting Impressions, 1990; The Complete Essays, 1991. *Address:* 12 Regent's Park Terrace, NW1 7ED. *Clubs:* Savile, Beefsteak. *Died 20 March 1997.*

PROCTOR, David Victor; Research Associate and Consultant, National Maritime Museum, since 1989; *b* 1 March 1930; *s* of Comdr Victor William Lake Proctor, RN and Marjorie Proctor (*née* Weeks); *m* 1st, 1959, Margaret Graham (marr. diss. 1984); three *s*; 2nd, 1984, Marion Clara Calver; one step *s* five step *d. Educ:* Dauntsey's Sch.; Clare Coll., Cambridge (MA; DipEd 1955); Imperial Coll., London (DIC). Shipbroking, 1953–54; teacher: Lycée de Brest, France, 1955–56; Clifton Coll., Bristol, 1956–62; National Maritime Museum: Educn Officer, 1962–72; Sec. and Educn Officer, 1972–74; Head of Educn and Res. Facilities, 1974–76; Head of Printed Books and Manuscripts Dept, 1976–87; Head of Printed, Manuscript and Technical Records Dept, 1987–89. International Congress of Maritime Museums: Sec. Gen., 1972–78; Mem. Exec. Council, 1978–81; Vice-Pres., 1981–84; Trustee, 1984–; Hon. Life Mem., 1997; International Commission for Maritime History: Sec. Gen., 1980–85; Mem. Exec. Council, 1985–90; Vice Pres., 1990–95; Fellow, 1996–. Chm., Gp for Educnl Services in Museums, 1971–75; Mem., Adv. Council, Internat. Council of Museums, 1983–95; Trustee: Madeleine Mainstone Trust, 1980–; Jane Austen Centre, 1987–94. Fellow, Huguenot Soc. of London, 1986–; Mem., Royal Belgian Marine Acad., 1998. *Publications:* Child of War, 1972; Music of the Sea, 1992; contribs to jls on museums, museum educn and hist. of science. *Recreations:* sailing, piano, walking, travel, DIY. *Address:* 6 Vange Mews, Rochester, Kent ME1 1RA. *T:* (01634) 849592. *Clubs:* Royal Cruising; Rochester Cruising.
Died 23 July 2000.

PROFUMO, Valerie Babette Louise; *see* Hobson, V. B. L.

PROOM, Major William Arthur, TD 1953; *b* 18 Dec. 1916; *s* of Arthur Henry Proom and Nesta Proom; *m* 1941, Nellie Lister; one *s* one *d. Educ:* Richmond Sch., Yorks; Keighley Technical Coll. Commnd TA, 1/6 Bn Duke of Wellington's Regt, 1938; served War: Iceland, 1940–42; REME/IEME, India and Burma, 1943–46; Major, retd. Mayor of Keighley, 1973; Member: W Yorks Metropolitan CC, 1974–81 (Chm., 1979–80); City of Bradford Metrop. Dist Council, 1975–79. Chm., NE Gas Consumers'

Council, 1973–77. *Recreations:* gardening, reading. *Address:* 5 Armstrong House, Front Street, Bamburgh NE69 7BJ.   *Died 3 Oct. 2000.*

PROOPS, (Rebecca) Marjorie, OBE 1969; journalist; *d* of Alfred and Martha Rayle; *m* 1935, Sidney Joseph Proops (*d* 1988); one *s. Educ:* Dalston Secondary Sch. Daily Mirror, 1939–45; Daily Herald, 1945–54; Daily Mirror, 1954–; Sunday Mirror, 1992–. Broadcaster, Television, 1960–. Member: Royal Commn on Gambling, 1976–78; Council for One Parent Families, 1969. Woman Journalist of the Year, 1969; Chairman's Award, British Press Awards, 1994. *Publications:* Pride, Prejudice & Proops, 1975; Dear Marje, 1976; *relevant publication:* Marje: the guilt and the gingerbread, by Angela Patmore, 1993. *Address:* Sherwood Close, SW13 0JD.
                                    Died 10 Nov. 1996.

PROUD, Sir John (Seymour), Kt 1978; mining engineer; director and chairman of companies; *b* 9 Aug. 1907; *s* of William James Proud and Hannah Seymour; *m* 1964, Laurine, *d* of M. Ferran. *Educ:* Univ. of Sydney (Bachelor of Engrg, Mining and Metallurgy). CEng, FIMM, FIEAust, FAusIMM. Chm., Newcastle Wallsend Coal Co., which merged with Peko Mines NL, 1960; Chm., Peko-Wallsend Investments Ltd, then Chm., Peko-Wallsend Ltd; retd from chair, 1978; Dir/Consultant, Peko-Wallsend Ltd, 1978–82. Chairman: Electrical Equipment Ltd (Group), 1978–82 (Dir, 1943–83); Oil Search Ltd, 1978–88 (Dir, 1974); Oil Co. of Australia NL, 1979–83; Dir, CSR Ltd, 1974–79. Fellow of Senate, Univ. of Sydney, 1974–83. Chm. Trustees, Lizard Island Reef Res. Foundn, 1978–87; Trustee, Aust. Museum, 1971–77. Hon. DEng Sydney, 1984; Hon LLD ANU, 1996. *Recreations:* yachting, pastoral activity. *Address:* 9 Finlay Road, Turramurra, NSW 2074, Australia. *Clubs:* Union, Royal Sydney Yacht Squadron, Royal Prince Alfred Yacht, American (Sydney).   *Died 7 Oct. 1997.*

PRYCE-JONES, Alan Payan, TD; book critic, author and journalist; *b* 18 Nov. 1908; *s* of late Col Henry Morris Pryce-Jones, CB, CVO, DSO, MC and Marion Vere, *d* of Lt-Col Hon. L. Payan Dawnay; *m* 1934, Thérèse (*d* 1953), *d* of late Baron Fould-Springer and Mrs Frank Wooster, Paris; one *s; m* 1968, Mrs Mary Jean Kempner Thorne (*d* 1969), *d* of late Daniel Kempner. *Educ:* Eton; Magdalen Coll., Oxford. Formerly Asst Editor, The London Mercury, 1928–32; subseq. Times Literary Supplement; Editor, Times Literary Supplement, 1948–59; Book critic: New York Herald Tribune, 1963–66; World Journal Tribune, 1967–68; Newsday, 1969–71; Theatre Critic, Theatre Arts, 1963–. Trustee, National Portrait Gallery, 1950–61; Director, Old Vic Trust, 1950–61; Member Council, Royal College of Music, 1956–61; Program Associate, The Humanities and Arts Program, Ford Foundation, NY, 1961–63. Served War of 1939–45, France, Italy, Austria; Lt-Col 1945. *Publications:* The Spring Journey, 1931; People in the South, 1932; Beethoven, 1933; 27 Poems, 1935; Private Opinion, 1936; Nelson, an opera, 1954; (with Robin Miller and Julian Slade) Vanity Fair, a musical play, 1962; The Bonus of Laughter (autobiog.), 1987. *Recreations:* music, travelling. *Address:* 46 John Street, Newport, RI 02840, USA. *Clubs:* Travellers, Garrick, Beefsteak; Knickerbocker, Century (New York); Artillery (Galveston, Texas).   *Died 22 Jan. 2000.*

PRYKE, Sir David Dudley, 3rd Bt *cr* 1926, of Wanstead, co. Essex; *b* 16 July 1912; *s* of Sir (William Robert) Dudley Pryke, 2nd Bt and Marjorie, *d* of H. Greenwood Brown, Leytonstone; *S* father, 1959; *m* 1945, Doreen Winifred, *er d* of late Ralph Bernard Wilkins; two *d. Educ:* St Lawrence Coll., Ramsgate. Liveryman, Turners' Company, 1961 (Master, 1985–86). *Heir: nephew*

Christopher Dudley Pryke [*b* 17 April 1946; *m* 1973, Angela Gay Meek (marr. diss. 1986); one *s*].
                                    Died 20 July 1998.

PUGH, Harold Valentine, CBE 1964; Chairman, Northern Ireland Joint Electricity Authority, 1967–70, retired; *b* 18 Oct. 1899; *s* of Henry John Valentine Pugh and Martha (*née* Bott); *m* 1934, Elizabeth Mary (*née* Harwood); two *s* one *d. Educ:* The High Sch., Murree, India; Manchester College of Technology. Trained Metropolitan-Vickers (asst engineer erection, 1925–30). Chief Engineer, Cory Bros, 1930–35; Deputy Superintendent and later Superintendent, Upper Boat Power Station, 1935–43; Generation Engineer, South Wales Power Company, 1943–44; Deputy Chief Engineer, Manchester Corporation Electricity Dept, 1944–48; Controller, British Electricity Authority, South Wales Division, 1948; Controller, British (later Central) Electricity Authority, London Division, 1951; Chairman: Eastern Electricity Board, 1957–63; South-Eastern Electricity Board, 1963–66. Dir, Aberdare Holdings, 1966–70. AMCT; FIEE; FIMechE. *Recreations:* gardening, golf. *Address:* Clontaff, Doggetts Wood Lane, Chalfont St Giles, Bucks HP8 4TH. *T:* Little Chalfont (01494) 2330.   *Died 6 Jan. 1996.*

PUGH, Roger Courtenay Beckwith, MD; Pathologist to St Peter's Hospitals and the Institute of Urology, London, 1955–82; *b* 23 July 1917; *y s* of late Dr Robert Pugh, Talgarth, Breconshire, and Margaret Louise Pugh (*née* Gough); *m* 1942, Winifred Dorothy, *yr d* of late Alfred Cooper and Margaret Cooper (*née* Evans); one *s* one *d. Educ:* Gresham's Sch., Holt; St Mary's Hospital (University of London). MRCS, LRCP 1940; MB, BS 1941; MD 1948; MCPath 1964, FRCPath 1967; FRCS 1983. House Surgeon, St Mary's Hospital and Sector Hospitals, 1940–42; War Service in RAF (Mediterranean theatre), 1942–46, Sqdn Leader, Registrar, Department of Pathology, St Mary's Hospital, 1946–48; Asst Pathologist and Lecturer in Pathology, St Mary's Hospital, 1948–51; Asst Morbid Anatomist, The Hospital for Sick Children, Great Ormond Street, 1951–54. Erasmus Wilson Demonstrator, RCS, 1959, 1961; Member: Board of Governors, St Peter's Hospitals, 1961–82; Pathological Society of Great Britain and Ireland; Assoc. of Clin. Pathologists (Marshall Medal, 1982); Internat. Society of Urology; Internat. Acad. of Pathology (former Pres., British Div.; Cunningham Medal, 1993); Hon. Member British Assoc. of Urological Surgeons (St Peter's Medal, 1981); FRSocMed (Hon. Mem., and former Pres., Sect. of Urology). *Publications:* (ed) Pathology of the Testis, 1976; various contributions to pathological, urological and paediatric journals. *Recreations:* gardening, photography. *Address:* 3 Waldron Gardens, Shortlands Road, Bromley, Kent BR2 0JR. *T:* (020) 8464 4240.
                                    Died 15 April 1999.

PUGSLEY, Sir Alfred Grenvile, Kt 1956; OBE 1944; DSc; FRS 1952; FEng 1976; Professor of Civil Engineering, 1944–68, then Emeritus, and Pro-Vice-Chancellor, 1961–64, University of Bristol (Hon. Fellow, 1986); *b* 13 May 1903; *s* of H. W. Pugsley, BA, FLS, London; *m* 1928, Kathleen M. Warner (*d* 1974); no *c. Educ:* Rutlish Sch.; London Univ. Civil Engineering Apprenticeship at Royal Arsenal, Woolwich, 1923–26; Technical Officer, at the Royal Airship Works, Cardington, 1926–31; Member scientific and technical staff at Royal Aircraft Establishment, Farnborough, 1931–45, being Head of Structural and Mechanical Engineering Dept there, 1941–45. Visiting Lecturer on aircraft structures at Imperial Coll., London, 1938–40. Chairman of Aeronautical Research Council, 1952–57; Member: Advisory Council on Scientific Policy, 1956–59; Tribunal of Inquiry on Ronan Point, 1968; Member of various scientific and professional institutions and cttees;

President: IStructE, 1957–58; Section G, British Assoc. for Advancement of Science, 1960; a Vice-Pres., ICE, 1971–73. Emeritus Mem., Smeatonian Soc. of Civil Engrs, 1989. Hon. FRAeS 1963; Hon. FICE 1981. Hon. DSc: Belfast, 1965; Cranfield, 1978; Birmingham, 1982; DUniv Surrey, 1968. Structural Engineers' Gold Medal, 1968; Civil Engineers' Ewing Gold Medal, 1979. *Publications:* The Theory of Suspension Bridges, 1957 (2nd edn 1968); The Safety of Structures, 1966; (ed and contrib.) The Works of Isambard Kingdom Brunel, 1976; numerous Reports and Memoranda of Aeronautical Research Council; papers in scientific journals and publications of professional engineering bodies; articles and reviews in engineering press. *Address:* St Angela's, 5 Litfield Place, Clifton Down, Bristol BS8 3LU. *Club:* Athenæum.
Died 7 March 1998.

PULLAN, John Marshall, MChir; FRCS; Hon. Surgeon, St Thomas' Hospital, London; late of King Edward VII Hospital, Bolingbroke Hospital, London and Royal Masonic Hospital, London; *b* 1 Aug. 1915; *e s* of late William Greaves Pullan and Kathleen, *d* of Alfred Marshall, Otley, Yorkshire; *m* 1940, Leila Diana, *d* of H. C. Craven-Veitch, surgeon; one *s* three *d. Educ:* Shrewsbury; King's Coll., Cambridge; St Thomas' Hospital, London. MA Cantab (1st Cl. Nat. Sci. Tripos) 1937; MB, BChir 1940; FRCS 1942; MChir 1945. Teacher in Surgery, Univ. of London; Examiner in Surgery, Univs of: London, 1956; Cambridge. Member: Court of Examiners, RCS, 1964; Board of Governors, St Thomas' Hospital. *Publications:* Section on Diseases of the Liver, Gall Bladder and Bile Ducts, in Textbook of British Surgery, ed Sir Henry Souttar, 1956; articles in surgical journals. *Address:* Palings, Warboys Road, Kingston Hill, Surrey KT2 7LS. *T:* (0181) 546 5310. *Clubs:* White's, Flyfishers', Boodle's.
Died 4 Jan. 1998.

PULLEN, Sir (William) Reginald (James), KCVO 1987 (CVO 1975; MVO 1966); JP; LLB; FCIS; Clerk to the Trustees, United Westminser Almshouses, since 1987; Deputy High Bailiff of Westminster, since 1988; *b* 17 Feb. 1922; *er s* of late William Pullen and Lillian Pullen (*née* Chinn), Falmouth; *m* 1948, Doreen Angela Hebron; two *d. Educ:* Falmouth Grammar School; King's College, London; private study. Served War of 1939–45; Flt Lt, RAFVR (admin and special duties), SE Asia. Westminster Abbey: Asst to Chief Accountant, 1947; Dep. Registrar, 1951; Receiver-Gen., 1959–87; Chapter Clerk, 1963–87; Registrar, 1964–84; Sec. Westminster Abbey Appeal, 1953. Westminster City Council, 1962–65. Jt. Hon. Treas., CCJ, 1988–91. Trustee: The Passage (RC) Day Centre for Homeless People, 1983–94; Abbey Community Centre, 1990–. JP Inner London, 1967. Liveryman, Worshipful Co. of Fishmongers; Freeman, Worshipful Co. of Wax Chandlers. KStJ 1987 (CStJ 1981; OStJ 1969). *Publication:* contrib. A House of Kings, 1966. *Recreations:* travel, dogwalking, gerentology. *Address:* 42 Rochester Row, SW1P 1BU. *T:* (0171) 828 3210. *Clubs:* Royal Air Force, MCC; Hurlingham.
Died 25 Sept. 1996.

PULLINGER, John Elphick; His Honour Judge Pullinger; a Circuit Judge, since 1982; *b* 27 Aug. 1930; *s* of late Reginald Edward Pullinger and Elsie Florence Pullinger (*née* Elphick); *m* 1956, Carette Maureen Stephens (marr. diss.); one *s* one *d*; *m* 1999, Natasha Jenner (*née* Tavoosi); one *s. Educ:* Friern Barnet Grammar Sch.; Quintin Sch.; London Sch. of Econs and Pol Science (LLB 1955). Official Solicitor's Office, 1948. Nat. Service, 1949–50. British Inst., Florence, 1953. Min. of Educn qualified teacher, 1955. Called to the Bar, Lincoln's Inn, 1958; Sir Thomas More Bursary Scholar, 1958. Legal Sec. to Lord Shrewsbury's Commn of Enquiry, 1958–59; Dep. Judge Advocate, 1965; AJAG, 1972–82; Judge

Advocate to NZ Force SE Asia, 1973–75; served in Germany, Mediterranean, Near East, ME and Far East; an Ethnic Minorities Adv. Commn Judge, 1998. Member: NSRA, 1977–; NRA, 1979–; Historical Breechloading Smallarms Assoc., 1984–; Internat. Soc. for Military Law and the Law of War, UK Gp, 1988–; HAC, 1950–; Burrswood Internat. Fellowship, 1994–; Wellcome Inst., 1997–; Denning Soc., Lincoln's Inn, 1998–. Vis. Lectr in Law, Coll. of Estate Management, Univ. of London, 1961–63. *Publication:* The Position of the British Serviceman under the Army and Air Force Acts 1955, 1975. *Recreations:* shooting, heraldry, bibliography. *Address:* 1 Essex Court, Temple, EC4Y 9AR.
Died 31 Dec. 2000.

PURCELL, Prof. Edward Mills, PhD; Gerhard Gade University Professor, Harvard University, 1960–80, then Emeritus; *b* 30 Aug. 1912; *s* of Edward A. Purcell and Mary Elizabeth Mills; *m* 1937, Beth C. Busser; two *s. Educ:* Purdue University; Harvard University. PhD Harvard, 1938. Instructor in Physics, Harvard, 1938–40; Radiation Laboratory, Mass Inst. of Technology, 1940–45; Associate Professor of Physics, Harvard, 1945–49; Professor of Physics, 1949–60. Senior Fellow, Society of Fellows, Harvard, 1950–71. Halley Lectr, Oxford Univ., 1982. Foreign Mem., Royal Soc., 1989. Hon. DEng Purdue, 1953; Hon. DSci Washington Univ., St Louis, 1963. (Jointly) Nobel Prize in Physics, 1952; Nat. Medal of Science, 1979. *Publications:* Principles of Microwave Circuits, 1948; Physics for Students of Science and Engineering, 1952; Electricity and Magnetism, 1965; papers in Physical Review, Astrophys. Jl, Biophys. Jl. *Address:* 5 Wright Street, Cambridge, MA 02138, USA. *T:* 547–9317.
Died 7 March 1997.

PURCELL, Harry, CBE 1982; Member (C) Wyre Forest District Council, since 1984; *b* 2 Dec. 1919; *s* of Charles and Lucy Purcell; *m* 1941, Eunice Mary Price; three *s* one *d. Educ:* Bewdley C of E Sch.; Kidderminster Coll. Joined TA, 1938; served War, 1939–46, Queen's Own Worcester Hussars; Transport Officer, Berlin, 1946–48. Carpet industry, 1949–60; self-employed, 1961. Formerly Mem., Kidderminster Bor. Council; Mayor of Kidderminster, 1967–68; Mem. (C) for Chaddesley Corbett, Hereford and Worcester CC, 1974–98 (Vice-Chm., 1989–90). Chairman: West Mercia Police Authority, 1979–82; National Police Negotiating Bd, 1978–82; Vice-Chm., ACC, 1982–85 (Chm., Police Cttee, 1977–81; Vice Chm., Personnel Cttee, 1990–); Mem., Home Office Race Relations Cttee, 1981–. Chm., Local Authorities Mutual Investment Trust, 1987–93; non-exec. Dir, Charities Official Investment Fund, 1988–93. *Recreations:* theatre, tennis, public service. *Address:* Meadowsmead, Woodrow, Chaddesley Corbett, near Kidderminster, Worcs DY10 4QG. *T:* (01562) 777347.
Died 9 Dec. 1998.

PURCELL, Rev. Canon William Ernest; author and broadcaster; Residentiary Canon of Worcester Cathedral, 1966–76; *b* 25 May 1909; *s* of Will and Gwladys Purcell; *m* 1939, Margaret Clegg; two *s* one *d. Educ:* Univ. of Wales (BA); Keble Coll., Oxford (MA); Queen's Coll., Birmingham. Deacon 1937, priest 1938; Curate: St John's, Ingrow, 1937–39; Dover Parish Church, 1939–43; Vicar: St Peter, Maidstone, 1944–47; Sutton Valence, 1947–53; Chaplain, HM Borstal Instn, East Sutton, 1947–53; Religious Broadcasting Organiser, BBC Midlands, 1953–66. *Publications:* These Thy Gods, 1950; Pilgrim's Programme, 1957; Onward Christian Soldier (biog. of S. Baring Gould), 1957; A Plain Man Looks At Himself, 1962; Woodbine Willie (biog. of G. Studdert Kennedy), 1962; This Is My Story, 1963; The Plain Man Looks At The Commandments, 1966; Fisher of Lambeth (biog. of Archbp of Canterbury), 1969; Portrait of Soper (biog. of Lord Soper), 1972; British Police in a Changing Society,

1974; A Time to Die, 1979; Pilgrim's England, 1981; The Christian in Retirement, 1982; Martyrs of Our Time, 1983; Seekers and Finders, 1985; The Anglican Spiritual Tradition, 1988. *Address:* Flat 3, Gretton Court, Girton, Cambridge CB3 0QN. *Club:* National Liberal.

Died 19 Sept. 1999.

PURDY, Robert John, CMG 1963; OBE 1954; Bursar, Gresham's School, Holt, 1965–81; retired from HM Overseas Civil Service, 1963; *b* 2 March 1916; 2nd *s* of late Lt-Col T. W. Purdy, Woodgate House, Aylsham, Norfolk; *m* 1957, Elizabeth (*née* Sharp); two *s* one *d*. *Educ:* Haileybury College; Jesus College, Cambridge (BA). Served 1940–46 with 81 West African Division Reconnaissance Regt, 3rd and 4th Burma Campaigns (despatches, Major). Appointed to Colonial Administrative Service, Northern Nigeria, 1939; promoted Resident, 1956, Senior Resident, Staff Grade, 1957; Resident, Adamawa Province, 1956; Senior Resident, Plateau Province, 1958–61; Senior Resident, Sokoto Province, 1961–63, retd. *Recreations:* shooting, fishing, gardening.

Address: Spratt's Green House, Aylsham, Norwich NR11 6TX. *T:* (01263) 732147.   *Died 18 March 1998.*

PYMAN, Lancelot Frank Lee, CMG 1961; HM Diplomatic Service, retired; *b* 8 Aug. 1910; *s* of late Dr F. L. Pyman, FRS, and Mrs I. C. Pyman; *m* 1936, Sarah Woods Gamble (*d* 1981). *Educ:* Dover College; King's College, Cambridge (Exhibitioner). Entered Levant Consular Service, 1933; various posts in Persia, 1933–38; Consul, Cernauti, Roumania, 1939–40; Vice-Consul, Beirut, Lebanon, 1940–41; served with HM Forces in Levant States, 1941; Asst Oriental Secretary, HM Embassy, Tehran, Dec. 1941–1944; Foreign Office, 1944–48; Consul, St Louis, Missouri, Dec. 1948–1949; Oriental Counsellor, Tehran, Dec. 1949–Sept. 1952; Counsellor, British Embassy, Rio de Janeiro, 1952–53; Consul-General, Tetuan, 1953–56; Counsellor, British Embassy, Rabat, 1956–57; HM Consul-General: Zagreb, 1957–61; Basra, March-Dec. 1961; Ambassador to the Somali Republic, 1961–63; Consul-General, San Francisco, 1963–66. *Address:* Knockroe, Delgany, Co. Wicklow, Ireland.   *Died 3 Aug. 1996.*

Q

QUICK, Norman, CBE 1984; DL; Life President, Quicks Group (formerly H. & J. Quick Group) plc, 1993 (Chairman, 1965–92; Managing Director, 1965–84); *b* 19 Nov. 1922; *s* of James and Jessie Quick; *m* 1949, Maureen Cynthia Chancellor; four *d. Educ:* Arnold Sch., Blackpool. FIMI. Served RNVR, Lieut 1941–46 (despatches, Mediterranean, 1943). H. & J. Quick Ltd to H. & J. Quick Group plc, 1939–. Non Executive Director: Williams & Glyn's Bank, 1979–85. Royal Bank of Scotland, 1985–90; Dir, Piccadilly Radio (formerly Greater Manchester Independent Radio), 1972–89 (Chm., 1980–88). Mem., NW Indust. Council. Pres., Stretford Cons. Assoc., 1974– (formerly Chm.). Mem., Lancs CC, 1954–57. Treasurer, 1975–80, Chm., 1980–83, Univ. of Manchester Council; Mem., Bd of Governors, Arnold Sch. Ltd, Blackpool, 1980–90. DL Greater Manchester, 1987, High Sheriff, 1990. Hon. MA Manchester, 1977; Hon. LLD Manchester, 1984. *Recreation:* Rugby. *Address:* Birkin House, Ashley, Altrincham, Cheshire WA14 3QL. *T:* (01565) 830175. *Clubs:* Royal Automobile; St James's (Manchester).

Died 19 April 1997.

QUINE, Prof. Willard Van Orman; American author; Professor of Philosophy, 1948, and Edgar Pierce Professor of Philosophy, 1956–78, Harvard University, then Emeritus Professor; *b* Akron, Ohio, 25 June 1908; *s* of Cloyd Robert Quine and Hattie (*née* Van Orman); *m* 1st, 1930, Naomi Clayton (marr. diss. 1947); two *d*; 2nd, 1948, Marjorie Boynton (*d* 1998); one *s* one *d. Educ:* Oberlin Coll., Ohio (AB); Harvard Univ. (AM, PhD). Lieut, then Lieut-Commander, USNR, active duty, 1942–46. Harvard: Sheldon Travelling Fellow, 1932–33 (Vienna, Prague, Warsaw); Jun. Fellow, Society of Fellows, 1933–36 (Sen. Fellow, 1949–78, Chairman, 1957–58); Instructor and Tutor in Philosophy, 1936–41; Associate Professor of Philosophy, 1941–48; Chairman, Dept of Philosophy, 1952–53. Consulting editor, Journal of Symbolic Logic, 1936–52; Vice-President, Association for Symbolic Logic, 1938–40, President, 1953–55; Vice-President, Eastern Division, American Philosophical Assoc., 1950, President, 1957; Fellow, Amer. Philos. Soc., 1957 (Mem., 1957; Councillor, 1966–68, 1982); Member: Acad. Internat. de Philosophie de Science, 1960; Institut International de Philosophie, 1983. FAAAS, 1945 (Councillor, 1950–53); Fellow, Nat. Acad. of Sciences, 1977. Corresponding Member: Instituto Brasileiro de Filosofia, 1963–; Institut de France, 1978–; Corresponding Fellow: British Acad., 1959; Norwegian Acad. of Scis, 1979. Trustee, Institute for Unity of Science, 1949–56; Syndic, Harvard University Press, 1951–53, 1954–56, 1959–60, 1962–66. George Eastman Visiting Prof., Oxford Univ., 1953–54; Visiting Professor: Universidade de São Paulo, Brazil, 1942; Univ. of Tokyo, 1959; Rockefeller Univ., 1968; Collège de France, 1969. A. T. Shearman Lecturer, University of London, 1954; Gavin David Young Lectr in Philosophy,

Univ. of Adelaide, 1959; John Dewey Lectr, Columbia Univ., 1968; Paul Carus Lectr, Amer. Philos. Assoc., 1971; Hägerström Lectr, Uppsala, 1973; Vis. Lectr, Calcutta, 1983. Member, Institute for Advanced Study, Princeton, USA, 1956–57. Fellow: Centre for Advanced Study in the Behavioural Sciences, Palo Alto, California, 1958–59; Centre for Advanced Studies, Wesleyan Univ., Conn, 1965; Sir Henry Saville Fellow, Merton Coll., Oxford, 1973–74. Hon. degrees: MA Oxon, 1953; DLitt Oxon, 1970; LittD: Oberlin, 1955; Akron, 1965; Washington, 1966; Temple, 1970; Cambridge, 1978; Ripon, 1983; LLD: Ohio State, 1957; Harvard, 1979; DèsL Lille, 1965; LHD: Chicago, 1967; Syracuse, 1981; DPh: Uppsala, 1980; Berne, 1982; Granada, 1986; Oldenburg, 1997. N. M. Butler Gold Medal, 1970; F. Polacky Gold Medal, Prague, 1991; Silver Medal, Charles Univ., Prague, 1993; Rolf Schock Prize, Sweden, 1993; Kyoto Prize, Japan, 1996. *Publications:* A System of Logistic, 1934; Mathematical Logic, 1940, rev. edn 1951; Elementary Logic, 1941, rev. edn 1965; O sentido da nova logica, 1944 (São Paulo); Methods of Logic, 1950, rev. edn 1982; From a Logical Point of View, 1953, rev. edn 1961; Word and Object, 1960; Set Theory and its Logic, 1963, rev. edn 1969; Ways of Paradox and Other Essays, 1966, rev. edn 1976; Selected Logic Papers, 1966, rev. edn 1995; Ontological Relativity and Other Essays, 1969; Philosophy of Logic, 1970; (with J. S. Ullian) The Web of Belief, 1970; The Roots of Reference, 1974; Theories and Things, 1981; The Time of My Life, 1985; (jtly) The Philosophy of W. V. Quine, 1986; La Scienza e i Dati di Senso, 1987; Quiddities, 1987; Pursuit of Truth, 1989; (jtly) Perspectives on Quine, 1989; The Logic of Sequences, 1990; From Stimulus to Science, 1995; contribs to Journal of Symbolic Logic, Journal of Philosophy, Philosophical Review, Mind, Rivista di Filosofia, Scientific American, NY Review of Books, Library of Living Philosophers. *Recreation:* travel. *Address:* 38 Chestnut Street, Boston, MA 02108, USA. *T:* (617) 7236754.

Died 25 Dec. 2000.

QUINLAN, Maj.-Gen. Henry, CB 1960; *b* 5 Jan. 1906; *s* of Dr Denis Quinlan, LRCP, LRCS (Edinburgh), Castletownroche, Co. Cork; *m* 1936, Euphemia Nancy, *d* of John Tallents Wynyard Brooke, Shanghai, and Altrincham, Cheshire; two *s* two *d. Educ:* Clongowes Wood Coll., Sallins, Co. Kildare; Nat. Univ. of Ireland (BDS 1926). FFDRCSI 1964. Royal Army Dental Corps; Lieut, 1927; Captain, 1930; Major, 1937; Lt-Col, 1947; Colonel, 1953; Maj.-Gen., 1958; Director Army Dental Service, 1958–63; QHDS 1954–64, retired. Colonel Comdt Royal Army Dental Corps, 1964–71. OStJ 1958. *Address:* White Bridges, Redlands Lane, Crondall, Hants GU10 5RF. *T:* (01252) 850239.

Died 29 Oct. 2000.

R

RADFORD, (Courtenay Arthur) Ralegh, OBE 1948; FBA 1956; *b* 7 Nov. 1900; *o s* of late Arthur Lock and Ada M. Radford; unmarried. *Educ:* St George's School, Harpenden; Exeter College, Oxford (BA 1921; MA 1937). Inspector of Ancient Monuments in Wales and Monmouthshire, 1929–34; Director of the British School at Rome, 1936–39. Member of Royal Commission on Ancient Monuments in Wales and Monmouthshire, 1935–46; Member of Royal Commission on Historical Monuments (England), 1953–76. Supervised excavations at Tintagel, Ditchley, Castle Dore, the Hurlers, Whithorn, Glastonbury, Birsay and elsewhere. FSA 1928 (Vice-Pres. 1954–58; Gold Medal, 1972); FRHistS 1930. President: Prehistoric Soc., 1954–58; Royal Archæological Inst., 1960–63; Cambrian Archæological Assoc., 1961; Soc. of Medieval Archæology, 1969–71. Hon. DLitt Glasgow, 1963; Univ. of Wales, 1963; Exeter, 1973; *Publications:* reports on the excavations at Tintagel, Ditchley, Whithorn, etc; various articles on archæological subjects. *Address:* Culmcott, Uffculme, Devon EX15 3AT. *Club:* Athenæum. *Died 27 Dec. 1998.*

RADICE, Edward Albert, CBE 1946; *b* 2 Jan. 1907; *s* of C. A. Radice, ICS and Alice Effie, DSc (Econ) (*née* Murray); *m* 1936, Joan Keeling (*d* 1991); one *s* one *d*. *Educ:* Winchester Coll.; Magdalen Coll., Oxford (1st in Maths Mods; 1st in Lit. Hum.; DPhil). Commonwealth Fund Fellow, Columbia Univ., New York, 1933–35; Assistant Professor of Economics, Wesleyan University, Middletown, Conn, 1937–39; League of Nations Secretariat, 1939; Ministry of Economic Warfare, 1940–44; HM Foreign Service, 1945–53; Min. of Defence, 1953–70 (Dir of Economic Intelligence, 1966–70); Senior Research Fellow, St Antony's Coll., Oxford, 1970–73. *Publications:* (jt) An American Experiment, 1936; Fundamental Issues in the United States, 1936; Savings in Great Britain, 1922–35, 1939; (contrib.) Communist Power in Europe 1944–1949, 1977; (jtly, also co-ed) The Economic History of Eastern Europe 1919–1975, Vols I and II, 1986; papers in Econometrica, Oxford Economic Papers, Economic History Review. *Address:* 2 Talbot Road, Oxford OX2 8LL. *T:* (01865) 515573.
Died 8 Nov. 1996.

RADICE, Italo de Lisle, CB 1969; Secretary and Comptroller General, National Debt Office, 1969–76; Appointed Member, Royal Patriotic Fund Corporation, 1969–91; *b* 2 March 1911; *s* of Charles Albert Radice, ICS, and Alice Effie (*née* Murray); *m* 1st, 1935, Betty Dawson (*d* 1985); three *s* (one *d* decd); 2nd, 1993, Marie Guise, SRCh, MChS. *Educ:* Blundell's School; Magdalen College, Oxford (demy). Admitted Solicitor, 1938; Public Trustee Office, 1939; Military Government, East and North Africa, Italy, and Germany, 1941–46; HM Treasury, 1946, Under-Secretary, 1961–68; Dir, Central Trustee Savings Bank Ltd, 1976–80. Comr for Income Tax, City of London, 1972–86. Cavaliere Ufficiale dell'Ordine al Merito (Italy), 1981. *Address:* Woodstock, 134 High Street, Kelvedon, Essex CO5 9JA.
Died 14 July 2000.

RADZINOWICZ, Sir Leon, Kt 1970; LLD; FBA 1973; Fellow of Trinity College, Cambridge, since 1948; Wolfson Professor of Criminology, University of Cambridge, 1959–73, and Director of the Institute of Criminology, 1960–72; Associate Fellow, Silliman College, Yale, since 1966; Adjunct Professor of Law and

Criminology, Columbia Law School, 1966–75; *b* Poland, 15 Aug. 1906; *né* Rabinowicz; naturalised British subject, 1947; *m* 1st, 1933, Irene Szereszewski (marr. diss. 1955); 2nd, 1958, Mary Ann (marr. diss. 1979), *d* of Gen. Nevins, Gettysburg, Pa, USA; one *s* one *d*; 3rd, 1979, Isolde Klarmann, *d* of late Prof. Emil and Elfriede Doernenburg, and *widow* of Prof. Adolf Klarmann, Philadelphia. *Educ:* Cracow, Paris, Geneva and Rome. University of Paris, 1924–25; Licencié en Droit, Univ. of Geneva, 1927; Doctor of Law, Rome, 1928; Doctor of Law, Cracow, 1929; LLD Cambridge, 1951. Lectr, Univ. of Geneva, 1928–31; reported on working of penal system in Belgium, 1930; Lectr, Free Univ. of Warsaw, 1932–36; came to England on behalf of Polish Ministry of Justice to report on working of English penal system, 1938; Asst Dir of Research, Univ. of Cambridge, 1946–49; Dir, Dept of Criminal Science, Univ. of Cambridge, 1949–59; Walter E. Meyer Research Prof. of Law, Yale Law Sch., 1962–63. Visiting Professor: Virginia Law Sch., 1968–75; Rutgers Univ., 1968–72, 1979–81; Univ. of Pennsylvania, 1970–73; John Jay Coll., CUNY, 1978–79; Benjamin Cardozo Law Sch., Yeshiva Univ., 1979–81; Univ. of Minnesota Law Sch., 1979; Overseer, Pennsylvania Law Sch. and Associate Trustee, Pennsylvania Univ., 1978–82. Mem., Conseil de Direction de l'Assoc. Intern. de Droit Pénal, Paris, 1947; Vice-Pres., Internat. Soc. of Social Defence, 1956–; Head of Social Defence Section, UN, New York, 1947–48. Member: Royal Commn on Capital Punishment, 1949–53; Royal Commn on Penal System in Eng. and Wales, 1964–66; Advisory Council on the Treatment of Offenders, Home Office, 1950–63; Adv. Council on the Penal System, Home Office, 1966–74; Jt Chm., Second UN Congress on Crime, 1955; Chief Rapporteur, 4th UN Congress on Crime, Kyoto, 1970; Hon. Vice-Chm., Fifth UN Congress on Crime, Geneva, 1975; Chm., Sub-Cttee on Maximum Security in Prisons, 1967–68; Mem. Advisory Council on the Penal System, 1966–74; first Pres., Brit. Acad. of Forensic Sciences, 1960–61, Hon. Vice-Pres., 1961–; first Chm. Council of Europe Sci. Cttee, Problems of Crime, 1963–70. Consultant: Ford Foundn and Bar Assoc., NYC, on teaching and res. in criminol., 1964–65; President's Nat. Commn on Violence, Washington, 1968–69; Min. of Justice, NSW, and Nat. Inst. of Criminology, Canberra, 1973; Hon. Vice-Pres., British Soc. of Criminology, 1978. Hon. QC 1999. For. Hon. Mem., Amer. Acad. of Arts and Sciences, 1973; Hon. Mem., Amer. Law Inst., 1981; Hon. Fellow, Imperial Police Coll., 1968. Hon. LLD: Leicester, 1965; Edinburgh, 1988. James Barr Ames Prize and Medal, Faculty of Harvard Law School, 1950; Bruce Smith Sr Award, Amer. Acad. Criminal Justice Sciences, 1976; Sellin-Glueck Award, Amer. Assoc. of Criminology, 1976. Coronation Medal, 1953. Chevalier de l'Ordre de Léopold (Belgium), 1930. *Publications:* History of English Criminal Law, Vol. I, 1948 (under auspices of Pilgrim Trust), Vols II and III, 1956, Vol. IV, 1968 (under auspices of Rockefeller Foundation), Vol. V (with R. Hood), 1986 (under auspices of Home Office and MacArthur Foundn); Sir James Fitzjames Stephen (Selden Soc. Lect.), 1957; In Search of Criminology, 1961 (Italian edn 1965; French edn 1965; Spanish edn 1971); The Need for Criminology, 1965; Ideology and Crime (Carpentier Lectures), 1966, (Italian edn 1968); The Dangerous Offender (Frank Newsam Memorial Lecture), 1968; (ed with Prof. M. E. Wolfgang) Crime and Justice, 3 vols, 1971, 2nd edn 1977; (with R. Hood) Criminology and the Administration of

Criminal Justice: a Bibliography, 1976 (Joseph L. Andrews Award, Amer. Assoc. of Law Libraries 1977); (with Joan King) The Growth of Crime, 1977 (trans. Italian, 1981); The Cambridge Institute of Criminology: the background and scope, 1988; The Roots of the International Association of Criminal Law and their Significance, 1991; Adventures in Criminology, 1999; (ed) English Studies in Criminal Science, latterly Cambridge Studies in Criminology, 52 vols (Vols I–VII with J. W. C. Turner); numerous articles in English and foreign periodicals. *Address:* Trinity College, Cambridge CB2 1TQ; The Quadrangle, Apt 2311, 3300 Darby Road, Haverford, PA 19041–1095, USA. *T:* (610) 6496803.

Died 29 Dec. 1999.

RAE, Allan Alexander Sinclair, CBE 1973; Chairman, CIBA-GEIGY PLC, 1972–90; *b* 26 Nov. 1925; *s* of John Rae and Rachel Margaret Sinclair; *m* 1st, 1955, Sheila Grace (*née* Saunders) (*d* 1985); two *s* one *d*; 2nd, 1986, Gertrud (*née* Dollinger). *Educ:* Ayr Acad.; Glasgow Univ. (LLB). Admitted Solicitor, 1948. Served Army, RA then JAG's Dept (Staff Captain), 1944–47. Partner, 1950, Sen. Partner, 1959, Crawford Bayley & Co., Bombay (Solicitors); Dir and Hd of Legal and Patents Dept, CIBA Ltd, Basle, 1964, Mem. Management Cttee, 1969; Mem. Exec. Cttee, CIBA-GEIGY Ltd, Basle and Chm., CIBA-GEIGY Gp of Cos in UK, 1972–90; Chm., Ilford Ltd, 1972–88; Director: The Clayton Aniline Co. Ltd, 1965–90 (Chm., 1965–87); CIBA-GEIGY Chemicals Ltd, 1965–90 (Chm., 1965–87); Gretag Ltd (formerly Gretag-CX Ltd), 1978–89 (Chm. 1978–87); ABB Power Ltd (formerly British Brown-Boveri Ltd), 1973–89; T & N plc (formerly Turner & Newall PLC), 1979–94; Brown Boveri Kent (Hldgs) Ltd, 1980–94; Mettler Instruments Ltd, 1985–89; Riggs AP Bank Ltd (formerly AP Bank Ltd), 1986–91. Internat. Consultant, Loxleys, Solicitors, 1990–. Member of Council: Chemical Industries Assoc., 1976–91 (Pres., 1986–88); CBI, 1980–; British Swiss Chamber of Commerce, 1965– (Pres., 1969–72). Vice-Chm., Business and Industry Adv. Cttee to OECD, 1986–94. *Recreations:* sailing, golf, ski-ing. *Address:* Bryn Dulas House, Llanddulas, Clwyd LL22 8NA. *Clubs:* Buck's; Royal Thames Yacht.   *Died 7 Feb. 1999.*

RAE, Henry Edward Grant; JP; Lord Provost, City of Aberdeen, 1984–88; Lord Lieutenant, City of Aberdeen, 1984–88; *b* 17 Aug. 1925; *s* of late James and Rachel Rae; *m* 1955, Margaret Raffan Burns; one *d*. *Educ:* Queen's Cross School, Aberdeen; Ruthrieston School, Aberdeen. Bus driver, with Grampian Regl Transport, 1948–85. Chairman: Aberdeen Dist Cttee, TGWU, 1969–82; Grampian and Northern Isles Dist Cttee, 1982–85. Councillor, Aberdeen City Council, 1974–96 (Convener, Libraries Cttee, 1977–80, Manpower Cttee, 1980–84). JP Aberdeen, 1984 (Chm., Justices' Cttee). OStJ 1987. *Address:* 78 Thistle Court, Aberdeen AB1 1ST. *T:* (01224) 630201.   *Died 27 June 1999.*

RAFAEL, Gideon; Ambassador of Israel, retired 1978; *b* Berlin, 5 March 1913; *s* of Max Rafael; *m* 1940, Nurit Weissberg; one *s* one *d*. *Educ:* Berlin Univ. Went to Israel, 1934; Member, kibbutz, 1934–43; Jewish Agency Polit. Dept, 1943; in charge of prep. of Jewish case for JA Polit. Dept, Nuremberg War Crimes Trial, 1945–46; Member: JA Commn to Anglo-American Commn of Enquiry, 1946, and of JA Mission to UN Special Commn for Palestine, 1947; Israel Perm. Deleg. to UN, 1951–52; Alt. Rep. to UN, 1953; Rep. at UN Gen. Assemblies, 1947–67; Counsellor in charge of ME and UN Affairs, Min. for Foreign Affairs, 1953–57; Ambassador to Belgium and Luxembourg, 1957–60, and to the European Economic Community, 1959; Head, Israel Delegn to 2nd Geneva Conf. on Maritime Law, 1960; Dep. Dir-Gen., Min. of Foreign Affairs, 1960–65; Perm. Rep. to UN and Internat.

Organizations in Geneva, 1965–66; Special Ambassador and Adviser to Foreign Minister, 1966–67; Perm. Rep. to UN, 1967; Dir-Gen., Min. for Foreign Affairs, 1967–71; Head, Israel Delegn to UNCTAD III, 1972; Sen. Polit. Adviser, Foreign Ministry, 1972–73; Ambassador to the Court of St James's, 1973–77, and non-resident Ambassador to Ireland, 1975–77; Sen. Advr to Foreign Minister, 1977–78. Visiting Professor: Woodrow Wilson Sch., Princeton Univ., 1988; Hamilton Coll., Clinton, NY, 1989. Bd Mem., Israel Cancer Soc., 1985–. *Publications:* Destination Peace: three decades of Israeli foreign policy, 1981; The Impact of the Six Day War, 1990; articles on foreign affairs in Israel and internat. periodicals. *Address:* Ministry for Foreign Affairs, Jerusalem, Israel.

Died 10 Feb. 1999.

RAFFERTY, Rt Rev. Mgr Kevin Lawrence; Titular Bishop of Ausuaga and Bishop Auxiliary to Archbishop of St Andrews and Edinburgh, since 1990; Parish Priest of SS John Cantius and Nicholas, Broxburn, since 1986; *b* 24 June 1933; *s* of John Rafferty and Catherine Quigg. *Educ:* Lisnascreaghog and St Adamnan's primary schs; St Columb's Coll., Derry; St Kieran's Coll., Kilkenny. Priest 1957; Assistant Priest: Linlithgow, 1957–67; St David's, Dalkeith, 1967–77; Chaplain, St David's High Sch., Dalkeith, 1967–73; Parish Priest, Our Lady, Star of the Sea, North Berwick, 1977–86; Dean of Midlothian and East Lothian, 1982–86. Mem., Coll. of Consultors of archdio., 1984; Vicar-General, archdio. St Andrews and Edinburgh, 1989–. Prelate of Honour to the Pope, 1989. *Recreations:* golf, football, music, reading. *Address:* SS John Cantius and Nicholas, 34 West Main Street, Broxburn, West Lothian EH52 5RJ. *T:* Broxburn (01506) 852040.   *Died 19 April 1996.*

RAFTERY, Peter Albert, CVO 1984 (MVO 1979); MBE 1972; HM Diplomatic Service, retired; *b* 8 June 1929; *s* of John Raftery and Mary (*née* Glynn); *m* 1st, 1949, Margaret Frances Hulse (decd); four *d*; 2nd, 1975, Fenella Jones. *Educ:* St Ignatius Coll., London. Nat. Service, 1947–49. India Office, 1946; CRO, 1949; New Delhi, 1950; Peshawar, 1956; Cape Town, 1959; Kuala Lumpur, 1963; Nairobi, 1964; Asst Political Agent, Bahrain, 1968; First Sec., FCO, 1973; Head of Chancery, Gaborone, 1976; Asst Head, E Africa Dept, FCO, 1980; Counsellor and Consul Gen., Amman, 1982–85; High Comr to Botswana, 1986–89. *Recreation:* croquet. *Address:* PO Box 170, Gaborone, Botswana.   *Died 10 June 1996.*

RAJAH, Arumugam Ponnu; consultant, Tan Rajah & Cheah, Singapore, since 1991; a Judge of the Supreme Court, Singapore, 1976–90; *b* Negri Sembilan, Malaysia, 23 July 1911; *m* Vijaya Lakshmi (*d* 1971); one *s* one *d*. *Educ:* St Paul's Inst., Seremban; Raffles Instn and Raffles Coll., Singapore; Lincoln Coll., Oxford Univ. (BA). Barrister-at-law, Lincoln's Inn. City Councillor, Singapore: nominated, 1947–49; elected, 1951–57; MLA for Farrer Park, Singapore, 1959–66: Chm., Public Accounts Cttee, 1959–63; Speaker, 1964–66; first High Comr for Singapore to UK, 1966–71; High Comr to Australia, 1971–73; practised law, Tan Rajah & Cheah, Singapore, 1973–76. Mem. Bd of Trustees, Singapore Improvement Trust, 1949–57; Mem., Raffles Coll. Council and Univ. of Malaya Council, 1955–63; Chm., Inst. of SE Asian Studies, 1975–84; Pro-Chancellor, Nat. Univ. of Singapore, 1975. Hon. LLD Nat. Univ. of Singapore, 1984. *Address:* 7–D Balmoral Road, Singapore 259790.

Died 28 Sept. 1999.

RAMPAL, Jean-Pierre Louis; Commandeur de la Légion d'Honneur et de l'Ordre National du Mérite; Commandeur des Arts et des Lettres; musician, concert flautist, conductor; *b* Marseilles, 7 Jan. 1922; *s* of Joseph Rampal and Andrée (*née* Roggero); *m* 1947, Françoise Bacqueyrisse; one *s* one *d*. *Educ:* Lycée Thiers; Facultés

des Sciences et de Médecine, Marseilles; Conservatoire Nat. Sup. de Musique, Paris. Flute Prizes, Marseilles and Paris. Professional flautist, 1945–; numerous internat. festivals, world wide tours; Prof. of Flute, Conservatoire Nat. Sup. de Musique, 1969–82; research in ancient music; conducting début, French Provinces, 1948, Paris, 1967; conducting career mostly in USA, parallel to soloist performances. Prix Edison, Netherlands, 1969; Prix Léonie Sonning, Denmark, 1978; Prix d'Honneur de Montreux, 1980. *Publication:* Music, My Life, 1991. *Recreations:* amateur cinema, tennis, diving. *Address:* (home) 15 avenue Mozart, 75016 Paris, France; (business) Bureau de Concerts de Valmalete, 75008 Paris, France.
Died 20 May 2000.

RAMSAY, Henry Thomas, CBE 1960; Director, Safety in Mines Research Establishment, Ministry of Technology (formerly Ministry of Power), Sheffield, 1954–70, retired; *b* 7 Dec. 1907; *s* of Henry Thomas and Florence Emily Ramsay, Gravesend, Kent; *m* 1953, Dora Gwenllian Burgoyne Davies (*d* 1979); one *s* one *d*; *m* 1983, Vivian Ducatel Prague, Bay St Louis, Miss. *Educ:* MSc London. On scientific staff, Research Labs, GEC, 1928–48; RAE, 1948–54. Chartered engineer; FInstP; FIMinE; Pres., Midland Inst. Mining Engrs, 1970–71. *Publications:* contrib. to: Trans of Instn of Electrical Engrs; Jl of Inst. of Mining Engrs; other technical jls. *Recreations:* reading, walking. *Died 11 July 1997.*

RAMSAY, Norman James Gemmill; Sheriff of South Strathclyde, Dumfries and Galloway at Kirkcudbright, Stranraer and Dumfries (formerly Dumfries and Galloway, Western Division), 1971–85, then Hon. Sheriff; *b* 26 Aug. 1916; *s* of late James and Christina Emma Ramsay; *m* 1952, Rachael Mary Berkeley Cox, *d* of late Sir Herbert Charles Fahie Cox, two *s*. *Educ:* Merchiston Castle Sch.; Edinburgh Univ. (MA, LLB). WS 1939, Advocate, Scotland, 1956. War Service, RN, 1940–46; Lieut (S), RNVR. Colonial Legal Service, Northern Rhodesia. Administrator-General, 1947; Resident Magistrate, 1956; Sen. Resident Magistrate, 1958; Puisne Judge of High Court, Northern Rhodesia, later Zambia, 1964–68. Mem., Victoria Falls Trust, 1950–58. *Address:* Mill of Borgue, Kirkcudbright DG6 4SY. *Died 23 Jan. 1999.*

RAMSAY, Thomas Anderson; retired; Post-Graduate Dean and Professor of Post-Graduate Medicine, University of Aberdeen, 1972–76; *b* 9 Feb. 1920; *s* of David Mitchell Ramsay and Ruth Bramfitt Ramsay; *m* 1949, Margaret Lilian Leggat Donald; one *s* two *d*. *Educ:* Glasgow Univ. (BSc, MB, ChB). FRCSGlas 1962; FFCM 1974; FRSH; FRCP 1983. Surg. Lieut, RNVR, 1945–47. Various posts in general and clinical hospital practice (mainly paediatric and orthopaedic surg.), 1943–56; Asst, later Dep. Sen. Admin. Med. Officer, NI Hospitals Authority, 1957–58; Dep. Sen., later Sen. Admin. Med. Officer, NE Metropolitan Reg. Hospital Bd, 1958–72; Dir of Post-Grad. Med. Educn, NE Region (Scotland), 1972–76; Regl Med. Officer, W Midlands RHA, 1976–79; Prof. of Post Graduate Med. Educn, Univ. of Warwick, 1980–83; Dir, Post Graduate Med. Educn, Coventry AHA, Warwicks Post Graduate Med. Centre, 1980–85. Vis. Prof. of Health Services Admin, London Sch. of Hygiene and Tropical Medicine, 1971–72; Vis. Prof., Health Services Admin, Univ. of Aston, 1979. Mem. Bd, Faculty of Community Medicine, 1972–. Governor, London Hosp., 1965–72. *Publications:* several papers in learned jls regarding post-graduate medical educn and community medicine. *Recreations:* travel, photography. *Address:* 26 Pinnaclehill Park, Kelso, Roxburghshire TD5 8HA. *T:* (01573) 226178. *Died 22 May 1998.*

RAMSEY, Sir Alfred (Ernest), Kt 1967; *b* Dagenham, 22 Jan. 1920; *s* of Herbert Henry Ramsey; *m* 1951, Victoria Phyllis Answorth, *d* of William Welch. *Educ:* Becontree

Heath School. Started playing for Southampton and was an International with them; transferred to Tottenham Hotspur, 1949; with Spurs (right back), 1949–51; they won the 2nd and 1st Division titles in successive seasons; Manager of Ipswich Town Football Club, which rose from 3rd Division to Championship of the League, 1955–63; Manager, FA World Cup Team, 1963–74. Played 31 times for England. *Address:* 41 Valley Road, Ipswich, Suffolk IP1 4EE. *Died 28 April 1999.*

RANCE, Gerald Francis Joseph, OBE 1985 (MBE 1968); HM Diplomatic Service, retired; *b* 20 Feb. 1927; *s* of Cecil Henry and Jane Carmel Rance; *m* 1949, Dorothy (*née* Keegan); one *d*. *Educ:* Brompton Oratory. HM Forces (RCMP), 1945–48; joined Foreign Service, 1948; Foreign Office, 1948–51; served Belgrade, Rome, Bucharest, Istanbul, Munich, Kabul, New York and Dallas; Inspectorate, FCO, 1973–77; Head of Chancery, Mbabane, 1977–79; First Sec. (Comm.), Nicosia, 1980–83; High Comr to Tonga, 1984–87. *Recreations:* golf, tennis, reading. *Address:* 1 Bruton Close, Chislehurst, Kent BR7 5SF. *Clubs:* Royal Commonwealth Society; Chislehurst Golf. *Died 8 Aug. 2000.*

RANDALL, William Edward, CBE 1978; DFC 1944; AFC 1945; Chairman, Chubb & Son Ltd, 1981–84 (Managing Director, 1971–81, Deputy Chairman, 1976–81); *b* 15 Dec. 1920; *s* of William George Randall and Jane Longdon (*née* Pannell); *m* 1st, 1943, Joan Dorothea Way; two *s* one *d*; 2nd, 1975, Iris Joyce Roads. *Educ:* Tollington Sch., London. FRSA. Served RAF, Flt Lieut, 1941–46. Commercial Union Assce Co., 1946–50; Chubb & Sons Lock and Safe Co., 1950; Man. Dir, 1965; Dir, Chubb & Son Ltd, 1965; Dir, Metal Closures Gp, 1976–86. Member: Home Office Standing Cttee on Crime Prevention, 1967–85; Exec. Cttee, British Digestive Foundn, 1982–86; Chairman: Council, British Security Industry Assoc., 1981–85; Airport Export Gp, NEDO, 1983. *Recreations:* reading, playing bridge. *Address:* Flat 8, Woodhouse, 10 The Avenue, Poole, Dorset BH13 6AG.
Died 22 May 1997.

RANDOLPH, His Honour John Hugh Edward; a Circuit Judge, 1972–87; *b* 14 Oct. 1913; *s* of late Charles Edward Randolph and Phyllis Randolph; *m* 1959, Anna Marjorie (*née* Thomson) (*d* 1999). *Educ:* Bradford Grammar Sch.; Leeds University. RAF, 1940–46. Called to the Bar, Middle Temple, 1946; practised on NE Circuit until 1965; Stipendiary Magistrate of Leeds, 1965–71. Deputy Chairman: E Riding QS, 1958–63; W Riding QS, 1963–71. *Recreation:* golf. *Died 22 Sept. 2000.*

RANDOLPH, Rev. Michael Richard Spencer; Editor-in-Chief, Reader's Digest (British Edition), 1957–88; *b* 2 Jan. 1925; *s* of late Leslie Richard Randolph and Gladys (*née* Keen); *m* 1952, Jenefer Scawen Blunt; two *s* two *d*. *Educ:* Merchant Taylors' Sch.; New Rochelle High Sch., NY, USA; Queen's Coll., Oxford; Canterbury Sch. of Ministry. Served RNVR, Intell. Staff Eastern Fleet, 1944–46, Sub-Lieut. Editorial staff, Amalgamated Press, 1948–52; Odham's Press, 1952–56; Reader's Digest, 1956–88. Press Mem., Press Council, 1975–88; Chm., Soc. of Magazine Editors, 1973. Ordained: deacon, 1990; priest, 1991. Asst Curate (Local NSM), 1990–94, Hon. Asst Priest, 1995–, Biddenden and Smarden. Pres., Weald of Kent Preservation Soc., 1988–. Mem. Smarden Parish Council, 1987–. FRSA 1962. *Recreation:* grandparenthood. *Address:* Little Smarden House, Smarden, Kent TN27 8NB. *Club:* Savile.
Died 29 June 1997.

RANGER, Sir Douglas, Kt 1978; FRCS; Otolaryngologist, The Middlesex Hospital, 1950–82; Dean, The Middlesex Hospital Medical School, 1974–83; Civil Consultant in Otolaryngology, Royal Air Force, 1965–83, then Hon.

Civil Consultant; *b* 5 Oct. 1916; *s* of William and Hatton Thomasina Ranger; *m* 1943, Betty, *d* of Captain Sydney Harold Draper and Elsie Draper; two *s. Educ:* Church of England Grammar Sch., Brisbane; The Middlesex Hosp. Med. Sch. (MB BS 1941). FRCS 1943. Surgical Registrar, The Middx Hosp., 1942–44; served War, Temp. Maj. RAMC and Surgical Specialist, 1945–48 (SEAC and MELF); Otolaryngologist, Mount Vernon Hosp., 1958–74. Hon. Sec., Brit. Assoc. of Otolaryngologists, 1965–71. Mem. Court of Examiners, 1966–72, Mem. Council, 1967–72, RCS; Pres., Assoc. of Head and Neck Oncologists of GB, 1974–77. Dir, Ferens Inst. of Otolaryngology, 1965–83; Cons. Adviser in Otolaryngology, DHSS, 1971–82. *Publications:* The Middlesex Hospital Medical School, Centenary to Sesquicentenary, 1985; papers and lectures on otolaryngological subjects, esp. with ref. to malignant disease. *Address:* Wisteria House, Bayshill Lane, Cheltenham, Glos GL50 3AX. *T:* (01242) 222865.

Died 22 Dec. 1997.

RANK, Joseph McArthur; President, Ranks Hovis McDougall Ltd, 1981–93; *b* 24 April 1918; *s* of late Rowland Rank and Margaret McArthur; *m* 1946, Hon. Moira, *d* of 3rd Baron Southborough and *widow* of Peter Anthony Stanley Woodwark (killed in action, 1943); one *s* one *d*, and one step *d. Educ:* Loretto. Joined Mark Mayhew Ltd, 1936. Served RAF, 1940–46; Personal Pilot to Air C-in-C, SEAC, 1945. Jt Man. Dir, Joseph Rank Ltd, 1955–65; Dep. Chm. and Chief Exec., Ranks Hovis McDougall Ltd, 1965–69, Chm., 1969–81. Pres., Nat. Assoc. of British and Irish Millers, 1957–58, Centenary Pres., 1978; Hon. Pres., Millers Mutual Assoc., 1991– (Chm., 1969–81); Chm. Council, British Nutrition Foundation, 1968–69. Dir, Royal Alexandra and Albert Sch., 1952, Chm., Governing Body, 1975–84; Council, Royal Warrant Holders Assoc., 1968–71. Mem., Shrievalty Assoc., 1974. First High Sheriff of East Sussex, 1974. Friend of the Royal Coll. of Physicians, 1967–. Hon. FRCP 1978. *Recreations:* boating, travelling.

Died 10 Feb. 1999.

RANKIN, Sir Alick (Michael), Kt 1992; CBE 1987; DL; Chairman, Scottish & Newcastle plc (formerly Scottish & Newcastle Breweries), 1989–97 (Chief Executive, 1983–91; Director, since 1974); Deputy Chairman: CGU plc, since 1998; Anglo American plc, since 1999; *b* 23 Jan. 1935; *s* of late Lt-Col (Arthur) Niall (Talbot) Rankin, FRPS, FRGS and of Lady Jean Rankin, DCVO; *m* 1st, 1958, Susan Margaret Dewhurst (marr. diss. 1976); one *s* three *d*: 2nd, 1976, Suzetta Barber (*née* Nelson). *Educ:* Ludgrove; Eton College. Scots Guards, 1954–56. Wood Gundy & Co., Investment Dealers, Toronto, 1956–59; Scottish & Newcastle Breweries: joined, 1960; Dir, Retail, Scottish Brewers, 1965–69; Chm. and Man. Dir, Waverley Vintners, 1969–76; Marketing Dir, 1977–82; Chm., Scottish Brewers, 1982–83; Dep. Chm., 1987–89. Chairman: Scottish Financial Enterprise, 1992–95; Christian Salvesen, 1992–97 (Dir, 1986–); Gen. Accident, 1997–98 (Dep. Chm., 1995–97); non-executive Director: Bank of Scotland plc, 1987–; Sears plc, 1991–98; Securities Trust of Scotland, 1991–; BAT Industries, 1993–95; James Finlay, 1994–. Chairman: The Brewers' Soc., 1989–90; Holyrood Brewery Foundn, 1990–96, Dir, Edinburgh Fest. Soc., 1996–. Mem., Royal Co. of Archers. FRSA 1992. DL Edinburgh, 1996. *Recreations:* fishing, shooting, golf, tennis, ornithology, oenology. *Address:* Tullimoy House, Glenalmond, Perthshire PH1 3SL. *T:* (01738) 800469. *Clubs:* Boodle's; New (Edinburgh); Hon. Co. of Edinburgh Golfers (Muirfield); Royal and Ancient Golf (St Andrews); I Zingari, Eton Ramblers Cricket.

Died 3 Aug. 1999.

RANKIN, James Deans, CBE 1983; PhD; Chief Inspector, Cruelty to Animals Act (1876), Home Office, 1976–83; *b* 17 Jan. 1918; *s* of late Andrew Christian Fleming Rankin and Catherine Sutherland (*née* Russell); *m* 1950, (Hilary) Jacqueline Bradshaw; two *d. Educ:* Hamilton Acad.; Glasgow Veterinary Coll. (MRCVS); Reading Univ. (PhD Microbiology). FIBiol. Gen. practice, 1941; Res. Officer, Min. of Agriculture and Fisheries, 1942; Principal Res. Officer, ARC, 1952; Inspector, Home Office, 1969. *Publications:* scientific contribs in standard works and in med. and veterinary jls. *Club:* Farmers'.

Died 26 June 2000.

RAPHAEL, Prof. Ralph Alexander, CBE 1982; PhD, DSc; ARCS, DIC; FRS 1962; FRSE, FRSC; Fellow of Christ's College, Professor of Organic Chemistry, and Head of Department of Organic and Inorganic Chemistry, Cambridge University, 1972–88, then Hon. Fellow and Professor Emeritus; *b* 1 Jan. 1921; *s* of Jack Raphael; *m* 1944, Prudence Marguerite Anne, *d* of Col P. J. Gaffikin, MC, MD; one *s* one *d. Educ:* Wesley College, Dublin; Tottenham County School; Imperial College of Science and Technology (PhD, DSc; FIC 1991). Chemist, May & Baker Ltd, 1943–46; ICI Research Fellow, Univ. of London, 1946–49; Lecturer in Organic Chemistry, Univ. of Glasgow, 1949–54; Professor of Organic Chemistry, Queen's University, Belfast, 1954–57; Regius Prof. of Chemistry, Glasgow Univ., 1957–72. Tilden Lectr, 1960, Corday-Morgan Vis. Lectr, 1963, Pedler Lectr, 1973, Chem. Soc.; Royal Soc. Vis. Prof., 1967; Pacific Coast Lectr, West Coast Univs tour from LA to Vancouver, 1979; Lady Davis Vis. Prof., Hebrew Univ. of Jerusalem, 1980; Sandin Lectr, Univ. of Alberta, 1985; Andrews Lectr, Univ. of NSW, 1985; Royal Soc. Kan Tong-Po Vis. Prof., Hong Kong Univ., 1989; Emilio Noelting Vis. Prof., Univ. de Haute Alsace, 1990. Vice-Pres. Chemical Soc., 1967–70; Member: Academic Adv. Bd, Warwick Univ., 1962–; Scientific Adv. Cttee, National Gall., 1986–. Hon. MRIA 1987. DUniv Stirling, 1982; Hon. DSc: East Anglia, 1986; QUB, 1989. Meldola Medallist, RIC, 1948; Chem. Soc. Ciba-Geigy Award for Synthetic Chemistry, 1975; Davy Medal, Royal Soc., 1981. *Publications:* Chemistry of Carbon Compounds, Vol. IIA, 1953; Acetylenic Compounds in Organic Synthesis, 1955; papers in Journal of Chemical Society. *Recreations:* music, bridge. *Address:* University Chemical Laboratory, Lensfield Road, Cambridge CB2 1EW. *T:* (01223) 336458; 4 Ivy Field, High Street, Barton, Cambs CB3 7BJ.

Died 27 April 1998.

RASCH, Sir Richard Guy Carne, 3rd Bt *cr* 1903, of Woodhill, Danbury, Essex; a Member of HM Body Guard, Honourable Corps of Gentlemen-at-Arms, 1968–88; *b* 10 Oct. 1918; *s* of Brigadier G. E. C. Rasch, CVO, DSO (*d* 1955) (*yr s* of 1st Bt), and Phyllis Dorothy Lindsay, *d* of Hon. Alwyn Greville, CVO; *S* uncle, 1963; *m* 1st, 1947, Anne Mary (marr. diss. 1959; she *d* 1989), *d* of late Major J. H. Dent-Brocklehurst; one *s* one *d*; 2nd, 1961, Fiona Mary, *d* of Robert Douglas Shaw. *Educ:* Eton; RMC, Sandhurst. Major, late Grenadier Guards. Served War of 1939–45; retired, 1951. *Recreations:* shooting, fishing. *Heir: s* Simon Anthony Carne Rasch [*b* 26 Feb. 1948; *m* 1987, Julia, *er d* of Major Michael Stourton; one *s* one *d*]. *Address:* 30 Ovington Square, SW3 1LR. *T:* 0171–589 9973; The Manor House, Lower Woodford, near Salisbury, Wilts SP4 6NQ. *Clubs:* White's, Pratt's, Cavalry and Guards.

Died 24 June 1996.

RASMINSKY, Louis, CC 1968; CBE 1946; Governor, Bank of Canada, 1961–73; *b* 1 Feb. 1908; *s* of David and Etta Rasminsky; *m* 1930, Lyla Rotenberg; one *s* one *d. Educ:* University of Toronto; London School of Economics (Hon. Fellow, 1960). Financial Section, League of Nations, 1930–39; Chairman, Foreign Exchange

Control Board, Canada, 1940–51; Deputy Governor, Bank of Canada, 1956–61. Executive Director: IMF, 1946–62; International Bank, 1950–62; Alternate Governor for Canada, IMF, 1969–73. Chm., Bd of Governors, Internat. Develt Res. Centre, 1973–78. Hon. LLD: Univ. of Toronto, 1953; Queen's Univ., 1967; Bishop's Univ., 1968; McMaster Univ., 1969; Yeshiva Univ., NY, 1970; Trent Univ., 1972; Concordia Univ., 1975; Univ. of Western Ontario, 1978; Univ. of British Columbia, 1979; Carleton Univ., 1987; Hon. DHL Hebrew Union Coll., 1963. Outstanding Achievement Award of Public Service of Canada, 1968; Vanier Medal, Inst. of Public Admin, 1974. *Recreations:* golf, fishing. *Address:* 20 Driveway, Apt 1006, Ottawa, ON K2P 1C8, Canada. *T:* (613) 5940150. *Clubs:* Rideau, Cercle Universitaire d'Ottawa (Ottawa); Five Lakes (Wakefield, PQ). *Died 15 Sept. 1998.*

RAVEN, Dame Kathleen (Annie), (Dame Kathleen Ingram), DBE 1968; FRCN 1986; SRN 1936; SCM 1938; Chief Nursing Officer in the Department of Health and Social Security (formerly Ministry of Health), 1958–72; *b* 9 Nov. 1910; *o d* of late Fredric William Raven and Annic Williams Raven (*née* Mason); *m* 1959, Prof. John Thornton Ingram, MD, FRCP (*d* 1972). *Educ:* Ulverston Grammar School; privately; St Bartholomew's Hosp., London; City of London Maternity Hospital. St Bartholomew's Hospital, 1937–49: Night Superintendent, Ward Sister, Administrative Sister, Assistant Matron, 1945–49; Matron, Gen. Infirmary, Leeds, 1949–57; Dep. Chief Nursing Officer, Min. of Health, 1957–58. Mem. Gen. Nursing Council for England and Wales, 1950–57; Mem. Council and Chm. Yorkshire Br., Royal Coll. of Nursing, 1950–57; Mem. Central Area Advisory Bd for Secondary Education, Leeds, 1953–57; Area Nursing Officer, Order of St John, 1953–57; Mem. Exec. Cttee, Assoc. of Hospital Matrons for England and Wales, 1955–57; Mem. Advisory Cttee for Sister Tutor's Diploma, Univ. of Hull, 1955–57; Internal Examr for Diploma of Nursing, Univ. of Leeds, 1950–57; Member: Area Nurse Trng Cttee, 1951–57; Area Cttee, Nat. Hosp. Service Reserve, 1950–57; Central Health Services Council, 1957–58; Council and Nursing Advisory Bd, British Red Cross Soc., 1958–72; Cttee of St John Ambulance Assoc., 1958–72; National Florence Nightingale Memorial Cttee of Great Britain and Northern Ireland, 1958–72; WHO Expert Advisory Panel on Nursing, 1961–79; WHO Fellow, 1960; a Vice-Pres., Royal Coll. of Nursing, 1972–. Civil Service Comr, 1972–80. Chief Nursing Adviser, Allied Med. Gp, 1974–86. Nursing missions to Saudi Arabia and Egypt, 1972–86. Member: Council, Distressed Gentlefolk's Aid Assoc., 1974–89 (Chm., F and GP Cttee, 1981–87); Court of Patrons, RCS, 1993–. Founder Gov., Aylesbury GS, 1985. Vice Pres., Med. Foundn, Epsom Coll., 1992–. Freedom, City of London, 1986. Hon. Freewoman, Worshipful Co. of Barbers, 1981. FRSA 1970. Hon. DLitt Keele, 1992; Hon. LLD Leeds, 1996. Officer (Sister) Order of St John, 1963. *Recreations:* painting, reading, travel. *Address:* Jesmond, Burcott, Wing, Leighton Buzzard, Bedfordshire LU7 0JU. *T:* (01296) 688244. *Club:* Royal Commonwealth Society.

Died 19 April 1999.

RAWLINGS, Margaret, (Lady Barlow); actress; *b* Osaka, Japan, 5 June 1906; *d* of Rev. G. W. Rawlings and Lilian Boddington; *m* 1st, 1927, Gabriel Toyne, actor (marr. diss. 1938); no *c*; 2nd, 1942, Sir Robert Barlow (*d* 1976); one *d. Educ:* Oxford High School for Girls; Lady Margaret Hall, Oxford. Left Oxford after one year, and joined the Macdona Players Bernard Shaw Repertory Company on tour, 1927; played Jennifer in the Doctor's Dilemma and many other parts; toured Canada with Maurice Colbourne, 1929; first London engagement Bianca Capello in The Venetian at Little Theatre in 1931, followed by New York; played Elizabeth Barrett Browning, in The Barretts of Wimpole Street in Australia and New Zealand; Oscar Wilde's Salome at Gate Theatre; Liza Kingdom, The Old Folks at Home, Queen's; Mary Fitton in This Side Idolatry, Lyric; Jean in The Greeks had a word for it, Liza Doolittle in Pygmalion and Ann in Man and Superman, Cambridge Theatre, 1935; Katie O'Shea in Parnell, Ethel Barrymore Theatre, New York 1935, later at New, London; Lady Macbeth for OUDS 1936; Mary and Lily in Black Limelight, St James's and Duke of York's, 1937–38; Helen in Trojan Women, Karen Selby in The Flashing Stream, Lyric, 1938–39, and in New York; revival of Liza in Pygmalion, Haymarket, 1939; You of all People, Apollo, 1939; A House in the Square, St Martin's, 1940; Mrs Dearth in Dear Brutus, 1941–42; Gwendolen Fairfax in the Importance of Being Earnest, Royal Command Perf., Haymarket, 1946; Titania in Purcell's Fairy Queen, Covent Garden, 1946; Vittoria Corombona in Webster's The White Devil, Duchess, 1947; Marceline in Jean-Jacques Bernard's The Unquiet Spirit, Arts, 1949; Germaine in A Woman in Love, tour and Embassy, 1949; The Purple Fig Tree, Piccadilly, 1950; Lady Macbeth, in Macbeth, Arts, 1950; Spring at Marino, Arts, 1951; Zabina in Tamburlaine, Old Vic, 1951–52; Lysistrata in The Apple Cart, Haymarket, 1953; Countess in The Dark is Light Enough, Salisbury and Windsor Repertory, 1955; Paulina and Mistress Ford, Old Vic, 1955–56; title rôle in Racine's Phèdre, Theatre in the Round, London and tour, 1957–58; Sappho in Sappho, Lyceum, Edinburgh, 1961; Ask Me No More, Windsor, 1962; title rôle in Racine's Phèdre, Cambridge Arts, 1963; Ella Rentheim in John Gabriel Borkman, Duchess, 1963; Jocasta in Œdipus, Playhouse (Nottingham), 1964; Gertrude in Hamlet, Ludlow Festival, 1965; Madame Torpe in Torpe's Hotel, Yvonne Arnaud Theatre, Guildford, 1965; Mrs Bridgenorth, in Getting Married, Strand, 1967; Carlotta, in A Song at Twilight, Windsor, 1968; Cats Play, Greenwich, 1973; Mixed Economy, King's Head Islington, 1977; Lord Arthur Saville's Crime, Malvern Fest. and tour, 1980; Uncle Vanya, Haymarket, 1982. One-woman performance, Empress Eugénic, May Fair, London, transf. to Vaudeville, UK tour and Dublin Fest., 1979; repeated at King's Lynn Fest., Riverside Theatre, London, New Univ. of Ulster, 1980; Cologne, Horsham, MacRobert Arts Centre, Stirling, Pitlochry Fest., New Univ. of Ulster, 1981; Spoleto Fest., Charleston, SC, 1983. *Films:* Roman Holiday; Beautiful Stranger; No Road Back; Hands of the Ripper; Dr Jekyll and Mr Hyde, 1989. *Television:* Criss Cross Quiz; Somerset Maugham Hour; Sunday Break; Compact; Maigret; Planemakers; solo performance, Black Limelight, Armchair Theatre, 1969; Wives and Daughters, 1971; Folio, 1983; innumerable radio broadcasts, incl. We Beg to Differ, Brains Trust, Desert Island Discs (an early castaway), plays (Tumbledown Dick, 1986; Golovliovo, 1988; Crown House (serial), 1988 (and on Radio 4, 1991, 1992)); poetry recitals; recordings of: Keats, Gerard Manley Hopkins, Alice in Wonderland; (Marlowe Soc.) King Lear, Pericles; New English Bible Gospels. *Publication:* (trans.) Racine's Phèdre, 1961 (US, 1962) (first professional prodn at Pearl Theatre, NY, 1993). *Recreation:* poetry. *Address:* Rocketer, Wendover, Aylesbury, Bucks HP22 6PR. *T:* Wendover (01296) 622234. *Died 19 May 1996.*

RAY, Robin; freelance broadcaster and writer; *b* 17 Sept. 1934; *s* of Ted Ray and Sybil (*née* Stevens); *m* 1960, Susan Stranks; one *s. Educ:* Highgate Sch.; RADA. London stage debut, The Changeling, 1960. Chief Technical Instructor, RADA, 1961–65; Associate Dir, Meadowbrook Theatre, Detroit, USA, 1965–66; writer and broadcaster of over 1000 progs for BBC, commercial radio and television, 1966–95; Artistic Dir, Performance Channel TV, 1996–97. Drama Critic, Punch, 1986–87; music adviser, Classic FM Radio, 1988–97. Consultant,

Nimbus Records, 1998. Deviser, Tomfoolery, Criterion Theatre, 1980; author, Café Puccini, Wyndham's Theatre, 1986; co-author/narrator, Let's Do It!, Chichester Fest., 1994. *Publications:* Time For Lovers (anthology), 1975; Robin Ray's Music Quiz, 1978; Favourite Hymns and Carols, 1982; Words on Music, 1984; (consultant ed.) Classic FM Music Guide to Classical Music, 1996. *Recreations:* music, cinema, reading, shopping. *Address:* c/o David Wilkinson Associates, 115 Hazlebury Road, SW6 2LX. *T:* (0171) 371 5188.

Died 29 Nov. 1998.

RAYNER, Baron *cr* 1983 (Life Peer), of Crowborough in the County of East Sussex; **Derek George Rayner,** Kt 1973; Chairman, 1984–91, Joint Managing Director, 1973–91, Marks and Spencer plc; *b* 30 March 1926; *o s* of George William Rayner and Hilda Jane (*née* Rant); unmarried. *Educ:* City Coll., Norwich; Selwyn Coll., Cambridge (Hon. Fellow 1983). Fellow, Inst. Purchasing and Supply, 1970. Nat. Service, commnd RAF Regt, 1946–48. Joined Marks & Spencer, 1953; Dir, 1967; Chief Exec., 1983–88. Special Adviser to HM Govt, 1970; Chief Exec., Procurement Executive, MoD, 1971–72. Mem., UK Permanent Security Commn, 1977–80. Dep. Chm., Civil Service Pay Bd, 1978–80. Member: Design Council, 1973–75; Council, RCA, 1973–76. Adviser to Prime Minister on improving efficiency and eliminating waste in Government, 1979–83. Chm., Coronary Artery Disease Res. Assoc. (CORDA), 1985–91. Pres., St Bartholomew's Hosp. Med. Coll., 1988–93. Trustee, Royal Botanic Gardens, Kew, Foundn, 1992–. Hon. DPhil Bar Ilan Univ., Israel, 1986; DUniv Surrey, 1991. Alexis de Tocqueville Gold Medal, Europ. Inst. of Public Admin, 1988. *Recreations:* gardening, music, food, travel. *Address:* c/o Michael House, 47 Baker Street, W1A 1DN. *Club:* Athenæum.   *Died 26 June 1998.*

RAZZALL, Leonard Humphrey; a Master of the Supreme Court (Taxing), 1954–81; *b* 13 Nov. 1912; *s* of Horace Razzall and Sarah Thompson, Scarborough; *m* 1st, 1936, Muriel (*d* 1968), *yr d* of late Pearson Knowles; two *s*; 2nd, 1975, Mary Elmore, *widow* of David Farrant Bland. *Educ:* Scarborough High Sch. Admitted solicitor, 1935; founded firm Humphrey Razzall & Co., 1938. Served in Royal Marines, 1941–46, Staff Captain; Staff Coll., Camberley (jsc). Contested (L) Scarborough and Whitby Division, 1945. Sometime Examr in High Court practice and procedure for solicitors final examination. *Publications:* A Man of Law's Tale, 1982; Law, Love and Laughter, 1984. *Recreations:* travel, cricket, book-collecting and book-selling, writing letters to The Times. *Address:* Lyle Park, 53 Putney Hill, SW15. *T:* (020) 8788 0471. *Clubs:* English-Speaking Union; Scarborough and Pickering Liberal.   *Died 26 Oct. 1999.*

READ, Gen. Sir (John) Antony (Jervis), GCB 1972 (KCB 1967; CB 1965); CBE 1959 (OBE 1957); DSO 1945; MC 1941; Governor of Royal Hospital, Chelsea, 1975–81; *b* 10 Sept. 1913; *e s* of late John Dale Read, Heathfield, Sussex; *m* 1947, Sheila, *e d* of late F. G. C. Morris, London, NW8; three *d. Educ:* Winchester; Sandhurst. Commissioned Oxford and Bucks LI, 1934; seconded to Gold Coast Regt, RWAFF, 1936; comd 81 (W African) Div. Reconnaissance Regt, 1943; comd 1 Gambia Regt, 1944; war service Kenya, Abyssinia, Somaliland, Burma; DAMS, War Office, 1947–49; Company Comd RMA Sandhurst, 1949–52; AA&QMG 11 Armd Div., 1953–54; comd 1 Oxford and Bucks LI, 1955–57; comd 3 Inf. Bde Gp, 1957–59; Comdt School of Infantry, 1959–62; GOC Northumbrian Area and 50 (Northumbrian) Division (TA), 1962–64; Vice-Quarter-Master-General, Min. of Defence, 1964–66; GOC-in-C, Western Comd, 1966–69; Quartermaster-General, 1969–72; Comdt, Royal Coll. of Defence Studies, 1973. ADC (Gen.) to the Queen,

1971–73. Colonel Commandant: Army Catering Corps, 1966–76; The Light Division, 1968–73; Small Arms School Corps, 1969–74; Hon. Col, Oxfordshire Royal Green Jackets Bn ACF, 1983–92. President: TA Rifle Assoc., 1972–90; Ex-Services Fellowship Centres, 1975–91; ACF Assoc., 1983–92 (Chm., 1973–82). Treas., Lord Kitchener Nat. Meml Fund, 1980–87. Governor: Royal Sch. for Daughters of Officers of the Army, 1966–83 (Chm., 1975–81); St Edward's Sch., Oxford, 1972–86; Special Comr, Duke of York's Royal Mil. Sch., 1974–90. *Address:* 8 Cherwood Close, Caversfield, Bicester, Oxon OX6 9RA. *T:* (01869) 252189. *Club:* Army and Navy.

Died 22 Sept. 2000.

READER HARRIS, Dame (Muriel) Diana, DBE 1972; Headmistress, Sherborne School for Girls, Dorset, 1950–75; *b* Hong Kong, 11 Oct. 1912; *er d* of late Montgomery Reader Harris. *Educ:* Sherborne School for Girls; University of London (external student). BA 1st Class Honours (English), 1934. Asst Mistress, Sherborne School for Girls, 1934, and House Mistress, 1938. Organised Public Schools and Clubs Camps for Girls, 1937–39; in charge of group evacuated from Sherborne to Canada, 1940; joined staff of National Association of Girls' Clubs, 1943; Chm. Christian Consultative Cttee, Nat. Assoc. of Mixed Clubs and Girls' Clubs, 1952–68, Vice-Pres., 1968; Chm. Outward Bound Girls' Courses, 1954–59; Mem. Council, Outward Bound Trust, 1956–64. Member: Women's Consultative Cttee, Min. of Labour, 1958–77; Women's Nat. Commn, 1976–78. Member: Dorset Educn Cttee, 1952–70; Exec. Cttee, Assoc. of Headmistresses, 1953–58, 1960 (Pres., 1964–66); Pres., Assoc. of Headmistresses of Boarding Schs, 1960–62; Member: Cttee on Agricl Colls, Min. of Agric., 1961–64; Schs Council, 1966–75. Member: Archbishop's Council on Evangelism, 1966–68; Panel on Broadcasting, Synod of C of E, 1975–86; Bd, Christian Aid, 1976–83 (Chm., 1978–83); Exec. Cttee and Assembly, BCC, 1977–83. Pres., CMS, 1969–82 (Mem., 1953–82, Chm., 1960–63, Exec. Cttee). Lay Canon, Salisbury Cathedral, 1987–92; King George's Jubilee Trust: Mem., Standing Res. and Adv. Cttee, 1949; Mem., Admin. Council, 1955–67; Member: Council, 1951–62, Exec. and Council, 1976–79, Nat. Youth Orch. of GB; ITA, 1956–60; Council, Westminster Abbey Choir Sch., 1976–88; Court, Royal Foundn of St Katharine, 1979–90 (Chm., 1981–88). Patron, Jt Educational Trust, 1986– (Chm., 1982–84, Trustee, 1975–86); President: Sch. Mistresses and Governesses Benevolent Instn, 1980–90; Time and Talents Assoc., 1981–92; British and For. Sch. Soc., 1982–91; Churches' Commn on Overseas Students, 1984–91. Governor: Godolphin Sch., Salisbury, 1975–86; St Michael's Sch., Limpsfield, 1975–83 (Chm., 1977–83). FRSA 1964 (Mem. Council, RSA, 1975–89; Chm., 1979–81; Vice-Pres., 1981–89; Vice-Pres. Emerita, 1989–); Mem., The Pilgrims, 1979–. Hon. FCP 1975. *Address:* 35 The Close, Salisbury, Wilts SP1 2EL. *T:* (01722) 326889.   *Died 7 Oct. 1996.*

REDDAWAY, (George Frank) Norman, CBE 1965 (MBE 1946); HM Diplomatic Service, retired; *b* 2 May 1918; *s* of late William Fiddian Reddaway and Kate Waterland Reddaway (*née* Sills); *m* 1944, Jean Brett, OBE; two *s* three *d. Educ:* Oundle School; King's College, Cambridge (Scholar Modern Langs, 1935; 1st Class Hons Mod. Langs Tripos Parts 1 and 2, 1937 and 1939). Served in Army, 1939–46; psc Camberley, 1944. Foreign Office, 1946; Private Sec. to Parly Under Sec. of State, 1947–49; Rome, 1949; Ottawa, 1952; Foreign Office, 1955; Imperial Defence College, 1960; Counsellor, Beirut, 1961; Counsellor, Office of the Political Adviser to the C-in-C, Far East, Singapore, 1965–66; Counsellor (Commercial), Khartoum, 1967–69; Asst Under-Sec. of State, FCO, 1970–74; Ambassador to Poland, 1974–78. Chm.,

International House (formerly English International), 1978–98; Dir, Catalytic International, 1978–89; Consultant: Badger Catalytic, 1989–94; Raytheon Engineers and Constructors, 1994–. Chm., British–Polish Council, 1996–98. Trustee, Thomson Foundn, 1978–. Commander, Order of Merit, Polish People's Republic, 1985. *Recreations:* international affairs, gardening, family history. *Address:* 51 Carlton Hill, NW8 0EL. *T:* (020) 7624 9238. *Clubs:* Athenæum, Royal Commonwealth Society, Polish Hearth. *Died 12 Oct. 1999.*

REDDY, (Neelam) Sanjiva; farmer and lemon grower; President of India, 1977–82; *b* 13 May 1913; *m* Nagaratnamma; one *s* three *d*. *Educ:* Adyar Arts Coll., Anantapur. Andhra Provincial Congress: Sec., Congress Cttee, 1936–46, Pres., 1951–52; Leader, Congress Legislature Party, 1953–64; Mem. and Sec., Madras Legislative Assembly, 1946; Mem., Indian Constituent Assembly, 1947; Minister for Prohibition, Housing and Forests, Madras Govt, 1949–51; Mem., Rajya Sabha, 1952–53; Andhra Pradesh: Mem., Legislative Assembly, 1953–64; Dep. Chief Minister, 1953–56; Chief Minister, 1956–57 and 1962–64; Pres., All-India Congress Party, 1960–62; Member: Rajya Sabha, 1964–67; Lok Sabha, 1967–71, and 1977; Minister: of Steel and Mines, 1964–65; of Transport, Aviation, Shipping and Tourism, 1966–67; Speaker of Lok Sabha, 1967–69, 1977. *Address:* Illure, Anantapur, Andhra Pradesh, India.
Died 1 June 1996.

REDMOND, Sir James, Kt 1979; FREng, FIEE; Director of Engineering, BBC, 1968–78; *b* 8 Nov. 1918; *s* of Patrick and Marion Redmond; *m* 1942, Joan Morris, one *s* one *d*. *Educ:* Graeme High Sch., Falkirk. Radio Officer, Merchant Navy, 1935–37 and 1939–45; BBC Television, Alexandra Palace, 1937–39; BBC: Installation Engr, 1949; Supt Engg Television Recording, 1960; Sen Supt Engg TV, 1963; Asst Dir of Engrg, 1967. Pres., Soc. of Electronic and Radio Technicians, 1970–75, Pres., IEE, 1978–79. Mem. Bd, Services Sound and Vision Corporation, 1983–90. Member: Council, Brunel Univ., 1980–88; Council, Open Univ., 1981–94. Hon. FIEE 1989. Hon. DTech Brunel, 1991; DUniv Open, 1995. *Recreation:* golf. *Address:* 43 Cholmeley Crescent, Highgate, N6 5EX. *T:* (020) 8340 1611. *Club:* Athenæum. *Died 17 Oct. 1999.*

REDMOND, Martin; MP (Lab) Don Valley, since 1983; *b* 15 Aug. 1937. *Educ:* Woodlands RC Sch.; Sheffield Univ. Mem., Doncaster Borough Council, 1975–83 (Chm. of Labour Gp and Leader of Council, 1982–83). Vice-Chm., Doncaster AHA. Mem., NUM. *Address:* House of Commons, SW1A 0AA. *Died 20 Jan. 1997.*

REED, Sir Nigel (Vernon), Kt 1970; CBE 1967 (MBE (mil.) 1945); TD 1950; Chief Justice of the Northern States of Nigeria, 1968–75; *b* 31 Oct. 1913; *s* of Vernon Herbert Reed, formerly MP and MLC New Zealand, and Eila Mabel Reed; *m* 1945, Ellen Elizabeth Langstaff; one *s* two *d*. *Educ:* Wanganui Collegiate School, NZ; Victoria University College, NZ (LLB); Jesus College, Cambridge (LLB). Called to the Bar, Lincoln's Inn, 1939. Military Service, 1939–45, Lt-Col 1944. Appointed to Colonial Legal Service, 1946; Magistrate, Nigeria, 1946; Chief Magistrate, Nigeria, 1951; Chief Registrar, 1955–56, Judge, 1956–64, High Court of the Northern Region of Nigeria; Sen. Puisne Judge, High Court of Northern Nigeria, 1964–68. Comr for Law Revision in States of N Nigeria, 1988. *Address:* 33 Bayview Road, Paihia, Bay of Islands, New Zealand. *Died 20 Sept. 1997.*

REED, (Robert) Oliver; actor; *b* 13 Feb. 1938; *s* of late Peter and Marcia Reed; *m* 1960, Kathleen Byrne (marr. diss. 1970); one *s*; one *d* by Jacquie Daryl; *m* 1985, Josephine Burge. *Educ:* Ewel Castle. Films included:

Oliver, 1967; Women In Love, 1969; The Devils, 1971; Three Musketeers, 1974; Tommy, 1975; The Prince and the Pauper, 1977; Lion of the Desert, Condorman, 1981; Venom, The Sting II, 1982; Second Chance, 1983; Captive, Castaway, 1986; The Adventures of Baron Munchausen, 1989; The Return of the Musketeers, 1989; Treasure Island, 1990; Prisoners of Honour, 1991; Funny Bones, 1995; Parting Shots, 1997. Return to Lonesome Dove (television series), 1993. *Publication:* Reed All About Me, 1979. *Recreations:* Rugby, racing. *Address:* c/o ICM, Oxford House, 76 Oxford Street, W1N 0AX.
Died 2 May 1999.

REED, Stanley William; Director, British Film Institute, 1964–72, Consultant on Regional Development, 1972–76; *b* 21 Jan. 1911; *s* of Sidney James Reed and Ellen Maria Patient; *m* 1937, Alicia Mary Chapman; three *d*. *Educ:* Stratford Grammar Sch.; Coll. of St Mark and St John, Chelsea. Teacher in E London schools, 1931–39; in charge of school evacuation parties, 1939–45; Teacher and Visual Aids Officer, West Ham Education Cttee, 1939–50; British Film Institute: Educn Officer, 1950–56; Sec., 1956–64. *Publications:* The Cinema, 1952; How Films are Made, 1955; A Guide to Good Viewing, 1961; Neighbourhood 15 (film, also Dir). *Recreations:* opera, exploring London's suburbs. *Address:* 54 Felstead Road, Wanstead, E11 2QL. *T:* 0181–989 6021. *Died 4 May 1996.*

REEKIE, Henry Enfield; Headmaster of Felsted School, 1951–68; *b* Hayfield, Derbyshire, 17 Oct. 1907; *s* of John Albert Reekie and Edith Dowson; *m* 1936, Pauline Rosalind, *d* of Eric W. Seeman; one *s* three *d*. *Educ:* Oundle; Clare College, Cambridge. RAFO, 1930–35. Asst Master, Felsted School, 1929, Housemaster, 1933, Senior Science Master, 1945; Headmaster, St Bees School, 1946. *Recreations:* ski-ing, gardening, travel. *Address:* 30 Town Mill, Kennet Place, Marlborough, Wilts SN8 1NS. *T:* (01672) 515596. *Died 3 Jan. 2000.*

REES, Arthur Morgan, CBE 1974 (OBE 1963); QPM 1970; DL; Chairman, St John's Staffordshire, since 1974; *b* 20 Nov. 1912; *s* of Thomas and Jane Rees, The Limes, Llangadog; *m* 1943, Dorothy Webb (*d* 1988); one *d*. *Educ:* Llandovery Coll.; St Catharine's Coll., Cambridge (BA 1935, MA 1939). Metropolitan Police, 1935–41; RAF (Pilot), 1941–46 (Subst. Sqdn Ldr; Actg Wing Comdr); Metropolitan Police, 1946–57; Chief Constable: Denbighshire, 1957–64; Staffordshire, 1964–77. Consultant Director: for Wales, Britannia Building Soc., 1983–88; Inter-Globe Security Services Ltd, 1986–88. Chm. (Founder), EPIC, ExPolice in Industry and Commerce, 1978, Life Pres., 1988. Life Mem., Midlands Sports Adv. Cttee, 1981; Chm., Queen's Silver Jubilee Appeal (Sport), 1976; Mem., King George's Jubilee Trust Council, 1973; Chm., The Prince's Trust Cttee (Sport and Leisure), 1981–88. Chm., British Karate Fedn, 1982; President: Welsh Karate Fedn; Staffs Playing Fields Assoc., 1985–; Dep. Pres., Staffs Assoc. of Boys' Clubs, 1975–; Chm., Staffs St John Ambulance Brigade, 1970. Trustee and Board of Governors, Llandovery College; Mem. Court, Univ. of Keele, 1981–84. Founder Pres., Eccleshall Rugby Football Club, 1980–. DL Staffs, 1967. KStJ 1977 (CStJ 1969). *Recreations:* former Rugby International for Wales (14 caps), Cambridge Rugby Blue, 1933 and 1934; played Welsh Schs Hockey Internationals, 1930; Pres., Crawshays Welsh Rugby XV, 1992– (Chm., 1960–92). *Address:* National Westminster Bank, Eccleshall, near Stafford ST21 6BP. *Clubs:* Royal Air Force; Hawks (Cambridge) (Vice-Chm. 1985, Chm. 1986). *Died 13 May 1998.*

REES, Sir (Charles William) Stanley, Kt 1962; TD 1949; DL; Judge of High Court of Justice, Family Division (formerly Probate, Divorce and Admiralty Division), 1962–77; *b* 30 Nov. 1907; *s* of Dr David Charles Rees,

MRCS, LRCP, and Myrtle May (née Dolley); *m* 1934, Jean Isabel Munro Wheildon (*d* 1985); one *s*. *Educ:* St Andrew's College, Grahamstown, S Africa; University College, Oxford (BA, BCL). Called to the Bar, Inner Temple, 1931, Bencher, 1962. 2nd Lieut 99th Regt AA RA (London Welsh), 1939; JAG's office in Home Commands, 1940–43; Lt-Col in charge JAG's Branch, HQ Palestine Command, 1944–45; released from military service as Hon. Lt-Col, 1945. QC 1957; Dep. Chm., 1959–64, Chm., 1964–71, E Sussex QS; Recorder of Croydon, 1961–62; Commissioner of Assize, Stafford, Dec. 1961. DL E Sussex (formerly Sussex), 1968. Chm., Statutory Cttee, Pharmaceutical Soc. of GB, 1980–81. Governor, Brighton College, 1954–83 (Pres., 1973–83; Vice Patron, 1983). *Recreation:* mountain walking. *Address:* Lark Rise, Lyoth Lane, Lindfield, Haywards Heath, W Sussex RH16 2QA. *Clubs:* United Oxford & Cambridge University; Sussex.

Died 2 Dec. 2000.

REES, Dr Richard John William, CMG 1979; FRCP, FRCPath; Head, Laboratory for Leprosy and Mycobacterial Research, and WHO Collaborating Centre for Reference and Research on *M. leprae*, National Institute for Medical Research, London, 1969–82; *b* 11 Aug. 1917; *s* of William and Gertrude Rees; *m* 1942, Kathleen Harris (*d* 1998); three *d*. *Educ:* East Sheen County Sch., London; Guy's Hosp., London (BSc 1939; MB, BS 1942). MRCS, LRCP 1941; FRCP 1983; MRCPath 1963, FRCPath 1964. Served War, 1942–46: Captain, RAMC Army Blood Transfusion Service, N Africa and Italy campaigns. House Surg. and Phys., Southern Hosp., Kent, 1941–42; Asst Clin. Pathologist, Guy's Hosp., 1946–49; Mem. of Scientific Staff, NIMR, 1949–69. Sec., MRC Leprosy Cttee, 1959–88; Consultant, US Japanese Co-op. Scientific Prog. on Leprosy, 1969–73. Chairman: LEPRA Med. Adv. Bd, 1963–87 (Mem. Exec. Cttee, 1964–87; Vice-Pres., 1987–); Acid Fast Club, 1960; Pres., Section of Comparative Medicine, RSM, 1975. Vice-Pres., Internat. Leprosy Assoc., 1988– (Mem. Council, 1963–88). Member: Trop. Medicine Res. Bd, 1968–72; 3rd WHO Expert Cttee on Leprosy, 1965; WHO IMMLEP Steering Cttee, 1974–90; WHO THELEP Steering Cttee, 1977–82. Almoth Wright Lectr, 1971; Erasmus Wilson Demonstration, RCS, 1973; 1st Clayton Meml Lectr, 1974; BMA Film, Silver Award, Leprosy, 1974. Member, Editorial Boards: Leprosy Review; Internat. Jl of Leprosy. Hon. Mem., RSM Comparative Medicine Section, 1982–. Manson Medal, RSTM&H, 1980. *Publications:* scientific papers on basic and applied studies in animals and man relevant to pathogenesis, immunology and chemotherapy of leprosy and tuberculosis. *Address:* 13 Bafford House, Newcourt Road, Charlton Kings, Glos GL53 8DQ. *T:* (01242) 574953.

Died 3 Oct. 1998.

REES, Sir Stanley; *see* Rees, Sir C. W. S.

REESE, Surg. Rear-Adm. (John) Mansel, CB 1962; OBE 1953; *b* 3 July 1906; *s* of late Dr D. W. Reese, and Mrs A. M. Reese; *m* 1946, Beryl (née Dunn) (*d* 1973); two *d* (and one *s* decd). *Educ:* Epsom Coll.; St Mary's Hosp. Med. Sch., London University. MRCS, LRCP 1930; DPH 1934. Entered Royal Navy, Jan. 1931; Naval Medical Officer of Health, Orkney and Shetland Comd, 1942–44; Naval MOH, Ceylon, 1944–46; Admiralty, 1947–53; Medical Officer i/c RN Hospital, Plymouth, 1960–63; QHP 1960–63. Surgeon Comdr, 1943; Surgeon Captain, 1954; Surgeon Rear-Adm., 1960; retd 1963. FRSTM&H. Sir Gilbert Blane Gold Medal, 1939. Member Gray's Inn, 1953. CStJ 1961. *Died 11 Sept. 1997.*

REESE, (John) Terence; bridge expert, author and journalist; *b* 28 Aug. 1913; *s* of John and Anne Reese; *m* 1970, Alwyn Sherrington. *Educ:* Bilton Grange; Bradfield

Coll. (top scholar); New Coll., Oxford (top class. scholar). Worked at Harrods, 1935–36; left to follow career as bridge expert and journalist; became bridge correspondent of the London Evening News, 1948, the Observer, 1950, the Lady, 1954, and the London Evening Standard, 1981. Winner of Championships, including: European Champion, 1948, 1949, 1954, 1963; World Champion Bridge Player, 1955; World Team Olympiad, 1960; World Pair Champion, 1961; World Pair Olympiad, 1962; winner of all top British Championships, including Gold Cup eight times and Masters Pairs seven times. Hon. Life Mem., English Bridge Union, 1993. *Publications include:* Reese on Play, 1948; The Expert Game, 1958; Play Bridge with Reese, 1960; Practical Bidding and Practical Play, 1973; (with Albert Dormer) The Complete Book of Bridge, 1973; Play These Hands With Me, 1976; Bridge at the Top (autobiog.), 1977; Teach Yourself Bridge, 1980; Bridge Tips by World Masters, 1980; (with Jeremy Flint) Trick 13 (fiction), 1980; (with David Bird) Miracles of Card Play, 1982; (with Roger Trézel) The Mistakes You Make in Bridge, 1984; (with Martin Hoffman) Play it again Sam, 1985; (with Julian Pottage) Positive Declarer's Play, 1986; Bridge for Ambitious Players, 1988; (with David Bird) Tricks of the Trade, 1989; (with Jeremy Flint) Bridge with the Professional Touch, 1991; Learn Bridge in Five Days, 1995; articles on bridge in magazines and periodicals. *Recreation:* golf.

Died 28 Jan. 1996.

REESE, Mansel; *see* Reese, J. M.

REESE, Terence; *see* Reese, J. T.

REEVE, Marjorie Frances, CBE 1944; TD 1950; JP; *b* 12 Dec. 1899; *d* of late Charles Fry, Bedford; *m* 1st, Lt-Cmdr J. K. Laughton, Royal Navy (*d* 1925); (one *s* decd); 2nd, Maj.-Gen. C. M. Wagstaff, CB, CMG, CIE, DSO (*d* 1934); 3rd, 1950, Maj.-Gen. J. T. W. Reeve, CB, CBE, DSO (*d* 1983). Joined ATS, 1938; served with BEF, and in Middle East and BAOR; late Controller ATS; i/c Public Welfare Section of Control Commission for Germany (BE), 1948–49; Principal in Board of Trade (Overseas), 1949–50. County Director, BRCS, 1953–57; Dep. Pres. Suffolk BRCS, 1957, Hon. Vice-Pres., 1977. Swedish Red Cross Medal in Silver, 1950; Badge of Honour (2nd Class) BRCS, 1970. JP W Suffolk, 1954. *Address:* Moorhouse Nursing Home, Hindhead, Surrey GU26 6RA. *T:* (01428) 604381. *Died 31 Jan. 1998.*

REICHSTEIN, Prof. Tadeus, Dr ing chem; Ordentlicher Professor, Head of Department of Organic Chemistry, University of Basel, 1946–60, then Emeritus; *b* Wloclawek, Poland, 20 July 1897; *s* of Isidor Reichstein and Gustava Brockmann; *m* 1927, Henriette Louise Quarles van Ufford; two *d*. *Educ:* Oberrealschule and Eidgenössische Technische Hochschule, Department of Chemistry, Zürich. Assistant, ETH, Zürich, 1922–34; Professor of Organic Chemistry, ETH, Zürich, 1934; Head of Department of Pharmacy, University of Basel, 1938. Dr *hc:* Sorbonne, Paris, 1947; Basel, 1951; Geneva, 1967; ETH, Zürich, 1967; Abidjan, 1967; London, 1968; Leeds, 1970. Marcel Benoît Prize, 1948; (jointly) Nobel Prize for Medicine, 1950; Cameron Prize, 1951; Copley Medal, Royal Soc., 1968; Dale Medal, Soc. for Endocrinology, 1975. Foreign Member: Royal Society, 1952; Linnean Society, 1974. Hon. Member: British Pteridological Soc., 1967; Amer. Fern Soc., 1974; Deutsche Botanische Gesellschaft, 1976; Schweizerische Botanische Gesellschaft, 1977. *Publications:* numerous papers. *Recreations:* botany (ferns), devoted gardener, mountain-climber. *Address:* Institut für Organische Chemie der Universität, St Johanns-Ring 19, 4056 Basel, Switzerland. *T:* (61) 3226060.

Died 1 Aug. 1996.

REID, Beryl Elizabeth, OBE 1986; actress; *b* 17 June 1920; *m* 1st, Bill Worsley (marr. diss. 1953); 2nd, 1954, Derek Franklin (marr. diss.). *Educ:* Lady Barne House Sch.; Withington High Sch.; Levenshulme High Sch., Manchester. First stage appearance, Bridlington, 1936; on London stage, 1951; appeared in variety, numerous sketches, revues and pantomimes, 1951–64. *Plays:* The Killing of Sister George, Duke of York's, 1965, NY, 1966 (Tony Award for Best Actress); Blithe Spirit, Globe, 1970; Entertaining Mr Sloane, Royal Court, Duke of York's, 1975; National Theatre: Spring Awakening, Romeo and Juliet, 1974; Il Campiello, Counting the Ways, 1976; The Way of the World, RSC, Aldwych, 1978; Born in the Gardens, Bristol Old Vic, 1979, Globe (SWET Award), 1980; The School for Scandal, Haymarket, and Duke of York's, 1983; A Little Bit on the Side, Yvonne Arnaud, Guildford, 1983; Gigi, Lyric, 1985. *Films include:* The Belles of St Trinians, Star, The Killing of Sister George, Entertaining Mr Sloane, No Sex Please—We're British!, Joseph Andrews, Carry On Emmanuelle, Yellowbeard, The Doctor and the Devils, Duel of Hearts, Comic Strip: Didn't You Kill My Brother? Frequent television and radio performances, including This is Your Life, and her own series on several occasions; Best TV actress award, BAFTA, 1983 (for Smiley's People). *Publications:* So Much Love (autobiog.), 1984; (with Eric Braun) The Cats Whiskers, 1986; (with Eric Braun) Beryl, Food and Friends, 1987; The Kingfisher Jump, 1991. *Recreations:* gardening, cooking. *Address:* Robert Luff, 294 Earls Court Road, SW5 9BB. *T:* (0171) 373 7003; James Sharkey Associates, 3rd Floor, 15 Golden Square, W1R 3AG.
Died 13 Oct. 1996.

REID, Rev. Canon Douglas William John; Rector of St Ninian's Episcopal Church, Glasgow, 1973–99; Dean of Glasgow and Galloway, 1987–96; *b* 15 Feb. 1934; *s* of Thomas Wood Reid and Catherine Henrietta Reid (*née* Ramsay); *m* 1964, Janet Cicely Nash; two *s. Educ:* Trinity Academy, Edinburgh; Episcopal Theological Coll., Edinburgh. Solicitor's clerk, Edinburgh, 1950–53; Army, 1953–55; industrial banking, 1956–60; theol coll., 1960–63; deacon 1963, priest 1964; Asst Curate, Holy Trinity, Ayr, 1963–68; Rector, St James, Glasgow, 1968–73. Canon, St Mary's Cathedral, Glasgow, 1979, Hon. Canon, 1999. *Recreations:* gardening, hill-walking, steam railways, reading. *Address:* St Ninian's Rectory, 32 Glencairn Drive, Glasgow G41 4PW. *T:* (0141) 423 1247.
Died 18 March 2000.

REID, James, OBE (mil.) 1968; VRD 1967; Director, Investments and Loans, Commission of European Communities, 1973–76; *b* 23 Nov. 1921; *s* of William Reid, MBE, and Dora Louisa Reid (*née* Smith); *m* 1949, Margaret James (*d* 1987); two *d. Educ:* City of London Sch.; Emmanuel Coll., Cambridge (MA). Served War, RN: RNVR (Sub Lieut), 1942–45; served RNVR and RNR (Comdr), 1953–72. Entered Northern Ireland Civil Service, 1948 (Asst Principal); Min. of Finance, 1948–61 and 1963–73; Min. of Commerce, 1961–63; Principal, 1953; Asst Sec., 1963; Sen. Asst Sec., 1971; Dep. Sec., 1972. *Recreations:* reading, music. *Address:* 4 Old School Court, King's Lynn, Norfolk PE30 1DB.
Died 28 Dec. 1999.

REILLY, Sir (D'Arcy) Patrick, GCMG 1968 (KCMG 1957; CMG 1949); OBE 1942; HM Diplomatic Service, retired; Chairman, Banque Nationale de Paris Ltd (formerly British and French Bank), 1969–80; *b* 17 March 1909; *s* of late Sir D'Arcy Reilly, Indian Civil Service and Margaret Florence, *d* of Alfred Thomas Wilkinson; *m* 1st, 1938, Rachel Mary (*d* 1984), *d* of late Brigadier-General Sir Percy Sykes, KCIE, CB, CMG; two *d*; 2nd, 1987, Ruth, *widow* of Sir Arthur Norrington. *Educ:* Winchester; New Coll., Oxford (1st class Hon. Mods 1930, Lit. Hum.

1932; Hon. Fellow, 1972). Laming Travelling Fellow, Queen's College, Oxford, 1932; Fellow of All Souls College, Oxford, 1932–39, 1969–; joined Diplomatic Service, 1933; Third Secretary, Tehran, 1935–38; Ministry of Economic Warfare, 1939–42; First Secretary, Algiers, 1943; Paris, 1944; Athens, 1945; Counsellor, HM Foreign Service, 1947; Counsellor at Athens, 1947–48; Imperial Defence College, 1949; Assistant Under-Secretary of State, Foreign Office, 1950–53; Minister in Paris, 1953–56; Dep. Under-Sec. of State, Foreign Office, 1956; Ambassador to the USSR, 1957–60; Dep. Under-Sec. of State, Foreign Office, 1960–64; Official Head of UK Delegation to UN Conference on Trade and Development, 1964; Ambassador to France, 1965–68. Pres., 1972–75, Vice-Pres., 1975–, London Chamber of Commerce and Industry (Chm., Standing Cttee for Common Market countries, 1969–72); Chairman: Overseas Policy Cttee, Assoc. of British Chambers of Commerce, 1970–72; London Univ. Management Cttee, British Inst. in Paris, 1970–79; Council, Bedford Coll., London Univ., 1970–75. Hon. DLitt Bath, 1982. Comdr Légion d'Honneur, 1979. *Address:* 75 Warrington Crescent, W9 1EH. *T:* (020) 7289 5384. *Club:* Athenæum.
Died 6 Oct. 1999.

REINES, Prof. Frederick, PhD; Emeritus Distinguished Professor of Physics, University of California, Irvine, since 1988; *b* 16 March 1918; *s* of Israel Reines and Gussie Reines (*née* Cohen); *m* 1940, Sylvia Samuels; one *s* one *d. Educ:* Stevens Inst. of Technology, Hoboken (ME MechEng 1939; MA Science 1941); New York Univ. (PhD Physics 1944). Staff Mem. and Gp Leader, Theoretical Div., Los Alamos Sci. Lab., 1944–59; Dir, Los Alamos Experiments, Op. Greenhouse, Eniwetok Atoll, 1951; Prof. and Dept Head, Physics Dept, Case Inst. of Technology, and Chm., Jt Case-Western Reserve High Energy Physics Program, 1959–66; Prof. of Physics, Univ. of California, Irvine, 1966–88 (Founding Dean, Phys. Scis, 1966–74). Hon. DEng Stevens Inst. of Technol., 1984. Awards include. J. Robert Oppenheimer Meml Prize, 1981; Nat. Medal of Science, 1985; Panofsky Prize, 1992; Franklin Medal, 1992; (jtly) Nobel Prize for Physics, 1995. *Publications:* papers on nuclear particles, neutrino interactions, supernovae, effects of nuclear weapons. *Address:* Department of Physics and Astronomy, University of California, Irvine, CA 92717, USA. *T:* (714) 8247036, *Fax:* (714) 8247478; *e-mail:* freines@uci.edu.
Died 26 Aug. 1998.

REISS, John Henry, OBE 1972; British Ambassador to Liberia, 1973–78, retired; *b* 26 March 1918; *s* of late Rev. Leopold Reiss and Dora Lillian (*née* Twisden-Bedford); *m* 1943, Dora Lily (*née* York); one *s* two *d. Educ:* Bradfield Coll.; St Thomas' Hosp. Served War, Army, 1939–42. Kenya Govt, 1945–59; Dir of Information, 1954–59; Commonwealth Office, 1959; Dir of Information Services: Johannesburg, 1961–63; Wellington, New Zealand, 1963–65; Foreign and Commonwealth Office, 1966–69; Dep. British Govt Representative, Antigua/St Kitts, 1969–73. *Recreations:* bridge, computing.
Died 1 Jan. 1996.

RELLY, Gavin Walter Hamilton; Director, Anglo American Corporation of South Africa Ltd, since 1966 (Deputy Chairman, 1977–82; Chairman, 1983–90); *b* 6 Feb. 1926; *s* of Cullis Hamilton Relly and Helen Relly; *m* 1951, Jane Margaret Glenton; one *s* two *d. Educ:* Diocesan Coll., Cape Town; Trinity Coll., Oxford (MA). Joined Anglo American Corp., 1949 (Sec. to H. F. Oppenheimer and then to Sir Ernest Oppenheimer); Manager, Chm.'s Office, 1958; elected to Bd of Corp., 1965; Chm., Exec. Cttee, 1978; Mem. Bd, Anglo American Industrial Corp., 1973–90 (Chm., 1973–83). Chm., AECI Ltd, 1983–93; Dir, Minerals & Resources Corp. Ltd, 1974–. Mem., South Africa Foundn, 1975– (Pres., 1981–82). Chm., Bd of

Trustees, WWF-SA, 1987–; Trustee: Univ. of S Africa Foundn, 1975–96; Univ. of the Witwatersrand Foundn, 1984–. Hon. LLD Rhodes, 1991; Hon. DComm Stellenbosch, 1993. *Recreations:* fishing, golf. *Address:* Anglo American Corporation of South Africa Ltd, PO Box 61587, Marshalltown, 2107, South Africa. *T:* (11) 6383234. *Clubs:* Rand, Country (Johannesburg).
Died 10 Jan. 1999.

RELTON, Stanley; HM Diplomatic Service, retired; Counsellor (Administration), British Embassy, Brussels, 1978–83; *b* 19 May 1923; *m* 1953, José Shakespeare; four *d*. Army, 1942–47. Joined HM Diplomatic Service, 1948: Haifa, 1949; Seoul, 1950; Tokyo, 1951; FCO, 1952–53; Vice-Consul, Stuttgart, 1954–57; Bremen, 1957–59; Consul, Rotterdam, 1959–61; Budapest, 1961–64; Second Sec., Buenos Aires, 1964–68; First Sec., Algiers, 1968–71; FCO, 1971–75; First Sec., Blantyre, Malaŵi, 1975–78. *Recreations:* music, chess. *Address:* 20A Waldegrave Park, Twickenham, Middx TW1 4TQ.
Died 1 Jan. 1998.

RENDALL, Peter Godfrey; Headmaster, Bembridge School, Isle of Wight, 1959–74; *b* 25 April 1909; *s* of Godfrey A. H. Rendall and Mary Whishaw Rendall (*née* Wilson); *m* 1944, Ann McKnight Kauffer (*d* 1996); two *s* one *d*. *Educ:* Rugby School; Corpus Christi College, Oxford. Served War of 1939–45, RAF, 1943–46, Flight-Lieut. Assistant Master: Felsted School, Essex, 1931–34; Upper Canada College, Toronto, 1934–35; Felsted School, Essex, 1935–43; Second Master, St Bees School, Cumberland, 1946–48; Headmaster, Achimota School, Gold Coast, 1949–54; Assistant Master, Lancing College, 1954–59. Clerk to Burford Town Council, 1977–85. Coronation Medal, 1953. *Recreations:* reading, gardening, carpentry, painting. *Address:* Chippings, The Hill, Burford, Oxon OX18 4RE. *T:* (01993) 822459. *Clubs:* Royal Commonwealth Society; Oxford Union Society.
Died 29 Nov. 1998.

RENDLESHAM, 8th Baron *cr* 1806 (Ire.); **Charles Anthony Hugh Thellusson;** Royal Corps of Signals; *b* 15 March 1915; *s* of Lt-Col Hon. Hugh Edmund Thellusson, DSO (3rd *s* of 5th Baron) and Gwynnydd Colleton, 5th *d* of Brig.-Gen. Sir Robert Augustus William Colleton, 9th Bt, CB; *S* uncle, 1943; *m* 1st, 1940, Margaret Elizabeth (marr. diss. 1947; she *m* 1962, Patrick P. C. Barthropp), *d* of Lt-Col Robin Rome, Monk's Hall, Glemsford; one *d*; 2nd, 1947, Clare (*d* 1987), *d* of Lt-Col D. H. G. McCririck; one *s* three *d*. *Educ:* Eton. **Heir:** *s* Hon. Charles William Brooke Thellusson [*b* 10 Jan. 1954; *m* 1st, 1983, Susan Fielding (marr. diss.); 2nd, 1988, Lucille Clare, *d* of Rev. Henry Ian Gordon Cumming; one *d*]. *Address:* 498 King's Road, SW10 0LE.
Died 9 Oct. 1999.

RENOUF, Sir Francis (Henry), Kt 1987; company chairman; *b* Wellington, NZ, 31 July 1918; *s* of Francis Charles Renouf and Mary Ellen (*née* Avery); *m* 1st, 1954, Ann Marie Harkin (marr. diss. 1985; she *d* 1998), *d* of Eamon Harkin; one *s* three *d*; 2nd, 1985, Mrs Susan Sangster (marr. diss. 1989), *d* of Hon. Sir John Rossiter, KBE; three step *d*; 3rd, 1991, Michele Ivan-Zadeh-Griaznoff (*née* Mainwaring) (marr. diss. 1996). *Educ:* Wellington Coll.; Victoria University Coll., Wellington (Levin Schol., 1932; MCom 1940); Oxford Univ. (DipEcon 1949). Served 2 NZEF, 1940–46 (Capt.). Stockbroker, 1950–87; Chairman: NZ United Corp. Ltd, 1960–83; Renouf Gp, 1960–87; Renouf Corp., 1983–87; Renouf Underwriters Pty. Officer's Cross, Order of Merit, Federal Republic of Germany, 1986. *Recreation:* lawn tennis (represented NZ Univs, 1938–40, Oxford Univ., 1948–49 (Oxford Blue); Pres., NZ LTA, 1985, 1986). *Address:* 3/260 Oriental Parade, Oriental Bay, Wellington, New Zealand.
Died 13 Sept. 1998.

RENOWDEN, Very Rev. Charles Raymond; Dean of St Asaph, 1971–92, then Dean Emeritus; *b* 27 Oct. 1923; *s* of Rev. Canon Charles Renowden; *m* 1951, Ruth Cecil Mary Collis; one *s* two *d*. *Educ:* Llandysil Grammar Sch.; St David's University Coll., Lampeter; Selwyn Coll., Cambridge. BA (Hons Philosophy, cl. I), Lampeter; BA, MA (Hons Theology, cl. I), Cambridge. Served War, Army, Intelligence Corps, in India and Japan, 1944–47. Cambridge Ordination Course; deacon, 1951, priest, 1952, Wales. Asst Curate, Hubberston, Milford Haven, 1951–55; St David's University College, Lampeter: Lectr in Philosophy and Theology, 1955–57; Head of Dept of Philosophy, 1957–69; Sen. Lectr in Philosophy and Theology, 1969–71. *Publications:* The Idea of Unity (monograph), 1965; New Patterns of Ministry, 1973; The Rôle of a Cathedral Today and Tomorrow, 1974; The Cathedral and the Festival: a partnership in music, 1993; A Genial Kind Divine, Watkin Herbert Williams 1845–1944, 1998; contributor to Theology, The Modern Churchman, Church Quarterly Review, Trivium, Province. *Recreations:* music, gardening, ornithology. *Address:* 17 Llys Idris, Elwy Park, St Asaph, Denbighshire LL17 0AJ. *T:* (01745) 584591.
Died 15 May 2000.

RENTON, Gordon Pearson; Director: R & D Communications Ltd, since 1990; Mediajet Ltd, 1987–93; Assistant Under-Secretary of State, Department of Trade and Industry, 1983–84; *b* 12 Dec. 1928; *s* of Herbert Renton and Annie (*née* Pearson); *m* 1st, 1952, Joan Mary Lucas (marr. diss. 1971); two *s*; 2nd, 1978, Sylvia Jones. *Educ:* King Edward VII Sch., Sheffield; Lincoln Coll., Oxford (Scholar; BA Lit. Hum.). Served Royal Signals, 1951–53. Teacher, W Riding, 1953–54; Asst Principal, Home Office, 1954; Asst Private Sec. to Home Sec. and Lord Privy Seal, 1959–60; Principal, 1960; Asst Sec., 1967; Asst Under-Sec. of State, 1978. Mem., Parole Bd, 1985–88. *Recreations:* music, gardening, sailing. *Address:* Bankers Mill House, Cefn Cribwr, Bridgend CF32 0DA. *T:* (01656) 749131. *Club:* Bristol Channel Yacht.
Died 12 Jan. 2000.

RESTIEAUX, Rt Rev. Cyril Edward; *b* 25 Feb. 1910; *s* of Joseph and Edith Restieaux. *Educ:* English Coll., Rome; Gregorian University. Ordained, 1932; Curate at Nottingham, 1933; Parish Priest at Matlock, 1936; Hon. Canon of Nottingham, 1948; Vicar-General of Nottingham, 1951; Provost and Domestic Prelate to HH Pope Pius XII, 1955; Bishop of Plymouth, 1955–86. *Publication:* Dedicated to Christ, 1989. *Address:* Stoodley Knowle, Anstey's Cove Road, Torquay TQ1 2JB.
Died 27 Feb. 1996.

REYES, Narciso Gallardo; Bintang Mahaputera, 1964; Order of Diplomatic Service Merit, 1972; President, Philippine Council for Foreign Relations, 1986–87; *b* Manila, 6 Feb. 1914; *m*. *Educ:* Univ. of Santo Tomás (AB). Mem., English Faculty, Univ. of Santo Tomás, 1935–36; Assoc. Ed., Philippines Commonweal, 1935–41; Nat. Language Faculty, Ateneo de Manila, 1939–41; Assoc. Ed., Manila Post, 1945–47; Assoc. News Ed., Evening News, Manila, 1947–48; Man. Ed., Philippine Newspaper Guild Organ, 1947–48; Dir, Philippine Information Agency, 1954–55; Minister-Counsellor, Bangkok, 1956; Public Relations Dir, SEATO, 1956–58; Minister, later Amb., Burma, 1958–62; Ambassador to: Indonesia, 1962–67; London, Stockholm, Oslo, Copenhagen, 1967–70; Permanent Rep. to UN, 1970–77; Philippine Ambassador to People's Republic of China, 1977–80; Sec. Gen., ASEAN, 1980–82. Mem. various delegns and missions, incl. sessions of UN; Philippine Rep. to UN Commn for Social Devt, 1967–72 (Vice-Chm., 1967; Chm., 1968); Special UN Rep. on Social Develt, 1968; Rep. to UN Human Rights Commn, 1970–72; Chairman: UNICEF Exec. Bd, 1972–74; UN

Gen. Assembly Finance and Economic Cttee, 1971; Pres., UNDP Governing Council, 1974; Vice-Pres., UN Environment Governing Council, 1975. Chm., External Educn Plans, 1988–89. Vice-Chm., Philippine Futuristics Soc. Editor, Foreign Relations Jl, 1986–. Outstanding Alumnus, Univ. of Santo Tomás, 1969. Dr of Laws (*hc*), Philippine Women's Univ., 1977. Gawad Mabini Award, Philippines, 1994. *Publications:* essays, poems and short stories. *Address:* 8 Lipa Road, Philamlife Homes, Quezon City, Manila, Philippines.   *Died 7 May 1996.*

REYNOLDS, James; Judge of the High Court, Eastern Region of Nigeria, 1956–63; *b* Belfast, May, 1908; *yr s* of late James Reynolds and Agnes Forde (*née* Cully); *m* 1946, Alexandra Mary Erskine Strain; two *s* two *d*. *Educ:* Belfast Royal Acad.; Queen's Univ., Belfast. Called to Bar of NI, 1931; practised at NI Bar, 1931–40; Colonial Legal Service as Crown Counsel in Hong Kong, 1940; Prisoner-of-war in Japanese hands, 1941–45; returned to Hong Kong, 1946; apptd District Judge, 1953. Chairman: Local Tribunal under Nat. Insce Acts, 1964–83; Industrial Tribunal, 1969–81.   *Died 14 March 1999.*

REYNOLDS, Prof. Leighton Durham, FBA 1987; Professor of Classical Languages and Literature, University of Oxford, 1996–97, then Emeritus; Fellow and Tutor in Classics, Brasenose College, Oxford, 1957–97, then Emeritus; *b* 11 Feb. 1930; *s* of Edgar James Reynolds and Hester Ann Reynolds (*née* Hale); *m* 1962, Susan Mary Buchanan, *d* of Prof. Sir Colin Buchanan, CBE; one *s* two *d*. *Educ:* Caerphilly Grammar Sch.; University Coll., Cardiff (BA 1st cl. Hons 1950); St John's Coll., Cambridge (BA 1st cl. Hons 1952; Craven Student, 1952; MA 1956); MA Oxon 1956. Flying Officer, RAF, 1952–54. Jun. Res. Fellow, Queen's Coll., Oxford, 1954–57. Visiting Professor: Cornell Univ., 1960, 1971; Univ. of Texas at Austin, 1967. Mem., Inst. for Advanced Study, Princeton, 1965, 1997. Editor, Classical Review, 1975–87. *Publications:* The Medieval Tradition of Seneca's Letters, 1965; (ed) Seneca, Epistulae Morales, 1965; (with N. G. Wilson) Scribes and Scholars, 1968, 3rd edn 1991; (ed) Seneca, Dialogi, 1977; (ed) Texts and Transmission: a survey of the Latin classics, 1983; (ed) Sallust, 1991; (ed) Cicero, De Finibus, 1998. *Recreations:* walking, camping, gardening, plant-hunting. *Address:* Winterslow Cottage, Lincombe Lane, Boars Hill, Oxford OX1 5DZ. *T:* (01865) 735741.

Died 4 Dec. 1999.

RHODES, Marion, RE 1953 (ARE 1941); etcher, painter in water colour and oils; *b* Huddersfield, Yorks, 17 May 1907; *d* of Samuel Rhodes and Mary Jane Mallinson. *Educ:* Greenhead High School, Huddersfield; Huddersfield Art School; Leeds College of Art; The Central School of Arts and Crafts, London. Art Teachers' Certificate (Univ. of Oxford), 1930. Teaching posts, 1930–67; pt-time Lecturer in Art at Berridge House Training Coll., 1947–55. Exhibited, 1934–: Royal Academy; Royal Scottish Academy; Mall Gall.; The Paris Salon (Honourable Mention, 1952; Bronze Medal, 1956; Silver Medal, 1961; Gold Medal, 1967); Walker Art Gall.; Towner Art Gall.; Atkinson Art Gall.; Southport, Brighton, Bradford, Leeds, Manchester and other provincial Art Galls; also USA and S Africa. Etching of Jordans' Hostel and drawing of The Meeting House purchased by Contemporary Art Soc. and presented to British Museum; other works in the Print Room, BM, and Print Room, V&A; work also purchased by Bradford Corp. Art Gall., Brighouse Art Gall., Huddersfield Art Gall., Stoke-on-Trent Educn Cttee's Loan Scheme, and South London (Camberwell) Library Committee; works reproduced. SGA 1936, Hon. Life Mem., 1969; Member, Manchester Acad. of Fine Art, 1955–81; Associate, Artistes Français, 1971–79; Hon. Mem., Tommasso Campanella Acad., Rome (Silver

Medal, 1970); Cert. of Merit, Dictionary of Internat. Biography, 1972; Mem., Accademia delle Arti e de Lavoro (Parma), 1979–82; Academic of Italy with Gold Medal, 1979. FAMS; FRSA. *Publication:* illustrations for Robert Harding's Snettisham, 1982. *Recreations:* gardening, geology. *Address:* 2 Goodwyn Avenue, Mill Hill, NW7 3RG. *T:* (0181) 959 2280. *Club:* English-Speaking Union.   *Died 6 Aug. 1998.*

RHODES JAMES, Sir Robert (Vidal), Kt 1991; DL; Chairman, History of Parliament Trust, 1983–92; *b* 10 April 1933; *y s* of late Lt-Col W. R. James, OBE, MC; *m* 1956, Angela Margaret Robertson, *er d* of late R. M. Robertson; four *d*. *Educ:* private schs in India; Sedbergh Sch.; Worcester Coll., Oxford. Asst Clerk, House of Commons, 1955–61; Senior Clerk, 1961–64; Fellow of All Souls Coll., Oxford, 1965–68, 1979–81; Dir, Inst. for Study of Internat. Organisation, Univ. of Sussex, 1968–73; Principal Officer, Exec. Office of Sec.-Gen. of UN, 1973–76. Consultant to UN Conf. on Human Environment, 1971–72; UK Mem., UN Sub-Commn on Prevention of Discrimination and Protection of Minorities, 1972–73. MP (C) Cambridge, Dec. 1976–1992. PPS, FCO, 1979–82; Mem., Chairmen's Panel, H of C, 1987–92. Conservative Party Liaison Officer for Higher and Further Educn, 1979–85 and 1987; Chm., Conservative Friends of Israel, 1989–95 (Pres., 1995–98). FRSL 1964; NATO Fellow, 1965; FRHistS 1973. Kratter Prof. of European History, Stanford Univ., Calif, 1968; Vis. Prof., Baylor Univ., Texas, 1992–; Professorial Fellow, Univ. of Sussex, 1973; Fellow, Wolfson Coll., Cambridge, 1991–. DL Cambs, 1993. Hon. DLitt Westminster Coll., Fulton, Missouri, 1986. *Publications:* Lord Randolph Churchill, 1959; An Introduction to the House of Commons, 1961 (John Llewelyn Rhys Memorial Prize); Rosebery, 1963 (Royal Society Lit. Award); Gallipoli, 1965; Standardization and Production of Military Equipment in NATO, 1967; Churchill: a study in failure, 1900–39, 1970; Ambitions and Realities: British politics 1964–70, 1972; Victor Cazalet: a portrait, 1976; The British Revolution 1880–1939, vol. I, 1976, vol. II, 1977, 1 vol. edn, 1978; Albert, Prince Consort, 1983; Anthony Eden, 1986; Bob Boothby: a portrait, 1991 (Angel Lit. Award, 1992); Henry Wellcome, 1994; A Spirit Undaunted: the political role of George VI, 1998; *edited:* Chips: The Diaries of Sir Henry Channon, 1967; Memoirs of a Conservative: J. C. C. Davidson's Memoirs and Papers, 1969; The Czechoslovak Crisis 1968, 1969; The Complete Speeches of Sir Winston Churchill, 1897–1963, 1974; *contributed:* Suez Ten Years After, 1967; Essays From Divers Hands, 1967; Churchill: four faces and the man, 1969; International Administration, 1971; The Prime Ministers, vol. II, 1975. *Address:* The Stone House, Great Gransden, near Sandy, Beds SG19 3AF. *T:* (01767) 677025. *Clubs:* Travellers, Grillion's; Cambridgeshire County.   *Died 20 May 1999.*

RHYMES, Rev. Canon Douglas Alfred; Canon Residentiary and Librarian, Southwark Cathedral, 1962–69, Hon. Canon, 1969, Canon Emeritus since 1984; *b* 26 March 1914; *s* of Peter Alfred and Jessie Rhymes; unmarried. *Educ:* King Edward VI School, Birmingham; Birmingham Univ.; Ripon Hall Theological College, Oxford. BA (2nd Cl. Hons 1st Div.) Philosophy 1939. Deacon 1940, priest 1941; Asst Curate, Dovercourt, Essex, 1940–43; Chaplain to the Forces, 1943–46; Asst Curate, Romford, Essex (in charge of St George's, Romford and St Thomas', Noak Hill), 1946–49; Priest-in-charge, Ascension, Chelmsford, 1949–50; Sacrist, Southwark Cathedral, 1950–54; Vicar, All Saints, New Eltham, SE9, 1954–62; Director of Lay Training, Diocese of Southwark, 1962–68; Vicar of St Giles, Camberwell, 1968–76; Parish Priest of Woldingham, 1976–84; Lectr in Ethics, Chichester Theol Coll., 1984–92. Proctor in Convocation and Mem. of Gen. Synod, 1975–85. *Publications:* (jtly)

Christianity and Communism, 1952; (jtly) Layman's Church, 1963; No New Morality, 1964; Prayer in the Secular City, 1967; Through Prayer to Reality, 1974; (jtly) Dropping the Bomb, 1985; Time Past to Time Future, 1993. *Recreations:* theatre, conversation, country walks. *Address:* Chillington Cottage, 7 Dukes Road, Fontwell, W Sussex BN18 0SP. *T:* Eastergate (01243) 543268.
Died 1 Jan. 1996.

RIABOUCHINSKA, Tatiana, (Mme Lichine); Ballerina of Russian Ballet; owns and operates the Lichine Ballet Academy, Beverly Hills; *b* 23 May 1916; *d* of Michael P. Riabouchinsky, Moscow, banker, and Tatiana Riabouchinska, Dancer of Moscow Imperial School of Dance; *m* 1942, David Lichine (*d* 1972); one *d*. *Educ:* Cour Fénelon, Paris. Trained first by her mother; then by Volinine (dancer of the Moscow Imperial Grand Theatre); then by Mathilde Kchesinska. First appeared as child dancer with Balieff's Chauve Souris in London, 1931; joined new Russian Ballet, 1932, and danced with them in nearly all countries of Western Europe, Australia and N and S America. Citizen of Honor, Beverly Hills, 1990. *Publications:* (contrib.) Garcia-Marquez, The Ballets Russes: Colonel de Basil's Ballets Russes de Monte Carlo 1932–52, 1991; contrib. to books on dancing by: Andre Levinson, Arnold L. Haskell, Irving Deakin, Rayner Heppenstall, Kay Ambrose, Prince Peter Lieven, Cyril W. Beaumont, Cyril Brahms, Adrian Stokes, A. V. Coton, Ninette de Valois, etc. *Address:* 965 Oakmont Drive, Los Angeles, CA 90049, USA; Lichine Ballet School, 405 North Foothill Road, Beverly Hills, CA 90210, USA.
Died 25 Aug. 2000.

RICHARDS, Archibald Banks, CA; retired; *b* 29 March 1911; *s* of late Charles Richards and Margaret Pollock Richards; *m* 1st, 1941, Edith Janet Sinclair (*d* 1987); one *s* one *d*; 2nd, 1990, Constance Mary Fleming Mason. *Educ:* Daniel Stewart's Coll., Edinburgh. Partner, A. T. Niven & Co., Chartered Accountants, Edinburgh, 1939–69, Touche Ross & Co., Chartered Accountants, 1964–78. Inst. of Chartered Accountants of Scotland: Mem., 1934; Mem. Council, 1968–73; Vice Pres., 1974–76; Pres., 1976–77. *Address:* 7 Midmar Gardens, Edinburgh EH10 6DY. *T:* 0131–447 1942.
Died 15 May 1996.

RICHARDS, Bertrand; see Richards, E. B. B.

RICHARDS, Charles Anthony Langdon, CMG 1958; *b* 18 April 1911; *s* of T. L. Richards, Bristol, musician; *m* 1937, Mary Edith Warren-Codrington; two *s*. *Educ:* Clifton Coll.; Brasenose Coll., Oxford. Appointed Colonial CS, Uganda, 1934; Major, 7th King's African Rifles, 1939–41; duties in Mauritius, 1941–46; District Officer, Uganda, 1946–50; Commissioner for Social Development, Tanganyika, 1950–53; Commissioner for Community Development, Uganda, 1953–54; Resident, Buganda, 1954–60; Minister of Local Government, Uganda, 1960–61. *Recreation:* gardening. *Address:* The Wall House, 4 Oak Drive, Highworth, Wilts SN6 7BP.
Died 7 Aug. 1996.

RICHARDS, His Honour (Edmund) Bertrand (Bamford); a Circuit Judge, 1972–86; *b* 14 Feb. 1913; *s* of Rev. Edmund Milo Richards, Llewesog Hall, Denbigh; *m* 2nd, 1966, Jane, *widow* of Edward Stephen Porter. *Educ:* Lancing Coll.; Corpus Christi Coll., Oxford. Served War, RA, 1940–46. Called to the Bar, Inner Temple, 1941. Dep. Chm., Denbighshire QS, 1964–71. Hon. Recorder of Ipswich, 1975. *Address:* Melton Towers, near Woodbridge, Suffolk IP12 1QE.
Died 29 Aug. 2000.

RICHARDS, Gordon Waugh; racehorse trainer, National Hunt, since 1964; *b* 7 Sept. 1930; *s* of Thomas Henry Richards and Gladys Florence Thompson; *m* 1st, Jean Charlton (decd); one *s* one *d*; 2nd, 1980, Joan Dacre Lacey, *d* of Hon. Henry Howard. *Educ:* Bath. Apprentice jockey, 1943; National Hunt jockey, 1950–63, trainer, 1964–; trained 2 Grand National winners: Lucius, 1978; Hello Dandy, 1984; trainer of more than 100 winners in a season, 1977–78, 1990–91 and 1992–93. *Recreations:* tennis, reading. *Address:* The Old Rectory, Greystoke, Penrith, Cumbria CA11 0TJ.
Died 29 Sept. 1998.

RICHARDS, Michael Anthony, CBiol, FIBiol 1985; MRCVS; Chief Inspector, Animals (Scientific Procedures) Act 1986 (formerly Cruelty to Animals Act (1876)), Home Office, 1982–87, retired; *b* 12 Oct. 1926; *s* of Edward Albert Richards and Clara Muriel (*née* Webb); *m* 1956, Sylvia Rosemary, *d* of Geoffrey Charles Pain, JP; two *d*. *Educ:* St Albans Coll., St George's Coll., and J. M. Estrada Coll., all in Buenos Aires; Royal Vet. Coll., London Univ. MRCVS 1953. Served Army, Intell. Corps, 1945–47. In general practice, 1953; Lectr in Vet. Medicine, Univ. of London, 1963–67; Lectr in Vet. Pathology, Univ. of Edinburgh, 1967–69; Home Office, 1969–87. *Publications:* scientific contribs to standard works and med. and vet. jls. *Recreation:* philately. *Address:* 10 Westfield Place, Forfar, Angus DD8 1HL. *T:* (01307) 461268.
Died 31 Dec. 1997.

RICHARDS, Lt-Comdr Richard Meredyth; JP; DL; Royal Navy, retired; Vice Lord-Lieutenant of Gwynedd, since 1985; *b* 27 Dec. 1920; *s* of late Major H. M. Richards, OBE, JP, VL and Mrs Mary Richards, MBE, MSc; *m* 1945, Pamela Watson; three *s* (one *d* decd). *Educ:* RNC, Dartmouth (Naval Cadet). Midshipman, 1939; Sub-Lt 1940; Lieut 1942; Lt-Comdr 1950; served in FAA, 1941–49; returned to gen. service, 1949; retd 1954 (to take over family estate). High Sheriff, Merioneth, 1960; DL Merioneth, 1967; JP Tal-y-Bont (Dolgellau), 1969. *Recreations:* fishing, shooting, sailing, ski-ing. *Address:* Caerynwch, Dolgellau, Gwynedd LL40 2RF. *T:* (01341) 422263.
Died 8 March 1999.

RICHARDSON, Elliot Lee; Partner, Milbank, Tweed, Hadley & McCloy, Washington DC, 1980–92; *b* 20 July 1920; *s* of Dr Edward P. and Clara Lee Richardson; *m* 1952, Anne F. Hazard; two *s* one *d*. *Educ:* Harvard Coll.; Harvard Law Sch. (AB *cum laude* 1941, LLB *cum laude* 1947, Harvard Univ.). Served with US Army, 1942–45 (Lieut): litter-bearer platoon ldr, 4th Inf. Div., Normandy Landing (Bronze Star, Purple Heart). Law clerk, 1947–49; Associate, Ropes, Gray, Best, Coolidge and Rugg, lawyers, Boston, 1949–53 and 1955–56; Asst to Senator Saltonstall, Washington, 1953 and 1954; Asst Sec. for Legislation of Dept of Health, Educn and Welfare, 1957–59 (Actg Sec., April-July 1958); US Attorney for Massachusetts, 1959–61; Special Asst to Attorney General of US, 1961; Partner, Ropes & Gray, 1961–62 and 1963–64; Lieut Governor of Mass, 1964; Attorney General of Mass, 1966; US Under Sec. of State, 1969–70; Sec. of Health, Educn and Welfare, 1970–73; Sec. of Defense, Jan.-May 1973; Attorney General of US, May-Oct. 1973, resigned; Ambassador to UK, 1975–76; Sec. of Commerce, 1976–77; Ambassador-at-large and Special Rep. of the US Pres. to the Law of the Sea Conf., 1977–80. Special Rep. of Pres. for multilateral assistance initiative for the Philippines, 1989–94; Personal Rep. of UN Sec. for monitoring electoral process in Nicaragua, 1989–90. Fellow, Woodrow Wilson Internat. Center for Scholars, 1973–74. Holder of numerous hon. degrees. Presidential Medal of Freedom, 1998. *Publications:* The Creative Balance, 1976; Reflections of a Radical Moderate, 1996; numerous articles on law, social services and govt policy. *Address:* 10450 Lottsford Road, Mitchellville, MD 20721, USA.
Died 31 Dec. 1999.

RICHARDSON, Maj.-Gen. Frank McLean, CB 1960; DSO 1941; OBE 1945; MD; FRCPE; Director Medical

Services, BAOR, 1956–61; *b* 3 March 1904; *s* of late Col Hugh Richardson, DSO, and Elizabeth Richardson; *m* 1944, Sylvia Innes, *d* of Col S. A. Innes, DSO; two *s* one *d*. *Educ:* Glenalmond; Edinburgh Univ. MB, ChB 1926; MD 1938. FRCPE 1986. Joined RAMC, 1927; Captain 1930; Major 1936; Lt-Col 1945; Col 1949; Brig. 1956; Maj.-Gen. 1957. Honorary Surgeon to the Queen, 1957–61. Hon. Col 51 (H) Div. Dist RAMC, TA, 1963–67. *Publications:* Napoleon: Bisexual Emperor, 1972; Napoleon's Death: an Inquest, 1974; Fighting Spirit: psychological factors in war, 1978; The Public and the Bomb, 1981; Mars without Venus: a study of some homosexual Generals, 1981; (with S. MacNeill) Piobaireachd and its Interpretation, 1987. *Address:* c/o Royal Bank of Scotland, Drummonds, 49 Charing Cross, SW1A 2DX; 4B Barnton Avenue West, Edinburgh EH4 6DE. *Died 28 Aug. 1996.*

RICHARDSON, Horace Vincent, OBE 1968; HM Diplomatic Service, retired; *b* 28 Oct. 1913; *s* of late Arthur John Alfred Richardson and Margaret Helena Jane Richardson (*née* Hooson); *m* 1942, Margery Tebbutt; two *s* one *d* (and one *d* decd). *Educ:* Abergele Grammar Sch.; King's Coll., London (LLB). Served with Army, 1940–45. LCC, 1931–35; Supreme Court of Judicature, 1935–47; FO, 1947–48; British Vice-Consul, Shanghai, 1948–50; Washington, 1950–53; 2nd Sec., Rome, 1953–56; FO, 1956–61; Consul, Philadelphia, 1961–63; FO, 1963–66; Consul, Cairo, 1966–68; 1st Sec., Washington, 1968–70; Head of Nationality and Treaty Dept, FCO, 1970–73. Rep. HM Govt at 9th and 10th Sessions of Hague Conf. of Private Internat. Law. FRGS. *Recreations:* golf, gardening. *Address:* 34 Friern Barnet Lane, N11 3LX. *T:* (020) 8368 1983. *Clubs:* MCC, Civil Service; Turf (Cairo); Highgate Golf. *Died 9 July 2000.*

RICHARDSON, Hugh Edward, CIE 1947; OBE 1944; *b* 22 Dec. 1905; *s* of Hugh Richardson, DSO, MD, and Elizabeth (*née* McLean); *m* 1951, Huldah (*née* Walker) (*d* 1995), *widow* of Maj.-Gen. T. G. Rennie, Black Watch (killed in action 1945). *Educ:* Trinity College, Glenalmond; Keble College, Oxford (Hon. Fellow, 1981). Entered Indian Civil Service, 1930; Jt Magistrate and Dep. Collector, Tamluk, Midnapore Dist, Bengal, 1932–34; entered Foreign and Political Service of Govt of India, 1934; Asst Pol Agent, Loralai, Baluchistan, 1934–35; British Trade Agent, Gyantse, and O i/c British Mission, Lhasa, 1936–40; service in NWFP, 1940–42; 1st Sec., Indian Agency-General in China, Chungking, 1942–43; Dep. Sec. to Govt of India, External Affairs Dept, 1944–45; British Trade Agent, Gyantse, and O i/c British Mission, Lhasa, 1946–47; Indian Trade Agent, Gyantse and O i/c Indian Mission, Lhasa, 1947–50; retd from ICS, 1950. Hon. FBA 1986. Hon. DLitt St Andrews, 1985. *Publications:* (with Sir Basil Gould) Tibetan Word Book, 1943; (trans) Ancient Historical Edicts at Lhasa, 1952; Tibet and its History, 1962; (with D. L. Snellgrove) A Cultural History of Tibet, 1968; A Corpus of Early Tibetan Inscriptions, 1985; Ceremonies of the Lhasa Year, 1993; High Peaks, Pure Earth, 1998. *Recreation:* golf. *Address:* c/o Abbey National, 145 Market Street, St Andrews KY16 9PZ. *Club:* Royal and Ancient Golf (St Andrews). *Died 3 Dec. 2000.*

RICHARDSON, John David Benbow, CBE 1988; MC 1942, and Bar 1943; President, Northern Rent Assessment Panel, since 1979 (Vice-President, 1968–79); *b* 6 April 1919; *s* of His Honour Judge Thomas Richardson, OBE, and Winifred Ernestine (*née* Templer); *m* 1946, Kathleen Mildred (*née* Price-Turner); four *s*. *Educ:* Harrow; Clare Coll., Cambridge. Called to Bar, Middle Temple, 1947. Served War of 1939–45, as Captain in King's Dragoon Guards (wounded; MC and Bar). ADC to Governor of South Australia (Lt-Gen. Sir Willoughby Norrie, later

Lord Norrie), 1946–47. Dep. Chm., Durham County Quarter Sessions, 1964–71, and Recorder, 1972–73. Mem., Police Complaints Bd, 1977–82. *Recreations:* fishing, gardening, golf. *Address:* The Old Vicarage, Nine Banks, Whitfield, near Hexham, Northumberland NE47 8DB. *T:* (01434) 345217. *Clubs:* MCC; Northern Counties (Newcastle upon Tyne). *Died 14 May 1997.*

RICHARDSON, John Eric, MS; FRCS; Surgeon: The London Hospital, 1949–81; The Royal Masonic Hospital, 1960–81; King Edward VII's Hospital for Officers, 1960–81; Prince of Wales Hospital, Tottenham, N15, 1958–65; former Consultant Surgeon to the Navy; *b* Loughborough, 24 Feb. 1916; *s* of late C. G. Richardson, MD, FRCS; *m* 1st, 1943, Elisabeth Jean (*d* 1991), *d* of late Rev. John Webster; one *s* one *d*; 2nd, 1994, Bettine, *widow* of R. O. B. Long. *Educ:* Clifton College; London Hospital. MB, BS London, 1939 (Hons and Distinction, Pathology); MRCS, LRCP 1939; Andrew Clarke Prize, London Hosp., 1939. Resident Appointments, London Hospital and Poplar Hospital, 1939–41; Surgeon Lieut RNVR, HMS Prince of Wales (Surgical Specialist), 1941–46; Surgical Registrar, London Hosp., 1946–47; Rockefeller Travelling Fellow, 1947–48; Research Fellow in Surgery, Harvard Univ., 1947–48; Fellow in Clinical Surgery, Massachusetts Gen. Hosp., Boston, Mass, 1947–48. Surgeon, St Andrews Hosp., Dollis Hill, 1965–73. Mem., Med. Appeal Tribunal, 1980–88. Hunterian Prof., RCS, 1953; Lettsomian Lectr, Med. Soc. of London, 1973. Pres., Med. Soc. of London, 1974–75. Examr in Surgery to Soc. of Apothecaries, London, 1959–67 and Univ. of London, 1962–63; 1965–66. Mem., Bd of Governors, London Hosp., 1964–73. *Publications:* contrib. to Lancet, BMJ and Brit. Jl of Surgery on gastro-enterology and endocrine disease. *Address:* 29 Abbey Mews, Amesbury Abbey, Amesbury, Wilts SP4 7EX. *T:* (01980) 624811.

Died 1 March 1998.

RICHARDSON, Robert Augustus; HM Chief Inspector of Schools, Department of Education and Science, 1968–72; *b* 2 Aug. 1912; *s* of late Ferdinand Augustus Richardson and Muriel Emma Richardson; *m* 1936, Elizabeth Gertrude Williamson; one *d*. *Educ:* Royal College of Art. Schoolmaster, 1934; Headmaster, Sidcup School of Art, 1937; served in Royal Navy, 1941–46; Principal: Folkestone Sch. of Art, 1946; Maidstone Coll. of Art, 1948. Dept of Education and Science: HM Inspector of Schools, 1958; HM Staff Inspector, 1966. ARCA 1934. *Recreations:* theatre, music. *Address:* Amber Cottage, Sigglesthorne, Hull, North Humberside HU11 5QA. *T:* Hornsea (01964) 534596. *Died 12 March 1996.*

RICHARDSON, William, CBE 1981; DL; CEng; FRINA; Chairman: Vickers Shipbuilding and Engineering Ltd, 1976–83 (Managing Director, 1969–76); Vosper Thornycroft (UK) Ltd, 1978–83; Barclay Curle Ltd, 1978–83; Brook Marine Ltd, 1981–83; Member Board, British Shipbuilders (from incorporation), 1977–83, Deputy Chairman 1981–83; Director, Vickers Cockatoo Dockyard Pty Ltd, Australia, 1977–84; *b* 15 Aug. 1916; *s* of Edwin Richardson, marine engr, and Hannah (*née* Remington); *m* 1941, Beatrice Marjorie Iliffe; one *s* one *d*. *Educ:* Ocean Road Boys' Sch., Walney Is, Barrow-in-Furness; Jun. Techn. and Techn. Colls, Barrow-in-Furness (part-time). HNC (Dist.) Naval Architecture; HNC (1st Cl.) Mech. Engrg. CIMgt (CBIM 1981; FBIM 1977); FInstD 1977–83. Vickers Ltd, Barrow-in-Furness: Shipbldg Apprentice, 1933–38; Techn. Dept, 1938–39; Admiralty Directorate of Aircraft Maintenance and Repair, UK and Far East, 1939–46; Vickers Ltd Barrow Shipyard: Techn. Depts, 1946–51; Asst Shipyard Manager, 1951–60; Dockside Outfitting Man., 1960–61; Dep. Shipyard Man., 1961–63; Shipyard Man., 1963–64; Dir and Gen. Man., 1964–66; Dir and Gen. Man., Vickers Ltd Naval Shipyard,

Newcastle upon Tyne, 1966–68; Dep. Man. Dir, Swan Hunter & Tyne Shipbldrs Ltd, 1968–69. Director: Slingsby Sailplanes, 1969–70 (co. then incorp. into Vickers Ltd); Vickers Oceanics, 1972–77; Chm., Clark & Standfield (subsid. of Vickers Gp), 1976–83; Dir, Vosper Shiprepairers, 1978–82. Dir of Trustees, 1976–, Mem. Res. Council and Office Bearer, 1976–78, BSRA; Mem. Exec. Council, 1969–77, Chm. Management Bd, 1976–78, SRNA; Pres. Brit. Productivity Assoc., Barrow and Dist, 1969–72; Shipbldg Ind. Rep., DIQAP, 1972–82; Mem., Shipbuilding Industry Trng Bd, 1979–82; Mem., NE Coast IES, 1967–. FRINA 1970 (ARINA 1950, MRINA 1955). Liveryman, Shipwrights' Co., 1978. DL Cumbria, 1982. Queen's Silver Jubilee Medal, 1977. *Publications:* papers on various aspects of UK shipbldg industry; contribs to techn. jls. *Recreations:* sailing, small-bore shooting, golf, fishing. *Address:* Sequoia, Sunbrick Lane, Baycliff, Ulverston, Cumbria LA12 9RQ. *T:* (01229) 869434. *Club:* National Small-Bore Rifle Association.

Died 17 Jan. 1999.

RICHES, Sir Derek (Martin Hurry), KCMG 1963 (CMG 1958); HM Diplomatic Service, retired; Ambassador to Lebanon, 1963–67; *b* 26 July 1912; *s* of late Claud Riches and Flora Martin; *m* 1942, Helen Barkley Hayes (*d* 1989), Poughkeepsie, NY, USA; one *d. Educ:* University College School; University College London. Appointed Probationer Vice-Consul, Beirut, Dec. 1934; subsequently promoted and held various appts, Ethiopia and Cairo; Foreign Office, 1944; promoted one of HM Consuls serving in FO, 1945; Kabul, 1948 (in charge, 1948 and 1949); Consul at Jedda, 1951 (Chargé d'Affaires, 1952); Officer Grade 6, Branch A, Foreign Service and apptd Trade Comr, Khartoum, 1953; attached to Imperial Defence College, 1955; returned to Foreign Office, 1955; Counsellor in the Foreign Office, Head of Eastern Department, 1955; British Ambassador in Libya, 1959–61; British Ambassador to the Congo, 1961–63. *Address:* 48 The Avenue, Kew Gardens, Surrey TW9 2AH.

Died 1 Oct. 1997.

RICHES, General Sir Ian (Hurry), KCB 1960 (CB 1959); DSO 1945; *b* 27 Sept. 1908; *s* of C. W. H. Riches; *m* 1936, Winifred Eleanor Layton; two *s. Educ:* University Coll. Sch., London. Joined Royal Marines, 1927; Major, 1946; Lt-Colonel, 1949; Colonel, 1953; Maj.-Gen., 1957; Lt-Gen., 1959; General, 1961. Maj.-Gen., RM, Portsmouth Group, 1957–59; Commandant-General, Royal Marines, 1959–62; Regional Dir of Civil Defence, 1964–68; Representative Col Comdt, 1967–68. *T:* Winchester (01962) 854067.

Died 23 Dec. 1996.

RICHES, Rt Rev. Kenneth, DD, STD; Bishop of Lincoln, 1956–74; *b* 20 Sept. 1908; *s* of Capt. A. G. Riches; *m* 1942, Kathleen Mary Dixon (JP 1964); two *s* one *d. Educ:* Royal Grammar Sch., Colchester; Corpus Christi Coll., Cambridge (Hon. Fellow, 1975). Deacon 1932, priest 1933; Curate: St Mary's, Portsea, 1932–35; St John's, East Dulwich, 1935–36; Chaplain and Librarian, Sidney Sussex Coll., Cambridge, 1936–42; Examining Chaplain to Bishops of Bradford and Wakefield, 1936; Rector of Bredfield with Boulge, Suffolk, and Dir of Service Ordination Candidates, 1942–45; Principal of Cuddesdon Theological Coll., Oxford, and Vicar of Cuddesdon, 1945–52; Hon. Canon of Portsmouth Cathedral, 1950–52; Bishop Suffragan of Dorchester, Archdeacon of Oxford and Canon of Christ Church, 1952–56; Asst Bishop of Louisiana, USA, 1976–77. Select Preacher: University of Cambridge, 1941, 1948, 1961, 1963; University of Oxford, 1954–55. Mem. Archbishops' Commission on Training for the Ministry, 1942; Sec. of Theol. Commn on the Church of Faith and Order Movement. Chm., Central Advisory Council for the Ministry, 1959–65. Visiting Lecturer, General Theological Seminary, New York, 1956

and 1962. Hon. Fellow: Sidney Sussex Coll., Cambridge, 1958; Lincoln Coll., Oxford, 1974. Editorial Sec., Cambridgeshire Syllabus, 1935; Editor, Cambridge Review, 1941–42. *Recreations:* gardening, antiques, country life. *Address:* Little Dingle, Dunwich, Saxmundham, Suffolk IP17 3EA. *T:* (01728) 648316.

Died 15 May 1999.

RICHMOND, Sir Alan (James), Kt 1969; engineering consultant, expert witness and arbitrator; *b* 12 Oct. 1919; *m* 1951, Sally Palmer (*née* Pain); one step *s* one step *d. Educ:* Berlin; Gland près Nyon, Switzerland; Wimbledon Tech. Coll.; Acton Tech. Coll.; Northampton Polytechnic, London. London Univ., BSc(Eng) 1945, PhD 1954. Trained and employed engineering industry, 1938–45; Lecturer, Battersea Polytechnic, 1946–55; Head of Engineering Dept, Welsh Coll. of Advanced Technology, 1955–58; Principal, Lanchester College of Technology, Coventry, 1959–69; Director, Lanchester Polytechnic, 1970–72; Principal, Strode Coll., Street, 1972–81; Associate Tutor, Further Education Staff Coll., Blagdon, Bristol, 1982–85. Chairman: Coventry Productivity Assoc., 1964–67; CNAA Mech./Prodn Engrg Subject Bd, 1965–68; CNAA Cttees for Sci. and Technology, 1968–72; Founder Chm., Cttee of Dirs of Polytechnics, 1970–72; Member: Home Office Deptl Cttee of Enquiry into Fire Service in GB, 1967–70; Open Univ. Planning Cttee, 1967–69; Open Univ. Council, 1969–71. FIMechE; FCIArb. Hon. DSc CNAA, 1972. *Publications:* (with W. J. Peck) Applied Thermodynamics Problems for Engineers, 1950; Problems in Heat Engines, 1957; various lectures, reviews and articles. *Recreations:* gardening, reading. *Address:* 5 The Orchard, Westfield Park South, Bath BA1 3HT. *T:* (01225) 333393. *Club:* Royal Commonwealth Society.

Died 11 April 1997.

RICHMOND, Rt Hon. Sir Clifford (Parris), KBE 1977; Kt 1972; PC 1973; Judge of the Court of Appeal of New Zealand, 1972–81, President, 1976–81; *b* 23 June 1914; *s* of Howard Parris Richmond, QC, and Elsie Wilhelmina (*née* MacTavish); *m* 1938, Valerie Jean Hamilton; two *s* one *d. Educ:* Wanganui Collegiate Sch.; Victoria and Auckland Univs. LLM (1st cl. Hons). Served War of 1939–45: 4 Field Regt 2NZEF, North Africa and Italy, 1942–45 (despatches, 1944). Partner, legal firm, Buddle Richmond & Co., Auckland; 1946–60; Judge of the Supreme Court of New Zealand, 1960–71. *Recreations:* golf, fishing. *Address:* 16 Glanville Terrace, Parnell, Auckland, New Zealand. *T:* (9) 3077104. *Club:* Northern (Auckland).

Died 29 Jan. 1997.

RICHMOND, Sir John (Frederick), 2nd Bt *cr* 1929, of Hollington, co. Sussex; *b* 12 Aug. 1924; *s* of Sir Frederick Henry Richmond, 1st Bt (formerly Chm. Debenham's Ltd and Harvey Nichols & Co. Ltd), and Dorothy Agnes (*d* 1982), *d* of Frances Joseph Sheppard; *S* father, 1953; *m* 1965, Mrs Anne Moreen Bentley (*d* 1997); one *d. Educ:* Eton; Jesus Coll., Cambridge. Lieut 10th Royal Hussars; seconded Provost Br., 1944–47. *Address:* Shimpling Park Farm, Bury St Edmunds, Suffolk IP29 4HY. *Club:* MCC.

Died 11 July 2000 (ext).

RICHTER, Sviatoslav Theofilovich; Hero of Socialist Labour, 1975; pianist; *b* Zhitomir, Ukraine, 20 March 1915; *m* Nina Dorliak. *Educ:* Moscow State Conservatoire. Gave first piano recital at age of nineteen and began to give concerts on a wide scale in 1942. Appeared at the Royal Albert Hall and the Royal Festival Hall, London, 1961; Royal Festival Hall, 1963, 1966, 1977, 1979, 1989, 1992. FRCM 1992. Hon. DMus Oxon, 1992. Awarded Lenin Prize, and also held the title of Peoples' Artist of the USSR; Order of Lenin, 1965; Order of October Revolution, 1991. *Recreations:* walking, ski-ing, painting.

Address: c/o Victor Hochhauser, 4 Oak Hill Way, NW3 7LR. *T:* (0171) 794 0987.
Died 1 Aug. 1997.

RICKETT, Sir Denis Hubert Fletcher, KCMG 1956 (CMG 1947); CB 1951; Director: Schroder International, 1974–79; De La Rue Co., 1974–77; Adviser, J. Henry Schroder Wagg & Co., 1974–79; *b* 27 July 1907; *s* of late Hubert Cecil Rickett, OBE, JP; *m* 1946, Ruth Pauline (MB, BS, MRCS, LRCP), *d* of late William Anderson Armstrong, JP; two *s* one *d. Educ:* Rugby School; Balliol College, Oxford (Schol. 1925; Jenkyns Exhibnr 1929; 1st cl. Hon. Mods 1927; 1st cl. Lit.Hum. 1929). Fellow of All Souls College, Oxford, 1929–49. Joined staff of Economic Advisory Council, 1931; Offices of War Cabinet, 1939; Principal Private Secretary to Rt Hon. Oliver Lyttelton, when Minister of Production, 1943–45; Personal Assistant (for work on Atomic Energy) to Rt Hon. Sir John Anderson, when Chancellor of the Exchequer, 1945; transferred to Treasury, 1947; Principal Private Secretary to the Rt Hon. C. R. Attlee, when Prime Minister, 1950–51; Economic Minister, British Embassy, Washington, and Head of UK Treasury and Supply Delegation, 1951–54; Third Secretary, HM Treasury, 1955–60, Second Secretary, 1960–68. Vice-Pres., World Bank, 1968–74. *Recreation:* music. *Address:* 9 The Close, Salisbury, Wilts SP1 2EB. *T:* (01722) 320125.*Clubs:* Athenæum, Brooks's. *Died 26 Feb. 1997.*

RICKETT, Sir Raymond (Mildmay Wilson), Kt 1990; CBE 1984; BSc, PhD; CChem, FRSC; Chairman, Mid Kent Health Care Trust, since 1992; *b* 17 March 1927; *s* of Mildmay Louis Rickett and Winifred Georgina Rickett; *m* 1958, Naomi Nishida; one *s* two *d. Educ:* Faversham Grammar Sch.; Medway Coll. of Technology (BSc London); Illinois Inst. of Technology (PhD). Royal Navy, 1946–48; Medway Coll. of Technology, 1953–55, Illinois Inst. of Technology, 1955–59; Plymouth Coll. of Technology, 1959; Lectr, Liverpool Coll. of Technology, 1960–62; Senr Lectr/Principal Lectr, West Ham Coll. of Technology, 1962–64; Head of Dept, Wolverhampton Coll. of Technology, 1965–66; Vice-Principal, Sir John Cass Coll., 1967–69; Vice-Provost, City of London Polytechnic, 1969–72; Dir, Middlesex Polytechnic, 1972–91; Chm., CNAA, 1991–93. Chairman: Cttee of Dirs of Polytechnics, 1980–82 and 1986–88; UK Nat. Commn for UNESCO Educn Adv. Cttee, 1983–85; IUPC, 1988–91; Cttee for Internat. Co-operation in Higher Educn, 1988–91; UK Erasmus Students Grants Council, 1988–93; Kent Council on Addiction, 1991–; Member: Oakes Cttee, 1977–78; Higher Educn Review Group for NI, 1978–82; NAB Bd, 1981–87; Open Univ. Council, 1983–93; Council for Industry and Higher Educn, 1985–91; British Council Bd, 1988–91; Erasmus (EEC) Adv. Cttee, 1988–90. Governor, Yehudi Menuhin Live Music Now Scheme, 1977–. Member: Council, Univ. of Kent, 1991–; Corp., Canterbury Coll., 1992–; Council, Strode Park Foundn, 1992–. Officer's Cross, Order of Merit (FRG), 1988. *Publications:* Experiments in Physical Chemistry (jtly), 1962, new edn 1968; 2 chapters in The Use of the Chemical Literature, 1962, 3rd edn 1992; articles on polytechnics in the national press and contribs to learned jls. *Recreations:* cricket, theatre-going, music. *Address:* 1 The Barn, Pontus Farm, Knockwood Lane, Molash, near Canterbury, Kent CT4 8HW. *Club:* Athenæum. *Died 6 April 1996.*

RICKETTS, (Anne) Theresa, (Lady Ricketts), CBE 1983; Chairman, National Association of Citizens' Advice Bureaux, 1979–84; *b* 12 April 1919; *d* of late Rt Hon. Sir (Richard) Stafford Cripps, CH, QC, FRS, and Dame Isobel Cripps, GBE; *m* 1945, Sir Robert Ricketts, 7th Bt; two *s* two *d. Educ:* Oxford University. Second Officer, WRNS, War of 1939–45. Joined Citizens' Advice Bureaux Service,

1962. Member: Electricity Consumers' Council, 1977–90; Council, Direct Mail Services Standards Board, 1983–92. *Recreations:* gardening, field botany. *Address:* Forwood House, Minchinhampton, Stroud, Glos GL6 9AB. *T:* (01453) 882160. *Club:* Royal Commonwealth Society.
Died 16 Jan. 1998.

RIDDELL-WEBSTER, John Alexander, MC 1943; farmer; Member (C) Tayside Regional Council, 1986–94; *b* 17 July 1921; *s* of Gen. Sir Thomas Riddell-Webster, GCB, DSO and Harriet Hill, *d* of Col Sir Alexander Sprot, 1st Bt; *m* 1960, Ruth, *d* of late S. P. L. A. Lithgow; two *s* one *d. Educ:* Harrow; Pembroke Coll., Cambridge. Seaforth Highlanders (Major), 1940–46. Joined Anglo-Iranian Oil Co., 1946; served in Iran, Iraq, Bahrain, Aden; Vice-Pres. Marketing, BP Canada, 1959; Dir, Shell-Mex and BP, 1965, Man. Dir, Marketing, 1971–75; Dir, BP Oil Ltd, 1975–82 (Dep. Man. Dir, 1976–80); Dir, Public Affairs, Scotland, BP, 1979–81. Mem. Cttee, AA, 1980–90; Mem. Exec. Cttee, Scottish Council (Develt and Industry), 1981–84; Member Council: Advertising Assoc., 1974–80; Inc. Soc. of British Advertisers, 1968–80; Royal Warrant Holders' Assoc. (Vice-Pres., 1979; Pres., 1980); British Road Fedn, 1971–80; Chm., Transport Action Scotland, 1982–98; Mem., Council for Vehicle Servicing and Repair, 1972–80 (Chm., 1975). Pres., Oil Industries Club, 1977–78. CIMgt. *Recreations:* shooting, fishing, gardening. *Address:* Lintrose, Coupar Angus, Perthshire PH13 9JQ. *T:* (01828) 627472. *Clubs:* New (Edinburgh); Royal Perth Golfing Society. *Died 15 April 1999.*

RIDGERS, John Nalton Sharpe; Deputy Chairman and Treasurer, Lloyd's Register of Shipping, 1973–78; Director, Smit International (UK) Ltd, 1974–84; *b* 10 June 1910; 4th *c* and *o s* of Sharpe Ridgers; *m* 1936, Barbara Mary, *o d* of Robert Cobb; five *d. Educ:* Wellington College. Entered Lloyd's, 1928; Underwriting Member, 1932. Member Cttee, Lloyd's Underwriters' Association, 1951–61, 1964–69, Chm. 1961; Member Joint Hull Cttee, 1957–69, Dep. Chm., 1968, Chm., 1969; Mem. Cttee of Lloyd's, 1957–60, 1962–65, Dep. Chm., 1962, Chm., 1963. Director: London Trust Co. Ltd, 1963–80; Arbuthnot Insurance Services Ltd, 1974–80; Danae Investment Trust Ltd, 1975–80. *Recreations:* snooker, carpentry. *Address:* 5 St Nicholas Court, Lime Tree Walk, Sevenoaks, Kent TN13 1TU. *T:* (01732) 455415.
Died 31 July 1999.

RIDLEY, Edward Alexander Keane, CB 1963; Principal Assistant Solicitor, Treasury Solicitor's Department, 1956–69, retired; *b* 16 April 1904; *s* of late Major Edward Keane Ridley, Dudswell House, near Berkhamsted, Herts, and Ethel Janet Ridley, *d* of Alexander Forbes Tweedie; unmarried. *Educ:* Wellington College; Keble College, Oxford. Admitted Solicitor, 1928. Entered Treasury Solicitor's Department, 1934. Hon. RCM 1977. *Publications:* Wind Instruments of European Art Music, 1975; Catalogue of Wind Instruments in the Museum of the Royal College of Music, 1982, with Addenda, 1998. *Recreation:* music. *Address:* c/o Coutts & Co., 440 Strand, WC2R 0QS. *Died 15 March 2000.*

RIDLEY, Philip Waller, CB 1978; CBE 1969; Deputy Secretary, Department of Industry, 1975–80; *b* 25 March 1921; *s* of Basil White Ridley and Frida (*née* Gutknecht); *m* 1942, Foye Robins; two *s* one *d. Educ:* Lewes County Grammar Sch.; Trinity Coll., Cambridge. Intelligence Corps, 1941–47 (Major); German Section, FO, 1948–51; Min. of Supply, 1951–55; BoT, 1955–56 and 1960–66; Atomic Energy Office, 1956–60; Counsellor (Commercial), British Embassy, Washington, 1966–70; Under-Sec., Dept of Industry, 1971–75. Dir, Avon Rubber Co., 1980–89. *Recreations:* music, gardening, ski-ing, walking. *Address:* Old Chimneys, Plumpton Green, Lewes, East Sussex BN8 4EN. *T:* Plumpton (01273) 890342. *Died 1 May 1996.*

RIGBY, Lt-Col Sir (Hugh) John (Macbeth), 2nd Bt *cr* 1929, of Long Durford, Rogate. co. Sussex; ERD and 2 clasps; Director, Executors of James Mills Ltd, retired 1977; *b* 1 Sept. 1914; *s* of Sir Hugh Mallinson Rigby, 1st Bt, and Flora (*d* 1970), *d* of Norman Macbeth; *S* father, 1944; *m* 1946, Mary Patricia Erskine Leacock (*d* 1988); four *s*. *Educ:* Rugby; Magdalene Coll., Cambridge (MA). Lt-Col RCT, retd, 1967. *Heir: s* Anthony John Rigby [*b* 3 Oct. 1946; *m* 1978, Mary, *e d* of R. G. Oliver, Park Moor Cottage, Pott Shrigley, Macclesfield; three *s* one *d*]. *Address:* 5 Park Street, Macclesfield, Cheshire SK11 6SR. *T:* (01625) 613959; Casa das Palmeiras, 8365 Armação de Pêra, Algarve, Portugal. *T:* (82) 312548.
Died 14 March 1999.

RIGBY, Norman Leslie; company chairman, retired; *b* 27 June 1920; *s* of Leslie Rigby and Elsie Lester Wright; *m* 1950, Mary Josephine Calderhead; two *d* (one *s* decd). *Educ:* Cowley Sch., St Helens. Served War, RAF, 1939–45, Intell. Officer to Free French Air Force. Management Trainee, Simon Engineering Group, 1946–48; Marketing Exec., Procter & Gamble Ltd, 1948–55; Marketing Dir, Macleans Ltd (Beecham Group), 1955–59; Nabisco Ltd: Marketing Dir, 1959; Man. Dir, 1960; Vice-Chm., 1962; Chm. 1964; Industrial Adviser, 1968–70, Co-ordinator of Industrial Advisers, HM Govt, 1969–70; Dir, Spillers Ltd, 1970–80 (Divl Man. Dir, 1977–80); Chm., Allan H. Williams Ltd and associated cos, 1981–82. *Recreations:* gardening, golf. *Address:* 38 West Common Way, Harpenden, Herts AL5 2LG. *T:* (01582) 715448. *Died 23 Dec. 1996.*

RIGBY, Reginald Francis, TD 1950 and Clasp 1952; Deputy Circuit Judge, 1973–77; a Recorder of the Crown Court, 1977–83; *b* Rudyard, Staffs, 22 June 1919; *s* of Reginald Rigby, FRIBA, FRICS, and Beatrice May Rigby, *d* of John Frederick Green, Woodbridge, Suffolk; *m* 1949, Joan Edwina, *d* of Samuel E. M. Simpson, Newcastle-under-Lyme, and Dorothy C. Simpson; one *s* (and one *s* decd). *Educ:* Manchester Grammar Sch.; Victoria Univ., Manchester. Solicitor, 1947 (Hons; John Peacock and George Hadfield Prizeman, Law Society Art Prize, 1962); practised Newcastle-under-Lyme; retired as Sen. Partner, Rigby Rowley Cooper & Co., 1984. Served War: commissioned 2nd Lieut 41 Bn, Royal Tank Corps, TA, 1939; served AFV Sch.; volunteered for maritime service: Captain in RASC motor boat companies in home coastal waters, India, Burma, Malaya and its Archipelago; demob. 1946; Major, Queen's Royal Rifles, The Staffordshire Yeomanry. Hon. Sec., North Staffs Forces Help Soc., 1964–84; Mem., Staffs War Pensions Cttee. Mem., Market Drayton RDC, 1966–71; Chm., Woore Parish Council, 1971–79. Pres., Uttoxeter Flyfishing Club, 1975–77; Mem., Birdsgrove Flyfishing Club, Ashbourne. Life Mem., Clan Morrison Soc. *Recreation:* fishing. *Address:* The Rookery, Woore, Salop CW3 9RG. *T:* (01630) 647414. *Clubs:* Army and Navy, Flyfishers'.
Died 18 Feb. 1999.

RILEY, Major John Roland Christopher; Chairman, Channel Islands Communications (TV) Group (formerly Channel Television), since 1982; *b* 4 July 1925; *s* of Christopher John Molesworth Riley and Bridget Maisie Hanbury; *m* 1956, Penelope Ann Harrison (*d* 1978); two *d*. *Educ:* Winchester College. Commissioned Coldstream Guards, 1943; served NW Europe, Palestine, Malaya; Instructor, Army Staff Coll., 1960–62; retired 1962; Elected Deputy, States of Jersey, 1963, Senator, 1975; retired from Govt, 1981. Director: Air UK, 1963–91; Jersey Gas Co., 1970–92; Chase Bank and Trust Co. (CI), 1975–91; Fuel Supplies CI, 1976–; Servisair Jersey,

1976–; Royal Trust Asset Management (CI) Ltd, 1980–92; Royal Trust Fund Management (CI) Ltd, 1984–92. *Recreations:* horse riding (Master Jersey Drag Hunt), yachting. *Address:* La Malzarderie, La Rue des Chataigniers, St John, Jersey, Channel Islands JE3 4DL. *T:* (01534) 861224. *Clubs:* Cavalry and Guards, Royal Yacht Squadron. *Died 17 May 1998.*

RILEY, Sir Ralph, Kt 1984; DSc; FRS 1967; Deputy Chairman, 1983–85, Secretary, 1978–85, Agricultural and Food Research Council; *b* 23 Oct. 1924; *y c* of Ralph and Clara Riley; *m* 1949, Joan Elizabeth Norrington; two *d*. *Educ:* Audenshaw Grammar Sch.; Univ. of Sheffield. Infantry soldier, 1943–47; Univ. of Sheffield, 1947–52; research worker, Plant Breeding Inst., Cambridge, 1952–78 (Head of Cytogenetics Dept, 1954–72; Dir, 1971–78). National Research Council/Nuffield Foundn Lectr at Canadian Univs, 1966; Special Prof. of Botany, Univ. of Nottingham, 1970–78. Fellow of Wolfson Coll., Cambridge, 1967–92, Emeritus Fellow, 1992–. Lectures: Sir Henry Tizard Meml, 1973; Holden, Univ. of Nottingham, 1975; Woodhull, Royal Instn, 1976; Bewley, Glasshouse Crops Res. Inst., 1980; Bernal, Birkbeck Coll., 1983. Sec., Internat. Genetics Fedn, 1973–78; Board Member: Internat. Rice Res. Inst., Manila, 1974–77; Internat. Centre Agricl Res. Dry Areas, Aleppo, 1989–93; Chairman: Rothamsted Experimental Station, 1990–; Bd, British Technol. Gp Ltd, 1984–; Sci. Adv. Cttee, Prog. Rice Biotech., Rockefeller Foundn, 1985–; UGC Working Pty on Vet. Educn., 1987–89; Mem., Tech. Adv. Cttee, Consultative Gp on Internat. Agricl Res., 1993–97. President: Genetical Soc., 1973–75; Sect. K, BAAS, 1979; Hon. Vice-Pres., 16th Internat. Congress of Genetics, Toronto, 1988, Pres., 17th Congress, Birmingham, 1993. Trustee, Lawes Agricl Trust, 1998–. Mem., NY Acad. Scis, 1995. For. Fellow, INSA, 1976; For. Correspondent, Acad. d'Agriculture de France, 1981; For. Associate, Nat. Acad. Scis, USA, 1982; Fellow, Indian Nat. Acad. of Agricl Sci., 1992–. Hon. FRASE 1980. Hon. DSc: Edinburgh, 1976; Hull, 1982; Cranfield, 1985; Hon. LLD Sheffield, 1984. William Bate Hardy Prize, Cambridge Phil Soc., 1969; Royal Medal, Royal Soc., 1981; Wolf Foundn Prize in Agriculture, 1986. *Publications:* scientific papers and articles on genetics of chromosome behaviour, plant cytogenetics and evolution and breeding of crop plants especially wheat. *Address:* 16 Gog Magog Way, Stapleford, Cambridge CB2 5BQ. *T:* (01223) 843845, *Fax:* (01223) 845825; *e-mail:* r.riley@cgnet.com. *Club:* Athenæum. *Died 27 Aug. 1999.*

RIMMER, Prof. Frederick William, CBE 1980; MA; FRSE; FRCO; FRSAMD; Gardiner Professor of Music, University of Glasgow, 1966–80, then Emeritus Professor; Director of Scottish Music Archive, 1968–80; *b* 21 Feb. 1914; 2nd *s* of William Rimmer and Amy Graham McMillan, Liverpool; *m* 1941, Joan Doreen, *d* of Major Alexander Hume Graham and Beatrice Cecilia Myles; two *s* one *d*. *Educ:* Quarry Bank High Sch., Liverpool; Durham Univ. (BMus 1939); Selwyn Coll., Cambridge (Organ Schol., 1946–48; BA 1948; MA 1954; Hon. Fellow, 1982); FRCO (Harding Prize), 1934. Served War: 11th Bn, The Lancashire Fusiliers, Middle East, 1941–45 (Major 1944). Sen. Lectr in Music, Homerton Coll., Cambridge, 1948–51; Cramb Lectr in Music, Univ. of Glasgow, 1951–56, Sen. Lectr, 1956–66, and Organist to the Univ., 1954–66. Henrietta Harvey Vis. Prof., Memorial Univ. of Newfoundland, 1977. A Dir of Scottish Opera, 1966–80; Chm., BBC's Scottish Music Adv. Cttee, 1972–77; Mem., Music Adv. Cttee, British Council, 1973–82, Scottish Adv. Cttee, 1979–82. Hon. DMus Durham, 1991. Special Award for services to contemp. music in Scotland, Composers' Guild of GB, 1975. *Publications:* contrib. to: A History of Scottish Music, 1973; Companion to Scottish Culture, 1981; articles on

20th century music, in: Tempo; Music Review; Organists' Review; compositions for solo organ: Five Preludes on Scottish Psalm Tunes, Pastorale and Toccata, Invenzione e Passacaglia Capricciosa, Ostinato Mesto, Fugato Giocoso, Variations on a theme of Paganini; for choir and organ: Sing we merrily; Christus natus est alleluia; O Lord, we beseech thee; O Blessed God in Trinity; Five carols of the Nativity; Magnificat and Nunc Dimittis; for solo soprano and organ: Of a Rose; Born is the Babe. *Recreations:* travel, reading, gardening. *Address:* Manor Farmhouse, 6 Mill Way, Grantchester, Cambridge CB3 9NB. *T:* (01223) 840716. *Died 3 July 1998.*

RING, Sir Lindsay (Roberts), GBE 1975; JP; Chairman, Ring & Brymer (Birchs) Ltd; Lord Mayor of London for 1975–76; *b* 1 May 1914; *y s* of George Arthur Ring and Helen Rhoda Mason Ring (*née* Stedman); *m* 1940, Hazel Doris, *d* of A. Trevor Nichols, CBE; two *s* one *d*. *Educ:* Dulwich Coll.; Mecklenburg, Germany. Served 1939–45, Europe and Middle East, Major RASC. Underwriting Member of Lloyd's, 1964. Fellow, Hotel and Catering Inst.; Chm., Hotel and Catering Trades Benevolent Assoc., 1962–71; Member: Bd of Verge of Royal Palaces, 1977–84; Gaming Bd for GB, 1977–83; NI Develt Agency, 1977–81. Chm., City of London (Arizona) Corp., 1981–84. Chancellor, City Univ., 1975–76. Governor, Farringtons Sch. Freeman, City of London, 1935; Member, Court of Assistants: Armourers' and Brasiers' Co. (Master 1972); Chartered Secretaries' and Administrators' Co. Common Councilman, City of London (Ward of Bishopsgate), 1964–68; Alderman (Ward of Vintry), 1968–84; Sheriff, City of London, 1967–68; Governor, Hon. Irish Soc., 1980–84. HM Lieut for City of London, JP Inner London, 1964. Hon. Col, 151 (Greater London) Regt, RCT(V). Hon. Burgess, Borough of Coleraine, NI. KStJ 1976. FCIS 1976. Hon. DSc City Univ., 1976; Hon. DLitt Ulster, 1978. Comdr, Legion of Honour, 1976, Order of Rio Branca (Brazil), 1976. *Address:* Chalvedune, Wilderness Road, Chislehurst, Kent, BR7 5EY. *Club.* City Livery. *Died 10 Aug. 1997.*

RINK, Margaret Joan; *see* Suttill, M. J.

RIPPON OF HEXHAM, Baron *cr* 1987 (Life Peer), of Hesleyside in the county of Northumberland; **(Aubrey) Geoffrey (Frederick) Rippon;** PC 1962; QC 1964; *b* 28 May 1924; *o s* of late A. E. S. Rippon; *m* 1946, Ann Leyland (OBE 1984), *d* of Donald Yorke, MC, Prenton, Birkenhead, Cheshire; one *s* three *d*. *Educ:* King's College, Taunton; Brasenose College, Oxford (Hulme Open Exhibitioner; MA; Hon. Fellow, 1972). Secretary and Librarian of the Oxford Union, 1942; Pres. Oxford University Conservative Assoc., 1942; Chm., Federation of University Conservative Associations, 1943. Called to the Bar, Middle Temple, 1948 (Robert Garraway Rice Pupillage Prizeman), Bencher, 1979. Member Surbiton Borough Council, 1945–54; Alderman, 1949–54; Mayor, 1951–52; Member: LCC (Chelsea), 1952–61 (Leader of Cons. Party on LCC, 1957–59); President: British Section (individual members), CEMR; British Sect., European League for Economic Co-operation; London Mayors' Assoc., 1968–71; Surrey Mayors' Assoc., 1974–76; Assoc. of District Councils, 1986–; Town and Country Planning Assoc., 1988–; Inst. of Credit Management, 1992–. Admiral of the Manx Herring Fleet, 1971–74. Chm. Conservative National Advisory Committee on Local Government, 1957–59, Pres., 1972–74; Vice-Pres., Council of Europe's Local Government Conference, 1957 and 1958. Contested (C) Shoreditch and Finsbury, 1950 and 1951; MP (C): Norwich South, 1955–64; Hexham, 1966–87. PPS to Minister of Housing and Local Govt, 1956–57, Minister of Defence, 1957–59; Parly Sec., Min. of Aviation, 1959–61; Jt Parly Sec., Min. of Housing and Local Govt, Oct. 1961–July 1962; Minister of Public

Building and Works, 1962–64 (Cabinet, 1963–64); Chief Opposition Spokesman on housing, local govt and land, 1966–68, on defence, 1968–70; Minister of Technology (incorporating Mins of Industry, Fuel and Power, Aviation and Supply), 1970; Chancellor of the Duchy of Lancaster, 1970–72 (resp. for negotiating Britain's entry into the EEC); Sec. of State for the Environment (incorporating Mins of Trans., Housing, Land, Local Govt, Public Bldg and Works), 1972–74; Chief Opposition Spokesman on Foreign and Commonwealth affairs, 1974–75. Chm., Parly Foreign and Commonwealth Affairs Cttee, 1979–81; Leader: Cons. Party Delegn to Council of Europe and WEU, 1967–70; Cons. Gp, European Parlt, 1977–79; Chm., Council of Ministers, EFTA, 1970–72. Chairman: Hansard Soc. Commn on Legislative Process, 1992; H of L Cttee on Scrutiny of Legislation, 1992–95. Chairman: Dun and Bradstreet Ltd, 1976–96; Britannia Arrow Hldgs, subseq. Invesco MIM, 1977–89 (Pres., 1989–93); Brassey's Defence Publishers, 1977–; Singer & Friedlander Hldgs, 1984–87; Robert Fraser and Partners, 1985–91; Michael Page Plc, 1987–95; UniChem, 1990–; Guerisle Investment Trust, 1992–; Holland, Hannen & Cubitts, 1965–69; Dep. Chm., Drake & Gorham, 1969–70; Director: Fairey Co. Ltd, 1965–70; Bristol Aeroplane Co., 1965–69; Hotung Estates, 1974–75; Groupe Bruxelles Lambert, 1982–90; Maxwell Communications Corp., 1986–92; Acer Group Ltd, 1991–93 (Chm., 1992–93). Mem. Council (formerly Court), London Univ., 1958– (Chm., Court, 1991–94, Council (1st Chm.), 1994–95); First Pro-Chancellor, London Univ., 1994–95. FCIArb; FRSA; Hon. Mem., Rating and Valuation Assoc. Hon. LLD London, 1989. Knight Grand Cross, Royal Order of North Star (Sweden); Grand Cross, Order of Merit (Liechtenstein). *Publications:* (co-author) Forward from Victory, 1943; The Rent Act, 1957; various pamphlets and articles on foreign affairs, local government and legal subjects. *Recreations:* watching cricket, travel. *Address:* The Old Vicarage, Broomfield, near Bridgwater, Somerset; 1 Essex Court, Temple, EC4Y 9AR; 4 Breams Buildings, EC4A 1AQ. *T:* (0171) 353 5835. *Clubs:* Whites, Pratt's, MCC. *Died 28 Jan. 1997.*

RISK, William Symington, CA; Chairman, Fleming and Ferguson Ltd, 1980–87; *b* 15 Sept. 1909; *er s* of late William Risk and Agnes Hetherington Symington, Glasgow; *m* 1937, Isobel Brown McLay; one *s* one *d*. *Educ:* Glasgow Academy; Glasgow Univ.; Edinburgh Univ. (BCom). FCMA 1944; JDipMA 1969. Served War, with Admiralty, on torpedo production at RN Torpedo Factory, at Greenock and elsewhere, 1940–45. Partner, Robson, Morrow & Co., 1945–53; Managing Director: H. W. Nevill Ltd (Nevill's Bread), 1953; Aerated Bread Co. Ltd, 1956; Chm., The London Multiple Bakers' Alliance, 1958–59; Regional Dir for Southern England, British Bakeries Ltd, 1960; Industrial Consultant, Hambros Bank Ltd, 1963; Chm., Martin-Black Ltd, 1976–79. Inst. of Chartered Accountants of Scotland: Mem. Exam. Bd, 1951–55; Mem. Council, 1963–68; Pres., 1974–75; Jt Dip. in Management Accounting Services, and First Chm. of Bd, 1966; Inst. of Cost and Management Accountants: Mem. Council, 1952–70; Pres. of Inst., 1960–61; Gold Medal of Inst., for services to the Inst. and the profession, 1965. Mem. Bd of Governors, Queen Charlotte's Hosp., 1970–80. *Publications:* technical papers on accountancy and management subjects; papers to internat. Congress of Accountants (London, 1952, Paris, 1967). *Recreation:* reading. *Clubs:* Caledonian (Edinburgh); Royal Scottish Automobile (Glasgow). *Died 31 Oct. 1996.*

RISNESS, Eric John, CBE 1982; FREng, FIEE; Managing Director, STC Technology Ltd, 1987–90; *b* 27 July 1927; *s* of Kristen Riisnaes and Ethel Agnes (*née* Weeks); *m* 1952, Colleen Edwina Armstrong; two *s* two *d*. *Educ:* Stratford Grammar School, London; Corpus Christi

College, Cambridge (MA, PhD). Royal Naval Scientific Service, Admiralty Research Lab., 1954; Naval Staff Coll., 1959; Admiralty Underwater Weapons Estabt, 1961; RCDS 1970; Ministry of Defence: Defence Science, 1974; Underwater Research, 1975; Sting Ray Torpedo Project, 1977; Underwater Weapons Projects, 1979; Admiralty Surface Weapons Estabt, 1980; Dir of Naval Analysis, 1982; Dir-Gen., Surface Weapons Projects, 1983; Man. Dir, Admiralty Res. Estabt, Portland, 1984–87. FREng (FEng 1990). *Recreations:* music, genealogy, golf. *Address:* 8 Orchard Road, Shalford, Guildford, Surrey GU4 8ER. *T:* (01483) 534581.   *Died 8 June 2000.*

RITCHIE, Alexander James Otway; Chairman, Union Discount Co. of London plc, 1970–90; *b* 5 May 1928; *s* of Charles Henry Ritchie and Marjorie Alice Ritchie (*née* Stewart); *m* 1953, Joanna Willink Fletcher; two *s* (one *d* decd). *Educ:* Stowe; St John's Coll., Cambridge (MA). Joined Glyn, Mills and Co., 1951 (Dir, 1964); Exec. Dir, Williams & Glyn's Bank, 1970; resigned Williams & Glyn's Bank, 1977; Dep. Chm., Grindlays Bank plc, 1977–83, Chief Exec. 1980–83; Dep. Chm., Grindlays Holdings, 1978–83; Chairman: Grindlays Bank, 1984–87; ANZ Hldgs (UK), 1985–87; Dep. Chm., Italian Internat. Bank, 1989–93 (Dir, 1986–93). Director: Australian and New Zealand Banking Gp, 1984–87; European Investment Bank, 1986–93; Debenham Tewson & Chinnocks Holdings plc, 1987–93; Archdale Holdings, 1991–97. Mem., London Cttee, Ottoman Bank, 1966–97; Mem., Export Guarantees Adv. Council, 1977–82 (Dep. Chm., 1980–81). Dir, Bath Abbey Trust, 1991–. Chairman of Governors: Windlesham House Sch., 1986–93; Downe House Sch., 1991–95 (Gov., 1988–98). *Address:* 54 Sydney Buildings, Bath BA2 6DB.

Died 23 Aug. 2000.

RITCHIE, Anthony Elliot, CBE 1978; MD; FRSE; Secretary and Treasurer, 1969–86, Trustee, since 1987, Carnegie Trust for the Universities of Scotland; *b* 30 March 1915; *s* of late Prof. James Ritchie, CBE, PRSE and Jessie Jane, *y d* of Walter Elliot, Galashiels; *m* 1941, Elizabeth Lambie Knox, MB, ChB, *y d* of John Knox, Dunfermline; one *s* three *d. Educ:* Edinburgh Academy; Aberdeen Univ. (MA 1933; BSc 1936, with Hunter Memorial Prize); Edinburgh Univ. (MB, ChB 1940); MD with Gold Medal Thesis, 1945. Carnegie Research Scholar, Physiology Dept, Edin. Univ., 1940–41; Asst Lectr 1941; Lectr 1942; senior lecturer grade, 1946. Lecturer in Electrotherapy, Edin. Royal Infirmary, 1943–48, 1972; Chandos Prof. of Physiology, Univ. of St Andrews, 1948–69, Dean, Faculty of Science, 1961–66. Hon. Physiologist Gogarburn Nerve Injuries Hospital, 1941–46; Hon. Consultant in Electrotherapy, Scot. E Regional Hospital Board, 1950–69. Scientific Adviser, Civil Defence, 1961–80; Adv. Cttee on Med. Research, Scotland, 1961, Vice-Chm., 1967–69; Chairman: Scottish Cttee on Science Educn, 1970–78; Blood Transfusion Adv. Gp, 1970–80; Scottish Universities Entrance Bd, 1963–69; St Leonard's Sch., St Andrews, 1968–69; Mem., Council for Applied Science in Scotland, 1978–86; Mem., British Library Bd, 1973–80; Trustee, Nat. Library of Scotland, 1974–95. Mem., Cttee of Inquiry into Teachers' Pay. Examiner, Chartered Soc. of Physiotherapy, Pharmaceutical Soc. of Great Britain, and RCSE. Royal Society of Edinburgh: Fellow, 1951; Council, 1957–60, 1979–80; Sec. to Ordinary Meetings, 1960–65, Vice-Pres., 1965–66, 1976–79; Gen. Sec., 1966–76. RAMC (TA) commission, 1942–44. Hon. FCSP 1970; Hon. FRCPE 1986. Hon. DSc St Andrews, 1972; Hon. LLD Strathclyde, 1985. Ellis Prize in Physiol., 1941; Gunning Victoria Jubilee Prize, RSE, 1943; Honeyman Gillespie Lectr, Edin. Univ., 1944; Bicentenary Medal, RSE, 1983. *Publications:* (with J. Lenman) Clinical Electromyography, 1976, 4th edn 1987; medical and

scientific papers on nerve injury diagnosis and medical electronics. *Recreations:* reading, hill walking, motor cars. *Address:* 12 Ravelston Park, Edinburgh EH4 3DX. *T:* (0131) 332 6560. *Clubs:* Caledonian; New (Edinburgh).

Died 14 Sept. 1997.

RITCHIE, James Walter, MC 1942, and Bar 1943; Director, Inchcape & Co. Ltd, 1972–84, retired; *b* 12 Jan. 1920; *s* of late Sir Adam Ritchie and Vivienne, *o d* of late Benjamin Plunkett Lentaigne, Judge of High Court, Burma; *m* 1951, Penelope June (*née* Forbes); two *s* two *d. Educ:* Ampleforth Coll.; Clare Coll., Cambridge. Gordon Highlanders. *Recreations:* hunting, fishing, golf. *Address:* Lockeridge Down, Lockeridge, near Marlborough, Wilts SN8 4EL. *T:* (01672) 861244. *Clubs:* Oriental; Muthaiga Country (Nairobi).   *Died 23 Sept. 1998.*

RIVERDALE, 2nd Baron *cr* 1935, of Sheffield, co. York; **Robert Arthur Balfour;** Bt 1929; DL; President, Balfour Darwins Ltd, 1969–75 (Chairman, 1961–69); *b* Sheffield, 1 Sept. 1901; *er s* of 1st Baron Riverdale, GBE and Frances Josephine Keighley, *d* of Charles Henry Bingham; *S* father, 1957; *m* 1st, 1926, Nancy Marguerite (*d* 1928), *d* of late Rear-Adm. Mark Rundle, DSO; (one *s* decd); 2nd, 1933, Christian Mary (*d* 1991), *er d* of late Major Rowland Hill; one *s* one *d. Educ:* Aysgarth; Oundle. MRINA. Served with RNVR, 1940–45, attaining rank of Lt-Comdr. Joined Arthur Balfour & Co. Ltd, 1918; Dir, 1924; Man. Dir, 1949; Chm. and Man. Dir, 1957–61; Exec. Chm., 1961–69. Director: National Provincial Bank, Main Central Bd, 1964–69 (Local Bd, 1949–69); National Westminster Bank, E Region, 1969–71; Light Trades House Ltd, 1956–65; Yorkshire Television, 1967–73. The Association of British Chambers of Commerce: Mem. Exec. Council, 1950; Vice-Pres., 1952–54; Dep. Pres., 1954–57; Pres., 1957–58; Chm., Overseas Cttee, 1953–57. President: Nat. Fedn of Engineers' Tool Manufacturers, 1951–57 (Hon. Vice-Pres., 1957–; Representative on Gauge and Tool Adv. Council, 1946–64); Sheffield Chamber of Commerce, 1950 (Jt Hon. Sec., 1957); Milling Cutter and Reamer Trade Assoc., 1936–54 (Vice-Pres., 1954–57); Twist Drill Traders' Assoc., 1946–55; Chm., British Council, Aust. Assoc. of British Manufacturers, 1954–57 (Vice-Chm., 1957–65; Hon. Mem., 1965–); Member: Management and Tech. Cttee, High Speed Steel Assoc., 1947–65; British Nat. Cttee of Internat. Chamber of Commerce Adv. Cttee, 1957–58; Nat. Production Adv. Cttee, 1957–58; Consultative Cttee for Industry, 1957–58; Standing Cttee, Crucible and High Speed Steel Conf., 1951–64; Western Hemisphere Exports Council (formerly Dollar Exports Council), 1957–61; Governor, Sheffield Savings Bank, 1948–58 (Patron, 1958–); Master Cutler, 1946; Trustee, Sheffield Town Trust, 1958–; Town Collector, Sheffield, 1974–; Guardian of Standard of Wrought Plate within City of Sheffield, 1948–; Belgian Consul for Sheffield area, 1945–. JP City of Sheffield, 1950–66 (Pres., S Yorks Br. Magistrates' Assoc., 1971–); DL S Yorks (formerly WR Yorks and City and County of York), 1959. Pres., Derwent Fly Fishing Club. A Churchman and a Conservative. Chevalier of Order of the Crown, Belgium, 1956; La Médaille Civique de première classe; Officier de l'Ordre de Leopold II, 1971. *Publications:* Squeeze the Trigger Gently, 1990; A Life, a Sail, a Changing Sea, 1995. *Recreations:* yachting, yacht designing, shooting, stalking, fishing. *Heir: g s* Anthony Robert Balfour, *b* 26 Feb. 1960. *Address:* Ropes, Grindleford, via Sheffield S30 1HX. *T:* (01433) 630408. *Clubs:* Royal Cruising (Commodore, 1962–66); Sheffield (Sheffield).   *Died 26 June 1998.*

RIVETT-DRAKE, Brig. Dame Jean (Elizabeth), DBE 1964 (MBE 1947); JP; DL; Mayor of Hove, 1977–78; Lay Member, Press Council, 1973–78; Director, Women's Royal Army Corps, 1961–64, retired; *b* 13 July 1909; *d* of

Comdr Bertram Gregory Drake and Dora Rivett-Drake; changed name from Drake to Rivett-Drake by deed-poll, 1937. Served War of 1939–45 (despatches, 1946). Hon. ADC to the Queen, 1961–64. Member: Hove Borough Council, 1966–84; East Sussex CC, 1973–77 (Mem. Educn and Social Services Cttees, AHA). JP 1965; DL E Sussex, 1983. *Address:* 9 Kestrel Close, Hove, East Sussex BN3 6NS. *T:* (01273) 505839; c/o Barclays Bank, PO Box 358, Brighton BN1 1SF. *Club:* English-Speaking Union.   *Died 8 Aug. 1999.*

ROARK, Helen Wills; artist; former international tennis player; *b* California, 1905; *d* of Dr Clarence A. Wills, surgeon and Catherine A. Wills; *m* 1st, 1929, Frederick Schander Moody (marr. diss. 1937); 2nd, 1939, Aidan Roark. *Educ:* Anna Head School, Berkeley, California; University of California; Phi Beta Kappa (Scholarship Society). *Publications:* three books on tennis; Mystery Book, 1939; articles in various magazines and periodicals. *Recreations:* American Lawn Tennis Championship, 1923–24–25–27–28–29 and 1931; English Lawn Tennis Championship, 1927–28–29–30–32–33–35–38; French, 1927–28–29–30; held exhibitions of drawing and paintings at Cooling Galleries, London, 1929 (drawings); Grand Central Art Galleries, New York, 1930 (drawings), 1936 (flower paintings in oil); Berheim-Jenne Galleries, Paris, 1932 (etchings). *Clubs:* All England Lawn Tennis; Colony, West Side Lawn Tennis (New York); Burlingame Country (California).   *Died 1 Jan. 1998.*

ROBARTS, Basil; Director, 1964–85, and Chief General Manager, 1963 75, Norwich Union Insurance Group; *b* 13 Jan. 1915; *s* of late Henry Ernest Robarts and Beatrice Katie (*née* Stevens); *m* 1941, Sheila Margaret Cooper Thwaites; one *s* one *d. Educ:* Gresham's Sch., Holt. Served Army, 1939–45 (Lt-Col, RA). Joined Norwich Union Life Insce Soc., 1934, Gen. Man. and Actuary, 1953. Institute of Actuaries: FIA 1939; Treas., 1965–67; Gen. Commissioner of Income Tax, 1958–90; Chm., British Insce Assoc., 1969–71. Trustee, Charities Official Investment Fund, 1977–85. *Recreation:* music. *Address:* 466B Unthank Road, Norwich NR4 7QJ. *T:* (01603) 451135.   *Died 21 Aug. 1997.*

ROBB, Prof. James Christie; Professor of Physical Chemistry, 1957–84, and Head of Department of Chemistry, 1981–84, University of Birmingham; *b* 23 April 1924; *s* of James M. Robb, Rocklands, The House of Daviot, Inverurie, Aberdeenshire; *m* 1951, Joyce Irene Morley; three *d. Educ:* Daviot School; Inverurie Academy; Aberdeen University (BSc Hons 1945, PhD 1948); DSc Birmingham, 1954. DSIR Senior Research Award, Aberdeen, 1948–50; ICI Fellow, Birmingham Univ., 1950–51; on Birmingham Univ. staff, 1951–84. A Guardian of Birmingham Assay Office, 1980–95. Mem. Council, Birmingham Civic Soc., 1981–93. Pres., Birmingham Rotary Club, 1982–83. *Publications:* scientific contribs to Proc. Royal Soc., Trans Faraday Soc., etc. *Recreations:* motoring, photography, computing. *Address:* 32 Coleshill Close, Hunt End, Redditch, Worcs B97 5UN.   *Died 8 Dec. 1999.*

ROBBINS, Harold; writer; *b* 21 May 1916; *né* Francis Kane; *m* Muriel Ling (decd); *m* Lillian Machnivitz (marr. diss.); *m* Yvonne; one *d*; *m* Grace Palermo (marr. diss.); one *d*; *m* 1992, Jann Stapp. *Educ:* New York. Formerly sugar exporter, film publicist, film impresario, etc. *Publications:* The Dream Merchants, 1949; 79 Park Avenue, 1955; A Stone for Danny Fisher, 1955; Never Leave Me, 1956; Never Love a Stranger, 1958; Stiletto, 1960; The Carpetbaggers, 1961; Where Love Has Gone, 1964; The Adventurers, 1966; The Inheritors, 1969; The Betsy, 1971 (filmed 1978); The Pirate, 1974; The Lonely Lady, 1976; Dreams Die First, 1977; Memories of Another Day, 1979; Goodbye, Janette, 1981; Spellbinder, 1982;

Descent from Xanadu, 1984; The Storyteller, 1985; The Piranhas, 1991; The Raiders, 1995; The Stallion, 1996; Tycoon, 1997. *Address:* c/o Simon and Schuster, 1230 6th Avenue, New York, NY 10020, USA.
                               Died 14 Oct. 1997.

ROBBINS, Jerome; choreographer and director; Co-Ballet Master in Chief, New York City Ballet, 1983–89 (Ballet Master, 1969–83; Associate Artistic Director, 1949–59); Founder Choreographer, Ballets: USA, 1958–61; *b* New York, 11 Oct. 1918; *s* of Harry and Lena Robbins. *Educ:* Woodrow Wilson High School, Weehawken, NJ; New York University. Studied ballet with Antony Tudor and Eugene Loring, and modern, Spanish and oriental dance. First stage experience with Sandor-Sorel Dance Center, New York, 1937; dancer in chorus of American musicals, 1938–40; Ballet Theatre, 1940–44 (soloist 1941), London season, 1946; formed own company, Ballets: USA, 1958. Ballets performed by cos which included Amer. Ballet Theatre, Australian Ballet, Dance Theatre of Harlem, Nat. Ballet of Canada, Kirov Ballet, Royal Ballet, Paris Opera Ballet, Royal Danish Ballet. Member: NY State Council on the Arts/Dance Panel, 1973–77; Nat. Council on the Arts, 1974–80. Hon. Mem., AAIL, 1985. Hon. degrees: Ohio, 1974; CUNY, 1980; Hon. DFA New York, 1985. City of Paris Award, 1971; Handel Medallion, NYC, 1976; Kennedy Center Honoree, 1981, and many other awards. Chevalier: Order of Arts and Letters (France), 1964; Légion d'Honneur (France), 1993. *Ballets include:* (for Ballet Theater) Fancy Free, 1944; (for Concert Varieties) Interplay, 1945; (for New York City Ballet) Age of Anxiety, 1950; The Cage, 1951; Afternoon of a Faun, 1953; Fanfare, 1953; The Concert, 1956; (for American Ballet Theater) Les Noces, 1965; Dances at a Gathering, 1969; In the Night, 1970; The Goldberg Variations, 1971; Watermill, 1972; Requiem Canticles, 1972; An Evening's Waltzes, 1973; Dybbuk (later The Dybbuk Variations, then renamed Suite of Dances), 1974; Concerto in G (later in G Major), 1975; Ma Mère l'Oye (later Mother Goose), 1975; Chansons Madécasses, 1975; The Four Seasons, 1979; Opus 19, The Dreamer, 1979; Rondo, 1981; Piano Pieces, 1981; The Gershwin Concerto, 1982; Four Chamber Works, 1982; Glass Pieces, 1983; I'm Old Fashioned, 1983; Antique Epigraphs, 1984; (for School of American Ballet) 2 and 3 Part Inventions, 1994; (with Twyla Tharp) Brahms/Handel, 1984; Eight Lines, 1985; In Memory Of, 1985; Quiet City, 1986; Piccolo Balleto, 1986; Ives, Songs, 1988; (with Mikhail Baryshnikov) A Suite of Dances, 1994; (for Ballets: USA) NY Export: Opus Jazz, 1958; Moves, 1959; (for Star Spangled Gala) Other Dances, 1976. *Musicals include:* On the Town, 1945; Billion Dollar Baby, 1946 (Donaldson award); High Button Shoes, 1947 (Donaldson and Tony awards); Miss Liberty, 1949; Call Me Madam, 1950; The King and I, 1951 (Donaldson award); Two's Company, 1952 (Donaldson award); Peter Pan, 1954; Bells Are Ringing, 1956; West Side Story, 1957 (Tony, Evening Standard, Laurel and two Academy awards); Gypsy, 1959; Fiddler on the Roof, 1964 (two Tony awards and Drama Critics' award); Jerome Robbins's Broadway, NY, 1989. Directed and choreographed films, drama and TV (incl. Peter Pan with Mary Martin, 1955 (Emmy award)). *Address:* c/o New York City Ballet, New York State Theater, Lincoln Center, New York, NY 10023, USA.
                              Died 29 July 1998.

ROBENS OF WOLDINGHAM, Baron *cr* 1961 (Life Peer), of Woldingham, co. Surrey; **Alfred Robens;** PC 1951; President, Snamprogetti, since 1988 (Chairman, 1980–88); Chairman, Alfred Robens Associates, since 1984; Director, Times Newspapers Holdings Ltd, 1980–83 (Times Newspapers Ltd, 1967–80); *b* 18 Dec. 1910; *s* of George and Edith Robens; *m* 1937, Eva, *d* of Fred and Elizabeth Powell. *Educ:* Manchester Secondary Sch. Official of

Union of Distributive and Allied Workers, 1935–45; Manchester City Councillor, 1942–45. MP (Lab) Wansbeck Div. of Northumberland, 1945–50, and for Blyth, 1950–60. Parliamentary Private Secretary to Minister of Transport, 1945–47; Parliamentary Secretary, Ministry of Fuel and Power, 1947–51; Minister of Labour and National Service, April-Oct. 1951. Chairman: National Coal Bd, 1961–71; Vickers Ltd, 1971–79; St Regis Internat., 1976–81; MLH Consultants, 1971–81; Johnson Matthey PLC, 1971–83 (Hon. Pres., 1983–); St Regis Newspapers, Bolton, 1975–80 (Dir, 1976); Director: Bank of England, 1966–81; St Regis Paper Co. (NY), 1976–80; Trust House Forte Ltd, 1971–86; British Fuel Co., 1967–87; AAH, 1971; AMI (Europe) Ltd, 1981. Chairman: Foundation on Automation and Employment, 1962; Cttee on Safety and Health of people at their place of work, 1970–72; Engrg Industries Council, 1976–80; Member: NEDC, 1962–71; Royal Commn on Trade Unions and Employers' Assocs, 1965–68. President: Advertising Assoc., 1963–68; Incorporated Soc. of British Advertisers, 1973–76; Chairman: Jt Steering Cttee for Malta, 1967; Jt Econ. Mission to Malta, 1967. Member: Council of Manchester Business School, 1964–79 (Dep. Chm., 1964–70; Chm., 1970–79); Court of Governors, LSE, 1965; Chancellor, Univ. of Surrey, 1966–77. Governor, Queen Elizabeth Training Coll. for the Disabled, 1951–80; Chairman: Bd of Govs, Guy's Hosp., 1965–74; Guy's Hosp. Medical and Dental Sch., 1974–82; Fellow, Manchester Coll. of Science and Technology, 1965; Hon. FRCR 1975. Hon. DCL: Univ. of Newcastle upon Tyne, 1964; Manchester Univ., 1974; Hon. LLD: Leicester, 1966; London, 1971. Hon. MInstM 1968; Hon. FIOB 1974. Mackintosh Medal, Advertising Assoc., 1970; Albert Medal, RSA, 1977. *Publications:* Engineering and Economic Progress, 1965; Industry and Government, 1970; Human Engineering, 1970; Ten Year Stint, 1972; sundry articles to magazines, journals and newspapers. *Address:* House of Lords, SW1A 0PW.

Died 27 June 1999.

ROBERTS, Arthur Loten, OBE 1971; Emeritus Professor, University of Leeds (Livesey Professor of Coal Gas and Fuel Industries, 1947–71; Chairman of the Houldsworth School of Applied Science, 1956–70); Pro-Vice-Chancellor, University of Leeds, 1967–69; *b* 1 April 1906; *s* of Arthur James Roberts, Hull, and Alice Maude Loten, Hornsea, E Yorks; *m* 1941, Katherine Mary Hargrove (*d* 1982); one *s* one *d. Educ:* Christ's Hospital; Univ. of Leeds (BSc 1928, PhD 1930). Assistant Lecturer, Lecturer, Senior Lecturer, Leeds Univ. Part-time Mem., North-Eastern Area Gas Board, 1950–71; Mem., Gas Corp. Res. Cttee (formerly Gas Council Research Cttee), 1951–79; Hon. Sec., Advisory Research Cttee of Gas Council and University, 1947–71; Chm., former Joint Refractories Cttee of British Ceramic Research Assoc. and the Gas Corporation; Pres. British Ceramic Society, 1957–58; Member of Technology Sub-Cttee, UGC, 1960–69. FRIC, FInstF. Hon. FICeram; Hon. FIGasE, Hon. FIChemE. *Publications:* numerous contributions to chemical, ceramic and fuel jls. *Recreations:* painting, pianoforte, garden. *Address:* Hillside, 6 King's Road, Bramhope, Leeds, W Yorks LS16 9JN. *T:* (0113) 267 4977.

Died 1 March 2000.

ROBERTS, Sir Bryan Clieve, KCMG 1973 (CMG 1964); QC; JP; Chairman, Commonwealth Magistrates' and Judges' Association (formerly Commonwealth Magistrates' Association), 1979–94 (Life Vice-President, 1994); *b* 22 March 1923; *s* of late Herbert Roberts, MA, and Doris Evelyn Clieve; *m* 1st, 1958, Pamela Dorothy Campbell (marr. diss. 1975); 2nd, 1976, Brigitte Patricia Reilly-Morrison (marr. diss. 1985); 3rd, 1985, Barbara Forter, *e d* of J. N. Wood, CBE. *Educ:* Whitgift School; Magdalen Coll., Oxford (MA). Served War of 1939–45:

commissioned in RA and RHA, 1941–46; active service in Normandy, Belgium, Holland and Germany, 1944–45. Called to Bar, Gray's Inn, 1950; in chambers in Temple, 1950–51; Treasury Solicitor's Dept, 1951–53; Crown Counsel, N Rhodesia, 1953–60; Dir of Public Prosecutions, N Rhodesia, 1960–61; QC (Fedn of Rhodesia and Nyasaland) 1961; Nyasaland: Solicitor-General, 1961–64; Minister of Justice, 1962–63; Mem., Legislative Council, 1961–63; Attorney-Gen. of Malawi, 1964–72; Perm. Sec. to Office of the President, Sec. to the Cabinet, and Head of Malawi Civil Service, 1965–72; Chairman: Malawi Army Council; Nat. Security and Intell. Council; Nat. Develt and Planning Council, 1966–72. Lord Chancellor's Office, 1973–82 (Under Sec., 1977–82). A Metropolitan Stipendiary Magistrate, 1982–93. JP Inner London, 1975 (Dep. Chm., South Westminster Bench, 1977–82). Officer of the Order of Menelik II of Ethiopia, 1965; Comdr, Nat. Order of Republic of Malagasy, 1969. *Address:* 3 Caroline Place, W2 4AW; Stonebarrow Lodge, Charmouth, Dorset. *Club:* Oriental. *Died 6 Dec. 1996.*

ROBERTS, Rt Rev. (David) John, OSB; Abbot of Downside, 1974–90; *b* 31 March 1919; *s* of Albert Edward and Elizabeth Minnith Roberts. *Educ:* Downside School; Trinity Coll., Cambridge (MA). Royal Sussex Regt, Oct. 1939–Nov. 1945 (POW Germany, May 1940–April 1945). Entered monastery, Feb. 1946; ordained, 1951; House Master, Downside School, 1953–62; Novice Master, 1962–66; Prior, 1966–74. Titular Abbot of St Albans, 1990. *Address:* Downside Abbey, Stratton-on-the-Fosse, Bath BA3 4RH. *Died 1 Feb. 2000.*

ROBERTS, Rev. Canon Edward Eric; JP; Canon Emeritus of Southwell, since 1980; *b* 29 April 1911; *o s* of late Edward Thomas Roberts and Charlotte Roberts, Liverpool; *m* 1938, Sybil Mary (*née* Curren); two *d. Educ:* Univ. of Liverpool; St Augustine's Coll., Canterbury. Youth Officer: City of Oxford LEA, 1938–43; Wallasey CB, LEA, 1943–44; Training Officer, Church of England Youth Council, 1944–52; Southwell Diocesan Director: of Further Educn, 1952–61; of Educn, 1961–68. Deacon 1961, priest 1962; Canon, 1964; Canon Residentiary, Vice-Provost of Southwell Cathedral and Personal Chaplain to Bishop of Southwell, 1969–79; Ecumenical Officer, Diocese of Southwell, 1973–79. Sec., Nottingham Council of Churches, 1980–84. JP: City of Nottingham, 1958–77; Gwynedd, 1977–. *Recreation:* photography. *Address:* Queen Elizabeth Court, Clarence Drive, Llandudno LL30 1TR. *T:* (01492) 860843.

Died 16 Jan. 2000.

ROBERTS, Rt Rev. Eric Matthias; Bishop of St David's, 1971–81; *b* 18 Feb. 1914; *s* of Richard and Jane Roberts; *m* 1944, Nancy Jane Roberts (*née* Davies); two *s. Educ:* Friars Sch., Bangor; University Coll., Bangor; St Edmund Hall, Oxon (MA); St Michael's Coll., Llandaff. Deacon 1938, priest 1939; Curate, Penmaenmawr, 1938–40; Sub-Warden, St Michael's Coll., Llandaff, 1940–47; Vicar: Port Talbot, 1947–56; Roath, 1956–65; Archdeacon of Margam, 1965–71. ChStJ 1973. *Address:* 2 Tudor Close, Westbourne Road, Penarth, South Glamorgan CF64 5BR. *Died 29 March 1997.*

ROBERTS, Sir Frank (Kenyon), GCMG 1963 (KCMG 1953; CMG 1946); GCVO 1965; HM Diplomatic Service, retired; Director: Hoechst (UK); Daimler-Benz (UK); Vice-President: European Atlantic Group, since 1983 (Chairman, 1970–73; President, 1973–83); Atlantic Treaty Association, since 1973 (President, 1969–73); Atlantic Council of UK (formerly British Atlantic Committee), since 1982 (President, 1968–81); *b* Buenos Aires, 27 Oct. 1907; *s* of Henry George Roberts, Preston, and Gertrude Kenyon, Blackburn; *m* 1937, Celeste Leila Beatrix (*d* 1990), *d* of late Sir Said Shoucair Pasha, Cairo, Financial Adviser to Sudan Government; no *c. Educ:* Bedales;

Rugby; Trinity College, Cambridge (Scholar). Entered Foreign Office, 1930; served HM Embassy, Paris, 1932–35 and at HM Embassy, Cairo, 1935–37; Foreign Office, 1937–45; Chargé d'Affaires to Czechoslovak Govt, 1943; British Minister in Moscow, 1945–47; Principal Private Secretary to Secretary of State for Foreign Affairs, 1947–49; Deputy High Comr in India, 1949–51; Deputy-Under Secretary of State, Foreign Office, 1951–54; HM Ambassador to Yugoslavia, 1954–57; United Kingdom Permanent Representative on the North Atlantic Council, 1957–60; Ambassador: to the USSR, 1960–62; to the Federal Republic of Germany, 1963–68. Vice-Pres., British-German Chamber of Commerce in UK, 1974– (Pres., 1971–74); Mem. Governing Body, Internat. Chamber of Commerce, 1978. UK Mem., FCO Review Cttee on Overseas Representation, 1968–69. Pres., British-German Assoc.; Vice-Pres., Britain-Russia Centre. Hon. LLD Manchester, 1991. Grand Cross, German Order of Merit, 1965. *Publication:* Dealing with Dictators, 1991. *Address:* 25 Kensington Court Gardens, W8 5QF. *Clubs:* Brooks's, Royal Automobile. *Died 7 Jan. 1998.*

ROBERTS, Brig. Sir Geoffrey Paul H.; *see* Hardy-Roberts.

ROBERTS, Maj.-Gen. (George) Philip (Bradley), CB 1945; DSO 1942; MC 1941; late RTR; *b* 5 Nov. 1906; *s* of Lt-Col William Bradley Roberts, DSO; *m* 1st, 1936, Désirée (*d* 1979), *d* of Major A. B. Godfray, Jersey; two *s* two *d*; 2nd, 1980, Annie Cornelia, *d* of Lt-Col F. E. W. Toussieng, Kt of Dannebrog, and *widow* of Brig. J. K. Greenwood, OBE. *Educ:* Marlborough; RMC, Sandhurst. 2nd Lieut Royal Tank Corps, 1926; served War of 1939–45 (MC, DSO and two Bars, CB, despatches thrice, Officier Légion d'Honneur, Croix de Guerre avec palmes); Adjt 6 RTR 1939; DAQMG 7th Armed Div., Bde Maj. 4th Armed Bde, GSO II 7th Armed Div., AQMG 30 Corps, CO 3 RTR 1939–41; Comd 22nd Armed Bde, Comd 26th Armed Bde, Comd 30th Armed Bde, 1941–43; Commander 11th Armoured Div., 1943–46; Comdr 7th Armoured Div., 1947–48; Dir, Royal Armoured Corps, War Office, 1948–49; retired pay, 1949. Hon. Col Kent and County of London Yeomanry Squadron, The Royal Yeomanry Regt, T&AVR, 1963–70. JP County of Kent, 1960–70. *Publication:* From the Desert to the Baltic, 1987. *Address:* Greenbank, West Street, Mayfield, E Sussex TN20 6DS; c/o Royal Bank of Scotland, Drummonds Branch, 49 Charing Cross, Admiralty Arch, SW1A 2DX. *Club:* Army and Navy. *Died 5 Nov. 1997.*

ROBERTS, Rt Rev. John; *see* Roberts, Rt Rev. D. J.

ROBERTS, Prof. John Eric, DSc; CPhys; FInstP; Emeritus Professor of Physics, University of London, 1969; Physicist to Middlesex Hospital, 1946–70; Consultant Adviser in Physics, Department of Health and Social Security, 1960–71; *b* Leeds, 5 Sept. 1907; *e s* of late James J. Roberts, Normanton, Yorks; *m* 1932, Sarah (*d* 1996), *o d* of late Thomas Raybould, Normanton, Yorks; two *d*. *Educ:* Normanton Grammar School; University of Leeds (Brown Scholar; BSc (Physics Hons) 1928; Univ. Res. Schol., 1928; PhD 1930; DSc 1944). FInstP 1938; CPhys 1985. Research Assistant in Physics, University of Leeds, 1930–32; Assistant Physicist, Royal Cancer Hospital, 1932–37; Senior Asst Physicist, Middlesex Hosp., 1937–46; Joel Prof. of Physics Applied to Medicine, Univ. of London, 1946–69; Regional Adviser to the ME, Internat. Atomic Energy Agency, 1963–64. Pres., British Inst. of Radiology, 1951–52; Pres. Hospital Physicists Assoc., 1950–51; Editor, Physics in Medicine and Biology, 1956–60; Editor, British Jl of Radiology, 1964–67. Hon. Mem., Royal Coll. of Radiologists; Hon. FIPEM. *Publications:* Nuclear War and Peace, 1956; What Must I Believe?, 1989; An Incoherence of Churches and Chapels, 1993; Meandering in Medical Physics, 1998; scientific

papers in various journals. *Address:* Badgeworth Court, Badgeworth, Cheltenham, Glos GL51 5UL. *T:* (01452) 715015. *Died 14 Oct. 1998.*

ROBERTS, Air Vice-Marshal John Frederick, CB 1967; CBE 1960 (OBE 1954); *b* 24 Feb. 1913; *y s* of late W. J. Roberts, Pontardawe; *m* 1st, 1942, Mary Winifred (*d* 1968), *d* of late J. E. Newns; one *s*; 2nd, 1976, Mrs P. J. Hull, *d* of A. Stiles. *Educ:* Pontardawe Grammar Sch., Glam. Chartered Accountant, 1936. Joined RAF, 1938; service in Middle East, 1942–45 (despatches); Mem. Directing Staff, RAF Staff Coll., Bracknell, 1954–56; SASO, RAF Record Office, 1958–60; Dep. Comptroller, Allied Forces Central Europe, 1960–62; Stn Comdr RAF Uxbridge, 1963; Dir of Personal Services I, Min. of Def. (Air), 1964–65; Dir-Gen. of Ground Training (RAF), 1966–68; retd, 1968; with Deloitte & Co., Chartered Accountants, Swansea, 1969–78. *Recreations:* cricket, golf, cabinet-making. *Address:* 1 Lon Cadog, Sketty, Swansea SA2 0TS. *T:* Swansea (01792) 203763. *Clubs:* Royal Air Force, MCC; Pontardawe Golf (Pres., 1978–88). *Died 20 April 1996.*

ROBERTS, Prof. Michael, FBA 1960; Director, Institute for Social and Economic Research, Rhodes University, 1974–76; Professor of Modern History, The Queen's University, Belfast, 1954–73; Dean of the Faculty of Arts, 1957–60; *b* 21 May 1908; *s* of Arthur Roberts and Hannah Elizabeth Landless; *m* 1941, Ann McKinnon Morton (decd); one *d*. *Educ:* Brighton Coll.; Worcester Coll., Oxford. Gladstone Meml Prizeman, 1931; A. M. P. Read Scholar (Oxford), 1932; DPhil Oxford, 1935. Procter Vis. Fellow, Princeton Univ., USA, 1931–32; Lectr, Merton Coll., Oxford, 1932–34; Asst Lectr, Univ. of Liverpool, 1934–35; Prof. of Modern History, Rhodes Univ., S Africa, 1935–53. Lieut, SA Intelligence Corps, 1942–44. British Council Representative, Stockholm, 1944–46. Public Orator, Rhodes Univ., 1951–53; Hugh Le May Vis. Fellow, Rhodes Univ., 1960–61; Lectures: A. L. Smith, Balliol Coll., Oxford, 1962; Enid Muir Meml, Univ. of Newcastle upon Tyne, 1965; Creighton in History, Univ. of London, 1965; Stenton, Univ. of Reading, 1969; James Ford special, Oxford Univ., 1973; Wiles, QUB, 1977. Hon. Fellow, Worcester Coll., Oxford, 1966; Vis. Fellow, All Souls Coll., Oxford, 1968–69; Leverhulme Faculty Fellow in European Studies, 1973; Vis. Fellow, Pomona Coll., Claremont, Calif, 1978; Vis. Fellow, Trevelyan Coll., Univ. of Durham, 1981. MRIA 1968. Foreign Member: Royal Swedish Acad. of Letters, History and Antiquities; Royal Swedish Academy of Science; Hon. Mem. Samfundet för utgivande av handskrifter rörande Skandinaviens historia. FRHistS; Fil dr (*hc*) Stockholm, 1960; Hon. DLit QUB, 1977; Hon. DLitt Rhodes, 1988. Kungens medalj i Serafimerband (Sweden), 1981. Chevalier, Order of North Star (Sweden), 1954. *Publications:* The Whig Party, 1807–1812, 1939; (with A. E. G. Trollip) The South African Opposition, 1939–1945, 1947; Gustavus Adolphus: a History of Sweden, 1611–1632, Vol. I, 1953, Vol. II, 1958; Essays in Swedish History, 1967; The Early Vasas: a History of Sweden 1523–1611, 1968; Sweden as a Great Power 1611–1697, 1968; Sverige och Europa, 1969; Gustav Vasa, 1970; (contrib.) Studies in Diplomatic History in Memory of D. B. Horn, 1970; Gustavus Adolphus and the Rise of Sweden, 1973, 2nd edn 1992; (ed) Sweden's Age of Greatness, 1973; Macartney in Russia, 1974; The Swedish Imperial Experience 1560–1718, 1979; British Diplomacy and Swedish Politics, 1758–1773, 1980; Sverige som Stormakt, 1980; (contrib.) L'Età dei Luni, 1985; The Age of Liberty: Sweden 1719–1772, 1986; (ed and trans.) Swedish Diplomats at Cromwell's Court, 1988; From Axel Oxenstierna to Charles XII, four studies, 1991; (trans.) The Journals and Letters of Johan August Wahlberg 1838–1856, 1994; Frihetstiden, 1995; trans. from Swedish of works by Nils Ahnlund, F. G. Bengtsson, Gunnar Wennerberg (Gluntarne), Birger Sjöberg (Fridas bok), Carl Michael Bellman (Epistles and Songs, I-III), Anna Maria Lenngren; articles in New Cambridge Mod. Hist., EHR, History, Historical Jl, Past and Present, Scandia, Karolinska Förbundets Årsbok, South African Archives Yearbook, etc. *Recreation:* music. *Address:* 1 Allen Street, Grahamstown, CP 6140, South Africa. *T:* Grahamstown 24855. *Died 31 Dec. 1996.*

ROBERTS, Maj.-Gen. Philip; *see* Roberts, Maj.-Gen. G. P. B.

ROBERTS-JONES, Ivor, CBE 1975; RA 1973 (ARA 1969); sculptor; Teacher of sculpture, Goldsmiths' College School of Art, 1946-68; *b* 2 Nov. 1913; *s* of William and Florence Robert-Jones; *m* 1940, Monica Florence Booth; (one *s* one *d* decd). *Educ:* Oswestry Grammar Sch.; Worksop Coll.; Goldsmiths' Coll. Art Sch.; Royal Academy Schs. Served in RA, 1939-46; active service in Arakan, Burma. One-man Exhibitions of Sculpture: Beaux Arts Gall., 1957; Oriel, Welsh Arts Council Gall., Cardiff 1978; Eisteddfod, 1983; exhibited at: The John Moore, Leicester Galls, Royal Academy, Arts Council travelling exhibitions, Jubilee Exhibn of Modern British Sculpture, Battersea Park, 1977, etc. Works purchased by: Tate Gall.; National Portrait Gall.; Arts Council of Gt Brit.; Welsh Arts Council; Beaverbrook Foundation, New Brunswick; Nat. Mus. of Wales; also in many private collections. Public commissions: Winston Churchill, Parliament Square; Augustus John Memorial, Fordingbridge; Saint Francis, Lady Chapel, Ardleigh, Essex; Apsley Cherry Garrard, Wheathampstead; Winston Churchill, Oslo, 1975; Winston Churchill, New Orleans, 1977; Earl Attlee, Members' Lobby, House of Commons, 1979; Janus Rider (equestrian group), Harlech Castle, 1982; Rupert Brooke memorial, Rugby, 1988; Field Marshal Lord Slim, Whitehall, 1990; Field Marshal Lord Alanbrooke, Whitehall, 1993. Best known portraits included: Paul Claudel, Somerset Maugham, Yehudi Menuhin, The Duke of Edinburgh, Geraint Evans, Speaker George Thomas, Sir James Callaghan. Hon. LLD Wales, 1983. *Publications:* poetry published in Welsh Review, Poets of the Forties, etc; sculpture illustr. in: British Art since 1900 by John Rothenstein; British Sculptors, 1947; Architectural Review, etc. *Address:* The Bridles, Hall Lane, Shimpling, near Diss, Norfolk IP21 4UH. *T:* (01379) 740204. *Died 9 Dec. 1996.*

ROBERTSON, Dr Alan, CBE 1982; PhD; CChem, FRSC; Vice-President, National Waterways Museum, since 1994; *b* 15 Aug. 1920; *s* of William Arthur Robertson and Clarice Firby Robertson; *m* 1948, Dorothy Eileen Freeman; two *s* one *d. Educ:* Middlesbrough High Sch.; BSc London; University Coll., Durham (PhD); Balliol Coll., Oxford (PhD 1947). CChem, FRSC 1970. ICI, 1936-82: variety of posts in research and works management; served on Boards of Dyestuffs Div., Mond Div., ICI Australia and ICI USA; Dep. Chm., Organics Div., 1965-73; Chm., Plant Protection Div., 1973-75; Main Bd Dir, 1975-82 (Agricl Product Dir, Management Services Dir, and Territorial Dir, Pacific and Far East). Chm., Agricultural Genetics Co., 1983-89. Vice-Chm., British Waterways Bd, 1983-89; Chm. Council of Management, Nat. Waterways Mus. Trust, 1989-94. Dir, First Step Housing Co. Ltd, 1990-. Royal Society of Chemistry: Mem. Council, 1978-81; Chm., Environment Gp, 1978-81; Chm., Indust. Div., 1978-81; Industrial Medal, 1982. Chairman: Eur. Chemical Industry Ecology and Toxicology Centre, 1978-83; British Nutrition Foundn, 1981-83 (Mem. Council, 1983-95; Gov. Emeritus, 1996); Member: NEDC for Paper and Paper Bd Industry, 1964-67; Teijin Agrochemicals Bd, 1975-82; British Industrial Biol Res. Assoc. Council, 1980-82; London

Bd, Halifax Bldg Soc., 1980-83; Kao Atlas Bd, 1975-82; Indust. Cttee, C of E Bd for Social Responsibility, 1980-86; Council, China Soc., 1985-; Vice-President: Heulwen Trust, 1986-; Pestalozzi Children's Village Trust, 1994- (Mem. Council, 1985-94); Mem. Court and Dep. Chm. of Council, UMIST, 1968-73; Governor, Lister Inst. of Preventive Medicine, 1985-. *Publications:* scientific papers in learned jls. *Recreations:* most sports (latterly non-active), gardening, industrial archaeology, biographical history, all matters oriental, children's and old people's welfare. *Address:* Woodlands, Tennyson's Lane, Haslemere, Surrey GU27 3AF. *T:* (01428) 644196. *Club:* Oriental. *Died 9 Jan. 1997.*

ROBERTSON, Prof. Anne Strachan, DLitt; FRSE; FSA, FSAScot; Titular Professor of Roman Archaeology, Glasgow University, 1974-75, retired; *d* of John Anderson Robertson and Margaret Purden. *Educ:* Hillhead High Sch.; Glasgow High Sch. for Girls; Glasgow Univ. (MA, DLitt); London Univ. (MA). FRSE 1975; FMA 1958; FRNS 1937; FSA 1958; FSAScot 1941. Glasgow University: Dalrymple Lectr in Archaeol., 1939; Under-Keeper, Hunterian Museum and Curator, Hunter Coin Cabinet, 1952; Reader in Roman Archaeol., Keeper of Cultural Collections and of Hunter Coin Cabinet, Hunterian Museum, 1964; Keeper of Roman Collections and of Hunter Coin Cabinet, 1974. Hon. Mem., Internat. Numismatic Commn, 1986; Corresp. Mem., Amer. Numismatic Soc., 1995. Silver Medal, RNS, 1964; Silver Huntington Medal, Amer. Numismatic Soc., 1970. *Publications:* An Antonine Fort: Golden Hill, Duntocher, 1957; The Antonine Wall, 1960, 4th edn 1990; Sylloge of Anglo-Saxon Coins in the Hunter Coin Cabinet, 1961; Catalogue of Roman Imperial Coins in the Hunter Coin Cabinet: Vol. 1, 1962; Vol. 2, 1971; Vol. 3, 1977; Vol. 4, 1978; Vol. 5, 1982; The Roman Fort at Castledykes, 1964; Birrens (Blatobulgium), 1975; contrib. to Britannia, Numismatic Chron., Proc. Soc. of Antiquaries of Scotland. *Recreations:* reading, writing, photography, walking, gardening. *Address:* 31 Upper Glenburn Road, Bearsden, Glasgow G61 4BN. *T:* (0141) 942 1136. *Died 4 Oct. 1997.*

ROBERTSON, Charles Robert Suttie; Member, Management Committee of The Distillers Company plc, 1970-82, retired; chartered accountant; *b* 23 Nov. 1920; *s* of late David Young McLellan Robertson and Doris May Beaumont; *m* 1949, Shona MacGregor Riddel (*d* 1985), *d* of late Robert Riddel, MC, and Phyllis Mary Stewart; one *s. Educ:* Dollar Academy. Joined DCL group, 1949; appointed: Managing Director, Scottish Malt Distillers, 1960; Sec., DCL, 1966, Finance Director, 1967. *Recreation:* reading. *Address:* The Arch, Edzell, Angus DD9 7TF. *T:* (01356) 648484. *Died 2 Jan. 1999.*

ROBERTSON, David Lars Manwaring, CVO 1990; Director, Kleinwort Benson Group plc, 1970-87; *b* 29 Jan. 1917; *m* 1939, Pamela Lauderdale Meares; three *s. Educ:* Rugby; University Coll., Oxford. Served Welsh Guards, 1940-45. Man. Dir, Charterhouse Finance Corp. Ltd, 1945-55; joined Kleinwort, Sons & Co. Ltd, 1955; Dir, Kleinwort, Benson Ltd, 1955-81; Chairman: MK Electric Group plc, 1975-87; Provident Mutual Life Assurance Assoc., 1973-89; Provident Mutual Managed Pensions Funds Ltd, 1974-89; Dir, Berry Bros and Rudd. JP Crowborough, 1971-87. *Recreation:* fishing. *Address:* 12 Lennox Gardens Mews, SW1X 0DP. *Clubs:* Boodle's, MCC. *Died 16 March 1999.*

ROBERTSON, (Harold) Rocke, CC 1969; MD, CM; FRCSCan, FRCSE, FACS, FRSC; Principal and Vice-Chancellor of McGill University, 1962-70; *b* 4 Aug. 1912; *s* of Harold Bruce Robertson and Helen McGregor Rogers; *m* 1937, Beatrice Roslyn Arnold; three *s* one *d. Educ:* St Michael's Sch., Victoria, BC; Ecole Nouvelle,

Switzerland; Brentwood College, Victoria, BC; McGill University. Montreal Gen. Hospital: rotating, 1936; pathology, 1937–38; Clin. Asst in Surg., Royal Infirmary, Edinburgh, 1938–39; Demonstr in Anat., Middx Hosp. Med. Sch., 1939; Jun. Asst in Surg., Montreal Gen. Hosp., 1939–40; Royal Canadian Army Medical Corps, 1940–45; Chief of Surgery: Shaughnessy Hosp., DVA, Vancouver, 1945–59 (Prof. of Surg., Univ. of BC, 1950–59); Vancouver Gen. Hosp., 1950–59; Montreal Gen. Hosp., 1959–62 (Prof. of Surg., McGill University, 1959–62). Member: Nat. Research Council, 1964; Science Council of Canada, 1976–82. Pres., Traffic Injury Res. Foundn, 1969–72, 1977–79; Hon. Pres., Mont St Hilaire Nature Conservation Centre, 1974–. Hon. DCL Bishop's Univ., 1963; Hon. LLD: Manitoba, 1964; Toronto, 1964; Victoria, 1964; Glasgow, 1965; Michigan, 1967; Dartmouth, 1967; Sir George Williams, 1970; McGill, 1970; Hon. DSc: Brit. Columbia, 1964; Memorial, 1968; Jefferson Med. Coll., 1969; Dr de l'Univ., Montreal, 1965. FRSA 1963. *Publications:* article on wounds, Encyclopædia Britannica; numerous contribs to scientific journals and text books. *Recreations:* tennis, fishing, gardening, golf. *Died 8 Feb. 1998.*

ROBERTSON, James Geddes, CMG 1961; formerly Under-Secretary, Department of the Environment, and Chairman, Northern Economic Planning Board, 1965–71, retired; *b* 29 Nov. 1910; *s* of late Captain A. M. Robertson and Elspeth Duncan Robertson, Portsoy, Banffshire; *m* 1939, Marion Mitchell Black (decd); *one s one d. Educ:* Fordyce Academy, Banffshire; George Watson's College, Edinburgh; Edinburgh University. Kitchener Schol., 1928–32; MA 1st cl. Hons History (Edinburgh), 1932. Entered Ministry of Labour as Third Class Officer, 1933; Principal, 1943; on exchange to Commonwealth Dept of Labour and Nat. Service, Australia, 1947–49; Asst Sec., Min of Labour, 1956–63; Member of Government Delegations to Governing Body and Conference of ILO, 1956–60, and Social Cttee, Council of Europe, 1953 61; Safety and Health Dept, 1961–63; Training Department, 1963–65. Member: Industrial Tribunals Panel, 1971–73; Northern Rent Scrutiny Bd, 1973–74; Rent Assessment Panel for Scotland, 1975–81. Served War of 1939–45: RAF, 1942–45. *Address:* 1/1 Wyvern Park, The Grange, Edinburgh EH9 2JY. *T:* (0131) 662 4367.
Died 4 Aug. 2000.

ROBERTSON, Jean, CBE 1986; RRC 1981; Matron-in-Chief, Queen Alexandra's Royal Naval Nursing Service, 1983–86; Director of Defence Nursing Services, Ministry of Defence, and Director of Royal Naval Nursing Services, 1985–86; working voluntarily for Queen Elizabeth Foundation for the Disabled, since 1989; *b* 21 Sept. 1928; *d* of late Alexander Robertson and Jean Robertson (*née* McCartney). *Educ:* Mary Erskine's School for Girls, Edinburgh. Registered Sick Children's Nurse, 1948; General Nurse, 1951; Ward Sister, Edinburgh Sick Children's Hospital, 1953; QARNNS 1955; QHNS, 1983–86. SSStJ 1981. *Recreations:* reading, swimming, knitting, making soft toys. *Address:* 14 The Haven, Alverstoke, Hants PO12 2BD. *T:* Gosport (01705) 582301. *Died 26 Aug. 1996.*

ROBERTSON, Comdt Dame Nancy (Margaret), DBE 1957 (CBE 1953; OBE 1946); Director of Women's Royal Naval Service, 1954–58, retired; *b* 1 March 1909; *er d* of Rev. William Cowper Robertson and Jessie Katharine (*née* McGregor). *Educ:* Esdaile School, Edinburgh; Paris. Secretarial work, London and Paris, 1928–39; WRNS, 1939. *Recreations:* needlework, bridge. *Address:* 10 Park View Court, Park View Road, Berkhamsted, Herts HP4 3ES. *Died 26 Dec. 2000.*

ROBERTSON, Prof. Noel Farnie, CBE 1978; PhD; FRSE; Professor of Agriculture and Rural Economy, University of Edinburgh, and Principal, East of Scotland College of Agriculture, 1969–83; *b* 24 Dec. 1923; *o s* of late James Robertson and Catherine Landles Robertson (*née* Brown); *m* 1948, Doreen Colina Gardner; two *s* two *d. Educ:* Trinity Academy, Edinburgh; University of Edinburgh (BSc, PhD); Trinity College, Cambridge (MA). Plant Pathologist, West African Cacao Research Institute, 1946–48; Lecturer in Botany, University of Cambridge, 1948–59; Prof. of Botany, Univ. of Hull, 1959–69. Pres., British Mycol Soc., 1965. Trustee, Royal Botanic Garden, Edinburgh, 1986–92. Chm. of Governors, Scottish Crop Res. Inst., 1983–89 (Governor, 1973–). *Publications:* (with I. J. Fleming) Britain's First Chair of Agriculture at the University of Edinburgh 1790–1990, 1990; (with Kenneth Blaxter) From Dearth to Plenty: the second agricultural revolution 1936–1986, 1995; (with D. S. Ingram) The Natural History of Plant Disease, 1999. *Address:* Woodend, Juniper Bank, Walkerburn, Peeblesshire EH43 6DE. *T:* (01896) 870523. *Club:* Farmers'. *Died 2 July 1999.*

ROBERTSON, Robert, CBE 1967; JP; FEIS; Member, Strathclyde Regional Council, 1974–86; *b* 15 Aug. 1909; *s* of late Rev. William Robertson, MA; *m* 1938, Jean, *d* of late James Moffatt, MA, Invermay, Broomhill, Glasgow; *one s one d. Educ:* Forres Academy; Royal Technical Coll., Glasgow. Civil Engr, retd 1969. Mem., Eastwood Dist Council, 1952–58; Chm., Renfrewshire Educn Cttee, 1962–73; Convener, Renfrewshire County Council, 1973–75 (Mem., 1958); Mem., Convention of Scottish Local Authorities, 1975–86. Chm., Sec. of State's Cttee on Supply and Trng of Teachers for Further Educn, 1962–78; Chm., Nat. Cttee for Inservice Trng of Teachers, 1965–78. Chm., E Renfrewshire Con. Assoc., 1971–74. Mem. Scottish Council for: Research in Educn, 1962–80; Commercial Admin and Professional Educn, 1960–69; Development of Industry, 1973–75. Chm., Sch. of Further Educn for training of teachers in Scotland, 1969–83. Governor: Jordanhill Coll. of Educn, 1966–83; Watt Memorial and Reid Kerr Colls, 1966–75, 1977–86. Member: Scottish Nat. School Camps Assoc., 1975–80; Scottish Assoc. of Young Farmers' Clubs, 1975–83; Glasgow Educnl Trust, 1978–86; Hutchison Educnl Trust, 1978–86; Council, Glasgow Coll. of Bldg and Printing, 1978–86. FEIS, at Stirling Univ., 1970; Hon. Warden, Co. of Renfrew, Ont, Canada, 1970. JP Renfrewshire, 1958. *Publication:* The Training of Teachers in Further Education (Robertson Report), HMSO, 1965. *Recreations:* fishing, painting. *Address:* 24 Broadwood Park, Alloway, Ayrshire KA7 4UR. *T:* Alloway (01292) 443820; Castlehill, Maybole, Ayrshire KA19 8JT. *T:* Dunure (01292) 500337. *Club:* RNVR (Scotland).
Died 21 Sept. 1996.

ROBERTSON, Rocke; *see* Robertson, H. R.

ROBINS, Prof. Robert Henry, FBA 1986; Professor of General Linguistics, 1966–86, then Emeritus, and Dean, Faculty of Arts, 1984–86, University of London; Head of Department of Phonetics and Linguistics, School of Oriental and African Studies, University of London, 1970–85; *b* 1 July 1921; *s* of John Norman Robins, medical practitioner, and Muriel Winifred (*née* Porter); *m* 1953, Sheila Marie Fynn (*d* 1983). *Educ:* Tonbridge Sch.; New Coll., Oxford, 1940–41 and 1945–48 (MA 1948); DLit London, 1968. Served war, RAF Intelligence, 1942–45. Lectr in Linguistics, Sch. of Oriental and African Studies, London, 1948–55; Reader in General Linguistics, Univ. of London, 1955–65. Mem. Senate, Univ. of London, 1980–85. Research Fellow, Univ. of California, 1951; Visiting Professor: Washington, 1963; Hawaii, 1968; Minnesota, 1971; Florida, 1975; Salzburg, 1977, 1979; Leverhulme Emeritus Fellow, 1990–91. President: Societas Linguistica Europaea, 1974; CIPL, 1977–97

(British Rep., 1970–77); Philological Soc., 1988–92 (Hon. Sec., 1961–88). Mem., Academia Europaea, 1991. Hon. Mem., Linguistic Soc. of Amer., 1981. *Publications:* Ancient and Mediaeval Grammatical Theory in Europe, 1951; The Yurok Language, 1958; General Linguistics: an introductory survey, 1964; A Short History of Linguistics, 1967; Diversions of Bloomsbury, 1970; Ideen- und Problemgeschichte der Sprachwissenschaft, 1973; System and Structure in Sundanese, 1983; The Byzantine Grammarians: their place in history, 1993; Texts and Contexts: selected papers on the history of linguistics, 1998; articles in Language, TPS, BSOAS, Lingua, Foundations of Language, Man, etc. *Recreations:* gardening, travel. *Address:* 65 Dome Hill, Caterham, Surrey CR3 6EF. *T:* (01883) 343778. *Clubs:* Athenæum, Royal Commonwealth Society. *Died 21 April 2000.*

ROBINSON, Air Vice-Marshal Bruce, CB 1968; CBE 1953; Air Officer Commanding No 24 Group, Royal Air Force, 1965–67; retired, 1967; *b* 19 Jan. 1912; *s* of late Dr G. Burton Robinson, Cannington, Somerset; *m* 1940, Elizabeth Ann Compton, *d* of Air Commodore D. F. Lucking; one *s* one *d. Educ:* King's School, Bruton. Commissioned in SRO, The Somerset Light Infty, 1931–33; commissioned in RAF, 1933; No 16 (Army Co-op. Sqdn), 1934–37; Specialist Engineer course, 1937–39; served War of 1939–45: Technical duties in Fighter and Bomber Commands, UK Senior Technical Staff Officer, Rhodesian Air Training Group, 1946–48; on loan to Indian Air Force (Director of Technical Services), 1951–53; Commandant, No 1 Radio School, RAF Locking, 1953–55; Sen. RAF Officer at Wright Patterson Air Force Base, Dayton, Ohio, 1958–60; Commandant No 1 Sch. of Technical Training, RAF Halton, Bucks, 1961–63; Director of RAF Aircraft Development, Min. of Aviation, 1963–65. *Recreations:* golf, painting, writing.
Died 20 May 1998.

ROBINSON, Clifton Eugene Bancroft, CBE 1985 (OBE 1973); JP; a Deputy-Chairman, Commission for Racial Equality, 1977–85; *b* 5 Oct. 1926; *s* of Theodore Emanuel and Lafrance Robinson; *m* (marr. diss.); one *s* three *d*; *m* 1977, Margaret Ann Ennever. *Educ:* Kingston Technical Coll., Jamaica; Birmingham Univ.; Leicester Univ.; Lancaster Coll. of Educn. BA, DipEd. Served War, RAF, 1944–49. Teacher: Mellor Sch., Leicester, 1951–61; i/c Special Educn Unit, St Peter's Sch., Leicester, 1961–64; Dep. Headteacher, Charnwood Sch., Leicester, 1964–68; Headteacher: St Peter's Sch., Leicester, 1968–70; Uplands Sch., Leicester, 1970–77. A Vice-Pres., Internat. Friendship League; President: Leicester United Caribbean Assoc.; Roots Coll. JP Leicester, 1974. *Recreations:* music (mainly classical), walking; when there was time, gardening. *Address:* 83 Numa Court, Justin Close, Brentford, Middlesex TW8 8QF.
Died 11 March 1996.

ROBINSON, John Armstrong, CMG 1969; HM Diplomatic Service, retired; Ambassador to Israel, 1980–81; *b* 18 Dec. 1925; *m* 1952, Marianne Berger; one *s* one *d.* HM Forces, 1944–46; Foreign Office, 1949–50; Second Secretary, Delhi, 1950–52; Foreign Office, 1952–53; Helsinki, 1953–56; Second, later First Secretary, Paris, 1956–58; Foreign Office, 1958–61; First Secretary in UK Delegation to European Communities, Brussels, 1962–67; Counsellor, Foreign Office, 1967; Head of European Economic Integration Dept, FCO, 1968–70; appointed Member of team of nine officials for negotiations on British entry into the Common Market, Brussels, 1970–71; Asst Under-Sec. of State, FCO, 1971–73; Ambassador to Algeria, 1974–77; Minister, Washington, 1977–80. *Address:* Mont-Riant 2, 2000 Neuchâtel, Switzerland.
Died 16 Jan. 1998.

ROBINSON, Rev. Canon Joseph, FKC; Master of the Temple, 1980–98; *b* 23 Feb. 1927; *er s* of Thomas and Maggie Robinson; *m* 1953, Anne Antrobus; two *s* two *d. Educ:* Upholland Grammar Sch., Lancs; King's Coll., London (BD 1st cl. Hons; AKC (1st cl.) 1951; MTh 1958; FKC 1973). Deacon, 1952; priest, 1953; Curate, All Hallows, Tottenham, 1952–55; Minor Canon of St Paul's Cathedral, 1956–68; Sacrist, 1958–68; Lectr in Hebrew and Old Testament Studies, King's Coll., London, 1959–68; Canterbury Cathedral: Canon Residentiary, 1968–80, then Canon Emeritus; Librarian, 1968–73; Treasurer, 1972–80; Exam. Chaplain to Archbishop of Canterbury, 1968–80. Golden Lectr, 1963; St Antholin Lectr, 1964–67. Chaplain, Worshipful Co. of Cutlers, 1963–; Sub Chaplain, Order of St John of Jerusalem, 1965–. Hon. Bencher, Inner Temple, 1994. *Publications:* The Cambridge Bible Commentary on 1 Kings, 1972, 2 Kings, 1976; articles in Church Quarterly Review, Expository Times, Church Times; many reviews in various jls. *Recreations:* reading, gardening. *Address:* The Master's House, The Temple, EC4Y 7BB. *T:* (020) 7353 8559. *Club:* Athenæum. *Died 21 June 1999.*

ROBINSON, Kathleen Marian, (Mrs Vincent F. Sherry; Kathleen M. Sherry); MD; FRCS, FRCOG; Hon. Obstetrician and Hon. Gynæcologist, Royal Free Hospital; Hon. Obstetrician, Queen Charlotte's Hospital; *b* 25 May 1911; *d* of late James Robinson and Ruth Robinson (*née* Edmeston); *m* 1946, Vincent Francis Sherry; one *s* one *d* (and one *d* decd). *Educ:* Penrhos College, Colwyn Bay; Royal Free Hospital School of Medicine, London University. MB, BS 1936; MRCS, LRCP 1936; MD London, 1940; FRCS 1940; MRCOG 1941; FRCOG 1953. Formerly: House Surgeon, Royal Free Hospital, Samaritan Hospital, Royal Marsden Hospital, Queen Charlotte's Hospital; Resident Obstetrician, Queen Charlotte's Hospital; Consultant Obstetrician and Gynaecologist, Royal Free Hosp. Recognised Teacher of the London University. FRSocMed; FRHS. *Publications:* contributor to Queen Charlotte's Text Book of Obstetrics, also to Practical Motherhood and Parentcraft. *Recreations:* gardening, cooking, travel. *Address:* 17 Herondale Avenue, SW18 3JN. *T:* (0181) 874 8588.
Died 22 Nov. 1998.

ROBINSON, Rt Hon. Sir Kenneth, Kt 1983; PC 1964; Hon. DLitt; FCIT; Chairman, Arts Council of Great Britain, 1977–82; *b* Warrington, Lancs, 19 March 1911; *s* of late Clarence Robinson, MRCS, LRCP; *m* 1941, Helen Elizabeth Edwards (*d* 1993); one *d. Educ:* Oundle Sch. Insurance Broker at Lloyd's, 1927–40; served War of 1939–45, RN 1941–46; Ord. Seaman, 1941; commissioned, 1942; Lieut-Comdr RNVR, 1944; served Home Fleet, Mediterranean, Far East and Pacific; Company Secretary, 1946–49. MP (Lab) St Pancras N, 1949–70; Asst Whip (unpaid), 1950–51, an Opposition Whip, 1951–54; Minister of Health, 1964–68; Minister for Planning and Land, Min. of Housing and Local Govt, 1968–69. Dir, Social Policy, 1970–72, Man. Dir (Personnel and Social Policy Div.), 1972–74, British Steel Corp.; Chm., LTE, 1975–78. Chairman: English National Opera, 1972–77; Young Concert Artists Trust, 1983–90; Carnegie Council Arts and Disabled People, 1985–87; Jt Treas., RSA, 1983–88. Trustee, Imperial War Mus., 1978–84. Hon. FRCGP; Hon. MRCP 1989; Hon. DLitt Liverpool, 1980. *Publications:* Wilkie Collins, a Biography, 1951; Policy for Mental Health, 1958; Patterns of Care, 1961; Look at Parliament, 1962. *Recreations:* looking at paintings, reading, listening to music. *Address:* 12 Grove Terrace, NW5 1PH. *Died 16 Feb. 1996.*

ROBINSON, Lloyd; *see* Robinson, T. L.

ROBINSON, Group Captain Marcus, CB 1956; AFC 1941 and Bar 1944; AE 1942; DL; Chairman, Robinson,

Dunn & Co. Ltd and subsidiary companies, 1966–77, retired; *b* 27 May 1912; *s* of Wilson and Eileen Robinson; *m* 1st, 1941, Mrs Mary Playfair (marr. diss. 1951); 2nd, 1953, Mrs Joan E. G. O. Weatherlake (*née* Carter) (decd); one *s* one *d*. *Educ:* Rossall. Commissioned AAF, 602 Sqdn, 1934; Squadron Ldr, 1940, commanding 616 Squadron; Wing Comdr, 1942; Group Capt., 1945; re-formed 602 Squadron, 1946; Member, Air Advisory Council, Air Ministry, 1952–56; Chairman Glasgow T&AFA, 1953–56. Chairman Glasgow Rating Valuation Appeals Cttee, 1963–74 (Dep. Chm., 1958–63). A Vice-Pres., Earl Haig Fund, Scotland, 1978– (Chm., 1974–78). DL Glasgow, 1953. Silver Jubilee Medal, 1977. *Recreations:* ski-ing, sailing. *Address:* Rockfort, Helensburgh, Argyll G84 7BA. *Club:* Royal Northern and Clyde Yacht (Rhu). *Died 25 March 1999.*

ROBINSON, Mollie Patricia, (Mrs Clare Robinson); *see* Panter-Downes, M. P.

ROBINSON, Sir Niall Bryan L.; *see* Lynch-Robinson.

ROBINSON, Oliver John; Editor, Good Housekeeping, 1947–65, Editor-in-Chief, 1965–67; *b* 7 April 1908; *s* of late W. Heath and Josephine Constance Robinson; *m* 1933, Evelyn Anne Laidler. *Educ:* Cranleigh Sch. Art Editor, Good Housekeeping, 1930; Art Editor, Nash's, 1933. Temporary commission, Queen's Royal Regt, 1941; Camouflage Development and Training Centre, 1942; Staff Officer, War Office, 1944. *Address:* 92 Charlbert Court, Eamont Street, NW8 7DA. *T:* 0171–722 0723. *Club:* Savage. *Died 26 June 1996.*

ROBINSON, Prof. Ronald Edward, CBE 1970, DFC 1944; Beit Professor of the History of the British Commonwealth, Oxford University, and Fellow of Balliol College, Oxford, 1971–87, then Professor and Fellow Emeritus; Director, University of Oxford Development Records Project, 1978–87; *b* 3 Sept. 1920; *s* of William Edward and Ada Theresa Robinson, Clapham, *m* 1940, Alice Josephine Denny; two *s* two *d*. *Educ:* Battersea Grammar Sch.; St John's Coll., Cambridge (Major Scholar in History, 1939; BA 1946, PhD 1949). Flt Lieut, 58 Bomber Sqn, RAF, 1942–45. Research Officer, African Studies Branch, Colonial Office, 1947–49; Lectr in History, 1953–66, Smuts Reader in History of the British Commonwealth, 1966–71, Univ. of Cambridge; Tutor 1961–66, Fellow 1949–71, St John's Coll., Cambridge; Chm., Faculty Bd of Modern Hist., Oxford, 1974–76, Vice-Chm., 1979–87. Inst. for Advanced Studies, Princeton, 1959–60. Mem., Bridges Cttee on Trng in Public Administration, 1961–62; Chm., Cambridge Confs on Problems of Developing Countries, 1961–70. UK observer, Zimbabwe election, 1980. *Publications:* Africa and the Victorians, 1961; Developing the Third World, 1971; (ed jtly) Bismarck, Europe and Africa, 1988; Railway Imperialism, 1991; articles in Cambridge History of the British Empire, Vol. III, 1959, and The New Cambridge Modern History, Vol. XI, 1963; reports on Problems of Developing Countries, 1963–71; articles and reviews in learned jls. *Recreation:* room cricket. *Address:* c/o Balliol College, Oxford. *Clubs:* Royal Commonwealth Society; Hawks (Cambridge); Gridiron (Oxford). *Died 19 June 1999.*

ROBINSON, Stanley Scott, MBE 1944; TD 1950; BL; SSC; Sheriff of Grampian, Highland and Islands (formerly Inverness (including Western Isles), Ross, Cromarty, Moray and Nairn), 1973–83; retired; *b* 27 March 1913; *s* of late William Scott Robinson, engineer, and Christina Douglas Robinson; *m* 1937, Helen Annan Hardie; three *s*. *Educ:* Boroughmuir Sch., Edinburgh; Edinburgh Univ. Admitted as solicitor, 1935; Solicitor in the Supreme Courts. Commissioned in TA, 1935; served War: France and Belgium, 1939–40, Captain RA; France, Holland and

Germany, 1944–45 (despatches twice); Major, RA, 1943; Lt-Col, 1948. Solicitor in gen. practice in Montrose, Angus, 1935–72 (except during war service). Hon. Sheriff: of Perth and Angus, 1970–72; of Inverness, 1984. Mem. Council of Law Society of Scotland, 1963–72 (Vice-Pres., 1971–72); Dean, Soc. of Solicitors of Angus, 1970–72. *Publications:* The Law of Interdict, 1987; The Law of Game and Fishing in Scotland, 1989; contribs to Stair Memorial Encyclopaedia and Jl of Law Society of Scotland. *Recreations:* golf, bowling, military history. *Address:* Flat 3, Drumallin House, Drummond Road, Inverness IV2 4NB. *T:* (01463) 233488.
Died 10 Aug. 1997.

ROBINSON, Thomas Lloyd, TD; Honorary President, The Dickinson Robinson Group Ltd, 1988–92 (Chairman, 1974–77, Deputy Chairman, 1968); *b* 21 Dec. 1912; *s* of late Thomas Rosser Robinson and Rebe Francis-Watkins; *m* 1939, Pamela Rosemary Foster; one *s* two *d*. *Educ:* Wycliffe Coll. Served War, 1939–45: Royal Warwickshire Regt, 61 Div., and SHAEF; Staff Coll., Camberley. Director, E. S. & A. Robinson Ltd, 1952; Jt Managing Dir, 1958; Dep. Chm., E. S. & A. Robinson (Holdings) Ltd, 1963; Director: Bristol Waterworks Co., 1978–84; Van Leer Groep, Holland, 1977–81; Legal & General Assurance Society (later Legal & General Group plc), 1970–83 (Vice-Chm., 1978–83); Chm., Legal & General South and Western Advisory Bd, 1972–84. Chm., Council of Governors, Wycliffe Coll., 1970–83, Pres., 1988–; Mem. Council, Univ. of Bristol, 1977–94; Pro-Chancellor, 1983–94. Master, Soc. of Merchant Venturers, Bristol, 1977–78. High Sheriff, Avon, 1979–80. President: Glos CCC, 1980–83, Warwicks Old County Cricketers Assoc., 1989. Hon. LLD Bristol, 1985. *Recreations:* music, reading, snooker, backgammon. *Address:* Lechlade, 23 Druid Stoke Avenue, Stoke Bishop, Bristol BS9 1DB. *T:* Bristol (0117) 968 1957. *Clubs:* Army and Navy, MCC; Royal and Ancient (St Andrews); Clifton (Bristol).
Died 2 Aug. 1996.

ROBOTHAM, Hon. Sir Lascelles (Lister), Kt 1987; Justice of Appeal, Belize, since 1992; *b* 22 Oct. 1923; *s* of Vivian Constantine Robotham and Ethline Blanche Robotham; *m* 1949, Gloria Angela Stiebel; one *s* one *d*. *Educ:* Calabar Coll., Jamaica. Called to the Bar, Lincoln's Inn, 1955, Hon. Bencher, 1988. Crown Counsel, Jamaica, 1955–58; Dep. Dir of Public Prosecutions, 1958–62; Resident Magistrate, 1962–64; Puisne Judge, 1964–76; Justice of Appeal, Jamaica, 1976–79; Justice of Appeal, Eastern Caribbean Supreme Court, 1979–84; Pres., Eastern Caribbean Court of Appeal, 1984–91; Chief Justice, Eastern Caribbean Supreme Court, 1984–91. *Recreations:* reading, gardening, cricket. *Address:* PO Box 1950, Castries, St Lucia, West Indies. *T:* (home) 28566.
Died 19 Feb. 1996.

ROBSON OF KIDDINGTON, Baroness *cr* 1974 (Life Peer), of Kiddington, co. Oxfordshire; **Inga-Stina Robson;** JP; Chairman, South-West Thames Regional Health Authority, 1974–82; *b* 20 Aug. 1919; *d* of Erik R. Arvidsson and Lilly A. Arvidsson (*née* Danielson); *m* 1940, Sir Lawrence W. Robson (*d* 1982); one *s* two *d*. *Educ:* Stockholm, Sweden. Swedish Foreign Office, 1939–40; Min. of Information, 1942–43. Contested (L) Eye Div., 1955 and 1959, Gloucester City, 1964 and 1966. President: Women's Liberal Fedn, 1968–69 and 1969–70; Liberal Party Orgn, 1970–71; Chm., Liberal Party Environment Panel, 1971–77. Chairman: Bd of Governors, Queen Charlotte's and Chelsea Hosps, 1970–84; Midwife Teachers Training Coll.; Nat. Assoc. of Leagues of Hosp. Friends, 1985–94; Member: Bd of Governors, University Coll. Hosp., 1966–74; Council, Surrey Univ., 1974. Pres., Anglo-Swedish Soc., 1992– (Chm., 1983–92). JP Oxfordshire, 1955. *Recreations:* sailing, skiing. *Address:*

The Dower House, Kiddington, Woodstock, Oxon OX20 1BU. *Died 9 Feb. 1999.*

ROBSON, William Michael; Deputy Chairman, The Standard Bank Ltd, 1965–83 (Director, 1960–83); *b* 31 Dec. 1912; *e s* of late Col the Hon. Harold Burge Robson, TD, DL, JP, Pinewood Hill, Witley, Surrey and Ysolt Robson (*née* Leroy-Lewis); *m* 1st, 1939, Audrey Isobel Wales (*d* 1964), *d* of late Major William Dick, Low Gosforth Hall, Northumberland; two *s* one *d*; 2nd, 1965, Frances Mary Wyville, *d* of late James Anderson Ramage Dawson, Balado House, Kinross, and *widow* of Andrew Alexander Nigel Buchanan. *Educ:* Eton; New College, Oxford. Served War of 1939–45: with Grenadier Guards (Major 1944), England and Europe BAOR. A Vice-Chm., Victoria League for Commonwealth Friendship, 1962–65. Director: Booker McConnell Ltd, 1955–78 (Chm., Booker Pensions, 1957–78); United Rum Merchants Ltd, 1965–78; British South Africa Co., 1961–66 (Vice-Chm., Jt East & Central African Bd, 1956–63); Antony Gibbs & Sons (Insurance) Ltd, 1946–48, 1973–76; Antony Gibbs (Insurance Holdings), 1976–80; Antony Gibbs, Sage Ltd, 1976–80; Anton Underwriting Agencies Ltd, 1977–82; Chm., Standard Bank Finance & Develt Corp. Ltd, 1966–73; Deputy Chairman: The Chartered Bank, 1974–83; Standard and Chartered Banking Gp Ltd, 1974–83 (Dir, 1970–83). Mem., BNEC, Africa, 1965–71 (Dep. Chm., 1970–71). High Sheriff of Kent, 1970. Liveryman, Vintners' Co., 1953. Mem. Council of The Shrievalty Assoc., 1971–76. *Club:* Brooks's.
Died 16 Jan. 1998.

ROCHE, Hon. Thomas Gabriel; QC 1955; Recorder of the City of Worcester, 1959–71; *b* 11 May 1909; *yr s* of Baron Roche, PC and Elfreda Gabriel, *d* of John Fenwick. *Educ:* Rugby; Wadham Coll., Oxford. Called to the Bar, Inner Temple, 1932. Served War of 1939–45 (Lt-Col 1944, despatches). Church Commissioner, 1961–65; Member, Monopolies Commission, 1966–69. *Address:* Chadlington, Oxford. *Club:* United Oxford & Cambridge University. *Died 27 May 1998.*

RODGER, Allan George, OBE 1944; Under-Secretary, Scottish Education Department, 1959–63, retired; *b* Kirkcaldy, 7 Jan. 1902; *s* of Allan Rodger, schoolmaster, and Annie Venters; *m* 1930, Barbara Melville Simpson (*d* 1991); one *s* one *d*. *Educ:* Pathhead Primary School, Kirkcaldy; Kirkcaldy High School; Edinburgh University (MA (Hons) Maths, BSc, MEd, Dip. Geog.). Teacher, Viewforth School, Kirkcaldy, 1926–29; Lecturer, Moray House Training Coll. and Univ. Dept of Educn (Edinburgh), 1929–35; HM Inspector of Schools, 1935–45, with special duties in regard to geography, special schools, and training colleges (seconded to special administrative duties in Education Dept, 1939–45); Asst Secretary, Scottish Educn Dept, 1945–59. Served on Educational Commission for Govts of Uganda and Kenya, 1961. Chairman of various Govt Cttees on Scottish Educn matters. *Publications:* contrib. to Jl of Educational Psychology and other educational journals. *Recreations:* reading, music. *Died 10 Oct. 1996.*

RODGERS, George; Library Officer, Labour Party Headquarters, 1988–90, retired; *b* 7 Nov. 1925; *s* of George and Lettitia Georgina Rodgers; *m* 1952, Joan, *d* of James Patrick and Elizabeth Graham; one *s* two *d*. *Educ:* St Margaret's and Holy Trinity, Liverpool; St Michael's, Sylvester, Rupert Road and Longview, Huyton. Co-operative Soc., Whiston, Lancs, 1939–43. Served War, RN, 1943–46 (War Medals, France, Germany Star). White's, Engrs, Widnes, 1946–50; with Civil Engineers: Eave's, Blackpool, 1950–53; Costain, Liverpool, 1953–54; Brit. Insulated Callender Cables, 1954–74. Mem., Huyton UDC, 1964–74 (Chm., Educn Cttee, 1969–73; Chm., Local Authority, 1973–74); Mem.

Liverpool Regional Hosp. Bd, 1967–74. MP (Lab) Chorley, Feb. 1974–1979. Chm., NW Region Lab MPs, 1975–79. Contested (Lab) Pendle, 1983. Sales Organiser, 1980, Circulation and Promotion Manager, 1980–87, Labour Weekly; Campaigns Officer, PLP, 1988. *Publication:* (with Ivor Clemitson) A Life to Live: beyond full employment, 1981. *Recreations:* cycling, political history, amateur boxing (spectator). *Address:* 32 Willoughby Road, Huyton, Liverpool L14 6XB. *T:* (0151) 489 1913. *Club:* Labour (Huyton).
Died 15 Feb. 2000.

RODGERS, Sir (John Fairlie) Tobias, 2nd Bt *cr* 1964, of Groombridge, Kent; antiquarian bookseller, publisher and journalist; *b* 2 July 1940; *s* of Sir John Rodgers, 1st Bt and Betsy (*née* Aikin-Sneath); *S* father, 1993. *Educ:* Eton; Worcester Coll., Oxford. *Recreations:* travelling, reading, bridge, tennis. *Heir: b* (Andrew) Piers (Wingate) Rodgers [*b* 24 Oct. 1944; *m* 1979, Marie Agathe Houette; two *s*]. *Address:* 34 Warwick Avenue, W9 2PT. *T:* (0171) 286 4376. *Clubs:* Brooks's, Garrick, Pratt's.
Died 19 Jan. 1997.

ROE, Rt Rev. (William) Gordon; Bishop Suffragan of Huntingdon, 1980–97; *b* 5 Jan. 1932; *s* of William Henry and Dorothy Myrtle Roe; *m* 1953, Mary Andreen; two *s* two *d. Educ:* Bournemouth School; Jesus Coll., Oxford (MA, DipTh (with distinction), DPhil); St Stephen's House, Oxford. Deacon 1958, priest 1959; Curate of Bournemouth, 1958–61; Priest-in-charge of St Michael's, Abingdon, 1961–69; Vice-Principal of St Chad's Coll., Durham, 1969–74; Vicar of St Oswald's, Durham, 1974–80; RD of Durham, 1974–80; Chaplain of Collingwood Coll., Durham, 1974–80; Hon. Canon of Durham Cathedral, 1979–80. Co-Chm., Meissen Commn, 1991–96. DUniv Anglia Poly. Univ., 1996. *Publications:* Lamennais and England, 1966; (with A. Hutchings) J. B. Dykes, Priest and Musician, 1976. *Recreations:* French literature, painting. *Address:* 8 Eldon Road, Bournemouth, Dorset BH9 2RT. *T:* (01202) 535127.
Died 19 July 1999.

ROGERS, Betty Evelyn, (Mrs P. E. Rogers); *see* Box, B. E.

ROGERS, Rev. Edward; General Secretary, Methodist Division of Social Responsibility (formerly Christian Citizenship Department), 1950–75; *b* 4 Jan. 1909; *s* of Capt. E. E. Rogers, Fleetwood; *m* 1st, 1937, Edith May (decd), *o d* of A. L. Sutton, Plaistow; 2nd, 1979, Lucy Eveline Howlett. *Educ:* Baines's Poulton-Le-Fylde Grammar School; Manchester University; Hartley Methodist Coll. Kitchener Scholar, Shuttleworth Scholar, Hulme Hall, Manchester; MA (Econ. and Pol.) 1931, BD 1933, Manchester Univ. Methodist Circuit Minister: East London Mission, Bakewell, Birmingham (Sutton Park), Southport, 1933–50. Editorial Dir, Methodist Newspaper Co., 1949–97; Organising Dir, Methodist Relief Fund, 1953–75; Chairman, Inter-Church Aid and Refugee Service, British Council of Churches, 1960–64; Pres., Methodist Conf., 1960; Moderator, Free Church Federal Council, 1968 (Chm., Exec., 1974–80); Vice-Pres., British Council of Churches, 1971–74. Chairman: Standing Commn on Migration, 1964–70; Churches Cttee on Gambling Legislation, 1967–73; Exec. Council, UK Immigrants Adv. Service, 1970; Community and Race Relations Unit, 1971–75; Avec Board, 1977–89; Select Committee on Cruelty to Animals, 1963. Lectures: Fernley, 1951; Ainslie, 1952; Beckly, 1957; Peake 1971. *Publications:* First Easter, 1948; A Commentary on Communism, 1951; Programme for Peace, 1954; God's Business, 1957; That They Might Have Life, 1958; The Christian Approach to the Communist, 1959; Church Government, 1964; Living Standards, 1964; Law, Morality and Gospel, 1969; Search for Security, 1973; Plundered

Planet, 1973; Money, 1976; Thinking About Human Rights, 1978; Changing Humanity: genetic engineering, 1989. *Recreations:* travel, indiscriminate reading. *Address:* 49 Fernhurst Road, Croydon, Surrey CR0 7OJ. *T:* (0181) 656 1729. *Died 27 Oct. 1997.*

ROGERS, George Theodore; Under-Secretary, Department of Trade, 1974–79; *b* 26 Feb. 1919; *s* of late George James and Margaret Lilian Rogers; *m* 1944, Mary Katherine Stedman; three *s* two *d. Educ:* Portsmouth Grammar Sch.; Keble Coll., Oxford (Open Schol. in Classics). Served War, Indian Infy, Burma, 1939–45; resumed univ. educn (PPE), 1945–48; Min. of Supply/Min. of Aviation, 1948–65; NATO Defence Coll., 1953–54; Univ. Grants Cttee, 1965–68; Min. of Technology, 1968–70; DTI, 1970–74; Under-Sec., 1973. *Recreations:* gardening, travel. *Address:* 39 Sandy Lane, Cheam, Surrey SM2 7PQ. *T:* (0181) 642 6428.

Died 24 Feb. 1999.

ROGERS, Henry Augustus, OBE 1976 (MBE 1967); HM Diplomatic Service, retired; *b* 11 Dec. 1918; *s* of Henry Augustus Rogers and Evelyn Mary Rogers (*née* Casey); *m* 1947, Margaret May Stainsby; three *s. Educ:* The Fox Sch.; West Kensington Central Sch., London, W. With Solicitors, Wedlake Letts & Birds, Temple, prior to war. Joined RNVR, 1938; served: Mediterranean, HMSs Argus, St Angelo (Malta) and Aurora, 1939–43; RMS Queen Elizabeth, N Atlantic, 1943–45. Joined Foreign Office, 1945; Buenos Aires, 1946; Havana, 1953; Vice-Consul, Guatemala City, 1954; Vice-Consul, Los Angeles, 1958; Second Sec., Belgrade, 1961; FO, 1963; Second Sec., Kaduna, Nigeria, 1965; took charge of British interests in Kano, Oct. 1966 during seriously deteriorating local tribal situation; First Sec., Head of Chancery and Consul, Tegucigalpa, 1967; FCO, 1971; Consul, Luanda, Angola, 1973; Consul-Gen., Brisbane, 1976–77; FCO, 1978, Malta GC 50th Anniv. Medal, 1992. *Recreations:* reading, classical literature and modern history, art (the Impressionists), music. *Address:* 18 Carew Views, 30/36 Carew Road, Eastbourne, East Sussex BN21 2JL. *T:* (01323) 730915. *Died 19 Feb. 1999.*

ROGERS, Thomas Edward, CMG 1960; MBE 1945; HM Diplomatic Service, retired; *b* 28 Dec. 1912; *s* of T. E. Rogers, MBE and Lucy Jane Browne; *m* 1950, Eileen Mary, *d* of R. J. Speechley; no *c. Educ:* Bedford Sch.; Emmanuel Coll., Cambridge (Exhibnr); School of Oriental Studies, London. Apptd to Indian Civil Service, 1936, and to Indian Political Service, 1941; served in Bengal, 1937–41; in Persia and Persian Gulf, 1941–45; Political Agent, Quetta, 1947; Dep. Sec. (Cabinet Secretariat), Pakistan Govt, 1947–48; entered Foreign Service, 1948: FO, 1948–50; Bogotá, 1950–53; jssc, 1953–54; Counsellor (Comm.), Madrid, 1954–58; Counsellor (Econ.), Belgrade, 1958–62; Minister (Econ.), Buenos Aires, 1963–66; Dep. UK High Comr, Canada, 1966–70, Actg High Comr, 1967–68; Ambassador to Colombia, 1970–73. Chm., Anglo-Colombian Soc., 1981–88. Great Cross of St Carlos, Colombia, 1974. *Publication:* Great Game Grand Game (memoirs), 1991. *Recreation:* travel. *Address:* Chintens, Firway, Grayshott, Hindhead, Surrey GU26 6JQ. *Club:* United Oxford & Cambridge University.

Died 26 Nov. 1999.

ROLAND, Nicholas; *see* Walmsley, Arnold Robert.

ROLFE, Rear-Adm. Henry Cuthbert Norris, CB 1959; *b* 1908; *s* of Benedict Hugh Rolfe, MA Oxon; *m* 1931, Mary Monica Fox (*d* 1996); one *s* two *d. Educ:* Pangbourne Nautical College. Joined Royal Navy, 1925; served War of 1939–45: HMS Hermes, 1939; South-East Asia, 1944; Staff of Director of Air Warfare, Admiralty, 1947; commanded HMS Veryan Bay, 1948; service with Royal Canadian Navy, 1949; commanded: HMS Vengeance,

1952; RN Air Station, Culdrose, 1952; HMS Centaur, 1954–56; RN Air Station, Ford, 1956–57; Asst Chief of Naval Staff (Warfare) 1957–60; Regional Director, Northern Region, Commonwealth Graves Commission, 1961–64, retd. Naval ADC to the Queen, 1957; Rear-Admiral, 1957. Liveryman, Worshipful Company of Coachmakers and Coach Harnessmakers, 1962. *Address:* 43 Nuns Road, Winchester, Hants SO23 7EF.

Died 21 April 1997.

ROLL, Rev. Sir James (William Cecil), 4th Bt *cr* 1921, of The Chestnuts, Wanstead, Essex; Vicar of St John's, Becontree, 1958–83, retired; *b* 1 June 1912; *s* of Sir Cecil Ernest Roll, 3rd Bt, and Mildred Kate (*d* 1926), *d* of William Wells, Snaresbrook; *S* father, 1938; unmarried. *Educ:* Chigwell School, Essex; Pembroke College, Oxford; Chichester Theological College. Deacon, 1937, priest, 1938; Curate, East Ham Parish Church, 1944 58. *Heir:* none. *Address:* 82 Leighcliff Road, Leigh on Sea, Essex SS9 1DN. *T:* (01702) 713050.

Died 13 Feb. 1998 (ext).

ROLLO, 13th Lord *cr* 1651; **Eric John Stapylton Rollo;** Baron Dunning 1869; JP; *b* 3 Dec. 1915; *s* of 12th Lord Rollo and Helen Maud (*d* 1928), *o c* of Frederick Chetwynd Stapylton, Hatton Hill, Windlesham, Surrey; *S* father, 1947; *m* 1938, Suzanne Hatton; two *s* one *d. Educ:* Eton. Served War of 1939–45, Grenadier Guards, retiring with rank of Captain. JP Perthshire, 1962. *Heir:* s Master of Rollo [*b* 31 March 1943; *m* 1971, Felicity Lamb; three *s*]. *Address:* Pitcairns, Dunning, Perthshire PH2 9BX. *T:* (01764) 684202. *Died 25 Sept. 1997.*

ROLO, Cyril Felix, CMG 1975; OBE 1959; HM Diplomatic Service, retired; *b* 13 Feb. 1918; *s* of late I. J. Rolo and Linda (*née* Suares); *m* 1948, Marie Luise Christine (*née* Baeurle); one *s. Educ:* Charterhouse; Oriel Coll., Oxford (MA). Served with Armed Forces, 1940–46 (Major): Oxford and Bucks LI, later on Gen. Staff: Western Desert, E Africa, Italy, Austria. Joined HM Foreign (subseq. Diplomatic) Service, 1946: Allied Commn for Austria, 1947–48; 2nd Sec., Rome, 1948–50; Political Adviser's Office, Berlin, 1950–52; FO, 1952–57; 1st Sec., Vienna, 1957–62; FO (subseq. FCO), 1962–76; Counsellor, 1971. *Recreations:* travel, golf, reading. *Address:* 12 Roxburghe Mansions, 32 Kensington Court, W8 5BQ. *T:* (020) 7937 4696. *Clubs:* Travellers; Sunningdale Golf.

Died 20 April 2000.

ROPER, John Charles Abercromby, CMG 1969; MC; HM Diplomatic Service, retired; *b* 8 June 1915; *s* of late Charles Roper, MD, and Ethel Emily Roper; *m* 1st, 1945, Mrs Valerie Armstrong-MacDonnell (marr. diss.); two *d*; 2nd, 1960, Kathryn (*d* 1984), *d* of late Edgar Bibas, New York; 3rd, 1986, Phoebe, *d* of late R. B. Foster, London and New York. *Educ:* Harrow; Gonville and Caius Coll., Cambridge (BA 1937); Princeton Univ. (Commonwealth Fellow). Served 1939–46, Scots Guards and Special Forces, Major (MC). HM Diplomatic Service, 1946; Athens, 1947–51; Foreign Office, 1951–54; Washington, 1954–59; seconded to Min. of Defence and apptd Dep. Commandant (Civil) of NATO Defence College, Paris, 1960–62; Asst Sec., Cabinet Office, 1962–64; Counsellor, UK Delegn to OECD, 1964–70; Ambassador to Luxembourg, 1970–75. *Address:* Tenuta di Monteverdi, 58048 Paganico, Provincia di Grosseto, Italy. *Club:* Special Forces. *Died 14 Oct. 1998.*

ROPNER, John Raymond; Consultant, Ropner PLC, and other companies; *b* 8 May 1903; *s* of William Ropner; *m* 1928, Joan Redhead; two *s* one *d. Educ:* Harrow; Clare College, Cambridge (BAEcon 1925). Durham Heavy Bde, RA (TA), 1922–28. Joined Sir R. Ropner & Co. Ltd, 1925; Ministry of War Transport, North Western Europe, 1944–45. High Sheriff of Durham, 1958. Member,

Shipping Advisory Panel, 1962. Order of Oranje-Nassau, 1947. *Recreations:* gardening, fishing; formerly golf (Cambridge blue, 1925). *Address:* The Limes, Dalton, Richmond, N Yorkshire DL11 7XJ. *T:* (01833) 21447.

Died 10 Nov. 1996.

ROSE, Bernard William George, OBE 1980; MusB Cantab 1938, MA Oxon, Cantab 1944, DMus Oxon 1955; FRCO; Fellow, Organist, Informator Choristarum, Magdalen College, Oxford, 1957–81, Vice-President, 1973 and 1974, Emeritus Fellow since 1981; University Lecturer in Music, 1950–81; Choragus in the University, 1958–63; *b* Little Hallingbury, Herts, 9 May 1916; *s* of William and Jessie Rose; *m* 1939, Molly Daphne, OBE, JP, DL, 5th *d* of D. G. Marshall, MBE, Cambridge; three *s. Educ:* Salisbury Cathedral Sch.; Royal Coll. of Music; St Catharine's Coll., Cambridge. Organ Scholar, St Catharine's, Cambridge, 1935–39; Stewart of Rannoch Scholar in Sacred Music, Cambridge, 1935–39; Organist, and Conductor of the Eaglesfield Musical Soc., The Queen's Coll., Oxford, 1939–57, Fellow, 1949. Served with 4th Co. of London Yeomanry (Sharpshooters), 1941–44, Adjutant 1942 (PoW 1943–44). Conductor, Oxford Orchestral Soc., 1971–74. Mem. Council, Royal Coll. of Organists (Pres. 1974–76). *Publications:* Catharine: an ode, 1973; (ed) Early English Church Music, Vols 5, 9, 14, 27, 37 and 39; various church music compositions and edns of church music; edns of Anthems of Thomas Tomkins; Hallische Händel Ausgabe, 'Susanna'; contrib. Proc. Royal Musical Assoc., 1955; reviews in Music and Letters, articles in Musical Times. *Recreations:* DIY, bowls. *Address:* Bampton House, Bampton, Oxford OX18 2JX. *T:* (01993) 850135.

Died 21 Nov. 1996.

ROSE, Eliot Joseph Benn, (Jim), CBE 1979; Chairman, Penguin Books, 1973–80; Director, Pearson Longman, 1974–81; *b* 7 June 1909; *s* of late Colonel E. A. Rose, CBE, and Dula, *e d* of Eliot Lewis, JP; *m* 1946, Susan Pamela Gibson; one *s* one *d. Educ:* Rugby; New College, Oxford. Served War of 1939–45, RAF, Wing-Comdr. Literary Editor, The Observer, 1948–51; Director: International Press Institute, Zürich, 1951–62; Survey of Race Relations in Britain, 1963–69; Editorial Dir, Westminster Press Ltd, 1970–74. Chm., Inter-Action Trust, 1968–84; Co-founder, Runnymede Trust, 1968 (Chm., 1980–90); Mem., Cttee of Inquiry into educn of children from ethnic minority groups, 1979–81; Special Consultant to Unicef, 1981. Trustee, Writers and Scholars Educnl Trust, 1978. Sidney Ball Meml Lectr, Oxford, 1970. Legion of Merit (US). *Publication:* (with Nicholas Deakin) Colour and Citizenship, 1969. *Address:* 37 Pembroke Square, W8 6PE. *T:* (020) 7937 3772; Rocks Farm, Groombridge, Tunbridge Wells, Kent TN3 9PG. *T:* (01892) 864223. *Club:* Garrick.

Died 21 May 1999.

ROSE, Jim; *see* Rose, E. J. B.

ROSIER, Air Chief Marshal Sir Frederick (Ernest), GCB 1972 (KCB 1966; CB 1961); CBE 1955 (OBE 1943); DSO 1942; RAF, retired; *b* 13 Oct. 1915; *s* of E. G. Rosier; *m* 1939, Hettie Denise Blackwell; three *s* one *d. Educ:* Grove Park School, Wrexham. Commissioned RAF, 1935; 43 (F) Sqdn, 1936–39; served War of 1939–45 in France, UK, Western Desert and Europe; OC Horsham St Faith, 1947; exchange duties with USAF, 1948–50; Instructor at Jt Services Staff College, 1950–52; Gp Capt. Operations at Central Fighter Establishment, 1952–54; Gp Capt. Plans at Fighter Command, 1955–56; ADC to the Queen, 1956–58; idc 1957; Director of Joint Plans, Air Ministry, 1958; Chm. Joint Planning Staff, 1959–61; AOC Air Forces Middle East, 1961–63; Senior Air Staff Officer, HQ Transport Command, 1964–66; Air Officer C-in-C, RAF, Fighter Command, 1966–68; UK Mem., Permanent

Military Deputies Group, Central Treaty Organisation, Ankara, 1968–70; Dep. C-in-C, Allied Forces Central Europe, 1970–73; Air ADC to the Queen, 1972–73. Mil. Advr and Dir, British Aircraft Corp. (Preston) Ltd, 1973–77; Director i/c BAC Ltd, Saudi Arabia, 1977–80. Commander: Order of Orange Nassau, 1947; Order of Polonia Restituta, 1985. *Address:* Ty Haul, Sun Bank, Llangollen, N Wales LL20 7UH. *T:* (01978) 861068; Flat 286, Latymer Court, Hammersmith, W6 7LD. *T:* (0181) 741 0765. *Club:* Royal Air Force.

Died 10 Sept. 1998.

ROSKELL, Prof. John Smith, MA, DPhil; FBA 1968; Professor of Medieval History, University of Manchester, 1962–79, then Professor Emeritus; *b* Norden, Rochdale, 2 July 1913; *s* of John Edmund and Lucy A. Roskell; *m* 1942, Evelyn Liddle (*d* 1989); one *s* one *d. Educ:* Rochdale Municipal Secondary School; Accrington Grammar Sch.; University of Manchester; Balliol College, Oxford. Asst Lecturer in History, Manchester University, 1938, Lecturer, 1945, Senior Lecturer, 1950–52; Professor of Medieval History, University of Nottingham, 1952–62. President: Lancashire Parish Register Soc., 1962–84; Chetham Soc., 1972–84; Feoffee, Chetham's Hosp. and Liby, Manchester, 1963–90. Royal Navy, 1940–45; Lieut RNVR, 1942–45. *Publications:* The Knights of the Shire of the County Palatine of Lancaster (1377–1460), Chetham Society, 1937; The Commons in the Parliament of 1422, 1954; The Commons and their Speakers in English Parliaments, 1376–1523, 1965; (ed with F. Taylor) Gesta Henrici Quinti, 1975; Parliament and Politics in Late Medieval England (3 vols), 1981–83; The Impeachment of Michael de la Pole, Earl of Suffolk, in 1386, 1984; (ed jtly) History of Parliament, The House of Commons 1386–1421, 1993. *Address:* 42 Barcheston Road, Cheadle, Cheshire SK8 1LL. *T:* (0161) 428 4630.

Died 1 May 1998.

ROSKILL, Baron *cr* 1980 (Life Peer), of Newtown in the County of Hampshire; **Eustace Wentworth Roskill,** Kt 1962; PC 1971; DL; a Lord of Appeal in Ordinary 1980–86; *b* 6 Feb. 1911; *y s* of late John Roskill, KC and Sybil Mary Wentworth, *d* of Ashton Wentworth Dilke, MP; *m* 1947, Elisabeth Wallace Jackson, 3rd *d* of late Thomas Frame Jackson, Buenos Aires; one *s* two *d. Educ:* Winchester College (Exhibnr; Fellow, 1981–86); Exeter Coll., Oxford (Exhibnr). 1st Cl. hons, Hon. Sch. of Mod. Hist. Oxford, BA 1932; MA 1936. Harmsworth Law Schol., Middle Temple, 1932; called to Bar, Middle Temple, 1933, Bencher 1961, Reader 1978, Dep. Treasurer 1979, Treasurer 1980; Hon. Bencher of The Inner Temple, 1980. Worked at Ministries of Shipping and War Transport, 1939–45. QC 1953. Dep. Chm. Hants QS, 1951–60, Chm. 1960–71; Comr of Assize (Birmingham), 1961; Judge of the High Court of Justice, Queen's Bench Division, 1962–71; a Lord Justice of Appeal, 1971–80. Vice-Chm., Parole Bd, 1967–69; Chm., Commn on Third London Airport, 1968–70. Pres., Senate of Four Inns of Court, 1972–74, Hon. Mem., 1974; Life Mem., Canadian Bar Assoc., 1974. Chairman: Average Adjusters Assoc., 1977–78; London Internat. Arbitration Trust, 1981–88; Fraud Trials Cttee, 1983–85; Take-over Panel Appeal Cttee, 1987–93. Chairman: Horris Hill Prep. Sch. Trust, 1957–64; Barristers' Benevolent Assoc., 1960–62. Hon. Fellow, Exeter College, Oxford, 1963. Hampshire: JP 1950; DL 1972. *Recreations:* music, swimming, gardening. *Address:* Heatherfield, Newtown, Newbury, Berks RG20 9DB. *T:* (01635) 40606; New Court, Temple, EC4Y 9BE. *T:* (0171) 353 8870; House of Lords, SW1A 0PW. *Club:* Reform. *Died 4 Oct. 1996.*

ROSS, Sir Archibald (David Manisty), KCMG 1961 (CMG 1953); HM Diplomatic Service, retired; *b* 12 Oct. 1911; *s* of late J. A. Ross, Indian Civil Service, and

Dorothea, *e d* of late G. Eldon Manisty, Indian Civil Service; *m* 1939, Mary Melville, *d* of Melville Macfadyen; one *s* one *d* (and one *s* decd). *Educ:* Winchester; New College, Oxford (MA). 1st Class Hon. Mods 1932, Lit. Hum. 1934; Gaisford Greek Verse Prize, 1932; Laming Travelling Fellow, Queen's College, 1934–35. Entered Foreign Office, 1936; Berlin, 1939; Stockholm, 1939–44; Foreign Office, 1944–47; Tehran, 1947–50; Counsellor, Foreign Office, 1950–53; HM Minister, Rome, 1953–56; Assistant Under Secretary of State for Foreign Affairs, 1956–60; Ambassador to Portugal, 1961–66; Ambassador to Sweden, 1966–71. Chairman: Alfa-Laval Co., 1972–82; Saab (GB), 1972–82; Scania (GB), 1972–82; Ericsson Information Systems, 1981–85. Mem. Council, RASE, 1980–85. Grand Cross, Order of the North Star, Sweden, 1981. *Address:* 17 Ennismore Gardens, SW7 1AA. *Clubs:* Travellers'; Leander.   *Died 25 Jan. 1996.*

ROSS, (Claud) Richard, CB 1973; Hon. Vice-President, European Investment Bank, since 1989 (Vice-President, and Vice-Chairman Board of Directors, 1978–89); *b* 24 March 1924; *o s* of late Claud Frederick Ross and Frances Muriel Ross, Steyning, Sussex; *m* 1954, Leslie Beatrice, *d* of late Oliver Arnell and Dr H. M. Arnell, Kitale, Kenya; two *d. Educ:* Ardingly Coll.; Hertford Coll., Oxford (Open Schol., Mod. Hist.). 1st cl. PPE, 1950; MA. Fellow of Hertford Coll., 1951–63; Lectr in Economics, Oxford Univ., 1951–52 and 1955–63; Economic Advr to HM Treasury, 1952–55; Junior Proctor, Oxford Univ., 1958–59; Bursar, Hertford Coll., 1959–63; Prof. of Economics and Dean, School of Social Studies, Univ. of East Anglia, 1963–68 (Pro-Vice-Chancellor, 1964–68); Special Consultant, OECD, Paris, 1968–71; Dep. Sec., Central Policy Review Staff, Cabinet Office, 1971–78. Adviser, Bankers' Mission to India and Pakistan, 1960; represented HM Treasury on OECD Working Party on Policies for Economic Growth, 1961–68; Leader, British Economic Mission to Tanzania, 1965; Member: East Anglia Regional Economic Planning Council, 1966–69 (Dep. Chm., 1967–69); Jt Mission for Malta, 1967. Chm., Population Panel, 1972–73. *Publications:* Financial and Physical Problems of Development in the Gold Coast (with D. Seers), 1952; articles on economics. *Address:* 2a Oliver's Wharf, 64 Wapping High Street, E1 9PJ.
                          Died 21 Feb. 1996.

ROSS, His Honour James; QC 1966; a Senior Circuit Judge, 1985–87 (a Circuit Judge (formerly a Judge of County Courts), 1971–87); *b* 22 March 1913; *s* of John Stuart Ross, FRCSE; *m* 1939, Clare Margaret (*d* 1993), *d* of Alderman Robert Cort-Cox, Stratford-on-Avon; one *d. Educ:* Glenalmond; Exeter Coll., Oxford. BA Oxon 1934. Admitted Solicitor, 1938; called to Bar, Gray's Inn, 1945. Legal Member, Mental Health Review Tribunal, Birmingham Region, 1962; Deputy Chairman, Agricultural Land Tribunal, East Midland Area, 1963; Dep. Chm. QS, Parts of Lindsey, 1968–71; Recorder of Coventry, 1968–71; Hon. Recorder: Coventry, 1978–85; City of Birmingham, 1985–87. Mem., Parole Bd, 1974–76. *Club:* Bar Yacht.   *Died 17 Aug. 1996.*

ROSS, James Alexander, MBE (mil.) 1944; MD; FRCSEd, FRCSGlas; Professor of Anatomy, King Saud University, Riyadh, 1983–84, retired; *b* 25 June 1911; *s* of James McMath Ross and Bessie Hopper Flint; *m* 1940, Catherine Elizabeth (*d* 1988), *d* of Clark Booth Curtis; one *s* one *d* (and two *d* decd). *Educ:* Merchiston Castle Sch.; Edinburgh Univ. MB ChB Edin., 1934, MD Edin., 1947; FRCSEd 1938, FRCSGlas 1965. Served War: RAMC, 1939–45: France, ME, Europe; then Lt-Col RAMC, RARO, 1953–55. Surgeon, Leith Hosp., 1946–61, and Royal Infirmary, Edinburgh, 1947–61; Surgeon, Eastern Gen. Hosp., 1961–76 and Edenhall Hosp., 1970–76. Hon. Sec., Royal Coll. of Surgeons of Edinburgh, 1960–68, Vice-

Pres., 1971–73, Pres., 1973–76; Pres., Edinburgh Harveian Soc., 1977–78; Vice-Pres., Internat. Fedn of Surgical Colls, 1975–81. Hon. Cons. Surgeon to Army in Scotland, 1970–76. Lectures: McCombe, RCSE, 1977; Mason Brown Meml, RCSE, 1978; Hutchinson, Edinburgh Univ., 1979; Mitchiner Meml, RAMC, 1979; Douglas Guthrie Hist. of Medicine, RCSE, 1983. Hon. FRCSI 1976; Hon. FRACS 1977; Hon. FDSRCSE 1983; Hon. Fellow: Coll. of Physicians and Surgeons, Pakistan, 1976; Sri Lanka Coll. of Surgeons, 1976; Hong Kong Surgical Soc., 1976. Governor, Merchiston Castle Sch., 1964–76. Guthrie Medallist, RAMC, 1976; Farquharson Award (teaching of anatomy and surgery), RCSE, 1986. *Publications:* Memoirs of an Army Surgeon, 1948; (jtly) Manual of Surgical Anatomy, 1964; (jtly) Behaviour of the Human Ureter, in Health and Disease, 1972; The Edinburgh School of Surgery after Lister, 1978; Memoirs of an Edinburgh Surgeon, 1988. *Recreations:* walking, swimming, watching cricket. *Address:* Cluny Lodge, 10–16 Cluny Drive, Edinburgh EH10 6DP.
                          Died 12 April 1997.

ROSS, Leonard Q.; *see* Rosten, L. C.

ROSS, Rear-Adm. Maurice James, CB 1962; DSC 1940; Assistant Chief of Naval Staff (Warfare), 1960–63; retired; *b* 31 Oct. 1908; *s* of Basil James Ross and Avis Mary (*née* Wilkinson); *m* 1946, Helen Matheson McCall (*d* 1996); one *d. Educ:* Charterhouse. Entered Royal Navy, 1927; specialised in gunnery, 1935; Comdr, 1943; Captain, 1951; Rear-Adm., 1960. Master, Gardeners' Company, 1983. *Publications:* Ross in the Antarctic 1839–1843, 1982; Polar Pioneers: John Ross and James Clark Ross, 1994; Chippenham: an East Anglian village, 1995. *Address:* The School House, Chippenham, Ely, Cambs CB7 5PP. *Club:* Army and Navy.
                          Died 27 Oct. 1996.

ROSS, Richard; *see* Ross, C. R.

ROSSER, Prof. Rachel Mary, FRCP, FRCPsych; Professor of Psychiatry, University College London Medical School (formerly University College and Middlesex School of Medicine, London), since 1984 (Head of Department, 1984–93); *b* 9 Oct. 1941; *d* of late John Rosser and of Madge Rosser; *m* 1967, Vincent Challacombe Watts, OBE; one *s* one *d. Educ:* King's High Sch., Warwick; Newnham Coll., Cambridge (MA); St Thomas's Hosp. Med. Sch. (MB, BChir). PhD London 1980. Res. Registrar, Dept of Medicine, Guy's Hosp., 1969–71; Registrar, Maudsley Hosp., 1971–74; Sen. Registrar, Maudsley and Hammersmith Hosps, 1974–76; Sen. Lectr 1976–82, Reader 1983–84, Charing Cross Hosp. Vis. academic posts, Green, Greyfriars and Nuffield Colls, Oxford, 1993–94. Pres., Soc. for Psychosomatic Research, 1984–86; Mem. Council, Internat. Coll. of Psychosomatic Medicine, 1983– (Treas., 1983–92). Mem. Adv. Bd, Health Ministries Assoc., USA. Dir, Churches' Council for Health and Healing, 1996–. *Publications:* (jtly) Health Care Priorities, 1980; Mind Made Disease, 1981; (jtly) Quality of Life: assessment and application, 1988; sci. papers on psychotherapy, psychosomatics, disaster aftermath. *Address:* Department of Psychiatry, Middlesex Hospital, Mortimer Street, W1A 8NN. *T:* (0171) 380 9475.   *Died 10 July 1998.*

ROSTEN, Leo Calvin, (Leonard Q. Ross); author and social scientist; *b* 11 April 1908; *s* of Samuel C. and Ida F. Rosten; *m* 1st, 1935, Priscilla Ann Mead (decd); one *s* two *d*; 2nd, 1960, Gertrude Zimmerman. *Educ:* University of Chicago (PhD); London School of Economics (Hon. Fellow, 1975). Research Assistant, Political Science Dept, Univ. of Chicago, 1933–35; Fellow, Social Science Research Council, 1934–36; Grants from Rockefeller Foundation and Carnegie Corporation, 1938–40; Dir,

Motion Picture Research Project, 1939–41; Spec. Consultant, Nat. Defense Advisory Commn, Washington, 1939; Chief, Motion Picture Div., Office of Facts and Figures, Washington, 1941–42; Dep. Dir, Office of War Information, Washington, 1942–45; Special Consultant, Sec. of War, Washington, 1945; special mission to France, Germany, England, 1945. Faculty Associate, Columbia Univ., 1953–; Lectr in Political Science, Yale Univ., 1955, New School for Social Research, NY, 1959. Ford Vis. Prof. in Pol Sci., Univ. of California (Berkeley), USA, 1960–61. Wrote film screenplays: Sleep, My Love; The Velvet Touch; Walk East on Beacon; The Dark Corner, etc. Member: Amer. Acad. of Political and Social Science; Amer. Assoc. for Advancement of Science; Nat. Acad. of Lit. and the Arts; Authors League of America; Authors Guild of America; Educnl Policies Cttee of Nat. Educnl Assoc. Phi Beta Kappa, 1929; Freedom Foundation's Award, 1955; George Polk Meml Award, 1955; Distinguished Alumnus Award, Univ. of Chicago, 1970. Hon. DHL: Univ. of Rochester, 1973; Hebrew Union Theol Coll., 1980. *Publications:* The Education of H*y*m*a*n K*a*p*l*a*n, 1937; The Washington Correspondents, 1937; The Strangest Places, 1939; Hollywood: The Movie Colony, The Movie Makers, 1941; The Dark Corner, 1945; (ed) Guide To The Religions of America, 1957; The Return of H*y*m*a*n K*a*p*l*a*n, 1959; Captain Newman, MD, 1961; The Story Behind the Painting, 1961; The Many Worlds of Leo Rosten, 1964; The Leo Rosten Bedside Book, 1965; A Most Private Intrigue, 1967; The Joys of Yiddish, 1968; A Trumpet for Reason, 1970; People I have Loved, Known or Admired, 1970; Rome Wasn't Burned in a Day, 1971; Leo Rosten's Treasury of Jewish Quotations, 1973; Dear "Herm", 1974; (ed) The Look Book, 1975; The 3.10 to Anywhere, 1976; O Kaplan! My Kaplan!, 1976; The Power of Positive Nonsense, 1977; Passions and Prejudices, 1978; (ed) Infinite Riches: Gems from a Lifetime of Reading, 1979; Silky!, 1979; King Silky!, 1980; Hooray for Yiddish!, 1983; Carnival of Wit, 1984; Leo Rosten's Giant Book of Laughter, 1985; The Joys of Yinglish, 1989; contrib. learned journals. *Recreations:* photography, travel. *Address:* 36 Sutton Place South, NY 10022, USA. *Clubs:* Savile, Reform, Garrick; Cosmos (Washington); Chaos, Round Table (New York). *Died 19 Feb. 1997.*

ROTHERHAM, Air Vice-Marshal John Kevitt, CB 1962; CBE 1960; Director-General (Engineering), Royal Air Force, 1967–69; retired; *b* 28 Dec. 1910; *s* of Colonel Ewan Rotherham; *m* 1st, 1936, Joan Catherine Penrose (*d* 1940); one *d*; 2nd, 1941, Margot Susan Hayter. *Educ:* Uppingham; Exeter College, Oxford. Joined RAF with Univ. perm. commn, 1933; 17 (F) Sqdn, 1934; 605 (B) Sqdn, 1936; School of Aeronautical Engineering, Henlow, 1936; post-grad. course, Imperial Coll., 1938; 43 (M) Group, 1939; Kidbrooke, 1940; MAP, 1941; 41 (M) Group, 1942; HQ Flying Training Comd, 1946; exchange posting with USAF, 1947; Air Ministry, 1948; Joint Services Staff Coll., 1951; No 205 Group, Middle East, 1952; Air Ministry, 1954; seconded to Pakistan Air Force, 1957; Senior Technical Staff Officer, Transport Command, RAF, 1960–63; AOC No 24 (Training) Group, Technical Training Command, RAF, 1963–65; Senior Tech. Staff Officer, Bomber Command, 1965–67. AFRAeS 1949, FRAeS 1967. *Recreation:* fishing. *Address:* Herons, Westbrook Field, Bosham, Chichester, Sussex PO18 8JP. *T:* (01243) 573346. *Clubs:* Royal Air Force; Bosham Sailing. *Died 14 May 1998.*

ROTHERMERE, 3rd Viscount *cr* 1919, of Hemsted, co. Kent; **Vere Harold Esmond Harmsworth;** Bt 1910; Baron 1914; Chairman: Daily Mail and General Trust plc, since 1978; Associated Newspapers Holdings Ltd, since 1970; *b* 27 Aug. 1925; *s* of 2nd Viscount Rothermere and Margaret Hunam (*d* 1991), *d* of late William Redhead; *S*

father, 1978; *m* 1st, 1957, Mrs Patricia Evelyn Beverley Brooks (*d* 1992), *d* of John William Matthews, FIAS; one *s* two *d*, and one step *d*; 2nd, 1993, Maiko Joeong-shun Lee. *Educ:* Eton; Kent Sch., Conn, USA. With Anglo Canadian Paper Mills, Quebec, 1948–50; Associated Newspapers Ltd, 1951–92; launched: new Daily Mail, 1971; Mail on Sunday, 1982. Trustee, Reuters. Pres., Euromoney Publications plc. Pres., Commonwealth Press Union, 1983–89 (Chm., UK Section, 1976); Pres., London Press Club, 1976–81; Patron, London Sch. of Journalism, 1980–. Mem., Ct of Benefactors, Oxford Univ., 1993–. FRSA, FIMgt. Commander: Order of Merit (Italy); Order of Lion (Finland); Order of Southern Cross (Brazil); Order of White Rose (Finland), 1995; Order of Merit, Middle Cross with Star (Hungary), 1996. *Recreations:* painting, sailing, reading. *Heir: s* Hon. Harold Jonathan Esmond Vere Harmsworth [*b* 3 Dec. 1967; *m* 1993, Claudia, *d* of T. J. Clemence; one *s* one *d*]. *Address:* 36 rue du Sentier, Paris, France. *Clubs:* Boodle's, Beefsteak; Royal Yacht Squadron; Brook (New York City); Travellers', Cercle de l'Union Interalliée (Paris). *Died 1 Sept. 1998.*

ROTHERWICK, 2nd Baron *cr* 1939, of Tylney, Southampton; **Herbert Robin Cayzer;** Bt 1924; *b* 5 Dec. 1912; *s* of 1st Baron Rotherwick and Freda Penelope, *d* of Col William Hans Rathborne; *S* father, 1958; *m* 1952, Sarah-Jane (*d* 1978), *o d* of Sir Michael Nial Slade, 6th Bt; three *s* one *d*. *Educ:* Eton; Christ Church, Oxford (BA). Supplementary Reserve Royal Scots Greys, 1938; served War of 1939–45 with them in Middle East. Former Deputy Chairman British & Commonwealth Shipping Co. Ltd, and Director of other and associated companies. *Heir: s* Hon. (Herbert) Robin Cayzer, Lieut Life Guards (T&AVR) [*b* 12 March 1954; *m* 1982, Sara, *o d* of R. J. McAlpine, Swettenham Hall, Cheshire; two *s* one *d*]. *Address:* Cornbury Park, Charlbury, Oxfordshire OX7 3EH. *T:* Charlbury (01608) 810311. *Club:* White's. *Died 11 June 1996.*

ROTHNIE, Sir Alan (Keir), KCVO 1980; CMG 1967; HM Diplomatic Service, retired; *b* 2 May 1920; *s* of late John and Dora Rothnie, Aberdeen; *m* 1953, Anne Cadogan Harris, *d* of late Euan Cadogan Harris; two *s* one *d*. *Educ:* Montrose Acad.; St Andrews University. Served RNVR, 1939–45. Entered Diplomatic Service, 1945; Foreign Office, 1945–46; 3rd Sec., HM Legation, Vienna, 1946–48; 2nd Sec., HM Embassy, Bangkok, 1949–50; FO, 1951–53; 1st Sec. HM Embassy, Madrid, 1953–55; Asst Political Agent, Kuwait, 1956–58; FO, 1958–60; Middle East Centre for Arab Studies, Shemlan, 1960–62 (Chargé d'Affaires, HM Embassy, Kuwait, 1961); Commercial Counsellor: HM Embassy, Baghdad, 1963–64; HM Embassy, Moscow, 1965–68; Consul-Gen., Chicago, 1969–72; Ambassador to Saudi Arabia, 1972–76, to Switzerland, 1976–80. Chm., Newsbrief Ltd, 1985–90. Hon. LLD St Andrews, 1981. *Recreations:* rural. *Address:* Little Job's Cross, Rolvenden Layne, Kent TN17 4PP. *T:* (01580) 241350. *Died 24 April 1997.*

ROTHSCHILD, Baron Robert, Grand Officier de l'Ordre de Leopold (Belgium); Hon. KCMG 1963; Belgian Ambassador to the Court of St James's, 1973–76; *b* 16 Dec. 1911; *s* of Bernard Rothschild and Marianne von Rynveld; *m* 1st, 1937, Renée Mattman (marr. diss. 1967); one *d*; 2nd, 1977, Mary Plunkett-Drax. *Educ:* Univ. of Brussels (DrRerPol). Entered Belgian Foreign Office: Brussels, 1937; Lisbon, 1942; Chungking, China, 1944; Shanghai, 1946; Washington, 1950; Paris, NATO, 1952; Brussels, 1954; Ambassador to Yugoslavia, 1958; Head of Mission, Katanga, Congo, 1960; Brussels, 1960; Ambassador to: Switzerland, 1964; France, 1966. *Publications:* La Chute de Chiang Kai-Shek, 1973 (Paris); Les Chemins de Munich, 1988 (Paris); Un Phenix nommé Europe, 1997 (Brussels). *Recreations:* gardening, travel.

Address: 43 Ranelagh Grove, SW1W 8PB; 1 Rue E. Dereume, Rixensart 1330, Belgium.
Died 3 Dec. 1998.

ROTHWELL, Sheila Gwendoline; Director, Centre for Employment Policy Studies, Henley Administrative Staff College, 1979–96; *b* 22 Aug. 1935; *d* of Reginald Herbert Paine and Joyce Margaret Paine; *m* 1958, Miles Rothwell (marr. diss. 1968); one *s* one *d*; *m* 1985, Graham L. Reid, CB. *Educ:* Wyggeston Sch., Leicester; Westfield Coll., Univ. of London (BA Hons History, 1956); LSE (MScEcon Indust. Relations, 1972). Teaching and res., London, Trinidad and Barbados, 1958–68; Res. Officer/Lectr, Indust. Relations Dept, LSE, 1969–75; Asst Sec. (Negotiations), National Union of Bank Employees, 1975–76; Asst Chief Exec., Equal Opportunities Commn, 1976–78. Res. Sec. to House of Lords Select Cttee on Anti-Discrimination Bill, 1972–73. Member: Williams Cttee on Obscenity and Film Censorship, 1978–79; ACAS Panel of Arbitrators, 1988– (ACAS Indep. Expert on Equal Pay, 1984–87); Dep. Chm., Central Arbitration Cttee, 1992–. Chm. Governors, Henley (Tertiary) Coll., 1989–94. *Publications:* Labour Turnover, 1980; (ed) Strategic Planning for Human Resources, 1991; contrib. Internat. Labour Rev., and Brit. Jl of Indust. Relations. *Recreations:* cinema, opera, walking, sketching. *Address:* 4 The Gardens, Fingest, Henley, Oxon RG9 6QF.
Died 4 April 1997.

ROUS, Lt.-Gen. Hon. Sir William (Edward), KCB 1992; OBE 1981 (MBE 1974); Chairman, Kingston Hospital NHS Trust, since 1996; *b* 22 Feb. 1939; *s* of 5th Earl of Stradbroke and Pamela Catherine Mabell, *d* of Captain Hon. Edward James Kay-Shuttleworth; *m* 1970, Judith Rosemary Persse; two *s*. *Educ:* Harrow; Royal Military Academy, Sandhurst. Commissioned Coldstream Guards, 1959; Comd 2nd Bn Coldstream Guards, 1979–81, Comd 1st Inf. Brigade, 1983–84; Dir of Public Relations (Army), 1985–87; GOC 4th Armoured Div., BAOR, 1987–89; Comdt, Staff Coll., Camberley, 1989–91; Military Sec., MoD, 1991–94; QMG and Mcm., Army Bd, MoD, 1994–96. Col, Coldstream Guards, 1994–. Chairman: British Greyhound Racing Bd, 1998–; Retired Greyhound Trust, 1998–. Managing Trustee, BLESMA, 1994–. *Address:* RHQ Coldstream Guards, Wellington Barracks, SW1E 6HQ.
Died 25 May 1999.

ROUSE, E(dward) Clive, MBE 1946; medieval archæologist, retired; specialist in mural and panel paintings; lecturer; *b* 15 Oct. 1901; *s* of late Edward Foxwell Rouse, Stroud, Gloucestershire and Acton, Middlesex, and Frances Sarah Rouse (*née* Sams). *Educ:* Gresham's School; St Martin's School of Art. On leaving school studied art and medieval antiquities, 1920–21. FSA 1937 (Mem. of Council, 1943–44); FRSA 1968. President: Royal Archæological Institute, 1969–72 (Vice-Pres., 1965); Bucks Archaeological Soc., 1969–79. Liveryman, Fishmongers' Company, 1962. Served War of 1939–45, RAFVR (Intelligence); Flight-Lt, 1941–45; MBE for special services at Central Interpretation Unit, Medmenham. Hon. MA Oxon, 1969; Hon. DLitt Sussex, 1983. *Publications:* The Old Towns of England, 1936 (twice reprinted); Discovering Wall Paintings, 1968 (reprinted); (jointly) Guide to Buckinghamshire, 1935; contributor to: The Beauty of Britain, 1935; Collins' Guide to English Parish Churches, 1958; papers in Archæologia, Antiquaries' Journal, Archæological Journal, and publications of many county archæological societies. *Recreations:* reading, bird watching. *Address:* Oakfield, North Park, Gerrards Cross, Bucks SL9 8JR. *T:* (01753) 882595.
Died 28 July 1997.

ROWAN, Carl Thomas; Syndicated columnist, correspondent, Chicago Sun-Times; radio and TV commentator, Post-Newsweek Broadcasting; Roving Editor, Reader's Digest; *b* 11 Aug. 1925; *s* of Thomas D. and Johnnie B. Rowan; *m* 1950, Vivien Murphy; two *s* one *d*. *Educ:* Tennessee State University; Washburn University; Oberlin Coll.; University of Minnesota. Mem. Staff of Minneapolis Tribune, 1948–61; Dept of State, 1961–63; US Ambassador to Finland, 1963–64; Director, United States Information Agency, Washington, DC, 1964–65. Hon. DLitt: Simpson Coll., 1957; Hamline Univ., 1958; Oberlin Coll., 1962; Dr of Humane Letters: Washburn Univ., 1964; Talladega Coll., 1965; St Olaf Coll., 1966; Knoxville Coll., 1966; Rhode Island Coll., 1970; Maine Univ., 1971; American Univ., 1980; Hon. LLD: Howard Univ., 1964; Alfred Univ., 1964; Temple Univ., 1964; Atlanta Univ., 1965; Allegheny Coll., 1966; Colby Coll., 1968; Clark Univ., 1971; Notre Dame, 1973; Dr of Public Admin, Morgan State Coll., 1964; Dr of Letters: Wooster Coll., 1968; Miami Univ., 1982; Drexel Inst. of Technology; Dr of Science Georgetown Med. Sch., 1982. *Publications:* South of Freedom, 1953; The Pitiful and the Proud, 1956; Go South to Sorrow, 1957; Wait Till Next Year, 1960; Between Us Blacks, 1974; Breaking Barriers (memoir), 1991; Dream Makers, Dream Breakers: the world of Justice Thurgood Marshall, 1993. *Recreations:* tennis, golf, bowling, singing and dancing. *Address:* c/o Little, Brown & Co., 34 Beacon Street, Boston, MA 02108, USA. *Clubs:* Federal City, Indian Spring (Washington, DC).
Died 23 Sept. 2000.

ROWAN-LEGG, Allan Aubrey; President, Edcom Ltd, Canada, since 1985 (Vice President, Western Region, 1976–85); *b* 19 May 1912; *m* 1944, Daphne M. Ker; three *d*. Dir, Vice-Pres. and Gen. Sales Man., Interlake Fuel Oil Ltd, and Interlake Steel Products, 1955–57; Pres. and Dir, Superior Propane Ltd, Northern Propane Gas Co, 1957–63; Dir, Vice-Pres. and Gen. Man., Garlock of Canada Ltd, and Yale Rubber Mfg Co. of Canada Ltd, 1963–64; Regional Dir for Ont, Canadian Corp. for 1967 World Exhibn, 1964–67; Agent General for Ontario in UK and Europe, 1967 72; Man. Dir, Canada Permanent Mortgage Corp. and Canada Permanent Trust Co., 1973–75; Dir, Wedgewood Estates, 1989. Chm. and Pres., Art Gallery of Greater Victoria, BC, 1980, then ex officio, 1980–83. Dir, Internat. Probus Club, 1994–. Liveryman, Painter-Stainers' Co., 1969; Freeman of City of London, 1969. Canada Centennial Medal. *Recreation:* travelling. *Address:* #9–2200 Arbutus Cove Lane 477–0017, Victoria, BC V8N 6J9, Canada. *Clubs:* Union, Victoria, Harbourside Rotary (Pioneer Rotarian, 1950; Hon. Dir and Hon. Mem., 1988) (Victoria, BC).
Died 26 June 1998.

ROWE, Sir Jeremy, Kt 1991; CBE 1980; Deputy Chairman, Abbey National plc (formerly Abbey National Building Society), 1978–89; Chairman: Peterborough Development Corporation, 1981–88; Family Assurance Society, 1986–93; *b* 31 Oct. 1928; *s* of Charles William Dell Rowe and Alison (*née* Barford); *m* 1957, Susan Mary (*née* Johnstone); four *d*. *Educ:* Wellesley House Sch.; Uppingham Sch.; Trinity Coll., Cambridge (MA (Hons) Hist.). English-Speaking Union Scholarship to USA, 1952. Joined London Brick Co. Ltd as trainee, 1952; Personal Asst to Chm., 1954; Dir and Sales Manager, 1963–67; Man. Dir, 1967–70; Dep. Chm. and Man. Dir, 1970–79; Man. Dir, 1979–82 and Chm., 1979–84; Director: West End Bd, Sun Alliance Insce Co. Ltd, 1978–; John Maunders Group plc, 1984–; Telephone Rentals plc, 1984–89. Chm., Occupational Pensions Bd, 1987–93. *Recreations:* tennis, shooting, reading, music. *Address:* Woodside House, Peasmarsh, near Rye, Sussex TN31 6YD. *Clubs:* All England Lawn Tennis; Rye Golf.
Died 28 Sept. 1996.

ROWLAND, Air Marshal Sir James (Anthony), AC 1987; KBE 1977; DFC 1944; AFC 1953; CEng, FRAeS, FIEAust; Governor of New South Wales, 1981–89;

Chairman: Thomson Radar Australia Corp., since 1996 (Director, 1993–96); Zylotech Pty Ltd, since 1997; *b* 1 Nov. 1922; *s* of Louis Claude Rowland and Elsie Jean Rowland; *m* 1955, Faye Alison (*née* Doughton); one *d*. *Educ:* Cranbrook Sch., Sydney; St Paul's Coll., Univ. of Sydney (BE Aero). CEng, FRAeS 1969; FIEAust 1978; FTSE (FTS 1988). Served War, Pilot, RAAF and RAF Bomber Comd, 1942–45. Sydney Univ., 1940–41 and 1946–47; Empire Test Pilots' Sch., Farnborough, 1949; Chief Test Pilot, RAAF R&D Unit, 1951–54; Staff Coll., 1956; Staff and unit posts, incl. OC R&D, 1957–60; RAAF Mirage Mission, Paris, 1961–64; CO No 1 Aircraft Depot, 1966; Sen. Engr SO, Ops Comd, 1968–69; RCDS, 1971; Dir Gen., Aircraft Engrg, RAAF, 1972; Air Mem. for Technical Services, 1973; Chief of Air Staff, RAAF, 1975–79. Chm., Preston Group Pty, 1991–95; Director: Angus & Coote Ltd, 1989–; Focus Books Ltd, later Focus Publishing Ltd, 1990–97; Thomson CSF Pacific Hldgs, 1996–99. Member: Admin. Appeals Tribunal, 1979–80; Police Board of NSW, 1989–92. Chairman: NSW Air Transport Council, 1989–; Aerospace Foundn, 1992–. Consultant, OFEMA Australia, 1980. Pres., Royal Humane Soc. of NSW, 1990. Chancellor, Univ. of Sydney, 1990–91. Hon. DEng Sydney, 1983. KStJ 1981. *Publications:* contribs to professional jls. *Recreations:* surfing, reading, golf. *Address:* 17 Pindari Avenue, Mosman, NSW 2088, Australia. *Clubs:* Royal Air Force; Australian, Royal Automobile, Union (Sydney).

Died 27 May 1999.

ROWLEY, John Charles, CMG 1977; Director, Crown Agents Board of Management, 1980–84, retired; *b* 29 Sept. 1919; *s* of John Ernest Rowley and Edith Muriel (*née* Aldridge); *m* 1st, 1945, Pamela Hilda Godfrey (marr. diss. 1971); two *d*; 2nd, 1972, Anne Patricia Dening; one *s*. *Educ:* Ilford; King's College, London (LLB 1948, Upper Second Cl. Hons). RAF, 1940–46, pilot, Flt-Lt; Iceland, 1944 (despatches). Inland Revenue, 1938–40 and 1946–64; Min. of Overseas Development, 1964–79: Head, Middle East Develt Div., Beirut, Lebanon and Amman, Jordan, 1971–79; Crown Agents Regional Controller for Middle East, 1979–80. *Recreations:* choral singing, sailing. *Address:* 43 Half Moon Lane, SE24 9JX.

Died 26 April 2000.

ROWLEY, John Vincent d'Alessio; General Manager, Bracknell New Town Development Corporation, 1955–73; *b* 12 Sept. 1907; 2nd *s* of late Ven. Hugh Rowley, Archdeacon of Kingwilliamstown, S Africa; *m* 1st, 1936, Violet Maud (*d* 1969), *d* of S. H. Day, Grahamstown, S Africa; one *s*; 2nd, 1972, (Kathleen) Mary Hawkesworth (*née* Pullom). *Educ:* St Andrews Coll., Grahamstown; Trinity Coll., Oxford (Rhodes Schol.). BA 1929; Oxford Univ. Rugby XV, 1929. Entered Sudan Political Service, 1930; Asst District Comr and District Comr, 1930–49; seconded Sudan Defence Force, 1940–42; Dep. Gov., Kordofan Province, 1950–52; Asst Financial Sec., 1952–53; Governor, Darfur Province, 1953–55. Chm., South Hill Park Arts Centre Trust, 1979. *Recreations:* music, gardening, golf. *Address:* The Spring, Stanford Dingley, near Bradfield, Berks RG7 6LX. *T:* (01734) 744270. *Club:* United Oxford & Cambridge University.

Died 30 Nov. 1996.

ROWLEY, Sir Joshua Francis, 7th Bt *cr* 1786, of Tendring Hall, Suffolk; JP; Lord-Lieutenant of Suffolk, 1978–94; *b* 31 Dec. 1920; *o s* of Lt-Col Sir Charles Rowley, 6th Bt, TD and Margery Frances Bacon (*d* 1977); *S* father, 1962; *m* 1959, Hon. Celia Ella Vere Monckton, 2nd *d* of 8th Viscount Galway; one *d*. *Educ:* Eton; Trinity College, Cambridge. Grenadier Guards, 1940–46. Deputy Secretary, National Trust, 1952–55. Chairman: W Suffolk CC, 1971–74; Suffolk CC, 1976–78; DL 1968, High Sheriff 1971, Vice Lord-Lieutenant, 1973–78, JP 1978,

Suffolk. Hon. DCL UEA, 1991. *Address:* Holbecks, Hadleigh, Ipswich, Suffolk IP7 5PF. *T:* (01473) 823211. *Clubs:* Boodle's, Pratt's, MCC.

Died 21 Feb. 1997.

ROWSE, Alfred Leslie, CH 1997; MA, DLitt; FBA 1958; Emeritus Fellow of All Souls College, Oxford; *b* St Austell, Cornwall, 4 Dec. 1903; *s* of Richard Rowse and Ann Vanson. *Educ:* Elementary and Grammar Schools, St Austell; Christ Church, Oxford (Douglas Jerrold Scholar in English Literature). Sen. Res. Associate, Huntington Library, Calif, 1962–69. Fellow of the Royal Society of Literature; President of the English Association, 1952. Raleigh Lecturer, British Academy, 1957; Trevelyan Lecturer, Cambridge, 1958; Beatty Memorial Lecturer, McGill University, 1963. Pres., Shakespeare Club, Stratford-upon-Avon, 1970–71. Benson Medal, RSL, 1982. *Publications:* Politics and the Younger Generation, 1931; Mr Keynes and the Labour Movement, 1936; Sir Richard Grenville of the Revenge, 1937; Tudor Cornwall, 1941; Poems of a Decade, 1931–41, 1941; A Cornish Childhood, 1942; The Spirit of English History, 1943; Poems Chiefly Cornish, 1944; The English Spirit: Essays in History and Literature, 1944, rev. edn 1966; West Country Stories, 1945; The Use of History, 1946; Poems of Deliverance, 1946; The End of an Epoch, 1947; The England of Elizabeth, 1950; The English Past, 1951 (rev. edn, as Times, Persons, Places, 1965); translation and completion of Lucien Romier's History of France, 1953; The Expansion of Elizabethan England, 1955; The Early Churchills, 1956; The Later Churchills, 1958; Poems Partly American, 1958; The Elizabethans and America, 1959; St Austell: Church, Town, Parish, 1960; All Souls and Appeasement, 1961; Ralegh and the Throckmortons, 1962; William Shakespeare: a Biography, 1963; Christopher Marlowe: a Biography, 1964; A Cornishman at Oxford, 1965; Shakespeare's Southampton: Patron of Virginia, 1965; Bosworth Field and the Wars of the Roses, 1966; Poems of Cornwall and America, 1967; Cornish Stories, 1967; A Cornish Anthology, 1968; The Cornish in America, 1969; The Elizabethan Renaissance: the Life of the Society, 1971; The Elizabethan Renaissance: the Cultural Achievement, 1972; Strange Encounter (poems), 1972; The Tower of London in the History of the Nation, 1972; Westminster Abbey in the History of the Nation, 1972; Shakespeare's Sonnets: a modern edition, 1973, rev. edn with introduction and prose versions, 1984; Shakespeare the Man, 1973, rev. edn, 1987; Simon Forman: Sex and Society in Shakespeare's Age, 1974; Windsor Castle in the History of England, 1974; (with John Betjeman) Victorian and Edwardian Cornwall, 1974; Oxford in the History of the Nation, 1975; Discoveries and Reviews, 1975; Jonathan Swift: Major Prophet, 1975; A Cornishman Abroad, 1976; Brown Buck: a Californian fantasy, 1976; Matthew Arnold: Poet and Prophet, 1976; Shakespeare the Elizabethan, 1977; Homosexuals in History: ambivalence in society, literature and the arts, 1977; Heritage of Britain, 1977; Milton the Puritan: Portrait of a Mind, 1977; The Road to Oxford: poems, 1978; (ed) The Poems of Shakespeare's Dark Lady, 1978; The Byrons and Trevanions, 1978; The Annotated Shakespeare, 3 vols (introds to vols and plays), 1978; A Man of the Thirties, 1979; Portraits and Views, 1979; Story of Britain, 1979; (ed) A Man of Singular Virtue: Roper's Life of Sir Thomas More, 1980; Memories of Men and Women, 1980; Shakespeare's Globe, 1980; A Life: Collected Poems, 1981; Eminent Elizabethans, 1983; Shakespeare's Characters: a complete guide, 1984; Night at the Carn, and Other Stories, 1984; Prefaces to Shakespeare's Plays, 1984; Shakespeare's Self-Portrait: passages chosen from his work, with notes, 1984; Glimpses of the Great, 1985; (ed) The Contemporary Shakespeare, 1985–87; Reflections on the Puritan Revolution, 1986;

The Little Land of Cornwall, 1986; Stories from Trenarren, 1986; A Quartet of Cornish Cats, 1986; The Poet Auden, 1987; Court and Country: studies in Tudor social history, 1987; Froude the Historian, 1988; Quiller Couch: portrait of Q, 1988; Shakespeare the Man, 1988; (ed and introd) Froude, Spanish Story of the Armada, 1988; A. L. Rowse's Cornwall, 1988; Friends and Contemporaries, 1989; Transatlantic: Later Poems, 1989; The Controversial Colensos: South Africa and New Zealand, 1989; Discovering Shakespeare, 1989; Selected Poems, 1990; Prompting the Age: Poems Early and Late, 1990; Four Caroline Portraits, 1993; (ed) The Sayings of Shakespeare, 1993; All Souls in my Time, 1993; The Regicides and the Puritan Revolution, 1995; Historians I Have Known, 1995; My View of Shakespeare, 1996. *Address:* Trenarren House, St Austell, Cornwall PL26 6BH. *Club:* Athenæum.   *Died 3 Oct. 1997.*

ROXBEE COX, family name of **Baron Kings Norton.**

RUBIN, His Honour Kenneth Warnell Reginald; DL; a Circuit Judge, 1972–92; *b* 8 March 1920; *s* of late Albert Reginald Rubin and Mary Eales Rubin; *m* 1948, Jeanne Marie Louise de Wilde (*d* 1991); one *s* two *d*. *Educ:* King's College Sch., Wimbledon; King's Coll., London (LLB). Served HM Forces, 1939–45. Called to the Bar, Gray's Inn, 1948. DL Surrey, 1989. *Address:* Tyrrellswood, Shere Road, West Horsley, Surrey KT24 6ER. *T:* (01483) 282848.   *Died 18 May 2000.*

RUBNER, Benjamin Barnett, (Ben); General Secretary, Furniture, Timber and Allied Trades Union, 1976–86; *b* 30 Sept. 1921; *s* of Charles and Lily Rubner; *m* 1952, Amelia Sonia Bagnari (*d* 1980); one *s* one *d*; *m* 1986, Patricia Elder, widow. *Educ:* Mansford Street Central Sch., Bethnal Green, E2. Apprentice cabinet maker, 1935. Served war in armed forces, Royal Corps of Signals: N Africa, Italy, Sicily, 1941–46. Mem. Cttee, Trade Union Br., 1937; Shop Steward, Sec., Chm. and Convenor, London Furniture Workers Shop Stewards Council, 1947–52; National Union of Furniture Trade Operatives: London Dist Cttee, 1954; Gen. Exec. Council, 1958; London Dist Organiser, 1959; Nat. Trade Organiser, 1963; Asst Gen. Sec., FTAT, 1973–76. London Delegate, 1955–58, full-time Officer Deleg., 1974–77, TUC. Mcm., Central Arbitration Cttee, ACAS, 1977. *Recreations:* music (opera, light and grand), chess, table tennis, swimming, Scrabble, golf. *Address:* 6 Oak Avenue, Bricket Wood, St Albans, Herts AL2 3LG. *Club:* Cambridge and Bethnal Green Old Boys.   *Died 21 Sept. 1998.*

RUDDEN, James; Advisory Head Teacher on Secondary Reorganisation, Inner London Education Authority, 1976–78, retired; President: National Association of Head Teachers, 1971; London Head Teachers Association, 1969; Metropolitan Catholic Teachers Association, 1964; *b* 11 Dec. 1911; *s* of Bernard and Mary Rudden; *m* 1937, Eileen Finlay (*d* 1992); one *s* four *d*. *Educ:* Carlisle Grammar Sch.; St Mary's Coll., Twickenham (BSc (Special, Geo.) London Univ.); Teacher's Cert., London Univ. Asst Teacher, Carlisle, 1933–47; served War, RAF Educn Officer, 1940–45; First Head: St Cuthbert's Sec. Mod. Sch., Cleator, 1948–52; St Thomas More Sec. Mod. Sch., Tottenham, 1952–59; Bishop Thomas Grant Comprehensive Sch., Streatham, 1959–75. External Examnr for BEd, Avery Hill Coll. Chairman: London Comprehensive Head Teachers Conf., 1974–75; Southwark Diocesan Schs Commn; Governing Body of Schs Council; Adv. Council for Supply and Trng of Teachers. KSG 1969. *Publications:* numerous articles on educnl topics in educational and national press. *Recreation:* indulgence in retirement pursuits.
Died 16 Nov. 2000.

RUGAMBWA, HE Cardinal Laurean; RC Archbishop of Dar-es-Salaam, 1969–92, then Emeritus; *b* Bukongo, 12 July 1912; *s* of Domitian Rushubirwa and Asteria Mukaboshezi. *Educ:* Rutabo, Rubya Seminary; Katigondo Seminary; Univ. of Propaganda, Rome (DCL 1951). Priest 1943; Bishop of Rutabo, 1952–60; Cardinal 1960; Bishop of Bukoba, 1960–69. Member: Knights of Columbus; Knights of St Peter Claver. Hon. Dr of Laws: Notre Dame, 1961; St Joseph's Coll., Philadelphia, 1961; Rosary Hill Coll., Buffalo, 1965; Hon. DHL New Rochelle, 1961; Hon. Dr Civil and Canon Law, Georgetown Univ. (Jesuits), 1961; Giving of the Scroll, Catholic Univ. of America, 1961. *Address:* Archbishop's House, PO Box 167, Dar-es-Salaam, Tanzania, East Africa.
Died 8 Dec. 1997.

RUGGE-PRICE, Sir Charles Keith Napier; *see* Price.

RUGGLES-BRISE, Captain Guy Edward, TD; DL; *b* 15 June 1914; *s* of late Col Sir Edward Archibald Ruggles-Brise, 1st Bt, MC, TD, DL, JP, MP, and Agatha, *e d* of J. H. Gurney, DL, JP, Keswick Hall, Norfolk; *b* and *heir pres.* of Sir John Ruggles-Brise, 2nd Bt, CB, OBE; *m* 1st, 1940, Elizabeth (*d* 1988), *o d* of James Knox, Smithstone House, Kilwinning, Ayrshire; three *s*; 2nd, 1994, Christine Margaret Fothergill-Spencer, *o d* of late Lieut J. A. Fothergill. *Educ:* Eton. Captain 104th (Essex Yeo.) Field Bde RHA (TA), No 7 Commando; served War of 1939–45 (POW). DL 1967, High Sheriff 1967, Essex. *Recreations:* field sports. *Address:* Pitkeathly, Cole End Lane, Wimbish, Saffron Walden, Essex CB10 2UT. *T:* (01799) 521215; Ledgowan Lodge, Achnasheen, Ross-shire IV22 2EH. *T:* (01445) 720245. *Club:* City of London.
Died 14 Nov. 2000.

RUIZ SOLER, Antonio, (Antonio); Cross of the Order of Isabella the Catholic, 1951; Comdr Order of Civil Merit, 1964; Spanish dancer; Director, Ballet Nacional Español; *b* Seville, 4 Nov. 1921. Studied at the Realito Dance Academy. First stage appearance at the age of eight; subsequently toured North and South America, Southern and Western Europe, and Scandinavia; first stage appearance in Great Britain, Edinburgh Festival, 1950; London début, Cambridge Theatre, 1951; formed Ballet Company, 1953; début in Generalife Theatre, Granada, presenting his Ballet in Europe, S and N America. Also appeared in many festivals in Spain. Appearances with Ballet in London: Stoll, 1954; Palace, 1956; Coliseum, 1958; Royalty, 1960; Drury Lane, 1963; Coliseum, 1975. Gala perf. in Washington to President Kennedy, Ed Sullivan Show in New York, appearances Europe, 1963; Festivals of Spain, 1964–65; Madrid Season, 1965; N Amer. tour, 1965; Ed Sullivan Show, 1965. Appeared on TV. Golden Medal, Fine Arts, 1952; Gold Medal, Swedish Acad. of Dancing, 1963; Medal of Min. of Information and Tourism, Madrid, 1963; Golden Medal, Spanish Inst., NY, 1979. *Address:* Coslada 7, Madrid, Spain.
Died 5 Feb. 1996.

RULE, David Charles; Dean of Postgraduate Dental Studies, Thames Postgraduate Medical and Dental Education (formerly British Postgraduate Medical Federation), since 1990; *b* 17 April 1937; *s* of Cyril George Leonard Rule and Ivy Rule; *m* 1972, Linda Marion Meyer; two *d*. *Educ:* Univ. of Birmingham (BDS). FDS RCS, MCCDRCS, DOrthRCS. Qualified Dental Surgeon, 1959; RADC, 1960–63; Eastman Dental Hosp., 1964: successively Registrar, Lectr, Sen. Registrar; Consultant, 1970–. Member: GDC, 1991–; Bd, Faculty of Dental Surgery, RCS, 1989– (Vice Dean, 1999–2000). President: British Paedontic Soc., 1988–89; British Soc. of Dentistry for the Handicapped, 1980; Internat. Assoc. of Dentistry for the Handicapped, 1990–92. *Recreation:*

sailing. *Address:* 7 Malmains Way, Beckenham, Kent BR2 6SA. *T:* (020) 8650 1895. *Club:* MCC.
Died 29 Aug. 2000.

RUMBLE, Captain John Bertram, RN (retired); Director General, Royal Over-Seas League, 1979–91; *b* 30 Oct. 1928; *s* of late Major and Mrs Rumble; *m* 1st, 1953, Jennifer (marr. diss. 1992), *d* of late Col R. H. Wilson, CIE, MC, and Ella Wilson; one *s* three *d*; 2nd, 1992, Mrs Elizabeth Villiers. *Educ:* Sherborne Sch. FBIM 1980, FIIM 1980. Special Entry Cadet into Royal Navy, 1946; HMS Magpie, 1950–51; ADC (Lieut) to Governor of Malta, 1952–53; specialised in Communications, 1954; HMS Maidstone, 1955–56; Staff, BRNC Dartmouth, 1956–57; Exchange Service with RCN, 1957–59; Signal Officer, HMS Ark Royal, 1959–61; Comdr 1962; RN sc 1963; CO HMS Torquay, 1964–65; Staff Communications Officer to C-in-C EASTLANT, 1966–67; Exec. Officer, HMS Hermes, 1967–69; Captain 1970; Staff Dir, Gen. Weapons, 1970–71; CO HMS Fearless, 1974–75; Asst Chief of Staff Communications (as Cdre), C-in-C SOUTH, 1976–77; MoD (Intelligence), 1977–79. Younger Brother, Trinity House, 1977; Member: Council, Mayfair, Piccadilly and St James's Assoc., 1979–91 (Chm., 1988–90); Jt Commonwealth Societies Council, 1980–91. Pres., Colchester Sea Cadets, 1994–. *Recreations:* shooting, sailing, fishing, music, theatre. *Address:* White Horse Cottage, School Street, Stoke-by-Nayland, Suffolk CO6 4QY. *T:* and *Fax:* Colchester (01206) 262325. *Clubs:* Farmers', Royal Over-Seas League (Hon.); Stour Sailing.
Died 2 July 1996.

RUNCIE, Baron *cr* 1991 (Life Peer), of Cuddesdon in the County of Oxfordshire; **Rt Rev. and Rt Hon. Robert Alexander Kennedy Runcie,** MC 1945; PC 1980; Royal Victorian Chain, 1991; Archbishop of Canterbury, 1980–91; Hon. Assistant Bishop of St Albans, since 1991; High Steward of the University of Cambridge, since 1991; *b* 2 Oct. 1921; *s* of Robert Dalziel Runcie and Anne Runcie; *m* 1957, Angela Rosalind, *d* of J. W. Cecil Turner; one *s* one *d*. *Educ:* Merchant Taylors', Crosby; Brasenose Coll., Oxford (Squire Minor Schol.; BA 1st cl. Hons Lit. Hum.; MA 1948; Hon. Fellow, 1979); Westcott House, Cambridge. Served Scots Guards, War of 1939–45 (MC). Deacon, 1950, priest, 1951; Curate, All Saints, Gosforth, 1950–52; Chaplain, Westcott House, Cambridge, 1953–54, Vice-Principal, 1954–56; Fellow, Dean and Asst Tutor of Trinity Hall, Cambridge, 1956–60, Hon. Fellow 1975; Vicar of Cuddesdon and Principal of Cuddesdon Coll., 1960–69; Bishop of St Albans, 1970–80. Canon and Prebendary of Lincoln, 1969. Hon. Bencher, Gray's Inn, 1980. Chm., BBC and IBA Central Religious Adv. Cttee, 1973–79. Teape Lectr, St Stephen's Coll., Delhi, 1962; William Noble Lectr, Harvard, 1986. Select Preacher: Cambridge, 1957 and 1975; Oxford, 1959 and 1973. Anglican Chm., Anglican-Orthodox Jt Doctrinal Commn, 1973–80. Pres., Classical Assoc., 1991–92. Freeman: St Albans, 1979; City of London, 1981; Canterbury, 1984. FKC 1981; Hon. Fellow: Merton Coll., Oxford, 1991; Gonville and Caius Coll., Cambridge, 1997. Hon. DD: Oxon, 1980; Cantab, 1981; New Raday Coll., Budapest, 1987; S Carolina, 1987; St Andrews, 1989; Yale, 1989; Univ. of the South, Sewanee, 1981; Trinity Coll., Toronto, 1986; Hon. DLitt Keele, 1981; Hon. LittD Liverpool, 1983; Hon. DCL West Indies, 1984; Hon. degree Berkeley Divinity Sch., USA, 1986; Hon. DrLitt Rikkyo, Japan, 1987. Council on Christian Unity's Patron of Christian Unity Award, Yale Univ., 1986; Order of St Vladimir Class II, Russian Orthodox Church, 1975; Cross of Order of the Holy Sepulchre, Greek Orthodox Church, 1986. *Publications:* (ed) Cathedral and City: St Albans Ancient and Modern, 1978; Windows onto God, 1983; Seasons of the Spirit, 1983; One Light for One World, 1988; Authority in Crisis? an Anglican response, 1988; The Unity We

Seek, 1989. *Recreations:* opera, reading history and novels, owning Berkshire pigs. *Address:* 26a Jennings Road, St Albans, Herts AL1 4PD. *T:* (01727) 848021, *Fax:* (01727) 842319. *Clubs:* Athenæum, Cavalry and Guards, MCC, Lord's Taverners, Saints and Sinners.
Died 11 July 2000.

RUNCIMAN, Hon. Sir James Cochran Stevenson Runciman, (Hon. Sir Steven), CH 1984; Kt 1958; CLit 1987; FBA 1957; FSA; *b* 7 July 1903; 2nd *s* of 1st Viscount Runciman of Doxford, PC and Hilda, JP, 5th *d* of James C. Stevenson, formerly MP South Shields. *Educ:* Eton (King's Schol.); Trinity College, Cambridge (Schol.; MA). Fellow of Trinity College, Cambridge, 1927–38 (Hon. Fellow 1965); Lecturer at the University of Cambridge, 1932–38; Press Attaché, British Legation, Sofia, 1940; British Embassy, Cairo, 1941; Professor of Byzantine Art and History in Univ. of Istanbul, 1942–45; Rep., Brit. Council in Greece, 1945–47. Lectures: Waynflete, Magdalen Coll., Oxford, 1953–54; Gifford, St Andrews, 1960–62; Birkbeck, Trinity Coll., Cambridge, 1966; Wiles, Queen's Univ., Belfast, 1968; Robb, Auckland, 1970; Regents', Los Angeles, California, 1971; Weir, Cincinnati, 1973. Alexander White Prof., Chicago, 1963. Mem. Advisory Council, Victoria and Albert Museum, 1957–71; Pres., British Inst. of Archæology at Ankara, 1960–75; Chairman: Anglo-Hellenic League, 1951–67; Nat. Trust for Greece, 1977–84; Councillor Emeritus, Nat. Trust for Scotland, 1985–; Trustee: British Museum, 1960–67; Scottish Nat. Museum of Antiquities, 1972–77; Hon. Vice-Pres., RHistS, 1967–; Vice-Pres., London Library, 1974; Hon. Pres., Internat. Cttee for Byzantine Studies, 1976; Pres., Friends of Mt Athos, 1992; Chm., Friends of Scottish Ballet, 1984–88. FSA 1964. For. Mem., American Philosophical Soc.; Corresp. Mem., Real Academia de Historia, Madrid. Hon. MRIA 1979. Hon. LittD Cambridge, 1955; Hon. LLD Glasgow, 1955; Hon. DLitt: Durham, 1956; St Andrews, 1969; Oxon, 1971; Birmingham, 1973; New York, 1984; Hon. LitD London, 1966; Hon. DPhil Salonika, 1951; Hon. DD Wabash, USA, 1962; Hon. DHL Chicago, 1963; Hon. DHum Ball State Univ., 1972; Hon. PhilD Sofia, 1983. Wolfson Literary Award, 1982; David Livingstone Medal, RSGS, 1992; Onassis Foundn Internat. Award for Culture, 1997. Knight Commander, Order of the Phœnix (Greece), 1961; Order of the Madara Horseman, 1st cl. (Bulgaria), 1993. *Publications:* The Emperor Romanus Lecapenus, 1929; The First Bulgarian Empire, 1930; Byzantine Civilization, 1933; The Medieval Manichee, 1947; A History of the Crusades, Vol. I, 1951 (illustrated edn, as The First Crusade, 1980), Vol. II, 1952, Vol. III, 1954; The Eastern Schism, 1955; The Sicilian Vespers, 1958; The White Rajahs, 1960; The Fall of Constantinople, 1453, 1965; The Great Church in Captivity, 1968; The Last Byzantine Renaissance, 1970; The Orthodox Churches and the Secular State, 1972; Byzantine Style and Civilisation, 1975; The Byzantine Theocracy, 1977; Mistra, 1980; A Traveller's Alphabet, 1991; contributions to various historical journals. *Address:* Elshieshields, Lockerbie, Dumfriesshire DG11 1LY. *Club:* Athenæum.
Died 1 Nov. 2000.

RUSHTON, William George; actor, author, cartoonist and broadcaster; *b* 18 Aug. 1937; *s* of John and Veronica Rushton; *m* 1968, Arlene Dorgan; one *s*, and two step *s*. *Educ:* Shrewsbury Sch. Founder/Editor, Private Eye, 1961. Stage début in The Bed-sitting Room, by Spike Milligan, Marlowe Theatre, Canterbury, 1961; Gulliver's Travels, Mermaid, 1971, 1979; Pass the Butler, by Eric Idle, Globe, 1982; Tales from a Long Room, Hammersmith, 1988; *films:* Nothing but the Best, 1963; Those Magnificent Men in their Flying Machines, 1964, and several others; *television* includes: That Was the Week that Was, 1962; Up Sunday, 1975–78; Celebrity Squares,

1979–80; numerous Jackanory progs; *radio* includes: I'm Sorry I Haven't a Clue, 1976–; much other broadcasting in UK and Australia. FZS. *Publications:* written and illustrated: William Rushton's Dirty Book, 1964; How to Play Football: the art of dirty play, 1968; The Day of the Grocer, 1971; The Geranium of Flüt, 1975; Superpig, 1976; Pigsticking: a joy for life, 1977; The Reluctant Euro, 1980; The Filth Amendment, 1981; W. G. Grace's Last Case, 1984; Willie Rushton's Great Moments of History, 1985; The Alternative Gardener: a compost of quips for the green-fingered, 1986; Marylebone Versus the Rest of the World, 1987; (ed) Spy Thatcher, 1987; Every Cat in the Book, 1993; Humphrey, the Nine Lives of the Number Ten Cat, 1995; illustrations for many others. *Recreations:* losing weight, gaining weight, parking. *Address:* Wallgrave Road, SW5 0RL. *Clubs:* Tatty Bogle's, Lord's Taverners; Surrey CCC.

Died 11 Dec. 1996.

RUSSELL, Sir Charles Ian, 3rd Bt *cr* 1916, of Littleworth Corner, Burnham, co. Buckingham; Partner, Charles Russell & Co., 1947–83; retired; Captain, Royal Horse Artillery (despatches); *b* 13 March 1918; *s* of Captain Sir Alec Charles Russell, 2nd Bt, and Monica (who *m* 2nd, 1942, Brig. John Victor Faviell, CBE, MC; she *d* 1978), *d* of Hon. Sir Charles Russell, 1st Bt; *S* father, 1938; *m* 1947, Rosemary (*d* 1996), *er d* of late Sir John Prestige; one *s* one *d*. *Educ:* Beaumont College; University College, Oxford. Admitted Solicitor, 1947. *Recreation:* golf. *Heir:* *s* Charles Dominic Russell [*b* 28 May 1956; *m* 1986, Sarah Jane Murray Chandor (marr. diss. 1995), *o d* of Anthony Chandor, Haslemere, Surrey; one *s*] *Address:* 22 Mullings Court, Cirencester, Glos GL7 2AW. *Clubs:* Garrick, Army and Navy; Royal St George's.

Died 26 Sept. 1997.

RUSSELL, Rev. Prof. Edward Augustine; Principal, Union Theological College, Belfast, 1981–87; Professor of New Testament (originally at Presbyterian College, Belfast), 1961–87, Emeritus 1987; *b* 29 Nov. 1916; *s* of William Russell and Annie (*née* Sudway); *m* 1st, 1948, Emily Frances Stevenson (*d* 1978); two *s* one *d*; 2nd, 1979, Joan Evelyn Rufli (*née* Craig). *Educ:* Royal Belfast Academical Instn; London Univ. (BA, BD, MTh); Magee UC, 1942–43; Presbyterian Coll., Belfast, 1943–44, 1945–46; New Coll., Edinburgh, 1944–45. Research at Göttingen Univ. Ordained to Ministry of Presbyterian Church in Ireland, 1948; Minister: Donacloney, 1948–53; Mountpottinger Churches, 1953–61. External Examiner, Glasgow Univ., 1968, 1972–73; extra-mural Lectr, QUB, 1972–. Vis. Prof., Southwest Univ., Memphis, 1980. Member of various clerical associations. Ed., Irish Biblical Studies, 1979–87. Hon. DD Presbyterian Theol Faculty of Ireland, 1966. *Publications:* contribs to: Studia Evangelica VI, Berlin 1973; Ministry and the Church, 1977; Studia Biblica vol. II, Sheffield 1980; Studia Evangelica VII, Berlin 1982; Proc. Irish Biblical Assoc., *et al. Recreations:* music, golf, painting, languages, bird-watching. *Address:* 30 Glenshesk Road, Ballycastle, N Ireland BT54 6PH.

Died 20 March 1997.

RUSSELL, Martin Guthrie, CBE 1970; Children's Division, Home Office, later Department of Health and Social Security, 1964–74; *b* 7 May 1914; *s* of William James Russell and Bessie Gertrude Meades; *m* 1951, Moira May Eynon, *d* of Capt. Richard Threlfell; one *d*. *Educ:* Alleyn's School; Sidney Sussex Coll., Cambridge (MA). Asst Principal, Home Office, 1937; Asst Private Sec. to Lord Privy Seal, 1942; Principal, Home Office, 1942; seconded to Treasury, 1949–51 and 1952–54; Asst Sec. 1950; Estabt Officer, 1954, Dep. Chm., 1960–64, Prison Commn. In charge of Interdepartmental Social Work Gp, 1969–70. *Recreations:* gardening, enjoying retirement. *Address:* 23 Sutton Lane, Banstead, Surrey

SM7 3QX. *T:* Burgh Heath (01737) 354397. *Club:* United Oxford & Cambridge University.

Died 3 March 1996.

RUSSELL, Sir Spencer (Thomas), Kt 1988; FCA; FCIS; FNZIM; Governor, Reserve Bank of New Zealand, 1984–88, retired; non-executive Chairman, National Bank of New Zealand, since 1992; *b* 5 Oct. 1923; *s* of Thomas Spencer Russell and Ann Jane Russell; *m* 1953, Ainsley (*née* Coull); three *s*. *Educ:* Wanganui Collegiate School. Served War, NZ Division, 1942–45. Joined National Bank of New Zealand, 1946; International Manager, 1956; Asst Gen. Man., 1960; Chief London Man., 1973; Chief Exec. and Dir, 1976. *Publications:* numerous articles in professional jls. *Recreations:* golf, gardening. *Address:* 6 Challenger Street, St Heliers, Auckland 5, New Zealand. *Clubs:* Wellington; Northern (Auckland); Wellington Golf.

Died 7 July 1995.

RUTHERFORD, Prof. Andrew, CBE 1993; Vice-Chancellor, University of London, 1994–97; Warden of Goldsmiths' College, 1984–92, and Professor, 1988–92, then Emeritus, University of London; *b* Helmsdale, Sutherland, 23 July 1929; *s* of Thomas Armstrong Rutherford and Christian P. Rutherford (*née* Russell); *m* 1953, Nancy Milroy Browning, MA, *d* of Dr Arthur Browning and Dr Jean G. Browning (*née* Thomson); two *s* one *d*. *Educ:* Helmsdale Sch.; George Watson's Boys' Coll.; Univ. of Edinburgh; Merton Coll., Oxford. MA Edinburgh Univ., First Cl. Hons Eng. Lang. and Lit., James Elliott Prize, and Vans Dunlop Schol., 1951; Carnegie Schol., 1953; BLitt Oxford, 1959. Commnd Seaforth Highlanders, serving with Somaliland Scouts, 1952–53; 11th Bn Seaforth Highlanders (TA), 1953–58. Asst Lectr in English, Univ. of Edinburgh, 1955; Lectr, 1956–64; Vis. Assoc. Prof., Univ. of Rochester (NY), 1963, University of Aberdeen: Sen. Lectr, 1964; Second Prof. of English, 1965–68; Regius (Chalmers) Prof. of Eng. Lit., 1968–84; Mem. Court, 1978–84; Dean, Faculty of Arts and Soc. Scis, 1979–82; Sen. Vice-Principal, 1982–84. Mem. Court, Univ. of London, 1990–92; Hon. Fellow, Goldsmiths' Coll., 1992. Lectures: Byron Foundn, Nottingham Univ., 1964; Chatterton, British Acad., 1965; Stevenson, Edinburgh Univ., 1967. Chairman: English Bd, CNAA, 1966–73; Literature Adv. Cttee, British Council, 1987–; Pres., Internat. Assoc. of Univ. Profs of English, 1978–80. Mem., BBC Gen. Adv. Council, 1979–84; Trustee: Learning from Experience Trust, 1986–92; Courtauld Trust, 1994–97. British Council lecture tours in Europe, India and S America. Freeman, City of London, 1990; Freeman, 1990, Liveryman, 1991, Goldsmiths' Co. Hon. DLitt SUNY, 1990; DUniv Athens, 1993; Hon. LLD Aberdeen, 1995. *Publications:* Byron: a Critical Study, 1961; (ed) Kipling's Mind and Art, 1964; (ed) Byron: the Critical Heritage, 1970; (ed) 20th Century Interpretations of A Passage to India, 1970; (ed) Kipling, A Sahibs' War and other stories, 1971; (ed) Kipling, Friendly Brook and other stories, 1971; The Literature of War, 1979, 2nd edn 1989; (ed) Early Verse by Rudyard Kipling, 1986; (ed) Kipling, Plain Tales from the Hills, 1987; (ed) Kipling, Selected Stories, 1987; (ed) Kipling, War Stories and Poems, 1990; (ed) Byron: Augustan and Romantic, 1990; (ed) The Sayings of Rudyard Kipling, 1994; articles in learned journals. *Address:* Saltoun Hall, Pencaitland, E Lothian EH34 5DS. *Clubs:* Athenæum; New (Edinburgh).

Died 13 Jan. 1998.

RUTHERFORD, (Gordon) Malcolm; Obituaries Editor, Financial Times, since 1995; *b* 21 Aug. 1939; *s* of late Gordon Brown Rutherford and Bertha Brown Rutherford; *m* 1st, 1965, Susan Tyler (marr. diss. 1969); one *d*; 2nd, 1970, Elizabeth Maitland Pelen; three *d*. *Educ:* Newcastle Royal Grammar Sch.; Balliol Coll., Oxford. Arts Editor 1962, Foreign Editor 1964, The Spectator; founded the

Newsletter, Latin America, 1965; Financial Times: Diplomatic Correspondent, 1967–69; Chief German Correspondent, 1969–74; Defence Specialist, 1974–77; Asst Editor, 1977–93; Chief political commentator, 1977–88; Chief theatre critic, 1990–94. Mem. of Council, Chatham House, 1994–. Founding Mem., Media Law Group, 1983; Co-Founder, West-West Agenda, 1988. *Publications:* Can We Save the Common Market?, 1981, 2nd edn 1983; (ed) A Peer without Equal: memoirs of an editor, 1997. *Recreations:* travel, tennis, bridge. *Address:* 89 Bedford Gardens, W8 7EQ. *T:* (020) 7229 2063. *Club:* Travellers. *Died 14 Dec. 1999.*

RUTHERFORD, Vice-Adm. Malcolm Graham, CBE 1991; Director, Defence Systems, GEC-Marconi, 1996; *b* Tunbridge Wells, 21 March 1941; *s* of (Herman) Graham Rutherford, CBE, QPM and late Dorothy Weaver; *m* 1969, Fleur Margaret Ann Smith; one *s* one *d. Educ:* New Coll. Sch., Oxford; Gordonstoun; London Univ. (BSc (Elec. Engrg) 1964); RNC Greenwich (Nuclear Reactor Engrg Dip. 1969). Italian Interpreter, 1968. FIEE 1986; EurIng 1989. Served HM Submarines, Thermopylae, Conqueror, Sceptre, 1967–78; ndc 1978; HMS Glamorgan, 1984; Dir, Tactical Weapons System Upholder Class Subs, 1986–88; Capt., HMS Collingwood, 1988–90; Dir, Personnel, MoD, 1990–92; Naval Sec., 1992–94; DCDS (Systems), MoD, 1994–95, and Chief Naval Engr Officer, 1994–96 (Ldr, Study Team, Engrg Structure in RN, 1995–96). President: RNRM Mountaineering Club, 1985–96; RN Winter Sports Assoc., 1993–96; Mem., Higher Management Cttee, Jt Services Everest Expedns, 1988, 1992. FRGS 1996. Freeman, City of London, 1996. *Recreations:* mountaineering, ski-ing, squash, cycling, running (London and NY marathons, 1989), photography, writing. *Clubs:* Garrick, Alpine; Escorts Squash Rackets; Alresford Golf. *Died 6 June 1997.*

RUTLAND, 10th Duke of, *cr* 1703; **Charles John Robert Manners,** CBE 1962; Marquess of Granby 1703; Earl of Rutland 1525; Baron Manners of Haddon 1679; Baron Roos of Belvoir 1896; Captain Grenadier Guards; *b* 28 May 1919; *e s* of 9th Duke of Rutland and Kathleen (*d* 1989), 3rd *d* of late F. J. Tennant; *S* father, 1940; *m* 1946, Anne Bairstow Cumming (marr. diss. 1956), *e d* of late Major Cumming Bell, Binham Lodge, Edgerton, Huddersfield; one *d*; *m* 1958, Frances Helen, *d* of late Charles Sweeny and Margaret, Duchess of Argyll; two *s* one *d* (and one *s* decd). *Educ:* Eton; Trinity Coll., Cambridge. Owned 18,000 acres; minerals in Leicestershire and Derbyshire; picture gallery at Belvoir Castle. Chairman: E Midlands Economic Planning Council, 1971–74; Leicestershire County Council, 1974–77. *Heir:* s Marquis of Granby, *b* 8 May 1959. *Address:* Belvoir Castle, Grantham NG32 1PD; Haddon Hall, Derbys DE4 1LA. *Died 3 Jan. 1999.*

RUTTER, Air Vice-Marshal Norman Colpoy Simpson, CB 1965; CBE 1945; Senior Technical Staff Officer, Bomber Command, 1961–65; *b* 9 June 1909; *s* of Rufus John Rutter; *m* 1936, Irene Sophia (*d* 1983), *d* of late Colonel A. M. Lloyd; one *s* one *d.* Air Cdre, 1957; Air Officer Commanding and Commandant of the Royal Air Force Technical College, Henlow, 1959–61. idc; jssc; psa. CEng, FIMechE; FRAeS. *Address:* 37 Meadow Road, Pinner, Middx HA5 1EB. *Died 9 Oct. 1998.*

RYBCZYNSKI, Tadeusz Mieczyslaw, FCIB; *b* 21 May 1923; *s* of Karol Rybczynski and Helena (*née* Sawicka); *m* 1951, Helena Perucka; one *d. Educ:* primary and secondary schs, Lwow, Poland; LSE, Univ. of London (BCom, MScEcon). FCIB (FIB 1966). Lloyds Bank, 1949–53; Lazard Brothers & Co. Ltd, 1954–88; Dir, Lazard Securities Ltd, 1969–86; Econ. Advr, Lazard Brothers & Co. Ltd, 1973–88; Dir, Euro-Canadian Internat. Investment Management, then Sund and Wrigley & Co.

Ltd, 1987–93. Visiting Professor: Univ. of Surrey, 1968–74; City Univ., 1974–. Chm., Soc. of Business Economists, 1962–75 (Fellow, 1988). Member: Monopolies and Mergers Commn, 1978–81; Council of Management and Exec. Cttee, NIESR, 1968– (also Governor); Exec. Cttee and Council, Inst. of Fiscal Studies, 1988–. Dir, European Council for Trade Promotion, 1994–95. Vice-Pres., Sect. F (Econs), BAAS, 1995–; Member: Council, REconS, 1969– (Treas., 1974–87; Vice-Pres., 1987–); Governing Body, Trade Policy Res. Centre, 1968–; Cttee, Foreign Affairs Club, 1968–85; Adv. Bd in Banking and Finance, Univ. of Aston Management Centre, 1973–82; Sci. Cttee, Centre for Monetary and Banking Studies, Univ. of Geneva, 1973–; Court, Brunel Univ., 1976–79; Trustee, Centre for Res. for Post-Communist Econs, 1983–. Mem. Cttee, Round Table, 1981– (Treas., 1981–94). Hon. DSc City Univ., 1990. Harms Award, Inst. for Economic Research, Univ. of Kiel, 1983; Abramson Award, Nat. Assoc. of Business Economists, USA, 1980. *Publications:* (ed) A New Era in Competition, 1973; (jtly) The Necessary Institutional Framework to Transform Formerly Planned Economies, 1994; *contributed* to: Comparative Banking, 1960, 3rd edn 1969; Long Range Planning, Paris and New York, 1967; (also ed jtly) The Economist in Business, 1967; Readings in International Economics, 1968; (also ed) Value Added Tax—the UK position and the European experience, 1969; Money in Britain 1959–69, 1970; Problems of Investment, 1971; Users of Economics, 1972; (also ed) The Economics of the Oil Crisis, 1976; Financial Management Handbook, 1977; The International Monetary System 1971–80, 1983; International Lending in a Fragile World Economy, 1983; Securities Markets & Investment Banking in the UK, 1988; Financial Markets, Regulation and Supervision, 1991; St Petersburg-Leningrad Papers, 1991; The New European Financial Marketplace, 1994; The Changing Face of European Banks and Securities Markets, 1994; Government and Markets, 1994; Investment Banking Theory and Practice, 1996; Institutions Governing Financial Markets, 1997; articles in serious jls, and in academic and bank revs. *Recreations:* opera, ballet, history, international affairs, travel. *Address:* 2 Windyridge Close, Parkside Avenue, SW19 5HB. *T:* (0181) 946 7363. *Club:* Reform. *Died 18 Dec. 1998.*

RYCROFT, Sir (Richard) Newton, 7th Bt *cr* 1784, of Calton, Yorkshire; *b* 23 Jan. 1918; *yr s* of Sir Nelson Edward Oliver Rycroft, 6th Bt, and Ethel Sylvia (*d* 1952), *d* of late Robert Nurton, Odcombe, Yeovil; *S* father, 1958; *m* 1947, Ann, *d* of late Hugh Bellingham-Smith, Alfriston, Sussex, and Mrs Harvey Robarts; two *d. Educ:* Winchester; Christ Church, Oxford (BA). Served War of 1939–45: Bedfordshire and Hertfordshire Regt, on special service work in Balkans (Major, despatches); Knight's Cross of Royal Order of Phœnix with Swords (Greece). *Heir:* cousin Richard John Rycroft, *b* 15 June 1946. *Address:* Winalls Wood House, Stuckton, Fordingbridge, Hampshire SP6 2HQ. *T:* (01425) 652263. *Died 12 Jan. 1999.*

RYDER OF WARSAW, Baroness *cr* 1979 (Life Peer), of Warsaw in Poland and of Cavendish in the County of Suffolk; **Margaret Susan, (Sue), Ryder,** CMG 1976; OBE 1957; Founder and Social Worker, Sue Ryder Foundation for the Sick and Disabled of all Age Groups; *b* 3 July 1923; *d* of late Charles and Elizabeth Ryder; *m* 1959, Geoffrey Leonard Cheshire (Baron Cheshire, VC, OM, DSO, DFC) (*d* 1992); one *s* one *d. Educ:* Benenden Sch., Kent. Served War of 1939–45 with FANY and with Special Ops Executive. Co-Founder, Ryder-Cheshire Foundn; Pres., Leonard Cheshire; Trustee, National Meml Arboretum. Hon. Fellow, Liverpool John Moores Univ., 1998. Hon. LLD: Liverpool, 1973; Exeter, 1980; London,

1981; Leeds, 1984; Cambridge, 1989; Hon. DLitt Reading, 1982; Hon. DCL Kent, 1986; DU Essex, 1993. Polish Humanitarian Award, 1996. Commander's Cross of Order of Polonia Restituta (Poland), 1992 (Officer's Cross, 1965); Medal of Yugoslav Flag with Gold Wreath and Diploma, 1971; Golden Order of Merit, Polish People's Republic, 1976; Order of Smile (Poland), 1981; Order of Merit (Poland), 1992. *Publications:* Remembrance (annual leaflet of the Sue Ryder Foundation); And the Morrow is Theirs (autobiog.), 1975; Child of My Love (autobiog.), 1986, rev. edn 1998. *Address:* PO Box 5259, Sue Ryder Home, Cavendish, Sudbury, Suffolk CO10 8AN.

Died 2 Nov. 2000.

RYLANDS, George Humphrey Wolferstan, CH 1987; CBE 1961; Fellow of King's College, Cambridge (sometime Dean, Bursar, College Lecturer, and Director of Studies); University Lecturer in English Literature, retired; *b* 23 Oct. 1902; *s* of Thomas Kirkland Rylands. *Educ:* Eton (King's Scholar); King's Coll., Cambridge (Scholar; MA). Chm. of Directors and Trustees of the Arts Theatre, Cambridge, 1946–82; Governor of the Old Vic, 1945–78; Chm. of Apollo Soc., 1946–72. Member: Cheltenham Coll. Council, 1946–76; Council of RADA. Directed Hamlet with Sir John Gielgud, 1945; recordings of the Shakespeare canon and the English poets, for the British Council. Hon. LittD Cambridge, 1976; Hon. DLitt Durham, 1988. *Publications:* Words and Poetry, 1928; Poems, 1931; Shakespeare the Poet (in a Companion to Shakespeare Studies), 1934; The Ages of Man, a Shakespeare Anthology, 1939; Shakespeare's Poetic Energy (British Academy Lecture, 1951); Quoth the Raven "Nevermore": an anthology, 1984; Croaked the Raven: one NO more, 1988; College Verse, 1989. *Address:* King's College, Cambridge CB2 1ST. *T:* (01223) 350411. *Clubs:* Athenæum, Garrick.

Died 16 Jan. 1999.

S

SABIN, Howard Westcott; Legal Adviser to Associated Newspapers Group Ltd, 1972–84; Chairman, William Morris Rolling Mills Ltd (formerly William Morris & Son (Birmingham) Ltd), since 1985; *b* 19 Oct. 1916; *s* of late John Howard Sabin and Octavia Roads (*née* Scruby); *m* 1st, 1942, Joan Eunice Noble (marr. diss. 1959); two *s* one *d*; 2nd, 1959, Janet Eileen Baillie. *Educ:* Shrewsbury; St John's Coll., Cambridge. MA (Hons in History and Law). Lieut, RNVR, 1939–46 (despatches 1944). Called to the Bar, Middle Temple, 1946. Counsel for Post Office (Midland Circuit), 1964; Assistant Recorder, Portsmouth, 1966, Bournemouth, 1967; Dep. Chm., Bedfordshire QS, 1968–72. *Recreations:* golf, swimming, music. *Address:* 40 Wynnstay Gardens, W8 6UT. *T:* 0171–937 9247. *Club:* Hadley Wood Golf.   *Died 9 Feb. 1996.*

SACKWOOD, Dr Mark; Regional Medical Officer, Northern Regional Health Authority, 1973–86, retired; *b* London, 18 Jan. 1926; *s* of Philip and Frances Sackwood; *m* 1953, Anne Harper Wilson; one *s* two *d*. *Educ:* King's Coll., London; Westminster Hosp. Med. School; MB, BS London, 1949. LRCP, MRCS 1949; DPH, DRCOG; FFCM. Various hosp. appts, South of England, 1949–58; mil. service, Far East, 1951–53; subseq. admin. med. appts, Middlesbrough and Newcastle upon Tyne, incl. Dep. Sen. Admin. MO with Newcastle RHB, 1968–73. *Recreations:* walking, reading, music. *Address:* 11 The Chesters, Beaumont Park, Whitley Bay, Tyne and Wear NE25 9UA. *T:* (0191) 252 7401.
    Died 1 March 2000.

SAINSBURY, Baron *cr* 1962 (Life Peer), of Drury Lane, Borough of Holborn; **Alan John Sainsbury;** Joint President of J. Sainsbury plc, since 1967 (Chairman, 1956–67); *b* 13 Aug. 1902; *er s* of John Benjamin and Mabel Miriam Sainsbury; *m* 1st, 1925, Doreen Davan Adams (marr. diss. 1939; she *d* 1985); three *s*; 2nd, 1944, Anne Elizabeth Lewy (*d* 1988); one *d*. *Educ:* Haileybury. Joined grocery and provision firm of J. Sainsbury, Ltd (founded by his grandparents), 1921. Served on many war-time consultative committees of Ministry of Food; Member: Williams' Committee on Milk Distribution, 1947–48; Food Research Advisory Cttee, 1960–70 (Chm., 1965–70); NEDC Cttee for the Distributive Trades, 1964–68; Exec. Cttee, PEP, 1970–76; House of Lords Select Cttee on the European Communities, 1978–81; Chm., Cttee of Inquiry into Relationship of Pharmaceutical Industry with National Health Service, 1965–67. President: Multiple Shops' Fedn, 1963–65; Grocers' Inst., 1963–66; Internat. Assoc. of Chain Stores, 1965–68; Royal Inst. of Public Health and Hygiene, 1965–70; Pestalozzi Children's Village Trust, 1963–93; Distributive Trades Educn and Trng Council, 1975–83; a Vice-President: Assoc. of Agriculture, 1965–73; Royal Society for the Encouragement of Arts, Manufactures and Commerce, 1962–66; Mem., Court of Univ. of Essex, 1966–76; Governor, City Literary Inst., 1967–69; Chairman of Trustees: Overseas Students Adv. Bureau; Uganda Asian Relief Trust, 1972–74; Vice-President: World Development Movement; Internat. Voluntary Service, 1977–81; Parly Gp for World Govt, 1982–. Contested (L) Sudbury Div. of Suffolk, Gen. Elections of 1929, 1931 and 1935; joined Labour Party, 1945, SDP, 1981. Hon. Fellow, Inst. of Food Sci. and Technology. *Address:* J. Sainsbury plc, Stamford House, Stamford Street, SE1 9LL.   *Died 21 Oct. 1998.*

SAINSBURY, Sir Robert (James), Kt 1967 (for services to the arts); Joint President, J. Sainsbury plc; *b* 24 Oct. 1906; *s* of late John Benjamin Sainsbury and Mabel Miriam (*née* Van den Bergh); *m* 1937, Lisa Ingeborg (*née* Van den Bergh; second cousin); one *s* two *d* (and one *d* decd). *Educ:* Haileybury Coll.; Pembroke Coll., Cambridge (MA; Hon. Fellow, 1983). ACA 1930, FCA 1935. Joined J. Sainsbury Ltd, 1930; Dir, 1934; Jt Gen. Man., 1938; Dep. Chm., 1956; Chm., 1967; Jt Pres., 1969. Formerly Mem., Art Panel of Arts Council; Member: Mgt Cttee, Courtauld Inst. of Art, Univ. of London, 1979–82; Vis. Cttee to Primitive Art Dept, Metropolitan Mus. of Art, New York, until 1986; Pres., British Assoc. of Friends of Museums, 1985–. Trustee, Tate Gall., 1959–73 (Vice-Chm. 1967; Chm., 1969). Founder, with wife, Sainsbury Centre for Visual Arts, UEA, 1978. Hon. Treasurer, Inst. of Med. Social Workers, 1948–71; Governor, St Thomas' Hospital, 1939–68. Hon. Freeman, City of Norwich, 1999. Hon. FRIBA 1986. Hon. Dr RCA, 1976; Hon. LittD East Anglia, 1977; Hon. LLD Liverpool, 1988.
    Died 2 April 2000.

ST AUBYN, Sir (John) Arscott M.; *see* Molesworth-St Aubyn.

ST JOHN, Maj.-Gen. Roger Ellis Tudor, CB 1965; MC 1944; *b* Hexham on Tyne, 4 Oct. 1911; *s* of late Major B. T. St John, Craigveigh, Aboyne, Aberdeenshire; *m* 1943, Rosemary Jean Douglas Vickers, Englefield Green, Surrey; one *s* three *d*. *Educ:* Wellington College; RMC Sandhurst. Joined Fifth Fusiliers, 1931; served War of 1939–45 (despatches, MC), in Hong Kong, UK and NW Europe; Bde Major 11 Armoured Div., 1944–45; GSO 2 Instructor Camberley Staff Coll., 1945–46; AA&QMG 1st Division, Tripoli, 1948–50; comd 1st Bn Royal Northumberland Fusiliers, 1953–55 (despatches), Mau Mau Rebellion; AMS Mil. Secretary's Branch, War Office, 1955–57; Comdr 11 Inf. Bde Group, BAOR, 1957–60; Asst Comdt, Camberley Staff Coll., 1960–62; Comdr, British Army Staff, Military Member, British Defence Staffs, and Military Attaché, Washington, 1963–65; President, Regular Army Commissions Board, 1965–67; retired, 1967. Colonel, Royal Northumberland Fusiliers, 1965–68. Personnel Adminr, Urwick, Orr and Partners Ltd, Management Consultants, 1967–73. *Address:* Harelaw, Gorse Hill Road, Virginia Water, Surrey GU25 4AS.   *Died 15 Oct. 1998.*

ST OSWALD, 5th Baron *cr* 1885, of Nostell, co. York; **Derek Edward Anthony Winn;** DL; *b* 9 July 1919; *s* of 3rd Baron St Oswald and Eve Carew (*d* 1976), *d* of Charles Greene; *S* brother, 1984; *m* 1954, (Charlotte) Denise (Eileen), *d* of Wilfred Haig Loyd; one *s* one *d*. *Educ:* Stowe. Joined 60th Rifles, KRRC, as 2nd Lieut, 1938; Parachute Regt, 1942; served N Africa (wounded); Malayan Police, 1948–51. Film Producer, 1953–67. Farm owner, Nostell Priory. President: Wakefield Parachute Regt, 1985–; Wakefield Hospice, 1985–; Wakefield Multiple Sclerosis Soc., 1985–. DL W Yorks, 1987. *Publication:* I Served Caesar, 1972. *Recreation:* shooting. *Heir: s* Hon. Charles Rowland Andrew Winn [*b* 22 July 1959; *m* 1985, Louise Alexandra, *yr d* of Stewart Scott; one *s* one *d*]. *Address:* Nostell Priory, Wakefield, Yorks WF4 1QE. *T:* (01924) 862394; 36 Broad Street, Ludlow, Shropshire SY8 1NL. *Clubs:* Lansdowne, Special Forces.
    Died 18 March 1999.

SALAM, Prof. Abdus, Hon. KBE 1989; Sitara-i-Pakistan, 1959; Order of Nishan-i-Imtiaz, Pakistan, 1979; PhD; FRS 1959; Professor of Theoretical Physics, 1957–93, Fellow, since 1994, Imperial College, University of London; Director, 1964–94, President, since 1994, International Centre for Theoretical Physics, Trieste; *b* 29 Jan. 1926; *m* 1st; one *s* three *d*; *m* 2nd; one *s* one *d. Educ:* Govt Coll., Lahore, Pakistan (MA); St John's Coll., Cambridge (BA, PhD). Fellow, St John's Coll., Cambridge, 1951–56 (Hon. Fellow, 1972); Professor of Mathematics, Government College, Lahore, 1951–54; Lecturer in Mathematics, University of Cambridge, 1954–56. Sci. Advr to Pres. of Pakistan, 1961–74. Made contributions to the theory of elementary particles. Member: UN Adv. Cttee on Science and Technology, 1964–75 (Chm., 1971–72); South Commn, 1987–; Vice-Pres., IUPAP, 1972–78. Founding Mem. and Pres., Third World Acad. of Scis, 1983; (first elected) Pres., Third World Network of Scientific Orgns, 1988–; Fellow: Royal Swedish Acad. of Sciences, 1970; APS, 1993; For. Mem., USSR Acad. of Scis, 1971. Hon. DSc, universities in: Punjab (Lahore), 1957; Edinburgh, 1971; Trieste and Islamabad, 1979; Lima, Cuzco, Caracas, Wroclow, Yarmouk and Istanbul, 1980; Amritsar, Aligarh, Banaras, Chittagong, Bristol and Maiduguri, 1981; Philippines, 1982; Khartoum and Madrid, 1983; New York (City Coll.) and Nairobi, 1984; Cuyo, La Plata and Göteborg, 1985; Sofia, Glasgow, Hefei and London (City Univ.), 1986; Punjab (Chandigarh), Benin, Exeter and Colombo, 1987; Gent, 1988; Bendel State and Ghana, 1990; Warwick, Dakar and Tucaman, 1991; Lagos, S Carolina, W Indies, St Petersburg, 1992; Gulbarga and Dhaka, 1993; Hon. ScD Cambridge, 1985. Hopkins Prize, Cambridge Philosophical Soc., 1957; Adams Prize, Cambridge Univ., 1958; Maxwell Medal and Prize, IPPS, 1961; Hughes Medal, Royal Society, 1964; Atoms for Peace Award, 1968; Oppenheimer Prize and Medal, 1971; Guthrie Medal and Prize, IPPS, 1976; Matteuci Medal, Accad. Naz. di XL, Rome, 1978, John Torrence Tate Medal, Amer. Inst. of Physics, 1978; Royal Medal, Royal Society, 1978; (jtly) Nobel Prize for Physics, 1979; Einstein Medal, UNESCO, Paris, 1979; Josef Stefan Medal, Josef Stefan Inst., Ljubljana, 1980; Gold Medal for outstanding contrib. to physics, Czechoslovak Acad. of Scis, Prague, 1981; Peace Medal, Charles Univ., Prague, 1981; Lomonosov Gold Medal, USSR Acad. of Scis, 1983; Genoa Internat. Develt of People's Prize, 1988; Edinburgh Medal and Prize, 1989; Ettore Majorana Erice Science for Peace Prize, 1989; Copley Medal, Royal Soc., 1990; Cataluña Internat. Prize, Spain, 1990; Internat. Leocino d'Oro Prize, Italy, 1993. Order of Andres Bello (Venezuela), 1980; Order of Istiqlal (Jordan), 1980; Cavaliere di Gran Croce, Order of Merit (Italy), 1989. *Publications:* (ed with E. P. Wigner) Aspects of Quantum Mechanics, 1972; Ideals and Realities: selected essays, 1984, 3rd edn 1989; Science and Education in Pakistan, 1987; (with Ergin Sezgin) Supergravity in Diverse Dimensions, Vols I and II, 1988; (ed) From a Life of Physics, 1989; Unification of Fundamental Forces: the first of the 1988 Dirac Memorial Lectures, 1990; Science and Technology: challenge for the South, 1992; Renaissance of Sciences in Islamic Countries, 1994; papers on physics of elementary particles and on scientific and educnl policies for developing countries and Pakistan; *relevant publications:* Abdus Salam, by Dr Abdul Ghani, 1982; Abdus Salam, by Jagjit Singh, 1992; Selected Papers of Abdus Salam (with commentary), 1994. *Address:* International Centre for Theoretical Physics, PO Box 586, 34100 Trieste, Italy.   *Died 21 Nov. 1996.*

SALMON, Dame Nancy (Marion); *see* Snagge, Dame N. M.

SALMON, Thomas David; Assistant to Speaker's Counsel, House of Commons, 1980–86; retired; *b* 1 Nov. 1916; *s*

of late Rev. Thomas Salmon and Isabel Salmon (*née* Littleton), North Stoneham, Hants; *m* 1950, (Morris) Patricia (Reyner) Turner, Ilford, Essex; one *s* two *d. Educ:* Winchester Coll.; Christ Church, Oxford (MA). Served War of 1939–45: Captain 133 Field Regt RA (despatches). Temp. Asst Principal, Cabinet Office, 1946. Admitted Solicitor, 1949; entered Treasury Solicitor's Dept, 1951; transf. to Bd of Trade, 1966; Under-Sec. (Legal), Solicitors' Dept, Depts of Industry and Trade, 1973–80. *Recreations:* walking, study of history and languages, gardening. *Address:* Tenures, 23 Sole Farm Road, Great Bookham, Surrey KT23 3DW. *T:* (01372) 452837.
Died 2 Sept. 1997.

SALMON, Col William Alexander, (Alec), OBE 1956; Assistant Ecclesiastical Secretary to the Lord Chancellor, 1964–77, and to the Prime Minister, 1964–77, retired; *b* 16 Nov. 1910; *o s* of late Lt-Col W. H. B. Salmon, late IA; *m* 1939, Jean Barbara Macmillan (*d* 1982), *o d* of late J. V. Macmillan, OBE, DD (Bishop of Guildford, 1934–49); one *s* two *d. Educ:* Haileybury College; RMC, Sandhurst. Commissioned 2nd Lieut HLI 1930; ADC to Governor of Sind, 1936–38; served during War of 1939–45: France, 1939; Middle East, Italy, Greece, Bde Major, 1942; GSO2 HQ Aegean Force, 1943; CO, 2nd Bn Beds and Herts Regt, 1945–46; CO, 2nd Bn Royal Irish Fusiliers, 1946–47; GSO1 (Trng), HQ Scottish Command, 1947–49; Chief of Staff to Lt-Gen. Glubb Pasha, HQ Arab Legion, 1950–53; CO 1st Bn HLI, 1953–55; Col GS (O and T Div.), SHAPE, 1957–59; AQMG (QAE2), The War Office, 1959–62; AAG (Adjt Gen. 14), The War Office, 1962–63; retd 1963. Life Governor, Haileybury and Imperial Service Coll., 1965. Order of El Istiqlal (2nd Cl.) (Hashemite Kingdom of Jordan), 1953. *Publication:* Churches and Royal Patronage, 1983. *Recreations:* shooting, fishing, gardening. *Address:* Balcombe Place, Balcombe, Haywards Heath, West Sussex RH17 6QT
Died 2 Nov. 2000.

SAMBROOK, Gordon Hartley, CBE 1986; Chairman, Iron Trades Employers' Insurance Association, and Iron Trades Insurance Co. Ltd (formerly Iron Trades Mutual Insurance Co.), since 1984; *b* 9 Jan. 1930; *m* 1956, Patricia Joan Mary Havard; one *s. Educ:* Sheffield Univ. (BA Hons, DipEd). Graduate Apprentice, United Steel, 1954; United Steel Cos, 1954–68; British Steel Corporation: General Manager, Rotherham, 1972; Dir, Tinplate Gp, 1973–75; Man. Dir, Personnel, 1975–77; Man. Dir, Commercial, 1977–80; Dir, 1978–90; Chief Exec., 1980–89, Chm., 1980–90; BSC General Steels, later General Steels. Director: Allied Steel & Wire Ltd, 1981–87; United Merchant Bar PLC, 1985–90; United Engineering Steels Ltd, 1986–92; Tuscaloosa Steel Corp., 1985–91. Chm. of Council, Steel Construction Inst., 1990–94.   *Died 4 Feb. 1996.*

SANDFORD, Herbert Henry, OBE 1963; DFM 1942; Member for Chelsea, and Opposition Chief Whip, Inner London Education Authority, 1986–90; *b* 19 Nov. 1916; *s* of Herbert Charles Sandford and Grace Ellen (*née* Onley); *m* 1st, 1938, Irene Lucy (*née* Porter) (marr. diss. 1944); 2nd, 1948, Jessie Irene (*née* Gray). *Educ:* Minchendon Secondary Sch., Southgate. Served War, Pathfinder Sqdns, RAF, 1939–45. Elected to St Marylebone Metrop. Bor. Council, 1953; Chm., Works Cttee. City of Westminster: Councillor, Lords Ward, 1964–68; Alderman, 1968–78; Dep. Leader of Council, 1975–76; Chairman: Traffic Cttee, 1964–67; Highways and Traffic Cttee, 1967–68; Highways Cttee, 1971–72 (Vice-Chm., 1969–71); Highways and Works Cttee, 1972–75; special sub-cttee of Highways and Town Planning Cttees on redevelt of Piccadilly Circus, 1972–76; Member: Policy Cttee, 1972–74; Town Planning Cttee, 1971–76; Road Safety Cttee, 1972–74; Road Safety Adv.

Cttee, 1974–76; Co-ord. Cttee, 1974–75; Housing Management Cttee, 1975–77; London Transport Passenger Cttee, 1974–76. Greater London Council: Mem. (C) for St Marylebone, 1976–86; Dep. Chm., 1985–86; Chm., Central Area Planning Cttee, 1977–81; Member: Public Services Safety Cttee, 1977–81; Covent Garden Cttee, 1977–81; Thames Water Regional Land Drainage Cttee, 1978–82; Leading Opposition Mem., Technical Services Cttee, 1983–86; Dep. Spokesman, Finance Cttee, 1983–86. Opposition Spokesman, Staff and Gen. Cttee, 1982–86, Staff Cttee, 1986–90, Gen. Purposes Cttee, 1986–90, ILEA. Chm., Grove End Housing Assoc., Ltd, 1986– (Dir, 1976–). Chairman: St Marylebone Sea Cadet Corps, 1953; St Marylebone Boy Scouts Assoc., 1958–64. Treasurer, Wiltons Music Hall Trust, 1982–. Governor: St John's Hosp. for Skin Diseases, 1973–76; London Inst., 1986–90; Chm. Bd of Governors, Abercorn Place Sch., 1992–. *Recreations:* golf, bridge, Yoga. *Address:* 5 Elmfield House, Carlton Hill, NW8 9XB. *T:* (0171) 624 9694. *Clubs:* Royal Air Force; Hampstead Golf (Captain, 1996–97). *Died 11 March 1999.*

SANDFORD SMITH, Richard Henry, FCIS; Chairman, Eastern Gas Region (formerly Eastern Gas Board), 1970–73; *b* 29 March 1909; *s* of late Dr H. Sandford Smith; *m* 1936, Dorothy Hewitt (*d* 1998), *y d* of late Rev. J. F. Hewitt; one *s. Educ:* Haileybury Coll. London Stock Exchange, 1926. Qualified as Chartered Secretary and awarded Sir Ernest Clarke Prize, 1932. Joined Gas Light & Coke Co., 1932; Sec., SE Gas Corp. Ltd, 1939–49; Sec., SE Gas Bd, 1949–56 (Dep. Chm., 1956–69). *Recreations:* theatre, gardening. *Address:* 60 The Marlowes, St John's Wood Park, NW8 6NA. *Club:* Savile. *Died 10 May 2000.*

SANDYS, Julian George Winston; QC 1983; *b* 19 Sept. 1936; *s* of Baron Duncan-Sandys, CH, PC and 1st wife Diana, *d* of late Rt Hon. Sir Winston Churchill, KG, OM, CH, PC; *m* 1970, Elisabeth Jane, *o d* of late John Besley Martin, CBE; three *s* one *d. Educ:* Eton; Salem; Trinity Coll., Melbourne. 2nd Lieut 4th Hussars, 1955; Captain, QRIH (AER), 1964. Called to the Bar, Inner Temple, 1959. Member: Midland Circuit, 1960–76; Western Circuit, 1982–89; Gray's Inn, 1970–. Contested (C) Ashfield, Notts, 1959. *Publication:* Regulation S, 1995. *Recreations:* flying, computers

Died 15 Aug. 1997.

SANKEY, Guy Richard; QC 1991; a Recorder, since 1992; *b* 2 April 1944; *s* of Graham and Joan Sankey; *m* 1969, Pauline Mace Lamotte; three *d. Educ:* Marlborough College; New College, Oxford (MA). Called to the Bar, Inner Temple, 1966. Junior Counsel to the Crown, Common Law, 1987–91. *Recreations:* golf, ski-ing, tennis. *Address:* 1 Temple Gardens, Temple, EC4Y 9BB. *Club:* Denham Golf. *Died 4 May 2000.*

SARGAN, Prof. John Denis, FBA 1981; Emeritus Professor, London School of Economics and Political Science, since 1984 (Tooke Professor of Economic Science and Statistics, 1982–84; Professor of Econometrics, 1964–84); *b* 23 Aug. 1924; *s* of H. and G. A. Sargan; *m* 1953, Phyllis Mary Millard; two *s* one *d. Educ:* Doncaster Grammar Sch.; St John's Coll., Cambridge. Asst. Lectr, Lectr and Reader, Leeds Univ., 1948–63; Reader, 1963–64, Hon. Fellow, 1991, LSE. Fellow, Amer. Acad. of Arts and Scis, 1987. Dr *hc* Univ. Carlos III, Madrid, 1993. *Address:* 49 Dukes Avenue, Theydon Bois, Essex CM16 7HQ. *Died 13 April 1996.*

SARGANT, Sir (Henry) Edmund, Kt 1969; President of the Law Society, 1968–69; Partner in Radcliffes and Co., 1930–71, and Senior Partner for twenty years; *b* 24 May 1906; *s* of Rt Hon. Sir Charles Henry Sargant, Lord Justice of Appeal, and Amelia Julia Sargant, RRC; *m* 1st, 1930,

Mary Kathleen Lemmey (*d* 1979); one *s*; 2nd, 1981, Evelyn Noel (*née* Arnold-Wallinger). *Educ:* Rugby School; Trinity College, Cambridge (MA). 3rd Cl. Hons Solicitors' final examination; admitted 1930. Served War of 1939–45 in RAF, Provost and Security Branch (W Africa; Middle East; Acting Wing Comdr). Member Council, Law Society, 1951–75; Chm., Disciplinary Cttee of Architects Registration Council, 1964, 1965, 1966. Master, Worshipful Co. of Merchant Taylors, 1954. *Address:* 902 Keyes House, Dolphin Square, SW1V 3NB. *Club:* United Oxford and Cambridge University.

Died 4 March 1998.

SARGEAUNT, Henry Anthony, CB 1961; OBE 1949; Scientific Consultant, United Nations, New York, 1968–69; *b* 11 June 1907; *o s* of Lt-Col Henry Sargeaunt and Norah Ierne Carden; *m* 1939, Winifred Doris Parkinson; two *s* one *d. Educ:* Clifton Coll.; University Coll., Reading (London Univ.); Cambridge Univ. Rhodes Research Grant, 1939–42; served with HM Forces, 1944–46: France, 1944; Staff Capt. with 21 Army Group, 1944; Supt Operational Research Group (ORG) (W&E), Min. of Supply, 1946; Supt, Army ORG, 1947–50; Dep. Scientific Adviser, 1950–52, Scientific Adviser, to Army Council, 1952–55; Asst Scientific Adviser to Supreme Allied Commander in Europe, 1955–57; Dep. Science Adviser, NATO, 1958–59; re-apptd Scientific Adviser to Army Council, 1959; Dep. Chief Scientist (B), War Office, 1960–62; Chief Scientific Adviser, Home Office, 1962–67. *Recreations:* yachting, horse-racing, bird-watching. *Address:* Coombe Grange, Coombe Lane, Sway, Lymington, Hants SO41 6BP. *T:* (01590) 682519.

Died 8 April 1997.

SARRAUTE, Nathalie; writer; *b* Ivanowo, Russia, 18 July 1900; *d* of Ilya Tcherniak and Pauline (*née* Chatounowski); *m* 1925, Raymond Sarraute (*d* 1985); three *d. Educ:* Sorbonne; Ecole de Droit de Paris; Oxford Univ. Dr *hc:* TCD, 1976; Univ. of Kent at Canterbury, 1980; Oxford Univ., 1991. Grand Prix National, 1982. *Publications:* Tropismes, 1939 (trans. Tropisms, 1964); Portrait d'un inconnu, 1948 (Portrait of a Man Unknown, 1959); Martereau, 1953 (trans. 1964); L'Ere du soupçon, 1956 (The Age of Suspicion, 1964); Le Planétarium, 1959 (The Planetarium, 1962); Les Fruits d'or, 1963 (The Golden Fruits, 1965) (Prix international de Littérature, 1964); Entre la vie et la mort, 1968 (Between Life and Death, 1969); Vous les entendez?, 1972 (Do You Hear Them?, 1973); "disent les imbéciles", 1976 ("fools say", 1977); L'usage de la parole, 1980 (The Use of Speech, 1983); Enfance, 1983 (Childhood, 1984) (Prix Grinzane Cavour, 1984); Tu ne t'aimes pas, 1989 (You Don't Love Yourself, 1990); ICI, 1995; Pléiade, 1996; *plays:* Le Silence, Le Mensonge, 1967 (Silence and The Lie, 1969); Isma, 1970 (Izzum, 1975); C'est beau, 1973 (It is Beautiful, 1978); Elle est là, 1978 (It is There, 1980); Collected Plays, 1981; Pour un oui ou pour un non, 1982; *essays:* Paul Valéry et l'enfant d'éléphant, Flaubert le précurseur, 1986; Ouvrez, 1997. *Address:* 12 avenue Pierre I de Serbie, 75116 Paris, France. *T:* 47205828. *Died 19 Oct. 1999.*

SATCHELL, Edward William John, (Jack), CEng, FIEE; RCNC; Director of Engineering (Ships), 1973–76; *b* 23 Sept. 1916; *s* of Horsey John Robert Satchell and Ethel Satchell (*née* Chandler); *m* 1941, Stella Grace Cook; one *d. Educ:* Esplanade House Sch., Southsea; Royal Dockyard Sch., Portsmouth; RNC, Greenwich. Electrical Apprentice, Portsmouth Dockyard, 1932; Probationary Asst Electrical Engr, 1936; Asst Electrical Engr, 1939; Electrical Engr, 1943; Suptg Electrical Engr, 1955; served with British Naval Mission in USA, 1951–53; Warship Electrical Supt, Scotland, 1958–61; Dep. Admty Repair Manager, Malta, 1961–64; Dep. Elec. Engrg Manager, Devonport, 1964–66; Asst Dir of Electrical Engineering, 1966; Dep.

Dir of Elec. Engrg, 1970; Head of RN Engrng Service, 1973–75; Dep. Head, RCNC (L), 1975–76; retired 1976. *Recreations:* reading, gardening, bird watching. *Address:* 6 Badminton Gardens, Bath BA1 2XS. *T:* (01225) 426974. *Died 26 Nov. 1998.*

SAUNDERS, Basil; public relations consultant; Director, Charles Barker Traverse-Healy (formerly Traverse-Healy & Regester Ltd), 1984–90; *b* 12 Aug. 1925; *s* of late Comdr J. E. Saunders, RN and Marjorie Saunders; *m* 1957, Betty Smith (*d* 1997); two *s* four *d*. *Educ:* Merchant Taylors'; Wadham Coll., Oxford (MA). FIPR. Sub-Lt, RNVR, 1944–46. Assistant d'Anglais, Collège de Tarascon, 1950–51; writer, General Electric Co. (USA), 1952–53; PRO, BIM, 1954–57; Public Relations Exec., Pritchard, Wood and Partners, 1957–63; Head of Public Relations Services, Wellcome Foundn Ltd, 1963–78; Dir-Gen., Aslib, 1978–80; Public Relations Officer, Arts Council, 1981. Consultant, Traverse-Healy Ltd, 1981–84. *Publications:* Crackle of Thorns (verse), 1968; (jtly) Bluff Your Way in PR, 1991; short stories in magazines and on radio; backpagers in Manchester Guardian; reviews, articles, etc. *Recreation:* throwing things away. *Address:* 18 Dartmouth Park Avenue, NW5 1JN. *T:* (0171) 485 4672. *Club:* Savile.   *Died 10 May 1998.*

SAUNDERS, Christopher Thomas, CMG 1953; Fellow, Sussex European Research Centre, since 1973, Hon. Fellow, Science Policy Research Unit, since 1993 (Fellow, 1973–93), University of Sussex; *b* 5 Nov. 1907; *s* of Thomas Beckenn Avening Saunders, clergyman, and Mary Theodora Slater; *m* 1947, Cornelia Jacomijntje Gielstra; one *s*. *Educ:* Craig School, Windermere; St Edward's School; Christ Church, Oxford (BA 1929; MA 1932). Social Survey of Merseyside, Univ. of Liverpool, 1930–33; Economic Research Dept, Univ. of Manchester, 1933–35; Joint Committee of Cotton Trade Organisations, Manchester, 1935–40; Cotton Control, 1940–44; Combined Production and Resources Board, Washington, 1944–45; Min. of Labour, 1945–47; Central Statistical Office, 1947–57; Dir, Nat. Inst. of Econ. and Social Research, 1957–64; Economist, UN Econ. Commn for Europe, 1965–72. *Publications:* (with M. P. Ashley) Red Oxford, 1929; (collaborated in) Social Survey of Merseyside, 1934; Seasonal Variations in Employment, 1936; From Free Trade to Integration?, 1975; Winners and Losers, 1977; Engineering in Britain, West Germany and France, 1978; (with D. Marsden) Pay Inequalities in the European Community, 1981; (ed) The Political Economy of New and Old Industrial Countries, 1981; (ed jtly) Europe's Industries, 1983; (ed) 15 volumes in East-West European Economic Interaction Workshop Papers, 1977–91; articles in Economic Jl, Jl of Royal Statistical Soc., The Manchester School. *Recreations:* walking and other forms of travel, painting. *Address:* Flat 17, 4 Gillsland Road, Edinburgh EH10 5BW. *Club:* Reform. *Died 13 Jan. 2000.*

SAUNDERS, Michael Lawrence, CB 1990; HM Procurator General, Treasury Solicitor and Queen's Proctor, since 1995; *b* 13 April 1944; *s* of Samuel Reuben Saunders and Doris Saunders; *m* 1970, Anna Stobo; one *s* one *d*. *Educ:* Clifton College; Birmingham University (LLB Hons); Jesus College, Cambridge (LLB Hons). Called to the Bar, Gray's Inn, 1971, Bencher, 1995. Third Sec., Hague Conf. on Private Internat. Law (Permt Bureau), 1966–68; Second Sec., 1968–72; Senior Legal Assistant: DTI, 1972–73; Treasury Solicitor's Dept (Energy Branch), 1973–76; Law Officers' Dept, 1976–79; Asst Treasury Solicitor (Cabinet Office European Secretariat Asst Legal Adviser), 1979–83; Asst Legal Sec., 1983–86, Legal Sec., 1986–89, Law Officers' Dept; Solicitor to HM Customs and Excise, 1989–92; Legal Advr to Home Office and NI Office, 1992–95. Hon. QC 1996. *Publications:* contribs to jls on

internat. law. *Address:* Queen Anne's Chambers, 28 Broadway, SW1H 9JS.   *Died 17 Dec. 1996.*

SAUZIER, Sir (André) Guy, Kt 1973; CBE 1959; ED; retired; General Overseas Representative of Mauritius Chamber of Agriculture, 1959–79; Minister Plenipotentiary, Mauritius Mission to EEC, 1972–79; *b* 20 Oct. 1910; *s* of J. Adrien Sauzier, Mauritius; *m* 1936, Thérèse (decd), *d* of Henri Mallac; six *s* two *d*. *Educ:* Royal Coll., Mauritius. Served War of 1939–45; late Major, Mauritius TF. A nominated Member of the Legislative Council, Mauritius, 1949–57; Member, Mauritius Political Delegn to the UK, 1955; Minister of Works and Communications, 1957–59. Represented Mauritius at the Coronation, 1953. *Address:* 15 Marloes Road, W8 6LQ.   *Died 23 Sept. 1998.*

SAVA, George, (**George Alexis Milkomanovich Milkomane**); author and consulting surgeon; *b* 15 Oct. 1903; *s* of Col Ivan Alexandrovitch Bankoff and Countess Maria Ignatiev; *nephew* of Prince Alexander Milkomanovich Milkomane; naturalised British subject in 1938; *m* 1939, Jannette Hollingdale; two *s* two *d*; one *s* by Melanie Lowy. *Educ:* Public Schools in Bulgaria and Russia. Entered Russian Imperial Naval Academy in 1913; after the Revolution studied in various medical schools, Univ. of Paris, Florence, Rome, Munich, Berlin and Bonn; domiciled in UK, 1932–; further medical education at Manchester, Glasgow and Edinburgh; Research scholarships in medicine and surgery, University of Rome, Libero Docente (Professorship) of Univ. of Rome, 1954. Grand Chevalier of the Crown of Bulgaria; Commendatore dell' Ordine al Merito Della Repubblica Italiana, 1961. *Publications: autobiog. medical:* The Healing Knife, 1937; Beauty from the Surgeon's Knife, 1938; A Surgeon's Destiny, 1939; Donkey's Serenade, 1940; Twice the Clock Round, 1941; A Ring at the Door, 1941; Surgeon's Symphony, 1944; They come by Appointment, 1946; The Knife Heals Again, 1948; The Way of a Surgeon, 1949; Strange Cases, 1950; A Doctor's Odyssey, 1951; Patients' Progress, 1952; A Surgeon Remembers, 1953; Surgeon Under Capricorn, 1954; The Lure of Surgery, 1955; A Surgeon at Large, 1957; Surgery and Crime, 1957; All this and Surgery too, 1958; Surgery Holds the Door, 1960; A Surgeon in Rome, 1961; A Surgeon in California, 1962; Appointments in Rome, 1963; A Surgeon in New Zealand, 1964; A Surgeon in Cyprus, 1965; A Surgeon in Australia, 1966; Sex, Surgery, People, 1967; The Gates of Heaven are Narrow, 1968; Bitter-Sweet Surgery, 1969; One Russian's Story, 1970; A Stranger in Harley Street, 1970; A Surgeon and his Knife, 1978; Living with your Psoriasis (essays), 1978; *political and historical books:* Rasputin Speaks, 1941; Valley of Forgotten People, 1942; The Chetniks, 1943; School for War, 1943; They Stayed in London, 1943; Russia Triumphant, 1944; A Tale of Ten Cities, 1944; War Without Guns, 1944; Caught by Revolution, 1952; *novels:* Land Fit for Heroes, 1945; Link of Two Hearts, 1945; Gissy, 1946; Call it Life, 1946; Boy in Samarkand, 1950; Flight from the Palace, 1953; Pursuit in the Desert, 1955; The Emperor Story, 1959; Punishment Deferred, 1966; Man Without Label, 1967; Alias Dr Holtzman, 1968; City of Cain, 1969; The Imperfect Surgeon, 1969; Nothing Sacred, 1970; Of Guilt Possessed, 1970; A Skeleton for My Mate, 1971; The Beloved Nemesis, 1971; On the Wings of Angels, 1972; The Sins of Andrea, 1972; Tell Your Grief Softly, 1972; Cocaine for Breakfast, 1973; Return from the Valley, 1973; Sheilah of Buckleigh Manor, 1974; Every Sweet Hath Its Sour, 1974; The Way of the Healing Knife, 1976; Mary Mary Quite Contrary, 1977; Crusader's Clinic, 1977; Pretty Polly, 1977; No Man is Perfect, 1978; A Stranger in his Skull, 1979; Secret Surgeon, 1979; Crimson Eclipse, 1980; Innocence on Trial, 1981; The Price of Prejudice, 1982; The Killer Microbes, 1982; Betrayal in Style, 1983;

Double Identity, 1984; A Smile Through Tears, 1985; Bill of Indictment, 1986; Rose By Any Other Name, 1987; The Roses Bloom Again, 1988; also wrote numerous novels as George Borodin. *Recreations:* tennis, golf, riding, aviation. *Address:* c/o A. P. Watt Ltd, 20 John Street, WC1N 2DL. *Died 15 March 1996.*

SAWYER, John Stanley, FRS 1962; Director of Research, Meteorological Office, 1965–76; *b* 19 June 1916; *s* of late Arthur Stanley Sawyer and Emily Florence Sawyer (*née* Frost); *m* 1951, Betty Vera Beeching (*née* Tooke), *widow*; one *d. Educ:* Latymer Upper Sch., Hammersmith; Jesus Coll., Cambridge (MA). Entered Meteorological Office, 1937. Mem., NERC, 1975–81. Pres., Commn for Atmospheric Sciences, World Meteorological Organisation, 1968–73 (IMO Prize, 1973); Pres., Royal Meteorological Soc., 1963–65 (Hugh Robert Mill Medal, 1956; Buchan Prize, 1962; Symons Medal, 1971). *Publications:* Ways of the Weather, 1958; scientific papers largely in Qly Jl Royal Met. Soc. *Address:* 16 Tanfield Park, Wickham, Hants PO17 5NP. *T:* (01329) 833409.
Died 19 Sept. 2000.

SAYERS, Maj.-Gen. (Matthew Herbert) Patrick, OBE 1945; MD; FRCPath; Major-General, Army Medical Services (retired); Consulting Pathologist, Employment Medical Advisory Service, Department of Employment and Health and Safety Executive, 1967–75; *b* 17 Jan. 1908; *s* of late Herbert John Ireland Sayers, musician, and Julia Alice Sayers (*née* Tabb), musician; *m* 1935, Moira (*d* 1995), *d* of Robert Dougall; two *s* one *d. Educ:* St Joseph's Coll., SE19; Whitgift School; St Thomas' Hospital, London; MB, BS 1933, MD 1961, London. MRCS, LRCP 1932; FRCPath (FCPath 1964). Commissioned Lieutenant RAMC, 1935; served India and Far East, 1936–46 (despatches, 1946): Asst Dir of Pathology, HQ 14th Army, 1943–44; Dep. Dir of Pathology, Allied Land Forces, SE Asia, 1945; Asst Dir-Gen., War Office, 1948; OC The David Bruce Laboratories, 1949–52 and 1955–61; Asst Dir of Pathology, Middle East Land Forces, 1953–55; Editor, Journal RAMC, 1955–61; Dep. Dir of Pathology, Far East Land Forces, 1961–64; Dir of Army Pathology and Consulting Pathologist to the Army, 1964–67. QHP, 1965–67. Mem., Johnson Socs of London and Lichfield. CStJ 1968. *Publications:* contribs (jtly) to scientific jls on scrub typhus, immunology and industrial medicine. *Recreations:* formerly gardening, music, cricket, field sports. *Address:* Generals Meadow, St Clare Road, Walmer, Kent CT14 7PY. *T:* (01304) 363526. *Clubs:* Army and Navy, MCC. *Died 12 Jan. 2000.*

SCADDING, Prof. John Guyett, MD; FRCP; Emeritus Professor of Medicine in the University of London; Hon. Consulting Physician, Brompton and Hammersmith Hospitals; *b* 30 Aug. 1907; *e s* of John William Scadding and Jessima Alice Guyett; *m* 1940, Mabel Pennington; one *s* two *d. Educ:* Mercers' School; Middlesex Hospital Medical School, University of London (MB, BS 1930; MD 1932 (University Gold Medal)). MRCS, LRCP 1929, MRCP 1932, FRCP 1941. Resident appts, Middx Hosp., Connaught Hosp., Walthamstow, and Brompton Hosp., 1930–35; First Asst, Dept of Med., Brit. Postgrad. Med. Sch., 1935; RAMC, 1940–45 (Lt-Col, O i/c Med. Div.); Phys., Hammersmith Hosp., Royal Postgrad. Med. Sch., 1946–72; Physician, Brompton Hosp., 1939–72; Institute of Diseases of the Chest: Dean, 1946–60; Dir of Studies, 1950–62; Prof. of Medicine, 1962–72. Hon. Cons. in Diseases of the Chest to the Army, 1953–72 (Guthrie Medal, 1973). Visiting Professor: Univ. Oklahoma, 1963; Stanford Univ. and Univ. Colorado, 1965; McMaster Univ., 1973; Univ. Manitoba, 1974; Univ. Chicago, 1976; Dalhousie Univ., 1977. Mem., Central Health Services Council, and Standing Medical Advisory Cttee, 1954–66;

Mem., Clinical Research Board, 1960–65. Royal College of Physicians: Bradshaw Lectr, 1949; Mitchell Lectr, 1960; Tudor Edwards Lectr, 1970; Lumleian Lectr, 1973; Councillor, 1949–52; Censor, 1968–70; Second Vice-Pres., 1971–72; Moxon Medal, 1975. Lettsomian Lectr, Med. Soc. of London, 1955. Editor, Thorax, 1946–59. President: British Tuberculosis Assoc., 1959–61; Section of Medicine, RSM, 1969–71; Thoracic Soc., 1971–72. Fellow: RPMS, 1993; Imperial Coll. Sch. of Medicine, 1999. Dr *hc* Reims, 1978. *Publications:* Sarcoidosis, 1967, 2nd edn 1985; contributions to textbooks, and articles, mainly on respiratory diseases, in medical journals. *Recreations:* music, pottering about. *Address:* 18 Seagrave Road, Beaconsfield, Bucks HP9 1SU. *T:* (01494) 676033. *Club:* Athenæum. *Died 10 Nov. 1999.*

SCARSDALE, 3rd Viscount *cr* 1911; **Francis John Nathaniel Curzon;** Bt (Scot.) 1636, (Eng.) 1641; Baron Scarsdale 1761; late Captain, Scots Guards; *b* 28 July 1924; *o s* of late Hon. Francis Nathaniel Curzon, 3rd *s* of 4th Baron Scarsdale, and Winifred Phyllis (*née* Combe); *S* cousin, 1977; *m* 1st, 1948, Solange (marr. diss. 1967; she *d* 1974), *yr d* of late Oscar Hanse, Mont-sur-Marchienne, Belgium; two *s* one *d*; 2nd, 1968, Helene Gladys Frances, *o d* of late Major William Ferguson Thomson, Kinellar, Aberdeenshire; two *s. Educ:* Eton. *Recreations:* racing, shooting, piping, photography. *Heir: s* Hon. Peter Ghislain Nathaniel Curzon [*b* 6 March 1949; *m* 1983, Mrs Karen Osborne (marr. diss. 1996); one *d*]. *Address:* Kedleston Hall, Derby DE22 5JH. *T:* (01332) 840386; Tullich, Strathcarron, Ross-shire.
Died 2 Aug. 2000.

SCHAPIRO, Meyer; University Professor, Columbia University, 1965–73, then Emeritus Professor; *b* Shavly, Lithuania, 23 Sept. 1904; *s* of Nathan Menahem Schapiro and Fege Edelman; *m* 1928, Dr Lillian Milgram; one *s* one *d. Educ:* Boys' High Sch., Brooklyn; Columbia University. PhD Columbia, 1929. Columbia University: Lectr, Dept of Art History and Archæology, 1928; Asst Prof., 1936; Assoc. Prof., 1948; Prof., 1952; University Prof., 1965. Visiting Lecturer: Institute of Fine Arts, NY University, 1931–36; New School for Social Research, NY, 1938–50; Visiting Professor: Univ. of London, 1947, 1957; Univ. of Jerusalem, 1961; Messenger Lectr, Cornell Univ., 1960; Patten Lectr, Indiana Univ., 1961; Charles Eliot Norton Prof., Harvard Univ., 1966–67; Slade Prof. of Fine Art, Oxford Univ., 1968; Vis. Lectr, Collège de France, 1974. Guggenheim Fellow, 1939, 1943; Fellow: Amer. Acad. of Arts and Sciences, 1952; Inst. for Advanced Study in Behavioral Sciences, Palo Alto, 1962–63; Amer. Philosophical Soc., 1969; Mediaeval Acad., 1970; Amer. Inst. of Arts and Letters, 1976; Corresponding FBA, 1990. Hon. degrees: Columbia Univ.; Harvard Univ.; Yale Univ.; Jewish Theological Seminary, NY; New Sch. for Social Research; Univ. of Hartford. Bd of Editors: Jl of History of Ideas; Semiotica. Distinguished Award, Amer. Council of Learned Socs, 1960; Mitchell Prize, 1979; Aby M. Warburg Prize, Hamburg, 1985. *Publications:* The Romanesque Sculpture of Moissac, 1931; Van Gogh, 1950; Cézanne, 1952; The Parma Ildefonsus, 1964; Words and Pictures, 1973; Selected Papers: vol. I, Romanesque Art, 1976; vol. II, Modern Art, 1978; vol. III, Late Antique, Early Christian and Medieval Art, 1980; Style, Artiste et Société, 1983; articles in collective books and in Art Bulletin, Gazette des Beaux-Arts, Jl Warburg and Courtauld Insts, Jl History of Ideas, Jl Architectural Historians, Kritische Berichte, Amer. Jl Sociology, Partisan Review, Encounter, etc. *Address:* RR1, Box 92, South Londonderry, VT 05155–9601, USA. *Died 3 March 1996.*

SCHAWLOW, Prof. Arthur Leonard, PhD; J. G. Jackson—C. J. Wood Professor of Physics, Stanford

University, 1961–91, then Professor Emeritus; *b* Mt Vernon, New York, 5 May 1921; *s* of Arthur Schawlow and Helen Schawlow (*née* Mason); *m* 1951, Aurelia Keith Townes (*d* 1991); one *s* two *d*. *Educ:* Univ. of Toronto, Canada. BA 1941, MA 1942, PhD 1949. Postdoctoral Fellow and Research Associate, Columbia Univ., 1949–51; Research Physicist, Bell Telephone Laboratories, 1951–61. Visiting Assoc. Prof., Columbia Univ., 1960. Hon. MRIA 1991. Hon. DSc: Ghent, 1968; Bradford, 1970; Alabama, 1984; TCD, 1986; Hon. LLD Toronto, 1970; Hon. DTech Lund, 1988; Hon. DSL Victoria Univ., Toronto, 1993. Ballantine Medal, Franklin Inst., 1962; Liebmann Prize, Inst. of Electrical and Electronic Engrs, 1963; Thomas Young Medal and Prize (GB), 1963; California Scientist of the Year, 1973; Ives Medal, Optical Soc. of America, 1975; Marconi Internat. Fellowship, 1977; (jtly) Nobel Prize in Physics, 1981; Arthur L. Schawlow Medal, Laser Inst. of America, 1982; US Nat. Medal of Science, 1991; Arata Award, High Temperature Soc. of Japan, 1994; Ronald H. Brown Amer. Innovator Award, 1996. *Publications:* (with C. H. Townes) Microwave Spectroscopy, 1955; many contribs to learned journals. *Recreation:* jazz music. *Address:* Department of Physics, Stanford University, Stanford, CA 94305–4060, USA. *T:* (415) 7234356.   *Died 28 April 1999.*

SCHEMBRI, His Honour Carmelo; Chief Justice of Malta and President of the Constitutional Court, Court of Appeal and Court of Criminal Appeal, 1981–87; *b* 2 Sept. 1922; *s* of Joseph Schembri and Lucia (*née* Tabone Adami); *m* 1949, Helen (*née* Holland); six *s* five *d*. *Educ:* The Lyceum, Malta; Royal Univ. of Malta (LLD 1946). Called to the Bar, 1947. Elected Mem., Malta Legislative Assembly (Nationalist Party), 1950; Dep. Speaker and Chm., Cttees until dissolution of Assembly, 1951; returned to Parliament in General Election, 1951 and re-elected Dep. Speaker and Chm. Cttees; Minister of Educn, 1952–53; Asst Crown Counsel and Officer i/c Inland Revenue Dept, Gozo, 1954–62; Magistrate: for Gozo, 1962–68; Malta, 1968–78; Judge of Superior Courts, 1978–81. Coronation Medal 1953. *Recreations:* football, woodwork, collecting match boxes. *Address:* 2 Holland Court, Bisazza Street, Sliema, Malta.

Died 8 Oct. 1997.

SCHERER, Prof. Jacques, DèsL; Professor, University of Paris-III, 1979–83, then Emeritus; *b* 24 Feb. 1912; *s* of Maurice Scherer and Madeleine Franck; *m* 1965, Colette Bié. *Educ:* Ecole Normale Supérieure; Sorbonne Univ., Paris (Agrégé des Lettres, Docteur ès Lettres). Prof. of French Literature, Univ. of Nancy, 1946–54; Prof. of French Literature and Theatre, Sorbonne Univ., 1954–73; Marshal Foch Prof. of French Literature and Fellow of All Souls Coll., Univ. of Oxford, 1973–79. *Publications:* L'expression littéraire dans l'œuvre de Mallarmé, 1947; La dramaturgie classique en France, 1950; La dramaturgie de Beaumarchais, 1954; Le 'Livre' de Mallarmé, 1957, new edn 1977; Structures de Tartuffe, 1966; Sur le Dom Juan de Molière, 1967; Le cardinal et l'orang-outang, essai sur Diderot, 1972; Théâtre du XVIIe siècle, 1975, vols I and II (ed jtly), 1987; Grammaire de Mallarmé, 1977; Racine et/ou la cérémonie, 1982; Le théâtre de Corneille, 1984; Dramaturgies d'Œdipe, 1987; Le théâtre en Afrique noire francophone, 1992; Dramaturgies de vrai-faux, 1994. *Address:* 11 rue de la Colonie, 75013 Paris, France.   *Died 4 June 1997.*

SCHILLING, Prof. Richard Selwyn Francis, CBE 1975; MD, DSc; FRCP, FFPHM, FFOM; DPH; Professor of Occupational Health, London School of Hygiene and Tropical Medicine, University of London, 1960–76, then Emeritus (Hon. Fellow 1979); Director, TUC Centenary Institute of Occupational Health, 1968–76; *b* 9 Jan. 1911; *s* of late George Schilling and Florence Louise Schilling,

Kessingland, Suffolk; *m* 1937, Heather Maude Elinor Norman; one *s* two *d*. *Educ:* Epsom College; St Thomas' Hospital. MD 1947, DPH 1947, DSc 1964, London. FRCP 1962; FFOM 1980; FFPHM 1990. Served War of 1939–45, Captain RAMC, France and Belgium, 1939–40. Obstetric House Physician, St Thomas' Hosp., 1935; House Physician, Addenbrooke's Hosp., Cambridge, 1936; Asst Industrial MO, ICI (Metals) Ltd, Birmingham, 1937; Medical Inspector of Factories, 1939–42; Sec. Industrial Health Research Board of Med. Research Council, 1942–46; Nuffield Fellow in Industrial Health, 1946–47; Reader in Occupational Health, Univ. of Manchester, 1947–56; WHO Consultant, 1956–69. Lectures: Milroy, RCP, 1956; Mackenzie, BMA, 1956; Cantor, RSA, 1963; C.-E. A. Winslow, Yale Univ., 1963; Ernestine Henry, RCP, 1970. Former Vice-Pres., Perm. Commn, Internat. Assoc. Occupational Health. Former President: Assoc. of Industrial Medical Officers; British Occupational Hygiene Soc.; Occup. Med. Sect. of Royal Soc. Med. Member: Committee of Inquiry into Trawler Safety, 1968; Royal Commn on Civil Liability and Compensation for Personal Injury, 1973–78. Hon. Mem., Amer. Occupational Med. Assoc., 1986. Hon. FRSocMed 1976; Hon. DIH, Soc. of Apothecaries, 1988; Hon. FFOMI 1990; Hon. Fellow, UMDS, 1994. *Publications:* (ed) Modern Trends in Occupational Health, 1960; (ed) Occupational Health Practice, 1973, 2nd edn 1981; original papers on byssinosis (respiratory disease of textile workers) and other subjects in occupational health in BMJ, Lancet, Brit. Jl of Industrial Medicine, and foreign journals. *Recreation:* fishing. *Address:* 11c Prior Bolton Street, N1 2NX. *T:* (0171) 359 1627.   *Died 30 Sept. 1997.*

SCHNITTKE, Alfred Garriyevich; composer; *b* Engels, Saratov Region, Russia, 24 Nov. 1934; *s* of Harry Schnittke and Maria Vogel; *m* 1st, 1956, Galina Koltsina (marr. diss. 1958); 2nd, 1961, Irina Katnycva; one *s*, *Edut*, Moscow Conservatory. Teacher of Instrumentation, polyphony and composition, Moscow Conservatory, 1961–71; teacher, Hochschule for Music and the Arts, Hamburg, 1989–. Member: Russian Composers' Union; Film Makers' Union; W Berlin Acad. of Fine Arts; Royal Swedish Music Acad.; Corresp. Mem., Bavarian Acad. of Fine Arts; Hon. Mem., Hamburg Acad. of Fine Arts. State Prize, RSFSR, 1986. Compositions include: 8 symphonies, 4 violin concertos, 5 concerti grossi, 2 concertos for viola and orchestra, 2 concertos for 'cello and orchestra; Peer Gynt (ballet); Life with an Idiot (opera); choral music, chamber music, film and theatre music. *Publications:* musicological articles. *Address:* Beim Andreasbrunnen 5, Hamburg, Germany; Vavilova 48, Apt 419, 117333 Moscow, Russia.   *Died 3 Aug. 1998.*

SCHOFIELD, Bertram, CBE 1959; MA, PhD, LittD; Keeper of Manuscripts and Egerton Librarian, British Museum, 1956–61; *b* 13 June 1896; *s* of George Craven Schofield, Southport; *m* 1928, Edith (*d* 1981), *d* of Arthur William and Edith Emily Thomas; one *s* two *d*. *Educ:* University Sch., Southport; University of Liverpool (Charles Beard and University Fellow); Sorbonne, Ecole des Chartes and Ecole des Hautes Etudes, Paris; Emmanuel College, Cambridge (Open Research Student). Served European War, with Royal Wilts Yeomanry, 1917–19; seconded to Min. of Economic Warfare, 1940–42, and for special duties with Inter-Services Intelligence and Combined Ops, HQ, 1942–44. Asst Keeper, Dept of MSS, British Museum, 1922; Deputy-Keeper, 1947; Keeper, 1956. Member: Bd of Studies in Palæography, University of London; Committee of Inst. of Historical Research, 1951–61; Council of Royal Historical Society, 1956–59; Canterbury and York Society; Vice-Pres. British Records Assoc., 1956–61; Governor, North London Collegiate School and Camden High Sch. for Girls, 1955–64. *Publications:* Muchelney Memoranda (Somerset Record

Soc.), 1927; (with A. J. Collins) Legal and Manorial Formularies, 1933; The Knyvett Letters, 1949; (contrib.) Studies presented to Sir Hilary Jenkinson, 1957; contrib. to Musical Quarterly, Music Review, Music and Letters. British Museum Quarterly, Musik in Geschichte und Gegenwart, etc. *Recreations:* gardening, music. *Address:* c/o 19 Apsley Road, Oxford OX2 7QX. *T:* (01865) 557532. *Died 15 May 1998.*

SCHOLES, Alwyn Denton; Senior Puisne Judge, Hong Kong, 1970–71 (Acting Chief Justice, 1970); *b* 16 Dec. 1910; *s* of Denton Scholes and Mrs Scholes (*née* Birch); *m* 1939, Juliet Angela Ierne Pyne; one *s* four *d. Educ:* Cheltenham College; Selwyn College, Cambridge. Legal Tripos Parts I and II, Cantab, 1932, 1933; MA 1933. Called to the Bar, 1934; practised at the Bar in London and on Midland Circuit, 1934–38; apptd District Magistrate, Gold Coast, 1938; Acting Crown Counsel and Solicitor General, Gold Coast, 1941; apptd Magistrate, Hong Kong, 1948; First Magistrate: Kowloon, 1949; Hong Kong, 1949; appointed District Judge, Hong Kong, 1953, Puisne Judge, Hong Kong, 1958; Comr, Supreme Ct of State of Brunei, 1964–67, 1968–71. Pres. or Mem., Hong Kong Full Ct of Appeal, on occasions, 1949–71. Member: Sidmouth Parochial Church Council, 1972–82; Ottery Deanery Synod, 1973–82. Governor, St Nicholas Sch., Sidmouth, 1984–89. *Recreations:* walking, gardening. *Address:* West Hayes, Convent Road, Sidmouth, Devon EX10 8RL. *Club:* Royal Commonwealth Society.
Died 9 Jan. 1997.

SCHULTZ, Prof. Theodore William, PhD; Charles L. Hutchinson Distinguished Service Professor of Economics, University of Chicago, 1952–72, then Emeritus; *b* 30 April 1902; *s* of Henry E. Schultz and Anna Elizabeth Weiss; *m* Esther Florence Werth; one *s* two *d. Educ:* South Dakota State Coll. (BS); Univ. of Wisconsin (MS, PhD). Iowa State College: Faculty of Economics, 1930–43; Head, Dept of Economics and Sociology, 1934–43; University of Chicago: Prof. of Economics, from 1943; Chairman, Dept of Economics, 1946–61. Hon. LLD: Grinnell Coll., 1949; Michigan State, 1962; Illinois, 1968; Wisconsin, 1968; Catholic Univ. of Chile, 1979; Dijon, 1981; N Carolina State Univ., 1984. Francis A. Walker Medal, Amer. Econ. Assoc., 1972; Leonard Elmhirst Medal, Internat. Agricl Econ. Assoc., 1976; Nobel Prize for Economic Science, 1979. *Publications:* Redirecting Farm Policy, 1943; Agriculture in an Unstable Economy, 1945; The Economic Organization of Agriculture, 1953; The Economic Value of Education, 1963; Transforming Traditional Agriculture, 1964; Economic Growth and Agriculture, 1968; Investment in Human Capital: role of education and research, 1971; Human Resources: policy issues and research opportunities, 1972; (ed) Distortions of Agricultural Incentives, 1978; Investing in People: the economics of population quality, 1981; Restoring Economic Equilibrium: human capital in the modernizing economy, 1990; The Economics of Being Poor, 1993; Origins of Increasing Returns, 1993. *Address:* 5620 South Kimbark Avenue, Chicago, IL 60637, USA. *T:* (312) 4936083. *Died 26 Feb. 1998.*

SCHUMANN, Maurice, Hon. GCMG 1972; Chevalier de la Légion d'Honneur; Compagnon de la Libération; Croix de Guerre (1939–45); Senator from the Department of the Nord, since 1974; Vice-President of the Senate, 1977–92; Member, Académie Française, since 1974; writer and broadcaster; *b* Paris, 10 April 1911; *s* of Julien Schumann and Thérèse Michel; *m* 1944, Lucie Daniel; three *d. Educ:* Lycées of Janson-de-Sailly and Henry IV; Faculty of Letters, Univ. of Paris (Licencié ès Lettres). Attached to l'Agence Havas in London and later Paris, 1935–39; Chief Official Broadcaster, BBC French Service, 1940–44;

Liaison Officer with Allied Expeditionary Forces at end of war; Mem. Provisional Consultative Assembly, Nov. 1944–July 1945; Deputy for Nord, 1945–67 and 1968–73; Mem. Constituent Assemblies, Oct. 1945–May 1946 and June-Nov. 1946. Chm., Popular Republican Movement (MRP); Deputy of this group, 1945–73 (Pres., 1945–49; Hon. Pres., 1949–); Dep. Minister for Foreign Affairs, 1951–54; Pres., For. Affairs Cttee of Nat. Assembly, 1959; Minister of State (Prime Minister's Office), April-May 1962; Minister of State, in charge of scientific res. and atomic and spacial questions, 1967–68; Minister of State for Social Affairs, 1968–69; Minister for Foreign Affairs, 1969–73. Chm., Commn on Cultural Affairs, 1986–. Has been Pres. of various organisations, incl. Internat. Movement for Atlantic Union, 1966–. Associate Prof., Faculté Catholique de Lille, 1975–. Pres., Assoc. des Ecrivains catholiques, 1980–. Mem. Editl Bd, Le Revue des Deux Mondes, 1984–. Hon. LLD: Cantab, 1972; St Andrews, 1974; Hon. Dr Oxon, 1972. *Publications:* Le Germanisme en marche, 1938; Mussolini, 1939; Les problèmes Ukrainiens et la paix européenne, 1939; Honneur et Patrie, 1945; Le vrai malaise des intellectuels de gauche, 1957; La Mort née de leur propre vie: essai sur Péguy, Simone Weil et Gandhi, 1974; Un Certain 18 Juin, 1980 (Prix Aujourd'hui); Qui a tué le duc d'Enghien?, 1984; Une grande Imprudence, 1986; *novels:* Le Rendezvous avec quelqu'un, 1962; Les Flots roulant au loin, 1973; La Communication, 1974; Angoisse et Certitude, 1978 (Grand Prix de Littérature Catholique); Le Concerto en Ut Majeur, 1982; La victoire et la nuit, 1989; Bergson où le retour de Dieu, 1995; chapters in: Mazarin, 1960; Talleyrand, 1962; Clemenceau, 1974; many articles etc (under pseudonym of André Sidobre) to L'Aube (Paris daily), Le Temps présent and La Vie catholique, etc. *Address:* 53 avenue du Maréchal-Lyautey, Paris 16e, France. *Died 10 Feb. 1998.*

SCHUSTER, Sir (Felix) James (Moncrieff), 3rd Bt *cr* 1906, of Collingham Road, Royal Borough of Kensington; OBE 1955; TD; Senior Partner, Sheppards and Chase, 1970–75, retired; *b* 8 Jan. 1913; *o s* of Sir Victor Schuster, 2nd Bt, and Lucy, *d* of W. B. Skene, Pitlour-Halyards, Fife; *S* father, 1962; *m* 1937, Ragna (*d* 1995), *er d* of late Direktor Ole Sundø, Copenhagen; two *d. Educ:* Winchester. Served War of 1939–45, with The Rifle Brigade (Middle East and Combined Operations); Lt-Col comdg London Rifle Brigade Rangers (RB), TA, 1952; Bt-Colonel, 1955. Hon. Col, 5th Bn Royal Green Jackets, 1970–75. *Heir:* none. *Address:* Piltdown Cottage, Piltdown, Uckfield, East Sussex TN22 3XB. *T:* Newick (01825) 722916. *Clubs:* Naval and Military, Lansdowne.
Died 12 March 1996 (ext).

SCIAMA, Prof. Dennis William Siahou, PhD; FRS 1983; Professor of Astrophysics, International School of Advanced Studies, Trieste, since 1983; Consultant, International Centre for Theoretical Physics, Trieste, since 1983; *b* 18 Nov. 1926; *s* of Abraham and Nelly Sciama; *m* 1959, Lidia Dina; two *d. Educ:* Malvern Coll.; Trinity Coll., Cambridge (MA, PhD). Fellow, Trinity Coll., Cambridge, 1952–56; Mem., Inst. for Advanced Study, Princeton, 1954–55; Agassiz Fellow, Harvard Univ., 1955–56; Res. Associate, KCL, 1958–60; Lectr in Maths, 1961–70, and Fellow of Peterhouse, 1963–70, Cambridge Univ.; Sen. Res. Fellow, 1970–85, Emeritus Fellow, 1985–, All Souls Coll., Oxford; Extraordinary Fellow, Churchill Coll., Cambridge, 1986–94. Vis. Prof., Cornell Univ., 1960–61; Luce Prof., Mount Holyoke Coll., 1977–78; Prof. of Physics, Univ. of Texas at Austin, 1978–83. Foreign Member: Amer. Philosophical Soc., 1981; Amer. Acad. of Arts and Scis, 1982; Accademia Nazionale dei Lincei, 1984. Guthrie Medal, Inst. of Physics, 1991. *Publications:* The Unity of the Universe, 1959; The Physical Foundations of General Relativity,

1969; Modern Cosmology, 1971, 2nd edn 1975; Modern Cosmology and the Dark Matter Problem, 1993; contribs to physics and astronomy jls. *Address:* 7 Park Town, Oxford OX2 6SN. *T:* (01865) 559441.

Died 19 Dec. 1999.

SCOPES, Sir Leonard Arthur, KCVO 1961; CMG 1957; OBE 1946; HM Diplomatic Service, retired; *b* 19 March 1912; *s* of late Arthur Edward Scopes and Jessie Russell Hendry; *m* 1938, Brunhilde Slater Rolfe; two *s* two *d*. *Educ:* St Dunstan's College; Gonville and Caius College, Cambridge (MA). Joined HM Consular Service, 1933; Vice-Consul: Antwerp, 1933; Saigon, 1935; Canton, 1937; Acting Consul, Surabaya, 1941; Vice-Consul, Lourenço Marques, 1942; Consul, Skoplje and Ljubljana, 1945; Commercial Secretary, Bogotà, 1947; Assistant in United Nations (Economic and Social) Department of Foreign Office, 1950; Counsellor, Djakarta, 1952; Foreign Service Inspector, 1954; Ambassador to Nepal, 1957–62; Ambassador to Paraguay, 1962–67; Mem., UN Jt Inspection Unit, Geneva, 1968–71. *Recreation:* retirement. *Address:* 2 Whaddon Hall Mews, Milton Keynes, Bucks MK17 0NA. *Died 30 June 1997.*

SCOTT, David; *b* 6 Sept. 1916; *er s* of Sir Basil Scott and late Gertrude, MBE, 2nd *d* of Henry Villiers Stuart, Dromana, sometime MP for Co. Waterford; *m* 1951, Hester Mary, MA, *y d* of late Gilbert Ogilvy Winton and Pencaitland; one *s* three *d*. *Educ:* Stowe; New College, Oxford (MA). War Service 1939–45: Argyll and Sutherland Highlanders (SR), Reconnaissance Corps and Highland Light Infantry; T/Capt., 1941; Asst to Political Adviser for Khuzistan, Iran, 1944; Actg Vice Consul, Ahwaz, 1944–45. Clerk, House of Commons, 1946; Deputy Principal Clerk, 1962; Clerk of Standing Cttees, 1966–70; Clerk of Select Cttees, 1970–73, Clerk of Private Bills, an Examiner of Petitions for Private Bills and Taxing Officer, House of Commons, 1974–77; retired 1977. Mem., Cttee on Canons, General Synod, Scottish Episcopal Church, 1983–91. *Recreation:* fishing. *Address:* 6a Stafford House, Maida Avenue, W2 1TE. *T:* 0171–723 8398; Glenaros, Aros, Isle of Mull PA72 6JP. *T:* Aros (01680) 300337. *Died 5 March 1996.*

SCOTT, Ven. David; Archdeacon of Stow, 1975–89; Chaplain to the Queen, 1983–94; *b* 19 June 1924; *m* Christine; one *s* one *d*. *Educ:* Trinity Hall, Cambridge (BA 1950; MA 1954); Cuddesdon Theological College. Deacon 1952, priest 1953, dio. Portsmouth; Curate of St Mark, Portsea, 1952–58; Asst Chaplain, Univ. of London, 1958–59; PC, Old Brumby, 1959–66; Vicar of Boston, Lincs, 1966–75; Rural Dean of Holland East, 1971–75; Surrogate, 1972–75; Vicar of Hackthorn with Cold Hanworth, 1975–89; Priest-in-Charge of North and South Carlton, 1978–89; Canon and Prebendary of Lincoln Cathedral, 1971–89. Mem. Gen. Synod, 1978–80, 1983–85, 1985–89. *Address:* 4 Honing Drive, Southwell, Notts NG25 0LB. *T:* Southwell (01636) 813900.

Died 31 Aug. 1996.

SCOTT, Donald; *see* Scott, W. D.

SCOTT, Hardiman; *see* Scott, P. H.

SCOTT, Jack Hardiman; *see* Scott, P. H.

SCOTT, Prof. James Alexander, CBE 1986; Regional Medical Officer, Trent Regional Health Authority, 1973–88, retired; Special Professor of Health Care Planning, Nottingham University, since 1974; Professor Associate in Health Service Planning, Department of Community Medicine, Sheffield University, since 1988; *b* 3 July 1931; *s* of Thomas Scott, MA Oxon and Margaret L. Scott; *m* 1957, Margaret Olive Slinger, BA, SRN; one *s* two *d*. *Educ:* Doncaster Grammar Sch.; Trinity Coll., Dublin Univ. BA 1953; MB, BCh, BAO 1955; MA, MD

1965; FFCM 1974; FRCP 1985. Pathologist, Sir Patrick Dun's Hosp., Dublin, 1957–59; Registrar in Clinical Pathology, United Sheffield Hosps, 1959–61; Trainee, later Asst and Principal Asst Sen. MO, Sheffield RHB, 1961–70; Sen. Lectr in Community Medicine, Nottingham Univ., 1967–71; Sen. Admin. MO, Sheffield RHB, 1971–73. Chm., English Regional MOs Gp, 1978–80; Pres., Hospital Cttee, EEC, 1980–86. Member: Health Services Res. Cttee, MRC, 1986–88; Nat. Cttee for Review of Blood Transfusion Service, 1986–87; Chm., Med. Adv. Cttee, Family Health Services Appeal Unit, 1992–94. Treas., Fac. of Community Medicine, RCP, 1984–86. Chm., Bd of Govs, Mid-Trent Coll. of Nursing and Midwifery, 1989–95. Masur Fellow, Nuffield Provincial Hospitals Trust, 1983. QHP, 1980–83. Hon. LLD Sheffield, 1983. *Publications:* contrib. Lancet. *Recreation:* stamp collecting. *Address:* 5 Slayleigh Lane, Sheffield S10 3RE. *T:* (0114) 230 2238; La Gardelle, 24260 Le Bugue, Dordogne, France. *Died 7 May 1997.*

SCOTT, (Peter) Hardiman, OBE 1989; Chief Assistant to Director General BBC, 1975–80; *b* King's Lynn, 2 April 1920; named Jack Hardiman Scott at birth; *s* of Thomas Hardiman Scott and Dorothy Constance Smith; *m* 1st, 1942, Sheilah Stewart Roberts (marr. diss.); two *s*; 2nd, Patricia Mary, (Sue), Windle. *Educ:* Grammar Sch.; privately. Northampton Chronicle and Echo series, 1939; then various provincial newspapers; Associated Press, and finally Hants and Sussex News, when began freelance broadcasting, 1948; joined BBC; Asst News Editor Midland Region, 1950; gen. reporting staff, London, 1954; various foreign assignments, incl. Suez war; BBC's first Polit. Corresp., 1960; subseq. first Polit. Editor until 1975. Member: Study Gp on Future of Broadcasting in Zimbabwe, 1980; Broadcasting Complaints Commn, 1981–89. Pres., Suffolk Poetry Soc., 1979–99. *Publications:* Secret Sussex, 1949; (ed) How Shall I Vote?, 1976; Many a Summer, 1991; *poems:* Adam and Eve and Us, 1946; When the Words are Gone, 1972; Part of Silence, 1984; (ed) Selected Poems of Sir Thomas Wyatt, 1996; Where Shadows Fall, 1998; *novels:* Within the Centre, 1946; The Lonely River, 1950; Text for Murder, 1951; Operation 10, 1982; No Exit, 1984; Deadly Nature, 1985; (with Becky Allan) Bait of Lies, 1986; contribs to: TV and Elections, 1977; BBC Guide to Parliament, 1979; Politics and the Media, 1980. *Recreations:* poetry, paintings, listening to music, conservation, East Anglia. *Address:* 4 Butchers Lane, Boxford, Sudbury, Suffolk CO10 5DZ. *T:* (01787) 210320. *Died 15 Sept. 1999.*

SCOTT, Robert, CBE 1976; Director, Wolverhampton Polytechnic, 1969–77, retired; *b* 7 July 1913; 2nd *s* of H. Scott, Westhoughton, Bolton; *m* 1940, Dorothy M. Howell, Westhoughton; one *s* one *d*. *Educ:* Hindley and Abram Grammar Sch., Lancs; Univ. of Liverpool; St John's Coll., Cambridge (Wrangler; MA). BSc 1st cl. hons 1934, DipEd 1937, Liverpool; BA Cantab, 1936. Asst Master, Newton-le-Willows Grammar Sch., 1937–41; Army and WO Staff, 1941–46; Scientific Civil Service at RMCS Shrivenham, 1946–54; Vice-Principal, Bolton Techn. Coll., 1954–57; Principal, Wolverhampton and Staffs Coll. of Technology, 1958–69. *Recreations:* motoring, reading. *Address:* 25 Market Road, Battle, E Sussex TN33 0XA. *T:* (01424) 774328. *Died 22 Feb. 1996.*

SCOTT, Robin; *see* Scutt, R. H.

SCOTT, Ronald, OBE 1981; musician; *b* 28 Jan. 1927; *s* of Joseph Schatt, (Jock Scott), and Sylvia Rosenbloom; one *s* one *d*. *Educ:* Jews' Infant Sch., Aldgate, E1; Benthal Road Elementary Sch., N16; Central Foundation Sch., Cowper St, E1. Musician (Tenor Saxophone), 1943–. Opened Ronnie Scott's Club, 1959 (Director, with Pete King); opened second Ronnie Scott's Club, Birmingham,

1991. *Publication:* (with Michael Hennessey) Some of My Best Friends are Blues, 1979; *relevant publication:* Let's Join Hands and Contact the Living (biography), by John Fordham, 1989. *Recreation:* motor sport. *Address:* 47 Frith Street, W1V 5TE. *T:* (0171) 439 0747. *Club:* just his own. *Died 23 Dec. 1996.*

SCOTT, William Clifford Munro, MD; Consulting Psychiatrist, Montreal Children's Hospital, and Montreal General Hospital; *b* 11 March 1903; *o s* of late Rev. Robert Smyth Scott and Katherine Munro Hopper; *m* 1934, Emmy Luise (marr. diss.), *er d* of late Hugo Böcking; two *s*; *m* 1970, Evelyn Freeman Fitch. *Educ:* Parkdale Collegiate, Toronto; University of Toronto. BSc (Med.), MD (Tor.), DPM (London), LMSSA. James H. Richardson Fellow, Department of Anat., 1922–24; Lectr in Anat. and Physiol., Margaret Eaton Sch. of Phys. Educ., Toronto, 1923–25; Post-Grad. Educ. in Psychiatry: Johns Hopkins Med. Sch., 1928–29; Boston Psychopathic Hosp., Harvard Univ. Med. Sch., 1929–30; Commonwealth Fund Fellow, Dept of Psychiatry, Harvard Univ., 1930–33; studied at Nat. Hosp., Queen Sq., London, 1931–32, and at Inst of Psycho-Analysis, London, 1931–33. Staff positions Maudsley Hosp., 1933–35, Cassel Hosp., 1935–38; private practice, 1938–. EMS Psychiatrist, Min. of Health, London, Sheffield and S Wales, 1939–46; Psychiatric Cons. to St Dunstan's, 1945. Mem. Cttee of Management, Inst. of Psychiatry (Univ. of London), 1951–53; Med. Dir London Clinic of Psycho-Analysis, 1947–53; Senior Psychotherapist, Bethlem Royal Hosp. and Maudsley Hosp., 1948–54; Teacher Inst. of Psychiatry (Univ. of London), 1948–54; Associate Professor in charge of Training in Psycho-Analysis, Department of Psychiatry, McGill University, Montreal, 1954–59; Post-Grad. Teacher (Psychiatry and Psycho-Analysis), 1945. Chm. Psychotherapy and Social Psychiatry Section, Roy. Medico-Psychological Assoc., 1952–54; Pres. Brit. Psycho-Analytical Soc., 1953–54; Mem. Bd Dirs, Inst. of Psycho-Analysis, 1947–54 (Chm. 1954); Director of Canadian Inst. of Psycho-Analysis, 1965–67. FRCPsych; FBPsS; ex-Chm. Med. Sect. and Mem. Council, Brit. Psychological Soc.; ex-Mem. Cttee Sect. Psychiatry; Roy. Soc. Med.; Amer. Psychiatric Assoc.; Vice-Pres., Psychiatric Sect., BMA, 1952 and 1955; ex-Asst Ed. Internat. Jl Psycho-Analysis; ex-Asst Ed., Brit. Jl Med. Psychology. Mem., Montreal AAA. *Publications:* chiefly in Brit. Jl of Med. Psychol. and Internat. Jl of Psycho-Analysis. *Recreations:* people, books. *Address:* 488 Mount Pleasant, Westmount, Quebec H3Y 3H3, Canada. *Died 19 Jan. 1997.*

SCOTT, (William) Donald, CBE 1968; MA (Oxon); BSc (Yale); *b* 22 May 1903; *s* of late Reverend William Scott and Sara Jane (*née* Platt); *m* 1928, Muriel Barbara, *d* of late Louis F. Rothschild, NYC; two *s* one *d. Educ:* Taunton Sch., Taunton; University College, Oxford (open scholar); Yale University, USA (Henry P. Davison Scholar). Hercules Powder Co., USA and Rotterdam, 1926–28; British Paint & Lacquer Co., Cowley, Oxford, 1928–35; ICI Ltd: Nobel Div., 1935–41; Dyestuffs Div., 1941–43; Southern Sales Region, Dep. Regional Manager, 1943–45; Regional Manager, 1945–51; Billingham Div., Jt Man. Dir, 1951–55; Main Board Director, 1954–65, Director, 1952–60, and Chairman, 1956–60, Scottish Agricultural Industries Ltd; Dir, Canadian Industries Ltd, 1957–62. Chm., Home Grown Cereals Authority, 1965–68; Director: Glaxo Group Ltd, 1965–68; Laporte Industries Ltd, 1965–68. Mem., Western Hemisphere Exports Council, 1961–64. FRSA 1968. *Recreations:* cricket, golf. *Address:* 42 Cumberland Terrace, Regent's Park, NW1 4HP. *Died 2 Aug. 1996.*

SCOTT, Rev. William G.; *see* Gardiner-Scott.

SCOTT ELLIOT, Maj.-Gen. James, CB 1954; CBE 1945 (OBE 1940); DSO 1943, Bar 1944; HM Lieutenant of the County of Dumfries, 1962–67; *b* 6 Nov. 1902; *s* of late Lt-Col W. Scott Elliot, DSO and Marie Theresa Scott Elliot (*née* Lyon); *m* 1st, 1932, Cecil Margaret Du Buisson; one *s* two *d*; 2nd, 1971, Mrs Fay Courtauld. *Educ:* Wellington College; Sandhurst. 2nd Lieut KOSB, 1923; Capt. Argyll and Sutherland Highlanders, 1936; psc 1937–38; served in Egypt, China, India, Malta, Palestine; War of 1939–45: France, N Africa, Sicily, Italy; Major, 1940; Temp. Lt-Col 1941; Temp. Brig. 1944; despatches, 1945; Germany, 1946–47; War Office, 1948–49; Maj.-Gen., 1954; GOC 51st (Highland) Division and Highland Dist, 1952–56; retd, 1956. Colonel King's Own Scottish Borderers, 1954–61. Mem. (Ind.) for Caerlaverock, Dumfriesshire CC, 1958–67. President: Dumfries and Galloway Natural History and Antiquarian Soc., 1962–65; Soc. of Antiquaries of Scotland, 1965–67; Brit. Soc. of Dowsers, 1966–75. *Publication:* Dowsing One Man's Way, 1977. *Address:* 14 King Street, Emsworth, Hants PO10 7AZ. *T:* Emsworth (01243) 372401. *Died 12 Sept. 1996.*

SCOTT-MALDEN, Air Vice-Marshal (Francis) David (Stephen), DSO 1942; DFC 1941; RAF, retired; *b* 26 Dec. 1919; *s* of late Gilbert Scott Scott-Malden and Phyllis Dorothy Wilkinson; *m* 1955, Anne Elizabeth Watson; two *s* two *d. Educ:* Winchester Coll. (Scholar; Goddard Scholar, 1938); King's Coll., Cambridge (Scholar, Sir William Browne Medal for Greek Verse, 1939). Joined Cambridge University Air Squadron, Nov. 1938; called up into RAFVR as Pilot Officer, Oct. 1939; flying on operations, 1940–42, as Pilot Officer, Flight Lt, Squadron Leader, and Wing Comdr (DFC and Bar, DSO, Norwegian War Cross); visited International Youth Assembly at Washington, DC, as rep. of English Universities, and toured USA as member of United Nations delegation, Sept.-Nov. 1942; RAF Selection Board (Dep. Pres.), 1946; on staff of RAF College, 1946–48; Central Fighter Establishment, 1948; RAF Staff Coll., Bracknell, 1951; psa; RAF Flying Coll., 1954–55; pfc; Jt Planning Staff, Min. of Defence, 1955–57; Group Capt. 1958; Imperial Defence College, 1957–59; idc; Dep. Dir Plans, Air Ministry, 1959–61; Air Cdre 1962; ACAS (Policy), 1965–66; Air Vice-Marshal, 1965. Comdr, Order of Orange Nassau (Netherlands), 1945. Department of Transport, 1966–78. *Recreation:* fishing. *Address:* Wiggons Farm, Helions Bumpstead, Haverhill, Suffolk CB9 7AD. *T:* (01440) 730697. *Died 2 March 2000.*

SCOTT-MONCRIEFF, William; Under-Secretary for Finance (Health), Department of Health and Social Security, 1977–82; *b* 22 Aug. 1922; *s* of Major R. Scott-Moncrieff and Mrs R. Scott-Moncrieff; *m* 1950, Dora Rosemary Knollys; two *d. Educ:* Trinity Coll., Glenalmond; Emmanuel Coll., Cambridge (BA Mech. Sciences). Served RE, 1941–65 (Lt-Col); DHSS (formerly Min. of Social Security), 1965–82. *Recreation:* fishing. *Address:* Combe Cottage, Chiddingfold, Surrey GU8 4XL. *T:* (01428) 682937. *Died 29 Aug. 1997.*

SCRIVENOR, Sir Thomas (Vaisey), Kt 1960; CMG 1956; *b* 28 Aug. 1908; *e s* of late John Brooke Scrivenor, ISO, formerly Dir of Geological Survey, Malaya; *m* 1934, Mary Elizabeth Neatby; one *s* three *d. Educ:* King's School, Canterbury; Oriel College, Oxford (MA). Temp. Assistant Principal, Colonial Office, 1930–33; Assistant District Officer, Tanganyika, 1934–37; Assistant District Commissioner, Palestine, 1937–43; Assistant Lt-Governor, Malta, 1943–44; Principal, Colonial Office, 1944–46; Principal Asst Sec., Palestine, 1946–48; Civil Service Comr, Nigeria, 1948–53; Deputy High Commissioner for Basutoland, the Bechuanaland

Protectorate, and Swaziland, 1953–60, Sec. to Exec. Council of Commonwealth Agricl Bureaux, 1961–73. *Address:* The Old Prebendal House, Shipton under Wychwood, Oxon OX7 6BQ. *T:* (01993) 831888.
Died 20 Dec. 1998.

SCUSE, Dennis George, MBE 1957; TD 1946; Managing Director, Dennis Scuse Ltd, PR Consultants in Radio and TV, 1976–87; *b* 19 May 1921; *yr s* of late Charles H. and Katherine Scuse; *m* 1948, Joyce Evelyn, *yr d* of late Frank and Frances Burt; one *s*. *Educ:* Park Sch., Ilford; Mercers' Sch., London. Joined Martins Bank, 1937. TA (RA), 1938; mobilised, Sept. 1939; served War, commissioned 78th (HAA) Regt, RA, 1940; Air Defence of Gt Britain, 1940–41; Command Entertainment Officer, Ceylon Army Comd, 1942; subseq. 65th (HAA) Regt, in MELF and CMF, 1943–44; joined Army Broadcasting Service, CMF: commanded stations in Bari, Rome and Athens, 1945–46; demobilised, Sept. 1946; joined Overseas Div. BBC and seconded to War Office for Forces Broadcasting Service in Benghasi and Canal Zone; Chief Programme Officer, 1947–48; Asst Dir, British Forces Network, Germany, 1949–50; Dir, 1950–57; introduced "Two-Way Family Favourites", 1952–57; Sen. Planning Asst, BBC-TV, 1958–59; Chief Asst (Light Entertainment), BBC-TV, 1960; Chief Asst (TV), BBC New York Office, Sept. 1960; BBC Rep. in USA, July 1962; Gen. Manager, BBC-TV Enterprises, 1963–72, and BBC Radio Enterprises, 1968–72; Trident Management Ltd, 1972; Man. Dir, Trident Internat. TV Enterprises Ltd, 1972–76. Consultant, Hanson Trust, 1984–89. *Publications:* numerous articles on broadcasting, television programme exports, etc. *Recreations:* journalism, watching television. *Address:* 2 York House, Courtlands, Sheen Road, Richmond, Surrey TW10 5BD. *T:* (0181) 948 4737. *Club:* Royal Greenjackets. *Died 30 April 1998.*

SCUTT, Robin Hugh, (Robin Scott), CBE 1976; television producer; Member: International Council, Monte Carlo Television Festival, 1989–97; Programme Advisory Committee, London Weekend Television, 1990–94; *b* Sandgate, Kent, 24 Oct. 1920; *s* of late Rev. A. O. Scutt, MA and Freda M. Scutt (*née* Palmer); *m* 1st, 1943, Judy Watson (marr. diss. 1960); two *s*; 2nd, 1961, Patricia A. M. Smith. *Educ:* Fonthill; Bryanston; British Inst., Paris; Jesus Coll., Cambridge (MA Mod. Lang.). Served Intell. Corps, 1941–42 (invalided out). BBC Eur. Service (French Section), 1942; BBC TV Outside Broadcasts Producer, 1955; BBC Paris Rep., 1958; Gen. Man., Trans Europe Television, 1962; rejoined BBC TV Outside Broadcasts, 1963; Asst Head of BBC TV Presentation (BBC1), 1966; Controller: BBC Radio 1 and 2, 1967–68; BBC 2, 1969–74; Development TV, 1974–77; Dep. Man. Dir, BBC TV, 1977–80; Dir, LWT, 1981–90; Dir of Production, NVC Arts, 1991–94. Chm., New Technologies Working Party, Broadcast Res. Unit, BFI, 1981–83. TV Producer for National Video Corp.: Tales of Hoffmann, Peter Grimes, La Bohème, Fanciulla del West, Manon Lescaut, Die Fledermaus, Der Rosenkavalier, Nutcracker and Don Carlo, Covent Gdn, 1981–85; Ernani, Il Trittico, I Lombardi, Andrea Chenier, Aida, Madame Butterfly and Nabucco, La Scala, 1982–86; Otello, Turandot, Madame Butterfly, Tosca, Il Trovatore and Attila, Verona, 1982–85; Don Quixote, and ABT at the Met, and at San Francisco, Amer. Ballet Theatre, 1983–85; Natasha (Natalia Makarova), and Carols for Christmas, 1985; Napoli and La Sylphide, Royal Theatre Copenhagen, 1986–88; Boris Godunov, and The Golden Age, Bolshoi Theatre, 1987; Cinderella, 1987, Diaghilev Tribute, 1990, Paris Opera Ballet; Le Corsaire, 1989, Swan Lake, 1990, The Stone Flower, 1991, Coppelia, 1993, Kirov Ballet, St Petersburg; Life for the Tsar, and Mlada, Bolshoi Theatre, 1992; La Traviata, La Fenice, Venice, 1992; Maid of Orleans, Bolshoi Th., 1993; Billboards, Joffrey Ballet, NY, 1993;

Holy Russia at Christmas, Moscow, 1994; Russian Opera at the Bolshoi Theatre: the vintage years, 1995. FRTS 1978 (Gold Medallist, 1980); FRSA 1984. Officier de la Légion d'Honneur (France), 1983; Officier de l'Ordre du Mérite Culturel (Monaco), 1991. *Recreations:* music, theatre, gardening. *Address:* The Abbey Cottage, Cockfield, Suffolk IP30 0LY. *Club:* Garrick.
Died 7 Feb. 2000.

SEABORG, Prof. Glenn Theodore; University Professor of Chemistry, University of California, Berkeley, since 1971; *b* 19 April 1912; *s* of Herman Theodore and Selma Erickson Seaborg; *m* 1942, Helen Lucille Griggs; three *s* two *d* (and one *s* decd). *Educ:* Univ. of Calif, Los Angeles (BA); Univ. of Calif, Berkeley (PhD). University of California, Berkeley: Res. Associate (with Prof. Gilbert N. Lewis), Coll. of Chem., 1937–39; Instr, Dept of Chem., 1939–41, Asst Prof., 1941–45, Prof., 1945–71; Chancellor, 1958–61; Lawrence Berkeley Laboratory: Associate Dir, 1954–61, and 1972–; Dir, Nuclear Chem. Div., 1946–58, and 1972–75; Dir, Lawrence Hall of Science, 1982–; Head, Plutonium Chem. Metall. Lab., Univ. of Chicago, 1942–46; Chm., US Atomic Energy Commn, 1961–71. Member, US Delegns to: 3rd (Chm.) and 4th (Chm. and Pres.) UN Internat. Confs on Peaceful Uses of Atomic Energy, Geneva, 1964 and 1971; 5–15th annual Gen. Confs of Internat. Atomic Energy Agency, 1961–71; USSR, for signing of Memorandum on Cooperation in the Field of Utilization of Atomic Energy for Peaceful Purposes (Chm.), 1963; USSR, for signing of Limited Test Ban Treaty, 1963. Member: Nat. Council on Marine Resources and Engineering Development, 1966–71; Nat. Aeronautics and Space Council, 1961–71; Fed. Council for Science and Tech., 1961 71; Pres.'s Cttee on Manpower, 1964–69; Fed. Radiation Council, 1961–69; Nat. Sci. Bd, Nat. Sci. Foundn, 1960–61; Pres.'s Science Adv. Cttee, 1959 61; 1st Gen. Adv. Cttee, US Atomic Energy Commn, 1946–50; Commn on the Humanities, 1962–65; Scientific Adv. Bd, Robert A. Welch Foundn, 1957–; Bd of Dirs, Nat. Educnl TV and Radio Centre, 1958–64, 1967–70; Bd of Dirs, World Future Soc., 1969–; Nat. Programming Council for Public TV, 1970–72; Bd of Governors, Amer.-Swedish Hist. Foundn, 1972–; Steering Cttee, Chem. Educn Material Study (Chm.), 1959–74; Nat. Cttee on America's Goals and Resources, Nat. Planning Assoc., 1962 64; Council on Foreign Relations, 1965–; Bd of Trustees: Pacific Science Centre Foundn, 1962–; Science Service, 1965– (Pres., 1966–); Amer.-Scandinavian Foundn, 1968–; Educnl Broadcasting Corp., 1970–73; Amer. Assoc. for the Advancement of Science (Pres. 1972; Chm. 1973); Amer. Chem. Soc. (Pres., 1976); Chm. Bd, Swedish Council of America, 1978–. Mem. and Hon. Mem., Fellow and Hon. Fellow, numerous scientific and professional socs and instns, Argentina, German Dem. Republic., German Fed. Republic, Japan, Poland, Spain, Sweden, UK, USA, USSR; Foreign Mem., Royal Society, 1985; Hon. FRSC 1982. Held 50 hon. doctorates from univs and colls. Named one of America's 10 Outstanding Young Men, 1947. Member: Electoral Coll., Hall of Fame for Great Americans, 1969; Calif Inventors' Hall of Fame, 1983. Awards (1947–) included: Nobel Prize for Chemistry (jtly), 1951; Perkin Medal, Amer. Sect. Soc. Chem. Ind., 1957; Enrico Fermi Award, US AEC, 1959; Priestley Meml Award, 1960; Franklin Medal, Franklin Inst. of Philadelphia, 1963; Award in Pure Chem., 1947, Charles Lathrop Parsons Award, 1964, Amer. Chem. Soc.; Chem. Pioneer Award, 1968, Gold Medal Award, 1973, Amer. Inst. of Chemists; Arches of Science Award, Pacific Science Centre, Seattle, 1968; John R. Kuebler Award, Alpha Chi Sigma, 1978; Priestley Medal, Amer. Chem. Soc., 1979; Henry DeWolf Smyth Award, Amer. Nuclear Soc., 1982; Actinide Award, 1984; Great Swedish Heritage

Award, 1984. Officer, French Legion of Honour, 1973. Co-discoverer of: nuclear energy source isotopes Pu-239 and U-233; elements (1940–74): 94, plutonium; 95, americium; 96, curium; 97, berkelium; 98, californium; 99, einsteinium; 100, fermium; 101, mendelevium; 102, nobelium; element 106. *Publications:* (jtly) The Chemistry of the Actinide Elements, 1958, 2nd edn 1986; The Transuranium Elements (Silliman Lectures), 1958; (jtly) Elements of the Universe, 1958; Man-made Transuranium Elements, 1963; (jtly) Education and the Atom, 1964; (jtly) The Nuclear Properties of the Heavy Elements, 1964; (jtly) Oppenheimer, 1969; (jtly) Man and Atom, 1971; Nuclear Milestones, 1972; (ed) Transuranium Elements—Products of Modern Alchemy, 1978; Kennedy, Khrushchev and the Test Ban, 1981; (jtly) Nuclear Chemistry, 1982; Stemming the Tide: arms control Johnson years, 1987; (with W. D. Loveland) Elements Beyond Uranium, 1990; (with B. S. Loeb) The Atomic Energy Commission under Nixon, 1992; (with R. C. Colvig) Chancellor at Berkeley, 1994; The Plutonium Story: the journals of Professor Glenn T. Seaborg 1939–1946, 1994; A Scientist Speaks Out, 1996; contrib. numerous papers on nuclear chem. and nuclear physics, transuranium elements, high energy nuclear reactions and educn in Physical Rev., Jl Amer. Chm. Soc., Annual Rev. of Nuclear Science, etc. *Recreations:* golf, reading, hiking. *Address:* (business) Lawrence Berkeley Laboratory, University of California, Berkeley, CA 94720, USA; (home) 1154 Glen Road, Lafayette, CA 94549, USA. *Clubs:* Faculty (Univ. Calif, Berkeley); Commonwealth Club of California, Bohemian (San Francisco); Chemists (NY); Cosmos, University (Washington).

Died 25 Feb. 1999.

SEALE, Douglas Robert; producer, actor and director (stage); *b* 28 Oct. 1913; *s* of Robert Henry Seale and Margaret Seale (*née* Law); *m* 1st, 1939, (Daisy) Elaine Wodson (marr. diss. 1948); 2nd, 1950, Joan Barbara Grattan Geary (marr. diss. 1964); two *s*; 3rd, 1964, Zenaide Alma Trigg. *Educ:* Rutlish. Studied for stage at Royal Academy of Dramatic Art and became an actor; first appeared as Starling in The Drums Begin, Embassy, 1934; subseq. in repertory. Served in Army, 1940–46, commissioned in Royal Signals. Joined Shakespeare Memorial Theatre Company, Stratford-on-Avon seasons, 1946 and 1947; from 1948 produced at Birmingham Repertory Theatre, at The Bedford, Camden Town (under Donald Wolfit), and again at Birmingham where he became Director of Productions, 1950; later productions included: Figaro and Fidelio, Sadler's Wells; Shaw's Caesar and Cleopatra at Birmingham Rep. Theatre, 1956 (later presented at Théâtre Sarah Bernhardt, Paris, and Old Vic); season 1957: The Tempest, Univ. of BC, Vancouver; King John, Stratford-on-Avon; Richard III, Old Vic; Trilogy of Henry VI, Old Vic; season 1958: The World of the Wonderful Dark, for first Vancouver Festival; King Lear, Old Vic; Much Ado about Nothing, Stratford-on-Avon; Old Vic productions as Associate Director, 1958: Julius Caesar; Macbeth; 1959: Molière's Tartuffe; Pinero's The Magistrate; Dryden-Davenant-Purcell version of Shakespeare's The Tempest; St Joan; She Stoops to Conquer, 1960; Landscape with Figures, by Cecil Beaton, Dublin Festival, 1960; King John, Festival Theatre, Stratford, Ontario, 1960; Director of tours in Russia and Poland for Old Vic Theatre Co., 1961: prod The Importance of Being Earnest, New York, 1962; The Comedy of Errors, Henry V, Stratford, Connecticut, 1963; Artistic Director, Center Stage, Baltimore, Maryland, USA, 1965–67; directed and acted, Meadowbrook Theater, Rochester, Mich, 1968; co-producing Director, Goodman Theater, Chicago, 1969–72: productions included Soldiers, Marching Song, Heartbreak House (Jefferson award), The Tempest, Twelfth Night, own musical adaptation of Lady

Audley's Secret; directed and acted in Lady Audley's Secret, Washington and New York, 1972; Giovani, in Pirandello's Henry IV, New York, 1973; directed: King Lear, Marin Shakespeare Festival, San Francisco; Doll's House and Look Back in Anger, Cleveland, Getting Married, New Haven, 1973; Sorin in The Seagull, Seattle; Artistic Dir, Philadelphia Drama Guild, 1974–80; The Last Few Days of Willie Callendar, Philadelphia, 1979; Summer, Philadelphia, 1980; directed at Shaw Festival, Ontario: Too True to be Good, 1974; Caesar and Cleopatra, 1975; Lady Audley's Secret, 1978; Director: The Winslow Boy, NY, 1980, and tour; The Dresser, Witness for the Prosecution, Miami, 1982; acted in: Frankenstein, NY, 1980; The Dresser, NY, 1981; Noises Off, 1983; The Entertainer, NY, 1996; acted in *films:* Amadeus, 1983; Heaven Help Us, 1984; Haunted by her Past, 1987; Ernest Saves Christmas, 1988; Triplicity, 1989; I'm No Angel, 1990; Mr Destiny, 1990; Rescue Down Under (voice of Koala Bear), 1991; Aladdin (voice of Sultan), 1992; For Love or Money, 1992; acted in, *TV:* Lucy Arnaz Show (series), 1985; Amazing Stories, 1985; Rags to Riches (series), 1987). Regent's Prof., Univ. of Calif at Santa Barbara, Jan.-June 1965. Hon. DFA Washington Coll., Md, 1967. Mensa Annual Achievement Award, 1979. *Address:* Apt 14c, One University Place, New York, NY 10003, USA.   *Died 13 June 1999.*

SEALES, Peter Clinton; Chairman, PSL Associates; Partner, Sealpharma, since 1995; *b* 1 Nov. 1929; *s* of James Seales, solicitor, and Angela Seales; *m* 1955, Bernadette Rogers; one *d* (and one *d* decd). Called to the Bar, King's Inns, 1953. Group Marketing Dir, Raleigh Industries Ltd, 1962–74; Dir, E Midlands Electricity Board, 1972–74; Man. Dir, Potterton International, and Chm. overseas subsidiaries in France, Belgium, Germany, Holland and Japan, 1974–76; International Marketing Dir, Ever Ready Holdings, 1977; Chief Executive: Sea Fish Industry Authority, 1982–83; Operation Raleigh, 1984–85; Consultant to Saatchi & Saatchi Compton, 1984; Group Marketing Dir, Wassen Internat. Ltd, 1986–92; Consultant, Gazzoni 1907 SpA, 1995– (Dir for Internat. Develts, 1992–95); Dir, Jephson Housing Assoc. Gp, 1994–; Consultant Director: Qualitec UK Ltd, 1995–; Custom Pharmaceuticals Ltd, 1995–. Hon. Council Mem., Operation Innervator, 1987–. Mem., Finance Cttee, Warwicks BRCS, 1994–. FInstD 1972. *Recreations:* sailing, music. *Clubs:* Wig and Pen; Real Tennis (Leamington Spa).   *Died 26 Jan. 1998.*

SEATON, Colin Robert; Chairman: Medical Appeal Tribunals, since 1989; Disability Appeal Tribunals, since 1992; Barrister-at-law; *b* 21 Nov. 1928; 2nd *s* of late Arthur William Robert Seaton and Helen Amelia Seaton (*née* Stone); *m* 1952, Betty (*née* Gosling); two *s*. *Educ:* Wallington County Grammar Sch. for Boys; Worcester Coll., Oxford (BA 1953; MA 1956). Royal Air Force, 1947–49. Called to Bar, Inner Temple, 1956 (Profumo Prize, 1953, 1954); schoolmaster for LCC, 1953–57; Solicitor's Dept, Ministries of Health and Housing and Local Govt, also Dept of the Environment, 1957–71; Sec. (Master) of Nat. Industrial Relations Court, 1971–74; Under Sec., Lord Chancellor's Dept, 1974–88; Circuit Administrator: Northern Circuit, 1974–82; SE Circuit, 1982–83; Head, Legislation Gp, 1983–88. Sec., Lord Chancellor's Law Reform Cttee, 1983–88; Sec. to Univ. Comrs, 1988–94. *Publication:* Aspects of the National Health Service Acts, 1966. *Recreations:* photography, reading. *Address:* 62 The Vale, Coulsdon, Surrey CR5 2AW. *T:* (0181) 668 5538. *Club:* Civil Service.

Died 24 Sept. 1997.

SEEAR, Baroness *cr* 1971 (Life Peer), of Paddington, City of Westminster; **Beatrice Nancy Seear;** PC 1985; formerly Reader in Personnel Management, University of

London, The London School of Economics, retired 1978, Hon. Fellow, 1980; Deputy Leader, Liberal Democrats (formerly Social & Liberal Democrats), House of Lords, since 1988 (Liberal Leader, 1984–88); *b* 7 Aug. 1913; *d* of late Herbert Charles Seear and Beatrice Maud Catchpole. *Educ:* Croydon High Sch.; Newnham Coll., Cambridge (Hon. Fellow, 1983); London Sch. of Economics and Political Science. BA (Cambridge Hist. Tripos). Personnel Officer, C. & J. Clark Ltd, shoe manufacturers, 1936–46; seconded as Mem. (pt-time), staff of Production Efficiency Bd at Min. of Aircraft Production, 1943–45; Teacher at London School of Economics, 1946–78. Vis. Prof. of Personnel Management, City Univ., 1980–87. Pres., Lib. Pty, 1964–65; contested (L): Hornchurch, 1950, 1951; Truro, 1955, 1959; Epping, 1964; Rochdale, 1966; Wakefield, 1970. Member: Hansard Soc. Commn on Electoral Reform, 1975–76; Top Salaries Review Body, 1971–84. Chm., Council, Morley Coll. President: BSI, 1974–77; Women's Liberal Fedn, 1974; Fawcett Soc., 1970–85; Inst. of Personnel Management, 1977–79; Carers Nat. Assoc. Mem. Council, Industrial Soc., 1972–84. Hon. LLD: Leeds, 1979; Exeter, 1989; Hon. DLit Bath, 1982. *Publications:* (with P. Jephcott and J. H. Smith) Married Women Working, 1962; (with V. Roberts and J. Brock) A Career for Women in Industry?, 1964; Industrial Social Services, 1964; The Position of Women in Industry, 1967; The Re-Entry of Women into Employment, 1971. *Recreations:* travel, gardening. *Address:* 189b Kennington Road, SE11 6ST. *T:* (0171) 587 0205. *Clubs:* Royal Commonwealth Society, National Liberal.
Died 23 April 1997.

SEENEY, Noel Conway; Commissioner of Stamp Duties, Queensland, 1975–86; *b* 7 April 1926; *s* of Percy Matthew Mark Seeney and Wilhelmina Augusta Zanow; *m* 1949, Valrae Muriel Uhlmann, two *d*. *Educ:* Teachers' Coll., Brisbane; Univ. of Queensland (BCom). Assoc. Accountancy; ACP, London. Teacher, 1944; Dep Principal, Secondary Sch., 1960; Principal 1964; Official Sec., Office of Agent-General for Qld in London, 1969; Agent-General for Qld in London, 1973. *Recreations:* golf, tennis. *Address:* 20 Nawarra Street, Indooroopilly, Qld 4068, Australia. *Clubs:* United Service (Brisbane); Indooroopilly Golf.
Died 23 March 1996.

SELBY, 4th Viscount *cr* 1905; **Michael Guy John Gully;** *b* 15 Aug. 1942; *s* of 3rd Viscount Selby and Veronica (*d* 1996), *er d* of late J. George and Mrs Briscoe-George; *S* father, 1959; *m* 1965, Mary Theresa, *d* of late Capt. Thomas Powell, London, SW7; one *s* one *d*. *Heir: s* Hon. Edward Thomas William Gully [*b* 21 Sept. 1967; *m* 1992, Charlotte, *yr d* of Rolph Brege; one *s*].
Died 10 Jan. 1997.

SELBY, Ralph Walford, CMG 1961; HM Diplomatic Service, retired; *b* 20 March 1915; *e s* of late Sir Walford Selby, KCMG, CB, CVO and Dorothy, *d* of William Orme Carter, Hurst Green and Bournemouth; *m* 1947, Julianna Snell (*d* 1994); three *d*. *Educ:* Eton; Christ Church, Oxford. Entered HM Diplomatic Service, Sept. 1938; served in Foreign Office until Oct. 1939; enlisted in Army and served with Grenadier Guards, March 1940–Feb. 1945, when returned to Foreign Office; seconded to Treasury for service in India as First Secretary in Office of High Commissioner for UK, Sept. 1947; transferred to The Hague, 1950; returned to FO, 1953–56; transf. to Tokyo as Counsellor, 1956, to Copenhagen in 1958, to Djakarta in 1961, to Warsaw in 1964; Chargé d'Affaires in 1952, 1958, 1959, 1960, 1961, 1962, 1964, 1965, 1969, 1970; Consul-Gen., Boston, 1966–69; Minister, British Embassy, Rome, 1969–72; Ambassador to Norway,

1972–75. *Address:* Mengeham House, Mengham Lane, Hayling Island, Hants PO11 9JX.
Died 21 Feb. 1997.

SELF, Hugh Michael; QC 1973; a Recorder, 1975–93; *b* 19 March 1921; *s* of Sir (Albert) Henry Self, KCB, KCMG, KBE and Rosalind Audrey, *d* of Sir John Lonsdale Otter, Brighton; *m* 1950, Penelope Ann, *d* of late John Drinkwater, poet and dramatist, and Daisy (*née* Kennedy), violinist; two *d*. *Educ:* Lancing Coll.; Worcester Coll., Oxford (BA). Royal Navy, 1942–46; Lieut RNVR 1946. Called to the Bar, Lincoln's Inn, 1951, Bencher, 1980. *Recreations:* golf, walking in England, literature. *Address:* 59 Maresfield Gardens, Hampstead, NW3 5TE. *T:* (0171) 435 8311. *Club:* Savile.
Died 28 May 1998.

SELF, Prof. Peter John Otter; Emeritus Professor of Public Administration, University of London; Visiting Fellow, Australian National University, since 1984; *b* 7 June 1919; *s* of Sir (Albert) Henry Self, KCB, KCMG, KBE and Rosalind Audrey, *d* of Sir John Lonsdale Otter, Brighton; *m* 1st, 1950, Diana Mary Pitt (marr. diss.); 2nd, 1959, Elaine Rosenbloom Adams (marr. diss.); two *s*; 3rd, 1981, Sandra Guerita Gough (*née* Moiseiwitsch) (*d* 1996). *Educ:* Lancing Coll.; Balliol Coll., Oxford (MA). Editorial staff of The Economist, 1944–62; Extra-mural Lectr, London Univ., 1944–49; Lectr in Public Administration, LSE, 1948–61; Reader in Political Science, LSE, 1961–63; Prof. of Public Admin, Univ. of London, 1963–82; Sen. Res. Fellow, ANU, 1982–84. Dir of Studies (Administration), Civil Service Dept, 1969–70. Chm., Australian Govt Inquiry into Local Govt Finance, 1984–85. Mem. Exec. and Council, 1954, Vice-Chm. Exec., 1955, Chm. Exec., 1961–69, Chm. Council, 1979 82, Town and Country Planning Assoc.; Mem., SE Regional Economic Planning Council, 1966–79. Hon. MRTPI. *Publications:* Regionalism, 1949; Cities in Flood: the Problems of Urban Growth, 1957; (with H. Storing) The State and the Farmer, 1962; Administrative Theories and Politics, 1972; Econocrats and the Policy Process, 1976, Planning the Urban Region, 1982; Political Theories of Modern Government, 1985; Government by the Market?, 1993; numerous articles on administration, politics and planning. *Recreations:* walking, golf, story-telling. *Address:* 7 Hobbs Street, O'Connor, ACT 2602, Australia. *T:* (2) 62477383. *Club:* Reform.
Died 29 March 1999.

SELLY, Susan, (Mrs Clifford Selly); *see* Strange, S.

SELWYN, John Sidney Augustus, OBE 1962 (MBE 1939); HM Diplomatic Service, retired; *b* 17 Oct. 1908; *s* of Rev. A. L. H. Selwyn; *m* 1932, Cicely Georgina Armour (marr. diss. 1952); one *s* one *d* (and one *d* decd); *m* 1952, Janette Bruce Mullin (*d* 1968); one *s*; *m* 1969, Phyllis Varcoe; *m* 1971, Sonja Fischer; one *d*. *Educ:* St Lawrence College, Ramsgate; Royal Military Coll., Sandhurst. Entered the Indian Police, 1928; served in NWF Campaigns, 1930, 1937 and 1941; Major, 12th Frontier Force Regt, active service in Burma, 1942–46; Allied Control Commission, Germany, 1946–48; entered Diplomatic Service, 1948; served in Bucharest, Lisbon, London, Lima, Santos, Beirut; Consul-General: Berlin, 1963; Strasbourg, 1964–68; Vice-Consul, Calais, 1969–73. *Recreation:* walking. *Club:* Civil Service.
Died 7 March 2000.

SEMMENCE, Dr Adrian Murdoch, CB 1986; Civil Service Medical Adviser, 1979–86, retired; Medical Officer, Health Control Unit, Heathrow Airport, 1993–96; *b* 5 April 1926; *e s* of late Adrian George Semmence, MA, and Henrietta Scorgie Semmence, MA (*née* Murdoch); *m* 1949, Joan, *o d* of Hugh Wood and Bobbie (*née* Weatherill); four *s* one *d*. *Educ:* Robert Gordon's Coll.; Univ. of Aberdeen (MB, ChB 1953; MD 1957); Univ. of London (MSc 1972); DObstRCOG 1954; FRCGP 1972;

DIH 1972; FFOM 1983. Served War, RN 1943–47, in mine-sweeping and Destroyer flotillas in Mediterranean and Channel (able seaman torpedoman). General Practitioner, E Yorks, Berks and Oxon, 1954–76; Upjohn Fellow, Univ. of Edinburgh, 1967; Nuffield Travelling Fellow, 1969–70; Unit of Clinical Epidemiology, Univ. of Oxford, 1970–76; Principal MO, CSD, 1976–79. FRSocMed (Pres. Sect. of Occupational Med., 1985–86). *Recreations:* pottering, rumination. *Address:* 3 Terrington Close, Abingdon OX14 1PQ. *Clubs:* Royal Society of Medicine; Frilford Heath Golf (Abingdon).

Died 27 Aug. 1999.

SENDALL, Bernard Charles, CBE 1952; Deputy Director-General, Independent Broadcasting Authority (formerly Independent Television Authority), 1955–77; *b* 30 April 1913; *s* of late William Sendall, Malvern, Worcestershire; *m* 1963, Barbara Mary, *d* of late Ambrose Coviello, DCM, FRAM; one step *s. Educ:* Magdalen College, Oxford; Harvard University. Entered Civil Service in the Admiralty, 1935; Principal Private Secretary to Minister of Information 1941–45; Controller (Home), Central Office of Information, 1946–49; Controller, Festival of Britain Office, 1949–51; Assistant Secretary, Admiralty, 1951–55. *Publication:* Independent Television in Britain, vol. I, 1982, vol. II, 1983. *Address:* 144 Montagu Mansions, York Street, W1H 1LA.

Died 25 May 1996.

SERBY, John Edward, CB 1958; CBE 1951; FRAeS; consultant; *b* 15 March 1902; *s* of Francis Serby; *m* 1933, Clarice Lilian (*née* Hawes); one *d. Educ:* Haberdashers' Aske's School; Emmanuel College, Cambridge (BA). Junior Scientific Officer, Admiralty, 1927–30; Scientific Officer, RAE, 1930–38; Headquarters, MAP, 1938–50; Deputy Director, Royal Aircraft Establishment, Farnborough, 1950–54; Dir-Gen. of Guided Weapons, Min. of Aviation, 1954–61; Dep. Controller Guided Weapons, Ministry of Aviation, 1961–63. *Recreation:* gardening. *Address:* Overwey, Bishopsmead, Farnham, Surrey GU9 0HQ. *T:* (01252) 713526.

Died 30 Jan. 1997.

SESSFORD, Rt Rev. George Minshull; Bishop of Moray, Ross and Caithness, 1970–93; *b* Aintree, Lancs, 7 Nov. 1928; *o s* of Charles Walter Sessford and Eliza Annie (*née* Minshull); *m* 1st, 1952, Norah (*d* 1985), *y d* of David Henry Hughes and Ellen (*née* Whitely); three *d;* 2nd, 1987, Joan Gwendoline Myra Black, *widow* of Rev. C. W. Black. *Educ:* Warbreck Primary Sch.; Oulton High and Liverpool Collegiate Schs; St Andrews Univ. (MA); Lincoln Theol Coll. Deacon 1953, priest 1954; Curate, St Mary's Cathedral, Glasgow, 1953; Chaplain, Glasgow Univ., 1955; Priest-in-Charge, Cumbernauld New Town, 1958; Rector, Forres, Moray, 1966. *Recreations:* Lanchester motor cars, donkey breeding, sailing. *Address:* Caladh No Sith, 33 Mellon Charles, Aultbea, Wester Ross IV22 2JL. *T:* Aultbea (01445) 731303.

Died 21 July 1996.

SETON, Sir James (Christall), 12th Bt *cr* 1683 (NS), of Pitmedden, Aberdeenshire; *b* 21 Jan. 1913; *s* of Christall Dougal Seton (*d* 1969), *g s* of Sir William Coote Seton, 7th Bt, and Sara Johnson Moore (*d* 1958); *S* kinsman, Sir Robert James Seton, 11th Bt, 1993; *m* 1939, Evelyn, *d* of Ray Hafer. Served US Army, 1943–46 (Corp.). Freemason (Patron, Eastern Star Chapter, 1961). *Recreations:* formerly golf, later hand weaving, calligraphy. *Heir:* nephew Charles Wallace Seton [*b* 25 Aug. 1948; *m* 1974, Rebecca, *d* of Robert Lawry]. *Address:* Otterbein Home, 585 North State Route 741, Lebanon, OH 45036–9551, USA. *Died 4 April 1998.*

SEYMOUR, Comdr Sir Michael Culme-, 5th Bt *cr* 1809, of Highmount, co. Limerick and Friery Park, Devonshire;

Royal Navy, retired; *b* 26 April 1909; *o s* of Vice-Admiral Sir Michael Culme-Seymour, 4th Bt, KCB, MVO and Florence Agnes Louisa (*d* 1956), *y d* of late A. L. Nugent; *S* father, 1925; *m* 1948, Lady (Mary) Faith Nesbitt (*d* 1983), *er d* of 9th Earl of Sandwich; (two *s* decd) one step *d* (adopted). ADC to Governor-General of Canada, 1933–35; served War of 1939–45 (despatches); served Imperial Defence College, 1946–47; retired from RN, 1947. Succeeded Rev. Wentworth Watson to the Rockingham Castle estates, 1925, and transferred them to his nephew, Comdr L. M. M. Saunders Watson, RN, 1967. Farmer and landowner. JP Northants, 1949; Mem. Northants CC, 1948–55; DL Northants, 1958–71; High Sheriff of Northants, 1966. Bledisloe Gold Medal for Landowners, 1972. *Heir:* cousin Michael Patrick Culme-Seymour [*b* 28 April 1962; *m* 1986, Karin Fleig; two *s*]. *Address:* Wytherston, Powerstock, Bridport, Dorset DT6 3TQ. *T:* (01308) 485211. *Club:* Brooks's.

Died 13 Oct. 1999.

SHACKLOCK, Constance, OBE 1971; FRAM 1953; international opera and concert singer; Professor, Royal Academy of Music, 1968–84; *b* 16 April 1913; *e d* of Randolph and Hilda Shacklock, Nottingham; *m* 1947, Eric Mitchell (*d* 1965). *Educ:* Huntingdon Street Secondary School, Nottingham; RAM (LRAM 1940). CEMA, 1943–45. Principal mezzo-soprano, Covent Garden, 1946–56. Outstanding rôles: Carmen, Amneris (Aida), Octavian (Der Rosenkavalier), Brangaene (Tristan und Isolde). Guest artist: Wagner Society, Holland, 1949; Berlin State Opera, 1951; Edinburgh Festival, 1954; Berlin Festival, 1956; Teatro Colon, Buenos Aires, 1956; Bolshoi Theatre, Moscow, 1957; Kirov Theatre, Leningrad, 1957; Elizabethan Theatre Trust, Sydney, 1958; Liège Opera, 1960; London production of The Sound of Music, 1961–66. President: English Singers and Speakers, 1978–79; Royal Acad. of Music, 1979–80; Royal Borough of Kingston Arts Fest., 1988–; Life Pres., Assoc. of Teachers of Singing, 1995. DUniv Kingston, 1993. *Recreations:* gardening, reading, tapestry. *Address:* East Dorincourt, Kingston Vale, SW15 3RN.

Died 29 June 1999.

SHAKESPEARE, Sir William (Geoffrey), 2nd Bt *cr* 1942, of Lakenham, City of Norwich; Medical Adviser to Buckinghamshire Adoption Panel, since 1987; General Practitioner, Aylesbury, 1968–87; Hospital Practitioner, Mental Subnormality, Manor House Hospital, Aylesbury, since 1972; *b* 12 Oct. 1927; *s* of Rt Hon. Sir Geoffrey Hithersay Shakespeare, 1st Bt, and Aimée Constance (*d* 1950), *d* of Walter Loveridge; *S* father, 1980; *m* 1964, Susan Mary, *d* of A. D. Raffel, Colombo, Ceylon; two *s. Educ:* Radley; Clare Coll., Cambridge (BA Hons Nat. Scis, MA 1957); St George's Hospital. MB BChir Camb. 1958; DCH Eng. 1961. Boston Children's Hosp., USA, 1963–64; Paediatric Registrar, Stoke Mandeville Hosp., 1964–66. Mem., Snowdon Working Party, Integration of Handicapped, 1974–76. Vice-President: Physically Handicapped & Able-Bodied, 1977–; Restricted Growth Assoc. (formerly Assoc. for Res. into Restricted Growth), 1982–. Member BMA. Trustee, Shakespeare Globe Trust, 1992–. *Heir:* s Thomas William Shakespeare, *b* 11 May 1966. *Address:* Manor Cottage, Stoke Mandeville, Bucks HP22 5XA. *Clubs:* MCC; Leander.

Died 12 March 1996.

SHAND, Sir James, Kt 1999; MBE 1962; accordionist and Scottish country dance band leader; *b* 28 Jan. 1908; *m* 1936, Anne G. Anderson; two *s. Educ:* East Wemyss, Fife. Formed the Jimmy Shand Band, 1945. First recording, 1933; first radio perf., 1934; subseq. numerous radio and television brodcasts incl. The White Heather Club. Over 330 compositions. Hon. MA Dundee. *Relevant* *publication:* The Jimmy Shand Story, by Ian Cameron, 1998. *Address:* Windy Edge, Auchtermuchty, Fife KY14 7HP.   *Died 23 Dec. 2000.*

SHAPLAND, Sir William (Arthur), Kt 1982; Trustee, Bernard Sunley Charitable Foundation; *b* 20 Oct. 1912; *s* of late Arthur Frederick Shapland and Alice Maud (*née* Jackson); *m* 1943, Madeline Annie (*née* Amiss); two *d*. *Educ:* Tollington Sch., Muswell Hill. Incorporated Accountant, 1936; Chartered Accountant, 1946. Allan Charlesworth & Co., Chartered Accountants, London, Cambridge and Rangoon, 1929–55; Blackwood Hodge, 1955–83 (Chm., 1965–83). Waynflete Fellow, Magdalen Coll., Oxford, 1981; Hon. Fellow, St Catherine's College, Oxford, 1982. Hon. FRCS 1978. Past Master, Paviors' Co. KStJ 1987 (OStJ 1981). Hon. DSc Buckingham, 1983; Hon. DLitt Leicester, 1985. *Recreations:* golf, gardening, travel. *Address:* 44 Beech Drive, N2 9NY. *T:* (0181) 883 5073.   *Died 1 Oct. 1997.*

SHARMA, Dr Shanker Dayal; President of India, 1992–97; *b* 19 Aug. 1918; *m* Vimala Sharma; two *s* one *d*. *Educ:* Lucknow Univ. (MA, LLM); Fitzwilliam Coll., Cambridge (PhD). Called to the Bar, Lincoln's Inn. Lawyer, 1940–; Mem., All India Congress Cttee, 1952–84; Pres., Bhopal State Congress Cttee, 1950–52; Chief Minister, Bhopal, 1952–56; Minister, Madhya Pradesh Govt, 1956–67; Gen. Sec., Indian Nat. Congress, 1968–72 (Pres., 1972–74); Mem., Lokh Sabha, 1971–77 and 1980–84; Minister of Communications, 1974–77; Governor, Andhra Pradesh, 1985, Punjab, 1985–86; suspended from Congress Party (I), 1986; Vice Pres. of India, 1987–92. Editor in Chief, Light and Learning, Ilm-au-Noor; Editor, Lucknow Law Jl. Hon. DPA London; Hon. LLD: Vikram and Bhopal Univs; Cantab, 1993. *Publication:* Congress Approach to International Affairs. *Address:* c/o Rashtrapati Bhavan, New Delhi 110004, India.   *Died 26 Dec. 1999.*

SHARP, Christopher; *see* Sharp, J. C.

SHARP, Sir George, Kt 1976; OBE 1969; JP; DL; Managing Trustee, Municipal Mutual Insurance Co. Ltd, 1979–91; Chairman, Glenrothes Development Corporation, 1978–86 (Vice-Chairman, 1973–78); *b* 8 April 1919; *s* of Angus Sharp and Mary S. McNee; *m* 1948, Elsie May Rodger, *o d* of David Porter Rodger and Williamina S. Young; one *s*. *Educ:* Thornton Public Sch.; Buckhaven High Sch. Engine driver, 1962; PRO, 1962–69. Fife County Council: Mem., 1945–75; Chm., Water and Drainage Cttee, 1955–61; Chm., Finance Cttee, 1961–72; Convener, 1972–75; Convener, Fife Regional Council, 1974–78. President: Assoc. of County Councils, 1972–74; Convention of Scottish Local Authorities, 1975–78. Chairman: Kirkcaldy Dist Council, 1958–75; Fife and Kinross Water Bd, 1967–75; Forth River Purification Bd, 1955–67 and 1975–78; Scottish River Purification Adv. Cttee, 1967–75; Scottish Tourist Consultative Council, 1979–83. Vice-Chairman: Forth Road Bridge Cttee, 1972–78; Tay Road Bridge Cttee, 1972–78. Member: Scottish Water Adv. Cttee, 1962–69; Cttee of Enquiry into Salmon and Trout Fishing, 1963; Potato Marketing Bd, 1965–71; Scottish Valuation Adv. Cttee, 1972; Cttee of Enquiry into Local Govt Finance, 1974–76; Scottish Develt Agency, 1975–80; Royal Commn on Legal Services in Scotland, 1978–80; Econ. and Soc. Cttee, EEC, 1982–86. Director: Grampian Television, 1975–89; National Girobank Scotland, 1985–90. JP Fife, 1975; DL Fife, 1978. *Recreations:* golf, gardening. *Address:* Strathlea, 56 Station Road, Thornton, Fife KY1 4AY. *T:* (01592) 774347.   *Died 24 June 2000.*

SHARP, Lt-Col Granville Maynard, MA; *b* 5 Jan. 1906; *s* of Walter Sharp, Cleckheaton, Yorks; *m* 1935, Margaret, *d* of Dr J. H. Vincent, Wembley Hill; two *d*. *Educ:* Cleckheaton Grammar School; Ashville College,

Harrogate; St John's College, Cambridge (MA Hons Economics). Lecturer in Economics at West Riding Technical Institutes, 1929–34; Chairman, Spenborough Housing and Town Planning Committee, 1935–39; Hon. Secretary, Spen Valley Divisional Labour Party, 1936–39; Battery Capt. 68 Anti-Tank Regt RA, 1939–42; Staff Capt. and DAQMG Belfast Area, 1942–43; Senior British Staff Officer, Economics Section, Allied Control Commission, Italy, 1943–44; Chief Economics and Supply Officer, Military Govt, Austria, 1944–45. MP (Lab) Spen Valley Div. of West Riding of Yorks, 1945–50; PPS to Minister of Civil Aviation, 1946, to Minister of Works, 1947–50. Chairman, Select Cttee of Estimates Sub-Cttee, 1946–48. Keymer Parish Councillor, 1969–83 (Vice-Chm., 1976–80); CC E Sussex, 1970–74; CC W Sussex, 1973–85 (Chm., Rts of Way Cttee, 1974–83); Member: Cuckfield RDC, 1971–74; Mid-Sussex DC, 1973–76. *Recreations:* swimming, singing, scything, Sussex Downs; attempting to preserve the local rural environment by every practical means, from collecting litter and clearing Rights of Way to chivvying authority (Queen Mother's Tidy Britain Award Certificate, 1989). *Address:* 31 Wilmington Close, Hassocks, West Sussex BN6 8QB. *T:* (01273) 842294.   *Died 8 Aug. 1997.*

SHARP, (James) Christopher, CBE 1993; solicitor; Managing Director, Northern Rock Building Society, since 1985; *b* 24 Dec. 1939; *s* of late Stanley Sharp and Annie (*née* Owrid); *m* 1963, Mary Bromfield; one *s* two *d*. *Educ:* Stockport Grammar Sch.; Pembroke Coll., Oxford (MA). FCIB (FCBSI 1989). Salop CC, 1963–68; admitted solicitor, 1965; G. H. Morgan and Co., Solicitors, Shrewsbury, 1968–70; Northern Rock Building Soc., 1970–. CIMgt (CBIM 1989). *Recreations:* reading, resting, walking. *Address:* Northern Rock House, Gosforth, Newcastle upon Tyne, NE3 4PL. *T:* (0191) 285 7191. *Club:* Northern Counties (Newcastle upon Tyne).
                                                                                                 Died 8 May 1997.

SHARP, J(ohn) M(ichael) Cartwright; Secretary of Law Commission, 1968–78; *b* 11 Aug. 1918; *s* of W. H. Cartwright Sharp, KC, and Dorothy (*née* Shelton). *Educ:* Rossall Sch.; Lincoln Coll., Oxford. Royal Artillery, 1940–46. Called to the Bar, Middle Temple, 1947. Lord Chancellor's Office, 1951–65; Legal Sec. to Law Officers, 1965; Asst Solicitor, Law Commn, 1966. *Recreations:* travel, reading. *Address:* The Quadrangle, Morden College, Blackheath SE3 0PW. *T:* (020) 8305 1278. *Club:* Reform.   *Died 21 July 2000.*

SHARP, Michael Cartwright; *see* Sharp, J. M. C.

SHARP, Sir Milton Reginald, 3rd Bt, *cr* 1920, of Heckmondwike, co. York; Captain, REME, TA; *b* 21 Nov. 1909; *s* of Sir Milton Sharp, 2nd Bt, and Gertrude (*d* 1940), *d* of John Earl, London; *S* father, 1941; *m* 1st, 1935, Dorothy Mary, *yr d* of Bernard R. McCarrick, Ballina, Ireland; 2nd, 1951, Marie-Louise de Vignon, Paris. *Educ:* Shrewsbury; Trinity Hall, Cambridge. *Heir:* cousin Samuel Christopher Reginald Sharp [*b* 25 April 1936; *m* 1st, 1958, Sheila Moody (marr. diss. 1967); 2nd, 1969, Anna Rossi].   *Died 4 May 1996.*

SHARPE, Hon. Sir John (Henry), Kt 1977; CBE 1972; JP; *b* 8 Nov. 1921; *s* of Harry Sharpe; *m* 1948, Eileen Margaret, *d* of George Morrow, BC, Canada; one *s* one *d*. *Educ:* Warwick Acad., Warwick, Bermuda; Mount Allison Commercial Coll., Sackville, New Brunswick. Served War of 1939–45: Pilot Officer, with Bomber Comd, NW Europe, RCAF, attached RAF. Chm., Purvis Ltd (Importers), Bermuda. MP Warwick W, Bermuda, 1963–93; Minister of Finance, 1968–75; Dep. Leader of Govt, 1971–75; Premier of Bermuda, 1975–77, resigned; Minister: of Transport, May–Dec. 1980; of Marine and Air Services, 1980–82; of Home Affairs, 1982–88; of

Legislative and Delegated Affairs, 1988–90; of Labour and Home Affairs, 1990–92; of Delegated and Legislative Affairs, 1990–93. Formerly Member several Parliamentary Select Cttees, and of Bd of Educn, Bermuda; also Dep. Chm., Central Planning Authority and Defence Bd. Delegate to Constitutional Conf., London, 1966. Mem., War Veterans Assoc., Bermuda; Warden, Anglican Church. Hon. Life Vice Pres., Bermuda FA. *Address:* Uplands, Harbour Road, Warwick West, Bermuda; PO Box WK 223, Warwick WKBX, Bermuda.
Died 11 July 1999.

SHARPE, Peter Samuel, QPM 1994; Chief Constable of Hertfordshire, 1994–2000; *b* 21 Nov. 1944; *s* of Arthur Samuel Sharpe and May Elizabeth Sharpe (*née* Eade); *m* 1985, Julia Anne Richens; one *s. Educ:* Varndean Grammar Sch., Brighton. Sussex Police: constable, Brighton Borough Police, 1963, rising to rank of Chief Superintendent, 1988–89; Mem. staff, Police Staff Coll., Bramshill, 1983–84; Surrey Police: Asst Chief Constable, 1989–91; Dep. Chief Constable, 1991–94. Chm., Air Support Sub-Cttee, 1996–99, Vice-Chm., Gen. Policing Cttee, 1997–99, ACPO. *Recreations:* cricket (Chm., British Police Cricket Section), golf. *Club:* XL.
Died 1 Dec. 2000.

SHARPE, William, OBE 1967; HM Diplomatic Service, retired; Overseas Relations Adviser, Potato Marketing Board, 1979–89; *b* 9 Dec. 1923; *s* of late William Joseph Sharpe and of Phoebe Irene (*née* Standen); *m* 1959, Marie-Antoinette Rodesch; one *s. Educ:* High Sch., Chichester; London Univ. BA (Hons), MA, BSc Econ (Hons). Served RAF, 1943–47. Joined Foreign (subseq. Diplomatic) Service, 1947; Foreign Office 1947–52; Cologne and Bonn, 1952–54; Leopoldville, 1954–57; UK Mission to UN, New York, 1957–61; Foreign Office, 1961–66; Milan, 1966–70; FCO, 1971–72; Kuwait, 1972–75; Consul-Gen., Berlin, 1975–78. *Recreations:* reading, music, walking. *Address:* 15 Regis Avenue, Aldwick Bay, Bognor Regis, Sussex PO21 4HQ.
Died 22 June 1999.

SHAW, Sir (John) Giles (Dunkerley), Kt 1987; *b* 16 Nov. 1931; *y s* of Hugh D. Shaw; *m* 1962, Dione Patricia Crosthwaite Ellison; one *s* two *d. Educ:* Sedbergh Sch.; St. John's Coll., Cambridge (MA). President of the Union, Cambridge, 1954. Joined Rowntree & Co. Ltd, 1955; Marketing Dir, Confectionery Div., Rowntree Mackintosh Ltd, 1970–74. Served on Flaxton RDC, 1957–64. Contested (C) Kingston upon Hull West, 1966. MP (C) Pudsey, Feb. 1974–1997. Parliamentary Under-Secretary of State: NI Office, 1979–81; DoE, 1981–83; Dept of Energy, 1983–84; Minister of State: Home Office, 1984–86; DTI, 1986–87. Mem., House of Commons Select Cttee on Nationalised Industries, 1976–79; Chm., Select Cttee on Sci. and Technol., 1992–97; Member: Speaker's Panel of Chairmen, 1988–97; H of C Privileges Cttee, 1994–97; Intelligence and Security Cttee, 1994–97; Vice-Chm., Cons. Prices and Consumer Affairs Cttee, 1978–79; Joint-Sec., All Party Wool Textile Group, 1978–79; Treasurer, 1922 Cttee, 1988–97. Chm. Govs, Sedbergh Sch., 1992–97. Trustee, Yorks Historic Churches Trust, 1998–. *Recreations:* ornithology, fishing. *Address:* Barn Court, Hovingham, York YO62 4LY. *Club:* United Oxford & Cambridge University.
Died 12 April 2000.

SHAW, Dr Robert Macdonald, CB 1968; Deputy Chief Medical Officer, Department of Health and Social Security (formerly Ministry of Health), 1965–77; *b* 16 Sept. 1912; *s* of late Peter Macdonald and Ellen Shaw; *m* 1941, Grace Helen Stringfellow; two *s* one *d. Educ:* Mill Hill School; Victoria Univ. of Manchester (MB, BCh). Miscellaneous hospital appointments, etc, 1936–39; Emergency Commission, RAMC, 1939–45; Asst County MOH, Essex,

1945–48; Department of Health and Social Security (formerly Ministry of Health), 1948–77. QHP 1971–74. *Address:* The Lodge, Tor Bryan, Ingatestone, Essex CM4 9HJ.
Died 9 Nov. 2000.

SHEARER, Rt Hon. Ian Hamilton; *see* Avonside, Rt Hon. Lord.

SHEERIN, John Declan; His Honour Judge Sheerin; a Circuit Judge, since 1982; *b* 29 Nov. 1932; *s* of late John Patrick Sheerin and Agnes Mary Sheerin; *m* 1958, Helen Suzanne (*née* LeRoux); two *s* two *d. Educ:* Wimbledon Coll.; London Sch. of Econs and Pol Science (LLB 1954). Served RAF, 1958–60 (Flying Officer). Admitted solicitor, 1957; Partner, Greene & Greene, 1962–82; a Recorder of the Crown Court, 1979–82. Resident Judge, Cambridge. *Recreation:* golf. *Address:* c/o Crown Court, Downing Street, Cambridge CB2 3DS. *Clubs:* Flempton Golf, Hunstanton Golf.
Died 10 Sept. 1999.

SHEPHARD, Air Cdre Harold Montague, CBE 1974 (OBE 1959); Provost Marshal (Royal Air Force) and Director of Security, 1971–74, retired; *b* 15 Aug. 1918; *s* of late Rev. Leonard B. Shephard; *m* 1939, Margaret Isobel (*née* Girdlestone); one *s* one *d. Educ:* St John's, Leatherhead. Metropolitan Police (CID), 1937–41. Served War, RAF, 1941; commissioned for Provost duties, 1943; seconded Public Safety Br., CCG, 1945; Wing Comdr, Special Investigation Br., BAFO, 1947–50; OC, RAF Police Sch., 1951–52; Dep. Asst Provost Marshal, Hong Kong; Provost Marshal I, Air Ministry; Command Provost Marshal, Cyprus; OC, 4 RAF Police District; Provost Marshal 4, Air Ministry; Comdt, RAF Police Depot, Debden, 1963–64; CPM, FEAF, 1964–67; Comdt, Police Depot, 1967–69; Comd Provost and Security Officer, RAF Germany, 1969–71; Air Cdre, 1971. MBIM. *Recreations:* watching all sports, reading, writing to newspapers. *Address:* 6 Bennetts Mews, Tenterden, Kent TN30 6JN. *Club:* Royal Air Force.
Died 4 Feb. 2000.

SHEPHEARD, Maj.-Gen. Joseph Kenneth, CB 1962; DSO 1943, and Bar, 1945; OBE 1949; *b* 15 Nov. 1908; *s* of late J. D. Shepheard, Poole and Bournemouth; *m* 1939, Maureen, *d* of late Capt. R. McG. Bowen-Colthurst, Oak Grove, County Cork; three *d. Educ:* Monmouth School; RMA Woolwich; Christ's Coll., Cambridge (BA Hons). Commissioned RE, 1928; served in India with King George V's Own Bengal Sappers and Miners, 1933–38; served in France with BEF as Adjt 4 Div. RE, 1939–40; Staff College, Camberley, 1940; Bde Major 161 (Essex) Inf. Bde in UK, Sierra Leone and Western Desert, 1940–41; Bde Major 18 Indian Inf. Bde in Iraq, 1941; GSO1 4 Indian Div. in N Africa and Italy, 1942–44; Comd 6 Assault Regt RE, Normandy to Baltic, 1944–46; JSSC, Latimer, Bucks, 1947; GSO1, FARELF, 1948–49; Staff Officer to Dir of Operations, Malaya, 1950; Comd 27 Fd Enrg Regt and CRE 6 Armd Div., 1951–53; Defence Research Policy Staff, 1953–56; Imperial Defence Coll., 1957; CCRE 1 (Br.) Corps in Germany, 1958–60; Chief of Staff, Northern Comd, 1960–62; Chief Engineer, Northern Army Group and BAOR, 1962–64. Col Comdt, RE, 1967–72. Gen. Sec., The Officers' Assoc., 1966–74. *Address:* Comfrey Cottage, Fields Farm Lane, Layer-de-la-Haye, Colchester, Essex CO2 0JN.
Died 11 May 1997.

SHEPHERD, Rear-Adm. Charles William Haimes, CB 1972; CBE 1968 (OBE 1958); *b* 10 Dec. 1917; *s* of William Henry Haimes Shepherd and Florence (*née* Hayter); *m* 1940, Myra Betty Joan Major (*d* 1988); one *s. Educ:* Public Central Sch., Plymouth; HMS Fisgard and RNC Greenwich. Entered RN as Artificer Apprentice, 1933; specialised Engrg Officer, 1940; served War of 1939–45 in HMS Repulse, Hero, Royal Sovereigh, Gambia (RNZN); Staff of C-in-C Pacific (Sydney); R&D, Guided

Weapons, 1946–49 and 1954–58 incl. Flotilla Eng Officer 3rd Tng Flotilla (HMS Crispin), 1949–51; Sen. Officers War Course, 1961–62; Tech. Dir, UK Polaris Weapon System, 1962–68; Dir Project Teams (Submarines), and Dep. Asst Controller (Polaris), MoD (Navy), 1968–71; Dep. Controller (Polaris), MoD, 1971–73. Sub-Lt 1940; Lieut 1941; Lt-Comdr 1949; Comdr 1952; Captain 1960; Rear-Adm. 1970; retired 1974. Past Pres., Plymouth Albion RFC. *Address:* 12 Underhill Road, Stoke, Plymouth PL3 4BP. *T:* (01752) 556888. *Clubs:* Royal Plymouth Corinthian Yacht, Plymouth Albion Rugby.
Died 24 Feb. 1998.

SHEPHERD, George Anthony, CMG 1986; HM Diplomatic Service, retired; *b* 8 Sept. 1931; *m* 1961, Sarah Eirlys Adamson; one *s* two *d. Educ:* Blundell's School; RMA Sandhurst. Served 4th Royal Tank Regt, in Egypt and BAOR, 1951–57; Trucial Oman Scouts, 1957–59; 2nd RTR, 1959–60; Durham Univ., 1960–61; Federal Regular Army, Aden, 1961–64; 2nd RTR, 1965; Asst Defence Adviser, British High Commission, Lagos, 1967–69; retd as Major RTR, 1969; 1st Secretary, FCO, Bahrain, Dubai and Islamabad, 1969–82; Counsellor, British High Commn, New Delhi, 1982–86; FCO, 1986. Life Member, Fauna Preservation Soc., 1964; Mem., Anglo Yemeni Soc., 1993–. *Publications:* Arabian Adventure, 1961; Flight of the Unicorns, 1964. *Recreations:* walking, bird watching, poetry. *Address:* c/o Foreign and Commonwealth Office, SW1A 2AH. *Club:* Army and Navy.   *Died 20 Feb. 1996.*

SHEPHERD, Sir Peter (Malcolm), Kt 1976; CBE 1967; DL; FCIOB; CIMgt; Director: Shepherd Building Group Ltd (Chairman, 1958–86); Shepherd Construction Ltd, since 1940 (Chairman, 1958–88); *b* 18 Oct. 1916, *s* of Alderman Frederick Welton Shepherd and Mrs Martha Eleanor Shepherd; *m* 1940, Patricia Mary Welton; four *s. Educ:* Nunthorpe and Rossall Schs, Chairman Wool, Jute and Flax ITB, 1964–74; Jt Cttee, Textile ITBs, 1966–74; Construction ITB, 1973–76; Mem. Council, CBI, 1976–89. Chartered Inst. of Building: Pres., 1964–65; Member: Nat. Council, 1956–87; Professional Practice Bd, 1963– (Chm. 1963–75; Vice-Chm., 1975–88); Mem., Bd of Bldg Educn, 1957–75 (Chm. 1965–68). British Inst. of Management: Mem., Nat. Council, 1965–71; Mem., Bd of Fellows, 1969–73; Founder Chm., Yorks and N Lincs Adv. Bd, 1969–71. Mem., President's Consult. Cttee, Building Employers Confedn (formerly Nat. Fedn of Building Trades Employers), 1956–89; Mem. Council, Fedn of Civil Engrg Contractors, 1952–60; Founder Mem., Technician Education Council, 1973–79. Chm., York and N Yorks Scanner Trust, 1979–. Mem., Co. of Merchant Adventurers of City of York (Governor, 1984–85). Mem. Court, York Univ., 1976–; Governor, St Peter's Sch., York, 1970–92. DL N Yorks, 1981. FCIOB (Hon. Fellow, 1987); Hon. Fellow, Leeds Metropolitan Univ. (formerly Leeds Poly.), 1987. Hon. DSc Heriot-Watt, 1979; DUniv York, 1981. *Recreation:* sailing. *Address:* Galtres House, Rawcliffe Lane, York YO3 6NP. *T:* York (01904) 624250. *Club:* Yorkshire (York).   *Died 6 Jan. 1996.*

SHERFIELD, 1st Baron *cr* 1964, of Sherfield-on-Lodden, Southampton; **Roger Mellor Makins,** GCB 1960 (KCB 1953); GCMG 1955 (KCMG 1949; CMG 1944); DL; FRS 1986; Chancellor of Reading University, 1970–92, Chancellor Emeritus, since 1992; *b* 3 Feb. 1904; *e s* of late Brigadier-General Sir Ernest Makins, KBE, CB, DSO and Florence, *d* of Sir James Mellor; *m* 1934, Alice (*d* 1985), *e d* of late Hon. Dwight F. Davis; two *s* four *d. Educ:* Winchester; Christ Church, Oxford. First Class Honours in History, 1925. Fellow of All Souls College, 1925–39 and 1957–. Called to Bar, Inner Temple, 1927; Foreign Office, 1928; served Washington, 1931–34, Oslo, 1934; Foreign Office, 1934; Assistant Adviser on League of Nations Affairs, 1937; Sec. Intergovernmental Cttee on Refugees from Germany, 1938–39; Adviser on League of Nations Affairs, 1939; Acting First Secretary, 1939; Acting Counsellor, 1940; Adviser to British Delegation, International Labour Conference, New York, 1941; served on Staff of Resident Minister in West Africa, 1942; Counsellor, 1942; Asst to Resident Minister at Allied Force Headquarters, Mediterranean, 1943–44; Minister at British Embassy, Washington, 1945–47; UK rep. on United Nations Interim Commission for Food and Agriculture, 1945; Asst Under-Sec. of State, FO, 1947–48, Dep. Under-Sec. of State, 1948–52; British Ambassador to the United States, 1953–56; Joint Permanent Secretary of the Treasury, 1956–59; Chm., UKAEA, 1960–64. Chairman: Hill, Samuel Group, 1966–70; Finance for Industry Ltd, 1973–74; Finance Corp. for Industry Ltd, 1973–74; Industrial & Commercial Finance Corp., 1964–74; Estate Duties Investment Trust, 1966–73; Ship Mortgage Finance Co., 1966–74; Technical Develt Capital, 1966–74; A. C. Cossor, 1968–82; Raytheon Europe Internat. Co., 1970–82; Wells Fargo Ltd, 1972–84, and other companies; Director: Times Publishing Co., 1964–67; Badger Ltd, 1981–83; Mem., Wells Fargo Bank Adv. Council, 1973 (Chm., 1974–86). Pres., BSI, 1970–73. Pres., Parly and Scientific Cttee, 1969–73; Chm., H of L Select Cttee on Science and Technology, 1984–87. Vice-Chm., The Ditchley Foundn, 1965–74 (Chm., 1962–65); Pres., Centre for Internat. Briefing, 1972–85; Mem., Foundn for Science and Technology, 1990–. Chm., Governing Body and Fellow of Imperial Coll. of Science and Technology, 1962–74; Fellow, Winchester College, 1962–79 (Warden, 1974–79). Chairman: Marshall Aid Commemoration Commn, 1965–73; Lindemann Trust Fellowship Cttee, 1973–83; Mem. of Council, Royal Albert Hall, 1959–87; Trustee, The Times Trust, 1968–73. DL Hants, 1978. Attlee Foundn Lectr, 1986. Hon. Student, Christ Church, Oxford, 1973; Hon. FICE 1964; Hon. DCL Oxford; Hon. DLitt Reading; Hon. LLD: Sheffield; London, Hon. DL North Carolina; and other American universities and colleges. Benjamin Franklin Medal, RSA, 1982. *Publications:* (ed) Economic and Social Consequences of Nuclear Energy, 1972; Lord Penney (Royal Soc. biographical memoir), 1994; lectures and articles on science policy. *Recreations:* gardening, travel. *Heir: s* Hon. Christopher James Makins [*b* 23 July 1942; *m* 1976, Wendy Cortesi]. *Address:* 81 Onslow Square, SW7 3LT; Ham Farm House, Ramsdell, Tadley, Hants RG26 5SD. *Clubs:* Boodle's, Pratt's, MCC.
Died 9 Nov. 1996.

SHERIDAN, Cecil Majella, CMG 1961; company director, 1984–93; *b* 9 Dec. 1911; *s* of late J. P. Sheridan, Liverpool, and Mrs Sheridan (*née* Myerscough), Preston, Lancs; *m* 1949, Monica, *d* of H. F. Ereaut, MBE, Jersey, CI; two *s* one *d. Educ:* Ampleforth College, York. Admitted Solicitor, 1934; called to the Bar, Inner Temple, 1952. Practised as solicitor in Liverpool (Messrs Yates, Sheridan & Co.), 1934–40. Served in RAFVR, General Duties Pilot, 1940–46; resigned with hon. rank of Squadron Leader. Joined Colonial Legal Service, 1946; Crown Counsel and Dep. Public Prosecutor, Malayan Union, 1946–48; Legal Adviser, Malay States of Pahang, Kelantan, Trengganu and Selangor and Settlement of Penang, 1948–55; Legal Draftsman, Fedn of Malaya, 1955–57; Solicitor-General, Fedn of Malaya, 1957–59; Attorney-General, Fedn of Malaya, 1959–63; Attorney-General, Malaysia, retd. Mem., (Fedn of Malaya) Inter-Governmental Cttees for Borneo Territories and Singapore, 1962–63. Chm. Traffic Comrs, E Midland Traffic Area, 1965–81, Dep. Chm., 1981–82. Pres., British Assoc. of Malaysia, 1964–65. Chm., Malaysia Housing Soc., 1964–65. Associate Mem., Commonwealth Parly Assoc. (UK Branch). Hon. PMN

(Malaysia), 1963. *Address:* Roselea Cottage, 65 Main Street, Queniborough, Leicester LE7 3DB.
Died 22 May 2000.

SHERLOCK, Dr Alexander, CBE 1989; medical practitioner; *b* 14 Feb. 1922; *s* of Thomas Sherlock, MM, and Evelyn M. Sherlock (*née* Alexander); *m* 1st, 1945, Clarice C. Scarff (*d* 1975); one *s* two *d*; 2nd, 1976, Eileen Hall; one step *d*. *Educ:* Magdalen College Sch., Oxford; Stowmarket Grammar Sch.; London Hospital. MB BS (Hons) 1945. Ho. Phys., Ho. Surg., London Hosp.; RAF, 1946–48; medical practitioner, Felixstowe, and consultant/adviser to many organisations in matters of occupational health, safety and welfare. Called to the Bar, Gray's Inn, 1961. Member: Felixstowe UDC, 1960–74; E Suffolk CC, 1966–74; Suffolk CC, 1974–79 (Chairman, Fire and Public Protection Cttee, 1977–79). MEP (C) SW Essex, 1979–89; former Mem. of Envmt Cttee (Eur. Democratic (C) Leader) and Develt Cttee; spokesman on Envmt, Health and Consumer Protection, 1979–89. Vice-President: Inst. of Trading Officers, 1981–; Assoc. of Envmtl Health Officers, 1981–; Soc. of Dist Councils, 1981–. FRSA. OStJ 1974. *Recreation:* gardening. *Address:* 16 Victoria Road, Felixstowe, Suffolk IP11 7PT. *T:* (01394) 284503. *Club:* Royal Air Force.
Died 18 Feb. 1999.

SHERLOCK, Sir Philip (Manderson), KBE 1967 (CBE 1953); Vice President, Caribbean Resources Development Foundation Inc., since 1983; Consultant to Vice-Chancellor, University of the West Indies, since 1989; *b* Jamaica, 25 Feb. 1902; *s* of Rev. Terence Sherlock, Methodist Minister, and Adina Sherlock; *m* 1942, Grace Marjorye Verity; two *s* one *d*. *Educ:* Calabar High Sch., Jamaica. Headmaster, Wolmer's Boys' Sch., Jamaica, 1933–38; Sec., Inst. of Jamaica, 1939–44; Educn Officer, Jamaica Welfare, 1944–47; Dir, Extra-Mural Dept, University Coll. of West Indies, 1947–60, also Vice-Principal, University Coll. of W Indies, 1952–62; Pro-Vice-Chancellor, Univ. of West Indies, 1962, Vice-Chancellor, 1963–69; Sec.-Gen., Assoc. of Caribbean Univs & Res. Insts, 1969–89; Sec., Assoc. of Caribbean Univs Foundn, 1979–83. Hon. LLD: Leeds, 1959; Carleton, 1967; St Andrews, 1968; Hon. DCL New Brunswick, 1966; Hon. DLitt: Acadia, 1966; Miami, 1971; Univ. of WI, 1972; Florida, 1975. Order of Andres Bello with collar (Venezuela), 1978; Order of Merit, 1989. *Publications:* Anansi the Spider Man, 1956; (with John Parry) Short History of the West Indies, 1956, 4th edn 1987; Caribbean Citizen, 1957; West Indian Story, 1960; Three Finger Jack, 1961; Jamaica, a Junior History, 1966; West Indian Folk Tales, 1966; West Indies, 1966; Land and People of the West Indies, 1967; Belize, a Junior History, 1969; The Iguana's Tail, 1969; West Indian Nations, 1973; Ears and Tails and Common Sense, 1974; Shout for Freedom, 1976; Norman Manley, a biography, 1980; Keeping Company with Jamaica, 1984; The University of the West Indies, 1990; (with Dr Hazel Bennett) The Story of the Jamaican People, 1998; educational books and articles. *Recreations:* reading, writing, cooking. *Address:* Office of the Vice-Chancellor, University of the West Indies, Mona Campus, Kingston 7, Jamaica. *Club:* National Liberal.
Died 4 Dec. 2000.

SHERRY, Kathleen Marian, (Mrs Vincent Sherry); *see* Robinson, K. M.

SHERSBY, Sir (Julian) Michael, Kt 1995; MP (C) Uxbridge, since Dec. 1972; *b* Ickenham, 17 Feb. 1933; *s* of William Henry and Elinor Shersby; *m* 1958, Barbara Joan, *d* of John Henry Barrow; one *s* one *d*. *Educ:* John Lyon Sch., Harrow-on-the-Hill. Mem., Paddington Borough Council, 1959–64; Mem., Westminster City Council, 1964–71; Deputy Lord Mayor of Westminster,

1967–68. Chm., Uxbridge Div. Young Conservatives, 1951–52; Conservative and Unionist Party Organisation, 1952–58; Sec., Assoc. of Specialised Film Producers, 1958–62; Dir, British Industrial Film Assoc., 1962–66; Dir, 1966–77, Dir-Gen., 1977–88, Sugar Bureau (formerly British Sugar Bureau); Sec., UK Sugar Industry Assoc., 1978–88, Parly Advr, 1988–95; Treas., World Sugar Res. Orgn, 1982–. PPS to Minister of Aerospace and Shipping, DTI, 1974; Member: Speaker's Panel of Chairmen, 1983–; Public Accounts Cttee, 1983–. Parly Advr to Police Fedn, 1989–; promoted Private Member's Bills: Town and Country Amenities Act, 1974; Parks Regulation (Amendment) Act, 1974; Stock Exchange (Completion of Bargains) Act, 1976; Gaming (Amendment) Act, 1980; Copyright Act (1956) Amendment Act, 1982; British Nationality (Falkland Islands) Act, 1983; Firearms (Amendment) Act, 1994. Jt Sec., 1977–80, Vice-Pres., 1980–83, Parly and Scientific Cttee. Chm., Falkland Is Gp, 1982–, Mem. Exec. Cttee, UK Br., 1988–, CPA. Pres., London Green Belt Council, 1989–. Mem. Court, Brunel Univ., 1975–; Pres., Abbeyfield Uxbridge Soc., 1975–. FIPR 1994. DUniv Brunel, 1994. *Recreations:* theatre, fishing, travel. *Address:* House of Commons, SW1A 0AA. *T:* (0171) 219 5023; Bay Lodge, 36 Harefield Road, Uxbridge, Middx UB8 1PH. *T:* (01895) 239465, *Fax:* (01895) 253105. *Clubs:* Carlton; Conservative (Uxbridge).
Died 8 May 1997.

SHIELDS, John Sinclair; *b* 4 Feb. 1903; *s* of Rev. W. H. Shields and Margaret Louisa (*née* Sinclair); *m* 1st, 1924, Norah Fane Smith; three *d*; 2nd, 1963, Mrs Noreen Moultrie, *widow* of Comdr John Moultrie. *Educ:* Charterhouse; Lincoln Coll., Oxford (MA). Headmaster: Wem Grammar School, 1934–47; Queen Mary's School, Basingstoke, 1947–56; Headmaster, Peter Symonds' School, Winchester, 1957–63. Vice-Pres. Classical Assoc., 1958; Mem., Broadcasting Cttee, 1960. *Recreations:* golf, gardening. *Address:* Rodmore Farm Cottage, Kings Stag, Sturminster Newton, Dorset DT10 2BE. *T:* (01963) 23018.
Died 23 Dec. 1997.

SHIELL, James Wyllie, BSc; FICE; chartered civil engineer, retired; *b* 20 Aug. 1912; *yr s* of late George Douglas Shiell, farmer, Rennieston, Jedburgh and Janet Gladstone Wyllie; *m* 1941, Maureen Cameron Macpherson Hunter, *d* of late Thomas Hunter, Leeds; two *s*. *Educ:* Jedburgh Grammar and Kelso High Schools; Edinburgh Univ. Municipal engrg posts in Edinburgh, Southampton, Sunderland and Leeds, 1934–39; Sen. Engr on Staff of J. D. & D. M. Watson, Consulting Engrs, Westminster, 1939–43 and 1945–47; Civil Engr on wartime service with Admty, 1943–45; Sen. Engr, Min. of Agriculture, 1947–49; Engrg Inspector, Dept of Health for Scotland, 1949–62; Dep. Chief Engr, Scottish Development Dept, 1962–68; Under Sec. and Chief Engr, Scottish Development Dept, 1968–75. Hon. FCIWEM. *Recreations:* walking with friends, listening to radio and tapes. *Address:* 25 Mortonhall Road, Edinburgh EH9 2HS. *T:* (0131) 667 8528.
Died 17 June 1997.

SHILLINGFORD, Prof. John Parsons, CBE 1988; MD; FRCP, FACC; Sir John McMichael Professor of Cardiovascular Medicine, Royal Postgraduate Medical School, London University, 1976–79, then Emeritus Professor (Director, Cardiovascular Research Unit, and Professor of Angiocardiology, 1966–76); Consultant Medical Director, British Heart Foundation, 1981–86; *b* 15 April 1914; *s* of Victor Shillingford and Ethel Eugenie Parsons; *m* 1947, Doris Margaret Franklin (*d* 1997); two *s* one *d*. *Educ:* Bishops Stortford; Harvard Univ. (MD 1943); London Hosp. Med. Sch. (MD 1948). FRCP 1960; FACC 1966. Rockefeller Student, Harvard Med. Sch., 1939–42; House appts, Presbyterian Hosp., New York, and London Hosp., 1943–45; Med. First Asst, London

Hosp., 1945–52, Sen. Lectr Royal Postgrad. Med. Sch., 1958–62. Sec., Brit. Cardiac Soc., 1963–70; Chm. Org. Cttee, Sixth World Congress Cardiology, 1970. Member: Assoc. Physicians Gt Brit.; Med. Res. Soc.; Med. Soc. London; Royal Soc. Med. (Pres., Sect. Experimental Med., 1968); Comité Recherche Médicale, EEC; various cttees, Brit. Heart Foundn. Hon. Member: Hellenic Cardiac Soc.; Cardiac Soc. of Yugoslavia; Polish Cardiac Soc.; Cardiological Soc. of India; French Cardiac Soc.; Corresp. Mem., Australian Cardiac Soc. Hon. FACP. Editor, Cardiovascular Research. Visiting Prof., Australian Heart Foundn, 1965; Lumleian Lectr, RCP, 1972; lectured extensively in Europe, USA, S America, Africa, Middle East. James Berry Prize, RCS. *Publications:* numerous scientific papers, mainly on heart disease and coronary thrombosis. *Recreations:* gardening, music. *Address:* 5 Chester Close, Queens Ride, Barnes, SW13 0JE. *T:* (020) 8789 3629. *Club:* Hurlingham.

Died 16 Sept. 1999.

SHILLITO, Charles Henry; Under-Secretary, Ministry of Agriculture, Fisheries and Food, 1974–82; *b* 8 Jan. 1922; *s* of Charles Cawthorne and Florence Shillito; *m* 1947, Elizabeth Jean (*née* Bull); two *d*. *Educ:* Hugh Bell Sch., Middlesbrough. Clerk, Min. of Agriculture and Fisheries, 1938; War Service, Lieut RNVR, 1941–46; Principal, MAFF, 1957; Asst Sec. 1966; Section Head, Nat. Econ. Devel. Office, 1966–69 (on secondment). Hon. ARCVS 1986; Hon. Mem., BVA, 1989. *Recreations:* gardening, nautical pursuits. *Address:* 62 Downs Road, Coulsdon, Surrey CR5 1AB. *T:* (01737) 553392.

Died 4 Aug. 1998.

SHIRLEY, David Andrew; a Special Commissioner of Income Tax, since 1988; *b* 23 Nov. 1926; *er s* of Rev. Canon F. J. Shirley, DD (Oxon), FSA, and Dorothy, *d* of John Howard, Aberfeldy; *m* 1st, 1955, Dorothy Evelyn Finn (*d* 1969); 2nd, 1973, (Alysia) Rosemary (*d* 1993), *d* of Col Gerald Tillimer-Thompson, Cayton Park, Wargrave; 3rd, 1997, Catherine Mary (*née* Macbeth), *widow* of Sir William Morton, CBE. *Educ:* Winchester Coll.; New Coll., Oxford (2nd Cl. Jurisprudence). 2nd Lieut Black Watch, 1946; ADC to Gov. of NW Frontier Province, 1947–48; Captain Black Watch (TA). Called to the Bar, Lincoln's Inn (Cholmeley Schol.), 1951; (*ad eundem*) Inner Temple, 1964; Bencher, Lincoln's Inn, 1978. Part-time Chm., VAT Tribunal, 1978–. *Recreations:* hunting, ski-ing, silviculture. *Address:* Flore Fields, Flore, Northampton NN7 4JX. *T:* (01327) 340226.

Died 25 Feb. 1999.

SHIRLEY, Philip Hammond; retired; *b* 4 Oct. 1912; *s* of Frank Shillito Shirley and Annie Lucy (*née* Hammond); *m* 1st, 1936, Marie Edna Walsh (*d* 1972); one *s* one *d*; 2nd, 1973, Norma Jones. *Educ:* Sydney Church of England Grammar School (Shore). Qualified in Australia as Chartered Accountant, 1934; with Peat Marwick Mitchell & Co., Chartered Accountants, London, 1937–49; with Unilever, 1951–58: Chief Accountant, 1952–58; Chm. Batchelors Foods Ltd, 1958–61; Mem. BR Bd, 1962–67 (Vice-Chm. Bd, 1964–67); Dep. Chm., Cunard Steamship Co., 1968–71; Chief Commissioner of Public Transport, NSW, 1972–75. *Address:* 11, 25 Belmont Avenue, Wollstonecraft, NSW 2065, Australia.

Died 12 May 1998.

SHORT, Rt Rev. Hedley Vicars Roycraft; retired 1985; *b* 24 Jan. 1914; *s* of Hedley Vicars Short and Martha Hallam Parke; *m* 1953, Elizabeth Frances Louise Shirley; one *s* four *d*. *Educ:* Trinity College, Univ. of Toronto (BA, LTh, BD). Deacon, 1943, priest, 1944, Assistant Curate St Michael and All Angels, Toronto; Junior Chaplain, Coventry Cathedral, England, 1946–47; Lecturer, Trinity Coll., Toronto, 1947–51, Dean of Residence, 1949–51; Rector, Cochrane, Ont, 1951–56; Rector, St Barnabas, St

Catharines, Ont, 1956–63; Canon, Christ's Church Cathedral, Hamilton, Ont, 1962; Dean of Saskatchewan, 1963–70; Archdeacon of Prince Albert, 1966–70; Bishop of Saskatchewan, 1970–85. Member of General Synod, 1955–83; Examining Chaplain successively to Bishops of Moosonee, Niagara and Saskatchewan. Mem., Northern Develt Adv. Council, Province of Saskatchewan, 1987–88. Pres. Council, Coll. of Emmanuel and St Chad, Saskatoon, 1974–80; Chm., Natonum Community Coll., Prince Albert, 1974–76; Chancellor, 1975–80, Hon. Fellow, 1980, Univ. of Emmanuel Coll. Hon. DD: Trinity Coll., Toronto, 1964; Emmanuel Coll., Saskatoon, 1983. *Publication:* (contrib.) Eucharistic Dimensions, 1977. *Recreations:* music, sketching, reading. *Address:* 355 19th Street W, Prince Albert, Saskatchewan S6V 4C8, Canada.

Died 25 Feb. 1996.

SHOTTON, Prof. Edward; Professor of Pharmaceutics, University of London, 1956–77, then Emeritus; *b* 15 July 1910; *s* of Ernest Richard and Maud Shotton; *m* 1943, Mary Constance Louise Marchant; one *d*. *Educ:* Smethwick (Junior) Technical School; Birkbeck College, University of London. PhC 1933; BSc (London), 1939; PhD (London), 1955; FRIC 1949. Pharmaceutical research and development work at Burroughs, Wellcome & Co., Dartford, 1939–48; Sen. Lecturer in Pharmaceutics, Univ. of London, 1948–56. Chairman, British Pharmaceutical Conference, 1966. Hon. ACT Birmingham, 1961. *Publications:* (with K. Ridgway) Physical Pharmaceutics, 1974; research papers, mainly in Jl of Pharmacy and Pharmacology. *Recreations:* gardening, cricket, fly-fishing. *Address:* 1 Henniker Road, Debenham, Stowmarket, Suffolk IP14 6PY. *T:* (01728) 860542. *Club:* Athenaeum.

Died 22 May 1998.

SHUTE, Prof. Charles Cameron Donald, MD; Professor of Histology, Cambridge University, 1969–84, then Emeritus; Life Fellow of Christ's College, Cambridge, 1957; *b* 23 May 1917; *s* of late Cameron Deane Shute; *m* 1st, 1947, Patricia Cameron (*d* 1952), *d* of F. H. Doran; 2nd, 1954, Lydia May (Wendy) (*née* Harwood) (marr diss. 1980); one *s* three *d*; 3rd, 1980, Rosemary Gay Robins. *Educ:* Eton; King's Coll., Cambridge; Middlesex Hosp., London. MA, MB, BChir Cambridge, 1945; MD Cambridge, 1958. Resident posts at Middlesex Hosp., 1945–47; RAMC (otologist), 1947–49; Demonstrator and Lectr in Anatomy, London Hosp. Med. Coll., 1951; Univ. Demonstrator and Lectr, Cambridge, 1952–69; Univ. Reader in Neuroanatomy, Cambridge, 1969. *Publications:* The McCollough Effect, 1979; (with R. G. Robins) The Rhind Mathematical Papyrus, 1987; papers in biological and Egyptological jls. *Recreation:* Egyptology. *Address:* 400 Princeton Way NE, Atlanta, GA 30307, USA. *T:* (404) 6339452.

Died 2 Jan. 1999.

SIDDONS, (Arthur) Harold (Makins), FRCS, FRCP; Hon. Consulting Surgeon, St George's Hospital; *b* 17 Jan. 1911; *s* of late A. W. Siddons, Housemaster, Harrow School; *m* 1st, 1939, Joan Richardson Anderson (*née* McConnell) *d* 1949); one *s* one *d*; 2nd, 1956, Eleanor Mary Oliver (*née* Hunter) (*d* 1970); 3rd, 1971, Margaret Christine Beardmore (*née* Smith) (*d* 1997). *Educ:* Harrow; Jesus College, Cambridge (MB, BCh 1935; MChir 1940); St George's Hosp. FRCS 1937; FRCP 1968. Surgeon, St George's Hospital, 1941; Consultant General and Thoracic Surgeon, St George's Hosp. and others, 1948–76. Served RAF Medical Branch, 1942–46. Member of Court of Examiners, Royal College of Surgeons of England, 1958–63. *Publications:* Cardiac Pacemakers, 1967; sections on lung surgery in various textbooks. *Recreations:* travel, gardens, birds. *Address:* 43a Waverley Lane, Farnham, Surrey GU9 8BH.

Died 6 April 2000.

SIDWELL, (John William) Martindale, FRAM, FRCO; Organist and Choirmaster, Hampstead Parish Church,

1945–92; Organist and Director of Music, St Clement Danes (Central Church of the Royal Air Force), 1957–92; Conductor: Martindale Sidwell Choir, since 1956; St Clement Danes Chorale, 1983–92; *b* 23 Feb. 1916; *s* of John William Sidwell, Little Packington, Warwicks, and Mary Martindale, Liverpool; *m* 1944, Barbara Anne (*née* Hill) (pianist, harpsichordist and Prof. of Piano and Harpsichord, Royal Coll. of Music, under the name Barbara Hill); two *s. Educ:* Wells Cathedral Sch., Somerset; Royal Academy of Music. Sub-Organist, Wells Cathedral, 1932. Served War of 1939–45, Royal Engineers. Organist, Holy Trinity Church, Leamington Spa, and Director of Music, Warwick School, 1943, also at same time Conductor of Royal Leamington Spa Bach Choir; Conductor, Hampstead Choral Soc., 1946–81; Founder 1967, and Director and Conductor, 1967–81, London Bach Orch.; Conductor, St Clement's Orch., 1983–87. Prof., RSCM, 1958–66; Prof. of Organ, RAM, 1963–84. Mem. Council, RCO, 1966–. Harriet Cohen International Bach Medal, 1967. Frequent broadcasts as conductor and as organ recitalist, 1944–. *Address:* 1 Frognal Gardens, Hampstead, NW3 6UY. *T:* (0171) 435 9210. *Clubs:* Savage, Wig and Pen.

Died 20 Feb. 1998.

SIE, Sir Banja T.; *see* Tejan-Sie.

SILKIN, Jon, FRSL 1986; poet; *b* 2 Dec. 1930; *s* of late Dora Rubenstein and Joseph Silkin, solicitor; three *s* one *d* (one *s* decd); *m* 1974, Lorna Tracy (American writer and co-editor of Stand) (marr. diss. 1995). *Educ:* Wycliffe Coll.; Dulwich Coll.; Univ. of Leeds (BA Hons Eng. Lit. 1962). Journalist, 1947; Nat. Service, teaching in Educn Corps, Army; subseq. six years as manual labourer, London and two years teaching English to foreign students. Founded magazine Stand, 1952. Several poetry-reading tours, USA; Vis. Lectr, Denison Univ., Ohio; taught at Writers' Workshop, Univ. of Iowa, 1968–69 and 1991; Visiting Writer: for Australian Council for the Arts, 1974; College of Idaho, Caldwell, 1978; Mishkenot Sha'ananim, Jerusalem, 1980; Bingham Vis. Poet, Univ. of Louisville, 1981; Elliston Poet-in-Residence, Univ. of Cincinnati, 1983; Distinguished Writer in Residence, The Amer. Univ., 1989; Residency, Dumfries and Galloway Arts, 1990; Lectr in English and Amer. Literature, Tsukuba Univ., Japan, 1991–94. C. Day Lewis Fellowship, 1976–77. Vis. Speaker, World Congress of Poets: Korea, 1979; Madrid, 1982; Corfu, 1985; Florence, 1986. *Publications:* The Peaceable Kingdom, 1954, reprint 1976; The Two Freedoms, 1958; The Re-ordering of the Stones, 1961; Nature with Man, 1965 (Geoffrey Faber Meml Prize, 1966); (with Murphy and Tarn) Penguin Modern Poets 7, 1965; Poems New and Selected, 1966; Killhope Wheel, 1971; Amana Grass, 1971; Out of Battle: the poetry of the Great War, 1972, 2nd edn 1996; (ed) Poetry of the Committed Individual, 1973; The Principle of Water, 1974; The Little Time-keeper, 1976; (ed) Penguin Book of First World War Poetry, 1979; (ed with Peter Redgrove) New Poetry, 1979; The Psalms with Their Spoils, 1980; Selected Poems, 1980, rev. and enl. edn 1988; (ed jtly) Stand One, 1984; Gurney (verse play), 1985; (ed) Wilfred Owen: the Collected Poems, 1985; The Ship's Pasture (poems), 1986; (with Jon Glover) The Penguin Book of First World War Prose, 1989; The Lensbreakers, 1992; Selected Poems, 1994; (ed) The War Poems of Wilfred Owen, 1994; The Life of Metrical and Free Verse in Twentieth Century Poetry, 1997. *Recreation:* travelling. *Address:* 13 Queens Terrace, Newcastle upon Tyne NE2 2PJ. *T:* (0191) 281 2614.

Died 25 Nov. 1997.

SILLITOE, Leslie Richard, OBE 1977; JP; General Secretary, Ceramic and Allied Trades Union, 1975–80, then Life Member; *b* 30 Aug. 1915; *s* of Leonard Richard Sillitoe and Ellen (*née* Sutton); *m* 1939, Lucy (*née* Goulding); two *d. Educ:* St George's and St Giles' Sch., Newcastle, Staffs; Stoke-on-Trent School of Art; WEA, N Staffs Technical Coll. Modeller and mouldmaker on leaving school. Served War, Royal Artillery, sen. noncommnd officer, 1939–46. Ceramic and Allied Trades Union: General President, 1961–63; Organiser, 1963; Asst Gen. Sec., 1967. Dep. Chm., Ceramics, Glass and Mineral Products Industry Trng Bd, 1977–82; Chm., Nat. Jt Council for Ceramic Industry, 1975–81. Member: Industrial Tribunals, 1971–84; VAT Tribunals, 1973–91. Chm., N Staffs Manpower Services Cttee, 1975–83; Life Mem., N Staffs Trades Council (Pres., 1963–81); Member: N Staffs Tourist Assoc.; N Staffs Medical Inst.; Staffordshire Soc.; Pottery & Glass Benevolent Inst. (Vice-Pres., 1980–); N Staffs Community Health Council, 1975–85; Staffordshire War Pensions Cttee, 1980–; N Staffs Special Adventure Playground Cttee, 1985–; Council, Univ. of Keele, 1976–85, 1989– (Mem. Court, 1976–); BBC Local Radio Council, 1978–81; Wetley Moor Jt Cttee, 1989–; Mem. Bd of Management, and Custodian Trustee, N Staffs Trustee Savings Bank; Vice-President: N Staffs District WEA, 1976–86; Muscular Dystrophy N Staffs Gp, 1978–; Pres., Staffordshire Lads and Dads Assoc., 1981–82, Vice-Pres. 1982–; Sec. and Treas., Ceramic Ind. Welfare Soc., 1971–81. Mem., Staffs Develt Assoc., 1977–81. Mem., Magistrates' Assoc.; Gideons Internat. Mem., Stoke-on-Trent District Council, 1953–83, 1986– (Vice-Chm., Museums Cttee); Lord Mayor, Stoke-on-Trent, 1981–82, Dep. Lord Mayor 1982–83. Mem., W Midland TAVRA, 1979–; Chairman: Friends of the Staffordshire Regt (N Staffs), 1982–; N Staffs Normandy Veterans' Assoc., 1986–; John Baskerfield VC Meml Cttee, 1996–. Governor: St Peter's High Sch., Penkhull, 1975–; Cauldon Coll. of Further Educn, Stoke-on-Trent, 1976–; Thistley Hough High Sch., Penkhull, 1982–86; Stoke Harpfield Primary Sch., 1982–; St Augustine's Primary Sch., Stoke, 1990–96. Pres., Longton Rotary Club, 1987–88. Former Member: Boy Scouts; St John's Ambulance Brigade. Territorial Efficient Service Medal, 1944. JP Stoke-on-Trent, 1963. Freeman, City of Stoke-on-Trent, 1993. *Publication:* foreword to The History of the Potters Union, 1977. *Recreations:* walking, photography, swimming, history. *Address:* 19 Sillitoe Place, Penkhull, Stoke-on-Trent ST4 5DQ. *T:* (01782) 847866.

Died 8 Oct. 1996.

SILVER, Prof. Robert Simpson, CBE 1967; FRSE; FIMechE; FInstP; James Watt Professor of Mechanical Engineering, University of Glasgow, 1967–79; *b* Montrose, Angus, 13 March 1913; *s* of Alexander Clark Silver and Isabella Simpson; *m* 1937, Jean McIntyre Bruce (*d* 1988), *er d* of Alexander and Elizabeth Bruce (*née* Livingstone); two *s. Educ:* Montrose Academy; University of Glasgow. MA 1932; BSc (1st Class Hons Nat. Phil) 1934; PhD 1938; DSc 1945. Research Physicist, ICI (Explosives), 1936–39; Head of Research, G. & J. Weir Ltd, 1939–46; Asst Director, Gas Research Board, 1947–48; Director of Research, Federated Foundries Ltd, 1948–54; Chief Designer, John Brown Land Boilers Ltd, 1954–56; Chief of Development and Research, G. & J. Weir Ltd, 1956–62 (Director 1958); Prof. of Mech. Engrg, Heriot-Watt Coll. (later Univ.), 1962–66. FInstP 1942; MIMechE 1953; FRSE 1963. Hon. DSc Strathclyde, 1984. Foreign Associate, Nat. Acad. of Engineering, USA, 1979. Unesco Prize for Science, 1968. *Publications:* An Introduction to Thermodynamics, 1971; The Bruce, Robert I King of Scots (play), 1986, revd edn as The Hert o Scotland, 1994; Conflict and Contexts: poems of the quarter-century 1930–1955, 1992; papers on physics and engineering, with special emphasis on thermo-dynamics, desalination, combustion, phase-change, and heat transfer; also on philosophy of science and education. *Recreations:*

fishing, music, theatre, Scottish history and affairs. *Address:* 5 Panmure Street, Montrose, Angus DD10 8EZ. *T:* (01674) 77793. *Died 21 April 1997.*

SILVERLEAF, Alexander, CB 1980; FEng 1981; FRINA, FICE, FCIT; Co-ordinator, International Transport Group (INTRA), since 1981; *b* 29 Oct. 1920; *m* 1950, Helen Marion Scott; two *d. Educ:* Kilburn Grammar Sch., London; Glasgow Univ. (BSc 1941). Wm Denny and Bros Ltd, Shipbuilders, Dumbarton, 1937–51: Student apprentice, 1937–41; Head, Design Office, 1947–51; National Physical Laboratory, 1951–71: Superintendent, Ship Div., 1962–67; Dep. Dir, 1966–71; Dir, Transport and Road Res. Lab., 1971–80. Chm., UK Council for Computing Develt, 1981–86. Hon. FIHT. *Publications:* papers in Trans Royal Instn Naval Architects and other technical jls. *Address:* 64 Fairfax Road, Teddington, Middx TW11 9BZ. *T:* (0181) 977 6261. *Club:* Athenæum. *Died 13 May 1997.*

SILVERMAN, Julius; Barrister-at-law; *b* Leeds, 8 Dec. 1905; *s* of Nathan Silverman; *m* 1959, Eva Price. *Educ:* Central High School, Leeds (Matriculated). Entered Gray's Inn as student in 1928; called to Bar, 1931; joined Midland Circuit, 1933, practised in Birmingham. Birmingham City Councillor, 1934–45. Contested Moseley Division, 1935. MP (Lab) Birmingham, Erdington, 1945–55 and 1974–83, Birmingham, Aston, 1955–74. Apptd Chm., by Birmingham City Council, of Handsworth Inquiry (into disturbances in Handsworth), 1985 (report published by Council, 1986). Chm., India League, 1971. Freeman, City of Birmingham, 1982. Hon. Fellow, Univ. of Central England (formerly City of Birmingham Poly.), 1987. Padma Bhushan (India), 1990. *Publication:* (contrib.) Centenary History of the Indian National Congress, 1986. *Address:* c/o 49 Viceroy Close, Bristol Road, Birmingham B5 7US. *Died 21 Sept. 1996.*

SIMEON, Sir John Edmund Barrington, 7th Bt *cr* 1815, of Grazeley, Berkshire; Civil Servant in Department of Social Welfare, Provincial Government, British Columbia, retired 1975; *b* 1 March 1911; *s* of Sir John Walter Barrington Simeon, 6th Bt, and Adelaide Jane (*d* 1934), *e d* of late Col Hon. E. A. Holmes-à-Court; *S* father, 1957; *m* 1937, Anne Robina Mary Dean; one *s* two *d. Educ:* Eton; Christ Church, Oxford. Motor business, 1931–39. Served with RAF, 1939–43; invalided, rank of Flight Lt, 1943. Civil Servant, Ministry of Agriculture, 1943–51. Took up residence in Vancouver, Canada, 1951. *Recreations:* sailing, painting. *Heir: s* Richard Edmund Barrington Simeon, PhD Yale, Professor of Political Science and Law, Toronto Univ. [*b* 2 March 1943; *m* 1st, 1966, Agnes Joan (marr. diss. 1989), *d* of George Frederick Weld; one *s* one *d;* 2nd, 1993, Maryetta Cheney]. *Address:* c/o Jerome & Co., Solicitors, 98 High Street, Newport, Isle of Wight PO30 1BD. *Died 6 Dec. 1999.*

SIMEON, John Power Barrington, OBE 1978; HM Diplomatic Service, retired; *b* 15 Nov. 1929; *o s* of late Cornwall Barrington Simeon and Ellaline Margery Mary (*née* Le Poer Power, Clonmel, Co. Tipperary); *m* 1st, 1951, Margareta Valborg Johanna Ahlstrom (marr. diss. 1955); 2nd, 1966, Norma Fill (*née* Dopson) (*d* 1969); one *s;* 3rd, 1970, Carina Renate Elisabeth Schüller. *Educ:* Beaumont Coll.; RMA, Sandhurst. Commnd 2nd Lieut Royal Corps of Signals, 1949; Lieut 1951; resigned, 1952. Ferrous and non-ferrous metal broker, London and Europe, 1953–57; Rank Organisation: served in Germany, Thailand, Singapore, India, ME, N Africa, Hong Kong and London, 1957–65; entered HM Diplomatic Service, 1965; First Sec. (Commercial): Colombo, 1967; Bonn, 1968–70; First Sec., and sometime Actg High Comr, Port of Spain, 1970–73; FCO, 1973–75; Dep. High Comr and Head of Post, Ibadan, Nigeria, 1975–79; Counsellor, 1978; HM Consul-General: Berlin, 1979–81; Hamburg,

1981–84. *Recreations:* travel, photography, reading, music. *Address:* 4 Cliff Road, Dovercourt, Harwich, Essex CO12 3PP. *T:* (01255) 552820.
Died 16 Nov. 2000.

SIMMONS, Prof. Jack, OBE 1999; Professor of History, University of Leicester, 1947–75, then Professor Emeritus (Pro-Vice-Chancellor, 1960–63; Public Orator, 1965–68); *b* 30 Aug. 1915; *o c* of Seymour Francis Simmons and Katharine Lillias, *d* of Thomas Finch, MB, Babbacombe, Devon. *Educ:* Westminster Sch.; Christ Church, Oxford. Beit Lectr in the History of the British Empire, Oxford Univ., 1943–47. FSA. Mem., Adv. Council, Science Museum, 1969–84; Chm., Nat. Railway Museum Cttee, York, 1981–84; Leicestershire Archæological and Historical Society: Hon. Editor, 1948–61; Pres. 1966–77. Chm., Leicester Local Broadcasting Council, 1967–70. Jt Editor, The Journal of Transport History, 1953–73; Editor: A Visual History of Modern Britain; Classical County Histories. *Publications:* African Discovery: an Anthology of Exploration (ed with Margery Perham), 1942; Southey, 1945; Edition of Southey's Letters from England, 1951; Journeys in England: an Anthology, 1951; Parish and Empire, 1952; Livingstone and Africa, 1955; New University, 1958; The Railways of Britain, 1961, 3rd edn 1986; Transport, 1962; Britain and the World, 1965; St Pancras Station, 1968; Transport Museums, 1970; A Devon Anthology, 1971; (ed) Memoirs of a Station Master, 1973; Leicester Past and Present (2 vols), 1974; (ed) Rail 150: the Stockton and Darlington Railway and What Followed, 1975; The Railway in England and Wales 1830–1914, 1978; A Selective Guide to England, 1979; Dandy Cart to Diesel: the National Railway Museum, 1981; (cd) F. R. Conder, The Men who Built Railways, 1983; Image of the Train, pt 1 1985, pt 2 1993; The Railway in Town and Country 1830–1914, 1986; The Victorian Railway, 1991; Railways: an Anthology, 1991; The Express Train and Other Railway Studies, 1994; (ed with Gordon Biddle) The Oxford Companion to British Railway History, 1997. *Address:* Flat 6, 36 Victoria Park Road, Leicester LE2 1XB. *Died 3 Sept. 2000.*

SIMON, Prof. Ulrich Ernst, DD; Professor of Christian Literature, 1972–80, Dean, 1978–80, King's College, London; *b* 21 Sept. 1913; *s* of James and Anna Simon; *m* 1949, Joan Edith Raynor Westlake; two *s* one *d. Educ:* Grunewald Gymnasium, Berlin; King's Coll., London. BD, MTh, DD, FKC. Ordained deacon in Church of England, 1938, priest 1939; Univ. Lectr, KCL, 1945; Reader, 1960. *Publications:* Theology of Crisis, 1948; Theology of Salvation, 1953; Heaven in the Christian Tradition, 1958; The Ascent to Heaven, 1961; The End is not Yet, 1964; Theology Observed, 1966; A Theology of Auschwitz, 1967 (paperback 1978); The Trial of Man, 1973; Story and Faith, 1975; Sitting in Judgment, 1978; Atonement, 1987; Pity and Terror, 1989. *Recreations:* gardening, chamber music, walking. *Address:* 22 Collingwood Avenue, N10 3ED. *T:* (0181) 883 4852.
Died 31 July 1997.

SIMON, Hon. William Edward; Chairman, William E. Simon & Sons, Inc., New Jersey, Los Angeles and Hong Kong, since 1988; *b* 27 Nov. 1927; *s* of Charles Simon and Eleanor Kearns; *m* 1st, 1950, Carol Girard (*d* 1995); two *s* five *d;* 2nd, 1996, Tonia Adams Donnelley. *Educ:* Newark Academy, NJ; Lafayette Coll. (BA). Joined Union Securities, NYC, 1952, Asst Vice-Pres. and Manager of firm's Municipal Trading Dept, 1955–57; Vice Pres., Weeden & Co., 1957–64; Sen. Partner and Mem. Exec. Cttee, Salomon Brothers, NYC, 1964–72. Dep. Sec., US Treasury Dept, and Administrator, Federal Energy Office, 1973–74; Secretary of the Treasury, 1974–77. Sen. Cons., Booz Allen & Hamilton Inc., 1977–79; Sen. Advr, Blyth Eastman Dillon & Co. Inc., 1977–80; Dep. Chm., Olayan

Investments Co. Estabt, 1980; Chairman: Crescent Diversified Ltd, 1980; Wesray Corp., 1981–86, then Emeritus; Wesray Capital Corp., 1984–86; Co-Chairman: WSPG International Inc., 1987–92; WSPG Partners, LP, 1990–92. Director: East Hampton Beach Preservation Soc.; Hoover Instn. Member: Covenant House; Board of Directors: Atlantic Council of US; Citizens Network for Foreign Affairs; Gerald R. Ford Foundn; Internat. Foundn for Educn and Self-Help; Kissinger Assoc.; Malta Human Services Foundn; Richard Nixon Liby and Birthplace Foundn; World Cup 1994 Organizing Cttee; US Olympic Cttee (former Pres.); Dir Emeritus, Nat. Football Hall of Fame. Mem., Amer. Assoc. of SMO Malta. Chm., Investment Cttee, Academic Develt Fund, USAF Acad.; Mem., Exec. Adv. Council, William E. Simon Grad. Sch. of Business Admin, Univ. of Rochester. Pres., John M. Olin Foundn, 1977–; Trustee: John M. Templeton Foundn; Heritage Foundn; US Olympic Foundn (former Chm.); Sen. Trustee, Univ. of Rochester; former Trustee: Lafayette Coll.; Boston Univ.; Hon. Trustee, Adelphi Univ. Life Gov., NY Hosp. Hon. LLD: Lafayette Coll., 1973; Pepperdine Univ., 1975; Manhattanville Coll., 1978; Washington, Boston, 1980; Washington Coll., Rider Coll., Seton Hall, Fairleigh Dickenson, 1984; Rutgers, Rochester, 1985; Hon. DCL Jacksonville Univ., 1976; Hon. PhD Tel Aviv, 1976; Hon. Scriptural Degree, Israel Torah Res. Inst., 1976; Hon. DSc New England Coll., 1977; Dr of Humanics, Springfield, 1986; Hon. Dr of Econs Hanyang Univ., Seoul, Korea, 1988; Hon. Dr Soc. Scis, Pontifical Univ. of St Thomas Aquinas, 1999. Numerous honours and awards. *Publications:* A Time for Truth, 1978; A Time for Action, 1980. *Address:* William E. Simon & Sons Inc., 310 South Street, PO Box 1913, Morristown, NJ 07962–1913, USA. *Clubs:* Sunningdale Golf; Links, Bond, Municipal Bond, Explorers (Hon. Dir); Pilgrims of US, New York Yacht (New York, NY); Maidstone (East Hampton, NY); Alfalfa (Washington, DC); Balboa Bay, Bel-Air Country (Calif); Morris County Golf (Convent Station, NJ); Rolling Rock (Pa); Oahu Country (Hawaii); Bohemian (San Francisco).
Died 3 June 2000.

SIMPSON, Alan, MA, DPhil; President and Professor of History, Vassar College, Poughkeepsie, NY, 1964–77; *b* Gateshead, Durham, England, 23 July 1912; *s* of George Hardwick Simpson and Isabella Simpson (*née* Graham); *m* 1938, Mary McQueen McEldowney, Chicago Heights, Ill; one *s* two *d. Educ:* Worcester Coll., Oxford (BA); Merton Coll., Oxford (MA, DPhil); Harvard Univ. (Commonwealth Fellow). Served War of 1939–45, RA, Major. Sen. Lectr in Modern British History and American History, Univ. of St Andrews, and Lectr in Constitutional Law, Law Sch., University Coll., Dundee, 1938–46; Asst Prof. of History, 1946–54, Associate Prof., 1954–59, Thomas E. Donnelley Prof. of History and Dean of the College, 1959–64, Univ. of Chicago. Member Board of Trustees: Colonial Williamsburg; Salve Regina Coll., Newport; Old Dartmouth Hist. Soc.; Mem., Amer. Antiquarian Soc.; Mem. Council of the Inst. of Early Amer. History and Culture, Williamsburg, Va, 1957–60; formerly Member: Midwest Conf. of British Historians (Co-Founder, 1954; Sec., 1954–61); Commn on Academic Affairs and Bd of Dirs, Amer. Council on Educn; Commn on Liberal Learning, Assoc. of Amer. Colls; Hudson River Valley Commn. LHD: Nat. Coll. of Educn, Evanston; Univ. of Rochester; LLD Knox Coll. *Publications:* (co ed) The People Shall Judge: Readings in the Formation of American Policy, 1949; Puritanism in Old and New England, 1955; The Wealth of the Gentry, 1540–1660: East Anglian Studies, 1961; (co-ed with Mary Simpson) Diary of King Philip's War, by Benjamin Church, 1975; (with Mary Simpson) I Too Am Here: selections from the letters of Jane Welsh Carlyle, 1977; (with Mary Simpson)

Jean Webster, Storyteller, 1984; The Mysteries of the "Frenchman's Map" of Williamsburg, Virginia, 1984; The Legends of Carter's Grove, 1993; (with Mary Simpson) Compton-Land Revisited: new looks at an old puzzle, 1994. *Address:* 1523 Wilmette Avenue, Wilmette, IL 60091–2450, USA. *Club:* Century (New York).
Died 15 May 1998.

SIMPSON, Angus; *see* Simpson, A. J. D.

SIMPSON, Athol John Dundas, (Angus), OBE 1976; Director of North American Operations, Crown Agents for Oversea Governments and Administrations, 1985–92; *b* 4 May 1932; *s* of John Simpson and Helen Murray Simpson (*née* Cubie); *m* 1956, Ricki Ellen Carter (*d* 1997); one *s* two *d. Educ:* Reigate Grammar Sch. Joined Crown Agents, 1950; served Royal Air Force, 1951–53; Crown Agents' Representative in E Africa, 1965–69; seconded as Managing Director, Millbank Technical Services (Iran) Ltd, 1973–77; returned to Bd appt as Dir of Marketing and Development with Crown Agents, 1977; Dir, Crown Agents, 1978–85. *Recreations:* Rugby football, golf, reading. *Address:* 66 Archel Road, West Kensington, W14 9QP. *T:* (020) 7381 0759. *Clubs:* Travellers; International (Washington, DC). *Died 10 Aug. 1999.*

SIMPSON, Esther Eleanor, MD; FRCP, FRCPCH, FFPHM; former Senior Principal Medical Officer, Department of Education and Science, and Department of Health and Social Security, retired 1979; *b* 28 May 1919. *Educ:* Kendal High Sch.; London Univ. (MD 1947). DPH 1958; FRCP 1970; FFPHM (FFCM 1974); FRCPCH 1997. Medical Officer, London County Council, then to Province of Natal Centre, Inst. of Child Health; joined Medical Br., Min. of Education, 1961. Hon. FRCSLT (Hon. FCST 1984). *Recreations:* music, reading, walking. *Address:* 19 Belsize Lane, NW3 5AG. *T:* (020) 7794 5623. *Died 17 July 1999.*

SIMPSON, John Liddle, CMG 1958; TD 1950; QC 1980; *b* 9 Oct. 1912; *s* of late James Simpson; *m* 1st, 1939, Nellie Lavender Mussett (*d* 1944); 2nd, 1959, Ursula Vaughan Washington (*nee* Rigby). *Educ:* George Watson's Coll.; Edinburgh Univ. (MA, DLitt). Barrister, Middle Temple, 1937. Served War of 1939–45; GSO1, 1945. Principal, Control Office for Germany and Austria, 1946; Senior Legal Assistant, FO (German Section), 1948; transferred to Foreign (later Diplomatic) Service and promoted Counsellor, 1954; Legal Counsellor, FO, 1954–59 and 1961–68; Legal Adviser, United Kingdom Mission to the United Nations, New York, 1959–61; Dep. Legal Adviser, 1968–71, Second Legal Adviser (Dep. Under-Sec. of State), 1971–72, FCO; returned to practice at the Bar, 1973. Elected alternate Pres. of Arbitral Tribunals, Internat. Telecommunications Satellite Org., 1974 and 1976; Mem., Dubai/Sharjah Boundary Court of Arbitration, 1978–81; Chm., UNESCO Appeals Bd, 1980–85. Freeman, City of London, 1976. *Publications:* Germany and the North Atlantic Community: a Legal Survey (with M. E. Bathurst), 1956; International Arbitration: Law and Practice (with Hazel Fox), 1959; articles and notes in legal journals. *Address:* 137a Ashley Gardens, Thirleby Road, SW1P 1HN. *T:* 0171–834 4814; 5 Paper Buildings, Temple, EC4Y 7HB. *T:* 0171–583 9275. *Died 8 June 1996.*

SIMPSON, Kenneth John, CMG 1961; HM Diplomatic Service, retired; *b* 5 Feb. 1914; *s* of Bernard and Ann Simpson, Millhouses, Sheffield; *m* 1939, Harriet, (Shan), Hughes; three *s. Educ:* Downing College, Cambridge. Entered HM Foreign (later Diplomatic) Service, 1937; lastly Consul-Gen., Hanoi and Stuttgart, Inspector, Diplomatic Service and Counsellor, FCO. *Address:* 33

The Westerings, Tye Green, Cressing, Braintree, Essex CM7 8HQ. *T:* (01376) 321565.

Died 9 Feb. 1998.

SIMPSON, Oliver, CB 1977; PhD; FInstP; Chief Scientist, Deputy Under-Secretary of State, Home Office, 1974–83; *b* 28 Oct. 1924; *y s* of late Sir George C. Simpson, KCB, FRS, and Dorothy (*née* Stephen); *m* 1946, Joan (*d* 1993), *d* of late Walter and Maud Morgan; one *s* (and one *s* decd). *Educ:* Highgate Sch.; Trinity Coll., Cambridge (MA; PhD 1949). War Service: Admiralty Research Laboratory, Teddington, on submarine detection, 1944–46. Research Scholar, 1946–49, Fellow, 1949–53, Trinity Coll., Cambridge; Asst Prof. of Physics, Univ. of Michigan, USA, 1949–52; Imperial Chemical Industries Fellow in Dept. of Theoretical Chemistry, Cambridge, 1952–53; joined Services Electronics Research Laboratory, Admty, 1953, Head of Solid State Physics, 1956–63; Supt, Basic Physics Div., Nat. Physical Laboratory, 1964–66; Dep. Dir, Nat. Physical Laboratory, 1966–69; Under-Sec., Cabinet Office, 1969–74. *Publications:* articles in scientific jls on infra-red detectors, semiconductors, fluorescence and standards of measurement. *Club:* Athenæum. *Died 12 Feb. 2000.*

SIMPSON, Ven. Rennie, LVO 1974; MA Lambeth 1970; Archdeacon of Macclesfield, 1978–85, Emeritus since 1986; Rector of Gawsworth, 1978–85; Chaplain to the Queen, 1982–90; *b* 13 Jan. 1920; *o s* of late Doctor Taylor Simpson and May Simpson, Rishton; *m* 1949, Margaret, *er d* of late Herbert and Olive Hardy, South Kirkby; one *s* one *d*. *Educ:* Blackburn Tech. Coll.; Kelham Theol College. Deacon 1945, priest 1946; Curate of S Elmsall, Yorks, 1945–49; Succentor of Blackburn Cath., 1949 52; Sacrist and Minor Canon of St Paul's Cath., 1952–58, Hon. Minor Canon, 1958–, Jun. Cardinal, 1954 55, Sen. Cardinal, 1955 58; Vicar of John Keble Church, Mill Hill, 1958–63; Precentor, 1963 74, Acting Sacrist, 1973–74 Westminster Abbey; Canon Residentiary, 1974–78, Vice-Dean, 1975–78, Chester Cathedral. Chaplain, RNVR, 1953 55; Dep. Chaplain, Gt Ormond St Hosp., 1954–58; Asst Chaplain, 1956–64, Officiating Chaplain, 1964–, Sub-Prelate, 1973–, Order of St John of Jerusalem; Deputy Priest to the Queen, 1956–67; Priest-in-Ordinary to the Queen, 1967–74. Life Governor, Imperial Cancer Research Fund, 1963. Liveryman of Waxchandlers' Co. and Freeman of City of London, 1955; Hon. Chaplain, Worshipful Soc. of Apothecaries of London, 1984–85. Jt Hon. Treas., Corp. Sons of the Clergy, 1967–74; Governor: King's School, Chester, 1974–78; King's Sch., Macclesfield, 1979–85. *Recreations:* football, cricket, theatre. *Address:* 18 Roseberry Green, North Stainley, Ripon, N Yorks HG4 3HZ. *Died 9 Jan. 1997.*

SIMPSON, Rt Hon. Dr Robert; PC (NI) 1970; *b* 3 July 1923; *er s* of Samuel and Agnes Simpson, Craigbilly, Ballymena; *m* 1954, Dorothy Isobel, 2nd *d* of Dr Robert Strawbridge, MA, DD, and Anne Strawbridge; two *s* one *d*. *Educ:* Ballymena Academy; Queen's University, Belfast. MB, BCh, BAO 1946; Founder Mem., RCGP; LRCPI (Occupational Medicine), 1980. House Surgeon, Belfast City Hosp., 1947; Resident Anaesthetist, Royal Infirmary, Leicester, 1948; GP, Ballymena, Co. Antrim, 1949–; Medical Correspondent: Belfast Telegraph, Irish Times (Dublin), Evening News (Edinburgh) and Leicester Mercury; Medical Representative, NI, Europ Assistance; Medical Officer, Flexibox Ltd, Ballymena, Northern Dairies Ltd. Founder Chm., Ballymena Round Table, 1951. NI Deleg. to CPA Conf. in NZ and Australia, 1965. MP (U) Mid-Antrim, Parlt of N Ireland, 1953–72; Minister of Community Relations, N Ireland, 1969–71. Vice-Pres., Co. Antrim Agricl Assoc., 1960–; Vice-Pres., Ballymena Musical Fest. Assoc., 1989–. *Publications:* contribs to newspapers and magazines on medical, country and travel subjects, *Recreations:* gardening, trees, the countryside. *Address:* Random Cottage, Craigbilly, Ballymena, Co. Antrim BT42 4HL. *T:* (01266) 653105. *Club:* Royal Overseas League. *Died 8 April 1997.*

SIMPSON, Robert Wilfred Levick, DMus; composer; BBC Music Producer, 1951–80; *b* Leamington, Warwickshire, 2 March 1921; *s* of Robert Warren Simpson (British) and Helena Hendrika Govaars (Dutch); *m* 1946, Bessie Fraser (*d* 1981); *m* 1982, Angela Musgrave. *Educ:* Westminster City Sch.; studied with Herbert Howells. DMus (Dunelm) 1952. Holder of: Carl Nielsen Gold Medal (Denmark), 1956; Medal of Honor of Bruckner Soc. of America, 1962. Mem., British Astronomical Assoc.; FRAS. *Compositions:* Symphonies: No 1, 1951 (recorded); No 2, 1956 (recorded); No 3, 1962 (recorded); No 4, 1972 (recorded); No 5, 1972; Nos 6 and 7, 1977 (recorded); No 8, 1981; No 9, 1986 (recorded); No 10, 1988 (recorded); No 11, 1990; Concertos: Piano, 1967; Flute, 1989; Cello, 1991; String Quartets: No 1, 1952 (recorded); No 2, 1953 (recorded); No 3, 1954 (recorded); No 4, 1973 (recorded); No 5, 1974 (recorded); No 6, 1975 (recorded); No 7, 1977 (recorded); No 8, 1979 (recorded); No 9, 1982 (recorded); No 10 (For Peace), 1983 (recorded); No 11, 1984 (recorded); No 12, 1987 (recorded); No 13, 1989; No 14, 1990; No 15, 1991; Piano Sonata, 1946; Variations and Finale on a Theme of Haydn, for piano, 1948; Variations and Finale on a Theme of Beethoven for piano, 1990; Allegro Deciso, for string orchestra (from String Quartet No 3); Canzona for Brass, 1958 (recorded); Variations and Fugue for recorder and string quartet, 1959; Incidental Music to Ibsen's The Pretenders, 1965; Trio for clarinet, cello and piano, 1967; Quintet for clarinet and strings, 1968 (recorded); Energy, Symphonic Study for brass band (test piece for 1971 World Championship) (recorded); Incidental Music to Milton's Samson Agonistes, 1974; *Media morte in vita sumus* (Motet for choir, brass, and timpani), 1975; Quartet for horn, violin, cello and piano, 1976; Volcano, for brass band, 1979 (test piece for Nat. Championship, 1979) (recorded); Sonata for two pianos, 1980; Quintet for double basses, clarinet and bass clarinet, 1981 (also for string trio, clarinet and bass clarinet); The Four Temperaments, for brass band, 1982 (recorded); Variations on a theme of Carl Nielsen, for orchestra, 1983; Trio for horn, violin and piano, 1984; Sonata for violin and piano, 1984; Eppur si muove, for organ, 1985; Introduction and Allegro on a bass by Max Reger, for brass band, 1986 (recorded); Tempi, for a cappella choir, 1987; String Quintet, 1987 (recorded); String Trio (Prelude and Fugue), 1987; Quintet for Brass, 1989; Vortex, for brass band, 1989 (recorded); Variations and Fugue on a theme of Bach, for string orch., 1991; String Quintet No 2, 1994. *Publications:* Carl Nielsen, Symphonist, 1952, rev. edn 1977; The Essence of Bruckner, 1966, rev. edn 1992; (ed) The Symphony, 1966; The Proms and Natural Justice, 1981; numerous articles in various jls and three BBC booklets (Bruckner and the Symphony, Sibelius and Nielsen, and The Beethoven Symphonies); contrib. to: Enc. Brit.; Musik in Geschichte und Gegenwart. *Recreation:* astronomy. *Address:* Síocháin, Killelton, near Camp, Tralee, Co. Kerry, Eire. *T:* (66) 30213. *Died 21 Nov. 1997.*

SIMPSON-ORLEBAR, Sir Michael (Keith Orlebar), KCMG 1991 (CMG 1982); HM Diplomatic Service, retired; Director-General, The Hispanic and Luso Brazilian Council (Canning House), 1992–96; *b* 5 Feb. 1932; *s* of late Aubrey Orlebar Simpson, Royal Artillery and Laura Violet, *d* of Captain Frederick Keith-Jones; *m* 1964, Rosita Duarte Triana; two *s* one *d*. *Educ:* Eton; Christ Church, Oxford (MA). 1st Lieut, KRRC, 1950–51. Joined Foreign Service, 1954; 3rd Sec., Tehran, 1955–57; FO, 1957–62; Private Sec. to Parly Under-Sec. of State, 1960–62; 1st Sec. (Commercial) and Consul, Bogotá, 1962–65;

seconded to Urwick, Orr and Partners Ltd, 1966; FO, 1966–68; 1st Sec., Paris, 1969–72; Counsellor (Commercial), Tehran, 1972–76; Head of UN Dept, FCO, 1977–80; Minister, HM Embassy, Rome, 1980–83; Head of British Interests Section, Tehran, 1983–85; Ambassador to Portugal, 1986–89; Ambassador to Mexico, 1989–92. Dir, Murray Emerging Economies Trust plc, 1994–. Chm., British Mexican Soc., 1992–95. Order of the Aztec Eagle, 1st Cl. (Mexico), 1994. *Recreations:* gardening, fishing. *Address:* Tudor House, 111 High Street, Needham Market, Suffolk IP6 8DQ. *T:* (01449) 720156.

Died 2 Jan. 2000.

SINATRA, Francis Albert, (Frank); singer, actor, composer, film producer, publisher; *b* Hoboken, New Jersey, USA, 12 Dec. 1915; *s* of late Natalie and Martin Sinatra; *m* 1st, 1939, Nancy Barbato (marr. diss. 1951); one *s* two *d*; 2nd 1951, Ava Gardner (marr. diss. 1957); 3rd, 1966, Mia Farrow (marr. diss. 1968); 4th, 1976, Barbara Marx. *Educ:* Demarest High School, New Jersey. Started in radio, 1936; then became band singer with orchestras; subseq. composed numerous popular songs; recorded over 100 albums (Grammy lifetime achievement award, 1994). Owner music publishing companies, etc. First appearance in films, 1941. *Films include:* Las Vegas Nights, 1941; Anchors Aweigh, 1945; On the Town, 1949; From Here to Eternity (Oscar for best supporting actor), 1953; The Tender Trap, Guys and Dolls, The Man with the Golden Arm, 1955; High Society, Johnny Concho, 1956; The Joker is Wild, Pal Joey, 1957; Kings Go Forth, Some Came Running, 1958; A Hole in the Head, 1959; Ocean's 11, 1960; The Devil at Four O'Clock, 1961; Sergeants Three, The Manchurian Candidate, 1962; Come Blow Your Horn, Four for Texas, 1963; Robin and the Seven Hoods, 1964; None But the Brave, Marriage on the Rocks, Von Ryan's Express, 1965; Assault on a Queen, 1966; The Naked Runner, Tony Rome, 1967; The Detective, Lady in Cement, 1968; Dirty Dingus Magee, 1970; The First Deadly Sin, 1980; Cannonball Run II, 1984. Jean Hersholt Humanitarian Award, 1971. *Address:* Scoop Marketing, 3701 Wilshire Boulevard, Los Angeles, CA 90010, USA. *Died 14 May 1998.*

SINCLAIR, Sir Ronald Ormiston, KBE 1963; Kt 1956; President, Court of Appeal: for the Bahamas and for Bermuda, 1965–70; for British Honduras, 1968–70; Chairman, Industrial Tribunals (England and Wales), 1966–69; *b* 2 May 1903; *yr s* of Rev. W. A. Sinclair, Auckland, NZ; *m* 1935, Ellen Isabel Entrican; two *s*. *Educ:* New Plymouth Boys' High School, NZ; Auckland University College, NZ; Balliol College, Oxford. Barrister and Solicitor of Supreme Court of New Zealand, 1924; LLM (NZ) (Hons) 1925; Barrister-at-Law, Middle Temple, 1939. Administrative Service, Nigeria, 1931; Magistrate, Nigeria, 1936; Resident Magistrate, Northern Rhodesia, 1938; Puisne Judge, Tanganyika, 1946; Chief Justice, Nyasaland, 1953–55; Vice-President, East African Court of Appeal, 1956–57, Pres., 1962–64; Chief Justice of Kenya, 1957–62. *Address:* 158 Victoria Avenue, Remuera, Auckland, New Zealand. *Died 11 Nov. 1996.*

SINGER, Alfred Ernst; Chairman, Landorne Corporation; *b* 15 Nov. 1924; *s* of late Dr Robert Singer and Mrs Charlotte Singer; *m* 1st, 1951, Gwendoline Doris Barnett (*d* 1985); one *s* one *d*; 2nd, 1988, Christine Annette McCarron (*née* Evans). *Educ:* Halesowen Grammar Sch. Served War of 1939–45: Army, 1943–47. Subseq. professional and exec. posts with Callingham, Brown & Co., Bunzl Pulp & Paper Ltd, David Brown Tractors Ltd; Rank Xerox Ltd, 1963–70 (Dir, 1967); Tesco Stores (Holdings) Ltd, 1970–73 (Dep. Managing Dir); Man. Dir (Giro), PO Corp., 1973–76; Chairman: PO Staff Superannuation Fund, 1977–79; Cannon Assurance Ltd, 1980–86; London American Growth Trust, 1985–95.

Chairman: Long Range Planning Soc., 1970–73; Council, Assoc. of Certified Accountants, 1972–81 (Vice-Pres., 1979–80); Mem., Cttee for Industrial Technologies, DTI, 1972–76; National Economic Develt Council: Chm., Electronic Computers Sector Working Party; Member: Electronics EDC; Food and Drink Manufacturing Industry EDC, 1976–77. Governor, Centre for Environmental Studies, 1979–85 (Chm., 1981–85). *Address:* York Cottage, Lower Chedworth, Cheltenham, Glos GL54 4AN. *T:* (01285) 720523. *Clubs:* Athenæum, MCC.

Died 27 Aug. 1999.

SINHA, 5th Baron *cr* 1919, of Raipur; **Anindo Kumar Sinha;** *b* 18 May 1930; *s* of 2nd Baron Sinha and his 2nd wife, Nirpuama, *yr d* of Rai Bahadur Lalit Mohan Chatterjee; *S* nephew, 1992; *m* 1965, Lolita, *d* of late Deb Kumar Das; two *s* two *d*. *Educ:* Charterhouse. *Heir: s* Hon. Arup Kumar Sinha [*b* 23 April 1966; *m* 1993, Deborah Jane Tidswell (marr. diss. 1995)]. *Address:* 2 Highfield Road, Billericay, Essex CM11 2PF.

Died 18 Jan. 1999.

SKELTON, Prof. Robin, FRSL; author; Professor of English, 1966–91, and Founder Chairman of Department of Creative Writing, 1973–76, University of Victoria, British Columbia, then Professor Emeritus; *b* 12 Oct. 1925; *o s* of Cyril Frederick William and Eliza Skelton; *m* 1957, Sylvia Mary Jarrett; one *s* two *d*. *Educ:* Pocklington Grammar Sch., 1936–43; Christ's Coll., Cambridge, 1943–44; Univ. of Leeds, 1947–51. BA 1950, MA 1951. Served RAF, 1944–47. Asst Lectr in English, Univ. of Manchester, 1951; Lectr, 1954; Associate Prof. of English, Univ. of Victoria, BC, 1963–66, Dir, Creative Writing Programme, 1967–73. Managing Dir, The Lotus Press, 1950–52; Examiner for NUJMB, 1954–58; Chm. of Examrs in English, 'O' Level, 1958–60; Co-founder and Chm., Peterloo Gp, Manchester, 1957–60; Founding Mem. and Hon. Sec., Manchester Inst. of Contemporary Arts, 1960–63; Gen. Editor, OUP edn of Works of J. M. Synge, 1962–68. Centenary Lectr at Univ. of Massachusetts, 1962–63; Visiting Prof., Univ. of Michigan, Ann Arbor, 1967. Founder and co-Editor, Malahat Review, 1967–71, Editor 1972–83; Dir, Pharos Press, 1972–; Editor, Sono Nis Press, 1976–83. Mem. Bd of Dirs, Art Gall. of Greater Victoria, BC, 1968–69, 1970–73; Founder Member: Victoria Soc. of Limners, 1972– (Pres., 1996–97); Hawthorne Soc. of Arts and Letters, 1993 (Hon. Sec., 1993–). FRSL 1966. Chm., Writers' Union of Canada, 1982 (first Vice-Chm., 1981). DLit Univ. of Victoria, BC, 1997. *Publications: poetry* Patmos and Other Poems, 1955; Third Day Lucky, 1958; Two Ballads of the Muse, 1960; Begging the Dialect, 1960; The Dark Window, 1962; A Valedictory Poem, 1963; An Irish Gathering, 1964; A Ballad of Billy Barker, 1965; Inscriptions, 1967; Because of This, 1968; The Hold of Our Hands, 1968; Selected Poems, 1947–67, 1968; An Irish Album, 1969; Georges Zuk, Selected Verse, 1969; Answers, 1969; The Hunting Dark, 1971; Two Hundred Poems from the Greek Anthology, 1971; A Different Mountain, 1971; A Private Speech, 1971; Remembering Synge, 1971; Three for Herself, 1972; Musebook, 1972; Country Songs, 1973; Timelight, 1974; Georges Zuk: The Underwear of the Unicorn, 1975; Callsigns, 1976; Because of Love, 1977; Landmarks, 1979; Collected Shorter Poems 1947–1977, 1981; Limits, 1981; De Nihilo, 1982; Zuk, 1982; Wordsong, 1983; Distances, 1985; The Collected Longer Poems 1947–1977, 1985; Openings, 1988; Words for Witches, 1990; Popping Fuchsias, 1992; A Formal Music, 1993; Islands, 1993; Briefly Singing, 1994; I Am Me, 1994; Wrestling the Angel, 1994; A Way of Walking, 1994; The Edge of Time, 1995; Lens of Crystal, 1996; One Leaf Shaking, 1996; A Further Spring, 1996; *prose:* John Ruskin: the Final Years, 1955; The Poetic Pattern, 1956; (ed) Cavalier Poets, 1960; Poetry (in Teach Yourself series), 1963; The Writings of J. M. Synge, 1971; J. M Synge and His World, 1971; The Practice of Poetry, 1971; J. M. Synge (Irish Writers series), 1972; The Poet's Calling, 1975; Poetic Truth, 1978; Spellcraft, 1978; They Call It The Cariboo, 1980; Talismanic Magic, 1985; The Memoirs of a Literary Blockhead (autobiog.), 1988; Portrait of My Father, 1989; (with Jean Kozocari) A Gathering of Ghosts, 1989; Celtic Contraries, 1990; The Magical Practice of Talismans, 1991; *fiction:* The Man who sang in his Sleep, 1984; The Parrot who Could, 1987; Telling the Tale, 1987; The Fires of the Kindred, 1987; Hanky Panky, 1990; Higgledy Piggledy, 1992; *drama:* The Paper Cage, 1982; *edited texts:* J. M. Synge: Translations, 1961; Four Plays and the Aran Islands, 1962; Collected Poems, 1962; Riders to the Sea, 1969; Translations of Petrarch, 1971; Edward Thomas, Selected Poems, 1962; Selected Poems of Byron, 1965; David Gascoyne, Collected Poems, 1965; David Gascoyne, Collected Verse Translations (with Alan Clodd), 1970; Jack B. Yeats, Collected Plays, 1971; (also trans.) George Faludy, Selected Poems, 1985; (also trans.) George Faludy, Corpses Brats and Cricket Music, 1987; The Selected Writings of Jack B. Yeats, 1991; (also trans.) Georg Trakl, Dark Seasons: a selection of poems translated from the German, 1994; *anthologies:* Leeds University Poetry, 1949, 1950; Viewpoint, 1962; Six Irish Poets, 1962; Poetry of the Thirties, 1964; Five Poets of the Pacific Northwest, 1964; Poetry of the Forties, 1968; The Cavalier Poets, 1970; Six Poets of British Columbia, 1980; Earth, Air, Fire and Water (with Margaret Blackwood), 1990, *symposia:* The World of W. B. Yeats (with Ann Saddlemyer), 1965; Irish Renaissance (with David R. Clark), 1965; Herbert Read: a memorial symposium, 1970; *posthumous publication:* The Shapes of Our Singing, 1999. *Recreations:* book collecting, art collecting, making collages, stone carving, philately. *Address:* 1255 Victoria Avenue, Victoria, BC V8S 4P3, Canada. *T:* (250) 5927032. *Fax:* (250) 5921064. *Died 22 Aug. 1997.*

SKEMP, Terence Rowland Frazer, CB 1973; QC 1984; Barrister-at-law; *b* 14 Feb. 1915; *s* of Frank Whittingham Skemp and Dorothy Frazer; *m* 1939, Dorothy Norman Pringle; one *s* two *d. Educ:* Charterhouse; Christ Church, Oxford. Called to Bar, Gray's Inn, 1938. Served War, Army, 1939–46. Entered Parliamentary Counsel Office, 1946; Parliamentary Counsel, 1964; Second Parly Counsel, 1973–80; Counsel to the Speaker, 1980–85. *Address:* 997 Finchley Road, NW11 7HB.
Died 15 March 1996.

SKILLINGTON, William Patrick Denny, CB 1964; a Deputy Secretary, Department of the Environment (formerly Ministry of Public Building and Works), 1966–73; Housing Commissioner, for Clay Cross Urban District Council, 1973–74; *b* 13 Feb. 1912; *s* of late S. J. Skillington, Leicester; *m* 1941, Dorin Kahn (*d* 1996), Sydney, Australia; two *d. Educ:* Malvern College; Exeter College, Oxford (BA 1935, MA 1939). Articled to Clerk of Leicestershire CC, 1936–39. Commissioned in Royal Welch Fusiliers (SR), 1933; served War of 1939–45 (despatches); regimental officer in France and Belgium, and on staff in Sicily, Italy and Greece; AA&QMG; Lt-Col. Entered Min. of Works as Principal, 1946; Asst Sec., 1952; Under-Sec. (Dir of Establishments), Min. of Public Building and Works, 1956–64; Asst Under-Sec. of State, Home Office, 1964–66. *Address:* 95a S Mark's Road, Henley-on-Thames, Oxon RG9 1LP. *T:* (01491) 573756. *Clubs:* United Oxford & Cambridge University; Phyllis Court (Henley). *Died 25 March 1998.*

SKYNNER, (Augustus Charles) Robin, FRCPsych; consultant psychiatrist in private practice; writer; *b* 16 Aug. 1922; *e s* of Reginald C. A. Skynner and Mary F. Skynner (*née* Johns); *m* 1st, 1948, Geraldine Annella (*née*

Foley) (marr. diss. 1959); 2nd, 1959, Prudence Mary (*née* Fawcett) (*d* 1987); one *s* one *d. Educ:* St Austell County Sch.; Blundell's Sch.; UCL and UCH (Trotter Medal in Clin. Surgery; MB BS 1952; DPM 1957). FRCPsych 1978. War service, 1940–46, RAF, as pilot, Flight-Lieut. Postgrad. med. trng at Inst. of Psych. and Maudsley Hosp.; consultant psychiatric posts, 1959–, incl. Physician-in-Charge, Dept of Psych., Queen Elizabeth Hosp. for Children, 1965–70; Sen. Tutor in Psychotherapy, Inst. of Psych. and Hon. Consultant, Maudsley Hosp., 1971–82. Founder Mem., RCPsych, 1971; Joint Founder: Inst. of Group Analysis, 1969; Inst. of Family Therapy, 1977 (Chm., 1977–79); Mem. Council, Tavistock Inst. of Med. Psychology, 1988–92. FRSA. *Publications:* One Flesh, Separate Persons, 1976; (with John Cleese) Families and How to Survive Them, 1983; Explorations with Families, 1987; Institutes and How to Survive Them, 1989; (with John Cleese) Life and How to Survive It, 1993; Family Matters, 1995. *Recreations:* wind-surfing, country pursuits. *Address:* 88 Montagu Mansions, W1H 1LF. *T:* (020) 7935 3103. *Club:* Royal Society of Medicine.
Died 24 Sept. 2000.

SLATCHER, William Kenneth, CMG 1983; CVO 1975; HM Diplomatic Service, retired; High Commissioner in Guyana and non-resident Ambassador to Suriname, 1982–85, *b* 12 April 1926; *s* of John William and Ada Slatcher; *m* 1948, Erica Marjorie Konigs; one *s* one *d. Educ:* St John's Coll., Oxford. Royal Artillery, 1950–57; HM Diplomatic Service, 1958: Peking, 1959–60; Tokyo, 1961–63; Paris, 1965–68; New Delhi, 1968–71; Tokyo, 1974–77; Consul-Gen., Osaka, 1977–80; Head of Consular Dept, FCO, 1980–82. *Recreations:* travelling, oriental art and history, reading. *Address:* Jardin aux Fontaines, 9 rue Nazareth, 34090 Montpellier, France. *Club:* Royal Commonwealth Society. *Died 31 July 1997.*

SLATER, Gordon Charles Henry, CMG 1964; CBE 1956; Director, Branch Office in London of International Labour Office, 1964–70; Under-Secretary, Ministry of Labour, in the Overseas Department, 1960–64, retired; *b* 14 Dec. 1903; *s* of Matthew and Florence Slater; *m* 1928, Doris Primrose Hammond; one *s* one *d.* Entered Ministry of Labour, 1928, as Third Class Officer; Assistant Secretary, Organisation and Establishments, 1945, Disabled Persons Branch, 1949; Secretary of National Advisory Council on Employment of Disabled Persons, 1949–56; Sec. of Piercy Committee on Rehabilitation of Disabled, 1953–56; Under-Sec., Ministry of Labour, 1958. Member Governing Body, ILO, 1961–64; UK Govt delegate, Internat. Labour Conf., 1961–64. Mem. Berkshire CC, 1970–81, Vice-Chm., 1977–79. *Address:* Cookham House, Berries Road, Cookham, Maidenhead, Berks SL6 9SD. *T:* (01628) 526779. *Died 5 Nov. 1997.*

SLATER, Leonard, CBE 1976; JP; DL; *b* 23 July 1908; *s* of S. M. Slater, Oldham, and Heysham, Lancs; *m* 1943, Olga Patricia George (*d* 1983); two *s. Educ:* Hulme Grammar School, Oldham; St Catharine's College, Cambridge (MA 1932). British Guiana Expedn, 1929; research at Cambridge, 1930–32; Lecturer in Geography, Univ. of Rangoon, 1932–37; Geography Master, Repton School, 1937; University of Durham: Lectr, Geography Dept, 1939; Reader, 1948; Pro-Vice-Chancellor, 1969–73; Master, University Coll., Durham, 1953–73. Mem. Peterlee Develt Corp., 1956–63; Chairman: Durham Hosp. Management Cttee, 1961–73; Durham AHA, 1973–77; Mem., Newcastle Regional Hosp. Bd, 1965–69 and 1971–74. JP 1961, DL 1978, Durham. Served War, 1940–45; RE (Survey) in UK, India and SE Asia; Lt-Col 1944 and Hon. Lt-Col 1946. *Publications:* articles in geographical periodicals. *Recreations:* formerly travel, tennis, golf. *Address:* Beddell House, Sherburn Hospital, Durham DH1 2SE. *Died 5 Jan. 1999.*

SLINGER, William, CBE 1991; *b* 27 Oct. 1917; *yr s* of late William and Maud Slinger, Newcastle, Co. Down; *m* 1944, Muriel, *o d* of late R. J. Johnston, Belfast; three *d. Educ:* Methodist Coll., Belfast; Queen's Univ., Belfast (BComSc). Entered Northern Ireland Civil Service, 1937; Private Secretary: to Minister of Labour, 1942–43 and 1945–46; to Minister of Public Security, 1944; Sec. to Nat. Arbitration Tribunal (NI), 1946–48; Principal, Min. of Labour and Nat. Insurance, Industrial Relations Div., 1954–60; Asst Sec. and Head of Industrial Relations Div., 1961–69; Sec., Dept of Community Relations, 1969–75; Dep. Sec., Dept of Educn for NI, 1975–77. CIMgt. *Recreations:* gardening, walking. *Address:* Cairnfield, Circular Road, Belfast BT4 2GD. *T:* (01232) 768240. *Clubs:* Ulster Reform (Belfast); Civil Service (N Ireland).
Died 26 Sept. 1998.

SLOAN, Norman Alexander; QC (Scot.) 1953; Legal Adviser, British Shipbuilders, 1978–81; *b* 27 Jan. 1914; *s* of George Scott Sloan and Margaret Hutcheson Smith; *m* 1st, 1944, Peggy Perry (*d* 1982); two *s* one *d*; 2nd, 1983, Norma Olsen (*d* 1985); 3rd, 1988, Beryl Maureen Hogg, Dublin. *Educ:* Glasgow Academy; Glasgow University (BL). Solicitor, 1935; admitted to Faculty of Advocates, 1939. Served in RNVR, 1940–46. Lecturer in Industrial Law, Edinburgh University, 1946–51; Standing Counsel to Department of Health for Scotland, 1946–51; Advocate-Depute, 1951–53. Director: The Shipbuilding Employers' Federation, 1955–68; Shipbuilders and Repairers Nat. Assoc., 1968–72; Swan Hunter Group Ltd, 1973–77; Swan Hunter Shipbuilders Ltd, 1973–78. *Recreations:* golf, gardening. *Address:* Timbers, 1 Mapleleaf, Coldwaltham, Pulborough, West Sussex RH20 1LN.
Died 22 March 1999.

SMALLWOOD, Air Chief Marshal Sir Denis (Graham), GBE 1975 (CBE 1961; MBE 1951); KCB 1969 (CB 1966); DSO 1944; DFC 1942; idc; jssc; psc; aws; FRSA; FRAeS; Military Adviser to British Aerospace, 1977–83; *b* 13 Aug. 1918; *s* of Frederick William Smallwood, Moseley, Birmingham; *m* 1940, Frances Jeanne (*d* 1992), *d* of Walter Needham; one *s* one *d. Educ:* King Edward VI School, Birmingham. Joined Royal Air Force, 1938; Asst Adjt and Flying Instructor No 605 (County of Warwick) Sqdn, RAuxAF, 1938–39; served War of 1939–45, Fighter Command, as a fighter pilot in Nos 247 and 87 Hurricane Sqns, 1940–42, and Spitfire Wing Leader, 1943–44; Asst Sec., COS Cttee, 1946–49; Directing Staff, JSSC, 1950–52; OC RAF Biggin Hill, 1953–55; Directing Staff, IDC, 1956; Group Captain, 1957; commanded RAF Guided Missiles Station, Lincs, 1959–61; AOC and Commandant, RAF Coll. of Air Warfare, Manby, 1961–62; ACAS (Ops), 1962–65; AOC No 3 Gp, RAF Bomber Comd, 1965–67; SASO, Bomber Comd, 1967–68; Dep. C-in-C, Strike Comd, 1968–69; AOC-in-C, NEAF, Comdr, British Forces Near East, and Administrator, Sovereign Base Area, Cyprus, 1969–70; Vice-Chief of the Air Staff, 1970–74; C-in-C, RAF Strike Command, 1974–76, and C-in-C, UK Air Forces, 1975–76. ADC to the Queen, 1959–64. Life Vice-Pres., Air League, 1984 (Pres., 1981–84, Chm., 1978–81). Patron: Philip Green Meml Trust; PACE, 1990–; Museum of Aviation, 1997. Freeman, City of London, 1976; Liveryman, GAPAN, 1975. *Recreations:* shooting, gun dog training, walking, swimming, sailing. *Address:* 27 Swinnerton House, Phyllis Court Drive, Henley-on-Thames, Oxon RG9 2HU. *Clubs:* Royal Air Force, Les Ambassadeurs.
Died 26 July 1997.

SMART, (Raymond) Jack; DL; formerly Managing Director, Bus and Truck Group, British Leyland, retired; *b* 1 Aug. 1917; *s* of Frank Smart and Emily Rose Smart; *m* 1942, Jessie Alice Tyrrell; one *s* one *d. Educ:* Redhill Technical Coll. (HNC). Apprentice Prodn Engr, Lanston

Monotype Corp., 1933–38; Aeronautical Inspection Directorate, Air Min., 1939–40; Rotol Airscrews/Dowty Rotol, 1940–59: successively Chief Inspector, Prodn Controller, Works Manager; Man. Dir, British Light Steel Pressings (subsidiary of Rootes Motors Ltd), 1960–65; British Leyland (formerly BM Corp.): Man. Dir, Truck Div., 1966–72; Gp Manufg Dir, 1972–76; Gp Exec. Dir and Dep. Man. Dir, 1976–79; Man. Dir, Aveling Barford Holdings Ltd, 1979–80; non-exec. Dir, Marshall Sons & Co. Ltd, 1981–84. DL W Yorks, 1987. *Recreations:* Rugby Union, gardening. *Address:* 17 Whitecroft Park, Northfield Road, Nailsworth, Glos GL6 0NS. *T:* (01453) 835634.
Died 29 Jan. 1998.

SMEALL, James Leathley; JP; MA; Principal, Saint Luke's College, Exeter, 1945–72; *b* 16 June 1907; *s* of late William Francis Smeall, MB, BCh (Edin.), and Ethel Mary Leathley; *m* 1936, Joan Rachel Harris (*d* 1984); one *d. Educ:* Sorbonne; Queens' College, Cambridge (Scholar). Class I English Tripos, Class II Division 1 Anthropological and Archæological Tripos. Assistant Master, Merchiston, 1929–30; Staff, Royal Naval College, Dartmouth, 1930–34; Housemaster, Bradfield College, 1934–36; Head of the English Department, Epsom College, 1936–39; Headmaster, Chesterfield Grammar School, 1939–45. Commissioned RAFVR, 1941–44. Mayor of Exeter, 1965–66; President: Exeter Civic Soc., 1980–87; Exeter and Dist Br., ESU, 1983–88. Hon. LLD Exeter, 1988. *Publication:* English Satire, Parody and Burlesque, 1952. *Recreations:* gardening, travel. *Address:* Follett Orchard, Topsham, Exeter EX3 0JP. *T:* (01392) 873892.
Died 24 Feb. 1998.

SMITH, Baron *cr* 1978 (Life Peer), of Marlow in the County of Buckinghamshire; **Rodney Smith,** KBE 1975; MS; FRCS; Hon. Consulting Surgeon: St George's Hospital, London, 1978; Royal Prince Alfred Hospital, Sydney, NSW; Wimbledon Hospital; Examiner in Surgery, University of London; External Examiner in Surgery, Universities of Cambridge, Birmingham and Hong Kong; former Advisor in Surgery to Department of Health and Social Security; Hon. Consultant in Surgery to the Army, 1972, Emeritus Consultant, 1980; *b* 10 May 1914; *o s* of Dr Edwin Smith and Edith Catherine (*née* Dyer); *m* 1st, 1938, Mary Rodwell (marr. diss. 1971); three *s* one *d*; 2nd, 1971, Susan Fry. *Educ:* Westminster Sch.; London Univ. (St Thomas' Hospital). MB, BS London, MRCS, LRCP 1937; FRCS 1939; MS London, 1941. Surgical Registrar, Middlesex Hospital, 1939–41; Surgeon RAMC, 1941–45; appointed Surgeon, St George's Hospital 1946. Royal College of Surgeons: Hunterian Professor, 1947 and 1952; Arris and Gale Lecturer, 1959; Jacksonian Prizewinner, 1951; Penrose May Tutor in Surgery, 1957–63; Dean, Inst. of Basic Medical Sciences, 1966–71; Mem., Ct of Examiners, 1963–69, Chm. Feb.-July 1969; Mem. Council, 1965–78; Pres., 1973–77; Mem. Ct of Patrons; Hunterian Orator, 1975. President: Brit. Assoc. Surg. Oncologists; Harveian Soc., 1965; Pancreatic Soc., GB and Ire., 1976; Royal Soc. Med., 1978–80; London Med. Orchestra. Chairman: ASCAB; Conf. of Med. Royal Coll. UK, 1976–78; Armed Forces Med. Adv. Bd, 1980–84. Member: Council, Brit. Empire Cancer Campaign; Exec., Internat. Fedn Surg. Colls. Trustee, Wolfson Foundn; Governor, Motability. Vis. Lectr to S Africa Assoc. of Surgeons, 1957; McIlrath Guest Prof. in Surgery, Royal Prince Alfred Hosp., Sydney, NSW, 1966; Vis. Prof., Surg. Unit, Univ. of Illinois, Chicago, 1978; Visiting Professor of Surgery: Jackson Univ., Miss, 1979; Johns Hopkins Hosp., Baltimore, 1979; Flint Univ., Mich, 1979. Lectures: first Datuk Abdul Majid Ismail Oration and Gold Medal, Malaysian Assoc. of Surgeons, 1972; Robert Whitmarsh Oration, Providence, 1972; Cheselden, St Thomas' Hosp., 1975; Philip Mitchiner, 1976; Balfour, Toronto, 1976; Colles, RCSI, 1976; Faltin (and Medal),

Helsinki, 1976; Bradshaw, RCP, 1977; Sir Robert Bradlaw, Faculty of Dental Surgery, RCS, 1978; Sir Ernest Finch Meml, Sheffield, 1978; Telford Meml, Manchester, 1978; Annual Oration Med. Soc. of London, 1978; Sir William MacEwen Meml, Glasgow, 1978; Eisenberg, Boston, 1978; Judd, Minneapolis, 1979; first Samuel Jason Mixter, New England Surgical Soc., 1985. Hon. Member: Soc. of Grad. Surgeons of LA County Hosp., 1965; Finnish Surgical Soc., 1976; Surgical Res. Soc., 1976; Surgical Soc. of Phoenix, Arizona; Soc. Surg. Alimentary Tract; Hellenic Surg. Soc.; Kentucky Surg. Soc., 1979; Internat. Biliary Assoc., 1977. Hon. Fellow: Amer. Assoc. Surg.; Assoc. Clin. Anat.; Surgical Res. Soc., 1977; Assoc. of Surgeons of France, 1979; Philadelphia Acad. of Surg., 1979; Acad. de Chirurgie de Paris, 1981; Hon. FRACS 1957; Hon. FRCSEd 1975; Hon. FACS 1975; Hon. FRCSCan 1976; Hon. FRCSI 1976; Hon. FRCS S Africa 1976; Hon. FDS; Hon. FRSocMed 1981; Hon. FRCPSGlas 1982. Hon. DSc: Exeter, 1974; Leeds, 1976; Hon. MD Zürich Univ., 1979. Biennial Prize, Internat. Soc. of Surgery, 1975; Gimbernat Surg. Prize, Surg. Soc. of Barcelona, 1980; Gold Medal, BMA, 1982. Hon. Freeman, Worshipful Co. of Barbers. *Publications:* Acute Intestinal Obstruction, 1947; Surgery of Pancreatic Neoplasms, 1951; Progress in Clinical Surgery, 1953, 1961, 1969; (ed with C. G. Rob) Operative Surgery: 8 vols, 1956–57; 14 vols, 1968–69; Surgery of the Gallbladder and Bile Ducts, 1965; Clinical Surgery (Vols 1–14), 1965–67; papers in learned journals on pancreatic surgery, general abdominal surgery, intestinal obstruction. *Recreations:* music, painting, cricket, golf, bridge. *Address:* 135 Harley Street, W1N 1DJ. *T:* (0171) 935 1714. *Club:* MCC.
Died 1 July 1998.

SMITH, Alan Guy E.; *see* Elliot-Smith.

SMITH, Alan Oliver, QPM 1986; DL; Chief Constable of Derbyshire, 1985–90; *b* 9 Sept. 1929; *s* of Thomas Allen and Lily Oliver; *m* 1950, Jane (*née* Elliott); one *d*. *Educ:* elementary schools, Birmingham; Guiseley and Bradford Tech. Coll.; courses at Police Staff Coll., 1964, 1973, 1979. Constable to Supt, Bradford City Police, 1952–74; Supt and Chief Supt, W Yorks Metropolitan Police, 1974–79; Comdt, Bishopgarth Detective Training Sch., 1977–79; Asst Chief Constable, W Yorks, 1979–83; Dep. Chief Constable, Derbyshire Constabulary, 1983–84 (Acting Chief Constable, June 1984–Dec. 1985). Vice-President: Derbys Assoc. of Boys' Clubs, 1988–93; Wirksworth Br., Royal British Legion, 1988–; Derby and Dist Br., RSPCA, 1988–93; Chm., Ashbourne and Dovedale Br., Children's Soc., 1991–93. Formerly Mem., NE Consultative Cttee, Commn for Racial Equality; Mem., Professional Adv. Cttee, NSPCC, 1980–91; Mem., St John Council for Derbyshire, 1986– (formerly Hon. County Dir, St John Ambulance, S and W Yorks). DL, Derbyshire, 1992. OStJ 1988. *Recreation:* landscape artist (various exhibns; works in permt collections, Calderdale Authy, Leeds City Council, Bradford Univ.). *Address:* c/o Constabulary HQ, Butterley Hall, Ripley, Derbyshire DE5 3RS. *Died 18 April 1998.*

SMITH, Alastair Macleod M.; *see* Macleod-Smith.

SMITH, Brian A.; *see* Abel-Smith.

SMITH, Ven. (Brian) John; Archdeacon of Wilts, 1980–98, then Emeritus; *b* 21 Sept. 1933; *s* of Stanley and Doris Jessie Smith; *m* 1965, Jean Margaret, *d* of Frank and Beryl Hanning; one *s* two *d*. *Educ:* St Marylebone Grammar School; Mill Hill School; St John's Coll., Durham; Salisbury Theological Coll. Army, 1952–55; professional photographer, 1956–62. Ordained deacon 1965, priest 1966; Curate of All Saints', Whitstable, 1965–69; Vicar of Woodford, Wilsford and Durnford, and Religious Drama Adviser to Diocese of Salisbury, 1969–76; Vicar

of Mere, West Knoyle and Maiden Bradley, 1976–80; RD of Heytesbury, 1977–80; Vicar of Bishop's Cannings, All Cannings and Etchilhampton, 1980–83; Non-residentiary Canon, Salisbury Cath., 1980–98; Team Vicar, Redhorn, Salisbury, 1990–98. Member: Gen. Synod of C of E, 1985–90; Council of RADIUS (Religious Drama Soc. of GB), 1971–76; various cttees, Diocese of Salisbury, 1969–98; Chm., Diocesan Christian Stewardship Cttee, 1983–91. Author of a number of plays. *Publication:* contrib. to Religious Drama. *Recreations:* drama, photography, travel. *Address:* Cranmer House, 2 Long Ridings, Chippenham, Wilts SN15 1PL. *T:* (01249) 652454. *Died 22 June 2000.*

SMITH, Brian Percival, CEng, FIProdE; independent business consultant; *b* 3 Oct. 1919; *s* of Percival Smith and Hilda Judge; *m* 1942, Phoebe (Tina) Ginno; one *s*. *Educ:* Erith, Woolwich; London Univ. (BSc). Apprentice, 1936–41, Manager, 1941–46, Royal Ordnance Factories; Gen. Manager, Cumbrian Tool Co., 1946–49; PA Management Consultants: Consultant, 1949–59; Dir, R&D, 1959–66; Man. Dir, 1966–72; Chm. of Bd, 1972–76. Mem., CAA, 1981–84. Mem., Adv. Bd, LEK Partnership, 1987–92. Mem., Design Council, 1975–80; Vice-Pres., Royal Soc. of Arts, 1976–80. Prof. of Design Management, RCA, 1977–81. Member Council: BIM, 1972–74; Instn of Prodn Engrs, 1972 (Pres., 1973–74). CIMgt. *Publications:* Leadership in Management, 1968; Bureaucracy in Management, 1969; Management Style, 1973; Going into Europe, Why and How, 1975; The Morality and Management of Design, 1977. *Recreations:* painting, writing, listening to music. *Address:* 4 Cliff Road, Eastbourne, East Sussex BN20 7RU. *T:* (01323) 731870. *Died 29 Nov. 2000.*

SMITH, Prof. (Christopher) Colin; Professor of Spanish, University of Cambridge, 1975–90; *b* 17 Sept. 1927; *s* of Alfred Edward Smith and Dorothy May Berry; *m* 1954, Ruth Margaret Barnes; three *d* (one *s* decd). *Educ:* Varndean Grammar Sch., Brighton, St Catharine's Coll., Cambridge (MA, PhD, LittD). BA 1st cl. hons 1950. Dept of Spanish, Univ. of Leeds: Asst Lectr, 1953; Lectr, 1956; Sen. Lectr, 1964; Sub-Dean of Arts, etc, 1963–67; Cambridge University: Univ. Lectr in Spanish, 1968; Fellow, St Catharine's Coll., 1968–, Professorial Fellow, 1975–90, Tutor 1970; Chm. Faculty of Mod. and Med. Langs, 1973. Pres., Modern Humanities Res. Assoc., 1996. Hon. Vice-Consul of Spain, Cambridge, 1983–. Corresp. Mem., Royal Spanish Acad. of the Language, 1993. Comendador de número de la Orden de Isabel la Católica (Spain), 1988. General Editor, Modern Language Review, 1976–81 (Hispanic Editor, 1974–81). *Publications:* Spanish Ballads, 1964; (ed) Poema de mio Cid, 1972 (Spanish edn 1976); Collins' Spanish-English, English-Spanish Dictionary, 1971, 3rd edn 1992 (Spanish edn 1972); Estudios cidianos, 1977; (with A. L. F. Rivet) Place-names of Roman Britain, 1979; The Making of the Poema de mio Cid, 1983 (Spanish edn 1985); Christians and Moors in Spain, vol. I, 1988, vol. II, 1989; contrib. Bull. Hispanic Studies, Mod. Lang. Rev., Bull. Hispanique, etc. *Recreations:* theatre, opera, natural history (especially entomology), archaeology. *Address:* 56 Girton Road, Cambridge CB3 0LL. *T:* (01223) 276214.
Died 16 Feb. 1997.

SMITH, Claude C.; *see* Croxton-Smith.

SMITH, Colin; *see* Smith, Christopher C.

SMITH, Very Rev. David MacIntyre Bell Armour; Minister at Logie Kirk, Stirling, 1965–89; Moderator of the General Assembly of the Church of Scotland, 1985–86; *b* 5 April 1923; *s* of Frederick Smith and Matilda Shearer; *m* 1960, Mary Kulvear Cumming; three *s*. *Educ:* Monkton Combe School; Peebles High School; St Andrews Univ.

(MA 1947, BD 1950; Cook and Macfarlan Scholar). Served as Pilot, RAF, 1942–45. Warrender Church, Edinburgh, 1951–60; Old Partick Parish, Glasgow, 1960–65. Member: Stirlingshire Education Cttee, 1969–79; Central Region Educn Cttee, 1986–94; Chm., Church of Scotland Bd of Education, 1979–83. DUniv Stirling, 1983. *Recreations:* gardening, philately. *Address:* 34 Annfield Gardens, Stirling FK8 2BJ. *T:* (01786) 475085. *Died 22 Nov. 1997.*

SMITH, Donald MacKeen; Agent General of Nova Scotia, in London, 1980–91; *b* 26 Nov. 1923; *s* of Leonard Vernard and Lena Smith (*née* MacKeen); *m* 1949, Helen Elizabeth (*d* 1987), *d* of late Lt-Col David Guildford; three *d. Educ:* Halifax Public Schs; King's College Sch.; Dalhousie Univ., Nova Scotia. Served Canadian Armored Corps, 1942–45; 18th Armored Car Regt, 1944–45. J. E. Morse and Co. Ltd, Halifax: salesman, 1946; Vice-Pres., Director, 1951; Pres., 1956. Pres., Tea Council of Canada, 1975–78; Vice-Pres. and Dir, Tea and Coffee Assoc. of Canada, 1960–78. Member, Executive Council of Nova Scotia, 1960–69; MLA Nova Scotia (Halifax Citadel), 1960–70; Minister of Mines, Minister in Charge of Liquor Control Act, 1960–69. *Recreations:* swimming, sailing, fishing, walking. *Address:* PO Box 442, Station M, Halifax, Nova Scotia B3J 2P8, Canada; 1 Park Place, 1049 South Park Street, Halifax, NS B3H 2W5, Canada. *Clubs:* Royal Automobile; Saraguay; Halifax, Royal Nova Scotia Yacht Squadron (Halifax). *Died 16 Feb. 1998.*

SMITH, Eileen S.; *see* Stamers-Smith.

SMITH, Gerard Thomas C.; *see* Corley Smith.

SMITH, Sir Howard (Frank Trayton), GCMG 1981 (KCMG 1976; CMG 1966); HM Diplomatic Service, retired; *b* 15 Oct. 1919; *s* of Frank Howard Smith; *m* 1st, 1943, Winifred Mary Cropper (*d* 1982); one *d;* 2nd, 1983, Mary Penney (*d* 1996). *Educ:* Sidney Sussex Coll., Cambridge. Employed in FO, 1939; apptd Foreign Service, 1946; served Oslo; transf. Washington, 2nd Sec. (Inf.), 1950; 1st Sec., Dec. 1950; 1st Sec. and Consul, Caracas, 1953; FO, 1956; Counsellor: Moscow, 1961–63; Foreign Office, 1964–68; Ambassador to Czechoslovakia, 1968–71; UK Rep. in NI, 1971–72; Dep. Sec., Cabinet Office, on secondment, 1972–75; Ambassador in Moscow, 1976–78. *Club:* Travellers'. *Died 7 May 1996.*

SMITH, Captain Humphry Gilbert B.; *see* Boys-Smith.

SMITH, James Aikman, TD; Sheriff of Lothian and Borders (formerly the Lothians and Peebles) at Edinburgh, 1968–76; Hon. Sheriff, 1976; *b* 13 June 1914; *s* of Rev. W. J. Smith, DD; *m* 1947, Ann, *d* of Norman A. Millar, FRICS, Glasgow; three *d. Educ:* Glasgow Academy; The Queen's Coll., Oxford; Edinburgh Univ. BA (Oxford) 1936; LLB (Edinburgh) 1939; Mem. of Faculty of Advocates, 1939. Served War of 1939–45 (despatches): Royal Artillery, 1939–46; Lt-Col 1944. Sheriff-Substitute: of Renfrew and Argyll, 1948–52; of Roxburgh, Berwick and Selkirk, 1952–57; of Aberdeen, Kincardine and Banff, 1957–68. Pres., Sheriffs-Substitute Assoc., 1969; Pres., Sheriffs' Assoc., 1971–72. Member Departmental Cttee on Probation Service, 1959–62. Chm., Edinburgh and E of Scotland Br., English-Speaking Union, 1971. Bronze Star (US), 1945. *Publications:* occasional articles in legal journals. *Address:* 16 Murrayfield Avenue, Edinburgh EH12 6AX. *Club:* New (Edinburgh).
Died 12 March 1996.

SMITH, James Archibald Bruce, CBE 1981; British Council Representative, Indonesia, 1978–83; *b* 12 Sept. 1929; *s* of James Thom Smith and Anna Tyrie; *m* 1957, Anne Elizabeth Whittle; three *d. Educ:* Forfar Acad.; Edinburgh Univ. (MA 1952); Sch. of Econs, Dundee (BScEcon 1953); Jesus Coll., Cambridge. RAF, 1953–55.

HMOCS, Dist Officer, Kenya, 1956–62; British Council, 1962–83: Asst, Edinburgh, 1962–65; Asst Rep., Tanzania, 1965–66; Reg. Dir, Kumasi, Ghana, 1966–69; Rep., Sierra Leone, 1969–72; seconded to ODM, 1973–75; Dir, Personnel Dept, 1975–77; Controller, Personnel and Staff Recruitment Div., 1977–78. *Recreations:* Angusiana, reading, walking, collecting. *Address:* Calluna, West Hemming Street, Letham, Angus DD8 2PU. *T:* Forfar (01307) 818212. *Died 1 March 1996.*

SMITH, Janet Buchanan A.; *see* Adam Smith.

SMITH, Rear-Adm. John Edward D.; *see* Dyer-Smith.

SMITH, Sir John Kenneth N.; *see* Newson-Smith.

SMITH, John Roger B.; *see* Bickford Smith.

SMITH, Lawrence Delpré; Senior Puisne Judge of the Supreme Court of Sarawak, North Borneo and Brunei, 1951–64, retired; *b* 29 Oct. 1905; *m;* one *s* three *d. Educ:* Christ's Hospital; Hertford College, Oxford; Gray's Inn. Colonial Administrative Service, 1929; Colonial Legal Service, 1934; Tanganyika, 1929; Palestine, 1946; Gambia, 1948. *Address:* 34 The Avenue, Muswell Hill, N10 2QL. *T:* 0181–883 7198. *Died 2 Feb. 1996.*

SMITH, Prof. Michael, CC 1995; OBC 1994; FRS 1986; FRSC 1981; Peter Wall Distinguished Professor of Biotechnology, University of British Columbia, since 1994; *b* 26 April 1932; *s* of Rowland Smith and Mary Agnes Smith; *m* 1960, Helen Wood, *d* of Herbert Read Christie and Edith Germaine (*née* Wood); two *s* one *d. Educ:* Arnold Sch., Blackpool; Manchester Univ. (BSc Chemistry, PhD). Post-doctoral fellowship, Brit. Columbia Res. Council, 1956–60; Res. Associate, Inst. for Enzyme Res., Univ. of Wisconsin, 1960–61; Hd, Chemistry Sect., Vancouver Lab., Fisheries Res. Bd of Canada, 1961–66; University of British Columbia: Associate Prof., 1966–70, Prof., 1970–97, Univ. Prof. Emeritus, 1998–, Dept of Biochem.; Dir, Biotechnology Lab., 1987–96. Career Investigator, MRC of Canada, 1966–. Nobel Prize for Chemistry (jtly), 1993. *Recreations:* ski-ing, hiking, sailing. *Address:* University of British Columbia, Biotechnology Laboratory, Room 237 Wesbrook Building, 6174 University Boulevard, Vancouver, BC V6T 1Z3, Canada. *Clubs:* Faculty (Univ. of British Columbia); Royal Vancouver Yacht.
Died 4 Oct. 2000.

SMITH, Philip; Deputy Director Warship Design (Electrical), Ministry of Defence (Navy), 1969–73, retired; *b* 19 May 1913; *m* 1940, Joan Mary Harker; one *s* one *d. Educ:* Bishop Wordsworth's Sch., Salisbury; Bristol Univ. (BSc First Cl. Hons). CEng, FIEE, FIMechE; RCNC. Graduate Trainee Apprentice, BTH Co., 1934–37; Outside Construction Engrg, BTH Co., 1937–38; Central Electricity Bd, 1938–39; Admty (Electrical Engrg Dept) (later MoD Navy), 1939–73; past service at Chatham Dockyard and Dockyard Dept, HQ; Electrical Engrg Design Divs; Head of Electrical Dept, Admty Engrg Laboratory, West Drayton. *Recreations:* horticulture, painting. *Address:* Myrfield, Summer Lane, Combe Down, Bath BA2 7EU. *T:* (01225) 833408. *Club:* Bath Golf.
Died 26 March 1999.

SMITH, Philip George, CBE 1973; Director, Metal Market & Exchange Co. Ltd, 1954–92 (Chairman, 1967–84); Adviser, Triland Metals Ltd, since 1984; *b* 10 Sept. 1911; *m* 1937, Phyllis Mary, *d* of Adrianus Emck; one *d* (one *s* decd). *Educ:* St Lawrence Coll., Ramsgate; Royal School of Mines, London. ARSM, BSc (Eng). Director: Bassett Smith & Co. Ltd, 1946–75; Bardyke Chemicals Ltd, 1968–90; (non-exec.), Comfin (Commodity & Finance) Co. Ltd, 1978–82. Mem. Cttee, London Metal Exchange, 1949–64 (Chm. 1954–64); Adviser to Dept of Trade and

Industry, 1958 86; part-time Mem., Sugar Bd, 1967–76. *Address:* 67B Camlet Way, Hadley Wood, Barnet EN4 0NL. *Died 9 Nov. 1998.*

SMITH, Richard; *see* Smith, W. R.

SMITH, Richard Henry S.; *see* Sandford Smith.

SMITH, Ronald George, CBE 1973; Member, British Steel Corporation, 1967–77 (Managing Director (Personnel and Social Policy), 1967–72); formed British Steel Corporation (Industry) Ltd and was first Chairman, 1974–77; *b* 15 July 1915; *s* of Henry Sidney Smith and Bertha Clara (*née* Barnwell); *m* 1940, Daisy Hope (*d* 1974), *d* of Herbert Leggatt Nicholson; one *d. Educ:* Workers' Education Association. Post Office Messenger, 1929; Postman, 1934; Postal and Telegraph Officer, 1951; Treasurer, Union of Post Office Workers, 1953; Gen. Sec., Union of Post Office Workers, 1957–66. General Council, TUC, 1957–66; Civil Service National Whitley Council, 1957–66 (Vice-Chm., Post Office Dept, 1959–66); Exec. Cttee, Postal, Telegraph and Telephone International, 1957–66. Member: Cttee on Grants to Students, 1958–60; Development Areas, Treasury Advisory Cttee, 1959–60; Cttee on Company Law, 1960–62; National Economic Development Council, 1962–66; Court of Enquiry into Ford Motor Co. Dispute, 1963; Cttee of Enquiry into Pay, etc, of London Transport Bus Staff, 1963–64; Organising Cttee for Nat. Steel Corp., 1966; (part-time) Associated British Ports Hldgs plc (formerly BTDB), 1978–86. President, Postal, Telegraph and Telephone Internat., 1966. Director, BOAC, 1964–70. *Recreations:* photography, golf. *Address:* 3 Beech Grove, Epsom, Surrey KT18 5UD. *Club:* Kingswood Golf and Country. *Died 20 Oct. 1999.*

SMITH, Simon Harcourt N.; *see* Nowell-Smith.

SMITH, Adm. Sir Victor (Alfred Trumper), AC 1975; KBE 1969 (CBE 1963); CB 1968; DSC 1941; Chairman, Australian Chiefs of Staff Committee, 1970–75; Military Adviser to SEATO, 1970–74; *b* 9 May 1913; *s* of George Smith; *m* 1944, Nanette Suzanne Harrison; three *s. Educ:* Royal Australian Naval College. Sub-Lieut, 1935; Lieut, 1936; Lieut-Commander, 1944; Commander, 1947; Captain, 1953; Rear-Admiral, 1963; Vice-Admiral, 1968; Chief of Naval Staff and First Naval Member, Aust. Commonwealth Naval Bd, 1968–70; Admiral, 1970. *Recreation:* walking. *Address:* Fishburn Street, Red Hill, ACT 2603, Australia. *T:* (2) 62958942. *Died 13 July 1998.*

SMITH, (Walter) Richard; Regional Chairman of Industrial Tribunals, 1976–92; *b* 12 Oct. 1926; *s* of Walter Richard and Ivy Millicent Smith; *m* 1959, Jean Monica Law; one *s* one *d. Educ:* Bromsgrove Sch.; Birmingham Univ. (LLB). Called to the Bar, Gray's Inn, 1954. A Chairman of Industrial Tribunals, 1971. *Died 15 Feb. 1997.*

SMITH, William W.; *see* Wenban-Smith.

SMITHERS, Prof. Geoffrey Victor; Professor of English Language, University of Durham, 1960–74, then Emeritus; *b* 5 May 1909; *s* of William Henry and Agnes Madeline Smithers; *m* 1953, Jean Buglass Hay McDonald; three *s* one *d. Educ:* Durban High School; Natal University College; Hertford College, Oxford (Rhodes Schol. for Natal, 1930; 1st Cl. in Final Hon. School of English, Oxford, 1933). Assistant Lecturer: King's Coll., London, 1936; University Coll., London, 1938; Lectr in English Language, 1940, Senior Lecturer in English Language, 1950, Reader in Medieval English, 1954, Univ. of Oxford, and professorial Fellow of Merton Coll., 1954. *Publications:* 2nd edn of C. Brown's Religious Lyrics of the Fourteenth Century, 1952; Kyng Alisaunder, Vol. I 1952, Vol. II 1957; (with J. A. W. Bennett and N. Davis)

Early Middle English Verse and Prose, 1966, rev. edn 1974; Havelok, 1987; contribs to vols in honour of M. Schlauch, G. N. Garmonsway, D. Meritt, A. McIntosh and N. Davis; papers in Med. Æv., English and Germanic Studies, Archivum Linguisticum, Rev. Eng. Studies, Shakespeare Survey, Durham Univ. Jl, Neuphilologische Mitteilungen, Notes and Queries. *Recreation:* music. *Died 7 May 2000.*

SMYTH, Reginald; cartoonist (as Reginald Smythe); contracted to Mirror Publications, since 1955; *b* 10 July 1917; *s* of Richard Oliver Smyth and Florence Pearce; *m* 1949, Vera Toyne (*d* 1997); *m* Jean. *Educ:* Galleys Field Sch., Hartlepool, Cleveland. Served Army, Royal Northumberland Fusiliers, 1936–45. Civil Service, 1945–55. Creator, Andy Capp daily comic strip, 1956–. Best Brit. Cartoon Strip Awards, 1961–65; Premio Cartoon Award, Lucca, 1969; Best Cartoonist Award, Genoa, 1973; Best Strip Cartoon, USA Cartoonist Assoc., 1974; Italian Strip Award, Derthona, 1978. *Publications:* annual World of Andy Capp book, 1957–; annual Andy Capp books (USA), 1968–. *Address:* 96 Caledonian Road, Hartlepool, Cleveland TS25 5LB. *Died 13 June 1998.*

SMYTHE, Patricia Rosemary K.; *see* Koechlin-Smythe.

SMYTHE, Captain Quentin George Murray, VC 1942; Officer Instructor, Department of Defence, South Africa, 1970–81, retired; *b* 6 Aug. 1916; *s* of Edric Murray Smythe and *g s* of 1st Administrator of Natal (Hon. Charles Smythe, Methven Castle, Perthshire, Scotland); *m* 1945, Dale Griffiths (marr. diss. 1970), Capetown; three *s* one *d*; *m* 1970, Margaret Joan Shatwell (*d* 1980); *m* 1984, Patricia Stamper. *Educ:* Estcourt High Sch. Went through Abyssinian Campaign with Regt, Natal Carabineers; Sgt at Alem Hanza, Egypt (VC). *Recreations:* bowls, fishing, shooting. *Address:* 76 Agulhas, 3 Topham Road, Doonside 4126, Natal, Republic of South Africa. *Died 21 Oct. 1997.*

SMYTHE, Reginald; *see* Smyth, R.

SNAGGE, John Derrick Mordaunt, OBE 1944; *b* 8 May 1904; 2nd *s* of His Honour Sir Mordaunt Snagge and Gwendaline, *y d* of Rt Hon. Sir John Colomb, KCMG; 1st, 1936, Eileen Mary (*d* 1979), *e d* of late H. P. Joscelyne; 2nd, 1983, Joan Mary (*d* 1992), *e d* of late William Wilson. *Educ:* Winchester College; Pembroke College, Oxford. Assistant Station Director BBC, Stoke-on-Trent, 1924; Announcer London (Savoy Hill), 1928; Commentator, Oxford and Cambridge Boat Race, 1931–80; Assistant Outside Broadcast Department, 1933; Assistant Director Outside Broadcasts, 1939; Presentation Director BBC, 1939–45; Head of Presentation (Home Service), 1945–57; Head of Presentation (Sound) BBC, 1957–63; Special Duties, BBC, 1963–65; retired from BBC 1965. Chairman of the Lord's Taverners, 1956, 1960, 1961; President, 1952, 1964; Secretary, 1965–67; Trustee, 1970–76. *Publication:* (with Michael Barsley) Those Vintage Years of Radio, 1972. *Recreation:* fishing. *Address:* Delgaty, Village Road, Dorney, near Windsor, Berks SL4 6QJ. *T:* Burnham (01628) 661303. *Clubs:* MCC, Lord's Taverners, Sportsman's, Leander. *Died 25 March 1996.*

SNAGGE, Dame Nancy (Marion), DBE 1955 (OBE 1945); *b* 2 May 1906; *d* of late Henry Thomas Salmon; *m* 1962, Thomas Geoffrey Mordaunt Snagge, DSC (*d* 1984), *e s* of His Honour Sir Mordaunt Snagge. *Educ:* Notting Hill High Sch. Joined the WAAF on its inception, March 1939; served as a commnd officer in the WAAF and WRAF from Sept. 1939; Director Women's Royal Air Force, 1950–56, retired as Air Commandant. ADC to King George VI, 1950–52; ADC to the Queen, 1952–56.

Address: The Dower House, Headbourne Worthy, Winchester, Hants SO23 7JG. *T:* (01962) 886067.
Died 9 Oct. 1999.

SNAPE, Thomas Peter, OBE 1988; General Secretary, Secondary Heads Association and Headmasters' Conference, 1983–88; *b* 4 June 1925; *s* of Charles Snape and Jane Elizabeth Middleton; *m* 1951, Anne Christina McColl; three *d* (one *s* decd). *Educ:* Cockburn High Sch., Leeds; Exeter Coll., Oxford (MA). PCE London Univ. Asst Master, grammar and comprehensive schs, 1950–60; Headmaster: Settle High Sch., Yorks, 1960–64; King Edward VI Grammar Sch., Totnes, 1964–66; King Edward VI Comprehensive Sch., Totnes, 1966–83; Warden, Totnes Community Coll., 1971–83. Leverhulme Res. Fellow, USA, 1970. Member: Consultative Cttee, Assessment of Performance Unit, 1975–84; Teacher Educn Accreditation Council, 1984–86. Chm., Leechwell Press, 1989–92. Chm. of Govs, St Dunstan's Abbey, Plymouth, 1993–97. FRSA 1989. JP Devon, 1975, Inner London 1983. *Publications:* Ten Sites in Totnes, 1990; chapters in edited works; sections of Open University readers; contrib. learned jls. *Address:* 10 Chalcot Square, NW1 8YB. *Club:* East India.
Died 30 April 1997.

SNEDDON, Prof. Ian Naismith, OBE 1969; DSc; FRS 1983; FRSE; CMath, FIMA; Emeritus Professor of Mathematics, University of Glasgow, 1985; *b* 8 Dec. 1919; *o s* of Naismith Sneddon and Mary Ann Cameron; *m* 1943, Mary Campbell Macgregor; two *s* one *d. Educ:* Hyndland School, Glasgow; University of Glasgow (DSc); Trinity College, Cambridge (Senior Scholar, 1941; MA). Scientific Officer, Ministry of Supply, 1942–45; research worker, H. H. Wills Physical Lab., Univ. of Bristol, 1945–46; Lecturer in Natural Philosophy, Univ. of Glasgow, 1946–50; Professor of Mathematics in University Coll. of N Staffordshire, 1950–56 (Senior Tutor of the College, 1954–56); Simson Prof. of Mathematics, Univ. of Glasgow, 1956–85 (Dean of Faculty of Science, 1970–72; Senate Assessor on Univ. Court, 1973–77). Visiting Professor: Duke Univ., North Carolina, 1959 and 1960; Michigan State Univ., 1967; Univ. of California, Berkeley, 1979; La Trobe Univ., 1984; Strathclyde Univ., 1985–91; Georgia Inst. of Technol., 1986; Adjunct Prof., North Carolina State Univ., 1965–72; Visiting Lecturer: Univ. of Palermo, 1953 and 1980; Serbian Acad. of Sciences, 1958; Univ. of Warsaw, 1959, 1973, 1975; Canadian Mathematical Congress, 1961; Polish Acad. of Sciences, 1962; US Midwest Mechanics Research Seminar, 1963 and 1981; Univ. of Zagreb, 1964; Univ. of Calgary, 1968; Indiana Univ., 1970–80; Kuwait Univ., 1972; CISM, Udine, 1972, 1974; Britton Lectr, McMaster Univ., 1979; Huber Lectr, Polish Acad. of Sciences, 1980. NSF Distinguished Vis. Scientist, State Univ., New York, 1969. Member: various govt scientific cttees, 1950–80; Adv. Council on Scientific Research and Tech. Development, Min. of Supply, 1953–56, Min. of Defence, 1965–68; Univs Science and Technology Bd, SRC, 1965–69; Adv. Council of Scottish Opera, 1972–92 (Vice-Chm., 1979–92); Bd of Scottish Nat. Orch., 1976–83; Bd of Citizens Theatre, Glasgow, 1975–97; BBC Central Music Adv. Cttee, 1978–85; Chm., BBC Scottish Music Adv. Cttee, 1978–85; Mem. Council, Scottish Soc. of Composers, 1981–83; Vice-Pres., RSE, 1966–69 and 1979–82. Pres., Scottish-Polish Cultural Assoc., 1970–84. Mem., Polish Academy of Sciences. Kelvin Medal, Univ. of Glasgow, 1948; Makdougall-Brisbane Prize, RSE, 1956–58; Soc. of Engrg Sci. Medal, 1979. Hon. Fellow, Soc. of Engrg Sci., USA, 1977; Foreign Mem., Acad. of Scis, Turin. Hon. DSc: Warsaw, 1973; Heriot-Watt, 1982; Hull, 1983; Strathclyde, 1994. Comdr's Cross, Order of Polonia Restituta, 1969; Comdr, Order of Merit (Poland), 1979; Medal of Cultural Merit (Poland), 1983. Mem., Order of Long-Leaf Pine, USA,

1964. *Publications:* (with N. F. Mott) Wave Mechanics and Its Applications, 1948; Fourier Transforms, 1951; Special Functions of Mathematical Physics and Chemistry, 1956; The Elements of Partial Differential Equations, 1956; (with J. G. Defares) Introduction to the Mathematics of Biology and Medicine, 1960; Fourier Series, 1961; Zagadnienie Szczelin w Teorii Sprezystasci, 1962; Mixed Boundary Value Problems in Potential Theory, 1966; (with M. Lowengrub) Crack Problems in the Mathematical Theory of Elasticity, 1969; An Introduction to the Use of Integral Transforms, 1972; Metoda Transformacji Calkowych w Mieszanych Zogadnieniach Brzegowych, 1974; The Linear Theory of Thermoelasticity, 1974; (ed) Encyclopedic Dictionary of Mathematics for Engineers, 1976; (with G. Eason, W. Nowacki and Z. Olesiak) Integral Transform Methods in Elasticity, 1977; (with E. L. Ince) The Solution of Ordinary Differential Equations, 1987; articles in Handbuch der Physik, 1956–58; scientific papers on quantum theory of nuclei, theory of elasticity, and boundary value problems in jls. *Recreations:* music, painting, photography. *Address:* 19 Crown Terrace, Glasgow G12 9ES. *T:* (0141) 339 4114. *Club:* Glasgow Art.
Died 4 Nov. 2000.

SNEDDON, Robert, CMG 1976; MBE 1945; HM Diplomatic Service, retired; *b* 8 June 1920; *m* 1945, Kathleen Margaret Smith; two *d. Educ:* Dalziel High Sch., Motherwell; Kettering Grammar Sch.; University Coll., Nottingham. HM Forces, 1940–46: 8th Army, ME and Italy, 1942–45; 30 Corps, Germany (Major), 1945–46. Joined Foreign (subseq. Diplomatic) Service, 1946; 3rd Sec., Warsaw, 1946; 2nd Sec., Stockholm, 1950; FO, 1954; 1st Sec., Oslo, 1956; 1st Sec., Berlin, 1961; FO, 1963; Counsellor, Bonn, 1969; FCO, 1971, retired 1977. *Recreation:* music. *Address:* Windrose, Church Road, Horsell, Woking, Surrey GU21 4QS. *T:* (01483) 765745.
Died 12 March 1997.

SNELL, Dr George Davis; geneticist; *b* Bradford, Mass, 19 Dec. 1903; *s* of Cullen Bryant and Katharine Davis Snell; *m* 1937, Rhoda Carson (*d* 1994); three *s. Educ:* Dartmouth Coll. (BS 1926); Harvard Univ. (MS 1928; ScD 1930). Instr in Zoology, Dartmouth Coll., 1929–30, Brown Univ., 1930–31; Res. Fellow, Texas Univ., 1931–33; Asst Prof., Washington Univ., St Louis, 1933–34; Jackson Laboratory: Res. Associate, 1935–56; Sen. Staff Scientist, 1957–73, then Emeritus. Guggenheim Fellow, Texas Univ., 1953–54. Mem., Allergy and Immunology Study Sect., NIH, 1958–62. Member: Amer. Acad. of Arts and Scis; Nat. Acad. of Scis; French Acad. of Scis (foreign associate); Amer. Philosophical Soc., 1982; Hon. Member: British Transplantation Soc.; British Soc. for Immunology, 1983. Hon. MD Charles Univ., Prague, 1967; Hon. DSc: Dartmouth, 1974; Gustavus Adolphus Coll., 1981; Bates Coll., 1981; Ohio State Univ., 1984; Hon. LLD: Univ. of Maine, 1981; Colby Coll., 1982. Bertner Foundn Award, 1962; Gregor Mendel Medal, Czechoslovak Acad. of Scis, 1967; Gairdner Foundn Award, 1976; Prize in Medicine, Wolf Foundn, 1978; (jt) Nobel Prize for Physiology or Medicine, 1980. *Publications:* (ed) The Biology of the Laboratory Mouse, 1941; (jtly) Histocompatibility, 1976; Search for a Rational Ethic, 1988; contribs to learned jls. *Address:* The Jackson Laboratory, Bar Harbor, ME 04609, USA; 21 Atlantic Avenue, Bar Harbor, ME 04609, USA.
Died 6 June 1996.

SNELLGROVE, (John) Anthony; HM Diplomatic Service, retired; Secretary, British Brush Manufacturers' Association, 1977–89; *b* 29 Jan. 1922; *s* of late John Snellgrove and Anne Mary Priscilla (*née* Brown); *m* 1956, Rose Jeanne Marie Suzanne (*née* Paris); two *d. Educ:* Wimbledon Coll.; Stonyhurst Coll.; Peterhouse, Cambridge (1940–41 and 1945–48; BA and MA). Served War, Royal Navy, latterly as temp. actg Lieut, RNVR,

1941–45. Asst Principal, Colonial Office, 1948–49; joined Foreign Service, Oct. 1949; 2nd Sec., Prague, 1950–51; FO (Econ. Relations Dept), 1951–53; HM Vice-Consul, Tamsui (Formosa), 1953–56; 1st Sec., 1954; FO (SE Asia Dept and UN (E&S) Dept), 1956–59; 1st Sec., Bangkok, 1959–62; 1st Sec. and Consul, Mogadishu (Somali Republic), 1962–63; FO (Arabian and European Econ. Org. Depts), 1963–66; 1st Sec., Holy See, 1967–71; Counsellor, 1971; Dep. Sec.-Gen. (Economic), CENTO, 1971–73; Counsellor and Head of Chancery, Carácas, 1973–75, retired, 1977. *Recreations:* music, bridge.

Died 24 Dec. 1999.

SNELLING, Sir Arthur (Wendell), KCMG 1960 (CMG 1954); KCVO 1962; HM Diplomatic Service, retired; *b* 7 May 1914; *s* of Arthur and Ellen Snelling; *m* 1939, Frieda, *d* of late Lt-Col F. C. Barnes; one *s*. *Educ:* Ackworth Sch., Yorks; University Coll., London (BSc Econ.). Study Gp Sec., Royal Inst. of Internat. Affairs, 1934–36; Dominions Office, 1936; Private Sec. to Parly Under-Sec., 1939; Joint Sec. to UK Delegn to Internat. Monetary Conference, Bretton Woods, USA, 1944; accompanied 1st Baron Keynes on missions to USA and Canada, 1943 and 1944; Dep. High Comr for UK in New Zealand, 1947–50, in S Africa, 1953–55; Assistant Under-Secretary of State, Commonwealth Relations Office, 1956–59; British High Comr in Ghana, 1959–61; Dep. Under-Sec. of State, FCO (formerly CRO), 1961–69; Ambassador to South Africa, 1970–73. Dir, Gordon and Gotch Holdings Ltd, 1973–81. Fellow, UCL, 1970; Mem., College Council, UCL, 1976–86. Vice-Pres., UK-S Africa Trade Assoc., 1974–80; Mem., Ciskei Commn, 1978–80. *Address:* 19 Albany Park Road, Kingston-upon-Thames, Surrey KT2 5SW. *T:* 0181-549 4160. *Club:* Reform.

Died 25 June 1996.

SNOW, Thomas Maitland, CMG 1934; *b* 21 May 1890; *s* of Thomas Snow, Cleve, Exeter, and Edith Banbury; *m* 1st, 1927, Phyllis Annette Malcolmson; two *s* (and one *s* decd); 2nd, 1949, Sylvia, *d* of W. Delmar, Buda-Pest. *Educ:* Winchester; New Coll., Oxford. 1st Secretary, HM Diplomatic Service, 1923; Counsellor, 1930; Minister: to Cuba, 1935–37; to Finland, 1937–40; to Colombia, 1941–44 (Ambassador, 1944–45); to Switzerland, 1946–49; retired, 1950. *Recreation:* metaphysics. *Address:* Chemin des Vuarennes 35, 1820 Montreux, Switzerland.

Died 24 Jan. 1997.

SNOWDEN, Rt Rev. John Samuel Philip; Bishop of Cariboo, 1974–91. *Educ:* Anglican Theological Coll., Vancouver (LTh 1951); Univ. of British Columbia (BA 1956). Deacon 1951, priest 1952; Curate: Kaslo-Kokanee, 1951–53; Oak Bay, 1953–57; Nanaimo, 1957–60; Incumbent of St Timothy, Vancouver, 1960–64; Priest Pastoral, Christ Church Cathedral, Vancouver, 1964–66; Rector of St Timothy, Edmonton, 1966–71; Dean and Rector of St Paul's Cathedral, Kamloops, 1971–74. Domestic Chaplain to Bishop of Cariboo, 1971–73.

Died 27 Sept. 1996.

SOANE, Leslie James, OBE 1985; CEng, MICE; FCIT, FIMgt; Member of Board and Director, Railway Heritage Trust, since 1985; *b* 15 Jan. 1926; *s* of Arthur Edward Soane and Florence May Herring; *m* 1950, Joan Edith Mayo; one *s* one *d*. *Educ:* Watford Central Sch.; London Univ. Railways Civil Engineer posts: London Midland Region, 1948–55; Eastern Region, 1955–62; LMR, 1962–71; Chief Civil Engr, Western Region, 1971–75; Dep. Gen. Manager, WR, 1975–77; Gen. Manager, Scottish Region, 1977–83; Man. Dir (Reorganisation), BRB, 1983–85. Lt-Col, then Col, Engr and Logistic (formerly Transport) Staff Corps, RE (TA), 1985–. FRSA. *Recreations:* theatre, reading, golf.

Died 30 Oct. 1999.

SOLOMON, Sir David (Arnold), Kt 1973; MBE 1944; *b* 13 Nov. 1907; *s* of Richard Solomon and Sarah Annie Solomon (*née* Simpson); *m* 1935, Marjorie Miles (*d* 1990); two *s* one *d*. *Educ:* Leys Sch., Cambridge; Liverpool Univ. Qualified a Solicitor, 1933; became Mem. Liverpool Stock Exchange, 1935; practised as a Stockbroker until retirement, March 1969. Chairman: Liverpool RHB, 1968–73; Community Health Council, SE Cumbria, 1973–76. Served War of 1939–45, RAF (MBE). *Recreation:* music. *Address:* Green Lane End, Spittal, Fangfoss, York YO4 5QR.

Died 25 July 1997.

SOLOMON, Jonathan Hilali Moïse; Director: Commonwealth Partnership for Technology Management, since 1995; China Infonet, since 1998; Intelligent Engineering, since 1998; Millicom International Cellular SA, since 1999; *b* 3 March 1939; *s* of Samuel and Moselle Solomon; *m* 1966, Hester McFarland; one *s*. *Educ:* Clifton College; King's College, Cambridge (BA Hons, MA). Research worker, Supervisor and Tutor, Cambridge and London Univs, 1960–63, 1965. Entered Home Civil Service, 1963; Asst Private Sec. to Pres. of Board of Trade, 1966–67; Principal, Companies Div., BoT, transferred to DTI, 1970; to HM Treasury, 1972; Asst Sec., Dept of Prices and Consumer Protection, 1974; returned to Dept of Industry, Electronics Divs, 1977–80; Under-Sec., Telecomns (formerly Posts and Telecomns) Div., DoI, 1980–84; Under Sec., Quality and Educn Div., DTI, 1984–85; Cable and Wireless: Dir of Special Projects, 1985–87; Mem., Ct of Dirs, 1987–97; Dir, Corporate Strategy, 1987–89; Dir, Strategy and Corporate Business Develt, 1989–97; Special Advr to Bd, 1997–98. Director: Internat. Digital Communications, Japan, 1987–97; Tele 2, Nahodka and Sakhalin Telecom, 1991–97; Hong Kong Telecom, 1996–97; Thus, 1999–; Flag Telecom, 1999–. Head UK Delegn, ITU Plenipotentiary Conf., Nairobi, 1982. Member Editorial Board: Telecommunications Policy, 1984–; Utilities Policy, 1990–. *Publications:* contribs to journals such as Platon, Contemporary Review, New Outlook, Frontier, Tablet, Telecommunications Policy. *Recreations:* sport, futurology, writing. *Address:* 12 Kidderpore Gardens, NW3 7SR. *T:* (020) 7794 6230. *Clubs:* English-Speaking Union, Royal Automobile.

Died 21 May 2000.

SOLTI, Sir Georg, KBE 1971 (Hon. CBE 1968); Artistic Director, Salzburg Easter Festival, 1992 and 1993; Music Director, Chicago Symphony Orchestra, 1969–91, Music Director Laureate, since 1991; Principal Conductor and Artistic Director, London Philharmonic Orchestra, 1979–83, then Conductor Emeritus; *b* Budapest, 21 Oct. 1912; *s* of Mor Stern Solti and Teresa Rosenbaum; adopted British nationality, 1972; *m* 1st, 1946, Hedwig Oeschli; 2nd, 1967, Anne Valerie Pitts; two *d*. *Educ:* High School of Music, Budapest. Studied with Kodály, Bartók, and Dohnányi. Conductor and pianist, State Opera, Budapest, 1930–39; first prize, as pianist, Concours Internationale, Geneva, 1942; Musical Director, Bavarian State Opera, 1946–52; Musical Director, Frankfurt Opera, and Permanent Conductor, Museums Concerts, Frankfurt, 1952–61; Musical Director: Covent Garden Opera Co., 1961–71 (Music Director Laureate, Royal Opera, 1992); Orchestre de Paris, 1972–75. Guest Conductor: Berlin, Salzburg, Vienna, Munich, Paris, London (first conducted London Philharmonic Orchestra, 1947; Covent Garden début, 1959), Glyndebourne Festival, Edinburgh Festival, Bayreuth Festival, San Francisco, New York, Los Angeles, Chicago, etc. Made numerous recordings (many of which received international awards or prizes, incl. Grand Prix Mondiale du Disque (14 times), and 32 Grammy Awards (incl. special Trustees Grammy Award for recording of The Ring Cycle and Grammy Lifetime Achievement Award), Nat. Acad. of Recorded Arts and Scis). Hon. FRCM, 1980; Hon. Prof., Baden-Württemberg, 1985.

Hon. Fellow, Jesus Coll., Oxford, 1990. Hon. DMus: Leeds, 1971; Oxon, 1972; Yale Univ., 1974; Harvard, 1979; Furman, 1983; Surrey, 1983; London, 1986; Hon. Dr DePaul, 1975. Médaille de Vermeil, Ville de Paris, 1985; Loyola-Mellon Humanities Award, 1987; Medal of Merit, City of Chicago, 1987; Gold Medal, Royal Philharmonic Soc., 1989; Frankfurt Music Prize, 1992; Kennedy Center Award, 1993; Hans Richter Medal, Vienna Philharmonic Orch., 1993; Von Bülow Medal, Berlin Philharmonic Orch., 1993. Kt Commander's Cross, OM (FRG), 1987; Order of the Flag (Hungarian People's Republic), 1987; Commander, Order of Leopold (Belgium), 1993; Middle Cross, Order of Merit with Star (Republic of Hungary), 1993; Grosses Verdienstskreuz mit Stern und Schulterband (Germany), 1993; Ordem Militar de Santiago de Espada (Portugal), 1994; Comdr, Order of Arts and Letters (France), 1995; Kt Grand Cross, OM (Italy), 1996. *Posthumous publication:* Solti on Solti (memoirs), 1997. *Address:* Chalet Haut Pré, Villars s. Ollon, 1884, Switzerland. *Club:* Athenæum.

Died 5 Sept. 1997.

SOMERSCALES, Thomas Lawrence, CBE 1970; General Secretary, Joint Committee of the Order of St John of Jerusalem and the British Red Cross Society, 1960–78; *b* 1 July 1913; *s* of Wilfred Somerscales; *m* 1941, Ann Teresa, *d* of Robert Victor Kearney; three *s* one *d*. *Educ:* Riley High Sch., Hull. FCA 1939. KStJ 1978. Finance Sec., Jt Cttee, Order of St John of Jerusalem and BRCS, 1953–60. Mem., Adv. Council, ITA, 1964–67. *Address:* The Dormer House, The Rookery, Alveston, Stratford-upon-Avon CV31 1QP. *Died 16 Nov. 1996.*

SOMERSET FRY, (Peter George Robin) Plantagenet; author and journalist, since 1955; *b* 3 Jan. 1931; *s* of late Comdr Peter K. Ll. Fry, OBE, RN, and Ruth Emily (*née* Marriott), LRAM; *m* 1st, 1952, Audrey Anne (*née* Russell) (marr. diss. 1957); 2nd, 1958, Daphne Diana Elizabeth Caroline Yorke (*d* 1961); 3rd, 1961, Hon. Mrs Leri Butler (marr. diss. 1973, she *d* 1985); 4th, 1974, Pamela Fiona Ileene (author: Horses, 1981; A Soldier in Wellington's Army, 1987), *d* of late Col H. M. Whitcombe, MBE. *Educ:* Lancing; St Thomas's Hosp. Med. Sch., London; St Catherine's Coll., Oxford (Sec. Oxford Union, Hilary 1956). Mem. editorial staff: Atomics and Nuclear Energy, 1957–58; The Tatler and Bystander, 1958; public relations, 1960–64; Information Officer: Incorp. Assoc. of Architects and Surveyors, 1965–67; MPBW, 1967–70; Head of Inf. Services, COSIRA, 1970–74; Editor of Books, HM Stationery Office, 1975–80. Gen. Editor, Macmillan History in Pictures Series, 1977–80. Vis. Scholar, 1980–84, Sen. Mem., 1984–, Observer Mem., Governing Body, 1992–, Wolfson Coll., Cambridge. Mem. Council, East Anglian Writers, 1977–82; Co-founder, Congress of Indep. Archaeologists, 1985; Founder and Hon. Secretary: Little Bardfield Village Community Trust, 1971–74; Daphne Somerset Fry Meml Trust for Kidney Disease Res., 1961–; Burgh Soc., 1978–80. FRSA 1966. *Publications:* Mysteries of History, 1957; The Cankered Rose, 1959; Rulers of Britain, 1967, 3rd edn 1973; They Made History, 1970, 2nd edn 1973; The World of Antiques, 1970, 4th edn 1972; Antique Furniture, 1971, 2nd edn 1972; Constantinople, 1970; The Wonderful Story of the Jews, 1970; Children's History of the World, 1972, 12th edn 1995; Answer Book of History, 1972, 2nd edn 1973; Zebra Book of Famous Men, 1972; Zebra Book of Famous Women, 1972; Collecting Inexpensive Antiques, 1973, 5th edn 1980; Zebra Book of Castles, 1974; Great Caesar, 1974; British Mediaeval Castles, 1974; 1000 Great Lives, 1975, 8th edn 1984; Questions, 1976; 2,000 Years of British Life, 1976; Chequers: the country home of Britain's Prime Ministers, 1977 (official history); 3,000 Questions and Answers, 1977, 14th edn 1995; Boudicca, 1978; David & Charles Book of Castles,

1980, 3rd edn 1996; Fountains Abbey (official souvenir guide), 1980; Beautiful Britain, 1981; (with Fiona Somerset Fry) History of Scotland, 1982, 4th edn 1995; Revolt Against Rome, 1982; Great Cathedrals, 1982; (ed) Longman Pocket History Dictionary, 1983; Roman Britain: history and sites, 1984; Battle Abbey and the Battle of Hastings (official souvenir guide), 1984, 2nd edn 1990; 3,000 More Questions and Answers, 1984, 2nd edn 1995; Antiques, 1985, 2nd edn 1992; Rievaulx Abbey (official souvenir guide), 1986; Children's Illustrated Dictionary, 1987; (with Fiona Somerset Fry) History of Ireland, 1988, 4th edn 1995; 1000 Great People Through the Ages, 1989; Kings & Queens of England & Scotland, 1990, 6th edn 1995; The Tower of London, 1990; Handbook of Antique Furniture, 1992; The Dorling Kindersley History of the World, 1994, 2nd edn 1994. *Recreations:* studying 18th Century French furniture, Roman history, visiting British, Irish and European castles. *Address:* Wood Cottage, Wattisfield, via Diss, Suffolk IP22 1NE. *T:* Stanton (01359) 251324.

Died 10 Sept. 1996.

SONDES, 5th Earl *cr* 1880; **Henry George Herbert Milles-Lade;** Baron Sondes, 1760; Viscount Throwley, 1880; *b* 1 May 1940; *o s* of 4th Earl Sondes, and Pamela (*d* 1967), *d* of Col H. McDougall; *S* father, 1970; *m* 1st, 1968, Primrose Creswell (marr. diss. 1969), *d* of late Lawrence Stopford Llewellyn Cotter; 2nd, 1976, Sissy Fürstin zu Salm-Reifferscheidt-Raitz (marr. diss. 1981); 3rd, 1981, Sharon McCluskey (marr. diss. 1984); 4th, 1986, Phyllis Kane Schmertz. *Educ:* Eton; La Rosey. Vice Chm., Gillingham FC, 1985–. *Recreations:* shooting, skiing, the Turf. *Address:* Stringman's Farm, Faversham, Kent ME13 0LA. *T:* (01227) 730336. *Club:* Brook's.

Died 2 Dec. 1996 (ext).

SOPER, Baron, *cr* 1965 (Life Peer), of Kingsway in the London Borough of Camden; **Rev. Donald Oliver Soper,** PhD; Methodist Minister; President of the Methodist Conference, 1953, Superintendent, West London Mission, Kingsway Hall, 1936–78; *b* 31 Jan. 1903; *s* of late Ernest and Caroline Soper; *m* 1929, Marie Dean (*d* 1994), *d* of late Arthur Dean, Norbury; four *d*. *Educ:* Aske's School, Hatcham; St Catharine's College, Cambridge (MA; Hon. Fellow, 1966); Wesley House, Cambridge; London School of Economics, London University (PhD). Minister, South London Mission, 1926–29; Central London Mission, 1929–36. Chm., Shelter, 1974–78. President, League against Cruel Sports. Life FTCL 1995. Hon. DD Cambridge, 1988. Peace Award, World Methodist Council, 1981. *Publications:* Christianity and its Critics; Popular Fallacies about the Christian Faith; Will Christianity Work?; Practical Christianity To-day; Questions and Answers in Ceylon; All His Grace (Methodist Lent Book for 1957); It is Hard to Work for God; The Advocacy of the Gospel; Tower Hill 12.30; Aflame with Faith; Christian Politics; Calling for Action, 1984. *Recreations:* music, open air speaking. *Address:* 19 Thayer Street, W1M 5LJ. *Died 22 Dec. 1998.*

SOPWITH, Sir Charles (Ronald), Kt 1966; Second Counsel to Chairman of Committees, House of Lords, 1974–82; *b* 12 Nov. 1905; *s* of Alfred Sopwith, S Shields, Co. Durham; *m* 1946, Ivy Violet (*d* 1968), *d* of Frederick Leonard Yeates, Gidea Park, Essex. *Educ:* S Shields High School. Chartered Accountant, 1928; Solicitor, 1938. Assistant Director, Press Censorship, 1943–45; Assistant Solicitor, 1952–56, Principal Asst Solicitor, 1956–61, Solicitor, 1963–70, Board of Inland Revenue; Public Trustee, 1961–63; Deputy Sec., Cabinet Office, 1970–72. Hon. FRAM, 1984. *Recreations:* music, reading history. *Address:* Kilfillan House, Græmesdyke Road, Berkhamsted, Herts HP4 3LZ. *Club:* Reform.

Died 15 Nov. 1996.

SORRELL, Alec Albert; Director of Statistics, Department of the Environment, 1981–82, retired; *b* 20 July 1925; *s* of Albert Edward Sorrell and Jessie (*née* Morris); *m* 1962, Eileen Joan Orchard; one *s*. *Educ:* George Gascoigne Sch., Walthamstow; SW Essex Technical College. BSc (Econ). Statistical Officer, MAP, 1945; Board of Trade: Asst Statistician, 1950; Statistician, 1954; Chief Statistician, 1966; Chief Statistician: Min. of Technology, 1969; Dept of Trade and Industry, 1970; Central Statistical Office, 1971; Asst Dir, Central Statistical Office, Cabinet Office, 1972–78; Principal Dir of Statistics, Depts of the Environment and Transport, 1978–81. *Publications:* various articles in trade, professional and learned jls. *Recreations:* walking, reading, music, gardening. *Address:* Ranelagh, Stewarts Road, Week St Mary, Holsworthy, Devon EX22 6XA. *T:* Week St Mary (01288) 341436.
Died 30 July 1996.

SOUTHERN, Sir Robert, Kt 1970; CBE 1953; General Secretary, Co-operative Union Ltd, 1948–72; *b* 17 March 1907; *s* of Job Southern and Margaret (*née* Tonge); *m* 1933, Lena Chapman; one *s* one *d*. *Educ:* Stand Grammar Sch.; Co-operative Coll.; Manchester University. Joined Co-operative Wholesale Soc., 1923; Bank Dept, 1925–29; Personal Asst to Gen. Sec., Co-operative Union Ltd, 1929; Asst Gen. Sec., 1946, Actg Gen. Sec., 1947, Co-op. Union Ltd. *Publication:* Handbook to the Industrial and Provident Societies' Act, 1938. *Address:* Spurr House, Pole Lane, Unsworth, Bury, Lancs BL9 8QL.
Died 8 Sept. 1999.

SOUTHEY, Sir Robert (John), Kt 1976; AO 1993; CMG 1970; Federal President, Liberal Party of Australia, 1970–75; Chairman, National Council, Australian Ballet 1991–95 (Chairman, Australian Ballet, 1980–90); *b* 20 March 1922; *s* of Allen Hope Southey and Ethel Thorpe McComas, MBE; *m* 1st, 1946, Valerie Janet Cotton (*d* 1977), *y d* of late Hon. Sir Francis Grenville Clarke, KBE, MLC; five *s*, 2nd, 1982, Marigold Merlyn Bailleu, *yr d* of late Sidney and Dame Merlyn Myer, DBE, and *widow* of Ross Shelmerdine, CMG, OBE. *Educ:* Geelong Grammar Sch.; Magdalen Coll., Oxford (BA, 1st cl. PPE 1948; MA). Coldstream Guards, 1941–46 (Captain 1944; served N Africa, Italy). Wm Haughton & Co. Ltd: Dir 1953; Man. Dir, 1959–75; Chm. 1968–80; Chm., General Accident Insurance Co. Australia Ltd, later NZI Insurance Australia Ltd, 1987–92; Director: ICL Australia Pty Ltd, 1961–72, 1977–90; BP Australia Holdings Ltd, 1962–91; Kinnears Ltd, 1975–84; National Westminster Finance Australia Ltd, 1983–85; Nat West Australia Bank Ltd, 1985–87; Kawasaki (Australia) Pty Ltd, 1986–; Chairman: McArthur Shipping (Vic.) Pty Ltd, 1974–81; Australian Adv. Council, General Accident Assurance Corp. PLC, 1978–89. Mem. Executive, Liberal Party, 1966–82; Victorian State Pres., Liberal Party, 1966–70. Chm. of Council, Geelong Grammar Sch., 1966–72; Pres., Geelong Grammar Foundn, 1975–88; Chm. Australian Adv. Cttee, Nuffield Foundn, 1970–81; Mem., Rhodes Scholarship Selection Cttee, Victoria, 1973–76. *Publication:* (with C. J. Puplick) Liberal Thinking, 1980. *Recreations:* fishing, music. *Address:* 16 Horsburgh Grove, Armadale, Vic 3143, Australia. *Clubs:* Cavalry and Guards, MCC; Melbourne (Melbourne); Vincent's (Oxford); Leander.
Died 29 Sept. 1998.

SOUTHGATE, Very Rev. John Eliot; Dean of York, 1984–94, then Dean Emeritus; *b* 2 Sept. 1926; *m* 1958, Patricia Mary Plumb; two *s* one *d*. *Educ:* City of Norwich Sch.; Durham Univ. (BA 1953, DipTh 1955). Ordained deacon 1955, priest 1956; Vicar of Plumstead, 1962–66; Rector of Old Charlton, 1966–72; Dean of Greenwich, 1968–72; York Diocesan Sec. for Mission and Evangelism, 1972–81, and Vicar of Harome, 1972–77; Archdeacon of Cleveland, 1974–84. A Church Comr, 1987–94. Chm.,

Assoc. of English Cathedrals, 1990–94. DUniv York, 1989. *Recreations:* music, sailing. *Address:* 39 Churchfields, Hethersett, Norwich NR9 3PH. *T:* (01603) 812116.
Died 18 Dec. 1999.

SOUTHWARD, Sir Ralph, KCVO 1975; Apothecary to the Household of Queen Elizabeth the Queen Mother, 1966–86, to the Household of HRH the Duke of Gloucester, 1966–75, to HM Household, 1964–74, to HM the Queen, 1972–74; *b* 2 Jan. 1908; *s* of Henry Stalker Southward; *m* 1935, Evelyn, *d* of J. G. Tassell; four *s*. *Educ:* High School of Glasgow; Glasgow Univ. MB, ChB (Glasgow) 1930; MRCP 1939; FRCP 1970. Formerly: Western Infirmary, and Royal Hospital for Sick Children, Glasgow; Postgraduate Medical School, Hammersmith, London. Served War of 1939–45: Medical Officer, 215 Field Ambulance, North Africa, 1940–41; Medical Specialist, Egypt, India and Ceylon, and Lieut-Colonel in charge Medical Division, 1942–43; Colonel Comdg Combined General Hospital, 1944–45. Hon. Freeman, Worshipful Soc. of Apothecaries of London, 1975. *Recreations:* trout and salmon fishing, golf, travel. *Address:* 9 Devonshire Place, W1N 1PB. *T:* (0171) 935 7969; Amerden Priory, Amerden Lane, Taplow, Maidenhead, Berks SL6 0EE. *T:* (01628) 23525.
Died 16 Oct. 1997.

SOUTHWOOD, Captain Horace Gerald, CBE 1966; DSC 1941; Royal Navy; Managing Director, Silley, Cox & Co. Ltd, Falmouth Docks, 1974–78; Chairman, Falmouth Group, 1976–78; *b* 19 April 1912; *s* of late Horace George Southwood; *m* 1936, Ruby Edith Hayes; two *s* one *d*. *Educ:* HMS Fisgard, RN Coll., Greenwich. Joined RN, 1927; HMS Revolution, Medit. Stn, 1932–34, HMS Barham, 1934–35; RN Coll., Greenwich, 1935–36; HMS Royal Oak, Home Fleet, 1936–38; specialised in Submarines, 1938; HMS Lucia, 1938–39; HM Submarine, Regent, 1939–41, China and Medit. (despatches, 1941, DSC); HMS Medway, Medit., 1941–42; HM Submarine, Amphion (first of Class), 1943–45. HMS Dolphin, 1946–48; HMS Vengeance, 1948–49; Comdr, 1948; HMS Glory, 1949–51; HMS Forth, 1951–52; Admty, Whitehall, 1952–54; HM Dockyard, Portsmouth (Dep. Man.), 1954–58; jssc, 1958–59; Capt., 1958; Chief Engr, Singapore, 1959–62; Sen. Officers' War Course, 1962; Manager, Engrg Dept, HM Dockyard, Portsmouth, 1963–67; Gen. Manager, HM Dockyard, Devonport, 1967–72, retd. Management Consultant, Productivity and Management Services Ltd, 1972–74. CEng, FIMechE. *Recreations:* sailing, fishing, golf, caravanning. *Address:* Dolphin Cottage, Riverside, Newton Ferrers, Devon PL8 1AA. *T:* (01752) 872401. *Clubs:* Royal Western Yacht (Plymouth); Yealm Yacht (Newton Ferrers).
Died 13 March 1997.

SOUTHWORTH, Sir Frederick, Kt 1965; QC (Bahamas) 1952; Chief Justice, Malawi, 1964–70, retired; *b* Blackburn, Lancs, 9 May 1910; *s* of late Harper Southworth, Blackburn, Lancs; *m* 1942, Margaret, *d* of James Rice, Monaghan, Ireland; three *d*. *Educ:* Queen Elizabeth's Grammar Sch., Blackburn; Exeter Coll., Oxford. Called to the Bar, Gray's Inn, 1936. War of 1939–45; commissioned 1939; served with South Lancashire Regiment and Lancashire Fusiliers, and with Department of the Judge Advocate General in India, 1939–46; Hon. Colonel, Crown Counsel, Palestine, 1946–47; Crown Counsel, Tanganyika, 1947–51; Attorney-General, Bahamas, 1951–55; Acting Governor, July-Aug. 1952; Acting Chief Justice, July-Oct. 1954; Puisne Judge, Nyasaland, 1955–64; Acting Governor-General, Malawi, 1964 and 1965. *Publications:* Specimen Charges, in use in the courts of Tanzania, Zanzibar, Kenya and Uganda; The Southworth Commission Report: an inquiry into allegations made by the international press against the Nyasaland Police, 1960. *Address:* 40 Waverley Lane, Farnham, Surrey GU9 8BJ.

Died 22 Feb. 1999.

SOWDEN, John Percival; Chairman, Costain Group Ltd (formerly Richard Costain Ltd), 1972–80 (Director, 1967–82); Regional Director, Central London and City of London Regional Boards, Lloyds Bank, 1980–87; *b* 6 Jan. 1917; *s* of Percy Sowden and Gertrude Sowden (*née* Moss); *m* 1st, 1940, Ruth Dorothy Keane (marr. diss. 1969); one *s*; 2nd, 1969, Joyce Diana Timson. *Educ:* Silcoates Sch., Wakefield, Yorks; The Grammar Sch., Hebden Bridge, Yorks; City and Guilds Coll., Imperial Coll. of Science (BScEng, ACGI; FCGI 1973). FIStructE. Served War: commnd RE, with service in UK, ME and Italy, 1939–46 (despatches, 1943). Joined Richard Costain Ltd, 1948; Site Project Manager on various construction projects, incl. Festival of Britain, Apapa Wharf, Nigeria, and Bridgetown Harbour, Barbados, 1948–60; Joint Managing Director: Richard Costain (Associates) Ltd, 1961–62; Costain-Blankevoort Internat. Dredging Co. Ltd, 1963–65; Richard Costain Ltd: Manager, Civil Engrg Div., 1965–69; Board Member, 1967; Chief Executive, Internat. Area, 1969–70; Group Chief Executive, 1970–75. Member, Governing Body, Imperial Coll. of Science and Technology, 1971, Fellow, 1980. FRSA 1983. *Recreations:* reading, joinery. *Address:* Below Star Cottage, East Tytherley Road, Lockerley, Romsey, Hants SO5 0LW. *T:* (01794) 341172. *Club:* Royal Automobile.

Died 4 Nov. 1997.

SPAREY, John Raymond, MA; Director (Association of Municipal Engineers), Institution of Civil Engineers, 1984–85; Secretary-General, International Federation of Municipal Engineers, 1979–85; *b* 28 July 1924; *s* of late Henry Sparey and Lilian May (*née* Coles); *m* 1950, Audrie Kathleen (marr. diss. 1991), *d* of late Col E. J. W. Porter, OBE, TD, Portsmouth; two *s* one *d. Educ:* City of Bath Sch.; King's Coll., London; Trinity Coll., Cambridge (BA 1950; MA 1954). Royal Naval Scientific Service, 1944–47; Asst Secretary, Assoc. of Certified Accountants, 1952–69; Royal Institution of Chartered Surveyors: Dep. Sec., 1969–70; Sec. for Educn and Membership, 1970–74; Sec., Planning and Development Div., 1976; Sec., Instn of Municipal Engrs, 1977–84. *Recreations:* gardening, sailing. *Address:* 10 Elms Avenue, Great Shelford, Cambridge CB2 5LN. *T:* (01223) 844572. *Club:* Seaview Yacht (Seaview, IoW).   *Died 29 Sept. 1997.*

SPARKS, Rev. Hedley Frederick Davis, DD Oxon, 1949; FBA 1959; ATCL 1927; Oriel Professor of the Interpretation of Holy Scripture, University of Oxford, 1952–76; *b* 14 Nov. 1908; *s* of late Rev. Frederick Sparks and Blanche Barnes Sparks (formerly Jackson); *m* 1953, Margaret Joan, *d* of late C. H. Davy; two *s* one *d. Educ:* St Edmund's Sch., Canterbury; BNC, Oxford (Colquitt Exhibnr, 1927; BA 1st Cl. Theol., 1930; Sen. Hulme Schol., 1930; Hon. Fellow, 1987); Ripon Hall, Oxford. Ordained deacon, 1933, priest, 1934; Curate of St Martin and All Saints, Oxford, and Chaplain of Ripon Hall, 1933–36; Lectr in Theol., 1936–46, and Censor of Hatfield Coll., 1940–46, Univ. of Durham; Prof. of Theol., 1946–52, and Dean, Faculty of Arts, 1949–52, Univ. of Birmingham; Rector of Wytham, 1961–68. Hon. DD: St Andrews, 1963; Birmingham, 1983. Hon. Fellow, Oriel Coll., Oxford, 1980. Jt Editor, Jl of Theol Studies, 1954–77. *Publications:* The Old Testament in the Christian Church, 1944; The Formation of the New Testament, 1952; A Synopsis of the Gospels, part I: The Synoptic Gospels with the Johannine Parallels, 1964, 2nd edn 1970; part II: The Gospel according to St John with the Synoptic Parallels, 1974, combined volume edn, 1977; (ed) The Apocryphal Old Testament, 1984; (ed jointly): Novum Testamentum Domini Nostri Iesu Christi Latine secundum editionem Sancti Hieronymi, Part ii, fasc. 5, 1937, fasc. 6, 1939, fasc. 7, 1941, Part iii, fasc. 2, 1949, fasc. 3, 1953; Biblia Sacra iuxta Vulgatam versionem, 1969, 4th edn 1994; (contributed): The Bible in its Ancient and English Versions, 1940, 2nd edn 1954; Studies in the Gospels, 1955; The Cambridge History of the Bible, vol. 1, 1970, 2nd edn, 1975. *Recreations:* music, railways. *Address:* 14 Longport, Canterbury, Kent CT1 1PE. *T:* (01227) 766265.   *Died 22 Nov. 1996.*

SPEAR, Harold Cumming, CBE 1976; Member, Electricity Council, 1972–76; *b* 26 Oct. 1909; *yr s* of late Rev. Edwin A. and Elizabeth Spear; *m* 1935, Gwendolen (*née* Richards); one *s* one *d. Educ:* Kingswood Sch., Bath. Asst to Employment Manager, Gramophone Co. Ltd, 1928–33; Labour and Welfare Supervisor, Mitcham Works Ltd, 1933–35; Employment Supervisor, Hoover Ltd, 1935–38; Personnel Manager, Sperry Gyroscope Co. Ltd, 1938–40; appts with British Overseas Airways Corp., finally as Chief Personnel Officer, 1941–59; Dir of Personnel Management, Central Electricity Generating Bd, 1959–72; Mem., Central Arbitration Cttee, 1976–85. Pres., Inst. of Personnel Management, 1969–71; CIPM. *Recreation:* golf. *Address:* The Almonry, Newlands, Pershore, Worcs WR10 1BW. *Club:* Roehampton.

Died 2 June 1997.

SPEARMAN, Clement, CBE 1979; HM Diplomatic Service, retired; Ambassador and Consul-General to the Dominican Republic, 1975–79; *b* 10 Sept. 1919; *y s* of late Edward and Clara Spearman; *m* 1950, Olwen Regina Morgan; one *s* two *d. Educ:* Cardiff High School. RN (Air Arm), 1942–46. Entered Foreign (subseq. Diplomatic) Service, 1947; 3rd Sec., Brussels, 1948–49; 2nd Sec., FO, 1949–51; HM Consul, Skoplje, 1951–53; FO, 1953–56; 1st Sec., Buenos Aires, 1956–60; FO, 1960–62; Counsellor, CENTO, Ankara, 1962–65; Reykjavik, 1965–69; FCO, 1969–71; Manila, 1971–74; Toronto, 1974–75. *Recreations:* tennis, swimming. *Address:* 56 Riverview Gardens, SW13 9QZ. *T:* (0181) 748 9339. *Clubs:* Naval, Roehampton.   *Died 3 Feb. 1997.*

SPEED, Sir Robert (William Arney), Kt 1954; CB 1946; QC 1963; Counsel to the Speaker, 1960–80; *b* 18 July 1905; *s* of late Sir Edwin Arney Speed and Ada Frances, *d* of Rev. William Ross, formerly Rector of Haddington; *m* 1929, Phyllis (*d* 1991), *d* of Rev. P. Armitage; (one *s* one *d* decd). *Educ:* Rugby; Trinity College, Cambridge. Called to the Bar, Inner Temple, 1928; Bencher, 1961. Principal Assistant Solicitor, Office of HM Procurator-General and Treasury Solicitor, 1945–48; Solicitor to the Board of Trade, 1948–60. *Address:* Upper Culham, Wargrave, Berks RG10 8NR. *T:* (01491) 574271. *Club:* United Oxford & Cambridge University.

Died 13 Aug. 1999.

SPEIGHT, Johnny; writer; *b* 2 June 1920; *s* of John and Johanna Speight; *m* 1956, Constance Beatrice Barrett; two *s* one *d. Educ:* St Helen's RC School. Wrote for: Arthur Haynes Show; Morecambe and Wise Show; Peter Sellers; Till Death Us Do Part (Screenwriters Guild Award, 1966, 1967, 1968); The Lady is a Tramp (Pye TV Award, 1982); In Sickness and in Health; with Ray Galton: Tea Ladies, 1979; Spooner's Patch, 1979. *Plays:* Compartment (Screenwriters Guild Award, 1962); Playmates; Salesman; Knackers Yard; If There Weren't any Blacks You Would Have to Invent Them (Prague Festival Award, 1969). Evening Standard Drama Award for Best Comedy; Lifetime Achievement Award, Writers' Guild of GB, 1996. *Publications:* It Stands to Reason, 1974; The Thoughts of Chairman Alf, 1974; The Garnett Chronicles, 1986; For Richer, for Poorer, 1991; various scripts. *Recreation:* golf. *Address:* Fouracres, Heronsgate, Chorleywood, Herts WD3 5DP. *Clubs:* Stage Golf, Variety Golf, Pinner Hill Golf.   *Died 5 July 1998.*

SPEIR, Sir Rupert (Malise), Kt 1964; *b* 10 Sept. 1910; *y s* of late Guy Thomas Speir and Mary Lucy Fletcher, Saltoun. *Educ:* Eton Coll.; Pembroke Coll., Cambridge (BA). Admitted Solicitor, 1936. Served in Army throughout War of 1939–45; commissioned in Intelligence Corps, Sept. 1939; retired with rank of Lt-Col, 1945. Contested (C) Linlithgow, 1945, Leek, 1950; MP (C) Hexham Div. of Northumberland, 1951–66, retired. Sponsor of: Litter Act, 1958; Noise Abatement Act, 1960; Local Government (Financial Provisions) Act, 1963; Parliamentary Private Secretary: to Minister of State for Foreign Affairs and to Parly Sec., CRO, 1956–59; to Parly and Fin. Sec., Admty and to Civil Lord of Admty, 1952–56. Special Mem., Hops Marketing Board, 1958. Hon. Fellow, Inst. of Public Cleansing; Vice-Pres., Keep Britain Tidy Group. *Recreations:* golf, shooting. *Address:* Birtley Hall, Hexham, Northumberland NE48 3HL. *T:* (01434) 230275. *Died 16 Sept. 1998.*

SPEIRS, William James McLaren; HM Diplomatic Service, retired; *b* 22 Nov. 1924; *s* of late Alec McLaren Speirs and Olivia (*née* Petersen) *m* 1952, Jane Downing; two *s* one *d* (and one *d* decd). *Educ:* Clifton Coll.; Jesus Coll., Cambridge. Served Royal Signals, 1943–47; ADC to Governor of Singapore, 1946–47. HM Diplomatic Service, 1948–79: Rangoon, 1950; Jakarta, 1953; Berlin, 1957; Munich, 1963; Tel Aviv, 1970; Counsellor, FCO, 1979. Gp Security Adviser, Gallaher Ltd, 1979–85; Sen. Advr, Sultanate of Oman, 1986–94. *Recreations:* walking, collecting topographical books. *Address:* 24 Kingswood Firs, Grayshott, Hindhead, Surrey GU26 6ET. *Clubs:* Army and Navy, Special Forces.

Died 17 May 1998.

SPENCER, Alan Douglas, CIMgt; Chairman, 1977–80 and Managing Director, 1977–79, Boots The Chemist Ltd; Director: Owen Owen plc, 1980–86; Johnson Wax (UK) Ltd, 1981–90; *b* 22 Aug. 1920; *s* of Thomas and Laura Spencer; *m* 1944, Dorothy Joan Harper; two *d*. *Educ:* Prince Henry's Grammar Sch., Evesham. FBIM 1975, Command Gloucester Regt, 1940, served war with Green Howards, 1940–45; Instr, Sch. of Infantry, 1945–47. Joined Boots Co., 1938; rejoined 1947; Dir, 1963–81, Man. Dir, 1975, Vice-Chm., 1978–80, Boots Co. Ltd. Mem., E Midlands Electricity Bd, 1976–86. Pres., British Retailers' Assoc., 1983–84 (British Multiple Retailers Assoc., 1981–83). Governor, Trent Coll., 1979–90. *Recreation:* shooting. *Address:* Oakwood, Grange Road, Edwalton, Nottingham NG12 4BT. *T:* (0115) 923 1722.

Died 7 March 2000.

SPENCER, Cyril; Executive Chairman, Burton Group Ltd, 1979–81; *b* 31 Aug. 1924; *s* of Isaac and Lily Spencer; *m* 1971, Wendy Lois Sutton; two *s* one *d*, and two step *s* one step *d*. *Educ:* Christ Coll., Finchley; London Univ. (BSc). Joined Evans (Outsizes) Ltd, 1946: Managing Director, 1956; Chairman, 1969; takeover of Evans by Burton Group Ltd, 1971; Head of Womenswear, 1972; Group Man. Dir and Chief Exec., 1976. Chm., Waring and Gillow, 1985–88. *Recreations:* tennis, swimming, golf. *Address:* 6 Haversham Place, Merton Lane, N6 6NG.

Died 3 Oct. 1999.

SPITZER, Prof. Lyman, Jr, BA; PhD; Professor of Astronomy, 1947–82 (Charles A. Young Professor, 1952–82), Princeton University; Chairman of Astrophysical Sciences Department, and Director of Observatory, Princeton University, 1947–79; *b* 26 June 1914; *s* of Lyman Spitzer and Blanche B. (*née* Brumback); *m* 1940, Doreen D. Canaday; one *s* three *d*. *Educ:* Phillips Academy, Andover; Yale Univ. (BA); Cambridge Univ., England; Princeton Univ. (PhD). Instructor in Physics and Astronomy, Yale Univ., 1939–42; Scientist, Special Studies Group, Columbia Univ. Div. of War Research, 1942–44; Dir, Sonar Analysis Group, Columbia Univ. Div. of War Research, 1944–46; Assoc. Prof. of Astrophysics, Yale Univ., 1946–47. Princeton University: Dir Project Matterhorn, 1953–61; Chm. Exec. Cttee, Plasma Physics Lab., 1961–66; Chm. Res. Bd, 1967–72; Principal Investigator, Princeton telescope on Copernicus satellite. Chm., Space Telescope Inst. Council, 1981–90. Member: Nat. Acad. of Sciences; American Academy of Arts and Sciences; American Philosophical Society; Internat. Acad. of Astronautics; Corresp. Member, Société Royale des Sciences, Liège; Foreign Mem., Royal Soc., 1990; Foreign Associate, Royal Astronomical Soc.; Pres., American Astronomical Soc., 1959–61. Hon. Dr of Science: Yale Univ., 1958; Case Inst. of Technology, 1961; Harvard, 1975; Princeton, 1984; Hon. Dr of Laws, Toledo Univ., 1963. Rittenhouse Medal, Franklin Inst., 1957; NASA Medal, 1972; Bruce Medal, Astron. Soc. of the Pacific, 1973; Draper Medal, Nat. Acad. of Scis, 1974; Maxwell Prize, Amer. Physical Soc., 1975; Schwarzschild Medal, Deutsche Astron. Ges., 1975; Dist. Public Service Medal, NASA, 1976; Gold Medal, RAS, 1978; Nat. Medal of Science, 1980; Janssen Medal, Soc. Astron. de France, 1980; Franklin Medal, Franklin Inst., 1980; Crafoord Prize, Royal Swedish Acad. Sci., 1985; Madison Medal, Princeton Univ., 1989; Franklin Medal, Amer. Philosophical Soc., 1991. *Publications:* (ed) Physics of Sound in the Sea, 1946; Physics of Fully Ionized Gases, 1956 (2nd edn 1962); Diffuse Matter in Space, 1968; Physical Processes in the Interstellar Medium, 1978; Searching between the Stars, 1982; Dynamical Evolution of Globular Clusters, 1987; Dreams, Stars and Electrons, 1997; papers in Astrophysical Jl, Monthly Notices of Royal Astronomical Soc., Physical Review, Physics of Fluids, on interstellar matter, stellar dynamics, plasma physics, space astronomy, etc. *Recreations:* ski-ing, mountain climbing. *Address:* 659 Lake Drive, Princeton, NJ 08540, USA. *T:* (609) 9243007. *Clubs:* Alpine; American Alpine. *Died 31 March 1997.*

SPOCK, Dr Benjamin McLane; Professor of Child Development, Western Reserve University, USA, 1955–67, then lecturing, writing and working for peace; *b* New Haven, Connecticut, 2 May 1903; *s* of Benjamin Ives Spock and Mildred Louise (*née* Stoughton); *m* 1st, 1927, Jane Davenport Cheney (marr. diss. 1975); two *s*; 2nd, 1976, Mary Morgan; one step *d*. *Educ:* Yale Univ. (BA); Yale Medical Sch.; Coll. Physicians and Surgeons, Columbia Univ. (MD). Served, 1944–46 in US Navy. In practice (pediatrics), 1933–47: Cornell Med. Coll.; NY Hospital; NYC Health Dept; on staff of Rochester (Minn) Child Health Inst., Mayo Clinic, University of Minnesota, 1947–51; Prof. of Child Development, University of Pittsburgh, 1951–55. *Publications:* The Pocket Book of Baby and Child Care (also published as The Common Sense Book of Baby and Child Care), 1946, 7th edn as Dr Spock's Baby and Child Care, 1998; (with John Reinhart and Wayne Miller) A Baby's First Year, 1955; (with Miriam E. Lowenberg) Feeding Your Baby and Child, 1955; Dr Spock Talks with Mothers, 1961; Problems of Parents, 1962; (with Marion Lerrigo) Caring for Your Disabled Child, 1964; (with Mitchell Zimmerman) Dr Spock on Vietnam, 1968; Decent and Indecent: our personal and political behaviour, 1970; A Young Person's Guide to Life and Love, 1971; Raising Children in a Difficult Time, 1974 (UK as Bringing Up Children in a Difficult Time, 1974); Dr Spock on Parenting, 1987; (with Mary Morgan) Spock on Spock, 1989; A Better World for Our Children, 1994; *relevant publications:* The Trial of Doctor Spock, by Jessica Mitford, 1969; Dr Spock: biography of a conservative radical, by Lynn Z. Bloom, 1972. *Address:* PO Box 1268, Camden, ME 04843–1268, USA. *Died 15 March 1998.*

SPREULL, Prof. James Spreull Andrew; William Dick Professor of Veterinary Surgery at the University of

Edinburgh, 1959–78, then Emeritus; *b* 2 May 1908; *s* of late Lt-Col Andrew Spreull, DSO, TD, MRCVS, and Effie Andrew Spreull; *m* 1951, Kirsten Brummerstedt-Hansen; three *s*. *Educ:* Dundee High Sch.; Edinburgh Univ. (PhD); Royal Dick Veterinary Coll. (MRCVS). Royal Dick Veterinary College: Demonstrator of Anatomy, 1930–34, Lecturer in Applied Anatomy, 1931–34; engaged in general practice in Dundee, 1934–59. FRSE 1965. *Publications:* various contributions to veterinary journals. *Recreations:* agriculture, fishing, badminton, antiques. *Address:* 2 Marlee Road, Broughty Ferry, Dundee DD5 3HA. *T:* (01382) 775916. *Died 16 May 1998.*

SPRING, Frank Stuart, DSc (Manchester), PhD (Liverpool), FRS 1952; FRSC; Director, Laporte Industries Ltd, London, W1, 1959–71; *b* 5 Sept. 1907; 3rd *s* of John Spring and Isabella Spring, Crosby, Liverpool; *m* 1932, Mary, 2nd *d* of Rev. John Mackintosh, MA and Mabelle Mackintosh, Heswall; one *s* one *d*. *Educ:* Waterloo Grammar Sch.; University of Liverpool. United Alkali Research Scholar, University of Liverpool, 1928–29; University Fellow, Liverpool, 1929–30; Assistant Lecturer, Lecturer and Senior Lecturer in Chemistry, University of Manchester, 1930–46; Freeland Professor of Chemistry, The Royal College of Science and Technology, Glasgow, 1946–59. Tilden Lecturer, Chemical Society, 1950. Hon. DSc: Salford, 1967; Strathclyde, 1981. *Publications:* papers (mostly jtly) in chemical journals. *Address:* Flat 26, 1 Hyde Park Square, W2 2JZ. *T:* (0171) 262 8174. *Died 1 March 1997.*

SPRINGER, Tobias; a Metropolitan Stipendiary Magistrate, 1963–82; Barrister-at-law; *b* 3 April 1907; *o c* of late Samuel Springer, MBE; *m* 1937, Stella Rauchwerger. *Educ:* Mill Hill Sch.; Caius Coll., Cambridge (Law Tripos 1928). Called to the Bar, Gray's Inn, 1929; practised London and SE Circuit. Served War of 1939–45: 60th Rifles, 1940–45; Lt-Col GSO1, GHQ, H Forces, 1944. Returned to practise at Bar, 1945. Actg Dep. Chm., Co. London Sessions, periods 1962, 1963; sometime Dep. Circuit Judge. Life Governor: Mill Hill School; Metropolitan Hosp. Freedom, City of London, 1982. *Recreations:* travel, reading. *Address:* 82 Cholmley Gardens, Fortune Green Road, NW6 1UN. *T:* (020) 7435 0817. *Club:* Old Mill Hillians.

Died 17 Aug. 2000.

SPRINGETT, Jack Allan, CBE 1978; MA (Cantab); Education Officer, Association of Metropolitan Authorities, 1980–82; *b* 1 Feb. 1916; *s* of Arthur John and Agnes Springett; *m* 1950, Patricia Winifred Singleton; three *s* one *d*. *Educ:* Windsor Grammar Sch.; Fitzwilliam House, Cambridge. Served War, Royal Signals and Gen. Staff, 1940–46. Asst Master, Christ's Hospital, Horsham, 1938–47; Administrative Asst, North Riding, 1947–52; Asst Educn Officer, Birmingham, 1952–62; Dep. Educn Officer, Essex, 1962–73; County Educn Officer, Essex, 1973–80. *Address:* 3 Roxwell Road, Chelmsford, Essex CM1 2LY. *T:* Chelmsford (01245) 258669.

Died 15 March 1996.

SPRY, Sir John (Farley), Kt 1975; President, British Antarctic Territory Court of Appeal, since 1991; *b* 11 March 1910; *s* of Joseph Farley Spry and Fanny Seagrave Treloar Spry; *m* 1st (marr. diss. 1940); one *s* one *d*; 2nd, Stella Marie (*née* Fichat) (*d* 1995). *Educ:* Perse School; Peterhouse, Cambridge (MA). Solicitor, 1935; Asst Registrar of Titles and Conveyancer, Uganda, 1936–44; Chief Inspector of Land Registration, Palestine, 1944; Asst Director of Land Registration, Palestine, 1944–48; Registrar-General, Tanganyika 1948–50, Kenya 1950–52; Tanganyika: Registrar-Gen., 1952–56; Legal Draftsman, 1956–60; Principal Sec., Public Service Commn, 1960–61; Puisne Judge, 1961–64; Justice of Appeal, Court of Appeal for Eastern Africa, 1964–70, Vice-President, 1970–75;

Chm., Pensions Appeal Tribunals, 1975–76; Gibraltar: Chief Justice, 1976–80; Justice of Appeal, 1980–83; Pres., Court of Appeal, 1983–91; Comr for Revision of Laws of Gibraltar, 1981–85; Chief Justice: British Indian Ocean Territory, 1981–87; St Helena and its Dependencies, 1983–92. *Publications:* Sea Shells of Dar es Salaam, Part I, 1961 (3rd edn 1968), Part II, 1964; Civil Procedure in East Africa, 1969; Civil Law of Defamation in East Africa, 1976. *Address:* 15 De Vere Gardens, W8 5AN.

Died 17 May 1999.

STABLER, Arthur Fletcher; Board Member, Theatre Royal Trust Ltd, since 1987; *b* 7 Nov. 1919; *s* of Edward and Maggie Stabler; *m* 1948, Margaret Stabler; two *s*. *Educ:* Cruddas Park Sch. Engineer apprenticeship, Vickers Armstrong, 1935–39. Served War, Royal Northumberland Fusiliers, 1939–46. With Vickers Armstrong, 1946–78. Mem., Supplementary Benefits Commn, 1976–79. Newcastle upon Tyne: City Councillor, 1963–97; Dep. Lord Mayor, 1982–83; Lord Mayor, 1983–84; Chairman: Housing Renewals, 1975–76; Arts and Recreation, 1976–77; Case Work Sub-Cttee, 1974–77; Tenancy Relations Sub-Cttee, 1975–77; Community Develt Sub-Cttee, 1975–76; Town Moor Sub-Cttee, 1976–77; Personnel Sub-Cttee, 1982–; Area Housing Cttee, 1984–85; Priority Area Sub-Cttee, 1984–85; Health Adv. Cttee, 1986–87; District HA Jt Consultative Cttee; Festival Cttee, 1987–88; Public Works Cttee, 1987–88; Vice-Chairman: Social Services Cttee, 1974–76; Housing Management Cttee, 1975–76; Tyneside Summer Exhibn Cttee, 1982–; Tyne and Wear Jt Fire and Civil Defence Cttee, 1986–89; Cityworks Cttee, 1989. Chm., Axwell Park Community Homes, 1978–79; Mem., numerous Tenants' Assocs. Chm., Newcastle upon Tyne Central Labour Party, 1965–78. Pres., No 6 Br., AUEW. Chm., Westerhope Golf Club Jt Sub-Cttee, 1976–77. President: Newcastle upon Tyne and District Allotments and Garden Council, 1980–; Elswick Park Bowling Club, 1980–; Cttee, Tyne Wear Polish Solidarity Club, 1981–. Life Mem., High Pitt Social Club; Hon. Member: Casino Royal Club, 1980; St Joseph's Club, 1983; Royal British Legion Club, 1983. *Publication:* Gannin Along the Scotswood Road, 1976. *Recreations:* social work, local history. *Address:* 207 Cruddas Park House, Elswick, Newcastle upon Tyne NE4 7RG. *T:* (0191) 273 2362. *Clubs:* Pineapple CIU, Polish White Eagle, Ryton Social, Tyneside Irish (Hon.), Maddison's (Hon.) (Newcastle upon Tyne). *Died 3 May 1997.*

STAFFORD-CLARK, Dr David, MD; FRCP, FRCPsych; Consultant Emeritus, Guy's Hospital and Joint Hospitals, Institute of Psychiatry, University of London; Physician in Charge, Department of Psychological Medicine, and Director of The York Clinic, Guy's Hospital, 1954–73; Chairman, Psychiatric Division, Guy's Group, 1973–74; Consultant Physician, Bethlem Royal and Maudsley Hospitals and the Institute of Psychiatry, 1954–73; *b* 17 March 1916; *s* of Francis and Cordelia Susan Stafford Clark; *m* 1941, Dorothy Stewart (*née* Oldfield); three *s* one *d*. *Educ:* Felsted; University of London; Guy's Hospital. MB, BS 1939; MD 1947; DPM 1948. MRCS, LRCP, 1939; MRCP 1946; FRCP 1958. Served War of 1939–45, RAFVR; trained as medical parachutist (despatches twice); demobilised 1945. Nuffield Med. Fellow, Guy's Hosp., 1946; 3 years postgrad. trng appts, Inst. of Psychiatry, Maudsley Hosp.; Registrar, Nat. Hosp., Queen Sq., 1948; Resident, Massachusetts Gen. Hosp., Dept of Psychiatry, and Teaching Clinical Fellow, Harvard Med. School, 1949; First Asst, Professorial Unit, Maudsley Hosp., 1950; Consultant Staff, Guy's Hosp., 1950; Lecturership, Psychology (Faculty of Letters), Reading Univ., 1950–54. Mem. Assoc. for Research in Mental and Nervous Disorders, NY, 1950–53; Consultant, British Near East Forces, BMH Dhekelia and Princess Mary's

Hosp., Akrotiri, Cyprus, 1975–80. Hon. Vis. Prof., Johns Hopkins Univ., USA, 1964; Gifford Lectr and Vis. Prof., St Andrews Univ., 1978. Member: Archbishop of Canterbury's Commn on Divine Healing; Council, Royal Medico-Psychological Assoc.; Council, Medico-Legal Soc.; Examr, RCP and Cambridge MD; Editorial Bds, Guy's Hosp. Reports, and Mod. Med. of Gt Britain. Acted as adviser to various motion picture companies (Universal International, etc) on medical aspects of their productions; also acted as adviser and director on a large number of medical programmes on radio, and both BBC and Independent Television, including the "Lifeline" series of programmes for the BBC, and documentary programmes for ITV on the emotional and intellectual growth of normal children, and the life and work of Freud; author of Brain and Behaviour series in Adult Education Television Programmes on BBC2; Mind and Motive series, 1966. Mem., NY Acad. of Sciences; Foundn Fellow, RCPsych, 1972, Hon. Fellow, 1976; FRSocMed. Hon. Pres., Guy's Hosp. RUFC, 1972; Hon. Mem., Cambridge RUFC, 1972. FRSA (Silver Medal), 1959; Hon. RCM 1966. Gate Prize for Poetry, 1933. *Publications: poetry:* Autumn Shadow, 1941; Sound in the Sky, 1944; *novel:* Soldier Without a Rifle, 1979; *medical:* Psychiatry Today, 1951; Psychiatry for Students, 1964, 7th (rev.) edn, 1989; What Freud Really Said, 1965; Five Questions in Search of an Answer, 1970; chapters in: Emergencies in Medical Practice, 1st edn 1948–3rd edn 1952; Compendium of Emergencies, 1st and 2nd edns; Case Histories in Psychosomatic Medicine, 1952; Taylor's Medical Jurisprudence, 12th edn, 1965; Schizophrenia: Somatic Aspects, 1st edn, 1957; Frontiers in General Hospital Psychiatry, 1961; A Short Textbook of Medicine, 1963; The Pathology and Treatment of Sexual Deviation, 1964; Modern Trends in Psychological Medicine, 1970; Psychiatric Treatment, Concepts of, in Encyclopædia Britannica, 200th anniv. edn, 1973; contributions to various medical textbooks and to medical and scientific jls. *Recreations:* travel, reading, writing, making and watching films, theatre. *Club:* Royal Air Force.
Died 9 Sept. 1999.

STAIR, 13th Earl of, *cr* 1703; **John Aymer Dalrymple,** KCVO 1978 (CVO 1964); MBE 1941; Bt 1664 and 1698 (Scot.); Viscount Stair, Lord Glenluce and Stranraer, 1690; Viscount Dalrymple, Lord Newliston, 1703; Baron Oxenfoord (UK) 1841; Colonel (retired) Scots Guards; Lord-Lieutenant of Wigtown, 1961–81; Captain General of the Queen's Body Guard for Scotland, Royal Company of Archers, 1973–88; *b* 9 Oct. 1906; *e s* of 12th Earl of Stair, KT, DSO, and Violet Evelyn (*née* Harford) (*d* 1968); *S* father, 1961; *m* 1960, Davina, DL, *d* of late Hon. Sir David Bowes-Lyon, KCVO; three *s. Educ:* Eton; Sandhurst. Bde Major, 3rd (London) Infantry Bde and Regimental Adjt Scots Guards, 1935–38; served Middle East, 1941; Bde Major, 16th Inf. Bde (despatches, MBE), Lt-Col 1942; commanded 1st Scots Guards, 1942–43; AMS Headquarters AAI, 1944; Comd Trg Bn Scots Guards, 1945; Comd 2nd Scots Guards, 1946–49; Comd Scots Guards, Temp. Colonel, 1949–52; retired, 1953; retired as Hon. Colonel Scots Guards, 1953. *Heir: s* Viscount Dalrymple, *b* 4 Sept. 1961. *Address:* Lochinch Castle, Stranraer, Wigtownshire DG9 8RT. *Club:* Cavalry and Guards.   *Died 26 Feb. 1996.*

STAMERS-SMITH, Eileen, MA; Headmistress, Malvern Girls' College, 1984–85; *b* 17 April 1929; *d* of Charles and May Fairey; *m* 1970, Henry Arthur Stamers-Smith, CBE, MA (*d* 1982). *Educ:* Castleford Grammar Sch., Yorks; Lady Margaret Hall, Oxford (BA Hons English Lang. and Lit., Cl. II, 1951; MA; DipEd). Assistant English Teacher: Abbeydale Girls' Grammar Sch., Sheffield, 1952–57; Cheltenham Ladies' Coll., 1957–67; Headmistress, Bermuda Girls' High Sch., 1967–71. Tutor/

lecturer in garden history, art history and English literature for Dept for Continuing Educn, Univ. of Oxford, Denman Coll., WI, WEA, English Sch. of Gardening, Inchbald Sch. of Design, V&A, etc, 1985–; Guest Lecturer: Swan's Hellenic Art Treasures Tours, 1990, 1992; Page & Moy, 1993. Member Council: Garden Hist. Soc., 1987– (Newsletter Editor, 1987–96); Kipling Soc., 1996–; Editor, Garden Hist. Soc. Jl, 1989. *Publications:* monographs on the gardens of Lady Margaret Hall, Oxford, 1879–1929, 1991, 1929–1949, 1993, 1949–1990s, 1998; articles in Garden Hist. Soc. Jl and Newsletter, The Northern Gardener, HORTUS and Kipling Soc. Jl. *Recreations:* music, garden history, Venice, photography, gardening, collecting books. *Address:* 8 Mavor Close, Old Woodstock, Oxon OX20 1YL. *T:* (01993) 811383.
Died 20 Oct. 1998.

STANBURY, Prof. Sydney William, MD; FRCP; Professor of Medicine, University of Manchester, 1965–84, then Emeritus; *b* 21 April 1919; *s* of F. A. W. Stanbury and A. B. Stanbury (*née* Rowe); *m* 1943, Helen, *d* of Harry and Patty Jackson; one *s* four *d. Educ:* Hulme Grammar Sch., Oldham; Manchester Univ. MB, ChB (1st Cl. Hons) 1942; MD (Gold Medal) 1948; MRCP 1947, FRCP 1958. Served RAMC, Burma and India, 1944–47. Beit Meml Res. Fellow, 1948–51; Rockefeller Travelling Fellow, 1951–52; Registrar, Lectr and Reader, Dept of Medicine, Manchester Royal Infirmary, 1947–65; Consultant Phys., United Manchester Hosps, 1959. Member: Assoc. of Physicians; Bone and Tooth Soc. Visiting Professor: John Howard Means, Massachusetts Gen. Hosp., Boston, 1958; Henry M. Winans, Univ. of Texas, Dallas, 1958; W. T. Connoll, Queen's Univ., Kingston, Ont, 1978; Weild Lectr, RCPSG, 1958; Lumleian Lectr, RCP, 1981; Vis. Lectr, Univ. of Washington, Mayo Clinic, etc. *Publications:* contrib. European and American med. books and jls on renal function, electrolyte metabolism, metabolic bone disease and vitamin D metabolism. *Recreation:* gardening. *Address:* Halaman, Gillan, Manaccan, Helston, Cornwall TR12 6HL. *T:* Manaccan (01326) 231586.   *Died 29 Feb. 1996.*

STANIFORTH, John Arthur Reginald, CBE 1969; Director: Constructors John Brown, 1947–84 (Chief Executive and Deputy Chairman, 1958–84); John Brown & Co., Ltd, 1965–84; John Brown Engineering (Clydebank) Ltd, 1968–84 (Chairman, 1970–77); *b* 19 Sept. 1912; *o s* of Captain Staniforth, MC, Anston House, Anston, Yorks; *m* 1936, Penelope Cecile, *y d* of Maj.-Gen. Sir Henry Freeland; one *d* (one *s* decd). *Educ:* Marlborough Coll. With John Brown Group, 1929–84. Mem., Export Guarantees Adv. Council, 1971–76, Dep. Chm., 1975–76. Founder Chm., British Chemical Engrg Contractors Assoc., 1965–68; former Chm., Oil and Chemical Plant Assoc. Dir, St Wilfrid's Hospice (South Coast), 1981–92. Governor, Bryanston Sch., 1962–92. *Recreations:* golf, fishing. *Address:* 11 The Holdens, Old Bosham, West Sussex PO18 8LN. *T:* Bosham (01243) 572401. *Clubs:* MCC (Hon. Mem., 1991); Goodwood Golf and Country (Hon. Mem., 1994).   *Died 28 Aug. 1996.*

STANLEY PRICE, His Honour Peter; QC 1956; a Circuit Judge (formerly a Judge of the Central Criminal Court), 1969–83; President, National Reference Tribunal for the Coal Mining Industry, 1979–83; Judge of the Chancery Court of York, 1967–83; *b* 27 Nov. 1911; *s* of late Herbert Stanley Price and Gertrude Rangeley Stanley Price (*née* Wightman); *m* 1st, 1946, Harriett Ella Theresa (*d* 1948), *o d* of late Rev. R. E. Pownall; two *s*; 2nd, 1950, Margaret Jane, *o d* of late Samuel Milkins (she *m* 1937, William Hebditch, RAF; he *d* 1941); one *d*, one step *s. Educ:* Cheltenham; Exeter College, Oxford (1st cl. Final Hons Sch. of Jurisprudence, 1933). Barrister, Inner Temple, 1936, Bencher, 1963. Served War of 1939–45, Lieut (S)

RNVR. Recorder of Pontefract, 1954, of York, 1955, of Kingston-upon-Hull, 1958, of Sheffield, 1965–69. Dep. Chm., N Riding QS, 1955–58, 1970–71, Chm., 1958–70; Judge of Appeal, Jersey and Guernsey, 1964–69; Solicitor-General, County Palatine of Durham, 1965–69. Pres., Nat. Reference Tribunal, Officials Conciliation Scheme, 1967–79. *Recreations:* birds and trees, gardening, shooting. *Address:* Church Hill, Great Ouseburn, York YO26 9RH. *T:* (01423) 330252. *Club:* Brooks's.
Died 28 Sept. 1998.

STAPLES, Sir Gerald (James Arland), 16th Bt *cr* 1628, of Lissan, co. Tyrone; *b* 2 Dec. 1909; *s* of Thomas Staples (*d* 1963; *nephew* of Sir Nathaniel Alexander Staples, 10th Bt); *S* brother, 1997; *m* 1951, Henrietta Owen, *d* of Arland Ussher; two *d. Heir: b* Richard Molesworth Staples [*b* 11 June 1914; *m* 1954, Marjorie Charlotte (*née* Jefcoate) (*d* 1998)]. *Died 22 Sept. 1999.*

STAPLES, Sir Thomas, 15th Bt *cr* 1628 (Ire.), of Lissan, Co. Tyrone; *b* 9 Feb. 1905; *s* of Thomas Staples (*d* 1963) (nephew of 10th Bt) and Mary Ussher (*d* 1966), *d* of Frederick Greer; *S* cousin, 1989; *m* 1952, Frances Ann Irvine (*d* 1981). *Heir: b* Gerald James Arland Staples [*b* 2 Dec. 1909; *m* 1951, Henrietta Owen, *d* of Arland Ussher; two *d*]. *Address:* 219, 3051 Shelbourne Street, Victoria, BC V8R 6T2, Canada. *Died 19 Dec. 1997.*

STAVELEY, Martin Samuel, CMG 1966; CVO 1966; CBE 1962 (MBE 1955); *b* 3 Oct. 1921; fourth *s* of late Herbert Samuel Staveley and Edith Ellen Staveley (*née* Shepherd); *m* 1942, Edith Eileen Baker; one *s* two *d. Educ:* Stamford School; Trinity College, Oxford. Appointed Cadet, Colonial Administrative Service, Nigeria, 1942; Secretary, Development and Welfare Organisation in the West Indies, 1946–57; Secretary to Governor-General, Federation of the West Indies, 1958–62; Administrator, British Virgin Islands, 1962–67; HM Diplomatic Service, 1967–74; Home Civil Service, 1974–84. *Address:* Stonewall Cottage, Brinton, Norfolk NR24 2QF. *Died 20 June 1998.*

STAVELEY, Admiral of the Fleet Sir William (Doveton Minet), GCB 1984 (KCB 1981); DL; Chairman, Chatham Historic Dockyard Trust, since 1991 (Trustee, since 1988); *b* 10 Nov. 1928; *s* of late Adm. Cecil Minet Staveley, CB, CMG, and Margaret Adela (*née* Sturdee); *m* 1954, Bettina Kirstine Shuter; one *s* one *d. Educ:* West Downs, Winchester; RN Colls, Dartmouth and Greenwich. Entered Royal Navy as Cadet, 1942; Midshipman, HMS Ajax, Mediterranean, 1946–47; Sub-Lieut/Lieut, HM Ships Nigeria and Bermuda, S Atlantic, 1949–51; Flag Lieut to Adm. Sir George Creasy, C-in-C Home Fleet, HM Ships Indomitable and Vanguard, 1952–54; Staff, Britannia, RNC, Dartmouth, 1954–56; HM Yacht Britannia, 1957; First Lieut, HMS Cavalier, Far East, 1958–59; Lt-Comdr, 1958; RN Staff Coll., 1959; Staff, C-in-C Nore and Flag Officer Medway, 1959–61; Comdr 1961; Sen. Officer, 104th and 6th Minesweeping Sqdn, HMS Houghton, Far East, 1962–63; Comdr, Sea Trng, Staff of Flag Officer, Sea Trng, Portland, 1964–66; comd HMS Zulu, ME and Home Station, 1967; Captain 1967; Asst Dir, Naval Plans, Naval Staff, 1967–70; Command: HM Ships Intrepid, Far and ME, 1970–72; Albion, Home Station, 1972; RCDS, 1973; Dir of Naval Plans, Naval Staff, 1974–76; Flag Officer, Second Flotilla, 1976–77; Flag Officer, Carriers and Amphibious Ships, and NATO Commander, Carrier Striking Group Two, 1977–78; Chief of Staff to C-in-C Fleet, 1978–80; Vice-Chief of Naval Staff, 1980–82; C-in-C, Fleet, and Allied C-in-C, Channel and E Atlantic, 1982–85; First Sea Lord and Chief of Naval Staff, 1985–89; First and Principal Naval ADC to the Queen, 1985–89. Chairman: Royal London Hosp. and Associated Community Services NHS Trust, 1991–92 (Special Trustee, Royal London Hosp., 1992); NE Thames RHA,

1993–94; N Thames RHA, 1994–96; Mem., NHS Policy Bd, 1994–96. Chairman: Combined Services Equitation Assoc., 1980–82; Council, British Horse Soc., 1982; Member: London Adv. Cttee, English Heritage, 1990–; RHS; Royal Nat. Rose Soc.; Gen. Council, King Edward VII Hosp. Fund for London, 1993–96. Trustee, Florence Nightingale Mus. Trust, 1988–93. President, Kent Branch: Royal British Legion, 1991–; CPRE, 1997–; a Vice Pres., Falkland Is Assoc., 1991. Dir, British Sch. of Osteopathy, 1990–96 (Chm., 1992–96). Mem. Court, 1988–, Council, 1992–, Univ. of Kent; Governor, Sutton Valence Sch., 1990–92. A Younger Brother of Trinity House, 1973. CIMgt (CBIM 1983). Freeman, City of London, 1987; Liveryman and Hon. Freeman, Shipwrights' Co., 1987. DL Kent, 1992. *Recreations:* country sports, gardening. *Address:* Chatham Historic Dockyard Trust, The Historic Dockyard, Chatham, Kent ME4 4TE. *T:* (01634) 812551, *Fax:* (01634) 826918. *Clubs:* Boodle's; Royal Naval Sailing Association. *Died 14 Oct. 1997.*

STEDMAN, Baroness *cr* 1974 (Life Peer), of Longthorpe, Peterborough; **Phyllis Stedman,** OBE 1965; *b* 14 July 1916; *o d* of Percy and Emmie Adams; *m* 1941, Henry William Stedman (*d* 1989), OBE 1981. *Educ:* County Grammar Sch., Peterborough. Branch Librarian, Peterborough City Council, 1934–41; Group Officer, National Fire Service, 1942–45. Baroness-in-Waiting (a Govt Whip), 1975–79; Parly Under-Sec. of State, DoE, 1979; Govt spokesman for Transport, the Environment, Educn and Trade, 1975–79; Opposition spokesman on the environment, local govt, new towns and transport, 1979–81; Leader of SDP in House of Lords, 1988–91 (Mem., 1981–91, SDP Whip, 1982–86, SDP Chief Whip, 1986–88); cross-bencher, 1992–. County Councillor: Soke of Peterborough, 1946–65; Huntingdon and Peterborough, 1965–74; Cambridgeshire, 1974–76; Vice-Chm., Cambridgeshire County Council, 1974–76. Member: Board, Peterborough Development Corp., 1972–76; IBA, 1974–75; Board, Hereward Radio, 1979–85; Exec. Mem., Tripscope, 1994–; Vice-Chm., Nat. PHAB, 1978–; Vice-Pres., ACC, 1986–. Mem. Exec. Council, Fire Services Nat. Benevolent Fund, 1976–. *Address:* 1 Grovelands, Thorpe Road, Peterborough PE3 6AQ. *T:* Peterborough (01733) 61109. *Died 8 June 1996.*

STEEL, Prof. Robert Walter, CBE 1983; Principal, University College of Swansea, 1974–82; Vice-Chancellor, 1979–81, Emeritus Professor 1982, University of Wales; *b* 31 July 1915; *er s* of late Frederick Grabham and Winifred Barry Steel; *m* 1940, Eileen Margaret, *er d* of late Arthur Ernest and Evelyn Beatrice Page, Bournemouth; one *s* two *d. Educ:* Great Yarmouth Grammar Sch.; Cambridge and County High School for Boys; Jesus College, Oxford (Open Exhibitioner in Geography; BSc, MA). RGS Essay Prize, 1936; Drapers' Co. Research Scholarship for Geography, 1937–39, for work in Sierra Leone; Departmental Lectr in Geography, Univ. of Oxford, 1939–47; Naval Intelligence Div., Admiralty, 1940–45; attached to Sociological Dept of W African Inst. of Arts, Industry and Social Science as geographer to Ashanti Social Survey, Gold Coast, 1945–46; University of Oxford: Univ. Lectr in Commonwealth Geography, 1947–56; Lectr in Geography, St Peter's Hall, 1951–56; Official Fellow and Tutor in Geography, Jesus Coll., 1954–56 (Supernumary Welsh Fellow, 1974–75 and 1979–80; Hon. Fellow 1982); Univ. of Liverpool: John Rankin Prof. of Geography, 1957–74; Dean, Faculty of Arts, 1965–68; Pro-Vice-Chancellor, 1971–73. Murchison Grant, RGS, 1948; Council RGS, 1949–53, 1968–71; Inst. of Brit. Geographers: Council, 1947–60; Actg Sec., 1948, Asst Sec., 1949–50; Hon. Editor of Publications, 1950–60; Vice-Pres., 1966–67, Pres. 1968, Hon. Mem. 1974; President: Section E (Geography), BAAS, 1966; African

Studies Assoc. of the UK, 1970–71 (Vice-Pres., 1969–70); Geographical Assoc., 1973 (Hon. Mem. 1982); Glamorgan Trust for Nature Conservation, 1982–86. Dir, Commonwealth Geographical Bureau, 1972–81; Member: Inter-Univ. Council for Higher Educn Overseas, 1974–81; Welsh Adv. Cttee, British Council, 1978–90; Cttee for Internat. Co-operation in Higher Educn, British Council (Higher Educn Div.), 1981–85; Chairman: Universities Council for Adult Educn, 1976–80; Governors, Westhill Coll., Birmingham, 1981–95; Bd, Wales Adv. Body for Local Authority Higher Educn, 1982–86; Swansea Festival of Music and the Arts, 1982–95; Lower Swansea Valley Develt Gp, 1979–88; Swansea Civic Soc., 1988–97; Commonwealth Human Ecology Council, 1988–90; Pres., Council for Church and Associated Colls, 1990–94 (Vice-Chm., 1988–90); Mcm., ESRC, 1983–86 (Chm., Internat. Activities Cttee, 1985–86). Member Council: National Univ. of Lesotho, 1981–85; Univ. of Swaziland, 1987–91. Vice-Pres., Royal African Soc., 1977–; Council, Nat. Inst. of Adult Educn, 1977–80; Vice-Pres., WEA, S Wales, 1997–. Vis. Prof., Univ. of Ghana, 1964; Canadian Commonwealth Vis. Fellow, Carleton Univ., 1970. Fellow, Selly Oak Colls, Birmingham, 1995. Hon. Fellow: UC Swansea, 1991; Trinity Coll., Carmarthen, 1995. Hon. DSc Salford, 1977; Hon. LLD: Wales, 1983; Liverpool, 1985; Birmingham, 1995; DUniv Open, 1987. *Publications:* (ed with A. F. Martin, and contrib.) The Oxford Region: a Scientific and Historical Survey, 1954; (ed with C. A. Fisher, and contrib.) Geographical Essays on British Tropical Lands, 1956; (ed with R. M. Prothero, and contrib.) Geographers and the Tropics: Liverpool Essays, 1964; (ed with R. Lawton, and contrib.) Liverpool Essays on Geography: a Jubilee Collection, 1967; (with Eileen M. Steel) Africa, 1974, 3rd edn 1982; (ed) Human Ecology and Hong Kong: report for the Commonwealth Human Ecology Council, 1975; The Institute of British Geographers, the First Fifty Years, 1984; (contrib. and ed) British Geography 1918–1945, 1987; articles, mainly on tropical Africa, in Geographical Jl and other geog. jls. *Recreations:* walking, gardening, music. *Address:* 12 Cambridge Road, Langland, Swansea SA3 4PE. *T:* (01792) 369087. *Club:* Royal Commonwealth Society.
Died 29 Dec. 1997.

STEELE, Frank Fenwick, OBE 1969; *b* 11 Feb. 1923; *s* of Frank Robert and Mary Fenwick Steele; *m* 1944, (Evelyn) Angela Scott; one *s* one *d*. *Educ:* St Peter's Sch., York; Emmanuel Coll., Cambridge (MA). Army, 1943–47. HM Colonial Service, Uganda, 1948–50; joined HM Diplomatic Service, 1951; FO, 1951; Vice-Consul, Basra, 1951; Third, later Second Sec., Tripoli, 1953; Foreign Office, 1956; Second Sec., Beirut, 1958; FO, 1961; First Secretary: Amman, 1965; Nairobi, 1968; Counsellor and Dep. UK Rep., Belfast, 1971; FCO, 1973; resigned 1975; joined Kleinwort, Benson as Adviser, 1975; Dir, and Hd of Export Finance Dept, Kleinwort Benson, 1985–87; Dir, cos in Cluff group, 1979–87; Chm., Network Television Ltd, 1981–87; consultant, 1987–96. Mem., Export Promotion Cttee, CBI, 1983–87. Dir, Arab British Chamber of Commerce, 1978–87; Member Council: Anglo-Jordanian Soc., 1980–88; Royal Soc. for Asian Affairs, 1981–88 (Vice-Pres., 1985–88); Royal Asiatic Soc., 1986–90 (Mem., 1988–90); Royal Geographical Soc., 1990–95 (Mem., F and GP Cttee, 1986–95; Vice-Pres., 1993–95); Mem. Cttee, Mount Everest Foundn, 1990–95. Trustee, Prostate Cancer Charity, 1996–. *Publications:* articles on Tibet. *Recreation:* travel. *Address:* 9 Ashley Gardens, SW1P 1QD. *T:* (0171) 834 7596. *Clubs:* Beefsteak, Shikar, Travellers'.
Died 20 Nov. 1997.

STEER, Rt Rev. Stanley Charles; Bishop of Saskatoon, 1950–70; *b* 2 June 1900; *s* of S. E. and E. G. Steer; *m* 1936, Marjorie Slater. *Educ:* Guildford Grammar Sch.;

Univ. of Saskatchewan (BA); Oxford Univ. (MA). Missionary at Vanderhoof, BC, 1929; Chaplain, St Mark's Church, Alexandria, 1931; Chaplain, University Coll., Oxford, 1932–33; St John's Hall, Univ. of London: Tutor, 1933; Vice-Principal, 1936; Chaplain, The Mercers' Company, City of London, 1937; Principal, Emmanuel Coll., Saskatoon, 1941; Hon. Canon of St John's Cathedral, Saskatoon, and CF (R of O), 1943. Hon. DD: Wycliffe Coll., Toronto, 1947; Emmanuel Coll., Saskatoon, 1952; St Chad's Coll., Regina, 1964. *Recreation:* tennis. *Address:* 2383 Lincoln Road, Victoria, BC V8R 6A3, Canada. *T:* (604) 5929888.
Died 10 Dec. 1997.

STEINER, Rear-Adm. Ottokar Harold Mojmir St John, CB 1967; Assistant Chief of Defence Staff, 1966–68, retired; *b* 8 July 1916; *e s* of late O. F. Steiner; *m* 1st, 1940, Evelyn Mary Young (marr. diss. 1975; she *d* 1994); one *s* one *d*; 2nd, 1975, Eleanor, *widow* of Sqdn Leader W. J. H. Powell, RAF. *Educ:* St Paul's School. Special entry cadet, RN, 1935; served War of 1939–45 (despatches twice), HMS Ilex, Havelock, Frobisher, Superb; Naval Staff Course, 1947; Staff of C-in-C, Far East Fleet, 1948–50; Comdr 1950; jssc 1953; HMS Ceylon, 1953–54; NATO Defence Coll., 1955; HMS Daedalus, 1955–56; Capt. 1956; Admiralty, 1956–58; in comd HMS Saintes and Capt. (D) 3rd Destroyer Sqdn, 1958–60; Naval Adviser to UK High Commission, Canada, 1960–62; Senior Offrs War Course, 1962; in comd HMS Centaur, 1963–65; ADC to the Queen, 1965; Rear-Adm., 1966. Chm., Whitbread Round the World Race, 1972–82; Transglobe Expedition (Capt. of ship to Antarctica), 1979–80. Vice-Pres., Shipwrecked Fishermen and Mariners Royal Benevolent Soc. Freeman, City of London; Liveryman, Coachmakers' and Coach Harness Makers' Co. *Recreations:* sailing, golf. *Clubs:* Royal Cruising; Isle of Wight Motor Yacht (Adm.); Royal Naval Sailing Association; Union (Malta).
Died 27 Dec. 1998.

STENHOUSE, John Godwyn, TD with bar; FCIB; Chairman, Stenhouse Holdings plc, 1978–80 (Director, 1947–84); retired; *b* 16 Nov. 1908; *s* of Alexander Rennie Stenhouse and Hughina Cowan Stenhouse; *m* 1st, 1936, Margaret Constance Thornton (*d* 1965); two *d*; 2nd, 1967, Jean Ann Bennie (*née* Finlayson); one step *s*. *Educ:* Warristo Sch., Moffat; Kelvinside Acad., Glasgow. With an insurance co., 1927; joined A. R. Stenhouse & Partners, Ltd, Insurance Brokers (later Stenhouse Holdings Ltd), 1931. *Recreations:* sailing, mechanical engineering. *Address:* 2 St Germains, Bearsden, Glasgow G61 2RS. *T:* (0141) 942 0151. *Club:* Royal Scottish Automobile (Glasgow).
Died 30 May 1997.

STENHOUSE, Sir Nicol, Kt 1962; *b* 14 Feb. 1911; 2nd *s* of late John Stenhouse, Shanghai, China, and Tring, Hertfordshire; *m* 1951, Barbara Heath Wilson (*d* 1991); two *s* one *d*. *Educ:* Repton. Joined Andrew Yule & Co. Ltd, Calcutta, India, 1937; Managing Director, 1953–59; Chairman and Senior Managing Director, 1959–62. President: Bengal Chamber of Commerce and Industry, Calcutta, 1961–62; Associated Chambers of Commerce of India, Calcutta, 1961–62. *Recreation:* gardening. *Address:* 3 St Mary's Court, Sixpenny Handley, near Salisbury, Wilts SP5 5PH.
Died 20 March 1998.

STENING, Sir George (Grafton Lees), Kt 1968; ED; Hon. Gynæcological Consultant, Royal Prince Alfred Hospital, Sydney, since 1964 (Hon. Gynæcological Surgeon, 1948–64); Emeritus Consultant, St Luke's Hospital, Sydney (Board Director, 1970–84); *b* 16 Feb. 1904; *s* of George Smith Stening and Muriel Grafton Lees; *m* 1935, Kathleen Mary Packer, DStJ; one *s* one *d*. *Educ:* Sydney High Sch.; Univ. of Sydney. MB, BS (Syd.) 1927 (Hons Cl. II); FRCSEd 1931; FRACS 1935; FRCOG 1947; FRACOG, 1980. Carnegie Trav. Fellow, 1948. Served War of 1939–45: Middle East, New Guinea, Australia;

OC, 3rd Aust. Surgical Team, Libyan Desert, 1941; CO, 2/11 Aust. Gen. Hosp., 1941–44; CO, 113 Aust. Gen. Hosp., 1945. Hon. Col, RAAMC. GCStJ 1971; Chancellor, Order of St John, in Australia, 1961–82. Pres., Sen. Golfers' Soc. of Aust., 1974. *Publication:* A Text Book of Gynæcology (co-author), 1948. *Recreations:* golf, yachting. *Address:* 2/22 Wolseley Road, Point Piper, NSW 2027, Australia. *Clubs:* Royal Sydney Golf (Sydney); Australian Jockey.   *Died 17 July 1996.*

STEPHENS, Air Comdt Dame Anne, DBE 1961 (MBE 1946); Hon. Aide-de-camp to the Queen, 1960–63; Director, Women's Royal Air Force, 1960–63; *b* 4 Nov. 1912; *d* of late General Sir Reginald Byng Stephens, KCB, CMG and Lady (Eleanore Dorothea) Stephens. *Educ:* privately. Joined WAAF, 1939; served in UK, Belgium and Germany, 1939–45; command WRAF Depot, Hawkinge, 1950–52; promoted Group Officer, 1951; Inspector WRAF, 1952–54; Deputy Director, 1954–57; Staff Officer, HQ 2nd TAF, 1957–59; promoted Air Commandant, 1960. *Address:* The Forge, Sibford Ferris, Banbury, Oxfordshire OX15 5RG. *T:* (01295) 780452.
       Died 26 July 2000.

STEPHENSON, Prof. Gordon, CBE 1967; FRIBA, FRTPI, LFRAIA, LFRAPI, FLI, DistTP; Professor Emeritus of Architecture, University of Western Australia; *b* 6 June 1908; *s* of Francis E. and Eva E. Stephenson, Liverpool; *m* 1938, Flora Bartlett Crockett (*d* 1979), Boston, USA; three *d*. *Educ:* Liverpool Institute; University of Liverpool; University of Paris; Massachusetts Institute of Technology. Elmes Scholar, Univ. of Liverpool, 1925–30; Holt Scholar, 1928; First Cl. Hons in Architecture, 1930; Chadwick Scholar at Brit. Inst. in Paris and Univ. of Paris, 1930–32; BArch; MCP (MIT). Lecturer and Studio Instructor in Architecture, University of Liverpool, 1932–36; Commonwealth Fellow and Medallist, Massachusetts Inst. of Technology, 1936–38; Studio Master, Architectural Assoc., School of Architecture, 1939–40; Lever Professor of Civic Design, School of Architecture, University of Liverpool, 1948–53; Professor of Town and Regional Planning in the University of Toronto, Canada, 1955–60; Prof. of Architecture, Univ. of WA, 1960–72. Architectural and Planning practice: asst to Corbett, Harrison and McMurray, NY City, 1929; asst to Le Corbusier and Pierre Jeanneret, Paris, 1930–32; Div. Architect, with W. G. Holford, on Royal Ordnance Factory work, 1940–42; Research Officer, Sen. Research Officer, and Chief Planning Officer, Min. of Works and Planning, and Min. of Town and Country Planning, 1942–47; seconded to assist Sir Patrick Abercrombie on Greater London Plan, 1943–44; partner, Stephenson, Young and Partners, 1949–53; Cnslt Architect, Univ. of WA, 1960–69; in partnership with R. J. Ferguson, as architects and planners for Murdoch Univ., WA, 1972–76; in private practice, houses, militia camp, university bldgs, community centre, housing schemes, town and regional planning studies. Mem., Nat. Capital Planning Cttee, Canberra, 1967–73; Consultant, Perth Northwestern Suburbs Railway Project, 1989–90. Editor, Town Planning Review, 1949–54. Hon. MCIP 1960. Hon. LLD Univ. of WA, 1976; Hon. DArch Univ. of Melbourne, 1984; Hon. DSc Flinders Univ., 1987; DUniv Murdoch Univ., 1988. *Publications:* (with Flora Stephenson) Community Centres, 1941; (with F. R. S. Yorke) Planning for Reconstruction, 1944; (with J. A. Hepburn) Plan for the Metropolitan Region of Perth and Fremantle, 1955; A Redevelopment Study of Halifax, Nova Scotia, 1957; (with G. G. Muirhead) A Planning Study of Kingston, Ontario, 1959; The Design of Central Perth, 1975; Joondalup Regional Centre, 1977; Planning for the University of Western Australia: 1914–70, 1986; On a Human Scale, 1992; Compassionate Town Planning, 1995; articles and papers in British, Australian, Canadian technical professional jls. *Recreations:* architectural

practice, drawing, travel. *Address:* Unit 55, 14 Albert Street, St Louis Estate, Claremont, WA 6010, Australia. *T:* (9) 3852309.   *Died 29 March 1997.*

STEPHENSON, (James) Ian (Love), RA 1986 (ARA 1975); painter; *b* 11 Jan. 1934; *o s* of James Stephenson and May (*née* Emery); *m* 1959, Kate, *o d* of James Brown; one *s* one *d*. *Educ:* King Edward VII School of Art, King's Coll., Univ. of Durham, Newcastle upon Tyne (3 prizes; Hatton Schol.; BA Dunelm 1956, 1st Class Hons in Fine Art). Tutorial Student, 1956–57, Studio Demonstrator, 1957–58, King's Coll., Newcastle upon Tyne (pioneered 1st foundn course in UK dedicated to new creativity in art); Boise Schol. (Italy), Univ. of London, 1958–59; Vis. Lectr, Polytechnic Sch. of Art, London, 1959–62; Vis. Painter, Chelsea Sch. of Art, 1959–66; Dir, Foundn Studies, Dept of Fine Art, Univ. of Newcastle, 1966–70 (introd 1st academic syllabus alternating between perceptual and conceptual studies in the UK); Dir, Postgrad. Painting, Chelsea Sch. of Art, 1970–89 (attained Master's Degree status, 1974, the only CNAA Fine Art MA course in UK approved in nationwide survey, 1977–78); Internat. Course Leader, Voss Summer Sch., 1979. Member: Visual Arts Panel, Northern Arts Assoc., Newcastle, 1967–70; Fine Art Panel, NCDAD, 1972–74; Perm. Cttee, New Contemp. Assoc., 1973–75 (revived annual nat. student exhibns); Fine Art Board, CNAA, 1974–75; Adv. Cttee, Nat. Exhibn of Children's Art, Manchester, 1975–92; Working Party, RA Jubilee Exhibn, 1976–77; Selection Cttee, Arts Council Awards, 1977–78; Painting Faculty, Rome and Abbey Major Scholarships, 1978–82; Recommending Cttee, Chantrey Bequest, 1979–80. RA Steward, Artists' Gen. Benevolent Instn, 1979–80; Fine Art Advr, Canterbury Art Coll., 1974–79; 1st Specialist Advr, CNAA, 1980–83; Boise Scholarship Cttee, UCL, 1983; Cttee Chm., David Murray Studentship Fund, 1990. Examiner: Birmingham Poly., 1972–73; Portsmouth Poly., 1973–76; London Univ., 1975–83 (Sen. Postgrad. Examiner); Leicester Poly., 1976–78; Ulster Poly., 1979–82; Canterbury Art Coll., 1981–83; Newcastle Poly., 1982–85; Kingston Poly., 1985–88; Edinburgh Art Coll., 1989–96. Juror: Contemporary Art, Portsmouth, 1966; Fedn N Art Socs, Newcastle, 1966; Pernod Competition, Northern Arts Assoc., Newcastle, 1970; Yorkshire Artists' Exhibn, Leeds, 1971; Open Field, SAA, Reading, 1972; N Young Contemps, Manchester, 1973; British Painting, London, 1974; Winsor & Newton Award, Birmingham, 1975; Second Chance Charity Exhibn, London, 1977; RA Summer Exhibn, London, 1980, 1989, 1990, 1997, 1998 (Chief Hanger, 1998); JM 12 Exhibn, Liverpool, 1980. Vice-Pres., Sunderland Arts Centre, 1982–86. Hon. Member: CAS, 1980–81; Accademia Italia, 1980–; Mark Twain Soc., 1978–. *Exhibitions included:* British Painting in the Sixties, London, 1963; Mostra di Pittura Contemporanea, Amsterdam and Europe, 1964–65; 9o Biennio, Lugano, 1966; 5e Biennale and 18e Salon, Paris, 1967; Recent British Painting, London and world tour, 1967–75; Junge Generation Grossbritannien, Berlin, 1968; Retrospective, Newcastle, 1970; La Peinture Anglaise Aujourd'hui, Paris, 1973; Elf Englische Zeichner, Baden Baden and Bremen, 1973; Recente Britse Tekenkunst, Antwerp, 1973; 13a Bienal, São Paulo and Latin America, 1975; Arte Inglese Oggi, Milan, 1976; Retrospective, London and Bristol, 1977; Englische Kunst der Gegenwart, Bregenz, 1977; British Painting 1952–77, London, 1977; Color en la Pintura Britanica, Rio de Janeiro and Latin America, 1977–79; Abstract Paintings from UK, Washington, 1978; Retrospective, Birmingham and Cardiff, 1978; Royal Acad. of Arts, Edinburgh, 1979–80; Art Anglais d'Aujourd'hui, Geneva, 1980; British Art 1940–80, London, 1980; Colour in British Painting, Hong Kong and Far East, 1980–81; Contemporary British Drawings, Tel-Aviv and Near East,

1980–82; The Deck of Cards, Athens and Arabia, 1980–82; A Taste of British Art Today, Brussels, 1982; Arteder Muestra Internaçional, Bilbao, 1982; La Couleur en la Peinture Britannique, Luxembourg and Bucharest, 1982–83; 7th, 8th and 9th Internat. Print Biennales, Bradford, 1982, 1984 and 1986; 15a Bienale, Ljubljana, 1983; Peintiadau Prydeinig 1946–72, Penarth, 1985; Ready Steady Go, London and UK, 1992–93; Raphael Cartoons Re-opening, London, 1996; *illustrations included:* Cubism and After (BBC film), 1962; Contemporary British Art, 1965; Private View, 1965; Blow Up (film), 1966; Art of Our Time, 1967; Recent British Painting, 1968; Adventure in Art, 1969; In Vogue, 1975; Painting in Britain 1525–1975, 1976; British Painting, 1976; Contemporary Artists, 1977, 1983, 1989 and 1995; Contemporary British Artists, 1979; Tendenze e Testimonianze, 1983; Dictionary of 20th Century British Artists, 1991; *work in collections:* Arnolfini Trust, Arts Council, Birmingham and Bristol City Art Galls, British Council, BP Chemicals and Co., Bury Art Gall., Contemp. Art Soc., Creasey Lit. Museum, DoE, Economist Newspaper, Granada TV, Gulbenkian Foundn, Hatton Gall., Hunterian Museum, Kettle's Yard, Leeds City Art Gall., Leicestershire Educn Authority, Madison Art Center, Marzotto Roma, Nat. West. Bank, Northern Arts Assoc., Nuffield Foundn, Queen Elizabeth II Conf. Centre, Stuyvesant Foundn, Sunderland Art Gall., Tate Gall., Unilever Ltd, Union Bank of Switzerland, V&A Museum, Victoria Nat. Gall., Welsh Nat. Museum, Whitworth Art Gall. Hon. DLitt Dunelm, 1999. *Prizes included:* Junior Section, Moores Exhibn, Liverpool, 1957; European Selection, Premio Marzotto, Valdagno, 1964; First, Northern Painters' Exhibn, 1966. *Address:* c/o Royal Academy of Arts, Piccadilly, W1V 0DS.
Died 25 Aug. 2000.

STEPHENSON, Rt Hon. Sir John (Frederick Eustace), Kt 1962; PC 1971; a Lord Justice of Appeal, 1971–85; *b* 28 March 1910; 2nd *s* of late Sir Guy Stephenson, CB, and of Gwendolen, *d* of Rt Hon. John Gilbert Talbot, PC, MP; *m* 1951, (Frances) Rose, *yr d* of Baron Asquith of Bishopstone, PC; two *s* two *d. Educ:* Winchester College (Schol.); New Coll., Oxford (Schol.; Hon. Fellow, 1979). 1st Cl. Hon. Mods. 1930, 1st Cl. Lit. Hum. 1932, BA 1932, MA 1956. Called to the Bar, Inner Temple (Entrance Scholarship), 1934; Bencher, 1962. Sapper RE (TA), 1938; War Office, 1940; Intelligence Corps, Captain 1943, Major 1944 and Lt-Col 1946; Middle East and NW Europe; Regional Intelligence Officer, Hamburg, 1946. Recorder of Bridgwater, 1954–59; Recorder of Winchester, 1959–62; Chancellor of the Diocese: of Peterborough, 1956–62; of Winchester, 1958–62; QC 1960; Dep. Chm., Dorset QS, 1962–71; Judge of Queen's Bench Div., High Court of Justice, 1962–71. *Publication:* A Royal Correspondence, 1938. *Address:* 26 Doneraile Street, SW6 6EN. *T:* (0171) 736 6782. *Clubs:* Hurlingham, MCC; Royal Wimbledon Golf.
Died 1 Nov. 1998.

STEVENS, Richard William, RDI 1973; BSc; FCSD; FCIBS; Partner, Richard Stevens Design Associates, 1987–94; *b* 1 Oct. 1924; *s* of William Edward Stevens and Caroline Alice (*née* Mills); *m* 1947, Anne Clara Hammond (*d* 1994); one *s* one *d. Educ:* Dorking County Grammar Sch.; Regent St Polytechnic (BSc). FCSD (FSIAD 1960); FCIBS 1977. Designer, then Chief Designer, Atlas Lighting Ltd, 1954–63; Industrial Design Manager, Standard Telephones and Cables Ltd, 1963–69; Design Manager, Post Office Telecommunications (later British Telecom), 1969–83. Pres., SIAD, 1972–73; Treasurer, ICSID, 1975–77. Gold Medal, Milan Triennale, 1957; three Design Centre Awards, London. *Recreations:*

gardening, music, photography, walking. *Address:* Hazel Cottage, Ewood Lane, Newdigate, Dorking, Surrey RH5 5AR.
Died 21 March 1997.

STEVENS, Prof. Thomas Stevens, FRS 1963; FRSE 1964; Emeritus Professor of Chemistry, University of Sheffield; *b* 8 Oct. 1900; *o c* of John Stevens and Jane E. Stevens (*née* Irving); *m* 1949, Janet Wilson Forsyth (*d* 1994); no *c. Educ:* Paisley Grammar School; Glasgow Academy; Universities of Glasgow and Oxford. DPhil 1925. Assistant in Chemistry, Univ. of Glasgow, 1921–23, Lecturer, 1925–47; Ramsay Memorial Fellow, Oxford, 1923–25; Sen. Lectr in Organic Chemistry, Univ. of Sheffield, 1947–49, Reader, 1949–63, Prof., 1963–66. Visiting Prof. of Chemistry, Univ. of Strathclyde, 1966–67. Hon. DSc Glasgow, 1985. *Publications:* (with W. E. Watts) Selected Molecular Rearrangements, 1973; contrib. to Elsevier-Rodd, Chemistry of Carbon Compounds, 1957–60; papers in scientific jls. *Recreation:* unsophisticated bridge. *Address:* 313 Albert Drive, Glasgow G41 5RP. *T:* (0141) 423 6928.
Died 12 Nov. 2000.

STEVENSON, Vice-Adm. Sir (Hugh) David, AC 1976; KBE 1977 (CBE 1970); Royal Australian Navy, retired; *b* 24 Aug. 1918; *s* of late Rt Rev. William Henry Webster Stevenson, Bishop of Grafton, NSW, and Mrs Katherine Saumarez Stevenson; *m* 1st, 1944, Myra Joyce Clarke (*d* 1978); one *s* one *d*; 2nd, 1979, Margaret Wheeler Wright. *Educ:* Southport Sch., Qld; RAN Coll. psc RN 1956; idc 1966. Commnd, 1938; served War: Mediterranean, East Indies, Pacific; minesweeping post, SW Pacific; specialised in navigation, 1944 (HM Navigation Sch.); Commands: HMAS Tobruk and 10th Destroyer Sqdn, 1959–60; HMNZS Royalist, 1960–61; HMAS Sydney 1964; HMAS Melbourne, 1965–66; Dir of Plans, 1962–63; Naval Officer i/c W Australian area, 1967; Dep. Chief of Naval Staff, 1968–69; Comdr Aust. Fleet, 1970–71; Chief of: Naval Personnel, 1972–73, Naval Staff, 1973–76; retd 1976. Comdr 1952; Captain 1958; Cdre 1967; Rear-Adm. 1968; Vice-Adm. 1973. Chm. for Territories, Queen Elizabeth Jubilee Fund for Young Australians, 1977; Patron, N Class Destroyers Assoc. (Qld), 1992–. *Publication:* (contrib.) The Use of Radar at Sea, 1952. *Recreations:* reading, opera, bridge. *Address:* PO Box 297, Main Beach, Qld 4217, Australia. *T:* (7) 55271910, *Fax:* (7) 55271920. *Clubs:* United Service (Brisbane); Twin Towns RSL (Tweed Heads).
Died 26 Oct. 1998.

STEWARD, Stanley Feargus, CBE 1947; FIEE; Director, George Thurlow and Sons (Holdings) Ltd; Chairman, ERA Technology Ltd, 1983–84; *b* 9 July 1904; *s* of late Arthur Robert and Minnie Elizabeth Steward, Mundesley, Norfolk; *m* 1929, Phyllis Winifred, *d* of late J. Thurlow, Stowmarket, Suffolk; one *s* one *d. Educ:* The Paston Sch., North Walsham, Norfolk. Was apprenticed to East Anglian Engineering Co. (subseq. Bull Motors Ltd) and held positions of Chief Designer, Sales Manager and Managing Dir; Ministry of Supply: Electrical Adviser to Machine Tool Control, 1940; Director of Industrial Electrical Equipment, 1941–44; Dir Gen. of Machine Tools, 1944–45; Chairman: Machine Tool Advisory Council, 1946–47; Gauge & Tool Advisory Council, 1946–47; South Western Electricity Board, 1948–55; Man. Dir, Lancashire Dynamo Holdings Ltd, 1956–59 (Chm., 1957–58); Man. Dir, BEAMA, 1959–71. Dir, E. R. & F. Turner, Ltd, Ipswich, 1944–48. Former Chm., Lancashire Dynamo and Crypto Ltd, Lancashire Dynamo Electronic Products Ltd and Lancashire Dynamo Group Sales; Chairman: William Steward (Holdings) Ltd and William Steward & Co. Ltd, 1970–80; Thurlow, Nunn & Sons Ltd, 1970–84; Dir, Bull Motors Ltd, 1981–85. Member: British Electricity Authority, 1952–53; Elect. Engineering EDC, 1962–71; Machine Tool EDC, 1971–80; Chm., British Electrical Development Assoc., 1954; President: Ipswich and District Electrical Assoc., 1964–67, 1972–78; Electrical Industries Club, 1966–67; Assoc. of Supervisory and Exec. Engineers, 1970–74; Electrical and Electronic Industries Benevolent Assoc., 1971–72; Instn of Engineers-in-Charge, 1982–84; Pres., Exec. Cttee, Organisme de Liaison des Industries Metalliques Europeénes, 1963–67. Freeman of City of London; Master, Worshipful Company of Glaziers and Painters of Glass, 1964. *Publications:* Electricity and Food Production, 1953; British Electrical Manufacture in the National Economy, 1961; Twenty Five Years of South Western Electricity, 1973; The Story of the Dynamicables, 1983; The Story of Electrex, 1984; regular 'Personal View' contribs to Electrical Review and other jls. *Recreations:* books, music, watching cricket. *Address:* 41 Fairacres, Roehampton Lane, SW15 5LX. *T:* (020) 8876 2457.

Died 23 Oct. 1999.

STEWART, Campbell; *see* Stewart, W. A. C.

STEWART, Duncan Montgomery; Principal of Lady Margaret Hall, Oxford, 1979–95; *b* 14 Feb. 1930; *s* of William Montgomery Stewart and Mary Pauline (*née* Checkley); *m* 1961, Valerie Mary Grace, *er d* of Major E. H. T. Boileau, Rampisham, Dorset; one *s* one *d*. *Educ:* Greymouth Technical High Sch.; Christ's Coll., NZ; Canterbury University Coll., NZ (MA 1st Cl. French 1951, 1st Cl. Latin 1952; Pres., Students' Assoc., 1952); Rhodes Scholar, 1953; Queen's Coll., Oxford (1st Cl. Hons Mod. Langs 1955). Oxford University: Lectr, 1955, Fellow, 1956–79, Wadham Coll.; Mem., Gen. Bd of Faculties, 1972–79, 1985–88 (Vice-Chm., 1976–78); Mem., Hebdomadal Council, 1976–91; Vice-Chm., Libraries Bd, 1979–85; Curator, Bodleian Liby, 1979–83; Rhodes Trustee, 1986–; Sen. Mem., Univ. Wine Tasting Soc., 1974–85. Oxford Chm., Oxford and Cambridge Schs Exam. Bd, 1986–91. *Publications:* articles and revs on French Literature, esp. later medieval. *Recreations:* opera, wine. *Address:* 12 Dunstan Road, Oxford OX3 9BY; Place de la Résistance, 82270 Montpezat de Quercy, Tarn et Garonne, France. *Died 22 May 1996.*

STEWART, Ewen; Sheriff at Wick, Caithness, 1962–92, at Dornoch, Sutherland and Tain, Ross and Cromarty, 1977–92, and at Stornoway, Western Isles, 1990–92; *b* 22 April 1926; *o s* of late Duncan Stewart and Kate Blunt; *g s* of late Ewen Stewart, Kinlocheil; *m* 1959, Norma Porteous Hollands (*d* 1992), *d* of late William Charteris Hollands, Earlston; one *d*. *Educ:* Edinburgh University (BSc (Agric.) 1945; MA (Econ.) 1950; LLB 1952). Asst Agricultural Economist, East of Scotland Coll. of Agriculture, 1946–49; practised at Scottish Bar, 1952–62; Lectr on Agricultural Law, Univ. of Edinburgh, 1957–62; former Standing Junior Counsel, Min. of Fuel and Power. Parly Cand. (Lab) Banffshire, 1962. *Address:* 16 Bignold Court, George Street, Wick, Caithness KW1 4DL.

Died 9 Oct. 2000.

STEWART, James Maitland, DFC with 2 oak leaf clusters (US); Air Medal with 3 oak leaf clusters; DSM (US); actor, stage and film; *b* Indiana, Pa, 20 May 1908; *s* of Alexander Maitland Stewart and Elizabeth Ruth (*née* Jackson); *m* 1949, Gloria McLean (*d* 1994); two *s* twin *d*. *Educ:* Mercersburg Academy, Pa; Princeton University (BS Arch.). War Service, 1942–45: Lt-Col Air Corps; Europe, 1943–45 (Air Medal, DFC); Colonel, 1945; USAF Reserve: Brig.-Gen. 1959; Dir, Air Force Assoc. First New York appearance, Carry Nation, 1932; subseq. played in Goodbye Again, Spring in Autumn, All Good Americans, Yellow Jack, Divided by Three, Page Miss Glory, A Journey by Night; Harvey (Broadway), 1970, (Prince of Wales), 1975. Entered films, 1935; *films include:* Murder Man, Next Time We Love, Seventh Heaven, You Can't Take It With You, Made for Each Other, Vivacious Lady, The Shopworn Angel, Mr Smith Goes to Washington, Destry Rides Again, No Time for Comedy, Philadelphia Story, The Shop around the Corner, Pot o' Gold, Ziegfeld Girl, Come Live with Me, It's a Wonderful Life, Magic Town, On Our Merry Way, You Gotta Stay Happy, Call Northside 777, Rope, The Stratton Story, Malaya, The Jackpot, Harvey, Winchester '73, Broken Arrow, No Highway in the Sky, Bend of the River, Carbine Williams, The Greatest Show on Earth, Thunder Bay, Naked Spur, The Glenn Miller Story, Rear Window, The Man from Laramie, The Far Country, Strategic Air Command, The Man Who Knew Too Much, Night Passage, Spirit of St Louis, Midnight Story, Vertigo, Bell, Book and Candle, Anatomy of a Murder, The FBI Story, The Mountain Road, The Man Who Shot Liberty Valance, Mr Hobbs Takes a Vacation, Take her, She's Mine, Cheyenne Autumn, Shenandoah, The Rare Breed, Firecreek, Bandalero, The Cheyenne Social Club, Fool's Parade, Dynamite Man from Glory Jail, The Shootist, Airport 77, The Big Sleep, Magic of Lassie. Held many awards including: five Academy Award nominations; Oscar award as best actor of the year; Hon. Oscar Award; two NY Film Critics best actor awards; Venice Film Festival best actor award; France's Victoire Trophy for best actor; Screen Actors Guild award. Hon. degrees include: DLitt, Pennsylvania; MA, Princeton. *Address:* 9201 Wilshire Boulevard, Suite 204, Beverly Hills, CA 90210, USA. *Died 2 July 1997.*

STEWART, Kenneth Albert; Member (Lab) Merseyside West, European Parliament, since 1984; *b* Liverpool, 28 July 1925; *m* 1946, Margaret Robertson Vass; one *s* two *d*. *Educ:* local schs. Parachute Regt (Sgt). Former joiner. Former Member: Merseyside CC; Liverpool CC (Chm., Housing Cttee); former Chm. and Sec., Liverpool West Derby Labour Party. *Address:* 26 Tiptree Close, off Burghill Road, Croxteth Park, Liverpool L12 0BW.

Died 2 Sept. 1996.

STEWART, Sir Ronald (Compton), 2nd Bt *cr* 1937, of Stewartby, co. Bedford; DL; Chairman, London Brick Co. Ltd, 1966–79; *b* 14 Aug. 1903; *s* of Sir (Percy) Malcolm Stewart, 1st Bt, OBE, and Cordelia (*d* 1906), *d* of late Rt Hon. Sir Joseph Compton Rickett, DL, MP; *S* father, 1951; *m* 1936, Cynthia, OBE, JP (*d* 1987), *d* of Harold Farmiloe. *Educ:* Rugby; Jesus College, Cambridge. High Sheriff of Bedfordshire, 1954, DL 1974. *Heir:* none. *Address:* Maulden Grange, Maulden, Bedfordshire MK45 2AU.

Died 26 Jan. 1999 (ext).

STEWART, Prof. (William Alexander) Campbell, DL; MA, PhD; Vice-Chancellor, University of Keele, 1967–79; *b* Glasgow, 17 Dec. 1915; *s* of late Thomas Stewart, Glasgow, and Helen Fraser, Elgin, Morayshire; *m* 1947, Ella Elizabeth Burnett, Edinburgh; one *s* one *d*. *Educ:* Colfe's Grammar Sch., London; University Coll., and Inst. of Education, Univ. of London. Exhibitioner, University Coll., London., 1934–37; BA 1937; MA 1941; PhD 1947; Diploma in Education, 1938; Fellow, UCL, 1975–. Sen. English Master: and Housemaster, Friends' School, Saffron Walden, Essex, 1938–43; Abbotsholme School, Derbyshire, 1943–44 (Member of Governing Body, 1960–80; Chm., Council, 1974–80); Asst Lectr and Lectr in Education, University Coll., Nottingham, 1944–47; Lectr in Education, Univ. of Wales (Cardiff), 1947–50; Prof. of Education, Univ. of Keele (formerly UC of N Staffs), 1950–67, Prof. Emeritus, 1979. Vis. Prof., McGill Univ., 1957, Univ. of Calif, Los Angeles 1959; Simon Vis. Prof., Univ. of Manchester, 1962–63; Prestige Fellow, NZ Univs, 1969; Hon. Vis. Professorial Fellow, 1979–84, Privy Council Mem. of Univ. Court, 1980–, Univ. of Sussex. Chairman: YMCA Educn Cttee, 1962–67; Nat. Adv. Council for Child Care, 1968–71; Univs Council for Adult Educn, 1969–73; Council, Roehampton Inst. of Higher Educn, 1979–88 (Fellow, 1988); Member: Inter-

Univ. and Polytech. Council for Higher Education Overseas; Commonwealth Univ. Interchange Council, 1968–80; Adv. Council, Supply and Training of Teachers, 1974–78; US-UK Educnl Commn, 1977–81; Council: Univ. of Sierra Leone, 1968–83; Open Univ., 1973–80. Fellow, Internat. Inst. of Art and Letters. DL Stafford, 1973. Hon. DLitt: Ulster, 1973; Keele, 1981. *Publications:* Quakers and Education, 1953; (ed with J. Eros) Systematic Sociology of Karl Mannheim, 1957; (with K. Mannheim) An Introduction to the Sociology of Education, 1962; (contrib.) The American College (ed Sanford), 1962; The Educational Innovators, Vol. 1 (with W. P. McCann), 1967, Vol. 2, 1968; Progressives and Radicals in English Education 1750–1970, 1972; Higher Education in Postwar Britain, 1989. *Recreations:* talking and listening, theatre, music. *Address:* Flat 4, 74 Westgate, Chichester, West Sussex PO19 3HH. *T:* (01243) 785528. *Clubs:* Oriental; Federation House (Stoke on Trent).

Died 23 April 1997.

STEWART, Rt Rev. William Allen; Bishop Suffragan of Taunton, since 1997; *b* 19 Sept. 1943; *s* of William Stewart and Betty Hele Sandeman-Allen; *m* 1969, Janet Margaret Andrews; two *s* two *d. Educ:* Uppingham Sch.; Trinity Coll., Cambridge (MA); Cranmer Hall, Durham (DipTh). Ordained deacon, 1968, priest, 1969; Assistant Curate: Eccleshall, Sheffield, 1968–72; St Mary, Cheltenham, 1972–74; Vicar, St James, Gloucester, 1974–80; Priest-in-charge, All Saints, Gloucester, 1978–80; Rector, St Mary Magdalene, Upton, Torquay, 1980–85; Vicar, St Mark, Oulton Broad, 1985–87. Rural Dean, of Lothingland, 1992–97; Hon. Canon of Norwich Cathedral, 1994–97. *Recreations:* singing, cricket, Rugby, football, walking. *Address:* Sherford Farm House, Sherford, Taunton TA1 3RF. *T:* (01823) 288759.

Died 24 March 1998.

STIBBE, Philip Godfrey, MA; Head Master of Norwich School, 1975–84; *b* 20 July 1921; *m* 1956, Mary Joy, *d* of late Canon C. G. Thornton; two *s* one *d. Educ:* Mill Hill Sch.; Merton Coll., Oxford (MA). Served War of 1939–45; joined Royal Sussex Regt, 1941; seconded King's (Liverpool) Regt, 1942; 1st Wingate Expedn into Burma (wounded, despatches), 1943; POW, 1943–45. Asst Master, 1948–75, Housemaster, 1953–74, Bradfield Coll. JP Norwich, 1979–84. *Publication:* Return via Rangoon, 1947, repr. 1994. *Recreations:* people, places, books. *Address:* 29A Bracondale, Norwich NR1 2AT. *T:* (01603) 630704. *Died 17 Jan. 1997.*

STIRLING, Hamish; Sheriff of South Strathclyde, Dumfries and Galloway, since 1992; *b* 9 July 1938; *s* of late James Stirling, DSc, FRSE and Anne Wood Stirling; *m* 1963, Margaret Davidson Bottomley, RGN; two *s* one *d. Educ:* Liverpool Coll.; Robert Gordon's Coll., Aberdeen; Aberdeen Univ. (MA 1959; LLB 1961). Solicitor Assistant, Elgin, 1961–62; Procurator Fiscal Depute: Dundee, 1963–70; Borders, 1970–74; Glasgow, 1974–75; admitted to Faculty of Advocates, 1976. *Recreations:* golf, foreign travel, gardening, bridge, classic sports cars. *Address:* Sheriff's Chambers, Hamilton Sheriff Court, 4 Beckford Street, Hamilton ML3 6AA. *T:* (01698) 282957. *Died 21 July 1998.*

STOATE, Richard Charles; Circuit Administrator, Midland and Oxford Circuit, since 1995; *b* 5 Nov. 1952; *s* of Alvan Charles Stoate and Maisie Stoate (*née* Russell), Walton-on-Thames, Surrey; *m* 1976, Gaenor Brown (marr. diss. 1996); one *s* one *d*; partner, 1991, Samantha Jayne Maybury; one *d. Educ:* King's Coll. Sch., Wimbledon; Christ's Coll., Cambridge (BA 1st cl. Hons Law 1974; MA; Bachelor Scholar). Called to the Bar, Middle Temple, 1975 (Harmsworth Major Exhibnr and Harmsworth Major Scholar). Legal staff, Law Commn, 1976–79; Lord Chancellor's Department: Legal Assistant: Family Law

Div., 1979–80; Legal Aid Div., 1980–81; Sen. Legal Assistant, EC & Internat. Law Div., 1981–83; Prin. Private Sec. to Lord Chancellor, 1983–87; Head of Judicial Appts Div., 1987–90; Head of Criminal Business and Court Service Resources Div., 1990–92; Head of Criminal Policy Div., Home Office, 1992–95. *Recreations:* cricket, squash, watching Rugby, theatre. *Address:* Midland and Oxford Circuit Office, The Priory Courts, 33 Bull Street, Birmingham B4 6DW. *T:* (0121) 681 3200. *Clubs:* Olinda Vandals Cricket, Surrey County Cricket, Lancashire County Cricket. *Died 18 Sept. 1996.*

STOCK, Prof. Francis Edgar, CBE 1977 (OBE 1961); FRCS, FACS; Principal and Vice-Chancellor of the University of Natal, South Africa, 1970–77; then Emeritus Professor; *b* 5 July 1914; *o s* of late Edgar Stephen and Olive Blanche Stock; *m* 1939, Gwendoline Mary Thomas; two *s* one *d. Educ:* Colfe's Grammar Sch., Lewisham; King's Coll., London (Sambrooke schol.); King's Coll. Hosp., London (Jelf Medal, Todd Medal and Prize in Clin. Med.; Hygiene and Psychological Med. Prizes; AKC); Univ. of Edinburgh. MB, BS (Lond.), 1938; DTM&H (Edin.), 1940. FRCS 1939; FACS 1951. Ho. Surg., Cancer Research Registrar, Radium Registrar, King's Coll. Hosp., 1938–39; MO, Colonial Med. Service, Nigeria, 1940–45; Lectr and Asst to Prof. of Surg., Univ. of Liverpool, 1946–48; Prof. of Surgery, Univ. of Hong Kong, 1948–63; Cons. in Surg. to Hong Kong Govt, Brit. Mil. Hosps in Hong Kong, and Ruttonjee Sanatorium, 1948–63; Dean, Fac. of Med., Univ. of Hong Kong, 1957–62; Med. Council, Hong Kong, 1957–60; Pro-Vice-Chancellor, Univ. of Hong Kong, 1959–63; McIlrath Guest Prof., Royal Prince Alfred Hosp., Sydney, NSW, 1960 (Hon. Cons. Surg., 1960–); Prof. of Surg., Univ. of Liverpool, 1964–70; Cons. Surg., Liverpool Royal Infirmary and Liverpool Regional Hosp. Bd, 1964–70; Dean, Fac. of Med., Univ. of Liverpool, 1969–70. Cons. Surg., RN, 1949–70; Visiting Prof. or Lectr, Univs of Alberta, Edinburgh, Qld, Singapore, W Australia, QUB, State Univ. of NY; Brit. Council Lectr in Thailand, Burma, Fiji, Mauritius. Hunterian Prof., RCS, 1948 and 1951. Member: BMA (Council, 1964–69; Bd of Science and Educn, 1978–80); Bd of Governors, United Liverpool Hosps, 1967–70; Med. Adv. Council and Chm. Techn. Adv. Cttee on Surg., Liverpool Reg. Hosp. Bd, 1964–70; Gen. Med. Council, 1969–70; Med. Appeals Tribunals, Liverpool and N Wales, 1966–70; Council, Edgewood Coll. of Education, 1976–77; Univs Adv. Council, 1976; Cttee of Univ. Principals, 1970–77 (Chm., 1976–77). Examr in Surgery: to Univs of Edinburgh, Glasgow, Liverpool, Hong Kong, Malaya, Singapore and NUI, at various times, 1949–70; to Soc. of Apothecaries, 1958–60; Mem. Ct of Examrs, RCS, 1965–69. Sen. Fellow, Assoc. of Surgeons of GB and Ire.; Sen. Mem. Pan Pacific Surg. Assoc. (past Mem. Council and Bd of Trustees). Mem., Board of Control, Nat. Inst. of Metallurgy, 1975–77. Liveryman, Soc. of Apothecaries. Hon. FACCP. *Publications:* Surgical Principles (with J. Moroney), 1968; chapters in: Surgery of Liver and Bile Ducts (ed Smith and Sherlock); Clinical Surgery (ed Rob and Smith); Scientific Foundations of Surgery (ed Wells and Kyle); Abdominal Operations (ed Maingot), and others; numerous articles in scientific jls. *Recreations:* swimming (Univ. of London colours, 1934, Kent Co. colours, 1935), sailing (Pres., Hong Kong Yacht Racing Assoc., 1961–63, Vice-Pres., Far East Yacht Racing Fedn, 1961–62), gardening, photography, music. *Address:* Clos des Arbres, Rue de la Retraite, St Saviour, Jersey, CI JE2 7SW. *T:* (01534) 858009. *Clubs:* Royal Over-Seas League; Royal Hong Kong Yacht (Cdre, 1957–63). *Died 26 Sept. 1997.*

STOCKER, Rt Hon. Sir John (Dexter), Kt 1973; MC; TD; PC 1986; a Lord Justice of Appeal, 1986–92; *b* 7 Oct. 1918; *s* of late John Augustus Stocker and Emma Eyre

Stocker (*née* Kettle), Hampstead; *m* 1956, Margaret Mary Hegarty (*d* 1987); no *c*. *Educ:* Westminster Sch.; London University. 2nd Lieut Queen's Own Royal West Kent Regt, 1939; France, 1940; Middle East, 1942–43; Italy, 1943–46; Maj. 1943; Lt-Col 1945. LLB London 1947. Called to Bar, Middle Temple, 1948, Master of the Bench, 1971. QC 1965; a Recorder, 1972–73; Judge of the High Court, Queen's Bench Div., 1973–86; Presiding Judge, SE Circuit, 1976–79. *Recreations:* golf, cricket. *Address:* 20 Parkside Gardens, Wimbledon, SW19 5EU. *Clubs:* Naval and Military, Army and Navy, MCC; Royal Wimbledon Golf. *Died 27 Dec. 1996.*

STOCKWELL, Air Cdre Edmund Arthur, CB 1967; MA; Command Education Officer, Royal Air Force Training Command, 1968–72, retired; *b* 15 Dec. 1911; *e s* of Arthur Davenport Stockwell, Dewsbury; *m* 1st, 1937, Pearl Arber; two *d* (one *s* decd); 2nd, 1955, Lillian Gertrude Moore (*d* 1965), OBE, MRCP; two *s*; 3rd, 1970, Mrs Kathleen, (Betty), Clarke, Chesham. *Educ:* Wheelwright Grammar School; Balliol Coll., Oxford (Williams Exhibnr; BA 1933; MA 1939). Entered RAF Educational Service, Cranwell, 1935; RAF Educn in India, 1936; Punjab and NW Frontier, 1936–38; RAFVR (Admin and Special Duties), 1939; Lahore, Simla, Delhi, 1939–44; Group Educn Officer, No 6 (RCAF) Group, 1944; Air Min., 1944–48; OC, RAF Sch. of Educn, 1948–51; Comd Educn Officer, Coastal Comd, 1951–53; Comd Educn Officer, Far East Air Force, 1953–55; Principal Educn Officer, Halton, 1956–59; Comd Educn Officer, Maintenance Comd, 1959–62; Dep. Dir of Educational Services, Air Min., 1962–64; Comd Educn Officer, Flying Trng Comd, 1964–68. Group Captain, 1954; Air Commodore, 1964. FRAeS 1963. *Recreations:* golf, gardening. *Address:* 95 Newland, Sherborne, Dorset DT9 3AS. *T:* (01935) 815689. *Died 8 May 2000.*

STOGDON, Norman Francis; a Recorder of the Crown Court, 1972–83; *b* 14 June 1909; *s* of late F. R. Stogdon and L. Stogdon (*née* Reynolds); *m* 1959, Yvonne (*née* Jaques). *Educ:* Harrow; Brasenose Coll., Oxford (BA, BCL). Called to Bar, Middle Temple, 1932. War Service, Army, 1939–45: served with Royal Fusiliers, King's African Rifles, 1941–45; Staff Officer; sc Middle East 1944. Part-time Chairman: Mental Health Tribunal, 1960–81; Industrial Tribunal, 1975–83. Contested (Lab): Gosport, 1951; Banbury and N Oxford, 1955. ACIArb 1984. *Publications:* contrib. 2nd, 3rd and 4th edns Halsbury's Laws of England. *Recreations:* golf, ski-ing. *Address:* The Cloisters, Temple, EC4Y 7AA. *T:* 0171–353 2548. *Club:* Moor Park Golf. *Died 13 July 1996.*

STONE, Sir Alexander, Kt 1994; OBE 1988; Chairman, Combined Capital Ltd, since 1978; Founder, and Chairman, since 1967, Alexander Stone Foundation; *b* 21 April 1907; *s* of Morris Stone and Rebecca (*née* Silverstone); *m* 1988, (Phyllis) Bette Fenton. *Educ:* Hutcheson's Grammar Sch., Glasgow; Univ. of Glasgow (BL). Estd Alexander Stone & Co., Lawyers, Glasgow, 1934; Chm., British Bank of Commerce Ltd, 1956–74; Director: Samuel Montague Ltd, 1961–65; James Finlay Corp. Ltd, 1975–79. Mem., CIB Scotland, 1991. Chm., Adv. Bd for Scotland and N of Eng., Bank Leumi, 1994–. Mem., Glasgow Univ. Investment Adv. Cttee, 1989–. Chm., Friends of Scottish Cons. Party, 1989–. Vice-Pres., Scottish Council for Spastics, 1984–. Hon. Life Mem., Law Soc. of Scotland, 1989. Hon. LLD Glasgow, 1986; Hon. DLitt Strathclyde, 1989. *Recreations:* reading, collecting antiquarian books, charitable activities. *Address:* The Moss, 69 St Andrews Drive, Glasgow G41 4HP. *T:* (0141) 423 7223. *Club:* Western (Glasgow). *Died 15 March 1998.*

STONE, Prof. Lawrence; Dodge Professor of History, 1963–90, and Director, Shelby Cullom Davis Center for Historical Studies, 1968–90, Princeton University; *b* 4 Dec. 1919; *s* of Lawrence Frederick Stone and Mabel Julia Annie Stone; *m* 1943, Jeanne Caecilia, *d* of Prof. Robert Fawtier, Membre de l'Institut, Paris; one *s* one *d*. *Educ:* Charterhouse School, 1933–38; Sorbonne, Paris, 1938; Christ Church, Oxford, 1938–40, 1945–46 (MA). Lieut RNVR, 1940–45. Bryce Research Student, Oxford Univ., 1946–47; Lectr, University Coll., Oxford, 1947–50; Fellow, Wadham Coll., Oxford, 1950–63 (Hon. Fellow, 1983); Mem. Inst. for Advanced Study, Princeton, 1960–61; Chm., Dept of History, Princeton Univ., 1967–70. Mem., Amer. Philosophical Soc., 1970. Fellow, Amer. Acad. of Arts and Sciences, 1968; Corresp. FBA 1983. Hon. DHL: Chicago, 1979; Pennsylvania, 1986; Hon. DLitt: Edinburgh, 1983; Glasgow, 1993; Oxford, 1994; Princeton, 1995. *Publications:* Anatomy of the Elizabethan Aristocracy, 1948; Sculpture in Britain: The Middle Ages, 1955; An Elizabethan: Sir Horatio Palavicino, 1956; The Crisis of the Aristocracy, 1558–1641, 1965; The Causes of the English Revolution, 1529–1642, 1972; Family and Fortune: Studies in Aristocratic Finance in the 16th and 17th Centuries, 1973; (ed) The University in Society, 1975; (ed) Schooling and Society, 1977; Family, Sex and Marriage in England 1500–1800, 1977; The Past and the Present, 1981; An Open Elite? England 1540–1880, 1984; The Past and the Present Revisited, 1987; Road to Divorce: England 1530–1987, 1990; Uncertain Unions: marriage in England 1660–1753, 1992; Broken Lives: separation and divorce in England 1660–1857, 1993; (ed) An Imperial State at War: Britain from 1689 to 1815, 1994; numerous articles in History, Economic History Review, Past and Present, Archæological Jl, English Historical Review, Bulletin of the Inst. for Historical Research, Malone Soc., Comparative Studies in Society and History, History Today, etc. *Address:* 266 Moore Street, Princeton, NJ 08540, USA. *T:* (609) 9212717; 231A Woodstock Road, Oxford OX2 7AD. *T:* (01865) 59174.

Died 16 June 1999.

STORAR, Leonore Elizabeth Therese; retired; *b* 3 May 1920. Served HM Forces, 1942–46. Min. of Works, 1947; joined CRO, 1948; First Sec., Delhi and Calcutta, 1951–53; Salisbury, 1956–58; Colombo, 1960–62; Counsellor, 1963; Head of General and Migration Dept, CRO, 1962; Dep. Consul-Gen., NY, 1967; Consul-Gen., Boston, 1969; Head of Commonwealth Co-ordination Dept, FCO, 1971–75; Dir, Colombo Plan Bureau, Colombo, Sri Lanka, 1976–78. *Address:* Lavender Cottage, Dippenhall Street, Crondall, Farnham, Surrey GU10 5PF.

Died 5 Sept. 1997.

STORMONTH DARLING, Sir James Carlisle, (Sir Jamie), Kt 1983; CBE 1972; MC 1945; TD; WS; Vice-President Emeritus, The National Trust for Scotland, since 1986 (Secretary, 1949–71, then Director, 1971–83, as chief executive); *b* 18 July 1918; *s* of late Robert Stormonth Darling, Writer to the Signet, Rosebank, Kelso, Roxburghshire, and Beryl Madeleine Sayer, Battle, Sussex; *m* 1948, Mary Finella (BEM 1945), DL, *d* of late Lt-Gen. Sir James Gammell, KCB, DSO, MC; one *s* two *d*. *Educ:* Winchester Coll.; Christ Church, Oxford (BA 1939, MA 1972); Edinburgh Univ. (LLB 1949). 2nd Lieut KOSB (TA), 1938; War Service, 1939–46, in KOSB and 52nd (Lowland) Reconnaissance Regt, RAC, of which Lt-Col comdg in 1945 (TD). Admitted Writer to the Signet, 1949. Member, Queen's Body Guard for Scotland (Royal Company of Archers), 1958–. Mem., Ancient Monuments Bd for Scotland, 1983–93. Dir, Scottish Widows Fund and Life Assce Soc., 1981–89. Vice–President: Scotland's Gardens Scheme, 1983–; Scottish Conservation Projects Trust, 1989–97 (Pres., 1984–89); Trustee: Scottish Churches Architectural Heritage Trust, 1983–; Edinburgh Old Town Charitable Trust, 1990– (Chm., 1985–91);

Vice-Chm. and Trustee, Scotland's Churches Scheme, 1994–98; Chm., Edinburgh Old Town Trust, 1985–91. Patron: Edinburgh Green Belt Trust, 1993–; Woodland Trust, 1993–. Hon. FRIAS 1982. DUniv Stirling, 1983; Hon. LLD Aberdeen, 1984. *Address:* Chapelhill House, Dirleton, East Lothian EH39 5HG. *T:* (01620) 850296. *Clubs:* New, Hon. Co. of Edinburgh Golfers (Edinburgh).
Died 17 April 2000.

STOTT, Rt Hon. Lord; George Gordon Stott; PC 1964; Senator of College of Justice in Scotland, 1967–84; *b* 22 Dec. 1909; *s* of Rev. Dr G. Gordon Stott; *m* 1947, Nancy, *d* of A. D. Braggins; one *s* one *d. Educ:* Cramond Sch.; Edinburgh Acad.; Edinburgh Univ. Advocate 1936; QC (Scot.) 1950; Advocate-Depute, 1947–51; Sheriff of Roxburgh, Berwick and Selkirk, 1961–64; Lord Advocate, 1964–67. Editor, Edinburgh Clarion, 1939–44. Member, Monopolies Commission, 1949–56. *Publications:* Lord Advocate's Diary, 1991; Judge's Diary, 1995. *Address:* 12 Midmar Gardens, Edinburgh. *T:* (0131) 447 4251.
Died 12 April 1999.

STOTT, Rt Hon. George Gordon; *see* Stott, Rt Hon. Lord.

STOTT, Roger, CBE 1979; MP (Lab) Wigan, since 1983 (Westhoughton, May 1973–1983); *b* 7 Aug. 1943; *s* of Richard and Edith Stott; *m* 1st, 1969, Irene Mills (marr. diss. 1982); two *s*; 2nd, 1985, Gillian Pye, Wigan; one *s* one *d. Educ:* Rochdale Tech. Coll. Served in Merchant Navy, 1959–64; Post Office Telephone Engineer, 1964–73. PPS to Sec. of State for Industry, 1975–76, to the Prime Minister, 1976–79, to Leader of the Opposition, 1979; opposition spokesman on transport, 1980–83, 1984–86, on trade and industry, with special responsibility for IT, 1983–89, on NI, 1990–97. Member: Select Cttee on Agriculture, 1980–81; Nat. Heritage Select Cttee, 1996–. Mem., British–Irish Inter-Parly Body, 1991–. *Recreations:* cricket, gardening, Rugby League. *Address:* House of Commons, SW1A 0AA; 26 Spelding Drive, Standish Lower Ground, Wigan WN6 8LW.
Died 8 Aug. 1999.

STOW, Sir John Montague, GCMG 1966 (KCMG 1959; CMG 1950); KCVO 1966; Governor-General of Barbados, 1966–67; retired, 1967; *b* 3 Oct. 1911; *s* of Sir Alexander Stow, KCIE, OBE and Violet, *d* of Sir John Benton, KCIE; *m* 1939, Beatrice Tryhorne; two *s. Educ:* Harrow School; Pembroke College, Cambridge. Administrative Officer, Nigeria, 1934; Secretariat, Gambia, 1938; Chief Sec., Windward Islands, 1944; Administrator, St Lucia, BWI, 1947; Dir of Establishments, Kenya, 1952–55; Chief Sec., Jamaica, 1955–59; Governor and C-in-C Barbados, 1959–66. With Stewart, Wrightson Ltd, 1967–77; Dir, Buckmaster Management Co. Ltd, 1981–83. Chm., Commonwealth Soc. for Deaf, 1983–85. KStJ 1959. *Recreations:* cricket, tennis. *Address:* 26a Tregunter Road, SW10 9LH. *T:* (0171) 370 1921. *Clubs:* Caledonian, MCC.
Died 16 March 1997.

STOY, Prof. Philip Joseph; Professor of Dentistry, Queen's University of Belfast, 1948–73, then Professor Emeritus; *b* 19 Jan. 1906; *m* 1945, Isabella Mary Beatrice Crispin; two *s. Educ:* Wolverhampton School; Birmingham Univ. (Queen's Scholar, 1929; BDS (Hons) 1932). LDS RCS 1931; FDS RCS 1947; FFDRCSI 1963. Lectr in Dental Mechanics, Univ. of Bristol, 1934; Lectr in Dental Surgery, Univ. of Bristol, 1940. Hon. MD QUB, 1987. *Publications:* articles in British Dental Journal, Dental Record. *Recreations:* reading, painting, dental history, chess. *Address:* Westward Ho!, 57 Imperial Road, Exmouth, Devon EX8 1DQ. *T:* (01395) 265113.
Died 15 Jan. 2000.

STRACHAN, Michael Francis, CBE 1980 (MBE 1945); FRSE 1979; Chairman, Ben Line Steamers Ltd and Ben Line Containers Ltd, 1970–82; Director, Bank of Scotland,

1972–90; *b* 23 Oct. 1919; *s* of Francis William Strachan and Violet Blackwell (*née* Palmer); *m* 1948, Iris Hemingway; two *s* two *d. Educ:* Rugby Sch. (Scholar); Corpus Christi Coll., Cambridge (Exhibnr, MA). Served in Army, 1939–46; demobilised 1946 (Lt-Col). Joined Wm Thomson & Co., Edinburgh, Managers of Ben Line, 1946; Partner, 1950–64; Jt Man. Dir, Ben Line Steamers Ltd, 1964. Chm., Associated Container Transportation Ltd, 1971–75. Trustee: Nat. Galleries of Scotland, 1972–74; Nat. Library of Scotland, 1974– (Chm., 1974–90); Carnegie Trust for Univs of Scotland, 1976–. Member of Queen's Body Guard for Scotland (Royal Co. of Archers). *Publications:* The Life and Adventures of Thomas Coryate, 1962; (ed jtly) The East India Company Journals of Captain William Keeling and Master Thomas Bonner, 1615–1617, 1971; Sir Thomas Roe (1581–1644), A Life, 1989; (contrib.) Oxford Book of Military Anecdotes, 1987; The Ben Line 1825–1982, 1992; Esmond S. de Beer (1895–1990), Scholar and Benefactor, 1995; contrib. New DNB; articles in Blackwood's, Hakluyt Society's Hakluyt and Purchas Handbooks, History Today, Jl Soc. for Nautical Research, The Oldie. *Recreations:* country pursuits, silviculture. *Address:* Glenhighton, Broughton, by Biggar ML12 6JF. *Club:* New (Edinburgh).
Died 30 Nov. 2000.

STRADLING, Rt Rev. Leslie Edward, MA; *b* 11 Feb. 1908; *er s* of late Rev. W. H. Stradling; unmarried. *Educ:* King Edward VII Sch., Sheffield; The Queen's Coll., Oxford; Westcott House, Cambridge. Deacon 1933, priest 1934; Curate of St Paul's, Lorrimore Square, 1933–38; Vicar of St Luke's Camberwell, 1938–43; of St Anne's, Wandsworth, 1943–45; Bishop of Masasi, 1945–52; Bishop of South West Tanganyika, 1952–61; Bishop of Johannesburg, 1961–74. Hon. DCL Bishops' Univ., Lennoxville, Canada, 1968. *Publications:* A Bishop on Safari, 1960; The Acts through Modern Eyes, 1963; An Open Door, 1966; A Bishop at Prayer, 1971; Praying Now, 1976; Praying the Psalms, 1977; Show Me Your Ways, 1996. *Address:* Brachead House, Auburn Road, Kenilworth 7700, Republic of South Africa. *Club:* City and Civil Service (Cape Town).
Died 8 Jan. 1998.

STRAKER, Sir Michael (Ian Bowstead), Kt 1984; CBE 1973; JP; DL; farmer, since 1951; Chairman, Go-Ahead Group plc, since 1987; *b* 10 March 1928; *s* of late Edward Charles Straker and Margaret Alice Bridget Straker. *Educ:* Eton. Served in Coldstream Guards, 1946–50. Dir, Newcastle and Gateshead Water Co., 1975–82 (Chm., 1979–82); Chairman: Northumbrian Water Authy, later Northumbrian Water Group plc, 1982–93; Aycliffe and Peterlee Devlt Corps, 1980–88; Member, Board: Port of Tyne Authority, 1986–; British Shipbuilders, 1990. Chairman: Newcastle upon Tyne AHA(T), 1973–81; Newcastle Univ. HMC, 1971; Mem. Newcastle Univ. Court and Council, 1972– (Chm. Council, 1983–93). Mem. Council, RASE, 1970–86. Chm., Northern Area Conservative Assoc., 1969–72. High Sheriff of Northumberland, 1977; JP 1962, DL 1988, Northumberland. Hon. DCL Newcastle, 1987. *Address:* High Warden, Hexham, Northumberland NE46 4SR. *T:* (01434) 602083. *Club:* Northern Counties (Newcastle upon Tyne).
Died 28 Aug. 1998.

STRANG, William John, CBE 1973; PhD; FRS 1977; FREng; FRAeS; Deputy Technical Director, British Aerospace, Aircraft Group, 1978–83, retired; *b* 29 June 1921; *s* of late John F. Strang and Violet Strang (*née* Terrell); *m* 1946, Margaret Nicholas Howells; three *s* one *d. Educ:* Torquay Grammar Sch.; King's Coll., London Univ. (BSc). FREng (FEng 1977). Bristol Aeroplane Co., Ltd, Stress Office, 1939–46; King's Coll., London Univ., 1946–48; Aeronautical Research Lab., Melbourne, Aust.,

1948–51; Bristol Aeroplane Co. Ltd: Dep. Head, Guided Weapons Dept, 1951–52; Head of Aerodynamics and Flight Research, 1952–55; Chief Designer, 1955–60; British Aircraft Corporation: Dir and Chief Engr, 1960–67, Technical Dir, 1967–71, Filton Div.; Technical Dir, Concorde, 1966–77; Technical Dir, Commercial Aircraft Div., 1971–77. Chm., Airworthiness Requirements Bd, 1983–90 (Mem., 1979–90). *Address:* Manor Barn, Manor Lane, Wedmore BS28 4EL. *T:* (01934) 712134.

Died 14 Sept. 1999.

STRANGE, Prof. Susan, (Mrs Clifford Selly); Professor of International Relations, Warwick University, since 1993; *b* 9 June 1923; *d* of Col Louis Strange and Marjorie Beath; *m* 1st, 1942, Dr Denis Merritt (marr. diss. 1955; he *d* 1993); one *s* one *d*; 2nd, 1955, Clifford Selly; two *s* one *d* (and one *s* decd). *Educ:* Royal Sch., Bath; Université de Caen; London Sch. of Econs (BScEcon). The Economist, 1944–46; The Observer, 1946–57 (Washington, UN, and Econ. Corresp.); Lectr in Internat. Relations, University Coll., London, 1949–64; Res. Fellow, RIIA, 1965–76; German Marshall Fund Fellow, 1976–78; Montague Burton Prof. of Internat. Relns, LSE, 1978–88; Prof. of Internat. Relns, European Univ. Inst., Florence, 1989–93. *Publications:* Sterling and British Policy, 1971; International Monetary Relations, 1976; (ed with R. Tooze) The International Politics of Surplus Capacity, 1981; (ed) Paths to International Political Economy, 1984; Casino Capitalism, 1986; States and Markets, 1988; (with J. Stopford) Rival States, Rival Firms, 1991; The Retreat of the State, 1996; *posthumous publication:* Mad Money, 1998. *Recreations:* cooking, gardening, tennis. *Address:* Weedon Hill House, Aylesbury, Bucks HP22 4DP. *T:* (01296) 27772. *Died 25 Oct. 1998.*

STRATTON, Ven. Basil; Archdeacon of Stafford and Canon Residentiary of Lichfield Cathedral, 1959–74, Archdeacon Emeritus, since 1974; Chaplain to the Queen, 1965–76; *b* 27 April 1906; *s* of Rev. Samuel Henry Stratton and Kate Mabel Stratton; *m* 1934, Euphemia Frances Stuart; one *s* three *d*. *Educ:* Lincoln School; Hatfield College, Durham University (BA 1929, MA 1932). Deacon 1930, priest 1931; Curate, St Stephen's, Grimsby, 1930–32; SPG Missionary, India, 1932–34; Indian Ecclesiastical Establishment, 1935–47; Chaplain to the Forces on service in Iraq, India, Burma and Malaya, 1941–46 (despatches); officiated as Chaplain-General in India, 1946; Vicar of Figheldean with Milston, Wilts, 1948–53; Vicar of Market Drayton, Shropshire, 1953–59. *Address:* Kenilworth Manor Nursing Home, Thickthorn Orchards, Kenilworth CV8 2AF.

Died 9 May 2000.

STREETEN, Frank; *see* Streeten, R. H.

STREETEN, Reginald Hawkins, (Frank), CBE 1991; Head of Statute Law Revision, Law Commission, 1978–93; *b* 19 March 1928; *s* of late Reginald Craufurd Streeten, BA, LLB and Olive Gladys Streeten (*née* Palmer); *m* 1962, Bodile Westergren, Lappland, Sweden; two *s*. *Educ:* Grey Coll., S Africa; Rhodes University Coll., Univ. of S Africa (BA, LLB). Called to the Bar, S Rhodesia, 1959. Registrar to Justice Steyn, Supreme Court, Cape Town, 1948–52; Crown Counsel and Legal Draftsman, S Rhodesia and Fedn of Rhodesia and Nyasaland, 1952–63; Jun. Counsel for Fed. Govt at inquiry into aircraft accident involving late Dag Hammarskjöld, 1961; Parly Draftsman, Zambia, 1964–66; Mem. Legal Staff, 1967–93, Sec., 1981–82, Law Commn. Legal Mem., Med. Council of S Rhodesia, 1959–63. Lawyer Mem., Dept of Transport Deregulation Rev. Gp, 1993–94. Legal Consultant, Home Office, 1994–96. *Recreation:* church organist. *Address:* 32 Holme Chase, St George's Avenue, Weybridge, Surrey KT13 0BZ.

Died 4 April 1997.

STREETER, His Honour John Stuart; DL; a Circuit Judge, 1972–86 (Deputy Chairman 1967–71, Chairman 1971, Kent Quarter Sessions); *b* 20 May 1920; *yr s* of late Wilfrid A. Streeter, osteopath, and Mrs R. L. Streeter; *m* 1956, (Margaret) Nancy Richardson; one *s* two *d*. *Educ:* Sherborne. Served War of 1939–45 (despatches): Captain, Royal Scots Fusiliers, 1940–46. Called to Bar, Gray's Inn, 1947. Post Office Counsel SE Circuit, 1957; Treasury Counsel, London Sessions, 1959; Part-time Dep. Chm., Kent Quarter Sessions, 1963. Pres., Sherborne House Probation Centre, Bermondsey, 1993. Pres., Old Shirburnian Soc., 1990. DL Kent, 1986. *Recreation:* gardening. *Address:* Playstole, Sissinghurst, Cranbrook, Kent TN17 2JN. *T:* (01580) 712847.

Died 10 Dec. 1996.

STRINGER, Donald Arthur, OBE 1975; Deputy Chairman, Associated British Ports (formerly British Transport Docks Board), 1982–85 (Member, 1969–85; Deputy Managing Director, 1967–71 and 1978–82; Joint Managing Director, 1982–85); *b* 15 June 1912; *s* of late Harry William Stringer and Helen Stringer; *m* 1945, Hazel Handley; one *s* one *d*. *Educ:* Dorking High Sch.; Borden Grammar Sch. FCIT; FILT; CIMgt. Joined Southern Railway Co., 1938; service with RAF, 1941–46; Docks Manager: Fleetwood, 1957–58; East Coast Scottish Ports, 1958–62; Chief Docks Manager, Southampton, 1963–67, Port Director, 1970–77. Chairman: ABP (formerly BTDB) Bds, Southampton, 1972–85, Humber, 1978–85; Southampton Cargo Handling Co. Ltd, 1968–85; Nat. Assoc. of Port Employers, 1982–85 (Mem. Exec. Cttee, 1964–85); Mem., National Dock Labour Bd, 1976–85; Past Pres., Southampton Chamber of Commerce. Col, Engr and Logistic Staff Corps, RE (TA). *Recreation:* gardening. *Address:* Hillcrest, Pinehurst Road, Bassett, Southampton SO16 7FZ. *T:* (023) 8076 8887. *Clubs:* Army and Navy; Royal Southampton Yacht.

Died 16 July 2000.

STROUD, Dorothy Nancy, MBE 1968; Assistant Curator, Sir John Soane's Museum, 1945–84; *b* London, 11 Jan. 1910; *o c* of late Alfred and Nancy Stroud, London. *Educ:* Claremont, Eastbourne; Edgbaston High Sch. On staff of: Country Life, 1930–41; National Monuments Record, 1941–45. Vice-Pres., Garden History Soc., 1982–; Mem., Historic Buildings Council, 1974–82. FSA 1951; Hon. RIBA, 1975. *Publications:* Capability Brown, 1950, new edn 1975; The Thurloe Estate, 1959; The Architecture of Sir John Soane, 1961; Humphry Repton, 1962; Henry Holland, 1966; George Dance, 1971; The South Kensington Estate of Henry Smith's Charity, 1975; Sir John Soane, Architect, 1984. *Address:* 24 Onslow Square, SW7 3NS. *Died 27 Dec. 1997.*

STUART; *see* Mackenzie-Stuart.

STUART OF FINDHORN, 2nd Viscount *cr* 1959, of Findhorn, co. Moray; **David Randolph Moray Stuart;** *b* 20 June 1924; *s* of 1st Viscount Stuart of Findhorn, CH, MVO, MC, PC, and Lady Rachel Cavendish, OBE (*d* 1977), 4th *d* of 9th Duke of Devonshire; *S* father, 1971; *m* 1st, 1945, Grizel Mary Wilfreda (*d* 1948), *d* of D. T. Fyfe and *widow* of Michael Gillilan; one *s*; 2nd, 1951, Marian Emelia (marr. diss. 1979), *d* of Gerald H. Wilson; one *s* three *d*; 3rd, 1979, Margaret Anne, *yr d* of Comdr Peter Du Cane, CBE, RN. *Educ:* Eton; Cirencester Agricultural College. FRICS. Page of Honour to HM George VI, 1937–39. Served KRRC LI, 1942–47; later RWF Major, TA. DL Caernarvonshire (retired). *Heir:* s Hon. (James) Dominic Stuart [*b* 25 March 1948; *m* 1979, Yvonne Lucienne, *d* of Edgar Després, Ottawa]. *Address:* Findhorn, Forres, Moray IV36 0YE. *Died 24 Nov. 1999.*

STUART, (Henry) Francis (Montgomery); *b* Queensland, Australia, 29 April 1902; *s* of Henry and Elizabeth Stuart,

Co. Antrim, Ireland; *m* 1st, 1920, Iseult Gonne (*d* 1954); one *s* one *d*; 2nd, 1954, Gertrude, (Madeleine), Meiszner (*d* 1986); 3rd, 1987, Finola Graham. *Educ:* Rugby. First book, poems, which received an American prize and also award of the Royal Irish Academy, published at age of 21; first novel published in 1931 at age of 29; contributor to various newspapers and periodicals. *Publications: novels:* Women and God, 1931; Pigeon Irish, 1932; The Coloured Dome, 1933; Try the Sky, 1933; Glory, 1934; The Pillar of Cloud, 1948; Redemption, 1949; The Flowering Cross, 1950; Good Friday's Daughter, 1951; The Chariot, 1953; The Pilgrimage, 1955; Victors and Vanquished, 1958; Angels of Providence, 1959; Black List, Section H, 1971; Memorial, 1973; A Hole in the Head, 1977; The High Consistory, 1980; Faillandia, 1985; The Abandoned Snail Shell, 1987; A Compendium of Lovers, 1990; King David Dances, 1997; *short stories:* Selected Stories, 1983; *poetry:* We Have Kept the Faith, 1923; Night Pilot, 1988; Collected Poems, 1992; Arrow of Anguish, 1995; *autobiography:* Things to Live For, 1936. *Recreation:* horse-racing. *Address:* 2 Highfield Park, Dublin 14, Ireland.   *Died 2 Feb. 2000.*

STUART-HARRIS, Sir Charles (Herbert), Kt 1970; CBE 1961; MD; FRCP; Fogarty Scholar-in-Residence, National Institutes of Health, Bethesda, Maryland, USA, 1979–80; Postgraduate Dean of Medicine, University of Sheffield, 1972–77, Professor of Medicine, 1946–72, then Emeritus Professor; Physician, United Sheffield Hospitals, 1946–74; *b* 12 July 1909; *s* of late Dr and Mrs Herbert Harris, Birmingham; *m* 1937, Marjorie, *y d* of late Mr and Mrs F. Robinson, Dulwich; two *s* one *d. Educ:* King Edward's School, Birmingham; St Bartholomew's Hospital Medical School. MB, BS London 1931 (Gold Medal); MD 1933 (Gold Medal); FRCP 1944. House-Physician and Demonstrator in Pathology, St Bartholomew's Hosp.; First Asst, Dept of Medicine, Brit. Postgrad. Medical Sch., 1935; Sir Henry Royce Research Fellow, Univ. of London, 1935; Foulerton Research Fellow, Royal Society, 1938; War Service, 1939–46: Specialist Pathologist Comdg Mobile Bacteriological Command and Field Laboratories; Colonel RAMC, 1945. Goulstonian Lectr, Royal College of Physicians, 1944; Sir Arthur Sims Commonwealth Travelling Prof., 1962. Visiting Professor of Medicine: Albany Medical Coll., New York, 1953; Vanderbilt Univ., Tennessee, 1961; Univ. of Southern California, Los Angeles, 1962; Croonian Lectr, Royal Coll. of Physicians, 1962; Henry Cohen Lectr, Hebrew Univ. of Jerusalem, 1966; Waring Prof., Univ. of Colorado and Stanford Univ., Calif, 1967; Harveian Orator, RCP, 1974. Member: MRC, 1957–61; Public Health Lab. Service Bd, 1954–66; UGC 1968–77 (Chm., Med. Sub-Cttee, 1973–77); UPGC, Hong Kong, 1978–84. Pres., Assoc. of Physicians of GB and Ireland, 1971. Hon. Member: Assoc. of Amer. Physicians; Infectious Diseases Soc. of Amer. Hon. DSc: Hull, 1973; Sheffield, 1978. *Publications:* (co-author) Chronic bronchitis, emphysema and cor pulmonale, 1957; Influenza and other virus infections of the respiratory tract, 1965; (co-author) Virus and Rickettsial Diseases, 1967, (co-author) Influenza—the Viruses and the Disease, 1976, 2nd edn 1985; (contrib.) Topley and Wilson, Principles of Bacteriology, Virology and Immunity, vol. 4, Virology, 8th edn 1990; papers in med. and scientific jls on influenza, typhus and bronchitis. *Recreation:* music. *Address:* 28 Whitworth Road, Sheffield S10 3HD. *T:* Sheffield (0114) 230 1200.   *Died 23 Feb. 1996.*

STUBBLEFIELD, Sir (Cyril) James, Kt 1965; DSc; FRS 1944; FGS; FZS; Director, Geological Survey of Great Britain and Museum of Practical Geology, 1960–66; Director, Geological Survey in Northern Ireland, 1960–66; *b* Cambridge, 6 Sept. 1901; *s* of James and Jane Stubblefield; *m* 1932, Muriel Elizabeth, *d* of L. R. Yakchee; two *s. Educ:* The Perse Sch.; Chelsea

Polytechnic; Royal College of Science, London (Royal Scholar; ARCS); London Univ. (Geology Scholar, 1921; DSc). Demonstrator in Geology, Imperial College of Science and Technology, 1923–28; Warden of pioneer Imperial Coll. Hostel, 1926–28; apptd Geological Survey as Geologist, 1928; Chief Palæontologist, 1947–53; Asst Director, 1953–60. Mem., Anglo-French Commn of Surveillance, Channel Tunnel, 1964–67. Pres., Geological Soc. of London, 1958–60; Bigsby Medallist, 1941; Murchison Medallist, 1955. Sec. of Palæontographical Soc., 1934–48; Pres., 1966–71; Hon. Mem., 1974. Member Council, Brit. Assoc. for Advancement of Science, 1946–52, 1958–63; Pres. Section C (Geology), 1954. Pres. Cambrian Subcommn, Internat. Geol Union's Commn on Stratigraphy, 1964–72; Pres. Internat. Congress Carboniferous Stratigraphy and Geology, 6th Session, Sheffield, 1967, and Editor, 4 vol. Compte rendu, 1968–72. Vice-Pres. International Paleontological Union, 1948–56. Corresp., Palaeontol Soc., USA, 1950; Corresp. Mem., Geol Soc., Sweden, 1952; Senckenbergische Naturforschende Gesellschaft, 1957. Member: Gov. Body (later Council), Chelsea Coll. of Science and Technology, 1958–82; Council, Royal Soc., 1960–62. Hon. Fellow: Palynol Soc. of India, 1961; Chelsea Coll., 1985; KCL, 1985. Fellow Imperial Coll., 1962; Hon. Member: Geologists' Assoc., 1973; Liverpool Geol Soc., 1960; Petroleum Exploration Soc. GB, 1966; For. Corresp., Geol Soc., France, 1963, For. Vice-Pres., 1966. Hon. DSc Southampton, 1965. *Publications:* (ed jtly) Handbook of the Geology of Great Britain, 1929; (revised) Introduction to Palæontology (A. Morley Davies), 3rd edn 1961; papers in journals, on Palæozoic fossils and rocks; also contributions to: Geological Survey Memoirs; Trilobita, Zoological Record, 1938–51, 1965–77. *Address:* 35 Kent Avenue, Ealing, W13 8BE. *T:* (020) 8997 5051.
                                    Died 23 Oct. 1999.

STUBBS, Sir James (Wilfrid), KCVO 1979 (LVO 1946); Grand Secretary, United Grand Lodge of England, 1958–80; *b* 13 Aug. 1910; *s* of Rev. Wilfrid Thomas Stubbs and Muriel Elizabeth (*née* Pope); *m* Richenda Katherine Theodora Streatfeild (*d* 1995); one *s* (and one *d* decd). *Educ:* Charterhouse (Junior and Senior Scholar); Brasenose Coll., Oxford (Scholar; MA). Assistant Master, St Paul's Sch., London, 1934–46. Served War, Royal Signals, 1941–46: Captain 1941, Major 1945, Lt-Col 1946 (2nd Lieut, SR, 1932, Lieut 1935). Asst Grand Scc., United Grand Lodge of England, 1948–54; Dep. Grand Sec., 1954–58. *Publications:* Grand Lodge 1717–1967, 1967; The Four Corners, 1983; Freemasonry in My Life, 1985. *Recreations:* family history, travel. *Address:* The Albany, 7 London Road, Headington, Oxford OX3 7SW.
                                    Died 7 March 2000.

STUNGO, Adrian Paul; Chief Executive, Local Government Commission for England, since 1996; *b* 12 April 1940; *s* of Ellis and Claudine Stungo; *m* 1965, Ruth Halliday; one *s* one *d* (and one *s* decd). *Educ:* Michael Hall Sch.; Edinburgh Coll. of Art; Edinburgh Univ. (BArch 1964); University Coll. London (DipTP 1972); FRTPI 1980. Architectl Asst, Roland Wedgwood & Partners, 1964–65; Architect/Planner: Wilson & Womersley, 1965–68, 1971–72; Colin Buchanan and Partners, France, 1968–71; GLC, 1973–74; Asst Dir of Develt (Planning), Tower Hamlets LBC, 1974–83; London Borough of Bromley: Asst Chief Exec. and Hd of Land Resources, 1983–87; Dir of Land and Gen. Services, 1987–95; Dir of Corporate Affairs, 1995–96. Vis. Lectr, Univ. of Paris, 1971–73. Adviser: AMA, 1973–83; Nat. Develt Control Forum, 1973–83; Member: Council, RTPI, 1982–86; Standing Adv. Cttee, Trunk Road Assessment, 1985–87; Mem. Council, S London TEC, 1993–96. *Publications:* articles and papers. *Recreations:* walking, tennis, gardening, opera. *Address:* Local Government

Commission for England, Dolphyn Court, Great Turnstile, Lincoln's Inn Fields, WC1V 7JU. *T:* (0171) 430 8441.
Died 16 Feb. 1998.

STUTTAFORD, Sir William (Royden), Kt 1995; CBE 1989 (OBE 1983); Director, Amvescap (formerly Invesco) plc, 1993–98; *b* 21 Nov. 1928; *s* of Dr William Joseph Edward Stuttaford and Mary Marjorie Dean Stuttaford; *m* 1st, 1958, Sarah Jane Legge; two *s* two *d*; 2nd, 1974, Susan d'Esterre Grahame (*née* Curteis). *Educ:* Gresham's Sch., Holt; Trinity Coll., Oxford (MA Nat. Scis). 2nd Lieut, 10th Royal Hussars (PWO), 1952–53. Mem. Stock Exchange, 1959–92; Chairman: Framlington Unit Management, 1974–87; Framlington Gp, 1983–89; Senior Partner, Laurence, Prust & Co., 1983–86. Director: Brown Shipley Hldgs, 1990–93; Towry Law, 1993–98. Chm., Unit Trust Assoc., 1987–89. Chairman: Conservative Political Centre, 1978–81; Eastern Area Cons. Council, 1986–89; Pres., Nat. Union of Cons. and Unionist Assocs, 1994–95 (Jt Vice-Chm., 1991–94). *Address:* Moulshams Manor, Great Wigborough, Colchester, Essex CO5 7RL. *T:* (01206) 735330. *Club:* Cavalry and Guards.
Died 2 Jan. 1999.

STYLE, Lt-Comdr Sir Godfrey (William), Kt 1973; CBE 1961; DSC 1941; RN; an External Member of Lloyd's, since 1943; formerly: Governor, Queen Elizabeth's Foundation; Director, Star Centre for Youth, Cheltenham; also formerly Member of a number of allied advisory bodies and panels; *b* 3 April 1915; *er s* of Brig.-Gen. R. C. Style (*y s* of Sir William Henry Marsham Style, 9th Bt), and Hélène Pauline, *d* of Herman Greverus Kleinwort; *m* 1st, 1942, Jill Elizabeth Caruth (marr. diss. 1951); one *s* two *d*; 2nd, 1951, Sigrid Elisabeth Julin (*née* Carlberg) (*d* 1985); one *s;* 3rd, 1986, Valerie Beauclerk (*née* Hulton-Sams), *widow* of W. D. McClure. *Educ:* Eton. Joined Royal Navy as a Regular Officer, 1933; served in Royal Yacht Victoria and Albert, 1938; served War: Flag-Lieut to C-in-C, Home Fleet, 1939–41 (despatches, DSC, 1941); wounded, 1942, in Mediterranean; despatches, 1943; invalided from Royal Navy, due to war wounds and injuries, 1945. Dep. Underwriter at Lloyd's, 1945–55. Mem., National Advisory Council on Employment of Disabled People, 1944–74 (Chm., 1963–74). Mem. Council, Sir Oswald Stoll Foundn, 1975–84. *Recreations:* the field sports, horticulture, lapidary work. *Club:* Naval and Military.
Died 20 April 2000.

STYLES, Fredrick William, BEM 1943; Director, Royal Arsenal Co-operative Society, 1968–84 (Chairman, 1975–79); *b* 18 Dec. 1914; *s* of Henry Albert Styles and Mabel Louise (*née* Sherwood); *m* 1942, Mary Gwendoline Harrison; one *s* three *d*. *Educ:* LCC elementary sch.; London Univ. (Dipl. economics); NCLC (Dipls Local and Central Govt). Salesman, Co-op, 1929–39. RAFVR Air Sea Rescue Service, 1939–46: Royal Humane Soc. Silver Medal, 1939; BEM for gallantry, 1943. Trade union official, NUPE (London divisional officer), 1946–52; social worker, hospital, 1952–58; social worker, LCC and GLC, 1958–68. Mem. Exec., 1973, Vice-Chm., 1974–79, Chm., 1979–80, Bexley and Greenwich AHA. Mem. (Lab) Greenwich, GLC, 1974–81; Mem., Greenwich Borough Council, 1971–78; Mem., 1971–81, Vice-Chm., 1974–75, Chm., 1975–76, ILEA; Chm. Staff and General Cttee, ILEA, 1977–81; Chm., ILEA schools, 1983–92 (Vice Chm., 1976–83): Nansen (partially sighted), latterly incorporated into Hawthorn Cottage (physically handicapped), and Rose Cottage (educationally sub-normal). Chm., Co-operative Metropolitan Industrial Relations Cttee, 1979–85 (Exec. Mem., 1970; Vice-Chm., 1973); first Chm., Heronsgate Community Centre, Thamesmead, 1982–92; Sen. Vice-Chm. 1986–, Chm., 1988–, Governors, Greenwich Univ. (formerly Thames Polytechnic); Chm. Governors, Avery Hill Teachers Trng

Coll. (incorporated in Thames Polytechnic, 1986), 1971–86; Governor: Woolwich Coll., 1971–92 (Vice-Chm., 1983–92); Thameside Inst., 1971–92 (Vice Chm., 1983–87, Chm., 1987). DUniv Greenwich, 1995. *Recreations:* problems, people, pensioners, politics. *Address:* 49 Court Farm Road, Mottingham, SE9 4JN. *T:* (0181) 857 1508.
Died 8 June 1998.

STYLES, Dr William McNeil, OBE 1995; FRCGP; Chairman, Royal College of General Practitioners, 1993–96; Principal in General Practice, since 1969; *b* 22 March 1941; *s* of Sydney James Styles and Mary McCallum Styles; *m* 1967, Jill Manderson; one *s* three *d*. *Educ:* City of Bath Boys' Sch.; St Catharine's Coll., Cambridge (MA); St Mary's Hosp. Med. Sch., London. MB, BChir. FRCGP 1980. Regl Advr in General Practice, NW Thames RHA, 1983–. Royal College of General Practitioners: Hon. Sec., 1983–89; Chm., Commn on Primary Care, 1992–. Hon. Sec., Jt Cttee on Postgrad. Trng for General Practice, 1984–93. Mem. Council, and Chm., GP Adv. Bd, Med. Protection Soc., 1990–. *Publications:* papers on medical educn for general practice. *Recreations:* reading, horse-riding, family. *Address:* The Grove Health Centre, 95 Goldhawk Road, W12 8EJ; 86 Park Road, Chiswick, W4 3HL. *T:* 0181–995 2952.
Died 8 March 1996.

SUBRAMANIAM, Chidambaram; Chairman, Rajaji International Institute of Public Affairs and Administration, since 1980; President, Madras Voluntary Health Services, since 1987; Governor of Maharashtra, Bombay, 1990–93; *b* 30 Jan. 1910; *s* of Chidambara Gounder and Valliammal; *m* 1945, Sakuntala; one *s* two *d*. *Educ:* Madras Univ. (BA, LLB). Set up legal practice, Coimbatore, 1936; took active part in freedom movt, imprisoned 1932, 1941 and again 1942; Pres., District Congress Committee, Coimbatore; Mem. Working Cttee of State Congress Cttee; Member: Constituent Assembly of India, 1946–51; Madras Legislative Assembly, 1952–62; Minister of Finance, Educn and Law, Govt of Madras, 1952–62; Mem., Lok Sabha, 1962–67, 1971–; Minister of Steel, 1962–63; Minister of Steel, Mines and Heavy Engrg, 1963–64; Minister of Food and Agric., 1964–66; Minister of Food, Agriculture, Community Develt and Co-operation, 1966–67; Chm. Cttee on Aeronautics Industry, 1967–69; Interim Pres., Indian Nat. Congress, July-Dec. 1969; Chm., Nat. Commn on Agric., 1970; Minister of Planning and Dep. Chm., Planning Commn, 1971; also i/c Dept of Science and Technology; Minister of Industrial Develt, Science and Technology, 1972–74 (also Agric., temp., 1974); Minister of Finance, 1974–77; Minister of Defence, 1979–80. Hon. Pres., Internat. Inst. of Public Enterprises, Ljubljana, 1985–87; Pres., Bharatiya Vidya Bhavan, Bombay, 1985–. Hon. DLitt: Wattair; Sri Venkateswara; Madurai; Madras; Annamalai; Hon. LLD Andhra. Jawaharlal Nehru Award, 1991. *Publications:* Nan Sendra Sila Nadugal (travelogues), 1961; War on Poverty, 1963; Ulagam Sutrinen (in Tamil); India of My Dreams (in English), 1972; Strategy Statement for Fighting Protein Hunger in Developing Countries; The New Strategy in Indian Agriculture, 1979; Hand of Destiny (memoirs): vol. 1, The Turning Point, 1993, vol. 2, The Green Revolution, 1995. *Recreation:* yoga. *Address:* River View, Kotturpuram, Madras 600085, India. *T:* (44) 414208. *Clubs:* Cosmopolitan, Gymkhana (Madras); Cosmopolitan (Coimbatore).
Died 7 Nov. 2000.

SUCKSDORFF, Mrs Åke; *see* Jonzen, Karin.

SUENENS, His Eminence Cardinal Leo Joseph, DTheol, DPhil; Cardinal since 1962; Archbishop of Malines-Brussels and Primate of Belgium, 1961–79; *b* Ixelles (Brussels), 16 July 1904. *Educ:* primary sch., Inst. of Marist Brothers, Brussels; secondary sch., St Mary's High

Sch., Brussels; Gregorian Univ., Rome (BCL, DPhil, DTheol). Priest, 1927; Teacher, St Mary's High Sch., Brussels, 1929; Prof. of Philosophy, Diocesan Seminary, Malines, 1930; Vice-Rector, Cath. Univ. of Louvain, 1940; Vicar-Gen., Archdio. of Malines, 1945; Auxiliary Bp to Archbp of Malines, 1945. Moderator of Second Vatican Council, 1962–65; Pres., Belgian Bishops' Conf.; Internat. Pastoral Delegate for Catholic Charismatic Renewal. Templeton Prize for Religion, 1976. *Publications:* Une héroïne de l'apostolat: Edel Quinn, 1952, 4th edn 1954 (English trans. 1952); Que faut-il penser du Réarmement moral?, 1953 (The Right View on Moral Rearmament, 1953); Théologie de l'apostolat de la Légion de Marie, 1954, 7th edn 1957 (Theology of the Apostolate of the Legion of Mary, 1951); L'Eglise en état de mission, 1955, 4th edn 1957; (ed) The Gospel to Every Creature, 1955; La Question scolaire, 1956; Quelle est Celle-ci?, 1957; (ed) Mary the Mother of God, 1957; Un problème crucial: amour et maîtrise de soi, 5th edn 1959 (Love and Control, 1961); Vie quotidienne, vie chrétienne, 2nd edn 1962 (Christian Life Day by Day, 1961); La Promotion apostolique de la religieuse, 1962 (The Nun in the World, 1962); The Church in Dialogue, 1965; La Coresponsabilité dans l'Eglise d'aujourd'hui, 1968 (Co-responsibility in the Church, 1968); (ed with Archbishop Ramsey) L'Avenir de l'Eglise, 1971 (The Future of the Christian Church, 1971); Une nouvelle Pentecôte, 1974 (A New Pentecost?, 1975); Ways of the Spirit, 1976; (with Archbishop Ramsey) Come Holy Spirit, 1976; Essays on Renewal, 1976; Your God?, 1978; Pour l'Eglise de demain, 1979; Open the Frontiers, 1980; La Promesse légionnaire, 1982; Renewal and the Powers of Darkness, 1982; Nature and Grace, 1986; Itinéraire spirituel, 1990 (Spiritual Journey, 1990); Souvenirs et Espérances, 1991 (Memories and Hopes, 1992); Les Imprévus du Dieu, 1993. *Address:* Boulevard de Smet de Mayer 570, 1020 Bruxelles, Belgium. *T:* (2) 4791950.

Died 6 May 1996.

SUFFIAN, Tun Mohamed, SSM 1975 (PSM 1967), SPCM 1978; SPMK 1989; DIMP 1969; JMN 1961; PJK 1963; Judge, Administrative Tribunal, World Bank, Washington DC, 1985–94; Vice President, International Labour Organisation Administrative Tribunal, Geneva, 1987–92 (Judge, 1986–87); *b* 12 Nov. 1917; *s* of late Haji Mohamed Hashim and Zaharah binti Ibrahim; *m* 1946, Dora Evelina Grange (*d* 1997). *Educ:* Gonville and Caius Coll., Cambridge (MA Hons, LLM); SOAS; LSE. Called to the Bar, Middle Temple, 1941 (Hon. Bencher, 1984). All India Radio, New Delhi, 1942–45; BBC, London, 1945–46; Malayan Civil Service, 1948; Malayan Judicial and Legal Service, 1949–61; Solicitor General, 1959; High Court Judge, 1961; Federal Judge, 1968; Chief Justice of Malaya, 1973; Lord Pres., Federal Court, 1974–82. Advr, Standard Chartered Bank in Malaysia, 1982–90. Pro-Chancellor, Univ. of Malaya, 1963–86. President: Commonwealth Magistrates Assoc., 1979–85; Asean Law Assoc., 1982–84. Pres., Malaysian Br., Royal Asiatic Soc., 1978–92. Fellow, Univ. Coll. at Buckingham, 1979. Hon. LLD: Singapore, 1975; Buckingham, 1983; Hon. DLitt Malaya, 1975; DUniv Murdoch, WA, 1988. Ramon Magsaysay Foundn Award for Government Service, 1975. SMB 1959. *Publications:* Malayan Constitution (official trans.), 1963; An Introduction to the Constitution of Malaysia, 1972, 2nd edn 1976; (ed jtly) The Constitution of Malaysia: its development 1957–1977, 1978; Introduction to the Legal System of Malaysia, 1987, 2nd edn 1989. *Recreations:* gardening, swimming, reading. *Address:* (home) 4 Lorong Duta 3, Taman Duta, 50480 Kuala Lumpur, Malaysia; (office) 1 Jalan Ampang, 3rd floor, 50450 Kuala Lumpur, Malaysia. *T:* (3) 2013439, *Fax:* (3) 2018979. *Clubs:* Lake, Bankers' (Kuala Lumpur). *Died 26 Sept. 2000.*

SUFFIELD, Sir (Henry John) Lester, Kt 1973; Head of Defence Sales, Ministry of Defence, 1969–76; *b* 28 April 1911; *m* 1940, Elizabeth Mary White (*d* 1985); one *s* one *d*. *Educ:* Camberwell Central, LCC. Served with RASC, 1939–45 (Major). LNER, 1926–35; Morris Motors, 1935–38 and 1945–52; Pres., British Motor Corp., Canada and USA, 1952–64; Dep. Man. Dir, British Motor Corp., Birmingham, 1964–68; Sales Dir, British Leyland Motor Corp., 1968–69. Freeman of City of London, 1978; Liveryman, Coachmakers' and Coach Harness Makers' Co. *Recreation:* golf. *Address:* 16 Glebe Court, Fleet, Hants GU13 8NJ. *T:* (01252) 616861. *Clubs:* Royal Automobile; Royal Wimbledon Golf.

Died 23 April 1999.

SUGDEN, Maj.-Gen. Francis George, CB 1991; CBE 1989 (OBE 1980); Lieutenant Governor and Secretary, Royal Hospital, Chelsea, since 1992; *b* IOM, 27 July 1938; *s* of Maj.-Gen. Sir Henry H. C. Sugden, KBE, CB, DSO and Joan Morgan Sugden (*née* Francis); *m* 1964, Elizabeth Blackburn Bradbury; two *s* one *d*. *Educ:* Wellington Coll. Commnd RE, 1958; service on Christmas Is, in England and Germany; sc 1970; GSO2 Defence Secretariat 6, MoD, 1971–72; OC 4 Field Sqn RE, BAOR, 1973–74; GSO2 RE HQ 1 (BR) Corps, 1974–77; GSO1 Staff of CDS, MoD, 1977–78; CO 22 Engr Regt, UK and Rhodesia, 1978–80; Col GS HQ 1 (BR) Corps, 1980–83; RCDS, 1984; Comdr Engr HQ 1 (BR) Corps and Comdr Hameln Garrison, 1985–86; GS Dir, MoD, 1986–89; COS, HQ BAOR, 1989–91. Chm., Management Cttee, Royal Homes for Officers' Widows and Daughters, 1994–. Member: Council, SSAFA, 1994–; Exec. Cttee, Royal Patriotic Fund, 1995–. Zimbabwe Independence Medal, 1980. *Recreations:* golf, gardening, ski-ing.

Died 6 Aug. 1997.

SULLIVAN, Sir Desmond (John), Kt 1985; Chief District Court Judge, New Zealand, 1979–85, retired; Member, Treaty of Waitangi Tribunal, since 1986; *b* 3 March 1920; *s* of Patrick James Sullivan and Annie Sullivan; *m* 1947, Phyllis Maude Mahon; two *s* four *d* (and one *s* decd). *Educ:* Timaru Marist Bros Sch.; Timaru Boys' High Sch.; Canterbury Univ. (LLB). Served NZ Army and Navy, 1940–45. Barrister and solicitor: Westport, 1949–59; Palmerston North, 1960–66; Stipendiary Magistrate, Wellington, 1966–79. Member, Westport Bor. Council, 1955–59; Chairman: NZ Council for Recreation and Sport, 1973–76; Film Industry Board, 1962–85. *Publication:* (jtly) Violence in the Community, 1975. *Recreations:* golf, swimming, reading. *Address:* 208 Whites Line East, Lower Hutt, New Zealand. *T:* (4) 5695440.

Died 6 Sept. 1996.

SULLIVAN, Tod; management consultant; *b* 3 Jan. 1934; *s* of Timothy William and Elizabeth Sullivan; *m* 1963, Patricia Norma Roughsedge; one *s* three *d*. *Educ:* Fanshawe Crescent Sch., Dagenham. Merchant Navy, 1950–52; RAF, 1952–55; electrician, 1955–60; children's journalist, 1960–68; Industrial Relations Officer: ATV, 1968–71; CIR, 1971–72; Gen. Sec., Union of Kodak Workers, 1973–74 (until transfer of engagements to TGWU); Nat. Sec., Admin., Clerical, Tech. and Supervisory Staffs, TGWU, 1974–92; Exec. Sec., Immigration Appeals Adv. Service, 1993. *Recreations:* good reading, good music, good bridge, poor golf. *Address:* Windchimes, 48 Westlands, Pickering, N Yorks YO18 7HJ. *Died 4 May 1997.*

SUMMERFIELD, Sir John (Crampton), Kt 1973; CBE 1966 (OBE 1961); Judge of the Grand Court and Chief Justice of the Cayman Islands, 1977–87, retired; *b* 20 Sept. 1920; *s* of late Arthur Fred Summerfield and Lilian Winifred Summerfield (*née* Staas); *m* 1945, Patricia Sandra Musgrave; two *s* two *d*. *Educ:* Lucton Sch., Herefordshire. Called to Bar, Gray's Inn, 1949. Served War, 1939–46:

East Africa, Abyssinia, Somaliland, Madagascar; Captain, Royal Signals. Crown Counsel, Tanganyika (later Tanzania), 1949; Legal Draftsman, 1953; Dep. Legal Sec., E African High Commission, 1958. Attorney-Gen., Bermuda, 1962; QC (Bermuda) 1963; MEC, 1962–68, and MLC, 1962–68, Bermuda; Chief Justice of Bermuda 1972–77; Judge of Supreme Court, Turks and Caicos Islands, 1977–82; Justice of Appeal for Bermuda, 1979–87; Pres., Ct of Appeal for Belize, 1982–84. *Publications:* Preparation of Revised Laws of Bermuda, 1963 and 1971 edns. *Recreations:* photography, chess, sailing. *Address:* 3 The Corniche, Sandgate, Folkestone, Kent CT20 3TA. *Club:* Royal Commonwealth Society.
Died 4 April 1997.

SUTCLIFFE, Geoffrey Scott, OBE 1944; TD 1952; *b* 12 June 1912; *o s* of late John Walton Sutcliffe and Alice Mary Sutcliffe (*née* Scott); *m* 1st, 1946, Mary Sylvia (*d* 1984), *d* of late George Herbert Kay; two *s* one *d*; 2nd, 1990, Gillian Patricia Ann Billings. *Educ:* Repton. TA 2nd Lieut, 1939; Lt-Col, 1943; GSO1, AFHQ, N Africa and Italy; served France and Belgium, 1940; N Africa and Italy, 1943–45 (despatches, OBE). Ferodo Ltd, 1932: Works Dir, 1947; Home Sales Dir, 1952; Man. Dir, 1955; Chm., 1956–67; Turner & Newall Ltd: Dir, 1957–75; Jt Man. Dir, 1963–74; Dep. Chm., 1967–74. *Recreations:* gardening, reading. *Address:* Crosswinds, 25b Coopers Drive, Bridport, Dorset DT6 4JU.
Died 15 Feb. 1999.

SUTHERLAND, 6th Duke of, *cr* 1833; **John Sutherland Egerton,** TD; DL; Bt 1620; Baron Gower 1703; Earl Gower, Viscount Trentham 1746; Marquess of Stafford 1786; Viscount Brackley and Earl of Ellesmere 1846; *b* 10 May 1915; *o s* of 4th Earl of Ellesmere, MVO and Violet (*d* 1976), *e d* of 4th Earl of Durham; *S* father, 1944; *S* kinsman as Duke of Sutherland, 1963; *m* 1st, 1939, Lady Diana Percy (*d* 1978), *yr d* of 8th Duke of Northumberland; 2nd, 1979, Evelyn, *e d* of late Major Robert Moubray. Served War of 1939–45 (prisoner). DL Berwickshire, 1955. *Heir: c* Francis Ronald Egerton [*b* 18 Feb. 1940; *m* 1974, Victoria Mary, *d* of Maj.-Gen. Edward Alexander Wilmot Williams, CB, CBE, MC; two *s*]. *Address:* Mertoun, St Boswell's, Melrose, Roxburghshire TD6 0EA; Lingay Cottage, Hall Farm, Newmarket CB8 0TX. *Clubs:* White's, Turf; Jockey (Newmarket).
Died 21 Sept. 2000.

SUTHERLAND, Anthony Frederic Arthur; Under-Secretary, Department of Employment, retired; *b* 19 Oct. 1916; *e s* of Bertram and Grace Sutherland; *m* 1940, Betty Josephine Glass (decd); one *s* two *d*. *Educ:* Christ's Hosp.; Gonville and Caius Coll., Cambridge (Classical Schol.). 1st cl. hons Classics, 1938; MA 1944. HM Forces, 1940–45 (Major, Middx Regt). Asst Prin., Min. of Labour, 1938; Prin., 1943; Priv. Sec. to Ministers of Labour, 1948–53; Counsellor (Labour), British Embassy, Rome, 1953–55; Asst Sec., 1955; Imp. Def. Coll., 1960; Under-Sec., 1967. Coronation Medal, 1953; Silver Jubilee Medal, 1977. *Recreations:* philately, bird watching. *Address:* 53 Wieland Road, Northwood, Middx HA6 3QX. *T:* Northwood (01923) 822078. *Club:* Civil Service. *Died 25 Feb. 1996.*

SUTHERLAND, Sir James (Runcieman), Kt 1992; MA, BLitt; FBA 1953; Emeritus Professor of Modern English Literature, University College, London (Lord Northcliffe Professor, 1951–67); *b* Aberdeen, 26 April 1900; *s* of Henry Edward Sutherland, stockbroker; *m* 1st, 1931, Helen (*d* 1975) *d* of Will H. Dircks; 2nd, 1977, Eve Betts, *widow* of Ernest Betts. *Educ:* Aberdeen Grammar Sch.; Univ. of Aberdeen; Oxford Univ. Chancellor's English Essay Prize, Oxford, 1925; BLitt Oxford, 1927. Lecturer in English: Univ. of Saskatchewan, 1921–23; Merton Coll., Oxford, 1923–25; University College, Southampton,

1925; University of Glasgow, 1925–30; Senior Lecturer in English, University College, London, 1930–36; Professor of English Literature, Birkbeck College, London, 1936–44; Prof. of English Language and Literature, Queen Mary College, London, 1944–51. Public Orator, University of London, 1957–62; Warton Lecturer on English Poetry to the British Academy, 1944; editor of The Review of English Studies, 1940–47. Visiting Professor: Harvard Univ., 1947; Indiana Univ., 1950–51; UCLA, 1967–68; Mellon Prof., Univ. of Pittsburgh, 1965; Berg Prof., NY Univ., 1969–70. Sir Walter Scott Lectures, Edinburgh University, 1952; Clark Lectures, Cambridge University, 1956; Alexander Lectures, Toronto University, 1956; W. P. Ker Memorial Lecture, Glasgow Univ., 1962; Clark Library Fellow, Univ. of California, Los Angeles, 1962–63. Hon. Mem. Modern Language Assoc. of America, 1960. Hon. LLD Aberdeen, 1955; Hon. DLitt Edinburgh, 1968; Hon. Doctor, Liège, 1974. *Publications:* Leucocholy (poems), 1926; Jasper Weeple, 1930; The Medium of Poetry, 1934; Defoe, 1937; Background for Queen Anne, 1939; (ed) The Dunciad, 1943; English in the Universities, 1945; A Preface to Eighteenth Century Poetry, 1948; The English Critic, 1952; The Oxford Book of English Talk, 1953; On English Prose, 1957; English Satire, 1958; English Literature of the late Seventeenth Century, 1969; Daniel Defoe: a critical study, 1971; (ed) Lucy Hutchinson's Memoirs of the Life of Colonel Hutchinson, 1973; (ed) The Oxford Book of Literary Anecdotes, 1975; The Restoration Newspaper and its Development, 1986; editions of plays by Nicholas Rowe, Thomas Dekker, John Dryden, William Shakespeare; contributions to various literary journals. *Recreations:* fishing, second-hand book catalogues. *Address:* Oaken Holt Residential Home, Farmoor, Eynsham, Oxford OX2 9NL. *Died 24 Feb. 1996.*

SUTHERLAND, Prof. (Norman) Stuart, DPhil; Professor of Experimental Psychology, University of Sussex, 1965–92, then Professor Emeritus; *b* 26 March 1927; *s* of Norman McLeod Sutherland; *m* 1956, Jose Louise Fogden; two *d*. *Educ:* Magdalen Coll., Oxford (BA Hons Lit. Hum. 1949 and PPP 1953; John Locke Scholar 1953; MA; DPhil). Fellow; Magdalen Coll., Oxford, 1954–58; Merton Coll., Oxford, 1962–64; Univ. Lectr in Exper. Psychol., Oxford, 1960–64. Vis. Prof., MIT, 1961–62, 1964–65. Director: William Schlackman Ltd, 1968–81; Deedland Ltd, 1987–. *Publications:* Shape Discrimination by Animals, 1959; (ed jtly) Animal Discrimination Learning, 1969; (with N. J. Mackintosh) Mechanisms of Animal Discrimination Learning, 1971; Breakdown: a personal crisis and a medical dilemma, 1976, 3rd edn 1998; (ed) Tutorial Essays in Psychology, vol. 1, 1977, vol. 2, 1979; Discovering the Human Mind, 1982; Men Change Too, 1987; Macmillan Dictionary of Psychology, 1989, 2nd edn 1996; Irrationality: the enemy within, 1992; scientific papers mainly on perception and learning. *Address:* Centre for Research on Perception and Cognition, Sussex University, Brighton BN1 9QG. *T:* (01273) 678304.
Died 8 Nov. 1998.

SUTTIE, Sir (George) Philip Grant-, 8th Bt *cr* 1702, of Balgone, Haddingtonshire; *b* 20 Dec. 1938; *o s* of late Major George Donald Grant-Suttie (*g s* of 5th Bt) and Marjorie Neville, *d* of Capt. C. E. Carter, RN, Newfoundland; *S* cousin, 1947; *m* 1962, Elspeth Mary (marr. diss. 1969), *e d* of Maj.-Gen. R. E. Urquhart, CB, DSO; one *s*. *Educ:* Sussex Composite High School, NB, Canada; Macdonald College, McGill University, Montreal. *Recreations:* flying, fishing, farming, forestry. *Heir: s* James Edward Grant-Suttie [*b* 29 May 1965; *m* 1st, 1989, Emma Jane (marr. diss. 1996), *yr d* of Peter Craig; 2nd, 1997, Sarah Jane Smale; one *s*]. *Address:* (seat) Balgone, North Berwick EH39 5PB; The Granary,

Sheriff Hall, North Berwick, East Lothian EH39 5PB. *T:* (01620) 892569, *Fax:* (01620) 894913.
Died 7 Nov. 1997.

SUTTILL, Dr Margaret Joan, (Mrs G. A. Rink); *d* of Ernest Montrose and Caroline Hyde; *m* 1st, 1935, F. A. Suttill, DSO, LLB (*d* 1945); two *s*; 2nd, 1949, G. A. Rink, QC (*d* 1983). *Educ:* Royal Free Hospital Medical School. MB, BS 1935; MRCP 1972. Director, Medical Dept, 1948–76, and Chief Medical Advr, 1976–78, British Council, retired. Vice Pres. and Mem. Court, DGAA, 1995– (Mem. Council, 1984–95). *Recreations:* music, reading, walking, consumer problems. *Address:* 173 Oakwood Court, W14 8JE. *T:* 0171–602 2143.
Died 12 Sept. 1996.

SUTTON, Robert William, CB 1962; OBE 1946; Superintendent and Chief Scientific Officer, Services Electronics Research Laboratories, Baldock, Herts, 1946–70, retired; *b* 13 Nov. 1905; *s* of late William Sutton; *m* 1951, Elizabeth Mary, *d* of George Maurice Wright, CBE, Chelmsford; one *s* two *d*. *Educ:* Brighton College; Royal College of Science, London University. Formerly with Ferranti Ltd, and then with E. K. Cole Ltd until 1938; Admiralty, 1939–68. *Address:* 32 High Street, Cottenham, Cambridge CB4 4SA.
Died 14 Dec. 1997.

SWAINE, Edward Thomas William, CMG 1968; MBE 1952; Director, Exhibitions Division, Central Office of Information, 1961–71, retired; *b* 17 July 1907; *s* of Edward James Swaine; *m* 1942, Ruby Louise (*née* Ticehurst) (*d* 1974). Entered Govt Service, Min. of Information, 1940; Festival of Britain, 1948–52; Dir of Exhibns, British Pavilion, Montreal World Exhibn, 1967; UK Dep. Comr-Gen. and Dir of Exhibns, Japan World Exhibn, 1970. *Address:* 6/12 Northwood Hall, Highgate, N6 5PN. *T:* (020) 8340 4392.
Died 8 Jan. 2000.

SWALES, Prof. John Douglas, MD, FRCP, Professor of Medicine, University of Leicester, since 1974; *b* 19 Oct. 1935; *s* of Frank Swales and Doris Agnes Swales (*née* Hude); *m* 1967, Kathleen Patricia Townsend; one *s* one *d*. *Educ:* Wyggeston Grammar Sch.; Clare Coll., Cambridge (Passingham Prize 1957; BA double 1st cl. hons; MA; MB BChir 1961; MD 1971). FRCP 1977. House Officer, 1961–62, Registrar, 1964–68, Westminster Hosp.; Res. Fellow, RPMS, 1968–70; Sen. Lectr in Medicine, Manchester Univ., 1970–73; Dir of R&D, DoH, 1996–98 (on leave of absence). Mem., MRC, 1995–98. Pres., British Hypertension Soc., 1982–84; Mem. Council, British Heart Foundn, 1999–. Trustee, Hypertension Trust, 1996–; Gov., PPP HealthCare Charitable Trust, 1999–. Bradshaw Lectr, 1987, Croonian Lectr, 1991, Harveian Orator, 1995, RCP; Lloyd-Roberts Lectr, RSM, 1998; Hall Lectr, Univ. of Sheffield, 2000. Founder FMedSci 1998. Fellow, Amer. High Blood Pressure Council, 1982. Hon. Fellow, Australian High Blood Pressure Res. Council, 1981. Editor: Clinical Science, 1980–82; Jl of Hypertension, 1983–87; Jl of RSM, 1994–96. *Publications:* Sodium Metabolism in Disease, 1975; Clinical Hypertension, 1979; Platt versus Pickering: an episode in recent medical history, 1985; Textbook of Hypertension, 1994 (Medical Writers Award for best textbook of the year, 1995); Manual of Hypertension, 1995. *Recreation:* bibliophile. *Address:* 21 Morland Avenue, Leicester LE2 2PF. *T:* (0116) 270 7161; Clinical Sciences Building, Royal Infirmary, Leicester LE2 7LX. *T:* (0116) 252 3182. *Club:* Athenæum.
Died 17 Oct. 2000.

SWALLOW, Sir William, Kt 1967; FIMechE; *b* 2 Jan. 1905; *s* of William Turner Swallow, Gomersal, Yorks; *m* 1929, Kathleen Lucy Smith; no *c*. *Educ:* Batley and Huddersfield Technical Colleges. Draughtsman, Karrier Motors Ltd, 1923; senior draughtsman, chief body designer, Short Bros, 1926; Gilford Motors Ltd, 1930; development engineer, Pressed Steel Co., 1932; chief production engineer, Short Bros, 1943; development engineer, General Motors Overseas Operations, New York, 1947; i/c manufacturing staff, General Motors Ltd, 1948; Gen. Man., A. C. Sphinx Spark Plug Div. of Gen. Motors Ltd, 1950; Managing Director, General Motors Ltd, 1953, Chairman, 1958; Chm., Vauxhall Motors Ltd, Luton, Beds, 1961–66 (Man. Dir, 1961–65). Mem., Advisory Council on Technology, 1968–70; Chairman: NPL Adv. Bd, 1969; Shipbuilding and Shiprepairing Council, 1967–71; EDC for Hotel and Catering Industry, 1966–72; Shipbuilding Industry Bd, 1966–71. Governor, Ashridge Coll., 1965–72. ARAeS; MSAE. President: SMMT, 1964–65 (Dep. Pres. 1966–67); Inst. Road Tspt Engrs, 1966–68. *Address:* Alderton Lodge, Ashridge Park, Berkhamsted, Herts HP4 1NA. *T:* (01442) 842284.
Died 6 Aug. 1997.

SWANTON, Ernest William, CBE 1994 (OBE 1965); author; Cricket and Rugby football Correspondent to the Daily Telegraph, retired 1975; BBC Commentator, 1934–75; *b* 11 Feb. 1907; *s* of late William Swanton; *m* 1958, Ann (*d* 1998), *d* of late R. H. de Montmorency and *widow* of G. H. Carbutt. *Educ:* Cranleigh. Evening Standard, 1927–39. Served 1939–46; captured at Singapore, 1942; POW Siam, 1942–45; Actg Major Bedfordshire Yeomanry (RA). Joined Daily Telegraph staff, 1946; covered 20 Test tours to Australia, W Indies, S Africa, New Zealand and India. Played Cricket for Middlesex, 1937–38; managed own XI to West Indies, 1956 and 1961 and to Malaya and Far East, 1964. Pres., The Cricketer, 1988– (Editorial Director, 1967–88). Hon. Life Vice Pres., MCC, 1989 (Mem. Cttee, 1975–84). Mem. Cttee, Kent CCC, 1971–91 (Pres., 1981); President: Sandwich Town CC, 1976–; Cricket Soc., 1976–83; Forty Club, 1983–86. *Publications:* (with H. S. Altham) A History of Cricket, 1938, 4th edn 1962; Denis Compton, A Cricket Sketch, 1948; Elusive Victory, 1951; Cricket and The Clock, 1952; Best Cricket Stories, 1953; West Indian Adventure, 1954; Victory in Australia, 1954/5, 1955; Report from South Africa, 1957; West Indies Revisited, 1960; The Ashes in Suspense, 1963; Cricket from all Angles, 1968; Sort of a Cricket Person (memoirs), 1972; Swanton in Australia, 1975; Follow On (memoirs), 1977; As I Said at the Time: a lifetime of cricket, 1983; Gubby Allen: Man of Cricket, 1985; (with C. H. Taylor) Kent Cricket: a photographic history 1744–1984, 1985; Back Page Cricket, 1987; The Essential E. W. Swanton (anthol.), 1990; Arabs in Aspic, 1993; (jtly) Last Over, 1996; Cricketers of My Time, 1999; General Editor, The World of Cricket, 1966, revised as Barclays World of Cricket, 1980, 3rd edn 1986. *Recreations:* cricket, golf. *Address:* Delf House, Sandwich, Kent CT13 9HB. *Clubs:* Army and Navy, MCC; Vincent's (Oxford); Royal St George's Golf.
Died 22 Jan. 2000.

SWASH, Stanley Victor, MC 1917 and Bar 1918; *b* 29 Feb. 1896; British; *s* of A. W. Swash, JP and Sylvia Swash; *m* 1924, Florence Kathleen Moore (marr. diss. 1955); three *s* one *d*; *m* 1955, Jane Henderson. *Educ:* Llandovery College; St John's College, Oxford (MA Mathematics). Called to the Bar, Lincoln's Inn, 1938. Served European War, 1915–19, RFA; short period in Ministry of Pensions; served Royal Navy as Lieut Instr., 1921–24; worked in Woolworth Company, 1924–55; Director, 1939, Chairman, 1951–55; retired 1955. OC 57 County of London Home Guard Battalion, Lieut-Colonel, 1940–45. Chairman, Horticultural Marketing Advisory Council, 1958; Member Milk Marketing Board, 1957–63; Chm. BOAC/MEA Cttee of Enquiry, 1963–64. *Recreations:* swimming, bridge. *Address:* Park Avenue, St Andrews, Malta. *Club:* United Oxford & Cambridge University.
Died 3 Jan. 1997.

SWAYTHLING, 4th Baron *cr* 1907, of Swaythling, co. Southampton; **David Charles Samuel Montagu;** Bt 1894; Chairman, Rothmans International, 1988–98; *b* 6 Aug. 1928; *e s* of 3rd Baron Swaythling, OBE, and Mary Violet, *e d* of Major Walter Henry Levy, DSO; *S* father, 1990; *m* 1951, Christiane Françoise, (Ninette), *d* of Edgar Dreyfus, Paris; one *s* one *d* (and one *d* decd). *Educ:* Eton; Trinity Coll., Cambridge. Exec. Dir, 1954, Chm., 1970–73, Samuel Montagu & Co. Ltd; Chm. and Chief Exec., Orion Bank, 1974–79; Chm., Ailsa Investment Trust plc, 1981–88; Director: J. Rothschild Holdings PLC, 1983–89; The Telegraph plc, 1985–96; Chelsfield plc, 1993–98. Mem., Bd of Banking Supervision, Bank of England, 1990–96. Dir, British Horseracing Bd, 1993–97. *Recreations:* shooting, racing, theatre. *Heir: s* Hon. Charles Edgar Samuel Montagu [*b* 20 Feb. 1954; *m* 1996, Hon. Angela, *d* of Baron Rawlinson of Ewell, PC, QC; one *d*]. *Address:* 14 Craven Hill Mews, Devonshire Terrace, W2 3DY. *T:* (0171) 724 7860; (office) 15 Hill Street, W1X 7FB. *T:* (0171) 491 4366. *Clubs:* White's, Portland, Pratt's. *Died 1 July 1998.*

SWEANEY, William Douglas, CMG 1965; retired 1972, as Establishment Officer, Overseas Development Administration, Foreign and Commonwealth Office; *b* 12 Nov. 1912; *s* of late Lt-Comdr William Sweaney, MBE, RN, and Elizabeth Bridson; *m* 1939, Dorothy Beatrice Parsons; one *s*. *Educ:* Gillingham County Sch.; London Sch. of Economics. BSc(Econ). Clerical Officer, Inland Revenue (Special Comrs of Income Tax), 1929; Officer of Customs and Excise, 1932; seconded to Colonial Office, 1943 (promoted Surveyor of Customs and Excise *in absentia*); transferred to Colonial Office, 1948; Principal, 1948; Private Sec. to Minister of State for Colonial Affairs, 1953; Asst Sec., 1955; Dept of Technical Co-operation, 1961; ODM, later ODA, FCO, 1964–72; Establishment Officer, 1965. Panel of Chairmen, Agricl Dwelling House Adv. Cttees, 1977–86. *Recreations:* travel, ornithology. *Address:* 1 Beech Hurst Close, Haywards Heath, West Sussex RH16 4AE. *T:* Haywards Heath (01444) 450341. *Died 15 Aug. 1996.*

SWIFT, Michael Charles, MC 1943; Member, Economic and Social Committee of the European Communities, 1983–86; Secretary-General, British Bankers' Association, 1978–82; *b* 29 Aug. 1921; *s* of late Comdr C. C. Swift, OBE, RN; *m* 1957, (Dorothy) Jill, *d* of late R. G. Bundey; one *s* one *d*. *Educ:* Radley College. Served War, Royal Artillery (Captain), 1940–45. Bank of England, 1946–58; Committee of London Clearing Bankers, 1958–75; Dep. Sec., British Bankers' Assoc., 1975–78. UK Rep., European Communities Banking Fedn Central Cttee, 1978–82, Chm. 1980–82. Gen. Comr for City of London, 1982–87. *Recreations:* golf, birdwatching. *Club:* Royal West Norfolk Golf. *Died 2 June 1999.*

SWINBURNE, Nora; *see* Swinburne Johnson, Elinore.

SWINBURNE JOHNSON, Elinore, (Nora Swinburne); actress; retired from stage and films, 1975; *b* Bath, 24 July 1902; *d* of H. Swinburne Johnson; *m* 1st, Francis Lister (marr. diss.); one *s*; 2nd, Edward Ashley-Cooper (marr. diss.); 3rd, 1946, Esmond Knight (*d* 1987). *Educ:* Rossholme College, Weston-super-Mare; Royal Academy of Dramatic Art. First West End appearance, 1916; went to America, 1923; returned to London stage, 1924; New York, again, 1930; continuous successes in London, from 1931; went into management, 1938, in addition to acting; played as Diana Wentworth in The Years Between (which ran for more than a year), Wyndhams, 1945; Red Letter Day, Garrick; A Woman of No Importance, Savoy, 1953; The Lost Generation, Garrick, 1955; Fool's Paradise, Apollo, 1959; Music at Midnight, Westminster, 1962; All Good Children, Hampstead, 1964; Family Reunion, 1973,

The Cocktail Party, 1975, Royal Exchange, Manchester. *Films included:* Jassy, Good Time Girl, The Blind Goddess, Fanny by Gaslight, They Knew Mr Knight, Quartet, Christopher Columbus, My Daughter Joy, The River (made in India), Quo Vadis, Helen of Troy (made in Italy), Third Man on the Mountain, Conspiracy of Hearts, Music at Midnight, Interlude, Anne of the Thousand Days. Appeared on television (incl. Forsyte Saga, Post Mortem, Kate serial, Fall of Eagles). *Address:* 52 Cranmer Court, SW3 3HW. *Died 1 May 2000.*

SWINGLER, Bryan Edwin, CBE 1979; British Council Representative in France, 1980–84, retired; *b* 20 Sept. 1924; *s* of late George Edwin Swingler, Birmingham, and Mary Eliza Frayne; *m* 1954, Herta (*d* 1993), *er d* of late Edwin Jaeger, Schoenlinde; one *d*. *Educ:* King Edward's Sch., Birmingham; Peterhouse, Cambridge (Sen. Schol.); Charles Univ., Prague. BA 1948, MA 1953. Served War, Royal Navy (Leading Signalman), 1943–46. Apptd to British Council, 1949; Vienna, 1949–52; Lahore, 1952–55; Karachi, 1955–56; Oslo, 1956–59; Berlin, 1959–61; Cologne, 1961–63; Dir, Scholarships, 1963–67; Dep. Controller, Commonwealth Div., 1967–68; Rep. Indonesia, Djakarta, 1968–71; Controller Finance, 1972–73; Controller, Home, 1973–75; Asst Dir-Gen., 1975–77; Head of British Council Div., India, and Minister (Educn), British High Commn, New Delhi, 1977–80. Vice-Chm., British Council Staff Assoc., 1965–67; Member: British-Austrian Mixed Commn, 1973–77; British-French Mixed Commn, 1976–77, 1980–84. *Recreations:* tending Rebel a border terrier, reading, writing, arithmetic, music, painting, oriental ceramics. *Address:* Brackenside Granary, Bowsden, Berwick-upon-Tweed TD15 2TQ. *T:* Lowick (01289) 388302; 5 quai Commandant Mages, 34300 Agde, France. *T:* 67944621. *Club:* Travellers'. *Died 8 Jan. 1996.*

SWISS, Sir Rodney (Geoffrey), Kt 1975; OBE 1964; JP; FDSRCS; President, General Dental Council, 1974–79 (Member, 1957–79); *b* 4 Aug. 1904; *e s* of Henry H. Swiss, Devonport, Devon, and Emma Jane Swiss (*née* Williams); *m* 1928, Muriel Alberta Gledhill (*d* 1985). *Educ:* Plymouth Coll.; Dean Close Sch., Cheltenham; Guy's Hosp. LDSRCS 1926, FDSRCS 1978. General dental practice, Harrow, Middx, 1930–69 (Hon. dental surgeon, Harrow Hosp., 1935–67). NHS Middx Exec. Council, 1947–74 (Chm., 1970–71); Chm., Visiting Cttee and Bd of Visitors, Wormwood Scrubs Prison, 1958–63; Mem., Central Health Services Council, 1964–74; Chairman: Standing Dental Advisory Cttee, 1964–74; Hendon Juvenile Court, 1959–64; Gore Petty Sessional Div., 1965–67 and 1970–74; Management Cttee, Sch. for Dental Auxiliaries, 1972–74. JP Middx area, 1949. *Publications:* contribs to dental press. *Recreation:* philately. *Address:* Shrublands, 23 West Way, Pinner, Middx HA5 3NX. *Died 11 July 1996.*

SWYNNERTON, Sir Roger (John Massy), Kt 1976; CMG 1959; OBE 1951; MC 1941; former consultant in tropical agriculture and development; Director, Booker Agriculture International Ltd, 1976–88; *b* S Rhodesia, 16 Jan. 1911; *s* of late C. F. M. Swynnerton, CMG, formerly Dir, Tsetse Research, Tanganyika, and N. A. G. Swynnerton (*née* Watt Smyth); *m* 1943, Grizel Beryl Miller, *d* of late R. W. R. Miller, CMG, formerly Member for Agriculture and Natural Resources, Tanganyika; two *s*. *Educ:* Lancing Coll.; Gonville and Caius Coll., Cambridge (BA Hons 1932; DipAgric 1933); Imperial Coll. of Tropical Agriculture, Trinidad (AICTA 1934). OC CU OTC Artillery Bty, 1932–33; TARO, 1933–60; served War, 1939–42, with 1/6 Bn KAR (Temp. Capt. and Adjt, 1941–42); Abyssinian Campaign. Entered Colonial

Agricultural Service as Agricl Officer and Sen. Agricl Officer, 1934–50, in Tanganyika Territory; seconded to Malta on Agric. duty, 1942–43; transferred to Kenya on promotion, Asst Director of Agric., 1951, Dep. Dir, 1954, Director, 1956–60; Permanent Sec., Min. of Agriculture, 1960–62; Temp. Minister for Agriculture, Animal Husbandry and Water Resources, 1961, retd 1963. Nominated Member of Kenya Legislative Council, 1956–61. Mem. Advisory Cttee on Development of Economic Resources of S Rhodesia, 1961–62; Agricl Adviser and Mem. Exec. Management Bd, Commonwealth Develt Corp., 1962–76. Vis. Lectr, 1977–88, and Mem. Adv. Bd, Inst. of Irrigation Studies, 1980–88, Southampton Univ. President: Swinnerton Family Soc., 1982–; Tropical Agriculture Assoc., 1983–89. *Publications:* All About KNCU Coffee, 1948; A Plan to Intensify the Development of African Agriculture in Kenya, 1954; various agricultural and scientific papers. *Address:* Cherry House, 2 Vincent Road, Stoke D'Abernon, Cobham, Surrey KT11 3JB. *Clubs:* Royal Commonwealth Society, Royal Over-Seas League.
Died 30 Dec. 2000.

SYKES, Bonar Hugh Charles; farmer; Counsellor in HM Diplomatic Service, retired; *b* 20 Dec. 1922; *s* of late Sir Frederick Sykes, GCSI, GCIE, GBE, KCB, CMG, and of Isabel, *d* of Andrew Bonar Law; *m* 1949, Mary, *d* of late Sir Eric Phipps, GCB, GCMG, GCVO, and of Frances Phipps; four *s. Educ:* Eton; The Queen's Coll., Oxford. War service in Navy (Lieut RNVR), 1942–46. Trainee with Ford Motor Co. (Tractor Div.), 1948–49; joined Foreign Service, 1949: served in Prague, Bonn, Tehran, Ottawa, FCO; retired 1970. Pres , Wiltshire Archaeological and Natural History Soc., 1975–85 (Trustee, 1947–97). Chm., Bd of Visitors of Erlestoke Prison, 1983–85 (Mem., 1977–87); Member: Area Museums Council (SW), 1976–86, Council, Museums Assoc , 1981–84. Victoria County History Cttee, Wilts, 1985–. FSA 1986. High Sheriff, Wilts, 1988. *Address:* Conock Manor, Devizes, Wiltshire SN10 3QQ. *T:* (01380) 840227.
Died 1 April 1998.

SYKES, Prof. Keble Watson; Vice-Principal, 1978–86, Professor of Physical Chemistry, 1956–86, Queen Mary College, University of London; then Emeritus Professor; *b* 7 Jan. 1921; *s* of Watson and Victoria May Sykes; *m* 1950, Elizabeth Margaret Ewing Forsyth; three *d* (one *s* decd). *Educ:* Seascale Preparatory Sch.; St Bees Sch.; The Queen's Coll., Oxford. MA, BSc, DPhil (Oxon). ICI Research Fellow, Physical Chemistry Lab., Oxford, 1945–48; Lecturer, 1948–51, and Senior Lecturer in Chemistry, 1951–56, University Coll. of Swansea, Univ. of Wales; Head of Chemistry Dept, 1959–78, and Dean, Fac. of Science, 1970–73, QMC, subseq. QMW London (Fellow, 1987). Mem., Physical Scis Subcttee, UGC, 1980–85. Hon. Sec. Chemical Soc. of London, 1960–66, Vice-Pres., 1966–69, Mem. Council, 1977–80. Member Council, Westfield College, University of London, 1962–77; Governor, Highgate Sch., 1986–91. *Publications:* scientific papers in journals of Royal Society, Faraday Soc. and Chem. Soc. *Address:* 58 Wood Vale, Muswell Hill, N10 3DN. *T:* (0181) 883 1502.
Died 24 May 1997.

SYME, Dr James, FRCP, FRCPE, FRCPGlas; Consultant Paediatrician, Edinburgh, 1965–94, retired; *b* 25 Aug. 1930; *s* of James Wilson Syme and Christina Kay Syme (*née* Marshall); *m* 1956, Pamela McCormick; one *s* one *d. Educ:* University of Edinburgh (MB ChB). FRCPE 1967; FRCPGlas 1978; FRCP 1991. House Officer posts, 1954–55; Captain, RAMC, 1955–57; Royal Infirmary, Edinburgh, 1957–62; Senior Registrar in Paediatrics, Glasgow, 1962–65. Royal College of Physicians of Edinburgh: Secretary, 1971–75; Mem. Council, 1976–85;

Vice Pres., 1985–89. Chm., Part II MRCP Bd of three Royal Colls of Physicians of UK, 1989–95. External examnr, London, Glasgow, Dundee, Nigeria, Hong Kong, Dublin, Singapore. Hon. FRCPCH 1997. *Publications:* contribs to Textbook of Paediatrics (Forfar & Arneil), 1st edn, 1973 to 5th edn, 1997; papers in med. jls on paediatric topics. *Recreations:* travel, visiting churches, gardening. *Address:* Holme Barn, Airton, by Skipton, North Yorks BD23 4AL. *T:* (01729) 830579. *Clubs:* New, Aesculapian, Harveian Society (Edinburgh).
Died 12 June 1999.

SYMMERS, Prof. William St Clair, senior; MD; Emeritus Professor of Histopathology, University of London, since 1986; *b* 16 Aug. 1917; *s* of William St Clair Symmers, Columbia, S Carolina (Musgrave Professor of Pathology and Bacteriology, QUB) and Marion Latimer (*née* Macredie), Sydney, NSW; *m* 1941, Jean Noble (*d* 1990), *d* of Kenyon and Elizabeth Wright, Paisley, Renfrewshire; one *s. Educ:* Royal Belfast Academical Instn; Queen's Univ. of Belfast (MB, BCh, BAO 1939; Johnson Symington Medal in Anatomy, 1936; Sinclair Medal in Surgery, 1939; MD 1946); PhD Birmingham, 1953; DSc London, 1979. FRCP 1959; FRCPI 1978; FRCPE 1979; FRCS 1979; FRCSE; FRCPA 1967; FRCPath (FCPath 1963); FFPath, RCPI 1982. Surg.-Lieut, RNVR, 1940–46. Demonstrator in Pathology and pupil of Prof. G. Payling Wright, Guy's Hosp. Med. Sch., 1946–47; Registrar in Clinical Pathology, Guy's Hosp., 1946–47; Deptl Demonstrator of Pathology, Univ. of Oxford, 1947; Sen. Asst Pathologist, 1947–48, Consultant, 1948, Radcliffe Infirmary, Oxford; Sen. Lectr in Pathology, Univ. of Birmingham, 1948–53; Prof. of Morbid Anatomy, later of Histopathology, Univ. of London at Charing Cross Hosp. Med. Sch., 1953–82. Hon. Consultant Pathologist: United Birmingham Hosps, 1948–53; Birmingham Regional Hosp Bd, 1949–53; Charing Cross Hosp , 1953–82 (Hon. Consulting Pathologist, 1983–). Pres., Section of Pathology, RSM, 1969–70. Hon. FRCPA 1980; Hon. FACP 1982. Hon. DSc QUB, 1990. Dr Dhayagude Meml Prize, Seth GS Med. Sch., Univ. of Bombay, 1967; Yamagiwa Medal, Univ. of Tokyo, 1969; Scott-Heron Medal, Royal Victoria Hosp., Belfast, 1975; Morgagni Medal, Univ. of Padua, 1979. *Publications:* (ed with Prof. G. Payling Wright) Systemic Pathology, 1966, (ed) 2nd edn, 6 vols, 1976–80, (gen. editor) 3rd edn, 13 vols, 1986–98; Curiosa, 1974; Exotica, 1984. *Address:* Woodbine Cottage, 10 Kingsmeadows Road, Peebles, Scotland EH45 9EN. *T:* (01721) 723100.
Died 25 Oct. 2000.

SYMONDS, Ronald Charters, CB 1975; *b* 25 June 1916; *e s* of Sir Charles Symonds, KBE, CB, and Janet Palmer (*née* Poulton); *m* 1939, Pamela Painton (*d* 1996); one *s* one *d* (and one *s* decd). *Educ:* Rugby Sch.; New Coll., Oxford. Military Service, 1939–45. British Council, 1938–39 and 1946–51; War Office, later MoD, 1951–76, retired. Advr, Royal Commn on Gambling, 1976–78. Consultant, ICI Ltd, 1978–81. United States Bronze Star, 1948. *Recreations:* walking, ornithology. *Address:* 28 Gibson Square, N1 0RD.
Died 21 Dec. 1997.

SYTHES, Percy Arthur, CB 1980; Comptroller and Auditor General for Northern Ireland, 1974–80, retired; *b* 21 Dec. 1915; *s* of William Sythes and Alice Maud Grice; *m* 1941, Doreen Smyth Fitzsimmons; three *d. Educ:* Campbell Coll., Belfast; Trinity Coll., Dublin (Exhibr, Scholar; BA (Mod. Lit.), 1st cl. hons Gold Medal 1938; Vice-Chancellor's Prizeman 1939). Assistant Master: Royal Sch., Dungannon, 1939; Portadown Coll., 1940. Royal Artillery, 1940–46 (Major); GSO2, 1946. Asst Principal, NI Civil Service, 1946; Asst Sec., 1963; Dep. Sec., 1971. Chm., Bd of Governors, Strathearn Sch., 1982–91 (Mem.,

1966–91). *Recreations:* gardens, family. *Address:* Malory, 37 Tweskard Park, Belfast BT4 2JZ. *T:* (028) 9076 3310.
Died 9 May 1999.

SZEMERÉNYI, Prof. Oswald John Louis, DrPhil (Budapest); FBA 1982; Professor of Indo-European and General Linguistics, University of Freiburg-im-Breisgau, 1965–81, then Emeritus Professor; *b* London, 7 Sept. 1913; *m* 1940, Elizabeth Kövér; one *s. Educ:* Madách Imre Gimnázium; University of Budapest. Classics Master in Beregszász and Mátyásföld, 1939–41; Lecturer in Greek, 1942–45, Reader, 1946, Professor of Comparative Indo-European Philology in University of Budapest, 1947–48; returned to England, Oct. 1948; employed in industry, 1949–52; Research Fellow, Bedford Coll., London, 1952–53; Asst Lecturer, 1953–54, Lecturer, 1954–58, Reader, 1958–60, in Greek at Bedford College; Professor of Comparative Philology, University College, London, 1960–65. Collitz Prof., Linguistic Inst., USA, 1963; Vis. Prof., Seattle, 1964. Corresp. Mem., Hungarian Acad. of Scis, 1948 (restitution, 1989), Ordinary Mem., 1991; Hon. Mem., Linguistic Soc. of Amer., 1989.

Publications: The Indo-European liquid sonants in Latin, 1941; Studies in the Indo-European System of Numerals, 1960; Trends and Tasks in Comparative Philology, 1962; Syncope in Greek and Indo-European, 1964; Einführung in die vergleichende Sprachwissenschaft, 1970 (trans. Spanish, 1978, Russian, 1980, Italian, 1985), 4th edn 1991; Richtungen der modernen Sprachwissenschaft, part I, 1971 (trans. Spanish, 1979), part II, 1982 (trans. Spanish, 1986); (contrib.) Comparative Linguistics, in, Current Trends in Linguistics 9, 1972; The Kinship Terminology of the Indo-European Languages, 1978; Four Old Iranian Ethnic Names, 1980; An den Quellen des Lateinischen Wortschatzes, 1989; Scripta Minora: selected essays in Indo-European, Greek and Latin, I–III, 1987, IV, 1991, V, 1992; Summing up a Life, 1992; contribs to British and foreign learned jls; *festschriften:* Studies in Diachronic, Synchronic and Typological Linguistics, ed Bela Brogyanyi, 1979; General Linguistics, Historical Philology I–III, ed B. Brogyanyi and R. Lipp, 1992–93. *Recreation:* motoring. *Address:* Caspar Schrenk Weg 14, 79117 Freiburg-im-Breisgau, Germany. *T:* (761) 66117.
Died 29 Dec. 1996.

T

TAIT, Sir James (Sharp), Kt 1969; PhD; CEng, FIEE; Vice-Chancellor and Principal, The City University, 1966–74, retired (formerly Northampton College of Advanced Technology, London, of which he was Principal, 1957–66); *b* 13 June 1912; *s* of William Blyth Tait and Helen Sharp; *m* 1939, Mary C. Linton; two *s* one *d*. *Educ:* Royal Technical College, Glasgow; Glasgow Univ. (BScEng, PhD). Lecturer, Royal Technical Coll., Glasgow, 1935–46; Head of Electrical Engineering Department: Portsmouth Municipal Coll., 1946–47; Northampton Polytechnic, EC1, 1947–51; Principal, Woolwich Polytechnic, SE18, 1951–56. Member: Adv. Council on Scientific Policy, 1959–62; National Electronics Council, 1964–76, Hon. Mem., 1976. Pres., Inst. of Information Scientists, 1970–72. Hon. Fellow: Inst. of Measurement and Control, 1970; Inst. of Inf. Scientists, 1973. Hon. LLD Strathclyde, 1967; Hon. DSc City, 1974. *Recreation:* open-air pursuits. *Address:* 23 Trowlock Avenue, Teddington, Middx TW11 9QT. *T:* (0181) 977 6541.
Died 18 Feb. 1998.

TAIT, Sir Peter, KBE 1975 (OBE 1967); JP; *b* Wellington, NZ, 5 Sept. 1915; *s* of John Oliver Tait and Barbara Ann Isbister; *m* 1946, Lilian Jean Dunn; one *s* one *d*. *Educ:* Wellington Coll., NZ. MP (National Party) Napier, 1951–54; Mayor, City of Napier, 1956–74; Pres., NZ Municipal Assoc., 1968–69. Chairman: Napier Fire Bd, 1956–75; Hawke's Bay Airport Authority, 1962–74. Freeman, City of Napier. JP 1956. *Recreations:* bowls, gardening. *Clubs:* Lions, (Hon.) Cosmopolitan (Napier).
Died 31 Jan. 1998.

TALBOT, Vice-Adm. Sir (Arthur Allison) FitzRoy, KBE 1964; CB 1961; DSO 1940 and Bar 1942; DL; Commander-in-Chief, Plymouth, 1965–67; retired; *b* 22 Oct. 1909; *s* of late Henry FitzRoy George Talbot, Captain Royal Navy, and Susan Blair Athol Allison; *m* 1st, 1940, Joyce Gertrude Linley (*d* 1981); two *d*; 2nd, 1983, Lady (Elizabeth) Durlacher (*d* 1995). *Educ:* RN College, Dartmouth. Served War of 1939–45: Comd 10th Anti-Submarine Striking Force, North Sea, 1939, and 3rd Motor Gun-boat Flotilla, Channel, 1940–41 (DSO); Comd HMS Whitshed, East Coast, 1942 (Bar to DSO); Comd HMS Teazer, Mediterranean, 1943–44; Comdr 1945; Chief Staff Officer to Commodore Western Isles, 1945; Staff Officer Ops to C-in-C Brit. Pacific Fleet and Far East Station, 1947–48; Comd HMS Alert, 1949; Capt. 1950; Naval Attaché, Moscow and Helsinki, 1951–53; Imperial Defence College, 1954; Capt. (D) 3rd Destroyer Squadron, 1955–57; Commodore RN Barracks Portsmouth, 1957–59; Rear-Adm. 1960; Flag Officer: Arabian Seas and Persian Gulf, 1960–61; Middle East, 1961–62; Vice-Adm. 1962; Commander-in-Chief, S Atlantic and S America, 1963–65. DL Somerset, 1973. *Recreations:* riding, shooting. *Club:* Army and Navy.
Died 16 June 1998.

TALBOT, Godfrey Walker, LVO 1960; OBE 1946; author, broadcaster, lecturer, journalist; Senior News Reporter and Commentator on staff of British Broadcasting Corporation, 1946–69; official BBC observer accredited to Buckingham Palace, 1948–69; *b* 8 Oct. 1908; *s* of Frank Talbot and Kate Bertha Talbot (*née* Walker); *m* 1933, Bess, *d* of Robert and Clara Owen, Bradford House, Wigan; one *s* (and one *s* decd). *Educ:* Leeds Grammar School. Joined editorial staff on The Yorkshire Post, 1928; Editor of The Manchester City News, 1932–34; editorial staff, Daily Dispatch, 1934–37; joined BBC, 1937; War of 1939–45: BBC war correspondent overseas, 1941–45 (despatches, OBE); organised BBC Home Reporting Unit, as Chief Reporter, after the war. BBC Commentator, Royal Commonwealth Tour, 1953–54, and other overseas visits by HM the Queen. Pres., Queen's English Soc., 1982–. *Publications:* Speaking from the Desert, 1944; Ten Seconds from Now, 1973; Queen Elizabeth the Queen Mother, 1973; Permission to Speak, 1976; Royal Heritage, 1977; Royalty Annual, 1952, 1953, 1954, 1955, 1956; The Country Life Book of Queen Elizabeth The Queen Mother, 1978, 3rd edn 1989; The Country Life Book of the Royal Family, 1980, new edn 1983; Forty Years The Queen, 1992. *Recreation:* keeping quiet. *Address:* Hill House, 48–50 Park Road, Kenley, Surrey CR8 5AR. *T:* (020) 8660 9336. *Club:* Royal Over-Seas League (Vice-Chm., 1985–96; Vice-Pres., 1996–).
Died 3 Sept. 2000.

TALBOT, Very Rev. Maurice John; Dean Emeritus of Limerick; *b* 29 March 1912; 2nd *s* of late Very Rev. Joseph Talbot, sometime Dean of Cashel; *m* 1st, 1942, Elisabeth Enid Westropp (*d* 1975); four *s*; 2nd, 1980, Reta Soames. *Educ:* St Columba's College; Trinity College, Dublin (MA). Deacon 1935, priest 1936; Curate of Nantenan, 1935; Rector of Rathkeale, 1942; Rector of Killarney, 1952; Dean of Limerick, 1954–71; Prebendary of Taney, St Patrick's Nat. Cathedral, Dublin; Bishop's Curate, Kilmallock Union of Parishes, 1971–73; Rector of Drumcliffe, 1980–84. *Publications:* Pictorial Guide to St Mary's Cathedral, Limerick, 1969; contrib. to North Munster Studies, 1967; The Monuments of St Mary's Cathedral, 1976. *Recreations:* tennis, shooting, fishing. *Address:* 4 Meadow Close, Caherdavin, Limerick, Ireland.
Died 17 June 1999.

TANNER, Prof. Paul Antony, (Tony); Professor of English and American Literature, since 1989, and Fellow of King's College, since 1960, University of Cambridge; *b* 18 March 1935; *s* of late Arthur Bertram Tanner, MBE and of Susan Williamson; *m* 1st, Marcia Albright (marr. diss.); 2nd, 1979, Nadia Fusini. *Educ:* Raynes Park County Grammar Sch.; Jesus Coll., Cambridge (MA, PhD). ACLS Fellow, Univ. of California, Berkeley, 1962–63; Univ. Lectr, Cambridge, 1966–80; Fellow, Center for Advanced Studies in Behavioral Sciences, Stanford, 1974–75; Reader in Amer. Lit., Cambridge Univ., 1980–89. *Publications:* Henry James and the Art of Non fiction, 1955; The Reign of Wonder, 1965; City of Words, 1970; Adultery in the Novel, 1979; Thomas Pynchon, 1982; Henry James, 1985; Jane Austen, 1986; Scenes of Nature, Signs of Men, 1987; Venice Desired, 1992. *Recreations:* travelling, talking. *Address:* King's College, Cambridge CB2 1ST. *T:* (01223) 350411.
Died 5 Dec. 1998.

TATE, Francis Herbert; Vice-Chairman, Tate & Lyle Ltd, 1962–78; *b* 3 April 1913; 2nd *s* of late Alfred Herbert Tate and Elsie Tate (*née* Jelf Petit); *g g s* of Sir Henry Tate, 1st Bt, founder of Henry Tate & Sons (later Tate & Lyle, Ltd) and donor of the Tate Gallery; *m* 1937, Esther, *d* of Sir (John) Bromhead Matthews, JP, KC, and Lady (Annette Amelia) Matthews, JP; one *s* two *d*. *Educ:* private tutor; Christ Church Oxford (BA 1934, MA 1963). Called to the Bar, Inner Temple, 1937. War Service, 1940–46, Royal Corps of Military Police (Lt-Col). Joined Tate & Lyle Ltd, 1946; Man. Dir, 1949. Chairman: British Sugar Bureau, 1966–78; Council, London Chamber of Commerce,

1962–64 (Vice-Pres., 1964–); Federation of Commonwealth Chambers of Commerce, 1964–69. Dir, Lloyds Bank, Southern Region, 1977–83; a Managing Trustee, Bustamente Foundn, 1979–. General Comr for Income Tax, Woking Div., 1980–88. Dep. Chm., Royal Commonwealth Soc. for the Blind, 1984–89; Chm. Central Council, Royal Commonwealth Soc., 1969–72; Mem. Council, Australia Soc., 1974–78. Governor, Commonwealth Inst., 1975–88. Master of Mercers' Company, 1967–68. *Recreations:* golf (played for Oxford, 1934–35), motoring. *Address:* Little Wissett, Hook Heath, Woking, Surrey GU22 0QG. *T:* (01483) 760532. *Club:* Woking Golf (Pres., 1986–). *Died 12 Jan. 1998.*

TATTON BROWN, William Eden, CB 1965; ARIBA; retired architect; *b* 13 Oct. 1910; *s* of Eden Tatton-Brown, Chichester; *m* 1936, Aileen Hope Johnston Sparrow; two *s* one *d* (and one *d* decd). *Educ:* Wellington Coll.; King's Coll., Cambridge (MA); Architectural Association School, London; School of Planning, London. Special Final Examination of Town Planning Institute. Chief Design Asst, Messrs Tecton, Architects, 1934–38; private practice, 1938–40; Finsbury Borough Council, 1940–41; served in HM Forces, Major, Royal Engineers, 1941–46; Asst Regional Planning Officer, Min. of Town and Country Planning, 1946–48; Dep. County Architect, Herts CC, 1948–59; Chief Architect, Min. of Health, later Dept of Health and Social Security, 1959–71. Steuben-Corning Research Fellowship, Travelling Scholarship to USA, 1957. Guest Lectr, Internat. Hosp. Conferences: Finland, 1966; Holland, 1967; Australia, 1967; Düsseldorf, 1969; Tunisia, 1969; Sweden, 1970; Canada, 1970; S Africa, 1971; WHO Commn to Madrid, 1968. Lecturer and broadcaster. *Publications:* (with Paul James) Hospitals: design and development, 1986; contributor to technical and national press. *Recreation:* painting. *Address:* 47 Lansdowne Road, W11 2LG. *T:* (0171) 727 4529.
Died 2 Feb. 1997.

TAYLER, Prof. Roger John, OBE 1990; PhD; FRS 1995; Professor of Astronomy, University of Sussex, 1967–96; *b* 25 Oct. 1929; *s* of Richard Henry Tayler and Frances Florence Bessie Tayler (*née* Redrup); *m* 1955, Moya Elizabeth Fry. *Educ:* Solihull Sch.; Clare Coll., Cambridge (MA, PhD). Commonwealth Fund Fellow, CIT and Princeton, 1953–54; AEA Harwell and Culham, 1955–61; Dept of Applied Maths and Theoretical Physics, Cambridge Univ., and Fellow, Corpus Christi Coll., Cambridge, 1961–67. Gresham Prof. of Astronomy, 1969–75. Royal Astronomical Society: Sec., 1971–79; Treas., 1979–87; Pres., 1989–90. *Publications:* The Stars: their structure and evolution, 1970, 2nd edn 1994; The Origin of the Chemical Elements, 1972; Galaxies: structure and evolution, 1978, 2nd edn 1993; (ed) History of the Astronomical Society, vol. 2, 1987; The Hidden Universe, 1991; (ed) Stellar Astrophysics, 1992; The Sun as a Star, 1996. *Recreations:* walking, gardening. *Address:* 17 Prince Edward's Road, Lewes, East Sussex BN7 1BJ. *T:* (01273) 472181. *Died 23 Jan. 1997.*

TAYLOR, Lady; (May Doris) Charity Taylor; Assistant Director and Inspector of Prisons (Women), 1959–66, retired; Member, BBC General Advisory Council, 1964–67; President, Newfoundland and Labrador Social Welfare Council, 1968–71; *b* Sept. 1914; *d* of W. George and Emma Clifford; *m* 1939, Stephen J. L. Taylor (later Baron Taylor) (*d* 1988; two *s* one *d*. *Educ:* The Grammar School, Huntingdon; London (Royal Free Hospital) School of Medicine for Women (MB, BS 1937). MRCS, LRCP 1937. House Surgeon: Royal Free Hospital; Elizabeth Garrett Anderson Hospital; HM Prison, Holloway: Assistant Medical Officer; Medical Officer; Governor, 1945–59. *Recreation:* conversation.
Died 4 Jan. 1998.

TAYLOR OF GOSFORTH, Baron *cr* 1992 (Life Peer), of Embleton in the County of Northumberland; **Peter Murray Taylor,** Kt 1980; PC 1988; Lord Chief Justice of England, 1992–96; *b* 1 May 1930; *s* of Herman Louis Taylor, medical practitioner and Raie Helena Taylor (*née* Shockett); *m* 1956, Irene Shirley (*d* 1995), *d* of Lionel and Mary Harris; one *s* three *d*. *Educ:* Newcastle upon Tyne Royal Grammar Sch.; Pembroke Coll., Cambridge (Exhibr; Hon. Fellow, 1992). Called to Bar, Inner Temple, 1954, Bencher, 1975; QC 1967; Vice-Chm. of the Bar, 1978–79, Chm., 1979–80. Recorder of: Huddersfield, 1969–70; Teesside, 1970–71; Dep. Chm., Northumberland QS, 1970–71; a Recorder of the Crown Court, 1972–80; a Judge of the High Court of Justice, QBD, 1980–88. North Eastern Circuit: Leader, 1975–80; Presiding Judge, 1984–88; a Lord Justice of Appeal, 1988–92. Pres., Inns of Court Council, 1990–92. Chm., Inquiry into Hillsborough Football Club Disaster, 1989. Controller, Royal Opera House Develt Land Trust, 1990–96. Chm., Trinity Coll. of Music, 1991–92. Hon. Bencher, Middle Temple, 1995; Hon. Member: Amer. Bar Assoc., 1980; Canadian Bar Assoc., 1980. Hon. LLD: Newcastle upon Tyne, 1990; Liverpool, 1993; Northumbria, 1993; Nottingham, 1994; Leeds, 1995; Hon. DCL City, 1996. *Recreation:* music. *Address:* House of Lords, SW1A 0PW. *Club:* Garrick. *Died 28 April 1997.*

TAYLOR, Brian Hyde; Secretary General, Committee of Vice-Chancellors and Principals, 1983–88; *b* 18 Aug. 1931; *s* of late Robert E. Taylor and Ivy Taylor (*née* Wash), Woodford, Essex; *m* 1960, Audrey Anne Barnes; two *s*. *Educ:* Buckhurst Hill County High Sch.; SW Essex Technical Coll.; LSE (BSc (Econ)). Nat. Service, commnd RASC, 1954–56. Clerk, Corp. of Lloyd's, 1947–48; Personal Asst to Principal, Univ. of London, 1956–59; administrative posts, Univ. of London, 1959–66; Asst Sec., ACU (and Vice-Chancellors Cttee), 1966; Exec. Sec., Cttee of Vice-Chancellors and Principals, 1973; Sec., Univ. Authorities Panel, 1980. Mem., Bd of Dirs, Busoga Trust, 1990–96; Treasurer, Council for Educn in Commonwealth, 1991–98. Gov., Kingston Coll. of Further Educn, 1982–90. *Publication:* Writing From Experience, 2000. *Recreations:* travel (Mem., Travelers' Century Club), browsing in bookshops. *Address:* Sylverstone, Ashley Park Road, Walton-on-Thames, Surrey KT12 1JN. *T:* (01932) 225397. *Club:* Athenæum.
Died 27 June 2000.

TAYLOR, Dr Charity; *see* Taylor, Lady.

TAYLOR, Derek, CBE 1992; FREng; Managing Director, NNC Ltd (formerly National Nuclear Corporation), 1987–94; Director: Taylor Moore Graphics, since 1995; Canute Services (formerly Tatton Management Services), since 1994; *b* 25 April 1930; *s* of Ambrose and Joyce Taylor; *m* 1955, Lorna Margaret Ross; two *s* one *d*. *Educ:* Egerton Boys' School, Knutsford; Salford Royal Tech. Coll. FIMechE; FREng (FEng 1988); FINucE 1988. Engineer, Ministry of Supply, 1951; UKAEA, 1955; Asst Chief Engineer, UKAEA, 1968; Eng Manager, Nuclear Power Gp, 1969; Project Gen. Manager, Nuclear Power Co., 1980; Project Dir, Nat. Nuclear Corp., 1984–87. Chm., Eur. Nuclear Assistance Consortium, 1992–95; Mem., Eur. Scientific and Tech. Cttee, 1991–. Non-exec. Dir, PWR Power Projects Ltd, 1988–94. *Publications:* papers on nuclear engineering. *Recreations:* golf, gardening. *Address:* 68 Glebelands Road, Knutsford, Cheshire WA16 9DZ. *T:* (01565) 633907.
Died 5 July 2000.

TAYLOR, Eric W., RE 1948 (ARE 1935); printmaker, painter and sculptor; *b* 6 Aug. 1909; *s* of Thomas John and Ethel Annie Taylor; *m* 1939, Alfreda Marjorie Hurren; one *s* one *d*. *Educ:* William Ellis School, Hampstead; Royal College of Art, South Kensington (ARCA 1934).

ASIA (Ed) 1965. Worked for 3 years in London Studio; then as a free-lance illustrator; won British Inst. Scholarship, 1932; runner-up in Prix de Rome, 1934, while at Royal College of Art. Art Instructor Camberwell School of Art, 1936–39; Willesden School of Art, 1936–49; Central School of Art, 1948–49; Head of the Design School, Leeds Coll. of Art, 1949–56, Principal, 1956–69, Organiser and Administrator of revolutionary Leeds Basic Course which played considerable part in changing whole direction of British art education; Asst Dir, Leeds Polytechnic, 1969–71; disagreed with organization of Art Faculties in Polytechnics and returned to work as full-time artist, 1971. Leverhulme Research Awards, 1958–59, visiting Colleges of Art in Austria, Germany, Holland, Denmark and Italy; study of Mosaics, Italy, 1965, prior to execution of large mural on Leeds Meirion Centre. Exhibited: Royal Academy; Royal Scottish Academy; Doncaster Art Gallery; New York; Brooklyn; Chicago; London Group; New English Art Club. Pictures in permanent collections of Stockholm Art Gallery, Art Inst. of Chicago, Washington Art Gallery, Imperial War Museum, V&A and British Museum Print Rooms, Ashmolean Mus., Leeds Art Gall., Bradford Art Gall., Inst. of Contemp. History, Wiener Liby, Kirkleatham Old Hall Mus., Redcar, Leeds Univ, Art Gall. and Liby (collection of prints, war drawings and paintings, presented 1997); War pictures bought by Nat. Gall. Adv. Cttee for Imperial War Mus., 1945. Logan Prize for best Etching in International Exhibition of Etching and Engraving at Art Institute of Chicago, 1937; selected by British Council to exhibit in Scandinavian Exhibition, 1940, S America, 1942–44, Spain and Portugal, 1942–44, Turkey, 1943–45, Iceland, 1943, Mexico, 1943–45, China, 1945, Czechoslovakia, 1948, and Rotterdam, 1948; picture purchased by British Council, 1948; print selected by Royal Soc. of Painter Etchers for presentation to Print Collections Club, 1947. Representative exhibitions: Wakefield Art Gall., 1960; Goosewell Gall., Menston, 1972, 1973, 1976; Middlesbrough Art Gall., 1972; Northern Artists Gall., Harrogate, 1977; Linton Ct Gall., Settle, 1983; Design Innovation Centre, Leeds, 1992; retrospective, Leeds Univ. Art Gall., 1994; group exhibn, Staithes Gall., Nottingham, and Scarborough Art Gall., 1994. Extensive experimental ceramic work, 1980–. Examiner: Bristol Univ., 1948–51; Durham Univ., 1971–74; Min. of Educn NDD Pictorial Subjects, 1957–59. British Representative Speaker, International Design Conference, Karachi, 1962. Volunteered for RA, Nov. 1939; Instructor at Northern Command Camouflage School, 1941–43; Royal Engineers, France and Germany, 1943–45; Normandy Landing, Falaise Gap, Battle of Caen, crossings of Rhine and Maas; Instructing for Educational Corps Germany, 1946; Designer and Supervisor, Lubeck Sch. of Art for the Services, 1946. Mem. of Senefelder Club, 1947. *Publications:* etchings published in Fine Prints of the Year, 1935, 1936, 1937, and in 1939 and 1940 issues of Print Collectors Quarterly. *Address:* Linton Springs Farm, Sicklinghall Road, near Wetherby, W Yorks LS22 4AQ. *T:* (01937) 588143.

Died 23 Feb. 1999.

TAYLOR, Frank, CBE 1969; QFSM 1965; fire consultant; Chief Fire Officer, Merseyside County Fire Brigade, 1974–76, retired; *b* 6 April 1915; *s* of Percy and Beatrice Taylor; *m* 1940, Nancy (*née* Hefford); two *s* two *d*; *m* 1976, Florence Mary Latham. *Educ:* Council Sch., Sheffield. Fireman, Sheffield Fire Bde, 1935–41; Instr, NFS West Riding, 1941–42; Company Officer up to Station Officer (ops), NFS in Yorkshire, 1942–49; Chief Officer, Western Fire Authority, NI, 1949–51; Divl Officer NI Fire Authority, 1951–57; Dep. Chief Officer, 1958–60,

Chief Officer, 1960–6?, Belfast; Chief Fire Officer, Liverpool Fire Bde, 1962–74. *Recreations:* football, gardening. *Died 20 May 1999.*

TAYLOR, Dr Frank; Deputy Director and Principal Keeper, The John Rylands University Library of Manchester, 1972–77; Hon. Lecturer in Manuscript Studies, University of Manchester, 1967–77; *b* 16 June 1910; *s* of J. and M. J. Taylor. *Educ:* Univ. of Manchester (MA, PhD). FSA. Served with RN, 1942–46: Lieut, RNVR, 1943–46. Research for Cttee on History of Parlt, 1934–35; Keeper of Western Manuscripts, 1935–49, Keeper of Manuscripts, 1949–72, Librarian, 1970–72, John Rylands Library. Jt Hon. Sec., Lancs Parish Record Soc., 1937–56, Hon. Sec., 1956–82; Registrar of Research, Soc. of Architectural Historians, 1978–82. Member: British Acad. Oriental Documents Cttee, 1974–80; British Acad. Medieval Latin Dictionary Cttee, 1973–83. Editor, Bulletin of the John Rylands Univ. Liby of Manchester, 1948–87. *Publications:* The Chronicle of John Strecche for the Reign of Henry 5, 1932; An Early Seventeenth Century Calendar of Records Preserved in Westminster Palace Treasury, 1939; The Parish Registers of Aughton, 1541–1764, 1942; (contrib.) Some Twentieth Century Interpretations of Boswell's Life of Johnson, ed J. L. Clifford, 1970; The Oriental Manuscript Collections in the John Rylands Library, 1972; (ed with J. S. Roskell) Gesta Henrici Quinti, 1975; (with G. A. Matheson) Hand-List of Personal Papers from the Muniments of the Earl of Crawford and Balcarres, 1976; rev. edn of M. R. James's Descriptive Catalogue of Latin Manuscripts in the John Rylands Library (1921), 1980; (ed) Society of Architectural Historians, Research Register No 5, 1981; The John Rylands University Library of Manchester, 1982; various Calendars of Western Manuscripts and Charter Room collections in the Rylands Library, 1937–77; articles in Bulletin of John Rylands Library, Indian Archives. *Died 3 March 2000.*

TAYLOR, Lt-Comdr Horace; *see* Taylor, Lt-Comdr W. H.

TAYLOR, John William Ransom, OBE 1991; author; Editor Emeritus, Jane's All the World's Aircraft, since 1990; *b* 8 June 1922; *s* of late Victor Charles Taylor and Florence Hilda Taylor (*née* Ransom); *m* 1946, Doris Alice Haddrick; one *s* one *d*. *Educ:* Ely Cathedral Choir Sch.; Soham Grammar Sch., Cambs. FRAeS, FRHistS, AFAIAA. Design Dept, Hawker Aircraft Ltd, 1941–47; Editorial Publicity Officer, Fairey Aviation Gp, 1947–55; Jane's All the World's Aircraft: Editl Asst, 1955; Asst Compiler, 1956–59; Editor, 1959–84; Editor-in-Chief, 1985–89. Air Corresp., Meccano Magazine, 1943–72; Editor, Air BP Magazine, British Petroleum, 1956–72; Jt Editor, Guinness Book of Air Facts and Feats, 1974–83; Contributing Editor: Air Force Magazine (USA), 1971–97; Jane's Defence Weekly (formerly Jane's Defence Review), 1980–87; Specialist Correspondent, Jane's Intelligence Review (formerly Soviet Intelligence Review), 1989–97. Member: Académie Nat. de l'Air et de l'Espace, France, 1985–; CFS Assoc. (Hon. Mem., 1987–). Pres., Chiltern Aviation Soc.; Vice-President: Guild of Aviation Artists; Croydon Airport Soc.; Surbiton Scout Assoc.; Gov., Horse Rangers Assoc. Warden, Christ Church, Surbiton Hill, 1976–80. Freeman, 1983, Liveryman, 1987, GAPAN; Freeman, City of London, 1987. Hon. DEng Kingston, 1993. C. P. Robertson Memorial Trophy, 1959; Cert. of Honour, Commn of Bibliography, History and Arts, Aero Club de France, 1971; Order of Merit, World Aerospace Educn Organization, 1981; Tissandier Diploma, FAI, 1990; Lauren D. Lyman Award, Aviation Space Writers Assoc., USA, 1990. *Publications:* (with M. F. Allward) Spitfire, 1946; Aircraft Annual, 1949–75; Civil Aircraft Markings, 1950–78; Wings for Tomorrow, 1951; Military

Aircraft Recognition, 1952–79; Civil Airliner Recognition, 1953–79; Picture History of Flight, 1955; Science in the Atomic Age, 1956; Rockets and Space Travel, 1956; Best Flying Stories, 1956; Jane's All the World's Aircraft, 1956–89; Helicopters Work Like This, 1957; Royal Air Force, 1957; Fleet Air Arm, 1957; Jet Planes Work Like This, 1957; Russian Aircraft, 1957; Rockets and Missiles, 1958; CFS, Birthplace of Air Power, 1958, rev. edn 1987; Rockets and Spacecraft Work Like This; British Airports, 1959; US Military Aircraft, 1959; Warplanes of the World, 1959, rev. as Military Aircraft of the World; BP Book of Flight Today, 1960; Westland 50, 1965; Encyclopaedia of World Aircraft, 1966; Aircraft Aircraft, 1967, 4th edn 1974; Pictorial History of the Royal Air Force, 3 vols, 1968–71, rev. 1980; Into the '70s with the Royal Air Force, 1969; Combat Aircraft of the World, 1969; Light Plane Recognition, 1970; Civil Aircraft of the World, 1970–79; The Lore of Flight, 1971; Rockets and Missiles, 1971; (with G. Swanborough) British Civil Aircraft Register, 1971; (with M. J. H. Taylor) Missiles of the World, 1972–79; (with D. Mondey) Spies in the Sky, 1972; (with K. Munson) History of Aviation, 1973, 2nd edn 1978; Jane's Aircraft Pocket Books, 1973–87; History of Aerial Warfare, 1974; (with S. H. H. Young) Passenger Aircraft and Airlines, 1975; Jets, 1976; (with M. J. H. Taylor) Helicopters of the World, 1976–79; (with Air Vice-Marshal R. A. Mason) Aircraft, Strategy and Operations of the Soviet Air Force, 1986; Soviet Wings, 1991; (with M. F. Allward) The de Havilland Aircraft Company, 1996; Fairey Aviation, 1997; Sikorsky, 1998; This Century of Flight, 1999. *Recreations:* historical studies, travel. *Address:* 36 Alexandra Drive, Surbiton, Surrey KT5 9AF. *T:* (020) 8399 5435. *Clubs:* City Livery, Royal Aero, Royal Air Force (Hon.); Avro 504 (Manchester). *Died 12 Dec. 1999.*

TAYLOR, Keith Henry, CBE 2000; PhD; FREng; Chairman and Chief Executive, Esso UK plc, 1993–2000 (Managing Director, 1985–93); *b* 25 Oct. 1938; *s* of George Henry Philip Taylor and Vera May (*née* Jones); *m* 1964, Adelaide Lines; one *s* one *d*. *Educ:* King Edward VI Sch., Stratford upon Avon; Birmingham Univ. (BSc, PhD Chem. Engrg). FREng (FEng 1994). Joined Esso, 1964, holding variety of positions in Refining, Research, Marine and Planning Functions of Co., 1964–80; Division Operations Manager, Exxon Co. USA, New Orleans, 1980; Production Manager, Esso Exploration and Production UK Ltd, London, 1982; Exec. Asst to Chm., Exxon Corp., New York, 1984. Pres., UKOOA, 1988–89; Vice Pres., Inst. of Petroleum, 1991–94; Mem., Offshore Industry Adv. Bd, 1989–94. Mem. Bd, Lloyd's Register of Shipping, 1994–99. Member: Adv. Council, Prince's Youth Business Trust, 1993–2000; Council, Inst. of Business Ethics, 1993–2000; Bd, HEFCE, 1997–99; Council, Centre for Marine and Petroleum Technol., 1997–99; Council, Royal Acad. of Engrg, 1997–2000. Gov., NIESR, 1993–2000. FIChemE 1991 (Pres., 1995–97). Hon. FICE, 1998. Hon. DEng Birmingham, 1996. *Died 17 Sept. 2000.*

TAYLOR, Peter, FCIS; Clerk of Convocation, 1991–96, Esquire Bedell, 1994–98, University of London; *b* 5 Jan. 1924; *s* of late Frederick and Doris Taylor; *m* 1948, Jeannette (*née* Evans); two *d*. *Educ:* Salt Boys' High Sch., Saltaire, Yorks; Bradford Technical Coll. (BSc(Econ) London, 1949). FCIS 1959. Served War, FAA, 1942–46. WR Treasurer's Dept, 1940–50; Registrar, Lincoln Technical Coll., 1950–58; Secretary: Wolverhampton and Staffs Coll. of Technol., 1959–60; Chelsea Coll., Univ. of London, 1961–77; Clerk of Senate, Univ. of London, 1977–89. Pres., Assoc. of Coll. Registrars, 1970–72. Mem. Council, Univ. of London, 1996–; Governor, Heythrop Coll., 1996–. Treas., Soc. for Promotion of Hellenic

Studies, 1989–93. Hon. FKC, 1985. *Address:* April Cottage, 52 Wattleton Road, Beaconsfield, Bucks HP9 1SD. *Died 6 Dec. 1999.*

TAYLOR, (Robert) Ronald, CBE 1971; FIM; former Chairman: Robert Taylor (Holdings) Ltd (formerly Robert Taylor Ironfounders (Holdings) Ltd); Forth Alloys Ltd; *b* 25 Aug. 1916; *e s* of late Robert Taylor, ironfounder, Larbert; *m* 1941, Margaret, *d* of late William Purdie, Coatbridge; two *s* two *d*. *Educ:* High Sch., Stirling. FIM 1970. Chm., Glenrothes Develt Corp., 1964–78 (Dep. Chm., 1960–64). Rep. of Sec. of State for Scotland to Scottish Council Develt and Industry, 1966–82 (Fellow of Council, 1986). Chm. Council, British Cast Iron Res. Assoc., 1970–71; Member: Extra Parly Panel, 1967–87; Scottish Industrial Adv. Bd, 1978–83. Mem. Court, St Andrews Univ., 1968–71; Trustee and Mem., Exec. Cttee, Carnegie Trust for Scottish Univs, 1976–85. E. J. Fox Gold Medal, Inst. of British Foundrymen, 1967. *Recreations:* fishing, stalking, golf. *Address:* Beoraid, Caledonian Crescent, Auchterarder, Perthshire PH3 1NG. *Club:* Army and Navy. *Died 11 April 1999.*

TAYLOR, Selwyn Francis, DM; FRCS; Dean, 1965–74, then Emeritus, and Fellow, Royal Postgraduate Medical School, London; Senior Lecturer in Surgery, and Surgeon, Hammersmith Hospital; *b* Sale, Cheshire, 16 Sept. 1913; *s* of late Alfred Petre Taylor and Emily Taylor, Salcombe, Devon; *m* 1939, Ruth Margaret (*d* 1999), 2nd *d* of late Sir Alfred Howitt, CVO; one *s* one *d*. *Educ:* Peter Symonds, Winchester; Keble College, Oxford (BA Hons 1936; MA; MCh 1946; DM 1959); King's College Hospital, London (Burney Yeo Schol., 1936). MRCS, LRCP 1939; FRCS 1940. Surgical Registrar, King's Coll. Hosp., 1946–47; Oxford Univ. George Herbert Hunt Travelling Schol., Stockholm, 1947; Rockefeller Travelling Fellow in Surgery, 1948–49; Research Fellow, Harvard Univ., and Fellow in Clin. Surgery, Massachusetts Gen. Hosp., Boston, Mass, USA, 1948–49. RNVR, 1940–46; Surgeon Lt-Comdr; Surgeon Specialist, Kintyre, East Indies, Australia; Surgeon: Belgrave Hosp. for Children, 1946–65; Hammersmith Hosp., 1947–78; King's Coll. Hospital, 1951–65. Emeritus Consultant to Royal Navy; Member, Armed Forces Medical Advisory Board. Examiner in Surgery, Universities of Oxford, London, Manchester, Leeds, National University of Ireland, West Indies, Makerere and Society of Apothecaries. Bradshaw Lectr, RCS, 1977; Legg Meml Lectr, KCH, 1979; Keats Lectr, Soc. of Apothecaries, 1987. President: Harveian Soc., 1969; Internat. Assoc. Endocrine Surgeons, 1979–81; Member: Council, RCS, 1966– (Senior Vice-Pres., 1976–77 and 1977–78; Joll Prize, 1976); GMC, 1974–83; Surgical Research Soc.; Internat. Soc. for Surgery; Fellow Assoc. Surgeons of GB; FRSocMed; Hon. FRCSE 1976; Hon. FCS(SoAf) 1978; Corresp. Fellow Amer. Thyroid Assoc.; Pres., London Thyroid Club and Sec., Fourth Internat. Goitre Conference. Mem., Senate of London Univ., 1970–75. Chm., Heinemann Medical Books, 1972–83. *Publications:* books and papers on surgical subjects and thyroid physiology. *Recreations:* sailing, tennis, wine. *Address:* Trippets, Bosham, West Sussex PO18 8JE. *T:* (01243) 573387. *Clubs:* Garrick, Hurlingham; Bosham Sailing.
Died 13 Jan. 2000.

TAYLOR, Maj.-Gen. Walter Reynell, CB 1981; Director, EST Ltd; *b* 5 April 1928; *s* of Col Richard Reynell Taylor and Margaret Catherine Taylor (*née* Holme); *m* 1st, 1954, Doreen Myrtle Dodge; one *s* one *d*; 2nd, 1982, Mrs Rosemary Gardner (*née* Breed); one *s*. *Educ:* Wellington; RMC, Sandhurst. Commanded: 4th/7th Royal Dragoon Guards, 1969–71; 12 Mechanised Bde, 1972–74; rcds 1975; Brig., Mil. Operations, MoD, 1976–78; Administrator, Sovereign Base Areas of Cyprus, 1978–80;

COS, HQ BAOR, 1980–84. Dir, ME Centre for Management Studies, Nicosia, Cyprus, 1984–86. *Recreation:* sailing. *Address:* Blake's Farm, Halse, Taunton TA4 3AG. *Clubs:* Special Forces; Royal Armoured Corps Yacht. *Died 22 Jan. 1996.*

TAYLOR, Lt-Comdr (William) Horace, GC 1941; MBE 1973; RNR; Commissioner of the Scout Association, 1946–74; *b* 23 Oct. 1908; *s* of William Arthur Taylor; *m* 1946, Joan Isabel Skaife d'Ingerthorpe (decd); one *s* three *d. Educ:* Manchester Grammar Sch. Junior Partner, 1929; Managing Dir, 1937. Served War: Dept of Torpedoes and Mines, Admiralty, 1940 (despatches, 1941); Founder Mem., Naval Clearance Divers, HMS Vernon (D), 1944. Travelling Commissioner for Sea Scouts of UK, 1946; Field Commissioner for SW England, Scout Association, 1952–74, Estate Manager, 1975–84. *Recreations:* scouting, boating, music. *Address:* Inchmarlo House, Banchory, Kincardineshire AB31 4AL. *T:* (01330) 824981. *Clubs:* Naval; Manchester Cruising Association. *Died 16 Jan. 1999.*

TEBBLE, Norman, DSc; FRSE; CBiol, FIBiol; marine biologist and biogeographer; *b* 17 Aug. 1924; 3rd *s* of late Robert Soulsby Tebble and Jane Ann (*née* Graham); *m* 1954, Mary Olivia Archer, *o d* of H. B. and J. I. Archer, Kenilworth; two *s* one *d. Educ:* Bedlington Grammar School; St Andrews Univ. (BSc 1st cl. Hons Zool. 1950; DSc 1968); MA Oxford (Merton Coll.), 1971. FIBiol 1971, CBiol 1979; FRSE 1976. St Andrews Univ. Air Squadron, 1942–43; Pilot, RAFVR, Canada, India and Burma, 1943–46. Scientific Officer, British Museum (Natural History), 1950, Curator of Annelida; John Murray Travelling Student in Oceanography, Royal Soc., 1958; Vis. Curator, Univ. of California, Scripps Inst. of Oceanography, 1959; Curator of Molluscs, British Museum, 1961; Univ. Lecturer in Zoology and Curator, zoological collection, Univ. of Oxford, 1968, Curator, Oxford Univ. Museum, 1969; Dir, Royal Scottish Museum, 1971–84 (incorporating Mus. of Flight, E Fortune Airfield, 1973; Biggar Gasworks, 1974; Mus. of Costume, New Abbey, 1982). Member Council: Marine Biological Assoc., UK, 1963–66; Museums Assoc., 1972–75 (Vice-Pres., 1976–77; Pres., 1977–78); Mem., Tyne and Wear Museums Cttee, 1986–92. *Publications:* Polychaete Fauna of Gold Coast (Ghana), 1955; Distribution of Pelagic Polychaetes—South Atlantic, 1960; Distribution of Pelagic Polychaetes—North Pacific, 1962; (ed jtly) Speciation in the Sea, 1963; British Bivalve Seashells, 1966, 2nd edn 1976; (ed jtly) Bibliography of British Fauna and Flora, 1967; scientific papers on systematics of polychaeta and mollusca. *Recreations:* Tebbel-Tebble genealogy, ornithology, going forth about the Forth with grandchildren. *Address:* Vale Bank, 48 Forth Street, North Berwick, E Lothian EH39 4JQ. *T:* (01620) 892595. *Died 23 July 1998.*

TEESDALE, Edmund Brinsley, CMG 1964; MC 1945; DPhil; *b* 30 Sept. 1915; *s* of late John Herman Teesdale and Winifred Mary (*née* Gull); *m* 1947, Joyce, *d* of late Walter Mills and Mrs J. T. Murray; three *d. Educ:* Lancing; Trinity College, Oxford. DPhil CNAA, 1987. Entered Colonial Administrative Service, Hong Kong, 1938; Active War Service in Hong Kong, China, India, 1941–45; subsequently various administrative posts in Hong Kong; Colonial Secretary, Hong Kong, 1963–65. Dir, Assoc. of British Pharmaceutical Industry, 1965–76. *Publications:* The Queen's Gunstonemaker, 1984; Gunfounding in the Weald in the Sixteenth Century, 1991. *Recreations:* gardening, swimming, reading. *Address:* The Hogge House, Buxted, East Sussex TN22 4AY. *Died 5 March 1997.*

TE HEUHEU, Sir Hepi (Hoani), KBE 1979; New Zealand sheep and cattle farmer; Paramount Chief of Ngati-

Tuwharetoa tribe of Maoris; *b* 1919; *m* Pauline Hinepoto; six *c.* Chairman: Tuwharetoa Maori Trust Board; Puketapu 3A Block (near Taupo); Rotoaira Lake Trust; Rotoaira Forest Trust; Tauranga-Taupo Trust; Motutere Point Trust; Turamakina Tribal Cttee; Lake Taupo Forest Trust; Oraukura 3 Block; Hauhungaroa 1C Block; Waihi Pukawa Block; Mem., Tongariro National Park Board (great grandson of original donor). OStJ. *Address:* Prince of Wales Drive, Waihi Village, Lake Taupo, New Zealand. *Died 31 July 1997.*

TEJAN-SIE, Sir Banja, GCMG 1970 (CMG 1967); Governor-General of Sierra Leone, 1970–71 (Acting Governor-General, 1968–70); international business and legal consultant; *b* 7 Aug. 1917; *s* of late Alpha Ahmed Tejan-Sie; *m* 1946, Admira Stapleton; three *s* one *d. Educ:* Bo Sch., Freetown; Prince of Wales Sch., Freetown; LSE, London University. Called to the Bar, Lincoln's Inn, 1951. Station Clerk, Sierra Leone Railway, 1938–39; Nurse, Medical Dept, 1940–46; Ed., West African Students' Union, 1948–51; Nat. Vice-Pres., Sierra Leone People's Party, 1953–56; Police Magistrate: Eastern Province, 1955; Northern Province, 1958; Sen. Police Magistrate, NE and S Provinces, 1961; Speaker, Sierra Leone House of Representatives, 1962–67; Chief Justice of Sierra Leone, 1967–70. Mem. Keith Lucas Commn on Electoral Reform, 1954. Hon. Sec. Sierra Leone Bar Assoc., 1957–58. Chm. Bd of Management, Cheshire Foundn, Sierra Leone, 1966. Led delegations and paid official visits to many countries throughout the world. Hon. Treasurer, Internat. African Inst., London, 1978–. Pres., Freetown Golf Club, 1970. GCON (Nigeria), 1970; Grand Band, Order of Star of Africa (Liberia), 1969; Special Grand Cordon, Order of propitious clouds (Taiwan), 1970; Grand Cordon, Order of Knighthood of Pioneers (Liberia), 1970; Order of Cedar (Lebanon), 1970. *Recreations:* music, reading. *Address:* 3 Tracy Avenue, NW2 4AT. *T:* (020) 8452 2324. *Club:* Royal Commonwealth Society. *Died 8 Aug. 2000.*

TELFORD BEASLEY, John, CBE 1988; Chairman, PS Ltd, since 1991; Director, MGM Assurance, since 1987; *b* 26 March 1929; *s* of James George and Florence Telford Beasley; *m* (marr. diss.); one *s* two *d. Educ:* Watford Grammar School; Open Univ. (BA). Dep. Chm., Cadbury Ltd, 1970–73; Chm., Cadbury Schweppes Food Ltd, 1973–75; Dir, Cadbury Schweppes, 1973–77; Chm., Schweppes Ltd, 1975–77; Regional Pres., Warner Lamber Co., 1977–84; Dir, LRT, 1984–92; Chm., London Buses Ltd, 1985–92. *Recreations:* golf, cricket. *Address:* 3 Monmouth Square, Winchester, Hants SO22 4HY. *Died 24 March 1998.*

TEMPLE, His Honour Sir (Ernest) Sanderson, Kt 1988; MBE 1946; QC 1969; a Circuit Judge, 1977–91; Honorary Recorder of Kendal, since 1972, of Liverpool, 1978–91, and of Lancaster, since 1987; *b* 23 May 1921; *o s* of Ernest Temple, Oxenholme House, Kendal; *m* 1st, 1946, June Debonnaire (*d* 1995), *o d* of W. M. Saunders, JP, Wennington Hall, Lancaster; one *s* two *d*; 2nd, 1996, Patricia Margaret Shrubsole, *yr d* of late J. B. Smalley, JP, CA, Cark-in-Cartmel, and widow of Paul Patrick Shrubsole. *Educ:* Kendal School; Queen's Coll., Oxford (MA). Served in Border Regt in India and Burma, attaining temp. rank of Lt-Col (despatches, 1945). Barrister-at-Law, Gray's Inn, 1943. Joined Northern Circuit, 1946; Dep. Recorder of Salford, 1962–65; Dep. Chm., Agricultural Land Tribunal (Northern), 1966–69; Chm., Westmorland QS, 1969–71 (Dep. Chm., 1967); a Recorder of the Crown Court, 1972–77. Mem., Bar Council, 1965. Chairman: Arnside/Silverdale Landscape Trust, 1987–; NW Area Point-to-Point Assoc., 1987–; Cumbria and N Lancs Bridleways Socs; Pres., British Harness Racing Club, 1991–; Patron, British Mule Soc. Jt Master, Vale of Lune

Hunt, 1963–85. Hon. FICW. Hon. Citizen of Kendal, 1992. *Recreations:* farming, horses. *Address:* Yealand Hall, Yealand Redmayne, near Carnforth, Lancs LA5 9TD. *T:* (01524) 781200.   *Died 7 Aug. 1999.*

TEMPLE, Rt Rev. Frederick Stephen; Hon. Assistant Bishop, Diocese of Bristol, since 1983; *b* 24 Nov. 1916; *s* of Frederick Charles and Frances Temple; *m* 1947, Joan Catharine Webb; one *s* one *d* (and one *s* decd). *Educ:* Rugby; Balliol Coll., Oxford; Trinity Hall, Cambridge; Westcott House, Cambridge. Deacon, 1947, priest, 1948; Curate, St Mary's, Arnold, Notts, 1947–49; Curate, Newark Parish Church, 1949–51; Rector, St Agnes, Birch, Manchester, 1951–53; Dean of Hong Kong, 1953–59; Senior Chaplain to the Archbishop of Canterbury, 1959–61; Vicar of St Mary's, Portsea, 1961–70; Archdeacon of Swindon, 1970–73; Bishop Suffragan of Malmesbury, 1973–83. Proctor, Canterbury Convocation, 1964; Hon. Canon, Portsmouth Cathedral, 1965. *Publication:* (ed) William Temple, Some Lambeth Letters, 1942–44, 1963. *Recreations:* theatre, television. *Address:* 7 The Barton, Wood Street, Wootton Bassett, Wilts SN4 7BG. *T:* (01793) 851227.   *Died 26 Nov. 2000.*

TEMPLE, Sir Rawden (John Afamado), Kt 1980; CBE 1964; QC 1951; Chief Social Security (formerly National Insurance) Commissioner, 1975–81 (a National Insurance Commissioner, 1969); a Referee under Child Benefit Act 1975, since 1976; *b* 24 May 1908; *s* of Elie Raphael Afoumado and Bertha Afoumado; *né* Nessim Sabatai Afoumado; *m* 1936, Margaret Jessie Wiseman (*d* 1980), *d* of late Sir James Gunson, CMG, CBE; two *s*. *Educ:* King Edward's School, Birmingham; The Queen's College, Oxford (BA 1930; BCL, 1931). Called to the Bar, Inner Temple, 1931; Master of the Bench, 1960 (Reader, 1982; Treasurer, 1983). Vice-Chairman, General Council of the Bar, 1960–64. Mem., Industrial Injuries Adv. Council, 1981–84. War Service, 1941–45. Liveryman, Worshipful Company of Pattenmakers, 1948. *Address:* 3 North King's Bench Walk, Temple, EC4Y 7DQ.

Died 31 May 2000.

TEMPLE, Sir Sanderson; *see* Temple, Sir E. S.

TENNANT, Sir Peter (Frank Dalrymple), Kt 1972; CMG 1958; OBE 1945; Director-General, British National Export Council, 1965–71; Industrial Adviser, Barclays Bank International Ltd, 1972–81; Director: Prudential Assurance Company Ltd, 1973–81; Prudential Corporation plc, 1979–86; C. Tennant Sons & Company Ltd, 1972–80; Anglo-Romanian Bank, 1973–81; Northern Engineering Industries (International) Ltd, 1979–82; International Energy Bank, 1981–84; *b* 29 Nov. 1910; *s* of G. F. D. Tennant and Barbara Tennant (*née* Beck); *m* 1st, 1934, Hellis (marr. diss. 1952), *d* of Professor Fellenius, Stockholm; one *s* two *d*; 2nd, 1953, Galina Bosley (*d* 1995), *d* of K. Grunberg, Helsinki; one step *s*. *Educ:* Marlborough; Trinity College, Cambridge. Sen. Mod. Languages Scholar, Trinity College, Cambridge, 1929; Cholmondeley Studentship, Lincoln's Inn; 1st Cl. Hons Mod. Langs Tripos, 1931; BA 1931, MA 1936, Cambridge. Cambridge Scandinavian Studentship, Oslo, Copenhagen, Stockholm, 1932–33; Fellow Queens' College, Cambridge, and University Lecturer, Scandinavian Languages, 1933; Press Attaché, British Legation, Stockholm, 1939–45; Information Counsellor, British Embassy, Paris, 1945–50; Deputy Commandant, British Sector, Berlin, 1950–52; resigned Foreign Service to become Overseas Director, FBI, 1952–63; Deputy Director-General, FBI, 1963–65. Special Advr, CBI, 1964–65. Mem., Council of Industrial Design, 1954–71; Acting Chm., Wilton Park Academic Council, 1969–71; Mem. Bd, Centre for Internat. Briefing, Farnham Castle, 1954–72; Chm., Gabbitas Thring Educational Trust, 1971–91; Pres., London Chamber of Commerce and

Industry, 1978–79 (Chm., 1976–78); Chm., British Cttee, European Cultural Foundn, 1975–90; Mem., Impact Foundn Council, 1974–91; Trustee, Heinz Koeppler Trust, 1985–. Vis. Fellow, St Cross Coll., Oxford, 1982. MA Oxford, 1982. *Publications:* Ibsen's Dramatic Technique, 1947; The Scandinavian Book, 1952; (in Swedish) Touchlines of War, 1989, English edn 1992. *Recreations:* writing, talking, painting, travel, languages, sailing, country life. *Address:* Blue Anchor House, Linchmere Road, Haslemere, Surrey GU27 3QF. *T:* (01428) 643124. *Club:* Travellers'.   *Died 22 Dec. 1996.*

TENNSTEDT, Klaus; Principal Conductor and Music Director, The London Philharmonic, 1983–87, Conductor Laureate, 1987–94; *b* 6 June 1926; *s* of Hermann and Agnes Tennstedt; *m* 1960, Ingeborg Fischer. *Educ:* Leipzig Conservatory (violin, piano). Conductor at: Landersoper, Dresden, 1958–62; Staatstheater, Schwerin, 1962–70; Operhaus, Kiel, 1972–76; guest conductor with Boston, Chicago, New York Philharmonic, Cleveland, Philadelphia, Berlin and Israel Philharmonic Orchestras. Hon. RAM, 1990. Hon. DMus: Colgate Hamilton, NY State, 1984; Oxford, 1994. Officer's Cross, Order of Merit (FRG), 1986. *Recreations:* astronomy, hot air ballooning. *Address:* Rothenbaumchaussee 132–134, 20149 Hamburg, Germany.   *Died 11 Jan. 1998.*

TEŌ, Sir (Fiatau) Penitala, GCMG 1979; GCVO 1982; ISO 1970; MBE 1956; Governor-General of Tuvalu, 1978–86; *b* 23 July 1911; *s* of Teō Veli, Niutao, and Tilesa Samuelu, Funafuti; *m* 1st, 1931, Muniara Apelu, Vaitupu; one *d* (one *s* decd); 2nd, 1949, Uimai Tofiga, Nanumaga; eight *s* three *d* (and one *d* decd). *Educ:* Elisefou, Vaitupu, Tuvalu. Asst Sch. Master, Elisefou, 1930–32; Clerk and Ellice Interpreter: Dist Admin, Funafuti, 1932–37; Resident Comr's Office, Ocean Is., 1937–42; under Japanese Occupation (Ocean Is. and Tarawa), 1942–43 (1939–45 Star, Pacific Star and War Medal); re-joined Res. Comr's Office, 1943 (i/c Labour Force), Special Clerk 1944; Asst Admin. Officer and Mem., Gilbert and Ellice Is Defence Force (2nd Lieut), 1944; Asst and Actg Dist Officer for Ellice Is, 1944–50; transf. to Tarawa to re-organise Information Office, 1953; Acting Colony Marine Supt, 1953; Dep. Comr for Western Pacific, 1960; Officer i/c, Betio, 1960; Lands Officer for Gilbert and Ellice Is, 1960–62; District Commissioner: Ocean Is., 1963; (acting) Gilbert and Ellice Is, 1965; Ellice Is, 1967–69; Asst and Actg Supt of Labour, British Phosphate Comrs, Ocean Is., 1971–78. ADC to High Comr of Western Pacific during tours, 1954 and 1957; Dist Officer for visit of Prince Philip to Vaitupu Is., Ellice Is, 1959; ADC to Res. Comr, 1963. Represented Gilbert and Ellice Is at confs, and Festival of Britain, 1951. Scout Medal of Merit, 1971. Coronation Medal, 1953. *Recreations:* formerly fishing, cricket, football, Rugby, local games. *Address:* Alapi, Funafuti, Tuvalu, S Pacific.   *Died 1998.*

TERESA, Mother, (Agnes Gonxha Bojaxhiu), MC; Hon. OM 1983; Hon. OBE 1978; Padma Shri, 1962; Bharat Ratna (Jewel of India), 1980; Roman Catholic nun; *b* Skopje, Yugoslavia, 27 Aug. 1910; *d* of Albanian parents. *Educ:* government school in Yugoslavia. Joined Sisters of Loretto, Rathfarnam, Ireland, 1929; trained at Loretto insts in Ireland and India; came to Calcutta, 1929; Principal, St Mary's High School, Calcutta. Founded the Missionaries of Charity (Sisters), 1950, Missionary Brothers of Charity, 1963, the Internat. Co-Workers of Mother Teresa, 1969, Missionaries of Charity, Sisters Contemplatives, 1976, Brothers of the Word Contemplatives, 1979, and Missionaries of Charity Fathers, 1983, to give free service to the poor and the unwanted, irrespective of caste, creed, nationality, race or place; she set up: slum schools; orphanages; Nirmol Hridoy (Pure Heart) Homes for sick and dying street cases; Shishu Bhavan Homes for unwanted, crippled and mentally-retarded children; mobile gen. clinics and centres for malnourished; mobile clinics and rehabilitation centres for leprosy patients; homes for drug addicts and alcoholics; night shelters for the homeless. Hon. DD Cambridge, 1977; Hon. DrMed: Catholic Univ. of Sacred Heart, Rome, 1981; Catholic Univ. of Louvain, 1982. Ramón Magsaysay Internat. Award, 1962; Pope John XXIII Peace Prize, 1971; Kennedy Internat. Award, 1971; Jawaharlal Nehru Internat. Award, 1972; Templeton Foundation Prize, 1973; first Albert Schweitzer Internat. Prize, 1975; Nobel Peace Prize, 1979, and many other awards too numerous to mention. Hon. Citizen, Assisi, 1982. *Publications:* Gift for God, 1975; Heart of Joy, 1988; Living the Word, 1990; Loving Jesus, 1991; A Simple Path (compilation), 1995; *relevant publications* include: Something Beautiful for God, by Malcolm Muggeridge; Mother Teresa, her people and her works, by Desmond Doig; Such a Vision of the Street, by Eileen Egan. *Address:* 54A Acharya Jagadish Chandra Bose Road, Calcutta 700016, India. *T:* (33) 297115.

Died 5 Sept. 1997.

TERRINGTON, 4th Baron *cr* 1918, of Huddersfield, co. York; **James Allen David Woodhouse;** former Member, Stock Exchange; Partner in Sheppards and Chase, 1952–80; *b* 30 Dec. 1915; *er s* of 3rd Baron Terrington, KBE, and Valerie (*née* Phillips) (*d* 1958), Leyden's House, Edenbridge, Kent; *S* father, 1961; *m* 1942, Suzanne, *y d* of Colonel T. S. Irwin, DL, JP, late Royal Dragoons, Justicetown, Carlisle, and Mill House, Holton, Suffolk; three *d. Educ:* Winchester; Royal Military College, Sandhurst. Commnd Royal Norfolk Regiment, TA, 1936. Farming in Norfolk, 1936–39. Served War of 1939–45 in India, North Africa (1st Army, Tunisia) and Middle East (wounded); ADC to GOC Madras, 1940; Staff Coll., Haifa, 1944; psc 1944; GSOII, Allied Force HQ Algiers, Ninth Army, Lebanon, Middle East, and War Office, Military Operations; GSO, India (during Partition), 1947; retired as Major, 1948; joined Queen's Westminster Rifles (KRRC), TA. Joined Messrs Chase Henderson and Tennant, 1949 (later Sheppards). Deputy Chairman of Cttees, House of Lords, 1961–63; Mem., Select Cttee on Commodity Prices, 1976. Member: Ecclesiastical Cttee, 1979–; Exec. Cttee, Wider Shareownership Council, 1981– (former Dep. Chm. of Council); Dep. Chm., Nat. Listening Library (Talking Books for the Disabled), 1977–. Vice-Pres., Small Farmers' Assoc., 1986–. Mem. Internat. Adv. Bd, American Univ., Washington DC, 1985–. *Heir: b* Hon. (Christopher) Montague Woodhouse, DSO, OBE [*b* 11 May 1917; *m* 1945, Lady Davina (*d* 1995), *d* of 2nd Earl of Lytton, KG, GCSI, GCIE, PC and *widow* of 5th Earl of Erne; two *s* one *d*]. *Address:* 3 Whitelands House, Cheltenham Terrace, SW3 4QX. *Club:* Boodle's.

Died 6 May 1998.

TETLEY, Sir Herbert, KBE 1965; CB 1958; Government Actuary, 1958–73; *b* 23 April 1908; *s* of Albert Tetley, Leeds; *m* 1941, Agnes Maclean Macfarlane Macphee; one *s. Educ:* Leeds Grammar School; The Queen's College, Oxford. Hastings Scholar, Queen's College, 1927–30; 1st Cl. Hons Mods (Mathematics), 1928; 1st Cl. Final Hons School of Mathematics, 1930. Fellow of Institute of Actuaries, 1934; Fellow of Royal Statistical Society. Served with London Life Assoc., 1930–36; Scottish Provident Instn, 1936–38; National Provident Instn, 1938–51 (Joint Actuary); joined Government Actuary's Dept as Principal Actuary, 1951; Deputy Government Actuary, 1953. Chairman: Civil Service Insurance Soc., 1961–73; Cttee on Economics Road Research Board, 1962–65; Cttee on Road Traffic Research, 1966–73. Pres., Inst. of Actuaries, 1964–66. *Publications:* Actuarial Statistics, Vol. I, 1946; (jtly) Statistics, An Intermediate Text Book, Vol. I, 1949, Vol. II, 1950. *Recreations:* gardening, music, fell-walking. *Address:* 37 Upper

Brighton Road, Surbiton, Surrey KT6 6QX. *T:* (0181) 399 3001.

Died 12 March 1999.

THIMANN, Prof. Kenneth Vivian; Professor of Biology, 1965–72, and Provost of Crown College, 1966–72, Emeritus Professor, recalled to duty 1972–87, University of California, Santa Cruz, Calif, USA; *b* 5 Aug. 1904; *s* of Phoebus Thimann and Muriel Kate Thimann (*née* Harding); naturalized American citizen; *m* 1929, Ann Mary Bateman, Sutton Bridge, Lincs; three *d. Educ:* Caterham Sch., Surrey; Imperial Coll., London. BSc, ARCS 1924; DIC 1925; PhD 1928. Beit Memorial Res. Fellow, 1927–29; Demonstr in Bacteriology, King's Coll. for Women, 1926–28; Instr in Biochem., Calif Inst. of Techn., 1930–35; Harvard University: Lectr on Botany, 1935; (Biology): Asst Prof., 1936, Associate Prof., 1939, Prof., 1946, and Higgins Prof., 1962–65, then Prof. Emeritus. Vis. Professor: Sorbonne, 1954; Univ. of Massachusetts, 1974; Univ. of Texas, 1976. Scientific Consultant, US Navy, 1942–45. Dir, Amer. Assoc. for Advancement of Science, 1968–71. Pres., XIth Internat. Botanical Congress, Seattle, USA, 1969; 2nd Nat. Biol Congress, Miami, 1971. Hon. AM Harvard, 1940; Hon. PhD Univ. of Basle, 1959; Hon. Doctor Univ. of Clermont-Ferrand, 1961; Hon. DSc Brown Univ., 1989. Fellow: Nat. Acad. of Scis (Councillor, 1967–71); Amer. Acad. of Arts and Scis; Amer. Philosophical Soc. (Councillor, 1973–76); and professional biological socs in USA and England; Foreign Member: Royal Society; Institut de France (Acad. des Sciences, Paris); Académie d'Agriculture; Accademia Nazionale dei Lincei (Rome); Leopoldina Akademie (Halle); Roumanian Academy (Bucharest); Botanical Societies of Japan and Netherlands. Silver Medal, Internat. Plant Growth Substance Assoc.; Balzan Prize, 1983. *Publications:* Phytohormones (with F. W. Went), 1937; The Action of Hormones in Plants and Invertebrates, 1948; The Life of Bacteria, 1955, 2nd edn 1963 (German edn 1964); L'Origine et les Fonctions des Auxines, 1956; The Natural Plant Hormones, 1972; Hormones in the Whole Life of Plants, 1977; (ed) Senescence in Plants, 1980; (with J. Langenheim) Botany: Plant Biology in relation to Human Affairs, 1981; over 300 papers in biological and biochemical jls. *Recreations:* music (piano), gardening. *Address:* The Quadrangle, 3300 Darby Road, Apt 3314, Haverford, PA 19041, USA. *Club:* Harvard Faculty (Cambridge, Mass).

Died 15 Jan. 1997.

THIRKETTLE, (William) Ellis, CBE 1959; Principal, London College of Printing, 1939–67; *b* 26 July 1904; *s* of William Edward Thirkettle; *m* 1930, Alva (*d* 1987), *d* of Thomas Tough Watson; two *s. Educ:* Tiffin School. Principal, Stow College of Printing, Glasgow, 1936–39. *Address:* Watermoor House, Cirencester, Glos GL7 1JR.

Died 25 Oct. 2000.

THIRLWALL, Air Vice-Marshal George Edwin, CB 1976; *b* 24 Dec. 1924; *s* of Albert and Clarice Editha Thirlwall; *m* 1st, 1949, Daphne Patricia Wynn Giles (*d* 1975); 2nd, 1977, Louisa Buck Russell (*née* Cranston). *Educ:* Sheffield Univ.; Cranfield Inst. of Technology. BEng, MSc. Joined RAF, 1950; OC RAF Sealand, 1969; Dir Air Guided Weapons, MoD, 1972; AO Ground Trng, RAF Trng Comd, 1974–76; AO Engineering, Strike Command, 1976–79. Director: Ceramics, Glass and Mineral ITB, 1979–82; Sand and Gravel Assoc., 1983–89. *Recreations:* gardening, golf. *Address:* Che Sara Sara, Gosmore Road, Hitchin, Herts SG4 9AR. *T:* (01462) 434182. *Club:* Royal Air Force.

Died 19 Oct. 2000.

THODE, Dr Henry George, CC 1967; MBE 1946; FRS 1954; FRSC 1943; FCIC 1948; Professor Emeritus, McMaster University, Canada, since 1979; *b* 10 Sept. 1910; Canadian; *s* of Charles Herman Thode and Zelma

Ann (*née* Jacoby); *m* 1935, Sadie Alicia Patrick; three *s*. *Educ:* University of Saskatchewan (BSc 1930, MSc 1932); University of Chicago (PhD 1934). Research Asst, Columbia Univ., 1936–38; Research Chemist, US Rubber Co., 1938; McMaster University: Asst Prof. of Chem., 1939–42; Assoc. Prof. of Chem., 1942–44; Prof. of Chem., 1944–79; Head, Department of Chemistry, 1948–52; Dir of Res., 1947–61; Principal of Hamilton Coll., 1949–63; Vice-Pres., 1957–61; Pres. and Vice-Chancellor, 1961–72. California Inst. of Technology, Pasadena, Calif: Nat. Science Foundn Sen. Foreign Res. Fellow, 1970; Sherman Fairchild Distinguished Scholar, 1977. National Research Council, War Research-Atomic Energy, 1943–45. Member: Nat. Research Council, 1943–45; Defence Research Bd, 1955–61; Commn on Atomic Weights (SAIC), IUPAC, 1965–73; Board of Governors, Ontario Research Foundn, 1955–82; Director: Atomic Energy of Canada Ltd, 1966–81; Stelco Inc., 1969–85. Hon. Fellow, Chemical Inst. of Canada, 1972; Shell Canada Merit Fellowship, 1974. Hon. DSc, Universities: Toronto, 1955; BC, Acadia, 1960; Laval, 1963; McGill, 1966; Queen's, 1967; York, 1972; McMaster, 1973; Hon. DSc Royal Mil. Coll., Canada, 1964; Hon. LLD: Saskatchewan, 1958; Regina, 1983. Medal of Chemical Inst. of Canada, 1957; Tory Medal, 1959, Centenary Medal, 1982, Sir William Dawson Medal, 1989, Royal Soc. of Canada; Arthur L. Day Medal, Geological Soc. of America, 1980; Montreal Medal, Chem. Inst. of Canada, 1993. Order of Ontario, 1989. *Publications:* numerous publications on nuclear chemistry, isotope chemistry, isotope abundances in terrestrial and extraterrestrial material, separation of isotopes, magnetic susceptibilities, electrical discharges in gases, sulphur concentrations and isotope ratios in lunar materials. *Recreations:* swimming, farming. *Address:* Department of Chemistry, Nuclear Research Building, McMaster University, 1280 Main Street West, Hamilton, Ontario L8S 4K1, Canada. *T:* (905) 5259140. *Club:* Rotary (Hamilton, Ont). *Died 22 March 1997.*

THODY, Prof. Philip Malcolm Waller; Professor of French Literature, University of Leeds, 1965–93, then Professor Emeritus; *b* Lincoln, 21 March 1928; *s* of Thomas Edwin Thody and Florence Ethel (*née* Hart); *m* 1954, Joyce Elizabeth Woodin; two *s* two *d. Educ:* Lincoln Sch.; King's Coll., Univ. of London. FIL 1982. Temp. Asst Lectr, Univ. of Birmingham, 1954–55; Asst Lectr, subseq. Lectr, QUB, 1956–65; Chairman: Dept of French, Univ. of Leeds, 1968–72, 1975–79, 1982–85, 1987–93; Bd of Faculties of Arts, Social Studies and Law, Univ. of Leeds, 1972–74. Visiting Professor: Univ. of Western Ontario, Canada, 1963–64; Berkeley Summer Sch., 1964; Harvard Summer Sch., 1968; Virginia Summer Sch., 1990; Stanford Univ., 1993–94; Centenary Vis. Prof., Adelaide Univ., 1974; Canterbury Vis. Fellow, Univ. of Canterbury, NZ, 1977, 1982; Vis. Fellow, Univ. of WA, 1988. Pres., Modern Languages Assoc., 1980, 1981. Officier dans l'Ordre des Palmes Académiques (France), 1981. *Publications:* Albert Camus, a study of his work, 1957; Jean-Paul Sartre, a literary and political study, 1960; Albert Camus, 1913–1960, 1961; Jean Genet, a study of his novels and plays, 1968; Jean Anouilh, 1968; Choderlos de Laclos, 1970; Jean-Paul Sartre, a biographical introduction, 1971; Aldous Huxley, a biographical introduction, 1973; Roland Barthes: a conservative estimate, 1977; A True Life Reader for Children and Parents, 1977; Dog Days in Babel (novel), 1979; (jtly) Faux Amis and Key Words, 1985; Marcel Proust, novelist, 1987; Albert Camus, novelist, 1989; French Caesarism from Napoleon 1[cf9]er to Charles de Gaulle, 1989; Jean-Paul Sartre, novelist, 1992; The Conservative Imagination, 1993; Le Franglais, 1995; Twentieth-Century Literature: critical issues and themes, 1996; An Historical Introduction to the European Union, 1997; Don't Do It, 1997; Roland

Barthes for Beginners, 1997; Jean-Paul Sartre for Beginners, 1998; The Fifth French Republic, 1998; Europe since 1945, 1998; contribs to French Studies, Times Literary Supplement, Times Higher Educational Supplement, Modern Languages Review, London Magazine, Twentieth Century, Encounter, Yorkshire Post. *Recreations:* talking, golf, Wodehouse inter-war first editions. *Address:* 6 The Nook, Primley Park, Alwoodley, Leeds LS17 7JU. *T:* (0113) 268 7350.

Died 15 June 1999.

THOMAS, Alston Havard Rees; Finance and Property Writer, Bristol Evening Post, 1985 (Diary Editor, 1970–85); *b* Dinas, Pembrokeshire, 8 July 1925. Trainee and reporter, West Wales Guardian, 1939–44; Dist Reporter, Wilts Times, 1944–46; joined Bristol Evening Post, 1946, successively Industrial, Speedway, Municipal, Ecclesiastical, Crime and Med. correspondent. Institute of Journalists: Mem., 1974–; Chm. Nat. Exec., 1981–84; Pres., 1985–86; Chm. SW Region, 1975–; Mem., Press Council, 1979–90. Mem., St John Council (Avon Co.), 1974–97. *Recreations:* Rugby Union, music, travel, gardening. *Address:* Havene, Maysmead Lane, Langford, N Somerset BS18 7HX. *T:* (01934) 862515.

Died 31 Aug. 1999.

THOMAS, Ambler Reginald, CMG 1951; Under-Secretary, Ministry of Overseas Development, retired 1975; *b* 12 Feb. 1913; *s* of late John Frederick Ivor Thomas, OBE, MICE, MIME and Elizabeth Thomas; *m* 1943, Diana Beresford Gresham; two *s* three *d. Educ:* Gresham's School, Holt; Corpus Christi College, Cambridge. Entered Home Civil Service as Asst Principal and apptd to Ministry of Agriculture and Fisheries, 1935; transferred to Colonial Office, 1936; Asst Private Sec. to Sec. of State for Colonies, 1938–39; Principal, Colonial Office, 1939; Asst Sec., 1946; Chief Sec. to Govt of Aden, 1947–49; Establishment and Organization Officer, Colonial Office, 1950–52; Assistant Under-Sec. of State, Colonial Office, 1952–64; Under-Sec., Min. of Overseas Develt, and Overseas Develt Administration, 1964–73. Member, Exec. Cttee, British Council, 1965–68. Chm., Commn of Inquiry into Gilbert Is Develt Authority, 1976. Mem., formerly Chm., Corona Club. *Address:* Champsland, North Chideock, Bridport, Dorset DT6 6JZ. *Club:* United Oxford & Cambridge University.

Died 30 Dec. 1996.

THOMAS, David Monro; retired; *b* 31 July 1915; *s* of late Henry Monro and Winifred Thomas, East Hagbourne, Berks; *m* 1948, Ursula Mary, *d* of late H. W. Liversidge; two *s* one *d. Educ:* St Edward's School, Oxford; St Edmund Hall, Oxford. Oxford House, 1937; Army, 1939, Major, Royal Welch Fusiliers; Head of Oxford House, 1946–48; Secretary of Greek House, 1948–51; Legal & General Assurance Soc. Ltd, 1951–75; YWCA, 1975–80: Co. Sec., 1977–80. *Address:* Watcombe Corner, Watlington, Oxford OX9 5QJ. *T:* Watlington (01491) 612403.

Died 13 Feb. 1996.

THOMAS, His Honour Dewi Alun, MBE; a Circuit Judge, 1972–90; *b* 3 Dec. 1917; *e s* of late Joshua and Martha Ann Thomas; *m* 1952, Doris Maureen Smith, barrister; one *s* one *d. Educ:* Christ Coll., Brecon; Jesus Coll., Oxford (MA). Served War of 1939–45 (MBE, despatches): mobilised with TA (RA), 1939; served Sicily, Italy, the Balkans; Major, No 2 Commando. Called to Bar, Inner Temple, 1951, Bencher 1969. *Recreations:* golf, watching Rugby football. *Address:* c/o Law Courts, Barker Road, Maidstone, Kent ME16 8EW.

Died 19 Jan. 1996.

THOMAS, Frank; *see* Thomas, J. F. P.

THOMAS, Sir Frederick William, Kt 1959; AE; Councillor, City of Melbourne, 1953–65 (Lord Mayor,

1957–59); *b* 27 June 1906; *s* of F. J. Thomas; *m* 1944, Coral Kirkwood Patrick; three *s*; *m* 1968, Dorothy Alexa Gordon (*d* 1997). *Educ:* Melbourne Grammar School. Served War of 1939–45, RAAF (Air Efficiency Award, two bars); Group Captain. Comdr Order of Orange Nassau with swords (Netherlands), 1943. *Recreation:* golf. *Address:* 35 Hitchcock Avenue, Barwon Heads, Vic 3227, Australia. *Clubs:* Naval and Military, Royal Automobile of Victoria (Melbourne); Barwon Heads Golf, Melbourne Cricket. *Died Feb. 1999.*

THOMAS, (John) Frank (Phillips); Telecommunications Consultant to British Telecom, international industry and commerce, retired; *b* 11 April 1920; *s* of late John and Catherine Myfanwy Phillips Thomas; *m* 1942, Edith V. Milne; one *s* one *d*. *Educ:* Christ's Coll., Finchley; Univ. of London (BSc). CEng, MIEE. Joined Post Office Research Dept, 1937; trans-oceanic telephone cable system develt, 1947–63; planning UK inland telephone network, 1963–69; Dep. Dir, London Telephone Region, 1969–71; Dep. Dir Engrg, Network Planning Dept, 1971; Dir, Network Planning Dept, 1972–79; Dir, Overseas Liaison and Consultancy Dept, Post Office, 1979–81. *Publications:* contrib. scientific and technical jls on telecommunications subjects. *Recreations:* fly fishing, automated horticulture. *Address:* 24 Moneyhill Road, Rickmansworth, Herts WD3 2EQ. *T:* (01923) 772992. *Club:* Rickmansworth Lawn Tennis (Vice-Pres.).
Died 14 Oct. 2000.

THOMAS, Adm. Sir Richard; *see* Thomas, Adm. Sir W. R. S.

THOMAS, Rev. Ronald Stuart; poet; *b* 29 March 1913; *m* 1940, Mildred E. Eldridge (*d* 1991); one *s*; *m* 1996, Elisabeth A., (Betty), Vernon. *Educ:* University of Wales (BA); St Michael's College, Llandaff. Ordained deacon, 1936, priest, 1937. Curate of Chirk, 1936–40; Curate of Hanmer, in charge of Talarn Green, 1940–42; Rector of Manafon, 1942–54; Vicar of Eglwysfach, 1954–67; Vicar of St Hywyn, Aberdaron, with St Mary, Bodferin, 1967–78, and Rector of Rhiw with Llanfaelrhys, 1972–78. First record, reading his own poems, 1977. Queen's Gold Medal for Poetry, 1964; Cholmondeley Award, 1978. *Publications: poems:* Stones of the Field (privately printed), 1947; Song at the Year's Turning, 1955 (Heinemann Award of the Royal Society of Literature, 1956); Poetry for Supper, 1958; Tares, 1961; Bread of Truth, 1963; Pietà, 1966; Not That He Brought Flowers, 1968; H'm, 1972; Selected Poems 1946–1968, 1974; Laboratories of the Spirit, 1976; Frequencies, 1978; Between Here and Now, 1981; Later Poems 1972–1982, 1983; Experimenting with an Amen, 1986; Welsh Airs, 1987; The Echoes Return Slow, 1988; Counterpoint, 1990; Mass for Hard Times, 1992; Collected Poems 1945–1990, 1993; No Truce with the Furies, 1995; *autobiography:* Neb, 1985; Autobiographies, 1997; *edited:* A Book of Country Verse, 1961; Penguin Book of Religious Verse, 1963; Edward Thomas, Selected Poems, 1964; George Herbert, A Choice of Verse, 1967; A Choice of Wordsworth's Verse, 1971. *Address:* Ty Main, Llanfrothen, Penrhyndeudraeth LL48 6SG.
Died 25 Sept. 2000.

THOMAS, Adm. Sir (William) Richard (Scott), KCB 1987; KCVO 1995; OBE 1974; Gentleman Usher of the Black Rod, and Serjeant-at-Arms, House of Lords, and Secretary to the Lord Great Chamberlain, 1992–95; *b* 22 March 1932; *s* of late Comdr William Scott Thomas, DSC, RN and Mary Hilda Bertha Hemelryk, Findon, Sussex; *m* 1959, Patricia Margaret, (Paddy), *d* of late Dr and Mrs J. H. Cullinan, Fressingfield, Suffolk; two *s* four *d* (and two *s* decd). *Educ:* Penryn Sch., Ross-on-Wye; Downside Sch., Bath. psc 1963, jssc 1966, rcds 1979. Midshipman, 1951–52; Sub-Lt and Lieut, 1953–62 (CO HM Ships

Buttress, Wolverton and Greetham); CO HMS Troubridge, 1966–68; Staff Officer Ops to Flag Officer First Flotilla and Flag Officer Scotland and NI, 1970–74; Directorate of Naval Plans, MoD, 1974–77; CO HMS Fearless, 1977–78; Dir of Office Appts (Seamen), 1980–83; Naval Sec., 1983–85; Flag Officer Second Flotilla, 1985–87; Dep. SACLANT, 1987–89; UK Mil. Rep. to NATO, 1989–92. Member: Cttee, Royal Humane Soc., 1992–; Council, Stroke Assoc., 1996–. Gov., ESU, 1996–. Pres., Havant Dist Scouts, 1992–. Kt Comdr Order of Pope Pius IX, 1995. *Recreation:* family. *Address:* 14 King Street, Emsworth, Hants PO10 7AZ.
Died 13 Dec. 1998.

THOMPSON, Ernest; *see* Thompson, R. E.

THOMPSON, Vice-Adm. Sir Hugh (Leslie Owen), KBE 1987; FEng 1989; FIMechE; Deputy Controller of the Navy and Chief Above-Water Systems Executive (formerly Deputy Controller Warships), Ministry of Defence, 1986–89; Chief Naval Engineer Officer, 1987–89; retired; *b* 2 April 1931; *s* of Hugh Thompson and Elsie Standish (*née* Owen); *m* 1st, 1957, Sheila Jean Finch (*d* 1974); one *s* two *d*; 2nd, 1977, Rosemary Ann (*née* Oliver). *Educ:* Royal Belfast Academical Institution; RNC Dartmouth; RNEC Manadon. Asst Dir, Submarines Mechanical, 1976–79; RCDS, 1980; Dep. Dir, Systems 1, 1981–83; Dir Gen., Marine Engineering, 1983–84; Dir Gen. Surface Ships, MoD, 1984–86. *Recreations:* railways, woodwork. *Clubs:* Army and Navy; Bath and County (Bath).
Died 11 Dec. 1996.

THOMPSON, Rear-Adm. John Yelverton, CB 1960; retired 1961; *b* 25 May 1909; *s* of late Sir John Perronet Thompson, KCSI, KCIE, and Lady (Ada Lucia) Thompson (*née* Tyrrell); *m* 1934, Barbara Helen Mary Aston Key (*d* 1996); two *s*. *Educ:* Mourne Grange, Kilkeel, Co. Down; RN College, Dartmouth. Midshipman, HMS Repulse and Berwick, 1926–29; Sub-Lieutenant, HMS Warspite, 1931, Lieutenant, HMS Queen Elizabeth, 1931–32, Restless 1933, Excellent 1933–34, Queen Elizabeth 1935, Glasgow 1936–39; Lieut-Commander, HMS Excellent 1939–41, Anson 1941–43; Commander: Admiralty, Naval Ordnance Dept, 1943–45; US Fifth Fleet, 1946; HMS Liverpool, 1947; HMS Newcastle, 1948; Captain: Ordnance Board, 1948–50; HMS Unicorn, 1951–52; Director, Gunnery Division, Naval Staff, 1952–54; Imperial Defence College, 1955; Commodore, Royal Naval Barracks, Portsmouth, 1956–57; Rear-Admiral: Admiralty Interview Boards, 1958; Adm. Superintendent, HM Dockyard, Chatham, 1958–61. ADC to the Queen, 1957. Governor, Aldenham Sch., 1967–73. DL: Hertfordshire, 1966–73; Cornwall, 1973–88. American Legion of Merit, 1953. *Address:* Redcot, Three Gates Lane, Haslemere, Surrey GU27 2LL. *Died 27 March 1998.*

THOMPSON, Sir Lionel; *see* Thompson, Sir T. L. T.

THOMPSON, Reginald Aubrey, CMG 1964; *b* 22 Nov. 1905; *s* of John and Alice Thompson, Mansfield; *m* 1932, Gwendoline Marian Jackson (*d* 1978); one *s*. *Educ:* Brunts Sch., Mansfield; University Coll., Nottingham. BSc London (1st Cl. Hons Chemistry), 1927. Research, Organic Chemistry, 1927–29; Science Master, various grammar schools, 1929–41; Scientific Civil Service, Min. of Supply, 1941–46; transf. to Admin. Class (Principal), 1946; Asst Sec., 1953; Assistant Secretary, Department of Education and Science (formerly Office of Minister of Science), 1956–64; Ministry of Technology, 1964; retd, 1966. Led UK Delegn at Confs on liability of operators of nuclear ships, Brussels Convention, 1962, on liability for nuclear damage, Vienna Convention, 1963. *Recreations:* reading, music, crosswords. *Address:* 81 Bentsbrook Park, North Holmwood, Dorking, Surrey RH5 4JL. *T:* (01306) 882289. *Died 2 April 1998.*

THOMPSON, Sir Richard (Hilton Marler), 1st Bt *cr* 1963, of Reculver, co. Kent; *b* Calcutta, India, 5 Oct. 1912; *s* of late Richard Smith Thompson and Kathleen Hilda (*née* Marler); *m* 1939, Anne Christabel de Vere, *d* of late Philip de Vere Annesley, MA, and Christabel Charlotte Annesley, BEM; one *s.* *Educ:* Malvern College. In business in India, Burma and Ceylon, 1930–40; travelled in Tibet, Persia, Iraq, Turkey, etc. Served in RNVR, 1940–46, volunteering as ordinary seaman; commissioned, 1941 (despatches, 1942); Lt-Comdr 1944. MP (C) Croydon West, 1950–55, Croydon South, 1955–66 and 1970–Feb. 1974. Assistant-Government Whip, 1952; Lord Commissioner of the Treasury, 1954; Vice-Chamberlain of HM Household, 1956; Parly Sec., Ministry of Health, 1957–59; Under-Secretary of State, CRO, 1959–60; Parly Sec., Ministry of Works, 1960–62. Mem., Public Accounts Cttee, 1973–74. A Cottonian family Trustee of the British Museum, 1951–63, a Prime Minister's Trustee, 1963–84; Trustees' representative on Council of Nat. Trust, 1978–84. Chm., Overseas Migration Bd, 1959; led UK delegation to ECAFE in Bangkok, 1960; signed Indus Waters Agreement with India, Pakistan and World Bank for UK, Sept. 1960; led UK Parly Delegn to Tanganyika, to present Speaker's chair, Jan. 1963. Chm., Capital and Counties Property Co., 1971–77, retired; Pres., British Property Fedn, 1976–77; Director, British Museum Publications Ltd. Chm., British Museum Society, 1970–74. *Recreations:* gardening, collecting, study of history. *Heir: s* Nicholas Annesley Marler Thompson [*b* 19 March 1947; *m* 1982, Venetia, *y d* of Mr and Mrs John Heathcote, Conington; three *s* one *d*]. *Address:* Rhodes House, Sellindge, Kent TN25 6JA. *Clubs:* Carlton, Army and Navy. *Died 15 July 1999.*

THOMPSON, Robert Henry Stewart, CBE 1973; DSc, DM; FRS 1974; FRCP, FRCPath; Courtauld Professor of Biochemistry, Middlesex Hospital Medical School, University of London, 1965–76, then Emeritus Professor; Trustee, Wellcome Trust, 1963–82; *b* 2 Feb. 1912; *s* of Dr Joseph Henry Thompson and Mary Eleanor Rutherford; *m* 1938, Inge Vilma Anita Gebert; one *s* two *d.* *Educ:* Epsom College; Trinity College, Oxford (MA); Guy's Hospital Medical School. DM 1942, DSc 1965, Oxford. FRCPath 1964; FRCP 1969. Millard Scholar, Trinity College, Oxford, 1930; Theodore Williams Scholar in Physiology, Oxford, 1932; 1st Class Animal Physiology, Oxford, 1933; Senior Demy, Magdalen College, Oxford, 1933; Univ. Scholar, Guy's Hosp. Med. School, 1933. Adrian Stokes Travelling Fellowship to Hosp. of Rockefeller Inst., New York, 1937–38; Gillson Research Scholar in Pathology, Soc. of Apothecaries of London, 1938; Fellow of University Coll., Oxford, 1938–47, Hon. Fellow, 1983; Demonstrator in Biochemistry, Oxford, 1938–47; Dean of Medical School, Oxford, 1946–47; Prof. of Chemical Pathology, Guy's Hosp. Medical School, Univ. of London, 1947–65. Secretary-General, International Union of Biochemistry, 1955–64; Hon. Sec. Royal Society of Medicine, 1958–64; Mem. of Medical Research Council, 1958–62; Mem., Bd of Governors, Middlesex Hosp., 1972–74. Vice-Pres., Epsom Coll. (Gov., 1982). Hon. Mem., Biochemical Soc., 1986. Radcliffe Prize for Medical Research, Oxford, 1943. Served War of 1939–45, Major, RAMC, 1944–46. *Publications:* (with C. W. Carter) Biochemistry in relation to Medicine, 1949; (ed with E. J. King) Biochemical Disorders in Human Disease, 1957; numerous papers on biochemical and pathological subjects in various scientific journals. *Recreation:* gardening. *Address:* 7 The Cedars, Milford, Godalming, Surrey GU8 5DH. *T:* (01483) 427516; Orchard's Almshouses, Launcells, N Cornwall EX23 9NG. *T:* (01288) 353817. *Club:* Athenæum. *Died 16 Jan. 1998.*

THOMPSON, (Russell) Ernest; Chief Executive, Society of Motor Manufacturers and Traders, since 1993; *b* 18 Feb. 1936; *s* of Russell Thompson and Madge Edith Mary Thompson; *m* 1958, Muriel June; one *s* one *d.* *Educ:* Brighton, Hove and Sussex Grammar Sch.; Corpus Christi Coll., Oxford (MA Mod. Hist.). Joined Ford Motor Co. Ltd, 1960: Director: Car Sales, 1973–82; Marketing, 1982–86; Sales, 1986–93. *Recreations:* golf, reading, walking. *Address:* Forbes House, Halkin Street, SW1X 7DS. *T:* (0171) 235 7000. *Died 17 Nov. 1998.*

THOMPSON, Sir (Thomas) Lionel (Tennyson), 5th Bt *cr* 1806, of Hartsbourne Manor, Hertfordshire; Barrister-at-law; *b* 19 June 1921; *s* of Lt-Col Sir Thomas Thompson, 4th Bt, MC, and Milicent Ellen Jean, *d* of late Edmund Charles Tennyson-d'Eyncourt, Bayons Manor, Lincolnshire; *S* father, 1964; *m* 1955, Mrs Margaret van Beers (marr. diss. 1962), *d* of late Walter Herbert Browne; one *s* one *d.* *Educ:* Eton. Served War of 1939–45: Royal Air Force Volunteer Reserve, 1940; Flying Officer, 1942 (invalided, 1944); Able Seaman, Royal Fleet Auxiliary, 1944–46. Awarded 1939–45 Star, Aircrew (Europe) Star, Defence and Victory Medals. Called to the Bar, Lincoln's Inn, 1952. *Recreations:* shooting, sailing, photography. *Heir: s* (Thomas d'Eyncourt) John Thompson, *b* 22 Dec. 1956. *Address:* 16 Old Buildings, Lincoln's Inn, WC2A 3UP. *T:* (020) 7405 7929. *Died 25 Sept. 1999.*

THOMSON, Sir Adam, Kt 1983; CBE 1976; Chairman and Chief Executive, British Caledonian Group (formerly The Caledonian Aviation Group plc), 1970–88 (formerly Airways Interests (Thomson) Ltd, Chairman and Managing Director, 1964–70); Chairman and Chief Executive, British Caledonian Airways Ltd, 1970–88; *b* 7 July 1926; *s* of Frank Thomson and Jemina Rodgers; *m* 1948, Dawn Elizabeth Burt; two *s.* *Educ:* Rutherglen Acad.; Coatbridge Coll.; Royal Technical Coll., Glasgow. Pilot; Fleet Air Arm, 1944–47; Flying Instructor/ Commercial Pilot, 1947–50; BEA, West African Airways, Britavia, 1951–59. Caledonian Airways: Man. Dir, 1961–64; Chm. and Man. Dir, 1964–70; Chairman: Caledonian Airmotive Ltd, 1978–87; Caledonian Hotel Holdings, 1971–87. Dep. Chm., Martin Currie Pacific Trust PLC, 1985–92; Director: Williams & Glyn's Bank Ltd, 1978–82; Royal Bank of Scotland Gp, 1982–91; Otis Elevators Ltd, 1978–84; MEPC plc, 1982–89. Chairman: Assoc. of European Airlines, 1977–78; Inst. of Directors, 1988–91 (Mem., 1977–). FRAeS; FCIT; FIMgt. Hon. LLD: Glasgow, 1979; Sussex, 1984; Strathclyde, 1986. Businessman of the Year, Hambro Award, 1970; first Scottish Free Enterprise Award, Aims for Freedom and Enterprise, 1976. *Publication:* High Risk: the politics of the air, 1990. *Recreations:* golf, sailing. *Address:* 5 Green Ridge, Westdene, Brighton BN1 5LT. *Died 23 May 2000.*

THOMSON, Francis Paul, OBE 1975; Consultant on Post Office and Bank Giro Systems, 1968–85; *b* Corstorphine, Scotland, 17 Dec. 1914; *y s* of late William George and Elizabeth Hannah Thomson, Goring-by-Sea; *m* 1954, E. Sylvia, *e d* of late Lokförare J. Erik Nilsson, Bollnäs, Sweden. *Educ:* Friends' Sch., Sibford Ferris; Sch. of Engrg, Polytechnic, London; in Denmark and Sweden. TV and radar research, 1935–42; Special Ops Exec., 1942–44; Sen. Planning Engr, Postwar research and reconstruction, communications industry; founded British Post Giro Campaign, 1946 and conducted Campaign to victory in Parlt, 1965; Lectr, Stockholm Univ. Extension, 1947–49; Founder, and Man. Editor, English Illustrated, 1950–61; techn. exports promotion with various firms, esp. electronic equipment, 1950–60; pioneered electronic language laboratory equipment and methods, 1930–; bank computerisation consultant, 1967–80. Governor, Watford Coll. of Technology, 1965–70 (Engrg and Sci. Dept Adv.

Cttee, 1972–91); Mem., Communication of Technical Information Adv. Cttee, CGLI; Advr to PO Users' Nat. Council's Giro Sub Cttee, 1975; Founder and first Hon. Sec., SW Herts Post Office Adv. Cttee, 1976–90; first British Cttee Mem., Internat. Centre for Ancient and Modern Tapestry (CITAM), Lausanne, 1974–80. Founder and Hon. Sec., St Andrews Residents' Assoc. (Watford). Mem., Soc. of Authors, 1990–; MIMgt; FIQA 1978. Hon. Fellow, Inst. of Scientific and Technical Communicators, 1975. Life Member: Corstorphine Trust; Anglo-Swedish Soc.; House of Gordon Assoc.; Friends of Chichester Cathedral; Voice of Listener & Viewer. Donated research papers, book copyrights and mss to Scottish univ. libraries, Royal Coll. of Art, V&A etc. *Publications:* Giro Credit Transfer Systems, 1964; Money in the Computer Age, 1968; (ed jtly) Banking Automation, 1971; (ed with E. S. Thomson) rev. repr. of A History of Tapestry (2nd edn), by W. G. Thomson, 1973; Tapestry: mirror of history, 1979; numerous papers in European and other learned jls. *Recreations:* gardening, archaeology, walking, Swedish hospitals and healthcare.   *Died 26 Feb. 1998.*

THOMSON, George Malcolm, OBE 1990; author and journalist; *b* Leith, Scotland, 2 Aug. 1899; *e s* of Charles Thomson, journalist, and Mary Arthur, *d* of John Eason; *m* 1926, Else (*d* 1957), *d* of Harald Ellefsen, Tœnsberg, Norway; one *s* one *d*; *m* 1963, Diana Van Cortlandt Robertson. *Educ:* Daniel Stewart's College, Edinburgh; Edinburgh University. Journalist, Evening Standard and Daily Express; Principal Private Sec. to 1st Baron Beaverbrook during 2nd World War. *Publications:* Caledonia, or the Future of the Scots, 1927; A Short History of Scotland, 1930; Crisis in Zanat, 1942; The Twelve Days, 1964; The Robbers Passing By, 1966; The Crime of Mary Stuart, 1967; Vote of Censure, 1968; A Kind of Justice, 1970; Sir Francis Drake, 1972; Lord Castlerosse, 1973; The North West Passage, 1975; Warrior Prince: Prince Rupert of the Rhine, 1976; The First Churchill: the life of John, 1st Duke of Marlborough, 1979; The Prime Ministers, 1980; The Ball at Glenkerran, 1982; Kronstadt '21, 1985. *Address:* 5 The Mount Square, NW3 6SY. *T:* 0171–435 8775. *Club:* Garrick.
          Died 20 May 1996.

THOMSON, Very Rev. Ian; *see* White-Thomson.

THOMSON, Ian Mackenzie, WS; President, Industrial Tribunals (Scotland), 1989–91; *b* 16 Feb. 1926; *s* of Donald Hugh Thomson and Doris Emma (*née* Moseley); *m* 1950, Elizabeth Marie Wallace; two *s* one *d. Educ:* George Watson's Coll.; Edinburgh Univ., 1947–50 (BL). Served Royal Navy, 1944–47. Admitted: Solicitor, 1951; Writer to the Signet, 1958; Partner, Davidson and Syme, WS, and after merger, Dundas and Wilson, CS, 1958–75; full-time Chm., Industrial Tribunals, 1975; Regl Chm., 1978; Temp. Sheriff, 1987. *Recreations:* swimming, walking, reading, occasional fishing. *Club:* Drumsheugh Baths (Edinburgh).   *Died 4 Nov. 2000.*

THOMSON, Prof. James Leonard, CBE 1955; Professor Emeritus in Civil Engineering, Royal Military College of Science, Shrivenham, since 1970; *b* 9 Aug. 1905; *s* of James Thomson, Liverpool. *Educ:* University of Manchester (BSc (Tech) 1st Cl. Hons and Stoney Prizeman); St John's College, Cambridge; Mather & Platt, Ltd, Manchester, 1923–26; Univ. of Manchester, 1926–30 (BA 1934, MA 1938). Lecturer, Technical College, Horwich, 1930–32; Whitworth Senior Scholar, 1931; St John's Coll., Cambridge, 1932–34; Research Engineer, ICI, Billingham-on-Tees, 1934–38; Lecturer, Dept of Civil and Mechanical Engineering, Univ. of London, King's College, 1938; seconded for War-time Service: Managing Engineer, HM Royal Ordnance Factory, Pembrey, Carms, 1940–42; Principal Technical Officer, School of Tank Technology, 1942–46; Royal Military College of Science,

Shrivenham: Prof. of Mechanical Engrg and Head of Dept of Civil and Mechanical Engrg, 1946–61; Prof. of Civil Engrg and Head of Dept of Civil Engrg, 1965–70; seconded to ME Technical Univ., Ankara, Turkey, 1961–65 : Consultant Dean and Mechanical Engrg Specialist; later Chief Technical Adviser for UNESCO project in Turkey. *Publications:* various scientific papers dealing with high pressure techniques. *Recreations:* mountaineering, sailing. *Address:* c/o 33 West Street, Bridport, Dorset DT6 3QW.   *Died 12 Jan. 1997.*

THOMSON, Sir John, KBE 1972; TD 1944; Chairman, Morland and Co. Ltd, 1979–83; Director: Barclays Bank Ltd, 1947–78 (Chairman, 1962–73); Union Discount Company of London Ltd, 1960–74; *b* 1908; *s* of late Guy Thomson, JP, Woodperry, Oxford; *m* 1st, 1935, Elizabeth, JP (*d* 1977), *d* of late Stanley Brotherhood, JP, Thornhaugh Hall, Peterborough; no *c*; 2nd, 1979, Eva Elizabeth (*d* 1993), *d* of Marcus Ralph Russell, and *widow* of Tom Dreaper. *Educ:* Winchester; Magdalen College, Oxford (MA). Commanded Oxfordshire Yeomanry Regt, RA (TA), 1942–44 and 1947–50. Deputy High Steward of Oxford University; a Curator of Oxford University Chest, 1949–74; Chairman: Nuffield Medical Benefaction, 1951–82 (Trustee, 1947–82); Nuffield Orthopædic Centre Trust, 1949–81. President, British Bankers' Association, 1964–66 (Vice-President, 1963–64); FIB. Mem. Royal Commn on Trade Unions and Employers' Assocs, 1965–68; Mem. BNEC, 1968–71. Hon. Fellow St Catherine's Coll., Oxford. Hon. Colonel: 299 Fd Regt RA (TA), 1964–67; Oxfordshire Territorials, 1967–75; Bt Col, 1950. DL Oxfordshire, 1947–57; High Sheriff of Oxfordshire, 1957; Vice-Lieut, 1957–63; Lord-Lieut, 1963–79. A Steward, Jockey Club, 1974–77. Hon. DCL Oxford, 1957. KStJ 1973. *Address:* Manor Farm House, Spelsbury, Oxford OX7 3LG. *T:* (01608) 810266. *Clubs:* Cavalry and Guards, Overseas Bankers' (Vice-Pres., 1969–; Pres., 1968–69).   *Died 2 Jan. 1998.*

THORNE, Maj.-Gen. Sir David (Calthrop), KBE 1983 (CBE 1979; OBE 1975); CVO 1995; Director General, Commonwealth Trust, later Royal Commonwealth Society, 1989–97; Project Director, National Skills Festival 2000, since 1998; *b* 13 Dec. 1933; *s* of Richard Everard Thorne and Audrey Ursula (*née* Bone); *m* 1962, Susan Anne Goldsmith; one *s* two *d. Educ:* St Edward's Sch., Oxford; RMA, Sandhurst. Staff Coll., Camberley, 1963; jssc 1967; Defence Intelligence Staff, MoD, 1968–70; Instructor, RAF Staff Coll., 1970–72; CO 1 Royal Anglian, 1972–74; Col, General Staff, MoD, 1975–77; Comdr, 3rd Inf. Bde, NI, 1978–79; RCDS 1980; VQMG, 1981–82; Comdr, British Forces Falkland Islands, July 1982–April 1983; Comdr, 1st Armoured Div., 1983–85; Dir of Infantry, 1986–88. Dep. Col, Royal Anglian Regt, 1981–86; Col Comdt, Queen's Div., 1986–88. Pres., Royal Anglian Regt Assoc., 1988–. Dir, W Suffolk Hosps NHS Trust, 1993–97. Pres., Norfolk CCC, 1993–95; Trustee: Falklands Conservation, 1996–; International Alert, 1998–. *Recreations:* cricket, butterfly collecting. *Address:* c/o Barclays Bank, 52 Abbeygate Street, Bury St Edmunds, Suffolk IP33 1LL. *Clubs:* Royal Commonwealth Society, MCC, Jesters.
          Died 23 April 2000.

THORNHILL, Lt-Col Edmund Basil, MC 1918; *b* 27 Feb. 1898; *e s* of late E. H. Thornhill, Manor House, Boxworth, Cambridge; *m* 1934, Diana Pearl Day Beales (*d* 1983), *d* of late Hubert G. D. Beales, Hambleden and Cambridge; two *s* one *d. Educ:* St Bees School; Royal Military Academy. 2nd Lieut Royal Artillery, 1916; served European War, 1914–18, France and Belgium (wounded, MC); served War of 1939–45, France, Western Desert (Eighth Army) and Italy (despatches); psc 1934; Lt-Col 1945; retd 1948. Chm., Cambs and I of Ely T&AFA,

1957–62. DL Cambs and Isle of Ely, 1956, Vice-Lieut, 1965–75. *Address:* Manor House, Boxworth, Cambridge CB3 8NF. *T:* (01954) 267209. *Club:* Army and Navy.
Died 18 April 1998.

THORNTON, Jack Edward Clive, CB 1978; OBE 1964 (MBE 1945); *b* 22 Nov. 1915; *s* of late Stanley Henry Thornton and Elizabeth Daisy (*née* Baxter); *m* 1st, 1946, Margaret, JP, *d* of late John David and Emily Copeland, Crewe, Cheshire; 2nd, Helen Ann Elizabeth Meixner. *Educ:* Solihull Sch.; Christ's Coll., Cambridge (Open Exhibnr 1936; BA 1938); Cert Ed 1939, MA 1942 Cantab. Served in RASC, 1939–46 (despatches, 1946); Lt-Col 1944. Teaching in UK, 1946–47; Asst, then Dep. Educn Officer, City of York, 1947–51; Asst Educn Officer, WR Yorks, 1951–54; Dep. Dir of Educn, Cumberland, 1954–62; Sec., Bureau for External Aid for Educn, Fed. Govt of Nigeria, 1962–64; Educn Consultant, IBRD, 1964–65; Adviser on Educn in W Africa and Controller Appts Div., British Council, 1965–68; Dep. Educn Adviser, 1968–70, Chief Educn Adviser and Under Sec., 1970–77, Ministry of Overseas Devolt (later Overseas Devolt Admin in FCO). Lectr, Dept of Educn in Developing Countries, Inst. of Educn, Univ. of London, 1978–79. Chm., PNEU World-wide Educn Service, 1979–90; Member: Exec. Cttee, Council for Educn in the Commonwealth, 1978– (Chm., 1979–85; Dep. Chm., 1985–90); Lloyd Foundn, 1981– (Vice-Chm., 1988–95); Educational Panel, Independent Schs Tribunal, 1978–; Charlotte Mason Coll. Higher Educn Corp., 1986–92; Trustee, Christopher Cox Meml Fund, 1983–. *Recreations:* books, conservation, gardens, mountains, music, railways, travel. *Address:* 131 Dalling Road, W6 0ET. *T:* 0181–748 7692; 15 Chepstow House, Chepstow Street, Manchester M1 5JF. *T:* 0161–237 1407. *Died 12 April 1996.*

THORNTON, Lt-Gen. Sir Leonard (Whitmore), KCB 1967 (CB 1962); CBE 1957 (OBE 1944); *b* Christchurch, 15 Oct. 1916; *s* of late Cuthbert John Thornton and Frances Caverhill Thornton; *m* 1st, 1942, Gladys Janet Sloman, Wellington; three *s*; 2nd, 1971, Ruth Leicester, Wellington. *Educ:* Christchurch Boys' High Sch.; Royal Military Coll., Duntroon, Australia. Commissioned in New Zealand Army, 1937; served War of 1939–45 (despatches twice, OBE), Middle East and Italy in 2nd New Zealand Expeditionary Force; Commander, Royal Artillery, 2 New Zealand Division; Commander, Tokyo Sub-area, 1946; Deputy Chief of General Staff, 1948; idc 1952; Head, New Zealand Joint Service Liaison Staff, 1953 and 1954; QMG, New Zealand, 1955; Adjutant-General, 1956–58; Chief, SEATO Planning Office, Thailand, 1958–59; Chief of General Staff, NZ, 1960–65; Chief of Defence Staff, NZ, 1965–71; Ambassador for New Zealand in S Vietnam and Khmer Republic, 1972–74. Chm., Alcoholic Liquor Adv. Council, 1977–83. *Recreation:* fishing. *Address:* 20 Beauchamp Street, Wellington 5, New Zealand. *Club:* Wellington (Wellington). *Died 10 June 1999.*

THOROLD, Captain Sir Anthony (Henry), 15th Bt *cr* 1642, of Marston, Lincolnshire; OBE 1942; DSC 1942, and Bar 1945; JP; Royal Navy, retired; *b* 7 Sept. 1903; *s* of Sir James (Ernest) Thorold, 14th Bt and Katharine Isabel Mary, *e d* of Rev. William Rolfe Tindal-Atkinson; *S* father, 1965; *m* 1939, Jocelyn Elaine Laura (*d* 1993), *er d* of late Sir Clifford Heathcote-Smith, KBE, CMG; one *s* two *d. Educ:* Royal Naval Colleges Osborne and Dartmouth. Entered RN, 1917; qualified as Navigating Officer, 1928; psc 1935; Commander, 1940; served in Mediterranean and Home Fleets, 1939–40; Staff Officer Operations to Flag Officer Commanding Force 'H', 1941–43; in command of Escort Groups in Western Approaches Comd, 1944–45; Captain, 1946; Naval Assistant Secretary in Cabinet Office and Ministry of Defence, 1945–48; Sen. Officer, Fishery Protection

Flotilla, 1949–50; Captain of HMS Dryad (Navigation and Direction Sch.), 1951–52; Commodore in Charge, Hong Kong, 1953–55; ADC to the Queen, 1955–56; retired, 1956. DL Lincs, 1959–95; JP Lincolnshire (Parts of Kesteven), 1961; High Sheriff of Lincolnshire, 1968. CC Kesteven, 1958–74; Leader, Lincs County Council, 1973–81. Chairman: Grantham Hospital Management Cttee, 1963–74; Lincoln Diocesan Trust and Board of Finance, 1966–71; Community Council of Lincs, 1974–81. *Recreation:* shooting. *Heir: s* (Anthony) Oliver Thorold [*b* 15 April 1945; *m* 1977, Genevra M., *y d* of John Richardson, Midlothian; one *s* one *d*]. *Address:* Syston Old Hall, Grantham, Lincs NG32 2BX. *T:* (01400) 250270. *Club:* Army and Navy.
Died 1 May 1999.

THRELFALL, Richard Ian; QC 1965; *b* 14 Jan. 1920; *s* of William Bernhard and Evelyn Alice Threlfall; *m* 1948, Annette, *d* of George C. H. Matthey; two *s* three *d* (and one *s* decd). *Educ:* Oundle; Gonville and Caius Coll., Cambridge. War service, 1940–45 (despatches twice); Indian Armoured Corps (Probyn's Horse) and Staff appointments. Barrister, Lincoln's Inn, 1947, Bencher 1973. FSA 1949. Mem. Court of Assistants, Worshipful Co. of Goldsmiths (Prime Warden, 1978–79). *Address:* Pebble Hill House, Limpsfield, Surrey RH8 0EA. *T:* (01883) 712452. *Died 6 Jan. 1997.*

THUILLIER, Maj.-Gen. Leslie de Malapert, (Pete), CB 1958; CVO 1966; OBE 1944; writer; freelance journalist; *b* 26 Sept. 1905; *s* of late Lt-Col L. C. Thuillier, Indian Army; *m* 1936, Barbara Leonard Rawlins; one *s* two *d. Educ:* Berkhamsted Sch.; Royal Military Academy, Woolwich. Commissioned as 2nd Lieut, Royal Corps of Signals, 1926; Lieut, 1929; Captain, 1937; Temp. Major, 1940; Temp. Lt-Col, 1941; Temp. Colonel, 1945; Colonel, 1949, Brigadier, 1951; Maj.-Gen., 1955. Staff Coll., Camberley, 1939; War Office, 1940–41; Middle East and Italy, 1941–45; Chief Signal Officer, Northern Ireland District, 1945–46; British Troops in Egypt, 1951–53; Northern Command, 1954–55; Director of Telecommunications, War Office, 1955–58; Asst Sec., Cabinet Office, 1958–67. Leader, UK Govtl Mission to USA to discuss experimental civil mil. satellite communications systems, 1960; Mem., UK Delegn to Internat. Conf. in Paris, Rome and London to discuss estabt of internat. communication satellite systems, 1963–65. Consultant, Airwork Services Ltd, 1969–84. *Recreation:* gardening. *Address:* The Red Barn, Patney, Devizes, Wilts SN10 3RA. *T:* (01380) 840669. *Club:* Naval and Military. *Died 21 March 1999.*

TILBERIS, Elizabeth Jane; Editor in Chief, Harper's Bazaar magazine, since 1992; *b* 7 Sept. 1947; *d* of Thomas Stuart-Black Kelly and Janet Storrie Kelly; *m* 1971, Andrew Tilberis; two adopted *s. Educ:* Malvern Girls' Coll.; Jacob Kramer Coll., Leeds; Leicester College of Art (BA Art and Design). Vogue Magazine: Fashion Asst, 1970; Fashion Editor, 1973; Exec. Fashion Editor, 1985; Fashion Dir, 1986; Editor in Chief, 1987–92. Dir, Condé Nast Publications, 1991–. *Publication:* No Time to Die (autobiog.), 1998. *Recreations:* gardening, music. *Address:* The Hearst Corp., 1700 Broadway, New York, NY 10019, USA. *Died 21 April 1999.*

TILLINGHAST, Charles Carpenter, Jr; aviation and financial consultant; *b* 30 Jan. 1911; *s* of Charles Carpenter Tillinghast and Adelaide Barrows Shaw; *m* 1935, Elizabeth Judd, (Lisette), Micoleau; one *s* three *d. Educ:* Horace Mann Sch.; Brown Univ. (PhB); Columbia Univ. (JD). Associate, Hughes, Schurman & Dwight, 1935–37; Dep. Asst Dist Attorney, NY County, 1938–40; Associate, Hughes, Richards, Hubbard & Ewing, 1940–42; Partner, Hughes, Hubbard and Ewing (and successor firm, Hughes, Hubbard, Blair & Reed), 1942–57; Vice-Pres. and Dir,

The Bendix Corp., 1957–61; Pres. and Chief Exec. Officer, Trans World Airlines Inc., 1961–69 (Director, 1961–81; Chm. and Chief Exec. Officer, 1969–76); Vice-Chm., White, Weld & Co. Inc., 1977–78; Man. Dir, Merrill Lynch White Weld Capital Markets Gp, 1978–83; Vice-Pres., Merrill Lynch Pierce Fenner & Smith Inc., 1978–84; Director: Amstar Corp., 1964–83; Merck & Co., 1962–83; Trustee: Mutual Life Ins. Co. of NY, 1966–84; Brown Univ., 1954–61, 1965–79 (Chancellor, 1968–79; Fellow, 1979–); Mem. IATA Executive Cttee, 1969–76. Hon. LHD South Dakota Sch. of Mines and Tech., 1959; Hon. LLD: Franklin Coll., 1963; Univ. of Redlands, 1964; Brown Univ., 1967; Drury Coll., 1967; William Jewell Coll., 1973. *Recreations:* golf, shooting, gardening, woodworking, reading, Philharmonic and opera. *Address:* 355 Blackstone Boulevard, Apt 530, Providence, RI 02906, USA. *T:* (401) 8616676. *Clubs:* Brown Faculty, Wings (NY); Hope (RI); Sakonnet Golf (USA).
Died 25 July 1998.

TILNEY, Dame Guinevere, DBE 1984; Adviser to Rt Hon. Margaret Thatcher, MP, 1975–83; UK Representative on United Nations Commission on Status of Women, 1970–73; *b* 8 Sept. 1916; *y d* of late Sir Hamilton Grant, 12th Bt, KCSI, KCIE, and Lady Grant; *m* 1st, 1944, Captain Lionel Hunter (*d* 1947), Princess Louise Dragoon Guards; one *s*; 2nd, 1954, Sir John Tilney, TD (*d* 1994). *Educ:* Westonbirt. WRNS, 1941–45; Private Sec. to Earl of Selborne, 1949–54; Vice-Chm., SE Lancs Br., British Empire Cancer Campaign, 1957–64; Founder Mem., 1st Chm., 1st Pres., Merseyside Conservative Ladies Luncheon Club, 1957–75, later 1st Hon. Life Mem.; Nat. Council of Women of Great Britain; Vice-Pres., 1958–61, Pres., 1961–68, Liverpool and Birkenhead Br.; Sen. Nat. Vice-Pres., 1966–68; Nat. Pres., 1968–70; Co-Chm., Women's Nat. Commn, 1969–71; Co-Chm., Women Caring Trust, 1972–75. Mem., North Thames Gas Consultative Council, 1967–69; Mem., BBC Gen. Adv. Council, 1967–76. DL: Co. Palatine of Lancaster, 1971–74; Co. Merseyside, 1974–76. *Recreations:* reading, making soup, writing. *Address:* 3 Victoria Square, SW1W 0QZ. *T:* (0171) 828 8674.   *Died 4 April 1997.*

TIMMS, Cecil, DEng, CEng, FIMechE, FIProdE; Engineering Consultant, Department of Trade and Industry, later Department of Industry, retired; *b* 13 Dec. 1911; *m* Mary (decd); *m* Susan; no *c*. *Educ:* Liverpool Univ. Head of Metrology, Mechanisms and Noise Control Div., 1950–61, Supt of Machinery Group, 1961–65, National Engrg Laboratory; Head of Machine Tools Branch, Min. of Technology, later DTI, 1965–73. *Publications:* contribs to Proc. IMechE, Metalworking Prod. and Prod. Engr. *Address:* Broom House, Ballsdown, Chiddingfold, Surrey GU8 4XJ. *T:* (01428) 682014.
Died 5 June 1998.

TIMMS, Ven. George Boorne; Archdeacon of Hackney, 1971–81, then Emeritus; Vicar of St Andrew, Holborn, 1965–81; *b* 4 Oct. 1910; *s* of late George Timms and Annie Elizabeth Timms (*née* Boorne); unmarried. *Educ:* Derby Sch.; St Edmund Hall, Oxford (MA); Coll. of the Resurrection, Mirfield. Deacon, 1935; priest, 1936; Curate: St Mary Magdalen, Coventry, 1935–38; St Bartholomew, Reading, 1938–49; Oxford Diocesan Inspector of Schools, 1944–49; Sacrist of Southwark Cath., 1949–52; Vicar of St Mary, Primrose Hill, NW3, 1952–65; Rural Dean of Hampstead, 1959–65; Prebendary of St Paul's Cathedral, 1964–71. Proctor in Conv., 1955–59, 1965–70, 1974–80; Member: Standing Cttee, Church Assembly, 1968–70; Anglican-Methodist Unity Commn, 1965–69. Dir of Ordination Trng, and Exam. Chap. to Bp of London, 1965–81; Chm., Alcuin Club, 1968–87. Pres., Sion Coll., 1980–81. Papal Medallion for services to Christian Unity, 1976. *Publications:* Dixit Cranmer, 1946; The Liturgical

Seasons, 1965; (contrib.) A Manual for Holy Week, 1967; (ed) English Praise, 1975; (jtly) The Cloud of Witnesses, 1982; (ed) The New English Hymnal, 1985. *Address:* Cleve Lodge, Minster-in-Thanet, Ramsgate, Kent CT12 4BA. *T:* (01843) 821777.   *Died 15 Nov. 1997.*

TINDAL-CARILL-WORSLEY, Air Cdre Geoffrey Nicolas Ernest, CB 1954; CBE 1943; Royal Air Force, retired; *b* 8 June 1908; *s* of late Philip Tindal-Carill-Worsley; *m* 1st, 1937, Berys Elizabeth Gilmour (marr. diss. 1951; she *d* 1962); one *s*; 2nd, 1951, Dorothy Mabel Murray Stanley-Turner (*d* 1995). *Educ:* Eton; RAF Coll., Cranwell. Commanding Officer, RAF Station, Halton, Bucks, 1954–56; Sen. Technical Staff Officer, Far East Air Force, 1956–59; Director of Technical Training, Air Ministry, 1959; retired 1960. *Recreation:* country life.
Died 28 April 1996.

TINDALE, Lawrence Victor Dolman, CBE 1971; CA, Chairman, North British Canadian Investment Trust, 1979–94; *b* 24 April 1921; *s* of late John Stephen and Alice Lilian Tindale; *m* 1946, Beatrice Mabel, (Betty), Barton (*d* 1996); one *s* (one *d* decd). Educ: Latymer Upper Sch., Hammersmith; Inst. of Chartered Accountants of Scotland. Apprenticed McClelland Ker, 1938. Served War, Army, in E Africa and Burma, 1941–45. Returned to McClelland Ker, and qualified, 1946; Partner, 1951; invited to join ICFC Ltd as Asst Gen. Manager, 1959; Dir and Gen. Manager, 1966–72; on secondment, DTI, as Dir of Industrial Development, 1972–74; Dep. Chm., FFI, subseq. Investors in Industry Gp, then 3i Gp, 1974–91. Member: DTI Cttee of Inquiry on Small Firms, 1969–71; Adv. Council on Energy Conservation, 1977 80; British Technology Gp (NRDC, 1974 91; NEB, 1981–91); Chm., EDC for Mechanical Engrg Industry, 1968–72. Director: Commodore Shipping Co. Ltd, 1969–; Guernsey Gas Light Co. Ltd, 1970–91; Investment Trust of Guernsey Ltd, 1970–94; Edbro plc (Chm.), 1974–91; Northern Engineering Industries plc, 1974–89 (Dep. Chm., 1986–89), Flextech (Holdings) Ltd, 1975–93 (Chm., 1984–86); London Atlantic Investment Trust plc (Chm.), 1977–91; Transpec Holdings Ltd, 1980–87; Dewrance MacNeil Ltd, 1980–88; British Caledonian Gp (formerly Caledonian Airways) plc, 1980–88; BNOC, 1980–84; Britoil, 1984–88; Penspen Ltd, 1985–89; Polly Peck (International) plc, 1985–91; Shandwick plc, 1985–92; C. & J. Clark, 1986–91 (Chm., 1986–91); Barnsley Partnership Ltd, 1991–. Mem. Council: Consumers' Assoc., 1970–87 (Vice Chm., 1981–85); BIM, 1974–84 (Chm. 1982–84; Vice-Pres., 1984–); Soc. for Protection of Ancient Buildings (Hon. Treasurer), 1974–; Mem., Management Cttee, Ex-Services Mental Welfare Soc. CIMgt; FRSA 1989. *Recreation:* opera. *Address:* 3 Amyand Park Gardens, Twickenham, TW1 3HS. *T:* (0181) 892 9457. *Clubs:* Reform; St James's (Manchester).   *Died 30 Oct. 1996.*

TINKER, Prof. Hugh Russell; Professor of Politics, University of Lancaster, 1977–82, then Emeritus; *b* 20 July 1921; *s* of late Clement Hugh Tinker and Gertrude Marian Tinker; *m* 1947, Elisabeth McKenzie (*née* Willis); two *s* (and one *s* killed in action). *Educ:* Taunton Sch.; Sidney Sussex Coll., Cambridge (BA Scholar; MA); PhD London. Indian Army, 1941–45; Indian civil admin, 1945–46. Lectr, Reader and Prof., SOAS, 1948–69; Dir, Inst. of Race Relations, 1970–72; Sen. Fellow, Inst. of Commonwealth Studies, Univ. of London, 1972–77. Vis. Prof., Univ. of Rangoon, 1954–55; Prof., Cornell Univ., USA, 1959. Vice-Pres., Ex-Services Campaign for Nuclear Disarmament. Contested (L): Barnet, 1964 and 1966; Morecambe and Lonsdale, 1979. *Publications:* The Foundations of Local Self-Government in India, Pakistan and Burma, 1954; The Union of Burma, a Study of the First Years of Independence, 1957, 4th edn 1967; India and Pakistan, a Political Analysis, 1962; Ballot Box and Bayonet, People and Government in Emergent Asian Countries, 1964; Reorientations, Studies on Asia in Transition, 1965; South Asia, a Short History, 1966; Experiment with Freedom, India and Pakistan 1947, 1967; (ed and wrote introduction) Henry Yule: Narrative of the Mission to the Court of Ava in 1855, 1969; A New System of Slavery: the export of Indian labour overseas 1830–1920, 1974; Separate and Unequal: India and the Indians in the British Commonwealth 1920–1950, 1976; The Banyan Tree: overseas emigrants from India, Pakistan and Bangladesh, 1977, 2nd edn 1996; Race, Conflict and the International Order: from Empire to United Nations, 1977; The Ordeal of Love: C. F. Andrews and India, 1979, 2nd edn 1998; A Message from the Falklands: the life and gallant death of David Tinker, 1982; (ed) Burma: the struggle for independence, vol. I 1944–1946, 1983, vol. II 1946–1948, 1984; Men Who Overturned Empires: fighters, dreamers, schemers, 1987; Viceroy: Curzon to Mountbatten, 1997. *Recreation:* pottering. *Address:* Montbegon, Hornby, near Lancaster LA2 8JZ.

Died 15 April 2000.

TINN, James; *b* 23 Aug. 1922; *s* of James Tinn and Nora (*née* Davie). *Educ:* Consett Elementary School; Ruskin College; Jesus College, Oxford (BA PPE). Cokeworker until 1953; Branch official, Nat. Union of Blastfurnacemen; full-time study for BA; Teacher, secondary modern school, 1958–64. MP (Lab): Cleveland, 1964–74; Redcar, 1974–87. PPS to Sec. of State for the Commonwealth (formerly for Commonwealth Relations), 1965–66, to Minister for Overseas Development, 1966–67; an Asst Govt Whip, 1976–79; an Opposition Whip, 1979–82. Mem. Exec. Cttee, CPA. *Address:* 1 Norfolk Road, Moorside, Consett, Co. Durham DH8 8DD. *T:* (01207) 509313. *Club:* United Oxford & Cambridge University. *Died 18 Nov. 1999.*

TIPPETT, Sir Michael (Kemp), OM 1983; CH 1979; Kt 1966; CBE 1959; composer; *b* 2 Jan. 1905; *s* of Henry William Tippett and Isabel Kemp. *Educ:* Stamford Grammar Sch.; Royal College of Music (Foley Scholar; FRCM 1961). Ran Choral and Dramatic Society, Oxted, Surrey, and taught French at Hazelwood School, till 1931; entered Adult Education work in music (LCC and Royal Arsenal Co-operative Soc. Educn Depts), 1932; Director of Music at Morley College, London, 1940–51. Sent to prison for 3 months as a conscientious objector, June 1943. A Child of Our Time first performed March 1944, broadcast Jan. 1945; 1st Symphony performed Nov. 1945 by Liverpool Philharmonic Society. Artistic Dir, Bath Festival, 1969–74. President: Kent Opera Company, 1979–; London Coll. of Music, 1983–. Hon. Mem., Amer. Acad. of Arts and Letters, 1973; Extraordinary Mem., Akad. der Künste, Berlin, 1976. Honorary degrees include: MusD Cambridge, 1964; DMus: Trinity Coll., Dublin, 1964; Leeds, 1965; Oxford, 1967; London, 1975; Keele, 1986; DUniv York, 1966; DLitt Warwick, 1974. Cobbett Medal for Chamber Music, 1948; Gold Medal, Royal Philharmonic Society, 1976; Prix de Composition Musicale, Fondation Prince Pierre de Monaco, 1984. Commandeur de l'Ordre des Arts et des Lettres (France), 1988. *Works include:* String Quartet No 1, 1935; Piano Sonata, 1937; Concerto for Double String Orchestra, 1939; oratorio, A Child of Our Time, 1941; Fantasia on a Theme of Handel for Piano and Orchestra, 1942; String Quartet, No 2, 1943; Symphony No 1, 1945; String Quartet No 3, 1946; Little Music for Strings, 1946; Suite in D, 1948; song cycle, The Heart's Assurance, 1951; opera, The Midsummer Marriage, 1952 (first performed 1955); Ritual Dances, excerpts from the opera for orchestra, 1953; Fantasia Concertante on a Theme of Corelli for String Orchestra, 1953 (commnd for Edinburgh Festival); Divertimento, 1955; Concerto for Piano and Orchestra,

1956 (commnd by City of Birmingham Symphony Orch.); Symphony No 2, 1957 (commnd by BBC); Crown of the Year (commnd by Badminton School), 1958; opera, King Priam (commnd by Koussevitsky Foundation of America), 1961; Magnificat and Nunc Dimittis (commnd by St John's Coll., Cambridge), 1961; Piano Sonata No 2, 1962; Incidental Music to The Tempest, 1962; Praeludium for Brass, Bells and Percussion, 1962 (commnd by BBC); cantata, The Vision of St Augustine, 1966; The Shires Suite, 1970; opera, The Knot Garden, 1970; Songs for Dov, 1970; Symphony No 3, 1972; Piano Sonata No 3, 1973; opera, The Ice Break, 1977; Symphony No 4, 1977 (commnd by Chicago SO); String Quartet No 4, 1979; Triple Concerto, 1979 (commnd by LSO with Ralph Vaughan Williams Trust); The Mask of Time, 1983 (commnd by Boston SO); The Blue Guitar, 1983 (commnd by Ambassador Internat. Cultural Foundn); Festal Brass with Blues, 1983 (commnd by Hong Kong Fest.); Piano Sonata No 4, 1984 (commnd by LA Philharmonic Assoc.); opera, New Year, 1989 (commnd by Houston Grand Opera, Glyndebourne Fest. Opera and BBC); Byzantium, for soprano solo and orchestra, 1989 (commnd by Chicago Symphony Orch. and Carnegie Hall for their centennials); String Quartet No 5, 1991 (commnd by Lindsay String Quartet); The Rose Lake, 1993 (commnd by LSO, Boston and Toronto SOs); Caliban's Song, 1995 (commnd by BBC). *Publications:* Moving into Aquarius, 1959, rev. edn 1974; Music of the Angels, 1980; Those Twentieth Century Blues (autobiog.), 1991; Tippett on Music, 1995. *Recreation:* walking. *Address:* 5 Thirsk Road, SW11 5SU. *T:* (0171) 228 0465, *Fax:* (0171) 738 2790.

Died 8 Jan. 1998.

TITCHELL, John, RA 1991 (ARA 1986); ARCA; professional painter, since 1951; *b* 6 Aug. 1926; *s* of Arthur Titchell and Elsie Catt; *m* 1947, Audrey Ward; one *s* one *d.* *Educ:* Crayford Elem. Sch.; Sidcup Sch. of Art; Royal Coll. of Art (ARCA 1951). *Recreations:* reading, listening to music. *Address:* Frith Farm, Pluckley, Ashford, Kent TN27 0SY. *Died 11 May 1998.*

TITCHENER, (John) Lanham (Bradbury), CMG 1955; OBE 1947; *b* 28 Nov. 1912; *s* of late Alfred Titchener and Alicia Marion Leonora Bradbury; *m* 1st, 1937, Catherine Law Clark (marr. diss. 1958) (decd); no *c*; 2nd, 1958, Rikke Marian Lehmann (*née* Bendixsen), *e d* of late Frederik Carl Bendixsen and Kammerherreinde Nina Grandjean, Vennerslund, Falster, Denmark; two step *s.* *Educ:* City of London Sch.; Royal College of Music. Nat. Council of Education of Canada, 1934; BBC 1938–43; War of 1939–45: served HM Forces, Jan.-Aug. 1943; Psychological Warfare Branch, Allied Force HQ, Algiers, 1943; 15th Army Group HQ, Italy, 1944–45; Asst Dep. Director, Political Warfare Div., SACSEA, 1945; Political Warfare Adviser to C-in-C, Netherlands East Indies, 1945–46; First Secretary, HM Foreign Service, 1947; served in FO until 1950, when transferred to HM Embassy, Moscow; then at HM Embassy, Ankara, 1953–54; Economic Counsellor, HM Embassy, Tehran, 1954–56, Chargé d'Affaires, 1955; resigned HM Foreign Service, 1957. *Recreations:* music, gardening, fishing. *Address:* 3 Impasse du Château, 06190 Roquebrune Village, France. *T:* 493350785; Weysesgade 13, 2100 Copenhagen, Denmark. *T:* 31200871. *Club:* Travellers'.

Died 26 Aug. 1998.

TITCHENER-BARRETT, Sir Dennis (Charles), Kt 1981; TD 1953, 2 bars; Chairman, Woodstock (London) Ltd (industrial minerals), 1962–89; *m* 1940, Joan Wilson; one *s* three *d.* Served War, RA, 1939–46; commanded 415 Coast Regt RA (TA), 1950–56; Mem., Kent T&AFA, 1950–56. An Underwriting Member of Lloyd's, 1977–. ILEA School Governor, 1956–73; Member: Gtr London Central Valuation Panel, 1964–75; Cons. Bd of Finance,

1968–75; Cons. Policy Gp for Gtr London, 1975–78; National Union of Conservative Associations: Mem., Central Council and Exec. Cttee, 1968–81; Treasurer, 1968–75, Chm., 1975–78, Vice-Pres., 1978–, Gtr London Area; Vice-Pres., Nat. Soc. of Cons. Agents, Gtr London Area, 1975–; Chm., S Kensington Cons. Assoc., 1954–57; Hon. Vice Pres., Kensington and Chelsea Cons. Assoc., 1996– (Trustee, 1975–94; Pres., 1975–89). Mem., RUSI, 1947–. Fellow, Inst. of Dirs, 1952. High Sheriff of Greater London, 1977–78. *Address:* 8 Launceston Place, W8 5RL. *T:* (0171) 937 0613. *Club:* Carlton.

Died 20 Sept. 1996.

TITFORD, Rear-Adm. Donald George, CEng, FRAeS; Deputy Controller of Aircraft, Ministry of Defence, 1976–78, retired; *b* 15 June 1925; *s* of late Percy Maurice Titford and Emily Hannah Titford (*née* McLaren). *Educ:* Highgate Sch.; Royal Naval Engineering Coll.; Coll. of Aeronautics, Cranfield. MSc. Entered RN as Cadet, 1943; Comdr 1959; Air Engr Officer, HMS Victorious, 1965; Captain 1967; comd, RN Air Station, Lee-on-Solent, 1972–74; Comd Engr Officer, Naval Air Comd, 1974–76. *Publication:* Moonrakers in my Family, 1995. *Recreation:* historical research. *Address:* Merry Hill, North Road, Bath BA2 6HD. *T:* (01225) 462132.

Died 16 Sept. 2000.

TOD, Sir John Hunter H.; *see* Hunter-Tod.

TODD, Baron *cr* 1962 (Life Peer), of Trumpington, Co. Cambridge; **Alexander Robertus Todd,** OM 1977; Kt 1954; DSc Glasgow; Dr phil. nat. Frankfurt; DPhil Oxon; MA Cantab; FRS 1942; FRSC; Master of Christ's College, Cambridge, 1963–78 (Fellow, 1944); Professor of Organic Chemistry, University of Cambridge, 1944–71; (first) Chancellor, University of Strathclyde, Glasgow, 1965–91 (Fellow, 1990); *b* Glasgow, 2 Oct. 1907; *e s* of Alexander Todd, JP, Glasgow, and Joan Ramsay, 3rd *d* of Robert Lowrie, Glasgow; *m* 1937, Alison Sarah (*d* 1987), *e d* of Sir Henry H. Dale, OM, GBE, FRS; one *s* two *d*. *Educ:* Allan Glen's Sch.; University of Glasgow. Carnegie Research Scholar, University of Glasgow, 1928–29; Univ. of Frankfurt a. M. 1929–31; 1851 Exhibition Senior Student, Univ. of Oxford, 1931–34; Assistant in Medical Chemistry, 1934–35, and Beit Memorial Research Fellow, 1935–36, University of Edinburgh; Member of Staff, Lister Institute of Preventive Medicine, London, 1936–38; Reader in Biochemistry, University of London, 1937–38; Sir Samuel Hall Professor of Chemistry and Director of Chemical Laboratories, University of Manchester, 1938–44. Visiting Lecturer, California Institute of Technology, USA, 1938; Visiting Professor: University of Chicago, 1948; University of Sydney, 1950; Mass Inst. Tech., 1954; Visitor, Hatfield Polytechnic, 1978–86. Chemical Society, Tilden Lecturer, 1941, Pedler Lecturer, 1946; Meldola Medal, 1936; Leverhulme Lecturer, Society of Chemical Industry, 1948; Bakerian Lectr, Royal Soc., 1954. Dir, Fisons Ltd, 1963–78. President: Chemical Soc., 1960–62; Internat. Union of Pure and Applied Chemistry, 1963–65; BAAS, 1969–70; Royal Soc., 1975–80; Soc. of Chem. Industry, 1981–82. Chairman: Adv. Council on Scientific Policy, 1952–64; Royal Commn on Medical Education, 1965–68; Board of Governors, United Cambridge Hospitals, 1969–74. Member Council, Royal Society, 1967–70; Mem., NRDC, 1968–76. Hon. Member French, German, Spanish, Belgian, Swiss, Japanese Chemical Societies; Foreign Member: Nat. Acad. Sciences, USA; American Acad. of Arts and Sciences; Akad. Naturforscher Halle; American Phil Soc.; Australian, Austrian, Indian, Iranian, Japanese, New York, Russian and Polish Academies of Science. Hon. Fellow: Australian Chem. Institute; Manchester College Technology; Royal Society Edinburgh. Chairman, Managing Trustees, Nuffield Foundation, 1973–79

(Trustee, 1950–79); Pres., Croucher Foundn (Hong Kong), 1988– (Trustee, 1979–; Chm., Trustees, 1980–88); Pres., Parly and Scientific Cttee, 1983–86. Lavoisier Medallist, French Chemical Society, 1948; Davy Medal of Royal Society, 1949; Royal Medal of Royal Society, 1955; Nobel Prize for Chemistry, 1957; Cannizzaro Medal, Italian Chemical Society, 1958; Paul Karrer Medal, Univ. Zürich, 1962; Stas Medal, Belgian Chemical Society, 1962; Longstaff Medal, Chemical Society, 1963; Copley Medal, Royal Society, 1970; Lomonosov Medal, USSR Acad. Sci., 1979; Copernicus Medal, Polish Acad. Sci., 1979; Hanbury Medal, Pharmaceutical Soc., 1986. Hon. FRCP 1975; Hon. FRCPSGlas 1980; Hon. FIMechE 1976. Hon. Fellow: Oriel Coll., Oxford, 1955; Churchill Coll., Cambridge, 1971; Darwin Coll., Cambridge, 1981. Hon. LLD: Glasgow, Melbourne, Edinburgh, Manchester, California, Hokkaido, Chinese Univ. of Hong Kong; Hon. Dr rer nat Kiel; Hon. DSc: London, Madrid, Exeter, Leicester, Aligarh, Sheffield, Wales, Yale, Strasbourg, Harvard, Liverpool, Adelaide, Strathclyde, Oxford, ANU, Paris, Warwick, Durham, Michigan, Cambridge, Widener, Philippines, Tufts, Hong Kong; Hon. DLitt Sydney. Pour le Mérite, German Federal Republic, 1966; Order of Rising Sun (Japan), 1978. Master, Salters' Company, 1961. *Publications:* A Time to Remember (autobiog.), 1983; numerous scientific papers in chemical and biochemical journals. *Recreations:* fishing, golf. *Address:* Christ's College, Cambridge CB2 3BU. *T:* (01223) 334900.

Died 10 Jan. 1997.

TOLSTOY, Dimitry, (Dimitry Tolstoy-Miloslavsky); QC 1959; Barrister-at-Law; *b* 8 Nov. 1912; *s* of late Michael Tolstoy-Miloslavsky and Eileen May Hamshaw; *m* 1st, 1934, Frieda Mary Wicksteed (marr. diss.); one *s* one *d*; 2nd, 1943, Natalie Deytrikh; one *s* one *d*. *Educ:* Wellington; Trinity Coll., Cambridge. President of Cambridge Union, 1935. Called to Bar, Gray's Inn, 1937. Lecturer in Divorce to Inns of Court, 1952–68. *Publications:* Tolstoy on Divorce, 1946–7th edn 1971; The Tolstoys: genealogy and origin, 1991, articles in legal periodicals.

Died 14 March 1997.

TOMLINSON, David Cecil MacAlister; actor; *b* 7 May 1917; *s* of C. S. Tomlinson, solicitor, Folkestone, Kent, and F. E. Tomlinson (*née* Sinclair-Thomson); *m* 1953, Audrey Freeman, actress; four *s*. *Educ:* Tonbridge Sch. Guardsman, Grenadier Guards, 1935–36; served War of 1939–45, Flight Lieut, Pilot, RAF; demobilised, 1946. Chief roles included: Henry, in The Little Hut, Lyric, 1950–53; Clive, in All for Mary, Duke of York's, 1954–55; David, in Dear Delinquent, Westminster and Aldwych, 1957–58; Tom, in The Ring of Truth, Savoy, 1959; Robert, in Boeing Boeing, Apollo, 1962; acted and directed: Mother's Boy (Nero), Globe, 1964; A Friend Indeed, Cambridge, 1966; The Impossible Years, Cambridge, 1966; On the Rocks (Prime Minister), Dublin Festival, 1969; A Friend Indeed, and A Song at Twilight, South Africa, 1973–74; The Turning Point, Duke of York's, 1974. First appeared in films, 1939; thereafter appeared in leading roles in over 50 films, including Three Men in a Boat, 1956. *Publication:* Luckier than Most (autobiog.), 1990. *Recreation:* putting my feet up. *Address:* Brook Cottage, Mursley, Bucks MK17 0RS. *Club:* Boodle's.

Died 24 June 2000.

TOMLINSON, Maj.-Gen. Michael John, CB 1981; OBE 1973 (MBE 1964); Secretary, The Dulverton Trust, 1984–94; Director Royal Artillery, 1981–84, retired; *b* 20 May 1929; *s* of late Sidney Tomlinson and Rose Hodges; *m* 1955, Patricia, *d* of late Lt-Col A. Rowland; one *s* one *d*. *Educ:* Skinners' Sch.; Royal Military Academy. Commissioned, RA, 1949; served in Brunei (despatches, 1962); GSO2 to Dir of Ops Borneo, 1962–64; DAMS, MoD, 1966–68; GSO1, Staff Coll. Camberley, 1968–70;

CO, 2 Field Regt RA, 1970–72; Col GS, Staff Coll. Camberley, 1972–73; CRA 3rd Div., 1973–75; Student, RCDS, 1976; Dep. Mil. Sec. (B), MoD, 1976–78; Dir of Manning, Army, 1978–79; Vice-Adjt Gen., 1979–81. Col Comdt, RA, 1982–91; Hon. Colonel: 2 Field Regt, RA, 1985–89; 104 Regt RA (Volunteers), 1985–87. FIMgt (FBIM 1984); FRSA 1985. *Recreations:* music, gardening. *Address:* c/o Lloyds Bank, 82 Mount Pleasant Road, Tunbridge Wells, Kent TN1 1RP. *Club:* Army and Navy.
Died 14 June 1997.

TOMS, Carl, OBE 1969; first Head of Design, and Associate Director, for the Young Vic at the National Theatre, since 1970; *b* 29 May 1927. *Educ:* High Oakham Sch., Mansfield, Nottingham; Mansfield College of Art; Royal Coll. of Art (Sen. Fellow, 1998); Old Vic Sch. Designing for theatre, films, opera, ballet, etc, on the London stage, 1957–; also for productions at Glyndebourne, Edinburgh Festival, Chichester Festival, and Aldeburgh (world première of Midsummer Night's Dream, 1960). *Theatre designs included:* Vivat! Vivat Regina!, Chichester and London, 1970, NY 1972; Sherlock Holmes, London, 1974, NY 1974 (Tony Award and Drama Desk Award for Theatre Design); Travesties, London, 1974, NY 1975, Vienna Burgtheater, 1976; Long Day's Journey into Night, LA 1977; Man and Superman, Malvern Festival and London, 1977; The Devil's Disciple, LA 1977, NY 1978; Look After Lulu, Chichester, 1978, Haymarket, 1978; Night and Day, Phoenix, 1978, NY, 1979; Stage Struck, Vaudeville, 1979; Windy City, Victoria Palace, 1982; The Real Thing, Strand, 1982; The Winslow Boy, Lyric, 1983; A Patriot for Me, Chichester and Haymarket, 1983, LA, 1984 (Hollywood Dramalogue Critics Award); The Hothouse, Vienna Burgtheater, 1983; Jeeves Takes Charge, NY, 1983; Hay Fever, Queen's, 1983; The Aspern Papers, 1984; Jumpers, Aldwych, 1985; The Dragon's Tail, Apollo, 1985; Blithe Spirit, Vaudeville, 1986; Wildfire, Phoenix, 1986; The Importance of Being Earnest, Royalty, 1987; Hapgood, Aldwych, 1988; The Browning Version, Royalty, 1988; Artist Descending a Staircase, Duke of York's, 1988; Richard II, Phoenix, 1988; Richard III, Phoenix, 1989; Hapgood, LA, 1989; Noël and Gertie, Comedy, 1989; Thark, Lyric, Hammersmith, 1989; Look Look!, Aldwych, 1990; The Silver King, Chichester, 1990; Private Lives, Aldwych, 1990; Painting Churches, Playhouse, 1991; Preserving Mr Panure, Chichester, 1991; It's Ralph, Comedy, 1991; Straight and Narrow, Wyndhams, 1992; An Ideal Husband, Globe, 1992; Separate Tables, Albery, 1993; She Stoops to Conquer, Queen's, 1993; Three Tall Women, Wyndham's, 1994; Indian Ink, Aldwych, 1995; A Delicate Balance, Haymarket, 1997; *for Royal Opera House, Covent Garden,* included: Gala perf. for State Visit of King and Queen of Nepal, 1960; Iphigénie en Tauride, 1961; Ballet Imperial, 1963; Swan Lake, 1963; Die Frau ohne Schatten (costumes), 1967; Fanfare for Europe, 1973; Queen's Silver Jubilee Gala, 1977; Fanfare for Elizabeth, 1986; *for London Festival Ballet:* Swan Lake, 1982; *for Sadler's Wells:* Cenerentola, 1959; The Barber of Seville, 1960; Our Man in Havana, 1963; *for English National Ballet:* Swan Lake, 1995; *for National Theatre:* Edward II, Love's Labour's Lost, 1968; Cyrano de Bergerac, 1970; For Services Rendered, 1979; Playbill, The Provok'd Wife, 1980 (SWET Designer of the Year award); The Second Mrs Tanqueray, On the Razzle, 1981; Rough Crossing, 1984; Brighton Beach Memoirs, Dalliance, The Magistrate, 1986; Six Characters in Search of an Author, Fathers and Sons, The Ting Tang Mine, 1987; *for RSC:* The Happiest Days of Your Life, 1984; The Man Who Came to Dinner, 1989; The Strange Case of Dr Jekyll and Mr Hyde, 1991; *for Vienna Nat. Theatre:* Travesties, 1977; She Stoops to Conquer, 1978; Betrayal, 1978; The Guardsman, 1979; Night and Day, 1980; *for Vienna State*

Opera: Macbeth, 1982; Faust, 1985; *for NY City Opera:* Die Meistersinger von Nürnberg, 1975; The Marriage of Figaro, 1977; The Voice of Ariadne, 1977; Der Freischutz, 1981; Rigoletto, 1988; *for NY Metropolitan Opera:* Thais, 1978; *for San Diego Opera Co.:* Norma, 1976; La Traviata, 1976; The Merry Widow, 1977; Hamlet, 1978; Romeo and Juliet, 1982; *for San Francisco Opera:* Peter Grimes, 1973; Thais, 1976; other productions included: The Italian Girl in Algiers (costumes), Geneva, 1984; Lucia di Lammermoor (costumes), Cologne Opera, 1985; Oberon, Edinburgh Fest. and Frankfurt, 1986; The Importance of Being Earnest, Royal Th., Copenhagen, 1987; Making it Better, Josephstadt Th., Vienna, 1991; Arcadia, Zurich, 1993; also designed for Old Vic, Young Vic, Welsh Nat. Opera, NY State Opera. Completed re-designing of: Theatre Royal, Windsor, 1965; Theatre Royal, Bath, 1982; Richmond Theatre, 1991; design consultant for Investiture of Prince of Wales, Caernarvon Castle, 1969. Designed sets and costumes for numerous films; work included decoration of restaurants, hotels, houses, etc; also designed exhibns, programmes, cards, etc. FRSA 1987. *Publications:* Winter's Tale (designs for stage prodn), 1975; Scapino (designs for stage prodn), 1975. *Recreations:* gardening, travel. *Address:* Old Manor Farmhouse, Didmarton, Badminton, Glos GL9 1DT.
Died 4 Aug. 1999.

TONKIN, Hon. David Oliver, AO 1993; FRACO; Secretary-General, Commonwealth Parliamentary Association, 1986–92; *b* 20 July 1929; *s* of Oliver Athelstone Prisk Tonkin and Bertha Ida Louise (*née* Kennett); *m* 1954, Prudence Anne Juttner; three *s* three *d*. *Educ:* St Peter's Coll., Adelaide; Univ. of Adelaide (MB, BS 1953); Inst. of Ophthalmology, London (DO 1958). FRACO 1974. In private ophthalmic practice, 1958–70. Vis. staff, Royal Adelaide Hosp., 1958–68. Mem., Social Adv. Council, SA Govt, 1968–70; MLA (L) for Bragg, SA, 1970–83; Leader, Liberal Party of SA, 1975–82; Leader of the Opposition, 1975–79; Premier, Treasurer, Minister of State Development and of Ethnic Affairs, SA, 1979–82. Chm., Patient Care Review Cttee, Adelaide Children's Hosp., 1984–86. Chairman: State Opera of SA, 1985; SA Film Corp., 1994–99. Hon. Consul of Belgium for SA and NT, 1984–85. Governor: Commonwealth Trust, 1990–94; Royal Commonwealth Soc. for the Blind, 1990–94; Trustee, Vision Aid Overseas, 1990–93. Governor, Queen Elizabeth House, Oxford, 1986–94. Freeman, City of London, 1981; Liveryman, Spectacle Makers' Co., 1992. *Publications:* Sex Discrimination Bill, 1973; Patient Care Review: quality assurance in health care, 1985. *Recreations:* the family, music, film, theatre. *Address:* 5A Glenferrie Avenue, Myrtle Bank, SA 5064, Australia. *T:* (8) 83790419, *Fax:* (8) 83795001. *Club:* Adelaide.
Died 2 Oct. 2000.

TONYPANDY, 1st Viscount *cr* 1983, of Rhondda in the County of Mid Glamorgan; **Thomas George Thomas;** PC 1968; *b* 29 Jan. 1909; *s* of Zacharia and Emma Jane Thomas. *Educ:* University Coll., Southampton. Schoolmaster. MP (Lab): Cardiff Central, 1945–50; Cardiff West, 1950–83; Speaker of the House of Commons, 1976–83; PPS to Minister of Civil Aviation, 1951; Mem., Chairman's Panel, H of C, 1951–64; Jt Parly Under-Sec. of State, Home Office, 1964–66; Minister of State: Welsh Office, 1966–67; Commonwealth Office, 1967–68; Secretary of State for Wales, 1968–70; Dep. Speaker and Chm. of Ways and Means, House of Commons, 1974–76. First Chm., Welsh Parly Grand Cttee, 1951; Chairman: Welsh PLP, 1950–51; Jt Commonwealth Societies' Council, 1984–87. Chm., Bank of Wales, 1985–91. Vice-Pres., Methodist Conf., 1960–61; President: Nat. Brotherhood Movement, 1955; Luton Methodist Industrial Coll., 1982; College of Preceptors, 1984–87; National Children's Home, 1990–95 (Chm.,

1983–89), A Vice Pres., Cancer Relief Macmillan Fund, 1994–. Life Governor, ICRF, 1994. Hon. Mem., Ct of Assts, Blacksmiths' Co., 1980. Freeman: Borough of Rhondda, 1970; City of Cardiff, 1975; City of London, 1980; Hon. Freeman: Paphos, Cyprus, 1989; Port Talbot, 1990. Hon. Master Bencher, Gray's Inn, 1982; Hon. Fellow: UC Cardiff, 1972; College of Preceptors, 1977; Polytechnic of Wales, 1982; St Hugh's Coll., Oxford, 1983; Hertford Coll., Oxford, 1983; Faculty of Bldg, 1983; Westminster Coll., Oxford, 1990; Trinity Coll., Carmarthen, 1994; Hon. Companion, Leicester Polytechnic, 1989. Hon. DCL Oxford, 1983; Hon. LLD: Asbury Coll., Kentucky, 1976; Southampton, 1977; Wales, 1977; Birmingham, 1978; Oklahoma, 1981; Liverpool, 1982; Leeds, 1983; Keele, 1984; Warwick, 1984; DUniv Open, 1984; Hon. DD Centenary Univ., Louisiana, 1982. William Hopkins Bronze Medal, St David's Soc., New York, 1982; Rhondda Rotary Paul Harris Award, 1992. Dato Setia Negara, Brunei, 1971; Grand Cross of the Peruvian Congress, 1982; Gold Medal for Democratic Services, State of Carinthia, Austria, 1982; Silver Medal of St Paul and St Barnabas, Cyprus, 1989. *Publications:* The Christian Heritage in Politics, 1960; George Thomas, Mr Speaker, 1985; My Wales, 1986. *Heir:* none. *Address:* House of Lords, SW1A 0AA. *Clubs:* Travellers', Reform, English-Speaking Union, United Oxford & Cambridge University; County (Cardiff).

Died 22 Sept. 1997 (ext).

TOOTH, Geoffrey Cuthbert, MD; MRCP; Visiting Scientist, National Institute of Mental Health, USA, 1968–71; *b* 1 Sept. 1908; *s* of late Howard Henry Tooth, CB, CMG, MD, FRCP, and Helen Katherine Tooth, OBE (*née* Chilver), *m* 1st, 1934, Princess Olga Galitzine (*d* 1955), *d* of Prince Alexander Galitzine, MD; 2nd, 1958, HSH Princess Xenia of Russia, *d* of Prince Andrew of Russia. *Educ:* Rugby Sch.; St John's Coll., Cambridge; St Bartholomew's Hosp., Johns Hopkins Hosp., Baltimore, Md, USA. MRCS, LRCP 1934; MA Cantab 1935; MD Cantab 1946, DPM 1944; MRCP 1965. Asst Psychiatrist, Maudsley Hosp., 1937–39; Surg. Lt-Comdr, RNVR, Neuropsychiatric Specialist, 1939–45; Colonial Social Science Research Fellow, 1946–53; Comr, Bd of Control, 1954–60; transf. to Min. of Health, and retd as Sen. PMO, Head of Mental Health Section, Med. Div., 1968. Mem. Expert Advisory Panel (Mental Health), WHO. *Publications:* Studies in Mental Illness in the Gold Coast, 1950; various reports to learned societies; articles and papers in med. jls. *Recreations:* sailing, gardening, metal work, photography. *Address:* Grand Prouillac, Plazac, 24580 Rouffignac, France.				*Died 18 Feb. 1998.*

TORNARITIS, Criton George; QC (Cyprus); Attorney-General of the Republic of Cyprus, 1960–84 (Attorney-General, Cyprus, 1952); Special Legal Adviser of the President of the Republic of Cyprus; *b* 27 May 1902; *m* 1934, Mary (*née* Pitta) (*d* 1973); one *s. Educ:* Gymnasium of Limassol; Athens University (LLB Hons); Gray's Inn. Advocate of the Supreme Court of Cyprus, 1924; District Judge, Cyprus, 1940; President, District Court, Cyprus, 1942; Solicitor-General of Cyprus, 1944; Attorney-General, Cyprus, 1952. Attached to Legal Div. of the Colonial Office, 1955; seconded as Commissioner for Consolidation of the Cyprus Legislation, 1956; Legal Adviser to Greek-Cypriot Delegation on the Mixed Constitutional Commission, 1959; Greek-Cypriot delegate to Ankara for initialling of Constitution of Republic of Cyprus, 1960. Prize of Academy of Athens, 1984. *Publications:* The Laws of Cyprus, rev. edn 1959; The Individual as a Subject of International Law, 1972; The Turkish Invasion of Cyprus and legal problems arising therefrom, 1975; The European Convention of Human Rights in the Legal Order of the Republic of Cyprus, 1975; The Ecclesiastical Courts especially in Cyprus, 1976; Cyprus and its

Constitutional and other Legal Problems, 1977, 2nd edn 1980; Federalism and Regionalism in the Contemporary World, 1979; The State Law of the Republic of Cyprus, 1982; Constitutional Review of the Laws in the Republic of Cyprus, 1983; The Legal System in the Republic of Cyprus, 1984; The Legal Position of the Church in the Republic of Cyprus, 1989; contributions to legal journals and periodicals. *Recreations:* walking, reading. *Address:* 11 Penelope Delta Street, Nicosia, Cyprus. *T:* (2) 376252.				*Died 1 March 1997.*

TORNEY, Thomas William; JP; *b* London, 2 July 1915; *m* (wife decd); one *d*; *m* 2nd, 1987. *Educ:* elementary school. Joined Labour Party, 1930; Election Agent: Wembley North, 1945; Derbyshire West, 1964. Derby and Dist Area Organizer, USDAW, 1946–70. Member: North Midland Regional Joint Apprenticeship Council for catering industry, 1946–68 (Past Chm.); Local Appeals Tribunal, Min. of Social Security, 1946–68. MP (Lab) Bradford South, 1970–87. Member: Parly Select Cttee on Race Relations and Immigration, 1970–79; Parly Select Cttee on Agriculture, 1979–87; Chm., PLP Gp on Agriculture, Fish and Food, 1981–87. Especially interested in education, social security, industrial relations, agriculture and food. JP Derby, 1969. Chevalier, Commanderie of GB, Confrérie des Chevaliers du Sacavan d'Anjou, 1976.				*Died 21 Oct. 1998.*

TOUT, Herbert, CMG 1946; MA; Reader in Political Economy, University College, London, 1947–68, retired; *b* Manchester, 20 April 1904; *e s* of Professor T. F. Tout, Manchester University, and Mary Johnstone; unmarried. *Educ:* Sherborne School; Hertford College, Oxford. Instructor in Economics, University of Minnesota, USA, 1929–35; Assistant Lecturer, University College, London, 1936; Colston Research Fellow and Director of University of Bristol Social Survey, 1936–38; Lecturer, University of Bristol, 1938–47; Temp. Principal, Board of Trade, 1940–41, Assistant Secretary, 1941–45. *Recreation:* reading. *Address:* Brooklands Nursing Home, Wych Cross, East Sussex RH18 5JN. *T:* (01825) 712005.				*Died 21 Jan. 1997.*

TOVELL, Laurence, FCA; Chief Inspector of Audit, Department of the Environment, 1977–79; *b* 6 March 1919; *s* of William Henry Tovell and Margaret Tovell (*née* Mahoney); *m* 1945, Iris Joan (*née* Lee); two *s* one *d. Educ:* Devonport High School. Entered Civil Service as Audit Assistant, District Audit Service, 1938; District Auditor, No 4 Audit District, Birmingham, 1962. Served War, 1940–46; Lieut RNVR, 1942–46. *Recreation:* do-it-yourself. *Address:* White Lions, Links Road, Bramley, Guildford, Surrey GU5 0AL. *T:* (01483) 892702.				*Died 31 Aug. 1998.*

TOWNSEND, Rear-Adm. Sir Leslie (William), KCVO 1981; CBE 1973; Member: Lord Chancellor's Panel of Independent Inspectors, 1982–94; Lord Chancellor's Services Pensions Appeals Tribunal, 1985–96; *b* 22 Feb. 1924; *s* of Seaman Gunner William Bligh Townsend and Ellen (*née* Alford); *m* 1947, Marjorie Bennett; one *s* three *d. Educ:* Regent's Park School, Southampton. Joined RN, 1942; served in HMS Durban, 1942–43; commissioned, 1943; HM Ships Spurwing, Astraea, Liverpool, Duke of York, Ceres, 1944–53; HMS Ceylon, 1956–58; Secretary to ACNS, 1959, to VCNS, 1967, to First Sea Lord, 1970; MA to CDS, 1971–73, to Chm. NATO Mil. Cttee, 1974; Dir, Naval and WRNS Officers' Appointments, 1977; Rear-Adm. 1979; Defence Services Sec., 1979–82. Life Vice Pres., RN Benevolent Soc. *Recreations:* fishing, cooking. *Address:* 8 King Charles Street, Old Portsmouth, Hants PO1 2BS. *T:* (01705) 844508. *Clubs:* Army and Navy; Royal Naval and Royal Albert Yacht.

Died 13 Jan. 1999.

TOWNSING, Sir Kenneth (Joseph), Kt 1982; CMG 1971; ISO 1966; Director: Western Mining Corporation Ltd, 1975–87; Central Norseman Gold Corporation, 1982–87; *b* 25 July 1914; *s* of J. W. and L. A. Townsing; *m* 1942, Frances Olive Daniel; two *s* one *d. Educ:* Perth Boys' Sch.; Univ. of Western Australia. Served War, AIF (Middle East), 1940–46, Major. Treasury Officer, 1933–39; Public Service Inspector, 1946–49; Sec., Public Service Commissioner's Office, 1949–52; Dep. Under Treasurer, 1952–57; Public Service Comr, 1958–59; Under Treasurer (Permanent Head), 1959–75. Chm., Salaries and Allowances Tribunal, 1975–84. Mem. Senate, Univ. of Western Australia, 1954–70 (Chm. Finance Cttee, 1956–70; Pro-Chancellor, 1968–70); Comr, Rural and Industries Bank, 1959–65; Member: Jackson Cttee on Tertiary Educn, 1967; Tertiary Educn Commn, 1971–74; Past Mem. numerous other Bds and Cttees. Fellow, W Australian Museum, 1975; Hon. Zoo Associate, 1979. FCPA. Hon. LLD Univ. of W Australia, 1971; DUniv Murdoch, 1982. *Recreation:* gardening. *Address:* 22 Robin Street, Mount Lawley, WA 6050, Australia. *T:* (8) 92721393. *Club:* University House (Perth).
Died 24 Aug. 1997.

TRANTER, Nigel Godwin, OBE 1983; novelist and author since 1936; *b* Glasgow, 23 Nov. 1909; *yr s* of Gilbert T. Tranter and Eleanor A. Cass; *m* 1933, May Jean Campbell Grieve (*d* 1979); one *d* (one *s* decd). *Educ:* St James Episcopal Sch., Edinburgh; George Heriot's Sch., Edinburgh. Served War of 1939–45, RASC and RA. Accountancy trng, then in small family insce co., until could live on writing, after war service; much and actively interested in Scottish public affairs. Chm., Scottish Convention, Edinburgh Br., 1948–51; Vice-Convener, Scottish Covenant Assoc., 1951–55; Pres., E Lothian Liberal Assoc., 1960–76; Chm., Nat. Forth Road Bridge Cttee, 1953–57; Pres., Scottish PEN, 1962–66, Hon. Pres., 1973–; Chm., Soc. of Authors, Scotland, 1966–72; Pres., E Lothian Wildfowlers' Assoc., 1952–73; Chm., St Andrew Soc. of E Lothian, 1966–; Chm., Nat. Book League, Scotland, 1972–77; Hon. Vice-Pres., Scottish Assoc. of Teachers of History, 1989; Hon. Pres., Saltire Soc., 1991; Mem., Cttee of Aberlady Bay Nature Reserve, 1953–76, etc. Hon. Member: Mark Twain Soc. of Amer., 1976; Scottish Soc. of Memphis, Tennessee, 1995; Marquis of Montrose Soc., 1996; Scottish Liby Assoc., 1997; Clan Scott Soc., 1997. Hon. Freeman, Blackstone, Va, 1980. Hon. MA Edinburgh, 1971; Hon. DLitt Strathclyde, 1990. Scot of the Year, BBC Radio Scotland, 1989. Chevalier, Order of St Lazarus of Jerusalem, 1961 (Vice-Chancellor of the Order, Scotland, 1980, Chancellor, 1986). *Publications: fiction:* 87 novels, from Trespass, 1937, including: Bridal Path, 1952; Macgregor's Gathering, 1957; the Master of Gray trilogy: The Master of Gray, 1961, The Courtesan, 1963, Past Master, 1965; Chain of Destiny, 1964; the Robert the Bruce trilogy: The Steps to the Empty Throne, 1969, The Path of the Hero King, 1970, The Price of the King's Peace, 1971; The Young Montrose, 1972; Montrose: the Captain General, 1973; The Wisest Fool, 1974; The Wallace, 1975; the Stewart trilogy: Lords of Misrule, 1976, A Folly of Princes, 1977, The Captive Crown, 1977; Macbeth the King, 1978; Margaret the Queen, 1979; David the Prince, 1980; True Thomas, 1981; The Patriot, 1982; Lord of the Isles, 1983; Unicorn Rampant, 1984; the James V trilogy: The Riven Realm, 1984, James, By the Grace of God, 1985, Rough Wooing, 1986; Columba, 1987; Cache Down, 1987; Flowers of Chivalry, 1988; Mail Royal, 1989; Warden of the Queen's March, 1989; Kenneth, 1990; Crusader, 1991; Children of the Mist, 1992; Druid Sacrifice, 1993; Tapestry of the Boar, 1993; Price of a Princess, 1994; Lord in Waiting, 1994; Highness in Hiding, 1995; Honours Even, 1995; A Rage of Regents, 1996; Poetic Justice, 1996; The

Marchman, 1997; The Lion's Whelp, 1997; High Kings and Vikings, 1998; Sword of State, 1999; Envoy Extraordinary, 1999; 12 children's novels; *non-fiction:* The Fortalices and Early Mansions of Southern Scotland, 1935; The Fortified House in Scotland (5 vols), 1962–71; Pegasus Book of Scotland, 1964; Outlaw of the Highlands: Rob Roy, 1965; Land of the Scots, 1968; Portrait of the Border Country, 1972; Portrait of the Lothians, 1979; The Queen's Scotland Series: The Heartland: Clackmannan, Perth and Stirlingshire, 1971; The Eastern Counties: Aberdeen, Angus and Kincardineshire, 1972; The North East: Banff, Moray, Nairn, East Inverness and Easter Ross, 1974; Argyll and Bute, 1977; Nigel Tranter's Scotland, 1981; Scottish Castles: tales and traditions, 1982, rev. edn 1993; Scotland of Robert the Bruce, 1986; The Story of Scotland, 1987; Footbridge to Enchantment, 1992; contribs to many jls, on Scots history, topography, castellated architecture, etc; *posthumous publication:* Courting Favour (novel), 2000. *Recreations:* walking, historical research, helping to restore Scottish castles. *Address:* 2 Goose Green Mews, Gullane, East Lothian EH31 2BN. *T:* (01620) 842026. *Club:* PEN.
Died 9 Jan. 2000.

TRAPNELL, John Arthur; Under-Secretary, Departments of Trade and Industry, 1973–77; *b* 7 Sept. 1913; *s* of Arthur Westicote Trapnell and Helen Trapnell (*née* Alles); *m* 1939, Winifred Chadwick Rushton; two *d. Educ:* privately; Law Soc.'s Sch. of Law. Admitted Solicitor 1938; private practice until 1940; served HM Army, 1940–46: commnd Som LI, 1943; served with 82nd W African Div. (Major); Civil Service, 1946; Board of Trade, Solicitors Dept. Mem. Law Soc. *Recreations:* golf, bridge. *Address:* 29 Connaught Road, New Malden, Surrey KT3 3PZ. *T:* (0181) 942 3183. *Died 30 Jan. 1997.*

TRAVERS, Basil Holmes, AM 1983; OBE 1943; MA; BLitt; FACE; FRSA; FAIM; Headmaster of Sydney Church of England Grammar School, North Sydney, NSW, 1959–84; *b* 7 July 1919; *s* of Col R. J. A. Travers, DSO and Dorothy Mabel Travers, *d* of Maj.-Gen. William Holmes, CMG, DSO; *m* 1942, Margaret Emily Marr; three *d. Educ:* Sydney Church of England Grammar Sch.; Sydney Univ. (BA); New Coll., Oxford (MA, BLitt). Rhodes Scholar for NSW, 1940. Served War of 1939–45 (despatches, OBE); AIF, 2/2 Australian Infantry Battalion; ADC to Maj.-Gen. Sir I. G. Mackay, 1940; Brigade Major, 15 Aust. Inf. Bde, 1943–44; psc 1944; GSO 2, HQ, 2 Aust. Corps, 1944–45. Assistant Master, Wellington Coll., Berks, England, 1948–49; Assistant Master, Cranbrook Sch., Sydney, 1950–52; Headmaster, Launceston Church Grammar Sch., Launceston, Tasmania, 1953–58. Chm., Headmasters' Conf. of Australia, 1971–73. Member: Soldiers' Children Education Board, 1959–97; NSW Cttee, Duke of Edinburgh's Award Scheme in Australia, 1959–88 (Chm., 1979–84). Lt-Col commanding 12 Inf. Bn (CMF), 1955–58; Col Comdt, Royal Australian Army Educn Corps, 1984–88. *Publications:* Let's Talk Rugger, 1949; The Captain General, 1952. *Recreations:* cricket (Oxford Blue, 1946, 1948), swimming, rugby (Oxford Blue, 1946, 1947), athletics (Half Blue, 1947); also Sydney Blue, football, cricket; Rugby Union International for England, 1947, 1948, 1949; represented NSW, 1950. *Address:* 19 Edward Street, Gordon, NSW 2072, Australia. *T:* (2) 94984661. *Club:* Rugby Union (Sydney).
Died 18 Dec. 1998.

TRAVERS, Sir Thomas (à Beckett), Kt 1972; Consulting Ophthalmologist, Royal Melbourne Hospital, 1962–63 (Hon. Ophthalmologist, 1946–62); *b* 16 Aug. 1902; *s* of late Walter Travers, Warragul, Vic and Isabelle Travers; *m* 1949, Mercy, (Tone), *d* of H. Smith and *widow* of R. S. Burnard; no *c. Educ:* Melbourne Grammar School. MB, BS 1925, DSc 1941, Melbourne; MRCP 1928; DOMS

London 1928; FRACS. Asst Ophthalmologist, Alfred Hosp., 1930–39; Consultant, RAAF, 1939–45. *Publications:* various on strabismus. *Recreation:* gardening. *Address:* 6 Barrup Street, Carlton, Vic 3053, Australia. *T:* (3) 93476286. *Club:* Melbourne (Melbourne). *Died 16 March 1999.*

TREASE, (Robert) Geoffrey, FRSL; *b* 11 Aug. 1909; *s* of George Albert Trease and Florence (*née* Dale); *m* 1933, Marian Haselden Granger Boyer (*d* 1989); one *d. Educ:* Nottingham High Sch.; Queen's Coll., Oxford (schol.). Chm., 1972–73, Mem. Council, 1974–, Society of Authors. FRSL 1979. *Publications:* Walking in England, 1935; Such Divinity, 1939; Only Natural, 1940; Tales Out of School, 1949; Snared Nightingale, 1957; So Wild the Heart, 1959; The Italian Story, 1963; The Grand Tour, 1967; (ed) Matthew Todd's Journal, 1968; Nottingham, a biography, 1970; The Condottieri, 1970; A Whiff of Burnt Boats, an early autobiography, 1971; Samuel Pepys and his World, 1972; Laughter at the Door, a continued autobiography, 1974; London, a concise history, 1975; Portrait of a Cavalier: William Cavendish, first Duke of Newcastle, 1979; *for young readers:* Bows Against the Barons, 1934; Cue for Treason, 1940; Trumpets in the West, 1947; The Hills of Varna, 1948; No Boats on Bannermere, 1949; The Seven Queens of England, 1953; This Is Your Century, 1965; The Red Towers of Granada, 1966; Byron, a Poet Dangerous to Know, 1969; A Masque for the Queen, 1970; Horsemen on the Hills, 1971; D. H. Lawrence: the Phoenix and the Flame, 1973; Popinjay Stairs, 1973; Days to Remember, 1973; The Iron Tsar, 1975; The Chocolate Boy, 1975; When the Drums Beat, 1976; Violet for Bonaparte, 1976; The Field of the Forty Footsteps, 1977; Mandeville, 1980; A Wood by Moonlight and Other Stories, 1981; Saraband for Shadows, 1982; The Cormorant Venture, 1984; The Edwardian Era, 1986; Tomorrow is a Stranger, 1987; The Arpino Assignment, 1988; A Flight of Angels, 1988; Shadow Under the Sea, 1990; Calabrian Quest, 1990; Aunt Augusta's Elephant, 1991; Song for a Tattered Flag, 1992; Fire on the Wind, 1993; Bring Out the Banners, 1994; No Horn at Midnight, 1994; Curse on the Sea, 1996; Danger in the Wings, 1997; Cloak for a Spy, 1997, and many others; *plays:* After the Tempest, 1938 (Welwyn Fest. award); Colony, 1939. *Recreations:* walking, the theatre. *Died 27 Jan. 1998.*

TRESIDDER, Gerald Charles, FRCS; Lecturer, Department of Anatomy, University of Leicester, 1980–91, retired; *b* Rawalpindi, 5 Dec. 1912; *s* of late Lt-Col A. G. Tresidder, CIE, MD, MS, FRCS and Lilian Annie, *d* of Thomas Henry Trelease, JP, Falmouth; *m* 1940, Marguerite Bell; one *s* two *d. Educ:* Haileybury; Queen Mary College and The London Hospital Medical College, Univ. of London. LRCP, MRCS 1937; MB, BS London 1938; FRCS 1946. Surgical Specialist, Major, Indian Medical Service, 1940–46. Surgeon, 1951–64, Urologist, 1964–76, at The London Hospital; Lectr in Surgery and part-time Sen. Lectr in Anatomy, The London Hosp. Med. Coll., 1951–76; Senior Lectr, Human Morphology, Univ. of Southampton, 1976–80. Past Pres., Section of Urology, RSocMed; Senior Mem., British Assoc. of Urological Surgeons; Sen. Fellow, British Assoc. of Clinical Anatomists; formerly Examr in Anatomy for Primary FRCS and FRCSE. *Publications:* contributions to: Rob and Smith's Operative Surgery; Smith and Aitkenhead's Textbook of Anaesthesia, 1985; British Jl of Surgery; British Jl of Urology; Lancet; BMJ. *Recreations:* walking, talking. *Address:* Woodspring, 4 Penny Long Lane, Derby DE22 1AW. *T:* Derby (01332) 558026. *Died 3 May 1996.*

TREVELYAN, Sir George (Lowthian), 4th Bt *cr* 1874, of Wallington, Northumberland; Hon. President, Wrekin Trust (Founder, 1971; Director, 1971–86); *b* 5 Nov. 1906; *e s* of Rt Hon. Sir Charles Philips Trevelyan, 3rd Bt and Mary Katharine, *y d* of Sir Hugh Bell, 2nd Bt; *S* father, 1958; *m* 1940, Editha Helen (*d* 1994), *d* of Col John Lindsay-Smith; one adopted *d. Educ:* Sidcot School; Trinity College, Cambridge (MA). Worked as artist-craftsman with Peter Waals workshops, fine furniture, 1929–31; trained and worked in F. M. Alexander re-education method, 1932–36; taught at Gordonstoun School and Abinger Hill School, 1936–41. Served War, 1941–45, Captain, Home Guard Training; taught No 1 Army Coll., Newbattle Abbey, 1945–47. Principal, Shropshire Adult College, Attingham Park, Shrewsbury, 1947–71; mounted and ran Wrekin Trust courses, 1971–86; latterly, lecture tours on holistic themes. *Publications:* A Vision of the Aquarian Age, 1977; The Active Eye in Architecture, 1977; Magic Casements, 1980; Operation Redemption, 1981; Summons to a High Crusade, 1986; Exploration into God, 1991. *Heir: b* Geoffrey Washington Trevelyan [*b* 4 July 1920; *m* 1947, Gillian Isabel, *d* of late Alexander Wood; one *s* one *d*]. *Address:* The Barn, Hawkesbury, near Badminton, Avon GL9 1BW. *T:* Chipping Sodbury (01454) 238359. *Died 7 Feb. 1996.*

TREVELYAN, Sir Norman Irving, 10th Bt *cr* 1662, of Nettlecombe, Somerset; *b* 29 Jan. 1915; *s* of Edward Walter Trevelyan (*d* 1947), and of Kathleen E. H., *d* of William Irving; *S* kinsman, Sir Willoughby John Trevelyan, 9th Bt, 1976; *m* 1951, Jennifer Mary, *d* of Arthur E. Riddett, Burgh Heath, Surrey; two *s* one *d. Educ:* The Cate School, Carpinteria, California (grad. 1932); Harvard Univ., Cambridge, Mass (grad. 1936). *Heir: s* Edward Norman Trevelyan, *b* 14 Aug. 1955. *Address:* 1041 Adella Avenue, Coronado, CA 92118, USA. *Died 16 Jan. 1996.*

TREVOR, 4th Baron *cr* 1880, of Brynkinalt, co. Denbigh; **Charles Edwin Hill-Trevor;** JP; *b* 13 Aug. 1928; *e s* of 3rd Baron and Phyllis May, 2nd *d* of J. A. Sims, Ings House, Kirton-in-Lindsey, Lincolnshire; *S* father, 1950; *m* 1967, Susan Janet Elizabeth, *o d* of Dr Ronald Bence; two *s. Educ:* Shrewsbury. Royal Forestry Society: Mem. Council and Trustee; Chm., N Wales Div. Trustee, Robert Jones and Agnes Hunt Orthopaedic Hosp. Inst. Cttee. JP Clwyd (formerly Denbighshire) 1959; Chm., Berwyn PSD. CStJ. *Recreations:* shooting, fishing. *Heir: s* Hon. Marke Charles Hill-Trevor, *b* 8 Jan. 1970. *Address:* Brynkinalt, Chirk, Wrexham, Clwyd LL14 5NS. *T:* (01691) 773425; Auch, Bridge of Orchy, Argyllshire. *T:* (01838) 400282. *Clubs:* East India, Flyfishers'. *Died 1 Jan. 1997.*

TREVOR, Meriol; author; *b* 15 April 1919; *d* of Lt-Col Arthur Prescott Trevor and Lucy M. E. Trevor (*née* Dimmock). *Educ:* Perse Girls' Sch., Cambridge; St Hugh's Coll., Oxford. FRSL. *Publications: novels:* The Last of Britain, 1956; The New People, 1957; A Narrow Place, 1958; Shadows and Images, 1960; The City and the World, 1970; The Holy Images, 1971; The Fugitives, 1973; The Two Kingdoms, 1973; The Marked Man, 1974; The Enemy at Home, 1974; The Forgotten Country, 1975; The Fortunate Marriage, 1976; The Treacherous Paths, 1976; The Civil Prisoners, 1977; The Fortunes of Peace, 1978; The Wanton Fires, 1979; The Sun with a Face, 1984; The Golden Palaces, 1986; *poems:* Midsummer, Midwinter, 1957; *biography:* John Henry Newman, vol. 1, The Pillar of the Cloud, 1962, vol. 2, Light in Winter, 1962 (James Tait Black Meml Prize), shortened version in one vol. as Newman's Journey, 1974, repr. with new introd., 1996; Apostle of Rome, 1966; Pope John, 1967; Prophets and Guardians, 1969; The Arnolds, 1973; The Shadow of a Crown: the life story of James II of England

and VII of Scotland, 1988; also books for children. *Address:* 41 Fitzroy House, Pulteney Street, Bath BA2 4DW. *Died 12 Jan. 2000.*

TRICKETT, (Mabel) Rachel; Principal, St Hugh's College, Oxford, 1973–91; *b* 20 Dec. 1923. *Educ:* Lady Margaret Hall, Oxford (BA Hons 1st Cl. in English 1945; MA 1947; Hon. Fellow, 1978). Asst to Curator, Manchester City Art Galleries, 1945–46; Asst Lectr in English, Univ. of Hull, 1946–49; Commonwealth Fund Fellow, Yale Univ., 1949–50; Lectr in English, Hull Univ., 1950–54; Fellow and Tutor in English, St Hugh's Coll., Oxford, 1954–73, Hon. Fellow, 1991. *Publications:* The Honest Muse (a study in Augustan verse), 1967; *novels:* The Return Home, 1952; The Course of Love, 1954; Point of Honour, 1958; A Changing Place, 1962; The Elders, 1966; A Visit to Timon, 1970. *Address:* Flat 4, 18 Norham Gardens, Oxford OX2 6QB. *T:* (01865) 556121.

Died 24 June 1999.

TRIMLESTOWN, 20th Baron *cr* 1461 (Ire.), of Trimlestown, co. Meath; **Anthony Edward Barnewall;** *b* 2 Feb. 1928; *s* of 19th Baron and Muriel (*d* 1937), *d* of Edward Oskar Schneider; *S* father, 1990; *m* 1st, 1963, Lorna Margaret Marion (marr. diss. 1973; she *d* 1988), *d* of late Douglas Ramsay; 2nd, 1977, Mary Wonderly, *e d* of late Judge Thomas F. McAllister, Grand Rapids, Mich. *Educ:* Ampleforth. Irish Guards, 1946–48. Naval architect with Jack Jones, 1949–53; European Sales Exec., P&O Shipping Co., 1965–74. *Recreation:* travel. *Heir:* b Hon. Raymond Charles Barnewall, *b* 29 Dec. 1930. *Address:* PO Box 215, Ada, MI 49301, USA.

Died 19 Aug. 1997.

TRUDEAU, Rt Hon. Pierre Elliott, CC 1985; CH 1984; PC (Can.); QC (Can.) 1969; FRSC; Prime Minister of Canada, 1968–79 and 1980–84; Leader of Liberal Party of Canada, 1968–84; Senior Consultant, Heenan Blaikie, since 1984; *b* Montreal, 18 Oct. 1919; *s* of Charles-Emile Trudeau and Grace Elliott; *m* 1971, Margaret Joan (marr. diss. 1984), *d* of late James Sinclair and of Kathleen Bernard; two *s* (and one *s* decd). *Educ:* Jean-de-Brébeuf College, Montreal; University of Montreal; Harvard University; Ecole des Sciences Politiques, Paris; London School of Economics (Hon. Fellow, 1969). Called to the Bar: Quebec, 1944; Ontario, 1967; practised law, Quebec; co-founder of review Cité Libre; Associate Professor of Law, University of Montreal, 1961–65. MP (L) Mount Royal, Montreal, 1965–84. Parliamentary Secretary to Prime Minister, Jan. 1966–April 1967; Minister of Justice and Attorney General, April 1967–July 1968; Leader of the Opposition, 1979. Founding Member, Montreal Civil Liberties Union. Freeman of City of London, 1975. Hon. Dean, Faculty of Law, Univ. of Poitiers, 1975. Hon. degrees and awards from many universities in Canada, US, Japan, Macau. *Publications:* La Grève de l'Amiante, 1956; (with Jacques Hébert) Deux Innocents en Chine Rouge, 1961 (Two Innocents in Red China, 1969); Le Fédéralisme et la Société canadienne-française, 1968 (Federalism and the French Canadians, 1968); Réponses, 1968; Memoirs, 1993; (with Ivan Head) The Canadian Way: shaping Canada's foreign policy 1968–84, 1995; Against the Current, 1996. *Recreations:* swimming, skiing, flying, scuba diving, canoeing. *Address:* c/o Heenan Blaikie, 1250 boulevard René-Lévesque Ouest, Bureau 2500, Montreal, QC H3B 4Y1, Canada.

Died 28 Sept. 2000.

TRUEMAN, Prof. Edwin Royden; Beyer Professor of Zoology, University of Manchester, 1974–82, then Emeritus; *b* 7 Jan. 1922; *s* of late Sir Arthur Trueman, KBE, FRS, and Lady (Florence Kate) Trueman (*née* Offler); *m* 1945, Doreen Burt; two *d. Educ:* Bristol Grammar Sch.; Univ. of Glasgow (DSc); MSc Manchester. Technical Officer (Radar), RAF, 1942–46. Asst Lectr and Lectr, 1946–58, Sen. Lectr and Reader, 1958–68, Univ. of Hull (Dean, Faculty of Science, 1954–57); Prof. of Zoology, Univ. of Manchester, 1969–74. R. T. French Vis. Prof., Univ. of Rochester, NY, 1960–61; Nuffield Travelling Fellowship in Tropical Marine Biology, Univ. of West Indies, Jamaica, 1968–69; Leverhulme Emeritus Fellowship, 1983–85. *Publications:* Locomotion of Soft-bodied Animals, 1975; (ed) Aspects of Animal Movement, 1980; (ed) vols 10–12 of series The Mollusca, 1985–88; articles on animal locomotion, littoral physiology and Mollusca. *Address:* Burwood, Chestnut Way, Stoke Mandeville, Bucks HP22 5UY. *T:* (01296) 612544.

Died 26 Feb. 2000.

TUBBS, Ralph, OBE 1952; FRIBA; architect; *b* 9 Jan. 1912; *s* of late Sydney W. Tubbs and Mabel Frost; *m* 1946, Mary Taberner; two *s* one *d. Educ:* Mill Hill School; Architectural Assoc. School (Hons Dip.). Sec. MARS Group (Modern Architectural Research), 1939; Member: Council and Executive Committee of RIBA, 1944–50, re-elected Council, 1951; Vice-Pres. Architectural Assoc., 1945–47; Associate Institute of Landscape Architects, 1942–. Member, Presentation Panel and Design Group for 1951 Festival of Britain, and architect of Dome of Discovery in London Exhibn (then the largest dome in world, 365 ft diam.). Other works include: Baden-Powell House for Boy Scouts' Assoc., London; Indian Students' Union building, Fitzroy Sq., London; Granada TV Centre and Studios, Manchester; Cambridge Inst. Educn; Halls of residence for University Coll., London; residential areas at Harlow and Basildon New Towns; industrial buildings. Architect for new Charing Cross Hospital and Med. Sch., London; Consultant for Hospital Develt, Jersey, CI. Pres., British Entomological and Natural Hist. Soc., 1977; Vice-Pres., Royal Entomol Soc. of London, 1982–84. *Publications:* Living in Cities, 1942; The Englishman Builds, 1945. *Recreation:* study of the natural world. *Address:* 9 Lingfield Road, Wimbledon, SW19 4QA. *T:* (0181) 946 2010. *Died 23 Nov. 1996.*

TUCKER, Herbert Harold, OBE 1965; HM Diplomatic Service, retired; Secretary, Roberts Centre; Consultant, Dulverton Trust, since 1989; *b* 4 Dec. 1925; *o s* of late Francis and Mary Ann Tucker; *m* 1948, Mary Stewart Dunlop; three *s. Educ:* Queen Elizabeth's, Lincs; Rossington Main, Yorks. Western Morning News, Sheffield Telegraph, Nottingham Journal, Daily Telegraph, 1944–51; Economic Information Unit, Treasury, 1948–49; FO, later FCO, 1951; Counsellor (Information) and Dir, British Information Services, Canberra, 1974–78; Consul-General, Vancouver, 1979–83; Disarmament Information Coordinator, FCO, 1983–84. Consultant, Centre for Security and Conflict Studies, 1986–89. *Publication:* (ed) Combating the Terrorists, 1988. *Recreations:* gardening, reading, watercolouring. *Address:* Pullens Cottage, Leigh Hill Road, Cobham, Surrey KT11 2HX. *T:* Cobham (01932) 864461. *Clubs:* Travellers', Commonwealth Trust. *Died 30 Aug. 1996.*

TUDBALL, Peter Colum, CBE 1993; Chairman, Baltic Exchange, 1991–94 (Hon. Member, since 1994); *b* 5 July 1933; *s* of Colum Tudball and Annie (*née* Critchett); *m* 1960, Carole Maureen Thompson (*d* 1995); one *s* two *d. Educ:* Cardiff High Sch. Mem., Baltic Exchange, 1954. Chm., Energy Capital Investment Co., 1995–; Director: Greig Middleton & Co. Ltd, 1987–; American Port Services plc, 1995–; Royal Olympic Cruise Lines, 1998–. Chm., London Missions to Seamen, 1993–. Mem. Council, Epsom Coll., 1997–. Prime Warden, Shipwrights' Co., 1999–2000. *Recreations:* sport, acting, walking, theatre. *Address:* Cleaver House, Headley, Surrey KT18 6NR. *T:* (01372) 377314. *Clubs:* London Capital; Cardiff and County (Cardiff). *Died 11 June 2000.*

TUDHOPE, David Hamilton, CMG 1984; DFC 1944, and Bar 1944; Chairman, National Bank of New Zealand, 1983–92; *b* 9 Nov. 1921; *s* of William and Sybil Tudhope; *m* 1946, Georgina Charity Lee; two *s* two *d*. *Educ:* Wanganui Collegiate Sch., NZ; King's Coll., Cambridge (MA, LLB). Served War, 1941–45: Pilot RNZAF, UK (Flt Lieut) (DFC and Bar, Pathfinder Force, Bomber Comd). Barrister and solicitor, NZ, 1947–49; Shell Oil, NZ, 1949–60; Gen. Manager, Shell Oil Rhodesia, N Rhodesia and Nyasaland, 1960–62; Area Co-ordinator, Shell London, 1962–67; Chm. and Chief Exec., Shell Interests in NZ, 1967–81; Chm., Shell BP & Todd Oil Services, 1967–81; Chm. (in rotation), NZ Oil Refinery, 1969, 1974, 1980, and Maui Development, 1975, 1980; Chm., National Mutual Life Assoc., 1983–88; Director: Shell Holdings Ltd, 1981–87; Commercial Union Insurance, 1982–88; Steel & Tube, 1986–93. Dep. Chm., Crown Corp., 1984–86. Chm., Pukeiti Rhododendron Trust, 1981–90. *Recreations:* gardening, golf. *Address:* 7 Cluny Avenue, Kelburn, Wellington, New Zealand. *T:* Wellington (4) 4759358. *Club:* Wellington (Pres., 1992–94).   *Died 5 Sept. 1996.*

TU'IPELEHAKE, HRH Prince Fatafehi, Hon. KBE 1977 (Hon. CBE 1966); Prime Minister of Tonga, 1965–91, and former Minister for Agriculture, Fisheries and Forests, and Marine Affairs; *b* 7 Jan. 1922; *s* of HRH Prince Viliami Tupoulahi Tungi and HM Queen Salote of Tonga; *m* 1947, Princess Melenaite Topou Moheofo (*d* 1992); two *s* four *d*. *Educ:* Newington College, Sydney; Gatton Agricultural College, Queensland. Governor of Vava'u, 1949–51. Chm., Commodities Board. 'Uluafi Medal, 1982. *Address:* Palace Office, PO Box 6, Nuku'alofa, Tonga.   *Died 10 April 1999.*

TUNC, Prof. André Robert; Croix de Guerre 1940; Officier de la Légion d'Honneur 1984; Professor, University of Paris, since 1958; *b* 3 May 1917; *s* of Gaston Tunc and Gervaise (*née* Letourneur); *m* 1941, Suzanne Fortin. *Educ:* Law Sch., Paris. LLB 1937, LLM 1941; Agrégé des Facultés de Droit, 1943. Prof., Univ. of Grenoble, 1943–47; Counsellor, Internat. Monetary Fund, 1947–50; Prof., Univ. of Grenoble, 1950–58; Legal Adviser, UN Economic Commn for Europe, 1957–58. Hon. Doctorates: Free Univ. of Brussels, 1958; Cath. Univ. of Louvain, 1968; LLD Cambridge, 1986; DCL: Oxford, 1970; Stockholm, 1978; Geneva, 1984; Gent, 1986; Saarbrück, 1988; MA Cantab, 1972. Corresp. FBA 1974; Corresp. Fellow, Royal Acad. of Belgium, 1978; Foreign Member: Royal Acad. of the Netherlands, 1980; Amer. Acad. of Arts and Scis, 1982; Istituto Lombardo, 1993; Accademia Nazionale dei Lincei, 1997. Officier de l'Ordre d'Orange-Nassau (Netherlands), 1965. *Publications:* Le contrat de garde, 1941; Le particulier au service de l'ordre public, 1942; (with Suzanne Tunc) Le Système constitutionnel des Etats-Unis d'Amérique, 2 vols, 1953, 1954; (with Suzanne Tunc) Le droit des Etats-Unis d'Amérique, 1955; (with François Givord) (tome 8) Le louage: Contrats civils, du Traité pratique de droit civil français de Planiol et Ripert, 2nd edn 1956; (jtly) Traité théorique et pratique de la responsabilité civile de Henri et Léon Mazeaud, vols, 1957, 1958, 1960, 5th edn, and 6th edn (Vol. I) 1965; Les Etats-Unis—comment ils sont gouvernés, 1958, 3rd edn 1974; Dans un monde qui souffre, 1962, 4th edn 1968; Le droit des Etats-Unis (Que sais-je?), 1964, 5th edn 1989; La sécurité routière, 1965; Le droit anglais des sociétés anonymes, 1971, 4th edn 1998; Traffic Accident Compensation: Law and Proposals (Internat. Encycl. of Comparative Law, Vol. XI: Torts, chap. 14), 1971; Introd. to Vol. XI: Torts (Internat. Encycl. of Comparative Law), 1974; (jtly) La cour judiciaire suprême: une enquête comparative, 1978; La responsabilité civile, 1981, 2nd edn 1990; (jtly) Pour une loi sur les accidents de la circulation, 1981; Le droit américain des sociétés anonymes, 1985;

Jalons, dits et écrits d'André Tunc, 1991; articles in various legal periodicals. *Address:* 112 rue de Vaugirard, 75006 Paris, France.   *Died 10 Sept. 1999.*

TUOHY, John Francis, (Frank), FRSL; novelist, short story writer; *b* 2 May 1925; *s* of late Patrick Gerald Tuohy and Dorothy Marion (*née* Annandale). *Educ:* Stowe Sch.; King's College, Cambridge. Prof. of English Language and Literature, Univ. of São Paulo, 1950–56; Contract Prof., Jagiellonian Univ., Cracow, Poland, 1958–60; Visiting Professor: Waseda Univ., Tokyo, 1964–67; Rikkyo Univ., Tokyo, 1983–89; Writer-in-Residence, Purdue Univ., Indiana, 1970–71, 1976, 1980. FRSL 1965. Hon. DLitt Purdue, 1987. Bennett Award, Hudson Review, USA, 1994. *Publications:* The Animal Game, 1957; The Warm Nights of January, 1960; The Admiral and the Nuns (short stories), 1962 (Katherine Mansfield Memorial Prize); The Ice Saints (James Tait Black and Geoffrey Faber Memorial Prizes), 1964; Portugal, 1970; Fingers in the Door (short stories), 1970 (E. M. Forster Meml Award, 1972); Yeats: a biographical study, 1976; Live Bait (short stories), 1978 (Heinemann Award, 1979); Collected Stories, 1984. *Recreation:* travel. *Address:* Shatwell Cottage, Yarlington, near Wincanton, Somerset BA9 8DL.   *Died 11 April 1999.*

TURNBULL, Sir Richard (Gordon), GCMG 1962 (KCMG 1958; CMG 1953); *b* 7 July 1909; *s* of Richard Francis Turnbull; *m* 1939, Beatrice (*d* 1986), *d* of John Wilson, Glasgow; two *s* one *d*. *Educ:* University College School, London; University College, London (Fellow); Magdalene Coll., Cambridge (Hon. Fellow, 1970). Colonial Administrative Service, Kenya: District Officer, 1931–48; Provincial Comr, 1948–53; Minister for Internal Security and Defence, 1954; Chief Secretary, Kenya, 1955–58; Governor and C-in-C, Tanganyika, 1958–61; Governor-General and Commander-in-Chief, 1961–62; Chairman, Central Land Board, Kenya, 1963–64; High Commissioner for Aden and the Protectorate of South Arabia, 1965–67. KStJ 1958. *Address:* Friars Neuk, Jedburgh, Roxburghshire TD8 6BN. *T:* (01835) 862389.
                                    Died 21 Dec. 1998.

TURNER, Air Vice-Marshal Cameron Archer, CB 1968; CBE 1960 (OBE 1947); Royal New Zealand Air Force, retired; *b* Wanganui, NZ, 29 Aug. 1915; *s* of James Oswald Turner and Vida Cathrine Turner; *m* 1941, Josephine Mary, *d* of George Richardson; two *s*. *Educ:* New Plymouth Boys' High Sch.; Victoria University of Wellington; Massey Univ., Palmerston North, NZ. CEng, FIEE, FRAeS. Commn RAF, 1936–39; commn RNZAF, 1940; served War of 1939–45, UK, NZ, and Pacific; comd RNZAF Station Nausori, Fiji, 1944; comd RNZAF Station, Guadalcanal, Solomon Islands, 1944; Director of Signals, 1945–47; psa 1947; RNZAF Liaison Officer, Melbourne, Australia, 1948–50; comd RNZAF Station, Taieri, NZ, 1950–52; Director of Organization, HQ, RNZAF, 1953–56; comd RNZAF Station Ohakea, NZ, 1956–58; Asst Chief of Air Staff, HQ, RNZAF, 1958; Air Member for Personnel, HQ, RNZAF, 1959; idc 1960; AOC HQ, RNZAF, London, 1961–63; Air Member for Supply, HQ, RNZAF, 1964–65; Chief of Air Staff, HQ RNZAF, 1966–69. Dir, NZ Inventions Develt Authority, 1969–76. Pres., RNZAF Assoc., 1972–81. *Recreations:* fishing, Polynesian and religious studies. *Address:* 37a Parkvale Road, Wellington 5, New Zealand. *T:* (4) 4766063. *Club:* Wellington (Wellington).   *Died 26 Nov. 1999.*

TURNER, Prof. Herbert Arthur (Frederick), PhD; Montague Burton Professor of Industrial Relations, University of Cambridge, 1963–83, then Professor Emeritus; Fellow of Churchill College, Cambridge, since 1963; *b* 11 Dec. 1919; *s* of Frederick and May Turner; *m* 1st, 1949, Jane Paterson Smith Scott; two *s* one *d*; *m* 2nd; one *d*; *m* 4th, Evelyne Hanquart-Turner; one *s* one *d*.

Educ: Henry Thornton Sch., Clapham; LSE (Leverhulme Schol., then Leverhulme Res. Student, 1936–40; BSc (Econ) 1939); PhD Manchester, 1960; MA Cantab. Army, then naval staff, 1940–44. Member, Trades Union Congress Research and Economic Department, 1944; Assistant Education Secretary, TUC, 1947; Lecturer, 1950, Senior Lecturer, 1959, University of Manchester; Council of Europe Res. Fellow, 1957–58; Montague Burton Professor of Industrial Relations, University of Leeds, 1961–63. Mem., NBPI, 1967–71. Visiting Professor: Lusaka, 1969; Harvard and MIT, 1971–72; Sydney Univ., 1976–77; Hong Kong Univ., 1978–79 and 1985–87; Monash Univ., 1982; Bombay and Lucknow Univs, 1983; South China Univ. of Technology, 1986; Zhongshan Univ., 1987; Leverhulme Sen. Res. Fellow, 1985–88. Sometime Adviser to Govts of Congo, Zaïre, Egypt, Tanzania, Fiji, Papua New Guinea, Zambia and other developing countries; Chm., Incomes Policies Commn of E African Community, 1973; ILO Adviser: Malawi, 1967; Iran, 1975; Labour Adviser, UNECA, 1980; World Bank Consultant, China, 1988. *Publications:* Arbitration, 1951; Wage Policy Abroad, 1956; Trade Union Growth, Structure and Policy, 1962; Wages: the Problems for Underdeveloped Countries, 1965, 2nd edn 1968; Prices, Wages and Incomes Policies, 1966; Labour Relations in the Motor Industry, 1967; Is Britain Really Strike-Prone?, 1969; Do Trade Unions Cause Inflation?, 1972, 3rd edn 1978; Management Characteristics and Labour Conflict, 1978; The Last Colony: labour in Hong Kong, 1980; The ILO and Hong Kong, 1986; Between Two Societies: Hong Kong labour in transition, 1990; Studies of Labour in Hong Kong, 1991; various reports of ILO, monographs, papers and articles on labour economics and statistics, industrial relations, developing countries. *Recreations:* minimal but mostly excusable. *Address:* Churchill College, Cambridge CB3 0DS; 129 Route de Bourgogne, Veneux-les-Sablons 77250, France. *Club:* United Oxford & Cambridge University.

Died 2 Dec. 1998.

TURNER, Lloyd Charles; livestock farmer, Kent, since 1986; Director, Messenger Nationwide, since 1988; Assistant Editor, Today, since 1990; *b* 2 Oct. 1938; *s* of Charles Thomas and Lily Turner; *m* 1st, 1961, Rosemary Munday (marr. diss. 1966); 2nd, 1967, Jennifer Anne Cox (marr. diss. 1972); 3rd, 1973, Jill Marguerite King. *Educ:* Giants Creek Primary Sch., Australia; The Armidale Sch., Armidale, Australia. Newcastle Morning Herald, Australia: Cadet journalist, 1956; Chief Crime Reporter, 1960; Features Editor, 1961; Picture Editor, 1962; Asst Editor, 1964; Industrial Correspondent, Manchester Evening News, 1968; Daily Express: Sub-Editor, 1968; Asst Chief Sub-Editor, 1974; Dep. Chief Sub-Editor, 1975; Asst Night Editor, 1976; Dep. Night Editor, 1977; Night Editor, 1979; Editor: The Daily Star, subseq. The Star, 1980–87; The Post, 1988; Editor-in-Chief, Messenger TV, 1988; Director: Express Newspapers plc, 1982–87; Daily Star plc, 1982–87. CPU Scholar, 1966. Pres., Australian Journalists Assoc. (Provincial), 1962–65; Chm., (Father), Daily Express/Sunday Express NUJ Chapel, 1969–74. Hon. Mem., NSPCC, 1989. *Recreations:* gardening, horse-racing. *Address:* 1 Virginia Street, E1 9BS. *Clubs:* St James's; Journalists' (Sydney).

Died 12 Sept. 1996.

TURNER, Surg. Rear-Adm. Philip Stanley, CB 1963; QHDS 1960–64; Director of Dental Services, Royal Navy, Admiralty, 1961–64; *b* 31 Oct. 1905; *s* of Frank Overy Turner and Ellen Mary Turner, Langton Green, Tunbridge Wells; *m* 1934, Marguerite Donnelly (*d* 1990); one *d* (one *s* decd). *Educ:* Cranbrook Coll.; Guy's Hospital. LDS, RCS 1927. Surgeon Lieut (D) Royal Navy, 1928; Surgeon Captain (D) 1955; Surgeon Rear-Admiral (D), 1961. Senior Specialist in Dental Surgery, 1946–61. Served in:

HMS Ramillies, Vanguard, Implacable, Indomitable; HMHS Maine, Tjitjalengka; RN Hospitals Haslar, Plymouth; RN Barracks Portsmouth, etc; Naval HQ, Malta. Foundation Fellow, British Assoc. of Oral Surgeons, 1962.   *Died 13 Jan. 1997.*

TURNER, Theodora, OBE 1961; ARRC 1944; Matron of St Thomas' Hospital and Superintendent of Nightingale Training School, 1955–65; *b* 5 Aug. 1907; *er d* of H. E. M. Turner. *Educ:* Godolphin School, Salisbury; Edinburgh School of Domestic Economy. Ward Sister, St Thomas' Hosp., 1935–38; Administrative Course, Florence Nightingale Internat. Foundn, 1938–39; QAIMNS Reserve, Italy and E Mediterranean, 1939–45; Administrative Sister, St Thomas' Hosp., 1946–47; Matron Royal Infirmary, Liverpool, 1948–53; Education Officer, Educn Centre, Royal College of Nursing, Birmingham, 1953–55. President: Florence Nightingale Internat. Nurses Assoc., 1971–74; Royal Coll. of Nursing and Nat. Council of Nurses of UK, 1966–68. Mem., Argyll and Clyde Health Bd, 1974–75.   *Died 24 Aug. 1999.*

TURNER CAIN, Maj.-Gen. George Robert, CB 1967; CBE 1963; DSO 1945; President, Anglia Maltings (Holdings) Ltd, since 1982 (Chairman, 1976–82); Chairman: Anglia Maltings Ltd, 1976–82; F. & G. Smith Ltd, 1962–82; Walpole & Wright Ltd, 1968–82; Director: Crisp Maltings Ltd, 1967–82; Crisp Malt Products Ltd, 1968–82; Edme Ltd, 1972–82; *b* 16 Feb. 1912; *s* of late Wing Comdr G. Turner Cain; *m* 1938, Lamorna Maturin, *d* of late Col G. B. Hingston; one *s* one *d*. *Educ:* Norwich Sch.; RMC Sandhurst. 2nd Lieut Norfolk Regt, 1932; 1st Bn Royal Norfolk Regt, India, 1933–38; Waziristan Campaign, 1937; served War of 1939–45 with 1st Royal Norfolk and 1st Hereford Regt, BLA, 1944–45; Comd 1st Royal Norfolk Regt, Berlin, 1947–48; Hong Kong and UK, 1953–55; Comd Tactical Wing, School of Infantry, 1955–57; Comd 1st Federal Inf. Bde, Malaya, in operations in Malaya, 1957–59; BGS, HQ, BAOR, 1961; Maj.-Gen. Administration, GHQ FARELF, 1964–67, retired; ADC, 1961–64. Dep. Col, Royal Anglian Regt, 1971–74. Croix de Guerre avec Palm, 1945; Star of Kedah (Malaya), 1959. *Recreation:* shooting. *Address:* Holbreck, Hollow Lane, Stiffkey, Wells-next-the-Sea, Norfolk NR23 1QG.

Died 11 July 1996.

TURPIN, Maj.-Gen. Patrick George, CB 1962; OBE 1943; FCIT; *b* 27 April 1911; 3rd *s* of late Rev. J. J. Turpin, MA, BD, late Vicar of Misterton, Somerset; *m* 1947, Cherry Leslie Joy, *d* of late Major K. S. Grove, York and Lancaster Regiment; one *s* one *d*. *Educ:* Haileybury Coll., Hertford; Exeter College, Oxford (Sen. Classical Schol.). BA (Hons) Oxford (Lit. Hum.), 1933; MA 1963. Commd RASC, 2nd Lieut 1933; Lieut 1936; Capt. 1941; Major 1946; Lt-Col 1949; Col 1953; Brig. 1959; Maj.-Gen. 1960; psc 1941; jssc 1949; idc 1955. Served War of 1939–45 (despatches twice, OBE): Adjt, 1939–40; AQMG, 30 Corps, W Desert, 1943; AA&QMG, 5th Div., Italy, 1943–44; DA&QMG (Brig.), 1 Corps, BLA, 1945; Brig. A, 21 Army Gp, 1945–46; Comd 6 Training Bn, RASC, 1947; ADS&T, WO, 1948; AA&QMG (Plans), HQ, British Troops in Egypt, 1950; GSO1 (instructor), Jt Services Staff Coll., 1951–53; ADS&T (Col), WO, 1953–54; DAG, HQ, BAOR, 1956–59; Brig. i/c Admin, 17 Gurkha Div., Malaya, 1959–60; DST, 1960–63; Dir of Movements, MoD (Army), 1963–66. Col Comdt, Royal Corps of Transport, 1965–71; Col Gurkha Army Service Corps, 1960–65; Col Gurkha Transport Regt, 1965–73. Sec.-Gen., Assoc. of British Travel Agents, 1966–69. Pres., Army Lawn Tennis Assoc., 1968–73. Governor, Royal Sch. for Daughters of Officers of the Army, Bath, 1963–83. FCIT (MInstT 1961). *Publication:* The Turn of the Wheel, 1988. *Recreations:* lawn tennis (Somerset County Champion, 1948, Army Colours, 1952), squash

rackets (Bucks County Colours, 1952), golf. *Clubs:* Oxford Union Society; All England Lawn Tennis; International Lawn Tennis; Escorts Squash Rackets.
Died 14 Sept. 1996.

TUZO, Gen. Sir Harry (Craufurd), GCB 1973 (KCB 1971); OBE 1961; MC 1945; *b* 26 Aug. 1917; *s* of John Atkinson Tuzo and Annie Katherine (*née* Craufurd); *m* 1943, Monica Patience Salter; one *d. Educ:* Wellington Coll.; Oriel Coll., Oxford (BA 1939; MA 1970; Hon. Fellow 1977). Regimental Service, Royal Artillery, 1939–45; Staff appts, Far East, 1946–49; Royal Horse Artillery, 1950–51 and 1954–58; Staff at Sch. of Infantry, 1951–53; GSO1, War Office, 1958–60; CO, 3rd Regt, RHA, 1960–62; Asst Comdt, Sandhurst, 1962–63; Comdr, 51 Gurkha Infantry Bde, 1963–65; Imp. Def. Coll., 1966; Maj.-Gen. 1966; Chief of Staff, BAOR, 1967–69; Director, RA, 1969–71; Lt-Gen. 1971; GOC and Dir of Operations, NI, 1971–73; Gen. 1973; Comdr Northern Army Gp and C-in-C BAOR, 1973–76; Dep. Supreme Allied Comdr, Europe, 1976–78. ADC (Gen.) to the Queen, 1974–77. Colonel Commandant: RA, 1971–83; RHA, 1976–83; Master Gunner, St James's Park, 1977–83. Chm., Marconi Space and Defence Systems, 1979–83; Dir, Oceonics, 1988–91. Chm., RUSI, 1980–83; Member: Council, IISS, 1978–87; Council, Inst. for Study of Conflict, later Res. Inst. for Study of Conflict and Terrorism, 1979–91. Chairman: Fermoy Centre Foundn, Kings Lynn, 1982–87; Imperial War Mus. Redevelt Appeal, 1984–88; Council, Pensthorpe Waterfowl Trust, 1988–96; Pres., Norfolk Soc., CPRE, 1987–92. DL Norfolk, 1983–96. Dato Setia Negeri Brunei, 1965. *Recreations:* gardening, music, theatre. *Club:* Army and Navy.
Died 7 Aug. 1998.

TWEEDSMUIR, 2nd Baron *cr* 1935, of Elsfield, Oxford; **John Norman Stuart Buchan,** CBE 1964 (OBE (mil.) 1943); CD 1964; FREI; Lieutenant-Colonel Canadian Infantry Corps, retired; *b* 25 Nov. 1911; *e s* of 1st Baron Tweedsmuir, GCMG, GCVO, CH, PC and Susan Charlotte (*d* 1977), *d* of Hon. Norman Grosvenor; *S* father, 1940; *m* 1st, 1948, Priscilla Jean Fortescue, later Baroness Tweedsmuir of Belhelvie, PC (*d* 1978); one *d*; 2nd, 1980, Jean Margherita, *widow* of Sir Francis Grant, 12th Bt. *Educ:* Eton; Brasenose Coll., Oxford (BA 1933; MA 1987). Asst District Comr, Uganda Protectorate, 1934–36; joined Hudson's Bay Company, 1937; wintered in their service at Cape Dorset, Baffin Land, Canadian Arctic, 1938–39; served War of 1939–45 in Canadian Army (wounded, despatches twice, OBE (mil.) 1945, Order of Orange-Nassau, with swords); comd Hastings and Prince Edward Regt in Sicily and Italy, 1943; Hon. Col, 1955–60. Rector of Aberdeen Univ., 1948–51. Chm., Joint East and Central African Board, 1950–52; UK Delegate: UN Assembly, 1951–52; Council of Europe, 1952; Pres., Commonwealth and British Empire Chambers of Commerce, 1955–57; a Governor: Commonwealth Inst., 1958–77, Trustee, 1977–; Ditchley Foundn; Pres., Inst. of Export, 1964–67; Mem. Board, BOAC, 1955–64; Chairman: Advertising Standards Authority, 1971–74; Council on Tribunals, 1973–80. Mem., Scottish Cttee, Nature Conservancy, 1971–73. President: Institute of Rural Life at Home and Overseas, 1951–85; British Schools Exploring Society, 1964–85; Chm., British Rheumatism and Arthritis Assoc., 1971–78, Pres., 1978–86. Chancellor, Primrose League, 1969–75. FRSA. Hon. LLD: Aberdeen, 1949; Queen's (Canada), 1955. *Publications:* (part author) St Kilda papers, 1931; Hudson's Bay Trader, 1951; Always a Countryman, 1953; One Man's Happiness, 1968. *Recreations:* fishing, shooting, falconry. *Heir: b* Hon. William de l'Aigle Buchan, RAFVR [*b* 10 Jan. 1916; *m* 1st, Nesta (marr. diss. 1946), *o d* of Lt-Col C. D. Crozier; one *d*; 2nd, 1946, Barbara (marr. diss. 1960), 2nd *d* of E. N. Ensor, late of

Hong Kong; three *s* three *d*; 3rd, 1960, Sauré Cynthia Mary, *y d* of late Major G. E. Tatchell, Royal Lincolnshire Regt; one *s*]. *Address:* Kingston House, Kingston Bagpuize, Oxon OX13 5AX. *T:* Longworth (01865) 820259. *Clubs:* Carlton, Travellers', Flyfishers'.
Died 20 June 1996.

TWISLETON-WYKEHAM-FIENNES, Sir John (Saye Wingfield), KCB 1970 (CB 1953); QC 1972; First Parliamentary Counsel, 1968–72, retired; *b* 14 April 1911; *s* of Gerard Yorke Twisleton-Wykeham-Fiennes and Gwendolen (*née* Gisborne); *m* 1937, Sylvia Beatrice (*d* 1979), *d* of Rev. C. R. L. McDowall; two *s* one *d. Educ:* Winchester; Balliol College, Oxford. Called to Bar, Middle Temple, 1936; Bencher, 1969. Joined Parliamentary Counsel Office, 1939; Second Parly Counsel, Treasury, 1956–68; Parliamentary Counsel, Malaya, 1962–63 (Colombo Plan); with Law Commission, 1965–66. *Address:* Mill House, Preston, Sudbury, Suffolk CO10 9ND.
Died 21 April 1996.

TWIST, Henry Aloysius, CMG 1966; OBE 1947; *b* 18 June 1914; *s* of John Twist, Preston; *m* 1941, (Mary) Monica, *yr d* of Nicholas Mulhall, Manchester; one *s* one *d. Educ:* Liverpool Univ. (BA). Senior Classics Master, St Chad's Coll., Wolverhampton, 1936–40; Lecturer in English, South Staffordshire High School of Commerce, 1939–40. Served War of 1939–45 with RASC and RAEC, 1940–46; released with rank of Lt-Col, 1946. Principal, Dominions Office, 1946; Official Secretary, British High Commission in Ceylon, 1948–49; British High Commission in Australia, 1949–52; Commonwealth Relations Office, 1952–54; Secretariat, Commonwealth Economic Conference, London, 1952; Deputy High Commissioner for the United Kingdom in Bombay, 1954–57; Assistant Secretary, Commonwealth Relations Office, 1957–60; British Deputy High Commissioner, Kaduna, Northern Region, Federation of Nigeria, 1960–62; Commonwealth Service representative on the 1963 Course at Imperial Defence College; Commonwealth Office, 1964; Asst Under-Sec., 1966; Dep. High Comr, 1966–70, Minister (Commercial), 1968–70, Rawalpindi; retired 1970. Dir of Studies, RIPA, 1973–82. *Recreation:* gardening. *Address:* Pine Lodge, Woodham Lane, Woking, Surrey GU21 5SP. *Club:* Royal Commonwealth Society.
Died 8 Sept. 1997.

TYE, James; Director-General, British Safety Council, since 1968; *b* 21 Dec. 1921; *s* of late Benjamin and Rose Tye; *m* 1950, Mrs Rosalie Hooker; one *s* one *d. Educ:* Upper Hornsey LCC Sch. Served War of 1939–45; RAF, 1940–46. Advertising agent and contractor, 1946–50; Managing Dir, 1950–62: Sky Press Ltd; Safety Publications Ltd; joined British Safety Council as Exec. Dir, 1962. Chairman: Bd of Governors, Internat. Inst. of Safety Management, 1975–; British Wellness Council, 1990–. FIMgt; Hon. Vice-Pres., Inst. of Occupational Safety and Health; Member: Amer. Soc. of Safety Engineers; Amer. Safety Management Soc.; Vice-Pres., Jamaica Safety Council; Fellow, Inst. of Accident Prevention, Zambia. FRSA. Freeman, City of London, 1976; Liveryman, Worshipful Co. of Basketmakers; Mem., Guild of Freemen of City of London. Inducted, US Safety Hall of Fame, 1995. *Publications:* Communicating the Safety Message, 1968; Management Introduction to Total Loss Control, 1971; Safety-Uncensored (with K. Ullyett), 1971; (with Bowes Egan) The Management Guide to Product Liability, 1979; *handbooks:* Industrial Safety Digest, 1953; Skilful Driving, 1952; Advanced Driving, 1954; International Nautical Safety Code (with Uffa Fox), 1961; Why Imprison Untrained Drivers?, 1980; Workplace Wellness; Papers and Reports to Parly Groups and British Safety Council Members on: product liability, training safety officers, vehicle seat belts, anti-jack knife devices for articulated vehicles, lifejackets and buoyancy aids, motorway safety barriers, Britain's filthy beaches, back pain, insurance costs, safety in fairgrounds, dangers of mini fire extinguishers, drip feed oil heaters, and children's flammable nightwear, vehicle recall procedures, need for a nat. vehicle defects hotline, brain injuries caused by boxing and recommendations to improve the rules, pollution caused by diesel engines, safe toys, introduction of defensive driving techniques, risk management — stress at work, increased risk of accidents thereof, use of colour in envmt to promote safety and productivity, dangers of smoke masks, fire prevention — recommendations to industry. *Recreations:* squash, badminton, ski-ing, golf, sailing. *Address:* 55 Hartington Road, Chiswick, W4 3TS. *T:* 0181–995 3206. *Clubs:* City Livery, Royal Automobile.   *Died 21 July 1996.*

TYE, Walter, CBE 1966 (OBE 1948); CEng; *b* 12 Dec. 1912; *s* of Walter and Alice Tye; *m* 1939, Eileen Mary Whitmore; one *s* one *d. Educ:* Woodbridge Sch.; London Univ. (BScEng). Fairey Aviation Co., 1934; RAE, 1935–38; Air Registration Bd, 1938–39; RAE, 1939–44; Air Registration Bd, 1944–72 (Chief Techn. Officer, 1946, Chief Exec., 1969); Mem., CAA (Controller Safety), 1972–74. Hon. FRAeS; Hon. DSc Cranfield Inst. of Technology, 1972. *Publications:* articles, lectures and contrib. Jl RAeS. *Address:* 12 Bramble Rise, Cobham, Surrey KT11 2HP. *T:* (01932) 863692.
                    Died 13 May 1998.

TYLER, Brig. Arthur Catchmay, CBE 1960; MC 1945; DL; a Military Knight of Windsor, since 1978 (Supernumerary, 1991); *b* 20 Aug. 1913; 4th *s* of Hugh Griffin Tyler and Muriel Tyler (*née* Barnes); *m* 1938, Sheila, *d* of James Kinloch, Meigle, Perthshire; three *s* one *d. Educ:* Allhallows Sch.; RMC, Sandhurst. Commissioned, The Welch Regt, 1933; served War of 1939–45: Africa, India and Burma (despatches); Staff Coll., 1946; JSSC, 1951; Sec., BJSM, Washington, 1952–54; Bt Lt-Col, 1953; Comd 4th (Carms) Bn The Welch Regt, 1954–57; Col, 1957; AAG, War Office, 1957–60; Brig. 1960; Senior UK Liaison Officer and Military Adviser to High Commissioner, Canada, 1960–63; Asst Chief of Staff (Ops and Plans), Allied Forces Central Europe, 1963–65. Sec., Council, TA&VR Assocs, 1967–72. Hon. Col, 7th(V) Bn, The Queen's Regt, T&AVR, 1971–75. Governor, Allhallows Sch., 1968, Chm., 1977–80. DL Surrey, 1968. *Address:* Kenwith Castle Nursing Home, Abbotsham, Bideford, Devon EX39 5BE.   *Died 6 Oct. 1998.*

TYLER, Cyril, DSc, PhD, FRSC; Professor of Physiology and Biochemistry, 1958–76, then Emeritus, and Deputy Vice-Chancellor, 1968–76, Reading University; *b* 26 Jan. 1911; *er s* of John and Annie Tyler; *m* 1st, 1939, Myra Eileen (*d* 1971), *d* of George and Rosa Batten; two *s* one *d* 2nd, 1971, Rita Patricia, *d* of Sidney and Lilian Jones. *Educ:* Ossett Grammar Sch.; Univ. of Leeds (BSc 1st Class Hons 1933; PhD 1935; DSc 1959). Lectr in Agricultural Chemistry, RAC, Cirencester, 1935–39; University of Reading: Lecturer in Agricultural Chemistry, 1939–47; Professor, 1947–58; Dean of the Faculty of Agriculture, 1959–62. Playing Mem., Glos CCC, 1936–39. *Publications:* Organic Chemistry for Students of

Agriculture, 1946; Animal Nutrition (2nd edn), 1964; Wilhelm von Nathusius 1821–1899 on Avian Eggshells, 1964; numerous papers on poultry metabolism and egg shells in scientific journals. *Recreations:* gardening, history of animal nutrition. *Address:* 22 Belle Avenue, Reading, Berks RG6 2BL.   *Died 25 Jan. 1996.*

TYNDALE-BISCOE, Rear-Adm. Alec Julian, CB 1959; OBE 1946; lately Chairman of Blaw Knox Ltd; *b* 10 Aug. 1906; *s* of late Lt-Col A. A. T. Tyndale-Biscoe, Aubrey House, Keyhaven, Lymington, Hants; *m* 1st, 1939, Emma Winifred Haselden (*d* 1974); four *d*; 2nd, 1974, Hugolyne Cotton Cooke, *widow* of Captain Geoffrey Cotton Cooke. *Educ:* RN Colleges Osborne and Dartmouth. Entered RN, 1920; served War, 1939–46; HMS Vanguard, 1947–49; Captain, 1949; Asst Engineer-in-Chief, Fleet, 1950–53; Comdg RN Air Station, Anthorn, 1953–55; Fleet Engr Officer, Mediterranean, 1955–57; Rear-Adm. 1957; Flag-Officer Reserve Aircraft, 1957–59, retired. *Address:* Bunces Farm Gardens, Birch Grove, Haywards Heath, West Sussex RH17 7BT.   *Died 26 April 1997.*

TYRWHITT, Brig. Dame Mary (Joan Caroline), DBE 1949 (OBE 1946); TD; *b* 27 Dec. 1903; *d* of Admiral of the Fleet Sir Reginald Tyrwhitt, 1st Bt, GCB, DSO and Angela, *d* of Matthew Corbally, JP, Swords, Ireland; unmarried. Senior Controller, 1946 (rank altered to Brigadier, 1950); Director, ATS, 1946–49, Women's Royal Army Corps, 1949–50, retired Dec. 1950; Hon. ADC to the King, 1949–50. *Address:* 12A Tiddington Court, Tiddington, Stratford-on-Avon CV37 7AP.
                    Died 13 Feb. 1997.

TYSON, Dr Alan Walker, CBE 1989; FBA 1978; musicologist; Fellow of All Souls College, Oxford, 1952–94, Senior Research Fellow, 1971–94; *b* 27 Oct. 1926; *e s* of Henry Alan Maurice Tyson and Dorothy (*née* Walker). *Educ:* Rugby School; Magdalen College, Oxford (BA 1951, MA 1952); University College Hospital Medical School, London (MB, BS 1965). MRCPsych 1972. Vis. Lectr in Psychiatry, Montefiore Hosp., NY, 1967–68; Lectr in Psychopathology and Developmental Psychology, Oxford Univ., 1968–70. Vis. Prof. of Music, Columbia Univ., 1969; James P. R. Lyell Reader in Bibliography, Oxford Univ., 1973–74; Ernest Bloch Prof. of Music, Univ. of California at Berkeley, 1977–78; Mem., Inst. for Advanced Study, Princeton, 1983–84; Vis. Prof. of Music, Graduate Center, City Univ. of New York, 1985. Hon. Mem., British Psychoanalytical Soc., 1989–. Hon. DLitt St Andrews, 1989. On editorial staff, Standard Edition of Freud's Works, 1952–74. *Publications:* The Authentic English Editions of Beethoven, 1963; (with O. W. Neighbour) English Music Publishers' Plate Numbers, 1965; (ed) Selected Letters of Beethoven, 1967; Thematic Catalogue of the Works of Muzio Clementi, 1967; (ed) Beethoven Studies, Vol. 1, 1973, Vol. 2, 1977, Vol. 3, 1982; (with D. Johnson and R. Winter) The Beethoven Sketchbooks, 1985; Mozart: studies of the autograph scores, 1987; (with A. Rosenthal) Mozart's Thematic Catalogue: a facsimile, 1990; Mozart: Wasserzeichen-Katalog (Catalogue of Watermarks in Mozart's autographs), 1992. *Address:* c/o Stanecroft, Jarvis Lane, Steyning, West Sussex BN44 3GL.
                    Died 10 Nov. 2000.

U

UBEE, Air Vice-Marshal Sydney Richard, CB 1952; AFC 1939; Royal Air Force, retired; Air Officer Commanding No 2 Group, 2nd Tactical Air Force, Germany, 1955–58; *b* 5 March 1903; *s* of late Edward Joseph Ubee, London; *m* 1942, Marjorie Doris (*d* 1954), *d* of George Clement-Parker, Newport, Mon; two step *s*. *Educ:* Beaufoy Technical Institute. Joined RAF, 1927, with short service commission; permanent commission, 1932; test pilot, Royal Aircraft Establishment, Farnborough, 1933–37; served in India, Iraq, Burma, and Ceylon, 1937–43; Airborne Forces Experimental Establishment, 1943–45; Comdg Officer, Experimental Flying, RAE Farnborough, 1946–47; Commandant Empire Test Pilots' Sch., Cranfield, Bucks, and Farnborough, 1947–48; Deputy Director Operational Requirements, Air Min., 1948–51; Commandant RAF Flying Coll., Manby, 1951–54; Director-General of Personnel (II), Air Ministry, 1954–55. *Address:* Harwood Lodge, 100 Lodge Hill Road, Lower Bourne, Farnham, Surrey GU10 3RD. *Club:* Royal Air Force. *Died 7 July 1998.*

ud-DIN, Rt Rev. Khair-; Church Missionary Society Mission Partner in Britain, 1990–92; *b* 7 Feb. 1921; *s* of Sharam-ud-Din and Barkat Bibi; *m* 1963, Daphne Dionys. *Educ:* Punjab Univ., Lahore (BA Hons Oriental Langs); theol studies in India, Canada, UK. Ordained deacon, 1948, priest, 1949. Mem., St John's Divinity Sch., 1952. Pattoki, Okara and Clarkabad mission dists, Punjab, 1948 64; Vicar St John's, Peshawar, 1964–68; Cath. Church of the Resurrection, Lahore, 1968–77, Associate Priest, St Martin in the Bullring, Birmingham, 1973; Archdeacon of Lahore and Dean of Frontier Regions, Lahore Dio., 1977–82; Bishop of Peshawar, 1982–90. Official rep. of Danish Missionary Soc. in Pakistan, as Dean of Frontier Regions. Radio and TV broadcaster in Pakistan. Reviewer of books of poetry and prose in oriental lit., 1969–85. Hon. DD Theol Seminary, Gujranwala, Pakistan, 1987. Gold Medallist for outstanding servs in Dio. Lahore, 1979. *Publications:* Guidebook for Youth Workers, 1966; (ed) Sunday Sch. courses, 1962–66. *Recreations:* gardening, antiques. *Address:* 60 St Leonard's Road, Headington, Oxford OX3 8AB. *Club:* St Clement's Family Centre (Oxford).
Died 18 Jan. 1997.

UDOMA, Hon. Sir (Egbert) Udo, CFR 1978; Kt 1964; Justice, Supreme Court of Nigeria, Lagos, 1969–82, retired; Commissioner for Law Reform, Cross River State, Nigeria, 1985–88; *b* 21 June 1917; *s* of Chief Udoma Inam, Ihekwe Ntanaran Akama, Opobo (later Ikot Abasi, Akwa Ibom State), Nigeria, and Adiaha Edem; *m* 1950, Grace Bassey; six *s* one *d* (and one *s* decd). *Educ:* Methodist Coll., Uzuakoli, Nigeria; Trinity Coll., Dublin; St Catherine's Coll., Oxford. BA 1942; LLB 1942; PhD 1944; MA 1945. President, Dublin Univ. Philosophical Society, 1942–43. Called to Bar, Gray's Inn, 1945; practised as Barrister-at-law in Nigeria, 1946–61. Nat. Pres., Ibibio State Union, 1947–61; Member, House of Representatives, Nigeria, 1952–59; Judge of High Court of Federal Territory of Lagos, Nigeria, 1961–63. Chief Justice, High Court, Uganda, 1963–69; Acting Gov.-Gen., Uganda, 1963; Chm., Constituent Assembly for Nigerian Constitution, 1977–78; Dir, Seminar for Judges, 1980–82. Member Nigeria Marketing Board and Director Nigeria Marketing Co. Board, 1952–54; Member Managing Cttee, West African Inst. for Oil Palm Research, 1953–63. Vice-President, Nigeria Bar Assoc., 1957–61; Member: Internat.

Commn of Jurists; World Assoc. of Judges. Vice-President, Uganda Sports Union, 1964; Chairman, Board of Trustees, King George V Memorial Fund, 1964–69. Chancellor, Ahmadu Bello Univ., Zaria, 1972–75. Patron, Nigerian Soc. of Internat. Law, 1968–82; Mem., Nigerian Inst. of Internat. Affairs, 1979–. Grand Patron, Ikot Abasi dio. Methodist church, 1993. LLD *hc*: Ibadan, 1967; Zaria, 1972; TCD, 1973. Awarded title of Obong Ikpa Isong Ibibio, 1961. Kt of John Wesley, Methodist Conf., Nigeria, 1994. *Publications:* The Lion and the Oil Palm and other essays, 1943; (jtly) The Human Right to Individual Freedom—a Symposium on World Habeas Corpus, ed by Luis Kutner, 1970; The Story of the Ibibio Union, 1987; History and the Law of the Constitution of Nigeria, 1994. *Recreations:* billiards, tennis, gardening. *Address:* Mfut Itiat Enin, 8 Dr Udoma Street, PO Box 47, Ikot Abasi, Akwa Ibom State, Nigeria, West Africa. *Clubs:* Island, Metropolitan (Lagos); Yoruba Tennis (Vice-Patron, 1982–) (Lagos). *Died 2 Feb. 1998.*

UGLOW, Euan Ernest Richard; artist, painter; *b* 10 March 1932; *s* of Ernest and Elizabeth Uglow; *m* 1963, Clare O'Brien (marr. diss.). *Educ:* Camberwell Sch. of Art; Slade Sch. of Fine Art. Trustee, Nat. Gall., 1990–95; Art Advr, Arts Council. Examr, CNAA Bd, 1982–86. Fellow, UCL, 1983. Hon. Fellow, London Inst., 1998. *One-man exhibitions:* Beaux Arts Gall., 1961; Retrospective, Whitechapel Art Gall., 1974; Browse & Darby, 1977, 1983, 1989, 1991, 1997; Whitechapel Art Gall., 1989; Salander O'Reilly Gall., NY, 1993. *Recreations:* claret and conversation. *Address:* c/o Browse & Darby Ltd, 19 Cork Street, W1X 2LP. *T:* (020) 7734 7984. *Club:* Garrick. *Died 31 Aug. 2000.*

ULANOVA, Galina Sergeyevna; Order of Lenin, 1953, 1970; Hero of Socialist Labour, 1974, 1980; People's Artist of the USSR, 1951; Order of Red Banner of Labour, 1939, 1951, 1959, 1967; Order of People's Friendship, 1986; Badge of Honour, 1940; Prima Ballerina, Bolshoi Theatre, Moscow, 1944–60, retired; ballet-mistress at the Bolshoi Theatre since 1963; *b* 8 Jan. 1910; *d* of Sergei Nikolaevich Ulanov and Maria Feodorovna Romanova (dancers at Mariinsky Theatre, St Petersburg). *Educ:* State School of Choreography, Leningrad. Kirov Theatre of Opera and Ballet, Leningrad, 1928–44 (début, 1928); danced Odette-Odile in Swan Lake, 1929; Raimonda, 1931; Solweig in The Ice Maiden, 1931; danced Diane Mirelle in first performance of Flames of Paris, 1932; Giselle, 1933; Masha in The Nutcracker Suite, 1933; The Fountain of Bakhchisarai, as Maria, 1934; Lost Illusions, as Coralie, 1936; Romeo and Juliet, as Juliet, 1940; with Bolshoi: Cinderella, as Cinderella, 1945; Parasha in The Bronze Horseman, 1949; Tao Hua in The Red Poppy, 1950; Katerina in The Stone Flower, 1954. Visited London with the Bolshoi Theatre Ballet, 1956. Member, Academies of Arts of USA, GB and France. Winner of first Anna Pavlova Prize; awarded State Prize, 1941; for Cinderella, 1946; for Romeo and Juliet, 1947; for Red Poppy, 1950; awarded Lenin prize for outstanding achievement in ballet, 1957. FRAD 1963. *Address:* Bolshoi Theatre, Moscow, Russia. *Clubs:* Union of Theatrical Workers, Central House of Workers in the Arts. *Died 21 March 1998.*

UNWIN, Rayner Stephens, CBE 1977; Chairman, Unwin Enterprises, since 1986; Director, Allen and Unwin Australia, since 1990; *b* 23 Dec. 1925; *s* of late Sir Stanley

Unwin, KCMG, and Mary (*née* Storr); *m* 1952, Carol Margaret, *d* of Harold Curwen; one *s* three *d. Educ:* Abbotsholme Sch.; Trinity Coll., Oxford (MA); Harvard, USA (MA). Sub-Lt, RNVR, 1944–47. Entered George Allen & Unwin Ltd, 1951; Chm., 1968–86; Chm., 1986–88, Vice-Chm., 1988–90, Unwin Hyman. Mem. Council, Publishers' Assoc., 1965–85 (Treasurer, 1969; Pres., 1971; Vice-Pres., 1973); Chm., British Council Publishers' Adv. Cttee, 1981–88; Dir, Book House Training Centre, 1976–. Pres., Book Trade Benevolent Soc., 1989–95; Vice-Pres., Book Trust, 1991–. Trustee, Nat. Life Story Collection, 1998–. Chm., Little Missenden Festival, 1981–88. *Publications:* The Rural Muse, 1954; The Defeat of John Hawkins, 1960; A Winter away from Home, 1995; George Allen & Unwin: a remembrancer, 1999. *Recreations:* mountains, birds, gardens. *Address:* Limes Cottage, Little Missenden, near Amersham, Bucks HP7 0RG. *T:* (01494) 862900. *Club:* Garrick.

Died 23 Nov. 2000.

URWIN, Charles Henry, (Harry); Associate Fellow, Industrial Relations Research Unit, Warwick University, since 1981; Member, TUC General Council, 1969–80; Deputy General-Secretary, Transport and General Workers Union, 1969–80; Chairman, TUC Employment Policy and Organisation Committee, 1973–80; *b* 24 Feb. 1915; *s* of Thomas and Lydia Urwin; *m* 1941, Hilda Pinfold; one *d. Educ:* Durham County Council Sch. Convenor, Machine Tool Industry, until 1947; Coventry Dist Officer, TGWU, 1947–59; Coventry Dist Sec., Confedn of Shipbuilding and Engineering Unions, 1954–59; Regional Officer, TGWU, 1959–69. Member: Industrial Develt Adv. Bd, Industry Act, 1972–79; Sir Don Ryder Inquiry, British Leyland Motor Corp., 1974–75; Manpower Services Commn, 1974–79; Nat. Enterprise Bd, 1975–79; Energy Commn, 1977–79; Council, ACAS, 1978–80; Standing Cttee on Pay Comparability, 1979–80. *Recreation:* swimming. *Address:* 4 Leacliffe Way, Aldridge, Walsall WS9 0PW.

Died 9 Feb. 1996.

USBORNE, Henry Charles, MA; Founder, Parliamentary Group for World Government, 1946; *b* 16 Jan. 1909; *s* of Charles Frederick Usborne and Janet Lefroy; *m* 1936; two *s* two *d. Educ:* Bradfield; Corpus Christi, Cambridge. MP (Lab) Yardley Div. of Birmingham, 1950–59 (Acock's Green Div. of Birmingham, 1945–50). JP Worcs, 1964–79. *Address:* Totterdown, Evesham, Worcs WR11 5JP.

Died 16 March 1996.

USHER, Sir (William) John (Tevenar), 7th Bt *cr* 1899, of Norton, Ratho, Midlothian, and of Wells, Hobkirk, Roxburghshire; *b* 18 April 1940; *er s* of William Dove Usher (*d* 1969), 5th *s* of Sir Robert Usher, 2nd Bt, and of Christa Elizabeth, *d* of Bruno von Tevenar; *S* kinsman, 1994; *m* 1st, 1962, Rosemary Margaret (marr. diss. 1990), *d* of Col Sir Reginald Douglas Henry Houldsworth, 4th Bt, OBE, TD; two *s* one *d*; 2nd, 1992, Georgina Elizabeth, *d* of Charles Manclark. *Educ:* Uppingham. *Heir: s* Andrew John Usher [*b* 8 Feb. 1963; *m* 1987, Charlotte Louise Alexandra, *o d* of R. B. Eldridge; two *s*]. *Address:* 7 Thorngate Road, Hayfields, Pietermaritzburg 3201, South Africa.

Died 25 July 1998.

V

VAES, Baron Robert, Hon. KCMG 1966; LLD; Grand Officer, Order of Leopold, Belgium; Director of Sotheby's, since 1984; *b* Antwerp, 9 Jan. 1919; created Baron, 1985; *s* of Louis Vaes; *m* 1947, Anne Albers; one *d*. *Educ:* Brussels Univ. (LLD; special degree in Commercial and Maritime Law). Joined Diplomatic Service, 1946: postings to Washington, Paris, Hong Kong, London, Rome and Madrid; Personal Private Sec. to Minister of Foreign Trade, 1958–60; Dir-Gen. of Polit. Affairs, 1964–66; Permanent Under-Sec., Min. of For. Affairs, For. Trade and Develt Cooperation, 1966–72; Ambassador: to Spain, 1972–76; to UK, 1976–84. Numerous foreign decorations including: Grand Officer, Legion of Honour (France); Grand Cross, Order of Isabela la Católica (Spain). *Recreation:* bridge. *Address:* 45 Gloucester Square, W2 2TQ. *Clubs:* White's, Pratt's, Anglo-Belgian; Royal Yacht of Belgium. *Died 2 March 2000.*

VALDAR, Colin Gordon; consultant editor; *b* 18 Dec. 1918; 3rd *s* of Lionel and Mary Valdar; *m* 1st, 1940, Evelyn Margaret Barriff (marr. diss.); two *s*; 2nd, Jill (*née* Davis). *Educ:* Haberdashers' Aske's Hampstead School. Free-lance journalist, 1936–39. Served War of 1939–45, Royal Engineers, 1939–42. Successively Production Editor, Features Editor, Asst Editor, Sunday Pictorial, 1942–46; Features Editor, Daily Express, 1946–51; Asst Editor, Daily Express, 1951–53; Editor, Sunday Pictorial, 1953–59; Editor, Daily Sketch, 1959–62; Director, Sunday Pictorial Newspapers Ltd, 1957–59; Director, Daily Sketch and Daily Graphic Ltd, 1959–62; Chm., Bouverie Publishing Co., 1964–83. Founded UK Press Gazette, 1965. *Address:* 2A Ratcliffe Wharf, 18–22 Narrow Street, E14 8DQ. *T:* 0171-791 2155.

Died 11 Jan. 1996.

van den BOGAERDE, Sir Derek Jules Gaspard Ulric Niven, (Sir Dirk Bogarde), Kt 1992; actor and writer; *b* 28 March 1921; *s* of Ulric Jules van den Bogaerde and Margaret (*née* Niven). *Educ:* University College School; Allan Glen's (Scotland). Served War of 1939–45: Queen's Royal Regt, 1940–46, Europe and Far East, and Air Photographic Intelligence. Reviewer, Daily Telegraph, 1988–95. Hon. DLitt: St Andrews, 1985; Sussex, 1993. Commandeur de l'Ordre des Arts et des Lettres, 1990 (Chevalier, 1982). *Theatre:* Cliff, in Power Without Glory, New Lindsey, transf. Fortune, 1947; Orpheus, in Point of Departure, 1950; Nicky, in The Vortex, 1953; Alberto, in Summertime, 1955–56; Jezebel, Oxford Playhouse, 1958, etc. *Films,* 1947–, included: Hunted, Appointment in London, They Who Dare, The Sleeping Tiger, Doctor in the House, Doctor at Sea, Doctor at Large, Simba, The Spanish Gardener, Cast a Dark Shadow, Ill Met by Moonlight, The Blue Lamp, So Long at the Fair, Quartet, A Tale of Two Cities (Sidney Carton), The Wind Cannot Read, The Doctor's Dilemma, Libel, Song Without End, The Angel Wore Red, The Singer Not The Song, Victim, HMS Defiant, The Password is Courage, The Lonely Stage, The Mindbenders, The Servant, Doctor in Distress, Hot Enough for June, The High Bright Sun, King and Country, Darling . . ., Modesty Blaise, Accident, Our Mother's House, Mister Sebastian, The Fixer, Oh What A Lovely War, Götterdämmerung, Justine, Death in Venice, Upon This Rock, Le Serpent, The Night Porter, Permission To Kill, Providence, A Bridge Too Far, Despair, These Foolish Things; *television:* The Patricia Neal Story (USA), 1981 (film); May We Borrow Your Husband? (also adapted), 1986 (play); The Vision, 1987 (film); By Myself

(series), 1992; *radio* included Galsworthy in serial, The Forsyte Chronicles, 1990–91; No Man's Land, 1992. *Publications: autobiography:* A Postillion Struck by Lightning, 1977; Snakes and Ladders, 1978; An Orderly Man, 1983; Backcloth, 1986; A Particular Friendship, 1989; The Great Meadow, 1992; A Short Walk From Harrods, 1993; Cleared for Take Off, 1995; *novels:* A Gentle Occupation, 1980; Voices in the Garden, 1981 (televised 1993); West of Sunset, 1984; Jericho, 1992; A Period of Adjustment, 1994; Closing Ranks, 1997; For the Time Being, 1998. *Address:* c/o JAA, 27 Floral Street, WC2E 3DP. *Died 8 May 1999.*

VAN der KISTE, Wing Comdr Robert Edgar Guy, DSO 1941; OBE 1957; Royal Auxiliary Air Force, retired; Director, Plymouth Incorporated Chamber of Trade and Commerce, 1974–80 (Secretary, 1964–74); *b* 20 July 1912; *y s* of late Lt-Col F. W. Van der Kiste, DSO and Evelyn Grace, *d* of Gen. R. Y. Shipley, CB, Royal Fusiliers; *m* 1939, Nancy Kathleen, *er d* of Alec George Holman, MRCS, LRCP, and Grace Kathleen Brown; one *s* two *d* (and one *s* decd). *Educ:* Cheltenham College. Commissioned Royal Air Force, 1936; served War of 1939–45 (despatches, DSO); retired, 1959. Commanded No 3 MHQ Unit, Royal Auxiliary Air Force. *Recreations:* watching other people working, sleeping. *Address:* Lavandou, Moorland Park, South Brent, Devon TQ10 9AR. *Died 29 Sept. 1999.*

van der POST, Sir Laurens (Jan), Kt 1981; CBE 1947; writer, farmer, soldier, explorer, conservationist; Trustee, World Wilderness Foundation, since 1974, *b* Philippolis, S Africa, 13 Dec. 1906; *s* of late C. W. H. van der Post, Chairman of Orange Free State Republic Volksraad, and M. M. Lubbe, Boesmansfontein, Wolwekop, and Stilton; *m* 1st, 1928, Marjorie Wendt (marr. diss. 1947; she *d* 1995); one *d* (one *s* decd); 2nd, 1949, Ingaret Giffard. Served War of 1939–45: Ethiopia; North Africa; Syria; Dutch East Indies; Java; commanded 43 Special Military Mission, Prisoner of War 1943–45, thereafter Lord Mountbatten's Military-Political Officer, attached to 15 Indian Army Corps, Java, and subseq. to British Minister, Batavia, until 1947. Thereafter undertook several missions for British Government and Colonial Development Corp. in Africa, including Government Mission to Kalahari, 1952. FRSL. Hon. DLitt: Natal, 1964; Liverpool, 1976; Rhodes, 1978; St Andrews, 1980; Calgary, 1995; DUniv Surrey, 1971; Hon. LLD Dundee, 1989. *Films:* The Lost World of the Kalahari, 1956; A Region of Shadow, 1971; The Story of Carl Gustav Jung, 1971; All Africa Within Us, 1975; Shakespeare in Perspective—The Tempest, 1976; Zulu Wilderness: Black Umfolozi Re-discovered, 1979. *Publications:* In a Province, 1934; Venture to the Interior, 1952 (Book Society choice and Amy Woolf Memorial Prize); A Bar of Shadow, 1952 (repr., 1972); The Face Beside the Fire, 1953; Flamingo Feather, 1955 (German Book Society choice); The Dark Eye in Africa, 1955; Creative Pattern in Primitive Man, 1956; The Lost World of the Kalahari, 1958 (American Literary Guild Choice), rev. edn with long epilogue, The Great and Little Memory, 1988; The Heart of the Hunter, 1961; The Seed and the Sower, 1963 (South African CNA Award for best work published in 1963; filmed, 1983, as Merry Christmas, Mr Lawrence); Journey into Russia, 1964; A Portrait of all The Russias, 1967; The Hunter and the Whale, 1967 (CNA and Yorkshire Post Fiction Awards); A Portrait of Japan, 1968; The Night of the New Moon, 1970; A Story

like the Wind, 1972; A Far Off Place, 1974 (filmed, 1993); A Mantis Carol, 1975; Jung and the Story of Our Time, 1976; First Catch Your Eland: a taste of Africa, 1977; Yet Being Someone Other, 1982; (with Jane Taylor) Testament to the Bushmen, 1984; About Blady: a pattern out of time, 1991; The Voice of the Thunder, 1993; Feather Fall (anthology), 1994; The Admiral's Baby, 1996; *relevant publication:* A Walk with a White Bushman: Laurens van der Post in conversation with Jean-Marc Pottiez, 1986; *posthumous publication:* The Secret River, 1997. *Recreations:* walking, climbing, ski-ing, tennis, studying grasses, cooking in winter. *Address:* lived in London.
Died 16 Dec. 1996.

van EYCK, Aldo Ernest; Officer, Order of House of Orange; architect in private practice; *b* 16 March 1918; *s* of Peter Nicolaas van Eyck and Nellie Estelle van Eyck-Benjamins; *m* 1943, Hannie van Roojen; one *s* one *d.* *Educ:* Federal Sch. of Technology, Zürich. Private practice, 1951–, with Theo Bosch, 1971–82, with wife Hannie, 1983–; Prof. of Architecture, Delft Univ. of Technology, 1966–85; Paul Philip Cret Prof. of Architecture, Pennsylvania Univ., Philadelphia, 1979–84. Hon. FAIA 1981; Hon. RIAS 1985; Hon. Fellow, Bund Deutscher Arch. 1983; Hon. FRIBA 1988; Hon. Fellow: Royal Acad., Belgium, 1981; Royal Soc. of Architects in Holland, 1994. Hon. degrees from Dutch, Canadian and US Univs. Wihuri Internat. Culture Prize, Finland, 1982; Royal Gold Medal for Arch., RIBA, 1990; Medal for Science and Art, Austria, 1991; Ikea Prize, Holland, 1992; (jtly) Silver Cube, Royal Soc. of Architects in Holland, 1994; Internat. Prize for Architecture, Wolf Foundn, 1997. *Publications: essays:* Steps towards a configurative discipline, 1962; Miracles of moderation, 1968; Rats, Posts and other Pests, 1981 (RIBA annual discourse). *Recreations:* world-wide travel, lecturing. *Address:* Entrepotdok 23–24, 1018 AD Amsterdam, Holland. *T:* (20) 6230947. *Died 14 Jan. 1999.*

van LENNEP, Jonkheer Emile; Commander, Order of the Netherlands Lion; Commander, Order of Orange Nassau; Minister of State, since 1986; Secretary-General, OECD, 1969–84; *b* 20 Jan. 1915; *s* of Louis Henri van Lennep and Catharina Hillegonda Enschede; *m* 1941, Alexa Alison Labberton (decd); two *s* two *d.* Univ. of Amsterdam. Foreign Exchange Inst., 1940–45; Netherlands Bank, 1945–48; Financial Counsellor, High Representative of the Crown, Indonesia, 1948–50; Netherlands Bank, 1950–51; Treasurer-General, Ministry of Finance, The Netherlands, 1951–69. Chairman: Monetary Cttee, EEC, 1958–69; Working Party No 3, OECD, 1962–69; Mem., Board Directors, KLM (Airline), 1951–69. KStJ. Grand Cross or Grand Officer in various foreign orders. *Address:* Ruychrocklaan 444, 2597 EJ The Hague, Netherlands. *Club:* Haagsche (The Hague). *Died 3 Oct. 1996.*

VANNECK, Air Cdre Hon. Sir Peter Beckford Rutgers, GBE 1977 (OBE (mil.) 1963); CB 1973; AFC 1955; AE 1954; JP; DL; *b* 7 Jan. 1922; *y s* of 5th Baron Huntingfield, KCMG and Margaret Eleanor, *d* of Judge Ernest Crosby, NY; *m* 1st, 1943, Cordelia (marr. diss. 1984), *y d* of Captain R. H. Errington, RN (retd); one *d* (and one *d* decd); 2nd, 1984, Mrs Elizabeth Forbes; one step *s* one step *d.* *Educ:* Geelong Grammar Sch.; Stowe Sch. (Scholar); Trinity Coll., Cambridge (MA); Harvard; IEng; MIAgrE. Cadet, RN, 1939; served in Nelson, King George V, Eskimo, 55th LCA Flot., Wren, MTB 696 (in comd), 771 Sqdn and 807 Sqdn FAA, resigned 1949; Cambridge Univ. Air Sqdn, 1949; 601 (Co. of London) Sqdn RAuxAF, 1950–57 (101 Sqdn Mass. Air Nat. Guard, 1953); 3619 (Co. of Suffolk) Fighter Control Unit, 1958–61 (in comd 1959–61); No 1 Maritime HQ Unit, 1961–63; Group Captain, 1963; Inspector RAuxAF, 1963–73, Hon. Inspector-General 1974–83; ADC to the Queen, 1963–73;

Hon. Air Cdre, No 1 (Co. Hertford) Maritime HQ Unit, RAuxAF, 1973–87. Gentleman Usher to the Queen, 1967–79. Mem., Stock Exchange Council, 1968–79 (Dep. Chm., 1973–75). MEP (C) Cleveland, 1979–84, Cleveland and Yorks N, 1984–89; contested (C) Cleveland and Yorks N, EP, 1989. European Parliament: Mem., Energy, Res. and Technology Cttee, 1979–89; Vice-Chm., Political Affairs Cttee, 1984–89. Prime Warden, Fishmongers' Co., 1981–82; Past Master: Gunmakers' Co., 1977 and 1988; Guild of Air Pilots and Air Navigators, 1976–77; Freeman, Watermen's and Lightermen's Co., 1978; Alderman of Cordwainer Ward, City of London, 1969–79; Sheriff, City of London, 1974–75; Lord Mayor of London, 1977–78. Member: Ipswich Gp Hosps Bd, 1956–62; City and E London AHA, 1973–77; Gov. Body, Brit. Post Graduate Medical Fedn, Univ. of London, 1963–71; St Bartholomew's Hosp. Bd of Governors, 1971–73; Special Trustee, St Bartholomew's Hosp., 1974–82. Pres., Anglo-Netherlands Soc., 1989–99. Trustee: RAF Museum, 1976–87; Royal Academy Trust, 1981–87; Governor, RSC, 1974–87. President: Gun Trades Assoc., 1976–87; Stock Exchange Ski Club, 1977–87. FRSA 1995. Churchwarden of St Mary-le-Bow, 1969–84. Supernumerary JP City of London; DL Greater London, 1970; High Sheriff, Suffolk, 1979. Hon. DSc City Univ. KStJ (former Mem., Chapter General). Commander, Legion of Honour (France), 1981; Grand Officer, Order of the Crown (Belgium), 1983; Officer, Order of Orange Nassau (Netherlands), 1999. *Recreations:* sailing, bad bridge. *Address:* 10 Brompton Square, SW3 2AA; Red House, Sudbourne, Woodbridge, Suffolk IP12 2AT. *Clubs:* White's, Pratt's; Stock Exchange Ski; Royal Yacht Squadron, Royal London Yacht (Commodore, 1977–78); Bembridge Sailing, Island Sailing, Orford Sailing; Seawanhaka Corinthian Yacht (US).
Died 2 Aug. 1999.

van STRAUBENZEE, Sir William (Radcliffe), Kt 1981; MBE 1954; *b* 27 Jan. 1924; *o s* of late Brig. A. B. van Straubenzee, DSO, MC and Margaret Joan, 3rd *d* of A. N. Radcliffe, Kensington Square, W8, and Bag Park, Widecombe-in-the-Moor, Newton Abbot, S Devon. *Educ:* Westminster. Served War of 1939–45: five years with Royal Artillery (Major); Regimental and Staff appointments, including two years in Far East. Admitted a Solicitor, 1952. Chairman, Young Conservative Nat. Advisory Cttee, 1951–53. Contested Wandsworth (Clapham), 1955. MP (C) Wokingham, 1959–87. PPS to Minister of Educn (Sir David Eccles), 1960–62; Jt Parly Under-Sec. of State, Dept of Educn and Science, 1970–72; Minister of State, NI Office, 1972–74. Chairman: Select Cttee on Assistance to Private Members, 1975–77; Select Cttee on Educn and the Arts, 1984–87; Cons. Parly Educn Cttee, 1979–83. Mem. Exec. Cttee, 1922 Cttee, 1979–87. Member of Richmond (Surrey) Borough Council, 1955–58. Chairman: United and Cecil Club, 1965–68 (Hon. Sec., 1952–59); Westminster House Boys' Club, Camberwell, 1965–68 (Hon. Sec., 1952–65); Nat. Council for Drama Training, 1976–81. Hon. Sec., Fedn of Conservative Students, 1965–71, Vice-Pres., 1974. Member: House of Laity, Church Assembly, 1965–70; General Synod, 1975–85; Chairman: Dioceses Commn, 1978–86; Commn on Sen. Church Appts, 1988–92; Second Church Estates Commissioner, 1979–87. Patron of Living of Rockbourne, Hants. Freeman: Wokingham, 1980; Bracknell, 1994. Hon. DEd E London, 1995. *Recreations:* walking, reading. *Address:* 36 Ebury Street, SW1W 0LU. *T:* (020) 7730 0001. *Clubs:* Carlton, Garrick. *Died 2 Nov. 1999.*

VAREY, Prof. John Earl, PhD, LittD; FBA 1985; Principal, Westfield College, 1984–89, and Professor of Spanish, 1963–89, then Emeritus, London University; *b* 26 Aug. 1922; *s* of Harold Varey and Dorothy Halstead Varey; *m*

1948, Cicely Rainford Virgo; two *s* one *d* (and one *s* decd). *Educ:* Blackburn Grammar Sch.; Emmanuel Coll., Cambridge. MA 1948; PhD 1951; LittD 1981. Navigator, Bomber and Transport Commands, RAF, 1942–45. Westfield College: Lectr in Spanish, 1952; Reader, 1957; Actg Principal, 1983. Leverhulme Trust Fellow, 1970–71 and 1976; Visiting Professor: Univ. of Indiana, 1970, 1971; Purdue Univ., 1977. Pres., Assoc. of Hispanists of GB and Ireland, 1979–81. Corresp. Mem., Spanish Royal Acad., 1981; Hon. Mem., Instituto de Estudios Madrileños, 1988. Hon. Fellow, QMW, 1989. Hijo ilustre de Madrid, 1980. Co-founder, Tamesis Books Ltd, 1963; Partner, Editorial Támesis SL, 1992; Gen. Editor, Colección Támesis, 1963– (Chm., 1992–95). Hon. Dr Univ. Valencia, 1989. *Publications:* Historia de los títeres en España, 1957; (with N. D. Shergold) Los autos sacramentales en Madrid en la época de Calderón: 1637–1681, 1961; (ed) Galdós Studies, 1970; (ed with N. D. Shergold and Jack Sage) Juan Vélez de Guevara: Los celos hacen estrellas, 1970; Pérez Galdós: Doña Perfecta, 1971, 2nd edn 1993 (Spanish trans., 1989); (with N. D. Shergold, C. J. Davis and others) Fuentes para la historia del teatro en España, 26 vols, 1971–; (with D. W. Cruickshank) The Comedias of Calderón, 19 vols, 1973; (ed with J. M. Ruano) Lope de Vega: Peribáñez y el Comendador de Ocaña, 1980; Cosmovisión y escenografía: el teatro español en el Siglo de Oro, 1988; contrib. Bull. of Hispanic Studies, etc. *Recreation:* travel. *Address:* 38 Platt's Lane, NW3 7NT. *T:* (0171) 435 1764. *Died 28 March 1999.*

VAUGHAN, Frankie, (Frank Ableson), CBE 1997 (OBE 1965); DL; entertainer; *b* Liverpool, 3 Feb. 1928; *s* of Isaac Ableson and Leah Ableson; *m* 1951, Stella Shock; two *s* one *d*. *Educ:* Boys' Nat. Sch., Lancaster; Lancaster Coll. of Art (ATD). Professional singing début, 1951; record hits included: Green Door; Garden of Eden (British no 1, 1957); Tower of Strength (British no 1, 1961); theatre, concert and cabaret perfs worldwide, incl numerous Royal Comd Performances; Julian Marsh in 42nd Street, Drury Lane, 1986; *films* included: These Dangerous Years, 1957; Wonderful Things, 1958; The Lady is a Square, 1958; The Heart of a Man, 1959; Let's Make Love, 1961; The Right Approach, 1962; It's All Over Town, 1964. Patron, Nat. Boys' Clubs, 1987–; Dep. Pres., NABC–Clubs for Young People (formerly Nat. Assoc. of Boys' Clubs), 1975–. King Rat, Grand Order of Water Rats, 1968, 1998. Freeman, City of London, 1983; Liveryman, Co. of Carmen, 1988. DL Bucks, 1993. Hon. Fellow, Liverpool Poly., 1988. *Recreations:* golf, fishing. *Address:* c/o 68 Old Brompton Road, SW7 3LQ. *Died 17 Sept. 1999.*

VAUGHAN, William Randal; Founder and Proprietor, W. R. Vaughan Associates Ltd (formerly W. R. Vaughan Ltd), since 1945; *b* 11 March 1912; *m* 1945, K. A. Headland; three *s* one *d*. *Educ:* Centaur Trade School, Coventry. FIProdE. Apprenticed, Alfred Herbert Ltd, 1926; Coventry Gauge & Tool Co. Ltd, 1933; A. C. Wickman Ltd, 1934; A. Pattison Ltd, 1942; C. G. Wade Ltd, London, 1943. Chairman, Machine Tool Industry Research Assoc., 1974–83 (Vice-Pres., 1983–); President, Machine Tool Trades Assoc., 1977–79. Member of Lloyd's. *Recreations:* squash, skiing, sailing, flying. *Address:* Rowley Bank, Rowley Lane, Arkley, Barnet, Herts EN5 3HS. *T:* (0181) 441 4800. *Clubs:* Lansdowne, Royal Automobile. *Died 16 Sept. 1998.*

VAVASOUR, Comdr Sir Geoffrey William, 5th Bt *cr* 1828, of Haslewood, Yorkshire; DSC 1943; RN (retired); a Director of W. M. Still & Sons, 1962–80, retired; *b* 5 Sept. 1914; *s* of Captain Sir Leonard Vavasour, 4th Bt, RN, and Ellice Margaret Nelson; *S* father, 1961; *m* 1st, 1940, Joan Robb (marr. diss. 1947); two *d*; 2nd, 1971, Marcia Christine, *d* of late Marshall Lodge, Batley, Yorks.

Educ: RNC Dartmouth. *Heir: kinsman* Eric Michael Joseph Marmaduke Vavasour [*b* 3 Jan 1953; *m* 1976, Isabelle, *d* of André van Hille; two *s* one *d*]. *Address:* 8 Bede House, Manor Fields, Putney, SW15 3LT. *Club:* All England Lawn Tennis. *Died 28 July 1997.*

VEREY, Michael John, TD 1945; *b* 12 Oct. 1912; *yr s* of late Henry Edward and Lucy Alice Verey; *m* 1947, Sylvia Mary (*d* 2000), widow of Charles Bartlet and *d* of Lt-Col Denis Wilson and Mary Henrietta Wilson; two *s* one *d*. *Educ:* Eton; Trinity College, Cambridge (MA). Served War of 1939–45, Warwickshire Yeomanry; campaigns in Iraq, Syria, Persia, Western Desert, Italy; Lt Col comdg, 1944. Joined Helbert, Wagg & Co. Ltd, 1934; Chairman: J. Henry Schroder Wagg & Co. Ltd, 1972–73 (Dep. Chm., 1966–72); Schroders Ltd, 1973–77. Chairman: Accepting Houses Cttee, 1974–77; Broadstone Investment Trust Ltd, 1962–83; Brixton Estate Ltd, 1971–83; Trustees, Charities Official Investment Fund, 1974–83; American Energy Investments Ltd, 1981–83; Director: Rothschild Investment Trust, 1961–70; British Petroleum Co. Ltd, 1974–82; The Boots Co. (Vice-Chm., 1978–83); Commercial Union Assurance Co. Ltd (Vice-Chm., 1975–78; Dep. Chm., 1978–82); BI International, and other cos. Mem., Covent Garden Market Authority, 1961 66. Trustee: Manor Charitable Trust, 1951–90; Baring Foundn, 1988–91. High Sheriff of Berkshire, 1968. Pres., Warwickshire Yeomanry Regtl Assoc., 1976–86. *Recreations:* gardening, travel. *Address:* The Lodge, Little Bowden, Pangbourne, Berks RG8 8JR. *T:* (0118) 984 2210. *Club:* Boodle's. *Died 13 Oct. 2000.*

VERNIER-PALLIEZ, Bernard Maurice Alexandre; Commandeur de la Légion d'Honneur; Croix de Guerre; Médaille de la Résistance; Ambassadeur de France, 1904; *b* 2 March 1918; *s* of Maurice Vernier and Marie-Thérèse Palliez; *m* 1952, Denise Silet-Pathe; one *s* three *d*. *Educ:* Ecole des Hautes Etudes Commerciales; Ecole Libre des Sciences Politiques. Licencié en Droit. Joined Régie Nationale des Usines, Renault, 1945 (dealing with personnel and trade unions); Sécretaire Général, RNUR, 1948 67; Directeur Général Adjoint, RNUR, 1967–71; Président Directeur Général, SAVIEM, 1967–74; Délégué Général aux Vehicules Industriels, Cars et Bus à la RNUR, Président du Directoire de Berliet, and Vice-Président du Conseil de Surveillance de SAVIEM, Jan.-Dec. 1975; Président Directeur Général, RNUR, 1975–81; Ambassador to Washington, 1982–84. Dir, Public Affairs for Europe, International Distillers and Vintners, 1987–98; Mem., American International Gp Adv. Bd, 1985–. *Address:* 25 Grande Rue, 78170 La Celle St-Cloud, France. *T:* (1) 39693011. *Died 18 Dec. 1999.*

VERNON, 10th Baron *cr* 1762; **John Lawrance Vernon;** *b* 1 Feb. 1923; *s* of 9th Baron Vernon and Violet (*d* 1978), *d* of Col Charles Herbert Clay; *S* father, 1963; *m* 1st, 1955, Sheila Jean (marr. diss. 1982), *d* of W. Marshall Clark, Johannesburg; one *d* (and one *d* decd); 2nd, 1982, Sally, *d* of Robin Stratford, QC, and former wife of Sir Jeremy Tennyson-d'Eyncourt, 3rd Bt. *Educ:* Eton; Magdalen Coll., Oxford. Served in Scots Guards, 1942–46, retiring with rank of Captain. Called to the Bar, Lincoln's Inn, 1949. Served in various Government Departments, 1950–61; attached to Colonial Office (for service in Kenya), 1957–58. Chm., Population Concern, 1984–89. JP Derbyshire, 1965–77. *Heir: kinsman* Anthony William Vernon-Harcourt [*b* 29 Oct. 1939; *m* 1966, Cherry Stanhope, *er d* of T. J. Corbin; three *s* one *d*]. *Address:* Sudbury House, Sudbury, Ashbourne, Derbyshire DE6 5HT. *Club:* Boodle's. *Died 19 Aug. 2000.*

VERNON, James William, CMG 1964; retired; *b* 19 Nov. 1915; *s* of late John Alfred Vernon; *m* 1941, Betty Désirée, *d* of Gordon E. Nathan; one *s* one *d*. *Educ:* Wallasey Grammar Sch.; Emmanuel Coll., Cambridge (Scholar; BA

1937 (Senior Wrangler); MA 1940). Entered Civil Service, Ministry of Food, 1939; Flt Lieut, RAF, 1943; Wing Comdr (despatches), 1945; Principal Scientific Officer, Ministry of Works, 1945–48; Principal, 1948–54, Assistant Secretary, 1954–64, Colonial Office; Economic Adviser, British High Commission, Lusaka, 1966; Asst Under-Sec. of State, DEA, 1966–69; Under-Sec., Min. of Housing and Local Govt, later DoE, 1969–72. Called to the Bar, Inner Temple, 1975. Queen's Commendation for Brave Conduct, 1955. *Recreations:* gardening, computer science, chaos. *Address:* 20 Grove Hill, Topsham, Devon EX3 0EG.   *Died 17 May 1999.*

VESEY, Sir (Nathaniel) Henry (Peniston), Kt 1965; CBE 1953; Chairman, H. A. & E. Smith Ltd, 1939, then Hon. Chairman; Chairman, Bank of N. T. Butterfield & Son Ltd, 1970–86; Member of House of Assembly, Bermuda, 1938–72; *b* 1 June 1901; *s* of late Hon. Nathaniel Vesey, Devonshire, Bermuda; *m* 1920, Louise Marie, *d* of late Captain J. A. Stubbs, Shelly Bay, Bermuda; two *s. Educ:* Saltus Grammar Sch. Chairman: Food and Supplies Control Board, 1941–42; Board of Trade, 1943; Finance Cttee of House of Assembly, 1943–44; Bermuda Trade Development Board, 1945–56, 1960–69; Board of Civil Aviation, 1957–59; Board of Agriculture, 1957–59. MEC, 1948–57. Mem. Executive Council for Tourism and Trade, 1968–69. *Recreations:* fishing, golf. *Address:* Windward, Shelly Bay, Bermuda FL BX. *T:* 2930186. *Clubs:* Naval and Military; Royal Bermuda Yacht, Mid Ocean, Coral Beach (Bermuda).   *Died 19 April 1997.*

VICK, Sir (Francis) Arthur, Kt 1973; OBE 1945; PhD; FIEE, FInstP; MRIA; President and Vice-Chancellor, Queen's University of Belfast, 1966–76; Pro-Chancellor, University of Warwick, 1977–92 (Chairman of Council, 1977–90); *b* 5 June 1911; *s* of late Wallace Devenport Vick and Clara (*née* Taylor); *m* 1943, Elizabeth Dorothy Story (*d* 1989); one *d. Educ:* Waverley Grammar School, Birmingham; Birmingham Univ. Asst Lectr in Physics, University Coll., London, 1936–39, Lectr, 1939–44; Asst Dir of Scientific Research, Min. of Supply, 1939–44; Lectr in Physics, Manchester Univ., 1944–47, Sen. Lectr, 1947–50; Prof. of Physics, University Coll. of N Staffs, 1950–59 (Vice-Principal, 1950–54, Actg Principal, 1952–53); Dep. Dir, AERE, Harwell, 1959–60, Dir, 1960–64; Dir of Research Group, UKAEA, 1961–64; Mem. for Research, 1964–66. Institute of Physics: Mem. Bd, 1946–51; Chm., Manchester and District Branch, 1948–51; Vice-Pres., 1953–56; Hon. Sec., 1956–60. Chairman: Manchester Fedn of Scientific Societies, 1949–51; Naval Educn Adv. Cttee, 1964–70; Academic Adv. Council, MoD, 1969–76; Standing Conf. on Univ. Entrance, 1968–75. Pres., Assoc. of Teachers in Colls and Depts of Educn, 1964–72, Hon. Mem., 1972; Vice-Pres., Arts Council of NI, 1966–76. Member: Adv. Council on Bldg Research, Min. of Works, 1955–59; Scientific Adv. Council, Min. of Supply, 1956–59; UGC, 1959–66; Colonial Univ. Grants Adv. Cttee, 1960–65; Adv. Council on Research and Develt, Min. of Power, 1960–63; Nuclear Safety Adv. Cttee, Min. of Power, 1960–66; Governing Body, Nat. Inst. for Research in Nuclear Science, 1964–65. MRIA 1973. Hon. DSc: Keele, 1972; NUI, 1976; Birmingham, 1988; Warwick, 1993; Hon. LLD: Dublin, 1973; Belfast, 1977; Hon. DCL Kent, 1977. Kt Comdr, Liberian Humane Order of African Redemption, 1962. *Publications:* various scientific papers and contributions to books. *Recreations:* music, gardening, using tools. *Address:* Fieldhead Cottage, Fieldhead Lane, Myton Road, Warwick CV34 6QF. *T:* (01926) 491822. *Club:* Savile.   *Died 2 Sept. 1998.*

VICK, His Honour Richard (William); a Circuit Judge (formerly County Court Judge), 1969–89; Senior Circuit Judge in England and Wales, 1987–89; Judge,

Wandsworth County Court, 1985–89; Honorary Recorder of Guildford, since 1973; *b* 9 Dec. 1917; *s* of late Richard William Vick, JP, and Hilda Josephine (*née* Carlton), Windsor, Berks; *m* 1st, 1947, Judith Jean Warren (*d* 1974), *d* of Denis Franklin Warren; one *s* two *d*; 2nd, 1975, Mrs Joan Chesney Frost, BA (*d* 1994), *d* of Arthur Blaney Powe, MA, Sydney, Australia. *Educ:* Stowe; Jesus Coll., Cambridge (BA Hons). Served in RNVR, 1939–46: i/c Coastal Forces, Western Approaches, Mediterranean and N Sea. Called to Bar, Inner Temple, 1940. Partner, R. W. Vick Jr & Co., Lloyd's Insurance Brokers, 1944–46; Associate Mem. of Lloyd's, 1944–46; Deputy Chairman: W Kent QS, 1960–62; Kent QS, 1962–65; QS for Middx Area of Gtr London, 1965–69; Resident Judge, 1978–83, Liaison Judge for Magistrates, 1979–83, Kingston Gp of Courts. Chm., London Gp of County Court Judges, 1983–89. Vice-Chm., Surrey Magistrates Soc., 1972–83; Member: Magistrates' Courts Cttee; Probation Cttee, 1972–83; Circuit Adviser, Judicial Studies Bd, 1981–83. *Publication:* The Administration of Civil Justice in England and Wales, 1967. *Recreations:* sailing, swimming, bridge. *Address:* 18 Ibis Lane, Chiswick, W4 3UP. *Clubs:* Savage; Hawks (Cambridge); Bar Yacht; Royal Naval Sailing Association (Portsmouth).
                                   Died 1 April 1997.

VICKERS, Thomas Douglas, CMG 1956; *b* 25 Sept. 1916; 2nd *s* of late Ronald Vickers, Scaitcliffe, Englefield Green, Surrey; *m* 1951, Margaret Awdry, *o c* of late E. A. Headley, Wagga, NSW; one *s* one *d. Educ:* Eton; King's Coll., Cambridge (MA Hons). Served War of 1939–45; Coldstream Guards, 1940–45. Cadet, Colonial Administrative Service, 1938; Colonial Office, 1938–40 and 1945–50; Gold Coast, 1950–53; Colonial Secretary, British Honduras, 1953–60; Chief Secretary, Mauritius, 1960–67, Dep. Governor, 1967–68; retired from HMOCS, 1968; Head of Personnel Services, Imperial Cancer Research Fund, 1969–81. *Address:* Wood End, Worplesdon, Surrey GU3 3RJ. *T:* (01483) 233468. *Club:* Army and Navy.   *Died 21 May 1999.*

VIELER, Geoffrey Herbert, FCA; Member of Board, Post Office Corporation, 1969–71; *b* 21 Aug. 1910; *s* of late Herbert Charles Stuart Vieler, Huddersfield, and Emily Mary; *m* 1934, Phyllis Violet (*d* 1993); one *d. Educ:* Fairway Sch., Bexhill-on-Sea. With Vale & West, Chartered Accountants, Reading, 1927–41 (qual. 1932); War Service, 1941–46: commnd RAOC, 1943, Major 1945; joined Binder Hamlyn, Chartered Accountants, 1946, Partner 1959–69; Managing Dir, Posts and National Giro, 1969–71. Member: Techn. Adv. Cttee, Inst. of Chartered Accountants in England and Wales, 1967–74; Special Cttee, Tax Law Consultative Bodies, 1986–91. Chm., London Chartered Accountants, 1976–77; Chm., Taxation Cttee, ABCC, 1985–91. *Address:* Robins Wood, Monks Drive, South Ascot, Berks SL5 9BB.
                                   Died 28 Nov. 1997.

VILLIERS, Viscount; George Henry Child Villiers; guitarist and composer; *b* 29 Aug. 1948; *s* and *heir* of 9th Earl of Jersey and third wife, Bianca Maria Adriana Luciana, *er d* of late Enrico Mottironi, Turin; *m* 1st, 1969, Verna (marr. diss. 1973), 2nd *d* of K. A. Stott, St Mary, Jersey; one *d*; 2nd, 1974, Sandra (marr. diss. 1988), step *d* of H. Briginshaw, Feremina, St Martin, Guernsey; one *s* two *d*; 3rd, 1992, Stephanie Louise, *d* of J. J. Penman; one *s. Educ:* Eton; Millfield. Late The Royal Hussars (PWO). Leader, George Villiers Express. Recordings: Magical Dance, 1988; Dawn, 1989; No Dog Required, 1995. *Publication:* (ed) Classic Duets for Guitar. *Heir:* *s* Hon. George Francis William Child Villiers, *b* 5 Feb. 1976.
                                   Died 19 March 1998.

von BITTENFELD, Hans Heinrich H.; *see* Herwarth von Bittenfeld.

von CLEMM, (Frederick) Michael; Chairman and Chief Executive, Highmount Capital, since 1993; President, Templeton College, University of Oxford, since 1996; *b* 18 March 1935; *s* of Werner Conrad Clemm von Hohenberg and Veronica Rudge Green; *m* 1956, Louisa Bronson Hunnewell; two *d. Educ:* Harvard College (AB *cum laude* 1956); Harvard Graduate School of Arts and Sciences; Corpus Christi College, Oxford (MLitt 1959, DPhil 1962; Hon. Fellow 1996). Staff journalist, Boston Globe, 1959–60; First National City Bank, 1962–67; Faculty, Harvard Graduate Sch. of Business Administration, 1967–71; Chm., 1971–89, Pres., 1990–93, Roux Restaurants; White Weld & Co.: Exec. Dir, 1971–75; Man. Dir, 1975–78; Dep. Chm., 1976; Chm., Credit Suisse First Boston Ltd, 1978–86; Exec. Vice Pres., Merrill Lynch & Co. Inc., 1986–93; Chm., Merrill Lynch Capital Markets, 1986–93; Director: The India Fund, 1987–; Merrill Lynch Capital Partners, 1989–; Liberty Mutual Insce Gp, 1993– (Mem., Exec. Cttee, 1993–); Liberty Financial Co., 1993–; Rust International, 1993–95 (Member: Compensation Cttee; Audit Cttee); Eastman Chemical, 1993– (Chm., Finance Cttee); Nycomed ASA; Molson Cos, 1997–. Member Advisory Board: E African Develt Bank, 1979–; Creditanstalt Bankverein, Vienna, 1986–93. President: Foundn for Preservation of the Archaeol Heritage, USA, 1979–87; ESU of US, 1991–94; Vice-Pres., City of London Archaeol Trust, 1979–; Member: Court of The Mary Rose, 1982–; Adv. Bd, Royal Acad. of Arts, 1986–; Council, Compton Verney Opera Project, 1986–; Corp., Massachusetts Gen. Hosp., 1980–; Nat. Tanglewood Cttee, 1986–91; US–Japan Business Council, 1982–; US–Korea Business Council, 1988– (Chm.); Vis. Cttee, Harvard Univ. Grad. Sch. of Design, 1983–89 (Co-Chm., Resources Council, 1985–89); Cttee on Univ. Resources, Harvard Univ., 1986–; Vis. Cttee, Harvard Univ. Sch. of Public Health, 1990–; Bd of Fellows, Harvard Med. Sch., 1990–. Trustee and Hon. Treasurer, British Museum Develt Trust, 1979–94; Trustee: Gen. Hosp. Corp., 1988–; NY Historical Soc., 1989–92. *Publications:* contribs to Economic Botany, 1963, Harvard Business Review, 1971, Public Utilities Fortnightly, Euromoney and Jl of Comparative Corporate Law and Securities. *Recreations:* collecting Michelin Guide stars (with Albert and Michel Roux), collecting airline boarding cards. *Address:* (office) 2 Drayson Mews, W8 4LY. *T:* (0171) 499 7812. *Clubs:* White's, Boodle's; Porcellian (Trustee, 1988–) (Cambridge, Mass); Brook (NY). *Died 6 Nov. 1997.*

W

WADDELL, Sir Alexander (Nicol Anton), KCMG 1959 (CMG 1955); DSC 1944; HM Overseas Civil Service, retired; *b* 8 Nov. 1913; *yr s* of late Rev. Alexander Waddell, Eassie, Angus, Scotland, and Effie Thompson Anton Waddell; *m* 1949, Jean Margot Lesbia, *d* of late W. E. Masters. *Educ:* Fettes Coll., Edinburgh; Edinburgh Univ. (MA); Gonville and Caius Coll., Cambridge. Colonial Administrative Service, 1937; British Solomon Islands Protectorate: Cadet, 1937; District Officer, 1938; District Commissioner, 1945; Acting Resident Commissioner, 1945; Malayan Civil Service, 1946; Principal Asst Secretary, North Borneo, 1947–52 (Acting Dep. Chief Secretary, periods, 1947–51); Colonial Secretary, Gambia, 1952–56; Colonial Secretary, Sierra Leone, 1956–58; Dep. Governor, Sierra Leone, 1958–60; Governor and Commander-in-Chief of Sarawak, 1960–63; UK Comr, British Phosphate Commissioners, 1965–77. Mem., Panel of Independent Inspectors, Dept of the Environment, 1979–85. On Naval Service (Coastwatcher), 1942–44, Lieut, RANVR; on Military Service, 1945–47, Lt-Col, Gen. List (British Mil. Administration). *Recreations:* hill walking, golf, gardening. *Address:* Pilgrim Cottage, Ashton Keynes, Wilts SN6 6PD. *Clubs:* Royal Commonwealth Society, East India, Devonshire, Sports and Public Schools. *Died 14 June 1999.*

WADDILOVE, Lewis Edgar, CBE 1978 (OBE 1965); JP; Deputy Chairman, Housing Corporation, 1978–83 (Member since 1968); Director, Joseph Rowntree Memorial Trust, 1961–79 (Executive Officer of the Trust, 1946–61); *b* 5 Sept. 1914; *s* of Alfred and Edith Waddilove; *m* 1st, 1940, Louise Power (*d* 1967); one *s* one *d*; 2nd, 1969, Maureen Piper. *Educ:* Westcliff High Sch.; Univ. of London (DPA). Admin. Officer, LCC Educn Dept, 1936–38; Govt Evacuation Scheme, Min. of Health, 1938–43; Friends Ambulance Unit, Middle East, 1943–45 (Exec. Chm., 1946). Chairman: Friends Service Council, 1961–67; Nat. Fedn of Housing Assocs (formerly Socs), 1965–73 and 1977–79 (Vice-Pres., 1982–90); Member: Cttee on Housing in Greater London (Milner Holland), 1963–65; Nat. Cttee for Commonwealth Immigrants, 1966–68; Social Science Research Council, 1967–71; Public Schools Commn, 1968–70; Central Housing Advisory Cttee, 1960–75; Standing Cttee, Centre for Socio-Legal Studies at Oxford, 1972–75; Legal Aid Advisory Cttee, 1972–78; Adv. Cttee on Rent Rebates and Rent Allowances, 1975–81; Cttee on Voluntary Organisations, 1974–78; Working Party on Housing Cooperatives, 1974–76; Central Appeals Adv. Cttee (BBC and IBA), 1974–84 (Chm., 1978–84); Chairman: Advisory Cttee on Fair Rents, 1973–74; Advisory Cttee on Housing Cooperatives, 1976–79; York City Charities, 1957–65 and 1972–88; York Univ. Council, 1977–87; Personal Social Services Council, 1977–80; Coal Mining Subsidence Compensation Review Cttee, 1983–84; Trustee, Shelter, 1966–74 (Chm. 1970–72). Presiding Clerk, 4th World Conf. of Friends, in N Carolina, 1967. Governor, Co. of Merchant Adventurers, City of York, 1978–79. Governor: Leighton Park Sch., 1951–71; Bootham and The Mount Schs., 1972–81 (Chm. 1974–81). JP York, 1968. DUniv: Brunel, 1978; York, 1987. *Publications:* One Man's Vision, 1954; Housing Associations (PEP), 1962; Private Philanthropy and Public Welfare, 1983; various articles in technical jls. *Address:* 14 Rowan Avenue, New Earswick, York YO32 4AT. *T:* (01904) 768696.

Died 21 Aug. 2000.

WADDINGTON, Gerald Eugene, CBE 1975; QC (Cayman Islands) 1971; Attorney General of the Cayman Islands, 1970–77; *b* 31 Jan. 1909; *o s* of Walter George Waddington and Una Blanche Waddington (*née* Hammond); *m* 1935, Hylda Kathleen (*née* Allen); one *s* one *d*. *Educ:* Jamaica Coll.; Wolmer's Sch., Jamaica. Solicitor, Supreme Court, Jamaica, 1932; LLB (London) 1949; Solicitor, Supreme Court, England, 1950; called to the Bar, Gray's Inn, 1957. Deputy Clerk of Courts, Jamaica, 1939; Asst Crown Solicitor, Jamaica, 1943–48; Resident Magistrate, 1948–58; Puisne Judge, 1959–64; Judge of the Court of Appeal, Jamaica, 1964–70, retired. Joint Ed., West Indian Law Reports. Vice-Pres. Nat. Rifle Assoc. Chm. St John Council for Jamaica. CStJ 1962, KStJ 1970. *Recreation:* shooting (Member of Jamaica Rifle Team to Bisley, 1937, 1950, 1953, 1956, 1957, 1960, 1963, 1965, 1967, 1968; Captain, 1950, 1953, 1957, 1967; Captain, WI Rifle Team, 1960). *Address:* 41 Pretty Street, Stittsville, Ontario K2S 1N5, Canada. *Died 6 March 1996.*

WADE, Maj.-Gen. (Douglas) Ashton (Lofft), CB 1946; OBE 1941; MC 1918; BA; CEng; MIEE; *b* 13 March 1898; 2nd *s* of C. S. D. Wade, solicitor, Saffron Walden, Essex; *m* 1st, 1926, Heather Mary Patricia Bulmer (*d* 1968), Sowerby, Thirsk, Yorkshire; one *d*; 2nd, 1972, Cynthia Halliday (*née* Allen). *Educ:* St Lawrence Coll., Ramsgate; Royal Military Acad., Woolwich; Clare Coll., Cambridge. Commnd into Royal Artillery, 1916; served European War, France, Italy and S Russia; seconded RE, 1918–21; transferred to Royal Signals, 1921; Staff Coll., Camberley, 1933–34; DAQMG India, 1937–40; GSO 1, GHQ, BEF and GHQ Home Forces, 1940–41; AA&QMG 2nd Division, 1941–42; Dep. Ajt-General, India, 1942–44; Comdr, Madras Area, India, 1944–47; GOC Malaya District, 1947–48; Mem., Indian Armed Forces Nationalisation Cttee, 1947; Special Appointment War Office, 1948–49; retired, 1950; Telecommunications Attaché, British Embassy, Washington, 1951–54; Sen. Planning Engineer, Independent Television Authority, 1954–60; Regional Officer, East Anglia, Independent Television Authority, 1960–64. Technical Consultant: Inter-University Research Unit, Cambridge, 1965–69; WRVS Headquarters, 1970–75. Chm., South East Forum for closed circuit TV in educn, 1967–73. Chm., Royal Signals Institute, 1957–63; National Vice-Chairman Dunkirk Veterans' Association, 1962–67, National Chairman, 1967–74. *Publications:* A Life on the Line (autobiog.), 1988; contributed to various Services publications, including RUSI Journal, United Services Journal (India), and Brassey's Annual. *Recreations:* gardening, writing. *Address:* Phoenix Cottage, 6 Church Street, Old Catton, Norwich NR6 7DS. *T:* Norwich (01603) 425755. *Died 14 Jan. 1996.*

WADE, Maj.-Gen. Ronald Eustace, CB 1961; CBE 1956; retired; *b* 28 Oct. 1905; *s* of late Rev. E. V. Wade and Marcia Wade; *m* 1933, Doris, *d* of late C. K. Ross, Kojonup, WA; one *s* one *d*. *Educ:* Melbourne Church of England Grammar Sch.; RMC, Duntroon, ACT. Commissioned, 1927; attached 4/7 DG (India), 1928–29; Adjutant 10 LH and 9 LH, 1930–38; Captain, 1935; Major, 1940; served War of 1939–45, Lieut-Colonel (CO 2/10 Aust. Armd Regt), 1942; Colonel (Colonel A, Adv. LHQ, Morotai), 1945; Colonel Q, AHQ, Melbourne, 1946; idc 1948; Director of Cadets, 1949; Director of Quartering, 1950–51; Director of Personal Services, 1951–52; Military Secretary, 1952–53; Comd 11 Inf. Bde (Brig.), 1953–55;

Maj.-General (Head Aust. Joint Service Staff, Washington), 1956–57; Adjutant-General, 1957–60; GOC Northern Command, 1961–62, retired, 1962. *Address:* Windsor, 1/20 Comer Street, Como, WA 6152, Australia.
Died 12 Aug. 1995.

WAHLSTRÖM, General Jarl Holger; International Leader of The Salvation Army, 1981–86; *b* 9 July 1918; *s* of Rafael Alexander Wahlström and Aina Maria Wahlström (*née* Dahlberg); *m* 1944, Maire Helfrid Nyberg; two *s* one *d*. *Educ:* Salvation Army International Training Coll. Salvation Army, Finland: Corps Officer, 1939–45; Scout Organizer, 1945–52; Private Sec. to Territorial Commander, 1952–54; Youth Sec., 1954–60; Divisional Comdr, 1960–63; Principal, Training Coll., 1963–68; Chief Secretary, 1968–72; Territorial Comdr, 1976–80; Salvation Army, Canada and Bermuda: Chief Secretary, 1972–76; Salvation Army, Sweden: Territorial Comdr, 1981. Hon. DHL Western Illinois, 1985. Cross of Liberty, IV cl. (Finland), 1941; Knight, Order of the Finnish Lion, 1964; Order of Civil Merit, and Mugunghwa Medal (Korea), 1983; Comdr, Order of the White Rose (Finland), 1989. *Publications:* (autobiog.) Matkalaulu (Finnish edn), En Vallfartssång (Swedish edn), 1989; contribs to Salvation Army papers and magazines, English, Finnish, Swedish. *Recreation:* music. *Address:* Borgströminkuja 1 A 10, 00840 Helsinki, Finland. *T:* (0) 6982413. *Club:* Rotary. *Died 3 Dec. 1999.*

WAIN, Prof. (Ralph) Louis, CBE 1968; DSc, PhD; FRS 1960, FRSC; Hon. Professor of Chemistry, University of Kent, since 1977 and Emeritus Professor, University of London, since 1978; Professor of Agricultural Chemistry, University of London, 1950–78, and Head of Department of Physical Sciences at Wye College (University of London), 1945–78; Hon. Director, Agricultural Research Council Unit on Plant Growth Substances and Systemic Fungicides, 1953–78; Fellow of Wye College, since 1981; *b* 29 May 1911; 2nd *s* of late George Wain, Hyde, Cheshire; *m* 1940, Joan Bowker; one *s* one *d*. *Educ:* County Grammar Sch., Hyde, Cheshire; University of Sheffield (First Class Hons Chemistry, 1932; MSc 1933; PhD 1935; Hon. DSc 1977); DSc London, 1949. Town Trustees Fellow, University of Sheffield, 1934; Research Assistant, University of Manchester, 1935–37; Lecturer in Chemistry, Wye Coll., 1937–39; Research Chemist, Long Ashton Research Station (University of Bristol), 1939–45; Rockefeller Fellow, 1950 and 1962. Vice-President, Royal Institute of Chemistry, 1961–64, 1975–78; Member: Governing Body, Glasshouse Crops Res. Inst., 1953–71; E African Natural Resources Res. Council, 1963; Manager, Royal Instn, 1971–74. Chm., AFRC Wain Fellowships Cttee, 1976. NZ Prestige Fellowship, 1973; Leverhulme Emeritus Fellowship, 1978. Lectures: Sir Thomas Middleton Meml, London, 1955; Frankland Meml, Birmingham, 1965; Benjamin Minge Duggar Meml, Alabama, 1966; Amos Meml, E Malling, 1969; Masters Meml, London, 1973; Sir Jesse Boot Foundn, Nottingham, 1974; Ronald Slack Meml, London, 1975; Extramural Centenary, London Univ., 1976; Vis. Lectr, Pontifical Acad. Scis, 1976; Douglas Wills, Bristol, 1977; Gooding Meml, London, 1978; Drummond Meml, London, 1979; John Dalton, Manchester, 1979; Holden, Nottingham, 1984; Hannaford Meml, Adelaide, 1985. Nuffield Vis. Prof., Ibadan Univ., 1959; Vis. Prof., Cornell Univ., 1966; Royal Soc. Vis. Prof. to Jordan, 1960, Sudan, 1965, Czechoslovakia, 1968, Mexico, 1971, China, 1973 and 1982, Romania, 1974, Poland, 1976, Bulgaria, 1978, Israel, 1979, Hungary, 1980, West Indies and Philippines, 1981, Hong Kong, 1984, 1988, Indonesia, 1989, S Korea, 1990, Japan 1991, Australia 1992, Taiwan 1993. Elected to Académie Internationale de Lutèce, 1980. Pruthivi Gold Medal, 1957; RASE Research Medal, 1960; John Scott Award, 1963; Flintoff Medal, Chem. Soc., 1969; Internat.

Award, Amer. Chem. Soc., 1972; Internat. Medal for Research on Plant Growth Substances, 1973; John Jeyes Gold Medal and Award, Chem. Soc., 1976; Royal Instn Actonian Award, 1977; Mullard Award and Medal, Royal Soc., 1988. Hon. DAgricSci, Ghent, 1963; Hon. DSc: Kent, 1976; Lausanne, 1977. *Publications:* numerous research publications in Annals of Applied Biology, Journal of Agric. Science, Journal of Chemical Society, Berichte der Deutschen Chemischen Gesellschaft, Proc. Royal Society, etc. *Recreations:* painting, travel. *Address:* Crown Point, Scotton Street, Wye, Ashford, Kent TN25 5BZ. *T:* (01233) 812157. *Died 14 Dec. 2000.*

WAINWRIGHT, Edwin, BEM 1957; *b* 12 Aug. 1908; *s* of John Wainwright and Ellen (*née* Hodgson); *m* 1938, Dorothy Metcalfe; two *s* two *d*. *Educ:* Darfield Council School; Wombwell and Barnsley Technical Colleges. WEA student for 20 years. Started work at 14, at Darfield Main Colliery; Nat. Union of Mineworkers: Member Branch Cttee, 1933–39; Delegate, 1939–48; Branch Sec., 1948–59; Member, Nat. Exec. Cttee, 1952–59. Member, Wombwell UDC, 1939–59. Sec./Agent, Dearne Valley Labour Party, 1951–59. MP (Lab) Dearne Valley, S Yorks, Oct. 1959–1983; Mem., Select Cttee on Energy, 1979–83. Secretary: PLP Trade Union Gp, 1966–83; Yorkshire Gp of PLP, 1966–83. *Recreations:* gardening, reading. *Address:* 20 Dovecliffe Road, Wombwell, near Barnsley, South Yorks S73 8UE. *T:* (01226) 752153.
Died 22 Jan. 1998.

WAKEFIELD, Rev. Gordon Stevens; Principal of the Queen's College, Birmingham, 1979–87; Director, Alister Hardy Research Centre, Oxford, 1989–92; *b* 15 Jan. 1921; *s* of Ernest and Lucy Wakefield, *m* 1949, Beryl Dimes; one *s* three *d*. *Educ:* Crewe County Sec. School; Univ. of Manchester; Fitzwilliam Coll. and Wesley House, Cambridge (MA); St Catherine's Coll., Oxford (MLitt). Methodist Circuit Minister in Edgware, Woodstock, Stockport, Newcastle upon Tyne, Bristol, 1944–63; Methodist Connexional Editor, 1963–72; Chairman, Manchester and Stockport Methodist District, 1971–79; Chaplain, Westminster Coll., Oxford, 1988–89. Fernley-Hartley Lectr, 1957; Select Preacher: Univ. of Oxford, 1971 and 1982; Cambridge, 1988. Recognized Lectr, Univ. of Birmingham, 1979–87. Member, Joint Liturgical Group (Chairman, 1978–84). DD Lambeth, 1986. *Publications:* Puritan Devotion, 1957; (with Hetley Price) Unity at the Local Level, 1965; Methodist Devotion, 1966; The Life of the Spirit in the World of Today, 1969; On the Edge of the Mystery, 1969; Robert Newton Flew, 1971; Fire of Love, 1976; (ed, with biographical introdns of E. C. Hoskyns and F. N. Davey) Crucifixion—Resurrection, 1981; (ed) Dictionary of Christian Spirituality, 1983; Kindly Light, 1984; The Liturgy of St John, 1985; John Wesley, 1990; Bunyan the Christian, 1992; An Outline of Christian Worship, 1998; Medicines for the Heart, 1999; Methodist Spirituality, 1999; T. S. Gregory, 2000; contribs to theological jls and symposia. *Recreations:* watching and talking cricket, churches and cathedrals. *Address:* 56 Wissage Road, Lichfield WS13 6SW. *T:* (01543) 414029. *Died 11 Sept. 2000.*

WALD, Prof. George; Professor of Biology, 1948–77, Higgins Professor of Biology, 1968–77, then Emeritus Professor, Harvard University; *b* 18 Nov. 1906; *s* of Isaac Wald and Ernestine (*née* Rosenmann); *m* 1st, 1931, Frances Kingsley (marr. diss.); two *s*; 2nd, 1958, Ruth Hubbard; one *s* one *d*. *Educ:* Washington Square Coll. of New York Univ. (BS); Columbia Univ. (PhD). Nat. Research Council Fellowship, 1932–34; Harvard University: Instr and Tutor in Biology, 1934–39; Faculty Instr, 1939–44; Associate Prof., 1944–48. Nobel Prize in Physiology and Medicine (jointly), 1967. Vice-Pres., People's Permanent Tribunal, Rome (Pres., internat.

tribunals on El Salvador, Philippines, Afghanistan, Zaire, Guatemala). Wrote and lectured on cold war, arms race, human rights, nuclear power and weapons; developed World-Third World relations. Many hon. doctorates from univs in USA and abroad. Guest, China Assoc. for Friendship with Foreign Peoples, Jan.-Feb. 1972; US/Japan Distinguished Scientist Exchange, 1973. *Publications:* (co-author) General Education in a Free Society; (co-author) Twenty-six Afternoons of Biology; many sci. papers on the biochemistry and physiology of vision and on biochem. evolution in Jl of Gen. Physiology, Nature, Science, Jl of Opt. Soc. of Amer., etc. *Recreations:* art, archæology. *Address:* 21 Lakeview Avenue, Cambridge, MA 02138–3325, USA. *T:* (617) 8687748.
Died 12 Aug. 1997.

WALKER, Bobby; *see* Walker, W. B. S.

WALKER, Sir Colin (John Shedlock), Kt 1991; OBE 1981; Chairman, National Blood Authority, 1993–98; *b* 7 Oct. 1934; *s* of Arthur John Walker and Olave Gertrude Walker; *m* 1963, Wendy Elizabeth Ellis; two *s. Educ:* St Edward's Sch., Oxford; Royal Agricultural Coll., Cirencester. Landowner, farmer and businessman. Chm., Harwich Haven Authority (formerly Harbour Bd), 1988–. Mem., 1985–88, Vice-Chm., 1991–93, Central Blood Labs Authority; Chairman: E Suffolk HA, 1986–87; E Anglian RHA, 1987–94 (Mem., 1983–86). Chm., All Party European Movement in Suffolk, 1979–81; various posts, incl. Chm., Constituency Cons. Assoc., 1968–88. Mem., Suffolk CC, 1976–80. Chm. of Govs, Orwell Park Sch., 1991–97. *Recreations:* shooting, gardening, reading, forestry, conservation. *Address:* Blomvyle Hall, Hacheston, Woodbridge, Suffolk IP13 0DY. *T:* (01728) 746756, *Fax:* (01728) 747737. *Club:* Royal Over-Seas League.
Died 1 Sept. 1999.

WALKER, Paul Francis; Marketing Consultant: Academy of Medical Sciences, since 1998; Royal College of Pathologists, 1991–97; *b* 22 April 1932; *s* of Robert Philip Sebastian Walker and Nora (*née* Parsons); *m* 1961, Sally Jonquil Taylor; three *s. Educ:* Stonyhurst Coll.; London Univ. BBC studio manager and announcer, 1953–55; TV producer and Internat. Exec., J. Walter Thompson, 1955–72; Educn Dir, Help The Aged, 1972–73; Exec. Dir, Muscular Dystrophy Gp of GB and NI, 1973–91 (Vice-Pres., 1998–). Mem., English Cttee, Internat. Year of Disabled People, 1981. Founder Trustee, Stackpole Trust, 1981–98; Trustee: Child Rescue International, 1986–98; Patrick Foundn, 1987–. Pres., Neuromuscular Centre, 1992–95. *Recreations:* bridge, snooker. *Address:* The Quarry, Quarry Road, Oxted, Surrey RH8 9HF. *T:* (01883) 712834.
Died 29 Sept. 1999.

WALKER, Walter Basil Scarlett, (Bobby), MA; FCA; Deputy UK Senior Partner, Peat, Marwick, Mitchell & Co., 1979–82; *b* 19 Dec. 1915; *s* of James and Hilda Walker, Southport; *m* 1945, Teresa Mary Louise John (decd); one *d* (and one *s* decd). *Educ:* Rugby Sch.; Clare Coll., Cambridge (MA). Joined Peat, Marwick, Mitchell & Co., 1937, leaving temporarily, 1939, to join RNVR; service in Home Fleet, incl. convoys to Russia and Malta, 1940–42; finally, Asst Sec. to British Naval C-in-C in Germany; Lt-Comdr; returned to Peat, Marwick, Mitchell & Co., 1946, becoming a partner, 1956. Mem. (part-time), UKAEA, 1972–81. Governor, Royal Ballet, Covent Garden, 1980–90. *Recreations:* ballet, gardening, golf. *Address:* 11 Sloane Avenue, SW3 3JD. *T:* (0171) 589 4133; Coles, Privett, near Alton, Hants GU34 3PH. *T:* (01730) 828223. *Club:* Royal Automobile.
Died 25 Dec. 1996.

WALL, Major Sir Patrick (Henry Bligh), Kt 1981; MC 1945; VRD 1957; Royal Marines, retired; *b* 19 Oct. 1916; *s* of Henry Benedict Wall and Gladys Eleanor Finney; *m*

1953, Sheila Elizabeth Putnam (*d* 1983); one *d. Educ:* Downside. Commissioned in RM, 1935 (specialised in naval gunnery); served in HM Ships, support craft, with RM Commandos and US Navy; Actg Major, 1943; RN Staff Coll., 1945; Joint Services Staff Coll., 1947; Major, 1949; CO 47 Commando RMFVR, 1951–57; Comr for Sea Scouts in London, 1950–66. Westminster City Council, 1953–62. Contested Cleveland Division (Yorks), 1951 and 1952. MP (C): Haltemprice Div. of Hull, Feb. 1954–1955; Haltemprice Div. of E Yorks, 1955–83; Beverley, 1983–87, retd. Parliamentary Private Secretary to: Minister of Agriculture, Fisheries and Food, 1955–57; Chancellor of the Exchequer, 1958–59. Mem., Select Cttee on Defence, 1980–83. Chm. Mediterranean Group of Conservative Commonwealth Council, 1954–67; Chm. Cons. Parly East and Central Africa Cttee, 1956–59; Vice-Chairman: Conservative Commonwealth Affairs Cttee, 1960–68; Cons. Overseas Bureau, 1963–73; Cons. Defence Cttee, 1965–77; Vice-Chm. or Treasurer, IPU, 1974–82 (Chairman: British-Maltese, Anglo-Bahrain, Anglo-South African, Anglo-Taiwan Groups; Vice-Chm., Anglo-Portuguese Gp; Treasurer, Anglo-Korean Gp); North Atlantic Assembly: Leader, British Delegn, 1979–87; Pres., 1983–85; Chm., Mil. Cttee, 1978–81; Chm., Cons./Christian Democrat Gp, 1977–87. Mem. Defence Cttee, WEU and Council of Europe, 1972–75. Chairman: Cons. Fisheries Sub-Cttee, 1962–83; Africa Centre, 1961–65; Joint East and Central Africa Board, 1965–75; Cons. Southern Africa Group, 1970–78; Cons. Africa Sub-Cttee, 1979–83; RM Parly Group, 1956–87; British Rep. at 17th General Assembly of UN, 1962. Chm., Monday Club, 1978–80. Pres., Yorks Area Young Conservatives, 1955–60. Pres., British UFO Res. Assoc.; Vice-Pres., British Sub-Aqua Club, 1955–87. FIJ 1989. Freeman of Beverley, 1989. Kt, SMO Malta; USA Legion of Merit, 1945; Gold Star of Taiwan, 1988. *Publications:* Royal Marine Pocket Book, 1944; Student Power, 1968; Defence Policy, 1969; Overseas Aid, 1969; The Soviet Maritime Threat, 1973; The Indian Ocean and the Threat to the West, 1975; Prelude to Detente, 1975; Southern Oceans and the Security of the Free World, 1977; co-author of a number of political pamphlets. *Recreation:* ship and aircraft models. *Address:* Lordington Park, Lordington, near Chichester, West Sussex PO18 9DX. *T:* (01243) 370989. *Club:* Royal Naval Sailing Association.
Died 15 May 1998.

WALLACE OF CAMPSIE, Baron *cr* 1974 (Life Peer), of Newlands, Glasgow; **George Wallace;** JP; DL; Life President, Wallace, Cameron (Holdings) Ltd, 1981 (President, 1977–81); Director, Smith & Nephew Associated Companies Ltd, 1973–77; *b* 13 Feb. 1915; *s* of John Wallace and Mary Pollock; *m* 1977, Irene Alice Langdon Phipps, *er d* of Ernest Phipps, Glasgow. *Educ:* Queen's Park Secondary Sch., Glasgow; Glasgow Univ. Estd Wallace, Cameron & Co. Ltd, 1948, Chm., 1950–77. Solicitor before the Supreme Courts, 1950–; Hon. Sheriff at Hamilton, 1971–. Chm., E Kilbride and Stonehouse Devlt Corp., 1969–75; Mem. Bd, S of Scotland Electricity Bd, 1966–68; founder Mem. Bd, Scottish Devlt Agency, 1975–78; Chm., E Kilbride Business Centre, 1984–89. Pres., Glasgow Chamber of Commerce, 1974–76; Vice-Pres., Scottish Assoc. of Youth Clubs, 1971–; Chm., Adv. Bd (Strathclyde) Salvation Army, 1972–90; Mem. Court, Univ. of Strathclyde, 1973–74; Hon. Pres., Town and Country Planning Assoc. (Scottish Sect.), 1969–; Chm., Scottish Exec. Cttee, Brit. Heart Foundn, 1973–76; Chm., Britannia Cttee, British Sailors' Soc., 1967–77; Vice-Chm., Scottish Retirement Council, 1975–; Hon. Pres., Lanarkshire Samaritans, 1984–97. FRSA 1970; FSAScot 1990; FCIM (FInstM 1968); FIMgt (FBIM 1990). Hon. Mem., Royal Faculty of Procurators, 1997. JP 1968, DL 1971, Glasgow. Hon. LLD Strathclyde, 1993. KStJ 1976.

Recreation: reading. *Address:* 14 Fernleigh Road, Newlands, Glasgow G43 2UE. *T:* (0141) 637 3337. *Club:* Royal Scottish Automobile (Glasgow).

Died 23 Dec. 1997.

WALLER, Rt Hon. Sir George (Stanley), Kt 1965; OBE 1945; PC 1976; a Lord Justice of Appeal, 1976–84; *b* 3 Aug. 1911; *s* of late James Stanley and Ann Waller; *m* 1936, Elizabeth Margery, *d* of 1st Baron Hacking; two *s* one *d. Educ:* Oundle; Queens' Coll., Cambridge (Hon. Fellow 1974). Called to the Bar, Gray's Inn, 1934, Bencher, 1961, Treasurer, 1978. RAFO, 1931–36; served War of 1939–45, in RAFVR, Coastal Command; 502 Sqdn, 1940–41; Wing Comdr, 1943 (despatches). Chm., Northern Dist Valuation Bd, 1948–55; QC 1954; Recorder of Doncaster, 1953–54, of Sunderland, 1954–55, of Bradford, 1955–57, of Sheffield, 1957–61, and of Leeds, 1961–65; a Judge of the High Court, Queen's Bench Div., 1965–76; Presiding Judge, NE Circuit, 1973–76. Solicitor-General of the County Palatine of Durham, 1957–61; Attorney-General of the County Palatine of Durham, 1961–65. Member: Criminal Injuries Compensation Board, 1964–65; General Council of the Bar, 1958–62 and 1963–65; Parole Bd, 1969–72 (Vice-Chm., 1971–72); Adv. Council on the Penal System, 1970–73 and 1974–78; Criminal Law Revision Cttee, 1977–85; Chm., Policy Adv. Cttee on Sexual Offences, 1977–85. President: Inns of Court and Bar, 1979–80; British Acad. of Forensic Sciences, 1983–84. *Address:* Hatchway, Hatch Lane, Kingsley Green, Haslemere, Surrey GU27 3LJ. *T:* (01428) 644629. *Clubs:* Army and Navy; Hawks (Cambridge).

Died 5 Feb. 1999.

WALLS, Prof. Daniel Frank, FRS 1992; FRSNZ; Professor of Physics, University of Auckland, since 1987; *b* 13 Sept. 1942; *s* of James Reginald Walls and Barbara Gertrude Walls (*née* Leddra); *m* 1968, Fari Khoy (marr. diss. 1986); one *s*; partner, since 1989, Pamela Christine Maude King. *Educ:* Univ. of Auckland (MSc); Harvard Univ. (PhD). Asst Prof., Univ. of Stuttgart, 1970; Postdoctoral Fellow, Univ. of Auckland, 1971; University of Waikato: Sen. Lectr, 1972; Reader, 1976; Prof., 1980. FAPS; Fellow, Optical Soc. of America. Hector Medal, RSNZ, 1988; Einstein Medal for Laser Science, USA, 1990; Paul Dirac Medal, Inst. of Physics, 1995. *Publications:* numerous papers on quantum optics in learned jls. *Recreations:* skiing, swimming, tramping. *Address:* 75A Selwyn Avenue, Mission Bay, Auckland, New Zealand.

Died 12 May 1999.

WALMSLEY, (Arnold) Robert, CMG 1963; MBE 1946; HM Diplomatic Service, retired; *b* 29 Aug. 1912; *s* of late Rev. Canon A. M. Walmsley; *m* 1944, Frances Councell de Mouilpied. *Educ:* Rossall Sch.; Hertford Coll., Oxford (1st Class Maths Mods, 1st Class Modern Greats). Private Sec. to Julius Meinl, Vienna, 1935–38; Foreign Office, 1939–45; established in Foreign Service, 1946; Foreign Office, 1946–50; British Consul in Jerusalem, 1950–54; Foreign Office, 1954–63; Head of Arabian Dept, 1961; Counsellor, Khartoum, 1963–65; Dir, Middle East Centre of Arab Studies, Lebanon, 1965–69. Order of the Two Niles (Sudan), 1965. *Publications:* (as Nicholas Roland) The Great One, 1967; Natural Causes, 1969; Who Came by Night, 1971. *Address:* 10 Park Lane, Saffron Walden, Essex CB10 1DA. *Club:* Travellers.

Died 23 May 2000.

WALMSLEY, Prof. Robert, TD 1984; MD; FRCPE, FRCSE, FRSE; Bute Professor of Anatomy, University of St Andrews, 1946–73; *b* 24 Aug. 1906; *s* of late Thomas Walmsley, Supt Marine Engr; *m* 1939, Isabel Mary, *e d* of James Mathieson, Aberdeen; two *s. Educ:* Greenock Acad.; Univ. of Edinburgh; Carnegie Inst. of Embryology, Baltimore, USA. MB, ChB (Edinburgh); MD (Edinburgh) with Gold Medal, 1937. Demonstrator, Lectr and Senior

Lectr on Anatomy, Univ. of Edinburgh, 1931–46; Goodsir Fellowship in Anatomy, 1933; Rockefeller Fellowship, 1935–36; served as Pathologist in RAMC in UK and MEF, 1939–44. Struthers Lectr, Royal Coll. of Surgeons, Edinburgh, 1952; Fulbright Advanced Scholarship, 1960; Pres., Edinburgh Harveian Soc., 1963–64. Vis. Prof. of Anatomy: George Washington Univ., USA, 1960; Auckland, NZ, 1967. Formerly: Master, St Salvator's Coll.; Chm. Council, St Leonards and St Katherines Schs; Hon. Pres., British Medical Students Assoc.; External Examiner in Anatomy, Cambridge, Edinburgh, Durham, Glasgow, Aberdeen, Liverpool, Singapore, Kingston (WI), Accra, etc. Life Mem. Anatomical Soc. Hon. Fellow, British Assoc. of Clinical Anatomists, 1980. Hon. DSc St Andrews, 1972. First Farquharson Award, RCSEd, 1974. *Publications:* (jtly) Manual of Surgical Anatomy, 1964; (jtly) Clinical Anatomy of the Heart, 1978; (co-reviser) Jamieson's Illustrations Regional Anatomy, 1981; contribs to various jls, on heart, bone and joints, and on whales. *Recreation:* gardening. *Address:* 45 Kilrymont Road, St Andrews, Fife KY16 8DE. *T:* (01334) 472879.

Died 24 Aug. 1998.

WALSH, Sir Alan, Kt 1977; DSc; FRS 1969; consultant spectroscopist; *b* 19 Dec. 1916; *s* of late Thomas Haworth and Betsy Alice Walsh, Hoddlesden, Lancs; *m* 1949, Audrey Dale Hutchinson; two *s. Educ:* Darwen Grammar Sch.; Manchester Univ. BSc 1938; MSc (Tech.) 1946; DSc 1960. FAA 1958. British Non-Ferrous Metals Research Assoc., 1939–42 and 1944–46; Min. of Aircraft Production, 1943; Div. of Chemical Physics, CSIRO, Melbourne, 1946–77 (Asst Chief of Div., 1961–77). Einstein Memorial Lectr, Australian Inst. of Physics, 1967; Pres., Australian Inst. of Physics, 1967–69. Hon. Member: Soc. of Analytical Chemistry, 1969; Royal Soc. NZ, 1975. Foreign Mem., Royal Acad. of Sciences, Stockholm, 1969. FTS 1982. Hon. FCS 1973; Hon. FAIP 1981; Hon. Mem., Japan Soc. of Analytical Chemistry, 1981. Hon. DSc: Monash, 1970, Manchester, 1984. Britannica Australia Science Award, 1966; Research Medal, Royal Soc. of Victoria, 1968; Talanta Gold Medal, 1969; Maurice Hasler Award, Soc. of Applied Spectroscopy, USA, 1972; James Cook Medal, Royal Soc. of NSW, 1975; Torbern Bergman Medal, Swedish Chem. Soc., 1976; Royal Medal, Royal Soc., 1976; John Scott Award, City of Philadelphia, 1977; Matthew Flinders Medal, Aust. Acad. of Science, 1980; Robert Boyle Medal, RSC, 1982; K. L. Sutherland Medal, Aust. Acad. of Technol Sciences, 1982; Inaugural CSI Award, Colloquium Spectroscopicum Internationale, 1991. *Publications:* papers in learned jls. *Address:* 43A Carpenter Street, Brighton, Vic 3186, Australia. *T:* (3) 95924897. *Club:* Metropolitan Golf (Melbourne).

Died 3 Aug. 1998.

WALSH, Brian; DL; QC 1977; **His Honour Judge Walsh;** a Senior Circuit Judge and Recorder of Leeds, since 1996; *b* 17 June 1935; *er s* of late Percy Walsh and Sheila (*née* Frais), Leeds; *m* 1964, Susan Margaret, *d* of late Eli (Kay) Frieze and Doris Frieze; two *d. Educ:* Sheikh Bagh Sch., Srinagar, Kashmir; Leeds Grammar Sch. (Head Boy, 1954); Gonville and Caius Coll., Cambridge (BA, LLB; MA 1992). Pres., Cambridge Union Soc., 1959. Served RAF (Pilot Officer), 1954–56. Called to the Bar, Middle Temple, 1961 (Blackstone Scholar, Harmsworth Scholar); Bencher, 1986. Joined North Eastern Circuit, 1961, Leader, 1990–94; a Recorder, 1972–96. Member: Circuit Exec. Cttee, 1980–96; Gen. Council of the Bar, 1982–84, and 1990–96; Mental Health Review Tribunal, 1986–. Chm., W Yorks Criminal Justice Liaison Cttee, 1996–. Mem. Court, Leeds Univ., 1988–; Vice-Pres., Yorks CCC, 1993– (Mem. Cttee, 1984–93, Chm., 1986–91); Governor: Leeds Grammar Sch., 1977–; Leeds Girls' High Sch., 1978–96; Chm., Leeds Grammar Sch./Leeds Girls' High Sch. Foundn, 1997–; Pres., Old Leodiensian Assoc., 1983–85.

DL W Yorks, 1998. *Recreations:* golf, cricket, eating. *Address:* Leeds Combined Court Centre, 1 Oxford Row, Leeds LS1 3BG. *T:* (0113) 283 0040.

Died 23 Sept. 2000.

WALSH, Lt-Gen. Geoffrey, CBE 1944; DSO 1943; CD; *b* 19 Aug. 1909; *s* of late H. L. Walsh; *m* 1935, Gwynn Abigail Currie; one *s*. *Educ:* Royal Military Coll., Kingston; McGill Univ. (BEng (EE)). DSc(Mil) RMC, Kingston, 1971. Chief Engineer, 1st Canadian Army, 1944–45 (mentioned in despatches (twice) 1945); DQMG, 1945–46; Comdr Northwest Highway System, 1946–48; Comdr Eastern Ontario Area, 1948–51; Comdr 27 Bde (Europe), 1951–52; DGMT, 1953–55; QMG, 1955–58; GOC, Western Command, 1958–61; Chief of the General Staff, Canada, 1961–64; Vice Chief of the Defence Staff, Canada, 1964–65. Col Comdt, Royal Canadian Army Cadets and Cadet Services of Canada, 1970–73. Legion of Merit (US); Comdr of Orange Order of Nassau (Netherlands). *Recreations:* golf, fishing, philately. *Address:* 201 Northcote Place, Rockcliffe Park, Ottawa, ON K1M 0Y7, Canada. *Clubs:* RMC, Royal Ottawa Golf (Ottawa); USI (Ottawa and Edmonton).

Died 3 April 1999.

WALSH, James Mark, CMG 1956; OBE 1948; HM Diplomatic Service; Consul-General, Zürich, 1962–68; *b* 18 Aug. 1909; *s* of Mark Walsh and Emily (*née* Porter); *m* 1st, 1937, Mireille Loir (*d* 1966); one *s*; 2nd, 1967, Bertha Hoch. *Educ:* Mayfield Coll., Sussex; King's Coll., London. BA (Hons) 1929; LLB 1932. Called to the Bar, Lincoln's Inn, 1932; passed an examination and appointed to Foreign Service, 1932; Vice-Consul: Paris, 1932–33, Rotterdam, 1933–34; Judge of HBM Consular Court, Alexandria, Egypt, 1934–38; Acting Consul-General, Barcelona, 1939; Vice-Consul, Philadelphia, 1939–44; Consul, Antwerp, 1944–45; First Secretary, British Legation: Helsinki, 1945–46; Budapest, 1946–48; Dep. Consul-General, New York, 1948–50; Counsellor (Commercial), Ankara, 1950–54, and Berne, 1954–59; Consul-General, Jerusalem, 1959–62. *Recreations:* painting, golf. *Address:* Fairfield, The Paddock, Haslemere, Surrey GU27 1HB. *T:* (01428) 652089. *Died 27 June 1997.*

WALSH, Prof. William; Professor of Commonwealth Literature, 1972–84, then Emeritus, and Acting Vice-Chancellor, 1981–83, University of Leeds; Douglas Grant Fellow in Commonwealth Literature in the School of English, since 1969; Chairman, School of English, 1973–78; *b* 23 Feb. 1916; *e s* of William and Elizabeth Walsh; *m* 1945, May Watson; one *s* one *d*. *Educ:* Downing Coll., Cambridge; University of London. Schoolmaster, 1943–51; Senior English Master, Raynes Park County Grammar Sch., 1945–51; Lecturer in Education, University Coll. of N Staffordshire, 1951–53; Lecturer in Education, Univ. of Edinburgh, 1953–57; Prof. of Education, and Head of Dept of Education, Univ. of Leeds, 1957–72, Chm., Sch. of Education, 1969–72; Chm., Bd of combined Faculties of Arts, Economics, Social Studies and Law, Univ. of Leeds, 1964–66; Pro-Vice-Chancellor, Univ. of Leeds, 1965–67. Chm. Bd of Adult Educn, 1969–77; Member: IBA Adult Educn Cttee, 1974–76; IBA Educn Adv. Cttee, 1976–81; Bd of Foundn for Canadian Studies in UK, 1981–. Dir, Yorkshire TV, 1967–86; Trustee, Edward Boyle Meml Trust, 1981–. Vis. Prof., ANU, 1968; Australian Commonwealth Vis. Fellow, 1970; Vis. Prof., Canadian Univs, 1973; Leverhulme Emeritus Fellow, 1986–88. Hon. LLD Leeds, 1984. *Publications:* Use of Imagination, 1959; A Human Idiom, 1964; Coleridge: the Work and the Relevance, 1967; A Manifold Voice, 1970; R. K. Narayan, 1972; V. S. Naipaul, 1972; Commonwealth Literature, 1973; Readings in Commonwealth Literature, 1973; D. J. Enright: poet of humanism, 1974; Patrick White: Voss, 1976; Patrick

White's Fiction, 1977; F. R. Leavis, 1981; Introduction to Keats, 1981; R. K. Narayan: a critical appreciation, 1982; Indian Literature in English, 1990; contributions to: From Blake to Byron, 1957; Young Writers, Young Readers, 1960; Speaking of the Famous, 1962; F. R. Leavis—Some Aspects of his Work, 1963; The Teaching of English Literature Overseas, 1963; Higher Education: patterns of change in the 1970s, 1972; Literatures of the World in English, 1974; Considerations, 1977; Indo-English Literature, 1977; Perspectives on Mulk Raj Anand, 1978; Awakened Conscience, 1978; The Study of Education, vol. 1, 1980; The Twofold Voice: essays in honour of Ramesh Mohan, 1982; Life by Other Means: essays on D. J. Enright, 1990; Edward Boyle: his life by his friends, 1991; papers and essays on literary and educational topics in British and American journals. *Address:* 27 Moor Drive, Headingley, Leeds LS6 4BY. *T:* Leeds (0113) 275 5705.

Died 23 June 1996.

WALSH-ATKINS, Leonard Brian, CMG 1962; CVO 1961; Assistant Under-Secretary of State, Commonwealth Relations Office, 1962; retired 1970; *b* 15 March 1915; *o c* of late Leonard and Gladys Atkins; step *s* of late Geoffrey Walsh, CMG, CBE; *m* 1st, 1940, Marguerite Black (marr. diss. 1968); three *s*; 2nd, 1969, Margaret Eva, *d* of Sidney Gould Ashford, and formerly wife of Baron Runcorn, PC, TD. *Educ:* Charterhouse (Scholar); Hertford Coll., Oxford (Scholar; BA 1937). Asst Principal, India Office, 1937; Fleet Air Arm, 1940–45; Lieut-Comdr (A), RNVR (despatches); Burma Office, 1945–47; Commonwealth Relations Office, 1947; Counsellor, Dublin, 1953–56; idc 1957; Dep. High Comr, Pakistan, 1959–61. The Abbeyfield Society, 1971–89 (Nat. Vice Chm., 1984–88); Dep. Chm., Nat. Fedn of Housing Assocs, 1984–86. *Address:* Berkeley Cottage, Mayfield, E Sussex TN20 6AU. *Died 28 April 1997.*

WALTERS, Very Rev. Derrick; *see* Walters, Very Rev. R. D. C.

WALTERS, Peter Ernest, CMG 1965; Group Staff Manager, Courage Ltd, 1967–78 (Staff Manager, Courage, Barclay and Simonds Ltd, 1967); Member, London (South) Industrial Tribunal, 1978–82; *b* 9 Oct. 1913; *s* of Ernest Helm Walters and Kathleen Walters (*née* Farrer-Baynes); *m* 1943, Ayesha Margaret (*d* 1996), *d* of Alfred and Winifred Bunker; three *d*. *Educ:* Windlesham House Sch. Emigrated to Kenya, 1931. Army Service, 1939–45; commissioned KAR, 1940; Major 1944. Cadet, Colonial Admin. Service, Kenya, 1945; Dist Comr, 1948; Provincial Comr, Northern Prov., 1959; Civil Sec., Eastern Region, Kenya, 1963–65; retd from Colonial Service, 1965; Principal, Min. of Aviation (London), 1965–67. Member Management Committee: Southern Housing Gp, 1983–96; Coastal Counties Housing Assoc., 1983–96; CAB, Dorking, 1986–96. *Address:* Honeywood House, Rowhook, Horsham, West Sussex RH12 3QD. *Club:* Nairobi (Kenya). *Died 17 Oct. 1999.*

WALTERS, Very Rev. (Rhys) Derrick (Chamberlain), OBE 1994; Dean of Liverpool, 1983–99; *b* 10 March 1932; *s* of Ivor Chamberlain Walters and Rosamund Grace Walters (*née* Jackson); *m* 1959, Joan Trollope (*née* Fisher); two *s*. *Educ:* Gowerton Boys' Grammar School; London School of Economics (BScSoc 1955); Ripon Hall, Oxford. Deacon 1957, priest 1958; Curate, Manselton, Swansea, 1957–58; Anglican Chaplain, University College, Swansea and Curate, St Mary's, 1958–62; Vicar of All Saints, Totley, 1962–67; Vicar of St Mary's, Boulton by Derby, 1967–74; Diocesan Missioner, Diocese of Salisbury, 1974–82; Vicar of Burcombe, 1974–79; Non-residentiary Canon of Salisbury, 1978; Residentiary Canon and Treasurer of Salisbury Cathedral, 1979–82. Hon. Fellow, Liverpool John Moores Univ. (formerly Liverpool Poly.), 1988. *Recreations:* escapist literature, croquet, classical music. *Address:* Lady Chapel Close, Liverpool L1 7BZ. *Died 5 April 2000.*

WALTON, Anthony Michael; QC 1970; *b* 4 May 1925; *y s* of Henry Herbert Walton and Clara Martha Walton, Dulwich; *m* 1955, Jean Frederica, *o d* of William Montague Hey, Bedford; one *s*. *Educ:* Dulwich College (Scholar); Hertford College, Oxford (Scholar; pupil to W. L. Ferrar (maths) and C. H. S. Fifoot (law); BA 1946; BCL 1950; MA 1950). Pres., Oxford Union Society, Trinity Term 1945. Nat. Service as physicist. Called to the Bar, Middle Temple, 1950 (Bencher, 1978; Master Reader, Autumn, 1996); pupil to Lord Justice Winn. Interested in education. Liveryman, Worshipful Co. of Gunmakers. Freeman, City of London, 1968. *Publications:* (ed) (Asst to Hon. H. Fletcher Moulton) Digest of the Patent, Design, Trade Mark and Other Cases, 1959; (ed) Russell on Arbitration, 17th edn 1963–20th edn 1982; (with Hugh Laddie) Patent Law of Europe and the United Kingdom, 1978. *Address:* 62 Kingsmead Road, SW2 3JG.

Died 18 Nov. 2000.

WALTON, Sir John Robert, Kt 1971; retired; Director, Waltons Ltd Group, Australia (Managing Director, 1951–72; Chairman, 1961–72); Chairman, FNCB-Waltons Corp. Ltd, Australia, 1966–75; *b* 7 Feb. 1904; *s* of John Thomas Walton; *m* 1938, Peggy Everley Gamble; one *s* one *d*. *Educ:* Scots Coll., Sydney. National Cash Register Co Pty Ltd, 1930: NSW Manager, 1934; Managing Director in Australia, 1946–51. *Recreations:* gardening, swimming, golf, reading. *Address:* 9A Longwood, 5 Thornton Street, Darling Point, NSW 2027, Australia. *Clubs:* Rotary, Royal Sydney Golf, American National, Tattersall's (all in Sydney).

Died 13 Jan. 1998.

WANI, Most Rev. Silvanus; *b* July 1916; *s* of late Mana Ada Wani and Daa Miriam; *m* 1936, Penina Yopa Wani, six *s* two *d* (and two *s* decd). *Educ:* Kampala Normal School, Makerere (Teacher's Cert.). Teaching, Arua Primary School, 1936–39; student, Buwalasi Theol Coll., 1940–42; ordained as one of first two priests in West Nile District, 1943; Chaplain, King's African Rifles, 1944–46; Parish Priest: Arua, 1947–50; Koboko, 1951–60; Canon and Rural Dean, Koboko, 1953–60; attended Oak Hill Theological Coll., 1955–56; Diocesan Secretary/Treasurer, N Uganda Diocese, 1961–64; student (Christianity and Islam), St George's Coll., Jerusalem, 1963–64; Asst Bishop, later full Bishop, N Uganda, 1964; Bishop of Madi/West Nile Diocese, 1969; Dean, Province of Church of Uganda, Rwanda, Burundi and Boga Zaire, 1974–77; Archbishop of Uganda (also of Rwanda, Burundi and Boga Zaire, 1977–80) and Bishop of Kampala, 1977–83; retd, on health and age grounds, to home area, 1983. Chaplain Gen. to Uganda Armed Forces, 1964–78. *Recreations:* reading, walking, gardening. *Address:* c/o PO Box 370, Arua, Uganda. *Died 4 Feb. 1998.*

WARD, Ven. Arthur Frederick; Archdeacon of Exeter, 1970–81, Archdeacon Emeritus since 1981; Canon Residentiary of Exeter Cathedral, 1970–81, Precentor, 1972–81; *b* 23 April 1912; *s* of William Thomas and Annie Florence Ward, Corbridge, Northumberland; *m* 1937, Margaret Melrose, Tynemouth, Northumberland; two *d*. *Educ:* Durham Choir School; Newcastle upon Tyne Royal Grammar School; Durham University; Ridley Hall, Cambridge. Deacon 1935, priest 1936; Curate, Byker Parish Church, Newcastle, 1935–40; Rector of Harpurhey, North Manchester, 1940–44; Vicar of Nelson, 1944–55; Vicar of Christ Church, Paignton, 1955–62; Archdeacon of Barnstaple and Rector of Shirwell with Loxhore, Devon, 1962–70. *Recreations:* gardening, cricket, touring. *Address:* Melrose, Christow, Devon EX6 7LY. *T:* (01647) 252498. *Died 30 Sept. 1998.*

WARD, Bill; *see* Ward, I. W.

WARD, Edmund Fisher, CBE 1972; architect; *b* 29 Sept. 1912; *m* Marjorie; one *d*. Formerly Partner, then Consultant, Gollins Melvin Ward Partnership. Member, Royal Fine Art Commission, 1974–83.

Died 27 March 1998.

WARD, Ivor William, (Bill), OBE 1968; independent televison producer and director, since 1982; Deputy Managing Director, Associated Television (Network) Ltd, 1974–77; *b* 19 Jan. 1916; *s* of Stanley James Ward and Emily Ward; *m* 1st, 1940, Patricia Aston; two *s* one *d*; 2nd, 1970, Betty Nichols; one step *s*; 3rd, 1988, Sandra Calkins Hastie. *Educ:* Hoe Grammar Sch., Plymouth. Asst Engr, BBC Radio Plymouth, 1932; Technical Asst, BBC Experimental TV Service, Alexandra Palace, 1936; Maintenance Engr, BBC TV London, 1937; Instructor Radar, REME and Military Coll. of Science, 1939–45; Studio Manager, BBC TV, 1946; Producer, BBC TV, 1947–55; Head of Light Entertainment, ATV (Network), ITV, 1955–61; Production Controller, ATV, 1961–63; Executive Controller and Production Controller, ATV, 1963–67; Director of Programmes, ATV, 1968–76; Head of Operations Group, European Broadcasting Union: World Cup 1978, 1977–78; Moscow Olympics 1980, 1978–82. Chm., ITV Network Sports Cttee, 1972–77; Exec. producer, Highway series, ITV, 1983. FRTS 1989; FRSA. *Recreations:* sport, golf, fishing, motor sport and motor cars, photography, music. *Address:* Nichols Nyman Cottage, North Tawton, Devon EX20 2BR.

Died 21 Oct. 1999.

WARD, Prof. John Clive, FRS 1965; Professor, Macquarie University, Sydney, NSW, 1967–84, then Emeritus; *b* 1 Aug. 1924; *s* of Joseph William Ward and Winifred Palmer; *m* 1965, Catherine Levin. *Educ:* Bishops Stortford Coll.; Merton Coll., Oxford (Hon. Fellow, 1995). Member, Inst. for Advanced Study, Princeton, 1951–52, 1955–56, 1960–61; Professor of Physics: Carnegie Inst. of Technology, Pittsburgh, 1959–60; The Johns Hopkins University, Baltimore, 1961–66. Hughes Medal, Royal Soc., 1983. *Publications:* various articles on particle theory and statistical mechanics. *Recreations:* travel, music. *Address:* 3477 Arbutus Drive South, Cobble Hill, BC V0R 1L1, Canada. *Died 6 May 2000.*

WARD, Air Vice-Marshal Peter Alexander; *b* 26 Jan. 1930; *s* of Arthur Charles Ward and Laura Mary (*née* Squires); *m* 1963, Patricia Louise (*née* Robertson); two *s*. *Educ:* Woking Grammar School. Joined RAF, 1947; Flying and Staff appointments; OC 511 Sqdn, 1968–70; jssc 1970; ndc 1971; Station Comdr, RAF Brize Norton, 1974–75; Senior Air Staff Officer, HQ 38 Group, 1976–79; rcds 1979; Dir Gen., RAF Training, 1980–82; Dep. COS (Ops), HQ Allied Air Forces Central Europe, 1982–84. Gen. Manager, Bromley HA, 1985–87. Director: Corps of Commissionaires Management; OEF Management Services; Vice-Chm., Regular Forces Employment Assoc.; Mem., Royal Patriotic Fund Corp. Chm., St Barbe Foundn, 1994–; Trustee, Lymington Mus. Trust, 1994–. Gov., Bromley Coll., 1986–. *Address:* Swiss Cottage, Lower Buckland Road, Lymington, Hampshire SO41 9DU.

Died 20 Nov. 1996.

WARD, Thomas William, RE 1955; RWS 1957; sometime Course Director, Illustration, Harrow College of Technology and Art; painter in water colour and oil colour, draughtsman, engraver, illustrator; *b* 8 Nov. 1918; *s* of John B. Ward, Master Stationer, and Lilly B. Ward (*née* Hunt), Sheffield; *m* Joan Palmer, ARCA, *d* of F. N. Palmer, Blackheath; one *s* one *d*. *Educ:* Nether Edge Grammar Sch., Sheffield; Sheffield Coll. of Art (part-time); Royal Coll. of Art, 1946–49 (ARCA 1949; Silver Medal, 1949); Postgrad. Scholarship, RCA, 1949–50. Cadet, Merchant

Service, 1935–36; stationer, 1936–39; Military service, 1939–46: commissioned N Staffs Regt, 1942; GSO3, 1944–46. *One man exhibitions included:* Walker Gall., 1957, 1960; Wakefield City Art Gall., 1962; Shipley Art Gall., 1962; Middlesbrough Art Gall., 1963; St John's Coll., York, 1965; Bohun Gall., Henley, 1974; Digby Gall., Colchester, 1981; Coach House Gall., CI, 1987; Wherry Quay Gall., Ipswich, 1992; Grove House, Ipswich, 1993; Mansion House Gall., Ipswich, 1995; retrospective, Chappel Galls, 1995. *Group exhibitions included:* Leicester Gall.; Kensington Gall.; Zwemmer Gall.; Bohun Gall; Bankside Gall., 1987; Chappel Gall., Essex, 1995. *Open exhibitions included:* RA, RSA, NEAC, London Group, RSMA, and in Japan, USA, S Africa, NZ. *Important purchases included:* S London Art Gall.; V&A; Nat. Gall. of NZ; Leicester, Oxford and Durham Univs; Arts Council; Contemp. Art Soc.; Bowes Mus.; Graves Art Gall.; Rochdale Art Gall.; Lord Clark. *Illustrations included:* Colman Prentis Varley; Shell Mex; Editions Lausanne; books for Country Life, Conway Maritime Press, MAP. Designer of theatre properties, Tom Arnold Ice Show. *Recreation:* sailing. *Address:* Hollydene, Ipswich Road, Holbrook, Ipswich IP9 2QT.

Died 4 Aug. 2000.

WARDE, His Honour John Robins; a Circuit Judge, 1977–90; *b* 25 April 1920; (Guardian) A. W. Ormond, CBE, FRCS; *m* 1941, Edna Holliday Gipson; three *s*. *Educ:* Radley Coll., Abingdon, Berks; Corpus Christi Coll., Oxford (MA). Served War, 1940–45: Lieut, RA; awarded C-in-C's cert. for outstanding good service in the campaign in NW Europe. Admitted a solicitor, 1950; Partner in Waugh and Co., Solicitors, Haywards Heath and East Grinstead, Sussex, 1960–70; a Recorder of the Crown Court, 1972–77; Registrar of Clerkenwell County Court, 1970–77. Member: Devon CC, 1946–49; Devon Agricl Exec. Cttee, 1948–53; West Regional Advisory Council of BBC, 1950–53. Liveryman, Gardeners' Co., 1983. *Recreations:* mountaineering, watching cricket, listening to music. *Address:* 14 Clifton Terrace, Brighton, East Sussex BN1 3HA. *T:* (01273) 326642. *Clubs:* Law Society, MCC; Forty; Swiss Alpine.

Died 14 June 1999.

WARDLE, Sir Thomas (Edward Jewell), Kt 1970; Lord Mayor of Perth, Western Australia, 1967–72; *b* 18 Aug. 1912; *s* of Walter Wardle and Lily Wardle (*née* Jewell); *m* 1940, Hulda May Olson; one *s* one *d. Educ:* Perth Boys' Sch., Western Australia. Member: King's Park Bd, 1970–81; Bd, Churchland Teachers Coll., 1973–78; Chairman: Trustees, WA Museum, 1973–82; Aboriginal Loans Commn, 1974–80; Pres., Nat. Trust of WA, 1971–82. Hon. LLD Univ. of WA, 1973. Commendatore, Order of Merit (Italy), 1970. *Recreations:* boating, fishing. *Address:* 3 Kent Street, Bicton, WA 6157, Australia. *Club:* Returned Services League (Western Australia).

Died 11 Feb. 1997.

WARE, Martin, FRCP; Editor, British Medical Journal, 1966–75; *b* 1 Aug. 1915; *o s* of late Canon Martin Stewart Ware and Margaret Isabel (*née* Baker, later Baker Wilbraham); *m* 1938, Winifred Elsie Boyce; two *s* three *d. Educ:* Eton; St Bartholomew's Hospital. MB, BS (London) 1939; MRCP 1945; FRCP 1967; MSc (Wales) 1978; BA (Open) 1989. House-surgeon, St Bartholomew's Hosp., 1939; served with RAMC, attached to Royal W African Frontier Force, 1940–45; HQ staff, Medical Research Council, 1946–50; editorial staff, British Medical Jl, 1950–75; research in micropalaeontology, UCW, Aberystwyth, 1975–84. Vice-President: BMA; Internat. Union of Med. Press, 1966–75. *Recreations:* bird watching, reading, Alpines. *Address:* 4 Ellis Close, Cottenham, Cambs CB4 4UN. *T:* (01954) 251428.

Died 23 Sept. 1998.

WAREING, Prof. Philip Frank, OBE 1986; PhD, DSc London; FRS 1969; Professor of Botany, University College of Wales, Aberystwyth, 1958–81, then Emeritus; *b* 27 April 1914; *e s* of late Frank Wareing; *m* 1939, Helen Clark; one *s* one *d* (and one *d* decd). *Educ:* Watford Grammar School; Birkbeck Coll., Univ. of London. Exec. Officer, Inland Revenue, 1931–41; Captain, REME, 1942–46; Lectr, Bedford Coll., Univ. of London, 1947–50; Lectr, then Sen. Lectr, Univ. of Manchester, 1950–58. Man. Dir, Hortotec Ltd, 1985–91. Member: Nature Conservancy, 1965–68; Water Resources Board, 1968–71; Chm. Res. Adv. Cttee, Forestry Commn, 1972–86. President: Sect. K, British Assoc., 1970; Internat. Plant Growth Substances Assoc., 1982–85; Mem. Council, Royal Soc., 1972. Mem., Leopoldina Acad. of Science, 1971. *Publications:* (with I. D. J. Phillips) Control of Growth and Differentiation in Plants, 1970, 3rd edn as Growth and Differentiation in Plants, 1981; (ed with C. F. Graham) Development Control of Animals and Plants, 1976, 2nd edn 1984; various papers on plant physiology in scientific journals. *Recreation:* gardening. *Address:* Brynrhedyn, Cae Melyn, Aberystwyth, Dyfed SY23 2HA. *T:* Aberystwyth (01970) 623910.

Died 29 March 1996.

WARMINGTON, Sir (Marshall Denham) Malcolm, 4th Bt *cr* 1908, of Pembridge Square, Royal Borough of Kensington; *b* 5 Jan. 1934; *s* of Sir Marshall George Clitheroe Warmington, 3rd Bt and his 1st wife Mollie Warmington (*née* Kennard); *S* father, 1995. *Educ:* privately. *Heir: half-b* David Marshall Warmington [*b* 14 Feb. 1944; *m* 1st, 1966, Susan Mary Chapman; two *s*; 2nd, 1981, Eileen Victoria Johnston]. *Address:* c/o D. M. Warmington, 139 Highlands Heath, Putney, SW15 3TZ.

Died 23 Nov. 1996.

WARREN, Sir Brian; *see* Warren, Sir H. B. S.

WARREN, Frederick Lloyd, PhD, DSc; Professor of Biochemistry, London Hospital Medical College, 1952–78, then Emeritus; *b* 2 Oct. 1911; *s* of Frederick James and Edith Agnes Warren; *m* 1st, 1949, Natalia Vera Peierls (*née* Ladan) (marr. diss. 1958); two *s* one *d*; 2nd, 1961, Ruth Natallé Jacobs. *Educ:* Bristol Grammar Sch.; Exeter Coll., Oxford (BSc, MA); PhD, DSc London. Demonstrator, Biochem. Dept, Oxford, 1932–34; Sir Halley Stewart Res. Fellow, Chester Beatty Research Institute, Royal Cancer Hospital, 1934–46; Laura de Saliceto Student, University of London, 1937–42; Anna Fuller Research Student, 1942–46; Senior Lecturer in Biochemistry, St Mary's Hospital Medical School, 1946–48; Reader in Biochemistry, University College, London, 1948–52. *Publications:* papers and articles in scientific journals. *Address:* 5 River View, Enfield, Middx EN2 6PX. *T:* (020) 8366 0674.

Died 11 Aug. 1999.

WARREN, Sir (Harold) Brian (Seymour), Kt 1974; physician; *b* 19 Dec. 1914; *er s* of late Harold Warren, St Ives, Hunts and Marian Jessie Emlyn; *m* 1st, 1942, Dame Alice Josephine Mary Taylor Barnes (marr. diss. 1964); one *s* two *d*; 2nd, 1964, Elizabeth Anne (*d* 1983), *y d* of late Walter William Marsh, Wordsley, Staffs; two *s. Educ:* Bishop's Stortford Coll.; University Coll. London; University Coll. Hosp. MRCS, LRCP. Pres., Univ. of London Union, 1937–38. House Phys. and House Surg., UCH, 1942. War service with RAMC, RMO 1st Bn Gren. Gds and DADMS Gds Div., 1942–46 (despatches). Mem., Westminster City Council, 1955–64 and 1968–78; rep. West Woolwich on LCC, 1955–58, County Alderman 1961–62. Contested (C) Brixton Div. of Lambeth, 1959. Personal Phys. to Prime Minister, 1970–74. Mem., Westminster, Chelsea and Kensington AHA, 1975–77. Visitor and Mem. Emergency Bed Service Cttee, King Edward's Hosp. Fund for London, 1966–72; Mem.

Governing Body, Westminster Hosp., 1970–74; Mem. Council, King Edward VII's Hosp. for Officers (Surg.-Apothecary, 1952–80). Pres., Chelsea Clinical Soc., 1955–56. Mem., Develt Cttee, BTA, 1978–87. Liveryman, Apothecaries' Soc., 1950; Freeman, City of London. *Publications:* contrib. Encycl. Gen. Practice. *Recreations:* reading, gardening, travel, listening to music. *Address:* 94 Oakley Street, SW3 5NR. *T:* 0171–351 6462. *Club:* Pratt's.   *Died 18 Aug. 1996.*

WARREN, Dame Josephine; *see* Barnes, Dame A. J. M. T.

WARWICK, 8th Earl of, *cr* 1759; **David Robin Francis Guy Greville;** Baron Brooke 1621; Earl Brooke 1746; *b* 15 May 1934; *s* of 7th Earl of Warwick and Rose, *d* of late D. C. Bingham; *S* father, 1984; *m* 1956, Sarah Anne (marr. diss. 1967), *d* of late Alfred Chester Beatty and Mrs Pamela Neilson; one *s* one *d. Educ:* Eton. Life Guards, 1952; Warwicks Yeo. (TA), 1954. *Heir: s* Lord Brooke [*b* 30 Jan. 1957; *m* 1981, Susan McKinlay Cobbold (marr. diss.); one *s*]. *Clubs:* White's; The Brook (NY); Eagle Ski (Gstaad).   *Died 20 Jan. 1996.*

WARWICK, Captain William Eldon, CBE 1971; RD; Royal Navy Reserve, retired; Commodore, Cunard Line Ltd, 1970–75; First Master, RMS Queen Elizabeth 2, 1966–72; *b* 12 Nov. 1912; *e s* of Eldon Warwick, architect and Gertrude Florence Gent; *m* 1939, Evelyn King (*née* Williams); three *s. Educ:* Birkenhead Sch.; HMTS Conway. Joined Merchant Service, 1928, serving in Indian Ocean and Red Sea; awarded Master Mariner's Certificate, 1936; joined Cunard White Star as Jun. Officer (Lancastria), 1937; first cargo command, Alsatia, 1954; first passenger command, Carinthia, 1958; followed by command of almost all the passenger liners in Cunard fleet. Commissioned in RNR, 1937; mobilized in RN War Service, 1939, in Coastal Forces and Corvettes in North Atlantic, Russian Convoys and Normandy Landings, 1939–46 (despatches, 1946); promoted Captain RNR, 1960; retd RNR, 1965. Treas., Internat. Fedn of Shipmasters' Assocs., 1973–92. Younger Brother of Trinity House; Liveryman, Hon. Co. of Master Mariners (Master, 1976–77); Freeman of City of London. *Recreations:* reading, music. *Address:* 50 Algarth Road, Pocklington, York YO4 2HJ. *T:* (01759) 306534. *Club:* Naval.   *Died 27 Feb. 1999.*

WASTIE, Winston Victor, CB 1962; OBE 1946 (MBE 1937); Under-Secretary, Ministry of Public Building and Works, Scotland, 1959–62, retired; *b* 5 March 1900; *s* of Harry Wastie; *m* 1924, Charmbury Billows (*d* 1986); one *d. Educ:* Greenwich Secondary Sch. Civil Service, New Scotland Yard, 1915–42; Chief Licensing Officer, Civil Building Control, Ministry of Works, 1942–46; Assistant Secretary, Scottish HQ, Ministry of Works, 1946–59; Under-Secretary, 1959. *Recreations:* bridge, gardening, sport. *Address:* North Hill, 9 Clifford Avenue, Ilkley, West Yorks LS29 0AS.   *Died 10 May 1996.*

WATERHOUSE, Dr Douglas Frew, AO 1980; CMG 1970; FRS 1967; FAA; FRACI; FTSE; Chief of Division of Entomology, Commonwealth Scientific and Industrial Research Organization, 1960–81, Hon. Research Fellow, since 1981; *b* 3 June 1916; *s* of late Prof. E. G. Waterhouse, CMG, OBE, and Janet Frew Kellie, MA; *m* 1944, Allison Dawn, *d* of J. H. Calthorpe; three *s* one *d. Educ:* Sydney C of E Grammar Sch.; Univ. of Sydney (BSc Hons, University Medal, MSc, DSc); Cambridge Univ. FRACI 1948; FAA 1954; FTSE 1998. Served War of 1939–45, Captain, AAMC Medical Entomology. Joined Research Staff, CSIRO, 1938; Asst Chief, Div. of Entomology, 1953–60. Biological Secretary, Australian Acad. of Science, 1961–66; Chairman: Council, Canberra Coll. of Advanced Educn, 1969–84; Council for Internat.

Congresses of Entomology, 1968–84 (Hon. Mem., 1984); Nat. Sci. Summer Sch., Aust. Industry Develt Corp., 1985–88; Pres., ACT Br., Nat. Trust of Australia, 1984–88. Corresp. Mem., Brazilian Acad. of Sciences, 1974; Hon. For. Mem., All-Union Entomological Soc. of USSR, 1979; For. Mem., Russian (formerly USSR) Acad. of Science, 1982; Foreign Assoc., US Nat. Acad. of Scis, 1983. Hon. FRES 1972. Hon. DSc ANU, 1978. David Syme Research Prize, 1953; Mueller Medal, ANZAAS, 1972; Farrer Medal, Farrer Meml Trust, 1973; Medal, 10th Internat. Congress of Plant Protection, 1983; Principal Bicentennial Contrib. to Agriculture Award, 1988. *Publications:* (jtly) Butterflies of Australia, 1972, rev. edn 1981; (jtly) Biological Control: Pacific prospects, 1987, Supplement 1 (jtly), 1989, Suppl. 2, 1993; Major Pests and Weeds of Southeast Asia, 1993; Biological Control of Weeds: Southeast Asian prospects, 1994; Major Pests and Weeds of Agriculture and Forestry Plantations in the Oceanic Pacific, 1997; Biological Control of Insect Pests: Southeast Asian prospects, 1998; numerous articles on insect physiology, biochemistry, ecology and biological control of insects. *Recreations:* gardening, fishing, gyotaku. *Address:* 60 National Circuit, Deakin, ACT 2600, Australia. *T:* (6) 2731772. *Club:* Commonwealth (Canberra).   *Died Dec. 2000.*

WATERS, Denise Jeanne Marie Lebreton, (Mrs Frank Waters); *see* Brown, D. J. M. L.

WATERS, Montague; QC 1968; *b* 28 Feb. 1917; *s* of Elias Wasserman, BSc, and Rose Waters; *m* 1st, 1940, Jessica Freedman (*d* 1988); three *s*; 2nd, 1991, Georgia Heather Schaverien. *Educ:* Central Foundation Sch., City of London; London University (LLB Hons 1938) Solicitor of the Supreme Court, 1939; called to the Bar, Inner Temple, 1946. Military Service, KRRC, Intelligence Corps and Dept of HM Judge Advocate General, 1940–46 (Defence and Victory Medals, 1939–45 Star); released from HM Forces with rank of Major (Legal Staff), 1946. Tutor, Legal Affairs, Univ. of the Third Age, Bournemouth Br., 1992–. Governor, Central Foundation Schools, 1968. Freeman, City of London, 1962. *Recreations:* theatre, sport, bridge, poetry. *Address:* 48 Keverstone Court, Manor Road, Bournemouth, Dorset BH1 3BY. *T:* (01202) 309966.   *Died 19 Oct. 1999.*

WATKIN, Rt Rev. Abbot (Christopher) Aelred (Paul); titular Abbot of Glastonbury; Headmaster of Downside School, 1962–75; *b* 23 Feb. 1918; *s* of late Edward Ingram Watkin and Helena Watkin (*née* Shepheard). *Educ:* Blackfriars Sch., Laxton; Christ's Coll., Cambridge (1st class Parts I and II, historical Tripos). Ordained priest, 1943. Housemaster at Downside Sch., 1948–62. Mayor of Beccles, 1979. FRHistS 1946; FSA 1950; FRSA 1969. *Publications:* Wells Cathedral Miscellany, 1943; (ed) Great Chartulary of Glastonbury, 3 vols, 1946–58; (ed) Registrum Archidiaconatus Norwyci, 2 vols, 1946–48; Heart of the World, 1954; The Enemies of Love, 1958; Resurrection is Now, 1975; Through the Church's Year, 1991; articles in Eng. Hist. Rev., Cambridge Hist. Journal, Victoria County History of Wilts, etc. *Address:* Downside Abbey, Stratton-on-the-Fosse, Bath BA3 4RH. *T:* (01761) 232295.   *Died 2 May 1997.*

WATKIN WILLIAMS, Sir Peter, Kt 1963; *b* 8 July 1911; *s* of late Robert Thesiger Watkin Williams, late Master of the Supreme Court, and Mary Watkin Williams; *m* 1938, Jane Dickinson (*née* Wilkin); two *d. Educ:* Sherborne; Pembroke Coll., Cambridge. Partner in Hansons, legal practitioners, Shanghai, 1937–40; served War of 1939–45, Rhodesia and Middle East, 1940–46; Resident Magistrate, Uganda, 1946–55; Puisne Judge, Trinidad and Tobago, 1955–58; Puisne Judge, Sierra Leone, 1958–61; Plebiscite Judge, Cameroons, 1961; Chief Justice of Basutoland, Bechuanaland and Swaziland, and President of the Court of Appeal, 1961–65; High Court Judge, Malawi, 1967–69; Chief Justice of Malawi, 1969–70. *Recreation:* fishing. *Address:* Lower East Horner, Stockland, Honiton, Devon EX14 9EY. *Died 26 March 1996.*

WATSON, Sir Duncan; *see* Watson, Sir N. D.

WATSON, Sir Michael M.; *see* Milne-Watson.

WATSON, Sir (Noel) Duncan, KCMG 1967 (CMG 1960); HM Diplomatic Service, retired; *b* 16 Dec. 1915; *s* of late Harry and Mary Noel Watson, Bradford, Yorks; *m* 1951, Aileen Bryans (*d* 1980), *d* of late Charles Bell, Dublin. *Educ:* Bradford Grammar School; New College, Oxford. Colonial Administrative Service: Admin. Officer, Cyprus, 1938–43; Assistant Colonial Secretary, Trinidad, 1943–45; Principal, Colonial Office (secondment), 1946; transferred to Home Civil Service, 1947; Principal Private Sec. to Sec. of State for the Colonies, 1947–50; Asst Secretary: CO, 1950–62, Central African Office, 1962–63; Under-Secretary, 1963; Asst Under-Sec. of State, CO and CRO, 1964–67; Political Adviser to C-in-C Far East, 1967–70; High Comr in Malta, 1970–72; Dep. Under-Sec. of State, FCO, 1972–75. Mem., Central Council, Royal Commonwealth Soc., 1975– (Dep. Chm., 1983–87). *Address:* Sconce, Steels Lane, Oxshott, Surrey KT22 0QH. *Clubs:* Travellers, Royal Commonwealth Society; Leander. *Died 8 July 1999.*

WATSON, Dr Reginald Gordon Harry, (Rex), CB 1987; CChem, FRSC; Director, Building Research Establishment, Department of the Environment, 1983–88; *b* 3 Nov. 1928; *s* of Gordon Henry and Winifred Catherine Watson; *m* 1st, 1951, Molly Joyce Groom (*d* 1989); one *s* two *d*; 2nd, 1995, Pamela Mary Katherine Webley (*née* O'Connor). *Educ:* Chislehurst and Sidcup Grammar Sch.; Imperial Coll., London (Royal Schol.; BSc (1st cl. Hons Chem.), PhD; DIC; ARCS). Res. Worker (Fuel Cells), Dept of Chemical Engrg, Univ. of Cambridge, 1951–56; joined Royal Naval Scientific Service, 1956, as Sen. Scientific Officer, Admty Materials Lab.; Head of Chemical Engrg Div., 1958–66; Naval Staff Course, 1962; Individual Merit Sen. Principal Scientific Officer, 1965; Director: Naval R&D Admin, 1967–69; Admty Materials Lab., 1969–74; Chemical Defence Estab., Porton Down, 1974–83. *Publications:* papers on electrochemistry, chemical engineering and materials science. *Recreations:* photography, natural history, sailing. *Address:* 39 Old Pound Close, Lytchett Matravers, Poole, Dorset BH16 6BW. *T:* (01202) 621828. *Died 27 Feb. 2000.*

WATSON, Rt Rev. Richard Charles Challinor; Hon. Assistant Bishop, Diocese of Oxford, since 1988; *b* 16 Feb. 1923; *o s* of Col Francis W. Watson, CB, MC, TD, DL, Aylesbury, Bucks, and 1st wife, Alice Madelein, *d* of Arthur Collings-Wells, JP, Caddington Hall, Herts; *m* 1955, Anna (*d* 1996), *er d* of Rt Rev. C. M. Chavasse, OBE, MC, MA, DD (Bishop of Rochester, 1940–60); one *s* one *d*. *Educ:* Rugby; New Coll., Oxford (Scholar; BA Hons Lang. and Lit., 1948, Theology, 1949); Westcott House, Cambridge, 1950–51. Served Indian Artillery, Lieut and Capt. RA, 1942–45. Deacon 1951, priest 1952; Curate of Stratford, London E, 1952–53; Tutor and Chaplain, Wycliffe Hall, Oxford, 1954–57; Chaplain of Wadham Coll. and Chaplain of Oxford Pastorate, 1957–61; Vicar of Hornchurch, 1962–70; Asst Rural Dean of Havering, 1967–70; Rector of Burnley, 1970–77; Bishop Suffragan of Burnley, 1970–87; Hon. Canon of Blackburn Cathedral, 1970–87. Examining Chaplain to Bishop Rochester, 1956–61, to Bishop of Chelmsford, 1962–70. *Recreations:* reading, gardening. *Address:* 6 Church Road, Thame, Oxon OX9 3AJ. *T:* (01844) 213853. *Died 1 March 1998.*

WATSON, Thomas Yirrell, CMG 1955; MBE 1943; *b* 27 May 1906; *s* of William Scott Watson and Edith Rose Watson (*née* Yirrell); *m* 1st, 1935, Margaret Alice (*d* 1978), *d* of late J. J. Watson; one *d*; 2nd, 1984, Katharine Margaret, *d* of late James Kay and *widow* of W. J. Mill Irving, OBE. *Educ:* Aberdeen Grammar Sch.; Aberdeen Univ. (BSc); Cambridge Univ. (Diploma in Agricultural Science); Pretoria Univ., South Africa. Colonial Agricultural Scholar, 1929–31; Agricultural Officer, Kenya, 1931–43; Senior Agricultural Officer, Kenya, 1943–48; Dep. Director of Agriculture, Uganda, 1948–51; Director of Agriculture, Uganda, 1951–53; Secretary for Agriculture and Natural Resources, Uganda, 1954–55; Minister of Natural Resources, Uganda, 1955–56. General Manager, Uganda Lint Cotton Marketing Board, 1951–53; MEC and MLC, Uganda, 1951–56. Member: Commission of Inquiry into Land and Population Problems, Fiji, 1959–60; Economic Development Commn, Zanzibar, 1961; Commission of Inquiry into Cotton Ginning Industry, Uganda, 1962; Commissioner, Burley Tobacco Industry Inquiry, Malawi, 1964. Coronation Medal, 1953. *Address:* 2 Lennox Milne Court, Haddington, East Lothian EH41 4DF. *T:* Haddington (01620) 824490. *Died 16 Feb. 1996.*

WATT, Andrew, CBE 1963; Forestry Commissioner, 1965–69; *b* 10 Nov. 1909; 2nd surv. *s* of late James Watt, LLD, WS, and Menie Watt; *m* 1943, Helen McGuffog (*d* 1969); two *s* one *d*. *Educ:* Winchester; Magdalen Coll., Oxford. BA 1931. District Officer, Forestry Commn, 1934; Divisional Officer, 1940; Conservator, 1946; Director of Forestry for Scotland, 1957–63; Director of Forest Research, 1963–65. *Address:* 7A Ravelston Park, Edinburgh EH4 3DX. *T:* 0131–332 1084. *Died 18 July 1996.*

WATTS, Rachel Mary; *see* Rosser, R. M.

WAY, Sir Richard (George Kitchener), KCB 1961 (CB 1957); CBE 1952; Principal, King's College London, 1975–80; *b* 15 Sept. 1914; *s* of Frederick and Clara Way; *m* 1947, Ursula Joan Starr; one *s* two *d*. *Educ:* Polytechnic Secondary Sch., London. Joined Civil Service as Exec. Officer, 1933; Higher Executive Officer, 1940; Principal, 1942; Asst Secretary, 1946; Asst Under-Secretary of State, 1954; Deputy Under-Secretary of State, War Office, 1955–57; Dep. Secretary, Ministry of Defence, 1957–58; Dep. Secretary, Ministry of Supply, 1958–59; Permanent Under-Secretary of State, War Office, 1960–63; Permanent Secretary, Ministry of Aviation, 1963–66. Dep. Chm., Lansing Bagnall Ltd, 1966–67; Chm. 1967–69; Chm., LTE, 1970–74. Chairman, EDC Machine Tool Industry, 1967–70; Member (part-time) Board of: BOAC, 1967–73; Dobson Park Industries Ltd, 1975–85. Chm., Council of Roedean Sch., 1969–74; Chm., Royal Commn for the Exhibn of 1851, 1978–87. London Zoological Society: Mem. Council, 1977–82 and 1984–87; Vice-Pres., 1979–82 and 1984–87; Treasurer, 1983–84. CStJ 1974. FKC 1975. Hon. DSc Loughborough, 1986. Coronation Medal, 1953. American Medal of Freedom (with bronze palm), 1946. *Address:* The Old Forge, Shalden, Alton, Hants GU34 4DX. *T:* (01420) 82383. *Club:* Brooks's. *Died 2 Oct. 1998.*

WAYMOUTH, Charity, PhD; Senior Staff Scientist, The Jackson Laboratory, Bar Harbor, Maine, 1963–81, then Emeritus; *b* 29 April 1915; *o d* of Charles Sydney Herbert Waymouth, Major, The Dorsetshire Regt, and Ada Curror Scott Dalgleish; unmarried. *Educ:* Royal School for Daughters of Officers of the Army, Bath; University of London (BSc); University of Aberdeen (PhD). Biochemist, City of Manchester General Hospitals, 1938–41; Research Fellow, University of Aberdeen, 1944; Beit Memorial Fellow for Medical Research, 1944–46; Member of scientific staff and head of tissue culture dept, Chester Beatty Research Institute for Cancer Research (University of London), 1947–52; British Empire Cancer Campaign-

American Cancer Society Exchange Fellow, 1952–53; The Jackson Laboratory: Staff Scientist, 1952–63; Asst Dir (Training), 1969–72; Asst Dir (Research), 1976–77; Associate Dir (Scientific Affairs), 1977–80; Dir *ad interim*, 1980–81. Mem. Bd of Dirs, W. Alton Jones Cell Sci. Center, 1979–82. Rose Morgan Vis. Prof., Univ. of Kansas, 1971. Member: Tissue Culture Association (President, 1960–62; Editor-in-Chief, 1968–75; Mem. Council, 1980–84); various British and American professional and learned societies. Hon. Life Member and Hon. Director, Psora Society (Canada). Episcopal Church of the USA: Vice-Chm., Clergy Deployment Bd, 1971–79, and Exec. Council, 1967–70; Deputy, Gen. Convention, 1970, 1973, 1976, 1979, 1982, 1985, 1988; Member, Diocesan Council, 1962–70, 1971–76, and Standing Cttee, 1984–87, Dio. of Maine; Chm., Cttee on the State of the Church, 1976–79; Mem., Standing Commn on Health, 1988–91. DD *hc* Gen. Theol Seminary, NY, 1979; Hon. ScD Bowdoin College, 1982. *Publications:* numerous papers in scientific journals, on nucleic acids and on tissue culture and cell nutrition. *Recreations:* reading, gardening.   *Died 31 Oct. 2000.*

WEBB, Anthony Michael Francis, CMG 1963; QC (Kenya) 1961; JP; *b* 27 Dec. 1914; *s* of late Sir (Ambrose) Henry Webb and Agnes, *d* of Michael Gunn, late of Dublin; *m* 1948, Diana Mary, *e d* of late Capt. Graham Farley, Indian Army, and Mrs Herbert Browne (*née* Pyper); one *s* one *d. Educ:* Ampleforth; Magdalen Coll., Oxford (MA). Barrister-at-Law, Gray's Inn, 1939. Served War, 1939–46, Major, GSO2, The Queen's Bays. Colonial Legal Service (HMOCS), 1947–64, Malaya and Kenya; MLC Kenya, 1958–63; Attorney General and Minister for Legal Affairs, Kenya, 1961–63; Sec., Nat. Adv. Council on Trng of Magistrates, and Trng Officer, 1964–73, Dep. Sec. of Commns, 1969–75, Head of Court Business, 1975–77, Lord Chancellor's Office; retd 1977. A Chm. of Indust. Tribunals, 1978–87. Member of Council of Kenya Lawn Tennis Association, 1957–63. JP, Kent, 1966. *Publication:* The Natzweiler Trial (ed). *Address:* 19 Crittle's Court, Wadhurst, E Sussex TN5 6BY. *T:* (01892) 782399. *Club:* Special Forces.

Died 5 March 1998.

WEBB, Kaye, MBE 1974; Chairman and Founder of Puffin Club (for children), since 1967; Director, Unicorn Children's Theatre, since 1972; Managing Director, Kaye Webb Ltd, since 1973; *b* 26 Jan. 1914; *d* of Arthur Webb and Kathleen Stevens, journalists; *m* 1st, 1936, Christopher Brierley; 2nd, 1941, Andrew Hunter; 3rd, 1946, Ronald Searle, RDI (marr. diss. 1967); one *s* one *d.* Entered journalism via Picturegoer, 1931; joined Picture Post, 1938; Asst Editor, Lilliput, 1941–47; Theatre Corresp., The Leader, 1947–49; Feature Writer, News Chronicle, 1949–55; Editor of children's magazine Elizabethan, 1955–58; Theatre Critic to National Review, 1957–58; Children's Editor, Puffin Books, and Publishing Dir, Children's Div., Penguin Books Ltd, 1961–79; Editor, Puffin Post, 1967–81. Children's Advisor, Goldcrest TV, 1978–84; Mem. UK Branch, UNICEF. Eleanor Farjeon Award for services to Children's Literature, 1969. *Publications:* (ed) C. Fry, Experience of Critics, 1952; (ed) Penguin Patrick Campbell; (ed) The Friday Miracle; (ed) The St Trinian's Story, 1959; Puffins Pleasure; (ed) I Like This Poem, 1979; (ed) Lilliput Goes to War, 1985; (ed) I Like This Story, 1986; Round About Six, 1991; Meet my Friends, 1991; Family Tree, 1994; (with Ronald Searle): Paris Sketchbook, 1950, rev. edn 1957; Looking at London, 1953; Refugees 1960, 1960; (with Treld Bicknell) 1st and 2nd Puffin Annuals. *Recreations:* children and their interests, theatre. *Address:* 8 Lampard House, Maida Avenue, W2 1SS. *T:* 0171–262 4695.

Died 16 Jan. 1996.

WEBER, (Edmund) Derek (Craig); Editor, The Geographical Magazine, 1967–81; *b* 29 April 1921; 3rd *s* of late R. J. C. and B. M. Weber; *m* 1953, Molly Patricia (*d* 1994), *d* of late R. O. and Ellen Podger; one *s* four *d. Educ:* Bristol Grammar School. Journalist on newspapers in Swindon, Bristol and Bath, and on magazines in London from 1937 until 1953, except for War Service in RAF, 1940–46; The Geographical Magazine: Art Editor, 1953; Assoc. Editor, 1965. Hon. FRGS 1980. Hon. Life Member: IBG, 1981; NUJ, 1981. Hon. MA Open, 1982. *Address:* 32 London Road, Maldon, Essex CM9 6HD. *T:* (01621) 852871. *Club:* Savage.   *Died 23 Dec. 1996.*

WEBSTER, John Alexander R.; *see* Riddell-Webster.

WEDGWOOD, Dame (Cicely) Veronica, OM 1969; DBE 1968 (CBE 1956); FRHistS; FBA 1975; historian; *b* 20 July 1910; *d* of Sir Ralph Wedgwood, 1st Bt, CB, CMG and Iris Veronica, *d* of Albert H. Pawson, Leeds. *Educ:* privately; Lady Margaret Hall, Oxford. 1st Class Mod. Hist. 1931. Mem., Royal Commn on Historical MSS, 1953–78. President: English Assoc., 1955–56; English Centre of Internat. Pen Club, 1951–57; Society of Authors, 1972–77; Member: Arts Council, 1958–61; Arts Council Literature Panel, 1965–67; Institute for Advanced Study, Princeton, USA, 1953–68; Adv. Council, V&A Museum, 1960–69; Trustee, Nat. Gall., 1962–68, 1969–76. Special Lecturer, UCL, 1962–91. Hon. Member: Amer. Acad. of Arts and Letters, 1966; Amer. Acad. of Arts and Scis, 1973; Amer. Philosophical Soc., 1973; Amer. Hist. Soc. 1973. Hon. Fellow: Lady Margaret Hall, Oxford, 1962; UCL, 1965; LSE 1975. Hon. LLD Glasgow; Hon. LittD Sheffield; Hon. DLitt: Smith College; Harvard; Oxford; Keele; Sussex; Liverpool. Hon. Bencher, Middle Temple, 1978. Officer, Order of Orange-Nassau (Netherlands), 1946; Goethe Medal, 1958. *Publications:* Strafford, 1935 (revd edn, as Thomas Wentworth, 1961); The Thirty Years' War, 1938; Oliver Cromwell 1939, rev edn 1973; Charles V by Carl Brandi (trans.), 1939; William the Silent, 1944 (James Tait Black Prize for 1944); Auto da Fé by Elias Canetti (trans.), 1946; Velvet Studies, 1946, Richelieu and the French Monarchy, 1949; Seventeenth Century Literature, 1950; Montrose, 1952; The King's Peace, 1955; The King's War, 1958; Truth and Opinion, 1960; Poetry and Politics, 1960; The Trial of Charles I, 1964 (in USA as A Coffin for King Charles, 1964); Milton and his World, 1969; The Political Career of Rubens, 1975; The Spoils of Time, vol. 1, 1984; History and Hope: collected essays, 1987. *Address:* 17 Ashley Court, Morpeth Terrace, SW1P 1EN.   *Died 9 March 1997.*

WEEKS, Alan Frederick; Governor, Sports Aid Foundation, since 1983; *b* 8 Sept. 1923; *s* of late Captain Frederick Charles Weeks, MN, and Ada Frances Weeks; *m* 1947, Barbara Jane (*née* Huckle); one *s* (and one *s* one *d* decd). *Educ:* Brighton, Hove and Sussex Grammar School. Served: MN, Cadet, 1939–41; RNR, Midshipman to Lieut, 1941–46. PRO, Sports Stadium, Brighton, 1946–65; Sec., Brighton Tigers Ice Hockey Club, 1946–65; Dir, London Lions Ice Hockey Club, 1973–74; first Director, Sports Aid Foundn, 1976–83. BBC Commentator: Ice Hockey, 1951–88; Football, 1956–78; Ice Skating, 1958–96; Gymnastics, 1962–89; Swimming, 1971–90; Presenter: Summer Grandstand, 1959–62; Olympics, 1960, 1964; BBC Commentator: Winter Olympics: 1964, 1968, 1972, 1976, 1980, 1984, 1988, 1992, 1994; Olympics: 1968, 1972, 1976, 1980, 1984, 1988; World Cup: 1966, 1970, 1974, 1978; Commonwealth Games: 1970, 1974, 1978, 1982, 1986; Presenter, Pot Black, 1970–84. Life Mem., Nat. Skating Assoc. of GB, 1984 (Chm. Trustees, 1993–); Mem. Council, British Ice Hockey Assoc., 1983–; inducted British Ice Hockey Hall of Fame, 1988. Life Pres., Brighton and Hove Entertainment Managers' Assoc.,

1985. Hon. Mem., Amateur Swimming Assoc., 1990. *Recreation:* swimming. *Address:* c/o API Personality Management, 141–143 Drury Lane, WC2B 5TB. *Club:* Lord's Taverners. *Died 11 June 1996.*

WEIGALL, Peter Raymond; Managing Director, P. R. Weigall & Co. Ltd, 1976–84; *b* 24 Feb. 1922; *s* of Henry Stuart Brome Weigall and Madeleine Bezard; *m* 1950, Nancy, *d* of Alexander Webster, CIE, and Margaret Webster; one *s* one *d. Educ:* Lycée Janson, Paris; Edinburgh Univ. (BSc). Served War, Captain, RE, 1942–46. Henry Wiggin & Co. Ltd, Birmingham, 1949–51; Petrochemicals Ltd, London, 1951–54; Chemical Industry Admin, Shell Petroleum Co., London, 1954–58; Chemicals Manager, Shell Sekiyu, Tokyo, 1958–63; Shell Internat. Chemical Co., London, 1964–69; Managing Dir, Monteshell, Milan, 1970–73; Industrial Advr to HM Govt, DTI, 1973–75. Member: Movement of Exports EDC, 1974–75; Chemicals EDC, 1974–75; Motor Vehicle Distribution and Repair EDC, 1974–75; Mergers Panel, Office of Fair Trading, 1974–75. *Recreations:* sailing, skiing. *Club:* Royal Engineer Yacht.
Died 8 Aug. 1999.

WEIGH, Brian, CBE 1982; QPM 1976; HM Inspector of Constabulary for South-West England and part of East Anglia, 1983–88; *b* 22 Sept. 1926; *s* of late Edwin Walter Weigh and Ellen Weigh; *m* 1952, Audrey; one *d. Educ:* St Joseph's Coll., Blackpool, Lancs; Queen's Univ., Belfast. All ranks to Supt, Metrop. Police, 1948–67; Asst Chief Constable, 1967–69, Dep. Chief Constable, 1969–74, Somerset and Bath Constab.; Chief Constable: Gloucestershire Constab., 1975–79; Avon and Somerset Constab., 1979–83 (Dep. Chief Constable, 1974–75). Pres., County of Avon Special Olympics, 1982–; Mem., Royal Life Saving Soc. (UK Pres., 1989–92). *Recreations:* walking, gardening, golf. *Address:* c/o Bridge House, Sion Place, Clifton Down, Bristol BS8 4XA.
Died 8 Feb. 1997.

WEIGHILL, Air Cdre Robert Harold George, CBE 1973; DFC 1944; Secretary, Rugby Football Union, 1973–86; *b* 9 Sept. 1920; *s* of late Harold James and Elsie Weighill, Heswall, Cheshire; *m* 1946, Beryl (*d* 1981), *d* of late W. Y. Hodgson, Bromborough, Cheshire; two *s* (one *d* decd). *Educ:* Wirral Grammar Sch., Bebington, Cheshire. Served War: RAF, 1941; No 2 FR Sqdn, 1942–44; No 19 F Sqdn, 1944–45; Sqdn Comdr, RAF Coll., Cranwell, 1948–52; Student, RAF Staff Coll., 1952; CO, No 2 FR Sqdn and 138 F Wing, 1953–57; student, JSSC, 1959; Directing Staff, Imperial Defence Coll., 1959–61; CO, RAF, Cottesmore, 1961–64; Gp Captain Ops, RAF Germany, 1964–67; Asst Comdt, RAF Coll. of Air Warfare, 1967–68; Comdt, RAF Halton, 1968–73. ADC to the Queen, 1968–73. Hon. Secretary: Internat. Rugby Football Bd, 1986–88; Five Nation Rugby Cttee, 1986–. *Recreations:* Rugby (Harlequins, Barbarians, Cheshire, RAF, Combined Services, England), squash, swimming. *Address:* 3 Bridle Manor, Halton, Aylesbury, Bucks HP22 5PQ. *T:* (01296) 625172. *Clubs:* Royal Air Force, East India, Devonshire, Sports and Public Schools. *Died 27 Oct. 2000.*

WEIGHT, Prof. Carel Victor Morlais, CH 1995; CBE 1961; RA 1965 (ARA 1955); Hon. RBA 1972 (RBA 1934); Hon. RWS 1985; practising artist (painter); Professor Emeritus, since 1973, Senior Fellow, since 1984, Royal College of Art; *b* London, 10 Sept. 1908; *s* of Sidney Louis and Blanche H. C. Weight; British; *m* 1990, Helen Roeder. *Educ:* Sloane School; Goldsmiths' Coll., Univ. of London (Sen. County Scholarship, 1933; Hon. Fellow, 1990). Official War Artist, 1945. Royal College of Art: Teacher of Painting, 1947; Fellow, 1956; Prof. of Painting, 1957–73. First exhibited at Royal Acad., 1931; first one-man show, Cooling Galls, 1934; 2nd and 3rd exhibns, Picture Hire Ltd, 1936 and 1938; one-man shows:

Leicester Galls, 1946, 1952, 1968; Zwemmer Gall., 1956, 1959, 1961, 1965; Agnew's, 1959; Russell Cotes Gall., Bournemouth, 1962; Fieldbourne Galleries, 1972; New Grafton Gall., 1974, 1976; exhibited in: 60 Paintings for 1951; (by invitation) exhibns of Contemporary British Art in provinces and overseas, incl. USSR, 1957; retrospective exhibitions: Reading Museum and Art Gallery, 1970; RCA, 1973; Royal Acad., 1982; Bernard Jacobson Gall., 1988; Imperial War Mus., 1995; exhibn, Tate Gall., 1992–93; travelling exhibn, Newport, Llandudno, London (Christie's), 1993. Work purchased by: Chantry Bequest for Tate Gall., 1955, 1956, 1957, 1963, 1968; Walker Art Gall., Liverpool; Southampton, Hastings and Oldham Art Galls, etc; Art Gall., Melbourne; Nat. Gall., Adelaide; Arts Council; New Coll., Oxford; Contemporary Art Soc.; V&A Museum. Mural for: Festival of Britain, 1951; Manchester Cathedral, 1963. Picture, Transfiguration, presented by Roman Catholics to the Pope. Member: London Group, 1950; West of England Acad.; Fine Arts Panel, Arts Council, 1951–57; Rome Faculty of Art, 1960. Mem., Cttee of Enquiry into the Economic Situation of the Visual Artist (Gulbenkian Foundn), 1978. Vice-Pres., Artists' Gen. Benevolent Inst., 1980. Trustee, RA, 1975–84. DUniv Heriot-Watt, 1983; Dr *hc* Edinburgh, 1983. *Recreations:* music, reading. *Address:* 33 Spencer Road, SW18 2SP. *T:* (0171) 228 6928. *Club:* Chelsea Arts. *Died 13 Aug. 1997.*

WEIR, Very Rev. Andrew John, (Jack), MSc; Clerk of Assembly and General Secretary, The Presbyterian Church in Ireland, 1964–85, Emeritus since 1985; *b* 24 March 1919; *s* of Rev. Andrew Weir and Margaret Weir, Missionaries to Manchuria of the Presbyterian Church in Ireland. *Educ:* Campbell Coll., Belfast; Queen's Univ., Belfast (BD, MSc); New Coll., Edinburgh; Presbyterian Coll., Belfast. Ordained, 1944; Missionary to China, 1945–51; Minister, Trinity Presbyterian Church, Letterkenny, Co. Donegal, 1952–62; Asst Clerk of Assembly and Home Mission Convener, The Presbyterian Church in Ireland, 1962–64. Moderator of the General Assembly, The Presbyterian Church in Ireland, 1976–77. Hon. DD: Presbyterian Theol Faculty, Ireland, 1972; QUB, 1990. *Address:* 62 Towell House, 57 Kings Road, Belfast BT5 7BS. *T:* (028) 9079 5153.
Died 18 Sept. 2000.

WELBY-EVERARD, Maj.-Gen. Sir Christopher Earle, KBE 1965 (OBE 1945); CB 1961; DL; *b* 9 Aug. 1909; *s* of late E. E. E. Welby-Everard, Gosberton House, near Spalding, Lincolnshire; *m* 1938, Sybil Juliet Wake Shorrock (*d* 1994); two *s. Educ:* Charterhouse; CCC, Oxford. Gazetted The Lincolnshire Regt, 1930; OC 2 Lincolns, 1944; GSO1, 49 (WR) Inf. Div., 1944–46; GSO1 GHQ, MELF, 1946–48; OC 1 Royal Lincolnshire Regt, 1949–51; Comd 264 Scottish Beach Bde and 157 (L) Inf. Bde, 1954–57; BGS (Ops), HQ, BAOR, and HQ Northern Army Group, 1957–59; Chief of Staff, HQ Allied Forces, Northern Europe, 1959–61; GOC Nigerian Army, 1962–65; retd. DL Lincolnshire, 1966; High Sheriff of Lincolnshire, 1974. *Recreations:* shooting, cricket. *Address:* The Manor House, Sapperton, Sleaford, Lincolnshire NG34 0TB. *T:* Ingoldsby (01476) 585273. *Clubs:* Army and Navy; Free Foresters.
Died 10 May 1996.

WELCH, Colin; see Welch, J. C. R.

WELCH, David, CBE 1999; horticultural consultant and writer; Chief Executive, The Royal Parks, 1992–2000; *b* 13 Dec. 1933; *s* of late Thomas Welch and Eleanor (*née* Foster); *m* 1960, Eva Doring; three *s* one *d.* Horticultural Officer, Blackpool CB, 1959–63; Hd, Parks and Recreation Dept, Borough of Bebington, Cheshire, 1963–67; Dir, Leisure and Recreation, City of Aberdeen, 1967–89; Consultant, 1989–92. President: Inst. Parks and

Recreation, 1977–78; Inst. Leisure and Amenity Mgt, 1992–93; Inst. Hort., 1992–94; RHS of Aberdeen, 1987–94. Member Council: Royal Nat. Rose Soc., 1982– (Vice Pres., 1998–); NPFA, 1995–. Associate of Honour, RHS, 1990. Liveryman, Gardeners' Co., 1998. Hon. LLD Aberdeen, 1990. Scottish Horticultural Medal, Royal Caledonian Horticultural Soc., 1973. *Publications:* Roses, 1988; Managing Urban Parks, 1990; Managing the Public Use of Open Space, 1995. *Recreations:* walking, theatre, after dinner speaking, horticultural writing. *Address·* The Chanonry, Aberdeen AB24 1RN. *Club:* Royal Northern and University (Aberdeen).   *Died 18 Sept. 2000.*

WELCH, (James) Colin (Ross); freelance columnist and book critic; *b* 23 April 1924; *s* of James William Welch and Irene Margherita (*née* Paton), Ickleton Abbey, Cambridgeshire; *m* 1950, Sybil Russell; one *s* one *d. Educ:* Stowe Sch. (schol.); Peterhouse, Cambridge (major schol., BA Hons). Commissioned Royal Warwickshire Regt, 1942; served NW Europe, twice wounded. Glasgow Herald, 1948; Colonial Office, 1949; Daily Telegraph: leader writer, columnist (Peter Simple, with Michael Wharton), parliamentary sketch writer, 1950–64; Dep. Editor, 1964–80; regular column, 1981–83; Editor-in-Chief, Chief Executive magazine, 1980–82; parly sketch-writer, Daily Mail, 1984–92; columnist and critic for The Times (formerly for The Independent, Spectator, American Spectator, National Review). Granada Journalist of the Year, 1974; Specialist Writer, British Press Awards, 1986. Knight's Cross, Order of Polonia Restituta, 1972. *Publications:* (ed) Sir Frederick Ponsonby, Recollections of Three Reigns, 1951; (trans. with Sybil Welch) Nestroy, Liberty Comes to Krähwinkel, 1954 (BBC); articles in Encounter, Spectator, New Statesman, American Spectator, etc; contribs to symposia, incl. The Future that Doesn't Work, 1977 (New York); *posthumous publication:* The Odd Thing About the Colonel & Other Pieces, 1997. *Address:* 4 Goddard's Lane, Aldbourne, Wilts SN8 2DL. *T:* (01672) 40010.
          Died 27 Jan. 1997.

WELCH, Rt Rev. Neville; *see* Welch, Rt Rev. W. N.

WELCH, Robert Radford, MBE 1979; RDI 1965; FCSD (FSIAD 1962); designer and silversmith; *b* 21 May 1929, *m* 1959, Patricia Marguerite Hinksman; two *s* one *d. Educ:* Hanley Castle Grammar Sch.; Malvern Sch. of Art; Birmingham Coll. of Art; Royal Coll. of Art (DesRCA; Hon. Fellow, 1972). Started own workshop in Chipping Campden, 1955; opened Robert Welch Studio Shop, Chipping Campden, 1969, and second Studio Shop, Warwick, 1991. Major retrospective exhibn for 40th anniv. of workshop and design studio, Cheltenham, Manchester and Birmingham Art Galls, 1995–96. Visiting Lecturer: Central Sch. of Art and Design, 1957–63; RCA, 1963–71; visited India by invitation of All India Handicraft Bd, 1975. Design Consultant to Old Hall Tableware, 1955–83. Silver commns for various clients, incl. civic plate, university colls, Goldsmiths' Hall, Canterbury Cathedral, V&A Museum, and British Govt Gift to St Lucia; tableware for British Ambassador's residence, Manila; British Museum; Silver Trust for No 10 Downing St; design commns in Denmark, Germany, USA, Japan and Korea. Liveryman, Goldsmiths' Co., 1982. FRSA 1967. DUniv UCE, 1998. *Publications:* Design in a Cotswold Workshop (with Alan Crawford), 1973; Hand and Machine, 1986. *Recreations:* drawing, painting. *Address:* Lower High Street, Chipping Campden, Glos GL55 6DY. *T:* (01386) 840522.   *Died 15 March 2000.*

WELCH, Rt Rev. (William) Neville; *b* 30 April 1906; *s* of Thomas William and Agnes Maud Welch; *m* 1935, Kathleen Margaret Beattie (*d* 1998); two *s* two *d. Educ:* Dean Close Sch., Cheltenham; Keble Coll., Oxford (MA); Wycliffe Hall, Oxford. Deacon 1929, priest 1930;

Assistant Curate: Kidderminster, 1929–32, St Michael's, St Albans, 1932–34; Organising Sec., Missions to Seamen, 1934–39; Vicar of Grays, 1939–43; Officiating Chaplain, Training Ship Exmouth, 1939–40; Vicar of Ilford, 1943–53; Rural Dean of Barking, 1948–53; Vicar of Great Burstead, 1953–56; Archdeacon of Southend, 1953–72; Bishop Suffragan of Bradwell, 1968–73. Proctor in Convocation, 1945 and 1950; Hon. Canon of Chelmsford, 1951–53. *Address:* 59 Moorfield Court, Newland Street, Witham, Essex CM8 1AE. *T:* (01376) 503681.
          Died 3 Feb. 1999.

WELLESLEY, Julian Valerian; Chairman, East Sussex, Brighton and Hove Health Authority, since 1996; *b* 9 Aug. 1933; *s* of late Gerald Valerian Wellesley, MC, and Elizabeth Thornton Harvey; *m* 1965, Elizabeth Joan Hall; one *s* one *d*, and three step *d. Educ:* Royal Naval Colleges, Dartmouth (schol.) and Greenwich. Royal Navy, 1947–61: America and West Indies, 1955–56; Far East, 1957–58; Navigation Specialist, 1959. Joined Charles Barker Group, 1961: a Dir, 1963; Dep. Chm., 1975; Chm., 1978–83; Consultant, TSB Gp, 1984; Director: Horizon Travel, 1984–87; Chatsworth Food Ltd, 1986–90; E. & R. Garrould Ltd, 1988–90. Dir, Assoc. of Lloyd's Mems, 1985–91. Mem., 1986–90, Chm., 1990–93, Eastbourne HA; Chm., East Sussex HA, 1993–96. Vice-Chm., Wealden Cons. Assoc., 1988–91. Chm. Govs, Uplands Community Coll., 1994– (Gov., 1991–). FIPA 1976. *Recreations:* family, gardening, opera, playing tennis and bridge, watching cricket. *Address:* Tidebrook Manor, Wadhurst, Sussex TN5 6PD. *Clubs:* Brooks's, MCC; Sussex.   *Died 13 Sept. 1996.*

WELLS, Sir Charles Maltby, 2nd Bt *cr* 1944, of Felmersham, co. Bedford; TD 1960; *b* 24 July 1908; *e s* of Sir Richard Wells, 1st Bt, and Mary Dorothy Maltby (*d* 1956); *S* father, 1956; *m* 1935, Katharine Boulton, *d* of Frank Boteler Kenrick, Toronto; two *s. Educ:* Bedford School; Pembroke College, Cambridge. Joined RE (TA), 1933; Capt. 1939; served War of 1939–45: 54th (EA) Div., 1939–41; Lt-Col 1941; 76th Div., 1941–43; British Army Staff, Washington, 1943–45. *Heir: s* Christopher Charles Wells [*b* 12 Aug. 1936; *m* 1st, 1960, Elizabeth Florence Vaughan (marr. diss. 1983), *d* of I. F. Griffiths, Outremont, Quebec; two *s* two *d*; 2nd, 1985, Lynda Anne Cormack; one *s*]. *Address:* 41 Sherwood Avenue, Toronto, Ont M4P 2A6, Canada.   *Died 23 June 1996.*

WELLS, John Campbell; writer, actor and director; *b* 17 Nov. 1936; *s* of Eric George Wells and Dorothy Amy Thompson; *m* 1982, Teresa (*née* Chancellor); one *d. Educ:* Eastbourne Coll.; St Edmund Hall, Oxford. Taught: English at Landerziehungsheim Schondorf am Ammersee, 1958–59; French and German at Eton, 1961–63; Co-Editor, Private Eye, 1964–67; Afterthought column, The Spectator, 1966–68. *Author of: revues, etc (also performer):* Never Too Late, 1960, Late Night Final, 1961 (both jtly), Edinburgh Fest.; A Man Apart (jtly), 1968, Changing Scenes, 1969, BBC Radio; Charlie's Grants (jtly), 1970, Up Sunday, 1973–74, The End of the Pier Show (jtly), 1975, BBC TV; Return to Leeds (jtly), Yorkshire TV, 1974; In the Looking Glass (jtly), 1976; Frontiers—East/West Germany (documentary), BBC TV, 1990; *plays:* (with Claud Cockburn) Listen to the Knocking Bird, Nottingham Playhouse, 1965; (with Richard Ingrams) Mrs Wilson's Diary, R. Royal, Stratford East, transf. Criterion, 1968; The Projector, 1970, and Cranford, 1970, Th. Royal, Stratford East; (with Barry Fantoni) Lionel, New London, 1977; (with Julius Gellner) The Immortal Haydon, Mermaid, 1978; The Peace, Scottish Opera Go Round, 1978; (with Robert Morley) A Picture of Innocence, Brighton, 1979; Anyone for Denis?, Whitehall, 1981–82 (also title rôle); Alice in Wonderland, Lyric, Hammersmith, 1986; A Brand from the Burning

(also dir.), RSC, 1995; *television plays:* The Scriblerus Club, 1967; Voltaire in England, 1968; Orpheus in the Underground, 1977; The Arnolfini Marriage, 1978; *film:* (jtly) Princess Caraboo (also acted), 1994; *radio play adaptations:* Alice in Wonderland, 1978; Alice Through the Looking Glass, 1980; *translations:* Danton's Death, 1971, The Marriage of Figaro, 1974, NT; The Barber of Seville, and A Mother's Guilt, 1984, BBC Radio; Women All Over, Edinburgh, 1984; La Vie Parisienne, Scottish Opera, 1986 (also dir, Glasgow, 1987); The Magic Flute, City of Birmingham Touring Opera, 1988; The Merry Widow, Scottish Opera, 1989; Cyrano de Bergerac, Theatre Royal, Haymarket, 1992; La Belle Hélène, Scottish Opera, 1995. *Actor:* An Italian Straw Hat, Lyric, Hammersmith, 1961; Murderous Angels, Paris, 1971; Private Lives, Newcastle, 1972; Jumpers, 1973, Design for Living, 1974, Nottingham Playhouse; Bartholomew Fair, Round House, 1978; Greystoke (film), 1984; The Philanthropist, Chichester Fest., 1985; Rude Health, Channel Four, 1985–86; Bartholomew Fair, NT, 1988; Dunrulin', BBC TV, 1990; The Philanthropist, Wyndham's, 1991; Travels With My Aunt, Wyndham's, 1992, Sydney Fest., 1994; Beatrice and Benedict (narrator), Glyndebourne Opera, RFH, 1993; The Chamber, BBC TV, 1995; Chalk, BBC TV, 1996; *director:* (with Jonathan Miller) Candide, Glasgow, 1988; The Mikado, D'Oyly Carte, Savoy Theatre and tour, 1989; The Bold Fisherman, TVS, 1991. *Publications:* The Exploding Present, 1971; (with John Fortune) A Melon for Ecstacy, 1971; Masterpieces, 1982; Fifty Glorious Years, 1984; Rude Words: a history of the London Library, 1991; Princess Caraboo: her true story, 1994; with Richard Ingrams: Mrs Wilson's Diary, 1965; Mrs Wilson's 2nd Diary, 1966; Dear Bill: the collected letters of Denis Thatcher, 1980; The Other Half: further letters of Denis Thatcher, 1981; One for the Road, 1982; My Round!, 1983; Down the Hatch, 1985; Just the One, 1986; The Best of Dear Bill, 1986; Mud in Your Eye, 1987; Number 10, 1989; *posthumous publication:* The House of Lords: an anecdotal history, 1998. *Recreations:* walking, talking. *Address:* 1A Scarsdale Villas, W8 6PT. *T:* (0171) 937 0534.
Died 11 Jan. 1998.

WELMAN, Douglas Pole, CBE 1966; *b* 22 June 1902; *s* of late Col Arthur Pole Welman and Fanny Vaughan Johnston, *d* of Thomas Ramsay Dennis (she *m* 2nd, Adm. Sir Percy Scott, 1st Bt, KCB, KCVO); *m* 1st, 1929, Denise, *d* of Charles Steers Peel; one *d*; 2nd, 1946, Betty Marjorie, *d* of late Henry Huth. *Educ:* Tonbridge Sch.; Faraday House Engineering Coll. DFH, CEng, FIMechE, FIEE, CIGasE. Asst Engr, Preece Cardew & Ryder, 1926–28; Resident Engr, Grenada, 1928–29, Grenada and St Vincent, 1930; Chief Engr, Windward Islands, 1930–32; consulting practice, London, 1932–37; Man. Dir of Foster, Yates and Thom Limited, Heavy Precision Engineers, 1937–50; Chairman of number of wartime committees in Lancashire including Armaments Production, Emergency Services Organisation, and Ministry of Production; went to Ministry of Aircraft Production at request of Minister as Director of Engine Production, 1942; Deputy Director-General, 1943; Control of Directorate-Gen. including Propeller and Accessory Production, 1944; Part Time Member North Western Gas Board, 1949, Chairman, 1950–64; Chairman, Southern Gas Board, 1964–67; Member, Gas Council, 1950–67; Chm. and Man. Dir, Allspeeds Holdings Ltd, 1967–72. Member, Ct of Govs, Univ. of Manchester Inst. of Sci. and Techn., 1956–64, 1968–72 (Mem. Council, 1960–64, 1968–72). CStJ 1968 (OStJ 1964). FRSA. *Publications:* articles and papers on company management. *Recreations:* sailing, fishing. *Address:* 11 St Michael's Gardens, St Cross, Winchester SO23 9JD. *T:* Winchester (01962) 868091. *Club:* Royal Thames Yacht.
Died 19 Aug. 1996.

WENBAN-SMITH, William, CMG 1960; CBE 1957; *b* 8 June 1908; *o s* of late Frederick Wenban-Smith, Worthing; *m* 1935, Ruth Orme, *e d* of late S. B. B. McElderry, CMG; three *s* two *d*. *Educ:* Bradfield; King's Coll., Cambridge (MA). Colonial Administrative Service, 1931–61: Cadet, Zanzibar, 1931; Administrative Officer, Grade II, 1933; Asst Dist Officer, Tanganyika, 1935; Dist Officer, 1943; Sen. Dist Officer, 1951 (acted on various occasions as Resident Magistrate, Comr for Co-op. Development, Provincial Comr, and Sec. for Finance); Dir of Establishments, 1953; Minister for Social Services, 1958; Minister for Education and Labour, 1959–61; Chairman, Public Service Commission and Speaker, Legislative Council, Nyasaland, 1961–63; HM Diplomatic Service, Kuala Lumpur, 1964–69. *Publication:* Walks in the New Forest, 1975. *Recreation:* music. *Address:* Lane End, School Lane, Lymington, Hants SO41 9EJ. *T:* (01590) 679343. *Club:* Royal Commonwealth Society.
Died 4 Jan. 2000.

WENHAM, Brian George; media consultant and journalist; *b* 9 Feb. 1937; *s* of late George Frederick Wenham and of Harriet Wenham, London; *m* 1966, Elisabeth Downing, *d* of Keith and Margery Woolley; two *d*. *Educ:* Royal Masonic Sch., Bushey; St John's Coll., Oxon. Television journalist, Independent Television News, 1962–69; Editor, Panorama, BBC, 1969–71; Head of Current Affairs Gp, 1971–78; Controller, BBC 2, 1978–82; Dir of Programmes, BBC TV, 1983–85; Man. Dir, BBC Radio, 1985–87; Chm, UK Radio Developments, 1993–; Director: Renaissance Films, 1990–; Carlton Television, 1991–; English Touring Opera, 1991–. FRTS 1986. *Publication:* (ed) The Third Age of Broadcasting, 1982. *Address:* Red Cottage, Wey Road, Weybridge, Surrey KT13 8HW. *T:* (01932) 843313.
Died 8 May 1997.

WERNHAM, Prof. Richard Bruce, FBA 1995; Professor of Modern History, Oxford University, 1951–72; Fellow of Worcester College, Oxford, 1951–72; then Professor and Fellow Emeritus; *b* 11 Oct. 1906; *o s* of Richard George and Eleanor Mary Wernham; *m* 1939, Isobel Hendry Macmillan (*d* 1987), Vancouver BC; one *d. Educ:* Newbury Grammar School; Exeter College, Oxford (MA). Research Asst, Inst. of Historical Research, London Univ., 1929–30; Temp. Asst, Public Record Office, 1930–32; Editor, PRO, State Papers, Foreign Series, 1932; Lecturer in Modern History, University Coll., London, 1933–34; Fellow of Trinity College, Oxford, 1934–51, Senior Tutor, 1940–41 and 1948–51; University Lecturer in Modern History, Oxford, 1941–51; Examiner in Final Honour School of Modern History, Oxford, 1946–48. Visiting Professor: Univ. of S Carolina, 1958; Univ. of California, Berkeley, 1965–66; Una's Lectr, Berkeley, 1978. Served in RAF, 1941–45. *Publications:* Before the Armada: the Growth of English Foreign Policy 1485–1588, 1966; (ed) Vol III, New Cambridge Modern History: The Counter-Reformation and Price Revolution, 1559–1610, 1968; The Making of Elizabethan Policy, 1980; After the Armada: Elizabethan England and the Struggle for Western Europe 1588–95, 1984; (ed) Expedition of Sir John Norris and Sir Francis Drake to Spain and Portugal, 1589, 1988; The Return of the Armadas: the last years of the Elizabethan war with Spain, 1994; Calendars of State Papers, Foreign Series, Elizabeth; articles in English Hist. Review, History, Trans Royal Hist. Soc., Encyclopædia Britannica. *Address:* 63 Hill Head Road, Hill Head, Fareham, Hants PO14 3JL.
Died 17 April 1999.

WEST, Rt Rev. Francis Horner; *b* 9 Jan. 1909; *o s* of Sydney Hague and Mary West, St Albans, Herts; *m* 1947, Beryl Elaine, 2nd *d* of late Rev. W. A. Renwick, Smallbridge, Rochdale; one *s* one *d. Educ:* Berkhamsted School; Magdalene Coll., Cambridge (Exhibitioner; MA 1934); Ridley Hall, Cambridge. Deacon 1933, priest 1934;

Curate, St Agnes, Leeds, 1933–36; Chaplain, Ridley Hall, Cambridge, 1936–38; Vicar of Starbeck, Yorks, 1938–42; served War of 1939–45, as CF with BEF, MEF, CMF and SEAC, 1939–46 (despatches, 1945); Director of Service Ordination Candidates, 1946–47; Vicar of Upton, Notts, 1947–51; Archdeacon of Newark, 1947–62; Vicar of East Retford, 1951–55; Bishop Suffragan of Taunton, 1962–77; Prebendary of Wells, 1962–77; Rector of Dinder, Somerset, 1962–71. Select Preacher, Cambridge Univ., 1962. Visitor, Croft House School, 1968–79. *Publications:* Rude Forefathers, the Story of an English Village, 1600–1666, 1949, reprinted 1989; The Great North Road in Nottinghamshire, 1956; Sparrows of the Spirit, 1957; The Country Parish Today and Tomorrow, 1960; F. R. B.: a portrait of Bishop F. R. Barry, 1980; The Story of a Wiltshire Country Church, 1987. *Recreation:* gardening. *Address:* 11 Castle Street, Aldbourne, Marlborough, Wilts SN8 2DA. *T:* (01672) 540630.   *Died 2 Jan. 1999.*

WEST, Morris Langlo, AO 1997 (AM 1985); novelist; *b* Melbourne, 26 April 1916; *s* of Charles Langlo West and Florence Guilfoyle Hanlon; *m* 1st, 1941 (marr. diss.); one *s*; 2nd, 1953, Joyce Lawford; three *s* one *d*. *Educ:* Melbourne Univ. (BA 1937). Taught modern langs and maths, NSW and Tas, 1933–39. Served, Lieutenant, AIF, South Pacific, 1939–43. Sec. to Rt Hon. William Morris Hughes, former PM of Australia, 1943. FRSL; Fellow, World Acad. of Art and Science. Hon. DLitt: Univ. of Santa Clara, 1969; Mercy Coll., NY, 1982; Univ. of Western Sydney, 1993; ANU, Canberra, 1995. Internat. Dag Hammarskjöld Prize (Grand Collar of Merit), 1978; Lloyd O'Neil Award, Australian Publishers Assoc., 1997. *Publications:* Gallows on the Sand, 1955; Kundu, 1956; Children of the Sun, 1957; The Crooked Road, 1957 (UK, as The Big Story); The Concubine, 1958; Backlash, 1958 (UK, as The Second Victory); The Devil's Advocate, 1959 (National Brotherhood Award, National Council of Christians and Jews 1960; James Tait Black Memorial Prize, 1960; RSL Heinemann Award, 1960; filmed 1977); The Naked Country, 1960; Daughter of Silence (novel and play), 1961; The Shoes of the Fisherman, 1963; The Ambassador, 1965; The Tower of Babel, 1968; The Heretic, a Play in Three Acts, 1970; (with R. Francis) Scandal in the Assembly, 1970; Summer of the Red Wolf, 1971; The Salamander, 1973; Harlequin, 1974; The Navigator, 1976; Proteus, 1979; The Clowns of God, 1981 (Universe Literary Prize, 1981); The World is Made of Glass, 1983 (play 1984); Cassidy, 1986; Masterclass, 1988; Lazarus, 1990; The Ringmaster, 1991; The Lovers, 1993; Vanishing Point, 1996; A View from the Ridge, 1996; Images & Inscriptions, 1997; Eminence, 1998. *Address:* PO Box 102, Avalon, NSW 2107, Australia. *Clubs:* Australian, Royal Prince Alfred Yacht (Sydney).
                    Died 9 Oct. 1999.

WESTOLL, James; DL; *b* 26 July 1918; *s* of late James Westoll, Glingerbank, Longtown; *m* 1946, Sylvia Jane Luxmoore, MBE, *d* of late Rt Hon. Lord Justice Luxmoore, Bilsington, Kent; two *s* two *d*. *Educ:* Eton; Trinity College, Cambridge (MA). Served War of 1939–45: Major, The Border Regiment (despatches). Called to the Bar, Lincoln's Inn, 1952. Deputy Chm., Cumberland Quarter Sessions, 1960–71. Member, NW Electricity Board, 1959–66. Cumberland County Council: CC 1947; CA 1959–74; Chm., 1958–74; Chm., Cumbria Local Govt Reorganisation Jt Cttee, 1973; Chm., Cumbria CC, 1973–76. DL 1963, High Sheriff 1964, Cumberland. Warden, 1973–75, Master, 1983–84, Clothworkers' Company. Hon. LLD Leeds, 1984. KStJ 1983. *Publication:* Complete Illustrated Check List of the Birds of the World, 1998. *Recreations:* gardening, shooting. *Address:* Dykeside, Longtown, Carlisle, Cumbria CA6 5ND. *T:* (01228) 791235. *Clubs:* Boodle's, Farmers'.
                    Died 7 Feb. 1999.

WESTON, Bertram John, CMG 1960; OBE 1957; retired from the public service; Estate Factor to British Union Trust Ltd, 1964–81; *b* 30 March 1907; *o s* of late J. G. Weston, Kennington, Kent; *m* 1932, Irene Carey; two *d*. *Educ:* Ashford Grammar School; Sidney Sussex College, Cambridge (MA); Pretoria University, SA (MSc Agric.); Cornell University, USA (Post Grad.). Horticulturist, Cyprus, 1931; Asst Comr, Nicosia (on secondment), 1937; Administrative Officer, 1939; War Service, 1940–43 (Major); Commissioner for development and post-war construction, Cyprus, 1943; Commissioner, 1946; Administrative Officer Class I, 1951; Senior Administrative Officer, 1954; Senior Commissioner, 1958; Government Sec., St Helena, 1960–63; acted as Governor and C-in-C, St Helena, at various times during this period. *Recreations:* lawn tennis, gardening, watching cricket and other sports. *Address:* 10 Westfield Close, Uphill, Weston-super-Mare BS23 4XQ. *Club:* Royal Commonwealth Society.   *Died 11 Sept. 1997.*

WESTON, Rear-Adm. Charles Arthur Winfield, CB 1978; Admiral President, Royal Naval College, Greenwich, 1976–78; Appeals Secretary, King Edward VII's Hospital for Officers, 1979–87; *b* 12 July 1922; *s* of late Charles Winfield Weston and of Edith Alice Weston; *m* 1946, Jeanie Findlay Miller; one *s* one *d*. *Educ:* Merchant Taylors' Sch. Entered RN as Special Entry Cadet, 1940; HM Ships: Glasgow, 1940; Durban, 1942; Staff of C-in-C Mediterranean, as Sec. to Captain of the Fleet, 1944–45 (despatches 1945); Sec. to Cdre in Charge Sheerness, 1946–47, to Flag Captain Home Fleet, HMS Duke of York, 1947–48; Loan Service, RAN, 1948–50; HM Ships: St Vincent, 1952–53; Ceres, 1954–55; Decoy, 1956; Sec. to Dep. Chief of Naval Personnel, (Trng and Manning), 1957–58, to DG Trng, 1959; CO HMS Jufair, 1960; Supply Officer, St Vincent, 1961–62; Sec. to Fleet Comdr Far East Fleet, 1963–64, to Second Sea Lord, 1965–67; sowc 1968; Chief Staff Officer (Q) to C-in-C Naval Home Comd, 1969–70; Dir, Naval Physical Trng and Sport, 1971; Director Defence Admin Planning Staff, 1972–74; Dir of Quartering (Navy), 1975. ADC to the Queen, 1976. Rear-Adm. 1976. Liveryman, 1979–93; Freeman, 1993, Shipwrights' Co. *Recreations:* golf, gardening, music, watching cricket. *Address:* Flinten Barn, Little Thornage, Holt, Norfolk NR25 7JD. *T:* (01263) 713523. *Clubs:* MCC; Norfolk (Norwich); Sheringham Golf.   *Died 27 March 1998.*

WESTON, Geoffrey Harold, CBE 1975; retired; Deputy Health Service Commissioner for England, Scotland and for Wales, 1977–82; *b* 11 Sept. 1920; *s* of George and Florence Mary Weston; *m* 1953, Monica Mary Grace Comyns; three *d*. *Educ:* Wolverhampton Sch. War Service, 1940–46. Gp Sec., Reading and Dist Hosp. Management Cttee, 1955–65; Board Sec., NW Metropolitan Regional Hosp. Bd, 1965–73; Regional Administrator, NW Thames RHA, 1973–76. Member: Salmon Cttee, 1963–65; Whitley Councils: Mem. Management side of Optical Council, 1955–65, and of Nurses and Midwives Council, 1966–76; Mem., Working Party on Collab. between Local Govt and Nat. Health Service, 1973–74. Institute of Health Service Administrators: Pres., 1970; Mem., Nat. and Reg. Councils, 1959–78 (Vice-Chm. of Council, 1968, Chm. 1969). Bd Mem., London and Provincial Nursing Services Ltd, 1973–90; Member: Mental Health Review Tribunal, 1982–93; Oxford RHA, 1983–89; Trustee, Goring Day Centre, 1978–89. Vice-Chm., Goring Decorative and Fine Arts Soc., 1990–93 (Treas., 1987–89); Mem., Goring and Streatley Probus Club, 1987–. Parish Councillor, Goring, 1979–87. *Recreations:* travel, dining with friends. *Address:* 15 Hill Gardens, Streatley, near Reading, Berks RG8 9QF. *T:* (01491) 872881. *Club:* Royal Air Force.
                    Died 30 Sept. 1999.

WESTON, Dr John Carruthers; General Manager, Northampton Development Corporation, 1969–77; *b* 15 May 1917; *o s* of John Albert and May Carruthers Weston; *m* 1943, Mary Standish Lester; two *s*. *Educ:* Univ. of Nottingham. Admiralty Research, 1940–46; Plessey Co., 1946–47; Building Research Station, 1947–64; Chief Exec. Operational Div., Nat. Building Agency, 1964–65; Dir, Building Research Station, MPBW, 1966–69. *Recreations:* gardening, music, walking, reading, living.
Died 26 March 1999.

WESTWOOD, Rt Rev. William John; Bishop of Peterborough, 1984–95; *b* 28 Dec. 1925; *s* of Ernest and Charlotte Westwood; *m* 1954, Shirley Ann, *yr d* of Dr Norman Jennings; one *s* one *d*. *Educ:* Grove Park Grammar Sch., Wrexham; Emmanuel Coll., Cambridge (Exhibnr 1944; MA; Hon. Fellow 1989); Westcott House, Cambridge. Soldier, 1944–47. Deacon 1952, priest 1953; Curate of Hull, 1952–57; Rector of Lowestoft, 1957–65; Vicar of S Peter Mancroft, Norwich, 1965–75; Hon. Canon, Norwich Cathedral, 1969–75; Rural Dean of Norwich, 1966–70, City Dean, 1970–73; Area Bishop of Edmonton, 1975–84. Member: General Synod, 1970–75 and 1977–95; Archbishop's Commission on Church and State, 1966–70; Church Commissioner, 1973–78 and 1985–92; Chm., C of E Cttee for Communications, 1979–86; Member: Press Council, 1975–81; IBA Panel of Religious Advisers, 1983–87; Video Consultative Council, 1985–89; Broadcasting Standards Council, 1988–92; HEA, 1992–98; Volunteering Partnership, 1995–96. President: Nat. Deaf-Blind League, 1991–95; E of England Agricl Soc., 1994. Chm., Emmanuel Soc., 1989–96. Chm. Governors, Coll. of All Saints, Tottenham, 1976–78; Member Court: Univ. of Leicester, 1985–95; Nene Coll., Northampton, 1990–95. Trustee: Oakham Sch., 1984–94; Uppingham Sch., 1984–95 (Chm., Trustees, 1994–95); Brooke Weston City Technol. Coll., Corby, 1992–95. Pres., English Churches Housing (formerly Church Housing Assoc.), 1985–95; Chairman: Lowestoft Church and Town Charities, 1957–65; Norwich Housing Soc., 1969–74; Cotman Housing Assoc., Norwich, 1972–75. Freeman, City of London, 1977. Hon. LLD Leicester, 1991. *Recreations:* the countryside, art galleries, wine bars. *Address:* 102 Thwaite Street, Cottingham, East Yorks HU16 4RQ. *T:* (01482) 876263.
Died 15 Sept. 1999.

WETHERED, Joyce, (Lady Heathcoat Amory); *b* 17 Nov. 1901; *o d* of Newton and Marian Wethered, Brook, Surrey; *m* 1937, Major Sir John Heathcoat Amory, 3rd Bt (*d* 1972). *Educ:* privately. Learned golf playing with brother Roger, during holidays at Dornoch; Ladies Open Amateur Golf Champion 1922, 1924, 1925, 1929, runner-up 1921; English Ladies' Golf Champion, 1920–24; runner-up French Ladies' Championship, 1921; English International (golf), 1921–25 and 1929; First Curtis Cup, 1929 (Captain); GB *v* France, 1931; GB *v* USA, 1932 (Captain); won Worplesdon Mixed Foursomes 8 times between 1922 and 1936 with 7 diff. partners, and with husband runners-up, 1948; professional golf adviser to Fortnum & Mason, 1933–37; tour of USA, exhibn matches, 1935; reinstated as amateur, 1946. 1st Pres., English Ladies' Golf Assoc., 1951; Pres. and Hon. Life Mem., Worplesden Golf; Hall of Fame, USA. With husband, created gardens at Knightshayes Court (later Nat. Trust). VMH. *Publications:* Golf from Two Sides (with Roger Wethered), 1922; 3 chapters in The Game of Golf (Lonsdale Library), 1931; Golfing Memories and Methods, 1933; contribs to numerous books and jls. *Recreations:* gardening, reading, needlework. *Address:* Knightshayes House, Tiverton, Devon EX16 7RQ.
Died 18 Nov. 1997.

WETHERELL, Alan Marmaduke, PhD; FRS 1971; Senior Physicist, CERN (European Organisation for Nuclear Research), Geneva, 1963–97 (Division Leader, Experimental Physics Division, 1981–84); *b* 31 Dec. 1932; *s* of Marmaduke and Margaret Edna Wetherell; *m* 1957, Alison Morag Dunn (*d* 1974); one *s*; *m* 1996, Mrs Linda Hardwick (*née* Darby). *Educ:* Univ. of Liverpool (BSc, PhD). Demonstrator in Physics, Univ. of Liverpool, 1956–57; Commonwealth Fund Fellow, California Inst. of Technology, Pasadena, Calif, 1957–59; Physicist, CERN, 1959–63. Vis. Prof., Dept of Physics, Univ. of Liverpool, 1981–. *Publications:* scientific papers in Proc. Phys. Soc., Proc. Royal Soc., Physical Review, Physical Review Letters, Physics Letters, Nuovo Cimento, Nuclear Physics, Nuclear Instruments and Methods, Yadernaya Fizika, Uspekhi Fizicheski Nauk. *Recreation:* ski-ing. *Address:* 27 Chemin de la Vendée, 1213 Petit Lancy, Geneva, Switzerland. *T:* (22) 7928742.
Died 13 Sept. 1998.

WHALE, Rev. John Seldon, MA (Oxon); DD (Glasgow); *b* 19 Dec. 1896; *s* of Rev. John Whale and Alice Emily Seldon; *m* Mary, *d* of Rev. H. C. Carter, MA; two *s* one *d* (and one *s* one *d* decd). *Educ:* Caterham School, Surrey; St Catherine's Society and Mansfield College, Oxford; 1st Class Hons Sch. of Mod. Hist. 1922; Magdalene College, Cambridge, 1933. Minister of Bowdon Downs Congregational Church, Manchester, 1925–29; Mackennal Professor of Ecclesiastical History, Mansfield College, Oxford, and Tutor in Modern History, St Catherine's, 1929–33; President of Cheshunt College, Cambridge, 1933–44; Headmaster of Mill Hill School, 1944–51; Visiting Professor of Christian Theology, Drew Univ., Madison, NJ, USA, 1951–53. Moderator of Free Church Federal Council, 1942–43; Select Preacher, Univ. of Cambridge, 1943, 1957; Warrack Lecturer, 1944; Russell Lecturer (Auburn and New York), 1936 and 1948; Alden Tuthill Lecturer, Chicago, 1952; Greene Lecturer, Andover, 1952; Currie Lecturer, Austin, Texas, 1953; Hill Lectr, St Olaf Coll., Minnesota, 1954; Visiting Lecturer, Univ. of Toronto, 1957; Danforth Scholar, USA, 1958; Sir D. Owen Evans Lectures, Aberystwyth, 1958; Visiting Professor, Univ. of Chicago, 1959; Senior Fellow of Council of Humanities, Princeton Univ., 1960. *Publications:* The Christian Answer to the Problem of Evil, 1936; What is a Living Church?, 1937; This Christian Faith, 1938; Facing the Facts, 1940; Christian Doctrine, 1941; The Protestant Tradition, 1955; Victor and Victim: the Christian doctrine of Redemption, 1960; Christian Reunion: historic divisions reconsidered, 1971; The Coming Dark Age, 1973 (Eng. trans. of Roberto Vacca's Il Medioevo Prossimo Venturo, 1972). *Address:* Struan Lodge, 54 Balgreen Avenue, Edinburgh EH12 5SU. *T:* (0131) 337 4614.
Died 17 Sept. 1997.

WHARTON, Baroness (11th in line) *cr* 1544–45; **Myrtle Olive Felix, (Ziki), Robertson;** *b* 20 Feb. 1934; *d* of David George Arbuthnot (*d* 1985) and Baroness Wharton, 10th in line (*d* 1974); *S* to Barony of mother (called out of abeyance, 1990); *m* 1958, Henry McLeod Robertson (*d* 1996); three *s* one *d*. Co-Vice Chairman: All Party Media Gp, 1994–; All Party Animal Welfare Gp, 1996–; All Party Photographic Gp, 1997–; elected Mem., H of L, 1999. Vice Pres., RSPCA, 1997–; Co Vice Pres., Pet Adv. Cttee, 1995–. Hon. Associate, BVA, 1995. LRPS. *Publication:* (jtly) Parliament in Pictures, 1999. *Recreations:* animal welfare, photography, ski-ing, opera. *Heir: s* Hon. Myles Christopher David Robertson [*b* 1 Oct. 1964; *m* 1998, Caroline Laura, *d* of John David Jeffrey]. *Address:* c/o House of Lords, SW1A 0PW.
Died 15 May 2000.

WHATLEY, William Henry Potts, OBE 1986; General Secretary, Union of Shop Distributive and Allied Workers,

1979–85; *b* 16 Dec. 1922; *s* of Arthur John and Ethel Whatley; *m* 1946, Margaret Ann Harrison. *Educ:* Gosforth Secondary School. Clerk, CWS, Newcastle upon Tyne, 1938; War Service, RAF, War of 1939–45; Area Organiser, USDAW, Bristol, 1948; National Officer, 1966; Chief Organising Officer, 1976. Member: TUC General Council, 1979–85; TUC Economic Cttee, 1979; Pres., EURO-FIET, 1982–87. *Recreations:* gardening, reading. *Address:* 72 St Martin's Road, Ashton-on-Mersey, Sale, Cheshire M33 5PZ. *T:* (0161) 973 3772.

Died 4 Sept. 1997.

WHEELER, Rt Rev. Gordon; *see* Wheeler, W. G.

WHEELER, Hon. Sir Kenneth (Henry), Kt 1976; JP; Speaker of the Victorian Parliament, Australia, 1973–79; *b* 7 Sept. 1912; *s* of William Henry Wheeler and Alma Nellie Wheeler; *m* 1934, Hazel Jean Collins; one *s* one *d.* *Educ:* Mernda State Sch., Vic. Grazier and retail dairyman for 19 years. Municipal Councillor, 1950–59; Mayor, City of Coburg, Vic, 1955–56; elected to Parliament of Victoria for Essendon, 1958. Member: CPA; Victorian Parly Former Mems Assoc.; Life Mem., Coburg FC. Life Governor: Essendon Hosp.; Essendon Lions Club. *Recreations:* golf, football, exhibition of horses. *Address:* St Ann's, 33 Wattle Road, Hawthorn, Vic 3122, Australia. *Clubs:* Essendon; Coburg Rotary; Royal-Park Golf; Royal Automobile of Victoria. *Died 10 May 1996.*

WHEELER, Rt Rev. (William) Gordon, MA Oxon; RC Bishop of Leeds, 1966–85, then Bishop Emeritus; *b* 5 May 1910; *o s* of late Frederick Wheeler and Marjorie (*née* Upjohn). *Educ:* Manchester Grammar Sch.; University Coll. and St Stephen's House, Oxford; Beda Coll., Rome. Ordained deacon 1933, priest 1934; Curate, St Bartholomew's, Brighton, 1933; Curate, St Mary and All Saints, Chesterfield, 1934; Asst Chaplain, Lancing Coll., 1935; received into Roman Catholic Church at Downside, 1936; Beda Coll., Rome, 1936–40; ordained priest, 1940; Asst, St Edmund's, Lower Edmonton, 1940–44; Chaplain of Westminster Cathedral and Editor of Westminster Cathedral Chronicle, 1944–50; Chaplain to the Catholics in the University, London, 1950–54, and Ecclesiastical Adviser to the Union of Catholic Students, 1953–60; Privy Chamberlain to HH The Pope, 1952; Hon. Canon of Westminster, 1954, Administrator of Cathedral, 1954–65; created Domestic Prelate to HH Pope Pius XII, 1955; Grand Cross Conventual Chaplain to the British Association of the Sovereign and Military Order of Malta, 1986; Coadjutor Bishop of Middlesbrough, 1964–66; present at 2nd Vatican Council, Rome, 1964 and 1965. Hon. DD Leeds. *Publications:* (ed and contrib.) Homage to Newman, 1945; (contrib.) Richard Challoner, 1947; (contrib.) The English Catholics, 1950; In Truth and Love (memoirs), 1990; More Truth and Love (memoirs), 1994; contribs to Dublin Review, The Tablet, Clergy Review, etc. *Address:* Mount St Joseph's, Shire Oak Road, Leeds LS6 2DE. *Died 20 Feb. 1998.*

WHEELER, William Henry, CMG 1959; PhD; Chairman, Mark Laboratories Ltd, since 1960; *b* Petersfield, Hants, 5 March 1907; *s* of John William and Ellen Wheeler; *m* 1937, Mary Inkpen (decd); no *c.* *Educ:* St Catharine's Coll., Cambridge (BA); Imperial Coll. of Science (DIC 1930; PhD 1932). Beit Memorial Research Fellow, Imperial Coll., 1931. Man. British Automatic Refrigerators, London, 1935; Government Scientific Service, 1937; Dir, Guided Weapons Research & Development, 1950; Head of UK Ministry of Supply Staff and Scientific Adviser to UK High Commission, Australia, 1955; Director of Explosives Research, Waltham Abbey, 1959–61; Man. Dir, 1961–82, and Dep. Chm., 1968–82, Urquhart Engineering Co. Ltd; Chairman: Urquhart Engineering Co. (Pty) Ltd, 1971–82; Urquhart Engineering GmbH, 1973–82; Dep. Chm., Steam and Combustion

Engineering Ltd, 1973–82; Chm., Process Combustion Corp., USA, 1970–82. *Publications:* papers on combustion and detonation in Proc. and Trans Royal Society, and on rocket propellants in Nature, Proc. of Inst. of Fuel and Instn of Chemical Engineers; papers on the mechanism of cavitation erosion for DSIR and American Soc. of Mechanical Engineers. *Recreation:* private research laboratory. *Address:* 9 Bulstrode Court, Oxford Road, Gerrards Cross, Bucks SL9 7RR.

Died 23 June 2000.

WHISTLER, Sir (Alan Charles) Laurence, Kt 2000; CBE 1973 (OBE 1955); engraver on glass; writer; *b* 21 Jan. 1912; *s* of Henry Whistler and Helen (*née* Ward); *yr b* of late Rex Whistler; *m* 1st, 1939, Jill (*d* 1944), *d* of Sir Ralph Furse, KCMG, DSO; one *s* one *d*; 2nd, 1950, Theresa (marr. diss. 1986), *yr sister* of Jill Furse; one *s* one *d;* 3rd, 1987, Carol Dawson (marr. diss. 1991), *d* of John Dudley Groves, CB, OBE. *Educ:* Stowe; Balliol College, Oxford (BA; MA 1985; Hon. Fellow 1974). Chancellor's Essay Prize, 1934. Served War of 1939–45: private soldier, 1940; commissioned in The Rifle Brigade, 1941; Captain 1942. King's Gold Medal for Poetry, 1935 (first award); Atlantic Award for Literature, 1945. First Pres., Guild of Glass Engravers, 1975–80. Hon. DLitt Oxon, 1993. *Work on glass included:* goblets, etc, in point-engraving and drill, and engraved church windows and panels at: Sherborne Abbey; Moreton, Dorset; Checkendon, Oxon; Ilton, Som; Eastbury, Berks (window to Edward and Helen Thomas); Guards' Chapel, London; Stowe, Bucks; St Hugh's Coll., Oxford; Ashmansworth, Berks; Steep, Hants (windows to Edward Thomas); Hannington, Hants; Yalding, Kent (windows to Edmund Blunden); Thornham Parva, Suffolk; Salisbury Cathedral; Curry Rivel, Som; Wootton St Lawrence, Hants; panel to Jacqueline du Pré, St Hilda's Coll., Oxford. *Exhibitions:* Agnews, Bond Street, 1969; Marble Hill, Twickenham, 1972; Corning Museum, USA, 1974; Ashmolean, 1976, 1985; Sotheby's, 1992; (with Simon Whistler) S Wilts Mus., Salisbury, 1993. *Publications included:* Sir John Vanbrugh (biography), 1938; The English Festivals, 1947; Rex Whistler, His Life and His Drawings, 1948; The World's Room (collected poems), 1949; The Engraved Glass of Laurence Whistler, 1952; Rex Whistler: the Königsmark Drawings, 1952; The Imagination of Vanbrugh and his Fellow Artists, 1954; The View From This Window (poems), 1956; Engraved Glass, 1952–58, 1959; (with Ronald Fuller) The Work of Rex Whistler, 1960; Audible Silence (poems), 1961; The Initials in the Heart: the story of a marriage, 1964, rev. edn 1975; To Celebrate Her Living (poems), 1967; Pictures on Glass, 1972; The Image on the Glass, 1975; Scenes and Signs on Glass, 1985; The Laughter and the Urn: the life of Rex Whistler, 1985; Enter (poems), 1987; Point Engraving on Glass, 1992. *Address:* Scriber's Cottage, High Street, Watlington, Oxford OX9 5PY.

Died 19 Dec. 2000.

WHISTON, Peter Rice, RSA 1977; ARIBA; FRIAS; consultant architect, since 1977; *b* 19 Oct. 1912; *s* of Thomas Whiston and Marie Barrett; *m* 1947, Kathleen Anne Parker (*d* 1983); one *s* four *d.* *Educ:* Holy Cross Acad.; Sch. of Architecture, Edinburgh Coll. of Art. RIBA Silver Medallist for Recognised Schs, 1937. Served War, Staff Captain RE, 1940–45. Articled, City Architect, Edinburgh, 1930–35; Partner, Dick Peddie McKay & Jamieson, 1937–38; Chief Architect, SSHA, 1946–49; ecclesiological practice, 1950–77; Sen. Lectr, Sch. of Architecture, ECA, 1950–69; Dir, Arch. Conservation Studies, Heriot Watt Univ., 1969–77. Visiting Lectr, Internat. Centre for Conservation, Rome, 1971. *Works included:* Cistercian Abbey at Nunraw; St Margaret's, St Mark's and St Paul's, Edin.; St Columba, Cupar; St Mary Magdalene's, Perth; St Ninian's and St Leonard's, Dundee;

Our Lady, Mother of the Church, Edin.; Corpus Christi, Glasgow; St Mark's, Rutherglen; St Bernadette's, Tullibody. Awarded Papal Knighthood of St Gregory for services to architecture, 1969. *Recreations:* travel, sketching, painting. *Address:* Grange Lodge, Grange Road, North Berwick, East Lothian EH39 4QT.

Died 24 Jan. 1999.

WHITAKER, Sir James Herbert Ingham, 3rd Bt *cr* 1936, of Babworth, Nottinghamshire; OBE 1996; Vice-Chairman, Halifax Building Society, 1973–94; *b* 27 July 1925; *s* of late Maj.-Gen. Sir John Whitaker, 2nd Bt, CB, CBE, and Lady (Pamela) Whitaker (*née* Snowden); *S* father, 1957; *m* 1948, Mary Elisabeth Lander Urling Clark (*née* Johnston) (*d* 1998), *widow* of Captain D. Urling Clark, MC; one *s* one *d. Educ:* Eton. Coldstream Guards, 1944; served in North West Europe; retired, 1947. Formerly Dir, Governing Body, Atlantic Coll. High Sheriff of Notts, 1969–70. *Recreation:* shooting. *Heir: s* John James Ingham Whitaker, BSc, FCA, AMIEE [*b* 23 Oct. 1952; *m* 1981, Janey, *d* of L. J. R. Starke, New Zealand; one *s* three *d*]. *Address:* Garden House, Babworth, Retford, Notts DN22 8EW. *T:* (01777) 703454; Auchnafree, Dunkeld, Perthshire PH8 0EH.

Died 13 Jan. 1999.

WHITBY, Prof. (Lionel) Gordon, FRSE, FRCP, FRCPE, FRCPath; Professor of Clinical Chemistry, University of Edinburgh, 1963–91, Emeritus Professor since 1991; Biochemist-in-charge, Royal Infirmary of Edinburgh, 1963–91; *b* London, 18 July 1926; *s* of Sir Lionel Whitby, CVO, MC, TD (Regius Prof. of Physic and Master of Downing Coll., Cambridge) and Ethel Whitby, 2nd *d* of James Murgatroyd, Shelf, Yorks; *m* 1949, Joan Hunter Sanderson; one *s* two *d. Educ:* Eton; King's Coll., Cambridge (MA, PhD 1951; MB BChir 1956; MD 1961); Middlesex Hosp. Fellow of King's College, Cambridge, 1951–55; W. A. Meek Schol., Univ. of Cambridge, 1951; Murchison Schol., RCP, 1958; Registrar and Asst Lectr in Chem. Path., Hammersmith Hosp. and Postgrad. Med. Sch. of London, 1958–60; Rockefeller Trav. Res. Fellow, Nat. Insts of Health, Bethesda, Md, USA, 1959; Univ. Biochemist to Addenbrooke's Hosp., 1960–63, and Fellow of Peterhouse, 1961–62, Cambridge; University of Edinburgh: Dean of Faculty of Medicine, 1969–72 and 1983–86; Curator of Patronage, 1978–91; Vice-Principal, 1979–83. Chm., Scottish Sub-Cttee, Adv. Cttee on Distinction Awards, 1991–92 and 1993–96 (Mem., 1989–92); Member: Standing Adv. Cttee, Lab. Services, SHHD, 1965–72; Laboratory Develt Adv. Group, DHSS, 1972–76; Scientific Services Adv. Gp, SHHD, 1974–77; Screening Sub-Cttee of Standing Medical Adv. Cttee, 1975–81; Training Cttee, RCPath, 1977–79; Med. Lab. Technicians Bd, 1978–94; GMC, 1986–91; Adv. Council, British Library, 1986–91. Guest Lectr, Amer. Chem. Soc., 1966; Vis. Prof. of Chemical Pathology, RPMS, 1974. Vice-Pres., RSE, 1983–86. Trustee, Nat. Library of Scotland, 1982–91. *Publications:* (ed jtly) Principles and Practice of Medical Computing, 1971; (jtly) Lecture Notes on Clinical Chemistry, 1975, 5th edn, as Lecture Notes on Clinical Biochemistry, 1993; (jtly) Multiple Choice Questions on Clinical Chemistry, 1981; scientific papers on flavinglucosides, catecholamines and metabolites, several aspects of clin. chem., and early detection of disease by chemical tests. *Recreations:* gardening, photography. *Address:* 51 Dick Place, Edinburgh EH9 2JA. *T:* (0131) 667 4358. *Died 12 March 2000.*

WHITE, Baroness *cr* 1970 (Life Peer), of Rhymney, co. Monmouth; **Eirene Lloyd White;** a Deputy Speaker, House of Lords, 1979–89; *b* 7 Nov. 1909; *d* of late Dr Thomas Jones, CH and Eirene Theodora, *d* of R. J. Lloyd; *m* 1948, John Cameron White (*d* 1968). *Educ:* St Paul's Girls' Sch.; Somerville Coll., Oxford (Hon. Fellow, 1966).

Ministry of Labour officer, 1933–37 and 1941–45; Political Correspondent, Manchester Evening News, 1945–49. Contested (Lab) Flintshire, 1945; MP (Lab) East Flint, 1950–70. Parly Secretary, Colonial Office, 1964–66; Minister of State for Foreign Affairs, 1966–67; Minister of State, Welsh Office, 1967–70. Mem., Nat. Exec. Cttee of Labour Party, 1947–53, 1958–72 (Chm., 1968–69). Chm., Select Cttee on Eur. Communities, and Principal Dep. Chm. of Cttees, H of L, 1979–82; Dep. Chm., Parly Scientific Cttee, 1986–89. Member: Royal Commn on Environmental Pollution, 1974–81; British Waterways Bd, 1974–80. Governor: National Library of Wales, 1950–70; Brit. Film Inst. and National Film Theatre, 1959–64; Indep. Mem., Cinematograph Films Council, 1946–64. Chairman, Fabian Society, 1958–59. President: Nursery School Assoc., 1964–66; Council for Protection of Rural Wales, 1974–89; former Pres., Nat. Council of Women (Wales); Lord President's nominee, Council, UCW, Aberystwyth, 1973–77, Court (elected), 1977–85; Member: UGC, 1977–80; Council, UCNW Bangor, 1977–80; Council, Univ. of Wales Coll. of Cardiff (formerly UWIST), 1981–93 (Chm., 1983–88; Pres., 1987–88; Vice-Pres., 1988–93); Chm., Coleg Harlech, 1974–84. Chairman: Internat. Cttee, Nat. Council of Social Service, 1973–77; Adv. Cttee on Oil Pollution at sea, 1974–78; Land Authority for Wales, 1975–80; Dep. Chm., Metrication Bd, 1972–76; Vice-President: Commonwealth Countries League; Commonwealth Youth Exchange Council, 1976–79; Council for National Parks, 1985–; TCPA, 1983–91. Hon. MRTPI 1987. Hon. Fellow, Univ. of Wales, Cardiff, 1989. Hon. LLD: Wales, 1979; Queen's Univ., Belfast, 1981; Bath, 1983. *Publication:* The Ladies of Gregynog, 1985. *Address:* 22 Bailey Court, Hereford Road, Abergavenny, Gwent NP7 5PQ. *T:* (01873) 859032. *Died 23 Dec. 1999.*

WHITE, Raymond Walter Ralph, CMG 1982; Chairman, New Zealand Advisory Board, Westpac Banking Corporation, 1991–95; *b* 23 June 1923; *s* of Henry Underhill White and Ethel Annie White; *m* 1946, Nola Colleen Adin; one *s* two *d. Educ:* Palmerston North Technical High Sch.; Victoria Univ. FCA 1981; FCIS 1968; FBINZ 1982. Dep. Governor, 1967–77, Governor, 1977–82, Reserve Bank of NZ. Chairman: BP New Zealand, 1984–92; Australian Guarantee Corp (NZ) Ltd, 1991–93; Director: NZ Guardian Trust Co., 1983–91; Alcan Australia Ltd, 1988–95; NZ Adv. Bd, ICI, 1990–93. *Recreations:* golf, tennis, gardening. *Address:* 63 Chatsworth Road, Silverstream, New Zealand. *T:* Wellington (4) 282084. *Club:* Wellington (NZ).

Died 14 April 1998.

WHITE, Richard Hamilton Hayden; Director, Special Projects, Lord Chancellor's Department, since 1998; *b* 9 Aug. 1939; *s* of late Charles Henry Hayden White and Helen Margherita Hamilton White. *Educ:* Sutton Valence Sch.; Trinity Coll., Oxford (MA). Admitted solicitor, 1963. Asst Solicitor, Freshfields, 1963–67; Lectr in Law, later Sen. Lectr, Univ. of Birmingham, 1967–74; Lord Chancellor's Department, 1974–: Temp. Legal Advr, then Sen. Legal Advr; Asst Solicitor, 1981; Under Sec. and Head of Legal Gp, 1992; Legal Advr, 1995. Secretary: Rev. Body on Chancery Div., report pubd 1981; Civil Justice Rev., report pubd 1988. *Publications:* (contributed): Social Needs and Legal Action, 1973; Legal Services in Birmingham, 1975; Lawyers in their Social Setting, 1976; Rechtsbedürfnis und Rechtshilfe, 1978; EEC Conventions on Jurisdiction and Enforcement of Judgments, 1992. *Recreations:* rural pursuits, Sicily. *Address:* Lord Chancellor's Department, Selborne House, 54/60 Victoria Street, SW1E 6QW. *T:* (0171) 210 3530.

Died 4 Aug. 1998.

WHITE, Roger Lowrey; JP; Managing Director, Research Information Services (Westminster) Ltd, 1975–93; Associate Director, Cargill Attwood International, since 1971; *b* 1 June 1928; *o s* of late George Frederick White and Dorothy Jeanette White; *m* 1962, Angela Mary (*née* Orman), company director. *Educ:* St Joseph's Coll., Beulah Hill. National Vice-Chm., Young Conservatives, 1958–59; Founder Mem., Conservative Commonwealth Council; Mem. Council, London Borough of Bromley, 1964–68. MP (C) Gravesend, 1970–Feb. 1974. Gen. Comr of Taxes, 1991–95. Member: National Asthma Campaign (formerly Asthma Research) Council, 1973–95; London Crime Stoppers Bd, 1989– (Dep. Chm., 1992–95). Freeman, City of London, 1953; Liveryman, Worshipful Co. of Makers of Playing Cards, 1975–95. JP Inner London Area, 1965; Chm., E Central Div. of Inner London Magistrates, 1989–91 (Dep. Chm., 1986–89). *Recreations:* golf, fishing. *Address:* 9 Dartmoor Drive, Huntingdon, Cambs PE18 8XT. *Club:* English-Speaking Union.
Died 16 Feb. 2000.

WHITE, Sir Thomas Astley Woollaston, 5th Bt *cr* 1802, of Wallingwells, Nottinghamshire; JP; Hon. Sheriff for Wigtownshire, since 1963; *b* 13 May 1904; *s* of Sir Archibald Woollaston White, 4th Bt, and late Gladys Becher Love, *d* of Rev. E. A. B. Pitman; *S* father, 1945; *m* 1935, Daphne Margaret, *er d* of late Lt-Col F. R. I. Athill, CMG, OBE; one *d*. *Educ:* Wellington College. FRICS. JP Wigtownshire, 1952. *Heir: nephew* Nicholas Peter Archibald White [*b* 2 March 1939; *m* 1970, Susan Irene, *d* of G. W. D. Pollock; two *s* one *d*]. *Address:* Ha Hill, Torhousemuir, Wigtown, Newton Stewart DG8 9DJ. *T:* Wigtown (01988) 402238. *Died 20 May 1996.*

WHITE-THOMSON, Very Rev. Ian Hugh; Dean of Canterbury, 1963–76; *b* 18 Dec. 1904; *m* 1954, Wendy Ernesta Woolliams; two *s* two *d*. *Educ:* Harrow; Brasenose Coll., Oxford; Cuddesdon Coll. Deacon, 1929; priest, 1930; Curacy, St Mary's, Ashford, Kent, 1929–34; Rector of S Martin's with St Paul's, Canterbury, 1934–39; Chaplain to Archbishops of Canterbury, 1939–47; Vicar of Folkestone, 1947–54; Archdeacon of Northumberland and Canon of Newcastle, 1955–63; Chaplain to King George VI, 1947–52, to the Queen, 1952–63; Examining Chaplain to Bishop of Newcastle, 1955–63. Hon. Canon of Canterbury Cathedral, 1950. Governor, Harrow School, 1947–62, 1965–70. Freeman, City of Canterbury, 1976. Hon. DCL Univ. of Kent at Canterbury, 1971. *Address:* Camphill, Harville Road, Wye, Ashford, Kent TN25 5EY. *T:* (01233) 812210. *Died 11 Jan. 1997.*

WHITEHEAD, George Sydney, CMG 1966; LVO 1961; HM Diplomatic Service, retired; re-employed in Foreign and Commonwealth Office (Security Department), 1976–81; *b* 15 Nov. 1915; *s* of William George and Annie Sabina Whitehead; *m* 1948, Constance Mary Hart (*née* Vale); one *d*, and one step *d*. *Educ:* Harrow County Sch.; London Sch. of Economics. Armed Forces (Royal Artillery), 1940–45. India Office, 1934; Private Sec. to Parly Under-Sec. of State for India and Burma, 1945–46; British Embassy, Rangoon, 1947; CRO, 1948–52; British High Commn, Canberra, 1952–55; Counsellor, British High Commn, Calcutta, 1958–61; Inspector, Commonwealth Service, 1961–64; Inspector, Diplomatic Service, 1965; Head of Asia Economic Dept, CO, 1966–67; Head of Commonwealth Trade Dept, CO, 1967–68; Head of Commodities Dept, FCO, 1968–69; Dep. High Comr and Minister (Commercial), Ottawa, 1970–72; Asst Under-Sec. of State, 1972–75, Dep. Chief Clerk, 1973–75, FCO. Vice-Pres., RIPA, 1985– (Mem. Council, 1977–84). *Recreations:* gardening, reading, walking. *Address:* Victoria House, Victoria Road,

Aldeburgh, Suffolk IP15 5EG. *T:* (01728) 453671. *Clubs:* Civil Service, Victory Services; Middlesex County Cricket. *Died 21 Oct. 1998.*

WHITELAW, 1st Viscount *cr* 1983, of Penrith in the County of Cumbria; **William Stephen Ian Whitelaw,** KT 1990; CH 1974; MC; PC 1967; DL; farmer and landowner; *b* 28 June 1918; *s* of late W. A. Whitelaw, Monkland, Nairn, and Helen, *d* of Maj.-Gen. F. S. Russell, CMG; *m* 1943, Cecilia Doriel, 2nd *d* of late Major Mark Sprot, Riddell, Melrose, Roxburghshire; four *d*. *Educ:* Winchester Coll.; Trinity Coll., Camb. Reg. Officer, Scots Guards; Emergency Commn, 1939; resigned Commn, 1947. MP (C) Penrith and the Border Div. of Cumberland, 1955–83; PPS to Pres. of BOT, 1956, to Chancellor of the Exchequer, 1957–58; Asst Govt Whip, 1959–61; a Lord Comr of the Treasury, 1961–62; Parly Sec., Min. of Labour, 1962–64; Chief Opposition Whip, 1964–70; Lord Pres. of Council and Leader, House of Commons, 1970–72; Secretary of State for: N Ireland, 1972–73; Employment, 1973–74; Chm., Conservative Party, 1974–75; Dep. Leader of the Opposition and spokesman on home affairs, 1975–79; Home Secretary, 1979–83; Lord President of the Council and Leader, H of L, 1983–88. Visiting Fellow, Nuffield Coll., Oxford, 1970. DL Dunbartonshire, 1952–66; DL Cumbria, formerly Cumberland, 1967. *Publication:* The Whitelaw Memoirs, 1989. *Recreations:* golf, shooting. *Heir:* none. *Address:* House of Lords, SW1A 0AA. *Clubs:* White's, Carlton (Chm., 1986–92); Royal and Ancient (Captain 1969–70). *Died 1 July 1999 (ext).*

WHITELEY, Maj.-Gen. Gerald Abson, CB 1969; OBE 1952; *b* 4 March 1915; *s* of late Harry Whitcley, Walton Park, Bexhill; *m* 1943, Ellen Hanna (*d* 1973). *Educ:* Workbop Coll.; Emmanuel Coll., Cambridge (MA). Solicitor, 1938. Commissioned, RA, 1940; Maj., DJAG's Staff, MF, 1942–45; AAG, Mil. Dept, JAG's Office, WO, 1945–48; Asst Dir of Army Legal Services: FARELF, 1948–51; WO, 1952–53; Northern Army Gp, 1953–54; MELF, 1954–57; BAOR, 1957–60; Dep. Dir of Army Legal Services, BAOR, 1960–62; Col, Legal Staff, WO, 1962–64; Dir of Army Legal Services, MoD, 1964–69. *Recreations:* photography, walking. *Address:* 8 Kemnal Park, Haslemere, Surrey GU27 2LF. *T:* (01428) 642803. *Club:* Army and Navy. *Died 5 Jan. 1997.*

WHITEMAN, (Elizabeth) Anne (Osborn); JP; DPhil; FRHistS, FSA; Tutor in Modern History 1946–85, Fellow 1948–85, and Vice-Principal 1971–81, Lady Margaret Hall, Oxford; *b* 10 Feb. 1918; *d* of Harry Whitmore Whiteman and Dorothy May (*née* Austin). *Educ:* St Albans High Sch.; Somerville Coll., Oxford (MA 1945, DPhil 1951). FRHistS 1954; FSA 1958. Served War, WAAF, 1940–45: served in N Africa and Italy (mentioned in despatches, 1943). Rep. of Women's Colls, Oxford Univ., 1960–61. Member: Hebdomadal Council, Oxford Univ., 1968–85; Academic Planning Bd, Univ. of Warwick, 1961–65; UGC, 1976–83. Trustee, Ruskin Sch. of Drawing, 1974–77. JP City of Oxford, 1962. *Publications:* (contrib.) Victoria County History, Wilts, Vol. III, 1956; (contrib.) New Cambridge Modern History, Vol. V, 1961; (contrib.) From Uniformity to Unity, ed Chadwick and Nuttall, 1962; (ed with J. S. Bromley and P. G. M. Dickson, and contrib.) Statesmen, Scholars and Merchants: Essays in eighteenth-century History presented to Dame Lucy Sutherland, 1973; (ed with Mary Clapinson) The Compton Census of 1676, 1986; contrib. hist. jls. *Address:* 5 Observatory Street, Oxford OX2 6EW. *T:* (01865) 511009. *Died 11 May 2000.*

WHITFIELD, Rev. George Joshua Newbold; General Secretary, Church of England Board of Education, 1969–74; *b* 2 June 1909; *s* of late Joshua Newbold and Eva Whitfield; *m* 1937, Dr Audrey Priscilla Dence (*d*

1999), *d* of late Rev. A. T. Dence; two *s* two *d. Educ:*
Bede Grammar Sch., Sunderland; King's Coll., Univ. of
London (BA 1st cl. Hons English and AKC, 1930 (Barry
Prizeman); MA 1935); Bishops' Coll., Cheshunt. Asst
Master, Trin. Sch., Croydon, 1931–34; Senior English
Master: Doncaster Grammar Sch., 1934–36; Hymers Coll.,
Hull, 1937–43; Headmaster: Tavistock Grammar Sch.,
1943–46; Stockport Sch., 1946–50; Hampton Sch.,
1950–68 (Whitfield Building opened 1990). Chief Examr
in English, Univ. of Durham Sch. Exams Bd, 1940–43.
Ordained deacon, 1962; priest, 1963; Curate, St Mary,
Hampton, 1962–74. Member: Duke of Edinburgh's Award
Adv. Cttee, 1960–66; Headmasters' Conf., 1964–68;
Corporation of Church House, 1974–; Pres., Headmasters'
Assoc., 1967; Chm., Exeter Diocesan Educn Cttee,
1981–88. *Publications:* (ed) Teaching Poetry, 1937; An
Introduction to Drama, 1938; God and Man in the Old
Testament, 1949; (ed) Poetry in the Sixth Form, 1950;
Philosophy and Religion, 1955; (jtly) Christliche
Erziehung in Europa, Band I, England, 1975. *Recreations:*
gardening, photography. *Address:* Linksway, Douglas
Avenue, Exmouth, Devon EX8 2EY.

Died 28 Oct. 2000.

WHITLEY, Air Marshal Sir John (René), KBE 1956
(CBE 1945); CB 1946; DSO 1943; AFC 1937, Bar, 1956;
b 7 Sept. 1905; *s* of late A. Whitley, Condette, Pas de
Calais, France; *m* 1st, 1932, Barbara Liscombe (*d* 1965);
three *s* (and one *s* decd); 2nd, 1967, Alison (*d* 1986), *d* of
Sir Nigel Campbell and *widow* of John Howard Russell;
three step *s. Educ:* Haileybury. Entered Royal Air Force
with a short-service commission, 1926; Permanent
Commission, 1931; served in India, 1932–37; served in
Bomber Command, 1937–45, as a Squadron Comdr,
Station Comdr, Base Comdr and AOC 4 Group; HQ
ACSEA Singapore, 1945; HQ India and Base Comdr,
Karachi, 1946–47; Director of Organisation
(Establishments), Air Ministry, 1948 and 1949; Imperial
Defence College, 1950; AOA, 2nd Tactical Air Force,
1951 and 1952; AOC No 1 (Bomber) Group, 1953–56;
Air Member for Personnel, 1957–59; Inspector-General,
RAF, 1959–62; Controller, RAF Benevolent Fund,
1962–68, retd. *Address:* The Grange, Steep, Petersfield,
Hampshire GU32 2DB. *Died 26 Dec. 1997.*

WHITTLE, Air Cdre Sir Frank, OM 1986; KBE 1948
(CBE 1944); CB 1947; MA Cantab; RDI 1985; FRS 1947;
FEng; RAF, retired; *b* 1 June 1907; *s* of M. Whittle; *m*
1930, Dorothy Mary Lee (marr. diss. 1976; she *d* 1996);
two *s*; *m* 1976, Hazel S. Hall. *Educ:* Leamington Coll.;
No 4 Apprentices' Wing, RAF Cranwell; RAF Coll.,
Cranwell; Peterhouse, Cambridge (Mechanical Sciences
Tripos, BA 1st Cl. Hons). No 4 Apprentices' Wing, RAF
Cranwell, 1923–26; Flight Cadet, RAF Coll., Cranwell,
1926–28 (Abdy-Gerrard-Fellowes Memorial Prize); Pilot
Officer, 111 (Fighter) Sqdn, 1928–29; Flying Instructors'
Course, Central Flying Sch., 1929; Flying Instructor, No
2 Flying Training Sch., RAF Digby, 1930; Test Pilot,
Marine Aircraft Experimental Estab., RAF Felixstowe,
1931–32; RAF Sch. of Aeronautical Engrg, Henlow,
1932–34; Officer i/c Engine Test, Engine Repair Section,
Henlow, 1934 (6 mths); Cambridge Univ., 1934–37 (Post-
Graduate year, 1936–37); Special Duty List, attached
Power Jets Ltd for develt of aircraft gas turbine for jet
propulsion, 1937–46; War Course, RAF Staff Coll., 1943;
Technical Adviser to Controller of Supplies (Air), Min. of
Supply, 1946–48; retd RAF, 1948. Hon. Technical
Adviser: Jet Aircraft, BOAC, 1948–52; Shell Gp, 1953–57;
Consultant, Bristol Siddeley Engines/Rolls Royce on turbo
drill project, 1961–70. Mem. Faculty, US Naval Acad.,
Annapolis, Maryland, 1977–. Partnered Flt-Lt G. E.
Campbell in Crazy Flying RAF Display, Hendon, 1930;
1st flights of Gloster jet-propelled aeroplane with Whittle
engine, May 1941. Freeman of Royal Leamington Spa,

1944. Hon. FRAeS; Hon. FAeSI; Hon. FIMechE; Founder
Fellow, Fellowship of Engineering, 1976. Hon. Mem.,
Franklin Inst.; Hon. FAIAA; Hon. Mem., Société Royale
Belge des Ingénieurs; Hon. Foreign Mem., Amer. Acad.
Arts and Scis, 1976; For. Assoc., US Nat. Acad. of Engrg,
1978; Hon. Fellow, Soc. of Experimental Test Pilots,
USA; Hon. MEIC. Hon. Fellow, Peterhouse. Hon. DSc:
Oxon; Manchester; Leicester; Bath; Warwick; Exeter;
Cranfield Inst. of Technology, 1987; Hon. LLD Edinburgh;
Hon. ScD Cantab; Hon. DTech: Trondheim;
Loughborough, 1987. James Alfred Ewing Medal, ICE,
1944; Gold Medal, RAeS, 1944; James Clayton Prize,
IMechE, 1946; Daniel Guggenheim Medal, USA, 1946;
Kelvin Gold Medal, 1947; Melchett Medal, 1949; Rumford
Medal, Royal Soc., 1950; Gold Medal, Fédn Aéronautique
Internat., 1951; Churchill Gold Medal, Soc. of Engineers,
1952; Albert Gold Medal, Soc. of Arts, 1952; Franklin
Medal, USA, 1956; John Scott Award, 1957; Goddard
Award, USA, 1965; Coventry Award of Merit, 1966;
International Communications (Christopher Columbus)
Prize, City of Genoa, 1966; Tony Jannus Award, Greater
Tampa Chamber of Commerce, 1969; James Watt Internat.
Gold Medal, IMechE, 1977; Nat. Air and Space Mus.
Trophy, 1986; (first) Prince Philip Medal, Fellowship of
Engrg, 1991; Charles Stark Draper Prize, Nat. Acad. of
Engrng, 1991. Comdr, US Legion of Merit, 1946.
Publications: Jet, 1953; Gas Turbine Aero-
Thermodynamics, 1981. *Clubs:* Royal Air Force; Wings
(New York). *Died 8 Aug. 1996.*

WHITTUCK, Gerald Saumarez, CB 1959; *b* 13 Oct. 1912;
s of late Francis Gerald Whittuck; *m* 1938, Catherine
McCrea (*d* 1992); two *s. Educ:* Cheltenham; Clare Coll.,
Cambridge. Air Ministry, 1935; Private Secretary to
Secretary of State, 1944–46; Asst Under-Secretary of
State: Air Ministry, 1955–63; War Office, 1963–64; MoD,
1964–71; Dir, Greenwich Hosp., 1971–74. Mem., Royal
Patriotic Fund Corp., 1971–74. *Address:* 15A Greenaway
Gardens, NW3 7DH. *T:* (0171) 435 3742.

Died 7 Sept. 1997.

WHITWORTH, Hugh Hope Aston, MBE 1945; Lay
Assistant to the Archbishop of Canterbury, 1969–78; *b* 21
May 1914; *s* of Sidney Alexander Whitworth and Elsie
Hope Aston; *m* 1st, 1944, Elizabeth Jean Boyes (*d* 1961);
two *s* one *d*; 2nd, 1961, Catherine Helen Bell (*d* 1986).
Educ: Bromsgrove Sch.; Pembroke Coll., Cambridge
(BA). Indian Civil Service, Bombay Province, 1937–47;
Administrator, Ahmedabad Municipality, 1942–44;
Collector and District Magistrate, Nasik, 1945–46; Board
of Trade, 1947–55; Scottish Home Dept, 1955; Asst Sec.,
1957; Under-Sec., Scottish Home and Health Dept,
1968–69. *Recreations:* travel, gardening. *Address:* 7
Walpole Gardens, Strawberry Hill, Twickenham TW2
5SL. *T:* 0181–894 4590. *Club:* Commonwealth Trust.

Died 13 Feb. 1996.

WICKBERG, Gen. Erik E.; Comdr of the Order of Vasa
(Sweden), 1970; General of the Salvation Army, 1969–74;
b 6 July 1904; *s* of David Wickberg, Commissioner,
Salvation Army, and Betty (*née* Lundblad); *m* 1st, 1929,
Ens. Frieda de Groot (*d* 1930); 2nd, 1932, Captain
Margarete Dietrich (*d* 1976); two *s* two *d*; 3rd, 1977,
Major Eivor Lindberg. *Educ:* Uppsala; Berlin; Stockholm.
Salvation Army Internat. Training Coll., 1924–25, and
Staff Coll., 1926; commissioned, 1925; appts in Scotland,
Berlin, London; Divisional Commander, Uppsala,
1946–48; Chief Secretary, Switzerland, 1948–53; Chief
Secretary, Sweden, 1953–57; Territorial Commander,
Germany, 1957–61; Chief of the Staff, Internat. HQ,
London, 1961–69; elected General of the Salvation Army,
July 1969; assumed international leadership, Sept. 1969.
Hon. LLD Choong Ang Univ., Seoul, 1970. Order of
Moo-Koong-Wha, Korea, 1970; Grosses Verdienstkreuz,

Germany, 1971; The King's Golden Medal (Sweden), 1980. *Publications:* In Darkest England Now, 1974; Inkallad (autobiography, in Swedish), 1978; Uppdraget (The Charge: my way to preaching, in Swedish), 1990; articles in Salvation Army periodicals and Year Book. *Recreations:* reading, fishing, chess. *Address:* c/o The Salvation Army, Box 5090, 10242 Stockholm, Sweden.
Died 26 April 1996.

WICKS, David Vaughan, RE 1961 (ARE 1950); Technical Artist, Bank of England Printing Works, 1954–79, retired, Consultant, 1979–85; *b* 20 Dec. 1918; British; *m* 1948, Margaret Gwyneth Downs (*d* 1990); one *s* one *d* (and one *s* decd). *Educ:* Wychwood, Bournemouth; Cranleigh School, Surrey. Polytechnic School of Art, 1936, silver medal for figure composition, 1938, 1939. Radio Officer, Merchant Navy, 1940–46. Royal College of Art, Engraving School, 1946–49, Diploma, ARCA Engraving; taught Processes of Engraving at RCA, 1949–54. *Recreations:* gardening, bowls. *Address:* Flat 92, Orchard Court, The Avenue, Egham, Surrey TW20 9HA.
Died 28 April 1996.

WICKS, Sir James (Albert), Kt 1978; JP; Wanganui Computer Centre Privacy Commissioner, 1978–83; Acting District Court Judge, 1980–81; *b* 14 June 1910; *s* of Henry James Wilmont Wicks and Melanie de Rohan Wicks (*née* Staunton); *m* 1942 Lorna Margaret de la Cour; one *s* one *d*. *Educ:* Christchurch Boys' High Sch.; Canterbury Univ., NZ. LLM (Hons) Univ. of New Zealand. Admitted Barrister and Solicitor of Supreme Court of NZ, 1932; Notary Public, 1951. In practice as barrister and solicitor, Christchurch, 1945–61; Stipendiary Magistrate, 1961–78. Lectr in Trustee Law, Canterbury Univ., 1946–55. Council, Canterbury Dist Law Soc., 1954–61. JP 1963; Chairman: Magistrates' Courts' Rules Cttee, 1967–78; NZ Magistrates' Exec., 1973–78; Dept of Justice's Editorial Bd, 1968–78; various Appeal Boards and Statutory Cttees, 1965–78; Teachers' Disciplinary Bd, 1978–82; Cttee of Inquiry into the Administration of the Electoral Act, 1979; Public Service Appeal Bd, 1982; conducted inquiry into alleged improper political interference in administration of the State Services Commn, 1986. Consultant to Govt of Niue on legal, judicial and law enforcement systems and policies, 1983. Mem. Bd of Dirs, Nat. Soc. on Alcoholism and Drug Dependence, NZ Inc., 1985–88. *Publications:* papers to Australian Inst. of Criminology, 1974, and Commonwealth Magistrates' Conf., Kuala Lumpur, 1975; contribs to NZ Law Jl, Commonwealth Judicial Jl. *Address:* 29 Glen Road, Kelburn, Wellington 5, New Zealand. *T:* (4) 4759204. *Club:* Canterbury (Christchurch, NZ). *Died 1996.*

WICKS, Rt Rev. Ralph Edwin, OBE 1982; ED 1964; Bishop of the Southern Region, Diocese of Brisbane, 1985–88; *b* 16 Aug. 1921; *s* of Charles Thomas Wicks and Florence Maud Wicks (*née* White); *m* 1st, 1946, Gladys Hawgood (*d* 1981); one *s* one *d*; 2nd, 1988, Patricia Henderson. *Educ:* East State Sch. and State High Sch., Toowoomba, Qld; St Francis Theological Coll., Brisbane, Qld (LTh). Mem., Qld Public Service (Educn Dept) 1936–41; Theological Student, 1941–44; Assistant Curate: Holy Trinity Ch., Fortitude Valley, Brisbane, 1944–47; St James' Ch., Toowoomba, Qld, 1947–48; Rector: Holy Trinity Ch., Goondiwindi, Qld, 1949–54; Holy Trinity Ch., Fortitude Valley, Brisbane, 1954–63; St James' Church, Toowoomba, Qld, 1963–72; Archdeacon of Darling Downs, Qld, 1972–73; Asst Bishop of Brisbane, 1973–85; Rector of St Andrew's Parish, Caloundra, and Commissary to Archbishop of Brisbane, 1983–85. Hon. Canon of St John's Cath., Brisbane, 1968. Chaplain to the Australian Army, 1949–70. *Recreations:* reading, gardening, music. *Address:* 1/9 The Esplanade, Mudjimba, Qld 4564, Australia. *Died 11 Sept. 1997.*

WIDDECOMBE, James Murray, CB 1968; OBE 1959; Director-General, Supplies and Transport (Naval), Ministry of Defence, 1968–70, retired; *b* 7 Jan. 1910; *s* of late Charles Frederick Widdecombe and Alice Widdecombe; *m* 1936, Rita Noreen Plummer; one *s* one *d*. *Educ:* Devonport High Sch. Asst Naval Armament Supply Officer, Portsmouth, Holton Heath and Chatham, 1929–35; Dep. Naval Armt Supply Officer, Chatham, 1936; OC, RN Armt Depot, Gibraltar, 1936–40; Naval Armt Supply Officer: Admty, 1940–43; Levant, 1943–44; served War, Capt. (SP) RNVR; Sen. Armt Supply Officer: Staff of C-in-C, Med., 1944–46; Admty, 1946–50; Asst Dir of Armt Supply, Admty, 1950–51, and 1956–59; Suptg Naval Armt Supply Officer, Portsmouth, 1951–53; Prin. Naval Armt Supply Officer, Staff of C-in-C, Far East, 1953–56; Dep. Dir of Armt Supply, Admiralty, 1959–61; Dir of Victualling, Admty, 1961–66; Head of RN Supply and Transport Service, MoD, 1966–68; special duties, Management Services, MoD, 1970–73. Gen. Sec., CS Retirement Fellowship, 1973–79. FIMgt; FCIPS. *Recreations:* golf, gardening, amateur dramatics. *Address:* 1 Manor Close, Haslemere, Surrey GU27 1PP. *T:* (01428) 642899. *Club:* Navy Department Golfing Society (Pres.).
Died 24 Feb. 1999.

WIDDOWSON, Dr Elsie May, CH 1993; CBE 1979; FRS 1976; Department of Medicine, Addenbrooke's Hospital, Cambridge, 1972–88; *b* 21 Oct. 1906; *d* of Thomas Henry Widdowson and Rose Widdowson. *Educ:* Imperial Coll., London (BSc, PhD; FIC 1994); DSc London, 1948. Courtauld Inst. of Biochemistry, Middx Hosp., 1931–33; KCH, London, 1933–38; Cambridge University: Dept of Exper. Medicine, 1938–66; Infant Nutrition Res. Div., 1966–72. President: Nutrition Soc., 1977–80; Neonatal Soc., 1978–81; British Nutrition Foundn, 1986–96. Hon. FRCP 1994; Hon. Fellow, Amer. Inst. of Nutrition, 1995. Hon DSc: Manchester, 1974; Salford, 1995 James Spence Medal, British Paediatric Assoc., 1981; 2nd Bristol Myers Award for Distinguished Achievement in Nutrition Res., 1982; 1st European Nutrition Award, Fedn of European Nutrition Socs, 1983; Rank Prize Funds Prize for Nutrition, 1984; McCollum Award, E. V. McCollum Commemorative Cttee, USA, 1985; Atwater Award, USA Agricl Res. Service, 1986; Nutritia Internat. Award, Nutricia Res. Foundn, 1988; 1st Edna and Robert Langholz Internat. Nutrition Award, 1992. *Publications:* (with R. A. McCance) The Composition of Foods, 1940, 2nd edn 1967; (with R. A. McCance) Breads White and Brown: Their Place in Thought and Social History, 1956; contrib. Proc. Royal Soc., Jl Physiol., Biochem. Jl, Brit. Jl Nut., Arch. Dis. Child., Lancet, BMJ, Nature, Biol. Neonate, Nut. Metabol., and Ped. Res. *Address:* Orchard House, 9 Boot Lane, Barrington, Cambridge CB2 5RA. *T:* (01223) 870219. *Died 14 June 2000.*

WIGAN, Sir Alan (Lewis), 5th Bt *cr* 1898, of Clare Lawn, Mortlake, Surrey and Purland Chase, Ross, Herefordshire; *b* 19 Nov. 1913; *second s* of Sir Roderick Grey Wigan, 3rd Bt, and Ina (*d* 1977), *o c* of Lewis D. Wigan, Brandon Park, Suffolk; *S* brother, 1979; *m* 1950, Robina, *d* of Sir Iain Colquhoun, 7th Bt, KT, DSO; one *s* one *d*. *Educ:* Eton; Magdalen College, Oxford. Commissioned Suppl. Reserve, KRRC, 1936; served with KRRC, 1939–46; wounded and taken prisoner, Calais, 1940. Director, Charrington & Co. (Brewers) 1939–70. Master, Brewers' Co., 1958–59. *Recreations:* shooting, fishing, golf. *Heir:* *s* Michael Iain Wigan [*b* 3 Oct. 1951; *m* 1st, 1984, Frances (marr. diss. 1985), *d* of late Flt-Lt Angus Barr Faucett and of Mrs Antony Reid; 2nd, 1989, Julia, *d* of John de Courcy Ling, CBE; two *s* one *d*]. *Address:* Badingham House, Badingham, Woodbridge, Suffolk IP13 8JP. *T:* Badingham (01728) 638664; Moorburn, The Lake, Kirkcudbright DG6 4XL. *T:* Kirkcudbright (01557) 30623. *Club:* Army and Navy. *Died 3 May 1996.*

WIGRAM, Rev. Canon Sir Clifford Woolmore, 7th Bt *cr* 1805, of Walthamstow, Essex; Vicar of Marston St Lawrence with Warkworth, near Banbury, 1945–83, also of Thenford, 1975–83; Non-Residentiary Canon of Peterborough Cathedral, 1973–83, Canon Emeritus since 1983; *b* 24 Jan. 1911; *er s* of late Robert Ainger Wigram and Evelyn Dorothy, *d* of C. W. E. Henslowe; *S* uncle, 1935; *m* 1948, Christobel Joan Marriott (*d* 1983), *d* of late William Winter Goode. *Educ:* Winchester; Trinity Coll., Cambridge. Deacon 1934, priest 1935; Asst Priest at St Ann's, Brondesbury, 1934–37; Chaplain, Ely Theological College, 1937–40; Curate: Long Ashton, 1940–42; St John the Baptist, Holland Road, Kensington, 1942–45. *Heir: b* Major Edward Robert Woolmore Wigram, Indian Army [*b* 19 July 1913; *m* 1944, Viva Ann (*d* 1997), *d* of late Douglas Bailey, Laughton Lodge, near Lewes, Sussex; one *d*]. *Address:* 8 Emden House, Barton Lane, Headington, Oxford OX3 9JU.

Died 11 Dec. 2000.

WIGRAM, Derek Roland, MA, BSc (Econ); Headmaster of Monkton Combe School, near Bath, 1946–68; *b* 18 March 1908; *er s* of late Roland Lewis Wigram and Mildred (*née* Willock); *m* 1944, Catharine Mary, *d* of late Very Rev. W. R. Inge, KCVO, DD, former Dean of St Paul's; one *s* one *d*. *Educ:* Marlborough Coll.; Peterhouse, Cambridge (Scholar). 1st Class Hons Classical Tripos, 1929; 2nd Class Hons Economics and Political Science, London, 1943. Assistant Master and Careers Master, Whitgift School, Croydon, 1929–36; House Master and Careers Master, Bryanston School, 1936–46. Hon. Associate Mem., Headmasters' Conf. (Chm., 1963–64); Vice-Pres., CMS (Chm., Exec. Cttee, 1956–58, 1969–72); Patron, Oxford Conf. in Education; Vice Pres. and Trustee of Lee Abbey; Founder Mem., Coll. of Preachers, 1962. Bishops' Inspector of Theological Colls (Mem. Archbishops' Commn, 1970–71). *Publication:* (Jt Editor) Hymns for Church and School, 1964. *Address:* The Old Schoolhouse, The Common, Swardeston, Norwich NR14 8EB. *T:* Mulbarton (01508) 578060.

Died 6 Feb. 1996.

WILCOX, Desmond John; independent television producer/reporter; journalist and author; *b* 21 May 1931; *e s* of late John Wallace Wilcox and Alice May Wilcox; *m* 1st 1954, Patsy (*née* Price) (marr. diss.); one *s* two *d*; 2nd, 1977, Esther Rantzen; one *s* two *d*. *Educ:* Cheltenham Grammar Sch.; Christ's Coll., London; Outward Bound Sea Sch. Sail training apprentice, 1947; Deckhand, Merchant Marine, 1948; Reporter, weekly papers, 1949; commissioned Army, National Service, 1949–51; News Agency reporter, 1951–52; Reporter and Foreign Correspondent, Daily Mirror, incl. New York Bureau and UN, 1952–60; Reporter, This Week, ITV, 1960–65; joined BBC 1965: Co-Editor/Presenter, Man Alive, 1965; formed Man Alive Unit, 1968; Head of General Features, BBC TV, 1972–80; Writer/Presenter, Americans, TV documentary, 1979; Presenter/Chm., Where it Matters, ITV discussion series, 1981; Producer/Presenter TV series: The Visit, BBC, 1982–91 (TV Radio Industries Club Award for Best Documentary, 1984, 1986), ITV, 1993; The Marriage, BBC, 1986; Black in Blue, BBC, 1990, 1992; A Day in the Life, ITV, 1993; Presenter, 60 Minutes, BBC TV, 1983–84. Mem. Council, BAFTA, 1997–. Man. Dir, Desmond Wilcox Productions Ltd, 1994–; Chm., Man Alive Gp, 1994–. Trustee: Conservation Foundn, 1982–; The Walk Fund (Walk Again Limb Kinetics), 1984–; Mem. of Bd, Disfigurement Guidance Centre, 1988–; Mem. Council, Queen's Coll., Harley St; Patron: Wessex Heartbeat (Wessex Cardiac Trust); All Hear Cochlear Implant Charity; CHIT (Children's Head Injury Trust); Headway; Harefield Hosp. Fund; British Deaf Assoc.; TIME (Transplants in Mind); Lin Berwick Trust; Chm., Defeating Deafness—Hearing Res. Trust, 1996–.

FInstD; FRSA 2000. SFTA Award for best factual programme series, 1967; Richard Dimbleby Award, SFTA, for most important personal contrib. in factual television, 1971. *Publications:* (jtly) Explorers, 1975; Americans, 1978; (with Esther Rantzen) Kill the Chocolate Biscuit: or Behind the Screen, 1981; (with Esther Rantzen) Baby Love, 1985; Return Visit, 1991. *Recreations:* riding, gardening, television. *Address:* c/o Noel Gay Artists, 19 Denmark Street, WC2H 8NA. *T:* (020) 7836 3941. *Clubs:* Arts, Groucho.

Died 6 Sept. 2000.

WILD, Major Hon. Gerald Percy, AM 1980; MBE 1941; company director; Agent-General for Western Australia in London, 1965–71; *b* 2 Jan. 1908; *m* 1944, Virginia Mary Baxter; two *s* one *d*. *Educ:* Shoreham Grammar Sch., Sussex; Chivers Acad., Portsmouth, Hants. Served War of 1939–45 (despatches, MBE): Middle East, Greece, Crete, Syria, New Guinea and Moratai, Netherlands East Indies (Major). Elected MLA for Western Australia, 1947; Minister for Housing and Forests, 1950–53; Minister for Works and Water Supplies and Labour (WA), 1959–65. JP Perth (WA), 1953. *Recreations:* golf, tennis, cricket, football. *Address:* 5 Hellam Grove, Booragoon, WA 6154, Australia. *Clubs:* East India, Devonshire, Sports and Public Schools; West Australian Turf (WA).

Died 9 Oct. 1996.

WILES, Sir Donald (Alonzo), KA 1984; CMG 1965; OBE 1960; Consultant to Barbados National Trust, since 1985; *b* 8 Jan. 1912; *s* of Donald Alonzo Wiles and Millicent Wiles; *m* 1938, Amelia Elsie Pemberton; two *d*. *Educ:* Harrison Coll., Barbados; Univs of London, Toronto, Oxford. Member of Staff of Harrison College, Barbados, 1931–45; Public Librarian, Barbados, 1945–50; Asst Colonial Secretary, Barbados, 1950–54; Permanent Secretary, Barbados, 1954–60; Administrator, Montserrat, 1960–64; Administrative Sec., Da Costa & Musson Ltd, 1965–79. Exec. Dir, Barbados Nat. Trust, 1980–84. *Recreations:* swimming, hiking, tennis. *Address:* Casa Loma, Sunrise Drive, Pine Gardens, St Michael, Barbados. *T:* 4266875.

Died 21 Nov. 1999.

WILES, Prof. Peter John de la Fosse, FBA 1990; Professor of Russian Social and Economic Studies, University of London, 1965–85, then Emeritus Professor of Sovietological Economics; *b* 25 Nov. 1919; *m* 1st, 1945, Elizabeth Coppin (marr. diss. 1960); one *s* two *d*; 2nd, 1960, Carolyn Stedman. *Educ:* Lambrook Sch.; Winchester Coll.; New Coll., Oxford. Royal Artillery, 1940–45 (despatches twice; mainly attached Intelligence Corps). Fellow, All Souls Coll., Oxford, 1947–48; Fellow, New Coll., Oxford, 1948–60; Prof., Brandeis Univ., USA, 1960–63; Research Associate, Institutet för Internationell Ekonomi, Stockholm, 1963–64. Visiting Professor: Columbia Univ., USA, 1958; City Coll. of New York, 1964 and 1967; Collège de France, 1972; Ecole des Sciences Politiques, 1979; Univ. of Windsor, Ont, 1986. *Publications:* Price, Cost and Output, 1956, 2nd edn 1962; The Political Economy of Communism, 1962; Communist International Economics, 1968; (ed) The Prediction of Communist Economic Performance, 1971; Economic Institutions Compared, 1977; Die Parallelwirtschaft, 1981; The Black Market; (ed) The New Communist Third World, 1981; (ed with Guy Routh) Economics in Disarray, 1985; article, Cost Inflation and the State of Economic Theory, Econ. Jl, 1973. *Recreation:* listening to Radio 3. *Address:* 23 Ridgmount Gardens, WC1E 7AR.

Died 11 July 1997.

WILKIE, Prof. Douglas Robert, FRS 1971; Jodrell Research Professor of Physiology in the University of London, 1979–88, then Emeritus Research Professor of Experimental Physiology; *b* 2 Oct. 1922; *s* of Robert M. Wilkie and Lilian Creed; *m* 1949, June Rosalind Hill (marr. diss. 1982; she *d* 1996); one *s*. *Educ:* Medical

Student, University Coll. London, 1940–42 (Fellow, 1972); Yale Univ. (MD), 1942–43; University Coll. Hosp., MB, BS 1944. MRCP 1945; FRCP 1972. Lectr, Dept of Physiology, UCL, 1948; Inst. of Aviation Medicine, Farnborough (Mil. Service), 1948–50; London University: Locke Research Fellowship (Royal Soc.), UCL, 1951–54; Readership in Experimental Physiology, UCL, 1954–65; Prof. of Experimental Physiology, 1965–69; Jodrell Prof., and Head of Physiology Dept, UCL, 1969–79. SRC Sen. Res. Fellowship, 1978. *Publications:* Muscle, 1968; 130 contribs to learned jls, etc, mainly research on energetics of muscular contraction, and attempts to explain thermodynamics simply, and, latterly, application of nuclear magnetic resonance in medicine. *Recreations:* sailing, friends, photography. *Address:* 2 Wychwood End, Stanhope Road, N6 5ND. *T:* (0171) 272 4024.

Died 21 May 1998.

WILKIN, (Frederick) John, CBE 1978 (OBE 1968); DFM 1943; President, National Incorporated Beneficent Society, since 1995 (Member of Council, since 1973); Chairman, The Wickenby Register (12 and 626 Squadrons Association), since 1983; *b* 15 Aug. 1916; *s* of late George Wilkin and Rosetta Christina Wilkin; *m* 1st, 1943, Marjorie Joan Wilson (*d* 1972); one *d*; 2nd, 1975, Laura Elizabeth Eason (*d* 1993); one *s* one *d*. *Educ:* Southwark Central Sch.; Morley Coll., London. Served RAF, 1940–46: Navigator (12, 101 and 156 Sqdns); Permanent Award Pathfinder Badge. Asst Accountant, House of Commons, 1955, Chief Accountant, 1962–80; Secretary: House of Commons Members' Fund, 1962–81; Parliamentary Contributory Pension Fund, 1965–80; Head of Admin Dept, House of Commons, 1980–81. Associate Mem. of Special Trustees, Charing Cross and Westminster Hosps, 1979–91; Vice-Chm., Hammersmith and Fulham DHA, 1982–83. Mem., Guild of Freemen of City of London. *Recreations:* gardening, watching sport; formerly cricket, cycling, table tennis. *Address:* 14 Forest Ridge, Beckenham, Kent BR3 3NH. *T:* (0181) 650 5261. *Club:* Royal Air Force. *Died 4 Aug. 1997.*

WILKINSON, Prof. Sir Geoffrey, Kt 1976; FRS 1965; Sir Edward Frankland Professor of Inorganic Chemistry, University of London, 1956–88, then Emeritus; Senior Research Fellow, Imperial College, since 1988; *b* 14 July 1921; *s* of Henry and Ruth Wilkinson; *m* 1951, Lise Sølver, *o d* of Rektor Prof. Svend Aa. Schou, Copenhagen; two *d*. *Educ:* Todmorden Secondary Sch. (Royal Scholar, 1939); Imperial Coll., London; USA. Junior Scientific Officer, Nat. Res. Council, Atomic Energy Div., Canada, 1943–46; Research Fellow: Radiation Lab., Univ. of Calif, Berkeley, Calif, USA, 1946–50; Chemistry Dept, Mass Inst. of Technology, Cambridge, Mass, USA, 1950–51; Asst Prof. of Chemistry, Harvard Univ., Cambridge, Mass, 1951–56; Prof. of Inorganic Chemistry at Imperial Coll., Univ. of London, 1956, Sir Edward Frankland Prof. 1978. Arthur D. Little Visiting Prof., MIT, 1967; Lectures: William Draper Harkins' Meml, Univ. of Chicago, 1968; Leermakers, Wesleyan Univ., 1975; (first) Mond, Chem. Soc., 1980; (first) Sir Edward Frankland, RSC, 1983; Tovborg Jensen, Univ. of Copenhagen, 1992. John Simon Guggenheim Fellow, 1954. Foreign Member: Royal Danish Acad. of Science and Arts (math.-phys section), 1968; Amer. Acad. of Arts and Sciences, 1970; Foreign Assoc., Nat. Acad. of Scis, 1975; Centennial Foreign Fellow, Amer. Chem. Soc., 1976. Hon. Fellow: Lady Margaret Hall, Oxford, 1984; UMIST, 1989. Hon. DSc: Edinburgh, 1975; Granada, 1976; Columbia, 1978; Bath, 1980; Essex, 1989; Oxford, 1996. American Chem. Soc. Award in Inorganic Chemistry, 1965; Lavoisier Medal, Société Chimique de France, 1968; Chem. Soc. Award for Transition Metal Chemistry, 1972; (jtly) Nobel Prize for Chemistry, 1973; Consejero de Honor, Spanish Council for Scientific Res., 1974; Hiroshima Univ Medal, 1978;

Royal Medal, Royal Soc., 1981; Galileo Medal, Univ. of Pisa, 1983; Longstaff Medal RSC, 1987; Medal, Univ. of Camerino, Italy, 1989; Messel Medal, SCI, 1990. Hon. Citizen Award, Todmorden Town Council, 1990. *Publications:* (jtly) Advanced Inorganic Chemistry: a Comprehensive Text, 1962, 5th edn 1988; Basic Inorganic Chemistry, 1976, 3rd edn 1995; numerous in Physical Review, Journal of the American Chemical Society, etc. *Address:* Chemistry Department, Imperial College, SW7 2AY. *T:* (0171) 594 5764. *Died 26 Sept. 1996.*

WILKINSON, Dr John Frederick, FRCP, MD, PhD; CChem, FRSC; author; consulting physician; Consulting Haematologist, United Manchester Hospitals; late Director of Department of Hæmatology, University and Royal Infirmary of Manchester; *b* Oldham, 10 June 1897; *s* of John Frederick Wilkinson, Oldham and Stockport, and Annie, *d* of late Rev. E. Wareham, DD, Rector of Heaton Mersey; *m* 1964, Marion Crossfield, Major WRAC (marr. diss. 1995). *Educ:* Arnold School, Blackpool; University of Manchester; Manchester Royal Infirmary. Served European War, 1916–19, RNAS, RN, and later attached Tank Corps, France; also served on Vindictive at Zeebrugge, 1918, and ballotted for Victoria Cross award. Chemical research, Manchester University, 1919–28, medical research, 1929, Graduate Scholarship (Chemistry), 1920; Dalton Research Scholarship; Sir Clement Royds Research Fellowship; Medical (Graduate) Scholarship, 1923; Hon. Demonstrator in Crystallography; Research Asst in Physiology; Sidney Renshaw Physiology Prizeman; Gold Medal for Dissertation in Med., 1931, University of Manchester. Late Reader in Hæmatology, and Lecturer in Systematic Medicine, Univ. of Manchester; late Hon. Consulting Hæmatologist, The Christie Cancer Hospital, Holt Radium Institute and The Duchess of York Hospital for Babies, Manchester. Hon. Fellow and Editor, Manchester Medical Society. Formerly President, European Hæmatological Soc.; Life Councillor, International Hæmatological Soc. Regional Transfusion Officer, and Regional Adviser on Resuscitation, Ministry of Health, NW Region, 1940–46. RCP Lectures: Oliver Sharpey, 1948; Samuel Gee, 1977. Worshipful Society of Apothecaries, London: Liveryman, 1948; Osler Lectr, 1981; Hon. Fellow 1982 (Faculty of History and Philosophy of Medicine and Pharmacy). Freeman, City of London, 1949. Hon. DSc Bradford, 1976. *Publications:* sections on Blood Diseases, Anæmias and Leukæmias in British Encyclopædia of Medical Practice, 1936, 1950, and yearly supplements 1951–, and in Encyclopædia of General Practice, 1964; section on Emergencies in Blood Diseases, in Medical Emergencies, 1948; (ed) Modern Trends in Diseases of the Blood, 1955, 1975; The Diagnosis and Treatment of Blood Diseases, 1973; (ed) section in Clinical Surgery, 1967; scientific and medical publications in English and foreign journals, etc, 1920–91; articles on antiques, Old English and continental apothecaries' drug jars, etc, in miscellaneous medical and art jls, 1970–91. *Recreations:* motoring, antiques, travel, zoos, tropical fish keeping, lecturing, Scouting since 1908. *Address:* Pax Meadow, Hall Lane, Mobberley, Knutsford, Cheshire WA16 7AE. *T:* (01565) 872111.

Died 13 Aug. 1998.

WILKINSON, Sir Peter (Allix), KCMG 1970 (CMG 1960); DSO 1944; OBE 1944; HM Diplomatic Service, retired; *b* 15 April 1914; *s* of late Captain Osborn Cecil Wilkinson (killed in action, 1915) and Esmé, *d* of late Sir Alexander Wilson; *m* 1945, Mary Theresa (*d* 1984), *d* of late Algernon Villiers; two *d*. *Educ:* Rugby; Corpus Christi Coll., Cambridge. Commissioned in 2nd Bn Royal Fusiliers, 1935; active service in Poland (despatches), France, ME, Italy, Balkans and Central Europe; commanded No 6 Special Force (SOE), 1943–45; retired with rank of Lt-Col, 1947; entered HM Foreign Service, appointed 1st Secretary at British Legation, Vienna, 1947; 1st Secretary at British Embassy, Washington, 1952; Secretary-General of Heads of Government Meeting at Geneva, 1955; Counsellor, HM Embassy, Bonn, 1955; Counsellor, Foreign Office, 1960–63; Under-Secretary, Cabinet Office, 1963–64; Senior Civilian Instructor at the Imperial Defence Coll., 1964–66; Ambassador to Vietnam, 1966–67; Under-Secretary, Foreign Office, 1967–68; Chief of Administration, HM Diplomatic Service, 1968–70; Ambassador to Vienna, 1970–71; Co-ordinator of Intelligence, Cabinet Office, 1972–73. Cross of Valour (Poland), 1940; Order of White Lion (IV Class) (Czechoslovakia), 1945; Order of Jugoslav Banner (Hon.), 1984. *Publication:* (with J. Bright-Astley) Gubbins and SOE, 1993; Foreign Fields: the story of an SOE operative, 1997. *Recreations:* gardening, sailing, fishing. *Address:* 28 High Street, Charing, Kent TN27 0HX. *T:* (01233) 712306. *Clubs:* White's, Army and Navy.

Died 16 June 2000.

WILKINSON, Sir William (Henry Nairn), Kt 1989; Chairman, Nature Conservancy Council, 1983–91; *b* 22 July 1932; *e s* of late Denys and Gillian Wilkinson, Eton College; *m* 1964, Katharine Louise Frederica, *er d* of late F. W. H. Loudon and of Lady Prudence Loudon; one *s* two *d*. *Educ:* Eton Coll. (King's Schol.); Trinity Coll., Cambridge (Major Scholar; MA). President: London Wildlife Trust, 1992–; British Trust for Ornithology, 1993–; Vice-President: RSPB, 1991–; Plantlife, 1991–; Kent Trust for Nature Conservation, 1991–; British Butterfly Conservation Soc., 1993–; Chm., West Palaearctic Birds Ltd, 1987–; Member of Council: Wildfowl and Wetlands Trust, 1991–; Game Conservancy, 1993–. Chm., TSL Thermal Syndicate plc, 1984–88 (Dir, 1976–88); Director: Kleinwort Benson Ltd, 1973–85; John Mowlem and Co. plc, 1977–87; Mem., CEGB, 1986–89. Mem. Council, Winston Churchill Meml Trust, 1985–93. FRSA. *Publications:* papers for ornithological conferences. *Recreations:* ornithology, opera and music, archaeology. *Address:* 119 Castelnau, Barnes, SW13 9EL; Pill House, Llanmadoc, Gower, West Glamorgan SA3 1DB. *Club:* Brooks's. *Died 12 April 1996.*

WILKS, Jim; *see* Wilks, S. D.

WILKS, Stanley David, (Jim), CB 1979; MIEx; Consultant Director, Strategy International, since 1992; Deputy Chairman, The Development Group, since 1993; *b* 1 Aug. 1920; *m* 1947, Dorothy Irene Adamthwaite; one *s* one *d*. *Educ:* Polytechnic Sch., London. Royal Armoured Corps, 1939–46; service with 48th Bn, Royal Tank Regt; 3rd Carabiniers, Imphal, 1944. Home Office, 1946–50; Board of Trade, later Dept of Trade and Industry, 1950–80: posts included 1st Sec., British Embassy, Washington, 1950–53; GATT, non-ferrous metals, ECGD, airports policy; Chief Exec., BOTB, 1975–80. Deputy Chairman, Technology Transfer Gp, 1981–89; Trade Network Internat., 1989 (Chm., Export Network, 1986–89); Director: Matthew Hall Internat. Develt, subseq. Matthew Hall Business Develt, 1981–89; Hadson Petroleum Internat., 1981–91; Hadson Corp., 1985–93; Associated Gas Supplies, 1988–90; Regl Dir, James Hallam, 1984–. Vice-Chm., Internat. Tin Council, 1968–69; Chm., Tech. Help for Exporters Management Cttee, BSI, 1982–88. Commodore, UK Wayfarer Assoc., 1993–96 (Chm., 1982–89). MIEx 1981. *Recreations:* dinghy racing, ski-ing. *Address:* 6 Foxgrove Avenue, Beckenham, Kent BR3 5BA. *Clubs:* Civil Service; Medway Yacht (Rochester); Aldenham Sailing. *Died 25 Dec. 1997.*

WILLATT, Sir (Robert) Hugh, Kt 1972; Secretary General of the Arts Council of Great Britain, 1968–75 (Member, 1958–68); *b* 25 April 1909; *s* of Robert John Willatt, OBE, JP; *m* 1945, Evelyn Gibbs (*d* 1991), ARE, ARCA, (Rome Scholar); no *c*. *Educ:* Repton; Pembroke Coll., Oxford

(MA). Admitted a Solicitor, 1934; Partner, Hunt, Dickins and Willatt, Nottingham, and later Partner in Lewis, Silkin & Partners, Westminster. Served War of 1939–45, in RAF. Member BBC Midland Regional Adv. Council, 1953–58; Member Arts Council Drama Panel, 1955–68 (Chairman, 1960–68). Pres., Riverside Studios, Hammersmith, 1983– (Chm., 1976–82); Vice-Pres., English Stage Co. (Royal Court Theatre), 1993– (Mem., 1976–92); Chm. Bd, Nat. Opera Studio, 1977–93; Member Board: National Theatre, 1964–68; Mercury Trust Ltd (Ballet Rambert) (Chm.), 1961–67; Nottingham Theatre Trust Ltd, 1949–60; Visiting Arts Unit (Chm., 1977–83). Trustee, Shakespeare's Birthplace, 1968–94. FRSA 1974. Hon. MA, University of Nottingham. *Address:* 4 St Peter's Wharf, Hammersmith Terrace, W6 9UD. *Clubs:* Garrick, Arts. *Died 18 Oct. 1996.*

WILLIAMS, Catrin Mary, FRCS; Consultant Ear, Nose and Throat Surgeon, Clwyd Health Authority (North), 1956–86; Chairman, Wales Council for the Deaf, 1986–88; *b* 19 May 1922; *d* of late Alderman Richard Williams, JP, Pwllheli, and Mrs Margaret Williams; unmarried. *Educ:* Pwllheli Grammar Sch.; Welsh National Sch. of Medicine (BSc 1942, MB, BCh 1945). FRCS 1948. Co-Chm., Women's National Commn, 1981–83; Chm., Wales Women's European Network. Pres., Medical Women's Fedn, 1973–74; Founding Vice-Pres., Gymdeithas Feddygol Gymraeg (Welsh Med. Soc.), 1975–79; Vice-Chm., Meniere's Soc., 1986–90, Chm., 1990–; Member: Exec. Cttee, Wales Council for the Disabled, 1988–; Regl Vice-Pres., Med. Women's Internat. Assoc., 1992– (Procedure Advr, 1984–92); Trustee, RNID, 1992– (Mem. Council and Exec. Cttee, 1986–92). *Recreations:* reading, embroidery. *Address:* Gwrych House, Abergele, Clwyd LL22 8EU. *T:* (01745) 832256.

Died 9 Oct. 1998.

WILLIAMS, Cecil Beaumont, (Monty), CHB 1980; OBE 1963; retired; Executive Director, Da Costa & Musson Ltd, Barbados, 1980–91; *b* 8 March 1926; *s* of George Cuthbert and Violet Irene Williams; *m* 1952, Dorothy Marshall; two *s* one *d*. *Educ:* Harrison Coll., Barbados; Durham Univ. (BA, DipEd); Oxford Univ. Asst Master, Harrison Coll., 1948–54. Asst Sec., Govt Personnel Dept, and Min. of Trade, Industry and Labour (Barbados), 1954–56; Permanent Secretary: Min. of Educn, 1958; Min. of Trade, Industry and Labour, 1958–63; Dir, Economic Planning Unit, 1964–65; Manager, Industrial Develt Corp., 1966–67; High Comr to Canada, 1967–70; Permanent Sec., Min. of External Affairs, 1971–74; Ambassador to USA and Perm. Rep. to OAS, 1974–75; High Comr in UK, 1976–79. *Recreations:* music, tennis, reading, gardening. *Address:* Moonshine Hall, St George, Barbados. *Died 19 Sept. 1998.*

WILLIAMS, Hon. Sir Edward (Stratten), KCMG 1983; KBE 1981; QC (Aust.) 1965; *b* 29 Dec. 1921; *s* of Edward Stratten and Zilla Claudia Williams; *m* 1949, Dorothy May Murray; three *s* four *d* (and one *s* decd). *Educ:* Yungaburra State Sch., Qld; Mt Carmel Coll., Charters Towers, Qld; Univ. of London (LLB Hons). Served RAAF, UK and Aust., 1942–46. Barrister-at-Law, Qld, 1946; Justice of Supreme Court of Qld, 1971–84. Judge, Fiji Court of Appeal, 1993–96. Chairman: Parole Board of Qld, 1976–83; Qld Corrective Services Commn Bd, 1989–90; Royal Commissioner, Aust. Royal Commn of Inquiry into Drugs, 1977–80; Member, Internat. Narcotics Control Board (UN), 1982–87. Comr-Gen., Expo 88, Brisbane, 1984–88; Director: Elders IXL Ltd, then Fosters Brewing Gp, 1984–91; Aust. Hydrocarbons NL, 1985–94. Chairman, Commonwealth Games Foundn Brisbane (1982), 1976–83. Pres., Playground and Recreation Assoc. of Qld, 1971–94. Mem., Anti-Cancer Council, 1983–95, Trustee, 1987–95, Queensland Cancer Fund. Chm. of

Trustees, Eagle Farm Racecourse, 1996–98. Australian of the Year, 1982; Queenslander of the Year, 1983. *Publications:* Report of Australian Royal Commission of Inquiry into Drugs and associated reports. *Recreations:* horse racing, gardening, golf. *Address:* 150 Adelaide Street East, Clayfield, Qld 4011, Australia. *T:* (7) 32624802, *Fax:* (7) 32627610. *Clubs:* Brisbane, United Services, Tattersall's, Queensland Turf (Chairman, 1980–91), Brisbane Turf, Far North Queensland Amateur Turf, Rugby Union (all Queensland).

Died 10 Jan. 1999.

WILLIAMS, Edward Taylor, CMG 1962; MICE; retired as General Manager, Malayan Railway; civil engineering railway consultant with Kennedy Henderson Ltd (formerly Henderson, Busby partnership), consulting engineers and economists, since 1965; *b* Bolton, Lancashire, 15 Oct. 1911; *s* of Edward and Harriet Williams; *m* 1940, Ethel Gertrude Bradley (*d* 1983); one step *s* one step *d*. *Educ:* Accrington Grammar School; Manchester College of Technology. Pupil engineer, LMS, 1929–36; Asst Civil Engr, Sudan Rly, 1936–38; Civil Engr, Metropolitan Water Board, 1939–41; Malayan Rly, 1941–62 (Gen. Man. 1959–62); Rly Advr, Saudi Govt Railroad, 1963–65. Interned in Singapore, in Changi and Sime Road, 1941–45. *Recreation:* travel. *Address:* 20 Sundial Lodge, Park Hill Road, Torquay, Devon TQ1 2EA.

Died 29 June 1997.

WILLIAMS, Prof. Glanville Llewelyn; QC 1968; FBA 1957; Fellow of Jesus College, Cambridge, 1955–78, Hon. Fellow, 1978, and Rouse Ball Professor of English Law in the University of Cambridge, 1968–78, later Professor Emeritus (Reader, 1957–65; Professor, 1965), *b* 15 Feb. 1911; *s* of late B. E. Williams, Bridgend, Glam; *m* 1939, Lorna Margaret, *d* of late F. W. Lawfield, Cambridge; one *s*. *Educ:* Cowbridge; University College of Wales, Aberystwyth; St John's Coll., Cambridge. PhD Cantab, 1936; LLD Cantab, 1946. Called to the Bar, 1935. Research Fellow of St John's Coll., Cambridge, 1936–42; Reader in English Law and successively Professor of Public Law and Quain Professor of Jurisprudence, University of London, 1945–55. Carpentier Lecturer in Columbia Univ., 1956; Cohen Lecturer in Hebrew University of Jerusalem, 1957; first Walter E. Meyer Visiting Research Professor, New York Univ., 1959–60; Charles Inglis Thompson Guest Professor, University of Colorado, 1965; Vis. Prof., Univ. of Washington, 1969. Special Consultant to the American Law Institute's Model Penal Code, 1956–58; Member: Standing Cttee on Criminal Law Revision, 1959–80; Law Commn's Working Party on Codification of Criminal Law, 1967; Cttee on Mentally Abnormal Offenders, 1972. Pres., Abortion Law Reform Assoc., 1962–; Vice-Pres., Voluntary Euthanasia, 1985–. Hon. Bencher, Middle Temple, 1966. Fellow, Galton Inst.; For. Hon. Mem., Amer. Acad. of Arts and Sci., 1985; Hon. Life Mem., Soc. for Reform of Criminal Law, 1992. Ames Prize, Harvard, 1963; (joint) Swiney Prize, RSA, 1964. Hon. LLD: Nottingham, 1963; Wales, 1974; Glasgow, 1980; Sussex, 1987; Hon. DCL Durham, 1984; Hon. LittD Cantab, 1995. *Publications:* Liability for Animals, 1939; chapters in McElroy's Impossibility of Performance, 1941; The Law Reform (Frustrated Contracts) Act (1943), 1944; Learning the Law, 1945, 11th edn 1982; Crown Proceedings, 1948; Joint Obligations, 1949; Joint Torts and Contributory Negligence, 1950; Speedhand Shorthand, 1952, 8th edn 1980; Criminal Law: The General Part, 1953, 2nd edn 1961; The Proof of Guilt, 1955, 3rd edn 1963; The Sanctity of Life and the Criminal Law, American edn 1956, English edn 1958; The Mental Element in Crime, 1965; (with B. A. Hepple) Foundations of the Law of Tort, 1976, 2nd edn 1984; Textbook of Criminal Law, 1978, 3rd edn 1995; articles in legal periodicals. *Address:*

Merrion Gate, Conley Lane, Cambridge CB2 2HB. *T:* (01223) 841175. *Died 10 April 1997.*

WILLIAMS, Harri Llwyd H.; *see* Hudson-Williams.

WILLIAMS, Ian Malcolm Gordon, CBE 1960 (OBE 1954; MBE 1945); *b* 7 May 1914; *s* of late Thomas and Mabel Williams. *Educ:* Tatterford Sch., Norfolk; Leeds Univ.; Gonville and Caius Coll., Cambridge. President, Leeds University Students' Union, 1939. Volunteered Military Service, Sept. 1939; Officer Cadet, 123 OCTU; commnd Royal Regt of Artillery, March 1940; NW Frontier of India and Burma, 1940–45, as Major, RA, and Mountain Artillery, Indian Army (despatches, MBE). Staff Officer, Hong Kong Planning Unit, 1946; Adjutant, Hong Kong Defence Force, 1946. Entered Colonial Administrative Service, 1946; District Officer and Asst Colonial Secretary, Hong Kong, 1946–49; at Colonial Office, 1949–51; Senior Asst Secretary, Secretariat, Cyprus, 1951–53; Commissioner: of Paphos, 1953–55, of Larnaca, 1955–57, of Limassol, 1957–60; Chief Officer, Sovereign Base Areas of Akrotiri and Dhekelia, 1960–64; Member Administrator's Advisory Board; UK Chairman, Joint Consultative Board, 1960–64; Min. of Technology, 1965–67; DoE, 1967–71; Programme Dir, UN/Thai Programme for Drug Abuse Control in Thailand, 1972–79. Comdr, Most Noble Order of the Crown of Thailand, 1981. *Recreations:* art, Cypriot archæology, swimming. *Address:* White House, Adderbury, near Banbury, Oxfordshire OX17 3NL. *Club:* East India, Devonshire, Sports and Public Schools. *Died 13 Jan. 1997.*

WILLIAMS, Prof. John Ellis Caerwyn, FBA 1978; FSA; Professor of Irish, University College of Wales, Aberystwyth, 1965–79, then Professor Emeritus; Director of Centre for Advanced Welsh and Celtic Studies, Aberystwyth, 1978–85; *b* 17 Jan. 1912; *s* of John R. Williams and Maria Williams; *m* 1946, Gwen Watkins. *Educ:* Ystalyfera Int. County Sch.; University Coll. of N Wales, Bangor (BA Hons Latin 1933, Welsh 1934; MA); Nat. Univ. of Ireland, Dublin; TCD; United Theol Coll, Aberystwyth (BD 1944); Theol Coll., Bala. Research Lectr, UC of N Wales, Bangor, 1937–39; Fellow, Univ. of Wales, 1939–41; Lectr, 1945–51, Sen. Lectr, 1951–53, Prof. of Welsh, 1953–65, UC of N Wales. Leverhulme Fellow, 1963–64; Vis. Prof. Celtic, UCLA, 1968; Summer Sch., Harvard, 1968; Lectures: O'Donnell, in Celtic Studies, Oxford Univ., 1979–80; Dr Daniel Williams, Aberystwyth, 1983; Sir John Morris Jones, Oxford, 1983; R. T. Jenkins, Bangor, 1983. Pres., Welsh Acad., 1989–98 (Chm., 1965–75); Mem., Council for Name Studies in GB and Ireland, 1965–. Cons. Editor, Univ. of Wales Welsh Dict. Fasc. xxiii–; Chm., Editorial Cttee, Welsh Acad. Dict., 1976–95; Editor: Y Traethodydd, 1965–; Ysgrifau Beirniadol, i–xxv; Studia Celtica, i–xxvii (Cons. Editor, Studia Celtica, xxviii–); Llên y Llenor, 1983–; Llyfryddiaeth yr Iaith Gymraeg, 1988; Cerddi Waldo Williams, 1992. FSA 1975; Hon. MRIA 1990; Hon. DLitt: Celt., Univ. of Ireland, 1967; Univ. of Wales, 1983. Derek Allen Prize, British Acad., 1985. *Publications:* (trans.) Ystoriau ac Ysgrifau Pádraic Ó Conaire, 1947; (trans.) Yr Ebol Glas, 1954; Traddodiad Llenyddol Iwerddon, 1958; (trans.) Aderyn y Gwirionedd, 1961; Edward Jones, Maes-y-Plwm, 1963; (ed) Llên a Llafar Môn, 1963; (trans.) I. Williams, Canu Taliesin (Poems of Taliesin), 1968; The Court Poet in Medieval Ireland, 1971; Y Storïwr Gwyddeleg a'i Chwedlau, 1972; Beirdd y Tywysogion—Arolwg 1970, in Llên Cymru, and separately 1972; (ed) Literature in Celtic Countries, 1971; (trans.) Jakez Riou, An Ti Satanazet (Diawl yn y Tŷ), 1972; Canu Crefyddol y Gogynfeirdd (Darlith Goffa Henry Lewis), 1976; The Poets of the Welsh Princes, 1978, 2nd edn 1994; Cerddi'r Gogynfeirdd i Wragedd a Merched, 1979; (with Máirín Ní Mhuiríosa) Traidisiún

Liteartha Na nGael, 1979; Geiriadurwyr y Gymraeg yng nghyfnod y Dadeni, 1983; Y Dardd Celtaidd, 1991; (with Patrick Ford) The Irish Literary Tradition, 1992; Diwylliant a Dysg, 1996; The Court Poet in Medieval Wales, 1997; contribs to Encyclopaedia Britannica, Princeton Encyclopedia of Poetry and Poetics, Bull. Bd of Celt. Studies, Celtica, Études Celt., Llên Cymru, Proc. of British Acad., etc. *Recreation:* walking. *Address:* Centre for Advanced Welsh and Celtic Studies, National Library of Wales, Aberystwyth SY23 3HH. *T:* (01970) 626717; Iwerydd, 6 Pant-y-Rhos, Aberystwyth, Dyfed SY23 3QE. *T:* (01970) 612959. *Died 10 June 1999.*

WILLIAMS, John M(eredith), CBE 1988; Chairman, Welsh Development Agency, 1982–88; *b* 20 Oct. 1926; *s* of Gwynne Evan Owen Williams and Cicely Mary Innes; *m* 1953, Jean Constance (*née* Emerson); two *d*. *Educ:* Sherborne Sch., Dorset; Trinity Hall, Cambridge. Dir, BOC Gp, 1969–78; Chm., Newman Industries Ltd, 1980–82; Director: Stone-Platt Industries Ltd, 1981–82; Harland and Wolff Ltd, 1982–89. Mem., Milk Marketing Bd, 1984–94. *Address:* 95 Hurlingham Court, Ranelagh Gardens, SW6 3UR. *T:* (0171) 731 0686; Victuals Grove, St Briavels, Lydney, Glos GL15 6RW. *T:* (01594) 530494. *Clubs:* Hurlingham, Himalayan.

Died 16 Sept. 1997.

WILLIAMS, Sir John (Robert), KCMG 1982 (CMG 1973); HM Diplomatic Service, retired; Chairman, Board of Governors, Commonwealth Institute, 1984–87; *b* 15 Sept. 1922; *s* of late Sydney James Williams, Salisbury; *m* 1958, Helga Elizabeth, *d* of Frederick Konow Lund, Bergen; two *s* two *d*. *Educ:* Sheen County School; Fitzwilliam House, Cambridge (Hon. Fellow 1984). Served War of 1939–45, with 1st Bn King's African Rifles in East Africa and Burma Campaign (Captain). Joined Colonial Office as Asst Principal, 1949; First Secretary, UK High Commission, New Delhi, 1956; Commonwealth Relations Office, 1958; Deputy High Commissioner in North Malaya, 1959–63; Counsellor, New Delhi, 1963–66; Commonwealth Office, 1966; Private Sec. to Commonwealth Secretary, 1967; Diplomatic Service Inspectorate, 1968; High Comr, Suva, 1970–74; Minister, Lagos, 1974–79 and concurrently Ambassador (non-resident) to Benin, 1976–79; Asst Under-Sec. of State, FCO, 1979; High Comr in Kenya, 1979–82; Perm. British Rep. to UN Environment Prog. and to UN Centre for Human Settlements, 1979–82. Mem. Gen. Council, Royal Over-Seas League, 1983–87 (Vice Pres., 1995–). Chm., Salisbury and S Wilts Museum, 1989–95. *Recreations:* music, gardening. *Address:* Eton House, Hanging Langford, Salisbury SP3 4NN. *Club:* United Oxford & Cambridge University. *Died 24 March 2000.*

WILLIAMS, Ven. Leslie Arthur, MA; Archdeacon of Bristol, 1967–79; *b* 14 May 1909; *s* of Arthur and Susan Williams; *m* 1937, Margaret Mary, *d* of Richard Crocker; one *s* one *d*. *Educ:* Knutsford; Downing Coll., Cambridge. Deacon 1934, priest 1935; Curate of Holy Trinity, Bristol, 1934–37; Licensed to officiate, St Andrew the Great, Cambridge, 1937–40; Curate in Charge, St Peter, Lowden, Chippenham, 1940–42; Chaplain, RAFVR, 1942–46; Curate, Stoke Bishop, 1946–47; Vicar: Corsham, Wilts, 1947–53; Bishopston, Bristol, 1953–60; Stoke Bishop, Bristol, 1960–67. Rural Dean of Clifton, 1966–67; Hon. Canon of Bristol, 1958. *Recreation:* gardening. *Address:* St Monica Home, Westbury on Trym, Bristol BS9 3UN. *Clubs:* Hawks (Cambridge); Savage (Bristol).

Died 2 July 1996.

WILLIAMS, Michael Edward John; Golf Correspondent, Daily Telegraph, since 1971; *b* 19 Oct. 1933; *s* of Edward Williams and Norah Marguerite Williams (*née* Skinner); *m* 1959, Judith Ann Sanderson; one *s* three *d*. *Educ:* Ipswich Sch. Sports reporter, E Anglian Daily Times,

1950–57; sports sub-ed., Evening Standard, 1957–59; news ed., Stratford Express (London), 1959–60; Sports sub-ed., Daily Telegraph, 1960–63; sports columnist, Sunday Telegraph, 1963–71. Chm., Assoc. of Golf Writers, 1987–92. Chelmsford Golf Club: Capt., 1968; Centenary Capt., 1993. Ed., Royal & Ancient Golfers' Handbook, 1993–. *Publications:* History of Golf, 1985; Grand Slam Golf, 1988; Official History of the Ryder Cup, 1989. *Recreations:* golf, snooker, bowls. *Address:* Fairlight, 45 Birch Lane, Stock, Ingatestone, Essex CM4 9NB. *Clubs:* Royal & Ancient (St Andrews), Chelmsford Golf, Aldeburgh Golf; Old Ipswichians (Pres., 1991).

Died 17 April 1997.

WILLIAMS, Monty; *see* Williams, C. B.

WILLIAMS, Owen Lenn; retired; Regional Financial and Development Adviser, St Vincent, West Indies, 1976–78; *b* 4 March 1914; *s* of Richard Owen Williams and Frances Daisy Williams (*née* Lenn); *m* 1959, Gisela Frucht (*d* 1991). *Educ:* St Albans Sch.; London University. Asst Principal, Export Credit Guarantee Dept, 1938; Asst Principal, Treasury, 1939; UK High Commn, Ottawa, 1941; Principal, Treasury, 1945; Asst Treasury Representative, UK High Commn, New Delhi, 1953; Treasury Rep., UK High Commn, Karachi, 1955; Economic and Financial Adviser, Leeward Islands, 1957; Perm. Sec., Min. of Finance, Eastern Nigeria, 1959; Asst Sec., Treasury, 1962; Counsellor, UK Delegn to OECD, 1968–73; Gen. Fiscal Adviser to Minister of Finance, Sierra Leone, 1974–75. *Recreations:* music, travel. *Address:* c/o National Westminster Bank, Stag Place, Victoria, SW1E 5NW. *Died 16 July 1997.*

WILLIAMS, Sir Peter W.; *see* Watkin Williams.

WILLIAMS, Trevor Illtyd, MA, BSc, DPhil; CChem, FRSC; FRHistS; scientific writer and historian; *b* 16 July 1921; *s* of Illtyd Williams and Alma Mathilde Sohlberg; *m* 1st, 1945 (marr. diss. 1952); 2nd, 1952, Sylvia Irène Armstead; four *s* one *d*. *Educ:* Clifton College; Queen's College, Oxford (scholar and exhibnr). Nuffield Research Scholar, Sir William Dunn Sch. of Pathology, Oxford, 1942–45; Endeavour: Deputy Editor, 1945–54; Editor, 1954–74, 1977–95 (Consulting Scientific Editor, 1974–76); Editor Emeritus, 1996–; Jt Editor, Annals of Science, 1966–74; Editor, Outlook on Agriculture, 1982–89. Academic Relations Advr, ICI Ltd, 1962–74. Chairman: Soc. for the Study of Alchemy and Early Chemistry, 1967–86; World List of Scientific Periodicals, 1966–88; Adv. Cttee on the Selection of Low-priced Books for Overseas, 1982–84; Member: Steering Cttee, English Language Book Soc., 1984–90; Adv. Council, Science Museum, 1972–84; Council, University Coll., Swansea, 1965–83. Vis. Fellow, ANU, 1981; Leverhulme Fellow, 1985. Dexter Award, Amer. Chem. Soc., for contribs to the history of chemistry, 1976. *Publications:* An Introduction to Chromatography, 1946; Drugs from Plants, 1947; (ed) The Soil and the Sea, 1949; The Chemical Industry Past and Present, 1953; The Elements of Chromatography, 1954; (ed jtly) A History of Technology, 1954–58; (with T. K. Derry) A Short History of Technology, 1960; Science and Technology (Ch. III, Vol. XI, New Cambridge Mod. History); (ed) Alexander Findlay's A Hundred Years of Chemistry, 3rd rev. edn 1965; (ed) A Biographical Dictionary of Scientists, 1968, 4th edn 1994; Alfred Bernhard Nobel, 1973; James Cook, 1974; Man the Chemist, 1976; (ed) A History of Technology, Vols VI and VII: The Twentieth Century, 1978; (ed) Industrial Research in the United Kingdom, 1980; A History of the British Gas Industry, 1981; A Short History of Twentieth Century Technology, 1982; (ed) European Research Centres, 1982; Florey: penicillin and after, 1984; The Triumph of Invention, 1987; Robert Robinson, Chemist Extraordinary, 1990; Science:

invention and discovery in the twentieth century, 1990; Our Scientific Heritage: an A–Z of Great Britain and Ireland, 1996; numerous articles on scientific subjects, especially history of science and technology. *Recreations:* gardening, hill walking. *Address:* 20 Blenheim Drive, Oxford OX2 8DG. *T:* (01865) 558591. *Club:* Athenæum.
Died 12 Oct. 1996.

WILLIAMS, Walter Gordon Mason, CB 1983; FRICS; Deputy Chief Valuer, 1979–83; *b* 10 June 1923; *s* of Rees John Williams, DSO and Gladys Maud Williams; *m* 1950, Gwyneth Joyce Lawrence; two *d. Educ:* Cardiff High Sch. ARICS 1948, FRICS 1975. Joined Valuation Office, Inland Revenue, 1947; Superintending Valuer (N Midlands), 1969–73; Asst Chief Valuer, 1973–79. Vice Pres., London Rent Assessment Panel, 1984–94. *Address:* 33A Sydenham Hill, SE26 6SH. *T:* (020) 8670 8580.
Died 6 March 2000.

WILLIAMS-WYNNE, Col John Francis, CBE 1972; DSO 1945; JP; FRAgS; Vice Lord-Lieutenant of Gwynedd, 1980–85 (Lieutenant, 1974–80; HM Lieutenant of Merioneth, 1957–74); Constable of Harlech Castle since 1964; *b* 9 June 1908; *s* of late Major F. R. Williams-Wynn, CB, and Beatrice (*née* Cooper); *m* 1938, Margaret Gwendolen (*d* 1991), DL Gwynedd, *d* of late Rev. George Roper and Mrs G. S. White; one *s* two *d. Educ:* Oundle; Magdalene College, Cambridge (MA Mech. Sciences). Commissioned in RA 1929; served NW Frontier, 1936; served War of 1939–45; psc Camberley; Brigade Major, RA ? Div., 1940–41; 2 i/c 114 Fd Regt, 1942; GSO2 HQ Ceylon Comd, 1942; comd 160 Jungle Field Regt, RA, 1943–44; GSO1, GHQ India, 1945; GSO1, War Office, 1946–48; retd 1948; comd 636 (Royal Welch) LAA Regt, RA, TA, 1951–54; Subs. Col 1954; Hon. Col 7th (Cadet) Bn RWF, 1964–74. Contested (C) Merioneth, 1950. JP 1950, DL 1953, VL 1954, Merioneth. Chairman, Advisory Cttee, Min. of Agric. Experimental Husbandry Farm, Trawscoed, 1955–76. Part-time Mem., Merseyside and N Wales Electricity Bd, 1953–65; National Parks Comr, 1961–66; Forestry Comr, 1963–65; Member: Regional Adv. Cttee N Wales Conservancy Forestry Commission, 1950–63; County Agric. Exec. Cttee, 1955–63 and 1967–71; Gwynedd River Board, 1957–63; Forestry Cttee of GB, 1966–76; Home Grown Timber Advisory Cttee, 1966–76; Prince of Wales's Cttee for Wales, 1970–79; President: Timber Growers Organisation, 1974–76; Royal Welsh Agric. Soc., 1968 (Chm. Council, 1971–77); Chairman: Agricl Adv. Cttee, BBC Wales, 1974–79; Flying Farmers' Assoc., 1974–82. Pres., Merioneth Br., CLA, 1979. Member: Airline Users Cttee, CAA, 1973–79; Sch. of Agric. Cttee, University Coll. N Wales, 1982. *Recreations:* farming, forestry, flying. *Address:* Peniarth, Tywyn-Merioneth, Gwynedd LL36 9UD. *T:* (01654) 710328. *Clubs:* Army and Navy, Pratt's.
Died 20 Jan. 1998.

WILLIAMSON, Frank Edger, QPM 1966; *b* 24 Feb. 1917; *s* of John and Mary Williamson; *m* 1943, Margaret Beaumont; one *d. Educ:* Northampton Grammar Sch. Manchester City Police, 1936–61; Chief Constable: Carlisle, 1961–63; Cumbria Constabulary, 1963–67; HM Inspector of Constabulary, 1967–72. OStJ 1967. *Address:* Eagle Cottage, Alderley Park, Nether Alderley, Macclesfield, Cheshire SK10 4TD. *T:* (01625) 583135.
Died 25 Dec. 1998.

WILLIAMSON, Sir Nicholas Frederick Hedworth, 11th Bt *cr* 1642, of East Markham, Nottinghamshire; *b* 26 Oct. 1937; *s* of late Maj. William Hedworth Williamson (killed in action, 1942) and Diana Mary, *d* of late Brig.-Gen. Hon. Charles Lambton, DSO (she *m* 2nd, 1945, 1st Baron Hailes, GBE, CH, PC); *S* uncle, 1946. *Heir:* none. *Address:* Abbey Croft, Mortimer, Reading, Berks RG7 3PE. *T:* (01734) 332324.
Died 31 Dec. 2000 (ext).

WILLIS, Hon Sir Eric (Archibald), KBE 1975; CMG 1974; *b* 15 Jan. 1922; *s* of Archibald Clarence Willis and Vida Mabel Willis (*née* Buttenshaw); *m* 1st, 1951, Norma Dorothy Thompson (*née* Knight) (marr. diss. 1982); two *d*; 2nd, 1982, Lynn Anitra Ward (*née* Roberts) (marr. diss. 1992). *Educ:* Murwillumbah High Sch., NSW; Univ. of Sydney (BA Hons). MLA (L) Earlwood, NSW, 1950–78; Dep. Leader, NSW Parly Liberal Party, 1959–75, Leader, 1976–77; Minister for Labour and Industry, Chief Secretary and Minister for Tourism, 1965–71; Chief Sec. and Minister for Tourism and Sport, 1971–72; Minister for Education, 1972–76; Premier and Treasurer, NSW, 1976; Leader of the Opposition, NSW Parlt, 1976–77. Exec. Sec., Royal Australian Coll. of Ophthalmologists, 1978–83; Exec. Dir, Arthritis Foundn of NSW, 1984–91. *Recreation:* reading. *Address:* 5/94 Kurraba Road, Neutral Bay, NSW 2089, Australia. *T:* (2) 99093432.
Died 10 May 1999.

WILLIS, Frank William; Director of Advertising and Sponsorship, Independent Television Commission, since 1991; *b* 6 April 1947; *s* of late Prof. F. M. Willis and of J. C. Willis; *m* 1972, Jennifer Carol Arnold; two *d. Educ:* Bradford Grammar School; Magdalen Coll., Oxford (BA, BPhil). HM Diplomatic Service, 1971; Moscow, 1972–74; Ecole Nationale d'Administration, 1974–75; First Sec., FCO, 1975–79; Dept of Trade, later DTI, 1980; Asst Sec., Consumer Affairs Div., DTI, 1984; Controller of Advertising, IBA, 1987–90. *Recreations:* shopping in Muswell Hill, moors and mountains, wine. *Address:* ITC, 33 Foley Street, W1P 7LB.
Died 16 March 1999.

WILLIS, Gaspard; *see* Willis, R. W. G.

WILLIS, His Honour John Brooke; a Circuit Judge (formerly County Court Judge), 1965–80; Barrister-at-law; *b* 3 July 1906; *yr s* of William Brooke Willis and Maud Mary Willis, Rotherham; *m* 1929, Mary Margaret Coward (marr. diss. 1946); one *s* one *d*; *m* 1964, Terona Ann Steel (formerly Hood); two *d. Educ:* Bedford Modern Sch.; Sheffield Univ. Called to the Bar, Middle Temple, 1938, North Eastern Circuit. Served War of 1939–45: RAFVR, 1940–45, Sqdn Leader. Recorder, Rotherham, 1955–59, Huddersfield, 1959–65; Dep. Chm., W Riding of Yorks QS, 1958–71. Chairman, Medical Appeal Tribunal under the National Insurance (Industrial Injuries) Acts, 1953–65. *Address:* 14 Larchwood, Woodlands Drive, Rawdon, Leeds LS19 6JZ.
Died 17 July 1996.

WILLIS, John Trueman, DFC; DFM 1942; housing consultant; *b* 27 Oct. 1918; *s* of Gordon and Ethel Willis, Headington, Oxford; *m* 1947, Audrey Joan, *d* of Aubrey and Gertrude Gurden, Headington, Oxford; one *s* one *d. Educ:* Oxford High Sch., Oxford. Estates Management, Magdalen Coll., Oxford, 1935–36; Industrial Trng, Lockheed Hydraulic Brake Co., Leamington Spa, 1937–38; served War of 1939–45: Pilot on 14 Sqdn RAF, Middle East, 1940–42; PoW Stalag Luft III, Germany, 1943–45; Estates Management, 1946–64, Estates Sec., 1953–65, Magdalen Coll., Oxford; Rent Officer for Oxford, 1965–67; Sec., Housing Societies Charitable Trust, 1968–69; Director: Shelter, 1971–72 (Housing Dir, 1969–70); Liverpool Housing Trust, 1973–75; Castle Rock Housing Assoc., 1976–78. Director: Kingdomwide Ltd, 1981–92; Kingdomwide Housing Trust, 1982; Kingdomwide Develt Ltd, 1982. Member: NEDO Housing Strategy Cttee, 1975–78; Management Cttees, North British Housing Assoc., S Yorks Area, 1996–, SW Area, 1996–. Promoted housing conf., Planning for Home Work, 1984. ICSA. *Publication:* Housing and Poverty Report, 1970. *Recreations:* diminishing. *Address:* 36 Kings Court, The Kings Gap, Hoylake, Wirral, Merseyside L47 1JE. *T:* (0151) 632 3873.
Died 16 Aug. 1998.

WILLIS, Rear-Adm. Kenneth Henry George, CB 1981; Director General, Home Farm Trust Ltd, Bristol, 1982–88, retired; *m*; three *d. Educ:* Royal Naval Engineering Coll.; Royal Naval Coll.; Jesus Coll., Cambridge (BA 1949). Joined RN 1944; served at sea and in shore weapons depts; Resident Officer, Polaris Executive, Clyde Submarine Base, 1965–68; i/c training, HMS Collingwood, 1969–70; Asst Dir, Underwater Weapon Dept, 1970; sowc 1974; Dep. Dir, RN Staff Coll., Greenwich, 1975–76, Dir, 1976; CO HMS Collingwood, 1976–79; C of S to C-in-C, Naval Home Command, 1979–81, retired. Trustee, Foundn Trust for Mentally Handicapped, 1987–. MInstD. FRSA. *Address:* c/o Barclays Bank, 1 Manvers Street, Bath. *Club:* Bath and County (Bath). *Died 28 July 1998.*

WILLIS, (Robert William) Gaspard, MA; Founder and Headmaster of Copford Glebe School, 1958–69, Principal, 1969–72, retired; *b* 22 Nov. 1905; *s* of Rev. W. N. Willis, founder and Headmaster for 38 years of Ascham St Vincent's, Eastbourne, and Sophia Caroline Baker; *m* 1930, Ernestine Ruth Kimber (decd); two *s* two *d. Educ:* Ascham St Vincent's, Eastbourne; Eton Coll. (Foundation Scholar); Corpus Christi Coll., Cambridge (Scholar). Assistant Master at Malvern Coll., Worcs, 1927–39 (Mathematics and Classics); Senior Mathematical Master at The King's School, Macclesfield, Cheshire, 1939–41; Headmaster of Sir William Turner's School (Coatham School), Redcar, 1941–53; Headmaster of English High School for Boys, Istanbul, Turkey, 1953–57. Hon. Fellow, Huguenot Soc. of London. Hon. Life Mem., Gainsborough's House Soc., Sudbury. Reader, 1935–92. *Publication:* A Centenary History of Ascham 1889–1989, 1989. *Address:* East Hill House, East Hill Drive, Liss, Hants GU33 7RR. *Died 13 Nov. 1997.*

WILLIS, His Honour Roger Blenkiron, TD; a Circuit Judge (formerly County Court Judge), 1959–81; *b* 22 June 1906; *s* of late William Outhwaite Willis, KC, and Margaret Alice (*née* Blenkiron); *m* 1933, Joan Eleanor Amy Good (*d* 1990); two *d. Educ:* Charterhouse School; Emmanuel Coll., Cambridge. Barrister, Inner Temple, Nov. 1930. Joined Middlesex Yeomanry (TA), 1938; served War of 1939–45. *Address:* 18 Turners Reach House, 9 Chelsea Embankment, SW3. *Clubs:* Garrick, MCC. *Died 6 April 1996.*

WILLMOTT, Peter; Senior Fellow, Institute of Community Studies, since 1997; *b* 18 Sept. 1923; *s* of Benjamin Merriman Willmott and Dorothy Willmott (*née* Waymouth); *m* 1948, Phyllis Mary Noble; two *s. Educ:* Tollington Sch., London; Ruskin Coll., Oxford; BScSoc (external) London. Research Asst, Labour Party, 1948–54; Institute of Community Studies: Res. Officer, 1954–60; Dep. Dir, 1960–64; Co-Dir, 1964–78; Dir, Centre for Environmental Studies, 1978–80; Head of Central Policy Unit, GLC, 1981–83; Sen. Fellow, PSI, 1983–97. Visiting Professor: Bartlett Sch. of Architecture and Planning, UCL, 1972–83; Ecole Pratique des Hautes Etudes, Paris, 1972; LSE, 1983–88; Regents' Lectr, Univ. of California, 1982. Hon. LitD Univ. of Orleans, 1990. Editor, Policy Studies, 1988–95. *Publications:* (with Michael Young) Family and Kinship in East London, 1957; (with Michael Young) Family and Class in a London Suburb, 1960; The Evolution of a Community, 1963; Adolescent Boys of East London, 1966; (with Michael Young) The Symmetrical Family, 1973; (ed) Sharing Inflation? Poverty Report, 1976; (with Graeme Shankland and David Jordan) Inner London: policies for dispersal and balance, 1977; (with Charles Madge) Inner City Poverty in Paris and London, 1981; (with Roger Mitton and Phyllis Willmott) Unemployment, Poverty and Social Policy in Europe, 1983; Community in Social Policy, 1984; Social Networks, Informal Care and Public Policy, 1986; Friendship

Networks and Social Support, 1987; (with Alan Murie) Polarisation and Social Housing, 1988; Community Initiatives: patterns and prospects, 1989; (ed) Urban Trends 1, 1992; (ed) Urban Trends 2, 1994. *Address:* 27 Kingsley Place, N6 5EA. *T:* (020) 8245 3408. *Died 8 April 2000.*

WILLOUGHBY, Ven. David Albert; Archdeacon of the Isle of Man, 1982–96; Vicar of St George's with All Saints, Douglas, 1980–96; *b* 8 Feb. 1931; *s* of John Robert and Jane May Willoughby; *m* 1959, Brenda Mary (*née* Watson); two *s. Educ:* Bradford Grammar School; St John's Coll., Univ. of Durham (BA, DipTh). Deacon 1957, priest 1958; Assistant Curate: St Peter's, Shipley, 1957–60; Barnoldswick with Bracewell, 1960–62; Rector of St Chad's, New Moston, Manchester, 1962–72; Vicar of Marown, Isle of Man, 1972–80; Rural Dean of Douglas, 1980–82. Chaplain: Noble's Hospital, Douglas, 1980–; Tynwald, 1996–; Mem. Gen. Synod, 1982–96; Church Commissioner for IOM, 1982–96. *Recreations:* competition singing, involvement in light entertainment. *Address:* 19 Glen Vine Park, Glen Vine, Isle of Man IM4 4EZ. *T:* (01624) 852493. *Died 17 June 1998.*

WILLS, Colin Spencer, FCA; Chairman, Visiting Arts Office of Great Britain and Northern Ireland, since 1990; Director: Breadwinners (London) Ltd, since 1987; Rhinegold Publishing Ltd, since 1991; *b* 25 June 1937; *s* of Sir John Spencer Wills and late Elizabeth Drusilla Alice Clare Garcke. *Educ:* Eton; Queens' Coll., Cambridge (MA). FCA 1967. Qualified, 1962; worked in USA, 1963–64; Rediffusion Television, 1964–68; Dep. Gen. Man., ATV Network, Birmingham, 1968–69; employed by British Electric Traction, 1970–88 as Managing Director: Humphries Holdings plc, 1977–85; A-R Television, 1972–88; Director: Thames Television, 1970–91; Euston Films, 1972–91; Wembley Stadium, 1974–84; ENO, 1975–87; BAFTA, 1980–94. Governor: English Nat. Ballet, 1988–94; English Nat. Ballet Sch., 1988–. *Recreations:* music, opera, travel, country pursuits. *Address:* 12 Campden Hill Square, W8 7LB. *T:* (0171) 727 0534; Old Brick Farm, Burwash, East Sussex TN19 7DG. *T:* (01435) 882234. *Club:* White's. *Died 28 Oct. 1997.*

WILLS, Sir (Hugh) David (Hamilton), Kt 1980; CBE 1971 (MBE 1946); TD 1964; DL; *b* 19 June 1917; 2nd *s* of late Frederick Noel Hamilton Wills and Margery Hamilton Sinclair; *m* 1949, Eva Helen, JP, *d* of late Major A. T. McMorrough Kavanagh, MC; one *d* (one *s* decd). *Educ:* Eton; Magdalen Coll., Oxford. Served War of 1939–45 with Queen's Own Cameron Highlanders (TA): France 1940, Aruba 1941; GSO 3 (Ops) GHQ Home Forces, 1942–43; GSO 2 (Ops) Southern Command, 1943–44. Chairman of Trustees, Rendcomb Coll., 1955–83; Founder and Chm., Ditchley Foundation, 1972–83; Mem. Governing Body, Atlantic Coll., 1963–73, 1980–. High Sheriff Oxfordshire, 1961, DL 1967. *Recreations:* fishing, racing. *Address:* Sandford Park, Sandford St Martin, Oxford OX7 7AJ. *T:* (01608) 683238. *Died 10 Dec. 1999.*

WILLS, Sir John Vernon, 4th Bt *cr* 1923, of Blagdon, co. Somerset; KCVO 1998; TD; JP; FRICS; Lord-Lieutenant and Keeper of the Rolls of Somerset, since 1994; President, Bristol and West Building Society, since 1993 (Director, 1969–93; Vice-Chairman, 1982–88; Chairman, 1988–93); Chairman, Bristol Waterworks Co., later Bristol Water Holdings, 1986–98 (Director, 1964–73; Deputy Chairman, 1983–86); Director, since 1973, Deputy Chairman, since 1978, Bristol United Press plc (formerly Bristol Evening Post); *b* 3 July 1928; *s* of Sir George Vernon Proctor Wills, 2nd Bt, and Lady Nellie Jeannie, ARRC, JP, *y d* of late J. T. Rutherford, Abergavenny; *S* brother, 1945; *m* 1953, Diana Veronica Cecil, (Jane), DStJ, *o d* of Douglas

R. M. Baker, Winsford, Somerset; four *s*. *Educ:* Eton. Served Coldstream Guards, 1946–49; Lt-Col Comdg N Somerset and Bristol Yeomanry, 1965–67; Bt Col 1967; later TARO; Hon. Col, 37th (Wessex and Welsh) Signal Regt, T&AVR, 1975–87; Hon. Capt., RNR, 1988. Chm., Wessex Water Authy, 1973–82; Mem., Nat. Water Council, 1973–82; Chm., Bristol Marketing Bd, 1984–86. Local Dir, Barclays Bank, 1981–87. Pro-Chancellor, Univ. of Bath, 1979–. Pres., Royal Bath and West Southern Counties Soc., 1980. Member of Somerset CC. Lord-Lieutenant of Avon, 1974–96; Keeper of the Rolls, Avon Commn of Peace, 1974–97. JP 1962, DL 1968, High Sheriff, 1968, Somerset. KStJ 1978. Hon. LLD Bristol, 1986; Hon. DLitt Bath, 1993. *Heir: s* David James Vernon Wills, *b* 2 Jan. 1955. *Address:* Langford Court, near Bristol BS18 7DA. *T:* (01934) 862338. *Club:* Cavalry and Guards. *Died 26 Aug. 1998.*

WILLS-MOODY, Helen; *see* Roark, H. W.

WILMINGTON, Joseph Robert; JP; Chairman and Managing Director, Wilmington Employment Agencies Ltd, since 1966; *b* 21 April 1932; *s* of Joseph R. Wilmington and Magtilda Susanna Wilmington; *m* Anne; two *s*. *Educ:* Alsop High Sch., Liverpool; London Sch. of Economics. Chm., Liverpool Liberal Party, 1965–67. Liverpool City Council: Mem., 1962; Chairman: Personnel Cttee; Markets Cttee; Chief Whip; Lord Mayor of Liverpool, 1974–75. Chm., NW Fedn of Employment Consultants; Mem. Nat. Exec., Fedn of Employment Consultants; Mem. Inst. Employment Consultants. JP Liverpool, 1976. *Recreations:* koi keeping, music and the arts. *Address:* Jordaan, New Mill Stile, Church Road, Woolton, Liverpool L25 6DA. *T:* (0151) 428 5817. *Died 2 Feb. 1999.*

WILSON OF LANGSIDE, Baron *cr* 1969 (Life Peer), of Broughton, in co. of City of Edinburgh; **Henry Stephen Wilson;** PC 1967; QC (Scot.) 1965; *b* 21 March 1916; *s* of James Wilson, solicitor, Glasgow, and Margaret Wilson (*née* Young); *m* 1942, Jessie Forrester Waters (*d* 1996); no *c*. *Educ:* High School, Glasgow; Univ. of Glasgow (MA, LLB). Joined Army, 1939; commd 1940; Regl Officer, HLI and RAC, 1940–46. Called to Scottish Bar, 1946; Advocate-Depute, 1948–51; Sheriff-Substitute: Greenock, 1955–56; Glasgow, 1956–65; Solicitor-General for Scotland, 1965–67; Lord Advocate, 1967–70; Dir, Scottish Courts Administration, 1971–74; Sheriff Principal of Glasgow and Strathkelvin, 1975–77. Contested (Lab) Dumfriesshire, 1950, 1955, W Edinburgh, 1951; Mem. SDP, 1981–92. Cross-bencher. *Recreations:* hill walking, gardening. *Club:* Western (Glasgow). *Died 23 Nov. 1997.*

WILSON, Brian Harvey, CBE 1972 (MBE 1944); solicitor, retired; Town Clerk and Chief Executive, London Borough of Camden, 1965–77 (Town Clerk, Hampstead, 1956–65); *b* 4 Sept. 1915; *o s* of Sydney John Wilson, MC, and Bessie Mildred (*née* Scott); *m* 1941, Constance Jane (*née* Gee); one *s*. *Educ:* Manchester Grammar Sch.; Corpus Christi Coll., Cambridge (Exhibitioner; MA, LLB). Admitted solicitor, 1941; Chief Asst Solicitor, Warrington, 1946–48; Dep. Town Clerk: Grimsby, 1948–53; Ilford, 1953–56. Hon. Clerk to Housing and Works Cttee, London Boroughs Assoc., 1965–79; Chm., Metropolitan Housing Trust, 1978–85. Chm., Royal Inst. of Public Administration, 1973–75. Member: Uganda Resettlement Board, 1972–73; DoE Study Gp on Agrément, 1978. Chairman: Public Examn, Glos Structure Plan, 1980; Indep. Inquiry into death of Maria Mehmedagi, 1981; GLC Independent Inquiry into financial terms of GLC housing transferred to London Boroughs and Districts, 1984–85. *Address:* Victoria House, Church Path, Shipton-under-Wychwood, Oxon OX7 6BQ. *T:* (01993) 830695. *Died 21 May 2000.*

WILSON, Christopher Maynard, DIC, PhD; Director, Inspec Group Ltd, since 1992; *b* 19 Dec. 1928; *s* of late George Henry Cyril Wilson and of Adelaide Flora Marie Wilson; *m* 1953, Elizabeth Ursula Canning; one *s* two *d*. *Educ:* King Edward VII Sch., Sheffield; Worksop Coll., Notts; Imperial Coll., London Univ. (BSc, ARCS, DIC, PhD). National Service, RAF, 1947–49. Ferranti Computers, 1953–63; Ferranti merged with ICT, 1963, ICT merged with English Electric Computers to become ICL, 1968; Manager, UK Sales, 1968–70; Director: Marketing and Product Strategy, 1970–72; Internat. Div., 1972–77; Man. Dir, International Computers Ltd, 1977–81; Chm., Exxel Consultants Ltd, 1982–86; Man. Dir, Ansafone Corp., 1984–86. *Recreations:* squash, tennis, gardening, golf. *Address:* Tiles Cottage, Forest Road, Winkfield Row, near Bracknell, Berks RG42 7NR. *Died 18 May 1997.*

WILSON, Clifford; Professor of Medicine, University of London, at the London Hospital and Director, Medical Unit, The London Hospital, 1946–71, then Emeritus Professor; *b* 27 Jan. 1906; *m* 1936, Kathleen Hebden (decd); one *s* one *d*. *Educ:* Balliol College, Oxford (Brackenbury Scholar, 1924; 1st Class Final Hons School of Nat. Sciences, 1928; BM BCh 1933; DM 1936). MRCS 1931; FRCP 1951 (MRCP 1946). House Physician, etc, London Hospital, 1931–34; Rockefeller Travelling Fellow, 1934–35; Research Fellow, Harvard Univ.; Asst Director, Medical Unit, London Hosp., 1938; Univ. Reader in Medicine, London Hosp., 1940; Major RAMC, Medical Research Section, 1942–45. President Renal Association, 1963–64. Examiner MRCP, 1960–; Censor, RCP, 1964–66; Senior Censor and Senior Vice-Pres., 1967–68. Dean, Faculty of Medicine, Univ. of London, 1968–71. Hon. Fellow, London Hosp. Medical Coll., 1986. *Publications:* sections on renal diseases and diseases of the arteries in Price's Text Book of Medicine; papers on renal disease, hypertension, arterial disease and other medical subjects, 1930–70. *Died 10 Nov. 1997.*

WILSON, (Gerald) Roy; Under Secretary and Deputy Director of Savings, Department for National Savings, 1986–89, retired; *b* 11 Jan. 1930; *s* of late Fred Wilson and Elsie Wilson (*née* Morrison); *m* 1st, 1965, Doreen Chadderton (*d* 1990); one *s* one *d*; 2nd, 1990, Patricia Henderson (*née* Ive). *Educ:* High School, Oldham. Min. of Works, 1947; HM Stationery Office, 1949; Post Office Savings Dept, 1957; PO HQ, 1963; National Girobank, 1966; Dept for National Savings, 1969–89; Controller (Asst Sec.), Savings Certificate and SAYE Office, Durham, 1978–86. FIMgt; Mensa. *Recreations:* swimming, reading, drawing, photography, travel. *Address:* 6 West Farm Court, Broompark, Durham DH7 7RN. *Clubs:* Civil Service; Rotary; Probus (Durham); Durham City Swimming, Durham City Cricket. *Died 25 Dec. 1997.*

WILSON, Gordon Wallace, CB 1986; Under Secretary, Ministry of Agriculture, Fisheries and Food, 1975–86, retired; *b* 14 July 1926; *s* of late John Wallace Wilson and Mrs Joyce Elizabeth Grace Sherwood-Smith; *m* 1951, Gillian Maxwell (*née* Wood) (*d* 1998); three *s*. *Educ:* King's Sch., Bruton; Queen's Coll., Oxford (BA PPE). Entered Civil Service (War Office), 1950; Principal Private Sec. to Sec. of State for War, 1962; Asst Sec., MoD, 1964; Dir, Centre of Admin Studies, HM Treasury, 1965; Asst Sec., DEA, 1968; HM Treasury, 1969. *Recreations:* tennis, gardening, sketching, recording vernacular architecture. *Died 25 Sept. 2000.*

WILSON, Harold Arthur Cooper B.; *see* Bird-Wilson.

WILSON, Harry; *see* Wilson of Langside, Baron.

WILSON, Sir John (Foster), Kt 1975; CBE 1965 (OBE 1955); Director, Royal Commonwealth Society for the

Blind, 1950–83, Vice-President 1983; Senior Consultant, United Nations Development Programme, since 1983; President, International Agency for the Prevention of Blindness, 1974–83; *b* 20 Jan. 1919; *s* of late Rev. George Henry Wilson, Buxton, Derbys; *m* 1944, Chloe Jean McDermid (OBE 1981); two *d*. *Educ:* Worcester College for the Blind; St Catherine's Coll., Oxford (MA Jurisprudence, Dipl. Public and Social Administration; Hon. Fellow, 1984). Asst Secretary, Royal National Inst. for the Blind, 1941–49; Member, Colonial Office Delegation investigating blindness in Africa, 1946–47. Proposed formation of Royal Commonwealth Society for Blind; became its first Director, 1950; extensive tours in Africa, Asia, Near and Far East, Caribbean and N America, 1952–67; formulated Asian plan for the Blind, 1963, and African Plan for the Blind, 1966. Pres., Internat. Agency for the Prevention of Blindness, 1974–83; established UN Initiative Against Avoidable Disability IMPACT, 1983 (Chm., Internat. Council, 1991–). Hon. DCL Oxford, 1995. Helen Keller International Award, 1970; Lions Internat. Humanitarian Award, 1978; World Humanity Award, 1979; Albert Lasker Award, 1979; Richard T. Hewitt Award, RSM, 1991; Albert Schweitzer Internat. Prize, 1993. *Publications:* Blindness in African and Middle East Territories, 1948; Ghana's Handicapped Citizens, 1961; Travelling Blind, 1963; (ed) World Blindness and its Prevention, 1980; Disability Prevention—the Global Challenge, 1980, 2nd edn 1984; various on Commonwealth affairs and disability. *Recreations:* current affairs, travel, writing, tape-recording, wine-making. *Address:* 22 The Cliff, Roedean, Brighton, East Sussex BN2 5RE. *T:* (01273) 607667, *Fax:* (01273) 679624.
Died 24 Nov. 1999.

WILSON, Prof. John Stuart Gladstone, MA, DipCom; Professor of Economics and Commerce in the University of Hull, 1959–82, then Emeritus Professor; Head of Department, 1959–71, and 1974–77; *b* 18 Aug. 1916; *s* of Herbert Gladstone Wilson and Mary Buchanan Wilson (*née* Wylie); *m* 1943, Beryl Margaret Gibson, *d* of Alexander Millar Gibson and Bertha Noble Gibson; no *c*. *Educ:* University of Western Australia (1st Cl. Hons Econs, 1941). Lecturer in Economics: University of Tasmania, 1941–43; Sydney, 1944–45; Canberra, 1946–47; LSE, 1948–49; Reader in Economics, with special reference to Money and Banking, Univ. of London, 1950–59; Dean, Faculty of Social Sciences and Law, Univ. of Hull, 1962–65; Chairman, Centre for S-E Asian Studies, Univ. of Hull, 1963–66. Hackett Research Student, 1947; Leverhulme Research Award, 1955; SSRC Grant for comparative study of banking policy and structure, 1977–81; Leverhulme Emeritus Fellow, 1983–84. Economic Survey of New Hebrides on behalf of Colonial Office, 1958–59; Consultant, Trade and Payments Dept, OECD, 1965–66; Consultant with Harvard Advisory Development Service in Liberia, 1967; headed Enquiry into Sources of Capital and Credit to UK Agriculture, 1970–73; Consultant, Directorate Gen. for Agric., EEC, 1974–75; Specialist Adviser, H of C Select Cttee on Nationalised Industries, 1976; Consultant, Cttee on Financial Markets, OECD, 1979–81; Dir, Centre for Jt Study of Economics, Politics and Sociology, 1980–82; Mem. Cttee of Management, Inst. of Commonwealth Studies, London, 1960–77, Hon. Life Mem., 1980; Governor, SOAS, London, 1963–92. Member: Yorkshire Council for Further Education, 1963–67; Nat. Advisory Council on Education for Industry and Commerce, 1964–66; Languages Bd, CNAA, 1978–83. Société Universitaire Européenne de Recherches Financières: Mem., Steering Cttee, 1964–69; Sec.-Gen., 1968–72; Mem. Council, 1970–91; Pres., 1973–75; Vice-Pres., 1977–83. Editor, Yorkshire Bulletin of Economic and Social Research, 1964–67; Mem., Editorial Adv. Bd,

Modern Asian Studies, 1966–89. *Publications:* French Banking Structure and Credit Policy, 1957; Economic Environment and Development Programmes, 1960; Monetary Policy and the Development of Money Markets, 1966; Economic Survey of the New Hebrides, 1966; (ed with C. R. Whittlesey) Essays in Money and Banking in Honour of R. S. Sayers, 1968; Availability of Capital and Credit to United Kingdom Agriculture, 1973; (ed with C. F. Scheffer) Multinational Enterprises—Financial and Monetary Aspects, 1974; Credit to Agriculture—United Kingdom, 1975; The London Money Markets, 1976, 2nd edn 1989; (ed with J. E. Wadsworth and H. Fournier) The Development of Financial Institutions in Europe, 1956–1976, 1977; Industrial Banking: a comparative survey, 1978; Banking Policy and Structure: a comparative analysis, 1986; (ed) Managing Bank Assets and Liabilities, 1988; Money Markets: the international perspective, 1993; contributions to: Banking in the British Commonwealth (ed R. S. Sayers), 1952; Banking in Western Europe (ed R. S. Sayers), 1962; A Decade of the Commonwealth, 1955–64 (ed W. B. Hamilton and others), 1966; International Encyclopaedia of the Social Sciences, 1968; Encyclopaedia Britannica, 15th edn 1974; New Palgrave Dictionary of Money and Finance, 1992; Economica, Economic Journal, Journal of Political Econ., Economic Record, Banca Nazionale del Lavoro Quarterly Rev. *Recreations:* gardening, theatre, art galleries, travel, photography. *Address:* Department of Economics, The University, Hull, North Humberside HU6 7RX. *Club:* Reform.
Died 5 June 1996.

WILSON, Sir Reginald (Holmes), Kt 1951; CA; FCIT; Director of business and finance companies; *b* 10 July 1905; *o s* of Alexander Wilson and Emily Holmes Wilson; *m* 1st, 1930, Rose Marie von Arnim; one *s* one *d*; 2nd, 1938, Sonia Havell. *Educ:* St Peter's Sch., Panchgani; St Lawrence, Ramsgate; London Univ. (BCom). Partner in Whinney Murray & Co., 1937–72; HM Treasury, 1940; Principal Assistant Secretary, Ministry of Shipping, 1941; Director of Finance, Ministry of War Transport, 1941; Under-Secretary, Ministry of Transport, 1945; returned to City, 1946; Joint Financial Adviser, Ministry of Transport, 1946; Member of Royal Commission on Press, 1946; Vice-Chairman, Hemel Hempstead Development Corporation, 1946–56; Adviser on Special Matters, CCG, 1947. British Transport Commission: Comptroller, 1947–53; Member, 1953–62; Chm. E Area Board, 1955–60; Chm. London Midland Area Board, 1960–62; Dep. Chm. and Man. Dir, Transport Holding Co., 1962–67; Chairman: Transport Holding Co., 1967–70; Nat. Freight Corp., 1969–70; Transport Develt Gp, 1971–74 (Dep. Chm., 1970–71); Thos Cook & Son Ltd, 1967–76. Mem., Cttee of Enquiry into Civil Air Transport, 1967–69. Chm., Bd for Simplification of Internat. Trade Procedures, 1976–79. Award of Merit, Inst. Transport, 1953; President, Inst. Transport, 1957–58. Governor, LSE, 1954–58; Chairman, Board of Governors: Hospitals for Diseases of the Chest, 1960–71; National Heart Hospital, 1968–71; National Heart and Chest Hospitals, 1971–80; Chm., Cardiothoracic Inst., 1960–80; UK Rep., Council of Management, Internat. Hosp. Fedn, 1973–79. CIMgt. *Publications:* various papers on transport matters. *Recreations:* music, walking. *Address:* 49 Gloucester Square, W2 2TQ. *Club:* Athenæum.
Died 1 Jan. 1999.

WILSON, Sir Roland, KBE 1965 (CBE 1941); Kt 1955; Chairman: Commonwealth Banking Corporation, 1966–75; Qantas Airways Ltd, 1966–73; Wentworth Hotel, 1966–73; Director: The MLC Ltd, 1969–79; ICI Australia, 1967–74; economic and financial consultant; *b* Ulverstone, Tasmania, 7 April 1904; *s* of Thomas Wilson; *m* 1930, Valeska (*d* 1971), *d* of William Thompson; *m* 1975, Joyce, *d* of Clarence Henry Chivers. *Educ:*

Devonport High School; Univ. of Tasmania; Oriel College, Oxford; Chicago University. Rhodes Scholar for Tasmania, 1925; BCom 1926, Univ. of Tasmania; Dip. in Economics and Political Science 1926, and DPhil 1929, Oxon; Commonwealth Fund Fellow, 1928, and PhD 1930, Chicago. Pitt Cobbett Lecturer in Economics, Univ. of Tasmania, 1930–32; Director of Tutorial Classes, Univ. of Tasmania, 1931–32; Asst Commonwealth Statistician and Economist, 1932; Economist, Statistician's Branch, Commonwealth Treasury, 1933; Commonwealth Statistician and Economic Adviser to the Treasury, Commonwealth of Australia, 1936–40 and 1946–51; Sec. to Dept Labour and Nat. Service, 1941–46; Chairman Economic and Employment Commission, United Nations, 1948–49; Secretary to Treasury, Commonwealth of Australia, 1951–66; Member Bd: Commonwealth Bank of Australia, 1951–59; Reserve Bank of Australia, 1960–66; Qantas Empire Airways, 1954–66; Commonwealth Banking Corp., 1960–75. Hon. Fellow, Acad. of Social Scis in Australia, 1972. Hon. LLD Tasmania, 1969. Distinguished Fellow Award, Econ. Soc. of Australia, 1988. *Publications:* Capital Imports and the Terms of Trade, 1931; Public and Private Investment in Australia, 1939; Facts and Fancies of Productivity, 1946. *Address:* 64 Empire Circuit, Forrest, Canberra, ACT 2603, Australia. *T:* (6) 2952560. *Club:* Commonwealth (Canberra). *Died 25 Oct. 1996.*

WILSON, Roy; *see* Wilson, G. R.

WILSON, Thomas Marcus; Assistant Under-Secretary, Ministry of Defence (Procurement Executive), 1971–73; retired; *b* 15 April 1913; *s* of Reverend C. Wilson; *m* 1939, Norah Boyes (*née* Sinclair) (*d* 1984); no *c*. *Educ:* Manchester Grammar School; Jesus College, Cambridge. Asst Principal, Customs and Excise, 1936; Private Secretary: to Board of Customs and Excise, 1939; to Chm. Bd, 1940; Principal, 1941; lent to Treasury, 1942; lent to Office of Lord President of Council, 1946; Asst Sec., 1947; seconded: Min. of Food, 1949; Min. of Supply, 1953, Under-Sec., 1962, and Prin. Scientific and Civil Aviation Advr to Brit. High Comr in Australia, also Head of Defence Research and Supply Staff, 1962–64; Under-Secretary: Min. of Aviation, 1964–67; Min. of Technology, 1967–70; Min. of Aviation Supply, 1970–71; MoD, 1971–73. *Recreations:* reading, music, painting, travel, especially in France. *Address:* Flat 6, 21 Queen Square, Bath BA1 2HX. *Died 1 Dec. 1996.*

WILSON, Rt Rev. William Gilbert, PhD; Bishop of Kilmore, Elphin and Ardagh, 1981–93; *b* 23 Jan. 1918; *s* of Adam and Rebecca R. Wilson; *m* 1944, Peggy Muriel Busby; three *s* three *d*. *Educ:* Belfast Royal Academy; Trinity Coll., Dublin (BA 1939; MA, BD 1944; PhD 1949). Deacon 1941, priest 1942; Curate Assistant, St Mary Magdalene, Belfast, 1941–44; Curate, St Comgall's, Bangor, 1944–47; Rector of Armoy with Loughguile, 1947–76; Prebendary of Cairncastle in Chapter of St Saviour's, Connor, 1964–76; Dean of Connor, 1976–81; Rector of Lisburn Cathedral, 1976–81; Clerical Hon. Sec. of Connor Synod and Council, 1956–81. *Publications:* A Guild of Youth Handbook, 1944; Church Teaching, A Church of Ireland Handbook, 1954, revised edn 1970; How the Church of Ireland is Governed, 1964; (jtly) Anglican Teaching—An Exposition of the Thirty-nine Articles, 1964; The Church of Ireland after 1970—Advance or Retreat?, 1968; The Church of Ireland—Why Conservative?, 1970; Is there a Life after Death?, 1974; A Critique of 'Authority in the Church', 1977; Irish Churchwardens' Handbook, 1979 (expanded, revised and rewritten edn of 1901 pubn); The Faith of an Anglican, 1980; The Way of the Church, 1982; Should we have Women Deacons?, 1984; Why no Women Priests?, 1988; Towards Accepting Women Priests, 1989;

contribs to Jl of Theol Studies and The Church Qly Review. *Recreations:* gardening, woodworking. *Address:* 24 Pennington Park, Cairnshill Road, Belfast BT8 4GJ. *T:* (01232) 701742. *Died 21 June 1999.*

WILTON, 7th Earl of, *cr* 1801; **Seymour William Arthur John Egerton;** Viscount Grey de Wilton 1801; *b* 29 May 1921; *s* of 6th Earl of Wilton and Brenda (*d* 1930), *d* of late Sir William Petersen, KBE; *S* father, 1927; *m* 1962, Mrs Diana Naylor Leyland. *Heir:* (by special remainder) *kinsman* 6th Baron Ebury [*b* 8 Feb. 1934; *m* 1st, 1957, Gillian Elfrida (marr. diss. 1962), *d* of Martin Soames, London; 2nd, 1963, Kyra (marr. diss. 1973), *d* of late L. L. Aslin; 3rd, 1974, Suzanne Jean, *d* of Graham Suckling, Christchurch, NZ; one *d*]. *Address:* Chapel House, Shurlock Row, Reading RG10 0PS. *Club:* White's. *Died 1 Oct. 1999.*

WINCHILSEA, 16th Earl of, *cr* 1628, **AND NOTTINGHAM,** 11th Earl of, *cr* 1681; **Christopher Denys Stormont Finch Hatton;** Bt 1611; Viscount Maidstone 1623; Bt 1660; Baron Finch, 1674; Custodian of Royal Manor of Wye; *b* 17 Nov. 1936; *er s* of 15th Earl and Countess Gladys Széchényi (she *m* 1954, Arthur Talbot Peterson, and *d* 1978), 3rd *d* of Count László Széchényi; *S* father, 1950; *m* 1962, Shirley, *e d* of late Bernard Hatfield, Wylde Green, Sutton Coldfield; one *s* one *d*. *Heir: s* Viscount Maidstone, *b* 7 Oct. 1967. *Address:* South Cadbury House, South Cadbury, Yeovil, Somerset BA22 7HA. *Died 26 June 1999.*

WINCKLES, Kenneth, MBE 1945; FCA; Director and Group Assistant Managing Director, Rank Organisation, 1953–67; *b* 17 June 1918; *s* of Frank and Emily Winckles; *m* 1941, Peggy Joan Hodges; one *s* one *d*. *Educ:* Lower School of John Lyon, Harrow. Served War, Army, 1939–46, demobilised Lt-Col. Company Secretary, Scribbans-Kemp Ltd, 1947–48; Rank Organisation, 1948–67. Managing Dir, Theatre Div.; Dir, Southern Television Ltd; Dir, Rank-Xerox Ltd; Chm., Odeon Theatres (Canada) Ltd; Chm., Visnews Ltd; Chm and Man. Dir, United Artists Corp, 1967–69; Man. Dir, Cunard Line Ltd, 1969–70; Dir, Hill Samuel Gp Ltd, 1971–80; Dep. Chm., ITL Information Technology plc, 1981–89. Director: Horserace Totalisator Bd, 1974–76; CAA, 1978–80. *Publications:* The Practice of Successful Business Management, 1986; Funding Your Business, 1988. *Recreations:* swimming, gardening, music. *Died 23 July 1999.*

WINFIELD, Peter Stevens, FRICS; Senior Partner, Healey & Baker, London, Amsterdam, Brussels, New York, Paris, St Helier, Jersey, 1975–88, Consultant, 1988–97; *b* 24 March 1927; *s* of late Harold Stevens Winfield and Susan Cooper; *m* 1955, Mary Gabrielle Kenrick (*d* 1999); four *s* two *d*. *Educ:* Sloane Sch., Chelsea; West London College of Commerce. Served Royal Artillery, 1944–48. Joined Healey & Baker, 1951. Chairman: London Auction Mart Ltd, 1980–92 (Dir, 1970–92); Letinvest plc, 1987–94; Director: Manders plc (formerly Manders (Holdings) plc), 1987–97; Golden Square Properties Ltd, 1990–96. Member: Lloyd's of London, 1978–; Property Investment Cttee of Save & Prosper Gp Ltd, 1980–97; Horserace Totalisator Bd, 1981–92. Dir, Kingston Theatre Trust, 1990–. Special Trustee: Guy's Hosp., 1974–97 (Gov., 1973–74); St Thomas' Hosp., 1996–97. Liveryman: Worshipful Company of Farriers, 1967; Worshipful Company of Feltmakers, 1972 (Asst to the Court, 1979–; Master, 1990–91). Variety Club Lifetime Achievement Award, 1995. *Recreations:* horseracing, cricket. *Address:* 29 St George Street, W1A 3BG. *T:* (020) 7629 9292. *Clubs:* Buck's, Royal Automobile, United & Cecil, MCC. *Died 11 Nov. 1999.*

WINGFIELD DIGBY, Simon; *see* Digby, K. S. D. W.

WINGFIELD DIGBY, Ven. Stephen Basil, MBE 1944; Archdeacon of Sarum, 1968–79; Canon Residentiary, 1968–79, and Treasurer, 1971–79, Salisbury Cathedral; *b* 10 Nov. 1910; *m* 1940, Barbara Hatton Budge (*d* 1987); three *s* one *d. Educ:* Marlborough Coll.; Christ Church, Oxford; Wycliffe Hall, Oxford. Asst Master, Kenton Coll., Kenya, 1933–36; deacon 1936, priest 1937; Curate, St Paul's, Salisbury, 1936–38; Priest-in-Charge, St George's, Oakdale, Poole, 1938–47; Vicar of Sherborne with Castleton and Lillington, 1947–68. RD of Sherborne and Canon of Salisbury Cathedral, 1954–68. CF (temp.), 1939–45; SCF, 7th Armoured Div., 1943–45. *Recreations:* fishing, gardening. *Address:* Eastbury House, Long Street, Sherborne, Dorset DT9 3BZ. *T:* Sherborne (01935) 812876.   *Died 22 Jan. 1996.*

WINTER, Rt Rev. Allen Ernest; Bishop of St Arnaud, 1951–73; *b* 8 Dec. 1903; *o s* of Ernest Thomas and Margaret Winter, Malvern, Vic; *m* 1939, Eunice Eleanor, 3rd *d* of Albert and Eleanor Sambell; three *s* two *d. Educ:* Melbourne C of E Grammar School; Trinity Coll., Univ. of Melbourne (BA 1926; MA 1928); University Coll., Oxford (BA 1932; MA 1951); Australian College of Theology (ThL 1927; ThD 1951 *iur. dig.*). Deacon, 1927, priest, 1928, Melbourne; Curate, Christ Church, S Yarra, 1927–29; on leave, Oxford, 1929–32; Curate, St James', Ivanhoe, 1932–35; Minister of Sunshine, 1935–39; Incumbent of St Luke's, Brighton, Melb., 1939–48; Chaplain, AIF, 1942–46; Incumbent of Christ Church, Essendon, 1948–49; Canon-Residentiary and Rector of All Saints' Cathedral, Bathurst, 1949–51; Chaplain, St John's Coll., Morpeth, NSW, 1974. *Address:* Wynnstay Nursing Home, 21 Wynnstay Street, Armadale, Vic 3143, Australia.   *Died 8 July 1997.*

WINTER, Charles Milne, CBE 1990; FIBScot; a Vice-Chairman, Royal Bank of Scotland Group plc, 1992–93 (Director, 1981–93); *b* 21 July 1933; *s* of David and Annie Winter; *m* 1957, Audrey Hynd; one *s* one *d. Educ:* Harris Acad., Dundee. FIBScot 1979. Served RAF, 1951–53. Joined The Royal Bank of Scotland, 1949; Exec. Dir, 1981–86; Man. Dir, 1982–85; Dep. Gp Chief Exec., 1985; Gp Chief Exec., 1985. Dir, Williams & Glyn's Bank, 1982–85 (Man. Dir, March-Oct. 1985). President: Inst. of Bankers in Scotland, 1981–83; Edinburgh Chamber of Commerce and Manufactures, 1992–94; Chm., Cttee of Scottish Clearing Bankers, 1983–85, 1989–91; Dir-Gen., The Scottish Chamber of Commerce, 1995. *Recreations:* golf, choral music. *Club:* Royal and Ancient Golf (St Andrews).   *Died 15 May 1996.*

WINTOUR, Charles Vere, CBE 1978 (MBE (mil.) 1945); journalist; *b* 18 May 1917; *s* of late Maj.-Gen. Fitzgerald Wintour, CB, CBE and Alice Jane Blanche, *d* of Major J. F. Foster, Louth, Ireland; *m* 1st, 1940, Eleanor Trego Baker (marr. diss. 1979; she *d* 1996), *er d* of Prof. R. J. Baker, Harvard Univ.; two *s* two *d* (and one *s* decd); 2nd 1979, Mrs Audrey Slaughter. *Educ:* Oundle Sch.; Peterhouse, Cambridge (BA 1939; MA 1946). Royal Norfolk Regt, 1940; GSO2 Headquarters of Chief of Staff to the Supreme Allied Commander (Designate) and SHAEF, 1943–45 (despatches). Joined Evening Standard, 1946: Dep. Editor, 1954–57; Editor, 1959–76 and 1978–80; Managing Dir, 1978–79; Chm., 1968–80; Asst Editor, Sunday Express, 1952–54; Managing Editor, Daily Express, 1957–59, Managing Dir, 1977–78; Editor: Sunday Express Magazine, 1981–82; UK Press Gazette, 1985–86; Editorial Consultant, London Daily News, 1986–87; Ombudsman, Sunday Times, 1990–95. Director: Evening Standard Co. Ltd, 1959–82; Express (formerly Beaverbrook) Newspapers Ltd, 1964–82; TV-am (News) Ltd, 1982–84; Wintour Publications, 1984–85. Mem., Press Council, 1979–81; Pres., Media Soc., 1989–91. Wilts Rep., NACF, 1995–. Croix de Guerre (France),

1945; Bronze Star (US), 1945. *Publications:* Pressures on the Press, 1972; The Rise and Fall of Fleet Street, 1989. *Recreations:* theatre-going, reading newspapers. *Address:* 60 East Hatch, Tisbury, Wilts SP3 6PH. *T:* (01747) 870880. *Club:* Garrick.   *Died 4 Nov. 1999.*

WISE, Audrey; MP (Lab) Preston, since 1987; *b* 4 Jan. 1935; *d* of George and Elsie Crawford Brown; *m* 1953, John Wise; one *s* one *d.* Shorthand typist. MP (Lab) Coventry South West, Feb. 1974–1979. Contested (Lab) Woolwich, 1983. Mem., Labour Party NEC, 1982–87. Pres., USDAW, 1991–97. *Publications:* Women and the Struggle for Workers' Control, 1973; Eyewitness in Revolutionary Portugal, 1975. *Recreations:* family life, gardening. *Address:* House of Commons, SW1A 0AA.
                                Died 2 Sept. 2000.

WISE, Ernie; *see* Wiseman, Ernest.

WISE, Very Rev. Randolph George, VRD 1964; Dean of Peterborough, 1981–92, Dean Emeritus, since 1997; *b* 20 Jan. 1925; *s* of George and Agnes Lucy Wise; *m* 1951, Hazel Hebe Simpson; four *d. Educ:* St Olave's and St Saviour's Grammar School; Queen's Coll., Oxford (MA); Lincoln Theological Coll.; Ealing Technical Coll. (DMS); Leicester Univ. (MA 1996). Served RNVR, 1943–47. Deacon 1951, priest 1952; Assistant Curate: Lady Margaret, Walworth, 1951–53; Stocksbridge, Sheffield, 1953–55; Vicar of Lady Margaret, Walworth, 1955–60; Vicar of Stocksbridge, 1960–66; Bishop of London's Industrial Chaplaincy, 1966–76; Guild Vicar, St Botolph, Aldersgate, 1972–76; Rector of Notting Hill, 1976–81. Member of Plaisterers' Company. *Recreation:* music. *Address:* 2 Derwent Drive, Oakham, Leics LE15 6SA. *T:* (01572) 756263. *Club:* Naval.   *Died 9 Sept. 1999.*

WISEMAN, Ernest, (Ernie Wise), OBE 1976; *b* 27 Nov. 1925; *s* of Harry and Connie Wiseman; *m* 1953, Doreen Blyth. *Educ:* Council School. Career in show business: radio, variety, TV, films; first double act (with Eric Morecambe), at Empire Theatre, Liverpool, 1941; first radio broadcast, 1943; *television:* BBC and ITV series, 1955–84 (SFTA Best Light Entertainment Award, 1973); series sold to Time Life, USA, 1980; Morecambe and Wise Tribute Show, Bring Me Sunshine, 1984; The Best of Morecambe and Wise, BBC, 1984; What's My Line, 1985; Too Close for Comfort, 1985; Los Angilla's, 1985; The Importance of Being Ernie, 1993; *stage:* The Mystery of Edwin Drood, Savoy, 1987; Run for Your Wife, Criterion, 1988; Sleeping Beauty, Theatre Royal, Windsor, 1992; *films:* The Intelligence Men, 1964; That Riviera Touch, 1965; The Magnificent Two, 1966; (for TV) Night Train to Murder, 1983. *Awards:* BAFTA (formerly SFTA), 1963, 1971, 1972, 1973, 1977; Silver Heart, 1964; Water Rats, 1970; Radio Industries, 1971, 1972; Sun Newspaper, 1973; Sun, 1974; Water Rats Distinguished Services, 1974; TV Times Hall of Fame Award, 1980–81; Commendation, 1981, Special Mention, 1982, HM Queen Mother's Award, Keep Britain Tidy; Best Dressed Man Award, 1983; Variety Club of GB award for work for deprived children, 1983; TV Times Award, 1985. Telethon for Children's Charity, NZ, 1985. Freeman, City of London, 1976. *Publications:* (with E. Morecambe): Eric and Ernie: an autobiography of Morecambe and Wise, 1973; Scripts of Morecambe and Wise, 1974; Morecambe and Wise Special, 1977; There's No Answer to That, 1981; Still on My Way to Hollywood (autobiog.), 1990. *Recreations:* boating, tennis, swimming, jogging. *Address:* c/o Ian Kennedy, 174–178 North Gower Street, NW1 2NA.   *Died 21 March 1999.*

WITHERINGTON, Giles Somerville Gwynne; Member of Assembly, Save the Children Fund, since 1991 (Member of Council, 1980–91; Chairman, 1982–87); *b* 7 June 1919; *s* of Iltid Gwynne Witherington and Alice Isabel Gage

Spicer; *m* 1951, Rowena Ann Spencer Lynch; one *s* three *d. Educ:* Charterhouse; University Coll., Oxford (MA). War Service, Royal Artillery, UK, N Africa, Italy, 1939–46 (despatches). Joined Spicers Ltd, 1946, Jt Managing Director, 1960; joined Reed International Ltd: Director, 1963; Dep. Chm., 1976; retired, 1982. Mem. Council, Textile Conservation Centre, 1984–92 (Chm. of Trustees of the Friends, 1984–91). Hon. LLD Birmingham, 1983. *Recreations:* shooting, gardening, modern art, travel. *Address:* Bishops, Widdington, Saffron Walden, Essex CB11 3SQ; Flat 2, 11 Netherton Grove, SW10 9TQ. *Club:* Arts. *Died 17 July 1996.*

WITHERS, John Keppel Ingold D.; *see* Douglas-Withers.

WITHY, George; retired journalist; Assistant Editor (night), Liverpool Echo, 1972–89; *b* Birkenhead, 15 May 1924; *er s* of George Withy and Alma Elizabeth Withy (*née* Stankley); *m* 1950, Dorothy Betty, *e c* of Bertram Allen and Dorothy Gray, Northfield, Birmingham; two *d. Educ:* Birkenhead Park High Sch. Served War, Royal Artillery, Britain and NW Europe, 1942–47. Trainee and Reporter, Birkenhead News, 1940; Chief Reporter, Redditch Indicator, 1948; District Reporter, Birmingham Post and Mail, 1950; Editor, Redditch Indicator, 1952; joined Liverpool Daily Post 1960: successively Sub-Editor, Dep. Chief Sub-Editor, Asst News Editor, Chief Sub-Editor; Chief Sub-Editor, Liverpool Echo, 1970; Rugby Writer, Liverpool Daily Post and Liverpool Echo, 1968–93. Institute of Journalists, 1962: successively Sec. and Chm., Liverpool District; Convenor, NW Region; Chm., Salaries and Conditions Bd, 1973–89; Vice-Pres. and then Pres., 1975; Fellow 1975; Life FCIJ, 1998. Chm., Nat. Council for the Trng of Journalists, 1974, 1982 (Mem., 1970; Vice-Chm., 1973), 1981; Chm., North-West Adv. Trng Cttee, 1974–76, 1983–85); Mem., Newspaper Trng Cttee, Printing and Publishing Industry Trng Bd; Mem., Press Council, 1973–79. *Recreations:* gardening, reading, philately. *Address:* 3 Woodside Road, Irby, Wirral, Merseyside L61 4UL. *T:* (0151) 648 2809.
Died 17 Nov. 1998.

WITNEY, Kenneth Percy, CVO 1976; *b* 19 March 1916; *s* of late Rev. Thomas and Dr Myfanwy Witney, S India; *m* 1947, Joan Tait (decd); one *s* one *d. Educ:* Eltham Coll.; Wadham Coll., Oxford (Schol.; BA Hons Mod. History, 1938; MA 1975); Univ. of Kent (DipArch 1990). Min. of Home Security, 1940; Private Sec. to Parly Under-Sec., 1942–44; Home Office, 1945; Asst Private Sec. to Home Sec., 1945–47; Colonial Office (Police Div.), 1955–57; Asst Sec., Home Office, 1957; Asst Under-Sec. of State, Home Office, 1969–76. Special Consultant to Royal Commn on Gambling, 1976–78. Chm., Kent Fedn of Amenity Socs, 1982–85. *Publications:* The Jutish Forest, 1976; The Kingdom of Kent, 1982; contribs to Econ. Hist. Rev., Archaeologia Cantiana, Agricl Hist. Rev. *Recreations:* local history, gardening. *Address:* 1 Loampits Close, Tonbridge, Kent TN9 1PX. *T:* (01732) 352971.
Died 7 Sept. 1999.

WITT, Rt Rev. Howell Arthur John; Bishop of Bathurst, 1981–89; *b* 12 July 1920; *s* of Thomas Leyshon Witt and Harriet Jane Witt; *m* 1949, Gertrude Doreen Edwards (*d* 1983); three *s* two *d. Educ:* Newport Sec. Sch.; Leeds Univ.; Coll. of the Resurrection, Mirfield. Deacon 1944; priest 1945; Assistant Curate: Usk, Mon, 1944–47; St George's, Camberwell, 1948–49; Chaplain, Woomera, S Australia, 1949–54; Rector, St Mary Magdalene's, Adelaide, 1954–57; Priest in charge of Elizabeth, 1957–65; Missioner of St Peter's Coll. Mission, 1954–65; Bishop of North-West Australia, 1965–81. *Publication:* Bush Bishop (autobiography), 1980. *Recreation:* script writing. *Address:* Unit 20, DGV, 99 McCabe Street, Mosman Park, WA 6012, Australia. *Club:* Public Schools (Adelaide).
Died 8 July 1998.

WOLKIND, Jack, CBE 1978; Chairman, World Trade Centre in London Ltd, 1991–95; *b* 16 Feb. 1920; *s* of Samuel and Golda Wolkind; *m* 1945, Bena Sternfeld; two *s* one *d. Educ:* Mile End Central Sch.; King's Coll., London. LLB Hons, LLM (London). Admitted Solicitor, 1953. Army service to 1945. Dep. Town Clerk and Solicitor, Stepney Borough Council, 1952–65; Chief Exec. (formerly Town Clerk), Tower Hamlets, 1964–85; Chief Exec., St Katharine by the Tower Ltd, 1990–91 (Dir, 1985–93). Mem., London Residuary Body, 1985–96. Chm., Claredale Housing Assoc. Ltd, 1987–. Governor: Toynbee Hall, 1981–; QMC, Univ. of London, 1981–90 (Fellow, 1985). FRSA 1980; Fellow, Guildhall Univ. (formerly City of London Poly.), 1985. *Recreations:* reading, music. *Died 6 March 1997.*

WOLVERSON COPE, F(rederick); *see* Cope.

WOOD, Prof. Derek Rawlins, FIBiol; Dean of Faculty of Medicine and Professor of Applied Pharmacology, University of Leeds, 1969–86, then Professor Emeritus; *b* 16 May 1921; *s* of Frederick Charles Wood and Ruth Dorothy (*née* Rawlins); *m* 1945, Mary Elizabeth Caldwell; two *s* two *d* (and one *s* decd). *Educ:* Wm Hulme's Grammar Sch., Manchester; Brasenose Coll. and Radcliffe Infirmary, Oxford. BM BCh, BSc, MA Oxford. House Physician, Radcliffe Inf., 1945; Demonstrator, Pharmacology, Oxford, 1945–46; Lectr 1946, Sen. Lectr 1952–57, Pharmacology, Univ. of Sheffield; J. H. Hunt Travelling Schol., 1949; J. H. Brown Fellow, Pharmacol., Yale, 1955–56; Associate Prof., Pharmacol., McGill Univ., 1957–60; Prof. and Head of Dept of Pharmacol., Univ. of Leeds, 1960–69. Hon. Sec., 1952–57, Hon. Treas., 1964–70, Hon. Mem., 1994, Brit. Pharmacol. Soc.; Member: Stag Jt Commn on Classification of Proprietary Remedies, 1964–69; British Nat. Formulary Cttee, 1967–74; Adv. Commn on Pesticides, 1968–70; Brit. Pharmacopoeia Commn, 1969–70; UMC 1969–86; Gen. Dental Council, 1971–86; Leeds Reg. Hosp. Bd, 1969–74; Bd of Governors, United Leeds Hosps, 1969–74; Leeds AHA (T), 1974–82; Leeds DHA, West and East, 1982–84. Exec. Sec., University Hosps Assoc., 1988–91 (Chm., 1978–81). Mem. Court, Univs of Bradford, 1970–91, and Sheffield, 1966–79. Hon. MPS. *Publications:* Dental Pharmacology and Therapeutics (with L. E. Francis), 1961; contribs to Brit. Jl Pharmacol., Jl Physiol., and others. *Recreations:* gardening, music. *Address:* 5 Spring Terrace, Lothersdale, Keighley, W Yorks BD20 8HA. *T:* (01535) 632593. *Died 21 June 1997.*

WOOD, Kenneth Maynard; consultant; *b* 4 Oct. 1916; *s* of late Frederick Cavendish Wood and Agnes Maynard; *m* 1st, 1944, Laurie Marion McKinlay (*d* 1976); two *s* two *d*; 2nd, 1978, Patricia Rose; three step *s*. *Educ:* Bromley County School. Cadet, Merchant Navy, 1930–34; electrical and mechanical engineering, 1934–37; started own company radio, television and radar development, 1937–39; sold business and joined RAF, transferred for development of electronic equipment, 1939–46; started Kenwood Manufacturing Co. Ltd, 1946; Managing Director, 1946 until take-over by Thorn Electrical Industries Ltd, 1968; Chm. and Man. Dir, Dawson-Keith Group of Companies, 1972–80; Chm, Hydrotech Systems Ltd, 1984–87. Fellow, Inst. of Ophthalmology. *Recreation:* golf. *Address:* Dellwood Cottage, Wheatsheaf Enclosure, Liphook, Hants GU30 7EH. *T:* (01428) 723108. *Died 19 Oct. 1997.*

WOOD, Walter; Town Clerk, City of Birmingham, 1972–74; *b* Bolton, 11 Jan. 1914; *s* of Walter Scott Wood; *m* 1939, Hilda Maude, *d* of Albert Forrester; two *s*. *Educ:* Canon Slade Sch., Bolton; Victoria Univ., Manchester (LLB). Served with RAF, 1940–45. Admitted solicitor, 1937 (Daniel Reardon and Clabon prizeman); Legal Associate Member, RTPI, 1948. Asst Solicitor, Bradford,

1937, Swansea, 1939; Dep. Town Clerk, Grimsby, 1947; Principal Asst Solicitor, Sheffield, 1948; Asst Town Clerk, Birmingham, 1952; Dep. Town Clerk, Birmingham, 1960. Panel Inspector, DoE, 1974–85. Governor, Solihull Sch., 1974–84. Pres., Birmingham Law Soc., 1976. Pres., West Midland Rent Assessment Panel, 1980–84. *Recreations:* swimming, philately. *Address:* 43 Sandgate Road, Hall Green, Birmingham B28 0UN. *T:* (0121) 744 1195.

Died 14 June 1997.

WOODBINE PARISH, Sir David (Elmer), Kt 1980; CBE 1964; Chairman, City and Guilds of London Institute, 1967–79 (Council Member, 1954; Life Vice-President, 1979); *b* 29 June 1911; *o s* of late Walter Woodbine Parish and Audrey Makins; *m* 1939, Mona Blair McGarel, BA (Arch), ARIBA (*d* 1991), *o d* of late Charles McGarel Johnston, Glynn, Co. Antrim; two *d*. *Educ:* Sandroyd; Eton; Lausanne, Switzerland. Chm. and Man. Dir, Holliday and Greenwood Ltd, 1953–59 (Dir., 1937–59); Chm., Bovis Ltd, 1959–66; Dep. Chm., Marine and General Mutual Life Assurance Soc., 1976–86 (Dir, 1971–86). President: London Master Builders Assoc., 1952; Nat. Fedn of Building Trades Employers, 1960; Vice-Pres., Internat. Fedn of European Contractors of Building and Public Works, 1967–71; Member: Regional Adv. Council for Technological Educn, London and Home Counties, 1952–69; Architects Registration Council, 1952–72; Nat. Adv. Council for Educn in Industry and Commerce, 1953–78; BIM Council, 1953–62, Bd of Fellows, 1966–72; Nat. Council for Technological Awards, 1955–61; Bd of Building Educn, 1955–66; Building Res. Bd, 1957–60; Industrial Training Council, 1958–64; Council, British Employers' Confedn, 1959–65; Council Foundn for Management Educn, 1959–65; British Productivity Council, 1961–70 (Chm., Educn and Trng Cttee, 1963–70); Human Sciences Cttee, SRC, 1963–66; Construction Industry Training Bd, 1964–70. Chairman: UK Nat. Cttee, Internat. Apprentice Competition, 1962–70; MPBW Working Party on Res. and Information, 1963; Nat. Examinations Bd for Supervisory Studies, 1964–73; Mem., Nat. Jt Consult. Cttee of Architects, Quantity Surveyors and Builders, 1958–70 (Chm. 1966–68); Chm., Dept of Health and Social Security Cttee of Inquiry on Hosp. Building Maintenance and Minor Capital Works, 1968–70; Chm., Jt Mission Hosp. Equip. Bd (ECHO), 1973–78. Member: Court, Russia Co., 1937–84; Court, City Univ., 1967–72; Bd of Governors, The Polytechnic, Regent Street, 1967–70, Court, Polytechnic of Central London, 1970–76; Governing Body, Imperial Coll. of Science and Technology, 1971–81. Vice-Chm., Bd of Governors, St Thomas' Hosp., 1967–74 (Chm., Rebuilding Cttee, 1968–76); Chairman: Council, St Thomas's Hosp. Med. Sch., 1970–82; St Thomas' Dist Educn Adv. Council, 1974–81; Florence Nightingale Museum Trust, 1982–86; Member: Nightingale Fund Council, 1974–84; Bd of Governors, Bethlem Royal Hosp. and Maudsley Hosp., 1975–78; Council of Governors, Utd Medical and Dental Schs of Guy's and St Thomas's Hosps, 1982–85. Chm., Sussex Area, Royal Sch. of Church Music, 1981–85. Master, Clothworkers' Co., 1974–75 (Warden, 1962–64; Chm., Angel Court Develt, 1969–80). Mem. Bd of Govs, Clothworkers' Foundation, 1977–97. FCIOB (FIOB 1940); FRSA 1953; CIMgt (FBIM 1957); FIC 1976; Hon. FCGI 1979. Hon. LLD Leeds, 1975. *Publications:* contribs to technical jls concerned with construction. *Recreations:* garden, music. *Address:* The Glebe Barn, Pulborough, West Sussex RH20 2AF. *T:* (01798) 872613. *Club:* Boodle's.

Died 12 Nov. 1998.

WOODFIELD, Sir Philip (John), KCB 1983 (CB 1974); CBE 1963; Chairman, Irish Soldiers and Sailors Land Trust, 1986–99; *b* 30 Aug. 1923; *s* of late Ralph and Ruth Woodfield; *m* 1958, Diana Margaret, *d* of late Sydney and

Margaret Herington; three *d*. *Educ:* Alleyn's Sch., Dulwich; King's Coll., London. Served War of 1939–45: Royal Artillery, 1942–47 (Captain). Entered Home Office, 1950; Asst Private Secretary to Home Secretary, 1952; Federal Government of Nigeria, 1955–57; Home Office, 1957–60; Private Secretary to the Prime Minister, 1961–65; Asst Sec., 1965–67, Asst Under-Sec. of State, 1967–72, Home Office; Deputy Sec., NI Office, 1972–74, Home Office, 1974–81; Perm. Under-Sec. of State, NI Office, 1981–83. Secretary to: Commonwealth Immigration Mission, 1965; Lord Mountbatten's inquiry into prison security, Nov.-Dec. 1966; Chairman: Scrutiny of Supervision of Charities, 1987; Review of British Transport Police, 1987–88; Review of WRVS, 1991. Chm., London and Metropolitan Govt Staff Commn, 1984–91. Mem., Royal Commn on Criminal Justice, 1991–93. Staff Cllr for Security and Intelligence Services, 1987–95. *Recreation:* music. *Address:* c/o Lloyds TSB, 7 Pall Mall, SW1Y 5NA. *Clubs:* Garrick, Beefsteak.

Died 17 Sept. 2000.

WOODHAM, Prof. Ronald Ernest; Professor of Music, Reading University, 1951–77; *b* 8 Feb. 1912; *s* of Ernest Victor Woodham, Beckenham, Kent; *m* 1949, Kathleen Isabel, *e d* of P. J. Malone; three *s*. *Educ:* Sherborne Sch.; Royal College of Music, London; Christ Church, Oxford. BA, DMus; FRCO, ARCM. Served in RASC, in Middle East and Italy, 1939–45 (despatches). Assistant Director of Music, 1936, Acting Director of Music, 1946, Bradfield Coll.; Director of Music, Sherborne Sch., 1946; Cramb Lecturer in Music, Glasgow Univ., 1947–51. *Address:* 8 Sutton Gardens, St Peter Street, Winchester, Hants SO23 8HP.

Died 14 April 1998.

WOODLOCK, Jack Terence; Under-Secretary, Department of Health and Social Security, 1969–79, retired; *b* 10 July 1919; *s* of late James Patrick and Florence Woodlock; *m* 1941, Joan Mary Taylor; three *s* one *d*. *Educ:* Bromley Grammar School. Entered Civil Service, 1936; served in Royal Artillery, 1939–45; Ministry of Health, 1945; Asst Principal 1946; Principal 1950; Principal Private Sec. to Minister, 1958–59; Asst Sec. 1959. *Recreation:* historical studies. *Address:* 3 Parkside Mews, Hurst Road, Horsham, W Sussex RH12 2SA.

Died 15 June 1998.

WOODROW, David, CBE 1979; retired solicitor; *b* 16 March 1920; *s* of late Sydney Melson Woodrow and Edith Constance (*née* Farmer); *m* 1st, 1950, Marie-Armande (marr. diss.; she *d* 1989), *d* of late Benjamin Barrios, Hon. KBE, and Lady (Armande) Ovey; two *d*; 2nd, 1983, Mary Miley, *d* of late Rupert Alexander Whitamore and Sally Whitamore. *Educ:* Shrewsbury; Trinity Coll., Oxford. Commnd Royal Artillery, 1940; served SE Asia; POW Java and Japan, 1942–45. Admitted Solicitor, 1949. Chairman: Reading and District HMC, 1966–72; Oxford Regional Hosp. Bd, 1972–74; RHA, 1973–78; NHS Nat. Staff Cttee, Administrative and Clerical Staff, 1975–79. *Recreations:* painting and looking at pictures. *Address:* Dobsons, Brightwell-cum-Sotwell, Wallingford, Oxon OX10 0RH. *T:* (01491) 836170. *Club:* Leander (Henley-on-Thames).

Died 22 Nov. 1999.

WOODROW, Gayford William; HM Diplomatic Service, retired; Consul, Algeciras, 1982–85; *b* 21 Feb. 1922; *s* of William Alexander Woodrow and Charlotte Louise (*née* Ellis); *m* 1946, Janine Suzanne Marcelle Jannot; one *s*. *Educ:* Brockley County School. Served War, RAF, 1941–46. Foreign Office, 1946; Caracas, 1949; Vice Consul: Barcelona, 1952; Panama, 1954; Consul: Cairo, 1960; Alexandria, 1961; First Sec. and Consul, Warsaw, 1962; Consul: Valencia, 1965; Jerusalem, 1969; First Sec., Ottawa, 1976; Consul General, Tangier, 1978–80; Asst, Consular Dept, FCO, 1980–81. *Recreations:* walking, swimming, history. *Address:* Apartment 3, Pitt House, Chudleigh, Devon TQ13 0EL.

Died 8 March 1999.

WOODRUFF, Philip; *see* Mason, P.

WOODS, Maj.-Gen. Charles William, CB 1970; MBE 1952; MC 1944; Chairman, Douglas Haig Memorial Homes, 1975–87; *b* 21 March 1917; *s* of late Captain F. W. U. Woods and Mrs M. E. Woods, Gosbrook House, Binfield Heath, Henley-on-Thames; *m* 1940, Angela Helen Clay (*d* 1996); one *d* (one *s* decd). *Educ:* Uppingham Sch.; Trinity Coll., Cambridge (MA). Commnd into Corps of Royal Engineers, 1938; served War of 1939–45, N Africa, Sicily, Italy, NW Europe (D Landings with 50th Div.); Staff Coll., Camberley, 1946; served in Korea, 1951–52; comd 35 Corps Engineer Regt, BAOR, 1959–60; Dep. Military Secretary, 1964–67; Dir of Manning (Army), 1967–70. Col Comdt, RE, 1973–78. Chm., RE Assoc., 1971–77. *Recreations:* sailing, ski-ing. *Address:* 6 Grove Pastures, Lymington, Hants SO41 9RG. *T:* (01590) 673445. *Clubs:* Royal Ocean Racing, Royal Cruising, Ski Club of Great Britain; Royal Lymington Yacht, Royal Engineer Yacht; Island Sailing (Cowes).

Died 28 Dec. 1996.

WOODS, Rt Rev. Robert Wilmer, (Robin), KCMG 1989; KCVO 1971; Assistant Bishop, Diocese of Gloucester, since 1982; Prelate of the Most Distinguished Order of St Michael and St George, 1971–89; *b* 15 Feb. 1914; *s* of late Rt Rev. Edward Woods, Bishop of Lichfield, and Clemence (*née* Barclay); *m* 1942, Henrietta Marion (JP 1966), *d* of late K. H. Wilson; two *s* three *d*. *Educ:* Gresham's Sch., Holt; Trinity Coll., Cambridge (MA). Asst Sec., Student Christian Movement, 1937–42; deacon 1938, priest 1939, Curate, St Edmund the King, Lombard Street, 1938–39; Hoddesdon, 1939–42; Chaplain to the Forces, 1942–46 (despatches, 1944); Vicar of South Wigston, Leicester, 1946–51; Archdeacon of Singapore and Vicar of St Andrew's Cathedral, 1951–58; Archdeacon of Sheffield and Rector of Tankersley, 1958–62; Dean of Windsor, 1962–70; Domestic Chaplain to the Queen, 1962–70; Register of the Most Noble Order of the Garter, 1962–70; Bishop of Worcester, 1970–81. Secretary, Anglican/Methodist Commn for Unity, 1965–74; Member: Council, Duke of Edinburgh's Award Scheme, 1968; Public Schools Commn, 1968–70; Governor, Haileybury Coll.; Visitor, Malvern Coll., 1970–81; Pres, Queen's Coll., Birmingham, and Chm. Council, 1970–85; Chairman: Windsor Festival Co., 1969–71; Churches Television Centre, 1969–79; Dir, Christian Aid, 1969. Chm., Birmingham and Hereford and Worcester Bd, MSC, 1976–83. *Publication:* Robin Woods: an autobiography, 1986. *Recreations:* shooting, painting. *Address:* Torse End, Tirley, Gloucester GL19 4EU. *T:* (01452) 780327.

Died 20 Oct. 1997.

WOODWARD, Prof. C(omer) Vann; Sterling Professor of History, Yale University, 1961–77, then Emeritus Professor; *b* 13 Nov. 1908; *s* of Hugh Allison Woodward and Bess (*née* Vann); *m* 1937, Glenn Boyd MacLeod; one *s. Educ:* Emory Univ. (PhB); Universities of Columbia (MA), North Carolina (PhD). Asst Professor of History, University of Florida, 1937–39; Visiting Asst Professor of History, University of Virginia, 1939–40; Associate Professor of History: Scripps Coll., 1940–43; Johns Hopkins University, 1946; Professor of American History, Johns Hopkins Univ., 1947–61. Served with US Naval Reserve, 1943–46. Commonwealth Lecturer, UCL, 1954; Harold Vyvyan Harmsworth Professor of American History, University of Oxford, 1954–55. Corresp. Fellow: British Academy, 1972; RHistS, 1978. Member: American Academy of Arts and Sciences (Vice-Pres., 1988–89); American Philosophical Society; Amer. Acad. of Arts and Letters; American Historical Assoc. (President, 1969);

Orgn of American Historians (President, 1968–69). Hon. MA Oxon, 1954; hon. doctoral degrees from univs of Arkansas, Brandeis, Cambridge, Colgate, Columbia, Dartmouth, Emory, Florida, Henderson, Hendrix, Johns Hopkins, Michigan, N Carolina, Northwestern, Pennsylvania, Princeton, Rutgers, Tulane, Washington and Lee, William and Mary, and Rhodes Coll. Literary Award, Amer. Acad. and Inst. of Arts and Letters, 1954; Gold Medal for History, 1990. *Publications:* Tom Watson: Agrarian Rebel, 1938; The Battle for Leyte Gulf, 1947; Origins of the New South (1877–1913), 1951 (Bancroft Prize, 1952); Reunion and Reaction, 1951; The Strange Career of Jim Crow, 1955; The Burden of Southern History, 1960; American Counterpoint, 1971; Thinking Back, 1986; The Future of the Past, 1989; The Old World's New World, 1991; (ed) The Comparative Approach to American History, 1968; (ed) Mary Chesnut's Civil War, 1981 (Pulitzer Prize, 1982). *Address:* 83 Rogers Road, Hamden, CT 06517, USA.

Died 17 Dec. 1999.

WOODWARD, Geoffrey Frederick, RIBA; Assistant Director General of Design Services, Property Services Agency, Department of the Environment, 1983–84; *b* 29 June 1924; *s* of Joseph Frederick and Edith Mary Woodward; *m* 1953, Elizabeth Marjory McCubbin; four *s. Educ:* Wirral Grammar School for Boys; Trinity College, Cambridge Univ.; School of Architecture, Liverpool Univ. (BArch). jssc 1963. Architects' Department: Hertfordshire CC, 1952–56; British Transport Commn, 1956–60; Directorate of Army Works, 1960–63; Directorate of Research & Development, Min. of Public Building and Works, 1963–67; Directorate of Works (Married Quarters), MPBW, 1967–70; Directorate of Works (Navy Home), PSA, 1970–71; Director of Works (Navy Home), PSA, 1971–75; Director, Directorate General of Design Services, Design Office, 1975–78; Under Sec., PSA, DoE, 1978; Dir of Architectural Services, 1978–81; Dir, Diplomatic and Post Office Services, 1981–83. *Recreations:* motoring, walking. *Address:* Little Orchard, Cuddington Way, Cheam, Sutton, Surrey SM2 7JA. *T:* (0181) 643 1964. *Died 11 June 1997.*

WOODWARD, Rev. Max Wakerley; Methodist Minister, retired 1973; *b* 29 Jan. 1908; *s* of Alfred Woodward, Methodist Minister, and Mabel (*née* Wakerley); *m* 1934, Kathleen May Beaty; three *s* one *d. Educ:* Orme Sch., Newcastle; Kingswood Sch., Bath; Handsworth Coll., Birmingham. Missionary to Ceylon, 1929–42; Chaplain, Royal Navy, 1942–46; Minister: Leamington Spa, 1946–50; Finsbury Park, 1950–54; Harrow, 1954–58; Wesley's Chapel, London, 1958–64; Secretary, World Methodist Council, 1964–69; Minister, Bromley, Kent, 1969–73. Exchange Preacher, Univ. Methodist Church, Baton Rouge, La, 1957. Dir, Methodist Newspaper Co. Ltd, 1962–84. *Publication:* One At London, 1966. *Recreations:* gardening, stamp collecting. *Address:* 6a Field End Road, Pinner, Middx HA5 2QL. *T:* 0181–429 0608. *Died 19 April 1996.*

WOOF, Robert Edward; Member and former Official, National Union of Mineworkers; *b* 24 Oct. 1911; *m* Mary Bell (*d* 1971); one *d. Educ:* elementary school. Began work in the mines at an early age, subsequently coal face worker. Member of the Labour Party, 1937–; MP (Lab) Blaydon, Co. Durham, Feb. 1956–1979. Member Durham County Council, 1947–56. *Address:* 10 Ramsay Road, Chopwell, Newcastle upon Tyne NE17 7AG.

Died 27 Nov. 1997.

WOOLF, Sir John, Kt 1975; film and television producer; Founder and Chairman, Romulus Films Ltd, since 1948; Chairman, British & American Investment Trust Plc (formerly British & American Film Holdings Plc), since 1982; *b* 15 March 1913; *s* of Charles M. and Vera Woolf;

m 1st, 1937, Dorothy Vernon (marr. diss.); 2nd, 1946, Edna Romney (marr. diss.); 3rd, 1955, Ann Saville, *d* of Victor Saville, film director; one *s* (and one *s* decd). *Educ:* Institut Montana, Switzerland. War of 1939–45 (Bronze Star (USA), 1945): Asst Dir, Army Kinematography, War Office (Lt Col), 1944–45. Co-founder and Executive Director, Anglia TV Group PLC (responsible for Drama Dept), 1958–83. Member: Cinematograph Films Council, 1969–79; Bd of Governors, Services Sound & Vision Corp. (formerly Services Kinema Corp.), 1974–83; Dir, First Leisure Corp. Plc, 1982–97; Mem. Exec. Cttee and Trustee, Cinema and Television Benevolent Fund, 1964–97 (first Life Vice-Pres., 1997). Freeman, City of London, 1982. FRSA 1978. Romulus prodns won 13 Oscars in various categories; films produced by Romulus Group included: The African Queen, Pandora and the Flying Dutchman, Moulin Rouge, I am a Camera, Carrington VC, The Bespoke Overcoat (Academy Award for Best Short Film, 1956), Beat the Devil, Story of Esther Costello, Room at the Top, Wrong Arm of the Law, The L-Shaped Room, Term of Trial, Life at the Top, Oliver!, Day of the Jackal, The Odessa File; TV productions for Anglia included: over 100 plays and the series Orson Welles' Great Mysteries, and Tales of the Unexpected. Personal awards included: British Film Academy Award for Best Film of 1958, Room at the Top; Oscar and Golden Globe for Best Film of 1969, Oliver!; nominated Producer of the Year, Producers Guild of America, 1968; special awards for contribution to British film industry from Cinematograph Exhibitors Assoc., 1969, Variety Club of GB, 1974. *Address:* 214 The Chambers, Chelsea Harbour, SW10 0XF. *T:* (020) 7376 3791, *Fax:* (020) 7352 7457.
Died 28 June 1999.

WOOLFORD, Harry Russell Halkerston, OBE 1970; Consultant, formerly Chief Restorer, National Gallery of Scotland; *b* 23 May 1905; *s* of H. Woolford, engineer; *m* 1932, Nancy Philip; one *d. Educ:* Edinburgh. Studied art at Edinburgh Coll. of Art (Painting and Drawing) and RSA Life School (Carnegie Travelling Scholarship, 1928), London, Paris and Italy; afterwards specialized in picture restoration. FMA; FIIC. Hon. Mem., Assoc. of British Picture Restorers, 1970. Hon. MA Dundee, 1976. *Address:* 7a Barntongate Avenue, Barnton, Edinburgh EH4 8BD. *T:* (0131) 339 6861. *Club:* Scottish Arts.
Died 29 Aug. 1999.

WOOLFSON, Mark; Consultant and Director of Consortium, Pollution Control Consultants, 1972–87; a Partner, Posford Duvivier (formerly Posford Pavry & Partners), 1972–90, retired; *b* 10 Nov. 1911; *s* of Victor Woolfson and Sarah (*née* Kixman); *m* 1940, Queenie Carlis; two *d. Educ:* City of London. CEng, FIMechE, FIEE. Student Engr, Lancashire Dynamo & Crypto, until 1936; Engr, ASEA Electric Ltd, 1936–40; War Service, RNVR, 1940–46 (Lt-Comdr); MPBW, later DoE, 1946–71, Chief Mech. and Elect. Engineer, 1969–71. *Publications:* papers in Jls of Instns of Civil, Mechanical and Elect. Engrs. *Recreations:* gardening, golf. *Address:* 1 Highlawn House, Sudbury Hill, Harrow-on-the-Hill HA1 3NY. *T:* (020) 8422 1599.
Died 13 Sept. 2000.

WOOLHOUSE, Prof. Harold William; Director, Waite Agricultural Research Institute, and Dean, Faculty of Agricultural and Natural Resource Sciences, University of Adelaide, 1990–95, then Professor Emeritus, University of Adelaide; *b* 12 July 1932; *s* of William Everson Woolhouse and Frances Ella Woolhouse; *m* 1959, Leonie Marie Sherwood; two *s* one *d. Educ:* Univ. of Reading (BSc); Univ. of Adelaide (PhD). Lecturer and Sen. Lectr, Sheffield Univ., 1960–69; Professor of Botany, Leeds Univ., 1969–80; Dir, John Innes Inst., and Prof. of Biological Scis, UEA, 1980–86; Dir of Res., AFRC Inst.

of Plant Sci. Res., and Hon. Prof., UEA, 1987–90. Vis. Professor, USC, Los Angeles, 1968; Andrew D. White Professor at Large, Cornell Univ., 1983–89. Hon. DSc UEA, 1990. *Publications:* research papers on plant senescence, photosynthesis, metal toxicity and tolerance, and physiology of adaptation. *Recreations:* poetry, music, poultry breeding, gardening. *Address:* Old Sun House, 65 Damgate Street, Wymondham, Norfolk NR18 0BH.
Died 19 June 1996.

WOOLLASTON, Sir (Mountford) Tosswill, Kt 1979; painter (abandoned other occupations, 1966); *b* 11 April 1910; *s* of John Reginald Woollaston and Charlotte Kathleen Frances (*née* Tosswill); *m* 1936, Edith Winifred Alexander (*d* 1987); three *s* one *d. Educ:* Huinga Primary; Stratford (NZ) Secondary; brief brushes with art schools, Christchurch, 1931; King Edward Technical Coll., Dunedin, 1932. Member, The Group, Christchurch, 1935–; a few private but enthusiastic supporters; work featured in Art in New Zealand, 1937; the doldrums, 1950s; Auckland City Art Gallery began purchasing work, 1958, other galleries followed; overseas travel grant, NZ Arts Council, 1961; reputation increased; Govt purchases for embassies overseas, early sixties; Peter McLeavey, Dealer, Wellington, took over selling, 1967. *Publications:* The Faraway Hills, 1962; Erua (48 drawings of a boy, with text—Paul), 1966; Sage Tea (autobiog.), 1981. *Recreation:* gardening. *Address:* Kelling Road, Upper Moutere, Nelson, New Zealand.
Died 31 Aug. 1998.

WORDIE, Sir John (Stewart), Kt 1981; CBE 1975; VRD 1963; barrister-at-law; *b* 15 Jan. 1924; *s* of late Sir James Mann Wordie, CBE, Hon. LLD, and of Lady Wordie (*née* Henderson); *m* 1955, Patricia Gladys Kynoch, Keith, Banffshire, *d* of Lt-Col G. B. Kynoch, CBE, TD, DL; four *s. Educ:* Winchester Coll.; St John's Coll., Cambridge (MA; LLM). Served RNVR, 1942–46; Comdr RNR, 1967; Comdr London Div. RNR, 1969–71. Cambridge, 1946–49. Called to the Bar, Inner Temple, 1950; in practice at the Bar, 1951–86. Chairman: Burnham and Pelham Cttees, 1966–87; Soulbury Cttee, 1966; Wages Councils, 1956–93; Mem., Agricultural Wages Bd for England and Wales, 1974–95; Dep. Chm. and Mem., Central Arbitration Cttee, 1976–91; Mem. Council, ACAS, 1986–90. Chm., Nat. Jt Council for Lectures in Further Educn, 1980–93. Mem. Court of Assistants, Salters' Co., 1971–, Master, 1975. *Recreations:* shooting, sailing and boating, athletics, tennis. *Address:* Dodington House, Breamore, Fordingbridge, Hants SP6 2EH. *T:* (01725) 512317. *Clubs:* Travellers, Army and Navy, Royal Ocean Racing; Hawks (Cambridge); Royal Tennis Court (Hampton Court); Clyde Corinthian Yacht.
Died 21 Jan. 1997.

WORLOCK, Most Rev. Derek John Harford; Archbishop of Liverpool (RC) and Metropolitan of Northern Province with Suffragen Sees, Hallam, Hexham, Lancaster, Leeds, Middlesbrough and Salford, since 1976; **Most Rev. Derek John Harford Worlock,** CH 1996; *b* 4 Feb. 1920; 2nd *s* of Captain Harford Worlock and Dora (*née* Hoblyn). *Educ:* St Edmund's Coll., Ware, Herts. Ordained RC priest, 1944; Curate, Our Lady of Victories, Kensington, 1944–45; Private Secretary to Archbishop of Westminster, 1945–64; Rector and Rural Dean, Church of SS Mary and Michael London, E1, 1964–65; Bishop of Portsmouth, 1965–76. Privy Chamberlain to Pope Pius XII, 1949–53; Domestic Prelate of the Pope, 1953–65; *Peritus* at Vatican Council II, 1963–65; Consultor to Council of Laity, 1967–76; Episcopal Secretary to RC Bishops' Conference, 1967–76, Vice-Pres., 1979–. Member: Synod Council, 1976–77; Holy See's Laity Council, 1977– (formerly Mem., Cttee for the Family); English delegate to Internat. Synod of Bishops, 1974, 1977, 1980, 1983, 1987 and 1990. Chm., Nat. Pastoral Congress, 1980. Freedom, City of Liverpool, 1995. Hon. Fellow, Portsmouth Polytechnic, 1988. Hon. LLD Liverpool, 1981; Hon. DTech Liverpool Polytechnic, 1987; Hon. DD Cambridge, 1990. Knight Commander of Holy Sepulchre of Jerusalem, 1966. *Publications:* Seek Ye First (compiler), 1949; Take One at Bedtime (anthology), 1962; English Bishops at the Council, 1965; Turn and Turn Again, 1971; Give Me Your Hand, 1977; Bread Upon the Waters, 1991; with Rt Rev. D. Sheppard: Better Together, 1988; With Christ in the Wilderness, 1990; With Hope in Our Hearts, 1994. *Address:* Archbishop's House, 87 Green Lane, Mossley Hill, Liverpool L18 2EP. *T:* 0151–722 2379.

Died 8 Feb. 1996.

WORSLEY, Air Cdre Geoffrey Nicolas Ernest T. C.; *see* Tindal-Carill-Worsley.

WRAIGHT, Sir John (Richard), KBE 1976; CMG 1962; HM Diplomatic Service, retired; company consultant and company director, since 1976; *b* 4 June 1916; *s* of late Richard George Wraight; *m* 1947, Marquita, (Maggie), Elliott. *Educ:* Selhurst Grammar Sch.; London Univ. extension courses at SSEES. Served War of 1939–45 with Honourable Artillery Company and RHA, Western Desert and Libya; Balkans Section, Ministry of Economic Warfare Mission in the Middle East, Cairo, 1944; Economic Warfare Adviser, HQ Mediterranean Allied Air Forces, Italy, June-Dec. 1944. Worked in City of London, 1933–39; Foreign Office, 1945; Special Assistant to Chief of UNRRA Operations in Europe, 1946 (special missions to Vienna, Prague and Belgrade); entered Foreign (subseq. Diplomatic) Service, 1947; British Embassy: Athens, 1948; Tel Aviv, 1950 (negotiated first British financial agreement with new state); Washington, 1953; Asst Head of Economic Relations Dept, Foreign Office, 1957; Counsellor (Commercial) Cairo, 1959 (helped to restore trade links after Suez); Brussels and Luxembourg, 1962 (UK Comr on Tripartite Commn for Restitution of Monetary Gold, Brussels, 1962–68); Minister and Consul-General, Milan, 1968–73; Ambassador to Switzerland, 1973–76. Internat. consultant to Phillips & Drew, 1976–88. Pres., Greater London SW Scout County, 1977–. Commander of the Order of the Crown (Belgium), 1966. *Publications:* The Food Situation in Austria, 1946; The Swiss and the British, 1987; The Swiss in London, 1991. *Recreations:* music, reading history, birdwatching. *Address:* 35 Jameson Street, W8 7SH.

Died 23 April 1997.

WRIGHT, Hon. Alison Elizabeth; Director General, British Invisibles, 1991–97; *b* 5 Jan. 1945; *d* of Baron Franks, OM, GCMG, KCB, KCVO, CBE, FBA and late Barbara Mary Tanner; *m* 1973, Stanley Harris Wright. *Educ:* Headington School, Oxford; Downe House, Newbury; St Anne's College Oxford (BA PPE). Research Officer, Overseas Development Institute, 1965–69; research in Spain, 1970–72; business advr on Spain and Portugal, 1972–87; Managing Consultant, Ernst & Whinney, then Ernst & Young, 1988–90. Member: Heilbron Cttee on Law of Rape, 1975; Top Salaries Review Body, Nov. 1984, resigned April 1985; Commonwealth Develt Corp., 1984–94; CSO Adv. Cttee, 1992–99; Adv. Council, NCVO, 1994–; Adv. Panel, NIESR Eur. Financial Markets Prog., 1995–99; Adv. Council, Centre for Study of Financial Innovation, 1996–99. Member Council: ODI, 1988–95; British Consultants Bureau, 1993–97; City Univ., 1994–97. JP Inner London, 1978–91; Mem., Inner London Exec. Cttee, Magistrates' Assoc., 1980–82. Trustee, Marshall Plan of the Mind, BBC, 1992–99. *Publications:* The Less Developed Countries in World Trade (with M. Zammit Cutajar), 1969; The Spanish Economy 1959–1976, 1977; contribs to Economist Intelligence Unit, Encyclopaedia Britannica and other publications. *Recreations:* reading, theatre. *Address:* 6

Holly Place, Holly Walk, NW3 6QU, *T:* (020) 7435 0237. *Club:* Capital. *Died 19 June 2000.*

WRIGHT, Arthur Francis Stevenson, MBE 1945; FRIBA, FRIAS; architect principal in private practice, since 1949, consultant, since 1983; *b* 15 Feb. 1918; *s* of Arthur and Alice Wright; *m* 1946, Catherine Grey Linton; one *d*. *Educ:* Morgan Academy; College of Art, Dundee (DipArch 1948). Served War, Royal Engineers (Major), 1940–46. FRIBA 1956; FRIAS 1954 (Pres., 1975–77); FCIOB (FIOB 1974); FCIArb (FIArb 1976). Chm., Jt Standing Cttee of Architects, Surveyors and Builders in Scotland, 1973–75. *Recreations:* fishing, golf. *Address:* Thorvale, Castlegate, Ceres, Fife KY15 5NG. *T:* (01334) 82540. *Died 12 Feb. 1997.*

WRIGHT, David; *see* Wright, W. D.

WRIGHT, Judith Arundell (Mrs J. P. McKinney); writer; *b* 31 May 1915; *d* of late Phillip Arundell Wright, CMG, and Ethel Mabel (*née* Bigg); *m* J. P. McKinney (*d* 1966); one *d*. *Educ:* NSW Correspondence Sch.; New England Girls' Sch.; Sydney Univ. Secretarial work, 1938–42; Univ. Statistician, Univ. of Queensland, 1945–48. Creative Arts Fellow, ANU, 1974; Australia Council Senior Writers' Fellowship, 1977. FAHA 1970. Hon. Dr of Letters: New England, 1963; ANU, 1981; Griffith, 1988; Hon. DLitt: Sydney, 1976; Monash, 1977; Hon. LittD Melbourne, 1988. Encyclopædia Britannica Writer's Award, 1965; Robert Frost Medallion, Fellowship of Australian Writers, 1975; Asan World Prize, Asan Meml Assoc., 1984; NSW Premier's Special Prize for Poetry, 1991; Queen's Gold Medal for Poetry, 1992; Human Rights Poetry Award, 1994. *Publications: verse:* The Moving Image, 1946; Woman to Man, 1950; The Gateway, 1953; The Oxford Book of Australian Verse, 1954; The Two Fires, 1955; New Land New Language (anthology), 1956; Birds, 1960; Five Senses, 1963; The Other Half, 1966; Collected Poems, 1971; Alive, 1972; Fourth Quarter, 1976; The Double Tree, 1978; Phantom Dwelling, 1985; A Human Pattern, 1990, Collected Poems 1942–1985, 1994; *prose:* The Generations of Men, 1955; Preoccupations in Australian Poetry, 1964; The Nature of Love, 1966; Because I Was Invited, 1975; Charles Harpur, 1977; The Coral Battleground, 1977; The Cry for the Dead, 1981; We Call for a Treaty, 1985; Born of The Conquerors, 1991; Going on Talking, 1992; Half a Lifetime, 1999; five books for children; also critical essays and monographs. *Recreation:* gardening. *Address:* 1/17 Devonport Street, Lyons, ACT 2606, Australia.

Died 25 June 2000.

WRIGHT, Prof. Verna, FRCP; Professor of Rheumatology, University of Leeds, 1970–94, then Emeritus; Consultant Physician in Rheumatology, Leeds Area Health Authority (A) Teaching, and Yorkshire Regional Health Authority, 1964–94; Co-Director, Bioengineering Group for Study of Human Joints, University of Leeds, 1964–94; *b* 31 Dec. 1928; *s* of Thomas William and Nancy Eleanor Wright; *m* 1953, Esther Margaret Brown; five *s* four *d*. *Educ:* Bedford Sch.; Univ. of Liverpool (MB ChB 1953, MD 1956). FRCP 1970 (MRCP 1958). House Officer, Broadgreen Hosp., Liverpool, 1953–54; Sen. Ho. Officer, Stoke Mandeville Hosp., 1954–56; Research Asst, Dept of Clin. Medicine, Univ. of Leeds, 1956–58; Research Fellow, Div. of Applied Physiology, Johns Hopkins Hosp., Baltimore, 1958–59; Lectr, Dept of Clin. Med., Univ. of Leeds, 1960–64; Sen. Lectr, Dept of Medicine, Univ. of Leeds, 1964–70. Adv. Fellow to World Fedn of Occupational Therapists, 1980–. President: Heberden Soc., 1976–77; British Assoc. for Rheumatology and Rehabilitation, 1978–80; Soc. for Research in Rehabilitation, 1978; Soc. for Back Pain Research, 1977–79; Arthritis and Rheumatism Council: Chairman: Standing Cttee for Academic Develt and Res., 1989–93;

Exec. and Finance Cttee, 1993–. Member, Johns Hopkins Soc. for Scholars, USA, 1978–. Lectures: Casson Meml, Assoc. of Occupational Therapists, 1979; John Gibson Flemming, Royal Infirmary, Glasgow, 1984; Phillip Ellman, RSocMed, 1985; Kodama Meml, Japanese Rheumatism Assoc., Tokyo, 1986; C. W. Stewart Meml, Maryland Univ., 1988; John Matheson Shaw, RCPE, 1988; Heberden Oration, British Soc. of Rheumatology, 1985. Hon. Member: Canadian Rheumatism Assoc., 1978; Brazilian Soc. for Rheumatology, 1978; Hellenic Soc. of Rheumatology, 1981; Amer. Rheumatism Assoc., 1985; RSocMed, 1994. Elizabeth Fink Award, Nat. Ankylosing Spondylitis Soc., 1987. *Publications:* Lubrication and Wear in Joints, 1969; (with J. M. H. Moll) Seronegative Polyarthritis, 1976; Clinics in Rheumatic Diseases: Osteoarthrosis, 1976; (with I. Haslock) Rheumatism for Nurses and Remedial Therapists, 1977; (with D. Dowson) Evaluation of Artificial Joints, 1977; (with D. Dowson) Introduction to the Biomechanics of Joints and Joint Replacement, 1981; The Relevance of Christianity in a Scientific Age, 1981; (with H. A. Bird) Applied Drug Therapy of the Rheumatic Diseases, 1982; Topical Reviews in Rheumatic Disorders, vol. 2, 1982; Clinics in Rheumatic Diseases: osteoarthritis, 1982; Clinics in Rheumatic Diseases: measurement of joint movement, 1982; Bone and Joint Disease in the Elderly, 1983; (with R. A. Dickson) Integrated Clinical Science: musculo-skeletal disease, 1984; Personal Peace in a Nuclear Age, 1985; Arthritis and Joint Replacement (family doctor bklt), 1987; Pain, Clinical Rheumatology, International Practice and Research, 1987; (with A. Harvey) Diagnostic Picture Tests in Rheumatology, 1987; (with E. L. Radin) Mechanics of Human Joints: physiology, pathophysiology and treatment, 1993; (with P. S. Helliwell) Psoriatic Arthritis, 1994. *Recreations:* interdenominational Christian youth work, voracious reader. *Address:* Inglehurst, Park Drive, Harrogate HG2 9AY. *T:* (01423) 502326, *Fax:* (01423) 521981.

Died 31 Jan. 1998.

WRIGHT, Vincent, PhD; FBA 1995; Fellow of Nuffield College, Oxford, since 1977; *b* 6 Aug. 1937; *s* of Walter Hogarth Wright and Mary Teresa Kinsella. *Educ:* London Sch. of Economics (BSc Econ; PhD 1965); Inst d'Etudes Politiques, Paris. Lectr, Newcastle Univ., 1965–69; Vis. Fellow, St Antony's Coll., Oxford, 1969–70; Lectr, Sen. Lectr, and Reader, LSE, 1970–79; Prof., Eur. Univ. Inst., Florence, 1980–82 (on leave of absence); Einaudi Prof., Cornell Univ., 1988–89. Vis. Prof., Amer. and Eur. univs. Member, Academic Board: Inst d'Etudes Politiques, Bordeaux, 1993–; Res. Centre, Juan March Inst., Madrid, 1995–; Mem. Res. Council, Eur. Univ. Inst., Florence, 1997–. Chairman: Hist. Gp, Internat. Inst. of Admin. Scis, 1993–; Scientific Bd, Centre d'Etude de la Vie Politique Française, CNRS, Paris, 1994–. Officier, Ordre Nat. du Mérite (France), 1995. *Publications:* Le Conseil d'Etat sous le Second Empire, 1972; (jtly) Les Préfets du Second Empire, 1973; (jtly) Les Universités Britanniques, 1973; The Government and Politics of France, 1978, 3rd edn 1989; *edited:* (jtly) Local Government in Britain and France: problems and prospects, 1979 (trans. French 1982); (also contrib.) Continuity and Consensus in France, 1979; (also contrib.) Continuity and Change in France, 1984; (jtly) La Crise de la sidérurgie européenne 1974–1984, 1985; (jtly) Economic Policy and Policy Making under the Mitterrand Presidency, 1985; (jtly) The Political Management of Industrial Crisis: the case of steel 1974–1984, 1986; (jtly) Tensions in the Territorial Politics of Western Europe, 1987; (jtly) The Politics of Privatization in Western Europe, 1989; (also contrib.) The Representativity of Public Administration, 1991; Les privatisations en Europe: programmes et problèmes, 1993, rev. edn as Privatization in Western Europe, 1994; (jtly)

La Riforma Amministrativa in Europa, 1994; (jtly) The State in Western Europe: retreat or redefinition?, 1994; (jtly) La Recomposition de l'Etat en Europe, 1996; (jtly) Developments in West European Politics, 1997. *Address:* Nuffield College, Oxford OX1 1NF.

Died 8 July 1999.

WRIGHT, Prof. (William) David, DIC, DSc; ARCS; Professor of Applied Optics, Imperial College of Science and Technology, 1951–73; *b* 6 July 1906; *s* of late William John Wright and Grace Elizabeth Ansell; *m* 1932, Dorothy Mary Hudson (*d* 1990); two *s. Educ:* Southgate County Sch.; Imperial Coll. Research engineer at Westinghouse Electric and Manufacturing Co., Pittsburgh, USA, 1929–30; research and consultant physicist to Electric and Musical Industries, 1930–39. Lecturer and Reader in Technical Optics Section, Imperial Coll., 1931–51. Kern Prof. of Communications, Rochester Inst. of Technol., USA, 1984–85. Physical Society: Vice-Pres., 1948–50; Chairman: Colour Group, 1941–43; Optical Group, 1956–59; Sec., International Commn for Optics, 1953–66; Chm., Colour Group (GB), 1973–75; Pres., International Colour Assoc., 1967–69. Hon. DSc: City Univ., 1971; Waterloo, Canada, 1991. *Publications:* The Perception of Light, 1938; The Measurement of Colour, 1944, 4th edn 1969; Researches on Normal and Defective Colour Vision, 1946; Photometry and the Eye, 1950; The Rays are not Coloured, 1967; about 80 original scientific papers, mainly dealing with colour and vision. *Address:* c/o Dr S. J. Wright, 3 Pewley Bank, Guildford, Surrey GU1 3PU. *T:* (01483) 564021.

Died 4 June 1997.

WRIGLEY, Air Vice-Marshal Henry Bertram, CB 1962; CBE 1956; DL; Senior Technical Staff Officer, Royal Air Force Fighter Command, 1960–64, retired; Sales Manager Air Weapons, Hawker Siddeley Dynamics, 1964–76; *b* 24 Nov. 1909; *s* of Frederick William Wrigley and Anne Jeffreys, Seascale, Cumberland; *m* 1935, Audrey (*d* 1987), *d* of C. S. Boryer, Portsmouth; one *d. Educ:* Whitehaven Grammar Sch.; RAF Coll., Cranwell. 33 Squadron, 1930; HMS Glorious, 1931; HMS Eagle, 1933; long Signals Course, 1934; various signals appointments until 1937; RAF Signals Officer, HMS Glorious, 1938; served War of 1939–45, X Force, Norway, 1940; Fighter Command, 1940–43; HQ South East Asia, 1943–46; RAF Staff Coll., 1946; comd Northern Signals Area, 1947–50; jssc 1950; Inspector, Radio Services, 1950–52; Chief Signals Officer, 2nd TAF, 1952–54; Director of: Signals (I), Air Ministry, 1954–57; Guided Weapons (Air), Min. of Aviation, 1957–60. DL Hertfordshire, 1966. *Recreation:* gardening. *Address:* Boonwood, Turpin's Chase, Oaklands Rise, Welwyn, Herts AL6 0RA. *T:* (01438) 715231. *Club:* Royal Air Force.

Died 30 Dec. 1999.

WRIXON-BECHER, Major Sir William Fane; *see* Becher.

WUTTKE, Hans A., Dr jur; German banker, retired; Executive Vice President and Chief Executive, International Finance Corporation (World Bank Group), 1981–84; *b* Hamburg, 23 Oct. 1923; *m* 1st, 1957, Marina M. Schorsch (marr. diss. 1976); two *s* two *d*; 2nd, 1982, Jagoda M. Buić. *Educ:* Univs of Cologne and Salamanca. Dresdner Bank AG, 1949–54; Daimler-Benz AG, 1954–61; Partner, M. M. Warburg-Brinckmann, Wirtz and Co., Hamburg, 1961–75; Executive Director, S. G. Warburg and Co. Ltd, London, 1962–75; Man. Dir, Dresdner Bank AG, Frankfurt, 1975–80; Chm., Deutsch-Süd-Amerikanische Bank AG, 1975–80. Mem. Board several European companies; Mem. Bd, German Development Co., Cologne, 1962–80. Chm., East Asia Assoc., 1963–73. *Address:* 77 Cadogan Square, SW1X 0DY; (office) 6 Edith Grove, SW10 0NW. *T:* (020) 7376 5163, *Fax:* (020) 7376 5643.

Died 23 Feb. 2000.

WYATT OF WEEFORD, Baron cr 1987 (Life Peer), of Weeford in the county of Staffordshire; **Woodrow Lyle Wyatt**, Kt 1983; Chairman, Horserace Totalisator Board, 1976–97; b 4 July 1918; y s of late Robert Harvey Lyle Wyatt and Ethel Morgan; m 1st, 1939, Susan Cox (marr. diss. 1944); 2nd, 1948, Nora Robbins (marr. diss. 1956); 3rd, 1957, Lady Moorea Hastings (marr. diss., 1966), e d of 15th Earl of Huntingdon and Cristina, d of the Marchese Casati, Rome; one s; 4th, 1966, Veronica, widow of Baron Dr Laszlo Banszky Von Ambroz; one d. Educ: Eastbourne Coll.; Worcester Coll., Oxford (MA). Served throughout War of 1939–45 (despatches for Normandy); Major, 1944. Founder and Editor, English Story, 1940–50; Editorial Staff, New Statesman and Nation, 1947–48; weekly columnist: Reynolds News, 1949–61; Daily Mirror, 1965–73; Sunday Mirror, 1973–83; News of the World, 1983–; fortnightly columnist, The Times, 1983–. Began Panorama with Richard Dimbleby, 1955; under contract BBC TV, 1955–59; introduced non-heat-set web offset colour printing to England, 1962. MP (Lab) Aston Div. of Birmingham, 1945–55; contested (Lab) Grantham Div. of Lincolnshire, 1955; MP (Lab) Bosworth Div. of Leicester, 1959–70. Member of Parly Delegn to India, 1946; Personal Asst to Sir Stafford Cripps on Cabinet Mission to India, 1946; Parly Under-Sec. of State, and Financial Sec., War Office, May-Oct. 1951. Mem. Council, Zoological Soc. of London, 1968–71, 1973–77. Publications: (ed with introd.) English Story, 10 vols, 1940–50; The Jews at Home, 1950; Southwards from China, 1952; Into the Dangerous World, 1952; The Peril in Our Midst, 1956; Distinguished for Talent, 1958; (ed with introd.) 69 Short Stories by O'Henry, 1967; Turn Again, Westminster, 1973; The Exploits of Mr Saucy Squirrel, 1976; The Further Exploits of Mr Saucy Squirrel, 1977; What's Left of the Labour Party?, 1977; To the Point, 1981; Confessions of an Optimist (autobiog.), 1985; (ed with introd.) The Way We Lived Then: the English story in the 1940s, 1989; High Profiles (play), 1992. Address: House of Lords, SW1A 0PW. *Died 7 Dec. 1997.*

WYFOLD, 3rd Baron cr 1919, of Accrington; **Hermon Robert Fleming Hermon-Hodge**, ERD 1990; Bt 1902; Director, Robert Fleming Holdings, 1949–85, retired; formerly director other companies; b 26 June 1915; s of 2nd Baron Wyfold, DSO, MVO and Dorothy (d 1976), e d of late Robert Fleming, Joyce Grove, Oxford; S father, 1942. Educ: Eton; Le Rosey, Switzerland. Captain, Grenadier Guards (RARO), 1939–65. Heir: none. Address: c/o Robert Fleming Holdings, 25 Copthall Avenue, EC2R 7DR. T: (020) 7638 5858. Clubs: Carlton, Pratt's; Metropolitan (New York).

Died 8 April 1999 (ext).

WYLIE, (William) Derek, FRCP, FRCS, FRCA; Consulting Anaesthetist, St Thomas' Hospital, SE1; Consultant Anaesthetist, The Royal Masonic Hospital, 1959–82; Dean, St Thomas's Hospital Medical School, 1974–79; Adviser in Anaesthetics to the Health Service Commissioner, 1974–79; b 24 Oct. 1918; s of Edward and Mabel Wylie, Huddersfield; m 1945, Margaret Helen, 2nd d of F. W. Toms, Jersey, CI (formerly Dep. Inspector-Gen., Western Range, Indian Police); one s two d (and one s decd). Educ: Uppingham Sch.; Gonville and Caius Coll., Cambridge (MA; MB, BChir); St Thomas's Hosp. Med. Sch. MRCP 1945, FRCP 1967; FRCA (FFARCS 1953); FRCS 1972. Resident posts at St Thomas' Hosp., 1943–45; served RAFVR, 1945–47, Wing Comdr; apptd Hon. Staff, St Thomas' Hosp., 1946; Consultant, 1948; Sen. Cons. Anaesthetist, 1966–79; Cons. Anaesthetist, The National Hosp. for Nervous Diseases, 1950–67. Examiner: FFARCS, 1959–72; FFARCSI, 1966–78. Mem., Bd of Faculty of Anaesthetists, RCS, 1960–70 (Dean, 1967–69; Vice-Dean, 1965–66; Bernard Johnson Adviser in Postgraduate Studies, 1959–67; Faculty Medal,

1984); Mem. Council, RCS, 1967 69; FRSocMed (Mem. Council, 1962–72; Hon. Treas., 1964–70; Pres., Section of Anaesthetics, 1963); Mem., Bd of Governors, St Thomas' Hosp., 1969–74; Mem. Council, Med. Defence Union, 1962–92, Pres., 1982–88; Pres., Assoc. of Anaesthetists of GB and Ireland, 1980–82, Hon. Mem., 1984 (John Snow Silver Medal, 1988). Jenny Hartmann Lectr, Basle Univ., 1961; Clover Lectr and Medallist, RCS, 1974. Hon. FFARCSI, 1971; Hon. FANZCA (Hon. FFARACS, 1984). Henry Hill Hickman Medal, RSM, 1983. Hon. Citizen of Dallas, USA, 1963. Publications: The Practical Management of Pain in Labour, 1953; (ed with Dr H. C. Churchill-Davidson), A Practice of Anaesthesia, 1960, 3rd edn 1972; papers in specialist and gen. med. jls. Recreations: reading, travel, philately. Address: St John's Cottage, Nursery Lane, Fairwarp, Uckfield, East Sussex TN22 3BD. T: (01825) 712822. Club: Royal Automobile. *Died 30 Sept. 1998.*

WYNNE, Prof. Charles Gorrie, PhD; FRS 1970; Senior Visiting Fellow, Cambridge University Institute of Astronomy, since 1988; b 18 May 1911; s of C. H. and A. E. Wynne; m 1937, Jean Richardson; one s one d (and one s decd). Educ: Wyggeston Grammar Sch., Leicester; Exeter Coll., Oxford (Scholar; BA). Optical Designer, Taylor Taylor & Hobson Ltd, 1935–43; Wray (Optical Works) Ltd, 1943–60, latterly Director; Dir, Optical Design Gp, 1960–78, and Sen. Res. Fellow, 1978–87, Imperial Coll., London; Prof. of Optical Design, Univ. of London, 1969–78, then Emeritus. Vis. Prof. Univ. of Durham, 1987–90. Dir, IC Optical Systems, 1970– (Chm., 1975 88). Hon. Sec. (business), Physical Soc., 1947–60; Hon. Sec., Inst. of Physics and Physical Soc., 1960–66. Editor, Optica Acta, 1954–65. Thomas Young Medal, Inst. of Physics, 1971; Gold Medal, Royal Astronomical Soc., 1979; Rumford Medal, Royal Soc., 1982. Publications: scientific papers on aberration theory and optical instruments in Proc. Phys. Soc., Mon. Not. RAS, Astrophys. Jl, Optica Acta, etc. Address: 4 Holbein Close, Barton, Cambs CB3 7AQ. T: (01223) 263098.

Died 1 Oct. 1999.

WYNNE, Col John Francis W.; see Williams-Wynne.

WYNNE-EDWARDS, Vero Copner, CBE 1973; MA, DSc; FRS 1970; FRSE, FRSC; Regius Professor of Natural History, University of Aberdeen, 1946–74, Vice Principal, 1972–74; b 4 July 1906; 3rd s of late Rev. Canon John Rosindale Wynne-Edwards and Lilian Agnes Streatfeild; m 1929, Jeannie Campbell, e d of late Percy Morris, Devon County Architect; one s one d. Educ: Leeds Grammar Sch.; Rugby Sch.; New Coll., Oxford. 1st Class Hons in Natural Science (Zoology), Oxford, 1927. Senior Scholar of New Coll., 1927–29; Student Probationer, Marine Biological Laboratory, Plymouth, 1927–29; Assistant Lecturer in Zoology, Univ. of Bristol, 1929–30; Asst Prof. of Zoology, McGill Univ., Montreal, 1930–44; Associate Prof., 1944–46. Canadian representative, MacMillan Baffin Island expedition, 1937; Canadian Fisheries Research Board expeditions to Mackenzie River, 1944, and Yukon Territory, 1945; Baird expedition to Central Baffin Island, 1950. Visiting Prof. of Conservation, University of Louisville, Kentucky, 1959; Commonwealth Universities Interchange Fellow New Zealand, 1962; Leverhulme Emeritus Fellowship, 1978–80. Jt Editor, Journal of Applied Ecology, 1963–68. Member: Nature Conservancy, 1954–57; Red Deer Commn (Vice-Chm.), 1959–68; Royal Commn on Environmental Pollution, 1970–74; President: British Ornithologists' Union, 1965–70; Scottish Marine Biological Assoc., 1967–73; Section D, British Assoc., 1974; Chairman: NERC, 1968–71; DoE and Scottish Office Adv. Cttees on Protection of Birds, 1970–78; Scientific Authority for Animals, DoE, 1976–77. For. Mem., Societas Scientiarum

Fennica, 1965; Hon. Mem., British Ecological Soc., 1977; Hon. Fellow, Amer. Ornithologists' Union, 1991. Hon. FIBiol 1980. Hon. DUniv Stirling, 1974; Hon. LLD Aberdeen, 1976. Godman-Salvin Medal, British Ornithologists' Union, 1977; Neill Prize, RSE, 1977; Frink Medal, Zoological Soc., 1980. *Publications:* Animal Dispersion in relation to social behaviour, 1962; Evolution through Group Selection, 1986; (contrib.) Leaders in the Study of Animal Behaviour, ed D. A. Dewsbury, 1985; scientific papers on ornithology (esp. oceanic birds), animal populations. *Recreation:* natural history. *Address:* Ravelston, William Street, Torphins, via Banchory, Aberdeenshire AB31 4JR.　　　　　*Died 5 Jan. 1997.*

Y

YANG SHANGKUN; President of the People's Republic of China, 1988–93; *b* Tongnan County, Sichuan Province, 1907; *m* Li Bozhao (*d* 1985), playwright. *Educ:* Sun Yat-sen Univ., Moscow. Joined Communist Youth League, 1925, and Communist Party, 1926; formerly: Head of Propaganda Department: All-China Fedn of Trade Unions, Shanghai (also Sec. of Party Orgn); Communist Party's Jiangsu Provincial Cttee; Communist Party's Central Cttee; Editor, Red China newspaper; Dep. Head, Communist Party's sch., Jiangxi; Dir, Political Dept, First Front Army of Red Army; Dep. Dir, Gen. Pol Dept, Red Army; Pol Commisar, Third Red Army Corps; Long March, Oct. 1934–Oct. 1935; Chinese Communist Party's Central Committee: successively: Sec., N Bureau, 1937; Sec.-Gen., Mil. Commn, 1945; Dir, Gen. Office; Dep Sec.-Gen.; Alternate Mem. of Secretariat; Mem. Secretariat, Guangdong Provincial Party Cttee; removed from posts and imprisoned during Cultural Revolution, 1966–76; successively: Second Sec., Guangdong Provincial Party Cttee; Vice-Gov., Guangdong; First Sec., Guangzhou City Party Cttee; Chm., Guangzhou City Revolutionary Cttee; Vice-Chm. and Sec.-Gen., Standing Cttee, Nat. People's Congress, 1980; Exec. Vice-Chm., 1982, First Vice Chm., 1989, Mil. Commn of Party Central Cttee (Sec.-Gen., 1980–81); Mem., Pol Bureau, 1982–92. *Recreations:* sports, especially swimming.
Died 14 Sept. 1998.

YEOMAN, Philip Metcalfe, MD, FRCS. Consultant Orthopaedic Surgeon, Bath, 1964–88, retired; *b* 29 April 1923; *s* of William Yeoman, MD and Dorothy Young; *m* 1947, Idonea Evelyn Mary Scarrott; two *s* one *d. Educ:* Sedbergh; Cambridge (MA, MB BChir, MD); University Coll. Hosp. London. Flight Lieut, RAF Hosp., Ely, 1950–52. Lectr, Inst. of Orthopaedics, 1959–64. Member: Pensions Appeal Tribunals, 1986–; Professional and Linguistic Assessment Bd, 1987–. Hon. Consultant Surgeon, Royal British Legion, 1995–. External Examr in Surg., Univ. of Liverpool. Mem. Council, RCS, 1984–92 (Mem., Court of Examrs, 1980–; Hunterian Prof., 1983); Vice-Pres., British Orthopaedic Assoc., 1984–85 (Robert Jones Gold Medal, 1963; North American Travelling Fellow, 1964; Mem. Council, 1981–84); President: Section of Orthopaedics, RSocMed, 1983; North American Travelling Fellows, 1981–83. Mem., Internat. Skeletal Soc. Hugh Owen Thomas Meml Lectr, Liverpool, 1988. *Publications:* Orthopaedic Practice, 1995; chapters on peripheral nerve injuries, brachial plexus injuries, bone tumours, surgical management of rheumatoid arthritis of the cervical spine. *Recreations:* golf, gardening. *Address:* Broadmead, Monkton Combe, near Bath BA2 7JE. *T:* (01225) 723294. *Club:* Army and Navy.
Died 29 Nov. 1997.

YORK, Christopher; DL; *b* 27 July 1909; *s* of late Col Edward York; *m* 1934, Pauline Rosemary, *d* of late Sir Lionel Fletcher, CBE; one *s* three *d. Educ:* Eton; RMC Sandhurst. Joined The Royal Dragoons, India, 1930; retired, 1934, on to Supplementary Reserve; rejoined Regt, 1939, rank Major. Joined Land Agents Soc., 1934, and passed examinations, acting as Land Agent until elected MP; MP (U): Ripon Div. of WR, 1939–50; Harrogate Division, 1950–54. DL West Riding of Yorkshire, later N Yorkshire, 1954; High Sheriff of Yorkshire, 1966. Pres., RASE, 1979. Hon. Fellow, Royal Veterinary Coll., 1971. *Recreation:* writing. *Address:* South Park, Long Marston, York YO5 8LL. *TA* and *T:* (01904) 738357. *Clubs:* Boodle's, Carlton.
Died 13 March 1999.

YOUENS, Sir Peter (William), Kt 1965; CMG 1962; OBE 1960; *b* 29 April 1916; 2nd *s* of late Rev. Canon F. A. C. Youens and Dorothy Mary, *o d* of William and Annie Ross, Blackpool; *m* 1943, Diana Stephanie (*d* 1990), *d* of Edward Hawkins, Southacre, Norfolk; two *d. Educ:* King Edward VII's School, Sheffield; Wadham College, Oxford (MA 1938). Served War, RNVR, 1939–40, Sub Lieut. Joined Colonial Administrative Service, 1938; Cadet, Sierra Leone, 1939; Asst Dist Comr, 1942; Dist Comr, 1948; Colony Comr and Member, Sierra Leone Legislative Council, 1950; Asst Sec., Nyasaland, 1951; Dep. Chief Sec., 1953–63; Mem., Nyasaland Legislative Council, 1954–61; Secretary to the Prime Minister and to the Cabinet, Nyasaland, 1963–64, Malawi, 1964–66, retd. Exec. Dir, Lonrho Ltd, 1966–69, Non-Exec. Dir, 1980–81, Exec. Dir, 1981–94; Partner, John Tyzack & Partners Ltd, 1969–81. *Address:* Hill View, Primrose Hill Road, NW3 3AB. *Clubs:* East India, Devonshire, Sports and Public Schools; Vincent's (Oxford).
Died 6 May 2000.

YOUNG, (Basil) Alexander, FRNCM; retired as free-lance concert and opera singer; Head of Department of Vocal Studies, Royal Northern College of Music, Manchester, 1973–86; *b* London, 18 Oct. 1920; *m* 1948, Jean Anne Prewett; one *s* one *d. Educ.* secondary; (scholar) Royal Coll. of Music, London; studied in London with Prof Pollmann, of Vienna State Academy. FRNCM 1977. Served War HM Forces, 1941–46. First operatic role (tenor), as Scaramuccio in Strauss' Ariadne, Edin. Fest., with Glyndebourne Opera, 1950; parts at Glyndebourne, and began broadcasting for BBC, 1951 (subseq. incl. opera, oratorio, recitals, light music, etc); first appearances with English Opera Group, world Première of Lennox Berkeley's opera, A Dinner Engagement, 1954; also appeared at Royal Festival Hall, several times with Sir Thomas Beecham, in Mozart Requiem; at Sadler's Wells Opera, as Eisenstein in Die Fledermaus, 1959, and subsequently in many roles such as: Ramiro in La Cenerentola; title role in Count Ory; Almaviva in The Barber of Seville; notable roles included: Tom in Stravinsky's Rake's Progress (which he created for British audiences); David in Die Meistersinger; title role in Mozart's Idomeneo; at Covent Garden sang in: Strauss's Arabella; Britten's A Midsummer Night's Dream; oratorio roles included: Evangelist in Bach Passions; Elgar's Dream of Gerontius; Britten's War Requiem; was regularly engaged by Welsh National Opera and Scottish Opera. Had regular engagements with the BBC; sang in the USA, Canada, and most European countries, as well as frequently in Britain. Many commercial recordings, especially of Handel oratorios and operas, as well as The Rake's Progress conducted by the composer. Lieder recitals a speciality. *Recreations:* railway modelling, stamp collecting, photography.
Died 5 March 2000.

YOUNG, Lt-Gen. Sir David (Tod), KBE 1980; CB 1977; DFC 1952; General Officer Commanding Scotland and Governor of Edinburgh Castle, 1980–82; *b* 17 May 1926; *s* of late William Young and Davina Tod Young; *m* 1st, 1950, Joyce Marian Melville (*d* 1987); two *s*; 2nd, 1988, Joanna Myrtle Oyler (*née* Torin). *Educ:* George Watson's Coll., Edinburgh. Commissioned The Royal Scots (The Royal Regt), 1945 (Col, 1975–80); attached Glider Pilot Regt, 1949–52; Bt Lt-Col, 1964; Mil. Asst to Dep. Chief of Gen. Staff, MoD, 1964–67; commanded 1st Bn The Royal Scots (The Royal Regt), 1967–69; Col Gen. Staff, Staff Coll., 1969–70; Comdr, 12th Mechanized Bde, 1970–72; Dep. Mil. Sec., MoD, 1972–74; Comdr Land Forces, NI, 1975–77; Dir of Infantry, 1977–80. Colonel Commandant: Scottish Div., 1980–82; UDR, 1986–91; Hon. Col, NI Regt AAC, 1988–93. Pres., ACFA, Scotland, 1984–96. HM Comr, Queen Victoria Sch., Dunblane, 1980–82, 1984–93. Chm., Cairntech Ltd, Edinburgh, 1983–92 (Dir, 1992–96). Chm., St Mary's Cathedral Workshop Ltd, 1986–92 (Hon. Pres., 1993–). Mem. Scottish Cttee, 1983– (Chm., 1986–99), and Trustee, 1986–99, Marie Curie Cancer Care (formerly Marie Curie Meml Foundn); Vice Pres., Scottish Partnership Agency for Palliative and Cancer Care, 1993–98; Governor, St Columba's Hospice, Edinburgh, 1986–. *Recreations:* golf, spectator of sports. *Address:* c/o Adam & Co. plc, 22 Charlotte Square, Edinburgh EH2 4DF. *Clubs:* Royal Scots, New (Edinburgh). *Died 9 Jan. 2000.*

YOUNG, Frieda Margaret, OBE 1969; HM Diplomatic Service, retired; *b* 9 April 1913; *d* of Arthur Edward Young. *Educ:* Wyggeston Grammar Sch., Leicester; Wycombe Abbey Sch., Bucks; and in France and Germany. Home Office, 1937–39; Min. of Home Security, WWII; MOI, 1941–44; Paris, 1944–48; Tehran, 1948–51; Vienna, 1951–54; FO, 1954–57; First Secretary and Consul, Reykjavik, 1957–59; Consul, Cleveland, 1959–62; FO, 1962–65; Consul, Bergen, 1965–68; Consul-General, Rotterdam, 1968–73. *Recreations:* travel, bird-watching. *Address:* 6 Lady Street, Lavenham, Suffolk.
Died 10 Feb. 1998.

YOUNG, John Zachary, MA; FRS 1945; Professor of Anatomy, University College, London, 1945–74, then Emeritus (Hon. Fellow, 1975); engaged in research at Oxford University, Marine Biology Station, Plymouth, and Duke Marine Laboratory, Beaufort, N Carolina; *b* 18 March 1907; *s* of Philip Young and Constance Maria Lloyd; *m* 1931, Phyllis Elizabeth, *d* of A. J. Heaney; one *s* one *d*; *m* Raymonde Parsons; one *d*. *Educ:* Wells House, Malvern Wells; Marlborough Coll.; Magdalen Coll., Oxford (Demy). Senior Demy, Magdalen Coll., 1929, Christopher Welch Scholar, 1928, Naples Biological Scholar, 1928, 1929; Fellow of Magdalen Coll., Oxford, 1931–45 (Hon. Fellow, 1975); University Demonstrator in Zoology and Comparative Anatomy, Oxford, 1933–45; Rockefeller Fellow, 1936. Fullerton Professor of Physiology, Royal Institution, 1958–61. Pres., Marine Biol Assoc., 1976–86. Foreign Member: Amer. Acad. of Arts and Scis; Amer. Philosophical Soc.; Accademia dei Lincei. Hon. FBA 1986. Hon. DSc: Bristol, 1965; McGill, 1967; Durham, 1969; Bath, 1973; Duke, 1978; Oxford, 1979; Hon. LLD: Glasgow, 1975; Aberdeen, 1980. Royal Medal, Royal Society, 1967; Linnean Gold Medal, 1973; Jan Swammerdam Medal, Amsterdam Soc. for Natural Scis and Medicine, 1980. *Publications:* The Life of Vertebrates, 1950, 3rd edn 1981; Doubt and Certainty in

Science, 1951; The Life of Mammals, 1957; A Model of the Brain, 1964 (lectures); The Memory System of the Brain, 1966; An Introduction to the Study of Man, 1971; The Anatomy of the Nervous System of *Octopus vulgaris*, 1971; Programs of the Brain, 1978; Philosophy and the Brain, 1987; scientific papers, mostly on the nervous system. *Recreation:* walking. *Address:* 1 The Crossroads, Brill, Bucks HP18 9TL. *T:* (01844) 237412; Department of Experimental Psychology, South Parks Road, Oxford OX1 3UD. *T:* (01865) 271444, *Fax:* (01865) 310447.
Died 4 July 1997.

YOUNG, Sir Norman (Smith), Kt 1968; formerly Chairman: Pipelines Authority of South Australia; South Australian Brewing Co. Ltd; South Australian Oil and Gas Corporation Pty Ltd; News Ltd; Elder Smith Goldsbrough Mort Ltd; Bradmill Ltd; *b* 24 July 1911; *s* of Thomas and Margaret Young; *m* 1936, Jean Fairbairn Sincock (*d* 1996); two *s* one *d*. *Educ:* Norwood High Sch.; University of Adelaide. Member: Adelaide City Council, 1949–60; Municipal Tramways Trust, 1951–67 (Dep. Chairman); Royal Commn on Television, 1953–54; Bankruptcy Law Review Cttee, 1956–62. Fellow, Inst. of Chartered Accountants, 1933; FASA 1932; Associate in Commerce, University of Adelaide, 1930. *Publication:* Bankruptcy Practice in Australia, 1942. *Address:* 522 Greenhill Road, Hazelwood Park, SA 5006, Australia. *T:* (8) 83791684.
Died 17 May 1999.

YOUNG, Sir Robert Christopher M.; *see* Mackworth-Young.

YOUNG, Robert Henry; Consultant Orthopædic Surgeon, St George's Hospital, SW1, 1946–68; Hon. Consultant, St Peter's Hospital, Chertsey, 1939–68; *b* 6 Oct. 1903; *s* of James Allen Young and Constance Barrow Young; *m* 1st, 1929, Nancy Willcox; 2nd, 1961, Norma, *d* of Leslie Williams; two *s*. *Educ:* Sherborne Sch.; Emmanuel Coll., Cambridge; St Thomas' Hospital, SE1. *Publications:* numerous articles in leading medical journals. *Address:* Milestone Farm, Ash, near Martock, Somerset TA12 6PD. *Clubs:* United Oxford & Cambridge University, Buck's.
Died 8 Feb. 1997.

YOUNGER OF LECKIE, 3rd Viscount *cr* 1923, of Alloa, Clackmannanshire; **Edward George Younger,** OBE 1940; Bt 1911; Lord-Lieutenant, Stirling and Falkirk (formerly of County of Stirling), 1964–79; Colonel, Argyll and Sutherland Highlanders (TA); *b* 21 Nov. 1906; *er s* of 2nd Viscount Younger of Leckie, DSO and Maud (*d* 1957), *e d* of Sir John Gilmour, 1st Bt; *S* father, 1946; *m* 1930, Evelyn Margaret, MBE (*d* 1983), *e d* of late Alexander Logan McClure, KC; three *s* one *d*. *Educ:* Winchester; New Coll., Oxford. Served War of 1939–45 (OBE). *Heir: s* Baron Younger of Prestwick [*b* 22 Sept. 1931; *m* 1954, Diana Rhona, *er d* of Capt. G. S. Tuck, RN, Chichester; three *s* one *d*]. *Address:* Leckie, Gargunnock, Stirling FK8 3BN. *T:* (01786) 860281. *Club:* New (Edinburgh). *Died 25 June 1997.*

Z

ZEIDLER, Sir David (Ronald), AC 1990; Kt 1980; CBE 1971; FAA 1985; FRACI; FIChemE; FIEAust; FTS; Chairman and Managing Director, ICI Australia, 1973–80, retired; *b* 18 March 1918; *s* of Otto William and Hilda Maude Zeidler; *m* 1943, June Susie Broadhurst; four *d*. *Educ:* Scotch Coll., Melbourne; Melbourne Univ. (MSc). FTS 1976; FIEAust 1988. CSIRO, 1941–52; joined ICI Australia, 1952: Research Manager, 1953; Development Manager, 1959; Controller, Dyes and Fabrics Gp, 1962; Dir, 1963; Man. Dir, 1971; Dep. Chm., 1972. Chm., Metal Manufactures Ltd, 1980–88; Director: Amatil Ltd, 1979–89; Broken Hill Pty Co. Ltd, 1978–88; Commercial Bank of Australia Ltd, 1974–82; Westpac Banking Corp., 1982–91 (Dep. Chm., 1989–91); Australian Foundation Investment Co. Ltd, 1982–90; past Director: ICI New Zealand Ltd; IMI Australia Ltd. Vice-Pres., Walter and Eliza Hall Inst. of Med. Res., 1972–89; Dep. Chm., Queen's Silver Jubilee Trust, 1977–88. Chairman: Govt Inquiry into Elec. Generation and Power Sharing in SE Aust., 1980–81; Defence Industry Cttee, 1981–84; Member, or past Mem., cttees concerned with prof. qualifications, defence industry, educn and trng, internat. business co-operation. Member: Aust.-Japan Businessmen's Co-operation Cttee, 1978–80; Aust.-NZ Businessmen's Council Ltd, 1978–80; Sir Robert Menzies Meml Trust, 1978–80; Council, Aust. Acad. of Technol Scis, 1979–88 (Vice-Pres., 1970–71; Pres., 1983–88); Council, Science Museum of Victoria, 1964–82; Commerce and Industry Cttee, 1978–85, and Defence Industry Cttee, 1977–84 (Chm., 1981–84), Victorian Div. of Aust. Red Cross Soc.; Inst. of Dirs; Royal Society, Victoria; Royal Soc. for Encouragement of Arts, Manufrs and Commerce in London; Cook Society. Director: Schizophrenia Aust. Foundn, 1986–; Aust. Bicentennial Multicultural Foundn, 1988–; Vic. Govt Strategic Res. Foundn, 1988– (Dep. Chm., 1990–). Governor, Ian Clunies Ross Meml Foundn, 1984–. *Recreations:* tennis, ski-ing, golf. *Address:* 45/238 The Avenue, Parkville, Vic 3052, Australia. *T:* (3) 93875720. *Clubs:* Melbourne, Australian, Sciences (Melbourne); Australian (Sydney).
Died 16 March 1998.

ZIEGLER, Henri Alexandre Léonard; Ingénieur Général (Air); Grand Officier, Légion d'Honneur; Croix de Guerre (1939–45); Rosette de la Résistance; Hon. CVO; Hon. CBE; Legion of Merit (US); French aviation executive; *b* Limoges, 18 Nov. 1906; *s* of Charles Ziegler and Alix Mousnier-Buisson; *m* 1932, Gillette Rizzi; three *s* one *d*. *Educ:* Collège Stanislas, Paris; Ecole Polytechnique (Grad.); Ecole Nationale Supérieure de l'Aéronautique. Officer-Pilot in French Air Force, 1928 (5000 hours); Tech. Officer, Min. of Aviation, 1929; Dep. Dir of Flight Test Centre, 1938; Foreign Missions: Gt Britain, USA, Germany, Poland, USSR; War of 1939–45: Dep. Buying Mission, USA, Dec. 1939; French Resistance, 1941–44; Col and Chief of Staff, Forces Françaises de l'Intérieur (London), 1944. Dir-Gen., Air France, 1946–54; Dir of Cabinet: of J. Chaban-Delmas (Minister of Public Works, Transport and Tourism), 1954; of Gen. Cormiglion-Molignier (Minister of Public Works), 1955–56; Admin. Dir-Gen., Ateliers d'aviation Louis Breguet, 1957–67; Pres. Dir-Gen., Sud Aviation, 1968; Pres. Dir-Gen., Soc. Nationale Industrielle Aérospatiale, 1970–73; Pres., Airbus Industrie, 1970–74. Pres., Air-Alpes, 1961–76; Pres., Forum Atomique Européen, 1956–60; Admin. Inst. du Transport Aérien, 1969–77 (Hon. Mem. 1977); Pres., Union Syndicale des Industries Aérospatiales, 1971–74. Mem., Amicale des anciens des essais en vol. Hon. Fellow, Soc. of Experimental Test Pilots; Hon. FRAeS. *Publication:* La Grande Aventure de Concorde, 1976. *Recreation:* alpinism. *Address:* 55 boulevard Lannes, 75116 Paris, France. *T:* 45046153. *Club:* Aéro-Club de France (Paris). *Died 23 July 1998.*

ZINNEMANN, Fred; film director since 1934; *b* Austria, 29 April 1907; *s* of Dr Oskar Zinnemann, physician, and Anna F. Zinnemann; *m* 1936, Renée Bartlett; one *s*. *Educ:* Vienna Univ. (Law School). First film, The Wave (documentary) directed for Mexican Govt, 1934; initiated, with others, school of neo-realism in American cinema, directing among other films: The Seventh Cross, 1943; The Search, 1948; The Men, 1949; Teresa, 1950, High Noon, 1951; Member of the Wedding, 1952; From Here to Eternity, 1953; later films include: Oklahoma!, 1956; The Nun's Story, 1959, The Sundowners, 1960; Behold a Pale Horse, 1964; A Man for All Seasons, 1966, The Day of the Jackal, 1973, Julia, 1977; Five Days One Summer, 1982. Exhibn of photographs of NY taken in 1932, V&A Mus., 1992. Member: Amer. Film Inst. (co-founder and ex-trustee); Acad. of Motion Picture Arts; Directors' Guild of America (2nd Vice-Pres., 1960–64); Hon. Pres., Directors' Guild of Great Britain, 1983–87. Fellow: BAFTA, 1978; BFI, 1990. Hon. DLitt Durham, 1994. Awards include: Academy Award, Los Angeles, 1951, 1954, 1967; Film Critics' Award, NY, 1952, 1954, 1960, 1967; Golden Thistle Award, Edinburgh, 1965; Moscow Film Festival Award, 1965; D. W. Griffith Award, 1970; Donatello Award, Florence, 1978; US Congressional Lifetime Achievement Award, 1987; John Huston Award (1st recipient), Artists' Rights Foundn, LA, 1994. Gold Medal of City of Vienna, 1967. Order of Arts and Letters, France, 1982. *Publications:* Fred Zinnemann: an autobiography, 1992; article on directing films, Encyclopædia Britannica. *Recreations:* mountain climbing, chamber music. *Address:* 98 Mount Street, W1Y 5HF. *Club:* Sierra (San Francisco).
Died 14 March 1997.